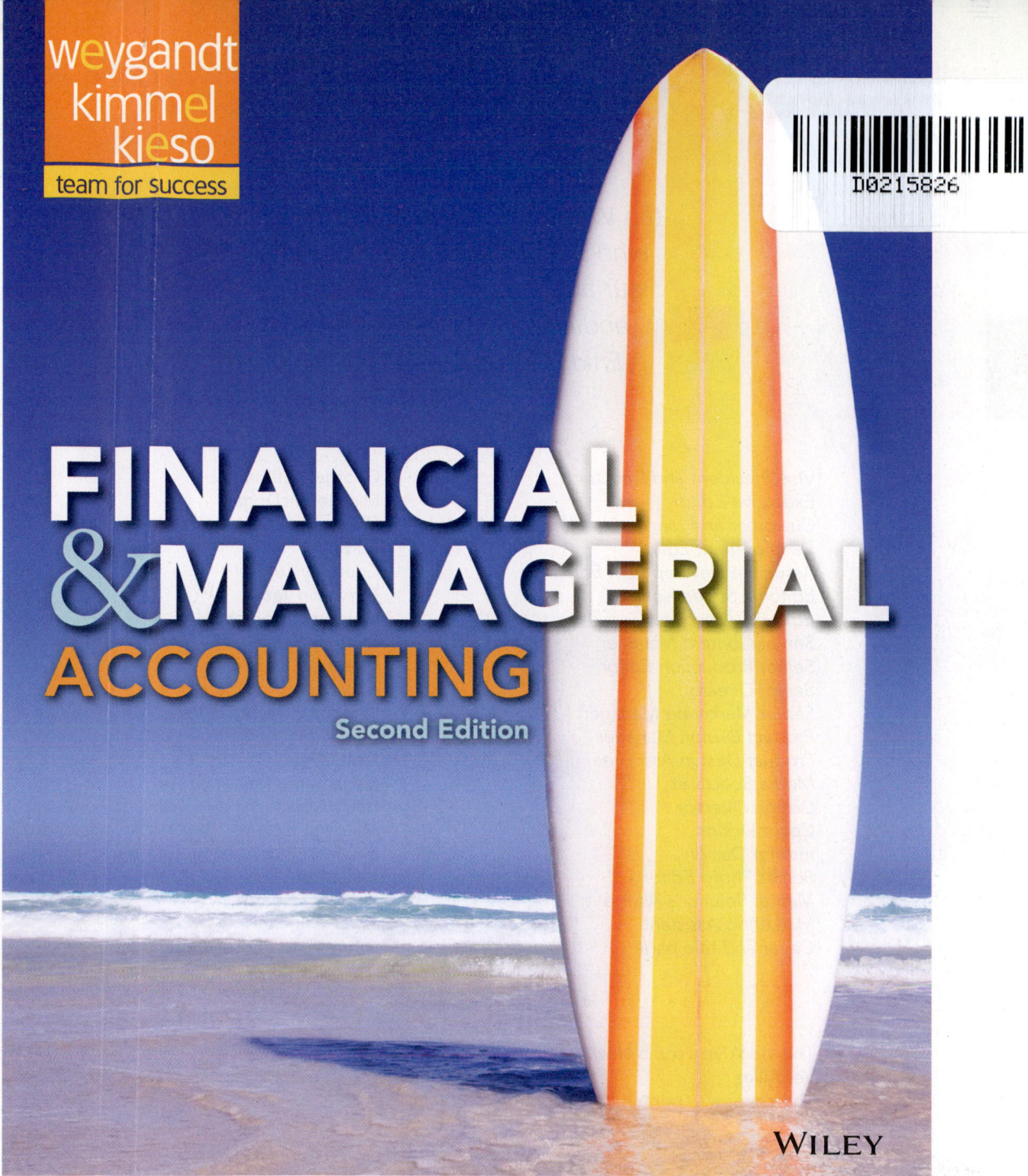

weygandt
kimmel
kieso
team for success

FINANCIAL & MANAGERIAL ACCOUNTING

Second Edition

WILEY

Jerry J. Weygandt PhD, CPA
University of Wisconsin—Madison
Madison, Wisconsin

Paul D. Kimmel PhD, CPA
University of Wisconsin—Milwaukee
Milwaukee, Wisconsin

Donald E. Kieso PhD, CPA
Northern Illinois University
DeKalb, Illinois

WILEY

DEDICATED TO

*the Wiley sales representatives
who sell our books and service
our adopters in a professional
and ethical manner, and to
Enid, Merlynn, and Donna*

Vice President and Director	George Hoffman
Executive Editor	Michael McDonald
Customer and Market Development Manager	Christopher DeJohn
Development Editor	Ed Brislin
Associate Development Editor	Courtney Luzzi
Editorial Supervisor	Terry Ann Tatro
Editorial Associate	Margaret Thompson
Senior Content Manager	Dorothy Sinclair
Senior Production Editor	Valerie A. Vargas
Senior Director	Amy Scholz
Senior Marketing Manager	Karolina Zarychta Honsa
Product Design Manager	Allison Morris
Product Design Associate	Matt Origoni
Media Specialist	Elena Santa Maria
Design Director	Harry Nolan
Cover Design	Maureen Eide
Interior Design	Maureen Eide/Kristine Carney
Senior Photo Editor	Mary Ann Price
Market Solutions Assistant	Elizabeth Kearns
Marketing Assistant	Anna Wilhelm
Cover and title page	John White Photos/Getty Images

This book was set in New Aster LT Std by Aptara®, Inc. and printed and bound by Quad Graphics/Versailles.
The cover was printed by Quad Graphics/Versailles.

Founded in 1807, John Wiley & Sons, Inc. has been a valued source of knowledge and understanding for more than 200 years, helping people around the world meet their needs and fulfill their aspirations. Our company is built on a foundation of principles that include responsibility to the communities we serve and where we live and work. In 2008, we launched a Corporate Citizenship Initiative, a global effort to address the environmental, social, economic, and ethical challenges we face in our business. Among the issues we are addressing are carbon impact, paper specifications and procurement, ethical conduct within our business and among our vendors, and community and charitable support. For more information, please visit our website: www.wiley.com/go/citizenship.

ISBN-13 978-1-118-33426-3

Binder-Ready Version ISBN 978-1-118-33841-4

Printed in the United States of America

10 9 8 7 6 5 4 3 2 1

Brief Contents

1 Accounting in Action 2
2 The Recording Process 48
3 Adjusting the Accounts 94
4 Completing the Accounting Cycle 150
5 Accounting for Merchandising Operations 204
6 Inventories 258
7 Fraud, Internal Control, and Cash 306
8 Accounting for Receivables 356
9 Plant Assets, Natural Resources, and Intangible Assets 396
10 Liabilities 444
11 Corporations: Organization, Stock Transactions, Dividends, and Retained Earnings 498
12 Investments 558
13 Statement of Cash Flows 598
14 Financial Statement Analysis 658
15 Managerial Accounting 710
16 Job Order Costing 752
17 Process Costing 794
18 Activity-Based Costing 838
19 Cost-Volume-Profit 884
20 Cost-Volume-Profit Analysis: Additional Issues 922
21 Incremental Analysis 972
22 Pricing 1012
23 Budgetary Planning 1056
24 Budgetary Control and Responsibility Accounting 1106
25 Standard Costs and Balanced Scorecard 1158
26 Planning for Capital Investments 1204

APPENDICES

A Specimen Financial Statements: Apple Inc.
B Specimen Financial Statements: PepsiCo, Inc.
C Specimen Financial Statements: The Coca-Cola Company
D Specimen Financial Statements: Amazon.com, Inc.
E Specimen Financial Statements: Wal-Mart Stores, Inc.
F Specimen Financial Statements: Louis Vuitton
G Time Value of Money
H Payroll Accounting*
I Subsidiary Ledgers and Special Journals*
J Other Significant Liabilities*
K Standards of Ethical Conduct for Managerial Accountants*

Cases for Managerial Decision-Making*

*Available at the book's companion website, **www.wiley.com/college/weygandt**.

From the **Authors**

Dear Student,

Why This Course? *Remember your biology course in high school? Did you have one of those "invisible man" models (or maybe something more high-tech than that) that gave you the opportunity to look "inside" the human body? This accounting course offers something similar. To understand a business, you have to understand the financial insides of a business organization. An accounting course will help you understand the essential financial components of businesses. Whether you are looking at a large multinational company like* Apple *or* Starbucks *or a single-owner software consulting business or coffee shop, knowing the fundamentals of accounting will help you understand what is happening. As an employee, a manager, an investor, a business owner, or a director of your own personal finances—any of which roles you will have at some point in your life—you will make better decisions for having taken this course.*

"Whether you are looking at a large multinational company like Apple or Starbucks or a single-owner software consulting business or coffee shop, knowing the fundamentals of accounting will help you understand what is happening."

Why This Book? *Hundreds of thousands of students have used this textbook. Your instructor has chosen it for you because of its trusted reputation. The authors have worked hard to keep the book fresh, timely, and accurate.*

How to Succeed? *We've asked many students and many instructors whether there is a secret for success in this course. The nearly unanimous answer turns out to be not much of a secret: "Do the homework." This is one course where doing is learning. The more time you spend on the homework assignments—using the various tools that this textbook provides—the more likely you are to learn the essential concepts, techniques, and methods of accounting. Besides the textbook itself, WileyPLUS and the book's companion website also offers various support resources.*

Good luck in this course. We hope you enjoy the experience and that you put to good use throughout a lifetime of success the knowledge you obtain in this course. We are sure you will not be disappointed.

Jerry J. Weygandt
Paul D. Kimmel
Donald E. Kieso

Author Commitment

Jerry Weygandt

Paul Kimmel

Don Kieso

JERRY J. WEYGANDT, PhD, CPA, is Arthur Andersen Alumni Emeritus Professor of Accounting at the University of Wisconsin—Madison. He holds a Ph.D. in accounting from the University of Illinois. Articles by Professor Weygandt have appeared in the *Accounting Review, Journal of Accounting Research, Accounting Horizons, Journal of Accountancy*, and other academic and professional journals. These articles have examined such financial reporting issues as accounting for price-level adjustments, pensions, convertible securities, stock option contracts, and interim reports. Professor Weygandt is author of other accounting and financial reporting books and is a member of the American Accounting Association, the American Institute of Certified Public Accountants, and the Wisconsin Society of Certified Public Accountants. He has served on numerous committees of the American Accounting Association and as a member of the editorial board of the Accounting Review; he also has served as President and Secretary-Treasurer of the American Accounting Association. In addition, he has been actively involved with the American Institute of Certified Public Accountants and has been a member of the Accounting Standards Executive Committee (AcSEC) of that organization. He has served on the FASB task force that examined the reporting issues related to accounting for income taxes and served as a trustee of the Financial Accounting Foundation. Professor Weygandt has received the Chancellor's Award for Excellence in Teaching and the Beta Gamma Sigma Dean's Teaching Award. He is on the board of directors of M & I Bank of Southern Wisconsin. He is the recipient of the Wisconsin Institute of CPA's Outstanding Educator's Award and the Lifetime Achievement Award. In 2001 he received the American Accounting Association's Outstanding Educator Award.

PAUL D. KIMMEL, PhD, CPA, received his bachelor's degree from the University of Minnesota and his doctorate in accounting from the University of Wisconsin. He is an Associate Professor at the University of Wisconsin—Milwaukee, and has public accounting experience with Deloitte & Touche (Minneapolis). He was the recipient of the UWM School of Business Advisory Council Teaching Award, the Reggie Taite Excellence in Teaching Award and a three-time winner of the Outstanding Teaching Assistant Award at the University of Wisconsin. He is also a recipient of the Elijah Watts Sells Award for Honorary Distinction for his results on the CPA exam. He is a member of the American Accounting Association and the Institute of Management Accountants and has published articles in *Accounting Review, Accounting Horizons, Advances in Management Accounting, Managerial Finance, Issues in Accounting Education, Journal of Accounting Education,* as well as other journals. His research interests include accounting for financial instruments and innovation in accounting education. He has published papers and given numerous talks on incorporating critical thinking into accounting education, and helped prepare a catalog of critical thinking resources for the Federated Schools of Accountancy.

DONALD E. KIESO, PhD, CPA, received his bachelor's degree from Aurora University and his doctorate in accounting from the University of Illinois. He has served as chairman of the Department of Accountancy and is currently the KPMG Emeritus Professor of Accountancy at Northern Illinois University. He has public accounting experience with Price Waterhouse & Co. (San Francisco and Chicago) and Arthur Andersen & Co. (Chicago) and research experience with the Research Division of the American Institute of Certified Public Accountants (New York). He has done post doctorate work as a Visiting Scholar at the University of California at Berkeley and is a recipient of NIU's Teaching Excellence Award and four Golden Apple Teaching Awards. Professor Kieso is the author of other accounting and business books and is a member of the American Accounting Association, the American Institute of Certified Public Accountants, and the Illinois CPA Society. He has served as a member of the Board of Directors of the Illinois CPA Society, then AACSB's Accounting Accreditation Committees, the State of Illinois Comptroller's Commission, as Secretary-Treasurer of the Federation of Schools of Accountancy, and as Secretary-Treasurer of the American Accounting Association. Professor Kieso is currently serving on the Board of Trustees and Executive Committee of Aurora University, as a member of the Board of Directors of Kishwaukee Community Hospital, and as Treasurer and Director of Valley West Community Hospital. From 1989 to 1993 he served as a charter member of the national Accounting Education Change Commission. He is the recipient of the Outstanding Accounting Educator Award from the Illinois CPA Society, the FSA's Joseph A. Silvoso Award of Merit, the NIU Foundation's Humanitarian Award for Service to Higher Education, a Distinguished Service Award from the Illinois CPA Society, and in 2003 an honorary doctorate from Aurora University.

Practice Made Simple

The Team for Success is focused on helping students get the most out of their accounting course by **making practice simple**. Both in the printed text and the online environment of *WileyPLUS*, new opportunities for self-guided practice allow students to check their knowledge of accounting concepts, skills, and problem-solving techniques as they receive individual feedback at the question, learning objective, and course level.

Personalized Practice

Based on cognitive science, **WileyPLUS with ORION** is a personalized, adaptive learning experience that gives students the practice they need to build proficiency on topics while using their study time most effectively. The adaptive engine is powered by hundreds of unique questions per chapter, giving students endless opportunities for practice throughout the course.

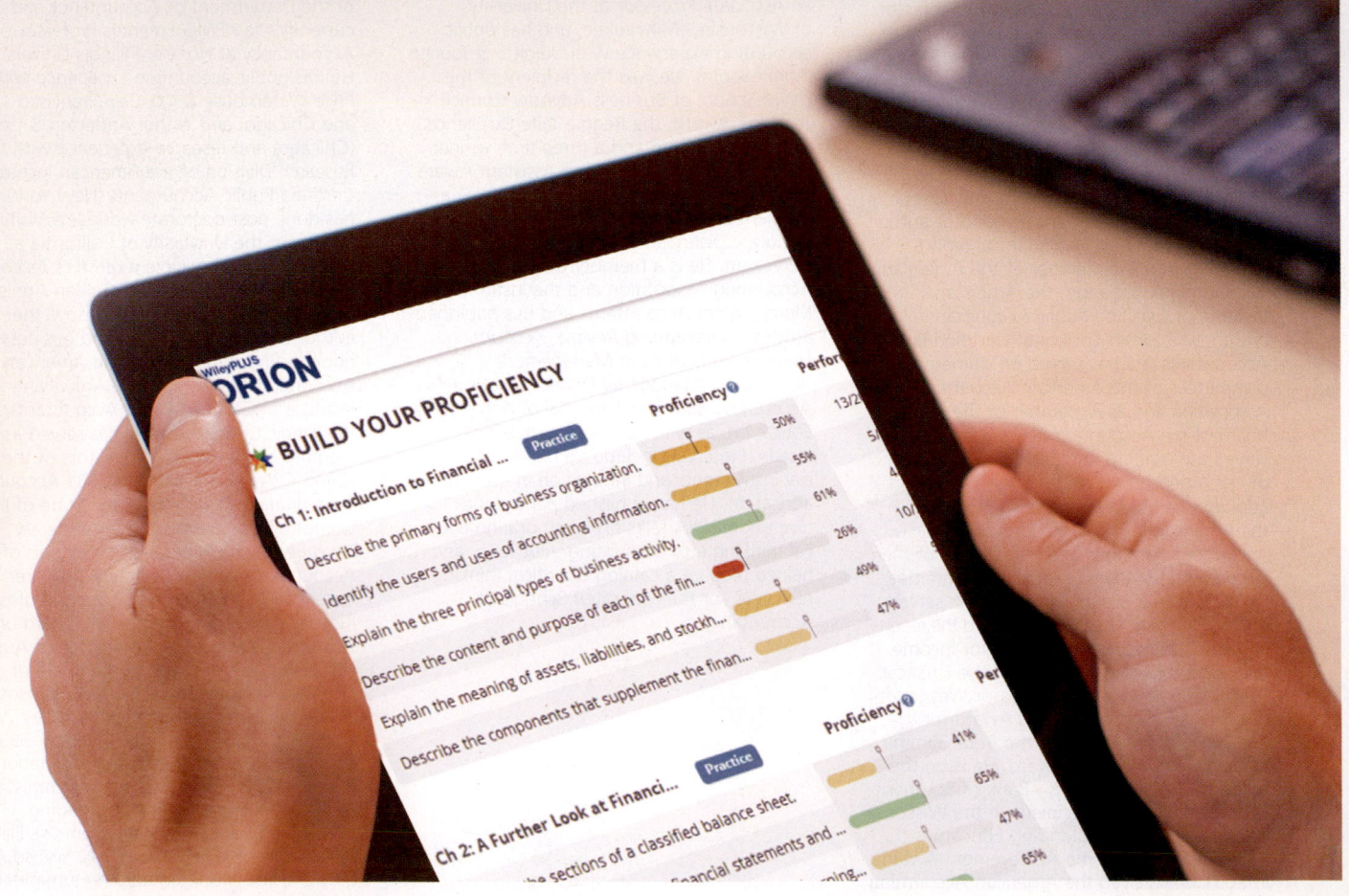

Streamlined Learning Objectives

Newly streamlined learning objectives help students make the best use of their time outside of class. Each learning objective is addressed by reading content, answering a variety of practice and assessment questions, and watching educational videos, so that no matter where students begin their work, the relevant resources and practice are readily accessible.

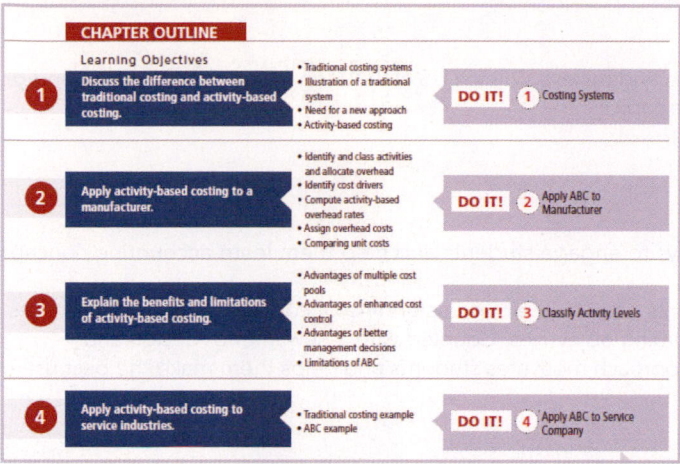

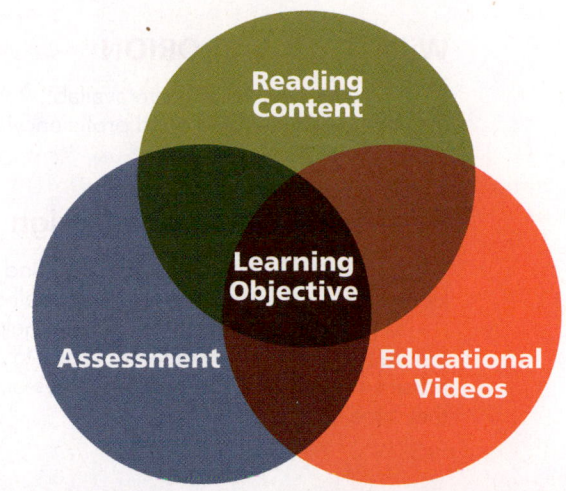

Review and Practice

A new section in the text and in **WileyPLUS** offers students more opportunities for self-guided practice.

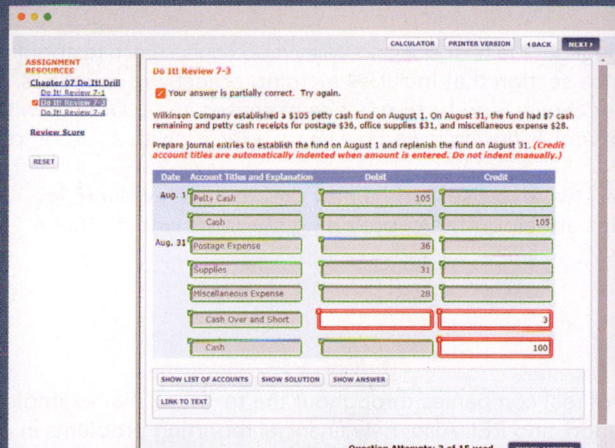

In the text, the new Review and Practice section includes:

- Learning Objectives Review
- Glossary Review
- Practice Multiple-Choice Questions and Solutions
- Practice Exercises and Solutions
- Practice Problem and Solution

In **WileyPLUS**, the new practice assignments include several Do ITs, Brief Exercises, Exercises, and Problems, giving students the opportunity to check their work or see the answer and solution after their final attempt.

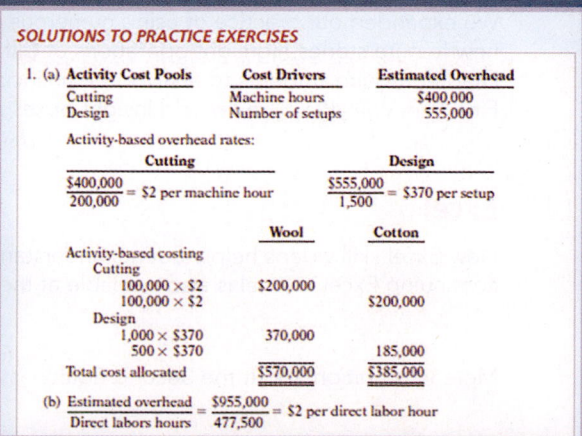

What's New?

WileyPLUS with ORION

Over 5,500 new questions are available for practice and review. WileyPLUS with Orion is an adaptive study and practice tool that helps students build proficiency in course topics.

Updated Content and Design

We scrutinized all chapter material to find new ways to engage students and help them learn accounting concepts. Homework problems were updated in all chapters.

A new learning objective structure helps students practice their understanding of concepts with **DO IT!** exercises before they move on to different topics in other learning objectives. Coupled with a new interior design and revised infographics, the new outcomes-oriented approach motivates students and helps them make the best use of their time.

WileyPLUS Videos

Over 250 videos are available in WileyPLUS. More than 80 of the videos are new to the Second Edition. The videos walk students through relevant homework problems and solutions, review important concepts, provide overviews of Excel skills, and explore topics in a real-world context.

Student Practice and Solutions

New practice opportunities with solutions are integrated throughout the textbook and WileyPLUS course. Each textbook chapter now provides students with a **Review and Practice** section that includes learning objective summaries, multiple-choice questions with feedback for each answer choice, and both practice exercises and problems with solutions. Also, each learning objective module in the textbook is now followed by a **DO IT!** exercise with an accompanying solution.

In **WileyPLUS**, two brief exercises, two **DO IT!** exercises, two exercises, and a new problem are available for practice with each chapter. These new practice questions are algorithmic, providing students with multiple opportunities for advanced practice.

Real World Context

We expanded our practice of using numerous examples of real companies throughout the textbook. For example, new feature stories highlight operations of Clif Bar, Groupon, and REI. Also, new financial reporting problems in each chapter require students to analyze the financial statements of Apple, Wal-Mart, Louis Vuitton, and Amazon.com. Finally, in WileyPLUS, real-world Insight boxes now have questions that can be assigned as homework.

Excel

New Excel skill videos help students understand Excel features they can apply in their accounting studies. A new continuing Excel tutorial is also available at the end of each managerial accounting chapter.

More information about the Second Edition is available on the book's website at **www.wiley.com/college/weygandt**.

Table of Contents

1 Accounting in Action 2

Knowing the Numbers: **Clif Bar 2**
LO 1: Identify the activities and users associated with accounting. 4
  Three Activities 4
  Who Uses Accounting Data? 5
LO 2: Explain the building blocks of accounting: ethics, principles, and assumptions. 7
  Ethics in Financial Reporting 7
  Generally Accepted Accounting Principles 9
  Measurement Principles 9
  Assumptions 9
LO 3: State the accounting equation, and define its components. 12
  Assets 12
  Liabilities 12
  Stockholders' Equity 12
LO 4: Analyze the effects of business transactions on the accounting equation. 14
  Transaction Analysis 15
  Summary of Transactions 19
LO 5: Describe the four financial statements and how they are prepared. 21
  Income Statement 21
  Retained Earnings Statement 21
  Balance Sheet 23
  Statement of Cash Flows 23
LO *6: APPENDIX 1A: Explain the career opportunities in accounting. 25
  Public Accounting 25
  Private Accounting 25
  Governmental Accounting 25
  Forensic Accounting 26
  "Show Me the Money" 26
A Look at IFRS 46

2 The Recording Process 48

Accidents Happen: **MF Global Holdings 48**
LO 1: Describe how accounts, debits, and credits are used to record business transactions. 50
  Debits and Credits 50
  Stockholders' Equity Relationships 54
  Summary of Debit/Credit Rules 54
LO 2: Indicate how a journal is used in the recording process. 55
  Steps in the Recording Process 55
  The Journal 56

LO 3: Explain how a ledger and posting help in the recording process. 58
  The Ledger 58
  Posting 60
  The Recording Process Illustrated 62
  Summary Illustration of Journalizing and Posting 67
LO 4: Prepare a trial balance. 69
  Limitations of a Trial Balance 69
  Locating Errors 70
  Dollar Signs and Underlining 70
A Look at IFRS 92

3 Adjusting the Accounts 94

Keeping Track of Groupons: **Groupon 94**
LO 1: Explain the accrual basis of accounting and the reasons for adjusting entries. 96
  Fiscal and Calendar Years 96
  Accrual- versus Cash-Basis Accounting 96
  Recognizing Revenues and Expenses 97
  The Need for Adjusting Entries 98
  Types of Adjusting Entries 98
LO 2: Prepare adjusting entries for deferrals. 100
  Prepaid Expenses 100
  Unearned Revenues 104
LO 3: Prepare adjusting entries for accruals. 106
  Accrued Revenues 106
  Accrued Expenses 108
  Summary of Basic Relationships 111
LO 4: Describe the nature and purpose of an adjusted trial balance. 113
  Preparing the Adjusted Trial Balance 113
  Preparing Financial Statements 114
LO *5: APPENDIX 3A: Prepare adjusting entries for the alternative treatment of deferrals. 117
  Prepaid Expenses 118
  Unearned Revenues 119
  Summary of Additional Adjustment Relationships 120
LO *6: APPENDIX 3B: Discuss financial reporting concepts. 120
  Qualities of Useful Information 120
  Assumptions in Financial Reporting 121
  Principles in Financial Reporting 122
  Cost Constraint 122
A Look at IFRS 148

4 Completing the Accounting Cycle 150

Everyone Likes to Win: **Rhino Foods 150**
LO 1: Prepare a worksheet. 152
Steps in Preparing a Worksheet 153
Preparing Financial Statements from a
Worksheet 155
Preparing Adjusting Entries from a Worksheet 157
LO 2: Prepare closing entries and a post-closing trial balance. 157
Preparing Closing Entries 158
Posting Closing Entries 160
Preparing a Post-Closing Trial Balance 162
LO 3: Explain the steps in the accounting cycle and how to prepare correcting entries. 165
Summary of the Accounting Cycle 165
Reversing Entries—An Optional Step 165
Correcting Entries—An Avoidable Step 166
LO 4: Identify the sections of a classified balance sheet. 168
Current Assets 168
Long-Term Investments 170
Property, Plant, and Equipment 170
Intangible Assets 170
Current Liabilities 171
Long-Term Liabilities 172
Stockholders' (Owners') Equity 172
LO *5: APPENDIX 4A: Prepare reversing entries. 174
Reversing Entries Example 174
A Look at IFRS 200

5 Accounting for Merchandising Operations 204

Buy Now, Vote Later: **REI 204**
LO 1: Describe merchandising operations and inventory systems. 206
Operating Cycles 206
Flow of Costs 207
LO 2: Record purchases under a perpetual inventory system. 209
Freight Costs 210
Purchase Returns and Allowances 212
Purchase Discounts 212
Summary of Purchasing Transactions 213
LO 3: Record sales under a perpetual inventory system. 214
Sales Returns and Allowances 215
Sales Discounts 216
LO 4: Apply the steps in the accounting cycle to a merchandising company. 218
Adjusting Entries 218

Closing Entries 218
Summary of Merchandising Entries 219
LO 5: Compare a multiple-step with a single-step income statement. 220
Multiple-Step Income Statement 220
Single-Step Income Statement 223
Classified Balance Sheet 224
LO *6: APPENDIX 5A: Prepare a worksheet for a merchandising company. 225
Using a Worksheet 225
LO *7: APPENDIX 5B: Record purchases and sales under a periodic inventory system. 227
Determining Cost of Goods Sold Under a Periodic System 227
Recording Merchandise Transactions 228
Recording Purchases of Merchandise 228
Recording Sales of Merchandise 229
Journalizing and Posting Closing Entries 229
Using a Worksheet 231
A Look at IFRS 256

6 Inventories 258

"Where Is That Spare Bulldozer Blade?": **Caterpillar 258**
LO 1: Discuss how to classify and determine inventory. 260
Classifying Inventory 260
Determining Inventory Quantities 261
LO 2: Apply inventory cost flow methods and discuss their financial effects. 264
Specific Identification 264
Cost Flow Assumptions 265
Financial Statement and Tax Effects of Cost Flow Methods 269
Using Inventory Cost Flow Methods Consistently 271
LO 3: Indicate the effects of inventory errors on the financial statements. 272
Income Statement Effects 272
Balance Sheet Effects 273
LO 4: Explain the statement presentation and analysis of inventory. 274
Presentation 274
Lower-of-Cost-or-Market 274
Analysis 275
LO *5: APPENDIX 6A: Apply the inventory cost flow methods to perpetual inventory records. 277
First-In, First-Out (FIFO) 278
Last-In, First-Out (LIFO) 278
Average-Cost 279
LO *6: APPENDIX 6B: Describe the two methods of estimating inventories. 280
Gross Profit Method 280
Retail Inventory Method 281
A Look at IFRS 304

7 Fraud, Internal Control, and Cash 306

Minding the Money in Madison: **Barriques 306**
LO 1: Discuss fraud and the principles of internal control. 308
Fraud 308
The Sarbanes-Oxley Act 308
Internal Control 309
Principles of Internal Control Activities 309
Limitations of Internal Control 316
LO 2: Apply internal control principles to cash. 317
Cash Receipts Controls 318
Cash Disbursements Controls 320
Petty Cash Fund 322
LO 3: Identify the control features of a bank account. 325
Making Bank Deposits 325
Writing Checks 326
Bank Statements 327
Reconciling the Bank Account 328
Electronic Funds Transfer (EFT) System 332
LO 4: Explain the reporting of cash. 333
Cash Equivalents 333
Restricted Cash 333
A Look at IFRS 354

8 Accounting for Receivables 356

A Dose of Careful Management Keeps Receivables Healthy: **Whitehall-Robins 356**
LO 1: Explain how companies recognize accounts receivable. 358
Types of Receivables 358
Recognizing Accounts Receivable 358
LO 2: Describe how companies value accounts receivable and record their disposition. 360
Valuing Accounts Receivable 360
Disposing of Accounts Receivable 366
LO 3: Explain how companies recognize notes receivable. 369
Determining the Maturity Date 369
Computing Interest 370
Recognizing Notes Receivable 371
LO 4: Describe how companies value notes receivable, record their disposition, and present and analyze receivables. 371
Valuing Notes Receivable 371
Disposing of Notes Receivable 372
Statement Presentation and Analysis 373
A Look at IFRS 393

9 Plant Assets, Natural Resources, and Intangible Assets 396

How Much for a Ride to the Beach?: **Rent-A-Wreck 396**
LO 1: Explain the accounting for plant asset expenditures. 398
Determining the Cost of Plant Assets 398
Expenditures During Useful Life 400
LO 2: Apply depreciation methods to plant assets. 402
Factors in Computing Depreciation 403
Depreciation Methods 403
Depreciation and Income Taxes 408
Revising Periodic Depreciation 408
LO 3: Explain how to account for the disposal of plant assets. 409
Retirement of Plant Assets 410
Sale of Plant Assets 410
LO 4: Describe how to account for natural resources and intangible assets. 412
Natural Resources 412
Depletion 412
Intangible Assets 414
Accounting for Intangible Assets 414
Research and Development Costs 416
LO 5: Discuss how plant assets, natural resources, and intangible assets are reported and analyzed. 417
Presentation 417
Analysis 418
LO *6: APPENDIX 9A: Explain how to account for the exchange of plant assets. 419
Loss Treatment 419
Gain Treatment 420
A Look at IFRS 441

10 Liabilities 444

Financing His Dreams: **Wilbert Murdock 444**
LO 1: Explain how to account for current liabilities. 446
What Is a Current Liability? 446
Notes Payable 446
Sales Taxes Payable 447
Payroll and Payroll Taxes Payable 448
Unearned Revenues 450
Current Maturities of Long-Term Debt 451
LO 2: Describe the major characteristics of bonds. 452
Types of Bonds 452
Issuing Procedures 452

Bond Trading 453
Determining the Market Price of a Bond 454
LO 3: Explain how to account for bond transactions. 456
Issuing Bonds at Face Value 456
Discount or Premium on Bonds 456
Issuing Bonds at a Discount 457
Issuing Bonds at a Premium 459
Redeeming and Converting Bonds 460
LO 4: Explain how to account for long-term notes payable. 462
LO 5: Discuss how liabilities are reported and analyzed. 464
Presentation 464
Use of Ratios 465
Debt and Equity Financing 466
LO *6: APPENDIX 10A: Apply the straight-line method of amortizing bond discount and bond premium. 468
Amortizing Bond Discount 468
Amortizing Bond Premium 469
LO *7: APPENDIX 10B: Apply the effective-interest method of amortizing bond discount and bond premium. 470
Amortizing Bond Discount 471
Amortizing Bond Premium 473
A Look at IFRS 495

11 Corporations: Organization, Stock Transactions, Dividends, and Retained Earnings 498

What's Cooking?: **Nike 498**
LO 1: Discuss the major characteristics of a corporation. 500
Characteristics of a Corporation 500
Forming a Corporation 502
Stockholder Rights 504
Stock Issue Considerations 504
Corporate Capital 507
LO 2: Explain how to account for the issuance of common and preferred stock. 509
Accounting for Common Stock 509
Accounting for Preferred Stock 511
LO 3: Explain how to account for treasury stock. 512
Purchase of Treasury Stock 512
Disposal of Treasury Stock 513
LO 4: Explain how to account for cash dividends. 515
Cash Dividends 515
Dividend Preferences 517
LO 5: Explain how to account for stock dividends and splits. 520
Stock Dividends 520
Stock Splits 522

LO 6: Discuss how stockholders' equity is reported and analyzed. 524
Retained Earnings 524
Statement Presentation and Analysis 528
LO *7: APPENDIX 11A: Describe the use and content of the stockholders' equity statement. 531
LO *8: APPENDIX 11B: Compute book value per share. 531
Book Value per Share 531
Book Value versus Market Price 532
A Look at IFRS 555

12 Investments 558

"Is There Anything Else We Can Buy?":
Time Warner 558
LO 1: Explain how to account for debt investments. 560
Why Corporations Invest 560
Accounting for Debt Investments 561
LO 2: Explain how to account for stock investments. 563
Holdings of Less than 20% 563
Holdings Between 20% and 50% 564
Holdings of More than 50% 566
LO 3: Discuss how debt and stock investments are reported in financial statements. 568
Categories of Securities 568
Balance Sheet Presentation 571
Presentation of Realized and Unrealized Gain or Loss 572
Classified Balance Sheet 573
LO *4: APPENDIX 12A: Describe the form and content of consolidated financial statements as well as how to prepare them. 575
Consolidated Balance Sheet 575
Consolidated Income Statement 578
A Look at IFRS 596

13 Statement of Cash Flows 598

Got Cash?: **Microsoft 598**
LO 1: Discuss the usefulness and format of the statement of cash flows. 600
Usefulness of the Statement of Cash Flows 600
Classification of Cash Flows 600
Significant Noncash Activities 601
Format of the Statement of Cash Flows 602
LO 2: Prepare a statement of cash flows using the indirect method. 603
Indirect and Direct Methods 604
Indirect Method—Computer Services Company 604
Step 1: Operating Activities 606

Summary of Conversion to Net Cash Provided by
Operating Activities—Indirect Method 609
Step 2: Investing and Financing Activities 610
Step 3: Net Change in Cash 611
LO 3: Analyze the statement of cash flows. 614
Free Cash Flow 614
**LO *4: APPENDIX 13A: Prepare a statement of
cash flows using the direct method. 616**
Step 1: Operating Activities 616
Step 2: Investing and Financing Activities 622
Step 3: Net Change in Cash 623
**LO *5: APPENDIX 13B: Use a worksheet to
prepare the statement of cash flows using the
indirect method. 623**
Preparing the Worksheet 624
**LO *6: APPENDIX 13C: Use the T-account approach
to prepare a statement of cash flows. 629**
A Look at IFRS 656

**14 Financial Statement
Analysis 658**

It Pays to Be Patient: Warren Buffett 658
**LO 1: Apply horizontal and vertical analysis to
financial statements. 660**
Need for Comparative Analysis 660
Tools of Analysis 660
Horizontal Analysis 661
Vertical Analysis 664
**LO 2: Analyze a company's performance using ratio
analysis. 666**
Liquidity Ratios 667
Profitability Ratios 670
Solvency Ratios 674
Summary of Ratios 676
LO 3: Apply the concept of sustainable income. 678
Discontinued Operations 679
Other Comprehensive Income 679
A Look at IFRS 707

15 Managerial Accounting 710

Just Add Water . . . and Paddle: Current Designs 710
**LO 1: Identify the features of managerial accounting
and the functions of management. 712**
Comparing Managerial and Financial
Accounting 712
Management Functions 712
Organizational Structure 714
**LO 2: Describe the classes of manufacturing costs
and the differences between product and period
costs. 716**
Manufacturing Costs 716
Product Versus Period Costs 718
Illustration of Cost Concepts 718

**LO 3: Demonstrate how to compute cost of goods
manufactured and prepare financial statements
for a manufacturer. 720**
Income Statement 720
Cost of Goods Manufactured 721
Cost of Goods Manufactured Schedule 722
Balance Sheet 722
**LO 4: Discuss trends in managerial
accounting. 724**
Service Industries 724
Focus on the Value Chain 725
Balanced Scorecard 726
Business Ethics 727
Corporate Social Responsibility 728

16 Job Order Costing 752

Profiting from the Silver Screen: Disney 752
**LO 1: Describe cost systems and the flow of costs
in a job order system. 754**
Process Cost System 754
Job Order Cost System 754
Job Order Cost Flow 755
Accumulating Manufacturing Costs 756
**LO 2: Use a job cost sheet to assign costs to work
in process. 758**
Raw Materials Costs 759
Factory Labor Costs 761
**LO 3: Demonstrate how to determine and use the
predetermined overhead rate. 763**
**LO 4: Prepare entries for manufacturing and service
jobs completed and sold. 766**
Assigning Costs to Finished Goods 766
Assigning Costs to Cost of Goods Sold 767
Summary of Job Order Cost Flows 767
Job Order Costing for Service Companies 769
Advantages and Disadvantages of Job Order
Costing 770
**LO 5: Distinguish between under- and overapplied
manufacturing overhead. 771**
Under- or Overapplied Manufacturing
Overhead 772

17 Process Costing 794

The Little Guy Who Could: Jones Soda Co. 794
**LO 1: Discuss the uses of a process cost
system and how it compares to a job order
system. 796**
Uses of Process Cost Systems 796
Process Costing for Service Companies 797
Similarities and Differences Between
Job Order Cost and Process Cost
Systems 797

LO 2: Explain the flow of costs in a process cost system and the journal entries to assign manufacturing costs. 799
Process Cost Flow 799
Assigning Manufacturing Costs—Journal Entries 799
LO 3: Compute equivalent units. 802
Weighted-Average Method 802
Refinements on the Weighted-Average Method 803
LO 4: Complete the four steps to prepare a production cost report. 805
Compute the Physical Unit Flow (Step 1) 806
Compute the Equivalent Units of Production (Step 2) 806
Compute Unit Production Costs (Step 3) 807
Prepare a Cost Reconciliation Schedule (Step 4) 808
Preparing the Production Cost Report 808
Costing Systems—Final Comments 809
LO *5: APPENDIX 17A: Compute equivalent units using the FIFO method. 810
Equivalent Units Under FIFO 810
Comprehensive Example 811
FIFO and Weighted-Average 815

18 Activity-Based Costing 838

Precor Is on Your Side 838
LO 1: Discuss the difference between traditional costing and activity-based costing. 840
Traditional Costing Systems 840
Illustration of a Traditional Costing System 840
The Need for a New Approach 841
Activity-Based Costing 841
LO 2: Apply activity-based costing to a manufacturer. 844
Identify and Classify Activities and Assign Overhead to Cost Pools (Step 1) 844
Identify Cost Drivers (Step 2) 844
Compute Activity-Based Overhead Rates (Step 3) 845
Allocate Overhead Costs to Products (Step 4) 845
Comparing Unit Costs 846
LO 3: Explain the benefits and limitations of activity-based costing. 849
The Advantage of Multiple Cost Pools 849
The Advantage of Enhanced Cost Control 850
The Advantage of Better Management Decisions 852
Some Limitations and Knowing When to Use ABC 853

LO 4: Apply activity-based costing to service industries. 854
Traditional Costing Example 855
Activity-Based Costing Example 856
LO *5: APPENDIX 18A: Explain just-in-time (JIT) processing. 858
Objective of JIT Processing 859
Elements of JIT Processing 859
Benefits of JIT Processing 859

19 Cost-Volume-Profit 884

Don't Worry—Just Get Big: Amazon.com 884
LO 1: Explain variable, fixed, and mixed costs and the relevant range. 886
Variable Costs 886
Fixed Costs 887
Relevant Range 888
Mixed Costs 889
LO 2: Apply the high-low method to determine the components of mixed costs. 890
High-Low Method 891
Importance of Identifying Variable and Fixed Costs 893
LO 3: Prepare a CVP income statement to determine contribution margin. 894
Basic Components 894
CVP Income Statement 894
LO 4: Compute the break-even point using three approaches. 898
Mathematical Equation 898
Contribution Margin Technique 899
Graphic Presentation 900
LO 5: Determine the sales required to earn target net income and determine margin of safety. 901
Target Net Income 901
Margin of Safety 903

20 Cost-Volume-Profit Analysis: Additional Issues 922

Not Even a Flood Could Stop It: Whole Foods Market 922
LO 1: Apply basic CVP concepts. 924
Basic Concepts 924
Basic Computations 925
CVP and Changes in the Business Environment 926
LO 2: Explain the term sales mix and its effects on break-even sales. 929
Break-Even Sales in Units 929
Break-Even Sales in Dollars 931

LO 3: Determine sales mix when a company has limited resources. 933

LO 4: Indicate how operating leverage affects profitability. 935
Effect on Contribution Margin Ratio 936
Effect on Break-Even Point 936
Effect on Margin of Safety Ratio 937
Operating Leverage 937

LO *5: APPENDIX 20A: Explain the differences between absorption costing and variable costing. 939
Example Comparing Absorption Costing with Variable Costing 939
Net Income Effects 941
Decision-Making Concerns 945
Potential Advantages of Variable Costing 947

21 Incremental Analysis 972

Keeping It Clean: Method Products 972

LO 1: Describe management's decision-making process and incremental analysis. 974
Incremental Analysis Approach 974
How Incremental Analysis Works 975
Qualitative Factors 976
Relationship of Incremental Analysis and Activity-Based Costing 976
Types of Incremental Analysis 977

LO 2: Analyze the relevant costs in accepting an order at a special price. 977

LO 3: Analyze the relevant costs in a make-or-buy decision. 979
Opportunity Cost 980

LO 4: Analyze the relevant costs in determining whether to sell or process materials further. 981
Single-Product Case 982
Multiple-Product Case 982

LO 5: Analyze the relevant costs to be considered in repairing, retaining, or replacing equipment. 985

LO 6: Analyze the relevant costs in deciding whether to eliminate an unprofitable segment or product. 986

22 Pricing 1012

They've Got Your Size—and Color: Zappos.com 1012

LO 1: Compute a target cost when the market determines a product price. 1014
Target Costing 1015

LO 2: Compute a target selling price using cost-plus pricing. 1016

Cost-Plus Pricing 1016
Variable-Cost Pricing 1019

LO 3: Use time-and-material pricing to determine the cost of services provided. 1020

LO 4: Determine a transfer price using the negotiated, cost-based, and market-based approaches. 1024
Negotiated Transfer Prices 1024
Cost-Based Transfer Prices 1027
Market-Based Transfer Prices 1028
Effect of Outsourcing on Transfer Pricing 1029
Transfers Between Divisions in Different Countries 1029

LO *5: APPENDIX 22A: Determine prices using absorption-cost pricing and variable-cost pricing. 1030
Absorption-Cost Pricing 1030
Variable-Cost Pricing 1032

LO *6: APPENDIX 22B: Explain issues involved in transferring goods between divisions in different countries. 1034

23 Budgetary Planning 1056

What's in Your Cupcake?: BabyCakes NYC 1056

LO 1: State the essentials of effective budgeting and the components of the master budget. 1058
Budgeting and Accounting 1058
The Benefits of Budgeting 1058
Essentials of Effective Budgeting 1058
The Master Budget 1061

LO 2: Prepare budgets for sales, production, and direct materials. 1063
Sales Budget 1063
Production Budget 1064
Direct Materials Budget 1065

LO 3: Prepare budgets for direct labor, manufacturing overhead, and selling and administrative expenses, and a budgeted income statement. 1068
Direct Labor Budget 1068
Manufacturing Overhead Budget 1069
Selling and Administrative Expense Budget 1070
Budgeted Income Statement 1070

LO 4: Prepare a cash budget and a budgeted balance sheet. 1072
Cash Budget 1072
Budgeted Balance Sheet 1075

LO 5: Apply budgeting principles to nonmanufacturing companies. 1077
Merchandisers 1077
Service Companies 1078
Not-for-Profit Organizations 1079

24 Budgetary Control and Responsibility Accounting 1106

Pumpkin Madeleines and a Movie: **Tribeca Grand Hotel 1106**

LO 1: Describe budgetary control and static budget reports. 1108
Budgetary Control 1108
Static Budget Reports 1109

LO 2: Prepare flexible budget reports. 1111
Why Flexible Budgets? 1111
Developing the Flexible Budget 1114
Flexible Budget—A Case Study 1114
Flexible Budget Reports 1116

LO 3: Apply responsibility accounting to cost and profit centers. 1118
Controllable versus Noncontrollable Revenues and Costs 1120
Principles of Performance Evaluation 1120
Responsibility Reporting System 1122
Types of Responsibility Centers 1124

LO 4: Evaluate performance in investment centers. 1127
Return on Investment (ROI) 1127
Responsibility Report 1128
Judgmental Factors in ROI 1129
Improving ROI 1129

LO *5: APPENDIX 24A: Explain the difference between ROI and residual income. 1131
Residual Income Compared to ROI 1132
Residual Income Weakness 1132

25 Standard Costs and Balanced Scorecard 1158

80,000 Different Caffeinated Combinations: **Starbucks 1158**

LO 1: Describe standard costs. 1160
Distinguishing Between Standards and Budgets 1161
Setting Standard Costs 1161

LO 2: Determine direct materials variances. 1165
Analyzing and Reporting Variances 1165
Direct Materials Variances 1166

LO 3: Determine direct labor and total manufacturing overhead variances. 1169
Direct Labor Variances 1169
Manufacturing Overhead Variances 1171

LO 4: Prepare variance reports and balanced scorecards. 1173
Reporting Variances 1173
Income Statement Presentation of Variances 1174
Balanced Scorecard 1175

LO *5: APPENDIX 25A: Identify the features of a standard cost accounting system. 1178
Journal Entries 1178
Ledger Accounts 1180

LO *6: APPENDIX 25B: Compute overhead controllable and volume variances. 1181
Overhead Controllable Variance 1181
Overhead Volume Variance 1182

26 Planning for Capital Investments 1204

Floating Hotels: **Holland America Line 1204**

LO 1: Describe capital budgeting inputs and apply the cash payback technique. 1206
Cash Flow Information 1206
Illustrative Data 1207
Cash Payback 1207

LO 2: Use the net present value method. 1209
Equal Annual Cash Flows 1210
Unequal Annual Cash Flows 1211
Choosing a Discount Rate 1212
Simplifying Assumptions 1213
Comprehensive Example 1213

LO 3: Identify capital budgeting challenges and refinements. 1214
Intangible Benefits 1214
Profitability Index for Mutually Exclusive Projects 1216
Risk Analysis 1218
Post-Audit of Investment Projects 1218

LO 4: Use the internal rate of return method. 1219
Comparing Discounted Cash Flow Methods 1221

LO 5: Use the annual rate of return method. 1222

A Specimen Financial Statements: Apple Inc. A-1

B Specimen Financial Statements: PepsiCo, Inc. B-1

C Specimen Financial Statements: The Coca-Cola Company C-1

D Specimen Financial Statements: Amazon.com, Inc. **D-1**

E Specimen Financial Statements: Wal-Mart Stores, Inc. **E-1**

F Specimen Financial Statements: Louis Vuitton **F-1**

G Time Value of Money **G-1**

LO 1: **Compute interest and future values. G-1**
Nature of Interest G-1
Future Value of a Single Amount G-3
Future Value of an Annuity G-4
LO 2: **Compute present values. G-7**
Present Value Variables G-7
Present Value of a Single Amount G-7
Present Value of an Annuity G-9
Time Periods and Discounting G-11
Present Value of a Long-Term Note or Bond G-11
LO 3: **Compute the present value in capital budgeting situations. G-14**
LO 4: **Use a financial calculator to solve time value of money problems. G-15**
Present Value of a Single Sum G-16
Present Value of an Annuity G-17
Useful Applications of the Financial Calculator G-17

H Payroll Accounting* **H-1**

LO 1: **Record the payroll for a pay period. H-1**
Determining the Payroll H-1
Recording the Payroll H-5
LO 2: **Record employer payroll taxes. H-7**
FICA Taxes H-7
Federal Unemployment Taxes H-8
State Unemployment Taxes H-8
Recording Employer Payroll Taxes H-9
Filing and Remitting Payroll Taxes H-9
LO 3: **Discuss the objectives of internal control for payroll. H-10**

I Subsidiary Ledgers and Special Journals* **I-1**

LO 1: **Describe the nature and purpose of a subsidiary ledger. I-1**
Subsidiary Ledger Example I-2
Advantages of Subsidiary Ledgers I-2
LO 2: **Record transactions in special journals. I-4**
Sales Journal I-4
Cash Receipts Journal I-7
Purchases Journal I-11
Cash Payments Journal I-13
Effects of Special Journals on the General Journal I-16
Cyber Security: A Final Comment I-17

J Other Significant Liabilities* **J-1**

LO 1: **Describe the accounting and disclosure requirements for contingent liabilities. J-1**
Recording a Contingent Liability J-2
Disclosure of Contingent Liabilities J-3
LO 2: **Discuss the accounting for lease liabilities and off-balance-sheet financing. J-3**
Operating Leases J-3
Capital Leases J-4
LO 3: **Discuss additional fringe benefits associated with employee compensation. J-5**
Paid Absences J-5
Postretirement Benefits J-6

K Standards of Ethical Conduct for Management Accountants* **K-1**

IMA Statement of Ethical Professional Practice K-1
Principles K-1
Standards K-1
Resolution of Ethical Conflict K-2

Cases for Managerial Decision-Making*

Company Index I-1
Subject Index I-5

*Available online at www.wiley.com/college/weygandt.

Acknowledgments

Financial and Managerial Accounting has benefited greatly from the input of focus group participants, manuscript reviewers, those who have sent comments by letter or e-mail, ancillary authors, and proofers. We greatly appreciate the constructive suggestions and innovative ideas of reviewers and the creativity and accuracy of the ancillary authors and checkers.

Second Edition

Shawn Abbott
College of the Siskiyous

Joseph Adamo
Cazenovia College

Pushpa Agrawal
University of Nebraska—Kearney

Sol Ahiarah
SUNY—Buffalo State

Lynn Almond
Virginia Polytechnic Institute

Elizabeth Ammann
Lindenwood University

Joe Atallah
Coastline Community College

Timothy Baker
California State University—Fresno

Lisa Banks
Mott Community College

Joyce Barden
DeVry University

Melody Barta
Evergreen Valley College

Jeffrey Beatty
Fresno City College

Linda Bell
Park University

David Bojarsky
California State University—Long Beach

Jack Borke
University of Wisconsin—Platteville

Anna Boulware
St. Charles Community College

Linda Bressler
University of Houston—Downtown

Ann K. Brooks
University of New Mexico

Robert Brown
Evergreen Valley College

Melodi Bunting
Edgewood College

Amy Chang
San Francisco State University

Sandy Cereola
James Madison University

James Chiafery
University of Massachusetts—Boston

Bea Chiang
The College of New Jersey

Cheryl Clark
Point Park University

Stephen Collins
University of Massachusetts—Lowell

Maxine Cohen
Bergen Community College

Arthur College
Evergreen Valley College

Solveg Cooper
Cuesta College

William Cooper
North Carolina A&T State University

Alan E. Davis
Community College of Philadelphia

Steven Day
Dixie State University

Michael Deschamps
MiraCosta College

Bettye Desselle
Texas Southern University

Cyril Dibie
Tarrant County College—Arlington

Jean Dunn
Rady School of Management at University of California—San Diego

Frank Ehresmann
Mercy College

Dennis Elam
Texas A&M University—San Antonio

James Emig
Villanova University

Jeanne Franco
Paradise Valley Community College

Patrick Geer
Hawkeye Community College

Andrew Griffith
Iona College

Jeffrey Haber
Iona College

John Hogan
Fisher College

M.A. Houston
Wright State University

Jeff Hsu
St. Louis Community College—Meramec

Janet Jamieson
University of Dubuque

Kevin Jones
Drexel University

Lynn Krausse
Bakersfield College

Jeffrey T. Kunz
Carroll University

Steven LaFave
Augsburg College

Suneel Maheshwari
Marshall University

Diane Marker
University of Toledo

Christian Mastilak
Xavier University

Josephine Mathias
Mercer County Community College

Michael J. MacDonald
University of Wisconsin—Whitewater

Edward McGinnis
American River College

Pam Meyer
University of Louisiana—Lafayette

Mary Michel
Manhattan College

Joan Miller
William Paterson University

Syed Moiz
University of Wisconsin—Platteville

Johnna Murray
University of Missouri—St. Louis

Lee Nicholas
University of Northern Iowa

Rosemary Nurre
College of San Mateo

Cindy Nye
Bellevue University

Obeua Parsons
Rider University

Gary Olsen
Carroll University

Glenn Pate
Palm Beach State College

Nori Pearson
Washington State University

Joe Pecore
Rady School of Management at University of California—San Diego

Timothy Peterson
Gustavus Adolphus College

Jim Resnik
Bergen Community College

We thank Benjamin Huegel and Teresa Speck of St. Mary's University for their extensive efforts in the preparation of the homework materials related to Current Designs. We also appreciate the considerable support provided to us by the following people at Current Designs: Mike Cichanowski, Jim Brown, Diane Buswell, and Jake Greseth. We also benefited from the assistance and suggestions provided to us by Joan Van Hise in the preparation of materials related to sustainability.

We appreciate the exemplary support and commitment given to us by executive editor Michael McDonald, senior marketing manager Karolina Zarychta Honsa, customer and product development manager Christopher DeJohn, development editor Ed Brislin, associate development editor Courtney Luzzi, market solutions assistant Elizabeth Kearns, marketing assistant Anna Wilhelm, editorial supervisor Terry Ann Tatro, editorial associate Margaret Thompson, product design manager Allie Morris, product design associate Matt Origoni, designers Maureen Eide and Kristine Carney, photo editor Mary Ann Price, indexer Steve Ingle, and Denise Showers at Aptara. All of these professionals provided innumerable services that helped the textbook take shape.

Finally, our thanks to Amy Scholz, Susan Elbe, George Hoffman, Tim Stookesberry, Douglas Reiner, Brent Gordon, Joe Heider, and Steve Smith for their support and leadership in Wiley's Global Education. We will appreciate suggestions and comments from users—instructors and students alike. You can send your thoughts and ideas about the textbook to us via email at: *AccountingAuthors@yahoo.com*.

Jerry J. Weygandt   Paul D. Kimmel   Donald E. Kieso
Madison, Wisconsin   Milwaukee, Wisconsin   DeKalb, Illinois

*The **Chapter Preview** describes the purpose of the chapter and highlights major topics.*

CHAPTER PREVIEW The Feature Story below about Clif Bar & Company highlights the importance of having good financial information and knowing how to use it to make effective business decisions. Whatever your pursuits or occupation, the need for financial information is inescapable. You cannot earn a living, spend money, buy on credit, make an investment, or pay taxes without receiving, using, or dispensing financial information. Good decision-making depends on good information. The purpose of this chapter is to show you that accounting is the system used to provide useful financial information.

*The **Feature Story** helps you picture how the chapter topic relates to the real world of accounting and business.*

FEATURE STORY

Knowing the Numbers

Many students who take this course do not plan to be accountants. If you are in that group, you might be thinking, "If I'm not going to be an accountant, why do I need to know accounting?" Well, consider this quote from Harold Geneen, the former chairman of IT&T: "To be good at your business, you have to know the numbers—cold." In business, accounting and financial statements are the means for communicating the numbers. If you don't know how to read financial statements, you can't really know your business.

Many businesses agree with this view. They see the value of their employees being able to read financial statements and understand how their actions affect the company's financial results. For example, consider Clif Bar & Company. The original Clif Bar® energy bar was created in 1990 by Gary Erickson and his mother in her kitchen. Today, the company has almost 300 employees.

Clif Bar is guided by what it calls its Five Aspirations—Sustaining Our Business, Our Brands, Our People, Our Community, and the Planet. Its website documents its efforts and accomplishments in these five areas. Just a few examples include the company's use of organic products to protect soil, water, and biodiversity; the "smart" solar array (the largest in North America), which provides nearly all the electrical needs for its 115,000-square foot building; and the incentives Clif

Bar provides to employees to reduce their personal environmental impact, such as $6,500 toward the purchase of an efficient car or $1,000 per year for eco-friendly improvements toward their homes.

One of the company's proudest moments was the creation of an employee stock ownership plan (ESOP) in 2010. This plan gives its employees 20% ownership of the company (Gary and his wife Kit own the other 80%). The ESOP also resulted in Clif Bar enacting an open-book management program, including the commitment to educate all employee-owners about its finances. Armed with this basic financial knowledge, employees are more aware of the financial impact of their actions, which leads to better decisions.

Many other companies have adopted this open-book management approach. But even in companies that do not practice open-book management, employers generally assume that managers in all areas of the company are "financially literate."

Taking this course will go a long way to making you financially literate. In this textbook, you will learn how to read and prepare financial statements, and how to use basic tools to evaluate financial results. Throughout this textbook, we attempt to increase your familiarity with financial reporting by providing numerous references, questions, and exercises that encourage you to explore the financial statements of well-known companies.

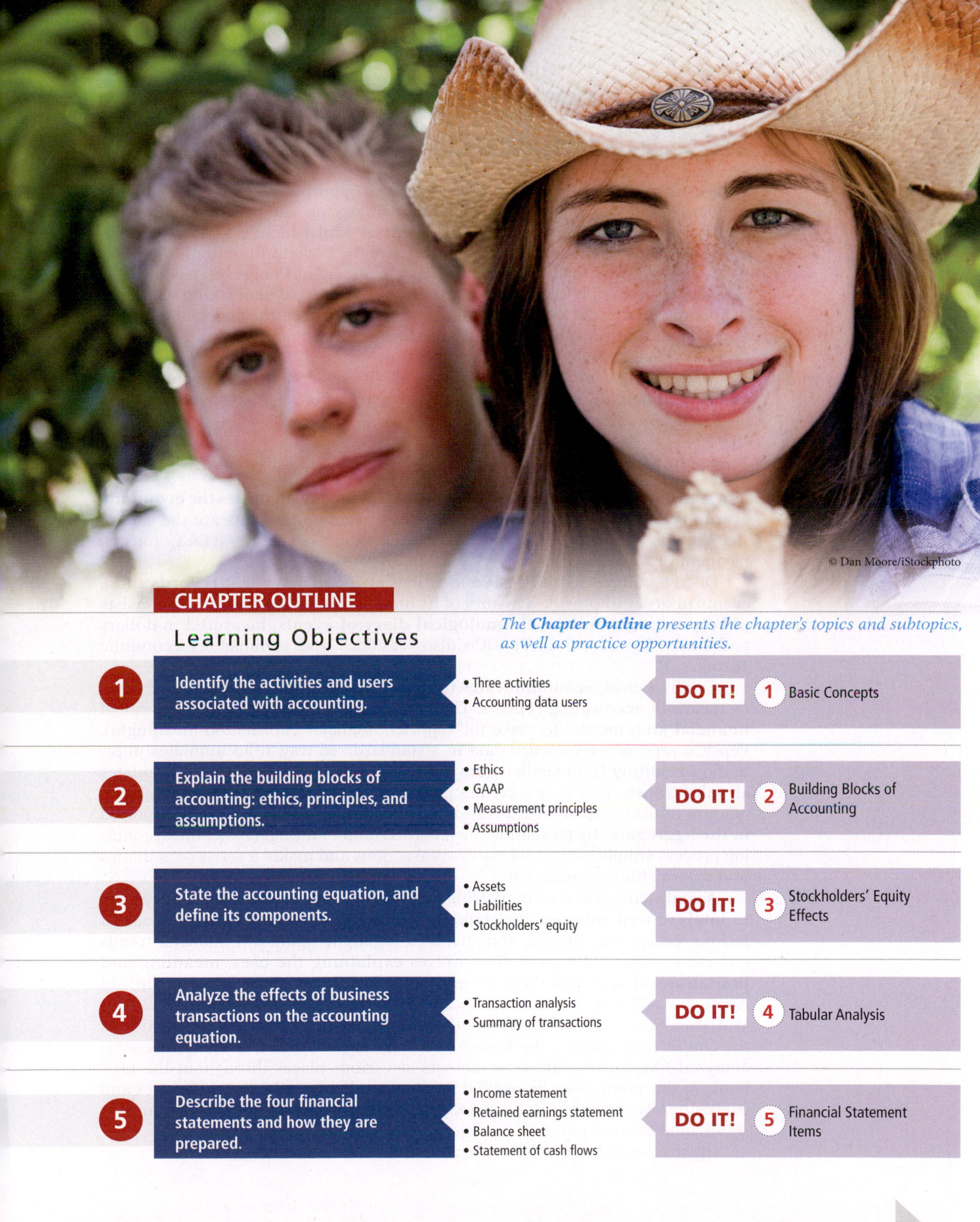

© Dan Moore/iStockphoto

CHAPTER OUTLINE

Learning Objectives

*The **Chapter Outline** presents the chapter's topics and subtopics, as well as practice opportunities.*

1 Identify the activities and users associated with accounting.
- Three activities
- Accounting data users

DO IT! 1 Basic Concepts

2 Explain the building blocks of accounting: ethics, principles, and assumptions.
- Ethics
- GAAP
- Measurement principles
- Assumptions

DO IT! 2 Building Blocks of Accounting

3 State the accounting equation, and define its components.
- Assets
- Liabilities
- Stockholders' equity

DO IT! 3 Stockholders' Equity Effects

4 Analyze the effects of business transactions on the accounting equation.
- Transaction analysis
- Summary of transactions

DO IT! 4 Tabular Analysis

5 Describe the four financial statements and how they are prepared.
- Income statement
- Retained earnings statement
- Balance sheet
- Statement of cash flows

DO IT! 5 Financial Statement Items

Go to the **REVIEW AND PRACTICE** section at the end of the chapter for a review of key concepts and practice applications with solutions.

Visit **WileyPLUS with ORION** for additional tutorials and practice opportunities.

Identify the activities and users associated with accounting.

Essential terms are printed in blue when they first appear, and are defined in the end-of-chapter Glossary Review.

What consistently ranks as one of the top career opportunities in business? What frequently rates among the most popular majors on campus? What was the undergraduate degree chosen by Nike founder Phil Knight, Home Depot co-founder Arthur Blank, former acting director of the Federal Bureau of Investigation (FBI) Thomas Pickard, and numerous members of Congress? Accounting.[1] Why did these people choose accounting? They wanted to understand what was happening financially to their organizations. Accounting is the financial information system that provides these insights. In short, to understand your organization, you have to know the numbers.

Accounting consists of three basic activities—it **identifies**, **records**, and **communicates** the economic events of an organization to interested users. Let's take a closer look at these three activities.

Three Activities

As a starting point to the accounting process, a company **identifies** the **economic events relevant to its business**. Examples of economic events are the sale of snack chips by PepsiCo, the provision of telephone services by AT&T, and the payment of wages by Facebook.

Once a company like PepsiCo identifies economic events, it **records** those events in order to provide a history of its financial activities. Recording consists of keeping a **systematic**, **chronological diary of events**, measured in dollars and cents. In recording, PepsiCo also classifies and summarizes economic events.

Finally, PepsiCo **communicates** the collected information to interested users by means of **accounting reports**. The most common of these reports are called **financial statements**. To make the reported financial information meaningful, PepsiCo reports the recorded data in a standardized way. It accumulates information resulting from similar transactions. For example, PepsiCo accumulates all sales transactions over a certain period of time and reports the data as one amount in the company's financial statements. Such data are said to be reported **in the aggregate**. By presenting the recorded data in the aggregate, the accounting process simplifies a multitude of transactions and makes a series of activities understandable and meaningful.

A vital element in communicating economic events is the accountant's ability to **analyze and interpret** the reported information. Analysis involves use of ratios, percentages, graphs, and charts to highlight significant financial trends and relationships. Interpretation involves **explaining the uses**, **meaning**, **and limitations of reported data**. Appendices A–E show the financial statements of Apple Inc., PepsiCo, Inc., The Coca-Cola Company, Amazon.com, Inc., and Wal-Mart Stores, Inc., respectively. (In addition, in the *A Look at IFRS* section at the end of each chapter, the French company Louis Vuitton Moët Hennessy is analyzed.) We refer to these statements at various places throughout the textbook. At this point, these financial statements probably strike you as complex and confusing. By the end of this course, you'll be surprised at your ability to understand, analyze, and interpret them.

Illustration 1-1 summarizes the activities of the accounting process.

---

[1]The appendix to this chapter describes job opportunities for accounting majors and explains why accounting is such a popular major.

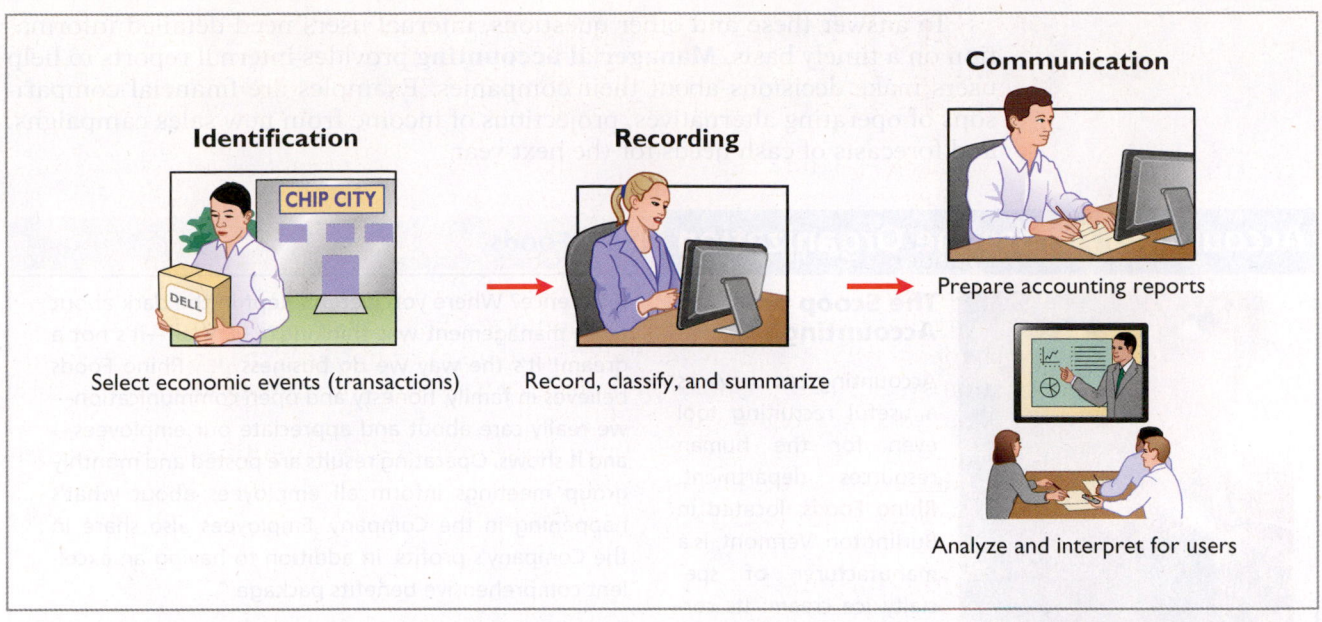

Identification

Select economic events (transactions)

Recording

Record, classify, and summarize

Communication

Prepare accounting reports

Analyze and interpret for users

Illustration 1-1
The activities of the accounting process

You should understand that the accounting process **includes** the bookkeeping function. **Bookkeeping** usually involves **only** the recording of economic events. It is therefore just one part of the accounting process. In total, accounting involves **the entire process of identifying**, **recording**, **and communicating economic events**.[2]

Who Uses Accounting Data

The financial information that users need depends upon the kinds of decisions they make. There are two broad groups of users of financial information: internal users and external users.

INTERNAL USERS

Internal users of accounting information are managers who plan, organize, and run the business. These include marketing managers, production supervisors, finance directors, and company officers. In running a business, internal users must answer many important questions, as shown in Illustration 1-2.

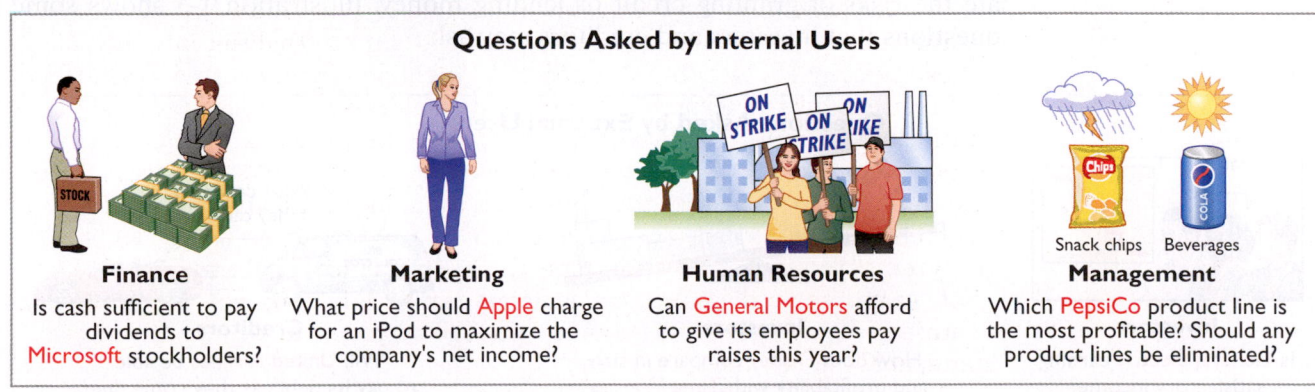

Questions Asked by Internal Users

Finance
Is cash sufficient to pay dividends to Microsoft stockholders?

Marketing
What price should Apple charge for an iPod to maximize the company's net income?

Human Resources
Can General Motors afford to give its employees pay raises this year?

Management
Snack chips   Beverages
Which PepsiCo product line is the most profitable? Should any product lines be eliminated?

Illustration 1-2
Questions that internal users ask

[2]The origins of accounting are generally attributed to the work of Luca Pacioli, an Italian Renaissance mathematician. Pacioli was a close friend and tutor to Leonardo da Vinci and a contemporary of Christopher Columbus. In his 1494 text *Summa de Arithmetica, Geometria, Proportione et Proportionalite*, Pacioli described a system to ensure that financial information was recorded efficiently and accurately.

To answer these and other questions, internal users need detailed information on a timely basis. **Managerial accounting** provides internal reports to help users make decisions about their companies. Examples are financial comparisons of operating alternatives, projections of income from new sales campaigns, and forecasts of cash needs for the next year.

Accounting Across the Organization Rhino Foods

© Agnieszka Pastuszak-Maksim/iStockphoto

The Scoop on Accounting

Accounting can serve as a useful recruiting tool even for the human resources department. Rhino Foods, located in Burlington, Vermont, is a manufacturer of specialty ice cream. Its corporate website includes the following:

"Wouldn't it be great to work where you were part of a team? Where your input and hard work made a difference? Where you weren't kept in the dark about what management was thinking? . . . Well—it's not a dream! It's the way we do business . . . Rhino Foods believes in family, honesty and open communication— we really care about and appreciate our employees— and it shows. Operating results are posted and monthly group meetings inform all employees about what's happening in the Company. Employees also share in the Company's profits, in addition to having an excellent comprehensive benefits package."

Source: www.rhinofoods.com/workforus/workforus.html.

What are the benefits to the company and its employees of making the financial statements available to all employees? (Go to **WileyPLUS** for this answer and additional questions.)

Accounting Across the Organization boxes demonstrate applications of accounting information in various business functions.

EXTERNAL USERS

External users are individuals and organizations outside a company who want financial information about the company. The two most common types of external users are investors and creditors. **Investors** (owners) use accounting information to decide whether to buy, hold, or sell ownership shares of a company. **Creditors** (such as suppliers and bankers) use accounting information to evaluate the risks of granting credit or lending money. Illustration 1-3 shows some questions that investors and creditors may ask.

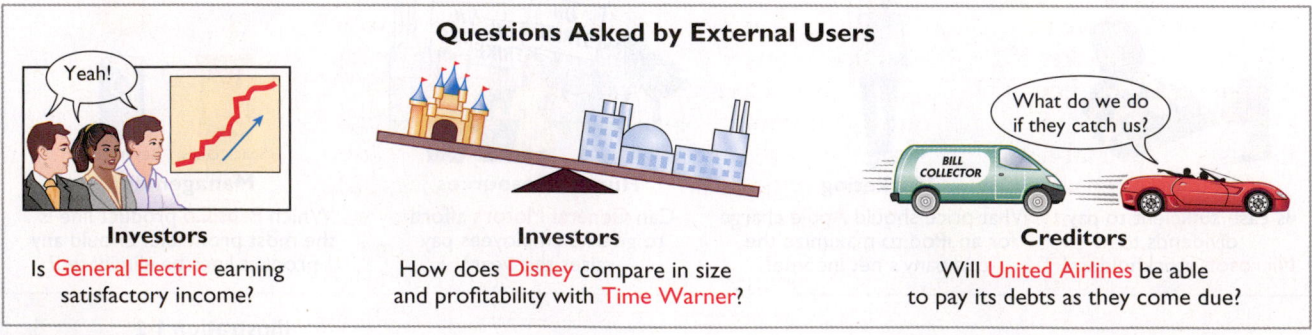

Questions Asked by External Users

Investors
Is General Electric earning satisfactory income?

Investors
How does Disney compare in size and profitability with Time Warner?

Creditors
Will United Airlines be able to pay its debts as they come due?

Illustration 1-3
Questions that external users ask

Financial accounting answers these questions. It provides economic and financial information for investors, creditors, and other external users. The information needs of external users vary considerably. **Taxing authorities**, such as the Internal Revenue Service, want to know whether the company complies with tax laws. **Regulatory agencies**, such as the Securities and Exchange

Commission or the Federal Trade Commission, want to know whether the company is operating within prescribed rules. **Customers** are interested in whether a company like Telsa will continue to honor product warranties and support its product lines. **Labor unions** such as the Major League Baseball Players Association want to know whether the owners have the ability to pay increased wages and benefits.

*The **DO IT!** exercises ask you to put newly acquired knowledge to work. They outline the **Action Plan** necessary to complete the exercise, and they show a **Solution**.*

DO IT! 1 Basic Concepts

Indicate whether each of the five statements presented below is true or false.

1. The three steps in the accounting process are identification, recording, and communication.
2. Bookkeeping encompasses all steps in the accounting process.
3. Accountants prepare, but do not interpret, financial reports.
4. The two most common types of external users are investors and company officers.
5. Managerial accounting activities focus on reports for internal users.

Solution

1. True.   2. False. Bookkeeping involves only the recording step.   3. False. Accountants analyze and interpret information in reports as part of the communication step.   4. False. The two most common types of external users are investors and creditors.   5. True.

Related exercise material: **E1-1, E1-2, and DO IT! 1-1.**

Action Plan
✔ Review the basic concepts discussed.
✔ Develop an understanding of the key terms used.

LEARNING OBJECTIVE **2**

Explain the building blocks of accounting: ethics, principles, and assumptions.

A doctor follows certain protocols in treating a patient's illness. An architect follows certain structural guidelines in designing a building. Similarly, an accountant follows certain standards in reporting financial information. These standards are based on specific principles and assumptions. For these standards to work, however, a fundamental business concept must be present—ethical behavior.

Ethics in Financial Reporting

People won't gamble in a casino if they think it is "rigged." Similarly, people won't play the stock market if they think stock prices are rigged. In recent years, the financial press has been full of articles about financial scandals at Enron, World-Com, HealthSouth, AIG, and other companies. As the scandals came to light, mistrust of financial reporting in general grew. One article in the *Wall Street Journal* noted that "repeated disclosures about questionable accounting practices have bruised investors' faith in the reliability of earnings reports, which in turn has sent stock prices tumbling." Imagine trying to carry on a business or invest money if you could not depend on the financial statements to be honestly prepared. Information would have no credibility. There is no doubt that a sound, well-functioning economy depends on accurate and dependable financial reporting.

United States regulators and lawmakers were very concerned that the economy would suffer if investors lost confidence in corporate accounting because of unethical financial reporting. In response, Congress passed the **Sarbanes-Oxley Act (SOX)**. Its intent is to reduce unethical corporate behavior and decrease the likelihood of future corporate scandals. As a result of SOX, top management must now certify the accuracy of financial information. In addition, penalties for

ETHICS NOTE

Circus-founder P.T. Barnum is alleged to have said, "Trust everyone, but cut the deck." What Sarbanes-Oxley does is to provide measures that (like cutting the deck of playing cards) help ensure that fraud will not occur.

Ethics Notes help sensitize you to some of the ethical issues in accounting.

fraudulent financial activity are much more severe. Also, SOX increased the independence requirements of the outside auditors who review the accuracy of corporate financial statements and increased the oversight role of boards of directors.

The standards of conduct by which actions are judged as right or wrong, honest or dishonest, fair or not fair, are **ethics**. Effective financial reporting depends on sound ethical behavior. To sensitize you to ethical situations in business and to give you practice at solving ethical dilemmas, we address ethics in a number of ways in this textbook:

1. A number of the *Feature Stories* and other parts of the textbook discuss the central importance of ethical behavior to financial reporting.

2. *Ethics Insight* boxes and marginal *Ethics Notes* highlight ethics situations and issues in actual business settings.

3. Many of the *People, Planet, and Profit Insight* boxes focus on ethical issues that companies face in measuring and reporting social and environmental issues.

4. At the end of the chapter, an *Ethics Case* simulates a business situation and asks you to put yourself in the position of a decision-maker in that case.

When analyzing these various ethics cases, as well as experiences in your own life, it is useful to apply the three steps outlined in Illustration 1-4.

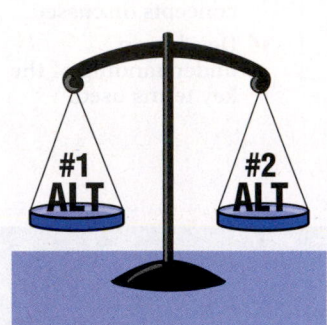

1. Recognize an ethical situation and the ethical issues involved.	**2. Identify and analyze the principal elements in the situation.**	**3. Identify the alternatives, and weigh the impact of each alternative on various stakeholders.**
Use your personal ethics to identify ethical situations and issues. Some businesses and professional organizations provide written codes of ethics for guidance in some business situations.	Identify the **stakeholders**—persons or groups who may be harmed or benefited. Ask the question: What are the responsibilities and obligations of the parties involved?	Select the most ethical alternative, considering all the consequences. Sometimes there will be one right answer. Other situations involve more than one right solution; these situations require an evaluation of each and a selection of the best alternative.

Illustration 1-4
Steps in analyzing ethics cases and situations

*Insight boxes provide examples of business situations from various perspectives—ethics, investor, international, and corporate social responsibility. Guideline answers to the critical thinking questions are available in **WileyPLUS** and at **www.wiley.com/college/weygandt**. Additional questions are offered in **WileyPLUS**.*

Ethics Insight | Dewey & LeBoeuf LLP

© Alliance/Shutterstock

I Felt the Pressure— Would You?

"I felt the pressure." That's what some of the employees of the now-defunct law firm of Dewey & LeBoeuf LLP indicated when they helped to overstate revenue and use accounting tricks to hide losses and cover up cash shortages. These employees worked for the former finance director and former chief financial officer (CFO) of the firm. Here are some of their comments:

• "I was instructed by the CFO to create invoices, knowing they would not be sent to clients. When I created these invoices, I knew that it was inappropriate."

• "I intentionally gave the auditors incorrect information in the course of the audit."

What happened here is that a small group of lower-level employees over a period of years carried out the instructions of their bosses. Their bosses, however, seemed to have no concern as evidenced by various e-mails with one another in which they referred to their financial manipulations as accounting tricks, cooking the books, and fake income.

Source: Ashby Jones, "Guilty Pleas of Dewey Staff Detail the Alleged Fraud," *Wall Street Journal* (March 28, 2014).

*Why did these employees lie, and what do you believe should be their penalty for these lies? (Go to **WileyPLUS** for this answer and additional questions.)*

Generally Accepted Accounting Principles

The accounting profession has developed standards that are generally accepted and universally practiced. This common set of standards is called **generally accepted accounting principles (GAAP)**. These standards indicate how to report economic events.

The primary accounting standard-setting body in the United States is the **Financial Accounting Standards Board (FASB)**. The **Securities and Exchange Commission (SEC)** is the agency of the U.S. government that oversees U.S. financial markets and accounting standard-setting bodies. The SEC relies on the FASB to develop accounting standards, which public companies must follow. Many countries outside of the United States have adopted the accounting standards issued by the **International Accounting Standards Board (IASB)**. These standards are called **International Financial Reporting Standards (IFRS)**.

As markets become more global, it is often desirable to compare the results of companies from different countries that report using different accounting standards. In order to increase comparability, in recent years the two standard-setting bodies have made efforts to reduce the differences between U.S. GAAP and IFRS. This process is referred to as **convergence**. As a result of these convergence efforts, it is likely that someday there will be a single set of high-quality accounting standards that are used by companies around the world. Because convergence is such an important issue, we highlight any major differences between GAAP and IFRS in *International Notes* (as shown in the margin here) and provide a more in-depth discussion in the *A Look at IRFS* section at the end of each chapter.

> ### International Note
>
> Over 100 countries use International Financial Reporting Standards (called IFRS). For example, all companies in the European Union follow international standards. The differences between U.S. and international standards are not generally significant.

International Notes highlight differences between U.S. and international accounting standards.

Measurement Principles

GAAP generally uses one of two measurement principles, the historical cost principle or the fair value principle. Selection of which principle to follow generally relates to trade-offs between relevance and faithful representation. **Relevance** means that financial information is capable of making a difference in a decision. **Faithful representation** means that the numbers and descriptions match what really existed or happened—they are factual.

Helpful Hint
Relevance and faithful representation are two primary qualities that make accounting information useful for decision-making.

Helpful Hints further clarify concepts being discussed.

HISTORICAL COST PRINCIPLE

The **historical cost principle** (or cost principle) dictates that companies record assets at their cost. This is true not only at the time the asset is purchased, but also over the time the asset is held. For example, if **Best Buy** purchases land for $360,000, the company initially reports it in its accounting records at $360,000. But what does Best Buy do if, by the end of the next year, the fair value of the land has increased to $400,000? Under the historical cost principle, it continues to report the land at $360,000.

FAIR VALUE PRINCIPLE

The **fair value principle** states that assets and liabilities should be reported at fair value (the price received to sell an asset or settle a liability). Fair value information may be more useful than historical cost for certain types of assets and liabilities. For example, certain investment securities are reported at fair value because market price information is usually readily available for these types of assets. In determining which measurement principle to use, companies weigh the factual nature of cost figures versus the relevance of fair value. In general, most companies choose to use cost. Only in situations where assets are actively traded, such as investment securities, do companies apply the fair value principle extensively.

Assumptions

Assumptions provide a foundation for the accounting process. Two main assumptions are the **monetary unit assumption** and the **economic entity assumption**.

MONETARY UNIT ASSUMPTION

The **monetary unit assumption** requires that companies include in the accounting records only transaction data that can be expressed in money terms. This assumption enables accounting to quantify (measure) economic events. The monetary unit assumption is vital to applying the historical cost principle.

This assumption prevents the inclusion of some relevant information in the accounting records. For example, the health of a company's owner, the quality of service, and the morale of employees are not included. The reason: Companies cannot quantify this information in money terms. Though this information is important, companies record only events that can be measured in money.

ECONOMIC ENTITY ASSUMPTION

An economic entity can be any organization or unit in society. It may be a company (such as Crocs, Inc.), a governmental unit (the state of Ohio), a municipality (Seattle), a school district (St. Louis District 48), or a church (Southern Baptist). The **economic entity assumption** requires that the activities of the entity be kept separate and distinct from the activities of its owner and all other economic entities. To illustrate, Sally Rider, owner of Sally's Boutique, must keep her personal living costs separate from the expenses of her business. Similarly, J. Crew and Gap Inc. are segregated into separate economic entities for accounting purposes.

PROPRIETORSHIP A business owned by one person is generally a **proprietorship**. The owner is often the manager/operator of the business. Small service-type businesses (plumbing companies, beauty salons, and auto repair shops), farms, and small retail stores (antique shops, clothing stores, and used-book stores) are often proprietorships. **Usually, only a relatively small amount of money (capital) is necessary to start in business as a proprietorship. The owner (proprietor) receives any profits, suffers any losses, and is personally liable for all debts of the business.** There is no legal distinction between the business as an economic unit and the owner, but the accounting records of the business activities are kept separate from the personal records and activities of the owner.

PARTNERSHIP A business owned by two or more persons associated as partners is a **partnership**. In most respects a partnership is like a proprietorship except that more than one owner is involved. Typically, a partnership agreement (written or oral) sets forth such terms as initial investment, duties of each partner, division of net income (or net loss), and settlement to be made upon death or withdrawal of a partner. Each partner generally has unlimited personal liability for the debts of the partnership. **Like a proprietorship, for accounting purposes the partnership transactions must be kept separate from the personal activities of the partners**. Partnerships are often used to organize retail and service-type businesses, including professional practices (lawyers, doctors, architects, and certified public accountants).

CORPORATION A business organized as a separate legal entity under state corporation law and having ownership divided into transferable shares of stock is a **corporation**. The holders of the shares (stockholders) **enjoy limited liability**; that is, they are not personally liable for the debts of the corporate entity. Stockholders **may transfer all or part of their ownership shares to other investors at any time** (i.e., sell their shares). The ease with which ownership can change adds to the attractiveness of investing in a corporation. Because ownership can be transferred without dissolving the corporation, the corporation **enjoys an unlimited life**.

Although the combined number of proprietorships and partnerships in the United States is more than five times the number of corporations, the revenue produced by corporations is eight times greater. Most of the largest companies in the United States—for example, **ExxonMobil**, **Ford**, **Wal-Mart Stores, Inc.**, **Citigroup**, and **Apple**—are corporations.

Accounting Across the Organization

Josef Volavka/iStockphoto

Spinning the Career Wheel

How will the study of accounting help you? A working knowledge of accounting is desirable for virtually every field of business. Some examples of how accounting is used in business careers include:

General management: Managers at **Ford Motors**, **Massachusetts General Hospital**, California State University—Fullerton, a **McDonald's** franchise, and a **Trek** bike shop all need to understand accounting data in order to make wise business decisions.

Marketing: Marketing specialists at **Procter & Gamble** must be sensitive to costs and benefits, which accounting helps them quantify and understand. Making a sale is meaningless unless it is a profitable sale.

Finance: Do you want to be a banker for **Citicorp**, an investment analyst for **Goldman Sachs**, or a stock broker for **Merrill Lynch**? These fields rely heavily on accounting knowledge to analyze financial statements. In fact, it is difficult to get a good job in a finance function without two or three courses in accounting.

Real estate: Are you interested in being a real estate broker for **Prudential Real Estate**? Because a third party—the bank—is almost always involved in financing a real estate transaction, brokers must understand the numbers involved: Can the buyer afford to make the payments to the bank? Does the cash flow from an industrial property justify the purchase price? What are the tax benefits of the purchase?

How might accounting help you? (Go to **WileyPLUS** for this answer and additional questions)

DO IT! 2   Building Blocks of Accounting

Indicate whether each of the five statements presented below is true or false. If false, indicate how to correct the statement.

1. Congress passed the Sarbanes-Oxley Act to reduce unethical behavior and decrease the likelihood of future corporate scandals.
2. The primary accounting standard-setting body in the United States is the Financial Accounting Standards Board (FASB).
3. The historical cost principle dictates that companies record assets at their cost. In later periods, however, the fair value of the asset must be used if fair value is higher than its cost.
4. Relevance means that financial information matches what really happened; the information is factual.
5. A business owner's personal expenses must be separated from expenses of the business to comply with accounting's economic entity assumption.

Solution

1. True. 2. True. 3. False. The historical cost principle dictates that companies record assets at their cost. Under the historical cost principle, the company must also use cost in later periods. 4. False. Faithful representation means that financial information matches what really happened; the information is factual. 5. True.

Related exercise material: **E1-3, E1-4, and DO IT! 1-2.**

Action Plan

✔ Review the discussion of ethics and financial reporting standards.

✔ Develop an understanding of the key terms used.

LEARNING OBJECTIVE **3** **State the accounting equation, and define its components.**

The two basic elements of a business are what it owns and what it owes. **Assets** are the resources a business owns. For example, Google has total assets of approximately $93.8 billion. Liabilities and stockholders' equity are the rights or claims against these resources. Thus, Google has $93.8 billion of claims against its $93.8 billion of assets. Claims of those to whom the company owes money (creditors) are called **liabilities**. Claims of owners are called **stockholders' equity**. Google has liabilities of $22.1 billion and stockholders' equity of $71.7 billion.

We can express the relationship of assets, liabilities, and stockholders' equity as an equation, as shown in Illustration 1-5.

Illustration 1-5
The basic accounting equation

Assets	=	Liabilities	+	Stockholders' Equity

This relationship is the **basic accounting equation**. Assets must equal the sum of liabilities and stockholders' equity. Liabilities appear before stockholders' equity in the basic accounting equation because they are paid first if a business is liquidated.

The accounting equation applies to all **economic entities** regardless of size, nature of business, or form of business organization. It applies to a small proprietorship such as a corner grocery store as well as to a giant corporation such as PepsiCo. The equation provides the **underlying framework** for recording and summarizing economic events.

Let's look in more detail at the categories in the basic accounting equation.

Assets

As noted above, **assets** are resources a business owns. The business uses its assets in carrying out such activities as production and sales. The common characteristic possessed by all assets is **the capacity to provide future services or benefits**. In a business, that service potential or future economic benefit eventually results in cash inflows (receipts). For example, consider Campus Pizza, a local restaurant. It owns a delivery truck that provides economic benefits from delivering pizzas. Other assets of Campus Pizza are tables, chairs, jukebox, cash register, oven, tableware, and, of course, cash.

Liabilities

Liabilities are claims against assets—that is, existing debts and obligations. Businesses of all sizes usually borrow money and purchase merchandise on credit. These economic activities result in payables of various sorts:

- Campus Pizza, for instance, purchases cheese, sausage, flour, and beverages on credit from suppliers. These obligations are called **accounts payable**.
- Campus Pizza also has a **note payable** to First National Bank for the money borrowed to purchase the delivery truck.
- Campus Pizza may also have **salaries and wages payable** to employees and **sales and real estate taxes payable** to the local government.

All of these persons or entities to whom Campus Pizza owes money are its **creditors**.

Creditors may legally force the liquidation of a business that does not pay its debts. In that case, the law requires that creditor claims be paid **before** ownership claims.

Stockholders' Equity

The ownership claim on a corporation's total assets is **stockholders' equity**. It is equal to total assets minus total liabilities. Here is why: The assets of a business are

Helpful Hint
In some situations, accountants use the term *owner's equity* and in others *owners' equity*. *Owner's* refers to one *owner* (the case with a sole proprietorship), and *owners'* refers to multiple owners (the case with partnerships). The term *stockholders' equity* refers to ownership in corporations.

claimed by either creditors or stockholders. To find out what belongs to stockholders, we subtract creditors' claims (the liabilities) from the assets. The remainder is the stockholders' claim on the assets—stockholders' equity. It is often referred to as **residual equity**—that is, the equity "left over" after creditors' claims are satisfied.

The stockholders' equity section of a corporation's balance sheet generally consists of (1) common stock and (2) retained earnings.

COMMON STOCK

A corporation may obtain funds by selling shares of stock to investors. **Common stock** is the term used to describe the total amount paid in by stockholders for the shares they purchase.

RETAINED EARNINGS

The **retained earnings** section of the balance sheet is determined by three items: revenues, expenses, and dividends.

REVENUES **Revenues are the gross increases in stockholders' equity resulting from business activities entered into for the purpose of earning income.** Generally, revenues result from selling merchandise, performing services, renting out property, and lending money.

Revenues usually result in an increase in an asset. They may arise from different sources and are called various names depending on the nature of the business. Campus Pizza, for instance, has two categories of sales revenues—pizza sales and beverage sales. Other titles for and sources of revenue common to many businesses are sales, fees, services, commissions, interest, dividends, royalties, and rent.

EXPENSES **Expenses** are the cost of assets consumed or services used in the process of earning revenue. **They are decreases in stockholders' equity that result from operating the business.** Like revenues, expenses take many forms and are called various names depending on the type of asset consumed or service used. For example, Campus Pizza recognizes the following types of expenses: cost of ingredients (flour, cheese, tomato paste, meat, mushrooms, etc.); cost of beverages; wages expense; utilities expense (electric, gas, and water expense); telephone expense; delivery expense (gasoline, repairs, licenses, etc.); supplies expense (napkins, detergents, aprons, etc.); rent expense; interest expense; and property tax expense.

DIVIDENDS Net income represents an increase in net assets which are then available to distribute to stockholders. The distribution of cash or other assets to stockholders is called a **dividend**. Dividends reduce retained earnings. However, dividends are **not an expense**. A corporation first determines its revenues and expenses and then computes net income or net loss. If it has net income and decides it has no better use for that income, a corporation may decide to distribute a dividend to its owners (the stockholders).

In summary, the principal sources (increases) of stockholders' equity are investments by stockholders and revenues from business operations. In contrast, reductions (decreases) in stockholders' equity result from expenses and dividends. These relationships are shown in Illustration 1-6.

Helpful Hint
The effect of revenues is positive—an increase in stockholders' equity coupled with an increase in assets or a decrease in liabilities.

Helpful Hint
The effect of expenses is negative—a decrease in stockholders' equity coupled with a decrease in assets or an increase in liabilities.

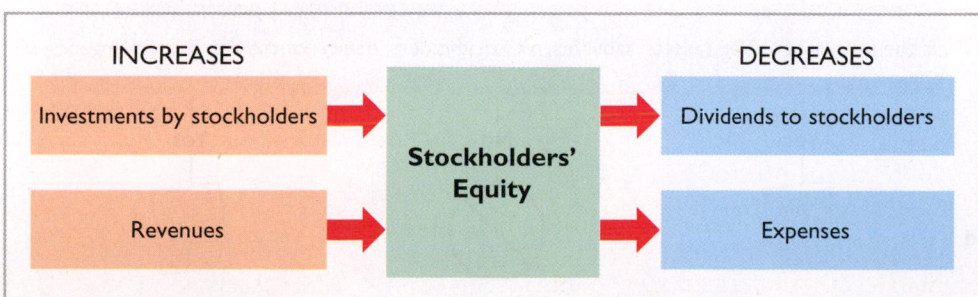

Illustration 1-6
Increases and decreases in stockholders' equity

DO IT! 3 — Stockholders' Equity Effects

Action Plan

✔ Understand the sources of revenue.

✔ Understand what causes expenses.

✔ Review the rules for changes in stockholders' equity.

✔ Recognize that dividends are distributions of cash or other assets to stockholders.

Classify the following items as issuance of stock (I), dividends (D), revenues (R), or expenses (E). Then indicate whether each item increases or decreases stockholders' equity.

(1) Rent Expense   (3) Dividends

(2) Service Revenue   (4) Salaries and Wages Expense

Solution

1. Rent Expense is an expense (E); it decreases stockholders' equity.   2. Service Revenue is a revenue (R); it increases stockholders' equity.   3. Dividends is a distribution to stockholders (D); it decreases stockholders' equity.   4. Salaries and Wages Expense is an expense (E); it decreases stockholders' equity.

Related exercise material: **BE1-1, BE1-2, BE1-3, BE1-4, BE1-5, BE1-8, BE1-9, E1-5, E1-6, and DO IT! 1-3.**

LEARNING OBJECTIVE 4

Analyze the effects of business transactions on the accounting equation.

Transactions (**business transactions**) are a business's economic events recorded by accountants. Transactions may be external or internal. **External transactions** involve economic events between the company and some outside enterprise. For example, Campus Pizza's purchase of cooking equipment from a supplier, payment of monthly rent to the landlord, and sale of pizzas to customers are external transactions. **Internal transactions** are economic events that occur entirely within one company. The use of cooking and cleaning supplies are internal transactions for Campus Pizza.

Companies carry on many activities that do not represent business transactions. Examples are hiring employees, responding to e-mails, talking with customers, and placing merchandise orders. Some of these activities may lead to business transactions: Employees will earn wages, and suppliers will deliver ordered merchandise. The company must analyze each event to find out if it affects the components of the accounting equation. If it does, the company will record the transaction. Illustration 1-7 demonstrates the transaction-identification process.

Illustration 1-7
Transaction-identification process

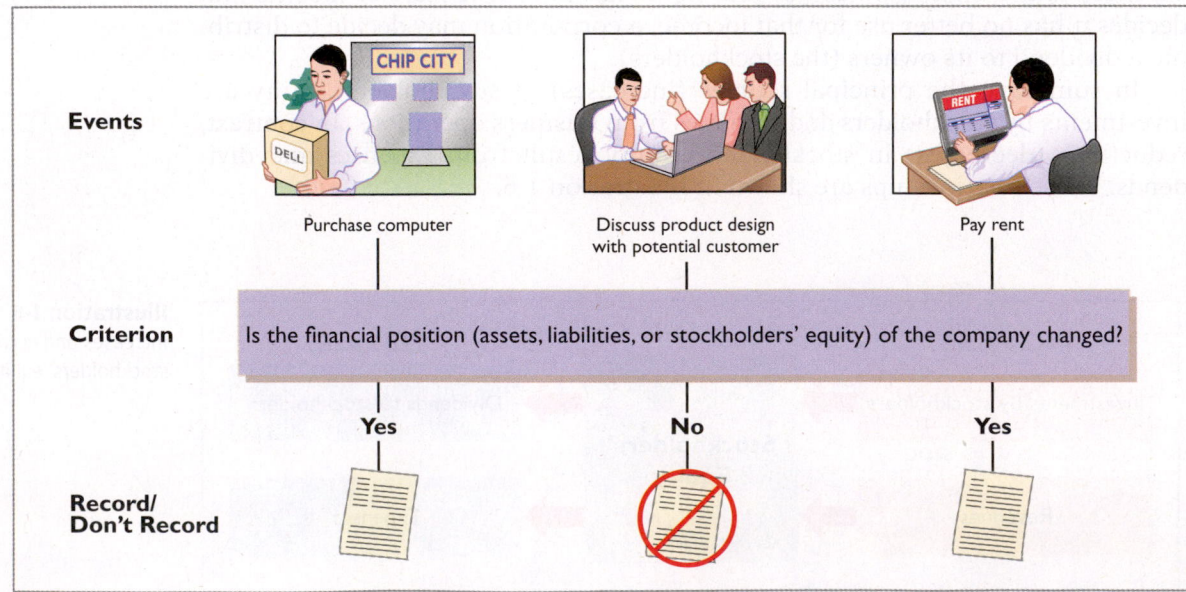

Each transaction must have a dual effect on the accounting equation. For example, if an asset is increased, there must be a corresponding (1) decrease in another asset, (2) increase in a specific liability, or (3) increase in stockholders' equity.

Two or more items could be affected. For example, as one asset is increased $10,000, another asset could decrease $6,000 and a liability could increase $4,000. Any change in a liability or ownership claim is subject to similar analysis.

Transaction Analysis

To demonstrate how to analyze transactions in terms of the accounting equation, we will review the business activities of Softbyte Inc., a smartphone app development business, during its first month of operations. As part of this analysis, we will expand the basic accounting equation. This will allow us to better illustrate the impact of transactions on stockholders' equity. Recall that stockholders' equity is comprised of two parts: common stock and retained earnings. Common stock is affected when the company issues new shares of stock in exchange for cash. Retained earnings is affected when the company earns revenue, incurs expenses, or pays dividends. Illustration 1-8 shows the **expanded accounting equation**.

Illustration 1-8
Expanded accounting equation

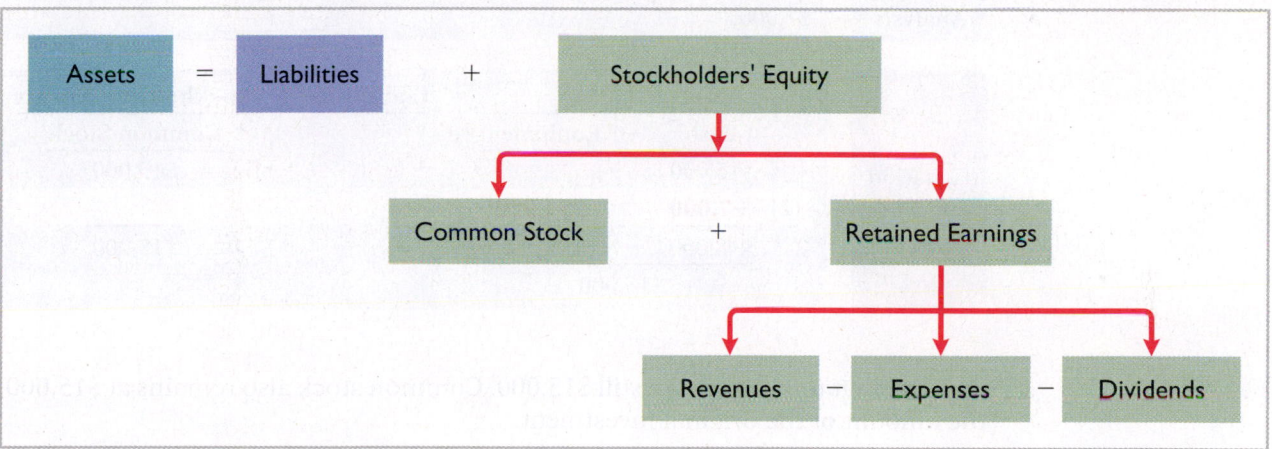

If you are tempted to skip ahead after you've read a few of the following transaction analyses, don't do it. Each has something unique to teach, something you'll need later. (We assure you that we've kept them to the minimum needed!)

TRANSACTION 1. INVESTMENT BY STOCKHOLDERS Ray and Barbara Neal start a smartphone app development company that they incorporate as Softbyte Inc. On September 1, 2017, they invest $15,000 cash in the business in exchange for $15,000 of common stock. The common stock indicates the ownership interest that the Neals have in Softbyte Inc. This transaction results in an equal increase in both assets and stockholders' equity.

Helpful Hint
Study these transactions until you are sure you understand them. They are not difficult, but understanding them is important to your success in this course. The ability to analyze transactions in terms of the basic accounting equation is essential in accounting.

Basic Analysis	The asset Cash increases $15,000, and stockholders' equity (identified as Common Stock) increases $15,000.

	Assets	**= Liabilities +**	**Stockholders' Equity**
Equation Analysis	Cash =		Common Stock
	(1) +$15,000 =		+$15,000 Issued Stock

Observe that the equality of the basic equation has been maintained. Note also that the source of the increase in stockholders' equity (in this case, issued stock) is indicated. Why does this matter? Because investments by stockholders do not represent revenues, and they are excluded in determining net income. Therefore, it is necessary to make clear that the increase is an investment rather than revenue from operations. Additional investments (i.e., investments made by stockholders after the corporation has been initially formed) have the same effect on stockholders' equity as the initial investment.

TRANSACTION 2. PURCHASE OF EQUIPMENT FOR CASH Softbyte Inc. purchases computer equipment for $7,000 cash. This transaction results in an equal increase and decrease in total assets, though the composition of assets changes.

Basic Analysis	The asset Cash decreases $7,000, and the asset Equipment increases $7,000.

	Assets		**= Liabilities +**	**Stockholders' Equity**
	Cash +	Equipment =		Common Stock
Equation Analysis	$15,000			$15,000
	(2) −7,000	+$7,000		
	$ 8,000 +	$ 7,000 =		$15,000
		$15,000		

Observe that total assets are still $15,000. Common stock also remains at $15,000, the amount of the original investment.

TRANSACTION 3. PURCHASE OF SUPPLIES ON CREDIT Softbyte Inc. purchases for $1,600 from Mobile Solutions headsets and other computer accessories expected to last several months. Mobile Solutions agrees to allow Softbyte to pay this bill in October. This transaction is a purchase on account (a credit purchase). Assets increase because of the expected future benefits of using the headsets and computer accessories, and liabilities increase by the amount due Mobile Solutions.

Basic Analysis	The asset Supplies increases $1,600, and the liability Accounts Payable increases $1,600.

	Assets			**= Liabilities +**		**Stockholders' Equity**
	Cash +	Supplies +	Equipment =	Accounts Payable	+	Common Stock
Equation Analysis	$8,000		$7,000			$15,000
	(3)	+$1,600		+$1,600		
	$8,000 +	$ 1,600 +	$7,000 =	$ 1,600	+	$15,000
		$16,600			$16,600	

Total assets are now $16,600. This total is matched by a $1,600 creditor's claim and a $15,000 ownership claim.

TRANSACTION 4. SERVICES PERFORMED FOR CASH Softbyte Inc. receives $1,200 cash from customers for app development services it has performed. This transaction represents Softbyte's principal revenue-producing activity. Recall that **revenue increases stockholders' equity**.

Basic Analysis	The asset Cash increases $1,200, and stockholders' equity increases $1,200 due to Service Revenue.

		Assets			= Liabilities +		Stockholders' Equity				
					Accounts		Common		Retained Earnings		
	Cash	+ Supplies +	Equipment =		Payable	+	Stock	+	Rev. −	Exp. −	Div.
	$8,000	$1,600	$7,000		$1,600		$15,000				
(4)	+1,200								+$1,200		Service Revenue
	$9,200 +	$1,600 +	$7,000	=	$1,600	+	$15,000	+	$ 1,200		
		$17,800					$17,800				

The two sides of the equation balance at $17,800. Service Revenue is included in determining Softbyte's net income.

Note that we do not have room to give details for each individual revenue and expense account in this illustration. Thus, revenues (and expenses when we get to them) are summarized under one column heading for Revenues and one for Expenses. However, it is important to keep track of the category (account) titles affected (e.g., Service Revenue) as they will be needed when we prepare financial statements later in the chapter.

TRANSACTION 5. PURCHASE OF ADVERTISING ON CREDIT Softbyte Inc. receives a bill for $250 from the *Daily News* for advertising on its online website but postpones payment until a later date. This transaction results in an increase in liabilities and a decrease in stockholders' equity.

Basic Analysis	The liability Accounts Payable increases $250, and stockholders' equity decreases $250 due to Advertising Expense.

		Assets			= Liabilities +		Stockholders' Equity				
					Accounts		Common		Retained Earnings		
	Cash	+ Supplies +	Equipment =		Payable	+	Stock	+	Rev. −	Exp. −	Div.
	$9,200	$1,600	$7,000		$1,600		$15,000		$1,200		
(5)					+250					−$250	Advertising Expense
	$9,200 +	$1,600 +	$7,000	=	$1,850	+	$15,000	+	$1,200 −	$ 250	
		$17,800					$17,800				

The two sides of the equation still balance at $17,800. Retained Earnings decreases when Softbyte incurs the expense. Expenses do not have to be paid in cash at the time they are incurred. When Softbyte pays at a later date, the liability Accounts Payable will decrease and the asset Cash will decrease (see Transaction 8). The cost of advertising is an expense (rather than an asset) because Softbyte has used the benefits. Advertising Expense is included in determining net income.

TRANSACTION 6. SERVICES PERFORMED FOR CASH AND CREDIT Softbyte Inc. performs $3,500 of app development services for customers. The company receives cash of $1,500 from customers, and it bills the balance of $2,000 on account. This transaction results in an equal increase in assets and stockholders' equity.

Basic Analysis	Three specific items are affected: The asset Cash increases $1,500, the asset Accounts Receivable increases $2,000, and stockholders' equity increases $3,500 due to Service Revenue.

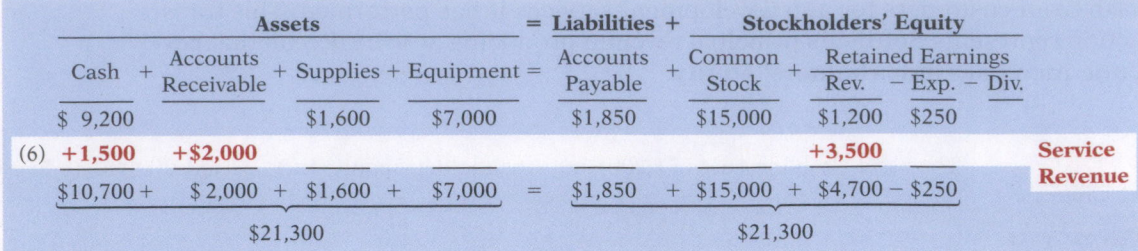

Equation Analysis

	Assets				= Liabilities +	Stockholders' Equity			
Cash +	Accounts Receivable	+ Supplies +	Equipment =		Accounts Payable	+ Common Stock +	Retained Earnings		
							Rev. −	Exp. −	Div.
$ 9,200		$1,600	$7,000		$1,850	$15,000	$1,200	$250	
(6) +1,500	+$2,000						+3,500		Service Revenue
$10,700 +	$ 2,000 +	$1,600 +	$7,000	=	$1,850	+ $15,000 +	$4,700 −	$250	
	$21,300					$21,300			

Softbyte recognizes $3,500 in revenues when it performs the service. In exchange for this service, it received $1,500 in Cash and Accounts Receivable of $2,000. This Accounts Receivable represents customers' promises to pay $2,000 to Softbyte in the future. When it later receives collections on account, Softbyte will increase Cash and will decrease Accounts Receivable (see Transaction 9).

TRANSACTION 7. PAYMENT OF EXPENSES Softbyte Inc. pays the following expenses in cash for September: office rent $600, salaries and wages of employees $900, and utilities $200. These payments result in an equal decrease in assets and stockholders' equity.

Basic Analysis	The asset Cash decreases $1,700, and stockholders' equity decreases $1,700 due to the following expenses: Rent Expense, Salaries and Wages Expense, and Utilities Expense.

Equation Analysis

	Assets				= Liabilities +	Stockholders' Equity			
Cash +	Accounts Receivable	+ Supplies +	Equipment =		Accounts Payable	+ Common Stock +	Retained Earnings		
							Rev. −	Exp. −	Div.
$10,700	$2,000	$1,600	$7,000		$1,850	$15,000	$4,700	$ 250	
(7) −1,700								−600	Rent Exp.
								−900	Sal./Wages Exp.
								−200	Utilities Exp.
$ 9,000 +	$2,000 +	$1,600 +	$7,000	=	$1,850	+ $15,000 +	$4,700 −	$1,950	
	$19,600					$19,600			

The two sides of the equation now balance at $19,600. Three lines are required in the analysis to indicate the different types of expenses that have been incurred.

TRANSACTION 8. PAYMENT OF ACCOUNTS PAYABLE Softbyte Inc. pays its $250 *Daily News* bill in cash. The company previously (in Transaction 5) recorded the bill as an increase in Accounts Payable and a decrease in stockholders' equity.

Basic Analysis	This cash payment "on account" decreases the asset Cash by $250 and also decreases the liability Accounts Payable by $250.

Equation Analysis

	Assets				= Liabilities +	Stockholders' Equity			
Cash +	Accounts Receivable	+ Supplies +	Equipment =		Accounts Payable	+ Common Stock +	Retained Earnings		
							Rev.	−Exp. −	Div.
$9,000	$2,000	$1,600	$7,000		$1,850	$15,000	$4,700	$1,950	
(8) −250					−250				
$8,750 +	$2,000 +	$1,600 +	$7,000	=	$1,600	+ $15,000 +	$4,700 −	$1,950	
	$19,350					$19,350			

Observe that the payment of a liability related to an expense that has previously been recorded does not affect stockholders' equity. Softbyte recorded the expense (in Transaction 5) and should not record it again.

TRANSACTION 9. RECEIPT OF CASH ON ACCOUNT Softbyte Inc. receives $600 in cash from customers who had been billed for services (in Transaction 6). Transaction 9 does not change total assets, but it changes the composition of those assets.

Basic Analysis	The asset Cash increases $600, and the asset Accounts Receivable decreases $600.

			Assets			= Liabilities +		Stockholders' Equity			
	Cash +	Accounts Receivable	+ Supplies +	Equipment =		Accounts Payable	+ Common Stock	+	Retained Earnings Rev. − Exp. − Div.		
	$8,750	$2,000	$1,600	$7,000		$1,600	$15,000		$4,700	$1,950	
(9)	+600	−600									
	$9,350 +	$1,400	+ $1,600 +	$7,000	=	$1,600	+ $15,000	+ $4,700	− $1,950		
			$19,350					$19,350			

Note that the collection of an account receivable for services previously billed and recorded does not affect stockholders' equity. Softbyte already recorded this revenue (in Transaction 6) and should not record it again.

TRANSACTION 10. DIVIDENDS The corporation pays a dividend of $1,300 in cash to Ray and Barbara Neal, the stockholders of Softbyte Inc. This transaction results in an equal decrease in assets and stockholders' equity.

Basic Analysis	The asset Cash decreases $1,300, and stockholders' equity decreases $1,300 due to dividends.

			Assets			= Liabilities +		Stockholders' Equity			
	Cash +	Accounts Receivable	+ Supplies +	Equipment =		Accounts Payable	+ Common Stock	+	Retained Earnings Rev. − Exp. − Div.		
	$ 9,350	$1,400	$1,600	$7,000		$1,600	$15,000		$4,700	$1,950	
(10)	−1,300									−$1,300	**Dividends**
	$ 8,050 +	$1,400	+ $1,600 +	$7,000	=	$1,600	+ $15,000	+ $4,700	− $1,950	− $ 1,300	
			$18,050					$18,050			

Note that the dividend reduces retained earnings, which is part of stockholders' equity. **Dividends are not expenses**. Like stockholders' investments, dividends are excluded in determining net income.

Summary of Transactions

Illustration 1-9 (page 20) summarizes the September transactions of Softbyte Inc. to show their cumulative effect on the basic accounting equation. It also indicates the transaction number and the specific effects of each transaction. Finally, Illustration 1-9 demonstrates a number of significant facts:

1. Each transaction must be analyzed in terms of its effect on:
   (a) The three components of the basic accounting equation.
   (b) Specific types (kinds) of items within each component.

2. The two sides of the equation must always be equal.

3. The Common Stock and Retained Earnings columns indicate the causes of each change in the stockholders' claim on assets.

Trans-action		Assets			=	Liabilities +		Stockholders' Equity				
	Cash	+ Accounts Receivable	+ Supplies	+ Equipment =		Accounts Payable	+ Common Stock	+	Rev.	Retained Earnings − Exp.	− Div.	
(1)	+$15,000						+ $15,000					Issued Stock
(2)	−7,000			+$7,000								
(3)			+$1,600			+$1,600						
(4)	+1,200								+$1,200			Service Revenue
(5)						+250				−$250		Adver. Expense
(6)	+1,500	+$2,000							+3,500			Service Revenue
(7)	−1,700									−600		Rent Expense
										−900		Sal./Wages Exp.
										−200		Utilities Expense
(8)	−250					−250						
(9)	+600	−600										
(10)	−1,300										−$1,300	Dividends
	$ 8,050 +	$1,400 +	$1,600 +	$7,000 =		$1,600 +	$15,000 +		$4,700 −	$1,950 −	$1,300	
		$18,050						**$18,050**				

Illustration 1-9
Tabular summary of Softbyte Inc. transactions

There! You made it through transaction analysis. If you feel a bit shaky on any of the transactions, it might be a good idea at this point to get up, take a short break, and come back again for a brief (10- to 15-minute) review of the transactions, to make sure you understand them before you go on to the next section.

DO IT! 4 Tabular Analysis

Action Plan

✔ Analyze the effects of each transaction on the accounting equation.

✔ Use appropriate category names (not descriptions).

✔ Keep the accounting equation in balance.

Transactions made by Virmari & Co., a public accounting firm, for the month of August are shown below. Prepare a tabular analysis which shows the effects of these transactions on the expanded accounting equation, similar to that shown in Illustration 1-9.

1. Stockholders purchased shares of stock for $25,000 cash.
2. The company purchased $7,000 of office equipment on credit.
3. The company received $8,000 cash in exchange for services performed.
4. The company paid $850 for this month's rent.
5. The company paid a dividend of $1,000 in cash to stockholders.

Solution

Transaction	Assets		=	Liabilities +		Stockholders' Equity			
	Cash	+ Equipment =		Accounts Payable	+ Common Stock	+ Rev.	Retained Earnings − Exp.	− Div.	
(1)	+$25,000				+$25,000				
(2)		+$7,000		+$7,000					
(3)	+8,000					+$8,000			Service Revenue
(4)	−850						−$850		Rent Expense
(5)	−1,000							− $1,000	Dividends
	$31,150 +	$7,000 =		$7,000 +	$25,000 +	$8,000 −	$850 −	$1,000	
		$38,150				$38,150			

Related exercise material: **BE1-6, BE1-7, BE1-9, E1-6, E1-7, E1-8, and DO IT! 1-4.**

Describe the four financial statements and how they are prepared.

Companies prepare four financial statements from the summarized accounting data:

1. An **income statement** presents the revenues and expenses and resulting net income or net loss for a specific period of time.

2. A **retained earnings statement** summarizes the changes in retained earnings for a specific period of time.

3. A **balance sheet** reports the assets, liabilities, and stockholders' equity of a company at a specific date.

4. A **statement of cash flows** summarizes information about the cash inflows (receipts) and outflows (payments) for a specific period of time.

These statements provide relevant financial data for internal and external users. Illustration 1-10 (page 22) shows the financial statements of Softbyte Inc. Note that the statements shown in Illustration 1-10 are interrelated:

1. Net income of $2,750 on the **income statement** is added to the beginning balance of retained earnings in the **retained earnings statement**.

2. Retained earnings of $1,450 at the end of the reporting period shown in the **retained earnings statement** is reported on the **balance sheet**.

3. Cash of $8,050 on the **balance sheet** is reported on the **statement of cash flows**.

Also, explanatory notes and supporting schedules are an integral part of every set of financial statements. We illustrate these notes and schedules in later chapters of this textbook.

Be sure to carefully examine the format and content of each statement in Illustration 1-10. We describe the essential features of each in the following sections.

> **International Note**
>
> The primary types of financial statements required by GAAP and IFRS are the same. In practice, some format differences do exist in presentations employed by GAAP companies compared to IFRS companies.

> **Helpful Hint**
> The income statement, retained earnings statement, and statement of cash flows are all for a *period* of time, whereas the balance sheet is for a *point* in time.

Income Statement

The income statement reports the success or profitability of the company's operations over a specific period of time. For example, Softbyte Inc.'s income statement is dated "For the Month Ended September 30, 2017." It is prepared from the data appearing in the revenue and expense columns of Illustration 1-9 (page 20). The heading of the statement identifies the company, the type of statement, and the time period covered by the statement.

The income statement lists revenues first, followed by expenses. Finally, the statement shows net income (or net loss). When revenues exceed expenses, **net income** results. When expenses exceed revenues, a **net loss** results.

Although practice varies, we have chosen in our illustrations and homework solutions to list expenses in order of magnitude. (We will consider alternative formats for the income statement in later chapters.)

Note that the income statement does not include investment and dividend transactions between the stockholders and the business in measuring net income. For example, as explained earlier, the cash dividend from Softbyte Inc. was not regarded as a business expense. This type of transaction is considered a reduction of retained earnings, which causes a decrease in stockholders' equity.

> **Alternative Terminology**
> The income statement is sometimes referred to as the *statement of operations, earnings statement,* or *profit and loss statement.*
>
> *Alternative Terminology notes present synonymous terms that you may come across in practice.*

Retained Earnings Statement

Softbyte Inc.'s retained earnings statement reports the changes in retained earnings for a specific period of time. The time period is the same as that covered by the income statement ("For the Month Ended September 30, 2017"). Data for the

Illustration 1-10
Financial statements
and their interrelationships

Helpful Hint
The heading of each
statement identifies the
company, the type of
statement, and the
specific date or time
period covered by the
statement.

Helpful Hint
Note that final sums are
double-underlined, and
negative amounts (in
the statement of cash
flows) are presented in
parentheses.

Helpful Hint
The arrows in this
illustration show the
interrelationships of
the four financial
statements.
1. Net income is
computed first and is
needed to determine
the ending balance in
retained earnings.
2. The ending balance
in retained earnings is
needed in preparing
the balance sheet.
3. The cash shown on
the balance sheet is
needed in preparing
the statement of cash
flows.

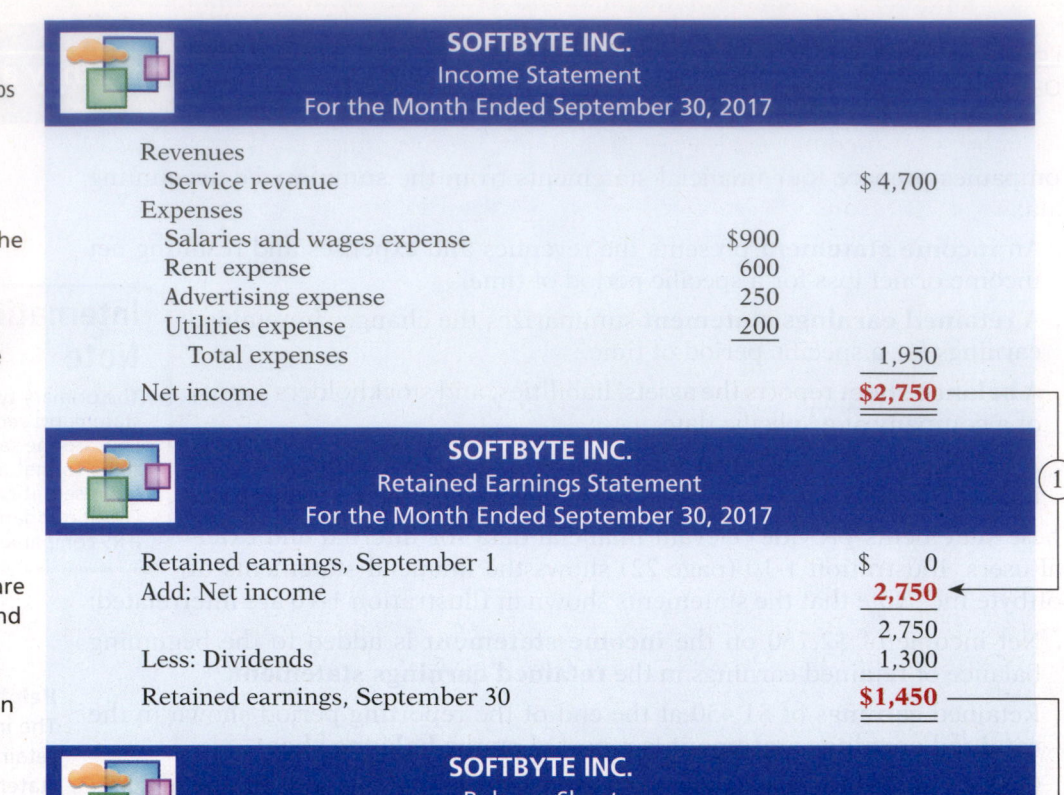

SOFTBYTE INC.
Income Statement
For the Month Ended September 30, 2017

Revenues		
Service revenue		$ 4,700
Expenses		
Salaries and wages expense	$900	
Rent expense	600	
Advertising expense	250	
Utilities expense	200	
Total expenses		1,950
Net income		$2,750

SOFTBYTE INC.
Retained Earnings Statement
For the Month Ended September 30, 2017

Retained earnings, September 1		$ 0
Add: Net income		2,750
		2,750
Less: Dividends		1,300
Retained earnings, September 30		$1,450

SOFTBYTE INC.
Balance Sheet
September 30, 2017

Assets

Cash		$ 8,050
Accounts receivable		1,400
Supplies		1,600
Equipment		7,000
Total assets		$18,050

Liabilities and Stockholders' Equity

Liabilities		
Accounts payable		$ 1,600
Stockholders' equity		
Common stock	$15,000	
Retained earnings	1,450	16,450
Total liabilities and stockholders' equity		$18,050

SOFTBYTE INC.
Statement of Cash Flows
For the Month Ended September 30, 2017

Cash flows from operating activities		
Cash receipts from revenues		$ 3,300
Cash payments for expenses		(1,950)
Net cash provided by operating activities		1,350
Cash flows from investing activities		
Purchase of equipment		(7,000)
Cash flows from financing activities		
Sale of common stock	$15,000	
Payment of cash dividends	(1,300)	13,700
Net increase in cash		8,050
Cash at the beginning of the period		0
Cash at the end of the period		$8,050

preparation of the retained earnings statement come from the retained earnings columns of the tabular summary (Illustration 1-9) and from the income statement (Illustration 1-10, page 22).

The first line of the statement shows the beginning retained earnings amount. Then come net income and dividends. The retained earnings ending balance is the final amount on the statement. The information provided by this statement indicates the reasons why retained earnings increased or decreased during the period. If there is a net loss, it is deducted with dividends in the retained earnings statement.

Balance Sheet

Softbyte Inc.'s balance sheet reports the assets, liabilities, and stockholders' equity at a specific date (September 30, 2017). The company prepares the balance sheet from the column headings and the month-end data shown in the last line of the tabular summary (Illustration 1-9).

Observe that the balance sheet lists assets at the top, followed by liabilities and stockholders' equity. Total assets must equal total liabilities and stockholders' equity. Softbyte Inc. reports only one liability, Accounts Payable, on its balance sheet. In most cases, there will be more than one liability. When two or more liabilities are involved, a customary way of listing is as shown in Illustration 1-11.

Illustration 1-11
Presentation of liabilities

Liabilities	
Notes payable	$ 10,000
Accounts payable	63,000
Salaries and wages payable	18,000
Total liabilities	**$91,000**

The balance sheet is like a snapshot of the company's financial condition at a specific moment in time (usually the month-end or year-end).

Statement of Cash Flows

The statement of cash flows provides information on the cash receipts and payments for a specific period of time. The statement of cash flows reports (1) the cash effects of a company's operations during a period, (2) its investing activities, (3) its financing activities, (4) the net increase or decrease in cash during the period, and (5) the cash amount at the end of the period.

Reporting the sources, uses, and change in cash is useful because investors, creditors, and others want to know what is happening to a company's most liquid resource. The statement of cash flows provides answers to the following simple but important questions.

1. Where did cash come from during the period?
2. What was cash used for during the period?
3. What was the change in the cash balance during the period?

As shown in Softbyte Inc.'s statement of cash flows in Illustration 1-10, cash increased $8,050 during the period. Net cash provided by operating activities increased cash $1,350. Cash flow from investing activities decreased cash $7,000, while cash flow from financing activities increased cash $13,700. At this time, you need not be concerned with how these amounts are determined. Chapter 13 will examine in detail how the statement is prepared.

Helpful Hint
Investing activities pertain to investments made by the company, not investments made by the owners.

People, Planet, and Profit Insight

Beyond Financial Statements

Should we expand our financial statements beyond the income statement, retained earnings statement, balance sheet, and statement of cash flows? Some believe we should take into account ecological and social performance, in addition to financial results, in evaluating a company. The argument is that a company's responsibility lies with anyone who is influenced by its actions. In other words, a company should be interested in benefiting many different parties, instead of only maximizing stockholders' interests.

A socially responsible business does not exploit or endanger any group of individuals. It follows fair trade practices, provides safe environments for workers, and bears responsibility for environmental damage. Granted, measurement of these factors is difficult. How to report this information is also controversial. But, many interesting and useful efforts are underway. Throughout this textbook, we provide additional insights into how companies are attempting to meet the challenge of measuring and reporting their contributions to society, as well as their financial results, to stockholders.

*Why might a company's stockholders be interested in its environmental and social performance? (Go to **WileyPLUS** for this answer and additional questions)*

DO IT! 5 Financial Statement Items

Presented below is selected information related to Flanagan Corporation at December 31, 2017. Flanagan reports financial information monthly.

Equipment	$10,000	Utilities Expense	$ 4,000
Cash	8,000	Accounts Receivable	9,000
Service Revenue	36,000	Salaries and Wages Expense	7,000
Rent Expense	11,000	Notes Payable	16,500
Accounts Payable	2,000	Dividends	5,000

(a) Determine the total assets of Flanagan at December 31, 2017.

(b) Determine the net income that Flanagan reported for December 2017.

(c) Determine the stockholders' equity of Flanagan at December 31, 2017.

Solution

Action Plan

✔ Remember the basic accounting equation: assets must equal liabilities plus stockholders' equity.

✔ Review previous financial statements to determine how total assets, net income, and stockholders' equity are computed.

(a) The total assets are $27,000, comprised of Cash $8,000, Accounts Receivable $9,000, and Equipment $10,000.

(b) Net income is $14,000, computed as follows.

Revenues		
Service revenue		$36,000
Expenses		
Rent expense	$11,000	
Salaries and wages expense	7,000	
Utilities expense	4,000	
Total expenses		22,000
Net income		$14,000

(c) The ending stockholders' equity of Flanagan Corporation is $8,500. By rewriting the accounting equation, we can compute stockholders' equity as assets minus liabilities, as follows.

Total assets [as computed in (a)]		$27,000
Less: Liabilities		
Notes payable	$16,500	
Accounts payable	2,000	18,500
Stockholders' equity		$ 8,500

Note that it is not possible to determine the corporation's stockholders' equity in any other way, because the beginning total for stockholders' equity is not provided.

Related exercise material: **BE1-10, BE1-11, E1-9, E1-10, E1-11, E1-12, E1-13, E1-14, E1-15, E1-16, E1-17, and DO IT! 1-5.**

APPENDIX 1A: Explain the career opportunities in accounting.

Why is accounting such a popular major and career choice? First, there are a lot of jobs. In many cities in recent years, the demand for accountants exceeded the supply. Not only are there a lot of jobs, but there are a wide array of opportunities. As one accounting organization observed, "accounting is one degree with 360 degrees of opportunity."

Accounting is also hot because it is obvious that accounting matters. Interest in accounting has increased, ironically, because of the attention caused by the accounting failures of companies such as **Enron** and **WorldCom**. These widely publicized scandals revealed the important role that accounting plays in society. Most people want to make a difference, and an accounting career provides many opportunities to contribute to society. Finally, the Sarbanes-Oxley Act (SOX) (see page 7) significantly increased the accounting and internal control requirements for corporations. This dramatically increased demand for professionals with accounting training.

Accountants are in such demand that it is not uncommon for accounting students to have accepted a job offer a year before graduation. As the following discussion reveals, the job options of people with accounting degrees are virtually unlimited.

Public Accounting

Individuals in **public accounting** offer expert service to the general public, in much the same way that doctors serve patients and lawyers serve clients. A major portion of public accounting involves **auditing**. In auditing, a certified public accountant (CPA) examines company financial statements and provides an opinion as to how accurately the financial statements present the company's results and financial position. Analysts, investors, and creditors rely heavily on these "audit opinions," which CPAs have the exclusive authority to issue.

Taxation is another major area of public accounting. The work that tax specialists perform includes tax advice and planning, preparing tax returns, and representing clients before governmental agencies such as the Internal Revenue Service.

A third area in public accounting is **management consulting**. It ranges from installing basic accounting software or highly complex enterprise resource planning systems, to performing support services for major marketing projects and merger and acquisition activities.

Many CPAs are entrepreneurs. They form small- or medium-sized practices that frequently specialize in tax or consulting services.

Private Accounting

Instead of working in public accounting, you might choose to be an employee of a for-profit company such as **Starbucks**, **Google**, or **PepsiCo**. In **private** (or **managerial**) **accounting**, you would be involved in activities such as cost accounting (finding the cost of producing specific products), budgeting, accounting information system design and support, and tax planning and preparation. You might also be a member of your company's internal audit team. In response to SOX, the internal auditors' job of reviewing the company's operations to ensure compliance with company policies and to increase efficiency has taken on increased importance.

Alternatively, many accountants work for not-for-profit organizations such as the **Red Cross** or the **Bill and Melinda Gates Foundation**, or for museums, libraries, or performing arts organizations.

Governmental Accounting

Another option is to pursue one of the many accounting opportunities in governmental agencies. For example, the Internal Revenue Service (IRS), Federal Bureau of Investigation (FBI), and the Securities and Exchange Commission (SEC) all employ accountants. The FBI has a stated goal that at least 15 percent of its new agents should be CPAs. There is also a very high demand for accounting educators at public colleges and universities and in state and local governments.

Forensic Accounting

Forensic accounting uses accounting, auditing, and investigative skills to conduct investigations into theft and fraud. It is listed among the top 20 career paths of the future. The job of forensic accountants is to catch the perpetrators of the estimated $600 billion per year of theft and fraud occurring at U.S. companies. This includes tracing money-laundering and identity-theft activities as well as tax evasion. Insurance companies hire forensic accountants to detect frauds such as arson, and law offices employ forensic accountants to identify marital assets in divorces. Forensic accountants often have FBI, IRS, or similar government experience.

"Show Me the Money"

How much can a new accountant make? Take a look at the average salaries for college graduates in public and private accounting. Keep in mind if you also have a CPA license, you'll make 10–15% more when you start out.

Illustration 1A-1

Salary estimates for jobs in public and corporate accounting

Employer	Jr. Level (0–3 yrs.)	Sr. Level (4–6 yrs.)
Public accounting (large firm)	$51,500–$74,250	$71,000–$92,250
Public accounting (small firm)	$42,500–$60,500	$57,000–$74,000
Corporate accounting (large company)	$41,750–$68,500	$67,000–$86,500
Corporate accounting (small company)	$37,000–$56,750	$52,750–$68,500

Serious earning potential over time gives CPAs great job security. Here are some examples of upper-level salaries for managers in corporate accounting. Note that geographic region, experience, education, CPA certification, and company size each play a role in determining salary.

Illustration 1A-2

Upper-level management salaries in corporate accounting

Position	Large Company	Small to Medium Company
Chief financial officer	$189,750–$411,000	$96,750–$190,500
Corporate controller	$128,000–$199,000	$82,750–$144,750
Tax manager	$100,250–$142,500	$79,500–$110,750

For up-to-date salary estimates, as well as a wealth of additional information regarding accounting as a career, check out **www.startheregoplaces.com.**

*The **Review and Practice** section provides opportunities for students to review key concepts and terms as well as complete multiple-choice questions, exercises, and a comprehensive problem. Detailed solutions are also included.*

REVIEW AND PRACTICE

LEARNING OBJECTIVES REVIEW

1 Identify the activities and users associated with accounting. Accounting is an information system that identifies, records, and communicates the economic events of an organization to interested users. The major users and uses of accounting are as follows. (a) Management uses accounting information to plan, organize, and run the business. (b) Investors (owners) decide whether to buy, hold, or sell their financial interests on the basis of accounting data. (c) Creditors (suppliers and bankers) evaluate the risks of granting credit or lending money on the basis of accounting information. Other groups that use accounting information are taxing authorities, regulatory agencies, customers, and labor unions.

❷ Explain the building blocks of accounting: ethics, principles, and assumptions. Ethics are the standards of conduct by which actions are judged as right or wrong. Effective financial reporting depends on sound ethical behavior. Generally accepted accounting principles are a common set of standards used by accountants. The primary accounting standard-setting body in the United States is the Financial Accounting Standards Board. The monetary unit assumption requires that companies include in the accounting records only transaction data that can be expressed in terms of money. The economic entity assumption requires that the activities of each economic entity be kept separate from the activities of its owner(s) and other economic entities.

❸ State the accounting equation, and define its components. The basic accounting equation is:

$$\text{Assets} = \text{Liabilities} + \text{Stockholders' Equity}$$

Assets are resources a business owns. Liabilities are creditorship claims on total assets. Stockholders' equity is the ownership claim on total assets.

The expanded accounting equation is:

$$\text{Assets} = \text{Liabilities} + \text{Common Stock}$$
$$+ \text{Revenues} - \text{Expenses} - \text{Dividends}$$

Common stock is affected when the company issues new shares of stock in exchange for cash. Revenues are increases in assets resulting from income-earning activities. Expenses are the costs of assets consumed or services used in the process of earning revenue. Dividends are payments the company makes to its stockholders.

❹ Analyze the effects of business transactions on the accounting equation. Each business transaction must have a dual effect on the accounting equation. For example, if an individual asset increases, there must be a corresponding (1) decrease in another asset, or (2) increase in a specific liability, or (3) increase in stockholders' equity.

❺ Describe the four financial statements and how they are prepared. An income statement presents the revenues and expenses and resulting net income or net loss for a specific period of time. A retained earnings statement summarizes the changes in retained earnings for a specific period of time. A balance sheet reports the assets, liabilities, and stockholders' equity at a specific date. A statement of cash flows summarizes information about the cash inflows (receipts) and outflows (payments) for a specific period of time.

*❻ Explain the career opportunities in accounting. Accounting offers many different jobs in fields such as public and private accounting, governmental accounting, and forensic accounting. Accounting is a popular major because there are many different types of jobs, with unlimited potential for career advancement.

GLOSSARY REVIEW

Accounting The information system that identifies, records, and communicates the economic events of an organization to interested users. (p. 4).

Assets Resources a business owns. (p. 12).

*Auditing The examination of financial statements by a certified public accountant in order to express an opinion as to how accurately the financial statements present the company's results and financial position. (p. 25).

Balance sheet A financial statement that reports the assets, liabilities, and stockholders' equity at a specific date. (p. 21).

Basic accounting equation Assets = Liabilities + Stockholders' Equity. (p. 12).

Bookkeeping A part of accounting that involves only the recording of economic events. (p. 5).

Common stock Term used to describe the total amount paid in by stockholders for the shares they purchase. (p. 13).

Convergence The process of reducing the differences between U.S. GAAP and IFRS. (p. 9).

Corporation A business organized as a separate legal entity under state corporation law, having ownership divided into transferable shares of stock. (p. 10).

Dividend A distribution by a corporation to its stockholders. (p. 13).

Economic entity assumption An assumption that requires that the activities of the entity be kept separate and distinct from the activities of its owner and all other economic entities. (p. 10).

Ethics The standards of conduct by which one's actions are judged as right or wrong, honest or dishonest, fair or not fair. (p. 8).

Expanded accounting equation Assets = Liabilities + Common stock + Revenues − Expenses − Dividends. (p. 15).

Expenses The cost of assets consumed or services used in the process of earning revenue. (p. 13).

Fair value principle An accounting principle stating that assets and liabilities should be reported at fair value (the price received to sell an asset or settle a liability). (p. 9).

Faithful representation Numbers and descriptions match what really existed or happened—they are factual. (p. 9).

Financial accounting The field of accounting that provides economic and financial information for investors, creditors, and other external users. (p. 6).

Financial Accounting Standards Board (FASB) A private organization that establishes generally accepted accounting principles in the United States (GAAP). (p. 9).

*Forensic accounting An area of accounting that uses accounting, auditing, and investigative skills to conduct investigations into theft and fraud. (p. 26).

Generally accepted accounting principles (GAAP) Common standards that indicate how to report economic events. (p. 9).

Historical cost principle An accounting principle that states that companies should record assets at their cost. (p. 9).

Income statement A financial statement that presents the revenues and expenses and resulting net income or net loss of a company for a specific period of time. (p. 21).

International Accounting Standards Board (IASB) An accounting standard-setting body that issues standards adopted by many countries outside of the United States. (p. 9).

International Financial Reporting Standards (IFRS) International accounting standards set by the International Accounting Standards Board (IASB). (p. 9).

Liabilities Creditor claims against total assets. (p. 12).

*Management consulting An area of public accounting ranging from development of accounting and computer systems to support services for marketing projects and merger and acquisition activities. (p. 25).

Managerial accounting The field of accounting that provides internal reports to help users make decisions about their companies. (p. 6).

Monetary unit assumption An assumption stating that companies include in the accounting records only transaction data that can be expressed in terms of money. (p. 10).

Net income The amount by which revenues exceed expenses. (p. 21).

Net loss The amount by which expenses exceed revenues. (p. 21).

Partnership A business owned by two or more persons associated as partners. (p. 10).

*Private (or managerial) accounting An area of accounting within a company that involves such activities as cost accounting, budgeting, design and support of accounting information systems, and tax planning and preparation. (p. 25).

Proprietorship A business owned by one person. (p. 10).

*Public accounting An area of accounting in which the accountant offers expert service to the general public. (p. 25).

Relevance Financial information that is capable of making a difference in a decision. (p. 9).

Retained earnings statement A financial statement that summarizes the changes in retained earnings for a specific period of time. (p. 21).

Revenues The gross increase in stockholders' equity resulting from business activities entered into for the purpose of earning income. (p. 13).

Sarbanes-Oxley Act (SOX) Law passed by Congress intended to reduce unethical corporate behavior. (p. 7).

Securities and Exchange Commission (SEC) A governmental agency that oversees U.S. financial markets and accounting standard-setting bodies. (p. 9).

Statement of cash flows A financial statement that summarizes information about the cash inflows (receipts) and cash outflows (payments) for a specific period of time. (p. 21).

Stockholders' equity The ownership claim on a corporation's total assets. (p. 12).

*Taxation An area of public accounting involving tax advice, tax planning, preparing tax returns, and representing clients before governmental agencies. (p. 25).

Transactions The economic events of a business that are recorded by accountants. (p. 14).

PRACTICE MULTIPLE-CHOICE QUESTIONS

(LO 1) **1.** Which of the following is **not** a step in the accounting process?
(a) Identification.   (c) Recording.
(b) Economic entity.   (d) Communication.

(LO 1) **2.** Which of the following statements about users of accounting information is **incorrect**?
(a) Management is an internal user.
(b) Taxing authorities are external users.
(c) Present creditors are external users.
(d) Regulatory authorities are internal users.

(LO 2) **3.** The historical cost principle states that:
(a) assets should be initially recorded at cost and adjusted when the fair value changes.
(b) activities of an entity are to be kept separate and distinct from its owner.
(c) assets should be recorded at their cost.
(d) only transaction data capable of being expressed in terms of money be included in the accounting records.

4. Which of the following statements about basic assumptions is **correct**? (LO 2)
(a) Basic assumptions are the same as accounting principles.
(b) The economic entity assumption states that there should be a particular unit of accountability.
(c) The monetary unit assumption enables accounting to measure employee morale.
(d) Partnerships are not economic entities.

5. The three types of business entities are: (LO 2)
(a) proprietorships, small businesses, and partnerships.
(b) proprietorships, partnerships, and corporations.
(c) proprietorships, partnerships, and large businesses.
(d) financial, manufacturing, and service companies.

6. Net income will result during a time period when: (LO 3)
(a) assets exceed liabilities.
(b) assets exceed revenues.
(c) expenses exceed revenues.
(d) revenues exceed expenses.

(LO 3) 7. As of December 31, 2017, Reed Company has assets of $3,500 and stockholders' equity of $1,500. What are the liabilities for Reed Company as of December 31, 2017?
- (a) $1,500.
- (b) $1,000.
- (c) $2,500.
- (d) $2,000.

(LO 4) 8. Performing services on account will have the following effects on the components of the basic accounting equation:
- (a) increase assets and decrease stockholders' equity.
- (b) increase assets and increase stockholders' equity.
- (c) increase assets and increase liabilities.
- (d) increase liabilities and increase stockholders' equity.

(LO 4) 9. Which of the following events is **not** recorded in the accounting records?
- (a) Equipment is purchased on account.
- (b) An employee is terminated.
- (c) A cash investment is made into the business.
- (d) The company pays a cash dividend.

(LO 4) 10. During 2017, Seisor Company's assets decreased $50,000 and its liabilities decreased $90,000. Its stockholders' equity therefore:
- (a) increased $40,000.
- (b) decreased $140,000.
- (c) decreased $40,000.
- (d) increased $140,000.

(LO 4) 11. Payment of an account payable affects the components of the accounting equation in the following way.
- (a) Decreases stockholders' equity and decreases liabilities.
- (b) Increases assets and decreases liabilities.
- (c) Decreases assets and increases stockholders' equity.
- (d) Decreases assets and decreases liabilities.

(LO 5) 12. Which of the following statements is **false**?
- (a) A statement of cash flows summarizes information about the cash inflows (receipts) and outflows (payments) for a specific period of time.
- (b) A balance sheet reports the assets, liabilities, and stockholders' equity at a specific date.
- (c) An income statement presents the revenues, expenses, changes in stockholders' equity, and resulting net income or net loss for a specific period of time.
- (d) A retained earnings statement summarizes the changes in retained earnings for a specific period of time.

(LO 5) 13. On the last day of the period, Alan Cesska Company buys a $900 machine on credit. This transaction will affect the:
- (a) income statement only.
- (b) balance sheet only.
- (c) income statement and retained earnings statement only.
- (d) income statement, retained earnings statement, and balance sheet.

(LO 5) 14. The financial statement that reports assets, liabilities, and stockholders' equity is the:
- (a) income statement.
- (b) retained earnings statement.
- (c) balance sheet.
- (d) statement of cash flows.

(LO 6) *15. Services performed by a public accountant include:
- (a) auditing, taxation, and management consulting.
- (b) auditing, budgeting, and management consulting.
- (c) auditing, budgeting, and cost accounting.
- (d) auditing, budgeting, and management consulting.

Solutions

1. (b) Economic entity is not one of the steps in the accounting process. The other choices are true because (a) identification is the first step in the accounting process, (c) recording is the second step in the accounting process, and (d) communication is the third and final step in the accounting process.

2. (d) Regulatory authorities are external, not internal, users of accounting information. The other choices are true statements.

3. (c) The historical cost principle states that assets should be recorded at their cost. The other choices are incorrect because (a) the historical cost principle does not say that assets should be adjusted for changes in fair value, (b) describes the economic entity assumption, and (d) describes the monetary unit assumption.

4. (b) The economic entity assumption states that there should be a particular unit of accountability. The other choices are incorrect because (a) basic assumptions are not the same as accounting principles, (c) the monetary unit assumption allows accounting to measure economic events, and (d) partnerships are economic entities.

5. (b) Proprietorships, partnerships, and corporations are the three types of business entities. Choices (a) and (c) are incorrect because small and large businesses only denote the sizes of businesses. Choice (d) is incorrect because financial, manufacturing, and service companies are types of businesses, not business entities.

6. (d) Net income results when revenues exceed expenses. The other choices are incorrect because (a) assets and liabilities are not used in the computation of net income; (b) revenues, not assets, are included in the computation of net income; and (c) when expenses exceed revenues, a net loss results.

7. (d) Using a variation of the basic accounting equation, Assets − Stockholders' equity = Liabilities, $3,500 − $1,500 = $2,000. Therefore, choices (a) $1,500, (b) $1,000, and (c) $2,500 are incorrect.

8. (b) When services are performed on account, assets are increased and stockholders' equity is increased. The other choices are incorrect because when services are performed on account (a) stockholders' equity is increased, not decreased; (c) liabilities are not affected; and (d) stockholders' equity is increased and liabilities are not affected.

9. (b) If an employee is terminated, this represents an activity of a company, not a business transaction. Assets, liabilities, and stockholders' equity are not affected. Thus, there is no effect on the accounting equation. The other choices are incorrect because they are all recorded: (a) when equipment is purchased on account, both assets and liabilities increase; (c) when a cash investment is made into a business, both assets and stockholders' equity increase; and (d) when a dividend is paid, both assets and stockholders' equity decrease.

10. (a) Using the basic accounting equation, Assets = Liabilities + Stockholders' equity, −$50,000 = −$90,000 + Stockholders' equity, so stockholders' equity increased $40,000, not (b) decreased $140,000, (c) decreased $40,000, or (d) increased $140,000.

11. (d) Payment of an account payable results in an equal decrease of assets (cash) and liabilities (accounts payable). The other choices are incorrect because payment of an account payable (a) does not affect stockholders' equity, (b) does not increase assets, and (c) does not affect stockholders' equity.

12. (c) An income statement represents the revenues, expenses, and the resulting net income or net loss for a specific period of time but not the changes in stockholders' equity. The other choices are true statements.

13. (b) This transaction will cause assets to increase by $900 and liabilities to increase by $900. The other choices are incorrect because this transaction (a) will have no effect on the income statement, (c) will have no effect on the income statement or the retained earnings statement, and (d) will affect the balance sheet but not the income statement or the retained earnings statement.

14. (c) The balance sheet is the statement that reports assets, liabilities and stockholders' equity. The other choices are incorrect because (a) the income statement reports revenues and expenses, (b) the retained earnings statement reports details about stockholders' equity, and (d) the statement of cash flows reports inflows and outflows of cash.

*15. (a) Auditing, taxation, and management consulting are all services performed by public accountants. The other choices are incorrect because public accountants do not perform budgeting or cost accounting.

PRACTICE EXERCISES

Analyze the effect of transactions
(LO 3, 4)

1. Selected transactions for Beale Lawn Care Company are listed below.

1. Sold common stock for cash to start business.
2. Paid monthly utilities.
3. Purchased land on account.
4. Billed customers for services performed.
5. Paid dividends.
6. Received cash from customers billed in (4).
7. Incurred utilities expense on account.
8. Purchased equipment for cash.
9. Received cash from customers when service was performed.

Instructions

List the numbers of the above transactions and describe the effect of each transaction on assets, liabilities, and stockholders' equity. For example, the first answer is (1) Increase in assets and increase in stockholders' equity.

Solution

1. 1. Increase in assets and increase in stockholders' equity.
   2. Decrease in assets and decrease in stockholders' equity.
   3. Increase in assets and increase in liabilities.
   4. Increase in assets and increase in stockholders' equity.
   5. Decrease in assets and decrease in stockholders' equity.
   6. Increase in assets and decrease in assets.
   7. Increase in liabilities and decrease in stockholders' equity.
   8. Increase in assets and decrease in assets.
   9. Increase in assets and increase in stockholders' equity.

Analyze the effect of transactions on assets, liabilities, and stockholders' equity.
(LO 3, 4)

2. Hayes Computer Timeshare Company entered into the following transactions during May 2017.

1. Purchased office equipment for $10,000 from Office Outfitters on account.
2. Paid $3,000 cash for May rent on storage space.
3. Received $12,000 cash from customers for contracts billed in April.

4. Performed services for Bayliss Construction Company for $4,000 cash.

5. Paid Southern Power Co. $10,000 cash for energy usage in May.

6. Stockholders invested an additional $30,000 in the business.

7. Paid Office Outfitters for the equipment purchased in (1) above.

8. Incurred advertising expense for May of $1,500 on account.

Instructions

Indicate with the appropriate letter whether each of the transactions above results in:

(a) An increase in assets and a decrease in assets.

(b) An increase in assets and an increase in stockholders' equity.

(c) An increase in assets and an increase in liabilities.

(d) A decrease in assets and a decrease in stockholders' equity.

(e) A decrease in assets and a decrease in liabilities.

(f) An increase in liabilities and a decrease in stockholders' equity.

(g) An increase in stockholders' equity and a decrease in liabilities.

Solution

2. 1. (c)	3. (a)	5. (d)	7. (e)
2. (d)	4. (b)	6. (b)	8. (f)

▮ PRACTICE PROBLEM

Legal Services Inc. was incorporated on July 1, 2017. During the first month of operations, the following transactions occurred.

Prepare a tabular presentation and financial statements.

(LO 4, 5)

1. Stockholders invested $10,000 in cash in exchange for common stock of Legal Services Inc.

2. Paid $800 for July rent on office space.

3. Purchased office equipment on account $3,000.

4. Performed legal services for clients for cash $1,500.

5. Borrowed $700 cash from a bank on a note payable.

6. Performed legal services for client on account $2,000.

7. Paid monthly expenses: salaries $500, utilities $300, and advertising $100.

Instructions

(a) Prepare a tabular summary of the transactions.

(b) Prepare the income statement, retained earnings statement, and balance sheet at July 31, 2017, for Legal Services Inc.

Solution

(a)

Trans-action	Cash	+	Accounts Receivable	+	Equipment	=	Notes Payable	+	Accounts Payable	+	Common Stock	+	Rev.	−	Exp.	−	Div.	
(1)	+$10,000					=					+$10,000							Issued Stock
(2)	−800														−$800			Rent Expense
(3)					+$3,000	=			+$3,000									
(4)	+1,500												+$1,500					Service Revenue
(5)	+700						+$700											
(6)			+$2,000										+2,000					Service Revenue
(7)	−500														−500			Sal./Wages Exp.
	−300														−300			Utilities Expense
	−100														−100			Advertising Expense
	$10,500	+	$2,000	+	$3,000	=	$700	+	$3,000	+	$10,000	+	$3,500	−	$1,700			
			$15,500								$15,500							

Assets = Liabilities + Stockholders' Equity

Retained Earnings

(b)

LEGAL SERVICES INC.
Income Statement
For the Month Ended July 31, 2017

Revenues		
Service revenue		$3,500
Expenses		
Rent expense	$800	
Salaries and wages expense	500	
Utilities expense	300	
Advertising expense	100	
Total expenses		1,700
Net income		$1,800

LEGAL SERVICES INC.
Retained Earnings Statement
For the Month Ended July 31, 2017

Retained earnings, July 1	$ –0–
Add: Net income	1,800
Retained earnings, July 31	$1,800

LEGAL SERVICES INC.
Balance Sheet
July 31, 2017

Assets

Cash	$10,500
Accounts receivable	2,000
Equipment	3,000
Total assets	$15,500

Liabilities and Stockholders' Equity

Liabilities		
Notes payable	$ 700	
Accounts payable	3,000	
Total liabilities		$ 3,700
Stockholders' equity		
Common stock	10,000	
Retained earnings	1,800	11,800
Total liabilities and stockholders' equity		$15,500

WileyPLUS Brief Exercises, Exercises, **DO IT!** Exercises, and Problems and many additional resources are available for practice in WileyPLUS

NOTE: All asterisked Questions, Exercises, and Problems relate to material in the appendix to the chapter.

QUESTIONS

1. "Accounting is ingrained in our society and it is vital to our economic system." Do you agree? Explain.
2. Identify and describe the steps in the accounting process.
3. (a) Who are internal users of accounting data?
   (b) How does accounting provide relevant data to these users?

4. What uses of financial accounting information are made by (a) investors and (b) creditors?
5. "Bookkeeping and accounting are the same." Do you agree? Explain.
6. Harper Travel Agency purchased land for $85,000 cash on December 10, 2017. At December 31, 2017, the land's value has increased to $93,000. What

amount should be reported for land on Harper's balance sheet at December 31, 2017? Explain.

7. What is the monetary unit assumption?

8. What is the economic entity assumption?

9. What are the three basic forms of profit-oriented business organizations?

10. Juana Perez is the owner of a successful printing shop. Recently, her business has been increasing, and Juana has been thinking about changing the organization of her business from a proprietorship to a corporation. Discuss some of the advantages Juana would enjoy if she were to incorporate her business.

11. What is the basic accounting equation?

12. (a) Define the terms assets, liabilities, and stockholders' equity.
(b) What items affect stockholders' equity?

13. Which of the following items are liabilities of jewelry stores?
(a) Cash.
(b) Accounts payable.
(c) Dividends.
(d) Accounts receivable.
(e) Supplies.
(f) Equipment.
(h) Service revenue.
(g) Salaries and wages payable.
(i) Rent expense.

14. Can a business enter into a transaction in which only the left side of the basic accounting equation is affected? If so, give an example.

15. Are the following events recorded in the accounting records? Explain your answer in each case.
(a) The president of the company dies.
(b) Supplies are purchased on account.
(c) An employee is fired.

16. Indicate how the following business transactions affect the basic accounting equation.
(a) Paid cash for janitorial services.
(b) Purchased equipment for cash.
(c) Invested cash in the business for stock.
(d) Paid accounts payable in full.

17. Listed below are some items found in the financial statements of Jonas Co. Indicate in which financial statement(s) the following items would appear.
(a) Service revenue.
(b) Equipment.
(c) Advertising expense.
(d) Accounts receivable.
(e) Retained earnings.
(f) Salaries and wages payable.

18. In February 2017, Rachel Paige invested an additional $10,000 in Drumlin Company. Drumlin's accountant, Liz Cooke, recorded this receipt as an increase in cash and revenues. Is this treatment appropriate? Why or why not?

19. "A company's net income appears directly on the income statement and the retained earnings statement, and it is included indirectly in the company's balance sheet." Do you agree? Explain.

20. Monique Enterprises had a stockholders' equity balance of $158,000 at the beginning of the period. At the end of the accounting period, the stockholders' equity balance was $198,000.
(a) Assuming no additional investment or distributions during the period, what is the net income for the period?
(b) Assuming an additional investment of $16,000 but no distributions during the period, what is the net income for the period?

21. Summarized operations for Lakeview Co. for the month of July are as follows.

Revenues recognized: for cash $30,000; on account $70,000.

Expenses incurred: for cash $26,000; on account $38,000.

Indicate for Lakeview Co. (a) the total revenues, (b) the total expenses, and (c) net income for the month of July.

22. The basic accounting equation is Assets = Liabilities + Stockholders' equity. Replacing the words in that equation with dollar amounts, what is Apple's accounting equation at September 28, 2013?

BRIEF EXERCISES

BE1-1 Presented below is the basic accounting equation. Determine the missing amounts.

Use basic accounting equation.

(LO 3)

Assets	=	Liabilities	+	Stockholders' Equity
(a) $78,000		$50,000		?
(b) ?		$45,000		$70,000
(c) $94,000		?		$60,000

BE1-2 Given the accounting equation, answer each of the following questions.

(a) The liabilities of Holland Company are $120,000 and its stockholders' equity is $232,000. What is the amount of Holland Company's total assets?

(b) The total assets of Holland Company are $190,000 and its stockholders' equity is $86,000. What is the amount of its total liabilities?

(c) The total assets of Holland Company are $600,000 and its liabilities are equal to one-half of its total assets. What is the amount of Holland Company's stockholders' equity?

Use basic accounting equation.

(LO 3)

BE1-3 At the beginning of the year, Canon Company had total assets of $870,000 and total liabilities of $500,000. Answer the following questions.

(a) If total assets increased $150,000 during the year and total liabilities decreased $80,000, what is the amount of stockholders' equity at the end of the year?

Use basic accounting equation.

(LO 3)

(b) During the year, total liabilities increased $100,000 and stockholders' equity decreased $66,000. What is the amount of total assets at the end of the year?

(c) If total assets decreased $80,000 and stockholders' equity increased $120,000 during the year, what is the amount of total liabilities at the end of the year?

Solve accounting equation.

(LO 3)

BE1-4 Use the accounting equation to answer each of the following questions.

(a) The liabilities of Olga Company are $90,000. Common stock account is $150,000; dividends are $40,000; revenues, $450,000; and expenses, $320,000. What is the amount of Olga Company's total assets?

(b) The total assets of Lafayette Company are $57,000. Common stock account is $23,000; dividends are $7,000; revenues, $50,000; and expenses, $35,000. What is the amount of the company's total liabilities?

(c) The total assets of Dierdorf Co. are $600,000 and its liabilities are equal to two-thirds of its total assets. What is the amount of Dierdorf Co.'s stockholders' equity?

Identify assets, liabilities, and stockholders' equity.

(LO 3)

BE1-5 Indicate whether each of the following items is an asset (A), liability (L), or part of stockholders' equity (SE).

_____ (a) Accounts receivable   _____ (d) Supplies
_____ (b) Salaries and wages payable _____ (e) Owner's investment
_____ (c) Equipment   _____ (f) Notes payable

Determine effect of transactions on basic accounting equation.

(LO 4)

BE1-6 Presented below are three business transactions. On a sheet of paper, list the letters (a), (b), and (c) with columns for assets, liabilities, and stockholders' equity. For each column, indicate whether the transactions increased (+), decreased (−), or had no effect (NE) on assets, liabilities, and stockholders' equity.

(a) Purchased supplies on account.
(b) Received cash for performing a service.
(c) Paid expenses in cash.

Determine effect of transactions on accounting equation.

(LO 4)

BE1-7 Follow the same format as BE1-6 above. Determine the effect on assets, liabilities, and stockholders' equity of the following three transactions.

(a) Stockholders invested cash in the business for common stock.
(b) Paid a cash dividend.
(c) Received cash from a customer who had previously been billed for services performed.

Classify items affecting stockholders' equity.

(LO 3)

BE1-8 Classify each of the following items as dividends (D), revenue (R), or expense (E).

_____ (a) Advertising expense   _____ (e) Dividends
_____ (b) Service revenue   _____ (f) Rent revenue
_____ (c) Insurance expense   _____ (g) Utilities expense
_____ (d) Salaries and wages expense

Determine effect of transactions on stockholders' equity.

(LO 4)

BE1-9 Presented below are three transactions. Mark each transaction as affecting common stock (C), dividends (D), revenue (R), expense (E), or not affecting stockholders' equity (NSE).

_____ (a) Received cash for services performed.
_____ (b) Paid cash to purchase equipment.
_____ (c) Paid employee salaries.

Prepare a balance sheet.

(LO 5)

BE1-10 In alphabetical order below are balance sheet items for Ellerby Company at December 31, 2017. Prepare a balance sheet, following the format of Illustration 1-10.

Accounts payable	$85,000
Accounts receivable	72,500
Cash	44,000
Common stock	31,500

Determine where items appear on financial statements.

(LO 5)

BE1-11 Indicate whether the following items would appear on the income statement (IS), balance sheet (BS), or retained earnings statement (RE).

_____ (a) Notes payable   _____ (d) Cash
_____ (b) Advertising expense _____ (e) Service revenue
_____ (c) Common stock   _____ (f) Dividends

DO IT! Exercises

DO IT! 1-1 Indicate whether each of the five statements presented below is true or false. If false, indicate how to correct the statement.

Review basic concepts.
(LO 1, 2)

1. The three steps in the accounting process are identification, recording, and examination.
2. The accounting process includes the bookkeeping function.
3. Managerial accounting provides reports to help investors and creditors evaluate a company.
4. The two most common types of external users are investors and creditors.
5. Internal users include human resources managers.

DO IT! 1-2 Indicate whether each of the five statements presented below is true or false. If false, indicate how to correct the statement.

Review basic concepts.
(LO 1, 2)

1. Congress passed the Sarbanes-Oxley Act to ensure that investors invest only in companies that will be profitable.
2. The standards of conduct by which actions are judged as loyal or disloyal are ethics.
3. The primary accounting standard-setting body in the United States is the Securities and Exchange Commission (SEC).
4. The historical cost principle dictates that companies record assets at their cost and continue to report them at their cost over the time the asset is held.
5. The monetary unit assumption requires that companies record only transactions that can be measured in money terms.

DO IT! 1-3 Classify the following items as issuance of stock (I), dividends (D), revenues (R), or expenses (E). Then indicate whether each item increases or decreases stockholders' equity.

Evaluate effects of transactions on stockholders' equity
(LO 3)

1. Dividends.
2. Rent revenue.
3. Advertising expense.
4. Stockholders invest cash in the business.

DO IT! 1-4 Transactions made by Morlan and Co., a law firm, for the month of March are shown below. Prepare a tabular analysis which shows the effects of these transactions on the accounting equation, similar to that shown in Illustration 1-9 (page 20).

Prepare tabular analysis.
(LO 4)

1. The company performed $23,000 of services for customers, on credit.
2. The company received $23,000 in cash from customers who had been billed for services (in transaction 1).
3. The company received a bill for $1,800 of advertising, but will not pay it until a later date.
4. The company paid a dividend of $5,000 in cash to stockholders.

DO IT! 1-5 Presented below is selected information related to Garryowen Company at December 31, 2017. Garryowen reports financial information monthly.

Determine specific amounts on the financial statements.
(LO 5)

Accounts Payable	$ 3,000	Salaries and Wages Expense	$16,500
Cash	9,000	Notes Payable	25,000
Advertising Expense	6,000	Rent Expense	9,800
Service Revenue	54,000	Accounts Receivable	13,500
Equipment	29,000	Dividends	7,500

(a) Determine the total assets of Garryowen Company at December 31, 2017.
(b) Determine the net income that Garryowen Company reported for December 2017.
(c) Determine the stockholders' equity of Garryowen Company at December 31, 2017.

EXERCISES

E1-1 Callison Company performs the following accounting tasks during the year.

Classify the three activities of accounting.
(LO 1)

_____ Analyzing and interpreting information.
_____ Classifying economic events.
_____ Explaining uses, meaning, and limitations of data.
_____ Keeping a systematic chronological diary of events.
_____ Measuring events in dollars and cents.
_____ Preparing accounting reports.
_____ Reporting information in a standard format.
_____ Selecting economic activities relevant to the company.
_____ Summarizing economic events.

Accounting is "an information system that **identifies**, **records**, and **communicates** the economic events of an organization to interested users."

Instructions

Categorize the accounting tasks performed by Callison as relating to either the identification (I), recording (R), or communication (C) aspects of accounting.

Identify users of accounting information.

(LO 1)

E1-2 (a) The following are users of financial statements.

_____ Customers	_____ Securities and Exchange Commission
_____ Internal Revenue Service	_____ Store manager
_____ Labor unions	_____ Suppliers
_____ Marketing manager	_____ Vice president of finance
_____ Production supervisor	

Instructions

Identify the users as being either **external users (E)** or **internal users (I)**.

(b) The following questions could be asked by an internal user or an external user.

_____ Can we afford to give our employees a pay raise?
_____ Did the company earn a satisfactory income?
_____ Do we need to borrow in the near future?
_____ How does the company's profitability compare to other companies?
_____ What does it cost us to manufacture each unit produced?
_____ Which product should we emphasize?
_____ Will the company be able to pay its short-term debts?

Instructions

Identify each of the questions as being more likely asked by an **internal user (I)** or an **external user (E)**.

Discuss ethics and the historical cost principle.

(LO 2)

E1-3 Sam Cresco, president of Cresco Company, has instructed Sharon Gross, the head of the accounting department for Cresco Company, to report the company's land in the company's accounting reports at its fair value of $170,000 instead of its cost of $100,000. Cresco says, "Showing the land at $170,000 will make our company look like a better investment when we try to attract new investors next month."

Instructions

Explain the ethical situation involved for Sharon Gross, identifying the stakeholders and the alternatives.

Use accounting concepts.

(LO 2)

E1-4 The following situations involve accounting principles and assumptions.

1. Tina Company owns buildings that are worth substantially more than they originally cost. In an effort to provide more relevant information, Tina reports the buildings at fair value in its accounting reports.
2. Fayette Company includes in its accounting records only transaction data that can be expressed in terms of money.
3. Omar Shariff, president of Omar's Oasis, records his personal living costs as expenses of Oasis.

Instructions

For each of the three situations, state if the accounting method used is correct or incorrect. If correct, identify which principle or assumption supports the method used. If incorrect, identify which principle or assumption has been violated.

Classify accounts as assets, liabilities, and stockholders' equity.

(LO 3)

E1-5 Bailey Cleaners has the following balance sheet items.

Accounts payable	Accounts receivable
Cash	Notes payable
Equipment	Salaries and wages payable
Supplies	Common stock

Instructions

Classify each item as an asset, liability, or stockholders' equity.

Analyze the effect of transactions.

(LO 4)

E1-6 Selected transactions for Verdent Lawn Care Company are as follows.

1. Sold common stock for cash to start business.
2. Paid monthly rent.

3. Purchased equipment on account.
4. Billed customers for services performed.
5. Paid dividends.
6. Received cash from customers billed in (4).
7. Incurred advertising expense on account.
8. Purchased additional equipment for cash.
9. Received cash from customers when service was performed.

Instructions

List the numbers of the above transactions and describe the effect of each transaction on assets, liabilities, and stockholders' equity. For example, the first answer is (1) Increase in assets and increase in stockholders' equity.

E1-7 Keystone Computer Timeshare Company entered into the following transactions during May 2017.

1. Purchased computers for $20,000 from Data Equipment on account.
2. Paid $3,000 cash for May rent on storage space.
3. Received $15,000 cash from customers for contracts billed in April.
4. Performed computer services for Ryan Construction Company for $2,700 cash.
5. Paid Midland Power Co. $11,000 cash for energy usage in May.
6. Stockholders invested an additional $32,000 in the business.
7. Paid Data Equipment for the computers purchased in (1) above.
8. Incurred advertising expense for May of $840 on account.

Analyze the effect of transactions on assets, liabilities, and stockholders' equity.

(LO 4)

Instructions

Indicate with the appropriate letter whether each of the transactions results in:

(a) An increase in assets and a decrease in assets.
(b) An increase in assets and an increase in stockholders' equity.
(c) An increase in assets and an increase in liabilities.
(d) A decrease in assets and a decrease in stockholders' equity.
(e) A decrease in assets and a decrease in liabilities.
(f) An increase in liabilities and a decrease in stockholders' equity.
(g) An increase in stockholders' equity and a decrease in liabilities.

E1-8 An analysis of the transactions made by Foley & Co., a certified public accounting firm, for the month of August is shown below. Each increase and decrease in stockholders' equity is explained.

Analyze transactions and compute net income.

(LO 4, 5)

	Assets				= Liabilities +	Stockholders' Equity				
Cash	+ Accounts Receivable	+ Supplies	+ Equipment =		Accounts Payable	+ Common Stock	+ Retained Earnings			
							Rev.	− Exp.	− Div.	
1. +$15,000						+$15,000				
2. −2,000			+$5,000		+$3,000					
3. −750		+$750								
4. +4,900	+$4,500						+$9,400			Service Revenue
5. −1,500					−1,500					
6. −2,000									−$2,000	
7. −850								−$850		Rent Expense
8. +450	−450									
9. −3,900								−3,900		Sal./Wages Expense
10.					+500			−500		Utilities Expense

Instructions

(a) ✏ Describe each transaction that occurred for the month.
(b) Determine how much stockholders' equity increased for the month.
(c) Compute the amount of net income for the month.

E1-9 An analysis of transactions for Foley & Co. was presented in E1–8. Assume that August is the company's first month of business.

Prepare financial statements.

(LO 5)

Instructions

Prepare an income statement and a retained earnings statement for August and a balance sheet at August 31, 2017.

Determine net income (or loss).

(LO 5)

E1-10 Toth Company had the following assets and liabilities on the dates indicated.

December 31	Total Assets	Total Liabilities
2016	$400,000	$260,000
2017	$480,000	$300,000
2018	$590,000	$400,000

Toth began business on January 1, 2016, with an investment of $100,000 from stockholders.

Instructions

From an analysis of the change in stockholders' equity during the year, compute the net income (or loss) for:

(a) 2016, assuming Toth paid $15,000 in dividends for the year.

(b) 2017, assuming stockholders made an additional investment of $50,000 and Toth paid no dividends in 2017.

(c) 2018, assuming stockholders made an additional investment of $15,000 and Toth paid dividends of $30,000 in 2018.

Analyze financial statement items.

(LO 5)

E1-11 Two items are omitted from each of the following summaries of balance sheet and income statement data for two corporations for the year 2017, Plunkett Co. and Herring Enterprises.

	Plunkett Co.	Herring Enterprises
Beginning of year:		
Total assets	$ 97,000	$122,000
Total liabilities	85,000	(c)
Total stockholders' equity	(a)	75,000
End of year:		
Total assets	160,000	180,000
Total liabilities	120,000	50,000
Total stockholders' equity	40,000	130,000
Changes during year in stockholders' equity:		
Additional investment	(b)	25,000
Dividends	15,000	(d)
Total revenues	215,000	100,000
Total expenses	175,000	55,000

Instructions

Determine the missing amounts.

Prepare income statement and retained earnings statement.

(LO 5)

E1-12 The following information relates to La Greca Co. for the year 2017.

Retained earnings, January 1, 2017	$48,000	Advertising expense	$ 1,800
Dividends during 2017	5,000	Rent expense	10,400
Service revenue	62,500	Utilities expense	3,100
Salaries and wages expense	28,000		

Instructions

After analyzing the data, prepare an income statement and a retained earnings statement for the year ending December 31, 2017.

Correct an incorrectly prepared balance sheet.

(LO 5)

E1-13 Robyn Howser is the bookkeeper for Madison Company. Robyn has been trying to determine the correct balance sheet for Madison Company. Madison's balance sheet is shown below.

MADISON COMPANY
Balance Sheet
December 31, 2017

Assets		Liabilities	
Cash	$14,000	Accounts payable	$15,000
Supplies	3,000	Accounts receivable	(8,500)
Equipment	48,000	Common stock	50,000
Dividends	9,000	Retained earnings	17,500
Total assets	$74,000	Total liabilities and stockholders' equity	$74,000

Instructions

Prepare a correct balance sheet.

E1-14 Wyco Park, a public camping ground near the Four Corners National Recreation Area, has compiled the following financial information as of December 31, 2017.

Compute net income and prepare a balance sheet.

(LO 5)

Revenues during 2017—camping fees	$140,000	Notes payable	$ 60,000
Revenues during 2017—general store	47,000	Expenses during 2017	150,000
Accounts payable	11,000	Supplies on hand	2,500
Cash on hand	20,000	Common stock	20,000
Original cost of equipment	105,500	Retained earnings	?
Fair value of equipment	140,000		

Instructions

(a) Determine Wyco Park's net income for 2017.

(b) Prepare a balance sheet for Wyco Park as of December 31, 2017.

E1-15 Presented below is financial information related to the 2017 operations of Louisa Cruise Company.

Prepare an income statement.

(LO 5)

Maintenance and repairs expense	$ 92,000
Utilities expense	10,000
Salaries and wages expense	142,000
Advertising expense	3,500
Ticket revenue	328,000

Instructions

Prepare the 2017 income statement for Louisa Cruise Company.

E1-16 Presented below is information related to Alexis and Ryans, Attorneys at Law.

Prepare a retained earnings statement.

(LO 5)

Retained earnings, January 1, 2017	$ 23,000
Legal service revenue—2017	340,000
Total expenses—2017	211,000
Assets, January 1, 2017	85,000
Liabilities, January 1, 2017	62,000
Assets, December 31, 2017	168,000
Liabilities, December 31, 2017	80,000
Dividends—2017	64,000

Instructions

Prepare the 2017 retained earnings statement for Alexis and Ryans, Attorneys at Law.

E1-17 This information is for Paulo Company for the year ended December 31, 2017.

Prepare a cash flow statement.

(LO 5)

Cash received from revenues from customers	$600,000
Cash received for issuance of common stock	280,000
Cash paid for new equipment	115,000
Cash dividends paid	18,000
Cash paid for expenses	430,000
Cash balance 1/1/17	30,000

Instructions

Prepare the 2017 statement of cash flows for Paulo Company.

EXERCISES: SET B AND CHALLENGE EXERCISES

Visit the book's companion website, at **www.wiley.com/college/weygandt**, and choose the Student Companion site to access Exercises: Set B and Challenge Exercises.

PROBLEMS: SET A

P1-1A Fredonia Repair Inc. was started on May 1. A summary of May transactions is presented below.

1. Stockholders invested $10,000 cash in the business in exchange for common stock.
2. Purchased equipment for $5,000 cash.
3. Paid $400 cash for May office rent.
4. Paid $300 cash for supplies.
5. Incurred $250 of advertising costs in the *Beacon News* on account.
6. Received $4,700 in cash from customers for repair service.
7. Declared and paid a $700 cash dividend.
8. Paid part-time employee salaries $1,000.
9. Paid utility bills $140.
10. Performed repair services worth $1,100 on account.
11. Collected cash of $120 for services billed in transaction (10).

Instructions

(a) Total assets $13,560

Check figures let you know if you are on the right track with your solution.

(b) Net income $4,010

(a) Prepare a tabular analysis of the transactions using the following column headings: Cash, Accounts Receivable, Supplies, Equipment, Accounts Payable, Common Stock, and Retained Earnings (with separate columns for Revenues, Expenses, and Dividends). Include margin explanations for any changes in Retained Earnings. Revenue is called Service Revenue.
(b) From an analysis of the Retained Earnings columns, compute the net income or net loss for May.

Analyze transactions and prepare income statement, retained earnings statement, and balance sheet.

(LO 3, 4, 5)

P1-2A On August 31, the balance sheet of La Brava Veterinary Clinic showed Cash $9,000, Accounts Receivable $1,700, Supplies $600, Equipment $6,000, Accounts Payable $3,600, Common Stock $13,000, and Retained Earnings $700. During September, the following transactions occurred.

1. Paid $2,900 cash for accounts payable due.
2. Collected $1,300 of accounts receivable.
3. Purchased additional equipment for $2,100, paying $800 in cash and the balance on account.
4. Recognized revenue of $7,300, of which $2,500 is collected in cash and the balance is due in October.
5. Declared and paid a $400 cash dividend.
6. Paid salaries $1,700, rent for September $900, and advertising expense $200.
7. Incurred utilities expense for month on account $170.
8. Received $10,000 from Capital Bank on a 6-month note payable.

Instructions

(a) Ending cash $15,900

(a) Prepare a tabular analysis of the September transactions beginning with August 31 balances. The column headings should be as follows: Cash + Accounts Receivable + Supplies + Equipment = Notes Payable + Accounts Payable + Common Stock + Retained Earnings + Revenues − Expenses − Dividends.

(b) Net income $4,330
    Total assets $29,800

(b) Prepare an income statement for September, a retained earnings statement for September, and a balance sheet at September 30.

Prepare income statement, retained earnings statement, and balance sheet.

(LO 5)

P1-3A On May 1, Nimbus Flying School, a company that provides flying lessons, was started with an investment of $45,000 cash in the business. Following are the assets and liabilities of the company on May 31, 2017, and the revenues and expenses for the month of May.

Cash	$ 4,650	Notes Payable	$28,000
Accounts Receivable	7,400	Rent Expense	900
Equipment	64,000	Maintenance and	
Service Revenue	6,800	Repairs Expense	350
Advertising Expense	500	Gasoline Expense	2,500
Accounts Payable	1,400	Utilities Expense	400

No additional investments were made in May, but the company paid dividends of $500 during the month.

Instructions

(a) Prepare an income statement and a retained earnings statement for the month of May and a balance sheet at May 31.

(b) Prepare an income statement and a retained earnings statement for May assuming the following data are not included above: (1) $900 worth of services were performed and billed but not collected at May 31, and (2) $1,500 of gasoline expense was incurred but not paid.

(a) Net income $2,150
Total assets $76,050

(b) Net income $1,550

P1-4A Nancy Tercek started a delivery service, Tercek Deliveries, on June 1, 2017. The following transactions occurred during the month of June.

Analyze transactions and prepare financial statements.
(LO 3, 4, 5)

June 1	Stockholders invested $10,000 cash in the business in exchange for common stock.
2	Purchased a used van for deliveries for $14,000. Nancy paid $2,000 cash and signed a note payable for the remaining balance.
3	Paid $500 for office rent for the month.
5	Performed $4,800 of services on account.
9	Declared and paid $300 in cash dividends.
12	Purchased supplies for $150 on account.
15	Received a cash payment of $1,250 for services performed on June 5.
17	Purchased gasoline for $100 on account.
20	Received a cash payment of $1,500 for services performed.
23	Made a cash payment of $500 on the note payable.
26	Paid $250 for utilities.
29	Paid for the gasoline purchased on account on June 17.
30	Paid $1,000 for employee salaries.

Instructions

(a) Show the effects of the previous transactions on the accounting equation using the following format.

(a) Total assets $25,800

		Assets			=	Liabilities		+	Stockholders' Equity			
Date	Cash +	Accounts Receivable	+ Supplies +	Equipment =		Notes Payable	+ Accounts Payable	+ Common Stock	+	Retained Earnings		
									Rev. −	Exp.	−	Div.

Include margin explanations for any changes in the Retained Earnings account in your analysis.

(b) Prepare an income statement for the month of June.

(c) Prepare a balance sheet at June 30, 2017.

(b) Net income $4,450
(c) Cash $8,100

P1-5A Financial statement information about four different companies is as follows.

Determine financial statement amounts and prepare retained earnings statement.
(LO 4, 5)

	Donatello Company	Leonardo Company	Michelangelo Company	Raphael Company
January 1, 2017				
Assets	$ 75,000	$110,000	(g)	$150,000
Liabilities	48,000	(d)	$ 75,000	(j)
Stockholders' equity	(a)	60,000	45,000	100,000
December 31, 2017				
Assets	(b)	137,000	200,000	(k)
Liabilities	55,000	75,000	(h)	80,000
Stockholders' equity	40,000	(e)	130,000	140,000
Stockholders' equity changes in year				
Additional investment	(c)	15,000	10,000	15,000
Dividends	6,000	(f)	14,000	10,000
Total revenues	350,000	420,000	(i)	500,000
Total expenses	335,000	382,000	342,000	(l)

Instructions

(a) Determine the missing amounts. (*Hint:* For example, to solve for (a), Assets − Liabilities = Stockholders' Equity = $27,000.)

(b) Prepare the retained earnings statement for Leonardo Company. Assume beginning retained earnings was $20,000.

(c) ———— Write a memorandum explaining the sequence for preparing financial statements and the interrelationship of the retained earnings statement to the income statement and balance sheet.

PROBLEMS: SET B AND SET C

Visit the book's website, at **www.wiley.com/college/weygandt**, and choose the Student Companion site to access Problems: Set B and Set C.

CONTINUING PROBLEM

The Cookie Creations problem starts in this chapter and continues through Chapter 14. You also can find this problem at the book's companion website.

COOKIE CREATIONS

© leungchopan/
Shutterstock

CC1 Natalie Koebel spent much of her childhood learning the art of cookie-making from her grandmother. They passed many happy hours mastering every type of cookie imaginable and later creating new recipes that were both healthy and delicious. Now at the start of her second year in college, Natalie is investigating various possibilities for starting her own business as part of the requirements of the entrepreneurship program in which she is enrolled.

A long-time friend insists that Natalie has to somehow include cookies in her business plan. After a series of brainstorming sessions, Natalie settles on the idea of operating a cookie-making school. She will start on a part-time basis and offer her services in people's homes. Now that she has started thinking about it, the possibilities seem endless. During the fall, she will concentrate on holiday cookies. She will offer individual lessons and group sessions (which will probably be more entertainment than education for the participants). Natalie also decides to include children in her target market.

The first difficult decision is coming up with the perfect name for her business. In the end, she settles on "Cookie Creations" and then moves on to more important issues.

Instructions
(a) What form of business organization—proprietorship, partnership, or corporation—do you recommend that Natalie use for her business? Discuss the benefits and weaknesses of each form and give the reasons for your choice.
(b) Will Natalie need accounting information? If yes, what information will she need and why? How often will she need this Information?
(c) Identify specific asset, liability, and stockholders' equity accounts that Cookie Creations will likely use to record its business transactions.
(d) Should Natalie open a separate bank account for the business? Why or why not?

BROADENING YOUR PERSPECTIVE

FINANCIAL REPORTING AND ANALYSIS

Financial Reporting Problem: Apple Inc.

BYP1-1 The financial statements of Apple Inc. for 2013 are presented in Appendix A. Instructions for accessing and using the company's complete annual report, including the notes to the financial statements, are also provided in Appendix A.

Instructions
Refer to Apple's financial statements and answer the following questions.
(a) What were Apple's total assets at September 28, 2013? At September 29, 2012?
(b) How much cash (and cash equivalents) did Apple have on September 28, 2013?
(c) What amount of accounts payable did Apple report on September 28, 2013? On September 29, 2012?
(d) What were Apple's net sales in 2011? In 2012? In 2013?
(e) What is the amount of the change in Apple's net income from 2012 to 2013?

Comparative Analysis Problem:
PepsiCo, Inc. vs. The Coca-Cola Company

BYP1-2 PepsiCo's financial statements are presented in Appendix B. Financial statements of The Coca-Cola Company are presented in Appendix C. Instructions for accessing and using the complete annual reports of PepsiCo and Coca-Cola, including the notes to the financial statements, are also provided in Appendices B and C, respectively.

Instructions

(a) Based on the information contained in these financial statements, determine the following for each company.
 (1) Total assets at December 28, 2013, for PepsiCo and for Coca-Cola at December 31, 2013.
 (2) Accounts (notes) receivable, net at December 28, 2013, for PepsiCo and at December 31, 2013, for Coca-Cola.
 (3) Net revenues for the year ended in 2013.
 (4) Net income for the year ended in 2013.
(b) What conclusions concerning the two companies can be drawn from these data?

Comparative Analysis Problem:
Amazon.com, Inc. vs. Wal-Mart Stores, Inc.

BYP1-3 Amazon.com, Inc.'s financial statements are presented in Appendix D. Financial statements of Wal-Mart Stores, Inc. are presented in Appendix E. Instructions for accessing and using the complete annual reports of Amazon and Wal-Mart, including the notes to the financial statements, are also provided in Appendices D and E, respectively.

Instructions

(a) Based on the information contained in these financial statements, determine the following for each company.
 (1) Total assets at December 31, 2013, for Amazon and for Wal-Mart at January 31, 2014.
 (2) Receivables (net) at December 31, 2013, for Amazon and for Wal-Mart at January 31, 2014.
 (3) Net sales (product only) for the year ended in 2013 (2014 for Wal-Mart).
 (4) Net income for the year ended in 2013 (2014 for Wal-Mart).
(b) What conclusions concerning these two companies can be drawn from these data?

Real-World Focus

BYP1-4 This exercise will familiarize you with skill requirements, job descriptions, and salaries for accounting careers.

Address: **www.careers-in-accounting.com**, or go to **www.wiley.com/college/weygandt**

Instructions
Go to the site shown above. Answer the following questions.

(a) What are the three broad areas of accounting (from "Skills and Talents")?
(b) List eight skills required in accounting.
(c) How do the three accounting areas differ in terms of these eight required skills?
(d) Explain one of the key job options in accounting.
(e) What is the overall salary range for a junior staff accountant?

CRITICAL THINKING

Decision-Making Across the Organization

BYP1-5 Kathy and James Mohr, local golf stars, opened the Chip-Shot Driving Range Company on March 1, 2017. They invested $25,000 cash and received common stock in exchange for their investment. A caddy shack was constructed for cash at a cost of $8,000, and $800 was spent on golf balls and golf clubs. The Mohrs leased five acres of land at a cost of $1,000 per month and paid the first month's rent. During the first month, advertising costs totaled $750, of which $150 was unpaid at March 31, and $400 was paid to members of the high-school golf team for retrieving golf balls. All revenues from customers were deposited in the company's bank account. On March 15, Kathy and James received a dividend of $1,000. A $100 utility bill was received on March 31 but was not paid. On March 31, the balance in the company's bank account was $18,900.

Kathy and James thought they had a pretty good first month of operations. But, their estimates of profitability ranged from a loss of $6,100 to net income of $2,450.

Instructions

With the class divided into groups, answer the following.

(a) How could the Mohrs have concluded that the business operated at a loss of $6,100? Was this a valid basis on which to determine net income?

(b) How could the Mohrs have concluded that the business operated at a net income of $2,450? (*Hint:* Prepare a balance sheet at March 31.) Was this a valid basis on which to determine net income?

(c) Without preparing an income statement, determine the actual net income for March.

(d) What was the revenue recognized in March?

Communication Activity

BYP1-6 Ashley Hirano, the bookkeeper for New York Company, has been trying to develop the correct balance sheet for the company. The company's balance sheet is shown below.

NEW YORK COMPANY			
Balance Sheet			
For the Month Ended December 31, 2017			
Assets		**Liabilities**	
Equipment	$25,500	Common stock	$26,000
Cash	9,000	Accounts receivable	(6,000)
Supplies	2,000	Retained earnings	(2,000)
Accounts payable	(8,000)	Notes payable	10,500
	$28,500		$28,500

Instructions

Explain to Ashley Hirano in a memo why the original balance sheet is incorrect, and what should be done to correct it.

Ethics Case

BYP1-7 After numerous campus interviews, Greg Thorpe, a senior at Great Northern College, received two office interview invitations from the Baltimore offices of two large firms. Both firms offered to cover his out-of-pocket expenses (travel, hotel, and meals). He scheduled the interviews for both firms on the same day, one in the morning and one in the afternoon. At the conclusion of each interview, he submitted to both firms his total out-of-pocket expenses for the trip to Baltimore: mileage $112 (280 miles at $0.40), hotel $130, meals $36, and parking and tolls $18, for a total of $296. He believes this approach is appropriate. If he had made two trips, his cost would have been two times $296. He is also certain that neither firm knew he had visited the other on that same trip. Within 10 days, Greg received two checks in the mail, each in the amount of $296.

Instructions

(a) Who are the stakeholders (affected parties) in this situation?

(b) What are the ethical issues in this case?

(c) What would you do in this situation?

All About You

BYP1-8 Some people are tempted to make their finances look worse to get financial aid. Companies sometimes also manage their financial numbers in order to accomplish certain goals. Earnings management is the planned timing of revenues, expenses, gains, and losses to smooth out bumps in net income. In managing earnings, companies' actions vary from being within the range of ethical activity to being both unethical and illegal attempts to mislead investors and creditors.

Instructions

Provide responses for each of the following questions.

(a) Discuss whether you think each of the following actions (adapted from **www.finaid.org/fafsa/maximize.phtml**) to increase the chances of receiving financial aid is ethical.

(1) Spend the student's assets and income first, before spending parents' assets and income.

(2) Accelerate necessary expenses to reduce available cash. For example, if you need a new car, buy it before applying for financial aid.

(3) State that a truly financially dependent child is independent.

(4) Have a parent take an unpaid leave of absence for long enough to get below the "threshold" level of income.

(b) What are some reasons why a **company** might want to overstate its earnings?

(c) What are some reasons why a **company** might want to understate its earnings?

(d) Under what circumstances might an otherwise ethical person decide to illegally overstate or understate earnings?

BYP1-9 When companies need money, they go to investors or creditors. Before investors or creditors will give a company cash, they want to know the company's financial position and performance. They want to see the company's financial statements—the balance sheet and the income statement. When students need money for school, they often apply for financial aid. When you apply for financial aid, you must submit your own version of a financial statement—the Free Application for Federal Student Aid (FAFSA) form.

Suppose you have $4,000 in cash and $4,000 in credit card bills. The more cash and other assets that you have, the less likely you are to get financial aid. Also, if you have a lot of consumer debt (credit card bills), schools are not more likely to loan you money. To increase your chances of receiving aid, should you use the cash to pay off your credit card bills and therefore make yourself look "worse off" to the financial aid decision-makers?

YES: You are playing within the rules. You are not hiding assets. You are simply restructuring your assets and liabilities to best conform with the preferences that are built into the federal aid formulas.

NO: You are engaging in a transaction solely to take advantage of a loophole in the federal aid rules. In doing so, you are potentially depriving someone who is actually worse off than you from receiving aid.

Instructions

Write a response indicating your position regarding this situation. Provide support for your view.

FASB Codification Activity

BYP1-10 The FASB has developed the Financial Accounting Standards Board Accounting Standards Codification (or more simply "the Codification"). The FASB's primary goal in developing the Codification is to provide in one place all the authoritative literature related to a particular topic. To provide easy access to the Codification, the FASB also developed the Financial Accounting Standards Board Codification Research System (CRS). CRS is an online, real-time database that provides easy access to the Codification. The Codification and the related CRS provide a topically organized structure, subdivided into topic, subtopics, sections, and paragraphs, using a numerical index system.

You may find this system useful in your present and future studies, and so we have provided an opportunity to use this online system as part of the *Broadening Your Perspective* section.

Instructions

Academic access to the FASB Codification is available through university subscriptions, obtained from the American Accounting Association (at **http://aaahq.org/FASB/Access.cfm**), for an annual fee of $250. This subscription covers an unlimited number of students within a single institution. Once this access has been obtained by your school, you should log in (at **http://aaahq.org/ascLogin.cfm**) and familiarize yourself with the resources that are accessible at the FASB Codification site.

Considering People, Planet, and Profit

BYP1-11 This chapter's Feature Story discusses the fact that although Clif Bar & Company is not a public company, it does share its financial information with its employees as part of its open-book management approach. Further, although it does not publicly share its financial information, it does provide a different form of an annual report to external users. In this report, the company provides information regarding its sustainability efforts.

Address: **www.issuu.com/clifbar/docs/clif_all_aspirations_2012**

Instructions

Access the 2012 annual report of Clif Bar & Company at the site shown above and then answer the following questions.

(a) What are the Five Aspirations?

(b) What was the company's 10-year compounded annual growth rate? What is the amount of 10-year organic purchases made by the company?

A Look at IFRS

LEARNING
OBJECTIVE **7**
Describe the impact of international accounting standards on U.S. financial reporting.

Most agree that there is a need for one set of international accounting standards. Here is why:

Multinational corporations. Today's companies view the entire world as their market. For example, Coca-Cola, Intel, and McDonald's generate more than 50% of their sales outside the United States. Many foreign companies, such as Toyota, Nestlé, and Sony, find their largest market to be the United States.

Mergers and acquisitions. The mergers between Fiat/Chrysler and Vodafone/Mannesmann suggest that we will see even more such business combinations of companies from different countries in the future.

Information technology. As communication barriers continue to topple through advances in technology, companies and individuals in different countries and markets are becoming more comfortable buying and selling goods and services from one another.

Financial markets. Financial markets are of international significance today. Whether it is currency, equity securities (stocks), bonds, or derivatives, there are active markets throughout the world trading these types of instruments.

Key Points

Following are the key similarities and differences between GAAP and IFRS as related to accounting fundamentals.

Similarities

- The basic techniques for recording business transactions are the same for U.S. and international companies.
- Both international and U.S. accounting standards emphasize transparency in financial reporting. Both sets of standards are primarily driven by meeting the needs of investors and creditors.
- The three most common forms of business organizations, proprietorships, partnerships, and corporations, are also found in countries that use international accounting standards.

Differences

- International standards are referred to as International Financial Reporting Standards (IFRS), developed by the International Accounting Standards Board. Accounting standards in the United States are referred to as generally accepted accounting principles (GAAP) and are developed by the Financial Accounting Standards Board.
- IFRS tends to be simpler in its accounting and disclosure requirements; some people say it is more "principles-based." GAAP is more detailed; some people say it is more "rules-based."
- The internal control standards applicable to Sarbanes-Oxley (SOX) apply only to large public companies listed on U.S. exchanges. There is continuing debate as to whether non-U.S. companies should have to comply with this extra layer of regulation.

Looking to the Future

Both the IASB and the FASB are hard at work developing standards that will lead to the elimination of major differences in the way certain transactions are accounted for and reported.

IFRS Practice

IFRS Self-Test Questions

1. Which of the following is **not** a reason why a single set of high-quality international accounting standards would be beneficial?
   (a) Mergers and acquisition activity.
   (b) Financial markets.
   (c) Multinational corporations.
   (d) GAAP is widely considered to be a superior reporting system.

2. The Sarbanes-Oxley Act determines:
   (a) international tax regulations.
   (b) internal control standards as enforced by the IASB.
   (c) internal control standards of U.S. publicly traded companies.
   (d) U.S. tax regulations.

3. IFRS is considered to be more:
   (a) principles-based and less rules-based than GAAP.
   (b) rules-based and less principles-based than GAAP.
   (c) detailed than GAAP.
   (d) None of the above.

IFRS Exercises

IFRS1-1 Who are the two key international players in the development of international accounting standards? Explain their role.

IFRS1-2 What is the benefit of a single set of high-quality accounting standards?

International Financial Reporting Problem: Louis Vuitton

IFRS1-3 The financial statements of **Louis Vuitton** are presented in Appendix F. Instructions for accessing and using the company's complete annual report, including the notes to its financial statements, are also provided in Appendix F.

Instructions

Visit Louis Vuitton's corporate website and answer the following questions from the company's 2013 annual report.

(a) What accounting firm performed the audit of Louis Vuitton's financial statements?
(b) What is the address of the company's corporate headquarters?
(c) What is the company's reporting currency?

Answers to IFRS Self-Test Questions
1. d   **2.** c   **3.** a

The Recording Process

In Chapter 1, we analyzed business transactions in terms of the accounting equation, and we presented the cumulative effects of these transactions in tabular form. Imagine a company like MF Global (as in the Feature Story below) using the same tabular format as Softbyte Inc. to keep track of its transactions. In a single day, MF Global engaged in thousands of business transactions. To record each transaction this way would be impractical, expensive, and unnecessary. Instead, companies use a set of procedures and records to keep track of transaction data more easily. This chapter introduces and illustrates these basic procedures and records.

FEATURE STORY

Accidents Happen

How organized are you financially? Take a short quiz. Answer yes or no to each question:

- Does your wallet contain so many cash machine receipts that you've been declared a walking fire hazard?

- Do you wait until your debit card is denied before checking the status of your funds?

- Was Aaron Rodgers (the quarterback for the Green Bay Packers) playing high school football the last time you verified the accuracy of your bank account?

If you think it is hard to keep track of the many transactions that make up your life, imagine how difficult it is for a big corporation to do so. Not only that, but now consider how important it is for a large company to have good accounting records, especially if it has control of your life savings. MF Global Holdings Ltd is such a company. As a big investment broker, it held billions of dollars of investments for clients. If you had your life savings invested at MF Global, you might be slightly displeased if you heard this from one of its representatives: "You know, I kind of remember an account

for someone with a name like yours—now what did we do with that?"

Unfortunately, that is almost exactly what happened to MF Global's clients shortly before it filed for bankruptcy. During the days immediately following the bankruptcy filing, regulators and auditors struggled to piece things together. In the words of one regulator, "Their books are a disaster . . . we're trying to figure out what numbers are real numbers." One company that considered buying an interest in MF Global walked away from the deal because it "couldn't get a sense of what was on the balance sheet." That company said the information that should have been instantly available instead took days to produce.

It now appears that MF Global did not properly segregate customer accounts from company accounts. And, because of its sloppy record-keeping, customers were not protected when the company had financial troubles. Total customer losses were approximately $1 billion. As you can see, accounting matters!

Source: S. Patterson and A. Lucchetti, "Inside the Hunt for MF Global Cash," *Wall Street Journal Online* (November 11, 2011).

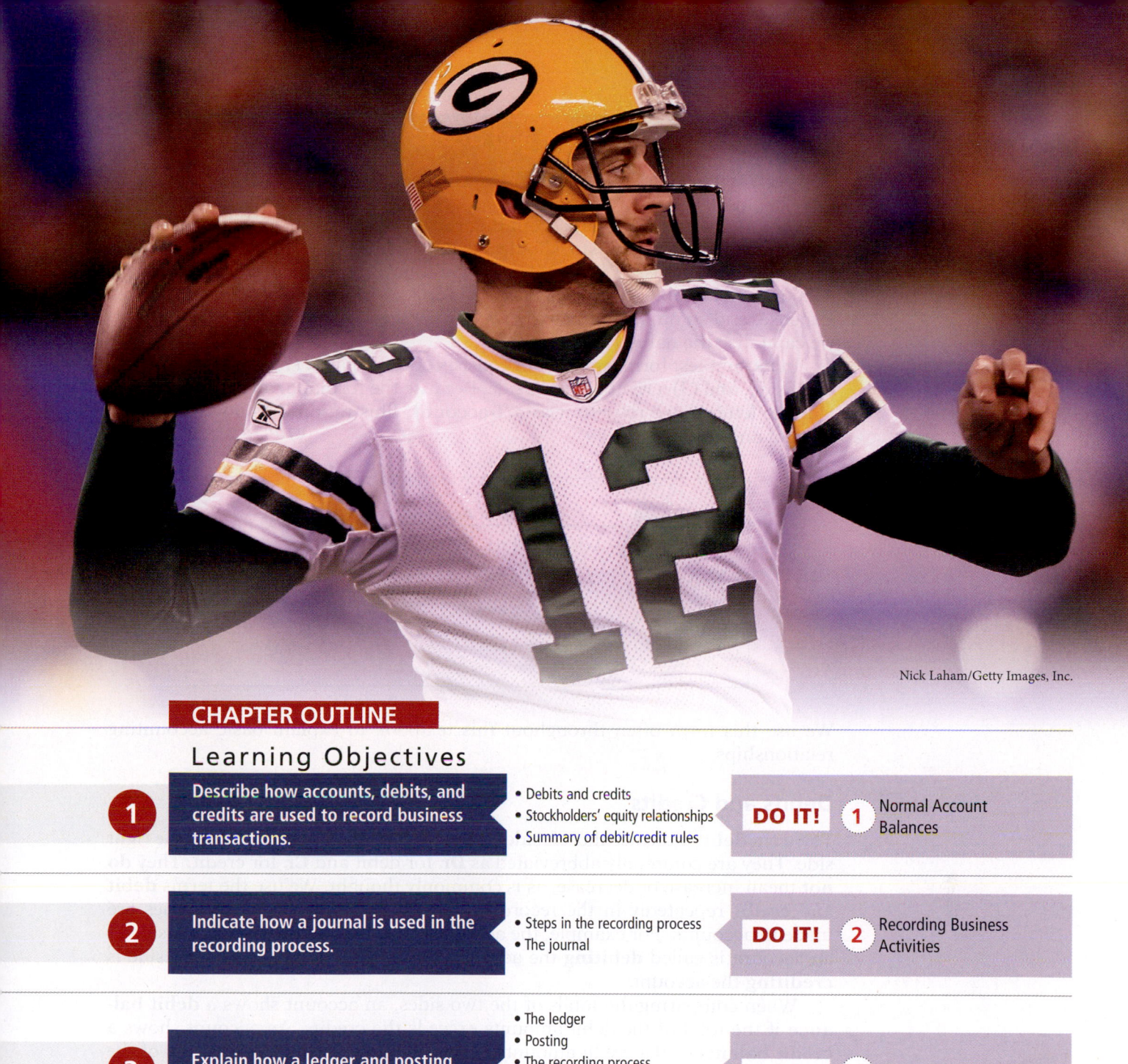

Nick Laham/Getty Images, Inc.

CHAPTER OUTLINE

Learning Objectives

1 Describe how accounts, debits, and credits are used to record business transactions.
- Debits and credits
- Stockholders' equity relationships
- Summary of debit/credit rules

DO IT! 1 Normal Account Balances

2 Indicate how a journal is used in the recording process.
- Steps in the recording process
- The journal

DO IT! 2 Recording Business Activities

3 Explain how a ledger and posting help in the recording process.
- The ledger
- Posting
- The recording process illustrated
- Summary illustration of journalizing and posting

DO IT! 3 Posting

4 Prepare a trial balance.
- Limitations of a trial balance
- Locating errors
- Dollar signs and underlining

DO IT! 4 Trial Balance

Go to the **REVIEW AND PRACTICE** section at the end of the chapter for a review of key concepts and practice applications with solutions.

Visit **WileyPLUS with ORION** for additional tutorials and practice opportunities.

An **account** is an individual accounting record of increases and decreases in a specific asset, liability, or stockholders' equity item. For example, Softbyte Inc. (the company discussed in Chapter 1) would have separate accounts for Cash, Accounts Receivable, Accounts Payable, Service Revenue, Salaries and Wages Expense, and so on. (Note that whenever we are referring to a specific account, we capitalize the name.)

In its simplest form, an account consists of three parts: (1) a title, (2) a left or debit side, and (3) a right or credit side. Because the format of an account resembles the letter T, we refer to it as a **T-account**. Illustration 2-1 shows the basic form of an account.

Illustration 2-1
Basic form of account

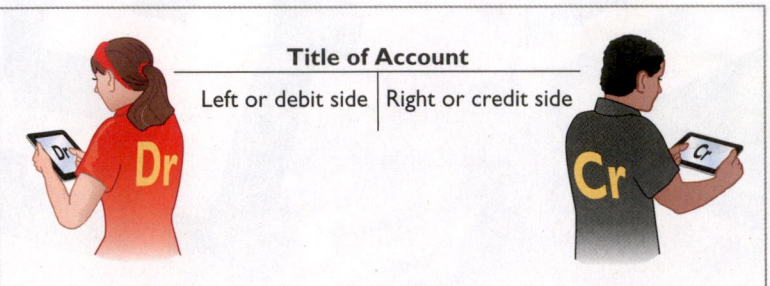

Title of Account

| Left or debit side | Right or credit side |

We use this form often throughout this textbook to explain basic accounting relationships.

Debits and Credits

The term **debit** indicates the left side of an account, and **credit** indicates the right side. They are commonly abbreviated as **Dr.** for debit and **Cr.** for credit. They **do not** mean increase or decrease, as is commonly thought. We use the terms **debit** and **credit** repeatedly in the recording process to describe **where** entries are made in accounts. For example, the act of entering an amount on the left side of an account is called **debiting** the account. Making an entry on the right side is **crediting** the account.

When comparing the totals of the two sides, an account shows a **debit balance** if the total of the debit amounts exceeds the credits. An account shows a **credit balance** if the credit amounts exceed the debits. Note the position of the debit side and credit side in Illustration 2-1.

The procedure of recording debits and credits in an account is shown in Illustration 2-2 for the transactions affecting the Cash account of Softbyte Inc. The data are taken from the Cash column of the tabular summary in Illustration 1-9 (page 20).

Illustration 2-2
Tabular summary and account form for Softbyte's Cash account

Tabular Summary

Cash
$15,000
−7,000
1,200
1,500
−1,700
−250
600
−1,300
$ 8,050

Account Form

Cash			
(Debits)	15,000	(Credits)	7,000
	1,200		1,700
	1,500		250
	600		1,300
Balance	8,050		
(Debit)			

Every positive item in the tabular summary represents a receipt of cash. Every negative amount represents a payment of cash. **Notice that in the account form, we record the increases in cash as debits and the decreases in cash as credits.** For example, the $15,000 receipt of cash (in red) is debited to Cash, and the −$7,000 payment of cash (in blue) is credited to Cash.

Having increases on one side and decreases on the other reduces recording errors and helps in determining the totals of each side of the account as well as the account balance. The balance is determined by netting the two sides (subtracting one amount from the other). The account balance, a debit of $8,050, indicates that Softbyte had $8,050 more increases than decreases in cash. In other words, Softbyte started with a balance of zero and now has $8,050 in its Cash account.

DEBIT AND CREDIT PROCEDURE

In Chapter 1, you learned the effect of a transaction on the basic accounting equation. Remember that each transaction must affect two or more accounts to keep the basic accounting equation in balance. In other words, for each transaction, debits must equal credits. The equality of debits and credits provides the basis for the **double-entry system** of recording transactions.

Under the double-entry system, the dual (two-sided) effect of each transaction is recorded in appropriate accounts. This system provides a logical method for recording transactions. As discussed in the Feature Story about MF Global, the double-entry system also helps ensure the accuracy of the recorded amounts as well as the detection of errors. If every transaction is recorded with equal debits and credits, the sum of all the debits to the accounts must equal the sum of all the credits.

The double-entry system for determining the equality of the accounting equation is much more efficient than the plus/minus procedure used in Chapter 1. The following discussion illustrates debit and credit procedures in the double-entry system.

> **International Note**
>
> Rules for accounting for specific events sometimes differ across countries. For example, European companies rely less on historical cost and more on fair value than U.S. companies. Despite the differences, the double-entry accounting system is the basis of accounting systems worldwide.

DR./CR. PROCEDURES FOR ASSETS AND LIABILITIES

In Illustration 2-2 for Softbyte Inc., increases in Cash—an asset—were entered on the left side, and decreases in Cash were entered on the right side. We know that both sides of the basic equation (Assets = Liabilities + Stockholders' Equity) must be equal. It therefore follows that increases and decreases in liabilities will have to be recorded **opposite from** increases and decreases in assets. Thus, increases in liabilities must be entered on the right or credit side, and decreases in liabilities must be entered on the left or debit side. The effects that debits and credits have on assets and liabilities are summarized in Illustration 2-3.

Debits	Credits
Increase assets	Decrease assets
Decrease liabilities	Increase liabilities

Illustration 2-3
Debit and credit effects—assets and liabilities

Asset accounts normally show debit balances. That is, debits to a specific asset account should exceed credits to that account. Likewise, **liability accounts normally show credit balances**. That is, credits to a liability account should exceed debits to that account. The **normal balance** of an account is on the side where an increase in the account is recorded. Illustration 2-4 shows the normal balances for assets and liabilities.

Assets		Liabilities	
Debit for increase	Credit for decrease	Debit for decrease	Credit for increase
Normal balance			**Normal balance**

Illustration 2-4
Normal balances—assets and liabilities

Knowing the normal balance in an account may help you trace errors. For example, a credit balance in an asset account such as Land or a debit balance in a liability account such as Salaries and Wages Payable usually indicates an error. Occasionally, though, an abnormal balance may be correct. The Cash account, for example, will have a credit balance when a company has overdrawn its bank balance (i.e., written a check that "bounced").

STOCKHOLDERS' EQUITY

As Chapter 1 indicated, there are five subdivisions of stockholders' equity: common stock, retained earnings, dividends, revenues, and expenses. In a double-entry system, companies keep accounts for each of these subdivisions, as explained below.

COMMON STOCK Companies issue **common stock** in exchange for the owners' investment paid in to the corporation. Credits increase the Common Stock account, and debits decrease it. For example, when an owner invests cash in the business in exchange for shares of the corporation's stock, the company debits (increases) Cash and credits (increases) Common Stock.

Illustration 2-5 shows the rules of debit and credit for the Common Stock account.

Illustration 2-5
Debit and credit effects—common stock

Debits	Credits
Decrease Common Stock	Increase Common Stock

Illustration 2-6 shows the normal balance for Common Stock.

Illustration 2-6
Normal balance—common stock

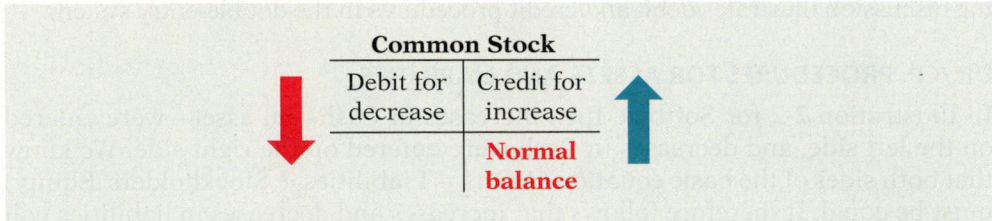

RETAINED EARNINGS **Retained earnings** is net income that is kept (retained) in the business. It represents the portion of stockholders' equity that the company has accumulated through the profitable operation of the business. Credits (net income) increase the Retained Earnings account, and debits (dividends or net losses) decrease it, as Illustration 2-7 shows.

Helpful Hint
The rules for debit and credit and the normal balances of common stock and retained earnings are the same as for liabilities.

Illustration 2-7
Debit and credit effects and normal balance—retained earnings

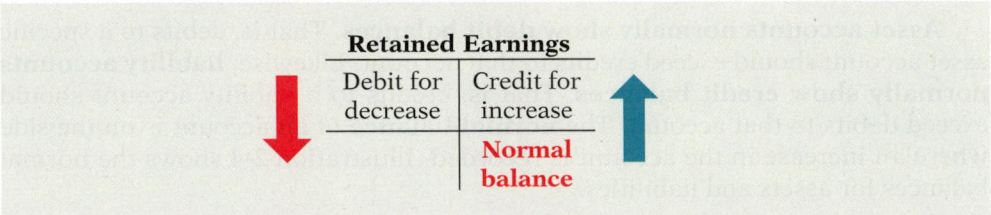

DIVIDENDS A **dividend** is a company's distribution to its stockholders on a pro rata (equal) basis. The most common form of a distribution is a **cash dividend**. Dividends reduce the stockholders' claims on retained earnings. Debits increase the Dividends account, and credits decrease it. Illustration 2-8 shows the normal balance for Dividends.

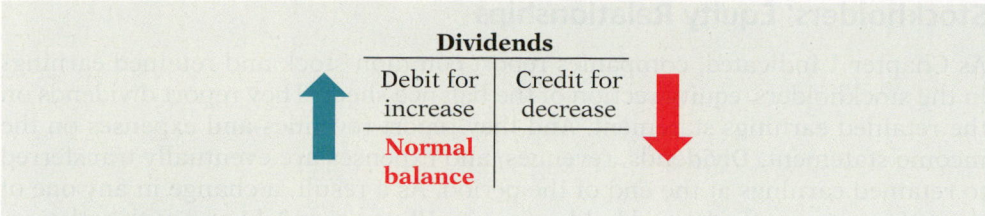

Illustration 2-8
Debit and credit effect and normal balance—dividends

Dividends	
Debit for increase	Credit for decrease
Normal balance	

Investor Insight | Chicago Cubs

Jonathan Daniel/Getty Images, Inc.

Keeping Score

The Chicago Cubs baseball team probably has these major revenue and expense accounts:

Revenues	Expenses
Admissions (ticket sales)	Players' salaries
Concessions	Administrative salaries
Television and radio	Travel
Advertising	Ballpark maintenance

Do you think that the Chicago Bears football team would be likely to have the same major revenue and expense accounts as the Cubs? (Go to **WileyPLUS** for this answer and additional questions.)

REVENUES AND EXPENSES The purpose of earning revenues is to benefit the stockholders of the business. When a company recognizes revenues, stockholders' equity increases. Revenues are a subdivision of stockholders' equity that provides information as to **why** stockholders' equity increased. Credits increase revenue accounts and debits decrease them. Therefore, **the effect of debits and credits on revenue accounts is the same as their effect on stockholders' equity**.

Expenses have the opposite effect. Expenses decrease stockholders' equity. Since expenses decrease net income and revenues increase it, it is logical that the increase and decrease sides of expense accounts should be the opposite of revenue accounts. Thus, expense accounts are increased by debits and decreased by credits. Illustration 2-9 shows the rules of debits and credits for revenues and expenses.

Helpful Hint
Because revenues increase stockholders' equity, a revenue account has the same debit/credit rules as the Common Stock account. Expenses have the opposite effect.

Debits	Credits
Decrease revenues	Increase revenues
Increase expenses	Decrease expenses

Illustration 2-9
Debit and credit effects—revenues and expenses

Credits to revenue accounts should exceed debits. Debits to expense accounts should exceed credits. Thus, revenue accounts normally show credit balances, and expense accounts normally show debit balances. Illustration 2-10 shows the normal balance for revenues and expenses.

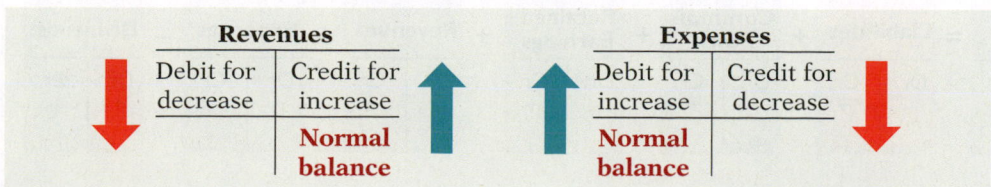

Illustration 2-10
Normal balances—revenues and expenses

Revenues		Expenses	
Debit for decrease	Credit for increase	Debit for increase	Credit for decrease
	Normal balance	**Normal balance**	

Stockholders' Equity Relationships

As Chapter 1 indicated, companies report common stock and retained earnings in the stockholders' equity section of the balance sheet. They report dividends on the retained earnings statement. And they report revenues and expenses on the income statement. Dividends, revenues, and expenses are eventually transferred to retained earnings at the end of the period. As a result, a change in any one of these three items affects stockholders' equity. Illustration 2-11 shows the relationships related to stockholders' equity.

Illustration 2-11
Stockholders' equity relationships

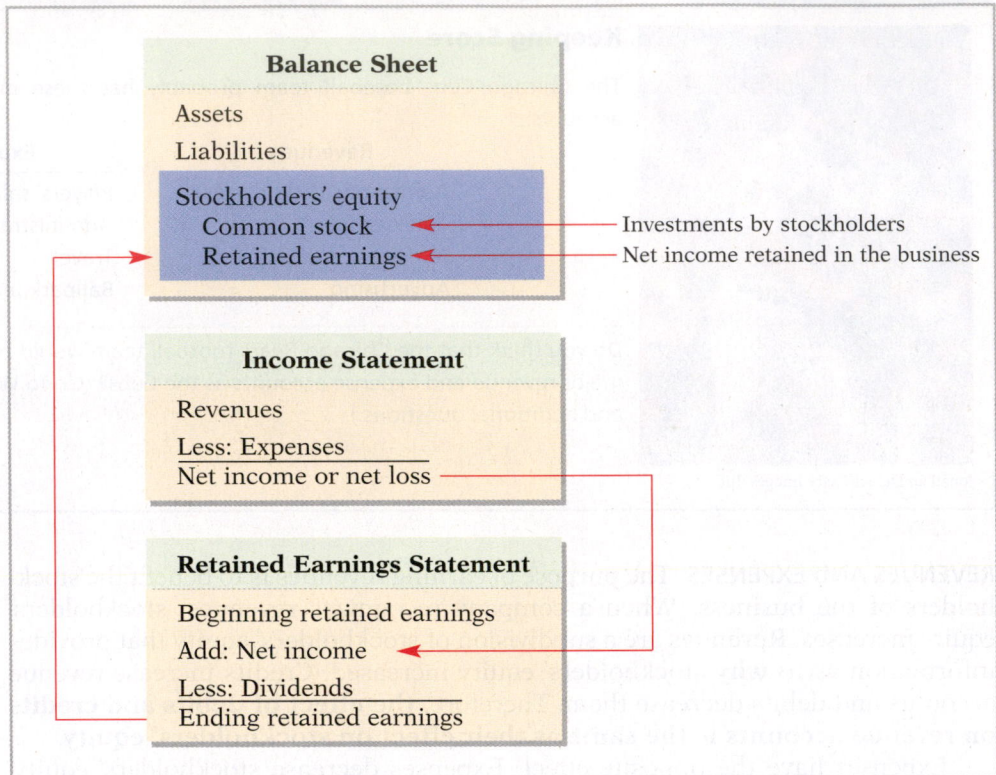

Summary of Debit/Credit Rules

Helpful Hint
You may want to bookmark Illustration 2-12. You probably will refer to it often.

Illustration 2-12 shows a summary of the debit/credit rules and effects on each type of account. Study this diagram carefully. It will help you understand the fundamentals of the double-entry system.

Illustration 2-12
Summary of debit/credit rules

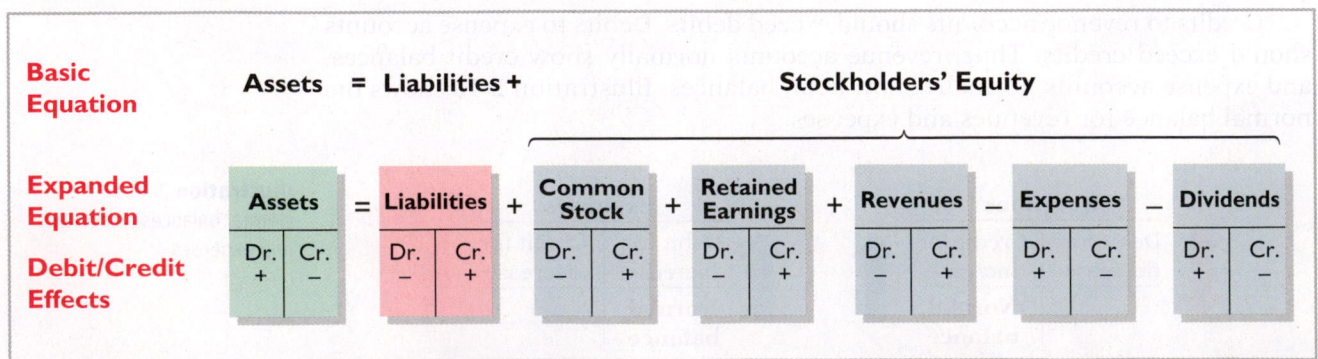

DO IT! 1   Normal Account Balances

Kate Browne, president of Hair It Is, Inc. has just rented space in a shopping mall in which she will open and operate a beauty salon. A friend has advised Kate to set up a double-entry set of accounting records in which to record all of her business transactions.

Identify the balance sheet accounts that Hair It Is, Inc. will likely use to record the transactions needed to establish and open the business. Also, indicate whether the normal balance of each account is a debit or a credit.

Solution

Hair It Is, Inc. would likely use the following accounts to record the transactions needed to ready the beauty salon for opening day:

Cash (debit balance)	Equipment (debit balance)
Supplies (debit balance)	Accounts Payable (credit balance)
Notes Payable (credit balance), if the business borrows money	Common Stock (credit balance)

Related exercise material: **BE2-1, BE2-2, E2-1, E2-2, E2-4, and** DO IT! **2-1.**

Action Plan

✔ Determine the types of accounts needed. Kate will need asset accounts for each different type of asset she invests in the business, and liability accounts for any debts she incurs.

✔ Understand the types of stockholders' equity accounts. When Kate begins the business, she will need only Common Stock. Later, she will need other stockholders' equity accounts.

LEARNING OBJECTIVE 2

Indicate how a journal is used in the recording process.

Steps in the Recording Process

Although it is possible to enter transaction information directly into the accounts without using a journal, few businesses do so. Practically every business uses three basic steps in the recording process:

1. Analyze each transaction for its effects on the accounts.
2. Enter the transaction information in a **journal**.
3. Transfer the journal information to the appropriate accounts in the **ledger**.[1]

The recording process begins with the transaction. **Business documents**, such as a sales receipt, a check, or a bill provide evidence of the transaction. The company analyzes this evidence to determine the transaction's effects on specific accounts. The company then enters the transaction in the journal. Finally, it transfers the journal entry to the designated accounts in the ledger. Illustration 2-13 shows the recording process.

ETHICS NOTE

International Outsourcing Services, LLC was accused of submitting fraudulent store coupons to companies for reimbursement of as much as $250 million. Use of proper business documents reduces the likelihood of fraudulent activity.

Illustration 2-13
The recording process

The Recording Process

Analyze each transaction   Enter transaction in a journal   Transfer journal information to ledger accounts

---

[1]We discuss here the manual recording process as we believe students should understand it first before learning and using a computerized system.

The steps in the recording process occur repeatedly. In Chapter 1, we illustrated the first step, the analysis of transactions, and will give further examples in this and later chapters. The other two steps in the recording process are explained in the next sections.

The Journal

Companies initially record transactions in chronological order (the order in which they occur). Thus, the **journal** is referred to as the book of original entry. For each transaction, the journal shows the debit and credit effects on specific accounts.

Companies may use various kinds of journals, but every company has the most basic form of journal, a **general journal**. Typically, a general journal has spaces for dates, account titles and explanations, references, and two amount columns. See the format of the journal in Illustration 2-14. *Whenever we use the term "journal" in this textbook, we mean the general journal unless we specify otherwise.*

The journal makes several significant contributions to the recording process:

1. It discloses in one place the **complete effects of a transaction**.

2. It provides a **chronological record** of transactions.

3. It helps to **prevent or locate errors** because the debit and credit amounts for each entry can be easily compared.

JOURNALIZING

Entering transaction data in the journal is known as **journalizing**. Companies make separate journal entries for each transaction. A complete entry consists of (1) the date of the transaction, (2) the accounts and amounts to be debited and credited, and (3) a brief explanation of the transaction.

Illustration 2-14 shows the technique of journalizing, using the first two transactions of Softbyte Inc. On September 1, stockholders invested $15,000 cash in the corporation in exchange for shares of stock, and Softbyte purchased computer equipment for $7,000 cash. The number J1 indicates that these two entries are recorded on the first page of the journal. Illustration 2-14 shows the standard form of journal entries for these two transactions. (The boxed numbers correspond to explanations in the list below the illustration.)

Illustration 2-14
Technique of journalizing

GENERAL JOURNAL					J1
Date	Account Titles and Explanation		Ref. ⑤	Debit	Credit
2017					
Sept. 1 ②	Cash			15,000	
① ③	Common Stock				15,000
④	(Issued shares of stock for cash)				
1	Equipment			7,000	
	Cash				7,000
	(Purchase of equipment for cash)				

① The date of the transaction is entered in the Date column.

② The debit account title (that is, the account to be debited) is entered first at the extreme left margin of the column headed "Account Titles and Explanation," and the amount of the debit is recorded in the Debit column.

③ The credit account title (that is, the account to be credited) is indented and entered on the next line in the column headed "Account Titles and Explanation," and the amount of the credit is recorded in the Credit column.

④ A brief explanation of the transaction appears on the line below the credit account title. A space is left between journal entries. The blank space separates individual journal entries and makes the entire journal easier to read.

5 The column titled Ref. (which stands for Reference) is left blank when the journal entry is made. This column is used later when the journal entries are transferred to the ledger accounts.

It is important to use correct and specific account titles in journalizing. Erroneous account titles lead to incorrect financial statements. However, some flexibility exists initially in selecting account titles. The main criterion is that each title must appropriately describe the content of the account. Once a company chooses the specific title to use, it should record under that account title all later transactions involving the account.[2]

SIMPLE AND COMPOUND ENTRIES

Some entries involve only two accounts, one debit and one credit. (See, for example, the entries in Illustration 2-14.) This type of entry is called a **simple entry**. Some transactions, however, require more than two accounts in journalizing. An entry that requires three or more accounts is a **compound entry**. To illustrate, assume that on July 1, Butler Company purchases a delivery truck costing $14,000. It pays $8,000 cash now and agrees to pay the remaining $6,000 on account (to be paid later). The compound entry is as follows.

Illustration 2-15
Compound journal entry

GENERAL JOURNAL				J1
Date	Account Titles and Explanation	Ref.	Debit	Credit
2017 July 1	Equipment		14,000	
	Cash			8,000
	Accounts Payable			6,000
	(Purchased truck for cash with balance on account)			

In a compound entry, the standard format requires that all debits be listed before the credits.

Accounting Across the Organization   Microsoft

Boosting Microsoft's Profits

© flyfloor/iStockphoto

Microsoft originally designed the Xbox 360 to have 256 megabytes of memory. But the design department said that amount of memory wouldn't support the best special effects. The purchasing department said that adding more memory would cost $30—which was 10% of the estimated selling price of $300. The marketing department, however, "determined that adding the memory would let Microsoft reduce marketing costs and attract more game developers, boosting royalty revenue. It would also extend the life of the console, generating more sales."

As a result of these changes, Xbox enjoyed great success. But, it does have competitors. Its newest video game console, Xbox One, is now in a battle with Sony's Playstation4 for market share. How to compete? First, Microsoft bundled the critically acclaimed *Titanfall* with its Xbox One. By including the game most Xbox One buyers were going to purchase anyway, Microsoft was making its console more attractive. In addition, retailers are also discounting the Xbox, which should get the momentum going for increased sales. What Microsoft is doing is making sure that Xbox One is the center of the home entertainment system in the long run, even if it suffers a bit of a hardware loss today.

Sources: Robert A. Guth, "New Xbox Aim for Microsoft: Profitability," *Wall Street Journal* (May 24, 2005), p. C1; and David Thier, "Will Microsoft Give the Xbox One a $50 Price Cut? *www.Forbes.com* (March 26, 2014).

In what ways is this Microsoft division using accounting to assist in its effort to become more profitable? (Go to **WileyPLUS** for this answer and additional questions.)

---

[2]*In homework problems, you should use specific account titles when they are given.* When account titles are not given, you may select account titles that identify the nature and content of each account. The account titles used in journalizing should not contain explanations such as Cash Paid or Cash Received.

DO IT! ② Recording Business Activities

As president and sole stockholder, Kate Browne engaged in the following activities in establishing her salon, Hair It Is, Inc.

1. Opened a bank account in the name of Hair It Is, Inc. and deposited $20,000 of her own money in this account in exchange for shares of common stock.

2. Purchased equipment on account (to be paid in 30 days) for a total cost of $4,800.

3. Interviewed three people for the position of hair stylist.

Prepare the entries to record the transactions.

Solution

The three activities would be recorded as follows.

1.	Cash	20,000	
	Common Stock		20,000
	(Issued shares of stock for cash)		
2.	Equipment	4,800	
	Accounts Payable		4,800
	(Purchase of equipment on account)		

3. No entry because no transaction has occurred.

Related exercise material: **BE2-3, BE2-4, BE2-5, BE2-6, E2-3, E2-5, E2-6, E2-7, and DO IT! 2-2.**

Action Plan

✔ Understand which activities need to be recorded and which do not. Any that affect assets, liabilities, or stockholders' equity should be recorded in a journal.

✔ Analyze the effects of transactions on asset, liability, and stockholders' equity accounts.

LEARNING OBJECTIVE ③ **Explain how a ledger and posting help in the recording process.**

The Ledger

The entire group of accounts maintained by a company is the **ledger**. The ledger provides the balance in each of the accounts as well as keeps track of changes in these balances.

Companies may use various kinds of ledgers, but every company has a general ledger. A **general ledger** contains all the asset, liability, and stockholders' equity accounts, as shown in Illustration 2-16 for J. Lind Company. *Whenever we use the term "ledger" in this textbook, we are referring to the general ledger unless we specify otherwise.*

Illustration 2-16
The general ledger, which contains all of a company's accounts

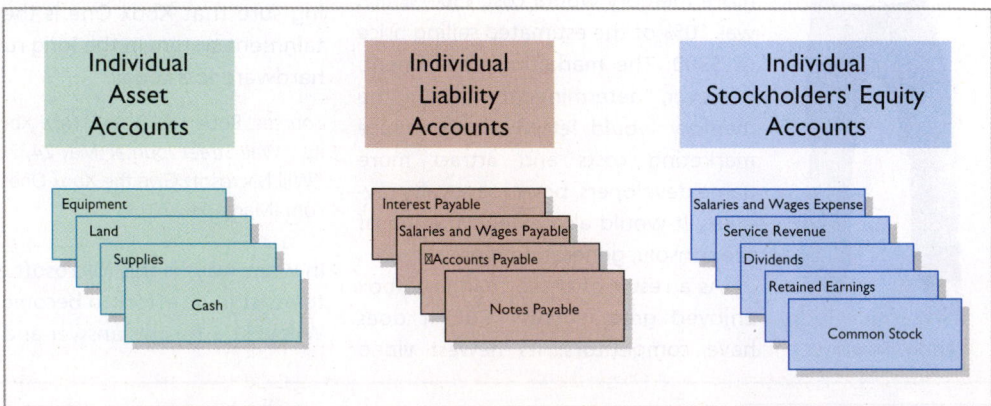

Individual Asset Accounts	Individual Liability Accounts	Individual Stockholders' Equity Accounts
Equipment Land Supplies Cash	Interest Payable Salaries and Wages Payable Accounts Payable Notes Payable	Salaries and Wages Expense Service Revenue Dividends Retained Earnings Common Stock

Companies arrange the ledger in the sequence in which they present the accounts in the financial statements, beginning with the balance sheet accounts. First in order are the asset accounts, followed by liability accounts, stockholders' equity accounts, revenues, and expenses. Each account is numbered for easier identification.

The ledger provides the balance in each of the accounts. For example, the Cash account shows the amount of cash available to meet current obligations. The Accounts Receivable account shows amounts due from customers. The Accounts Payable account shows amounts owed to creditors.

Ethics Insight   Credit Suisse Group

© Nuno Silva/iStockphoto

A Convenient Overstatement

Sometimes a company's investment securities suffer a permanent decline in value below their original cost. When this occurs, the company is supposed to reduce the recorded value of the securities on its balance sheet ("write-them down" in common financial lingo) and record a loss. It appears, however, that during the financial crisis of 2008, employees at some financial institutions chose to look the other way as the value of their investments skidded.

A number of Wall Street traders that worked for the investment bank Credit Suisse Group were charged with intentionally overstating the value of securities that had suffered declines of approximately $2.85 billion. One reason that they may have been reluctant to record the losses is out of fear that the company's shareholders and clients would panic if they saw the magnitude of the losses. However, personal self-interest might have been equally to blame—the bonuses of the traders were tied to the value of the investment securities.

Source: S. Pulliam, J. Eaglesham, and M. Siconolfi, "U.S. Plans Changes on Bond Fraud," *Wall Street Journal Online* (February 1, 2012).

What incentives might employees have had to overstate the value of these investment securities on the company's financial statements? (Go to **WileyPLUS** for this answer and additional questions.)

STANDARD FORM OF ACCOUNT

The simple T-account form used in accounting textbooks is often very useful for illustration purposes. However, in practice, the account forms used in ledgers are much more structured. Illustration 2-17 shows a typical form, using assumed data from a cash account.

CASH					NO. 101
Date	Explanation	Ref.	Debit	Credit	Balance
2017					
June 1			25,000		25,000
2				8,000	17,000
3			4,200		21,200
9			7,500		28,700
17				11,700	17,000
20				250	16,750
30				7,300	9,450

Illustration 2-17
Three-column form of account

This format is called the **three-column form of account**. It has three money columns—debit, credit, and balance. The balance in the account is determined after each transaction. Companies use the explanation space and reference columns to provide special information about the transaction.

Posting

Transferring journal entries to the ledger accounts is called **posting**. This phase of the recording process accumulates the effects of journalized transactions into the individual accounts. Posting involves the following steps.

1. In the **ledger**, in the appropriate columns of the account(s) debited, enter the date, journal page, and debit amount shown in the journal.
2. In the reference column of the **journal**, write the account number to which the debit amount was posted.
3. In the **ledger**, in the appropriate columns of the account(s) credited, enter the date, journal page, and credit amount shown in the journal.
4. In the reference column of the **journal**, write the account number to which the credit amount was posted.

Illustration 2-18 shows these four steps using Softbyte Inc.'s first journal entry. The boxed numbers indicate the sequence of the steps.

Illustration 2-18

Posting a journal entry

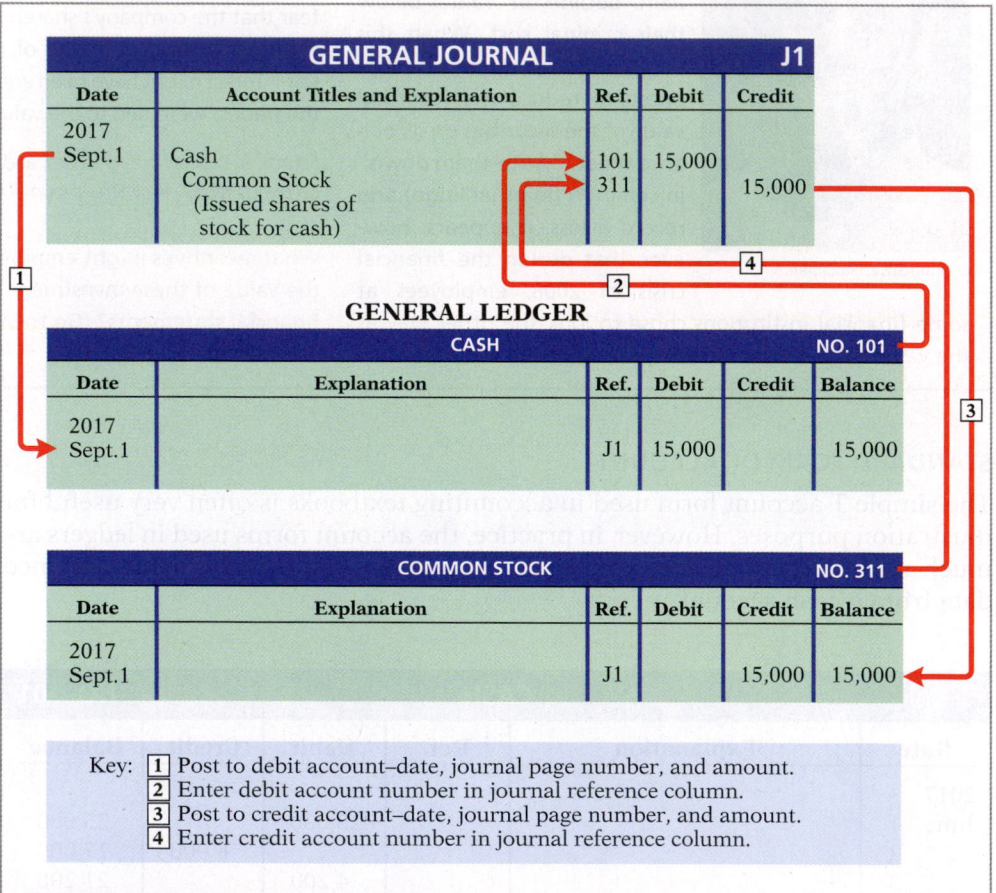

Key:
1 Post to debit account–date, journal page number, and amount.
2 Enter debit account number in journal reference column.
3 Post to credit account–date, journal page number, and amount.
4 Enter credit account number in journal reference column.

Posting should be performed in chronological order. That is, the company should post all the debits and credits of one journal entry before proceeding to the next journal entry. Postings should be made on a timely basis to ensure that the ledger is up-to-date.[3]

---

[3]In homework problems, you can journalize all transactions before posting any of the journal entries.

The reference column of a ledger account indicates the journal page from which the transaction was posted.[4] The explanation space of the ledger account is used infrequently because an explanation already appears in the journal.

CHART OF ACCOUNTS

The number and type of accounts differ for each company. The number of accounts depends on the amount of detail management desires. For example, the management of one company may want a single account for all types of utility expense. Another may keep separate expense accounts for each type of utility, such as gas, electricity, and water. Similarly, a small company like Softbyte Inc. will have fewer accounts than a corporate giant like Dell. Softbyte may be able to manage and report its activities in 20 to 30 accounts, while Dell may require thousands of accounts to keep track of its worldwide activities.

Most companies have a **chart of accounts**. This chart lists the accounts and the account numbers that identify their location in the ledger. The numbering system that identifies the accounts usually starts with the balance sheet accounts and follows with the income statement accounts.

In this and the next two chapters, we will be explaining the accounting for Pioneer Advertising Inc. (a service company). Accounts 101–199 indicate asset accounts; 200–299 indicate liabilities; 301–350 indicate stockholders' equity accounts; 400–499, revenues; 601–799, expenses; 800–899, other revenues; and 900–999, other expenses. Illustration 2-19 shows Pioneer's chart of accounts. Accounts listed in red are used in this chapter; accounts shown in black are explained in later chapters.

Helpful Hint
On the textbook's front endpapers, you also will find an expanded chart of accounts.

Illustration 2-19
Chart of accounts for Pioneer Advertising Inc.

PIONEER ADVERTISING INC.
Chart of Accounts

Assets	Stockholders' Equity
101 Cash	311 Common Stock
112 Accounts Receivable	320 Retained Earnings
126 Supplies	332 Dividends
130 Prepaid Insurance	350 Income Summary
157 Equipment	
158 Accumulated Depreciation— Equipment	**Revenues**
	400 Service Revenue
Liabilities	**Expenses**
200 Notes Payable	631 Supplies Expense
201 Accounts Payable	711 Depreciation Expense
209 Unearned Service Revenue	722 Insurance Expense
212 Salaries and Wages Payable	726 Salaries and Wages Expense
230 Interest Payable	729 Rent Expense
	732 Utilities Expense
	905 Interest Expense

You will notice that there are gaps in the numbering system of the chart of accounts for Pioneer. Companies leave gaps to permit the insertion of new accounts as needed during the life of the business.

---

[4]After the last entry has been posted, the accountant should scan the reference column **in the journal**, to confirm that all postings have been made.

The Recording Process Illustrated

Illustrations 2-20 through 2-29 show the basic steps in the recording process, using the October transactions of Pioneer Advertising Inc. A basic analysis, an equation analysis, and a debit-credit analysis precede the journal entry and posting of each transaction. For simplicity, we use the T-account form to show the posting instead of the standard account form.

Illustration 2-20
Investment of cash by stockholders

Cash Flows
+10,000

Helpful Hint
Follow these steps:

1. Determine what type of account is involved.
2. Determine what items increased or decreased and by how much.
3. Translate the increases and decreases into debits and credits.

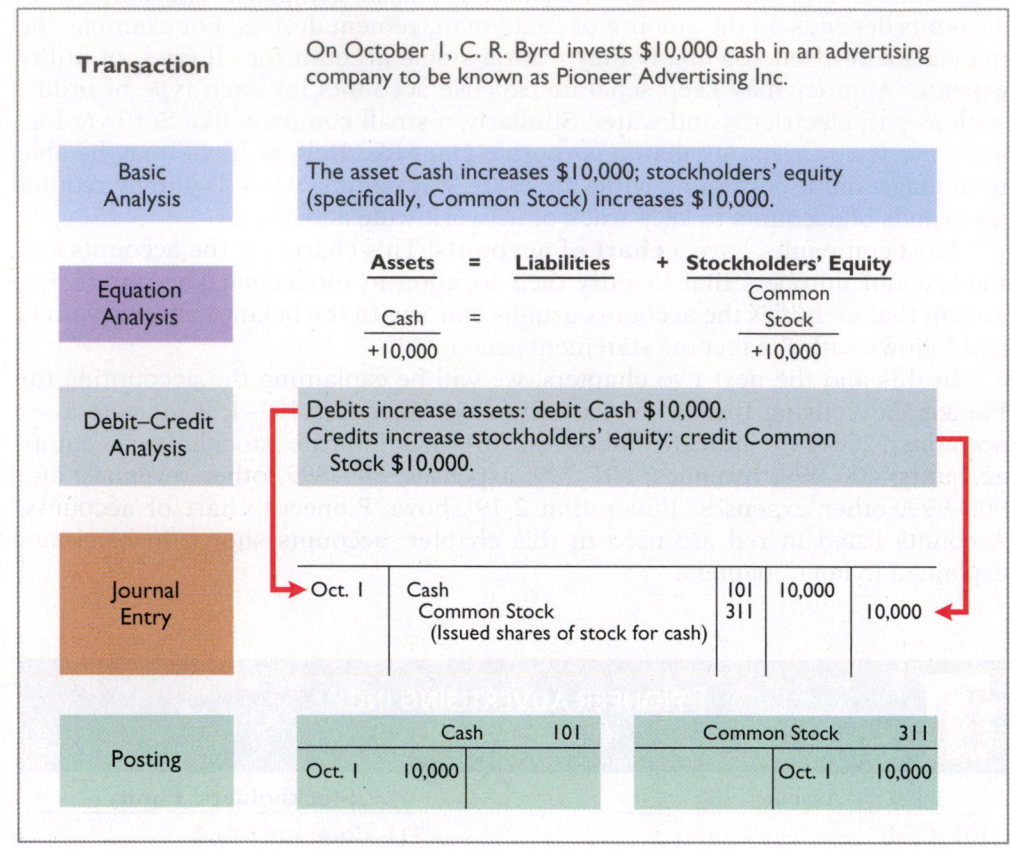

Transaction	On October 1, C. R. Byrd invests $10,000 cash in an advertising company to be known as Pioneer Advertising Inc.
Basic Analysis	The asset Cash increases $10,000; stockholders' equity (specifically, Common Stock) increases $10,000.

Equation Analysis

Assets	=	Liabilities	+	Stockholders' Equity
Cash	=			Common Stock
+10,000				+10,000

Debit–Credit Analysis
Debits increase assets: debit Cash $10,000.
Credits increase stockholders' equity: credit Common Stock $10,000.

Journal Entry

Oct. 1	Cash	101	10,000	
	Common Stock	311		10,000
	(Issued shares of stock for cash)			

Posting

Cash	101		Common Stock	311
Oct. 1 10,000				Oct. 1 10,000

Illustration 2-21
Purchase of office equipment

Cash Flows
no effect

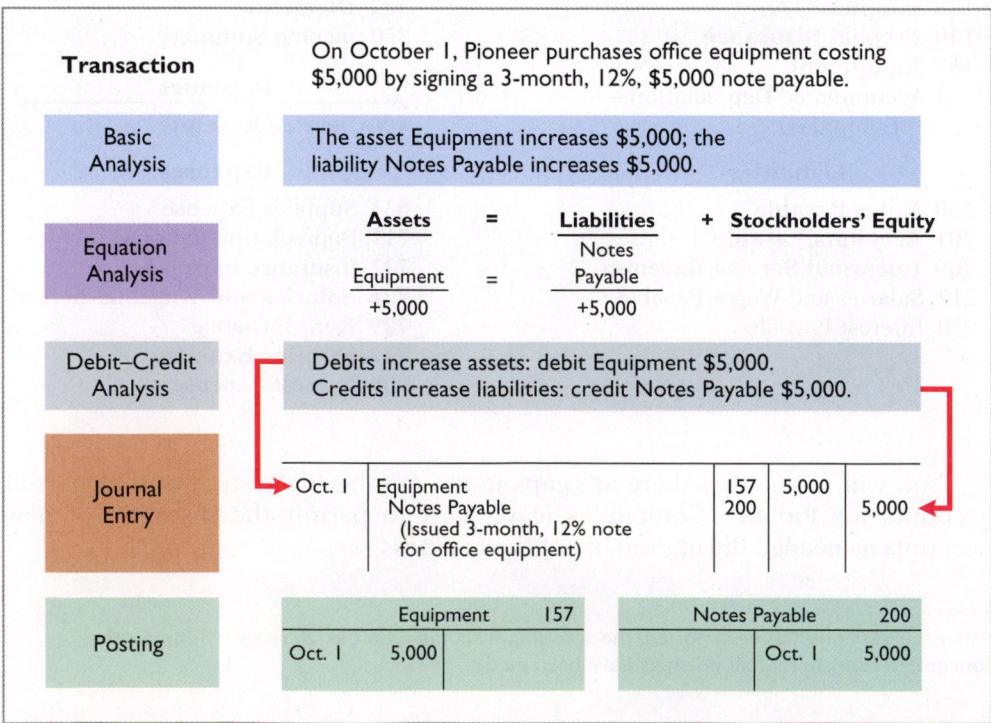

Transaction	On October 1, Pioneer purchases office equipment costing $5,000 by signing a 3-month, 12%, $5,000 note payable.
Basic Analysis	The asset Equipment increases $5,000; the liability Notes Payable increases $5,000.

Equation Analysis

Assets	=	Liabilities	+	Stockholders' Equity
		Notes		
Equipment	=	Payable		
+5,000		+5,000		

Debit–Credit Analysis
Debits increase assets: debit Equipment $5,000.
Credits increase liabilities: credit Notes Payable $5,000.

Journal Entry

Oct. 1	Equipment	157	5,000	
	Notes Payable	200		5,000
	(Issued 3-month, 12% note for office equipment)			

Posting

Equipment	157		Notes Payable	200
Oct. 1 5,000				Oct. 1 5,000

Illustration 2-22
Receipt of cash for future
service

Transaction

On October 2, Pioneer receives a $1,200 cash advance from R. Knox, a client, for advertising services that are expected to be completed by December 31.

Basic Analysis

The asset Cash increases $1,200; the liability Unearned Service Revenue increases $1,200 because the service has not been performed yet. That is, when Pioneer receives an advance payment, it should record an unearned revenue (a liability) in order to recognize the obligation that exists. Note also that although most liabilities have the word "payable" in their title, unearned revenue is considered a liability because the liability is satisfied by providing a product or performing a service.

Equation Analysis

Assets	=	Liabilities	+	Stockholders' Equity
		Unearned Service		
Cash	=	Revenue		
+1,200		+1,200		

Debit–Credit Analysis

Debits increase assets: debit Cash $1,200.
Credits increase liabilities: credit Unearned Service Revenue $1,200.

Journal Entry

Oct. 2	Cash	101	1,200	
	Unearned Service Revenue	209		1,200
	(Received cash from			
	R. Knox for future service)			

Posting

	Cash	101		Unearned Service Revenue	209
Oct. 1	10,000			Oct. 2	1,200
2	1,200				

Cash Flows
+1,200

Illustration 2-23
Payment of monthly rent

Transaction

On October 3, Pioneer pays office rent for October in cash, $900.

Basic Analysis

The expense account Rent Expense increases $900 because the payment pertains only to the current month; the asset Cash decreases $900.

Equation Analysis

Assets	=	Liabilities	+	Stockholders' Equity
				Rent
Cash	=			Expense
-900				-900

Debit–Credit Analysis

Debits increase expenses: debit Rent Expense $900.
Credits decrease assets: credit Cash $900.

Journal Entry

Oct. 3	Rent Expense	729	900	
	Cash	101		900
	(Paid October rent)			

Posting

	Cash	101			Rent Expense	729
Oct. 1	10,000	Oct. 3	900	Oct. 3	900	
2	1,200					

Cash Flows
−900

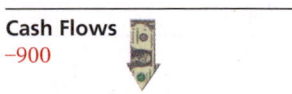

Illustration 2-24
Payment for insurance

Cash Flows
−600

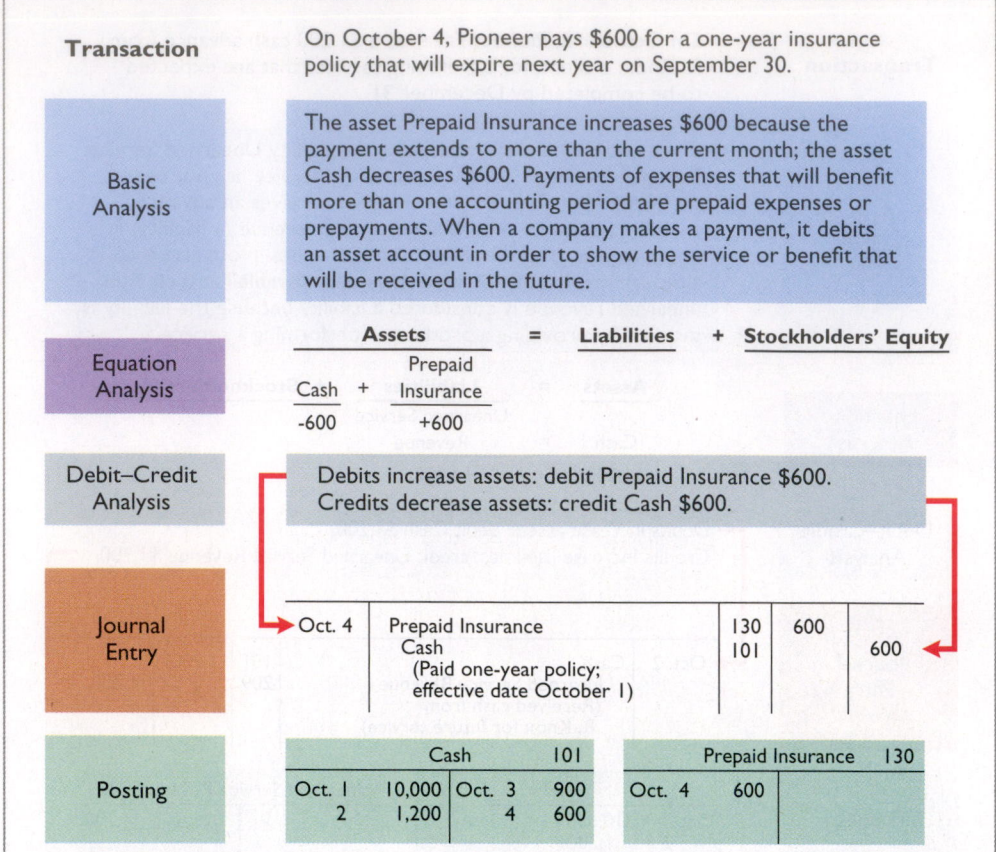

Transaction	On October 4, Pioneer pays $600 for a one-year insurance policy that will expire next year on September 30.
Basic Analysis	The asset Prepaid Insurance increases $600 because the payment extends to more than the current month; the asset Cash decreases $600. Payments of expenses that will benefit more than one accounting period are prepaid expenses or prepayments. When a company makes a payment, it debits an asset account in order to show the service or benefit that will be received in the future.

Equation Analysis

			=	Liabilities	+	Stockholders' Equity
	Cash	+	Prepaid Insurance			
	−600		+600			

Debit–Credit Analysis
Debits increase assets: debit Prepaid Insurance $600.
Credits decrease assets: credit Cash $600.

Journal Entry

Oct. 4	Prepaid Insurance	130	600	
	Cash	101		600
	(Paid one-year policy; effective date October 1)			

Posting

Cash			101		Prepaid Insurance	130
Oct. 1	10,000	Oct. 3	900	Oct. 4	600	
2	1,200	4	600			

Illustration 2-25
Purchase of supplies on credit

Cash Flows
no effect

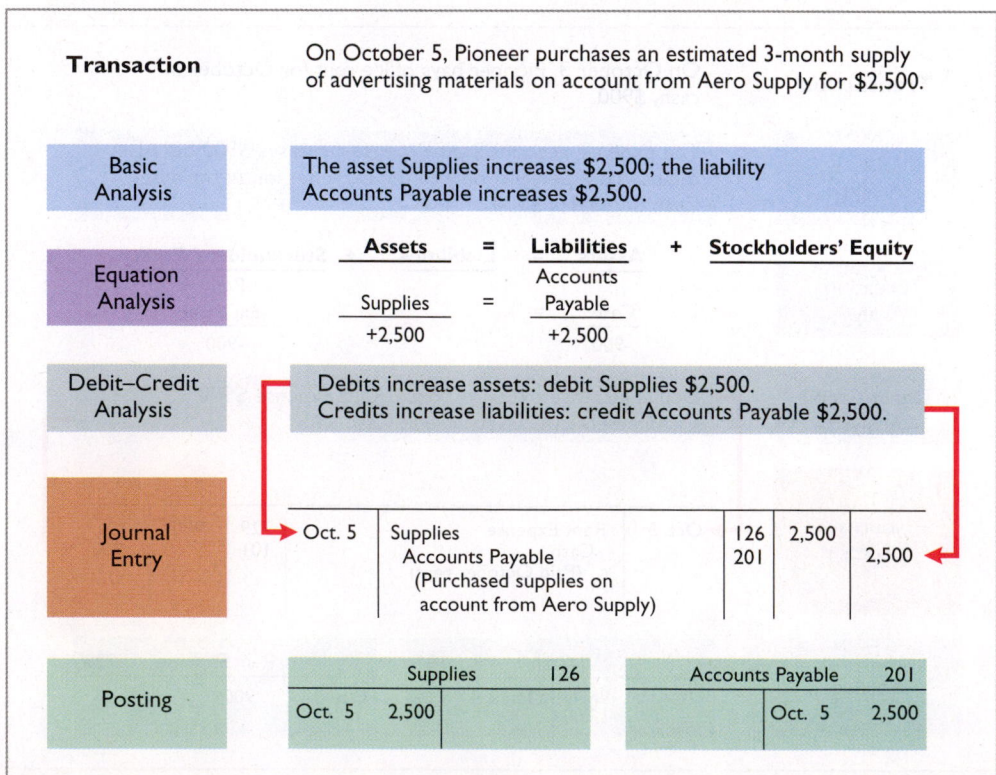

Transaction	On October 5, Pioneer purchases an estimated 3-month supply of advertising materials on account from Aero Supply for $2,500.
Basic Analysis	The asset Supplies increases $2,500; the liability Accounts Payable increases $2,500.

Equation Analysis

Assets	=	Liabilities	+	Stockholders' Equity
Supplies	=	Accounts Payable		
+2,500		+2,500		

Debit–Credit Analysis
Debits increase assets: debit Supplies $2,500.
Credits increase liabilities: credit Accounts Payable $2,500.

Journal Entry

Oct. 5	Supplies	126	2,500	
	Accounts Payable	201		2,500
	(Purchased supplies on account from Aero Supply)			

Posting

Supplies	126		Accounts Payable	201
Oct. 5	2,500		Oct. 5	2,500

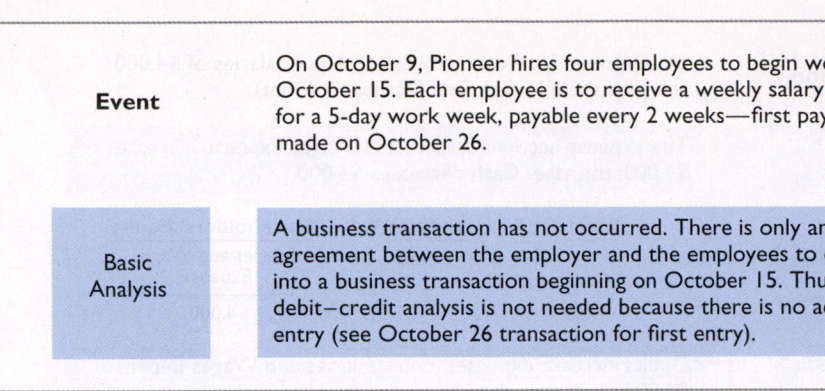

Illustration 2-26
Hiring of employees

Event	On October 9, Pioneer hires four employees to begin work on October 15. Each employee is to receive a weekly salary of $500 for a 5-day work week, payable every 2 weeks—first payment made on October 26.
Basic Analysis	A business transaction has not occurred. There is only an agreement between the employer and the employees to enter into a business transaction beginning on October 15. Thus, a debit–credit analysis is not needed because there is no accounting entry (see October 26 transaction for first entry).

Cash Flows
no effect

Illustration 2-27
Declaration and payment of dividend

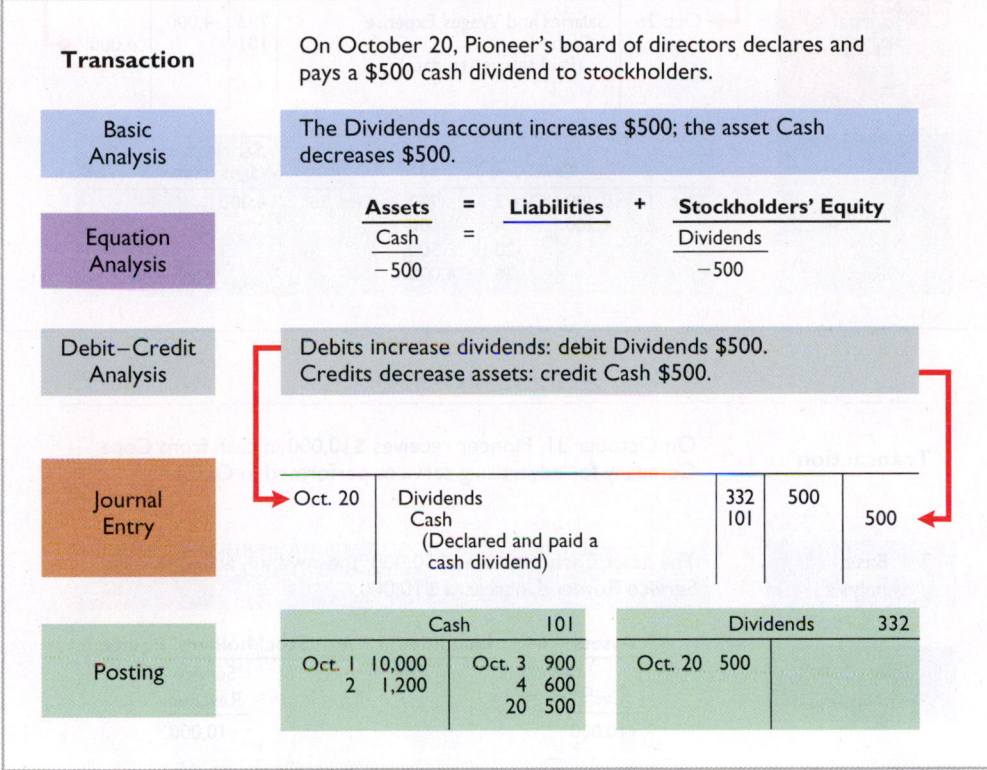

Transaction	On October 20, Pioneer's board of directors declares and pays a $500 cash dividend to stockholders.
Basic Analysis	The Dividends account increases $500; the asset Cash decreases $500.

Equation Analysis

Assets	=	Liabilities	+	Stockholders' Equity
Cash	=			Dividends
−500				−500

Debit–Credit Analysis

Debits increase dividends: debit Dividends $500.
Credits decrease assets: credit Cash $500.

Journal Entry

Oct. 20	Dividends	332	500	
	Cash	101		500
	(Declared and paid a cash dividend)			

Posting

Cash	101		Dividends	332
Oct. 1 10,000	Oct. 3 900		Oct. 20 500	
2 1,200	4 600			
	20 500			

Cash Flows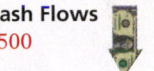
−500

Illustration 2-28
Payment of salaries

Cash Flows
–4,000

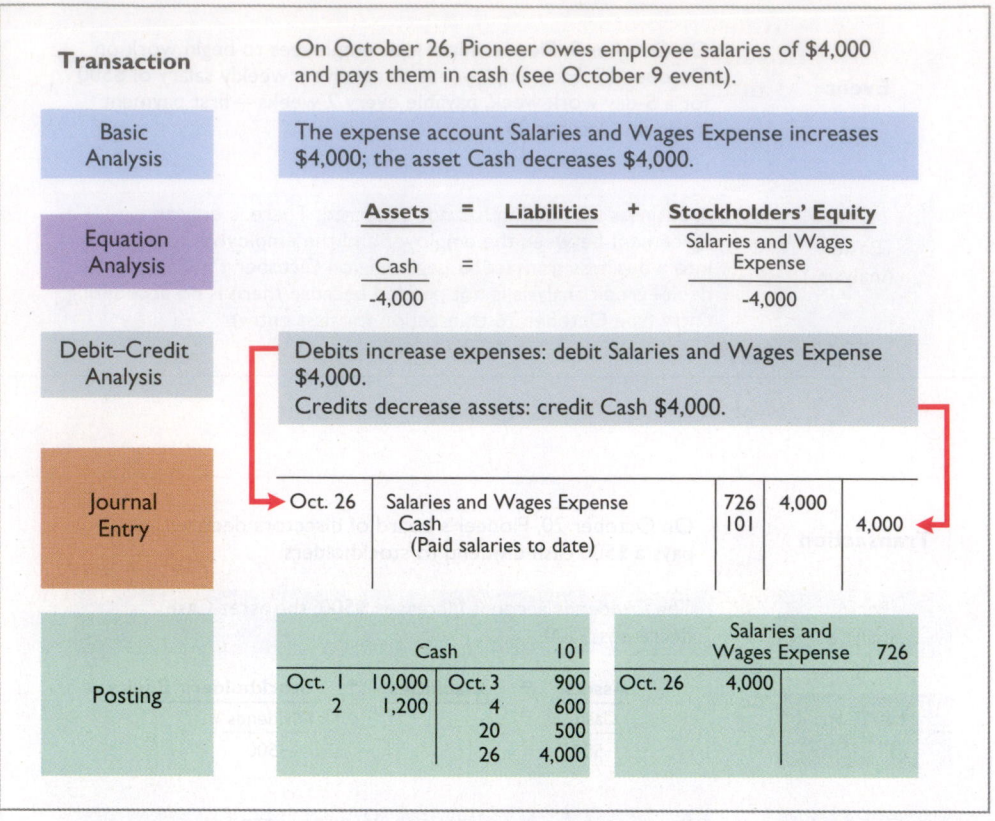

	Transaction	On October 26, Pioneer owes employee salaries of $4,000 and pays them in cash (see October 9 event).
Basic Analysis		The expense account Salaries and Wages Expense increases $4,000; the asset Cash decreases $4,000.
Equation Analysis		**Assets** = **Liabilities** + **Stockholders' Equity**
		Cash = ⟶ Salaries and Wages Expense
		–4,000 –4,000
Debit–Credit Analysis		Debits increase expenses: debit Salaries and Wages Expense $4,000. Credits decrease assets: credit Cash $4,000.
Journal Entry		Oct. 26 Salaries and Wages Expense 726 4,000
		Cash 101 4,000
		(Paid salaries to date)

Posting

Cash			101
Oct. 1	10,000	Oct. 3	900
2	1,200	4	600
		20	500
		26	4,000

Salaries and Wages Expense		726
Oct. 26	4,000	

Illustration 2-29
Receipt of cash for services performed

Cash Flows
+10,000

	Transaction	On October 31, Pioneer receives $10,000 in cash from Copa Company for advertising services performed in October.
Basic Analysis		The asset Cash increases $10,000; the revenue account Service Revenue increases $10,000.
Equation Analysis		**Assets** = **Liabilities** + **Stockholders' Equity**
		Cash = ⟶ Service Revenue
		+10,000 +10,000
Debit–Credit Analysis		Debits increase assets: debit Cash $10,000. Credits increase revenues: credit Service Revenue $10,000.
Journal Entry		Oct. 31 Cash 101 10,000
		Service Revenue 400 10,000
		(Received cash for services performed)

Posting

Cash			101
Oct. 1	10,000	Oct. 3	900
2	1,200	4	600
31	10,000	20	500
		26	4,000

Service Revenue		400
	Oct. 31	10,000

Study these transaction analyses carefully. **The purpose of transaction analysis is first to identify the type of account involved, and then to determine whether to make a debit or a credit to the account.** You should always perform this type of analysis before preparing a journal entry. Doing so will help you understand the journal entries discussed in this chapter as well as more complex journal entries in later chapters.

In addition, an Accounting Cycle Tutorial is available in *WileyPLUS*. It provides an interactive presentation of the steps in the accounting cycle, using the Pioneer example shown in Illustrations 2-20 through 2-29.

Summary Illustration of Journalizing and Posting

Illustration 2-30 shows the journal for Pioneer Advertising Inc. for October.

GENERAL JOURNAL				PAGE J1
Date	**Account Titles and Explanation**	**Ref.**	**Debit**	**Credit**
2017 Oct. 1	Cash	101	10,000	
	Common Stock	311		10,000
	(Issued shares of stock for cash)			
1	Equipment	157	5,000	
	Notes Payable	200		5,000
	(Issued 3-month, 12% note for office equipment)			
2	Cash	101	1,200	
	Unearned Service Revenue	209		1,200
	(Received cash from R. Knox for future service)			
3	Rent Expense	729	900	
	Cash	101		900
	(Paid October rent)			
4	Prepaid Insurance	130	600	
	Cash	101		600
	(Paid one-year policy; effective date October 1)			
5	Supplies	126	2,500	
	Accounts Payable	201		2,500
	(Purchased supplies on account from Aero Supply)			
20	Dividends	332	500	
	Cash	101		500
	(Declared and paid a cash dividend)			
26	Salaries and Wages Expense	726	4,000	
	Cash	101		4,000
	(Paid salaries to date)			
31	Cash	101	10,000	
	Service Revenue	400		10,000
	(Received cash for services performed)			

Illustration 2-30
General journal entries

Illustration 2-31
General ledger

Illustration 2-31 shows the ledger, with all balances in red.

GENERAL LEDGER						

Cash No. 101

Date	Explanation	Ref.	Debit	Credit	Balance
2017					
Oct. 1		J1	10,000		10,000
2		J1	1,200		11,200
3		J1		900	10,300
4		J1		600	9,700
20		J1		500	9,200
26		J1		4,000	5,200
31		J1	10,000		**15,200**

Supplies No. 126

Date	Explanation	Ref.	Debit	Credit	Balance
2017					
Oct. 5		J1	2,500		**2,500**

Prepaid Insurance No. 130

Date	Explanation	Ref.	Debit	Credit	Balance
2017					
Oct. 4		J1	600		**600**

Equipment No. 157

Date	Explanation	Ref.	Debit	Credit	Balance
2017					
Oct. 1		J1	5,000		**5,000**

Notes Payable No. 200

Date	Explanation	Ref.	Debit	Credit	Balance
2017					
Oct. 1		J1		5,000	**5,000**

Accounts Payable No. 201

Date	Explanation	Ref.	Debit	Credit	Balance
2017					
Oct. 5		J1		2,500	**2,500**

Unearned Service Revenue No. 209

Date	Explanation	Ref.	Debit	Credit	Balance
2017					
Oct. 2		J1		1,200	**1,200**

Common Stock No. 311

Date	Explanation	Ref.	Debit	Credit	Balance
2017					
Oct. 1		J1		10,000	**10,000**

Dividends No. 332

Date	Explanation	Ref.	Debit	Credit	Balance
2017					
Oct. 20		J1	500		**500**

Service Revenue No. 400

Date	Explanation	Ref.	Debit	Credit	Balance
2017					
Oct. 31		J1		10,000	**10,000**

Salaries and Wages Expense No. 726

Date	Explanation	Ref.	Debit	Credit	Balance
2017					
Oct. 26		J1	4,000		**4,000**

Rent Expense No. 729

Date	Explanation	Ref.	Debit	Credit	Balance
2017					
Oct. 3		J1	900		**900**

DO IT! 3 Posting

Kate Browne recorded the following transactions in a general journal during the month of March.

Mar. 4	Cash	2,280	
	Service Revenue		2,280
15	Salaries and Wages Expense	400	
	Cash		400
19	Utilities Expense	92	
	Cash		92

Post these entries to the Cash account of the general ledger to determine its ending balance. The beginning balance of Cash on March 1 was $600.

Action Plan

✔ Recall that posting involves transferring the journalized debits and credits to specific accounts in the ledger.

✔ Determine the ending balance by netting the total debits and credits.

Solution

	Cash		
3/1 Bal.	600	3/15	400
3/4	2,280	3/19	92
3/31 Bal.	2,388		

Related exercise material: **BE2-7, BE2-8, E2-8, E2-9, E2-12, and DO IT! 2-3.**

| LEARNING OBJECTIVE | **4** | **Prepare a trial balance.** |

A **trial balance** is a list of accounts and their balances at a given time. Customarily, companies prepare a trial balance at the end of an accounting period. They list accounts in the order in which they appear in the ledger. Debit balances appear in the left column and credit balances in the right column.

The trial balance proves the mathematical equality of debits and credits after posting. Under the double-entry system, this equality occurs when the sum of the debit account balances equals the sum of the credit account balances. **A trial balance may also uncover errors in journalizing and posting.** For example, a trial balance may well have detected the error at **MF Global** discussed in the Feature Story. **In addition, a trial balance is useful in the preparation of financial statements**, as we will explain in the next two chapters.

The steps for preparing a trial balance are:

1. List the account titles and their balances in the appropriate debit or credit column.
2. Total the debit and credit columns.
3. Prove the equality of the two columns.

Illustration 2-32 shows the trial balance prepared from Pioneer Advertising's ledger. Note that the total debits equal the total credits.

Illustration 2-32
A trial balance

PIONEER ADVERTISING INC.
Trial Balance
October 31, 2017

	Debit	Credit
Cash	$ 15,200	
Supplies	2,500	
Prepaid Insurance	600	
Equipment	5,000	
Notes Payable		$ 5,000
Accounts Payable		2,500
Unearned Service Revenue		1,200
Common Stock		10,000
Dividends	500	
Service Revenue		10,000
Salaries and Wages Expense	4,000	
Rent Expense	900	
	$28,700	**$28,700**

Helpful Hint
Note that the order of presentation in the trial balance is:
  Assets
  Liabilities
  Stockholders' equity
  Revenues
  Expenses

A trial balance is a necessary checkpoint for uncovering certain types of errors. For example, if only the debit portion of a journal entry has been posted, the trial balance would bring this error to light.

Limitations of a Trial Balance

A trial balance does not guarantee freedom from recording errors, however. Numerous errors may exist even though the totals of the trial balance columns agree. For example, the trial balance may balance even when:

1. A transaction is not journalized.
2. A correct journal entry is not posted.
3. A journal entry is posted twice.
4. Incorrect accounts are used in journalizing or posting.
5. Offsetting errors are made in recording the amount of a transaction.

ETHICS NOTE

An *error* is the result of an unintentional mistake; it is neither ethical nor unethical. An *irregularity* is an intentional misstatement, which *is* viewed as unethical.

As long as equal debits and credits are posted, even to the wrong account or in the wrong amount, the total debits will equal the total credits. **The trial balance does not prove that the company has recorded all transactions or that the ledger is correct.**

Locating Errors

Errors in a trial balance generally result from mathematical mistakes, incorrect postings, or simply transcribing data incorrectly. What do you do if you are faced with a trial balance that does not balance? First, determine the amount of the difference between the two columns of the trial balance. After this amount is known, the following steps are often helpful:

1. If the error is $1, $10, $100, or $1,000, re-add the trial balance columns and recompute the account balances.
2. If the error is divisible by 2, scan the trial balance to see whether a balance equal to half the error has been entered in the wrong column.
3. If the error is divisible by 9, retrace the account balances on the trial balance to see whether they are incorrectly copied from the ledger. For example, if a balance was $12 and it was listed as $21, a $9 error has been made. Reversing the order of numbers is called a **transposition error**.
4. If the error is not divisible by 2 or 9, scan the ledger to see whether an account balance in the amount of the error has been omitted from the trial balance, and scan the journal to see whether a posting of that amount has been omitted.

Dollar Signs and Underlining

Note that dollar signs do not appear in journals or ledgers. Dollar signs are typically used only in the trial balance and the financial statements. Generally, a dollar sign is shown only for the first item in the column and for the total of that column. A single line (a totaling rule) is placed under the column of figures to be added or subtracted. Total amounts are double-underlined to indicate they are final sums.

Investor Insight　Fannie Mae

Enviromatic/iStockphoto

Why Accuracy Matters

While most companies record transactions very carefully, the reality is that mistakes still happen. For example, bank regulators fined Bank One Corporation (now Chase) $1.8 million because they felt that the unreliability of the bank's accounting system caused it to violate regulatory requirements.

Also, in recent years Fannie Mae, the government-chartered mortgage association, announced a series of large accounting errors. These announcements caused alarm among investors, regulators, and politicians because they fear that the errors may suggest larger, undetected problems. This is important because the home-mortgage market depends on Fannie Mae to buy hundreds of billions of dollars of mortgages each year from banks, thus enabling the banks to issue new mortgages.

Finally, before a major overhaul of its accounting system, the financial records of Waste Management Inc. were in such disarray that of the company's 57,000 employees, 10,000 were receiving pay slips that were in error.

The Sarbanes-Oxley Act was created to minimize the occurrence of errors like these by increasing every employee's responsibility for accurate financial reporting.

In order for these companies to prepare and issue financial statements, their accounting equations (debits and credits) must have been in balance at year-end. How could these errors or misstatements have occurred? (Go to **WileyPLUS** for this answer and additional questions.)

DO IT! 4   Trial Balance

The following accounts come from the ledger of SnowGo Corporation at December 31, 2017.

157	Equipment	$88,000		311	Common Stock	$20,000
332	Dividends	8,000		212	Salaries and	
201	Accounts Payable	22,000			Wages Payable	2,000
726	Salaries and			200	Notes Payable	
	Wages Expense	42,000			(due in 3 months)	19,000
112	Accounts Receivable	4,000		732	Utilities Expense	3,000
400	Service Revenue	95,000		130	Prepaid Insurance	6,000
				101	Cash	7,000

Prepare a trial balance in good form.

Solution

SNOWGO CORPORATION
Trial Balance
December 31, 2017

	Debit	Credit
Cash	$ 7,000	
Accounts Receivable	4,000	
Prepaid Insurance	6,000	
Equipment	88,000	
Notes Payable		$ 19,000
Accounts Payable		22,000
Salaries and Wages Payable		2,000
Common Stock		20,000
Dividends	8,000	
Service Revenue		95,000
Utilities Expense	3,000	
Salaries and Wages Expense	42,000	
	$158,000	$158,000

Action Plan

✔ Determine normal balances and list accounts in the order they appear in the ledger.

✔ Accounts with debit balances appear in the left column, and those with credit balances in the right column.

✔ Total the debit and credit columns to prove equality.

Related exercise material: **BE2-9, BE2-10, E2-9, E2-10, E2-11, E2-13, E2-14, and DO IT! 2-4.**

REVIEW AND PRACTICE

LEARNING OBJECTIVES REVIEW

1 Describe how accounts, debits, and credits are used to record business transactions. An account is a record of increases and decreases in specific asset, liability, and stockholders' equity items. The terms debit and credit are synonymous with left and right. Assets, dividends, and expenses are increased by debits and decreased by credits. Liabilities, common stock, retained earnings, and revenues are increased by credits and decreased by debits.

2 Indicate how a journal is used in the recording process. The basic steps in the recording process are (a) analyze each transaction for its effects on the accounts, (b) enter the transaction information in a journal, and (c) transfer the journal information to the appropriate accounts in the ledger.

The initial accounting record of a transaction is entered in a journal before the data are entered in the accounts. A journal (a) discloses in one place the complete effects of a transaction, (b) provides a chronological record of transactions, and (c) prevents or locates errors because the debit and credit amounts for each entry can be easily compared.

3 **Explain how a ledger and posting help in the recording process.** The ledger is the entire group of accounts maintained by a company. The ledger provides the balance in each of the accounts as well as keeps track of changes in these balances. Posting is the transfer of journal entries to the ledger accounts. This phase of the recording process accumulates the effects of journalized transactions in the individual accounts.

4 **Prepare a trial balance.** A trial balance is a list of accounts and their balances at a given time. Its primary purpose is to prove the equality of debits and credits after posting. A trial balance also uncovers errors in journalizing and posting and is useful in preparing financial statements.

GLOSSARY REVIEW

Account A record of increases and decreases in specific asset, liability, or stockholders' equity items. (p. 50).

Chart of accounts A list of accounts and the account numbers that identify their location in the ledger. (p. 61).

Common stock Issued in exchange for the owners' investment paid in to corporation. (p. 52)

Compound entry A journal entry that involves three or more accounts. (p. 57).

Credit The right side of an account. (p. 50).

Debit The left side of an account. (p. 50).

Dividend A distribution by a corporation to its stockholders on a pro rata (equal) basis. (p. 52).

Double-entry system A system that records in appropriate accounts the dual effect of each transaction. (p. 51).

General journal The most basic form of journal. (p. 56).

General ledger A ledger that contains all asset, liability, and stockholders' equity accounts. (p. 58).

Journal An accounting record in which transactions are initially recorded in chronological order. (p. 56).

Journalizing The entering of transaction data in the journal. (p. 56).

Ledger The entire group of accounts maintained by a company. (p. 58).

Normal balance An account balance on the side where an increase in the account is recorded. (p. 51).

Posting The procedure of transferring journal entries to the ledger accounts. (p. 60).

Retained earnings Net income that is kept (retained) in the business. (p. 52).

Simple entry A journal entry that involves only two accounts. (p. 57).

T-account The basic form of an account. (p. 50).

Three-column form of account A form with columns for debit, credit, and balance amounts in an account. (p. 59).

Trial balance A list of accounts and their balances at a given time. (p. 69).

PRACTICE MULTIPLE-CHOICE QUESTIONS

(LO 1) **1.** Which of the following statements about an account is **true**?
  (a) The right side of an account is the debit or increase side.
  (b) An account is an individual accounting record of increases and decreases in specific asset, liability, and stockholders' equity items.
  (c) There are separate accounts for specific assets and liabilities but only one account for stockholders' equity items.
  (d) The left side of an account is the credit or decrease side.

(LO 1) **2.** Debits:
  (a) increase both assets and liabilities.
  (b) decrease both assets and liabilities.
  (c) increase assets and decrease liabilities.
  (d) decrease assets and increase liabilities.

(LO 1) **3.** A revenue account:
  (a) is increased by debits.
  (b) is decreased by credits.
  (c) has a normal balance of a debit.
  (d) is increased by credits.

4. Accounts that normally have debit balances are: (LO 1)
  (a) assets, expenses, and revenues.
  (b) assets, expenses, and common stock.
  (c) assets, liabilities, and dividends.
  (d) assets, dividends, and expenses.

5. The expanded accounting equation is: (LO 1)
  (a) Assets + Liabilities = Common Stock + Retained Earnings + Revenues + Expenses + Dividends.
  (b) Assets = Liabilities + Common Stock + Retained Earnings + Revenues − Expenses + Dividends.
  (c) Assets = Liabilities − Common Stock − Retained Earnings − Revenues − Expenses − Dividends.
  (d) Assets = Liabilities + Common Stock + Retained Earnings + Revenues − Expenses − Dividends.

6. Which of the following is **not** part of the recording (LO 1) process?
  (a) Analyzing transactions.
  (b) Preparing a trial balance.

(c) Entering transactions in a journal.

(d) Posting transactions.

(LO 2) **7.** Which of the following statements about a journal is **false**?

(a) It is not a book of original entry.

(b) It provides a chronological record of transactions.

(c) It helps to locate errors because the debit and credit amounts for each entry can be readily compared.

(d) It discloses in one place the complete effect of a transaction.

(LO 2) **8.** The purchase of supplies on account should result in:

(a) a debit to Supplies Expense and a credit to Cash.

(b) a debit to Supplies Expense and a credit to Accounts Payable.

(c) a debit to Supplies and a credit to Accounts Payable.

(d) a debit to Supplies and a credit to Accounts Receivable.

(LO 3) **9.** The order of the accounts in the ledger is:

(a) assets, revenues, expenses, liabilities, common stock, dividends.

(b) assets, liabilities, common stock, dividends, revenues, expenses.

(c) common stock, assets, revenues, expenses, liabilities, dividends.

(d) revenues, assets, expenses, liabilities, common stock, dividends.

(LO 3) **10.** A ledger:

(a) contains only asset and liability accounts.

(b) should show accounts in alphabetical order.

(c) is a collection of the entire group of accounts maintained by a company.

(d) is a book of original entry.

(LO 3) **11.** Posting:

(a) normally occurs before journalizing.

(b) transfers ledger transaction data to the journal.

(c) is an optional step in the recording process.

(d) transfers journal entries to ledger accounts.

(LO 3) **12.** Before posting a payment of $5,000, the Accounts Payable of Chola Corporation had a normal balance of $18,000. The balance after posting this transaction was:

(a) $13,000.   (c) $23,000.

(b) $5,000.   (d) Cannot be determined.

(LO 4) **13.** A trial balance:

(a) is a list of accounts with their balances at a given time.

(b) proves the mathematical accuracy of journalized transactions.

(c) will not balance if a correct journal entry is posted twice.

(d) proves that all transactions have been recorded.

(LO 4) **14.** A trial balance will not balance if:

(a) a correct journal entry is posted twice.

(b) the purchase of supplies on account is debited to Supplies and credited to Cash.

(c) a $100 cash dividend is debited to Dividends for $1,000 and credited to Cash for $100.

(d) a $450 payment on account is debited to Accounts Payable for $45 and credited to Cash for $45.

(LO 4) **15.** The trial balance of Stevens Corporation had accounts with the following normal balances: Cash $5,000, Service Revenue $85,000, Salaries and Wages Payable $4,000, Salaries and Wages Expense $40,000, Rent Expense $10,000, Common Stock $42,000, Dividends $13,000, and Equipment $61,000. In preparing a trial balance, the total in the debit column is:

(a) $116,000.   (c) $129,000.

(b) $118,000.   (d) $131,000.

Solutions

1. (b) An account is an individual accounting record of increases and decreases in specific asset, liability, and owner's equity items. The other choices are incorrect because (a) the right side of the account is the credit side, not the debit side, and can be the increase or the decrease side, depending on the specific classification account; (c) there are also separate accounts for different owner's equity items; and (d) the left side of the account is the debit side, not the credit side, and can be either the decrease or the increase side, depending on the specific classification account.

2. (c) Debits increase assets but they decrease liabilities. The other choices are incorrect because debits (a) decrease, not increase, liabilities; (b) increase, not decrease, assets; and (d) increase, not decrease, assets and decrease, not increase, liabilities.

3. (d) A revenue account is increased by credits. The other choices are incorrect because a revenue account (a) is increased by credits, not debits; (b) is decreased by debits, not credits; and (c) has a normal balance of a credit, not a debit.

4. (d) Assets, dividends, and expenses all have normal debit balances. The other choices are incorrect because (a) revenues have normal credit balances, (b) common stock has a normal credit balance, and (c) liabilities have normal credit balances.

5. (d) The expanded accounting equation is Assets = Liabilities + Common Stock + Retained Earnings + Revenues − Expenses − Dividends. The other choices are therefore incorrect.

6. (b) Preparing the trial balance is not part of the recording process. Choices (a) analyzing transactions, (c) entering transactions in a journal, and (d) posting transactions are all part of the recording process.

7. (a) The journal is a book of original entry. The other choices are true statements.

8. (c) The purchase of supplies on account results in a debit to Supplies and a credit to Accounts Payable. The other choices are incorrect because the purchase of supplies on account results in (a) a debit to Supplies, not Supplies Expense, and a credit to Accounts Payable, not Cash; (b) a debit to Supplies, not Supplies Expense; and (d) a credit to Accounts Payable, not Accounts Receivable.

9. (b) The correct order of the accounts in the ledger is assets, liabilities, common stock, dividends, revenues, expenses. The other choices are incorrect because they do not reflect this order. The order of the accounts in the ledger is (1) balance sheet accounts:

assets, liabilities, and stockholders' equity accounts (common stock and dividends), and then (2) income statement accounts: revenues and expenses.

10. (c) A ledger is a collection of all the accounts maintained by a company. The other choices are incorrect because a ledger (a) contains all account types—assets, liabilities, stockholders' equity, revenue, and expense accounts–not just asset and liability accounts; (b) usually shows accounts in account number order, not alphabetical order; and (d) is not a book of original entry because entries made in the ledger come from the journals (the books of original entry).

11. (d) Posting transfers journal entries to ledger accounts. The other choices are incorrect because posting (a) occurs after journalizing, (b) transfers journal transaction data to the ledger; and (c) is not an optional step in the recording process.

12. (a) The balance is $13,000 ($18,000 normal balance − $5,000 payment), not (b) $5,000 or (c) $23,000. Choice (d) is incorrect because the balance can be determined.

13. (a) A trial balance is a list of accounts with their balances at a given time. The other choices are incorrect because (b) the trial balance does not prove that journalized transactions are correct; (c) if a journal entry is posted twice, the trial balance will still balance; and (d) the trial balance does not prove that all transactions have been recorded.

14. (c) The trial balance will not balance in this case because the debit of $1,000 to Dividends is not equal to the credit of $100 to Cash. The other choices are incorrect because (a) if a correct journal entry is posted twice, the trial balance will still balance; (b) if the purchase of supplies on account is debited to Supplies and credited to Cash, Cash and Accounts Payable will be understated but the trial balance will still balance; and (d) since the debit and credit amounts are the same, the trial balance will still balance but both Accounts Payable and Cash will be overstated.

15. (c) The total debit column = $5,000 (Cash) + $40,000 (Salaries and Wages Expense) + $10,000 (Rent Expense) + $13,000 (Dividends) + $61,000 (Equipment) = $129,000, not (a) $116,000, (b) $118,000, or (d) $131,000.

PRACTICE EXERCISES

Analyze transactions and determine their effect on accounts.

(LO 1)

1. Presented below is information related to Conan Real Estate Agency.

Oct. 1 Arnold Conan begins business as a real estate agent with a cash investment of $18,000 in exchange for common stock.

     2 Hires an administrative assistant.

     3 Purchases office equipment for $1,700, on account.

     6 Sells a house and lot for B. Clinton; bills B. Clinton $4,200 for realty services performed.

    27 Pays $900 on the balance related to the transaction of October 3.

    30 Pays the administrative assistant $2,800 in salary for October.

Instructions

Journalize the transactions. (You may omit explanations.)

Solution

1.

	GENERAL JOURNAL			J1
Date	**Account Titles and Explanation**	**Ref.**	**Debit**	**Credit**
Oct. 1	Cash		18,000	
	Common Stock			18,000
2	No entry required			
3	Equipment		1,700	
	Accounts Payable			1,700
6	Accounts Receivable		4,200	
	Service Revenue			4,200
27	Accounts Payable		900	
	Cash			900
30	Salaries and Wages Expense		2,800	
	Cash			2,800

2. The T-accounts below summarize the ledger of Garfunkle Landscaping Company at the end of the first month of operations.

Journalize transactions from account data and prepare a trial balance.

(LO 2, 4)

Cash			No. 101
4/1	18,000	4/15	700
4/12	800	4/25	1,400
4/29	700		
4/30	1,200		

Accounts Receivable			No. 112
4/7	3,800	4/29	700

Supplies			No. 126
4/4	1,900		

Accounts Payable			No. 201
4/25	1,400	4/4	1,900

Unearned Service Revenue			No. 209
		4/30	1,200

Common Stock			No. 311
		4/1	18,000

Service Revenue			No. 400
		4/7	3,800
		4/12	800

Salaries and Wages Expense			No. 726
4/15	700		

Instructions

(a) Prepare the complete general journal (including explanations) from which the postings to Cash were made.

(b) Prepare a trial balance at April 30, 2017.

Solution

2. (a)

GENERAL JOURNAL				
Date	**Account Titles and Explanation**	**Ref.**	**Debit**	**Credit**
Apr. 1	Cash		18,000	
	Common Stock			18,000
	(Issued shares of stock for cash)			
12	Cash		800	
	Service Revenue			800
	(Received cash for services performed)			
15	Salaries and Wages Expense		700	
	Cash			700
	(Paid salaries to date)			
25	Accounts Payable		1,400	
	Cash			1,400
	(Paid creditors on account)			
29	Cash		700	
	Accounts Receivable			700
	(Received cash in payment of account)			
30	Cash		1,200	
	Unearned Service Revenue			1,200
	(Received cash for future services)			

(b)

GARFUNKLE LANDSCAPING COMPANY
Trial Balance
April 30, 2017

	Debit	Credit
Cash	$18,600	
Accounts Receivable	3,100	
Supplies	1,900	
Accounts Payable		$ 500
Unearned Service Revenue		1,200
Common Stock		18,000
Service Revenue		4,600
Salaries and Wages Expense	700	
	$24,300	$24,300

PRACTICE PROBLEM

Journalize transactions, post, and prepare a trial balance.

(LO 1, 2, 3, 4)

Bob Sample and other student investors opened Campus Laundromat Inc. on September 1, 2017. During the first month of operations, the following transactions occurred.

Sept. 1 Stockholders invested $20,000 cash in the business.
     2 The company paid $1,000 cash for store rent for September.
     3 Purchased washers and dryers for $25,000, paying $10,000 in cash and signing a $15,000, 6-month, 12% note payable.
     4 Paid $1,200 for a one-year accident insurance policy.
    10 Received a bill from the *Daily News* for advertising the opening of the laundromat $200.
    20 Declared and paid a cash dividend to stockholders $700.
    30 The company determined that cash receipts for laundry services for the month were $6,200.

The chart of accounts for the company is the same as that for Pioneer Advertising Inc. (Illustration 2-19, page 61), plus No. 610 Advertising Expense.

Instructions

(a) Journalize the September transactions. (Use J1 for the journal page number.)

(b) Open ledger accounts and post the September transactions.

(c) Prepare a trial balance at September 30, 2017.

Solution

(a)	GENERAL JOURNAL				J1
Date	**Account Titles and Explanation**	**Ref.**	**Debit**		**Credit**
2017					
Sept. 1	Cash	101	20,000		
	Common Stock	311			20,000
	(Stockholders' investment of cash in business)				
2	Rent Expense	729	1,000		
	Cash	101			1,000
	(Paid September rent)				
3	Equipment	157	25,000		
	Cash	101			10,000
	Notes Payable	200			15,000
	(Purchased laundry equipment for cash and 6-month, 12% note payable)				
4	Prepaid Insurance	130	1,200		
	Cash	101			1,200
	(Paid one-year insurance policy)				
10	Advertising Expense	610	200		
	Accounts Payable	201			200
	(Received bill from *Daily News* for advertising)				
20	Dividends	332	700		
	Cash	101			700
	(Declared and paid a cash dividend)				
30	Cash	101	6,200		
	Service Revenue	400			6,200
	(Received cash for services performed)				

(b) GENERAL LEDGER

	Cash					No. 101
Date	Explanation	Ref.	Debit	Credit	Balance	
2017						
Sept. 1		J1	20,000		20,000	
2		J1		1,000	19,000	
3		J1		10,000	9,000	
4		J1		1,200	7,800	
20		J1		700	7,100	
30		J1	6,200		13,300	

	Prepaid Insurance				No. 130
Date	Explanation	Ref.	Debit	Credit	Balance
2017					
Sept. 4		J1	1,200		1,200

	Equipment				No. 157
Date	Explanation	Ref.	Debit	Credit	Balance
2017					
Sept. 3		J1	25,000		25,000

(b)

GENERAL LEDGER (continued)

Notes Payable					No. 200
Date	Explanation	Ref.	Debit	Credit	Balance
2017					
Sept. 3		J1		15,000	15,000

Accounts Payable					No. 201
Date	Explanation	Ref.	Debit	Credit	Balance
2017					
Sept. 10		J1		200	200

Common Stock					No. 311
Date	Explanation	Ref.	Debit	Credit	Balance
2017					
Sept. 1		J1		20,000	20,000

Dividends					No. 332
Date	Explanation	Ref.	Debit	Credit	Balance
2017					
Sept. 20		J1	700		700

Service Revenue					No. 400
Date	Explanation	Ref.	Debit	Credit	Balance
2017					
Sept. 30		J1		6,200	6,200

Advertising Expense					No. 610
Date	Explanation	Ref.	Debit	Credit	Balance
2017					
Sept. 10		J1	200		200

Rent Expense					No. 729
Date	Explanation	Ref.	Debit	Credit	Balance
2017					
Sept. 2		J1	1,000		1,000

(c)

CAMPUS LAUNDROMAT INC.
Trial Balance
September 30, 2017

	Debit	Credit
Cash	$13,300	
Prepaid Insurance	1,200	
Equipment	25,000	
Notes Payable		$15,000
Accounts Payable		200
Common Stock		20,000
Dividends	700	
Service Revenue		6,200
Advertising Expense	200	
Rent Expense	1,000	
	$41,400	$41,400

WileyPLUS

Brief Exercises, Exercises, DO IT! Exercises, and Problems and many additional resources are available for practice in WileyPLUS

QUESTIONS

1. Describe the parts of a T-account.
2. "The terms debit and credit mean increase and decrease, respectively." Do you agree? Explain.
3. Tom Dingel, a fellow student, contends that the double-entry system means each transaction must be recorded twice. Is Tom correct? Explain.
4. Olga Conrad, a beginning accounting student, believes debit balances are favorable and credit balances are unfavorable. Is Olga correct? Discuss.
5. State the rules of debit and credit as applied to (a) asset accounts, (b) liability accounts, and (c) the stockholders' equity accounts (revenue, expenses, dividends, common stock, and retained earnings).
6. What is the normal balance for each of the following accounts? (a) Accounts Receivable. (b) Cash. (c) Dividends. (d) Accounts Payable. (e) Service Revenue. (f) Salaries and Wages Expense. (g) Common Stock.
7. Indicate whether each of the following accounts is an asset, a liability, or a stockholders' equity account and whether it has a normal debit or credit balance: (a) Accounts Receivable, (b) Accounts Payable, (c) Equipment, (d) Dividends, and (e) Supplies.

8. For the following transactions, indicate the account debited and the account credited.
   (a) Supplies are purchased on account.
   (b) Cash is received on signing a note payable.
   (c) Employees are paid salaries in cash.
9. Indicate whether the following accounts generally will have (a) debit entries only, (b) credit entries only, or (c) both debit and credit entries.
   (1) Cash.
   (2) Accounts Receivable.
   (3) Dividends.
   (4) Accounts Payable.
   (5) Salaries and Wages Expense.
   (6) Service Revenue.
10. What are the basic steps in the recording process?
11. What are the advantages of using a journal in the recording process?
12. (a) When entering a transaction in the journal, should the debit or credit be written first?
    (b) Which should be indented, the debit or credit?
13. Describe a compound entry, and provide an example.
14. (a) Should business transaction debits and credits be recorded directly in the ledger accounts?
    (b) What are the advantages of first recording transactions in the journal and then posting to the ledger?
15. The account number is entered as the last step in posting the amounts from the journal to the ledger. What is the advantage of this step?
16. Journalize the following business transactions.
    (a) Mark Stein invests $9,000 cash in the business in exchange for shares of common stock.

(b) Insurance of $800 is paid for the year.
(c) Supplies of $2,000 are purchased on account.
(d) Cash of $7,800 is received for services performed.
17. (a) What is a ledger?
    (b) What is a chart of accounts and why is it important?
18. What is a trial balance and what are its purposes?
19. Juan Kirby is confused about how accounting information flows through the accounting system. He believes the flow of information is as follows.
    (a) Debits and credits posted to the ledger.
    (b) Business transaction occurs.
    (c) Information entered in the journal.
    (d) Financial statements are prepared.
    (e) Trial balance is prepared.
    Is Juan correct? If not, indicate to Juan the proper flow of the information.
20. Two students are discussing the use of a trial balance. They wonder whether the following errors, each considered separately, would prevent the trial balance from balancing. What would you tell them?
    (a) The bookkeeper debited Cash for $600 and credited Salaries and Wages Expense for $600 for payment of wages.
    (b) Cash collected on account was debited to Cash for $900 and Service Revenue was credited for $90.
21. What are the normal balances for **Apple**'s Cash, Accounts Payable, and Interest Expense accounts?

BRIEF EXERCISES

Indicate debit and credit effects and normal balance.

(LO 1)

BE2-1 For each of the following accounts indicate the effects of (a) a debit and (b) a credit on the accounts and (c) the normal balance of the account.
1. Accounts Payable.
2. Advertising Expense.
3. Service Revenue.
4. Accounts Receivable.
5. Common Stock.
6. Dividends.

Identify accounts to be debited and credited.

(LO 1)

BE2-2 Transactions for the Sheldon Cooper Company, which provides welding services, for the month of June are presented below. Identify the accounts to be debited and credited for each transaction.

June 1 Sheldon Cooper invests $4,000 cash in exchange for shares of common stock in a small welding business.
      2 Purchases equipment on account for $1,200.
      3 $800 cash is paid to landlord for June rent.
     12 Bills P. Leonard $300 for welding work done on account.

Journalize transactions.

(LO 2)

BE2-3 Using the data in BE2-2, journalize the transactions. (You may omit explanations.)

Identify and explain steps in recording process.

(LO 2)

BE2-4 •———— Evan Saunders, a fellow student, is unclear about the basic steps in the recording process. Identify and briefly explain the steps in the order in which they occur.

Indicate basic and debit-credit analysis.

(LO 2)

BE2-5 Bombeck Inc. has the following transactions during August of the current year. Indicate (a) the effect on the accounting equation and (b) the debit-credit analysis illustrated on pages 62–66 of the textbook.

Aug. 1 Opens an office as a financial advisor, investing $5,000 in cash in exchange for common stock.
      4 Pays insurance in advance for 6 months, $1,800 cash.
     16 Receives $1,900 from clients for services performed.
     27 Pays secretary $1,000 salary.

BE2-6 Using the data in BE2-5, journalize the transactions. (You may omit explanations.)

Journalize transactions.

(LO 2)

BE2-7 Selected transactions for the Nikolai Company are presented in journal form below. Post the transactions to T-accounts. Make one T-account for each item and determine each account's ending balance.

Post journal entries to T-accounts.

(LO 3)

				J1
Date	Account Titles and Explanation	Ref.	Debit	Credit
May 5	Accounts Receivable		5,000	
	Service Revenue			5,000
	(Billed for services performed)			
12	Cash		2,100	
	Accounts Receivable			2,100
	(Received cash in payment of account)			
15	Cash		3,200	
	Service Revenue			3,200
	(Received cash for services performed)			

BE2-8 Selected journal entries for the Nikolai Company are presented in BE2-7. Post the transactions using the standard form of account.

Post journal entries to standard form of account.

(LO 3)

BE2-9 From the ledger balances given below, prepare a trial balance for the Favre Company at June 30, 2017. List the accounts in the order shown on page 69 of the textbook. All account balances are normal.

   Accounts Payable $7,000, Cash $5,200, Common Stock $20,000, Dividends $800, Equipment $17,000, Service Revenue $6,000, Accounts Receivable $3,000, Salaries and Wages Expense $6,000, and Rent Expense $1,000.

Prepare a trial balance.

(LO 4)

BE2-10 An inexperienced bookkeeper prepared the following trial balance. Prepare a correct trial balance, assuming all account balances are normal.

Prepare a correct trial balance.

(LO 4)

ERIKA COMPANY
Trial Balance
December 31, 2017

	Debit	Credit
Cash	$16,800	
Prepaid Insurance		$ 3,500
Accounts Payable		3,000
Unearned Service Revenue	4,200	
Common Stock		13,000
Dividends		4,500
Service Revenue		25,600
Salaries and Wages Expense	18,600	
Rent Expense		2,400
	$39,600	$52,000

DO IT! Exercises

DO IT! 2-1 James Mayaguez has just rented space in a strip mall. In this space, he will open a photography studio, to be called "Picture This!" A friend has advised James to set up a double-entry set of accounting records in which to record all of his business transactions.

   Identify the balance sheet accounts that James will likely need to record the transactions needed to open his business (a corporation). Indicate whether the normal balance of each account is a debit or credit.

Identify normal balances.

(LO 1)

Record business activities.

(LO 2)

DO IT! 2-2 James Mayaguez engaged in the following activities in establishing his photography studio, Picture This!:

1. Opened a bank account in the name of Picture This! and deposited $8,000 of his own money into this account in exchange for common stock.
2. Purchased photography supplies at a total cost of $1,600. The business paid $300 in cash and the balance is on account.
3. Obtained estimates on the cost of photography equipment from three different manufacturers.

In what form (type of record) should James record these three activities? Prepare the entries to record the transactions.

Post transactions.

(LO 3)

DO IT! 2-3 James Mayaguez recorded the following transactions during the month of April.

April 3	Cash	3,900	
	Service Revenue		3,900
April 16	Rent Expense	600	
	Cash		600
April 20	Salaries and Wages Expense	500	
	Cash		500

Post these entries to the Cash T-account of the general ledger to determine the ending balance in cash. The beginning balance in cash on April 1 was $1,600.

Prepare a trial balance.

(LO 4)

DO IT! 2-4 The following accounts are taken from the ledger of Chillin' Company at December 31, 2017.

200	Notes Payable	$20,000		101	Cash	$6,000
311	Common Stock	25,000		120	Supplies	5,000
157	Equipment	76,000		522	Rent Expense	2,000
332	Dividends	8,000		220	Salaries and	
726	Salaries and				Wages Payable	3,000
	Wages Expense	38,000		201	Accounts Payable	9,000
400	Service Revenue	86,000		112	Accounts Receivable	8,000

Prepare a trial balance in good form.

EXERCISES

Analyze statements about accounting and the recording process.

(LO 1)

E2-1 Faith Dillon as prepared the following list of statements about accounts.

1. An account is an accounting record of either a specific asset or a specific liability.
2. An account shows only increases, not decreases, in the item it relates to.
3. Some items, such as cash and accounts receivable, are combined into one account.
4. An account has a left, or credit side, and a right, or debit side.
5. A simple form of an account consisting of just the account title, the left side, and the right side, is called a T-account.

Instructions
Identify each statement as true or false. If false, indicate how to correct the statement.

Identify debits, credits, and normal balances.

(LO 1)

E2-2 Selected transactions for L. Takemoto, an interior decorating firm, in its first month of business, are shown below.

Jan.	2	Invested $15,000 cash in the business in exchange for common stock.
	3	Purchased used car for $8,200 cash for use in the business.
	9	Purchased supplies on account for $500.
	11	Billed customers $1,800 for services performed.
	16	Paid $200 cash for advertising.
	20	Received $780 cash from customers billed on January 11.
	23	Paid creditor $300 cash on balance owed.
	28	Declared and paid a $500 cash dividend.

Instructions
For each transaction indicate the following.

(a) The basic type of account debited and credited (asset, liability, stockholders' equity).
(b) The specific account debited and credited (Cash, Rent Expense, Service Revenue, etc.).

(c) Whether the specific account is increased or decreased.
(d) The normal balance of the specific account.

Use the following format, in which the January 2 transaction is given as an example.

	Account Debited				Account Credited			
Date	(a) Basic Type	(b) Specific Account	(c) Effect	(d) Normal Balance	(a) Basic Type	(b) Specific Account	(c) Effect	(d) Normal Balance
Jan. 2	Asset	Cash	Increase	Debit	Stockholders' Equity	Common Stock	Increase	Credit

E2-3 Data for L. Takemoto, interior decorating, are presented in E2-2.

Journalize transactions.
(LO 2)

Instructions
Journalize the transactions using journal page J1. (You may omit explanations.)

E2-4 Presented below is information related to Lexington Real Estate Agency.

Analyze transactions and determine their effect on accounts.
(LO 1)

Oct. 1 Diane Lexington begins business as a real estate agent with a cash investment of $20,000 in exchange for common stock.
     2 Hires an administrative assistant.
     3 Purchases office furniture for $2,300, on account.
     6 Sells a house and lot for N. Fennig; bills N. Fennig $3,600 for realty services performed.
    27 Pays $850 on the balance related to the transaction of October 3.
    30 Pays the administrative assistant $2,500 in salary for October.

Instructions
Prepare the debit-credit analysis for each transaction as illustrated on pages 62–66.

E2-5 Transaction data for Lexington Real Estate Agency are presented in E2-4.

Journalize transactions.
(LO 2)

Instructions
Journalize the transactions. (You may omit explanations.)

E2-6 Fredo Industries had the following transactions.

Analyze transactions and journalize.
(LO 1, 2)

1. Borrowed $5,000 from the bank by signing a note.
2. Paid $2,500 cash for a computer.
3. Purchased $450 of supplies on account.

Instructions
(a) Indicate what accounts are increased and decreased by each transaction.
(b) Journalize each transaction. (Omit explanations.)

E2-7 Leppard Enterprises had the following selected transactions.

Analyze transactions and journalize.
(LO 1, 2)

1. Kim Leppard invested $5,000 cash in the business in exchange for common stock.
2. Paid office rent of $950.
3. Performed consulting services and billed a client $4,700.
4. Declared and paid a $600 cash dividend.

Instructions
(a) Indicate the effect each transaction has on the accounting equation (Assets = Liabilities + Stockholders' Equity), using plus and minus signs.
(b) Journalize each transaction. (Omit explanations.)

E2-8 Meghan Selzer has prepared the following list of statements about the general ledger.

Analyze statements about the ledger.
(LO 3)

1. The general ledger contains all the asset and liability accounts, but no stockholders' equity accounts.
2. The general ledger is sometimes referred to as simply the ledger.
3. The accounts in the general ledger are arranged in alphabetical order.
4. Each account in the general ledger is numbered for easier identification.
5. The general ledger is a book of original entry.

Post journal entries and prepare a trial balance.

(LO 3, 4)

Instructions

Identify each statement as true or false. If false, indicate how to correct the statement.

E2-9 Selected transactions from the journal of Kati Tillman, investment broker, are presented below.

Date	Account Titles and Explanation	Ref.	Debit	Credit
Aug. 1	Cash		6,000	
	Common Stock			6,000
	(Investment of cash for stock)			
10	Cash		2,700	
	Service Revenue			2,700
	(Received cash for services performed)			
12	Equipment		5,000	
	Cash			800
	Notes Payable			4,200
	(Purchased office equipment for cash and notes payable)			
25	Account Receivable		1,600	
	Service Revenue			1,600
	(Billed clients for services performed)			
31	Cash		880	
	Accounts Receivable			880
	(Receipt of cash on account)			

Instructions

(a) Post the transactions to T-accounts.

(b) Prepare a trial balance at August 31, 2017.

Journalize transactions from account data and prepare a trial balance.

(LO 2, 4)

E2-10 The T-accounts below summarize the ledger of Santana Landscaping Company at the end of its first month of operations.

Cash		No. 101
4/1	10,000	4/15	720
4/12	900	4/25	1,500
4/29	400		
4/30	1,000		

Accounts Receivable		No. 112
4/7	3,200	4/29	400

Supplies		No. 126
4/4	1,800		

Accounts Payable		No. 201
4/25	1,500	4/4	1,800

Unearned Service Revenue		No. 209
		4/30	1,000

Common Stock		No. 311
		4/1	10,000

Service Revenue		No. 400
		4/7	3,200
		4/12	900

Salaries and Wages Expense		No. 726
4/15	720		

Instructions

(a) Prepare the complete general journal (including explanations) from which the postings to Cash were made.

(b) Prepare a trial balance at April 30, 2017.

E2-11 Presented below is the ledger for Higgs Co.

Cash			No. 101
10/1	5,000	10/4	400
10/10	730	10/12	1,500
10/10	3,000	10/15	280
10/20	500	10/30	300
10/25	2,000	10/31	500

Accounts Receivable			No. 112
10/6	800	10/20	500
10/20	910		

Supplies		No. 126
10/4	400	

Equipment		No. 157
10/3	2,000	

Notes Payable			No. 200
		10/10	3,000

Accounts Payable			No. 201
10/12	1,500	10/3	2,000

Common Stock			No. 311
		10/1	5,000
		10/25	2,000

Dividends		No. 332
10/30	300	

Service Revenue			No. 400
		10/6	800
		10/10	730
		10/20	910

Salaries and Wages Expense		No. 726
10/31	500	

Rent Expense		No. 729
10/15	280	

Instructions

(a) Reproduce the journal entries for the transactions that occurred on October 1, 10, and 20, and provide explanations for each.
(b) Determine the October 31 balance for each of the accounts above, and prepare a trial balance at October 31, 2017.

E2-12 Selected transactions for Alvarado Company during its first month in business are presented below.

Sept.	1	Invested $10,000 cash in the business in exchange for common stock.
	5	Purchased equipment for $12,000 paying $4,000 in cash and the balance on account.
	25	Paid $2,400 cash on balance owed for equipment.
	30	Declared and paid a $500 cash dividend.

Alvarado's chart of accounts shows No. 101 Cash, No. 157 Equipment, No. 201 Accounts Payable, No. 311 Common Stock, and No. 332 Dividends.

Instructions

(a) Journalize the transactions on page J1 of the journal. (Omit explanations.)
(b) Post the transactions using the standard account form.

E2-13 The bookkeeper for Brooks Equipment Repair made a number of errors in journalizing and posting, as described below.

1. A credit posting of $450 to Accounts Receivable was omitted.
2. A debit posting of $750 for Prepaid Insurance was debited to Insurance Expense.
3. A collection from a customer of $100 in payment of its account owed was journalized and posted as a debit to Cash $100 and a credit to Service Revenue $100.
4. A credit posting of $300 to Property Taxes Payable was made twice.
5. A cash purchase of supplies for $250 was journalized and posted as a debit to Supplies $25 and a credit to Cash $25.
6. A debit of $525 to Advertising Expense was posted as $552.

Instructions

For each error:

(a) Indicate whether the trial balance will balance.
(b) If the trial balance will not balance, indicate the amount of the difference.
(c) Indicate the trial balance column that will have the larger total.

Consider each error separately. Use the following form, in which error (1) is given as an example.

Error	(a) In Balance	(b) Difference	(c) Larger Column
(1)	No	$450	debit

Prepare a trial balance.

(LO 4)

E2-14 The accounts in the ledger of Time Is Money Delivery Service contain the following balances on July 31, 2017.

Accounts Receivable	$10,642	Prepaid Insurance	$ 1,968
Accounts Payable	8,396	Maintenance and Repairs Expense	961
Cash	?	Service Revenue	10,610
Equipment	49,360	Dividends	700
Gasoline Expense	758	Common Stock	40,000
Utilities Expense	523	Salaries and Wages Expense	4,428
Notes Payable	26,450	Salaries and Wages Payable	815
		Retained Earnings	4,636

Instructions

Prepare a trial balance with the accounts arranged as illustrated in the chapter and fill in the missing amount for Cash.

Identify cash flow activities.

(LO 4)

E2-15 The statement of cash flows classifies each transaction as an operating activity, an investing activity, or a financing activity. Operating activities are the types of activities the company performs to generate profits. Investing activities include the purchase of long-lived assets such as equipment or the purchase of investment securities. Financing activities are borrowing money, issuing shares of stock, and paying dividends.

Presented below are the following transactions.

1. Issued stock for $20,000 cash.
2. Issued note payable for $12,000 cash.
3. Purchased office equipment for $11,000 cash.
4. Received $15,000 cash for services performed.
5. Paid $1,000 cash for rent.
6. Paid $600 cash dividend to stockholders.
7. Paid $5,700 cash for salaries.

Instructions

Classify each of these transactions as operating, investing, or financing activities.

EXERCISES: SET B AND CHALLENGE EXERCISES

Visit the book's companion website, at **www.wiley.com/college/weygandt**, and choose the Student Companion site to access Exercises: Set B and Challenge Exercises.

PROBLEMS: SET A

Journalize a series of transactions.

(LO 1, 2)

P2-1A Grandview Park was started on April 1 by R. S. Francis and associates. The following selected events and transactions occurred during April.

Apr.	1	Stockholders invested $50,000 cash in the business in exchange for common stock.
	4	Purchased land costing $34,000 for cash.
	8	Incurred advertising expense of $1,800 on account.
	11	Paid salaries to employees $1,500.
	12	Hired park manager at a salary of $3,500 per month, effective May 1.
	13	Paid $2,400 cash for a one-year insurance policy.
	17	Declared and paid a $1,400 cash dividend.
	20	Received $5,700 in cash for admission fees.
	25	Sold 100 coupon books for $30 each. Each book contains 10 coupons that entitle the holder to one admission to the park.
	30	Received $8,900 in cash admission fees.
	30	Paid $840 on balance owed for advertising incurred on April 8.

Grandview uses the following accounts: Cash, Prepaid Insurance, Land, Accounts Payable, Unearned Service Revenue, Common Stock, Dividends, Service Revenue, Advertising Expense, and Salaries and Wages Expense.

Instructions
Journalize the April transactions.

P2-2A Julia Dumars is a licensed CPA. During the first month of operations of her business, Julia Dumars, Inc., the following events and transactions occurred.

Journalize transactions, post, and prepare a trial balance.

(LO 1, 2, 3, 4)

May	1	Stockholders invested $20,000 cash in exchange for common stock.
	2	Hired a secretary-receptionist at a salary of $2,000 per month.
	3	Purchased $1,500 of supplies on account from Vincent Supply Company.
	7	Paid office rent of $900 cash for the month.
	11	Completed a tax assignment and billed client $2,800 for services performed.
	12	Received $3,500 advance on a management consulting engagement.
	17	Received cash of $1,200 for services performed for Orville Co.
	31	Paid secretary-receptionist $2,000 salary for the month.
	31	Paid 40% of balance due Vincent Supply Company.

Julia uses the following chart of accounts: No. 101 Cash, No. 112 Accounts Receivable, No. 126 Supplies, No. 201 Accounts Payable, No. 209 Unearned Service Revenue, No. 311 Common Stock, No. 400 Service Revenue, No. 726 Salaries and Wages Expense, and No. 729 Rent Expense.

Instructions
(a) Journalize the transactions.
(b) Post to the ledger accounts.
(c) Prepare a trial balance on May 31, 2017.

(c) Trial balance totals $28,400

P2-3A Tom Zopf owns and manages a computer repair service, which had the following trial balance on December 31, 2016 (the end of its fiscal year).

Journalize and post transactions and prepare a trial balance.

(LO 1, 2, 3, 4)

TABLETTE REPAIR SERVICE, INC.
Trial Balance
December 31, 2016

	Debit	Credit
Cash	$ 8,000	
Accounts Receivable	15,000	
Supplies	11,000	
Prepaid Rent	3,000	
Equipment	21,000	
Accounts Payable		$17,000
Common Stock		30,000
Retained Earnings		11,000
	$58,000	$58,000

Summarized transactions for January 2017 were as follows.

1. Advertising costs, paid in cash, $1,000.
2. Additional supplies acquired on account $3,600.
3. Miscellaneous expenses, paid in cash, $1,700.
4. Cash collected from customers in payment of accounts receivable $13,000.
5. Cash paid to creditors for accounts payable due $14,400.
6. Repair services performed during January: for cash $5,000; on account $9,000.
7. Wages for January, paid in cash, $3,000.
8. Dividends during January were $1,600.

Instructions
(a) Open T-accounts for each of the accounts listed in the trial balance, and enter the opening balances for 2017.
(b) Prepare journal entries to record each of the January transactions. (Omit explanations.)
(c) Post the journal entries to the accounts in the ledger. (Add accounts as needed.)
(d) Prepare a trial balance as of January 31, 2017.

(d) Trial balance totals $61,200

Prepare a correct trial balance.

(LO 4)

P2-4A The trial balance of Dominic Company shown below does not balance.

DOMINIC COMPANY
Trial Balance
May 31, 2017

	Debit	Credit
Cash	$ 3,850	
Accounts Receivable		$ 2,750
Prepaid Insurance	700	
Equipment	12,000	
Accounts Payable		4,500
Unearned Service Revenue	560	
Common Stock		11,700
Service Revenue	8,690	
Salaries and Wages Expense	4,200	
Advertising Expense		1,100
Utilities Expense	800	
	$30,800	$20,050

Your review of the ledger reveals that each account has a normal balance. You also discover the following errors.

1. The totals of the debit sides of Prepaid Insurance, Accounts Payable, and Utilities Expense were each understated $100.
2. Transposition errors were made in Accounts Receivable and Service Revenue. Based on postings made, the correct balances were $2,570 and $8,960, respectively.
3. A debit posting to Salaries and Wages Expense of $200 was omitted.
4. A $1,000 cash dividend was debited to Common Stock for $1,000 and credited to Cash for $1,000.
5. A $520 purchase of supplies on account was debited to Equipment for $520 and credited to Cash for $520.
6. A cash payment of $450 for advertising was debited to Advertising Expense for $45 and credited to Cash for $45.
7. A collection from a customer for $420 was debited to Cash for $420 and credited to Accounts Payable for $420.

Instructions

Trial balance totals $26,720

Prepare a correct trial balance. Note that the chart of accounts includes the following: Dividends and Supplies. (*Hint:* It helps to prepare the correct journal entry for the transaction described and compare it to the mistake made.)

Journalize transactions, post, and prepare a trial balance.

(LO 1, 2, 3, 4)

P2-5A The Palace Theater opened on April 1. All facilities were completed on March 31. At this time, the ledger showed No. 101 Cash $6,000, No. 140 Land $12,000, No. 145 Buildings (concession stand, projection room, ticket booth, and screen) $8,000, No. 157 Equipment $6,000, No. 201 Accounts Payable $2,000, No. 275 Mortgage Payable $10,000, and No. 311 Common Stock $20,000. During April, the following events and transactions occurred.

Apr.	2	Paid film rental of $800 on first movie.
	3	Ordered two additional films at $950 each.
	9	Received $1,800 cash from admissions.
	10	Made $2,000 payment on mortgage and $1,000 for accounts payable due.
	11	Palace Theater contracted with Dever Company to operate the concession stand. Dever is to pay 18% of gross concession receipts (payable monthly) for the rental of the concession stand.
	12	Paid advertising expenses $320.
	20	Received one of the films ordered on April 3 and was billed $950. The film will be shown in April.
	25	Received $5,200 cash from admissions.
	29	Paid salaries $1,600.
	30	Received statement from Dever showing gross concession receipts of $1,000 and the balance due to The Palace Theater of $180 ($1,000 × 18%) for April. Dever paid one-half of the balance due and will remit the remainder on May 5.
	30	Prepaid $1,000 rental on special film to be run in May.

In addition to the accounts identified above, the chart of accounts shows No. 112 Accounts Receivable, No. 136 Prepaid Rent, No. 400 Service Revenue, No. 429 Rent Revenue, No. 610 Advertising Expense, No. 726 Salaries and Wages Expense, and No. 729 Rent Expense.

Instructions
(a) Enter the beginning balances in the ledger as of April 1. Insert a check mark (✓) in the reference column of the ledger for the beginning balance.
(b) Journalize the April transactions.
(c) Post the April journal entries to the ledger. Assume that all entries are posted from page 1 of the journal.
(d) Prepare a trial balance on April 30, 2017.

(d) Trial balance totals $37,130

PROBLEMS: SET B AND SET C

Visit the book's companion website, at **www.wiley.com/college/weygandt**, and choose the Student Companion site to access Problems: Set B and Set C.

CONTINUING PROBLEM

COOKIE CREATIONS

(*Note:* This is a continuation of the Cookie Creations problem from Chapter 1.)

CC2 After researching the different forms of business organization. Natalie Koebel decides to operate "Cookie Creations" as a corporation. She then starts the process of getting the business running.

Go to the book's companion website, **www.wiley.com/college/weygandt**, *to see the completion of this problem.*

© leungchopan/
Shutterstock

BROADENING YOUR *PERSPECTIVE*

FINANCIAL REPORTING AND ANALYSIS

Financial Reporting Problem: Apple Inc.

BYP2-1 The financial statements of Apple Inc. are presented in Appendix A. Instructions for accessing and using the company's complete annual report, including the notes to the financial statements, are also provided in Appendix A.

Apple's financial statements contain the following selected accounts, stated in millions of dollars.

Accounts Payable	Cash and Cash Equivalents
Accounts Receivable	Research and Development Expense
Property, Plant, and Equipment	Inventories

Instructions
(a) Answer the following questions.
   (1) What is the increase and decrease side for each account?
   (2) What is the normal balance for each account?
(b) Identify the probable other account in the transaction and the effect on that account when:
   (1) Accounts Receivable is decreased.
   (2) Accounts Payable is decreased.
   (3) Inventories are increased.
(c) Identify the other account(s) that ordinarily would be involved when:
   (1) Research and Development Expense is increased.
   (2) Property, Plant, and Equipment is increased.

Comparative Analysis Problem:
PepsiCo, Inc. vs. The Coca-Cola Company

BYP2-2 PepsiCo's financial statements are presented in Appendix B. Financial statements of The Coca-Cola Company are presented in Appendix C. Instructions for accessing and using the complete annual reports of PepsiCo and Coca-Cola, including the notes to the financial statements, are also provided in Appendices B and C, respectively.

Instructions

(a) Based on the information contained in the financial statements, determine the normal balance of the listed accounts for each company.

PepsiCo	Coca-Cola
1. Inventory	1. Accounts Receivable
2. Property, Plant, and Equipment	2. Cash and Cash Equivalents
3. Accounts Payable	3. Cost of Goods Sold (expense)
4. Interest Expense	4. Sales (revenue)

(b) Identify the other account ordinarily involved when:
  (1) Accounts Receivable is increased.
  (2) Salaries and Wages Payable is decreased.
  (3) Property, Plant, and Equipment is increased.
  (4) Interest Expense is increased.

Comparative Analysis Problem:
Amazon.com, Inc. vs. Wal-Mart Stores, Inc.

BYP2-3 Amazon.com, Inc.'s financial statements are presented in Appendix D. Financial statements of Wal-Mart Stores, Inc. are presented in Appendix E. Instructions for accessing and using the complete annual reports of Amazon and Wal-Mart, including the notes to the financial statements, are also provided in Appendices D and E, respectively.

Instructions

(a) Based on the information contained in the financial statements, determine the normal balance of the listed accounts for each company.

Amazon	Wal-Mart
1. Interest Expense	1. Product Revenues
2. Cash and Cash Equivalents	2. Inventories
3. Accounts Payable	3. Cost of Sales

(b) Identify the other account ordinarily involved when:
  (1) Accounts Receivable is increased.
  (2) Interest Expense is increased.
  (3) Salaries and Wages Payable is decreased.
  (4) Service Revenue is increased.

Real-World Focus

BYP2-4 Much information about specific companies is available on the Internet. Such information includes basic descriptions of the company's location, activities, industry, financial health, and financial performance.

Address: **biz.yahoo.com/i**, or go to **www.wiley.com/college/weygandt**

Steps

1. Type in a company name, or use the index to find a company name.
2. Choose **Profile**. Perform instructions (a)–(c) below.
3. Click on the company's specific industry to identify competitors. Perform instructions (d)–(g) below.

Instructions

Answer the following questions.

(a) What is the company's industry?
(b) What are the company's total sales?

(c) What is the company's net income?
(d) What are the names of four of the company's competitors?
(e) Choose one of these competitors.
(f) What is this competitor's name? What are its sales? What is its net income?
(g) Which of these two companies is larger by size of sales? Which one reported higher net income?

BYP2-5 The January 27, 2011, edition of the *New York Times* contains an article by Richard Sandomir entitled "N.F.L. Finances, as Seen Through Packers' Records." The article discusses the fact that the Green Bay Packers are the only NFL team that publicly publishes its annual report.

Instructions
Read the article and answer the following questions.

(a) Why are the Green Bay Packers the only professional football team to publish and distribute an annual report?
(b) Why is the football players' labor union particularly interested in the Packers' annual report?
(c) In addition to the players' labor union, what other outside party might be interested in the annual report?
(d) Even though the Packers' revenue increased in recent years, the company's operating profit fell significantly. How does the article explain this decline?

CRITICAL THINKING

Decision-Making Across the Organization

BYP2-6 Dyanna Craig operates Craig Riding Academy. The academy's primary sources of revenue are riding fees and lesson fees, which are paid on a cash basis. Dyanna also boards horses for owners, who are billed monthly for boarding fees. In a few cases, boarders pay in advance of expected use. For its revenue transactions, the academy maintains the following accounts: Cash, Accounts Receivable, and Service Revenue.

The academy owns 10 horses, a stable, a riding corral, riding equipment, and office equipment. These assets are accounted for in these accounts: Horses, Buildings, and Equipment.

The academy also maintains the following accounts: Supplies, Prepaid Insurance, Accounts Payable, Salaries and Wages Expense, Advertising Expense, Utilities Expense, and Maintenance and Repairs Expense.

Dyanna makes periodic withdrawals of cash dividends to stockholders. To record stockholders' equity in the business and dividends, three accounts are maintained: Common Stock, Retained Earnings, and Dividends.

During the first month of operations, an inexperienced bookkeeper was employed. Dyanna Craig asks you to review the following eight entries of the 50 entries made during the month. In each case, the explanation for the entry is correct.

May 1	Cash		18,000	
	Common Stock			18,000
	(Invested $18,000 cash in exchange for stock)			
5	Cash		250	
	Service Revenue			250
	(Received $250 cash for lessons provided)			
7	Cash		300	
	Service Revenue			300
	(Received $300 for boarding of horses beginning June 1)			
14	Equipment		80	
	Cash			800
	(Purchased desk and other office equipment for $800 cash)			
15	Salaries and Wages Expense		400	
	Cash			400
	(Issued dividend checks to stockholders)			
20	Cash		148	
	Service Revenue			184
	(Received $184 cash for riding fees)			

May 30	Maintenance and Repairs Expense		75	
	Accounts Payable			75
	(Received bill of $75 from carpenter for			
	repair services performed)			
31	Supplies		1,700	
	Cash			1,700
	(Purchased an estimated 2 months'			
	supply of feed and hay for $1,700 on account)			

Instructions

With the class divided into groups, answer the following.

(a) Identify each journal entry that is correct. For each journal entry that is incorrect, prepare the entry that should have been made by the bookkeeper.

(b) Which of the incorrect entries would prevent the trial balance from balancing?

(c) What was the correct net income for May, assuming the bookkeeper reported net income of $4,500 after posting all 50 entries?

(d) What was the correct cash balance at May 31, assuming the bookkeeper reported a balance of $12,475 after posting all 50 entries (and the only errors occurred in the items listed above)?

Communication Activity

BYP2-7 Keller's Maid Company offers home-cleaning service. Two recurring transactions for the company are billing customers for services performed and paying employee salaries. For example, on March 15, bills totaling $6,000 were sent to customers and $2,000 was paid in salaries to employees.

Instructions

Write a memo to your instructor that explains and illustrates the steps in the recording process for each of the March 15 transactions. Use the format illustrated in the textbook under the heading, "The Recording Process Illustrated" (p. 62).

Ethics Cases

BYP2-8 Meredith Ward is the assistant chief accountant at Frazier Company, a manufacturer of computer chips and cellular phones. The company presently has total sales of $20 million. It is the end of the first quarter. Meredith is hurriedly trying to prepare a trial balance so that quarterly financial statements can be prepared and released to management and the regulatory agencies. The total credits on the trial balance exceed the debits by $1,000. In order to meet the 4 p.m. deadline, Meredith decides to force the debits and credits into balance by adding the amount of the difference to the Equipment account. She chooses Equipment because it is one of the larger account balances; percentage-wise, it will be the least misstated. Meredith "plugs" the difference! She believes that the difference will not affect anyone's decisions. She wishes that she had another few days to find the error but realizes that the financial statements are already late.

Instructions

(a) Who are the stakeholders in this situation?

(b) What are the ethical issues involved in this case?

(c) What are Meredith's alternatives?

BYP2-9 If you haven't already done so, in the not-too-distant future you will prepare a résumé. In some ways, your résumé is like a company's annual report. Its purpose is to enable others to evaluate your past, in an effort to predict your future.

A résumé is your opportunity to create a positive first impression. It is important that it be impressive—but it should also be accurate. In order to increase their job prospects, some people are tempted to "inflate" their résumés by overstating the importance of some past accomplishments or positions. In fact, you might even think that "everybody does it" and that if you don't do it, you will be at a disadvantage.

David Edmondson, the president and CEO of well-known electronics retailer **Radio Shack**, overstated his accomplishments by claiming that he had earned a bachelor of science degree, when in fact he had not. Apparently, his employer had not done a background check to ensure the accuracy of his résumé. Should Radio Shack have fired him?

YES: Radio Shack is a publicly traded company. Investors, creditors, employees, and others doing business with the company will not trust it if its leader is known to have poor integrity. The "tone at the top" is vital to creating an ethical organization.

NO: Mr. Edmondson had been a Radio Shack employee for 11 years. He had served the company in a wide variety of positions, and had earned the position of CEO through exceptional performance. While the fact that he lied 11 years earlier on his résumé was unfortunate, his service since then made this past transgression irrelevant. In addition, the company was in the midst of a massive restructuring, which included closing 700 of its 7,000 stores. It could not afford additional upheaval at this time.

Instructions
Write a response indicating your position regarding this situation. Provide support for your view.

All About You

BYP2-10 Every company needs to plan in order to move forward. Its top management must consider where it wants the company to be in three to five years. Like a company, you need to think about where you want to be three to five years from now, and you need to start taking steps now in order to get there.

Instructions
Provide responses to each of the following items.

(a) Where would you like to be working in three to five years? Describe your plan for getting there by identifying between five and 10 specific steps that you need to take.
(b) In order to get the job you want, you will need a résumé. Your résumé is the equivalent of a company's annual report. It needs to provide relevant and reliable information about your past accomplishments so that employers can decide whether to "invest" in you. Do a search on the Internet to find a good résumé format. What are the basic elements of a résumé?
(c) A company's annual report provides information about a company's accomplishments. In order for investors to use the annual report, the information must be reliable; that is, users must have faith that the information is accurate and believable. How can you provide assurance that the information on your résumé is reliable?
(d) Prepare a résumé assuming that you have accomplished the five to 10 specific steps you identified in part (a). Also, provide evidence that would give assurance that the information is reliable.

Considering People, Planet, and Profit

BYP2-11 Auditors provide a type of certification of corporate financial statements. Certification is used in many other aspects of business as well. For example, it plays a critical role in the sustainability movement. The February 7, 2012, issue of the *New York Times* contained an article by S. Amanda Caudill entitled "Better Lives in Better Coffee," which discusses the role of certification in the coffee business.

Address: **http://scientistatwork.blogs.nytimes.com/2012/02/07/better-lives-in-better-coffee**

Instructions
Read the article and answer the following questions.

(a) The article mentions three different certification types that coffee growers can obtain from three different certification bodies. Using financial reporting as an example, what potential problems might the existence of multiple certification types present to coffee purchasers?
(b) According to the author, which certification is most common among coffee growers? What are the possible reasons for this?
(c) What social and environmental benefits are coffee certifications trying to achieve? Are there also potential financial benefits to the parties involved?

A Look at IFRS

LEARNING
OBJECTIVE **Compare the procedures for the accounting process under GAAP and IFRS.**

International companies use the same set of procedures and records to keep track of transaction data. Thus, the material in Chapter 2 dealing with the account, general rules of debit and credit, and steps in the recording process—the journal, ledger, and chart of accounts—is the same under both GAAP and IFRS.

Key Points

Following are the key similarities and differences between GAAP and IFRS as related to the recording process.

Similarities

- Transaction analysis is the same under IFRS and GAAP.
- Both the IASB and the FASB go beyond the basic definitions provided in the textbook for the key elements of financial statements, that is assets, liabilities, equity, revenues, and expenses. The implications of the expanded definitions are discussed in more advanced accounting courses.
- As shown in the textbook, dollar signs are typically used only in the trial balance and the financial statements. The same practice is followed under IFRS, using the currency of the country where the reporting company is headquartered.
- A trial balance under IFRS follows the same format as shown in the textbook.

Differences

- IFRS relies less on historical cost and more on fair value than do FASB standards.
- Internal controls are a system of checks and balances designed to prevent and detect fraud and errors. While most public U.S. companies have these systems in place, many non-U.S. companies have never completely documented the controls nor had an independent auditor attest to their effectiveness.

Looking to the Future

The basic recording process shown in this textbook is followed by companies around the globe. It is unlikely to change in the future. The definitional structure of assets, liabilities, equity, revenues, and expenses may change over time as the IASB and FASB evaluate their overall conceptual framework for establishing accounting standards.

IFRS Practice

IFRS Self-Test Questions

1. Which statement is **correct** regarding IFRS?
    (a) IFRS reverses the rules of debits and credits, that is, debits are on the right and credits are on the left.
    (b) IFRS uses the same process for recording transactions as GAAP.
    (c) The chart of accounts under IFRS is different because revenues follow assets.
    (d) None of the above statements are correct.

2. The expanded accounting equation under IFRS is as follows:
    (a) Assets = Liabilities + Common Stock + Retained Earnings + Revenues − Expenses + Dividends.
    (b) Assets + Liabilities = Common Stock + Retained Earnings + Revenues − Expenses − Dividends.
    (c) Assets = Liabilities + Common Stock + Retained Earnings + Revenues − Expenses − Dividends.
    (d) Assets = Liabilities + Common Stock + Retained Earnings − Revenues − Expenses − Dividends.

3. A trial balance:
   (a) is the same under IFRS and GAAP.
   (b) proves that transactions are recorded correctly.
   (c) proves that all transactions have been recorded.
   (d) will not balance if a correct journal entry is posted twice.

4. One difference between IFRS and GAAP is that:
   (a) GAAP uses accrual-accounting concepts and IFRS uses primarily the cash basis of accounting.
   (b) IFRS uses a different posting process than GAAP.
   (c) IFRS uses more fair value measurements than GAAP.
   (d) the limitations of a trial balance are different between IFRS and GAAP.

5. The general policy for using proper currency signs (dollar, yen, pound, etc.) is the same for both IFRS and this textbook. This policy is as follows:
   (a) Currency signs only appear in ledgers and journal entries.
   (b) Currency signs are only shown in the trial balance.
   (c) Currency signs are shown for all compound journal entries.
   (d) Currency signs are shown in trial balances and financial statements.

International Financial Reporting Problem: Louis Vuitton

IFRS2-1 The financial statements of **Louis Vuitton** are presented in Appendix F. Instructions for accessing and using the company's complete annual report, including the notes to its financial statements, are also provided in Appendix F.

Instructions

Describe in which statement each of the following items is reported, and the position in the statement (e.g., current asset).

(a) Other operating income and expense.
(b) Cash and cash equivalents.
(c) Trade accounts payable.
(d) Cost of net financial debt.

Answers to IFRS Self-Test Questions
1. b **2.** c **3.** a **4.** c **5.** d

3 Adjusting the Accounts

CHAPTER PREVIEW In Chapter 1, you learned a neat little formula: Net income = Revenues − Expenses. In Chapter 2, you learned some rules for recording revenue and expense transactions. Guess what? Things are not really that nice and neat. In fact, it is often difficult for companies to determine in what time period they should report some revenues and expenses. In other words, in measuring net income, timing is everything.

FEATURE STORY

Keeping Track of Groupons

Who doesn't like buying things at a discount? That's why it's not surprising that three years after it started as a company, Groupon was estimated to be worth $16 billion. This translates into an average increase in value of almost $15 million per day.

Now consider that Groupon had previously been estimated to be worth even more than that. What happened? Well, accounting regulators and investors began to question the way that Groupon had accounted for some of its transactions. But if Groupon sells only coupons ("groupons"), how hard can it be to accurately account for that? It turns out that accounting for coupons is not as easy as you might think.

First, consider what happens when Groupon makes a sale. Suppose it sells a groupon for $30 for Highrise Hamburgers. When it receives the $30 from the customer, it must turn over half of that amount ($15) to Highrise Hamburgers. So should Groupon record revenue for the full $30 or just $15? Until recently, Groupon recorded the full $30. But, in response to an SEC ruling on the issue, Groupon now records revenue of $15 instead.

A second issue is a matter of timing. When should Groupon record this $15 revenue? Should it record the revenue when it sells the groupon, or must it wait until the customer uses the groupon at Highrise Hamburgers? You can find the answer to

this question in the notes to Groupon's financial statements. It recognizes the revenue once "the number of customers who purchase the daily deal exceeds the predetermined threshold, the Groupon has been electronically delivered to the purchaser and a listing of Groupons sold has been made available to the merchant."

The accounting becomes even more complicated when you consider the company's loyalty programs. Groupon offers free or discounted groupons to its subscribers for doing things such as referring new customers or participating in promotions. These groupons are to be used for future purchases, yet the company must record the expense at the time the customer receives the groupon. The cost of these programs is huge for Groupon, so the timing of this expense can definitely affect its reported income.

The final kicker is that Groupon, like all other companies, must rely on many estimates in its financial reporting. For example, Groupon reports that "estimates are utilized for, but not limited to, stock-based compensation, income taxes, valuation of acquired goodwill and intangible assets, customer refunds, contingent liabilities and the depreciable lives of fixed assets." It concludes by saying that "actual results could differ materially from those estimates." So, next time you use a coupon, think about what that means for the company's accountants!

Rudy Archuleta/Redux Pictures

CHAPTER OUTLINE

Learning Objectives

1 Explain the accrual basis of accounting and the reasons for adjusting entries.

- Fiscal and calendar years
- Accrual- vs. cash-basis accounting
- Recognizing revenues and expenses
- Need for adjusting entries
- Types of adjusting entries

DO IT! 1 Timing Concepts

---

2 Prepare adjusting entries for deferrals.

- Prepaid expenses
- Unearned revenues

DO IT! 2 Adjusting Entries for Deferrals

---

3 Prepare adjusting entries for accruals.

- Accrued revenues
- Accrued expenses
- Summary of basic relationships

DO IT! 3 Adjusting Entries for Accruals

---

4 Describe the nature and purpose of an adjusted trial balance.

- Preparing the adjusted trial balance
- Preparing financial statements

DO IT! 4 Trial Balance

Go to the **REVIEW AND PRACTICE** section at the end of the chapter for a review of key concepts and practice applications with solutions.

Visit **WileyPLUS with ORION** for additional tutorials and practice opportunities.

LEARNING OBJECTIVE 1

Explain the accrual basis of accounting and the reasons for adjusting entries.

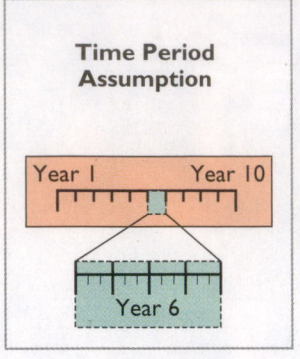

Time Period Assumption

Alternative Terminology
The time period assumption is also called the *periodicity assumption*.

If we could wait to prepare financial statements until a company ended its operations, no adjustments would be needed. At that point, we could easily determine its final balance sheet and the amount of lifetime income it earned.

However, most companies need immediate feedback about how well they are doing. For example, management usually wants monthly financial statements. The Internal Revenue Service requires all businesses to file annual tax returns. Therefore, **accountants divide the economic life of a business into artificial time periods**. This convenient assumption is referred to as the **time period assumption**.

Many business transactions affect more than one of these arbitrary time periods. For example, the airplanes purchased by **Southwest Airlines** five years ago are still in use today. We must determine the relevance of each business transaction to specific accounting periods. (How much of the cost of an airplane contributed to operations this year?)

Fiscal and Calendar Years

Both small and large companies prepare financial statements periodically in order to assess their financial condition and results of operations. **Accounting time periods are generally a month, a quarter, or a year.** Monthly and quarterly time periods are called **interim periods**. Most large companies must prepare both quarterly and annual financial statements.

An accounting time period that is one year in length is a **fiscal year**. A fiscal year usually begins with the first day of a month and ends 12 months later on the last day of a month. Many businesses use the **calendar year** (January 1 to December 31) as their accounting period. Some do not. Companies whose fiscal year differs from the calendar year include **Delta Air Lines**, June 30, and **The Walt Disney Company**, September 30. Sometimes a company's year-end will vary from year to year. For example, **PepsiCo**'s fiscal year ends on the Friday closest to December 31, which was December 29 in 2012 and December 28 in 2013.

Accrual- versus Cash-Basis Accounting

What you will learn in this chapter is **accrual-basis accounting**. Under the accrual basis, companies record transactions that change a company's financial statements **in the periods in which the events occur**. For example, using the accrual basis to determine net income means companies recognize revenues when they perform services (rather than when they receive cash). It also means recognizing expenses when incurred (rather than when paid).

An alternative to the accrual basis is the cash basis. Under **cash-basis accounting**, companies record revenue when they receive cash. They record an expense when they pay out cash. The cash basis seems appealing due to its simplicity, but it often produces misleading financial statements. It fails to record revenue for a company that has performed services but for which the company has not received the cash. As a result, the cash basis does not match expenses with revenues.

Accrual-basis accounting is therefore in accordance with generally accepted accounting principles (GAAP). Individuals and some small companies, however, do use cash-basis accounting. The cash basis is justified for small businesses because they often have few receivables and payables. Medium and large companies use accrual-basis accounting.

Recognizing Revenues and Expenses

It can be difficult to determine when to report revenues and expenses. The revenue recognition principle and the expense recognition principle help in this task.

REVENUE RECOGNITION PRINCIPLE

When a company agrees to perform a service or sell a product to a customer, it has a **performance obligation**. When the company meets this performance obligation, it recognizes revenue. The **revenue recognition principle** therefore requires that companies recognize revenue in the accounting period in which the performance obligation is satisfied. To illustrate, assume that Dave's Dry Cleaning cleans clothing on June 30 but customers do not claim and pay for their clothes until the first week of July. Dave's should record revenue in June when it performed the service (satisfied the performance obligation) rather than in July when it received the cash. At June 30, Dave's would report a receivable on its balance sheet and revenue in its income statement for the service performed.

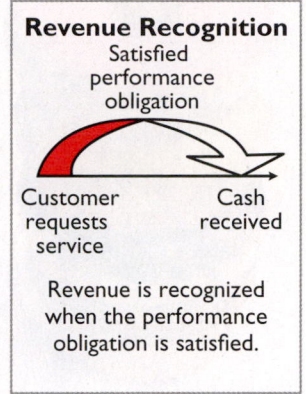

Revenue Recognition
Satisfied performance obligation

Customer requests service — Cash received

Revenue is recognized when the performance obligation is satisfied.

EXPENSE RECOGNITION PRINCIPLE

Accountants follow a simple rule in recognizing expenses: "Let the expenses follow the revenues." Thus, expense recognition is tied to revenue recognition. In the dry cleaning example, this means that Dave's should report the salary expense incurred in performing the June 30 cleaning service in the same period in which it recognizes the service revenue. The critical issue in expense recognition is when the expense makes its contribution to revenue. This may or may not be the same period in which the expense is paid. If Dave's does not pay the salary incurred on June 30 until July, it would report salaries payable on its June 30 balance sheet.

This practice of expense recognition is referred to as the **expense recognition principle** (often referred to as the **matching principle**). It dictates that efforts (expenses) be matched with results (revenues). Illustration 3-1 summarizes the revenue and expense recognition principles.

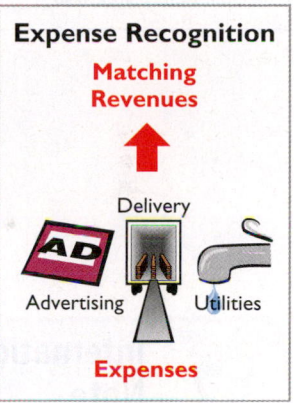

Expense Recognition

Matching Revenues

Delivery

Advertising   Utilities

Expenses

Illustration 3-1
GAAP relationships in revenue and expense recognition

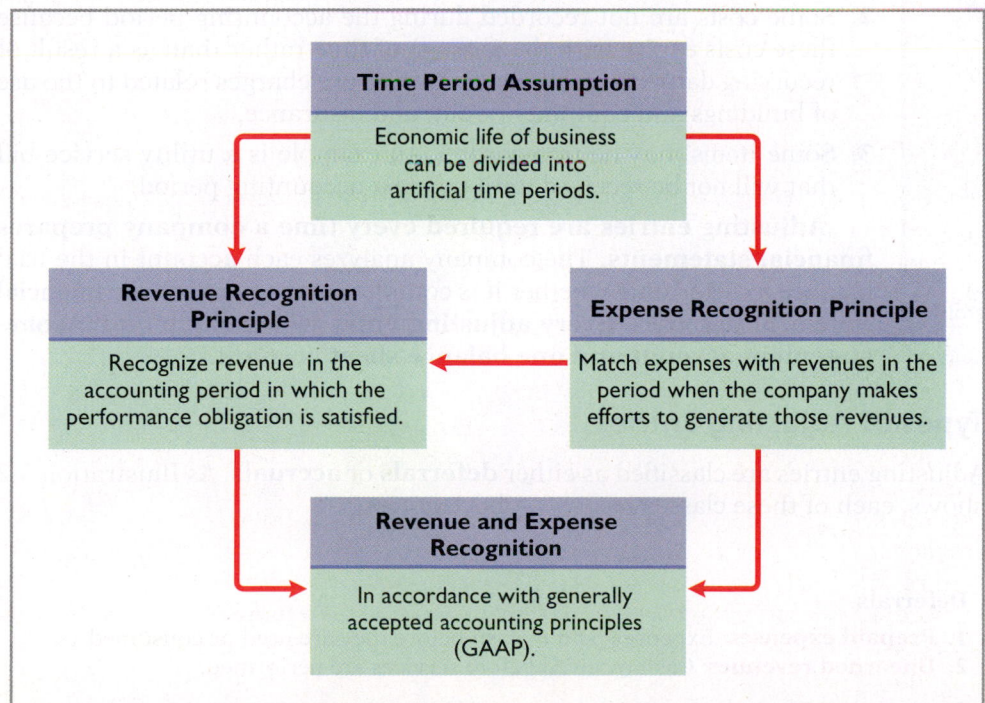

Time Period Assumption

Economic life of business can be divided into artificial time periods.

Revenue Recognition Principle

Recognize revenue in the accounting period in which the performance obligation is satisfied.

Expense Recognition Principle

Match expenses with revenues in the period when the company makes efforts to generate those revenues.

Revenue and Expense Recognition

In accordance with generally accepted accounting principles (GAAP).

© Dean Turner/iStockphoto

Cooking the Books?

Allegations of abuse of the revenue recognition principle have become all too common in recent years. For example, it was alleged that Krispy Kreme sometimes doubled the number of doughnuts shipped to wholesale customers at the end of a quarter to boost quarterly results. The customers shipped the unsold doughnuts back after the beginning of the next quarter for a refund. Conversely, Computer Associates International was accused of backdating sales—that is, reporting a sale in one period that did not actually occur until the next period in order to achieve the earlier period's sales targets.

What motivates sales executives and finance and accounting executives to participate in activities that result in inaccurate reporting of revenues? (Go to **WileyPLUS** for this answer and additional questions.)

The Need for Adjusting Entries

In order for revenues to be recorded in the period in which services are performed and for expenses to be recognized in the period in which they are incurred, companies make adjusting entries. **Adjusting entries ensure that the revenue recognition and expense recognition principles are followed.**

Adjusting entries are necessary because the **trial balance**—the first pulling together of the transaction data—may not contain up-to-date and complete data. This is true for several reasons:

1. Some events are not recorded daily because it is not efficient to do so. Examples are the use of supplies and the earning of wages by employees.

2. Some costs are not recorded during the accounting period because these costs expire with the passage of time rather than as a result of recurring daily transactions. Examples are charges related to the use of buildings and equipment, rent, and insurance.

3. Some items may be unrecorded. An example is a utility service bill that will not be received until the next accounting period.

Adjusting entries are required every time a company prepares financial statements. The company analyzes each account in the trial balance to determine whether it is complete and up-to-date for financial statement purposes. **Every adjusting entry will include one income statement account and one balance sheet account.**

International Note

Internal controls are a system of checks and balances designed to detect and prevent fraud and errors. The Sarbanes-Oxley Act requires U.S. companies to enhance their systems of internal control. However, many foreign companies do not have to meet strict internal control requirements. Some U.S. companies believe that this gives foreign firms an unfair advantage because developing and maintaining internal controls can be very expensive.

Types of Adjusting Entries

Adjusting entries are classified as either **deferrals** or **accruals**. As Illustration 3-2 shows, each of these classes has two subcategories.

Illustration 3-2
Categories of adjusting entries

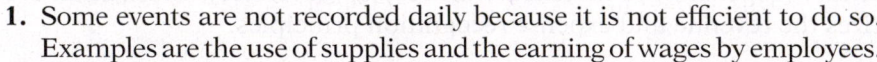

Deferrals:

1. **Prepaid expenses**: Expenses paid in cash before they are used or consumed.
2. **Unearned revenues**: Cash received before services are performed.

Accruals:

1. **Accrued revenues**: Revenues for services performed but not yet received in cash or recorded.
2. **Accrued expenses**: Expenses incurred but not yet paid in cash or recorded.

Subsequent sections give examples of each type of adjustment. Each example is based on the October 31 trial balance of Pioneer Advertising Inc. from Chapter 2, reproduced in Illustration 3-3.

Illustration 3-3
Trial balance

PIONEER ADVERTISING INC.
Trial Balance
October 31, 2017

	Debit	Credit
Cash	$ 15,200	
Supplies	2,500	
Prepaid Insurance	600	
Equipment	5,000	
Notes Payable		$ 5,000
Accounts Payable		2,500
Unearned Service Revenue		1,200
Common Stock		10,000
Retained Earnings		–0–
Dividends	500	
Service Revenue		10,000
Salaries and Wages Expense	4,000	
Rent Expense	900	
	$28,700	$28,700

We assume that Pioneer uses an accounting period of one month. Thus, monthly adjusting entries are made. The entries are dated October 31.

DO IT! 1 — Timing Concepts

Several timing concepts are discussed on pages 96–97. A list of concepts is provided in the left column below, with a description of the concept in the right column below. There are more descriptions provided than concepts. Match the description of the concept to the concept.

1. ____ Accrual-basis accounting.
2. ____ Calendar year.
3. ____ Time period assumption.
4. ____ Expense recognition principle.

(a) Monthly and quarterly time periods.

(b) Efforts (expenses) should be matched with results (revenues).

(c) Accountants divide the economic life of a business into artificial time periods.

(d) Companies record revenues when they receive cash and record expenses when they pay out cash.

(e) An accounting time period that starts on January 1 and ends on December 31.

(f) Companies record transactions in the period in which the events occur.

Action Plan

✔ Review the glossary terms identified on pages 123–124.

✔ Study carefully the revenue recognition principle, the expense recognition principle, and the time period assumption.

Solution

> **1.** f **2.** e **3.** c **4.** b

Related exercise material: **BE3-1, BE3-2, E3-1, E3-2, E3-3, and DO IT! 3-1**.

Prepare adjusting entries for deferrals.

To defer means to postpone or delay. **Deferrals** are expenses or revenues that are recognized at a date later than the point when cash was originally exchanged. The two types of deferrals are prepaid expenses and unearned revenues.

Prepaid Expenses

When companies record payments of expenses that will benefit more than one accounting period, they record an asset called **prepaid expenses** or **prepayments**. When expenses are prepaid, an asset account is increased (debited) to show the service or benefit that the company will receive in the future. Examples of common prepayments are insurance, supplies, advertising, and rent. In addition, companies make prepayments when they purchase buildings and equipment.

Prepaid expenses are costs that expire either with the passage of time (e.g., rent and insurance) **or through use** (e.g., supplies). The expiration of these costs does not require daily entries, which would be impractical and unnecessary. Accordingly, companies postpone the recognition of such cost expirations until they prepare financial statements. At each statement date, they make adjusting entries to record the expenses applicable to the current accounting period and to show the remaining amounts in the asset accounts.

Prior to adjustment, assets are overstated and expenses are understated. Therefore, as shown in Illustration 3-4, **an adjusting entry for prepaid expenses results in an increase (a debit) to an expense account and a decrease (a credit) to an asset account**.

Illustration 3-4
Adjusting entries for prepaid expenses

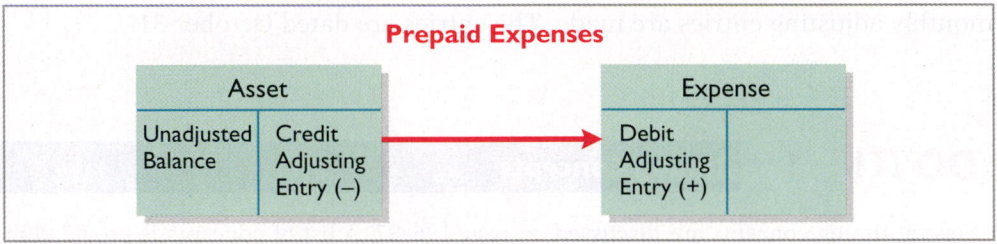

Let's look in more detail at some specific types of prepaid expenses, beginning with supplies.

SUPPLIES

Supplies

Oct. 5

Supplies purchased; record asset

Oct. 31
Supplies used; record supplies expense

The purchase of supplies, such as paper and envelopes, results in an increase (a debit) to an asset account. During the accounting period, the company uses supplies. Rather than record supplies expense as the supplies are used, companies recognize supplies expense at the **end** of the accounting period. At the end of the accounting period, the company counts the remaining supplies. As shown in Illustration 3-5, the difference between the unadjusted balance in the Supplies (asset) account and the actual cost of supplies on hand represents the supplies used (an expense) for that period.

Recall from Chapter 2 that Pioneer Advertising Inc. purchased supplies costing $2,500 on October 5. Pioneer recorded the purchase by increasing (debiting) the asset Supplies. This account shows a balance of $2,500 in the October 31 trial balance. An inventory count at the close of business on October 31 reveals that $1,000 of supplies are still on hand. Thus, the cost of supplies used is $1,500 ($2,500 − $1,000). This use of supplies decreases an asset, Supplies. It also decreases stockholders' equity by increasing an expense account, Supplies Expense. This is shown in Illustration 3-5.

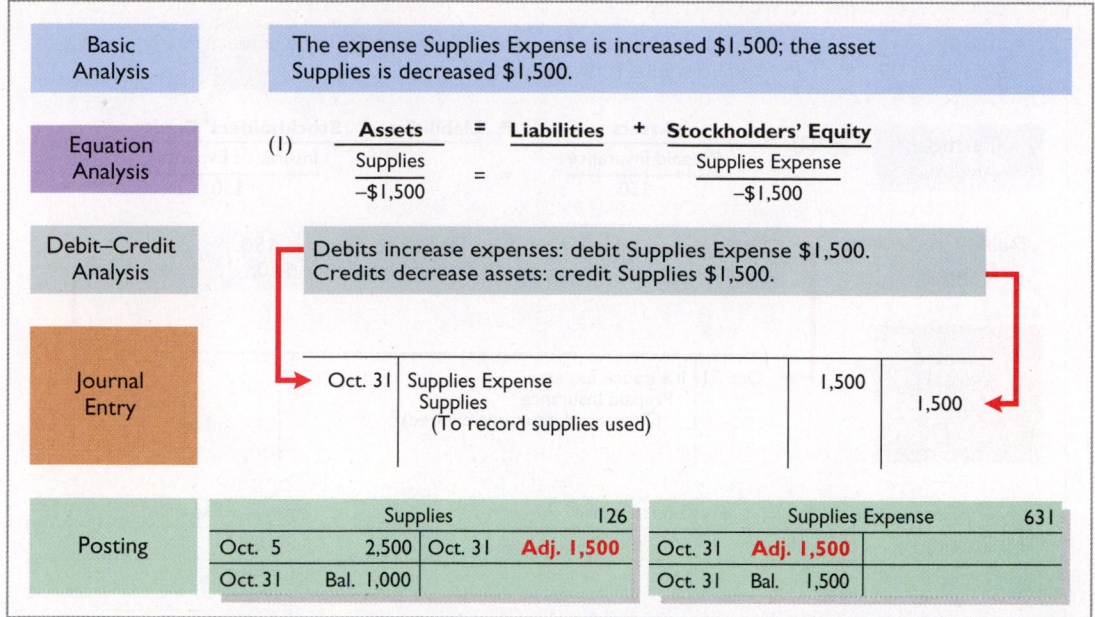

| Basic Analysis | The expense Supplies Expense is increased $1,500; the asset Supplies is decreased $1,500. |

Equation Analysis	(1)	**Assets**	**=**	**Liabilities**	**+**	**Stockholders' Equity**
		Supplies				Supplies Expense
		−$1,500	=			−$1,500

| Debit–Credit Analysis | Debits increase expenses: debit Supplies Expense $1,500. Credits decrease assets: credit Supplies $1,500. |

Journal Entry	Oct. 31	Supplies Expense		1,500	
		Supplies			1,500
		(To record supplies used)			

Posting

Supplies			126
Oct. 5	2,500	Oct. 31 Adj. 1,500	
Oct. 31	Bal. 1,000		

Supplies Expense			631
Oct. 31	Adj. 1,500		
Oct. 31	Bal. 1,500		

Illustration 3-5
Adjustment for supplies

After adjustment, the asset account Supplies shows a balance of $1,000, which is equal to the cost of supplies on hand at the statement date. In addition, Supplies Expense shows a balance of $1,500, which equals the cost of supplies used in October. **If Pioneer does not make the adjusting entry, October expenses are understated and net income is overstated by $1,500. Moreover, both assets and stockholders' equity will be overstated by $1,500 on the October 31 balance sheet.**

INSURANCE

Companies purchase insurance to protect themselves from losses due to fire, theft, and unforeseen events. Insurance must be paid in advance, often for more than one year. The cost of insurance (premiums) paid in advance is recorded as an increase (debit) in the asset account Prepaid Insurance. At the financial statement date, companies increase (debit) Insurance Expense and decrease (credit) Prepaid Insurance for the cost of insurance that has expired during the period.

On October 4, Pioneer Advertising paid $600 for a one-year fire insurance policy. Coverage began on October 1. Pioneer recorded the payment by increasing (debiting) Prepaid Insurance. This account shows a balance of $600 in the October 31 trial balance. Insurance of $50 ($600 ÷ 12) expires each month. The expiration of prepaid insurance decreases an asset, Prepaid Insurance. It also decreases stockholders' equity by increasing an expense account, Insurance Expense.

As shown in Illustration 3-6 (page 102), the asset Prepaid Insurance shows a balance of $550, which represents the unexpired cost for the remaining 11 months of coverage. At the same time, the balance in Insurance Expense equals the insurance cost that expired in October. **If Pioneer does not make this adjustment, October expenses are understated by $50 and net income is overstated by $50. Moreover, both assets and stockholders' equity will be overstated by $50 on the October 31 balance sheet.**

DEPRECIATION

A company typically owns a variety of assets that have long lives, such as buildings, equipment, and motor vehicles. The period of service is referred to as the **useful life** of the asset. Because a building is expected to be of service for many years, it is recorded as an asset, rather than an expense, on the date it is acquired.

Insurance

Oct. 4

Insurance purchased; record asset

Insurance Policy			
Oct	Nov	Dec	Jan
$50	$50	$50	$50
Feb	March	April	May
$50	$50	$50	$50
June	July	Aug	Sept
$50	$50	$50	$50
Insurance = $600/year			

Oct. 31
Insurance expired; record insurance expense

Illustration 3-6
Adjustment for insurance

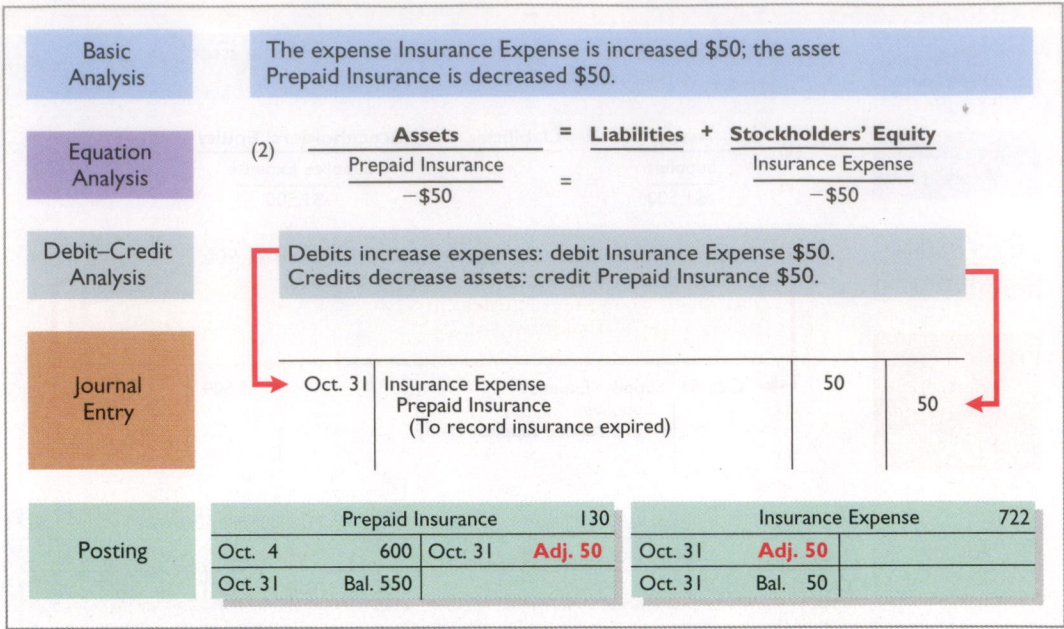

| | Basic Analysis | The expense Insurance Expense is increased $50; the asset Prepaid Insurance is decreased $50. |

| | Equation Analysis | (2) | **Assets** = **Liabilities** + **Stockholders' Equity** |

Prepaid Insurance / −$50 = / Insurance Expense / −$50

| | Debit–Credit Analysis | Debits increase expenses: debit Insurance Expense $50. Credits decrease assets: credit Prepaid Insurance $50. |

	Journal Entry	Oct. 31	Insurance Expense	50
			Prepaid Insurance		50
			(To record insurance expired)	

Posting

Prepaid Insurance			130
Oct. 4	600	Oct. 31 **Adj. 50**	
Oct. 31	Bal. 550		

Insurance Expense		722
Oct. 31 **Adj. 50**		
Oct. 31 Bal. 50		

Depreciation

Oct. 2

Equipment purchased; record asset

Equipment			
Oct $40	Nov $40	Dec $40	Jan $40
Feb $40	March $40	April $40	May $40
June $40	July $40	Aug $40	Sept $40
Depreciation = $480/year			

Oct. 31
Depreciation recognized; record depreciation expense

As explained in Chapter 1, companies record such assets **at cost**, as required by the historical cost principle. To follow the expense recognition principle, companies allocate a portion of this cost as an expense during each period of the asset's useful life. **Depreciation** is the process of allocating the cost of an asset to expense over its useful life.

NEED FOR ADJUSTMENT The acquisition of long-lived assets is essentially a long-term prepayment for the use of an asset. An adjusting entry for depreciation is needed to recognize the cost that has been used (an expense) during the period and to report the unused cost (an asset) at the end of the period. One very important point to understand: **Depreciation is an allocation concept, not a valuation concept.** That is, depreciation **allocates an asset's cost to the periods in which it is used. Depreciation does not attempt to report the actual change in the value of the asset.**

For Pioneer Advertising, assume that depreciation on the equipment is $480 a year, or $40 per month. As shown in Illustration 3-7, rather than decrease (credit) the asset account directly, Pioneer instead credits Accumulated Depreciation—Equipment. Accumulated Depreciation is called a **contra asset account**. Such an account is offset against an asset account on the balance sheet. Thus, the Accumulated Depreciation—Equipment account offsets the asset account Equipment. **This account keeps track of the total amount of depreciation expense taken over the life of the asset.** To keep the accounting equation in balance, Pioneer decreases stockholders' equity by increasing an expense account, Depreciation Expense.

The balance in the Accumulated Depreciation—Equipment account will increase $40 each month, and the balance in Equipment remains $5,000.

Helpful Hint
All contra accounts have increases, decreases, and normal balances opposite to the account to which they relate.

STATEMENT PRESENTATION As indicated, Accumulated Depreciation—Equipment is a contra asset account. It is offset against Equipment on the balance sheet. The normal balance of a contra asset account is a credit. A theoretical alternative to using a contra asset account would be to decrease (credit) the asset account by the amount of depreciation each period. But using the contra account is preferable for a simple reason: It discloses **both** the original cost of the equipment **and** the total cost that has been expensed to date. Thus, in the balance sheet,

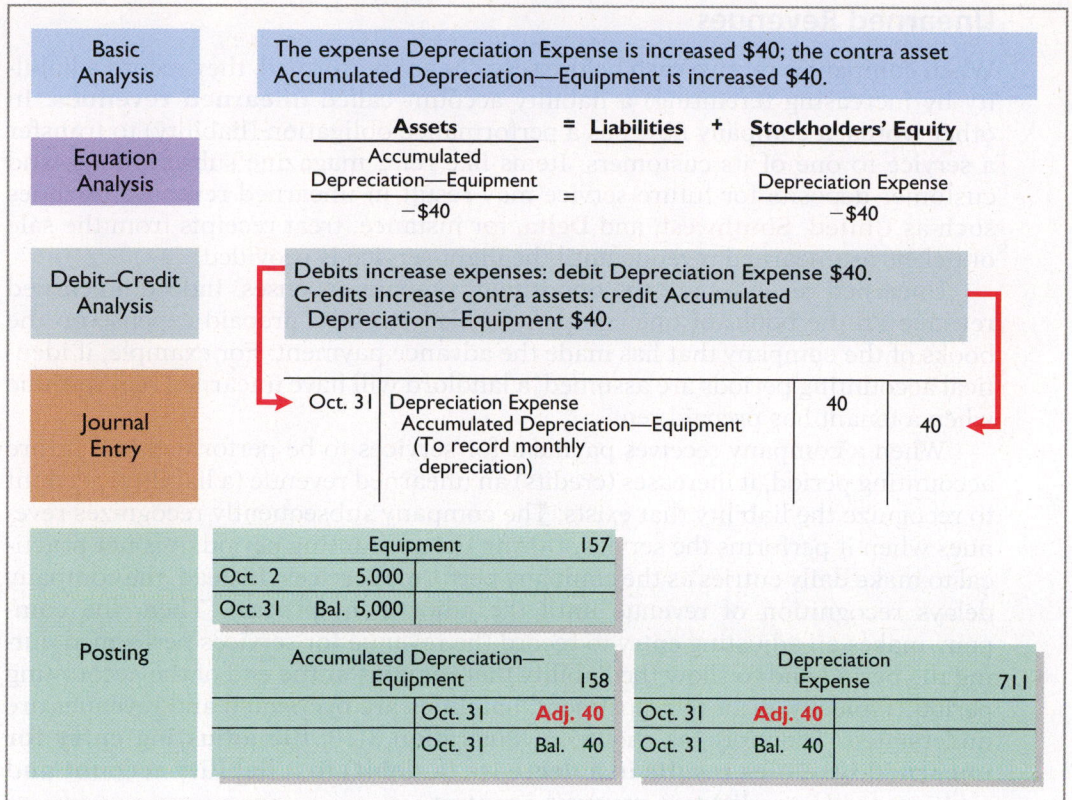

Illustration 3-7
Adjustment for depreciation

Pioneer deducts Accumulated Depreciation—Equipment from the related asset account, as shown in Illustration 3-8.

Equipment	$ 5,000
Less: Accumulated depreciation—equipment	40
	$4,960

Illustration 3-8
Balance sheet presentation of accumulated depreciation

Book value is the difference between the cost of any depreciable asset and its related accumulated depreciation. In Illustration 3-8, the book value of the equipment at the balance sheet date is $4,960. The book value and the fair value of the asset are generally two different values. As noted earlier, **the purpose of depreciation is not valuation but a means of cost allocation**.

Depreciation expense identifies the portion of an asset's cost that expired during the period (in this case, in October). The accounting equation shows that **without this adjusting entry, total assets, total stockholders' equity, and net income are overstated by $40 and depreciation expense is understated by $40**.

Illustration 3-9 summarizes the accounting for prepaid expenses.

Alternative Terminology
Book value is also referred to as *carrying value*.

ACCOUNTING FOR PREPAID EXPENSES

Examples	Reason for Adjustment	Accounts Before Adjustment	Adjusting Entry
Insurance, supplies, advertising, rent, depreciation	Prepaid expenses recorded in asset accounts have been used.	Assets overstated. Expenses understated.	Dr. Expenses Cr. Assets or Contra Assets

Illustration 3-9
Accounting for prepaid expenses

Unearned Revenues

When companies receive cash before services are performed, they record a liability by increasing (crediting) a liability account called **unearned revenues**. In other words, a company now has a performance obligation (liability) to transfer a service to one of its customers. Items like rent, magazine subscriptions, and customer deposits for future service may result in unearned revenues. Airlines such as United, Southwest, and Delta, for instance, treat receipts from the sale of tickets as unearned revenue until the flight service is provided.

Unearned revenues are the opposite of prepaid expenses. Indeed, unearned revenue on the books of one company is likely to be a prepaid expense on the books of the company that has made the advance payment. For example, if identical accounting periods are assumed, a landlord will have unearned rent revenue when a tenant has prepaid rent.

When a company receives payment for services to be performed in a future accounting period, it increases (credits) an unearned revenue (a liability) account to recognize the liability that exists. The company subsequently recognizes revenues when it performs the service. During the accounting period, it is not practical to make daily entries as the company performs services. Instead, the company delays recognition of revenue until the adjustment process. Then, the company makes an adjusting entry to record the revenue for services performed during the period and to show the liability that remains at the end of the accounting period. Typically, prior to adjustment, liabilities are overstated and revenues are understated. Therefore, as shown in Illustration 3-10, **the adjusting entry for unearned revenues results in a decrease (a debit) to a liability account and an increase (a credit) to a revenue account.**

Illustration 3-10
Adjusting entries for unearned revenues

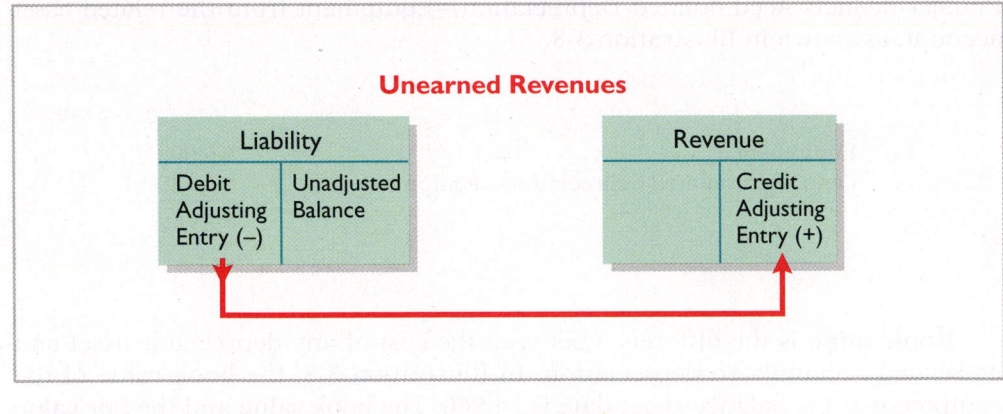

Pioneer Advertising received $1,200 on October 2 from R. Knox for advertising services expected to be completed by December 31. Pioneer credited the payment to Unearned Service Revenue. This liability account shows a balance of $1,200 in the October 31 trial balance. From an evaluation of the services Pioneer performed for Knox during October, the company determines that it should recognize $400 of revenue in October. The liability (Unearned Service Revenue) is therefore decreased, and stockholders' equity (Service Revenue) is increased.

As shown in Illustration 3-11, the liability Unearned Service Revenue now shows a balance of $800. That amount represents the remaining advertising services expected to be performed in the future. At the same time, Service Revenue shows total revenue recognized in October of $10,400. **Without this adjustment, revenues and net income are understated by $400 in the income statement. Moreover, liabilities will be overstated and stockholders' equity will be understated by $400 on the October 31 balance sheet.**

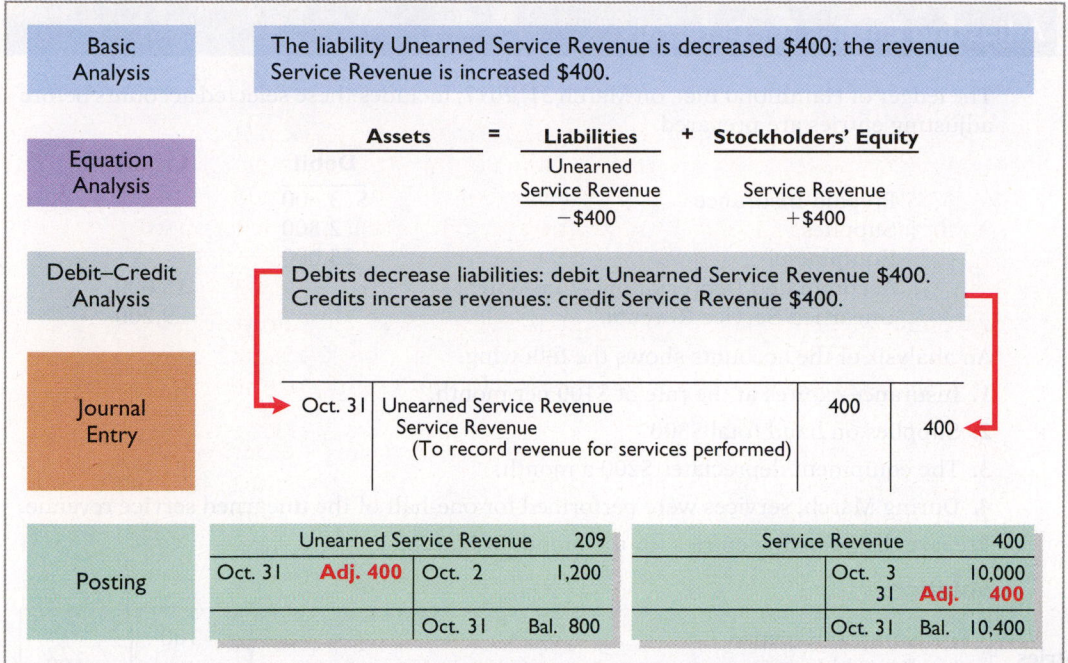

| Basic Analysis | The liability Unearned Service Revenue is decreased $400; the revenue Service Revenue is increased $400. |

Equation Analysis

$$\underline{\text{Assets}} = \underline{\text{Liabilities}} + \underline{\text{Stockholders' Equity}}$$

	Unearned Service Revenue	Service Revenue
	−$400	+$400

Debit–Credit Analysis

Debits decrease liabilities: debit Unearned Service Revenue $400.
Credits increase revenues: credit Service Revenue $400.

Journal Entry

Oct. 31	Unearned Service Revenue	400	
	Service Revenue		400
	(To record revenue for services performed)		

Posting

Unearned Service Revenue			209
Oct. 31	**Adj. 400**	Oct. 2	1,200
		Oct. 31	Bal. 800

Service Revenue			400
		Oct. 3	10,000
		31	**Adj. 400**
		Oct. 31	Bal. 10,400

Illustration 3-11
Service revenue accounts after adjustment

Illustration 3-12 summarizes the accounting for unearned revenues.

Illustration 3-12
Accounting for unearned revenues

ACCOUNTING FOR UNEARNED REVENUES

Examples	Reason for Adjustment	Accounts Before Adjustment	Adjusting Entry
Rent, magazine subscriptions, customer deposits for future service	Unearned revenues recorded in liability accounts are now recognized as revenue for services performed.	Liabilities overstated. Revenues understated.	Dr. Liabilities Cr. Revenues

Accounting Across the Organization   Best Buy

Turning Gift Cards into Revenue

Those of you who are marketing majors (and even most of you who are not) know that gift cards are among the hottest marketing tools in merchandising today. Customers purchase gift cards and give them to someone for later use. In a recent year, gift-card sales topped $95 billion.

Although these programs are popular with marketing executives, they create accounting questions. Should revenue be recorded at the time the gift card is sold, or when it is exercised? How should expired gift cards be accounted for? In a recent balance sheet, Best Buy reported unearned revenue related to gift cards of $428 million.

Source: Robert Berner, "Gift Cards: No Gift to Investors," *BusinessWeek* (March 14, 2005), p. 86.

Suppose that Robert Jones purchases a $100 gift card at Best Buy on December 24, 2016, and gives it to his wife, Mary Jones, on December 25, 2016. On January 3, 2017, Mary uses the card to purchase $100 worth of CDs. When do you think Best Buy should recognize revenue and why? (Go to **WileyPLUS** for this answer and additional questions.)

© Skip ODonnell/iStockphoto

DO IT! 2   Adjusting Entries for Deferrals

The ledger of Hammond Inc., on March 31, 2017, includes these selected accounts before adjusting entries are prepared.

	Debit	Credit
Prepaid Insurance	$ 3,600	
Supplies	2,800	
Equipment	25,000	
Accumulated Depreciation—Equipment		$5,000
Unearned Service Revenue		9,200

An analysis of the accounts shows the following.

1. Insurance expires at the rate of $100 per month.
2. Supplies on hand total $800.
3. The equipment depreciates $200 a month.
4. During March, services were performed for one-half of the unearned service revenue.

Prepare the adjusting entries for the month of March.

Action Plan

✔ Make adjusting entries at the end of the period for revenues recognized and expenses incurred in the period.

✔ Don't forget to make adjusting entries for deferrals. Failure to adjust for deferrals leads to overstatement of the asset or liability and understatement of the related expense or revenue.

Solution

1.	Insurance Expense	100	
	Prepaid Insurance		100
	(To record insurance expired)		
2.	Supplies Expense	2,000	
	Supplies		2,000
	(To record supplies used)		
3.	Depreciation Expense	200	
	Accumulated Depreciation—Equipment		200
	(To record monthly depreciation)		
4.	Unearned Service Revenue	4,600	
	Service Revenue		4,600
	(To record revenue for services performed)		

Related exercise material: **BE3-2, BE3-3, BE3-4, BE3-5, BE3-6,** and **DO IT! 3-2.**

LEARNING OBJECTIVE 3   Prepare adjusting entries for accruals.

The second category of adjusting entries is **accruals**. Prior to an accrual adjustment, the revenue account (and the related asset account) or the expense account (and the related liability account) are understated. Thus, the adjusting entry for accruals will **increase both a balance sheet and an income statement account**.

Accrued Revenues

Revenues for services performed but not yet recorded at the statement date are **accrued revenues**. Accrued revenues may accumulate (accrue) with the passing of time, as in the case of interest revenue. These are unrecorded because the earning of interest does not involve daily transactions. Companies do not record interest revenue on a daily basis because it is often impractical to do so. Accrued revenues also may result from services that have been performed but not yet billed nor collected, as in the case of commissions and fees. These may be unrecorded because only a portion of the total service has been performed and the clients will not be billed until the service has been completed.

An adjusting entry records the receivable that exists at the balance sheet date and the revenue for the services performed during the period. Prior to adjustment, both assets and revenues are understated. As shown in Illustration 3-13, **an adjusting entry for accrued revenues results in an increase (a debit) to an asset account and an increase (a credit) to a revenue account.**

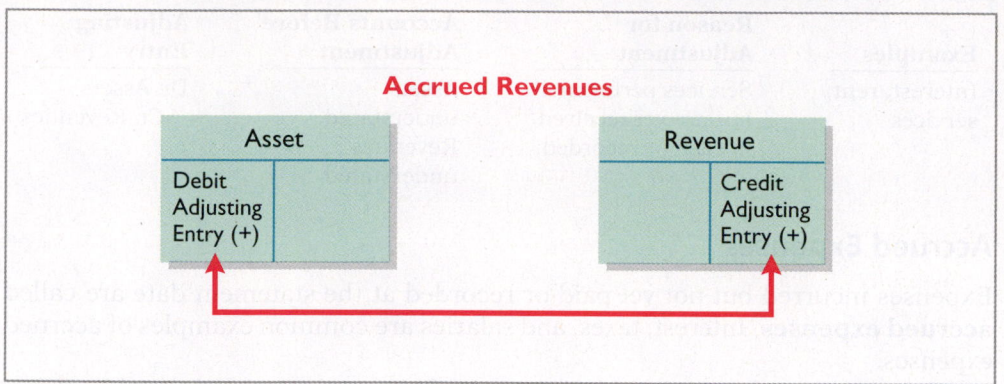

Illustration 3-13
Adjusting entries for accrued revenues

In October, Pioneer Advertising Inc. performed services worth $200 that were not billed to clients on or before October 31. Because these services are not billed, they are not recorded. The accrual of unrecorded service revenue increases an asset account, Accounts Receivable. It also increases stockholders' equity by increasing a revenue account, Service Revenue, as shown in Illustration 3-14.

Accrued Revenues

My fee is $200

Revenue and receivable are recorded for unbilled services

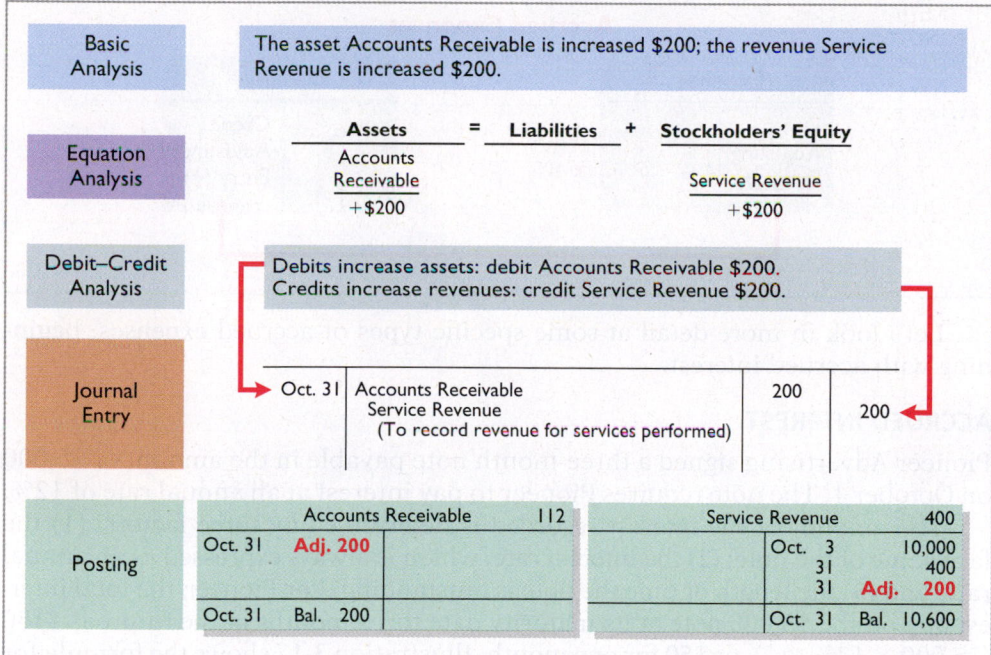

Illustration 3-14
Adjustment for accrued revenue

The asset Accounts Receivable shows that clients owe Pioneer $200 at the balance sheet date. The balance of $10,600 in Service Revenue represents the total revenue for services performed by Pioneer during the month ($10,000 + $400 + $200). **Without the adjusting entry, assets and stockholders' equity on the balance sheet and revenues and net income on the income statement are understated.**

On November 10, Pioneer receives cash of $200 for the services performed in October and makes the following entry.

Equation analyses summarize the effects of transactions on the three elements of the accounting equation, as well as the effect on cash flows.

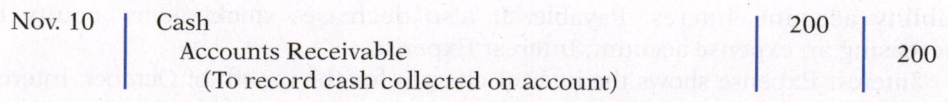

A	=	L	+	SE
+200				
−200				

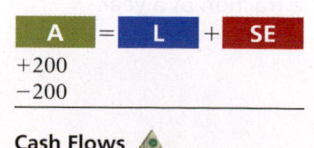

Cash Flows
+200

The company records the collection of the receivables by a debit (increase) to Cash and a credit (decrease) to Accounts Receivable.

Illustration 3-15 summarizes the accounting for accrued revenues.

ACCOUNTING FOR ACCRUED REVENUES			
Examples	**Reason for Adjustment**	**Accounts Before Adjustment**	**Adjusting Entry**
Interest, rent, services	Services performed but not yet received in cash or recorded.	Assets understated. Revenues understated.	Dr. Assets Cr. Revenues

Accrued Expenses

Expenses incurred but not yet paid or recorded at the statement date are called **accrued expenses**. Interest, taxes, and salaries are common examples of accrued expenses.

Companies make adjustments for accrued expenses to record the obligations that exist at the balance sheet date and to recognize the expenses that apply to the current accounting period. Prior to adjustment, both liabilities and expenses are understated. Therefore, as Illustration 3-16 shows, **an adjusting entry for accrued expenses results in an increase (a debit) to an expense account and an increase (a credit) to a liability account.**

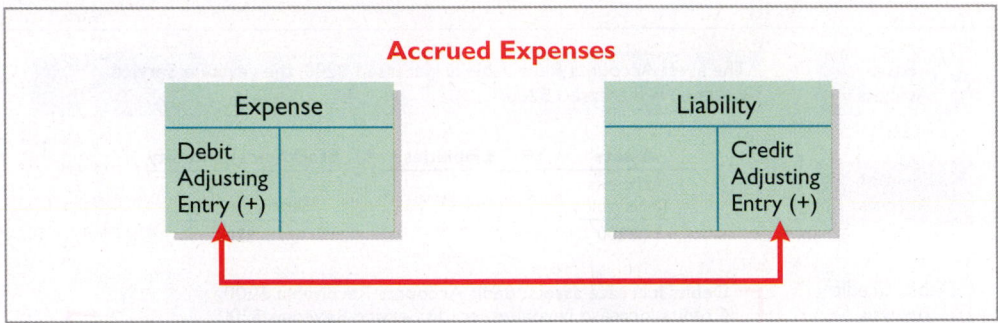

Let's look in more detail at some specific types of accrued expenses, beginning with accrued interest.

ACCRUED INTEREST

Pioneer Advertising signed a three-month note payable in the amount of $5,000 on October 1. The note requires Pioneer to pay interest at an annual rate of 12%.

The amount of the interest recorded is determined by three factors: (1) the face value of the note; (2) the interest rate, which is always expressed as an annual rate; and (3) the length of time the note is outstanding. For Pioneer, the total interest due on the $5,000 note at its maturity date three months in the future is $150 ($5,000 × 12% × $\frac{3}{12}$), or $50 for one month. Illustration 3-17 shows the formula for computing interest and its application to Pioneer for the month of October.

Face Value of Note	×	Annual Interest Rate	×	Time in Terms of One Year	×	Interest
$5,000	×	12%	×	$\frac{1}{12}$	=	$50

As Illustration 3-18 shows, the accrual of interest at October 31 increases a liability account, Interest Payable. It also decreases stockholders' equity by increasing an expense account, Interest Expense.

Interest Expense shows the interest charges for the month of October. Interest Payable shows the amount of interest the company owes at the statement date. Pioneer will not pay the interest until the note comes due at the end of three months. Companies use the Interest Payable account, instead of crediting Notes Payable, to

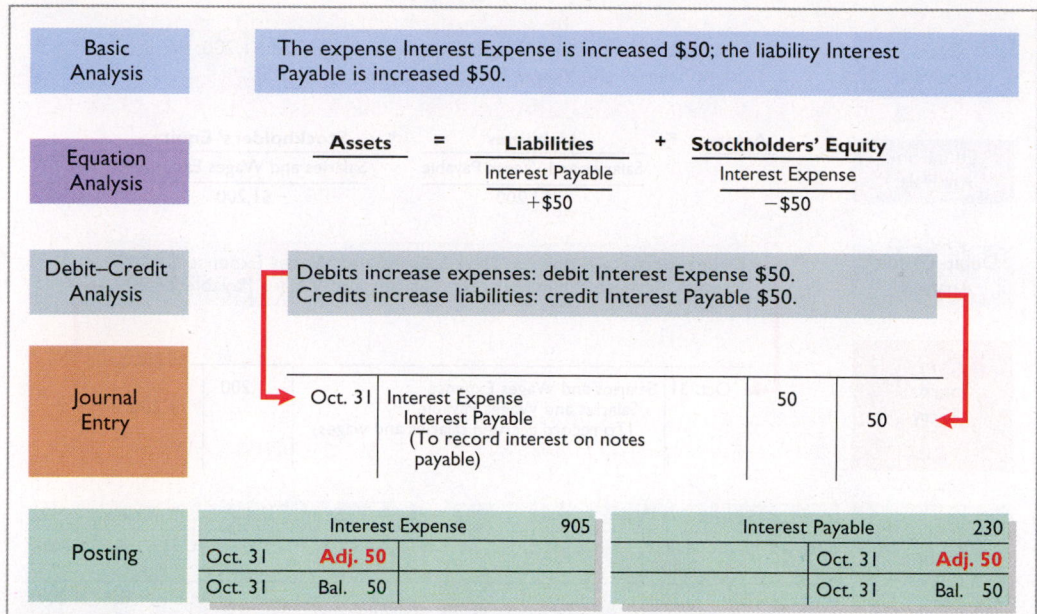

Illustration 3-18
Adjustment for accrued interest

disclose the two different types of obligations—interest and principal—in the accounts and statements. **Without this adjusting entry, liabilities and interest expense are understated, and net income and stockholders' equity are overstated.**

ACCRUED SALARIES AND WAGES

Companies pay for some types of expenses, such as employee salaries and wages, after the services have been performed. Pioneer Advertising paid salaries and wages on October 26 for its employees' first two weeks of work. The next payment of salaries will not occur until November 9. As Illustration 3-19 shows, three working days remain in October (October 29–31).

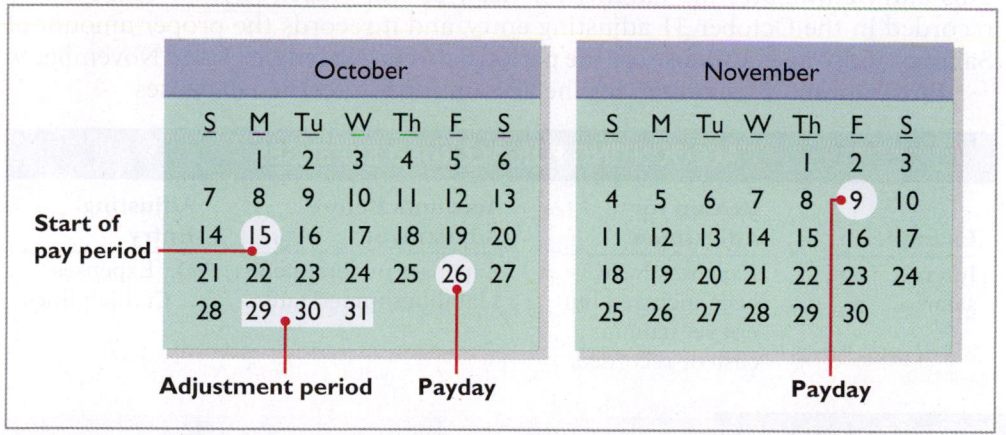

Illustration 3-19
Calendar showing Pioneer's pay periods

At October 31, the salaries and wages for these three days represent an accrued expense and a related liability to Pioneer. The employees receive total salaries and wages of $2,000 for a five-day work week, or $400 per day. Thus, accrued salaries and wages at October 31 are $1,200 ($400 × 3). This accrual increases a liability, Salaries and Wages Payable. It also decreases stockholders' equity by increasing an expense account, Salaries and Wages Expense, as shown in Illustration 3-20 (page 110).

After this adjustment, the balance in Salaries and Wages Expense of $5,200 (13 days × $400) is the actual salary and wages expense for October. The balance in Salaries and Wages Payable of $1,200 is the amount of the liability for salaries and wages Pioneer owes as of October 31. **Without the $1,200 adjustment for salaries and wages, Pioneer's expenses are understated $1,200 and its liabilities are understated $1,200.**

Illustration 3-20
Adjusting for accrued salaries and wages

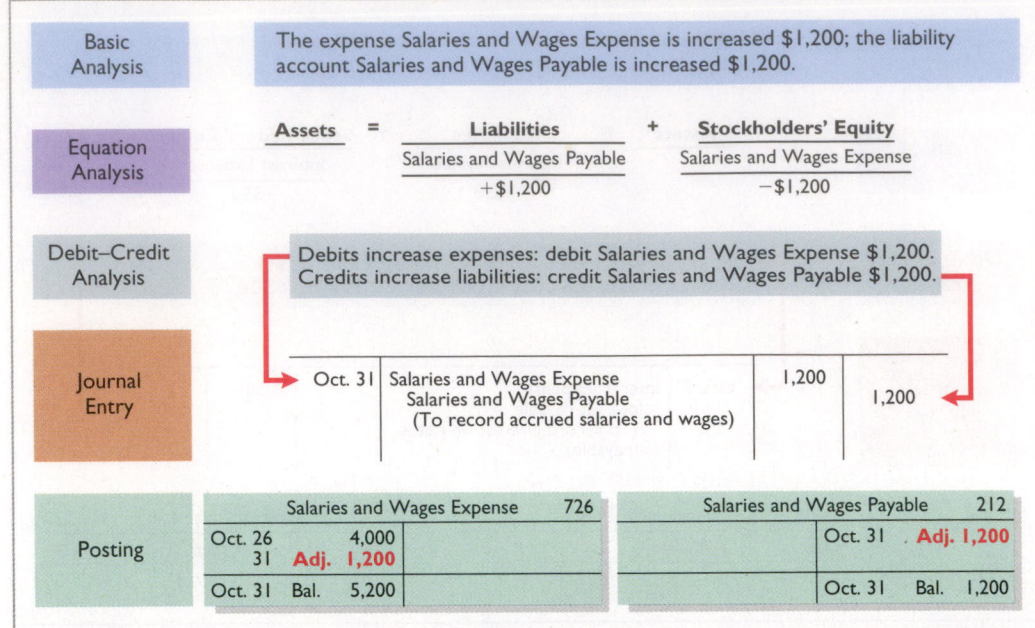

Basic Analysis	The expense Salaries and Wages Expense is increased $1,200; the liability account Salaries and Wages Payable is increased $1,200.

Equation Analysis

Assets	=	Liabilities	+	Stockholders' Equity
		Salaries and Wages Payable		Salaries and Wages Expense
		+$1,200		−$1,200

Debit–Credit Analysis

Debits increase expenses: debit Salaries and Wages Expense $1,200.
Credits increase liabilities: credit Salaries and Wages Payable $1,200.

Journal Entry

Oct. 31	Salaries and Wages Expense	1,200	
	Salaries and Wages Payable		1,200
	(To record accrued salaries and wages)		

Posting

Salaries and Wages Expense		726
Oct. 26	4,000	
31	**Adj. 1,200**	
Oct. 31 Bal.	5,200	

Salaries and Wages Payable		212
	Oct. 31	**Adj. 1,200**
	Oct. 31 Bal.	1,200

Pioneer pays salaries and wages every two weeks. Consequently, the next payday is November 9, when the company will again pay total salaries and wages of $4,000. The payment consists of $1,200 of salaries and wages payable at October 31 plus $2,800 of salaries and wages expense for November (7 working days, as shown in the November calendar × $400). Therefore, Pioneer makes the following entry on November 9.

A	=	L	+	SE
		−1,200		
				−2,800
−4,000				

Cash Flows
−4,000

Nov. 9	Salaries and Wages Payable	1,200	
	Salaries and Wages Expense	2,800	
	Cash		4,000
	(To record November 9 payroll)		

This entry eliminates the liability for Salaries and Wages Payable that Pioneer recorded in the October 31 adjusting entry, and it records the proper amount of Salaries and Wages Expense for the period between November 1 and November 9.

Illustration 3-21 summarizes the accounting for accrued expenses.

Illustration 3-21
Accounting for accrued expenses

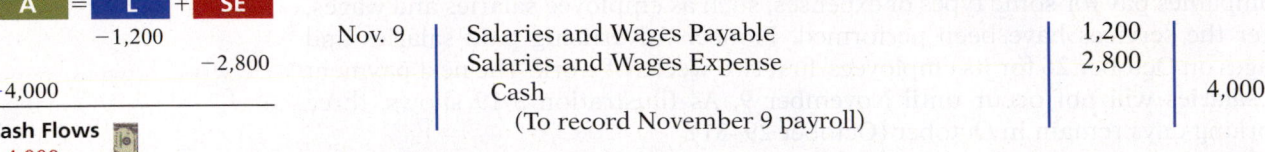

ACCOUNTING FOR ACCRUED EXPENSES			
Examples	**Reason for Adjustment**	**Accounts Before Adjustment**	**Adjusting Entry**
Interest, rent, salaries	Expenses have been incurred but not yet paid in cash or recorded.	Expenses understated. Liabilities understated.	Dr. Expenses Cr. Liabilities

People, Planet, and Profit Insight

© Nathan Gleave/iStockphoto

Got Junk?

Do you have an old computer or two that you no longer use? How about an old TV that needs replacing? Many people do. Approximately 163,000 computers and televisions become obsolete each day. Yet, in a recent year, only 11% of computers were recycled. It is estimated that 75% of all computers ever sold are sitting in storage somewhere, waiting to be disposed of. Each of these old TVs and computers is loaded with lead, cadmium, mercury, and other toxic chemicals. If you have one of these electronic gadgets, you have a responsibility, and a probable cost, for disposing of it. Companies have the same problem, but their discarded materials may include lead paint, asbestos, and other toxic chemicals.

What accounting issue might this cause for companies?
(Go to **WileyPLUS** for this answer and additional questions.)

Summary of Basic Relationships

Illustration 3-22 summarizes the four basic types of adjusting entries. Take some time to study and analyze the adjusting entries. Be sure to note that **each adjusting entry affects one balance sheet account and one income statement account**.

Type of Adjustment	Accounts Before Adjustment	Adjusting Entry

Prepaid expenses	Assets overstated
	Expenses understated
		Dr. Expenses
		  Cr. Assets or
		  Contra Assets

Unearned revenues	Liabilities overstated Revenues understated	Dr. Liabilities Cr. Revenues
Accrued revenues	Assets understated Revenues understated	Dr. Assets Cr. Revenues
Accrued expenses	Expenses understated Liabilities understated	Dr. Expenses Cr. Liabilities

Illustration 3-22
Summary of adjusting entries

Illustrations 3-23 (below) and 3-24 (on page 112) show the journalizing and posting of adjusting entries for Pioneer Advertising Inc. on October 31. The ledger identifies all adjustments by the reference J2 because they have been recorded on page 2 of the general journal. The company may insert a center caption "Adjusting Entries" between the last transaction entry and the first adjusting entry in the journal. When you review the general ledger in Illustration 3-24, note that the entries highlighted in color are the adjustments.

GENERAL JOURNAL				J2
Date	**Account Titles and Explanation**	**Ref.**	**Debit**	**Credit**
2017	*Adjusting Entries*			
Oct. 31	Supplies Expense	631	1,500	
	Supplies	126		1,500
	(To record supplies used)			
31	Insurance Expense	722	50	
	Prepaid Insurance	130		50
	(To record insurance expired)			
31	Depreciation Expense	711	40	
	Accumulated Depreciation—Equipment	158		40
	(To record monthly depreciation)			
31	Unearned Service Revenue	209	400	
	Service Revenue	400		400
	(To record revenue for services performed)			
31	Accounts Receivable	112	200	
	Service Revenue	400		200
	(To record revenue for services performed)			
31	Interest Expense	905	50	
	Interest Payable	230		50
	(To record interest on notes payable)			
31	Salaries and Wages Expense	726	1,200	
	Salaries and Wages Payable	212		1,200
	(To record accrued salaries and wages)			

Illustration 3-23
General journal showing adjusting entries

Helpful Hint
(1) Adjusting entries should not involve debits or credits to Cash.
(2) Evaluate whether the adjustment makes sense. For example, an adjustment to recognize supplies used should increase Supplies Expense.
(3) Double-check all computations.
(4) Each adjusting entry affects one balance sheet account and one income statement account.

Illustration 3-24
General ledger after adjustment

GENERAL LEDGER

Cash — No. 101

Date	Explanation	Ref.	Debit	Credit	Balance
2017					
Oct. 1		J1	10,000		10,000
2		J1	1,200		11,200
3		J1		900	10,300
4		J1		600	9,700
20		J1		500	9,200
26		J1		4,000	5,200
31		J1	10,000		15,200

Accounts Receivable — No. 112

Date	Explanation	Ref.	Debit	Credit	Balance
2017					
Oct. 31	Adj. entry	J2	200		200

Supplies — No. 126

Date	Explanation	Ref.	Debit	Credit	Balance
2017					
Oct. 5		J1	2,500		2,500
31	Adj. entry	J2		1,500	1,000

Prepaid Insurance — No. 130

Date	Explanation	Ref.	Debit	Credit	Balance
2017					
Oct. 4		J1	600		600
31	Adj. entry	J2		50	550

Equipment — No. 157

Date	Explanation	Ref.	Debit	Credit	Balance
2017					
Oct. 1		J1	5,000		5,000

Accumulated Depreciation—Equipment — No. 158

Date	Explanation	Ref.	Debit	Credit	Balance
2017					
Oct. 31	Adj. entry	J2		40	40

Notes Payable — No. 200

Date	Explanation	Ref.	Debit	Credit	Balance
2017					
Oct. 1		J1		5,000	5,000

Accounts Payable — No. 201

Date	Explanation	Ref.	Debit	Credit	Balance
2017					
Oct. 5		J1		2,500	2,500

Unearned Service Revenue — No. 209

Date	Explanation	Ref.	Debit	Credit	Balance
2017					
Oct. 2		J1		1,200	1,200
31	Adj. entry	J2	400		800

Salaries and Wages Payable — No. 212

Date	Explanation	Ref.	Debit	Credit	Balance
2017					
Oct. 31	Adj. entry	J2		1,200	1,200

Interest Payable — No. 230

Date	Explanation	Ref.	Debit	Credit	Balance
2017					
Oct. 31	Adj. entry	J2		50	50

Common Stock — No. 311

Date	Explanation	Ref.	Debit	Credit	Balance
2017					
Oct. 1		J1		10,000	10,000

Retained Earnings — No. 320

Date	Explanation	Ref.	Debit	Credit	Balance
2017					

Dividends — No. 332

Date	Explanation	Ref.	Debit	Credit	Balance
2017					
Oct. 20		J1	500		500

Service Revenue — No. 400

Date	Explanation	Ref.	Debit	Credit	Balance
2017					
Oct. 31		J1		10,000	10,000
31	Adj. entry	J2		400	10,400
31	Adj. entry	J2		200	10,600

Supplies Expense — No. 631

Date	Explanation	Ref.	Debit	Credit	Balance
2017					
Oct. 31	Adj. entry	J2	1,500		1,500

Depreciation Expense — No. 711

Date	Explanation	Ref.	Debit	Credit	Balance
2017					
Oct. 31	Adj. entry	J2	40		40

Insurance Expense — No. 722

Date	Explanation	Ref.	Debit	Credit	Balance
2017					
Oct. 31	Adj. entry	J2	50		50

Salaries and Wages Expense — No. 726

Date	Explanation	Ref.	Debit	Credit	Balance
2017					
Oct. 26		J1	4,000		4,000
31	Adj. entry	J2	1,200		5,200

Rent Expense — No. 729

Date	Explanation	Ref.	Debit	Credit	Balance
2017					
Oct. 3		J1	900		900

Interest Expense — No. 905

Date	Explanation	Ref.	Debit	Credit	Balance
2017					
Oct. 31	Adj. entry	J2	50		50

DO IT! 3   Adjusting Entries for Accruals

Micro Computer Services Inc. began operations on August 1, 2017. At the end of August 2017, management prepares monthly financial statements. The following information relates to August.

1. At August 31, the company owed its employees $800 in salaries and wages that will be paid on September 1.
2. On August 1, the company borrowed $30,000 from a local bank on a 15-year mortgage. The annual interest rate is 10%.
3. Revenue for services performed but unrecorded for August totaled $1,100.

Prepare the adjusting entries needed at August 31, 2017.

Solution

1. Salaries and Wages Expense	800	
Salaries and Wages Payable		800
(To record accrued salaries)		
2. Interest Expense	250	
Interest Payable		250
(To record accrued interest:		
$30{,}000 \times 10\% \times \frac{1}{12} = \$250$)		
3. Accounts Receivable	1,100	
Service Revenue		1,100
(To record revenue for services performed)		

Related exercise material: **BE3-7, E3-5, E3-6, E3-7, E3-8, E3-9, and**  **3-3.**

Action Plan

✔ Make adjusting entries at the end of the period to recognize revenues for services performed and for expenses incurred.

✔ Don't forget to make adjusting entries for accruals. Adjusting entries for accruals will increase both a balance sheet and an income statement account.

LEARNING OBJECTIVE 4   Describe the nature and purpose of an adjusted trial balance.

After a company has journalized and posted all adjusting entries, it prepares another trial balance from the ledger accounts. This trial balance is called an **adjusted trial balance**. It shows the balances of all accounts, including those adjusted, at the end of the accounting period. The purpose of an adjusted trial balance is to **prove the equality** of the total debit balances and the total credit balances in the ledger after all adjustments. Because the accounts contain all data needed for financial statements, the adjusted trial balance is the **primary basis for the preparation of financial statements**.

Preparing the Adjusted Trial Balance

Illustration 3-25 (page 114) presents the adjusted trial balance for Pioneer Advertising Inc. prepared from the ledger accounts in Illustration 3-24. The amounts affected by the adjusting entries are highlighted in color. Compare these amounts to those in the unadjusted trial balance in Illustration 3-3 (page 99). In this comparison, you will see that there are more accounts in the adjusted trial balance as a result of the adjusting entries made at the end of the month.

Illustration 3-25
Adjusted trial balance

PIONEER ADVERTISING INC. Adjusted Trial Balance October 31, 2017		
	Debit	**Credit**
Cash	$ 15,200	
Accounts Receivable	200	
Supplies	1,000	
Prepaid Insurance	550	
Equipment	5,000	
Accumulated Depreciation—Equipment		$ 40
Notes Payable		5,000
Accounts Payable		2,500
Interest Payable		50
Unearned Service Revenue		800
Salaries and Wages Payable		1,200
Common Stock		10,000
Retained Earnings		–0–
Dividends	500	
Service Revenue		10,600
Salaries and Wages Expense	5,200	
Supplies Expense	1,500	
Rent Expense	900	
Insurance Expense	50	
Interest Expense	50	
Depreciation Expense	40	
	$30,190	**$30,190**

Preparing Financial Statements

Companies can prepare financial statements directly from the adjusted trial balance. Illustrations 3-26 (page 115) and 3-27 (page 116) present the interrelationships of data in the adjusted trial balance and the financial statements.

As Illustration 3-26 shows, companies prepare the income statement from the revenue and expense accounts. Next, they use the Retained Earnings and Dividends accounts and the net income (or net loss) from the income statement to prepare the retained earnings statement.

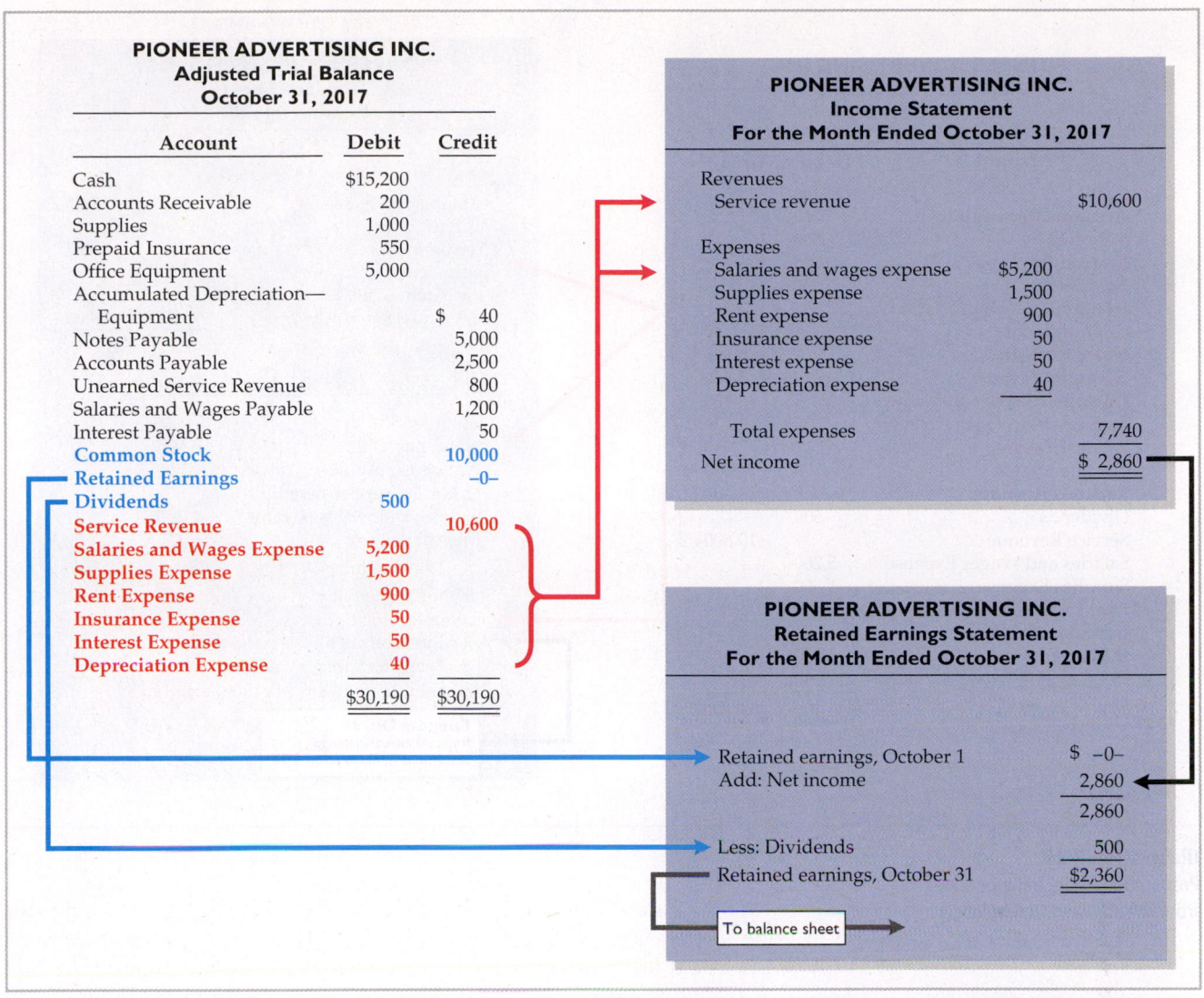

Illustration 3-26
Preparation of the income statement and retained earnings statement from the adjusted trial balance

As Illustration 3-27 (page 116) shows, companies then prepare the balance sheet from the asset and liability accounts and the ending retained earnings balance as reported in the retained earnings statement.

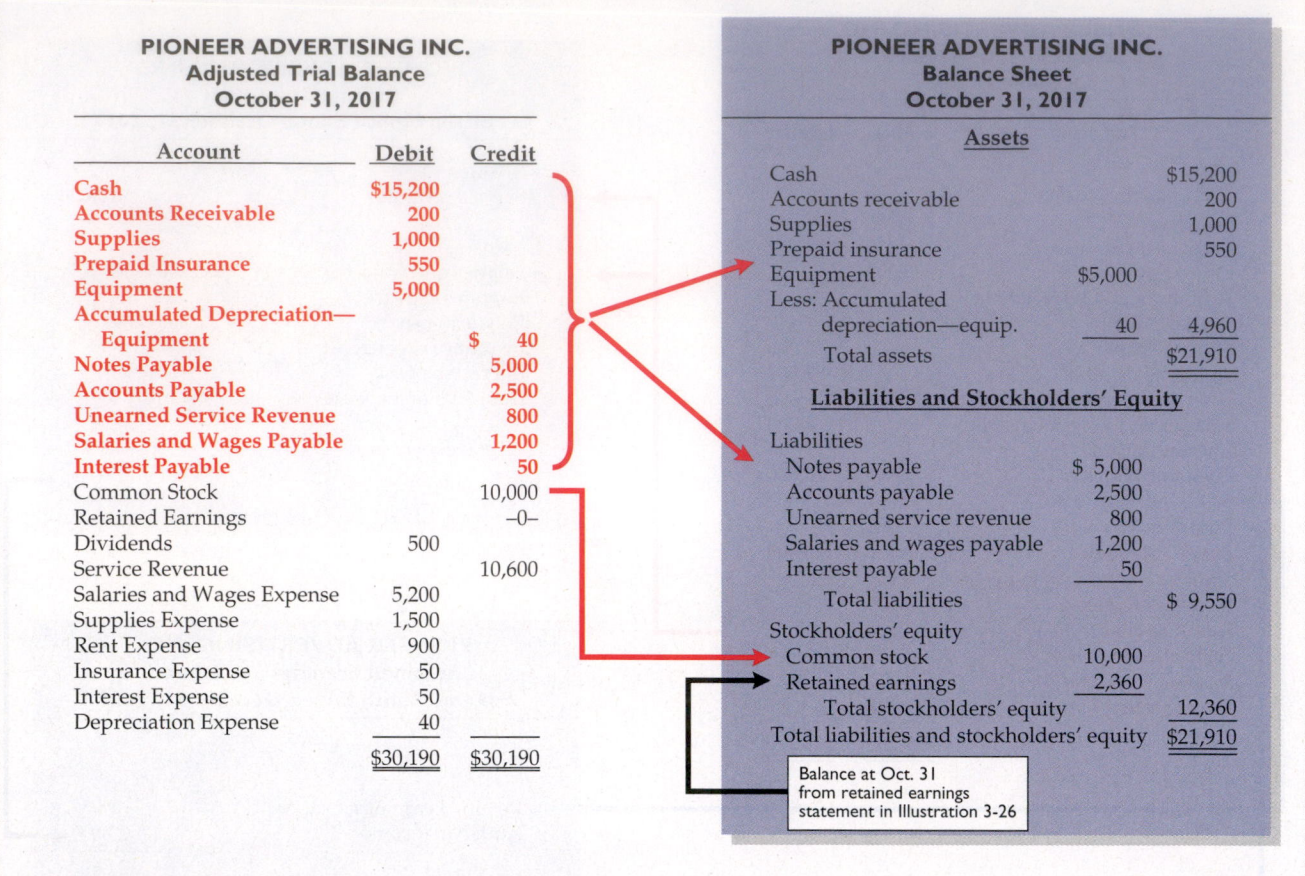

Illustration 3-27
Preparation of the balance sheet
from the adjusted trial balance

DO IT! 4 Trial Balance

Skolnick Co. was organized on April 1, 2017. The company prepares quarterly financial statements. The adjusted trial balance amounts at June 30 are shown below.

	Debit		Credit
Cash	$ 6,700	Accumulated Depreciation—	
Accounts Receivable	600	Equipment	$ 850
Prepaid Rent	900	Notes Payable	5,000
Supplies	1,000	Accounts Payable	1,510
Equipment	15,000	Salaries and Wages Payable	400
Dividends	600	Interest Payable	50
Salaries and Wages Expense	9,400	Unearned Rent Revenue	500
Rent Expense	1,500	Common Stock	14,000
Depreciation Expense	850	Service Revenue	14,200
Supplies Expense	200	Rent Revenue	800
Utilities Expense	510		
Interest Expense	50		
	$37,310		$37,310

(a) Determine the net income for the quarter April 1 to June 30.

(b) Determine the total assets and total liabilities at June 30, 2017, for Skolnick Co.

(c) Determine the amount that appears for retained earnings at June 30, 2017.

Solution

Action Plan

✔ In an adjusted trial balance, make sure all asset, liability, revenue, and expense accounts are properly stated.

✔ To determine the ending balance in Retained Earnings, add net income and subtract dividends.

(a) The net income is determined by adding revenues and subtracting expenses. The net income is computed as follows.

Revenues		
Service revenue	$14,200	
Rent revenue	800	
Total revenues		$15,000
Expenses		
Salaries and wages expense	9,400	
Rent expense	1,500	
Depreciation expense	850	
Utilities expense	510	
Supplies expense	200	
Interest expense	50	
Total expenses		12,510
Net income		$ 2,490

(b) Total assets and liabilities are computed as follows.

Assets			Liabilities	
Cash		$ 6,700	Notes payable	$5,000
Accounts receivable		600	Accounts payable	1,510
Supplies		1,000	Unearned rent	
Prepaid rent		900	revenue	500
Equipment	$15,000		Salaries and wages	
Less: Accumulated			payable	400
depreciation—			Interest payable	50
equipment	850	14,150		
Total assets		$23,350	Total liabilities	$7,460

(c)

Retained earnings, April 1	$ 0
Add: Net income	2,490
Less: Dividends	600
Retained earnings, June 30	$ 1,890

Related exercise material: **BE3-9, BE3-10, E3-11, E3-12, E3-13, and DO IT! 3-4.**

LEARNING OBJECTIVE 5

APPENDIX 3A: Prepare adjusting entries for the alternative treatment of deferrals.

In discussing adjusting entries for prepaid expenses and unearned revenues, we illustrated transactions for which companies made the initial entries to balance sheet accounts. In the case of prepaid expenses, the company debited the prepayment to an asset account. In the case of unearned revenue, the company credited a liability account to record the cash received.

Some companies use an alternative treatment. (1) When a company prepays an expense, it debits that amount to an expense account. (2) When it receives payment for future services, it credits the amount to a revenue account. In this appendix, we describe the circumstances that justify such entries and the different adjusting entries that may be required. This alternative treatment of prepaid expenses and unearned revenues has the same effect on the financial statements as the procedures described in the chapter.

Prepaid Expenses

Prepaid expenses become expired costs either through the passage of time (e.g., insurance) or through consumption (e.g., advertising supplies). If at the time of purchase the company expects to consume the supplies before the next financial statement date, **it may choose to debit (increase) an expense account rather than an asset account. This alternative treatment is simply more convenient.**

Assume that Pioneer Advertising Inc. expects that it will use before the end of the month all of the supplies purchased on October 5. A debit of $2,500 to Supplies Expense (rather than to the asset account Supplies) on October 5 will eliminate the need for an adjusting entry on October 31. At October 31, the Supplies Expense account will show a balance of $2,500, which is the cost of supplies used between October 5 and October 31.

But what if the company does not use all the supplies? For example, what if an inventory of $1,000 of advertising supplies remains on October 31? Obviously, the company would need to make an adjusting entry. Prior to adjustment, the expense account Supplies Expense is overstated $1,000, and the asset account Supplies is understated $1,000. Thus, Pioneer makes the following adjusting entry.

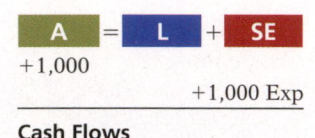

A = L + SE
+1,000
+1,000 Exp

Cash Flows
no effect

Oct. 31	Supplies	1,000	
	Supplies Expense		1,000
	(To record supplies inventory)		

After the company posts the adjusting entry, the accounts show the following:

Illustration 3A-1
Prepaid expenses accounts after adjustment

Supplies			Supplies Expense		
10/31 **Adj. 1,000**			10/5 2,500	10/31 **Adj. 1,000**	
			10/31 **Bal. 1,500**		

After adjustment, the asset account Supplies shows a balance of $1,000, which is equal to the cost of supplies on hand at October 31. In addition, Supplies Expense shows a balance of $1,500. This is equal to the cost of supplies used between October 5 and October 31. Without the adjusting entry, expenses are overstated and net income is understated by $1,000 in the October income statement. Also, both assets and stockholders' equity are understated by $1,000 on the October 31 balance sheet.

Illustration 3A-2 compares the entries and accounts for advertising supplies in the two adjustment approaches.

Illustration 3A-2
Adjustment approaches— a comparison

Prepayment Initially Debited to Asset Account (per chapter)			Prepayment Initially Debited to Expense Account (per appendix)		
Oct. 5 Supplies	2,500		Oct. 5 Supplies Expense	2,500	
Accounts Payable		2,500	Accounts Payable		2,500
Oct. 31 Supplies Expense	1,500		Oct. 31 Supplies	1,000	
Supplies		1,500	Supplies Expense		1,000

After Pioneer posts the entries, the accounts appear as follows.

Illustration 3A-3
Comparison of accounts

(per chapter) Supplies			(per appendix) Supplies		
10/5 2,500	10/31 **Adj. 1,500**		10/31 **Adj. 1,000**		
10/31 **Bal. 1,000**					

Supplies Expense			Supplies Expense		
10/31 **Adj. 1,500**			10/5 2,500	10/31 **Adj. 1,000**	
			10/31 **Bal. 1,500**		

Note that the account balances under each alternative are the same at October 31: Supplies $1,000 and Supplies Expense $1,500.

Unearned Revenues

Unearned revenues are recognized as revenue at the time services are performed. Similar to the case for prepaid expenses, companies may credit (increase) a revenue account when they receive cash for future services.

To illustrate, assume that Pioneer Advertising Inc. received $1,200 for future services on October 2. Pioneer expects to perform the services before October 31.[1] In such a case, the company credits Service Revenue. If Pioneer in fact performs the service before October 31, no adjustment is needed.

However, if at the statement date Pioneer has not performed $800 of the services, it would make an adjusting entry. Without the entry, the revenue account Service Revenue is overstated $800, and the liability account Unearned Service Revenue is understated $800. Thus, Pioneer makes the following adjusting entry.

Oct. 31	Service Revenue	800	
	Unearned Service Revenue		800
	(To record unearned service revenue)		

Helpful Hint
The required adjusted balances here are Service Revenue $400 and Unearned Service Revenue $800.

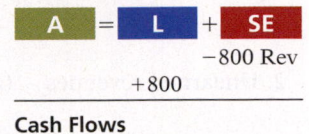

Cash Flows
no effect

After Pioneer posts the adjusting entry, the accounts show the following.

Unearned Service Revenue			Service Revenue			
	10/31 **Adj.** 800		10/31 **Adj.** 800	10/2	1,200	
				10/31 **Bal.** 400		

Illustration 3A-4
Unearned service revenue accounts after adjustment

The liability account Unearned Service Revenue shows a balance of $800. This equals the services that will be performed in the future. In addition, the balance in Service Revenue equals the services performed in October. Without the adjusting entry, both revenues and net income are overstated by $800 in the October income statement. Also, liabilities are understated by $800 and stockholders' equity is overstated by $800 on the October 31 balance sheet.

Illustration 3A-5 compares the entries and accounts for initially recording unearned service revenue in (1) a liability account or (2) a revenue account.

Unearned Service Revenue Initially Credited to Liability Account (per chapter)			Unearned Service Revenue Initially Credited to Revenue Account (per appendix)		
Oct. 2 Cash	1,200		Oct. 2 Cash	1,200	
Unearned Service Revenue		1,200	Service Revenue		1,200
Oct. 31 Unearned Service Revenue	400		Oct. 31 Service Revenue	800	
Service Revenue		400	Unearned Service Revenue		800

Illustration 3A-5
Adjustment approaches—a comparison

After Pioneer posts the entries, the accounts appear as follows.

(per chapter) Unearned Service Revenue			(per appendix) Unearned Service Revenue		
10/31 **Adj.** 400	10/2	1,200		10/31 **Adj.** 800	
	10/31 **Bal.** 800				

Service Revenue			Service Revenue		
	10/31 **Adj.** 400		10/31 **Adj.** 800	10/2	1,200
				10/31 **Bal.** 400	

Illustration 3A-6
Comparison of accounts

---

[1]This example focuses only on the alternative treatment of unearned revenues. For simplicity, we have ignored the entries to Service Revenue pertaining to the immediate recognition of revenue ($10,000) and the adjusting entry for accrued revenue ($200).

Note that the balances in the accounts are the same under the two alternatives: Unearned Service Revenue $800 and Service Revenue $400.

Illustration 3A-7
Summary of basic relationships for deferrals

Summary of Additional Adjustment Relationships

Illustration 3A-7 provides a summary of basic relationships for deferrals.

Type of Adjustment	Reason for Adjustment	Account Balances before Adjustment	Adjusting Entry
1. Prepaid expenses	(a) Prepaid expenses initially recorded in asset accounts have been used.	Assets overstated Expenses understated	Dr. Expenses Cr. Assets
	(b) **Prepaid expenses initially recorded in expense accounts have not been used.**	**Assets understated** **Expenses overstated**	**Dr. Assets** **Cr. Expenses**
2. Unearned revenues	(a) Unearned revenues initially recorded in liability accounts are now recognized as revenue.	Liabilities overstated Revenues understated	Dr. Liabilities Cr. Revenues
	(b) **Unearned revenues initially recorded in revenue accounts are still unearned.**	**Liabilities understated** **Revenues overstated**	**Dr. Revenues** **Cr. Liabilities**

Alternative adjusting entries **do not apply** to accrued revenues and accrued expenses because **no entries occur before companies make these types of adjusting entries**.

LEARNING OBJECTIVE *6

APPENDIX 3B: Discuss financial reporting concepts.

This appendix provides a summary of the concepts in action used in this textbook. In addition, it provides other useful concepts which accountants use as a basis for recording and reporting financial information.

Qualities of Useful Information

Recently, the FASB completed the first phase of a project in which it developed a conceptual framework to serve as the basis for future accounting standards. The framework begins by stating that the primary objective of financial reporting is to provide financial information that is **useful** to investors and creditors for making decisions about providing capital. Useful information should possess two fundamental qualities, relevance and faithful representation, as shown in Illustration 3B-1.

Illustration 3B-1
Fundamental qualities of useful information

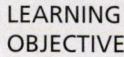

Tell me what I need to know.

BIG SHOT

Relevance Accounting information has **relevance** if it would make a difference in a business decision. Information is considered relevant if it provides information that has **predictive value**, that is, helps provide accurate expectations about the future, and has **confirmatory value**, that is, confirms or corrects prior expectations. **Materiality** is a company-specific aspect of relevance. An item is material when its **size** makes it likely to influence the decision of an investor or creditor.

Faithful Representation **Faithful representation** means that information accurately depicts what really happened. To provide a faithful representation, information must be **complete** (nothing important has been omitted), **neutral** (is not biased toward one position or another), and **free from error**.

ENHANCING QUALITIES

In addition to the two fundamental qualities, the FASB also describes a number of enhancing qualities of useful information. These include **comparability**, **consistency**, **verifiability**, **timeliness**, and **understandability**. In accounting, **comparability** results when different companies use the same accounting principles. Another characteristic that enhances comparability is consistency. **Consistency** means that a company uses the same accounting principles and methods from year to year. Information is **verifiable** if independent observers, using the same methods, obtain similar results. For accounting information to have relevance, it must be **timely**. That is, it must be available to decision-makers before it loses its capacity to influence decisions. For example, public companies like Google or Best Buy provide their annual reports to investors within 60 days of their year-end. Information has the quality of **understandability** if it is presented in a clear and concise fashion, so that reasonably informed users of that information can interpret it and comprehend its meaning.

Assumptions in Financial Reporting

To develop accounting standards, the FASB relies on some key assumptions, as shown in Illustration 3B-2. These include assumptions about the monetary unit, economic entity, time period, and going concern.

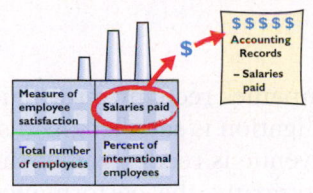

Monetary Unit Assumption The **monetary unit assumption** requires that only those things that can be expressed in money are included in the accounting records. This means that certain important information needed by investors, creditors, and managers, such as customer satisfaction, is not reported in the financial statements.

Economic Entity Assumption The **economic entity assumption** states that every economic entity can be separately identified and accounted for. In order to assess a company's performance and financial position accurately, it is important to not blur company transactions with personal transactions (especially those of its managers) or transactions of other companies.

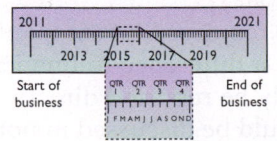

Time Period Assumption Notice that the income statement, retained earnings statement, and statement of cash flows all cover periods of one year, and the balance sheet is prepared at the end of each year. The **time period assumption** states that the life of a business can be divided into artificial time periods and that useful reports covering those periods can be prepared for the business.

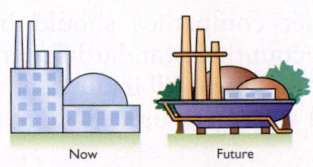

Going Concern Assumption The **going concern assumption** states that the business will remain in operation for the foreseeable future. Of course, many businesses do fail, but in general it is reasonable to assume that the business will continue operating.

Illustration 3B-2
Key assumptions in financial reporting

Principles in Financial Reporting

MEASUREMENT PRINCIPLES

GAAP generally uses one of two measurement principles, the historical cost principle or the fair value principle. Selection of which principle to follow generally relates to trade-offs between relevance and faithful representation.

HISTORICAL COST PRINCIPLE The **historical cost principle** (or cost principle, discussed in Chapter 1) dictates that companies record assets at their cost. This is true not only at the time the asset is purchased but also over the time the asset is held. For example, if land that was purchased for $30,000 increases in value to $40,000, it continues to be reported at $30,000.

FAIR VALUE PRINCIPLE The **fair value principle** (discussed in Chapter 1) indicates that assets and liabilities should be reported at fair value (the price received to sell an asset or settle a liability). Fair value information may be more useful than historical cost for certain types of assets and liabilities. For example, certain investment securities are reported at fair value because market price information is often readily available for these types of assets. In choosing between cost and fair value, two qualities that make accounting information useful for decision-making are used—relevance and faithful representation. In determining which measurement principle to use, the factual nature of cost figures are weighed versus the relevance of fair value. In general, most assets follow the historical cost principle because fair values may not be representationally faithful. Only in situations where assets are actively traded, such as investment securities, is the fair value principle applied.

REVENUE RECOGNITION PRINCIPLE

The **revenue recognition principle** requires that companies recognize revenue in the accounting period in which the performance obligation is satisfied. As discussed earlier in the chapter, in a service company, revenue is recognized at the time the service is performed. In a merchandising company, the performance obligation is generally satisfied when the goods transfer from the seller to the buyer (discussed in Chapter 5). At this point, the sales transaction is complete and the sales price established.

EXPENSE RECOGNITION PRINCIPLE

The **expense recognition principle** (often referred to as the matching principle, discussed earlier in the chapter) dictates that efforts (expenses) be matched with results (revenues). Thus, expenses follow revenues.

FULL DISCLOSURE PRINCIPLE

The **full disclosure principle** (discussed in Chapter 11) requires that companies disclose all circumstances and events that would make a difference to financial statement users. If an important item cannot reasonably be reported directly in one of the four types of financial statements, then it should be discussed in notes that accompany the statements.

Cost Constraint

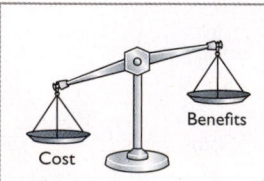

Providing information is costly. In deciding whether companies should be required to provide a certain type of information, accounting standard-setters consider the **cost constraint**. It weighs the cost that companies will incur to provide the information against the benefit that financial statement users will gain from having the information available.

REVIEW AND PRACTICE

LEARNING OBJECTIVES REVIEW

1 Explain the accrual basis of accounting and the reasons for adjusting entries. The time period assumption assumes that the economic life of a business is divided into artificial time periods. Accrual-basis accounting means that companies record events that change a company's financial statements in the periods in which those events occur, rather than in the periods in which the company receives or pays cash.

Companies make adjusting entries at the end of an accounting period. Such entries ensure that companies recognize revenues in the period in which the performance obligation is satisfied and recognize expenses in the period in which they are incurred. The major types of adjusting entries are deferrals (prepaid expenses and unearned revenues) and accruals (accrued revenues and accrued expenses).

2 Prepare adjusting entries for deferrals. Deferrals are either prepaid expenses or unearned revenues. Companies make adjusting entries for deferrals to record the portion of the prepayment that represents the expense incurred or the revenue for services performed in the current accounting period.

3 Prepare adjusting entries for accruals. Accruals are either accrued revenues or accrued expenses. Companies make adjusting entries for accruals to record revenues for services performed and expenses incurred in the current accounting period that have not been recognized through daily entries.

4 Describe the nature and purpose of an adjusted trial balance. An adjusted trial balance shows the balances of all accounts, including those that have been adjusted, at the end of an accounting period. Its purpose is to prove the equality of the total debit balances and total credit balances in the ledger after all adjustments.

*5 Prepare adjusting entries for the alternative treatment of deferrals. Companies may initially debit prepayments to an expense account. Likewise, they may credit unearned revenues to a revenue account. At the end of the period, these accounts may be overstated. The adjusting entries for prepaid expenses are a debit to an asset account and a credit to an expense account. Adjusting entries for unearned revenues are a debit to a revenue account and a credit to a liability account.

*6 Discuss financial reporting concepts. To be judged useful, information should have the primary characteristics of relevance and faithful representation. In addition, it should be comparable, consistent, verifiable, timely, and understandable.

The **monetary unit assumption** requires that companies include in the accounting records only transaction data that can be expressed in terms of money. The **economic entity assumption** states that economic events can be identified with a particular unit of accountability. The **time period assumption** states that the economic life of a business can be divided into artificial time periods and that meaningful accounting reports can be prepared for each period. The **going concern assumption** states that the company will continue in operation long enough to carry out its existing objectives and commitments.

The **historical cost principle** states that companies should record assets at their cost. The **fair value principle** indicates that assets and liabilities should be reported at fair value. The **revenue recognition principle** requires that companies recognize revenue in the accounting period in which the performance obligation is satisfied. The **expense recognition principle** dictates that efforts (expenses) be matched with results (revenues). The **full disclosure principle** requires that companies disclose circumstances and events that matter to financial statement users.

The **cost constraint** weighs the cost that companies incur to provide a type of information against its benefits to financial statement users.

GLOSSARY REVIEW

Accrual-basis accounting Accounting basis in which companies record transactions that change a company's financial statements in the periods in which the events occur. (p. 96).

Accruals Adjusting entries for either accrued revenues or accrued expenses. (p. 98).

Accrued expenses Expenses incurred but not yet paid in cash or recorded. (p. 108).

Accrued revenues Revenues for services performed but not yet received in cash or recorded. (p. 106).

Adjusted trial balance A list of accounts and their balances after the company has made all adjustments. (p. 113).

Adjusting entries Entries made at the end of an accounting period to ensure that companies follow the revenue recognition and expense recognition principles. (p. 98).

Book value The difference between the cost of a depreciable asset and its related accumulated depreciation. (p. 103).

Calendar year An accounting period that extends from January 1 to December 31. (p. 96).

Cash-basis accounting Accounting basis in which companies record revenue when they receive cash and an expense when they pay out cash. (p. 96).

*****Comparability** Ability to compare the accounting information of different companies because they use the same accounting principles. (p. 121).

*****Consistency** Use of the same accounting principles and methods from year to year within a company. (p. 121).

Contra asset account An account offset against an asset account on the balance sheet. (p. 102).

*****Cost constraint** Constraint that weighs the cost that companies will incur to provide the information against the benefit that financial statement users will gain from having the information available. (p. 122).

Deferrals Adjusting entries for either prepaid expenses or unearned revenues. (p. 98).

Depreciation The process of allocating the cost of an asset to expense over its useful life. (p. 102).

*****Economic entity assumption** An assumption that every economic entity can be separately identified and accounted for. (p. 121).

Expense recognition principle (matching principle) The principle that companies match efforts (expenses) with accomplishments (revenues). (pp. 97, 122).

*****Fair value principle** Assets and liabilities should be reported at fair value (the price received to sell an asset or settle a liability). (p. 122).

*****Faithful representation** Information that accurately depicts what really happened. (p. 120).

Fiscal year An accounting period that is one year in length. (p. 96).

*****Full disclosure principle** Accounting principle that dictates that companies disclose circumstances and events that make a difference to financial statement users. (p. 122).

*****Going concern assumption** The assumption that the company will continue in operation for the foreseeable future. (p. 121).

*****Historical cost principle** An accounting principle that states that companies should record assets at their cost. (p. 122).

Interim periods Monthly or quarterly accounting time periods. (p. 96).

*****Materiality** A company-specific aspect of relevance. An item is material when its size makes it likely to influence the decision of an investor or creditor. (p. 120).

*****Monetary unit assumption** An assumption that requires that only those things that can be expressed in money are included in the accounting records. (p. 121).

Prepaid expenses (prepayments) Expenses paid in cash before they are used or consumed. (p. 100).

*****Relevance** The quality of information that indicates the information makes a difference in a decision. (p. 120).

Revenue recognition principle The principle that companies recognize revenue in the accounting period in which the performance obligation is satisfied. (pp. 97, 122).

*****Timely** Information that is available to decision-makers before it loses its capacity to influence decisions. (p. 121).

Time period assumption An assumption that accountants can divide the economic life of a business into artificial time periods. (pp. 96, 121).

*****Understandability** Information presented in a clear and concise fashion so that users can interpret it and comprehend its meaning. (p. 121).

Unearned revenues A liability recorded for cash received before services are performed. (p. 104).

Useful life The length of service of a long-lived asset. (p. 101).

*****Verifiable** The quality of information that occurs when independent observers, using the same methods, obtain similar results. (p. 121).

PRACTICE MULTIPLE-CHOICE QUESTIONS

(LO 1) 1. The revenue recognition principle states that:
(a) revenue should be recognized in the accounting period in which a performance obligation is satisfied.
(b) expenses should be matched with revenues.
(c) the economic life of a business can be divided into artificial time periods.
(d) the fiscal year should correspond with the calendar year.

(LO 1) 2. The time period assumption states that:
(a) companies must wait until the calendar year is completed to prepare financial statements.
(b) companies use the fiscal year to report financial information.

(c) the economic life of a business can be divided into artificial time periods.
(d) companies record information in the time period in which the events occur.

3. Which of the following statements about the accrual **(LO 1)** basis of accounting is **false**?
(a) Events that change a company's financial statements are recorded in the periods in which the events occur.
(b) Revenue is recognized in the period in which services are performed.
(c) This basis is in accord with generally accepted accounting principles.
(d) Revenue is recorded only when cash is received, and expense is recorded only when cash is paid.

(LO 1) 4. The principle or assumption dictating that efforts (expenses) be matched with accomplishments (revenues) is the:
(a) expense recognition principle.
(b) cost assumption.
(c) time period assumption.
(d) revenue recognition principle.

(LO 1) 5. Adjusting entries are made to ensure that:
(a) expenses are recognized in the period in which they are incurred.
(b) revenues are recorded in the period in which services are performed.
(c) balance sheet and income statement accounts have correct balances at the end of an accounting period.
(d) All the responses above are correct.

(LO 1) 6. Each of the following is a major type (or category) of adjusting entries **except**:
(a) prepaid expenses.
(b) accrued revenues.
(c) accrued expenses.
(d) recognized revenues.

(LO 2) 7. The trial balance shows Supplies $1,350 and Supplies Expense $0. If $600 of supplies are on hand at the end of the period, the adjusting entry is:

(a) Supplies	600	
Supplies Expense		600
(b) Supplies	750	
Supplies Expense		750
(c) Supplies Expense	750	
Supplies		750
(d) Supplies Expense	600	
Supplies		600

(LO 2) 8. Adjustments for prepaid expenses:
(a) decrease assets and increase revenues.
(b) decrease expenses and increase assets.
(c) decrease assets and increase expenses.
(d) decrease revenues and increase assets.

(LO 2) 9. Accumulated Depreciation is:
(a) a contra asset account.
(b) an expense account.
(c) a stockholders' equity account.
(d) a liability account.

(LO 2) 10. Rivera Company computes depreciation on delivery equipment at $1,000 for the month of June. The adjusting entry to record this depreciation is as follows.

(a) Depreciation Expense	1,000	
Accumulated Depreciation— Rivera Company		1,000
(b) Depreciation Expense	1,000	
Equipment		1,000
(c) Depreciation Expense	1,000	
Accumulated Depreciation— Equipment		1,000
(d) Equipment Expense	1,000	
Accumulated Depreciation— Equipment		1,000

11. Adjustments for unearned revenues: **(LO 2)**
(a) decrease liabilities and increase revenues.
(b) have an assets-and-revenues-account relationship.
(c) increase assets and increase revenues.
(d) decrease revenues and decrease assets.

12. Adjustments for accrued revenues: **(LO 3)**
(a) have a liabilities-and-revenues-account relationship.
(b) have an assets-and-revenues-account relationship.
(c) decrease assets and revenues.
(d) decrease liabilities and increase revenues.

13. Anika Wilson earned a salary of $400 for the last week **(LO 3)** of September. She will be paid on October 1. The adjusting entry for Anika's employer at September 30 is:
(a) No entry is required.

(b) Salaries and Wages Expense	400	
Salaries and Wages Payable		400
(c) Salaries and Wages Expense	400	
Cash		400
(d) Salaries and Wages Payable	400	
Cash		400

14. Which of the following statements is **incorrect** concerning the adjusted trial balance? **(LO 4)**
(a) An adjusted trial balance proves the equality of the total debit balances and the total credit balances in the ledger after all adjustments are made.
(b) The adjusted trial balance provides the primary basis for the preparation of financial statements.
(c) The adjusted trial balance lists the account balances segregated by assets and liabilities.
(d) The adjusted trial balance is prepared after the adjusting entries have been journalized and posted.

*15. The trial balance shows Supplies $0 and Supplies **(LO 5)** Expense $1,500. If $800 of supplies are on hand at the end of the period, the adjusting entry is:
(a) debit Supplies $800 and credit Supplies Expense $800.
(b) debit Supplies Expense $800 and credit Supplies $800.
(c) debit Supplies $700 and credit Supplies Expense $700.
(d) debit Supplies Expense $700 and credit Supplies $700.

*16. Neutrality is an ingredient of: **(LO 6)**

	Faithful Representation	**Relevance**
(a)	Yes	Yes
(b)	No	No
(c)	Yes	No
(d)	No	Yes

*17. Which item is a constraint in financial accounting? **(LO 6)**
(a) Comparability. (c) Cost.
(b) Materiality. (d) Consistency.

Solutions

1. **(a)** Revenue should be recognized in the accounting period in which a performance obligation is satisfied. The other choices are incorrect because (b) defines the expense recognition principle, (c) describes the time period assumption, and (d) a company's fiscal year does not need to correspond with the calendar year.

2. (c) The economic life of a business can be divided into artificial time periods. The other choices are incorrect because (a) companies report their activities on a more frequent basis and not necessarily based on a calendar year; (b) companies report financial information more frequently than annually, such as monthly or quarterly, in order to evaluate results of operations; and (d) this statement describes accrual-basis accounting.

3. (d) Under the accrual basis of accounting, revenue is recognized when the performance obligation is satisfied, not when cash is received, and expense is recognized when incurred, not when cash is paid. The other choices are true statements.

4. (a) The expense recognition principle dictates that expense be matched with revenues. The other choices are incorrect because (b) there is no cost assumption, but the historical cost principle states that assets should be recorded at their cost; (c) the time period assumption states that the economic life of a business can be divided into artificial time periods; and (d) the revenue recognition principle indicates that revenue should be recognized in the accounting period in which a performance obligation is satisfied.

5. (d) Adjusting entries are made for the reasons noted in choices (a), (b), and (c). The other choices are true statements, but (d) is the better answer.

6. (d) Unearned revenues, not recognized revenues, are one of the major categories of adjusting entries. The other choices all list one of the major categories of adjusting entries.

7. (c) Debiting Supplies Expense for $750 and crediting Supplies for $750 will decrease Supplies and increase Supplies Expense. The other choices are incorrect because (a) will increase Supplies and decrease Supplies Expense and also for the wrong amounts, (b) will increase Supplies and decrease Supplies Expense, and (d) will cause Supplies to have an incorrect balance of $750 ($1,350 − $600) and Supplies Expense to have an incorrect balance of $600 ($0 + $600).

8. (c) Adjustments for prepaid expenses decrease assets and increase expenses. The other choices are incorrect because an adjusting entry for prepaid expenses (a) increases expenses, not revenues; (b) increases, not decreases, expenses and decreases, not increases, assets; and (d) increases, not decreases, revenues and decreases, not increases, assets.

9. (a) Accumulated Depreciation is a contra asset account; it is offset against an asset account on the balance sheet. The other choices are incorrect because Accumulated Depreciation is not (b) an expense account nor located on the income statement, (c) a stockholders' equity account, or (d) a liability account.

10. (c) The adjusting entry is to debit Depreciation Expense and credit Accumulated Depreciation—Equipment. The other choices are incorrect because (a) the contra asset account title includes the asset being depreciated, not the company name; (b) the credit should be to the contra asset account, not directly to the asset; and (d) the debit for this entry should be Depreciation Expense, not Equipment Expense.

11. (a) Adjustments for unearned revenues will consist of a debit (decrease) to unearned revenues (a liability) and a credit (increase) to a revenue account. Choices (b), (c), and (d) are incorrect because adjustments for unearned revenues will increase revenues but will have no effect on assets.

12. (b) Adjustments for accrued revenues will have an assets-and-revenues-account relationship. Choices (a) and (d) are incorrect because adjustments for accrued revenues have no effect on liabilities. Choice (c) is incorrect because these adjustments will increase, not decrease, both assets and revenues.

13. (b) The adjusting entry should be to debit Salaries and Wages Expense for $400 and credit Salaries and Wages Payable for $400. The other choices are incorrect because (a) if an adjusting entry is not made, the amount of money owed (liability) that is shown on the balance sheet will be understated and the amount of salaries and wages expense will also be understated; (c) the credit account is incorrect as adjusting entries never affect cash; and (d) the debit account should be Salaries and Wages Expense and the credit account should be Salaries and Wages Payable. Adjusting entries never affect cash.

14. (c) The accounts on the trial balance can be segregated by the balance in the account—either debit or credit—not whether they are assets or liabilities. All accounts in the ledger are included in the adjusted trial balance, not just assets and liabilities. The other choices are true statements.

*15. (a) This adjusting entry correctly states the Supplies account at $800 ($0 + $800) and the Supplies Expense account at $700 ($1,500 − $800). The other choices are incorrect because (b) will cause the Supplies account to have a credit balance (assets have a normal debit balance) and the Supplies Expense account to be stated at $2,300, which is too high; (c) will result in a $700 balance in the Supplies account ($100 too low) and an $800 balance in the Supplies Expense account ($100 too high); and (d) will cause the Supplies account to have a credit balance (assets have a normal debit balance) and the Supplies Expense account to be stated at $2,200, which is too high.

*16. (c) Neutrality is one of the enhancing qualities that makes information more representationally faithful, not relevant. Therefore, choices (a), (b), and (d) are incorrect.

*17. (c) Cost is a constraint in financial accounting. The other choices are all enhancing qualities of useful information.

■ PRACTICE EXERCISES

1. Wendy Penn, D.D.S., opened a dental practice on January 1, 2017. During the first month of operations, the following transactions occurred.

Prepare adjusting entries.

(LO 3, 4)

1. Performed services for patients totaling $785, which had not yet been recorded.

2. Utility expenses incurred but not paid prior to January 31 totaled $250.

3. Purchased dental equipment on January 1 for $90,000, paying $25,000 in cash and signing a $65,000, 3-year note payable. The equipment depreciates $500 per month. Interest is $550 per month.

4. Purchased a one-year malpractice insurance policy on January 1 for $15,000.

5. Purchased $1,700 of dental supplies. On January 31, determined that $300 of supplies were on hand.

Instructions

Prepare the adjusting entries on January 31. Account titles are Accumulated Depreciation—Equipment, Depreciation Expense, Service Revenue, Accounts Receivable, Insurance Expense, Interest Expense, Interest Payable, Prepaid Insurance, Supplies, Supplies Expense, Utilities Expense, and Utilities Payable.

Solution

1. Jan. 31	Accounts Receivable		785	
	Service Revenue			785
31	Utilities Expense		250	
	Accounts Payable			250
31	Depreciation Expense		500	
	Accumulated Depreciation—Equipment			500
31	Interest Expense		550	
	Interest Payable			550
31	Insurance Expense ($15,000 ÷ 12)		1,250	
	Prepaid Insurance			1,250
31	Supplies Expense ($1,700 − $300)		1,400	
	Supplies			1,400

2. The income statement of Bragg Co. for the month of July shows net income of $1,400 based on Service Revenue $5,500, Salaries and Wages Expense $2,300, Supplies Expense $1,200, and Utilities Expense $600. In reviewing the statement, you discover the following.

Prepare correct income statement.

(LO 2, 3, 4)

1. Insurance expired during July of $450 was omitted.

2. Supplies expense includes $300 of supplies that are still on hand at July 31.

3. Depreciation on equipment of $180 was omitted.

4. Accrued but unpaid salaries and wages at July 31 of $400 were not included.

5. Services performed but unrecorded totaled $600.

Instructions

Prepare a correct income statement for July 2017.

Solution

2.

BRAGG CO.		
Income Statement		
For the Month Ended July 31, 2017		
Revenues		
Service revenue ($5,500 + $600)		$6,100
Expenses		
Salaries and wages expense ($2,300 + $400)	$2,700	
Supplies expense ($1,200 − $300)	900	
Utilities expense	600	
Insurance expense	450	
Depreciation expense	180	
Total expenses		4,830
Net income		$1,270

PRACTICE PROBLEM

Prepare adjusting entries from selected data.

(LO 2, 3)

The Green Thumb Lawn Care Inc. began operations on April 1. At April 30, the trial balance shows the following balances for selected accounts.

Prepaid Insurance	$ 3,600
Equipment	28,000
Notes Payable	20,000
Unearned Service Revenue	4,200
Service Revenue	1,800

Analysis reveals the following additional data.

1. Prepaid insurance is the cost of a 2-year insurance policy, effective April 1.

2. Depreciation on the equipment is $500 per month.

3. The note payable is dated April 1. It is a 6-month, 12% note.

4. Seven customers paid for the company's 6-month lawn service package of $600 beginning in April. The company performed services for these customers in April.

5. Lawn services performed for other customers but not recorded at April 30 totaled $1,500.

Instructions

Prepare the adjusting entries for the month of April. Show computations.

Solution

	GENERAL JOURNAL			J1
Date	**Account Titles and Explanation**	**Ref.**	**Debit**	**Credit**
	Adjusting Entries			
Apr. 30	Insurance Expense		150	
	Prepaid Insurance			150
	(To record insurance expired:			
	$3,600 ÷ 24 = $150 per month)			
30	Depreciation Expense		500	
	Accumulated Depreciation—Equipment			500
	(To record monthly depreciation)			
30	Interest Expense		200	
	Interest Payable			200
	(To record interest on notes payable:			
	$20,000 × 12% × 1/12 = $200)			
30	Unearned Service Revenue		700	
	Service Revenue			700
	(To record revenue for services			
	performed: $600 ÷ 6 = $100;			
	$100 per month × 7 = $700)			
30	Accounts Receivable		1,500	
	Service Revenue			1,500
	(To record revenue for services			
	performed)			

WileyPLUS

Brief Exercises, Exercises, **DO IT!** Exercises, and Problems and many additional resources are available for practice in WileyPLUS

NOTE: All asterisked Questions, Exercises, and Problems relate to material in the appendices to the chapter.

QUESTIONS

1. (a) How does the time period assumption affect an accountant's analysis of business transactions?
   (b) Explain the terms fiscal year, calendar year, and interim periods.

2. Define two generally accepted accounting principles that relate to adjusting the accounts.

3. Susan Zupan, a lawyer, accepts a legal engagement in March, performs the work in April, and is paid in May. If Zupan's law firm prepares monthly financial statements, when should it recognize revenue from this engagement? Why?

4. Why do accrual-basis financial statements provide more useful information than cash-basis statements?

5. In completing the engagement in Question 3, Zupan pays no costs in March, $2,000 in April, and $2,500 in May (incurred in April). How much expense should the firm deduct from revenues in the month when it recognizes the revenue? Why?

6. "Adjusting entries are required by the historical cost principle of accounting." Do you agree? Explain.

7. Why may a trial balance not contain up-to-date and complete financial information?

8. Distinguish between the two categories of adjusting entries, and identify the types of adjustments applicable to each category.

9. What is the debit/credit effect of a prepaid expense adjusting entry?

10. "Depreciation is a valuation process that results in the reporting of the fair value of the asset." Do you agree? Explain.

11. Explain the differences between depreciation expense and accumulated depreciation.

12. J. Brownlee Company purchased equipment for $18,000. By the current balance sheet date, $6,000 had been depreciated. Indicate the balance sheet presentation of the data.

13. What is the debit/credit effect of an unearned revenue adjusting entry?

14. A company fails to recognize revenue for services performed but not yet received in cash or recorded. Which of the following accounts are involved in the adjusting entry: (a) asset, (b) liability, (c) revenue, or (d) expense? For the accounts selected, indicate whether they would be debited or credited in the entry.

15. A company fails to recognize an expense incurred but not paid. Indicate which of the following accounts is debited and which is credited in the adjusting entry: (a) asset, (b) liability, (c) revenue, or (d) expense.

16. A company makes an accrued revenue adjusting entry for $900 and an accrued expense adjusting entry for $700. How much was net income understated prior to these entries? Explain.

17. On January 9, a company pays $5,000 for salaries and wages of which $2,000 was reported as Salaries and Wages Payable on December 31. Give the entry to record the payment.

18. For each of the following items before adjustment, indicate the type of adjusting entry (prepaid expense, unearned revenue, accrued revenue, or accrued expense) that is needed to correct the misstatement. If an item could result in more than one type of adjusting entry, indicate each of the types.
    (a) Assets are understated.
    (b) Liabilities are overstated.
    (c) Liabilities are understated.
    (d) Expenses are understated.
    (e) Assets are overstated.
    (f) Revenue is understated.

19. One-half of the adjusting entry is given below. Indicate the account title for the other half of the entry.
    (a) Salaries and Wages Expense is debited.
    (b) Depreciation Expense is debited.
    (c) Interest Payable is credited.
    (d) Supplies is credited.
    (e) Accounts Receivable is debited.
    (f) Unearned Service Revenue is debited.

20. "An adjusting entry may affect more than one balance sheet or income statement account." Do you agree? Why or why not?

21. Why is it possible to prepare financial statements directly from an adjusted trial balance?

*22. Dashan Company debits Supplies Expense for all purchases of supplies and credits Rent Revenue for all advanced rentals. For each type of adjustment, give the adjusting entry.

*23. (a) What is the primary objective of financial reporting?
    (b) Identify the characteristics of useful accounting information.

*24. Dan Fineman, the president of King Company, is pleased. King substantially increased its net income in 2017 while keeping its unit inventory relatively the same. Howard Gross, chief accountant, cautions Dan, however. Gross says that since King changed its method of inventory valuation, there is a consistency problem and it is difficult to determine whether King is better off. Is Gross correct? Why or why not?

*25. What is the distinction between comparability and consistency?

*26. Describe the constraint inherent in the presentation of accounting information.

*27. Laurie Belk is president of Better Books. She has no accounting background. Belk cannot understand why fair value is not used as the basis for all accounting measurement and reporting. Discuss.

*28. What is the economic entity assumption? Give an example of its violation.

BRIEF EXERCISES

Indicate why adjusting entries are needed.

(LO 1)

BE3-1 The ledger of Jung Company includes the following accounts. Explain why each account may require adjustment.
(a) Prepaid Insurance.
(b) Depreciation Expense.
(c) Unearned Service Revenue.
(d) Interest Payable.

Identify the major types of adjusting entries.

(LO 1, 2, 3)

BE3-2 Moteki Company accumulates the following adjustment data at December 31. Indicate (a) the type of adjustment (prepaid expense, accrued revenue, and so on), and (b) the status of accounts before adjustment (overstated or understated).
1. Supplies of $100 are on hand.
2. Services performed but not recorded total $900.
3. Interest of $200 has accumulated on a note payable.
4. Rent collected in advance totaling $650 has been earned.

Prepare adjusting entry for supplies.

(LO 2)

BE3-3 Ritter Advertising Company's trial balance at December 31 shows Supplies $6,700 and Supplies Expense $0. On December 31, there are $2,500 of supplies on hand. Prepare the adjusting entry at December 31, and using T-accounts, enter the balances in the accounts, post the adjusting entry, and indicate the adjusted balance in each account.

Prepare adjusting entry for depreciation.

(LO 2)

BE3-4 At the end of its first year, the trial balance of Nygaard Company shows Equipment $30,000 and zero balances in Accumulated Depreciation—Equipment and Depreciation Expense. Depreciation for the year is estimated to be $4,000. Prepare the adjusting entry for depreciation at December 31, post the adjustments to T-accounts, and indicate the balance sheet presentation of the equipment at December 31.

Prepare adjusting entry for prepaid expense.

(LO 2)

BE3-5 On July 1, 2017, Dobbs Co. pays $14,400 to Kalter Insurance Co. for a 3-year insurance contract. Both companies have fiscal years ending December 31. For Dobbs Co., journalize and post the entry on July 1 and the adjusting entry on December 31.

Prepare adjusting entry for unearned revenue.

(LO 2)

BE3-6 Using the data in BE3-5, journalize and post the entry on July 1 and the adjusting entry on December 31 for Kalter Insurance Co. Kalter uses the accounts Unearned Service Revenue and Service Revenue.

Prepare adjusting entries for accruals.

(LO 3)

BE3-7 The bookkeeper for Bradbury Company asks you to prepare the following accrued adjusting entries at December 31.
1. Interest on notes payable of $400 is accrued.
2. Services performed but not recorded total $1,900.
3. Salaries earned by employees of $900 have not been recorded.

Use the following account titles: Service Revenue, Accounts Receivable, Interest Expense, Interest Payable, Salaries and Wages Expense, and Salaries and Wages Payable.

Analyze accounts in an unadjusted trial balance.

(LO 1, 2, 3)

BE3-8 The trial balance of Yewlett Company includes the following balance sheet accounts, which may require adjustment. For each account that requires adjustment, indicate (a) the type of adjusting entry (prepaid expense, unearned revenue, accrued revenue, or accrued expense) and (b) the related account in the adjusting entry.

Accounts Receivable	Interest Payable
Prepaid Insurance	Unearned Service Revenue
Accumulated Depreciation—Equipment	

Prepare an income statement from an adjusted trial balance.

(LO 4)

BE3-9 The adjusted trial balance of Parsons Company at December 31, 2017, includes the following accounts: Common Stock $15,600, Dividends $7,000, Service Revenue $37,000, Salaries and Wages Expense $16,000, Insurance Expense $2,000, Rent Expense $4,000, Supplies Expense $1,500, and Depreciation Expense $1,300. Prepare an income statement for the year.

BE3-10 Partial adjusted trial balance data for Parsons Company is presented in BE3-9. The balance in Common Stock is the balance as of January 1. Prepare a retained earnings statement for the year assuming net income is $12,200 for the year and Retained Earnings is $7,240 on January 1.

Prepare a retained earnings statement from an adjusted trial balance.

(LO 4)

*BE3-11 Mayes Company records all prepayments in income statement accounts At April 30, the trial balance shows Supplies Expense $2,800, Service Revenue $9,200, and zero balances in related balance sheet accounts. Prepare the adjusting entries at April 30 assuming (a) $700 of supplies on hand and (b) $3,000 of service revenue should be reported as unearned.

Prepare adjusting entries under alternative treatment of deferrals.

(LO 5)

*BE3-12 The accompanying chart shows the qualitative characteristics of useful accounting information. Fill in the blanks.

Identify characteristics of useful information.

(LO 6)

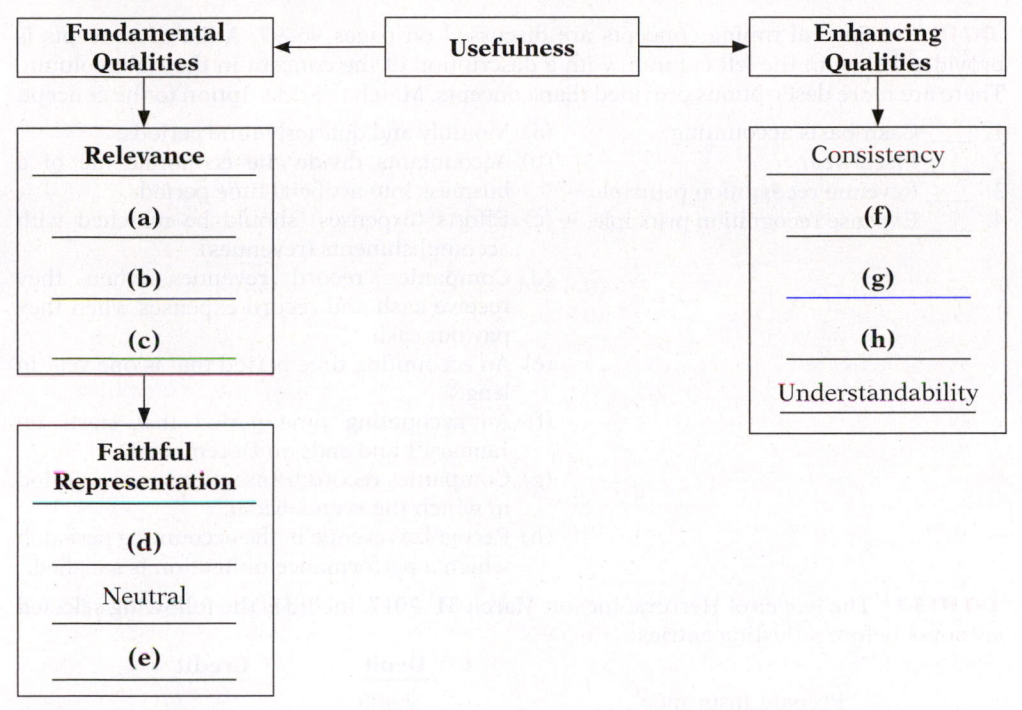

*BE3-13 Given the characteristics of useful accounting information, complete each of the following statements.
(a) For information to be _____, it should have predictive value, confirmatory value, and be material.
(b) _____ is the quality of information that gives assurance that the information accurately depicts what really happened.
(c) _____ means using the same accounting principles and methods from year to year within a company.

Identify characteristics of useful information.

(LO 6)

*BE3-14 Here are some qualitative characteristics of useful accounting information:
1. Predictive value   3. Verifiable
2. Neutral   4. Timely

Match each qualitative characteristic to one of the following statements.
_____ (a) Accounting information should help provide accurate expectations about future events.
_____ (b) Accounting information cannot be selected, prepared, or presented to favor one set of interested users over another.
_____ (c) The quality of information that occurs when independent observers, using the same methods, obtain similar results.
_____ (d) Accounting information must be available to decision-makers before it loses its capacity to influence their decisions.

Identify characteristics of useful information.

(LO 6)

Define full disclosure principle.

(LO 6)

*BE3-15 Select the response that completes the following statement correctly. The full disclosure principle dictates that:
(a) financial statements should disclose all assets at their cost.
(b) financial statements should disclose only those events that can be measured in currency.
(c) financial statements should disclose all events and circumstances that would matter to users of financial statements.
(d) financial statements should not be relied on unless an auditor has expressed an unqualified opinion on them.

DO IT! Exercises

Identify timing concepts.

(LO 1)

DO IT! 3-1 Several timing concepts are discussed on pages 96–97. A list of concepts is provided below in the left column, with a description of the concept in the right column. There are more descriptions provided than concepts. Match the description to the concept.

1. ____ Cash-basis accounting.
2. ____ Fiscal year.
3. ____ Revenue recognition principle.
4. ____ Expense recognition principle.

(a) Monthly and quarterly time periods.
(b) Accountants divide the economic life of a business into artificial time periods.
(c) Efforts (expenses) should be matched with accomplishments (revenues).
(d) Companies record revenues when they receive cash and record expenses when they pay out cash.
(e) An accounting time period that is one year in length.
(f) An accounting time period that starts on January 1 and ends on December 31.
(g) Companies record transactions in the period in which the events occur.
(h) Recognize revenue in the accounting period in which a performance obligation is satisfied.

Prepare adjusting entries for deferrals.

(LO 2)

DO IT! 3-2 The ledger of Herrera, Inc. on March 31, 2017, includes the following selected accounts before adjusting entries.

	Debit	Credit
Prepaid Insurance	2,400	
Supplies	2,500	
Equipment	30,000	
Unearned Service Revenue		9,000

An analysis of the accounts shows the following.

1. Insurance expires at the rate of $300 per month.
2. Supplies on hand total $1,100.
3. The equipment depreciates $500 per month.
4. During March, services were performed for two-fifths of the unearned service revenue.

Prepare the adjusting entries for the month of March.

Prepare adjusting entries for accruals.

(LO 3)

DO IT! 3-3 Javier Computer Services began operations in July 2017. At the end of the month, the company prepares monthly financial statements. It has the following information for the month.

1. At July 31, the company owed employees $1,300 in salaries that the company will pay in August.
2. On July 1, the company borrowed $20,000 from a local bank on a 10-year note. The annual interest rate is 12%.
3. Service revenue unrecorded in July totaled $2,400.

Prepare the adjusting entries needed at July 31, 2017.

DO IT! 3-4 Lumina Co. was organized on April 1, 2017. The company prepares quarterly financial statements. The adjusted trial balance amounts at June 30 are shown below.

Calculate amounts from trial balance.

(LO 4)

	Debit		Credit
Cash	$ 5,360	Accumulated Depreciation—	
Accounts Receivable	480	Equipment	$ 700
Prepaid Rent	720	Notes Payable	4,000
Supplies	920	Accounts Payable	790
Equipment	12,000	Salaries and Wages Payable	300
Dividends	500	Interest Payable	40
Salaries and Wages Expense	7,400	Unearned Rent Revenue	400
Rent Expense	1,200	Common Stock	11,200
Depreciation Expense	700	Service Revenue	11,360
Supplies Expense	160	Rent Revenue	1,100
Utilities Expense	410		$29,890
Interest Expense	40		
	$29,890		

(a) Determine the net income for the quarter April 1 to June 30.
(b) Determine the total assets and total liabilities at June 30, 2017, for Lumina Company.
(c) Determine the amount that appears for Retained Earnings at June 30, 2017.

EXERCISES

E3-1 Ian Muse has prepared the following list of statements about the time period assumption.

Explain the time period assumption.

(LO 1)

1. Adjusting entries would not be necessary if a company's life were not divided into artificial time periods.
2. The IRS requires companies to file annual tax returns.
3. Accountants divide the economic life of a business into artificial time periods, but each transaction affects only one of these periods.
4. Accounting time periods are generally a month, a quarter, or a year.
5. A time period lasting one year is called an interim period.
6. All fiscal years are calendar years, but not all calendar years are fiscal years.

Instructions
Identify each statement as true or false. If false, indicate how to correct the statement.

E3-2 On numerous occasions, proposals have surfaced to put the federal government on the accrual basis of accounting. This is no small issue. If this basis were used, it would mean that billions in unrecorded liabilities would have to be booked, and the federal deficit would increase substantially.

Distinguish between cash and accrual basis of accounting.

(LO 1)

Instructions
(a) What is the difference between accrual-basis accounting and cash-basis accounting?
(b) Why would politicians prefer the cash basis over the accrual basis?
(c) Write a letter to your senator explaining why the federal government should adopt the accrual basis of accounting.

E3-3 Primo Industries collected $105,000 from customers in 2017. Of the amount collected, $25,000 was for services performed in 2016. In addition, Primo performed services worth $40,000 in 2017, which will not be collected until 2018.

Compute cash and accrual accounting income.

(LO 1)

Primo Industries also paid $72,000 for expenses in 2017. Of the amount paid, $30,000 was for expenses incurred on account in 2016. In addition, Primo incurred $42,000 of expenses in 2017, which will not be paid until 2018.

Instructions
(a) Compute 2017 cash-basis net income.
(b) Compute 2017 accrual-basis net income.

Identify the type of adjusting entry needed.

(LO 1, 2, 3)

E3-4 Hart Corporation encounters the following situations:

1. Hart collects $1,300 from a customer in 2017 for services to be performed in 2018.
2. Hart incurs utility expense which is not yet paid in cash or recorded.
3. Hart's employees worked 3 days in 2017 but will not be paid until 2018.
4. Hart performs services for customers but has not yet received cash or recorded the transaction.
5. Hart paid $2,400 rent on December 1 for the 4 months starting December 1.
6. Hart received cash for future services and recorded a liability until the service was performed.
7. Hart performed consulting services for a client in December 2017. On December 31, it had not billed the client for services performed of $1,200.
8. Hart paid cash for an expense and recorded an asset until the item was used up.
9. Hart purchased $900 of supplies in 2017; at year-end, $400 of supplies remain unused.
10. Hart purchased equipment on January 1, 2017; the equipment will be used for 5 years.
11. Hart borrowed $10,000 on October 1, 2017, signing an 8% one-year note payable.

Instructions

Identify what type of adjusting entry (prepaid expense, unearned revenue, accrued expense, or accrued revenue) is needed in each situation at December 31, 2017.

Prepare adjusting entries from selected data.

(LO 2, 3)

E3-5 Verne Cova Company has the following balances in selected accounts on December 31, 2017.

Accounts Receivable	$ –0–
Accumulated Depreciation—Equipment	–0–
Equipment	7,000
Interest Payable	–0–
Notes Payable	10,000
Prepaid Insurance	2,100
Salaries and Wages Payable	–0–
Supplies	2,450
Unearned Service Revenue	30,000

All the accounts have normal balances. The information below has been gathered at December 31, 2017.

1. Verne Cova Company borrowed $10,000 by signing a 12%, one-year note on September 1, 2017.
2. A count of supplies on December 31, 2017, indicates that supplies of $900 are on hand.
3. Depreciation on the equipment for 2017 is $1,000.
4. Verne Cova Company paid $2,100 for 12 months of insurance coverage on June 1, 2017.
5. On December 1, 2017, Verne Cova collected $30,000 for consulting services to be performed from December 1, 2017, through March 31, 2018.
6. Verne Cova performed consulting services for a client in December 2017. The client will be billed $4,200.
7. Verne Cova Company pays its employees total salaries of $9,000 every Monday for the preceding 5-day week (Monday through Friday). On Monday, December 29, employees were paid for the week ending December 26. All employees worked the last 3 days of 2017.

Instructions

Prepare adjusting entries for the seven items described above.

Identify types of adjustments and account relationships.

(LO 1, 2, 3)

E3-6 Lei Company accumulates the following adjustment data at December 31.

1. Services performed but not recorded total $1,000.
2. Supplies of $300 have been used.
3. Utility expenses of $225 are unpaid.
4. Services related to unearned service revenue of $260 were performed.
5. Salaries of $800 are unpaid.
6. Prepaid insurance totaling $350 has expired.

Instructions

For each of the above items indicate the following.

(a) The type of adjustment (prepaid expense, unearned revenue, accrued revenue, or accrued expense).

(b) The status of accounts before adjustment (overstatement or understatement).

E3-7 The ledger of Perez Rental Agency on March 31 of the current year includes the selected accounts, shown below, before quarterly adjusting entries have been prepared.

Prepare adjusting entries from selected account data.
(LO 2, 3)

	Debit	Credit
Prepaid Insurance	$ 3,600	
Supplies	2,800	
Equipment	25,000	
Accumulated		
Depreciation—Equipment		$ 8,400
Notes Payable		20,000
Unearned Rent Revenue		10,200
Rent Revenue		60,000
Interest Expense	–0–	
Salaries and Wages Expense	14,000	

An analysis of the accounts shows the following.

1. The equipment depreciates $400 per month.
2. One-third of the unearned rent revenue was earned during the quarter.
3. Interest totaling $500 is accrued on the notes payable for the quarter.
4. Supplies on hand total $900.
5. Insurance expires at the rate of $200 per month.

Instructions
Prepare the adjusting entries at March 31, assuming that adjusting entries are made **quarterly**. Additional accounts are Depreciation Expense, Insurance Expense, Interest Payable, and Supplies Expense.

E3-8 Robin Shalit, D.D.S., opened a dental practice on January 1, 2017. During the first month of operations, the following transactions occurred.

Prepare adjusting entries.
(LO 2, 3)

1. Performed services for patients who had dental plan insurance. At January 31, $875 of such services were performed but not yet recorded.
2. Utility expenses incurred but not paid prior to January 31 totaled $650.
3. Purchased dental equipment on January 1 for $80,000, paying $20,000 in cash and signing a $60,000, 3-year note payable. The equipment depreciates $400 per month. Interest is $500 per month.
4. Purchased a one-year malpractice insurance policy on January 1 for $24,000.
5. Purchased $1,600 of dental supplies. On January 31, determined that $400 of supplies were on hand.

Instructions
Prepare the adjusting entries on January 31. Account titles are Accumulated Depreciation—Equipment, Depreciation Expense, Service Revenue, Accounts Receivable, Insurance Expense, Interest Expense, Interest Payable, Prepaid Insurance, Supplies, Supplies Expense, Utilities Expense, and Utilities Payable.

E3-9 The trial balance for Pioneer Advertising Inc. is shown in Illustration 3-3 (page 99). Instead of the adjusting entries shown in the text at October 31, assume the following adjustment data.

Prepare adjusting entries.
(LO 2, 3)

1. Supplies on hand at October 31 total $500.
2. Expired insurance for the month is $100.
3. Depreciation for the month is $50.
4. Services related to unearned service revenue in October worth $600 were performed.
5. Services performed but not recorded at October 31 are $300.
6. Interest accrued at October 31 is $95.
7. Accrued salaries at October 31 are $1,625.

Instructions
Prepare the adjusting entries for the items above.

E3-10 The income statement of Gopitkumar Co. for the month of July shows net income of $1,400 based on Service Revenue $5,500, Salaries and Wages Expense $2,300, Supplies Expense $1,200, and Utilities Expense $600. In reviewing the statement, you discover the following.

Prepare correct income statement.
(LO 1, 2, 3, 4)

1. Insurance expired during July of $400 was omitted.
2. Supplies expense includes $250 of supplies that are still on hand at July 31.
3. Depreciation on equipment of $150 was omitted.

4. Accrued but unpaid salaries and wages at July 31 of $300 were not included.
5. Services performed but unrecorded totaled $650.

Instructions
Prepare a correct income statement for July 2017.

Analyze adjusted data.

(LO 1, 2, 3, 4)

E3-11 A partial adjusted trial balance of Gehring Company at January 31, 2017, shows the following.

GEHRING COMPANY
Adjusted Trial Balance
January 31, 2017

	Debit	Credit
Supplies	$ 850	
Prepaid Insurance	2,400	
Salaries and Wages Payable		$ 800
Unearned Service Revenue		750
Supplies Expense	950	
Insurance Expense	400	
Salaries and Wages Expense	2,900	
Service Revenue		2,000

Instructions
Answer the following questions, assuming the year begins January 1.

(a) If the amount in Supplies Expense is the January 31 adjusting entry, and $1,000 of supplies was purchased in January, what was the balance in Supplies on January 1?
(b) If the amount in Insurance Expense is the January 31 adjusting entry, and the original insurance premium was for one year, what was the total premium and when was the policy purchased?
(c) If $3,500 of salaries was paid in January, what was the balance in Salaries and Wages Payable at December 31, 2016?

Journalize basic transactions and adjusting entries.

(LO 2, 3)

E3-12 Selected accounts of Koffman Company are as follows.

Supplies Expense

7/31	800	

Supplies

7/1 Bal.	1,100	7/31	800
7/10	650		

Salaries and Wages Payable

		7/31	1,200

Accounts Receivable

7/31	500	

Unearned Service Revenue

7/31	1,150	7/1 Bal.	1,500
		7/20	1,000

Salaries and Wages Expense

7/15	1,200	
7/31	1,200	

Service Revenue

		7/14	2,000
		7/31	1,150
		7/31	500

Instructions
After analyzing the accounts, journalize (a) the July transactions and (b) the adjusting entries that were made on July 31. (*Hint:* July transactions were for cash.)

E3-13 The trial balances before and after adjustment for Frinzi Company at the end of its fiscal year are presented below.

Prepare adjusting entries from analysis of trial balances.

(LO 2, 3, 4)

FRINZI COMPANY
Trial Balance
August 31, 2017

	Before Adjustment		After Adjustment	
	Dr.	**Cr.**	**Dr.**	**Cr.**
Cash	$10,400		$10,400	
Accounts Receivable	8,800		10,800	
Supplies	2,300		900	
Prepaid Insurance	4,000		2,500	
Equipment	14,000		14,000	
Accumulated Depreciation—Equipment		$ 3,600		$ 4,500
Accounts Payable		5,800		5,800
Salaries and Wages Payable		–0–		1,100
Unearned Rent Revenue		1,500		600
Common Stock		12,000		12,000
Retained Earnings		3,600		3,600
Service Revenue		34,000		36,000
Rent Revenue		11,000		11,900
Salaries and Wages Expense	17,000		18,100	
Supplies Expense	–0–		1,400	
Rent Expense	15,000		15,000	
Insurance Expense	–0–		1,500	
Depreciation Expense	–0–		900	
	$71,500	$71,500	$75,500	$75,500

Instructions

Prepare the adjusting entries that were made.

E3-14 The adjusted trial balance for Frinzi Company is given in E3-13.

Prepare financial statements from adjusted trial balance.

(LO 4)

Instructions

Prepare the income and retained earnings statements for the year and the balance sheet at August 31.

E3-15 The following data are taken from the comparative balance sheets of Cascade Billiards Club, which prepares its financial statements using the accrual basis of accounting.

Record transactions on accrual basis; convert revenue to cash receipts.

(LO 2, 3)

December 31	2017	2016
Accounts receivable from members	$14,000	$ 9,000
Unearned service revenue	17,000	25,000

Members are billed based upon their use of the club's facilities. Unearned service revenues arise from the sale of gift certificates, which members can apply to their future use of club facilities. The 2017 income statement for the club showed that service revenue of $161,000 was recorded during the year.

Instructions

(*Hint:* You will probably find it helpful to use T-accounts to analyze these data.)

(a) Prepare journal entries for each of the following events that took place during 2017.
  (1) Accounts receivable from 2016 were all collected.
  (2) Gift certificates outstanding at the end of 2016 were all redeemed.
  (3) An additional $38,000 worth of gift certificates were sold during 2017. A portion of these was used by the recipients during the year; the remainder was still outstanding at the end of 2017.
  (4) Services performed for members for 2017 were billed to members.
  (5) Accounts receivable for 2017 (i.e., those billed in item [4] above) were partially collected.

(b) Determine the amount of cash received by the club, with respect to member services, during 2017.

Journalize adjusting entries.

(LO 5)

*E3-16 Aaron Lynch Company has the following balances in selected accounts on December 31, 2017.

Service Revenue	$40,000
Insurance Expense	2,700
Supplies Expense	2,450

All the accounts have normal balances. Aaron Lynch Company debits prepayments to expense accounts when paid, and credits unearned revenues to revenue accounts when received. The following information below has been gathered at December 31, 2017.

1. Aaron Lynch Company paid $2,700 for 12 months of insurance coverage on June 1, 2017.
2. On December 1, 2017, Aaron Lynch Company collected $40,000 for consulting services to be performed from December 1, 2017, through March 31, 2018.
3. A count of supplies on December 31, 2017, indicates that supplies of $900 are on hand.

Instructions

Prepare the adjusting entries needed at December 31, 2017.

Journalize transactions and adjusting entries.

(LO 5)

*E3-17 At Cambridge Company, prepayments are debited to expense when paid, and unearned revenues are credited to revenue when cash is received. During January of the current year, the following transactions occurred.

Jan. 2   Paid $1,920 for fire insurance protection for the year.
     10   Paid $1,700 for supplies.
     15   Received $6,100 for services to be performed in the future.

On January 31, it is determined that $2,500 of the services were performed and that there are $650 of supplies on hand.

Instructions

(a) Journalize and post the January transactions. (Use T-accounts.)
(b) Journalize and post the adjusting entries at January 31.
(c) Determine the ending balance in each of the accounts.

Identify accounting assumptions and principles.

(LO 6)

*E3-18 Presented below are the assumptions and principles discussed in Appendix 3B.

1. Full disclosure principle.   4. Time period assumption.
2. Going concern assumption.   5. Historical cost principle.
3. Monetary unit assumption.   6. Economic entity assumption.

Instructions

Identify by number the accounting assumption or principle that is described below. Do not use a number more than once.

_____ (a) Is the rationale for why plant assets are not reported at liquidation value. (*Note:* Do not use the historical cost principle.)
_____ (b) Indicates that personal and business recordkeeping should be separately maintained.
_____ (c) Assumes that the monetary unit is the "measuring stick" used to report on financial performance.
_____ (d) Separates financial information into time periods for reporting purposes.
_____ (e) Measurement basis used when a reliable estimate of fair value is not available.
_____ (f) Dictates that companies should disclose all circumstances and events that make a difference to financial statement users.

Identify the assumption or principle that has been violated.

(LO 6)

*E3-19 Rosman Co. had three major business transactions during 2017.

(a) Reported at its fair value of $260,000 merchandise inventory with a cost of $208,000.
(b) The president of Rosman Co., Jay Rosman, purchased a truck for personal use and charged it to his Salaries and Wages Expense account.
(c) Rosman Co. wanted to make its 2017 income look better, so it added 2 more weeks to the year (a 54-week year). Previous years were 52 weeks.

Instructions

In each situation, identify the assumption or principle that has been violated, if any, and discuss what the company should have done.

*E3-20 The following characteristics, assumptions, principles, or constraint guide the FASB when it creates accounting standards.

Identify financial accounting concepts and principles.

(LO 6)

Relevance   Expense recognition principle
Faithful representation   Time period assumption
Comparability   Going concern assumption
Consistency   Historical cost principle
Monetary unit assumption   Full disclosure principle
Economic entity assumption   Materiality

Match each item above with a description below.

1. _____ Ability to easily evaluate one company's results relative to another's.
2. _____ Belief that a company will continue to operate for the foreseeable future.
3. _____ The judgment concerning whether an item's size is large enough to matter to decision-makers.
4. _____ The reporting of all information that would make a difference to financial statement users.
5. _____ The practice of preparing financial statements at regular intervals.
6. _____ The quality of information that indicates the information makes a difference in a decision.
7. _____ A belief that items should be reported on the balance sheet at the price that was paid to acquire them.
8. _____ A company's use of the same accounting principles and methods from year to year.
9. _____ Tracing accounting events to particular companies.
10. _____ The desire to minimize bias in financial statements.
11. _____ Reporting only those things that can be measured in monetary units.
12. _____ Dictates that efforts (expenses) be matched with results (revenues).

*E3-21 Net Nanny Software International Inc., headquartered in Vancouver, Canada, specializes in Internet safety and computer security products for both the home and commercial markets. In a recent balance sheet, it reported a deficit of US$5,678,288. It has reported only net losses since its inception. In spite of these losses, Net Nanny's shares of stock have traded anywhere from a high of $3.70 to a low of $0.32 on the Canadian Venture Exchange.

Comment on the objective and qualitative characteristics of accounting information.

(LO 6)

Net Nanny's financial statements have historically been prepared in Canadian dollars. Recently, the company adopted the U.S. dollar as its reporting currency.

Instructions

(a) What is the objective of financial reporting? How does this objective meet or not meet Net Nanny's investors' needs?
(b) Why would investors want to buy Net Nanny's shares if the company has consistently reported losses over the last few years? Include in your answer an assessment of the relevance of the information reported on Net Nanny's financial statements.
(c) Comment on how the change in reporting information from Canadian dollars to U.S. dollars likely affected the readers of Net Nanny's financial statements. Include in your answer an assessment of the comparability of the information.

*E3-22 A friend of yours, Ana Gehrig, recently completed an undergraduate degree in science and has just started working with an international biotechnology company. Ana tells you that the owners of the business are trying to secure new sources of financing which are needed in order for the company to proceed with development of a new health-care product. Ana said that her boss told her that the company must put together a report to present to potential investors.

Comment on the objective and qualitative characteristics of financial reporting.

(LO 6)

Ana thought that the company should include in this package the detailed scientific findings related to the Phase I clinical trials for this product. She said, "I know that the biotech industry sometimes has only a 10% success rate with new products, but if we report all the scientific findings, everyone will see what a sure success this is going to be! The president was talking about the importance of following some set of accounting principles. Why do we need to look at some accounting rules? What they need to realize is that we have scientific results that are quite encouraging, some of the most talented employees around, and the start of some really great customer relationships. We haven't made any sales yet, but we will. We just need the funds to get through all the clinical testing and get government approval for our product. Then these investors will be quite happy that they bought in to our company early!"

Instructions
(a) What is accounting information?
(b) Comment on how Ana's suggestions for what should be reported to prospective investors conforms to the qualitative characteristics of accounting information. Do you think that the things that Ana wants to include in the information for investors will conform to financial reporting guidelines?

EXERCISES: SET B AND CHALLENGE EXERCISES

Visit the book's companion website, at **www.wiley.com/college/weygandt**, and choose the Student Companion site to access Exercises: Set B and Challenge Exercises.

PROBLEMS: SET A

Prepare adjusting entries, post to ledger accounts, and prepare an adjusted trial balance.

(LO 2, 3, 4)

P3-1A Deanna Nardelli started her own consulting firm, Nardelli Consulting, on May 1, 2017. The trial balance at May 31 is as follows.

NARDELLI CONSULTING
Trial Balance
May 31, 2017

Account Number		Debit	Credit
101	Cash	$ 4,500	
112	Accounts Receivable	6,000	
126	Supplies	1,900	
130	Prepaid Insurance	3,600	
149	Equipment	11,400	
201	Accounts Payable		$ 2,200
209	Unearned Service Revenue		2,000
311	Common Stock		20,000
400	Service Revenue		7,500
726	Salaries and Wages Expense	3,400	
729	Rent Expense	900	
		$31,700	$31,700

In addition to those accounts listed on the trial balance, the chart of accounts for Nardelli Consulting also contains the following accounts and account numbers: No. 150 Accumulated Depreciation—Equipment, No. 212 Salaries and Wages Payable, No. 631 Supplies Expense, No. 717 Depreciation Expense, No. 722 Insurance Expense, and No. 732 Utilities Expense.

Other data:

1. $900 of supplies have been used during the month.
2. Utilities expense incurred but not paid on May 31, 2017, $250.
3. The insurance policy is for 2 years.
4. $400 of the balance in the unearned service revenue account remains unearned at the end of the month.
5. May 31 is a Wednesday, and employees are paid on Fridays. Nardelli Consulting has two employees, who are paid $900 each for a 5-day work week.
6. The equipment has a 5-year life with no salvage value. It is being depreciated at $190 per month for 60 months.
7. Invoices representing $1,700 of services performed during the month have not been recorded as of May 31.

Instructions
(a) Prepare the adjusting entries for the month of May. Use J4 as the page number for your journal.
(b) Enter the totals from the trial balance as beginning account balances and place a check mark in the posting reference column. Post the adjusting entries to the ledger accounts.
(c) Prepare an adjusted trial balance at May 31, 2017.

(c) Adj. trial balance $34,920

P3-2A The Skyline Motel opened for business on May 1, 2017. Its trial balance before adjustment on May 31 is as follows.

Prepare adjusting entries, post, and prepare adjusted trial balance and financial statements.

(LO 2, 3, 4)

SKYLINE MOTEL
Trial Balance
May 31, 2017

Account Number		Debit	Credit
101	Cash	$ 3,500	
126	Supplies	2,080	
130	Prepaid Insurance	2,400	
140	Land	12,000	
141	Buildings	60,000	
149	Equipment	15,000	
201	Accounts Payable		$11,180
208	Unearned Rent Revenue		3,300
275	Mortgage Payable		40,000
311	Common Stock		35,000
429	Rent Revenue		10,300
610	Advertising Expense	600	
726	Salaries and Wages Expense	3,300	
732	Utilities Expense	900	
		$99,780	$99,780

In addition to those accounts listed on the trial balance, the chart of accounts for Skyline Motel also contains the following accounts and account numbers: No. 142 Accumulated Depreciation—Buildings, No. 150 Accumulated Depreciation—Equipment, No. 212 Salaries and Wages Payable, No. 230 Interest Payable, No. 619 Depreciation Expense, No. 631 Supplies Expense, No. 718 Interest Expense, and No. 722 Insurance Expense.

Other data:

1. Prepaid insurance is a 1-year policy starting May 1, 2017.
2. A count of supplies shows $750 of unused supplies on May 31.
3. Annual depreciation is $3,000 on the buildings and $1,500 on equipment.
4. The mortgage interest rate is 12%. (The mortgage was taken out on May 1.)
5. Two-thirds of the unearned rent revenue has been earned.
6. Salaries of $750 are accrued and unpaid at May 31.

Instructions
(a) Journalize the adjusting entries on May 31.
(b) Prepare a ledger using the three-column form of account. Enter the trial balance amounts and post the adjusting entries. (Use J1 as the posting reference.)
(c) Prepare an adjusted trial balance on May 31.
(d) Prepare an income statement and a retained earnings statement for the month of May and a balance sheet at May 31.

(c) Adj. trial balance $101,305
(d) Net income $4,645
Ending retained earnings $4,645
Total assets $93,075

P3-3A Everett Co. was organized on July 1, 2017. Quarterly financial statements are prepared. The unadjusted and adjusted trial balances as of September 30 are shown on the next page.

Prepare adjusting entries and financial statements.

(LO 2, 3, 4)

EVERETT CO.
Trial Balance
September 30, 2017

	Unadjusted Dr.	Unadjusted Cr.	Adjusted Dr.	Adjusted Cr.
Cash	$ 8,700		$ 8,700	
Accounts Receivable	10,400		11,500	
Supplies	1,500		650	
Prepaid Rent	2,200		1,200	
Equipment	18,000		18,000	
Accumulated Depreciation—Equipment		$ –0–		$ 700
Notes Payable		10,000		10,000
Accounts Payable		2,500		2,500
Salaries and Wages Payable		–0–		725
Interest Payable		–0–		100
Unearned Rent Revenue		1,900		1,050
Common Stock		22,000		22,000
Dividends	1,600		1,600	
Service Revenue		16,000		17,100
Rent Revenue		1,410		2,260
Salaries and Wages Expense	8,000		8,725	
Rent Expense	1,900		2,900	
Depreciation Expense			700	
Supplies Expense			850	
Utilities Expense	1,510		1,510	
Interest Expense			100	
	$53,810	$53,810	$56,435	$56,435

Instructions

(a) Journalize the adjusting entries that were made.
(b) Prepare an income statement and a retained earnings statement for the 3 months ending September 30 and a balance sheet at September 30.
(c) If the note bears interest at 12%, how many months has it been outstanding?

(b) Net income $4,575
Ending retained
earnings $2,975
Total assets $39,350

Prepare adjusting entries.

(LO 2, 3)

1. Insurance expense $4,890

2. Rent revenue $84,000

3. Interest expense $1,800

4. Salaries and wages
   expense $2,000

P3-4A A review of the ledger of Carmel Company at December 31, 2017, produces the following data pertaining to the preparation of annual adjusting entries.

1. Prepaid Insurance $10,440. The company has separate insurance policies on its buildings and its motor vehicles. Policy B4564 on the building was purchased on April 1, 2016, for $7,920. The policy has a term of 3 years. Policy A2958 on the vehicles was purchased on January 1, 2017, for $4,500. This policy has a term of 2 years.

2. Unearned Rent Revenue $429,000. The company began subleasing office space in its new building on November 1. At December 31, the company had the following rental contracts that are paid in full for the entire term of the lease.

Date	Term (in months)	Monthly Rent	Number of Leases
Nov. 1	9	$5,000	5
Dec. 1	6	$8,500	4

3. Notes Payable $120,000. This balance consists of a note for 9 months at an annual interest rate of 9%, dated November 1.

4. Salaries and Wages Payable $0. There are eight salaried employees. Salaries are paid every Friday for the current week. Five employees receive a salary of $700 each per week, and three employees earn $500 each per week. Assume December 31 is a Tuesday. Employees do not work weekends. All employees worked the last 2 days of December.

Instructions

Prepare the adjusting entries at December 31, 2017.

P3-5A On November 1, 2017, the account balances of Schilling Equipment Repair were as follows.

No.		Debit	No.		Credit
101	Cash	$ 2,400	154	Accumulated Depreciation—Equipment	$ 2,000
112	Accounts Receivable	4,250	201	Accounts Payable	2,600
126	Supplies	1,800	209	Unearned Service Revenue	1,200
153	Equipment	12,000	212	Salaries and Wages Payable	700
			311	Common Stock	10,000
			320	Retained Earnings	3,950
		$20,450			$20,450

Journalize transactions and follow through accounting cycle to preparation of financial statements.

(LO 2, 3, 4)

 GLS

During November, the following summary transactions were completed.

Nov. 8 Paid $1,700 for salaries due employees, of which $700 is for October salaries.
   10 Received $3,420 cash from customers on account.
   12 Received $3,100 cash for services performed in November.
   15 Purchased equipment on account $2,000.
   17 Purchased supplies on account $700.
   20 Paid creditors on account $2,700.
   22 Paid November rent $400.
   25 Paid salaries $1,700.
   27 Performed services on account and billed customers $1,900 for these services.
   29 Received $600 from customers for future service.

Adjustment data consist of:

1. Supplies on hand $1,400.
2. Accrued salaries payable $350.
3. Depreciation for the month is $200.
4. Services related to unearned service revenue of $1,250 were performed.

Instructions

(a) Enter the November 1 balances in the ledger accounts.
(b) Journalize the November transactions.
(c) Post to the ledger accounts. Use J1 for the posting reference. Use the following additional accounts: No. 407 Service Revenue, No. 615 Depreciation Expense, No. 631 Supplies Expense, No. 726 Salaries and Wages Expense, and No. 729 Rent Expense.
(d) Prepare a trial balance at November 30.
(e) Journalize and post adjusting entries.
(f) Prepare an adjusted trial balance.
(g) Prepare an income statement and a retained earnings statement for November and a balance sheet at November 30.

(d) Trial balance $25,350
(f) Adj. trial balance $25,900
(g) Net income $1,500
   Ending retained earnings $5,450
   Total assets $18,950

*P3-6A Sommer Graphics Company was organized on January 1, 2017, by Krystal Sommer. At the end of the first 6 months of operations, the trial balance contained the accounts shown below.

Prepare adjusting entries, adjusted trial balance, and financial statements using Appendix 3A.

(LO 2, 3, 4, 5)

	Debit		Credit
Cash	$ 8,600	Notes Payable	$ 20,000
Accounts Receivable	14,000	Accounts Payable	9,000
Equipment	45,000	Common Stock	22,000
Insurance Expense	2,700	Sales Revenue	52,100
Salaries and Wages Expense	30,000	Service Revenue	6,000
Supplies Expense	3,700		
Advertising Expense	1,900		
Rent Expense	1,500		
Utilities Expense	1,700		
	$109,100		$109,100

Analysis reveals the following additional data.

1. The $3,700 balance in Supplies Expense represents supplies purchased in January. At June 30, $1,500 of supplies are on hand.
2. The note payable was issued on February 1. It is a 9%, 6-month note.
3. The balance in Insurance Expense is the premium on a one-year policy, dated March 1, 2017.
4. Service revenues are credited to revenue when received. At June 30, services revenue of $1,300 are unearned.
5. Revenue for services performed but unrecorded at June 30 totals $2,000.
6. Depreciation is $2,250 per year.

Instructions

(b) Adj. trial balance $112,975
(c) Net income $18,725
   Ending retained earnings
   $18,725
   Total assets $71,775

(a) Journalize the adjusting entries at June 30. (Assume adjustments are recorded every 6 months.)
(b) Prepare an adjusted trial balance.
(c) Prepare an income statement and a retained earnings statement for the 6 months ended June 30 and a balance sheet at June 30.

PROBLEMS: SET B AND SET C

Visit the book's companion website, at **www.wiley.com/college/weygandt**, and choose the Student Companion site to access Problems: Set B and Set C.

CONTINUING PROBLEM

© leungchopan/
Shutterstock

COOKIE CREATIONS

(*Note:* This is a continuation of the Cookie Creations problem from Chapters 1 and 2.)

CC3 It is the end of November and Natalie has been in touch with her grandmother. Her grandmother asked Natalie how well things went in her first month of business. Natalie, too, would like to know if she has been profitable or not during November. Natalie realizes that in order to determine Cookie Creations' income, she must first make adjustments.

Go to the book's companion website, **www.wiley.com/college/weygandt**, *to see the completion of this problem.*

BROADENING YOUR PERSPECTIVE

FINANCIAL REPORTING AND ANALYSIS

Financial Reporting Problem: Apple Inc.

BYP3-1 The financial statements of Apple Inc. are presented in Appendix A at the end of this textbook. Instructions for accessing and using the company's complete annual report, including the notes to the financial statements, are also provided in Appendix A.

Instructions

(a) Using the consolidated financial statements and related information, identify items that may result in adjusting entries for prepayments.
(b) Using the consolidated financial statements and related information, identify items that may result in adjusting entries for accruals.
(c) What has been the trend since 2011 for net income?

Comparative Analysis Problem:
PepsiCo, Inc. vs. The Coca-Cola Company

BYP3-2 PepsiCo's financial statements are presented in Appendix B. Financial statements of The Coca-Cola Company are presented in Appendix C. Instructions for accessing and using the complete annual reports of PepsiCo and Coca-Cola, including the notes to the financial statements, are also provided in Appendices B and C, respectively.

Instructions

Based on information contained in these financial statements, determine the following for each company.

(a) Net increase (decrease) in property, plant, and equipment (net) from 2012 to 2013.
(b) Increase (decrease) in selling, general, and administrative expenses from 2012 to 2013.
(c) Increase (decrease) in long-term debt (obligations) from 2012 to 2013.
(d) Increase (decrease) in net income from 2012 to 2013.
(e) Increase (decrease) in cash and cash equivalents from 2012 to 2013.

Comparative Analysis Problem:
Amazon.com, Inc. vs. Wal-Mart Stores, Inc.

BYP3-3 Amazon.com, Inc.'s financial statements are presented in Appendix D. Financial statements of Wal-Mart Stores, Inc. are presented in Appendix E. Instructions for accessing and using the complete annual reports of Amazon and Wal-Mart, including the notes to the financial statements, are also provided in Appendices D and E, respectively.

Instructions

Based on information contained in these financial statements, determine the following for each company.

1. (a) Increase (decrease) in interest expense from 2012 to 2013.
   (b) Increase (decrease) in net income from 2012 to 2013.
   (c) Increase (decrease) in cash flow from operations from 2012 to 2013.
2. Cash flow from operations and net income for each company is different. What are some possible reasons for these differences?

Real-World Focus

BYP3-4 No financial decision-maker should ever rely solely on the financial information reported in the annual report to make decisions. It is important to keep abreast of financial news. This activity demonstrates how to search for financial news on the Internet.

Address: **http://biz.yahoo.com/i**, or go to **www.wiley.com/college/weygandt**

Steps:
1. Type in either Wal-Mart, Target Corp., or Kmart.
2. Choose **News**.
3. Select an article that sounds interesting to you and that would be relevant to an investor in these companies.

Instructions
(a) What was the source of the article (e.g., Reuters, Businesswire, Prnewswire)?
(b) Assume that you are a personal financial planner and that one of your clients owns stock in the company. Write a brief memo to your client summarizing the article and explaining the implications of the article for their investment.

BYP3-5 The July 6, 2011, edition of the *Wall Street Journal Online* includes an article by Michael Rapoport entitled "U.S. Firms Clash Over Accounting Rules." The article discusses why some U.S. companies favored adoption of International Financial Reporting Standards (IFRS) while other companies opposed it.

Instructions
Read the article and answer the following questions.

(a) The articles says that the switch to IFRS tends to be favored by "larger companies, big accounting firms, and rule makers." What reasons are given for favoring the switch?

(b) What two reasons are given by many smaller companies that oppose the switch?
(c) What criticism of IFRS is raised with regard to regulated companies?
(d) Explain what is meant by "condorsement."

CRITICAL THINKING

Decision-Making Across the Organization

BYP3-6 Happy Camper Park, Inc. was organized on April 1, 2016, by Barbara Evans. Barbara is a good manager but a poor accountant. From the trial balance prepared by a part-time book-keeper, Barbara prepared the following income statement for the quarter that ended March 31, 2017.

HAPPY CAMPER PARK, INC.
Income Statement
For the Quarter Ended March 31, 2017

Revenues		
Rent revenue		$ 90,000
Operating expenses		
Advertising	$ 5,200	
Salaries and wages	29,800	
Utilities	900	
Depreciation	800	
Maintenance and repairs	4,000	
Total operating expenses		40,700
Net income		$ 49,300

Barbara thought that something was wrong with the statement because net income had never exceeded $20,000 in any one quarter. Knowing that you are an experienced accountant, she asks you to review the income statement and other data.

You first look at the trial balance. In addition to the account balances reported above in the income statement, the ledger contains the following additional selected balances at March 31, 2017.

Supplies	$ 6,200
Prepaid Insurance	7,200
Notes Payable	12,000

You then make inquiries and discover the following.

1. Rent revenues include advanced rentals for summer occupancy $15,000.
2. There were $1,700 of supplies on hand at March 31.
3. Prepaid insurance resulted from the payment of a one-year policy on January 1, 2017.
4. The mail on April 1, 2017, brought the following bills: advertising for week of March 24, $110; repairs made March 10, $260; and utilities, $180.
5. There are four employees who receive wages totaling $300 per day. At March 31, 2 days' salaries and wages have been incurred but not paid.
6. The note payable is a 3-month, 10% note dated January 1, 2017.

Instructions
With the class divided into groups, answer the following.

(a) Prepare a correct income statement for the quarter ended March 31, 2017.
(b) Explain to Barbara the generally accepted accounting principles that she did not recognize in preparing her income statement and their effect on her results.

Communication Activity

BYP3-7 In reviewing the accounts of Gloria Jean Co. at the end of the year, you discover that adjusting entries have not been made.

Instructions
Write a memo to Gloria Jean Hall, the owner of Gloria Jean Co., that explains the following: the nature and purpose of adjusting entries, why adjusting entries are needed, and the types of adjusting entries that may be made.

Ethics Case

BYP3-8 Kellner Company is a pesticide manufacturer. Its sales declined greatly this year due to the passage of legislation outlawing the sale of several of Kellner's chemical pesticides. In the coming year, Kellner will have environmentally safe and competitive chemicals to replace these discontinued products. Sales in the next year are expected to greatly exceed any prior year's. The decline in sales and profits appears to be a one-year aberration. But even so, the company president fears a large dip in the current year's profits. He believes that such a dip could cause a significant drop in the market price of Kellner's stock and make the company a takeover target.

To avoid this possibility, the company president calls in Melissa Ray, controller, to discuss this period's year-end adjusting entries. He urges her to accrue every possible revenue and to defer as many expenses as possible. He says to Melissa, "We need the revenues this year, and next year can easily absorb expenses deferred from this year. We can't let our stock price be hammered down!" Melissa didn't get around to recording the adjusting entries until January 17, but she dated the entries December 31 as if they were recorded then. Melissa also made every effort to comply with the president's request.

Instructions
(a) Who are the stakeholders in this situation?
(b) What are the ethical considerations of (1) the president's request and (2) Melissa dating the adjusting entries December 31?
(c) Can Melissa accrue revenues and defer expenses and still be ethical?

All About You

BYP3-9 Companies must report or disclose in their financial statements information about all liabilities, including potential liabilities related to environmental cleanup. There are many situations in which you will be asked to provide personal financial information about your assets, liabilities, revenue, and expenses. Sometimes you will face difficult decisions regarding what to disclose and how to disclose it.

Instructions
Suppose that you are putting together a loan application to purchase a home. Based on your income and assets, you qualify for the mortgage loan, but just barely. How would you address each of the following situations in reporting your financial position for the loan application? Provide responses for each of the following situations.

(a) You signed a guarantee for a bank loan that a friend took out for $20,000. If your friend doesn't pay, you will have to pay. Your friend has made all of the payments so far, and it appears he will be able to pay in the future.
(b) You were involved in an auto accident in which you were at fault. There is the possibility that you may have to pay as much as $50,000 as part of a settlement. The issue will not be resolved before the bank processes your mortgage request.
(c) The company for which you work isn't doing very well, and it has recently laid off employees. You are still employed, but it is quite possible that you will lose your job in the next few months.

Considering People, Planet, and Profit

BYP3-10 Many companies have potential pollution or environmental-disposal problems—not only for electronic gadgets, but also for the lead paint or asbestos they sold. How do we fit these issues into the accounting equation? Are these costs and related liabilities that companies should report?

YES: As more states impose laws holding companies responsible, and as more courts levy pollution-related fines, it becomes increasingly likely that companies will have to pay large amounts in the future.

NO: The amounts still are too difficult to estimate. Putting inaccurate estimates on the financial statements reduces their usefulness. Instead, why not charge the costs later, when the actual environmental cleanup or disposal occurs, at which time the company knows the actual cost?

Instructions
Write a response indicating your position regarding this situation. Provide support for your view.

FASB Codification Activity

BYP3-11 If your school has a subscription to the FASB Codification, go to **http://aaahq.org/asclogin. cfm** to log in and prepare responses to the following.

Instructions
Access the glossary ("Master Glossary") to answer the following.

(a) What is the definition of revenue?
(b) What is the definition of compensation?

 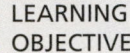

A Look at IFRS

| LEARNING OBJECTIVE **7** | **Compare the procedures for adjusting entries under GAAP and IFRS.** |

It is often difficult for companies to determine in what time period they should report particular revenues and expenses. Both the IASB and FASB are working on a joint project to develop a common conceptual framework that will enable companies to better use the same principles to record transactions consistently over time.

Key Points

Following are the key similarities and differences between GAAP and IFRS as related to accrual accounting.

Similarities

- In this chapter, you learned accrual-basis accounting applied under GAAP. Companies applying IFRS also use accrual-basis accounting to ensure that they record transactions that change a company's financial statements in the period in which events occur.
- Similar to GAAP, cash-basis accounting is not in accordance with IFRS.
- IFRS also divides the economic life of companies into artificial time periods. Under both GAAP and IFRS, this is referred to as the **time period assumption**.
- The **general** revenue recognition principle required by GAAP that is used in this textbook is similar to that used under IFRS.
- Revenue recognition fraud is a major issue in U.S. financial reporting. The same situation occurs in other countries, as evidenced by revenue recognition breakdowns at Dutch software company **Baan NV**, Japanese electronics giant **NEC**, and Dutch grocer **Ahold NV**.

Differences

- Under IFRS, revaluation (using fair value) of items such as land and buildings is permitted. IFRS allows depreciation based on revaluation of assets, which is not permitted under GAAP.
- The terminology used for revenues and gains, and expenses and losses, differs somewhat between IFRS and GAAP. For example, income under IFRS includes both revenues, which arise during the normal course of operating activities, and gains, which arise from activities outside of the normal sales of goods and services. The term income is not used this way under GAAP. Instead, under GAAP income refers to the net difference between revenues and expenses.
- Under IFRS, expenses include both those costs incurred in the normal course of operations as well as losses that are not part of normal operations. This is in contrast to GAAP, which defines each separately.

Looking to the Future

The IASB and FASB are completing a joint project on revenue recognition. The purpose of this project is to develop comprehensive guidance on when to recognize revenue. It is hoped that this approach will lead to more consistent accounting in this area. For more on this topic, see **www.fasb.org/project/revenue_recognition.shtml**.

IFRS Practice

IFRS Self-Test Questions

1. IFRS:
   (a) uses accrual accounting.
   (b) uses cash-basis accounting.
   (c) allows revenue to be recognized when a customer makes an order.
   (d) requires that revenue not be recognized until cash is received.

2. Which of the following statements is **false**?
   (a) IFRS employs the time period assumption.
   (b) IFRS employs accrual accounting.
   (c) IFRS requires that revenues and costs must be capable of being measured reliably.
   (d) IFRS uses the cash basis of accounting.

3. As a result of the revenue recognition project by the FASB and IASB:
   (a) revenue recognition places more emphasis on when the performance obligation is satisfied.
   (b) revenue recognition places more emphasis on when revenue is realized.
   (c) revenue recognition places more emphasis on when expenses are incurred.
   (d) revenue is no longer recorded unless cash has been received.

4. Which of the following is **false**?
   (a) Under IFRS, the term income describes both revenues and gains.
   (b) Under IFRS, the term expenses includes losses.
   (c) Under IFRS, companies do not engage in the adjusting process.
   (d) Under IFRS, revenue recognition fraud is a major issue.

5. Accrual-basis accounting:
   (a) is optional under IFRS.
   (b) results in companies recording transactions that change a company's financial statements in the period in which events occur.
   (c) has been eliminated as a result of the IASB/FASB joint project on revenue recognition.
   (d) is not consistent with the IASB conceptual framework.

International Financial Reporting Problem: Louis Vuitton

IFRS3-1 The financial statements of Louis Vuitton are presented in Appendix F. Instructions for accessing and using the company's complete annual report, including the notes to its financial statements, are also provided in Appendix F.

Instructions

Visit Louis Vuitton's corporate website and answer the following questions from Louis Vuitton's 2013 annual report.

(a) From the notes to the financial statements, how does the company determine the amount of revenue to record at the time of a sale?

(b) From the notes to the financial statements, how does the company determine the provision for product returns?

(c) Using the consolidated income statement and consolidated statement of financial position, identify items that may result in adjusting entries for deferrals.

(d) Using the consolidated income statement, identify two items that may result in adjusting entries for accruals.

Answers to IFRS Self-Test Questions
1. a   **2.** d   **3.** a   **4.** c   **5.** b

4 Completing the Accounting Cycle

CHAPTER PREVIEW As the Feature Story below highlights, at Rhino Foods, Inc., financial statements help employees understand what is happening in the business. In Chapter 3, we prepared financial statements directly from the adjusted trial balance. However, with so many details involved in the end-of-period accounting procedures, it is easy to make errors. One way to minimize errors in the records and to simplify the end-of-period procedures is to use a worksheet.

In this chapter, we will explain the role of the worksheet in accounting. We also will study the remaining steps in the accounting cycle, especially the closing process, again using Pioneer Advertising Inc. as an example. Then we will consider correcting entries and classified balance sheets.

FEATURE STORY

Everyone Likes to Win

When Ted Castle was a hockey coach at the University of Vermont, his players were self-motivated by their desire to win. Hockey was a game you usually either won or lost. But at Rhino Foods, Inc., a bakery-foods company he founded in Burlington, Vermont, he discovered that manufacturing-line workers were not so self-motivated. Ted thought, what if he turned the food-making business into a game, with rules, strategies, and trophies?

In a game, knowing the score is all-important. Ted felt that only if the employees know the score—know exactly how the business is doing daily, weekly, monthly—could he turn food-making into a game. But Rhino is a closely held, family-owned business, and its financial statements and profits were confidential. Ted wondered, should he open Rhino's books to the employees?

A consultant put Ted's concerns in perspective when he said, "Imagine you're playing touch football. You play for an hour or two, and the whole time I'm sitting there with a book, keeping score. All of a sudden I blow the whistle,

and I say, 'OK, that's it. Everybody go home.' I close my book and walk away. How would you feel?" Ted opened his books and revealed the financial statements to his employees.

The next step was to teach employees the rules and strategies of how to "win" at making food. The first lesson: "Your opponent at Rhino is expenses. You must cut and control expenses." Ted and his staff distilled those lessons into daily scorecards—production reports and income statements—that keep Rhino's employees up-to-date on the game. At noon each day, Ted posts the previous day's results at the entrance to the production room. Everyone checks whether they made or lost money on what they produced the day before. And it's not just an academic exercise: There's a bonus check for each employee at the end of every four-week "game" that meets profitability guidelines.

Rhino has flourished since the first game. Employment has increased from 20 to 130 people, while both revenues and profits have grown dramatically.

Comstock/Getty Images, Inc.

CHAPTER OUTLINE

Learning Objectives

1 **Prepare a worksheet.**
- Steps in preparing a worksheet
- Preparing financial statements from a worksheet
- Preparing adjusting entries from a worksheet

DO IT! **1** Worksheet

2 **Prepare closing entries and a post-closing trial balance.**
- Preparing closing entries
- Posting closing entries
- Preparing a post-closing trial balance

DO IT! **2** Closing Entries

3 **Explain the steps in the accounting cycle and how to prepare correcting entries.**
- Summary of the accounting cycle
- Reversing entries
- Correcting entries

DO IT! **3** Correcting Entries

4 **Identify the sections of a classified balance sheet.**
- Current assets
- Long-term investments
- Property, plant, and equipment
- Intangible assets
- Current liabilities
- Long-term liabilities
- Stockholders' (owners') equity

DO IT! **4** Balance Sheet Classifications

Go to the **REVIEW AND PRACTICE** section at the end of the chapter for a review of key concepts and practice applications with solutions.

Visit **WileyPLUS with ORION** for additional tutorials and practice opportunities.

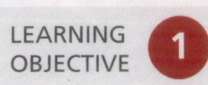

LEARNING OBJECTIVE 1

Prepare a worksheet.

A **worksheet** is a multiple-column form used in the adjustment process and in preparing financial statements. As its name suggests, the worksheet is a working tool. **It is not a permanent accounting record.** It is neither a journal nor a part of the general ledger. The worksheet is merely a device used in preparing adjusting entries and the financial statements. Companies generally computerize worksheets using an electronic spreadsheet program such as Excel.

Illustration 4-1 shows the basic form of a worksheet and the five steps for preparing it. Each step is performed in sequence. **The use of a worksheet is optional.** When a company chooses to use one, it prepares financial statements directly from the worksheet. It enters the adjustments in the worksheet columns and then journalizes and posts the adjustments after it has prepared the financial statements. Thus, worksheets make it possible to provide the financial statements to management and other interested parties at an earlier date.

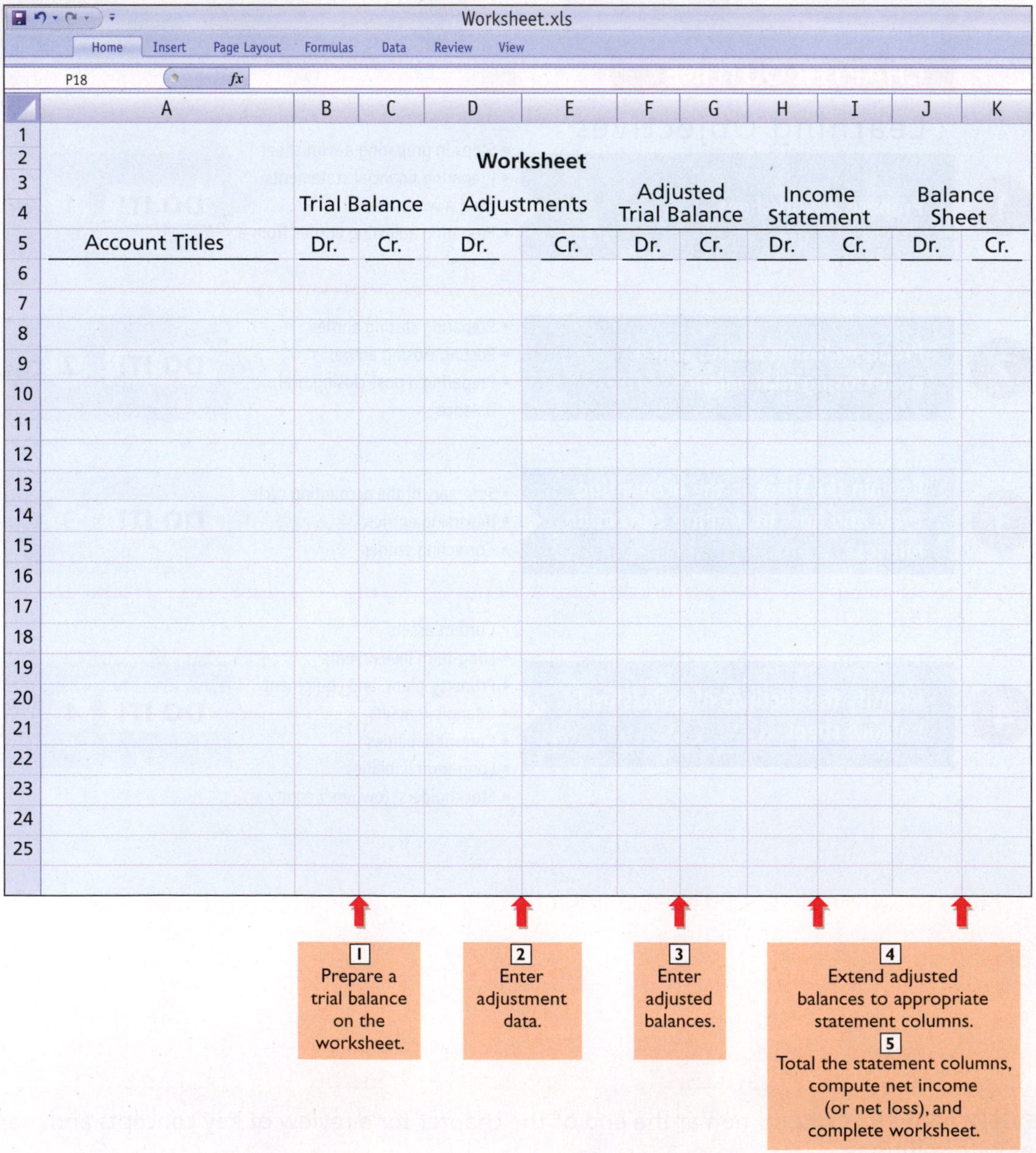

Worksheet.xls
Home
Insert
Page Layout
Formulas
Data
Review
View
P18
fx
A B C D E F G H I J K
Worksheet
Trial Balance
Adjustments
Adjusted Trial Balance
Income Statement
Balance Sheet
Account Titles
Dr. Cr. Dr. Cr. Dr. Cr. Dr. Cr. Dr. Cr.
1 Prepare a trial balance on the worksheet.
2 Enter adjustment data.
3 Enter adjusted balances.
4 Extend adjusted balances to appropriate statement columns.
5 Total the statement columns, compute net income (or net loss), and complete worksheet.

Illustration 4-1
Form and procedure for a worksheet

Steps in Preparing a Worksheet

We will use the October 31 trial balance and adjustment data of Pioneer Advertising Inc. from Chapter 3 to illustrate how to prepare a worksheet. We describe each step of the process and demonstrate these steps in Illustration 4-2 (page 154).

STEP 1. PREPARE A TRIAL BALANCE ON THE WORKSHEET

Enter all ledger accounts with balances in the account titles column. Enter debit and credit amounts from the ledger in the trial balance columns. Illustration 4-2 shows the worksheet trial balance for Pioneer Advertising Inc. This trial balance is the same one that appears in Illustration 2-32 (page 69) and Illustration 3-3 (page 99).

STEP 2. ENTER THE ADJUSTMENTS IN THE ADJUSTMENTS COLUMNS

When using a worksheet, enter all adjustments in the adjustments columns. In entering the adjustments, use applicable trial balance accounts. If additional accounts are needed, insert them on the lines immediately below the trial balance totals. A different letter identifies the debit and credit for each adjusting entry. The term used to describe this process is **keying**. **Companies do not journalize the adjustments until after they complete the worksheet and prepare the financial statements.**

The adjustments for Pioneer Advertising Inc. are the same as the adjustments in Illustration 3-23 (page 111). They are keyed in the adjustments columns of the worksheet as follows.

(a) Pioneer debits an additional account, Supplies Expense, $1,500 for the cost of supplies used, and credits Supplies $1,500.

(b) Pioneer debits an additional account, Insurance Expense, $50 for the insurance that has expired, and credits Prepaid Insurance $50.

(c) The company needs two additional depreciation accounts. It debits Depreciation Expense $40 for the month's depreciation, and credits Accumulated Depreciation—Equipment $40.

(d) Pioneer debits Unearned Service Revenue $400 for services performed, and credits Service Revenue $400.

(e) Pioneer debits an additional account, Accounts Receivable, $200 for services performed but not billed, and credits Service Revenue $200.

(f) The company needs two additional accounts relating to interest. It debits Interest Expense $50 for accrued interest, and credits Interest Payable $50.

(g) Pioneer debits Salaries and Wages Expense $1,200 for accrued salaries, and credits an additional account, Salaries and Wages Payable, $1,200.

After Pioneer has entered all the adjustments, the adjustments columns are totaled to prove their equality.

STEP 3. ENTER ADJUSTED BALANCES IN THE ADJUSTED TRIAL BALANCE COLUMNS

Pioneer determines the adjusted balance of an account by combining the amounts entered in the first four columns of the worksheet for each account. For example, the Prepaid Insurance account in the trial balance columns has a $600 debit balance and a $50 credit in the adjustments columns. The result is a $550 debit balance recorded in the adjusted trial balance columns. **For each account, the amount in the adjusted trial balance columns is the balance that will appear in the ledger after journalizing and posting the adjusting entries.** The balances in these columns are the same as those in the adjusted trial balance in Illustration 3-25 (page 114).

Illustration 4-2

Preparing a trial balance

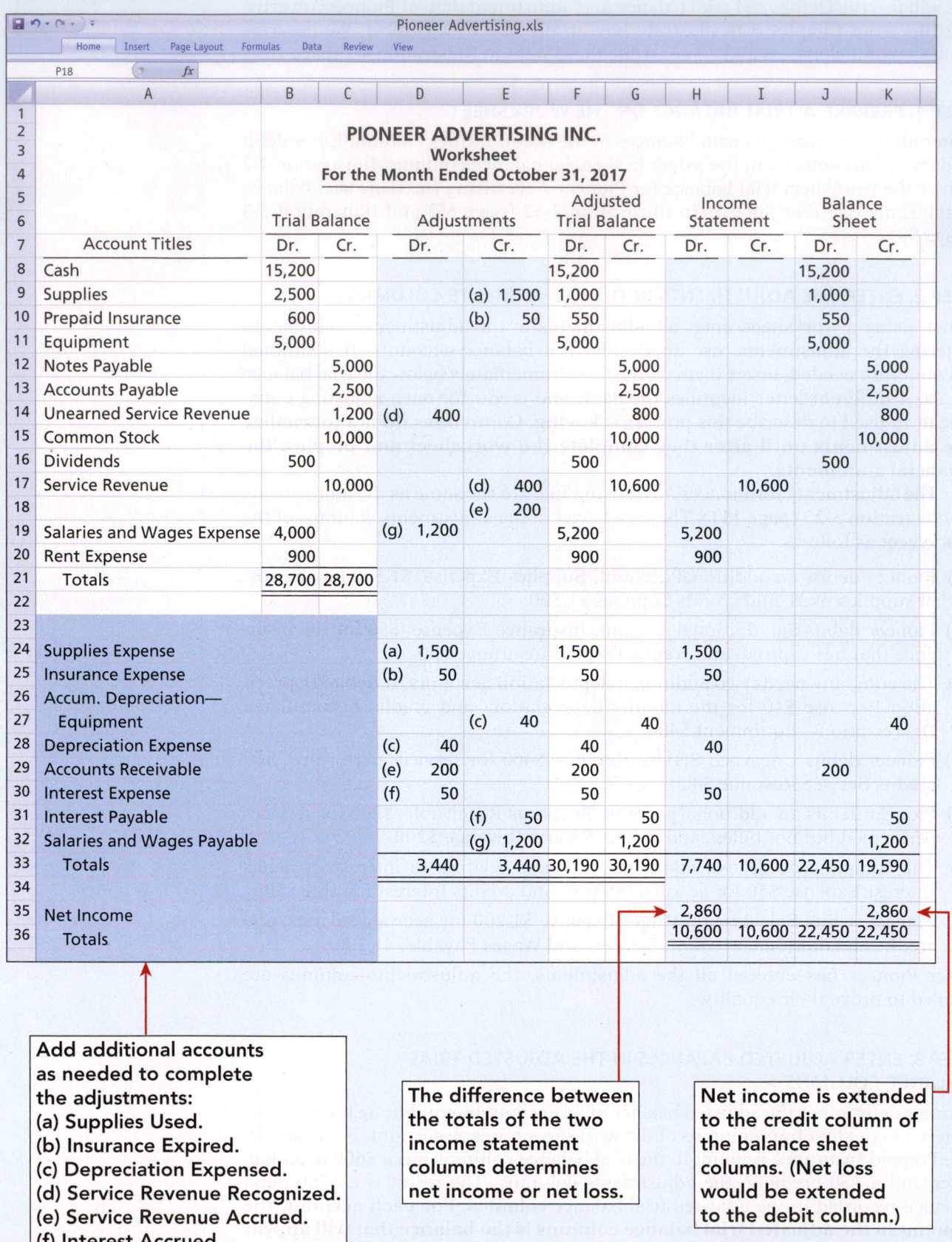

| Pioneer Advertising.xls |
| Home Insert Page Layout Formulas Data Review View |

PIONEER ADVERTISING INC.
Worksheet
For the Month Ended October 31, 2017

Account Titles	Trial Balance Dr.	Trial Balance Cr.	Adjustments Dr.	Adjustments Cr.	Adjusted Trial Balance Dr.	Adjusted Trial Balance Cr.	Income Statement Dr.	Income Statement Cr.	Balance Sheet Dr.	Balance Sheet Cr.
Cash	15,200				15,200				15,200	
Supplies	2,500			(a) 1,500	1,000				1,000	
Prepaid Insurance	600			(b) 50	550				550	
Equipment	5,000				5,000				5,000	
Notes Payable		5,000				5,000				5,000
Accounts Payable		2,500				2,500				2,500
Unearned Service Revenue		1,200	(d) 400			800				800
Common Stock		10,000				10,000				10,000
Dividends	500				500				500	
Service Revenue		10,000		(d) 400		10,600		10,600		
				(e) 200						
Salaries and Wages Expense	4,000		(g) 1,200		5,200		5,200			
Rent Expense	900				900		900			
Totals	28,700	28,700								
Supplies Expense			(a) 1,500		1,500		1,500			
Insurance Expense			(b) 50		50		50			
Accum. Depreciation—										
Equipment				(c) 40		40				40
Depreciation Expense			(c) 40		40		40			
Accounts Receivable			(e) 200		200				200	
Interest Expense			(f) 50		50		50			
Interest Payable				(f) 50		50				50
Salaries and Wages Payable				(g) 1,200		1,200				1,200
Totals			3,440	3,440	30,190	30,190	7,740	10,600	22,450	19,590
Net Income							2,860			2,860
Totals							10,600	10,600	22,450	22,450

Add additional accounts as needed to complete the adjustments:
(a) Supplies Used.
(b) Insurance Expired.
(c) Depreciation Expensed.
(d) Service Revenue Recognized.
(e) Service Revenue Accrued.
(f) Interest Accrued.
(g) Salaries Accrued.

The difference between the totals of the two income statement columns determines net income or net loss.

Net income is extended to the credit column of the balance sheet columns. (Net loss would be extended to the debit column.)

After Pioneer has entered all account balances in the adjusted trial balance columns, the columns are totaled to prove their equality. If the column totals do not agree, the financial statement columns will not balance and the financial statements will be incorrect.

STEP 4. EXTEND ADJUSTED TRIAL BALANCE AMOUNTS TO APPROPRIATE FINANCIAL STATEMENT COLUMNS

The fourth step is to extend adjusted trial balance amounts to the income statement and balance sheet columns of the worksheet. Pioneer enters balance sheet accounts in the appropriate balance sheet debit and credit columns. For instance, it enters Cash in the balance sheet debit column, and Notes Payable in the balance sheet credit column. Pioneer extends Accumulated Depreciation—Equipment to the balance sheet credit column. The reason is that accumulated depreciation is a contra asset account with a credit balance.

Pioneer extends the balances in Common Stock and Retained Earnings, if any, to the balance sheet credit column. In addition, it extends the balance in Dividends to the balance sheet debit column because it is a stockholders' equity account with a debit balance.

The company enters the expense and revenue accounts such as Salaries and Wages Expense and Service Revenue in the appropriate income statement columns.

Helpful Hint
Every adjusted trial balance amount must be extended to one of the four statement columns.

STEP 5. TOTAL THE STATEMENT COLUMNS, COMPUTE THE NET INCOME (OR NET LOSS), AND COMPLETE THE WORKSHEET

The company now must total each of the financial statement columns. The net income or net loss for the period is the difference between the totals of the two income statement columns. If total credits exceed total debits, the result is net income. In such a case, as shown in Illustration 4-2, the company inserts the words "Net Income" in the account titles space. It then enters the amount in the income statement debit column and the balance sheet credit column. **The debit amount balances the income statement columns; the credit amount balances the balance sheet columns.** In addition, the credit in the balance sheet column indicates the increase in stockholders' equity resulting from net income.

What if total debits exceed total credits in the income statement columns? In that case, the company has a net loss. It enters the amount of the net loss in the income statement credit column and the balance sheet debit column.

After entering the net income or net loss, the company determines new column totals. The totals shown in the debit and credit income statement columns will match. So will the totals shown in the debit and credit balance sheet columns. If either the income statement columns or the balance sheet columns are not equal after the net income or net loss has been entered, there is an error in the worksheet.

Preparing Financial Statements from a Worksheet

After a company has completed a worksheet, it has at hand all the data required for preparation of financial statements. The income statement is prepared from the income statement columns. The balance sheet and retained earnings statement are prepared from the balance sheet columns. Illustration 4-3 (page 156) shows the financial statements prepared from Pioneer Advertising's worksheet. At this point, the company has not journalized or posted adjusting entries. Therefore, ledger balances for some accounts are not the same as the financial statement amounts.

Illustration 4-3
Financial statements from a
worksheet

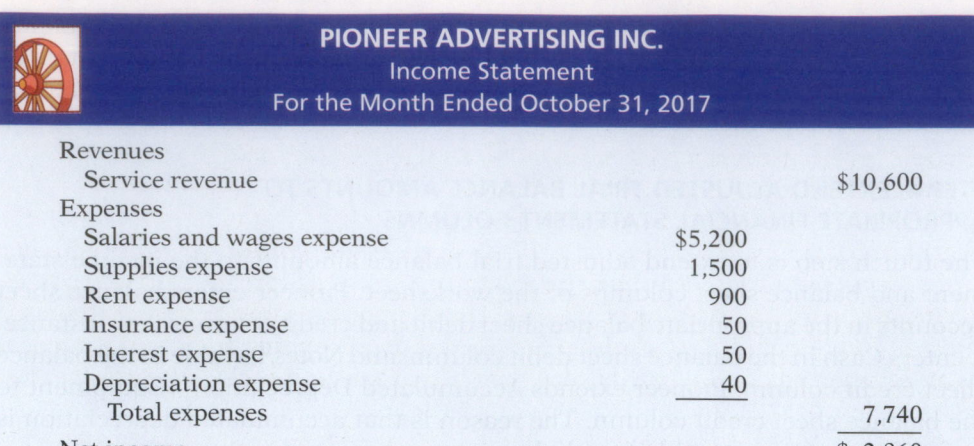

PIONEER ADVERTISING INC.
Income Statement
For the Month Ended October 31, 2017

Revenues		
Service revenue		$10,600
Expenses		
Salaries and wages expense	$5,200	
Supplies expense	1,500	
Rent expense	900	
Insurance expense	50	
Interest expense	50	
Depreciation expense	40	
Total expenses		7,740
Net income		$ 2,860

PIONEER ADVERTISING INC.
Retained Earnings Statement
For the Month Ended October 31, 2017

Retained earnings, October 1	$ –0–
Add: Net income	2,860
	2,860
Less: Dividends	500
Retained earnings, October 31	$2,360

PIONEER ADVERTISING INC.
Balance Sheet
October 31, 2017

Assets

Cash		$15,200
Accounts receivable		200
Supplies		1,000
Prepaid insurance		550
Equipment	$5,000	
Less: Accumulated depreciation—equipment	40	4,960
Total assets		$21,910

Liabilities and Stockholders' Equity

Liabilities		
Notes payable	$5,000	
Accounts payable	2,500	
Interest payable	50	
Unearned service revenue	800	
Salaries and wages payable	1,200	
Total liabilities		$ 9,550
Stockholders' equity		
Common stock	10,000	
Retained earnings	2,360	
Total stockholders' equity		12,360
Total liabilities and stockholders' equity		$21,910

The amount shown for common stock on the worksheet does not change from the beginning to the end of the period unless the company issues additional stock during the period. Because there was no balance in Pioneer's retained earnings, the account is not listed on the worksheet. Only after dividends and net income (or loss) are posted to retained earnings does this account have a balance at the end of the first year of the business.

Using a worksheet, companies can prepare financial statements before they journalize and post adjusting entries. **However, the completed worksheet is not a substitute for formal financial statements.** The format of the data in the financial statement columns of the worksheet is not the same as the format of the financial statements. **A worksheet is essentially a working tool of the accountant**; companies do not distribute it to management and other parties.

Preparing Adjusting Entries from a Worksheet

A worksheet is not a journal, and it cannot be used as a basis for posting to ledger accounts. To adjust the accounts, the company must journalize the adjustments and post them to the ledger. **The adjusting entries are prepared from the adjustments columns of the worksheet.** The reference letters in the adjustments columns and the explanations of the adjustments at the bottom of the worksheet help identify the adjusting entries. The journalizing and posting of adjusting entries **follow** the preparation of financial statements when a worksheet is used. The adjusting entries on October 31 for Pioneer Advertising Inc. are the same as those shown in Illustration 3-23 (page 111).

Helpful Hint
Note that writing the explanation of the adjustment at the bottom of the worksheet is not required

---

DO IT!   Worksheet

Susan Elbe is preparing a worksheet. Explain to Susan how she should extend the following adjusted trial balance accounts to the financial statement columns of the worksheet.

Cash	Dividends
Accumulated Depreciation—Equipment	Service Revenue
Accounts Payable	Salaries and Wages Expense

Solution

Income statement debit column—Salaries and Wages Expense
Income statement credit column—Service Revenue
Balance sheet debit column—Cash; Dividends
Balance sheet credit column—Accumulated Depreciation—Equipment; Accounts Payable

Related exercise material: **BE4-1, BE4-2, BE4-3, E4-1, E4-2, E4-5, E4-6, and DO IT! 4-1.**

Action Plan
✔ Balance sheet: Extend assets to debit column. Extend liabilities to credit column. Extend contra assets to credit column. Extend Dividends account to debit column.
✔ Income statement: Extend expenses to debit column. Extend revenues to credit column.

LEARNING OBJECTIVE 2   Prepare closing entries and a post-closing trial balance.

At the end of the accounting period, the company makes the accounts ready for the next period. This is called **closing the books**. In closing the books, the company distinguishes between temporary and permanent accounts.

Temporary accounts relate only to a given accounting period. They include all income statement accounts and the Dividends account. **The company closes all temporary accounts at the end of the period.**

In contrast, **permanent accounts** relate to one or more future accounting periods. They consist of all balance sheet accounts, including stockholders' equity accounts. **Permanent accounts are not closed from period to period.** Instead, the company carries forward the balances of permanent accounts into the next accounting period. Illustration 4-4 identifies the accounts in each category.

Illustration 4-4
Temporary versus permanent accounts

Alternative Terminology
Temporary accounts are sometimes called *nominal accounts*, and permanent accounts are sometimes called *real accounts*.

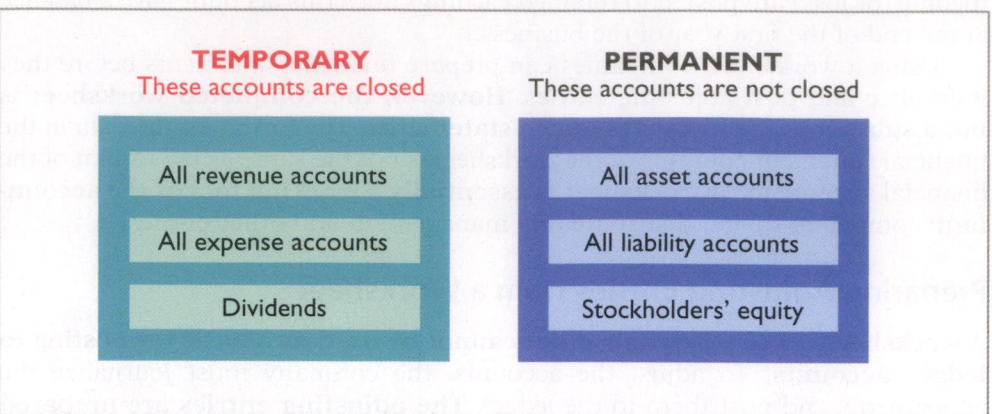

TEMPORARY
These accounts are closed

- All revenue accounts
- All expense accounts
- Dividends

PERMANENT
These accounts are not closed

- All asset accounts
- All liability accounts
- Stockholders' equity

Preparing Closing Entries

At the end of the accounting period, the company transfers temporary account balances to the permanent stockholders' equity account, Retained Earnings, by means of closing entries.

Closing entries formally recognize in the ledger the transfer of net income (or net loss) and Dividends to Retained Earnings. The retained earnings statement shows the results of these entries. **Closing entries also produce a zero balance in each temporary account.** The temporary accounts are then ready to accumulate data in the next accounting period separate from the data of prior periods. Permanent accounts are not closed.

Journalizing and posting closing entries is a required step in the accounting cycle (see Illustration 4-11 on page 165). The company performs this step after it has prepared financial statements. In contrast to the steps in the cycle that you have already studied, companies generally journalize and post closing entries **only at the end of the annual accounting period**. Thus, all temporary accounts will contain data for the entire year.

In preparing closing entries, companies could close each income statement account directly to Retained Earnings. However, to do so would result in excessive detail in the permanent Retained Earnings account. Instead, companies close the revenue and expense accounts to another temporary account, **Income Summary**, and they transfer the resulting net income or net loss from this account to Retained Earnings.

Companies **record closing entries in the general journal**. A center caption, Closing Entries, inserted in the journal between the last adjusting entry and the first closing entry, identifies these entries. Then the company posts the closing entries to the ledger accounts.

Companies generally prepare closing entries directly from the adjusted balances in the ledger. They could prepare separate closing entries for each nominal account, but the following four entries accomplish the desired result more efficiently:

1. Debit each revenue account for its balance, and credit Income Summary for total revenues.

2. Debit Income Summary for total expenses, and credit each expense account for its balance.

3. Debit Income Summary and credit Retained Earnings for the amount of net income.

4. Debit Retained Earnings for the balance in the Dividends account, and credit Dividends for the same amount.

Illustration 4-5 presents a diagram of the closing process. In it, the boxed numbers refer to the four entries required in the closing process.

Helpful Hint
The Dividends account is closed directly to Retained Earnings and *not* to Income Summary because dividends are not an expense.

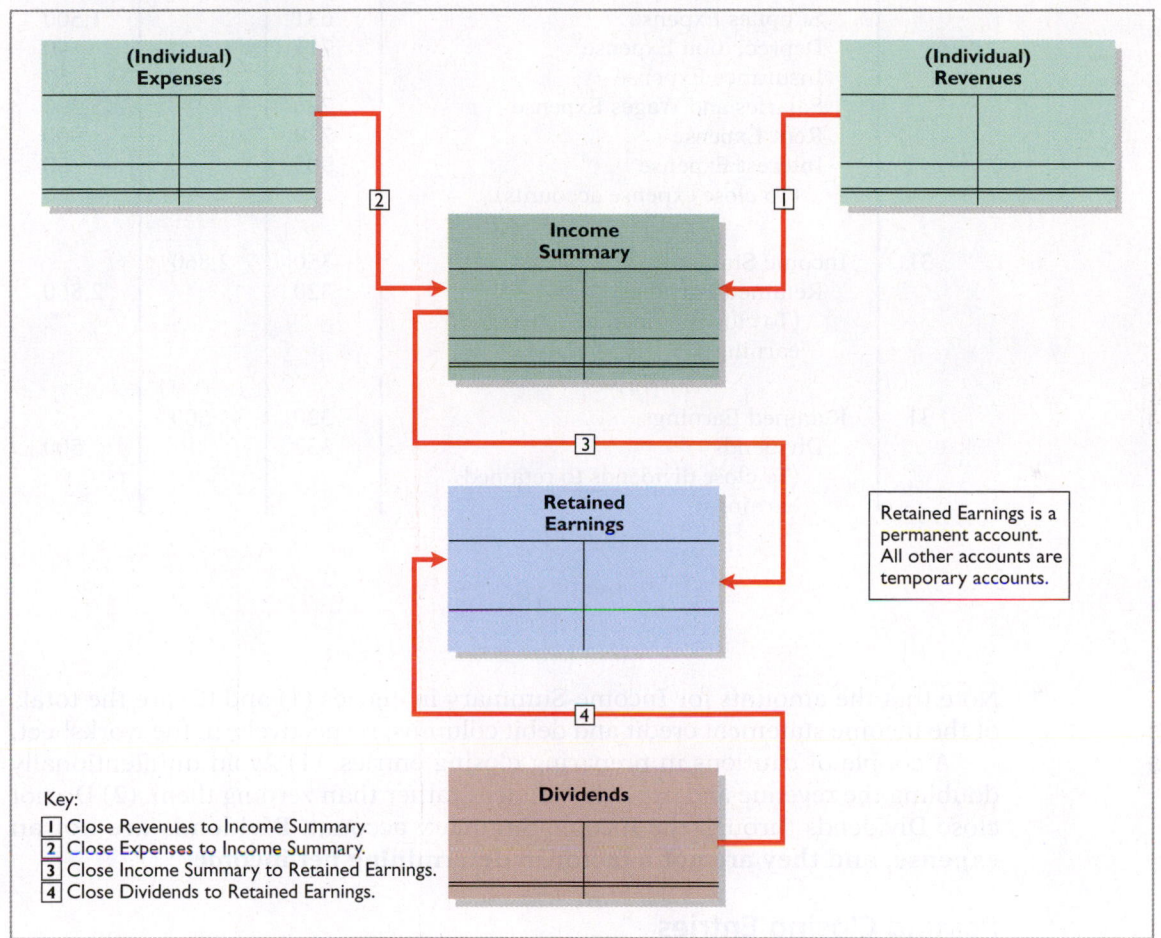

Key:
1 Close Revenues to Income Summary.
2 Close Expenses to Income Summary.
3 Close Income Summary to Retained Earnings.
4 Close Dividends to Retained Earnings.

Illustration 4-5
Diagram of closing process—corporation

If there were a net loss (because expenses exceeded revenues), entry 3 in Illustration 4-5 would be reversed: there would be a credit to Income Summary and a debit to Retained Earnings.

CLOSING ENTRIES ILLUSTRATED

In practice, companies generally prepare closing entries only at the end of the annual accounting period. However, to illustrate the journalizing and posting of closing entries, we will assume that Pioneer Advertising Inc. closes its books monthly. Illustration 4-6 (page 160) shows the closing entries at October 31. (The numbers in parentheses before each entry correspond to the four entries diagrammed in Illustration 4-5.)

	GENERAL JOURNAL			J3
Date	Account Titles and Explanation	Ref.	Debit	Credit
	Closing Entries			
2017	(1)			
Oct. 31	Service Revenue	400	10,600	
	Income Summary	350		10,600
	(To close revenue account)			
	(2)			
31	Income Summary	350	7,740	
	Supplies Expense	631		1,500
	Depreciation Expense	711		40
	Insurance Expense	722		50
	Salaries and Wages Expense	726		5,200
	Rent Expense	729		900
	Interest Expense	905		50
	(To close expense accounts)			
	(3)			
31	Income Summary	350	2,860	
	Retained Earnings	320		2,860
	(To close net income to retained earnings)			
	(4)			
31	Retained Earnings	320	500	
	Dividends	332		500
	(To close dividends to retained earnings)			

Note that the amounts for Income Summary in entries (1) and (2) are the totals of the income statement credit and debit columns, respectively, in the worksheet.

A couple of cautions in preparing closing entries. (1) Avoid unintentionally doubling the revenue and expense balances rather than zeroing them. (2) Do not close Dividends through the Income Summary account. **Dividends are not an expense, and they are not a factor in determining net income.**

Posting Closing Entries

Illustration 4-7 shows the posting of the closing entries and the underlining (ruling) of the accounts. Note that all temporary accounts have zero balances after posting the closing entries. In addition, you should realize that the balance in Retained Earnings represents the accumulated undistributed earnings of the corporation at the end of the accounting period. This balance is shown on the balance sheet and is the ending amount reported on the retained earnings statement, as shown in Illustration 4-3 (page 156). Pioneer Advertising uses the Income Summary account only in closing. It does not journalize and post entries to this account during the year.

As part of the closing process, Pioneer totals, balances, and double-underlines its temporary accounts—revenues, expenses, and Dividends, as shown in T-account form in Illustration 4-7. It does not close its permanent accounts—assets, liabilities, and stockholders' equity (Common Stock and Retained Earnings). Instead, Pioneer draws a single underline beneath the current-period entries for the permanent accounts. The account balance is then entered below the single underline and is carried forward to the next period (for example, see Retained Earnings).

Helpful Hint
The balance in Income Summary before it is closed must equal the net income or net loss for the period.

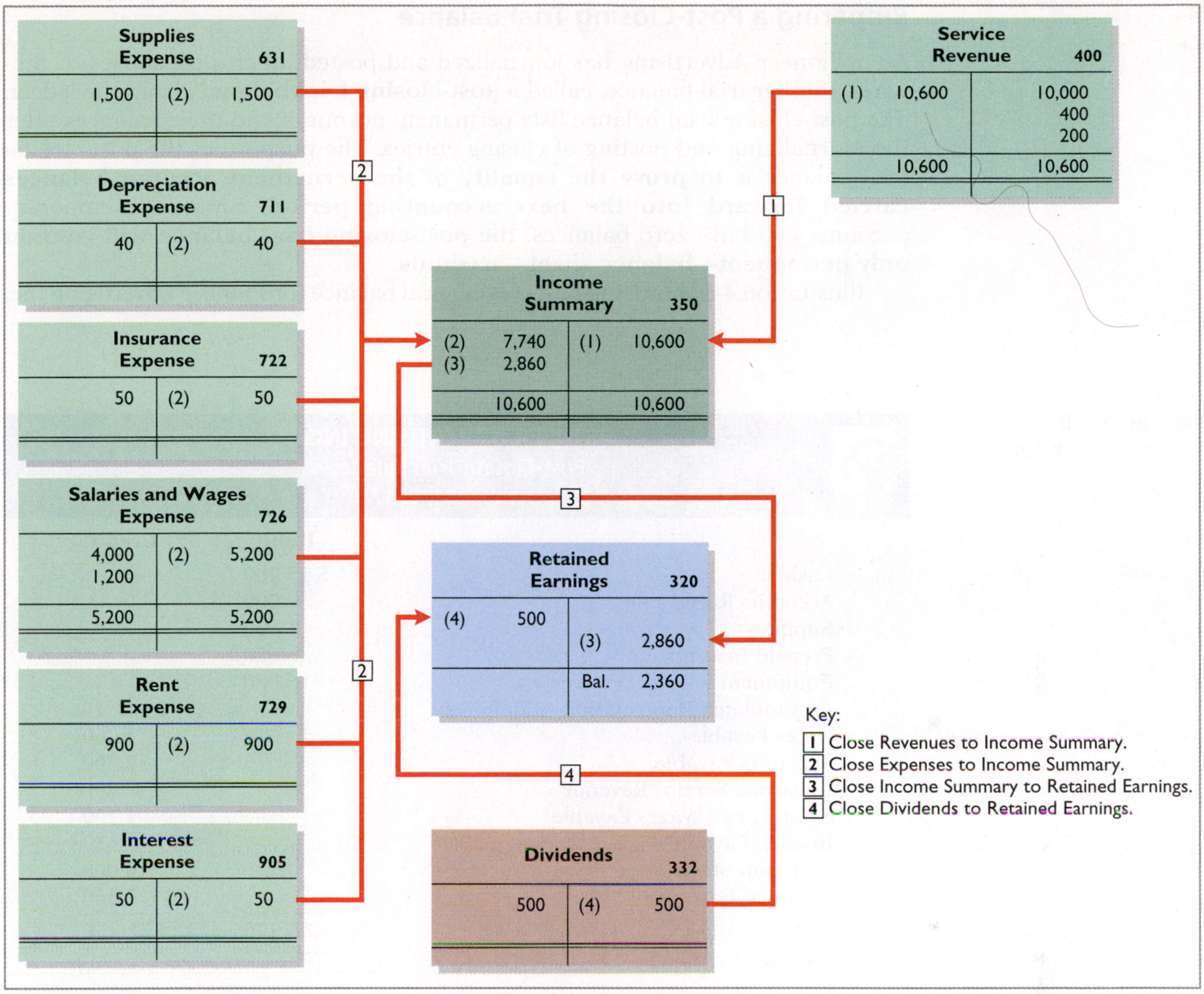

Supplies Expense		631				Service Revenue		400
1,500	(2)	1,500			(1)	10,600		10,000
								400
								200
						10,600		10,600

Depreciation Expense		711
40	(2)	40

Income Summary				350
(2)	7,740	(1)		10,600
(3)	2,860			
	10,600			10,600

Insurance Expense		722
50	(2)	50

Salaries and Wages Expense		726
4,000	(2)	5,200
1,200		
5,200		5,200

Retained Earnings			320
(4)	500		
		(3)	2,860
		Bal.	2,360

Rent Expense		729
900	(2)	900

Key:
1	Close Revenues to Income Summary.
2	Close Expenses to Income Summary.
3	Close Income Summary to Retained Earnings.
4	Close Dividends to Retained Earnings.

Interest Expense		905
50	(2)	50

Dividends		332
500	(4)	500

Illustration 4-7
Posting of closing entries

Accounting Across the Organization   Cisco Systems

© Steve Cole/iStockphoto

Cisco Performs the Virtual Close

Technology has dramatically shortened the closing process. Recent surveys have reported that the average company now takes only six to seven days to close, rather than the previous 20 days. But a few companies do much better. Cisco Systems can perform a "virtual close"—closing within 24 hours on any day in the quarter. The same is true at Lockheed Martin Corp., which improved its closing time by 85% in just the last few years. Not very long ago, it took 14 to 16 days. Managers at these companies emphasize that this increased speed has not reduced the accuracy and completeness of the data.

This is not just showing off. Knowing exactly where you are financially all of the time allows the company to respond faster than its competitors. It also means that the hundreds of people who used to spend 10 to 20 days a quarter tracking transactions can now be more usefully employed on things such as mining data for business intelligence to find new business opportunities.

Source: "Reporting Practices: Few Do It All," *Financial Executive* (November 2003), p. 11.

Who else benefits from a shorter closing process? (Go to **WileyPLUS** for this answer and additional questions.)

Preparing a Post-Closing Trial Balance

After Pioneer Advertising has journalized and posted all closing entries, it prepares another trial balance, called a **post-closing trial balance**, from the ledger. The post-closing trial balance lists permanent accounts and their balances after the journalizing and posting of closing entries. The purpose of the post-closing trial balance is **to prove the equality of the permanent account balances carried forward into the next accounting period**. Since all temporary accounts will have zero balances, **the post-closing trial balance will contain only permanent—balance sheet—accounts**.

Illustration 4-8 shows the post-closing trial balance for Pioneer Advertising Inc.

Illustration 4-8
Post-closing trial balance

PIONEER ADVERTISING INC.
Post-Closing Trial Balance
October 31, 2017

	Debit	Credit
Cash	$ 15,200	
Accounts Receivable	200	
Supplies	1,000	
Prepaid Insurance	550	
Equipment	5,000	
Accumulated Depreciation—Equipment		$ 40
Notes Payable		5,000
Accounts Payable		2,500
Unearned Service Revenue		800
Salaries and Wages Payable		1,200
Interest Payable		50
Common Stock		10,000
Retained Earnings		2,360
	$21,950	**$21,950**

Pioneer prepares the post-closing trial balance from the permanent accounts in the ledger. Illustration 4-9 shows the permanent accounts in Pioneer's general ledger.

(Permanent Accounts Only)

GENERAL LEDGER

Cash — No. 101

Date	Explanation	Ref.	Debit	Credit	Balance
2017					
Oct. 1		J1	10,000		10,000
2		J1	1,200		11,200
3		J1		900	10,300
4		J1		600	9,700
20		J1		500	9,200
26		J1		4,000	5,200
31		J1	10,000		**15,200**

Accounts Receivable — No. 112

Date	Explanation	Ref.	Debit	Credit	Balance
2017					
Oct. 31	Adj. entry	J2	**200**		**200**

Supplies — No. 126

Date	Explanation	Ref.	Debit	Credit	Balance
2017					
Oct. 5		J1	2,500		2,500
31	Adj. entry	J2		**1,500**	**1,000**

Prepaid Insurance — No. 130

Date	Explanation	Ref.	Debit	Credit	Balance
2017					
Oct. 4		J1	600		600
31	Adj. entry	J2		**50**	**550**

Equipment — No. 157

Date	Explanation	Ref.	Debit	Credit	Balance
2017					
Oct. 1		J1	5,000		**5,000**

Accumulated Depreciation—Equipment — No. 158

Date	Explanation	Ref.	Debit	Credit	Balance
2017					
Oct. 31	Adj. entry	J2		**40**	**40**

Notes Payable — No. 200

Date	Explanation	Ref.	Debit	Credit	Balance
2017					
Oct. 1		J1		5,000	**5,000**

Accounts Payable — No. 201

Date	Explanation	Ref.	Debit	Credit	Balance
2017					
Oct. 5		J1		2,500	**2,500**

Unearned Service Revenue — No. 209

Date	Explanation	Ref.	Debit	Credit	Balance
2017					
Oct. 2		J1		1,200	1,200
31	Adj. entry	J2	400		**800**

Salaries and Wages Payable — No. 212

Date	Explanation	Ref.	Debit	Credit	Balance
2017					
Oct. 31	Adj. entry	J2		**1,200**	**1,200**

Interest Payable — No. 230

Date	Explanation	Ref.	Debit	Credit	Balance
2017					
Oct. 31	Adj. entry	J2		**50**	**50**

Common Stock — No. 311

Date	Explanation	Ref.	Debit	Credit	Balance
2017					
Oct. 1		J1		10,000	**10,000**

Retained Earnings — No. 320

Date	Explanation	Ref.	Debit	Credit	Balance
2017					
Oct. 1					–0–
31	**Closing entry**	J3		2,860	**2,860**
31	**Closing entry**	J3	500		**2,360**

Note: The permanent accounts for Pioneer Advertising Inc. are shown here; the temporary accounts are shown in Illustration 4-10. Both permanent and temporary accounts are part of the general ledger; we segregated them here to aid in learning.

Illustration 4-9
General ledger, permanent accounts

A post-closing trial balance provides evidence that the company has properly journalized and posted the closing entries. It also shows that the accounting equation is in balance at the end of the accounting period. However, like the trial balance, it does not prove that Pioneer has recorded all transactions or that the ledger is correct. For example, the post-closing trial balance still will balance even if a transaction is not journalized and posted or if a transaction is journalized and posted twice.

The remaining accounts in the general ledger are temporary accounts, shown in Illustration 4-10 (page 164). After Pioneer correctly posts the closing entries, each temporary account has a zero balance. These accounts are double-underlined to finalize the closing process.

(Temporary Accounts Only)

GENERAL LEDGER

Dividends No. 332

Date	Explanation	Ref.	Debit	Credit	Balance
2017					
Oct. 20		J1	500		500
31	Closing entry	J3		500	–0–

Income Summary No. 350

Date	Explanation	Ref.	Debit	Credit	Balance
2017					
Oct. 31	Closing entry	J3		10,600	10,600
31	Closing entry	J3	7,740		2,860
31	Closing entry	J3	2,860		–0–

Service Revenue No. 400

Date	Explanation	Ref.	Debit	Credit	Balance
2017					
Oct. 31		J1		10,000	10,000
31	Adj. entry	J2		400	10,400
31	Adj. entry	J2		200	10,600
31	Closing entry	J3	10,600		–0–

Supplies Expense No. 631

Date	Explanation	Ref.	Debit	Credit	Balance
2017					
Oct. 31	Adj. entry	J2	1,500		1,500
31	Closing entry	J3		1,500	–0–

Depreciation Expense No. 711

Date	Explanation	Ref.	Debit	Credit	Balance
2017					
Oct. 31	Adj. entry	J2	40		40
31	Closing entry	J3		40	–0–

Insurance Expense No. 722

Date	Explanation	Ref.	Debit	Credit	Balance
2017					
Oct. 31	Adj. entry	J2	50		50
31	Closing entry	J3		50	–0–

Salaries and Wages Expense No. 726

Date	Explanation	Ref.	Debit	Credit	Balance
2017					
Oct. 26		J1	4,000		4,000
31	Adj. entry	J2	1,200		5,200
31	Closing entry	J3		5,200	–0–

Rent Expense No. 729

Date	Explanation	Ref.	Debit	Credit	Balance
2017					
Oct. 3		J1	900		900
31	Closing entry	J3		900	–0–

Interest Expense No. 905

Date	Explanation	Ref.	Debit	Credit	Balance
2017					
Oct. 31	Adj. entry	J2	50		50
31	Closing entry	J3		50	–0–

Note: The temporary accounts for Pioneer Advertising Inc. are shown here. Illustration 4-9 (page 163) shows the permanent accounts. Both permanent and temporary accounts are part of the general ledger; we segregate them here to aid in learning.

Illustration 4-10
General ledger, temporary accounts

DO IT! 2 Closing Entries

The worksheet for Hancock Company shows the following in the financial statement columns:

Dividends $15,000
Common stock $42,000
Net income $18,000

Prepare the closing entries at December 31 that affect stockholders' equity.

Solution

Action Plan

✔ Close Income Summary to Retained Earnings.

✔ Close Dividends to Retained Earnings.

Dec. 31	Income Summary	18,000	
	Retained Earnings		18,000
	(To close net income to retained earnings)		
31	Retained Earnings	15,000	
	Dividends		15,000
	(To close dividends to retained earnings)		

Related exercise material: **BE4-4, BE4-5, BE4-6, E4-4, E4-7, E4-8, E4-11, and DO IT! 4-2.**

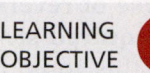

LEARNING OBJECTIVE **3** **Explain the steps in the accounting cycle and how to prepare correcting entries.**

Summary of the Accounting Cycle

Illustration 4-11 summarizes the steps in the accounting cycle. You can see that the cycle begins with the analysis of business transactions and ends with the preparation of a post-closing trial balance.

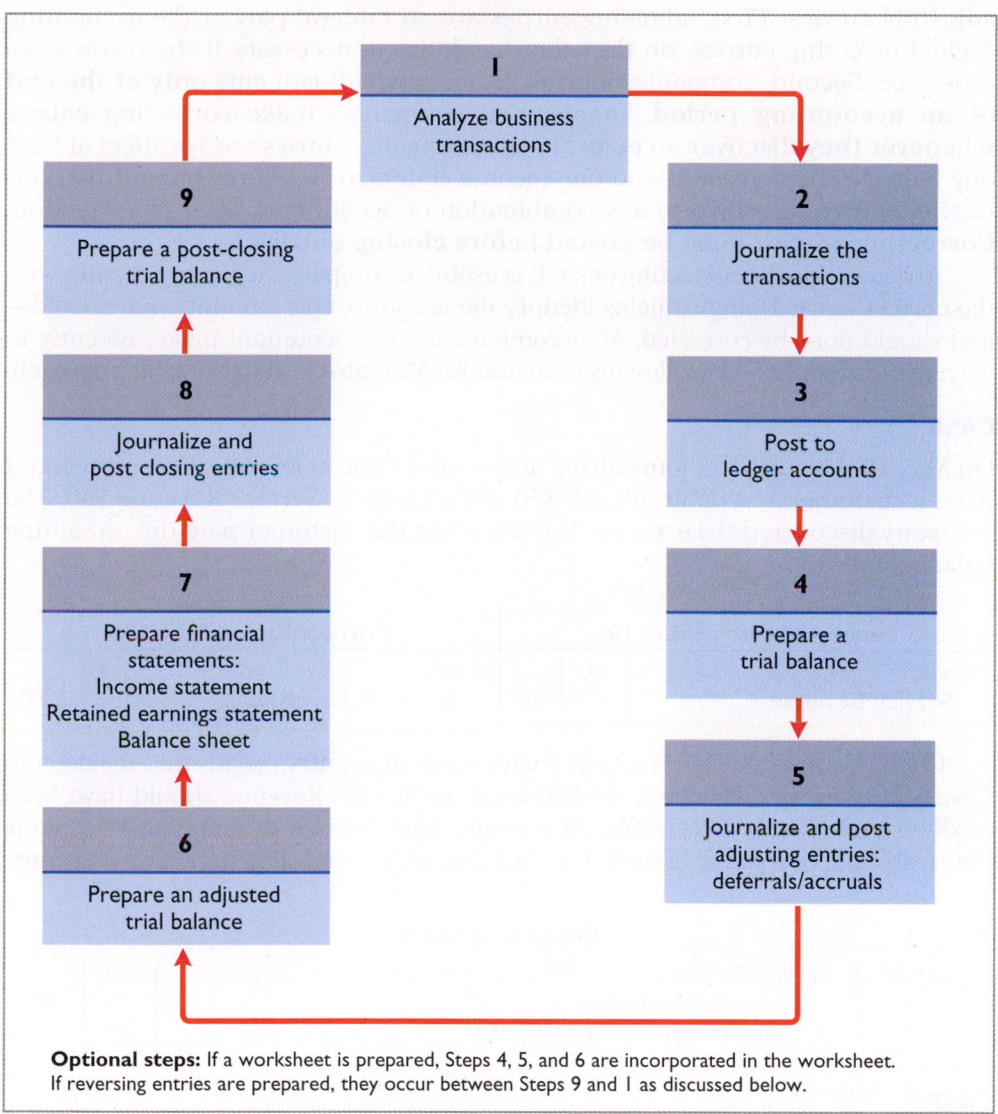

Illustration 4-11
Steps in the accounting cycle

Optional steps: If a worksheet is prepared, Steps 4, 5, and 6 are incorporated in the worksheet. If reversing entries are prepared, they occur between Steps 9 and 1 as discussed below.

Steps 1–3 may occur daily during the accounting period. Companies perform Steps 4–7 on a periodic basis, such as monthly, quarterly, or annually. Steps 8 and 9—closing entries and a post-closing trial balance—usually take place only at the end of a company's **annual** accounting period.

There are also two **optional steps** in the accounting cycle. As you have seen, companies may use a worksheet in preparing adjusting entries and financial statements. In addition, they may use reversing entries, as explained below.

Reversing Entries—An Optional Step

Some accountants prefer to reverse certain adjusting entries by making a **reversing entry** at the beginning of the next accounting period. A reversing entry is the exact opposite of the adjusting entry made in the previous period. **Use of reversing entries is an optional bookkeeping procedure; it is not a required step in the accounting cycle.** Accordingly, we have chosen to cover this topic in Appendix 4A at the end of this chapter.

Correcting Entries—An Avoidable Step

Unfortunately, errors may occur in the recording process. Companies should correct errors, **as soon as they discover them**, by journalizing and posting **correcting entries**. If the accounting records are free of errors, no correcting entries are needed.

You should recognize several differences between correcting entries and adjusting entries. First, adjusting entries are an integral part of the accounting cycle. Correcting entries, on the other hand, are unnecessary if the records are error-free. Second, companies journalize and post adjustments **only at the end of an accounting period**. In contrast, companies make correcting entries **whenever they discover an error**. Finally, adjusting entries always affect at least one balance sheet account and one income statement account. In contrast, correcting entries may involve any combination of accounts in need of correction. **Correcting entries must be posted before closing entries.**

To determine the correcting entry, it is useful to compare the incorrect entry with the correct entry. Doing so helps identify the accounts and amounts that should—and should not—be corrected. After comparison, the accountant makes an entry to correct the accounts. The following two cases for Mercato Co. illustrate this approach.

CASE 1

On May 10, Mercato Co. journalized and posted a $50 cash collection on account from a customer as a debit to Cash $50 and a credit to Service Revenue $50. The company discovered the error on May 20, when the customer paid the remaining balance in full.

Illustration 4-12
Comparison of entries

Incorrect Entry (May 10)			Correct Entry (May 10)		
Cash	50		Cash	50	
Service Revenue		50	Accounts Receivable		50

Comparison of the incorrect entry with the correct entry reveals that the debit to Cash $50 is correct. However, the $50 credit to Service Revenue should have been credited to Accounts Receivable. As a result, both Service Revenue and Accounts Receivable are overstated in the ledger. Mercato makes the following correcting entry.

Illustration 4-13
Correcting entry

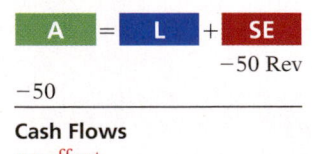

A = L + SE
−50   −50 Rev

Cash Flows
no effect

	Correcting Entry		
May 20	Service Revenue	50	
	Accounts Receivable		50
	(To correct entry of May 10)		

CASE 2

On May 18, Mercato purchased on account equipment costing $450. The transaction was journalized and posted as a debit to Equipment $45 and a credit to Accounts Payable $45. The error was discovered on June 3, when Mercato received the monthly statement for May from the creditor.

Illustration 4-14
Comparison of entries

Incorrect Entry (May 18)			Correct Entry (May 18)		
Equipment	45		Equipment	450	
Accounts Payable		45	Accounts Payable		450

Comparison of the two entries shows that two accounts are incorrect. Equipment is understated $405, and Accounts Payable is understated $405. Mercato makes the following correcting entry.

Correcting Entry			
June 3	Equipment	405	
	Accounts Payable		405
	(To correct entry of May 18)		

A	=	L	+	SE
+405				
				+405

Cash Flows
no effect

Illustration 4-15
Correcting entry

Instead of preparing a correcting entry, **it is possible to reverse the incorrect entry and then prepare the correct entry**. This approach will result in more entries and postings than a correcting entry, but it will accomplish the desired result.

Accounting Across the Organization   Yale Expresss

© Christian Lagereek/iStockphoto

Lost in Transportation

Yale Express, a short-haul trucking firm, turned over much of its cargo to local truckers to complete deliveries. Yale collected the entire delivery charge. When billed by the local trucker, Yale sent payment for the final phase to the local trucker. Yale used a cutoff period of 20 days into the next accounting period in making its adjusting entries for accrued liabilities. That is, it waited 20 days to receive the local truckers' bills to determine the amount of the unpaid but incurred delivery charges as of the balance sheet date.

On the other hand, Republic Carloading, a nationwide, long-distance freight forwarder, frequently did not receive transportation bills from truckers to whom it passed on cargo until months after the year-end. In making its year-end adjusting entries, Republic waited for months in order to include all of these outstanding transportation bills.

When Yale Express merged with Republic Carloading, Yale's vice president employed the 20-day cutoff procedure for both firms. As a result, millions of dollars of Republic's accrued transportation bills went unrecorded. When the company detected the error and made correcting entries, these and other errors changed a reported profit of $1.14 million into a loss of $1.88 million!

What might Yale Express's vice president have done to produce more accurate financial statements without waiting months for Republic's outstanding transportation bills? (Go to WileyPLUS for this answer and additional questions.)

DO IT! 3   Correcting Entries

Sanchez Company discovered the following errors made in January 2017.

1. A payment of Salaries and Wages Expense of $600 was debited to Supplies and credited to Cash, both for $600.
2. A collection of $3,000 from a client on account was debited to Cash $200 and credited to Service Revenue $200.
3. The purchase of supplies on account for $860 was debited to Supplies $680 and credited to Accounts Payable $680.

Correct the errors without reversing the incorrect entry.

Solution

1.	Salaries and Wages Expense	600	
	Supplies		600
2.	Service Revenue	200	
	Cash	2,800	
	Accounts Receivable		3,000
3.	Supplies ($860 − $680)	180	
	Accounts Payable		180

Action Plan

✔ Compare the incorrect entry with correct entry.

✔ After comparison, make an entry to correct the accounts.

Related exercise material: **BE4-9, E4-12, E4-13, and DO IT! 4-3**.

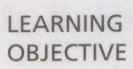

LEARNING
OBJECTIVE **4**

Identify the sections of a classified balance sheet.

The balance sheet presents a snapshot of a company's financial position at a point in time. To improve users' understanding of a company's financial position, companies often use a classified balance sheet. A **classified balance sheet** groups together similar assets and similar liabilities, using a number of standard classifications and sections. This is useful because items within a group have similar economic characteristics. A classified balance sheet generally contains the standard classifications listed in Illustration 4-16.

Illustration 4-16
Standard balance sheet classifications

Assets	Liabilities and Stockholders' Equity
Current assets	Current liabilities
Long-term investments	Long-term liabilities
Property, plant, and equipment	Stockholders' equity
Intangible assets	

These groupings help financial statement readers determine such things as (1) whether the company has enough assets to pay its debts as they come due, and (2) the claims of short- and long-term creditors on the company's total assets. Many of these groupings can be seen in the balance sheet of Franklin Corporation shown in Illustration 4-17. In the sections that follow, we explain each of these groupings.

Current Assets

Current assets are assets that a company expects to convert to cash or use up within one year or its operating cycle, whichever is longer. In Illustration 4-17, Franklin Corporation had current assets of $22,100. For most businesses, the cutoff for classification as current assets is one year from the balance sheet date. For example, accounts receivable are current assets because the company will collect them and convert them to cash within one year. Supplies is a current asset because the company expects to use them up in operations within one year.

Some companies use a period longer than one year to classify assets and liabilities as current because they have an operating cycle longer than one year. The **operating cycle** of a company is the average time that it takes to purchase inventory, sell it on account, and then collect cash from customers. For most businesses, this cycle takes less than a year so they use a one-year cutoff. But for some businesses, such as vineyards or airplane manufacturers, this period may be longer than a year. **Except where noted, we will assume that companies use one year to determine whether an asset or liability is current or long-term.**

Common types of current assets are (1) cash, (2) investments (such as short-term U.S. government securities), (3) receivables (notes receivable, accounts receivable, and interest receivable), (4) inventories, and (5) prepaid expenses (supplies and insurance). **On the balance sheet, companies usually list these items in the order in which they expect to convert them into cash.** Illustration 4-18 presents the current assets of **Southwest Airlines Co.**

FRANKLIN CORPORATION
Balance Sheet
October 31, 2017

Illustration 4-17
Classified balance sheet

Assets

Current assets
Cash	$ 6,600	
Debt investments	2,000	
Accounts receivable	7,000	
Notes receivable	1,000	
Inventory	3,000	
Supplies	2,100	
Prepaid insurance	400	
Total current assets		$22,100

Long-term investments
Stock investments	5,200	
Investment in real estate	2,000	7,200

Property, plant, and equipment
Land		10,000	
Equipment	$24,000		
Less: Accumulated depreciation— equipment	5,000	19,000	29,000

Intangible assets
Patents		3,100
Total assets		$61,400

Liabilities and Stockholders' Equity

Helpful Hint
Recall that the basic accounting equation is Assets = Liabilities + Stockholders' Equity.

Current liabilities
Notes payable	$11,000	
Accounts payable	2,100	
Unearned service revenue	900	
Salaries and wages payable	1,600	
Interest payable	450	
Total current liabilities		$16,050

Long-term liabilities
Mortgage payable	10,000	
Notes payable	1,300	
Total long-term liabilities		11,300
Total liabilities		27,350

Stockholders' equity
Common stock	20,000	
Retained earnings	14,050	
Total stockholders' equity		34,050
Total liabilities and stockholders' equity		$61,400

Real World

SOUTHWEST AIRLINES CO.
Balance Sheet (partial)
(in millions)

Illustration 4-18
Current assets section

Current assets
Cash and cash equivalents	$1,390
Short-term investments	369
Accounts receivable	241
Inventories	181
Prepaid expenses and other current assets	420
Total current assets	$2,601

Long-Term Investments

Alternative Terminology
Long-term investments are often referred to simply as *investments*.

Long-term investments are generally (1) investments in stocks and bonds of other companies that are normally held for many years, (2) long-term assets such as land or buildings that a company is not currently using in its operating activities, and (3) long-term notes receivable. In Illustration 4-17, Franklin Corporation reported total long-term investments of $7,200 on its balance sheet.

Yahoo! Inc. reported long-term investments in its balance sheet, as shown in Illustration 4-19.

Illustration 4-19
Long-term investments section

	YAHOO! INC. Balance Sheet (partial) (in thousands)	
Long-term investments		
Investments in securities		$90,266

Property, Plant, and Equipment

Alternative Terminology
Property, plant, and equipment is sometimes called *fixed assets* or *plant assets*.

Property, plant, and equipment are assets with relatively long useful lives that a company is currently using in operating the business. This category includes land, buildings, machinery and equipment, delivery equipment, and furniture. In Illustration 4-17, Franklin Corporation reported property, plant, and equipment of $29,000.

International Note

Recently, China adopted International Financial Reporting Standards (IFRS). This was done in an effort to reduce fraud and increase investor confidence in financial reports. Under these standards, many items, such as property, plant, and equipment, may be reported at current fair values rather than historical cost.

Depreciation is the practice of allocating the cost of assets to a number of years. Companies do this by systematically assigning a portion of an asset's cost as an expense each year (rather than expensing the full purchase price in the year of purchase). The assets that the company depreciates are reported on the balance sheet at cost less accumulated depreciation. The **accumulated depreciation** account shows the total amount of depreciation that the company has expensed thus far in the asset's life. In Illustration 4-17, Franklin Corporation reported accumulated depreciation of $5,000.

Illustration 4-20 presents the property, plant, and equipment of **Cooper Tire & Rubber Company**.

Illustration 4-20
Property, plant, and equipment section

	COOPER TIRE & RUBBER COMPANY Balance Sheet (partial) (in thousands)	
Property, plant, and equipment		
Land and land improvements	$ 41,553	
Buildings	298,706	
Machinery and equipment	1,636,091	
Molds, cores, and rings	268,158	$2,244,508
Less: Accumulated depreciation		1,252,692
		$ 991,816

Intangible Assets

Helpful Hint
Sometimes intangible assets are reported under a broader heading called "Other assets."

Many companies have long-lived assets that do not have physical substance yet often are very valuable. We call these assets **intangible assets**. One significant intangible asset is goodwill. Others include patents, copyrights, and trademarks or trade names that give the company **exclusive right** of use for a specified period of time. In Illustration 4-17, Franklin Corporation reported intangible assets of $3,100.

Illustration 4-21 shows the intangible assets of media giant Time Warner, Inc.

Illustration 4-21
Intangible assets section

TIME WARNER, INC. Balance Sheet (partial) (in millions)	
Intangible assets	
Goodwill	$40,953
Film library	2,690
Customer lists	2,540
Cable television franchises	38,048
Sports franchises	262
Brands, trademarks, and other intangible assets	8,313
	$92,806

(Real World)

People, Planet, and Profit Insight

Regaining Goodwill

© Gehringj/iStockphoto

After falling to unforeseen lows amidst scandals, recalls, and economic crises, the American public's positive perception of the reputation of corporate America is on the rise. Overall corporate reputation is experiencing rehabilitation as the American public gives high marks overall to corporate America, specific industries, and the largest number of individual companies in a dozen years. This is according to the findings of the *2011 Harris Interactive RQ Study*, which measures the reputations of the 60 most visible companies in the United States.

The survey focuses on six reputational dimensions that influence reputation and consumer behavior. Four of these dimensions, along with the five corporations that ranked highest within each, are as follows.

- **Social Responsibility:** (1) Whole Foods Market, (2) Johnson & Johnson, (3) Google, (4) The Walt Disney Company, (5) Procter & Gamble Co.

- **Emotional Appeal:** (1) Johnson & Johnson, (2) Amazon.com, (3) UPS, (4) General Mills, (5) Kraft Foods

- **Financial Performance:** (1) Google, (2) Berkshire Hathaway, (3) Apple, (4) Intel, (5) The Walt Disney Company

- **Products and Services:** (1) Intel Corporation, (2) 3M Company, (3) Johnson & Johnson, (4) Google, (5) Procter & Gamble Co.

Source: www.harrisinteractive.com.

Name two industries today which are probably rated low on the reputational characteristics of "being trusted" and "having high ethical standards." (Go to **WileyPLUS** for this answer and additional questions.)

Current Liabilities

In the liabilities and stockholders' equity section of the balance sheet, the first grouping is current liabilities. **Current liabilities** are obligations that the company is to pay within the coming year or its operating cycle, whichever is longer. Common examples are accounts payable, salaries and wages payable, notes payable, interest payable, and income taxes payable. Also included as current liabilities are current maturities of long-term obligations—payments to be made within the next year on long-term obligations. In Illustration 4-17, Franklin Corporation reported five different types of current liabilities, for a total of $16,050.

Illustration 4-22 (page 172) shows the current liabilities section adapted from the balance sheet of **Marcus Corporation**.

> **ETHICS NOTE**
>
> A company that has more current assets than current liabilities can increase the ratio of current assets to current liabilities by using cash to pay off some current liabilities. This gives the appearance of being more liquid. Do you think this move is ethical?

Illustration 4-22
Current liabilities section

Liquidity

Illiquidity

Real World	MARCUS CORPORATION	
	Balance Sheet (partial)	
	(in thousands)	
Current liabilities		
Notes payable		$ 239
Accounts payable		24,242
Current maturities of long-term debt		57,250
Other current liabilities		27,477
Income taxes payable		11,215
Salaries and wages payable		6,720
Total current liabilities		$127,143

Users of financial statements look closely at the relationship between current assets and current liabilities. This relationship is important in evaluating a company's **liquidity**—its ability to pay obligations expected to be due within the next year. When current assets exceed current liabilities, the likelihood for paying the liabilities is favorable. When the reverse is true, short-term creditors may not be paid, and the company may ultimately be forced into bankruptcy.

Accounting Across the Organization   REL Consultancy Group

© Jorge Salcedo/iStockphoto

Can a Company Be Too Liquid?

There actually is a point where a company can be too liquid—that is, it can have too much working capital (current assets less current liabilities). While it is important to be liquid enough to be able to pay short-term bills as they come due, a company does not want to tie up its cash in extra inventory or receivables that are not earning the company money.

By one estimate from the REL Consultancy Group, the thousand largest U.S. companies have on their books cumulative excess working capital of $764 billion. Based on this figure, companies could have reduced debt by 36% or increased net income by 9%. Given that managers throughout a company are interested in improving profitability, it is clear that they should have an eye toward managing working capital. They need to aim for a "Goldilocks solution"—not too much, not too little, but just right.

Source: K. Richardson, "Companies Fall Behind in Cash Management," *Wall Street Journal* (June 19, 2007).

*What can various company managers do to ensure that working capital is managed efficiently to maximize net income? (Go to **WileyPLUS** for this answer and additional questions.)*

Long-Term Liabilities

Long-term liabilities are obligations that a company expects to pay **after** one year. Liabilities in this category include bonds payable, mortgages payable, long-term notes payable, lease liabilities, and pension liabilities. Many companies report long-term debt maturing after one year as a single amount in the balance sheet and show the details of the debt in notes that accompany the financial statements. Others list the various types of long-term liabilities. In Illustration 4-17, Franklin Corporation reported long-term liabilities of $11,300.

Illustration 4-23 shows the long-term liabilities that **The Procter & Gamble Company** reported in its balance sheet.

Stockholders' (Owners') Equity

Alternative Terminology
Common stock is sometimes called *capital stock.*

The content of the owners' equity section varies with the form of business organization. In a proprietorship, there is one capital account. In a partnership, there is a capital account for each partner. Corporations divide owners' equity into two accounts—Common Stock (sometimes referred to as Capital Stock) and

Illustration 4-23
Long-term liabilities section

Real World	**THE PROCTER & GAMBLE COMPANY** Balance Sheet (partial) (in millions)	
Long-term liabilities		
Long-term debt		$23,375
Deferred income taxes		12,015
Other noncurrent liabilities		5,147
Total long-term liabilities		$40,537

Retained Earnings. Corporations record stockholders' investments in the company by debiting an asset account and crediting the Common Stock account. They record in the Retained Earnings account income retained for use in the business. Corporations combine the Common Stock and Retained Earnings accounts and report them on the balance sheet as **stockholders' equity**. (We discuss these corporation accounts in later chapters.) **Nordstrom, Inc.** recently reported its stockholders' equity section as follows.

Illustration 4-24
Stockholders' equity section

Real World	**NORDSTROM, INC.** Balance Sheet (partial) ($ in thousands)	
Stockholders' equity		
Common stock, 271,331 shares		$ 685,934
Retained earnings		1,406,747
Total stockholders' equity		$2,092,681

DO IT! 4 — Balance Sheet Classifications

The following accounts were taken from the financial statements of Callahan Company.

_____ Salaries and wages payable
_____ Service revenue
_____ Interest payable
_____ Goodwill
_____ Debt investments (short-term)
_____ Mortgage payable (due in 3 years)

_____ Stock investments (long-term)
_____ Equipment
_____ Accumulated depreciation—equipment
_____ Depreciation expense
_____ Common stock
_____ Unearned service revenue

Match each of the accounts to its proper balance sheet classification, shown below. If the item would not appear on a balance sheet, use "NA."

Current assets (CA)
Long-term investments (LTI)
Property, plant, and equipment (PPE)
Intangible assets (IA)

Current liabilities (CL)
Long-term liabilities (LTL)
Stockholders' equity (SE)

Solution

__CL__	Salaries and wages payable	__LTI__	Stock investments (long-term)
__NA__	Service revenue	__PPE__	Equipment
__CL__	Interest payable	__PPE__	Accumulated depreciation—equipment
__IA__	Goodwill		
__CA__	Debt investments (short-term)	__NA__	Depreciation expense
__LTL__	Mortgage payable (due in 3 years)	__SE__	Common stock
		__CL__	Unearned service revenue

Action Plan

✔ Analyze whether each financial statement item is an asset, liability, or stockholders' equity.

✔ Determine if asset and liability items are short-term or long-term.

Related exercise material: **BE4-11, E4-9, E4-14, E4-15, E4-16, E4-17, and DO IT! 4-4.**

APPENDIX 4A: Prepare reversing entries.

After preparing the financial statements and closing the books, it is often helpful to reverse some of the adjusting entries before recording the regular transactions of the next period. Such entries are **reversing entries**. Companies make **a reversing entry at the beginning of the next accounting period**. Each reversing entry **is the exact opposite of the adjusting entry made in the previous period**. The recording of reversing entries is an **optional step** in the accounting cycle.

The purpose of reversing entries is to simplify the recording of a subsequent transaction related to an adjusting entry. For example, in Chapter 3 (page 110), the payment of salaries after an adjusting entry resulted in two debits: one to Salaries and Wages Payable and the other to Salaries and Wages Expense. With reversing entries, the company can debit the entire subsequent payment to Salaries and Wages Expense. **The use of reversing entries does not change the amounts reported in the financial statements**. What it does is simplify the recording of subsequent transactions.

Reversing Entries Example

Companies most often use reversing entries to reverse two types of adjusting entries: accrued revenues and accrued expenses. To illustrate the optional use of reversing entries for accrued expenses, we will use the salaries expense transactions for Pioneer Advertising Inc. as illustrated in Chapters 2, 3, and 4. The transaction and adjustment data are as follows.

1. October 26 (initial salary entry): Pioneer pays $4,000 of salaries and wages earned between October 15 and October 26.

2. October 31 (adjusting entry): Salaries and wages earned between October 29 and October 31 are $1,200. The company will pay these in the November 9 payroll.

3. November 9 (subsequent salary entry): Salaries and wages paid are $4,000. Of this amount, $1,200 applied to accrued salaries and wages payable and $2,800 was earned between November 1 and November 9.

Illustration 4A-1
Comparative entries—not reversing vs. reversing

Illustration 4A-1 shows the entries with and without reversing entries.

Without Reversing Entries (per chapter)			With Reversing Entries (per appendix)		
Initial Salary Entry			*Initial Salary Entry*		
Oct. 26 │ Salaries and Wages Expense	4,000		Oct. 26 │ (Same entry)		
│ Cash		4,000			
Adjusting Entry			*Adjusting Entry*		
Oct. 31 │ Salaries and Wages Expense	1,200		Oct. 31 │ (Same entry)		
│ Salaries and Wages Payable		1,200			
Closing Entry			*Closing Entry*		
Oct. 31 │ Income Summary	5,200		Oct. 31 │ (Same entry)		
│ Salaries and Wages Expense		5,200			
Reversing Entry			*Reversing Entry*		
Nov. 1 │ No reversing entry is made.			Nov. 1 │ **Salaries and Wages Payable**	**1,200**	
			│ **Salaries and Wages Expense**		**1,200**
Subsequent Salary Entry			*Subsequent Salary Entry*		
Nov. 9 │ Salaries and Wages Payable	1,200		Nov. 9 │ **Salaries and Wages Expense**	**4,000**	
│ Salaries and Wages Expense	2,800		│ **Cash**		**4,000**
│ Cash		4,000			

The first three entries are the same whether or not Pioneer uses reversing entries. The last two entries are different. The November 1 **reversing entry** eliminates the $1,200 balance in Salaries and Wages Payable created by the October 31 adjusting entry. The reversing entry also creates a $1,200 credit balance in the Salaries and Wages Expense account. As you know, it is unusual for an expense account to have a credit balance. The balance is correct in this instance, though, because it anticipates that the entire amount of the first salaries and wages payment in the new accounting period will be debited to Salaries and Wages Expense. This debit will eliminate the credit balance. The resulting debit balance in the expense account will equal the salaries and wages expense incurred in the new accounting period ($2,800 in this example).

If Pioneer makes reversing entries, it can debit all cash payments of expenses to the expense account. This means that on November 9 (and every payday) Pioneer can debit Salaries and Wages Expense for the amount paid, without regard to any accrued salaries and wages payable. Being able to make the **same entry each time** simplifies the recording process. The company can record subsequent transactions as if the related adjusting entry had never been made.

Illustration 4A-2 shows the posting of the entries with reversing entries.

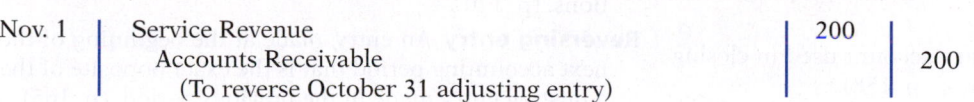

Salaries and Wages Expense					Salaries and Wages Payable			
10/26 Paid	4,000	10/31 Closing	5,200		**11/1 Reversing**	**1,200**	10/31 Adjusting	1,200
31 Adjusting	1,200							
	5,200		5,200					
11/9 Paid	4,000	**11/1 Reversing**	**1,200**					

Illustration 4A-2
Postings with reversing entries

A company can also use reversing entries for accrued revenue adjusting entries. For Pioneer, the adjusting entry was Accounts Receivable (Dr.) $200 and Service Revenue (Cr.) $200. Thus, the reversing entry on November 1 is:

Nov. 1	Service Revenue	200	
	Accounts Receivable		200
	(To reverse October 31 adjusting entry)		

A = L + SE
−200 Rev
−200

Cash Flows
no effect

When Pioneer collects the accrued service revenue, it debits Cash and credits Service Revenue.

REVIEW AND PRACTICE

LEARNING OBJECTIVES REVIEW

1 Prepare a worksheet. The steps in preparing a worksheet are as follows. (a) Prepare a trial balance on the worksheet. (b) Enter the adjustments in the adjustments columns. (c) Enter adjusted balances in the adjusted trial balance columns. (d) Extend adjusted trial balance amounts to appropriate financial statement columns. (e) Total the statement columns, compute net income (or net loss), and complete the worksheet.

2 Prepare closing entries and a post-closing trial balance. Closing the books occurs at the end of an accounting period. The process is to journalize and post closing entries and then underline and balance all accounts.

In closing the books, companies make separate entries to close revenues and expenses to Income Summary, Income Summary to Retained Earnings, and Dividends to Retained Earnings. Only temporary accounts are closed. A post-closing trial balance contains the balances in permanent accounts that are carried forward to the next accounting period. The purpose of this trial balance is to prove the equality of these balances.

3 **Explain the steps in the accounting cycle and how to prepare correcting entries.** The required steps in the accounting cycle are (1) analyze business transactions, (2) journalize the transactions, (3) post to ledger accounts, (4) prepare a trial balance, (5) journalize and post adjusting entries, (6) prepare an adjusted trial balance, (7) prepare financial statements, (8) journalize and post closing entries, and (9) prepare a post-closing trial balance.

One way to determine the correcting entry is to compare the incorrect entry with the correct entry.

After comparison, the company makes a correcting entry to correct the accounts. An alternative to a correcting entry is to reverse the incorrect entry and then prepare the correct entry.

4 **Identify the sections of a classified balance sheet.** A classified balance sheet categorizes assets as current assets; long-term investments; property, plant, and equipment; and intangibles. Liabilities are classified as either current or long-term. There is also a stockholders' (owners') equity section, which varies with the form of business organization.

*5 **Prepare reversing entries.** Reversing entries are the opposite of the adjusting entries made in the preceding period. Some companies choose to make reversing entries at the beginning of a new accounting period to simplify the recording of later transactions related to the adjusting entries. In most cases, only accrued adjusting entries are reversed.

GLOSSARY REVIEW

Classified balance sheet A balance sheet that contains standard classifications or sections. (p. 168).

Closing entries Entries made at the end of an accounting period to transfer the balances of temporary accounts to a permanent stockholders' equity account, Retained Earnings. (p. 158).

Correcting entries Entries to correct errors made in recording transactions. (p. 166).

Current assets Assets that a company expects to convert to cash or use up within one year. (p. 168).

Current liabilities Obligations that a company expects to pay within the coming year or its operating cycle, whichever is longer. (p. 171).

Income Summary A temporary account used in closing revenue and expense accounts. (p. 158).

Intangible assets Noncurrent assets that do not have physical substance. (p. 170).

Liquidity The ability of a company to pay obligations expected to be due within the next year. (p. 172).

Long-term investments Generally, (1) investments in stocks and bonds of other companies that companies normally hold for many years, and (2) long-term assets, such as land and buildings, not currently being used in operations. (p. 170).

Long-term liabilities Obligations that a company expects to pay after one year. (p. 172).

Operating cycle The average time that it takes to purchase inventory, sell it on account, and then collect cash from customers. (p. 168).

Permanent (real) accounts Accounts that relate to one or more future accounting periods. Consist of all balance sheet accounts. Balances are carried forward to the next accounting period. (p. 157).

Post-closing trial balance A list of permanent accounts and their balances after a company has journalized and posted closing entries. (p. 162).

Property, plant, and equipment Assets with relatively long useful lives and currently being used in operations. (p. 170).

Reversing entry An entry, made at the beginning of the next accounting period that is the exact opposite of the adjusting entry made in the previous period. (p. 165).

Stockholders' equity The ownership claim of shareholders on total assets. It is to a corporation what owner's equity is to a proprietorship. (p. 173).

Temporary (nominal) accounts Accounts that relate only to a given accounting period. Consist of all income statement accounts and the Dividends account. All temporary accounts are closed at the end of the accounting period. (p. 157).

Worksheet A multiple-column form that may be used in making adjusting entries and in preparing financial statements. (p. 152).

PRACTICE MULTIPLE-CHOICE QUESTIONS

(LO 1) **1.** Which of the following statements is **incorrect** concerning the worksheet?
(a) The worksheet is essentially a working tool of the accountant.

(b) The worksheet is distributed to management and other interested parties.
(c) The worksheet cannot be used as a basis for posting to ledger accounts.

(d) Financial statements can be prepared directly from the worksheet before journalizing and posting the adjusting entries.

(LO 1) 2. In a worksheet, net income is entered in the following columns:
(a) income statement (Dr) and balance sheet (Dr).
(b) income statement (Cr) and balance sheet (Dr).
(c) income statement (Dr) and balance sheet (Cr).
(d) income statement (Cr) and balance sheet (Cr).

(LO 1) 3. In the unadjusted trial balance of its worksheet for the year ended December 31, 2017, Knox Company reported Equipment of $120,000. The year-end adjusting entries require an adjustment of $15,000 for depreciation expense for the equipment. After the adjusted trial balance is completed, what amount should be shown in the financial statement columns?
(a) A debit of $105,000 for Equipment in the balance sheet column.
(b) A credit of $15,000 for Depreciation Expense—Equipment in the income statement column.
(c) A debit of $120,000 for Equipment in the balance sheet column.
(d) A debit of $15,000 for Accumulated Depreciation—Equipment in the balance sheet column.

(LO 2) 4. An account that will have a zero balance after closing entries have been journalized and posted is:
(a) Service Revenue.
(b) Supplies.
(c) Prepaid Insurance.
(d) Accumulated Depreciation—Equipment.

(LO 2) 5. When a net loss has occurred, Income Summary is:
(a) debited and Retained Earnings is credited.
(b) credited and Retained Earnings is debited.
(c) debited and Dividends is credited.
(d) credited and Dividends is debited.

(LO 2) 6. The closing process involves separate entries to close (1) expenses, (2) dividends, (3) revenues, and (4) income summary. The correct sequencing of the entries is:
(a) (4), (3), (2), (1).   (c) (3), (1), (4), (2).
(b) (1), (2), (3), (4).   (d) (3), (2), (1), (4).

(LO 2) 7. Which types of accounts will appear in the post-closing trial balance?
(a) Permanent (real) accounts.
(b) Temporary (nominal) accounts.
(c) Accounts shown in the income statement columns of a worksheet.
(d) None of these answer choices is correct.

(LO 3) 8. All of the following are required steps in the accounting cycle **except**:
(a) journalizing and posting closing entries.
(b) preparing financial statements.
(c) journalizing the transactions.
(d) preparing a worksheet.

(LO 3) 9. The proper order of the following steps in the accounting cycle is:
(a) prepare unadjusted trial balance, journalize transactions, post to ledger accounts, journalize and post adjusting entries.
(b) journalize transactions, prepare unadjusted trial balance, post to ledger accounts, journalize and post adjusting entries.
(c) journalize transactions, post to ledger accounts, prepare unadjusted trial balance, journalize and post adjusting entries.

(d) prepare unadjusted trial balance, journalize and post adjusting entries, journalize transactions, post to ledger accounts.

(LO 3) 10. When Ramirez Company purchased supplies worth $500, it incorrectly recorded a credit to Supplies for $5,000 and a debit to Cash for $5,000. Before correcting this error:
(a) Cash is overstated and Supplies is overstated.
(b) Cash is understated and Supplies is understated.
(c) Cash is understated and Supplies is overstated.
(d) Cash is overstated and Supplies is understated.

(LO 3) 11. Cash of $100 received at the time the service was performed was journalized and posted as a debit to Cash $100 and a credit to Accounts Receivable $100. Assuming the incorrect entry is not reversed, the correcting entry is:
(a) debit Service Revenue $100 and credit Accounts Receivable $100.
(b) debit Accounts Receivable $100 and credit Service Revenue $100.
(c) debit Cash $100 and credit Service Revenue $100.
(d) debit Accounts Receivable $100 and credit Cash $100.

(LO 4) 12. The correct order of presentation in a classified balance sheet for the following current assets is:
(a) accounts receivable, cash, prepaid insurance, inventory.
(b) cash, inventory, accounts receivable, prepaid insurance.
(c) cash, accounts receivable, inventory, prepaid insurance.
(d) inventory, cash, accounts receivable, prepaid insurance.

(LO 4) 13. A company has purchased a tract of land. It expects to build a production plant on the land in approximately 5 years. During the 5 years before construction, the land will be idle. The land should be reported as:
(a) property, plant, and equipment.
(b) land expense.
(c) a long-term investment.
(d) an intangible asset.

(LO 4) 14. In a classified balance sheet, assets are usually classified using the following categories:
(a) current assets; long-term assets; property, plant, and equipment; and intangible assets.
(b) current assets; long-term investments; property, plant, and equipment; and tangible assets.
(c) current assets; long-term investments; tangible assets; and intangible assets.
(d) current assets; long-term investments; property, plant, and equipment; and intangible assets.

(LO 4) 15. Current assets are listed:
(a) by expected conversion to cash.
(b) by importance.
(c) by longevity.
(d) alphabetically.

(LO 5) *16. On December 31, Kevin Hartman Company correctly made an adjusting entry to recognize $2,000 of accrued salaries payable. On January 8 of the next year, total salaries of $3,400 were paid. Assuming the correct reversing entry was made on January 1, the

entry on January 8 will result in a credit to Cash $3,400 and the following debit(s):
(a) Salaries and Wages Payable $1,400 and Salaries and Wages Expense $2,000.

(b) Salaries and Wages Payable $2,000 and Salaries and Wages Expense $1,400.
(c) Salaries and Wages Expense $3,400.
(d) Salaries and Wages Payable $3,400.

Solutions

1. (b) The worksheet is a working tool of the accountant; it is not distributed to management and other interested parties. The other choices are all true statements.

2. (c) Net income is entered in the Dr column of the income statement and the Cr column of the balance sheet. The other choices are incorrect because net income is entered in the (a) Cr (not Dr) column of the balance sheet, (b) Dr (not Cr) column of the income statement and in the Cr (not Dr) column of the balance sheet, and (d) Dr (not Cr) column of the income statement.

3. (c) A debit of $120,000 for Equipment would appear in the balance sheet column. The other choices are incorrect because (a) Equipment, less accumulated depreciation of $15,000, would total $105,000 under assets on the balance sheet, not on the worksheet; (b) a debit, not credit, for Depreciation Expense would appear in the income statement column; and (d) a credit, not debit, of $15,000 for Accumulated Depreciation—Equipment would appear in the balance sheet column.

4. (a) The Service Revenue account will have a zero balance after closing entries have been journalized and posted because it is a temporary account. The other choices are incorrect because (b) Supplies, (c) Prepaid Insurance, and (d) Accumulation Depreciation—Equipment are all permanent accounts and therefore not closed in the closing process.

5. (b) The effect of a net loss is a credit to Income Summary and a debit to Retained Earnings. The other choices are incorrect because (a) Income Summary is credited, not debited, and Retained Earnings is debited, not credited; (c) Income Summary is credited, not debited, and Dividends is not affected; and (d) Retained Earnings, not Dividends, is debited.

6. (c) The correct order is (3) revenues, (1) expenses, (4) income summary and (2) dividends. Therefore, choices (a), (b), and (d) are incorrect.

7. (a) Permanent accounts appear in the post-closing trial balance. The other choices are incorrect because (b) temporary accounts and (c) income statement accounts are closed to a zero balance and are therefore not included in the post-closing trial balance. Choice (d) is wrong as there is only one correct answer for this question.

8. (d) Preparing a worksheet is not a required step in the accounting cycle. The other choices are all required steps in the accounting cycle.

9. (c) The proper order of the steps in the accounting cycle is (1) journalize transactions, (2) post to ledger accounts, (3) prepare unadjusted trial balance, and (4) journalize and post adjusting entries. Therefore, choices (a), (b), and (d) are incorrect.

10. (d) This entry causes Cash to be overstated and Supplies to be understated. Supplies should have been debited (increasing supplies) and Cash should have been credited (decreasing cash). The other choices are incorrect because (a) Supplies is understated, not overstated; (b) Cash is overstated, not understated; and (c) Cash is overstated, not understated, and Supplies is understated, not overstated.

11. (b) The correcting entry is to debit Accounts Receivable $100 and credit Service Revenue $100. The other choices are incorrect because (a) Service Revenue should be credited, not debited, and Accounts Receivable should be debited, not credited; (c) Service Revenue should be credited for $100, and Cash should not be included in the correcting entry as it was recorded properly; and (d) Accounts Receivable should be debited for $100 and Cash should not be included in the correcting entry as it was recorded properly.

12. (c) Companies list current assets on balance sheet in the order of liquidity: cash, accounts receivable, inventory, and prepaid insurance. Therefore, choices (a), (b), and (d) are incorrect.

13. (c) Long-term investments include long-term assets such as land that a company is not currently using in its operating activities. The other choices are incorrect because (a) land would be reported as property, plant, and equipment only if it is being currently used in the business; (b) land is an asset, not an expense; and (d) land has physical substance and thus is a tangible property.

14. (d) These are the categories usually used in a classified balance sheet. The other choices are incorrect because the categories (a) "long-term assets" and (b) and (c) "tangible assets" are generally not used.

15. (a) Current assets are listed in order of their liquidity, not (b) by importance, (c) by longevity, or (d) alphabetically.

*16. (c) The use of reversing entries simplifies the recording of the first payroll following the end of the year by eliminating the need to make an entry to the Salaries and Wages Payable account. The other choices are incorrect because (a) Salaries and Wages Payable is not part of the payroll entry on January 8, and the debit to Salaries and Wages Expense should be for $3,400, not $2,000; and (b) and (d) the Salaries and Wages Expense account, not the Salaries and Wages Payable account, should be debited.

PRACTICE EXERCISES

1. Arapaho Company ended its fiscal year on July 31, 2017. The company's adjusted trial balance as of the end of its fiscal year is as shown below.

Journalize and post closing entries, and prepare a post-closing trial balance.

(LO 2)

ARAPAHO COMPANY
Adjusted Trial Balance
July 31, 2017

No.	Account Titles	Debit	Credit
101	Cash	$ 15,940	
112	Accounts Receivable	8,580	
157	Equipment	16,900	
158	Accumulated Depreciation—Equipment		$ 7,500
201	Accounts Payable		4,420
208	Unearned Rent Revenue		1,600
311	Common Stock		20,500
320	Retained Earnings		25,000
332	Dividends	14,000	
400	Service Revenue		64,000
429	Rent Revenue		5,500
711	Depreciation Expense	4,500	
726	Salaries and Wages Expense	54,700	
732	Utilities Expense	13,900	
		$128,520	$128,520

Instructions

(a) Prepare the closing entries using page J15 in a general journal.

(b) Post to Retained Earnings and No. 350 Income Summary accounts. (Use the three-column form.)

(c) Prepare a post-closing trial balance at July 31, 2017.

Solution

1. (a)

	GENERAL JOURNAL			J15
Date	**Account Titles**	**Ref.**	**Debit**	**Credit**
July 31	Service Revenue	400	64,000	
	Rent Revenue	429	5,500	
	Income Summary	350		69,500
	(To close revenue accounts)			
31	Income Summary	350	73,100	
	Depreciation Expense	711		4,500
	Salaries and Wages Expense	726		54,700
	Utilities Expense	732		13,900
	(To close expense accounts)			
31	Retained Earnings	320	3,600	
	Income Summary	350		3,600
	(To close net loss to retained earnings)			
31	Retained Earnings	320	14,000	
	Dividends	332		14,000
	(To close dividends to retained earnings)			

(b)

	Retained Earnings				No. 320
Date	**Explanation**	**Ref.**	**Debit**	**Credit**	**Balance**
July 31	Balance				25,000
31	Close net loss	J15	3,600		21,400
31	Close dividends	J15	14,000		7,400

	Income Summary				No. 350
Date	**Explanation**	**Ref.**	**Debit**	**Credit**	**Balance**
July 31	Close revenue	J15		69,500	69,500
31	Close expenses	J15	73,100		(3,600)
31	Close net loss	J15		3,600	0

(c)

ARAPAHO COMPANY Post-Closing Trial Balance July 31, 2017	Debit	Credit
Cash	$15,940	
Accounts Receivable	8,580	
Equipment	16,900	
Accumulated Depreciation—Equipment		$ 7,500
Accounts Payable		4,420
Unearned Rent Revenue		1,600
Common Stock		20,500
Retained Earnings		7,400
	$41,420	$41,420

Prepare financial statements.

(LO 4)

2. The adjusted trial balance for Arapaho Company is presented in **Practice Exercise 1**.

Instructions

(a) Prepare an income statement and a retained earnings statement for the year ended July 31, 2017.

(b) Prepare a classified balance sheet at July 31, 2017.

Solution

2. (a)

ARAPAHO COMPANY Income Statement For the Year Ended July 31, 2017		
Revenues		
Service revenue	$64,000	
Rent revenue	5,500	
Total revenues		$69,500
Expenses		
Salaries and wages expense	54,700	
Utilities expense	13,900	
Depreciation expense	4,500	
Total expenses		73,100
Net loss		($ 3,600)

ARAPAHO COMPANY Retained Earnings Statement For the Year Ended July 31, 2017		
Retained Earnings, August 1, 2016		$25,000
Less: Net loss	$ 3,600	
Dividends	14,000	17,600
Retained Earnings, July 31, 2017		$ 7,400

(b)

ARAPAHO COMPANY
Balance Sheet
July 31, 2017

Assets

Current assets		
Cash	$15,940	
Accounts receivable	8,580	
Total current assets		$24,520
Property, plant, and equipment		
Equipment	16,900	
Less: Accumulated depreciation—equipment	7,500	9,400
Total assets		$33,920

Liabilities and Stockholders' Equity

Current liabilities		
Accounts payable	$ 4,420	
Unearned rent revenue	1,600	
Total current liabilities		$ 6,020
Stockholders' equity		
Common stock	20,500	
Retained earnings	7,400	
Total stockholders' equity		27,900
Total liabilities and stockholders' equity		$33,920

■ PRACTICE PROBLEM

At the end of its first month of operations, Pampered Pet Service Inc. has the following unadjusted trial balance.

Prepare worksheet and classified balance sheet, and journalize closing entries.

(LO 1, 2, 4)

PAMPERED PET SERVICE INC.
August 31, 2017
Trial Balance

	Debit	Credit
Cash	$ 5,400	
Accounts Receivable	2,800	
Supplies	1,300	
Prepaid Insurance	2,400	
Equipment	60,000	
Notes Payable		$40,000
Accounts Payable		2,400
Common Stock		30,000
Dividends	1,000	
Service Revenue		4,900
Salaries and Wages Expense	3,200	
Utilities Expense	800	
Advertising Expense	400	
	$77,300	$77,300

Other data:

1. Insurance expires at the rate of $200 per month.
2. $1,000 of supplies are on hand at August 31.
3. Monthly depreciation on the equipment is $900.
4. Interest of $500 on the notes payable has accrued during August.

Instructions

(a) Prepare a worksheet.

(b) Prepare a classified balance sheet assuming $35,000 of the notes payable are long-term.

(c) Journalize the closing entries.

Solution

(a)

PAMPERED PET SERVICE INC.
Worksheet for the Month Ended August 31, 2017

Account Titles	Trial Balance Dr.	Trial Balance Cr.	Adjustments Dr.	Adjustments Cr.	Adjusted Trial Balance Dr.	Adjusted Trial Balance Cr.	Income Statement Dr.	Income Statement Cr.	Balance Sheet Dr.	Balance Sheet Cr.
Cash	5,400				5,400				5,400	
Accounts Receivable	2,800				2,800				2,800	
Supplies	1,300			(b) 300	1,000				1,000	
Prepaid Insurance	2,400			(a) 200	2,200				2,200	
Equipment	60,000				60,000				60,000	
Notes Payable		40,000				40,000				40,000
Accounts Payable		2,400				2,400				2,400
Common Stock		30,000				30,000				30,000
Dividends	1,000				1,000				1,000	
Service Revenue		4,900				4,900		4,900		
Salaries and Wages Expense	3,200				3,200		3,200			
Utilities Expense	800				800		800			
Advertising Expense	400				400		400			
Totals	77,300	77,300								
Insurance Expense			(a) 200		200		200			
Supplies Expense			(b) 300		300		300			
Depreciation Expense			(c) 900		900		900			
Accumulated Depreciation— Equipment				(c) 900		900				900
Interest Expense			(d) 500		500		500			
Interest Payable				(d) 500		500				500
Totals			1,900	1,900	78,700	78,700	6,300	4,900	72,400	73,800
Net Loss								1,400	1,400	
Totals							6,300	6,300	73,800	73,800

Explanation: (a) insurance expired, (b) supplies used, (c) depreciation expensed, and (d) interest accrued.

(b)

PAMPERED PET SERVICE INC.
Balance Sheet
August 31, 2017

Assets

Current assets		
Cash	$ 5,400	
Accounts receivable	2,800	
Supplies	1,000	
Prepaid insurance	2,200	
Total current assets		$11,400
Property, plant, and equipment		
Equipment	60,000	
Less: Accumulated depreciation—equipment	900	59,100
Total assets		$70,500

Liabilities and Stockholders' Equity

Current liabilities		
Notes payable	$ 5,000	
Accounts payable	2,400	
Interest payable	500	
Total current liabilities		$ 7,900
Long-term liabilities		
Notes payable		35,000
Total liabilities		42,900
Stockholders' equity		
Common stock	30,000	
Retained earnings	(2,400)*	
Total stockholders' equity		27,600
Total liabilities and stockholders' equity		$70,500

*Net loss $1,400, plus dividends of $1,000.

(c)

Aug. 31		Service Revenue	4,900	
		Income Summary		4,900
		(To close revenue account)		
	31	Income Summary	6,300	
		Salaries and Wages Expense		3,200
		Depreciation Expense		900
		Utilities Expense		800
		Interest Expense		500
		Advertising Expense		400
		Supplies Expense		300
		Insurance Expense		200
		(To close expense accounts)		
	31	Retained Earnings	1,400	
		Income Summary		1,400
		(To close net loss to retained earnings)		
	31	Retained Earnings	1,000	
		Dividends		1,000
		(To close dividends to retained earnings)		

WileyPLUS

Brief Exercises, Exercises, **DO IT!** Exercises, and Problems and many additional resources are available for practice in WileyPLUS

NOTE: All asterisked Questions, Exercises, and Problems relate to material in the appendix to the chapter.

QUESTIONS

1. "A worksheet is a permanent accounting record and its use is required in the accounting cycle." Do you agree? Explain.
2. Explain the purpose of the worksheet.
3. What is the relationship, if any, between the amount shown in the adjusted trial balance column for an account and that account's ledger balance?
4. If a company's revenues are $125,000 and its expenses are $113,000, in which financial statement columns of the worksheet will the net income of $12,000 appear? When expenses exceed revenues, in which columns will the difference appear?
5. Why is it necessary to prepare formal financial statements if all of the data are in the statement columns of the worksheet?
6. Identify the account(s) debited and credited in each of the four closing entries, assuming the company has net income for the year.
7. Describe the nature of the Income Summary account and identify the types of summary data that may be posted to this account.
8. What are the content and purpose of a post-closing trial balance?
9. Which of the following accounts would not appear in the post-closing trial balance? Interest Payable; Equipment; Depreciation Expense; Dividends; Unearned Service Revenue; Accumulated Depreciation—Equipment; and Service Revenue.
10. Distinguish between a reversing entry and an adjusting entry. Are reversing entries required?
11. Indicate, in the sequence in which they are made, the three required steps in the accounting cycle that involve journalizing.
12. Identify, in the sequence in which they are prepared, the three trial balances that are often used to report financial information about a company.
13. How do correcting entries differ from adjusting entries?
14. What standard classifications are used in preparing a classified balance sheet?
15. What is meant by the term "operating cycle?"
16. Define current assets. What basis is used for arranging individual items within the current assets section?
17. Distinguish between long-term investments and property, plant, and equipment.
18. (a) What is the term used to describe the owners' equity section of a corporation? (b) Identify the two owners' equity accounts in a corporation and indicate the purpose of each.
19. Using **Apple**'s annual report, determine its current liabilities at September 29, 2012, and September 28, 2013. Were current liabilities higher or lower than current assets in these two years?
*20. Cigale Company prepares reversing entries. If the adjusting entry for interest payable is reversed, what type of an account balance, if any, will there be in Interest Payable and Interest Expense after the reversing entry is posted?
*21. At December 31, accrued salaries payable totaled $3,500. On January 10, total salaries of $8,000 are paid. (a) Assume that reversing entries are made at January 1. Give the January 10 entry, and indicate the Salaries and Wages Expense account balance after the entry is posted. (b) Repeat part (a) assuming reversing entries are not made.

BRIEF EXERCISES

List the steps in preparing a worksheet.

(LO 1)

BE4-1 The steps in using a worksheet are presented in random order below. List the steps in the proper order by placing numbers 1–5 in the blank spaces.
(a) _____ Prepare a trial balance on the worksheet.
(b) _____ Enter adjusted balances.
(c) _____ Extend adjusted balances to appropriate statement columns.
(d) _____ Total the statement columns, compute net income (loss), and complete the worksheet.
(e) _____ Enter adjustment data.

Prepare partial worksheet.

(LO 1)

BE4-2 The ledger of Clayton Company includes the following unadjusted balances: Prepaid Insurance $3,000, Service Revenue $58,000, and Salaries and Wages Expense $25,000. Adjusting entries are required for (a) expired insurance $1,800; (b) services performed $1,100, but unbilled and uncollected; and (c) accrued salaries payable $800.

Enter the unadjusted balances and adjustments into a worksheet and complete the worksheet for all accounts. (Note: You will need to add the following accounts: Accounts Receivable, Salaries and Wages Payable, and Insurance Expense.)

BE4-3 The following selected accounts appear in the adjusted trial balance columns of the worksheet for Goulet Company: Accumulated Depreciation—Equipment; Depreciation Expense; Common Stock; Dividends; Service Revenue; Supplies; and Accounts Payable. Indicate the financial statement column (income statement Dr., balance sheet Cr., etc.) to which each balance should be extended.

Identify worksheet columns for selected accounts.
(LO 1)

BE4-4 The ledger of Rios Company contains the following balances: Retained Earnings $30,000; Dividends $2,000; Service Revenue $50,000; Salaries and Wages Expense $27,000; and Supplies Expense $7,000. Prepare the closing entries at December 31.

Prepare closing entries from ledger balances.
(LO 2)

BE4-5 Using the data in BE4-4, enter the balances in T-accounts, post the closing entries, and underline and balance the accounts.

Post closing entries; underline and balance T-accounts.
(LO 2)

BE4-6 The income statement for Weeping Willow Golf Club for the month ending July 31 shows Service Revenue $16,400, Salaries and Wages Expense $8,200, Maintenance and Repairs Expense $2,500, and Net Income $5,700. Prepare the entries to close the revenue and expense accounts. Post the entries to the revenue and expense accounts, and complete the closing process for these accounts using the three-column form of account.

Journalize and post closing entries using the three-column form of account.
(LO 2)

BE4-7 Using the data in BE4-3, identify the accounts that would be included in a post-closing trial balance.

Identify post-closing trial balance accounts.
(LO 2)

BE4-8 The steps in the accounting cycle are listed in random order below. List the steps in proper sequence, assuming no worksheet is prepared, by placing numbers 1–9 in the blank spaces.

List the required steps in the accounting cycle in sequence.
(LO 3)

(a) _____ Prepare a trial balance.
(b) _____ Journalize the transactions.
(c) _____ Journalize and post closing entries.
(d) _____ Prepare financial statements.
(e) _____ Journalize and post adjusting entries.
(f) _____ Post to ledger accounts.
(g) _____ Prepare a post-closing trial balance.
(h) _____ Prepare an adjusted trial balance.
(i) _____ Analyze business transactions.

BE4-9 At Creighton Company, the following errors were discovered after the transactions had been journalized and posted. Prepare the correcting entries.

Prepare correcting entries.
(LO 3)

1. A collection on account from a customer for $870 was recorded as a debit to Cash $870 and a credit to Service Revenue $870.
2. The purchase of store supplies on account for $1,570 was recorded as a debit to Supplies $1,750 and a credit to Accounts Payable $1,750.

BE4-10 The balance sheet debit column of the worksheet for Hamidi Company includes the following accounts: Accounts Receivable $12,500, Prepaid Insurance $3,600, Cash $4,100, Supplies $5,200, and Debt Investments (short-term) $6,700. Prepare the current assets section of the balance sheet, listing the accounts in proper sequence.

Prepare the current assets section of a balance sheet.
(LO 4)

BE4-11 The following are the major balance sheet classifications:

Classify accounts on balance sheet.
(LO 4)

Current assets (CA)
Long-term investments (LTI)
Property, plant, and equipment (PPE)
Intangible assets (IA)

Current liabilities (CL)
Long-term liabilities (LTL)
Stockholders' equity (SE)

Match each of the following accounts to its proper balance sheet classification.

_____ Accounts payable	_____ Income taxes payable
_____ Accounts receivable	_____ Debt investments (long-term)
_____ Accumulated depreciation—buildings	_____ Land
_____ Buildings	_____ Inventory
_____ Cash	_____ Patents
_____ Copyrights	_____ Supplies

Prepare reversing entries.

(LO 5)

*BE4-12 At October 31, Burgess Company made an accrued expense adjusting entry of $2,100 for salaries. Prepare the reversing entry on November 1, and indicate the balances in Salaries and Wages Payable and Salaries and Wages Expense after posting the reversing entry.

DO IT! Exercises

Prepare a worksheet.

(LO 1)

DO IT! 4-1 Bradley Decker is preparing a worksheet. Explain to Bradley how he should extend the following adjusted trial balance accounts to the financial statement columns of the worksheet.

Service Revenue	Accounts Receivable
Notes Payable	Accumulated Depreciation
Common Stock	Utilities Expense

Prepare closing entries.

(LO 2)

DO IT! 4-2 The worksheet for Tsai Company shows the following in the financial statement columns.

Dividends	$22,000
Common Stock	70,000
Net income	41,000

Prepare the closing entries at December 31 that affect stockholders' equity.

Prepare correcting entries.

(LO 3)

DO IT! 4-3 Hanson Company has an inexperienced accountant. During the first months on the job, the accountant made the following errors in journalizing transactions. All entries were posted as made.

1. The purchase of supplies for $650 cash was debited to Equipment $210 and credited to Cash $210.
2. A $500 withdrawal of cash for B. Hanson's personal use was debited to Salaries and Wages Expense $900 and credited to Cash $900.
3. A payment on account of $820 to a creditor was debited to Accounts Payable $280 and credited to Cash $280.

Prepare the correcting entries.

Match accounts to balance sheet classifications.

(LO 4)

DO IT! 4-4 The following accounts were taken from the financial statements of Lee Company.

_____ Interest revenue	_____ Common stock
_____ Utilities payable	_____ Accumulated depreciation—equipment
_____ Accounts payable	_____ Equipment
_____ Supplies	_____ Salaries and wages expense
_____ Bonds payable	_____ Debt investments (long-term)
_____ Goodwill	_____ Unearned rent revenue

Match each of the accounts to its proper balance sheet classification, as shown below. If the item would not appear on a balance sheet, use "NA."

Current assets (CA)	Current liabilities (CL)
Long-term investments (LTI)	Long-term liabilities (LTL)
Property, plant, and equipment (PPE)	Stockholders' equity (SE)
Intangible assets (IA)	

EXERCISES

E4-1 The trial balance columns of the worksheet for Nanduri Company at June 30, 2017, are as follows.

Complete the worksheet.
(LO 1)

NANDURI COMPANY
Worksheet
For the Month Ended June 30, 2017

Account Titles	Trial Balance Dr.	Trial Balance Cr.
Cash	2,320	
Accounts Receivable	2,440	
Supplies	1,880	
Accounts Payable		1,120
Unearned Service Revenue		240
Common Stock		3,600
Service Revenue		2,400
Salaries and Wages Expense	560	
Miscellaneous Expense	160	
	7,360	7,360

Other data:

1. A physical count reveals $500 of supplies on hand.
2. $100 of the unearned revenue is still unearned at month-end.
3. Accrued salaries are $210.

Instructions
Enter the trial balance on a worksheet and complete the worksheet.

E4-2 The adjusted trial balance columns of the worksheet for DeSousa Company are as follows.

Complete the worksheet.
(LO 1)

DESOUSA COMPANY
Worksheet (partial)
For the Month Ended April 30, 2017

Account Titles	Adjusted Trial Balance Dr.	Adjusted Trial Balance Cr.	Income Statement Dr.	Income Statement Cr.	Balance Sheet Dr.	Balance Sheet Cr.
Cash	10,000					
Accounts Receivable	7,840					
Prepaid Rent	2,280					
Equipment	23,050					
Accumulated Depreciation—Equip.		4,921				
Notes Payable		5,700				
Accounts Payable		4,920				
Common Stock		20,000				
Retained Earnings		7,960				
Dividends	3,650					
Service Revenue		15,590				
Salaries and Wages Expense	10,840					
Rent Expense	760					
Depreciation Expense	671					
Interest Expense	57					
Interest Payable		57				
Totals	59,148	59,148				

Instructions
Complete the worksheet.

Prepare financial statements from worksheet.

(LO 1, 4)

E4-3 Worksheet data for DeSousa Company are presented in E4-2.

Instructions

Prepare an income statement, a retained earnings statement, and a classified balance sheet.

Journalize and post closing entries and prepare a post-closing trial balance.

(LO 2)

E4-4 Worksheet data for DeSousa Company are presented in E4-2.

Instructions

(a) Journalize the closing entries at April 30.
(b) Post the closing entries to Income Summary and Retained Earnings. (Use T-accounts.)
(c) Prepare a post-closing trial balance at April 30.

Prepare adjusting entries from a worksheet, and extend balances to worksheet columns.

(LO 1)

E4-5 The adjustments columns of the worksheet for Misra Company are shown below.

	Adjustments	
Account Titles	**Debit**	**Credit**
Accounts Receivable	1,100	
Prepaid Insurance		300
Accumulated Depreciation—Equipment		900
Salaries and Wages Payable		500
Service Revenue		1,100
Salaries and Wages Expense	500	
Insurance Expense	300	
Depreciation Expense	900	
	2,800	2,800

Instructions

(a) Prepare the adjusting entries.
(b) Assuming the adjusted trial balance amount for each account is normal, indicate the financial statement column to which each balance should be extended.

Derive adjusting entries from worksheet data.

(LO 1)

E4-6 Selected worksheet data for Elsayed Company are presented below.

	Trial Balance		Adjusted Trial Balance	
Account Titles	**Dr.**	**Cr.**	**Dr.**	**Cr.**
Accounts Receivable	?		34,000	
Prepaid Insurance	26,000		20,000	
Supplies	7,000		?	
Accumulated Depreciation—Equipment		12,000		?
Salaries and Wages Payable		?		5,600
Service Revenue		88,000		97,000
Insurance Expense			?	
Depreciation Expense			10,000	
Supplies Expense			4,500	
Salaries and Wages Expense	?		49,000	

Instructions

(a) Fill in the missing amounts.
(b) Prepare the adjusting entries that were made.

Prepare closing entries, and prepare a post-closing trial balance.

(LO 2)

E4-7 Kay Magill Company had the following adjusted trial balance.

KAY MAGILL COMPANY
Adjusted Trial Balance
For the Month Ended June 30, 2017

Account Titles	Adjusted Trial Balance Debit	Adjusted Trial Balance Credit
Cash	$ 3,712	
Accounts Receivable	3,904	
Supplies	480	
Accounts Payable		$ 1,556
Unearned Service Revenue		160
Common Stock		4,000
Retained Earnings		1,760
Dividends	628	
Service Revenue		4,300
Salaries and Wages Expense	1,344	
Miscellaneous Expense	256	
Supplies Expense	1,900	
Salaries and Wages Payable		448
	$12,224	$12,224

Instructions
(a) Prepare closing entries at June 30, 2017.
(b) Prepare a post-closing trial balance.

E4-8 Plevin Company ended its fiscal year on July 31, 2017. The company's adjusted trial balance as of the end of its fiscal year is shown below.

Journalize and post closing entries, and prepare a post-closing trial balance.

(LO 2)

PLEVIN COMPANY
Adjusted Trial Balance
July 31, 2017

No.	Account Titles	Debit	Credit
101	Cash	$ 9,840	
112	Accounts Receivable	8,780	
157	Equipment	15,900	
158	Accumulated Depreciation—Equip.		$ 7,400
201	Accounts Payable		4,220
208	Unearned Rent Revenue		1,800
311	Common Stock		20,000
320	Retained Earnings		25,200
332	Dividends	16,000	
400	Service Revenue		64,000
429	Rent Revenue		6,500
711	Depreciation Expense	8,000	
726	Salaries and Wages Expense	55,700	
732	Utilities Expense	14,900	
		$129,120	$129,120

Instructions
(a) Prepare the closing entries using page J15.
(b) Post to the Retained Earnings and No. 350 Income Summary accounts. (Use the three-column form.)
(c) Prepare a post-closing trial balance at July 31.

E4-9 The adjusted trial balance for Plevin Company is presented in E4-8.

Prepare financial statements.

(LO 4)

Instructions
(a) Prepare an income statement and a retained earnings statement for the year.
(b) Prepare a classified balance sheet at July 31.

Answer questions related to the accounting cycle.

(LO 3)

E4-10 Janis Engle has prepared the following list of statements about the accounting cycle.

1. "Journalize the transactions" is the first step in the accounting cycle.
2. Reversing entries are a required step in the accounting cycle.
3. Correcting entries do not have to be part of the accounting cycle.
4. If a worksheet is prepared, some steps of the accounting cycle are incorporated into the worksheet.
5. The accounting cycle begins with the analysis of business transactions and ends with the preparation of a post-closing trial balance.
6. All steps of the accounting cycle occur daily during the accounting period.
7. The step of "post to the ledger accounts" occurs before the step of "journalize the transactions."
8. Closing entries must be prepared before financial statements can be prepared.

Instructions

Identify each statement as true or false. If false, indicate how to correct the statement.

Prepare closing entries.

(LO 2)

E4-11 Selected accounts for Heather's Salon are presented below. All June 30 postings are from closing entries.

Salaries and Wages Expense				Service Revenue				Retained Earnings				
6/10	3,200	6/30	8,800	6/30	18,100	6/15	9,700	6/30	2,500	6/1	12,000
6/28	5,600					6/24	8,400			6/30	5,000
										Bal.	14,500

Supplies Expense				Rent Expense				Dividends				
6/12	600	6/30	1,300	6/1	3,000	6/30	3,000	6/13	1,000	6/30	2,500
6/24	700							6/25	1,500		

Instructions

(a) Prepare the closing entries that were made.

(b) Post the closing entries to Income Summary.

Prepare correcting entries.

(LO 3)

E4-12 Andrew Clark Company discovered the following errors made in January 2017.

1. A payment of Salaries and Wages Expense of $700 was debited to Equipment and credited to Cash, both for $700.
2. A collection of $1,000 from a client on account was debited to Cash $100 and credited to Service Revenue $100.
3. The purchase of equipment on account for $760 was debited to Equipment $670 and credited to Accounts Payable $670.

Instructions

(a) Correct the errors by reversing the incorrect entry and preparing the correct entry.

(b) Correct the errors without reversing the incorrect entry.

Prepare correcting entries.

(LO 3)

E4-13 Keenan Company has an inexperienced accountant. During the first 2 weeks on the job, the accountant made the following errors in journalizing transactions. All entries were posted as made.

1. A payment on account of $840 to a creditor was debited to Accounts Payable $480 and credited to Cash $480.
2. The purchase of supplies on account for $560 was debited to Equipment $56 and credited to Accounts Payable $56.
3. A $500 cash dividend was debited to Salaries and Wages Expense $500 and credited to Cash $500.

Instructions

Prepare the correcting entries.

Prepare a classified balance sheet.

(LO 4)

E4-14 The adjusted trial balance for Martell Bowling Alley at December 31, 2017, contains the following accounts.

	Debit		Credit
Buildings	$128,800	Common Stock	$ 90,000
Accounts Receivable	14,520	Retained Earnings	25,000
Prepaid Insurance	4,680	Accumulated Depreciation—Buildings	42,600
Cash	18,040	Accounts Payable	12,300
Equipment	62,400	Notes Payable	97,780
Land	67,000	Accumulated Depreciation—Equipment	18,720
Insurance Expense	780	Interest Payable	2,600
Depreciation Expense	7,360	Service Revenue	17,180
Interest Expense	2,600		$306,180
	$306,180		

Instructions

(a) Prepare a classified balance sheet; assume that $22,000 of the note payable will be paid in 2018.

(b) ━━━━━ Comment on the liquidity of the company.

E4-15 The following are the major balance sheet classifications.

Classify accounts on balance sheet.

(LO 4)

Current assets (CA)	Current liabilities (CL)
Long-term investments (LTI)	Long-term liabilities (LTL)
Property, plant, and equipment (PPE)	Stockholders' equity (SE)
Intangible assets (IA)	

Instructions

Classify each of the following accounts taken from Raman Company's balance sheet.

_____	Accounts payable	_____	Accumulated depreciation—equipment
_____	Accounts receivable	_____	Buildings
_____	Cash	_____	Land (in use)
_____	Common stock	_____	Notes payable (due in 2 years)
_____	Patents	_____	Supplies
_____	Salaries and wages payable	_____	Equipment
_____	Inventory	_____	Prepaid expenses
_____	Stock investments		
	(to be sold in 7 months)		

E4-16 The following items were taken from the financial statements of D. Gygi Company. (All amounts are in thousands.)

Prepare a classified balance sheet.

(LO 4)

Long-term debt	$ 1,000	Accumulated depreciation—equipment	$ 5,655
Prepaid insurance	880	Accounts payable	1,444
Equipment	11,500	Notes payable (due after 2018)	400
Stock investments (long-term)	264	Common stock	10,000
Debt investments (short-term)	3,690	Retained earnings	2,955
Notes payable (due in 2018)	500	Accounts receivable	1,696
Cash	2,668	Inventory	1,256

Instructions

Prepare a classified balance sheet in good form as of December 31, 2017.

E4-17 These financial statement items are for Norsted Company at year-end, July 31, 2017.

Prepare financial statements.

(LO 4)

Salaries and wages payable	$ 2,080	Notes payable (long-term)	$ 1,800
Salaries and wages expense	51,700	Cash	14,200
Utilities expense	22,600	Accounts receivable	9,780
Equipment	30,400	Accumulated depreciation—equipment	6,000
Accounts payable	4,100	Dividends	3,000
Service revenue	62,000	Depreciation expense	4,000
Rent revenue	8,500	Retained earnings (beginning of the year)	21,200
Common stock	30,000		

Instructions

(a) Prepare an income statement and a retained earnings statement for the year.

(b) Prepare a classified balance sheet at July 31.

Use reversing entries.
(LO 5)

*E4-18 Reblin Company pays salaries of $12,000 every Monday for the preceding 5-day week (Monday through Friday). Assume December 31 falls on a Tuesday, so Reblin's employees have worked 2 days without being paid.

Instructions

(a) Assume the company does not use reversing entries. Prepare the December 31 adjusting entry and the entry on Monday, January 6, when Reblin pays the payroll.

(b) Assume the company does use reversing entries. Prepare the December 31 adjusting entry, the January 1 reversing entry, and the entry on Monday, January 6, when Reblin pays the payroll.

Prepare closing and reversing entries.
(LO 2, 5)

*E4-19 On December 31, the adjusted trial balance of Cisneros Employment Agency shows the following selected data.

Accounts Receivable	$24,500	Service Revenue	$92,500
Interest Expense	8,300	Interest Payable	2,000

Analysis shows that adjusting entries were made to (1) accrue $5,000 of service revenue and (2) accrue $2,000 interest expense.

Instructions

(a) Prepare the closing entries for the temporary accounts shown above at December 31.

(b) Prepare the reversing entries on January 1.

(c) Post the entries in (a) and (b), excluding the Income Summary account. Underline and balance the accounts. (Use T-accounts.)

(d) Prepare the entries to record (1) the collection of the accrued revenue on January 10 and (2) the payment of all interest due ($3,000) on January 15.

(e) Post the entries in (d) to the temporary accounts.

EXERCISES: SET B AND CHALLENGE EXERCISES

Visit the book's companion website, at **www.wiley.com/college/weygandt**, and choose the Student Companion site to access Exercises: Set B and Challenge Exercises.

PROBLEMS: SET A

Prepare a worksheet, financial statements, and adjusting and closing entries.
(LO 1, 2, 4)

P4-1A The trial balance columns of the worksheet for Lampert Roofing at March 31, 2017, are as follows.

LAMPERT ROOFING
Worksheet
For the Month Ended March 31, 2017

	Trial Balance	
Account Titles	Dr.	Cr.
Cash	4,500	
Accounts Receivable	3,200	
Supplies	2,000	
Equipment	11,000	
Accumulated Depreciation—Equipment		1,250
Accounts Payable		2,500
Unearned Service Revenue		550
Common Stock		10,000
Retained Earnings		2,900
Dividends	1,100	
Service Revenue		6,300
Salaries and Wages Expense	1,300	
Miscellaneous Expense	400	
	23,500	23,500

Other data:

1. A physical count reveals only $550 of roofing supplies on hand.
2. Depreciation for March is $250.
3. Unearned service revenue amounted to $210 at March 31.
4. Accrued salaries are $700.

Instructions

(a) Enter the trial balance on a worksheet and complete the worksheet.
(b) Prepare an income statement and a retained earnings statement for the month of March and a classified balance sheet at March 31.
(c) Journalize the adjusting entries from the adjustments columns of the worksheet.
(d) Journalize the closing entries from the financial statement columns of the worksheet.

(a) Adjusted trial balance
$24,450
(b) Net income $2,540
Total assets $17,750

P4-2A The adjusted trial balance columns of the worksheet for Alshwer Company are as follows.

Complete worksheet; prepare financial statements, closing entries, and post-closing trial balance.

(LO 1, 2, 4)

ALSHWER COMPANY
Worksheet
For the Year Ended December 31, 2017

Account No.	Account Titles	Adjusted Trial Balance	
		Dr.	Cr.
101	Cash	5,300	
112	Accounts Receivable	10,800	
126	Supplies	1,500	
130	Prepaid Insurance	2,000	
157	Equipment	27,000	
158	Accumulated Depreciation—Equipment		5,600
200	Notes Payable		15,000
201	Accounts Payable		6,100
212	Salaries and Wages Payable		2,400
230	Interest Payable		600
311	Common Stock		10,000
320	Retained Earnings		3,000
332	Dividends	7,000	
400	Service Revenue		61,000
610	Advertising Expense	8,400	
631	Supplies Expense	4,000	
711	Depreciation Expense	5,600	
722	Insurance Expense	3,500	
726	Salaries and Wages Expense	28,000	
905	Interest Expense	600	
	Totals	103,700	103,700

Instructions

(a) Complete the worksheet by extending the balances to the financial statement columns.
(b) Prepare an income statement, a retained earnings statement, and a classified balance sheet. (*Note:* $5,000 of the notes payable become due in 2018.)
(c) Prepare the closing entries. Use J14 for the journal page.
(d) Post the closing entries. (Use the three-column form of account.) Income Summary is No. 350.
(e) Prepare a post-closing trial balance.

(a) Net income $10,900
(b) Current assets $19,600
Current liabilities $14,100
(e) Post-closing trial balance
$46,600

P4-3A The completed financial statement columns of the worksheet for Fleming Company are shown on the next page.

Prepare financial statements, closing entries, and post-closing trial balance.

(LO 1, 2, 4)

FLEMING COMPANY
Worksheet
For the Year Ended December 31, 2017

Account No.	Account Titles	Income Statement Dr.	Income Statement Cr.	Balance Sheet Dr.	Balance Sheet Cr.
101	Cash			8,900	
112	Accounts Receivable			10,800	
130	Prepaid Insurance			2,800	
157	Equipment			24,000	
158	Accumulated Depreciation—Equip.				4,500
201	Accounts Payable				9,000
212	Salaries and Wages Payable				2,400
311	Common Stock				12,000
320	Retained Earnings				7,500
332	Dividends			11,000	
400	Service Revenue		60,000		
622	Maintenance and Repairs Expense	1,600			
711	Depreciation Expense	3,100			
722	Insurance Expense	1,800			
726	Salaries and Wages Expense	30,000			
732	Utilities Expense	1,400			
	Totals	37,900	60,000	57,500	35,400
	Net Income	22,100			22,100
		60,000	60,000	57,500	57,500

Instructions

(a) Prepare an income statement, a retained earnings statement, and a classified balance sheet.
(b) Prepare the closing entries.
(c) Post the closing entries and underline and balance the accounts. (Use T-accounts.) Income Summary is account No. 350.
(d) Prepare a post-closing trial balance.

(a) Ending retained earnings $18,600
Total current assets $22,500

(d) Post-closing trial balance $46,500

Complete worksheet; prepare classified balance sheet, entries, and post-closing trial balance.

(LO 1, 2, 4)

P4-4A Jarmuz Management Services began business on January 1, 2017, with a capital investment of $90,000. The company manages condominiums for owners (service revenue) and rents space in its own office building (rent revenue). The trial balance and adjusted trial balance columns of the worksheet at the end of 2017 are as follows.

JARMUZ MANAGEMENT SERVICES
Worksheet
For the Year Ended December 31, 2017

Account Titles	Trial Balance Dr.	Trial Balance Cr.	Adjusted Trial Balance Dr.	Adjusted Trial Balance Cr.
Cash	13,800		13,800	
Accounts Receivable	28,300		28,300	
Prepaid Insurance	3,600		2,400	
Land	67,000		67,000	
Buildings	127,000		127,000	
Equipment	59,000		59,000	
Accounts Payable		12,500		12,500
Unearned Rent Revenue		6,000		1,500
Mortgage Payable		120,000		120,000
Common Stock		90,000		90,000
Retained Earnings		54,000		54,000
Dividends	22,000		22,000	
Service Revenue		90,700		90,700
Rent Revenue		29,000		33,500
Salaries and Wages Expense	42,000		42,000	
Advertising Expense	20,500		20,500	
Utilities Expense	19,000		19,000	
Totals	402,200	402,200		

| | Trial Balance | | Adjusted Trial Balance | |
Account Titles	Dr.	Cr.	Dr.	Cr.
Insurance Expense	1,200			
Depreciation Expense	6,600			
Accumulated Depreciation—Buildings		3,000		
Accumulated Depreciation—Equipment		3,600		
Interest Expense	10,000			
Interest Payable		10,000		
Totals	418,800	418,800		

Instructions
(a) Prepare a complete worksheet.
(b) Prepare a classified balance sheet. (*Note:* $30,000 of the mortgage note payable is due for payment next year.)
(c) Journalize the adjusting entries.
(d) Journalize the closing entries.
(e) Prepare a post-closing trial balance.

(a) Net income $24,900
(b) Total current assets $44,500

(e) Post-closing trial balance $297,500

P4-5A Heidi Jara opened Jara's Cleaning Service on July 1, 2017. During July, the following transactions were completed.

Complete all steps in accounting cycle.

(LO 1, 2, 4)

GLS

July 1 Stockholders invested $20,000 cash in the business in exchange for common stock.
1 Purchased used truck for $9,000, paying $4,000 cash and the balance on account.
3 Purchased cleaning supplies for $2,100 on account.
5 Paid $1,800 cash on a 1-year insurance policy effective July 1.
12 Billed customers $4,500 for cleaning services.
18 Paid $1,500 cash on amount owed on truck and $1,400 on amount owed on cleaning supplies.
20 Paid $2,500 cash for employee salaries.
21 Collected $3,400 cash from customers billed on July 12.
25 Billed customers $6,000 for cleaning services.
31 Paid $350 for the monthly gasoline bill for the truck.
31 Paid a $5,600 cash dividend.

The chart of accounts for Jara's Cleaning Service contains the following accounts: No. 101 Cash, No. 112 Accounts Receivable, No. 126 Supplies, No. 130 Prepaid Insurance, No. 157 Equipment, No. 158 Accumulated Depreciation—Equipment, No. 201 Accounts Payable, No. 212 Salaries and Wages Payable, No. 311 Common Stock, No. 320 Retained Earnings, No. 332 Dividends, No. 350 Income Summary, No. 400 Service Revenue, No. 631 Supplies Expense, No. 633 Gasoline Expense, No. 711 Depreciation Expense, No. 722 Insurance Expense, and No. 726 Salaries and Wages Expense.

Instructions
(a) Journalize and post the July transactions. Use page J1 for the journal and the three-column form of account.
(b) Prepare a trial balance at July 31 on a worksheet.
(c) Enter the following adjustments on the worksheet and complete the worksheet.
   (1) Unbilled and uncollected revenue for services performed at July 31 were $2,700.
   (2) Depreciation on equipment for the month was $500.
   (3) One-twelfth of the insurance expired.
   (4) An inventory count shows $600 of cleaning supplies on hand at July 31.
   (5) Accrued but unpaid employee salaries were $1,000.
(d) Prepare an income statement and a retained earnings statement for July and a classified balance sheet at July 31.
(e) Journalize and post adjusting entries. Use page J2 for the journal.
(f) Journalize and post closing entries and complete the closing process. Use page J3 for the journal.
(g) Prepare a post-closing trial balance at July 31.

(b) Trial balance $34,700
(c) Adjusted trial balance $38,900

(d) Net income $7,200
Total assets $26,800

(g) Post-closing trial balance $27,300

Analyze errors and prepare correcting entries and trial balance.

(LO 3)

P4-6A Dao Vang, CPA, was retained by Universal Cable to prepare financial statements for April 2017. Vang accumulated all the ledger balances per Universal's records and found the following.

UNIVERSAL CABLE
Trial Balance
April 30, 2017

	Debit	Credit
Cash	$ 4,100	
Accounts Receivable	3,200	
Supplies	800	
Equipment	10,600	
Accumulated Depreciation—Equip.		$ 1,350
Accounts Payable		2,100
Salaries and Wages Payable		700
Unearned Service Revenue		890
Common Stock		10,000
Retained Earnings		2,900
Service Revenue		5,450
Salaries and Wages Expense	3,300	
Advertising Expense	600	
Miscellaneous Expense	290	
Depreciation Expense	500	
	$23,390	$23,390

Dao Vang reviewed the records and found the following errors.

1. Cash received from a customer on account was recorded as $950 instead of $590.
2. A payment of $75 for advertising expense was entered as a debit to Miscellaneous Expense $75 and a credit to Cash $75.
3. The first salary payment this month was for $1,900, which included $700 of salaries payable on March 31. The payment was recorded as a debit to Salaries and Wages Expense $1,900 and a credit to Cash $1,900. (No reversing entries were made on April 1.)
4. The purchase on account of a printer costing $310 was recorded as a debit to Supplies and a credit to Accounts Payable for $310.
5. A cash payment of repair expense on equipment for $96 was recorded as a debit to Equipment $69 and a credit to Cash $69.

Instructions

(a) Prepare an analysis of each error showing (1) the incorrect entry, (2) the correct entry, and (3) the correcting entry. Items 4 and 5 occurred on April 30, 2017.

(b) Trial balance $22,690

(b) Prepare a correct trial balance.

PROBLEMS: SET B AND SET C

Visit the book's companion website, at **www.wiley.com/college/weygandt**, and choose the Student Companion site to access Problems: Set B and Set C.

COMPREHENSIVE PROBLEM: CHAPTERS 2 TO 4

CP4 Kristin Malone opened Kristin's Maids Cleaning Service on July 1, 2017. During July, the company completed the following transactions.

July	1	Stockholders invested $14,000 cash in the business in exchange for common stock.
	1	Purchased a used truck for $10,000, paying $3,000 cash and the balance on account.
	3	Purchased cleaning supplies for $800 on account.
	5	Paid $1,800 on a 1-year insurance policy, effective July 1.
	12	Billed customers $3,800 for cleaning services.

18	Paid $1,000 of amount owed on truck, and $400 of amount owed on cleaning supplies.
20	Paid $1,600 for employee salaries.
21	Collected $1,400 from customers billed on July 12.
25	Billed customers $1,500 for cleaning services.
31	Paid gasoline for the month on the truck, $400.
31	Declared and paid a $600 cash dividend.

The chart of accounts for Kristin's Maids Cleaning Service contains the following accounts: No. 101 Cash, No. 112 Accounts Receivable, No. 126 Supplies, No. 130 Prepaid Insurance, No. 157 Equipment, No. 158 Accumulated Depreciation—Equipment, No. 201 Accounts Payable, No. 212 Salaries and Wages Payable, No. 311 Common Stock, No. 320 Retained Earnings, No. 332 Dividends, No. 350 Income Summary, No. 400 Service Revenue, No. 631 Supplies Expense, No. 633 Gasoline Expense, No. 711 Depreciation Expense, No. 722 Insurance Expense, and No. 726 Salaries and Wages Expense.

Instructions

(a) Journalize and post the July transactions. Use page J1 for the journal.

(b) Prepare a trial balance at July 31 on a worksheet.

(b) Trial balance $25,700

(c) Enter the following adjustments on the worksheet, and complete the worksheet.

   (1) Unbilled fees for services performed at July 31 were $1,300.

   (2) Depreciation on equipment for the month was $200.

   (3) One-twelfth of the insurance expired.

   (4) An inventory count shows $100 of cleaning supplies on hand at July 31.

   (5) Accrued but unpaid employee salaries were $500.

(d) Prepare an income statement and a retained earnings statement for July, and a classified balance sheet at July 31, 2017.

(d) Net income $3,050
Total assets $23,350

(e) Journalize and post the adjusting entries. Use page J2 for the journal.

(f) Journalize and post the closing entries, and complete the closing process. Use page J3 for the journal.

(g) Prepare a post-closing trial balance at July 31.

(g) Post-closing trial balance $23,550

▮ CONTINUING PROBLEM

COOKIE CREATIONS

© leungchopan/
Shutterstock

(*Note:* This is a continuation of the Cookie Creations problem from Chapters 1 through 3.)

CC4 Natalie had a very busy December. At the end of the month, after journalizing and posting the December transactions and adjusting entries, Natalie then prepared an adjusted trial balance.

*Go to the book's companion website, **www.wiley.com/college/weygandt**, to see the completion of this problem.*

BROADENING YOUR *PERSPECTIVE*

FINANCIAL REPORTING AND ANALYSIS

Financial Reporting Problem: Apple Inc.

BYP4-1 The financial statements of Apple Inc. are presented in Appendix A at the end of this textbook. Instructions for accessing and using the company's complete annual report, including the notes to the financial statements, are also provided in Appendix A.

Instructions

Answer the questions below using Apple's Consolidated Balance Sheets.

(a) What were Apple's total current assets at September 28, 2013, and September 29, 2012?

(b) Are assets that Apple included under current assets listed in proper order? Explain.

(c) How are Apple's assets classified?
(d) What was Apple's "Cash and cash equivalents" at September 28, 2013?
(e) What were Apple's total current liabilities at September 28, 2013, and September 29, 2012?

Comparative Analysis Problem:
PepsiCo, Inc. vs. The Coca-Cola Company

BYP4-2 PepsiCo's financial statements are presented in Appendix B. Financial statements of The Coca-Cola Company are presented in Appendix C. Instructions for accessing and using the complete annual reports of PepsiCo and Coca-Cola, including the notes to the financial statements, are also provided in Appendices B and C, respectively.

Instructions
(a) Based on the information contained in these financial statements, determine each of the following for PepsiCo at December 28, 2013, and for Coca-Cola at December 31, 2013.
   (1) Total current assets.
   (2) Net amount of property, plant, and equipment (land, buildings, and equipment).
   (3) Total current liabilities.
   (4) Total equity.
(b) What conclusions concerning the companies' respective financial positions can be drawn?

Comparative Analysis Problem:
Amazon.com, Inc. vs. Wal-Mart Stores, Inc.

BYP4-3 Amazon.com, Inc.'s financial statements are presented in Appendix D. Financial statements of Wal-Mart Stores, Inc. are presented in Appendix E. Instructions for accessing and using the complete annual reports of Amazon and Wal-Mart, including the notes to the financial statements, are also provided in Appendices D and E, respectively.

Instructions
(a) Based on the information contained in these financial statements, determine the following for Amazon at December 31, 2013, and Wal-Mart at January 31, 2014.
   (1) Total current assets.
   (2) Net amount of property and equipment (fixed assets), net.
   (3) Total current liabilities.
   (4) Total equity.
(b) What conclusions concerning these two companies can be drawn from these data?

Real-World Focus

BYP4-4 Numerous companies have established home pages on the Internet, e.g., the soda companies Capt'n Eli Root Beer Company (www.captneli.com/rootbeer.php) and Cheerwine (www.cheerwine.com).

Instructions
Examine the home pages of any two companies and answer the following questions.

(a) What type of information is available?
(b) Is any accounting-related information presented?
(c) Would you describe the home page as informative, promotional, or both? Why?

CRITICAL THINKING

Decision-Making Across the Organization

BYP4-5 Whitegloves Janitorial Service was started 2 years ago by Lynn Sanders. Because business has been exceptionally good, Lynn decided on July 1, 2017, to expand operations by acquiring an additional truck and hiring two more assistants. To finance the expansion, Lynn obtained on July 1, 2017, a $25,000, 10% bank loan, payable $10,000 on July 1, 2018, and the balance on July 1, 2019. The terms of the loan require the borrower to have $10,000 more current assets than current liabilities at December 31, 2017. If these terms are not met, the bank loan will be refinanced at 15% interest. At December 31, 2017, the accountant for Whitegloves Janitorial Service Inc. prepared the following balance sheet.

WHITEGLOVES JANITORIAL SERVICE
Balance Sheet
December 31, 2017

Assets			Liabilities and Stockholders' Equity		
Current assets			Current liabilities		
Cash	$ 6,500		Notes payable	$10,000	
Accounts receivable	9,000		Accounts payable	2,500	
Supplies	5,200		Total current liabilities		$12,500
Prepaid insurance	4,800		Long-term liability		
Total current assets		$25,500	Notes payable		15,000
Property, plant, and equipment			Total liabilities		27,500
Equipment (net)	22,000		Stockholders' equity		
Delivery trucks (net)	34,000		Common stock	30,000	
Total property, plant, and			Retained earnings	24,000	
equipment		56,000	Total stockholders' equity		54,000
Total assets		$81,500	Total liabilities and		
			stockholders' equity		$81,500

Lynn presented the balance sheet to the bank's loan officer on January 2, 2018, confident that the company had met the terms of the loan. The loan officer was not impressed. She said, "We need financial statements audited by a CPA." A CPA was hired and immediately realized that the balance sheet had been prepared from a trial balance and not from an adjusted trial balance. The adjustment data at the balance sheet date consisted of the following.

1. Unbilled janitorial services performed were $3,700.
2. Janitorial supplies on hand were $2,500.
3. Prepaid insurance was a 3-year policy dated January 1, 2017.
4. December expenses incurred but unpaid at December 31, $500.
5. Interest on the bank loan was not recorded.
6. The amounts for property, plant, and equipment presented in the balance sheet were reported net of accumulated depreciation (cost less accumulated depreciation). These amounts were $4,000 for cleaning equipment and $5,000 for delivery trucks as of January 1, 2017. Depreciation for 2017 was $2,000 for cleaning equipment and $5,000 for delivery trucks.

Instructions
With the class divided into groups, answer the following.

(a) Prepare a correct balance sheet.
(b) Were the terms of the bank loan met? Explain.

Communication Activity

BYP4-6 The accounting cycle is important in understanding the accounting process.

Instructions
Write a memo to your instructor that lists the steps of the accounting cycle in the order they should be completed. End with a paragraph that explains the optional steps in the cycle.

Ethics Case

BYP4-7 As the controller of Take No Prisoners Perfume Company, you discover a misstatement that overstated net income in the prior year's financial statements. The misleading financial statements appear in the company's annual report which was issued to banks and other creditors less than a month ago. After much thought about the consequences of telling the president, Jeb Wilde, about this misstatement, you gather your courage to inform him. Jeb says, "Hey! What they don't know won't hurt them. But, just so we set the record straight, we'll adjust this year's financial statements for last year's misstatement. We can absorb that misstatement better in this year than in last year anyway! Just don't make such a mistake again."

Instructions
(a) Who are the stakeholders in this situation?
(b) What are the ethical issues in this situation?
(c) What would you do as a controller in this situation?

All About You

BYP4-8 Companies prepare balance sheets in order to know their financial position at a specific point in time. This enables them to make a comparison to their position at previous points in time, and gives them a basis for planning for the future. In order to evaluate your financial position, you need to prepare a personal balance sheet. Assume that you have compiled the following information regarding your finances. (*Note:* Some of the items might not be used in your personal balance sheet.)

Amount owed on student loan balance (long-term)	$ 5,000
Balance in checking account	1,200
Certificate of deposit (6-month)	3,000
Annual earnings from part-time job	11,300
Automobile	7,000
Balance on automobile loan (current portion)	1,500
Balance on automobile loan (long-term portion)	4,000
Home computer	800
Amount owed to you by younger brother	300
Balance in money market account	1,800
Annual tuition	6,400
Video and stereo equipment	1,250
Balance owed on credit card (current portion)	150
Balance owed on credit card (long-term portion)	1,650

Instructions

Prepare a personal balance sheet using the format you have learned for a classified balance sheet for a company. For the equity account, use Owner's Equity.

FASB Codification Activity

BYP4-9 If your school has a subscription to the FASB Codification, go to **http://aaahq.org/ascLogin.cfm** to log in and prepare responses to the following.

Instructions

(a) Access the glossary ("Master Glossary") at the FASB Codification website to answer the following.
  (1) What is the definition of current assets?
  (2) What is the definition of current liabilities?
(b) A company wants to offset its accounts payable against its cash account and show a cash amount net of accounts payable on its balance sheet. Identify the criteria (found in the FASB Codification) under which a company has the right of set off. Does the company have the right to offset accounts payable against the cash account?

A Look at IFRS

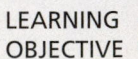 **LEARNING OBJECTIVE** **6**   Compare the procedures for the closing process under GAAP and IFRS.

The classified balance sheet, although generally required internationally, contains certain variations in format when reporting under IFRS.

Key Points

Following are the key similarities and differences between GAAP and IFRS related to the closing process and the financial statements.

Similarities

- The procedures of the closing process are applicable to all companies, whether they are using IFRS or GAAP.
- IFRS generally requires a classified statement of financial position similar to the classified balance sheet under GAAP.

- IFRS follows the same guidelines as this textbook for distinguishing between current and noncurrent assets and liabilities.

Differences

- IFRS recommends but does not require the use of the title "statement of financial position" rather than balance sheet.

- The format of statement of financial position information is often presented differently under IFRS. Although no specific format is required, many companies that follow IFRS present statement of financial position information in this order:
  - ◆ Non-current assets
  - ◆ Current assets
  - ◆ Equity
  - ◆ Non-current liabilities
  - ◆ Current liabilities

- Under IFRS, current assets are usually listed in the reverse order of liquidity. For example, under GAAP cash is listed first, but under IFRS it is listed last.

- IFRS has many differences in terminology from what are shown in your textbook. For example, in the sample statement of financial position illustrated below, notice in the investment category that stock is called shares.

FRANKLIN CORPORATION
Statement of Financial Position
October 31, 2017

Assets

Intangible assets

Patents			$ 3,100

Property, plant, and equipment

Land		$10,000	
Equipment	$24,000		
Less: Accumulated depreciation	5,000	19,000	29,000

Long-term investments

Share investments		5,200	
Investment in real estate		2,000	7,200

Current assets

Prepaid insurance	400	
Supplies	2,100	
Inventory	3,000	
Notes receivable	1,000	
Accounts receivable	7,000	
Debt investments	2,000	
Cash	6,600	22,100
Total assets		$61,400

Equity and Liabilities

Equity

Share capital	$34,050

Non-current liabilities

Mortgage payable	$10,000	
Notes payable	1,300	11,300

Current liabilities

Notes payable	11,000	
Accounts payable	2,100	
Salaries and wages payable	1,600	
Unearned service revenue	900	
Interest payable	450	16,050
Total equity and liabilities		$61,400

- Both GAAP and IFRS are increasing the use of fair value to report assets. However, at this point IFRS has adopted it more broadly. As examples, under IFRS companies can apply fair value to property, plant, and equipment, and in some cases intangible assets.

Looking to the Future

The IASB and the FASB are working on a project to converge their standards related to financial statement presentation. A key feature of the proposed framework is that each of the statements will be organized in the same format, to separate an entity's financing activities from its operating and investing activities and, further, to separate financing activities into transactions with owners and creditors. Thus, the same classifications used in the statement of financial position would also be used in the income statement and the statement of cash flows. The project has three phases. You can follow the joint financial presentation project at the following link: **http://www.fasb.org/project/financial_statement_presentation.shtml**.

IFRS Practice

IFRS Self-Test Questions

1. A company has purchased a tract of land and expects to build a production plant on the land in approximately 5 years. During the 5 years before construction, the land will be idle. Under IFRS, the land should be reported as:
   (a) land expense.
   (b) property, plant, and equipment.
   (c) an intangible asset.
   (d) a long-term investment.

2. Current assets under IFRS are listed generally:
   (a) by importance.
   (b) in the reverse order of their expected conversion to cash.
   (c) by longevity.
   (d) alphabetically.

3. Companies that use IFRS:
   (a) may report all their assets on the statement of financial position at fair value.
   (b) may offset assets against liabilities and show net assets and net liabilities on their statements of financial position, rather than the underlying detailed line items.
   (c) may report non-current assets before current assets on the statement of financial position.
   (d) do not have any guidelines as to what should be reported on the statement of financial position.

4. Companies that follow IFRS to prepare a statement of financial position generally use the following order of classification:
   (a) current assets, current liabilities, non-current assets, non-current liabilities, equity.
   (b) non-current assets, non-current liabilities, current assets, current liabilities, equity.
   (c) non-current assets, current assets, equity, non-current liabilities, current liabilities.
   (d) equity, non-current assets, current assets, non-current liabilities, current liabilities.

IFRS Exercises

IFRS4-1 In what ways does the format of a statement of financial of position under IFRS often differ from a balance sheet presented under GAAP?

IFRS4-2 What term is commonly used under IFRS in reference to the balance sheet?

IFRS4-3 The statement of financial position for Sundell Company includes the following accounts (in British pounds): Accounts Receivable £12,500, Prepaid Insurance £3,600, Cash £15,400, Supplies £5,200, and Debt Investments (short-term) £6,700. Prepare the current assets section of the statement of financial position, listing the accounts in proper sequence.

IFRS4-4 The following information is available for Lessila Bowling Alley at December 31, 2017.

Buildings	$128,800	Share Capital	$115,000
Accounts Receivable	14,520	Accumulated Depreciation—Buildings	42,600
Prepaid Insurance	4,680	Accounts Payable	12,300
Cash	18,040	Notes Payable	97,780
Equipment	62,400	Accumulated Depreciation—Equipment	18,720
Land	64,000	Interest Payable	2,600
Insurance Expense	780	Bowling Revenues	14,180
Depreciation Expense	7,360		
Interest Expense	2,600		

Prepare a classified statement of financial position. Assume that $13,900 of the notes payable will be paid in 2018.

International Comparative Analysis Problem: Apple vs. Louis Vuitton

IFRS4-5 The financial statements of Louis Vuitton are presented in Appendix F. Instructions for accessing and using the company's complete annual report, including the notes to its financial statements, are also provided in Appendix F.

Instructions
Identify five differences in the format of the statement of financial position used by Louis Vuitton compared to a company, such as Apple, that follows GAAP. (Apple's financial statements are available in Appendix A.)

Answers to IFRS Self-Test Questions
1. d 2. b 3. c 4. c

5 Accounting for Merchandising Operations

CHAPTER PREVIEW Merchandising is one of the largest and most influential industries in the United States. It is likely that a number of you will work for a merchandiser. Therefore, understanding the financial statements of merchandising companies is important. In this chapter, you will learn the basics about reporting merchandising transactions. In addition, you will learn how to prepare and analyze a commonly used form of the income statement—the multiple-step income statement.

FEATURE STORY

Buy Now, Vote Later

Have you ever shopped for outdoor gear at an REI (Recreational Equipment Incorporated) store? If so, you might have been surprised if a salesclerk asked if you were a member. A member? What do you mean a member? You soon realize that REI might not be your typical store. In fact, there's a lot about REI that makes it different.

REI is a consumer cooperative, or "co-op" for short. To figure out what that means, consider this quote from the company's annual stewardship report:

> As a cooperative, the Company is owned by its members. Each member is entitled to one vote in the election of the Company's Board of Directors. Since January 1, 2008, the nonrefundable, nontransferable, one-time membership fee has been 20 dollars. As of December 31, 2010, there were approximately 10.8 million members.

Voting rights? Now that's something you don't get from shopping at Walmart. REI members get other benefits as well, including sharing in the company's profits through a dividend at the end of the year, which can be used for purchases at REI stores during the next two years. The more you spend, the bigger your dividend.

Since REI is a co-op, you might also wonder whether management's incentives might be a little different than at other stores. For example, is management still concerned about making a profit? The answer is yes, as it ensures the long-term viability of the company. At the same time, REI's members want the company to be run efficiently, so that prices remain low. In order for its members to evaluate just how well management is doing, REI publishes an audited annual report, just like publicly traded companies do. So, while profit maximization might not be the ultimate goal for REI, the accounting and reporting issues are similar to those of a typical corporation.

How well is this business model working for REI? Well, it has consistently been rated as one of the best places to work in the United States by *Fortune* magazine. It is one of only five companies named each year since the list was created in 1998. Also, REI had sustainable business practices long before social responsibility became popular at other companies. As the CEO's stewardship report states, "we reduced the absolute amount of energy we use despite opening four new stores and growing our business; we grew the amount of FSC-certified paper we use to 58.4 percent of our total paper footprint—including our cash register receipt paper; we facilitated 2.2 million volunteer hours and we provided $3.7 million to more than 330 conservation and recreation nonprofits."

So, while REI, like other retailers, closely monitors its financial results, it also strives to succeed in other areas. And, with over 10 million votes at stake, REI's management knows that it has to deliver.

© omgimages/iStockphoto

CHAPTER OUTLINE

Learning Objectives

1 Describe merchandising operations and inventory systems.
- Operating cycles
- Flow of costs

DO IT! 1 Merchandising Operations and Inventory Systems

2 Record purchases under a perpetual inventory system.
- Freight costs
- Purchase returns and allowances
- Purchase discounts
- Summary of purchasing transactions

DO IT! 2 Purchase Transactions

3 Record sales under a perpetual inventory system.
- Sales returns and allowances
- Sales discounts

DO IT! 3 Sales Transactions

4 Apply the steps in the accounting cycle to a merchandising company.
- Adjusting entries
- Closing entries
- Summary of merchandising entries

DO IT! 4 Closing Entries

5 Compare a multiple-step with a single-step income statement.
- Multiple-step income statement
- Single-step income statement
- Classified balance sheet

DO IT! 5 Financial Statement Classifications

Go to the **REVIEW AND PRACTICE** section at the end of the chapter for a review of key concepts and practice applications with solutions.

Visit **WileyPLUS with ORION** for additional tutorials and practice opportunities.

Describe merchandising operations and inventory systems.

REI, Wal-Mart Stores, Inc., and Amazon.com are called merchandising companies because they buy and sell merchandise rather than perform services as their primary source of revenue. Merchandising companies that purchase and sell directly to consumers are called **retailers**. Merchandising companies that sell to retailers are known as **wholesalers**. For example, retailer Walgreens might buy goods from wholesaler McKesson. Retailer Office Depot might buy office supplies from wholesaler United Stationers. The primary source of revenues for merchandising companies is the sale of merchandise, often referred to simply as **sales revenue** or **sales**. A merchandising company has two categories of expenses: cost of goods sold and operating expenses.

Cost of goods sold is the total cost of merchandise sold during the period. This expense is directly related to the revenue recognized from the sale of goods. Illustration 5-1 shows the income measurement process for a merchandising company. The items in the two blue boxes are unique to a merchandising company; they are not used by a service company.

Illustration 5-1
Income measurement process for a merchandising company

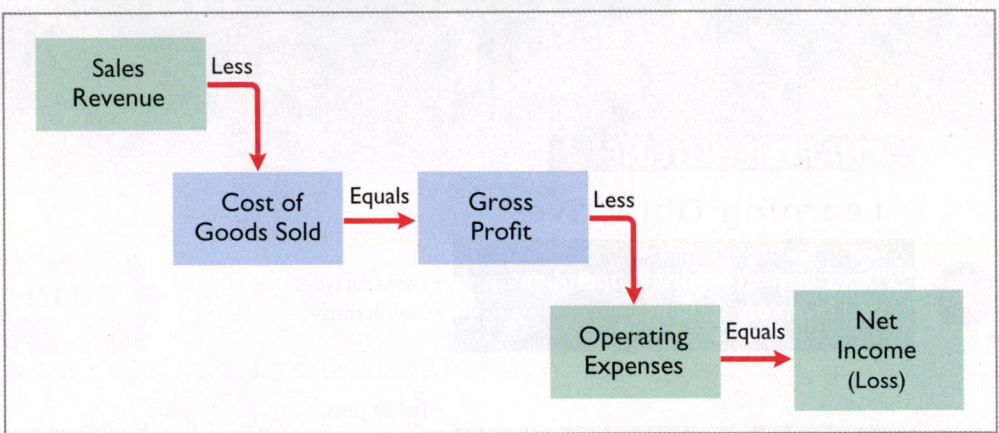

Operating Cycles

The operating cycle of a merchandising company ordinarily is longer than that of a service company. The purchase of merchandise inventory and its eventual sale lengthen the cycle. Illustration 5-2 shows the operating cycle of a service company.

Illustration 5-2
Operating cycle for a service company

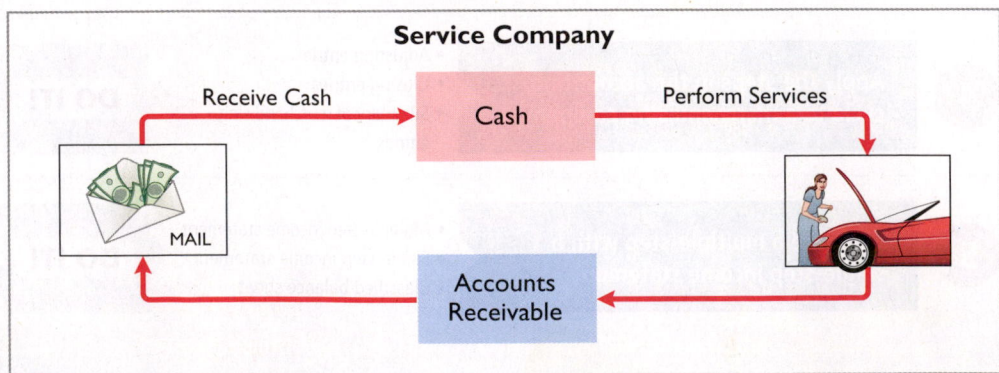

Illustration 5-3 shows the operating cycle of a merchandising company.

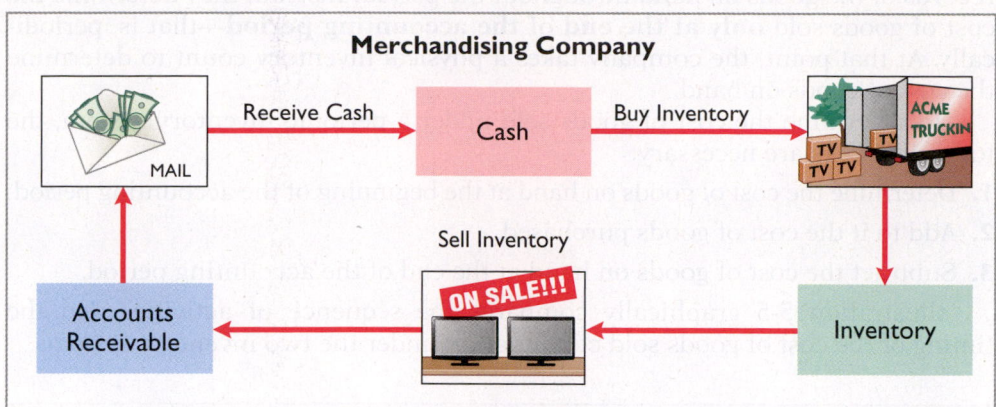

Illustration 5-3
Operating cycle for a merchandising company

Note that the added asset account for a merchandising company is the Inventory account. Companies report inventory as a current asset on the balance sheet.

Flow of Costs

The flow of costs for a merchandising company is as follows. Beginning inventory plus the cost of goods purchased is the cost of goods available for sale. As goods are sold, they are assigned to cost of goods sold. Those goods that are not sold by the end of the accounting period represent ending inventory. Illustration 5-4 describes these relationships. Companies use one of two systems to account for inventory: a **perpetual inventory system** or a **periodic inventory system**.

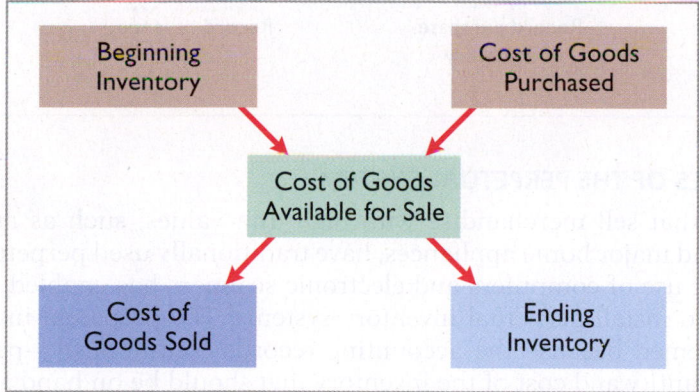

Illustration 5-4
Flow of costs

PERPETUAL SYSTEM

In a **perpetual inventory system**, companies keep detailed records of the cost of each inventory purchase and sale. These records continuously—perpetually— show the inventory that should be on hand for every item. For example, a Ford dealership has separate inventory records for each automobile, truck, and van on its lot and showroom floor. Similarly, a Kroger grocery store uses bar codes and optical scanners to keep a daily running record of every box of cereal and every jar of jelly that it buys and sells. Under a perpetual inventory system, a company determines the cost of goods sold **each time a sale occurs**.

Helpful Hint
For control purposes, companies take a physical inventory count under the perpetual system, even though it is not needed to determine cost of goods sold.

PERIODIC SYSTEM

In a **periodic inventory system**, companies do not keep detailed inventory records of the goods on hand throughout the period. Instead, they determine the cost of goods sold **only at the end of the accounting period**—that is, periodically. At that point, the company takes a physical inventory count to determine the cost of goods on hand.

To determine the cost of goods sold under a periodic inventory system, the following steps are necessary:

1. Determine the cost of goods on hand at the beginning of the accounting period.

2. Add to it the cost of goods purchased.

3. Subtract the cost of goods on hand at the end of the accounting period.

Illustration 5-5 graphically compares the sequence of activities and the timing of the cost of goods sold computation under the two inventory systems.

Illustration 5-5
Comparing perpetual and periodic inventory systems

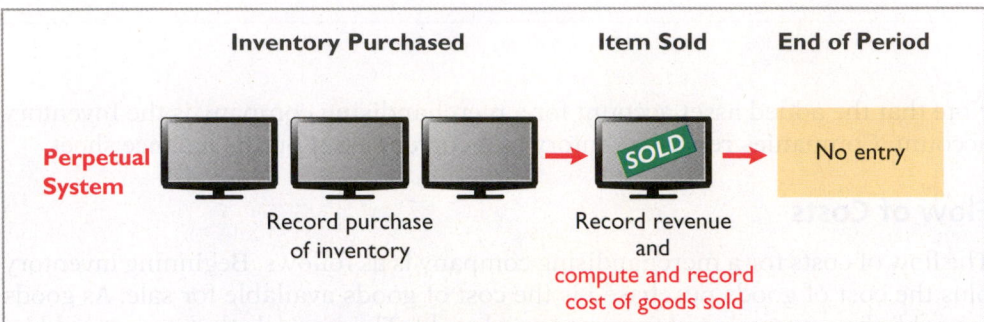

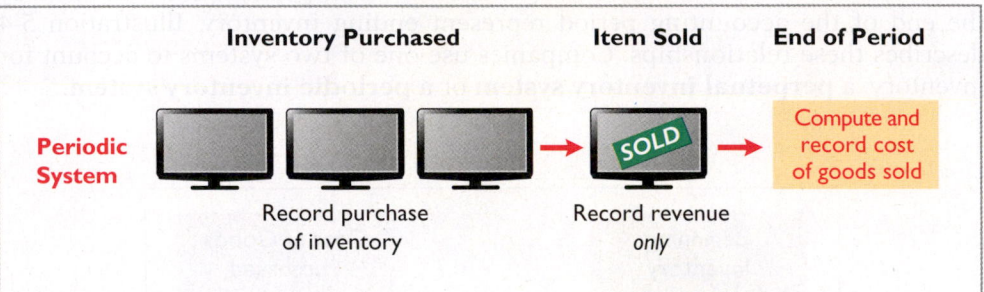

ADVANTAGES OF THE PERPETUAL SYSTEM

Companies that sell merchandise with high unit values, such as automobiles, furniture, and major home appliances, have traditionally used perpetual systems. The growing use of computers and electronic scanners has enabled many more companies to install perpetual inventory systems. The perpetual inventory system is so named because the accounting records continuously—perpetually—show the quantity and cost of the inventory that should be on hand at any time.

A perpetual inventory system provides better control over inventories than a periodic system. Since the inventory records show the quantities that should be on hand, the company can count the goods at any time to see whether the amount of goods actually on hand agrees with the inventory records. If shortages are uncovered, the company can investigate immediately. Although a perpetual inventory system requires both additional clerical work and expense to maintain the subsidiary records, a computerized system can minimize this cost. Much of Amazon.com's success is attributed to its sophisticated inventory system.

Some businesses find it either unnecessary or uneconomical to invest in a sophisticated, computerized perpetual inventory system such as Amazon's. Many small merchandising businesses find that basic accounting software provides some of the essential benefits of a perpetual inventory system. Also, managers of some small businesses still find that they can control their merchandise and manage day-to-day operations using a periodic inventory system.

Because of the widespread use of the perpetual inventory system, we illustrate it in this chapter. We discuss and illustrate the periodic system in Appendix 5B.

DO IT!   1   Merchandising Operations and Inventory Systems

Indicate whether the following statements are true or false.

1. The primary source of revenue for a merchandising company results from performing services for customers.
2. The operating cycle of a service company is usually shorter than that of a merchandising company.
3. Sales revenue less cost of goods sold equals gross profit.
4. Ending inventory plus the cost of goods purchased equals cost of goods available for sale.

Solution

> 1. False. The primary source of revenue for a service company results from performing services for customers.   2. True.   3. True.   4. False. Beginning inventory plus the cost of goods purchased equals cost of goods available for sale.

Related exercise material: **BE5-1, BE5-2, E5-1, and DO IT! 5-1.**

Action Plan

✔ Review merchandising concepts.
✔ Understand the flow of costs in a merchandising company.

LEARNING OBJECTIVE   2   Record purchases under a perpetual inventory system.

Companies purchase inventory using cash or credit (on account). They normally record purchases when they receive the goods from the seller. Every purchase should be supported by business documents that provide written evidence of the transaction. Each cash purchase should be supported by a canceled check or a cash register receipt indicating the items purchased and amounts paid. Companies record cash purchases by an increase in Inventory and a decrease in Cash.

A **purchase invoice** should support each credit purchase. This invoice indicates the total purchase price and other relevant information. However, the purchaser does not prepare a separate purchase invoice. Instead, the purchaser uses as a purchase invoice a copy of the sales invoice sent by the seller. In Illustration 5-6 (page 210), for example, Sauk Stereo (the buyer) uses as a purchase invoice the sales invoice prepared by PW Audio Supply, Inc. (the seller).

Illustration 5-6
Sales invoice used as purchase invoice by Sauk Stereo

Helpful Hint
To better understand the contents of this invoice, identify these items:
1. Seller
2. Invoice date
3. Purchaser
4. Salesperson
5. Credit terms
6. Freight terms
7. Goods sold: catalog number, description, quantity, price per unit
8. Total invoice amount

INVOICE NO. 731

PW AUDIO SUPPLY, INC.
27 CIRCLE DRIVE
HARDING, MICHIGAN 48281

S O L D	Firm Name ___Sauk Stereo___
	Attention of ___James Hoover, Purchasing Agent___
T O	Address ___125 Main Street___
	Chelsea Illinois 60915
	City State Zip

Date 5/4/17	Salesperson Malone	Terms 2/10, n/30	FOB Shipping Point		
Catalog No.	Description		Quantity	Price	Amount
X572Y9820	Printed Circuit Board-prototype		1	2,300	$2,300
A2547Z45	Production Model Circuits		5	300	1,500

IMPORTANT: ALL RETURNS MUST BE MADE WITHIN 10 DAYS   **TOTAL** $3,800

Sauk Stereo makes the following journal entry to record its purchase from PW Audio Supply. The entry increases (debits) Inventory and increases (credits) Accounts Payable.

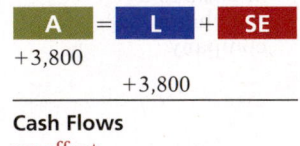

A = L + SE
+3,800
      +3,800

Cash Flows
no effect

May 4	Inventory	3,800	
	Accounts Payable		3,800
	(To record goods purchased on account from PW Audio Supply)		

Under the perpetual inventory system, companies record purchases of merchandise for sale in the Inventory account. Thus, **REI** would increase (debit) Inventory for clothing, sporting goods, and anything else purchased for resale to customers.

Not all purchases are debited to Inventory, however. Companies record purchases of assets acquired for use and not for resale, such as supplies, equipment, and similar items, as increases to specific asset accounts rather than to Inventory. For example, to record the purchase of materials used to make shelf signs or for cash register receipt paper, REI would increase (debit) Supplies.

Freight Costs

The sales agreement should indicate who—the seller or the buyer—is to pay for transporting the goods to the buyer's place of business. When a common carrier such as a railroad, trucking company, or airline transports the goods, the carrier prepares a freight bill in accord with the sales agreement.

Freight terms are expressed as either FOB shipping point or FOB destination. The letters FOB mean **free on board**. Thus, **FOB shipping point** means that the seller places the goods free on board the carrier, and the buyer pays the freight costs. Conversely, **FOB destination** means that the seller places the goods free on board to the buyer's place of business, and the seller pays the freight. For example, the sales invoice in Illustration 5-6 indicates FOB shipping point. Thus, the buyer (Sauk Stereo) pays the freight charges. Illustration 5-7 illustrates these shipping terms.

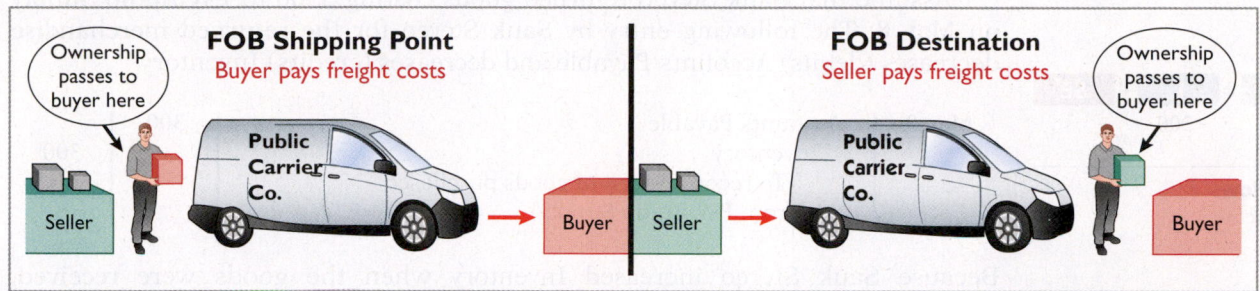

Illustration 5-7
Shipping terms

FREIGHT COSTS INCURRED BY THE BUYER

When the buyer incurs the transportation costs, these costs are considered part of the cost of purchasing inventory. Therefore, the buyer debits (increases) the Inventory account. For example, if Sauk Stereo (the buyer) pays Public Carrier Co. $150 for freight charges on May 6, the entry on Sauk Stereo's books is:

May 6	Inventory	150	
	Cash		150
	(To record payment of freight on		
	goods purchased)		

Thus, any freight costs incurred by the buyer are part of the cost of merchandise purchased. The reason: Inventory cost should include all costs to acquire the inventory, including freight necessary to deliver the goods to the buyer. Companies recognize these costs as cost of goods sold when inventory is sold.

FREIGHT COSTS INCURRED BY THE SELLER

In contrast, **freight costs incurred by the seller on outgoing merchandise are an operating expense to the seller**. These costs increase an expense account titled Freight-Out (sometimes called Delivery Expense). For example, if the freight terms on the invoice in Illustration 5-6 had required PW Audio Supply (the seller) to pay the freight charges, the entry by PW Audio Supply would be:

May 4	Freight-Out (or Delivery Expense)	150	
	Cash		150
	(To record payment of freight on		
	goods sold)		

When the seller pays the freight charges, the seller will usually establish a higher invoice price for the goods to cover the shipping expense.

Purchase Returns and Allowances

A purchaser may be dissatisfied with the merchandise received because the goods are damaged or defective, of inferior quality, or do not meet the purchaser's specifications. In such cases, the purchaser may return the goods to the seller for credit if the sale was made on credit, or for a cash refund if the purchase was for cash. This transaction is known as a **purchase return**. Alternatively, the purchaser may choose to keep the merchandise if the seller is willing to grant an allowance (deduction) from the purchase price. This transaction is known as a **purchase allowance**.

Assume that Sauk Stereo returned goods costing $300 to PW Audio Supply on May 8. The following entry by Sauk Stereo for the returned merchandise decreases (debits) Accounts Payable and decreases (credits) Inventory.

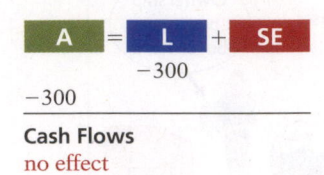

Cash Flows
no effect

May 8	Accounts Payable	300	
	Inventory		300
	(To record return of goods purchased from PW Audio Supply)		

Because Sauk Stereo increased Inventory when the goods were received, Inventory is decreased when Sauk Stereo returns the goods.

Suppose instead that Sauk Stereo chose to keep the goods after being granted a $50 allowance (reduction in price). It would reduce (debit) Accounts Payable and reduce (credit) Inventory for $50.

Purchase Discounts

The credit terms of a purchase on account may permit the buyer to claim a cash discount for prompt payment. The buyer calls this cash discount a **purchase discount**. This incentive offers advantages to both parties. The purchaser saves money, and the seller is able to shorten the operating cycle by converting the accounts receivable into cash.

Credit terms specify the amount of the cash discount and time period in which it is offered. They also indicate the time period in which the purchaser is expected to pay the full invoice price. In the sales invoice in Illustration 5-6 (page 210), credit terms are 2/10, n/30, which is read "two-ten, net thirty." This means that the buyer may take a 2% cash discount on the invoice price, less ("net of") any returns or allowances, if payment is made within 10 days of the invoice date (the **discount period**). Otherwise, the invoice price, less any returns or allowances, is due 30 days from the invoice date.

Alternatively, the discount period may extend to a specified number of days following the month in which the sale occurs. For example, 1/10 EOM (end of month) means that a 1% discount is available if the invoice is paid within the first 10 days of the next month.

When the seller elects not to offer a cash discount for prompt payment, credit terms will specify only the maximum time period for paying the balance due. For example, the invoice may state the time period as n/30, n/60, or n/10 EOM. This means, respectively, that the buyer must pay the net amount in 30 days, 60 days, or within the first 10 days of the next month.

When the buyer pays an invoice within the discount period, the amount of the discount decreases Inventory. Why? Because companies record inventory at cost, and by paying within the discount period, the buyer has reduced its cost. To illustrate, assume Sauk Stereo pays the balance due of $3,500 (gross invoice price of $3,800 less purchase returns and allowances of $300) on May 14, the last day of the discount period. The cash discount is $70 ($3,500 × 2%), and Sauk Stereo pays $3,430 ($3,500 − $70). The entry Sauk Stereo makes to record its May 14 payment decreases (debits) Accounts Payable by the amount of the gross invoice price, reduces (credits) Inventory by the $70 discount, and reduces (credits) Cash by the net amount owed.

Helpful Hint
The term *net* in "net 30" means the remaining amount due after subtracting any sales returns and allowances and partial payments.

May 14	Accounts Payable	3,500	
	Cash		3,430
	Inventory		70
	(To record payment within discount period)		

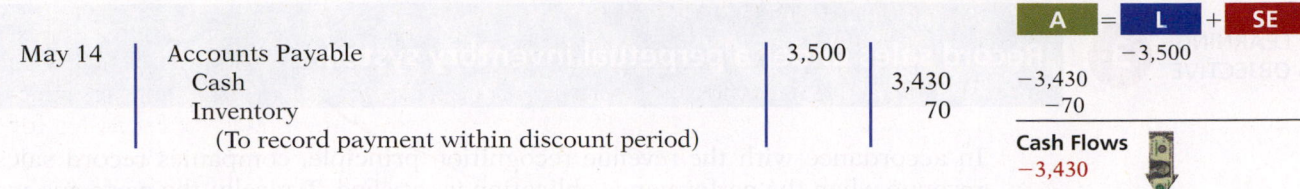

If Sauk Stereo failed to take the discount and instead made full payment of $3,500 on June 3, it would debit Accounts Payable and credit Cash for $3,500 each.

June 3	Accounts Payable	3,500	
	Cash		3,500
	(To record payment with no discount taken)		

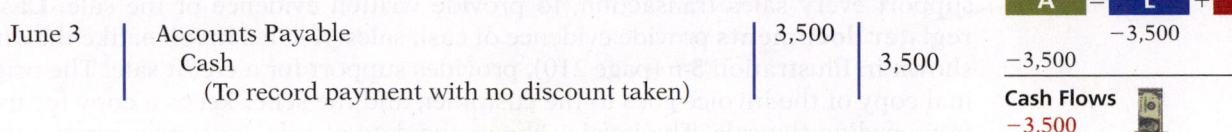

A merchandising company usually should take all available discounts. Passing up the discount may be viewed as **paying interest** for use of the money. For example, passing up the discount offered by PW Audio Supply would be comparable to Sauk Stereo paying an interest rate of 2% for the use of $3,500 for 20 days. This is the equivalent of an annual interest rate of approximately 36.5% (2% × 365/20). Obviously, it would be better for Sauk Stereo to borrow at prevailing bank interest rates of 6% to 10% than to lose the discount.

Summary of Purchasing Transactions

The following T-account (with transaction descriptions in red) provides a summary of the effect of the previous transactions on Inventory. Sauk Stereo originally purchased $3,800 worth of inventory for resale. It then returned $300 of goods. It paid $150 in freight charges, and finally, it received a $70 discount off the balance owed because it paid within the discount period. This results in a balance in Inventory of $3,580.

		Inventory			
Purchase	May 4	3,800	May 8	300	**Purchase return**
Freight-in	6	150	14	70	**Purchase discount**
Balance		3,580			

DO IT! 2   Purchase Transactions

On September 5, De La Hoya Company buys merchandise on account from Junot Diaz Company. The selling price of the goods is $1,500, and the cost to Diaz Company was $800. On September 8, De La Hoya returns defective goods with a selling price of $200. Record the transactions on the books of De La Hoya Company.

Solution

Sept. 5	Inventory	1,500	
	Accounts Payable		1,500
	(To record goods purchased on account)		
8	Accounts Payable	200	
	Inventory		200
	(To record return of defective goods)		

Action Plan
✔ Purchaser records goods at cost.
✔ When goods are returned, purchaser reduces Inventory.

Related exercise material: **BE5-3, BE5-5, E5-2, E5-3, E5-4, and DO IT! 5-2.**

LEARNING
OBJECTIVE **3**

Record sales under a perpetual inventory system.

In accordance with the revenue recognition principle, companies record sales revenue when the performance obligation is satisfied. Typically, the performance obligation is satisfied when the goods transfer from the seller to the buyer. At this point, the sales transaction is complete and the sales price established.

Sales may be made on credit or for cash. A **business document** should support every sales transaction, to provide written evidence of the sale. **Cash register documents** provide evidence of cash sales. A **sales invoice**, like the one shown in Illustration 5-6 (page 210), provides support for a credit sale. The original copy of the invoice goes to the customer, and the seller keeps a copy for use in recording the sale. The invoice shows the date of sale, customer name, total sales price, and other relevant information.

The seller makes two entries for each sale. **The first entry records the sale**: The seller increases (debits) Cash (or Accounts Receivable if a credit sale) and also increases (credits) Sales Revenue. **The second entry records the cost of the merchandise sold**: The seller increases (debits) Cost of Goods Sold and also decreases (credits) Inventory for the cost of those goods. As a result, the Inventory account will show at all times the amount of inventory that should be on hand.

To illustrate a credit sales transaction, PW Audio Supply, Inc. records its May 4 sale of $3,800 to Sauk Stereo (see Illustration 5-6) as follows (assume the merchandise cost PW Audio Supply $2,400).

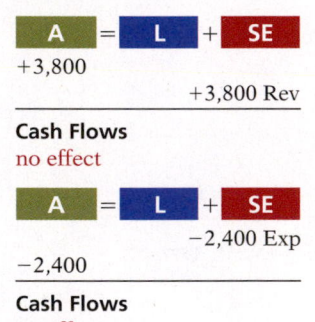

A	=	L	+	SE
+3,800				
				+3,800 Rev

Cash Flows
no effect

A	=	L	+	SE
				−2,400 Exp
−2,400				

Cash Flows
no effect

Date	Account	Debit	Credit
May 4	Accounts Receivable	3,800	
	Sales Revenue		3,800
	(To record credit sale to Sauk Stereo per invoice #731)		
4	Cost of Goods Sold	2,400	
	Inventory		2,400
	(To record cost of merchandise sold on invoice #731 to Sauk Stereo)		

For internal decision-making purposes, merchandising companies may use more than one sales account. For example, PW Audio Supply may decide to keep separate sales accounts for its sales of TVs, Blu-ray players, and headsets. REI might use separate accounts for camping gear, children's clothing, and ski equipment—or it might have even more narrowly defined accounts. By using separate sales accounts for major product lines, rather than a single combined sales account, company management can more closely monitor sales trends and respond more strategically to changes in sales patterns. For example, if TV sales are increasing while Blu-ray player sales are decreasing, PW Audio Supply might reevaluate both its advertising and pricing policies on these items to ensure they are optimal.

On its income statement presented to outside investors, a merchandising company normally would provide only a single sales figure—the sum of all of its individual sales accounts. This is done for two reasons. First, providing detail on all of its individual sales accounts would add considerable length to its income statement. Second, companies do not want their competitors to know the details of their operating results. However, **Microsoft** recently expanded its disclosure of revenue from three to five types. The reason: The additional categories enabled financial statement users to better evaluate the growth of the company's consumer and Internet businesses.

ETHICS NOTE

Many companies are trying to improve the quality of their financial reporting. For example, General Electric now provides more detail on its revenues and operating profits.

ANATOMY OF A FRAUD[1]

Holly Harmon was a cashier at a national superstore for only a short while when she began stealing merchandise using three methods. Under the first method, her husband or friends took UPC labels from cheaper items and put them on more expensive items. Holly then scanned the goods at the register. Using the second method, Holly scanned an item at the register but then voided the sale and left the merchandise in the shopping cart. A third approach was to put goods into large plastic containers. She scanned the plastic containers but not the goods within them. One day, Holly did not call in sick or show up for work. In such instances, the company reviews past surveillance tapes to look for suspicious activity by employees. This enabled the store to observe the thefts and to identify the participants.

Total take: $12,000

THE MISSING CONTROLS

Human resource controls. A background check would have revealed Holly's previous criminal record. She would not have been hired as a cashier.

Physical controls. Software can flag high numbers of voided transactions or a high number of sales of low-priced goods. Random comparisons of video records with cash register records can ensure that the goods reported as sold on the register are the same goods that are shown being purchased on the video recording. Finally, employees should be aware that they are being monitored.

Source: Adapted from Wells, *Fraud Casebook* (2007), pp. 251–259.

Sales Returns and Allowances

We now look at the "flip side" of purchase returns and allowances, which the seller records as **sales returns and allowances**. These are transactions where the seller either accepts goods back from the buyer (a return) or grants a reduction in the purchase price (an allowance) so the buyer will keep the goods. PW Audio Supply's entries to record credit for returned goods involve (1) an increase (debit) in Sales Returns and Allowances (a contra account to Sales Revenue) and a decrease (credit) in Accounts Receivable at the $300 selling price, and (2) an increase (debit) in Inventory (assume a $140 cost) and a decrease (credit) in Cost of Goods Sold, as shown below (assuming that the goods were not defective).

May 8	Sales Returns and Allowances	300	
	Accounts Receivable		300
	(To record credit granted to Sauk Stereo for returned goods)		
8	Inventory	140	
	Cost of Goods Sold		140
	(To record cost of goods returned)		

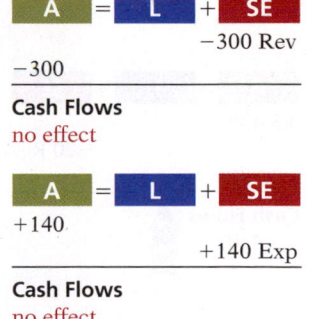

A = L + SE
−300   −300 Rev
Cash Flows no effect

A = L + SE
+140   +140 Exp
Cash Flows no effect

If Sauk Stereo returns goods because they are damaged or defective, then PW Audio Supply's entry to Inventory and Cost of Goods Sold should be for the fair value of the returned goods, rather than their cost. For example, if the returned goods were defective and had a fair value of $50, PW Audio Supply would debit Inventory for $50 and credit Cost of Goods Sold for $50.

What happens if the goods are not returned but the seller grants the buyer an allowance by reducing the purchase price? In this case, the seller debits Sales Returns and Allowances and credits Accounts Receivable for the amount of the allowance. An allowance has no impact on Inventory or Cost of Goods Sold.

[1]The "Anatomy of a Fraud" stories in this textbook are adapted from *Fraud Casebook: Lessons from the Bad Side of Business,* edited by Joseph T. Wells (Hoboken, NJ: John Wiley & Sons, Inc., 2007). Used by permission. The names of some of the people and organization in the stories are fictitious, but the facts in the stories are true.

Sales Returns and Allowances is a **contra revenue account** to Sales Revenue. This means that it is offset against a revenue account on the income statement. The normal balance of Sales Returns and Allowances is a debit. Companies use a contra account, instead of debiting Sales Revenue, to disclose in the accounts and in the income statement the amount of sales returns and allowances. Disclosure of this information is important to management. Excessive returns and allowances may suggest problems—inferior merchandise, inefficiencies in filling orders, errors in billing customers, or delivery or shipment mistakes. Moreover, a decrease (debit) recorded directly to Sales Revenue would obscure the relative importance of sales returns and allowances as a percentage of sales. It also could distort comparisons between total sales in different accounting periods.

Sales Discounts

As mentioned in our discussion of purchase transactions, the seller may offer the customer a cash discount—called by the seller a **sales discount**—for the prompt payment of the balance due. Like a purchase discount, a sales discount is based on the invoice price less returns and allowances, if any. The seller increases (debits) the Sales Discounts account for discounts that are taken. For example, PW Audio Supply makes the following entry to record the cash receipt on May 14 from Sauk Stereo within the discount period.

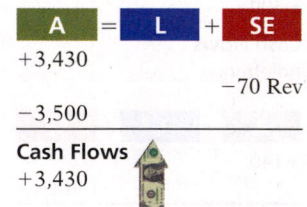

A	=	L	+	SE
+3,430				
				−70 Rev
−3,500				

Cash Flows
+3,430

May 14	Cash	3,430	
	Sales Discounts	70	
	Accounts Receivable		3,500
	(To record collection within 2/10, n/30		
	discount period from Sauk Stereo)		

Like Sales Returns and Allowances, Sales Discounts is a **contra revenue account** to Sales Revenue. Its normal balance is a debit. PW Audio Supply uses this account, instead of debiting Sales Revenue, to disclose the amount of cash discounts taken by customers. If Sauk Stereo does not take the discount, PW Audio Supply increases (debits) Cash for $3,500 and decreases (credits) Accounts Receivable for the same amount at the date of collection.

The following T-accounts summarize the three sales-related transactions and show their combined effect on net sales.

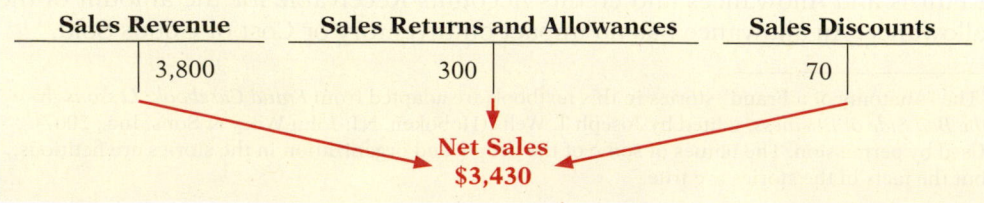

Sales Revenue	Sales Returns and Allowances	Sales Discounts
3,800	300	70

Net Sales $3,430

People, Planet, and Profit Insight   PepsiCo

Helen Sessions/Alamy

Selling Green

Here is a question an executive of PepsiCo was asked: Should PepsiCo market green? The executive indicated that the company should, as he believes it's the No. 1 thing consumers all over the world care about. Here are some of his thoughts on this issue:

"Sun Chips are part of the food business I run. It's a 'healthy snack.' We decided that Sun Chips, if it's a healthy snack, should be made in facilities that have a net-zero footprint. In other words, I want off the electric grid everywhere we make Sun Chips. We did that. Sun Chips should be made in a facility that puts back more water than it uses. It does that. And we partnered with our suppliers and came out with the world's first compostable chip package.

Now, there was an issue with this package: It was louder than the New York subway, louder than jet engines taking off. What would a company that's committed to green do: walk away or stay committed? If your people are passionate, they're going to fix it for you as long as you stay committed. Six months later, the compostable bag has half the noise of our current package.

So the view today is: we should market green, we should be proud to do it . . . it has to be a 360-degree process, both internal and external. And if you do that, you can monetize environmental sustainability for the shareholders."

Source: "Four Problems—and Solutions," *Wall Street Journal* (March 7, 2011), p. R2.

*What is meant by "monetize environmental sustainability" for shareholders? (Go to **WileyPLUS** for this answer and additional questions.)*

DO IT! 3 Sales Transactions

On September 5, De La Hoya Company buys merchandise on account from Junot Diaz Company. The selling price of the goods is $1,500, and the cost to Diaz Company was $800. On September 8, De La Hoya returns defective goods with a selling price of $200 and a fair value of $30. Record the transactions on the books of Junot Diaz Company.

Solution

Sept. 5	Accounts Receivable	1,500	
	Sales Revenue		1,500
	(To record credit sale)		
5	Cost of Goods Sold	800	
	Inventory		800
	(To record cost of goods sold on account)		
8	Sales Returns and Allowances	200	
	Accounts Receivable		200
	(To record credit granted for receipt of returned goods)		
8	Inventory	30	
	Cost of Goods Sold		30
	(To record fair value of goods returned)		

Action Plan

✔ Seller records both the sale and the cost of goods sold at the time of the sale.

✔ When goods are returned, the seller records the return in a contra account, Sales Returns and Allowances, and reduces Accounts Receivable.

✔ Any goods returned increase Inventory and reduce Cost of Goods Sold. Defective or damaged inventory is recorded at fair value (scrap value).

Related exercise material: **BE5-3, BE5-4, E5-3, E5-4, E5-5, and** **5-3.**

LEARNING
OBJECTIVE **4**

Apply the steps in the accounting cycle to a merchandising company.

Up to this point, we have illustrated the basic entries for transactions relating to purchases and sales in a perpetual inventory system. Now we consider the remaining steps in the accounting cycle for a merchandising company. Each of the required steps described in Chapter 4 for service companies apply to merchandising companies. Appendix 5A to this chapter shows the use of a worksheet by a merchandiser (an optional step).

Adjusting Entries

A merchandising company generally has the same types of adjusting entries as a service company. However, a merchandiser using a perpetual system will require one additional adjustment to make the records agree with the actual inventory on hand. Here's why: At the end of each period, for control purposes, a merchandising company that uses a perpetual system will take a physical count of its goods on hand. The company's unadjusted balance in Inventory usually does not agree with the actual amount of inventory on hand. The perpetual inventory records may be incorrect due to recording errors, theft, or waste. Thus, the company needs to adjust the perpetual records to make the recorded inventory amount agree with the inventory on hand. **This involves adjusting Inventory and Cost of Goods Sold.**

For example, suppose that PW Audio Supply, Inc. has an unadjusted balance of $40,500 in Inventory. Through a physical count, PW Audio Supply determines that its actual merchandise inventory at December 31 is $40,000. The company would make an adjusting entry as follows.

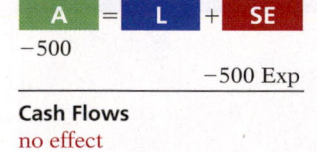

−500

−500 Exp

Cash Flows
no effect

Dec. 31	Cost of Goods Sold	500	
	Inventory		500
	(To adjust inventory to physical count)		

Closing Entries

A merchandising company, like a service company, closes to Income Summary all accounts that affect net income. In journalizing, the company credits all temporary accounts with debit balances, and debits all temporary accounts with credit balances, as shown below and on the next page for PW Audio Supply. Note that PW Audio Supply closes Cost of Goods Sold to Income Summary.

Helpful Hint
The easiest way to prepare the first two closing entries is to identify the temporary accounts by their balances and then prepare one entry for the credits and one for the debits.

Dec. 31	Sales Revenue	480,000	
	Income Summary		480,000
	(To close income statement accounts with credit balances)		
31	Income Summary	450,000	
	Sales Returns and Allowances		12,000
	Sales Discounts		8,000
	Cost of Goods Sold		316,000
	Salaries and Wages Expense		64,000
	Freight-Out		7,000
	Advertising Expense		16,000
	Utilities Expense		17,000
	Depreciation Expense		8,000
	Insurance Expense		2,000
	(To close income statement accounts with debit balances)		

31	Income Summary	30,000	
	Retained Earnings		30,000
	(To close net income to retained earnings)		
31	Retained Earnings	15,000	
	Dividends		15,000
	(To close dividends to retained earnings)		

After PW Audio Supply has posted the closing entries, all temporary accounts have zero balances. Also, Retained Earnings has a balance that is carried over to the next period.

Summary of Merchandising Entries

Illustration 5-8 summarizes the entries for the merchandising accounts using a perpetual inventory system.

Illustration 5-8
Daily recurring and adjusting and closing entries

	Transactions	Daily Recurring Entries	Dr.	Cr.
Sales Transactions	Selling merchandise to customers.	Cash or Accounts Receivable	XX	
		Sales Revenue		XX
		Cost of Goods Sold	XX	
		Inventory		XX
	Granting sales returns or allowances to customers.	Sales Returns and Allowances	XX	
		Cash or Accounts Receivable		XX
		Inventory	XX	
		Cost of Goods Sold		XX
	Paying freight costs on sales; FOB destination.	Freight-Out	XX	
		Cash		XX
	Receiving payment from customers within discount period.	Cash	XX	
		Sales Discounts	XX	
		Accounts Receivable		XX
Purchase Transactions	Purchasing merchandise for resale.	Inventory	XX	
		Cash or Accounts Payable		XX
	Paying freight costs on merchandise purchased; FOB shipping point.	Inventory	XX	
		Cash		XX
	Receiving purchase returns or allowances from suppliers.	Cash or Accounts Payable	XX	
		Inventory		XX
	Paying suppliers within discount period.	Accounts Payable	XX	
		Inventory		XX
		Cash		XX

	Events	Adjusting and Closing Entries	Dr.	Cr.
	Adjust because book amount is higher than the inventory amount determined to be on hand.	Cost of Goods Sold	XX	
		Inventory		XX
	Closing temporary accounts with credit balances.	Sales Revenue	XX	
		Income Summary		XX
	Closing temporary accounts with debit balances.	Income Summary	XX	
		Sales Returns and Allowances		XX
		Sales Discounts		XX
		Cost of Goods Sold		XX
		Freight-Out		XX
		Expenses		XX

DO IT! 4 Closing Entries

The trial balance of Celine's Sports Wear Shop at December 31 shows Inventory $25,000, Sales Revenue $162,400, Sales Returns and Allowances $4,800, Sales Discounts $3,600, Cost of Goods Sold $110,000, Rent Revenue $6,000, Freight-Out $1,800, Rent Expense $8,800, and Salaries and Wages Expense $22,000. Prepare the closing entries for the above accounts.

Solution

Action Plan

✔ Close all temporary accounts with credit balances to Income Summary by debiting these accounts.

✔ Close all temporary accounts with debit balances, except dividends, to Income Summary by crediting these accounts.

The two closing entries are:

Dec. 31	Sales Revenue	162,400	
	Rent Revenue	6,000	
	Income Summary		168,400
	(To close accounts with credit balances)		
31	Income Summary	151,000	
	Cost of Goods Sold		110,000
	Sales Returns and Allowances		4,800
	Sales Discounts		3,600
	Freight-Out		1,800
	Rent Expense		8,800
	Salaries and Wages Expense		22,000
	(To close accounts with debit balances)		

Related exercise material: **BE5-6, BE5-7, E5-6, E5-7, E5-8, and DO IT! 5-4.**

 LEARNING OBJECTIVE 5 **Compare a multiple-step with a single-step income statement.**

Merchandising companies widely use the classified balance sheet introduced in Chapter 4 and one of two forms for the income statement. This section explains the use of these financial statements by merchandisers.

Multiple-Step Income Statement

The **multiple-step income statement** is so named because it shows several steps in determining net income. Two of these steps relate to the company's principal operating activities. A multiple-step statement also distinguishes between **operating** and **nonoperating activities**. Finally, the statement highlights intermediate components of income and shows subgroupings of expenses.

INCOME STATEMENT PRESENTATION OF SALES

The multiple-step income statement begins by presenting **sales revenue**. It then deducts contra revenue accounts—sales returns and allowances and sales discounts—from sales revenue to arrive at **net sales**. Illustration 5-9 presents the sales section for PW Audio Supply, Inc., using assumed data.

Illustration 5-9
Computation of net sales

PW AUDIO SUPPLY, INC.		
Income Statement (partial)		
Sales		
Sales revenue		$ 480,000
Less: Sales returns and allowances	$12,000	
Sales discounts	8,000	20,000
Net sales		**$460,000**

GROSS PROFIT

From Illustration 5-1, you learned that companies deduct cost of goods sold from sales revenue to determine **gross profit**. For this computation, companies use **net sales** (which takes into consideration Sales Returns and Allowances and Sales Discounts) as the amount of sales revenue. On the basis of the sales data in Illustration 5-9 (net sales of $460,000) and cost of goods sold under the perpetual inventory system (assume $316,000), PW Audio Supply's gross profit is $144,000, computed as follows.

Alternative Terminology
Gross profit is sometimes referred to as *gross margin*.

Net sales	$ 460,000
Cost of goods sold	316,000
Gross profit	**$144,000**

Illustration 5-10
Computation of gross profit

We also can express a company's gross profit as a percentage, called the **gross profit rate**. To do so, we divide the amount of gross profit by net sales. For PW Audio Supply, the **gross profit rate** is 31.3%, computed as follows.

Gross Profit	÷	Net Sales	=	Gross Profit Rate
$144,000	÷	$460,000	=	31.3%

Illustration 5-11
Gross profit rate formula and computation

Analysts generally consider the gross profit **rate** to be more useful than the gross profit **amount**. The rate expresses a more meaningful (qualitative) relationship between net sales and gross profit. For example, a gross profit of $1,000,000 may sound impressive. But if it is the result of a gross profit rate of only 7%, it is not so impressive. The gross profit rate tells how many cents of each sales dollar go to gross profit.

Gross profit represents the **merchandising profit** of a company. It is not a measure of the overall profitability because operating expenses are not yet deducted. But managers and other interested parties closely watch the amount and trend of gross profit. They compare current gross profit with amounts reported in past periods. They also compare the company's gross profit rate with rates of competitors and with industry averages. Such comparisons provide information about the effectiveness of a company's purchasing function and the soundness of its pricing policies.

OPERATING EXPENSES AND NET INCOME

Operating expenses are the next component in measuring net income for a merchandising company. They are the expenses incurred in the process of earning sales revenue. These expenses are similar in merchandising and service companies. At PW Audio Supply, operating expenses were $114,000. The company determines its net income by subtracting operating expenses from gross profit. Thus, net income is $30,000, as shown below.

Gross profit	$144,000
Operating expenses	114,000
Net income	$ 30,000

Illustration 5-12
Operating expenses in computing net income

The net income amount is the so-called "bottom line" of a company's income statement.

NONOPERATING ACTIVITIES

Nonoperating activities consist of various revenues and expenses and gains and losses that are unrelated to the company's main line of operations. When nonoperating items are included, the label "**Income from operations**" (or "Operating income") precedes them. This label clearly identifies the results of the company's normal operations, an amount determined by subtracting cost of goods sold and operating expenses from net sales. The results of nonoperating activities are shown in the categories "**Other revenues and gains**" and "**Other expenses and losses**." Illustration 5-13 lists examples of each.

Illustration 5-13
Other items of nonoperating activities

Other Revenues and Gains
Interest revenue from notes receivable and marketable securities.
Dividend revenue from investments in common stock.
Rent revenue from subleasing a portion of the store.
Gain from the sale of property, plant, and equipment.
Other Expenses and Losses
Interest expense on notes and loans payable.
Casualty losses from recurring causes, such as vandalism and accidents.
Loss from the sale or abandonment of property, plant, and equipment.
Loss from strikes by employees and suppliers.

ETHICS NOTE

Companies manage earnings in various ways. ConAgra Foods recorded a non-recurring gain for $186 million from the sale of Pilgrim's Pride stock to help meet an earnings projection for the quarter.

Merchandising companies report the nonoperating activities in the income statement immediately after the company's operating activities. Illustration 5-14 shows these sections for PW Audio Supply, Inc., using assumed data.

Illustration 5-14
Multiple-step income statement

PW AUDIO SUPPLY, INC.
Income Statement
For the Year Ended December 31, 2017

Sales			
Sales revenue			$480,000
Less: Sales returns and allowances	$12,000		
Sales discounts	8,000		20,000
Net sales			460,000
Cost of goods sold			316,000
Gross profit			144,000
Operating expenses			
Salaries and wages expense		64,000	
Utilities expense		17,000	
Advertising expense		16,000	
Depreciation expense		8,000	
Freight-out		7,000	
Insurance expense		2,000	
Total operating expenses			114,000
Income from operations			30,000
Other revenues and gains			
Interest revenue		3,000	
Gain on disposal of plant assets		600	3,600
Other expenses and losses			
Interest expense		1,800	
Casualty loss from vandalism		200	2,000
Net income			$ 31,600

Calculation of gross profit

Calculation of income from operations

Results of nonoperating activities

The distinction between operating and nonoperating activities is crucial to many external users of financial data. These users view operating income as sustainable and many nonoperating activities as non-recurring. Therefore, when forecasting next year's income, analysts put the most weight on this year's operating income and less weight on this year's nonoperating activities.

Single-Step Income Statement

Another income statement format is the **single-step income statement**. The statement is so named because only one step—subtracting total expenses from total revenues—is required in determining net income.

In a single-step statement, all data are classified into two categories: (1) **revenues**, which include both operating revenues and other revenues and gains; and (2) **expenses**, which include cost of goods sold, operating expenses, and other expenses and losses. Illustration 5-15 shows a single-step statement for PW Audio Supply, Inc.

Illustration 5-15
Single-step income statement

PW AUDIO SUPPLY, INC.
Income Statement
For the Year Ended December 31, 2017

Revenues		
Net sales		$460,000
Interest revenue		3,000
Gain on disposal of plant assets		600
Total revenues		463,600
Expenses		
Cost of goods sold	$316,000	
Operating expenses	114,000	
Interest expense	1,800	
Casualty loss from vandalism	200	
Total expenses		432,000
Net income		$ 31,600

There are two primary reasons for using the single-step format. (1) A company does not realize any type of profit or income until total revenues exceed total expenses, so it makes sense to divide the statement into these two categories. (2) The format is simpler and easier to read. *For homework problems, however, you should use the single-step format only when specifically instructed to do so.*

Classified Balance Sheet

In the balance sheet, merchandising companies report inventory as a current asset immediately below accounts receivable. Recall from Chapter 4 that companies generally list current asset items in the order of their closeness to cash (liquidity). Inventory is less close to cash than accounts receivable because the goods must first be sold and then collection made from the customer. Illustration 5-16 presents the assets section of a classified balance sheet for PW Audio Supply, Inc.

Illustration 5-16
Assets section of a classified balance sheet

PW AUDIO SUPPLY, INC.
Balance Sheet (Partial)
December 31, 2017

Assets

Current assets		
Cash		$ 9,500
Accounts receivable		16,100
Inventory		40,000
Prepaid insurance		1,800
Total current assets		67,400
Property, plant, and equipment		
Equipment	$80,000	
Less: Accumulated depreciation—equipment	24,000	56,000
Total assets		$123,400

Helpful Hint
The $40,000 is the cost of the inventory on hand, not its expected selling price.

DO IT!　5　Financial Statement Classifications

You are presented with the following list of accounts from the adjusted trial balance for merchandiser Gorman Company. Indicate in which financial statement and under what classification each of the following would be reported.

Accounts Payable
Accounts Receivable
Accumulated Depreciation—Buildings
Accumulated Depreciation—Equipment
Advertising Expense
Buildings
Cash
Common Stock
Depreciation Expense
Dividends
Equipment
Freight-Out
Gain on Disposal of Plant Assets

Insurance Expense
Interest Expense
Interest Payable
Inventory
Land
Notes Payable (due in 3 years)
Property Taxes Payable
Salaries and Wages Expense
Salaries and Wages Payable
Sales Returns and Allowances
Sales Revenue
Utilities Expense

Action Plan

✔ Review the major sections of the income statement: sales, cost of goods sold, operating expenses, other revenues and gains, and other expenses and losses.

✔ Add net income and investments to beginning retained earnings and deduct dividends to arrive at ending retained earnings in the retained earnings statement.

Solution

Account	Financial Statement	Classification
Accounts Payable	Balance sheet	Current liabilities
Accounts Receivable	Balance sheet	Current assets
Accumulated Depreciation—Buildings	Balance sheet	Property, plant, and equipment
Accumulated Depreciation—Equipment	Balance sheet	Property, plant, and equipment
Advertising Expense	Income statement	Operating expenses
Buildings	Balance sheet	Property, plant, and equipment
Cash	Balance sheet	Current assets
Common Stock	Balance sheet	Stockholders' equity
Depreciation Expense	Income statement	Operating expenses

Dividends	Retained earnings statement	Deduction section
Equipment	Balance sheet	Property, plant, and equipment
Freight-Out	Income statement	Operating expenses
Gain on Disposal of Plant Assets	Income statement	Other revenues and gains
Insurance Expense	Income statement	Operating expenses
Interest Expense	Income statement	Other expenses and losses
Interest Payable	Balance sheet	Current liabilities
Inventory	Balance sheet	Current assets
Land	Balance sheet	Property, plant, and equipment
Notes Payable (due in 3 years)	Balance sheet	Long-term liabilities
Property Taxes Payable	Balance sheet	Current liabilities
Salaries and Wages Expense	Income statement	Operating expenses
Salaries and Wages Payable	Balance sheet	Current liabilities
Sales Returns and Allowances	Income statement	Sales
Sales Revenue	Income statement	Sales
Utilities Expense	Income statement	Operating expenses

Action Plan (cont'd)

✔ Review the major sections of the balance sheet, income statement, and retained earnings statement.

Related exercise material: **BE5-8, BE5-9, E5-9, E5-10, E5-12, E5-13, E5-14, and DO IT! 5-5.**

APPENDIX 5A: Prepare a worksheet for a merchandising company.

Using a Worksheet

As indicated in Chapter 4, a worksheet enables companies to prepare financial statements before they journalize and post adjusting entries. The steps in preparing a worksheet for a merchandising company are the same as for a service company (see pages 153–155). Illustration 5A-1 (page 226) shows the worksheet for PW Audio Supply, Inc. (excluding nonoperating items). The unique accounts for a merchandiser using a **perpetual inventory system** are in red.

TRIAL BALANCE COLUMNS

Data for the trial balance come from the ledger balances of PW Audio Supply at December 31. The amount shown for Inventory, $40,500, is the year-end inventory amount from the perpetual inventory system.

ADJUSTMENTS COLUMNS

A merchandising company generally has the same types of adjustments as a service company. As you see in the worksheet, adjustments (b), (c), and (d) are for insurance, depreciation, and salaries and wages. Pioneer Advertising Inc., as illustrated in Chapters 3 and 4, also had these adjustments. Adjustment (a) was required to adjust the perpetual inventory carrying amount to the actual count.

After PW Audio Supply enters all adjustments data on the worksheet, it establishes the equality of the adjustments column totals. It then extends the balances in all accounts to the adjusted trial balance columns.

ADJUSTED TRIAL BALANCE

The adjusted trial balance shows the balance of all accounts after adjustment at the end of the accounting period.

INCOME STATEMENT COLUMNS

Next, the merchandising company transfers the accounts and balances that affect the income statement from the adjusted trial balance columns to the income statement columns. PW Audio Supply shows Sales Revenue of $480,000 in the

			PW Audio Supply.xls						

Home   Insert   Page Layout   Formulas   Data   Review   View

P18   fx

	A	B	C	D	E	F	G	H	I	J	K
1											
2						PW AUDIO SUPPLY, INC.					
3						Worksheet					
4						For the Year Ended December 31, 2017					
5		Trial Balance		Adjustments		Adjusted Trial Balance		Income Statement		Balance Sheet	
6											
7	Accounts	Dr.	Cr.	Dr.	Cr.	Dr.	Cr.	Dr.	Cr.	Dr.	Cr.
8	Cash	9,500				9,500				9,500	
9	Accounts Receivable	16,100				16,100				16,100	
10	Inventory	40,500			(a) 500	40,000				40,000	
11	Prepaid Insurance	3,800			(b) 2,000	1,800				1,800	
12	Equipment	80,000				80,000				80,000	
13	Accumulated Depreciation— Equipment		16,000		(c) 8,000		24,000				24,000
14	Accounts Payable		20,400				20,400				20,400
15	Common Stock		50,000				50,000				50,000
16	Retained Earnings		33,000				33,000				33,000
17	Dividends	15,000				15,000				15,000	
18	Sales Revenue		480,000				480,000		480,000		
19	Sales Returns and Allowances	12,000				12,000		12,000			
20	Sales Discounts	8,000				8,000		8,000			
21	Cost of Goods Sold	315,500		(a) 500		316,000		316,000			
22	Freight-Out	7,000				7,000		7,000			
23	Advertising Expense	16,000				16,000		16,000			
24	Salaries and Wages Expense	59,000		(d) 5,000		64,000		64,000			
25	Utilities Expense	17,000				17,000		17,000			
26	Totals	599,400	599,400								
27	Insurance Expense			(b) 2,000		2,000		2,000			
28	Depreciation Expense			(c) 8,000		8,000		8,000			
29	Salaries and Wages Payable				(d) 5,000		5,000				5,000
30	Totals			15,500	15,500	612,400	612,400	450,000	480,000	162,400	132,400
31	Net Income							30,000			30,000
32	Totals							480,000	480,000	162,400	162,400
33											
34											

Key: (a) Adjustment to inventory on hand. (b) Insurance expired. (c) Depreciation expense. (d) Salaries and wages accrued.

Illustration 5A-1

Worksheet for merchandising company—perpetual inventory system

credit column. It shows the contra revenue accounts Sales Returns and Allowances $12,000 and Sales Discounts $8,000 in the debit column. The difference of $460,000 is the net sales shown on the income statement (Illustration 5-14, page 222).

Finally, the company totals all the credits in the income statement column and compares those totals to the total of the debits in the income statement column. If the credits exceed the debits, the company has net income. PW Audio Supply has net income of $30,000. If the debits exceed the credits, the company would report a net loss.

BALANCE SHEET COLUMNS

The major difference between the balance sheets of a service company and a merchandiser is inventory. PW Audio Supply shows the ending inventory amount of $40,000 in the balance sheet debit column. The information to prepare the retained earnings statement is also found in these columns. That is, the retained earnings beginning balance is $33,000. Dividends are $15,000. Net income results when the total of the debit column exceeds the total of the credit column in the balance sheet columns. A net loss results when the total of the credits exceeds the total of the debit balances.

APPENDIX 5B: Record purchases and sales under a periodic inventory system.

As described in this chapter, companies may use one of two basic systems of accounting for inventories: (1) the perpetual inventory system or (2) the periodic inventory system. In the chapter, we focused on the characteristics of the perpetual inventory system. In this appendix, we discuss and illustrate the **periodic inventory system**. One key difference between the two systems is the point at which the company computes cost of goods sold. For a visual reminder of this difference, refer back to Illustration 5-5 (on page 208).

Determining Cost of Goods Sold Under a Periodic System

Determining cost of goods sold is different when a periodic inventory system is used rather than a perpetual system. As you have seen, a company using a **perpetual system** makes an entry to record cost of goods sold and to reduce inventory each time a sale is made. A company using a **periodic system** does not determine cost of goods sold until the end of the period. At the end of the period, the company performs a count to determine the ending balance of inventory. It then **calculates cost of goods sold by subtracting ending inventory from the cost of goods available for sale**. Goods available for sale is the sum of beginning inventory plus purchases, as shown in Illustration 5B-1.

Beginning Inventory
+ Cost of Goods Purchased
Cost of Goods Available for Sale
− Ending Inventory
Cost of Goods Sold

Illustration 5B-1
Basic formula for cost of goods sold using the periodic system

Another difference between the two approaches is that the perpetual system directly adjusts the Inventory account for any transaction that affects inventory (such as freight costs, returns, and discounts). The periodic system does not do this. Instead, it creates different accounts for purchases, freight costs, returns, and discounts. These various accounts are shown in Illustration 5B-2, which presents the calculation of cost of goods sold for PW Audio Supply, Inc., using the periodic approach.

PW AUDIO SUPPLY, INC.
Cost of Goods Sold
For the Year Ended December 31, 2017

Cost of goods sold		
Inventory, January 1		$ 36,000
Purchases	$325,000	
Less: Purchase returns and allowances	$10,400	
Purchase discounts	6,800	17,200
Net purchases		307,800
Add: Freight-in		12,200
Cost of goods purchased		320,000
Cost of goods available for sale		356,000
Less: Inventory, December 31		40,000
Cost of goods sold		**$316,000**

Illustration 5B-2
Cost of goods sold for a merchandiser using a periodic inventory system

Helpful Hint
The far right column identifies the primary items that make up cost of goods sold of $316,000. The middle column explains cost of goods purchased of $320,000. The left column reports contra purchase items of $17,200.

Note that the basic elements from Illustration 5B-1 are highlighted in Illustration 5B-2. You will learn more in Chapter 6 about how to determine cost of goods sold using the periodic system.

The use of the periodic inventory system does not affect the form of presentation in the balance sheet. As under the perpetual system, a company reports inventory in the current assets section.

Recording Merchandise Transactions

In a **periodic inventory system**, companies record revenues from the sale of merchandise when sales are made, just as in a perpetual system. Unlike the perpetual system, however, companies **do not attempt on the date of sale to record the cost of the merchandise sold**. Instead, they take a physical inventory count at the **end of the period** to determine (1) the cost of the merchandise then on hand and (2) the cost of the goods sold during the period. And, **under a periodic system**, **companies record purchases of merchandise in the Purchases account rather than in the Inventory account**. Also, in a periodic system, purchase returns and allowances, purchase discounts, and freight costs on purchases are recorded in separate accounts.

To illustrate the recording of merchandise transactions under a periodic inventory system, we will use purchase/sales transactions between PW Audio Supply, Inc. and Sauk Stereo, as illustrated for the perpetual inventory system in this chapter.

Recording Purchases of Merchandise

Helpful Hint
Be careful not to debit purchases of equipment or supplies to a Purchases account.

On the basis of the sales invoice (Illustration 5-6, shown on page 210) and receipt of the merchandise ordered from PW Audio Supply, Sauk Stereo records the $3,800 purchase as follows.

May 4	Purchases	3,800	
	Accounts Payable		3,800
	(To record goods purchased on account		
	from PW Audio Supply)		

Purchases is a temporary account whose normal balance is a debit.

FREIGHT COSTS

Alternative Terminology
Freight-In is also called *Transportation-In.*

When the purchaser directly incurs the freight costs, it debits the account Freight-In (or Transportation-In). For example, if Sauk Stereo pays Public Carrier Co. $150 for freight charges on its purchase from PW Audio Supply on May 6, the entry on Sauk Stereo's books is:

May 6	Freight-In (Transportation-In)	150	
	Cash		150
	(To record payment of freight on goods		
	purchased)		

Like Purchases, Freight-In is a temporary account whose normal balance is a debit. **Freight-In is part of cost of goods purchased.** The reason is that cost of goods purchased should include any freight charges necessary to bring the goods to the purchaser. Freight costs are not subject to a purchase discount. Purchase discounts apply only to the invoice cost of the merchandise.

PURCHASE RETURNS AND ALLOWANCES

Sauk Stereo returns $300 of goods to PW Audio Supply and prepares the following entry to recognize the return.

May 8	Accounts Payable	300	
	Purchase Returns and Allowances		300
	(To record return of goods purchased		
	from PW Audio Supply)		

Purchase Returns and Allowances is a temporary account whose normal balance is a credit.

PURCHASE DISCOUNTS

On May 14, Sauk Stereo pays the balance due on account to PW Audio Supply, taking the 2% cash discount allowed by PW Audio Supply for payment within 10 days. Sauk Stereo records the payment and discount as follows.

May 14	Accounts Payable ($3,800 − $300)	3,500	
	Purchase Discounts ($3,500 × .02)		70
	Cash		3,430
	(To record payment within the discount period)		

Purchase Discounts is a temporary account whose normal balance is a credit.

Recording Sales of Merchandise

The seller, PW Audio Supply, records the sale of $3,800 of merchandise to Sauk Stereo on May 4 (sales invoice No. 731, Illustration 5-6, page 210) as follows.

May 4	Accounts Receivable	3,800	
	Sales Revenue		3,800
	(To record credit sales per invoice #731 to Sauk Stereo)		

SALES RETURNS AND ALLOWANCES

To record the returned goods received from Sauk Stereo on May 8, PW Audio Supply records the $300 sales return as follows.

May 8	Sales Returns and Allowances	300	
	Accounts Receivable		300
	(To record credit granted to Sauk Stereo for returned goods)		

SALES DISCOUNTS

On May 14, PW Audio Supply receives payment of $3,430 on account from Sauk Stereo. PW Audio Supply honors the 2% cash discount and records the payment of Sauk Stereo's account receivable in full as follows.

May 14	Cash	3,430	
	Sales Discounts ($3,500 × .02)	70	
	Accounts Receivable ($3,800 − $300)		3,500
	(To record collection within 2/10, n/30 discount period from Sauk Stereo)		

COMPARISON OF ENTRIES—PERPETUAL VS. PERIODIC

Illustration 5B-3 (page 230) summarizes the periodic inventory entries shown in this appendix and compares them to the perpetual system entries from the chapter. Entries that differ in the two systems are shown in color.

Journalizing and Posting Closing Entries

For a merchandising company, like a service company, all accounts that affect the determination of net income are closed to Income Summary. Data for the preparation of closing entries may be obtained from the income statement columns of the worksheet. In journalizing, all debit column amounts are credited, and all credit columns amounts are debited. To close the merchandise inventory in a periodic inventory system:

ENTRIES ON SAUK STEREO'S BOOKS				
Transaction	Perpetual Inventory System		Periodic Inventory System	
May 4 Purchase of merchandise on credit.	Inventory **3,800** Accounts Payable	3,800	Purchases **3,800** Accounts Payable	3,800
6 Freight costs on purchases.	Inventory **150** Cash	150	Freight-In **150** Cash	150
8 Purchase returns and allowances.	Accounts Payable 300 Inventory	**300**	Accounts Payable 300 Purchase Returns and Allowances	**300**
14 Payment on account with a discount.	Accounts Payable 3,500 Cash Inventory	3,430 **70**	Accounts Payable 3,500 Cash Purchase Discounts	3,430 **70**

ENTRIES ON PW AUDIO SUPPLY'S BOOKS				
Transaction	Perpetual Inventory System		Periodic Inventory System	
May 4 Sale of merchandise on credit.	Accounts Receivable 3,800 Sales Revenue	3,800	Accounts Receivable 3,800 Sales Revenue	3,800
	Cost of Goods Sold **2,400** Inventory	**2,400**	No entry for cost of goods sold	
8 Return of merchandise sold.	Sales Returns and Allowances 300 Accounts Receivable	300	Sales Returns and Allowances 300 Accounts Receivable	300
	Inventory **140** Cost of Goods Sold	**140**	No entry	
14 Cash received on account with a discount.	Cash 3,430 Sales Discounts 70 Accounts Receivable	3,500	Cash 3,430 Sales Discounts 70 Accounts Receivable	3,500

Illustration 5B-3
Comparison of entries for perpetual and periodic inventory systems

1. The beginning inventory balance is debited to Income Summary and credited to Inventory.
2. The ending inventory balance is debited to Inventory and credited to Income Summary.

The two entries for PW Audio Supply are as follows.

(1)

Dec. 31	Income Summary	36,000	
	Inventory		36,000
	(To close beginning inventory)		

(2)

31	Inventory	40,000	
	Income Summary		40,000
	(To record ending inventory)		

After posting, the Inventory and Income Summary accounts will show the following.

Illustration 5B-4
Posting closing entries for merchandise inventory

Inventory				Income Summary			
1/1	Bal.	36,000	12/31 Close **36,000**	12/31 Close **36,000**		12/31 Close **40,000**	
12/31	Close	**40,000**					
12/31	Bal.	40,000					

Often, the closing of Inventory is included with other closing entries, as shown on the next page for PW Audio Supply. (*Close Inventory with other accounts in homework problems unless stated otherwise.*)

Dec. 31	Inventory (Dec. 31)	40,000	
	Sales Revenue	480,000	
	Purchase Returns and Allowances	10,400	
	Purchase Discounts	6,800	
	Income Summary		537,200
	(To record ending inventory and close		
	accounts with credit balances)		
31	Income Summary	507,200	
	Inventory (Jan. 1)		36,000
	Sales Returns and Allowances		12,000
	Sales Discounts		8,000
	Purchases		325,000
	Freight-In		12,200
	Salaries and Wages Expense		64,000
	Freight-Out		7,000
	Advertising Expense		16,000
	Utilities Expense		17,000
	Depreciation Expense		8,000
	Insurance Expense		2,000
	(To close beginning inventory and		
	other income statement accounts with		
	debit balances)		
31	Income Summary	30,000	
	Retained Earnings		30,000
	(To transfer net income to		
	retained earnings)		
31	Retained Earnings	15,000	
	Dividends		15,000
	(To close dividends to retained earnings)		

Helpful Hint
Except for merchandise inventory, the easiest way to prepare the first two closing entries is to identify the temporary accounts by their balances and then prepare one entry for the credits and one for the debits.

After the closing entries are posted, all temporary accounts have zero balances. In addition, Retained Earnings has a credit balance of $48,000: beginning balance + net income − dividends ($33,000 + $30,000 − $15,000).

Using a Worksheet

As indicated in Chapter 4, a worksheet enables companies to prepare financial statements before journalizing and posting adjusting entries. The steps in preparing a worksheet for a merchandising company are the same as they are for a service company (see pages 153–155).

TRIAL BALANCE COLUMNS

Data for the trial balance come from the ledger balances of PW Audio Supply at December 31. The amount shown for Inventory, $36,000, is the beginning inventory amount from the periodic inventory system.

ADJUSTMENTS COLUMNS

A merchandising company generally has the same types of adjustments as a service company. As you see in the worksheet in Illustration 5B-5 (page 232), adjustments (a), (b), and (c) are for insurance, depreciation, and salaries and wages. These adjustments were also required for Pioneer Advertising Inc., as illustrated in Chapters 3 and 4. The unique accounts for a merchandiser using a **periodic inventory system** are shown in capital red letters. Note, however, that the worksheet excludes nonoperating items.

After all adjustment data are entered on the worksheet, the equality of the adjustment column totals is established. The balances in all accounts are then extended to the adjusted trial balance columns.

INCOME STATEMENT COLUMNS

Next, PW Audio Supply transfers the accounts and balances that affect the income statement from the adjusted trial balance columns to the income statement columns.

	PW Audio Supply.xls
Home Insert Page Layout Formulas Data Review View	
P18 _fx_	

PW AUDIO SUPPLY, INC.
Worksheet
For the Year Ended December 31, 2017

	Trial Balance		Adjustments		Adjusted Trial Balance		Income Statement		Balance Sheet	
Accounts	Dr.	Cr.	Dr.	Cr.	Dr.	Cr.	Dr.	Cr.	Dr.	Cr.
Cash	9,500				9,500				9,500	
Accounts Receivable	16,100				16,100				16,100	
INVENTORY	36,000				36,000		36,000	40,000	40,000	
Prepaid Insurance	3,800			(a) 2,000	1,800				1,800	
Equipment	80,000				80,000				80,000	
Accumulated Depreciation—Equipment		16,000		(b) 8,000		24,000				24,000
Accounts Payable		20,400				20,400				20,400
Common Stock		50,000				50,000				50,000
Retained Earnings		33,000				33,000				33,000
Dividends	15,000				15,000				15,000	
SALES REVENUE		480,000				480,000		480,000		
SALES RETURNS AND ALLOWANCES	12,000				12,000		12,000			
SALES DISCOUNTS	8,000				8,000		8,000			
PURCHASES	325,000				325,000		325,000			
PURCHASE RETURNS AND ALLOWANCES		10,400				10,400		10,400		
PURCHASE DISCOUNTS		6,800				6,800		6,800		
FREIGHT-IN	12,200				12,200		12,200			
Freight-Out	7,000				7,000		7,000			
Advertising Expense	16,000				16,000		16,000			
Salaries and Wages Expense	59,000		(c) 5,000		64,000		64,000			
Utilities Expense	17,000				17,000		17,000			
Totals	616,600	616,600								
Insurance Expense			(a) 2,000		2,000		2,000			
Depreciation Expense			(b) 8,000		8,000		8,000			
Salaries and Wages Payable				(c) 5,000		5,000				5,000
Totals			15,000	15,000	629,600	629,600	507,200	537,200	162,400	132,400
Net Income							30,000			30,000
Totals							537,200	537,200	162,400	162,400

Key: (a) Insurance expired. (b) Depreciation expense. (c) Salaries and wages accrued.

Illustration 5B-5
Worksheet for merchandising company—periodic inventory system

The company shows Sales Revenue of $480,000 in the credit column. It shows the contra revenue accounts, Sales Returns and Allowances of $12,000 and Sales Discounts of $8,000, in the debit column. The difference of $460,000 is the net sales shown on the income statement (Illustration 5-9, page 220). Similarly, Purchases of $325,000 and Freight-In of $12,200 are extended to the debit column. The contra purchase accounts, Purchase Returns and Allowances of $10,400 and Purchase Discounts of $6,800, are extended to the credit columns.

The worksheet procedures for the Inventory account merit specific comment. The procedures are shown on the next page.

1. The beginning balance, $36,000, is extended from the adjusted trial balance column to the **income statement debit column**. From there, it can be added in reporting cost of goods available for sale in the income statement.

2. The ending inventory, $40,000, is added to the worksheet by an **income statement credit and a balance sheet debit**. The credit makes it possible to deduct ending inventory from the cost of goods available for sale in the income statement to determine cost of goods sold. The debit means the ending inventory can be reported as an asset on the balance sheet.

These two procedures are specifically illustrated below:

	Income Statement		Balance Sheet	
	Dr.	Cr.	Dr.	Cr.
Inventory	(1) 36,000	40,000 ←——— (2) ——→ 40,000		

Illustration 5B-6
Worksheet procedures for inventories

The computation for cost of goods sold, taken from the income statement column in Illustration 5B-5, is as follows.

Debit Column		Credit Column	
Beginning inventory	$ 36,000	Ending inventory	$40,000
Purchases	325,000	Purchase returns and allowances	10,400
Freight-in	12,200	Purchase discounts	6,800
Total debits	373,200	Total credits	$57,200
Less: Total credits	57,200		
Cost of goods sold	**$316,000**		

Illustration 5B-7
Computation of cost of goods sold from worksheet columns

Helpful Hint
In a periodic system, cost of goods sold is a computation—it is not a separate account with a balance.

Finally, PW Audio Supply totals all the credits in the income statement column and compares these totals to the total of the debits in the income statement column. If the credits exceed the debits, the company has net income. PW Audio Supply has net income of $30,000. If the debits exceed the credits, the company would report a net loss.

BALANCE SHEET COLUMNS

The major difference between the balance sheets of a service company and a merchandising company is inventory. PW Audio Supply shows ending inventory of $40,000 in the balance sheet debit column. The information to prepare the retained earnings statement is also found in these columns. That is, the retained earnings beginning balance is $33,000. Dividends are $15,000. Net income results when the total of the debit column exceeds the total of the credit column in the balance sheet columns. A net loss results when the total of the credits exceeds the total of the debit balances.

REVIEW AND PRACTICE

LEARNING OBJECTIVES REVIEW

❶ Describe merchandising operations and inventory systems. Because of inventory, a merchandising company has sales revenue, cost of goods sold, and gross profit. To account for inventory, a merchandising company must choose between a perpetual and a periodic inventory system.

❷ Record purchases under a perpetual inventory system. The company debits the Inventory account for all purchases of merchandise and freight-in, and credits it for purchase discounts and purchase returns and allowances.

❸ Record sales under a perpetual inventory system. When a merchandising company sells inventory, it debits Accounts Receivable (or Cash) and credits Sales Revenue for the **selling price** of the merchandise. At the same time, it debits Cost of Goods Sold and credits Inventory for the **cost** of the inventory items sold. Sales Returns and Allowances and Sales Discounts are debited and are contra revenue accounts.

❹ Apply the steps in the accounting cycle to a merchandising company. Each of the required steps in the accounting cycle for a service company applies to a merchandising company. A worksheet is again an optional step. Under a perpetual inventory system, the company must adjust the Inventory account to agree with the physical count.

❺ Compare a multiple-step with a single-step income statement. A multiple-step income statement shows numerous steps in determining net income, including nonoperating activities sections. A single-step income statement classifies all data under two categories, revenues or expenses, and determines net income in one step.

∗❻ Prepare a worksheet for a merchandising company. The steps in preparing a worksheet for a merchandising company are the same as for a service company. The unique accounts for a merchandiser are Inventory, Sales Revenue, Sales Returns and Allowances, Sales Discounts, and Cost of Goods Sold.

∗❼ Record purchases and sales under a periodic inventory system. In recording purchases under a periodic system, companies must make entries for (a) cash and credit purchases, (b) purchase returns and allowances, (c) purchase discounts, and (d) freight costs. In recording sales, companies must make entries for (a) cash and credit sales, (b) sales returns and allowances, and (c) sales discounts.

GLOSSARY REVIEW

Contra revenue account An account that is offset against a revenue account on the income statement. (p. 216).

Cost of goods sold The total cost of merchandise sold during the period. (p. 206).

FOB destination Freight terms indicating that the seller places the goods free on board to the buyer's place of business, and the seller pays the freight. (p. 211).

FOB shipping point Freight terms indicating that the seller places goods free on board the carrier, and the buyer pays the freight costs. (p. 211).

Gross profit The excess of net sales over the cost of goods sold. (p. 221).

Gross profit rate Gross profit expressed as a percentage, by dividing the amount of gross profit by net sales. (p. 221).

Income from operations Income from a company's principal operating activity; determined by subtracting cost of goods sold and operating expenses from net sales. (p. 221).

Multiple-step income statement An income statement that shows several steps in determining net income. (p. 220).

Net sales Sales revenue less sales returns and allowances and less sales discounts. (p. 220).

Nonoperating activities Various revenues, expenses, gains, and losses that are unrelated to a company's main line of operations. (p. 221).

Operating expenses Expenses incurred in the process of earning sales revenue. (p. 221).

Other expenses and losses A nonoperating-activities section of the income statement that shows expenses and losses unrelated to the company's main line of operations. (p. 222).

Other revenues and gains A nonoperating-activities section of the income statement that shows revenues and gains unrelated to the company's main line of operations. (p. 222).

Periodic inventory system An inventory system under which the company does not keep detailed inventory records throughout the accounting period but determines the cost of goods sold only at the end of an accounting period. (p. 208).

Perpetual inventory system An inventory system under which the company keeps detailed records of the cost of each inventory purchase and sale, and the records continuously show the inventory that should be on hand. (p. 207).

Purchase allowance A deduction made to the selling price of merchandise, granted by the seller so that the buyer will keep the merchandise. (p. 212).

Purchase discount A cash discount claimed by a buyer for prompt payment of a balance due. (p. 212).

Purchase invoice A document that supports each credit purchase. (p. 209).

Purchase return A return of goods from the buyer to the seller for a cash or credit refund. (p. 212).

Sales discount A reduction given by a seller for prompt payment of a credit sale. (p. 216).

Sales invoice A document that supports each credit sale. (p. 214).

Sales returns and allowances Purchase returns and allowances from the seller's perspective. See *Purchase return* and *Purchase allowance*, above. (p. 215).

Sales revenue (Sales) The primary source of revenue in a merchandising company. (p. 206).

Single-step income statement An income statement that shows only one step in determining net income. (p. 223).

PRACTICE MULTIPLE-CHOICE QUESTIONS

(LO 1)   **1.** Gross profit will result if:
(a) operating expenses are less than net income.
(b) sales revenues are greater than operating expenses.
(c) sales revenues are greater than cost of goods sold.
(d) operating expenses are greater than cost of goods sold.

(LO 2)   **2.** Under a perpetual inventory system, when goods are purchased for resale by a company:
(a) purchases on account are debited to Inventory.
(b) purchases on account are debited to Purchases.
(c) purchase returns are debited to Purchase Returns and Allowances.
(d) freight costs are debited to Freight-Out.

(LO 3)   **3.** The sales accounts that normally have a debit balance are:
(a) Sales Discounts.
(b) Sales Returns and Allowances.
(c) Both (a) and (b).
(d) Neither (a) nor (b).

(LO 3)   **4.** A credit sale of $750 is made on June 13, terms 2/10, net/30. A return of $50 is granted on June 16. The amount received as payment in full on June 23 is:
(a) $700.   (c) $685.
(b) $686.   (d) $650.

(LO 2)   **5.** Which of the following accounts will normally appear in the ledger of a merchandising company that uses a perpetual inventory system?
(a) Purchases.   (c) Cost of Goods Sold.
(b) Freight-In.   (d) Purchase Discounts.

(LO 3)   **6.** To record the sale of goods for cash in a perpetual inventory system:
(a) only one journal entry is necessary to record cost of goods sold and reduction of inventory.
(b) only one journal entry is necessary to record the receipt of cash and the sales revenue.
(c) two journal entries are necessary: one to record the receipt of cash and sales revenue, and one to record the cost of goods sold and reduction of inventory.
(d) two journal entries are necessary: one to record the receipt of cash and reduction of inventory, and one to record the cost of goods sold and sales revenue.

(LO 4)   **7.** The steps in the accounting cycle for a merchandising company are the same as those in a service company **except**:
(a) an additional adjusting journal entry for inventory may be needed in a merchandising company.
(b) closing journal entries are not required for a merchandising company.
(c) a post-closing trial balance is not required for a merchandising company.
(d) a multiple-step income statement is required for a merchandising company.

8. The multiple-step income statement for a merchandising company shows each of the following features **except**: **(LO 5)**
(a) gross profit.
(b) cost of goods sold.
(c) a sales section.
(d) an investing activities section.

9. If sales revenues are $400,000, cost of goods sold is $310,000, and operating expenses are $60,000, the gross profit is: **(LO 5)**
(a) $30,000.   (c) $340,000.
(b) $90,000.   (d) $400,000.

10. A single-step income statement: **(LO 5)**
(a) reports gross profit.
(b) does not report cost of goods sold.
(c) reports sales revenue and "Other revenues and gains" in the revenues section of the income statement.
(d) reports operating income separately.

11. Which of the following appears on both a single-step and a multiple-step income statement? **(LO 5)**
(a) Inventory.
(b) Gross profit.
(c) Income from operations.
(d) Cost of goods sold.

*12. In a worksheet using a perpetual inventory system, Inventory is shown in the following columns: **(LO 6)**
(a) adjusted trial balance debit and balance sheet debit.
(b) income statement debit and balance sheet debit.
(c) income statement credit and balance sheet debit.
(d) income statement credit and adjusted trial balance debit.

*13. In determining cost of goods sold in a periodic system: **(LO 7)**
(a) purchase discounts are deducted from net purchases.
(b) freight-out is added to net purchases.
(c) purchase returns and allowances are deducted from net purchases.
(d) freight-in is added to net purchases.

*14. If beginning inventory is $60,000, cost of goods purchased is $380,000, and ending inventory is $50,000, cost of goods sold is: **(LO 7)**
(a) $390,000.   (c) $330,000.
(b) $370,000.   (d) $420,000.

*15. When goods are purchased for resale by a company using a periodic inventory system: **(LO 7)**
(a) purchases on account are debited to Inventory.
(b) purchases on account are debited to Purchases.
(c) purchase returns are debited to Purchase Returns and Allowances.
(d) freight costs are debited to Purchases.

Solutions

1. (c) Gross profit will result if sales revenues are greater than cost of goods sold. The other choices are incorrect because (a) operating expenses and net income are not used in the computation of gross profit; (b) gross profit results when sales revenues are greater than cost of goods sold, not operating expenses; and (d) gross profit results when sales revenues, not operating expenses, are greater than cost of goods sold.

2. (a) Under a perpetual inventory system, when a company purchases goods for resale, purchases on account are debited to the Inventory account, not (b) Purchases or (c) Purchase Returns and Allowances. Choice (d) is incorrect because freight costs are also debited to the Inventory account, not the Freight-Out account.

3. (c) Both Sales Discounts and Sales Returns and Allowances normally have a debit balance. Choices (a) and (b) are both correct, but (c) is the better answer. Choice (d) is incorrect as both (a) and (b), not neither, are correct.

4. (b) The full amount of $686 is paid within 10 days of the purchase ($750 − $50) – [($750 − $50) × 2%]. The other choices are incorrect because (a) does not consider the discount of $14; (c) the amount of the discount is based upon the amount after the return is granted ($700 × 2%), not the amount before the return of merchandise ($750 × 2%); and (d) does not constitute payment in full on June 23.

5. (c) The Cost of Goods Sold account normally appears in the ledger of a merchandising company using a perpetual inventory system. The other choices are incorrect because (a) the Purchases account, (b) the Freight-In account, and (d) the Purchase Discounts account all appear in the ledger of a merchandising company that uses a periodic inventory system.

6. (c) Two journal entries are necessary: one to record the receipt of cash and sales revenue, and one to record the cost of goods sold and reduction of inventory. The other choices are incorrect because (a) only considers the recognition of the expense and ignores the revenue, (b) only considers the recognition of revenue and leaves out the expense or cost of merchandise sold, and (d) the receipt of cash and sales revenue, not reduction of inventory, are paired together, and the cost of goods sold and reduction of inventory, not sales revenue, are paired together.

7. (a) An additional adjusting journal entry for inventory may be needed in a merchandising company to adjust for a physical inventory count, but it is not needed for a service company. The other choices are incorrect because (b) closing journal entries and (c) a post-closing trial balance are required for both types of companies. Choice (d) is incorrect because while a multiple-step income statement is not required for a merchandising company, it is useful to distinguish income generated from operating the business versus income or loss from nonrecurring nonoperating items.

8. (d) An investing activities section appears on the statement of cash flows, not on a multiple-step income statement. Choices (a) gross profit, (b) cost of goods sold, and (c) a sales section are all features of a multiple-step income statement.

9. (b) Gross profit = Sales revenue ($400,000) − Cost of goods sold ($310,000) = $90,000, not (a) $30,000, (c) $340,000, or (d) $400,000.

10. (c) Both sales revenue and "Other revenues and gains" are reported in the revenues section of a single-step income statement. The other choices are incorrect because (a) gross profit is not reported on a single-step income statement, (b) cost of goods sold is included in the expenses section of a single-step income statement, and (d) income from operations is not shown separately on a single-step income statement.

11. (d) Cost of goods sold appears on both a single-step and a multiple-step income statement. The other choices are incorrect because (a) inventory does not appear on either a single-step or a multiple-step income statement and (b) gross profit and (c) income from operations appear on a multiple-step income statement but not on a single-step income statement.

12 (a) In a worksheet using a perpetual inventory system, inventory is shown in the adjusted trial balance debit column and in the balance sheet debit column. The other choices are incorrect because the Inventory account is not shown in the income statement columns.

*13. (d) In determining cost of goods sold in a periodic system, freight-in is added to net purchases. The other choices are incorrect because (a) purchase discounts are deducted from purchases, not net purchases; (b) freight-out is a cost of sales, not a cost of purchases; and (c) purchase returns and allowances are deducted from purchases, not net purchases.

*14. (a) Beginning inventory ($60,000) + Cost of goods purchased ($380,000) − Ending inventory ($50,000) = Cost of goods sold ($390,000), not (b) $370,000, (c) $330,000, or (d) $420,000.

*15. (b) Purchases for resale are debited to the Purchases account. The other choices are incorrect because (a) purchases on account are debited to Purchases, not Inventory; (c) Purchase Returns and Allowances are always credited; and (d) freight costs are debited to Freight-In, not Purchases.

PRACTICE EXERCISES

Prepare purchase and sales entries.

(LO 2, 3)

1. On June 10, Vareen Company purchased $8,000 of merchandise from Harrah Company, FOB shipping point, terms 3/10, n/30. Vareen pays the freight costs of $400 on June 11. Damaged goods totaling $300 are returned to Harrah for credit on June 12. The fair value of these goods in $70. On June 19, Vareen pays Harrah Company in full, less the purchase discount. Both companies use a perpetual inventory system.

Instructions

(a) Prepare separate entries for each transaction on the books of Vareen Company.

(b) Prepare separate entries for each transaction for Harrah Company. The merchandise purchased by Vareen on June 10 had cost Harrah $4,800.

Solution

1. (a)

June 10	Inventory		8,000	
	Accounts Payable			8,000
11	Inventory		400	
	Cash			400
12	Accounts Payable		300	
	Inventory			300
19	Accounts Payable ($8,000 − $300)		7,700	
	Inventory			
	($7,700 × 3%)			231
	Cash ($7,700 − $231)			7,469

(b)

June 10	Accounts Receivable		8,000	
	Sales Revenue			8,000
	Cost of Goods Sold		4,800	
	Inventory			4,800
12	Sales Returns and Allowances		300	
	Accounts Receivable			300
	Inventory		70	
	Cost of Goods Sold			70
19	Cash ($7,700 − $231)		7,469	
	Sales Discounts ($7,700 × 3%)		231	
	Accounts Receivable			
	($8,000 − $300)			7,700

2. In its income statement for the year ended December 31, 2017, Marten Company reported the following condensed data.

Prepare multiple-step and single-step income statements.

(LO 5)

Interest expense	$ 70,000	Net sales	$2,200,000
Operating expenses	725,000	Interest revenue	25,000
Cost of goods sold	1,300,000	Loss on disposal of plant assets	17,000

Instructions

(a) Prepare a multiple-step income statement.
(b) Prepare a single-step income statement.

Solution

2. (a)

MARTEN COMPANY
Income Statement
For the Year Ended December 31, 2017

Net sales			$2,200,000
Cost of goods sold			1,300,000
Gross profit			900,000
Operating expenses			725,000
Income from operations			175,000
Other revenues and gains			
Interest revenue		$25,000	
Other expenses and losses			
Interest expense	$70,000		
Loss on disposal of plant assets	17,000	87,000	(62,000)
Net income			$ 113,000

(b)

MARTEN COMPANY		
Income Statement		
For the Year Ended December 31, 2017		
Revenues		
Net sales		$2,200,000
Interest revenue		25,000
Total revenues		2,225,000
Expenses		
Cost of goods sold	$1,300,000	
Operating expenses	725,000	
Interest expense	70,000	
Loss on disposal of plant assets	17,000	
Total expenses		2,112,000
Net income		$ 113,000

PRACTICE PROBLEM

Prepare a multiple-step income statement.

(LO 5)

The adjusted trial balance columns of Falcetto Company's worksheet for the year ended December 31, 2017, are as follows.

	Debit		Credit
Cash	14,500	Accumulated Depreciation—	
Accounts Receivable	11,100	Equipment	18,000
Inventory	29,000	Notes Payable	25,000
Prepaid Insurance	2,500	Accounts Payable	10,600
Equipment	95,000	Common Stock	50,000
Dividends	12,000	Retained Earnings	31,000
Sales Returns and Allowances	6,700	Sales Revenue	536,800
Sales Discounts	5,000	Interest Revenue	2,500
Cost of Goods Sold	363,400		673,900
Freight-Out	7,600		
Advertising Expense	12,000		
Salaries and Wages Expense	56,000		
Utilities Expense	18,000		
Rent Expense	24,000		
Depreciation Expense	9,000		
Insurance Expense	4,500		
Interest Expense	3,600		
	673,900		

Instructions

Prepare a multiple-step income statement for Falcetto Company.

Solution

FALCETTO COMPANY		
Income Statement		
For the Year Ended December 31, 2017		
Sales		
Sales revenue		$536,800
Less: Sales returns and allowances	$ 6,700	
Sales discounts	5,000	11,700
Net sales		525,100
Cost of goods sold		363,400
Gross profit		161,700

Operating expenses		
Salaries and wages expense	56,000	
Rent expense	24,000	
Utilities expense	18,000	
Advertising expense	12,000	
Depreciation expense	9,000	
Freight-out	7,600	
Insurance expense	4,500	
Total operating expenses		131,100
Income from operations		30,600
Other revenues and gains		
Interest revenue	2,500	
Other expenses and losses		
Interest expense	3,600	1,100
Net income		$ 29,500

WileyPLUS

Brief Exercises, Exercises, **DO IT!** Exercises, and Problems and many additional resources are available for practice in WileyPLUS

NOTE: All asterisked Questions, Exercises, and Problems relate to material in the appendices to the chapter.

QUESTIONS

1. (a) "The steps in the accounting cycle for a merchandising company are different from the accounting cycle for a service company." Do you agree or disagree? (b) Is the measurement of net income for a merchandising company conceptually the same as for a service company? Explain.

2. Why is the normal operating cycle for a merchandising company likely to be longer than for a service company?

3. What components of revenues and expenses are different between merchandising and service companies?

4. How does income measurement differ between a merchandising and a service company?

5. When is cost of goods sold determined in a perpetual inventory system?

6. Distinguish between FOB shipping point and FOB destination. Identify the freight terms that will result in a debit to Inventory by the buyer and a debit to Freight-Out by the seller.

7. Explain the meaning of the credit terms 2/10, n/30.

8. Goods costing $2,000 are purchased on account on July 15 with credit terms of 2/10, n/30. On July 18, a $200 credit memo is received from the supplier for damaged goods. Give the journal entry on July 24 to record payment of the balance due within the discount period using a perpetual inventory system.

9. Ming Xu believes revenues from credit sales may be recorded before they are collected in cash. Do you agree? Explain.

10. (a) What is the primary source document for recording (1) cash sales and (2) credit sales? (b) Using XXs for amounts, give the journal entry for each of the transactions in part (a).

11. A credit sale is made on July 10 for $900, terms 2/10, n/30. On July 12, $100 of goods are returned for credit. Give the journal entry on July 19 to record the receipt of the balance due within the discount period.

12. Explain why the Inventory account will usually require adjustment at year-end.

13. Prepare the closing entries for the Sales Revenue account, assuming a balance of $200,000 and the Cost of Goods Sold account with a $145,000 balance.

14. What merchandising account(s) will appear in the post-closing trial balance?

15. Minnick Co. has sales revenue of $105,000, cost of goods sold of $70,000, and operating expenses of $20,000. What is its gross profit and its gross profit rate?

16. Paul Scott Company reports net sales of $800,000, gross profit of $370,000, and net income of $240,000. What are its operating expenses?

17. Identify the distinguishing features of an income statement for a merchandising company.

18. Identify the sections of a multiple-step income statement that relate to (a) operating activities, and (b) nonoperating activities.

19. How does the single-step form of income statement differ from the multiple-step form?

20. Determine Apple's gross profit rate for 2013 and 2012. Indicate whether it increased or decreased from 2012 to 2013.

*21. Indicate the columns of the worksheet in a perpetual system in which (a) inventory and (b) cost of goods sold will be shown.

*22. Identify the accounts that are added to or deducted from Purchases in a periodic system to determine the cost of goods purchased. For each account, indicate whether it is added or deducted.

*23. Goods costing $3,000 are purchased on account on July 15 with credit terms of 2/10, n/30. On July 18, a $200 credit was received from the supplier for damaged goods. Give the journal entry on July 24 to record payment of the balance due within the discount period, assuming a periodic inventory system.

BRIEF EXERCISES

Compute missing amounts in determining cost of goods sold.

(LO 1)

BE5-1 Presented below are the components in determining cost of goods sold. Determine the missing amounts.

	Beginning Inventory	Purchases	Cost of Goods Available for Sale	Ending Inventory	Cost of Goods Sold
(a)	$80,000	$100,000	?	?	$120,000
(b)	$50,000	?	$115,000	$35,000	?
(c)	?	$110,000	$160,000	$29,000	?

Compute missing amounts in determining net income.

(LO 1)

BE5-2 Presented below are the components in Gates Company's income statement. Determine the missing amounts.

	Sales Revenue	Cost of Goods Sold	Gross Profit	Operating Expenses	Net Income
(a)	$ 75,000	?	$30,000	?	$10,800
(b)	$108,000	$70,000	?	?	$29,500
(c)	?	$83,900	$79,600	$39,500	?

Journalize perpetual inventory entries.

(LO 2, 3)

BE5-3 Radomir Company buys merchandise on account from Lemke Company. The selling price of the goods is $780, and the cost of the goods is $470. Both companies use perpetual inventory systems. Journalize the transaction on the books of both companies.

Journalize sales transactions.

(LO 3)

BE5-4 Prepare the journal entries to record the following transactions on Kwang Company's books using a perpetual inventory system.

(a) On March 2, Kwang Company sold $900,000 of merchandise to Sensat Company, terms 2/10, n/30. The cost of the merchandise sold was $620,000.

(b) On March 6, Sensat Company returned $90,000 of the merchandise purchased on March 2. The cost of the returned merchandise was $62,000.

(c) On March 12, Kwang Company received the balance due from Sensat Company.

Journalize purchase transactions.

(LO 2)

BE5-5 From the information in BE5-4, prepare the journal entries to record these transactions on Sensat Company's books under a perpetual inventory system.

Prepare adjusting entry for inventory.

(LO 4)

BE5-6 At year-end, the perpetual inventory records of Litwin Company showed merchandise inventory of $98,000. The company determined, however, that its actual inventory on hand was $95,700. Record the necessary adjusting entry.

Prepare closing entries for accounts.

(LO 4)

BE5-7 Hudson Company has the following account balances: Sales Revenue $195,000, Sales Discounts $2,000, Cost of Goods Sold $117,000, and Inventory $40,000. Prepare the entries to record the closing of these items to Income Summary.

Prepare sales section of income statement.

(LO 5)

BE5-8 Arndt Company provides the following information for the month ended October 31, 2017; sales on credit $280,000, cash sales $100,000, sales discounts $5,000, and sales returns and allowances $11,000. Prepare the sales section of the income statement based on this information.

Contrast presentation in multiple-step and single-step income statements.

(LO 5)

BE5-9 Explain where each of the following items would appear on (1) a multiple-step income statement, and on (2) a single-step income statement: (a) gain on sale of equipment, (b) interest expense, (c) casualty loss from vandalism, and (d) cost of goods sold.

Compute net sales, gross profit, income from operations, and gross profit rate.

(LO 5)

BE5-10 Assume Kader Company has the following reported amounts: Sales revenue $510,000, Sales returns and allowances $15,000, Cost of goods sold $330,000, and Operating expenses $110,000. Compute the following: (a) net sales, (b) gross profit, (c) income from operations, and (d) gross profit rate. (Round to one decimal place.)

*BE5-11 Presented below is the format of the worksheet using the perpetual inventory system presented in Appendix 5A.

Identify worksheet columns for selected accounts.

(LO 6)

Trial Balance		Adjustments		Adjusted Trial Balance		Income Statement		Balance Sheet	
Dr.	Cr.	Dr.	Cr.	Dr.	Cr.	Dr.	Cr.	Dr.	Cr.

Indicate where the following items will appear on the worksheet: (a) Cash, (b) Inventory, (c) Sales revenue, and (d) Cost of goods sold.

Example:
Cash: Trial balance debit column; Adjusted trial balance debit column; and Balance sheet debit column.

*BE5-12 Assume that Gallant Company uses a periodic inventory system and has these account balances: Purchases $450,000, Purchase Returns and Allowances $13,000, Purchase Discounts $8,000, and Freight-In $16,000. Determine net purchases and cost of goods purchased.

Compute net purchases and cost of goods purchased.

(LO 7)

*BE5-13 Assume the same information as in BE5-12 and also that Gallant Company has beginning inventory of $60,000, ending inventory of $90,000, and net sales of $730,000. Determine the amounts to be reported for cost of goods sold and gross profit.

Compute cost of goods sold and gross profit.

(LO 7)

*BE5-14 Prepare the journal entries to record these transactions on Nimmer Company's books using a periodic inventory system.
(a) On March 2, Nimmer Company purchased $900,000 of merchandise from Sen Company, terms 2/10, n/30.
(b) On March 6, Nimmer Company returned $130,000 of the merchandise purchased on March 2.
(c) On March 12, Nimmer Company paid the balance due to Sen Company.

Journalize purchase transactions.

(LO 7)

*BE5-15 A. Hall Company has the following merchandise account balances: Sales Revenue $180,000, Sales Discounts $2,000, Purchases $120,000, and Purchases Returns and Allowances $30,000. In addition, it has a beginning inventory of $40,000 and an ending inventory of $30,000. Prepare the entries to record the closing of these items to Income Summary using the periodic inventory system.

Prepare closing entries for merchandise accounts.

(LO 7)

*BE5-16 Presented below is the format of the worksheet using the periodic inventory system presented in Appendix 5B.

Identify worksheet columns for selected accounts.

(LO 7)

Trial Balance		Adjustments		Adjusted Trial Balance		Income Statement		Balance Sheet	
Dr.	Cr.	Dr.	Cr.	Dr.	Cr.	Dr.	Cr.	Dr.	Cr.

Indicate where the following items will appear on the worksheet: (a) Cash, (b) Beginning inventory, (c) Accounts payable, and (d) Ending inventory.

Example
Cash: Trial balance debit column; Adjustment trial balance debit column; and Balance sheet debit column.

DO IT! Exercises

DO IT! 5-1 Indicate whether the following statements are true or false.

1. A merchandising company reports gross profit but a service company does not.
2. Under a periodic inventory system, a company determines the cost of goods sold each time a sale occurs.

Answer general questions about merchandisers.

(LO 1)

3. A service company is likely to use accounts receivable but a merchandising company is not likely to do so.
4. Under a periodic inventory system, the cost of goods on hand at the beginning of the accounting period plus the cost of goods purchased less the cost of goods on hand at the end of the accounting period equals cost of goods sold.

Record transactions of purchasing company.

(LO 2)

DO IT! 5-2 On October 5, Loomis Company buys merchandise on account from Brooke Company. The selling price of the goods is $5,000, and the cost to Brooke Company is $3,100. On October 8, Loomis returns defective goods with a selling price of $650 and a fair value of $100. Record the transactions on the books of Loomis Company.

Record transactions of selling company.

(LO 3)

DO IT! 5-3 Assume information similar to that in DO IT! 5-2: On October 5, Loomis Company buys merchandise on account from Brooke Company. The selling price of the goods is $5,000, and the cost to Brooke Company is $3,100. On October 8, Loomis returns defective goods with a selling price of $650 and a fair value of $100. Record the transactions on the books of Brooke Company.

Prepare closing entries for a merchandising company.

(LO 4)

DO IT! 5-4 The trial balance of Optique Boutique at December 31 shows Inventory $21,000, Sales Revenue $156,000, Sales Returns and Allowances $4,000, Sales Discounts $3,000, Cost of Goods Sold $92,400, Interest Revenue $5,000, Freight-Out $1,500, Utilities Expense $7,400, and Salaries and Wages Expense $19,500. Prepare the closing entries for Optique for these accounts.

Classify financial statement accounts.

(LO 5)

DO IT! 5-5 Estes Company is preparing its multiple-step income statement, retained earnings statement, and classified balance sheet. Using the column headings **Account**, **Financial Statement**, and **Classification**, indicate in which financial statement and under what classification each of the following would be reported.

Account	Financial Statement	Classification
Accounts Payable		
Accounts Receivable		
Accumulated Depreciation—Buildings		
Cash		
Casualty Loss from Vandalism		
Common Stock		
Cost of Goods Sold		
Depreciation Expense		
Dividends		
Equipment		
Freight-Out		
Insurance Expense		
Interest Payable		
Inventory		
Land		
Notes Payable (due in 5 years)		
Property Taxes Payable		
Salaries and Wages Expense		
Salaries and Wages Payable		
Sales Returns and Allowances		
Sales Revenue		
Unearned Rent Revenue		
Utilities Expense		

EXERCISES

Answer general questions about merchandisers.

(LO 1)

E5-1 Mr. Etemadi has prepared the following list of statements about service companies and merchandisers.

1. Measuring net income for a merchandiser is conceptually the same as for a service company.
2. For a merchandiser, sales less operating expenses is called gross profit.
3. For a merchandiser, the primary source of revenues is the sale of inventory.
4. Sales salaries and wages is an example of an operating expense.

5. The operating cycle of a merchandiser is the same as that of a service company.
6. In a perpetual inventory system, no detailed inventory records of goods on hand are maintained.
7. In a periodic inventory system, the cost of goods sold is determined only at the end of the accounting period.
8. A periodic inventory system provides better control over inventories than a perpetual system.

Instructions

Identify each statement as true or false. If false, indicate how to correct the statement.

E5-2 Information related to Harwick Co. is presented below.

1. On April 5, purchased merchandise from Botham Company for $23,000, terms 2/10, net/30, FOB shipping point.
2. On April 6, paid freight costs of $900 on merchandise purchased from Botham.
3. On April 7, purchased equipment on account for $26,000.
4. On April 8, returned damaged merchandise to Botham Company and was granted a $3,000 credit for returned merchandise.
5. On April 15, paid the amount due to Botham Company in full.

Journalize purchase transactions.

(LO 2)

Instructions

(a) Prepare the journal entries to record these transactions on the books of Harwick Co. under a perpetual inventory system.
(b) Assume that Harwick Co. paid the balance due to Botham Company on May 4 instead of April 15. Prepare the journal entry to record this payment.

E5-3 On September 1, Boylan Office Supply had an inventory of 30 calculators at a cost of $18 each. The company uses a perpetual inventory system. During September, the following transactions occurred.

Journalize perpetual inventory entries.

(LO 2, 3)

Sept. 6 Purchased with cash 80 calculators at $20 each from Guthrie Co. terms net/30.
    9 Paid freight of $80 on calculators purchased from Guthrie Co.
  10 Returned 3 calculators to Guthrie Co. for $63 credit (including freight) because they did not meet specifications.
  12 Sold 26 calculators costing $21 (including freight) for $31 each to Lee Book Store, terms n/30.
  14 Granted credit of $31 to Lee Book Store for the return of one calculator that was not ordered.
  20 Sold 30 calculators costing $21 for $32 each to Orr's Card Shop, terms n/30.

Instructions

Journalize the September transactions.

E5-4 On June 10, Tuzun Company purchased $8,000 of merchandise from Epps Company, FOB shipping point, terms 2/10, n/30. Tuzun pays the freight costs of $400 on June 11. Damaged goods totaling $300 are returned to Epps for credit on June 12. The fair value of these goods is $70. On June 19, Tuzun pays Epps Company in full, less the purchase discount. Both companies use a perpetual inventory system.

Prepare purchase and sale entries.

(LO 2, 3)

Instructions

(a) Prepare separate entries for each transaction on the books of Tuzun Company.
(b) Prepare separate entries for each transaction for Epps Company. The merchandise purchased by Tuzun on June 10 had cost Epps $4,800.

E5-5 Presented below are transactions related to Bogner Company.

Journalize sales transactions.

(LO 3)

1. On December 3, Bogner Company sold $570,000 of merchandise to Maris Co., terms 2/10, n/30, FOB shipping point. The cost of the merchandise sold was $350,000.
2. On December 8, Maris Co. was granted an allowance of $20,000 for merchandise purchased on December 3.
3. On December 13, Bogner Company received the balance due from Maris Co.

Instructions

(a) Prepare the journal entries to record these transactions on the books of Bogner Company using a perpetual inventory system.
(b) Assume that Bogner Company received the balance due from Maris Co. on January 2 of the following year instead of December 13. Prepare the journal entry to record the receipt of payment on January 2.

Prepare sales section and closing entries.

(LO 4, 5)

E5-6 The adjusted trial balance of Tsai Company shows the following data pertaining to sales at the end of its fiscal year October 31, 2017: Sales Revenue $820,000, Freight-Out $16,000, Sales Returns and Allowances $25,000, and Sales Discounts $13,000.

Instructions

(a) Prepare the sales section of the income statement.

(b) Prepare separate closing entries for (1) sales revenue, and (2) the contra accounts to sales revenue.

Prepare adjusting and closing entries.

(LO 4)

E5-7 Juan Morales Company had the following account balances at year-end: Cost of Goods Sold $60,000, Inventory $15,000, Operating Expenses $29,000, Sales Revenue $115,000, Sales Discounts $1,200, and Sales Returns and Allowances $1,700. A physical count of inventory determines that merchandise inventory on hand is $13,900.

Instructions

(a) Prepare the adjusting entry necessary as a result of the physical count.

(b) Prepare closing entries.

Prepare adjusting and closing entries.

(LO 4)

E5-8 Presented below is information related to Garland Co. for the month of January 2017.

Ending inventory per		Insurance expense	$ 12,000
perpetual records	$ 21,600	Rent expense	20,000
Ending inventory actually		Salaries and wages expense	55,000
on hand	21,000	Sales discounts	10,000
Cost of goods sold	218,000	Sales returns and allowances	13,000
Freight-out	7,000	Sales revenue	380,000

Instructions

(a) Prepare the necessary adjusting entry for inventory.

(b) Prepare the necessary closing entries.

Prepare multiple-step income statement.

(LO 5)

E5-9 Presented below is information for Furlow Company for the month of March 2017.

Cost of goods sold	$212,000	Rent expense	$ 32,000
Freight-out	7,000	Sales discounts	8,000
Insurance expense	6,000	Sales returns and allowances	13,000
Salaries and wages expense	58,000	Sales revenue	380,000

Instructions

(a) Prepare a multiple-step income statement.

(b) Compute the gross profit rate.

Prepare multiple-step and single-step income statements.

(LO 5)

E5-10 In its income statement for the year ended December 31, 2017, Lemere Company reported the following condensed data.

Operating expenses	$ 725,000	Interest revenue	$ 28,000
Cost of goods sold	1,289,000	Loss on disposal of plant assets	17,000
Interest expense	70,000	Net sales	2,200,000

Instructions

(a) Prepare a multiple-step income statement.

(b) Prepare a single-step income statement.

Prepare correcting entries for sales and purchases.

(LO 2, 3)

E5-11 An inexperienced accountant for Huang Company made the following errors in recording merchandising transactions.

1. A $195 refund to a customer for faulty merchandise was debited to Sales Revenue $195 and credited to Cash $195.
2. A $180 credit purchase of supplies was debited to Inventory $180 and credited to Cash $180.
3. A $215 sales discount was debited to Sales Revenue.
4. A cash payment of $20 for freight on merchandise purchases was debited to Freight-Out $200 and credited to Cash $200.

Instructions

Prepare separate correcting entries for each error, assuming that the incorrect entry is not reversed. (Omit explanations.)

E5-12 In 2017, Matt Cruz Company had net sales of $900,000 and cost of goods sold of $522,000. Operating expenses were $225,000, and interest expense was $11,000. Cruz prepares a multiple-step income statement.

Compute various income measures.

(LO 5)

Instructions
(a) Compute Cruz's gross profit.
(b) Compute the gross profit rate. Why is this rate computed by financial statement users?
(c) What is Cruz's income from operations and net income?
(d) If Cruz prepared a single-step income statement, what amount would it report for net income?
(e) In what section of its classified balance sheet should Cruz report inventory?

E5-13 Presented below is financial information for two different companies.

Compute missing amounts and compute gross profit rate.

(LO 5)

	May Company	Reed Company
Sales revenue	$90,000	$ (d)
Sales returns	(a)	5,000
Net sales	87,000	102,000
Cost of goods sold	56,000	(e)
Gross profit	(b)	41,500
Operating expenses	15,000	(f)
Net income	(c)	15,000

Instructions
(a) Determine the missing amounts.
(b) Determine the gross profit rates. (Round to one decimal place.)

E5-14 Financial information is presented below for three different companies.

Compute missing amounts.

(LO 5)

	Allen Cosmetics	Bast Grocery	Corr Wholesalers
Sales revenue	$90,000	$ (e)	$122,000
Sales returns and allowances	(a)	5,000	12,000
Net sales	86,000	95,000	(i)
Cost of goods sold	56,000	(f)	(j)
Gross profit	(b)	38,000	24,000
Operating expenses	15,000	(g)	18,000
Income from operations	(c)	(h)	(k)
Other expenses and losses	4,000	7,000	(l)
Net income	(d)	11,000	5,000

Instructions
Determine the missing amounts.

*E5-15 Presented below are selected accounts for Salazar Company as reported in the worksheet using a perpetual inventory system at the end of May 2017.

Complete worksheet using a perpetual inventory system.

(LO 6)

Accounts	Adjusted Trial Balance		Income Statement		Balance Sheet	
	Dr.	Cr.	Dr.	Cr.	Dr.	Cr.
Cash	11,000					
Inventory	76,000					
Sales Revenue		480,000				
Sales Returns and Allowances	10,000					
Sales Discounts	9,000					
Cost of Goods Sold	300,000					

Instructions
Complete the worksheet by extending amounts reported in the adjusted trial balance to the appropriate columns in the worksheet. Do not total individual columns.

*E5-16 The trial balance columns of the worksheet using a perpetual inventory system for Marquez Company at June 30, 2017, are as follows.

Prepare a worksheet using a perpetual inventory system.

(LO 6)

MARQUEZ COMPANY
Worksheet
For the Month Ended June 30, 2017

Account Titles	Trial Balance	
	Debit	Credit
Cash	1,920	
Accounts Receivable	2,440	
Inventory	11,640	
Accounts Payable		1,120
Common Stock		3,500
Sales Revenue		42,500
Cost of Goods Sold	20,560	
Operating Expenses	10,560	
	47,120	47,120

Other data:
Operating expenses incurred on account, but not yet recorded, total $1,500.

Instructions
Enter the trial balance on a worksheet and complete the worksheet.

Prepare cost of goods sold section.

(LO 7)

*E5-17 The trial balance of D. Savage Company at the end of its fiscal year, August 31, 2017, includes these accounts: Inventory $17,200, Purchases $149,000, Sales Revenue $190,000, Freight-In $5,000, Sales Returns and Allowances $3,000, Freight-Out $1,000, and Purchase Returns and Allowances $2,000. The ending inventory is $23,000.

Instructions
Prepare a cost of goods sold section for the year ending August 31 (periodic inventory).

Compute various income statement items.

(LO 7)

*E5-18 On January 1, 2017, Christel Madan Corporation had inventory of $50,000. At December 31, 2017, Christel Madan had the following account balances.

Freight-in	$ 4,000
Purchases	509,000
Purchase discounts	6,000
Purchase returns and allowances	2,000
Sales revenue	840,000
Sales discounts	5,000
Sales returns and allowances	10,000

At December 31, 2017, Christel Madan determines that its ending inventory is $60,000.

Instructions
(a) Compute Christel Madan's 2017 gross profit.
(b) Compute Christel Madan's 2017 operating expenses if net income is $130,000 and there are no nonoperating activities.

Prepare cost of goods sold section.

(LO 7)

*E5-19 Below is a series of cost of goods sold sections for companies B, F, L, and R.

	B	F	L	R
Beginning inventory	$ 150	$ 70	$1,000	$ (j)
Purchases	1,620	1,060	(g)	43,590
Purchase returns and allowances	40	(d)	290	(k)
Net purchases	(a)	1,030	6,210	41,090
Freight-in	110	(e)	(h)	2,240
Cost of goods purchased	(b)	1,280	7,940	(l)
Cost of goods available for sale	1,840	1,350	(i)	49,530
Ending inventory	310	(f)	1,450	6,230
Cost of goods sold	(c)	1,230	7,490	43,300

Instruction

Fill in the lettered blanks to complete the cost of goods sold sections.

*E5-20 This information relates to Rana Co.

1. On April 5, purchased merchandise from Craig Company for $25,000, terms 2/10, net/30, FOB shipping point.
2. On April 6, paid freight costs of $900 on merchandise purchased from Craig Company.
3. On April 7, purchased equipment on account for $30,000.
4. On April 8, returned some of April 5 merchandise, which cost $2,800, to Craig Company.
5. On April 15, paid the amount due to Craig Company in full.

Journalize purchase transactions.

(LO 7)

Instructions

(a) Prepare the journal entries to record these transactions on the books of Rana Co. using a periodic inventory system.

(b) Assume that Rana Co. paid the balance due to Craig Company on May 4 instead of April 15. Prepare the journal entry to record this payment.

*E5-21 Presented below is information related to Lor Co.

1. On April 5, purchased merchandise from Garcia Company for $19,000, terms 2/10, net/30, FOB shipping point.
2. On April 6, paid freight costs of $800 on merchandise purchased from Garcia.
3. On April 7, purchased equipment on account from Holifield Mfg. Co. for $23,000.
4. On April 8, returned merchandise, which cost $4,000, to Garcia Company.
5. On April 15, paid the amount due to Garcia Company in full.

Journalize purchase transactions.

(LO 7)

Instructions

(a) Prepare the journal entries to record the preceding transactions on the books of Lor Co. using a periodic inventory system.

(b) Assume that Lor Co. paid the balance due to Garcia Company on May 4 instead of April 15. Prepare the journal entry to record this payment.

*E5-22 Presented below are selected accounts for B. Midler Company as reported in the worksheet at the end of May 2017. Ending inventory is $75,000.

Complete worksheet.

(LO 7)

Accounts	Adjusted Trial Balance		Income Statement		Balance Sheet	
	Dr.	Cr.	Dr.	Cr.	Dr.	Cr.
Cash	9,000					
Inventory	80,000					
Purchases	240,000					
Purchase Returns and Allowances		30,000				
Sales Revenue		450,000				
Sales Returns and Allowances	10,000					
Sales Discounts	5,000					
Rent Expense	42,000					

Instructions

Complete the worksheet by extending amounts reported in the adjusted trial balance to the appropriate columns in the worksheet. The company uses the periodic inventory system.

EXERCISES: SET B AND CHALLENGE EXERCISES

Visit the book's companion website, at **www.wiley.com/college/weygandt**, and choose the Student Companion site to access Exercises: Set B and Challenge Exercises.

PROBLEMS: SET A

Journalize purchase and sales transactions under a perpetual inventory system.

(LO 2, 3)

P5-1A Powell's Book Warehouse distributes hardcover books to retail stores and extends credit terms of 2/10, n/30 to all of its customers. At the end of May, Powell's inventory consisted of books purchased for $1,800. During June, the following merchandising transactions occurred.

June 1 Purchased books on account for $1,600 from Kline Publishers, FOB destination, terms 2/10, n/30. The appropriate party also made a cash payment of $50 for the freight on this date.

3 Sold books on account to Reading Rainbow for $2,500. The cost of the books sold was $1,440.

6 Received $100 credit for books returned to Kline Publishers.

9 Paid Kline Publishers in full, less discount.

15 Received payment in full from Reading Rainbow.

17 Sold books on account to Blanco Books for $1,800. The cost of the books sold was $1,080.

20 Purchased books on account for $1,500 from Dietz Publishers, FOB destination, terms 2/15, n/30. The appropriate party also made a cash payment of $50 for the freight on this date.

24 Received payment in full from Blanco Books.

26 Paid Dietz Publishers in full, less discount.

28 Sold books on account to Reddy Bookstore for $1,400. The cost of the books sold was $850.

30 Granted Reddy Bookstore $120 credit for books returned costing $72.

Powell's Book Warehouse's chart of accounts includes the following: No. 101 Cash, No. 112 Accounts Receivable, No. 120 Inventory, No. 201 Accounts Payable, No. 401 Sales Revenue, No. 412 Sales Returns and Allowances, No. 414 Sales Discounts, and No. 505 Cost of Goods Sold.

Instructions

Journalize the transactions for the month of June for Powell's Book Warehouse using a perpetual inventory system.

Journalize, post, and prepare a partial income statement.

(LO 2, 3, 5)

P5-2A Latona Hardware Store completed the following merchandising transactions in the month of May. At the beginning of May, the ledger of Latona showed Cash of $5,000 and Common Stock of $5,000.

May 1 Purchased merchandise on account from Gray's Wholesale Supply $4,200, terms 2/10, n/30.

2 Sold merchandise on account $2,100, terms 1/10, n/30. The cost of the merchandise sold was $1,300.

5 Received credit from Gray's Wholesale Supply for merchandise returned $300.

9 Received collections in full, less discounts, from customers billed on sales of $2,100 on May 2.

10 Paid Gray's Wholesale Supply in full, less discount.

11 Purchased supplies for cash $400.

12 Purchased merchandise for cash $1,400.

15 Received refund for poor quality merchandise from supplier on cash purchase $150.

17 Purchased merchandise from Amland Distributors $1,300, FOB shipping point, terms 2/10, n/30.

19 Paid freight on May 17 purchase $130.

24 Sold merchandise for cash $3,200. The merchandise sold had a cost of $2,000.

25 Purchased merchandise from Horvath, Inc. $620, FOB destination, terms 2/10, n/30.

27 Paid Amland Distributors in full, less discount.

29 Made refunds to cash customers for defective merchandise $70. The returned merchandise had a fair value of $30.

31 Sold merchandise on account $1,000 terms n/30. The cost of the merchandise sold was $560.

Latona Hardware's chart of accounts includes the following: No. 101 Cash, No. 112 Accounts Receivable, No. 120 Inventory, No. 126 Supplies, No. 201 Accounts Payable, No. 311 Common Stock, No. 401 Sales Revenue, No. 412 Sales Returns and Allowances, No. 414 Sales Discounts, and No. 505 Cost of Goods Sold.

Instructions
(a) Journalize the transactions using a perpetual inventory system.
(b) Enter the beginning cash and common stock balances and post the transactions. (Use J1 for the journal reference.)
(c) Prepare an income statement through gross profit for the month of May 2017.

(c) Gross profit $2,379

P5-3A The Deluxe Store is located in midtown Madison. During the past several years, net income has been declining because of suburban shopping centers. At the end of the company's fiscal year on November 30, 2017, the following accounts appeared in two of its trial balances.

Prepare financial statements and adjusting and closing entries.

(LO 4, 5)

	Unadjusted	Adjusted		Unadjusted	Adjusted
Accounts Payable	$ 25,200	$ 25,200	Inventory	$ 29,000	$ 29,000
Accounts Receivable	30,500	30,500	Notes Payable	37,000	37,000
Accumulated Depr.—Equip.	34,000	45,000	Prepaid Insurance	10,500	3,500
Cash	26,000	26,000	Property Tax Expense		2,500
Common Stock	40,000	40,000	Property Taxes Payable		2,500
Cost of Goods Sold	507,000	507,000	Rent Expense	15,000	15,000
Dividends	10,000	10,000	Retained Earnings	61,700	61,700
Freight-Out	6,500	6,500	Salaries and Wages Expense	96,000	96,000
Equipment	146,000	146,000	Sales Commissions Expense	6,500	11,000
Depreciation Expense		11,000	Sales Commissions Payable		4,500
Insurance Expense		7,000	Sales Returns and Allowances	8,000	8,000
Interest Expense	6,400	6,400	Sales Revenue	700,000	700,000
Interest Revenue	8,000	8,000	Utilities Expense	8,500	8,500

Instructions
(a) Prepare a multiple-step income statement, a retained earnings statement, and a classified balance sheet. Notes payable are due in 2020.
(b) Journalize the adjusting entries that were made.
(c) Journalize the closing entries that are necessary.

(a) Net income $29,100
Retained earnings $80,800
Total assets $190,000

P5-4A Adam Nichols, a former disc golf star, operates Adam's Discorama. At the beginning of the current season on April 1, the ledger of Adam's Discorama showed Cash $1,800, Inventory $2,500, and Common Stock $4,300. The following transactions were completed during April.

Journalize, post, and prepare a trial balance.

(LO 2, 3, 4)

Apr.	5	Purchased golf discs, bags, and other inventory on account from Rayford Co. $1,200, FOB shipping point, terms 2/10, n/60.
	7	Paid freight on the Rayford purchase $50.
	9	Received credit from Rayford Co. for merchandise returned $100.
	10	Sold merchandise on account for $900, terms n/30. The merchandise sold had a cost of $540.
	12	Purchased disc golf shirts and other accessories on account from Galaxy Sportswear $670, terms 1/10, n/30.
	14	Paid Rayford Co. in full, less discount.
	17	Received credit from Galaxy Sportswear for merchandise returned $70.
	20	Made sales on account for $610, terms n/30. The cost of the merchandise sold was $370.
	21	Paid Galaxy Sportswear in full, less discount.
	27	Granted an allowance to customers for clothing that was flawed $20.
	30	Received payments on account from customers $900.

The chart of accounts for the store includes the following: No. 101 Cash, No. 112 Accounts Receivable, No. 120 Inventory, No. 201 Accounts Payable, No. 311 Common Stock, No. 401 Sales Revenue, No. 412 Sales Returns and Allowances, and No. 505 Cost of Goods Sold.

Instructions

(a) Journalize the April transactions using a perpetual inventory system.

(b) Enter the beginning balances in the ledger accounts and post the April transactions. (Use J1 for the journal reference.)

(c) Prepare a trial balance on April 30, 2017.

(c) Total debits $5,810

Complete accounting cycle beginning with a worksheet.

(LO 4, 5, 6)

*P5-5A The trial balance of Valdez Fashion Center contained the following accounts at November 30, the end of the company's fiscal year.

VALDEZ FASHION CENTER
Trial Balance
November 30, 2017

	Debit	Credit
Cash	$ 8,700	
Accounts Receivable	30,700	
Inventory	44,700	
Supplies	6,200	
Equipment	133,000	
Accumulated Depreciation—Equipment		$ 28,000
Notes Payable		51,000
Accounts Payable		48,500
Common Stock		50,000
Retained Earnings		40,000
Dividends	12,000	
Sales Revenue		755,200
Sales Returns and Allowances	8,800	
Cost of Goods Sold	497,400	
Salaries and Wages Expense	140,000	
Advertising Expense	24,400	
Utilities Expense	14,000	
Maintenance and Repairs Expense	12,100	
Freight-Out	16,700	
Rent Expense	24,000	
Totals	$972,700	$972,700

Adjustment data:

1. Supplies on hand totaled $2,000.
2. Depreciation is $11,500 on the equipment.
3. Interest of $4,000 is accrued on notes payable at November 30.
4. Inventory actually on hand is $44,400.

Instructions

(a) Adj. trial balance $988,200
Net loss $2,200

(b) Gross profit $248,700
Total assets $179,300

(a) Enter the trial balance on a worksheet, and complete the worksheet.

(b) Prepare a multiple-step income statement and a retained earnings statement for the year, and a classified balance sheet as of November 30, 2017. Notes payable of $20,000 are due in January 2018.

(c) Journalize the adjusting entries.

(d) Journalize the closing entries.

(e) Prepare a post-closing trial balance.

Determine cost of goods sold and gross profit under periodic approach.

(LO 5, 7)

*P5-6A At the end of Dayton Department Store's fiscal year on November 30, 2017, these accounts appeared in its adjusted trial balance.

Freight-In	$ 7,500
Inventory	40,000
Purchases	585,000
Purchase Discounts	6,300
Purchase Returns and Allowances	2,700
Sales Revenue	1,000,000
Sales Returns and Allowances	20,000

Additional facts:

1. Merchandise inventory on November 30, 2017, is $52,600.
2. Dayton Department Store uses a periodic system.

Instructions

Prepare an income statement through gross profit for the year ended November 30, 2017.

*P5-7A Alana Inc. operates a retail operation that purchases and sells home entertainment products. The company purchases all merchandise inventory on credit and uses a periodic inventory system. The Accounts Payable account is used for recording inventory purchases only; all other current liabilities are accrued in separate accounts. You are provided with the following selected information for the fiscal years 2014 through 2017, inclusive.

Calculate missing amounts and assess profitability.

(LO 5, 7)

	2014	2015	2016	2017
Income Statement Data				
Sales revenue		$55,000	$ (e)	$47,000
Cost of goods sold		(a)	13,800	14,300
Gross profit		38,300	35,200	(i)
Operating expenses		34,900	(f)	28,600
Net income		$ (b)	$ 2,500	$ (j)
Balance Sheet Data				
Inventory	$7,200	$ (c)	$ 8,100	$ (k)
Accounts payable	3,200	3,600	2,500	(l)
Additional Information				
Purchases of merchandise inventory on account		$14,200	$ (g)	$13,200
Cash payments to suppliers		(d)	(h)	13,600

Instructions

(a) Calculate the missing amounts.

(b) Sales declined over the 3-year fiscal period, 2015–2017. Does that mean that profitability necessarily also declined? Explain, computing the gross profit rate and the profit margin (Net income ÷ Sales revenue) for each fiscal year to help support your answer. (Round to one decimal place.)

*P5-8A At the beginning of the current season on April 1, the ledger of Kokott Pro Shop showed Cash $3,000, Inventory $4,000, and Common Stock $7,000. These transactions occurred during April 2017.

Journalize, post, and prepare trial balance and partial income statement using periodic approach.

(LO 7)

Apr.	5	Purchased golf bags, clubs, and balls on account from Hogan Co. $1,200, FOB shipping point, terms 2/10, n/60.
	7	Paid freight on Hogan Co. purchases $50.
	9	Received credit from Hogan Co. for merchandise returned $100.
	10	Sold merchandise on account to customers $600, terms n/30.
	12	Purchased golf shoes, sweaters, and other accessories on account from Duffer Sportswear $450, terms 1/10, n/30.
	14	Paid Hogan Co. in full.
	17	Received credit from Duffer Sportswear for merchandise returned $50.
	20	Made sales on account to customers $600, terms n/30.
	21	Paid Duffer Sportswear in full.
	27	Granted credit to customers for clothing that had flaws $35.
	30	Received payments on account from customers $600.

The chart of accounts for the pro shop includes Cash, Accounts Receivable, Inventory, Accounts Payable, Common Stock, Sales Revenue, Sales Returns and Allowances, Purchases, Purchase Returns and Allowances, Purchase Discounts, and Freight-In.

Instructions

(a) Journalize the April transactions using a periodic inventory system.

(b) Using T-accounts, enter the beginning balances in the ledger accounts and post the April transactions.

(c) Prepare a trial balance on April 30, 2017.

(d) Prepare an income statement through gross profit, assuming merchandise inventory on hand at April 30 is $4,824.

PROBLEMS: SET B AND SET C

Visit the book's companion website, at **www.wiley.com/college/weygandt**, and choose the Student Companion site to access Problems: Set B and Set C.

COMPREHENSIVE PROBLEM

CP5 On December 1, 2017, Prosen Distributing Company had the following account balances.

	Debit		Credit
Cash	$ 7,200	Accumulated Depreciation—	
Accounts Receivable	4,600	Equipment	$ 2,200
Inventory	12,000	Accounts Payable	4,500
Supplies	1,200	Salaries and Wages Payable	1,000
Equipment	22,000	Common Stock	30,000
	$47,000	Retained Earnings	9,300
			$47,000

During December, the company completed the following summary transactions.

Dec.　6　Paid $1,600 for salaries and wages due employees, of which $600 is for December and $1,000 is for November salaries and wages payable.
　　　8　Received $1,900 cash from customers in payment of account (no discount allowed).
　　10　Sold merchandise for cash $6,300. The cost of the merchandise sold was $4,100.
　　13　Purchased merchandise on account from Maglio Co. $9,000, terms 2/10, n/30.
　　15　Purchased supplies for cash $2,000.
　　18　Sold merchandise on account $12,000, terms 3/10, n/30. The cost of the merchandise sold was $8,000.
　　20　Paid salaries and wages $1,800.
　　23　Paid Maglio Co. in full, less discount.
　　27　Received collections in full, less discounts, from customers billed on December 18.

Adjustment data:

1. Accrued salaries and wages payable $800.
2. Depreciation $200 per month.
3. Supplies on hand $1,500.

Instructions
(a) Journalize the December transactions using a perpetual inventory system.
(b) Enter the December 1 balances in the ledger T-accounts and post the December transactions. Use Cost of Goods Sold, Depreciation Expense, Salaries and Wages Expense, Sales Revenue, Sales Discounts, and Supplies Expense.
(c) Journalize and post adjusting entries.

(d) Totals $65,300
(d) Prepare an adjusted trial balance.

(e) Net income $740
(e) Prepare an income statement and a retained earnings statement for December and a classified balance sheet at December 31.

CONTINUING PROBLEM

COOKIE CREATIONS

(*Note:* This is a continuation of the Cookie Creations problem from Chapters 1 through 4.)

CC5 Because Natalie has had such a successful first few months, she is considering other opportunities to develop her business. One opportunity is the sale of fine European mixers. The owner of Kzinski Supply Company has approached Natalie to become the exclusive U.S. distributor of these fine mixers. The current cost of a mixer is approximately $525 (U.S.), and Natalie would sell each one for $1,050. Natalie comes to you for advice on how to account for these mixers.

Go to the book's companion website, **www.wiley.com/college/weygandt**, *to see the completion of this problem.*

BROADENING YOUR *PERSPECTIVE*

FINANCIAL REPORTING AND ANALYSIS

Financial Reporting Problem: Apple Inc.

BYP5-1 The financial statements of Apple Inc. are presented in Appendix A at the end of this textbook. Instructions for accessing and using the company's complete annual report, including the notes to the financial statements, are also provided in Appendix A.

Instructions

Answer the following questions using Apple's Consolidated Statement of Income.

(a) What was the percentage change in (1) sales and in (2) net income from 2011 to 2012 and from 2012 to 2013?
(b) What was the company's gross profit rate in 2011, 2012, and 2013?
(c) What was the company's percentage of net income to net sales in 2011, 2012, and 2013? Comment on any trend in this percentage.

Comparative Analysis Problem:
PepsiCo, Inc. vs. The Coca-Cola Company

BYP5-2 PepsiCo's financial statements are presented in Appendix B. Financial statements of The Coca-Cola Company are presented in Appendix C. Instructions for accessing and using the complete annual reports of PepsiCo and Coca-Cola, including the notes to the financial statements, are also provided in Appendices B and C, respectively.

Instructions

(a) Based on the information contained in these financial statements, determine each of the following for each company.
    (1) Gross profit for 2013.
    (2) Gross profit rate for 2013.
    (3) Operating income for 2013.
    (4) Percentage change in operating income from 2012 to 2013.
(b) What conclusions concerning the relative profitability of the two companies can you draw from these data?

Comparative Analysis Problem:
Amazon.com, Inc. vs. Wal-Mart Stores, Inc.

BYP5-3 Amazon.com, Inc.'s financial statements are presented in Appendix D. Financial statements of Wal-Mart Stores, Inc. are presented in Appendix E. (Use Wal-Mart's January 31, 2014, financial statements for comparative purposes.) Instructions for accessing and using the complete annual reports of Amazon and Wal-Mart, including the notes to the financial statements, are also provided in Appendices D and E, respectively.

Instructions

(a) Based on the information contained in these financial statements, determine each of the following for each company. Use Amazon's net product sales to compute gross profit information.
    (1) Gross profit for 2013.
    (2) Gross profit rate for 2013.
    (3) Operating income for 2013.
    (4) Percentage change in operating income from 2012 to 2013.
(b) What conclusions concerning the relative profitability of the two companies can you draw from these data?

Real-World Focus

BYP5-4 No financial decision-maker should ever rely solely on the financial information reported in the annual report to make decisions. It is important to keep abreast of financial news. This activity demonstrates how to search for financial news on the Internet.

Address: **biz.yahoo.com/i**, or go to **www.wiley.com/college/weygandt**

Steps:
1. Type in either PepsiCo or Coca-Cola.
2. Choose **News**.
3. Select an article that sounds interesting to you.

Instructions
(a) What was the source of the article (e.g., Reuters, Businesswire, PR Newswire)?
(b) Assume that you are a personal financial planner and that one of your clients owns stock in the company. Write a brief memo to your client, summarizing the article and explaining the implications of the article for his or her investment.

CRITICAL THINKING

Decision-Making Across the Organization

BYP5-5 Three years ago, Dana Mann and her brother-in-law Eric Boldt opened Family Department Store. For the first two years, business was good, but the following condensed income results for 2016 were disappointing.

FAMILY DEPARTMENT STORE
Income Statement
For The Year Ended December 31, 2016

Net sales		$700,000
Cost of goods sold		553,000
Gross profit		147,000
Operating expenses		
Selling expenses	$100,000	
Administrative expenses	20,000	120,000
Net income		$ 27,000

Dana believes the problem lies in the relatively low gross profit rate (gross profit divided by net sales) of 21%. Eric believes the problem is that operating expenses are too high.

Dana thinks the gross profit rate can be improved by making both of the following changes. She does not anticipate that these changes will have any effect on operating expenses.

1. Increase average selling prices by 17%. This increase is expected to lower sales volume so that total sales will increase only 6%.
2. Buy merchandise in larger quantities and take all purchase discounts. These changes are expected to increase the gross profit rate by 3 percentage points.

Eric thinks expenses can be cut by making both of the following changes. He feels that these changes will not have any effect on net sales.

1. Cut sales salaries of $60,000 in half and give sales personnel a commission of 2% of net sales.
2. Reduce store deliveries to one day per week rather than twice a week. This change will reduce delivery expenses of $30,000 by 40%.

Dana and Eric come to you for help in deciding the best way to improve net income.

Instructions
With the class divided into groups, answer the following.

(a) Prepare a condensed income statement for 2017, assuming (1) Dana's changes are implemented and (2) Eric's ideas are adopted.
(b) What is your recommendation to Dana and Eric?
(c) Prepare a condensed income statement for 2017, assuming both sets of proposed changes are made.

Communication Activity

BYP5-6 The following situation is in chronological order.

1. Connor decides to buy a surfboard.
2. He calls Surfing USA Co. to inquire about its surfboards.

3. Two days later, he requests Surfing USA Co. to make a surfboard.
4. Three days later, Surfing USA Co. sends him a purchase order to fill out.
5. He sends back the purchase order.
6. Surfing USA Co. receives the completed purchase order.
7. Surfing USA Co. completes the surfboard.
8. Connor picks up the surfboard.
9. Surfing USA Co. bills Connor.
10. Surfing USA Co. receives payment from Connor.

Instructions

In a memo to the president of Surfing USA Co., answer the following.

(a) When should Surfing USA Co. record the sale?
(b) Suppose that with his purchase order, Connor is required to make a down payment. Would that change your answer?

Ethics Case

BYP5-7 Jacquie Boynton was just hired as the assistant treasurer of Key West Stores. The company is a specialty chain store with nine retail stores concentrated in one metropolitan area. Among other things, the payment of all invoices is centralized in one of the departments Jacquie will manage. Her primary responsibility is to maintain the company's high credit rating by paying all bills when due and to take advantage of all cash discounts.

Phelan Carter, the former assistant treasurer who has been promoted to treasurer, is training Jacquie in her new duties. He instructs Jacquie that she is to continue the practice of preparing all checks "net of discount" and dating the checks the last day of the discount period. "But," Phelan continues, "we always hold the checks at least 4 days beyond the discount period before mailing them. That way, we get another 4 days of interest on our money. Most of our creditors need our business and don't complain. And, if they scream about our missing the discount period, we blame it on the mail room or the post office. We've only lost one discount out of every hundred we take that way. I think everybody does it. By the way, welcome to our team!"

Instructions

(a) What are the ethical considerations in this case?
(b) Who are the stakeholders that are harmed or benefitted in this situation?
(c) Should Jacquie continue the practice started by Phelan? Does she have any choice?

All About You

BYP5-8 There are many situations in business where it is difficult to determine the proper period in which to record revenue. Suppose that after graduation with a degree in finance, you take a job as a manager at a consumer electronics store called Impact Electronics. The company has expanded rapidly in order to compete with **Best Buy**. Impact has also begun selling gift cards for its electronic products. The cards are available in any dollar amount and allow the holder of the card to purchase an item for up to 2 years from the time the card is purchased. If the card is not used during that 2 years, it expires.

Instructions

Answer the following questions.

At what point should the revenue from the gift cards be recognized? Should the revenue be recognized at the time the card is sold, or should it be recorded when the card is redeemed? Explain the reasoning to support your answers.

FASB Codification Activity

BYP5-9 If your school has a subscription to the FASB Codification, go to **http://aaahq.org/ascLogin.cfm** to log in and prepare responses to the following.

Instructions

(a) Access the glossary ("Master Glossary") to answer the following:
   (1) What is the definition provided for inventory?
   (2) What is a customer?
(b) What guidance does the Codification provide concerning reporting inventories above cost?

A Look at IFRS

LEARNING OBJECTIVE **8**   **Compare the accounting for merchandising under GAAP and IFRS.**

The basic accounting entries for merchandising are the same under both GAAP and IFRS. The income statement is a required statement under both sets of standards. The basic format is similar although some differences do exist.

Key Points

Following are the key similarities and differences between GAAP and IFRS related to inventories.

Similarities

- Under both GAAP and IFRS, a company can choose to use either a perpetual or a periodic inventory system.
- The definition of inventories is basically the same under GAAP and IFRS.
- As indicated above, the basic accounting entries for merchandising are the same under both GAAP and IFRS.
- Both GAAP and IFRS require that income statement information be presented for multiple years. For example, IFRS requires that 2 years of income statement information be presented, whereas GAAP requires 3 years.

Differences

- Under GAAP, Companies generally classify income statement items by function. Classification by function leads to descriptions like administration, distribution, and manufacturing. Under IFRS, companies must classify expenses either by nature or by function. Classification by nature leads to descriptions such as the following: salaries, depreciation expense, and utilities expense. If a company uses the functional-expense method on the income statement, disclosure by nature is required in the notes to the financial statements.
- Presentation of the income statement under GAAP follows either a single-step or multiple-step format. IFRS does not mention a single-step or multiple-step approach.
- Under IFRS, revaluation of land, buildings, and intangible assets is permitted. The initial gains and losses resulting from this revaluation are reported as adjustments to equity, often referred to as **other comprehensive income**. The effect of this difference is that the use of IFRS result in more transactions affecting equity (other comprehensive income) but not net income.

Looking to the Future

The IASB and FASB are working on a project that would rework the structure of financial statements. Specifically, this project will address the issue of how to classify various items in the income statement. A main goal of this new approach is to provide information that better represents how businesses are run. In addition, this approach draws attention away from just one number—net income. It will adopt major groupings similar to those currently used by the statement of cash flows (operating, investing, and financing), so that numbers can be more readily traced across statements. For example, the amount of income that is generated by operations would be traceable to the assets and liabilities used to generate the income. Finally, this approach would also provide detail, beyond that currently seen in most statements (either GAAP or IFRS), by requiring that line items be presented both by function and by nature. The new financial statement format was heavily influenced by suggestions from financial statement analysts.

IFRS Practice

IFRS Self-Test Questions

1. Which of the following would **not** be included in the definition of inventory under IFRS?
   (a) Photocopy paper held for sale by an office-supply store.
   (b) Stereo equipment held for sale by an electronics store.
   (c) Used office equipment held for sale by the human relations department of a plastics company.
   (d) All of the above would meet the definition.

2. Which of the following would **not** be a line item of a company reporting costs by nature?
   (a) Depreciation expense.   (c) Interest expense.
   (b) Salaries expense.   (d) Manufacturing expense.

3. Which of the following would **not** be a line item of a company reporting costs by function?
   (a) Administration.   (c) Utilities expense.
   (b) Manufacturing.   (d) Distribution.

4. Which of the following statements is **false**?
   (a) IFRS specifically requires use of a multiple-step income statement.
   (b) Under IFRS, companies can use either a perpetual or periodic system.
   (c) The proposed new format for financial statements was heavily influenced by the suggestions of financial statement analysts.
   (d) The new income statement format will try to de-emphasize the focus on the "net income" line item.

IFRS Exercises

IFRS5-1 Explain the difference between the "nature-of-expense" and "function-of-expense" classifications.

IFRS5-2 For each of the following income statement line items, state whether the item is a "by nature" expense item or a "by function" expense item.

_____ Cost of goods sold	_____ Utilities expense
_____ Depreciation expense	_____ Delivery expense
_____ Salaries and wages expense	_____ General and administrative expenses
_____ Selling expenses	

IFRS5-3 Matilda Company reported the following amounts (in euros) in 2017: Net income, €150,000; Unrealized gain related to revaluation of buildings, €10,000; and Unrealized loss on non-trading securities, €(35,000). Determine Matilda's total comprehensive income for 2017.

International Financial Reporting Problem: Louis Vuitton

IFRS5-4 The financial statements of Louis Vuitton are presented in Appendix F. Instructions for accessing and using the company's complete annual report, including the notes to its financial statements, are also provided in Appendix F.

Instructions
Use Louis Vuitton's annual report to answer the following questions.

(a) Does Louis Vuitton use a multiple-step or a single-step income statement format? Explain how you made your determination.
(b) Instead of "interest expense," what label does Louis Vuitton use for interest costs that it incurs?
(c) Using the notes to the company's financial statements, determine the following:
   (1) Composition of the inventory.
   (2) Amount of inventory (gross) before impairment.

Answers to IFRS Self-Test Questions
1. c   **2.** d   **3.** c   **4.** a

6 Inventories

CHAPTER PREVIEW In the previous chapter, we discussed the accounting for merchandise inventory using a perpetual inventory system. In this chapter, we explain the methods used to calculate the cost of inventory on hand at the balance sheet date and the cost of goods sold.

FEATURE STORY

"Where Is That Spare Bulldozer Blade?"

Let's talk inventory—big, bulldozer-size inventory. Caterpillar Inc. is the world's largest manufacturer of construction and mining equipment, diesel and natural gas engines, and industrial gas turbines. It sells its products in over 200 countries, making it one of the most successful U.S. exporters. More than 70% of its productive assets are located domestically, and nearly 50% of its sales are foreign.

In the past, Caterpillar's profitability suffered, but today it is very successful. A big part of this turnaround can be attributed to effective management of its inventory. Imagine what it costs Caterpillar to have too many bulldozers sitting around in inventory—a situation the company definitely wants to avoid. Yet Caterpillar must also make sure it has enough inventory to meet demand.

At one time during a 7-year period, Caterpillar's sales increased by 100% while its inventory increased by only 50%. To achieve this dramatic reduction in the amount of resources tied up in inventory while continuing to meet customers' needs, Caterpillar used a two-pronged approach. First, it completed a factory modernization program, which greatly increased its production efficiency. The program reduced by 60% the amount of inventory the company processes at any one time. It also reduced by an incredible 75% the time it takes to manufacture a part.

Second, Caterpillar dramatically improved its parts distribution system. It ships more than 100,000 items daily from its 23 distribution centers strategically located around the world (10 million square feet of warehouse space—remember, we're talking bulldozers). The company can virtually guarantee that it can get any part to anywhere in the world within 24 hours.

These changes led to record exports, profits, and revenues for Caterpillar. It would seem that things couldn't be better. But industry analysts, as well as the company's managers, thought otherwise. In order to maintain Caterpillar's position as the industry leader, management began another major overhaul of inventory production and inventory management processes. The goal: to cut the number of repairs in half, increase productivity by 20%, and increase inventory turnover by 40%.

In short, Caterpillar's ability to manage its inventory has been a key reason for its past success and will very likely play a huge part in its future profitability as well.

James Porter/Workbook/Getty Images, Inc.

CHAPTER OUTLINE

Learning Objectives

1 Discuss how to classify and determine inventory.
- Classifying inventory
- Determine inventory quantities

DO IT! 1 Rules of Ownership

2 Apply inventory cost flow methods and discuss their financial effects.
- Specific identification
- Cost flow assumptions
- Financial statement and tax effects
- Using cost flow methods consistently

DO IT! 2 Cost Flow Methods

3 Indicate the effects of inventory errors on the financial statements.
- Income statement effects
- Balance sheet effects

DO IT! 3 Inventory Errors

4 Explain the statement presentation and analysis of inventory.
- Presentation
- Lower-of-cost-or-market
- Analysis

DO IT! 4 LCM and Inventory Turnover

Go to the **REVIEW AND PRACTICE** section at the end of the chapter for a review of key concepts and practice applications with solutions.

Visit **WileyPLUS with ORION** for additional tutorials and practice opportunities.

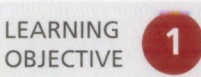

Discuss how to classify and determine inventory.

Two important steps in the reporting of inventory at the end of the accounting period are the classification of inventory based on its degree of completeness and the determination of inventory amounts.

Classifying Inventory

How a company classifies its inventory depends on whether the firm is a merchandiser or a manufacturer. In a **merchandising** company, such as those described in Chapter 5, inventory consists of many different items. For example, in a grocery store, canned goods, dairy products, meats, and produce are just a few of the inventory items on hand. These items have two common characteristics: (1) they are owned by the company, and (2) they are in a form ready for sale to customers in the ordinary course of business. Thus, merchandisers need only one inventory classification, **merchandise inventory**, to describe the many different items that make up the total inventory.

In a **manufacturing** company, some inventory may not yet be ready for sale. As a result, manufacturers usually classify inventory into three categories: finished goods, work in process, and raw materials. **Finished goods inventory** is manufactured items that are completed and ready for sale. **Work in process** is that portion of manufactured inventory that has been placed into the production process but is not yet complete. **Raw materials** are the basic goods that will be used in production but have not yet been placed into production.

For example, Caterpillar classifies earth-moving tractors completed and ready for sale as **finished goods**. It classifies the tractors on the assembly line in various stages of production as **work in process**. The steel, glass, tires, and other components that are on hand waiting to be used in the production of tractors are identified as **raw materials**. Illustration 6-1 shows an adapted excerpt from Note 7 of Caterpillar's annual report.

Helpful Hint
Regardless of the classification, companies report all inventories under Current Assets on the balance sheet.

Illustration 6-1
Composition of Caterpillar's inventory

(millions of dollars)	December 31		
	2013	**2012**	**2011**
Raw materials	$ 2,966	$ 3,573	$ 3,766
Work-in-process	2,589	2,920	2,959
Finished goods	6,785	8,767	7,562
Other	285	287	257
Total inventories	**$12,625**	**$15,547**	**$14,544**

By observing the levels and changes in the levels of these three inventory types, financial statement users can gain insight into management's production plans. For example, low levels of raw materials and high levels of finished goods suggest that management believes it has enough inventory on hand and production will be slowing down—perhaps in anticipation of a recession. Conversely, high levels of raw materials and low levels of finished goods probably signal that management is planning to step up production.

Many companies have significantly lowered inventory levels and costs using **just-in-time (JIT) inventory** methods. Under a just-in-time method, companies manufacture or purchase goods only when needed for use. **Dell** is famous for having developed a system for making computers in response to individual customer requests. Even though it makes each computer to meet each customer's particular specifications, Dell is able to assemble the computer and put it on a truck in less than 48 hours. The success of the JIT system depends on reliable suppliers. By integrating its information systems with those of its suppliers, Dell reduced its inventories to nearly zero. This is a huge advantage in an industry where products become obsolete nearly overnight.

The accounting concepts discussed in this chapter apply to the inventory classifications of both merchandising and manufacturing companies. Our focus here is on merchandise inventory.

Determining Inventory Quantities

No matter whether they are using a periodic or perpetual inventory system, all companies need to determine inventory quantities at the end of the accounting period. If using a perpetual system, companies take a physical inventory for the following reasons:

1. To check the accuracy of their perpetual inventory records.
2. To determine the amount of inventory lost due to wasted raw materials, shoplifting, or employee theft.

Companies using a periodic inventory system take a physical inventory for **two different purposes**: to determine the inventory on hand at the balance sheet date, and to determine the cost of goods sold for the period.

Determining inventory quantities involves two steps: (1) taking a physical inventory of goods on hand and (2) determining the ownership of goods.

TAKING A PHYSICAL INVENTORY

Companies take a physical inventory at the end of the accounting period. Taking a physical inventory involves actually counting, weighing, or measuring each kind of inventory on hand. In many companies, taking an inventory is a formidable task. Retailers such as Target, True Value Hardware, or Home Depot have thousands of different inventory items. An inventory count is generally more accurate when goods are not being sold or received during the counting. Consequently, companies often "take inventory" when the business is closed or when business is slow. Many retailers close early on a chosen day in January—after the holiday sales and returns, when inventories are at their lowest level—to count inventory. Wal-Mart Stores, Inc., for example, has a year-end of January 31.

ETHICS NOTE

In a famous fraud, a salad oil company filled its storage tanks mostly with water. The oil rose to the top, so auditors thought the tanks were full of oil. The company also said it had more tanks than it really did: It repainted numbers on the tanks to confuse auditors.

Ethics Insight   Leslie Fay

Falsifying Inventory to Boost Income

Managers at women's apparel maker Leslie Fay were convicted of falsifying inventory records to boost net income—and consequently to boost management bonuses. In another case, executives at Craig Consumer Electronics were accused of defrauding lenders by manipulating inventory records. The indictment said the company classified "defective goods as new or refurbished" and claimed that it owned certain shipments "from overseas suppliers" when, in fact, Craig either did not own the shipments or the shipments did not exist.

What effect does an overstatement of inventory have on a company's financial statements? (Go to WileyPLUS for this answer and additional questions.)

DETERMINING OWNERSHIP OF GOODS

One challenge in computing inventory quantities is determining what inventory a company owns. To determine ownership of goods, two questions must be answered: Do all of the goods included in the count belong to the company? Does the company own any goods that were not included in the count?

GOODS IN TRANSIT A complication in determining ownership is **goods in transit** (on board a truck, train, ship, or plane) at the end of the period. The company may have purchased goods that have not yet been received, or it may have sold goods that have not yet been delivered. To arrive at an accurate count, the company must determine ownership of these goods.

Goods in transit should be included in the inventory of the company that has legal title to the goods. Legal title is determined by the terms of the sale, as shown in Illustration 6-2 and described below.

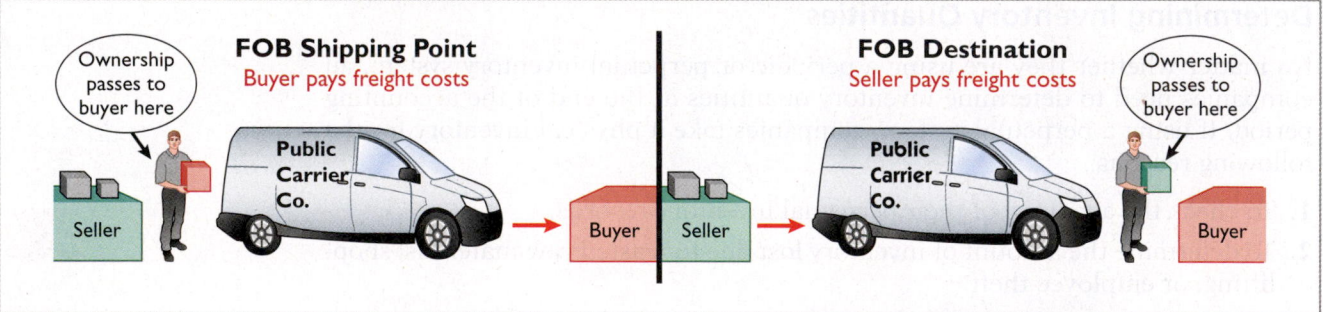

Illustration 6-2
Terms of sale

1. When the terms are **FOB (free on board) shipping point**, ownership of the goods passes to the buyer when the public carrier accepts the goods from the seller.

2. When the terms are **FOB destination**, ownership of the goods remains with the seller until the goods reach the buyer.

If goods in transit at the statement date are ignored, inventory quantities may be seriously miscounted. Assume, for example, that Hargrove Company has 20,000 units of inventory on hand on December 31. It also has the following goods in transit:

1. Sales of 1,500 units shipped December 31 FOB destination.

2. Purchases of 2,500 units shipped FOB shipping point by the seller on December 31.

Hargrove has legal title to both the 1,500 units sold and the 2,500 units purchased. If the company ignores the units in transit, it would understate inventory quantities by 4,000 units (1,500 + 2,500).

As we will see later in the chapter, inaccurate inventory counts affect not only the inventory amount shown on the balance sheet but also the cost of goods sold calculation on the income statement.

CONSIGNED GOODS In some lines of business, it is common to hold the goods of other parties and try to sell the goods for them for a fee, but without taking ownership of the goods. These are called **consigned goods**.

For example, you might have a used car that you would like to sell. If you take the item to a dealer, the dealer might be willing to put the car on its lot and charge you a commission if it is sold. Under this agreement, the dealer **would not take ownership** of the car, which would still belong to you. Therefore, if an inventory count were taken, the car would not be included in the dealer's inventory because the dealer does not own it.

Many car, boat, and antique dealers sell goods on consignment to keep their inventory costs down and to avoid the risk of purchasing an item that they will not be able to sell. Today, even some manufacturers are making consignment agreements with their suppliers in order to keep their inventory levels low.

ANATOMY OF A FRAUD

Ted Nickerson, CEO of clock manufacturer Dally Industries, was feared by all of his employees. Ted also had expensive tastes. To support this habit, Ted took out large loans, which he collateralized with his shares of Dally Industries stock. If the price of Dally's stock fell, he was required to provide the bank with more shares of stock. To achieve target net income figures and thus maintain the stock price, Ted coerced employees in the company to alter inventory figures. Inventory quantities were manipulated by changing the amounts on inventory control tags after the year-end physical inventory count. For example, if a tag said there were 20 units of a particular item, the tag was changed to 220. Similarly, the unit costs that were used to determine the value of ending inventory were increased from, for example, $125 per unit to $1,250. Both of these fraudulent changes had the effect of increasing the amount of reported ending inventory. This reduced cost of goods sold and increased net income.

Total take: $245,000

THE MISSING CONTROL

Independent internal verification. The company should have spot-checked its inventory records periodically, verifying that the number of units in the records agreed with the amount on hand and that the unit costs agreed with vendor price sheets.

Source: Adapted from Wells, *Fraud Casebook* (2007), pp. 502–509.

DO IT! 1   Rules of Ownership

Hasbeen Company completed its inventory count. It arrived at a total inventory value of $200,000. As a new member of Hasbeen's accounting department, you have been given the information listed below. Discuss how this information affects the reported cost of inventory.

1. Hasbeen included in the inventory goods held on consignment for Falls Co., costing $15,000.

2. The company did not include in the count purchased goods of $10,000 which were in transit (terms: FOB shipping point).

3. The company did not include in the count sold inventory with a cost of $12,000 which was in transit (terms: FOB shipping point).

Solution

> The goods of $15,000 held on consignment should be deducted from the inventory count. The goods of $10,000 purchased FOB shipping point should be added to the inventory count. Sold goods of $12,000 which were in transit FOB shipping point should not be included in the ending inventory. Thus, inventory should be carried at $195,000 ($200,000 − $15,000 + $10,000).

Action Plan

✔ Apply the rules of ownership to goods held on consignment.

✔ Apply the rules of ownership to goods in transit.

Related exercise material: **BE6-1, BE6-2, E6-1, E6-2, and** **6-1.**

Apply inventory cost flow methods and discuss their financial effects.

Inventory is accounted for at cost. Cost includes all expenditures necessary to acquire goods and place them in a condition ready for sale. For example, freight costs incurred to acquire inventory are added to the cost of inventory, but the cost of shipping goods to a customer are a selling expense.

After a company has determined the quantity of units of inventory, it applies unit costs to the quantities to compute the total cost of the inventory and the cost of goods sold. This process can be complicated if a company has purchased inventory items at different times and at different prices.

For example, assume that Crivitz TV Company purchases three identical 50-inch TVs on different dates at costs of $700, $750, and $800. During the year, Crivitz sold two sets at $1,200 each. These facts are summarized in Illustration 6-3.

Illustration 6-3
Data for inventory costing example

Purchases			
February 3	1 TV	at	$700
March 5	1 TV	at	$750
May 22	1 TV	at	$800
Sales			
June 1	2 TVs	for	$2,400 ($1,200 × 2)

Cost of goods sold will differ depending on which two TVs the company sold. For example, it might be $1,450 ($700 + $750), or $1,500 ($700 + $800), or $1,550 ($750 + $800). In this section, we discuss alternative costing methods available to Crivitz.

Specific Identification

If Crivitz can positively identify which particular units it sold and which are still in ending inventory, it can use the **specific identification method** of inventory costing. For example, if Crivitz sold the TVs it purchased on February 3 and May 22, then its cost of goods sold is $1,500 ($700 + $800), and its ending inventory is $750 (see Illustration 6-4). Using this method, companies can accurately determine ending inventory and cost of goods sold.

Illustration 6-4
Specific identification method

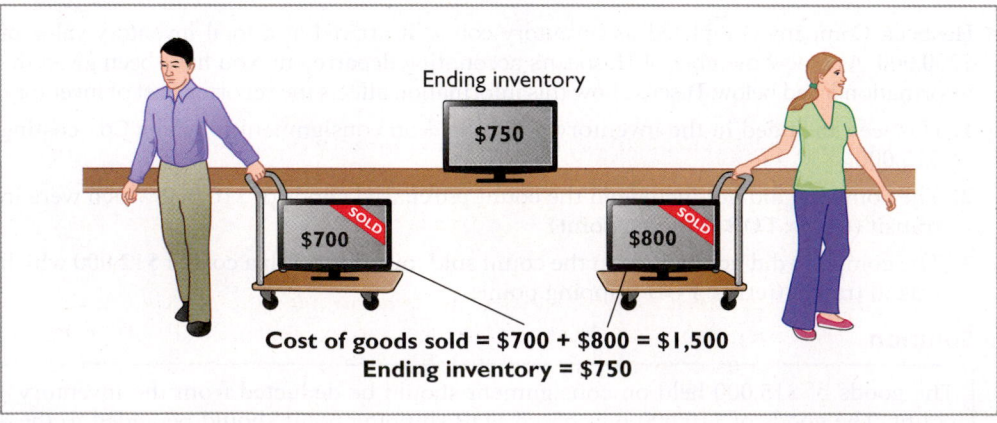

Ending inventory
$750

SOLD $700   SOLD $800

Cost of goods sold = $700 + $800 = $1,500
Ending inventory = $750

Specific identification requires that companies keep records of the original cost of each individual inventory item. Historically, specific identification was possible only when a company sold a limited variety of high-unit-cost items that could be identified clearly from the time of purchase through the time of sale. Examples of such products are cars, pianos, or expensive antiques.

Today, bar coding, electronic product codes, and radio frequency identification make it theoretically possible to do specific identification with nearly any type of product. The reality is, however, that this practice is still relatively rare. Instead, rather than keep track of the cost of each particular item sold, most companies make assumptions, called **cost flow assumptions**, about which units were sold.

Cost Flow Assumptions

Because specific identification is often impractical, other cost flow methods are permitted. These differ from specific identification in that they **assume** flows of costs that may be unrelated to the physical flow of goods. There are three assumed cost flow methods:

1. First-in, first-out (FIFO)
2. Last-in, first-out (LIFO)
3. Average-cost

There is no accounting requirement that the cost flow assumption be consistent with the physical movement of the goods. Company management selects the appropriate cost flow method.

To demonstrate the three cost flow methods, we will use a **periodic** inventory system. We assume a periodic system because **very few companies use perpetual LIFO, FIFO, or average-cost** to cost their inventory and related cost of goods sold. Instead, companies that use perpetual systems often use an assumed cost (called a standard cost) to record cost of goods sold at the time of sale. Then, at the end of the period when they count their inventory, they **recalculate cost of goods sold using periodic FIFO, LIFO, or average-cost** as shown in this chapter and adjust cost of goods sold to this recalculated number.[1]

To illustrate the three inventory cost flow methods, we will use the data for Houston Electronics' Astro condensers, shown in Illustration 6-5.

	HOUSTON ELECTRONICS Astro Condensers			
Date	**Explanation**	**Units**	**Unit Cost**	**Total Cost**
Jan. 1	Beginning inventory	100	$10	$ 1,000
Apr. 15	Purchase	200	11	2,200
Aug. 24	Purchase	300	12	3,600
Nov. 27	Purchase	400	13	5,200
	Total units available for sale	1,000		$12,000
	Units in ending inventory	(450)		
	Units sold	550		

Illustration 6-5
Data for Houston Electronics

The cost of goods sold formula in a periodic system is:

> **(Beginning Inventory + Purchases) − Ending Inventory = Cost of Goods Sold**

Houston Electronics had a total of 1,000 units available to sell during the period (beginning inventory plus purchases). The total cost of these 1,000 units is $12,000, referred to as **cost of goods available for sale**. A physical inventory

---

[1]Also, some companies use a perpetual system to keep track of units, but they do not make an entry for perpetual cost of goods sold. In addition, firms that employ LIFO tend to use **dollar-value LIFO**, a method discussed in upper-level courses. FIFO periodic and FIFO perpetual give the same result. Therefore, companies should not incur the additional cost to use FIFO perpetual. Few companies use perpetual average-cost because of the added cost of record-keeping. Finally, for instructional purposes, we believe it is easier to demonstrate the cost flow assumptions under the periodic system, which makes it more pedagogically appropriate.

taken at December 31 determined that there were 450 units in ending inventory. Therefore, Houston sold 550 units (1,000 − 450) during the period. To determine the cost of the 550 units that were sold (the cost of goods sold), we assign a cost to the ending inventory and subtract that value from the cost of goods available for sale. The value assigned to the ending inventory **will depend on which cost flow method we use**. No matter which cost flow assumption we use, though, the sum of cost of goods sold plus the cost of the ending inventory must equal the cost of goods available for sale—in this case, $12,000.

FIRST-IN, FIRST-OUT (FIFO)

The **first-in, first-out (FIFO) method** assumes that the **earliest goods** purchased are the first to be sold. FIFO often parallels the actual physical flow of merchandise. That is, it generally is good business practice to sell the oldest units first. Under the FIFO method, therefore, the **costs** of the earliest goods purchased are the first to be recognized in determining cost of goods sold. (This does not necessarily mean that the oldest units **are** sold first, but that the costs of the oldest units are **recognized** first. In a bin of picture hangers at the hardware store, for example, no one really knows, nor would it matter, which hangers are sold first.) Illustration 6-6 shows the allocation of the cost of goods available for sale at Houston Electronics under FIFO.

Illustration 6-6
Allocation of costs—
FIFO method

Helpful Hint
Note the sequencing of the allocation: (1) compute ending inventory, and (2) determine cost of goods sold.

Helpful Hint
Another way of thinking about the calculation of FIFO ending inventory is the **LISH assumption**—last in still here.

	COST OF GOODS AVAILABLE FOR SALE			
Date	**Explanation**	**Units**	**Unit Cost**	**Total Cost**
Jan. 1	Beginning inventory	100	$10	$ 1,000
Apr. 15	Purchase	200	11	2,200
Aug. 24	Purchase	300	12	3,600
Nov. 27	Purchase	400	13	5,200
	Total	1,000		**$12,000**

	STEP 1: ENDING INVENTORY			STEP 2: COST OF GOODS SOLD	
Date	**Units**	**Unit Cost**	**Total Cost**		
Nov. 27	400	$13	$ 5,200	Cost of goods available for sale	$12,000
Aug. 24	50	12	600	Less: Ending inventory	5,800
Total	450		**$5,800**	Cost of goods sold	**$ 6,200**

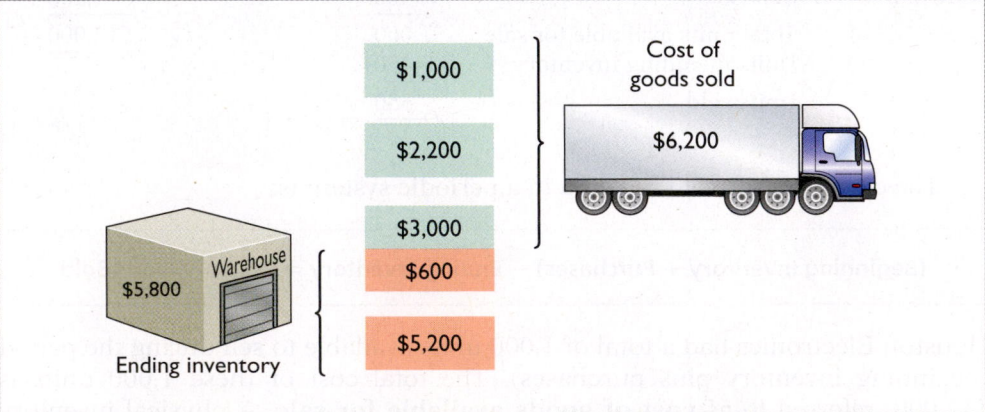

Under FIFO, since it is assumed that the first goods purchased were the first goods sold, ending inventory is based on the prices of the most recent units purchased. That is, **under FIFO, companies obtain the cost of the ending inventory by taking the unit cost of the most recent purchase and working backward until all units of inventory have been costed**. In this example, Houston Electronics prices the 450 units of ending inventory using the **most recent** prices. The last purchase was 400 units at $13 on November 27. The remaining 50 units are priced using the unit cost of the second most recent purchase, $12, on August 24. Next, Houston Electronics calculates cost of goods sold by subtracting the cost of the units **not sold** (ending inventory) from the cost of all goods available for sale.

Illustration 6-7 demonstrates that companies also can calculate cost of goods sold by pricing the 550 units sold using the prices of the first 550 units acquired. Note that of the 300 units purchased on August 24, only 250 units are assumed sold. This agrees with our calculation of the cost of ending inventory, where 50 of these units were assumed unsold and thus included in ending inventory.

Date	Units	Unit Cost	Total Cost
Jan. 1	100	$10	$ 1,000
Apr. 15	200	11	2,200
Aug. 24	250	12	3,000
Total	550		**$6,200**

Illustration 6-7
Proof of cost of goods sold

LAST-IN, FIRST-OUT (LIFO)

The **last-in, first-out (LIFO) method** assumes that the **latest goods** purchased are the first to be sold. LIFO seldom coincides with the actual physical flow of inventory. (Exceptions include goods stored in piles, such as coal or hay, where goods are removed from the top of the pile as they are sold.) Under the LIFO method, the **costs** of the latest goods purchased are the first to be recognized in determining cost of goods sold. Illustration 6-8 shows the allocation of the cost of goods available for sale at Houston Electronics under LIFO.

Illustration 6-8
Allocation of costs— LIFO method

COST OF GOODS AVAILABLE FOR SALE				
Date	Explanation	Units	Unit Cost	Total Cost
Jan. 1	Beginning inventory	100	$10	$ 1,000
Apr. 15	Purchase	200	11	2,200
Aug. 24	Purchase	300	12	3,600
Nov. 27	Purchase	400	13	5,200
	Total	1,000		**$12,000**

STEP 1: ENDING INVENTORY				STEP 2: COST OF GOODS SOLD	
Date	Units	Unit Cost	Total Cost		
Jan. 1	100	$10	$ 1,000	Cost of goods available for sale	$12,000
Apr. 15	200	11	2,200	Less: Ending inventory	5,000
Aug. 24	150	12	1,800	Cost of goods sold	**$ 7,000**
Total	450		**$5,000**		

Helpful Hint
Another way of thinking about the calculation of LIFO ending inventory is the **FISH assumption**—first in still here.

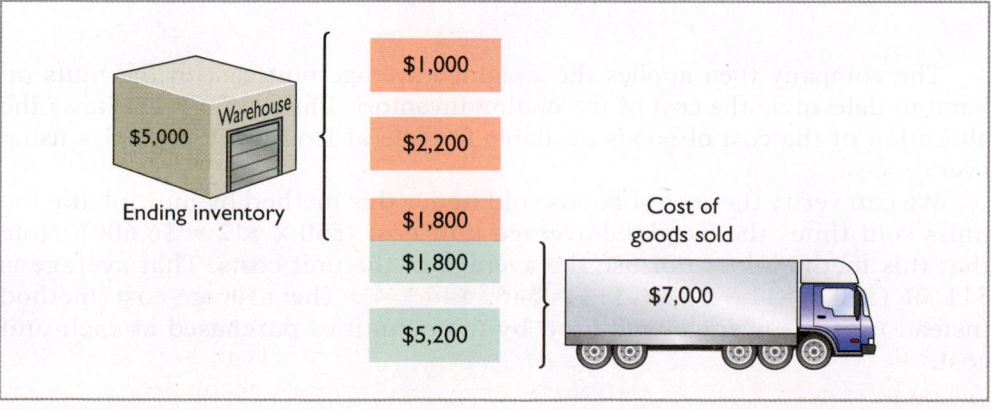

Under LIFO, since it is assumed that the first goods sold were those that were most recently purchased, ending inventory is based on the prices of the oldest units purchased. That is, **under LIFO, companies obtain the cost of the ending inventory by taking the unit cost of the earliest goods available for sale and working forward until all units of inventory have been costed**. In this example, Houston Electronics prices the 450 units of ending inventory using the **earliest** prices. The first purchase was 100 units at $10 in the January 1 beginning inventory. Then, 200 units were purchased at $11. The remaining 150 units needed are priced at $12 per unit (August 24 purchase). Next, Houston Electronics calculates cost of goods sold by subtracting the cost of the units **not sold** (ending inventory) from the cost of all goods available for sale.

Illustration 6-9 demonstrates that companies also can calculate cost of goods sold by pricing the 550 units sold using the prices of the last 550 units acquired. Note that of the 300 units purchased on August 24, only 150 units are assumed sold. This agrees with our calculation of the cost of ending inventory, where 150 of these units were assumed unsold and thus included in ending inventory.

Illustration 6-9
Proof of cost of goods sold

Date	Units	Unit Cost	Total Cost
Nov. 27	400	$13	$ 5,200
Aug. 24	150	12	1,800
Total	550		**$7,000**

Under a periodic inventory system, which we are using here, **all goods purchased during the period are assumed to be available for the first sale, regardless of the date of purchase**.

AVERAGE-COST

The **average-cost method** allocates the cost of goods available for sale on the basis of the **weighted-average unit cost** incurred. The average-cost method assumes that goods are similar in nature. Illustration 6-10 presents the formula and a sample computation of the weighted-average unit cost.

Illustration 6-10
Formula for weighted-average unit cost

Cost of Goods Available for Sale	÷	Total Units Available for Sale	=	Weighted-Average Unit Cost
$12,000	÷	1,000	=	$12

The company then applies the weighted-average unit cost to the units on hand to determine the cost of the ending inventory. Illustration 6-11 shows the allocation of the cost of goods available for sale at Houston Electronics using average-cost.

We can verify the cost of goods sold under this method by multiplying the units sold times the weighted-average unit cost (550 × $12 = $6,600). Note that this method does **not** use the average of the unit costs. That average is $11.50 ($10 + $11 + $12 + $13 = $46; $46 ÷ 4). The average-cost method instead uses the average **weighted by** the quantities purchased at each unit cost.

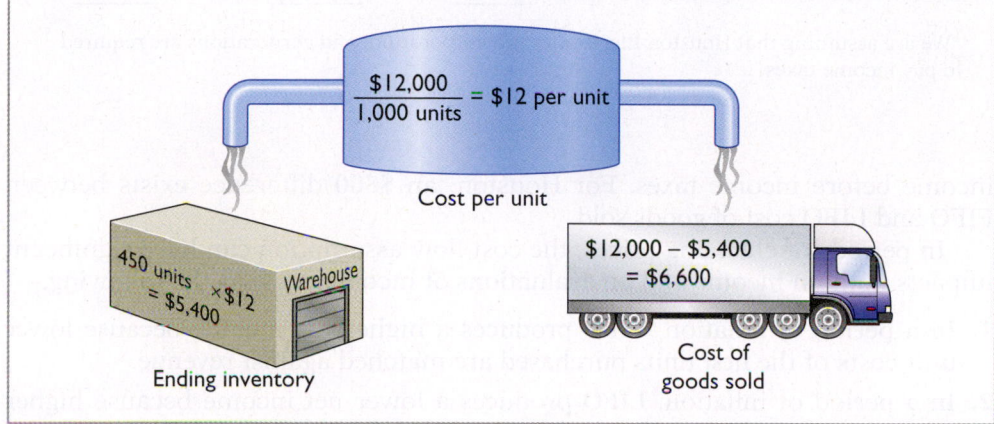

COST OF GOODS AVAILABLE FOR SALE				
Date	Explanation	Units	Unit Cost	Total Cost
Jan. 1	Beginning inventory	100	$10	$ 1,000
Apr. 15	Purchase	200	11	2,200
Aug. 24	Purchase	300	12	3,600
Nov. 27	Purchase	400	13	5,200
	Total	1,000		$12,000

STEP 1: ENDING INVENTORY			STEP 2: COST OF GOODS SOLD	
$12,000 ÷ 1,000 = $12			Cost of goods available for sale	$12,000
			Less: Ending inventory	5,400
Units	Unit Cost	Total Cost	Cost of goods sold	$ 6,600
450	$12	$5,400		

$$\frac{\$12,000}{1,000 \text{ units}} = \$12 \text{ per unit}$$

Cost per unit

450 units × $12 = $5,400
Warehouse

Ending inventory

$12,000 − $5,400 = $6,600

Cost of goods sold

Illustration 6-11
Allocation of costs—average-cost method

Financial Statement and Tax Effects of Cost Flow Methods

Each of the three assumed cost flow methods is acceptable for use. For example, **Reebok International Ltd.** and **Wendy's International** currently use the FIFO method of inventory costing. **Campbell Soup Company**, **Kroger**, and **Walgreen Drugs** use LIFO for part or all of their inventory. **Bristol-Myers Squibb**, **Starbucks**, and **Motorola** use the average-cost method. In fact, a company may also use more than one cost flow method at the same time. **Stanley Black & Decker Manufacturing Company**, for example, uses LIFO for domestic inventories and FIFO for foreign inventories. Illustration 6-12 (in the margin) shows the use of the three cost flow methods in 500 large U.S. companies.

The reasons companies adopt different inventory cost flow methods are varied, but they usually involve one of three factors: (1) income statement effects, (2) balance sheet effects, or (3) tax effects.

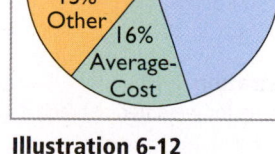

Illustration 6-12
Use of cost flow methods in major U.S. companies

INCOME STATEMENT EFFECTS

To understand why companies might choose a particular cost flow method, let's examine the effects of the different cost flow assumptions on the financial statements of Houston Electronics. The condensed income statements in Illustration 6-13 (page 270) assume that Houston sold its 550 units for $18,500, had operating expenses of $9,000, and is subject to an income tax rate of 30%.

Note the cost of goods available for sale ($12,000) is the same under each of the three inventory cost flow methods. However, the ending inventories and the costs of goods sold are different. This difference is due to the unit costs that the company allocated to cost of goods sold and to ending inventory. Each dollar of difference in ending inventory results in a corresponding dollar difference in

Illustration 6-13
Comparative effects of cost
flow methods

HOUSTON ELECTRONICS Condensed Income Statements			
	FIFO	**LIFO**	**Average-Cost**
Sales revenue	$18,500	$18,500	$18,500
Beginning inventory	1,000	1,000	1,000
Purchases	11,000	11,000	11,000
Cost of goods available for sale	12,000	12,000	12,000
Ending inventory	**5,800**	**5,000**	**5,400**
Cost of goods sold	6,200	7,000	6,600
Gross profit	12,300	11,500	11,900
Operating expenses	9,000	9,000	9,000
Income before income taxes*	3,300	2,500	2,900
Income tax expense (30%)	990	750	870
Net income	**$ 2,310**	**$ 1,750**	**$ 2,030**

*We are assuming that Houston Electronics is a corporation, and corporations are required to pay income taxes.

income before income taxes. For Houston, an $800 difference exists between FIFO and LIFO cost of goods sold.

In periods of changing prices, the cost flow assumption can have significant impacts both on income and on evaluations of income, such as the following.

1. In a period of inflation, FIFO produces a higher net income because lower unit costs of the first units purchased are matched against revenue.

2. In a period of inflation, LIFO produces a lower net income because higher unit costs of the last goods purchased are matched against revenue.

3. If prices are falling, the results from the use of FIFO and LIFO are reversed. FIFO will report the lowest net income and LIFO the highest.

4. Regardless of whether prices are rising or falling, average-cost produces net income between FIFO and LIFO.

As shown in the Houston example (Illustration 6-13), in a period of rising prices FIFO reports the highest net income ($2,310) and LIFO the lowest ($1,750); average-cost falls between these two amounts ($2,030).

To management, higher net income is an advantage. It causes external users to view the company more favorably. In addition, management bonuses, if based on net income, will be higher. Therefore, when prices are rising (which is usually the case), companies tend to prefer FIFO because it results in higher net income.

Others believe that LIFO presents a more realistic net income number. That is, LIFO matches the more recent costs against current revenues to provide a better measure of net income. During periods of inflation, many challenge the quality of non-LIFO earnings, noting that failing to match current costs against current revenues leads to an understatement of cost of goods sold and an over-statement of net income. As some indicate, net income computed using FIFO creates **"paper or phantom profits"**—that is, earnings that do not really exist.

BALANCE SHEET EFFECTS

A major advantage of the FIFO method is that in a period of inflation, the costs allocated to ending inventory will approximate their current cost. For example, for Houston Electronics, 400 of the 450 units in the ending inventory are costed under FIFO at the higher November 27 unit cost of $13.

Conversely, a major shortcoming of the LIFO method is that in a period of inflation, the costs allocated to ending inventory may be significantly understated in terms of current cost. The understatement becomes greater over prolonged periods of inflation if the inventory includes goods purchased in one or more prior accounting periods. For example, **Caterpillar** has used LIFO for more than 50 years. Its balance sheet shows ending inventory of $14,544 million. But the inventory's actual current cost if FIFO had been used is $16,966 million.

TAX EFFECTS

We have seen that both inventory on the balance sheet and net income on the income statement are higher when companies use FIFO in a period of inflation. Yet, many companies have selected LIFO. Why? The reason is that LIFO results in the lowest income taxes (because of lower net income) during times of rising prices. For example, at Houston Electronics, income taxes are $750 under LIFO, compared to $990 under FIFO. The tax savings of $240 makes more cash available for use in the business.

Helpful Hint
A tax rule, often referred to as the **LIFO conformity rule**, requires that if companies use LIFO for tax purposes they must also use it for financial reporting purposes. This means that if a company chooses the LIFO method to reduce its tax bills, it will also have to report lower net income in its financial statements.

Using Inventory Cost Flow Methods Consistently

Whatever cost flow method a company chooses, it should use that method consistently from one accounting period to another. This approach is often referred to as the **consistency concept**, which means that a company uses the same accounting principles and methods from year to year. Consistent application enhances the comparability of financial statements over successive time periods. In contrast, using the FIFO method one year and the LIFO method the next year would make it difficult to compare the net incomes of the two years.

Although consistent application is preferred, it does not mean that a company may never change its inventory costing method. When a company adopts a different method, it should disclose in the financial statements the change and its effects on net income. Illustration 6-14 shows a typical disclosure, using information from recent financial statements of **Quaker Oats** (now a unit of **PepsiCo**).

Illustration 6-14
Disclosure of change in cost flow method

Real World	**QUAKER OATS** Notes to the Financial Statements

Note 1: Effective July 1, the Company adopted the LIFO cost flow assumption for valuing the majority of U.S. Grocery Products inventories. The Company believes that the use of the LIFO method better matches current costs with current revenues. The effect of this change on the current year was to decrease net income by $16.0 million.

International Insight   ExxonMobil Corporation

Bloomberg/Getty Images

Is LIFO Fair?

ExxonMobil Corporation, like many U.S. companies, uses LIFO to value its inventory for financial reporting and tax purposes. In one recent year, this resulted in a cost of goods sold figure that was $5.6 billion higher than under FIFO. By increasing cost of goods sold, ExxonMobil reduces net income, which reduces taxes. Critics say that LIFO provides an unfair "tax dodge." As Congress looks for more sources of tax revenue, some lawmakers favor the elimination of LIFO. Supporters of LIFO argue that the method is conceptually sound because it matches current costs with current revenues. In addition, they point out that this matching provides protection against inflation.

International accounting standards do not allow the use of LIFO. Because of this, the net income of foreign oil companies such as **BP** and **Royal Dutch Shell** are not directly comparable to U.S. companies, which makes analysis difficult.

Source: David Reilly, "Big Oil's Accounting Methods Fuel Criticism," *Wall Street Journal* (August 8, 2006), p. C1.

What are the arguments for and against the use of LIFO? (Go to **WileyPLUS** for this answer and additional questions.)

DO IT! 2 Cost Flow Methods

The accounting records of Shumway Ag Implements show the following data.

Beginning inventory	4,000 units at $ 3
Purchases	6,000 units at $ 4
Sales	7,000 units at $12

Determine the cost of goods sold during the period under a periodic inventory system using (a) the FIFO method, (b) the LIFO method, and (c) the average-cost method.

Action Plan

✔ Understand the periodic inventory system.

✔ Allocate costs between goods sold and goods on hand (ending inventory) for each cost flow method.

✔ Compute cost of goods sold for each method.

Solution

Cost of goods available for sale = (4,000 × $3) + (6,000 × $4) = $36,000

Ending inventory = 10,000 − 7,000 = 3,000 units

(a) FIFO: $36,000 − (3,000 × $4) = $24,000

(b) LIFO: $36,000 − (3,000 × $3) = $27,000

(c) Average cost per unit: [(4,000 @ $3) + (6,000 @ $4)] ÷ 10,000 = $3.60
Average-cost: $36,000 − (3,000 × $3.60) = $25,200

Related exercise material: **BE6-3, BE6-4, BE6-5, E6-3, E6-4, E6-5, E6-6, E6-7, E6-8, and DO IT! 6-2.**

LEARNING OBJECTIVE 3

Indicate the effects of inventory errors on the financial statements.

Unfortunately, errors occasionally occur in accounting for inventory. In some cases, errors are caused by failure to count or price the inventory correctly. In other cases, errors occur because companies do not properly recognize the transfer of legal title to goods that are in transit. When errors occur, they affect both the income statement and the balance sheet.

Income Statement Effects

Under a periodic inventory system, both the beginning and ending inventories appear in the income statement. The ending inventory of one period automatically becomes the beginning inventory of the next period. Thus, inventory errors affect the computation of cost of goods sold and net income in two periods.

The effects on cost of goods sold can be computed by first entering incorrect data in the formula in Illustration 6-15 and then substituting the correct data.

Illustration 6-15
Formula for cost of goods sold

Beginning Inventory	+	Cost of Goods Purchased	−	Ending Inventory	=	Cost of Goods Sold

> **ETHICS NOTE**
>
> Inventory fraud increases during recessions. Such fraud includes pricing inventory at amounts in excess of its actual value, or claiming to have inventory when no inventory exists. Inventory fraud usually overstates ending inventory, thereby understating cost of goods sold and creating higher income.

If the error understates **beginning** inventory, cost of goods sold will be understated. If the error understates **ending** inventory, cost of goods sold will be overstated. Illustration 6-16 shows the effects of inventory errors on the current year's income statement.

So far, the effects of inventory errors are fairly straightforward. Now, though, comes the (at first) surprising part: An error in the ending inventory of the current period will have a **reverse effect on net income of the next accounting period**. Illustration 6-17 shows this effect. As you study the illustration, you will see that the reverse effect comes from the fact that understating ending inventory in 2016 results in understating beginning inventory in 2017 and overstating net income in 2017.

Illustration 6-16
Effects of inventory errors on current year's income statement

When Inventory Error:	Cost of Goods Sold Is:	Net Income Is:
Understates beginning inventory	Understated	Overstated
Overstates beginning inventory	Overstated	Understated
Understates ending inventory	Overstated	Understated
Overstates ending inventory	Understated	Overstated

SAMPLE COMPANY
Condensed Income Statements

	2016				2017			
	Incorrect		Correct		Incorrect		Correct	
Sales revenue		$80,000		$80,000		$90,000		$90,000
Beginning inventory	$20,000		$20,000		**$12,000**		**$15,000**	
Cost of goods purchased	40,000		40,000		68,000		68,000	
Cost of goods available for sale	60,000		60,000		80,000		83,000	
Ending inventory	**12,000**		**15,000**		23,000		23,000	
Cost of goods sold		48,000		45,000		57,000		60,000
Gross profit		32,000		35,000		33,000		30,000
Operating expenses		10,000		10,000		20,000		20,000
Net income		$22,000		$25,000		$13,000		$10,000

$(3,000)
Net income understated

$3,000
Net income overstated

The errors cancel. Thus, the combined total income for the 2-year period is correct.

Illustration 6-17
Effects of inventory errors on two years' income statements

Over the two years, though, total net income is correct because the errors **offset each other**. Notice that total income using incorrect data is $35,000 ($22,000 + $13,000), which is the same as the total income of $35,000 ($25,000 + $10,000) using correct data. Also note in this example that an error in the beginning inventory does not result in a corresponding error in the ending inventory for that period. The correctness of the ending inventory depends entirely on the accuracy of taking and costing the inventory at the balance sheet date under the periodic inventory system.

Balance Sheet Effects

Companies can determine the effect of ending inventory errors on the balance sheet by using the basic accounting equation: Assets = Liabilities + Stockholders' Equity. Errors in the ending inventory have the effects shown in Illustration 6-18.

Illustration 6-18
Effects of ending inventory errors on balance sheet

Ending Inventory Error	Assets	Liabilities	Stockholders' Equity
Overstated	Overstated	No effect	Overstated
Understated	Understated	No effect	Understated

The effect of an error in ending inventory on the subsequent period was shown in Illustration 6-17. Recall that if the error is not corrected, the combined total net income for the two periods would be correct. Thus, total stockholders' equity reported on the balance sheet at the end of 2017 will also be correct.

DO IT! 3 | Inventory Errors

Action Plan

✔ An ending inventory error in one period will have an equal and opposite effect on cost of goods sold and net income in the next period.

✔ After two years, the errors have offset each other.

Visual Company overstated its 2016 ending inventory by $22,000. Determine the impact this error has on ending inventory, cost of goods sold, and stockholders' equity in 2016 and 2017.

Solution

	2016	2017
Ending inventory	$22,000 overstated	No effect
Cost of goods sold	$22,000 understated	$22,000 overstated
Stockholders' equity	$22,000 overstated	No effect

Related exercise material: **BE6-6, E6-9, E6-10, and DO IT! 6-3.**

LEARNING OBJECTIVE 4

Explain the statement presentation and analysis of inventory.

Presentation

As indicated in Chapter 5, inventory is classified in the balance sheet as a current asset immediately below receivables. In a multiple-step income statement, cost of goods sold is subtracted from net sales. There also should be disclosure of (1) the major inventory classifications, (2) the basis of accounting (cost, or lower-of-cost-or-market), and (3) the cost method (FIFO, LIFO, or average-cost).

Wal-Mart Stores, Inc., for example, in its January 31, 2014, balance sheet reported inventories of $44,858 million under current assets. The accompanying notes to the financial statements, as shown in Illustration 6-19, disclosed the following information.

Illustration 6-19
Inventory disclosures by Wal-Mart

WAL-MART STORES, INC.
Notes to the Financial Statements

Note 1. Summary of Significant Accounting Policies

Inventories

The Company values inventories at the lower of cost or market as determined primarily by the retail method of accounting, using the last-in, first-out ("LIFO") method for substantially all of the WalMart U.S. segment's inventories. The WalMart International segment's inventories are primarily valued by the retail method of accounting, using the first-in, first-out ("FIFO") method. The retail method of accounting results in inventory being valued at the lower of cost or market since permanent markdowns are currently taken as a reduction of the retail value of inventory. The Sam's Club segment's inventories are valued based on the weighted-average cost using the LIFO method. At January 31, 2014 and 2013, the Company's inventories valued at LIFO approximate those inventories as if they were valued at FIFO.

As indicated in this note, Wal-Mart values its inventories at the lower-of-cost-or-market using LIFO and FIFO.

Lower-of-Cost-or-Market

The value of inventory for companies selling high-technology or fashion goods can drop very quickly due to continual changes in technology or fashion. These circumstances sometimes call for inventory valuation methods other than those presented so far. For example, at one time purchasing managers at **Ford** decided to make a large purchase of palladium, a precious metal used in vehicle emission devices. They made this purchase because they feared a future shortage. The shortage did not materialize, and by the end of the year the price of palladium had plummeted. Ford's inventory was then worth $1 billion less than its original cost. Do you think Ford's inventory should have been stated at cost, in accordance with the historical cost principle, or at its lower replacement cost?

International Note

Under U.S. GAAP, companies cannot reverse inventory write-downs if inventory increases in value in subsequent periods. IFRS permits companies to reverse write-downs in some circumstances.

As you probably reasoned, this situation requires a departure from the cost basis of accounting. This is done by valuing the inventory at the **lower-of-cost-or-market (LCM)** in the period in which the price decline occurs. LCM is a basis whereby inventory is stated at the lower of either its cost or market value as determined by current replacement cost. LCM is an example of the accounting convention of **conservatism**. Conservatism means that the approach adopted among accounting alternatives is the method that is least likely to overstate assets and net income.

Companies apply LCM to the items in inventory after they have used one of the cost flow methods (specific identification, FIFO, LIFO, or average-cost) to determine cost. Under the LCM basis, market is defined as **current replacement cost**, not selling price. For a merchandising company, current replacement cost is the cost of purchasing the same goods at the present time from the usual suppliers in the usual quantities. Current replacement cost is used because a decline in the replacement cost of an item usually leads to a decline in the selling price of the item.

To illustrate the application of LCM, assume that Ken Tuckie TV has the following lines of merchandise with costs and market values as indicated. LCM produces the results shown in Illustration 6-20. Note that the amounts shown in the final column are the lower-of-cost-or-market amounts for each item.

	Units	Cost per Unit	Market per Unit	Lower-of-Cost-or-Market	
Flat-screen TVs	100	$600	**$550**	$ 55,000	($550 × 100)
Satellite radios	500	**90**	104	45,000	($90 × 500)
Blu-ray players	850	50	**48**	40,800	($48 × 850)
CDs	3,000	**5**	6	15,000	($5 × 3,000)
Total inventory				$155,800	

Illustration 6-20
Computation of lower-of-cost-or-market

Analysis

The amount of inventory carried by a company has significant economic consequences. And inventory management is a double-edged sword that requires constant attention. On the one hand, management wants to have a great variety and quantity available so that customers have a wide selection and items are always in stock. But, such a policy may incur high carrying costs (e.g., investment, storage, insurance, obsolescence, and damage). On the other hand, low inventory levels lead to stock-outs and lost sales. Common ratios used to manage and evaluate inventory levels are inventory turnover and a related measure, days in inventory.

Inventory turnover measures the number of times on average the inventory is sold during the period. Its purpose is to measure the liquidity of the inventory. The inventory turnover is computed by dividing cost of goods sold by the average inventory during the period. Unless seasonal factors are significant, average inventory can be computed from the beginning and ending inventory balances. For example, **Wal-Mart** reported in its 2014 annual report a beginning inventory of $43,803 million, an ending inventory of $44,858 million, and cost of goods sold for the year ended January 31, 2014, of $358,069 million. The inventory turnover formula and computation for Wal-Mart are shown on the next page.

Illustration 6-21
Inventory turnover formula
and computation for Wal-Mart

Cost of Goods Sold	÷	Average Inventory	=	Inventory Turnover
$358,069	÷	$\dfrac{\$44{,}858 + \$43{,}803}{2}$	=	**8.1 times**

A variant of the inventory turnover is **days in inventory**. This measures the average number of days inventory is held. It is calculated as 365 divided by the inventory turnover. For example, Wal-Mart's inventory turnover of 8.1 times divided into 365 is 45.1 days. This is the approximate time that it takes a company to sell the inventory once it arrives at the store.

There are typical levels of inventory in every industry. Companies that are able to keep their inventory at lower levels and higher turnovers and still satisfy customer needs are the most successful.

Accounting Across the Organization · Sony

© Dmitry Kutlayev/iStockphoto

Too Many TVs or Too Few?

Financial analysts closely monitored the inventory management practices of companies during the recent recession. For example, some analysts following Sony expressed concern because the company built up its inventory of televisions in an attempt to sell 25 million liquid crystal display (LCD) TVs—a 60% increase over the prior year. A year earlier, Sony had cut its inventory levels so that its quarterly days in inventory was down to 38 days, compared to 61 days for the same quarter a year before that. But now, as a result of its inventory build-up, days in inventory rose to 59 days. While management was saying that it didn't think that Sony's inventory levels were now too high, analysts were concerned that the company would have to engage in very heavy discounting in order to sell off its inventory. Analysts noted that the losses from discounting can be "punishing."

Source: Daisuke Wakabayashi, "Sony Pledges to Corral Inventory," *Wall Street Journal Online* (November 2, 2010).

For Sony, what are the advantages and disadvantages of having a low days in inventory measure? (Go to **WileyPLUS** for this answer and additional questions.)

DO IT! 4 · LCM and Inventory Turnover

(a) Tracy Company sells three different types of home heating stoves (gas, wood, and pellet). The cost and market value of its inventory of stoves are as follows.

	Cost	Market
Gas	$ 84,000	$ 79,000
Wood	250,000	280,000
Pellet	112,000	101,000

Determine the value of the company's inventory under the lower-of-cost-or-market approach.

Action Plan

✔ Determine whether cost or market value is lower for each inventory type.

✔ Sum the lowest value of each inventory type to determine the total value of inventory.

Solution

The lowest value for each inventory type is gas $79,000, wood $250,000, and pellet $101,000. The total inventory value is the sum of these amounts, $430,000.

(b) Early in 2017, Westmoreland Company switched to a just-in-time inventory system. Its sales revenue, cost of goods sold, and inventory amounts for 2016 and 2017 are shown below.

	2016	2017
Sales revenue	$2,000,000	$1,800,000
Cost of goods sold	1,000,000	910,000
Beginning inventory	290,000	210,000
Ending inventory	210,000	50,000

Determine the inventory turnover and days in inventory for 2016 and 2017. Discuss the changes in the amount of inventory, the inventory turnover and days in inventory, and the amount of sales across the two years.

Solution

	2016	2017
Inventory turnover	$\dfrac{\$1,000,000}{(\$290,000 + \$210,000)/2} = 4$	$\dfrac{\$910,000}{(\$210,000 + \$50,000)/2} = 7$
Days in inventory	$365 \div 4 = 91.3$ days	$365 \div 7 = 52.1$ days

The company experienced a very significant decline in its ending inventory as a result of the just-in-time inventory. This decline improved its inventory turnover and its days in inventory. However, its sales declined by 10%. It is possible that this decline was caused by the dramatic reduction in the amount of inventory that was on hand, which increased the likelihood of "stock-outs." To determine the optimal inventory level, management must weigh the benefits of reduced inventory against the potential lost sales caused by stock-outs.

Related exercise material: **BE6-7, BE6-8, E6-9, E6-11, E6-12, E6-13, E6-14, and** DO IT! **6-4.**

Action Plan

✔ To find the inventory turnover, divide cost of goods sold by average inventory.

✔ To determine days in inventory, divide 365 days by the inventory turnover.

✔ Just-in-time inventory reduces the amount of inventory on hand, which reduces carrying costs. Reducing inventory levels by too much has potential negative implications for sales.

LEARNING OBJECTIVE *5

APPENDIX 6A: Apply the inventory cost flow methods to perpetual inventory records.

What inventory cost flow methods can companies employ if they use a perpetual inventory system? Simple—they can use any of the inventory cost flow methods described in the chapter. To illustrate the application of the three assumed cost flow methods (FIFO, LIFO, and average-cost), we will use the data shown in Illustration 6A-1 and in this chapter for Houston Electronics' Astro condensers.

Illustration 6A-1
Inventoriable units and costs

HOUSTON ELECTRONICS
Astro Condensers

Date	Explanation	Units	Unit Cost	Total Cost	Balance in Units
1/1	Beginning inventory	100	$10	$ 1,000	100
4/15	Purchases	200	11	2,200	300
8/24	Purchases	300	12	3,600	600
9/10	Sale	550			50
11/27	Purchases	400	13	5,200	450
				$12,000	

First-In, First-Out (FIFO)

Under perpetual FIFO, the company charges to cost of goods sold the cost of the earliest goods on hand **prior to each sale**. Therefore, the cost of goods sold on September 10 consists of the units on hand January 1 and the units purchased April 15 and August 24. Illustration 6A-2 shows the inventory under a FIFO method perpetual system.

Illustration 6A-2
Perpetual system—FIFO

Date	Purchases		Cost of Goods Sold	Balance (in units and cost)	
January 1				(100 @ $10)	$ 1,000
April 15	(200 @ $11)	$2,200		(100 @ $10) (200 @ $11)	} $ 3,200
August 24	(300 @ $12)	$3,600		(100 @ $10) (200 @ $11) (300 @ $12)	} $ 6,800
September 10			(100 @ $10) (200 @ $11) (250 @ $12)	(50 @ $12)	$ 600
			$6,200		
November 27	(400 @ $13)	$5,200		(50 @ $12) (400 @ $13)	} **$5,800**

Cost of goods sold → **$6,200**

Ending inventory → **$5,800**

The ending inventory in this situation is $5,800, and the cost of goods sold is $6,200 [(100 @ $10) + (200 @ $11) + (250 @ $12)].

Compare Illustrations 6-6 (page 266) and 6A-2. You can see that the results under FIFO in a perpetual system are the **same as in a periodic system**. In both cases, the ending inventory is $5,800 and cost of goods sold is $6,200. Regardless of the system, the first costs in are the costs assigned to cost of goods sold.

Last-In, First-Out (LIFO)

Under the LIFO method using a perpetual system, the company charges to cost of goods sold the cost of the most recent purchase prior to sale. Therefore, the cost of the goods sold on September 10 consists of all the units from the August 24 and April 15 purchases plus 50 of the units in beginning inventory. Illustration 6A-3 shows the computation of the ending inventory under the LIFO method.

Illustration 6A-3
Perpetual system—LIFO

Date	Purchases		Cost of Goods Sold	Balance (in units and cost)	
January 1				(100 @ $10)	$ 1,000
April 15	(200 @ $11)	$2,200		(100 @ $10) (200 @ $11)	} $ 3,200
August 24	(300 @ $12)	$3,600		(100 @ $10) (200 @ $11) (300 @ $12)	} $ 6,800
September 10			(300 @ $12) (200 @ $11) (50 @ $10)	(50 @ $10)	$ 500
			$6,300		
November 27	(400 @ $13)	$5,200		(50 @ $10) (400 @ $13)	} **$5,700**

Cost of goods sold → **$6,300**

Ending inventory → **$5,700**

The use of LIFO in a perpetual system will usually produce cost allocations that differ from those using LIFO in a periodic system. In a perpetual system, the company allocates the latest units purchased **prior to each sale** to cost of goods sold. In contrast, in a periodic system, the latest units purchased **during the period** are allocated to cost of goods sold. Thus, when a purchase is made after the last sale, the LIFO periodic system will apply this purchase to the previous sale. Compare Illustrations 6-8 (page 267) and 6A-3. Illustration 6-8 shows that the 400 units at $13 purchased on November 27 applied to the sale of 550 units on September 10. Under the LIFO perpetual system in Illustration 6A-3, the 400 units at $13 purchased on November 27 are all applied to the ending inventory.

The ending inventory in this LIFO perpetual illustration is $5,700, and cost of goods sold is $6,300, as compared to the LIFO periodic Illustration 6-8 (page 267) where the ending inventory is $5,000 and cost of goods sold is $7,000.

Average-Cost

The average-cost method in a perpetual inventory system is called the **moving-average method**. Under this method, the company computes a new average **after each purchase**, by dividing the cost of goods available for sale by the units on hand. The average cost is then applied to (1) the units sold, to determine the cost of goods sold, and (2) the remaining units on hand, to determine the ending inventory amount. Illustration 6A-4 shows the application of the moving-average cost method by Houston Electronics (computations of the moving-average unit cost are shown after Illustration 6A-4).

Date	Purchases	Cost of Goods Sold	Balance (in units and cost)	
January 1			(100 @ $10)	$1,000
April 15	(200 @ $11) $2,200		(300 @ $10.667)	$3,200
August 24	(300 @ $12) $3,600		(600 @ $11.333)	$6,800
September 10		(550 @ $11.333)	(50 @ $11.333)	$567
		$6,233		
November 27	(400 @ $13) $5,200		(450 @ $12.816)	**$5,767**

Illustration 6A-4
Perpetual system—moving-average method

Cost of goods sold

Ending inventory

As indicated, Houston Electronics computes **a new average each time it makes a purchase**.

1. On April 15, after Houston buys 200 units for $2,200, a total of 300 units costing $3,200 ($1,000 + $2,200) are on hand. The average unit cost is $10.667 ($3,200 ÷ 300).

2. On August 24, after Houston buys 300 units for $3,600, a total of 600 units costing $6,800 ($1,000 + $2,200 + $3,600) are on hand. The average cost per unit is $11.333 ($6,800 ÷ 600).

3. On September 10, to compute cost of goods sold, Houston uses this unit cost of $11.333 in costing sales until it makes another purchase, when the company computes a new unit cost. Accordingly, the unit cost of the 550 units sold on September 10 is $11.333, and the total cost of goods sold is $6,233.

4. On November 27, following the purchase of 400 units for $5,200, there are 450 units on hand costing $5,767 ($567 + $5,200) with a new average cost of $12.816 ($5,767 ÷ 450).

Compare this moving-average cost under the perpetual inventory system to Illustration 6-11 (page 269) showing the average-cost method under a periodic inventory system.

APPENDIX 6B: Describe the two methods of estimating inventories.

In the chapter, we assumed that a company would be able to physically count its inventory. What if it cannot? What if the inventory were destroyed by fire or flood, for example? In that case, the company would use an estimate.

Two circumstances explain why companies sometimes estimate inventories. First, a casualty such as fire, flood, or earthquake may make it impossible to take a physical inventory. Second, managers may want monthly or quarterly financial statements, but a physical inventory is taken only annually. The need for estimating inventories occurs primarily with a periodic inventory system because of the absence of perpetual inventory records.

There are two widely used methods of estimating inventories: (1) the gross profit method, and (2) the retail inventory method.

Gross Profit Method

The **gross profit method** estimates the cost of ending inventory by applying a gross profit rate to net sales. This method is relatively simple but effective. Accountants, auditors, and managers frequently use the gross profit method to test the reasonableness of the ending inventory amount. It will detect large errors.

To use this method, a company needs to know its net sales, cost of goods available for sale, and gross profit rate. The company then can estimate its gross profit for the period. Illustration 6B-1 shows the formulas for using the gross profit method.

Illustration 6B-1
Gross profit method formulas

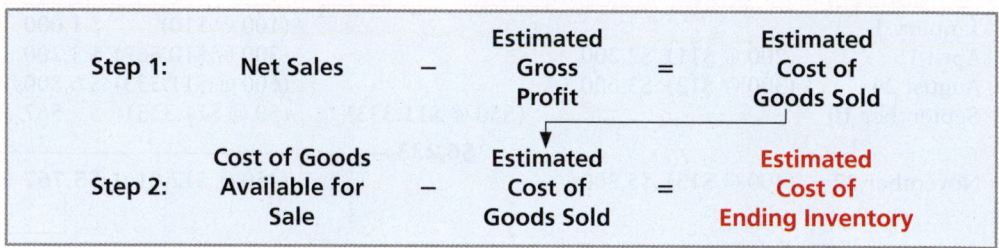

Step 1:	**Net Sales**	−	**Estimated Gross Profit**	=	**Estimated Cost of Goods Sold**	
Step 2:	**Cost of Goods Available for Sale**	−	**Estimated Cost of Goods Sold**	=	**Estimated Cost of Ending Inventory**	

To illustrate, assume that Kishwaukee Company wishes to prepare an income statement for the month of January. Its records show net sales of $200,000, beginning inventory $40,000, and cost of goods purchased $120,000. In the preceding year, the company realized a 30% gross profit rate. It expects to earn the same rate this year. Given these facts and assumptions, Kishwaukee can compute the estimated cost of the ending inventory at January 31 under the gross profit method as follows.

Illustration 6B-2
Example of gross profit method

Step 1:	
Net sales	$ 200,000
Less: Estimated gross profit (30% × $200,000)	60,000
Estimated cost of goods sold	**$140,000**
Step 2:	
Beginning inventory	$ 40,000
Cost of goods purchased	120,000
Cost of goods available for sale	160,000
Less: Estimated cost of goods sold	140,000
Estimated cost of ending inventory	**$ 20,000**

The gross profit method is based on the assumption that the gross profit rate will remain constant. But, it may not remain constant, due to a change in merchandising policies or in market conditions. In such cases, the company should adjust the rate to reflect current operating conditions. In some cases, companies can obtain a more accurate estimate by applying this method on a department or product-line basis.

Note that companies should not use the gross profit method to prepare financial statements at the end of the year. These statements should be based on a physical inventory count.

Retail Inventory Method

A retail store such as **Home Depot**, **Ace Hardware**, or **Walmart** has thousands of different types of merchandise at low unit costs. In such cases, it is difficult and time-consuming to apply unit costs to inventory quantities. An alternative is to use the **retail inventory method** to estimate the cost of inventory. Most retail companies can establish a relationship between cost and sales price. The company then applies the cost-to-retail percentage to the ending inventory at retail prices to determine inventory at cost.

Under the retail inventory method, a company's records must show both the cost and retail value of the goods available for sale. Illustration 6B-3 presents the formulas for using the retail inventory method.

Step 1:	Goods Available for Sale at Retail	−	Net Sales	=	Ending Inventory at Retail
Step 2:	Goods Available for Sale at Cost	÷	Goods Available for Sale at Retail	=	Cost-to-Retail Ratio
Step 3:	Ending Inventory at Retail	×	Cost-to-Retail Ratio	=	Estimated Cost of Ending Inventory

Illustration 6B-3
Retail inventory method formulas

We can demonstrate the logic of the retail method by using unit-cost data. Assume that Ortiz Inc. has marked 10 units purchased at $7 to sell for $10 per unit. Thus, the cost-to-retail ratio is 70% ($70 ÷ $100). If four units remain unsold, their retail value is $40 (4 × $10), and their cost is $28 ($40 × 70%). This amount agrees with the total cost of goods on hand on a per unit basis (4 × $7).

Illustration 6B-4 shows application of the retail method for Valley West. Note that it is not necessary to take a physical inventory to determine the estimated cost of goods on hand at any given time.

	At Cost	At Retail
Beginning inventory	$14,000	$ 21,500
Goods purchased	61,000	78,500
Goods available for sale	$75,000	100,000
Less: Net sales		70,000
Step (1) Ending inventory at retail =		**$ 30,000**

Step (2) Cost-to-retail ratio = $75,000 ÷ $100,000 = 75%
Step (3) Estimated cost of ending inventory = $30,000 × 75% = $22,500

Illustration 6B-4
Application of retail inventory method

The retail inventory method also facilitates taking a physical inventory at the end of the year. Valley West can value the goods on hand at the prices marked on the merchandise, and then apply the cost-to-retail ratio to the goods on hand at retail to determine the ending inventory at cost.

Helpful Hint
In determining inventory at retail, companies use selling prices of the units.

The major disadvantage of the retail method is that it is an averaging technique. Thus, it may produce an incorrect inventory valuation if the mix of the ending inventory is not representative of the mix in the goods available for sale. Assume, for example, that the cost-to-retail ratio of 75% for Valley West consists of equal proportions of inventory items that have cost-to-retail ratios of 70%, 75%, and 80%. If the ending inventory contains only items with a 70% ratio, an incorrect inventory cost will result. Companies can minimize this problem by applying the retail method on a department or product-line basis.

REVIEW AND PRACTICE

LEARNING OBJECTIVES REVIEW

1 Discuss how to classify and determine inventory. Merchandisers need only one inventory classification, merchandise inventory, to describe the different items that make up total inventory. Manufacturers, on the other hand, usually classify inventory into three categories: finished goods, work in process, and raw materials. To determine inventory quantities, manufacturers (1) take a physical inventory of goods on hand and (2) determine the ownership of goods in transit or on consignment.

2 Apply inventory cost flow methods and discuss their financial effects. The primary basis of accounting for inventories is cost. Cost of goods available for sale includes (a) cost of beginning inventory and (b) cost of goods purchased. The inventory cost flow methods are specific identification and three assumed cost flow methods—FIFO, LIFO, and average-cost.

When prices are rising, the first-in, first-out (FIFO) method results in lower cost of goods sold and higher net income than the other methods. The last-in, first-out (LIFO) method results in the lowest income taxes. The reverse is true when prices are falling. In the balance sheet, FIFO results in an ending inventory that is closest to current value. Inventory under LIFO is the farthest from current value.

3 Indicate the effects of inventory errors on the financial statements. In the income statement of the current year: (a) If beginning inventory is understated, net income is overstated. The reverse occurs if beginning inventory is overstated. (b) If ending inventory is overstated, net income is overstated. If ending inventory is understated, net income is understated. In the following period, its effect on net income for that period is reversed, and total net income for the two years will be correct.

In the balance sheet: Ending inventory errors will have the same effect on total assets and total stockholders' equity and no effect on liabilities.

4 Explain the statement presentation and analysis of inventory. Inventory is classified in the balance sheet as a current asset immediately below receivables. There also should be disclosure of (1) the major inventory classifications, (2) the basis of accounting, and (3) the cost method.

Companies use the lower-of-cost-or-market (LCM) basis when the current replacement cost (market) is less than cost. Under LCM, companies recognize the loss in the period in which the price decline occurs.

The inventory turnover is cost of goods sold divided by average inventory. To convert it to average days in inventory, divide 365 days by the inventory turnover.

*5 Apply the inventory cost flow methods to perpetual inventory records. Under FIFO and a perpetual inventory system, companies charge to cost of goods sold the cost of the earliest goods on hand prior to each sale. Under LIFO and a perpetual system, companies charge to cost of goods sold the cost of the most recent purchase prior to sale. Under the moving-average (average-cost) method and a perpetual system, companies compute a new average cost after each purchase.

*6 Describe the two methods of estimating inventories. The two methods of estimating inventories are the gross profit method and the retail inventory method. Under the gross profit method, companies apply a gross profit rate to net sales to determine estimated cost of goods sold. They then subtract estimated cost of goods sold from cost of goods available for sale to determine the estimated cost of the ending inventory.

Under the retail inventory method, companies compute a cost-to-retail ratio by dividing the cost of goods available for sale by the retail value of the goods available for sale. They then apply this ratio to the ending inventory at retail to determine the estimated cost of the ending inventory.

GLOSSARY REVIEW

Average-cost method Inventory costing method that uses the weighted-average unit cost to allocate to ending inventory and cost of goods sold the cost of goods available for sale. (p. 268).

Consigned goods Goods held for sale by one party although ownership of the goods is retained by another party. (p. 263).

Consistency concept Dictates that a company use the same accounting principles and methods from year to year. (p. 271).

Current replacement cost The current cost to replace an inventory item. (p. 275).

Days in inventory Measure of the average number of days inventory is held; calculated as 365 divided by inventory turnover. (p. 276).

Finished goods inventory Manufactured items that are completed and ready for sale. (p. 260).

First-in, first-out (FIFO) method Inventory costing method that assumes that the costs of the earliest goods purchased are the first to be recognized as cost of goods sold. (p. 266).

FOB (free on board) destination Freight terms indicating that ownership of the goods remains with the seller until the goods reach the buyer. (p. 262).

FOB (free on board) shipping point Freight terms indicating that ownership of the goods passes to the buyer when the public carrier accepts the goods from the seller. (p. 262).

*Gross profit method A method for estimating the cost of the ending inventory by applying a gross profit rate to net sales and subtracting estimated cost of goods sold from cost of goods available for sale. (p. 280).

Inventory turnover A ratio that measures the number of times on average the inventory sold during the period; computed by dividing cost of goods sold by the average inventory during the period. (p. 275).

Just-in-time (JIT) inventory Inventory system in which companies manufacture or purchase goods only when needed for use. (p. 260).

Last-in, first-out (LIFO) method Inventory costing method that assumes the costs of the latest units purchased are the first to be allocated to cost of goods sold. (p. 267).

Lower-of-cost-or-market (LCM) A basis whereby inventory is stated at the lower of either its cost or its market value as determined by current replacement cost. (p. 275).

*Moving-average method A new average is computed after each purchase, by dividing the cost of goods available for sale by the units on hand. (p. 279).

Raw materials Basic goods that will be used in production but have not yet been placed into production. (p. 260).

*Retail inventory method A method for estimating the cost of the ending inventory by applying a cost-to-retail ratio to the ending inventory at retail. (p. 281).

Specific identification method An actual physical flow costing method in which items still in inventory are specifically costed to arrive at the total cost of the ending inventory. (p. 264).

Weighted-average unit cost Average cost that is weighted by the number of units purchased at each unit cost. (p. 268).

Work in process That portion of manufactured inventory that has been placed into the production process but is not yet complete. (p. 260).

PRACTICE MULTIPLE-CHOICE QUESTIONS

(LO 1) **1.** Which of the following should **not** be included in the physical inventory of a company?
(a) Goods held on consignment from another company.
(b) Goods shipped on consignment to another company.
(c) Goods in transit from another company shipped FOB shipping point.
(d) None of the above.

(LO 1) **2.** As a result of a thorough physical inventory, Railway Company determined that it had inventory worth $180,000 at December 31, 2017. This count did not take into consideration the following facts: Rogers Consignment store currently has goods worth $35,000 on its sales floor that belong to Railway but are being sold on consignment by Rogers. The selling price of these goods is $50,000. Railway purchased $13,000 of goods that were shipped on December 27, FOB destination, that will be received by Railway on January 3. Determine the correct amount of inventory that Railway should report.
(a) $230,000.   (c) $228,000.
(b) $215,000.   (d) $193,000.

3. Cost of goods available for sale consists of two elements: **(LO 2)** beginning inventory and:
(a) ending inventory.
(b) cost of goods purchased.
(c) cost of goods sold.
(d) All of the answer choices are correct.

4. Poppins Company has the following: **(LO 2)**

	Units	Unit Cost
Inventory, Jan. 1	8,000	$11
Purchase, June 19	13,000	12
Purchase, Nov. 8	5,000	13

If Poppins has 9,000 units on hand at December 31, the cost of the ending inventory under FIFO is:
(a) $99,000.   (c) $113,000.
(b) $108,000.   (d) $117,000.

5. Using the data in Question 4 above, the cost of the **(LO 2)** ending inventory under LIFO is:
(a) $113,000.   (c) $99,000.
(b) $108,000.   (d) $100,000.

(LO 2) **6.** Hansel Electronics has the following:

	Units	Unit Cost
Inventory, Jan. 1	5,000	$ 8
Purchase, April 2	15,000	$10
Purchase, Aug. 28	20,000	$12

If Hansel has 7,000 units on hand at December 31, the cost of ending inventory under the average-cost method is:
(a) $84,000.   (c) $56,000.
(b) $70,000.   (d) $75,250.

(LO 2) **7.** In periods of rising prices, LIFO will produce:
(a) higher net income than FIFO.
(b) the same net income as FIFO.
(c) lower net income than FIFO.
(d) higher net income than average-cost.

(LO 2) **8.** Factors that affect the selection of an inventory costing method do **not** include:
(a) tax effects.
(b) balance sheet effects.
(c) income statement effects.
(d) perpetual vs. periodic inventory system.

(LO 3) **9.** Falk Company's ending inventory is understated $4,000. The effects of this error on the current year's cost of goods sold and net income, respectively, are:
(a) understated, overstated.
(b) overstated, understated.
(c) overstated, overstated.
(d) understated, understated.

(LO 3) **10.** Pauline Company overstated its inventory by $15,000 at December 31, 2016. It did not correct the error in 2016 or 2017. As a result, Pauline's stockholders' equity was:
(a) overstated at December 31, 2016, and understated at December 31, 2017.
(b) overstated at December 31, 2016, and properly stated at December 31, 2017.
(c) understated at December 31, 2016, and understated at December 31, 2017.

(d) overstated at December 31, 2016, and overstated at December 31, 2017.

11. Norton Company purchased 1,000 widgets and has **(LO 4)** 200 widgets in its ending inventory at a cost of $91 each and a current replacement cost of $80 each. The ending inventory under lower-of-cost-or-market is:
(a) $91,000.   (c) $18,200.
(b) $80,000.   (d) $16,000.

12. Santana Company had beginning inventory of **(LO 4)** $80,000, ending inventory of $110,000, cost of goods sold of $285,000, and sales of $475,000. Santana's days in inventory is:
(a) 73 days.   (c) 102.5 days.
(b) 121.7 days.   (d) 84.5 days.

13. Which of these would cause the inventory turnover to **(LO 4)** increase the most?
(a) Increasing the amount of inventory on hand.
(b) Keeping the amount of inventory on hand constant but increasing sales.
(c) Keeping the amount of inventory on hand constant but decreasing sales.
(d) Decreasing the amount of inventory on hand and increasing sales.

*14. In a perpetual inventory system: **(LO 5)**
(a) LIFO cost of goods sold will be the same as in a periodic inventory system.
(b) average costs are a simple average of unit costs incurred.
(c) a new average is computed under the average-cost method after each sale.
(d) FIFO cost of goods sold will be the same as in a periodic inventory system.

*15. King Company has sales of $150,000 and cost of **(LO 6)** goods available for sale of $135,000. If the gross profit rate is 30%, the estimated cost of the ending inventory under the gross profit method is:
(a) $15,000.   (c) $45,000.
(b) $30,000.   (d) $75,000.

Solutions

1. (a) Goods held on consignment should not be included because another company has title (ownership) to the goods. The other choices are incorrect because (b) goods shipped on consignment to another company and (c) goods in transit from another company shipped FOB shipping point should be included in a company's ending inventory. Choice (d) is incorrect as there is a correct answer for this question.

2. (b) The inventory held on consignment by Rogers should be included in Railway's inventory balance at cost ($35,000). The purchased goods of $13,000 should not be included in inventory until January 3 because the goods are shipped FOB destination. Therefore, the correct amount of inventory is $215,000 ($180,000 + $35,000), not (a) $230,000, (c) $228,000, or (d) $193,000.

3. (b) Cost of goods available for sale consists of beginning inventory and cost of goods purchased, not (a) ending inventory or (c) cost of goods sold. Therefore, choice (d) is also incorrect.

4. (c) Under FIFO, ending inventory will consist of 5,000 units from the Nov. 8 purchase and 4,000 units from the June 19 purchase. Therefore, ending inventory is (5,000 × $13) + (4,000 × $12) = $113,000, not (a) $99,000, (b) $108,000, or (d) $117,000.

5. (d) Under LIFO, ending inventory will consist of 8,000 units from the inventory at Jan. 1 and 1,000 units from the June 19 purchase. Therefore, ending inventory is (8,000 × $11) + (1,000 × $12) = $100,000, not (a) $113,000, (b) $108,000, or (c) $99,000.

6. (d) Under the average-cost method, total cost of goods available for sale needs to be calculated in order to determine average cost per unit. The total cost of goods available is $430,000 = (5,000 × $8) + (15,000 × $10) + (20,000 × $12). The average cost per unit = ($430,000/40,000 total units available for sale) = $10.75. Therefore, ending inventory is ($10.75 × 7,000) = $75,250, not (a) $84,000, (b) $70,000, or (c) $56,000.

7. (c) In periods of rising prices, LIFO will produce lower net income than FIFO, not (a) higher than FIFO or (b) the same as FIFO. Choice (d) is incorrect because in periods of rising prices, LIFO will produce lower net income than average-cost. LIFO therefore charges the highest inventory cost against revenues in a period of rising prices.

8. (d) Perpetual vs. periodic inventory system is not one of the factors that affect the selection of an inventory costing method. The other choices are incorrect because (a) tax effects, (b) balance sheet effects, and (c) income statement effects all affect the selection of an inventory costing method.

9. (b) Because ending inventory is too low, cost of goods sold will be too high (overstated) and since cost of goods sold (an expense) is too high, net income will be too low (understated). Therefore, the other choices are incorrect.

10. (b) Stockholders' equity is overstated by $15,000 at December 31, 2016, and is properly stated at December 31, 2017. An ending inventory error in one period will have an equal and opposite effect on cost of goods sold and net income in the next period; after two years, the errors have offset each other. The other choices are incorrect because stockholders' equity (a) is properly stated, not understand, at December 31, 2017; (c) is overstated, not understated, by $15,000 at December 31, 2016, and is properly stated, not understated, at December 31, 2017; and (d) is properly stated at December 31, 2017, not overstated.

11. (d) Under the LCM basis, "market" is defined as the current replacement cost. Therefore, ending inventory would be valued at 200 widgets × $80 each = $16,000, not (a) $91,000, (b) $80,000, or (c) $18,200.

12. (b) Santana's days in inventory = 365/Inventory turnover = 365/[$285,000/($80,000 + $110,000)/2)] = 121.7 days, not (a) 73 days, (c) 102.5 days, or (d) 84.5 days.

13. (d) Decreasing the amount of inventory on hand will cause the denominator to decrease, causing inventory turnover to increase. Increasing sales will cause the numerator of the ratio to increase (higher sales means higher COGS), thus causing inventory turn-over to increase even more. The other choices are incorrect because (a) increasing the amount of inventory on hand causes the denominator of the ratio to increase while the numerator stays the same, causing inventory turnover to decrease; (b) keeping the amount of inventory on hand constant but increasing sales will cause inventory turnover to increase because the numerator of the ratio will increase (higher sales means higher COGS) while the denominator stays the same, which will result in a lesser inventory increase than decreasing amount of inventory on hand and increasing sales; and (c) keeping the amount of inventory on hand constant but decreasing sales will cause inventory turnover to decrease because the numerator of the ratio will decrease (lower sales means lower COGS) while the denominator stays the same.

*****14. (d)** FIFO cost of goods sold is the same under both a periodic and a perpetual inventory system. The other choices are incorrect because (a) LIFO cost of goods sold is not the same under a periodic and a perpetual inventory system; (b) average costs are based on a moving average of unit costs, not an average of unit costs; and (c) a new average is computed under the average-cost method after each purchase, not sale.

*****15. (b)** COGS = Sales ($150,000) − Gross profit ($150,000 × 30%) = $105,000. Ending inventory = Cost of goods available for sale ($135,000) − COGS ($105,000) = $30,000, not (a) $15,000, (c) $45,000, or (d) $75,000.

PRACTICE EXERCISES

1. Mika Sorbino, an auditor with Martinez CPAs, is performing a review of Sergei Company's inventory account. Sergei's did not have a good year and top management is under pressure to boost reported income. According to its records, the inventory balance at year-end was $650,000. However, the following information was not considered when determining that amount.

Determine the correct inventory amount.

(LO 1)

1. Included in the company's count were goods with a cost of $200,000 that the company is holding on consignment. The goods belong to Bosnia Corporation.

2. The physical count did not include goods purchased by Sergei with a cost of $40,000 that were shipped FOB shipping point on December 28 and did not arrive at Sergei's warehouse until January 3.

3. Included in the inventory account was $15,000 of office supplies that were stored in the warehouse and were to be used by the company's supervisors and managers during the coming year.

4. The company received an order on December 28 that was boxed and was sitting on the loading dock awaiting pick-up on December 31. The shipper picked up the goods on January 1 and delivered them on January 6. The shipping terms were FOB shipping point. The goods had a selling price of $40,000 and a cost of $30,000. The goods were not included in the count because they were sitting on the dock.

5. On December 29, Sergei shipped goods with a selling price of $80,000 and a cost of $60,000 to Oman Sales Corporation FOB shipping point. The goods arrived on January 3. Oman Sales had only ordered goods with a selling price of $10,000 and a cost of $8,000. However, a Sergei's sales manager had authorized the shipment and said that if Oman wanted to ship the goods back next week, it could.

6. Included in the count was $30,000 of goods that were parts for a machine that the company no longer made. Given the high-tech nature of Sergei's products, it was unlikely that these obsolete parts had any other use. However, management would prefer to keep them on the books at cost, "since that is what we paid for them, after all."

Instructions

Prepare a schedule to determine the correct inventory amount. Provide explanations for each item above, saying why you did or did not make an adjustment for each item.

Solution

1. Ending inventory—as reported	$650,000
1. Subtract from inventory: The goods belong to Bosnia Corporation. Sergei is merely holding them as a consignee.	(200,000)
2. Add to inventory: The goods belong to Sergei when they were shipped.	40,000
3. Subtract from inventory: Office supplies should be carried in a separate account. They are not considered inventory held for resale.	(15,000)
4. Add to inventory: The goods belong to Sergei until they are shipped (Jan. 1).	30,000
5. Add to inventory: Oman Sales ordered goods with a cost of $8,000. Sergei should record the corresponding sales revenue of $10,000. Sergei's decision to ship extra "unordered" goods does not constitute a sale. The manager's statement that Oman could ship the goods back indicates that Sergei knows this over-shipment is not a legitimate sale. The manager acted unethically in an attempt to improve Sergei's reported income by overshipping.	52,000
6. Subtract from inventory: GAAP require that inventory be valued at the lower-of-cost-or-market. Obsolete parts should be adjusted from cost to zero if they have no other use.	(30,000)
Correct inventory	$527,000

Determine effects of inventory errors.

(LO 3)

2. Abel's Hardware reported cost of goods sold as follows.

	2016	2017
Beginning inventory	$ 20,000	$ 30,000
Cost of goods purchased	150,000	175,000
Cost of goods available for sale	170,000	205,000
Ending inventory	(30,000)	(35,000)
Cost of goods sold	$140,000	$170,000

Abel's made two errors: (1) 2016 ending inventory was overstated $2,500, and (2) 2017 ending inventory was understated $5,500.

Instructions

Compute the correct cost of goods sold for each year.

Solution

2.

	2016	2017
Beginning inventory	$ 20,000	$ 27,500
Cost of goods purchased	150,000	175,000
Cost of goods available for sale	170,000	202,500
Corrected ending inventory	(27,500)[a]	(40,500)[b]
Coat of goods sold	$142,500	$162,000

[a]$30,000 − $2,500 = $27,500; [b]$35,000 + $5,500 = $40,500

PRACTICE PROBLEMS

1. Gerald D. Englehart Company has the following inventory, purchases, and sales data for the month of March.

Compute inventory and cost of goods sold using three cost flow methods in a periodic inventory system.

(LO 2)

Inventory:	March 1	200 units @ $4.00	$ 800
Purchases:	March 10	500 units @ $4.50	2,250
	March 20	400 units @ $4.75	1,900
	March 30	300 units @ $5.00	1,500
Sales:	March 15	500 units	
	March 25	400 units	

The physical inventory count on March 31 shows 500 units on hand.

Instructions

Under a **periodic inventory system**, determine the cost of inventory on hand at March 31 and the cost of goods sold for March under (a) FIFO, (b) LIFO, and (c) average-cost.

Solution

1. The cost of goods available for sale is $6,450, as follows.

Inventory:		200 units @ $4.00	$ 800
Purchases:	March 10	500 units @ $4.50	2,250
	March 20	400 units @ $4.75	1,900
	March 30	300 units @ $5.00	1,500
Total:		1,400	$6,450

Under a **periodic inventory system**, the cost of goods sold under each cost flow method is as follows.

(a)   **FIFO Method**

Ending inventory:

Date	Units	Unit Cost	Total Cost	
March 30	300	$5.00	$1,500	
March 20	200	4.75	950	$2,450

Cost of goods sold: $6,450 − $2,450 = $4,000

(b)   **LIFO Method**

Ending inventory:

Date	Units	Unit Cost	Total Cost	
March 1	200	$4.00	$ 800	
March 10	300	4.50	1,350	$2,150

Cost of goods sold: $6,450 − $2,150 = $4,300

(c)   **Average-Cost Method**

Average unit cost: $6,450 ÷ 1,400 = $4.607
Ending inventory: 500 × $4.607 = $2,303.50

Cost of goods sold: $6,450 − $2,303.50 = $4,146.50

*2. Practice Problem 1 showed cost of goods sold computations under a periodic inventory system. Now let's assume that Gerald D. Englehart Company uses a perpetual inventory system. The company has the same inventory, purchases, and sales data for the month of March as shown earlier:

Compute inventory and cost of goods sold using three cost flow methods in a perpetual inventory system.

(LO 5)

Inventory: March 1	200 units @ $4.00	$ 800
Purchases:		
March 10	500 units @ $4.50	2,250
March 20	400 units @ $4.75	1,900
March 30	300 units @ $5.00	1,500
Sales:		
March 15	500 units	
March 25	400 units	

The physical inventory count on March 31 shows 500 units on hand.

Instructions

Under a **perpetual inventory system**, determine the cost of inventory on hand at March 31 and the cost of goods sold for March under (a) FIFO, (b) LIFO, and (c) moving-average cost.

Solution

2. The cost of goods available for sale is $6,450, as follows.

Inventory:	200 units @ $4.00	$ 800
Purchases: March 10	500 units @ $4.50	2,250
March 20	400 units @ $4.75	1,900
March 30	300 units @ $5.00	1,500
Total:	1,400	$6,450

Under a **perpetual inventory system**, the cost of goods sold under each cost flow method is as follows.

(a)   **FIFO Method**

Date	Purchases	Cost of Goods Sold	Balance
March 1			(200 @ $4.00) $ 800
March 10	(500 @ $4.50) $2,250		(200 @ $4.00) (500 @ $4.50) } $3,050
March 15		(200 @ $4.00) (300 @ $4.50) $2,150	(200 @ $4.50) $ 900
March 20	(400 @ $4.75) $1,900		(200 @ $4.50) (400 @ $4.75) } $2,800
March 25		(200 @ $4.50) (200 @ $4.75) $1,850	(200 @ $4.75) $ 950
March 30	(300 @ $5.00) $1,500		(200 @ $4.75) (300 @ $5.00) } $2,450
Ending inventory $2,450		Cost of goods sold: $2,150 + $1,850 = $4,000	

(b)   **LIFO Method**

Date	Purchases	Cost of Goods Sold	Balance
March 1			(200 @ $4.00) $ 800
March 10	(500 @ $4.50) $2,250		(200 @ $4.00) (500 @ $4.50) } $3,050
March 15		(500 @ $4.50) $2,250	(200 @ $4.00) $ 800
March 20	(400 @ $4.75) $1,900		(200 @ $4.00) (400 @ $4.75) } $2,700
March 25		(400 @ $4.75) $1,900	(200 @ $4.00) $ 800
March 30	(300 @ $5.00) $1,500		(200 @ $4.00) (300 @ $5.00) } $2,300
Ending inventory $2,300		Cost of goods sold: $2,250 + $1,900 = $4,150	

(c)   **Moving-Average Cost Method**

Date	Purchases	Cost of Goods Sold	Balance
March 1			(200 @ $ 4.00) $ 800
March 10	(500 @ $4.50) $2,250		(700 @ $4.357) $3,050
March 15		(500 @ $4.357) $2,179	(200 @ $4.357) $ 871
March 20	(400 @ $4.75) $1,900		(600 @ $4.618) $2,771
March 25		(400 @ $4.618) $1,847	(200 @ $4.618) $ 924
March 30	(300 @ $5.00) $1,500		(500 @ $4.848) $2,424
Ending inventory $2,424		Cost of goods sold: $2,179 + $1,847 = $4,026	

WileyPLUS

Brief Exercises, Exercises, **DO IT!** Exercises, and Problems and many additional resources are available for practice in WileyPLUS

NOTE: All asterisked Questions, Exercises, and Problems relate to material in the appendices to the chapter.

QUESTIONS

1. "The key to successful business operations is effective inventory management." Do you agree? Explain.

2. An item must possess two characteristics to be classified as inventory by a merchandiser. What are these two characteristics?

3. Your friend Theo Dolan has been hired to help take the physical inventory in Silker Hardware Store. Explain to Theo Dolan what this job will entail.

4. (a) Rochelle Company ships merchandise to Jay Company on December 30. The merchandise reaches the buyer on January 6. Indicate the terms of sale that will result in the goods being included in (1) Rochelle's December 31 inventory, and (2) Jay's December 31 inventory.

    (b) Under what circumstances should Rochelle Company include consigned goods in its inventory?

5. Katz Hat Shop received a shipment of hats for which it paid the wholesaler $2,970. The price of the hats was $3,000, but Katz was given a $30 cash discount and required to pay freight charges of $50. In addition, Katz paid $130 to cover the travel expenses of an employee who negotiated the purchase of the hats. What amount will Katz record for inventory? Why?

6. Explain the difference between the terms FOB shipping point and FOB destination.

7. Kyle Ebert believes that the allocation of inventoriable costs should be based on the actual physical flow of the goods. Explain to Kyle why this may be both impractical and inappropriate.

8. What is a major advantage and a major disadvantage of the specific identification method of inventory costing?

9. "The selection of an inventory cost flow method is a decision made by accountants." Do you agree? Explain. Once a method has been selected, what accounting requirement applies?

10. Which assumed inventory cost flow method:
    (a) usually parallels the actual physical flow of merchandise?
    (b) assumes that goods available for sale during an accounting period are identical?
    (c) assumes that the latest units purchased are the first to be sold?

11. In a period of rising prices, the inventory reported in Gumby Company's balance sheet is close to the current cost of the inventory. Pokey Company's inventory is considerably below its current cost. Identify the inventory cost flow method being used by each company. Which company has probably been reporting the higher gross profit?

12. Davey Company has been using the FIFO cost flow method during a prolonged period of rising prices. During the same time period, Davey has been paying out all of its net income as dividends. What adverse effects may result from this policy?

13. Josh Kuchin is studying for the next accounting mid-term examination. What should Josh know about (a) departing from the cost basis of accounting for inventories and (b) the meaning of "market" in the lower-of-cost-or-market method?

14. Taylor Entertainment Center has 5 televisions on hand at the balance sheet date. Each costs $400. The current replacement cost is $380 per unit. Under the lower-of-cost-or-market basis of accounting for inventories, what value should be reported for the televisions on the balance sheet? Why?

15. Bonnie Stores has 20 toasters on hand at the balance sheet date. Each costs $27. The current replacement cost is $30 per unit. Under the lower-of-cost-or-market basis of accounting for inventories, what value should Bonnie report for the toasters on the balance sheet? Why?

16. Kuzu Company discovers in 2017 that its ending inventory at December 31, 2016, was $7,000 understated. What effect will this error have on (a) 2016 net income, (b) 2017 net income, and (c) the combined net income for the 2 years?

17. Ryder Company's balance sheet shows Inventory $162,800. What additional disclosures should be made?

18. Under what circumstances might inventory turnover be too high? That is, what possible negative consequences might occur?

19. What inventory cost flow does **Apple** use for its inventories? (*Hint:* You will need to examine the notes for Apple's financial statements.)

*20. "When perpetual inventory records are kept, the results under the FIFO and LIFO methods are the same as they would be in a periodic inventory system." Do you agree? Explain.

*21. How does the average-cost method of inventory costing differ between a perpetual inventory system and a periodic inventory system?

*22. When is it necessary to estimate inventories?

*23. Both the gross profit method and the retail inventory method are based on averages. For each method, indicate the average used, how it is determined, and how it is applied.

*24. Wiggins Company has net sales of $400,000 and cost of goods available for sale of $300,000. If the gross profit rate is 35%, what is the estimated cost of the ending inventory? Show computations.

*25. Emporia Shoe Shop had goods available for sale in 2017 with a retail price of $120,000. The cost of these goods was $84,000. If sales during the period were $80,000, what is the estimated cost of ending inventory using the retail inventory method?

BRIEF EXERCISES

Identify items to be included in taking a physical inventory.

(LO 1)

BE6-1 Farley Company identifies the following items for possible inclusion in the taking of a physical inventory. Indicate whether each item should be included or excluded from the inventory taking.

(a) Goods shipped on consignment by Farley to another company.
(b) Goods in transit from a supplier shipped FOB destination.
(c) Goods sold but being held for customer pickup.
(d) Goods held on consignment from another company.

Determine ending inventory amount.

(LO 1)

BE6-2 Stallman Company took a physical inventory on December 31 and determined that goods costing $200,000 were on hand. Not included in the physical count were $25,000 of goods purchased from Pelzer Corporation, FOB shipping point, and $22,000 of goods sold to Alvarez Company for $30,000, FOB destination. Both the Pelzer purchase and the Alvarez sale were in transit at year-end. What amount should Stallman report as its December 31 inventory?

Compute ending inventory using FIFO and LIFO.

(LO 2)

BE6-3 In its first month of operations, Bethke Company made three purchases of merchandise in the following sequence: (1) 300 units at $6, (2) 400 units at $7, and (3) 200 units at $8. Assuming there are 360 units on hand, compute the cost of the ending inventory under the (a) FIFO method and (b) LIFO method. Bethke uses a periodic inventory system.

Compute the ending inventory using average-cost.

(LO 2)

BE6-4 Data for Bethke Company are presented in BE6-3. Compute the cost of the ending inventory under the average-cost method, assuming there are 360 units on hand. (Round average cost per unit to nearest cent.)

Explain the financial statement effect of inventory cost flow assumptions.

(LO 2)

BE6-5 The management of Svetlana Corp. is considering the effects of inventory-costing methods on its financial statements and its income tax expense. Assuming that the price the company pays for inventory is increasing, which method will:

(a) Provide the highest net income?
(b) Provide the highest ending inventory?
(c) Result in the lowest income tax expense?
(d) Result in the most stable earnings over a number of years?

Determine correct income statement amounts.

(LO 3)

BE6-6 Pettit Company reports net income of $90,000 in 2017. However, ending inventory was understated $7,000. What is the correct net income for 2017? What effect, if any, will this error have on total assets as reported in the balance sheet at December 31, 2017?

Determine the LCM valuation using inventory categories.

(LO 4)

BE6-7 Central Appliance Center accumulates the following cost and market data at December 31.

Inventory Categories	Cost Data	Market Data
Cameras	$12,000	$12,100
Camcorders	9,500	9,700
Blu-ray players	14,000	12,800

Compute the lower-of-cost-or-market for the company's total inventory.

Compute inventory turnover and days in inventory.

(LO 4)

BE6-8 At December 31, 2017, the following information was available for A. Kamble Company: ending inventory $40,000, beginning inventory $60,000, cost of goods sold $270,000, and sales revenue $380,000. Calculate inventory turnover and days in inventory for A. Kamble Company.

Apply cost flow methods to perpetual inventory records.

(LO 5)

*BE6-9 Gregory Department Store uses a perpetual inventory system. Data for product E2-D2 include the following purchases.

Date	Number of Units	Unit Price
May 7	50	$10
July 28	30	13

On June 1, Gregory sold 26 units, and on August 27, 40 more units. Prepare the perpetual inventory schedule for the above transactions using (a) FIFO, (b) LIFO, and (c) moving-average cost. (Round average cost per unit to nearest cent.)

*BE6-10 At May 31, Suarez Company has net sales of $330,000 and cost of goods available for sale of $230,000. Compute the estimated cost of the ending inventory, assuming the gross profit rate is 35%.

Apply the gross profit method.
(LO 6)

*BE6-11 On June 30, Calico Fabrics has the following data pertaining to the retail inventory method. Goods available for sale: at cost $38,000; at retail $50,000; net sales $40,000; and ending inventory at retail $10,000. Compute the estimated cost of the ending inventory using the retail inventory method.

Apply the retail inventory method.
(LO 6)

DO IT! Exercises

DO IT! 6-1 Gomez Company just took its physical inventory. The count of inventory items on hand at the company's business locations resulted in a total inventory cost of $300,000. In reviewing the details of the count and related inventory transactions, you have discovered the following.

Apply rules of ownership to determine inventory cost.
(LO 1)

1. Gomez has sent inventory costing $26,000 on consignment to Kako Company. All of this inventory was at Kako's showrooms on December 31.
2. The company did not include in the count inventory (cost, $20,000) that was sold on December 28, terms FOB shipping point. The goods were in transit on December 31.
3. The company did not include in the count inventory (cost, $17,000) that was purchased with terms of FOB shipping point. The goods were in transit on December 31.

Compute the correct December 31 inventory.

DO IT! 6-2 The accounting records of Old Towne Electronics show the following data.

Beginning inventory	3,000 units at $5
Purchases	8,000 units at $7
Sales	9,400 units at $10

Compute cost of goods sold under different cost flow methods.
(LO 2)

Determine cost of goods sold during the period under a periodic inventory system using (a) the FIFO method, (b) the LIFO method, and (c) the average-cost method. (Round unit cost to nearest tenth of a cent.)

DO IT! 6-3 Janus Company understated its 2016 ending inventory by $31,000. Determine the impact this error has on ending inventory, cost of goods sold, and stockholders' equity in 2016 and 2017.

Determine effect of inventory error.
(LO 3)

DO IT! 6-4 (a) Moberg Company sells three different categories of tools (small, medium, and large). The cost and market value of its inventory of tools are as follows.

Compute inventory value under LCM and assess inventory level.
(LO 4)

	Cost	Market
Small	$ 64,000	$ 73,000
Medium	290,000	260,000
Large	152,000	171,000

Determine the value of the company's inventory under the lower-of-cost-or-market approach. (b) Early in 2017, Chien Company switched to a just-in-time inventory system. Its sales revenue, cost of goods sold, and inventory amounts for 2016 and 2017 are shown below.

	2016	2017
Sales revenue	$3,120,000	$3,713,000
Cost of goods sold	1,200,000	1,425,000
Beginning inventory	180,000	220,000
Ending inventory	220,000	100,000

Determine the inventory turnover and days in inventory for 2016 and 2017. Discuss the changes in the amount of inventory, the inventory turnover and days in inventory, and the amount of sales revenue across the two years.

Determine the correct inventory amount.

(LO 1)

E6-1 Tri-State Bank and Trust is considering giving Josef Company a loan. Before doing so, management decides that further discussions with Josef's accountant may be desirable. One area of particular concern is the inventory account, which has a year-end balance of $297,000. Discussions with the accountant reveal the following.

1. Josef sold goods costing $38,000 to Sorci Company, FOB shipping point, on December 28. The goods are not expected to arrive at Sorci until January 12. The goods were not included in the physical inventory because they were not in the warehouse.
2. The physical count of the inventory did not include goods costing $95,000 that were shipped to Josef FOB destination on December 27 and were still in transit at year-end.
3. Josef received goods costing $22,000 on January 2. The goods were shipped FOB shipping point on December 26 by Solita Co. The goods were not included in the physical count.
4. Josef sold goods costing $35,000 to Natali Co., FOB destination, on December 30. The goods were received at Natali on January 8. They were not included in Josef's physical inventory.
5. Josef received goods costing $44,000 on January 2 that were shipped FOB destination on December 29. The shipment was a rush order that was supposed to arrive December 31. This purchase was included in the ending inventory of $297,000.

Instructions

Determine the correct inventory amount on December 31.

Determine the correct inventory amount.

(LO 1)

E6-2 Rachel Warren, an auditor with Laplante CPAs, is performing a review of Schuda Company's inventory account. Schuda did not have a good year, and top management is under pressure to boost reported income. According to its records, the inventory balance at year-end was $740,000. However, the following information was not considered when determining that amount.

1. Included in the company's count were goods with a cost of $250,000 that the company is holding on consignment. The goods belong to Harmon Corporation.
2. The physical count did not include goods purchased by Schuda with a cost of $40,000 that were shipped FOB destination on December 28 and did not arrive at Schuda's warehouse until January 3.
3. Included in the inventory account was $14,000 of office supplies that were stored in the warehouse and were to be used by the company's supervisors and managers during the coming year.
4. The company received an order on December 29 that was boxed and sitting on the loading dock awaiting pick-up on December 31. The shipper picked up the goods on January 1 and delivered them on January 6. The shipping terms were FOB shipping point. The goods had a selling price of $40,000 and a cost of $28,000. The goods were not included in the count because they were sitting on the dock.
5. On December 29, Schuda shipped goods with a selling price of $80,000 and a cost of $60,000 to Reza Sales Corporation FOB shipping point. The goods arrived on January 3. Reza had only ordered goods with a selling price of $10,000 and a cost of $8,000. However, a sales manager at Schuda had authorized the shipment and said that if Reza wanted to ship the goods back next week, it could.
6. Included in the count was $40,000 of goods that were parts for a machine that the company no longer made. Given the high-tech nature of Schuda's products, it was unlikely that these obsolete parts had any other use. However, management would prefer to keep them on the books at cost, "since that is what we paid for them, after all."

Instructions

Prepare a schedule to determine the correct inventory amount. Provide explanations for each item above, saying why you did or did not make an adjustment for each item.

Calculate cost of goods sold using specific identification and FIFO.

(LO 2)

E6-3 On December 1, Marzion Electronics Ltd. has three DVD players left in stock. All are identical, all are priced to sell at $150. One of the three DVD players left in stock, with serial #1012, was purchased on June 1 at a cost of $100. Another, with serial #1045, was purchased on November 1 for $90. The last player, serial #1056, was purchased on November 30 for $80.

Instructions

(a) Calculate the cost of goods sold using the FIFO periodic inventory method assuming that two of the three players were sold by the end of December, Marzion Electronics' year-end.

(b) If Marzion Electronics used the specific identification method instead of the FIFO method, how might it alter its earnings by "selectively choosing" which particular players to sell to the two customers? What would Marzion's cost of goods sold be if the company wished to minimize earnings? Maximize earnings?

(c) Which of the two inventory methods do you recommend that Marzion use? Explain why.

E6-4 Linda's Boards sells a snowboard, Xpert, that is popular with snowboard enthusiasts. Information relating to Linda's purchases of Xpert snowboards during September is shown below. During the same month, 121 Xpert snowboards were sold. Linda's uses a periodic inventory system.

Compute inventory and cost of goods sold using FIFO and LIFO.

(LO 2)

Date	Explanation	Units	Unit Cost	Total Cost
Sept. 1	Inventory	26	$ 97	$ 2,522
Sept. 12	Purchases	45	102	4,590
Sept. 19	Purchases	20	104	2,080
Sept. 26	Purchases	50	105	5,250
	Totals	141		$14,442

Instructions

(a) Compute the ending inventory at September 30 and cost of goods sold using the FIFO and LIFO methods. Prove the amount allocated to cost of goods sold under each method.

(b) For both FIFO and LIFO, calculate the sum of ending inventory and cost of goods sold. What do you notice about the answers you found for each method?

E6-5 Xiong Co. uses a periodic inventory system. Its records show the following for the month of May, in which 65 units were sold.

Compute inventory and cost of goods sold using FIFO and LIFO.

(LO 2)

		Units	Unit Cost	Total Cost
May 1	Inventory	30	$ 8	$240
15	Purchases	25	11	275
24	Purchases	35	12	420
	Totals	90		$935

Instructions

Compute the ending inventory at May 31 and cost of goods sold using the FIFO and LIFO methods. Prove the amount allocated to cost of goods sold under each method.

E6-6 Kaleta Company reports the following for the month of June.

Compute inventory and cost of goods sold using FIFO and LIFO.

(LO 2)

		Units	Unit Cost	Total Cost
June 1	Inventory	200	$5	$1,000
12	Purchase	400	6	2,400
23	Purchase	300	7	2,100
30	Inventory	100		

Instructions

(a) Compute the cost of the ending inventory and the cost of goods sold under (1) FIFO and (2) LIFO.

(b) Which costing method gives the higher ending inventory? Why?

(c) Which method results in the higher cost of goods sold? Why?

E6-7 Lisa Company had 100 units in beginning inventory at a total cost of $10,000. The company purchased 200 units at a total cost of $26,000. At the end of the year, Lisa had 80 units in ending inventory.

Compute inventory under FIFO, LIFO, and average-cost.

(LO 2)

Instructions

(a) Compute the cost of the ending inventory and the cost of goods sold under (1) FIFO, (2) LIFO, and (3) average-cost.

(b) Which cost flow method would result in the highest net income?

(c) Which cost flow method would result in inventories approximating current cost in the balance sheet?

(d) Which cost flow method would result in Lisa paying the least taxes in the first year?

Compute inventory and cost of goods sold using average-cost.

(LO 2)

E6-8 Inventory data for Kaleta Company are presented in E6-6.

Instructions

(a) Compute the cost of the ending inventory and the cost of goods sold using the average-cost method. (Round average cost per unit to nearest cent.)

(b) Will the results in (a) be higher or lower than the results under (1) FIFO and (2) LIFO?

(c) Why is the average unit cost not $6?

Determine effects of inventory errors.

(LO 3)

E6-9 Hamid's Hardware reported cost of goods sold as follows.

	2016	2017
Beginning inventory	$ 20,000	$ 30,000
Cost of goods purchased	150,000	175,000
Cost of goods available for sale	170,000	205,000
Ending inventory	30,000	35,000
Cost of goods sold	$140,000	$170,000

Hamid's made two errors: (1) 2016 ending inventory was overstated $3,000, and (2) 2017 ending inventory was understated $6,000.

Instructions

Compute the correct cost of goods sold for each year.

Prepare correct income statements.

(LO 3)

E6-10 Rulix Watch Company reported the following income statement data for a 2-year period.

	2016	2017
Sales revenue	$220,000	$250,000
Cost of goods sold		
Beginning inventory	32,000	44,000
Cost of goods purchased	173,000	202,000
Cost of goods available for sale	205,000	246,000
Ending inventory	44,000	52,000
Cost of goods sold	161,000	194,000
Gross profit	$ 59,000	$ 56,000

Rulix uses a periodic inventory system. The inventories at January 1, 2016, and December 31, 2017, are correct. However, the ending inventory at December 31, 2016, was overstated $6,000.

Instructions

(a) Prepare correct income statement data for the 2 years.

(b) What is the cumulative effect of the inventory error on total gross profit for the 2 years?

(c) ✏ Explain in a letter to the president of Rulix Watch Company what has happened, i.e., the nature of the error and its effect on the financial statements.

Determine ending inventory under LCM.

(LO 4)

E6-11 Optix Camera Shop uses the lower-of-cost-or-market basis for its inventory. The following data are available at December 31.

Item	Units	Unit Cost	Market
Cameras:			
Minolta	5	$170	$156
Canon	6	150	152
Light meters:			
Vivitar	12	125	115
Kodak	14	120	135

Instructions
Determine the amount of the ending inventory by applying the lower-of-cost-or-market basis.

E6-12 Serebin Company applied FIFO to its inventory and got the following results for its ending inventory.

Cameras	100 units at a cost per unit of $65
Blu-rays players	150 units at a cost per unit of $75
iPods	125 units at a cost per unit of $80

The cost of purchasing units at year-end was cameras $71, Blu-ray players $67, and iPods $78.

Compute lower-of-cost-or-market.

(LO 4)

Instructions
Determine the amount of ending inventory at lower-of-cost-or-market.

E6-13 This information is available for Quick's Photo Corporation for 2015, 2016, and 2017.

	2015	2016	2017
Beginning inventory	$ 100,000	$ 300,000	$ 400,000
Ending inventory	300,000	400,000	480,000
Cost of goods sold	900,000	1,120,000	1,300,000
Sales revenue	1,200,000	1,600,000	1,900,000

Compute inventory turnover, days in inventory, and gross profit rate.

(LO 4)

Instructions
Calculate inventory turnover, days in inventory, and gross profit rate (from Chapter 5) for Quick's Photo Corporation for 2015, 2016, and 2017. Comment on any trends.

E6-14 The cost of goods sold computations for Alpha Company and Omega Company are shown below.

Compute inventory turnover and days in inventory.

(LO 4)

	Alpha Company	Omega Company
Beginning inventory	$ 45,000	$ 71,000
Cost of goods purchased	200,000	290,000
Cost of goods available for sale	245,000	361,000
Ending inventory	55,000	69,000
Cost of goods sold	$190,000	$292,000

Instructions
(a) Compute inventory turnover and days in inventory for each company.
(b) Which company moves its inventory more quickly?

*****E6-15** Bufford Appliance uses a perpetual inventory system. For its flat-screen television sets, the January 1 inventory was 3 sets at $600 each. On January 10, Bufford purchased 6 units at $660 each. The company sold 2 units on January 8 and 4 units on January 15.

Apply cost flow methods to perpetual records.

(LO 5)

Instructions
Compute the ending inventory under (a) FIFO, (b) LIFO, and (c) moving-average cost. (Round average cost per unit to nearest cent.)

*****E6-16** Kaleta Company reports the following for the month of June.

Calculate inventory and cost of goods sold using three cost flow methods in a perpetual inventory system.

(LO 5)

Date	Explanation	Units	Unit Cost	Total Cost
June 1	Inventory	200	$5	$1,000
12	Purchase	400	6	2,400
23	Purchase	300	7	2,100
30	Inventory	100		

Instructions
(a) Calculate the cost of the ending inventory and the cost of goods sold for each cost flow assumption, using a perpetual inventory system. Assume a sale of 440 units occurred on June 15 for a selling price of $8 and a sale of 360 units on June 27 for $9. (Round average cost per unit to 3 decimal places.)

(b) How do the results differ from E6-6 and E6-8?

(c) Why is the average unit cost not $6 [($5 + $6 + $7) ÷ 3 = $6]?

Apply cost flow methods to perpetual records.

(LO 5)

*E6-17 Information about Linda's Boards is presented in E6-4. Additional data regarding Linda's sales of Xpert snowboards are provided below. Assume that Linda's uses a perpetual inventory system.

Date		Units	Unit Price	Total Revenue
Sept. 5	Sale	12	$199	$ 2,388
Sept. 16	Sale	50	199	9,950
Sept. 29	Sale	59	209	12,331
	Totals	121		$24,669

Instructions

(a) Compute ending inventory at September 30 using FIFO, LIFO, and moving-average cost. (Round average cost per unit to nearest cent.)

(b) Compare ending inventory using a perpetual inventory system to ending inventory using a periodic inventory system (from E6-4).

(c) Which inventory cost flow method (FIFO, LIFO) gives the same ending inventory value under both periodic and perpetual? Which method gives different ending inventory values?

Use the gross profit method to estimate inventory.

(LO 6)

*E6-18 Brenda Company reported the following information for November and December 2017.

	November	December
Cost of goods purchased	$536,000	$ 610,000
Inventory, beginning-of-month	130,000	120,000
Inventory, end-of-month	120,000	?
Sales revenue	840,000	1,000,000

Brenda's ending inventory at December 31 was destroyed in a fire.

Instructions

(a) Compute the gross profit rate for November.

(b) Using the gross profit rate for November, determine the estimated cost of inventory lost in the fire.

Determine merchandise lost using the gross profit method of estimating inventory.

(LO 6)

*E6-19 The inventory of Hauser Company was destroyed by fire on March 1. From an examination of the accounting records, the following data for the first 2 months of the year are obtained: Sales Revenue $51,000, Sales Returns and Allowances $1,000, Purchases $31,200, Freight-In $1,200, and Purchase Returns and Allowances $1,400.

Instructions

Determine the merchandise lost by fire, assuming:

(a) A beginning inventory of $20,000 and a gross profit rate of 40% on net sales.

(b) A beginning inventory of $30,000 and a gross profit rate of 30% on net sales.

Determine ending inventory at cost using retail method.

(LO 6)

*E6-20 Gepetto Shoe Store uses the retail inventory method for its two departments, Women's Shoes and Men's Shoes. The following information for each department is obtained.

Item	Women's Shoes	Men's Shoes
Beginning inventory at cost	$ 25,000	$ 45,000
Cost of goods purchased at cost	110,000	136,300
Net sales	178,000	185,000
Beginning inventory at retail	46,000	60,000
Cost of goods purchased at retail	179,000	185,000

Instructions

Compute the estimated cost of the ending inventory for each department under the retail inventory method.

EXERCISES: SET B AND CHALLENGE EXERCISES

Visit the book's companion website, at **www.wiley.com/college/weygandt**, and choose the Student Companion site to access Exercises: Set B and Challenge Exercises.

PROBLEMS: SET A

P6-1A Austin Limited is trying to determine the value of its ending inventory as of February 28, 2017, the company's year-end. The following transactions occurred, and the accountant asked your help in determining whether they should be recorded or not.

Determine items and amounts to be recorded in inventory.

(LO 1)

(a) On February 26, Austin shipped goods costing $800 to a customer and charged the customer $1,000. The goods were shipped with terms FOB shipping point and the receiving report indicates that the customer received the goods on March 2.

(b) On February 26, Louis Inc. shipped goods to Austin under terms FOB shipping point. The invoice price was $450 plus $30 for freight. The receiving report indicates that the goods were received by Austin on March 2.

(c) Austin had $650 of inventory isolated in the warehouse. The inventory is designated for a customer who has requested that the goods be shipped on March 10.

(d) Also included in Austin's warehouse is $700 of inventory that Ryhn Producers shipped to Austin on consignment.

(e) On February 26, Austin issued a purchase order to acquire goods costing $900. The goods were shipped with terms FOB destination on February 27. Austin received the goods on March 2.

(f) On February 26, Austin shipped goods to a customer under terms FOB destination. The invoice price was $350; the cost of the items was $200. The receiving report indicates that the goods were received by the customer on March 2.

Instructions
For each of the preceding transactions, specify whether the item in question should be included in ending inventory, and if so, at what amount.

P6-2A Express Distribution markets CDs of the performing artist Fishe. At the beginning of October, Express had in beginning inventory 2,000 of Fishe's CDs with a unit cost of $7. During October, Express made the following purchases of Fishe's CDs.

Determine cost of goods sold and ending inventory using FIFO, LIFO, and average-cost with analysis.

(LO 2)

Oct. 3 2,500 @ $8	Oct. 19 3,000 @ $10
Oct. 9 3,500 @ $9	Oct. 25 4,000 @ $11

During October, 10,900 units were sold. Express uses a periodic inventory system.

Instructions
(a) Determine the cost of goods available for sale.
(b) Determine (1) the ending inventory and (2) the cost of goods sold under each of the assumed cost flow methods (FIFO, LIFO, and average-cost). Prove the accuracy of the cost of goods sold under the FIFO and LIFO methods.
(c) Which cost flow method results in (1) the highest inventory amount for the balance sheet and (2) the highest cost of goods sold for the income statement?

(b) (2) Cost of goods sold:
FIFO $ 94,500
LIFO $108,700
Average $101,370

P6-3A Ziad Company had a beginning inventory on January 1 of 150 units of Product 4-18-15 at a cost of $20 per unit. During the year, the following purchases were made.

Determine cost of goods sold and ending inventory using FIFO, LIFO, and average-cost with analysis.

(LO 2)

Mar. 15 400 units at $23	Sept. 4 350 units at $26
July 20 250 units at $24	Dec. 2 100 units at $29

1,000 units were sold. Ziad Company uses a periodic inventory system.

Instructions
(a) Determine the cost of goods available for sale.
(b) Determine (1) the ending inventory, and (2) the cost of goods sold under each of the assumed cost flow methods (FIFO, LIFO, and average-cost). Prove the accuracy of the cost of goods sold under the FIFO and LIFO methods.
(c) Which cost flow method results in (1) the highest inventory amount for the balance sheet, and (2) the highest cost of goods sold for the income statement?

(b) (2) Cost of goods sold:
FIFO $23,400
LIFO $24,900
Average $24,160

*Compute ending inventory,
prepare income statements,
and answer questions using
FIFO and LIFO.*

(LO 2)

P6-4A The management of Felipe Inc. is reevaluating the appropriateness of using its present inventory cost flow method, which is average-cost. The company requests your help in determining the results of operations for 2017 if either the FIFO or the LIFO method had been used. For 2017, the accounting records show these data:

Inventories		Purchases and Sales	
Beginning (7,000 units)	$14,000	Total net sales (180,000 units)	$747,000
Ending (17,000 units)		Total cost of goods purchased (190,000 units)	466,000

Purchases were made quarterly as follows.

Quarter	Units	Unit Cost	Total Cost
1	50,000	$2.20	$110,000
2	40,000	2.35	94,000
3	40,000	2.50	100,000
4	60,000	2.70	162,000
	190,000		$466,000

Operating expenses were $130,000, and the company's income tax rate is 40%.

Instructions

(a) Gross profit:
FIFO $312,900
LIFO $303,000

(a) Prepare comparative condensed income statements for 2017 under FIFO and LIFO. (Show computations of ending inventory.)

(b) ——— Answer the following questions for management.

(1) Which cost flow method (FIFO or LIFO) produces the more meaningful inventory amount for the balance sheet? Why?

(2) Which cost flow method (FIFO or LIFO) produces the more meaningful net income? Why?

(3) Which cost flow method (FIFO or LIFO) is more likely to approximate the actual physical flow of goods? Why?

(4) How much more cash will be available for management under LIFO than under FIFO? Why?

(5) Will gross profit under the average-cost method be higher or lower than FIFO? Than LIFO? (*Note:* It is not necessary to quantify your answer.)

*Calculate ending inventory,
cost of goods sold, gross
profit, and gross profit rate
under periodic method;
compare results.*

(LO 2)

P6-5A You are provided with the following information for Najera Inc. for the month ended June 30, 2017. Najera uses the periodic method for inventory.

Date	Description	Quantity	Unit Cost or Selling Price
June 1	Beginning inventory	40	$40
June 4	Purchase	135	44
June 10	Sale	110	70
June 11	Sale return	15	70
June 18	Purchase	55	46
June 18	Purchase return	10	46
June 25	Sale	65	75
June 28	Purchase	30	50

Instructions

(a) (iii) Gross profit:
LIFO $4,215
FIFO $4,645
Average $4,414.60

(a) Calculate (i) ending inventory, (ii) cost of goods sold, (iii) gross profit, and (iv) gross profit rate under each of the following methods.

(1) LIFO.   (2) FIFO.   (3) Average-cost.

(b) Compare results for the three cost flow assumptions.

*Compare specific
identification, FIFO, and
LIFO under periodic method;
use cost flow assumption to
justify price increase.*

(LO 2)

P6-6A You are provided with the following information for Barton Inc. Barton Inc. uses the periodic method of accounting for its inventory transactions.

March 1	Beginning inventory 2,000 liters at a cost of 60¢ per liter.
March 3	Purchased 2,500 liters at a cost of 65¢ per liter.
March 5	Sold 2,300 liters for $1.05 per liter.
March 10	Purchased 4,000 liters at a cost of 72¢ per liter.
March 20	Purchased 2,500 liters at a cost of 80¢ per liter.
March 30	Sold 5,200 liters for $1.25 per liter.

Instructions

(a) Prepare partial income statements through gross profit, and calculate the value of ending inventory that would be reported on the balance sheet, under each of the following cost flow assumptions. (Round ending inventory and cost of goods sold to the nearest dollar.)

    (1) Specific identification method assuming:

        (i) The March 5 sale consisted of 1,000 liters from the March 1 beginning inventory and 1,300 liters from the March 3 purchase; and

        (ii) The March 30 sale consisted of the following number of units sold from beginning inventory and each purchase: 450 liters from March 1; 550 liters from March 3; 2,900 liters from March 10; and 1,300 liters from March 20.

    (2) FIFO.

    (3) LIFO.

(b) How can companies use a cost flow method to justify price increases? Which cost flow method would best support an argument to increase prices?

(a) Gross profit:
(1) Specific identification
$3,715

(2) FIFO $3,930
(3) LIFO $3,385

P6-7A The management of Sherlynn Co. asks your help in determining the comparative effects of the FIFO and LIFO inventory cost flow methods. For 2017, the accounting records provide the following data.

Compute ending inventory, prepare income statements, and answer questions using FIFO and LIFO.

(LO 2)

Inventory, January 1 (10,000 units)	$ 45,000
Cost of 100,000 units purchased	532,000
Selling price of 80,000 units sold	700,000
Operating expenses	140,000

Units purchased consisted of 35,000 units at $5.10 on May 10; 35,000 units at $5.30 on August 15; and 30,000 units at $5.60 on November 20. Income taxes are 30%.

Instructions

(a) Prepare comparative condensed income statements for 2017 under FIFO and LIFO. (Show computations of ending inventory.)

(b) ————— Answer the following questions for management.

    (1) Which inventory cost flow method produces the most meaningful inventory amount for the balance sheet? Why?

    (2) Which inventory cost flow method produces the most meaningful net income? Why?

    (3) Which inventory cost flow method is most likely to approximate actual physical flow of the goods? Why?

    (4) How much additional cash will be available for management under LIFO than under FIFO? Why?

    (5) How much of the gross profit under FIFO is illusory in comparison with the gross profit under LIFO?

(a) Net income:
FIFO $105,700
LIFO $91,000

*P6-8A Mercer Inc. is a retailer operating in British Columbia. Mercer uses the perpetual inventory method. All sales returns from customers result in the goods being returned to inventory; the inventory is not damaged. Assume that there are no credit transactions; all amounts are settled in cash. You are provided with the following information for Mercer Inc. for the month of January 2017.

Calculate cost of goods sold and ending inventory under LIFO, FIFO, and moving-average cost under the perpetual system; compare gross profit under each assumption.

(LO 5)

Date	Description	Quantity	Unit Cost or Selling Price
January 1	Beginning inventory	100	$15
January 5	Purchase	140	18
January 8	Sale	110	28
January 10	Sale return	10	28
January 15	Purchase	55	20
January 16	Purchase return	5	20
January 20	Sale	90	32
January 25	Purchase	20	22

(a) (iii) Gross profit:

LIFO	$2,160
FIFO	$2,560
Average	$2,421

Instructions

(a) For each of the following cost flow assumptions, calculate (i) cost of goods sold, (ii) ending inventory, and (iii) gross profit.
  (1) LIFO.
  (2) FIFO.
  (3) Moving-average cost. (Round average cost per unit to 3 decimal places.)
(b) Compare results for the three cost flow assumptions.

Determine ending inventory under a perpetual inventory system.

(LO 5)

*P6-9A Terando Co. began operations on July 1. It uses a perpetual inventory system. During July, the company had the following purchases and sales.

Date	Purchases Units	Unit Cost	Sales Units
July 1	5	$120	
July 6			4
July 11	7	$136	
July 14			3
July 21	8	$147	
July 27			6

Instructions

(a) Ending inventory:

FIFO	$1,029
Average	$994
LIFO	$958

(a) Determine the ending inventory under a perpetual inventory system using (1) FIFO, (2) moving-average cost, and (3) LIFO.
(b) Which costing method produces the highest ending inventory valuation?

Compute gross profit rate and inventory loss using gross profit method.

(LO 6)

*P6-10A Suzuki Company lost all of its inventory in a fire on December 26, 2017. The accounting records showed the following gross profit data for November and December.

	November	December (to 12/26)
Net sales	$600,000	$700,000
Beginning inventory	32,000	36,000
Purchases	389,000	420,000
Purchase returns and allowances	13,300	14,900
Purchase discounts	8,500	9,500
Freight-in	8,800	9,900
Ending inventory	36,000	?

Suzuki is fully insured for fire losses but must prepare a report for the insurance company.

Instructions

(a) Gross profit rate 38%

(a) Compute the gross profit rate for November.
(b) Using the gross profit rate for November, determine the estimated cost of the inventory lost in the fire.

Compute ending inventory using retail method.

(LO 6)

*P6-11A Dixon Books uses the retail inventory method to estimate its monthly ending inventories. The following information is available for two of its departments at October 31, 2017.

	Hardcovers Cost	Hardcovers Retail	Paperbacks Cost	Paperbacks Retail
Beginning inventory	$ 420,000	$ 700,000	$ 280,000	$ 360,000
Purchases	2,135,000	3,200,000	1,155,000	1,540,000
Freight-in	24,000		12,000	
Purchase discounts	44,000		22,000	
Net sales		3,100,000		1,570,000

At December 31, Dixon Books takes a physical inventory at retail. The actual retail values of the inventories in each department are Hardcovers $790,000 and Paperbacks $335,000.

Instructions

(a) Hardcovers: end. inv. $520,000

(a) Determine the estimated cost of the ending inventory for each department at **October 31**, 2017, using the retail inventory method.
(b) Compute the ending inventory at cost for each department at **December 31**, assuming the cost-to-retail ratios for the year are 65% for Hardcovers and 75% for Paperbacks.

PROBLEMS: SET B AND SET C

Visit the book's companion website, at **www.wiley.com/college/weygandt**, and choose the Student Companion site to access Problems: Set B and Set C.

COMPREHENSIVE PROBLEM

CP6 On December 1, 2017, Matthias Company had the account balances shown below.

	Debit		Credit
Cash	$ 4,800	Accumulated Depreciation—Equipment	$ 1,500
Accounts Receivable	3,900	Accounts Payable	3,000
Inventory	1,800*	Common Stock	20,000
Equipment	21,000	Retained Earnings	7,000
	$31,500		$31,500

*(3,000 × $0.60)

The following transactions occurred during December.

Dec. 3 Purchased 4,000 units of inventory on account at a cost of $0.72 per unit.
    5 Sold 4,400 units of inventory on account for $0.90 per unit. (It sold 3,000 of the $0.60 units and 1,400 of the $0.72.)
    7 Granted the December 5 customer $180 credit for 200 units of inventory returned costing $120. These units were returned to inventory.
    17 Purchased 2,200 units of inventory for cash at $0.80 each.
    22 Sold 2,000 units of inventory on account for $0.95 per unit. (It sold 2,000 of the $0.72 units.)

Adjustment data:

1. Accrued salaries payable $400.
2. Depreciation $200 per month.

Instructions

(a) Journalize the December transactions and adjusting entries, assuming Matthias uses the perpetual inventory method.
(b) Enter the December 1 balances in the ledger T-accounts and post the December transactions. In addition to the accounts mentioned above, use the following additional accounts: Cost of Goods Sold, Depreciation Expense, Salaries and Wages Expense, Salaries and Wages Payable, Sales Revenue, and Sales Returns and Allowances.
(c) Prepare an adjusted trial balance as of December 31, 2017.
(d) Prepare an income statement for December 2017 and a classified balance sheet at December 31, 2017.
(e) Compute ending inventory and cost of goods sold under FIFO, assuming Matthias Company uses the periodic inventory system.
(f) Compute ending inventory and cost of goods sold under LIFO, assuming Matthias Company uses the periodic inventory system.

CONTINUING PROBLEM

COOKIE CREATIONS

(*Note:* This is a continuation of the Cookie Creations problem from Chapters 1 through 5.)

CC6 Natalie is busy establishing both divisions of her business (cookie classes and mixer sales) and completing her business degree. Her goals for the next 11 months are to sell one mixer per month and to give two to three classes per week.

The cost of the fine European mixers is expected to increase. Natalie has just negotiated new terms with Kzinski that include shipping costs in the negotiated purchase price (mixers will be shipped FOB destination). Natalie must choose a cost flow assumption for her mixer inventory.

Go to the book's companion website, **www.wiley.com/college/weygandt**, *to see the completion of this problem.*

© leungchopan/
Shutterstock

FINANCIAL REPORTING AND ANALYSIS

Financial Reporting Problem: Apple Inc.

BYP6-1 The notes that accompany a company's financial statements provide informative details that would clutter the amounts and descriptions presented in the statements. Refer to the financial statements of Apple Inc. in Appendix A as well as its annual report. Instructions for accessing and using the company's complete annual report, including the notes to the financial statements, are also provided in Appendix A.

Instructions

Answer the following questions. Complete the requirements in millions of dollars, as shown in Apple's annual report.

(a) What did Apple report for the amount of inventories in its consolidated balance sheet at September 29, 2012? At September 28, 2013?

(b) Compute the dollar amount of change and the percentage change in inventories between 2012 and 2013. Compute inventory as a percentage of current assets at September 28, 2013.

(c) How does Apple value its inventories? Which inventory cost flow method does Apple use? (See Notes to the Financial Statements.)

(d) What is the cost of sales (cost of goods sold) reported by Apple for 2013, 2012, and 2011? Compute the percentage of cost of sales to net sales in 2013.

Comparative Analysis Problem:
PepsiCo, Inc. vs. The Coca-Cola Company

BYP6-2 PepsiCo's financial statements are presented in Appendix B. Financial statements of The Coca-Cola Company are presented in Appendix C. Instructions for accessing and using the complete annual reports of PepsiCo and Coca-Cola, including the notes to the financial statements, are also provided in Appendices B and C, respectively.

Instructions

(a) Based on the information contained in these financial statements, compute the following 2013 ratios for each company.

(1) Inventory turnover.

(2) Days in inventory.

(b) What conclusions concerning the management of the inventory can you draw from these data?

Comparative Analysis Problem:
Amazon.com, Inc. vs. Wal-Mart Stores, Inc.

BYP6-3 Amazon.com, Inc.'s financial statements are presented in Appendix D. Financial statements of Wal-Mart Stores, Inc. are presented in Appendix E. Instructions for accessing and using the complete annual reports of Amazon and Wal-Mart, including the notes to the financial statements, are also provided in Appendices D and E, respectively.

Instructions

(a) Based on the information contained in these financial statements, compute the following 2013 ratios for each company.

(1) Inventory turnover.

(2) Days in inventory.

(b) What conclusions concerning the management of the inventory can you draw from these data?

Real-World Focus

BYP6-4 A company's annual report usually will identify the inventory method used. Knowing that, you can analyze the effects of the inventory method on the income statement and balance sheet.

Address: **www.cisco.com**, or go to **www.wiley.com/college/weygandt**

Instructions

Answer the following questions based on the current year's annual report on Cisco's website.

(a) At Cisco's fiscal year-end, what was the inventory on the balance sheet?

(b) How has this changed from the previous fiscal year-end?

(c) How much of the inventory was finished goods?
(d) What inventory method does Cisco use?

CRITICAL THINKING

Decision-Making Across the Organization

BYP6-5 On April 10, 2017, fire damaged the office and warehouse of Corvet Company. Most of the accounting records were destroyed, but the following account balances were determined as of March 31, 2017: Inventory (January 1, 2017), $80,000; Sales Revenue (January 1–March 31, 2017), $180,000; Purchases (January 1–March 31, 2017), $94,000.

The company's fiscal year ends on December 31. It uses a periodic inventory system.

From an analysis of the April bank statement, you discover cancelled checks of $4,200 for cash purchases during the period April 1–10. Deposits during the same period totaled $18,500. Of that amount, 60% were collections on accounts receivable, and the balance was cash sales.

Correspondence with the company's principal suppliers revealed $12,400 of purchases on account from April 1 to April 10. Of that amount, $1,600 was for merchandise in transit on April 10 that was shipped FOB destination.

Correspondence with the company's principal customers produced acknowledgments of credit sales totaling $37,000 from April 1 to April 10. It was estimated that $5,600 of credit sales will never be acknowledged or recovered from customers.

Corvet Company reached an agreement with the insurance company that its fire-loss claim should be based on the average of the gross profit rates for the preceding 2 years. The financial statements for 2015 and 2016 showed the following data.

	2016	**2015**
Net sales	$600,000	$480,000
Cost of goods purchased	404,000	356,000
Beginning inventory	60,000	40,000
Ending inventory	80,000	60,000

Inventory with a cost of $17,000 was salvaged from the fire.

Instructions
With the class divided into groups, answer the following.

(a) Determine the balances in (1) Sales Revenue and (2) Purchases at April 10.
*(b) Determine the average gross profit rate for the years 2015 and 2016. (*Hint:* Find the gross profit rate for each year and divide the sum by 2.)
*(c) Determine the inventory loss as a result of the fire, using the gross profit method.

Communication Activity

BYP6-6 You are the controller of Small Toys Inc. Marta Johns, the president, recently mentioned to you that she found an error in the 2016 financial statements which she believes has corrected itself. She determined, in discussions with the Purchasing Department, that 2016 ending inventory was overstated by $1 million. Marta says that the 2017 ending inventory is correct. Thus, she assumes that 2017 income is correct. Marta says to you, "What happened has happened—there's no point in worrying about it anymore."

Instructions
You conclude that Marta is incorrect. Write a brief, tactful memo to Marta, clarifying the situation.

Ethics Case

BYP6-7 R. J. Graziano Wholesale Corp. uses the LIFO method of inventory costing. In the current year, profit at R. J. Graziano is running unusually high. The corporate tax rate is also high this year, but it is scheduled to decline significantly next year. In an effort to lower the current year's net income and to take advantage of the changing income tax rate, the president of R. J. Graziano Wholesale instructs the plant accountant to recommend to the purchasing department a large purchase of inventory for delivery 3 days before the end of the year. The price of the inventory to be purchased has doubled during the year, and the purchase will represent a major portion of the ending inventory value.

Instructions
(a) What is the effect of this transaction on this year's and next year's income statement and income tax expense? Why?
(b) If R. J. Graziano Wholesale had been using the FIFO method of inventory costing, would the president give the same directive?

(c) Should the plant accountant order the inventory purchase to lower income? What are the ethical implications of this order?

All About You

BYP6-8 Some of the largest business frauds ever perpetrated have involved the misstatement of inventory. Two classics were at **Leslie Fay** and **McKesson Corporation**.

Instructions

There is considerable information regarding inventory frauds available on the Internet. Search for information about one of the two cases mentioned above, or inventory fraud at any other company, and prepare a short explanation of the nature of the inventory fraud.

FASB Codification Activity

BYP6-9 If your school has a subscription to the FASB Codification, go to **http://aaahq.org/ascLogin.cfm** to log in and prepare responses to the following.

Instructions

(a) The primary basis for accounting for inventories is cost. How is cost defined in the Codification?
(b) What does the Codification state regarding the use of consistency in the selection or employment of a basis for inventory?

A Look at IFRS

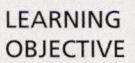 **LEARNING OBJECTIVE 7** | **Compare the accounting for inventories under GAAP and IFRS.**

The major IFRS requirements related to accounting and reporting for inventories are the same as GAAP. The major differences are that IFRS prohibits the use of the LIFO cost flow assumption and determines market in the lower-of-cost-or-market inventory valuation differently.

Relevant Facts

Following are the key similarities and differences between GAAP and IFRS related inventories.

Similarities

- IFRS and GAAP account for inventory acquisitions at historical cost and value inventory at the lower-of-cost-or-market subsequent to acquisition.
- Who owns the goods—goods in transit or consigned goods—as well as the costs to include in inventory are essentially accounted for the same under IFRS and GAAP.

Differences

- The requirements for accounting for and reporting inventories are more principles-based under IFRS. That is, GAAP provides more detailed guidelines in inventory accounting.
- A major difference between IFRS and GAAP relates to the LIFO cost flow assumption. GAAP permits the use of LIFO for inventory valuation. IFRS prohibits its use. FIFO and average-cost are the only two acceptable cost flow assumptions permitted under IFRS. Both sets of standards permit specific identification where appropriate.
- In the lower-of-cost-or-market test for inventory valuation, IFRS defines market as net realizable value. GAAP, on the other hand, defines market as replacement cost.

Looking to the Future

One convergence issue that will be difficult to resolve relates to the use of the LIFO cost flow assumption. As indicated, IFRS specifically prohibits its use. Conversely, the LIFO cost flow assumption is widely used in the United States because of its favorable tax advantages. In addition, many argue that LIFO from a financial reporting point of view provides a better matching of current costs against revenue and, therefore, enables companies to compute a more realistic income.

IFRS Practice

IFRS Self-Test Questions

1. Which of the following should **not** be included in the inventory of a company using IFRS?
   (a) Goods held on consignment from another company.
   (b) Goods shipped on consignment to another company.
   (c) Goods in transit from another company shipped FOB shipping point.
   (d) None of the above.

2. Which method of inventory costing is prohibited under IFRS?
   (a) Specific identification.   (c) FIFO.
   (b) LIFO.   (d) Average-cost.

IFRS Exercises

IFRS6-1 Briefly describe some of the similarities and differences between GAAP and IFRS with respect to the accounting for inventories.

IFRS6-2 LaTour Inc. is based in France and prepares its financial statements (in euros) in accordance with IFRS. In 2017, it reported cost of goods sold of €578 million and average inventory of €154 million. Briefly discuss how analysis of LaTour's inventory turnover (and comparisons to a company using GAAP) might be affected by differences in inventory accounting between IFRS and GAAP.

International Financial Reporting Problem: Louis Vuitton

IFRS6-3 The financial statements of Louis Vuitton are presented in Appendix F. Instructions for accessing and using the company's complete annual report, including the notes to its financial statements, are also provided in Appendix F.

Instructions
Using the notes to the company's financial statements, answer the following questions.

(a) What cost flow assumption does the company use to value inventory?
(b) What amount of goods purchased for retail and finished products did the company report at December 31, 2013?

Answers to IFRS Self-Test Questions
1. a   **2.** b

7 Fraud, Internal Control, and Cash

CHAPTER PREVIEW As the Feature Story about recording cash sales at Barriques indicates below, control of cash is important to ensure that fraud does not occur. Companies also need controls to safeguard other types of assets. For example, Barriques undoubtedly has controls to prevent the theft of food and supplies, and controls to prevent the theft of tableware and dishes from its kitchen.

In this chapter, we explain the essential features of an internal control system and how it prevents fraud. We also describe how those controls apply to a specific asset—cash. The applications include some controls with which you may be already familiar, such as the use of a bank.

FEATURE STORY

Minding the Money in Madison

For many years, Barriques in Madison, Wisconsin, has been named the city's favorite coffeehouse. Barriques not only does a booming business in coffee but also has wonderful baked goods, delicious sandwiches, and a fine selection of wines.

"Our customer base ranges from college students to neighborhood residents as well as visitors to our capital city," says bookkeeper Kerry Stoppleworth, who joined the company shortly after it was founded in 1998. "We are unique because we have customers who come in early on their way to work for a cup of coffee and then will stop back after work to pick up a bottle of wine for dinner. We stay very busy throughout all three parts of the day."

Like most businesses where purchases are low-cost and high-volume, cash control has to be simple. "We use a computerized point-of-sale (POS) system to keep track of our inventory and allow us to efficiently ring through an order for a customer," explains Stoppleworth. "You can either scan a barcode for an item or enter in a code for items that don't have a barcode such as cups of coffee or bakery items." The POS system also automatically tracks sales by department and maintains an electronic journal of all the sales transactions that occur during the day.

"There are two POS stations at each store, and throughout the day any of the staff may operate them," says Stoppleworth. At the end of the day, each POS station is reconciled separately. The staff counts the cash in the drawer and enters this amount into the closing totals in the POS system. The POS system then compares the cash and credit amounts, less the cash being carried forward to the next day (the float), to the shift total in the electronic journal. If there are discrepancies, a recount is done and the journal is reviewed transaction by transaction to identify the problem. The staff then creates a deposit ticket for the cash less the float and puts this in a drop safe with the electronic journal summary report for the manager to review and take to the bank the next day. Ultimately, the bookkeeper reviews all of these documents as well as the deposit receipt that the bank produces to make sure they are all in agreement.

As Stoppleworth concludes, "We keep the closing process and accounting simple so that our staff can concentrate on taking care of our customers and making great coffee and food."

© James Pauls/iStockphoto

CHAPTER OUTLINE

Learning Objectives

1 Discuss fraud and the principles of internal control.

- Fraud
- The Sarbanes-Oxley Act
- Internal control
- Principles of internal control activities
- Limitations of internal control

DO IT! **1** Control Activities

2 Apply internal control principles to cash.

- Cash receipts controls
- Cash disbursements controls
- Petty cash fund

DO IT! **2a** Control over Cash Receipts
2b Petty Cash Fund

3 Identify the control features of a bank account.

- Making bank deposits
- Writing checks
- Bank statements
- Reconciling the bank account
- EFT system

DO IT! **3** Bank Reconciliation

4 Explain the reporting of cash.

- Cash equivalents
- Restricted cash

DO IT! **4** Reporting Cash

Go to the **REVIEW AND PRACTICE** section at the end of the chapter for a review of key concepts and practice applications with solutions.

Visit **WileyPLUS with ORION** for additional tutorials and practice opportunities.

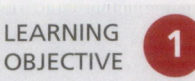

Discuss fraud and the principles of internal control.

The Feature Story describes many of the internal control procedures used by **Barriques**. These procedures are necessary to discourage employees from fraudulent activities.

Fraud

A **fraud** is a dishonest act by an employee that results in personal benefit to the employee at a cost to the employer. Examples of fraud reported in the financial press include the following.

- A bookkeeper in a small company diverted $750,000 of bill payments to a personal bank account over a three-year period.
- A shipping clerk with 28 years of service shipped $125,000 of merchandise to himself.
- A computer operator embezzled $21 million from **Wells Fargo Bank** over a two-year period.
- A church treasurer "borrowed" $150,000 of church funds to finance a friend's business dealings.

Why does fraud occur? The three main factors that contribute to fraudulent activity are depicted by the **fraud triangle** in Illustration 7-1 (in the margin).

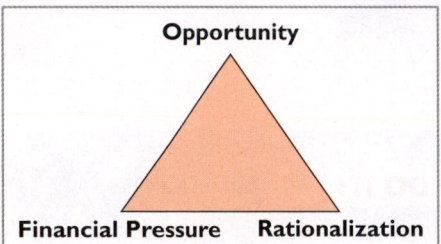

Illustration 7-1
Fraud triangle

The most important element of the fraud triangle is **opportunity**. For an employee to commit fraud, the workplace environment must provide opportunities that an employee can take advantage of. Opportunities occur when the workplace lacks sufficient controls to deter and detect fraud. For example, inadequate monitoring of employee actions can create opportunities for theft and can embolden employees because they believe they will not be caught.

A second factor that contributes to fraud is **financial pressure**. Employees sometimes commit fraud because of personal financial problems caused by too much debt. Or, they might commit fraud because they want to lead a lifestyle that they cannot afford on their current salary.

The third factor that contributes to fraud is **rationalization**. In order to justify their fraud, employees rationalize their dishonest actions. For example, employees sometimes justify fraud because they believe they are underpaid while the employer is making lots of money. Employees feel justified in stealing because they believe they deserve to be paid more.

The Sarbanes-Oxley Act

What can be done to prevent or to detect fraud? After numerous corporate scandals came to light in the early 2000s, Congress addressed this issue by passing the **Sarbanes-Oxley Act (SOX)**. Under SOX, all publicly traded U.S. corporations are required to maintain an adequate system of internal control. Corporate executives and boards of directors must ensure that these controls are reliable and effective. In addition, independent outside auditors must attest to the adequacy of the internal control system. Companies that fail to comply are subject to fines, and company officers can be imprisoned. SOX also created the Public Company Accounting Oversight Board (PCAOB) to establish auditing standards and regulate auditor activity.

One poll found that 60% of investors believe that SOX helps safeguard their stock investments. Many say they would be unlikely to invest in a company that fails to follow SOX requirements. Although some corporate executives have criticized the time and expense involved in following the SOX requirements, SOX appears to be working well. For example, the chief accounting officer of

Eli Lily noted that SOX triggered a comprehensive review of how the company documents its controls. This review uncovered redundancies and pointed out controls that needed to be added. In short, it added up to time and money well spent.

Internal Control

Internal control is a process designed to provide reasonable assurance regarding the achievement of objectives related to operations, reporting, and compliance. In more detail, it consists of all the related methods and measures adopted within an organization to safeguard assets, enhance the reliability of accounting records, increase efficiency of operations, and ensure compliance with laws and regulations. Internal control systems have five primary components as listed below.[1]

- **A control environment.** It is the responsibility of top management to make it clear that the organization values integrity and that unethical activity will not be tolerated. This component is often referred to as the "tone at the top."

- **Risk assessment.** Companies must identify and analyze the various factors that create risk for the business and must determine how to manage these risks.

- **Control activities.** To reduce the occurrence of fraud, management must design policies and procedures to address the specific risks faced by the company.

- **Information and communication.** The internal control system must capture and communicate all pertinent information both down and up the organization, as well as communicate information to appropriate external parties.

- **Monitoring.** Internal control systems must be monitored periodically for their adequacy. Significant deficiencies need to be reported to top management and/or the board of directors.

People, Planet, and Profit Insight

© Karl Dolenc/iStockphoto

And the Controls Are . . .

Internal controls are important for an effective financial reporting system. The same is true for sustainability reporting. An effective system of internal controls for sustainability reporting will help in the following ways: (1) prevent the unauthorized use of data; (2) provide reasonable assurance that the information is accurate, valid, and complete; and (3) report information that is consistent with overall sustainability accounting policies. With these types of controls, users will have the confidence that they can use the sustainability information effectively.

Some regulators are calling for even more assurance through audits of this information. Companies that potentially can cause environmental damage through greenhouse gases, as well as companies in the mining and extractive industries, are subject to reporting requirements. And, as demand for more information in the sustainability area expands, the need for audits of this information will grow.

Why is sustainability information important to investors? (Go to **WileyPLUS** *for this answer and additional questions.)*

Principles of Internal Control Activities

Each of the five components of an internal control system is important. Here, we will focus on one component, the control activities. The reason? These activities are the backbone of the company's efforts to address the risks it faces, such as fraud.

---

[1]The Committee of Sponsoring Organizations of the Treadway Commission, "Internal Control—Integrated Framework," *www.coso.org/documents/990025P_executive_summary_final_may20_e.pdf.*

The specific control activities used by a company will vary, depending on management's assessment of the risks faced. This assessment is heavily influenced by the size and nature of the company.

The six principles of control activities are as follows.

- Establishment of responsibility
- Segregation of duties
- Documentation procedures
- Physical controls
- Independent internal verification
- Human resource controls

We explain these principles in the following sections. You should recognize that they apply to most companies and are relevant to both manual and computerized accounting systems.

ESTABLISHMENT OF RESPONSIBILITY

It's your shift now. I'm turning in my cash drawer and heading home.

Transfer of cash drawers

An essential principle of internal control is to assign responsibility to specific employees. **Control is most effective when only one person is responsible for a given task.**

To illustrate, assume that the cash on hand at the end of the day in a **Safeway** supermarket is $10 short of the cash entered in the cash register. If only one person has operated the register, the shift manager can quickly determine responsibility for the shortage. If two or more individuals have worked the register, it may be impossible to determine who is responsible for the error.

Many retailers solve this problem by having registers with multiple drawers. This makes it possible for more than one person to operate a register but still allows identification of a particular employee with a specific drawer. Only the signed-in cashier has access to his or her drawer.

Establishing responsibility often requires limiting access only to authorized personnel, and then identifying those personnel. For example, the automated systems used by many companies have mechanisms such as identifying passcodes that keep track of who made a journal entry, who entered a sale, or who went into an inventory storeroom at a particular time. Use of identifying passcodes enables the company to establish responsibility by identifying the particular employee who carried out the activity.

ANATOMY OF A FRAUD

Maureen Frugali was a training supervisor for claims processing at Colossal Healthcare. As a standard part of the claims-processing training program, Maureen created fictitious claims for use by trainees. These fictitious claims were then sent to the accounts payable department. After the training claims had been processed, she was to notify Accounts Payable of all fictitious claims, so that they would not be paid. However, she did not inform Accounts Payable about every fictitious claim. She created some fictitious claims for entities that she controlled (that is, she would receive the payment), and she let Accounts Payable pay her.

Total take: $11 million

THE MISSING CONTROL

Establishment of responsibility. The healthcare company did not adequately restrict the responsibility for authorizing and approving claims transactions. The training supervisor should not have been authorized to create claims in the company's "live" system.

Source: Adapted from Wells, *Fraud Casebook* (2007), pp. 61–70.

SEGREGATION OF DUTIES

Segregation of duties is indispensable in an internal control system. There are two common applications of this principle:

1. Different individuals should be responsible for related activities.
2. The responsibility for recordkeeping for an asset should be separate from the physical custody of that asset.

The rationale for segregation of duties is this: **The work of one employee should, without a duplication of effort, provide a reliable basis for evaluating the work of another employee.** For example, the personnel that design and program computerized systems should not be assigned duties related to day-to-day use of the system. Otherwise, they could design the system to benefit them personally and conceal the fraud through day-to-day use.

SEGREGATION OF RELATED ACTIVITIES Making one individual responsible for related activities increases the potential for errors and irregularities. Instead, companies should, for example, assign related **purchasing activities** to different individuals. Related purchasing activities include ordering merchandise, order approval, receiving goods, authorizing payment, and paying for goods or services. Various frauds are possible when one person handles related purchasing activities:

- If a purchasing agent is allowed to order goods without obtaining supervisory approval, the likelihood of the purchasing agent receiving kickbacks from suppliers increases.
- If an employee who orders goods also handles the invoice and receipt of the goods, as well as payment authorization, he or she might authorize payment for a fictitious invoice.

These abuses are less likely to occur when companies divide the purchasing tasks.

Similarly, companies should assign related **sales activities** to different individuals. Related selling activities include making a sale, shipping (or delivering) the goods to the customer, billing the customer, and receiving payment. Various frauds are possible when one person handles related sales activities:

- If a salesperson can make a sale without obtaining supervisory approval, he or she might make sales at unauthorized prices to increase sales commissions.
- A shipping clerk who also has access to accounting records could ship goods to himself.
- A billing clerk who handles billing and receipt could understate the amount billed for sales made to friends and relatives.

These abuses are less likely to occur when companies divide the sales tasks. The salespeople make the sale, the shipping department ships the goods on the basis of the sales order, and the billing department prepares the sales invoice after comparing the sales order with the report of goods shipped.

ANATOMY OF A FRAUD

Lawrence Fairbanks, the assistant vice-chancellor of communications at Aesop University, was allowed to make purchases of under $2,500 for his department without external approval. Unfortunately, he also sometimes bought items for himself, such as expensive antiques and other collectibles. How did he do it? He replaced the vendor invoices he received with fake vendor invoices that he created. The fake invoices had descriptions that were more consistent with the communications department's purchases. He submitted these fake invoices to the accounting department as the basis for their journal entries and to the accounts payable department as the basis for payment.

Total take: $475,000

THE MISSING CONTROL

Segregation of duties. The university had not properly segregated related purchasing activities. Lawrence was ordering items, receiving the items, and receiving the invoice. By receiving the invoice, he had control over the documents that were used to account for the purchase and thus was able to substitute a fake invoice.

Source: Adapted from Wells, *Fraud Casebook* (2007), pp. 3–15.

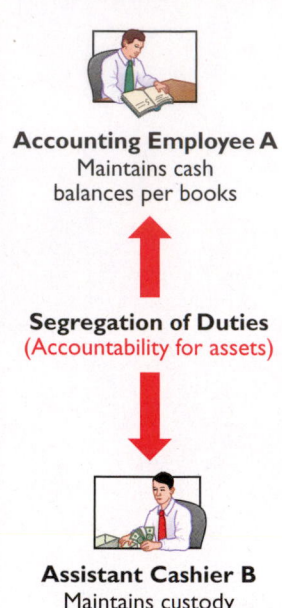

Accounting Employee A
Maintains cash
balances per books

Segregation of Duties
(Accountability for assets)

Assistant Cashier B
Maintains custody
of cash on hand

SEGREGATION OF RECORDKEEPING FROM PHYSICAL CUSTODY The accountant should have neither physical custody of the asset nor access to it. Likewise, the custodian of the asset should not maintain or have access to the accounting records. **The custodian of the asset is not likely to convert the asset to personal use when one employee maintains the record of the asset, and a different employee has physical custody of the asset.** The separation of accounting responsibility from the custody of assets is especially important for cash and inventories because these assets are very vulnerable to fraud.

ANATOMY OF A FRAUD

Angela Bauer was an accounts payable clerk for Aggasiz Construction Company. Angela prepared and issued checks to vendors and reconciled bank statements. She perpetrated a fraud in this way: She wrote checks for costs that the company had not actually incurred (e.g., fake taxes). A supervisor then approved and signed the checks. Before issuing the check, though, Angela would "white-out" the payee line on the check and change it to personal accounts that she controlled. She was able to conceal the theft because she also reconciled the bank account. That is, nobody else ever saw that the checks had been altered.

Total take: $570,000

THE MISSING CONTROL

Segregation of duties. Aggasiz Construction Company did not properly segregate recordkeeping from physical custody. Angela had physical custody of the checks, which essentially was control of the cash. She also had recordkeeping responsibility because she prepared the bank reconciliation.

Source: Adapted from Wells, *Fraud Casebook* (2007), pp. 100–107.

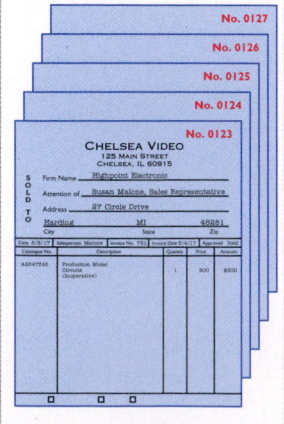

Prenumbered invoices

DOCUMENTATION PROCEDURES

Documents provide evidence that transactions and events have occurred. For example Barriques' point-of-sale terminals are networked with the company's computing and accounting records, which results in direct documentation.

Similarly, a shipping document indicates that the goods have been shipped, and a sales invoice indicates that the company has billed the customer for the goods. By requiring signatures (or initials) on the documents, the company can identify the individual(s) responsible for the transaction or event. Companies should document transactions when they occur.

Companies should establish procedures for documents. First, whenever possible, companies should use **prenumbered documents, and all documents should be accounted for**. Prenumbering helps to prevent a transaction from being recorded more than once, or conversely, from not being recorded at all. Second, the control system should require that employees **promptly forward source documents for accounting entries to the accounting department**. This control

measure helps to ensure timely recording of the transaction and contributes directly to the accuracy and reliability of the accounting records.

ANATOMY OF A FRAUD

To support their reimbursement requests for travel costs incurred, employees at Mod Fashions Corporation's design center were required to submit receipts. The receipts could include the detailed bill provided for a meal, the credit card receipt provided when the credit card payment is made, or a copy of the employee's monthly credit card bill that listed the item. A number of the designers who frequently traveled together came up with a fraud scheme: They submitted claims for the same expenses. For example, if they had a meal together that cost $200, one person submitted the detailed meal bill, another submitted the credit card receipt, and a third submitted a monthly credit card bill showing the meal as a line item. Thus, all three received a $200 reimbursement.

Total take: $75,000

THE MISSING CONTROL

Documentation procedures. Mod Fashions should require the original, detailed receipt. It should not accept photocopies, and it should not accept credit card statements. In addition, documentation procedures could be further improved by requiring the use of a corporate credit card (rather than a personal credit card) for all business expenses.

Source: Adapted from Wells, *Fraud Casebook* (2007), pp. 79–90.

PHYSICAL CONTROLS

Use of physical controls is essential. **Physical controls** relate to the safeguarding of assets and enhance the accuracy and reliability of the accounting records. Illustration 7-2 shows examples of these controls.

Illustration 7-2
Physical controls

Physical Controls

| Safes, vaults, and safety deposit boxes for cash and business papers | Locked warehouses and storage cabinets for inventories and records | Computer facilities with pass-key access or fingerprint or eyeball scans | Alarms to prevent break-ins | Television monitors and garment sensors to deter theft | Time clocks for recording time worked |

ANATOMY OF A FRAUD

At Centerstone Health, a large insurance company, the mailroom each day received insurance applications from prospective customers. Mailroom employees scanned the applications into electronic documents before the applications were processed. Once the applications were scanned, they could be accessed online by authorized employees.

Insurance agents at Centerstone Health earn commissions based upon successful applications. The sales agent's name is listed on the application. However, roughly 15% of the applications are from customers who did not work with a sales agent. Two friends—Alex, an employee in recordkeeping, and Parviz, a sales agent—thought up a way to perpetrate a fraud. Alex identified scanned applications that did not list a sales agent. After business hours, he entered the mailroom and found the hard-copy applications that did not show a sales agent. He wrote in Parviz's name as the sales agent and then rescanned the application for processing. Parviz received the commission, which the friends then split.

Total take: $240,000

THE MISSING CONTROL

Physical controls. Centerstone Health lacked two basic physical controls that could have prevented this fraud. First, the mailroom should have been locked during non-business hours, and access during business hours should have been tightly controlled. Second, the scanned applications supposedly could be accessed only by authorized employees using their passwords. However, the password for each employee was the same as the employee's user ID. Since employee user-ID numbers were available to all other employees, all employees knew all other employees' passwords. Unauthorized employees could access the scanned applications. Thus, Alex could enter the system using another employee's password and access the scanned applications.

Source: Adapted from Wells, *Fraud Casebook* (2007), pp. 316–326.

INDEPENDENT INTERNAL VERIFICATION

Most internal control systems provide for **independent internal verification**. This principle involves the review of data prepared by employees. To obtain maximum benefit from independent internal verification:

1. Companies should verify records periodically or on a surprise basis.

2. An employee who is independent of the personnel responsible for the information should make the verification.

3. Discrepancies and exceptions should be reported to a management level that can take appropriate corrective action.

Independent internal verification is especially useful in comparing recorded accountability with existing assets. The reconciliation of the electronic journal with the cash in the point-of-sale terminal at **Barriques** is an example of this internal control principle. Other common examples are the reconciliation of a company's cash balance per books with the cash balance per bank, and the verification of the perpetual inventory records through a count of physical inventory. Illustration 7-3 shows the relationship between this principle and the segregation of duties principle.

Illustration 7-3

Comparison of segregation of duties principle with independent internal verification principle

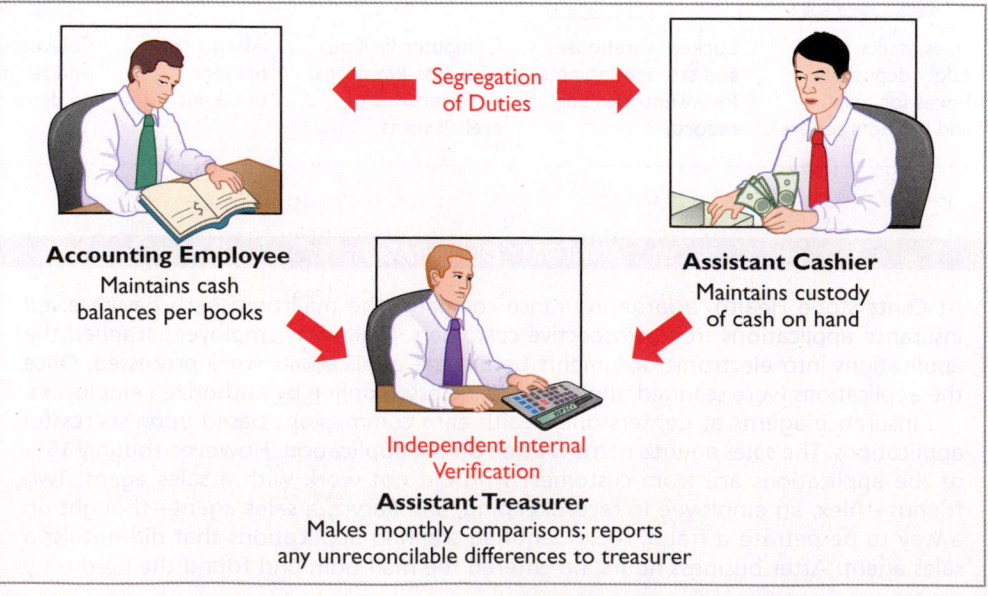

Segregation of Duties

Accounting Employee
Maintains cash balances per books

Assistant Cashier
Maintains custody of cash on hand

Independent Internal Verification

Assistant Treasurer
Makes monthly comparisons; reports any unreconcilable differences to treasurer

ANATOMY OF A FRAUD

Bobbi Jean Donnelly, the office manager for Mod Fashions Corporation's design center, was responsible for preparing the design center budget and reviewing expense reports submitted by design center employees. Her desire to upgrade her wardrobe got the better of her, and she enacted a fraud that involved filing expense-reimbursement requests for her own personal clothing purchases. Bobbi Jean was able to conceal the fraud because she was responsible for reviewing all expense reports, including her own. In addition, she sometimes was given ultimate responsibility for signing off on the expense reports when her boss was "too busy." Also, because she controlled the budget, when she submitted her expenses, she coded them to budget items that she knew were running under budget, so that they would not catch anyone's attention.

Total take: $275,000

THE MISSING CONTROL

Independent internal verification. Bobbi Jean's boss should have verified her expense reports. When asked what he thought her expenses for a year were, the boss said about $10,000. At $115,000 per year, her actual expenses were more than 10 times what would have been expected. However, because he was "too busy" to verify her expense reports or to review the budget, he never noticed.

Source: Adapted from Wells, *Fraud Casebook* (2007), pp. 79–90.

Large companies often assign independent internal verification to internal auditors. **Internal auditors** are company employees who continuously evaluate the effectiveness of the company's internal control systems. They review the activities of departments and individuals to determine whether prescribed internal controls are being followed. They also recommend improvements when needed. For example, WorldCom was at one time the second largest U.S. telecommunications company. The fraud that caused its bankruptcy (the largest ever when it occurred) involved billions of dollars. It was uncovered by an internal auditor.

HUMAN RESOURCE CONTROLS

Human resource control activities include the following.

1. **Bond employees who handle cash. Bonding** involves obtaining insurance protection against theft by employees. It contributes to the safeguarding of cash in two ways. First, the insurance company carefully screens all individuals before adding them to the policy and may reject risky applicants. Second, bonded employees know that the insurance company will vigorously prosecute all offenders.

2. **Rotate employees' duties and require employees to take vacations.** These measures deter employees from attempting thefts since they will not be able to permanently conceal their improper actions. Many banks, for example, have discovered employee thefts when the employee was on vacation or assigned to a new position.

3. **Conduct thorough background checks.** Many believe that the most important and inexpensive measure any business can take to reduce employee theft and fraud is for the human resources department to conduct thorough background checks. Two tips: (1) Check to see whether job applicants actually graduated from the schools they list. (2) Never use telephone numbers for previous employers provided by the applicant. Always look them up yourself.

ANATOMY OF A FRAUD

Ellen Lowry was the desk manager and Josephine Rodriguez was the head of housekeeping at the Excelsior Inn, a luxury hotel. The two best friends were so dedicated to their jobs that they never took vacations, and they frequently filled in for other employees. In fact, Ms. Rodriguez, whose job as head of housekeeping did not include cleaning rooms, often cleaned rooms herself, "just to help the staff keep up." These two "dedicated" employees, working as a team, found a way to earn a little more cash. Ellen, the desk manager, provided significant discounts to guests who paid with cash. She kept the cash and did not register the guest in the hotel's computerized system. Instead, she took the room out of circulation "due to routine maintenance." Because the room did not show up as being used, it did not receive a normal housekeeping assignment. Instead, Josephine, the head of housekeeping, cleaned the rooms during the guests' stay.

Total take: $95,000

THE MISSING CONTROL

Human resource controls. Ellen, the desk manager, had been fired by a previous employer after being accused of fraud. If the Excelsior Inn had conducted a thorough background check, it would not have hired her. The hotel fraud was detected when Ellen missed work for a few days due to illness. A system of mandatory vacations and rotating days off would have increased the chances of detecting the fraud before it became so large.

Source: Adapted from Wells, *Fraud Casebook* (2007), pp. 145–155.

Accounting Across the Organization

Stockbyte/Getty Images, Inc.

SOX Boosts the Role of Human Resources

Under SOX, a company needs to keep track of employees' degrees and certifications to ensure that employees continue to meet the specified requirements of a job. Also, to ensure proper employee supervision and proper separation of duties, companies must develop and monitor an organizational chart. When one corporation went through this exercise, it found that out of 17,000 employees, there were 400 people who did not report to anyone. The corporation also had 35 people who reported to each other. In addition, if an employee complains of an unfair firing and mentions financial issues at the company, HR should refer the case to the company audit committee and possibly to its legal counsel.

Why would unsupervised employees or employees who report to each other represent potential internal control threats? (Go to **WileyPLUS** *for this answer and additional questions.)*

Limitations of Internal Control

Companies generally design their systems of internal control to provide **reasonable assurance** of proper safeguarding of assets and reliability of the accounting records. The concept of reasonable assurance rests on the premise that the costs of establishing control procedures should not exceed their expected benefit.

To illustrate, consider shoplifting losses in retail stores. Stores could eliminate such losses by having a security guard stop and search customers as they leave the store. But store managers have concluded that the negative effects of such a procedure cannot be justified. Instead, they have attempted to control shoplifting losses by less costly procedures. They post signs saying, "We reserve the right to inspect all packages" and "All shoplifters will be prosecuted." They use hidden cameras and store detectives to monitor customer activity, and they install sensor equipment at exits.

The **human element** is an important factor in every system of internal control. A good system can become ineffective as a result of employee fatigue, carelessness, or indifference. For example, a receiving clerk may not bother to count goods received and may just "fudge" the counts. Occasionally, two or more individuals may work together to get around prescribed controls. Such **collusion** can significantly reduce the effectiveness of a system, eliminating the protection offered by segregation of duties. No system of internal control is perfect.

The **size of the business** also may impose limitations on internal control. Small companies often find it difficult to segregate duties or to provide for independent internal verification. A study by the Association of Certified Fraud Examiners (*Report to the Nation on Occupational Fraud and Abuse*) indicates that businesses with fewer than 100 employees are most at risk for employee theft. In fact, 29% of frauds occurred at companies with fewer than 100 employees. The median loss at small companies was $154,000, which was close to the median fraud at companies with more than 10,000 employees ($160,000). A $154,000 loss can threaten the very existence of a small company.

DO IT! 1   Control Activities

Identify which control activity is violated in each of the following situations, and explain how the situation creates an opportunity for a fraud.

1. The person with primary responsibility for reconciling the bank account and making all bank deposits is also the company's accountant.

2. Wellstone Company's treasurer received an award for distinguished service because he had not taken a vacation in 30 years.

3. In order to save money spent on order slips and to reduce time spent keeping track of order slips, a local bar/restaurant does not buy prenumbered order slips.

Solution

1. Violates the control activity of segregation of duties. Recordkeeping should be separate from physical custody. As a consequence, the employee could embezzle cash and make journal entries to hide the theft.

2. Violates the control activity of human resource controls. Key employees must take vacations. Otherwise, the treasurer, who manages the company's cash, might embezzle cash and use his position to conceal the theft.

3. Violates the control activity of documentation procedures. If prenumbered documents are not used, then it is virtually impossible to account for the documents. As a consequence, an employee could write up a dinner sale, receive the cash from the customer, and then throw away the order slip and keep the cash.

Related exercise material: **BE7-1, BE7-2, BE7-3, BE7-4, E7-1** and **DO IT! 7-1**.

Action Plan

✔ Familiarize yourself with each of the control activities summarized on page 310.

✔ Understand the nature of the frauds that each control activity is intended to address.

LEARNING OBJECTIVE 2   Apply internal control principles to cash.

Cash is the one asset that is readily convertible into any other type of asset. It also is easily concealed and transported, and is highly desired. Because of these characteristics, **cash is the asset most susceptible to fraudulent activities**. In addition, because of the large volume of cash transactions, numerous errors may occur in executing and recording them. To safeguard cash and to ensure the accuracy of the accounting records for cash, effective internal control over cash is critical.

Cash Receipts Controls

Illustration 7-4 shows how the internal control principles explained earlier apply to cash receipts transactions. As you might expect, companies vary considerably in how they apply these principles. To illustrate internal control over cash receipts, we will examine control activities for a retail store with both over-the-counter and mail receipts.

Illustration 7-4
Application of internal control principles to cash receipts

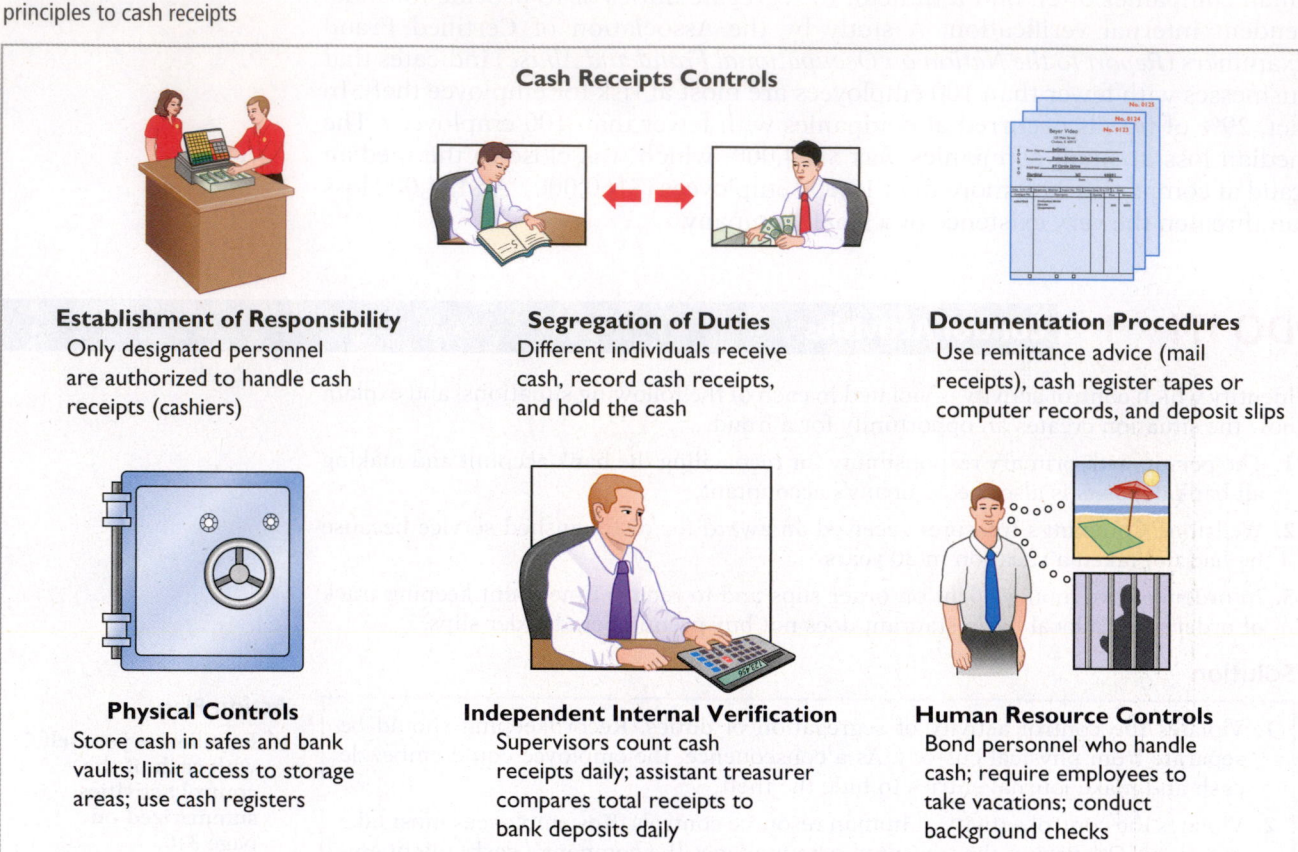

Cash Receipts Controls

Establishment of Responsibility
Only designated personnel are authorized to handle cash receipts (cashiers)

Segregation of Duties
Different individuals receive cash, record cash receipts, and hold the cash

Documentation Procedures
Use remittance advice (mail receipts), cash register tapes or computer records, and deposit slips

Physical Controls
Store cash in safes and bank vaults; limit access to storage areas; use cash registers

Independent Internal Verification
Supervisors count cash receipts daily; assistant treasurer compares total receipts to bank deposits daily

Human Resource Controls
Bond personnel who handle cash; require employees to take vacations; conduct background checks

OVER-THE-COUNTER RECEIPTS

In retail businesses, control of over-the-counter receipts centers on cash registers that are visible to customers. A cash sale is entered in a cash register (or point-of-sale terminal), with the amount clearly visible to the customer. This activity prevents the sales clerk from entering a lower amount and pocketing the difference. The customer receives an itemized cash register receipt slip and is expected to count the change received. (One weakness at **Barriques** in the Feature Story is that customers are only given a receipt if requested.) The cash register's tape is locked in the register until a supervisor removes it. This tape accumulates the daily transactions and totals.

At the end of the clerk's shift, the clerk counts the cash and sends the cash and the count to the cashier. The cashier counts the cash, prepares a deposit slip, and deposits the cash at the bank. The cashier also sends a duplicate of the deposit slip to the accounting department to indicate cash received. The supervisor removes the cash register tape and sends it to the accounting department as the basis for a journal entry to record the cash received. (For point-of-sale systems, the accounting department receives information on daily transactions and totals through the computer network.) Illustration 7-5 summarizes this process.

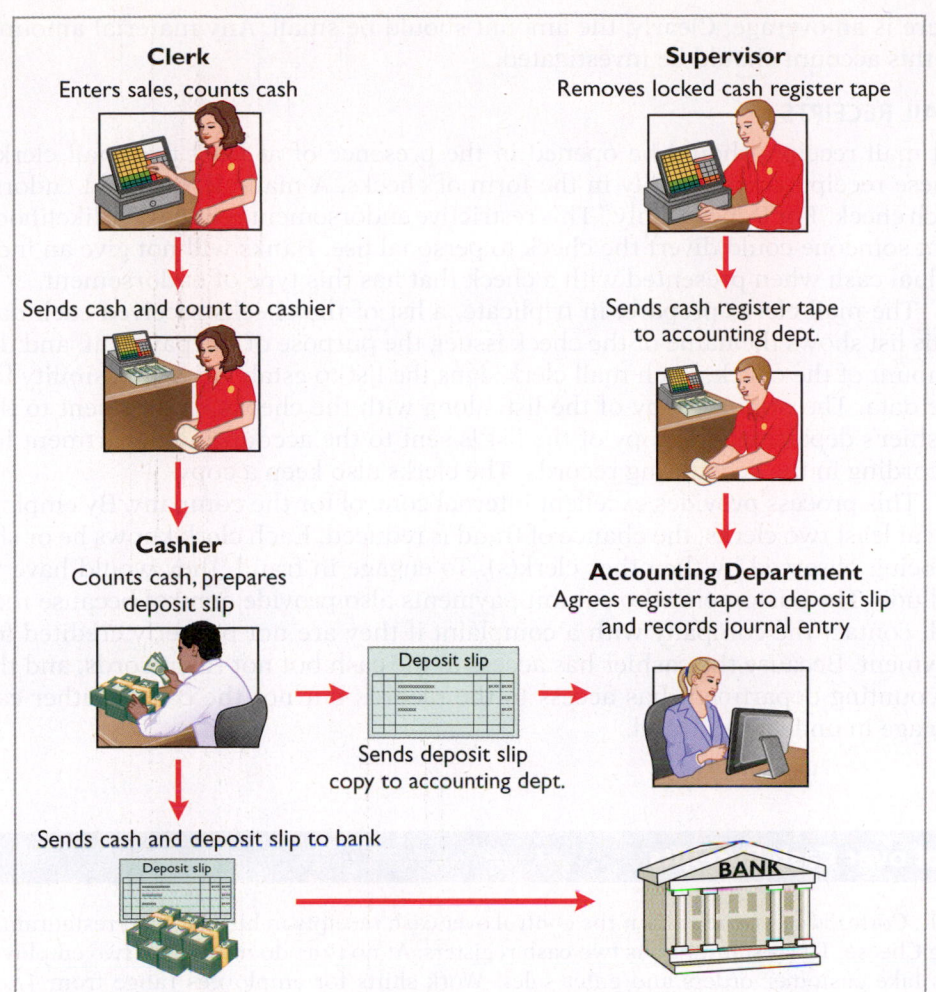

Illustration 7-5
Control of over-the-counter receipts

Helpful Hint
Flowcharts such as this one enhance the understanding of the flow of documents, the processing steps, and the internal control procedures.

This system for handling cash receipts uses an important internal control principle—segregation of recordkeeping from physical custody. The supervisor has access to the cash register tape but **not** to the cash. The clerk and the cashier have access to the cash but **not** to the register tape. In addition, the cash register tape provides documentation and enables independent internal verification. Use of these three principles of internal control (segregation of recordkeeping from physical custody, documentation, and independent internal verification) provides an effective system of internal control. Any attempt at fraudulent activity should be detected unless there is collusion among the employees.

In some instances, the amount deposited at the bank will not agree with the cash recorded in the accounting records based on the cash register tape. These differences often result because the clerk hands incorrect change back to the retail customer. In this case, the difference between the actual cash and the amount reported on the cash register tape is reported in a Cash Over and Short account. For example, suppose that the cash register tape indicated sales of $6,956.20 but the amount of cash was only $6,946.10. A cash shortfall of $10.10 exists. To account for this cash shortfall and related cash, the company makes the following entry.

Cash	6,946.10	
Cash Over and Short	10.10	
Sales Revenue		6,956.20
(To record cash shortfall)		

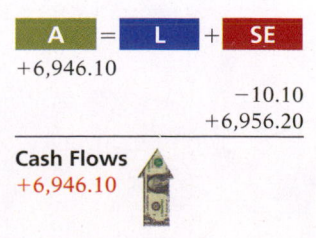

A = L + SE
+6,946.10
−10.10
+6,956.20

Cash Flows
+6,946.10

Cash Over and Short is an income statement item. It is reported as miscellaneous expense when there is a cash shortfall, and as miscellaneous revenue when there is an overage. Clearly, the amount should be small. Any material amounts in this account should be investigated.

MAIL RECEIPTS

All mail receipts should be opened in the presence of at least two mail clerks. These receipts are generally in the form of checks. A mail clerk should endorse each check "For Deposit Only." This restrictive endorsement reduces the likelihood that someone could divert the check to personal use. Banks will not give an individual cash when presented with a check that has this type of endorsement.

The mail clerks prepare, in triplicate, a list of the checks received each day. This list shows the name of the check issuer, the purpose of the payment, and the amount of the check. Each mail clerk signs the list to establish responsibility for the data. The original copy of the list, along with the checks, is then sent to the cashier's department. A copy of the list is sent to the accounting department for recording in the accounting records. The clerks also keep a copy.

This process provides excellent internal control for the company. By employing at least two clerks, the chance of fraud is reduced. Each clerk knows he or she is being observed by the other clerk(s). To engage in fraud, they would have to collude. The customers who submit payments also provide control because they will contact the company with a complaint if they are not properly credited for payment. Because the cashier has access to the cash but not the records, and the accounting department has access to the records but not the cash, neither can engage in undetected fraud.

DO IT! 2a   Control over Cash Receipts

L. R. Cortez is concerned about the control over cash receipts in his fast-food restaurant, Big Cheese. The restaurant has two cash registers. At no time do more than two employees take customer orders and enter sales. Work shifts for employees range from 4 to 8 hours. Cortez asks your help in installing a good system of internal control over cash receipts.

Action Plan

✔ Differentiate among the internal control principles of (1) establishing responsibility, (2) using physical controls, and (3) independent internal verification.

✔ Design an effective system of internal control over cash receipts.

Solution

Cortez should assign a separate cash register drawer to each employee at the start of each work shift, with register totals set at zero. Each employee should have access to only the assigned register drawer to enter all sales. Each customer should be given a receipt. At the end of the shift, the employee should do a cash count. A separate employee should compare the cash count with the register tape to be sure they agree. In addition, Cortez should install an automated system that would enable the company to compare orders entered in the register to orders processed by the kitchen.

Related exercise material: **BE7-5, BE7-6, BE7-7, E7-2, and DO IT! 7-2a.**

Cash Disbursements Controls

Companies disburse cash for a variety of reasons, such as to pay expenses and liabilities or to purchase assets. **Generally, internal control over cash disbursements is more effective when companies pay by check or electronic funds transfer (EFT) rather than by cash.** One exception is **payments for incidental amounts that are paid out of petty cash.**[2]

Companies generally issue checks only after following specified control procedures. Illustration 7-6 shows how principles of internal control apply to cash disbursements.

---

[2]We explain the operation of a petty cash fund on pages 322–324.

Cash Disbursements Controls

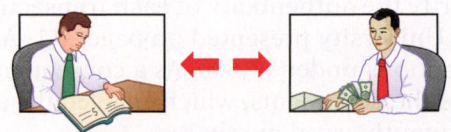
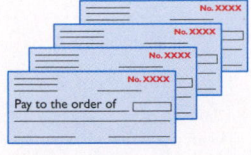

Establishment of Responsibility
Only designated personnel are authorized to sign checks (treasurer) and approve vendors

Segregation of Duties
Different individuals approve and make payments; check-signers do not record disbursements

Documentation Procedures
Use prenumbered checks and account for them in sequence; each check must have an approved invoice; require employees to use corporate credit cards for reimbursable expenses; stamp invoices "paid"

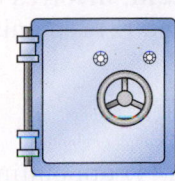

Physical Controls
Store blank checks in safes, with limited access; print check amounts by machine in indelible ink

Independent Internal Verification
Compare checks to invoices; reconcile bank statement monthly

Human Resource Controls
Bond personnel who handle cash; require employees to take vacations; conduct background checks

Illustration 7-6
Application of internal control principles to cash disbursements

VOUCHER SYSTEM CONTROLS

Most medium and large companies use vouchers as part of their internal control over cash disbursements. A **voucher system** is a network of approvals by authorized individuals, acting independently, to ensure that all disbursements by check are proper.

The system begins with the authorization to incur a cost or expense. It ends with the issuance of a check for the liability incurred. A **voucher** is an authorization form prepared for each expenditure. Companies require vouchers for all types of cash disbursements except those from petty cash.

The starting point in preparing a voucher is to fill in the appropriate information about the liability on the face of the voucher. The vendor's invoice provides most of the needed information. Then, an employee in the accounts payable department records the voucher (in a journal called a **voucher register**) and files it according to the date on which it is to be paid. The company issues and sends a check on that date, and stamps the voucher "paid." The paid voucher is sent to the accounting department for recording (in a journal called the **check register**). A voucher system involves two journal entries, one to record the liability when the voucher is issued and a second to pay the liability that relates to the voucher.

The use of a voucher system, whether done manually or electronically, improves internal control over cash disbursements. First, the authorization process inherent in a voucher system establishes responsibility. Each individual has responsibility to review the underlying documentation to ensure that it is correct. In addition, the voucher system keeps track of the documents that back up each transaction. By keeping these documents in one place, a supervisor can independently verify the authenticity of each transaction. Consider, for example, the case of Aesop University presented on page 311. Aesop did not use a voucher system for transactions under $2,500. As a consequence, there was no independent verification of the documents, which enabled the employee to submit fake invoices to hide his unauthorized purchases.

Petty Cash Fund

As you just learned, better internal control over cash disbursements is possible when companies make payments by check. However, using checks to pay small amounts is both impractical and a nuisance. For instance, a company would not want to write checks to pay for postage due, working lunches, or taxi fares. A common way of handling such payments, while maintaining satisfactory control, is to use a **petty cash fund** to pay relatively small amounts. The operation of a petty cash fund, often called an **imprest system**, involves (1) establishing the fund, (2) making payments from the fund, and (3) replenishing the fund.[3]

ESTABLISHING THE PETTY CASH FUND

Two essential steps in establishing a petty cash fund are (1) appointing a petty cash custodian who will be responsible for the fund, and (2) determining the size of the fund. Ordinarily, a company expects the amount in the fund to cover anticipated disbursements for a three- to four-week period.

To establish the fund, a company issues a check payable to the petty cash custodian for the stipulated amount. For example, if Laird Company decides to establish a $100 fund on March 1, the general journal entry is:

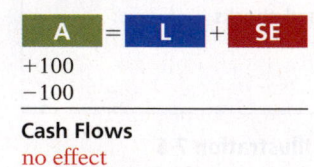

A = L + SE
+100
−100
―――――
Cash Flows
no effect

Mar. 1	Petty Cash	100	
	Cash		100
	(To establish a petty cash fund)		

The fund custodian cashes the check and places the proceeds in a locked petty cash box or drawer. Most petty cash funds are established on a fixed-amount basis. The company will make no additional entries to the Petty Cash account unless management changes the stipulated amount of the fund. For example, if Laird Company decides on July 1 to increase the size of the fund to $250, it would debit Petty Cash $150 and credit Cash $150.

MAKING PAYMENTS FROM THE PETTY CASH FUND

The petty cash custodian has the authority to make payments from the fund that conform to prescribed management policies. Usually, management limits the size of expenditures that come from petty cash. Likewise, it may not permit use of the fund for certain types of transactions (such as making short-term loans to employees).

Each payment from the fund must be documented on a prenumbered petty cash receipt (or petty cash voucher), as shown in Illustration 7-7. The signatures of both the fund custodian and the person receiving payment are required on the receipt. If other supporting documents such as a freight bill or invoice are available, they should be attached to the petty cash receipt.

ETHICS NOTE

Petty cash funds are authorized and legitimate. In contrast, "slush" funds are unauthorized and hidden (under the table).

Helpful Hint
The petty cash receipt satisfies two internal control procedures: (1) establishing responsibility (signature of custodian), and (2) documentation procedures.

---

[3]The term "imprest" means an advance of money for a designated purpose.

Illustration 7-7
Petty cash receipt

No. 7	LAIRD COMPANY
	Petty Cash Receipt

Date____3/6/17____

Paid to___Acme Express Agency___   Amount___$18.00___

For___Collect Express Charges___

CHARGE TO_____Freight-in_____

Approved   Received Payment

___L. A. Bird___ Custodian   ___R. E. Meins___

The petty cash custodian keeps the receipts in the petty cash box until the fund is replenished. The sum of the petty cash receipts and the money in the fund should equal the established total at all times. Management can (and should) make surprise counts at any time to determine whether the fund is being maintained correctly.

The company does not make an accounting entry to record a payment when it is made from petty cash. It is considered both inexpedient and unnecessary to do so. Instead, the company recognizes the accounting effects of each payment when it replenishes the fund.

REPLENISHING THE PETTY CASH FUND

When the money in the petty cash fund reaches a minimum level, the company replenishes the fund. The petty cash custodian initiates a request for reimbursement. The individual prepares a schedule (or summary) of the payments that have been made and sends the schedule, supported by petty cash receipts and other documentation, to the treasurer's office. The treasurer's office examines the receipts and supporting documents to verify that proper payments from the fund were made. The treasurer then approves the request and issues a check to restore the fund to its established amount. At the same time, all supporting documentation is stamped "paid" so that it cannot be submitted again for payment.

To illustrate, assume that on March 15 Laird's petty cash custodian requests a check for $87. The fund contains $13 cash and petty cash receipts for postage $44, freight-out $38, and miscellaneous expenses $5. The general journal entry to record the check is as follows.

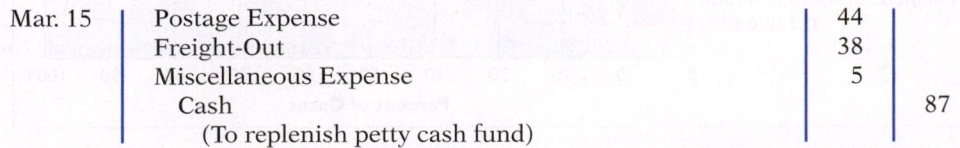

Mar. 15	Postage Expense	44	
	Freight-Out	38	
	Miscellaneous Expense	5	
	Cash		87
	(To replenish petty cash fund)		

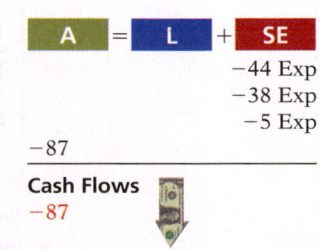

A	=	L	+	SE
				−44 Exp
				−38 Exp
				−5 Exp
−87				

Cash Flows
−87

Note that the reimbursement entry does not affect the Petty Cash account. Replenishment changes the composition of the fund by replacing the petty cash receipts with cash. It does not change the balance in the fund.

Occasionally, in replenishing a petty cash fund, the company may need to recognize a cash shortage or overage. This results when the total of the cash plus receipts in the petty cash box does not equal the established amount of the petty cash fund. To illustrate, assume that Laird's petty cash custodian has only $12 in

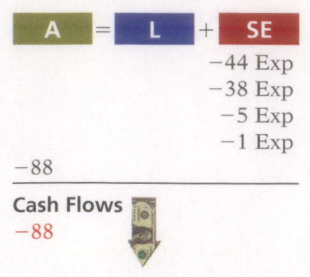

−44 Exp
−38 Exp
−5 Exp
−1 Exp

−88

Cash Flows
−88

cash in the fund plus the receipts as listed. The request for reimbursement would therefore be for $88, and Laird would make the following entry.

Mar. 15	Postage Expense	44	
	Freight-Out	38	
	Miscellaneous Expense	5	
	Cash Over and Short	1	
	Cash		88
	(To replenish petty cash fund)		

Conversely, if the custodian has $14 in cash, the reimbursement request would be for $86. The company would credit Cash Over and Short for $1 (overage). A company reports a debit balance in Cash Over and Short in the income statement as miscellaneous expense. It reports a credit balance in the account as miscellaneous revenue. The company closes Cash Over and Short to Income Summary at the end of the year.

Companies should replenish a petty cash fund at the end of the accounting period, regardless of the cash in the fund. Replenishment at this time is necessary in order to recognize the effects of the petty cash payments on the financial statements.

Helpful Hint
Cash over and short situations result from mathematical errors or from failure to keep accurate records.

Ethics Insight

© Chris Fernig/iStockphoto

How Employees Steal

Occupational fraud is using your own occupation for personal gain through the misuse or misapplication of the company's resources or assets. This type of fraud is one of three types:

1. **Asset misappropriation,** such as theft of cash on hand, fraudulent disbursements, false refunds, ghost employees, personal purchases, and fictitious employees. This fraud is the most common but the least costly.

2. **Corruption,** such as bribery, illegal gratuities, and economic extortion. This fraud generally falls in the middle between asset misappropriation and financial statement fraud as regards frequency and cost.

3. **Financial statement fraud,** such as fictitious revenues, concealed liabilities and expenses, improper disclosures, and improper asset values. This fraud occurs less frequently than other types of fraud but it is the most costly.

The graph below shows the frequency and the median loss for each type of occupational fraud.

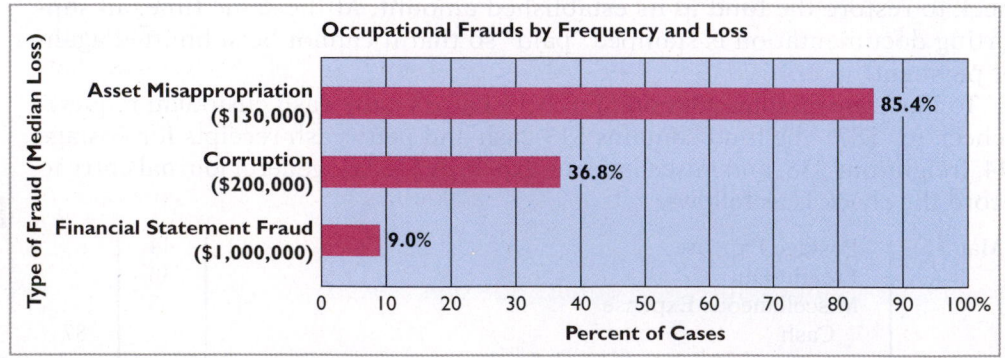

Source: 2014 Report to the Nations on Occupational Fraud and Abuse, Association of Certified Fraud Examiners, pp. 10–12.

How can companies reduce the likelihood of occupational fraud? (Go to **WileyPLUS** for this answer and additional questions.)

DO IT! 2b   Petty Cash Fund

Bateer Company established a $50 petty cash fund on July 1. On July 30, the fund had $12 cash remaining and petty cash receipts for postage $14, office supplies $10, and delivery expense $15. Prepare journal entries to establish the fund on July 1 and to replenish the fund on July 30.

Action Plan

✔ To establish the fund, set up a separate general ledger account.

✔ Determine how much cash is needed to replenish the fund: subtract the cash remaining from the petty cash fund balance.

✔ Total the petty cash receipts. Determine any cash over or short—the difference between the cash needed to replenish the fund and the total of the petty cash receipts.

✔ Record the expenses incurred according to the petty cash receipts when replenishing the fund.

Solution

July 1	Petty Cash	50	
	Cash		50
	(To establish petty cash fund)		
30	Postage Expense	14	
	Supplies	10	
	Delivery Expense	15	
	Cash Over and Short		1
	Cash ($50 − $12)		38
	(To replenish petty cash)		

Related exercise material: **BE7-9, E7-7, E7-8, and DO IT! 7-2b.**

LEARNING OBJECTIVE 3   Identify the control features of a bank account.

The use of a bank contributes significantly to good internal control over cash. A company can safeguard its cash by using a bank as a depository and as a clearinghouse for checks received and written. Use of a bank minimizes the amount of currency that a company must keep on hand. Also, use of a bank facilitates the control of cash because it creates a double record of all bank transactions—one by the company and the other by the bank. The asset account Cash maintained by the company should have the same balance as the bank's liability account for that company. A **bank reconciliation** compares the bank's balance with the company's balance and explains any differences to make them agree.

Many companies have more than one bank account. For efficiency of operations and better control, national retailers like **Wal-Mart Stores, Inc.** and **Target** may have regional bank accounts. Large companies, with tens of thousands of employees, may have a payroll bank account, as well as one or more general bank accounts. Also, a company may maintain several bank accounts in order to have more than one source for short-term loans when needed.

Making Bank Deposits

An authorized employee, such as the head cashier, should make a company's bank deposits. Each deposit must be documented by a deposit slip (ticket), as shown in Illustration 7-8 (page 326).

Deposit slips are prepared in duplicate. The bank retains the original; the depositor keeps the duplicate, machine-stamped by the bank to establish its authenticity.

Illustration 7-8
Deposit slip

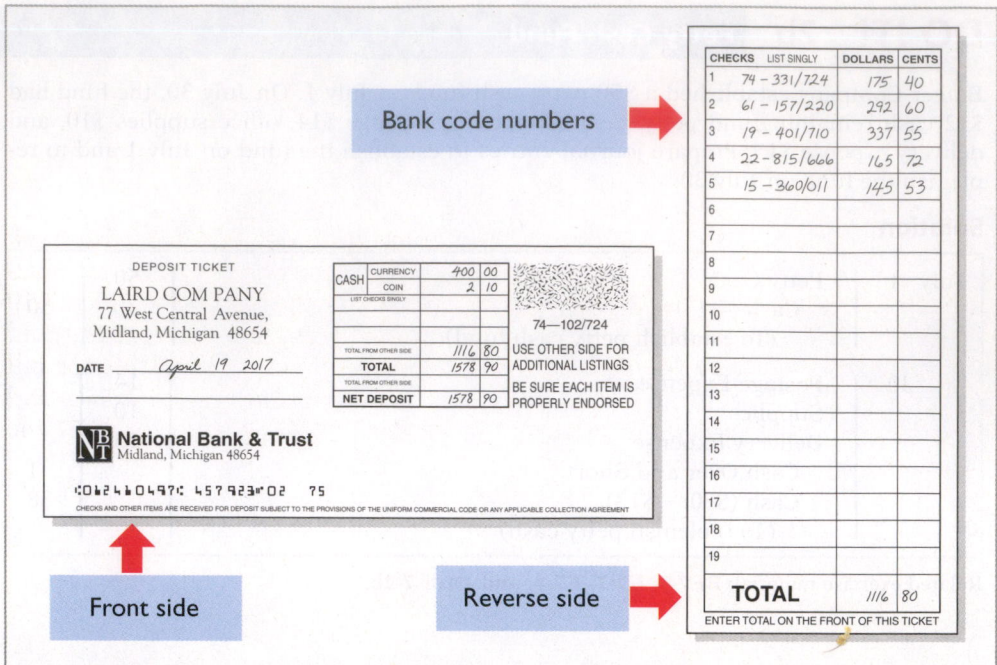

Writing Checks

A **check** is a written order signed by the depositor directing the bank to pay a specified sum of money to a designated recipient. There are three parties to a check: (1) the **maker** (or drawer) who issues the check, (2) the **bank** (or payer) on which the check is drawn, and (3) the **payee** to whom the check is payable. A check is a **negotiable instrument** that one party can transfer to another party by endorsement. Each check should be accompanied by an explanation of its purpose. In many companies, a remittance advice attached to the check, as shown in Illustration 7-9, explains the check's purpose.

Illustration 7-9
Check with remittance advice

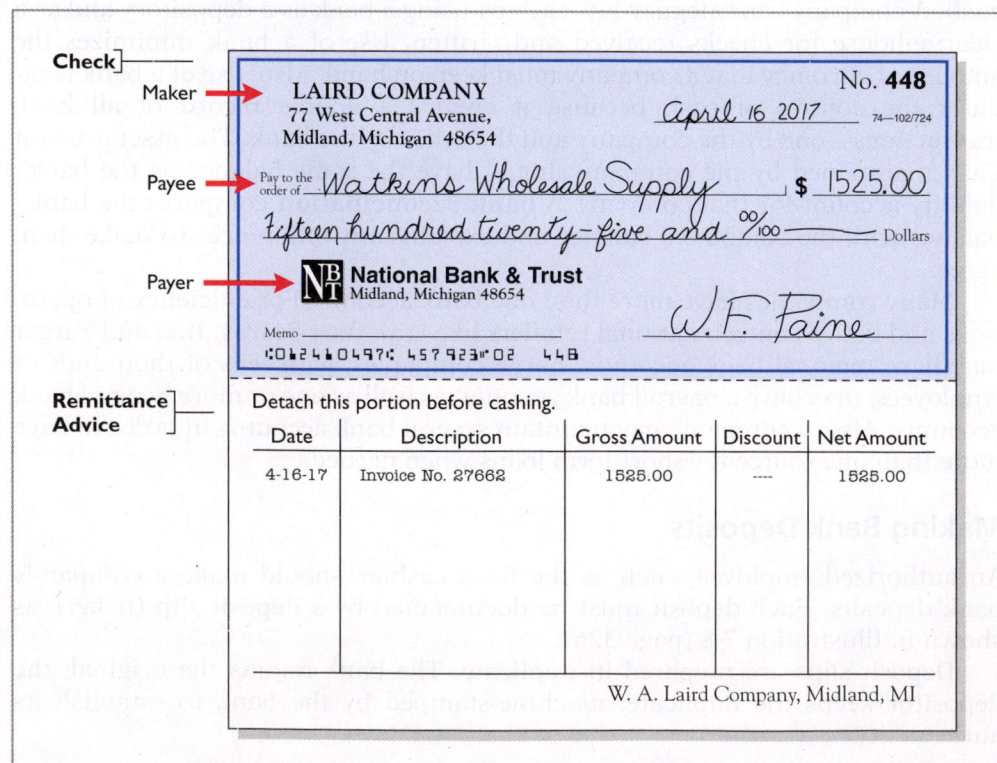

It is important to know the balance in the checking account at all times. To keep the balance current, the depositor should enter each deposit and check on running-balance memo forms (or online statements) provided by the bank or on the check stubs in the checkbook.

Bank Statements

If you have a personal checking account, you are probably familiar with bank statements. A **bank statement** shows the depositor's bank transactions and balances.[4] Each month, a depositor receives a statement from the bank. Illustration 7-10 presents a typical bank statement for Laird Company. It shows (1) checks paid and other debits (such as debit card transactions or direct withdrawals for bill payments) that reduce the balance in the depositor's account, (2) deposits and other credits that increase the balance in the depositor's account, and (3) the account balance after each day's transactions.

Helpful Hint
Essentially, the bank statement is a copy of the bank's records sent to the customer (or available online) for review.

Illustration 7-10
Bank statement

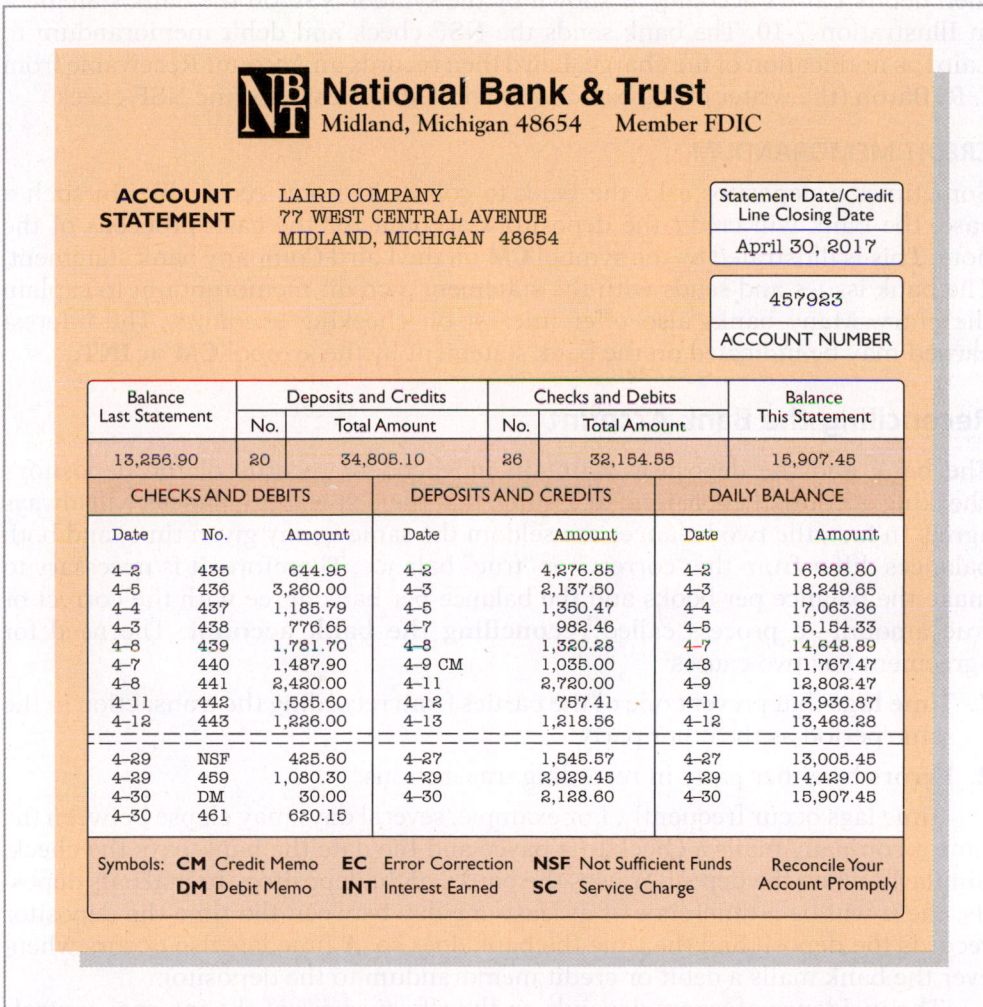

Helpful Hint
The bank *credits* to the customer's account every deposit it receives. The reverse occurs when the bank "pays" a check issued by a company on its checking account balance. Payment reduces the bank's liability. Thus, the bank *debits* check payments to the customer's account with the bank.

The bank statement lists in numerical sequence all "paid" checks, along with the date the check was paid and its amount. Upon paying a check, the bank stamps the check "paid"; a paid check is sometimes referred to as a **canceled** check. On the statement, the bank also includes memoranda explaining other debits and credits it made to the depositor's account.

[4]Our presentation assumes that the depositor makes all adjustments at the end of the month. In practice, a company may also make journal entries during the month as it reviews information from the bank regarding its account.

DEBIT MEMORANDUM

Some banks charge a monthly fee for their services. Often, they charge this fee only when the average monthly balance in a checking account falls below a specified amount. They identify the fee, called a **bank service charge**, on the bank statement by a symbol such as **SC**. The bank also sends with the statement a debit memorandum explaining the charge noted on the statement. Other debit memoranda may also be issued for other bank services such as the cost of printing checks, issuing traveler's checks, and wiring funds to other locations. The symbol **DM** is often used for such charges.

Banks also use a debit memorandum when a deposited check from a customer "bounces" because of insufficient funds. For example, assume that J. R. Baron, a customer of Laird Company, sends a check for $425.60 to Laird Company for services performed. Unfortunately, Baron does not have sufficient funds at its bank to pay for these services. In such a case, Baron's bank marks the check **NSF** (not sufficient funds) and returns it to Laird's (the depositor's) bank. Laird's bank then debits Laird's account, as shown by the symbol NSF on the bank statement in Illustration 7-10. The bank sends the NSF check and debit memorandum to Laird as notification of the charge. Laird then records an Account Receivable from J. R. Baron (the writer of the bad check) and reduces cash for the NSF check.

CREDIT MEMORANDUM

Sometimes a depositor asks the bank to collect its notes receivable. In such a case, the bank will credit the depositor's account for the cash proceeds of the note. This is illustrated by the symbol **CM** on the Laird Company bank statement. The bank issues and sends with the statement a credit memorandum to explain the entry. Many banks also offer interest on checking accounts. The interest earned may be indicated on the bank statement by the symbol **CM** or **INT**.

Reconciling the Bank Account

The bank and the depositor maintain independent records of the depositor's checking account. People tend to assume that the respective balances will always agree. In fact, the two balances are seldom the same at any given time, and both balances differ from the "correct" or "true" balance. Therefore, it is necessary to make the balance per books and the balance per bank agree with the correct or true amount—a process called **reconciling the bank account**. The need for agreement has two causes:

1. **Time lags** that prevent one of the parties from recording the transaction in the same period as the other party.
2. **Errors** by either party in recording transactions.

Time lags occur frequently. For example, several days may elapse between the time a company mails a check to a payee and the date the bank pays the check. Similarly, when the depositor uses the bank's night depository to make its deposits, there will be a difference of at least one day between the time the depositor records the deposit and the time the bank does so. A time lag also occurs whenever the bank mails a debit or credit memorandum to the depositor.

The incidence of errors depends on the effectiveness of the internal controls maintained by the company and the bank. Bank errors are infrequent. However, either party could accidentally record a $450 check as $45 or $540. In addition, the bank might mistakenly charge a check drawn by C. D. Berg to the account of C. D. Burg.

RECONCILIATION PROCEDURE

The bank reconciliation should be prepared by an employee who has no other responsibilities pertaining to cash. If a company fails to follow this internal control principle of independent internal verification, cash embezzlements may go unnoticed. For example, a cashier who prepares the reconciliation can embezzle cash and conceal the embezzlement by misstating the reconciliation. Thus, the bank accounts would reconcile, and the embezzlement would not be detected.

In reconciling the bank account, it is customary to reconcile the balance per books and balance per bank to their adjusted (correct or true) cash balances. The starting point in preparing the reconciliation is to enter the balance per bank statement and balance per books on the reconciliation schedule. The company then makes various adjustments, as shown in Illustration 7-11.

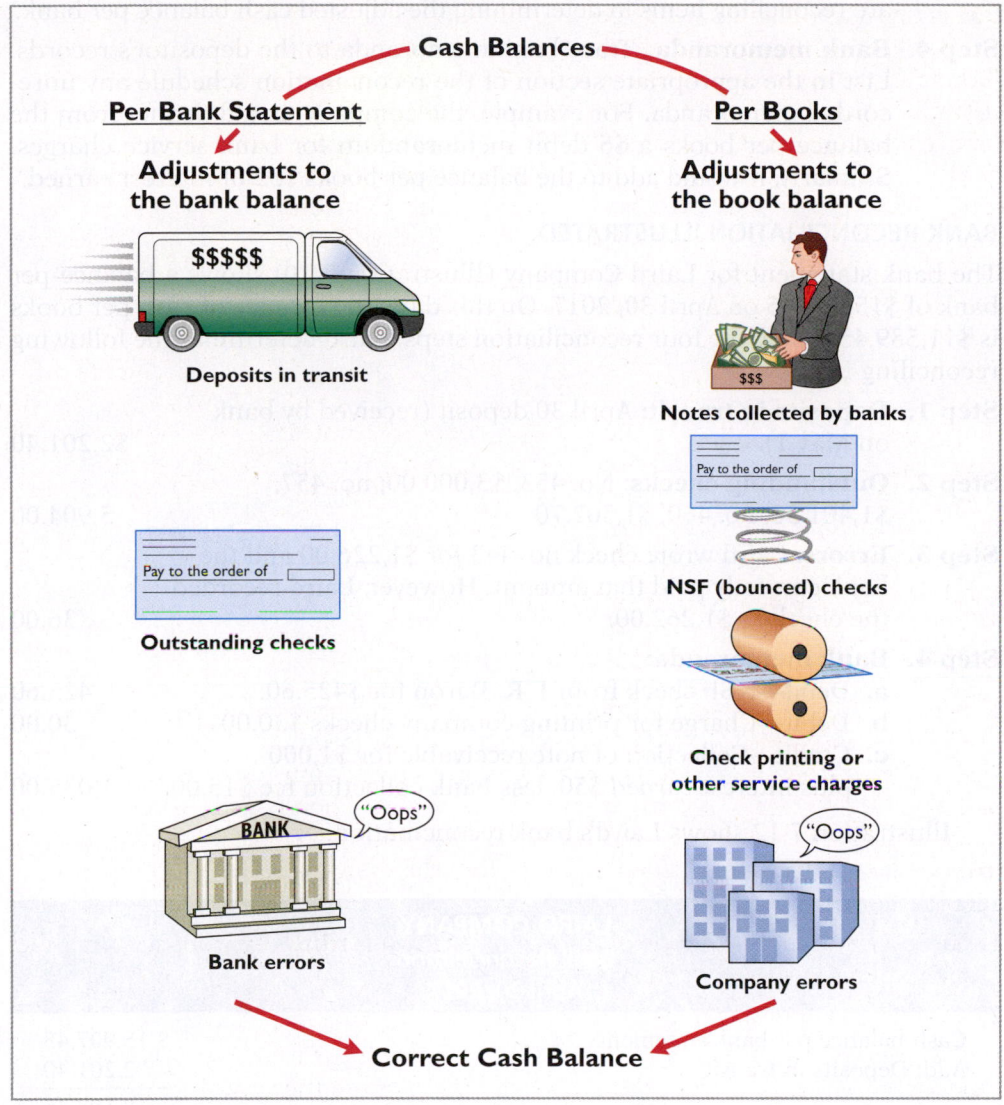

Illustration 7-11
Bank reconciliation adjustments

The following steps should reveal all the reconciling items that cause the difference between the two balances.

Step 1. Deposits in transit. Compare the individual deposits listed on the bank statement with deposits in transit from the preceding bank reconciliation and with the deposits per company records or duplicate deposit slips. Deposits recorded by the depositor that have not been recorded by the bank are the **deposits in transit**. Add these deposits to the balance per bank.

Step 2. Outstanding checks. Compare the paid checks shown on the bank statement with (a) checks outstanding from the previous bank reconciliation, and (b) checks issued by the company as recorded in the cash payments journal (or in the check register in your personal checkbook). Issued checks recorded by the company but that have not yet been paid by

Helpful Hint
Deposits in transit and outstanding checks are reconciling items because of time lags.

the bank are **outstanding checks**. Deduct outstanding checks from the balance per bank.

Step 3. Errors. Note any errors discovered in the foregoing steps and list them in the appropriate section of the reconciliation schedule. For example, if the company mistakenly recorded as $169 a paid check correctly written for $196, it would deduct the error of $27 from the balance per books. All errors made by the depositor are reconciling items in determining the adjusted cash balance per books. In contrast, all errors made by the bank are reconciling items in determining the adjusted cash balance per bank.

Step 4. Bank memoranda. Trace bank memoranda to the depositor's records. List in the appropriate section of the reconciliation schedule any unrecorded memoranda. For example, the company would deduct from the balance per books a $5 debit memorandum for bank service charges. Similarly, it would add to the balance per books $32 of interest earned.

BANK RECONCILIATION ILLUSTRATED

Helpful Hint
Note in the bank statement in Illustration 7-10 that checks no. 459 and 461 have been paid but check no. 460 is not listed. Thus, this check is outstanding. If a complete bank statement were shown, checks no. 453 and 457 would also not be listed. The amounts for these three checks are obtained from the company's cash payments records.

The bank statement for Laird Company (Illustration 7-10) shows a balance per bank of $15,907.45 on April 30, 2017. On this date, the balance of cash per books is $11,589.45. Using the four reconciliation steps, Laird determines the following reconciling items.

Step 1. Deposits in transit: April 30 deposit (received by bank on May 1). $2,201.40

Step 2. Outstanding checks: No. 453, $3,000.00; no. 457, $1,401.30; no. 460, $1,502.70.   5,904.00

Step 3. Errors: Laird wrote check no. 443 for $1,226.00 and the bank correctly paid that amount. However, Laird recorded the check as $1,262.00.   36.00

Step 4. Bank memoranda:
 a. Debit—NSF check from J. R. Baron for $425.60.   425.60
 b. Debit—Charge for printing company checks $30.00.   30.00
 c. Credit—Collection of note receivable for $1,000 plus interest earned $50, less bank collection fee $15.00.   1,035.00

Illustration 7-12 shows Laird's bank reconciliation.

Illustration 7-12
Bank reconciliation

Alternative Terminology
The terms *adjusted cash balance, true cash balance,* and *correct cash balance* are used interchangeably.

LAIRD COMPANY
Bank Reconciliation
April 30, 2017

Cash balance per bank statement		$ 15,907.45
Add: Deposits in transit		2,201.40
		18,108.85
Less: Outstanding checks		
No. 453	$3,000.00	
No. 457	1,401.30	
No. 460	1,502.70	5,904.00
Adjusted cash balance per bank		**$12,204.85** ←
Cash balance per books		$ 11,589.45
Add: Collection of note receivable $1,000, plus interest earned $50, less collection fee $15	$1,035.00	
Error in recording check no. 443	36.00	1,071.00
		12,660.45
Less: NSF check	425.60	
Bank service charge	30.00	455.60
Adjusted cash balance per books		**$12,204.85** ←

ENTRIES FROM BANK RECONCILIATION

The company records each reconciling item used to determine the **adjusted cash balance per books. If the company does not journalize and post these items, the Cash account will not show the correct balance.** Laird Company would make the following entries on April 30.

COLLECTION OF NOTE RECEIVABLE This entry involves four accounts. Assuming that the interest of $50 has not been accrued and the collection fee is charged to Miscellaneous Expense, the entry is:

Apr. 30	Cash	1,035.00	
	Miscellaneous Expense	15.00	
	Notes Receivable		1,000.00
	Interest Revenue		50.00
	(To record collection of note receivable by bank)		

BOOK ERROR The cash disbursements journal shows that check no. 443 was a payment on account to Andrea Company, a supplier. The correcting entry is:

Apr. 30	Cash	36.00	
	Accounts Payable—Andrea Company		36.00
	(To correct error in recording check no. 443)		

NSF CHECK As indicated earlier, an NSF check becomes an account receivable to the depositor. The entry is:

Apr. 30	Accounts Receivable—J. R. Baron	425.60	
	Cash		425.60
	(To record NSF check)		

BANK SERVICE CHARGES Depositors debit check printing charges (DM) and other bank service charges (SC) to Miscellaneous Expense because they are usually nominal in amount. The entry is:

Apr. 30	Miscellaneous Expense	30.00	
	Cash		30.00
	(To record charge for printing company checks)		

Instead of making four separate entries, Laird could combine them into one compound entry.

After Laird has posted the entries, the Cash account will show the following.

Cash			
Apr. 30 Bal.	11,589.45	Apr. 30	425.60
30	1,035.00	30	30.00
30	36.00		
Apr. 30 Bal.	**12,204.85**		

The adjusted cash balance in the ledger should agree with the adjusted cash balance per books in the bank reconciliation in Illustration 7-12 (page 330).

What entries does the bank make? If the company discovers any bank errors in preparing the reconciliation, it should notify the bank. The bank then can make the necessary corrections in its records. The bank does not make any entries for deposits in transit or outstanding checks. Only when these items reach the bank will the bank record these items.

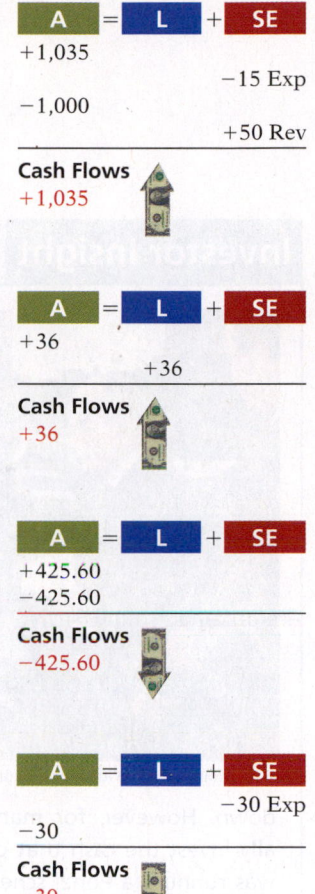

A = L + SE
+1,035
          −15 Exp
−1,000
          +50 Rev

Cash Flows
+1,035

A = L + SE
+36
     +36

Cash Flows
+36

A = L + SE
+425.60
−425.60

Cash Flows
−425.60

A = L + SE
          −30 Exp
−30

Cash Flows
−30

Illustration 7-13
Adjusted balance in Cash account

Electronic Funds Transfer (EFT) System

It is not surprising that companies and banks have developed approaches to transfer funds among parties without the use of paper (deposit tickets, checks, etc.). Such procedures, called **electronic funds transfers (EFT)**, are disbursement systems that use wire, telephone, or computers to transfer cash balances from one location to another. Use of EFT is quite common. For example, many employees receive no formal payroll checks from their employers. Instead, employers send electronic payroll data to the appropriate banks. Also, individuals and companies now frequently make regular payments such as those for house, car, and utilities by EFT.

EFT transactions normally result in better internal control since no cash or checks are handled by company employees. This does not mean that opportunities for fraud are eliminated. In fact, the same basic principles related to internal control apply to EFT transactions. For example, without proper segregation of duties and authorizations, an employee might be able to redirect electronic payments into a personal bank account and conceal the theft with fraudulent accounting entries.

Investor Insight

Mary Altaffer/©AP/Wide World Photos

Madoff's Ponzi Scheme

No recent fraud has generated more interest and rage than the one perpetrated by Bernard Madoff. Madoff was an elite New York investment fund manager who was highly regarded by securities regulators. Investors flocked to him because he delivered very steady returns of between 10% and 15%, no matter whether the market was going up or going down. However, for many years, Madoff did not actually invest the cash that people gave to him. Instead, he was running a Ponzi scheme: He paid returns to existing investors using cash received from new investors. As long as the size of his investment fund continued to grow from new investments at a rate that exceeded the amounts that he needed to pay out in returns, Madoff was able to operate his fraud smoothly.

To conceal his misdeeds, Madoff fabricated false investment statements that were provided to investors. In addition, Madoff hired an auditor that never verified the accuracy of the investment records but automatically issued unqualified opinions each year. Although a competing fund manager warned the SEC a number of times over a nearly 10-year period that he thought Madoff was engaged in fraud, the SEC never aggressively investigated the allegations. Investors, many of which were charitable organizations, lost more than $18 billion. Madoff was sentenced to a jail term of 150 years.

*How was Madoff able to conceal such a giant fraud? (Go to **WileyPLUS** for this answer and additional questions.)*

DO IT! 3 | Bank Reconciliation

Sally Kist owns Linen Kist Fabrics. Sally asks you to explain how she should treat the following reconciling items when reconciling the company's bank account: (1) a debit memorandum for an NSF check, (2) a credit memorandum for a note collected by the bank, (3) outstanding checks, and (4) a deposit in transit.

Solution

Action Plan

✔ Understand the purpose of a bank reconciliation.

✔ Identify time lags and explain how they cause reconciling items.

Sally should treat the reconciling items as follows.

(1) NSF check: Deduct from balance per books.

(2) Collection of note: Add to balance per books.

(3) Outstanding checks: Deduct from balance per bank.

(4) Deposit in transit: Add to balance per bank.

Related exercise material: **BE7-11, BE7-12, BE7-13, BE7-14, E7-9, E7-10, E7-11, E7-12, E7-13, and DO IT! 7-3.**

LEARNING OBJECTIVE 4   Explain the reporting of cash.

Cash consists of coins, currency (paper money), checks, money orders, and money on hand or on deposit in a bank or similar depository. Companies report cash in two different statements: the balance sheet and the statement of cash flows. The balance sheet reports the amount of cash available at a given point in time. The statement of cash flows shows the sources and uses of cash during a period of time. The statement of cash flows was introduced in Chapter 1 and will be discussed in much detail in Chapter 13. In this section, we discuss some important points regarding the presentation of cash in the balance sheet.

When presented in a balance sheet, cash on hand, cash in banks, and petty cash are often combined and reported simply as **Cash**. Because it is the most liquid asset owned by the company, cash is listed first in the current assets section of the balance sheet.

Cash Equivalents

Many companies use the designation "Cash and cash equivalents" in reporting cash. (See Illustration 7-14 for an example.) **Cash equivalents** are short-term, highly liquid investments that are both:

1. Readily convertible to known amounts of cash, and

2. So near their maturity that their market value is relatively insensitive to changes in interest rates. Generally, only investments with maturities of three months or less qualify under this definition.

Illustration 7-14
Balance sheet presentation of cash

Real World	DELTA AIR LINES, INC. Balance Sheet (partial) December 31, 2013 (in millions)	
Assets		
Current assets		
Cash and cash equivalents		$2,844
Short-term investments		959
Restricted cash		122

Examples of cash equivalents are Treasury bills, commercial paper (short-term corporate notes), and money market funds. All typically are purchased with cash that is in excess of immediate needs.

Occasionally, a company will have a net negative balance in its bank account. In this case, the company should report the negative balance among current liabilities. For example, farm equipment manufacturer **Ag-Chem** recently reported "Checks outstanding in excess of cash balances" of $2,145,000 among its current liabilities.

Restricted Cash

A company may have **restricted cash**, cash that is not available for general use but rather is restricted for a special purpose. For example, landfill companies are often required to maintain a fund of restricted cash to ensure they will have adequate resources to cover closing and clean-up costs at the end of a landfill site's useful life. **McKesson Corp.** recently reported restricted cash of $962 million to be paid out as the result of investor lawsuits.

Cash restricted in use should be reported separately on the balance sheet as restricted cash. If the company expects to use the restricted cash within the next year, it reports the amount as a current asset. When this is not the case, it reports the restricted funds as a noncurrent asset.

Illustration 7-14 shows restricted cash reported in the financial statements of **Delta Air Lines**. The company is required to maintain restricted cash as collateral to support insurance obligations related to workers' compensation claims. Delta does not have access to these funds for general use, and so it must report them separately, rather than as part of cash and cash equivalents.

DO IT! 4   Reporting Cash

Indicate whether each of the following statements is true or false.

1. Cash and cash equivalents are comprised of coins, currency (paper money), money orders, and NSF checks.

2. Restricted cash is classified as either a current asset or noncurrent asset, depending on the circumstances.

3. A company may have a negative balance in its bank account. In this case, it should offset this negative balance against cash and cash equivalents on the balance sheet.

4. Because cash and cash equivalents often includes short-term investments, accounts receivable should be reported as the first item on the balance sheet.

Action Plan

✔ Understand how companies present cash and restricted cash on the balance sheet.

✔ Review the designations of cash equivalents and restricted cash, and how companies typically handle them.

Solution

1. False. NSF checks should be reported as receivables, not cash and cash equivalents.
2. True.   3. False. Companies that have a negative balance in their bank accounts should report the negative balance as a current liability.   4. False. Cash equivalents are readily convertible to known amounts of cash, and so near maturity (less than 3 months) that they are considered more liquid than accounts receivable and therefore are reported before accounts receivable on the balance sheet.

Related exercise material: **E7-14, E7-15, and DO IT! 7-4.**

REVIEW AND PRACTICE

LEARNING OBJECTIVES REVIEW

1 **Discuss fraud and the principles of internal control.** A fraud is a dishonest act by an employee that results in personal benefit to the employee at a cost to the employer. The fraud triangle refers to the three factors that contribute to fraudulent activity by employees: opportunity, financial pressure, and rationalization. Internal control consists of all the related methods and measures adopted within an organization to safeguard its assets, enhance the reliability of its accounting records, increase efficiency of operations, and ensure compliance with laws and regulations.

The principles of internal control are establishment of responsibility, segregation of duties, documentation procedures, physical controls, independent internal verification, and human resource controls such as bonding and requiring employees to take vacations.

2 **Apply internal control principles to cash.** Internal controls over cash receipts include (a) designating specific personnel to handle cash; (b) assigning different individuals to receive cash, record cash, and maintain custody of cash; (c) using remittance advices for mail receipts, cash register tapes for over-the-counter receipts, and deposit slips for bank deposits; (d) using company safes and bank vaults to store cash with access limited to authorized personnel, and using cash registers in executing over-the-counter receipts; (e) making independent daily counts of register receipts and daily comparison of total receipts with total deposits; and (f) bonding personnel that handle cash and requiring them to take vacations.

Internal controls over cash disbursements include (a) having specific individuals such as the treasurer authorized to sign checks and approve vendors; (b) assigning different individuals to approve items for payment, make the payment, and record the payment; (c) using prenumbered checks and accounting for all checks, with each check supported by an approved invoice; (d) storing blank checks in a safe or vault with access restricted to authorized personnel, and using a check-writing machine to imprint amounts on checks; (e) comparing each check with the approved invoice before issuing the check, and making monthly reconciliations of bank and book balances; and (f) bonding personnel who handle cash, requiring employees to take vacations, and conducting background checks.

Companies operate a petty cash fund to pay relatively small amounts of cash. They must establish the fund, make payments from the fund, and replenish the fund when the cash in the fund reaches a minimum level.

3 Identify the control features of a bank account. A bank account contributes to good internal control by providing physical controls for the storage of cash. It minimizes the amount of currency that a company must keep on hand, and it creates a double record of a depositor's bank transactions. It is customary to reconcile the balance per books and balance per bank to their adjusted balances. The steps in the reconciling process are to determine deposits in transit, outstanding checks, errors by the depositor or the bank, and unrecorded bank memoranda.

4 Explain the reporting of cash. Companies list cash first in the current assets section of the balance sheet. In some cases, they report cash together with cash equivalents. Cash restricted for a special purpose is reported separately as a current asset or as a noncurrent asset, depending on when the cash is expected to be used.

GLOSSARY REVIEW

Bank reconciliation The process of comparing the bank's balance of an account with the company's balance and explaining any differences to make them agree. (p. 325).

Bank service charge A fee charged by a bank for the use of its services. (p. 328).

Bank statement A monthly statement from the bank that shows the depositor's bank transactions and balances. (p. 327).

Bonding Obtaining insurance protection against theft by employees. (p. 315).

Cash Resources that consist of coins, currency, checks, money orders, and money on hand or on deposit in a bank or similar depository. (p. 333).

Cash equivalents Short-term, highly liquid investments that can be converted to a specific amount of cash. (p. 333).

Check A written order signed by a bank depositor, directing the bank to pay a specified sum of money to a designated recipient. (p. 326).

Deposits in transit Deposits recorded by the depositor but not yet recorded by the bank. (p. 329).

Electronic funds transfer (EFT) A disbursement system that uses wire, telephone, or computers to transfer funds from one location to another. (p. 332).

Fraud A dishonest act by an employee that results in personal benefit to the employee at a cost to the employer. (p. 308).

Fraud triangle The three factors that contribute to fraudulent activity by employees: opportunity, financial pressure, and rationalization. (p. 308).

Internal auditors Company employees who continuously evaluate the effectiveness of the company's internal control system. (p. 315).

Internal control A process designed to provide reasonable assurance regarding the achievement of objectives related to operations, reporting, and compliance. (p. 309)

NSF check A check that is not paid by a bank because of insufficient funds in a customer's bank account. (p. 328).

Outstanding checks Checks issued and recorded by a company but not yet paid by the bank. (p. 330).

Petty cash fund A cash fund used to pay relatively small amounts. (p. 322).

Restricted cash Cash that must be used for a special purpose. (p. 333).

Sarbanes-Oxley Act (SOX) Regulations passed by Congress to try to reduce unethical corporate behavior. (p. 308).

Voucher An authorization form prepared for each payment in a voucher system. (p. 321).

Voucher system A network of approvals by authorized individuals acting independently to ensure that all disbursements by check are proper. (p. 321).

PRACTICE MULTIPLE-CHOICE QUESTIONS

(LO 1) **1.** Which of the following is **not** an element of the fraud triangle?
(a) Rationalization. (c) Segregation of duties.
(b) Financial pressure. (d) Opportunity.

2. An organization uses internal control to enhance the (LO 1) accuracy and reliability of accounting records and to:
(a) safeguard assets.
(b) prevent fraud.

(c) produce correct financial statements.

(d) deter employee dishonesty.

(LO 1) **3.** Which of the following was **not** a result of the Sarbanes-Oxley Act?

(a) Companies must file financial statements with the Internal Revenue Service.

(b) All publicly traded companies must maintain adequate internal controls.

(c) The Public Company Accounting Oversight Board was created to establish auditing standards and regulate auditor activity.

(d) Corporate executives and board of directors must ensure that controls are reliable and effective, and they can be fined or imprisoned for failure to do so.

(LO 1) **4.** The principles of internal control do **not** include:

(a) establishment of responsibility.

(b) documentation procedures.

(c) management responsibility.

(d) independent internal verification.

(LO 1) **5.** Physical controls do **not** include:

(a) safes and vaults to store cash.

(b) independent bank reconciliations.

(c) locked warehouses for inventories.

(d) bank safety deposit boxes for important papers.

(LO 1) **6.** Which of the following control activities is **not** relevant when a company uses a computerized (rather than manual) accounting system?

(a) Establishment of responsibility.

(b) Segregation of duties.

(c) Independent internal verification.

(d) All of these control activities are relevant to a computerized system.

(LO 2) **7.** Permitting only designated personnel to handle cash receipts is an application of the principle of:

(a) segregation of duties.

(b) establishment of responsibility.

(c) independent internal verification.

(d) human resource controls.

(LO 2) **8.** The use of prenumbered checks in disbursing cash is an application of the principle of:

(a) establishment of responsibility.

(b) segregation of duties.

(c) physical controls.

(d) documentation procedures.

(LO 2) **9.** A company writes a check to replenish a $100 petty cash fund when the fund contains receipts of $94 and $4 in cash. In recording the check, the company should:

(a) debit Cash Over and Short for $2.

(b) debit Petty Cash for $94.

(c) credit Cash for $94.

(d) credit Petty Cash for $2.

(LO 3) **10.** The control features of a bank account do **not** include:

(a) having bank auditors verify the correctness of the bank balance per books.

(b) minimizing the amount of cash that must be kept on hand.

(c) providing a double record of all bank transactions.

(d) safeguarding cash by using a bank as a depository.

(LO 3) **11.** In a bank reconciliation, deposits in transit are:

(a) deducted from the book balance.

(b) added to the book balance.

(c) added to the bank balance.

(d) deducted from the bank balance.

(LO 3) **12.** The reconciling item in a bank reconciliation that will result in an adjusting entry by the depositor is:

(a) outstanding checks.   (c) a bank error.

(b) deposit in transit.   (d) bank service charges.

(LO 4) **13.** Which of the following items in a cash drawer at November 30 is **not** cash?

(a) Money orders.

(b) Coins and currency.

(c) An NSF check.

(d) A customer check dated November 28.

(LO 4) **14.** Which of the following statements correctly describes the reporting of cash?

(a) Cash cannot be combined with cash equivalents.

(b) Restricted cash funds may be combined with cash.

(c) Cash is listed first in the current assets section.

(d) Restricted cash funds cannot be reported as a current asset.

Solutions

1. (c) Segregation of duties is not an element of the fraud triangle. The other choices are fraud triangle elements.

2. (a) Safeguarding assets is one of the purposes of using internal control. The other choices are incorrect because while internal control can help to (b) prevent fraud, (c) produce correct financial statements, and (d) deter employee dishonesty, it is not one of the main purposes of using it.

3. (a) Filing financial statements with the IRS is not a result of the Sarbanes-Oxley Act (SOX); SOX focuses on the prevention or detection of fraud. The other choices are results of SOX.

4. (c) Management responsibility is not one of the principles of internal control. The other choices are true statements.

5. (b) Independent bank reconciliations are not a physical control. The other choices are true statements.

6. (d) Establishment of responsibility, segregation of duties, and independent internal verification are all relevant to a computerized system.

7. (b) Permitting only designated personnel to handle cash receipts is an application of the principle of establishment of responsibility, not (a) segregation of duties, (c) independent internal verification, or (d) human resource controls.

8. (d) The use of prenumbered checks in disbursing cash is an application of the principle of documentation procedures, not (a) establishment of responsibility, (b) segregation of duties, or (c) physical controls.

9. (a) When this check is recorded, the company should debit Cash Over and Short for the shortage of $2 (total of the receipts plus cash in the drawer ($98) versus $100), not (b) debit Petty Cash for $94, (c) credit Cash for $94, or (d) credit Petty Cash for $2.

10. (a) Having bank auditors verify the correctness of the bank balance per books is not one of the control features of a bank account. The other choices are true statements.

11. (c) Deposits in transit are added to the bank balance on a bank reconciliation, not (a) deducted from the book balance, (b) added to the book balance, or (d) deducted from the bank balance.

12. (d) Because the depositor does not know the amount of the bank service charges until the bank statement is received, an adjusting entry must be made when the statement is received. The other choices are incorrect because (a) outstanding checks do not require an adjusting entry by the depositor because the checks have already been recorded in the depositor's books, (b) deposits in transit do not require an adjusting entry by the depositor because the deposits have already been recorded in the depositor's books, and (c) bank errors do not require an adjusting entry by the depositor, but the depositor does need to inform the bank of the error so it can be corrected.

13. (c) An NSF check should not be considered cash. The other choices are true statements.

14. (c) Cash is listed first in the current assets section. The other choices are incorrect because (a) cash and cash equivalents can be appropriately combined when reporting cash on the balance sheet, (b) restricted cash is not to be combined with cash when reporting cash on the balance sheet, and (d) restricted funds can be reported as current assets if they will be used within one year.

PRACTICE EXERCISES

1. Listed below are five procedures followed by Shepherd Company.

1. Total cash receipts are compared to bank deposits daily by someone who has no other cash responsibilities.
2. Time clocks are used for recording time worked by employees.
3. Employees are required to take vacations.
4. Any member of the sales department can approve credit sales.
5. Sam Hill ships goods to customers, bills customers, and receives payment from customers.

Indicate whether procedure is good or weak internal control.

(LO 1, 2)

Instructions

Indicate whether each procedure is an example of good internal control or of weak internal control. If it is an example of good internal control, indicate which internal control principle is being followed. If it is an example of weak internal control, indicate which internal control principle is violated. Use the table below.

Procedure	IC Good or Weak	Related Internal Control Principle
1.		
2.		
3.		
4.		
5.		

Solution

1.

Procedure	IC Good or Weak?	Related Internal Control Principle
1.	Good	Independent internal verification
2.	Good	Physical controls
3.	Good	Human resource controls
4.	Weak	Establishment of responsibility
5.	Weak	Segregation of duties

2. The information below relates to the Cash account in the ledger of Ansel Company.

Balance June 1—$17,150; Cash deposited—$64,000.
Balance June 30—$17,704; Checks written—$63,746.

Prepare bank reconciliation and adjusting entries.

(LO 3)

The June bank statement shows a balance of $16,422 on June 30 and the following memoranda.

Credits		Debits	
Collection of $1,500 note plus interest $30	$1,530	NSF check: Anne Adams	$425
Interest earned on checking account	$35	Safety deposit box rent	$55

At June 30, deposits in transit were $4,750, and outstanding checks totaled $2,383.

Instructions

(a) Prepare the bank reconciliation at June 30.

(b) Prepare the adjusting entries at June 30, assuming (1) the NSF check was from a customer on account, and (2) no interest had been accrued on the note.

Solution

2. (a)

ANSEL COMPANY
Bank Reconciliation
June 30

Cash balance per bank statement		$16,422
Add: Deposits in transit		4,750
		21,172
Less: Outstanding checks		2,383
Adjusted cash balance per bank		$18,789
Cash balance per books		$17,704
Add: Collection of note receivable ($1,500 + $30)	$1,530	
Interest earned	35	1,565
		19,269
Less: NSF check	425	
Safety deposit box rent	55	480
Adjusted cash balance per books		$18,789

(b)

June 30	Cash		1,530	
	Notes Receivable			1,500
	Interest Revenue			30
30	Cash		35	
	Interest Revenue			35
30	Accounts Receivable (Anne Adams)		425	
	Cash			425
30	Miscellaneous Expense		55	
	Cash			55

■ PRACTICE PROBLEM

Prepare bank reconciliation and journalize entries.

(LO 3)

Poorten Company's bank statement for May 2017 shows the following data.

Balance 5/1	$12,650	Balance 5/31		$14,280
Debit memorandum:		Credit memorandum:		
NSF check	$175	Collection of note receivable		$505

The cash balance per books at May 31 is $13,319. Your review of the data reveals the following.

1. The NSF check was from Copple Co., a customer.

2. The note collected by the bank was a $500, 3-month, 12% note. The bank charged a $10 collection fee. No interest has been accrued.

3. Outstanding checks at May 31 total $2,410.

4. Deposits in transit at May 31 total $1,752.

5. A Poorten Company check for $352, dated May 10, cleared the bank on May 25. The company recorded this check, which was a payment on account, for $325.

Instructions

(a) Prepare a bank reconciliation at May 31.

(b) Journalize the entries required by the reconciliation.

Solution

(a)

POORTEN COMPANY
Bank Reconciliation
May 31, 2017

Cash balance per bank statement		$14,280
Add: Deposits in transit		1,752
		16,032
Less: Outstanding checks		2,410
Adjusted cash balance per bank		$13,622
Cash balance per books		$13,319
Add: Collection of note receivable $500, plus $15		
interest, less collection fee $10		505
		13,824
Less: NSF check	$175	
Error in recording check	27	202
Adjusted cash balance per books		$13,622

(b)

May 31	Cash		505	
	Miscellaneous Expense		10	
	Notes Receivable			500
	Interest Revenue			15
	(To record collection of note by bank)			
31	Accounts Receivable—Copple Co.		175	
	Cash			175
	(To record NSF check from Copple Co.)			
31	Accounts Payable		27	
	Cash			27
	(To correct error in recording check)			

WileyPLUS Brief Exercises, Exercises, DO IT! Exercises, and Problems and many additional resources are available for practice in WileyPLUS

QUESTIONS

1. A local bank reported that it lost $150,000 as the result of an employee fraud. Edward Jasso is not clear on what is meant by an "employee fraud." Explain the meaning of fraud to Edward and give an example of frauds that might occur at a bank.

2. Fraud experts often say that there are three primary factors that contribute to employee fraud. Identify the three factors and explain what is meant by each.

3. Identify and describe the five components of a good internal control system.

4. "Internal control is concerned only with enhancing the accuracy of the accounting records." Do you agree? Explain.

5. What principles of internal control apply to most organizations?

6. At the corner grocery store, all sales clerks make change out of one cash register drawer. Is this a violation of internal control? Why?

7. Liz Kelso is reviewing the principle of segregation of duties. What are the two common applications of this principle?

8. How do documentation procedures contribute to good internal control?

9. What internal control objectives are met by physical controls?

10. (a) Explain the control principle of independent internal verification. (b) What practices are important in applying this principle?

11. The management of Nickle Company asks you, as the company accountant, to explain (a) the concept

of reasonable assurance in internal control and (b) the importance of the human factor in internal control.

12. Riverside Fertilizer Co. owns the following assets at the balance sheet date.

Cash in bank savings account	$ 8,000
Cash on hand	850
Cash refund due from the IRS	1,000
Checking account balance	14,000
Postdated checks	500

What amount should Riverside report as cash in the balance sheet?

13. What principle(s) of internal control is (are) involved in making daily cash counts of over-the-counter receipts?

14. Seaton Department Stores has just installed new electronic cash registers in its stores. How do cash registers improve internal control over cash receipts?

15. At Kellum Wholesale Company, two mail clerks open all mail receipts. How does this strengthen internal control?

16. "To have maximum effective internal control over cash disbursements, all payments should be made by check." Is this true? Explain.

17. Ken Deangelo Company's internal controls over cash disbursements provide for the treasurer to sign checks imprinted by a check-writing machine in indelible ink after comparing the check with the approved invoice. Identify the internal control principles that are present in these controls.

18. How do the principles of (a) physical controls and (b) documentation controls apply to cash disbursements?

19. (a) What is a voucher system? (b) What principles of internal control apply to a voucher system?

20. What is the essential feature of an electronic funds transfer (EFT) procedure?

21. (a) Identify the three activities that pertain to a petty cash fund, and indicate an internal control principle that is applicable to each activity. (b) When are journal entries required in the operation of a petty cash fund?

22. "The use of a bank contributes significantly to good internal control over cash." Is this true? Why or why not?

23. Anna Korte is confused about the lack of agreement between the cash balance per books and the balance per bank. Explain the causes for the lack of agreement to Anna, and give an example of each cause.

24. What are the four steps involved in finding differences between the balance per books and balance per bank?

25. Heather Kemp asks your help concerning an NSF check. Explain to Heather (a) what an NSF check is, (b) how it is treated in a bank reconciliation, and (c) whether it will require an adjusting entry.

26. (a) "Cash equivalents are the same as cash." Do you agree? Explain. (b) How should restricted cash funds be reported on the balance sheet?

27. At what amount does **Apple** report cash and cash equivalents in its 2013 consolidated balance sheet?

BRIEF EXERCISES

Identify fraud triangle concepts.

(LO 1)

BE7-1 Match each situation with the fraud triangle factor—opportunity, financial pressure, or rationalization—that best describes it.
1. An employee's monthly credit card payments are nearly 75% of his or her monthly earnings.
2. An employee earns minimum wage at a firm that has reported record earnings for each of the last five years.
3. An employee has an expensive gambling habit.
4. An employee has check-writing and -signing responsibilities for a small company, as well as reconciling the bank account.

Indicate internal control concepts.

(LO 1)

BE7-2 Shelly Eckert has prepared the following list of statements about internal control.
1. One of the objectives of internal control is to safeguard assets from employee theft, robbery, and unauthorized use.
2. One of the objectives of internal control is to enhance the accuracy and reliability of the accounting records.
3. No laws require U.S. corporations to maintain an adequate system of internal control.

Identify each statement as true or false. If false, indicate how to correct the statement.

Explain the importance of internal control.

(LO 1)

BE7-3 Jessica Mahan is the new owner of Penny Parking. She has heard about internal control but is not clear about its importance for her business. Explain to Jessica the four purposes of internal control and give her one application of each purpose for Penny Parking.

Identify internal control principles.

(LO 1)

BE7-4 The internal control procedures in Valentine Company provide that:
1. Employees who have physical custody of assets do not have access to the accounting records.
2. Each month, the assets on hand are compared to the accounting records by an internal auditor.
3. A prenumbered shipping document is prepared for each shipment of goods to customers.

Identify the principles of internal control that are being followed.

BE7-5 Rosenquist Company has the following internal control procedures over cash receipts. Identify the internal control principle that is applicable to each procedure.
1. All over-the-counter receipts are entered in cash registers.
2. All cashiers are bonded.
3. Daily cash counts are made by cashier department supervisors.
4. The duties of receiving cash, recording cash, and custody of cash are assigned to different individuals.
5. Only cashiers may operate cash registers.

Identify the internal control principles applicable to cash receipts.

(LO 2)

BE7-6 The cash register tape for Bluestem Industries reported sales of $6,871.50. Record the journal entry that would be necessary for each of the following situations. (a) Cash to be accounted for exceeds cash on hand by $50.75. (b) Cash on hand exceeds cash to be accounted for by $28.32.

Make journal entries for cash overage and shortfall.

(LO 2)

BE7-7 While examining cash receipts information, the accounting department determined the following information: opening cash balance $160, cash on hand $1,125.74, and cash sales per register tape $980.83. Prepare the required journal entry based upon the cash count sheet.

Make journal entry using cash count sheet.

(LO 2)

BE7-8 Pennington Company has the following internal control procedures over cash disbursements. Identify the internal control principle that is applicable to each procedure.
1. Company checks are prenumbered.
2. The bank statement is reconciled monthly by an internal auditor.
3. Blank checks are stored in a safe in the treasurer's office.
4. Only the treasurer or assistant treasurer may sign checks.
5. Check-signers are not allowed to record cash disbursement transactions.

Identify the internal control principles applicable to cash disbursements.

(LO 2)

BE7-9 On March 20, Dody's petty cash fund of $100 is replenished when the fund contains $9 in cash and receipts for postage $52, freight-out $26, and travel expense $10. Prepare the journal entry to record the replenishment of the petty cash fund.

Prepare entry to replenish a petty cash fund.

(LO 2)

BE7-10 Lance Bachman is uncertain about the control features of a bank account. Explain the control benefits of (a) a check and (b) a bank statement.

Identify the control features of a bank account.

(LO 3)

BE7-11 The following reconciling items are applicable to the bank reconciliation for Ellington Company: (1) outstanding checks, (2) bank debit memorandum for service charge, (3) bank credit memorandum for collecting a note for the depositor, and (4) deposits in transit. Indicate how each item should be shown on a bank reconciliation.

Indicate location of reconciling items in a bank reconciliation.

(LO 3)

BE7-12 Using the data in BE7-11, indicate (a) the items that will result in an adjustment to the depositor's records and (b) why the other items do not require adjustment.

Identify reconciling items that require adjusting entries.

(LO 3)

BE7-13 At July 31, Ramirez Company has the following bank information: cash balance per bank $7,420, outstanding checks $762, deposits in transit $1,620, and a bank service charge $20. Determine the adjusted cash balance per bank at July 31.

Prepare partial bank reconciliation.

(LO 3)

BE7-14 At August 31, Pratt Company has a cash balance per books of $9,500 and the following additional data from the bank statement: charge for printing Pratt Company checks $35, interest earned on checking account balance $40, and outstanding checks $800. Determine the adjusted cash balance per books at August 31.

Prepare partial bank reconciliation.

(LO 3)

BE7-15 Zhang Company has the following cash balances: Cash in Bank $15,742, Payroll Bank Account $6,000, and Plant Expansion Fund Cash $25,000 to be used two years from now. Explain how each balance should be reported on the balance sheet.

Explain the statement presentation of cash balances.

(LO 4)

DO IT! Exercises

Identify violations of control activities.

(LO 1)

DO IT! 7-1 Identify which control activity is violated in each of the following situations, and explain how the situation creates an opportunity for fraud or inappropriate accounting practices.

1. Once a month, the sales department sends sales invoices to the accounting department to be recorded.
2. Leah Hutcherson orders merchandise for Rice Lake Company; she also receives merchandise and authorizes payment for merchandise.
3. Several clerks at Great Foods use the same cash register drawer.

Design system of internal control over cash receipts.

(LO 2)

DO IT! 7-2a Gary Stanten is concerned with control over mail receipts at Gary's Sporting Goods. All mail receipts are opened by Al Krane. Al sends the checks to the accounting department, where they are stamped "For Deposit Only." The accounting department records and deposits the mail receipts weekly. Gary asks for your help in installing a good system of internal control over mail receipts.

Make journal entries for petty cash fund.

(LO 2)

DO IT! 7-2b Wilkinson Company established a $100 petty cash fund on August 1. On August 31, the fund had $7 cash remaining and petty cash receipts for postage $31, office supplies $42, and miscellaneous expense $16. Prepare journal entries to establish the fund on August 1 and replenish the fund on August 31.

Explain treatment of items in bank reconciliation.

(LO 3)

DO IT! 7-3 Roger Richman owns Richman Blankets. He asks you to explain how he should treat the following reconciling items when reconciling the company's bank account.

1. Outstanding checks.
2. A deposit in transit.
3. The bank charged to the company account a check written by another company.
4. A debit memorandum for a bank service charge.

Analyze statements about the reporting of cash.

(LO 4)

DO IT! 7-4 Indicate whether each of the following statements is true or false.

1. A company has the following assets at the end of the year: cash on hand $40,000, cash refund due from customer $30,000, and checking account balance $22,000. Cash and cash equivalents is therefore $62,000.
2. A company that has received NSF checks should report these checks as a current liability on the balance sheet.
3. Restricted cash that is a current asset is reported as part of cash and cash equivalents.
4. A company has cash in the bank of $50,000, petty cash of $400, and stock investments of $100,000. Total cash and cash equivalents is therefore $50,400.

EXERCISES

Identify the principles of internal control.

(LO 1)

E7-1 Eve Herschel is the owner of Herschel's Pizza. Herschel's is operated strictly on a carryout basis. Customers pick up their orders at a counter where a clerk exchanges the pizza for cash. While at the counter, the customer can see other employees making the pizzas and the large ovens in which the pizzas are baked.

Instructions
Identify the six principles of internal control and give an example of each principle that you might observe when picking up your pizza. (*Note:* It may not be possible to observe all the principles.)

Identify internal control weaknesses over cash receipts and suggest improvements.

(LO 1, 2)

E7-2 The following control procedures are used at Torres Company for over-the-counter cash receipts.

1. To minimize the risk of robbery, cash in excess of $100 is stored in an unlocked attaché case in the stockroom until it is deposited in the bank.
2. All over-the-counter receipts are processed by three clerks who use a cash register with a single cash drawer.
3. The company accountant makes the bank deposit and then records the day's receipts.

4. At the end of each day, the total receipts are counted by the cashier on duty and reconciled to the cash register total.
5. Cashiers are experienced; they are not bonded.

Instructions

(a) For each procedure, explain the weakness in internal control, and identify the control principle that is violated.
(b) For each weakness, suggest a change in procedure that will result in good internal control.

E7-3 The following control procedures are used in Mendy Lang's Boutique Shoppe for cash disbursements.

1. The company accountant prepares the bank reconciliation and reports any discrepancies to the owner.
2. The store manager personally approves all payments before signing and issuing checks.
3. Each week, 100 company checks are left in an unmarked envelope on a shelf behind the cash register.
4. After payment, bills are filed in a paid invoice folder.
5. The company checks are unnumbered.

Identify internal control weaknesses over cash disbursements and suggest improvements.

(LO 1, 2)

Instructions

(a) For each procedure, explain the weakness in internal control, and identify the internal control principle that is violated.
(b) For each weakness, suggest a change in the procedure that will result in good internal control.

E7-4 At Danner Company, checks are not prenumbered because both the purchasing agent and the treasurer are authorized to issue checks. Each signer has access to unissued checks kept in an unlocked file cabinet. The purchasing agent pays all bills pertaining to goods purchased for resale. Prior to payment, the purchasing agent determines that the goods have been received and verifies the mathematical accuracy of the vendor's invoice. After payment, the invoice is filed by the vendor name, and the purchasing agent records the payment in the cash disbursements journal. The treasurer pays all other bills following approval by authorized employees. After payment, the treasurer stamps all bills PAID, files them by payment date, and records the checks in the cash disbursements journal. Danner Company maintains one checking account that is reconciled by the treasurer.

Identify internal control weaknesses for cash disbursements and suggest improvements.

(LO 2)

Instructions

(a) List the weaknesses in internal control over cash disbursements.
(b) ✏——— Write a memo to the company treasurer indicating your recommendations for improvement.

E7-5 Listed below are five procedures followed by Eikenberry Company.

1. Several individuals operate the cash register using the same register drawer.
2. A monthly bank reconciliation is prepared by someone who has no other cash responsibilities.
3. Joe Cockrell writes checks and also records cash payment journal entries.
4. One individual orders inventory, while a different individual authorizes payments.
5. Unnumbered sales invoices from credit sales are forwarded to the accounting department every four weeks for recording.

Indicate whether procedure is good or weak internal control.

(LO 1, 2)

Instructions

Indicate whether each procedure is an example of good internal control or of weak internal control. If it is an example of good internal control, indicate which internal control principle is being followed. If it is an example of weak internal control, indicate which internal control principle is violated. Use the table below.

Procedure	IC Good or Weak?	Related Internal Control Principle
1.		
2.		
3.		
4.		
5.		

Indicate whether procedure is good or weak internal control.

(LO 1, 2)

E7-6 Listed below are five procedures followed by Gilmore Company.

1. Employees are required to take vacations.
2. Any member of the sales department can approve credit sales.
3. Paul Jaggard ships goods to customers, bills customers, and receives payment from customers.
4. Total cash receipts are compared to bank deposits daily by someone who has no other cash responsibilities.
5. Time clocks are used for recording time worked by employees.

Instructions

Indicate whether each procedure is an example of good internal control or of weak internal control. If it is an example of good internal control, indicate which internal control principle is being followed. If it is an example of weak internal control, indicate which internal control principle is violated. Use the table below.

Procedure	IC Good or Weak?	Related Internal Control Principle
1.		
2.		
3.		
4.		
5.		

Prepare journal entries for a petty cash fund.

(LO 2)

E7-7 Setterstrom Company established a petty cash fund on May 1, cashing a check for $100. The company reimbursed the fund on June 1 and July 1 with the following results.

June 1: Cash in fund $1.75. Receipts: delivery expense $31.25, postage expense $39.00, and miscellaneous expense $25.00.
July 1: Cash in fund $3.25. Receipts: delivery expense $21.00, entertainment expense $51.00, and miscellaneous expense $24.75.

On July 10, Setterstrom increased the fund from $100 to $130.

Instructions

Prepare journal entries for Setterstrom Company for May 1, June 1, July 1, and July 10.

Prepare journal entries for a petty cash fund.

(LO 2)

E7-8 Horvath Company uses an imprest petty cash system. The fund was established on March 1 with a balance of $100. During March, the following petty cash receipts were found in the petty cash box.

Date	Receipt No.	For	Amount
3/5	1	Stamp Inventory	$39
7	2	Freight-Out	21
9	3	Miscellaneous Expense	6
11	4	Travel Expense	24
14	5	Miscellaneous Expense	5

The fund was replenished on March 15 when the fund contained $2 in cash. On March 20, the amount in the fund was increased to $175.

Instructions

Journalize the entries in March that pertain to the operation of the petty cash fund.

Prepare bank reconciliation and adjusting entries.

(LO 3)

E7-9 Don Wyatt is unable to reconcile the bank balance at January 31. Don's reconciliation is as follows.

Cash balance per bank	$3,560.20
Add: NSF check	490.00
Less: Bank service charge	25.00
Adjusted balance per bank	$4,025.20
Cash balance per books	$3,875.20
Less: Deposits in transit	530.00
Add: Outstanding checks	730.00
Adjusted balance per books	$4,075.20

Instructions
(a) Prepare a correct bank reconciliation.
(b) Journalize the entries required by the reconciliation.

E7-10 On April 30, the bank reconciliation of Westbrook Company shows three outstanding checks: no. 254, $650; no. 255, $620; and no. 257, $410. The May bank statement and the May cash payments journal are shown as follows.

Determine outstanding checks.

(LO 3)

Bank Statement			Cash Payments Journal		
Checks Paid			Checks Issued		
Date	Check No.	Amount	Date	Check No.	Amount
5/4	254	$650	5/2	258	$159
5/2	257	410	5/5	259	275
5/17	258	159	5/10	260	890
5/12	259	275	5/15	261	500
5/20	261	500	5/22	262	750
5/29	263	480	5/24	263	480
5/30	262	750	5/29	264	560

Instructions
Using Step 2 in the reconciliation procedure, list the outstanding checks at May 31.

E7-11 The following information pertains to Crane Video Company.

1. Cash balance per bank, July 31, $7,263.
2. July bank service charge not recorded by the depositor $28.
3. Cash balance per books, July 31, $7,284.
4. Deposits in transit, July 31, $1,300.
5. Bank collected $700 note for Crane in July, plus interest $36, less fee $20. The collection has not been recorded by Crane, and no interest has been accrued.
6. Outstanding checks, July 31, $591.

Prepare bank reconciliation and adjusting entries.

(LO 3)

Instructions
(a) Prepare a bank reconciliation at July 31.
(b) Journalize the adjusting entries at July 31 on the books of Crane Video Company.

E7-12 The information below relates to the Cash account in the ledger of Minton Company.

> Balance September 1—$17,150; Cash deposited—$64,000.
> Balance September 30—$17,404; Checks written—$63,746.

Prepare bank reconciliation and adjusting entries.

(LO 3)

The September bank statement shows a balance of $16,422 on September 30 and the following memoranda.

Credits		Debits	
Collection of $2,500 note plus interest $30	$2,530	NSF check: Richard Nance	$425
Interest earned on checking account	$45	Safety deposit box rent	$65

At September 30, deposits in transit were $5,450, and outstanding checks totaled $2,383.

Instructions
(a) Prepare the bank reconciliation at September 30.
(b) Prepare the adjusting entries at September 30, assuming (1) the NSF check was from a customer on account, and (2) no interest had been accrued on the note.

E7-13 The cash records of Dawes Company show the following four situations.

1. The June 30 bank reconciliation indicated that deposits in transit total $920. During July, the general ledger account Cash shows deposits of $15,750, but the bank statement indicates that only $15,600 in deposits were received during the month.
2. The June 30 bank reconciliation also reported outstanding checks of $680. During the month of July, Dawes Company's books show that $17,200 of checks were issued. The bank statement showed that $16,400 of checks cleared the bank in July.

Compute deposits in transit and outstanding checks for two bank reconciliations.

(LO 3)

3. In September, deposits per the bank statement totaled $26,700, deposits per books were $26,400, and deposits in transit at September 30 were $2,100.
4. In September, cash disbursements per books were $23,700, checks clearing the bank were $25,000, and outstanding checks at September 30 were $2,100.

There were no bank debit or credit memoranda. No errors were made by either the bank or Dawes Company.

Instructions
Answer the following questions.

(a) In situation (1), what were the deposits in transit at July 31?
(b) In situation (2), what were the outstanding checks at July 31?
(c) In situation (3), what were the deposits in transit at August 31?
(d) In situation (4), what were the outstanding checks at August 31?

Show presentation of cash in financial statements.

(LO 4)

E7-14 Wynn Company has recorded the following items in its financial records.

Cash in bank	$ 42,000
Cash in plant expansion fund	100,000
Cash on hand	12,000
Highly liquid investments	34,000
Petty cash	500
Receivables from customers	89,000
Stock investments	61,000

The highly liquid investments had maturities of 3 months or less when they were purchased. The stock investments will be sold in the next 6 to 12 months. The plant expansion project will begin in 3 years.

Instructions
(a) What amount should Wynn report as "Cash and cash equivalents" on its balance sheet?
(b) Where should the items not included in part (a) be reported on the balance sheet?

EXERCISES: SET B AND CHALLENGE EXERCISES

Visit the book's companion website, at **www.wiley.com/college/weygandt**, and choose the Student Companion site to access Exercises: Set B and Challenge Exercises.

PROBLEMS: SET A

Identify internal control principles over cash disbursements.

(LO 1, 2)

P7-1A Bolz Office Supply Company recently changed its system of internal control over cash disbursements. The system includes the following features.

Instead of being unnumbered and manually prepared, all checks must now be pre-numbered and prepared by using the new accounts payable software purchased by the company. Before a check can be issued, each invoice must have the approval of Kathy Moon, the purchasing agent, and Robin Self, the receiving department supervisor. Checks must be signed by either Jennifer Edwards, the treasurer, or Rich Woodruff, the assistant treasurer. Before signing a check, the signer is expected to compare the amount of the check with the amount on the invoice.

After signing a check, the signer stamps the invoice PAID and inserts (within the stamp) the date, check number, and amount of the check. The "paid" invoice is then sent to the accounting department for recording.

Blank checks are stored in a safe in the treasurer's office. The combination to the safe is known only by the treasurer and assistant treasurer. Each month, the bank statement is reconciled with the bank balance per books by the assistant chief accountant. All employees who handle or account for cash are bonded.

Instructions
Identify the internal control principles and their application to cash disbursements of Bolz Office Supply Company.

P7-2A Forney Company maintains a petty cash fund for small expenditures. The following transactions occurred over a 2-month period.

Journalize and post petty cash fund transactions.

(LO 2)

July 1   Established petty cash fund by writing a check on Scranton Bank for $200.
     15   Replenished the petty cash fund by writing a check for $196.00. On this date, the fund consisted of $4.00 in cash and the following petty cash receipts: freight-out $92.00, postage expense $42.40, entertainment expense $46.60, and miscellaneous expense $11.20.
     31   Replenished the petty cash fund by writing a check for $192.00. At this date, the fund consisted of $8.00 in cash and the following petty cash receipts: freight-out $82.10, charitable contributions expense $45.00, postage expense $25.50, and miscellaneous expense $39.40.
Aug. 15   Replenished the petty cash fund by writing a check for $187.00. On this date, the fund consisted of $13.00 in cash and the following petty cash receipts: freight-out $77.60, entertainment expense $43.00, postage expense $33.00, and miscellaneous expense $37.00.
     16   Increased the amount of the petty cash fund to $300 by writing a check for $100.
     31   Replenished the petty cash fund by writing a check for $284.00. On this date, the fund consisted of $16 in cash and the following petty cash receipts: postage expense $140.00, travel expense $95.60, and freight-out $47.10.

Instructions
(a) Journalize the petty cash transactions.
(b) Post to the Petty Cash account.
(c) What internal control features exist in a petty cash fund?

(a) July 15, Cash short $3.80
(b) Aug. 31 balance $300

P7-3A On May 31, 2017, Reber Company had a cash balance per books of $6,781.50. The bank statement from New York State Bank on that date showed a balance of $6,404.60. A comparison of the statement with the Cash account revealed the following facts.

Prepare a bank reconciliation and adjusting entries.

(LO 3)

1. The statement included a debit memo of $40 for the printing of additional company checks.
2. Cash sales of $836.15 on May 12 were deposited in the bank. The cash receipts journal entry and the deposit slip were incorrectly made for $886.15. The bank credited Reber Company for the correct amount.
3. Outstanding checks at May 31 totaled $576.25. Deposits in transit were $2,416.15.
4. On May 18, the company issued check no. 1181 for $685 to Lynda Carsen on account. The check, which cleared the bank in May, was incorrectly journalized and posted by Reber Company for $658.
5. A $3,000 note receivable was collected by the bank for Reber Company on May 31 plus $80 interest. The bank charged a collection fee of $20. No interest has been accrued on the note.
6. Included with the canceled checks was a check issued by Stiner Company to Ted Cress for $800 that was incorrectly charged to Reber Company by the bank.
7. On May 31, the bank statement showed an NSF charge of $680 for a check issued by Sue Allison, a customer, to Reber Company on account.

Instructions
(a) Prepare the bank reconciliation at May 31, 2017.
(b) Prepare the necessary adjusting entries for Reber Company at May 31, 2017.

(a) Adjusted cash balance per bank $9,044.50

Prepare a bank reconciliation and adjusting entries from detailed data.

(LO 3)

P7-4A The bank portion of the bank reconciliation for Langer Company at November 30, 2017, was as follows.

LANGER COMPANY
Bank Reconciliation
November 30, 2017

Cash balance per bank		$14,367.90
Add: Deposits in transit		2,530.20
		16,898.10
Less: Outstanding checks		

Check Number	Check Amount	
3451	$2,260.40	
3470	720.10	
3471	844.50	
3472	1,426.80	
3474	1,050.00	6,301.80
Adjusted cash balance per bank		$10,596.30

The adjusted cash balance per bank agreed with the cash balance per books at November 30. The December bank statement showed the following checks and deposits.

Bank Statement

Checks			Deposits	
Date	**Number**	**Amount**	**Date**	**Amount**
12-1	3451	$ 2,260.40	12-1	$ 2,530.20
12-2	3471	844.50	12-4	1,211.60
12-7	3472	1,426.80	12-8	2,365.10
12-4	3475	1,640.70	12-16	2,672.70
12-8	3476	1,300.00	12-21	2,945.00
12-10	3477	2,130.00	12-26	2,567.30
12-15	3479	3,080.00	12-29	2,836.00
12-27	3480	600.00	12-30	1,025.00
12-30	3482	475.50	Total	$18,152.90
12-29	3483	1,140.00		
12-31	3485	540.80		
	Total	$15,438.70		

The cash records per books for December showed the following.

Cash Payments Journal							Cash Receipts Journal	
Date	**Number**	**Amount**	**Date**	**Number**	**Amount**		**Date**	**Amount**
12-1	3475	$1,640.70	12-20	3482	$ 475.50		12-3	$ 1,211.60
12-2	3476	1,300.00	12-22	3483	1,140.00		12-7	2,365.10
12-2	3477	2,130.00	12-23	3484	798.00		12-15	2,672.70
12-4	3478	621.30	12-24	3485	450.80		12-20	2,954.00
12-8	3479	3,080.00	12-30	3486	889.50		12-25	2,567.30
12-10	3480	600.00	Total		$13,933.20		12-28	2,836.00
12-17	3481	807.40					12-30	1,025.00
							12-31	1,690.40
							Total	$17,322.10

The bank statement contained two memoranda:

1. A credit of $5,145 for the collection of a $5,000 note for Langer Company plus interest of $160 and less a collection fee of $15. Langer Company has not accrued any interest on the note.

2. A debit of $572.80 for an NSF check written by L. Rees, a customer. At December 31, the check had not been redeposited in the bank.

At December 31, the cash balance per books was $12,485.20, and the cash balance per the bank statement was $20,154.30. The bank did not make any errors, but two errors were made by Langer Company.

Instructions

(a) Using the four steps in the reconciliation procedure, prepare a bank reconciliation at December 31.

(b) Prepare the adjusting entries based on the reconciliation. (*Hint:* The correction of any errors pertaining to recording checks should be made to Accounts Payable. The correction of any errors relating to recording cash receipts should be made to Accounts Receivable.)

(a) Adjusted balance per books $16,958.40

P7-5A Rodriguez Company maintains a checking account at the Imura Bank. At July 31, selected data from the ledger balance and the bank statement are shown below.

Prepare a bank reconciliation and adjusting entries.

(LO 3)

Cash in Bank

	Per Books	Per Bank
Balance, July 1	$17,600	$15,800
July receipts	81,400	
July credits		83,470
July disbursements	77,150	
July debits		74,756
Balance, July 31	$21,850	$24,514

Analysis of the bank data reveals that the credits consist of $79,000 of July deposits and a credit memorandum of $4,470 for the collection of a $4,400 note plus interest revenue of $70. The July debits per bank consist of checks cleared $74,700 and a debit memorandum of $56 for printing additional company checks.

You also discover the following errors involving July checks: (1) A check for $230 to a creditor on account that cleared the bank in July was journalized and posted as $320. (2) A salary check to an employee for $255 was recorded by the bank for $155.

The June 30 bank reconciliation contained only two reconciling items: deposits in transit $8,000 and outstanding checks of $6,200.

Instructions

(a) Prepare a bank reconciliation at July 31, 2017.

(b) Journalize the adjusting entries to be made by Rodriguez Company. Assume that interest on the note has not been accrued.

(a) Adjusted balance per books $26,354

P7-6A Rondelli Middle School wants to raise money for a new sound system for its auditorium. The primary fund-raising event is a dance at which the famous disc jockey D.J. Sound will play classic and not-so-classic dance tunes. Matt Ballester, the music and theater instructor, has been given the responsibility for coordinating the fund-raising efforts. This is Matt's first experience with fund-raising. He decides to put the eighth-grade choir in charge of the event; he will be a relatively passive observer.

Identify internal control weaknesses in cash receipts and cash disbursements.

(LO 1, 2)

Matt had 500 unnumbered tickets printed for the dance. He left the tickets in a box on his desk and told the choir students to take as many tickets as they thought they could sell for $5 each. In order to ensure that no extra tickets would be floating around, he told them to dispose of any unsold tickets. When the students received payment for the tickets, they were to bring the cash back to Matt and he would put it in a locked box in his desk drawer.

Some of the students were responsible for decorating the gymnasium for the dance. Matt gave each of them a key to the money box and told them that if they took money out to purchase materials, they should put a note in the box saying how much they took and what it was used for. After 2 weeks, the money box appeared to be getting full, so Matt asked Jeff Kenney to count the money, prepare a deposit slip, and deposit the money in a bank account Matt had opened.

The day of the dance, Matt wrote a check from the account to pay the DJ. D.J. Sound, however, said that he accepted only cash and did not give receipts. So Matt took $200 out of the cash box and gave it to D.J. At the dance, Matt had Sam Cooper working at the entrance to the gymnasium, collecting tickets from students, and selling tickets to those who had not prepurchased them. Matt estimated that 400 students attended the dance.

The following day, Matt closed out the bank account, which had $250 in it, and gave that amount plus the $180 in the cash box to Principal Finke. Principal Finke seemed surprised that, after generating roughly $2,000 in sales, the dance netted only $430 in cash. Matt did not know how to respond.

Instructions

Identify as many internal control weaknesses as you can in this scenario, and suggest how each could be addressed.

PROBLEMS: SET B AND SET C

Visit the book's companion website, at **www.wiley.com/college/weygandt**, and choose the Student Companion site to access Problems: Set B and Set C.

COMPREHENSIVE PROBLEM

CP7 On December 1, 2017, Fullerton Company had the following account balances.

	Debit		**Credit**
Cash	$18,200	Accumulated Depreciation—	
Notes Receivable	2,200	Equipment	$ 3,000
Accounts Receivable	7,500	Accounts Payable	6,100
Inventory	16,000	Common Stock	50,000
Prepaid Insurance	1,600	Retained Earnings	14,400
Equipment	28,000		$73,500
	$73,500		

During December, the company completed the following transactions.

Dec. 7 Received $3,600 cash from customers in payment of account (no discount allowed).
12 Purchased merchandise on account from Vance Co. $12,000, terms 1/10, n/30.
17 Sold merchandise on account $16,000, terms 2/10, n/30. The cost of the merchandise sold was $10,000.
19 Paid salaries $2,200.
22 Paid Vance Co. in full, less discount.
26 Received collections in full, less discounts, from customers billed on December 17.
31 Received $2,700 cash from customers in payment of account (no discount allowed).

Adjustment data:

1. Depreciation $200 per month.
2. Insurance expired $400.

Instructions

(a) Journalize the December transactions. (Assume a perpetual inventory system.)
(b) Enter the December 1 balances in the ledger T-accounts and post the December transactions. Use Cost of Goods Sold, Depreciation Expense, Insurance Expense, Salaries and Wages Expense, Sales Revenue, and Sales Discounts.
(c) The statement from Jackson County Bank on December 31 showed a balance of $26,130. A comparison of the bank statement with the Cash account revealed the following facts.
  1. The bank collected a note receivable of $2,200 for Fullerton Company on December 15.
  2. The December 31 receipts were deposited in a night deposit vault on December 31. These deposits were recorded by the bank in January.
  3. Checks outstanding on December 31 totaled $1,210.
  4. On December 31, the bank statement showed an NSF charge of $680 for a check received by the company from L. Bryan, a customer, on account.

  Prepare a bank reconciliation as of December 31 based on the available information. (*Hint:* The cash balance per books is $26,100. This can be proven by finding the balance in the Cash account from parts (a) and (b).)
(d) Journalize the adjusting entries resulting from the bank reconciliation and adjustment data.
(e) Post the adjusting entries to the ledger T-accounts.
(f) Prepare an adjusted trial balance.
(g) Prepare an income statement for December and a classified balance sheet at December 31.

CONTINUING PROBLEM

COOKIE CREATIONS

(*Note:* This is a continuation of the Cookie Creations problem from Chapters 1 through 6.)

CC7 Part 1 Natalie is struggling to keep up with the recording of her accounting transactions. She is spending a lot of time marketing and selling mixers and giving her cookie classes. Her friend John is an accounting student who runs his own accounting service. He has asked Natalie if she would like to have him do her accounting. John and Natalie meet and discuss her business.

Part 2 Natalie decides that she cannot afford to hire John to do her accounting. One way that she can ensure that her cash account does not have any errors and is accurate and up-to-date is to prepare a bank reconciliation at the end of each month. Natalie would like you to help her.

© leungchopan/
Shutterstock

Go to the book's companion website, **www.wiley.com/college/weygandt**, *to see the completion of this problem.*

Go to the book's companion website, www.wiley.com/college/weygandt, to see the completion of this problem.

BROADENING YOUR PERSPECTIVE

FINANCIAL REPORTING AND ANALYSIS

Financial Reporting Problem: Apple Inc.

BYP7-1 The financial statements of **Apple Inc.** are presented in Appendix A at the end of this textbook. Instructions for accessing and using the company's complete annual report, including the notes to the financial statements, are also provided in Appendix A.

Instructions
(a) What comments, if any, are made about cash in the report of the independent registered public accounting firm?
(b) What data about cash and cash equivalents are shown in the consolidated balance sheet?
(c) In its notes to Consolidated Financial Statements, how does Apple define cash equivalents?
(d) In management's Annual Report on Internal Control over Financial Reporting (Item 9A), what does Apple's management say about internal control?

Comparative Analysis Problem:
PepsiCo, Inc. vs. The Coca-Cola Company

BYP7-2 **PepsiCo**'s financial statements are presented in Appendix B. Financial statements of **The Coca-Cola Company** are presented in Appendix C. Instructions for accessing and using the complete annual reports of PepsiCo and Coca-Cola, including the notes to the financial statements, are also provided in Appendices B and C, respectively.

Instructions
(a) Based on the information contained in these financial statements, determine each of the following for each company:
  (1) Cash and cash equivalents balance at December 28, 2013, for PepsiCo and at December 31, 2013, for Coca-Cola.
  (2) Increase (decrease) in cash and cash equivalents from 2012 to 2013.
  (3) Cash provided by operating activities during the year ended December 2013 (from statement of cash flows).
(b) What conclusions concerning the management of cash can be drawn from these data?

Comparative Analysis Problem:
Amazon.com, Inc. vs. Wal-Mart Stores, Inc.

BYP7-3 **Amazon.com, Inc.**'s financial statements are presented in Appendix D. Financial statements of **Wal-Mart Stores, Inc.** are presented in Appendix E. Instructions for accessing and using the complete annual reports of Amazon and Wal-Mart, including the notes to the financial statements, are also provided in Appendices D and E, respectively.

Instructions

(a) Based on the information contained in these financial statements, determine each of the following for each company:
  (1) Cash and cash equivalents balance at December 31, 2013, for Amazon and at January 31, 2014, for Wal-Mart.
  (2) Increase (decrease) in cash and cash equivalents from 2012 to 2013.
  (3) Net cash provided by operating activities during the year ended December 31, 2013, for Amazon and January 31, 2014, for Wal-Mart from statement of cash flows.
(b) What conclusions concerning the management of cash can be drawn from these data?

Real-World Focus

BYP7-4 All organizations should have systems of internal control. Universities are no exception. This site discusses the basics of internal control in a university setting.

Address: **www.bc.edu/offices/audit/controls**, or go to **www.wiley.com/college/weygandt**

Steps: Go to the site shown above.

Instructions

The home page of this site provides links to pages that answer critical questions. Use these links to answer the following questions.

(a) In a university setting, who has responsibility for evaluating the adequacy of the system of internal control?
(b) What are some red flags indicating white collar crime?
(c) What role does an internal audit play at Boston College?
(d) What are two IT controls over computer operations?

CRITICAL THINKING

Decision-Making Across the Organization

BYP7-5 The board of trustees of a local church is concerned about the internal accounting controls for the offering collections made at weekly services. The trustees ask you to serve on a three-person audit team with the internal auditor of a local college and a CPA who has just joined the church.

At a meeting of the audit team and the board of trustees, you learn the following.

1. The church's board of trustees has delegated responsibility for the financial management and audit of the financial records to the finance committee. This group prepares the annual budget and approves major disbursements. It is not involved in collections or recordkeeping. No audit has been made in recent years because the same trusted employee has kept church records and served as financial secretary for 15 years. The church does not carry any fidelity insurance.

2. The collection at the weekly service is taken by a team of ushers who volunteer to serve one month. The ushers take the collection plates to a basement office at the rear of the church. They hand their plates to the head usher and return to the church service. After all plates have been turned in, the head usher counts the cash received. The head usher then places the cash in the church safe along with a notation of the amount counted. The head usher volunteers to serve for 3 months.

3. The next morning, the financial secretary opens the safe and recounts the collection. The secretary withholds $150–$200 in cash, depending on the cash expenditures expected for the week, and deposits the remainder of the collections in the bank. To facilitate the deposit, church members who contribute by check are asked to make their checks payable to "Cash."

4. Each month, the financial secretary reconciles the bank statement and submits a copy of the reconciliation to the board of trustees. The reconciliations have rarely contained any bank errors and have never shown any errors per books.

Instructions

With the class divided into groups, answer the following.

(a) Indicate the weaknesses in internal accounting control over the handling of collections.

(b) List the improvements in internal control procedures that you plan to make at the next meeting of the audit team for (1) the ushers, (2) the head usher, (3) the financial secretary, and (4) the finance committee.

(c) What church policies should be changed to improve internal control?

Communication Activity

BYP7-6 As a new auditor for the CPA firm of Eaton, Quayle, and Hale, you have been assigned to review the internal controls over mail cash receipts of Pritchard Company. Your review reveals the following. Checks are promptly endorsed "For Deposit Only," but no list of the checks is prepared by the person opening the mail. The mail is opened either by the cashier or by the employee who maintains the accounts receivable records. Mail receipts are deposited in the bank weekly by the cashier.

Instructions

Write a letter to Danny Peak, owner of Pritchard Company, explaining the weaknesses in internal control and your recommendations for improving the system.

Ethics Case

BYP7-7 You are the assistant controller in charge of general ledger accounting at Linbarger Bottling Company. Your company has a large loan from an insurance company. The loan agreement requires that the company's cash account balance be maintained at $200,000 or more, as reported monthly.

At June 30, the cash balance is $80,000, which you report to Lisa Infante, the financial vice president. Lisa excitedly instructs you to keep the cash receipts book open for one additional day for purposes of the June 30 report to the insurance company. Lisa says, "If we don't get that cash balance over $200,000, we'll default on our loan agreement. They could close us down, put us all out of our jobs!" Lisa continues, "I talked to Oconto Distributors (one of Linbarger's largest customers) this morning. They said they sent us a check for $150,000 yesterday. We should receive it tomorrow. If we include just that one check in our cash balance, we'll be in the clear. It's in the mail!"

Instructions

(a) Who will suffer negative effects if you do not comply with Lisa Infante's instructions? Who will suffer if you do comply?

(b) What are the ethical considerations in this case?

(c) What alternatives do you have?

All About You

BYP7-8 The print and electronic media are full of stories about potential security risks that may arise from your computer or smartphone. It is important to keep in mind, however, that there are also many other ways that your identity can be stolen. The federal government provides many resources to help protect you from identity thieves.

Instructions

Go to **http://onguardonline.gov/idtheft.html**, click **Video and Media**, and then click on **ID Theft Faceoff**. Complete the quiz provided there.

FASB Codification Activity

BYP7-9 If your school has a subscription to the FASB Codification, go to **http://aaahq.org/ascLogin. cfm** to log in and prepare responses to the following.

(a) How is cash defined in the Codification?

(b) How are cash equivalents defined in the Codification?

(c) What are the disclosure requirements related to cash and cash equivalents?

A Look at IFRS

  Compare the accounting for fraud, internal control, and cash under GAAP and IFRS.

Fraud can occur anywhere. Because the three main factors that contribute to fraud are universal in nature, the principles of internal control activities are used globally by companies. While Sarbanes-Oxley (SOX) does not apply to non-U.S. companies, most large international companies have internal controls similar to those indicated in the chapter. IFRS and GAAP are also very similar in accounting for cash. *IAS No. 1 (revised),* "Presentation of Financial Statements," is the only standard that discusses issues specifically related to cash.

Relevant Facts

Following are the key similarities and differences between GAAP and IFRS related to fraud, internal control, and cash.

Similarities

- The fraud triangle discussed in this chapter is applicable to all international companies. Some of the major frauds on an international basis are **Parmalat** (Italy), **Royal Ahold** (the Netherlands), and **Satyam Computer Services** (India).

- Rising economic crime poses a growing threat to companies, with 34% of all organizations worldwide being victims of fraud in a recent 12-month period.

- Accounting scandals both in the United States and internationally have re-ignited the debate over the relative merits of GAAP, which takes a "rules-based" approach to accounting, versus IFRS, which takes a "principles-based" approach. The FASB announced that it intends to introduce more principles-based standards.

- On a lighter note, at one time the Ig Nobel Prize in Economics went to the CEOs of those companies involved in the corporate accounting scandals of that year for "adapting the mathematical concept of imaginary numbers for use in the business world." A parody of the Nobel Prizes, the Ig Nobel Prizes (read Ignoble, as not noble) are given each year in early October for 10 achievements that "first make people laugh, and then make them think." Organized by the scientific humor magazine *Annals of Improbable Research* (*AIR*), they are presented by a group that includes genuine Nobel laureates at a ceremony at Harvard University's Sanders Theater (see **en.wikipedia.org/wiki/ Ig_Nobel_Prize**).

- Internal controls are a system of checks and balances designed to prevent and detect fraud and errors. While most companies have these systems in place, many have never completely documented them, nor had an independent auditor attest to their effectiveness. Both of these actions are required under SOX.

- Companies find that internal control review is a costly process but badly needed. One study estimates the cost of SOX compliance for U.S. companies at over $35 billion, with audit fees doubling in the first year of compliance. At the same time, examination of internal controls indicates lingering problems in the way companies operate. One study of first compliance with the internal-control testing provisions documented material weaknesses for about 13% of companies reporting in a two-year period (*PricewaterhouseCoopers' Global Economic Crime Survey*, 2005).

- The accounting and internal control procedures related to cash are essentially the same under both IFRS and this textbook. In addition, the definition used for cash equivalents is the same.

- Most companies report cash and cash equivalents together under IFRS, as shown in this textbook. In addition, IFRS follows the same accounting policies related to the reporting of restricted cash.

Differences

- The SOX internal control standards apply only to companies listed on U.S. exchanges. There is continuing debate over whether foreign issuers should have to comply with this extra layer of regulation.

Looking to the Future

Ethics has become a very important aspect of reporting. Different cultures have different perspectives on bribery and other questionable activities, and consequently penalties for engaging in such activities vary considerably across countries.

High-quality international accounting requires both high-quality accounting standards and high-quality auditing. Similar to the convergence of GAAP and IFRS, there is movement to improve international auditing standards. The International Auditing and Assurance Standards Board (IAASB) functions as an independent standard-setting body. It works to establish high-quality auditing and assurance and quality-control standards throughout the world. Whether the IAASB adopts internal control provisions similar to those in SOX remains to be seen. You can follow developments in the international audit arena at **http://www.ifac.org/iaasb/**.

IFRS Practice

IFRS Self-Test Questions

1. Non-U.S companies that follow IFRS:
   (a) do not normally use the principles of internal control activities described in this textbook.
   (b) often offset cash with accounts payable on the balance sheet.
   (c) are not required to follow SOX.
   (d) None of the above.

2. The Sarbanes-Oxley Act applies to:
   (a) all U.S. companies listed on U.S. exchanges.
   (b) all companies that list stock on any stock exchange in any country.
   (c) all European companies listed on European exchanges.
   (d) Both (a) and (c).

3. High-quality international accounting requires both high-quality accounting standards and:
   (a) a reconsideration of SOX to make it less onerous.
   (b) high-quality auditing standards.
   (c) government intervention to ensure that the public interest is protected.
   (d) the development of new principles of internal control activities.

IFRS Exercise

IFRS7-1 Some people argue that the internal control requirements of the Sarbanes-Oxley Act (SOX) put U.S. companies at a competitive disadvantage to companies outside the United States. Discuss the competitive implications (both pros and cons) of SOX.

International Financial Reporting Problem: Louis Vuitton

IFRS7-2 The financial statements of Louis Vuitton are presented in Appendix F. Instructions for accessing and using the company's complete annual report, including the notes to its financial statements, are also provided in Appendix F.

Instructions
Using the notes to the company's financial statements, what are Louis Vuitton's accounting policies related to cash and cash equivalents?

Answers to IFRS Self-Test Questions
1. c   **2.** a   **3.** b

8 Accounting for Receivables

CHAPTER PREVIEW As indicated in the Feature Story below, receivables are a significant asset for many pharmaceutical companies. Because a large portion of sales in the United States are credit sales, receivables are important to companies in other industries as well. As a consequence, companies must pay close attention to their receivables and manage them carefully. In this chapter, you will learn what journal entries companies make when they sell products, when they collect cash from those sales, and when they write off accounts they cannot collect.

FEATURE STORY

A Dose of Careful Management Keeps Receivables Healthy

"Sometimes you have to know when to be very tough, and sometimes you can give them a bit of a break," said Vivi Su. She wasn't talking about her children but about the customers of a subsidiary of former pharmaceutical company Whitehall-Robins, where she worked as supervisor of credit and collections.

For example, while the company's regular terms were 1/15, n/30 (1% discount if paid within 15 days), a customer might have asked for and received a few days of grace and still got the discount. Or a customer might have placed orders above its credit limit, in which case, depending on its payment history and the circumstances, Ms. Su might have authorized shipment of the goods anyway.

"It's not about drawing a line in the sand, and that's all," she explained. "You want a good relationship with your customers—but you also need to bring in the money."

"The money," in Whitehall-Robins' case, amounted to some $170 million in sales a year. Nearly all of it came in through the credit accounts Ms. Su managed. The process started with the decision to grant a customer an account in the first place. The sales rep gave the customer a credit application. "My department reviews this application very carefully; a customer needs to supply three good references, and we also run a check with a credit firm like Equifax. If we accept them, then based on their size and history, we assign a credit limit," Ms. Su explained.

Once accounts were established, "I get an aging report every single day," said Ms. Su. "The rule of thumb is that we should always have at least 85% of receivables current—meaning they were billed less than 30 days ago," she continued. "But we try to do even better than that—I like to see 90%."

At 15 days overdue, Whitehall-Robins phoned the client. After 45 days, Ms. Su noted, "I send a letter. Then a second notice is sent in writing. After the third and final notice, the client has 10 days to pay, and then I hand it over to a collection agency, and it's out of my hands."

Ms. Su's boss, Terry Norton, recorded an estimate for bad debts every year, based on a percentage of receivables. The percentage depended on the current aging history. He also calculated and monitored the company's accounts receivable turnover, which the company reported in its financial statements.

Ms. Su knew that she and Mr. Norton were crucial to the profitability of Whitehall-Robins. "Receivables are generally the second-largest asset of any company (after its capital assets)," she pointed out. "So it's no wonder we keep a very close eye on them."

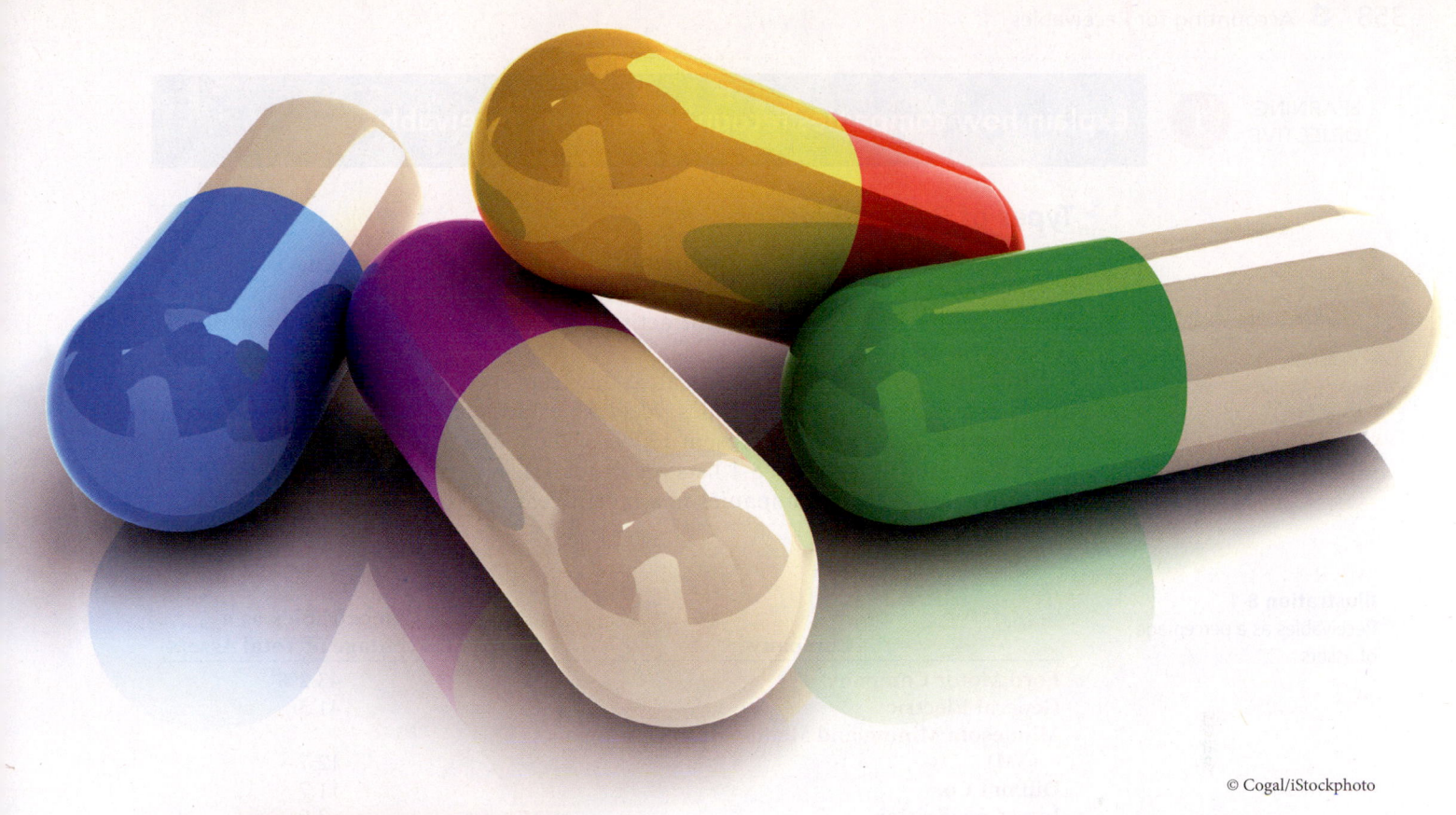

© Cogal/iStockphoto

CHAPTER OUTLINE

Learning Objectives

1 Explain how companies recognize accounts receivable.
- Types of receivables
- Recognizing accounts receivable

DO IT! 1 Recognizing Accounts Receivable

2 Describe how companies value accounts receivable and record their disposition.
- Valuing accounts receivable
- Disposing of accounts receivable

DO IT! 2 Uncollectible Accounts Receivable

3 Explain how companies recognize notes receivable.
- Determining the maturity date
- Computing interest
- Recognizing notes receivable

DO IT! 3 Recognizing Notes Receivable

4 Describe how companies value notes receivable, record their disposition, and present and analyze receivables.
- Valuing notes receivable
- Disposing of notes receivable
- Statement presentation and analysis

DO IT! 4 Analysis of Receivables

Go to the **REVIEW AND PRACTICE** section at the end of the chapter for a review of key concepts and practice applications with solutions.

Visit **WileyPLUS with ORION** for additional tutorials and practice opportunities.

Types of Receivables

The term **receivables** refers to amounts due from individuals and companies. Receivables are claims that are expected to be collected in cash. The management of receivables is a very important activity for any company that sells goods or services on credit.

Receivables are important because they represent one of a company's most liquid assets. For many companies, receivables are also one of the largest assets. For example, receivables represent 13.7% of the current assets of pharmaceutical giant **Rite Aid**. Illustration 8-1 lists receivables as a percentage of total assets for five other well-known companies in a recent year.

Illustration 8-1
Receivables as a percentage of assets

Company	Receivables as a Percentage of Total Assets
Ford Motor Company	43.2%
General Electric	41.5
Minnesota Mining and Manufacturing Company (3M)	12.7
DuPont Co.	11.7
Intel Corporation	3.9

The relative significance of a company's receivables as a percentage of its assets depends on various factors: its industry, the time of year, whether it extends long-term financing, and its credit policies. To reflect important differences among receivables, they are frequently classified as (1) accounts receivable, (2) notes receivable, and (3) other receivables.

Accounts receivable are amounts customers owe on account. They result from the sale of goods and services. Companies generally expect to collect accounts receivable within 30 to 60 days. They are usually the most significant type of claim held by a company.

Notes receivable are a written promise (as evidenced by a formal instrument) for amounts to be received. The note normally requires the collection of interest and extends for time periods of 60–90 days or longer. Notes and accounts receivable that result from sales transactions are often called **trade receivables**.

Other receivables include nontrade receivables such as interest receivable, loans to company officers, advances to employees, and income taxes refundable. These do not generally result from the operations of the business. Therefore, they are generally classified and reported as separate items in the balance sheet.

Recognizing Accounts Receivable

Recognizing accounts receivable is relatively straightforward. A service organization records a receivable when it performs a service on account. A merchandiser records accounts receivable at the point of sale of merchandise on account. When a merchandiser sells goods, it increases (debits) Accounts Receivable and increases (credits) Sales Revenue.

The seller may offer terms that encourage early payment by providing a discount. Sales returns also reduce receivables. The buyer might find some of the goods unacceptable and choose to return the unwanted goods.

To review, assume that Jordache Co. on July 1, 2017, sells merchandise on account to Polo Company for $1,000, terms 2/10, n/30. On July 5, Polo returns

ETHICS NOTE

Companies report receivables from employees separately in the financial statements. The reason: Sometimes these receivables are not the result of an "arm's-length" transaction.

ETHICS NOTE

In exchange for lower interest rates, some companies have eliminated the 25-day grace period before finance charges kick in. Be sure you read the fine print in any credit agreement you sign.

merchandise with a sales price of $100 to Jordache Co. On July 11, Jordache receives payment from Polo Company for the balance due. The journal entries to record these transactions on the books of Jordache Co. are as follows. **(Cost of goods sold entries are omitted.)**

July 1	Accounts Receivable—Polo Company	1,000	
	Sales Revenue		1,000
	(To record sales on account)		
July 5	Sales Returns and Allowances	100	
	Accounts Receivable—Polo Company		100
	(To record merchandise returned)		
July 11	Cash ($900 − $18)	882	
	Sales Discounts ($900 × .02)	18	
	Accounts Receivable—Polo Company		900
	(To record collection of accounts receivable)		

Helpful Hint
These entries are the same as those described in Chapter 5. For simplicity, we have omitted inventory and cost of goods sold from this set of journal entries and from end-of-chapter material.

Some retailers issue their own credit cards. When you use a retailer's credit card (**JCPenney**, for example), the retailer charges interest on the balance due if not paid within a specified period (usually 25–30 days).

To illustrate, assume that you use your JCPenney Company credit card to purchase clothing with a sales price of $300 on June 1, 2017. JCPenney will increase (debit) Accounts Receivable for $300 and increase (credit) Sales Revenue for $300 (cost of goods sold entry omitted) as follows.

June 1	Accounts Receivable	300	
	Sales Revenue		300
	(To record sale of merchandise)		

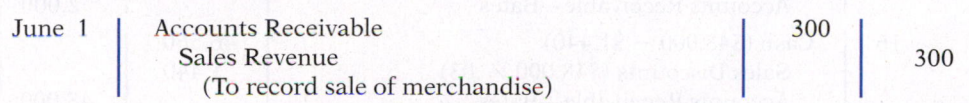

| A | = | L | + | SE |

+300
                                        +300 Rev

Cash Flows
no effect

Assuming that you owe $300 at the end of the month and JCPenney charges 1.5% per month on the balance due, the adjusting entry that JCPenney makes to record interest revenue of $4.50 ($300 × 1.5%) on June 30 is as follows.

June 30	Accounts Receivable	4.50	
	Interest Revenue		4.50
	(To record interest on amount due)		

| A | = | L | + | SE |

+4.50
                                        +4.50 Rev

Cash Flows
no effect

Interest revenue is often substantial for many retailers.

ANATOMY OF A FRAUD

Tasanee was the accounts receivable clerk for a large nonprofit foundation that provided performance and exhibition space for the performing and visual arts. Her responsibilities included activities normally assigned to an accounts receivable clerk, such as recording revenues from various sources (donations, facility rental fees, ticket revenue, and bar receipts). However, she was also responsible for handling all cash and checks from the time they were received until the time she deposited them, as well as preparing the bank reconciliation. Tasanee took advantage of her situation by falsifying bank deposits and bank reconciliations so that she could steal cash from the bar receipts. Since nobody else logged the donations or matched the donation receipts to pledges prior to Tasanee receiving them, she was able to off-set the cash that was stolen against donations that she received but didn't record. Her crime was made easier by the fact that her boss, the company's controller, only did a very superficial review of the bank reconciliation and thus didn't notice that some numbers had been cut out from other documents and taped onto the bank reconciliation.

DO IT! Recognizing Accounts Receivable

On May 1, Wilton sold merchandise on account to Bates for $50,000 terms 3/15, net 45. On May 4, Bates returns merchandise with a sales price of $2,000. On May 16, Wilton receives payment from Bates for the balance due. Prepare journal entries to record the May transactions on Wilton's books. (You may ignore cost of goods sold entries and explanations.)

Solution

Action Plan

✔ Prepare entry to record the receivable and related return.

✔ Compute the sales discount and related entry.

May 1	Accounts Receivable—Bates		50,000	
	Sales Revenue			50,000
4	Sales Returns and Allowances		2,000	
	Accounts Receivable—Bates			2,000
16	Cash ($48,000 − $1,440)		46,560	
	Sales Discounts ($48,000 × .03)		1,440	
	Accounts Receivable—Bates			48,000

Related exercise material: **BE8-1, BE8-2, E8-1, E8-2, and DO IT! 8-1.**

LEARNING OBJECTIVE 2

Describe how companies value accounts receivable and record their disposition.

Valuing Accounts Receivable

Once companies record receivables in the accounts, the next question is: How should they report receivables in the financial statements? Companies report accounts receivable on the balance sheet as an asset. But determining the **amount** to report is sometimes difficult because some receivables will become uncollectible.

Each customer must satisfy the credit requirements of the seller before the credit sale is approved. Inevitably, though, some accounts receivable become uncollectible. For example, a customer may not be able to pay because of a decline in its sales revenue due to a downturn in the economy. Similarly, individuals may be laid off from their jobs or faced with unexpected hospital bills. Companies record credit losses as **Bad Debt Expense** (or Uncollectible Accounts Expense). Such losses are a normal and necessary risk of doing business on a credit basis.

Alternative Terminology
You will sometimes see *Bad Debt Expense* called *Uncollectible Accounts Expense.*

When U.S. home prices fell, home foreclosures rose, and the economy in general slowed as a result of the financial crisis of 2008, lenders experienced huge increases in their bad debt expense. For example, during one quarter **Wachovia** (a large U.S. bank now owned by **Wells Fargo**) increased bad debt expense from

$108 million to $408 million. Similarly, **American Express** increased its bad debt expense by 70%.

Two methods are used in accounting for uncollectible accounts: (1) the direct write-off method and (2) the allowance method. The following sections explain these methods.

DIRECT WRITE-OFF METHOD FOR UNCOLLECTIBLE ACCOUNTS

Under the **direct write-off method**, when a company determines a particular account to be uncollectible, it charges the loss to Bad Debt Expense. Assume, for example, that Warden Co. writes off as uncollectible M. E. Doran's $200 balance on December 12. Warden's entry is as follows.

Dec. 12	Bad Debt Expense	200	
	Accounts Receivable—M. E. Doran		200
	(To record write-off of M. E. Doran account)		

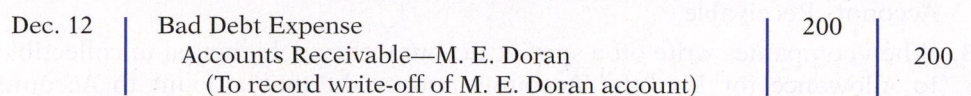

A = L + SE
−200   −200 Exp

Cash Flows
no effect

Under this method, Bad Debt Expense will show only **actual losses** from uncollectibles. The company will report accounts receivable at its gross amount.

Although this method is simple, its use can reduce the usefulness of both the income statement and balance sheet. Consider the following example. Assume that in 2017, Quick Buck Computer Company decided it could increase its revenues by offering computers to college students without requiring any money down and with no credit-approval process. On campuses across the country, it distributed one million computers with a selling price of $800 each. This increased Quick Buck's revenues and receivables by $800 million. The promotion was a huge success! The 2017 balance sheet and income statement looked great. Unfortunately, during 2018, nearly 40% of the customers defaulted on their loans. This made the 2018 income statement and balance sheet look terrible. Illustration 8-2 shows the effect of these events on the financial statements if the direct write-off method is used.

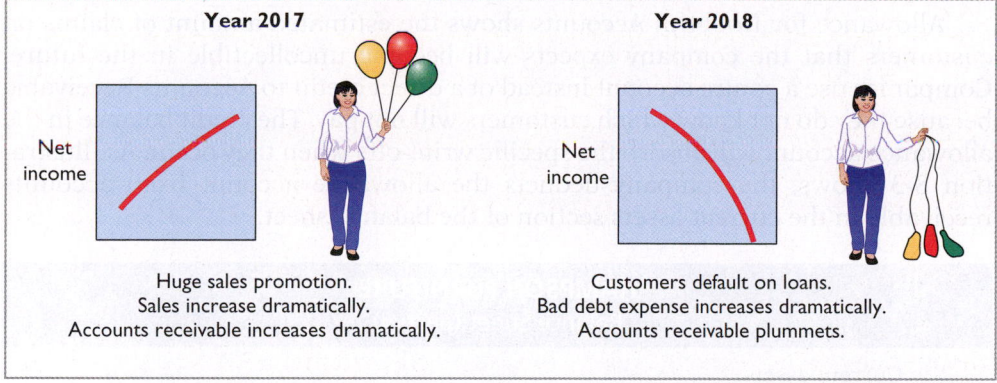

Illustration 8-2
Effects of direct write-off method

Under the direct write-off method, companies often record bad debt expense in a period different from the period in which they record the revenue. The method does not attempt to match bad debt expense to sales revenue in the income statement. Nor does the direct write-off method show accounts receivable in the balance sheet at the amount the company actually expects to receive. **Consequently, unless bad debt losses are insignificant, the direct write-off method is not acceptable for financial reporting purposes.**

ALLOWANCE METHOD FOR UNCOLLECTIBLE ACCOUNTS

The **allowance method** of accounting for bad debts involves estimating uncollectible accounts at the end of each period. This provides better matching on the income statement. It also ensures that companies state receivables on the balance sheet at their cash (net) realizable value. **Cash (net) realizable value** is the net amount the company expects to receive in cash. It excludes amounts that the company estimates it will not collect. Thus, this method reduces receivables in the balance sheet by the amount of estimated uncollectible receivables.

GAAP requires the allowance method for financial reporting purposes when bad debts are material in amount. This method has three essential features:

Helpful Hint
In this context, *material* means significant or important to financial statement users.

1. Companies **estimate** uncollectible accounts receivable. They match this estimated expense **against revenues** in the same accounting period in which they record the revenues.

2. Companies debit estimated uncollectibles to Bad Debt Expense and credit them to Allowance for Doubtful Accounts through an adjusting entry at the end of each period. Allowance for Doubtful Accounts is a contra account to Accounts Receivable.

3. When companies write off a specific account, they debit actual uncollectibles to Allowance for Doubtful Accounts and credit that amount to Accounts Receivable.

RECORDING ESTIMATED UNCOLLECTIBLES To illustrate the allowance method, assume that Hampson Furniture has credit sales of $1,200,000 in 2017. Of this amount, $200,000 remains uncollected at December 31. The credit manager estimates that $12,000 of these sales will be uncollectible. The adjusting entry to record the estimated uncollectibles increases (debits) Bad Debt Expense and increases (credits) Allowance for Doubtful Accounts, as follows.

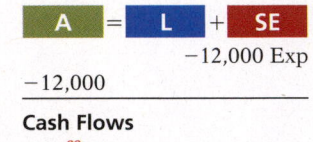

−12,000

Cash Flows
no effect

Dec. 31	Bad Debt Expense	12,000	
	Allowance for Doubtful Accounts		12,000
	(To record estimate of uncollectible		
	accounts)		

Hampson reports Bad Debt Expense in the income statement as an operating expense (usually as a selling expense). Thus, the estimated uncollectibles are matched with sales in 2017. Hampson records the expense in the same year it made the sales.

Allowance for Doubtful Accounts shows the estimated amount of claims on customers that the company expects will become uncollectible in the future. Companies use a contra account instead of a direct credit to Accounts Receivable because they do not know which customers will not pay. The credit balance in the allowance account will absorb the specific write-offs when they occur. As Illustration 8-3 shows, the company deducts the allowance account from accounts receivable in the current assets section of the balance sheet.

Illustration 8-3
Presentation of allowance for doubtful accounts

HAMPSON FURNITURE		
Balance Sheet (partial)		
Current assets		
Cash		$ 14,800
Accounts receivable	**$200,000**	
Less: Allowance for doubtful accounts	**12,000**	**188,000**
Inventory		310,000
Supplies		25,000
Total current assets		$ 537,800

Helpful Hint
Cash realizable value is sometimes referred to as *accounts receivable (net)*.

The amount of $188,000 in Illustration 8-3 represents the expected **cash realizable value** of the accounts receivable at the statement date. **Companies do not close Allowance for Doubtful Accounts at the end of the fiscal year.**

RECORDING THE WRITE-OFF OF AN UNCOLLECTIBLE ACCOUNT As described in the Feature Story, companies use various methods of collecting past-due accounts, such as letters, calls, and legal action. When they have exhausted all means of collecting a past-due account and collection appears impossible, the company writes off the account. In the credit card industry, for example, it is standard practice to write off accounts that are 210 days past due. To prevent premature or unauthorized write-offs, authorized management personnel should formally approve each write-off. To maintain segregation of duties, the employee authorized to write off accounts should not have daily responsibilities related to cash or receivables.

To illustrate a receivables write-off, assume that the financial vice president of Hampson Furniture authorizes a write-off of the $500 balance owed by R. A. Ware on March 1, 2018. The entry to record the write-off is as follows.

Mar. 1	Allowance for Doubtful Accounts		500	
	Accounts Receivable—R. A. Ware			500
	(Write-off of R. A. Ware account)			

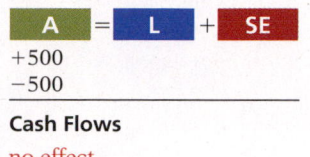

A = L + SE
+500
−500

Cash Flows
no effect

Bad Debt Expense does not increase when the write-off occurs. **Under the allowance method, companies debit every bad debt write-off to the allowance account rather than to Bad Debt Expense.** A debit to Bad Debt Expense would be incorrect because the company has already recognized the expense when it made the adjusting entry for estimated bad debts. Instead, the entry to record the write-off of an uncollectible account reduces both Accounts Receivable and Allowance for Doubtful Accounts. After posting, the general ledger accounts appear as shown in Illustration 8-4.

Accounts Receivable				Allowance for Doubtful Accounts			
Jan. 1 Bal. 200,000	Mar. 1	500		Mar. 1	500	Jan. 1 Bal.	12,000
Mar. 1 Bal. 199,500						Mar. 1 Bal.	11,500

Illustration 8-4
General ledger balances after write-off

A write-off affects **only balance sheet accounts**—not income statement accounts. The write-off of the account reduces both Accounts Receivable and Allowance for Doubtful Accounts. Cash realizable value in the balance sheet, therefore, remains the same, as Illustration 8-5 shows.

	Before Write-Off	After Write-Off
Accounts receivable	$ 200,000	$ 199,500
Allowance for doubtful accounts	12,000	11,500
Cash realizable value	**$188,000**	**$188,000**

Illustration 8-5
Cash realizable value comparison

RECOVERY OF AN UNCOLLECTIBLE ACCOUNT Occasionally, a company collects from a customer after it has written off the account as uncollectible. The company makes two entries to record the recovery of a bad debt. (1) It reverses the entry made in writing off the account. This reinstates the customer's account. (2) It journalizes the collection in the usual manner.

To illustrate, assume that on July 1, R. A. Ware pays the $500 amount that Hampson had written off on March 1. Hampson makes the following entries.

(1)

July 1	Accounts Receivable—R. A. Ware		500	
	Allowance for Doubtful Accounts			500
	(To reverse write-off of R. A. Ware account)			

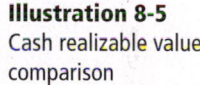

A = L + SE
+500
−500

Cash Flows
no effect

(2)

July 1	Cash		500	
	Accounts Receivable—R. A. Ware			500
	(To record collection from R. A. Ware)			

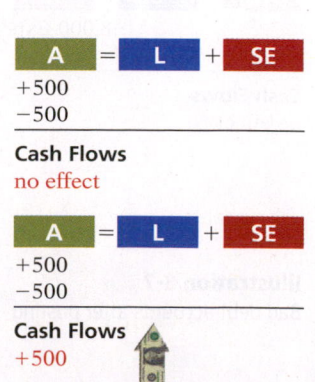

A = L + SE
+500
−500

Cash Flows
+500

Note that the recovery of a bad debt, like the write-off of a bad debt, affects **only balance sheet accounts**. The net effect of the two entries above is a debit to Cash and a credit to Allowance for Doubtful Accounts for $500. Accounts Receivable and Allowance for Doubtful Accounts both increase in entry (1) for two reasons. First, the company made an error in judgment when it wrote off the account receivable. Second, after R. A. Ware did pay, Accounts Receivable in the general ledger and Ware's account in the subsidiary ledger should show the collection for possible future credit purposes.

ESTIMATING THE ALLOWANCE For Hampson Furniture in Illustration 8-3, the amount of the expected uncollectibles was given. However, in "real life," companies must estimate that amount when they use the allowance method. Two bases are used to determine this amount: **(1) percentage of sales** and **(2) percentage of receivables**. Both bases are generally accepted. The choice is a management decision. It depends on the relative emphasis that management wishes to give to expenses and revenues on the one hand or to cash realizable value of the accounts receivable on the other. The choice is whether to emphasize income statement or balance sheet relationships. Illustration 8-6 compares the two bases.

Illustration 8-6
Comparison of bases for estimating uncollectibles

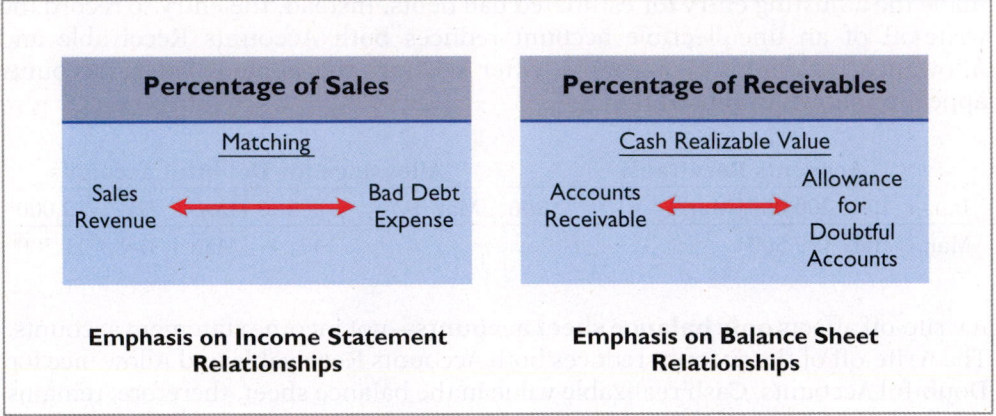

The percentage-of-sales basis results in a better matching of expenses with revenues—an income statement viewpoint. The percentage-of-receivables basis produces the better estimate of cash realizable value—a balance sheet viewpoint. Under both bases, the company must determine its past experience with bad debt losses.

Percentage-of-Sales In the **percentage-of-sales basis**, management estimates what percentage of credit sales will be uncollectible. This percentage is based on past experience and anticipated credit policy.

The company applies this percentage to either total credit sales or net credit sales of the current year. To illustrate, assume that Gonzalez Company elects to use the percentage-of-sales basis. It concludes that 1% of net credit sales will become uncollectible. If net credit sales for 2017 are $800,000, the estimated bad debt expense is $8,000 (1% × $800,000). The adjusting entry is as follows.

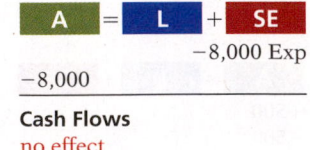

−8,000

Cash Flows
no effect

Dec. 31	Bad Debt Expense	8,000	
	Allowance for Doubtful Accounts		8,000
	(To record estimated bad debts for year)		

After the adjusting entry is posted, assuming the allowance account already has a credit balance of $1,723, the accounts of Gonzalez Company will show the following.

Illustration 8-7
Bad debt accounts after posting

Bad Debt Expense		Allowance for Doubtful Accounts	
Dec. 31 Adj. **8,000**			Jan. 1 Bal. 1,723
			Dec. 31 Adj. **8,000**
			Dec. 31 Bal. 9,723

This basis of estimating uncollectibles emphasizes the matching of expenses with revenues. As a result, Bad Debt Expense will show a direct percentage relationship to the sales base on which it is computed. **When the company makes the adjusting entry, it disregards the existing balance in Allowance for Doubtful Accounts.** The adjusted balance in this account should be a reasonable approximation of the realizable value of the receivables. If actual write-offs differ significantly from the amount estimated, the company should modify the percentage for future years.

Percentage-of-Receivables Under the **percentage-of-receivables basis**, management estimates what percentage of receivables will result in losses from uncollectible accounts. The company prepares an **aging schedule**, in which it classifies customer balances by the length of time they have been unpaid. Because of its emphasis on time, the analysis is often called **aging the accounts receivable**. In the Feature Story, Whitehall-Robins prepared an aging report daily.

After the company arranges the accounts by age, it determines the expected bad debt losses. It applies percentages based on past experience to the totals in each category. The longer a receivable is past due, the less likely it is to be collected. Thus, the estimated percentage of uncollectible debts increases as the number of days past due increases. Illustration 8-8 shows an aging schedule for Dart Company. Note that the estimated percentage uncollectible increases from 2% to 40% as the number of days past due increases.

Helpful Hint
Where appropriate, companies may use only a single percentage rate.

Illustration 8-8
Aging schedule

			Number of Days Past Due			
Customer	Total	Not Yet Due	1–30	31–60	61–90	Over 90
T. E. Adert	$ 600		$ 300		$ 200	$ 100
R. C. Bortz	300	$ 300				
B. A. Carl	450		200	$ 250		
O. L. Diker	700	500			200	
T. O. Ebbet	600			300		300
Others	36,950	26,200	5,200	2,450	1,600	1,500
	$39,600	$27,000	$5,700	$3,000	$2,000	$1,900
Estimated Percentage Uncollectible		2%	4%	10%	20%	40%
Total Estimated Bad Debts	$ 2,228	$ 540	$ 228	$ 300	$ 400	$ 760

Helpful Hint
The older categories have higher percentages because the longer an account is past due, the less likely it is to be collected.

Total estimated bad debts for Dart Company ($2,228) represent the amount of existing customer claims the company expects will become uncollectible in the future. This amount represents the **required balance** in Allowance for Doubtful Accounts at the balance sheet date. **The amount of the bad debt adjusting entry is the difference between the required balance and the existing balance in the allowance account.** If the trial balance shows Allowance for Doubtful Accounts with a credit balance of $528, the company will make an adjusting entry for $1,700 ($2,228 − $528), as shown here.

Dec. 31	Bad Debt Expense	1,700	
	Allowance for Doubtful Accounts		1,700
	(To adjust allowance account to total estimated uncollectibles)		

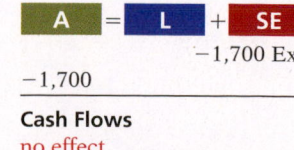

A = L + SE

−1,700 Exp

−1,700

Cash Flows
no effect

Illustration 8-9
Bad debt accounts after posting

After Dart posts its adjusting entry, its accounts will appear as follows.

Bad Debt Expense		Allowance for Doubtful Accounts	
Dec. 31 Adj. **1,700**			Bal. 528
			Dec. 31 Adj. **1,700**
			Bal. 2,228

Occasionally, the allowance account will have a **debit balance** prior to adjustment. This occurs when write-offs during the year have exceeded previous provisions for bad debts. In such a case, the company **adds the debit balance to the required balance** when it makes the adjusting entry. Thus, if there had been a $500 debit balance in the allowance account before adjustment, the adjusting entry would have been for $2,728 ($2,228 + $500) to arrive at a credit balance of $2,228 (see T-account in margin). The percentage-of-receivables basis will normally result in the better approximation of cash realizable value.

**Allowance
for Doubtful Accounts**

Dec. 31 **Unadj.**	Dec. 31 **Adj.** 2,728
Bal. 500	
	Dec. 31
	Bal. 2,228

Ethics Insight

© Christy Thompson/Shutterstock

Cookie Jar Allowances

There are many pressures on companies to achieve earnings targets. For managers, poor earnings can lead to dismissal or lack of promotion. It is not surprising then that management may be tempted to look for ways to boost their earnings number.

One way a company can achieve greater earnings is to lower its estimate of what is needed in its Allowance for Doubtful Accounts (sometimes referred to as "tapping the cooking jar"). For example, suppose a company has an Allowance for Doubtful Accounts of $10 million

and decides to reduce this balance to $9 million. As a result of this change, Bad Debt Expense decreases by $1 million and earnings increase by $1 million.

Large banks such as JP Morgan Chase, Wells Fargo, and Bank of America recently decreased their Allowance for Doubtful Accounts by over $4 billion. These reductions came at a time when these big banks were still suffering from lower mortgage lending and trading activity, both of which lead to lower earnings. They justified these reductions in the allowance balances by noting that credit quality and economic conditions had improved. This may be so, but it sure is great to have a cookie jar that might be tapped when a boost in earnings is needed.

How might investors determine that a company is managing its earnings? (Go to WileyPLUS for this answer and additional questions.)

Disposing of Accounts Receivable

In the normal course of events, companies collect accounts receivable in cash and remove the receivables from the books. However, as credit sales and receivables have grown in significance, the "normal course of events" has changed. Companies now frequently sell their receivables to another company for cash, thereby shortening the cash-to-cash operating cycle.

Companies sell receivables for two major reasons. First, **they may be the only reasonable source of cash**. When money is tight, companies may not be able to borrow money in the usual credit markets. Or if money is available, the cost of borrowing may be prohibitive.

A second reason for selling receivables is that **billing and collection are often time-consuming and costly**. It is often easier for a retailer to sell the receivables to another party with expertise in billing and collection matters. Credit card companies such as MasterCard, Visa, and Discover specialize in billing and collecting accounts receivable.

SALE OF RECEIVABLES

A common sale of receivables is a sale to a factor. A **factor** is a finance company or bank that buys receivables from businesses and then collects the payments directly from the customers. Factoring is a multibillion dollar business.

Factoring arrangements vary widely. Typically, the factor charges a commission to the company that is selling the receivables. This fee ranges from 1–3% of the amount of receivables purchased. To illustrate, assume that Hendredon Furniture factors $600,000 of receivables to Federal Factors. Federal Factors assesses a service charge of 2% of the amount of receivables sold. The journal entry to record the sale by Hendredon Furniture on April 2, 2017, is as follows.

Apr. 2	Cash	588,000	
	Service Charge Expense (2% × $600,000)	12,000	
	Accounts Receivable		600,000
	(To record the sale of accounts receivable)		

A = L + SE
+588,000
              −12,000 Exp
−600,000

Cash Flows
+588,000

If Hendredon often sells its receivables, it records the service charge expense as a selling expense. If the company infrequently sells receivables, it may report this amount in the "Other expenses and losses" section of the income statement.

CREDIT CARD SALES

Over one billion credit cards are in use in the United States—more than three credit cards for every man, woman, and child in this country. **Visa**, **MasterCard**, and **American Express** are the national credit cards that most individuals use. Three parties are involved when national credit cards are used in retail sales: (1) the credit card issuer, who is independent of the retailer; (2) the retailer; and (3) the customer. A retailer's acceptance of a national credit card is another form of selling (factoring) the receivable.

Illustration 8-10 shows the major advantages of national credit cards to the retailer. In exchange for these advantages, the retailer pays the credit card issuer a fee of 2–6% of the invoice price for its services.

Illustration 8-10
Advantages of credit cards to the retailer

ACCOUNTING FOR CREDIT CARD SALES The retailer generally considers sales from the use of national credit card sales as **cash sales**. The retailer must pay to the bank that issues the card a fee for processing the transactions. The retailer records the credit card slips in a similar manner as checks deposited from a cash sale.

To illustrate, Anita Ferreri purchases $1,000 of compact discs for her restaurant from Karen Kerr Music Co., using her Visa First Bank Card. First Bank charges a service fee of 3%. The entry to record this transaction by Karen Kerr Music on March 22, 2017, is as follows.

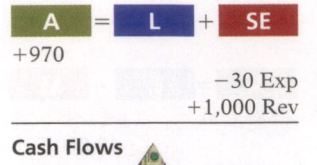

A = L + SE
+970
          −30 Exp
          +1,000 Rev

Cash Flows
+970

Mar. 22	Cash	970	
	Service Charge Expense	30	
	Sales Revenue		1,000
	(To record Visa credit card sales)		

Accounting Across the Organization Nordstrom

© Zibedik/iStockphoto

How Does a Credit Card Work?

Most of you know how to use a credit card, but do you know what happens in the transaction and how the transaction is processed? Suppose that you use a Visa card to purchase some new ties at Nordstrom. The salesperson swipes your card, which allows the information on the magnetic strip on the back of the card to be read. The salesperson then enters in the amount of the purchase. The machine contacts the Visa computer, which routes the call back to the bank that issued your Visa card. The issuing bank verifies that the account exists, that the card is not stolen, and that you have not exceeded your credit limit. At this point, the slip is printed, which you sign.

Visa acts as the clearing agent for the transaction. It transfers funds from the issuing bank to Nordstrom's bank account. Generally this transfer of funds, from sale to the receipt of funds in the merchant's account, takes two to three days.

In the meantime, Visa puts a pending charge on your account for the amount of the tie purchase; that amount counts immediately against your available credit limit. At the end of the billing period, Visa sends you an invoice (your credit card bill) which shows the various charges you made, and the amounts that Visa expended on your behalf, for the month. You then must "pay the piper" for your stylish new ties.

Assume that Nordstrom prepares a bank reconciliation at the end of each month. If some credit card sales have not been processed by the bank, how should Nordstrom treat these transactions on its bank reconciliation? (Go to WileyPLUS for this answer and additional questions.)

DO IT! 2 Uncollectible Accounts Receivable

Brule Co. has been in business for five years. The unadjusted trial balance at the end of the current year shows:

Accounts Receivable	$30,000 Dr.
Sales Revenue	$180,000 Cr.
Allowance for Doubtful Accounts	$2,000 Dr.

Brule estimates bad debts to be 10% of receivables. Prepare the entry necessary to adjust Allowance for Doubtful Accounts.

Action Plan

✔ Estimate the amount the company does not expect to collect.

✔ Consider the existing balance in the allowance account when using the percentage-of-receivables basis.

✔ Report receivables at their cash (net) realizable value.

Solution

The following entry should be made to bring the balance in Allowance for Doubtful Accounts up to a normal credit balance of $3,000 (10% × $30,000):

Bad Debt Expense [(10% × $30,000) + $2,000]	5,000	
Allowance for Doubtful Accounts		5,000
(To record estimate of uncollectible accounts)		

Related exercise material: **BE8-3, BE8-4, BE8-5, BE8-6, BE8-7, E8-3, E8-4, E8-5, E8-6, and DO IT! 8-2.**

Explain how companies recognize notes receivable.

Companies may also grant credit in exchange for a formal credit instrument known as a promissory note. A **promissory note** is a written promise to pay a specified amount of money on demand or at a definite time. Promissory notes may be used (1) when individuals and companies lend or borrow money, (2) when the amount of the transaction and the credit period exceed normal limits, or (3) in settlement of accounts receivable.

In a promissory note, the party making the promise to pay is called the **maker**. The party to whom payment is to be made is called the **payee**. The note may specifically identify the payee by name or may designate the payee simply as the bearer of the note.

In the note shown in Illustration 8-11, Calhoun Company is the maker and Wilma Company is the payee. To Wilma Company, the promissory note is a note receivable. To Calhoun Company, it is a note payable.

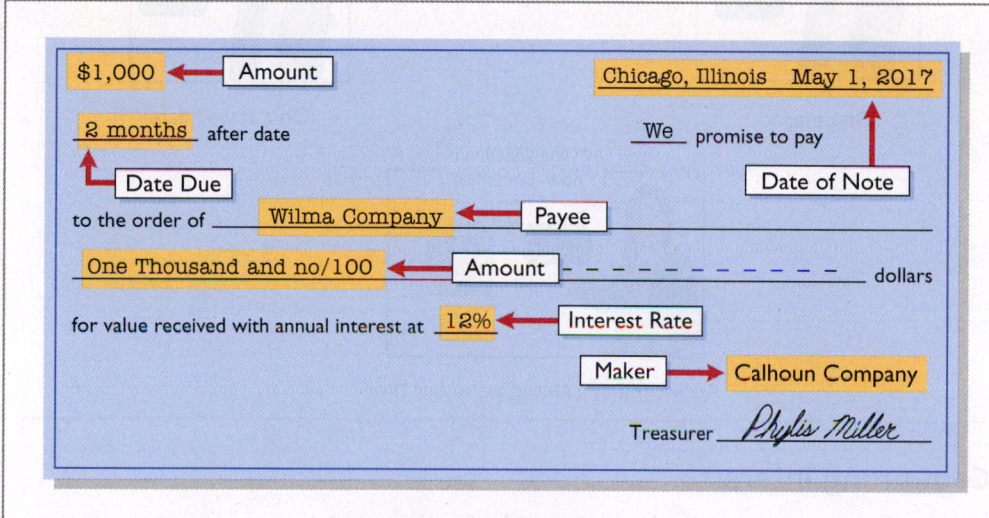

Illustration 8-11
Promissory note

Helpful Hint
For this note, the maker, Calhoun Company, debits Cash and credits Notes Payable. The payee, Wilma Company, debits Notes Receivable and credits Cash.

Notes receivable give the holder a stronger legal claim to assets than do accounts receivable. Like accounts receivable, notes receivable can be readily sold to another party. Promissory notes are negotiable instruments (as are checks), which means that they can be transferred to another party by endorsement.

Companies frequently accept notes receivable from customers who need to extend the payment of an outstanding account receivable. They often require such notes from high-risk customers. In some industries (such as the pleasure and sport boat industry), all credit sales are supported by notes. The majority of notes, however, originate from loans.

The basic issues in accounting for notes receivable are the same as those for accounts receivable. On the following pages, we look at these issues. Before we do, however, we need to consider two issues that do not apply to accounts receivable: determining the maturity date and computing interest.

Determining the Maturity Date

When the life of a note is expressed in terms of months, you find the date when it matures by counting the months from the date of issue. For example, the maturity date of a three-month note dated May 1 is August 1. A note drawn on the last day of a month matures on the last day of a subsequent month. That is, a July 31 note due in two months matures on September 30.

When the due date is stated in terms of days, you need to count the exact number of days to determine the maturity date. In counting, **omit the date the note is issued but include the due date**. For example, the maturity date of a 60-day note dated July 17 is September 15, computed as follows.

Illustration 8-12
Computation of maturity date

Term of note		60 days
July (31 − 17)	14	
August	31	45
Maturity date: September		**15**

Illustration 8-13 shows three ways of stating the maturity date of a promissory note.

Illustration 8-13
Maturity date of different notes

On demand

On a stated date

At the end of a stated period of time

Computing Interest

Illustration 8-14 gives the basic formula for computing interest on an interest-bearing note.

Illustration 8-14
Formula for computing interest

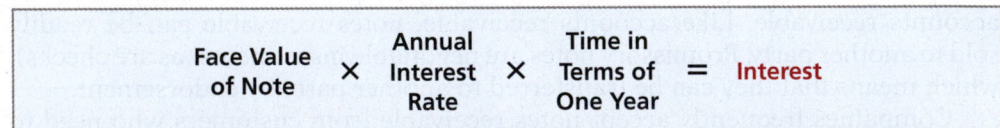

$$\text{Face Value of Note} \times \text{Annual Interest Rate} \times \text{Time in Terms of One Year} = \text{Interest}$$

Helpful Hint
The interest rate specified is the *annual* rate.

The interest rate specified in a note is an **annual** rate of interest. The time factor in the formula in Illustration 8-14 expresses the fraction of a year that the note is outstanding. When the maturity date is stated in days, the time factor is often the number of days divided by 360. When counting days, omit the date that the note is issued but include the due date. When the due date is stated in months, the time factor is the number of months divided by 12. Illustration 8-15 shows computation of interest for various time periods.

Illustration 8-15
Computation of interest

Terms of Note	Interest Computation				
	Face	× Rate	× Time	=	Interest
$ 730, 12%, 120 days	$ 730 ×	12%	× **120/360**	=	$ 29.20
$1,000, 9%, 6 months	$1,000 ×	9%	× **6/12**	=	$ 45.00
$2,000, 6%, 1 year	$2,000 ×	6%	× **1/1**	=	$120.00

There are different ways to calculate interest. For example, the computation in Illustration 8-15 assumes 360 days for the length of the year. Most financial instruments use 365 days to compute interest. *For homework problems, assume 360 days to simplify computations.*

Recognizing Notes Receivable

To illustrate the basic entry for notes receivable, we will use Calhoun Company's $1,000, two-month, 12% promissory note dated May 1. Assuming that Calhoun Company wrote the note to settle an open account, Wilma Company makes the following entry for the receipt of the note.

May 1	Notes Receivable	1,000	
	Accounts Receivable—Calhoun Company		1,000
	(To record acceptance of Calhoun Company note)		

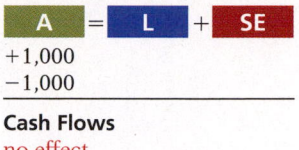

A = L + SE
+1,000
−1,000

Cash Flows
no effect

The company records the note receivable at its **face value**, the amount shown on the face of the note. No interest revenue is reported when the note is accepted because the revenue recognition principle does not recognize revenue until the performance obligation is satisfied. Interest is earned (accrued) as time passes.

If a company lends money using a note, the entry is a debit to Notes Receivable and a credit to Cash in the amount of the loan.

DO IT! 3   Recognizing Notes Receivable

Gambit Stores accepts from Leonard Co. a $3,400, 90-day, 6% note dated May 10 in settlement of Leonard's overdue account. (a) What is the maturity date of the note? (b) What is the interest payable at the maturity date?

Solution

(a) The maturity date is August 8, computed as follows.

Term of note:		90 days
May (31−10)	21	
June	30	
July	31	82
Maturity date: August		8

(b) The interest payable at the maturity date is $51, computed as follows.

Face	×	Rate	×	Time	=	Interest
$3,400	×	6%	×	90/360	=	$51

Action Plan

✔ Count the exact number of days to determine the maturity date. Omit the date the note is issued, but include the due date.

✔ Compute the accrued interest.

Related exercise material: **BE8-9, BE8-10, BE8-11, E8-10, E8-11, and DO IT! 8-3.**

LEARNING OBJECTIVE 4   **Describe how companies value notes receivable, record their disposition, and present and analyze receivables.**

Valuing Notes Receivable

Valuing short-term notes receivable is the same as valuing accounts receivable. Like accounts receivable, companies report short-term notes receivable at their **cash (net) realizable value**. The notes receivable allowance account is Allowance for Doubtful Accounts. The estimations involved in determining cash realizable value and in recording bad debt expense and the related allowance are done similarly to accounts receivable.

Disposing of Notes Receivable

Notes may be held to their maturity date, at which time the face value plus accrued interest is due. In some situations, the maker of the note defaults, and the payee must make an appropriate adjustment. In other situations, similar to accounts receivable, the holder of the note speeds up the conversion to cash by selling the receivables (as described later in this chapter).

HONOR OF NOTES RECEIVABLE

A note is **honored** when its maker pays in full at its maturity date. For each interest-bearing note, the **amount due at maturity** is the face value of the note plus interest for the length of time specified on the note.

To illustrate, assume that Wolder Co. lends Higley Co. $10,000 on June 1, accepting a five-month, 9% interest note. In this situation, interest is $375 ($10,000 × 9% × $\frac{5}{12}$). The amount due, **the maturity value**, is $10,375 ($10,000 + $375). To obtain payment, Wolder (the payee) must present the note either to Higley Co. (the maker) or to the maker's agent, such as a bank. If Wolder presents the note to Higley Co. on November 1, the maturity date, Wolder's entry to record the collection is as follows.

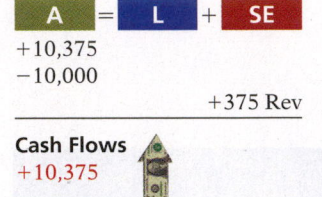

A = L + SE
+10,375
−10,000
+375 Rev

Cash Flows
+10,375

Nov. 1	Cash	10,375	
	Notes Receivable		10,000
	Interest Revenue ($10,000 × 9% × $\frac{5}{12}$)		375
	(To record collection of Higley note and interest)		

ACCRUAL OF INTEREST RECEIVABLE

Suppose instead that Wolder Co. prepares financial statements as of September 30. The timeline in Illustration 8-16 presents this situation.

Illustration 8-16
Timeline of interest earned

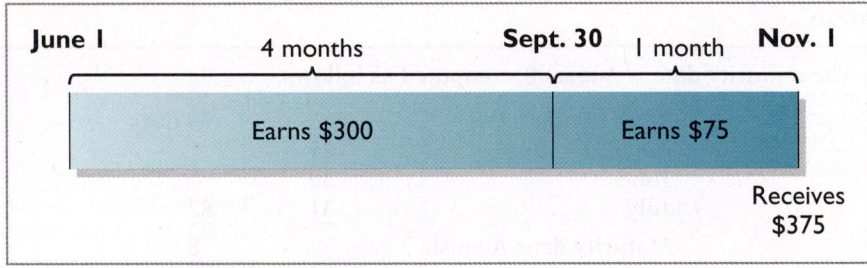

To reflect interest earned but not yet received, Wolder must accrue interest on September 30. In this case, the adjusting entry by Wolder is for four months of interest, or $300, as shown below.

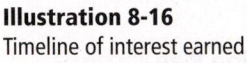

A = L + SE
+300
+300 Rev

Cash Flows
no effect

Sept. 30	Interest Receivable ($10,000 × 9% × $\frac{4}{12}$)	300	
	Interest Revenue		300
	(To accrue 4 months' interest on Higley note)		

At the note's maturity on November 1, Wolder receives $10,375. This amount represents repayment of the $10,000 note as well as five months of interest, or $375, as shown below. The $375 is comprised of the $300 Interest Receivable accrued on September 30 plus $75 earned during October. Wolder's entry to record the honoring of the Higley note on November 1 is as follows.

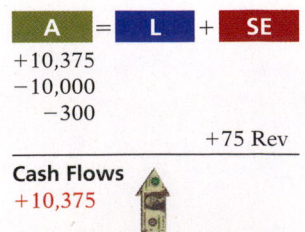

A = L + SE
+10,375
−10,000
−300
+75 Rev

Cash Flows
+10,375

Nov. 1	Cash [$10,000 + ($10,000 × 9% × $\frac{5}{12}$)]	10,375	
	Notes Receivable		10,000
	Interest Receivable		300
	Interest Revenue ($10,000 × 9% × $\frac{1}{12}$)		75
	(To record collection of Higley note and interest)		

In this case, Wolder credits Interest Receivable because the receivable was established in the adjusting entry on September 30.

DISHONOR OF NOTES RECEIVABLE

A **dishonored (defaulted) note** is a note that is not paid in full at maturity. A dishonored note receivable is no longer negotiable. However, the payee still has a claim against the maker of the note for both the note and the interest. Therefore, the note holder usually transfers the Notes Receivable account to an Accounts Receivable account.

To illustrate, assume that Higley Co. on November 1 indicates that it cannot pay at the present time. The entry to record the dishonor of the note depends on whether Wolder Co. expects eventual collection. If it does expect eventual collection, Wolder Co. debits the amount due (face value and interest) on the note to Accounts Receivable. It would make the following entry at the time the note is dishonored (assuming no previous accrual of interest).

Nov. 1	Accounts Receivable—Higley	10,375	
	Notes Receivable		10,000
	Interest Revenue		375
	(To record the dishonor of Higley note)		

A	=	L	+	SE

+10,375
−10,000

+375 Rev

Cash Flows
no effect

If instead on November 1 there is no hope of collection, the note holder would write off the face value of the note by debiting Allowance for Doubtful Accounts. No interest revenue would be recorded because collection will not occur.

SALE OF NOTES RECEIVABLE

The accounting for the sale of notes receivable is recorded similarly to the sale of accounts receivable. The accounting entries for the sale of notes receivable are left for a more advanced course.

Accounting Across the Organization   Countrywide Financial Corporation

© Andy Dean/iStockphoto

Bad Information Can Lead to Bad Loans

Many factors have contributed to the recent credit crisis. One significant factor that resulted in many bad loans was a failure by lenders to investigate loan customers sufficiently. For example, Countrywide Financial Corporation wrote many loans under its "Fast and Easy" loan program. That program allowed borrowers to provide little or no documentation for their income or their assets. Other lenders had similar programs, which earned the nickname "liars' loans." One study found that in these situations, 60% of applicants overstated their incomes by more than 50% in order to qualify for a loan. Critics of the banking industry say that because loan officers were compensated for loan volume and because banks were selling the loans to investors rather than holding them, the lenders had little incentive to investigate the borrowers' creditworthiness.

Sources: Glenn R. Simpson and James R. Hagerty, "Countrywide Loss Focuses Attention on Underwriting," *Wall Street Journal* (April 30, 2008), p. B1; and Michael Corkery, "Fraud Seen as Driver in Wave of Foreclosures," *Wall Street Journal* (December 21, 2007), p. A1.

What steps should the banks have taken to ensure the accuracy of financial information provided on loan applications? (Go to **WileyPLUS** for this answer and additional questions.)

Statement Presentation and Analysis

PRESENTATION

Companies should identify in the balance sheet or in the notes to the financial statements each of the major types of receivables. Short-term receivables appear in the current assets section of the balance sheet. Short-term investments appear before short-term receivables because these investments are more liquid (nearer to cash). Companies report both the gross amount of receivables and the allowance for doubtful accounts.

In a multiple-step income statement, companies report bad debt expense and service charge expense as selling expenses in the operating expenses section. Interest revenue appears under "Other revenues and gains" in the nonoperating activities section of the income statement.

ANALYSIS

Investors and corporate managers compute financial ratios to evaluate the liquidity of a company's accounts receivable. They use the **accounts receivable turnover** to assess the liquidity of the receivables. This ratio measures the number of times, on average, the company collects accounts receivable during the period. It is computed by dividing net credit sales (net sales less cash sales) by the average net accounts receivable during the year. Unless seasonal factors are significant, average net accounts receivable outstanding can be computed from the beginning and ending balances of net accounts receivable.

For example, in 2013 Cisco Systems had net sales of $38,029 million for the year. It had a beginning accounts receivable (net) balance of $4,369 million and an ending accounts receivable (net) balance of $5,470 million. Assuming that Cisco's sales were all on credit, its accounts receivable turnover is computed as follows.

Illustration 8-17
Accounts receivable turnover and computation

Net Credit Sales	÷	Average Net Accounts Receivable	=	Accounts Receivable Turnover
$38,029	÷	$\dfrac{\$4,369 + \$5,470}{2}$	=	7.7 times

The result indicates an accounts receivable turnover of 7.7 times per year. The higher the turnover, the more liquid the company's receivables.

A variant of the accounts receivable turnover that makes the liquidity even more evident is its conversion into an **average collection period** in terms of days. This is done by dividing the accounts receivable turnover into 365 days. For example, Cisco's turnover of 7.7 times is divided into 365 days, as shown in Illustration 8-18, to obtain approximately 47 days. This means that it takes Cisco 47 days to collect its accounts receivable.

Illustration 8-18
Average collection period for receivables formula and computation

Days in Year	÷	Accounts Receivable Turnover	=	Average Collection Period in Days
365 days	÷	7.7 times	=	47 days

Companies frequently use the average collection period to assess the effectiveness of a company's credit and collection policies. The general rule is that the collection period should not greatly exceed the credit term period (that is, the time allowed for payment).

DO IT! 4   Analysis of Receivables

In 2017, Phil Mickelson Company has net credit sales of $923,795 for the year. It had a beginning accounts receivable (net) balance of $38,275 and an ending accounts receivable (net) balance of $35,988. Compute Phil Mickelson Company's (a) accounts receivable turnover and (b) average collection period in days.

Solution

(a)

Net credit sales	÷	Average net accounts receivable	=	Accounts receivable turnover
$923,795	÷	$\dfrac{\$38,275 + \$35,988}{2}$	=	24.9 times

(b)

Days in year	÷	Accounts receivable turnover	=	Average collection period in days
365	÷	24.9 times	=	14.7 days

Related exercise material: **BE8-12, E8-14, and DO IT! 8-4.**

Action Plan

✔ Review the formula to compute the accounts receivable turnover.

✔ Make sure that both the beginning and ending accounts receivable balances are considered in the computation.

✔ Review the formula to compute the average collection period in days.

REVIEW AND PRACTICE

LEARNING OBJECTIVES REVIEW

1 Explain how companies recognize accounts receivable. Receivables are frequently classified as (1) accounts, (2) notes, and (3) other. Accounts receivable are amounts customers owe on account. Notes receivable are claims for which lenders issue formal instruments of credit as proof of the debt. Other receivables include nontrade receivables such as interest receivable, loans to company officers, advances to employees, and income taxes refundable.

Companies record accounts receivable when they perform a service on account or at the point of sale of merchandise on account. Accounts receivable are reduced by sales returns and allowances. Cash discounts reduce the amount received on accounts receivable. When interest is charged on a past due receivable, the company adds this interest to the accounts receivable balance and recognizes it as interest revenue.

2 Describe how companies value accounts receivable and record their disposition. There are two methods of accounting for uncollectible accounts: the allowance method and the direct write-off method. Companies may use either the percentage-of-sales or the percentage-of-receivables basis to estimate uncollectible accounts using the allowance method. The percentage-of-sales basis emphasizes the expense recognition (matching) principle. The percentage-of-receivables basis emphasizes the cash realizable value of the accounts receivable. An aging schedule is often used with this basis.

When a company collects an account receivable, it credits Accounts Receivable. When a company sells (factors) an account receivable, a service charge expense reduces the amount received.

3 Explain how companies recognize notes receivable. For a note stated in months, the maturity date is found by counting the months from the date of issue. For a note stated in days, the number of days is counted, omitting the issue date and counting the due date. The formula for computing interest is Face value × Interest rate × Time.

Companies record notes receivable at face value. In some cases, it is necessary to accrue interest prior to maturity. In this case, companies debit Interest Receivable and credit Interest Revenue.

4 Describe how companies value notes receivable, record their disposition, and present and analyze receivables. As with accounts receivable, companies report notes receivable at their cash (net) realizable value. The notes receivable allowance account is Allowance for Doubtful Accounts. The computation and estimations involved in valuing notes receivable at cash realizable value, and in recording the proper amount of bad debt expense and the related allowance, are similar to those for accounts receivable.

Notes can be held to maturity. At that time the face value plus accrued interest is due, and the note is removed from the accounts. In many cases, the holder of the note speeds up the conversion by selling the receivable to another party (a factor). In some situations, the maker of the note dishonors the note (defaults), in which case the company transfers the note and accrued interest to an account receivable or writes off the note.

Companies should identify in the balance sheet or in the notes to the financial statements each major type of receivable. Short-term receivables are considered current assets. Companies report the gross amount of receivables and the allowance for doubtful accounts. They report bad debt and service charge expenses in the multiple-step income statement as operating (selling) expenses. Interest revenue appears under other revenues and gains in the nonoperating activities section of the statement. Managers and investors evaluate accounts receivable for liquidity by computing a turnover ratio and an average collection period.

■ GLOSSARY REVIEW

Accounts receivable Amounts owed by customers on account. (p. 358).

Accounts receivable turnover A measure of the liquidity of accounts receivable; computed by dividing net credit sales by average net accounts receivable. (p. 374).

Aging the accounts receivable The analysis of customer balances by the length of time they have been unpaid. (p. 365).

Allowance method A method of accounting for bad debts that involves estimating uncollectible accounts at the end of each period. (p. 361).

Average collection period The average amount of time that a receivable is outstanding; calculated by dividing 365 days by the accounts receivable turnover. (p. 374).

Bad Debt Expense An expense account to record uncollectible receivables. (p. 360).

Cash (net) realizable value The net amount a company expects to receive in cash. (p. 361).

Direct write-off method A method of accounting for bad debts that involves expensing accounts at the time they are determined to be uncollectible. (p. 361).

Dishonored (defaulted) note A note that is not paid in full at maturity. (p. 373).

Factor A finance company or bank that buys receivables from businesses and then collects the payments directly from the customers. (p. 367).

Maker The party in a promissory note who is making the promise to pay. (p. 369).

Notes receivable Written promise (as evidenced by a formal instrument) for amounts to be received. (p. 358).

Other receivables Various forms of nontrade receivables, such as interest receivable and income taxes refundable. (p. 358).

Payee The party to whom payment of a promissory note is to be made. (p. 369).

Percentage-of-receivables basis Management estimates what percentage of receivables will result in losses from uncollectible accounts. (p. 365).

Percentage-of-sales basis Management estimates what percentage of credit sales will be uncollectible. (p. 364).

Promissory note A written promise to pay a specified amount of money on demand or at a definite time. (p. 369).

Receivables Amounts due from individuals and other companies. (p. 358).

Trade receivables Notes and accounts receivable that result from sales transactions. (p. 358).

■ PRACTICE MULTIPLE-CHOICE QUESTIONS

(LO 1) 1. Receivables are frequently classified as:
 (a) accounts receivable, company receivables, and other receivables.
 (b) accounts receivable, notes receivable, and employee receivables.
 (c) accounts receivable and general receivables.
 (d) accounts receivable, notes receivable, and other receivables.

(LO 1) 2. Buehler Company on June 15 sells merchandise on account to Chaz Co. for $1,000, terms 2/10, n/30. On June 20, Chaz Co. returns merchandise worth $300 to Buehler Company. On June 24, payment is received from Chaz Co. for the balance due. What is the amount of cash received?
 (a) $700.　　　　　　(c) $686.
 (b) $680.　　　　　　(d) None of the above.

(LO 2) 3. Which of the following approaches for bad debts is best described as a balance sheet method?
 (a) Percentage-of-receivables basis.
 (b) Direct write-off method.
 (c) Percentage-of-sales basis.
 (d) Both percentage-of-receivables basis and direct write-off method.

(LO 2) 4. Hughes Company has a credit balance of $5,000 in its Allowance for Doubtful Accounts before any adjustments are made at the end of the year. Based on review and aging of its accounts receivable at the end of the year, Hughes estimates that $60,000 of its receivables are uncollectible. The amount of bad debt expense which should be reported for the year is:
 (a) $5,000.　　　　　(c) $60,000.
 (b) $55,000.　　　　 (d) $65,000.

(LO 2) 5. Use the same information as in Question 4, except that Hughes has a debit balance of $5,000 in its Allowance for Doubtful Accounts before any adjustments are made at the end of the year. In this situation, the amount of bad debt expense that should be reported for the year is:
 (a) $5,000.　　　　　(c) $60,000.
 (b) $55,000.　　　　 (d) $65,000.

(LO 2) **6.** Net sales for the month are $800,000, and bad debts are expected to be 1.5% of net sales. The company uses the percentage-of-sales basis. If Allowance for Doubtful Accounts has a credit balance of $15,000 before adjustment, what is the balance after adjustment?
(a) $15,000. (c) $23,000.
(b) $27,000. (d) $31,000.

(LO 2) **7.** In 2017, Roso Carlson Company had net credit sales of $750,000. On January 1, 2017, Allowance for Doubtful Accounts had a credit balance of $18,000. During 2017, $30,000 of uncollectible accounts receivable were written off. Past experience indicates that 3% of net credit sales become uncollectible. What should be the adjusted balance of Allowance for Doubtful Accounts at December 31, 2017?
(a) $10,050. (c) $22,500.
(b) $10,500. (d) $40,500.

(LO 2) **8.** An analysis and aging of the accounts receivable of Prince Company at December 31 reveals the following data.

Accounts receivable	$800,000
Allowance for doubtful accounts per books before adjustment	50,000
Amounts expected to become uncollectible	65,000

The cash realizable value of the accounts receivable at December 31, after adjustment, is:
(a) $685,000. (c) $800,000.
(b) $750,000. (d) $735,000.

(LO 2) **9.** Which of the following statements about Visa credit card sales is **incorrect**?
(a) The credit card issuer makes the credit investigation of the customer.
(b) The retailer is not involved in the collection process.
(c) Two parties are involved.
(d) The retailer receives cash more quickly than it would from individual customers on account.

(LO 2) **10.** Blinka Retailers accepted $50,000 of Citibank Visa credit card charges for merchandise sold on July 1. Citibank charges 4% for its credit card use. The entry to record this transaction by Blinka Retailers will include a credit to Sales Revenue of $50,000 and a debit(s) to:
(a) Cash $48,000
    and Service Charge Expense $2,000
(b) Accounts Receivable $48,000
    and Service Charge Expense $2,000
(c) Cash $50,000
(d) Accounts Receivable $50,000

(LO 3) **11.** One of the following statements about promissory notes is incorrect. The **incorrect** statement is:
(a) The party making the promise to pay is called the maker.
(b) The party to whom payment is to be made is called the payee.
(c) A promissory note is not a negotiable instrument.
(d) A promissory note is often required from high-risk customers.

(LO 3) **12.** Foti Co. accepts a $1,000, 3-month, 6% promissory note in settlement of an account with Bartelt Co. The entry to record this transaction is as follows.

(a) Notes Receivable	1,015	
Accounts Receivable		1,015
(b) Notes Receivable	1,000	
Accounts Receivable		1,000
(c) Notes Receivable	1,000	
Sales Revenue		1,000
(d) Notes Receivable	1,030	
Accounts Receivable		1,030

(LO 4) **13.** Ginter Co. holds Kolar Inc.'s $10,000, 120-day, 9% note. The entry made by Ginter Co. when the note is collected, assuming no interest has been previously accrued, is:

(a) Cash	10,300	
Notes Receivable		10,300
(b) Cash	10,000	
Notes Receivable		10,000
(c) Accounts Receivable	10,300	
Notes Receivable		10,000
Interest Revenue		300
(d) Cash	10,300	
Notes Receivable		10,000
Interest Revenue		300

(LO 4) **14.** Accounts and notes receivable are reported in the current assets section of the balance sheet at:
(a) cash (net) realizable value.
(b) net book value.
(c) lower-of-cost-or-net realizable value.
(d) invoice cost.

(LO 4) **15.** Oliveras Company had net credit sales during the year of $800,000 and cost of goods sold of $500,000. The balance in accounts receivable at the beginning of the year was $100,000, and the end of the year it was $150,000. What were the accounts receivable turnover and the average collection period in days?
(a) 4.0 and 91.3 days.
(b) 5.3 and 68.9 days.
(c) 6.4 and 57 days.
(d) 8.0 and 45.6 days.

Solutions

1. (d) Receivables are frequently classified as accounts receivable, notes receivable, and other receivables. The other choices are incorrect because receivables are not frequently classified as (a) company receivables, (b) employee receivables, or (c) general receivables.

2. (c) Because payment is received within 10 days of the purchase, the cash received is $686 [[$1,000 − $300] − [($1,000 − $300) × 2%)]]. The other choices are incorrect because (a) $700 does not consider the 2% discount; (b) the amount of the discount is based upon the amount after the return is granted ($700 × 2%), not the amount before the return of merchandise ($1,000 × 2%); and (d) there is a correct answer.

3. (a) The percentage-of-receivables basis is a balance sheet method because it emphasizes the cash (net) realizable value of accounts receivable. The other choices are incorrect because (b) the direct write-off method is neither a balance sheet nor an income statement method for accounting for bad debts, (c) the percentage-of-sales basis is an income statement method because it results in a better matching of expenses with revenues, and (d) only the percentage-of-receivables basis is a balance sheet method, not the direct write-off method.

4. (b) By crediting Allowance for Doubtful Accounts for $55,000, the new balance will be the required balance of $60,000. This adjusting entry debits Bad Debt Expense for $55,000 and credits Allowance for Doubtful Accounts for $55,000, not (a) $5,000, (c) $60,000, or (d) $65,000.

5. (d) By crediting Allowance for Doubtful Accounts for $65,000, the new balance will be the required balance of $60,000. This adjusting entry debits Bad Debt Expense for $65,000 and credits Allowance for Doubtful Accounts for $65,000, not (a) $5,000, (b) $55,000, or (c) $60,000.

6. (b) Net sales times the percentage expected to default equals the amount of bad debt expense for the year ($800,000 × 1.5% = $12,000). Because this adjusting entry credits Allowance for Doubtful Accounts, the balance after adjustment is $27,000 ($15,000 + $12,000), not (a) $15,000, (c) $23,000, or (d) $31,000.

7. (b) The accounts written off during the year will result in a $30,000 debit to Allowance for Doubtful Accounts. The adjusting entry for bad debts will include a $22,500 credit ($750,000 × 3%) to Allowance for Doubtful Accounts. Combining the beginning balance of $18,000 credit, the $30,000 debit, and the $22,500 credit leaves a credit balance of $10,500 in the allowance account, not (a) $10,050, (c) $22,500, or (d) $40,500.

8. (d) Accounts Receivable less the expected uncollectible amount equals the cash realizable value of $735,000 ($800,000 − $65,000), not (a) $685,000, (b) $750,000, or (c) $800,000.

9. (c) There are three parties, not two, involved in Visa credit card sales: the credit card company, the retailer, and the customer. The other choices are true statements.

10. (a) Credit card sales are considered cash sales. Cash is debited $48,000 for the net amount received ($50,000 − $2,000 for credit card use fee), and Service Charge Expense is debited $2,000 for the 4% credit card use fee ($50,000 × 4%). The other choices are therefore incorrect.

11. (c) A promissory note is a negotiable instrument. The other choices are true statements.

12. (b) Notes Receivable is recorded at face value ($1,000). No interest on the note is recorded until it is earned. Accounts Receivable is credited because no new sales have been made. The other choices are therefore incorrect.

13. (d) Cash is debited for its maturity value [$10,000 + interest earned ($10,000 × 1/3 × 9%)], Notes Receivable credited for its face value, and Interest Revenue credited for the amount of interest earned. The other choices are therefore incorrect.

14. (a) Accounts Receivable is reported in the current assets section of the balance sheet at the gross amount less the allowance for doubtful accounts, not at (b) net book value, (c) lower-of-cost-or-net realizable value, or (d) invoice cost.

15. (c) The accounts receivable turnover is 6.4 [$800,000/($100,000 + $150,000)/2)]. The average collection period in days is 57 days (365/6.4). The other choices are therefore incorrect.

PRACTICE EXERCISES

Journalize entries to record allowance for doubtful accounts using two different bases.

(LO 2)

1. The ledger of J.C. Cobb Company at the end of the current year shows Accounts Receivable $150,000, Sales Revenue $850,000, and Sales Returns and Allowances $30,000.

Instructions

(a) If J.C. Cobb uses the direct write-off method to account for uncollectible accounts, journalize the adjusting entry at December 31, assuming J.C. Cobb determines that M. Jack's $1,500 balance is uncollectible.

(b) If Allowance for Doubtful Accounts has a credit balance of $2,400 in the trial balance, journalize the adjusting entry at December 31, assuming bad debts are expected to be (1) 1.5% of net sales, and (2) 10% of accounts receivable.

(c) If Allowance for Doubtful Accounts has a debit balance of $200 in the trial balance, journalize the adjusting entry at December 31, assuming bad debts are expected to be (1) 0.75% of net sales and (2) 6% of accounts receivable.

Solution

1. (a)	Dec. 31	Bad Debt Expense	1,500	
		Accounts Receivable—M. Jack		1,500
(b) (1)	Dec. 31	Bad Debt Expense	12,300	
		[($850,000 − $30,000) × 1.5%]		
		Allowance for Doubtful		
		Accounts		12,300
(2)	Dec. 31	Bad Debt Expense	12,600	
		Allowance for Doubtful Accounts		
		[($150,000 × 10%) − $2,400]		12,600

(c) (1) Dec. 31	Bad Debt Expense	6,150	
	[($850,000 − $30,000) × 0.75%]		
	Allowance for Doubtful		
	Accounts		6,150
(2) Dec. 31	Bad Debt Expense	9,200	
	Allowance for Doubtful Accounts		
	[($150,000 × 6%) + $200]		9,200

2. Troope Supply Co. has the following transactions related to notes receivable during the last 3 months of 2017.

Journalize entries for notes receivable transactions.

(LO 3, 4)

Oct. 1 Loaned $16,000 cash to Juan Vasquez on a 1-year, 10% note.

Dec. 11 Sold goods to A. Palmer, Inc., receiving a $6,750, 90-day, 8% note.

16 Received a $6,400, 6-month, 9% note in exchange for J. Nicholas's outstanding accounts receivable.

31 Accrued interest revenue on all notes receivable.

Instructions

(a) Journalize the transactions for Troup Supply Co.

(b) Record the collection of the Vasques note at its maturity in 2018.

Solution

2. (a)

			2017		
Oct. 1	Notes Receivable			16,000	
	Cash				16,000
Dec. 11	Notes Receivable			6,750	
	Sales Revenue				6,750
16	Notes Receivable			6,400	
	Accounts Receivable—Nicholas				6,400
31	Interest Receivable			454	
	Interest Revenue*				454

*Calculation of interest revenue:

Vasquez's note:	$16,000 × 10% × 3/12 =	$400
Palmer's note:	6,750 × 8% × 20/360 =	30
Nicholas's note:	6,400 × 9% × 15/360 =	24
	Total accrued interest	$454

(b)

		2018		
Oct. 1	Cash		17,600	
	Interest Receivable			400
	Interest Revenue**			1,200
	Notes Receivable			16,000

**($16,000 × 10% × 9/12)

▮ PRACTICE PROBLEM

The following selected transactions relate to Dylan Company.

Prepare entries for various receivables transactions.

(LO 1, 2, 3, 4)

Mar. 1 Sold $20,000 of merchandise to Potter Company, terms 2/10, n/30.

11 Received payment in full from Potter Company for balance due on existing accounts receivable.

12 Accepted Juno Company's $20,000, 6-month, 12% note for balance due.

13 Made Dylan Company credit card sales for $13,200.

15 Made Visa credit card sales totaling $6,700. A 3% service fee is charged by Visa.

Apr. 11 Sold accounts receivable of $8,000 to Harcot Factor. Harcot Factor assesses a service charge of 2% of the amount of receivables sold.

13 Received collections of $8,200 on Dylan Company credit card sales and added finance charges of 1.5% to the remaining balances.

May 10 Wrote off as uncollectible $16,000 of accounts receivable. Dylan uses the percentage-of-sales basis to estimate bad debts.

June 30   Credit sales recorded during the first 6 months total $2,000,000. The bad debt percentage is 1% of credit sales. At June 30, the balance in the allowance account is $3,500 before adjustment.

July   16   One of the accounts receivable written off in May was from J. Simon, who pays the amount due, $4,000, in full.

Instructions

Prepare the journal entries for the transactions. (Ignore entries for cost of goods sold.)

Solution

Mar. 1	Accounts Receivable—Potter	20,000	
	Sales Revenue		20,000
	(To record sales on account)		
11	Cash	19,600	
	Sales Discounts (2% × $20,000)	400	
	Accounts Receivable—Potter		20,000
	(To record collection of accounts receivable)		
12	Notes Receivable	20,000	
	Accounts Receivable—Juno		20,000
	(To record acceptance of Juno Company note)		
13	Accounts Receivable	13,200	
	Sales Revenue		13,200
	(To record company credit card sales)		
15	Cash	6,499	
	Service Charge Expense (3% × $6,700)	201	
	Sales Revenue		6,700
	(To record credit card sales)		
Apr. 11	Cash	7,840	
	Service Charge Expense (2% × $8,000)	160	
	Accounts Receivable		8,000
	(To record sale of receivables to factor)		
13	Cash	8,200	
	Accounts Receivable		8,200
	(To record collection of accounts receivable)		
	Accounts Receivable [($13,200 − $8,200) × 1.5%]	75	
	Interest Revenue		75
	(To record interest on amount due)		
May 10	Allowance for Doubtful Accounts	16,000	
	Accounts Receivable		16,000
	(To record write-off of accounts receivable)		
June 30	Bad Debt Expense ($2,000,000 × 1%)	20,000	
	Allowance for Doubtful Accounts		20,000
	(To record estimate of uncollectible accounts)		
July 16	Accounts Receivable—J. Simon	4,000	
	Allowance for Doubtful Accounts		4,000
	(To reverse write-off of accounts receivable)		
	Cash	4,000	
	Accounts Receivable—J. Simon		4,000
	(To record collection of accounts receivable)		

WileyPLUS

Brief Exercises, Exercises, **DO IT!** Exercises, and Problems and many additional resources are available for practice in WileyPLUS

QUESTIONS

1. What is the difference between an account receivable and a note receivable?
2. What are some common types of receivables other than accounts receivable and notes receivable?
3. **Texaco Oil Company** issues its own credit cards. Assume that Texaco charges you $40 interest on an unpaid balance. Prepare the journal entry that Texaco makes to record this revenue.
4. What are the essential features of the allowance method of accounting for bad debts?
5. Roger Holloway cannot understand why cash realizable value does not decrease when an uncollectible account is written off under the allowance method. Clarify this point for Roger.
6. Distinguish between the two bases that may be used in estimating uncollectible accounts.
7. Borke Company has a credit balance of $3,000 in Allowance for Doubtful Accounts. The estimated bad debt expense under the percentage-of-sales basis is $4,100. The total estimated uncollectibles under the percentage-of-receivables basis is $5,800. Prepare the adjusting entry under each basis.
8. How are bad debts accounted for under the direct write-off method? What are the disadvantages of this method?
9. Freida Company accepts both its own credit cards and national credit cards. What are the advantages of accepting both types of cards?
10. An article recently appeared in the *Wall Street Journal* indicating that companies are selling their receivables at a record rate. Why are companies selling their receivables?
11. Westside Textiles decides to sell $800,000 of its accounts receivable to First Factors Inc. First Factors assesses a service charge of 3% of the amount of receivables sold. Prepare the journal entry that Westside Textiles makes to record this sale.

12. Your roommate is uncertain about the advantages of a promissory note. Compare the advantages of a note receivable with those of an account receivable.
13. How may the maturity date of a promissory note be stated?
14. Indicate the maturity date of each of the following promissory notes:

Date of Note	Terms
(a) March 13	one year after date of note
(b) May 4	3 months after date
(c) June 20	30 days after date
(d) July 1	60 days after date

15. Compute the missing amounts for each of the following notes.

	Principal	Annual Interest Rate	Time	Total Interest
(a)	?	9%	120 days	$ 450
(b)	$30,000	10%	3 years	?
(c)	$60,000	?	5 months	$1,500
(d)	$45,000	8%	?	$1,200

16. In determining interest revenue, some financial institutions use 365 days per year and others use 360 days. Why might a financial institution use 360 days?
17. Jana Company dishonors a note at maturity. What are the options available to the lender?
18. **General Motors Corporation** has accounts receivable and notes receivable. How should the receivables be reported on the balance sheet?
19. The accounts receivable turnover is 8.14, and average net accounts receivable during the period is $400,000. What is the amount of net credit sales for the period?
20. What percentage does **Apple**'s 2013 allowance for doubtful accounts represent as a percentage of its gross receivables?

BRIEF EXERCISES

BE8-1 Presented below are three receivables transactions. Indicate whether these receivables are reported as accounts receivable, notes receivable, or other receivables on a balance sheet.
(a) Sold merchandise on account for $64,000 to a customer.
(b) Received a promissory note of $57,000 for services performed.
(c) Advanced $10,000 to an employee.

Identify different types of receivables.

(LO 1)

BE8-2 Record the following transactions on the books of RAS Co.
(a) On July 1, RAS Co. sold merchandise on account to Waegelein Inc. for $17,200, terms 2/10, n/30.
(b) On July 8, Waegelein Inc. returned merchandise worth $3,800 to RAS Co.
(c) On July 11, Waegelein Inc. paid for the merchandise.

Record basic accounts receivable transactions.

(LO 1)

Prepare entry for allowance method and partial balance sheet.

(LO 2, 4)

BE8-3 During its first year of operations, Gavin Company had credit sales of $3,000,000; $600,000 remained uncollected at year-end. The credit manager estimates that $31,000 of these receivables will become uncollectible.
(a) Prepare the journal entry to record the estimated uncollectibles.
(b) Prepare the current assets section of the balance sheet for Gavin Company. Assume that in addition to the receivables it has cash of $90,000, inventory of $130,000, and prepaid insurance of $7,500.

Prepare entry for write-off; determine cash realizable value.

(LO 2)

BE8-4 At the end of 2017, Carpenter Co. has accounts receivable of $700,000 and an allowance for doubtful accounts of $54,000. On January 24, 2018, the company learns that its receivable from Megan Gray is not collectible, and management authorizes a write-off of $6,200.
(a) Prepare the journal entry to record the write-off.
(b) What is the cash realizable value of the accounts receivable (1) before the write-off and (2) after the write-off?

Prepare entries for collection of bad debt write-off.

(LO 2)

BE8-5 Assume the same information as BE8-4. On March 4, 2018, Carpenter Co. receives payment of $6,200 in full from Megan Gray. Prepare the journal entries to record this transaction.

Prepare entry using percentage-of-sales method.

(LO 2)

BE8-6 Farr Co. elects to use the percentage-of-sales basis in 2017 to record bad debt expense. It estimates that 2% of net credit sales will become uncollectible. Sales revenues are $800,000 for 2017, sales returns and allowances are $40,000, and the allowance for doubtful accounts has a credit balance of $9,000. Prepare the adjusting entry to record bad debt expense in 2017.

Prepare entry using percentage-of-receivables method.

(LO 2)

BE8-7 Kingston Co. uses the percentage-of-receivables basis to record bad debt expense. It estimates that 1% of accounts receivable will become uncollectible. Accounts receivable are $420,000 at the end of the year, and the allowance for doubtful accounts has a credit balance of $1,500.
(a) Prepare the adjusting journal entry to record bad debt expense for the year.
(b) If the allowance for doubtful accounts had a debit balance of $800 instead of a credit balance of $1,500, determine the amount to be reported for bad debt expense.

Prepare entries to dispose of accounts receivable.

(LO 2)

BE8-8 Presented below are two independent transactions.
(a) Tony's Restaurant accepted a Visa card in payment of a $175 lunch bill. The bank charges a 4% fee. What entry should Tony's make?
(b) Larkin Company sold its accounts receivable of $60,000. What entry should Larkin make, given a service charge of 3% on the amount of receivables sold?

Compute interest and determine maturity dates on notes.

(LO 3)

BE8-9 Compute interest and find the maturity date for the following notes.

Date of Note	Principal	Interest Rate (%)	Terms
(a) June 10	$80,000	6%	60 days
(b) July 14	$64,000	7%	90 days
(c) April 27	$12,000	8%	75 days

Determine maturity dates and compute interest and rates on notes.

(LO 3)

BE8-10 Presented below are data on three promissory notes. Determine the missing amounts.

Date of Note	Terms	Maturity Date	Principal	Annual Interest Rate	Total Interest
(a) April 1	60 days	?	$600,000	6%	?
(b) July 2	30 days	?	90,000	?	$600
(c) March 7	6 months	?	120,000	10%	?

Prepare entry for note receivable exchanged for account receivable.

(LO 3)

BE8-11 On January 10, 2017, Perez Co. sold merchandise on account to Robertsen Co. for $15,600, n/30. On February 9, Robertsen Co. gave Perez Co. a 10% promissory note in settlement of this account. Prepare the journal entry to record the sale and the settlement of the account receivable.

BE8-12 The financial statements of Minnesota Mining and Manufacturing Company (3M) report net sales of $20.0 billion. Accounts receivable (net) are $2.7 billion at the beginning of the year and $2.8 billion at the end of the year. Compute 3M's accounts receivable turnover. Compute 3M's average collection period for accounts receivable in days.

Compute ratios to analyze receivables.

(LO 4)

DO IT! Exercises

DO IT! 8-1 On March 1, Lincoln sold merchandise on account to Amelia Company for $28,000, terms 1/10, net 45. On March 6, Amelia returns merchandise with a sales price of $1,000. On March 11, Lincoln receives payment from Amelia for the balance due. Prepare journal entries to record the March transactions on Lincoln's books. (You may ignore cost of goods sold entries and explanations.)

Prepare entries to recognize accounts receivable.

(LO 1)

DO IT! 8-2 Gonzalez Company has been in business for several years. At the end of the current year, the ledger shows:

Accounts Receivable	$ 310,000 Dr.
Sales Revenue	2,200,000 Cr.
Allowance for Doubtful Accounts	6,100 Cr.

Bad debts are estimated to be 5% of accounts receivable. Prepare the entry to adjust Allowance for Doubtful Accounts.

Prepare entry for uncollectible accounts.

(LO 2)

DO IT! 8-3 Gentry Wholesalers accepts from Benton Stores a $6,200, 4-month, 9% note dated May 31 in settlement of Benton's overdue account. (a) What is the maturity date of the note? (b) What is the interest payable at the maturity date?

Compute maturity date and interest on note.

(LO 3)

DO IT! 8-4 In 2017, Wainwright Company has net credit sales of $1,300,000 for the year. It had a beginning accounts receivable (net) balance of $101,000 and an ending accounts receivable (net) balance of $107,000. Compute Wainwright Company's (a) accounts receivable turnover and (b) average collection period in days.

Compute ratios for receivables.

(LO 4)

EXERCISES

E8-1 Presented below are selected transactions of Molina Company. Molina sells in large quantities to other companies and also sells its product in a small retail outlet.

Journalize entries related to accounts receivable.

(LO 1)

March	1	Sold merchandise on account to Dodson Company for $5,000, terms 2/10, n/30.
	3	Dodson Company returned merchandise worth $500 to Molina.
	9	Molina collected the amount due from Dodson Company from the March 1 sale.
	15	Molina sold merchandise for $400 in its retail outlet. The customer used his Molina credit card.
	31	Molina added 1.5% monthly interest to the customer's credit card balance.

Instructions
Prepare journal entries for the transactions above.

E8-2 Presented below are two independent situations.

Journalize entries for recognizing accounts receivable.

(LO 1)

(a) On January 6, Brumbaugh Co. sells merchandise on account to Pryor Inc. for $7,000, terms 2/10, n/30. On January 16, Pryor Inc. pays the amount due. Prepare the entries on Brumbaugh's books to record the sale and related collection.

(b) On January 10, Andrew Farley uses his Paltrow Co. credit card to purchase merchandise from Paltrow Co. for $9,000. On February 10, Farley is billed for the amount due of $9,000. On February 12, Farley pays $5,000 on the balance due. On March 10, Farley is billed for the amount due, including interest at 1% per month on the unpaid balance as of February 12. Prepare the entries on Paltrow Co.'s books related to the transactions that occurred on January 10, February 12, and March 10.

Journalize entries to record allowance for doubtful accounts using two different bases.

(LO 2)

E8-3 The ledger of Costello Company at the end of the current year shows Accounts Receivable $110,000, Sales Revenue $840,000, and Sales Returns and Allowances $20,000.

Instructions

(a) If Costello uses the direct write-off method to account for uncollectible accounts, journalize the adjusting entry at December 31, assuming Costello determines that L. Dole's $1,400 balance is uncollectible.

(b) If Allowance for Doubtful Accounts has a credit balance of $2,100 in the trial balance, journalize the adjusting entry at December 31, assuming bad debts are expected to be (1) 1% of net sales, and (2) 10% of accounts receivable.

(c) If Allowance for Doubtful Accounts has a debit balance of $200 in the trial balance, journalize the adjusting entry at December 31, assuming bad debts are expected to be (1) 0.75% of net sales and (2) 6% of accounts receivable.

E8-4 Menge Company has accounts receivable of $93,100 at March 31. Credit terms are 2/10, n/30. At March 31, Allowance for Doubtful Accounts has a credit balance of $1,200 prior to adjustment. The company uses the percentage-of-receivables basis for estimating uncollectible accounts. The company's estimate of bad debts is shown below.

Age of Accounts	Balance, March 31	Estimated Percentage Uncollectible
1–30 days	$60,000	2.0%
31–60 days	17,600	5.0%
61–90 days	8,500	20.0%
Over 90 days	7,000	50.0%
	$93,100	

Instructions

(a) Determine the total estimated uncollectibles.

(b) Prepare the adjusting entry at March 31 to record bad debt expense.

Journalize write-off and recovery.

(LO 2)

E8-5 At December 31, 2016, Finzelberg Company had a credit balance of $15,000 in Allowance for Doubtful Accounts. During 2017, Finzelberg wrote off accounts totaling $11,000. One of those accounts ($1,800) was later collected. At December 31, 2017, an aging schedule indicated that the balance in Allowance for Doubtful Accounts should be $19,000.

Instructions

Prepare journal entries to record the 2017 transactions of Finzelberg Company.

Journalize percentage-of-sales basis, write-off, recovery.

(LO 2)

E8-6 On December 31, 2017, Ling Co. estimated that 2% of its net sales of $450,000 will become uncollectible. The company recorded this amount as an addition to Allowance for Doubtful Accounts. On May 11, 2018, Ling Co. determined that the Jeff Shoemaker account was uncollectible and wrote off $1,100. On June 12, 2018, Shoemaker paid the amount previously written off.

Instructions

Prepare the journal entries on December 31, 2017, May 11, 2018, and June 12, 2018.

Journalize entries for the sale of accounts receivable.

(LO 2)

E8-7 Presented below are two independent situations.

(a) On March 3, Kitselman Appliances sells $650,000 of its receivables to Ervay Factors Inc. Ervay Factors assesses a finance charge of 3% of the amount of receivables sold. Prepare the entry on Kitselman Appliances' books to record the sale of the receivables.

(b) On May 10, Fillmore Company sold merchandise for $3,000 and accepted the customer's America Bank MasterCard. America Bank charges a 4% service charge for credit card sales. Prepare the entry on Fillmore Company's books to record the sale of merchandise.

E8-8 Presented below are two independent situations.

(a) On April 2, Jennifer Elston uses her JCPenney Company credit card to purchase merchandise from a JCPenney store for $1,500. On May 1, Elston is billed for the $1,500 amount due. Elston pays $500 on the balance due on May 3. Elston receives a bill dated June 1 for the amount due, including interest at 1.0% per month on the unpaid balance as of May 3. Prepare the entries on JCPenney Co.'s books related to the transactions that occurred on April 2, May 3, and June 1.

(b) On July 4, Spangler's Restaurant accepts a Visa card for a $200 dinner bill. Visa charges a 2% service fee. Prepare the entry on Spangler's books related to this transaction.

Journalize entries for credit card sales.

(LO 2)

E8-9 Colaw Stores accepts both its own and national credit cards. During the year, the following selected summary transactions occurred.

Jan.	15	Made Colaw credit card sales totaling $18,000. (There were no balances prior to January 15.)
	20	Made Visa credit card sales (service charge fee 2%) totaling $4,500.
Feb.	10	Collected $10,000 on Colaw credit card sales.
	15	Added finance charges of 1.5% to Colaw credit card account balances.

Instructions

Journalize the transactions for Colaw Stores.

Journalize credit card sales, and indicate the statement presentation of financing charges and service charge expense.

(LO 2)

E8-10 Elburn Supply Co. has the following transactions related to notes receivable during the last 2 months of 2017. The company does not make entries to accrue interest except at December 31.

Nov.	1	Loaned $30,000 cash to Manny Lopez on a 12 month, 10% note.
Dec.	11	Sold goods to Ralph Kremer, Inc., receiving a $6,750, 90-day, 8% note.
	16	Received a $4,000, 180 day, 9% note in exchange for Joe Fernetti's outstanding accounts receivable.
	31	Accrued interest revenue on all notes receivable.

Instructions

(a) Journalize the transactions for Elburn Supply Co.

(b) Record the collection of the Lopez note at its maturity in 2018.

Journalize entries for notes receivable transactions.

(LO 3)

E8-11 Record the following transactions for Redeker Co. in the general journal.

2017

May	1	Received a $9,000, 12-month, 10% note in exchange for Mark Chamber's outstanding accounts receivable.
Dec.	31	Accrued interest on the Chamber note.
Dec.	31	Closed the interest revenue account.

2018

May	1	Received principal plus interest on the Chamber note. (No interest has been accrued in 2018.)

Journalize entries for notes receivable.

(LO 3, 4)

E8-12 Vandiver Company had the following select transactions.

Apr.	1, 2017	Accepted Goodwin Company's 12-month, 12% note in settlement of a $30,000 account receivable.
July	1, 2017	Loaned $25,000 cash to Thomas Slocombe on a 9-month, 10% note.
Dec.	31, 2017	Accrued interest on all notes receivable.
Apr.	1, 2018	Received principal plus interest on the Goodwin note.
Apr.	1, 2018	Thomas Slocombe dishonored its note; Vandiver expects it will eventually collect.

Instructions

Prepare journal entries to record the transactions. Vandiver prepares adjusting entries once a year on December 31.

Prepare entries for notes receivable transactions.

(LO 3, 4)

Journalize entries for dishonor of notes receivable.

(LO 3, 4)

E8-13 On May 2, McLain Company lends $9,000 to Chang, Inc., issuing a 6-month, 9% note. At the maturity date, November 2, Chang indicates that it cannot pay.

Instructions
(a) Prepare the entry to record the issuance of the note.
(b) Prepare the entry to record the dishonor of the note, assuming that McLain Company expects collection will occur.
(c) Prepare the entry to record the dishonor of the note, assuming that McLain Company does not expect collection in the future.

Compute accounts receivable turnover and average collection period.

(LO 4)

E8-14 Kerwick Company had accounts receivable of $100,000 on January 1, 2017. The only transactions that affected accounts receivable during 2017 were net credit sales of $1,000,000, cash collections of $920,000, and accounts written off of $30,000.

Instructions
(a) Compute the ending balance of accounts receivable.
(b) Compute the accounts receivable turnover for 2017.
(c) Compute the average collection period in days.

EXERCISES: SET B AND CHALLENGE EXERCISES

Visit the book's companion website, at **www.wiley.com/college/weygandt**, and choose the Student Companion site to access Exercises: Set B and Challenge Exercises.

PROBLEMS: SET A

Prepare journal entries related to bad debt expense.

(LO 1, 2, 4)

P8-1A At December 31, 2016, House Co. reported the following information on its balance sheet.

Accounts receivable	$960,000
Less: Allowance for doubtful accounts	80,000

During 2017, the company had the following transactions related to receivables.

1. Sales on account	$3,700,000
2. Sales returns and allowances	50,000
3. Collections of accounts receivable	2,810,000
4. Write-offs of accounts receivable deemed uncollectible	90,000
5. Recovery of bad debts previously written off as uncollectible	29,000

Instructions
(a) Prepare the journal entries to record each of these five transactions. Assume that no cash discounts were taken on the collections of accounts receivable.

(b) Accounts receivable $1,710,000 ADA $19,000

(b) Enter the January 1, 2017, balances in Accounts Receivable and Allowance for Doubtful Accounts, post the entries to the two accounts (use T-accounts), and determine the balances.

(c) Bad debt expense $96,000

(c) Prepare the journal entry to record bad debt expense for 2017, assuming that an aging of accounts receivable indicates that expected bad debts are $115,000.
(d) Compute the accounts receivable turnover for 2017, assuming the expected bad debt information provided in (c).

Compute bad debt amounts.

(LO 2)

P8-2A Information related to Mingenback Company for 2017 is summarized below.

Total credit sales	$2,500,000
Accounts receivable at December 31	875,000
Bad debts written off	33,000

Instructions
(a) What amount of bad debt expense will Mingenback Company report if it uses the direct write-off method of accounting for bad debts?

(b) Assume that Mingenback Company estimates its bad debt expense to be 2% of credit sales. What amount of bad debt expense will Mingenback record if it has an Allowance for Doubtful Accounts credit balance of $4,000?

(c) Assume that Mingenback Company estimates its bad debt expense based on 6% of accounts receivable. What amount of bad debt expense will Mingenback record if it has an Allowance for Doubtful Accounts credit balance of $3,000?

(d) Assume the same facts as in (c), except that there is a $3,000 debit balance in Allowance for Doubtful Accounts. What amount of bad debt expense will Mingenback record?

(e) •——— What is the weakness of the direct write-off method of reporting bad debt expense?

P8-3A Presented below is an aging schedule for Halleran Company.

Journalize entries to record transactions related to bad debts.

(LO 2)

				Worksheet.xls			
Home	Insert	Page Layout	Formulas	Data	Review	View	
P18		*fx*					
	A	B	C	D	E	F	G
1				Number of Days Past Due			
2			Not				
3	Customer	Total	Yet Due	1–30	31–60	61–90	Over 90
4	Anders	$ 22,000		$10,000	$12,000		
5	Blake	40,000	$ 40,000				
6	Coulson	57,000	16,000	6,000		$35,000	
7	Deleon	34,000					$34,000
8	Others	132,000	96,000	16,000	14,000		6,000
9		$285,000	$152,000	$32,000	$26,000	$35,000	$40,000
10	Estimated Percentage Uncollectible		3%	6%	13%	25%	50%
11	Total Estimated Bad Debts	$ 38,610	$ 4,560	$ 1,920	$ 3,380	$ 8,750	$20,000
12							

At December 31, 2017, the unadjusted balance in Allowance for Doubtful Accounts is a credit of $12,000.

Instructions

(a) Journalize and post the adjusting entry for bad debts at December 31, 2017.

(b) Journalize and post to the allowance account the following events and transactions in the year 2018.

(1) On March 31, a $1,000 customer balance originating in 2017 is judged uncollectible.

(2) On May 31, a check for $1,000 is received from the customer whose account was written off as uncollectible on March 31.

(c) Journalize the adjusting entry for bad debts on December 31, 2018, assuming that the unadjusted balance in Allowance for Doubtful Accounts is a debit of $800 and the aging schedule indicates that total estimated bad debts will be $31,600.

(a) Bad debt expense $26,610

(c) Bad debt expense $32,400

P8-4A Rigney Inc. uses the allowance method to estimate uncollectible accounts receivable. The company produced the following aging of the accounts receivable at year-end.

Journalize transactions related to bad debts.

(LO 2)

				Worksheet.xls			
Home	Insert	Page Layout	Formulas	Data	Review	View	
P18		*fx*					
	A	B	C	D	E	F	G
1				Number of Days Outstanding			
2							
3		Total	0–30	31–60	61–90	91–120	Over 120
4	Accounts receivable	200,000	77,000	46,000	39,000	23,000	15,000
5	% uncollectible		1%	4%	5%	8%	20%
6	Estimated bad debts						
7							

(a) Tot. est. bad debts $9,400

Instructions

(a) Calculate the total estimated bad debts based on the above information.
(b) Prepare the year-end adjusting journal entry to record the bad debts using the aged uncollectible accounts receivable determined in (a). Assume the current balance in Allowance for Doubtful Accounts is a $8,000 debit.
(c) Of the above accounts, $5,000 is determined to be specifically uncollectible. Prepare the journal entry to write off the uncollectible account.
(d) The company collects $5,000 subsequently on a specific account that had previously been determined to be uncollectible in (c). Prepare the journal entry(ies) necessary to restore the account and record the cash collection.
(e) Comment on how your answers to (a)–(d) would change if Rigney Inc. used 4% of **total** accounts receivable rather than aging the accounts receivable. What are the advantages to the company of aging the accounts receivable rather than applying a percentage to total accounts receivable?

Journalize entries to record transactions related to bad debts.

(LO 2)

P8-5A At December 31, 2017, the trial balance of Darby Company contained the following amounts before adjustment.

	Debit	Credit
Accounts Receivable	$385,000	
Allowance for Doubtful Accounts		$ 1,000
Sales Revenue		970,000

Instructions

(a) Based on the information given, which method of accounting for bad debts is Darby Company using—the direct write-off method or the allowance method? How can you tell?
(b) Prepare the adjusting entry at December 31, 2017, for bad debt expense under each of the following independent assumptions.
(b) (2) $9,700
   (1) An aging schedule indicates that $11,750 of accounts receivable will be uncollectible.
   (2) The company estimates that 1% of sales will be uncollectible.
(c) Repeat part (b) assuming that instead of a credit balance there is a $1,000 debit balance in Allowance for Doubtful Accounts.
(d) During the next month, January 2018, a $3,000 account receivable is written off as uncollectible. Prepare the journal entry to record the write-off.
(e) Repeat part (d) assuming that Darby uses the direct write-off method instead of the allowance method in accounting for uncollectible accounts receivable.
(f) ✏—— What type of account is Allowance for Doubtful Accounts? How does it affect how accounts receivable is reported on the balance sheet at the end of the accounting period?

Prepare entries for various notes receivable transactions.

(LO 1, 2, 3, 4)

P8-6A Farwell Company closes its books monthly. On September 30, selected ledger account balances are:

Notes Receivable	$37,000
Interest Receivable	183

Notes Receivable include the following.

Date	Maker	Face	Term	Interest
Aug. 16	K. Goza Inc.	$12,000	60 days	8%
Aug. 25	Holt Co.	9,000	60 days	7%
Sept. 30	Noblitt Corp.	16,000	6 months	9%

Interest is computed using a 360-day year. During October, the following transactions were completed.

Oct. 7 Made sales of $6,900 on Farwell credit cards.
    12 Made sales of $900 on MasterCard credit cards. The credit card service charge is 3%.
    15 Added $460 to Farwell customer balances for finance charges on unpaid balances.
    15 Received payment in full from K. Goza Inc. on the amount due.
    24 Received notice that the Holt note has been dishonored. (Assume that Holt is expected to pay in the future.)

Instructions

(a) Journalize the October transactions and the October 31 adjusting entry for accrued interest receivable. There was no opening balance in accounts receivable.

(b) Enter the balances at October 1 in the receivable accounts. Post the entries to all of the receivable accounts.

(c) Show the balance sheet presentation of the receivable accounts at October 31.

(b) Accounts receivable $16,465

(c) Total receivables $32,585

P8-7A On January 1, 2017, Harter Company had Accounts Receivable $139,000, Notes Receivable $25,000, and Allowance for Doubtful Accounts $13,200. The note receivable is from Willingham Company. It is a 4-month, 9% note dated December 31, 2016. Harter Company prepares financial statements annually at December 31. During the year, the following selected transactions occurred.

Prepare entries for various receivable transactions.

(LO 1, 2, 3, 4)

Jan.	5	Sold $20,000 of merchandise to Sheldon Company, terms n/15.
	20	Accepted Sheldon Company's $20,000, 3-month, 8% note for balance due.
Feb.	18	Sold $8,000 of merchandise to Patwary Company and accepted Patwary's $8,000, 6-month, 9% note for the amount due.
Apr.	20	Collected Sheldon Company note in full.
	30	Received payment in full from Willingham Company on the amount due.
May	25	Accepted Potter Inc.'s $6,000, 3-month, 7% note in settlement of a past-due balance on account.
Aug.	18	Received payment in full from Patwary Company on note due.
	25	The Potter Inc. note was dishonored. Potter Inc. is not bankrupt; future payment is anticipated.
Sept.	1	Sold $12,000 of merchandise to Stanbrough Company and accepted a $12,000, 6-month, 10% note for the amount due.

Instructions

Journalize the transactions.

PROBLEMS: SET B AND SET C

Visit the book's companion website, at **www.wiley.com/college/weygandt**, and choose the Student Companion site to access Problems: Set B and Set C.

COMPREHENSIVE PROBLEM

CP8 Winter Company's balance sheet at December 31, 2016, is presented below.

WINTER COMPANY
Balance Sheet
December 31, 2016

Cash	$13,100	Accounts payable	$ 8,750
Accounts receivable	19,780	Common stock	20,000
Allowance for doubtful accounts	(800)	Retained earnings	12,730
Inventory	9,400		$41,480
	$41,480		

During January 2017, the following transactions occurred. Winter uses the perpetual inventory method.

Jan. 1 Winter accepted a 4-month, 8% note from Merando Company in payment of Merando's $1,200 account.
3 Winter wrote off as uncollectible the accounts of Inwood Corporation ($450) and Goza Company ($280).
8 Winter purchased $17,200 of inventory on account.
11 Winter sold for $28,000 on account inventory that cost $19,600.
15 Winter sold inventory that cost $700 to Mark Lauber for $1,000. Lauber charged this amount on his Visa First Bank card. The service fee charged Winter by First Bank is 3%.
17 Winter collected $22,900 from customers on account.
21 Winter paid $14,300 on accounts payable.
24 Winter received payment in full ($280) from Goza Company on the account written off on January 3.
27 Winter purchased supplies for $1,400 cash.
31 Winter paid other operating expenses, $3,718.

Adjustment data:

1. Interest is recorded for the month on the note from January 1.
2. Bad debts are expected to be 6% of the January 31, 2017, accounts receivable.
3. A count of supplies on January 31, 2017, reveals that $560 remains unused.

Instructions
(You may want to set up T-accounts to determine ending balances.)

(a) Prepare journal entries for the transactions listed above and adjusting entries. (Include entries for cost of goods sold using the perpetual system.)

(b) *Totals $74,765* (b) Prepare an adjusted trial balance at January 31, 2017.
(c) *Total assets $47,473* (c) Prepare an income statement and a retained earnings statement for the month ending January 31, 2017, and a balance sheet as of January 31, 2017.

CONTINUING PROBLEM

COOKIE CREATIONS

(*Note:* This is a continuation of the Cookie Creations problem from Chapters 1 through 7.)

CC8 One of Natalie's friends, Curtis Lesperance, runs a coffee shop where he sells specialty coffees and prepares and sells muffins and cookies. He is eager to buy one of Natalie's fine European mixers, which would enable him to make larger batches of muffins and cookies. However, Curtis cannot afford to pay for the mixer for at least 30 days. He asks Natalie if she would be willing to sell him the mixer on credit. Natalie comes to you for advice.

© leungchopan/ Shutterstock

*Go to the book's companion website, **www.wiley.com/college/weygandt**, to see the completion of this problem.*

BROADENING YOUR *PERSPECTIVE*

FINANCIAL REPORTING AND ANALYSIS

Financial Reporting Problem: RLF Company

BYP8-1 RLF Company sells office equipment and supplies to many organizations in the city and surrounding area on contract terms of 2/10, n/30. In the past, over 75% of the credit customers have taken advantage of the discount by paying within 10 days of the invoice date.

The number of customers taking the full 30 days to pay has increased within the last year. Current indications are that less than 60% of the customers are now taking the discount. Bad debts as a percentage of gross credit sales have risen from the 2.5% provided in past years to about 4.5% in the current year.

The company's Finance Committee has requested more information on the collections of accounts receivable. The controller responded to this request with the report reproduced below.

RLF COMPANY
Accounts Receivable Collections
May 31, 2017

The fact that some credit accounts will prove uncollectible is normal. Annual bad debt write-offs have been 2.5% of gross credit sales over the past 5 years. During the last fiscal year, this percentage increased to slightly less than 4.5%. The current Accounts Receivable balance is $1,400,000. The condition of this balance in terms of age and probability of collection is as follows.

Proportion of Total	Age Categories	Probability of Collection
60%	not yet due	98%
22%	less than 30 days past due	96%
9%	30 to 60 days past due	94%
5%	61 to 120 days past due	91%
$2^1/_2$%	121 to 180 days past due	75%
$1^1/_2$%	over 180 days past due	30%

Allowance for Doubtful Accounts had a credit balance of $29,500 on June 1, 2016. RLF has provided for a monthly bad debt expense accrual during the current fiscal year based on the assumption that 4.5% of gross credit sales will be uncollectible. Total gross credit sales for the 2016–2017 fiscal year amounted to $2,900,000. Write-offs of bad accounts during the year totaled $102,000.

Instructions
(a) Prepare an accounts receivable aging schedule for RLF Company using the age categories identified in the controller's report to the Finance Committee showing the following.
   (1) The amount of accounts receivable outstanding for each age category and in total.
   (2) The estimated amount that is uncollectible for each category and in total.
(b) Compute the amount of the year-end adjustment necessary to bring Allowance for Doubtful Accounts to the balance indicated by the age analysis. Then prepare the necessary journal entry to adjust the accounting records.
(c) In a recessionary environment with tight credit and high interest rates:
   (1) Identify steps RLF Company might consider to improve the accounts receivable situation.
   (2) Then evaluate each step identified in terms of the risks and costs involved.

Comparative Analysis Problem:
PepsiCo, Inc. vs. The Coca-Cola Company

BYP8-2 PepsiCo, Inc.'s financial statements are presented in Appendix B. Financial statements of The Coca-Cola Company are presented in Appendix C. Instructions for accessing and using the complete annual reports of PepsiCo and Coca-Cola, including the notes to the financial statements, are also provided in Appendices B and C, respectively.

Instructions
(a) Based on the information in these financial statements, compute the following 2013 ratios for each company. (Assume all sales are credit sales and that PepsiCo's receivables on its balance sheet are all trade receivables.)
   (1) Accounts receivable turnover.
   (2) Average collection period for receivables.
(b) What conclusions about managing accounts receivable can you draw from these data?

Comparative Analysis Problem:
Amazon.com, Inc. vs. Wal-Mart Stores, Inc.

BYP8-3 Amazon.com, Inc.'s financial statements are presented in Appendix D. Financial statements of Wal-Mart Stores, Inc. are presented in Appendix E. Instructions for accessing and using the complete annual reports of Amazon and Wal-Mart, including the notes to the financial statements, are also provided in Appendices D and E, respectively.

Instructions

(a) Based on the information in these financial statements, compute the following ratios for each company (for the most recent year shown). (Assume all sales are credit sales.)
   (1) Accounts receivable turnover.
   (2) Average collection period for receivables.
(b) What conclusions about managing accounts receivable can you draw from these data?

Real-World Focus

BYP8-4 Purpose: To learn more about factoring.

Address: **www.comcapfactoring.com**, or go to **www.wiley.com/college/weygandt**

Steps: Go to the website, click on **Invoice Factoring**, and answer the following questions.
(a) What are some of the benefits of factoring?
(b) What is the range of the percentages of the typical discount rate?
(c) If a company factors its receivables, what percentage of the value of the receivables can it expect to receive from the factor in the form of cash, and how quickly will it receive the cash?

CRITICAL THINKING

Decision-Making Across the Organization

BYP8-5 Carol and Sam Foyle own Campus Fashions. From its inception, Campus Fashions has sold merchandise on either a cash or credit basis, but no credit cards have been accepted. During the past several months, the Foyles have begun to question their sales policies. First, they have lost some sales because of refusing to accept credit cards. Second, representatives of two metropolitan banks have been persuasive in almost convincing them to accept their national credit cards. One bank, City National Bank, has stated that its credit card fee is 4%.

The Foyles decide that they should determine the cost of carrying their own credit sales. From the accounting records of the past 3 years, they accumulate the following data.

	2018	2017	2016
Net credit sales	$500,000	$550,000	$400,000
Collection agency fees for slow-paying customers	2,450	2,500	2,300
Salary of part-time accounts receivable clerk	4,100	4,100	4,100

Uncollectible account expense is 1.6% for net credit sales, billing and mailing costs 0.5%, and credit investigation fee on new customers is 0.15%.

Carol and Sam also determine that the average accounts receivable balance outstanding during the year is 5% of net credit sales. The Foyles estimate that they could earn an average of 8% annually on cash invested in other business opportunities.

Instructions

With the class divided into groups, answer the following.

(a) Prepare a table showing, for each year, total credit and collection expenses in dollars and as a percentage of net credit sales.
(b) Determine the net credit and collection expense in dollars and as a percentage of sales after considering the revenue not earned from other investment opportunities.
(c) Discuss both the financial and nonfinancial factors that are relevant to the decision.

Communication Activity

BYP8-6 Jill Epp, a friend of yours, overheard a discussion at work about changes her employer wants to make in accounting for uncollectible accounts. Jill knows little about accounting, and she asks you to help make sense of what she heard. Specifically, she asks you to explain the differences between the percentage-of-sales, percentage-of-receivables, and the direct write-off methods for uncollectible accounts.

Instructions

In a letter of one page (or less), explain to Jill the three methods of accounting for uncollectibles. Be sure to discuss differences among these methods.

Ethics Case

BYP8-7 The controller of Diaz Co. believes that the yearly allowance for doubtful accounts for Diaz Co. should be 2% of net credit sales. The president of Diaz Co., nervous that the stockholders might expect the company to sustain its 10% growth rate, suggests that the controller increase the allowance for doubtful accounts to 4%. The president thinks that the lower net income, which reflects a 6% growth rate, will be a more sustainable rate for Diaz Co.

Instructions

(a) Who are the stakeholders in this case?
(b) Does the president's request pose an ethical dilemma for the controller?
(c) Should the controller be concerned with Diaz Co.'s growth rate? Explain your answer.

All About You

BYP8-8 Credit card usage in the United States is substantial. Many startup companies use credit cards as a way to help meet short-term financial needs. The most common forms of debt for startups are use of credit cards and loans from relatives.

Suppose that you start up Brothers Sandwich Shop. You invested your savings of $20,000 and borrowed $70,000 from your relatives. Although sales in the first few months are good, you see that you may not have sufficient cash to pay expenses and maintain your inventory at acceptable levels, at least in the short term. You decide you may need to use one or more credit cards to fund the possible cash shortfall.

Instructions

(a) Go to the Internet and find two sources that provide insight into how to compare credit card terms.
(b) Develop a list, in descending order of importance, as to what features are most important to you in selecting a credit card for your business.
(c) Examine the features of your present credit card. (If you do not have a credit card, select a likely one online for this exercise.) Given your analysis above, what are the three major disadvantages of your present credit card?

FASB Codification Activity

BYP8-9 If your school has a subscription to the FASB Codification, go to **http://aaahq.org/ascLogin.cfm** to log in and prepare responses to the following.

(a) How are receivables defined in the Codification?
(b) What are the conditions under which losses from uncollectible receivables (Bad Debt Expense) should be reported?

 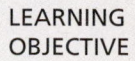

A Look at IFRS

LEARNING OBJECTIVE	5	**Compare the accounting for receivables under GAAP and IFRS.**

The basic accounting and reporting issues related to the recognition, measurement, and disposition of receivables are essentially the same between IFRS and GAAP.

Key Points

Following are the key similarities and differences between GAAP and IFRS related to the accounting for receivables.

Similarities

- The recording of receivables, recognition of sales returns and allowances and sales discounts, and the allowance method to record bad debts are the same between GAAP and IFRS.
- Both IFRS and GAAP often use the term impairment to indicate that a receivable or a percentage of receivables may not be collected.
- The FASB and IASB have worked to implement fair value measurement (the amount they currently could be sold for) for financial instruments, such as receivables. Both Boards have faced bitter opposition from various factions.

Differences

- Although IFRS implies that receivables with different characteristics should be reported separately, there is no standard that mandates this segregation.
- IFRS and GAAP differ in the criteria used to determine how to record a factoring transaction. IFRS uses a combination approach focused on risks and rewards and loss of control. GAAP uses loss of control as the primary criterion. In addition, IFRS permits partial derecognition of receivables; GAAP does not.

Looking to the Future

The question of recording fair values for financial instruments will continue to be an important issue to resolve as the Boards work toward convergence. Both the IASB and the FASB have indicated that they believe that financial statements would be more transparent and understandable if companies recorded and reported all financial instruments at fair value. That said, in *IFRS 9*, which was issued in 2009, the IASB created a split model, where some financial instruments are recorded at fair value, but other financial assets, such as loans and receivables, can be accounted for at amortized cost if certain criteria are met. Critics say that this can result in two companies with identical securities accounting for those securities in different ways. A proposal by the FASB would require that practically all equity instruments be reported at fair value, and that debt instruments may or may not be reported at fair value depending on whether certain criteria are met.

IFRS Practice

IFRS Self-Test Questions

1. Which of the following statements is **false?**
   - (a) Receivables include equity securities purchased by the company.
   - (b) Receivables include credit card receivables.
   - (c) Receivables include amounts owed by employees as a result of company loans to employees.
   - (d) Receivables include amounts resulting from transactions with customers.

2. In recording a factoring transaction:
   - (a) IFRS focuses on loss of control.
   - (b) GAAP focuses on loss of control and risks and rewards.
   - (c) IFRS and GAAP allow partial derecognition.
   - (d) IFRS allows partial derecognition.

3. Under IFRS:
   - (a) the entry to record estimated uncollected accounts is the same as GAAP.
   - (b) it is always acceptable to use the direct write-off method.
   - (c) all financial instruments are recorded at fair value.
   - (d) None of the above.

International Financial Reporting Problem: Louis Vuitton

IFRS8-1 The financial statements of Louis Vuitton are presented in Appendix F. Instructions for accessing and using the company's complete annual report, including the notes to its financial statements, are also provided in Appendix F.

Instructions

Use the company's annual report to answer the following questions.

(a) What is the accounting policy related to accounting for trade accounts receivable?

(b) According to the notes to the financial statements, what accounted for the difference between gross trade accounts receivable and net accounts receivable?

(c) According to the notes to the financial statements, what was the major reason why the balance in receivables increased relative to the previous year?

(d) Using information in the notes to the financial statements, determine what percentage the provision for impairment of receivables was as a percentage of total trade receivables for 2013 and 2012. How did the ratio change from 2012 to 2013, and what does this suggest about the company's receivables?

Answers to IFRS Self-Test Questions

1. a   **2.** d   **3.** a

9 Plant Assets, Natural Resources, and Intangible Assets

CHAPTER PREVIEW The accounting for long-term assets has important implications for a company's reported results. In this chapter, we explain the application of the historical cost principle of accounting to property, plant, and equipment, such as Rent-A-Wreck vehicles, as well as to natural resources and intangible assets, such as the "Rent-A-Wreck" trademark. We also describe the methods that companies may use to allocate an asset's cost over its useful life. In addition, we discuss the accounting for expenditures incurred during the useful life of assets, such as the cost of replacing tires and brake pads on rental cars.

FEATURE STORY

How Much for a Ride to the Beach?

It's spring break. Your plane has landed, you've finally found your bags, and you're dying to hit the beach—but first you need a "vehicular unit" to get you there. As you turn away from baggage claim, you see a long row of rental agency booths. Many are names that you know—Hertz, Avis, and Budget. But a booth at the far end catches your eye—Rent-A-Wreck. Now there's a company making a clear statement!

Any company that relies on equipment to generate revenues must make decisions about what kind of equipment to buy, how long to keep it, and how vigorously to maintain it. Rent-A-Wreck has decided to rent used rather than new cars and trucks. It rents these vehicles across the United States, Europe, and Asia. While the big-name agencies push vehicles with that "new car smell," Rent-A-Wreck competes on price.

Rent-A-Wreck's message is simple: Rent a used car and save some cash. It's not a message that appeals to everyone.

If you're a marketing executive wanting to impress a big client, you probably don't want to pull up in a Rent-A-Wreck car. But if you want to get from point A to point B for the minimum cash per mile, then Rent-A-Wreck is playing your tune. The company's message seems to be getting across to the right clientele. Revenues have increased significantly.

When you rent a car from Rent-A-Wreck, you are renting from an independent businessperson. This owner has paid a "franchise fee" for the right to use the Rent-A-Wreck name. In order to gain a franchise, he or she must meet financial and other criteria, and must agree to run the rental agency according to rules prescribed by Rent-A-Wreck. Some of these rules require that each franchise maintain its cars in a reasonable fashion. This ensures that, though you won't be cruising down Daytona Beach's Atlantic Avenue in a Mercedes convertible, you can be reasonably assured that you won't be calling a towtruck.

David Trood/Getty Images, Inc.

Learning Objectives

1 Explain the accounting for plant asset expenditures.
- Determining the cost of plant assets
- Expenditures during useful life

DO IT! **1** Cost of Plant Assets

2 Apply depreciation methods to plant assets.
- Factors in computing depreciation
- Depreciation methods
- Depreciation and income taxes
- Revising periodic depreciation

DO IT! **2a** Straight-Line Depreciation
2b Revised Depreciation

3 Explain how to account for the disposal of plant assets.
- Retirement of plant assets
- Sale of plant assets

DO IT! **3** Plant Asset Disposal

4 Describe how to account for natural resources and intangible assets.
- Natural resources
- Depletion
- Intangible assets
- Accounting for intangible assets
- Research and development costs

DO IT! **4** Classification Concepts

5 Discuss how plant assets, natural resources, and intangible assets are reported and analyzed.
- Presentation
- Analysis

DO IT! **5** Asset Turnover

Go to the **REVIEW AND PRACTICE** section at the end of the chapter for a review of key concepts and practice applications with solutions.

Visit **WileyPLUS with ORION** for additional tutorials and practice opportunities.

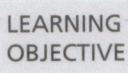

LEARNING
OBJECTIVE   **1**

Explain the accounting for plant asset expenditures.

Plant assets are resources that have three characteristics. They have a physical substance (a definite size and shape), are used in the operations of a business, and are not intended for sale to customers. They are also called **property, plant, and equipment**; **plant and equipment**; and **fixed assets**. These assets are expected to be of use to the company for a number of years. Except for land, plant assets decline in service potential over their useful lives.

Because plant assets play a key role in ongoing operations, companies keep plant assets in good operating condition. They also replace worn-out or outdated plant assets, and expand productive resources as needed. Many companies have substantial investments in plant assets. Illustration 9-1 shows the percentages of plant assets in relation to total assets of companies in a number of industries.

Illustration 9-1
Percentages of plant assets in relation to total assets

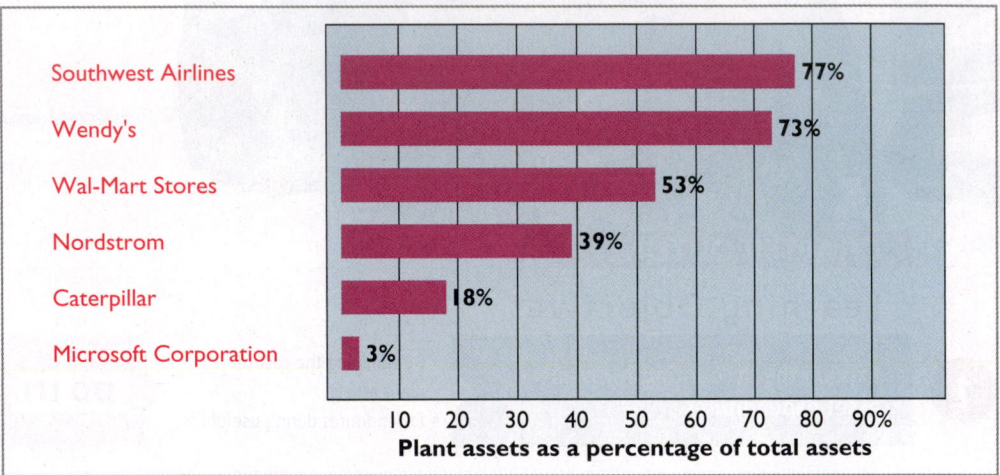

Determining the Cost of Plant Assets

The historical cost principle requires that companies record plant assets at cost. Thus, **Rent-A-Wreck** records its vehicles at cost. **Cost consists of all expenditures necessary to acquire the asset and make it ready for its intended use.** For example, the cost of factory machinery includes the purchase price, freight costs paid by the purchaser, and installation costs. Once cost is established, the company uses that amount as the basis of accounting for the plant asset over its useful life.

In the following sections, we explain the application of the historical cost principle to each of the major classes of plant assets.

LAND

Companies often use **land** as a building site for a manufacturing plant or office building. The cost of land includes (1) the cash purchase price, (2) closing costs such as title and attorney's fees, (3) real estate brokers' commissions, and (4) accrued property taxes and other liens assumed by the purchaser. For example, if the cash price is $50,000 and the purchaser agrees to pay accrued taxes of $5,000, the cost of the land is $55,000.

Companies record as debits (increases) to the Land account all necessary costs incurred to make land **ready for its intended use**. When a company acquires vacant land, these costs include expenditures for clearing, draining, filling, and grading. Sometimes the land has a building on it that must be removed before construction of a new building. In this case, the company debits to the Land account all demolition and removal costs, less any proceeds from salvaged materials.

Helpful Hint
Management's intended use is important in applying the historical cost principle.

To illustrate, assume that Hayes Company acquires real estate at a cash cost of $100,000. The property contains an old warehouse that is razed at a net cost of $6,000 ($7,500 in costs less $1,500 proceeds from salvaged materials). Additional expenditures are the attorney's fee, $1,000, and the real estate broker's commission, $8,000. The cost of the land is $115,000, computed as shown in Illustration 9-2.

Land	
Cash price of property	$ 100,000
Net removal cost of warehouse ($7,500 − $1,500)	6,000
Attorney's fee	1,000
Real estate broker's commission	8,000
Cost of land	**$115,000**

Illustration 9-2
Computation of cost of land

Hayes makes the following entry to record the acquisition of the land.

Land	115,000	
Cash		115,000
(To record purchase of land)		

A	=	L	+	SE

+115,000
−115,000

Cash Flows
−115,000

LAND IMPROVEMENTS

Land improvements are structural additions made to land. Examples are driveways, parking lots, fences, landscaping, and underground sprinklers. The cost of land improvements includes all expenditures necessary to make the improvements ready for their intended use. For example, the cost of a new parking lot for Home Depot includes the amount paid for paving, fencing, and lighting. Thus, Home Depot debits to Land Improvements the total of all of these costs.

Land improvements have limited useful lives. Even when well-maintained, they will eventually need to be replaced. As a result, companies expense (depreciate) the cost of land improvements over their useful lives.

BUILDINGS

Buildings are facilities used in operations, such as stores, offices, factories, warehouses, and airplane hangars. Companies debit to the Buildings account all necessary expenditures related to the purchase or construction of a building. When a building is **purchased**, such costs include the purchase price, closing costs (attorney's fee, title insurance, etc.), and the real estate broker's commission. Costs to make the building ready for its intended use include expenditures for remodeling and replacing or repairing the roof, floors, electrical wiring, and plumbing. When a new building is **constructed**, cost consists of the contract price plus payments for architects' fees, building permits, and excavation costs.

In addition, companies charge certain interest costs to the Buildings account. Interest costs incurred to finance the project are included in the cost of the building when a significant period of time is required to get the building ready for use. In these circumstances, interest costs are considered as necessary as materials and labor. However, the inclusion of interest costs in the cost of a constructed building is **limited to the construction period**. When construction has been completed, the company records subsequent interest payments on funds borrowed to finance the construction as debits (increases) to Interest Expense.

EQUIPMENT

Equipment includes assets used in operations, such as store check-out counters, office furniture, factory machinery, delivery trucks, and airplanes. The cost of equipment, such as Rent-A-Wreck vehicles, consists of the cash purchase price, sales taxes, freight charges, and insurance during transit paid by the purchaser. It also includes expenditures required in assembling, installing, and testing the unit. However, Rent-A-Wreck does not include motor vehicle licenses and accident insurance on company vehicles in the cost of equipment. These costs represent annual recurring expenditures and do not benefit future periods. Thus, they are treated as **expenses** as they are incurred.

To illustrate, assume Merten Company purchases factory machinery at a cash price of $50,000. Related expenditures are for sales taxes $3,000, insurance during shipping $500, and installation and testing $1,000. The cost of the factory machinery is $54,500, as computed in Illustration 9-3.

Illustration 9-3
Computation of cost of factory machinery

Factory Machinery	
Cash price	$ 50,000
Sales taxes	3,000
Insurance during shipping	500
Installation and testing	1,000
Cost of factory machinery	**$54,500**

Merten makes the following summary entry to record the purchase and related expenditures.

A = L + SE
+54,500
−54,500
Cash Flows
−54,500

Equipment	54,500	
Cash		54,500
(To record purchase of factory machinery)		

For another example, assume that Lenard Company purchases a delivery truck at a cash price of $22,000. Related expenditures consist of sales taxes $1,320, painting and lettering $500, motor vehicle license $80, and a three-year accident insurance policy $1,600. The cost of the delivery truck is $23,820, computed as follows.

Illustration 9-4
Computation of cost of delivery truck

Delivery Truck	
Cash price	$ 22,000
Sales taxes	1,320
Painting and lettering	500
Cost of delivery truck	**$23,820**

Lenard treats the cost of the motor vehicle license as an expense and the cost of the insurance policy as a prepaid asset. Thus, Lenard makes the following entry to record the purchase of the truck and related expenditures:

A = L + SE
+23,820
−80 Exp
+ 1,600
−25,500
Cash Flows
−25,500

Equipment	23,820	
License Expense	80	
Prepaid Insurance	1,600	
Cash		25,500
(To record purchase of delivery truck and related		
expenditures)		

Expenditures During Useful Life

During the useful life of a plant asset, a company may incur costs for ordinary repairs, additions, or improvements. **Ordinary repairs** are expenditures to **maintain** the operating efficiency and productive life of the unit. They usually are small amounts that occur frequently. Examples are motor tune-ups and oil changes, the painting of buildings, and the replacing of worn-out gears on machinery. Companies record such repairs as debits to Maintenance and Repairs Expense as they are incurred. Because they are immediately charged as an expense against revenues, these costs are often referred to as **revenue expenditures**.

In contrast, **additions and improvements** are costs incurred to **increase** the operating efficiency, productive capacity, or useful life of a plant asset. They are usually material in amount and occur infrequently. Additions and improvements increase the company's investment in productive facilities. Companies generally debit these amounts to the plant asset affected. They are often referred to as **capital expenditures**.

Companies must use good judgment in deciding between a revenue expenditure and capital expenditure. For example, assume that Rodriguez Co. purchases a number of wastepaper baskets. The proper accounting would appear to be to capitalize and then depreciate these wastepaper baskets over their useful lives. However, Rodriguez will generally expense these wastepaper baskets immediately. This practice is justified on the basis of **materiality**. Materiality refers to the impact of an item's size on a company's financial operations. The **materiality concept** states that if an item would not make a difference in decision-making, the company does not have to follow GAAP in reporting that item.

ANATOMY OF A FRAUD

Bernie Ebbers was the founder and CEO of the phone company WorldCom. The company engaged in a series of increasingly large, debt-financed acquisitions of other companies. These acquisitions made the company grow quickly, which made the stock price increase dramatically. However, because the acquired companies all had different accounting systems, WorldCom's financial records were a mess. When WorldCom's performance started to flatten out, Bernie coerced WorldCom's accountants to engage in a number of fraudulent activities to make net income look better than it really was and thus prop up the stock price. One of these frauds involved treating $7 billion of line costs as capital expenditures. The line costs, which were rental fees paid to other phone companies to use their phone lines, had always been properly expensed in previous years. Capitalization delayed expense recognition to future periods and thus boosted current-period profits.

Total take: $7 billion

THE MISSING CONTROLS

Documentation procedures. The company's accounting system was a disorganized collection of non-integrated systems, which resulted from a series of corporate acquisitions. Top management took advantage of this disorganization to conceal its fraudulent activities.

Independent internal verification. A fraud of this size should have been detected by a routine comparison of the actual physical assets with the list of physical assets shown in the accounting records.

Accounting Across the Organization

© Brian Raisbeck/iStockphoto

Many U.S. Firms Use Leases

Leasing is big business for U.S. companies. For example, business investment in equipment in a recent year totaled $800 billion. Leasing accounted for about 33% of all business investment ($264 billion).

Who does the most leasing? Interestingly, major banks such as Continental Bank, J.P. Morgan Leasing, and US Bancorp Equipment Finance are the major lessors. Also, many companies have established separate leasing companies, such as Boeing Capital Corporation, Dell Financial Services, and John Deere Capital Corporation. And, as an excellent example of the magnitude of leasing, leased planes account for nearly 40% of the U.S. fleet of commercial airlines. Leasing is also becoming more common in the hotel industry. Marriott, Hilton, and InterContinental are increasingly choosing to lease hotels that are owned by someone else.

Why might airline managers choose to lease rather than purchase their planes? (Go to WileyPLUS for this answer and additional questions.)

DO IT! 1   Cost of Plant Assets

Action Plan

✔ Identify expenditures made in order to get delivery equipment ready for its intended use.

✔ Treat operating costs as expenses.

Assume that Drummond Heating and Cooling Co. purchases a delivery truck for $15,000 cash, plus sales taxes of $900 and delivery costs of $500. The buyer also pays $200 for painting and lettering, $600 for an annual insurance policy, and $80 for a motor vehicle license. Explain how each of these costs would be accounted for.

Solution

The first four payments ($15,000, $900, $500, and $200) are expenditures necessary to make the truck ready for its intended use. Thus, the cost of the truck is $16,600. The payments for insurance and the license are operating costs and therefore are expensed.

Related exercise material: **BE9-1, BE9-2, BE9-3, E9-1, E9-2, E9-3, and DO IT! 9-1.**

LEARNING OBJECTIVE **2**   # Apply depreciation methods to plant assets.

As explained in Chapter 3, **depreciation** **is the process of allocating to expense the cost of a plant asset over its useful (service) life in a rational and systematic manner**. Cost allocation enables companies to properly match expenses with revenues in accordance with the expense recognition principle, as shown in Illustration 9-5.

Illustration 9-5
Depreciation as a cost allocation concept

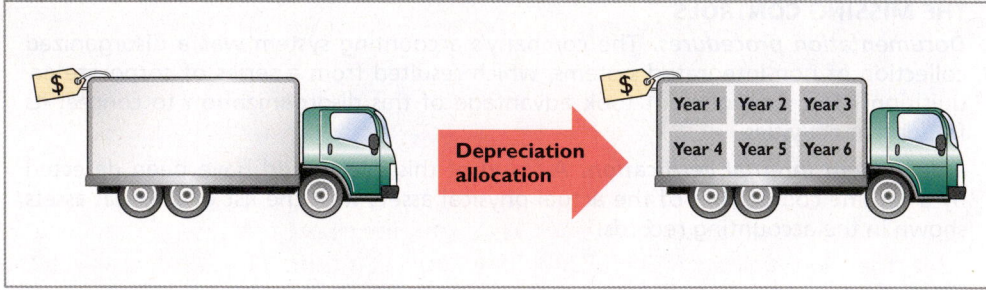

ETHICS NOTE

When a business is acquired, proper allocation of the purchase price to various asset classes is important since different depreciation treatments can materially affect income. For example, buildings are depreciated, but land is not.

It is important to understand that **depreciation is a process of cost allocation. It is not a process of asset valuation.** No attempt is made to measure the change in an asset's fair value during ownership. So, the **book value** (cost less accumulated depreciation) of a plant asset may be quite different from its fair value. In fact, if an asset is fully depreciated, it can have a zero book value but still have a fair value.

Depreciation applies to three classes of plant assets: land improvements, buildings, and equipment. Each asset in these classes is considered to be a **depreciable asset**. Why? Because the usefulness to the company and revenue-producing ability of each asset will decline over the asset's useful life. Depreciation **does not apply to land** because its usefulness and revenue-producing ability generally remain intact over time. In fact, in many cases, the usefulness of land is greater over time because of the scarcity of good land sites. Thus, **land is not a depreciable asset**.

During a depreciable asset's useful life, its revenue-producing ability declines because of **wear and tear**. A delivery truck that has been driven 100,000 miles will be less useful to a company than one driven only 800 miles.

Revenue-producing ability may also decline because of obsolescence. **Obsolescence** is the process of becoming out of date before the asset physically wears out. For example, major airlines moved from Chicago's Midway Airport to Chicago-O'Hare International Airport because Midway's runways were too short for jumbo jets. Similarly, many companies replace their computers long before they originally planned to do so because technological improvements make the old computers obsolete.

Recognizing depreciation on an asset does not result in an accumulation of cash for replacement of the asset. The balance in Accumulated Depreciation represents the total amount of the asset's cost that the company has charged to expense. It is not a cash fund.

Note that the concept of depreciation is consistent with the going concern assumption. The **going concern assumption** states that the company will continue in operation for the foreseeable future. If a company does not use a going concern assumption, then plant assets should be stated at their fair value. In that case, depreciation of these assets is not needed.

Factors in Computing Depreciation

Three factors affect the computation of depreciation, as shown in Illustration 9-6.

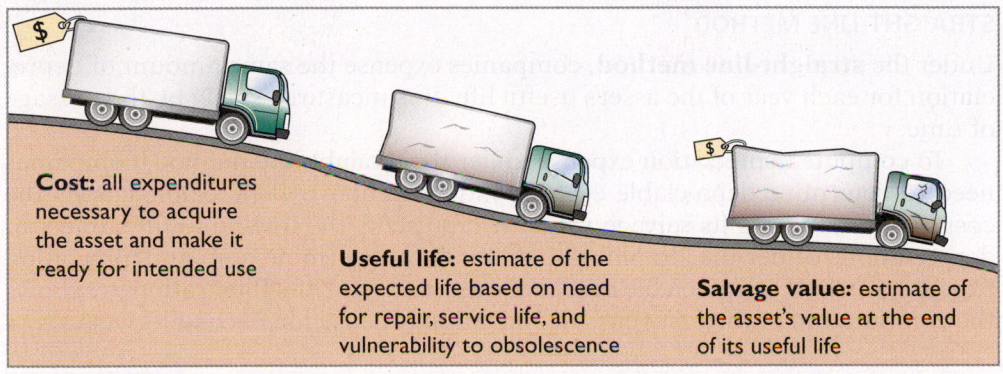

Cost: all expenditures necessary to acquire the asset and make it ready for intended use

Useful life: estimate of the expected life based on need for repair, service life, and vulnerability to obsolescence

Salvage value: estimate of the asset's value at the end of its useful life

Illustration 9-6
Three factors in computing depreciation

Helpful Hint
Depreciation expense is reported on the income statement. Accumulated depreciation is reported on the balance sheet as a deduction from plant assets.

1. **Cost.** Earlier, we explained the issues affecting the cost of a depreciable asset. Recall that companies record plant assets at cost, in accordance with the historical cost principle.

2. **Useful life.** **Useful life** is an estimate of the expected productive life, also called service life, of the asset for its owner. Useful life may be expressed in terms of time, units of activity (such as machine hours), or units of output. Useful life is an estimate. In making the estimate, management considers such factors as the intended use of the asset, its expected repair and maintenance, and its vulnerability to obsolescence. Past experience with similar assets is often helpful in deciding on expected useful life. We might reasonably expect Rent-A-Wreck and Avis to use different estimated useful lives for their vehicles.

3. **Salvage value.** **Salvage value** is an estimate of the asset's value at the end of its useful life. This value may be based on the asset's worth as scrap or on its expected trade-in value. Like useful life, salvage value is an estimate. In making the estimate, management considers how it plans to dispose of the asset and its experience with similar assets.

Alternative Terminology
Another term sometimes used for salvage value is *residual value*.

Depreciation Methods

Depreciation is generally computed using one of the following methods:

1. Straight-line
2. Units-of-activity
3. Declining-balance

Each method is acceptable under generally accepted accounting principles. Management selects the method(s) it believes to be appropriate. The objective is to select the method that best measures an asset's contribution to revenue over its useful life. Once a company chooses a method, it should apply it consistently over the useful life of the asset. Consistency enhances the comparability of financial statements. Depreciation affects the balance sheet through accumulated depreciation and the income statement through depreciation expense.

We will compare the three depreciation methods using the following data for a small delivery truck purchased by Barb's Florists on January 1, 2017.

Illustration 9-7
Delivery truck data

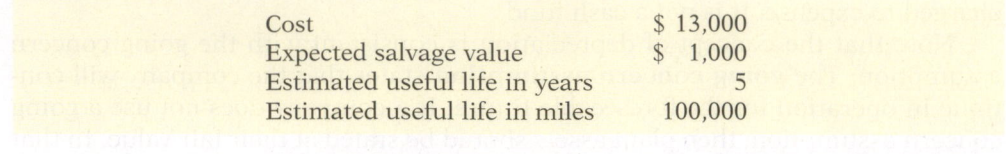

Cost	$ 13,000
Expected salvage value	$ 1,000
Estimated useful life in years	5
Estimated useful life in miles	100,000

Illustration 9-8 (in the margin) shows the use of the primary depreciation methods in a sample of the largest companies in the United States. No matter what method is used, the total amount depreciated over the useful life of the asset is its depreciable cost. **Depreciable cost** is equal to the cost of the asset less its salvage value.

STRAIGHT-LINE METHOD

Under the **straight-line method**, companies expense the same amount of depreciation for each year of the asset's useful life. It is measured solely by the passage of time.

To compute depreciation expense under the straight-line method, companies need to determine depreciable cost. As indicated above, depreciable cost is the cost of the asset less its salvage value. It represents the total amount subject to depreciation. Under the straight-line method, to determine annual depreciation expense, we divide depreciable cost by the asset's useful life. Illustration 9-9 shows the computation of the first year's depreciation expense for Barb's Florists.

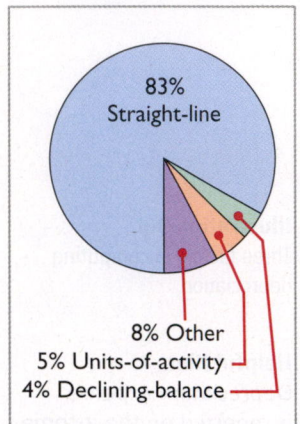

Illustration 9-8
Use of depreciation methods in large U.S. companies

Illustration 9-9
Formula for straight-line method

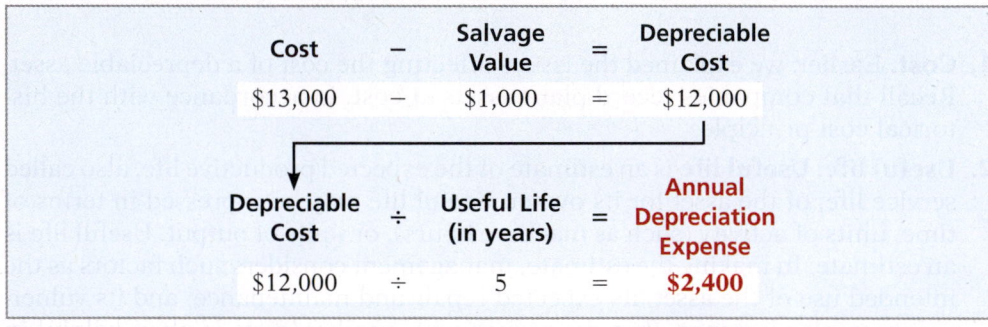

Alternatively, we also can compute an annual **rate** of depreciation. In this case, the rate is 20% (100% ÷ 5 years). When a company uses an annual straight-line rate, it applies the percentage rate to the depreciable cost of the asset. Illustration 9-10 shows a **depreciation schedule** using an annual rate.

Illustration 9-10
Straight-line depreciation schedule

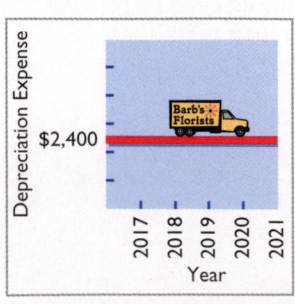

	BARB'S FLORISTS					
	Computation			**Annual**	**End of Year**	
Year	**Depreciable Cost**	×	**Depreciation Rate**	= **Depreciation Expense**	**Accumulated Depreciation**	**Book Value**
2017	$12,000		20%	**$2,400**	$ 2,400	$10,600*
2018	12,000		20	**2,400**	4,800	8,200
2019	12,000		20	**2,400**	7,200	5,800
2020	12,000		20	**2,400**	9,600	3,400
2021	12,000		20	**2,400**	12,000	**1,000**

*Book value = Cost − Accumulated depreciation = ($13,000 − $2,400).

Note that the depreciation expense of $2,400 is the same each year. The book value (computed as cost minus accumulated depreciation) at the end of the useful life is equal to the expected $1,000 salvage value.

What happens to these computations for an asset purchased **during** the year, rather than on January 1? In that case, it is necessary to **prorate the annual depreciation** on a time basis. If Barb's Florists had purchased the delivery truck on April 1, 2017, the company would own the truck for nine months of the first year (April–December). Thus, depreciation for 2017 would be $1,800 ($12,000 × 20% × 9/12 of a year).

The straight-line method predominates in practice. Such large companies as **Campbell Soup**, **Marriott**, and **General Mills** use the straight-line method. It is simple to apply, and it matches expenses with revenues when the use of the asset is reasonably uniform throughout the service life.

> ## DO IT! 2a Straight-Line Depreciation
>
> On January 1, 2017, Iron Mountain Ski Corporation purchased a new snow-grooming machine for $50,000. The machine is estimated to have a 10-year life with a $2,000 salvage value. What journal entry would Iron Mountain Ski Corporation make at December 31, 2017, if it uses the straight-line method of depreciation?
>
> ### Solution
>
> $$\text{Depreciation expense} = \frac{\text{Cost} - \text{Salvage value}}{\text{Useful life}} = \frac{\$50,000 - \$2,000}{10} = \$4,800$$
>
> The entry to record the first year's depreciation would be:
>
> | Dec. 31 | Depreciation Expense | 4,800 | |
> |---------|---------------------|-------|-------|
> | | Accumulated Depreciation—Equipment | | 4,800 |
> | | (To record annual depreciation on | | |
> | | snow-grooming machine) | | |
>
> **Action Plan**
>
> ✔ Calculate depreciable cost (Cost − Salvage value).
>
> ✔ Divide the depreciable cost by the asset's estimated useful life.
>
> Related exercise material: **BE9-4, BE9-5, E9-4, and DO IT! 9-2a.**

UNITS-OF-ACTIVITY METHOD

Under the **units-of-activity method**, useful life is expressed in terms of the total units of production or use expected from the asset, rather than as a time period. The units-of-activity method is ideally suited to factory machinery. Manufacturing companies can measure production in units of output or in machine hours. This method can also be used for such assets as delivery equipment (miles driven) and airplanes (hours in use). The units-of-activity method is generally not suitable for buildings or furniture because depreciation for these assets is more a function of time than of use.

To use this method, companies estimate the total units of activity for the entire useful life, and then divide these units into depreciable cost. The resulting number represents the depreciable cost per unit. The depreciable cost per unit is then applied to the units of activity during the year to determine the annual depreciation expense.

To illustrate, assume that Barb's Florists drives its delivery truck 15,000 miles in the first year. Illustration 9-11 (page 406) shows the units-of-activity formula and the computation of the first year's depreciation expense.

Alternative Terminology
Another term often used is the *units-of-production method.*

Helpful Hint
Under any method, depreciation stops when the asset's book value equals expected salvage value.

Illustration 9-11
Formula for units-of-activity method

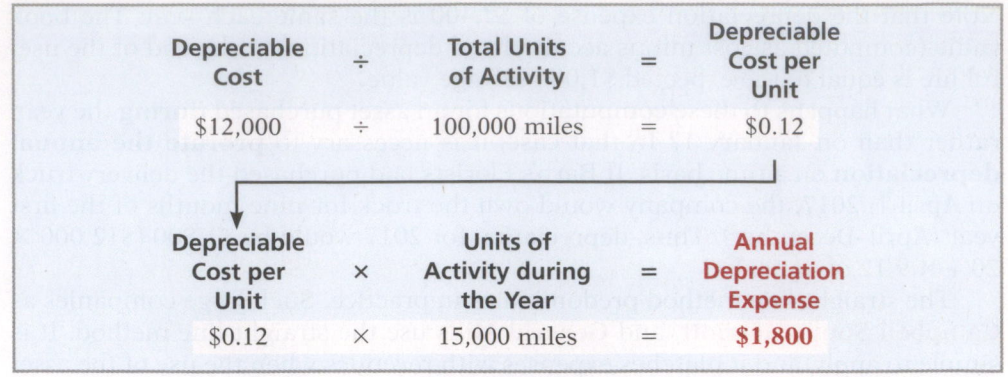

Depreciable Cost	÷	Total Units of Activity	=	Depreciable Cost per Unit
$12,000	÷	100,000 miles	=	$0.12

Depreciable Cost per Unit	×	Units of Activity during the Year	=	Annual Depreciation Expense
$0.12	×	15,000 miles	=	$1,800

The units-of-activity depreciation schedule, using assumed mileage, is as follows.

Illustration 9-12
Units-of-activity depreciation schedule

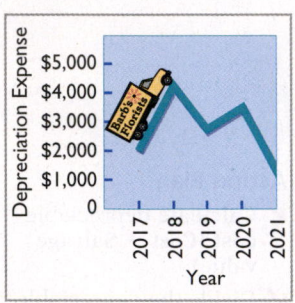

						BARB'S FLORISTS		
		Computation				**Annual**	**End of Year**	
Year	**Units of Activity**	×	**Depreciable Cost/Unit**	=		**Depreciation Expense**	**Accumulated Depreciation**	**Book Value**
2017	15,000		$0.12			**$1,800**	$ 1,800	$11,200*
2018	30,000		0.12			**3,600**	5,400	7,600
2019	20,000		0.12			**2,400**	7,800	5,200
2020	25,000		0.12			**3,000**	10,800	2,200
2021	10,000		0.12			**1,200**	12,000	**1,000**

*($13,000 − $1,800).

This method is easy to apply for assets purchased mid-year. In such a case, the company computes the depreciation using the productivity of the asset for the partial year.

The units-of-activity method is not nearly as popular as the straight-line method (see Illustration 9-8, page 404) primarily because it is often difficult for companies to reasonably estimate total activity. However, some very large companies, such as **Chevron** and **Boise Cascade** (a forestry company), do use this method. When the productivity of an asset varies significantly from one period to another, the units-of-activity method results in the best matching of expenses with revenues.

DECLINING-BALANCE METHOD

The **declining-balance method** produces a decreasing annual depreciation expense over the asset's useful life. The method is so named because the periodic depreciation is based on a **declining book value** (cost less accumulated depreciation) of the asset. With this method, companies compute annual depreciation expense by multiplying the book value at the beginning of the year by the declining-balance depreciation rate. **The depreciation rate remains constant from year to year, but the book value to which the rate is applied declines each year.**

At the beginning of the first year, book value is the cost of the asset. This is because the balance in accumulated depreciation at the beginning of the asset's useful life is zero. In subsequent years, book value is the difference between cost and accumulated depreciation to date. Unlike the other depreciation methods, the declining-balance method **ignores salvage value in determining the amount to which the declining-balance rate is applied**. Salvage value, however, does limit the total depreciation that can be taken. Depreciation stops when the asset's book value equals expected salvage value.

A common declining-balance rate is double the straight-line rate. The method is often called the **double-declining-balance method**. If Barb's Florists uses the double-declining-balance method, it uses a depreciation rate of 40% (2 × the straight-line rate of 20%). Illustration 9-13 shows the declining-balance formula and the computation of the first year's depreciation on the delivery truck.

Book Value at Beginning of Year	×	Declining-Balance Rate	=	Annual Depreciation Expense
$13,000	×	40%	=	**$5,200**

Illustration 9-13
Formula for declining-balance method

The depreciation schedule under this method is as follows.

Illustration 9-14
Double-declining-balance depreciation schedule

BARB'S FLORISTS

	Computation			Annual	End of Year	
Year	Book Value Beginning of Year	×	Depreciation Rate	= Depreciation Expense	Accumulated Depreciation	Book Value
2017	$13,000		40%	**$5,200**	$ 5,200	$7,800
2018	7,800		40	**3,120**	8,320	4,680
2019	4,680		40	**1,872**	10,192	2,808
2020	2,808		40	**1,123**	11,315	1,685
2021	1,685		40	**685***	12,000	**1,000**

*Computation of $674 ($1,685 × 40%) is adjusted to $685 in order for book value to equal salvage value.

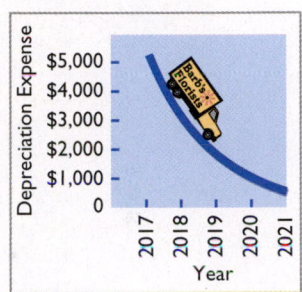

The delivery equipment is 69% depreciated ($8,320 ÷ $12,000) at the end of the second year. Under the straight-line method, the truck would be depreciated 40% ($4,800 ÷ $12,000) at that time. Because the declining-balance method produces higher depreciation expense in the early years than in the later years, it is considered an **accelerated-depreciation method**. The declining-balance method is compatible with the expense recognition principle. It matches the higher depreciation expense in early years with the higher benefits received in these years. It also recognizes lower depreciation expense in later years, when the asset's contribution to revenue is less. Some assets lose usefulness rapidly because of obsolescence. In these cases, the declining-balance method provides the most appropriate depreciation amount.

When a company purchases an asset during the year, it must prorate the first year's declining-balance depreciation on a time basis. For example, if Barb's Florists had purchased the truck on April 1, 2017, depreciation for 2017 would become $3,900 ($13,000 × 40% × 9/12). The book value at the beginning of 2018 is then $9,100 ($13,000 − $3,900), and the 2018 depreciation is $3,640 ($9,100 × 40%). Subsequent computations would follow from those amounts.

Helpful Hint
The method recommended for an asset that is expected to be significantly more productive in the first half of its useful life is the declining-balance method.

COMPARISON OF METHODS

Illustration 9-15 compares annual and total depreciation expense under each of the three methods for Barb's Florists.

Illustration 9-15
Comparison of depreciation methods

Year	Straight-Line	Units-of-Activity	Declining-Balance
2017	$ 2,400	$ 1,800	$ 5,200
2018	2,400	3,600	3,120
2019	2,400	2,400	1,872
2020	2,400	3,000	1,123
2021	2,400	1,200	685
	$12,000	$12,000	$12,000

Annual depreciation varies considerably among the methods, but **total depreciation expense is the same ($12,000) for the five-year period** under all three methods. Each method is acceptable in accounting because each recognizes in a rational and systematic manner the decline in service potential of the asset. Illustration 9-16 graphs the depreciation expense pattern under each method.

Illustration 9-16

Patterns of depreciation

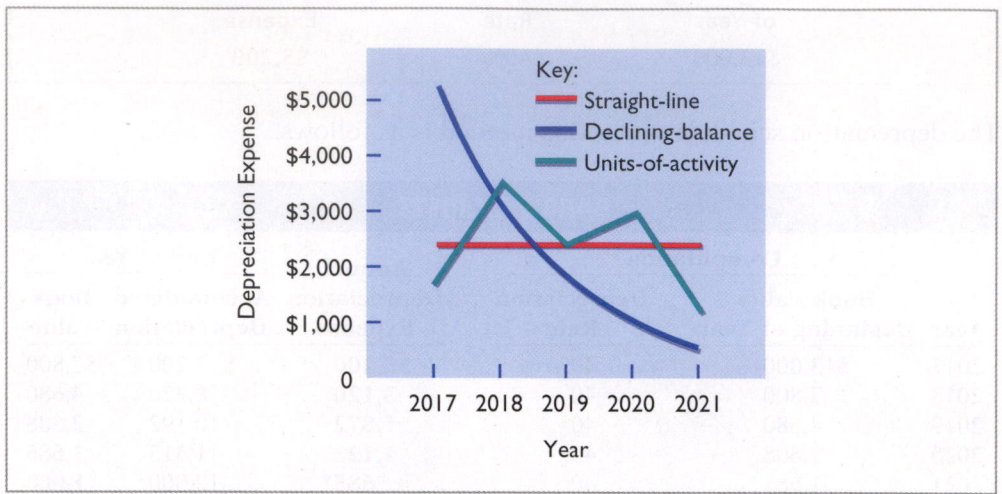

Depreciation and Income Taxes

The Internal Revenue Service (IRS) allows taxpayers to deduct depreciation expense when they compute taxable income. However, the IRS does not require taxpayers to use the same depreciation method on the tax return that is used in preparing financial statements.

Many corporations use straight-line in their financial statements to maximize net income. At the same time, they use a special accelerated-depreciation method on their tax returns to minimize their income taxes. Taxpayers must use on their tax returns either the straight-line method or a special accelerated-depreciation method called the **Modified Accelerated Cost Recovery System** (MACRS).

Revising Periodic Depreciation

Depreciation is one example of the use of estimation in the accounting process. Management should periodically review annual depreciation expense. If wear and tear or obsolescence indicate that annual depreciation estimates are inadequate or excessive, the company should change the amount of depreciation expense.

When a change in an estimate is required, the company makes the change in **current and future years**. **It does not change depreciation in prior periods.** The rationale is that continual restatement of prior periods would adversely affect confidence in financial statements.

Helpful Hint
Use a step-by-step approach: (1) determine new depreciable cost; (2) divide by remaining useful life.

To determine the new annual depreciation expense, the company first computes the asset's depreciable cost at the time of the revision. It then allocates the revised depreciable cost to the remaining useful life.

To illustrate, assume that Barb's Florists decides on January 1, 2020, to extend the useful life of the truck by one year (a total life of six years) and increase its salvage value to $2,200. The company has used the straight-line method to depreciate the asset to date. Depreciation per year was $2,400 [($13,000 − $1,000) ÷ 5]. Accumulated depreciation after three years (2017–2019) is $7,200 ($2,400 × 3), and book value is $5,800 ($13,000 − $7,200). The new annual depreciation is $1,200, computed as shown in Illustration 9-17.

Book value, 1/1/20	$ 5,800
Less: Salvage value	2,200
Depreciable cost	$ 3,600
Remaining useful life	3 years (2020–2022)
Revised annual depreciation ($3,600 ÷ 3)	**$ 1,200**

Illustration 9-17
Revised depreciation computation

Barb's Florists makes no entry for the change in estimate. On December 31, 2020, during the preparation of adjusting entries, it records depreciation expense of $1,200. Companies must describe in the financial statements significant changes in estimates.

DO IT! 2b   Revised Depreciation

Chambers Corporation purchased a piece of equipment for $36,000. It estimated a 6-year life and $6,000 salvage value. Thus, straight-line depreciation was $5,000 per year [($36,000 − $6,000) ÷ 6]. At the end of year three (before the depreciation adjustment), it estimated the new total life to be 10 years and the new salvage value to be $2,000. Compute the revised depreciation.

Solution

Original depreciation expense = [($36,000 − $6,000) ÷ 6] = $5,000
Accumulated depreciation after 2 years = 2 × $5,000 = $10,000
Book value = $36,000 − $10,000 = $26,000

Book value after 2 years of depreciation	$ 26,000
Less: New salvage value	2,000
Depreciable cost	$ 24,000
Remaining useful life	8 years
Revised annual depreciation ($24,000 ÷ 8)	$ 3,000

Action Plan
✔ Calculate depreciable cost.
✔ Divide depreciable cost by new remaining life.

Related exercise material: **BE9-8, E9-8, and** DO IT! **9-2b.**

LEARNING OBJECTIVE **3**   **Explain how to account for the disposal of plant assets.**

Companies dispose of plant assets that are no longer useful to them. Illustration 9-18 shows the three ways in which companies make plant asset disposals.

Illustration 9-18
Methods of plant asset disposal

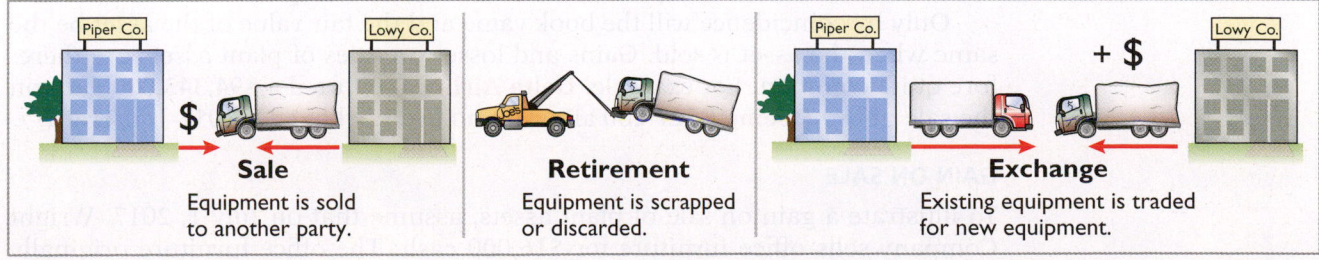

Sale
Equipment is sold to another party.

Retirement
Equipment is scrapped or discarded.

Exchange
Existing equipment is traded for new equipment.

Whatever the disposal method, the company must determine the book value of the plant asset at the disposal date to determine the gain or loss. Recall that the book value is the difference between the cost of the plant asset and the accumulated depreciation to date. If the disposal does not occur on the first day of the year, the company must record depreciation for the fraction of the year to the date of disposal. The company then eliminates the book value by reducing (debiting) Accumulated Depreciation for the total depreciation associated with that asset to the date of disposal and reducing (crediting) the asset account for the cost of the asset.

In this chapter, we examine the accounting for the retirement and sale of plant assets. In the appendix to the chapter, we discuss and illustrate the accounting for exchanges of plant assets.

Retirement of Plant Assets

To illustrate the retirement of plant assets, assume that Hobart Company retires its computer printers, which cost $32,000. The accumulated depreciation on these printers is $32,000. The equipment, therefore, is fully depreciated (zero book value). The entry to record this retirement is as follows.

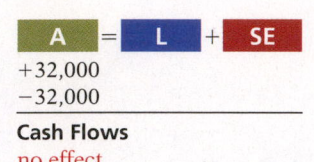

+32,000
−32,000

Cash Flows
no effect

Accumulated Depreciation—Equipment	32,000	
Equipment		32,000
(To record retirement of fully depreciated equipment)		

Helpful Hint
When disposing of a plant asset, the company removes all amounts related to the asset. This includes the original cost and the total depreciation to date in the accumulated depreciation account.

What happens if a fully depreciated plant asset is still useful to the company? In this case, the asset and its accumulated depreciation continue to be reported on the balance sheet, without further depreciation adjustment, until the company retires the asset. Reporting the asset and related accumulated depreciation on the balance sheet informs the financial statement reader that the asset is still in use. Once fully depreciated, no additional depreciation should be taken, even if an asset is still being used. In no situation can the accumulated depreciation on a plant asset exceed its cost.

If a company retires a plant asset before it is fully depreciated and no cash is received for scrap or salvage value, a loss on disposal occurs. For example, assume that Sunset Company discards delivery equipment that cost $18,000 and has accumulated depreciation of $14,000. The entry is as follows.

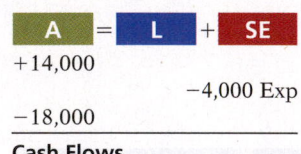

+14,000

−4,000 Exp

−18,000

Cash Flows
no effect

Accumulated Depreciation—Equipment	14,000	
Loss on Disposal of Plant Assets	4,000	
Equipment		18,000
(To record retirement of delivery equipment at a loss)		

Companies report a loss on disposal of plant assets in the "Other expenses and losses" section of the income statement.

Sale of Plant Assets

In a disposal by sale, the company compares the book value of the asset with the proceeds received from the sale. If the proceeds of the sale **exceed** the book value of the plant asset, **a gain on disposal occurs**. If the proceeds of the sale **are less than** the book value of the plant asset sold, **a loss on disposal occurs**.

Only by coincidence will the book value and the fair value of the asset be the same when the asset is sold. Gains and losses on sales of plant assets are therefore quite common. For example, **Delta Airlines** reported a $94,343,000 gain on the sale of five **Boeing** B727-200 aircraft and five **Lockheed** L-1011-1 aircraft.

GAIN ON SALE

To illustrate a gain on sale of plant assets, assume that on July 1, 2017, Wright Company sells office furniture for $16,000 cash. The office furniture originally cost $60,000. As of January 1, 2017, it had accumulated depreciation of $41,000. Depreciation for the first six months of 2017 is $8,000. Wright records depreciation expense and updates accumulated depreciation to July 1 with the following entry.

July 1	Depreciation Expense	8,000	
	Accumulated Depreciation—Equipment		8,000
	(To record depreciation expense for the first		
	6 months of 2017)		

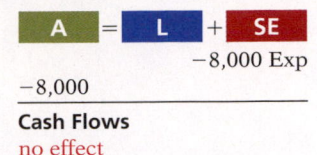

−8,000

Cash Flows
no effect

After the accumulated depreciation balance is updated, the company computes the gain or loss. The gain or loss is the difference between the proceeds from the sale and the book value at the date of disposal. Illustration 9-19 shows this computation for Wright Company, which has a gain on disposal of $5,000.

Cost of office furniture	$60,000
Less: Accumulated depreciation ($41,000 + $8,000)	49,000
Book value at date of disposal	11,000
Proceeds from sale	16,000
Gain on disposal of plant asset	**$ 5,000**

Illustration 9-19
Computation of gain on disposal

Wright records the sale and the gain on disposal of the plant asset as follows.

July 1	Cash	16,000	
	Accumulated Depreciation—Equipment	49,000	
	Equipment		60,000
	Gain on Disposal of Plant Assets		5,000
	(To record sale of office furniture		
	at a gain)		

+16,000
+49,000
−60,000

             +5,000 Rev

Cash Flows
+16,000

Companies report a gain on disposal of plant assets in the "Other revenues and gains" section of the income statement.

LOSS ON SALE

Assume that instead of selling the office furniture for $16,000, Wright sells it for $9,000. In this case, Wright computes a loss of $2,000 as follows.

Cost of office furniture	$60,000
Less: Accumulated depreciation	49,000
Book value at date of disposal	11,000
Proceeds from sale	9,000
Loss on disposal of plant asset	**$ 2,000**

Illustration 9-20
Computation of loss on disposal

Wright records the sale and the loss on disposal of the plant asset as follows.

July 1	Cash	9,000	
	Accumulated Depreciation—Equipment	49,000	
	Loss on Disposal of Plant Assets	2,000	
	Equipment		60,000
	(To record sale of office furniture at a loss)		

+ 9,000
+49,000

             −2,000 Exp

−60,000

Cash Flows
+9,000

Companies report a loss on disposal of plant assets in the "Other expenses and losses" section of the income statement.

DO IT! 3 Plant Asset Disposal

Overland Trucking has an old truck that cost $30,000, and it has accumulated depreciation of $16,000 on this truck. Overland has decided to sell the truck. (a) What entry would Overland Trucking make to record the sale of the truck for $17,000 cash? (b) What entry would Overland Trucking make to record the sale of the truck for $10,000 cash?

Solution

Action Plan

✔ At the time of disposal, determine the book value of the asset.

✔ Compare the asset's book value with the proceeds received to determine whether a gain or loss has occurred.

(a) Sale of truck for cash at a gain:		
Cash	17,000	
Accumulated Depreciation—Equipment	16,000	
Equipment		30,000
Gain on Disposal of Plant Assets		
[$17,000 − ($30,000 − $16,000)]		3,000
(To record sale of truck at a gain)		
(b) Sale of truck for cash at a loss:		
Cash	10,000	
Accumulated Depreciation—Equipment	16,000	
Loss on Disposal of Plant Assets		
[$10,000 − ($30,000 − $16,000)]	4,000	
Equipment		30,000
(To record sale of truck at a loss)		

Related exercise material: **BE9-9, BE9-10, E9-9, E9-10, and DO IT! 9-3.**

LEARNING OBJECTIVE 4

Describe how to account for natural resources and intangible assets.

Natural Resources

Helpful Hint
On a balance sheet, natural resources may be described more specifically as *timberlands, mineral deposits, oil reserves,* and so on.

Natural resources consist of standing timber and underground deposits of oil, gas, and minerals. These long-lived productive assets have two distinguishing characteristics: (1) they are physically extracted in operations (such as mining, cutting, or pumping), and (2) they are replaceable only by an act of nature.

The acquisition cost of a natural resource is the price needed to acquire the resource **and** prepare it for its intended use. For an already-discovered resource, such as an existing coal mine, cost is the price paid for the property.

Depletion

The allocation of the cost of natural resources in a rational and systematic manner over the resource's useful life is called **depletion**. (That is, depletion is to natural resources as depreciation is to plant assets.) **Companies generally use the units-of-activity method** (learned earlier in the chapter) **to compute depletion.** The reason is that **depletion generally is a function of the units extracted during the year**.

Under the units-of-activity method, companies divide the total cost of the natural resource minus salvage value by the number of units estimated to be in the resource. The result is a **depletion cost per unit**. To compute depletion, the cost per unit is then multiplied by the number of units extracted.

To illustrate, assume that Lane Coal Company invests $5 million in a mine estimated to have 1 million tons of coal and no salvage value. Illustration 9-21 shows the computation of the depletion cost per unit.

$$\frac{\text{Total Cost} - \text{Salvage Value}}{\text{Total Estimated Units Available}} = \text{Depletion Cost per Unit}$$
$$\frac{\$5,000,000}{\$1,000,000} = \$5.00 \text{ per ton}$$

Illustration 9-21
Computation of depletion cost per unit

If Lane extracts 250,000 tons in the first year, then the depletion for the year is $1,250,000 (250,000 tons × $5). It records the depletion as follows.

Inventory (coal)	1,250,000	
Accumulated Depletion		1,250,000

A	=	L	+	SE

+1,250,000
−1,250,000
_____

Cash Flows
no effect

Lane debits Inventory for the total depletion for the year and credits Accumulated Depletion to reduce the carrying value of the natural resource. Accumulated Depletion is a contra asset similar to Accumulated Depreciation. Lane credits Inventory when it sells the inventory and debits Cost of Goods Sold. The amount not sold remains in inventory and is reported in the current assets section of the balance sheet.

Some companies do not use an Accumulated Depletion account. In such cases, the company credits the amount of depletion directly to the natural resources account.

People, Planet, and Profit Insight | BHP Billiton

© Christian Uhrig/iStockphoto

Sustainability Report Please

Sustainability reports identify how the company is meeting its corporate social responsibilities. Many companies, both large and small, are now issuing these reports. For example, companies such as Disney, Best Buy, Microsoft, Ford, and ConocoPhilips issue these reports. Presented below is an adapted section of a recent BHP Billiton (a global mining, oil, and gas company) sustainability report on its environmental policies. These policies are to (1) take action to address the challenges of climate change, (2) set and achieve targets that reduce pollution, and (3) enhance biodiversity by assessing and considering ecological values and land-use aspects. Here is how BHP Billiton measures the success or failure of some of these policies:

Environment	Commentary	Target Date
We will maintain total greenhouse gas emissions below FY2006 levels.	FY2013 greenhouse gas emissions were lower than the FY2006 baseline.	30 June 2017
All operations to offset impacts to biodiversity and the related benefits derived from ecosystems.	Land and Biodiversity Management Plans were developed at all our operations.	Annual
We will finance the conservation and continuing management of areas of high biodiversity and ecosystem value.	Two projects of international conservation significance were established—the Five Rivers Conservation Project, in Australia, and the Valdivian Coastal Reserve Conservation Project, in Chile.	30 June 2017

In addition to the environment, BHP Billiton has sections in its sustainability report which discuss people, safety, health, and community.

Why do you believe companies issue sustainability reports? (Go to WileyPLUS for this answer and additional questions.)

Intangible Assets

Intangible assets are rights, privileges, and competitive advantages that result from the ownership of long-lived assets that do not possess physical substance. Evidence of intangibles may exist in the form of contracts or licenses. Intangibles may arise from the following sources:

1. Government grants, such as patents, copyrights, licenses, trademarks, and trade names.

2. Acquisition of another business, in which the purchase price includes a payment for **goodwill**.

3. Private monopolistic arrangements arising from contractual agreements, such as franchises and leases.

Some widely known intangibles are **Microsoft**'s patents, **McDonald's** franchises, **Apple**'s trade name iPod, J.K. Rowling's copyrights on the *Harry Potter* books, and the trademark **Rent-A-Wreck** in the Feature Story.

Accounting for Intangible Assets

Companies record intangible assets at cost. This cost consists of all expenditures necessary for the company to acquire the right, privilege, or competitive advantage. Intangibles are categorized as having either a limited life or an indefinite life. If an intangible has a **limited life**, the company allocates its cost over the asset's useful life using a process similar to depreciation. The process of allocating the cost of intangibles is referred to as **amortization**. The cost of intangible assets with **indefinite lives should not be amortized**.

> **Helpful Hint**
> *Amortization* is to intangibles what *depreciation* is to plant assets and *depletion* is to natural resources.

To record amortization of an intangible asset, a company increases (debits) Amortization Expense and decreases (credits) the specific intangible asset. (Unlike depreciation, no contra account, such as Accumulated Amortization, is usually used.)

Intangible assets are typically amortized on a straight-line basis. For example, the legal life of a patent is 20 years. Companies **amortize the cost of a patent over its 20-year life or its useful life, whichever is shorter**. To illustrate the computation of patent amortization, assume that National Labs purchases a patent at a cost of $60,000. If National estimates the useful life of the patent to be eight years, the annual amortization expense is $7,500 ($60,000 ÷ 8). National records the annual amortization as follows.

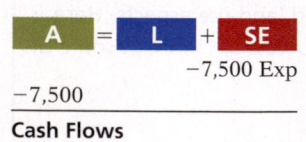

−7,500 Exp

−7,500

Cash Flows
no effect

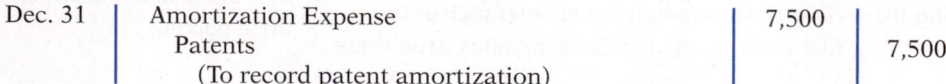

Dec. 31	Amortization Expense	7,500	
	Patents		7,500
	(To record patent amortization)		

Companies classify Amortization Expense as an operating expense in the income statement.

There is a difference between intangible assets and plant assets in determining cost. For plant assets, cost includes both the purchase price of the asset and the costs incurred in designing and constructing the asset. In contrast, the initial cost for an intangible asset includes **only the purchase price**. Companies expense any costs incurred in developing an intangible asset.

PATENTS

A **patent** is an exclusive right issued by the U.S. Patent Office that enables the recipient to manufacture, sell, or otherwise control an invention for a period of 20 years from the date of the grant. A patent is nonrenewable. But, companies can extend the legal life of a patent by obtaining new patents for improvements or other changes in the basic design. **The initial cost of a patent is the cash or cash equivalent price paid to acquire the patent.**

The saying, "A patent is only as good as the money you're prepared to spend defending it," is very true. Many patents are subject to litigation by competitors.

Any legal costs an owner incurs in successfully defending a patent in an infringement suit are considered necessary to establish the patent's validity. **The owner adds those costs to the Patents account and amortizes them over the remaining life of the patent.**

The patent holder amortizes the cost of a patent over its 20-year legal life or its useful life, whichever is shorter. Companies consider obsolescence and inadequacy in determining useful life. These factors may cause a patent to become economically ineffective before the end of its legal life.

COPYRIGHTS

The federal government grants **copyrights**, which give the owner the exclusive right to reproduce and sell an artistic or published work. Copyrights extend for the life of the creator plus 70 years. The cost of a copyright is the **cost of acquiring and defending it**. The cost may be only the small fee paid to the U.S. Copyright Office. Or, it may amount to much more if an infringement suit is involved.

The useful life of a copyright generally is significantly shorter than its legal life. Therefore, copyrights usually are amortized over a relatively short period of time.

TRADEMARKS AND TRADE NAMES

A **trademark** or **trade name** is a word, phrase, jingle, or symbol that identifies a particular enterprise or product. Trade names like Wheaties, Monopoly, Big Mac, Kleenex, Coca-Cola, and Jeep create immediate product identification. They also generally enhance the sale of the product. The creator or original user may obtain exclusive legal right to the trademark or trade name by registering it with the U.S. Patent Office. Such registration provides 20 years of protection. The registration may be renewed indefinitely as long as the trademark or trade name is in use.

If a company purchases the trademark or trade name, its cost is the purchase price. If a company develops and maintains the trademark or trade name, any costs related to these activities are expensed as incurred. Because trademarks and trade names have indefinite lives, they are not amortized.

FRANCHISES

When you fill up your tank at the corner Shell station, eat lunch at Subway, or rent a car from Rent-A-Wreck, you are dealing with franchises. A **franchise** is a contractual arrangement between a franchisor and a franchisee. The franchisor grants the franchisee the right to sell certain products, perform specific services, or use certain trademarks or trade names, usually within a designated geographic area.

Another type of franchise is a **license**. A license granted by a governmental body permits a company to use public property in performing its services. Examples are the use of city streets for a bus line or taxi service, the use of public land for telephone and electric lines, and the use of airwaves for radio or TV broadcasting. In a recent license agreement, FOX, CBS, and NBC agreed to pay $27.9 billion for the right to broadcast NFL football games over an eight-year period. Franchises and licenses may by granted for a definite period of time, an indefinite period, or perpetually.

When a company incurs costs in connection with the purchase of a franchise or license, it should recognize an intangible asset. Companies should amortize the cost of a limited-life franchise (or license) over its useful life. If the life is indefinite, the cost is not amortized. Annual payments made under a franchise agreement are recorded as **operating expenses** in the period in which they are incurred.

GOODWILL

Usually, the largest intangible asset that appears on a company's balance sheet is goodwill. **Goodwill** represents the value of all favorable attributes that relate to a company that are not attributable to any other specific asset. These include exceptional management, desirable location, good customer relations, skilled employees, high-quality products, and harmonious relations with labor unions. Goodwill is unique. Unlike assets such as investments and plant assets, which can be sold **individually** in the marketplace, goodwill can be identified only with the business **as a whole**.

If goodwill can be identified only with the business as a whole, how can its amount be determined? One could try to put a dollar value on the factors listed above (exceptional management, desirable location, and so on). But, the results would be very subjective, and such subjective valuations would not contribute to the reliability of financial statements. **Therefore, companies record goodwill only when an entire business is purchased. In that case, goodwill is the excess of cost over the fair value of the net assets (assets less liabilities) acquired.**

In recording the purchase of a business, the company debits (increases) the identifiable acquired assets, credits liabilities at their fair values, credits cash for the purchase price, and records the difference as goodwill. **Goodwill is not amortized** because it is considered to have an indefinite life. Companies report goodwill in the balance sheet under intangible assets.

Accounting Across the Organization   Google

We Want to Own Glass

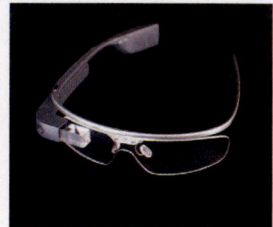

© Hattanas Kumchai/Shutterstock

Google, which has trademarked the term "Google Glass," now wants to trademark the term "Glass." Why? Because the simple word Glass has marketing advantages over the term Google Glass. It is easy to remember and is more universal. Regulators, however, are balking at Google's request. They say that the possible trademark is too similar to other existing or pending software trademarks that contain the word "glass." Also, regulators suggest that the term Glass is merely descriptive and therefore lacks trademark protection. For

example, regulators note that a company that makes salsa could not trademark the term "Spicy Salsa."

BorderStylo LLC, which developed a Web-browser extension called Write on Glass, has filed a notice of opposition to Google's request. Google is fighting back and has sent the trademark examiner a 1,928-page application defense.

Source: Jacob Gershman, "Google Wants to Own 'Glass'," *Wall Street Journal* (April 4, 2014), p. B5.

*If Google is successful in registering the term Glass, where will this trademark be reported on its financial statements? (Go to **WileyPLUS** for this answer and additional questions.)*

Research and Development Costs

Helpful Hint
Research and development (R&D) costs are not intangible assets. But because they may lead to patents and copyrights, we discuss them in this section.

Research and development costs are expenditures that may lead to patents, copyrights, new processes, and new products. Many companies spend considerable sums of money on research and development (R&D). For example, in a recent year, **IBM** spent over $5.1 billion on R&D.

Research and development costs present accounting problems. For one thing, it is sometimes difficult to assign the costs to specific projects. Also, there are uncertainties in identifying the extent and timing of future benefits. As a result, companies usually record R&D costs **as an expense when incurred**, whether the research and development is successful or not.

To illustrate, assume that Laser Scanner Company spent $3 million on R&D that resulted in two highly successful patents. It spent $20,000 on legal fees for the patents. The company would add the lawyers' fees to the Patents account. The R&D costs, however, cannot be included in the cost of the patents. Instead, the company would record the R&D costs as an expense when incurred.

Many disagree with this accounting approach. They argue that expensing R&D costs leads to understated assets and net income. Others, however, argue that capitalizing these costs will lead to highly speculative assets on the balance sheet. Who is right is difficult to determine.

DO IT! 4   Classification Concepts

Match the statement with the term most directly associated with it.

    Copyrights   Depletion
    Intangible assets   Franchises
    Research and development costs

1. _____ The allocation of the cost of a natural resource to expense in a rational and systematic manner.
2. _____ Rights, privileges, and competitive advantages that result from the ownership of long-lived assets that do not possess physical substance.
3. _____ An exclusive right granted by the federal government to reproduce and sell an artistic or published work.
4. _____ A right to sell certain products or services or to use certain trademarks or trade names within a designated geographic area.
5. _____ Costs incurred by a company that often lead to patents or new products. These costs must be expensed as incurred.

Solution

1. Depletion	4. Franchises
2. Intangible assets	5. Research and development costs
3. Copyrights	

Related exercise material: **BE9-11, BE9-12, E9-11, E9-12, E9-13, and DO IT! 9-4.**

Action Plan

✔ Know that the accounting for intangibles often depends on whether the item has a finite or indefinite life.

✔ Recognize the many similarities and differences between the accounting for natural resources, plant assets, and intangible assets.

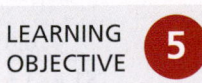

LEARNING OBJECTIVE **5**   **Discuss how plant assets, natural resources, and intangible assets are reported and analyzed.**

Presentation

Usually, companies combine plant assets and natural resources under "Property, plant, and equipment" in the balance sheet. They show intangibles separately. Companies disclose either in the balance sheet or the notes the balances of the major classes of assets, such as land, buildings, and equipment, and accumulated depreciation by major classes or in total. In addition, they should describe the depreciation and amortization methods that were used, as well as disclose the amount of depreciation and amortization expense for the period.

Illustration 9-22 (page 418) shows a typical financial statement presentation of property, plant, and equipment and intangibles for **The Procter & Gamble Company (P&G)** in its 2013 balance sheet. The notes to P&G's financial statements present greater details about the accounting for its long-term tangible and intangible assets.

Illustration 9-22
P&G's presentation of property, plant, and equipment, and intangible assets

THE PROCTER & GAMBLE COMPANY
Balance Sheet (partial)
(in millions)

Real World

	June 30	
	2013	2012
Property, plant, and equipment		
Buildings	$ 7,829	$ 7,324
Machinery and equipment	34,305	32,029
Land	878	880
	43,012	40,233
Accumulated depreciation	(21,346)	(19,856)
Net property, plant, and equipment	21,666	20,377
Goodwill and other intangible assets		
Goodwill	55,188	53,773
Trademarks and other intangible assets, net	31,572	30,988
Net goodwill and other intangible assets	$86,760	$84,761

Illustration 9-23 shows another comprehensive presentation of property, plant, and equipment from the balance sheet of **Owens-Illinois**. The notes to the financial statements of Owens-Illinois identify the major classes of property, plant, and equipment. They also indicate that depreciation and amortization are by the straight-line method, and depletion is by the units-of-activity method.

Illustration 9-23
Owens-Illinois' presentation of property, plant, and equipment, and intangible assets

OWENS-ILLINOIS, INC.
Balance Sheet (partial)
(in millions)

Real World

Property, plant, and equipment		
Timberlands, at cost, less accumulated depletion		$ 95.4
Buildings and equipment, at cost	$2,207.1	
Less: Accumulated depreciation	1,229.0	978.1
Total property, plant, and equipment		$1,073.5
Intangibles		
Patents		410.0
Total		$1,483.5

Analysis

Using ratios, we can analyze how efficiently a company uses its assets to generate sales. The **asset turnover** analyzes the productivity of a company's assets. It tells us how many dollars of sales a company generates for each dollar invested in assets. This ratio is computed by dividing net sales by average total assets for the period. Illustration 9-24 shows the computation of the asset turnover for **The Procter & Gamble Company**. P&G's net sales for 2013 were $84,167 million. Its total ending assets were $139,263 million, and beginning assets were $132,244 million.

Illustration 9-24
Asset turnover formula and computation

Net Sales	÷	Average Total Assets	=	Asset Turnover
$84,167	÷	$\dfrac{\$132{,}244 + \$139{,}263}{2}$	=	**.62 times**

Thus, each dollar invested in assets produced $0.62 in sales for P&G. If a company is using its assets efficiently, each dollar of assets will create a high amount of sales. This ratio varies greatly among different industries—from those that are asset-intensive (utilities) to those that are not (services).

DO IT! 5 | Asset Turnover

Paramour Company reported net income of $180,000, net sales of $420,000, and had total assets of $460,000 on January 1, 2017, and total assets on December 31, 2017, of $540,000 billion. Determine Paramour's asset turnover for 2017.

Solution

The asset turnover for Paramour Company is computed as follows.

Net Sales	÷	Average Total Assets	=	Asset Turnover
$420,000	÷	$\dfrac{\$460,000 + \$540,000}{2}$	=	.84

Related exercise material: **BE9-14, E9-14, and DO IT! 9-5.**

Action Plan

✔ Recognize that the asset turnover analyzes the productivity of a company's assets.

✔ Know the formula Net sales ÷ Average total assets equals Asset turnover.

LEARNING OBJECTIVE 6

APPENDIX 9A: Explain how to account for the exchange of plant assets.

Ordinarily, companies record a gain or loss on the exchange of plant assets. The rationale for recognizing a gain or loss is that most exchanges have **commercial substance**. An exchange has commercial substance if the future cash flows change as a result of the exchange.

To illustrate, Ramos Co. exchanges some of its equipment for land held by Brodhead Inc. It is likely that the timing and amount of the cash flows arising from the land will differ significantly from the cash flows arising from the equipment. As a result, both Ramos and Brodhead are in different economic positions. Therefore, **the exchange has commercial substance**, and the companies recognize a gain or loss in the exchange. Because most exchanges have commercial substance (even when similar assets are exchanged), we illustrate only this type of situation for both a loss and a gain.

Loss Treatment

To illustrate an exchange that results in a loss, assume that Roland Company exchanged a set of used trucks plus cash for a new semi-truck. The used trucks have a combined book value of $42,000 (cost $64,000 less $22,000 accumulated depreciation). Roland's purchasing agent, experienced in the secondhand market, indicates that the used trucks have a fair value of $26,000. In addition to the trucks, Roland must pay $17,000 for the semi-truck. Roland computes the cost of the semi-truck as follows.

Fair value of used trucks	$26,000
Cash paid	17,000
Cost of semi-truck	$43,000

Illustration 9A-1
Cost of semi-truck

Roland incurs a loss on disposal of plant assets of $16,000 on this exchange. The reason is that the book value of the used trucks is greater than the fair value of these trucks. The computation is as follows.

Illustration 9A-2
Computation of loss on disposal

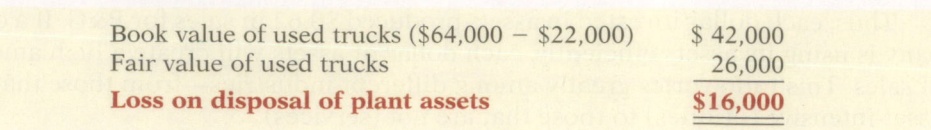

Book value of used trucks ($64,000 − $22,000)	$ 42,000
Fair value of used trucks	26,000
Loss on disposal of plant assets	**$16,000**

In recording an exchange at a loss, three steps are required: (1) eliminate the book value of the asset given up, (2) record the cost of the asset acquired, and (3) recognize the loss on disposal of plant assets. Roland Company thus records the exchange on the loss as follows.

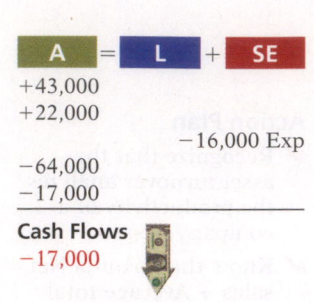

A = L + SE
+43,000
+22,000
　　　　−16,000 Exp
−64,000
−17,000

Cash Flows
−17,000

Equipment (new)	43,000	
Accumulated Depreciation—Equipment	22,000	
Loss on Disposal of Plant Assets	16,000	
Equipment (old)		64,000
Cash		17,000
(To record exchange of used trucks for semi-truck)		

Gain Treatment

To illustrate a gain situation, assume that Mark Express Delivery decides to exchange its old delivery equipment plus cash of $3,000 for new delivery equipment. The book value of the old delivery equipment is $12,000 (cost $40,000 less accumulated depreciation $28,000). The fair value of the old delivery equipment is $19,000.

The cost of the new asset is the fair value of the old asset exchanged plus any cash paid (or other consideration given up). The cost of the new delivery equipment is $22,000, computed as follows.

Illustration 9A-3
Cost of new delivery equipment

Fair value of old delivery equipment	$ 19,000
Cash paid	3,000
Cost of new delivery equipment	**$22,000**

A gain results when the fair value of the old delivery equipment is greater than its book value. For Mark Express, there is a gain of $7,000 on disposal of plant assets, computed as follows.

Illustration 9A-4
Computation of gain on disposal

Fair value of old delivery equipment	$19,000
Book value of old delivery equipment ($40,000 − $28,000)	12,000
Gain on disposal of plant assets	**$ 7,000**

Mark Express Delivery records the exchange as follows.

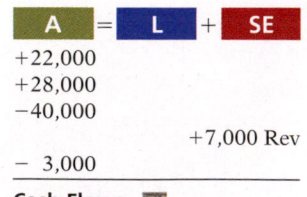

A = L + SE
+22,000
+28,000
−40,000
　　　　+7,000 Rev
− 3,000

Cash Flows
− 3,000

Equipment (new)	22,000	
Accumulated Depreciation—Equipment (old)	28,000	
Equipment (old)		40,000
Gain on Disposal of Plant Assets		7,000
Cash		3,000
(To record exchange of old delivery equipment for		
new delivery equipment)		

In recording an exchange at a gain, the following three steps are involved: (1) eliminate the book value of the asset given up, (2) record the cost of the asset acquired, and (3) recognize the gain on disposal of plant assets. Accounting for exchanges of plant assets becomes more complex if the transaction does not have commercial substance. This issue is discussed in more advanced accounting classes.

REVIEW AND PRACTICE

LEARNING OBJECTIVES REVIEW

① Explain the accounting for plant asset expenditures. The cost of plant assets includes all expenditures necessary to acquire the asset and make it ready for its intended use. Once cost is established, the company uses that amount as the basis of accounting for the plant assets over its useful life.

Companies incur revenue expenditures to maintain the operating efficiency and productive life of an asset. They debit these expenditures to Maintenance and Repairs Expense as incurred. Capital expenditures increase the operating efficiency, productive capacity, or expected useful life of the asset. Companies generally debit these expenditures to the plant asset affected.

② Apply depreciation methods to plant assets. Depreciation is the allocation of the cost of a plant asset to expense over its useful (service) life in a rational and systematic manner. Depreciation is not a process of valuation, nor is it a process that results in an accumulation of cash.

Three depreciation methods are:

Method	Effect on Annual Depreciation	Formula
Straight-line	Constant amount	Depreciable cost ÷ Useful life (in years)
Units-of-activity	Varying amount	Depreciable cost per unit × Units of activity during the year
Declining-balance	Decreasing amount	Book value at beginning of year × Declining-balance rate

Companies make revisions of periodic depreciation in present and future periods, not retroactively. They determine the new annual depreciation by dividing the depreciable cost at the time of the revision by the remaining useful life.

③ Explain how to account for the disposal of plant assets. The accounting for disposal of a plant asset through retirement or sale is as follows. (a) Eliminate the book value of the plant asset at the date of disposal. (b) Record cash proceeds, if any. (c) Account for the difference between the book value and the cash proceeds as a gain or loss on disposal.

④ Describe how to account for natural resources and intangible assets. Companies compute depletion cost per unit by dividing the total cost of the natural resource minus salvage value by the number of units estimated to be in the resource. They then multiply the depletion cost per unit by the number of units extracted and sold.

The process of allocating the cost of an intangible asset is referred to as amortization. The cost of intangible assets with indefinite lives is not amortized. Companies normally use the straight-line method for amortizing intangible assets.

⑤ Discuss how plant assets, natural resources, and intangible assets are reported and analyzed. Companies usually combine plant assets and natural resources under property, plant, and equipment. They show intangibles separately under intangible assets. Either within the balance sheet or in the notes, companies should disclose the balances of the major classes of assets, such as land, buildings, and equipment, and accumulated depreciation by major classes or in total. They also should describe the depreciation and amortization methods used, and should disclose the amount of depreciation and amortization expense for the period. The asset turnover measures the productivity of a company's assets in generating sales.

٭⑥ Explain how to account for the exchange of plant assets. Ordinarily, companies record a gain or loss on the exchange of plant assets. The rationale for recognizing a gain or loss is that most exchanges have commercial substance. An exchange has commercial substance if the future cash flows change as a result of the exchange.

GLOSSARY REVIEW

Accelerated-depreciation method Depreciation method that produces higher depreciation expense in the early years than in the later years. (p. 407).

Additions and improvements Costs incurred to increase the operating efficiency, productive capacity, or useful life of a plant asset. (p. 400).

Amortization The allocation of the cost of an intangible asset to expense over its useful life in a systematic and rational manner. (p. 414).

Asset turnover A measure of how efficiently a company uses its assets to generate sales; calculated as net sales divided by average total assets. (p. 418).

Capital expenditures Expenditures that increase the company's investment in productive facilities. (p. 401).

Copyrights Exclusive grant from the federal government that allows the owner to reproduce and sell an artistic or published work. (p. 415).

Declining-balance method Depreciation method that applies a constant rate to the declining book value of the asset and produces a decreasing annual depreciation expense over the useful life of the asset. (p. 406).

Depletion The allocation of the cost of a natural resource to expense in a rational and systematic manner over the resource's useful life. (p. 412).

Depreciable cost The cost of a plant asset less its salvage value. (p. 404).

Depreciation The process of allocating to expense the cost of a plant asset over its useful (service) life in a rational and systematic manner. (p. 402).

Franchise (license) A contractual arrangement under which the franchisor grants the franchisee the right to sell certain products, perform specific services, or use certain trademarks or trade names, usually within a designated geographic area. (p. 415).

Going concern assumption States that the company will continue in operation for the foreseeable future. (p. 403).

Goodwill The value of all favorable attributes that relate to a company that is not attributable to any other specific asset. (p. 415).

Intangible assets Rights, privileges, and competitive advantages that result from the ownership of long-lived assets that do not possess physical substance. (p. 414).

Materiality concept If an item would not make a difference in decision-making, a company does not have to follow GAAP in reporting it. (p. 401).

Natural resources Assets that consist of standing timber and underground deposits of oil, gas, and minerals. (p. 412).

Ordinary repairs Expenditures to maintain the operating efficiency and productive life of the unit. (p. 400).

Patent An exclusive right issued by the U.S. Patent Office that enables the recipient to manufacture, sell, or otherwise control an invention for a period of 20 years from the date of the grant. (p. 414).

Plant assets Tangible resources that are used in the operations of the business and are not intended for sale to customers. (p. 398).

Research and development (R&D) costs Expenditures that may lead to patents, copyrights, new processes, or new products. (p. 416).

Revenue expenditures Expenditures that are immediately charged against revenues as an expense. (p. 400).

Salvage value An estimate of an asset's value at the end of its useful life. (p. 403).

Straight-line method Depreciation method in which periodic depreciation is the same for each year of the asset's useful life. (p. 404).

Trademark (trade name) A word, phrase, jingle, or symbol that identifies a particular enterprise or product. (p. 415).

Units-of-activity method Depreciation method in which useful life is expressed in terms of the total units of production or use expected from an asset. (p. 405).

Useful life An estimate of the expected productive life, also called service life, of an asset. (p. 403).

▌ PRACTICE MULTIPLE-CHOICE QUESTIONS

(LO 1) **1.** Erin Danielle Company purchased equipment and incurred the following costs.

Cash price	$24,000
Sales taxes	1,200
Insurance during transit	200
Installation and testing	400
Total costs	$25,800

What amount should be recorded as the cost of the equipment?
(a) $24,000.   (c) $25,400.
(b) $25,200.   (d) $25,800.

(LO 1) **2.** Additions to plant assets are:
(a) revenue expenditures.
(b) debited to the Maintenance and Repairs Expense account.
(c) debited to the Purchases account.
(d) capital expenditures.

(LO 2) **3.** Depreciation is a process of:
(a) valuation.   (c) cash accumulation.
(b) cost allocation.   (d) appraisal.

(LO 2) **4.** Micah Bartlett Company purchased equipment on January 1, 2016, at a total invoice cost of $400,000. The equipment has an estimated salvage value of $10,000 and an estimated useful life of 5 years. The amount of accumulated depreciation at December 31,

2017, if the straight-line method of depreciation is used, is:
(a) $80,000.   (c) $78,000.
(b) $160,000.   (d) $156,000.

5. Ann Torbert purchased a truck for $11,000 on January **(LO 2)** 1, 2016. The truck will have an estimated salvage value of $1,000 at the end of 5 years. Using the units-of-activity method, the balance in accumulated depreciation at December 31, 2017, can be computed by the following formula:
(a) ($11,000 ÷ Total estimated activity) × Units of activity for 2017.
(b) ($10,000 ÷ Total estimated activity) × Units of activity for 2017.
(c) ($11,000 ÷ Total estimated activity) × Units of activity for 2016 and 2017.
(d) ($10,000 ÷ Total estimated activity) × Units of activity for 2016 and 2017.

6. Jefferson Company purchased a piece of equipment **(LO 2)** on January 1, 2017. The equipment cost $60,000 and has an estimated life of 8 years and a salvage value of $8,000. What was the depreciation expense for the asset for 2018 under the double-declining-balance method?
(a) $6,500.   (c) $15,000.
(b) $11,250.   (d) $6,562.

(LO 2) **7.** When there is a change in estimated depreciation:
  (a) previous depreciation should be corrected.
  (b) current and future years' depreciation should be revised.
  (c) only future years' depreciation should be revised.
  (d) None of the above.

(LO 2) **8.** Able Towing Company purchased a tow truck for $60,000 on January 1, 2015. It was originally depreciated on a straight-line basis over 10 years with an assumed salvage value of $12,000. On December 31, 2017, before adjusting entries had been made, the company decided to change the remaining estimated life to 4 years (including 2017) and the salvage value to $2,000. What was the depreciation expense for 2017?
  (a) $6,000.   (c) $15,000.
  (b) $4,800.   (d) $12,100.

(LO 3) **9.** Bennie Razor Company has decided to sell one of its old manufacturing machines on June 30, 2017. The machine was purchased for $80,000 on January 1, 2013, and was depreciated on a straight-line basis for 10 years assuming no salvage value. If the machine was sold for $26,000, what was the amount of the gain or loss recorded at the time of the sale?
  (a) $18,000.   (c) $22,000.
  (b) $54,000.   (d) $46,000.

(LO 4) **10.** Maggie Sharrer Company expects to extract 20 million tons of coal from a mine that cost $12 million. If no salvage value is expected and 2 million tons are mined in the first year, the entry to record depletion will include a:
  (a) debit to Accumulated Depletion of $2,000,000.
  (b) credit to Depletion Expense of $1,200,000.
  (c) debit to Inventory of $1,200,000.
  (d) credit to Accumulated Depletion of $2,000,000.

(LO 4) **11.** Which of the following statements is **false**?
  (a) If an intangible asset has a finite life, it should be amortized.
  (b) The amortization period of an intangible asset can exceed 20 years.
  (c) Goodwill is recorded only when a business is purchased.
  (d) Research and development costs are expensed when incurred, except when the research and development expenditures result in a successful patent.

(LO 4) **12.** Martha Beyerlein Company incurred $150,000 of research and development costs in its laboratory to develop a patent granted on January 2, 2017. On July 31, 2017, Beyerlein paid $35,000 for legal fees in a successful defense of the patent. The total amount debited to Patents through July 31, 2017, should be:
  (a) $150,000.   (c) $185,000.
  (b) $35,000.   (d) $170,000.

(LO 5) **13.** Indicate which of the following statements is **true**.
  (a) Since intangible assets lack physical substance, they need be disclosed only in the notes to the financial statements.
  (b) Goodwill should be reported as a contra account in the stockholders' equity section.
  (c) Totals of major classes of assets can be shown in the balance sheet, with asset details disclosed in the notes to the financial statements.
  (d) Intangible assets are typically combined with plant assets and natural resources, and shown in the property, plant, and equipment section.

(LO 5) **14.** Lake Coffee Company reported net sales of $180,000, net income of $54,000, beginning total assets of $200,000, and ending total assets of $300,000. What was the company's asset turnover?
  (a) 0.90.   (c) 0.72.
  (b) 0.20.   (d) 1.39.

(LO 6) ***15.** Schopenhauer Company exchanged an old machine, with a book value of $39,000 and a fair value of $35,000, and paid $10,000 cash for a similar new machine. The transaction has commercial substance. At what amount should the machine acquired in the exchange be recorded on Schopenhauer's books?
  (a) $45,000.   (c) $49,000.
  (b) $46,000.   (d) $50,000.

(LO 6) ***16.** In exchanges of assets in which the exchange has commercial substance:
  (a) neither gains nor losses are recognized immediately.
  (b) gains, but not losses, are recognized immediately.
  (c) losses, but not gains, are recognized immediately.
  (d) both gains and losses are recognized immediately.

Solutions

1. (d) All of the costs ($1,200 + $200 + $400) in addition to the cash price ($24,000) should be included in the cost of the equipment because they were necessary expenditures to acquire the asset and make it ready for its intended use. The other choices are therefore incorrect.

2. (d) When an addition is made to plant assets, it is intended to increase productive capacity, increase the assets' useful life, or increase the efficiency of the assets. This is called a capital expenditure. The other choices are incorrect because (a) additions to plant assets are not revenue expenditures because the additions will have a long-term useful life whereas revenue expenditures are minor repairs and maintenance that do not prolong the life of the assets; (b) additions to plant assets are debited to Plant Assets, not Maintenance and Repairs Expense, because the Maintenance and Repairs Expense account is used to record expenditures not intended to increase the life of the assets; and (c) additions to plant assets are debited to Plant Assets, not Purchases, because the Purchases account is used to record assets intended for resale (inventory).

3. (b) Depreciation is a process of allocating the cost of an asset over its useful life, not a process of (a) valuation, (c) cash accumulation, or (d) appraisal.

4. (d) Accumulated depreciation will be the sum of 2 years of depreciation expense. Annual depreciation for this asset is ($400,000 − $10,000)/5 = $78,000. The sum of 2 years' depreciation is therefore $156,000 ($78,000 + $78,000), not (a) $80,000, (b) $160,000, or (c) $78,000.

5. (d) The units-of-activity method takes salvage value into consideration; therefore, the depreciable cost is $10,000. This amount is divided by total estimated activity. The resulting number is multiplied by the units of activity used in 2016 and 2017 to compute the accumulated depreciation at the end of 2017, the second year of the asset's use. The other choices are therefore incorrect.

6. (b) For the double-declining method, the depreciation rate would be 25% or (1/8 × 2). For 2017, annual depreciation expense is $15,000 ($60,000 book value × 25%); for 2018, annual depreciation expense is $11,250 [($60,000 − $15,000) × 25%], not (a) $6,500, (c) $15,000, or (d) $6,562.

7. (b) When there is a change in estimated depreciation, the current and future years' depreciation computation should reflect the new estimates. The other choices are incorrect because (a) previous years' depreciation should not be adjusted when new estimates are made for depreciation, and (c) when there is a change in estimated depreciation, the current and future years' depreciation computation should reflect the new estimates. Choice (d) is wrong because there is a correct answer.

8. (d) First, calculate accumulated depreciation from January 1, 2015, through December 31, 2016, which is $9,600 [[($60,000 − $12,000)/10 years] × 2 years]. Next, calculate the revised depreciable cost, which is $48,400 ($60,000 − $9,600 − $2,000). Thus, the depreciation expense for 2017 is $12,100 ($48,400/4), not (a) $6,000, (b) $4,800, or (c) $15,000.

9. (a) First, the book value needs to be determined. The accumulated depreciation as of June 30, 2017, is $36,000 [($80,000/10) × 4.5 years]. Thus, the cost of the machine less accumulated depreciation equals $44,000 ($80,000 − $36,000). The loss recorded at the time of sale is $18,000 ($26,000 − $44,000), not (b) $54,000, (c) $22,000, or (d) $46,000.

10. (c) The amount of depletion is determined by computing the depletion per unit ($12 million/20 million tons = $0.60 per ton) and then multiplying that amount times the number of units extracted during the year (2 million tons × $0.60 = $1,200,000). This amount is debited to Inventory and credited to Accumulated Depletion. The other choices are therefore incorrect.

11. (d) Research and development (R&D) costs are expensed when incurred, regardless of whether the research and development expenditures result in a successful patent or not. The other choices are true statements.

12. (b) Because the $150,000 was spent developing the patent rather than buying it from another firm, it is debited to Research and Development Expense. Only the $35,000 spent on the successful defense can be debited to Patents, not (a) $150,000, (c) $185,000, or (d) $170,000.

13. (c) Reporting only totals of major classes of assets in the balance sheet is appropriate. Additional details can be shown in the notes to the financial statements. The other choices are false statements.

14. (c) Asset turnover = Net sales ($180,000)/Average total assets [($200,000 + $300,000)/2] = 0.72 times, not (a) 0.90, (b) 0.20, or (d) 1.39 times.

*15. (a) When an exchange has commercial substance, the debit to the new asset is equal to the fair value of the old asset plus the cash paid ($35,000 + $10,000 = $45,000), not (b) $46,000, (c) $49,000, or (d) $50,000.

*16. (d) Both gains and losses are recognized immediately when an exchange of assets has commercial substance. The other choices are therefore incorrect.

PRACTICE EXERCISES

Determine depreciation for partial periods.

(LO 2)

1. Winston Company purchased a new machine on October 1, 2017, at a cost of $120,000. The company estimated that the machine will have a salvage value of $12,000. The machine is expected to be used for 12,000 working hours during its 4-year life.

Instructions

Compute the depreciation expense under the following methods for the year indicated.

(a) Straight-line for 2017.

(b) Units-of-activity for 2017, assuming machine usage was 1,700 hours.

(c) Declining-balance using double the straight-line rate for 2017 and 2018.

Solution

1. (a) Straight-line method:

$$\left(\frac{\$120,000 - \$12,000}{4}\right) = \$27,000 \text{ per year}$$

2017 depreciation = $27,000 × 3/12 = $6,750

(b) Units-of-activity method:

$$\left(\frac{\$120,000 - \$12,000}{12,000}\right) = \$9 \text{ per hour}$$

2017 depreciation = 1,700 hours × $9 = $15,300

(c) Declining-balance method:

2017 depreciation = $120,000 × 50% × 3/12 = $15,000

Book value January 1, 2018 = $120,000 − $15,000 = $105,000

2018 depreciation = $105,000 × 50% = $52,500

2. Lake Company, organized in 2017, has the following transactions related to intangible assets.

1/2/17	Purchased patent (8-year life)	$560,000
4/1/17	Goodwill purchased (indefinite life)	360,000
7/1/17	10-year franchise; expiration date 7/1/2027	440,000
9/1/17	Research and development costs	185,000

Prepare entries to set up appropriate accounts for different intangibles; amortize intangible assets.

(LO 4)

Instructions

Prepare the necessary entries to record these intangibles. All costs incurred were for cash. Make the adjusting entries as of December 31, 2017, recording any necessary amortization and reflecting all balances accurately as of that date.

Solution

2.	1/2/17	Patents	560,000	
		Cash		560,000
	4/1/17	Goodwill	360,000	
		Cash		360,000
		(Part of the entry to record purchase of another company)		
	7/1/17	Franchises	440,000	
		Cash		440,000
	9/1/17	Research and Development Expense	185,000	
		Cash		185,000
	12/31/17	Amortization Expense	92,000	
		($560,000 ÷ 8) + [($440,000 ÷ 10) × 1/2]		
		Patents		70,000
		Franchises		22,000

Ending balances. 12/31/17:
Patents = $490,000 ($560,000 − $70,000)
Goodwill = $360,000
Franchises = $418,000 ($440,000 − $22,000)
R&D expense = $185,000

PRACTICE PROBLEMS

1. DuPage Company purchases a factory machine at a cost of $18,000 on January 1, 2017. DuPage expects the machine to have a salvage value of $2,000 at the end of its 4-year useful life.

During its useful life, the machine is expected to be used 160,000 hours. Actual annual hourly use was 2017, 40,000; 2018, 60,000; 2019, 35,000; and 2020, 25,000.

Compute depreciation under different methods.

(LO 2)

Instructions

Prepare depreciation schedules for the following methods: (a) straight-line, (b) units-of-activity, and (c) declining-balance using double the straight-line rate.

Solution

1. (a)

Straight-Line Method

	Computation			Annual	End of Year	
Year	Depreciable Cost*	×	Depreciation Rate	= Depreciation Expense	Accumulated Depreciation	Book Value
2017	$16,000		25%	$4,000	$ 4,000	$14,000**
2018	16,000		25%	4,000	8,000	10,000
2019	16,000		25%	4,000	12,000	6,000
2020	16,000		25%	4,000	16,000	2,000

*$18,000 − $2,000.
**$18,000 − $4,000.

(b)

Units-of-Activity Method

	Computation				Annual	End of Year	
Year	Units of Activity	×	Depreciable Cost/Unit	=	Depreciation Expense	Accumulated Depreciation	Book Value
2017	40,000		$0.10*		$4,000	$ 4,000	$14,000
2018	60,000		0.10		6,000	10,000	8,000
2019	35,000		0.10		3,500	13,500	4,500
2020	25,000		0.10		2,500	16,000	2,000

*($18,000 − $2,000) ÷ 160,000.

(c)

Declining-Balance Method

	Computation				Annual	End of Year	
Year	Book Value Beginning of Year	×	Depreciation Rate*	=	Depreciation Expense	Accumulated Depreciation	Book Value
2017	$18,000		50%		$9,000	$ 9,000	$9,000
2018	9,000		50%		4,500	13,500	4,500
2019	4,500		50%		2,250	15,750	2,250
2020	2,250		50%		250**	16,000	2,000

*¼ × 2.
**Adjusted to $250 because ending book value should not be less than expected salvage value.

Record disposal of plant asset.

(LO 3)

2. On January 1, 2017, Skyline Limousine Co. purchased a limo at an acquisition cost of $28,000. The vehicle has been depreciated by the straight-line method using a 4-year service life and a $4,000 salvage value. The company's fiscal year ends on December 31.

Instructions

Prepare the journal entry or entries to record the disposal of the limousine assuming that it was:

(a) Retired and scrapped with no salvage value on January 1, 2021.

(b) Sold for $5,000 on July 1, 2020.

Solution

2. (a) 1/1/21	Accumulated Depreciation—Equipment	24,000	
	Loss on Disposal of Plant Assets	4,000	
	Equipment		28,000
	(To record retirement of limousine)		
(b) 7/1/20	Depreciation Expense*	3,000	
	Accumulated Depreciation—Equipment		3,000
	(To record depreciation to date		
	of disposal)		
	Cash	5,000	
	Accumulated Depreciation—Equipment**	21,000	
	Loss on Disposal of Plant Assets	2,000	
	Equipment		28,000
	(To record sale of limousine)		

*[($28,000 − $4,000) ÷ 4] × $\frac{1}{2}$.
**[($28,000 − $4,000) ÷ 4] × 3 = $18,000; $18,000 + $3,000.

WileyPLUS

Brief Exercises, Exercises, **DO IT!** Exercises, and Problems and many additional resources are available for practice in WileyPLUS

NOTE: All asterisked Questions, Exercises, and Problems relate to material in the appendix to the chapter.

QUESTIONS

1. Sid Watney is uncertain about the applicability of the historical cost principle to plant assets. Explain the principle to Sid.

2. What are some examples of land improvements?

3. Lynn Company acquires the land and building owned by Noble Company. What types of costs may be incurred to make the asset ready for its intended use if Lynn Company wants to use (a) only the land, and (b) both the land and the building?

4. In a recent newspaper release, the president of Downs Company asserted that something has to be done about depreciation. The president said, "Depreciation does not come close to accumulating the cash needed to replace the asset at the end of its useful life." What is your response to the president?

5. Andrew is studying for the next accounting examination. He asks your help on two questions: (a) What is salvage value? (b) Is salvage value used in determining periodic depreciation under each depreciation method? Answer Andrew's questions.

6. Contrast the straight-line method and the units-of-activity method as to (a) useful life, and (b) the pattern of periodic depreciation over useful life.

7. Contrast the effects of the three depreciation methods on annual depreciation expense.

8. In the fourth year of an asset's 5-year useful life, the company decides that the asset will have a 6-year service life. How should the revision of depreciation be recorded? Why?

9. Distinguish between revenue expenditures and capital expenditures during useful life.

10. How is a gain or loss on the sale of a plant asset computed?

11. Romero Corporation owns a machine that is fully depreciated but is still being used. How should Romero account for this asset and report it in the financial statements?

12. What are natural resources, and what are their distinguishing characteristics?

13. Explain the concept of depletion and how it is computed.

14. What are the similarities and differences between the terms depreciation, depletion, and amortization?

15. Rowand Company hires an accounting intern who says that intangible assets should always be amortized over their legal lives. Is the intern correct? Explain.

16. Goodwill has been defined as the value of all favorable attributes that relate to a business. What types of attributes could result in goodwill?

17. Jimmy West, a business major, is working on a case problem for one of his classes. In the case problem, the company needs to raise cash to market a new product it developed. Ron Thayer, an engineering major, takes one look at the company's balance sheet and says, "This company has an awful lot of goodwill. Why don't you recommend that it sell some of it to raise cash?" How should Jimmy respond to Ron?

18. Under what conditions is goodwill recorded?

19. Often, research and development costs provide companies with benefits that last a number of years. (For example, these costs can lead to the development of a patent that will increase the company's income for many years.) However, generally accepted accounting principles require that such costs be recorded as an expense when incurred. Why?

20. **McDonald's Corporation** reports total average assets of $28.9 billion and net sales of $20.5 billion. What is the company's asset turnover?

21. Stark Corporation and Zuber Corporation operate in the same industry. Stark uses the straight-line method to account for depreciation; Zuber uses an accelerated method. Explain what complications might arise in trying to compare the results of these two companies.

22. Gomez Corporation uses straight-line depreciation for financial reporting purposes but an accelerated method for tax purposes. Is it acceptable to use different methods for the two purposes? What is Gomez's motivation for doing this?

23. You are comparing two companies in the same industry. You have determined that Ace Corp. depreciates its plant assets over a 40-year life, whereas Liu Corp. depreciates its plant assets over a 20-year life. Discuss the implications this has for comparing the results of the two companies.

24. Sosa Company is doing significant work to revitalize its warehouses. It is not sure whether it should capitalize these costs or expense them. What are the implications for current-year net income and future net income of expensing versus capitalizing these costs?

*25. When assets are exchanged in a transaction involving commercial substance, how is the gain or loss on disposal of plant assets computed?

*26. Unruh Refrigeration Company trades in an old machine on a new model when the fair value of the old machine is greater than its book value. The transaction has commercial substance. Should Unruh recognize a gain on disposal of plant assets? If the fair value of the old machine is less than its book value, should Unruh recognize a loss on disposal of plant assets?

BRIEF EXERCISES

Determine the cost of land.

(LO 1)

BE9-1 The following expenditures were incurred by McCoy Company in purchasing land: cash price $50,000, accrued taxes $3,000, attorneys' fees $2,500, real estate broker's commission $2,000, and clearing and grading $3,500. What is the cost of the land?

Determine the cost of a truck.

(LO 1)

BE9-2 Rich Castillo Company incurs the following expenditures in purchasing a truck: cash price $30,000, accident insurance $2,000, sales taxes $2,100, motor vehicle license $100, and painting and lettering $400. What is the cost of the truck?

Prepare entries for delivery truck costs.

(LO 1)

BE9-3 Flaherty Company had the following two transactions related to its delivery truck.

1. Paid $45 for an oil change.
2. Paid $400 to install a special gear unit, which increases the operating efficiency of the truck.

Prepare Flaherty's journal entries to record these two transactions.

Compute straight-line depreciation.

(LO 2)

BE9-4 Corales Company acquires a delivery truck at a cost of $38,000. The truck is expected to have a salvage value of $6,000 at the end of its 4-year useful life. Compute annual depreciation expense for the first and second years using the straight-line method.

Compute depreciation and evaluate treatment.

(LO 2)

BE9-5 Chisenhall Company purchased land and a building on January 1, 2017. Management's best estimate of the value of the land was $100,000 and of the building $200,000. However, management told the accounting department to record the land at $220,000 and the building at $80,000. The building is being depreciated on a straight-line basis over 15 years with no salvage value. Why do you suppose management requested this accounting treatment? Is it ethical?

Compute declining-balance depreciation.

(LO 2)

BE9-6 Depreciation information for Corales Company is given in BE9-4. Assuming the declining-balance depreciation rate is double the straight-line rate, compute annual depreciation for the first and second years under the declining-balance method.

Compute depreciation using the units-of-activity method.

(LO 2)

BE9-7 Rosco Taxi Service uses the units-of-activity method in computing depreciation on its taxicabs. Each cab is expected to be driven 150,000 miles. Taxi no. 10 cost $39,500 and is expected to have a salvage value of $500. Taxi no. 10 is driven 30,000 miles in year 1 and 20,000 miles in year 2. Compute the depreciation for each year.

Compute revised depreciation.

(LO 2)

BE9-8 On January 1, 2017, the Morgantown Company ledger shows Equipment $32,000 and Accumulated Depreciation—Equipment $9,000. The depreciation resulted from using the straight-line method with a useful life of 10 years and a salvage value of $2,000. On this date, the company concludes that the equipment has a remaining useful life of only 4 years with the same salvage value. Compute the revised annual depreciation.

Prepare entries for disposal by retirement.

(LO 3)

BE9-9 Prepare journal entries to record the following.

(a) Sound Tracker Company retires its delivery equipment, which cost $41,000. Accumulated depreciation is also $41,000 on this delivery equipment. No salvage value is received.
(b) Assume the same information as (a), except that accumulated depreciation is $37,000, instead of $41,000, on the delivery equipment.

Prepare entries for disposal by sale.

(LO 3)

BE9-10 Gunkelson Company sells equipment on September 30, 2017, for $18,000 cash. The equipment originally cost $72,000 and as of January 1, 2017, had accumulated depreciation of $42,000. Depreciation for the first 9 months of 2017 is $5,250. Prepare the journal entries to (a) update depreciation to September 30, 2017, and (b) record the sale of the equipment.

Prepare depletion entry and balance sheet presentation for natural resources.

(LO 4)

BE9-11 Franceour Mining Co. purchased for $7 million a mine that is estimated to have 35 million tons of ore and no salvage value. In the first year, 5 million tons of ore are extracted.

(a) Prepare the journal entry to record depletion for the first year.
(b) Show how this mine is reported on the balance sheet at the end of the first year.

BE9-12 Campanez Company purchases a patent for $140,000 on January 2, 2017. Its estimated useful life is 10 years.

(a) Prepare the journal entry to record amortization expense for the first year.
(b) Show how this patent is reported on the balance sheet at the end of the first year.

Prepare amortization expense entry and balance sheet presentation for intangibles.

(LO 4)

BE9-13 Information related to plant assets, natural resources, and intangibles at the end of 2017 for Dent Company is as follows: buildings $1,100,000, accumulated depreciation— buildings $600,000, goodwill $410,000, coal mine $500,000, and accumulated depletion— coal mine $108,000. Prepare a partial balance sheet of Dent Company for these items.

Classify long-lived assets on balance sheet.

(LO 5)

BE9-14 In a recent annual report, Target reported beginning total assets of $44.1 billion, ending total assets of $44.5 billion, and net sales of $63.4 billion. Compute Target's asset turnover.

Calculate asset turnover.

(LO 5)

*BE9-15 Olathe Company exchanges old delivery equipment for new delivery equipment. The book value of the old delivery equipment is $31,000 (cost $61,000 less accumulated depreciation $30,000). Its fair value is $24,000, and cash of $5,000 is paid. Prepare the entry to record the exchange, assuming the transaction has commercial substance.

Prepare entry for disposal by exchange.

(LO 6)

*BE9-16 Assume the same information as BE9-15, except that the fair value of the old delivery equipment is $33,000. Prepare the entry to record the exchange.

Prepare entry for disposal by exchange.

(LO 6)

DO IT! Exercises

DO IT! 9-1 Lofton Company purchased a delivery truck. The total cash payment was $27,900, including the following items.

Negotiated purchase price	$24,000
Installation of special shelving	1,100
Painting and lettering	900
Motor vehicle license	100
Annual insurance policy	500
Sales tax	1,300
Total paid	$27,900

Explain accounting for cost of plant assets.

(LO 1)

Explain how each of these costs would be accounted for.

DO IT! 9-2a On January 1, 2017, Emporia Country Club purchased a new riding mower for $15,000. The mower is expected to have an 8-year life with a $3,000 salvage value. What journal entry would Emporia make at December 31, 2017, if it uses straight-line depreciation?

Calculate depreciation expense and make journal entry.

(LO 2)

DO IT! 9-2b Pinewood Corporation purchased a piece of equipment for $70,000. It estimated an 8-year life and a $2,000 salvage value. At the end of year four (before the depreciation adjustment), it estimated the new total life to be 10 years and the new salvage value to be $6,000. Compute the revised depreciation.

Calculate revised depreciation.

(LO 2)

DO IT! 9-3 Napoli Manufacturing has old equipment that cost $52,000. The equipment has accumulated depreciation of $28,000. Napoli has decided to sell the equipment.

(a) What entry would Napoli make to record the sale of the equipment for $26,000 cash?
(b) What entry would Napoli make to record the sale of the equipment for $15,000 cash?

Make journal entries to record plant asset disposal.

(LO 3)

DO IT! 9-4 Match the statement with the term most directly associated with it.

Goodwill	Amortization
Intangible assets	Franchises
Research and development costs	

Match intangibles classifications concepts.

(LO 4)

1. _____ Rights, privileges, and competitive advantages that result from the ownership of long-lived assets that do not possess physical substance.

2. _____ The allocation of the cost of an intangible asset to expense in a rational and systematic manner.

3. _____ A right to sell certain products or services, or use certain trademarks or trade names, within a designated geographic area.

4. _____ Costs incurred by a company that often lead to patents or new products. These costs must be expensed as incurred.

5. _____ The excess of the cost of a company over the fair value of the net assets acquired.

Calculate asset turnover.

(LO 5)

DO IT! 9-5 For 2017, Sale Company reported beginning total assets of $300,000 and ending total assets of $340,000. Its net income for this period was $50,000, and its net sales were $400,000. Compute the company's asset turnover for 2017.

EXERCISES

Determine cost of plant acquisitions.

(LO 1)

E9-1 The following expenditures relating to plant assets were made by Prather Company during the first 2 months of 2017.

1. Paid $5,000 of accrued taxes at time plant site was acquired.
2. Paid $200 insurance to cover possible accident loss on new factory machinery while the machinery was in transit.
3. Paid $850 sales taxes on new delivery truck.
4. Paid $17,500 for parking lots and driveways on new plant site.
5. Paid $250 to have company name and advertising slogan painted on new delivery truck.
6. Paid $8,000 for installation of new factory machinery.
7. Paid $900 for one-year accident insurance policy on new delivery truck.
8. Paid $75 motor vehicle license fee on the new truck.

Instructions

(a) •————— Explain the application of the historical cost principle in determining the acquisition cost of plant assets.
(b) List the numbers of the foregoing transactions, and opposite each indicate the account title to which each expenditure should be debited.

Determine property, plant, and equipment costs.

(LO 1)

E9-2 Benedict Company incurred the following costs.

1. Sales tax on factory machinery purchased	$ 5,000
2. Painting of and lettering on truck immediately upon purchase	700
3. Installation and testing of factory machinery	2,000
4. Real estate broker's commission on land purchased	3,500
5. Insurance premium paid for first year's insurance on new truck	880
6. Cost of landscaping on property purchased	7,200
7. Cost of paving parking lot for new building constructed	17,900
8. Cost of clearing, draining, and filling land	13,300
9. Architect's fees on self-constructed building	10,000

Instructions

Indicate to which account Benedict would debit each of the costs.

Determine acquisition costs of land.

(LO 1)

E9-3 On March 1, 2017, Westmorlan Company acquired real estate on which it planned to construct a small office building. The company paid $75,000 in cash. An old warehouse on the property was razed at a cost of $8,600; the salvaged materials were sold for $1,700. Additional expenditures before construction began included $1,100 attorney's fee for work concerning the land purchase, $5,000 real estate broker's fee, $7,800 architect's fee, and $14,000 to put in driveways and a parking lot.

Instructions

(a) Determine the amount to be reported as the cost of the land.
(b) For each cost not used in part (a), indicate the account to be debited.

Understand depreciation concepts.

(LO 2)

E9-4 Tom Parkey has prepared the following list of statements about depreciation.

1. Depreciation is a process of asset valuation, not cost allocation.
2. Depreciation provides for the proper matching of expenses with revenues.
3. The book value of a plant asset should approximate its fair value.

4. Depreciation applies to three classes of plant assets: land, buildings, and equipment.
5. Depreciation does not apply to a building because its usefulness and revenue-producing ability generally remain intact over time.
6. The revenue-producing ability of a depreciable asset will decline due to wear and tear and to obsolescence.
7. Recognizing depreciation on an asset results in an accumulation of cash for replacement of the asset.
8. The balance in accumulated depreciation represents the total cost that has been charged to expense.
9. Depreciation expense and accumulated depreciation are reported on the income statement.
10. Four factors affect the computation of depreciation: cost, useful life, salvage value, and residual value.

Instructions
Identify each statement as true or false. If false, indicate how to correct the statement.

E9-5 Yello Bus Lines uses the units-of-activity method in depreciating its buses. One bus was purchased on January 1, 2017, at a cost of $148,000. Over its 4-year useful life, the bus is expected to be driven 100,000 miles. Salvage value is expected to be $8,000.

Compute depreciation under units-of-activity method.

(LO 2)

Instructions
(a) Compute the depreciable cost per unit.
(b) Prepare a depreciation schedule assuming actual mileage was: 2017, 26,000; 2018, 32,000; 2019, 25,000; and 2020, 17,000.

E9-6 Rottino Company purchased a new machine on October 1, 2017, at a cost of $150,000. The company estimated that the machine will have a salvage value of $12,000. The machine is expected to be used for 10,000 working hours during its 5-year life.

Determine depreciation for partial periods.

(LO 2)

Instructions
Compute the depreciation expense under the following methods for the year indicated.

(a) Straight-line for 2017.
(b) Units-of-activity for 2017, assuming machine usage was 1,700 hours.
(c) Declining-balance using double the straight-line rate for 2017 and 2018.

E9-7 Linton Company purchased a delivery truck for $34,000 on January 1, 2017. The truck has an expected salvage value of $2,000, and is expected to be driven 100,000 miles over its estimated useful life of 8 years. Actual miles driven were 15,000 in 2017 and 12,000 in 2018.

Compute depreciation using different methods.

(LO 2)

Instructions
(a) Compute depreciation expense for 2017 and 2018 using (1) the straight-line method, (2) the units-of-activity method, and (3) the double-declining-balance method.
(b) Assume that Linton uses the straight-line method.
(1) Prepare the journal entry to record 2017 depreciation.
(2) Show how the truck would be reported in the December 31, 2017, balance sheet.

E9-8 Terry Wade, the new controller of Hellickson Company, has reviewed the expected useful lives and salvage values of selected depreciable assets at the beginning of 2017. His findings are as follows.

Compute revised annual depreciation.

(LO 2)

Type of Asset	Date Acquired	Cost	Accumulated Depreciation 1/1/17	Useful Life in Years Old	Useful Life in Years Proposed	Salvage Value Old	Salvage Value Proposed
Building	1/1/11	$800,000	$114,000	40	50	$40,000	$26,000
Warehouse	1/1/12	100,000	19,000	25	20	5,000	6,000

All assets are depreciated by the straight-line method. Hellickson Company uses a calendar year in preparing annual financial statements. After discussion, management has agreed to accept Terry's proposed changes.

Instructions
(a) Compute the revised annual depreciation on each asset in 2017. (Show computations.)
(b) Prepare the entry (or entries) to record depreciation on the building in 2017.

Journalize entries for disposal of plant assets.

(LO 3)

E9-9 Presented below are selected transactions at Ridge Company for 2017.

Jan. 1   Retired a piece of machinery that was purchased on January 1, 2007. The machine cost $62,000 on that date. It had a useful life of 10 years with no salvage value.

June 30   Sold a computer that was purchased on January 1, 2014. The computer cost $45,000. It had a useful life of 5 years with no salvage value. The computer was sold for $14,000.

Dec. 31   Discarded a delivery truck that was purchased on January 1, 2013. The truck cost $33,000. It was depreciated based on a 6-year useful life with a $3,000 salvage value.

Instructions

Journalize all entries required on the above dates, including entries to update depreciation, where applicable, on assets disposed of. Ridge Company uses straight-line depreciation. (Assume depreciation is up to date as of December 31, 2016.)

Journalize entries for disposal of equipment.

(LO 3)

E9-10 Pryce Company owns equipment that cost $65,000 when purchased on January 1, 2014. It has been depreciated using the straight-line method based on an estimated salvage value of $5,000 and an estimated useful life of 5 years.

Instructions

Prepare Pryce Company's journal entries to record the sale of the equipment in these four independent situations.

(a) Sold for $31,000 on January 1, 2017.
(b) Sold for $31,000 on May 1, 2017.
(c) Sold for $11,000 on January 1, 2017.
(d) Sold for $11,000 on October 1, 2017.

Journalize entries for natural resources depletion.

(LO 4)

E9-11 On July 1, 2017, Friedman Inc. invested $720,000 in a mine estimated to have 900,000 tons of ore of uniform grade. During the last 6 months of 2017, 100,000 tons of ore were mined.

Instructions

(a) Prepare the journal entry to record depletion.
(b) Assume that the 100,000 tons of ore were mined, but only 80,000 units were sold. How are the costs applicable to the 20,000 unsold units reported?

Prepare adjusting entries for amortization.

(LO 4)

E9-12 The following are selected 2017 transactions of Pedigo Corporation.

Jan. 1   Purchased a small company and recorded goodwill of $150,000. Its useful life is indefinite.

May 1   Purchased for $75,000 a patent with an estimated useful life of 5 years and a legal life of 20 years.

Instructions

Prepare necessary adjusting entries at December 31 to record amortization required by the events above.

Prepare entries to set up appropriate accounts for different intangibles; amortize intangible assets.

(LO 4)

E9-13 Gill Company, organized in 2017, has the following transactions related to intangible assets.

1/2/17	Purchased patent (7-year life)	$595,000
4/1/17	Goodwill purchased (indefinite life)	360,000
7/1/17	10-year franchise; expiration date 7/1/2027	480,000
9/1/17	Research and development costs	185,000

Instructions

Prepare the necessary entries to record these intangibles. All costs incurred were for cash. Make the adjusting entries as of December 31, 2017, recording any necessary amortization and reflecting all balances accurately as of that date.

Calculate asset turnover.

(LO 5)

E9-14 During 2017, Paola Corporation reported net sales of $3,500,000 and net income of $1,500,000. Its balance sheet reported average total assets of $1,400,000.

Instructions

Calculate the asset turnover.

*E9-15 Presented below are two independent transactions. Both transactions have commercial substance.

Journalize entries for exchanges.

(LO 6)

1. Mercy Co. exchanged old trucks (cost $64,000 less $22,000 accumulated depreciation) plus cash of $17,000 for new trucks. The old trucks had a fair value of $38,000.
2. Pence Inc. trades its used machine (cost $12,000 less $4,000 accumulated depreciation) for a new machine. In addition to exchanging the old machine (which had a fair value of $11,000), Pence also paid cash of $3,000.

Instructions

(a) Prepare the entry to record the exchange of assets by Mercy Co.
(b) Prepare the entry to record the exchange of assets by Pence Inc.

*E9-16 Rizzo's Delivery Company and Overland's Express Delivery exchanged delivery trucks on January 1, 2017. Rizzo's truck cost $22,000. It has accumulated depreciation of $15,000 and a fair value of $3,000. Overland's truck cost $10,000. It has accumulated depreciation of $8,000 and a fair value of $3,000. The transaction has commercial substance.

Journalize entries for the exchange of plant assets.

(LO 6)

Instructions

(a) Journalize the exchange for Rizzo's Delivery Company.
(b) Journalize the exchange for Overland's Express Delivery.

EXERCISES: SET B AND CHALLENGE EXERCISES

Visit the book's companion website, at **www.wiley.com/college/weygandt**, and choose the Student Companion site to access Exercises: Set B and Challenge Exercises.

PROBLEMS: SET A

P9-1A Venable Company was organized on January 1. During the first year of operations, the following plant asset expenditures and receipts were recorded in random order.

Determine acquisition costs of land and building.

(LO 1)

	Debit
1. Cost of filling and grading the land	$ 4,000
2. Full payment to building contractor	690,000
3. Real estate taxes on land paid for the current year	5,000
4. Cost of real estate purchased as a plant site (land $100,000 and building $45,000)	145,000
5. Excavation costs for new building	35,000
6. Architect's fees on building plans	10,000
7. Accrued real estate taxes paid at time of purchase of real estate	2,000
8. Cost of parking lots and driveways	14,000
9. Cost of demolishing building to make land suitable for construction of new building	25,000
	$930,000
Credit	
10. Proceeds from salvage of demolished building	$ 3,500

Instructions

Analyze the foregoing transactions using the following column headings. Insert the number of each transaction in the Item column, and then insert the amounts in the other appropriate columns. For amounts entered in the Other Accounts column, also indicate the account titles.

Totals

Land $172,500
Buildings $735,000

Item	**Land**	**Buildings**	**Other Accounts**

P9-2A In recent years, Avery Transportation purchased three used buses. Because of frequent turnover in the accounting department, a different accountant selected the depreciation method for each bus, and various methods were selected. Information concerning the buses is shown on the next page.

Compute depreciation under different methods.

(LO 2)

Bus	Acquired	Cost	Salvage Value	Useful Life in Years	Depreciation Method
1	1/1/15	$ 96,000	$ 6,000	5	Straight-line
2	1/1/15	110,000	10,000	4	Declining-balance
3	1/1/16	92,000	8,000	5	Units-of-activity

For the declining-balance method, the company uses the double-declining rate. For the units-of-activity method, total miles are expected to be 120,000. Actual miles of use in the first 3 years were 2016, 24,000; 2017, 34,000; and 2018, 30,000.

Instructions

(a) Bus 2, 2016, $82,500

(a) Compute the amount of accumulated depreciation on each bus at December 31, 2017.

(b) If Bus 2 was purchased on April 1 instead of January 1, what is the depreciation expense for this bus in (1) 2015 and (2) 2016?

Compute depreciation under different methods.

(LO 2)

P9-3A On January 1, 2017, Evers Company purchased the following two machines for use in its production process.

Machine A: The cash price of this machine was $48,000. Related expenditures included: sales tax $1,700, shipping costs $150, insurance during shipping $80, installation and testing costs $70, and $100 of oil and lubricants to be used with the machinery during its first year of operations. Evers estimates that the useful life of the machine is 5 years with a $5,000 salvage value remaining at the end of that time period. Assume that the straight-line method of depreciation is used.

Machine B: The recorded cost of this machine was $180,000. Evers estimates that the useful life of the machine is 4 years with a $10,000 salvage value remaining at the end of that time period.

Instructions

(a) Prepare the following for Machine A.

(1) The journal entry to record its purchase on January 1, 2017.

(2) The journal entry to record annual depreciation at December 31, 2017.

(b) Calculate the amount of depreciation expense that Evers should record for Machine B each year of its useful life under the following assumptions.

(1) Evers uses the straight-line method of depreciation.

(b) (2) 2017 DDB depreciation $90,000

(2) Evers uses the declining-balance method. The rate used is twice the straight-line rate.

(3) Evers uses the units-of-activity method and estimates that the useful life of the machine is 125,000 units. Actual usage is as follows: 2017, 45,000 units; 2018, 35,000 units; 2019, 25,000 units; 2020, 20,000 units.

(c) Which method used to calculate depreciation on Machine B reports the highest amount of depreciation expense in year 1 (2017)? The highest amount in year 4 (2020)? The highest total amount over the 4-year period?

Calculate revisions to depreciation expense.

(LO 2)

P9-4A At the beginning of 2015, Mazzaro Company acquired equipment costing $120,000. It was estimated that this equipment would have a useful life of 6 years and a salvage value of $12,000 at that time. The straight-line method of depreciation was considered the most appropriate to use with this type of equipment. Depreciation is to be recorded at the end of each year.

During 2017 (the third year of the equipment's life), the company's engineers reconsidered their expectations and estimated that the equipment's useful life would probably be 7 years (in total) instead of 6 years. The estimated salvage value was not changed at that time. However, during 2020, the estimated salvage value was reduced to $5,000.

Instructions

Indicate how much depreciation expense should be recorded each year for this equipment, by completing the following table.

Year	Depreciation Expense	Accumulated Depreciation
2015		
2016		
2017		
2018		
2019		
2020		
2021		

2021 depreciation expense
$17,900

P9-5A At December 31, 2017, Grand Company reported the following as plant assets.

Land		$ 4,000,000
Buildings	$28,500,000	
Less: Accumulated depreciation—buildings	12,100,000	16,400,000
Equipment	48,000,000	
Less: Accumulated depreciation—equipment	5,000,000	43,000,000
Total plant assets		$63,400,000

During 2018, the following selected cash transactions occurred.

April 1 Purchased land for $2,130,000.
May 1 Sold equipment that cost $750,000 when purchased on January 1, 2014. The equipment was sold for $450,000.
June 1 Sold land purchased on June 1, 2008, for $1,500,000. The land cost $400,000.
July 1 Purchased equipment for $2,500,000.
Dec. 31 Retired equipment that cost $500,000 when purchased on December 31, 2008. The company received no proceeds related to salvage.

Instructions
(a) Journalize the above transactions. The company uses straight-line depreciation for buildings and equipment. The buildings are estimated to have a 50-year life and no salvage value. The equipment is estimated to have a 10-year useful life and no salvage value. Update depreciation on assets disposed of at the time of sale or retirement.
(b) Record adjusting entries for depreciation for 2018.
(c) Prepare the plant assets section of Grand's balance sheet at December 31, 2018.

Journalize a series of equipment transactions related to purchase, sale, retirement, and depreciation.

(LO 2, 3, 5)

(b) Depreciation Expense— Buildings $570,000; Equipment $4,800,000
(c) Total plant assets $61,760,000

P9-6A Ceda Co. has equipment that cost $80,000 and that has been depreciated $50,000.

Instructions
Record the disposal under the following assumptions.

(a) It was scrapped as having no value.
(b) It was sold for $21,000.
(c) It was sold for $31,000.

Record disposals.

(LO 4)

(b) $9,000 loss

P9-7A The intangible assets section of Sappelt Company at December 31, 2017, is presented below.

Patents ($70,000 cost less $7,000 amortization)	$63,000
Franchises ($48,000 cost less $19,200 amortization)	28,800
Total	$91,800

The patent was acquired in January 2017 and has a useful life of 10 years. The franchise was acquired in January 2014 and also has a useful life of 10 years. The following cash transactions may have affected intangible assets during 2018.

Jan. 2 Paid $27,000 legal costs to successfully defend the patent against infringement by another company.
Jan.–June Developed a new product, incurring $140,000 in research and development costs. A patent was granted for the product on July 1. Its useful life is equal to its legal life.
Sept. 1 Paid $50,000 to an extremely large defensive lineman to appear in commercials advertising the company's products. The commercials will air in September and October.
Oct. 1 Acquired a franchise for $140,000. The franchise has a useful life of 50 years.

Instructions
(a) Prepare journal entries to record the transactions above.
(b) Prepare journal entries to record the 2018 amortization expense.
(c) Prepare the intangible assets section of the balance sheet at December 31, 2018.

Prepare entries to record transactions related to acquisition and amortization of intangibles; prepare the intangible assets section.

(LO 4, 5)

(b) Amortization Expense (patents) $10,000 Amortization Expense (franchises) $5,500
(c) Total intangible assets $243,300

P9-8A Due to rapid turnover in the accounting department, a number of transactions involving intangible assets were improperly recorded by Goins Company in 2017.

1. Goins developed a new manufacturing process, incurring research and development costs of $136,000. The company also purchased a patent for $60,000. In early January,

Prepare entries to correct errors made in recording and amortizing intangible assets.

(LO 4)

Goins capitalized $196,000 as the cost of the patents. Patent amortization expense of $19,600 was recorded based on a 10-year useful life.

2. On July 1, 2017, Goins purchased a small company and as a result acquired goodwill of $92,000. Goins recorded a half-year's amortization in 2017, based on a 50-year life ($920 amortization). The goodwill has an indefinite life.

1. R&D Exp. $136,000

Instructions

Prepare all journal entries necessary to correct any errors made during 2017. Assume the books have not yet been closed for 2017.

Calculate and comment on asset turnover.

(LO 5)

P9-9A LaPorta Company and Lott Corporation, two corporations of roughly the same size, are both involved in the manufacture of in-line skates. Each company depreciates its plant assets using the straight-line approach. An investigation of their financial statements reveals the following information.

	LaPorta Co.	Lott Corp.
Net income	$ 800,000	$1,000,000
Sales revenue	1,300,000	1,180,000
Average total assets	2,500,000	2,000,000
Average plant assets	1,800,000	1,000,000

Instructions

(a) For each company, calculate the asset turnover.

(b) ━━━━━ Based on your calculations in part (a), comment on the relative effectiveness of the two companies in using their assets to generate sales and produce net income.

PROBLEMS: SET B AND SET C

Visit the book's companion website, at **www.wiley.com/college/weygandt**, and choose the Student Companion site to access Problems: Set B and Set C.

COMPREHENSIVE PROBLEM: CHAPTERS 3 TO 9

CP9 Hassellhouf Company's trial balance at December 31, 2017, is presented below and on page 437. All 2017 transactions have been recorded except for the items described on page 437.

	Debit	Credit
Cash	$ 28,000	
Accounts Receivable	36,800	
Notes Receivable	10,000	
Interest Receivable	–0–	
Inventory	36,200	
Prepaid Insurance	3,600	
Land	20,000	
Buildings	150,000	
Equipment	60,000	
Patents	9,000	
Allowance for Doubtful Accounts		$ 500
Accumulated Depreciation—Buildings		50,000
Accumulated Depreciation—Equipment		24,000
Accounts Payable		27,300
Salaries and Wages Payable		–0–
Unearned Rent Revenue		6,000
Notes Payable (due in 2018)		11,000
Interest Payable		–0–

	Debit	Credit
Notes Payable (due after 2018)		30,000
Common Stock		50,000
Retained Earnings		63,600
Dividends	12,000	
Sales Revenue		905,000
Interest Revenue		–0–
Rent Revenue		–0–
Gain on Disposal of Plant Assets		–0–
Bad Debt Expense	–0–	
Cost of Goods Sold	630,000	
Depreciation Expense	–0–	
Insurance Expense	–0–	
Interest Expense	–0–	
Other Operating Expenses	61,800	
Amortization Expense	–0–	
Salaries and Wages Expense	110,000	
Total	$1,167,400	$1,167,400

Unrecorded transactions:

1. On May 1, 2017, Hassellhouf purchased equipment for $21,200 plus sales taxes of $1,600 (all paid in cash).

2. On July 1, 2017, Hassellhouf sold for $3,500 equipment which originally cost $5,000. Accumulated depreciation on this equipment at January 1, 2017, was $1,800; 2017 depreciation prior to the sale of the equipment was $450.

3. On December 31, 2017, Hassellhouf sold on account $9,000 of inventory that cost $6,300.

4. Hassellhouf estimates that uncollectible accounts receivable at year-end is $3,500.

5. The note receivable is a one-year, 8% note dated April 1, 2017. No interest has been recorded.

6. The balance in prepaid insurance represents payment of a $3,600 6-month premium on September 1, 2017.

7. The building is being depreciated using the straight-line method over 30 years. The salvage value is $30,000.

8. The equipment owned prior to this year is being depreciated using the straight-line method over 5 years. The salvage value is 10% of cost.

9. The equipment purchased on May 1, 2017, is being depreciated using the straight-line method over 5 years, with a salvage value of $1,800.

10. The patent was acquired on January 1, 2017, and has a useful life of 10 years from that date.

11. Unpaid salaries and wages at December 31, 2017, total $5,200.

12. The unearned rent revenue of $6,000 was received on December 1, 2017, for 3 months' rent.

13. Both the short-term and long-term notes payable are dated January 1, 2017, and carry a 9% interest rate. All interest is payable in the next 12 months.

Instructions
(a) Prepare journal entries for the transactions listed above.
(b) Prepare an updated December 31, 2017, trial balance.
(c) Prepare a 2017 income statement and a retained earnings statement.
(d) Prepare a December 31, 2017, classified balance sheet.

(b) Totals
$1,205,040

(d) Total assets
$259,200

CONTINUING PROBLEM

COOKIE CREATIONS

(*Note:* This is a continuation of the Cookie Creations problem from Chapters 1 through 8.)

CC9 Natalie is also thinking of buying a van that will be used only for business. Natalie is concerned about the impact of the van's cost on her income statement and balance sheet. She has come to you for advice on calculating the van's depreciation.

Go to the book's companion website, **www.wiley.com/college/weygandt**, *to see the completion of this problem.*

© leungchopan/
Shutterstock

BROADENING YOUR *PERSPECTIVE*

FINANCIAL REPORTING AND ANALYSIS

Financial Reporting Problem: Apple Inc.

BYP9-1 The financial statements of Apple Inc. are presented in Appendix A. Instructions for accessing and using the company's complete annual report, including the notes to the financial statements, are also provided in Appendix A.

Instructions
Refer to Apple's financial statements and answer the following questions.

(a) What was the total cost and book value of property, plant, and equipment at September 28, 2013?
(b) What was the amount of depreciation and amortization expense for each of the three years 2011–2013?
(c) Using the statement of cash flows, what is the amount of capital spending in 2013 and 2012?
(d) Where does the company disclose its intangible assets, and what types of intangibles did it have at September 28, 2013?

Comparative Analysis Problem:
PepsiCo, Inc. vs. The Coca-Cola Company

BYP9-2 PepsiCo, Inc.'s financial statements are presented in Appendix B. Financial statements of The Coca-Cola Company are presented in Appendix C. Instructions for accessing and using the complete annual reports of PepsiCo and Coca-Cola, including the notes to the financial statements, are also provided in Appendices B and C, respectively.

Instructions
(a) Compute the asset turnover for each company for 2013.
(b) What conclusions concerning the efficiency of assets can be drawn from these data?

Comparative Analysis Problem:
Amazon.com, Inc. vs. Wal-Mart Stores, Inc.

BYP9-3 Amazon.com, Inc.'s financial statements are presented in Appendix D. Financial statements of Wal-Mart Stores, Inc. are presented in Appendix E. Instructions for accessing and using the complete annual reports of Amazon and Wal-Mart, including the notes to the financial statements, are also provided in Appendices D and E, respectively.

Instructions
(a) Compute the asset turnover for each company for 2013.
(b) What conclusions concerning the efficiency of assets can be drawn from these data?

Real-World Focus

BYP9-4 A company's annual report identifies the amount of its plant assets and the depreciation method used.

Address: www.annualreports.com, or go to **www.wiley.com/college/weygandt**

Steps
1. Select a particular company.
2. Search by company name.
3. Follow instructions below.

Instructions
Answer the following questions.

(a) What is the name of the company?
(b) What is the Internet address of the annual report?
(c) At fiscal year-end, what is the net amount of its plant assets?
(d) What is the accumulated depreciation?
(e) Which method of depreciation does the company use?

CRITICAL THINKING

Decision-Making Across the Organization

BYP9-5 Pinson Company and Estes Company are two proprietorships that are similar in many respects. One difference is that Pinson Company uses the straight-line method and Estes Company uses the declining-balance method at double the straight-line rate. On January 2, 2015, both companies acquired the depreciable assets shown below.

Asset	Cost	Salvage Value	Useful Life
Buildings	$360,000	$20,000	40 years
Equipment	130,000	10,000	10 years

Including the appropriate depreciation charges, annual net income for the companies in the years 2015, 2016, and 2017 and total income for the 3 years were as follows.

	2015	2016	2017	Total
Pinson Company	$84,000	$88,400	$90,000	$262,400
Estes Company	68,000	76,000	85,000	229,000

At December 31, 2017, the balance sheets of the two companies are similar except that Estes Company has more cash than Pinson Company.

Lynda Peace is interested in buying one of the companies. She comes to you for advice.

Instructions
With the class divided into groups, answer the following.

(a) Determine the annual and total depreciation recorded by each company during the 3 years.
(b) Assuming that Estes Company also uses the straight-line method of depreciation instead of the declining-balance method as in (a), prepare comparative income data for the 3 years.
(c) Which company should Lynda Peace buy? Why?

Communication Activity

BYP9-6 The chapter presented some concerns regarding the current accounting standards for research and development expenditures.

Instructions
Assume that you are either (a) the president of a company that is very dependent on ongoing research and development, writing a memo to the FASB complaining about the current accounting standards regarding research and development, or (b) the FASB member defending the current standards regarding research and development. Your memo should address the following questions.

1. By requiring expensing of R&D, do you think companies will spend less on R&D? Why or why not? What are the possible implications for the competitiveness of U.S. companies?
2. If a company makes a commitment to spend money for R&D, it must believe it has future benefits. Shouldn't these costs therefore be capitalized just like the purchase of any long-lived asset that is believed to have future benefits?

Ethics Case

BYP9-7 Turner Container Company is suffering declining sales of its principal product, nonbiodegradeable plastic cartons. The president, Robert Griffin, instructs his controller, Alexis Landrum, to lengthen asset lives to reduce depreciation expense. A processing line of automated plastic extruding equipment, purchased for $3.5 million in January 2017, was originally estimated to have a useful life of 8 years and a salvage value of $300,000. Depreciation has been recorded for 2 years on that basis. Robert wants the estimated life changed to 12 years total, and the straight-line method continued. Alexis is hesitant to make the change, believing it is unethical to increase net income in this manner. Robert says, "Hey, the life is only an estimate, and I've heard that our competition uses a 12-year life on their production equipment."

Instructions
(a) Who are the stakeholders in this situation?
(b) Is the change in asset life unethical, or is it simply a good business practice by an astute president?
(c) What is the effect of Robert Griffin's proposed change on income before taxes in the year of change?

All About You

BYP9-8 The Feature Story at the beginning of the chapter discussed the company **Rent-A-Wreck**. Note that the trade name Rent-A-Wreck is a very important asset to the company, as it creates immediate product identification. As indicated in the chapter, companies invest substantial sums to ensure that their product is well-known to the consumer. Test your knowledge of who owns some famous brands and their impact on the financial statements.

Instructions
(a) Provide an answer to the four multiple-choice questions below.
   (1) Which company owns both Taco Bell and Pizza Hut?
       (a) McDonald's.   (c) Yum Brands.
       (b) CKE.   (d) Wendy's.
   (2) Dairy Queen belongs to:
       (a) Breyer.   (c) GE.
       (b) Berkshire Hathaway.   (d) The Coca-Cola Company.
   (3) Philip Morris, the cigarette maker, is owned by:
       (a) Altria.   (c) Boeing.
       (b) GE.   (d) ExxonMobil.
   (4) AOL, a major Internet provider, belongs to:
       (a) Microsoft.   (c) NBC.
       (b) Cisco.   (d) Time Warner.
(b) How do you think the value of these brands is reported on the appropriate company's balance sheet?

FASB Codification Activity

BYP9-9 If your school has a subscription to the FASB Codification, go to **http://aaahq.org/ascLogin.cfm** to log in and prepare responses to the following.

(a) What does it mean to capitalize an item?
(b) What is the definition provided for an intangible asset?
(c) Your great-uncle, who is a CPA, is impressed that you are taking an accounting class. Based on his experience, he believes that depreciation is something that companies do based on past practice, not on the basis of authoritative guidance. Provide the authoritative literature to support the practice of fixed-asset depreciation.

A Look at IFRS

Compare the accounting for long-lived assets under GAAP and IFRS.

IFRS follows most of the same principles as GAAP in the accounting for property, plant, and equipment. There are, however, some significant differences in the implementation. IFRS allows the use of revaluation of property, plant, and equipment, and it also requires the use of component depreciation. In addition, there are some significant differences in the accounting for both intangible assets and impairments.

Key Points

The following are the key similarities and differences between GAAP and IFRS as related to the recording process for long-lived assets.

Similarities

- The definition for plant assets for both IFRS and GAAP is essentially the same.
- Both IFRS and GAAP follow the historical cost principle when accounting for property, plant, and equipment at date of acquisition. Cost consists of all expenditures necessary to acquire the asset and make it ready for its intended use.
- Under both IFRS and GAAP, interest costs incurred during construction are capitalized. Recently, IFRS converged to GAAP requirements in this area.
- IFRS also views depreciation as an allocation of cost over an asset's useful life. IFRS permits the same depreciation methods (e.g., straight-line, accelerated, and units-of-activity) as GAAP.
- Under both GAAP and IFRS, changes in the depreciation method used and changes in useful life are handled in current and future periods. Prior periods are not affected. GAAP recently conformed to international standards in the accounting for changes in depreciation methods.
- The accounting for subsequent expenditures (such as ordinary repairs and additions) are essentially the same under IFRS and GAAP.
- The accounting for plant asset disposals is essentially the same under IFRS and GAAP.
- Initial costs to acquire natural resources are essentially the same under IFRS and GAAP.
- The definition of intangible assets is essentially the same under IFRS and GAAP.
- The accounting for exchanges of nonmonetary assets has recently converged between IFRS and GAAP. GAAP now requires that gains on exchanges of nonmonetary assets be recognized if the exchange has commercial substance. This is the same framework used in IFRS.

Differences

- IFRS uses the term **residual value** rather than salvage value to refer to an owner's estimate of an asset's value at the end of its useful life for that owner.
- IFRS allows companies to revalue plant assets to fair value at the reporting date. Companies that choose to use the revaluation framework must follow revaluation procedures. If revaluation is used, it must be applied to all assets in a class of assets. Assets that are experiencing rapid price changes must be revalued on an annual basis, otherwise less frequent revaluation is acceptable.

- IFRS requires component depreciation. **Component depreciation** specifies that any significant parts of a depreciable asset that have different estimated useful lives should be separately depreciated. Component depreciation is allowed under GAAP but is seldom used.
- As in GAAP, under IFRS the costs associated with research and development are segregated into the two components. Costs in the research phase are always expensed under both IFRS and GAAP. Under IFRS, however, costs in the development phase are capitalized as Development Costs once technological feasibility is achieved.
- IFRS permits revaluation of intangible assets (except for goodwill). GAAP prohibits revaluation of intangible assets.

Looking to the Future

The IASB and FASB have identified a project that would consider expanded recognition of internally generated intangible assets. IFRS permits more recognition of intangibles compared to GAAP.

IFRS Practice

IFRS Self-Test Questions

1. Which of the following statements is **correct**?
    (a) Both IFRS and GAAP permit revaluation of property, plant, and equipment and intangible assets (except for goodwill).
    (b) IFRS permits revaluation of property, plant, and equipment and intangible assets (except for goodwill).
    (c) Both IFRS and GAAP permit revaluation of property, plant, and equipment but not intangible assets.
    (d) GAAP permits revaluation of property, plant, and equipment but not intangible assets.

2. Research and development costs are:
    (a) expensed under GAAP.
    (b) expensed under IFRS.
    (c) expensed under both GAAP and IFRS.
    (d) None of the above.

3. Under IFRS, value-in-use is defined as:
    (a) net realizable value.
    (b) fair value.
    (c) future cash flows discounted to present value.
    (d) total future undiscounted cash flows.

IFRS Exercises

IFRS9-1 What is component depreciation, and when must it be used?

IFRS9-2 What is revaluation of plant assets? When should revaluation be applied?

IFRS9-3 Some product development expenditures are recorded as development expenses and others as development costs. Explain the difference between these accounts and how a company decides which classification is appropriate.

International Financial Statement Analysis: Louis Vuitton

IFRS9-4 The financial statements of Louis Vuitton are presented in Appendix F. Instructions for accessing and using the company's complete annual report, including the notes to its financial statements, are also provided in Appendix F.

Instructions

Use the company's annual report to answer the following questions.

(a) According to the notes to the financial statements, what method or methods does the company use to depreciate "property, plant, and equipment?" What rate(s) does it use to depreciate property, plant, and equipment?

(b) Using the notes to the financial statements, identify the brands and trade names that are most significant to the company.

(c) Using the notes to the financial statements, determine (1) the balance in Accumulated Amortization and Impairment for intangible assets (other than goodwill), and (2) the balance in Accumulated Depreciation for property, plant, and equipment. (Round your amounts to the nearest thousand.)

Answers to IFRS Self-Test Questions
1. b   **2.** a

10 Liabilities

CHAPTER PREVIEW Inventor-entrepreneur Wilbert Murdock, as the Feature Story below notes, had to use multiple credit cards to finance his business ventures. Murdock's credit card debts would be classified as **current liabilities** because they are due every month. Yet, by making minimal payments and paying high interest each month, Murdock used this credit source long-term. Some credit card balances remain outstanding for years as they accumulate interest.

FEATURE STORY

Financing His Dreams

What would you do if you had a great idea for a new product but couldn't come up with the cash to get the business off the ground? Small businesses often cannot attract investors. Nor can they obtain traditional debt financing through bank loans or bond issuances. Instead, they often resort to unusual, and costly, forms of nontraditional financing.

Such was the case for Wilbert Murdock. Murdock grew up in a New York housing project and always had great ambitions. His entrepreneurial spirit led him into some business ventures that failed: a medical diagnostic tool, a device to eliminate carpal tunnel syndrome, custom-designed sneakers, and a device to keep people from falling asleep while driving.

Another idea was computerized golf clubs that analyze a golfer's swing and provide immediate feedback. Murdock saw great potential in the idea. Many golfers are willing to shell out considerable sums of money for devices that might improve their game. But Murdock had no cash to develop his product, and banks and other lenders had shied away.

Rather than give up, Murdock resorted to credit cards—in a big way. He quickly owed $25,000 to credit card companies.

While funding a business with credit cards might sound unusual, it isn't. A recent study found that one-third of businesses with fewer than 20 employees financed at least part of their operations with credit cards. As Murdock explained, credit cards are an appealing way to finance a start-up because "credit-card companies don't care how the money is spent." However, they do care how they are paid. And so Murdock faced high interest charges and a barrage of credit card collection letters.

Murdock's debt forced him to sacrifice nearly everything in order to keep his business afloat. His car stopped running, he barely had enough money to buy food, and he lived and worked out of a dimly lit apartment in his mother's basement. Through it all he tried to maintain a positive spirit, joking that, if he becomes successful, he might some day get to appear in an American Express commercial.

Source: Rodney Ho, "Banking on Plastic: To Finance a Dream, Many Entrepreneurs Binge on Credit Cards," *Wall Street Journal* (March 9, 1998), p. A1.

Cary Westfall/iStockphoto

CHAPTER OUTLINE

Learning Objectives

1 Explain how to account for current liabilities.

- What is a current liability?
- Notes payable
- Sales taxes payable
- Payroll and payroll taxes payable
- Unearned revenues
- Current maturities of long-term debt

DO IT!
- **1a** Wages and Payroll Taxes
- **1b** Current Liabilities

2 Describe the major characteristics of bonds.

- Types of bonds
- Issuing procedures
- Bond trading
- Determining the market price of a bond

DO IT!
- **2** Bond Terminology

3 Explain how to account for bond transactions.

- Issuing bonds at face value
- Discount or premium on bonds
- Issuing bonds at a discount
- Issuing bonds at a premium
- Redeeming and converting bonds

DO IT!
- **3a** Bond Issuance
- **3b** Bond Redemption

4 Explain how to account for long-term notes payable.

- Long-term notes payable
- Mortgage notes payable

DO IT!
- **4** Long-Term Notes

5 Discuss how liabilities are reported and analyzed.

- Presentation
- Use of ratios
- Debt and equity financing

DO IT!
- **5** Analyzing Liabilities

Go to the ***REVIEW AND PRACTICE*** section at the end of the chapter for a review of key concepts and practice applications with solutions.

Visit **WileyPLUS with ORION** for additional tutorials and practice opportunities.

What Is a Current Liability?

You have learned that liabilities are defined as "creditors' claims on total assets" and as "existing debts and obligations." Companies must settle or pay these claims, debts, and obligations at some time in the future by transferring assets or services. The future date on which they are due or payable (the maturity date) is a significant feature of liabilities.

As explained in Chapter 4, a **current liability** is a debt that a company expects to pay within one year or the operating cycle, whichever is longer. Debts that do not meet this criterion are **long-term liabilities**.

Financial statement users want to know whether a company's obligations are current or long-term. A company that has more current liabilities than current assets often lacks liquidity, or short-term debt-paying ability. In addition, users want to know the types of liabilities a company has. If a company declares bankruptcy, a specific, predetermined order of payment to creditors exists. Thus, the amount and type of liabilities are of critical importance.

The different types of current liabilities include notes payable, accounts payable, unearned revenues, and accrued liabilities such as taxes, salaries and wages, and interest payable. In the sections that follow, we discuss common types of current liabilities.

Helpful Hint
In previous chapters, we explained the entries for accounts payable and the adjusting entries for some current liabilities.

Notes Payable

Companies record obligations in the form of written notes as **notes payable**. Notes payable are often used instead of accounts payable because they give the lender formal proof of the obligation in case legal remedies are needed to collect the debt. Companies frequently issue notes payable to meet short-term financing needs. Notes payable usually require the borrower to pay interest.

Notes are issued for varying periods of time. **Those due for payment within one year of the balance sheet date are usually classified as current liabilities.**

To illustrate the accounting for notes payable, assume that First National Bank agrees to lend $100,000 on September 1, 2017, if Cole Williams Co. signs a $100,000, 12%, four-month note maturing on January 1. When a company issues an interest-bearing note, the amount of assets it receives upon issuance of the note generally equals the note's face value. Cole Williams therefore will receive $100,000 cash and will make the following journal entry.

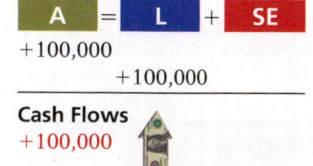

A	=	L	+	SE
+100,000				
		+100,000		

Cash Flows
+100,000

Sept. 1	Cash		100,000	
	Notes Payable			100,000
	(To record issuance of 12%, 4-month note to First National Bank)			

Interest accrues over the life of the note, and the company must periodically record that accrual. If Cole Williams prepares financial statements annually, it makes an adjusting entry at December 31 to recognize interest expense and interest payable of $4,000 ($100,000 × 12% × 4/12). Illustration 10-1 shows the formula for computing interest and its application to Cole Williams' note.

Illustration 10-1
Formula for computing interest

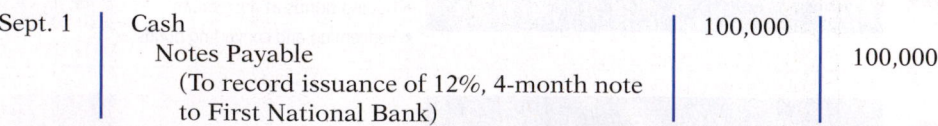

Face Value of Note	×	Annual Interest Rate	×	Time in Terms of One Year	=	Interest
$100,000	×	12%	×	4/12	=	$4,000

Cole Williams makes an adjusting entry as follows.

Dec. 31	Interest Expense	4,000	
	Interest Payable		4,000
	(To accrue interest for 4 months on		
	First National Bank note)		

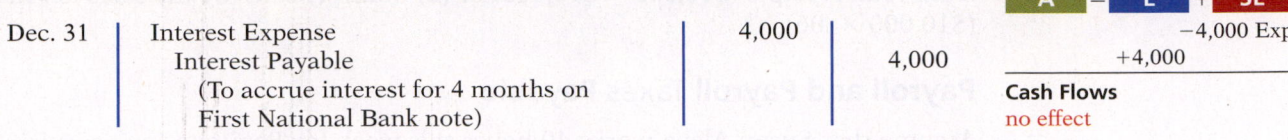

A = L + SE
−4,000 Exp
+4,000

Cash Flows
no effect

In the December 31 financial statements, the current liabilities section of the balance sheet will show notes payable $100,000 and interest payable $4,000. In addition, the company will report interest expense of $4,000 under "Other expenses and losses" in the income statement. If Cole Williams prepared financial statements monthly, the adjusting entry at the end of each month would be $1,000 ($100,000 × 12% × 1/12).

At maturity (January 1, 2018), Cole Williams must pay the face value of the note ($100,000) plus $4,000 interest ($100,000 × 12% × 4/12). It records payment of the note and accrued interest as follows.

Jan. 1	Notes Payable	100,000	
	Interest Payable	4,000	
	Cash		104,000
	(To record payment of First National Bank		
	interest-bearing note and accrued interest		
	at maturity)		

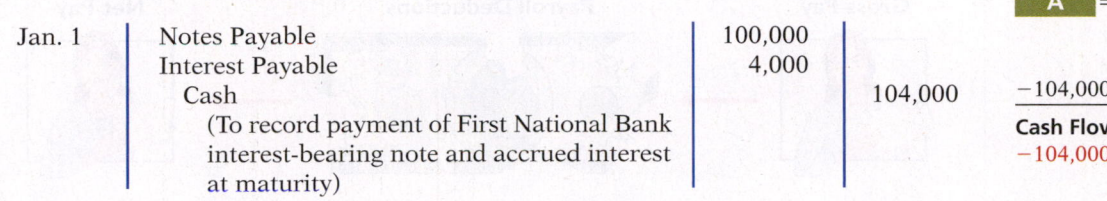

A = L + SE
−100,000
−4,000
−104,000

Cash Flows
−104,000

Sales Taxes Payable

Many of the products we purchase at retail stores are subject to sales taxes. Many states also are now collecting sales taxes on purchases made on the Internet as well. Sales taxes are expressed as a percentage of the sales price. The selling company collects the tax from the customer when the sale occurs. Periodically (usually monthly), the retailer remits the collections to the state's department of revenue. Collecting sales taxes is important. For example, the State of New York recently sued **Sprint Corporation** for $300 million for its alleged failure to collect sales taxes on phone calls.

Under most state sales tax laws, the selling company must enter separately in the cash register the amount of the sale and the amount of the sales tax collected. (Gasoline sales are a major exception.) The company then uses the cash register readings to credit Sales Revenue and Sales Taxes Payable. For example, if the March 25 cash register reading for Cooley Grocery shows sales of $10,000 and sales taxes of $600 (sales tax rate of 6%), the journal entry is as follows.

Helpful Hint
For point-of-sale systems, the company receives sales information through the computer network.

Mar. 25	Cash	10,600	
	Sales Revenue		10,000
	Sales Taxes Payable		600
	(To record daily sales and sales taxes)		

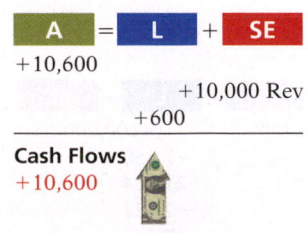

A = L + SE
+10,600
+10,000 Rev
+600

Cash Flows
+10,600

When the company remits the taxes to the taxing agency, it debits Sales Taxes Payable and credits Cash. The company does not report sales taxes as an expense. It simply forwards to the government the amount paid by the customers. Thus, Cooley Grocery serves only as a **collection agent** for the taxing authority.

Sometimes companies do not enter sales taxes separately in the cash register. To determine the amount of sales in such cases, divide total receipts by 100% plus the sales tax percentage. For example, assume that Cooley Grocery enters total receipts of $10,600. The receipts from the sales are equal to the sales price (100%) plus the tax percentage (6% of sales), or 1.06 times the sales total. We can compute the sales amount as follows.

$$\$10,600 \div 1.06 = \$10,000$$

Thus, we can find the sales tax amount of $600 by either (1) subtracting sales from total receipts ($10,600 − $10,000) or (2) multiply sales by the sales tax rate ($10,000 × .06).

Payroll and Payroll Taxes Payable

Assume that Susan Alena works 40 hours this week for Pepitone Inc., earning a wage of $10 per hour. Will Susan receive a $400 check at the end of the week? Not likely. The reason: Pepitone is required to withhold amounts from her wages to pay various governmental authorities. For example, Pepitone will withhold amounts for Social Security taxes[1] and for federal and state income taxes. If these withholdings total $100, Susan will receive a check for only $300. Illustration 10-2 summarizes the types of payroll deductions that normally occur for most companies.

Illustration 10-2
Payroll deductions

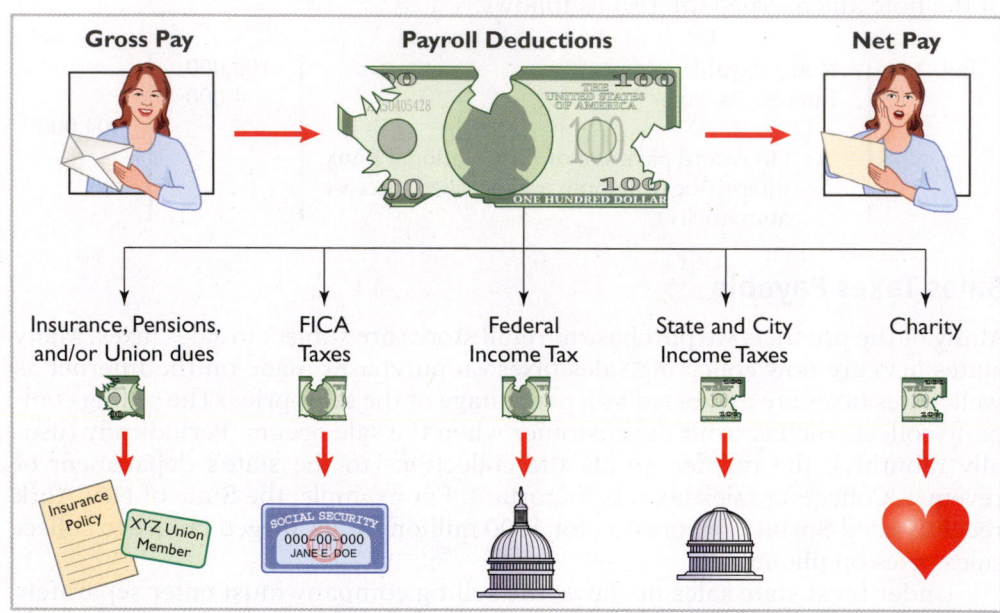

As a result of these deductions, companies withhold from employee pay-checks amounts that must be paid to other parties. Pepitone therefore has incurred a liability to pay these third parties and must report this liability in its balance sheet.

As a second illustration, assume that Cargo Corporation records its payroll for the week of March 7 with the journal entry shown below.

			A	=	L	+	SE

−100,000 Exp
+7,650
+21,864
+2,922
+67,564

Cash Flows
no effect

Mar. 7	Salaries and Wages Expense	100,000	
	FICA Taxes Payable		7,650
	Federal Income Taxes Payable		21,864
	State Income Taxes Payable		2,922
	Salaries and Wages Payable		67,564
	(To record payroll and withholding taxes for the week ending March 7)		

---

[1]Social Security taxes are commonly called FICA taxes. In 1937, Congress enacted the Federal Insurance Contribution Act (FICA). As can be seen in the journal entry and the payroll tax journal entry on the next page, the employee and employer must make equal contributions to Social Security. The Social Security rate in 2014 was 7.65%. *Our examples and homework use 7.65% for both.*

Cargo then records payment of this payroll on March 7 as follows.

Mar. 7	Salaries and Wages Payable	67,564	
	Cash		67,564
	(To record payment of the March 7 payroll)		

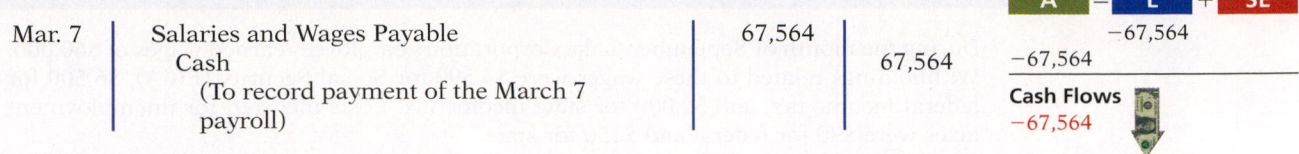

A = L + SE
−67,564
−67,564

Cash Flows
−67,564

In this case, Cargo reports $100,000 in salaries and wages expense. In addition, it reports liabilities for the salaries and wages payable as well as liabilities to governmental agencies. Rather than pay the employees $100,000, Cargo instead must withhold the taxes and make the tax payments directly. In summary, Cargo is essentially serving as a tax collector.

In addition to the liabilities incurred as a result of withholdings, employers also incur a second type of payroll-related liability. With every payroll, the employer incurs liabilities to pay various **payroll taxes** levied upon the employer. These payroll taxes include the **employer's share** of Social Security (FICA) taxes and state and federal unemployment taxes. Based on Cargo Corp.'s $100,000 payroll, the company would record the employer's expense and liability for these payroll taxes as follows.

Mar. 7	Payroll Tax Expense	13,850	
	FICA Taxes Payable		7,650
	Federal Unemployment Taxes Payable		800
	State Unemployment Taxes Payable		5,400
	(To record employer's payroll taxes on March 7 payroll)		

A = L + SE
−13,850 Exp
+7,650
+800
+5,400

Cash Flows
no effect

Companies classify the payroll and payroll tax liability accounts as current liabilities because they must be paid to employees or remitted to taxing authorities periodically and in the near term. Taxing authorities impose substantial fines and penalties on employers if the withholding and payroll taxes are not computed correctly and paid on time.

ANATOMY OF A FRAUD

Art was a custodial supervisor for a large school district. The district was supposed to employ between 35 and 40 regular custodians, as well as 3 or 4 substitute custodians to fill in when regular custodians were absent. Instead, in addition to the regular custodians, Art "hired" 77 substitutes. In fact, almost none of these people worked for the district. Instead, Art submitted time cards for these people, collected their checks at the district office, and personally distributed the checks to the "employees." If a substitute's check was for $1,200, that person would cash the check, keep $200, and pay Art $1,000.

Total take: $150,000

THE MISSING CONTROLS

Human resource controls. Thorough background checks should be performed. No employees should begin work until they have been approved by the Board of Education and entered into the payroll system. No employees should be entered into the payroll system until they have been approved by a supervisor. All paychecks should be distributed directly to employees at the official school locations by designated employees.

Independent internal verification. Budgets should be reviewed monthly to identify situations where actual costs significantly exceed budgeted amounts.

Source: Adapted from Wells, *Fraud Casebook* (2007), pp. 164–171.

DO IT! 1a — Wages and Payroll Taxes

During the month of September, Lake Corporation's employees earned wages of $60,000. Withholdings related to these wages were $4,590 for Social Security (FICA), $6,500 for federal income tax, and $2,000 for state income tax. Costs incurred for unemployment taxes were $90 for federal and $150 for state.

Prepare the September 30 journal entries for (a) salaries and wages expense and salaries and wages payable, assuming that all September wages will be paid in October, and (b) the company's payroll tax expense.

Solution

Action Plan

✔ Remember that wages earned are an expense to the company, but withholdings reduce the amount due to be paid to the employee.

✔ Payroll taxes are taxes the company incurs related to its employees.

(a) To determine wages payable, reduce wages expense by the withholdings for FICA, federal income tax, and state income tax.

Sept. 30	Salaries and Wages Expense	60,000	
	FICA Taxes Payable		4,590
	Federal Income Taxes Payable		6,500
	State Income Taxes Payable		2,000
	Salaries and Wages Payable		46,910

(b) Payroll taxes would be for the company's share of FICA, as well as for federal and state unemployment tax.

Sept. 30	Payroll Tax Expense	4,830	
	FICA Taxes Payable		4,590
	Federal Unemployment Taxes Payable		90
	State Unemployment Taxes Payable		150

Related exercise material: **BE10-5, BE10-6, E10-5, E10-6, and DO IT! 10-1a.**

Unearned Revenues

A magazine publisher, such as **Sports Illustrated**, receives customers' checks when they order magazines. An airline company, such as **Southwest Airlines**, often receives cash when it sells tickets for future flights. Season tickets for concerts, sporting events, and theater programs are also paid for in advance. How do companies account for unearned revenues that are received before goods are delivered or services are performed?

1. When a company receives the advance payment, it debits Cash and credits a current liability account identifying the source of the unearned revenue.

2. When the company recognizes revenue, it debits an unearned revenue account and credits a revenue account.

To illustrate, assume that Superior University sells 10,000 season football tickets at $50 each for its five-game home schedule. The university makes the following entry for the sale of season tickets.

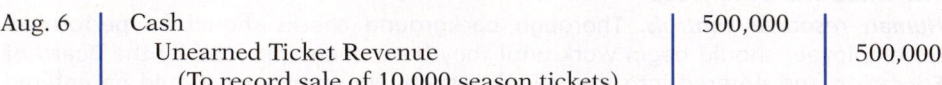

Aug. 6	Cash	500,000	
	Unearned Ticket Revenue		500,000
	(To record sale of 10,000 season tickets)		

As each game is completed, Superior records the recognition of revenue with the following entry.

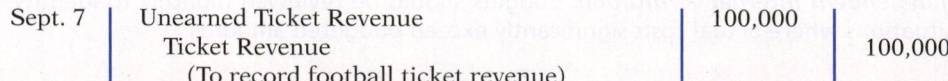

Sept. 7	Unearned Ticket Revenue	100,000	
	Ticket Revenue		100,000
	(To record football ticket revenue)		

The account Unearned Ticket Revenue represents unearned revenue, and Superior reports it as a current liability. As the school recognizes revenue, it

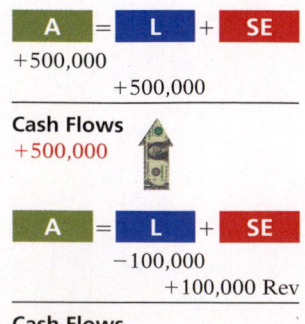

reclassifies the amount from unearned revenue to Ticket Revenue. Unearned revenue is substantial for some companies. In the airline industry, for example, tickets sold for future flights represent almost 50% of total current liabilities. At **United Air Lines**, unearned ticket revenue is its largest current liability, recently amounting to over $1 billion.

Illustration 10-3 shows specific unearned revenue and revenue accounts used in selected types of businesses.

Illustration 10-3
Unearned revenue and revenue accounts

Type of Business	Account Title	
	Unearned Revenue	**Revenue**
Airline	Unearned Ticket Revenue	Ticket Revenue
Magazine publisher	Unearned Subscription Revenue	Subscription Revenue
Hotel	Unearned Rent Revenue	Rent Revenue

Current Maturities of Long-Term Debt

Companies often have a portion of long-term debt that comes due in the current year. That amount is considered a current liability. As an example, assume that Wendy Construction issues a five-year, interest-bearing $25,000 note on January 1, 2017. This note specifies that each January 1, starting January 1, 2018, Wendy should pay $5,000 of the note. When the company prepares financial statements on December 31, 2017, it should report $5,000 as a current liability and $20,000 as a long-term liability. (The $5,000 amount is the portion of the note that is due to be paid within the next 12 months.) Companies often identify current maturities of long-term debt on the balance sheet as **long-term debt due within one year**. In a recent year, **General Motors** had $724 million of such debt.

It is not necessary to prepare an adjusting entry to recognize the current maturity of long-term debt. At the balance sheet date, all obligations due within one year are classified as current, and all other obligations as long-term.

DO IT! **1b**　**Current Liabilities**

You and several classmates are studying for the next accounting examination. They ask you to answer the following questions.

1. If cash is borrowed on a $50,000, 6-month, 12% note on September 1, how much interest expense would be incurred by December 31?

2. How is the sales tax amount determined when the cash register total includes sales taxes?

3. If $15,000 is collected in advance on November 1 for 3 months' rent, what amount of rent revenue should be recognized by December 31?

Solution

1. $50,000 × 12% × 4/12 = $2,000
2. First, divide the total cash register receipts by 100% plus the sales tax percentage to find the sales revenue amount. Second, subtract the sales revenue amount from the total cash register receipts to determine the sales taxes.
3. $15,000 × 2/3 = $10,000

Related exercise material: **BE10-1, BE10-2, BE10-3, BE10-4, E10-1, E10-2, E10-3, E10-4,** and **DO IT!** **10-1b.**

Action Plan

✔ Use the interest formula: Face value of note × Annual interest rate × Time in terms of one year.

✔ Divide total receipts by 100% plus the tax rate to determine sales revenue; then subtract sales revenue from the total receipts.

✔ Determine what fraction of the total unearned rent should be recognized this year.

Long-term liabilities are obligations that a company expects to pay more than one year in the future. In this section, we explain the accounting for the principal types of obligations reported in the long-term liabilities section of the balance sheet. These obligations often are in the form of bonds or long-term notes.

Bonds are a form of interest-bearing note payable issued by corporations, universities, and governmental agencies. Bonds, like common stock, are sold in small denominations (usually $1,000 or multiples of $1,000). As a result, bonds attract many investors. When a corporation issues bonds, it is borrowing money. The person who buys the bonds (the bondholder) is investing in bonds.

Types of Bonds

Bonds may have many different features. In the following sections, we describe the types of bonds commonly issued.

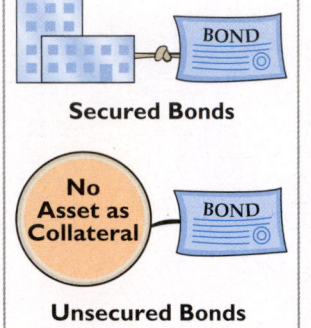

Secured Bonds

Unsecured Bonds

SECURED AND UNSECURED BONDS

Secured bonds have specific assets of the issuer pledged as collateral for the bonds. A bond secured by real estate, for example, is called a **mortgage bond**. A bond secured by specific assets set aside to redeem (retire) the bonds is called a **sinking fund bond**.

Unsecured bonds, also called **debenture bonds**, are issued against the general credit of the borrower. Companies with good credit ratings use these bonds extensively. For example, at one time, **DuPont** reported over $2 billion of debenture bonds outstanding.

CONVERTIBLE AND CALLABLE BONDS

Bonds that can be converted into common stock at the bondholder's option are **convertible bonds**. The conversion feature generally is attractive to bond buyers. Bonds that the issuing company can redeem (buy back) at a stated dollar amount prior to maturity are **callable bonds**. A call feature is included in nearly all corporate bond issues.

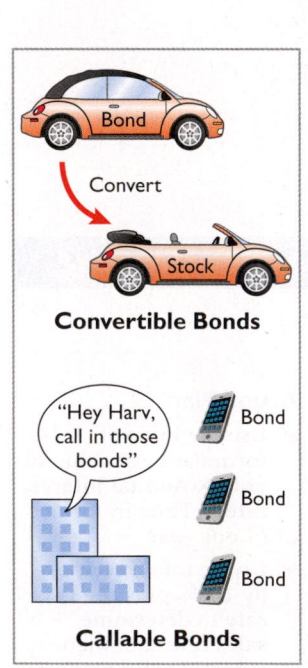

Convertible Bonds

Callable Bonds

Issuing Procedures

State laws grant corporations the power to issue bonds. Both the board of directors and stockholders usually must approve bond issues. **In authorizing the bond issue, the board of directors must stipulate the number of bonds to be authorized, total face value, and contractual interest rate.** The total bond authorization often exceeds the number of bonds the company originally issues. This gives the corporation the flexibility to issue more bonds, if needed, to meet future cash requirements.

The **face value** is the amount of principal due at the maturity date. The **maturity date** is the date that the final payment is due to the investor from the issuing company. The **contractual interest rate**, often referred to as the **stated rate**, is the rate used to determine the amount of cash interest the issuing company pays and the investor receives. Usually, the contractual rate is stated as an annual rate.

The terms of the bond issue are set forth in a legal document called a **bond indenture**. The indenture shows the terms and summarizes the rights of the bondholders and their trustees, and the obligations of the issuing company. The **trustee** (usually a financial institution) keeps records of each bondholder, maintains custody of unissued bonds, and holds conditional title to pledged property.

In addition, the issuing company arranges for the printing of **bond certificates**. The indenture and the certificate are separate documents. As shown in Illustration 10-4, a bond certificate provides the following information: name of the issuer, face value, contractual interest rate, and maturity date. An investment company that specializes in selling securities generally sells the bonds for the issuing company.

Illustration 10-4
Bond certificate

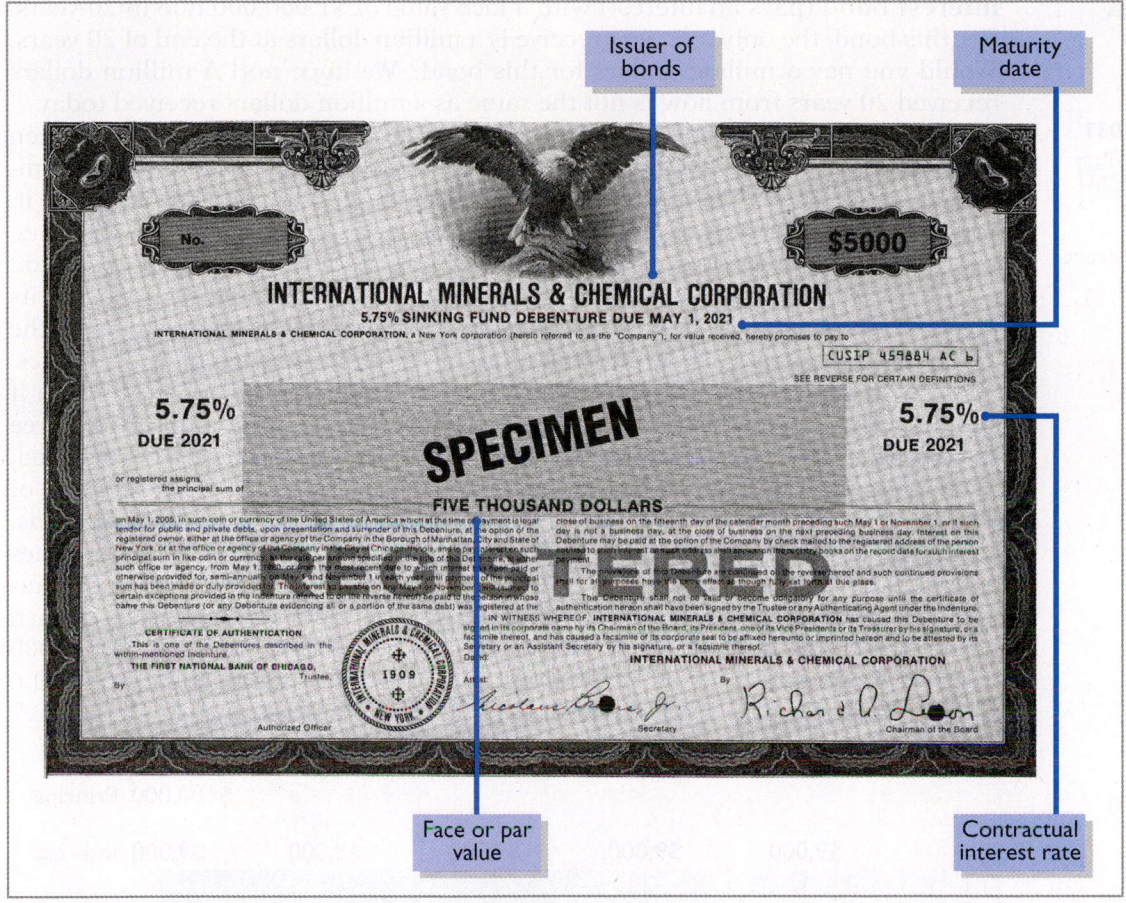

Bond Trading

Bondholders have the opportunity to convert their holdings into cash at any time by selling the bonds at the current market price on national securities exchanges. **Bond prices are quoted as a percentage of the face value of the bond, which is usually $1,000.** A $1,000 bond with a quoted price of 97 means that the selling price of the bond is 97% of face value, or $970. Newspapers and the financial press publish bond prices and trading activity daily, as shown in Illustration 10-5.

Illustration 10-5
Market information for bonds

Bonds	Maturity	Close	Yield	Est. Volume (000)
Boeing Co. 5.125	Feb. 15, 2017	96.595	5.747	33,965

This bond listing indicates that Boeing Co. has outstanding 5.125%, $1,000 bonds that mature in 2017. They currently yield a 5.747% return. On this day, $33,965,000 of these bonds were traded. At the close of trading, the price was 96.595% of face value, or $965.95.

A corporation makes journal entries **only when it issues or buys back bonds**, or when bondholders convert bonds into common stock. For example,

Helpful Hint
The price of a $1,000 bond trading at 95 1/4 is $952.50.

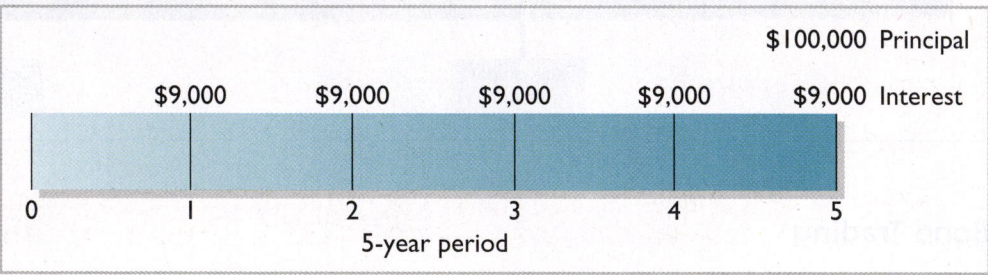

2017

$1 million

≠

2037

$1 million

Same dollars at different times are not equal.

DuPont **does not journalize** transactions between its bondholders and other investors. If Tom Smith sells his DuPont bonds to Faith Jones, DuPont does not journalize the transaction.

Determining the Market Price of a Bond

If you were an investor wanting to purchase a bond, how would you determine how much to pay? To be more specific, assume that Coronet, Inc. issues a **zero-interest bond** (pays no interest) with a face value of $1,000,000 due in 20 years. For this bond, the only cash you receive is a million dollars at the end of 20 years. Would you pay a million dollars for this bond? We hope not! A million dollars received 20 years from now is not the same as a million dollars received today.

The term **time value of money** is used to indicate the relationship between time and money—that a dollar received today is worth more than a dollar promised at some time in the future. If you had $1 million today, you would invest it. From that investment, you would earn interest such that at the end of 20 years, you would have much more than $1 million. Thus, if someone is going to pay you $1 million 20 years from now, you would want to find its equivalent today, or its present value. In other words, you would want to determine the value today of the amount to be received in the future after taking into account current interest rates.

The current market price (present value) of a bond is the value at which it should sell in the marketplace. Market price therefore is a function of the three factors that determine present value: (1) the dollar amounts to be received, (2) the length of time until the amounts are received, and (3) the market rate of interest. The **market interest rate** is the rate investors demand for loaning funds.

To illustrate, assume that Acropolis Company on January 1, 2017, issues $100,000 of 9% bonds, due in five years, with interest payable annually at year-end. The purchaser of the bonds would receive the following two types of cash payments: (1) **principal** of $100,000 to be paid at maturity, and (2) five $9,000 **interest payments** ($100,000 × 9%) over the term of the bonds. Illustration 10-6 shows a time diagram depicting both cash flows.

Illustration 10-6
Time diagram depicting cash flows

					$100,000 Principal
	$9,000	$9,000	$9,000	$9,000	$9,000 Interest

0   1   2   3   4   5

5-year period

The current market price of a bond is equal to the present value of all the future cash payments promised by the bond. Illustration 10-7 lists and totals the present values of these amounts, assuming the market rate of interest is 9%.

Illustration 10-7
Computing the market price of bonds

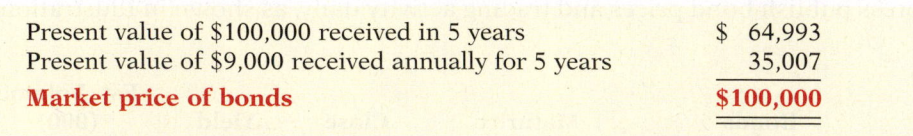

Present value of $100,000 received in 5 years	$ 64,993
Present value of $9,000 received annually for 5 years	35,007
Market price of bonds	**$100,000**

Tables are available to provide the present value numbers to be used, or these values can be determined mathematically or with financial calculators.[2] Appendix D, near the end of the textbook, provides further discussion of the concepts and the mechanics of the time value of money computations.

---

[2]For those knowledgeable in the use of present value tables, the computations in the example shown in Illustration 10-7 are $100,000 × .64993 = $64,993, and $9,000 × 3.88965 = $35,007 (rounded).

Investor Insight

© alphaspirit/Shutterstock

Running Hot!

Recently, the market for bonds was running hot. For example, consider these two large deals: Apple Inc. sold $17 billion of debt, which at the time was the largest corporate bond ever sold. But shortly thereafter, it was beat by Verizon Communications Inc., which sold $49 billion of debt. The following chart highlights the increased issuance of bonds.

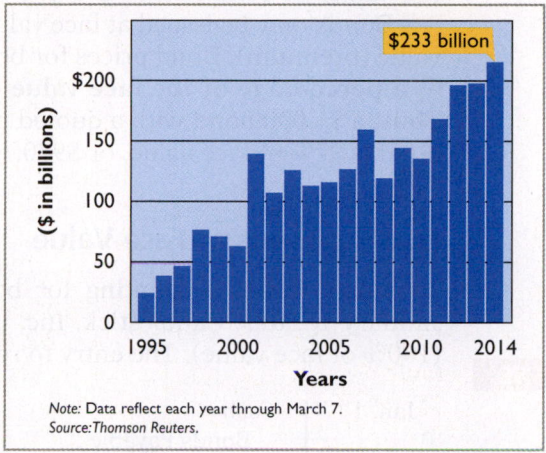

Note: Data reflect each year through March 7.
Source: Thomson Reuters.

As one expert noted about these increases, "Companies are taking advantage of this lower-rate environment in the limited period of time it is going to be around." An interesting aspect of these bond issuances is that companies, like Philip Morris International, Medtronic, Inc., and Simon Properties, are even selling 30-year bonds. These bond issuers are benefitting from "a massive sentiment shift," says one bond expert. The belief that the economy will recover is making investors more comfortable holding longer-term bonds, as they search for investments that offer better returns than U.S. Treasury bonds.

Sources: Vipal Monga, "The Big Number," *Wall Street Journal* (March 20, 2012), p. B5; and Mike Cherney, "Renewed Embrace of Bonds Sparks Boom," *Wall Street Journal* (March 8–9, 2014), p. B5.

What are the advantages for companies of issuing 30-years bonds instead of 5-year bonds? (Go to **WileyPLUS** for this answer and additional questions.)

DO IT! ② Bond Terminology

State whether each of the following statements is true or false. If false, indicate how to correct the statement.

_____ **1.** Mortgage bonds and sinking fund bonds are both examples of secured bonds.

_____ **2.** Unsecured bonds are also known as debenture bonds.

_____ **3.** The stated rate is the rate investors demand for loaning funds.

_____ **4.** The face value is the amount of principal the issuing company must pay at the maturity date.

_____ **5.** The market price of a bond is equal to its maturity value.

Solution

1. True. **2.** True. **3.** False. The stated rate is the contractual interest rate used to determine the amount of cash interest the borrower pays. **4.** True. **5.** False. The market price of a bond is the value at which it should sell in the marketplace. As a result, the market price of the bond and its maturity value are often different.

Action Plan

✔ Review the types of bonds and the basic terms associated with bonds.

Related exercise material: **E10-7 and DO IT! 10-2.**

Explain how to account for bond transactions.

As indicated earlier, a corporation records bond transactions when it issues (sells) or redeems (buys back) bonds and when bondholders convert bonds into common stock. If bondholders sell their bond investments to other investors, the issuing company receives no further money on the transaction, **nor does the issuing company journalize the transaction** (although it does keep records of the names of bondholders in some cases).

Bonds may be issued at face value, below face value (discount), or above face value (premium). Bond prices for both new issues and existing bonds are quoted as **a percentage of the face value of the bond**. **Face value is usually $1,000**. Thus, a $1,000 bond with a quoted price of 97 means that the selling price of the bond is 97% of face value, or $970.

Issuing Bonds at Face Value

To illustrate the accounting for bonds issued at face value, assume that on January 1, 2017, Candlestick, Inc. issues $100,000, five-year, 10% bonds at 100 (100% of face value). The entry to record the sale is as follows.

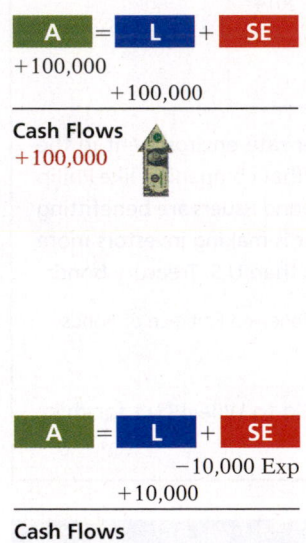

A = L + SE
+100,000
     +100,000

Cash Flows
+100,000

Jan. 1	Cash	100,000	
	Bonds Payable		100,000
	(To record sale of bonds at face value)		

Candlestick reports bonds payable in the long-term liabilities section of the balance sheet because the maturity date is January 1, 2022 (more than one year away).

Over the term (life) of the bonds, companies make entries to record bond interest. Interest on bonds payable is computed in the same manner as interest on notes payable, as explained on page 446. Assume that interest is payable annually on January 1 on the Candlestick bonds. In that case, Candlestick accrues interest of $10,000 ($100,000 × 10%) on December 31. At December 31, Candlestick recognizes the $10,000 of interest expense incurred with the following entry.

A = L + SE
          −10,000 Exp
     +10,000

Cash Flows
no effect

Dec. 31	Interest Expense	10,000	
	Interest Payable		10,000
	(To accrue bond interest)		

The company classifies interest payable as a current liability because it is scheduled for payment within the next year. When Candlestick pays the interest on January 1, 2018, it debits (decreases) Interest Payable and credits (decreases) Cash for $10,000.

Candlestick records the payment on January 1 as follows.

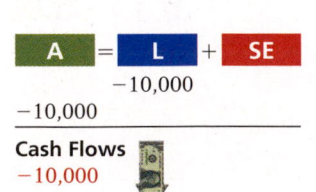

A = L + SE
     −10,000
−10,000

Cash Flows
−10,000

Jan. 1	Interest Payable	10,000	
	Cash		10,000
	(To record payment of bond interest)		

Discount or Premium on Bonds

The previous example assumed that the contractual (stated) interest rate and the market (effective) interest rate paid on the bonds were the same. Recall that the **contractual interest rate** is the rate applied to the face (par) value to arrive at the interest paid in a year. The **market interest rate** is the rate investors demand for loaning funds to the corporation. When the contractual interest rate and the market interest rate are the same, bonds sell **at face value (par value)**.

However, market interest rates change daily. The type of bond issued, the state of the economy, current industry conditions, and the company's performance all affect market interest rates. As a result, contractual and market interest rates often differ. To make bonds salable when the two rates differ, bonds sell below or above face value.

To illustrate, suppose that a company issues 10% bonds at a time when other bonds of similar risk are paying 12%. Investors will not be interested in buying the 10% bonds, so their value will fall below their face value. When a bond is sold for less than its face value, the difference between the face value of a bond and its selling price is called a **discount**. As a result of the decline in the bonds' selling price, the actual interest rate incurred by the company increases to the level of the current market interest rate.

Conversely, if the market rate of interest is **lower than** the contractual interest rate, investors will have to pay more than face value for the bonds. That is, if the market rate of interest is 8% but the contractual interest rate on the bonds is 10%, the price of the bonds will be bid up. When a bond is sold for more than its face value, the difference between the face value and its selling price is called a **premium**. Illustration 10-8 shows these relationships.

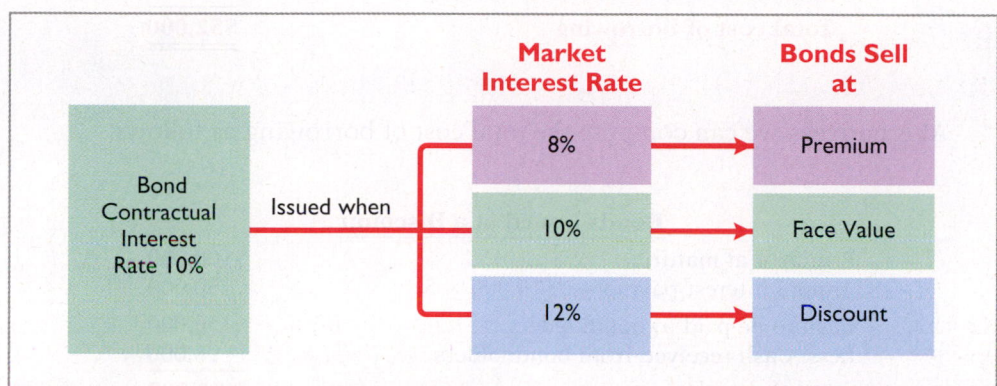

Illustration 10-8
Interest rates and bond prices

Issuance of bonds at an amount different from face value is quite common. By the time a company prints the bond certificates and markets the bonds, it will be a coincidence if the market rate and the contractual rate are the same. Thus, the issuance of bonds at a discount does not mean that the issuer's financial strength is suspect. Conversely, the sale of bonds at a premium does not indicate that the financial strength of the issuer is exceptional.

Issuing Bonds at a Discount

To illustrate issuance of bonds at a discount, assume that on January 1, 2017, Candlestick, Inc. sells $100,000, five-year, 10% bonds for $98,000 (98% of face value). Interest is payable annually on January 1. The entry to record the issuance is as follows.

Jan. 1	Cash	98,000	
	Discount on Bonds Payable	2,000	
	Bonds Payable		100,000
	(To record sale of bonds at a discount)		

Although Discount on Bonds Payable has a debit balance, **it is not an asset.** Rather, it is a **contra account**. This account is **deducted from bonds payable** on the balance sheet, as shown in Illustration 10-9.

Helpful Hint

Discount on Bonds Payable	
Increase	Decrease
Debit	Credit
↓	
Normal	
Balance	

A	=	L	+	SE
+98,000				
		−2,000		
		+100,000		

Cash Flows
+98,000

Illustration 10-9
Statement presentation of discount on bonds payable

CANDLESTICK, INC.
Balance Sheet (partial)

Long-term liabilities
  Bonds payable $100,000
  Less: Discount on bonds payable   **2,000** $98,000

Helpful Hint
Carrying value (book value) of bonds issued at a discount is determined by subtracting the balance of the discount account from the balance of the Bonds Payable account.

The $98,000 represents the **carrying (or book) value** of the bonds. On the date of issue, this amount equals the market price of the bonds.

The issuance of bonds below face value—at a discount—causes the total cost of borrowing to differ from the bond interest paid. That is, the issuing corporation must pay not only the contractual interest rate over the term of the bonds but also the face value (rather than the issuance price) at maturity. Therefore, the difference between the issuance price and face value of the bonds—the discount—is an **additional cost of borrowing**. The company records this additional cost as **interest expense** over the life of the bonds. The total cost of borrowing $98,000 for Candlestick, Inc. is therefore $52,000, computed as follows.

Illustration 10-10
Total cost of borrowing—bonds issued at a discount

Bonds Issued at a Discount	
Annual interest payments	
($100,000 × 10% = $10,000; $10,000 × 5)	$ 50,000
Add: Bond discount ($100,000 − $98,000)	2,000
Total cost of borrowing	**$52,000**

Alternatively, we can compute the total cost of borrowing as follows.

Illustration 10-11
Alternative computation of total cost of borrowing—bonds issued at a discount

Bonds Issued at a Discount	
Principal at maturity	$100,000
Annual interest payments ($10,000 × 5)	50,000
Cash to be paid to bondholders	150,000
Less: Cash received from bondholders	98,000
Total cost of borrowing	**$ 52,000**

To follow the expense recognition principle, companies allocate bond discount to expense in each period in which the bonds are outstanding. This is referred to as **amortizing the discount**. Amortization of the discount **increases** the amount of interest expense reported each period. That is, after the company amortizes the discount, the amount of interest expense it reports in a period will exceed the contractual amount. As shown in Illustration 10-10, for the bonds issued by Candlestick, Inc., total interest expense will exceed the contractual interest by $2,000 over the life of the bonds.

As the discount is amortized, its balance declines. As a consequence, the carrying value of the bonds will increase, until at maturity the carrying value of the bonds equals their face amount. This is shown in Illustration 10-12. Appendices 10A and 10B at the end of this chapter discuss procedures for amortizing bond discount.

Illustration 10-12
Amortization of bond discount

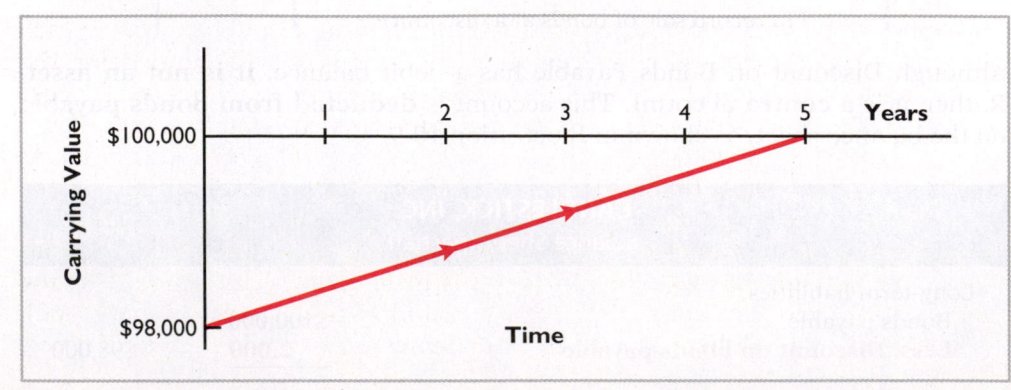

Issuing Bonds at a Premium

To illustrate the issuance of bonds at a premium, we now assume the Candlestick, Inc. bonds described above sell for $102,000 (102% of face value) rather than for $98,000. The entry to record the sale is as follows.

Jan. 1	Cash	102,000	
	Bonds Payable		100,000
	Premium on Bonds Payable		2,000
	(To record sale of bonds at a premium)		

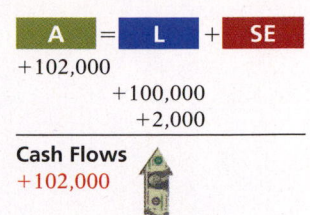

A	=	L	+	SE
+102,000				
		+100,000		
		+2,000		

Cash Flows
+102,000

Candlestick adds the premium on bonds payable **to the bonds payable amount** on the balance sheet, as shown in Illustration 10-13.

CANDLESTICK, INC.
Balance Sheet (partial)

Long-term liabilities		
Bonds payable	$100,000	
Add: Premium on bonds payable	**2,000**	**$102,000**

Illustration 10-13
Statement presentation of bond premium

The sale of bonds above face value causes the total cost of borrowing to be **less than the bond interest paid**. The reason: The borrower is not required to pay the bond premium at the maturity date of the bonds. Thus, the bond premium is considered to be **a reduction in the cost of borrowing** that reduces bond interest over the life of the bonds. The total cost of borrowing $102,000 for Candlestick, Inc. is shown in Illustrations 10-14 and 10-15.

Helpful Hint

Premium on Bonds Payable	
Decrease	Increase
Debit	Credit
	↓
	Normal
	Balance

Bonds Issued at a Premium

Annual interest payments		
($100,000 × 10% = $10,000; $10,000 × 5)	$ 50,000	
Less: Bond premium ($102,000 − $100,000)	2,000	
Total cost of borrowing	**$48,000**	

Illustration 10-14
Total cost of borrowing—bonds issued at a premium

Alternatively, we can compute the cost of borrowing as follows.

Bonds Issued at a Premium

Principal at maturity	$100,000
Annual interest payments ($10,000 × 5)	50,000
Cash to be paid to bondholders	150,000
Less: Cash received from bondholders	102,000
Total cost of borrowing	**$ 48,000**

Illustration 10-15
Alternative computation of total cost of borrowing—bonds issued at a premium

Similar to bond discount, companies allocate bond premium to expense in each period in which the bonds are outstanding. This is referred to as **amortizing the premium**. Amortization of the premium **decreases** the amount of interest expense reported each period. That is, after the company amortizes the premium, the amount of interest expense it reports in a period will be less than the contractual amount. As shown in Illustration 10-14, for the bonds issued by Candlestick, Inc., contractual interest will exceed the interest expense by $2,000 over the life of the bonds.

As the premium is amortized, its balance declines. As a consequence, the carrying value of the bonds will decrease, until at maturity the carrying value of the bonds equals their face amount. This is shown in Illustration 10-16 (page 460). Appendices 10A and 10B at the end of this chapter discuss procedures for amortizing bond premium.

Illustration 10-16
Amortization of bond premium

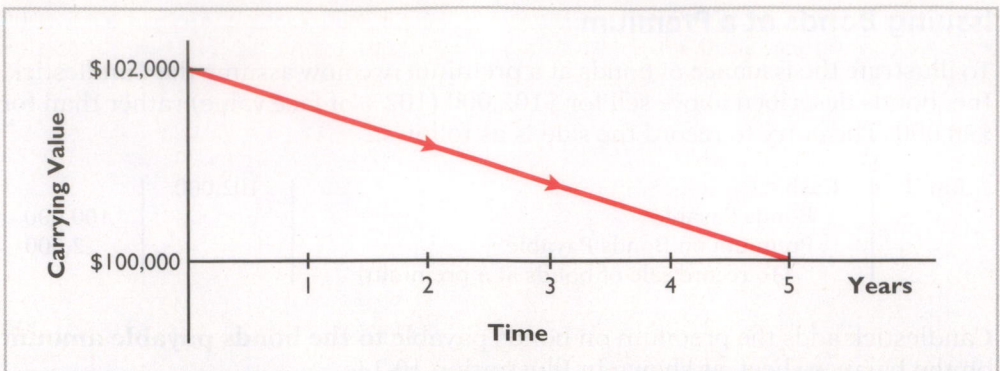

DO IT! 3a   Bond Issuance

Giant Corporation issues $200,000 of bonds for $189,000. (a) Prepare the journal entry to record the issuance of the bonds, and (b) show how the bonds would be reported on the balance sheet at the date of issuance.

Solution

Action Plan

✔ Record cash received, bonds payable at face value, and the difference as a discount or premium.

✔ Report discount as a deduction from bonds payable and premium as an addition to bonds payable.

(a)

Cash	189,000	
Discount on Bonds Payable	11,000	
Bonds Payable		200,000
(To record sale of bonds at a discount)		

(b)

Long-term liabilities		
Bonds payable	$200,000	
Less: Discount on bonds payable	11,000	$189,000

Related exercise material: **BE10-7, BE10-8, BE10-9, BE10-10, BE10-11, E10-8, E10-9, E10-10, and DO IT! 10-3a.**

Redeeming and Converting Bonds

REDEEMING BONDS AT MATURITY

Regardless of the issue price of bonds, the book value of the bonds at maturity will equal their face value. Assuming that the company pays and records separately the interest for the last interest period, Candlestick records the redemption of its bonds at maturity as follows.

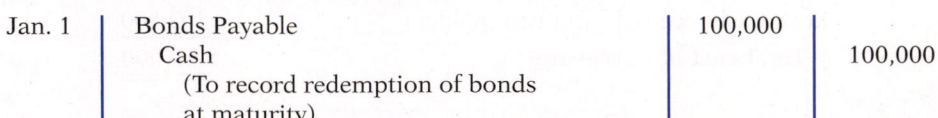

Jan. 1	Bonds Payable	100,000	
	Cash		100,000
	(To record redemption of bonds at maturity)		

REDEEMING BONDS BEFORE MATURITY

Bonds may be redeemed before maturity. A company may decide to redeem bonds before maturity to reduce interest cost and to remove debt from its balance sheet. A company should redeem debt early only if it has sufficient cash resources.

Helpful Hint
If a bond is redeemed prior to its maturity date and its carrying value exceeds its redemption price, this results in a gain.

When a company redeems bonds before maturity, it is necessary to (1) eliminate the carrying value of the bonds at the redemption date, (2) record the cash paid, and (3) recognize the gain or loss on redemption. The **carrying value** of the bonds is the face value of the bonds less any remaining bond discount or plus any remaining bond premium at the redemption date.

To illustrate, assume that Candlestick, Inc. has sold its bonds at a premium. At the end of the fourth period, Candlestick redeems these bonds at 103 after paying the annual interest. Assume that the carrying value of the bonds at the redemption date is $100,400 (principal $100,000 and premium $400). Candlestick records the redemption at the end of the fourth interest period (January 1, 2021) as follows.

Jan. 1	Bonds Payable	100,000	
	Premium on Bonds Payable	400	
	Loss on Bond Redemption	2,600	
	Cash		103,000
	(To record redemption of bonds at 103)		

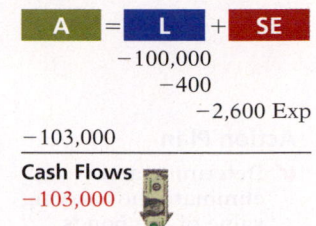

A = L + SE
−100,000
−400
−2,600 Exp
−103,000
Cash Flows
−103,000

Note that the loss of $2,600 is the difference between the cash paid of $103,000 and the carrying value of the bonds of $100,400.

CONVERTING BONDS INTO COMMON STOCK

Convertible bonds have features that are attractive both to bondholders and to the issuer. The conversion often gives bondholders an opportunity to benefit if the market price of the common stock increases substantially. Until conversion, though, the bondholder receives interest on the bond. For the issuer of convertible bonds, the bonds sell at a higher price and pay a lower rate of interest than comparable debt securities without the conversion option. Many corporations, such as Intel, Ford, and Wells Fargo, have convertible bonds outstanding.

When the issuing company records a conversion, the company ignores the current market prices of the bonds and stock. Instead, the company transfers the **carrying value** of the bonds to paid-in capital accounts. **No gain or loss is recognized.**

To illustrate, assume that on July 1, Saunders Associates converts $100,000 bonds sold at face value into 2,000 shares of $10 par value common stock. Both the bonds and the common stock have a market value of $130,000. Saunders makes the following entry to record the conversion.

Helpful Hint
When a company records issuance of common stock, it credits the par value of the shares to Common Stock. It also records in a separate paid-in capital account any excess that is above or below par value.

July 1	Bonds Payable	100,000	
	Common Stock		20,000
	Paid-in Capital in Excess of Par—		
	Common Stock		80,000
	(To record bond conversion)		

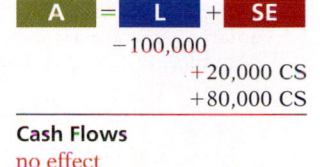

A = L + SE
−100,000
+20,000 CS
+80,000 CS
Cash Flows
no effect

Note that the company does not consider the current market value of the bonds and stock ($130,000) in making the entry. This method of recording the bond conversion is often referred to as the **carrying (or book) value method**.

People, Planet, and Profit Insight   Unilever

© CarpathianPrince/Shutterstock

How About Some Green Bonds?

Unilever recently began producing popular frozen treats such as Magnums and Cornettos, funded by green bonds. Green bonds are debt used to fund activities such as renewable-energy projects. In Unilever's case, the proceeds from the sale of green bonds are used to clean up the company's manufacturing operations and cut waste (such as related to energy consumption).

The use of green bonds has taken off as companies now have guidelines as to how to disclose and report on these green-bond proceeds. These standardized disclosures provide transparency as to how these bonds are used and their effect on overall profitability.

Investors are taking a strong interest in these bonds. Investing companies are installing socially responsible investing teams and have started to integrate sustainability into their investment processes. The disclosures of how companies are using the bond proceeds help investors to make better financial decisions.

Source: Ben Edwards, "Green Bonds Catch On." *Wall Street Journal* (April 3, 2014), p. C5.

Why might standardized disclosure help investors to better understand how proceeds from the sale or issuance of bonds are used? (Go to **WileyPLUS** for this answer and additional questions.)

DO IT! 3b　Bond Redemption

R & B Inc. issued $500,000, 10-year bonds at a discount. Prior to maturity, when the carrying value of the bonds is $496,000, the company redeems the bonds at 98. Prepare the entry to record the redemption of the bonds.

Solution

Action Plan

✔ Determine and eliminate the carrying value of the bonds.

✔ Record the cash paid.

✔ Compute and record the gain or loss (the difference between the first two items).

There is a gain on redemption. The cash paid, $490,000 ($500,000 × 98%), is less than the carrying value of $496,000. The entry is:

Bonds Payable	500,000	
Discount on Bonds Payable		4,000
Gain on Bond Redemption		6,000
Cash		490,000
(To record redemption of bonds at 98)		

Related exercise material: **BE10-12, E10-11, E10-12, and DO IT! 10-3b.**

LEARNING OBJECTIVE **4**　**Explain how to account for long-term notes payable.**

The use of notes payable in long-term debt financing is quite common. **Long-term notes payable** are similar to short-term interest-bearing notes payable except that the term of the notes exceeds one year. In periods of unstable interest rates, lenders may tie the interest rate on long-term notes to changes in the market rate for comparable loans.

A long-term note may be secured by a **mortgage** that pledges title to specific assets as security for a loan. Individuals widely use **mortgage notes payable** to purchase homes, and many small and some large companies use them to acquire plant assets. At one time, approximately 18% of **McDonald's** long-term debt related to mortgage notes on land, buildings, and improvements.

Like other long-term notes payable, the mortgage loan terms may stipulate either a **fixed** or an **adjustable** interest rate. The interest rate on a fixed-rate mortgage remains the same over the life of the mortgage. The interest rate on an adjustable-rate mortgage is adjusted periodically to reflect changes in the market rate of interest. Typically, the terms require the borrower to make equal installment payments over the term of the loan. Each payment consists of (1) interest on the unpaid balance of the loan and (2) a reduction of loan principal. While the total amount of the payment remains constant, the interest decreases each period, and the portion applied to the loan principal increases.

Companies initially record mortgage notes payable at face value. They subsequently make entries for each installment payment. To illustrate, assume that Porter Technology Inc. issues a $500,000, 8%, 20-year mortgage note on December 31, 2017, to obtain needed financing for a new research laboratory. The terms provide for annual installment payments of $50,926 (not including real estate taxes and insurance). The installment payment schedule for the first four years is as follows.

Illustration 10-17
Mortgage installment payment schedule

Interest Period	(A) Cash Payment	(B) Interest Expense (D) × 8%	(C) Reduction of Principal (A) − (B)	(D) Principal Balance (D) − (C)
Issue date				$500,000
1	$50,926	$40,000	$10,926	489,074
2	50,926	39,126	11,800	477,274
3	50,926	38,182	12,744	464,530
4	50,926	37,162	13,764	450,766

Porter records the mortgage loan on December 31, 2017, as follows.

Dec. 31	Cash	500,000	
	Mortgage Payable		500,000
	(To record mortgage loan)		

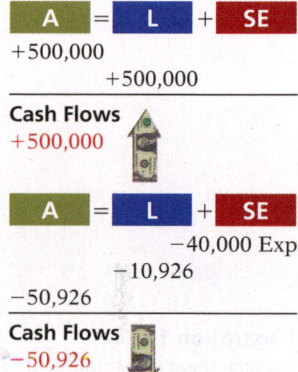

A = L + SE
+500,000
            +500,000
Cash Flows
+500,000

On December 31, 2018, Porter records the first installment payment as follows.

Dec. 31	Interest Expense	40,000	
	Mortgage Payable	10,926	
	Cash		50,926
	(To record annual payment on mortgage)		

A = L + SE
            −40,000 Exp
      −10,926
−50,926
Cash Flows
−50,926

In the balance sheet, the company reports the reduction in principal for the next year as a current liability, and it classifies the remaining unpaid principal balance as a long-term liability. At December 31, 2018, the total liability is $489,074. Of that amount, $11,800 is current and $477,274 ($489,074 − $11,800) is long-term.

DO IT!   4   Long-Term Notes

Cole Research issues a $250,000, 6%, 20-year mortgage note to obtain needed financing for a new lab. The terms call for annual payments of $21,796 each. Prepare the entries to record the mortgage loan and the first payment.

Solution

Cash		250,000	
Mortgage Payable			250,000
(To record mortgage loan)			
Interest Expense		15,000*	
Mortgage Payable		6,796	
Cash			21,796
(To record annual payment on mortgage)			

*Interest expense = $250,000 × 6% = $15,000

Action Plan

✔ Record the issuance of the note as a cash receipt and a liability.

✔ Each installment payment consists of interest and payment of principal.

Related exercise material: **BE10-13, E10-13, and DO IT! 10-4.**

Presentation

As indicated in Chapter 4, current liabilities are the first category under liabilities on the balance sheet. Each of the principal types of current liabilities is listed separately. In addition, companies disclose the terms of notes payable and other key information about the individual items in the notes to the financial statements.

Companies seldom list current liabilities in the order of liquidity. The reason is that varying maturity dates may exist for specific obligations such as notes payable. A more common method of presenting current liabilities is to list them by **order of magnitude**, with the largest ones first. Or, as a matter of custom, many companies show notes payable first and then accounts payable, regardless of amount. Then the remaining current liabilities are listed by magnitude. (*Use this approach in your homework.*) Illustration 10-18 provides an adapted excerpt from **Caterpillar Inc.**'s balance sheet, which illustrates its order of presentation.

Illustration 10-18
Balance sheet presentation of current liabilities

Real World	CATERPILLAR INC. Balance Sheet December 31, 2013 (in millions)	
Assets		
Current assets		$38,335
Property, plant and equipment (net)		17,075
Other long-term assets		29,486
Total assets		$84,896
Liabilities and Stockholders' Equity		
Current liabilities		
Short-term borrowings (notes payable)		$ 3,679
Accounts payable		6,560
Accrued expenses		3,493
Accrued wages, salaries, and employee benefits		1,622
Customer advances		2,360
Dividends payable		382
Other current liabilities		1,849
Long-term debt due within one year		7,352
Total current liabilities		27,297
Noncurrent liabilities		36,721
Total liabilities		64,018
Stockholders' equity		20,878
Total liabilities and stockholders' equity		$84,896

Helpful Hint
For other examples of current liabilities sections, refer to the **PepsiCo** and **Coca-Cola** balance sheets in Appendices B and C.

Companies report long-term liabilities in a separate section of the balance sheet immediately following current liabilities, as shown in Illustration 10-19. Alternatively, companies may present summary data in the balance sheet, with detailed data (interest rates, maturity dates, conversion privileges, and assets pledged as collateral) shown in a supporting schedule.

Illustration 10-19
Balance sheet presentation of long-term liabilities

LAX CORPORATION Balance Sheet (partial)		
Long-term liabilities		
Bonds payable 10% due in 2022	$1,000,000	
Less: Discount on bonds payable	80,000	$ 920,000
Mortgage payable, 11%, due in 2028 and secured by plant assets		500,000
Total long-term liabilities		$1,420,000

Companies report the current maturities of long-term debt under current liabilities if they are to be paid within one year or the operating cycle, whichever is longer.

Use of Ratios

Use of current and noncurrent classifications makes it possible to analyze a company's liquidity. **Liquidity** refers to the ability to pay maturing obligations and meet unexpected needs for cash. The relationship of current assets to current liabilities is critical in analyzing liquidity. We can express this relationship as a dollar amount (working capital) and as a ratio (the current ratio).

The excess of current assets over current liabilities is **working capital**. Illustration 10-20 shows the formula for the computation of **Caterpillar**'s working capital (dollar amounts in millions).

Illustration 10-20
Working capital formula and computation

Current Assets	−	Current Liabilities	=	Working Capital
$38,335	−	$27,297	=	**$11,038**

As an absolute dollar amount, working capital offers limited informational value. For example, $1 million of working capital may be more than needed for a small company but inadequate for a large corporation. Also, $1 million of working capital may be adequate for a company at one time but inadequate at another time.

The **current ratio** permits us to compare the liquidity of different-sized companies and of a single company at different times. The current ratio is calculated as current assets divided by current liabilities. Illustration 10-21 shows the formula for this ratio, along with its computation using Caterpillar's current asset and current liability data (dollar amounts in millions).

Illustration 10-21
Current ratio formula and computation

Current Assets	÷	Current Liabilities	=	Current Ratio
$38,335	÷	$27,297	=	**1.40:1**

Historically, companies and analysts considered a current ratio of 2:1 to be the standard for a good credit rating. In recent years, however, many healthy companies have maintained ratios well below 2:1 by improving management of their current assets and liabilities. Caterpillar's ratio of 1.40:1 is adequate but certainly below the standard of 2:1.

Next, we look at two ratios that provide information about a company's debt-paying ability and long-run solvency. Long-term creditors and stockholders are interested in a company's long-run solvency. Of particular interest is the company's ability to pay interest as it comes due and to repay the face value of the debt at maturity.

ETHICS NOTE

Some companies try to minimize the amount of debt reported on their balance sheet by not reporting certain types of commitments as liabilities. This subject is of intense interest in the financial community.

The **debt to assets ratio** measures the percentage of the total assets provided by creditors. It is computed by dividing total liabilities (both current and long-term liabilities) by total assets. To illustrate, we use data from a recent **Kellogg Company** annual report. The company reported total liabilities of $8,925 million, total assets of $11,200 million, interest expense of $295 million, income taxes of $476 million, and net income of $1,208 million. As shown in Illustration 10-22, Kellogg's debt to assets ratio is 79.7%. The higher the percentage of debt to assets, the greater the risk that the company may be unable to meet its maturing obligation.

Illustration 10-22
Debt to assets ratio

Total Liabilities	÷	Total Assets	=	Debt to Assets Ratio
$8,925	÷	$11,200	=	**79.7%**

Times interest earned indicates the company's ability to meet interest payments as they come due. It is computed by dividing the sum of net income, interest expense, and income tax expense by interest expense. As shown in Illustration 10-23, Kellogg's times interest earned is 6.71 times. This interest coverage is considered safe.

Illustration 10-23
Times interest earned

Net Income + Interest Expense + Income Tax Expense	÷	Interest Expense	=	Times Interest Earned
$1,208 + $295 + $476	÷	$295	=	**6.71 times**

Investor Insight

Paul Fleet/Alamy

"Covenant-Lite" Debt

In many corporate loans and bond issuances, the lending agreement specifies debt covenants. These covenants typically are specific financial measures, such as minimum levels of retained earnings, cash flows, times interest earned, or other measures that a company must maintain during the life of the loan. If the company violates a covenant, it is considered to have violated the loan agreement. The creditors can then demand immediate repayment, or they can renegotiate the loan's terms. Covenants protect lenders because they enable lenders to step in and try to get their money back before the borrower gets too deeply into trouble.

During the 1990s, most traditional loans specified between three to six covenants or "triggers." In more recent years, when lots of cash was available, lenders began reducing or completely eliminating covenants from loan agreements in order to be more competitive with other lenders. Lending to weaker companies on easy terms is now common as investors' appetite for higher-yielding debt grows stronger and the Federal Reserve keeps money flowing at ultralow rates. Since the 2008 financial crisis, companies have been able to borrow more without offering investors what were once considered standard protections against possible losses.

Sources: Cynthia Koons, "Risky Business: Growth of 'Covenant-Lite' Debt," *Wall Street Journal* (June 18, 2007), p. C2; and Katy Burne, "More Loans Come with Few Strings Attached," *Wall Street Journal* (June 12, 2014).

How can financial ratios such as those covered in this chapter provide protection for creditors? (Go to WileyPLUS for this answer and additional questions.)

Debt and Equity Financing

To obtain large amounts of long-term capital, corporate management has to decide whether to issue additional common stock (equity financing), bonds or notes (debt financing), or a combination of the two. This decision is important to both the company and to investors and creditors. The capital structure of a company provides clues as to the potential profit that can be achieved and the risks taken by the company. Debt financing offers these advantages over common stock, as shown in Illustration 10-24.

Bond Financing	Advantages
Ballot	1. **Stockholder control is not affected.** Bondholders do not have voting rights, so current owners (stockholders) retain full control of the company.
Tax Bill	2. **Tax savings result.** Bond interest is deductible for tax purposes; dividends on stock are not.
Income Statement EPS	3. **Earnings per share (EPS) may be higher.** Although bond interest expense reduces net income, earnings per share often is higher under bond financing because no additional shares of common stock are issued.

Illustration 10-24
Advantages of bond financing over common stock

As Illustration 10-24 shows, one reason to issue bonds is that they do not affect stockholder control. Because bondholders do not have voting rights, owners can raise capital with bonds and still maintain corporate control. In addition, bonds are attractive to corporations because the cost of bond interest is tax-deductible. As a result of this tax treatment, which stock dividends do not offer, bonds may result in a lower cost of financing than equity financing.

To illustrate another advantage of bond financing, assume that Microsystems, Inc. is considering two plans for financing the construction of a new $5 million plant. Plan A involves issuance of 200,000 shares of common stock at the current market price of $25 per share. Plan B involves issuance of $5 million, 8% bonds at face value. Income before interest and taxes on the new plant will be $1.5 million. Income taxes are expected to be 30%. Microsystems currently has 100,000 shares of common stock outstanding. Illustration 10-25 shows the alternative effects on earnings per share.

Helpful Hint
Besides corporations, governmental agencies and universities also issue bonds to raise capital.

	Plan A Issue Stock	Plan B Issue Bonds
Income before interest and taxes	$1,500,000	$1,500,000
Interest (8% × $5,000,000)	—	400,000
Income before income taxes	1,500,000	1,100,000
Income tax expense (30%)	450,000	330,000
Net income	$1,050,000	$ 770,000
Outstanding shares	300,000	100,000
Earnings per share	**$3.50**	**$7.70**

Illustration 10-25
Effects on earnings per share—stocks vs. bonds

Note that net income is $280,000 less ($1,050,000 − $770,000) with long-term debt financing (bonds). However, earnings per share is higher because there are 200,000 fewer shares of common stock outstanding.

One disadvantage in using bonds is that the company must **pay interest** on a periodic basis. In addition, the company must also **repay the principal** at the due date. A company with fluctuating earnings and a relatively weak cash position may have great difficulty making interest payments when earnings are low. Furthermore, when the economy, stock market, or a company's revenues stagnate, debt payments can gobble up cash quickly and limit a company's ability to meet its financial obligations.

DO IT! 5 | Analyzing Liabilities

Trout Company provides you with the following balance sheet information as of December 31, 2017.

Current assets	$10,500		Current liabilities	$ 8,000
Long-term assets	24,200		Long-term liabilities	16,000
Total assets	$34,700		Stockholders' equity	10,700
			Total liabilities and stockholders' equity	$34,700

In addition, Trout reported net income for 2017 of $14,000, income tax expense of $2,800, and interest expense of $900.

Instructions

Action Plan

✔ Use the formula for the current ratio: Current assets ÷ Current liabilities.

✔ Use the formula for working capital: Current assets − Current liabilities.

✔ Use the formula for the debt to assets ratio: Total liabilities ÷ Total assets.`

(a) Compute the current ratio and working capital for Trout for 2017.

(b) Assume that at the end of 2017, Trout used $2,000 cash to pay off $2,000 of accounts payable. How would the current ratio and working capital have changed?

(c) Compute the debt to assets ratio and the times interest earned for Trout for 2017.

Solution

(a) Current ratio is 1.31:1 ($10,500/$8,000). Working capital is $2,500 ($10,500 − $8,000).
(b) Current ratio is 1.42:1 ($8,500/$6,000). Working capital is $2,500 ($8,500 − $6,000).
(c) Debt to assets ratio is 69.2% ($24,000/$34,700). Times interest earned is 19.67 times [($14,000 + $2,800 + $900)/$900].

Related exercise material: **E10-16 and DO IT! 10-5.**

LEARNING OBJECTIVE *6

APPENDIX 10A: Apply the straight-line method of amortizing bond discount and bond premium.

Amortizing Bond Discount

To follow the expense recognition principle, companies allocate bond discount to expense in each period in which the bonds are outstanding. The **straight-line method of amortization** allocates the same amount to interest expense in each interest period. The calculation is presented in Illustration 10A-1.

Illustration 10A-1
Formula for straight-line method of bond discount amortization

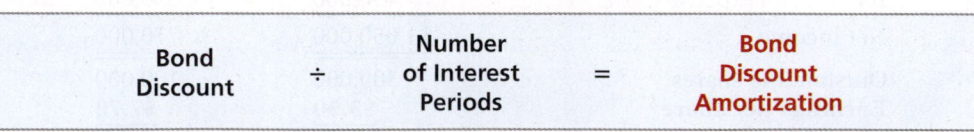

| Bond Discount | ÷ | Number of Interest Periods | = | Bond Discount Amortization |

In the Candlestick, Inc. example (page 457), the company sold $100,000, five-year, 10% bonds on January 1, 2017, for $98,000. This resulted in a $2,000 bond discount ($100,000 − $98,000). The bond discount amortization is $400 ($2,000 ÷ 5) for each of the five amortization periods. Candlestick records the first accrual of bond interest and the amortization of bond discount on December 31 as follows.

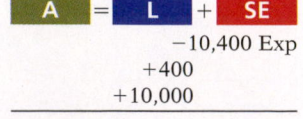

| A | = | L | + | SE |
| −10,400 Exp |
| +400 |
| +10,000 |

Cash Flows
no effect

Dec. 31	Interest Expense	10,400	
	Discount on Bonds Payable		400
	Interest Payable		10,000
	(To record accrued bond interest and amortization of bond discount)		

Over the term of the bonds, the balance in Discount on Bonds Payable will decrease annually by the same amount until it has a zero balance at the maturity date of the bonds. Thus, the carrying value of the bonds at maturity will be equal to the face value of the bonds.

Preparing a bond discount amortization schedule, as shown in Illustration 10A-2, is useful to determine interest expense, discount amortization, and the carrying value of the bond. As indicated, the interest expense recorded each period is $10,400. Also note that the carrying value of the bond increases $400 each period until it reaches its face value of $100,000 at the end of period 5.

Alternative Terminology
The amount in the Discount on Bonds Payable account is often referred to as *Unamortized Discount on Bonds Payable*.

Illustration 10A-2
Bond discount amortization schedule

		Candlestick Inc.xls			
Home Insert Page Layout Formulas Data Review View					
P18		*fx*			
	A	B	C	D	E	F

CANDLESTICK, INC.
Bond Discount Amortization Schedule
Straight-Line Method—Annual Interest Payments
$100,000 of 10%, 5-Year Bonds

Interest Periods	(A) Interest to Be Paid (10% × $100,000)	(B) Interest Expense to Be Recorded (A) + (C)	(C) Discount Amortization ($2,000 ÷ 5)	(D) Unamortized Discount (D) − (C)	(E) Bond Carrying Value ($100,000 − D)
Issue date				$2,000	$ 98,000
1	$10,000	$10,400	$ 400	1,600	98,400
2	10,000	10,400	400	1,200	98,800
3	10,000	10,400	400	800	99,200
4	10,000	10,400	400	400	99,600
5	10,000	10,400	400	0	100,000
	$50,000	$52,000	$2,000		

Column **(A)** remains constant because the face value of the bonds ($100,000) is multiplied by the annual contractual interest rate (10%) each period.

Column **(B)** is computed as the interest paid (Column A) plus the discount amortization (Column C).

Column **(C)** indicates the discount amortization each period.

Column **(D)** decreases each period by the same amount until it reaches zero at maturity.

Column **(E)** increases each period by the amount of discount amortization until it equals the face value at maturity.

Amortizing Bond Premium

The amortization of bond premium parallels that of bond discount. Illustration 10A-3 presents the formula for determining bond premium amortization under the straight-line method.

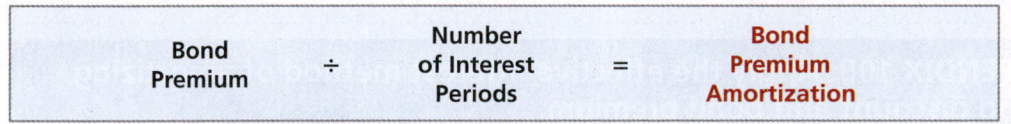

Bond Premium	÷	Number of Interest Periods	=	Bond Premium Amortization

Illustration 10A-3
Formula for straight-line method of bond premium amortization

Continuing our example, assume Candlestick, Inc., sells the bonds described above for $102,000, rather than $98,000 (see page 459). This results in a bond premium of $2,000 ($102,000 − $100,000). The premium amortization for each interest period is $400 ($2,000 ÷ 5). Candlestick records the first accrual of interest on December 31 as follows.

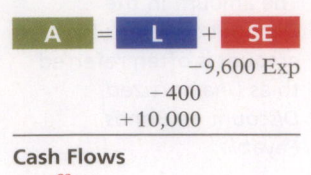

Cash Flows
no effect

Dec. 31	Interest Expense	9,600	
	Premium on Bonds Payable	400	
	Interest Payable		10,000
	(To record accrued bond interest and		
	amortization of bond premium)		

Over the term of the bonds, the balance in Premium on Bonds Payable will decrease annually by the same amount until it has a zero balance at maturity.

A bond premium amortization schedule, as shown in Illustration 10A-4, is useful to determine interest expense, premium amortization, and the carrying value of the bond. As indicated, the interest expense Candlestick records each period is $9,600. Note that the carrying value of the bond decreases $400 each period until it reaches its face value of $100,000 at the end of period 5.

Illustration 10A-4
Bond premium amortization schedule

CANDLESTICK, INC.
Bond Premium Amortization Schedule
Straight-Line Method—Annual Interest Payments
$100,000 of 10%, 5-Year Bonds

Interest Periods	(A) Interest to Be Paid (10% × $100,000)	(B) Interest Expense to Be Recorded (A) – (C)	(C) Premium Amortization ($2,000 ÷ 5)	(D) Unamortized Premium (D) – (C)	(E) Bond Carrying Value ($100,000 + D)
Issue date				$2,000	$102,000
1	$10,000	$ 9,600	$ 400	1,600	101,600
2	10,000	9,600	400	1,200	101,200
3	10,000	9,600	400	800	100,800
4	10,000	9,600	400	400	100,400
5	10,000	9,600	400	0	100,000
	$50,000	$48,000	$2,000		

Column **(A)** remains constant because the face value of the bonds ($100,000) is multiplied by the annual contractual interest rate (10%) each period.

Column **(B)** is computed as the interest paid (Column A) less the premium amortization (Column C).

Column **(C)** indicates the premium amortization each period.

Column **(D)** decreases each period by the same amount until it reaches zero at maturity.

Column **(E)** decreases each period by the amount of premium amortization until it equals the face value at maturity.

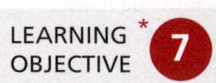

LEARNING *
OBJECTIVE **7**

APPENDIX 10B: Apply the effective-interest method of amortizing bond discount and bond premium.

To follow the expense recognition principle, companies allocate bond discount to expense in each period in which the bonds are outstanding. However, to completely comply with the expense recognition principle, interest expense as a percentage of carrying value should not change over the life of the bonds.

This percentage, referred to as the **effective-interest rate**, is established when the bonds are issued and remains constant in each interest period. Unlike the straight-line method, the effective-interest method of amortization accomplishes this result.

Under the **effective-interest method of amortization**, the amortization of bond discount or bond premium results in periodic interest expense equal to a constant percentage of the carrying value of the bonds. The effective-interest method results in **varying amounts** of amortization and interest expense per period but a **constant percentage rate**. In contrast, the straight-line method results in constant amounts of amortization and interest expense per period but a varying percentage rate.

Companies follow three steps under the effective-interest method:

1. Compute the **bond interest expense** by multiplying the carrying value of the bonds at the beginning of the interest period by the effective-interest rate.

2. Compute the **bond interest paid** (or accrued) by multiplying the face value of the bonds by the contractual interest rate.

3. Compute the **amortization amount** by determining the difference between the amounts computed in steps (1) and (2).

Illustration 10B-1 depicts these steps.

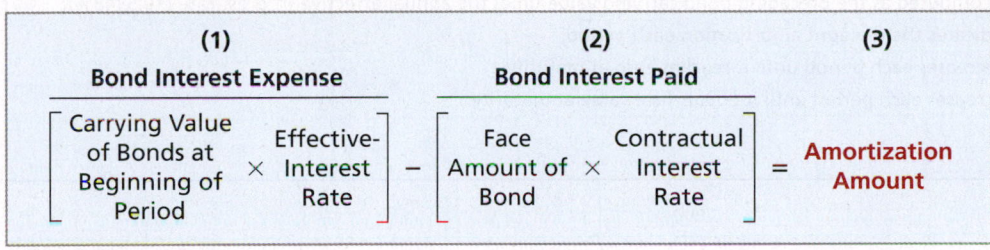

Illustration 10B-1
Computation of amortization using effective-interest method

Both the straight-line and effective-interest methods of amortization result in the same total amount of interest expense over the term of the bonds. Furthermore, interest expense each interest period is generally comparable in amount. However, **when the amounts are materially different**, generally accepted accounting principles (GAAP) require use of the effective-interest method.

Amortizing Bond Discount

In the Candlestick, Inc. example (page 457), the company sold $100,000, five-year, 10% bonds on January 1, 2017, for $98,000. This resulted in a $2,000 bond discount ($100,000 − $98,000). This discount results in an effective-interest rate of approximately 10.5348%. (The effective-interest rate can be computed using the techniques shown in Appendix G near the end of this textbook.)

Preparing a bond discount amortization schedule as shown in Illustration 10B-2 (page 472) facilitates the recording of interest expense and the discount amortization. Note that interest expense as a percentage of carrying value remains constant at 10.5348%.

Helpful Hint
Note that the amount of periodic interest expense increases over the life of the bonds when the effective-interest method is used for bonds issued at a discount. The reason is that a constant percentage is applied to an increasing bond carrying value to compute interest expense. The carrying value is increasing because of the amortization of the discount.

			Candlestick Inc.xls			
	Home	Insert	Page Layout Formulas Data Review View			
	P18		fx			

	A	B	C	D	E	F
1			**CANDLESTICK, INC.**			
2			**Bond Discount Amortization Schedule**			
3			**Effective-Interest Method—Annual Interest Payments**			
4			**10% Bonds Issued at 10.5348%**			
5						
6		(A)	(B)	(C)	(D)	(E)
7		Interest to	Interest Expense to Be Recorded	Discount	Unamortized	Bond
7	Interest	Be Paid	(10.5348% × Preceding	Amortization	Discount	Carrying Value
8	Periods	(10% × $100,000)	Bond Carrying Value)	(B) – (A)	(D) – (C)	($100,000 – D)
9	Issue date				$2,000	$ 98,000
10	1	$10,000	$10,324 (10.5348% × $98,000)	$ 324	1,676	98,324
11	2	10,000	10,358 (10.5348% × $98,324)	358	1,318	98,682
12	3	10,000	10,396 (10.5348% × $98,682)	396	922	99,078
13	4	10,000	10,438 (10.5348% × $99,078)	438	484	99,516
14	5	10,000	10,484 (10.5348% × $99,516)	484	–0–	100,000
15		$50,000	$52,000	$2,000		
16						
17	Column **(A)** remains constant because the face value of the bonds ($100,000) is multiplied by the annual contractual interest rate (10%) each period.					
18	Column **(B)** is computed as the preceding bond carrying value times the annual effective-interest rate (10.5348%).					
19	Column **(C)** indicates the discount amortization each period.					
20	Column **(D)** decreases each period until it reaches zero at maturity.					
21	Column **(E)** increases each period until it equals face value at maturity.					
22						
23						

Illustration 10B-2
Bond discount amortization schedule

For the first interest period, the computations of bond interest expense and the bond discount amortization are as follows.

Illustration 10B-3
Computation of bond discount amortization

Bond interest expense ($98,000 × 10.5348%)	$10,324
Less: Bond interest paid ($100,000 × 10%)	10,000
Bond discount amortization	**$ 324**

As a result, Candlestick, Inc. records the accrual of interest and amortization of bond discount on December 31 as follows.

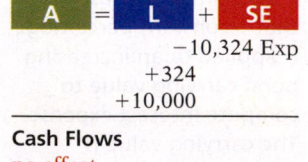

A = L + SE
−10,324 Exp
+324
+10,000

Cash Flows
no effect

Dec. 31	Interest Expense	10,324	
	Discount on Bonds Payable		324
	Interest Payable		10,000
	(To record accrued interest and		
	amortization of bond discount)		

For the second interest period, bond interest expense will be $10,358 ($98,324 × 10.5348%), and the discount amortization will be $358. At December 31, Candlestick makes the following adjusting entry.

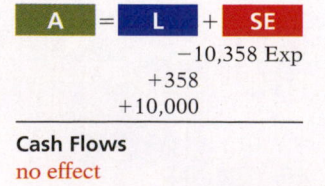

A = L + SE
−10,358 Exp
+358
+10,000

Cash Flows
no effect

Dec. 31	Interest Expense	10,358	
	Discount on Bonds Payable		358
	Interest Payable		10,000
	(To record accrued interest and		
	amortization of bond discount)		

Amortizing Bond Premium

Continuing our example, assume Candlestick, Inc. sells the bonds described above for $102,000 rather than $98,000 (see page 459). This would result in a bond premium of $2,000 ($102,000 − $100,000). This premium results in an effective-interest rate of approximately 9.4794%. (The effective-interest rate can be solved for using the techniques shown in Appendix G near the end of this textbook.) Illustration 10B-4 shows the bond premium amortization schedule.

Illustration 10B-4
Bond premium amortization schedule

	Candlestick Inc.xls				

	A	B	C	D	E	F
1			**CANDLESTICK, INC.**			
2			**Bond Premium Amortization Schedule**			
3			**Effective-Interest Method—Annual Interest Payments**			
4			**10% Bonds Issued at 9.4794%**			
5						
6		(A)	(B)	(C)	(D)	(E)
7	Interest	Interest to Be Paid	Interest Expense to Be Recorded (9.4794% × Preceding	Premium Amortization	Unamortized Premium	Bond Carrying Value
8	Periods	(10% × $100,000)	Bond Carrying Value)	(A) − (B)	(D) − (C)	($100,000 + D)
9	Issue date				$2,000	$102,000
10	1	$10,000	$ 9,669 (9.4794% × $102,000)	$ 331	1,669	101,669
11	2	10,000	9,638 (9.4794% × $101,669)	362	1,307	101,307
12	3	10,000	9,603 (9.4794% × $101,307)	397	910	100,910
13	4	10,000	9,566 (9.4794% × $100,910)	434	476	100,476
14	5	10,000	9,524 * (9.4794% × $100,476)	476*	–0–	100,000
15		$50,000	$48,000	$2,000		
16						
17	Column **(A)** remains constant because the face value of the bonds ($100,000) is multiplied by the contractual interest rate (10%) each period.					
18	Column **(B)** is computed as the carrying value of the bonds times the annual effective-interest rate (9.4794%).					
19	Column **(C)** indicates the premium amortization each period.					
20	Column **(D)** decreases each period until it reaches zero at maturity.					
21	Column **(E)** decreases each period until it equals face value at maturity.					
22						
23	*Rounded to eliminate remaining discount resulting from rounding the effective rate.					

For the first interest period, the computations of bond interest expense and the bond premium amortization are as follows.

Illustration 10B-5
Computation of bond premium amortization

Bond interest paid ($100,000 × 10%)	$10,000
Less: Bond interest expense ($102,000 × 9.4794%)	9,669
Bond premium amortization	**$ 331**

The entry Candlestick makes on December 31 is:

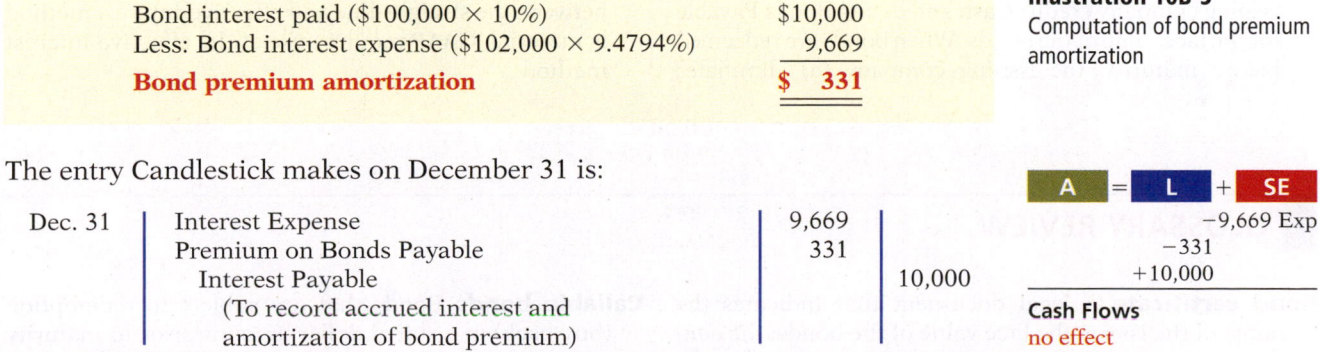

Dec. 31	Interest Expense	9,669	
	Premium on Bonds Payable	331	
	Interest Payable		10,000
	(To record accrued interest and amortization of bond premium)		

A = L + SE
−9,669 Exp
−331
+10,000

Cash Flows
no effect

For the second interest period, interest expense will be $9,638, and the premium amortization will be $362. Note that the amount of periodic interest expense decreases over the life of the bond when companies apply the effective-interest method to bonds issued at a premium. The reason is that a constant percentage is applied to a decreasing bond carrying value to compute interest expense. The carrying value is decreasing because of the amortization of the premium.

REVIEW AND PRACTICE

LEARNING OBJECTIVES REVIEW

1 Explain how to account for current liabilities. A current liability is a debt that a company expects to pay within one year or the operating cycle, whichever is longer. The major types of current liabilities are notes payable, accounts payable, sales taxes payable, unearned revenues, and accrued liabilities such as taxes, salaries and wages, and interest payable.

When a promissory note is interest-bearing, the amount of assets received upon the issuance of the note is generally equal to the face value of the note. Interest expense accrues over the life of the note. At maturity, the amount paid equals the face value of the note plus accrued interest.

Companies record sales taxes payable at the time the related sales occur. The company serves as a collection agent for the taxing authority. Sales taxes are not an expense to the company. Companies initially record unearned revenues in an unearned revenue account. As a company recognizes revenue, a transfer from unearned revenue to revenue occurs. Companies report the current maturities of long-term debt as a current liability in the balance sheet.

2 Describe the major characteristics of bonds. Bonds can have many different features and may be secured, unsecured, convertible, or callable. The terms of the bond issue are set forth in a bond indenture, and a bond certificate provides the specific information about the bond itself.

3 Explain how to account for bond transactions. When companies issue bonds, they debit Cash for the cash proceeds and credit Bonds Payable for the face value of the bonds. The account Premium on Bonds Payable shows a bond premium. Discount on Bonds Payable shows a bond discount.

When bondholders redeem bonds at maturity, the issuing company credits Cash and debits Bonds Payable for the face value of the bonds. When bonds are redeemed before maturity, the issuing company (a) eliminates the carrying value of the bonds at the redemption date, (b) records the cash paid, and (c) recognizes the gain or loss on redemption. When bonds are converted to common stock, the issuing company transfers the carrying (or book) value of the bonds to appropriate paid-in capital accounts. No gain or loss is recognized.

4 Explain how to account for long-term notes payable. Each payment consists of (1) interest on the unpaid balance of the loan and (2) a reduction of loan principal. The interest decreases each period, while the portion applied to the loan principal increases.

5 Describe how liabilities are reported and analyzed. Companies should report the nature and amount of each long-term debt in the balance sheet or in the notes accompanying the financial statements.

Companies may sell bonds to investors to raise long-term capital. Bonds offer the following advantages over common stock: (a) stockholder control is not affected, (b) tax savings result, and (c) earnings per share of common stock may be higher.

Stockholders and long-term creditors are interested in a company's long-run solvency. Debt to assets and times interest earned are two ratios that provide information about debt-paying ability and long-run solvency.

*6 Apply the straight-line method of amortizing bond discount and bond premium. The straight-line method of amortization results in a constant amount of amortization and interest expense per period.

*7 Apply the effective-interest method of amortizing bond discount and bond premium. The effective-interest method results in varying amounts of amortization and interest expense per period but a constant percentage rate of interest. When the difference between the straight-line and effective-interest method is material, GAAP requires use of the effective-interest method.

GLOSSARY REVIEW

Bond certificate A legal document that indicates the name of the issuer, the face value of the bonds, the contractual interest rate, and maturity date of the bonds. (p. 453).

Bond indenture A legal document that sets forth the terms of the bond issue. (p. 452).

Bonds A form of interest-bearing notes payable issued by corporations, universities, and governmental entities. (p. 452).

Callable bonds Bonds that are subject to redemption (buy back) at a stated dollar amount prior to maturity at the option of the issuer. (p. 452).

Contractual interest rate Rate used to determine the amount of cash interest the borrower pays and the investor receives. (p. 452).

Convertible bonds Bonds that permit bondholders to convert them into common stock at the bondholders' option. (p. 452).

Current ratio A measure of a company's liquidity; computed as current assets divided by current liabilities. (p. 465).

Debenture bonds Bonds issued against the general credit of the borrower. Also called unsecured bonds. (p. 452).

Debt to assets ratio A solvency measure that indicates the percentage of total assets provided by creditors; computed as total liabilities divided by total assets. (p. 466).

Discount (on a bond) The difference between the face value of a bond and its selling price, when the bond is sold for less than its face value. (p. 457).

*Effective-interest method of amortization A method of amortizing bond discount or bond premium that results in periodic interest expense equal to a constant percentage of the carrying value of the bonds. (p. 471).

*Effective-interest rate Rate established when bonds are issued that maintains a constant value for interest expense as a percentage of bond carrying value in each interest period. (p. 471).

Face value Amount of principal due at the maturity date of the bond. (p. 452).

Long-term liabilities Obligations expected to be paid more than one year in the future. (p. 452).

Market interest rate The rate investors demand for loaning funds to the corporation. (p. 454).

Maturity date The date on which the final payment on the bond is due from the bond issuer to the investor. (p. 452).

Mortgage bond A bond secured by real estate. (p. 452).

Mortgage notes payable A long-term note secured by a mortgage that pledges title to specific assets as security for a loan. (p. 462).

Notes payable Obligations in the form of written notes. (p. 446).

Premium (on a bond) The difference between the selling price and the face value of a bond, when the bond is sold for more than its face value. (p. 457).

Secured bonds Bonds that have specific assets of the issuer pledged as collateral. (p. 452).

Sinking fund bonds Bonds secured by specific assets set aside to redeem them. (p. 452).

*Straight-line method of amortization A method of amortizing bond discount or bond premium that allocates the same amount to interest expense in each interest period. (p. 468).

Times interest earned A solvency measure that indicates a company's ability to meet interest payments; computed by dividing the sum of net income, interest expense, and income tax expense by interest expense. (p. 466).

Time value of money The relationship between time and money. A dollar received today is worth more than a dollar promised at some time in the future. (p. 454).

Unsecured bonds Bonds issued against the general credit of the borrower. Also called debenture bonds. (p. 452).

Working capital A measure of a company's liquidity; computed as current assets minus current liabilities. (p. 465).

PRACTICE MULTIPLE-CHOICE QUESTIONS

(LO 1) **1.** The time period for classifying a liability as current is one year or the operating cycle, whichever is:
(a) longer.   (c) probable.
(b) shorter.   (d) possible.

(LO 1) **2.** To be classified as a current liability, a debt must be expected to be paid within:
(a) one year.
(b) the operating cycle.
(c) 2 years.
(d) (a) or (b), whichever is longer.

(LO 1) **3.** Maggie Sharrer Company borrows $88,500 on September 1, 2017, from Sandwich State Bank by signing an $88,500, 12%, one-year note. What is the accrued interest at December 31, 2017?
(a) $2,655.   (c) $4,425.
(b) $3,540.   (d) $10,620.

(LO 1) **4.** Becky Sherrick Company has total proceeds from sales of $4,515. If the proceeds include sales taxes of 5%, the amount to be credited to Sales Revenue is:
(a) $4,000.
(b) $4,300.
(c) $4,289.25.
(d) No correct answer given.

(LO 1) **5.** Employer payroll taxes do **not** include:
(a) federal unemployment taxes.
(b) state unemployment taxes.
(c) federal income taxes.
(d) FICA taxes.

6. Sensible Insurance Company collected a premium of (LO 1) $18,000 for a 1-year insurance policy on April 1. What amount should Sensible report as a current liability for Unearned Service Revenue at December 31?
(a) $0.   (c) $13,500.
(b) $4,500.   (d) $18,000.

7. The term used for bonds that are unsecured is: (LO 2)
(a) callable bonds.
(b) U.S. Treasury bonds.
(c) debenture bonds.
(d) convertible bonds.

8. Karson Inc. issues 10-year bonds with a maturity (LO 3) value of $200,000. If the bonds are issued at a premium, this indicates that:
(a) the contractual interest rate exceeds the market interest rate.
(b) the market interest rate exceeds the contractual interest rate.
(c) the contractual interest rate and the market interest rate are the same.
(d) no relationship exists between the two rates.

9. Gester Corporation redeems its $100,000 face value (LO 3) bonds at 105 on January 1, following the payment of annual interest. The carrying value of the bonds at the redemption date is $103,745. The entry to record the redemption will include a:

(a) credit of $3,745 to Loss on Bond Redemption.
(b) debit of $3,745 to Premium on Bonds Payable.
(c) credit of $1,255 to Gain on Bond Redemption.
(d) debit of $5,000 to Premium on Bonds Payable.

(LO 3) **10.** Colson Inc. converts $600,000 of bonds sold at face value into 10,000 shares of common stock, par value $1. Both the bonds and the stock have a market value of $760,000. What amount should be credited to Paid-in Capital in Excess of Par—Common Stock as a result of the conversion?

(a) $10,000.   (c) $600,000.
(b) $160,000.   (d) $590,000.

(LO 4) **11.** Andrews Inc. issues a $497,000, 10% 3-year mortgage note on January 1. The note will be paid in three annual installments of $200,000, each payable at the end of the year. What is the amount of interest expense that should be recognized by Andrews Inc. in the second year?

(a) $16,567.   (c) $34,670.
(b) $49,700.   (d) $346,700.

(LO 4) **12.** Howard Corporation issued a 20-year mortgage note payable on January 1, 2017. At December 31, 2017, the unpaid principal balance will be reported as:

(a) a current liability.
(b) a long-term liability.
(c) part current and part long-term liability.
(d) interest payable.

(LO 5) **13.** For 2017, Corn Flake Corporation reported net income of $300,000. Interest expense was $40,000 and income taxes were $100,000. The times interest earned was:

(a) 3 times.   (c) 7.5 times.
(b) 4.4 times.   (d) 11 times.

*14. On December 31, Hurley Corporation issues $500,000, (LO 6) 5-year, 12% bonds at 96 with interest payable on December 31, 2017. The entry on December 31, 2018, to record payment of bond interest and the amortization of bond discount using the straight-line method will include a:

(a) debit to Interest Expense $30,000.
(b) debit to Interest Expense $60,000.
(c) credit to Discount on Bonds Payable $4,000.
(d) credit to Discount on Bonds Payable $2,000.

*15. For the bonds issued in Question 14, what is the car- (LO 6) rying value of the bonds at the end of the third interest period?

(a) $492,000.   (c) $486,000.
(b) $488,000.   (d) $464,000.

*16. On January 1, Besalius Inc. issued $1,000,000, 9% (LO 7) bonds for $938,554. The market rate of interest for these bonds is 10%. Interest is payable annually on December 31. Besalius uses the effective-interest method of amortizing bond discount. At the end of the first year, Besalius should report unamortized bond discount of:

(a) $54,900.   (c) $51,610.
(b) $57,591.   (d) $51,000.

*17. Dias Corporation issued $1,000,000, 14%, 5-year (LO 7) bonds with interest payable annually on December 31. The bonds sold for $1,072,096. The market rate of interest for these bonds was 12%. On the first interest date, using the effective-interest method, the debit entry to Interest Expense is for:

(a) $120,000.   (c) $128,652.
(b) $125,581.   (d) $140,000.

Solutions

1. (a) The time period for classifying a liability as current is one year or the operating cycle, whichever is longer, not (b) shorter, (c) probable, or (d) possible.

2. (d) To be classified as a current liability, a debt must be expected to be paid within one year or the operating cycle. Choices (a) and (b) are both correct, but (d) is the better answer. Choice (c) is incorrect.

3. (b) Accrued interest at 12/31/17 is computed as the face value ($88,500) times the interest rate (12%) times the portion of the year the debt was outstanding (4 months out of 12), or $3,540 ($88,500 × 12% × $\frac{4}{12}$), not (a) $2,655, (c) $4,425, or (d) $10,620.

4. (b) Dividing the total proceeds ($4,515) by one plus the sales tax rate (1.05) will result in the amount of sales to be credited to the Sales Revenue account of $4,300 ($4,515 ÷ 1.05). The other choices are therefore incorrect.

5. (c) Federal income taxes are a payroll deduction, not an employer payroll tax. The employer is merely a collection agent. The other choices are all included in employer payroll taxes.

6. (b) The monthly premium is $1,500 or $18,000 divided by 12. Because Sensible has recognized 9 months of insurance revenue (April 1–December 31), 3 months' insurance premium is still unearned. The amount that Sensible should report as Unearned Service Revenue is therefore $4,500 (3 months × $1,500), not (a) $0, (c) $13,500, or (d) $18,000.

7. (c) Debenture bonds are not secured by any collateral. The other choices are incorrect because (a) callable bonds can be paid off or retired by the issuer before they reach their maturity date, (b) U.S. Treasury bonds are secured by the federal government, and (d) convertible bonds permit bondholders to convert them into common stock at the bondholders' option.

8. (a) When bonds are issued at a premium, this indicates that the contractual interest rate is higher than the market interest rate. The other choices are incorrect because (b) when the market interest rate exceeds the contractual interest rate, bonds are sold at a discount; (c) when the contractual interest rate and the market interest rate are the same, bonds will be issued at par; and (d) the relationship between the market rate of interest and the contractual rate of interest determines whether bonds are issued at par, a discount, or a premium.

9. (b) The entry to record the retirement of bonds will include a debit to Bonds Payable of $100,000, a debit to Premium on Bonds Payable of $3,745 ($103,745 − $100,000), a credit to Cash of $105,000 ($100,000 × 1.05) and a debit to Loss on Bond Redemption of $1,255 ($105,000 − $103,745). The other choices are therefore incorrect.

10. (d) First, the market value in this transaction is ignored. Bonds Payable will be debited for $600,000; Common Stock will be credited for $10,000 since this account is always credited for shares issued (10,000) times par value ($1). The remaining amount,

$590,000 ($600,000 − $10,000) is credited to Paid-in Capital in Excess of Par–Common Stock, not (a) $10,000, (b) $160,000, or (c) $600,000.

11. (c) In the first year, Andrews will recognize $49,700 of interest expense ($497,000 × 10%). After the first payment is made, the amount remaining on the note will be $346,700 [$497,000 principal − ($200,000 payment − $49,700 interest)]. The remaining balance ($346,700) is multiplied by the interest rate (10%) to compute the interest expense to be recognized for the second year, $34,670 ($346,700 × 10%), not (a) $16,567, (b) $49,700, or (d) $346,700.

12. (c) Howard Corporation reports the reduction in principal for the next year as a current liability, and it classifies the remaining unpaid principal balance as a long-term liability. The other choices are therefore incorrect.

13. (d) Times interest earned = Net income + Interest expense + Income tax expense ($300,000 + $40,000 + $100,000 = $440,000) divided by Interest expense ($40,000), which equals 11 times, not (a) 3, (b) 4.4, or (c) 7.5 times.

***14. (c)** [$500,000 − (96% × $500,000)] = $20,000; $20,000 ÷ 5 = $4,000 of discount to amortize annually. As a result, the entry would involve a credit to Discount on Bonds Payable $4,000. The other choices are therefore incorrect.

***15. (a)** The carrying value of bonds increases by the amount of the periodic discount amortization. Discount amortization using the straight-line method is $4,000 each period. Total discount amortization for three periods is $12,000 ($4,000 × 3 periods) which is added to the initial carrying value ($480,000) to arrive at $492,000, the carrying value at the end of the third interest period, not (b) $488,000, (c) $486,000, or (d) $464,000.

***16. (b)** The beginning balance of unamortized discount is $61,446 ($1,000,000 − $938,554). The discount amortization is $3,855, the difference between the cash interest payment of $90,000 ($1,000,000 × 9%) and the interest expense recorded of $93,855 ($938,554 × 10%). This discount amortization ($3,855) is then subtracted from the beginning balance of unamortized discount ($61,446), to arrive at a balance of $57,591 at the end of the first year, not (a) $54,900, (c) $51,610, or (d) $51,000.

***17. (c)** The debit to Interest Expense = $1,072,096 (initial carrying value of bond) × 12% (market rate) = $128,652, not (a) $120,000, (b) $125,581, or (d) $140,000.

PRACTICE EXERCISES

1. On June 1, JetSet Company borrows $150,000 from First Bank on a 6-month, $150,000, 8% note.

Prepare entries for interest-bearing notes.

(LO 1)

Instructions

(a) Prepare the entry on June 1.
(b) Prepare the adjusting entry on June 30.
(c) Prepare the entry at maturity (December 1), assuming monthly adjusting entries have been made through November 30.
(d) What was the total financing cost (interest expense)?

Solution

1. (a) June 1	Cash	150,000	
	Notes Payable		150,000
(b) June 30	Interest Expense	1,000	
	Interest Payable		
	($150,000 × 8% × 1/12)		1,000
(c) Dec. 1	Notes Payable	150,000	
	Interest Payable		
	($150,000 × 8% × 6/12)	6,000	
	Cash		156,000
(d) $6,000			

2. Global Airlines Company issued $900,000 of 8%, 10-year bonds on January 1, 2017, at face value. Interest is payable annually on January 1.

Prepare entries for bonds issued at face value.

(LO 3)

Instructions

Prepare the journal entries to record the following events.

(a) The issuance of the bonds.
(b) The accrual of interest on December 31.
(c) The payment of interest on January 1, 2018.
(d) The redemption of bonds at maturity, assuming interest for the last interest period has been paid and recorded.

Solution

2.   **January 1, 2017**

(a) Cash	900,000	
Bonds Payable		900,000

December 31, 2017

(b) Interest Expense	72,000	
Interest Payable ($900,000 × 8%)		72,000

January 1, 2018

(c) Interest Payable	72,000	
Cash		72,000

January 1, 2027

(d) Bonds Payable	900,000	
Cash		900,000

Prepare entries to record mortgage note and installment payments.

(LO 4)

3. Trawler Company borrowed $500,000 on December 31, 2017, by issuing a $500,000, 7% mortgage note payable. The terms call for annual installment payments of $80,000 on December 31.

Instructions

(a) Prepare the journal entries to record the mortgage loan and the first two installment payments.

(b) Indicate the amount of mortgage note payable to be reported as a current liability and as a long-term liability at December 31, 2018.

Solution

3.   **December 31, 2017**

(a) Cash	500,000	
Mortgage Payable		500,000

December 31, 2018

Interest Expense ($500,000 × 7%)	35,000	
Mortgage Payable	45,000	
Cash		80,000

December 31, 2019

Interest Expense [($500,000 − $45,000) × 7%]	31,850	
Mortgage Payable	48,150	
Cash		80,000

(b) Current: $48,150
    Long-term: $406,850 ($500,000 − $45,000 − $48,150)

PRACTICE PROBLEM

Prepare entries to record issuance of bonds and long-term notes, interest accrued, and bond redemption.

(LO 3, 4)

Snyder Software Inc. has successfully developed a new spreadsheet program. To produce and market the program, the company needed $1.9 million of additional financing. On January 1, 2017, Snyder borrowed money as follows.

1. Snyder issued $500,000, 11%, 10-year convertible bonds. The bonds sold at face value and pay annual interest on January 1. Each $1,000 bond is convertible into 30 shares of Snyder's $20 par value common stock.

2. Snyder issued $1 million, 10%, 10-year bonds at face value. Interest is payable on January 1.

3. Snyder also issued a $400,000, 6%, 15-year mortgage payable. The terms provide for annual installment payments of $41,185 on December 31.

Instructions

1. For the convertible bonds, prepare journal entries for:

   (a) The issuance of the bonds on January 1, 2017.

   (b) Interest expense on December 31, 2017.

(c) The payment of interest on January 1, 2018.

(d) The conversion of all bonds into common stock on January 1, 2018, when the market price of the common stock was $67 per share.

2. For the 10-year, 10% bonds:

(a) Journalize the issuance of the bonds on January 1, 2017.

(b) Prepare the journal entry for interest expense in 2017.

(c) Prepare the entry for the redemption of the bonds at 101 on January 1, 2020, after paying the interest due on this date.

3. For the mortgage payable:

(a) Prepare the entry for the issuance of the note on January 1, 2017.

(b) Prepare a payment schedule for the first four installment payments.

(c) Indicate the current and noncurrent amounts for the mortgage payable at December 31, 2017.

Solution

1. (a) 2017			
Jan. 1	Cash	500,000	
	Bonds Payable		500,000
	(To record issue of 11%, 10-year convertible bonds at face value)		
(b) Dec. 31	Interest Expense	55,000	
	Interest Payable ($500,000 × 11%)		55,000
	(To record accrual of annual bond interest)		
(c) 2018			
Jan. 1	Interest Payable	55,000	
	Cash		55,000
	(To record payment of accrued interest)		
(d) Jan. 1	Bonds Payable	500,000	
	Common Stock		300,000*
	Paid-in Capital in Excess of Par—Common Stock		200,000
	(To record conversion of bonds into common stock)		

*($500,000 ÷ $1,000 = 500 bonds; 500 × 30 = 15,000 shares; 15,000 × $20 = $300,000)

2. (a) 2017			
Jan. 1	Cash	1,000,000	
	Bonds Payable		1,000,000
	(To record issuance of bonds)		
(b) 2017			
Dec. 31	Interest Expense	100,000	
	Interest Payable ($1,000,000 × 10%)		100,000
	(To record accrual of annual interest)		
(c) 2020			
Jan. 1	Bonds Payable	1,000,000	
	Loss on Bond Redemption	10,000*	
	Cash		1,010,000
	(To record redemption of bonds at 101)		

*($1,010,000 − $1,000,000)

3. (a) 2017			
Jan. 1	Cash	400,000	
	Mortgage Payable		400,000
	(To record issuance of mortgage payable)		

(b) Interest Period	Cash Payment	Interest Expense	Reduction of Principal	Principal Balance
Issue date				$400,000
1	$41,185	$24,000	$17,185	382,815
2	41,185	22,969	18,216	364,599
3	41,185	21,876	19,309	345,290
4	41,185	20,717	20,468	324,822

(c) Current liability: $18,216
Long-term liability: $364,599

WileyPLUS

Brief Exercises, Exercises, **DO IT!** Exercises, and Problems and many additional resources are available for practice in WileyPLUS

NOTE: All asterisked Questions, Exercises, and Problems relate to material in the appendices to the chapter.

■ QUESTIONS

1. Lori Randle believes a current liability is a debt that can be expected to be paid in one year. Is Lori correct? Explain.

2. Petrocelli Company obtains $40,000 in cash by signing a 7%, 6-month, $40,000 note payable to First Bank on July 1. Petrocelli's fiscal year ends on September 30. What information should be reported for the note payable in the annual financial statements?

3. (a) Your roommate says, "Sales taxes are reported as an expense in the income statement." Do you agree? Explain.
   (b) Jensen Company has cash proceeds from sales of $8,400. This amount includes $400 of sales taxes. Give the entry to record the proceeds.

4. Ottawa University sold 15,000 season football tickets at $80 each for its six-game home schedule. What entries should be made (a) when the tickets were sold, and (b) after each game?

5. Identify three taxes commonly withheld by the employer from an employee's gross pay.

6. (a) What are long-term liabilities? Give three examples. (b) What is a bond?

7. Contrast the following types of bonds: (a) secured and unsecured, and (b) convertible and callable.

8. The following terms are important in issuing bonds: (a) face value, (b) contractual interest rate, (c) bond indenture, and (d) bond certificate. Explain each of these terms.

9. Describe the two major obligations incurred by a company when bonds are issued.

10. Assume that Remington Inc. sold bonds with a face value of $100,000 for $104,000. Was the market interest rate equal to, less than, or greater than the bonds' contractual interest rate? Explain.

11. If a 7%, 10-year, $800,000 bond is issued at face value and interest is paid annually, what is the amount of the interest payment at the end of the first period?

12. If the Bonds Payable account has a balance of $900,000 and the Discount on Bonds Payable account has a balance of $120,000, what is the carrying value of the bonds?

13. Which accounts are debited and which are credited if a bond issue originally sold at a premium is redeemed before maturity at 97 immediately following the payment of interest?

14. Rattigan Corporation is considering issuing a convertible bond. What is a convertible bond? Discuss the advantages of a convertible bond from the standpoint of (a) the bondholders and (b) the issuing corporation.

15. Rob Grier, a friend of yours, has recently purchased a home for $125,000, paying $25,000 down and the remainder financed by a 10.5%, 20-year mortgage, payable at $998.38 per month. At the end of the first month, Rob receives a statement from the bank indicating that only $123.38 of principal was paid during the month. At this rate, he calculates that it will take over 67 years to pay off the mortgage. Is he right? Discuss.

16. In general, what are the requirements for the financial statement presentation of long-term liabilities?

17. (a) As a source of long-term financing, what are the major advantages of bonds over common stock? (b) What are the major disadvantages in using bonds for long-term financing?

18. What is liquidity? What are two measures of liquidity?

*19. Explain the straight-line method of amortizing discount and premium on bonds payable.

*20. DeWeese Corporation issues $400,000 of 8%, 5-year bonds on January 1, 2017, at 105. Assuming that the straight-line method is used to amortize the premium, what is the total amount of interest expense for 2017?

*21. Kelli Deane is discussing the advantages of the effective-interest method of bond amortization with her accounting staff. What do you think Kelli is saying?

*22. Windsor Corporation issues $500,000 of 9%, 5-year bonds on January 1, 2017, at 104. If Windsor uses the effective-interest method in amortizing the premium, will the annual interest expense increase or decrease over the life of the bonds? Explain.

BRIEF EXERCISES

BE10-1 Jamison Company has the following obligations at December 31: (a) a note payable for $100,000 due in 2 years, (b) a 10-year mortgage payable of $300,000 payable in ten $30,000 annual payments, (c) interest payable of $15,000 on the mortgage, and (d) accounts payable of $60,000. For each obligation, indicate whether it should be classified as a current liability. (Assume an operating cycle of less than one year.)

Identify whether obligations are current liabilities.

(LO 1)

BE10-2 Peralta Company borrows $60,000 on July 1 from the bank by signing a $60,000, 10%, one-year note payable.
(a) Prepare the journal entry to record the proceeds of the note.
(b) Prepare the journal entry to record accrued interest at December 31, assuming adjusting entries are made only at the end of the year.

Prepare entries for an interest-bearing note payable.

(LO 1)

BE10-3 Coghlan Auto Supply does not segregate sales and sales taxes at the time of sale. The register total for March 16 is $16,380. All sales are subject to a 5% sales tax. Compute sales taxes payable, and make the entry to record sales taxes payable and sales revenue.

Compute and record sales taxes payable.

(LO 1)

BE10-4 Derby University sells 4,000 season basketball tickets at $210 each for its 12-game home schedule. Give the entry to record (a) the sale of the season tickets and (b) the revenue recognized by playing the first home game.

Prepare entries for unearned revenues.

(LO 1)

BE10-5 Beth Corbin's regular hourly wage rate is $16, and she receives an hourly rate of $24 for work in excess of 40 hours. During a January pay period, Beth works 45 hours. Beth's federal income tax withholding is $95, and she has no voluntary deductions. Compute Beth Corbin's gross earnings and net pay for the pay period.

Compute gross earnings and net pay.

(LO 1)

BE10-6 Data for Beth Corbin are presented in BE10-5. Prepare the journal entries to record (a) Beth's pay for the period and (b) the payment of Beth's wages. Use January 15 for the end of the pay period and the payment date.

Record a payroll and the payment of wages.

(LO 1)

BE10-7 Randle Inc. issues $300,000, 10-year, 8% bonds at 98. Prepare the journal entry to record the sale of these bonds on March 1, 2017.

Prepare entry for bonds issued.

(LO 3)

BE10-8 Price Company issues $400,000, 20-year, 7% bonds at 101. Prepare the journal entry to record the sale of these bonds on June 1, 2017.

Prepare entry for bonds issued.

(LO 3)

BE10-9 Meera Corporation issued 4,000, 8%, 5-year, $1,000 bonds dated January 1, 2017, at 100. Interest is paid each January 1.
(a) Prepare the journal entry to record the sale of these bonds on January 1, 2017.
(b) Prepare the adjusting journal entry on December 31, 2017, to record interest expense.
(c) Prepare the journal entry on January 1, 2018, to record interest paid.

Prepare entries for bonds issued at face value.

(LO 3)

BE10-10 Nasreen Company issues $2 million, 10-year, 8% bonds at 97, with interest payable each January 1.
(a) Prepare the journal entry to record the sale of these bonds on January 1, 2017.
(b) Assuming instead that the above bonds sold for 104, prepare the journal entry to record the sale of these bonds on January 1, 2017.

Prepare entries for bonds sold at a discount and a premium.

(LO 3)

BE10-11 Frankum Company has issued three different bonds during 2017. Interest is payable annually on each of these bonds.
1. On January 1, 2017, 1,000, 8%, 5-year, $1,000 bonds dated January 1, 2017, were issued at face value.
2. On July 1, $900,000, 9%, 5-year bonds dated July 1, 2017, were issued at 102.
3. On September 1, $400,000, 7%, 5-year bonds dated September 1, 2017, were issued at 98.

Prepare the journal entry to record each bond transaction at the date of issuance.

Prepare entries for bonds issued.

(LO 3)

Prepare entry for redemption of bonds.

(LO 3)

BE10-12 The balance sheet for Miley Consulting reports the following information on July 1, 2017.

Long-term liabilities		
Bonds payable	$1,000,000	
Less: Discount on bonds payable	60,000	$940,000

Miley decides to redeem these bonds at 101 after paying annual interest. Prepare the journal entry to record the redemption on July 1, 2017.

Prepare entries for long-term notes payable.

(LO 4)

BE10-13 Hanschu Inc. issues an $800,000, 10%, 10-year mortgage note on December 31, 2017, to obtain financing for a new building. The terms provide for annual installment payments of $130,196. Prepare the entry to record the mortgage loan on December 31, 2017, and the first installment payment on December 31, 2018.

Prepare statement presentation of long-term liabilities.

(LO 5)

BE10-14 Presented below are long-term liability items for Lind Company at December 31, 2017. Prepare the long-term liabilities section of the balance sheet for Lind Company.

Bonds payable, due 2019	$600,000
Notes payable, due 2022	80,000
Discount on bonds payable	45,000

Compare bond versus stock financing.

(LO 5)

BE10-15 Moby Inc. is considering two alternatives to finance its construction of a new $2 million plant.
(a) Issuance of 200,000 shares of common stock at the market price of $10 per share.
(b) Issuance of $2 million, 8% bonds at face value.

Complete the following table, and indicate which alternative is preferable.

	Issue Stock	Issue Bond
Income before interest and taxes	$700,000	$700,000
Interest expense from bonds	_____	_____
Income before income taxes		
Income tax expense (30%)	_____	_____
Net income	$ _____	$ _____
Outstanding shares		500,000
Earnings per share	_____	_____

Prepare entries for bonds issued at a discount.

(LO 6)

*BE10-16 Sweetwood Company issues $5 million, 10-year, 9% bonds at 96, with interest payable annually on January 1. The straight-line method is used to amortize bond discount.
(a) Prepare the journal entry to record the sale of these bonds on January 1, 2017.
(b) Prepare the adjusting journal entry to record interest expense and bond discount amortization on December 31, 2017.

Prepare entries for bonds issued at a premium.

(LO 6)

*BE10-17 Golden Inc. issues $4 million, 5-year, 10% bonds at 102, with interest payable annually January 1. The straight-line method is used to amortize bond premium.
(a) Prepare the journal entry to record the sale of these bonds on January 1, 2017.
(b) Prepare the adjusting journal entry to record interest expense and bond premium amortization on December 31, 2017.

Use effective-interest method of bond amortization.

(LO 7)

*BE10-18 Presented below is the partial bond discount amortization schedule for Gomez Corp. Gomez uses the effective-interest method of amortization.

Interest Periods	Interest to Be Paid	Interest Expense to Be Recorded	Discount Amortization	Unamortized Discount	Bond Carrying Value
Issue date				$38,609	$961,391
1	$45,000	$48,070	$3,070	35,539	964,461
2	45,000	48,223	3,223	32,316	967,684

(a) Prepare the journal entry to record the payment of interest and the discount amortization at the end of period 1.
(b) ———— Explain why interest expense is greater than interest paid.
(c) Explain why interest expense will increase each period.

DO IT! Exercises

DO IT! 10-1a During the month of February, Morrisey Corporation's employees earned wages of $74,000. Withholdings related to these wages were $5,661 for Social Security (FICA), $7,100 for federal income tax, and $1,900 for state income tax. Costs incurred for unemployment taxes were $110 for federal and $160 for state.

Prepare the February 28 journal entries for (a) salaries and wages expense and salaries and wages payable assuming that all February wages will be paid in March and (b) the company's payroll tax expense.

Prepare entries for payroll and payroll taxes.

(LO 1)

DO IT! 10-1b You and several classmates are studying for the next accounting examination. They ask you to answer the following questions:
1. If cash is borrowed on a $70,000, 9-month, 6% note on August 1, how much interest expense would be incurred by December 31?
2. The cash register total including sales taxes is $42,000, and the sales tax rate is 5%. What is the sales taxes payable?
3. If $45,000 is collected in advance on November 1 for 6-month magazine subscriptions, what amount of subscription revenue should be recognized by December 31?

Answer questions about current liabilities.

(LO 1)

DO IT! 10-2 State whether each of the following statements is true or false. If false, indicate how to correct the statement.
_____ 1. Mortgage bonds and sinking fund bonds are both examples of debenture bonds.
_____ 2. Convertible bonds are also known as callable bonds.
_____ 3. The market rate is the rate investors demand for loaning funds.
_____ 4. Annual interest on bonds is equal to the face value times the stated rate.
_____ 5. The present value of a bond is the value at which it should sell in the market.

Evaluate statements about bonds.

(LO 2)

DO IT! 10-3a Eubank Corporation issues $500,000 of bonds for $520,000. (a) Prepare the journal entry to record the issuance of the bonds, and (b) show how the bonds would be reported on the balance sheet at the date of issuance.

Prepare journal entry for bond issuance and show balance sheet presentation.

(LO 3)

DO IT! 10-3b Prater Corporation issued $400,000 of 10-year bonds at a discount. Prior to maturity, when the carrying value of the bonds was $390,000, the company redeemed the bonds at 99. Prepare the entry to record the redemption of the bonds.

Prepare entry for bond redemption.

(LO 3)

DO IT! 10-4 Detwiler Orchard issues a $700,000, 6%, 15-year mortgage note to obtain needed financing for a new lab. The terms call for annual payments of $72,074 each. Prepare the entries to record the mortgage loan and the first installment payment.

Prepare entries for mortgage note and installment payment on note.

(LO 4)

DO IT! 10-5 Grouper Company provides you with the following balance sheet information as of December 31, 2017.

Analyze liabilities.

(LO 5)

Current assets	$11,500	Current liabilities	$12,000
Long-term assets	26,500	Long-term liabilities	14,000
Total assets	$38,000	Stockholders' equity	12,000
		Total liabilities and stockholders' equity	$38,000

In addition, Grouper reported net income for 2017 of $16,000, income tax expense of $3,200, and interest expense of $1,300.
(a) Compute the current ratio and working capital for Grouper for 2017.
(b) Assume that at the end of 2017, Grouper used $3,000 cash to pay off $3,000 of accounts payable. How would the current ratio and working capital have changed?
(c) Compute the debt to assets ratio and the times interest earned ratio for Grouper for 2017.

EXERCISES

Prepare entries for interest-bearing notes.

(LO 1)

E10-1 C.S. Lewis Company had the following transactions involving notes payable.

July 1, 2017	Borrows $50,000 from First National Bank by signing a 9-month, 8% note.
Nov. 1, 2017	Borrows $60,000 from Lyon County State Bank by signing a 3-month, 6% note.
Dec. 31, 2017	Prepares adjusting entries.
Feb. 1, 2018	Pays principal and interest to Lyon County State Bank.
Apr. 1, 2018	Pays principal and interest to First National Bank.

Instructions
Prepare journal entries for each of the transactions.

Prepare entries for interest-bearing notes.

(LO 1)

E10-2 On June 1, Merando Company borrows $90,000 from First Bank on a 6-month, $90,000, 8% note.

Instructions
(a) Prepare the entry on June 1.
(b) Prepare the adjusting entry on June 30.
(c) Prepare the entry at maturity (December 1), assuming monthly adjusting entries have been made through November 30.
(d) What was the total financing cost (interest expense)?

Journalize sales and related taxes.

(LO 1)

E10-3 In performing accounting services for small businesses, you encounter the following situations pertaining to cash sales.

1. Poole Company enters sales and sales taxes separately in its cash register. On April 10, the register totals are sales $30,000 and sales taxes $1,500.
2. Waterman Company does not segregate sales and sales taxes. Its register total for April 15 is $25,680, which includes a 7% sales tax.

Instructions
Prepare the entry to record the sales transactions and related taxes for each client.

Journalize unearned subscription revenue.

(LO 1)

E10-4 Moreno Company publishes a monthly sports magazine, *Fishing Preview*. Subscriptions to the magazine cost $20 per year. During November 2017, Moreno sells 15,000 subscriptions beginning with the December issue. Moreno prepares financial statements quarterly and recognizes subscription revenue at the end of the quarter. The company uses the accounts Unearned Subscription Revenue and Subscription Revenue.

Instructions
(a) Prepare the entry in November for the receipt of the subscriptions.
(b) Prepare the adjusting entry at December 31, 2017, to record sales revenue recognized in December 2017.
(c) Prepare the adjusting entry at March 31, 2018, to record sales revenue recognized in the first quarter of 2018.

Calculate and record net pay.

(LO 1)

E10-5 Dan Noll's gross earnings for the week were $1,780, his federal income tax withholding was $303, and his FICA total was $136.

Instructions
(a) What was Noll's net pay for the week?
(b) Journalize the entry for the recording of his pay in the general journal. (*Note:* Use Salaries and Wages Payable: not Cash.)
(c) Record the issuing of the check for Noll's pay in the general journal.

Record accrual of payroll taxes.

(LO 1)

E10-6 According to the accountant of Ulster Inc., its payroll taxes for the week were as follows: $137.68 for FICA taxes, $13.77 for federal unemployment taxes, and $92.93 for state unemployment taxes.

Instructions
Journalize the entry to record the accrual of the payroll taxes.

E10-7 Nick Bosch has prepared the following list of statements about bonds.

1. Bonds are a form of interest-bearing notes payable.
2. Secured bonds have specific assets of the issuer pledged as collateral for the bonds.
3. Secured bonds are also known as debenture bonds.
4. A conversion feature may be added to bonds to make them more attractive to bond buyers.
5. The rate used to determine the amount of cash interest the borrower pays is called the stated rate.
6. Bond prices are usually quoted as a percentage of the face value of the bond.
7. The present value of a bond is the value at which it should sell in the marketplace.

Evaluate statements about bonds.

(LO 2)

Instructions

Identify each statement as true or false. If false, indicate how to correct the statement.

E10-8 On January 1, 2017, Klosterman Company issued $500,000, 10%, 10-year bonds at face value. Interest is payable annually on January 1.

Prepare entries for issuance of bonds, and payment and accrual of bond interest.

(LO 3)

Instructions

Prepare journal entries to record the following.

(a) The issuance of the bonds.
(b) The accrual of interest on December 31, 2017.
(c) The payment of interest on January 1, 2018.

E10-9 On January 1, 2017, Forrester Company issued $400,000, 8%, 5-year bonds at face value. Interest is payable annually on January 1.

Prepare entries for bonds issued at face value.

(LO 3)

Instructions

Prepare journal entries to record the following.

(a) The issuance of the bonds.
(b) The accrual of interest on December 31, 2017.
(c) The payment of interest on January 1, 2018.

E10-10 Whitmore Company issued $500,000 of 5-year, 8% bonds at 97 on January 1, 2017. The bonds pay interest annually.

Prepare entries to record issuance of bonds at discount and premium.

(LO 3)

Instructions

(a) (1) Prepare the journal entry to record the issuance of the bonds.
    (2) Compute the total cost of borrowing for these bonds.
(b) Repeat the requirements from part (a), assuming the bonds were issued at 105.

E10-11 The following section is taken from Ohlman Corp.'s balance sheet at December 31, 2016.

Prepare entries for bond interest and redemption.

(LO 3)

Current liabilities	
Interest payable	$ 112,000
Long-term liabilities	
Bonds payable, 7%, due January 1, 2021	1,600,000

Bond interest is payable annually on January 1. The bonds are callable on any interest date.

Instructions

(a) Journalize the payment of the bond interest on January 1, 2017.
(b) Assume that on January 1, 2017, after paying interest, Ohlman calls bonds having a face value of $600,000. The call price is 103. Record the redemption of the bonds.
(c) Prepare the entry to record the accrual of interest on December 31, 2017.

E10-12 Presented below and on page 486 are three independent situations.

Prepare entries for redemption of bonds and conversion of bonds into common stock.

(LO 3)

1. Longbine Corporation redeemed $130,000 face value, 12% bonds on June 30, 2017, at 102. The carrying value of the bonds at the redemption date was $117,500. The bonds pay annual interest, and the interest payment due on June 30, 2017, has been made and recorded.

2. Tastove Inc. redeemed $150,000 face value, 12.5% bonds on June 30, 2017, at 98. The carrying value of the bonds at the redemption date was $151,000. The bonds pay annual interest, and the interest payment due on June 30, 2017, has been made and recorded.

3. Precision Company has $80,000, 8%, 12-year convertible bonds outstanding. These bonds were sold at face value and pay annual interest on December 31 of each year. The bonds are convertible into 30 shares of Precision $5 par value common stock for each $1,000 worth of bonds. On December 31, 2017, after the bond interest has been paid, $20,000 face value bonds were converted. The market price of Precision common stock was $44 per share on December 31, 2017.

Instructions
For each independent situation above, prepare the appropriate journal entry for the redemption or conversion of the bonds.

Prepare entries to record mortgage note and payments.

(LO 4)

E10-13 Jernigan Co. receives $300,000 when it issues a $300,000, 10%, mortgage note payable to finance the construction of a building at December 31, 2017. The terms provide for annual installment payments of $50,000 on December 31.

Instructions
Prepare the journal entries to record the mortgage loan and the first two payments.

Prepare long-term liabilities section.

(LO 5)

E10-14 The adjusted trial balance for Karr Farm Corporation at the end of the current year contained the following accounts.

Interest Payable	$ 9,000
Bonds Payable, due 2021	180,000
Premium on Bonds Payable	32,000

Instructions
Prepare the long-term liabilities section of the balance sheet.

Compare two alternatives of financing—issuance of common stock vs. issuance of bonds.

(LO 5)

E10-15 Gilliland Airlines is considering two alternatives for the financing of a purchase of a fleet of airplanes. These two alternatives are:

1. Issue 90,000 shares of common stock at $30 per share. (Cash dividends have not been paid nor is the payment of any contemplated.)
2. Issue 10%, 10-year bonds at face value for $2,700,000.

It is estimated that the company will earn $800,000 before interest and taxes as a result of this purchase. The company has an estimated tax rate of 30% and has 120,000 shares of common stock outstanding prior to the new financing.

Instructions
Determine the effect on net income and earnings per share for these two methods of financing.

Calculate current ratio and working capital before and after paying accounts payable.

(LO 5)

E10-16 Suppose the following financial data were reported by **3M Company** for 2016 and 2017 (dollars in millions).

3M COMPANY
Balance Sheets (partial)

	2017	2016
Current assets		
Cash and cash equivalents	$ 3,040	$1,849
Accounts receivable, net	3,250	3,195
Inventories	2,639	3,013
Other current assets	1,866	1,541
Total current assets	$10,795	$9,598
Current liabilities	$ 4,897	$5,839

Instructions
(a) Calculate the current ratio and working capital for 3M for 2016 and 2017.
(b) Suppose that at the end of 2017, 3M management used $200 million cash to pay off $200 million of accounts payable. How would its current ratio and working capital have changed?

*E10-17 Adcock Company issued $600,000, 9%, 20-year bonds on January 1, 2017, at 103. Interest is payable annually on January 1. Adcock uses straight-line amortization for bond premium or discount.

Prepare entries to record issuance of bonds, payment of interest, amortization of premium, and redemption at maturity.

(LO 6)

Instructions

Prepare the journal entries to record the following.

(a) The issuance of the bonds.
(b) The accrual of interest and the premium amortization on December 31, 2017.
(c) The payment of interest on January 1, 2018.
(d) The redemption of the bonds at maturity, assuming interest for the last interest period has been paid and recorded.

*E10-18 Gridley Company issued $800,000, 11%, 10-year bonds on December 31, 2016, for $730,000. Interest is payable annually on December 31. Gridley Company uses the straight-line method to amortize bond premium or discount.

Prepare entries to record issuance of bonds, payment of interest, amortization of discount, and redemption at maturity.

(LO 6)

Instructions

Prepare the journal entries to record the following.

(a) The issuance of the bonds.
(b) The payment of interest and the discount amortization on December 31, 2017.
(c) The redemption of the bonds at maturity, assuming interest for the last interest period has been paid and recorded.

*E10-19 Lorance Corporation issued $400,000, 7%, 20-year bonds on January 1, 2017, for $360,727. This price resulted in an effective-interest rate of 8% on the bonds. Interest is payable annually on January 1. Lorance uses the effective-interest method to amortize bond premium or discount.

Prepare entries for issuance of bonds, payment of interest, and amortization of discount using effective-interest method.

(LO 7)

Instructions

Prepare the journal entries to record the following. (Round to the nearest dollar.)

(a) The issuance of the bonds.
(b) The accrual of interest and the discount amortization on December 31, 2017.
(c) The payment of interest on January 1, 2018.

*E10-20 LRNA Company issued $380,000, 7%, 10-year bonds on January 1, 2017, for $407,968. This price resulted in an effective-interest rate of 6% on the bonds. Interest is payable annually on January 1. LRNA uses the effective-interest method to amortize bond premium or discount.

Prepare entries of issuance of bonds, payment of interest, and amortization of discount using effective-interest method.

(LO 7)

Instructions

Prepare the journal entries to record the following. (Round to the nearest dollar.)

(a) The issuance of the bonds.
(b) The accrual of interest and the premium amortization on December 31, 2017.
(c) The payment of interest on January 1, 2018.

EXERCISES: SET B AND CHALLENGE EXERCISES

Visit the book's companion website, at **www.wiley.com/college/weygandt**, and choose the Student Companion site to access Exercises: Set B and Challenge Exercises.

PROBLEMS: SET A

*Prepare current liability
entries, adjusting entries, and
current liabilities section.*

(LO 1, 5)

P10-1A On January 1, 2017, the ledger of Accardo Company contains the following liability accounts.

Accounts Payable	$52,000
Sales Taxes Payable	7,700
Unearned Service Revenue	16,000

During January, the following selected transactions occurred.

Jan. 5 Sold merchandise for cash totaling $20,520, which includes 8% sales taxes.
12 Performed services for customers who had made advance payments of $10,000. (Credit Service Revenue.)
14 Paid state revenue department for sales taxes collected in December 2016 ($7,700).
20 Sold 900 units of a new product on credit at $50 per unit, plus 8% sales tax.
21 Borrowed $27,000 from Girard Bank on a 3-month, 8%, $27,000 note.
25 Sold merchandise for cash totaling $12,420, which includes 8% sales taxes.

Instructions
(a) Journalize the January transactions.
(b) Journalize the adjusting entry at January 31 for the outstanding note payable. (*Hint:* Use one-third of a month for the Girard Bank note.)

*(c) Current liability total
$91,100*

(c) Prepare the current liabilities section of the balance sheet at January 31, 2017. Assume no change in accounts payable.

*Journalize and post note
transactions; show balance
sheet presentation.*

(LO 1, 5)

P10-2A The following are selected transactions of Blanco Company. Blanco prepares financial statements **quarterly**.

Jan. 2 Purchased merchandise on account from Nunez Company, $30,000, terms 2/10, n/30. (Blanco uses the perpetual inventory system.)
Feb. 1 Issued a 9%, 2-month, $30,000 note to Nunez in payment of account.
Mar. 31 Accrued interest for 2 months on Nunez note.
Apr. 1 Paid face value and interest on Nunez note.
July 1 Purchased equipment from Marson Equipment paying $11,000 in cash and signing a 10%, 3-month, $60,000 note.
Sept. 30 Accrued interest for 3 months on Marson note.
Oct. 1 Paid face value and interest on Marson note.
Dec. 1 Borrowed $24,000 from the Paola Bank by issuing a 3-month, 8% note with a face value of $24,000.
Dec. 31 Recognized interest expense for 1 month on Paola Bank note.

Instructions
(a) Prepare journal entries for the listed transactions and events.
(b) Post to the accounts Notes Payable, Interest Payable, and Interest Expense.
(c) Show the balance sheet presentation of notes and interest payable at December 31.

(d) $2,110

(d) What is total interest expense for the year?

*Prepare entries to record
issuance of bonds,
interest accrual, and bond
redemption.*

(LO 3, 5)

P10-3A On May 1, 2017, Herron Corp. issued $600,000, 9%, 5-year bonds at face value. The bonds were dated May 1, 2017, and pay interest annually on May 1. Financial statements are prepared annually on December 31.

Instructions
(a) Prepare the journal entry to record the issuance of the bonds.
(b) Prepare the adjusting entry to record the accrual of interest on December 31, 2017.
(c) Show the balance sheet presentation on December 31, 2017.

(d) Int. exp. $18,000

(d) Prepare the journal entry to record payment of interest on May 1, 2018.
(e) Prepare the adjusting entry to record the accrual of interest on December 31, 2018.

(f) Loss $12,000

(f) Assume that on January 1, 2019, Herron pays the accrued bond interest and calls the bonds at 102. Record the payment of interest and redemption of the bonds.

*Prepare entries to record
issuance of bonds, interest
accrual, and bond redemption.*

(LO 3, 5)

P10-4A Kershaw Electric sold $6,000,000, 10%, 15-year bonds on January 1, 2017. The bonds were dated January 1, 2017, and paid interest on January 1. The bonds were sold at 98.

Instructions

(a) Prepare the journal entry to record the issuance of the bonds on January 1, 2017.

(b) At December 31, 2017, $8,000 of the Discount on Bonds Payable account has been amortized. Show the balance sheet presentation of the long-term liability at December 31, 2017.

(c) On January 1, 2019, when the carrying value of the bonds was $5,896,000, the company redeemed the bonds at 102. Record the redemption of the bonds assuming that interest for the period has already been paid.

(c) Loss $224,000

P10-5A Talkington Electronics issues a $400,000, 8%, 10-year mortgage note on December 31, 2016. The proceeds from the note are to be used in financing a new research laboratory. The terms of the note provide for annual installment payments, exclusive of real estate taxes and insurance, of $59,612. Payments are due on December 31.

Prepare installment payments schedule and journal entries for a mortgage note payable.

(LO 4, 5)

Instructions

(a) Prepare an installment payments schedule for the first 4 years.

(b) Prepare the entries for (1) the loan and (2) the first installment payment.

(c) Show how the total mortgage liability should be reported on the balance sheet at December 31, 2017.

(b) December 31 debit Mortgage Payable $27,612

(c) Current liability—2017 $29,821

*P10-6A Paris Electric sold $3,000,000, 10%, 10-year bonds on January 1, 2017. The bonds were dated January 1 and pay interest annually on January 1. Paris Electric uses the straight-line method to amortize bond premium or discount. The bonds were sold at 104.

Prepare entries to record issuance of bonds, interest accrual, and straight-line amortization for 2 years.

(LO 5, 6)

Instructions

(a) Prepare the journal entry to record the issuance of the bonds on January 1, 2017.

(b) Prepare a bond premium amortization schedule for the first 4 interest periods.

(c) Prepare the journal entries for interest and the amortization of the premium in 2017 and 2018.

(d) Show the balance sheet presentation of the bond liability at December 31, 2018.

(b) Amortization $12,000

(d) Premium on bonds payable $96,000

*P10-7A Saberhagen Company sold $3,500,000, 8%, 10-year bonds on January 1, 2017. The bonds were dated January 1, 2017, and pay interest annually on January 1. Saberhagen Company uses the straight-line method to amortize bond premium or discount.

Prepare entries to record issuance of bonds, interest, and straight-line amortization of bond premium and discount.

(LO 5, 6)

Instructions

(a) Prepare all the necessary journal entries to record the issuance of the bonds and bond interest expense for 2017, assuming that the bonds sold at 104.

(b) Prepare journal entries as in part (a) assuming that the bonds sold at 98.

(c) Show balance sheet presentation for the bonds at December 31, 2017, for both the requirements in (a) and (b).

(a) Amortization $14,000

(b) Amortization $7,000

(c) Premium on bonds payable $126,000
Discount on bonds payable $63,000

*P10-8A The following is taken from the Colaw Company balance sheet.

Prepare entries to record interest payments, straight-line premium amortization, and redemption of bonds.

(LO 6)

COLAW COMPANY
Balance Sheet (partial)
December 31, 2017

Current liabilities		
Interest payable (for 12 months from January 1 to December 31)		$ 210,000
Long-term liabilities		
Bonds payable, 7% due January 1, 2028	$3,000,000	
Add: Premium on bonds payable	200,000	3,200,000

Interest is payable annually on January 1. The bonds are callable on any annual interest date. Colaw uses straight-line amortization for any bond premium or discount. From December 31, 2017, the bonds will be outstanding for an additional 10 years (120 months).

Instructions

(a) Journalize the payment of bond interest on January 1, 2018.

(b) Prepare the entry to amortize bond premium and to accrue the interest due on December 31, 2018.

(b) Amortization $20,000

(c) Gain $60,000

(c) Assume that on January 1, 2019, after paying interest, Colaw Company calls bonds having a face value of $1,200,000. The call price is 101. Record the redemption of the bonds.

(d) Amortization $12,000

(d) Prepare the adjusting entry at December 31, 2019, to amortize bond premium and to accrue interest on the remaining bonds.

Prepare journal entries to record issuance of bonds, payment of interest, and amortization of bond discount using effective-interest method.

(LO 7)

(c) Interest
    Expense $100,051

*P10-9A On January 1, 2017, Lock Corporation issued $1,800,000 face value, 5%, 10-year bonds at $1,667,518. This price resulted in an effective-interest rate of 6% on the bonds. Lock uses the effective-interest method to amortize bond premium or discount. The bonds pay annual interest January 1.

Instructions
(Round all computations to the nearest dollar.)
(a) Prepare the journal entry to record the issuance of the bonds on January 1, 2017.
(b) Prepare an amortization table through December 31, 2019 (three interest periods) for this bond issue.
(c) Prepare the journal entry to record the accrual of interest and the amortization of the discount on December 31, 2017.
(d) Prepare the journal entry to record the payment of interest on January 1, 2018.
(e) Prepare the journal entry to record the accrual of interest and the amortization of the discount on December 31, 2018.

Prepare journal entries to record issuance of bonds, payment of interest, and effective-interest amortization, and balance sheet presentation.

(LO 5, 7)

(a) (4) Interest
    Expense $128,162

*P10-10A On January 1, 2017, Jade Company issued $2,000,000 face value, 7%, 10-year bonds at $2,147,202. This price resulted in a 6% effective-interest rate on the bonds. Jade uses the effective-interest method to amortize bond premium or discount. The bonds pay annual interest on each January 1.

Instructions
(a) Prepare the journal entries to record the following transactions.
    (1) The issuance of the bonds on January 1, 2017.
    (2) Accrual of interest and amortization of the premium on December 31, 2017.
    (3) The payment of interest on January 1, 2018.
    (4) Accrual of interest and amortization of the premium on December 31, 2018.
(b) Show the proper long-term liabilities balance sheet presentation for the liability for bonds payable at December 31, 2018.
(c) ◆━━━━ Provide the answers to the following questions in narrative form.
    (1) What amount of interest expense is reported for 2018?
    (2) Would the bond interest expense reported in 2018 be the same as, greater than, or less than the amount that would be reported if the straight-line method of amortization were used?

PROBLEMS: SET B AND SET C

Visit the book's companion website, at **www.wiley.com/college/weygandt**, and choose the Student Companion site to access Problems: Set B and Set C.

COMPREHENSIVE PROBLEMS

CP10-1 James Corporation's balance sheet at December 31, 2016, is presented below.

JAMES CORPORATION
Balance Sheet
December 31, 2016

Cash	$ 30,500	Accounts payable	$ 13,750
Inventory	25,750	Interest payable	2,500
Prepaid insurance	5,600	Bonds payable	50,000
Equipment	43,000	Common stock	20,000
	$104,850	Retained earnings	18,600
			$104,850

During 2017, the following transactions occurred.

1. James paid $2,500 interest on the bonds on January 1, 2017.
2. James purchased $241,100 of inventory on account.
3. James sold for $450,000 cash inventory which cost $250,000. James also collected $31,500 sales taxes.
4. James paid $230,000 on accounts payable.
5. James paid $2,500 interest on the bonds on July 1, 2017.
6. The prepaid insurance ($5,600) expired on July 31.
7. On August 1, James paid $12,000 for insurance coverage from August 1, 2017, through July 31, 2018.
8. James paid $24,000 sales taxes to the state.
9. Paid other operating expenses, $91,000.
10. Retired the bonds on December 31, 2017, by paying $47,000 plus $2,500 interest.
11. Issued $90,000 of 8% bonds on December 31, 2017, at 104. The bonds pay interest every December 31.

Adjustment data:
1. Recorded the insurance expired from item 7.
2. The equipment was acquired on December 31, 2016, and will be depreciated on a straight-line basis over 5 years with a $3,000 salvage value.
3. The income tax rate is 30%. (*Hint:* Prepare the income statement up to income before taxes and multiply by 30% to compute the amount.)

Instructions
(You may want to set up T-accounts to determine ending balances.)

(a) Prepare journal entries for the transactions listed above and adjusting entries.
(b) Prepare an adjusted trial balance at December 31, 2017.   (b) Totals $652,070
(c) Prepare an income statement and a retained earnings statement for the year ending December 31,   (c) N.I. $61,880
2017, and a classified balance sheet as of December 31, 2017.

CP10-2 Eastland Company and Westside Company are competing businesses. Both began operations 6 years ago and are quite similar in most respects. The current balance sheet data for the two companies are shown below.

	Eastland Company	Westside Company
Cash	$ 63,300	$ 48,400
Accounts receivable	304,700	302,500
Allowance for doubtful accounts	(13,600)	–0–
Inventory	463,900	515,200
Plant and equipment	255,300	257,300
Accumulated depreciation—plant and equipment	(112,650)	(189,850)
Total assets	$960,950	$933,550
Current liabilities	$440,200	$431,500
Long-term liabilities	78,000	82,000
Total liabilities	518,200	513,500
Stockholders' equity	442,750	420,050
Total liabilities and stockholders' equity	$960,950	$933,550

You have been engaged as a consultant to conduct a review of the two companies. Your goal is to determine which of them is in the stronger financial position.

Your review of their financial statements quickly reveals that the two companies have not followed the same accounting practices. The differences and your conclusions regarding them are summarized below.

1. Eastland Company has used the allowance method of accounting for bad debts. A review shows that the amount of its write-offs each year has been quite close to the allowances that have been provided. It therefore seems reasonable to have confidence in its current estimate of bad debts.

   Westside Company has used the direct write-off method for bad debts, and it has been somewhat slow to write off its uncollectible accounts. Based upon an aging analysis and review of its accounts receivable, it is estimated that $18,000 of its existing accounts will probably prove to be uncollectible.

2. Eastland Company has determined the cost of its merchandise inventory on a LIFO basis. The result is that its inventory appears on the balance sheet at an amount that is below its current replacement cost. Based upon a detailed physical examination of its merchandise on hand, the current replacement cost of its inventory is estimated at $513,000.

   Westside Company has used the FIFO method of valuing its merchandise inventory. Its ending inventory appears on the balance sheet at an amount that quite closely approximates its current replacement cost.

3. Eastland Company estimated a useful life of 12 years and a salvage value of $30,000 for its plant and equipment. It has been depreciating them on a straight-line basis.

   Westside Company has the same type of plant and equipment. However, it estimated a useful life of 10 years and a salvage value of $10,000. It has been depreciating its plant and equipment using the double-declining-balance method.

   Based upon engineering studies of these types of plant and equipment, you conclude that Westside's estimates and method for calculating depreciation are the more appropriate.

4. Among its current liabilities, Eastland has included the portions of long-term liabilities that become due within the next year. Westside has not done so.

   You find that $16,000 of Westside's $82,000 of long-term liabilities are due to be repaid in the current year.

Instructions

(a) Total assets:
    Eastland $934,325
    Westside $915,550

(a) Revise the balance sheets presented above so that the data are comparable and reflect the current financial position for each of the two companies.

(b) ✏ Prepare a brief report to your client stating your conclusions.

CONTINUING PROBLEM

COOKIE CREATIONS

(*Note:* This is a continuation of the Cookie Creations problem from Chapters 1 through 9.)

CC10 Recall that Cookie Creations sells fine European mixers that it purchases from Kzinski Supply Co. Kzinski warrants the mixers to be free of defects in material and workmanship for a period of one year from the date of original purchase. If the mixer has such a defect, Kzinski will repair or replace the mixer free of charge for parts and labor.

Go to the book's companion website, **www.wiley.com/college/weygandt**, *to see the completion of this problem.*

© leungchopan/
Shutterstock

BROADENING YOUR **PERSPECTIVE**

FINANCIAL REPORTING AND ANALYSIS

Financial Reporting Problem: Apple Inc.

BYP10-1 The financial statements of **Apple Inc.** are presented in Appendix A. Instructions for accessing and using the company's complete annual report, including the notes to the financial statements, are also provided in Appendix A.

Instructions

Refer to Apple's financial statements and answer the following questions about current and contingent liabilities and payroll costs.

(a) What were Apple's total current liabilities at September 28, 2013? What was the increase/decrease in Apple's total current liabilities from the prior year?

(b) In Apple's Note 10, the company explains the nature of its contingencies. Under what conditions does Apple recognize (record and report) liabilities for contingencies?

(c) What were the components of total current liabilities on September 28, 2013?

(d) What were Apple's total long-term liabilities at September 28, 2013? What was the increase/decrease in total long-term liabilities from the prior year?

(e) Determine whether Apple redeemed (bought back) any long-term liabilities during the fiscal year ended September 28, 2013.

Comparative Analysis Problem:
PepsiCo, Inc. vs. The Coca-Cola Company

BYP10-2 **PepsiCo, Inc.**'s financial statements are presented in Appendix B. Financial statements of **The Coca-Cola Company** are presented in Appendix C. Instructions for accessing and using the complete annual reports of PepsiCo and Coca-Cola, including the notes to the financial statements, are also provided in Appendices B and C, respectively.

Instructions

(a) At December 28, 2013, what was PepsiCo's largest current liability account? What were its total current liabilities? At December 31, 2013, what was Coca-Cola's largest current liability account? What were its total current liabilities?

(b) Based on information contained in those financial statements, compute the following 2013 values for each company:
   (1) Working capital.
   (2) Current ratio.

(c) What conclusions concerning the relative liquidity of these companies can be drawn from these data?

(d) Based on the information contained in these financial statements, compute the following 2013 ratios for each company.
   (1) Debt to assets.
   (2) Times interest earned.

(e) What conclusions concerning the companies' long-run solvency can be drawn from these ratios?

Comparative Analysis Problem:
Amazon.com, Inc. vs. Wal-Mart Stores, Inc.

BYP10-3 **Amazon.com, Inc.**'s financial statements are presented in Appendix D. Financial statements of **Wal-Mart Stores, Inc.** are presented in Appendix E. Instructions for accessing and using the complete annual reports of Amazon and Wal-Mart, including the notes to the financial statements, are also provided in Appendices D and E, respectively.

Instructions

(a) At December 31, 2013, what was Amazon's largest current liability account? What were its total current liabilities? At January 31, 2014, what was Wal-Mart's largest current liability account? What were its total current liabilities?

(b) Based on information in these financial statements, compute the following 2013 values for Amazon and 2014 values for Wal-Mart:
   (1) Working capital.
   (2) Current ratio.

(c) What conclusions concerning the relative liquidity of these companies can be drawn from these data?

(d) Based on the information contained in these financial statements, compute the following 2013 ratios for Amazon and 2014 ratios for Wal-Mart.
   (1) Debt to assets.
   (2) Times interest earned.

(e) What conclusions concerning the companies' long-run solvency can be drawn from these ratios?

Real-World Focus

BYP10-4 Bond or debt securities pay a stated rate of interest. This rate of interest is dependent on the risk associated with the investment. Also, bond prices change when the risks associated with those bonds change. **Standard & Poor's** provides ratings for companies that issue debt securities.

Address: **www.img.en25.com/Web/StandardandPoors/GuidetoCreditRatingsCriteria.pdf**, or go to **www.wiley.com/college/weygandt**

Instructions

Go to the website shown and answer the following questions.

(a) Explain the meaning of an "A" rating. Explain the meaning of a "C" rating.
(b) What types of things can cause a change in a company's credit rating?
(c) Explain the relationship between a company's credit rating and the merit of an investment in that company's bonds.

CRITICAL THINKING

Decision-Making Across the Organization

*BYP10-5 On January 1, 2015, Glover Corporation issued $2,400,000 of 5-year, 8% bonds at 95. The bonds pay interest annually on January 1. By January 1, 2017, the market rate of interest for bonds of risk similar to those of Glover Corporation had risen. As a result, the market value of these bonds was $2,000,000 on January 1, 2017—below their carrying value. Joanna Glover, president of the company, suggests repurchasing all of these bonds in the open market at the $2,000,000 price. To do so, the company will have to issue $2,000,000 (face value) of new 10-year, 11% bonds at par. The president asks you, as controller, "What is the feasibility of my proposed repurchase plan?"

Instructions

With the class divided into groups, answer the following.

(a) What is the carrying value of the outstanding Glover Corporation 5-year bonds on January 1, 2017? (Assume straight-line amortization.)
(b) Prepare the journal entry to redeem the 5-year bonds on January 1, 2017. Prepare the journal entry to issue the new 10-year bonds.
(c) Prepare a short memo to the president in response to her request for advice. List the economic factors that you believe should be considered for her repurchase proposal.

Communication Activity

BYP10-6 Sam Masasi, president of Masasi Corporation, is considering the issuance of bonds to finance an expansion of his business. He has asked you to (1) discuss the advantages of bonds over common stock financing, (2) indicate the types of bonds he might issue, and (3) explain the issuing procedures used in bond transactions.

Instructions

Write a memo to the president, answering his request.

Ethics Case

BYP10-7 Ken Iwig is the president, founder, and majority owner of Olathe Medical Corporation, an emerging medical technology products company. Olathe is in dire need of additional capital to keep operating and to bring several promising products to final development, testing, and production. Ken, as owner of 51% of the outstanding stock, manages the company's operations. He places heavy emphasis on research and development and on long-term growth. The other principal stockholder is Barb Lowery who, as a nonemployee investor, owns 40% of the stock. Barb would like to deemphasize the R&D functions and emphasize the marketing function, to maximize short-run sales and profits from existing products. She believes this strategy would raise the market price of Olathe's stock.

All of Ken's personal capital and borrowing power is tied up in his 51% stock ownership. He knows that any offering of additional shares of stock will dilute his controlling interest because he won't be able to participate in such an issuance. But, Barb has money and would likely buy enough shares to gain control of Olathe. She then would dictate the company's future direction, even if it meant replacing Ken as president and CEO.

The company already has considerable debt. Raising additional debt will be costly, will adversely affect Olathe's credit rating, and will increase the company's reported losses due to the growth in interest expense. Barb and the other minority stockholders express opposition to the assumption of additional debt, fearing the company will be pushed to the brink of bankruptcy. Wanting to maintain his control and to preserve the direction of "his" company, Ken is doing everything to avoid a stock issuance. He is contemplating a large issuance of bonds, even if it means the bonds are issued with a high effective-interest rate.

Instructions
(a) Who are the stakeholders in this situation?
(b) What are the ethical issues in this case?
(c) What would you do if you were Ken?

All About You

BYP10-8 Medical costs are substantial and rising. But will they be the most substantial expense over your lifetime? Not likely. Will it be housing or food? Again, not likely. The answer is taxes. On average, Americans work 107 days per year to afford their taxes. Companies, too, have large tax burdens. They look very hard at tax issues in deciding where to build their plants and where to locate their administrative headquarters.

Instructions
(a) Determine what your state income taxes are if your taxable income is $60,000 and you file as a single taxpayer in the state in which you live.
(b) Assume that you own a home worth $200,000 in your community and the tax rate is 2.1%. Compute the property taxes you would pay.
(c) Assume that the total gasoline bill for your automobile is $1,200 a year (300 gallons at $4 per gallon). What are the amounts of state and federal taxes that you pay on the $1,200?
(d) Assume that your purchases for the year total $9,000. Of this amount, $5,000 was for food and prescription drugs. What is the amount of sales tax you would pay on these purchases? (Many states do not levy a sales tax on food or prescription drugs. Does yours?)
(e) Determine what your Social Security taxes are if your income is $60,000.
(f) Determine what your federal income taxes are if your taxable income is $60,000 and you file as a single taxpayer.
(g) Determine your total taxes paid based on the above calculations, and determine the percentage of income that you would pay in taxes based on the following formula: Total taxes paid ÷ Total income.

BYP10-9 Numerous articles have been written that identify early warning signs that you might be getting into trouble with your personal debt load. You can find many good articles on this topic on the Internet.

Instructions
Find an article that identifies early warning signs of personal debt trouble. Write a summary of the article and bring your summary and the article to class to share.

FASB Codification Activity

BYP10-10 If your school has a subscription to the FASB Codification, go to **http://aaahq.org/ ascLogin.cfm** to log in and prepare responses to the following.
(a) What is the definition of current liabilities?
(b) What is the definition of long-term obligation?
(c) What guidance does the Codification provide for the disclosure of long-term liabilities?

A Look at IFRS

LEARNING OBJECTIVE 8   Compare the accounting for liabilities under GAAP and IFRS.

IFRS and GAAP have similar definitions of liabilities but have a different approach for recording certain liabilities.

Key Points

Following are the key similarities and differences between GAAP and IFRS as related to accounting for liabilities.

Similarities

- The basic definition of a liability under GAAP and IFRS is very similar. In a more technical way, liabilities are defined by the IASB as a present obligation of the entity arising from past events, the settlement of which is expected to result in an outflow from the entity of resources embodying economic benefits.

- The accounting for current liabilities such as notes payable, unearned revenue, and payroll taxes payable are similar between GAAP and IFRS.

- IFRS requires that companies classify liabilities as current or noncurrent on the face of the statement of financial position (balance sheet), except in industries where a **presentation** based on liquidity would be considered to provide more useful information (such as financial institutions). When current liabilities (also called short-term liabilities) are presented, they are generally presented in order of liquidity.

- Under IFRS, liabilities are classified as current if they are expected to be paid within 12 months.

- Similar to GAAP, items are normally reported in order of liquidity. Companies sometimes show liabilities before assets. Also, they will sometimes show long-term liabilities before current liabilities.

- The basic calculation for bond valuation is the same under GAAP and IFRS. In addition, the accounting for bond liability transactions is essentially the same between GAAP and IFRS.

- IFRS requires use of the effective-interest method for amortization of bond discounts and premiums. GAAP also requires the effective-interest method, except that it allows use of the straight-line method where the difference is not material. Under IFRS, companies do not use a premium or discount account but instead show the bond at its net amount. For example, if a $100,000 bond was issued at 97, under IFRS a company would record:

Cash	97,000	
Bonds Payable		97,000

Differences

- The accounting for convertible bonds differs between **IFRS** and **GAAP**. Unlike GAAP, IFRS splits the proceeds from the convertible bond between an equity component and a debt component. The equity conversion rights are reported in equity.

    To illustrate, assume that Harris Corp. issues convertible 7% bonds with a face value of $1,000,000 and receives $1,000,000. Comparable bonds without a conversion feature would have required a 9% rate of interest. To determine how much of the proceeds would be allocated to debt and how much to equity, the promised payments of the bond obligation would be discounted at the market rate of 9%. Suppose that this results in a present value of $850,000. The entry to record the issuance would be:

Cash	1,000,000	
Bonds Payable		850,000
Share Premium—Conversion Equity		150,000

- Under IFRS, companies sometimes will net current liabilities against current assets to show working capital on the face of the statement of financial position.

Looking to the Future

The FASB and IASB are currently involved in two projects, each of which has implications for the accounting for liabilities. One project is investigating approaches to differentiate between debt and equity instruments. The other project, the elements phase of the conceptual framework project, will evaluate the definitions of the fundamental building blocks of accounting. The results of these projects could change the classification of many debt and equity securities.

IFRS Practice

IFRS Self-Test Questions

1. Which of the following is **false**?
    (a) Under IFRS, current liabilities must always be presented before noncurrent liabilities.
    (b) Under IFRS, an item is a current liability if it will be paid within the next 12 months.
    (c) Under IFRS, current liabilities are sometimes netted against current assets on the statement of financial position.
    (d) Under IFRS, a liability is only recognized if it is a present obligation.

2. The accounting for bonds payable is:
   (a) essentially the same under IFRS and GAAP.
   (b) differs in that GAAP requires use of the straight-line method for amortization of bond premium and discount.
   (c) the same except that market prices may be different because the present value calculations are different between IFRS and GAAP.
   (d) not covered by IFRS.

3. Stevens Corporation issued 5% convertible bonds with a total face value of $3,000,000 for $3,000,000. If the bonds had not had a conversion feature, they would have sold for $2,600,000. Under IFRS, the entry to record the transaction would require a credit to:
   (a) Bonds Payable for $3,000,000.
   (b) Bonds Payable for $400,000.
   (c) Share Premium—Conversion Equity for $400,000.
   (d) Discount on Bonds Payable for $400,000.

4. Which of the following is **true** regarding accounting for amortization of bond discount and premium?
   (a) Both IFRS and GAAP must use the effective-interest method.
   (b) GAAP must use the effective-interest method, but IFRS may use either the effective-interest method or the straight-line method.
   (c) IFRS is required to use the effective-interest method.
   (d) GAAP is required to use the straight-line method.

5. The joint projects of the FASB and IASB could potentially:
   (a) change the definition of liabilities.
   (b) change the definition of equity.
   (c) change the definition of assets.
   (d) All of the above.

IFRS Exercises

IFRS10-1 Briefly describe some of the similarities and differences between GAAP and IFRS with respect to the accounting for liabilities.

IFRS10-2 Ratzlaff Company issues (in euros) €2 million, 10-year, 8% bonds at 97, with interest payable annually on January 1.

Instructions
(a) Prepare the journal entry to record the sale of these bonds on January 1, 2017.
(b) Assuming instead that the above bonds sold for 104, prepare the journal entry to record the sale of these bonds on January 1, 2017.

IFRS10-3 Archer Company issued (in pounds) £4,000,000 par value, 7% convertible bonds at 99 for cash. The net present value of the debt without the conversion feature is £3,800,000. Prepare the journal entry to record the issuance of the convertible bonds.

International Financial Statement Analysis: Louis Vuitton

IFRS10-4 The financial statements of Louis Vuitton are presented in Appendix F. Instructions for accessing and using the company's complete annual report, including the notes to its financial statements, are also provided in Appendix F.

Instructions
Use the company's annual report to answer the following questions.

(a) What were the total current liabilities for the company as of December 31, 2013? What portion of these current liabilities related to provisions?
(b) According to the notes to the financial statements, what is the composition of long-term gross borrowings?
(c) According to the accounting policy note to the financial statements, how are borrowings measured?
(d) Determine the amount of fixed-rate and adjustable-rate (floating) borrowings (gross) that the company reports.

Answers to IFRS Self-Test Questions
1. a **2.** a **3.** c **4.** c **5.** d

11

Corporations: Organization, Stock Transactions, Dividends, and Retained Earnings

CHAPTER PREVIEW Corporations like Nike and adidas have substantial resources at their disposal. In fact, the corporation is the dominant form of business organization in the United States in terms of sales, earnings, and number of employees. All of the 500 largest companies in the United States are corporations. In this chapter, we will explain the essential features of a corporation and the accounting for a corporation's capital stock transactions.

FEATURE STORY

What's Cooking?

What major U.S. corporation got its start 41 years ago with a waffle iron? *Hint:* It doesn't sell food. *Second hint:* Swoosh. *Third hint:* "Just do it." That's right, Nike. In 1971, Nike co-founder Bill Bowerman put a piece of rubber into a kitchen waffle iron, and its trademark sole was born. It seems fair to say that at Nike, "They don't make 'em like they used to."

Nike was co-founded by Bowerman and Phil Knight, a member of Bowerman's University of Oregon track team. Each began in the shoe business independently during the early 1960s. Bowerman got his start by making hand-crafted running shoes for his University of Oregon track team. Knight, after completing graduate school, started a small business importing low-cost, high-quality shoes from Japan. In 1964, the two joined forces, each contributing $500, and formed Blue Ribbon Sports, a partnership that marketed Japanese shoes.

It wasn't until 1971 that the company began manufacturing its own line of shoes. With the new shoes came a new corporate name–Nike–the Greek goddess of victory. It is hard to imagine that the company that now boasts a stable full of world-class athletes as promoters at one time had part-time employees selling shoes out of car trunks at track meets. Nike has achieved its success through relentless innovation combined with unbridled promotion.

By 1980, Nike was sufficiently established and issued its first stock to the public. That same year, it created a stock ownership program for its employees, allowing them to share in the company's success. Since then, Nike has enjoyed phenomenal growth, with 2014 sales reaching $27.8 billion and total dividends paid of $799 million.

Nike is not alone in its quest for the top of the sport shoe world. Reebok used to be Nike's arch rival (get it? "arch"), but then Reebok was acquired by the German company adidas. Now adidas pushes Nike every step of the way.

The shoe market is fickle, with new styles becoming popular almost daily and vast international markets still lying untapped. Whether one of these two giants does eventually take control of the pedi-planet remains to be seen. Meanwhile, the shareholders sit anxiously in the stands as this Olympic-size drama unfolds.

CHAPTER OUTLINE

Learning Objectives

1 Discuss the major characteristics of a corporation.
- Characteristics of a corporation
- Forming a corporation
- Stockholder rights
- Stock issue considerations
- Corporate capital

DO IT! **1a** Corporate Organization
1b Corporate Capital

2 Explain how to account for the issuance of common and preferred stock.
- Accounting for common stock
- Accounting for preferred stock

DO IT! **2** Issuance of Stock

3 Explain how to account for treasury stock.
- Purchase of treasury stock
- Disposal of treasury stock

DO IT! **3** Treasury Stock

4 Explain how to account for cash dividends.
- Cash dividends
- Dividend preferences

DO IT! **4** Dividends on Preferred and Common Stock

5 Explain how to account for stock dividends and splits.
- Stock dividends
- Stock splits

DO IT! **5** Stock Dividends and Stock Splits

6 Discuss how stockholders' equity is reported and analyzed.
- Retained earnings
- Statement presentation and analysis

DO IT! **6a** Retained Earnings Statement
6b Stockholders' Equity

Franck Fife/AFP/Getty Images, Inc.

Go to the **REVIEW AND PRACTICE** section at the end of the chapter for a review of key concepts and practice applications with solutions.

Visit **WileyPLUS with ORION** for additional tutorials and practice opportunities.

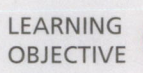

Discuss the major characteristics of a corporation.

In 1819, Chief Justice John Marshall defined a corporation as "an artificial being, invisible, intangible, and existing only in contemplation of law." This definition is the foundation for the prevailing legal interpretation that a **corporation** is an **entity separate and distinct from its owners**.

A corporation is created by law, and its continued existence depends upon the statutes of the state in which it is incorporated. As a legal entity, a corporation has most of the rights and privileges of a person. The major exceptions relate to privileges that only a living person can exercise, such as the right to vote or to hold public office. A corporation is subject to the same duties and responsibilities as a person. For example, it must abide by the laws, and it must pay taxes.

Two common ways to classify corporations are by **purpose** and by **ownership**. A corporation may be organized for the purpose of making a profit, or it may be not-for-profit. For-profit corporations include such well-known companies as **McDonald's**, **Nike**, **PepsiCo**, and **Google**. Not-for-profit corporations are organized for charitable, medical, or educational purposes. Examples are the **Salvation Army** and the **American Cancer Society**.

Classification by ownership differentiates publicly held and privately held corporations. A **publicly held corporation** may have thousands of stockholders. Its stock is regularly traded on a national securities exchange such as the New York Stock Exchange or NASDAQ. Examples are **IBM**, **Caterpillar**, and **Apple**.

Alternative Terminology
Privately held corporations are also referred to as *closely held corporations.*

In contrast, a **privately held corporation** usually has only a few stockholders, and does not offer its stock for sale to the general public. Privately held companies are generally much smaller than publicly held companies, although some notable exceptions exist. **Cargill Inc.**, a private corporation that trades in grain and other commodities, is one of the largest companies in the United States.

Characteristics of a Corporation

In 1964, when **Nike**'s founders Phil Knight and Bill Bowerman were just getting started in the running shoe business, they formed their original organization as a partnership. In 1968, they reorganized the company as a corporation. A number of characteristics distinguish corporations from proprietorships and partnerships. We explain the most important of these characteristics below.

SEPARATE LEGAL EXISTENCE

Stockholders
Legal existence separate from owners

As an entity separate and distinct from its owners, the corporation acts under its own name rather than in the name of its stockholders. Nike may buy, own, and sell property. It may borrow money, and it may enter into legally binding contracts in its own name. It may also sue or be sued, and it pays its own taxes.

In a partnership, the acts of the owners (partners) bind the partnership. In contrast, the acts of its owners (stockholders) do not bind the corporation unless such owners are **agents** of the corporation. For example, if you owned shares of Nike stock, you would not have the right to purchase inventory for the company unless you were designated as an agent of the corporation.

LIMITED LIABILITY OF STOCKHOLDERS

Stockholders
Limited liability of stockholders

Since a corporation is a separate legal entity, creditors have recourse only to corporate assets to satisfy their claims. The liability of stockholders is normally limited to their investment in the corporation. Creditors have no legal claim on the personal assets of the owners unless fraud has occurred. Even in the event of bankruptcy, stockholders' losses are generally limited to their capital investment in the corporation.

TRANSFERABLE OWNERSHIP RIGHTS

Shares of capital stock give ownership in a corporation. These shares are transferable units. Stockholders may dispose of part or all of their interest in a corporation simply by selling their stock. The transfer of an ownership interest in a partnership requires the consent of each owner. In contrast, the transfer of stock is entirely at the discretion of the stockholder. It does not require the approval of either the corporation or other stockholders.

Transferable ownership rights

The transfer of ownership rights between stockholders normally has no effect on the daily operating activities of the corporation. Nor does it affect the corporation's assets, liabilities, and total ownership equity. The transfer of these ownership rights is a transaction between individual owners. The company does not participate in the transfer of these ownership rights after the original sale of the capital stock.

ABILITY TO ACQUIRE CAPITAL

It is relatively easy for a corporation to obtain capital through the issuance of stock. Buying stock in a corporation is often attractive to an investor because a stockholder has limited liability and shares of stock are readily transferable. Also, numerous individuals can become stockholders by investing relatively small amounts of money.

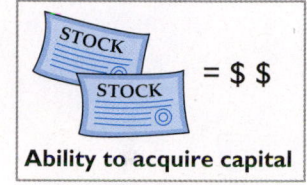

Ability to acquire capital

CONTINUOUS LIFE

The life of a corporation is stated in its charter. The life may be perpetual, or it may be limited to a specific number of years. If it is limited, the company can extend the life through renewal of the charter. Since a corporation is a separate legal entity, its continuance as a going concern is not affected by the withdrawal, death, or incapacity of a stockholder, employee, or officer. As a result, a successful company can have a continuous and perpetual life.

Continuous life

CORPORATION MANAGEMENT

Stockholders legally own the corporation. However, they manage the corporation indirectly through a board of directors they elect. Philip Knight is the chairman of the board for **Nike**. The board, in turn, formulates the operating policies for the company. The board also selects officers, such as a president and one or more vice presidents, to execute policy and to perform daily management functions. As a result of the Sarbanes-Oxley Act, the board is now required to monitor management's actions more closely. Many feel that the failures of **Enron**, **WorldCom**, and more recently **MF Global** could have been avoided by more diligent boards.

Illustration 11-1 (page 502) presents a typical organization chart showing the delegation of responsibility. The chief executive officer (CEO) has overall responsibility for managing the business. As the organization chart shows, the CEO delegates responsibility to other officers. The chief accounting officer is the **controller**. The controller's responsibilities include (1) maintaining the accounting records, (2) ensuring an adequate system of internal control, and (3) preparing financial statements, tax returns, and internal reports. The **treasurer** has custody of the corporation's funds and is responsible for maintaining the company's cash position.

The organizational structure of a corporation enables a company to hire professional managers to run the business. On the other hand, the separation of ownership and management often reduces an owner's ability to actively manage the company.

ETHICS NOTE

Managers who are not owners are often compensated based on the performance of the firm. They thus may be tempted to exaggerate firm performance by inflating income figures.

Illustration 11-1
Corporation organization chart

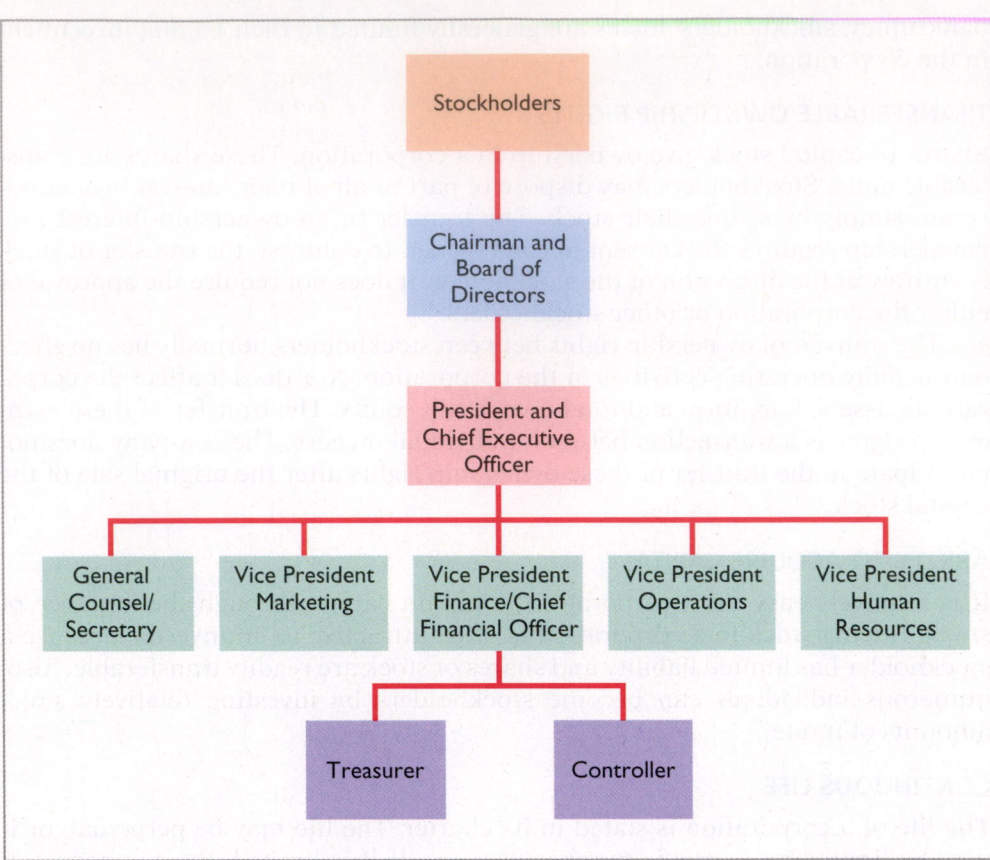

GOVERNMENT REGULATIONS

Government regulations

A corporation is subject to numerous state and federal regulations. For example, state laws usually prescribe the requirements for issuing stock, the distributions of earnings permitted to stockholders, and the acceptable methods for buying back and retiring stock. Federal securities laws govern the sale of capital stock to the general public. Also, most publicly held corporations are required to make extensive disclosure of their financial affairs to the Securities and Exchange Commission (SEC) through quarterly and annual reports (Forms 10Q and 10K). In addition, when a corporation lists its stock on organized securities exchanges, it must comply with the reporting requirements of these exchanges. Government regulations are designed to protect the owners of the corporation.

ADDITIONAL TAXES

Additional taxes

Owners of proprietorships and partnerships report their share of earnings on their personal income tax returns. The individual owner then pays taxes on this amount. Corporations, on the other hand, must pay federal and state income taxes **as a separate legal entity**. These taxes can be substantial. They can amount to as much as 40% of taxable income.

In addition, stockholders must pay taxes on cash dividends (pro rata distributions of net income). Thus, many argue that the government taxes corporate income **twice (double taxation)**—once at the corporate level and again at the individual level.

In summary, Illustration 11-2 shows the advantages and disadvantages of a corporation compared to a proprietorship and a partnership.

Forming a Corporation

A corporation is formed by grant of a state **charter**. The charter is a document that describes the name and purpose of the corporation, the types and number of shares of stock that are authorized to be issued, the names of the individuals that

Advantages	Disadvantages
Separate legal existence	Corporation management—separation of ownership and management
Limited liability of stockholders	
Transferable ownership rights	Government regulations
Ability to acquire capital	Additional taxes
Continuous life	
Corporation management—professional managers	

Illustration 11-2
Advantages and disadvantages of a corporation

formed the company, and the number of shares that these individuals agreed to purchase. Regardless of the number of states in which a corporation has operating divisions, it is incorporated in only one state.

It is to the company's advantage to incorporate in a state whose laws are favorable to the corporate form of business organization. For example, although **General Motors** has its headquarters in Michigan, it is incorporated in New Jersey. In fact, more and more corporations have been incorporating in states with rules that favor existing management. For example, **Gulf Oil** changed its state of incorporation to Delaware to thwart possible unfriendly takeovers. There, certain defensive tactics against takeovers can be approved by the board of directors alone, without a vote by shareholders.

Upon receipt of its charter from the state of incorporation, the corporation establishes **by-laws**. The by-laws establish the internal rules and procedures for conducting the affairs of the corporation. Corporations engaged in interstate commerce must also obtain a **license** from each state in which they do business. The license subjects the corporation's operating activities to the general corporation laws of the state.

Costs incurred in the formation of a corporation are called **organization costs**. These costs include legal and state fees, and promotional expenditures involved in the organization of the business. **Corporations expense organization costs as incurred.** Determining the amount and timing of future benefits is so difficult that it is standard procedure to take a conservative approach of expensing these costs immediately.

Alternative Terminology
The charter is often referred to as the *articles of incorporation.*

Accounting Across the Organization   Facebook

A Thousand Millionaires!

Traveling to space or embarking on an expedition to excavate lost Mayan ruins are normally the stuff of adventure novels. But for employees of Facebook, these and other lavish dreams moved closer to reality when the world's No. 1 online social network went public through an initial public offering (IPO) that may have created at least a thousand millionaires. The IPO was the largest in Internet history, valuing Facebook at over $104 billion.

With all these riches to be had, why did Mark Zuckerberg, the founder of Facebook, delay taking his company public?

Consider that the main motivation for issuing shares to the public is to raise money so you can grow your business. However, unlike a manufacturer or even an online retailer, Facebook doesn't need major physical resources, it doesn't have inventory, and it doesn't really need much money for marketing. So in the past, the company hasn't had much need for additional cash beyond what it was already generating on its own. Finally, as head of a closely held, nonpublic company, Zuckerberg was subject to far fewer regulations than a public company.

Source: "Status Update: I'm Rich! Facebook Flotation to Create 1,000 Millionaires Among Company's Rank and File," *Daily Mail Reporter* (February 1, 2012).

Jeff Chiu/AP/Wide World Photos

Why did Mark Zuckerberg, the CEO and founder of Facebook, delay taking his company's shares public through an initial public offering (IPO)? (Go to WileyPLUS for this answer and additional questions.)

Stockholder Rights

When chartered, the corporation may begin selling shares of stock. When a corporation has only one class of stock, it is **common stock**. Each share of common stock gives the stockholder the ownership rights pictured in Illustration 11-3. The articles of incorporation or the by-laws state the ownership rights of a share of stock.

Illustration 11-3
Ownership rights of stockholders

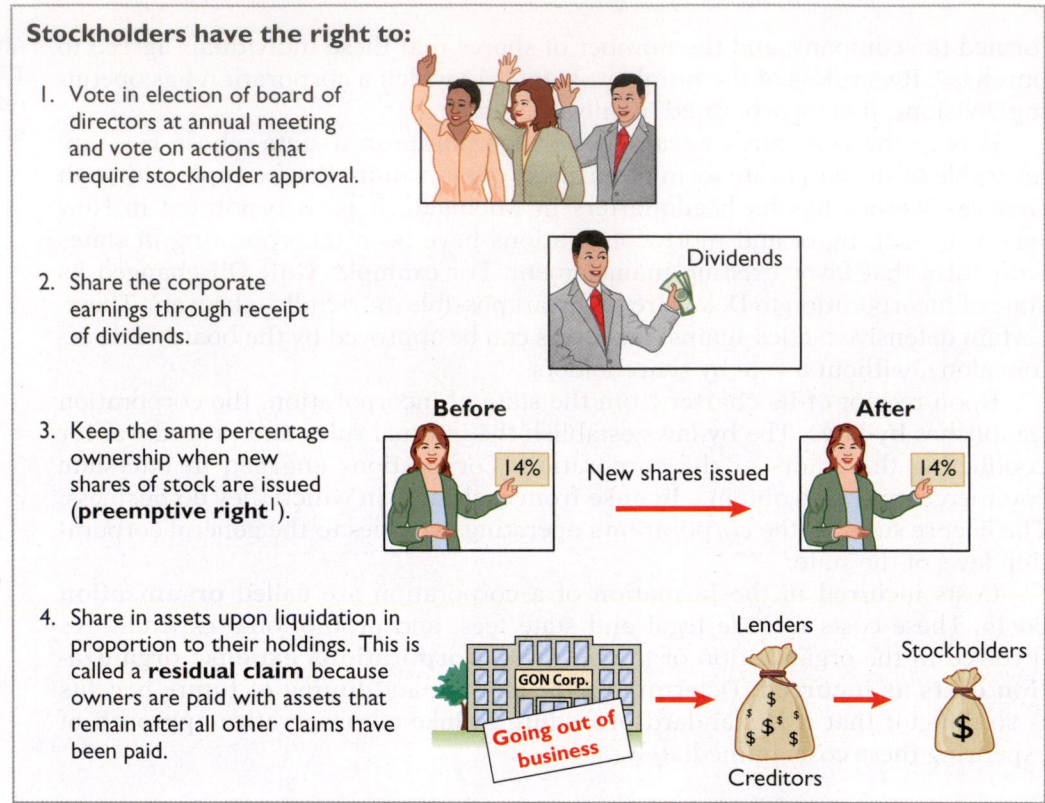

Stockholders have the right to:

1. Vote in election of board of directors at annual meeting and vote on actions that require stockholder approval.

2. Share the corporate earnings through receipt of dividends.

3. Keep the same percentage ownership when new shares of stock are issued (**preemptive right**[1]).

4. Share in assets upon liquidation in proportion to their holdings. This is called a **residual claim** because owners are paid with assets that remain after all other claims have been paid.

Proof of stock ownership is evidenced by a form known as a **stock certificate**. As Illustration 11-4 shows, the face of the certificate shows the name of the corporation, the stockholder's name, the class and special features of the stock, the number of shares owned, and the signatures of authorized corporate officials. Prenumbered certificates facilitate accountability. They may be issued for any quantity of shares.

Stock Issue Considerations

Although **Nike** incorporated in 1968, it did not sell stock to the public until 1980. At that time, Nike evidently decided it would benefit from the infusion of cash that a public sale would bring. When a corporation decides to issue stock, it must resolve a number of basic questions: How many shares should it authorize for sale? How should it issue the stock? What value should the corporation assign to the stock? We address these questions in the following sections.

---

[1]A number of companies have eliminated the preemptive right because they believe it makes an unnecessary and cumbersome demand on management. For example, by stockholder approval, **IBM** has dropped its preemptive right for stockholders.

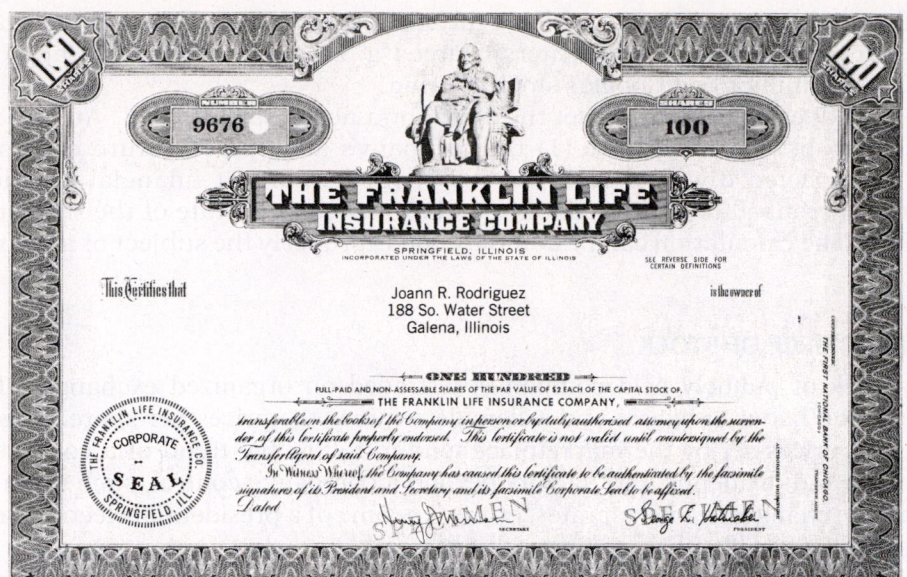

Illustration 11-4
A stock certificate

AUTHORIZED STOCK

The charter indicates the amount of stock that a corporation is **authorized** to sell. The total amount of **authorized stock** at the time of incorporation normally anticipates both initial and subsequent capital needs. As a result, the number of shares authorized generally exceeds the number initially sold. If it sells all authorized stock, a corporation must obtain consent of the state to amend its charter before it can issue additional shares.

The authorization of capital stock does not result in a formal accounting entry. The reason is that the event has no immediate effect on either corporate assets or stockholders' equity. However, the number of authorized shares is often reported in the stockholders' equity section. It is then simple to determine the number of unissued shares that the corporation can issue without amending the charter: subtract the total shares issued from the total authorized. For example, if **Advanced Micro** was authorized to sell 100,000 shares of common stock and issued 80,000 shares, 20,000 shares would remain unissued.

ISSUANCE OF STOCK

A corporation can issue common stock **directly** to investors. Alternatively, it can issue the stock **indirectly** through an investment banking firm that specializes in bringing securities to the attention of prospective investors. Direct issue is typical in closely held companies. Indirect issue is customary for a publicly held corporation.

In an indirect issue, the investment banking firm may agree to **underwrite** the entire stock issue. In this arrangement, the investment banker buys the stock from the corporation at a stipulated price and resells the shares to investors. The corporation thus avoids any risk of being unable to sell the shares. Also, it obtains immediate use of the cash received from the underwriter. The investment banking firm, in turn, assumes the risk of reselling the shares, in return for an underwriting fee.[2] For example, **Google** (the world's number-one Internet search engine)

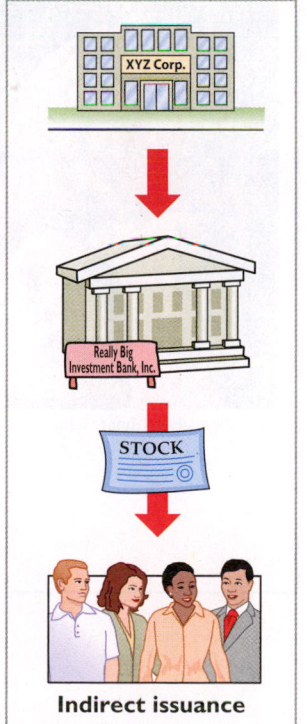

Indirect issuance

---

[2]Alternatively, the investment banking firm may agree only to enter into a **best-efforts contract** with the corporation. In such cases, the banker agrees to sell as many shares as possible at a specified price. The corporation bears the risk of unsold stock. Under a best-efforts arrangement, the banking firm is paid a fee or commission for its services.

used underwriters when it issued a highly successful initial public offering, raising $1.67 billion. The underwriters charged a 3% underwriting fee (approximately $50 million) on Google's stock offering.

How does a corporation set the price for a new issue of stock? Among the factors to be considered are (1) the company's anticipated future earnings, (2) its expected dividend rate per share, (3) its current financial position, (4) the current state of the economy, and (5) the current state of the securities market. The calculation can be complex and is properly the subject of a finance course.

MARKET PRICE OF STOCK

The stock of publicly held companies is traded on organized exchanges. The interaction between buyers and sellers determines the prices per share. In general, the prices set by the marketplace tend to follow the trend of a company's earnings and dividends. But, factors beyond a company's control, such as an oil embargo, changes in interest rates, or the outcome of a presidential election, may cause day-to-day fluctuations in market prices.

The trading of capital stock on securities exchanges involves the transfer of **already issued shares** from an existing stockholder to another investor. These transactions have **no impact** on a corporation's stockholders' equity.

Investor Insight Nike

How to Read Stock Quotes

Joe Robbins/Getty Images, Inc.

Organized exchanges trade the stock of publicly held companies at dollar prices per share established by the interaction between buyers and sellers. For each listed security, the financial press reports the high and low prices of the stock during the year, the total volume of stock traded on a given day, the high and low prices for the day, and the closing market price, with the net change for the day. Nike is listed on the New York Stock Exchange. Here is a listing for Nike:

	52 Weeks						
Stock	High	Low	Volume	High	Low	Close	Net Change
Nike	79.64	62.81	2,912,866	77.25	76.39	76.78	–0.35

These numbers indicate the following. The high and low market prices for the last 52 weeks have been $79.64 and $62.81. The trading volume for the day was 2,912,866 shares. The high, low, and closing prices for that date were $77.25, $76.39, and $76.78, respectively. The net change for the day was a decrease of $0.35 per share.

*For stocks traded on organized exchanges, how are the dollar prices per share established? What factors might influence the price of shares in the marketplace? (Go to **WileyPLUS** for this answer and additional questions.)*

PAR AND NO-PAR VALUE STOCKS

Par value stock is capital stock to which the charter has assigned a value per share. Years ago, par value determined the **legal capital** per share that a company must retain in the business for the protection of corporate creditors. That amount was not available for withdrawal by stockholders. Thus, in the past, most states required the corporation to sell its shares at par or above.

However, par value was often immaterial relative to the value of the company's stock—even at the time of issue. Thus, its usefulness as a protective device to creditors was questionable. For example, Loews Corporation's par value is $0.01 per share, yet a new issue in 2014 would have sold at a **market price** in the $44 per share range. Thus, par has no relationship with market price. In the vast majority of cases, it is an immaterial amount. As a consequence, today many states do not require a par value. Instead, they use other means to protect creditors.

No-par value stock is capital stock to which the charter has not assigned a value. No-par value stock is fairly common today. For example, Nike and Procter & Gamble both have no-par stock. In many states, the board of directors assigns a **stated value** to no-par shares.

DO IT! 1a   Corporate Organization

Indicate whether each of the following statements is true or false. If false, indicate how to correct the statement.

_____ **1.** Similar to partners in a partnership, stockholders of a corporation have unlimited liability.

_____ **2.** It is relatively easy for a corporation to obtain capital through the issuance of stock.

_____ **3.** The separation of ownership and management is an advantage of the corporate form of business.

_____ **4.** The journal entry to record the authorization of capital stock includes a credit to the appropriate capital stock account.

_____ **5.** All states require a par value per share for capital stock.

Solution

> **1.** False. The liability of stockholders is normally limited to their investment in the corporation.   **2.** True.   **3.** False. The separation of ownership and management is a disadvantage of the corporate form of business.   **4.** False. The authorization of capital stock does not result in a formal accounting entry.   **5.** False. Many states do not require a par value.

Related exercise material: **BE11-1, E11-1, E11-2, and DO IT! 11-1a.**

Action Plan

✔ Review the characteristics of a corporation and understand which are advantages and which are disadvantages.

✔ Understand that corporations raise capital through the issuance of stock, which can be par or no-par.

Corporate Capital

Owners' equity is identified by various names: **stockholders' equity**, **shareholders' equity**, or **corporate capital**. The stockholders' equity section of a corporation's balance sheet consists of two parts: (1) paid-in (contributed) capital and (2) retained earnings (earned capital).

The distinction between **paid-in capital** and **retained earnings** is important from both a legal and a financial point of view. Legally, corporations can make distributions of earnings (declare dividends) out of retained earnings in all states. However, in many states they cannot declare dividends out of paid-in capital. Management, stockholders, and others often look to retained earnings for the continued existence and growth of the corporation.

PAID-IN CAPITAL

Paid-in capital is the total amount of cash and other assets paid in to the corporation by stockholders in exchange for capital stock. As noted earlier, when a corporation has only one class of stock, it is **common stock**.

RETAINED EARNINGS

Retained earnings is net income that a corporation retains for future use. Net income is recorded in Retained Earnings by a closing entry that debits Income

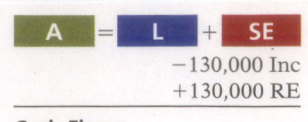

−130,000 Inc
+130,000 RE

Cash Flows
no effect

Summary and credits Retained Earnings. For example, assuming that net income for Delta Robotics in its first year of operations is $130,000, the closing entry is:

Income Summary	130,000	
Retained Earnings		130,000
(To close Income Summary and transfer net income		
to Retained Earnings)		

If Delta Robotics has a balance of $800,000 in common stock at the end of its first year, its stockholders' equity section is as follows.

Illustration 11-5
Stockholders' equity section

DELTA ROBOTICS
Balance Sheet (partial)

Stockholders' equity		
Paid-in capital		
Common stock	$800,000	
Retained earnings	130,000	
Total stockholders' equity		**$930,000**

Illustration 11-6 compares the owners' equity (stockholders' equity) accounts reported on a balance sheet for a proprietorship and a corporation.

Illustration 11-6
Comparison of owners' equity accounts

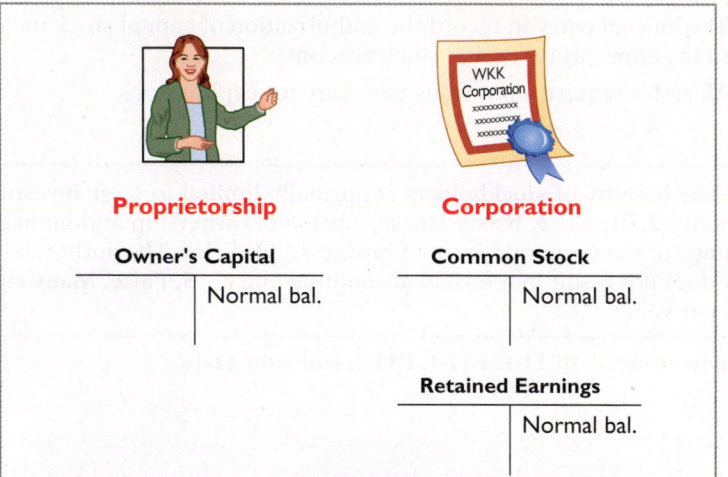

Proprietorship

Owner's Capital

	Normal bal.

Corporation

Common Stock

	Normal bal.

Retained Earnings

	Normal bal.

DO IT! 1b   Corporate Capital

At the end of its first year of operation, Doral Corporation has $750,000 of common stock and net income of $122,000. Prepare (a) the closing entry for net income and (b) the stockholders' equity section at year-end.

Solution

Action Plan

✔ Record net income in Retained Earnings by a closing entry in which Income Summary is debited and Retained Earnings is credited.

✔ In the stockholders' equity section, show (1) paid-in capital and (2) retained earnings.

(a)	Income Summary	122,000	
	Retained Earnings		122,000
	(To close Income Summary and transfer net		
	income to Retained Earnings)		
(b)	Stockholders' equity		
	Paid-in capital		
	Common stock	$750,000	
	Retained earnings	122,000	
	Total stockholders' equity		$872,000

Related exercise material: **DO IT!** **11-1b.**

LEARNING OBJECTIVE **2**

Explain how to account for the issuance of common and preferred stock.

Accounting for Common Stock

Let's now look at how to account for issues of common stock. The primary objectives in accounting for the issuance of common stock are (1) to identify the specific sources of paid-in capital, and (2) to maintain the distinction between paid-in capital and retained earnings. **The issuance of common stock affects only paid-in capital accounts.**

ISSUING PAR VALUE COMMON STOCK FOR CASH

As discussed earlier, par value does not indicate a stock's market price. Therefore, the cash proceeds from issuing par value stock may be equal to, greater than, or less than par value. When the company records issuance of common stock for cash, it credits the par value of the shares to Common Stock. It also records in a separate paid-in capital account the portion of the proceeds that is above or below par value.

To illustrate, assume that Hydro-Slide, Inc. issues 1,000 shares of $1 par value common stock at par for cash. The entry to record this transaction is:

Cash	1,000	
Common Stock		1,000
(To record issuance of 1,000 shares of $1 par		
common stock at par)		

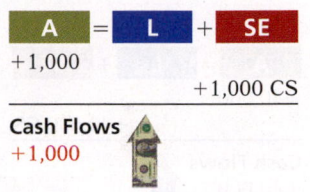

Now assume that Hydro-Slide issues an additional 1,000 shares of the $1 par value common stock for cash at $5 per share. The amount received above the par value, in this case $4 ($5 − $1), is credited to Paid-in Capital in Excess of Par—Common Stock. The entry is:

Cash	5,000	
Common Stock		1,000
Paid-in Capital in Excess of Par—Common Stock		4,000
(To record issuance of 1,000 shares of $1 par		
common stock)		

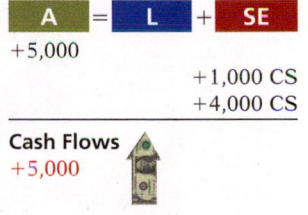

The total paid-in capital from these two transactions is $6,000, and the legal capital is $2,000. Assuming Hydro-Slide, Inc. has retained earnings of $27,000, Illustration 11-7 shows the company's stockholders' equity section.

Illustration 11-7
Stockholders' equity—paid-in capital in excess of par

HYDRO-SLIDE, INC.	
Balance Sheet (partial)	
Stockholders' equity	
Paid-in capital	
Common stock	$ 2,000
Paid-in capital in excess of par—	
common stock	**4,000**
Total paid-in capital	6,000
Retained earnings	27,000
Total stockholders' equity	$33,000

Alternative Terminology
Paid-in Capital in Excess of Par is also called *Premium on Stock*.

When a corporation issues stock for less than par value, it debits the account Paid-in Capital in Excess of Par—Common Stock if a credit balance exists in this account. If a credit balance does not exist, then the corporation debits to Retained Earnings the amount less than par. This situation occurs only rarely. Most states do not permit the sale of common stock below par value because stockholders may be held personally liable for the difference between the price paid upon original sale and par value.

ISSUING NO-PAR COMMON STOCK FOR CASH

When no-par common stock has a stated value, the entries are similar to those illustrated for par value stock. The corporation credits the stated value to Common Stock. Also, when the selling price of no-par stock exceeds stated value, the corporation credits the excess to Paid-in Capital in Excess of Stated Value—Common Stock.

For example, assume that instead of $1 par value stock, Hydro-Slide, Inc. has $5 stated value no-par stock and the company issues 5,000 shares at $8 per share for cash. The entry is:

A	=	L	+	SE
+40,000				
				+25,000 CS
				+15,000 CS

Cash Flows
+40,000

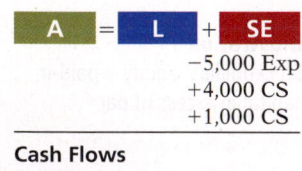

Cash	40,000	
Common Stock		25,000
Paid-in Capital in Excess of Stated Value—Common Stock		15,000
(To record issue of 5,000 shares of $5 stated		
value no-par stock)		

Hydro-Slide, Inc. reports Paid-in Capital in Excess of Stated Value—Common Stock as part of paid-in capital in the stockholders' equity section.

What happens when no-par stock does not have a stated value? In that case, the corporation credits the entire proceeds to Common Stock. Thus, if Hydro-Slide does not assign a stated value to its no-par stock, it records the issuance of the 5,000 shares at $8 per share for cash as follows.

A	=	L	+	SE
+40,000				
				+40,000 CS

Cash Flows
+40,000

Cash	40,000	
Common Stock		40,000
(To record issue of 5,000 shares of no-par stock)		

ISSUING COMMON STOCK FOR SERVICES OR NONCASH ASSETS

Corporations also may issue stock for services (compensation to attorneys or consultants) or for noncash assets (land, buildings, and equipment). In such cases, what cost should be recognized in the exchange transaction? To comply with the **historical cost principle**, in a noncash transaction **cost is the cash equivalent price**. Thus, **cost is either the fair value of the consideration given up or the fair value of the consideration received**, whichever is more clearly determinable.

To illustrate, assume that attorneys have helped Jordan Company incorporate. They have billed the company $5,000 for their services. They agree to accept 4,000 shares of $1 par value common stock in payment of their bill. At the time of the exchange, there is no established market price for the stock. In this case, the fair value of the consideration received, $5,000, is more clearly evident. Accordingly, Jordan Company makes the following entry.

A	=	L	+	SE
				−5,000 Exp
				+4,000 CS
				+1,000 CS

Cash Flows
no effect

Organization Expense	5,000	
Common Stock		4,000
Paid-in Capital in Excess of Par—Common Stock		1,000
(To record issuance of 4,000 shares of $1 par value		
stock to attorneys)		

As explained on page 503, organization costs are expensed as incurred.

In contrast, assume that Athletic Research Inc. is an existing publicly held corporation. Its $5 par value stock is actively traded at $8 per share. The company issues 10,000 shares of stock to acquire land recently advertised for sale at $90,000. The most clearly evident value in this noncash transaction is the market price of the consideration given, $80,000. The company records the transaction as follows.

A	=	L	+	SE
+80,000				
				+50,000 CS
				+30,000 CS

Cash Flows
no effect

Land	80,000	
Common Stock		50,000
Paid-in Capital in Excess of Par—Common Stock		30,000
(To record issuance of 10,000 shares of $5 par value		
stock for land)		

As illustrated in these examples, **the par value of the stock is never a factor in determining the cost of the assets or services received in noncash transactions**. This is also true of the stated value of no-par stock.

Accounting for Preferred Stock

To appeal to a larger segment of potential investors, a corporation may issue an additional class of stock, called preferred stock. **Preferred stock** has contractual provisions that give it some preference or priority over common stock. Typically, preferred stockholders have a priority as to (1) distributions of earnings (dividends) and (2) assets in the event of liquidation. However, they generally do not have voting rights.

Like common stock, corporations may issue preferred stock for cash or for noncash assets. The entries for these transactions are similar to the entries for common stock. When a corporation has more than one class of stock, each paid-in capital account title should identify the stock to which it relates. A company might have the following accounts: Preferred Stock, Common Stock, Paid-in Capital in Excess of Par—Preferred Stock, and Paid-in Capital in Excess of Par—Common Stock.

For example, if Stine Corporation issues 10,000 shares of $10 par value preferred stock for $12 cash per share, the entry to record the issuance is:

Cash	120,000	
Preferred Stock		100,000
Paid-in Capital in Excess of Par—Preferred Stock		20,000
(To record the issuance of 10,000 shares of $10 par value preferred stock)		

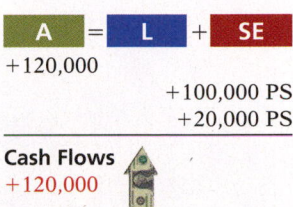

A = L + SE
+120,000
                +100,000 PS
                +20,000 PS

Cash Flows
+120,000

Preferred stock may have either a par value or no-par value. In the stockholders' equity section of the balance sheet, companies list preferred stock first because of its dividend and liquidation preferences over common stock.

DO IT! 2   Issuance of Stock

Cayman Corporation begins operations on March 1 by issuing 100,000 shares of $1 par value common stock for cash at $12 per share. On March 15, it issues 5,000 shares of common stock to attorneys in settlement of their bill of $50,000 for organization costs. On March 28, Cayman Corporation issues 1,500 shares of $10 par value preferred stock for cash at $30 per share. Journalize the issuance of the common and preferred shares, assuming the shares are not publicly traded.

Solution

Mar. 1	Cash	1,200,000	
	Common Stock (100,000 × $1)		100,000
	Paid-in Capital in Excess of Par—		
	Common Stock		1,100,000
	(To record issuance of 100,000 shares at $12 per share)		
Mar. 15	Organization Expense	50,000	
	Common Stock (5,000 × $1)		5,000
	Paid-in Capital in Excess of Par—		
	Common Stock		45,000
	(To record issuance of 5,000 shares for attorneys' fees)		
Mar. 28	Cash	45,000	
	Preferred Stock (1,500 × $10)		15,000
	Paid-in Capital in Excess of Par—		
	Preferred Stock		30,000
	(To record issuance of 1,500 shares at $30 per share)		

Action Plan

✔ In issuing shares for cash, credit Common Stock for par value per share.

✔ Credit any additional proceeds in excess of par to a separate paid-in capital account.

✔ When stock is issued for services, use the cash equivalent price.

✔ For the cash equivalent price, use either the fair value of what is given up or the fair value of what is received, whichever is more clearly determinable.

Related exercise material: **BE11-2, BE11-3, BE11-4, BE11-5, E11-3, E11-4, E11-8,** and **DO IT! 11-2.**

LEARNING OBJECTIVE 3

Explain how to account for treasury stock.

Treasury stock is a corporation's own stock that it has issued and subsequently reacquired from shareholders but not retired. A corporation may acquire treasury stock for various reasons:

Helpful Hint
Treasury shares do not have dividend rights or voting rights.

1. To reissue the shares to officers and employees under bonus and stock compensation plans.
2. To increase trading of the company's stock in the securities market. Companies expect that buying their own stock will signal that management believes the stock is underpriced, which they hope will enhance its market price.
3. To have additional shares available for use in the acquisition of other companies.
4. To reduce the number of shares outstanding and thereby increase earnings per share.

Another infrequent reason for purchasing shares is that management may want to eliminate hostile shareholders by buying them out.

Many corporations have treasury stock. For example, approximately 65% of U.S. companies have treasury stock. In a recent year, Nike purchased more than 6 million treasury shares.

Purchase of Treasury Stock

Companies generally account for treasury stock by **the cost method**. This method uses the cost of the shares purchased to value the treasury stock. Under the cost method, the company debits **Treasury Stock** for the **price paid to reacquire the shares**. When the company disposes of the shares, it credits to Treasury Stock **the same amount** it paid to reacquire the shares.

To illustrate, assume that on January 1, 2017, the stockholders' equity section of Mead, Inc. has 400,000 shares authorized and 100,000 shares of $5 par value common stock outstanding (all issued at par value) and Retained Earnings of $200,000. The stockholders' equity section before purchase of treasury stock is as follows.

Illustration 11-8
Stockholders' equity with no treasury stock

MEAD, INC.	
Balance Sheet (partial)	
Stockholders' equity	
Paid-in capital	
Common stock, $5 par value, 400,000 shares	
authorized, 100,000 shares issued and outstanding	$500,000
Retained earnings	200,000
Total stockholders' equity	$700,000

On February 1, 2017, Mead acquires 4,000 shares of its stock at $8 per share. The entry is as follows.

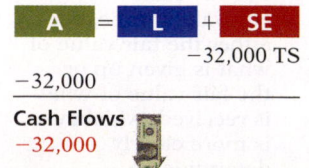

A	=	L	+	SE
				−32,000 TS
−32,000				

Cash Flows
−32,000

Feb. 1	Treasury Stock	32,000	
	Cash		32,000
	(To record purchase of 4,000 shares of		
	treasury stock at $8 per share)		

Mead debits Treasury Stock for the cost of the shares purchased ($32,000). Is the original paid-in capital account, Common Stock, affected? No, because the number of issued shares does not change.

In the stockholders' equity section of the balance sheet, Mead deducts treasury stock from total paid-in capital and retained earnings. Treasury Stock is a **contra stockholders' equity account**. Thus, the acquisition of treasury stock reduces stockholders' equity. The stockholders' equity section of Mead, Inc. after purchase of treasury stock is as follows.

Illustration 11-9
Stockholders' equity with treasury stock

MEAD, INC.	
Balance Sheet (partial)	
Stockholders' equity	
Paid-in capital	
Common stock, $5 par value, 400,000 shares authorized,	
100,000 shares issued, and 96,000 shares outstanding	$500,000
Retained earnings	200,000
Total paid-in capital and retained earnings	700,000
Less: Treasury stock (4,000 shares)	**32,000**
Total stockholders' equity	$668,000

Mead discloses in the balance sheet both the number of shares issued (100,000) and the number in the treasury (4,000). The difference is the number of shares of stock outstanding (96,000). The term **outstanding stock** means the number of shares of issued stock that are being held by stockholders.

Some maintain that companies should report treasury stock as an asset because it can be sold for cash. But under this reasoning, companies would also show unissued stock as an asset, which is clearly incorrect. Rather than being an asset, treasury stock reduces stockholder claims on corporate assets. This effect is correctly shown by reporting treasury stock as a deduction from total paid-in capital and retained earnings.

> **ETHICS NOTE**
>
> The purchase of treasury stock reduces the cushion (cash available) for creditors and preferred stockholders. A restriction for the cost of treasury stock purchased is often required. The restriction is usually applied to retained earnings.

Disposal of Treasury Stock

Treasury stock is usually sold or retired. The accounting for its sale differs when treasury stock is sold above cost than when it is sold below cost.

SALE OF TREASURY STOCK ABOVE COST

If the selling price of the treasury shares is equal to their cost, the company records the sale of the shares by a debit to Cash and a credit to Treasury Stock. When the selling price of the shares is greater than their cost, the company credits the difference to Paid-in Capital from Treasury Stock.

To illustrate, assume that on July 1, Mead, Inc. sells for $10 per share 1,000 of the 4,000 shares of its treasury stock previously acquired at $8 per share. The entry is as follows.

Helpful Hint
Treasury stock transactions are classified as capital stock transactions. As in the case when stock is issued, the income statement is not involved.

July 1	Cash	10,000	
	Treasury Stock		8,000
	Paid-in Capital from Treasury Stock		2,000
	(To record sale of 1,000 shares of treasury stock above cost)		

A	=	L	+	SE
+10,000				
				+8,000 TS
				+2,000 TS

Cash Flows
+10,000

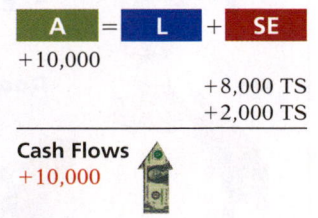

Mead does not record a $2,000 gain on sale of treasury stock because (1) gains on sales occur when **assets** are sold, and treasury stock is not an asset, and (2) a corporation does not realize a gain or suffer a loss from stock transactions with its own stockholders. Thus, companies should **not** include in net income any paid-in capital arising from the sale of treasury stock. Instead, they report Paid-in Capital from Treasury Stock separately on the balance sheet, as a part of paid-in capital.

SALE OF TREASURY STOCK BELOW COST

When a company sells treasury stock below its cost, it usually debits to Paid-in Capital from Treasury Stock the excess of cost over selling price. Thus, if Mead, Inc. sells an additional 800 shares of treasury stock on October 1 at $7 per share, it makes the following entry.

A	=	L	+	SE
+5,600				

−800 TS
+6,400 TS

Cash Flows
+5,600

Oct. 1	Cash		5,600	
	Paid-in Capital from Treasury Stock		800	
	Treasury Stock			6,400
	(To record sale of 800 shares of treasury			
	stock below cost)			

Observe the following from the two sales entries. (1) Mead credits Treasury Stock at cost in each entry. (2) Mead uses Paid-in Capital from Treasury Stock for the difference between cost and the resale price of the shares. (3) The original paid-in capital account, Common Stock, is not affected. **The sale of treasury stock increases both total assets and total stockholders' equity.**

After posting the foregoing entries, the treasury stock accounts will show the following balances on October 1.

Illustration 11-10
Treasury stock accounts

Treasury Stock				Paid-in Capital from Treasury Stock			
Feb. 1	32,000	July 1	8,000	Oct. 1	800	July 1	2,000
		Oct. 1	6,400			Oct. 1 Bal.	1,200
Oct. 1 Bal.	17,600						

When a company fully depletes the credit balance in Paid-in Capital from Treasury Stock, it debits to Retained Earnings any additional excess of cost over selling price. To illustrate, assume that Mead, Inc. sells its remaining 2,200 shares at $7 per share on December 1. The excess of cost over selling price is $2,200 [2,200 × ($8 − $7)]. In this case, Mead debits $1,200 of the excess to Paid-in Capital from Treasury Stock. It debits the remainder to Retained Earnings. The entry is:

A	=	L	+	SE
+15,400				

−1,200 TS
−1,000 RE
+17,600 TS

Cash Flows
+15,400

Dec. 1	Cash		15,400	
	Paid-in Capital from Treasury Stock		1,200	
	Retained Earnings		1,000	
	Treasury Stock			17,600
	(To record sale of 2,200 shares of treasury			
	stock at $7 per share)			

Accounting Across the Organization   Reebok

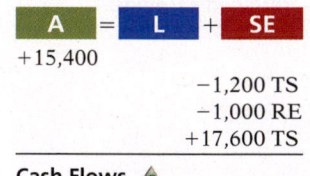

Han Myung-Gu/WireImage/
Getty Images, Inc.

Why Did Reebok Buy Its Own Stock?

In a bold (and some would say risky) move, Reebok at one time bought back nearly a third of its shares. This repurchase of shares dramatically reduced Reebok's available cash. In fact, the company borrowed significant funds to accomplish the repurchase. In a press release, management stated that it was repurchasing the shares because it believed its stock was severely underpriced.

The repurchase of so many shares was meant to signal management's belief in good future earnings.

Skeptics, however, suggested that Reebok's management was repurchasing shares to make it less likely that another company would acquire Reebok (in which case Reebok's top managers would likely lose their jobs). By depleting its cash, Reebok became a less attractive acquisition target. Acquiring companies like to purchase companies with large cash balances so they can pay off debt used in the acquisition.

What signal might a large stock repurchase send to investors regarding management's belief about the company's growth opportunities? (Go to **WileyPLUS** for this answer and additional questions.)

DO IT! 3   Treasury Stock

Santa Anita Inc. purchases 3,000 shares of its $50 par value common stock for $180,000 cash on July 1. It will hold the shares in the treasury until resold. On November 1, the corporation sells 1,000 shares of treasury stock for cash at $70 per share. Journalize the treasury stock transactions.

Solution

July 1	Treasury Stock	180,000	
	Cash		180,000
	(To record the purchase of 3,000 shares at $60 per share)		
Nov. 1	Cash	70,000	
	Treasury Stock		60,000
	Paid-in Capital from Treasury Stock		10,000
	(To record the sale of 1,000 shares at $70 per share)		

Related exercise material: **BE11-6, E11-5, E11-7, E11-9**, and **DO IT! 11-3.**

Action Plan

✔ Record the purchase of treasury stock at cost.

✔ When treasury stock is sold above its cost, credit the excess of the selling price over cost to Paid-in Capital from Treasury Stock.

✔ When treasury stock is sold below its cost, debit the excess of cost over selling price to Paid-in Capital from Treasury Stock.

LEARNING OBJECTIVE 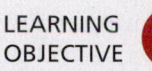 **4**   **Explain how to account for cash dividends.**

A **dividend** is a corporation's distribution of cash or stock to its stockholders on a pro rata (proportional to ownership) basis. Pro rata means that if you own 10% of the common shares, you will receive 10% of the dividend. Dividends can take four forms: cash, property, scrip (a promissory note to pay cash), or stock. Cash dividends predominate in practice although companies also declare stock dividends with some frequency. These two forms of dividends are therefore the focus of our discussion.

Investors are very interested in a company's dividend practices. In the financial press, **dividends are generally reported quarterly as a dollar amount per share**. (Sometimes they are reported on an annual basis.) For example, **Nike**'s **quarterly** dividend rate in the fourth quarter of 2013 was 24 cents per share. The dividend rate for the fourth quarter of 2013 for **GE** was 22 cents, and for **ConAgra Foods** it was 25 cents.

Cash Dividends

A **cash dividend** is a pro rata distribution of cash to stockholders. Cash dividends are not paid on treasury shares. For a corporation to pay a cash dividend, it must have the following.

1. **Retained earnings.** The legality of a cash dividend depends on the laws of the state in which the company is incorporated. Payment of cash dividends from retained earnings is legal in all states. In general, cash dividend distributions from only the balance in common stock (legal capital) are illegal.

   A dividend declared out of paid-in capital is termed a **liquidating dividend**. Such a dividend reduces or "liquidates" the amount originally paid in by stockholders. Statutes vary considerably with respect to cash dividends based on paid-in capital in excess of par or stated value. Many states permit such dividends.

2. **Adequate cash.** The legality of a dividend and the ability to pay a dividend are two different things. For example, **Nike**, with retained earnings of over

$5.6 billion, could legally declare a dividend of at least $5.6 billion. But Nike's cash balance is only $3.3 billion.

Before declaring a cash dividend, a company's board of directors must carefully consider both current and future demands on the company's cash resources. In some cases, current liabilities may make a cash dividend inappropriate. In other cases, a major plant expansion program may warrant only a relatively small dividend.

3. **Declared dividends.** A company does not pay dividends unless its board of directors decides to do so, at which point the board "declares" the dividend. The board of directors has full authority to determine the amount of income to distribute in the form of a dividend and the amount to retain in the business. Dividends do not accrue like interest on a note payable, and they are not a liability until declared.

The amount and timing of a dividend are important issues for management to consider. The payment of a large cash dividend could lead to liquidity problems for the company. On the other hand, a small dividend or a missed dividend may cause unhappiness among stockholders. Many stockholders expect to receive a reasonable cash payment from the company on a periodic basis. Many companies declare and pay cash dividends quarterly. On the other hand, a number of high-growth companies pay no dividends, preferring to conserve cash to finance future capital expenditures.

ENTRIES FOR CASH DIVIDENDS

Three dates are important in connection with dividends: (1) the declaration date, (2) the record date, and (3) the payment date. Normally, there are two to four weeks between each date. Companies make accounting entries on the declaration date and the payment date.

On the **declaration date**, the board of directors formally declares (authorizes) the cash dividend and announces it to stockholders. The declaration of a cash dividend **commits the corporation to a legal obligation**. The company must make an entry to recognize the increase in Cash Dividends and the increase in the liability Dividends Payable.

To illustrate, assume that on December 1, 2017, the directors of Media General declare a 50 cents per share cash dividend on 100,000 shares of $10 par value common stock. The dividend is $50,000 (100,000 × $0.50). The entry to record the declaration is:

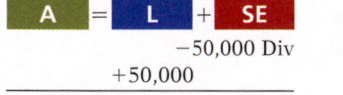

	Declaration Date		
Dec. 1	Cash Dividends	50,000	
	Dividends Payable		50,000
	(To record declaration of cash dividend)		

Cash Flows
no effect

Media General debits the account Cash Dividends. Cash dividends decrease retained earnings. We use the specific title Cash Dividends to differentiate it from other types of dividends, such as stock dividends. Dividends Payable is a current liability. It will normally be paid within the next several months. *For homework problems, you should use the Cash Dividends account for recording dividend declarations.*

At the **record date**, the company determines ownership of the outstanding shares for dividend purposes. The stockholders' records maintained by the corporation supply this information. In the interval between the declaration date and the record date, the corporation updates its stock ownership records. For Media General, the record date is December 22. No entry is required on this date because the corporation's liability recognized on the declaration date is unchanged.

Helpful Hint
The purpose of the record date is to identify the persons or entities that will receive the dividend, not to determine the amount of the dividend liability.

	Record Date		
Dec. 22	No entry		

On the **payment date**, the company makes cash dividend payments to the stockholders of record (as of December 22) and records the payment of the dividend. If January 20 is the payment date for Media General, the entry on that date is as follows.

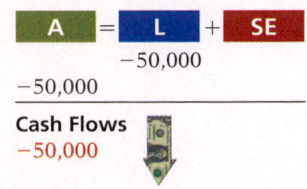

	Payment Date		
Jan. 20	Dividends Payable	50,000	
	Cash		50,000
	(To record payment of cash dividend)		

Note that payment of the dividend reduces both current assets and current liabilities. It has no effect on stockholders' equity. The cumulative effect of the declaration and payment of a cash dividend is to **decrease both stockholders' equity and total assets**. Illustration 11-11 summarizes the three important dates associated with dividends for Media General.

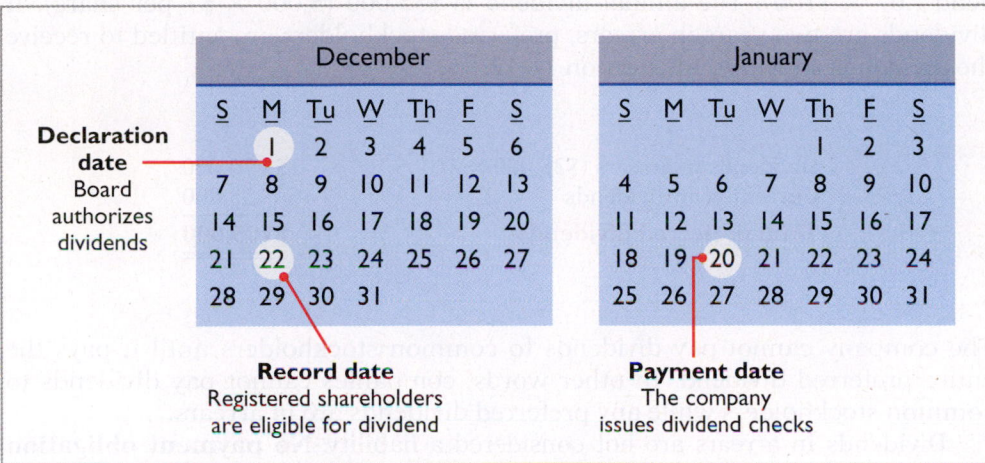

Illustration 11-11
Key dividend dates

When using a Cash Dividends account, Media General should transfer the balance of that account to Retained Earnings at the end of the year by a closing entry. The entry for Media General at closing is as follows.

	Retained Earnings	50,000	
	Cash Dividends		50,000
	(To close Cash Dividends to		
	Retained Earnings)		

Dividend Preferences

Preferred stockholders have the right to receive dividends before common stockholders. For example, if the dividend rate on preferred stock is $5 per share, common shareholders cannot receive any dividends in the current year until preferred stockholders have received $5 per share. The first claim to dividends does not, however, **guarantee** the payment of dividends. Dividends depend on many factors, such as adequate retained earnings and availability of cash. If a company does not pay dividends to preferred stockholders, it cannot pay dividends to common stockholders.

For preferred stock, companies state the per share dividend amount as a percentage of the par value or as a specified amount. For example, Earthlink specifies a 3% dividend on its $100 par value preferred. PepsiCo pays $4.56 per share on its no-par value stock.

I hope there's some money left when it's my turn.

Preferred   Common
stockholders   stockholders

Dividend preferences

Most preferred stocks also have a preference on corporate assets if the corporation fails. This feature provides security for the preferred stockholder. The preference to assets may be for the par value of the shares or for a specified liquidating value. For example, **Commonwealth Edison**'s preferred stock entitles its holders to receive $31.80 per share, plus accrued and unpaid dividends, in the event of liquidation. The liquidation preference establishes the respective claims of creditors and preferred stockholders in litigation involving bankruptcy lawsuits.

CUMULATIVE DIVIDEND

Preferred stock often contains a **cumulative dividend** feature. This feature stipulates that preferred stockholders must be paid both current-year dividends and any unpaid prior-year dividends before common stockholders are paid dividends. When preferred stock is cumulative, preferred dividends not declared in a given period are called **dividends in arrears**.

To illustrate, assume that Scientific Leasing has 5,000 shares of 7%, $100 par value, cumulative preferred stock outstanding. Each $100 share pays a $7 dividend (.07 × $100). The annual dividend is $35,000 (5,000 × $7 per share). If dividends are two years in arrears, preferred stockholders are entitled to receive the dividends shown in Illustration 11-12.

Illustration 11-12
Computation of total dividends to preferred stock

Dividends in arrears ($35,000 × 2)	$ 70,000
Current-year dividends	35,000
Total preferred dividends	**$105,000**

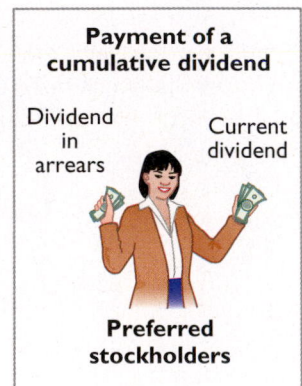

Payment of a cumulative dividend

Dividend in arrears

Current dividend

Preferred stockholders

The company cannot pay dividends to common stockholders until it pays the entire preferred dividend. In other words, companies cannot pay dividends to common stockholders while any preferred dividends are in arrears.

Dividends in arrears are not considered a liability. **No payment obligation exists until the board of directors formally declares that the corporation will pay a dividend.** However, companies should disclose in the notes to the financial statements the amount of dividends in arrears. Doing so enables investors to assess the potential impact of this commitment on the corporation's financial position.

The investment community does not look favorably on companies that are unable to meet their dividend obligations. As a financial officer noted in discussing one company's failure to pay its cumulative preferred dividend for a period of time, "Not meeting your obligations on something like that is a major black mark on your record."

ALLOCATING CASH DIVIDENDS BETWEEN PREFERRED AND COMMON STOCK

As indicated, preferred stock has priority over common stock in regard to dividends. Holders of cumulative preferred stock must be paid any unpaid prior-year dividends and their current year's dividend before common stockholders receive dividends.

To illustrate, assume that at December 31, 2017, IBR Inc. has 1,000 shares of 8%, $100 par value cumulative preferred stock. It also has 50,000 shares of $10 par value common stock outstanding. The dividend per share for preferred stock is $8 ($100 par value × 8%). The required annual dividend for preferred stock is therefore $8,000 (1,000 shares × $8). At December 31, 2017, the directors declare a $6,000 cash dividend. In this case, the entire dividend amount goes to preferred stockholders because of their dividend preference. The entry to record the declaration of the dividend is as follows.

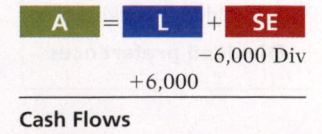

A = L + SE
−6,000 Div
+6,000

Cash Flows
no effect

Dec. 31	Cash Dividends	6,000	
	Dividends Payable		6,000
	(To record $6 per share cash dividend		
	to preferred stockholders)		

Because of the cumulative feature, dividends of $2 ($8 − $6) per share are in arrears on preferred stock for 2017. IBR must pay these dividends to preferred stockholders before it can pay any future dividends to common stockholders. IBR should disclose dividends in arrears in the financial statements.

At December 31, 2018, IBR declares a $50,000 cash dividend. The allocation of the dividend to the two classes of stock is as follows.

Total dividend		$50,000
Allocated to preferred stock		
Dividends in arrears, 2017 (1,000 × $2)	**$2,000**	
2018 dividend (1,000 × $8)	**8,000**	**10,000**
Remainder allocated to common stock		$40,000

Illustration 11-13
Allocating dividends to preferred and common stock

The entry to record the declaration of the dividend is as follows.

Dec. 31	Cash Dividends	50,000	
	Dividends Payable		50,000
	(To record declaration of cash dividends of $10,000 to preferred stock and $40,000 to common stock)		

A	=	L	+	SE
				−50,000 Div
		+50,000		

Cash Flows
no effect

If IBR's preferred stock is not cumulative, preferred stockholders receive only $8,000 in dividends in 2018. Common stockholders receive $42,000.

DO IT! 4   Dividends on Preferred and Common Stock

MasterMind Corporation has 2,000 shares of 6%, $100 par value preferred stock outstanding at December 31, 2017. At December 31, 2017, the company declared a $60,000 cash dividend. Determine the dividend paid to preferred stockholders and common stockholders under each of the following scenarios.

1. The preferred stock is noncumulative, and the company has not missed any dividends in previous years.

2. The preferred stock is noncumulative, and the company did not pay a dividend in each of the two previous years.

3. The preferred stock is cumulative, and the company did not pay a dividend in each of the two previous years.

Solution

1. The company has not missed past dividends and the preferred stock is noncumulative. Thus, the preferred stockholders are paid only this year's dividend. The dividend paid to preferred stockholders would be $12,000 (2,000 × .06 × $100). The dividend paid to common stockholders would be $48,000 ($60,000 − $12,000).

2. The preferred stock is noncumulative. Thus, past unpaid dividends do not have to be paid. The dividend paid to preferred stockholders would be $12,000 (2,000 × .06 × $100). The dividend paid to common stockholders would be $48,000 ($60,000 − $12,000).

3. The preferred stock is cumulative. Thus, dividends that have been missed (dividends in arrears) must be paid. The dividend paid to preferred stockholders would be $36,000 (3 × 2,000 × .06 × $100). Of the $36,000, $24,000 relates to dividends in arrears and $12,000 relates to the current dividend on preferred stocks. The dividend paid to common stockholders would be $24,000 ($60,000 − $36,000).

Related exercise material: **BE11-7, E11-6, E11-13, and 11-4.**

Action Plan

✔ Determine dividends on preferred shares by multiplying the dividend rate times the par value of the stock times the number of preferred shares.

✔ Understand the cumulative feature. If preferred stock is cumulative, then any missed dividends (dividends in arrears) and the current year's dividend must be paid to preferred stockholders before dividends are paid to common stockholders.

Stock Dividends

A **stock dividend** is a pro rata (proportional to ownership) distribution of the corporation's own stock to stockholders. Whereas a company pays cash in a cash dividend, a company issues shares of stock in a stock dividend. **A stock dividend results in a decrease in retained earnings and an increase in paid-in capital.** Unlike a cash dividend, a stock dividend does not decrease total stockholders' equity or total assets.

To illustrate, assume that you have a 2% ownership interest in Cetus Inc. That is, you own 20 of its 1,000 shares of common stock. If Cetus declares a 10% stock dividend, it would issue 100 shares (1,000 × 10%) of stock. You would receive two shares (2% × 100). Would your ownership interest change? No, it would remain at 2% (22 ÷ 1,100). **You now own more shares of stock, but your ownership interest has not changed.**

Cetus has disbursed no cash and has assumed no liabilities. What, then, are the purposes and benefits of a stock dividend? Corporations issue stock dividends generally for one or more of the following reasons.

1. To satisfy stockholders' dividend expectations without spending cash.

2. To increase the marketability of the corporation's stock. When the number of shares outstanding increases, the market price per share decreases. Decreasing the market price of the stock makes it easier for smaller investors to purchase the shares.

3. To emphasize that a company has permanently reinvested in the business a portion of stockholders' equity, which therefore is unavailable for cash dividends.

When the dividend is declared, the board of directors determines the size of the stock dividend and the value assigned to each dividend.

Generally, if the company issues a **small stock dividend** (less than 20–25% of the corporation's issued stock), the value assigned to the dividend is the fair value (market price) per share. This treatment is based on the assumption that a small stock dividend will have little effect on the market price of the shares previously outstanding. Thus, many stockholders consider small stock dividends to be distributions of earnings equal to the market price of the shares distributed. If a company issues a **large stock dividend** (greater than 20–25%), the price assigned to the dividend is the par or stated value. Small stock dividends predominate in practice. Thus, we will illustrate only entries for small stock dividends.

ENTRIES FOR STOCK DIVIDENDS

To illustrate the accounting for small stock dividends, assume that Medland Corporation has a balance of $300,000 in retained earnings. It declares a 10% stock dividend on its 50,000 shares of $10 par value common stock. The current market price of its stock is $15 per share. The number of shares to be issued is 5,000 (10% × 50,000). Therefore, the total amount to be debited to Stock Dividends is $75,000 (5,000 × $15). The entry to record the declaration of the stock dividend is as follows.

A	=	L	+	SE
−75,000 Div				
+50,000 CS				
+25,000 CS				

Cash Flows
no effect

Stock Dividends	75,000	
Common Stock Dividends Distributable		50,000
Paid-in Capital in Excess of Par—Common Stock		25,000
(To record declaration of 10% stock dividend)		

Medland debits Stock Dividends for the market price of the stock issued ($15 × 5,000). (Similar to Cash Dividends, Stock Dividends decrease retained earnings.) Medland also credits Common Stock Dividends Distributable for the par value of the dividend shares ($10 × 5,000) and credits Paid-in Capital in Excess of Par—Common Stock for the excess of the market price over par ($5 × 5,000).

Common Stock Dividends Distributable is a **stockholders' equity account**. It is not a liability because assets will not be used to pay the dividend. If the company prepares a balance sheet before it issues the dividend shares, it reports the distributable account under paid-in capital as shown in Illustration 11-14.

Paid-in capital	
Common stock	$500,000
Common stock dividends distributable	**50,000**
Paid-in capital in excess of par—common stock	25,000
Total paid-in capital	$575,000

Illustration 11-14
Statement presentation of common stock dividends distributable

When Medland issues the dividend shares, it debits Common Stock Dividends Distributable and credits Common Stock, as follows.

Common Stock Dividends Distributable	50,000	
Common Stock		50,000
(To record issuance of 5,000 shares in a stock dividend)		

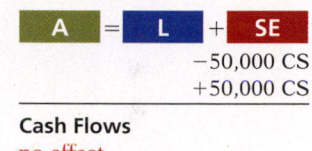

A = L + SE

−50,000 CS
+50,000 CS

Cash Flows
no effect

EFFECTS OF STOCK DIVIDENDS

How do stock dividends affect stockholders' equity? They **change the composition of stockholders' equity** because they transfer a portion of retained earnings to paid-in capital. However, **total stockholders' equity remains the same**. Stock dividends also have no effect on the par or stated value per share, but the number of shares outstanding increases. Illustration 11-15 shows these effects for Medland.

	Before Dividend	Change	After Dividend
Stockholders' equity			
Paid-in capital			
Common stock, $10 par	$ 500,000	$ 50,000	$ 550,000
Paid-in capital in excess of par	—	25,000	25,000
Total paid-in capital	500,000	+75,000	575,000
Retained earnings	300,000	−75,000	225,000
Total stockholders' equity	**$800,000**	**$ 0**	**$800,000**
Outstanding shares	**50,000**	**+5,000**	**55,000**
Par value per share	**$10.00**	**$0**	**$10.00**

Illustration 11-15
Stock dividend effects

In this example, total paid-in capital increases by $75,000 (50,000 shares × 10% × $15) and retained earnings decreases by the same amount. Note also that total stockholders' equity remains unchanged at $800,000. The number of shares increases by 5,000 (50,000 × 10%).

ANATOMY OF A FRAUD

The president, chief operating officer, and chief financial officer of SafeNet, a software encryption company, were each awarded employee stock options by the company's board of directors as part of their compensation package. Stock options enable an employee to buy a company's stock sometime in the future at the price that existed when the stock option was awarded. For example, suppose that you received stock options today, when the stock price of your company was $30. Three years later, if the stock price rose to $100, you could "exercise" your options and buy the stock for $30 per share, thereby making $70 per share. After being awarded their stock options, the three employees changed the award dates in the company's records to dates in the past, when the company's stock was trading at historical lows. For instance, using the previous example, they would choose a past date when the stock was selling for $10 per share, rather than the $30 price on the actual award date. This would increase the profit from exercising the options to $90 per share.

Total take: $1.7 million

THE MISSING CONTROL

Independent internal verification. The company's board of directors should have ensured that the awards were properly administered. For example, the date on the minutes from the board meeting could be compared to the dates that were recorded for the awards. In addition, the dates should again be confirmed upon exercise.

Stock Splits

Helpful Hint
A stock split changes the par value per share but does not affect any balances in stockholders' equity.

A **stock split**, like a stock dividend, involves issuance of additional shares to stockholders according to their percentage ownership. **However, a stock split results in a reduction in the par or stated value per share.** The purpose of a stock split is to increase the marketability of the stock by lowering its market price per share. This, in turn, makes it easier for the corporation to issue additional stock.

The effect of a split on market price is generally **inversely proportional** to the size of the split. For example, after a 2-for-1 stock split, the market price of Nike's stock fell from $111 to approximately $55. The lower market price stimulated market activity. Within one year, the stock was trading above $100 again. Illustration 11-16 shows the effect of a 4-for-1 stock split for stockholders.

Illustration 11-16
Effect of stock split for stockholders

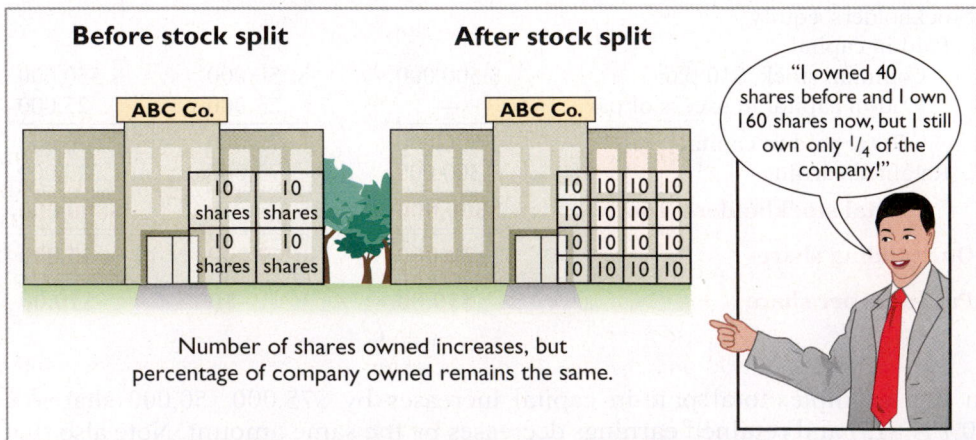

In a stock split, the company increases the number of shares in the same proportion that par or stated value per share decreases. For example, in a 2-for-1 split, the company exchanges one share of $10 par value stock for two shares of $5 par value stock. **A stock split does not have any effect on total paid-in capital, retained earnings, or total stockholders' equity.** However, the number of shares outstanding increases, and par value per share decreases. Illustration 11-17 shows these effects for Medland Corporation, assuming that it splits its 50,000 shares of common stock on a 2-for-1 basis.

Illustration 11-17
Stock split effects

	Before Stock Split	Change	After Stock Split
Stockholders' equity			
Paid-in capital			
Common stock,	$ 500,000		$ 500,000
Paid-in capital in excess of par—common stock	–0–		–0–
Total paid-in capital	500,000	$ 0	500,000
Retained earnings	300,000	0	300,000
Total stockholders' equity	**$800,000**	**$ 0**	**$800,000**
Outstanding shares	**50,000**	**+50,000**	**100,000**
Par value per share	**$10.00**	**−$5.00**	**$5.00**

A stock split does not affect the balances in any stockholders' equity accounts. Therefore, **a company does not need to journalize a stock split**.

Illustration 11-18 summarizes the differences between stock dividends and stock splits.

Illustration 11-18
Differences between the effects of stock dividends and stock splits

Item	Stock Dividend	Stock Split
Total paid-in capital	Increase	No change
Total retained earnings	Decrease	No change
Total par value (common stock)	Increase	No change
Par value per share	No change	Decrease
Outstanding shares	Increase	Increase
Total stockholders' equity	No change	No change

Investor Insight Berkshire Hathaway

Dietmar Klement/ iStockphoto

A No-Split Philosophy

Warren Buffett's company, Berkshire Hathaway, has two classes of shares. Until recently, the company had never split either class of stock. As a result, the class A stock had a market price of $97,000 and the class B sold for about $3,200 per share. Because the price per share is so high, the stock does not trade as frequently as the stock of other companies. Buffett has always opposed stock splits because he feels that a lower stock price attracts short-term investors. He appears to be correct. For example, while more than 6 million shares of IBM are exchanged on the average day, only about 1,000 class A shares of Berkshire are traded. Despite Buffett's aversion to splits, in order to accomplish a recent acquisition, Berkshire decided to split its class B shares 50 to 1.

Source: Scott Patterson, "Berkshire Nears Smaller Baby B's," *Wall Street Journal Online* (January 19, 2010).

Why does Warren Buffett usually oppose stock splits? (Go to **WileyPLUS** for this answer and additional questions.)

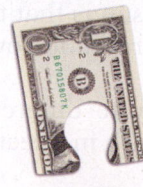

DO IT! 5 Stock Dividends and Stock Splits

Sing CD Company has had five years of record earnings. Due to this success, the market price of its 500,000 shares of $2 par value common stock has tripled from $15 per share to $45. During this period, paid-in capital remained the same at $2,000,000. Retained earnings increased from $1,500,000 to $10,000,000. President Joan Elbert is considering either a 10% stock dividend or a 2-for-1 stock split. She asks you to show the before-and-after effects of each option on retained earnings, total stockholders' equity, shares outstanding, and par value per share.

Action Plan

✔ Calculate the stock dividend's effect on retained earnings by multiplying the number of new shares times the market price of the stock (or par value for a large stock dividend).

✔ Recall that a stock dividend increases the number of shares without affecting total stockholders' equity.

✔ Recall that a stock split only increases the number of shares outstanding and decreases the par value per share.

Solution

The stock dividend amount is $2,250,000 [(500,000 × 10%) × $45]. The new balance in retained earnings is $7,750,000 ($10,000,000 − $2,250,000). The retained earnings balance after the stock split is the same as it was before the split: $10,000,000. Total stockholders' equity does not change. The effects on the stockholders' equity accounts are as follows.

	Original Balances	After Dividend	After Split
Paid-in capital	$ 2,000,000	$ 4,250,000	$ 2,000,000
Retained earnings	10,000,000	7,750,000	10,000,000
Total stockholders' equity	$12,000,000	$12,000,000	$12,000,000
Shares outstanding	500,000	550,000	1,000,000
Par value per share	$2.00	$2.00	$1.00

Related exercise material: **BE11-8, BE11-9, E11-14, E11-15**, and **DO IT! 11-5.**

LEARNING OBJECTIVE 6 **Discuss how stockholders' equity is reported and analyzed.**

Retained Earnings

Recall that **retained earnings** is net income that a company retains in the business. The balance in retained earnings is part of the stockholders' claim on the total assets of the corporation. It does not, however, represent a claim on any specific asset. Nor can the amount of retained earnings be associated with the balance of any asset account. For example, a $100,000 balance in retained earnings does not mean that there should be $100,000 in cash. The reason is that the company may have used the cash resulting from the excess of revenues over expenses to purchase buildings, equipment, and other assets.

To demonstrate that retained earnings and cash may be quite different, Illustration 11-19 shows recent amounts of retained earnings and cash in selected companies.

Illustration 11-19
Retained earnings and cash balances

	(in millions)	
Company	Retained Earnings	Cash
Facebook	$ 3,159	$3,323
Google	61,262	8,989
Nike, Inc.	5,695	3,337
Starbucks	4,130	2,576
Amazon.com	2,190	8,658

Remember that when a company has net income, it closes net income to retained earnings. The closing entry is a debit to Income Summary and a credit to Retained Earnings.

When a company has a **net loss** (expenses exceed revenues), it also closes this amount to retained earnings. The closing entry is a debit to Retained Earnings and a credit to Income Summary. To illustrate, assume that Rendle Corporation has a net loss of $400,000 in 2017. The closing entry to record this loss is as follows.

Retained Earnings	400,000	
Income Summary		400,000
(To close net loss to Retained Earnings)		

This closing entry is done even if it results in a debit balance in Retained Earnings. **Companies do not debit net losses to paid-in capital accounts.** To do so would destroy the distinction between paid-in and earned capital. If cumulative losses exceed cumulative income over a company's life, a debit balance in Retained Earnings results. A debit balance in Retained Earnings is identified as a **deficit**. A company reports a deficit as a deduction in the stockholders' equity section, as shown below.

Balance Sheet (partial)

Stockholders' equity	
Paid-in capital	
Common stock	$800,000
Retained earnings (deficit)	**(50,000)**
Total stockholders' equity	$750,000

Illustration 11-20
Stockholders' equity with deficit

RETAINED EARNINGS RESTRICTIONS

The balance in retained earnings is generally available for dividend declarations. In some cases, however, there may be **retained earnings restrictions**. These make a portion of the retained earnings balance currently unavailable for dividends. Restrictions result from one or more of the following causes.

1. **Legal restrictions.** Many states require a corporation to restrict retained earnings for the cost of treasury stock purchased. The restriction keeps intact the corporation's legal capital that is being temporarily held as treasury stock. When the company sells the treasury stock, the restriction is lifted.

2. **Contractual restrictions.** Long-term debt contracts may restrict retained earnings as a condition for the loan. The restriction limits the use of corporate assets for payment of dividends. Thus, it increases the likelihood that the corporation will be able to meet required loan payments.

3. **Voluntary restrictions.** The board of directors may voluntarily create retained earnings restrictions for specific purposes. For example, the board may authorize a restriction for future plant expansion. By reducing the amount of retained earnings available for dividends, the company makes more cash available for the planned expansion.

Companies generally disclose **retained earnings restrictions** in the notes to the financial statements. For example, as shown in Illustration 11-21 (page 526), **Tektronix Inc.**, a manufacturer of electronic measurement devices, had total retained earnings of $774 million, but the unrestricted portion was only $223.8 million.

Illustration 11-21
Disclosure of restriction

TEKTRONIX INC.
Notes to the Financial Statements

Certain of the Company's debt agreements require compliance with debt covenants. Management believes that the Company is in compliance with such requirements. The Company had unrestricted retained earnings of $223.8 million after meeting those requirements.

PRIOR PERIOD ADJUSTMENTS

Suppose that a corporation has closed its books and issued financial statements. The corporation then discovers that it made a material error in reporting net income of a prior year. How should the company record this situation in the accounts and report it in the financial statements?

The correction of an error in previously issued financial statements is known as a **prior period adjustment**. The company makes the correction directly to Retained Earnings because the effect of the error is now in this account. The net income for the prior period has been recorded in retained earnings through the journalizing and posting of closing entries.

To illustrate, assume that General Microwave discovers in 2017 that it understated depreciation expense on equipment in 2016 by $300,000 due to computational errors. These errors overstated both net income for 2016 and the current balance in retained earnings. The entry for the prior period adjustment, ignoring all tax effects, is as follows.

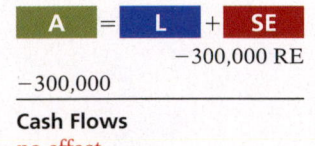

−300,000 RE
−300,000
Cash Flows
no effect

Retained Earnings	300,000	
Accumulated Depreciation—Equipment		300,000
(To adjust for understatement of depreciation in a prior period)		

A debit to an income statement account in 2017 is incorrect because the error pertains to a prior year.

Companies report prior period adjustments in the retained earnings statement. They add (or deduct, as the case may be) these adjustments from the beginning retained earnings balance. This results in an adjusted beginning balance. For example, assuming a beginning balance of $800,000 in retained earnings, General Microwave reports the prior period adjustment as follows.

Illustration 11-22
Statement presentation of prior period adjustments

GENERAL MICROWAVE
Retained Earnings Statement (partial)

Balance, January 1, as reported	$ 800,000
Correction for overstatement of net income in prior period (depreciation error)	**(300,000)**
Balance, January 1, as adjusted	$ 500,000

Again, reporting the correction in the current year's income statement would be incorrect because it applies to a prior year's income statement.

RETAINED EARNINGS STATEMENT

The **retained earnings statement** shows the changes in retained earnings during the year. The company prepares the statement from the Retained Earnings account. Illustration 11-23 shows (in T-account form) transactions that affect retained earnings.

Illustration 11-23
Debits and credits to retained earnings

Retained Earnings	
1. Net loss	1. Net income
2. Prior period adjustments for overstatement of net income	2. Prior period adjustments for understatement of net income
3. Cash dividends and stock dividends	
4. Some disposals of treasury stock	

As indicated, net income increases retained earnings, and a net loss decreases retained earnings. Prior period adjustments may either increase or decrease retained earnings. Both cash dividends and stock dividends decrease retained earnings. The circumstances under which treasury stock transactions decrease retained earnings are explained on page 514.

A complete retained earnings statement for Graber Inc., based on assumed data, is as follows.

Illustration 11-24
Retained earnings statement

GRABER INC.
Retained Earnings Statement
For the Year Ended December 31, 2017

Balance, January 1, as reported		$1,050,000
Correction for understatement of net income in prior period (inventory error)		50,000
Balance, January 1, as adjusted		1,100,000
Add: Net income		360,000
		1,460,000
Less: Cash dividends	$100,000	
Stock dividends	200,000	300,000
Balance, December 31		$1,160,000

DO IT! 6a Retained Earnings Statement

Vega Corporation has retained earnings of $5,130,000 on January 1, 2017. During the year, Vega earned $2,000,000 of net income. It declared and paid a $250,000 cash dividend. In 2017, Vega recorded an adjustment of $180,000 due to the understatement (from a mathematical error) of 2016 depreciation expense. Prepare a retained earnings statement for 2017.

Solution

VEGA CORPORATION
Retained Earnings Statement
For the Year Ended December 31, 2017

Balance, January 1, as reported	$5,130,000
Correction for overstatement of net income in prior period (depreciation error)	(180,000)
Balance, January 1, as adjusted	4,950,000
Add: Net income	2,000,000
	6,950,000
Less: Cash dividends	250,000
Balance, December 31	$6,700,000

Action Plan

✔ Recall that a retained earnings statement begins with retained earnings, as reported at the end of the previous year.

✔ Add or subtract any prior period adjustments to arrive at the adjusted beginning figure.

✔ Add net income and subtract dividends declared to arrive at the ending balance in retained earnings.

Related exercise material: **BE11-10, BE11-11, BE11-12, E11-17, E11-18, and DO IT! 11-6a.**

Statement Presentation and Analysis

In the stockholders' equity section of the balance sheet, paid-in capital and retained earnings are reported. The specific sources of paid-in capital are identified. Within paid-in capital, two classifications are recognized:

1. **Capital stock.** This category consists of preferred and common stock. Preferred stock is shown before common stock because of its preferential rights. Par value, shares authorized, shares issued, and shares outstanding are reported for each class of stock.

2. **Additional paid-in capital.** This includes the excess of amounts paid over par or stated value and paid-in capital from treasury stock.

PRESENTATION

Illustration 11-25 presents the stockholders' equity section of Graber Inc.'s balance sheet. Note the following: (1) "Common stock dividends distributable" is shown under "Capital stock" in "Paid-in capital" and (2) a note (Note R) discloses a retained earnings restriction.

Illustration 11-25

Comprehensive stockholders' equity section

GRABER INC.
Balance Sheet (partial)

Stockholders' equity		
Paid-in capital		
Capital stock		
9% Preferred stock, $100 par value, cumulative,		
callable at $120, 10,000 shares authorized,		
6,000 shares issued and outstanding		$ 600,000
Common stock, no par, $5 stated value,		
500,000 shares authorized, 400,000 shares		
issued and 390,000 shares outstanding	$2,000,000	
Common stock dividends distributable	**50,000**	2,050,000
Total capital stock		2,650,000
Additional paid-in capital		
In excess of par—preferred stock	30,000	
In excess of stated value—common stock	1,050,000	
Total additional paid-in capital		1,080,000
Total paid-in capital		3,730,000
Retained earnings **(see Note R)**		1,160,000
Total paid-in capital and retained earnings		4,890,000
Less: Treasury stock (10,000 common shares)		80,000
Total stockholders' equity		$4,810,000

Note R: Retained earnings is restricted for the cost of treasury stock, $80,000.

The stockholders' equity section of Graber Inc. in Illustration 11-25 includes most of the accounts discussed in this chapter. The disclosures pertaining to Graber's common stock indicate that the company issued 400,000 shares; 100,000 shares are unissued (500,000 authorized less 400,000 issued), and 390,000 shares are outstanding (400,000 issued less 10,000 shares in treasury).

Published annual reports often combine and report as a single amount the individual sources of additional paid-in capital, as shown in Illustration 11-26. In addition, authorized shares are sometimes not reported.

KELLOGG COMPANY
Balance Sheet (partial)
($ in millions)

Stockholders' equity		
Common stock, $0.25 par value, 1,000,000,000 shares authorized		
Issued: 418,669,193 shares		$ 105
Capital in excess of par value		388
Retained earnings		4,217
Treasury stock, at cost 28,618,052 shares		(1,357)
Accumulated other comprehensive income (loss)		(827)
Total stockholders' equity		$ 2,526

Illustration 11-26
Published stockholders' equity section

In practice, companies sometimes use the term "Capital surplus" in place of "Additional paid-in capital," and "Earned surplus" in place of "Retained earnings." The use of the term "surplus" suggests that the company has available an excess amount of funds. Such is not necessarily the case. Therefore, **the term "surplus" should not be employed in accounting**. Unfortunately, a number of companies still do use it.

Instead of presenting a detailed stockholders' equity section in the balance sheet and a retained earnings statement, many companies prepare a **stockholders' equity statement**. This statement shows the changes (1) in each stockholders' equity account and (2) in total that occurred during the year. Examples of stockholders' equity statements appear for **Apple** in Appendix A and for Hampton Corporation in an appendix to this chapter (Illustration 11A-1).

ANALYSIS

Investors and analysts can measure profitability from the viewpoint of the common stockholder by the **return on common stockholders' equity**. This ratio, as shown in Illustration 11-27, indicates how many dollars of net income the company earned for each dollar invested by the common stockholders. It is computed by dividing **net income available to common stockholders** (which is net income minus preferred dividends) by average common stockholders' equity.

To illustrate, **Walt Disney Company**'s beginning-of-the-year and end-of-the-year common stockholders' equity were $31,820 and $30,753 million, respectively. Its net income was $4,687 million, and no preferred stock was outstanding. The return on common stockholders' equity is computed as follows.

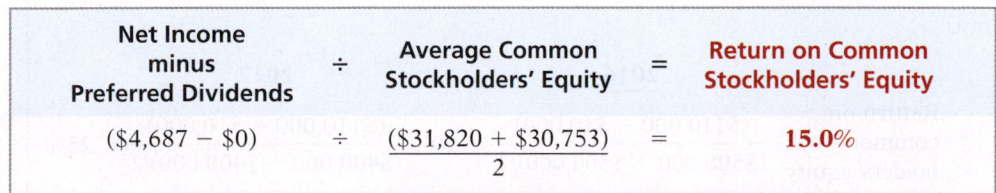

Net Income minus Preferred Dividends	÷	Average Common Stockholders' Equity	=	Return on Common Stockholders' Equity
($4,687 − $0)	÷	$\dfrac{(\$31{,}820 + \$30{,}753)}{2}$	=	15.0%

Illustration 11-27
Return on common stockholders' equity and computation

As shown above, if a company has preferred stock, we would deduct the amount of **preferred dividends** from the company's net income to compute income available to common stockholders. Also, the par value of preferred stock is deducted from total stockholders' equity when computing the average common stockholders' equity.

People, Planet, and Profit Insight

©Robert Churchill/iStockphoto

The Impact of Corporate Social Responsibility

A recent survey conducted by Institutional Shareholder Services, a proxy advisory firm, shows that 83% of investors now believe environmental and social factors can significantly impact shareholder value over the long term. This belief is clearly visible in the rising level of support for shareholder proposals requesting action related to social and environmental issues.

The following table shows that the number of corporate social responsibility (CSR)-related shareholder proposals

rose from 150 in 2000 to 191 in 2010. Moreover, those proposals received average voting support of 18.4% of votes cast versus just 7.5% a decade earlier.

Trends in Shareholder Proposals on Corporate Responsibility

	2000	2005	2010
Number of proposals voted	150	155	191
Average voting support	7.5%	9.9%	18.4%
Percent proposals receiving >10% support	16.7%	31.2%	52.1%

Source: Investor Responsibility Research Center, Ernst & Young, *Seven Questions CEOs and Boards Should Ask About: "Triple Bottom Line" Reporting.*

Why are CSR-related shareholder proposals increasing? (Go to **WileyPLUS** for this answer and additional questions.)

DO IT! 6b Stockholders' Equity

On January 1, 2017, Siena Corporation purchased 2,000 shares of treasury stock. Other information regarding Siena Corporation is provided below.

	2016	2017
Net income	$110,000	$110,000
Dividends on preferred stock	$10,000	$10,000
Dividends on common stock	$2,000	$1,600
Common stockholders' equity, beginning of year	$500,000	$400,000*
Common stockholders' equity, end of year	$500,000	$400,000

*Adjusted for purchase of treasury stock.

Compute (a) return on common stockholders' equity for each year, and (b) discuss its change from 2016 to 2017.

Action Plan

✔ Determine return on common stockholders' equity by dividing net income available to common stockholders by average common stockholders' equity.

Solution

(a)

	2016	**2017**
Return on common stockholders' equity	$\dfrac{(\$110,000 - \$10,000)}{(\$500,000 + \$500,000)/2} = 20\%$	$\dfrac{(\$110,000 - \$10,000)}{(\$400,000 + \$400,000)/2} = 25\%$

(b) Between 2016 and 2017, return on common stockholders' equity improved from 20% to 25%. While this would appear to be good news for the company's common stockholders, this increase should be carefully evaluated. It is important to note that net income did not change during this period. The increase in the ratio was due to the purchase of treasury shares, which reduced the denominator of the ratio. As the company repurchases its own shares, it becomes more reliant on debt and thus increases its risk.

Related exercise material: **E11-22 and DO IT! 11-6b.**

APPENDIX 11A: Describe the use and content of the stockholders' equity statement.

LEARNING OBJECTIVE *7

When balance sheets and income statements are presented by a corporation, changes in the separate accounts comprising stockholders' equity should also be disclosed. Disclosure of such changes is necessary to make the financial statements sufficiently informative for users. The disclosures may be made in an additional statement or in the notes to the financial statements.

Many corporations make the disclosures in a **stockholders' equity statement**. The statement shows the changes in **each** stockholders' equity account and in **total** stockholders' equity during the year. As shown in Illustration 11A-1, the stockholders' equity statement is prepared in columnar form. It contains columns for each account and for total stockholders' equity. The transactions are then identified and their effects are shown in the appropriate columns.

Illustration 11A-1
Stockholders' equity statement

HAMPTON CORPORATION
Stockholders' Equity Statement
For the Year Ended December 31, 2017

	Common Stock ($5 Par)	Paid-in Capital in Excess of Par—Common Stock	Retained Earnings	Treasury Stock	Total
Balance January 1	$300,000	$200,000	$650,000	$(34,000)	$1,116,000
Issued 5,000 shares of common stock at $15	25,000	50,000			75,000
Declared a $40,000 cash dividend			(40,000)		(40,000)
Purchased 2,000 shares for treasury at $16				(32,000)	(32,000)
Net income for year			240,000		240,000
Balance December 31	$325,000	$250,000	$850,000	$(66,000)	$1,359,000

In practice, additional columns are usually provided to show the number of shares of issued stock and treasury stock. The stockholders' equity statement for PepsiCo for a three-year period is shown in Appendix B. **When a stockholders' equity statement is presented, a retained earnings statement is not necessary** because the retained earnings column explains the changes in this account.

APPENDIX 11B: Compute book value per share.

LEARNING OBJECTIVE *8

Book Value per Share

You have learned about a number of per share amounts in this chapter. Another per share amount of some importance is **book value per share**. It represents **the equity a common stockholder has in the net assets of the corporation** from owning one share of stock. Remember that the net assets (total assets minus total liabilities) of a corporation must be equal to total stockholders' equity. Therefore, the formula for computing book value per share when a company has only one class of stock outstanding is as follows.

Illustration 11B-1
Book value per share formula

Total Stockholders' Equity	÷	Number of Common Shares Outstanding	=	Book Value per Share

Thus, if Marlo Corporation has total stockholders' equity of $1,500,000 (common stock $1,000,000 and retained earnings $500,000) and 50,000 shares of common stock outstanding, book value per share is $30 ($1,500,000 ÷ 50,000).

When a company has both preferred and common stock, the computation of book value is more complex. Since preferred stockholders have a prior claim on net assets over common stockholders, their equity must be deducted from total stockholders' equity. Then, we can determine the stockholders' equity that applies to the common stock. The computation of book value per share involves the following steps.

1. **Compute the preferred stock equity.** This equity is equal to the sum of the call price of preferred stock plus any cumulative dividends in arrears. If the preferred stock does not have a call price, the par value of the stock is used.

2. **Determine the common stock equity.** Subtract the preferred stock equity from total stockholders' equity.

3. **Determine book value per share.** Divide common stock equity by shares of common stock outstanding.

EXAMPLE

We will use the stockholders' equity section of Graber Inc. shown in Illustration 11-25 (page 528). Graber's preferred stock is callable at $120 per share and is cumulative. Assume that dividends on Graber's preferred stock were in arrears for one year, $54,000 (6,000 × $9). The computation of preferred stock equity (Step 1 in the preceding list) is shown below.

Illustration 11B-2
Computation of preferred stock equity—Step 1

Call price (6,000 shares × $120)	$ 720,000
Dividends in arrears (6,000 shares × $9)	54,000
Preferred stock equity	**$774,000**

The computation of book value (Steps 2 and 3) is as follows.

Illustration 11B-3
Computation of book value per share with preferred stock—Steps 2 and 3

Total stockholders' equity	$4,810,000
Less: **Preferred stock equity**	774,000
Common stock equity	**$4,036,000**
Shares of common stock outstanding	390,000
Book value per share ($4,036,000 ÷ 390,000)	**$10.35**

Note that we used the call price of $120 instead of the par value of $100. Note also that the paid-in capital in excess of par value of preferred stock, $30,000, **is not assigned to the preferred stock equity**. Preferred stockholders ordinarily do not have a right to amounts paid-in in excess of par value. Therefore, such amounts are assigned to the common stock equity in computing book value.

Book Value versus Market Price

Be sure you understand that **book value per share may not equal market price per share**. Book value generally is based on recorded costs. Market price reflects the subjective judgments of thousands of stockholders and prospective investors about a company's potential for future earnings and dividends. Market price per share may exceed book value per share, but that fact does not necessarily mean that the stock is overpriced. The correlation between book value and the annual range of a company's market price per share is often remote, as indicated by the following recent data.

Company	Book Value (year-end)	Market Range (for the year)
The Limited, Inc.	$13.38	$31.03–$22.89
H. J. Heinz Company	$ 7.48	$40.61–$34.53
Cisco Systems	$ 3.66	$21.24–$17.01
Wal-Mart Stores, Inc.	$12.79	$50.87–$42.31

Illustration 11B-4
Book value and market prices compared

Book value per share **is useful** in determining the trend of a stockholder's per share equity in a corporation. It is also significant in many contracts and in court cases where the rights of individual parties are based on cost information.

REVIEW AND PRACTICE

■ LEARNING OBJECTIVES REVIEW

❶ Discuss the major characteristics of a corporation. The major characteristics of a corporation are separate legal existence, limited liability of stockholders, transferable ownership rights, ability to acquire capital, continuous life, corporation management, government regulations, and additional taxes.

❷ Explain how to account for the issuance of common and preferred stock. When companies record the issuance of common stock for cash, they credit the par value of the shares to Common Stock. They record in a separate paid-in capital account the portion of the proceeds that is above or below par value. When no-par common stock has a stated value, the entries are similar to those for par value stock. When no-par stock does not have a stated value, companies credit the entire proceeds to Common Stock.

Preferred stock has contractual provisions that give it priority over common stock in certain areas. Typically, preferred stockholders have preferences (1) to dividends and (2) to assets in liquidation. They usually do not have voting rights.

❸ Explain how to account for treasury stock. The cost method is generally used in accounting for treasury stock. Under this approach, companies debit Treasury Stock at the price paid to reacquire the shares. They credit the same amount to Treasury Stock when they sell the shares. The difference between the sales price and cost is recorded in stockholders' equity accounts, not in income statement accounts.

❹ Explain how to account for cash dividends. Companies make entries for cash dividends at the declaration date and at the payment date. At the **declaration date**, the entry is debit Cash Dividends and credit

Dividends Payable. At the **payment date**, the entry is debit Dividends Payable and credit Cash.

❺ Explain how to account for stock dividends and splits. At the declaration date, the entry for a small stock dividend is debit Stock Dividends, credit Paid-in Capital in Excess of Par (or Stated Value)—Common Stock, and credit Common Stock Dividends Distributable. At the payment date, the entry for a small stock dividend is debit Common Stock Dividends Distributable and credit Common Stock. A stock split reduces the par or stated value per share and increases the number of shares but does not affect balances in stockholders' equity accounts.

❻ Discuss how stockholders' equity is reported and analyzed. Companies report each of the individual debits and credits to retained earnings in the retained earnings statement. Additions consist of net income and prior period adjustments to correct understatements of prior years' net income. Deductions consist of net loss, prior period adjustments to correct overstatements of prior years' net income, cash and stock dividends, and some disposals of treasury stock.

In the stockholders' equity section, paid-in capital and retained earnings are reported and specific sources of paid-in capital are identified. Within paid-in capital, two classifications are shown: capital stock and additional paid-in capital. If a corporation has treasury stock, the cost of treasury stock is deducted from total paid-in capital and retained earnings to obtain total stockholders' equity. One measure of profitability is the return on common stockholders' equity. It is calculated by dividing net income minus preferred dividends by average common stockholders' equity.

*❼ **Describe the use and content of the stockholders' equity statement.** Corporations must disclose changes in stockholders' equity accounts and may choose to do so by issuing a separate stockholders' equity statement. This statement, prepared in columnar form, shows changes in each stockholders' equity account and in total stockholders' equity during the accounting period. When this statement is presented, a retained earnings statement is not necessary.

*❽ **Compute book value per share.** Book value per share represents the equity a common stockholder has in the net assets of a corporation from owning one share of stock. When there is only common stock outstanding, the formula for computing book value is: Total stockholders' equity ÷ Number of common shares outstanding = Book value per share.

▌ GLOSSARY REVIEW

Authorized stock The amount of stock that a corporation is authorized to sell as indicated in its charter. (p. 505).

*__Book value per share__ The equity a common stockholder has in the net assets of the corporation from owning one share of stock. (p. 531).

Cash dividend A pro rata distribution of cash to stockholders. (p. 515).

Charter A document that is issued by the state to set forth important terms and features regarding the creation of a corporation. (p. 502).

Corporation A business organized as a legal entity separate and distinct from its owners under state corporation law. (p. 500).

Cumulative dividend A feature of preferred stock entitling the stockholder to receive current and unpaid prior-year dividends before common stockholders receive dividends. (p. 518).

Declaration date The date the board of directors formally declares (authorizes) a dividend and announces it to stockholders. (p. 516).

Deficit A debit balance in Retained Earnings. (p. 525).

Dividend A corporation's distribution of cash or stock to its stockholders on a pro rata (proportional) basis. (p. 515).

Liquidating dividend A dividend declared out of paid-in capital. (p. 515).

No-par value stock Capital stock that has not been assigned a value in the corporate charter. (p. 507).

Organization costs Costs incurred in the formation of a corporation. (p. 503).

Outstanding stock Capital stock that has been issued and is being held by stockholders. (p. 513).

Paid-in capital Total amount of cash and other assets paid in to the corporation by stockholders in exchange for capital stock. (p. 507).

Par value stock Capital stock that has been assigned a value per share in the corporate charter. (p. 506).

Payment date The date dividends are transferred to stockholders. (p. 517).

Preferred stock Capital stock that has some preferences over common stock. (p. 511).

Prior period adjustment The correction of an error in previously issued financial statements. (p. 526).

Privately held corporation A corporation that has only a few stockholders and whose stock is not available for sale to the general public. (p. 500).

Publicly held corporation A corporation that may have thousands of stockholders and whose stock is regularly traded on a national securities exchange. (p. 500).

Record date The date when ownership of outstanding shares is determined for dividend purposes. (p. 516).

Retained earnings Net income that the corporation retains for future use. (p. 507).

Retained earnings restrictions Circumstances that make a portion of retained earnings currently unavailable for dividends. (p. 525).

Retained earnings statement A financial statement that shows the changes in retained earnings during the year. (p. 526).

Return on common stockholders' equity A measure of profitability that shows how many dollars of net income were earned for each dollar invested by the owners; computed as net income minus preferred dividends divided by average common stockholders' equity. (p. 529).

Stated value The amount per share assigned by the board of directors to no-par value stock. (p. 507).

Stock dividend A pro rata distribution to stockholders of the corporation's own stock. (p. 520).

Stockholders' equity statement A statement that shows the changes in each stockholders' equity account and in total stockholders' equity during the year. (p. 529).

Stock split The issuance of additional shares of stock to stockholders according to their percentage ownership. It is accompanied by a reduction in the par or stated value per share. (p. 522).

Treasury stock A corporation's own stock that has been issued and subsequently reacquired from shareholders by the corporation but not retired. (p. 512).

PRACTICE MULTIPLE-CHOICE QUESTIONS

(LO 1) **1.** Which of the following is **not** a major advantage of a corporate form of organization?
(a) Separate legal existence.
(b) Continuous life.
(c) Government regulations.
(d) Transferable ownership rights.

(LO 1) **2.** A major disadvantage of a corporation is:
(a) limited liability of stockholders.
(b) additional taxes.
(c) transferable ownership rights.
(d) separate legal existence.

(LO 1) **3.** Which of the following statements is **false**?
(a) Ownership of common stock gives the owner a voting right.
(b) The stockholders' equity section begins with a paid-in capital section.
(c) The authorization of capital stock does not result in a formal accounting entry.
(d) Par value and market price of a company's stock are always the same.

(LO 2) **4.** ABC Corporation issues 1,000 shares of $10 par value common stock at $12 per share. In recording the transaction, credits are made to:
(a) Common Stock $10,000 and Paid-in Capital in Excess of Stated Value $2,000.
(b) Common Stock $12,000.
(c) Common Stock $10,000 and Paid-in Capital in Excess of Par $2,000.
(d) Common Stock $10,000 and Retained Earnings $2,000.

(LO 2) **5.** Preferred stock may have priority over common stock **except** in:
(a) dividends.
(b) assets in the event of liquidation.
(c) cumulative dividend features.
(d) voting.

(LO 3) **6.** XYZ, Inc. sells 100 shares of $5 par value treasury stock at $13 per share. If the cost of acquiring the shares was $10 per share, the entry for the sale should include credits to:
(a) Treasury Stock $1,000 and Paid-in Capital from Treasury Stock $300.
(b) Treasury Stock $500 and Paid-in Capital from Treasury Stock $800.
(c) Treasury Stock $1,000 and Retained Earnings $300.
(d) Treasury Stock $500 and Paid-in Capital in Excess of Par $800.

(LO 3) **7.** In the stockholders' equity section, the cost of treasury stock is deducted from:
(a) total paid-in capital and retained earnings.
(b) retained earnings.
(c) total stockholders' equity.
(d) common stock in paid-in capital.

(LO 4) **8.** M-Bot Corporation has 10,000 shares of 8%, $100 par value, cumulative preferred stock outstanding at December 31, 2017. No dividends were declared in 2015 or 2016. If M-Bot wants to pay $375,000 of dividends in 2017, common stockholders will receive:
(a) $0.
(b) $295,000.
(c) $215,000.
(d) $135,000.

9. Entries for cash dividends are required on the: (LO 4)
(a) declaration date and the payment date.
(b) record date and the payment date.
(c) declaration date, record date, and payment date.
(d) declaration date and the record date.

10. Which of the following statements about small stock (LO 5) dividends is **true**?
(a) A debit to Retained Earnings for the par value of the shares issued should be made.
(b) A small stock dividend decreases total stockholders' equity.
(c) Market price per share should be assigned to the dividend shares.
(d) A small stock dividend ordinarily will have an effect on par value per share of stock.

11. All **but one** of the following is reported in a retained (LO 6) earnings statement. The **exception** is:
(a) cash and stock dividends.
(b) net income and net loss.
(c) sales revenue.
(d) prior period adjustments.

12. A prior period adjustment is: (LO 6)
(a) reported in the income statement as a nontypical item.
(b) a correction of an error that is recorded directly to retained earnings.
(c) reported directly in the stockholders' equity section.
(d) reported in the retained earnings statement as an adjustment of the ending balance of retained earnings.

13. In the stockholders' equity section of the balance (LO 6) sheet, common stock:
(a) is listed before preferred stock.
(b) is added to total capital stock.
(c) is part of paid-in capital.
(d) is part of additional paid-in capital.

14. Which of the following is **not** reported under additional paid-in capital? (LO 6)
(a) Paid-in capital in excess of par.
(b) Common stock.
(c) Paid-in capital in excess of stated value.
(d) Paid-in capital from treasury stock.

15. Katie Inc. reported net income of $186,000 during (LO 6) 2017 and paid dividends of $26,000 on common stock. It also has 10,000 shares of 6%, $100 par value, noncumulative preferred stock outstanding and paid dividends of $60,000 on preferred stock. Common stockholders' equity was $1,200,000 on January 1, 2017, and $1,600,000 on December 31, 2017. The company's return on common stockholders' equity for 2017 is:
(a) 10.0%.
(c) 7.1%.
(b) 9.0%.
(d) 13.3%.

*16. When a stockholders' equity statement is presented, it (LO 7) is not necessary to prepare a (an):
(a) retained earnings statement.
(b) balance sheet.
(c) income statement.
(d) None of the above.

(LO 8)*17. The ledger of JFK, Inc. shows common stock, common treasury stock, and no preferred stock. For this company, the formula for computing book value per share is:

(a) total paid-in capital and retained earnings divided by the number of shares of common stock issued.

(b) common stock divided by the number of shares of common stock issued.

(c) total stockholders' equity divided by the number of shares of common stock outstanding.

(d) total stockholders' equity divided by the number of shares of common stock issued.

Solutions

1. (c) Government regulations are a disadvantage of a corporation. The other choices are advantages of a corporation.

2. (b) Additional taxes are a disadvantage of a corporation. The other choices are advantages of a corporation.

3. (d) Par value has no relationship with market price, and many states today do not require a par value. The other choices are true statements.

4. (c) Common Stock should be credited for $10,000 and Paid-in Capital in Excess of Par should be credited for $2,000. The stock is par value stock, not stated value stock, and this excess is contributed, not earned, capital. The other choices are therefore incorrect.

5. (d) Preferred stock usually does not have voting rights and therefore does not have priority over common stock on this issue. The other choices are true statements.

6. (a) Treasury Stock should be credited for $1,000 (100 shares × $10, the acquisition price). Paid-in Capital from Treasury Stock should be credited for the difference between the $1,000 and the cash received of $1,300 (100 shares × $13), or $300. The other choices are therefore incorrect.

7. (a) The cost of treasury stock is deducted from total paid-in capital and retained earnings. The other choices are therefore incorrect.

8. (d) The preferred stockholders will receive a total of $240,000 of dividends [dividends in arrears ($80,000 × 2 years) + current-year dividends ($80,000)]. If M-Bot wants to pay a total of $375,000 in 2017, then common stockholders will receive $135,000 ($375,000 − $240,000), not (a) $0, (b) $295,000, or (c) $215,000.

9. (a) Entries are required for dividends on the declaration date and the payment date, but not the record date. The other choices are therefore incorrect.

10. (c) Because the stock dividend is considered small, the fair value (market price), not the par value, is assigned to the shares. The other choices are incorrect because (a) a debit to Retained Earnings for the fair value of the shares issued should be made; (b) a small stock dividend changes the composition of total stockholders' equity, but does not change the total; and (d) a small stock dividend will have no effect on par value per share.

11. (c) Sales revenue is not reported on the retained earnings statement. The other choices are true statements.

12. (b) A prior period adjustment is a correction of an error that is recorded directly to retained earnings. The other choices are incorrect because a prior period adjustment is reported in the retained earnings statement, not in the (a) income statement or (c) stockholders' equity section of the balance sheet. Choice (d) is incorrect because the prior period adjustment is an adjustment of the beginning, not the ending, balance of retained earnings.

13. (c) Common stock is part of part-in capital. The other choices are incorrect because common stock (a) is listed after preferred stock, (b) is not added to total capital stock but is part of capital stock, and (d) is part of capital stock, not additional paid-in capital.

14. (b) Common stock is reported in the capital stock section of paid-in capital, not in the additional paid-in capital section. The other choices are true statements.

15. (b) Return on common stockholders' equity is Net income available to common stockholders divided by Average common stockholders' equity. Net income available to common stockholders is Net income less Preferred dividends = $126,000 [$186,000 − (10,000 × .06 × $100)]. The company's return on common stockholders' equity for the year is therefore 9.0% [$126,000/($1,200,000 + $1,600,000)/2)], not (a) 10.0%, (c) 7.1%, or (d) 13.3%.

*16. (a) When a stockholders' equity statement is presented a retained earnings statement is unnecessary as the information would be redundant. Choices (b) balance sheet and (c) income statement are required statements. Choice (d) is wrong because there is a correct answer given.

*17. (c) When a company has only one class of stock outstanding, Book value per share is Total stockholders' equity divided by Number of shares of common stock outstanding. The other choices are therefore incorrect.

▌ PRACTICE EXERCISES

Journalize issuance of common and preferred stock and purchase of treasury stock.

(LO 2, 3)

1. Maci Co. had the following transactions during the current period.

Mar.	2	Issued 5,000 shares of $5 par value common stock to attorneys in payment of a bill for $35,000 for services performed in helping the company to incorporate.
June	12	Issued 60,000 shares of $5 par value common stock for cash of $370,000.
July	11	Issued 1,000 shares of $100 par value preferred stock for cash at $112 per share.
Nov.	28	Purchased 2,000 shares of treasury stock for $70,000.

Instructions

Journalize the transactions.

Solution

1.	Mar. 2	Organization Expense	35,000	
		Common Stock (5,000 × $5)		25,000
		Paid-in Capital in Excess of Par—		
		Common Stock		10,000
	June 12	Cash	370,000	
		Common Stock (60,000 × $5)		300,000
		Paid-in Capital in Excess of Par—		
		Common Stock		70,000
	July 11	Cash (1,000 × $112)	112,000	
		Preferred Stock (1,000 × $100)		100,000
		Paid-in Capital in Excess of Par—		
		Preferred Stock (1,000 × $12)		12,000
	Nov. 28	Treasury Stock	70,000	
		Cash		70,000

2. On January 1, Chong Corporation had 95,000 shares of no-par common stock issued and outstanding. The stock has a stated value of $5 per share. During the year, the following occurred.

Journalize cash dividends; indicate statement presentation.

(LO 4, 6)

Apr. 1   Issued 25,000 additional shares of common stock for $17 per share.
June 15   Declared a cash dividend of $1 per share to stockholders of record on June 30.
July 10   Paid the $1 cash dividend.
Dec. 1   Issued 2,000 additional shares of common stock for $19 per share.
     15   Declared a cash dividend on outstanding shares of $1.20 per share to stockholders of record on December 31.

Instructions

(a) Prepare the entries, if any, on each of the three dividend dates.

(b) How are dividends and dividends payable reported in the financial statements prepared at December 31?

Solution

2. (a)	June 15	Cash Dividends (120,000 × $1)	120,000	
		Dividends Payable		120,000
	July 10	Dividends Payable	120,000	
		Cash		120,000
	Dec. 15	Cash Dividends (122,000 × $1.20)	146,400	
		Dividends Payable		146,400

(b) In the retained earnings statement, dividends of $266,400 will be deducted. In the balance sheet, Dividends Payable of $146,400 will be reported as a current liability.

3. On January 1, 2017, Rabb Corporation had retained earnings of $550,000. During the year, Rabb had the following selected transactions.

Prepare a retained earnings statement.

(LO 6)

1. Declared cash dividends $120,000.
2. Corrected overstatement of 2016 net income because of depreciation error $30,000.
3. Earned net income $320,000.
4. Declared stock dividends $60,000.

Instructions

Prepare a retained earnings statement for the year ended December 31, 2017.

Solution

3.

RABB CORPORATION		
Retained Earnings Statement		
For the Year Ended December 31, 2017		
Balance, January 1, as reported		$550,000
Correction for overstatement of 2016 net income (depreciation error)		(30,000)
Balance, January 1, as adjusted		520,000
Add: Net income		320,000
		840,000
Less: Cash dividends	$120,000	
Stock dividends	60,000	180,000
Balance, December 31		$660,000

PRACTICE PROBLEM

Journalize transactions and prepare stockholders' equity section.

(LO 2, 3, 6)

Rolman Corporation is authorized to issue 1,000,000 shares of $5 par value common stock. In its first year, the company has the following stock transactions.

Jan. 10   Issued 400,000 shares of stock at $8 per share.
July 1   Issued 100,000 shares of stock for land. The land had an asking price of $900,000. The stock is currently selling on a national exchange at $8.25 per share.
Sept. 1   Purchased 10,000 shares of common stock for the treasury at $9 per share.
Dec. 1   Sold 4,000 shares of the treasury stock at $10 per share.

Instructions

(a) Journalize the transactions.

(b) Prepare the stockholders' equity section assuming the company had retained earnings of $200,000 at December 31.

Solution

(a) Jan. 10	Cash	3,200,000	
	Common Stock		2,000,000
	Paid-in Capital in Excess of Par—Common Stock		1,200,000
	(To record issuance of 400,000 shares of $5 par value stock)		
July 1	Land	825,000	
	Common Stock		500,000
	Paid-in Capital in Excess of Par—Common Stock		325,000
	(To record issuance of 100,000 shares of $5 par value stock for land)		
Sept. 1	Treasury Stock	90,000	
	Cash		90,000
	(To record purchase of 10,000 shares of treasury stock at cost)		
Dec. 1	Cash	40,000	
	Treasury Stock		36,000
	Paid-in Capital from Treasury Stock		4,000
	(To record sale of 4,000 shares of treasury stock above cost)		

(b)

ROLMAN CORPORATION		
Balance Sheet (partial)		

Stockholders' equity		
Paid-in capital		
Capital stock		
Common stock, $5 par value, 1,000,000 shares authorized, 500,000 shares issued, 494,000 shares outstanding		$2,500,000
Additional paid-in capital		
In excess of par—common stock	$1,525,000	
From treasury stock	4,000	
Total additional paid-in capital		1,529,000
Total paid-in capital		4,029,000
Retained earnings		200,000
Total paid-in capital and retained earnings		4,229,000
Less: Treasury stock (6,000 shares)		54,000
Total stockholders' equity		$4,175,000

WileyPLUS

Brief Exercises, Exercises, **DO IT!** Exercises, and Problems and many additional resources are available for practice in WileyPLUS

NOTE: All asterisked Questions, Exercises, and Problems relate to material in the appendices to the chapter.

QUESTIONS

1. Mark Kemp, a student, asks your help in understanding the following characteristics of a corporation: (a) separate legal existence, (b) limited liability of stockholders, and (c) transferable ownership rights. Explain these characteristics to Mark.

2. (a) Your friend Katie Fehr cannot understand how the characteristic of corporation management is both an advantage and a disadvantage. Clarify this problem for Katie.
   (b) Identify and explain two other disadvantages of a corporation.

3. (a) The following terms pertain to the forming of a corporation: (1) charter, (2) by-laws, and (3) organization costs. Explain the terms.
   (b) Donna Fleming believes a corporation must be incorporated in the state in which its headquarters' office is located. Is Donna correct? Explain.

4. What are the basic ownership rights of common stockholders in the absence of restrictive provisions?

5. (a) What are the two principal components of stockholders' equity?
   (b) What is paid-in capital? Give three examples.

6. How does the balance sheet for a corporation differ from the balance sheet for a proprietorship?

7. The corporate charter of Luney Corporation allows the issuance of a maximum of 100,000 shares of common stock. During its first two years of operations, Luney sold 70,000 shares to shareholders and reacquired 7,000 of these shares. After these transactions, how many shares are authorized, issued, and outstanding?

8. Which is the better investment—common stock with a par value of $5 per share, or common stock with a par value of $20 per share? Why?

9. What factors help determine the market price of stock?

10. Why is common stock usually not issued at a price that is less than par value?

11. Land appraised at $80,000 is purchased by issuing 1,000 shares of $20 par value common stock. The market price of the shares at the time of the exchange, based on active trading in the securities market, is $95 per share. Should the land be recorded at $20,000, $80,000, or $95,000? Explain.

12. For what reasons might a company like IBM repurchase some of its stock (treasury stock)?

13. Meng, Inc. purchases 1,000 shares of its own previously issued $5 par common stock for $12,000. Assuming the shares are held in the treasury, what effect does this transaction have on (a) net income, (b) total assets, (c) total paid-in capital, and (d) total stockholders' equity?

14. The treasury stock purchased in Question 13 is resold by Meng, Inc. for $16,000. What effect does this transaction have on (a) net income, (b) total assets, (c) total paid-in capital, and (d) total stockholders' equity?

15. (a) What are the principal differences between common stock and preferred stock?
(b) Preferred stock may be cumulative. Discuss this feature.
(c) How are dividends in arrears presented in the financial statements?

16. Identify the events that result in credits and debits to retained earnings.

17. Indicate how each of the following accounts should be classified in the stockholders' equity section.
(a) Common stock.
(b) Paid-in capital in excess of par—common stock.
(c) Retained earnings.
(d) Treasury stock.
(e) Paid-in capital from treasury stock.
(f) Paid-in capital in excess of stated value—common stock.
(g) Preferred stock.

18. Jan Kimler maintains that adequate cash is the only requirement for the declaration of a cash dividend. Is Jan correct? Explain.

19. (a) Three dates are important in connection with cash dividends. Identify these dates, and explain their significance to the corporation and its stockholders.
(b) Identify the accounting entries that are made for a cash dividend and the date of each entry.

20. Contrast the effects of a cash dividend and a stock dividend on a corporation's balance sheet.

21. Rich Mordica asks, "Since stock dividends don't change anything, why declare them?" What is your answer to Rich?

22. Gorton Corporation has 30,000 shares of $10 par value common stock outstanding when it announces a 2-for-1 stock split. Before the split, the stock had a market price of $120 per share. After the split, how many shares of stock will be outstanding? What will be the approximate market price per share?

23. The board of directors is considering either a stock split or a stock dividend. They understand that total stockholders' equity will remain the same under either action. However, they are not sure of the different effects of the two types of actions on other aspects of stockholders' equity. Explain the differences to the directors.

24. What is a prior period adjustment, and how is it reported in the financial statements?

25. What is the purpose of a retained earnings restriction? Identify the possible causes of retained earnings restrictions.

***26.** What is the formula for computing book value per share when a corporation has only common stock?

***27.** Emko Inc.'s common stock has a par value of $1, a book value of $24, and a current market price of $18. Explain why these amounts are all different.

BRIEF EXERCISES

List the advantages and disadvantages of a corporation.
(LO 1)

BE11-1 Angie Baden is studying for her accounting midterm examination. Identify for Angie the advantages and disadvantages of the corporate form of business organization.

Prepare entries for issuance of par value common stock.
(LO 2)

BE11-2 On May 10, Jack Corporation issues 2,000 shares of $10 par value common stock for cash at $18 per share. Journalize the issuance of the stock.

Prepare entries for issuance of no-par value common stock.
(LO 2)

BE11-3 On June 1, Noonan Inc. issues 4,000 shares of no-par common stock at a cash price of $6 per share. Journalize the issuance of the shares assuming the stock has a stated value of $1 per share.

Prepare entries for issuance of stock in a noncash transaction.
(LO 2)

BE11-4 Lei Inc.'s $10 par value common stock is actively traded at a market price of $15 per share. Lei issues 5,000 shares to purchase land advertised for sale at $85,000. Journalize the issuance of the stock in acquiring the land.

Prepare entries for issuance of preferred stock.
(LO 2)

BE11-5 Garb Inc. issues 5,000 shares of $100 par value preferred stock for cash at $130 per share. Journalize the issuance of the preferred stock.

Prepare entries for treasury stock transactions.
(LO 3)

BE11-6 On July 1, Raney Corporation purchases 500 shares of its $5 par value common stock for the treasury at a cash price of $9 per share. On September 1, it sells 300 shares of the treasury stock for cash at $11 per share. Journalize the two treasury stock transactions.

Prepare entries for a cash dividend.
(LO 4)

BE11-7 Greenwood Corporation has 80,000 shares of common stock outstanding. It declares a $1 per share cash dividend on November 1 to stockholders of record on December 1. The dividend is paid on December 31. Prepare the entries on the appropriate dates to record the declaration and payment of the cash dividend.

BE11-8 Langley Corporation has 50,000 shares of $10 par value common stock outstanding. It declares a 15% stock dividend on December 1 when the market price per share is $16. The dividend shares are issued on December 31. Prepare the entries for the declaration and issuance of the stock dividend.

Prepare entries for a stock dividend.
(LO 5)

BE11-9 The stockholders' equity section of Pretzer Corporation consists of common stock ($10 par) $2,000,000 and retained earnings $500,000. A 10% stock dividend (20,000 shares) is declared when the market price per share is $14. Show the before-and-after effects of the dividend on the following.
(a) The components of stockholders' equity.
(b) Shares outstanding.
(c) Par value per share.

Show before-and-after effects of a stock dividend.
(LO 5)

BE11-10 For the year ending December 31, 2017, Soto Inc. reports net income $170,000 and dividends $85,000. Prepare the retained earnings statement for the year assuming the balance in retained earnings on January 1, 2017, was $220,000.

Prepare a retained earnings statement.
(LO 6)

BE11-11 The balance in retained earnings on January 1, 2017, for Palmer Inc. was $800,000. During the year, the corporation paid cash dividends of $90,000 and distributed a stock dividend of $8,000. In addition, the company determined that it had understated its depreciation expense in prior years by $50,000. Net income for 2017 was $120,000. Prepare the retained earnings statement for 2017.

Prepare a retained earnings statement.
(LO 6)

BE11-12 Pine Corporation has the following accounts at December 31: Common Stock, $10 par, 5,000 shares issued, $50,000; Paid-in Capital in Excess of Par—Common Stock $30,000; Retained Earnings $45,000; and Treasury Stock, 500 shares, $11,000. Prepare the stockholders' equity section of the balance sheet.

Prepare stockholders' equity section.
(LO 6)

*BE11-13 The balance sheet for Lauren Inc. shows the following: total paid-in capital and retained earnings $877,000, total stockholders' equity $817,000, common stock issued 44,000 shares, and common stock outstanding 38,000 shares. Compute the book value per share. (No preferred stock is outstanding.)

Compute book value per share.
(LO 8)

DO IT! Exercises

DO IT! 11-1a Indicate whether each of the following statements is true or false. If false, indicate how to correct the statement.

Analyze statements about corporate organization.
(LO 1)

_____ 1. The corporation is an entity separate and distinct from its owners.
_____ 2. The liability of stockholders is normally limited to their investment in the corporation.
_____ 3. The relative lack of government regulation is an advantage of the corporate form of business.
_____ 4. There is no journal entry to record the authorization of capital stock.
_____ 5. No-par value stock is quite rare today.

DO IT! 11-1b At the end of its first year of operation, Goss Corporation has $1,000,000 of common stock and net income of $236,000. Prepare (a) the closing entry for net income and (b) the stockholders' equity section at year-end.

Close net income and prepare stockholders' equity section.
(LO 1)

DO IT! 11-2 Beauty Island Corporation began operations on April 1 by issuing 60,000 shares of $5 par value common stock for cash at $13 per share. On April 19, it issued 2,000 shares of common stock to attorneys in settlement of their bill of $27,500 for organization costs. In addition, Beauty Island issued 1,000 shares of $1 par value preferred stock for $6 cash per share. Journalize the issuance of the common and preferred shares, assuming the shares are not publicly traded.

Journalize issuance of stock.
(LO 2)

Journalize treasury stock transactions.

(LO 3)

DO IT! 11-3   Fouts Corporation purchased 2,000 shares of its $10 par value common stock for $130,000 on August 1. It will hold these shares in the treasury until resold. On December 1, the corporation sold 1,200 shares of treasury stock for cash at $72 per share. Journalize the treasury stock transactions.

Determine dividends paid to preferred and commonstockholders.

(LO 4)

DO IT! 11-4   Herr Corporation has 3,000 shares of 7%, $100 par value preferred stock outstanding at December 31, 2017. At December 31, 2017, the company declared a $105,000 cash dividend. Determine the dividend paid to preferred stockholders and common stockholders under each of the following scenarios.

1. The preferred stock is noncumulative, and the company has not missed any dividends in previous years.
2. The preferred stock is noncumulative, and the company did not pay a dividend in each of the two previous years.
3. The preferred stock is cumulative, and the company did not pay a dividend in each of the two previous years.

Determine effects of stock dividend and stock split.

(LO 5)

DO IT! 11-5   Jurgens Company has had 4 years of net income. Due to this success, the market price of its 400,000 shares of $3 par value common stock has increased from $12 per share to $46. During this period, paid-in capital remained the same at $4,800,000. Retained earnings increased from $1,800,000 to $12,000,000. President E. Rife is considering either a 15% stock dividend or a 2-for-1 stock split. He asks you to show the before-and-after effects of each option on (a) retained earnings and (b) total stockholders' equity.

Prepare a retained earnings statement.

(LO 6)

DO IT! 11-6a   Foley Corporation has retained earnings of $3,100,000 on January 1, 2017. During the year, Foley earned $1,200,000 of net income. It declared and paid a $150,000 cash dividend. In 2017, Foley recorded an adjustment of $110,000 due to the overstatement (from mathematical error) of 2016 depreciation expense. Prepare a retained earnings statement for 2017.

Compute return on stockholders' equity and discuss changes.

(LO 6)

DO IT! 11-6b   On January 1, 2017, Vahsholtz Corporation purchased 5,000 shares of treasury stock. Other information regarding Vahsholtz Corporation is provided as follows.

	2016	2017
Net income	$100,000	$110,000
Dividends on preferred stock	$ 30,000	$ 30,000
Dividends on common stock	$ 20,000	$ 25,000
Weighted-average number of common shares outstanding	50,000	45,000
Common stockholders' equity beginning of year	$600,000	$750,000
Common stockholders' equity end of year	$750,000	$830,000

Compute (a) return on common stockholders' equity for each year, and (b) discuss the changes in each.

EXERCISES

Identify characteristics of a corporation.

(LO 1)

E11-1   Andrea has prepared the following list of statements about corporations.

1. A corporation is an entity separate and distinct from its owners.
2. As a legal entity, a corporation has most of the rights and privileges of a person.
3. Most of the largest U.S. corporations are privately held corporations.
4. Corporations may buy, own, and sell property; borrow money; enter into legally binding contracts; and sue and be sued.
5. The net income of a corporation is not taxed as a separate entity.
6. Creditors have a legal claim on the personal assets of the owners of a corporation if the corporation does not pay its debts.
7. The transfer of stock from one owner to another requires the approval of either the corporation or other stockholders.
8. The board of directors of a corporation legally owns the corporation.
9. The chief accounting officer of a corporation is the controller.
10. Corporations are subject to fewer state and federal regulations than partnerships or proprietorships.

Instructions
Identify each statement as true or false. If false, indicate how to correct the statement.

E11-2 Andrea (see E11-1) has studied the information you gave her in that exercise and has come to you with more statements about corporations.

Identify characteristics of a corporation.

(LO 1)

1. Corporation management is both an advantage and a disadvantage of a corporation compared to a proprietorship or a partnership.
2. Limited liability of stockholders, government regulations, and additional taxes are the major disadvantages of a corporation.
3. When a corporation is formed, organization costs are recorded as an asset.
4. Each share of common stock gives the stockholder the ownership rights to vote at stockholder meetings, share in corporate earnings, keep the same percentage ownership when new shares of stock are issued, and share in assets upon liquidation.
5. The number of issued shares is always greater than or equal to the number of authorized shares.
6. A journal entry is required for the authorization of capital stock.
7. Publicly held corporations usually issue stock directly to investors.
8. The trading of capital stock on a securities exchange involves the transfer of already issued shares from an existing stockholder to another investor.
9. The market price of common stock is usually the same as its par value.
10. Retained earnings is the total amount of cash and other assets paid in to the corporation by stockholders in exchange for capital stock.

Instructions
Identify each statement as true or false. If false, indicate how to correct the statement.

E11-3 During its first year of operations, Foyle Corporation had the following transactions pertaining to its common stock.

Journalize issuance of common stock.

(LO 2)

| Jan. 10 | Issued 70,000 shares for cash at $5 per share. |
| July 1 | Issued 40,000 shares for cash at $7 per share. |

Instructions
(a) Journalize the transactions, assuming that the common stock has a par value of $5 per share.
(b) Journalize the transactions, assuming that the common stock is no-par with a stated value of $1 per share.

E11-4 Osage Corporation issued 2,000 shares of stock.

Journalize issuance of common stock.

(LO 2)

Instructions
Prepare the entry for the issuance under the following assumptions.

(a) The stock had a par value of $5 per share and was issued for a total of $52,000.
(b) The stock had a stated value of $5 per share and was issued for a total of $52,000.
(c) The stock had no par or stated value and was issued for a total of $52,000.
(d) The stock had a par value of $5 per share and was issued to attorneys for services during incorporation valued at $52,000.
(e) The stock had a par value of $5 per share and was issued for land worth $52,000.

E11-5 Hodge Corporation issued 100,000 shares of $20 par value, cumulative, 6% preferred stock on January 1, 2016, for $2,300,000. In December 2018, Hodge declared its first dividend of $500,000.

Differentiate between preferred and common stock.

(LO 2, 4)

Instructions
(a) Prepare Hodge's journal entry to record the issuance of the preferred stock.
(b) If the preferred stock is **not** cumulative, how much of the $500,000 would be paid to **common** stockholders?
(c) If the preferred stock is cumulative, how much of the $500,000 would be paid to **common** stockholders?

Journalize noncash common stock transactions.

(LO 2)

E11-6 As an auditor for the CPA firm of Hinkson and Calvert, you encounter the following situations in auditing different clients.

1. LR Corporation is a closely held corporation whose stock is not publicly traded. On December 5, the corporation acquired land by issuing 5,000 shares of its $20 par value common stock. The owners' asking price for the land was $120,000, and the fair value of the land was $110,000.
2. Vera Corporation is a publicly held corporation whose common stock is traded on the securities markets. On June 1, it acquired land by issuing 20,000 shares of its $10 par value stock. At the time of the exchange, the land was advertised for sale at $250,000. The stock was selling at $11 per share.

Instructions
Prepare the journal entries for each of the situations above.

Journalize treasury stock transactions.

(LO 3)

E11-7 Rinehart Corporation purchased from its stockholders 5,000 shares of its own previously issued stock for $255,000. It later resold 2,000 shares for $54 per share, then 2,000 more shares for $49 per share, and finally 1,000 shares for $43 per share.

Instructions
Prepare journal entries for the purchase of the treasury stock and the three sales of treasury stock.

Journalize issuance of common and preferred stock and purchase of treasury stock.

(LO 2, 3)

E11-8 Quay Co. had the following transactions during the current period.

Mar. 2   Issued 5,000 shares of $5 par value common stock to attorneys in payment of a bill for $30,000 for services performed in helping the company to incorporate.
June 12   Issued 60,000 shares of $5 par value common stock for cash of $375,000.
July 11   Issued 1,000 shares of $100 par value preferred stock for cash at $110 per share.
Nov. 28   Purchased 2,000 shares of treasury stock for $80,000.

Instructions
Journalize the transactions.

Journalize treasury stock transactions.

(LO 3)

E11-9 On January 1, 2017, the stockholders' equity section of Newlin Corporation shows common stock ($5 par value) $1,500,000; paid-in capital in excess of par $1,000,000; and retained earnings $1,200,000. During the year, the following treasury stock transactions occurred.

Mar. 1   Purchased 50,000 shares for cash at $15 per share.
July 1   Sold 10,000 treasury shares for cash at $17 per share.
Sept. 1   Sold 8,000 treasury shares for cash at $14 per share.

Instructions
(a) Journalize the treasury stock transactions.
(b) Restate the entry for September 1, assuming the treasury shares were sold at $12 per share.

Journalize preferred stock transactions and indicate statement presentation.

(LO 2, 6)

E11-10 Tran Corporation is authorized to issue both preferred and common stock. The par value of the preferred is $50. During the first year of operations, the company had the following events and transactions pertaining to its preferred stock.

Feb. 1   Issued 20,000 shares for cash at $53 per share.
July 1   Issued 12,000 shares for cash at $57 per share.

Instructions
(a) Journalize the transactions.
(b) Post to the stockholders' equity accounts.
(c) Indicate the financial statement presentation of the related accounts.

Answer questions about stockholders' equity section.

(LO 2, 3, 6)

E11-11 The stockholders' equity section of Haley Corporation at December 31 is as follows.

HALEY CORPORATION
Balance Sheet (partial)

Paid-in capital	
Preferred stock, cumulative, 10,000 shares authorized, 6,000 shares issued and outstanding	$ 300,000
Common stock, no par, 750,000 shares authorized, 600,000 shares issued	1,200,000
Total paid-in capital	1,500,000
Retained earnings	1,858,000
Total paid-in capital and retained earnings	3,358,000
Less: Treasury stock (10,000 common shares)	64,000
Total stockholders' equity	$3,294,000

Instructions

From a review of the stockholders' equity section, as chief accountant, write a memo to the president of the company answering the following questions.

(a) How many shares of common stock are outstanding?
(b) Assuming there is a stated value, what is the stated value of the common stock?
(c) What is the par value of the preferred stock?
(d) If the annual dividend on preferred stock is $30,000, what is the dividend rate on preferred stock?
(e) If dividends of $60,000 were in arrears on preferred stock, what would be the balance in Retained Earnings?

E11-12 Gilliam Corporation recently hired a new accountant with extensive experience in accounting for partnerships. Because of the pressure of the new job, the accountant was unable to review his textbooks on the topic of corporation accounting. During the first month, the accountant made the following entries for the corporation's capital stock.

Prepare correct entries for capital stock transactions.

(LO 2, 3)

May 2	Cash	130,000	
	Capital Stock		130,000
	(Issued 10,000 shares of $10 par value common stock at $13 per share)		
10	Cash	600,000	
	Capital Stock		600,000
	(Issued 10,000 shares of $50 par value preferred stock at $60 per share)		
15	Capital Stock	15,000	
	Cash		15,000
	(Purchased 1,000 shares of common stock for the treasury at $15 per share)		
31	Cash	8,000	
	Capital Stock		5,000
	Gain on Sale of Stock		3,000
	(Sold 500 shares of treasury stock at $16 per share)		

Instructions

On the basis of the explanation for each entry, prepare the entry that should have been made for the capital stock transactions.

E11-13 On January 1, Guillen Corporation had 95,000 shares of no-par common stock issued and outstanding. The stock has a stated value of $5 per share. During the year, the following occurred.

Journalize cash dividends; indicate statement presentation.

(LO 4)

Apr. 1   Issued 25,000 additional shares of common stock for $17 per share.
June 15   Declared a cash dividend of $1 per share to stockholders of record on June 30.
July 10   Paid the $1 cash dividend.
Dec. 1   Issued 2,000 additional shares of common stock for $19 per share.
    15   Declared a cash dividend on outstanding shares of $1.20 per share to stockholders of record on December 31.

Instructions

(a) Prepare the entries, if any, on each of the three dividend dates.
(b) How are dividends and dividends payable reported in the financial statements prepared at December 31?

Journalize stock dividends.

(LO 5)

E11-14 On January 1, 2017, Frontier Corporation had $1,000,000 of common stock outstanding that was issued at par. It also had retained earnings of $750,000. The company issued 40,000 shares of common stock at par on July 1 and earned net income of $400,000 for the year.

Instructions

Journalize the declaration of a 15% stock dividend on December 10, 2017, for the following independent assumptions.

(a) Par value is $10, and market price is $18.
(b) Par value is $5, and market price is $20.

Compare effects of a stock dividend and a stock split.

(LO 5)

E11-15 On October 31, the stockholders' equity section of Heins Company consists of common stock $500,000 and retained earnings $900,000. Heins is considering the following two courses of action: (1) declaring a 5% stock dividend on the 50,000, $10 par value shares outstanding, or (2) effecting a 2-for-1 stock split that will reduce par value to $5 per share. The current market price is $14 per share.

Instructions

Prepare a tabular summary of the effects of the alternative actions on the components of stockholders' equity, outstanding shares, and par value per share. Use the following column headings: Before Action, After Stock Dividend, and After Stock Split.

Prepare correcting entries for dividends and a stock split.

(LO 4, 5)

E11-16 Before preparing financial statements for the current year, the chief accountant for Toso Company discovered the following errors in the accounts.

1. The declaration and payment of $50,000 cash dividend was recorded as a debit to Interest Expense $50,000 and a credit to Cash $50,000.
2. A 10% stock dividend (1,000 shares) was declared on the $10 par value stock when the market price per share was $18. The only entry made was Stock Dividends (Dr.) $10,000 and Dividend Payable (Cr.) $10,000. The shares have not been issued.
3. A 4-for-1 stock split involving the issue of 400,000 shares of $5 par value common stock for 100,000 shares of $20 par value common stock was recorded as a debit to Retained Earnings $2,000,000 and a credit to Common Stock $2,000,000.

Instructions

Prepare the correcting entries at December 31.

Prepare a retained earnings statement.

(LO 6)

E11-17 On January 1, 2017, Eddy Corporation had retained earnings of $650,000. During the year, Eddy had the following selected transactions.

1. Declared cash dividends $120,000.
2. Corrected overstatement of 2016 net income because of depreciation error $40,000.
3. Earned net income $350,000.
4. Declared stock dividends $90,000.

Instructions

Prepare a retained earnings statement for the year.

Prepare a retained earnings statement.

(LO 6)

E11-18 Newland Company reported retained earnings at December 31, 2016, of $310,000. Newland had 200,000 shares of common stock outstanding at the beginning of 2017.
   The following transactions occurred during 2017.

1. An error was discovered. In 2015, depreciation expense was recorded at $70,000, but the correct amount was $50,000.
2. A cash dividend of $0.50 per share was declared and paid.
3. A 5% stock dividend was declared and distributed when the market price per share was $15 per share.
4. Net income was $285,000.

Instructions

Prepare a retained earnings statement for 2017.

E11-19 The ledger of Rolling Hills Corporation contains the following accounts: Common Stock, Preferred Stock, Treasury Stock, Paid-in Capital in Excess of Par—Preferred Stock, Paid-in Capital in Excess of Stated Value—Common Stock, Paid-in Capital from Treasury Stock, and Retained Earnings.

Classify stockholders' equity accounts.

(LO 6)

Instructions

Classify each account using the following table headings.

| | Paid-in Capital | | | |
| | Capital | | Retained | |
Account	Stock	Additional	Earnings	Other

E11-20 The following accounts appear in the ledger of Horner Inc. after the books are closed at December 31.

Prepare a stockholders' equity section.

(LO 6)

Common Stock, no par, $1 stated value, 400,000 shares authorized;	
300,000 shares issued	$ 300,000
Common Stock Dividends Distributable	30,000
Paid-in Capital in Excess of Stated Value—Common Stock	1,200,000
Preferred Stock, $5 par value, 8%, 40,000 shares authorized;	
30,000 shares issued	150,000
Retained Earnings	800,000
Treasury Stock (10,000 common shares)	74,000
Paid-in Capital in Excess of Par—Preferred Stock	344,000

Instructions

Prepare the stockholders' equity section at December 31, assuming retained earnings is restricted for plant expansion in the amount of $100,000.

E11-21 Dirk Company reported the following balances at December 31, 2016: common stock $500,000, paid-in capital in excess of par value—common stock $100,000, and retained earnings $250,000. During 2017, the following transactions affected stockholders' equity.

Prepare a stockholders' equity section.

(LO 6)

1. Issued preferred stock with a par value of $125,000 for $200,000.
2. Purchased treasury stock (common) for $40,000.
3. Earned net income of $180,000.
4. Declared and paid cash dividends of $56,000.

Instructions

Prepare the stockholders' equity section of Dirk Company's December 31, 2017, balance sheet.

E11-22 In 2017, Pennington Corporation had net sales of $600,000 and cost of goods sold of $360,000. Operating expenses were $153,000, and interest expense was $7,500. The corporation's tax rate is 30%. The corporation declared preferred dividends of $15,000 in 2017, and its average common stockholders' equity during the year was $200,000.

Prepare an income statement and compute return on equity.

(LO 6)

Instructions

(a) Prepare an income statement for Pennington Corporation.
(b) Compute Pennington Corporation's return on common stockholders' equity for 2017.

*E11-23 A recent stockholders' equity section of **Aluminum Company of America (Alcoa)** showed the following (in alphabetical order): additional paid-in capital $6,101, common stock $925, preferred stock $56, retained earnings $7,428, and treasury stock $2,828. (All dollar data are in millions.)

Prepare a stockholders' equity section.

(LO 6, 8)

The preferred stock has 557,740 shares authorized, with a par value of $100 and an annual $3.75 per share cumulative dividend preference. At December 31 of the current year, 557,649 shares of preferred are issued and 546,024 shares are outstanding. There are 1.8 billion shares of $1 par value common stock authorized, of which 924.6 million are issued and 844.8 million are outstanding at December 31.

Instructions

(a) Prepare the stockholders' equity section of the current year, including disclosure of all relevant data.

(b) Compute the book value per share of common stock, assuming there are no preferred dividends in arrears. (Round to two decimals.)

Compute book value per share with preferred stock.

(LO 8)

*E11-24 At December 31, Gorden Corporation has total stockholders' equity of $3,200,000. Included in this total are preferred stock $500,000 and paid-in capital in excess of par—preferred stock $50,000. There are 10,000 shares of $50 par value, 8% cumulative preferred stock outstanding. At year-end, 200,000 shares of common stock are outstanding.

Instructions

Compute the book value per share of common stock under each of the following assumptions.

(a) There are no preferred dividends in arrears, and the preferred stock does not have a call price.

(b) Preferred dividends are one year in arrears, and the preferred stock has a call price of $60 per share.

EXERCISES: SET B AND CHALLENGE EXERCISES

Visit the book's companion website, at **www.wiley.com/college/weygandt**, and choose the Student Companion site to access Exercises: Set B and Challenge Exercises.

PROBLEMS: SET A

Journalize stock transactions, post, and prepare paid-in capital section.

(LO 2, 6)

P11-1A DeLong Corporation was organized on January 1, 2017. It is authorized to issue 10,000 shares of 8%, $100 par value preferred stock, and 500,000 shares of no-par common stock with a stated value of $2 per share. The following stock transactions were completed during the first year.

Jan. 10	Issued 80,000 shares of common stock for cash at $4 per share.
Mar. 1	Issued 5,000 shares of preferred stock for cash at $105 per share.
Apr. 1	Issued 24,000 shares of common stock for land. The asking price of the land was $90,000. The fair value of the land was $85,000.
May 1	Issued 80,000 shares of common stock for cash at $4.50 per share.
Aug. 1	Issued 10,000 shares of common stock to attorneys in payment of their bill of $30,000 for services performed in helping the company organize.
Sept. 1	Issued 10,000 shares of common stock for cash at $5 per share.
Nov. 1	Issued 1,000 shares of preferred stock for cash at $109 per share.

Instructions

(a) Journalize the transactions.

(c) Total paid-in capital $1,479,000

(b) Post to the stockholders' equity accounts. (Use J5 as the posting reference.)

(c) Prepare the paid-in capital section of stockholders' equity at December 31, 2017.

Journalize and post treasury stock transactions, and prepare stockholders' equity section.

(LO 3, 6)

P11-2A Fechter Corporation had the following stockholders' equity accounts on January 1, 2017: Common Stock ($5 par) $500,000, Paid-in Capital in Excess of Par—Common Stock $200,000, and Retained Earnings $100,000. In 2017, the company had the following treasury stock transactions.

Mar. 1	Purchased 5,000 shares at $8 per share.
June 1	Sold 1,000 shares at $12 per share.
Sept. 1	Sold 2,000 shares at $10 per share.
Dec. 1	Sold 1,000 shares at $7 per share.

Fechter Corporation uses the cost method of accounting for treasury stock. In 2017, the company reported net income of $30,000.

Instructions
(a) Journalize the treasury stock transactions, and prepare the closing entry at December 31, 2017, for net income.
(b) Open accounts for (1) Paid-in Capital from Treasury Stock, (2) Treasury Stock, and (3) Retained Earnings. Post to these accounts using J10 as the posting reference.
(c) Prepare the stockholders' equity section for Fechter Corporation at December 31, 2017.

(b) Treasury Stock $8,000
(c) Total stockholders' equity
$829,000

P11-3A The stockholders' equity accounts of Castle Corporation on January 1, 2017, were as follows.

Preferred Stock (8%, $50 par, cumulative, 10,000 shares authorized)	$ 400,000
Common Stock ($1 stated value, 2,000,000 shares authorized)	1,000,000
Paid-in Capital in Excess of Par—Preferred Stock	100,000
Paid-in Capital in Excess of Stated Value—Common Stock	1,450,000
Retained Earnings	1,816,000
Treasury Stock (10,000 common shares)	50,000

Journalize and post transactions, and prepare stockholders' equity section.

(LO 2, 3, 6)

During 2017, the corporation had the following transactions and events pertaining to its stockholders' equity.

Feb. 1   Issued 25,000 shares of common stock for $120,000.
Apr. 14 Sold 6,000 shares of treasury stock—common for $33,000.
Sept. 3 Issued 5,000 shares of common stock for a patent valued at $35,000.
Nov. 10 Purchased 1,000 shares of common stock for the treasury at a cost of $6,000.
Dec. 31 Determined that net income for the year was $452,000.

No dividends were declared during the year.

Instructions
(a) Journalize the transactions and the closing entry for net income.
(b) Enter the beginning balances in the accounts, and post the journal entries to the stockholders' equity accounts. (Use J5 for the posting reference.)
(c) Prepare a stockholders' equity section at December 31, 2017, including the disclosure of the preferred dividends in arrears.

(c) Total stockholders' equity
$5,350,000

P11-4A On January 1, 2017, Geffrey Corporation had the following stockholders' equity accounts.

Common Stock ($20 par value, 60,000 shares issued and outstanding)	$1,200,000
Paid-in Capital in Excess of Par—Common Stock	200,000
Retained Earnings	600,000

Prepare dividend entries and stockholders' equity section.

(LO 4, 5, 6)

During the year, the following transactions occurred.

Feb. 1   Declared a $1 cash dividend per share to stockholders of record on February 15, payable March 1.
Mar. 1   Paid the dividend declared in February.
Apr. 1   Announced a 2-for-1 stock split. Prior to the split, the market price per share was $36.
July 1   Declared a 10% stock dividend to stockholders of record on July 15, distributable July 31. On July 1, the market price of the stock was $13 per share.
      31 Issued the shares for the stock dividend.
Dec. 1   Declared a $0.50 per share dividend to stockholders of record on December 15, payable January 5, 2018.
      31 Determined that net income for the year was $350,000.

Instructions
(a) Journalize the transactions and the closing entries for net income and dividends.
(b) Enter the beginning balances, and post the entries to the stockholders' equity accounts. (*Note:* Open additional stockholders' equity accounts as needed.)
(c) Prepare a stockholders' equity section at December 31.

(c) Total stockholders' equity
$2,224,000

Prepare retained earnings statement and stockholders' equity section, and compute allocation of dividends.

(LO 4, 5, 6)

P11-5A The post-closing trial balance of Storey Corporation at December 31, 2017, contains the following stockholders' equity accounts.

Preferred Stock (15,000 shares issued)	$ 750,000
Common Stock (250,000 shares issued)	2,500,000
Paid-in Capital in Excess of Par—Preferred Stock	250,000
Paid-in Capital in Excess of Par—Common Stock	400,000
Common Stock Dividends Distributable	250,000
Retained Earnings	1,042,000

A review of the accounting records reveals the following.

1. No errors have been made in recording 2017 transactions or in preparing the closing entry for net income.
2. Preferred stock is $50 par, 6%, and cumulative; 15,000 shares have been outstanding since January 1, 2016.
3. Authorized stock is 20,000 shares of preferred, 500,000 shares of common with a $10 par value.
4. The January 1 balance in Retained Earnings was $1,170,000.
5. On July 1, 20,000 shares of common stock were issued for cash at $16 per share.
6. On September 1, the company discovered an understatement error of $90,000 in computing depreciation in 2016, which overstated net income. The net of tax effect of $63,000 was properly debited directly to Retained Earnings.
7. A cash dividend of $250,000 was declared and properly allocated to preferred and common stock on October 1. No dividends were paid to preferred stockholders in 2016.
8. On December 31, a 10% common stock dividend was declared out of retained earnings on common stock when the market price per share was $16.
9. Net income for the year was $585,000.
10. On December 31, 2017, the directors authorized disclosure of a $200,000 restriction of retained earnings for plant expansion. (Use Note X.)

Instructions
(a) Reproduce the Retained Earnings account (T-account) for 2017.
(b) Prepare a retained earnings statement for 2017.

(c) Total stockholders' equity
$5,192,000

(c) Prepare a stockholders' equity section at December 31, 2017.
(d) Compute the allocation of the cash dividend to preferred and common stock.

Prepare entries for stock transactions and prepare stockholders' equity section.

(LO 2, 3, 4, 5, 6)

P11-6A Irwin Corporation has been authorized to issue 20,000 shares of $100 par value, 10%, noncumulative preferred stock and 1,000,000 shares of no-par common stock. The corporation assigned a $2.50 stated value to the common stock. At December 31, 2017, the ledger contained the following balances pertaining to stockholders' equity.

Preferred Stock	$ 120,000
Paid-in Capital in Excess of Par—Preferred Stock	20,000
Common Stock	1,000,000
Paid-in Capital in Excess of Stated Value—Common Stock	1,800,000
Treasury Stock (1,000 common shares)	11,000
Paid-in Capital from Treasury Stock	1,500
Retained Earnings	82,000

The preferred stock was issued for land having a fair value of $140,000. All common stock issued was for cash. In November, 1,500 shares of common stock were purchased for the treasury at a per share cost of $11. In December, 500 shares of treasury stock were sold for $14 per share. No dividends were declared in 2017.

Instructions
(a) Prepare the journal entries for the:
   (1) Issuance of preferred stock for land.
   (2) Issuance of common stock for cash.
   (3) Purchase of common treasury stock for cash.
   (4) Sale of treasury stock for cash.

(b) Total stockholders' equity
$3,012,500

(b) Prepare the stockholders' equity section at December 31, 2017.

P11-7A On January 1, 2017, Primo Corporation had the following stockholders' equity accounts.

Prepare dividend entries and stockholders' equity section.

(LO 4, 5, 6)

Common Stock ($10 par value, 75,000 shares issued and outstanding)	$750,000
Paid-in Capital in Excess of Par—Common Stock	200,000
Retained Earnings	540,000

During the year, the following transactions occurred.

Jan. 15	Declared a $1 cash dividend per share to stockholders of record on January 31, payable February 15.
Feb. 15	Paid the dividend declared in January.
Apr. 15	Declared a 10% stock dividend to stockholders of record on April 30, distributable May 15. On April 15, the market price of the stock was $14 per share.
May 15	Issued the shares for the stock dividend.
July 1	Announced a 2-for-1 stock split. The market price per share prior to the announcement was $15. (The new par value is $5.)
Dec. 1	Declared a $0.60 per share cash dividend to stockholders of record on December 15, payable January 10, 2018.
31	Determined that net income for the year was $250,000.

Instructions

(a) Journalize the transactions and the closing entries for net income and dividends.
(b) Enter the beginning balances, and post the entries to the stockholders' equity accounts. (*Note:* Open additional stockholders' equity accounts as needed.)
(c) Prepare a stockholders' equity section at December 31.

(c) Total stockholders' equity
$1,566,000

*P11-8A The following stockholders' equity accounts arranged alphabetically are in the ledger of Westin Corporation at December 31, 2017.

Prepare stockholders' equity section; compute book value per share.

(LO 6, 8)

Common Stock ($10 stated value)	$1,500,000
Paid-in Capital from Treasury Stock	6,000
Paid-in Capital in Excess of Par—Preferred Stock	42,400
Paid-in Capital in Excess of Stated Value—Common Stock	690,000
Preferred Stock (8%, $100 par, noncumulative)	360,000
Retained Earnings	776,000
Treasury Stock—Common (7,000 shares)	92,000

Instructions

(a) Prepare a stockholders' equity section at December 31, 2017.
(b) Compute the book value per share of the common stock, assuming the preferred stock has a call price of $110 per share.

(a) Total stockholders' equity
$3,282,400

*P11-9A On January 1, 2017, Goodhue Inc. had the following stockholders' equity balances.

Prepare stockholders' equity statement.

(LO 6, 7)

Common Stock (400,000 shares issued)	$800,000
Paid-in Capital in Excess of Par—Common Stock	500,000
Common Stock Dividends Distributable	120,000
Retained Earnings	600,000

During 2017, the following transactions and events occurred.

1. Issued 60,000 shares of $2 par value common stock as a result of 15% stock dividend declared on December 15, 2016.
2. Issued 30,000 shares of common stock for cash at $4 per share.
3. Purchased 25,000 shares of common stock for the treasury at $5 per share.
4. Declared and paid a cash dividend of $111,000.
5. Sold 8,000 shares of treasury stock for cash at $5 per share.
6. Earned net income of $360,000.

Instructions

Prepare a stockholders' equity statement for the year.

Total stockholders' equity
$2,304,000

PROBLEMS: SET B AND SET C

Visit the book's companion website, at **www.wiley.com/college/weygandt**, and choose the Student Companion site to access Problems: Set B and Set C.

CONTINUING PROBLEM

COOKIE CREATIONS

(*Note:* This is a continuation of the Cookie Creations problem from Chapters 1 through 10.)

CC11 After establishing their company's fiscal year-end to be October 31, Natalie and Curtis began operating Cookie & Coffee Creations Inc. on November 1, 2017. On that date, they issued both preferred and common stock. After the first year of operations, Natalie and Curtis want to prepare financial information for the year.

Go to the book's companion website, **www.wiley.com/college/weygandt**, *to see the completion of this problem.*

© leungchopan/
Shutterstock

BROADENING YOUR PERSPECTIVE

FINANCIAL REPORTING AND ANALYSIS

Financial Reporting Problem: Apple Inc.

BYP11-1 The stockholders' equity section for Apple Inc. is shown in Appendix A. Instructions for accessing and using the company's complete annual report, including the notes to the financial statements, are also provided in Appendix A.

Instructions
(a) What is the par or stated value per share of Apple's common stock?
(b) What percentage of Apple's authorized common stock was issued at September 28, 2013?
(c) What amount, if any, did Apple declare in dividends on common stock in the year ended September 28, 2013?

Comparative Analysis Problem:
PepsiCo, Inc. vs. The Coca-Cola Company

BYP11-2 PepsiCo, Inc.'s financial statements are presented in Appendix B. Financial statements of The Coca-Cola Company are presented in Appendix C. Instructions for accessing and using the complete annual reports of PepsiCo and Coca-Cola, including the notes to the financial statements, are also provided in Appendices B and C, respectively.

Instructions
(a) What percentage of authorized shares was issued by Coca-Cola at December 31, 2013, and by PepsiCo at December 28, 2013?
(b) How many shares are held as treasury stock by Coca-Cola at December 31, 2013, and by PepsiCo at December 28, 2013?
(c) How many Coca-Cola common shares are outstanding at December 31, 2013? How many PepsiCo shares of common stock are outstanding at December 28, 2013?
(d) Compute earnings per share and return on common stockholders' equity for both companies for 2013. Assume PepsiCo's weighted-average shares were 1,541 million and Coca-Cola's weighted-average shares were 4,568 million. Can these measures be used to compare the profitability of the two companies? Why or why not?
(e) What was the total amount of dividends paid by each company in 2013?

Comparative Analysis Problem:
Amazon.com, Inc. vs. Wal-Mart Stores, Inc.

BYP11-3 Amazon.com, Inc.'s financial statements are presented in Appendix D. Financial statements of Wal-Mart Stores, Inc. are presented in Appendix E. Instructions for accessing and using the complete annual reports of Amazon and Wal-Mart, including the notes to the financial statements, are also provided in Appendices D and E, respectively. Wal-Mart has 11,000 million shares authorized.

Instructions

(a) What percentage of authorized shares was issued by Amazon at December 31, 2013, and by Wal-Mart at January 31, 2014?

(b) How many shares are held as treasury stock by Amazon at December 31, 2013, and by Wal-Mart at January 31, 2014?

(c) How many Amazon common shares are outstanding at December 31, 2013? How many Wal-Mart shares of common stock are outstanding at January 31, 2014?

(d) What are the basic earnings per share for both Amazon and Wal-Mart as of December 31, 2013, and January 31, 2014, respectively?

(e) What was the total amount of dividends, if any, paid by Amazon for the year ending December 31, 2013? What was the total dividends paid by Wal-Mart for the year ending January 31, 2014?

Real-World Focus

BYP11-4 Use the stockholders' equity section of an annual report and identify the major components.

Address: **www.annualreports.com**, or go to **www.wiley.com/college/weygandt**

Steps

1. From the Annual Reports Homepage, choose **Search by Alphabet**, and choose a letter.
2. Select a particular company.
3. Choose Annual Report.
4. Follow instructions below.

Instructions
Answer the following questions.

(a) What is the company's name?

(b) What classes of capital stock has the company issued?

(c) For each class of stock:
   (1) How many shares are authorized, issued, and/or outstanding?
   (2) What is the par value?

(d) What are the company's retained earnings?

(e) Has the company acquired treasury stock? How many shares?

CRITICAL THINKING

Decision-Making Across the Organization

BYP11-5 The stockholders' meeting for Percival Corporation has been in progress for some time. The chief financial officer for Percival is presently reviewing the company's financial statements and is explaining the items that comprise the stockholders' equity section of the balance sheet for the current year. The stockholders' equity section of Percival Corporation at December 31, 2017, is as follows.

PERCIVAL CORPORATION
Balance Sheet (partial)
December 31, 2017

Paid-in capital		
Capital stock		
Preferred stock, authorized 1,000,000 shares		
cumulative, $100 par value, $8 per share, 6,000		
shares issued and outstanding		$ 600,000
Common stock, authorized 5,000,000 shares, $1 par		
value, 3,000,000 shares issued, and 2,700,000 outstanding		3,000,000
Total capital stock		3,600,000
Additional paid-in capital		
In excess of par—preferred stock	$ 50,000	
In excess of par—common stock	25,000,000	
Total additional paid-in capital		25,050,000
Total paid-in capital		28,650,000
Retained earnings		900,000
Total paid-in capital and retained earnings		29,550,000
Less: Treasury stock (300,000 common shares)		9,300,000
Total stockholders' equity		$20,250,000

At the meeting, stockholders have raised a number of questions regarding the stockholders' equity section.

Instructions

With the class divided into groups, answer the following questions as if you were the chief financial officer for Percival Corporation.

(a) "What does the cumulative provision related to the preferred stock mean?"

(b) "I thought the common stock was presently selling at $29.75, but the company has the stock stated at $1 per share. How can that be?"

(c) "Why is the company buying back its common stock? Furthermore, the treasury stock has a debit balance because it is subtracted from stockholders' equity. Why is treasury stock not reported as an asset if it has a debit balance?"

Communication Activity

BYP11-6 Joe Moyer, your uncle, is an inventor who has decided to incorporate. Uncle Joe knows that you are an accounting major at U.N.O. In a recent letter to you, he ends with the question, "I'm filling out a state incorporation application. Can you tell me the difference in the following terms: (1) authorized stock, (2) issued stock, (3) outstanding stock, and (4) preferred stock?"

Instructions

In a brief note, differentiate for Uncle Joe among the four different stock terms. Write the letter to be friendly, yet professional.

Ethics Case

BYP11-7 The R&D division of Piqua Chemical Corp. has just developed a chemical for sterilizing the vicious Brazilian "killer bees" which are invading Mexico and the southern United States. The president of the company is anxious to get the chemical on the market to boost the company's profits. He believes his job is in jeopardy because of decreasing sales and profits. The company has an opportunity to sell this chemical in Central American countries, where the laws are much more relaxed than in the United States.

The director of Piqua's R&D division strongly recommends further testing in the laboratory for side-effects of this chemical on other insects, birds, animals, plants, and even humans. He cautions the president, "We could be sued from all sides if the chemical has tragic side-effects that we didn't even test for in the labs." The president answers, "We can't wait an additional year for your lab tests. We can avoid losses from such lawsuits by establishing a separate wholly owned corporation to shield Piqua Corp. from such lawsuits. We can't lose any more than our investment in the new corporation, and we'll invest in just the patent covering this chemical. We'll reap the benefits if the chemical works and is safe, and avoid the losses from lawsuits if it's a disaster." The following week, Piqua creates a new wholly owned corporation called Finlay Inc., sells the chemical patent to it for $10, and watches the spraying begin.

Instructions

(a) Who are the stakeholders in this situation?

(b) Are the president's motives and actions ethical?

(c) Can Piqua shield itself against losses of Finlay Inc.?

All About You

BYP11-8 A high percentage of Americans own stock in corporations. As a shareholder in a corporation, you will receive an annual report. One of the goals of this course is for you to learn how to navigate your way around an annual report.

Instructions

Use Apple's 2013 annual report (see Appendix A) to answer the following questions.

(a) What CPA firm performed the audit of Apple's financial statements?

(b) What was the amount of Apple's earnings per share in 2013?

(c) What were net sales in 2013?

(d) How much cash did Apple spend on capital expenditures in 2013?

(e) Over what life does the company depreciate its buildings?

(f) What were the proceeds from issuance of common stock in 2013?

FASB Codification Activity

BYP11-9 If your school has a subscription to the FASB Codification, go to **http://aaahq.org/ ascLogin.cfm** to log in and prepare responses to the following.

(a) What is the stock dividend?

(b) What is a stock split?

(c) At what percentage point does the issuance of additional shares qualify as a stock dividend, as opposed to a stock split?

A Look at IFRS

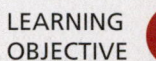 **LEARNING OBJECTIVE 9** 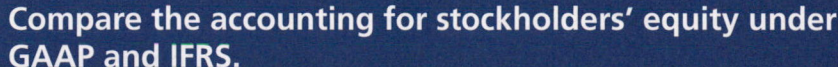 **Compare the accounting for stockholders' equity under GAAP and IFRS.**

The accounting for transactions related to stockholders' equity, such as issuance of shares and purchase of treasury stock, are similar under both IFRS and GAAP. Major differences relate to terminology used, introduction of items such as revaluation surplus, and presentation of stockholders' equity information.

Key Points

Following are the key similarities and differences between GAAP and IFRS as related to stockholders' equity, dividends, retained earnings, and income reporting.

Similarities

• Aside from the terminology used, the accounting transactions for the issuance of shares and the purchase of treasury stock are similar.

• Like GAAP, IFRS does not allow a company to record gains or losses on purchases of its own shares.

• The accounting related to prior period adjustment is essentially the same under IFRS and GAAP.

• The income statement using IFRS is called the **statement of comprehensive income**. A statement of comprehensive income is presented in a one- or two-statement format. The single-statement approach includes all items of income and expense, as well as each component of other comprehensive income or loss by its individual characteristic. In the two-statement approach, a traditional income statement is prepared. It is then followed by a statement of comprehensive income, which starts with net income or loss and then adds other comprehensive income or loss items. Regardless of which approach is reported, income tax expense is required to be reported.

• The computations related to earnings per share are essentially the same under IFRS and GAAP.

Differences

• Under IFRS, the term **reserves** is used to describe all equity accounts other than those arising from contributed (paid-in) capital. This would include, for example, reserves related to retained earnings, asset revaluations, and fair value differences.

• Many countries have a different mix of investor groups than in the United States. For example, in Germany, financial institutions like banks are not only major creditors of corporations but often are the largest corporate stockholders as well. In the United States, Asia, and the United Kingdom, many companies rely on substantial investment from private investors.

• There are often terminology differences for equity accounts. The following summarizes some of the common differences in terminology.

GAAP	IFRS
Common stock	Share capital—ordinary
Stockholders	Shareholders
Par value	Nominal or face value
Authorized stock	Authorized share capital
Preferred stock	Share capital—preference
Paid-in capital	Issued/allocated share capital
Paid-in capital in excess of par—common stock	Share premium—ordinary
Paid-in capital in excess of par—preferred stock	Share premium—preference
Retained earnings	Retained earnings or Retained profits
Retained earnings deficit	Accumulated losses
Accumulated other comprehensive income	General reserve and other reserve accounts

As an example of how similar transactions use different terminology under IFRS, consider the accounting for the issuance of 1,000 shares of $1 par value common stock for $5 per share. Under IFRS, the entry is as follows.

Cash	5,000	
Share Capital—Ordinary		1,000
Share Premium—Ordinary		4,000

- A major difference between IFRS and GAAP relates to the account Revaluation Surplus. Revaluation surplus arises under IFRS because companies are permitted to revalue their property, plant, and equipment to fair value under certain circumstances. This account is part of general reserves under IFRS and is not considered contributed capital.

- IFRS often uses terms such as **retained profits** or **accumulated profit or loss** to describe retained earnings. The term retained earnings is also often used.

- Equity is given various descriptions under IFRS, such as shareholders' equity, owners' equity, capital and reserves, and shareholders' funds.

Looking to the Future

The IASB and the FASB are currently working on a project related to financial statement presentation. An important part of this study is to determine whether certain line items, subtotals, and totals should be clearly defined and required to be displayed in the financial statements. For example, it is likely that the statement of stockholders' equity and its presentation will be examined closely.

Both the IASB and FASB are working toward convergence of any remaining differences related to earnings per share computations. This convergence will deal with highly technical changes beyond the scope of this textbook.

IFRS Practice

IFRS Self-Test Questions

1. Which of the following is **true**?
   - (a) In the United States, the primary corporate stockholders are financial institutions.
   - (b) Share capital means total assets under IFRS.
   - (c) The IASB and FASB are presently studying how financial statement information should be presented.
   - (d) The accounting for treasury stock differs extensively between GAAP and IFRS.

2. Under IFRS, the amount of capital received in excess of par value would be credited to:
   - (a) Retained Earnings.
   - (b) Contributed Capital.
   - (c) Share Premium.
   - (d) Par value is not used under IFRS.

3. Which of the following is **false**?
   - (a) Under GAAP, companies cannot record gains on transactions involving their own shares.
   - (b) Under IFRS, companies cannot record gains on transactions involving their own shares.
   - (c) Under IFRS, the statement of stockholders' equity is a required statement.
   - (d) Under IFRS, a company records a revaluation surplus when it experiences an increase in the price of its common stock.

4. Which of the following does **not** represent a pair of GAAP/IFRS-comparable terms?
   - (a) Additional paid-in capital/Share premium.
   - (b) Treasury stock/Repurchase reserve.
   - (c) Common stock/Share capital.
   - (d) Preferred stock/Preference shares.

5. The basic accounting for cash dividends and stock dividends:
    (a) is different under IFRS versus GAAP.
    (b) is the same under IFRS and GAAP.
    (c) differs only for the accounting for cash dividends between GAAP and IFRS.
    (d) differs only for the accounting for stock dividends between GAAP and IFRS.

6. Which item in **not** considered part of reserves?
    (a) Unrealized loss on available-for-sale investments.   (c) Retained earnings.
    (b) Revaluation surplus.   (d) Issued shares.

7. Under IFRS, a statement of comprehensive income must include:
    (a) accounts payable.   (c) income tax expense.
    (b) retained earnings.   (d) preference stock.

8. Which set of terms can be used to describe total stockholders' equity under IFRS?
    (a) Shareholders' equity, capital and reserves, other comprehensive income.
    (b) Capital and reserves, shareholders' equity, shareholders' funds.
    (c) Capital and reserves, retained earnings, shareholders' equity.
    (d) All of the answer choices are correct.

9. Earnings per share computations related to IFRS and GAAP:
    (a) are essentially similar.
    (b) result in an amount referred to as earnings per share.
    (c) must deduct preferred (preference) dividends when computing earnings per share.
    (d) All of the answer choices are correct.

IFRS Exercises

IFRS11-1 On May 10, Jaurez Corporation issues 1,000 shares of $10 par value ordinary shares for cash at $18 per share. Journalize the issuance of the shares.

IFRS11-2 Meenen Corporation has the following accounts at December 31 (in euros): Share Capital—Ordinary, €10 par, 5,000 shares issued, €50,000; Share Premium—Ordinary €10,000; Retained Earnings €45,000; and Treasury Shares—Ordinary, 500 shares, €11,000. Prepare the equity section of the statement of financial position (balance sheet).

IFRS11-3 Overton Co. had the following transactions during the current period.

Mar. 2   Issued 5,000 shares of $1 par value ordinary shares to attorneys in payment of a bill for $30,000 for services performed in helping the company to incorporate.
June 12   Issued 60,000 shares of $1 par value ordinary shares for cash of $375,000.
July 11   Issued 1,000 shares of $100 par value preference shares for cash at $110 per share.
Nov. 28   Purchased 2,000 treasury shares for $80,000.

Instructions
Journalize the above transactions.

International Financial Reporting Problem: Louis Vuitton

IFRS11-4 The financial statements of Louis Vuitton are presented in Appendix F. Instructions for accessing and using the company's complete annual report, including the notes to its financial statements, are also provided in Appendix F.

Instructions
Use the company's annual report to answer the following questions.

(a) Determine the following amounts at December 31, 2013: (1) total equity, (2) total revaluation reserve, and (3) number of treasury shares.
(b) Examine the equity section of the company's balance sheet. For each of the following, provide the comparable label that would be used under GAAP: (1) share capital, (2) share premium, and (3) net profit, group share.
(c) Did the company declare and pay any dividends for the year ended December 31, 2013?
(d) Compute the company's return on ordinary shareholders' equity for the year ended December 31, 2013.
(e) What was Louis Vuitton's earnings per share for the year ended December 31, 2013?

Answers to IFRS Self-Test Questions
1. c   **2.** c   **3.** d   **4.** b   **5.** b   **6.** d   **7.** c   **8.** b   **9.** d

12 Investments

CHAPTER PREVIEW Time Warner's management, as the Feature Story below indicates, believes in aggressive growth through investing in the stock of existing companies. Besides purchasing stock, companies also purchase other securities such as bonds issued by corporations or by governments. Companies can make investments for a short or long period of time, as a passive investment, or with the intent to control another company. As you will see in this chapter, the way in which a company accounts for its investments is determined by a number of factors.

FEATURE STORY

"Is There Anything Else We Can Buy?"

In a rapidly changing world, you must keep up or suffer the consequences. In business, change requires investment.

A case in point is found in the entertainment industry. Technology is bringing about innovations so quickly that it is nearly impossible to guess which will last and which will soon fade away. For example, will both satellite TV and cable TV survive? Or, will both be replaced by something else?

Consider the publishing industry as well. Will paper newspapers and magazines be replaced completely by online news? If you are a publisher, you have to make your best guess about what the future holds and invest accordingly.

Time Warner Inc. lives at the center of this arena. It is not an environment for the timid, and Time Warner's philosophy is anything but that. Instead, it might be characterized as, "If we can't beat you, we will buy you." Its mantra is "invest, invest, invest." A partial list of Time Warner's holdings gives an idea of its reach:

Magazines: *People, Time, Life, Sports Illustrated,* and *Fortune.*

Book publishers: Time-Life Books; Book-of-the-Month Club; Little, Brown & Co; and Sunset Books.

Television and movies: Warner Bros. ("The Big Bang Theory" and "The Mentalist"), HBO, and movies like *The Hobbit: The Battle of the Five Armies* and *Into the Storm.*

Broadcasting: TNT, CNN news, and Turner's library of thousands of classic movies.

Internet: America Online and AOL Anywhere.

Time Warner owns more information and entertainment copyrights and brands than any other company in the world.

Recently, Rupert Murdoch, chairman and CEO of 21st Century Fox, made an unsolicited $80 billion offer to buy the major media conglomerate. Murdoch's bid put "a positive light on Time Warner's assets," says one analyst. Murdoch eventually withdrew his bid, which resulted in driving down Time Warner's stock price. However, analysts expect the stock to eventually rebound as the long-term institutional investors start taking advantage of the lower price.

Source: Gene Marcial, "Why Time Warner Will Deliver Superb Growth and Valuation Despite Murdoch's Surrender," *Forbes* (August 6, 2014).

Robert Voets/CBS via Getty Images

CHAPTER OUTLINE

Learning Objectives

1 Explain how to account for debt investments.
- Why corporations invest
- Accounting for debt investments

DO IT! ① Debt Investments

2 Explain how to account for stock investments.
- Holdings of less than 20%
- Holdings between 20% and 50%
- Holdings of more than 50%

DO IT! ② Stock Investments

3 Discuss how debt and stock investments are reported in financial statements.
- Categories of securities
- Balance sheet presentation
- Presentation of realized and unrealized gain or loss
- Classified balance sheet

DO IT! ③a Trading and Available-for-Sale Securities
③b Financial Statement Presentation of Investments

Go to the **REVIEW AND PRACTICE** section at the end of the chapter for a review of key concepts and practice applications with solutions.

Visit **WileyPLUS with ORION** for additional tutorials and practice opportunities.

Explain how to account for debt investments.

Why Corporations Invest

Corporations purchase investments in debt or stock securities generally for one of three reasons. First, a corporation may **have excess cash** that it does not need for the immediate purchase of operating assets. For example, many companies experience seasonal fluctuations in sales. A Cape Cod marina has more sales in the spring and summer than in the fall and winter. The reverse is true for an Aspen ski shop. Thus, at the end of an operating cycle, many companies may have cash on hand that is temporarily idle until the start of another operating cycle. These companies may invest the excess funds to earn—through interest and dividends—a greater return than they would get by just holding the funds in the bank. Illustration 12-1 shows the role that such temporary investments play in the operating cycle.

Illustration 12-1

Temporary investments and the operating cycle

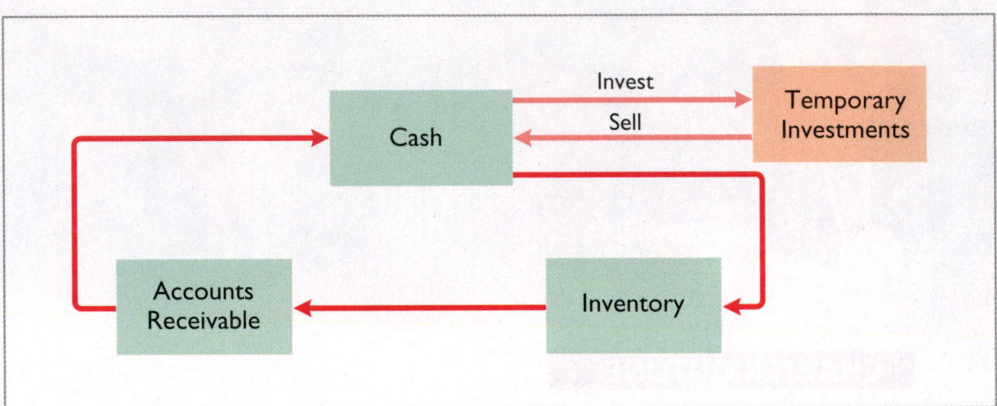

A second reason some companies such as banks purchase investments is to generate **earnings from investment income**. Although banks make most of their earnings by lending money, they also generate earnings by investing primarily in debt securities. Banks purchase investment securities because loan demand varies both seasonally and with changes in the economic climate. Thus, when loan demand is low, a bank must find other uses for its cash.

Some companies attempt to generate investment income through speculative investments. That is, they are speculating that the investment will increase in value and thus result in positive returns. Therefore, they invest mostly in the common stock of other corporations.

Third, companies also invest for **strategic reasons**. A company may purchase a noncontrolling interest in another company in a related industry in which it wishes to establish a presence. Or, a company can exercise some influence over one of its customers or suppliers by purchasing a significant, but not controlling, interest in that company. Another option is for a corporation to purchase a controlling interest in another company in order to enter a new industry without incurring the costs and risks associated with starting from scratch.

In summary, businesses invest in other companies for the reasons shown in Illustration 12-2.

Illustration 12-2
Why corporations invest

Reason	Typical Investment
To house excess cash until needed	Low-risk, highly liquid, short-term securities such as government-issued securities
To generate earnings *I need 1,000 Treasury bills by tonight*	Debt securities (banks and other financial institutions) and stock securities (mutual funds and pension funds)
To meet strategic goals	Stocks of companies in a related industry or in an unrelated industry that the company wishes to enter

Accounting for Debt Investments

Debt investments are investments in government and corporation bonds. In accounting for debt investments, companies make entries to record (1) the acquisition, (2) the interest revenue, and (3) the sale.

RECORDING ACQUISITION OF BONDS

At acquisition, debt investments are recorded at cost. Cost includes all expenditures necessary to acquire these investments, such as the price paid plus brokerage fees (commissions), if any.

For example, assume that Kuhl Corporation acquires 50 Doan Inc. 8%, 10-year, $1,000 bonds on January 1, 2017, for $50,000. Kuhl records the investment as:

Jan. 1	Debt Investments (50 × $1,000)	50,000	
	Cash		50,000
	(To record purchase of 50 Doan Inc. bonds)		

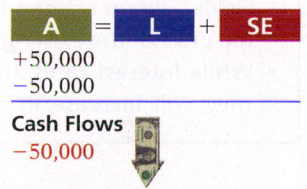

RECORDING BOND INTEREST

The Doan Inc. bonds pay interest of $4,000 annually on January 1 ($50,000 × 8%). If Kuhl Corporation's fiscal year ends on December 31, it accrues the interest of $4,000 earned since January 1. The adjusting entry is:

Dec. 31	Interest Receivable	4,000	
	Interest Revenue		4,000
	(To accrue interest on Doan Inc. bonds)		

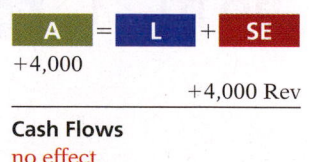

Kuhl reports Interest Receivable as a current asset in the balance sheet. It reports Interest Revenue under "Other revenues and gains" in the income statement.

Kuhl reports receipt of the interest on January 1 as follows.

Jan. 1	Cash	4,000	
	Interest Receivable		4,000
	(To record receipt of accrued interest)		

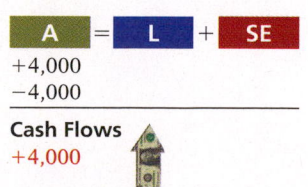

A credit to Interest Revenue at this time is incorrect because the company earned and accrued interest revenue in the **preceding** accounting period.

RECORDING SALE OF BONDS

When Kuhl sells the bonds, it credits the investment account for the cost of the bonds. Kuhl records as a gain or loss any difference between the net proceeds from the sale (sales price less brokerage fees) and the cost of the bonds.

Assume, for example, that Kuhl Corporation receives net proceeds of $54,000 on the sale of the Doan Inc. bonds on January 1, 2018, after receiving the interest due. Since the securities cost $50,000, the company realizes a gain of $4,000. It records the sale as:

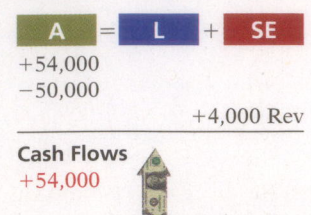

A = L + SE

+54,000
−50,000
              +4,000 Rev

Cash Flows
+54,000

Jan. 1	Cash	54,000	
	Debt Investments		50,000
	Gain on Sale of Debt Investments		4,000
	(To record sale of Doan Inc. bonds)		

Kuhl reports the gain on sale of debt investments under "Other revenues and gains" in the income statement and reports losses under "Other expenses and losses."

Investor Insight

© Jane0606/Shutterstock

Hey, I Thought It Was Safe!

It is often stated that bond investments are safer than stock investments. After all, with an investment in bonds, you are guaranteed return of principal and interest payments over the life of the bonds. However, here are some other factors you may want to consider:

- In 2013, the value of bonds fell by 2% due to interest rate risk. That is, when interest rates rise, it makes the yields paid on existing bonds less attractive. As a result, the price of the existing bond you are holding falls.
- While interest rates are currently low, it is likely that they will increase in the future. If you hold bonds,

there is a real possibility that the value of your bonds will be reduced.
- Credit risk also must be considered. Credit risk means that a company may not be able to pay back what it borrowed. Former bondholders in companies like General Motors, United Air Lines, and Eastman Kodak saw their bond values drop substantially when these companies declared bankruptcy.

An advantage of a bond investment over stock is that if you hold it to maturity, you will receive your principal and also interest payments over the life of the bond. But if you have to sell your bond investment before maturity, you may be facing a roller coaster regarding its value.

Why is the fluctuating value of bonds of concern if a company intends to hold them until maturity? (Go to WileyPLUS for this answer and additional questions.)

DO IT! ① Debt Investments

Waldo Corporation had the following transactions pertaining to debt investments.

Jan. 1, 2017   Purchased 30, $1,000 Hillary Co. 10% bonds for $30,000. Interest is payable annually on January 1.
Dec. 31, 2017   Accrued interest on Hillary Co. bonds in 2017.
Jan. 1, 2018   Received interest on Hillary Co. bonds.
Jan. 1, 2018   Sold 15 Hillary Co. bonds for $14,600.
Dec. 31, 2018   Accrued interest on Hillary Co. bonds in 2018.

Journalize the transactions.

Solution

Jan. 1 (2017)	Debt Investments	30,000	
	Cash		30,000
	(To record purchase of 30 Hillary Co. bonds)		
Dec. 31 (2017)	Interest Receivable	3,000	
	Interest Revenue ($30,000 × 10%)		3,000
	(To accrue interest on Hillary Co. bonds)		

Jan. 1 (2018)	Cash	3,000	
	Interest Receivable		3,000
	(To record receipt of interest on Hillary Co. bonds)		
Jan. 1 (2018)	Cash	14,600	
	Loss on Sale of Debt Investments	400	
	Debt Investments ($30,000 × 15/30)		15,000
	(To record sale of 15 Hillary Co. bonds)		
Dec. 31 (2018)	Interest Receivable	1,500	
	Interest Revenue ($15,000 × 10%)		1,500
	(To accrue interest on Hillary Co. bonds)		

Action Plan

✔ Record bond investments at cost.

✔ Record interest when accrued.

✔ When bonds are sold, credit the investment account for the cost of the bonds.

✔ Record any difference between the cost and the net proceeds as a gain or loss.

Related exercise material: **BE12-1, E12-2, E12-3, and DO IT! 12-1.**

LEARNING OBJECTIVE **2** **Explain how to account for stock investments.**

Stock investments are investments in the capital stock of other corporations. When a company holds stock (and/or debt) of several different corporations, the group of securities is identified as an **investment portfolio**.

The accounting for investments in common stock depends on the extent of the investor's influence over the operating and financial affairs of the issuing corporation (the **investee**). Illustration 12-3 shows the general guidelines.

Investor's Ownership Interest in Investee's Common Stock	Presumed Influence on Investee	Accounting Guidelines
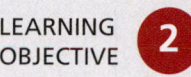 Less than 20%	Insignificant	Cost method
Between 20% and 50%	Significant	Equity method
More than 50%	Controlling	Consolidated financial statements

Illustration 12-3
Accounting guidelines for stock investments

Companies are required to use judgment instead of blindly following the guidelines.[1] We explain the application of each guideline next.

Holdings of Less than 20%

In accounting for stock investments of less than 20%, companies use the cost method. Under the **cost method**, companies record the investment at cost and recognize revenue only when cash dividends are received.

Helpful Hint
The entries for investments in common stock also apply to investments in preferred stock.

---

[1]Among the questions that are considered in determining an investor's influence are these: (1) Does the investor have representation on the investee's board? (2) Does the investor participate in the investee's policy-making process? (3) Are there material transactions between the investor and investee? (4) Is the common stock held by other stockholders concentrated or dispersed?

RECORDING ACQUISITION OF STOCK INVESTMENTS

At acquisition, stock investments are recorded at cost. Cost includes all expenditures necessary to acquire these investments, such as the price paid plus any brokerage fees (commissions), if any.

For example, assume that on July 1, 2017, Sanchez Corporation acquires 1,000 shares (10% ownership) of Beal Corporation common stock. Sanchez pays $40 per share. The entry for the purchase is:

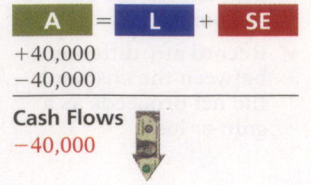

July 1	Stock Investments (1,000 × $40)	40,000	
	Cash		40,000
	(To record purchase of 1,000 shares of Beal Corporation common stock)		

RECORDING DIVIDENDS

During the time Sanchez owns the stock, it makes entries for any cash dividends received. If Sanchez receives a $2 per share dividend on December 31, the entry is:

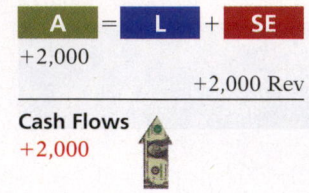

Dec. 31	Cash (1,000 × $2)	2,000	
	Dividend Revenue		2,000
	(To record receipt of a cash dividend)		

Sanchez reports Dividend Revenue under "Other revenues and gains" in the income statement. Unlike interest on notes and bonds, dividends do not accrue. Therefore, companies do not make adjusting entries to accrue dividends.

RECORDING SALE OF STOCK

When a company sells a stock investment, it recognizes as a gain or a loss the difference between the net proceeds from the sale (sales price less brokerage fees) and the cost of the stock.

Assume that Sanchez Corporation receives net proceeds of $39,000 on the sale of its Beal stock on February 10, 2018. Because the stock cost $40,000, Sanchez incurred a loss of $1,000. The entry to record the sale is:

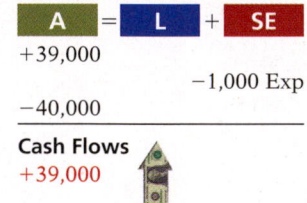

Feb. 10	Cash	39,000	
	Loss on Sale of Stock Investments	1,000	
	Stock Investments		40,000
	(To record sale of Beal common stock)		

Sanchez reports the loss under "Other expenses and losses" in the income statement. It would show a gain on sale under "Other revenues and gains."

Holdings Between 20% and 50%

When an investor company owns only a small portion of the shares of stock of another company, the investor cannot exercise control over the investee. But, when an investor owns between 20% and 50% of the common stock of a corporation, it is presumed that the investor has significant influence over the financial and operating activities of the investee. The investor probably has a representative on the investee's board of directors. Through that representative, the investor may exercise some control over the investee. The investee company in some sense becomes part of the investor company.

For example, even prior to purchasing all of **Turner Broadcasting**, **Time Warner** owned 20% of Turner. Because it exercised significant control over major decisions made by Turner, Time Warner used an approach called the equity method. Under the **equity method**, **the investor records its share of the net income of the investee in the year when it is earned**. An alternative might be to delay recognizing the investor's share of net income until the investee declares a cash dividend. But, that approach would ignore the fact that the investor and investee are, in some sense, one company, making the investor better off by the investee's earned income.

Under the equity method, the investor company initially records the investment in common stock at cost. After that, it **adjusts** the investment account annually to show the investor's equity in the investee. Each year, the investor does the following. (1) It increases (debits) the investment account and increases (credits) revenue for its share of the investee's net income.[2] (2) The investor also decreases (credits) the investment account for the amount of dividends received. The investment account is reduced for dividends received because payment of a dividend decreases the net assets of the investee.

Helpful Hint
Under the equity method, the investor recognizes revenue on the accrual basis, i.e., when it is earned by the investee.

RECORDING ACQUISITION OF STOCK

Assume that Milar Corporation acquires 30% of the common stock of Beck Company for $120,000 on January 1, 2017. The entry to record this transaction is:

Jan. 1	Stock Investments	120,000	
	Cash		120,000
	(To record purchase of Beck common stock)		

A	=	L	+	SE

+120,000
−120,000

Cash Flows
−120,000

RECORDING REVENUE AND DIVIDENDS

For 2017, Beck reports net income of $100,000. It declares and pays a $40,000 cash dividend. Milar records (1) its share of Beck's income, $30,000 (30% × $100,000), and (2) the reduction in the investment account for the dividends received, $12,000 ($40,000 × 30%). The entries are:

(1)

Dec. 31	Stock Investments	30,000	
	Revenue from Stock Investments		30,000
	(To record 30% equity in Beck's 2017 net income)		

A	=	L	+	SE

+30,000
            +30,000 Rev

Cash Flows
no effect

(2)

Dec. 31	Cash	12,000	
	Stock Investments		12,000
	(To record dividends received)		

A	=	L	+	SE

+12,000
−12,000

Cash Flows
+12,000

After Milar posts the transactions for the year, its investment and revenue accounts will show the following.

Stock Investments				Revenue from Stock Investments		
Jan. 1	120,000	Dec. 31	**12,000**		Dec. 31	**30,000**
Dec. 31	**30,000**					
Dec. 31 Bal.	138,000					

Illustration 12-4
Investment and revenue accounts after posting

During the year, the investment account increased $18,000. This increase of $18,000 is explained as follows: (1) Milar records a $30,000 increase in revenue from its stock investment in Beck, and (2) Milar records a $12,000 decrease due to dividends received from its stock investment in Beck.

---

[2]Conversely, the investor increases (debits) a loss account and decreases (credits) the investment account for its share of the investee's net loss.

Note that the difference between reported revenue under the cost method and reported revenue under the equity method can be significant. For example, Milar would report only $12,000 of dividend revenue (30% × $40,000) if it used the cost method.

Holdings of More than 50%

A company that owns more than 50% of the common stock of another entity is known as the **parent company**. The entity whose stock the parent company owns is called the **subsidiary (affiliated) company**. Because of its stock ownership, the parent company has a **controlling interest** in the subsidiary.

When a company owns more than 50% of the common stock of another company, it usually prepares **consolidated financial statements**. These statements present the total assets and liabilities controlled by the parent company. They also present the total revenues and expenses of the subsidiary companies. Companies prepare consolidated statements **in addition to** the financial statements for the parent and individual subsidiary companies.

As noted earlier, when Time Warner had a 20% investment in Turner, it reported this investment in a single line item—Other Investments. After the merger, Time Warner instead consolidated Turner's results with its own. Under this approach, Time Warner included Turner's individual assets and liabilities with its own. Its plant and equipment were added to Time Warner's plant and equipment, its receivables were added to Time Warner's receivables, and so on.

> **Helpful Hint**
>
> If parent (A) has three wholly owned subsidiaries (B, C, and D), there are four separate legal entities. From the viewpoint of the shareholders of the parent company, there is only one economic entity.

Accounting Across the Organization   Procter & Gamble Company

© Stígur Karlsson/iStockphoto

How Procter & Gamble Accounts for Gillette

Several years ago, Procter & Gamble Company acquired Gillette Company for $53.4 billion. The common stockholders of Procter & Gamble elect the board of directors of the company, who in turn select the officers and managers of the company. Procter & Gamble's board of directors controls the property owned by the corporation, which includes the common stock of Gillette. Thus, they are in a position to elect the board of directors of Gillette and, in effect, control its operations. These relationships are graphically illustrated here.

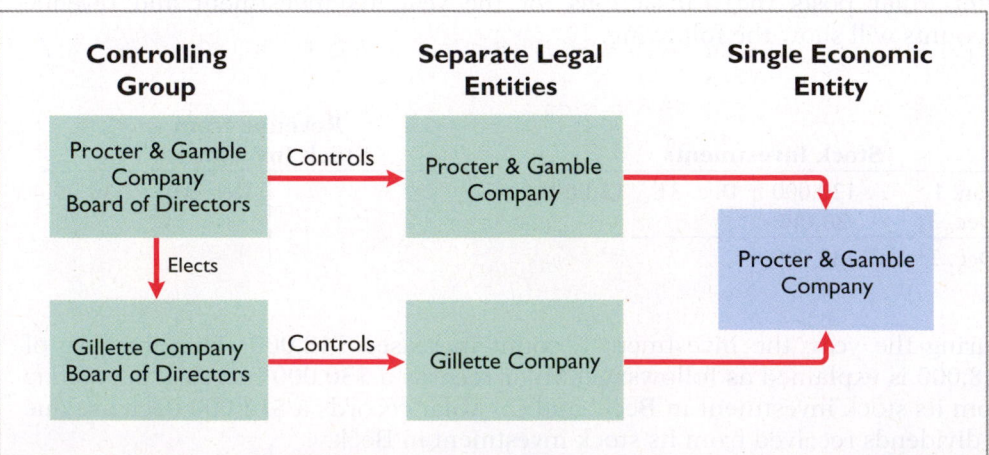

Where on Procter & Gamble's balance sheet will you find its investment in Gillette Company? (Go to **WileyPLUS** for this answer and additional questions.)

Consolidated statements are useful to the stockholders, board of directors, and management of the parent company. These statements indicate the magnitude and scope of operations of the companies under common control. For example, regulators and the courts undoubtedly used the consolidated statements of **AT&T** to determine whether a breakup of the company was in the public interest. Illustration 12-5 lists three companies that prepare consolidated statements and some of the companies they have owned.

PepsiCo	Cendant	The Disney Company
Frito-Lay	Howard Johnson	Capital Cities/ABC, Inc.
Tropicana	Ramada Inn	Disneyland, Disney World
Quaker Oats	Century 21	Mighty Ducks
Pepsi-Cola	Coldwell Banker	Anaheim Angels
Gatorade	Avis	ESPN

Illustration 12-5
Examples of consolidated companies and their subsidiaries

DO IT! 2 Stock Investments

Presented below are two independent situations.

1. Rho Jean Inc. acquired 5% of the 400,000 shares of common stock of Stillwater Corp. at a total cost of $6 per share on May 18, 2017. On August 30, Stillwater declared and paid a $75,000 dividend. On December 31, Stillwater reported net income of $244,000 for the year.

2. Debbie, Inc. obtained significant influence over North Sails by buying 40% of North Sails' 60,000 outstanding shares of common stock at a cost of $12 per share on January 1, 2017. On April 15, North Sails declared and paid a cash dividend of $45,000. On December 31, North Sails reported net income of $120,000 for the year.

Prepare all necessary journal entries for 2017 for (1) Rho Jean Inc. and (2) Debbie, Inc.

Solution

(1) May 18	Stock Investments (400,000 × 5% × $6)		120,000	
	Cash			120,000
	(To record purchase of 20,000 shares of Stillwater Co. stock)			
Aug. 30	Cash		3,750	
	Dividend Revenue ($75,000 × 5%)			3,750
	(To record receipt of cash dividend)			
(2) Jan. 1	Stock Investments (60,000 × 40% × $12)		288,000	
	Cash			288,000
	(To record purchase of 24,000 shares of North Sails' stock)			
Apr. 15	Cash		18,000	
	Stock Investments ($45,000 × 40%)			18,000
	(To record receipt of cash dividend)			
Dec. 31	Stock Investments ($120,000 × 40%)		48,000	
	Revenue from Stock Investments			48,000
	(To record 40% equity in North Sails' net income)			

Action Plan

✔ Presume that the investor has relatively little influence over the investee when an investor owns less than 20% of the common stock of another corporation. In this case, net income earned by the investee is not considered a proper basis for recognizing income from the investment by the investor.

✔ Presume significant influence for investments of 20%–50%. Therefore, record the investor's share of the net income of the investee.

Related exercise material: **BE12-2, BE12-3, E12-4, E12-5, E12-6, E12-7, E12-8, and DO IT! 12-2.**

Discuss how debt and stock investments are reported in financial statements.

The value of debt and stock investments may fluctuate greatly during the time they are held. For example, in one 12-month period, the stock price of **Time Warner** hit a high of $58.50 and a low of $9. In light of such price fluctuations, how should companies value investments at the balance sheet date? Valuation could be at cost, at fair value, or at the lower-of-cost-or-market value.

Many people argue that fair value offers the best approach because it represents the expected cash realizable value of securities. **Fair value** is the amount for which a security could be sold in a normal market. Others counter that unless a security is going to be sold soon, the fair value is not relevant because the price of the security will likely change again.

Categories of Securities

For purposes of valuation and reporting at a financial statement date, companies classify **debt investments** into three categories:

1. **Trading securities** are bought and held primarily for sale in the near term to generate income on short-term price differences.

2. **Available-for-sale securities** are held with the intent of selling them sometime in the future.

3. **Held-to-maturity securities** are debt securities that the investor has the intent and ability to hold to maturity.[3]

Stock investments are classified into two categories:

1. **Trading securities** (as defined above).

2. **Available-for-sale securities** (as defined above).

Stock investments have no maturity date. Therefore, they are never classified as held-to-maturity securities.

Illustration 12-6 shows the valuation guidelines for these securities. **These guidelines apply to all debt securities and all stock investments in which the holdings are less than 20%.**

Illustration 12-6
Valuation guidelines for securities

---

[3]This category is provided for completeness. The accounting and valuation issues related to held-to-maturity securities are discussed in more advanced accounting courses.

TRADING SECURITIES

Companies hold trading securities with the intention of selling them in a short period (generally less than a month). **Trading** means frequent buying and selling. As indicated in Illustration 12-7, companies adjust trading securities to fair value at the end of each period (an approach referred to as mark-to-market accounting). They report changes from cost as part of net income. The changes are reported as **unrealized gains or losses** because the securities have not been sold. The unrealized gain or loss is the difference between the **total cost** of trading securities and their **total fair value**. Companies classify trading securities as current assets.

Illustration 12-7 shows the cost and fair values for investments Pace Corporation classified as trading securities on December 31, 2017. Pace has an unrealized gain of $7,000 because total fair value of $147,000 is $7,000 greater than total cost of $140,000.

Illustration 12-7
Valuation of trading securities

Trading Securities, December 31, 2017			
Investments	**Cost**	**Fair Value**	**Unrealized Gain (Loss)**
Yorkville Company bonds	$ 50,000	$ 48,000	$(2,000)
Kodak Company stock	90,000	99,000	9,000
Total	$140,000	$147,000	**$ 7,000**

Pace records fair value and unrealized gain or loss through an adjusting entry at the time it prepares financial statements. In this entry, the company uses a valuation allowance account, Fair Value Adjustment—Trading, to record the difference between the total cost and the total fair value of the securities. The adjusting entry for Pace Corporation is:

Dec. 31	Fair Value Adjustment—Trading	7,000	
	Unrealized Gain—Income		7,000
	(To record unrealized gain on trading		
	securities)		

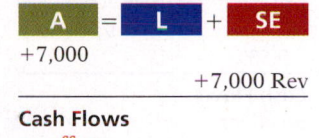

A = L + SE
+7,000
+7,000 Rev

Cash Flows
no effect

The use of a Fair Value Adjustment—Trading account enables Pace to maintain a record of the investment cost. It needs actual cost to determine the gain or loss realized when it sells the securities. Pace adds the debit balance (or subtracts a credit balance) of the Fair Value Adjustment—Trading account to the cost of the investments to arrive at a fair value for the trading securities.

The fair value of the securities is the amount Pace reports on its balance sheet. It reports the unrealized gain in the income statement in the "Other revenues and gains" section. The term "Income" in the account title indicates that the gain affects net income.

If the total cost of the trading securities is greater than total fair value, an unrealized loss has occurred. In such a case, the adjusting entry is a debit to Unrealized Loss—Income and a credit to Fair Value Adjustment—Trading. Companies report the unrealized loss under "Other expenses and losses" in the income statement.

The Fair Value Adjustment—Trading account is carried forward into future accounting periods. The company does not make any entry to the account until the end of each reporting period. At that time, the company adjusts the balance in the account to the difference between cost and fair value. For trading securities, it closes the Unrealized Gain (Loss)—Income account at the end of the reporting period.

AVAILABLE-FOR-SALE SECURITIES

As indicated earlier, companies hold available-for-sale securities with the intent of selling these investments sometime in the future. If the intent is to sell the securities within the next year or operating cycle, the investor classifies the securities as current assets in the balance sheet. Otherwise, it classifies them as long-term assets in the investments section of the balance sheet.

ETHICS NOTE

At one time, the SEC accused investment bank Morgan Stanley of overstating the value of certain bond investments by $75 million. The SEC stated that, in applying market value accounting, Morgan Stanley used its own more-optimistic assumptions rather than relying on external pricing sources.

ETHICS NOTE

Some managers seem to hold their available-for-sale securities that have experienced losses, while selling those that have gains, thus increasing income. Do you think this is ethical?

Companies report available-for-sale securities at fair value. The procedure for determining fair value and the unrealized gain or loss for these securities is the same as for trading securities. To illustrate, assume that Ingrao Corporation has two securities that it classifies as available-for-sale. Illustration 12-8 provides information on the cost, fair value, and amount of the unrealized gain or loss on December 31, 2017. There is an unrealized loss of $9,537 because total cost of $293,537 is $9,537 more than total fair value of $284,000.

Illustration 12-8
Valuation of available-for-sale securities

Available-for-Sale Securities, December 31, 2017			
Investments	Cost	Fair Value	Unrealized Gain (Loss)
Campbell Soup Corporation 8% bonds	$ 93,537	$103,600	$10,063
Hershey Company stock	200,000	180,400	(19,600)
Total	$293,537	$284,000	**$(9,537)**

Both the adjusting entry and the reporting of the unrealized gain or loss for Ingrao's available-for-sale securities differ from those illustrated for trading securities. The differences result because Ingrao does not expect to sell these securities in the near term. Thus, prior to actual sale it is more likely that changes in fair value may change either unrealized gains or losses. Therefore, Ingrao does not report an unrealized gain or loss in the income statement. Instead, it reports it as a **separate component of stockholders' equity**.

In the adjusting entry, Ingrao identifies the fair value adjustment account with available-for-sale securities, and it identifies the unrealized gain or loss account with stockholders' equity. Ingrao records the unrealized loss of $9,537 as follows.

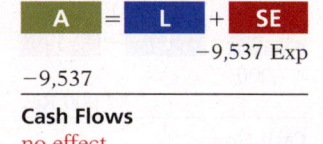

A = L + SE
−9,537 Exp
−9,537

Cash Flows
no effect

Dec. 31	Unrealized Gain or Loss—Equity	9,537	
	Fair Value Adjustment—Available-for-Sale		9,537
	(To record unrealized loss on available-for-sale securities)		

If total fair value exceeds total cost, Ingrao debits Fair Value Adjustment—Available-for-Sale and credits Unrealized Gain or Loss—Equity.

For available-for-sale securities, the company carries forward the Unrealized Gain or Loss—Equity account to future periods. At each future balance sheet date, Ingrao adjusts the Fair Value Adjustment—Available-for-Sale account and the Unrealized Gain or Loss—Equity account to show the difference between cost and fair value at that time.

Investor Insight

enciktepstudio/Shutterstock

Can Fair Value Be Unfair?

The FASB is considering proposals for how to account for financial instruments. The FASB at one time proposed that loans and receivables be accounted for at their fair value (the amount they could currently be sold for), as are most investments. The FASB believes that this would provide a more accurate view of a company's financial position. It might be especially useful as an early warning when a bank is in trouble because of poor-quality loans. But, banks argue that fair values are difficult to estimate accurately. They are also concerned that volatile fair values could cause large swings in a bank's reported net income.

Source: David Reilly, "Bank Face a Mark-to-Market Challenge," *Wall Street Journal Online* (March 15, 2010).

What are the arguments in favor of and against fair value accounting for loans and receivables? (Go to **WileyPLUS** for this answer and additional questions.)

DO IT! 3a — Trading and Available-for-Sale Securities

Some of Powderhorn Corporation's investment securities are classified as trading securities and some are classified as available-for-sale. The cost and fair value of each category at December 31, 2017, are shown below.

	Cost	Fair Value	Unrealized Gain (Loss)
Trading securities	$93,600	$94,900	$1,300
Available-for-sale securities	$48,800	$51,400	$2,600

At December 31, 2016, the Fair Value Adjustment—Trading account had a debit balance of $9,200, and the Fair Value Adjustment—Available-for-Sale account had a credit balance of $5,750. Prepare the required journal entries for each group of securities for December 31, 2017.

Solution

Trading securities:

Unrealized Loss—Income	7,900*	
Fair Value Adjustment—Trading		7,900
(To record unrealized loss on trading securities)		

    *$9,200 − $1,300

Available-for-sale securities:

Fair Value Adjustment—Available-for-Sale	8,350**	
Unrealized Gain or Loss—Equity		8,350
(To record unrealized gain on available-for-sale securities)		

    **$5,750 + $2,600

Related exercise material: **BE12-4, BE12-6, E12-8, E12-10, E12-11, E12-12, and DO IT! 12-3a.**

Action Plan

✔ Mark trading securities to fair value and report the adjustment in current-period income.

✔ Mark available-for-sale securities to fair value and report the adjustment as a separate component of stockholders' equity.

Balance Sheet Presentation

In the balance sheet, companies classify investments as either short-term or long-term.

SHORT-TERM INVESTMENTS

Short-term investments (also called **marketable securities**) are securities held by a company that are (1) **readily marketable** and (2) **intended to be converted into cash** within the next year or operating cycle, whichever is longer. Investments that do not meet **both criteria** are classified as **long-term investments**.

READILY MARKETABLE An investment is readily marketable when it can be sold easily whenever the need for cash arises. Short-term paper[4] meets this criterion. It can be readily sold to other investors. Stocks and bonds traded on organized securities exchanges, such as the New York Stock Exchange, are readily marketable. They can be bought and sold daily. In contrast, there may be only a limited market for the securities issued by small corporations, and no market for the securities of a privately held company.

INTENT TO CONVERT Intent to convert means that management intends to sell the investment within the next year or operating cycle, whichever is longer. Generally, this criterion is satisfied when the investment is considered a resource

Helpful Hint
Trading securities are always classified as short-term. Available-for-sale securities can be either short-term or long-term.

---

[4]**Short-term paper** includes (1) certificates of deposit (CDs) issued by banks, (2) money market certificates issued by banks and savings and loan associations, (3) Treasury bills issued by the U.S. government, and (4) commercial paper (notes) issued by corporations with good credit ratings.

that the investor will use whenever the need for cash arises. For example, a ski resort may invest idle cash during the summer months with the intent to sell the securities to buy supplies and equipment shortly before the winter season. This investment is considered short-term even if lack of snow cancels the next ski season and eliminates the need to convert the securities into cash as intended.

Because of their high liquidity, short-term investments appear immediately below Cash in the "Current assets" section of the balance sheet. They are reported at fair value. For example, Pace Corporation would report its trading securities as shown in Illustration 12-9.

Illustration 12-9
Presentation of short-term investments

PACE CORPORATION	
Balance Sheet (partial)	
Current assets	
Cash	$ 21,000
Short-term investments, at fair value	147,000

LONG-TERM INVESTMENTS

Companies generally report long-term investments in a separate section of the balance sheet immediately below "Current assets," as shown later in Illustration 12-12 (page 574). Long-term investments in available-for-sale securities are reported at fair value. Investments in common stock accounted for under the equity method are reported at equity.

Presentation of Realized and Unrealized Gain or Loss

Companies must present in the financial statements gains and losses on investments, whether realized or unrealized. In the income statement, companies report gains and losses in the nonoperating activities section under the categories listed in Illustration 12-10. Interest and dividend revenue are also reported in that section.

Illustration 12-10
Nonoperating items related to investments

Other Revenues and Gains	Other Expenses and Losses
Interest Revenue	Loss on Sale of Investments
Dividend Revenue	Unrealized Loss—Income
Gain on Sale of Investments	
Unrealized Gain—Income	

As indicated earlier, companies report an unrealized gain or loss on available-for-sale securities as a separate component of stockholders' equity. To illustrate, assume that Dawson Inc. has common stock of $3,000,000, retained earnings of $1,500,000, and an unrealized loss on available-for-sale securities of $100,000. Illustration 12-11 shows the balance sheet presentation of the unrealized loss.

Illustration 12-11
Unrealized loss in stockholders' equity section

DAWSON INC.	
Balance Sheet (partial)	
Stockholders' equity	
Common stock	$3,000,000
Retained earnings	1,500,000
Total paid-in capital and retained earnings	4,500,000
Less: Unrealized loss on available-for-sale securities	**100,000**
Total stockholders' equity	$4,400,000

Note that the presentation of the loss is similar to the presentation of the cost of treasury stock in the stockholders' equity section (it decreases stockholders' equity). An unrealized gain would be added to this section. Reporting the unrealized gain or loss in the stockholders' equity section serves two purposes. (1) It reduces the volatility of net income due to fluctuations in fair value. (2) It informs the financial statement user of the gain or loss that would occur if the securities were sold at fair value.

Companies must report items such as unrealized gains or losses on available-for-sale securities as part of a more inclusive measure called comprehensive income. Unrealized gains and losses on available-for-sale securities therefore affect comprehensive income (and stockholders' equity) but are not included in the computation of net income. We discuss comprehensive income more fully in Chapter 14.

Classified Balance Sheet

We have presented many sections of classified balance sheets in this and preceding chapters. The classified balance sheet in Illustration 12-12 (page 574) includes, in one place, key topics from previous chapters: the issuance of par value common stock, restrictions of retained earnings, and issuance of long-term bonds. From this chapter, the statement includes (highlighted in red) short-term and long-term investments. The investments in short-term securities are considered trading securities. The long-term investments in stock of less than 20%-owned companies are considered available-for-sale securities. Illustration 12-12 also includes a long-term investment reported at equity and descriptive notations within the statement, such as the cost flow method for valuing inventory and one note to the statement.

DO IT! 3b   Financial Statement Presentation of Investments

Identify where each of the following items would be reported in the financial statements.

1. Interest earned on investments in bonds.
2. Fair value adjustment—available-for-sale.
3. Unrealized loss on available-for-sale securities.
4. Gain on sale of investments in stock.
5. Unrealized gain on trading securities.

Use the following possible categories:

Balance sheet:

Current assets	Current liabilities
Investments	Long-term liabilities
Property, plant, and equipment	Stockholders' equity
Intangible assets	

Income statement:

Other revenues and gains	Other expenses and losses

Action Plan

✔ Classify investments as current assets if they will be held for less than one year.

✔ Report unrealized gains or losses on trading securities in income.

✔ Report unrealized gains or losses on available-for-sale securities in equity.

✔ Report realized gains or losses on investments in the income statement as "Other revenues and gains" or as "Other expenses and losses."

Solution

Item	Financial Statement	Category
1. Interest earned on investments in bonds	Income statement	Other revenues and gains
2. Fair value adjustment—available-for-sale	Balance sheet	Investments
3. Unrealized loss on available-for-sale securities	Balance sheet	Stockholders' equity
4. Gain on sale of investments in stock	Income statement	Other revenues and gains
5. Unrealized gain on trading securities	Income statement	Other revenues and gains

Related exercise material: **BE12-5, BE12-7, BE12-8, E12-10, E12-11, E12-12, and DO IT! 12-3b.**

Illustration 12-12
Classified balance sheet

PACE CORPORATION
Balance Sheet
December 31, 2017

Assets

Current assets			
Cash			$ 21,000
Short-term investments, at fair value			**147,000**
Accounts receivable		$ 84,000	
Less: Allowance for doubtful accounts		4,000	80,000
Inventory, at FIFO cost			43,000
Prepaid insurance			23,000
Total current assets			314,000
Investments			
Investment in stock of less than 20% owned companies, at fair value		**50,000**	
Investment in stock of 20–50% owned company, at equity		**150,000**	
Total investments			200,000
Property, plant, and equipment			
Land		200,000	
Buildings	$800,000		
Less: Accumulated depreciation—buildings	200,000	600,000	
Equipment	180,000		
Less: Accumulated depreciation—equipment	54,000	126,000	
Total property, plant, and equipment			926,000
Intangible assets			
Goodwill			270,000
Total assets			$1,710,000

Liabilities and Stockholders' Equity

Current liabilities			
Accounts payable			$ 185,000
Federal income taxes payable			60,000
Interest payable			10,000
Total current liabilities			255,000
Long-term liabilities			
Bonds payable, 10%, due 2024		$ 300,000	
Less: Discount on bonds		10,000	
Total long-term liabilities			290,000
Total liabilities			545,000
Stockholders' equity			
Paid-in capital			
Common stock, $10 par value, 200,000 shares authorized, 80,000 shares issued and outstanding		800,000	
Paid-in capital in excess of par— common stock		100,000	
Total paid-in capital		900,000	
Retained earnings (Note 1)		255,000	
Total paid-in capital and retained earnings		1,155,000	
Add: Unrealized gain on available-for-sale securities		**10,000**	
Total stockholders' equity			1,165,000
Total liabilities and stockholders' equity			$1,710,000

Note 1. Retained earnings of $100,000 is restricted for plant expansion.

LEARNING OBJECTIVE 4 *

APPENDIX 12A: Describe the form and content of consolidated financial statements as well as how to prepare them.

Most of the large U.S. corporations are holding companies that own other corporations. They therefore prepare **consolidated** financial statements that combine the separate companies.

Consolidated Balance Sheet

Companies prepare consolidated balance sheets from the individual balance sheets of their affiliated companies. They do not prepare consolidated statements from ledger accounts kept by the consolidated entity because only the separate legal entities maintain accounting records.

All items in the individual balance sheets are included in the consolidated balance sheet except amounts that pertain to transactions between the affiliated companies. Transactions between the affiliated companies are identified as **intercompany transactions**. The process of excluding these transactions in preparing consolidated statements is referred to as **intercompany eliminations**. These eliminations are necessary to avoid overstating assets, liabilities, and stockholders' equity in the consolidated balance sheet. For example, amounts owed by a subsidiary to a parent company and the related receivable reported by the parent company would be eliminated. The objective in a consolidated balance sheet is to show only obligations to and receivables from parties who are not part of the affiliated group of companies.

To illustrate, assume that on January 1, 2017, Powers Company pays $150,000 in cash for 100% of Serto Company's common stock. Powers Company records the investment at cost, as required by the historical cost principle. Illustration 12A-1 presents the separate balance sheets of the two companies immediately after the purchase, together with combined and consolidated data.[5] Powers Company obtains the balances in the "combined" column by adding the items in the separate balance sheets of the affiliated companies. The combined totals do not represent a consolidated balance sheet because there has been a double-counting of assets and stockholders' equity in the amount of $150,000.

> **Helpful Hint**
> Eliminations are aptly named because they eliminate duplicate data. They are not adjustments.

> **Illustration 12A-1**
> Combined and consolidated data

POWERS COMPANY AND SERTO COMPANY
Balance Sheet
January 1, 2017

Assets	Powers Company	Serto Company	Combined Data	Consolidated Data
Current assets	$ 50,000	$ 80,000	$130,000	**$130,000**
Investment in Serto Company common stock	150,000		150,000	**–0–**
Plant and equipment (net)	325,000	145,000	470,000	**470,000**
Total assets	$525,000	$225,000	$750,000	**$600,000**
Liabilities and Stockholders' Equity				
Current liabilities	$ 50,000	$ 75,000	$125,000	**$125,000**
Common stock	300,000	100,000	400,000	**300,000**
Retained earnings	175,000	50,000	225,000	**175,000**
Total liabilities and stockholders' equity	$525,000	$225,000	$750,000	**$600,000**

---

[5]We use condensed data throughout this material to keep details at a minimum.

The Investment in Serto Company common stock that appears on the balance sheet of Powers Company represents an interest in the net assets of Serto. As a result, there has been a double-counting of assets. Similarly, there has been a double-counting in stockholders' equity because the common stock of Serto Company is completely owned by the stockholders of Powers Company.

The balances in the consolidated data column are the amounts that should appear in the consolidated balance sheet. The double-counting has been eliminated by showing Investment in Serto Company at zero and by reporting only the common stock and retained earnings of Powers Company as stockholders' equity.

USE OF A WORKSHEET—COST EQUAL TO BOOK VALUE

The preparation of consolidated balance sheets is usually facilitated by the use of a worksheet. As shown in Illustration 12A-2, the worksheet for a consolidated balance sheet contains columns for (1) the balance sheet data for the separate legal entities, (2) intercompany eliminations, and (3) consolidated data. All data in the worksheet relate to the preceding example in which Powers Company acquires 100% ownership of Serto Company for $150,000. In this case, the cost of the investment, $150,000, is equal to the book value [$150,000 ($225,000 − $75,000)] of the subsidiary's net assets. The intercompany elimination results in a credit to the investment account maintained by Powers Company for its balance, $150,000, and debits to the Common Stock and Retained Earnings accounts of Serto Company for their respective balances, $100,000 and $50,000.

Illustration 12A-2
Worksheet—Cost equal to book value

	Powers Company.xls

Home Insert Page Layout Formulas Data Review View

P18   fx

	A	B	C	D	E	F
1		**POWERS COMPANY AND SUBSIDIARY**				
2		**Worksheet—Consolidated Balance Sheet**				
3		**January 1, 2017 (Acquisition Date)**				
4		Powers	Serto	Eliminations		Consolidated
5	Assets	Company	Company	Dr.	Cr.	Data
6	Current assets	50,000	80,000			130,000
7	Investment in Serto Company common					
8	stock	150,000			**150,000**	–0–
9	Plant and equipment (net)	325,000	145,000			470,000
10	Totals	525,000	225,000			600,000
11						
12						
13	Liabilities and Stockholders' Equity					
14	Current liabilities	50,000	75,000			125,000
15	Common stock—Powers Company	300,000				300,000
16	Common stock—Serto Company		100,000	**100,000**		–0–
17	Retained earnings—Powers Company	175,000				175,000
18	Retained earnings—Serto Company		50,000	**50,000**		–0–
19	Totals	525,000	225,000	150,000	150,000	600,000
20						

Helpful Hint
As is the case of the worksheets explained earlier in this textbook, consolidated worksheets are also optional.

It is important to recognize that companies make intercompany eliminations solely on the worksheet to present correct consolidated data. Neither of the affiliated companies journalizes or posts the eliminations. Therefore, eliminations do not affect the ledger accounts. Powers Company's investment account and Serto Company's common stock and retained earnings accounts are reported by the separate entities in preparing their own financial statements.

USE OF A WORKSHEET—COST ABOVE BOOK VALUE

The cost of acquiring the common stock of another company may be above or below its book value. The management of the parent company may pay more than book value for the stock. Why? Because it believes the fair values of identifiable assets such as land, buildings, and equipment are higher than their recorded book values. Or, it may believe the subsidiary's future earnings prospects warrant a payment for goodwill.

To illustrate, assume the same data used above, except that Powers Company pays $165,000 in cash for 100% of Serto's common stock. The excess of cost over book value is $15,000 ($165,000 − $150,000). Powers recognizes this amount separately in eliminating the parent company's investment account, as shown in Illustration 12A-3. Total assets and total liabilities and stockholders' equity are the same as in the preceding example ($600,000). However, in this case, total assets include $15,000 of excess of cost over book value of subsidiary. The disposition of the excess is explained in the next section.

Helpful Hint
The consolidated worksheet is another useful spreadsheet application. This is an easier worksheet to attempt since the required instructions are very straightforward.

Illustration 12A-3
Worksheet—Cost above book value

	Powers Company	Serto Company	Eliminations Dr.	Eliminations Cr.	Consolidated Data
POWERS COMPANY AND SUBSIDIARY Worksheet—Consolidated Balance Sheet January 1, 2017 (Acquisition Date)					
Assets					
Current assets	35,000	80,000			115,000
Investment in Serto Company common stock	165,000			165,000	–0–
Plant and equipment (net)	325,000	145,000			470,000
Excess of cost over book value of subsidiary			15,000		15,000
Totals	525,000	225,000			600,000
Liabilities and Stockholders' Equity					
Current liabilities	50,000	75,000			125,000
Common stock—Powers Company	300,000				300,000
Common stock—Serto Company		100,000	100,000		–0–
Retained earnings—Powers Company	175,000				175,000
Retained earnings—Serto Company		50,000	50,000		–0–
Totals	525,000	225,000	165,000	165,000	600,000

Note that a separate line is added to the worksheet for the excess of cost over book value of subsidiary.

CONTENT OF A CONSOLIDATED BALANCE SHEET

To illustrate a consolidated balance sheet, we will use the worksheet shown in Illustration 12A-3. This worksheet shows an excess of cost over book value of $15,000. In the consolidated balance sheet, Powers Company first allocates this amount to specific assets, such as plant and equipment and inventory, if their fair values on the acquisition date exceed their book values. Any remainder is considered to be goodwill. For Serto Company, assume that the fair value of the plant and equipment is $155,000. Thus, Powers allocates $10,000 of the excess of cost over book value to plant and equipment, and the remainder, $5,000, to goodwill. Illustration 12A-4 (page 578) shows the condensed consolidated balance sheet of Powers Company.

Illustration 12A-4
Consolidated balance sheet

POWERS COMPANY		
Consolidated Balance Sheet		
January 1, 2017		

Assets		
Current assets		$115,000
Plant and equipment (net)		480,000*
Goodwill		5,000
Total assets		$600,000

Liabilities and Stockholders' Equity		
Current liabilities		$125,000
Stockholders' equity		
Common stock	$300,000	
Retained earnings	175,000	475,000
Total liabilities and stockholders' equity		$600,000

*($470,000 + $10,000)

Through innovative financial restructuring, **The Coca-Cola Company** at one time eliminated a substantial amount of non-intercompany debt. It sold to the public 51% of two bottling companies. The "49% solution," as insiders call the strategy, enabled Coca-Cola to keep effective control over the businesses, and it swept $3 billion of debt from its consolidated balance sheet. (It no longer consolidated the two bottling companies.) At the same time, the new companies obtained independent access to equity markets to satisfy their own large appetites for capital.

Consolidated Income Statement

Affiliated companies also prepare a consolidated income statement. This statement shows the results of operations of affiliated companies as though they are one economic unit. This means that the statement shows only revenue and expense transactions between the consolidated entity and companies and individuals who are outside the affiliated group.

Consequently, all intercompany revenue and expense transactions must be eliminated. Intercompany transactions such as sales between affiliates and interest on loans charged by one affiliate to another must be eliminated. A worksheet facilitates the preparation of consolidated income statements in the same manner as it does for the balance sheet.

REVIEW AND PRACTICE

LEARNING OBJECTIVES REVIEW

❶ Explain how to account for debt investments. Companies record investments in debt securities when they purchase bonds, receive or accrue interest, and sell the bonds. They report gains or losses on the sale of bonds in the "Other revenues and gains" or "Other expenses and losses" sections of the income statement.

❷ Explain how to account for stock investments. Companies record investments in common stock when they purchase the stock, receive dividends, and sell the stock. When ownership is less than 20%, the cost method is used. When ownership is between 20%

and 50%, the equity method should be used. When ownership is more than 50%, companies prepare consolidated financial statements. Consolidated financial statements indicate the magnitude and scope of operations of the companies under common control.

❸ Discuss how debt and stock investments are reported in financial statements. Investments in debt securities are classified as trading, available-for-sale, or held-to-maturity securities for valuation and reporting purposes. Stock investments are classified either as trading or available-for-sale securities. Stock investments have no maturity date and therefore are never classified as held-to-maturity securities. Trading securities are reported as current assets at fair value, with changes from cost reported in net income. Available-for-sale securities are also reported at fair value, with the changes from cost reported in stockholders' equity. Available-for-sale securities are classified as short-term or long-term, depending on their expected future sale date.

Short-term investments are securities that are (a) readily marketable and (b) intended to be converted to cash within the next year or operating cycle, whichever is longer. Investments that do not meet both criteria are classified as long-term investments.

*❹ **Describe the form and content of consolidated financial statements as well as how to prepare them.** Consolidated financial statements are similar in form and content to the financial statements of an individual corporation. A consolidated balance sheet shows the assets and liabilities controlled by the parent company. A consolidated income statement shows the results of operations of affiliated companies as though they are one economic unit. The worksheet for a consolidated balance sheet contains columns for (a) the balance sheet data for the separate entities, (b) intercompany eliminations, and (c) consolidated data.

GLOSSARY REVIEW

Available-for-sale securities Securities that are held with the intent of selling them sometime in the future. (p. 568).

Consolidated financial statements Financial statements that present the assets and liabilities controlled by the parent company and the total revenues and expenses of the subsidiary companies. (p. 566).

Controlling interest Ownership of more than 50% of the common stock of another entity. (p. 566).

Cost method An accounting method in which the investment in common stock is recorded at cost, and revenue is recognized only when cash dividends are received. (p. 563).

Debt investments Investments in government and corporation bonds. (p. 561).

Equity method An accounting method in which the investment in common stock is initially recorded at cost, and the investment account is then adjusted annually to show the investor's equity in the investee. (p. 565).

Fair value Amount for which a security could be sold in a normal market. (p. 568).

Held-to-maturity securities Debt securities that the investor has the intent and ability to hold to their maturity date. (p. 568).

*****Intercompany eliminations** Eliminations made to exclude the effects of intercompany transactions in preparing consolidated statements. (p. 575).

*****Intercompany transactions** Transactions between affiliated companies. (p. 575).

Investment portfolio A group of stocks and/or debt securities in different corporations held for investment purposes. (p. 563).

Long-term investments Investments that are not readily marketable or that management does not intend to convert into cash within the next year or operating cycle, whichever is longer. (p. 571).

Parent company A company that owns more than 50% of the common stock of another entity. (p. 566).

Short-term investments Investments that are readily marketable and intended to be converted into cash within the next year or operating cycle, whichever is longer. (p. 571).

Stock investments Investments in the capital stock of other corporations. (p. 563).

Subsidiary (affiliated) company A company in which more than 50% of its stock is owned by another company. (p. 566).

Trading securities Securities bought and held primarily for sale in the near term to generate income on short-term price differences. (p. 568).

PRACTICE MULTIPLE-CHOICE QUESTIONS

(LO 1) **1.** Which of the following is **not** a primary reason why corporations invest in debt and equity securities?
(a) They wish to gain control of a competitor.
(b) They have excess cash.
(c) They wish to move into a new line of business.
(d) They are required to by law.

(LO 1) **2.** Debt investments are initially recorded at:
(a) cost.
(b) cost plus accrued interest.

(c) fair value.
(d) face value.

3. Hanes Company sells debt investments costing (LO 1) $26,000 for $28,000. In journalizing the sale, credits are to:
(a) Debt Investments and Loss on Sale of Debt Investments.
(b) Debt Investments and Gain on Sale of Debt Investments.

(c) Stock Investments and Gain on Sale of Stock Investments.

(d) No correct answer is given.

(LO 2) **4.** Pryor Company receives net proceeds of $42,000 on the sale of stock investments that cost $39,500. This transaction will result in reporting in the income statement a:

(a) loss of $2,500 under "Other expenses and losses."

(b) loss of $2,500 under "Operating expenses."

(c) gain of $2,500 under "Other revenues and gains."

(d) gain of $2,500 under "Operating revenues."

(LO 2) **5.** The equity method of accounting for long-term investments in stock should be used when the investor has significant influence over an investee and owns:

(a) between 20% and 50% of the investee's common stock.

(b) 20% or more of the investee's common stock.

(c) more than 50% of the investee's common stock.

(d) less than 20% of the investee's common stock.

(LO 2) **6.** Assume that Horicon Corp. acquired 25% of the common stock of Sheboygan Corp. on January 1, 2017, for $300,000. During 2017, Sheboygan Corp. reported net income of $160,000 and paid total dividends of $60,000. If Horicon uses the equity method to account for its investment, the balance in the investment account on December 31, 2017, will be:

(a) $300,000.   (c) $400,000.

(b) $325,000.   (d) $340,000.

(LO 2) **7.** Using the information in Question 6, what entry would Horicon make to record the receipt of the dividend from Sheboygan?

(a) Debit Cash and credit Revenue from Stock Investments.

(b) Debit Cash Dividends and credit Revenue from Stock Investments.

(c) Debit Cash and credit Stock Investments.

(d) Debit Cash and credit Dividend Revenue.

(LO 2) **8.** You have a controlling interest if:

(a) you own more than 20% of a company's stock.

(b) you are the president of the company.

(c) you use the equity method.

(d) you own more than 50% of a company's stock.

(LO 2) **9.** Which of the following statements is **false**? Consolidated financial statements are useful to:

(a) determine the profitability of specific subsidiaries.

(b) determine the total profitability of companies under common control.

(c) determine the breadth of a parent company's operations.

(d) determine the full extent of total obligations of companies under common control.

(LO 3) **10.** At the end of the first year of operations, the total cost of the trading securities portfolio is $120,000. Total fair value is $115,000. The financial statements should show:

(a) a reduction of an asset of $5,000 and a realized loss of $5,000.

(b) a reduction of an asset of $5,000 and an unrealized loss of $5,000 in the stockholders' equity section.

(c) a reduction of an asset of $5,000 in the current assets section and an unrealized loss of $5,000 in "Other expenses and losses."

(d) a reduction of an asset of $5,000 in the current assets section and a realized loss of $5,000 in "Other expenses and losses."

11. At December 31, 2017, the fair value of available-for- (LO 3) sale securities is $41,300 and the cost is $39,800. At January 1, 2017, there was a credit balance of $900 in the Fair Value Adjustment—Available-for-Sale account. The required adjusting entry would be:

(a) Debit Fair Value Adjustment—Available-for-Sale for $1,500 and credit Unrealized Gain or Loss—Equity for $1,500.

(b) Debit Fair Value Adjustment—Available-for-Sale for $600 and credit Unrealized Gain or Loss—Equity for $600.

(c) Debit Fair Value Adjustment—Available-for-Sale for $2,400 and credit Unrealized Gain or Loss—Equity for $2,400.

(d) Debit Unrealized Gain or Loss—Equity for $2,400 and credit Fair Value Adjustment—Available-for-Sale for $2,400.

12. If a company wants to increase its reported income by (LO 3) manipulating its investment accounts, which should it do?

(a) Sell its "winner" trading securities and hold its "loser" trading securities.

(b) Hold its "winner" trading securities and sell its "loser" trading securities.

(c) Sell its "winner" available-for-sale securities and hold its "loser" available-for-sale securities.

(d) Hold its "winner" available-for-sale securities and sell its "loser" available-for-sale securities.

13. In the balance sheet, a debit balance in Unrealized (LO 3) Gain or Loss—Equity is reported as a(n):

(a) increase to stockholders' equity.

(b) decrease to stockholders' equity.

(c) loss in the income statement.

(d) loss in the retained earnings statement.

14. Short-term debt investments must be readily market- (LO 3) able and expected to be sold within:

(a) 3 months from the date of purchase.

(b) the next year or operating cycle, whichever is shorter.

(c) the next year or operating cycle, whichever is longer.

(d) the operating cycle.

*15. Pate Company pays $175,000 for 100% of Sinko's (LO 4) common stock when Sinko's stockholders' equity consists of Common Stock $100,000 and Retained Earnings $60,000. In the worksheet for the consolidated balance sheet, the eliminations will include a:

(a) credit to Investment in Sinko Common Stock $160,000.

(b) credit to Excess of Book Value over Cost of Subsidiary $15,000.

(c) debit to Retained Earnings $75,000.

(d) debit to Excess of Cost over Book Value of Subsidiary $15,000.

*16. Which of the following statements about intercom- (LO 4) pany eliminations is **true**?

(a) They are not journalized or posted by any of the subsidiaries.

(b) They do not affect the ledger accounts of any of the subsidiaries.

(c) They are made solely on the worksheet to arrive at correct consolidated data.

(d) All of these statements are true.

(LO 4) *17. Which one of the following statements about consolidated income statements is **false**?
(a) A worksheet facilitates the preparation of the statement.
(b) The consolidated income statement shows the results of operations of affiliated companies as a single economic unit.
(c) All revenue and expense transactions between parent and subsidiary companies are eliminated.
(d) When a subsidiary is wholly owned, the form and content of the statement will differ from the income statement of an individual corporation.

Solutions

1. (d) Corporations are not required to by law to invest in debt and equity securities. The other choices are reasons why corporations invest in debt and equity securities.

2. (a) When debt investments are purchased, they are recorded at cost, not (b) cost plus accrued interest, (c) fair value, or (d) face value.

3. (b) Credits are made to Debt Investments $26,000 and Gain on Sale of Debt Investments $2,000 ($28,000 − $26,000). The other choices are therefore incorrect.

4. (c) Because the cash received ($42,000) is greater than the cost ($39,500), this sale results in a gain, not a loss, which will be reported under "Other revenues and gains" in the income statement. The other choices are therefore incorrect.

5. (a) The equity method is used when the investor can exercise significant influence and owns between 20% and 50% of the investee's common stock. The other choices are therefore incorrect.

6. (b) Horicon records the acquisition of the stock investment by debiting Stock Investments $300,000 and crediting Cash $300,000. Then, Horicon records (1) its share in Sheboygan Corp.'s net income ($160,000 × .25) by debiting Stock Investments $40,000 and crediting Revenue from Stock Investments $40,000 and (2) the reduction in the investment account for the dividends received ($60,000 × .25) by debiting Cash $15,000 and crediting Stock Investments $15,000. Thus, the balance in the investment account on December 31 will be $325,000 ($300,000 + $40,000 − $15,000), not (a) $300,000, (C) $400,000, or (d) $340,000.

7. (c) Horicon records the receipt of the dividend from Sheboygan by debiting Cash and crediting Stock Investments. The other choices are therefore incorrect.

8. (d) You have a controlling interest if you own more than 50% of a company's stock, not (a) 20% of a company's stock, (b) are president of the company, or (c) use the equity method.

9. (a) Consolidated financial statements are not useful in determining the profitability of specific subsidiaries (legal entities) because consolidated financial statements represent the result of the single economic entity. The other choices are true statements.

10. (c) The difference between the fair value ($115,000) and total cost ($120,000) of trading securities at the end of the first year would result in a reduction of an asset of $5,000 through the valuation allowance account in the current assets section and an unrealized loss of $5,000 in "Other expenses and losses." The other choices are therefore incorrect.

11. (c) In this case, there is an unrealized gain of $1,500 because total fair value of $41,300 is $1,500 greater than the total cost of $39,800. The desired balance in the market adjustment account is $1,500 debit. The required adjusting entry considers the existing credit balance of $900 and is a debit to Fair Value Adjustment—Available-for-Sale for $2,400 ($1,500 + $900) and a credit to Unrealized Gain or Loss—Equity for $2,400 ($1,500 + $900). The other choices are therefore incorrect.

12. (c) When a company sells its winners as related to available-for-sale securities, it has a realized gain that increases net income. Selling the winners will affect the balance in Unrealized Holding Gain or Loss—Equity, but any change in this balance does not affect net income. Choices (a) and (b) are incorrect because trading securities' gains and losses related to changes in valuation are reported in net income. Thus, when a company sells a trading security, it should have no effect on net income because the value change was recognized in net income previously. Choice (d) is incorrect because selling the losing available-for-sale securities will decrease net income.

13. (b) A debit balance in Unrealized Gain or Loss—Equity is reported on the balance sheet as a separate component of stockholders' equity, decreasing stockholders' equity. The other choices are therefore incorrect.

14. (c) Short-term investments are current assets that are expected to be consumed, sold, or converted to cash within one year or the operating cycle, whichever is longer. The other choices are therefore incorrect.

*15. (d) The eliminations will include a debit to Excess of Cost over Book Value of Subsidiary $15,000 ($175,000 − $160,000). The other choices are therefore incorrect.

*16. (d) All of the statements in choices (a), (b), and (c) are correct, so (d) is the best answer.

*17. (d) When a subsidiary is wholly owned, the form and content of the statement will be the same as, not different from, the income statement of an individual corporation. The other choices are true statements.

◼ PRACTICE EXERCISES

1. Bach Company purchased 70 Lester Company 6%, 10-year, $1,000 bonds on January 1, 2017, for $70,000. The bonds pay interest annually on January 1. On January 1, 2018, after receipt of interest, Bach Company sold 42 of the bonds for $39,100.

Journalize debt investment transactions, accrue interest, and record sale.

(LO 1)

Instructions

Prepare the journal entries to record the transactions described above.

Solution

1.

		January 1, 2017		
Debt Investments			70,000	
Cash				70,000
		December 31, 2017		
Interest Receivable			4,200	
Interest Revenue ($70,000 × 6%)				4,200
		January 1, 2018		
Cash			4,200	
Interest Receivable				4,200
		January 1, 2018		
Cash			39,100	
Loss On Sale of Debt Investments			2,900	
Debt Investments (42/70 × $70,000)				42,000

Journalize stock investment transactions.

(LO 2)

2. Cannon Company had the following transactions in 2017 pertaining to stock investments.

Feb. 1	Purchased 600 shares of Ronin common stock (2%) for $6,000 cash.
July 1	Received cash dividends of $1 per share on Ronin common stock.
Sept. 1	Sold 300 shares of Ronin common stock for $4,200.
Dec. 1	Received cash dividends of $1 per share on Ronin common stock.

Instructions

Journalize the transactions.

Solution

2.

		February 1, 2017		
Stock Investments (600 × $10)			6,000	
Cash				6,000
		July 1, 2017		
Cash (600 × $1)			600	
Dividend Revenue				600
		September 1, 2017		
Cash			4,200	
Stock Investments ($6,000 × 300/600)				3,000
Gain on Sale of Stock Investments				1,200
		December 1, 2017		
Cash (300 × $1)			300	
Dividend Revenue				300

Prepare adjusting entries for fair value, and indicate statement presentation for two classes of securities.

(LO 3)

3. Sunshine Company started business on January 1, 2017, and has the following data at December 31, 2017.

Securities	Cost	Fair Value
Trading	$120,000	$125,000
Available-for-sale	100,000	96,000

The available-for-sale securities are held as a long-term investment.

Instructions

(a) Prepare the adjusting entries to report each class of securities at fair value.

(b) Indicate the statement presentation of each class of securities and the related unrealized gain (loss) accounts.

Solution

3. (a)

December 31, 2017

Fair Value Adjustment—Trading		
($125,000 − $120,000)	5,000	
Unrealized Gain—Income		5,000
Unrealized Gain or Loss—Equity		
($100,000 − $96,000)	4,000	
Fair Value Adjustment—Available-for-Sale		4,000

(b)

Balance Sheet

Current assets	
Short-term investments, at fair value	$125,000
Investments	
Investments in stock of less than 20% owned	
companies, at fair value	96,000
Stockholders' equity	
Less: Unrealized loss on available-for-sale	
securities	$ 4,000

Income Statement

Other revenues and gains	
Unrealized gain on trading securities	$ 5,000

▌ PRACTICE PROBLEM

In its first year of operations, DeMarco Company had the following selected transactions in stock investments that are considered trading securities.

Journalize transactions and prepare adjusting entry to record fair value.

(LO 2, 3)

June 1   Purchased for cash 600 shares of Sanburg common stock at $24 per share.

July 1   Purchased for cash 800 shares of Cey Corporation common stock at $33 per share.

Sept. 1   Received a $1 per share cash dividend from Cey Corporation.

Nov. 1   Sold 200 shares of Sanburg common stock for cash at $27 per share.

Dec. 15 Received a $0.50 per share cash dividend on Sanburg common stock.

At December 31, the fair values per share were Sanburg $25 and Cey $30.

Instructions

(a) Journalize the transactions.

(b) Prepare the adjusting entry at December 31 to report the securities at fair value.

Solution

(a)			
June 1	Stock Investments	14,400	
	Cash (600 × $24)		14,400
	(To record purchase of 600 shares of		
	Sanburg common stock)		
July 1	Stock Investments	26,400	
	Cash (800 × $33)		26,400
	(To record purchase of 800 shares of		
	Cey common stock)		
Sept. 1	Cash (800 × $1.00)	800	
	Dividend Revenue		800
	(To record receipt of $1 per share cash		
	dividend from Cey Corporation)		
Nov. 1	Cash (200 × $27)	5,400	
	Stock Investments (200 × $24)		4,800
	Gain on Sale of Stock Investments		600
	(To record sale of 200 shares of Sanburg		
	common stock)		

Dec. 15	Cash [(600 − 200) × $0.50]	200	
	Dividend Revenue		200
	(To record receipt of $0.50 per share dividend from Sanburg)		
(b) Dec. 31	Unrealized Loss—Income	2,000	
	Fair Value Adjustment—Trading		2,000
	(To record unrealized loss on trading securities)		

Investment	Cost	Fair Value	Unrealized Gain (Loss)
Sanburg common stock	$ 9,600[a]	$10,000[b]	$ 400
Cey common stock	26,400[c]	24,000[d]	(2,400)
Total	$36,000	$34,000	$(2,000)

[a]400 × $24; [b]400 × $25; [c]800 × $33; [d]800 × $30

WileyPLUS

Brief Exercises, Exercises, **DO IT!** Exercises, and Problems and many additional resources are available for practice in WileyPLUS

NOTE: All asterisked Questions, Exercises, and Problems relate to material in the appendix to the chapter.

QUESTIONS

1. What are the reasons that corporations invest in securities?

2. (a) What is the cost of an investment in bonds? (b) When is interest on bonds recorded?

3. Alex Ramirez is confused about losses and gains on the sale of debt investments. Explain to Alex (a) how the gain or loss is computed, and (b) the statement presentation of the gains and losses.

4. Seibel Company sells Mayo's bonds costing $40,000 for $45,000. Seibel records a $5,000 gain on this sale. Is this correct? Explain.

5. What is the cost of an investment in stock?

6. To acquire Peoples Corporation stock, J. Rich pays $62,000 in cash. What entry should be made for this investment?

7. (a) When should a long-term investment in common stock be accounted for by the equity method? (b) When is revenue recognized under this method?

8. Ling Corporation uses the equity method to account for its ownership of 35% of the common stock of Gorman Packing. During 2017, Gorman reported a net income of $80,000 and declares and pays cash dividends of $10,000. What recognition should Ling Corporation give to these events?

9. What constitutes "significant influence" when an investor's financial interest is below the 50% level?

10. Distinguish between the cost and equity methods of accounting for investments in stocks.

11. What are consolidated financial statements?

12. What are the classification guidelines for investments at a balance sheet date?

13. Jill Hollern is the controller of Chavez Inc. At December 31, the company's investments in trading securities cost $74,000. They have a fair value of $72,000. Indicate how Jill would report these data in the financial statements prepared on December 31.

14. Using the data in Question 13, how would Jill report the data if the investments were long-term and the securities were classified as available-for-sale?

15. Culver Company's investments in available-for-sale securities at December 31 show total cost of $195,000 and total fair value of $205,000. Prepare the adjusting entry.

16. Using the data in Question 15, prepare the adjusting entry assuming the securities are classified as trading securities.

17. What is the proper statement presentation of the account Unrealized Loss—Equity?

18. What purposes are served by reporting Unrealized Gain or Loss—Equity in the stockholders' equity section?

19. Deering Wholesale Supply owns stock in Orr Corporation. Deering intends to hold the stock indefinitely because of some negative tax consequences if sold. Should the investment in Orr be classified as a short-term investment? Why or why not?

20. What does Apple state regarding its accounting policy involving consolidated financial statements?

*21. (a) What asset and stockholders' equity balances are eliminated in preparing a consolidated balance sheet for a parent and a wholly owned subsidiary? (b) Why are they eliminated?

*22. Roscoe Company pays $318,000 to purchase all the outstanding common stock of Lia Corporation. At the date of purchase, the net assets of Lia have a book value of $290,000. Roscoe's management allocates $20,000 of the excess cost to undervalued land on the books of Lia. What should be done with the rest of the excess?

BRIEF EXERCISES

BE12-1 Ownbey Corporation purchased debt investments for $52,000 on January 1, 2017. On July 1, 2017, Ownbey received cash interest of $2,340. Journalize the purchase and the receipt of interest. Assume that no interest has been accrued.

Journalize entries for debt investments.
(LO 1)

BE12-2 On August 1, Shaw Company buys 1,000 shares of Estrada common stock for $37,000 cash. On December 1, Shaw sells the stock investments for $40,000 in cash. Journalize the purchase and sale of the common stock.

Journalize entries for stock investments.
(LO 2)

BE12-3 Noler Company owns 25% of Lauer Company. For the current year, Lauer reports net income of $180,000 and declares and pays a $50,000 cash dividend. Record Noler's equity in Lauer's net income and the receipt of dividends from Lauer.

Record transactions under the equity method of accounting.
(LO 2)

BE12-4 The cost of the trading securities of Munoz Company at December 31, 2017, is $64,000. At December 31, 2017, the fair value of the securities is $59,000. Prepare the adjusting entry to record the securities at fair value.

Prepare adjusting entry using fair value.
(LO 3)

BE12-5 For the data presented in BE12-4, show the financial statement presentation of the trading securities and related accounts.

Indicate statement presentation using fair value.
(LO 3)

BE12-6 Godfrey Corporation holds, as a long-term investment, available-for-sale securities costing $72,000. At December 31, 2017, the fair value of the securities is $68,000. Prepare the adjusting entry to record the securities at fair value.

Prepare adjusting entry using fair value.
(LO 3)

BE12-7 For the data presented in BE12-6, show the financial statement presentation of the available-for-sale securities and related accounts. Assume the available-for-sale securities are noncurrent.

Indicate statement presentation using fair value.
(LO 3)

BE12-8 Kruger Corporation has the following long-term investments. (1) Common stock of Eidman Co. (10% ownership) held as available-for-sale securities, cost $108,000, fair value $115,000. (2) Common stock of Pickerill Inc. (30% ownership), cost $210,000, equity $260,000. Prepare the investments section of the balance sheet.

Prepare investments section of balance sheet.
(LO 3)

*BE12-9 Paula Company acquires 100% of the common stock of Shannon Company for $190,000 cash. On the acquisition date, Shannon's ledger shows Common Stock $120,000 and Retained Earnings $70,000. Complete the worksheet for the following accounts: Paula—Investment in Shannon Common Stock, Shannon—Common Stock, and Shannon—Retained Earnings.

Prepare partial consolidated worksheet when cost equals book value.
(LO 4)

*BE12-10 Data for the Paula and Shannon companies are given in BE12-9. Instead of paying $190,000, assume that Paula pays $200,000 to acquire the 100% interest in Shannon Company. Complete the worksheet for the accounts identified in BE12-9 and for the excess of cost over book value.

Prepare partial consolidated worksheet when cost exceeds book value.
(LO 4)

DO IT! Exercises

DO IT! 12-1 Kurtyka Corporation had the following transactions relating to debt investments:

Jan. 1, 2017   Purchased 50 $1,000, 10% Spiller Company bonds for $50,000. Interest is payable annually on January 1.

Dec. 31, 2017   Accrued interest on Spiller Company bonds.
Jan. 1, 2018   Received interest from Spiller Company bonds.
Jan. 1, 2018   Sold 30 Spiller Company bonds for $29,000.

(a) Journalize the transactions, and (b) prepare the adjusting entry for the accrual of interest on December 31, 2017.

Make journal entry for bond purchase and adjusting entry for interest accrual.
(LO 1)

Make journal entries for stock investments.

(LO 2)

DO IT! 12-2 Presented below are two independent situations:

1. Edelman Inc. acquired 10% of the 500,000 shares of common stock of Schuberger Corporation at a total cost of $11 per share on June 17, 2017. On September 3, Schuberger declared and paid a $160,000 dividend. On December 31, Schuberger reported net income of $550,000 for the year.

2. Wen Corporation obtained significant influence over Hunsaker Company by buying 30% of Hunsaker's 100,000 outstanding shares of common stock at a cost of $18 per share on January 1, 2017. On May 15, Hunsaker declared and paid a cash dividend of $150,000. On December 31, Hunsaker reported net income of $270,000 for the year.

Prepare all necessary journal entries for 2017 for (a) Edelman and (b) Wen.

Make journal entries for trading and available-for-sale securities.

(LO 3)

DO IT! 12-3a Some of Tollakson Corporation's investment securities are classified as trading securities and some are classified as available-for-sale. The cost and fair value of each category at December 31, 2017, were as follows.

	Cost	Fair Value	Unrealized Gain (Loss)
Trading securities	$96,300	$84,900	$(11,400)
Available-for-sale securities	$59,000	$63,200	$ 4,200

At December 31, 2016, the Fair Value Adjustment—Trading account had a debit balance of $3,200, and the Fair Value Adjustment—Available-for-Sale account had a credit balance of $5,750. Prepare the required journal entries for each group of securities for December 31, 2017.

Indicate financial statement presentation of investments.

(LO 3)

DO IT! 12-3b Identify where each of the following items would be reported in the financial statements.

1. Loss on sale of investments in stock.
2. Unrealized gain on available-for-sale securities.
3. Fair value adjustment—trading.
4. Interest earned on investments in bonds.
5. Unrealized loss on trading securities.

Use the following possible categories:

Balance sheet:

Current assets	Current liabilities
Investments	Long-term liabilities
Property, plant, and equipment	Stockholders' equity
Intangible assets	

Income statement:

Other revenues and gains	Other expenses and losses

EXERCISES

Understand debt and stock investments.

(LO 1)

E12-1 Mr. Taliaferro is studying for an accounting test and has developed the questions below about investments.

1. What are three reasons why companies purchase investments in debt or stock securities?
2. Why would a corporation have excess cash that it does not need for operations?
3. What is the typical investment when investing cash for short periods of time?
4. What are the typical investments when investing cash to generate earnings?
5. Why would a company invest in securities that provide no current cash flows?
6. What is the typical stock investment when investing cash for strategic reasons?

Instructions

Provide answers for Mr. Taliaferro.

Journalize debt investment transactions and accrue interest.

(LO 1)

E12-2 Jenek Corporation had the following transactions pertaining to debt investments.

1. Purchased 50 9%, $1,000 Leeds Co. bonds for $50,000 cash. Interest is payable annually on January 1, 2017.
2. Accrued interest on Leeds Co. bonds on December 31, 2017.
3. Received interest on Leeds Co. bonds on January 1, 2018.
4. Sold 30 Leeds Co. bonds for $33,000 on January 1, 2018.

Instructions
Journalize the transactions.

E12-3 Flynn Company purchased 70 Rinehart Company 6%, 10-year, $1,000 bonds on January 1, 2017 for $70,000. The bonds pay interest annually on January 1. On January 1, 2018, after receipt of interest, Flynn Company sold 40 of the bonds for $38,500.

Journalize debt investment transactions, accrue interest, and record sale.

(LO 1)

Instructions
Prepare the journal entries to record the transactions described above.

E12-4 Hulse Company had the following transactions pertaining to stock investments.

Feb.	1	Purchased 600 shares of Wade common stock (2%) for $7,200 cash.
July	1	Received cash dividends of $1 per share on Wade common stock.
Sept.	1	Sold 300 shares of Wade common stock for $4,300.
Dec.	1	Received cash dividends of $1 per share on Wade common stock.

Journalize stock investment transactions.

(LO 2)

Instructions
(a) Journalize the transactions.
(b) Explain how dividend revenue and the gain (loss) on sale should be reported in the income statement.

E12-5 Nosker Inc. had the following transactions pertaining to investments in common stock.

Jan.	1	Purchased 2,500 shares of Escalante Corporation common stock (5%) for $152,000 cash.
July	1	Received a cash dividend of $3 per share.
Dec.	1	Sold 500 shares of Escalante Corporation common stock for $32,000 cash.
Dec.	31	Received a cash dividend of $3 per share.

Journalize transactions for investments in stocks.

(LO 2)

Instructions
Journalize the transactions.

E12-6 On February 1, Rinehart Company purchased 500 shares (2% ownership) of Givens Company common stock for $32 per share. On March 20, Rinehart Company sold 100 shares of Givens stock for $2,900. Rinehart received a dividend of $1.00 per share on April 25. On June 15, Rinehart sold 200 shares of Givens stock for $7,600. On July 28, Rinehart received a dividend of $1.25 per share.

Journalize transactions for investments in stocks.

(LO 2)

Instructions
Prepare the journal entries to record the transactions described above.

E12-7 On January 1, Zabel Corporation purchased a 25% equity in Helbert Corporation for $180,000. At December 31, Helbert declared and paid a $60,000 cash dividend and reported net income of $200,000.

Journalize and post transactions, under the equity method.

(LO 2)

Instructions
(a) Journalize the transactions.
(b) Determine the amount to be reported as an investment in Helbert stock at December 31.

E12-8 Presented below are two independent situations.

1. Gambino Cosmetics acquired 10% of the 200,000 shares of common stock of Nevins Fashion at a total cost of $13 per share on March 18, 2017. On June 30, Nevins declared and paid a $60,000 dividend. On December 31, Nevins reported net income of $122,000 for the year. At December 31, the market price of Nevins Fashion was $15 per share. The stock is classified as available-for-sale.
2. Kanza, Inc., obtained significant influence over Rogan Corporation by buying 40% of Rogan's 30,000 outstanding shares of common stock at a total cost of $9 per share on January 1, 2017. On June 15, Rogan declared and paid a cash dividend of $30,000. On December 31, Rogan reported a net income of $80,000 for the year.

Journalize entries under cost and equity methods.

(LO 2, 3)

Instructions
Prepare all the necessary journal entries for 2017 for (a) Gambino Cosmetics and (b) Kanza, Inc.

E12-9 Agee Company purchased 70% of the outstanding common stock of Himes Corporation.

Understand the usefulness of consolidated statements.

(LO 2)

Instructions
(a) Explain the relationship between Agee Company and Himes Corporation.
(b) How should Agee account for its investment in Himes?
(c) Why is the accounting treatment described in (b) useful?

Prepare adjusting entry to record fair value, and indicate statement presentation.

(LO 3)

E12-10 At December 31, 2017, the trading securities for Storrer, Inc. are as follows.

Security	Cost	Fair Value
A	$17,500	$16,000
B	12,500	14,000
C	23,000	21,000
	$53,000	$51,000

Instructions
(a) Prepare the adjusting entry at December 31, 2017, to report the securities at fair value.
(b) Show the balance sheet and income statement presentation at December 31, 2017, after adjustment to fair value.

Prepare adjusting entry to record fair value, and indicate statement presentation.

(LO 3)

E12-11 Data for investments in stock classified as trading securities are presented in E12-10. Assume instead that the investments are classified as available-for-sale securities. They have the same cost and fair value. The securities are considered to be a long-term investment.

Instructions
(a) Prepare the adjusting entry at December 31, 2017, to report the securities at fair value.
(b) Show the statement presentation at December 31, 2017, after adjustment to fair value.
(c) ✎ E. Kretsinger, a member of the board of directors, does not understand the reporting of the unrealized gains or losses. Write a letter to Ms. Kretsinger explaining the reporting and the purposes that it serves.

Prepare adjusting entries for fair value, and indicate statement presentation for two classes of securities.

(LO 3)

E12-12 Uttinger Company has the following data at December 31, 2017.

Securities	Cost	Fair Value
Trading	$120,000	$126,000
Available-for-sale	100,000	96,000

The available-for-sale securities are held as a long-term investment.

Instructions
(a) Prepare the adjusting entries to report each class of securities at fair value.
(b) Indicate the statement presentation of each class of securities and the related unrealized gain (loss) accounts.

Prepare consolidated worksheet when cost exceeds book value.

(LO 4)

*****E12-13** On January 1, 2017, Lennon Corporation acquires 100% of Ono Inc. for $220,000 in cash. The condensed balance sheets of the two corporations immediately following the acquisition are shown below.

	Lennon Corporation	Ono Inc.
Current assets	$ 60,000	$ 50,000
Investment in Ono Inc. common stock	220,000	
Plant and equipment (net)	300,000	220,000
	$580,000	$270,000
Current liabilities	$180,000	$ 50,000
Common stock	230,000	80,000
Retained earnings	170,000	140,000
	$580,000	$270,000

Instructions
Prepare a worksheet for a consolidated balance sheet.

*E12-14 Data for the Lennon and Ono corporations are presented in E12-13. Assume that instead of paying $220,000 in cash for Ono Inc., Lennon Corporation pays $225,000 in cash. Thus, at the acquisition date, the assets of Lennon Corporation are current assets $55,000, investment in Ono Inc. common stock $225,000, and plant and equipment (net) $300,000.

Prepare consolidated worksheet when cost exceeds book value.

(LO 4)

Instructions
Prepare a worksheet for a consolidated balance sheet.

EXERCISES: SET B AND CHALLENGE EXERCISES

Visit the book's companion website, at **www.wiley.com/college/weygandt**, and choose the Student Companion site to access Exercises: Set B and Challenge Exercises.

PROBLEMS: SET A

P12-1A Vilander Carecenters Inc. provides financing and capital to the healthcare industry, with a particular focus on nursing homes for the elderly. The following selected transactions relate to bonds acquired as an investment by Vilander, whose fiscal year ends on December 31.

Journalize debt investment transactions and show financial statement presentation.

(LO 1, 3)

2017

Jan. 1   Purchased at face value $2,000,000 of Javier Nursing Centers, Inc., 10-year, 8% bonds dated January 1, 2017, directly from Javier.

Dec. 31   Accrual of interest at year-end on the Javier bonds.

(Assume that all intervening transactions and adjustments have been properly recorded and that the number of bonds owned has not changed from December 31, 2017, to December 31, 2019.)

2020

Jan. 1   Received the annual interest on the Javier bonds.

Jan. 1   Sold $1,000,000 Javier bonds at 106.

Dec. 31   Accrual of interest at year-end on the Javier bonds.

Instructions
(a) Journalize the listed transactions for the years 2017 and 2020.
(b) Assume that the fair value of the bonds at December 31, 2017, was $2,200,000. These bonds are classified as available-for-sale securities. Prepare the adjusting entry to record these bonds at fair value.
(c) Based on your analysis in part (b), show the balance sheet presentation of the bonds and interest receivable at December 31, 2017. Assume the investments are considered long-term. Indicate where any unrealized gain or loss is reported in the financial statements.

(a) Gain on sale of debt investment $60,000

P12-2A In January 2017, the management of Kinzie Company concludes that it has sufficient cash to permit some short-term investments in debt and stock securities. During the year, the following transactions occurred.

Journalize investment transactions, prepare adjusting entry, and show statement presentation.

(LO 1, 2, 3)

Feb. 1   Purchased 600 shares of Muninger common stock for $32,400.

Mar. 1   Purchased 800 shares of Tatman common stock for $20,000.

Apr. 1   Purchased 50 $1,000, 7% Yoakem bonds for $50,000. Interest is payable semiannually on April 1 and October 1.

July 1   Received a cash dividend of $0.60 per share on the Muninger common stock.

Aug. 1   Sold 200 shares of Muninger common stock at $58 per share.

Sept. 1   Received a $1 per share cash dividend on the Tatman common stock.

Oct. 1   Received the semiannual interest on the Yoakem bonds.

Oct. 1   Sold the Yoakem bonds for $49,000.

At December 31, the fair value of the Muninger common stock was $55 per share. The fair value of the Tatman common stock was $24 per share.

(a) Gain on sale of stock
investment $800

Instructions

(a) Journalize the transactions and post to the accounts Debt Investments and Stock Investments. (Post in T-account form.)

(b) Prepare the adjusting entry at December 31, 2017, to report the investments at fair value. All securities are considered to be trading securities.

(c) Show the balance sheet presentation of investments at December 31, 2017.

(d) Identify the income statement accounts and give the statement classification of each account.

Journalize transactions and adjusting entry for stock investments

(LO 2, 3)

P12-3A On December 31, 2017, Turnball Associates owned the following securities, held as a long-term investment. The securities are not held for influence or control of the investee.

Common Stock	Shares	Cost
Gehring Co.	2,000	$60,000
Wooderson Co.	5,000	45,000
Kitselton Co.	1,500	30,000

On December 31, 2017, the total fair value of the securities was equal to its cost. In 2018, the following transactions occurred.

Aug. 1   Received $0.50 per share cash dividend on Gehring Co. common stock.
Sept. 1   Sold 1,500 shares of Wooderson Co. common stock for cash at $8 per share.
Oct. 1   Sold 800 shares of Gehring Co. common stock for cash at $33 per share.
Nov. 1   Received $1 per share cash dividend on Kitselton Co. common stock.
Dec. 15   Received $0.50 per share cash dividend on Gehring Co. common stock.
     31   Received $1 per share annual cash dividend on Wooderson Co. common stock.

At December 31, the fair values per share of the common stocks were Gehring Co. $32, Wooderson Co. $8, and Kitselton Co. $18.

Instructions

(a) Journalize the 2018 transactions and post to the account Stock Investments. (Post in T-account form.)

(b) Unrealized loss $4,100

(b) Prepare the adjusting entry at December 31, 2018, to show the securities at fair value. The stock should be classified as available-for-sale securities.

(c) Show the balance sheet presentation of the investment-related accounts at December 31, 2018. At this date, Turnball Associates has common stock $1,500,000 and retained earnings $1,000,000.

Prepare entries under the cost and equity methods, and tabulate differences.

(LO 2)

P12-4A Heidebrecht Design acquired 20% of the outstanding common stock of Quayle Company on January 1, 2017, by paying $800,000 for the 30,000 shares. Quayle declared and paid $0.30 per share cash dividends on March 15, June 15, September 15, and December 15, 2017. Quayle reported net income of $320,000 for the year. At December 31, 2017, the market price of Quayle common stock was $34 per share.

Instructions

(a) Total dividend revenue $36,000

(a) Prepare the journal entries for Heidebrecht Design for 2017 assuming Heidebrecht Design cannot exercise significant influence over Quayle. Use the cost method and assume that Quayle common stock should be classified as a trading security.

(b) Revenue from stock investments $64,000

(b) Prepare the journal entries for Heidebrecht Design for 2017 assuming Heidebrecht Design can exercise significant influence over Quayle. Use the equity method.

(c) Indicate the balance sheet and income statement account balances at December 31, 2017, under each method of accounting.

Journalize stock investment transactions and show statement presentation.

(LO 2, 3)

P12-5A The following securities are in Frederick Company's portfolio of long-term available-for-sale securities at December 31, 2017.

	Cost
1,000 shares of Willhite Corporation common stock	$52,000
1,400 shares of Hutcherson Corporation common stock	84,000
1,200 shares of Downing Corporation preferred stock	33,600

On December 31, 2017, the total cost of the portfolio equaled total fair value. Frederick had the following transactions related to the securities during 2018.

Jan. 20   Sold all 1,000 shares of Willhite Corporation common stock at $55 per share.

28   Purchased 400 shares of $70 par value common stock of Liggett Corporation at $78 per share.

30   Received a cash dividend of $1.15 per share on Hutcherson Corporation common stock.

Feb. 8   Received cash dividends of $0.40 per share on Downing Corporation preferred stock.

18   Sold all 1,200 shares of Downing Corp. preferred stock at $27 per share.

July 30   Received a cash dividend of $1.00 per share on Hutcherson Corporation common stock.

Sept. 6   Purchased an additional 900 shares of $10 par value common stock of Liggett Corporation at $82 per share.

Dec. 1   Received a cash dividend of $1.50 per share on Liggett Corporation common stock.

At December 31, 2018, the fair values of the securities were:

Hutcherson Corporation common stock	$64 per share
Liggett Corporation common stock	$72 per share

Instructions

(a) Prepare journal entries to record the transactions.

(b) Post to the investment accounts. (Use T-accounts.)

(c) Prepare the adjusting entry at December 31, 2018 to report the portfolio at fair value.

(d) Show the balance sheet presentation at December 31, 2018, for the investment-related accounts.

(a) Loss on sale of stock investment $1,200

(c) Unrealized loss $5,800

P12-6A The following data, presented in alphabetical order, are taken from the records of Nieto Corporation.

Prepare a balance sheet.

(LO 3)

Accounts payable	$ 260,000
Accounts receivable	140,000
Accumulated depreciation—buildings	180,000
Accumulated depreciation—equipment	52,000
Allowance for doubtful accounts	6,000
Bonds payable (10%, due 2025)	500,000
Buildings	950,000
Cash	62,000
Common stock ($10 par value; 500,000 shares authorized, 150,000 shares issued)	1,500,000
Dividends payable	80,000
Equipment	275,000
Fair value adjustment—available-for-sale securities (Dr)	8,000
Goodwill	200,000
Income taxes payable	120,000
Inventory	170,000
Investment in Mara common stock (30% ownership), at equity	380,000
Investment in Sasse common stock (10% ownership), at cost	278,000
Land	390,000
Notes payable (due 2018)	70,000
Paid-in capital in excess of par—common stock	130,000
Premium on bonds payable	40,000
Prepaid insurance	16,000
Retained earnings	103,000
Short-term investments, at fair value (and cost)	180,000
Unrealized gain—available-for-sale securities	8,000

The investment in Sasse common stock is considered to be a long-term available-for-sale security.

Instructions

Prepare a classified balance sheet at December 31, 2017.

Total assets $2,811,000

Prepare consolidated worksheet and balance sheet when cost exceeds book value.

(LO 4)

*P12-7A Robinson Corporation purchased all the outstanding common stock of Hoffman Plastics, Inc. on December 31, 2017. Just before the purchase, the condensed balance sheets of the two companies appeared as follows.

	Robinson Corporation	Hoffman Plastics, Inc.
Current assets	$1,480,000	$ 435,500
Plant and equipment (net)	2,100,000	676,000
	$3,580,000	$1,111,500
Current liabilities	$ 578,000	$ 92,500
Common stock	1,950,000	525,000
Retained earnings	1,052,000	494,000
	$3,580,000	$1,111,500

Robinson used current assets of $1,225,000 to acquire the stock of Hoffman Plastics. The excess of this purchase price over the book value of Hoffman Plastics' net assets is determined to be attributable $86,000 to Hoffman Plastics' plant and equipment and the remainder to goodwill.

Instructions
(a) Prepare the entry for Robinson's acquisition of Hoffman Plastics, Inc. stock.

(b) Excess of cost over book value $120,000

(b) Prepare a consolidated worksheet at December 31, 2017.
(c) Prepare a consolidated balance sheet at December 31, 2017.

PROBLEMS: SET B AND SET C

Visit the book's companion website, at **www.wiley.com/college/weygandt**, and choose the Student Companion site to access Problems: Set B and Set C.

COMPREHENSIVE PROBLEM: CHAPTERS 11 TO 12

CP12 Part I   Debby Kauffman and her two colleagues, Jamie Hiatt and Ella Rincon, are personal trainers at an upscale health spa/resort in Tampa, Florida. They want to start a health club that specializes in health plans for people in the 50+ age range. The growing population in this age range and strong consumer interest in the health benefits of physical activity have convinced them they can profitably operate their own club. In addition to many other decisions, they need to determine what type of business organization they want. Jamie believes there are more advantages to the corporate form than a partnership, but he hasn't yet convinced Debby and Ella. They have come to you, a small-business consulting specialist, seeking information and advice regarding the choice of starting a partnership versus a corporation.

Instructions
(a) ⊷————— Prepare a memo (dated May 26, 2016) that describes the advantages and disadvantages of both partnerships and corporations. Advise Debby, Jamie, and Ella regarding which organizational form you believe would better serve their purposes. Make sure to include reasons supporting your advice.

Part II   After deciding to incorporate, each of the three investors receives 20,000 shares of $2 par common stock on June 12, 2016, in exchange for their co-owned building ($200,000 fair value) and $100,000 total cash they contributed to the business. The next decision that Debby, Jamie, and Ella need to make is how to obtain financing for renovation and equipment. They understand the difference between equity securities and debt securities, but do not understand the tax, net income, and earnings per share consequences of equity versus debt financing on the future of their business.

Instructions
(b) Prepare notes for a discussion with the three entrepreneurs in which you will compare the consequences of using equity versus debt financing. As part of your notes, show the differences in interest and tax expense assuming $1,400,000 is financed with common stock, and then alternatively with debt. Assume that when common stock is used, 140,000 shares will be issued. When debt is used, assume the interest rate on debt is 9%, the tax rate is 32%, and income before interest and taxes is $300,000. (You may want to use a computer spreadsheet.)

Part III   During the discussion about financing, Ella mentions that one of her clients, Timothy Hansen, has approached her about buying a significant interest in the new club. Having an interested investor sways the three to issue equity securities to provide the financing they need. On July 21, 2016, Mr. Hansen buys 90,000 shares at a price of $10 per share.

The club, LifePath Fitness, opens on January 12, 2017, and after a slow start begins to produce the revenue desired by the owners. The owners decide to pay themselves a stock dividend since cash has been less than abundant since they opened their doors. The 10% stock dividend is declared by the owners on July 27, 2017. The market price of the stock is $3 on the declaration date. The date of record is July 31, 2017 (there have been no changes in stock ownership since the initial issuance), and the issue date is August 15, 2017. By the middle of the fourth quarter of 2017, the cash flow of LifePath Fitness has improved to the point that the owners feel ready to pay themselves a cash dividend. They declare a $0.05 cash dividend on December 4, 2017. The record date is December 14, 2017, and the payment date is December 24, 2017.

Instructions

(c) (1) Record all of the transactions related to the common stock of LifePath Fitness during the years 2016 and 2017. (2) Indicate how many shares are issued and outstanding after the stock dividend is issued.

Part IV Since the club opened, a major concern has been the pool facilities. Although the existing pool is adequate, Debby, Jamie, and Ella all desire to make LifePath a cutting-edge facility. Until the end of 2017, financing concerns prevented this improvement. However, because there has been steady growth in clientele, revenue, and income since the third quarter of 2017, the owners have explored possible financing options. They are hesitant to issue stock and change the ownership mix because they have been able to work together as a team with great effectiveness. They have formulated a plan to issue secured term bonds to raise the needed $600,000 for the pool facilities. By the end of December 2017, everything was in place for the bond issue to go ahead. On January 1, 2018, the bonds were issued for $548,000. The bonds pay annual interest of 6% on January 1 of each year. The bonds mature in 10 years, and amortization is computed using the straight-line method.

Instructions

(d) Record (1) the issuance of the secured bonds, (2) the adjusting entry required at December 31, 2018, (3) the interest payment made on January 1, 2019 and (4) the interest accrual on December 31, 2019.

Part V Mr. Hansen's purchase of the stock of LifePath Fitness was done through his business. The stock investment has always been accounted for using the cost method on his firm's books. However, early in 2019 he decided to take his company public. He is preparing an IPO (initial public offering), and he needs to have the firm's financial statements audited. One of the issues to be resolved is to restate the stock investment in LifePath Fitness using the equity method since Mr. Hansen's ownership percentage is greater than 20%.

Instructions

(e) (1) Give the entries that would have been made on Hansen's books if the equity method of accounting for investments had been used from the initial investment through 2018. Assume the following data for LifePath.

	2016	2017	2018
Net income	$30,000	$70,000	$105,000
Total cash dividends	$ 2,100	$20,000	$ 50,000

(2) Compute the balance in the Stock Investments account (as it relates to LifePath Fitness) at the end of 2018.

CONTINUING PROBLEM

COOKIE CREATIONS

(*Note:* This is a continuation of the Cookie Creations problem from Chapters 1 through 11.)

CC12 Natalie has been approached by Ken Thornton, a shareholder of The Beanery Coffee Inc. Ken wants to retire and would like to sell his 1,000 shares in The Beanery, which represent 30% of all shares issued. The Beanery is currently operated by Ken's twin daughters, who each own 35% of the common shares. The Beanery not only operates a coffee shop but also roasts and sells beans to retailers under the name "Rocky Mountain Beanery."

Ken has met with Curtis and Natalie to discuss the business operation. All have concluded that there would be many advantages for Cookie & Coffee Creations Inc. to acquire an interest in The Beanery Coffee. Despite the apparent advantages, however, Natalie and Curtis are still not convinced that they should participate in this business venture.

© leungchopan/
Shutterstock

Go to the book's companion website, **www.wiley.com/college/weygandt**, *to see the completion of this problem.*

FINANCIAL REPORTING AND ANALYSIS

Financial Reporting Problem: Apple Inc.

BYP12-1 The annual report of Apple Inc. is presented in Appendix A. Instructions for accessing and using the company's complete annual report, including the notes to the financial statements, are also provided in Appendix A.

Instructions
(a) Determine the percentage increase for (1) short-term marketable securities from 2012 to 2013, and (2) long-term marketable securities from 2012 to 2013.
(b) Using Apple's consolidated statement of cash flows, determine:
   (1) Purchases of marketable securities during the current year.
   (2) How much was spent for business acquisitions, net of cash acquired during the current year.

Comparative Analysis Problem:
PepsiCo, Inc. vs. The Coca-Cola Company

BYP12-2 PepsiCo's financial statements are presented in Appendix B. Financial statements of The Coca-Cola Company are presented in Appendix C. Instructions for accessing and using the complete annual reports of PepsiCo and Coca-Cola, including the notes to the financial statements, are also provided in Appendices B and C, respectively.

Instructions
(a) Based on the information contained in these financial statements, determine the following for each company.
   (1) Net cash used in investing (investment) activities for the current year (from the statement of cash flows).
   (2) Cash used for capital expenditures during the current year.
(b) Each of PepsiCo's financial statements is labeled "consolidated." What has been consolidated? That is, from the contents of PepsiCo's annual report, identify by name the corporations that have been consolidated (parent and subsidiaries).

Comparative Analysis Problem:
Amazon.com, Inc. vs. Wal-Mart Stores, Inc.

BYP12-3 Amazon.com, Inc.'s financial statements are presented in Appendix D. Financial statements of Wal-Mart Stores, Inc. are presented in Appendix E. Instructions for accessing and using the complete annual reports of Amazon and Wal-Mart, including the notes to the financial statements, are also provided in Appendices D and E, respectively.

Instructions
(a) Based on the information contained in these financial statements, determine the following for each company.
   (1) Net cash used for investing (investment) activities for the current year (from the statement of cash flows).
   (2) Cash used for business acquisitions, net of cash acquired during the current year.
(b) Each of Amazon's financial statements is labeled "consolidated." What has been consolidated? That is, from the contents of Amazon's annual report, identify by name the corporations that have been consolidated (parent and subsidiaries).

Real-World Focus

BYP12-4 Most publicly traded companies are examined by numerous analysts. These analysts often don't agree about a company's future prospects. In this exercise, you will find analysts' ratings about companies and make comparisons over time and across companies in the same industry. You will also see to what extent the analysts experienced "earnings surprises." Earnings surprises can cause changes in stock prices.

Address: **biz.yahoo.com/i**, or go to **www.wiley.com/college/weygandt**

Steps
1. Choose a company.
2. Use the index to find the company's name.
3. Choose **Research**.

Instructions
(a) How many analysts rated the company?
(b) What percentage rated it a strong buy?
(c) What was the average rating for the week?
(d) Did the average rating improve or decline relative to the previous week?

CRITICAL THINKING

Decision-Making Across the Organization

BYP12-5 At the beginning of the question-and-answer portion of the annual stockholders' meeting of Neosho Corporation, stockholder John Linton asks, "Why did management sell the holdings in JMB Company at a loss when this company has been very profitable during the period Neosho held its stock?"

Since president Tony Cedeno has just concluded his speech on the recent success and bright future of Neosho, he is taken aback by this question and responds, "I remember we paid $1,300,000 for that stock some years ago. I am sure we sold that stock at a much higher price. You must be mistaken."

Linton retorts, "Well, right here in footnote number 7 to the annual report it shows that 240,000 shares, a 30% interest in JMB, were sold on the last day of the year. Also, it states that JMB earned $520,000 this year and paid out $160,000 in cash dividends. Further, a summary statement indicates that in past years, while Neosho held JMB stock, JMB earned $1,240,000 and paid out $440,000 in dividends. Finally, the income statement for this year shows a loss on the sale of JMB stock of $180,000. So, I doubt that I am mistaken."

Red-faced, president Cedeno turns to you.

Instructions
With the class divided into groups, answer the following.

(a) What dollar amount did Neosho receive upon the sale of the JMB stock?
(b) Explain why both stockholder Linton and president Cedeno are correct.

Communication Activity

BYP12-6 Fegan Corporation has purchased two securities for its portfolio. The first is a stock investment in Plummer Corporation, one of its suppliers. Fegan purchased 10% of Plummer with the intention of holding it for a number of years, but has no intention of purchasing more shares. The second investment was a purchase of debt securities. Fegan purchased the debt securities because its analysts believe that changes in market interest rates will cause these securities to increase in value in a short period of time. Fegan intends to sell the securities as soon as they have increased in value.

Instructions
Write a memo to Sam Nichols, the chief financial officer, explaining how to account for each of these investments. Explain what the implications for reported income are from this accounting treatment.

Ethics Case

BYP12-7 Harding Financial Services Company holds a large portfolio of debt and stock securities as an investment. The total fair value of the portfolio at December 31, 2017, is greater than total cost. Some securities have increased in value and others have decreased. Ann Bales, the financial vice president, and Kim Reeble, the controller, are in the process of classifying for the first time the securities in the portfolio.

Bales suggests classifying the securities that have increased in value as trading securities in order to increase net income for the year. She wants to classify the securities that have decreased in value as long-term available-for-sale securities, so that the decreases in value will not affect 2017 net income.

Reeble disagrees. She recommends classifying the securities that have decreased in value as trading securities and those that have increased in value as long-term available-for-sale securities. Reeble argues that the company is having a good earnings year and that recognizing the losses now will help to smooth income for this year. Moreover, for future years, when the company may not be as profitable, the company will have built-in gains.

Instructions

(a) Will classifying the securities as Bales and Reeble suggest actually affect earnings as each says it will?

(b) Is there anything unethical in what Bales and Reeble propose? Who are the stakeholders affected by their proposals?

(c) Assume that Bales and Reeble properly classify the portfolio. At year-end, Bales proposes to sell the securities that will increase 2017 net income, and Reeble proposes to sell the securities that will decrease 2017 net income. Is this unethical?

All About You

BYP12-8 The Securities and Exchange Commission (SEC) is the primary regulatory agency of U.S. financial markets. Its job is to ensure that the markets remain fair for all investors. The following SEC sites provide useful information for investors.

Address: **www.sec.gov/answers.shtml** and **http://www.sec.gov/investor/tools/quiz.htm,** or go to **www.wiley.com/college/weygandt**.

Instructions

(a) Go to the first SEC site and find the definition of the following terms.
   (i)   Ask price.
   (ii) Margin.
   (iii) Prospectus.
   (iv) Index fund.

(b) Go to the second SEC site and take the short quiz.

FASB Codification Activity

BYP12-9 If your school has a subscription to the FASB Codification, go to **http://aaahq.org/ ascLogin.cfm** to log in and prepare responses to the following.

(a) What is the definition of a trading security?

(b) What is the definition of an available-for-sale security?

(c) What is the definition of a held-to-maturity security?

A Look at IFRS

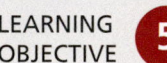

LEARNING OBJECTIVE 5 **Compare the accounting for investments under GAAP and IFRS.**

Until recently, when the IASB issued *IFRS 9*, the accounting and reporting for investments under IFRS and GAAP were for the most part very similar. However, *IFRS 9* introduces a new framework for classifying investments.

Key Points

Following are the similarities and differences between GAAP and IFRS as related to investments.

Similarities

- The basic accounting entries to record the acquisition of debt securities, the receipt of interest, and the sale of debt securities are the same under IFRS and GAAP.

- The basic accounting entries to record the acquisition of stock investments, the receipt of dividends, and the sale of stock securities are the same under IFRS and GAAP.

- Both IFRS and GAAP use the same criteria to determine whether the equity method of accounting should be used—that is, significant influence with a general guide of over 20% ownership, IFRS uses the term **associate investment** rather than equity investment to describe its investment under the equity method.

- Equity investments are generally recorded and reported at fair value under IFRS. Equity investments do not have a fixed interest or principal payment schedule and therefore cannot be accounted for at amortized cost. In general, equity investments are valued at fair value, with all gains and losses reported in income, similar to GAAP.

- Unrealized gains and losses related to available-for-sale securities are reported in other comprehensive income under GAAP and IFRS. These gains and losses that accumulate are then reported in the balance sheet.

Differences

- Under IFRS, both the investor and an associate company should follow the same accounting policies. As a result, in order to prepare financial information, adjustments are made to the associate's policies to conform to the investor's books. GAAP does not have that requirement.

- In general, IFRS requires that companies determine how to measure their financial assets based on two criteria:

  ◆ The company's business model for managing their financial assets; and

  ◆ The contractual cash flow characteristics of the financial asset.

  If a company has (1) a business model whose objective is to hold assets in order to collect contractual cash flows and (2) the contractual terms of the financial asset gives specified dates to cash flows that are solely payments of principal and interest on the principal amount outstanding, then the company should use cost (often referred to as amortized cost).

  For example, assume that Mitsubishi purchases a bond investment that it intends to hold to maturity (held-for-collection). Its business model for this type of investment is to collect interest and then principal at maturity. The payment dates for the interest rate and principal are stated on the bond. In this case, Mitsubishi accounts for the investment at cost. If, on the other hand, Mitsubishi purchased the bonds as part of a trading strategy to speculate on interest rate changes (a trading investment), then the debt investment is reported at fair value. As a result, only debt investments such as receivables, loans, and bond investments that meet the two criteria above are recorded at amortized cost. All other debt investments are recorded and reported at fair value.

Looking to the Future

As indicated earlier, the IASB has issued a new revised IFRS which deals with the accounting issues related to investment securities. The FASB is now in the final process of issuing a new standard in this area. It is likely that some differences will continue to exist between the IFRS and the FASB regarding investments.

IFRS Practice

IFRS Self-Test Questions

1. The following asset is **not** considered a financial asset under IFRS:
   (a) trading securities.
   (b) equity securities.
   (c) held-for-collection securities.
   (d) inventories.

2. Under IFRS, the equity method of accounting for long-term investments in common stock should be used when the investor has significant influence over an investee and owns:
   (a) between 20% and 50% of the investee's common stock.
   (b) 30% or more of the investee's common stock.
   (c) more than 50% of the investee's common stock.
   (d) less than 20% of the investee's common stock.

3. Under IFRS, the unrealized loss on trading investments should be reported:
   (a) as part of other comprehensive loss reducing net income.
   (b) on the income statement reducing net income.
   (c) as part of other comprehensive loss not affecting net income.
   (d) directly to stockholders' equity bypassing the income statement.

Answers to IFRS Self-Test Questions
1. d   **2.** a   **3.** b

13 Statement of Cash Flows

CHAPTER PREVIEW The balance sheet, income statement, and retained earnings statement do not always show the whole picture of the financial condition of a company or institution. In fact, looking at the financial statements of some well-known companies, a thoughtful investor might ask questions like these: How did Eastman Kodak finance cash dividends of $649 million in a year in which it earned only $17 million? How could United Air Lines purchase new planes that cost $1.9 billion in a year in which it reported a net loss of over $2 billion? How did the companies that spent a combined fantastic $3.4 trillion on mergers and acquisitions in a recent year finance those deals? Answers to these and similar questions can be found in this chapter, which presents the statement of cash flows.

FEATURE STORY

Got Cash?

Companies must be ready to respond to changes quickly in order to survive and thrive. This requires careful management of cash. One company that managed cash successfully in its early years was Microsoft. During those years, the company paid much of its payroll with stock options (rights to purchase company stock in the future at a given price) instead of cash. This conserved cash and turned more than a thousand of its employees into millionaires.

In recent years, Microsoft has had a different kind of cash problem. Now that it has reached a more "mature" stage in life, it generates so much cash—roughly $1 billion per month—that it cannot always figure out what to do with it. At one time, Microsoft had accumulated $60 billion.

The company said it was accumulating cash to invest in new opportunities, buy other companies, and pay off pending lawsuits. Microsoft's stockholders complained that holding all this cash was putting a drag on the company's profitability. Why? Because Microsoft had the cash invested in very low-yielding government securities. Stockholders felt that the company either should find new investment projects that would bring higher returns, or return some of the cash to stockholders.

Finally, Microsoft announced a plan to return cash to stockholders by paying a special one-time $32 billion

dividend. This special dividend was so large that, according to the U.S. Commerce Department, it caused total personal income in the United States to rise by 3.7% in one month—the largest increase ever recorded by the agency. (It also made the holiday season brighter, especially for retailers in the Seattle area.) Microsoft also doubled its regular annual dividend to $3.50 per share. Further, it announced that it would spend another $30 billion buying treasury stock.

Apple also has encountered this cash "problem." Recently, Apple had nearly $100 billion in liquid assets (cash, cash equivalents, and investment securities). The company was generating $37 billion of cash per year from its operating activities but spending only about $7 billion on plant assets and purchases of patents. Shareholders pressured Apple to unload some of this cash. In response, Apple announced that it would begin to pay a quarterly dividend of $2.65 per share and it would buy back up to $10 billion of its stock. Analysts noted that the dividend consumes only $10 billion of cash per year. This leaves Apple wallowing in cash. The rest of us should have such problems.

Source: "Business: An End to Growth? Microsoft's Cash Bonanza," *The Economist* (July 23, 2005), p. 61.

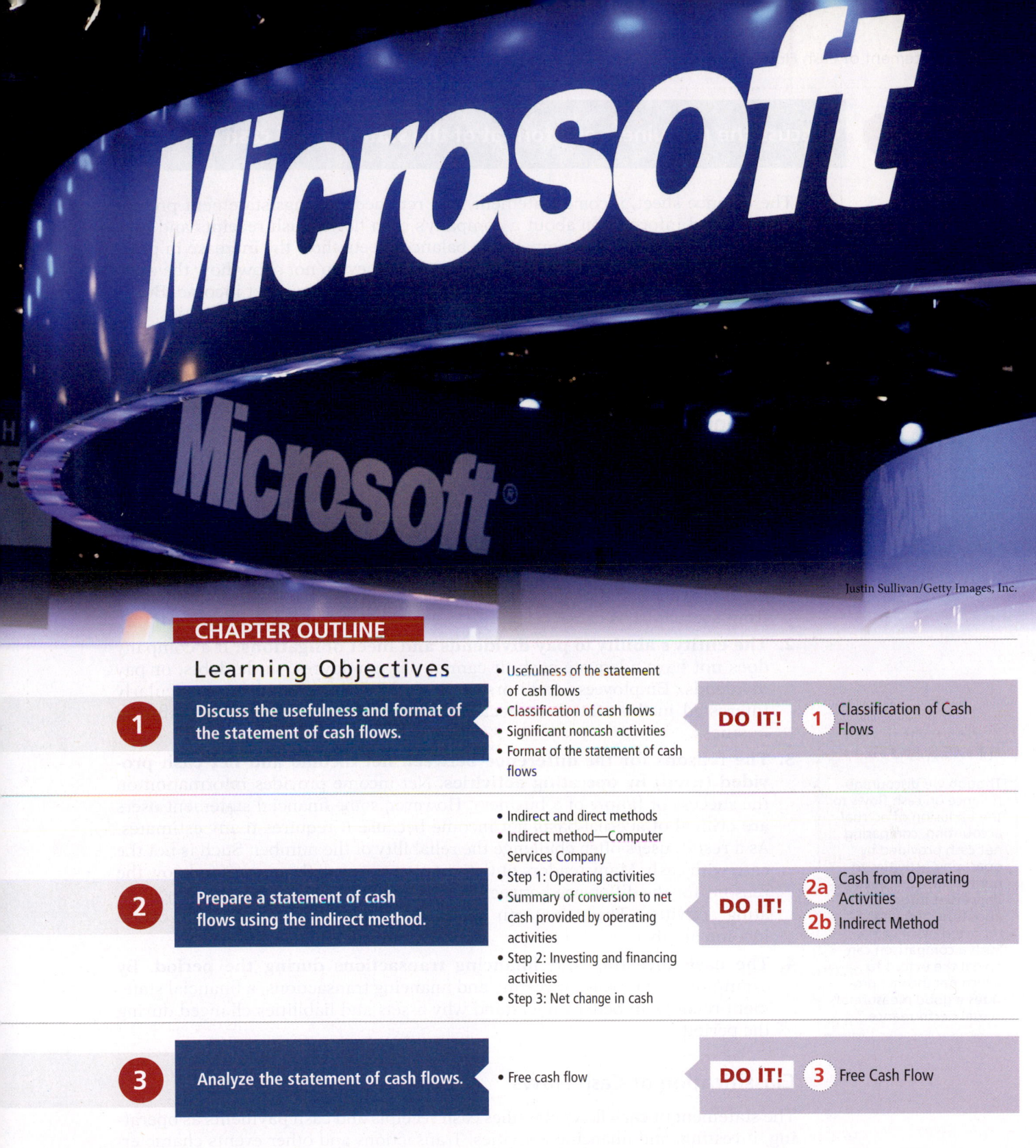

Justin Sullivan/Getty Images, Inc.

CHAPTER OUTLINE

Learning Objectives

1 Discuss the usefulness and format of the statement of cash flows.

- Usefulness of the statement of cash flows
- Classification of cash flows
- Significant noncash activities
- Format of the statement of cash flows

DO IT! **1** Classification of Cash Flows

2 Prepare a statement of cash flows using the indirect method.

- Indirect and direct methods
- Indirect method—Computer Services Company
- Step 1: Operating activities
- Summary of conversion to net cash provided by operating activities
- Step 2: Investing and financing activities
- Step 3: Net change in cash

DO IT! **2a** Cash from Operating Activities
2b Indirect Method

3 Analyze the statement of cash flows.

- Free cash flow

DO IT! **3** Free Cash Flow

Go to the **REVIEW AND PRACTICE** section at the end of the chapter for a review of key concepts and practice applications with solutions.

Visit **WileyPLUS with ORION** for additional tutorials and practice opportunities.

The balance sheet, income statement, and retained earnings statement provide only limited information about a company's cash flows (cash receipts and cash payments). For example, comparative balance sheets show the increase in property, plant, and equipment during the year. But, they do not show how the additions were financed or paid for. The income statement shows net income. But, it does not indicate the amount of cash generated by operating activities. The retained earnings statement shows cash dividends declared but not the cash dividends paid during the year. None of these statements presents a detailed summary of where cash came from and how it was used.

Usefulness of the Statement of Cash Flows

The **statement of cash flows** reports the cash receipts, cash payments, and net change in cash resulting from operating, investing, and financing activities during a period. The information in a statement of cash flows helps investors, creditors, and others assess the following.

1. **The entity's ability to generate future cash flows.** By examining relationships between items in the statement of cash flows, investors can better predict the amounts, timing, and uncertainty of future cash flows than they can from accrual-basis data.

2. **The entity's ability to pay dividends and meet obligations.** If a company does not have adequate cash, it cannot pay employees, settle debts, or pay dividends. Employees, creditors, and stockholders should be particularly interested in this statement because it alone shows the flows of cash in a business.

3. **The reasons for the difference between net income and net cash provided (used) by operating activities.** Net income provides information on the success or failure of a business. However, some financial statement users are critical of accrual-basis net income because it requires many estimates. As a result, users often challenge the reliability of the number. Such is not the case with cash. Many readers of the statement of cash flows want to know the reasons for the difference between net income and net cash provided by operating activities. Then, they can assess for themselves the reliability of the income number.

4. **The cash investing and financing transactions during the period.** By examining a company's investing and financing transactions, a financial statement reader can better understand why assets and liabilities changed during the period.

ETHICS NOTE

Though we discourage reliance on cash flows to the exclusion of accrual accounting, comparing net cash provided by operating activities to net income can reveal important information about the "quality" of reported net income. Such a comparison can reveal the extent to which net income provides a good measure of actual performance.

Classification of Cash Flows

The statement of cash flows classifies cash receipts and cash payments as operating, investing, and financing activities. Transactions and other events characteristic of each kind of activity are as follows.

1. **Operating activities** include the cash effects of transactions that create revenues and expenses. They thus enter into the determination of net income.

2. **Investing activities** include (a) acquiring and disposing of investments and property, plant, and equipment, and (b) lending money and collecting the loans.

3. **Financing activities** include (a) obtaining cash from issuing debt and repaying the amounts borrowed, and (b) obtaining cash from stockholders, repurchasing shares, and paying dividends.

The operating activities category is the most important. It shows the cash provided by company operations. This source of cash is generally considered to be the best measure of a company's ability to generate sufficient cash to continue as a going concern.

Illustration 13-1 lists typical cash receipts and cash payments within each of the three classifications. **Study the list carefully.** It will prove very useful in solving homework exercises and problems.

Illustration 13-1
Typical receipt and payment classifications

TYPES OF CASH INFLOWS AND OUTFLOWS

Operating activities—Income statement items
Cash inflows:
    From sale of goods or services.
    From interest received and dividends received.
Cash outflows:
    To suppliers for inventory.
    To employees for wages.
    To government for taxes.
    To lenders for interest.
    To others for expenses.

Investing activities—Changes in investments and long-term assets
Cash inflows:
    From sale of property, plant, and equipment.
    From sale of investments in debt or equity securities of other entities.
    From collection of principal on loans to other entities.
Cash outflows:
    To purchase property, plant, and equipment.
    To purchase investments in debt or equity securities of other entities.
    To make loans to other entities.

Investing activities

Financing activities—Changes in long-term liabilities and stockholders' equity
Cash inflows:
    From sale of common stock.
    From issuance of debt (bonds and notes).
Cash outflows:
    To stockholders as dividends.
    To redeem long-term debt or reacquire capital stock (treasury stock).

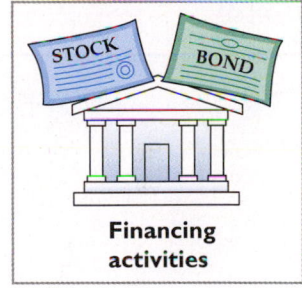

Financing activities

Note the following general guidelines:

1. Operating activities involve income statement items.

2. Investing activities involve cash flows resulting from changes in investments and long-term asset items.

3. Financing activities involve cash flows resulting from changes in long-term liability and stockholders' equity items.

Companies classify as operating activities some cash flows related to investing or financing activities. For example, receipts of investment revenue (interest and dividends) are classified as operating activities. So are payments of interest to lenders. Why are these considered operating activities? **Because companies report these items in the income statement, where results of operations are shown.**

Significant Noncash Activities

Not all of a company's significant activities involve cash. Examples of significant noncash activities are as follows.

1. Direct issuance of common stock to purchase assets.

2. Conversion of bonds into common stock.

3. Direct issuance of debt to purchase assets.

4. Exchanges of plant assets.

Helpful Hint
Do not include noncash investing and financing activities in the body of the statement of cash flows. Report this information in a separate schedule.

Companies do not report in the body of the statement of cash flows significant financing and investing activities that do not affect cash. Instead, they report these activities in either a **separate schedule** at the bottom of the statement of cash flows or in a **separate note or supplementary schedule** to the financial statements. The reporting of these noncash activities in a separate schedule satisfies the **full disclosure principle**.

In solving homework assignments, you should present significant noncash investing and financing activities in a separate schedule at the bottom of the statement of cash flows (see the last entry in Illustration 13-2 below).

Accounting Across the Organization   Target Corporation

Darren McCollester/Getty Images, Inc.

Net *What*?

Net income is not the same as net cash provided by operating activities. Below are some results from recent annual reports (dollars in millions), including Target Corporation. Note how the numbers differ greatly across the list even though all these companies engage in retail merchandising.

Company	Net Income	Net Cash Provided by Operating Activities
Kohl's Corporation	$ 889	$ 1,884
Wal-Mart Stores, Inc.	16,669	25,591
J. C. Penney Company, Inc.	(1,388)	(1,814)
Costco Wholesale Corp.	20,391	3,437
Target Corporation	1,971	6,520

In general, why do differences exist between net income and net cash provided by operating activities? (Go to **WileyPLUS** for this answer and additional questions.)

Format of the Statement of Cash Flows

The general format of the statement of cash flows presents the results of the three activities discussed previously—operating, investing, and financing—plus the significant noncash investing and financing activities. Illustration 13-2 shows a widely used form of the statement of cash flows.

Illustration 13-2
Format of statement of cash flows

COMPANY NAME Statement of Cash Flows For the Period Covered		
Cash flows from operating activities		
(List of individual items)	XX	
Net cash provided (used) by operating activities		XXX
Cash flows from investing activities		
(List of individual inflows and outflows)	XX	
Net cash provided (used) by investing activities		XXX
Cash flows from financing activities		
(List of individual inflows and outflows)	XX	
Net cash provided (used) by financing activities		XXX
Net increase (decrease) in cash		XXX
Cash at beginning of period		XXX
Cash at end of period		XXX
Noncash investing and financing activities		
(List of individual noncash transactions)		XXX

The cash flows from operating activities section always appears first, followed by the investing activities section and then the financing activities section. The sum of the operating, investing, and financing sections equals the net increase or decrease in cash for the period. This amount is added to the beginning cash balance to arrive at the ending cash balance—the same amount reported on the balance sheet.

DO IT! 1   Classification of Cash Flows

Action Plan

✔ Identify the three types of activities used to report all cash inflows and outflows.

During its first week, Duffy & Stevenson Company had these transactions.

1. Issued 100,000 shares of $5 par value common stock for $800,000 cash.
2. Borrowed $200,000 from Castle Bank, signing a 5-year note bearing 8% interest.
3. Purchased two semi-trailer trucks for $170,000 cash.
4. Paid employees $12,000 for salaries and wages.
5. Collected $20,000 cash for services performed.

Classify each of these transactions by type of cash flow activity.

✔ Report as operating activities the cash effects of transactions that create revenues and expenses and enter into the determination of net income.

Solution

1. Financing activity.	4. Operating activity.
2. Financing activity.	5. Operating activity.
3. Investing activity.	

✔ Report as investing activities transactions that (a) acquire and dispose of investments and long-term assets and (b) lend money and collect loans.

Related exercise material: **BE13-1, BE13-2, BE13-3, E13-1, E13-2, E13-3, and DO IT! 13-1.**

✔ Report as financing activities transactions that (a) obtain cash from issuing debt and repay the amounts borrowed and (b) obtain cash from stockholders and pay them dividends.

LEARNING OBJECTIVE **2**   **Prepare a statement of cash flows using the indirect method.**

Companies prepare the statement of cash flows differently from the three other basic financial statements. First, it is not prepared from an adjusted trial balance. It requires detailed information concerning the changes in account balances that occurred between two points in time. An adjusted trial balance will not provide the necessary data. Second, the statement of cash flows deals with cash receipts and payments. As a result, the company **adjusts** the effects of the use of accrual accounting **to determine cash flows**.

The information to prepare this statement usually comes from three sources:

- **Comparative balance sheets.** Information in the comparative balance sheets indicates the amount of the changes in assets, liabilities, and stockholders' equities from the beginning to the end of the period.

- **Current income statement.** Information in this statement helps determine the amount of net cash provided or used by operating activities during the period.

- **Additional information.** Such information includes transaction data that are needed to determine how cash was provided or used during the period.

Preparing the statement of cash flows from these data sources involves three major steps, explained in Illustration 13-3.

Illustration 13-3
Three major steps in preparing the statement of cash flows

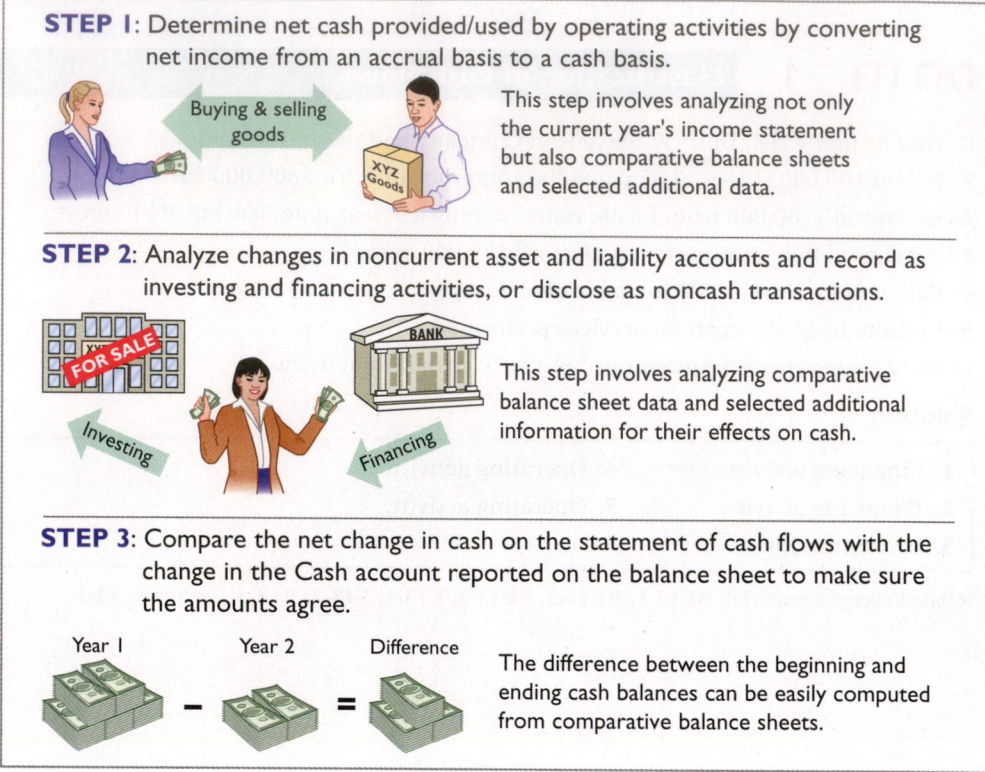

STEP 1: Determine net cash provided/used by operating activities by converting net income from an accrual basis to a cash basis.

Buying & selling goods

This step involves analyzing not only the current year's income statement but also comparative balance sheets and selected additional data.

STEP 2: Analyze changes in noncurrent asset and liability accounts and record as investing and financing activities, or disclose as noncash transactions.

FOR SALE

BANK

Investing

Financing

This step involves analyzing comparative balance sheet data and selected additional information for their effects on cash.

STEP 3: Compare the net change in cash on the statement of cash flows with the change in the Cash account reported on the balance sheet to make sure the amounts agree.

Year 1   Year 2   Difference

The difference between the beginning and ending cash balances can be easily computed from comparative balance sheets.

Indirect and Direct Methods

In order to perform Step 1, a company **must convert net income from an accrual basis to a cash basis**. This conversion may be done by either of two methods: (1) the indirect method or (2) the direct method. **Both methods arrive at the same amount** for "Net cash provided by operating activities." They differ in **how** they arrive at the amount.

The **indirect method** adjusts net income for items that do not affect cash. A great majority of companies use this method. Companies favor the indirect method for two reasons: (1) it is easier and less costly to prepare, and (2) it focuses on the differences between net income and net cash flow from operating activities.

The **direct method** shows operating cash receipts and payments. It is prepared by adjusting each item in the income statement from the accrual basis to the cash basis. The FASB has expressed a preference for the direct method but allows the use of either method.

The next section illustrates the more popular indirect method. Appendix 13A illustrates the direct method.

Indirect Method—Computer Services Company

To explain how to prepare a statement of cash flows using the indirect method, we use financial information from Computer Services Company. Illustration 13-4 presents Computer Services' current- and previous-year balance sheets, its current-year income statement, and related financial information for the current year.

COMPUTER SERVICES COMPANY
Comparative Balance Sheets
December 31

Assets	2017	2016	Change in Account Balance Increase/Decrease
Current assets			
Cash	$ 55,000	$ 33,000	$ 22,000 Increase
Accounts receivable	20,000	30,000	10,000 Decrease
Inventory	15,000	10,000	5,000 Increase
Prepaid expenses	5,000	1,000	4,000 Increase
Property, plant, and equipment			
Land	130,000	20,000	110,000 Increase
Buildings	160,000	40,000	120,000 Increase
Accumulated depreciation—buildings	(11,000)	(5,000)	6,000 Increase
Equipment	27,000	10,000	17,000 Increase
Accumulated depreciation—equipment	(3,000)	(1,000)	2,000 Increase
Total assets	$398,000	$138,000	

Liabilities and Stockholders' Equity

	2017	2016	
Current liabilities			
Accounts payable	$ 28,000	$ 12,000	$ 16,000 Increase
Income taxes payable	6,000	8,000	2,000 Decrease
Long-term liabilities			
Bonds payable	130,000	20,000	110,000 Increase
Stockholders' equity			
Common stock	70,000	50,000	20,000 Increase
Retained earnings	164,000	48,000	116,000 Increase
Total liabilities and stockholders' equity	$398,000	$138,000	

COMPUTER SERVICES COMPANY
Income Statement
For the Year Ended December 31, 2017

Sales revenue		$507,000
Cost of goods sold	$150,000	
Operating expenses (excluding depreciation)	111,000	
Depreciation expense	9,000	
Loss on disposal of equipment	3,000	
Interest expense	42,000	315,000
Income before income tax		192,000
Income tax expense		47,000
Net income		$145,000

Additional information for 2017:
1. Depreciation expense was comprised of $6,000 for building and $3,000 for equipment.
2. The company sold equipment with a book value of $7,000 (cost $8,000, less accumulated depreciation $1,000) for $4,000 cash.
3. Issued $110,000 of long-term bonds in direct exchange for land.
4. A building costing $120,000 was purchased for cash. Equipment costing $25,000 was also purchased for cash.
5. Issued common stock for $20,000 cash.
6. The company declared and paid a $29,000 cash dividend.

We now apply the three steps for preparing a statement of cash flows to the information provided for Computer Services Company.

Step 1: Operating Activities

DETERMINE NET CASH PROVIDED/USED BY OPERATING ACTIVITIES BY CONVERTING NET INCOME FROM AN ACCRUAL BASIS TO A CASH BASIS

To determine net cash provided by operating activities under the indirect method, companies **adjust net income in numerous ways**. A useful starting point is to understand **why** net income must be converted to net cash provided by operating activities.

Under generally accepted accounting principles, most companies use the accrual basis of accounting. This basis requires that companies record revenue when their performance obligation is satisfied and record expenses when incurred. Revenues include credit sales for which the company has not yet collected cash. Expenses incurred include some items that it has not yet paid in cash. Thus, under the accrual basis, net income is not the same as net cash provided by operating activities.

Therefore, under the **indirect method**, companies must adjust net income to convert certain items to the cash basis. The indirect method (or reconciliation method) starts with net income and converts it to net cash provided by operating activities. Illustration 13-5 lists the three types of adjustments.

Illustration 13-5
Three types of adjustments to convert net income to net cash provided by operating activities

Net Income	+/–	Adjustments	=	Net Cash Provided/ Used by Operating Activities

- **Add back noncash expenses**, such as depreciation expense and amortization expense.
- **Deduct gains and add losses** that resulted from investing and financing activities.
- **Analyze changes** to noncash current asset and current liability accounts.

Helpful Hint
Depreciation is similar to any other expense in that it reduces net income. It differs in that it does not involve a current cash outflow. That is why it must be *added back* to net income to arrive at net cash provided by operating activities.

We explain the three types of adjustments in the next three sections.

DEPRECIATION EXPENSE

Computer Services' income statement reports depreciation expense of $9,000. Although depreciation expense reduces net income, it does not reduce cash. In other words, depreciation expense is a noncash charge. The company must add it back to net income to arrive at net cash provided by operating activities. Computer Services reports depreciation expense in the statement of cash flows as shown below.

Illustration 13-6
Adjustment for depreciation

Cash flows from operating activities	
Net income	$145,000
Adjustments to reconcile net income to net cash provided by operating activities:	
Depreciation expense	9,000
Net cash provided by operating activities	$154,000

As the first adjustment to net income in the statement of cash flows, companies frequently list depreciation and similar noncash charges such as amortization of intangible assets, depletion expense, and bad debt expense.

LOSS ON DISPOSAL OF EQUIPMENT

Illustration 13-1 states that cash received from the sale (disposal) of plant assets is reported in the investing activities section. Because of this, **companies eliminate**

from net income all gains and losses related to the disposal of plant assets, to arrive at net cash provided by operating activities.

In our example, Computer Services' income statement reports a $3,000 loss on the disposal of equipment (book value $7,000, less $4,000 cash received from disposal of equipment). The company's loss of $3,000 should not be included in the operating activities section of the statement of cash flows. Illustration 13-7 shows that the $3,000 loss is eliminated by adding $3,000 back to net income to arrive at net cash provided by operating activities.

Illustration 13-7
Adjustment for loss on disposal of equipment

Cash flows from operating activities		
Net income		$145,000
Adjustments to reconcile net income to net cash provided by operating activities:		
Depreciation expense	$9,000	
Loss on disposal of equipment	**3,000**	12,000
Net cash provided by operating activities		$157,000

If a gain on disposal occurs, the company deducts the gain from net income in order to determine net cash provided by operating activities. **In the case of either a gain or a loss, companies report as a source of cash in the investing activities section of the statement of cash flows the actual amount of cash received from the sale.**

CHANGES TO NONCASH CURRENT ASSET AND CURRENT LIABILITY ACCOUNTS

A final adjustment in reconciling net income to net cash provided by operating activities involves examining all changes in current asset and current liability accounts. The accrual-accounting process records revenues in the period in which the performance obligation is satisfied and expenses are incurred. For example, Accounts Receivable reflects amounts owed to the company for sales that have been made but for which cash collections have not yet been received. Prepaid Insurance reflects insurance that has been paid for but which has not yet expired (therefore has not been expensed). Similarly, Salaries and Wages Payable reflects salaries and wages expense that has been incurred but has not been paid.

As a result, companies need to adjust net income for these accruals and prepayments to determine net cash provided by operating activities. Thus, they must analyze the change in each current asset and current liability account to determine its impact on net income and cash.

CHANGES IN NONCASH CURRENT ASSETS. The adjustments required for changes in noncash current asset accounts are as follows. **Deduct from net income increases in current asset accounts, and add to net income decreases in current asset accounts, to arrive at net cash provided by operating activities.** We observe these relationships by analyzing the accounts of Computer Services.

DECREASE IN ACCOUNTS RECEIVABLE Computer Services' accounts receivable decreased by $10,000 (from $30,000 to $20,000) during the period. For Computer Services, this means that cash receipts were $10,000 higher than sales revenue. The Accounts Receivable account in Illustration 13-8 shows that Computer Services had $507,000 in sales revenue (as reported on the income statement), but it collected $517,000 in cash.

Illustration 13-8
Analysis of accounts receivable

		Accounts Receivable		
1/1/17	Balance	30,000	**Receipts from customers**	517,000
	Sales revenue	**507,000**		
12/31/17	Balance	20,000		

As shown in Illustration 13-9 (below), to adjust net income to net cash provided by operating activities, the company adds to net income the decrease of $10,000 in accounts receivable. When the Accounts Receivable balance increases, cash receipts are lower than sales revenue earned under the accrual basis. Therefore, the company deducts from net income the amount of the increase in accounts receivable, to arrive at net cash provided by operating activities.

INCREASE IN INVENTORY Computer Services' inventory increased $5,000 (from $10,000 to $15,000) during the period. The change in the Inventory account reflects the difference between the amount of inventory purchased and the amount sold. For Computer Services, this means that the cost of merchandise purchased exceeded the cost of goods sold by $5,000. As a result, cost of goods sold does not reflect $5,000 of cash payments made for merchandise. The company deducts from net income this inventory increase of $5,000 during the period, to arrive at net cash provided by operating activities (see Illustration 13-9). If inventory decreases, the company adds to net income the amount of the change, to arrive at net cash provided by operating activities.

INCREASE IN PREPAID EXPENSES Computer Services' prepaid expenses increased during the period by $4,000. This means that cash paid for expenses is higher than expenses reported on an accrual basis. In other words, the company has made cash payments in the current period but will not charge expenses to income until future periods (as charges to the income statement). To adjust net income to net cash provided by operating activities, the company deducts from net income the $4,000 increase in prepaid expenses (see Illustration 13-9).

Illustration 13-9
Adjustments for changes in current asset accounts

Cash flows from operating activities		
Net income		$145,000
Adjustments to reconcile net income to net cash provided by operating activities:		
Depreciation expense	$ 9,000	
Loss on disposal of equipment	3,000	
Decrease in accounts receivable	10,000	
Increase in inventory	(5,000)	
Increase in prepaid expenses	(4,000)	13,000
Net cash provided by operating activities		$158,000

If prepaid expenses decrease, reported expenses are higher than the expenses paid. Therefore, the company adds to net income the decrease in prepaid expenses, to arrive at net cash provided by operating activities.

CHANGES IN CURRENT LIABILITIES. The adjustments required for changes in current liability accounts are as follows. **Add to net income increases in current liability accounts and deduct from net income decreases in current liability accounts, to arrive at net cash provided by operating activities.**

INCREASE IN ACCOUNTS PAYABLE For Computer Services, Accounts Payable increased by $16,000 (from $12,000 to $28,000) during the period. That means the company received $16,000 more in goods than it actually paid for. As shown in Illustration 13-10, to adjust net income to determine net cash provided by operating activities, the company adds to net income the $16,000 increase in Accounts Payable.

DECREASE IN INCOME TAXES PAYABLE When a company incurs income tax expense but has not yet paid its taxes, it records income taxes payable. A change in the Income Taxes Payable account reflects the difference between income tax expense incurred and income tax actually paid. Computer Services' Income Taxes Payable account decreased by $2,000. That means the $47,000 of income tax expense reported on the income statement was $2,000 less than the amount of taxes paid during the period of $49,000. As shown in Illustration 13-10, to adjust net income to a cash basis, the company must reduce net income by $2,000.

Cash flows from operating activities		
Net income		$145,000
Adjustments to reconcile net income to net cash		
provided by operating activities:		
Depreciation expense	$ 9,000	
Loss on disposal of equipment	3,000	
Decrease in accounts receivable	10,000	
Increase in inventory	(5,000)	
Increase in prepaid expenses	(4,000)	
Increase in accounts payable	**16,000**	
Decrease in income taxes payable	**(2,000)**	27,000
Net cash provided by operating activities		$172,000

Illustration 13-10
Adjustments for changes in current liability accounts

Illustration 13-10 shows that after starting with net income of $145,000, the sum of all of the adjustments to net income was $27,000. This resulted in net cash provided by operating activities of $172,000.

Summary of Conversion to Net Cash Provided by Operating Activities—Indirect Method

As shown in the previous illustrations, the statement of cash flows prepared by the indirect method starts with net income. It then adds or deducts items to arrive at net cash provided by operating activities. The required adjustments are of three types:

1. Noncash charges such as depreciation and amortization.
2. Gains and losses on the disposal of plant assets.
3. Changes in noncash current asset and current liability accounts.

Illustration 13-11 provides a summary of these changes and required adjustments.

Illustration 13-11
Adjustments required to convert net income to net cash provided by operating activities

		Adjustments Required to Convert Net Income to Net Cash Provided by Operating Activities
Noncash Charges	Depreciation expense	Add
	Amortization expense	Add
Gains and Losses	Loss on disposal of plant assets	Add
	Gain on disposal of plant assets	Deduct
Changes in Current Assets and Current Liabilities	Increase in current asset account	Deduct
	Decrease in current asset account	Add
	Increase in current liability account	Add
	Decrease in current liability account	Deduct

DO IT! 2a   Cash from Operating Activities

Josh's PhotoPlus reported net income of $73,000 for 2017. Included in the income statement were depreciation expense of $7,000 and a gain on disposal of equipment of $2,500. Josh's comparative balance sheets show the following balances.

	12/31/16	12/31/17
Accounts receivable	$17,000	$21,000
Accounts payable	6,000	2,200

Calculate net cash provided by operating activities for Josh's PhotoPlus.

Action Plan

✔ Add noncash charges such as depreciation back to net income to compute net cash provided by operating activities.

Action Plan (cont.)

✔ Deduct from net income gains on the disposal of plant assets, or add losses back to net income, to compute net cash provided by operating activities.

✔ Use changes in noncash current asset and current liability accounts to compute net cash provided by operating activities.

Solution

Cash flows from operating activities		
Net income		$73,000
Adjustments to reconcile net income to net cash provided by operating activities:		
Depreciation expense	$ 7,000	
Gain on disposal of equipment	(2,500)	
Increase in accounts receivable	(4,000)	
Decrease in accounts payable	(3,800)	(3,300)
Net cash provided by operating activities		$69,700

Related exercise material: **BE13-4, BE13-5, BE13-6, E13-4, E13-5, E13-6, and DO IT! 13-2.**

Step 2: Investing and Financing Activities

ANALYZE CHANGES IN NONCURRENT ASSET AND LIABILITY ACCOUNTS AND RECORD AS INVESTING AND FINANCING ACTIVITIES, OR AS NONCASH INVESTING AND FINANCING ACTIVITIES

INCREASE IN LAND As indicated from the change in the Land account and the additional information, Computer Services purchased land of $110,000 by directly exchanging bonds for land. The issuance of bonds payable for land has no effect on cash. But, it is a significant noncash investing and financing activity that merits disclosure in a separate schedule (see Illustration 13-13).

INCREASE IN BUILDINGS As the additional data indicate, Computer Services acquired an office building for $120,000 cash. This is a cash outflow reported in the investing activities section (see Illustration 13-13).

INCREASE IN EQUIPMENT The Equipment account increased $17,000. The additional information explains that this net increase resulted from two transactions: (1) a purchase of equipment of $25,000, and (2) the sale for $4,000 of equipment costing $8,000. These transactions are investing activities. The company should report each transaction separately. Thus, it reports the purchase of equipment as an outflow of cash for $25,000. It reports the sale as an inflow of cash for $4,000. The T-account below shows the reasons for the change in this account during the year.

Illustration 13-12
Analysis of equipment

Equipment			
1/1/17 Balance	10,000	Cost of equipment sold	8,000
Purchase of equipment	**25,000**		
12/31/17 Balance	27,000		

The following entry shows the details of the equipment sale transaction.

A	=	L	+	SE

+4,000
+1,000
                                        −3,000 Exp
−8,000

Cash		4,000	
Accumulated Depreciation—Equipment		1,000	
Loss on Disposal of Equipment		3,000	
Equipment			8,000

Cash Flows
+4,000

INCREASE IN BONDS PAYABLE The Bonds Payable account increased $110,000. As indicated in the additional information, the company acquired land from the issuance of these bonds. It reports this noncash transaction in a separate schedule at the bottom of the statement.

INCREASE IN COMMON STOCK The balance sheet reports an increase in Common Stock of $20,000. The additional information section notes that this increase resulted from the issuance of new shares of stock. This is a cash inflow reported in the financing activities section.

INCREASE IN RETAINED EARNINGS Retained earnings increased $116,000 during the year. This increase can be explained by two factors: (1) net income of $145,000 increased retained earnings, and (2) dividends of $29,000 decreased retained earnings. The company adjusts net income to net cash provided by operating activities in the operating activities section. Payment of the dividends (not the declaration) is a **cash outflow that the company reports as a financing activity**.

Helpful Hint
When companies issue stocks or bonds for cash, the actual proceeds will appear in the statement of cash flows as a financing inflow (rather than the par value of the stocks or face value of bonds).

STATEMENT OF CASH FLOWS—2017

Using the previous information, we can now prepare a statement of cash flows for 2017 for Computer Services Company as shown in Illustration 13-13.

Illustration 13-13
Statement of cash flows, 2017—indirect method

COMPUTER SERVICES COMPANY		
Statement of Cash Flows—Indirect Method		
For the Year Ended December 31, 2017		
Cash flows from operating activities		
Net income		$145,000
Adjustments to reconcile net income to net cash		
provided by operating activities:		
Depreciation expense	$ 9,000	
Loss on disposal of equipment	3,000	
Decrease in accounts receivable	10,000	
Increase in inventory	(5,000)	
Increase in prepaid expenses	(4,000)	
Increase in accounts payable	16,000	
Decrease in income taxes payable	(2,000)	27,000
Net cash provided by operating activities		172,000
Cash flows from investing activities		
Purchase of building	(120,000)	
Purchase of equipment	(25,000)	
Sale of equipment	4,000	
Net cash used by investing activities		(141,000)
Cash flows from financing activities		
Issuance of common stock	20,000	
Payment of cash dividends	(29,000)	
Net cash used by financing activities		(9,000)
Net increase in cash		22,000
Cash at beginning of period		33,000
Cash at end of period		$ 55,000
Noncash investing and financing activities		
Issuance of bonds payable to purchase land		$110,000

Helpful Hint
Note that in the investing and financing activities sections, positive numbers indicate cash inflows (receipts), and negative numbers indicate cash outflows (payments).

Step 3: Net Change in Cash

COMPARE THE NET CHANGE IN CASH ON THE STATEMENT OF CASH FLOWS WITH THE CHANGE IN THE CASH ACCOUNT REPORTED ON THE BALANCE SHEET TO MAKE SURE THE AMOUNTS AGREE

Illustration 13-13 indicates that the net change in cash during the period was an increase of $22,000. This agrees with the change in Cash account reported on the balance sheet in Illustration 13-4 (page 605).

Accounting Across the Organization

© Soubrette/iStockphoto

Burning Through Our Cash

Box (cloud storage), Cyan (game creator), Fireeye (cyber security), and Mobile Iron (mobile security of data) are a few of the tech companies that recently have issued or are about to issue stock to the public. Investors now have to determine whether these tech companies have viable products and high chances for success.

An important consideration in evaluating a tech company is determining its financial flexibility—its ability to withstand adversity if an economic setback occurs. One way to measure financial flexibility is to assess a company's cash burn rate, which determines how long its cash will hold out if the company is expending more cash than it is receiving.

Fireeye, for example, burned cash in excess of $50 million in 2013. But the company also had over $150 million as a cash cushion, so it would take over 30 months before it runs out of cash. And even though Box has a much lower cash burn rate than Fireeye, it still has over a year's cushion. Compare that to the tech companies in 2000, when over one-quarter of them were on track to run out of cash within a year. And many did. Fortunately, the tech companies of today seem to be better equipped to withstand an economic setback.

Source: Shira Ovide, "Tech Firms' Cash Hoards Cool Fears of a Meltdown," *Wall Street Journal* (May 14, 2014).

What implications does a company's cash burn rate have for its survival? (See WileyPLUS for this answer and additional questions.)

DO IT! 2b   Indirect Method

Use the information below and on page 613 to prepare a statement of cash flows using the indirect method.

REYNOLDS COMPANY
Comparative Balance Sheets
December 31

Assets	2017	2016	Change Increase/Decrease
Cash	$ 54,000	$ 37,000	$ 17,000 Increase
Accounts receivable	68,000	26,000	42,000 Increase
Inventory	54,000	–0–	54,000 Increase
Prepaid expenses	4,000	6,000	2,000 Decrease
Land	45,000	70,000	25,000 Decrease
Buildings	200,000	200,000	–0–
Accumulated depreciation—buildings	(21,000)	(11,000)	10,000 Increase
Equipment	193,000	68,000	125,000 Increase
Accumulated depreciation—equipment	(28,000)	(10,000)	18,000 Increase
Totals	$569,000	$386,000	
Liabilities and Stockholders' Equity			
Accounts payable	$ 23,000	$ 40,000	$ 17,000 Decrease
Accrued expenses payable	10,000	–0–	10,000 Increase
Bonds payable	110,000	150,000	40,000 Decrease
Common stock ($1 par)	220,000	60,000	160,000 Increase
Retained earnings	206,000	136,000	70,000 Increase
Totals	$569,000	$386,000	

REYNOLDS COMPANY
Income Statement
For the Year Ended December 31, 2017

Sales revenue		$890,000
Cost of goods sold	$465,000	
Operating expenses	221,000	
Interest expense	12,000	
Loss on disposal of equipment	2,000	700,000
Income before income taxes		190,000
Income tax expense		65,000
Net income		$125,000

Additional information:
1. Operating expenses include depreciation expense of $33,000 and charges from prepaid expenses of $2,000.
2. Land was sold at its book value for cash.
3. Cash dividends of $55,000 were declared and paid in 2017.
4. Interest expense of $12,000 was paid in cash.
5. Equipment with a cost of $166,000 was purchased for cash. Equipment with a cost of $41,000 and a book value of $36,000 was sold for $34,000 cash.
6. Bonds of $10,000 were redeemed at their face value for cash. Bonds of $30,000 were converted into common stock.
7. Common stock ($1 par) of $130,000 was issued for cash.
8. Accounts payable pertain to merchandise suppliers.

Solution

REYNOLDS COMPANY
Statement of Cash Flows—Indirect Method
For the Year Ended December 31, 2017

Cash flows from operating activities		
Net income		$ 125,000
Adjustments to reconcile net income to net		
cash provided by operating activities:		
Depreciation expense	$ 33,000	
Loss on disposal of equipment	2,000	
Increase in accounts receivable	(42,000)	
Increase in inventory	(54,000)	
Decrease in prepaid expenses	2,000	
Decrease in accounts payable	(17,000)	
Increase in accrued expenses payable	10,000	(66,000)
Net cash provided by operating activities		59,000
Cash flows from investing activities		
Sale of land	25,000	
Sale of equipment	34,000	
Purchase of equipment	(166,000)	
Net cash used by investing activities		(107,000)
Cash flows from financing activities		
Redemption of bonds	(10,000)	
Sale of common stock	130,000	
Payment of dividends	(55,000)	
Net cash provided by financing activities		65,000
Net increase in cash		17,000
Cash at beginning of period		37,000
Cash at end of period		$54,000
Noncash investing and financing activities		
Conversion of bonds into common stock		$30,000

Action Plan
✔ Determine net cash provided/used by operating activities by adjusting net income for items that did not affect cash.

✔ Determine net cash provided/used by investing activities and financing activities.

✔ Determine the net increase/decrease in cash.

Related exercise material: **BE13-4, BE13-5, BE13-6, BE13-7, E13-4, E13-5, E13-6, and E13-8.**

LEARNING OBJECTIVE **3**

Analyze the statement of cash flows.

Traditionally, investors and creditors used ratios based on accrual accounting. These days, cash-based ratios are gaining increased acceptance among analysts.

Free Cash Flow

In the statement of cash flows, net cash provided by operating activities is intended to indicate the cash-generating capability of a company. Analysts have noted, however, that **net cash provided by operating activities fails to take into account that a company must invest in new fixed assets** just to maintain its current level of operations. Companies also must at least **maintain dividends at current levels** to satisfy investors. The measurement of free cash flow provides additional insight regarding a company's cash-generating ability. **Free cash flow** describes the net cash provided by operating activities after adjustment for capital expenditures and dividends.

Consider the following example. Suppose that MPC produced and sold 10,000 personal computers this year. It reported $100,000 net cash provided by operating activities. In order to maintain production at 10,000 computers, MPC invested $15,000 in equipment. It chose to pay $5,000 in dividends. Its free cash flow was $80,000 ($100,000 − $15,000 − $5,000). The company could use this $80,000 either to purchase new assets to expand the business or to pay an $80,000 dividend and continue to produce 10,000 computers. In practice, free cash flow is often calculated with the formula in Illustration 13-14. (Alternative definitions also exist.)

Illustration 13-14
Free cash flow

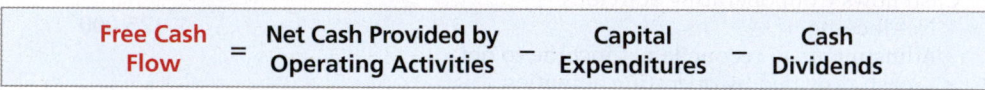

Free Cash Flow	=	Net Cash Provided by Operating Activities	−	Capital Expenditures	−	Cash Dividends

Illustration 13-15 provides basic information (in millions) excerpted from the 2013 statement of cash flows of Microsoft Corporation.

Illustration 13-15
Microsoft's cash flow information ($ in millions)

Real World	MICROSOFT CORPORATION Statement of Cash Flows (partial) 2013	

Cash provided by operating activities		$21,863
Cash flows from investing activities		
Additions to property and equipment	$ (4,257)	
Purchases of investments	(75,396)	
Sales of investments	52,464	
Acquisitions of companies	(1,584)	
Maturities of investments	5,130	
Other	(168)	
Cash used by investing activities		(23,811)
Cash paid for dividends		(7,455)

Microsoft's free cash flow is calculated as shown in Illustration 13-16.

Cash provided by operating activities	$21,863
Less: Expenditures on property, plant, and equipment	4,257
Dividends paid	7,455
Free cash flow	**$10,151**

Illustration 13-16
Calculation of Microsoft's free
cash flow ($ in millions)

Microsoft generated approximately $10.15 billion of free cash flow. This is a tremendous amount of cash generated in a single year. It is available for the acquisition of new assets, the retirement of stock or debt, or the payment of dividends. Also note that Microsoft's cash from operations of $21.8 billion is nearly identical to its 2013 net income of $21.9 billion. This lends additional credibility to Microsoft's income number as an indicator of potential future performance.

DO IT! 3 Free Cash Flow

Chicago Corporation issued the following statement of cash flows for 2017.

CHICAGO CORPORATION
Statement of Cash Flows—Indirect Method
For the Year Ended December 31, 2017

Cash flows from operating activities		
Net income		$ 19,000
Adjustments to reconcile net income to net cash		
provided by operating activities:		
Depreciation expense	$ 8,100	
Loss on disposal of plant assets	1,300	
Decrease in accounts receivable	6,900	
Increase in inventory	(4,000)	
Decrease in accounts payable	(2,000)	10,300
Net cash provided by operating activities		29,300
Cash flows from investing activities		
Sale of investments	1,100	
Purchase of equipment	(19,000)	
Net cash used by investing activities		(17,900)
Cash flows from financing activities		
Issuance of stock	10,000	
Payment on long-term note payable	(5,000)	
Payment for dividends	(9,000)	
Net cash used by financing activities		(4,000)
Net increase in cash		7,400
Cash at beginning of year		10,000
Cash at end of year		$ 17,400

(a) Compute free cash flow for Chicago Corporation. (b) Explain why free cash flow often provides better information than "Net cash provided by operating activities."

Action Plan

✔ Compute free cash flow as Net cash provided by operating activities − Capital expenditures − Cash dividends.

Solution

(a) Free cash flow = $29,300 − $19,000 − $9,000 = $1,300

(b) Net cash provided by operating activities fails to take into account that a company must invest in new plant assets just to maintain the current level of operations. Companies must also maintain dividends at current levels to satisfy investors. The measurement of free cash flow provides additional insight regarding a company's cash-generating ability.

Related exercise material: **BE13-8, BE13-9, BE13-10, BE13-11, E13-7, E13-9, and DO IT! 13-3.**

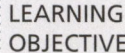

APPENDIX 13A: Prepare a statement of cash flows using the direct method.

To explain and illustrate the direct method for preparing a statement of cash flows, we use the transactions of Computer Services Company for 2017. Illustration 13A-1 presents information related to 2017 for the company.

To prepare a statement of cash flows under the direct approach, we apply the three steps outlined in Illustration 13-3 (page 604).

Step 1: Operating Activities

DETERMINE NET CASH PROVIDED/USED BY OPERATING ACTIVITIES BY CONVERTING NET INCOME FROM AN ACCRUAL BASIS TO A CASH BASIS

Under the **direct method**, companies compute net cash provided by operating activities by **adjusting each item in the income statement** from the accrual basis to the cash basis. To simplify and condense the operating activities section, companies **report only major classes of operating cash receipts and cash payments**. For these major classes, the difference between cash receipts and cash payments is the net cash provided by operating activities. These relationships are as shown in Illustration 13A-2 (page 618).

An efficient way to apply the direct method is to analyze the items reported in the income statement in the order in which they are listed. We then determine cash receipts and cash payments related to these revenues and expenses. The following presents the adjustments required to prepare a statement of cash flows for Computer Services Company using the direct approach.

CASH RECEIPTS FROM CUSTOMERS The income statement for Computer Services reported sales revenue from customers of $507,000. How much of that was cash receipts? To answer that, a company considers the change in accounts receivable during the year. When accounts receivable increase during the year, revenues on an accrual basis are higher than cash receipts from customers. Operations led to revenues, but not all of those revenues resulted in cash receipts.

To determine the amount of cash receipts, a company deducts from sales revenue the increase in accounts receivable. On the other hand, there may be a decrease in accounts receivable. That would occur if cash receipts from customers exceeded sales revenue. In that case, a company adds to sales revenue the decrease in accounts receivable. For Computer Services, accounts receivable decreased

COMPUTER SERVICES COMPANY
Comparative Balance Sheets
December 31

Assets	2017	2016	Change in Account Balance Increase/Decrease
Current assets			
Cash	$ 55,000	$ 33,000	$ 22,000 Increase
Accounts receivable	20,000	30,000	10,000 Decrease
Inventory	15,000	10,000	5,000 Increase
Prepaid expenses	5,000	1,000	4,000 Increase
Property, plant, and equipment			
Land	130,000	20,000	110,000 Increase
Buildings	160,000	40,000	120,000 Increase
Accumulated depreciation—buildings	(11,000)	(5,000)	6,000 Increase
Equipment	27,000	10,000	17,000 Increase
Accumulated depreciation—equipment	(3,000)	(1,000)	2,000 Increase
Total assets	$398,000	$138,000	

Liabilities and Stockholders' Equity			
Current liabilities			
Accounts payable	$ 28,000	$ 12,000	$ 16,000 Increase
Income taxes payable	6,000	8,000	2,000 Decrease
Long-term liabilities			
Bonds payable	130,000	20,000	110,000 Increase
Stockholders' equity			
Common stock	70,000	50,000	20,000 Increase
Retained earnings	164,000	48,000	116,000 Increase
Total liabilities and stockholders' equity	$398,000	$138,000	

COMPUTER SERVICES COMPANY
Income Statement
For the Year Ended December 31, 2017

Sales revenue		$507,000
Cost of goods sold	$150,000	
Operating expenses (excluding depreciation)	111,000	
Depreciation expense	9,000	
Loss on disposal of equipment	3,000	
Interest expense	42,000	315,000
Income before income tax		192,000
Income tax expense		47,000
Net income		$145,000

Additional information for 2017:

1. Depreciation expense was comprised of $6,000 for building and $3,000 for equipment.
2. The company sold equipment with a book value of $7,000 (cost $8,000, less accumulated depreciation $1,000) for $4,000 cash.
3. Issued $110,000 of long-term bonds in direct exchange for land.
4. A building costing $120,000 was purchased for cash. Equipment costing $25,000 was also purchased for cash.
5. Issued common stock for $20,000 cash.
6. The company declared and paid a $29,000 cash dividend.

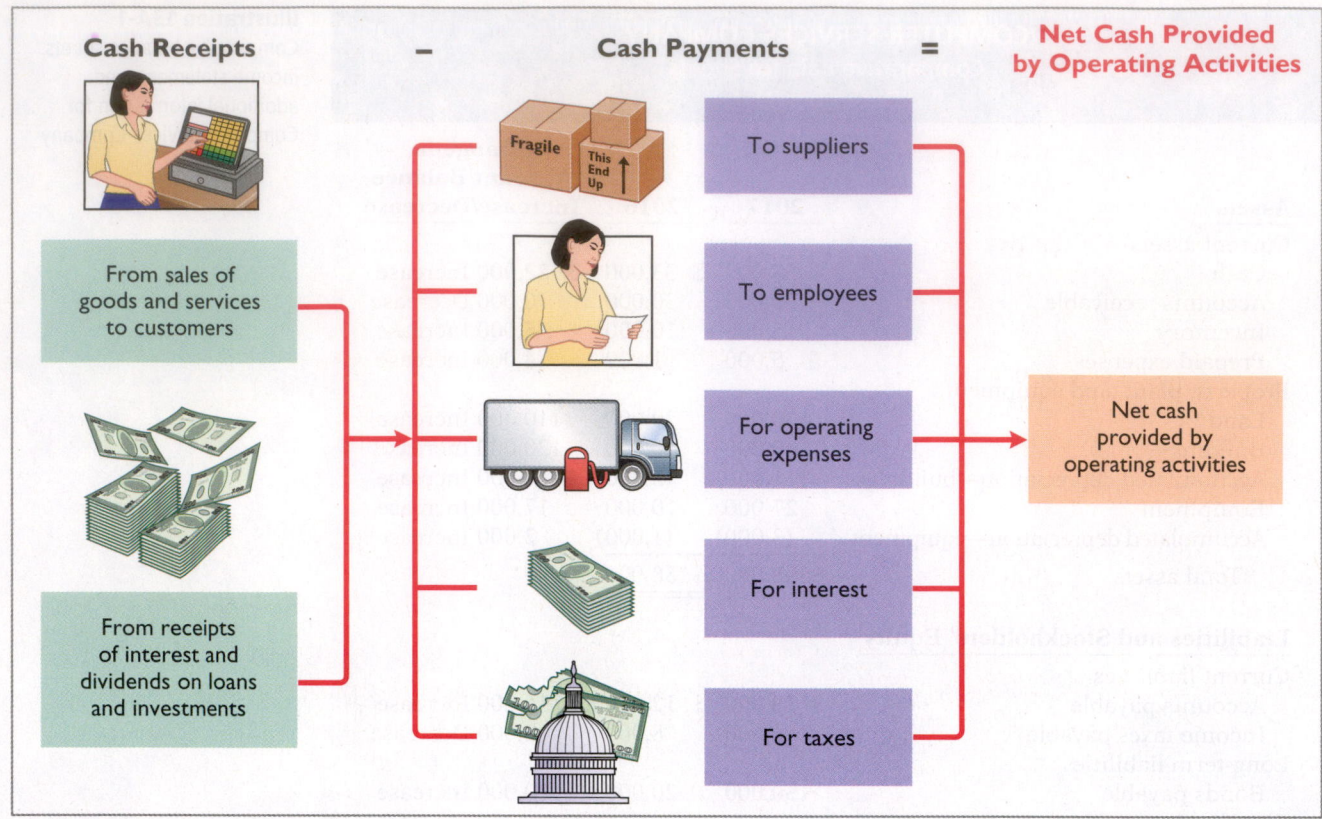

Illustration 13A-2
Major classes of cash receipts and payments

$10,000. Thus, cash receipts from customers were $517,000, computed as shown in Illustration 13A-3.

Illustration 13A-3
Computation of cash receipts from customers

Sales revenue	$ 507,000
Add: Decrease in accounts receivable	10,000
Cash receipts from customers	**$517,000**

Computer Services can also determine cash receipts from customers from an analysis of the Accounts Receivable account, as shown in Illustration 13A-4.

Illustration 13A-4
Analysis of accounts receivable

Helpful Hint
The T-account shows that sales revenue plus decrease in accounts receivable equals cash receipts.

Accounts Receivable				
1/1/17	Balance	30,000	**Receipts from customers**	**517,000**
	Sales revenue	507,000		
12/31/17	Balance	20,000		

Illustration 13A-5 shows the relationships among cash receipts from customers, sales revenue, and changes in accounts receivable.

Illustration 13A-5
Formula to compute cash receipts from customers—direct method

Cash Receipts from Customers	=	Sales Revenue	+ Decrease in Accounts Receivable
			or
			− Increase in Accounts Receivable

CASH PAYMENTS TO SUPPLIERS Computer Services reported cost of goods sold of $150,000 on its income statement. How much of that was cash payments to suppliers? To answer that, it is first necessary to find purchases for the year. To find purchases, a company adjusts cost of goods sold for the change in inventory. When inventory increases during the year, purchases for the year have exceeded cost of goods sold. As a result, to determine the amount of purchases, a company adds to cost of goods sold the increase in inventory.

In 2017, Computer Services' inventory increased $5,000. It computes purchases as follows.

Cost of goods sold	$ 150,000
Add: Increase in inventory	5,000
Purchases	**$155,000**

Illustration 13A-6
Computation of purchases

Computer Services can also determine purchases from an analysis of the Inventory account, as shown in Illustration 13A-7.

Illustration 13A-7
Analysis of inventory

Inventory			
1/1/17 Balance	10,000	Cost of goods sold	150,000
Purchases	**155,000**		
12/31/17 Balance	15,000		

After computing purchases, a company can determine cash payments to suppliers. This is done by adjusting purchases for the change in accounts payable. When accounts payable increase during the year, purchases on an accrual basis are higher than they are on a cash basis. As a result, to determine cash payments to suppliers, a company deducts from purchases the increase in accounts payable. On the other hand, if cash payments to suppliers exceed purchases, there will be a decrease in accounts payable. In that case, a company adds to purchases the decrease in accounts payable. For Computer Services, cash payments to suppliers were $139,000, computed as follows.

Purchases	$ 155,000
Deduct: Increase in accounts payable	16,000
Cash payments to suppliers	**$139,000**

Illustration 13A-8
Computation of cash payments to suppliers

Computer Services also can determine cash payments to suppliers from an analysis of the Accounts Payable account, as shown in Illustration 13A-9.

Illustration 13A-9
Analysis of accounts payable

Accounts Payable			
Payments to suppliers	**139,000**	1/1/17 Balance	12,000
		Purchases	155,000
		12/31/17 Balance	28,000

Helpful Hint
The T-account shows that purchases less increase in accounts payable equals payments to suppliers.

Illustration 13A-10 (page 620) shows the relationships among cash payments to suppliers, cost of goods sold, changes in inventory, and changes in accounts payable.

Illustration 13A-10
Formula to compute cash payments to suppliers—direct method

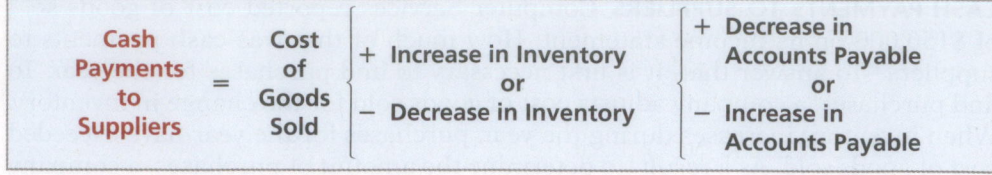

CASH PAYMENTS FOR OPERATING EXPENSES Computer Services reported on its income statement operating expenses of $111,000. How much of that amount was cash paid for operating expenses? To answer that, we need to adjust this amount for any changes in prepaid expenses and accrued expenses payable. For example, if prepaid expenses increased during the year, cash paid for operating expenses is higher than operating expenses reported on the income statement. To convert operating expenses to cash payments for operating expenses, a company adds the increase in prepaid expenses to operating expenses. On the other hand, if prepaid expenses decrease during the year, it deducts the decrease from operating expenses.

Companies must also adjust operating expenses for changes in accrued expenses payable. When accrued expenses payable increase during the year, operating expenses on an accrual basis are higher than they are in a cash basis. As a result, to determine cash payments for operating expenses, a company deducts from operating expenses an increase in accrued expenses payable. On the other hand, a company adds to operating expenses a decrease in accrued expenses payable because cash payments exceed operating expenses.

Computer Services' cash payments for operating expenses were $115,000, computed as follows.

Illustration 13A-11
Computation of cash payments for operating expenses

Operating expenses	$ 111,000
Add: Increase in prepaid expenses	4,000
Cash payments for operating expenses	**$115,000**

Illustration 13A-12 shows the relationships among cash payments for operating expenses, changes in prepaid expenses, and changes in accrued expenses payable.

Illustration 13A-12
Formula to compute cash payments for operating expenses—direct method

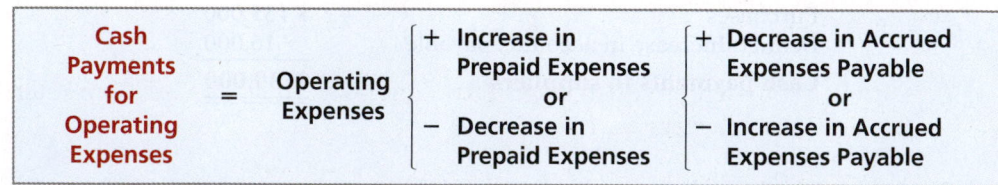

DEPRECIATION EXPENSE AND LOSS ON DISPOSAL OF EQUIPMENT Computer Services' depreciation expense in 2017 was $9,000. Depreciation expense is not shown on a statement of cash flows under the direct method because it is a non-cash charge. If the amount for operating expenses includes depreciation expense, operating expenses must be reduced by the amount of depreciation to determine cash payments for operating expenses.

The loss on disposal of equipment of $3,000 is also a noncash charge. The loss on disposal of equipment reduces net income, but it does not reduce cash. Thus, the loss on disposal of equipment is not shown on the statement of cash flows under the direct method.

Other charges to expense that do not require the use of cash, such as the amortization of intangible assets, depletion expense, and bad debt expense, are treated in the same manner as depreciation.

CASH PAYMENTS FOR INTEREST Computer Services reported on the income statement interest expense of $42,000. Since the balance sheet did not include an accrual for interest payable for 2016 or 2017, the amount reported as expense is the same as the amount of interest paid.

CASH PAYMENTS FOR INCOME TAXES Computer Services reported income tax expense of $47,000 on the income statement. Income taxes payable, however, decreased $2,000. This decrease means that income taxes paid were more than income taxes reported in the income statement. Cash payments for income taxes were therefore $49,000 as shown below.

Income tax expense	$ 47,000
Add: Decrease in income taxes payable	2,000
Cash payments for income taxes	**$49,000**

Illustration 13A-13
Computation of cash payments for income taxes

Computer Services can also determine cash payments for income taxes from an analysis of the Income Taxes Payable account, as shown in Illustration 13A-14.

Income Taxes Payable

Cash payments for income taxes	**49,000**	1/1/17	Balance	8,000
			Income tax expense	47,000
		12/31/17	Balance	6,000

Illustration 13A-14
Analysis of income taxes payable

Illustration 13A-15 shows the relationships among cash payments for income taxes, income tax expense, and changes in income taxes payable.

Cash Payments for Income Taxes	=	Income Tax Expense	+ Decrease in Income Taxes Payable or − Increase in Income Taxes Payable

Illustration 13A-15
Formula to compute cash payments for income taxes—direct method

The operating activities section of the statement of cash flows of Computer Services is shown in Illustration 13A-16.

Cash flows from operating activities		
Cash receipts from customers		$517,000
Less: Cash payments:		
To suppliers	$139,000	
For operating expenses	115,000	
For interest expense	42,000	
For income taxes	49,000	345,000
Net cash provided by operating activities		$172,000

Illustration 13A-16
Operating activities section of the statement of cash flows

When a company uses the direct method, it must also provide in a **separate schedule** (not shown here) the net cash flows from operating activities as computed under the indirect method.

Step 2: Investing and Financing Activities

ANALYZE CHANGES IN NONCURRENT ASSET AND LIABILITY ACCOUNTS AND RECORD AS INVESTING AND FINANCING ACTIVITIES, OR DISCLOSE AS NONCASH TRANSACTIONS

Helpful Hint
The investing and financing activities are measured and reported the same under both the direct and indirect methods.

INCREASE IN LAND As indicated from the change in the Land account and the additional information, Computer Services purchased land of $110,000 by directly exchanging bonds for land. The exchange of bonds payable for land has no effect on cash. But, it is a significant noncash investing and financing activity that merits disclosure in a separate schedule (see Illustration 13A-18).

INCREASE IN BUILDINGS As the additional data indicate, Computer Services acquired an office building for $120,000 cash. This is a cash outflow reported in the investing activities section (see Illustration 13A-18).

INCREASE IN EQUIPMENT The Equipment account increased $17,000. The additional information explains that this was a net increase that resulted from two transactions: (1) a purchase of equipment of $25,000, and (2) the sale for $4,000 of equipment costing $8,000. These transactions are investing activities. The company should report each transaction separately. The statement in Illustration 13A-18 reports the purchase of equipment as an outflow of cash for $25,000. It reports the sale as an inflow of cash for $4,000. The T-account below shows the reasons for the change in this account during the year.

Illustration 13A-17
Analysis of equipment

Equipment			
1/1/17 Balance	10,000	Cost of equipment sold	8,000
Purchase of equipment	**25,000**		
12/31/17 Balance	27,000		

The following entry shows the details of the equipment sale transaction.

A	=	L	+	SE
+4,000				
+1,000				
				−3,000 Exp
−8,000				

Cash Flows
+4,000

Cash	4,000	
Accumulated Depreciation—Equipment	1,000	
Loss on Disposal of Equipment	3,000	
Equipment		8,000

INCREASE IN BONDS PAYABLE The Bonds Payable account increased $110,000. As indicated in the additional information, the company acquired land by directly exchanging bonds for land. Illustration 13A-18 reports this noncash transaction in a separate schedule at the bottom of the statement.

Helpful Hint
When companies issue stocks or bonds for cash, the actual proceeds will appear in the statement of cash flows as a financing inflow (rather than the par value of the stocks or face value of bonds).

INCREASE IN COMMON STOCK The balance sheet reports an increase in Common Stock of $20,000. The additional information section notes that this increase resulted from the issuance of new shares of stock. This is a cash inflow reported in the financing activities section in Illustration 13A-18.

INCREASE IN RETAINED EARNINGS Retained earnings increased $116,000 during the year. This increase can be explained by two factors: (1) net income of $145,000 increased retained earnings, and (2) dividends of $29,000 decreased retained earnings. The company adjusts net income to net cash provided by operating activities in the operating activities section. **Payment** of the dividends (not the declaration) is a **cash outflow that the company reports as a financing activity in Illustration 13A-18.**

STATEMENT OF CASH FLOWS—2017

Illustration 13A-18 shows the statement of cash flows for Computer Services Company.

COMPUTER SERVICES COMPANY
Statement of Cash Flows—Direct Method
For the Year Ended December 31, 2017

Cash flows from operating activities		
Cash receipts from customers		$ 517,000
Less: Cash payments:		
To suppliers	$ 139,000	
For operating expenses	115,000	
For income taxes	49,000	
For interest expense	42,000	345,000
Net cash provided by operating activities		172,000
Cash flows from investing activities		
Sale of equipment	4,000	
Purchase of building	(120,000)	
Purchase of equipment	(25,000)	
Net cash used by investing activities		(141,000)
Cash flows from financing activities		
Issuance of common stock	20,000	
Payment of cash dividends	(29,000)	
Net cash used by financing activities		(9,000)
Net increase in cash		22,000
Cash at beginning of period		33,000
Cash at end of period		$ 55,000
Noncash investing and financing activities		
Issuance of bonds payable to purchase land		$ 110,000

Illustration 13A-18
Statement of cash flows, 2017—direct method

Step 3: Net Change in Cash

COMPARE THE NET CHANGE IN CASH ON THE STATEMENT OF CASH FLOWS WITH THE CHANGE IN THE CASH ACCOUNT REPORTED ON THE BALANCE SHEET TO MAKE SURE THE AMOUNTS AGREE

Illustration 13A-18 indicates that the net change in cash during the period was an increase of $22,000. This agrees with the change in balances in the Cash account reported on the balance sheets in Illustration 13A-1 (page 617).

LEARNING OBJECTIVE *5

APPENDIX 13B: Use a worksheet to prepare the statement of cash flows using the indirect method.

When preparing a statement of cash flows, companies may need to make numerous adjustments of net income. In such cases, they often use **a worksheet to assemble and classify the data that will appear on the statement**. The worksheet is merely an aid in preparing the statement. Its use is optional. Illustration 13B-1 (page 624) shows the skeleton format of the worksheet for preparation of the statement of cash flows.

The following guidelines are important in preparing a worksheet.

1. In the balance sheet accounts section, **list accounts with debit balances separately from those with credit balances**. This means, for example, that Accumulated Depreciation appears under credit balances and not as a contra account under debit balances. Enter the beginning and ending balances of each account in the appropriate columns. Enter as reconciling items in the two middle columns the transactions that caused the change in the account balance during the year.

Illustration 13B-1
Format of worksheet

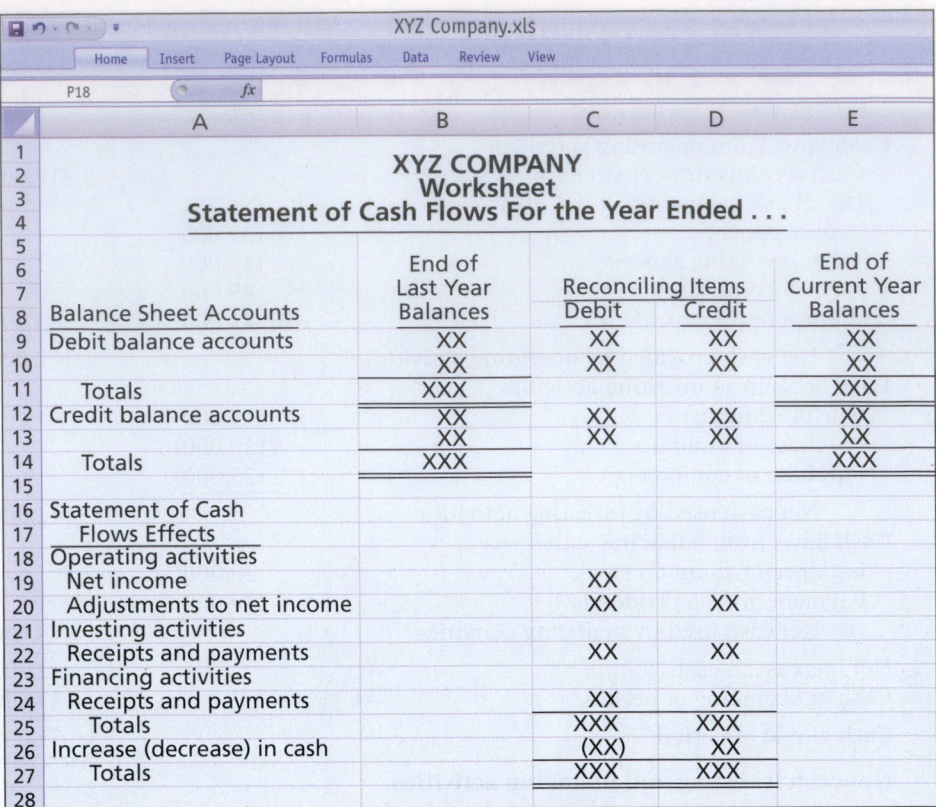

After all reconciling items have been entered, each line pertaining to a balance sheet account should "foot across." That is, the beginning balance plus or minus the reconciling item(s) must equal the ending balance. When this agreement exists for all balance sheet accounts, all changes in account balances have been reconciled.

2. The bottom portion of the worksheet consists of the operating, investing, and financing activities sections. It provides the information necessary to prepare the formal statement of cash flows. **Enter inflows of cash as debits in the reconciling columns. Enter outflows of cash as credits in the reconciling columns.** Thus, in this section, the sale of equipment for cash at book value appears as a debit under investing activities. Similarly, the purchase of land for cash appears as a credit under investing activities.

3. **The reconciling items shown in the worksheet are not entered in any journal or posted to any account.** They do not represent either adjustments or corrections of the balance sheet accounts. They are used only to facilitate the preparation of the statement of cash flows.

Preparing the Worksheet

As in the case of worksheets illustrated in earlier chapters, preparing a worksheet involves a series of prescribed steps. The steps in this case are:

1. Enter in the balance sheet accounts section the balance sheet accounts and their beginning and ending balances.

2. Enter in the reconciling columns of the worksheet the data that explain the changes in the balance sheet accounts other than cash and their effects on the statement of cash flows.

3. Enter on the cash line and at the bottom of the worksheet the increase or decrease in cash. This entry should enable the totals of the reconciling columns to be in agreement.

To illustrate the preparation of a worksheet, we will use the 2017 data for Computer Services Company. Your familiarity with these data (from the chapter) should help you understand the use of a worksheet. For ease of reference, the comparative balance sheets, income statement, and selected data for 2017 are presented in Illustration 13B-2.

Illustration 13B-2
Comparative balance sheets, income statement, and additional information for Computer Services Company

	Computer Services Company.xls			
	Home Insert Page Layout Formulas Data Review View			
	P18 fx			
	A	B	C	D
1	**COMPUTER SERVICES COMPANY**			
2	**Comparative Balance Sheets**			
3	**December 31**			
4				Change in
5				Account Balance
6	Assets	2017	2016	Increase/Decrease
7	Current assets			
8	Cash	$ 55,000	$ 33,000	$ 22,000 Increase
9	Accounts receivable	20,000	30,000	10,000 Decrease
10	Inventory	15,000	10,000	5,000 Increase
11	Prepaid expenses	5,000	1,000	4,000 Increase
12	Property, plant, and equipment			
13	Land	130,000	20,000	110,000 Increase
14	Buildings	160,000	40,000	120,000 Increase
15	Accumulated depreciation—buildings	(11,000)	(5,000)	6,000 Increase
16	Equipment	27,000	10,000	17,000 Increase
17	Accumulated depreciation—equipment	(3,000)	(1,000)	2,000 Increase
18	Total assets	$398,000	$138,000	
19				
20	Liabilities and Stockholders' Equity			
21	Current liabilities			
22	Accounts payable	$ 28,000	$ 12,000	$ 16,000 Increase
23	Income taxes payable	6,000	8,000	2,000 Decrease
24	Long-term liabilities			
25	Bonds payable	130,000	20,000	110,000 Increase
26	Stockholders' equity			
27	Common stock	70,000	50,000	20,000 Increase
28	Retained earnings	164,000	48,000	116,000 Increase
29	Total liabilities and stockholders' equity	$398,000	$138,000	

	Computer Services Company.xls			
	Home Insert Page Layout Formulas Data Review View			
	P18 fx			
	A	B	C	D
1	**COMPUTER SERVICES COMPANY**			
2	**Income Statement**			
3	**For the Year Ended December 31, 2017**			
4				
5	Sales revenue			$507,000
6	Cost of goods sold		$150,000	
7	Operating expenses (excluding depreciation)		111,000	
8	Depreciation expense		9,000	
9	Loss on disposal of equipment		3,000	
10	Interest expense		42,000	315,000
11	Income before income tax			192,000
12	Income tax expense			47,000
13	Net income			$145,000
14				

Additional information for 2017:
1. Depreciation expense was comprised of $6,000 for building and $3,000 for equipment.
2. The company sold equipment with a book value of $7,000 (cost $8,000, less accumulated depreciation $1,000) for $4,000 cash.
3. Issued $110,000 of long-term bonds in direct exchange for land.
4. A building costing $120,000 was purchased for cash. Equipment costing $25,000 was also purchased for cash.
5. Issued common stock for $20,000 cash.
6. The company declared and paid a $29,000 cash dividend.

DETERMINING THE RECONCILING ITEMS

Companies can use one of several approaches to determine the reconciling items. For example, they can first complete the changes affecting net cash provided by operating activities, and then can determine the effects of financing and investing transactions. Or, they can analyze the balance sheet accounts in the order in which they are listed on the worksheet. We will follow this latter approach for Computer Services, except for cash. As indicated in Step 3, **cash is handled last**.

ACCOUNTS RECEIVABLE The decrease of $10,000 in accounts receivable means that cash collections from sales revenue are higher than the sales revenue reported in the income statement. To convert net income to net cash provided by operating activities, we add the decrease of $10,000 to net income. The entry in the reconciling columns of the worksheet is:

| (a) | Operating—Decrease in Accounts Receivable | 10,000 | |
| | Accounts Receivable | | 10,000 |

INVENTORY Computer Services Company's inventory balance increases $5,000 during the period. The Inventory account reflects the difference between the amount of inventory that the company purchased and the amount that it sold. For Computer Services, this means that the cost of merchandise purchased exceeds the cost of goods sold by $5,000. As a result, cost of goods sold does not reflect $5,000 of cash payments made for merchandise. We deduct this inventory increase of $5,000 during the period from net income to arrive at net cash provided by operating activities. The worksheet entry is:

| (b) | Inventory | 5,000 | |
| | Operating—Increase in Inventory | | 5,000 |

PREPAID EXPENSES An increase of $4,000 in prepaid expenses means that expenses deducted in determining net income are less than expenses that were paid in cash. We deduct the increase of $4,000 from net income in determining net cash provided by operating activities. The worksheet entry is:

| (c) | Prepaid Expenses | 4,000 | |
| | Operating—Increase in Prepaid Expenses | | 4,000 |

Helpful Hint
These amounts are asterisked in the worksheet to indicate that they result from a significant noncash transaction.

LAND The increase in land of $110,000 resulted from a purchase through the issuance of long-term bonds. The company should report this transaction as a significant noncash investing and financing activity. The worksheet entry is:

| (d) | Land | 110,000 | |
| | Bonds Payable | | 110,000 |

BUILDINGS The cash purchase of a building for $120,000 is an investing activity cash outflow. The entry in the reconciling columns of the worksheet is:

| (e) | Buildings | 120,000 | |
| | Investing—Purchase of Building | | 120,000 |

EQUIPMENT The increase in equipment of $17,000 resulted from a cash purchase of $25,000 and the disposal of equipment costing $8,000. The book value of the equipment was $7,000, the cash proceeds were $4,000, and a loss of $3,000 was recorded. The worksheet entries are:

| (f) | Equipment | 25,000 | |
| | Investing—Purchase of Equipment | | 25,000 |

(g)	Investing—Sale of Equipment	4,000	
	Operating—Loss on Disposal of Equipment	3,000	
	Accumulated Depreciation—Equipment	1,000	
	Equipment		8,000

ACCOUNTS PAYABLE We must add the increase of $16,000 in accounts payable to net income to determine net cash provided by operating activities. The worksheet entry is:

| (h) | Operating—Increase in Accounts Payable | 16,000 | |
| | Accounts Payable | | 16,000 |

INCOME TAXES PAYABLE When a company incurs income tax expense but has not yet paid its taxes, it records income taxes payable. A change in the Income Taxes Payable account reflects the difference between income tax expense incurred and income tax actually paid. Computer Services' Income Taxes Payable account decreases by $2,000. That means the $47,000 of income tax expense reported on the income statement was $2,000 less than the amount of taxes paid during the period of $49,000. To adjust net income to a cash basis, we must reduce net income by $2,000. The worksheet entry is:

(i)	Income Taxes Payable	2,000	
	Operating—Decrease in Income Taxes		
	Payable		2,000

BONDS PAYABLE The increase of $110,000 in this account resulted from the issuance of bonds for land. This is a significant noncash investing and financing activity. Worksheet entry (d) above is the only entry necessary.

COMMON STOCK The balance sheet reports an increase in Common Stock of $20,000. The additional information section notes that this increase resulted from the issuance of new shares of stock. This is a cash inflow reported in the financing section. The worksheet entry is:

| (j) | Financing—Issuance of Common Stock | 20,000 | |
| | Common Stock | | 20,000 |

ACCUMULATED DEPRECIATION—BUILDINGS, AND ACCUMULATED DEPRECIATION— EQUIPMENT Increases in these accounts of $6,000 and $3,000, respectively, resulted from depreciation expense. Depreciation expense is a **noncash charge that we must add to net income** to determine net cash provided by operating activities. The worksheet entries are:

(k)	Operating—Depreciation Expense	6,000	
	Accumulated Depreciation—Buildings		6,000
(l)	Operating—Depreciation Expense	3,000	
	Accumulated Depreciation—Equipment		3,000

RETAINED EARNINGS The $116,000 increase in retained earnings resulted from net income of $145,000 and the declaration and payment of a $29,000 cash dividend. Net income is included in net cash provided by operating activities, and the dividends are a financing activity cash outflow. The entries in the reconciling columns of the worksheet are:

(m)	Operating—Net Income	145,000	
	Retained Earnings		145,000
(n)	Retained Earnings	29,000	
	Financing—Payment of Dividends		29,000

DISPOSITION OF CHANGE IN CASH The firm's cash increased $22,000 in 2017. The final entry on the worksheet, therefore, is:

(o)	Cash	22,000	
	Increase in Cash		22,000

As shown in the worksheet, we enter the increase in cash in the reconciling credit column as a **balancing** amount. This entry should complete the reconciliation of the changes in the balance sheet accounts. Also, it should permit the totals of the reconciling columns to be in agreement. When all changes have been explained and the reconciling columns are in agreement, the reconciling columns are ruled to complete the worksheet. The completed worksheet for Computer Services Company is shown in Illustration 13B-3.

Illustration 13B-3
Completed worksheet—indirect method

Computer Services Company.xls

COMPUTER SERVICES COMPANY
Worksheet
Statement of Cash Flows For the Year Ended December 31, 2017

Balance Sheet Accounts	Balance 12/31/16	Reconciling Items Debit	Credit	Balance 12/31/17
Debits				
Cash	33,000	(o) 22,000		55,000
Accounts Receivable	30,000		(a) 10,000	20,000
Inventory	10,000	(b) 5,000		15,000
Prepaid Expenses	1,000	(c) 4,000		5,000
Land	20,000	(d)110,000*		130,000
Buildings	40,000	(e)120,000		160,000
Equipment	10,000	(f) 25,000	(g) 8,000	27,000
Total	144,000			412,000
Credits				
Accounts Payable	12,000		(h) 16,000	28,000
Income Taxes Payable	8,000	(i) 2,000		6,000
Bonds Payable	20,000		(d)110,000*	130,000
Accumulated Depreciation—Buildings	5,000		(k) 6,000	11,000
Accumulated Depreciation—Equipment	1,000	(g) 1,000	(l) 3,000	3,000
Common Stock	50,000		(j) 20,000	70,000
Retained Earnings	48,000	(n) 29,000	(m)145,000	164,000
Total	144,000			412,000
Statement of Cash Flows Effects				
Operating activities				
Net income		(m)145,000		
Decrease in accounts receivable		(a) 10,000		
Increase in inventory			(b) 5,000	
Increase in prepaid expenses			(c) 4,000	
Increase in accounts payable		(h) 16,000		
Decrease in income taxes payable			(i) 2,000	
Depreciation expense		ſ(k) 6,000		
		₹(l) 3,000		
Loss on disposal of equipment		(g) 3,000		
Investing activities				
Purchase of building			(e)120,000	
Purchase of equipment			(f) 25,000	
Sale of equipment		(g) 4,000		
Financing activities				
Issuance of common stock		(j) 20,000		
Payment of dividends			(n) 29,000	
Totals		525,000	503,000	
Increase in cash			(o) 22,000	
Totals		525,000	525,000	

* Significant noncash investing and financing activity.

LEARNING OBJECTIVE **6**

APPENDIX 13C: Use the T-account approach to prepare a statement of cash flows.

Many people like to use T-accounts to provide structure to the preparation of a statement of cash flows. The use of T-accounts is based on the accounting equation that you learned in Chapter 1. The basic equation is:

> **Assets = Liabilities + Equity**

Now, let's rewrite the left-hand side as:

> **Cash + Noncash Assets = Liabilities + Equity**

Next, rewrite the equation by subtracting Noncash Assets from each side to isolate Cash on the left-hand side:

> **Cash = Liabilities + Equity − Noncash Assets**

Finally, if we insert the Δ symbol (which means "change in"), we have:

> **Δ Cash = Δ Liabilities + Δ Equity − Δ Noncash Assets**

What this means is that the change in cash is equal to the change in all of the other balance sheet accounts. Another way to think about this is that if we analyze the changes in all of the noncash balance sheet accounts, we will explain the change in the Cash account. This, of course, is exactly what we are trying to do with the statement of cash flows.

   To implement this approach, first prepare a large Cash T-account with sections for operating, investing, and financing activities. Then, prepare smaller T-accounts for all of the other noncash balance sheet accounts. Insert the beginning and ending balances for each of these accounts. Once you have done this, then walk through the steps outlined in Illustration 13-3 (page 604). As you walk through the steps, enter debit and credit amounts into the affected accounts. When all of the changes in the T-accounts have been explained, you are done. To demonstrate, we apply this approach to the example of Computer Services Company that is presented in the chapter. Each of the adjustments in Illustration 13C-1 (page 630) is numbered so you can follow them through the T-accounts.

1. Post net income as a debit to the operating section of the Cash T-account and a credit to Retained Earnings. Make sure to label all adjustments to the Cash T-account. It also helps to number each adjustment so you can trace all of them if you make an error.

2. Post depreciation expense as a debit to the operating section of Cash and a credit to each of the appropriate accumulated depreciation accounts.

3. Post any gains or losses on the sale of property, plant, and equipment. To do this, it is best to first prepare the journal entry that was recorded at the time of the sale and then post each element of the journal entry. For example, for Computer Services the entry was as follows.

Cash	4,000	
Accumulated Depreciation—Equipment	1,000	
Loss on Disposal of Equipment	3,000	
Equipment		8,000

Cash

Operating				
(1) Net income	145,000	5,000	Inventory (5)	
(2) Depreciation expense	9,000	4,000	Prepaid expenses (6)	
(3) Loss on equipment	3,000	2,000	Income taxes payable (8)	
(4) Accounts receivable	10,000			
(7) Accounts payable	16,000			
Net cash provided by operating activities	172,000			
Investing				
(3) Sold equipment	4,000	120,000	Purchased building (10)	
		25,000	Purchased equipment (11)	
		141,000	Net cash used by investing activities	
Financing				
(12) Issued common stock	20,000	29,000	Dividend paid (13)	
		9,000	Net cash used by financing activities	
	22,000			

Accounts Receivable		**Inventory**		**Prepaid Expenses**		**Land**	
30,000		10,000		1,000		20,000	
	10,000 (4)	(5) 5,000		(6) 4,000		(9) 110,000	
20,000		15,000		5,000		130,000	

Buildings		**Accumulated Depreciation—Buildings**		**Equipment**		**Accumulated Depreciation—Equipment**	
40,000			5,000	10,000			1,000
(10) 120,000			6,000 (2)	(11) 25,000	8,000 (3)	(3) 1,000	3,000 (2)
160,000			11,000	27,000			3,000

Accounts Payable		**Income Taxes Payable**		**Bonds Payable**		**Common Stock**		**Retained Earnings**	
	12,000		8,000		20,000		50,000		48,000
	16,000 (7)	(8) 2,000			110,000 (9)		20,000 (12)		145,000 (1)
	28,000		6,000		130,000		70,000	(13) 29,000	
									164,000

Illustration 13C-1

T-account approach

The $4,000 cash entry is a source of cash in the investing section of the Cash account. Accumulated Depreciation—Equipment is debited for $1,000. The Loss on Disposal of Equipment is a debit to the operating section of the Cash T-account. Finally, Equipment is credited for $8,000.

4–8. Next, post each of the changes to the noncash current asset and current liability accounts. For example, to explain the $10,000 decline in Computer Services' accounts receivable, credit Accounts Receivable for $10,000 and debit the operating section of the Cash T-account for $10,000.

9. Analyze the changes in the noncurrent accounts. Land was purchased by issuing bonds payable. This requires a debit to Land for $110,000 and a credit to Bonds Payable for $110,000. Note that this is a significant noncash event that requires disclosure at the bottom of the statement of cash flows.

10. Buildings is debited for $120,000, and the investing section of the Cash T-account is credited for $120,000 as a use of cash from investing.

11. Equipment is debited for $25,000 and the investing section of the Cash T-account is credited for $25,000 as a use of cash from investing.

12. Common Stock is credited for $20,000 for the issuance of shares of stock, and the financing section of the Cash T-account is debited for $20,000.

13. Retained Earnings is debited to reflect the payment of the $29,000 dividend, and the financing section of the Cash T-account is credited to reflect the use of Cash.

At this point, all of the changes in the noncash accounts have been explained. All that remains is to subtotal each section of the Cash T-account and compare the total change in cash with the change shown on the balance sheet. Once this is done, the information in the Cash T-account can be used to prepare a statement of cash flows.

REVIEW AND PRACTICE

LEARNING OBJECTIVES REVIEW

1 Discuss the usefulness and format of the statement of cash flows. The statement of cash flows provides information about the cash receipts, cash payments, and net change in cash resulting from the operating, investing, and financing activities of a company during the period. Operating activities include the cash effects of transactions that enter into the determination of net income. Investing activities involve cash flows resulting from changes in investments and long-term asset items. Financing activities involve cash flows resulting from changes in long-term liability and stockholders' equity items.

2 Prepare a statement of cash flows using the indirect method. The preparation of a statement of cash flows involves three major steps. (1) Determine net cash provided/used by operating activities by converting net income from an accrual basis to a cash basis. (2) Analyze changes in noncurrent asset and liability accounts and record as investing and financing activities, or disclose as noncash transactions. (3) Compare the net change in cash on the statement of cash flows with the change in the Cash account reported on the balance sheet to make sure the amounts agree.

3 Analyze the statement of cash flows. Free cash flow indicates the amount of cash a company generated during the current year that is available for the payment of additional dividends or for expansion.

*4 Prepare a statement of cash flows using the direct method. The preparation of the statement of cash flows involves three major steps. (1) Determine net cash provided/used by operating activities by converting net income from an accrual basis to a cash basis. (2) Analyze changes in noncurrent asset and liability

accounts and record as investing and financing activities, or disclose as noncash transactions. (3) Compare the net change in cash on the statement of cash flows with the change in the Cash account reported on the balance sheet to make sure the amounts agree. The direct method reports cash receipts less cash payments to arrive at net cash provided by operating activities.

*5 Use a worksheet to prepare the statement of cash flows using the indirect method. When there are numerous adjustments, a worksheet can be a helpful tool in preparing the statement of cash flows. Key guidelines for using a worksheet are as follows. (1) List accounts with debit balances separately from those with credit balances. (2) In the reconciling columns in the bottom portion of the worksheet, show cash inflows as debits and cash outflows as credits. (3) Do not enter reconciling items in any journal or account, but use them only to help prepare the statement of cash flows.

The steps in preparing the worksheet are as follows. (1) Enter beginning and ending balances of balance sheet accounts. (2) Enter debits and credits in reconciling columns. (3) Enter the increase or decrease in cash in two places as a balancing amount.

*6 Use the T-account approach to prepare a statement of cash flows. To use T-accounts to prepare the statement of cash flows: (1) prepare a large Cash T-account with sections for operating, investing, and financing activities; (2) prepare smaller T-accounts for all other noncash accounts; (3) insert beginning and ending balances for all accounts; and (4) follows the steps in Illustration 13-3 (page 604), entering debit and credit amounts as needed.

■ GLOSSARY REVIEW

***Direct method** A method of preparing a statement of cash flows that shows operating cash receipts and payments, making it more consistent with the objective of the statement of cash flows. (pp. 604, 616).

Financing activities Cash flow activities that include (a) obtaining cash from issuing debt and repaying the amounts borrowed and (b) obtaining cash from stockholders, repurchasing shares, and paying dividends. (p. 600).

Free cash flow Net cash provided by operating activities adjusted for capital expenditures and dividends paid. (p. 614).

Indirect method A method of preparing a statement of cash flows in which net income is adjusted for items that do not affect cash, to determine net cash provided by operating activities. (pp. 604, 606).

Investing activities Cash flow activities that include (a) purchasing and disposing of investments and property, plant, and equipment using cash and (b) lending money and collecting the loans. (p. 600).

Operating activities Cash flow activities that include the cash effects of transactions that create revenues and expenses and thus enter into the determination of net income. (p. 600).

Statement of cash flows A basic financial statement that provides information about the cash receipts, cash payments, and net change in cash during a period, resulting from operating, investing, and financing activities. (p. 600).

■ PRACTICE MULTIPLE-CHOICE QUESTIONS

(LO 1) **1.** Which of the following is **incorrect** about the statement of cash flows?
  (a) It is a fourth basic financial statement.
  (b) It provides information about cash receipts and cash payments of an entity during a period.
  (c) It reconciles the ending Cash account balance to the balance per the bank statement.
  (d) It provides information about the operating, investing, and financing activities of the business.

(LO 1) **2.** Which of the following is **not** reported in the statement of cash flows?
  (a) The net change in stockholders' equity during the year.
  (b) Cash payments for plant assets during the year.
  (c) Cash receipts from sales of plant assets during the year.
  (d) How acquisitions of plant assets during the year were financed.

(LO 1) **3.** The statement of cash flows classifies cash receipts and cash payments by these activities:
  (a) operating and nonoperating.
  (b) investing, financing, and operating.
  (c) financing, operating, and nonoperating.
  (d) investing, financing, and nonoperating.

(LO 1) **4.** Which is an example of a cash flow from an operating activity?
  (a) Payment of cash to lenders for interest.
  (b) Receipt of cash from the sale of common stock.
  (c) Payment of cash dividends to the company's stockholders.
  (d) None of the above.

(LO 1) **5.** Which is an example of a cash flow from an investing activity?
  (a) Receipt of cash from the issuance of bonds payable.
  (b) Payment of cash to repurchase outstanding common stock.
  (c) Receipt of cash from the sale of equipment.
  (d) Payment of cash to suppliers for inventory.

(LO 1) **6.** Cash dividends paid to stockholders are classified on the statement of cash flows as:
  (a) an operating activity.
  (b) an investing activity.
  (c) a combination of (a) and (b).
  (d) a financing activity.

(LO 1) **7.** Which is an example of a cash flow from a financing activity?
  (a) Receipt of cash from sale of land.
  (b) Issuance of debt for cash.
  (c) Purchase of equipment for cash.
  (d) None of the above.

(LO 1) **8.** Which of the following is **incorrect** about the statement of cash flows?
  (a) The direct method may be used to report net cash provided by operating activities.
  (b) The statement shows the net cash provided (used) for three categories of activity.
  (c) The operating section is the last section of the statement.
  (d) The indirect method may be used to report net cash provided by operating activities.

Use the indirect method to solve Questions 9 through 11.

(LO 2) **9.** Net income is $132,000, accounts payable increased $10,000 during the year, inventory decreased $6,000 during the year, and accounts receivable increased $12,000 during the year. Under the indirect method, what is net cash provided by operating activities?
  (a) $102,000.   (c) $124,000.
  (b) $112,000.   (d) $136,000.

(LO 2) **10.** Items that are added back to net income in determining net cash provided by operating activities under the indirect method do **not** include:
  (a) depreciation expense.
  (b) an increase in inventory.
  (c) amortization expense.
  (d) loss on disposal of equipment.

(LO 2)   **11.** The following data are available for Allen Clapp Corporation.

Net income	$200,000
Depreciation expense	40,000
Dividends paid	60,000
Gain on disposal of land	10,000
Decrease in accounts receivable	20,000
Decrease in accounts payable	30,000

Net cash provided by operating activities is:
(a) $160,000.   (c) $240,000.
(b) $220,000.   (d) $280,000.

(LO 2)   **12.** The following data are available for Orange Peels Corporation.

Proceeds from sale of land	$100,000
Proceeds from sale of equipment	50,000
Issuance of common stock	70,000
Purchase of equipment	30,000
Payment of cash dividends	60,000

Net cash provided by investing activities is:
(a) $120,000.   (c) $150,000.
(b) $130,000.   (d) $190,000.

(LO 2)   **13.** The following data are available for Something Strange!

Increase in accounts payable	$ 40,000
Increase in bonds payable	100,000
Sale of investment	50,000
Issuance of common stock	60,000
Payment of cash dividends	30,000

Net cash provided by financing activities is:
(a) $90,000.   (c) $160,000.
(b) $130,000.   (d) $170,000.

(LO 3)   **14.** The statement of cash flows should **not** be used to evaluate an entity's ability to:
(a) earn net income.
(b) generate future cash flows.
(c) pay dividends.
(d) meet obligations.

15. Free cash flow provides an indication of a company's (LO 3) ability to:
(a) generate net income.
(b) generate cash to pay dividends.
(c) generate cash to invest in new capital expenditures.
(d) Both (b) and (c).

Use the direct method to solve Questions 16 and 17.

*16. The beginning balance in accounts receivable is (LO 4) $44,000, the ending balance is $42,000, and sales during the period are $129,000. What are cash receipts from customers?
(a) $127,000.   (c) $131,000.
(b) $129,000.   (d) $141,000.

*17. Which of the following items is reported on a state- (LO 4) ment of cash flows prepared by the direct method?
(a) Loss on disposal of building.
(b) Increase in accounts receivable.
(c) Depreciation expense.
(d) Cash payments to suppliers.

*18. In a worksheet for the statement of cash flows, a (LO 5) decrease in accounts receivable is entered in the reconciling columns as a credit to Accounts Receivable and a debit in the:
(a) investing activities section.
(b) operating activities section.
(c) financing activities section.
(d) None of the above.

*19. In a worksheet for the statement of cash flows, a (LO 5) worksheet entry that includes a credit to accumulated depreciation will also include a:
(a) credit in the operating activities section and a debit in another section.
(b) debit in the operating activities section.
(c) debit in the investing activities section.
(d) debit in the financing activities section.

Solutions

1. (c) The statement of cash flows does not reconcile the ending cash balance to the balance per the bank statement. The other choices are true statements.

2. (a) The net change in stockholders' equity during the year is not reported in the statement of cash flows. The other choices are true statements.

3. (b) Operating, investing, and financing activities are the three classifications of cash receipts and cash payments used in the statement of cash flows. The other choices are therefore incorrect.

4. (a) Payment of cash to lenders for interest is an operating activity. The other choices are incorrect because (b) receipt of cash from the sale of common stock is a financing activity, (c) payment of cash dividends to the company's stockholders is a financing activity, and (d) there is a correct answer.

5. (c) Receipt of cash from the sale of equipment is an investing activity. The other choices are incorrect because (a) the receipt of cash from the issuance of bonds payable is a financing activity, (b) payment of cash to repurchase outstanding common stock is a financing activity, and (d) payment of cash to suppliers for inventory is an operating activity.

6. (d) Cash dividends paid to stockholders are classified as a financing activity, not (a) an operating activity, (b) an investing activity, or (c) a combination of (a) and (b).

7. (b) Issuance of debt for cash is a financing activity. The other choices are incorrect because (a) the receipt of cash for the sale of land is an investing activity, (c) the purchase of equipment for cash is an investing activity, and (d) there is a correct answer.

8. (c) The operating section of the statement of cash flows is the first, not the last, section of the statement. The other choices are true statements.

9. (d) Net cash provided by operating activities is computed by adjusting net income for the changes in the three current asset/current liability accounts listed. An increase in accounts payable ($10,000) and a decrease in inventory ($6,000) are added to net income ($132,000), while an increase in accounts receivable ($12,000) is subtracted from net income, or $132,000 + $10,000 + $6,000 − $12,000 = $136,000, not (a) $102,000, (b) $112,000, or (c) $124,000.

10. (b) An increase in inventory is subtracted, not added, to net income in determining net cash provided by operating activities. The other choices are incorrect because (a) depreciation expense, (c) amortization expense, and (d) loss on disposal of equipment are all added back to net income in determining net cash provided by operating activities.

11. (b) Net cash provided by operating activities is $220,000 (Net income $200,000 + Depreciation expense $40,000 − Gain on disposal of land $10,000 + Decrease in accounts receivable $20,000 − Decrease in accounts payable $30,000), not (a) $160,000, (c) $240,000, or (d) $280,000.

12. (a) Net cash provided by investing activities is $120,000 (Sale of land $100,000 + Sale of equipment $50,000 − Purchase of equipment $30,000), not (b) $130,000, (c) $150,000, or (d) $190,000. Issuance of common stock and payment of cash dividends are financing activities.

13. (b) Net cash provided by financing activities is $130,000 (Increase in bonds payable $100,000 + Issuance of common stock $60,000 − Payment of cash dividends $30,000), not (a) $90,000, (c) $160,000, or (d) $170,000. Increase in accounts payable is an operating activity and sale of investment is an investing activity.

14. (a) The statement of cash flows is not used to evaluate an entity's ability to earn net income. The other choices are true statements.

15. (d) Free cash flow provides an indication of a company's ability to generate cash to pay dividends and to invest in new capital expenditures. Choice (a) is incorrect because other measures besides free cash flow provide the best measure of a company's ability to earn net income. Choices (b) and (c) are true statements, but (d) is the better answer.

*16. **(c)** Cash collections from customers amount to $131,000 ($129,000 + $2,000). The other choices are therefore incorrect.

*17. **(d)** Cash payments to suppliers are reported on a statement of cash flows prepared by the direct method. The other choices are incorrect because (a) loss on disposal of building, (b) increase in accounts receivable, and (c) depreciation expense are reported in the operating activities section of the statement of cash flows when the indirect, not direct, method is used.

*18. **(b)** Because accounts receivable is a current asset, the debit belongs in the operating activities section of the worksheet, not in the (a) investing activities or (c) financing activities section. Choice (d) is incorrect as there is a right answer.

*19. **(b)** A worksheet entry that includes a credit to accumulated depreciation will also include a debit depreciation expense. This debit in the operating activities section of the statement of cash flows will be added to the net income to determine net cash provided by operating activities. The other choices are therefore incorrect.

PRACTICE EXERCISES

Prepare journal entries to determine effect on statement of cash flows.

(LO 2)

1. Furst Corporation had the following transactions.

1. Paid salaries of $14,000.
2. Issued 1,000 shares of $1 par value common stock for equipment worth $16,000.
3. Sold equipment (cost $10,000, accumulated depreciation $6,000) for $3,000.
4. Sold land (cost $12,000) for $16,000.
5. Issued another 1,000 shares of $1 par value common stock for $18,000.
6. Recorded depreciation of $20,000.

Instructions

For each transaction above, (a) prepare the journal entry, and (b) indicate how it would affect the statement of cash flows. Assume the indirect method.

Solution

1. 1. (a) Salaries and Wages Expense	14,000	
Cash		14,000

(b) Salaries and wages expense is not reported separately on the statement of cash flows. It is part of the computation of net income in the income statement and is included in the net income amount on the statement of cash flows.

2. (a) Equipment   16,000
        Common Stock   1,000
        Paid-in Capital in Excess of Par—Common Stock   15,000

   (b) The issuance of common stock for equipment ($16,000) is reported as a noncash financ-
       ing and investing activity at the bottom of the statement of cash flows.

3. (a) Cash   3,000
        Loss on Disposal of Plant Assets   1,000
        Accumulated Depreciation—Equipment   6,000
            Equipment   10,000

   (b) The cash receipt ($3,000) is reported in the investing section. The loss ($1,000) is added
       to net income in the operating section.

4. (a) Cash   16,000
        Land   12,000
        Gain on Disposal of Plant Assets   4,000

   (b) The cash receipt ($16,000) is reported in the investing section. The gain ($4,000) is
       deducted from net income in the operating section.

5. (a) Cash   18,000
        Common Stock   1,000
        Paid-in Capital in Excess of Par—Common Stock   17,000

   (b) The cash receipt ($18,000) is reported in the financing section.

6. (a) Depreciation Expense   20,000
        Accumulated Depreciation—Equipment   20,000

   (b) Depreciation expense ($20,000) is added to net income in the operating section.

2. Strong Corporation's comparative balance sheets are presented below.

Prepare statement of cash flows and compute free cash flow.

(LO 2, 3)

STRONG CORPORATION
Comparative Balance Sheets
December 31

	2017	2016
Cash	$ 28,200	$ 17,700
Accounts receivable	24,200	22,300
Investments	23,000	16,000
Equipment	60,000	70,000
Accumulated depreciation—equipment	(14,000)	(10,000)
Total	$121,400	$116,000
Accounts payable	$ 19,600	$ 11,100
Bonds payable	10,000	30,000
Common stock	60,000	45,000
Retained earnings	31,800	29,900
Total	$121,400	$116,000

Additional information:

1. Net income was $28,300. Dividends declared and paid were $26,400.
2. Equipment which cost $10,000 and had accumulated depreciation of $1,200 was sold for $4,300.
3. All other changes in noncurrent account balances had a direct effect on cash flows, except the change in accumulated depreciation.

Instructions

(a) Prepare a statement of cash flows for 2017 using the indirect method.
(b) Compute free cash flow.

Solution

2. (a)

STRONG CORPORATION
Statement of Cash Flows
For the Year Ended December 31, 2017

Cash flows from operating activities		
Net income		$ 28,300
Adjustments to reconcile net income to net cash provided by operating activities:		
Depreciation expense	$ 5,200*	
Loss on sale of equipment	4,500**	
Increase in accounts payable	8,500	
Increase in accounts receivable	(1,900)	16,300
Net cash provided by operating activities		44,600
Cash flows from investing activities		
Sale of equipment	4,300	
Purchase of investments	(7,000)	
Net cash used by investing activities		(2,700)
Cash flows from financing activities		
Issuance of common stock	15,000	
Retirement of bonds	(20,000)	
Payment of dividends	(26,400)	
Net cash used by financing activities		(31,400)
Net increase in cash		10,500
Cash at beginning of period		17,700
Cash at end of period		$ 28,200

*[$14,000 − ($10,000 − $1,200)]; **[$4,300 − ($10,000 − $1,200)]

(b) $44,600 − $0 − $26,400 = $18,200

PRACTICE PROBLEMS

Prepare statement of cash flows using indirect method.

(LO 2)

1. The income statement for the year ended December 31, 2017, for Kosinski Manufacturing Company contains the following condensed information.

KOSINSKI MANUFACTURING COMPANY
Income Statement
For the Year Ended December 31, 2017

Sales revenue		$6,583,000
Operating expenses (excluding depreciation)	$4,920,000	
Depreciation expense	880,000	5,800,000
Income before income taxes		783,000
Income tax expense		353,000
Net income		$ 430,000

Included in operating expenses is a $24,000 loss resulting from the sale of equipment for $270,000 cash. Equipment was purchased at a cost of $750,000.

The following balances are reported on Kosinski's comparative balance sheets at December 31.

KOSINSKI MANUFACTURING COMPANY		
Comparative Balance Sheets (partial)		
	2017	**2016**
Cash	$672,000	$130,000
Accounts receivable	775,000	610,000
Inventory	834,000	867,000
Accounts payable	521,000	501,000

Income tax expense of $353,000 represents the amount paid in 2017. Dividends declared and paid in 2017 totaled $200,000.

Instructions

Prepare the statement of cash flows using the indirect method.

Solution

1.

KOSINSKI MANUFACTURING COMPANY		
Statement of Cash Flows—Indirect Method		
For the Year Ended December 31, 2017		
Cash flows from operating activities		
Net income		$ 430,000
Adjustments to reconcile net income to net cash provided by operating activities:		
Depreciation expense	$ 880,000	
Loss on disposal of equipment	24,000	
Increase in accounts receivable	(165,000)	
Decrease in inventory	33,000	
Increase in accounts payable	20,000	792,000
Net cash provided by operating activities		1,222,000
Cash flows from investing activities		
Sale of equipment	270,000	
Purchase of equipment	(750,000)	
Net cash used by investing activities		(480,000)
Cash flows from financing activities		
Payment of cash dividends		(200,000)
Net increase in cash		542,000
Cash at beginning of period		130,000
Cash at end of period		$ 672,000

*2. The income statement for Kosinski Manufacturing Company contains the following condensed information.

Prepare statement of cash flows using direct method.

(LO 4)

KOSINSKI MANUFACTURING COMPANY		
Income Statement		
For the Year Ended December 31, 2017		
Sales revenue		$6,583,000
Operating expenses, excluding depreciation	$4,920,000	
Depreciation expense	880,000	5,800,000
Income before income taxes		783,000
Income tax expense		353,000
Net income		$ 430,000

Included in operating expenses is a $24,000 loss resulting from the sale of equipment for $270,000 cash. Equipment was purchased at a cost of $750,000. The following balances are reported on Kosinski's comparative balance sheet at December 31.

KOSINSKI MANUFACTURING COMPANY		
Comparative Balance Sheets (partial)		
	2017	**2016**
Cash	$672,000	$130,000
Accounts receivable	775,000	610,000
Inventory	834,000	867,000
Accounts payable	521,000	501,000

Income tax expense of $353,000 represents the amount paid in 2017. Dividends declared and paid in 2017 totaled $200,000.

Instructions

Prepare the statement of cash flows using the direct method.

Solution

2.

KOSINSKI MANUFACTURING COMPANY		
Statement of Cash Flows—Direct Method		
For the Year Ended December 31, 2017		
Cash flows from operating activities		
Cash collections from customers		$6,418,000*
Cash payments:		
For operating expenses	$4,843,000**	
For income taxes	353,000	5,196,000
Net cash provided by operating activities		1,222,000
Cash flows from investing activities		
Sale of equipment	270,000	
Purchase of equipment	(750,000)	
Net cash used by investing activities		(480,000)
Cash flows from financing activities		
Payment of cash dividends	(200,000)	
Net cash used by financing activities		(200,000)
Net increase in cash		542,000
Cash at beginning of period		130,000
Cash at end of period		$ 672,000
Direct-Method Computations:		
*Computation of cash collections from customers:		
Sales revenue		$6,583,000
Deduct: Increase in accounts receivable		(165,000)
Cash collections from customers		$6,418,000
**Computation of cash payments for operating expenses:		
Operating expenses		$4,920,000
Deduct: Loss on disposal of equipment		(24,000)
Deduct: Decrease in inventories		(33,000)
Deduct: Increase in accounts payable		(20,000)
Cash payments for operating expenses		$4,843,000

WileyPLUS

Brief Exercises, Exercises, DO IT! Exercises, and Problems and many additional resources are available for practice in WileyPLUS

NOTE: All asterisked Questions, Exercises, and Problems relate to material in the appendix to the chapter.

QUESTIONS

1. (a) What is a statement of cash flows?
   (b) Mark Paxson maintains that the statement of cash flows is an optional financial statement. Do you agree? Explain.

2. What questions about cash are answered by the statement of cash flows?

3. Distinguish among the three types of activities reported in the statement of cash flows.

4. (a) What are the major sources (inflows) of cash in a statement of cash flows?
   (b) What are the major uses (outflows) of cash?

5. Why is it important to disclose certain noncash transactions? How should they be disclosed?

6. Diane Hollowell and Terry Parmenter were discussing the format of the statement of cash flows of Snow Candy Co. At the bottom of Snow Candy's statement of cash flows was a separate section entitled "Noncash investing and financing activities." Give three examples of significant noncash transactions that would be reported in this section.

7. Why is it necessary to use comparative balance sheets, a current income statement, and certain transaction data in preparing a statement of cash flows?

8. Contrast the advantages and disadvantages of the direct and indirect methods of preparing the statement of cash flows. Are both methods acceptable? Which method is preferred by the FASB? Which method is more popular?

9. When the total cash inflows exceed the total cash outflows in the statement of cash flows, how and where is this excess identified?

10. Describe the indirect method for determining net cash provided (used) by operating activities.

11. Why is it necessary to convert accrual-basis net income to cash-basis income when preparing a statement of cash flows?

12. The president of Merando Company is puzzled. During the last year, the company experienced a net loss of $800,000, yet its cash increased $300,000 during the same period of time. Explain to the president how this could occur.

13. Identify five items that are adjustments to convert net income to net cash provided by operating activities under the indirect method.

14. Why and how is depreciation expense reported in a statement of cash flows prepared using the indirect method?

15. Why is the statement of cash flows useful?

16. During 2017, Doubleday Company converted $1,700,000 of its total $2,000,000 of bonds payable into common stock. Indicate how the transaction would be reported on a statement of cash flows, if at all.

17. In its 2013 statement of cash flows, what amount did Apple report for net cash (a) provided by operating activities, (b) used for investing activities, and (c) used for financing activities?

*18. Describe the direct method for determining net cash provided by operating activities.

*19. Give the formulas under the direct method for computing (a) cash receipts from customers and (b) cash payments to suppliers.

*20. Molino Inc. reported sales revenue of $2 million for 2017. Accounts receivable decreased $200,000 and accounts payable increased $300,000. Compute cash receipts from customers, assuming that the receivable and payable transactions related to operations.

*21. In the direct method, why is depreciation expense not reported in the cash flows from operating activities section?

*22. Why is it advantageous to use a worksheet when preparing a statement of cash flows? Is a worksheet required to prepare a statement of cash flows?

BRIEF EXERCISES

BE13-1 Each of the items below must be considered in preparing a statement of cash flows for Baskerville Co. for the year ended December 31, 2017. For each item, state how it should be shown in the statement of cash flows for 2017 and the indirect method is used.
(a) Issued bonds for $200,000 cash.
(b) Purchased equipment for $150,000 cash.
(c) Sold land costing $20,000 for $20,000 cash.
(d) Declared and paid a $50,000 cash dividend.

Indicate statement presentation of selected transactions.

(LO 1)

BE13-2 Classify each item as an operating, investing, or financing activity. Assume all items involve cash unless there is information to the contrary and the indirect method is used.
(a) Purchase of equipment.
(b) Proceeds from sale of building.
(c) Redemption of bonds.
(d) Depreciation.
(e) Payment of dividends.
(f) Issuance of common stock.

Classify items by activities.

(LO 1)

Identify financing activity transactions.

(LO 1)

BE13-3 The following T-account is a summary of the Cash account of Cuellar Company.

Cash (Summary Form)			
Balance, Jan. 1	8,000		
Receipts from customers	364,000	Payments for goods	200,000
Dividends on stock investments	6,000	Payments for operating expenses	140,000
Proceeds from sale of equipment	36,000	Interest paid	10,000
Proceeds from issuance of		Taxes paid	8,000
bonds payable	300,000	Dividends paid	50,000
Balance, Dec. 31	306,000		

What amount of net cash provided (used) by financing activities should be reported in the statement of cash flows?

Compute net cash provided by operating activities—indirect method.

(LO 2)

BE13-4 Telfer, Inc. reported net income of $2.8 million in 2017. Depreciation for the year was $160,000, accounts receivable decreased $350,000, and accounts payable decreased $280,000. Compute net cash provided by operating activities using the indirect method.

Compute net cash provided by operating activities—indirect method.

(LO 2)

BE13-5 The net income for Metz Co. for 2017 was $280,000. For 2017, depreciation on plant assets was $70,000, and the company incurred a loss on disposal of plant assets of $12,000. Compute net cash provided by operating activities under the indirect method.

Compute net cash provided by operating activities—indirect method.

(LO 2)

BE13-6 The comparative balance sheets for Montalvo Company show these changes in noncash current asset accounts: accounts receivable decrease $80,000, prepaid expenses increase $28,000, and inventories increase $30,000. Compute net cash provided by operating activities using the indirect method assuming that net income is $300,000.

Determine cash received from sale of equipment.

(LO 2)

BE13-7 The T-accounts for Equipment and the related Accumulated Depreciation—Equipment for Luo Company at the end of 2017 are shown here.

Equipment			
Beg. bal.	80,000	Disposals	22,000
Acquisitions	41,600		
End. bal.	99,600		

Accumulated Depreciation—Equipment			
Disposals	5,500	Beg. bal.	44,500
		Depr. exp.	12,000
		End. bal.	51,000

In addition, Luo Company's income statement reported a loss on the disposal of equipment of $6,500. What amount was reported on the statement of cash flows as "cash flow from sale of equipment"?

Calculate free cash flow.

(LO 3)

BE13-8 Assume that during 2017, **Cypress Semiconductor Corporation** reported net cash provided by operating activities of $155,793,000, net cash used in investing activities of $207,826,000 (including cash spent for plant assets of $132,280,000), and net cash used in financing activities of $33,372,000. Dividends of $5,000,000 were paid. Calculate free cash flow.

Calculate free cash flow.

(LO 3)

BE13-9 Hinck Corporation reported net cash provided by operating activities of $360,000, net cash used by investing activities of $250,000 (including cash spent for capital assets of $200,000), and net cash provided by financing activities of $70,000. Dividends of $140,000 were paid. Calculate free cash flow.

Calculate free cash flow.

(LO 3)

BE13-10 Suppose in a recent quarter, **Alliance Atlantis Communications Inc.** reported net cash provided by operating activities of $45,600,000 and revenues of $264,800,000. Cash spent on plant asset additions during the quarter was $1,600,000. No dividends were paid. Calculate free cash flow.

BE13-11 The management of Morrow Inc. is trying to decide whether it can increase its dividend. During the current year, it reported net income of $875,000. It had net cash provided by operating activities of $734,000, paid cash dividends of $70,000, and had capital expenditures of $280,000. Compute the company's free cash flow, and discuss whether an increase in the dividend appears warranted. What other factors should be considered?

Calculate and analyze free cash flow.

(LO 3)

*BE13-12 Suppose Columbia Sportswear Company had accounts receivable of $206,024,000 at the beginning of a recent year, and $267,653,000 at year-end. Sales revenue was $1,095,307,000 for the year. What is the amount of cash receipts from customers?

Compute receipts from customers—direct method.

(LO 4)

*BE13-13 Howell Corporation reported income tax expense of $340,000,000 on its 2017 income statement and income taxes payable of $297,000,000 at December 31, 2016, and $522,000,000 at December 31, 2017. What amount of cash payments were made for income taxes during 2017?

Compute cash payments for income taxes—direct method.

(LO 4)

*BE13-14 Sisson Corporation reports operating expenses of $80,000 excluding depreciation expense of $15,000 for 2017. During the year, prepaid expenses decreased $6,600 and accrued expenses payable increased $4,400. Compute the cash payments for operating expenses in 2017.

Compute cash payments for operating expenses—direct method.

(LO 4)

*BE13-15 During the year, prepaid expenses decreased $5,600, and accrued expenses increased $2,400. Indicate how the changes in prepaid expenses and accrued expenses payable should be entered in the reconciling columns of a worksheet. Assume that beginning balances were prepaid expenses $18,600 and accrued expenses payable $8,200.

Indicate entries in worksheet.

(LO 5)

DO IT! Exercises

DO IT! 13-1 Ragsdell Corporation had the following transactions.

1. Issued $200,000 of bonds payable.
2. Paid utilities expense.
3. Issued 500 shares of preferred stock for $45,000.
4. Sold land and a building for $250,000.
5. Lent $30,000 to Tegtmeier Corporation, receiving Tegtmeier's 1-year, 12% note.

Classify each of these transactions by type of cash flow activity (operating, investing, or financing).

Classify transactions by type of cash flow activity.

(LO 1)

DO IT! 13-2 Wise Photography reported net income of $130,000 for 2017. Included in the income statement were depreciation expense of $6,000, amortization expense of $2,000, and a gain on disposal of equipment of $3,600. Wise's comparative balance sheets show the following balances.

Calculate net cash from operating activities.

(LO 2)

	12/31/16	12/31/17
Accounts receivable	$27,000	$21,000
Accounts payable	6,000	9,200

Calculate net cash provided by operating activities for Wise Photography.

DO IT! 13-3 Obermeyer Corporation issued the following statement of cash flows for 2017.

Compute and discuss free cash flow.

(LO 3)

OBERMEYER CORPORATION
Statement of Cash Flows—Indirect Method
For the Year Ended December 31, 2017

Cash flows from operating activities		
Net income		$59,000
Adjustments to reconcile net income to net cash		
provided by operating activities:		
Depreciation expense	$ 9,100	
Loss on disposal of equipment	9,500	
Increase in inventory	(5,000)	
Decrease in accounts receivable	3,300	
Decrease in accounts payable	(2,200)	14,700
Net cash provided by operating activities		73,700
Cash flows from investing activities		
Sale of investments	3,100	
Purchase of equipment	(27,000)	
Net cash used by investing activities		(23,900)
Cash flows from financing activities		
Issuance of stock	20,000	
Payment on long-term note payable	(10,000)	
Payment for dividends	(15,000)	
Net cash used by financing activities		(5,000)
Net increase in cash		44,800
Cash at beginning of year		13,000
Cash at end of year		$57,800

(a) Compute free cash flow for Obermeyer Corporation. (b) Explain why free cash flow often provides better information than "Net cash provided by operating activities."

EXERCISES

Classify transactions by type of activity.

(LO 1)

E13-1 Tabares Corporation had these transactions during 2017.
(a) Issued $50,000 par value common stock for cash.
(b) Purchased a machine for $30,000, giving a long-term note in exchange.
(c) Issued $200,000 par value common stock upon conversion of bonds having a face value of $200,000.
(d) Declared and paid a cash dividend of $18,000.
(e) Sold a long-term investment with a cost of $15,000 for $15,000 cash.
(f) Collected $16,000 of accounts receivable.
(g) Paid $18,000 on accounts payable.

Instructions
Analyze the transactions and indicate whether each transaction resulted in a cash flow from operating activities, investing activities, financing activities, or noncash investing and financing activities.

Classify transactions by type of activity.

(LO 1)

E13-2 An analysis of comparative balance sheets, the current year's income statement, and the general ledger accounts of Wellman Corp. uncovered the following items. Assume all items involve cash unless there is information to the contrary.

(a) Payment of interest on notes payable.
(b) Exchange of land for patent.
(c) Sale of building at book value.
(d) Payment of dividends.
(e) Depreciation.
(f) Receipt of dividends on investment in stock.
(g) Receipt of interest on notes receivable.

(h) Issuance of common stock.
(i) Amortization of patent.
(j) Issuance of bonds for land.
(k) Purchase of land.
(l) Conversion of bonds into common stock.
(m) Sale of land at a loss.
(n) Retirement of bonds.

Instructions

Indicate how each item should be classified in the statement of cash flows using these four major classifications: operating activity (indirect method), investing activity, financing activity, and significant noncash investing and financing activity.

E13-3 Cushenberry Corporation had the following transactions.

1. Sold land (cost $12,000) for $15,000.
2. Issued common stock at par for $20,000.
3. Recorded depreciation on buildings for $17,000.
4. Paid salaries of $9,000.
5. Issued 1,000 shares of $1 par value common stock for equipment worth $8,000.
6. Sold equipment (cost $10,000, accumulated depreciation $7,000) for $1,200.

Prepare journal entry and determine effect on cash flows.

(LO 1)

Instructions

For each transaction above, (a) prepare the journal entry, and (b) indicate how it would affect the statement of cash flows using the indirect method.

E13-4 Gutierrez Company reported net income of $225,000 for 2017. Gutierrez also reported depreciation expense of $45,000 and a loss of $5,000 on the disposal of equipment. The comparative balance sheet shows a decrease in accounts receivable of $15,000 for the year, a $17,000 increase in accounts payable, and a $4,000 decrease in prepaid expenses.

Prepare the operating activities section—indirect method.

(LO 2)

Instructions

Prepare the operating activities section of the statement of cash flows for 2017. Use the indirect method.

E13-5 The current sections of Scoggin Inc.'s balance sheets at December 31, 2016 and 2017, are presented here. Scoggin's net income for 2017 was $153,000. Depreciation expense was $24,000.

Prepare the operating activities section—indirect method.

(LO 2)

	2017	2016
Current assets		
Cash	$105,000	$ 99,000
Accounts receivable	110,000	89,000
Inventory	158,000	172,000
Prepaid expenses	27,000	22,000
Total current assets	$400,000	$382,000
Current liabilities		
Accrued expenses payable	$ 15,000	$ 5,000
Accounts payable	85,000	92,000
Total current liabilities	$100,000	$ 97,000

Instructions

Prepare the net cash provided by operating activities section of the company's statement of cash flows for the year ended December 31, 2017, using the indirect method.

E13-6 The three accounts shown on page 644 appear in the general ledger of Herrick Corp. during 2017.

Prepare partial statement of cash flows—indirect method.

(LO 2)

Equipment

Date		Debit	Credit	Balance
Jan. 1	Balance			160,000
July 31	Purchase of equipment	70,000		230,000
Sept. 2	Cost of equipment constructed	53,000		283,000
Nov. 10	Cost of equipment sold		49,000	234,000

Accumulated Depreciation—Equipment

Date		Debit	Credit	Balance
Jan. 1	Balance			71,000
Nov. 10	Accumulated depreciation on equipment sold	30,000		41,000
Dec. 31	Depreciation for year		28,000	69,000

Retained Earnings

Date		Debit	Credit	Balance
Jan. 1	Balance			105,000
Aug. 23	Dividends (cash)	14,000		91,000
Dec. 31	Net income		77,000	168,000

Instructions

From the postings in the accounts, indicate how the information is reported on a statement of cash flows using the indirect method. The loss on disposal of equipment was $7,000. (*Hint:* Cost of equipment constructed is reported in the investing activities section as a decrease in cash of $53,000.)

Prepare statement of cash flows and compute free cash flow.

(LO 2, 3)

E13-7 Rojas Corporation's comparative balance sheets are presented below.

ROJAS CORPORATION
Comparative Balance Sheets
December 31

	2017	2016
Cash	$ 14,300	$ 10,700
Accounts receivable	21,200	23,400
Land	20,000	26,000
Buildings	70,000	70,000
Accumulated depreciation—buildings	(15,000)	(10,000)
Total	$110,500	$120,100
Accounts payable	$ 12,370	$ 31,100
Common stock	75,000	69,000
Retained earnings	23,130	20,000
Total	$110,500	$120,100

Additional information:

1. Net income was $22,630. Dividends declared and paid were $19,500.
2. No noncash investing and financing activities occurred during 2017.
3. The land was sold for cash of $4,900.

Instructions

(a) Prepare a statement of cash flows for 2017 using the indirect method.
(b) Compute free cash flow.

E13-8 Here are comparative balance sheets for Velo Company.

Prepare a statement of cash flows—indirect method.

(LO 2)

VELO COMPANY
Comparative Balance Sheets
December 31

Assets	2017	2016
Cash	$ 63,000	$ 22,000
Accounts receivable	85,000	76,000
Inventory	170,000	189,000
Land	75,000	100,000
Equipment	270,000	200,000
Accumulated depreciation—equipment	(66,000)	(32,000)
Total	$597,000	$555,000

Liabilities and Stockholders' Equity	2017	2016
Accounts payable	$ 39,000	$ 47,000
Bonds payable	150,000	200,000
Common stock ($1 par)	216,000	174,000
Retained earnings	192,000	134,000
Total	$597,000	$555,000

Additional information:

1. Net income for 2017 was $93,000.
2. Cash dividends of $35,000 were declared and paid.
3. Bonds payable amounting to $50,000 were redeemed for cash $50,000.
4. Common stock was issued for $42,000 cash.
5. No equipment was sold during 2017, but land was sold at cost.

Instructions
Prepare a statement of cash flows for 2017 using the indirect method.

E13-9 Rodriquez Corporation's comparative balance sheets are presented below.

Prepare statement of cash flows and compute free cash flow.

(LO 2, 3)

RODRIQUEZ CORPORATION
Comparative Balance Sheets
December 31

	2017	2016
Cash	$ 15,200	$ 17,700
Accounts receivable	25,200	22,300
Investments	20,000	16,000
Equipment	60,000	70,000
Accumulated depreciation—equipment	(14,000)	(10,000)
Total	$106,400	$116,000

	2017	2016
Accounts payable	$ 14,600	$ 11,100
Bonds payable	10,000	30,000
Common stock	50,000	45,000
Retained earnings	31,800	29,900
Total	$106,400	$116,000

Additional information:

1. Net income was $18,300. Dividends declared and paid were $16,400.
2. Equipment which cost $10,000 and had accumulated depreciation of $1,200 was sold for $3,300.
3. No noncash investing and financing activities occurred during 2017.

Instructions
(a) Prepare a statement of cash flows for 2017 using the indirect method.
(b) Compute free cash flow.

Compute net cash provided by operating activities—direct method.
(LO 4)

*E13-10 Macgregor Company completed its first year of operations on December 31, 2017. Its initial income statement showed that Macgregor had revenues of $192,000 and operating expenses of $78,000. Accounts receivable and accounts payable at year-end were $60,000 and $23,000, respectively. Assume that accounts payable related to operating expenses. Ignore income taxes.

Instructions
Compute net cash provided by operating activities using the direct method.

Compute cash payments—direct method.
(LO 4)

*E13-11 Suppose a recent income statement for McDonald's Corporation shows cost of goods sold $4,852.7 million and operating expenses (including depreciation expense of $1,201 million) $10,671.5 million. The comparative balance sheet for the year shows that inventory increased $18.1 million, prepaid expenses increased $56.3 million, accounts payable (merchandise suppliers) increased $136.9 million, and accrued expenses payable increased $160.9 million.

Instructions
Using the direct method, compute (a) cash payments to suppliers and (b) cash payments for operating expenses.

Compute cash flow from operating activities—direct method.
(LO 4)

*E13-12 The 2017 accounting records of Blocker Transport reveal these transactions and events.

Payment of interest	$ 10,000	Collection of accounts receivable	$182,000
Cash sales	48,000	Payment of salaries and wages	53,000
Receipt of dividend revenue	18,000	Depreciation expense	16,000
Payment of income taxes	12,000	Proceeds from sale of vehicles	12,000
Net income	38,000	Purchase of equipment for cash	22,000
Payment of accounts payable		Loss on disposal of vehicles	3,000
for merchandise	115,000	Payment of dividends	14,000
Payment for land	74,000	Payment of operating expenses	28,000

Instructions
Prepare the cash flows from operating activities section using the direct method. (Not all of the items will be used.)

Calculate cash flows—direct method.
(LO 4)

*E13-13 The following information is taken from the 2017 general ledger of Swisher Company.

Rent	Rent expense	$ 48,000
	Prepaid rent, January 1	5,900
	Prepaid rent, December 31	9,000
Salaries	Salaries and wages expense	$ 54,000
	Salaries and wages payable, January 1	10,000
	Salaries and wages payable, December 31	8,000
Sales	Sales revenue	$175,000
	Accounts receivable, January 1	16,000
	Accounts receivable, December 31	7,000

Instructions
In each case, compute the amount that should be reported in the operating activities section of the statement of cash flows under the direct method.

Prepare a worksheet.
(LO 5)

*E13-14 Comparative balance sheets for International Company are presented as follows.

INTERNATIONAL COMPANY
Comparative Balance Sheets
December 31

Assets	2017	2016
Cash	$ 73,000	$ 22,000
Accounts receivable	85,000	76,000
Inventory	180,000	189,000
Land	75,000	100,000
Equipment	250,000	200,000
Accumulated depreciation—equipment	(66,000)	(42,000)
Total	$597,000	$545,000

Liabilities and Stockholders' Equity		
Accounts payable	$ 34,000	$ 47,000
Bonds payable	150,000	200,000
Common stock ($1 par)	214,000	164,000
Retained earnings	199,000	134,000
Total	$597,000	$545,000

Additional information:

1. Net income for 2017 was $135,000.
2. Cash dividends of $70,000 were declared and paid.
3. Bonds payable amounting to $50,000 were redeemed for cash $50,000.
4. Common stock was issued for $50,000 cash.
5. Depreciation expense was $24,000.
6. Sales revenue for the year was $978,000.
7. Land was sold at cost, and equipment was purchased for cash.

Instructions

Prepare a worksheet for a statement of cash flows for 2017 using the indirect method. Enter the reconciling items directly on the worksheet, using letters to cross-reference each entry.

EXERCISES: SET B AND CHALLENGE EXERCISES

Visit the book's companion website, at **www.wiley.com/college/weygandt**, and choose the Student Companion site to access Exercises: Set B and Challenge Exercises.

PROBLEMS: SET A

P13-1A You are provided with the following transactions that took place during a recent fiscal year.

Distinguish among operating, investing, and financing activities.

(LO 1)

Transaction	Statement of Cash Flows Activity Affected	Cash Inflow, Outflow, or No Effect?
(a) Recorded depreciation expense on the plant assets.		
(b) Recorded and paid interest expense.		
(c) Recorded cash proceeds from a disposal of plant assets.		
(d) Acquired land by issuing common stock.		
(e) Paid a cash dividend to preferred stockholders.		
(f) Paid a cash dividend to common stockholders.		
(g) Recorded cash sales.		
(h) Recorded sales on account.		
(i) Purchased inventory for cash.		
(j) Purchased inventory on account.		

Instructions

Complete the table indicating whether each item (1) affects operating (O) activities, investing (I) activities, financing (F) activities, or is a noncash (NC) transaction reported in a separate schedule, and (2) represents a cash inflow or cash outflow or has no cash flow effect. Assume use of the indirect approach.

Determine cash flow effects of changes in equity accounts.

(LO 2)

P13-2A The following account balances relate to the stockholders' equity accounts of Kerbs Corp. at year-end.

	2017	2016
Common stock, 10,500 and 10,000 shares, respectively, for 2017 and 2016	$170,000	$140,000
Preferred stock, 5,000 shares	125,000	125,000
Retained earnings	300,000	250,000

A small stock dividend was declared and issued in 2017. The market value of the shares was $10,500. Cash dividends were $15,000 in both 2017 and 2016. The common stock has no par or stated value.

Instructions

(a) Net income $75,500

(a) What was the amount of net income reported by Kerbs Corp. in 2017?
(b) Determine the amounts of any cash inflows or outflows related to the common stock and dividend accounts in 2017.
(c) Indicate where each of the cash inflows or outflows identified in (b) would be classified on the statement of cash flows.

Prepare the operating activities section—indirect method.

(LO 2)

P13-3A The income statement of Whitlock Company is presented here.

WHITLOCK COMPANY
Income Statement
For the Year Ended November 30, 2017

Sales revenue		$7,700,000
Cost of goods sold		
Beginning inventory	$1,900,000	
Purchases	4,400,000	
Goods available for sale	6,300,000	
Ending inventory	1,400,000	
Total cost of goods sold		4,900,000
Gross profit		2,800,000
Operating expenses		1,150,000
Net income		$1,650,000

Additional information:

1. Accounts receivable increased $200,000 during the year, and inventory decreased $500,000.
2. Prepaid expenses increased $150,000 during the year.
3. Accounts payable to suppliers of merchandise decreased $340,000 during the year.
4. Accrued expenses payable decreased $100,000 during the year.
5. Operating expenses include depreciation expense of $70,000.

Instructions

Cash from operations $1,430,000

Prepare the operating activities section of the statement of cash flows for the year ended November 30, 2017, for Whitlock Company, using the indirect method.

Prepare the operating activities section—direct method.

(LO 4) Cash from operations $1,430,000

*P13-4A Data for Whitlock Company are presented in P13-3A.

Instructions

Prepare the operating activities section of the statement of cash flows using the direct method.

Prepare the operating activities section—indirect method.

(LO 2)

P13-5A Zumbrunn Company's income statement contained the following condensed information.

ZUMBRUNN COMPANY
Income Statement
For the Year Ended December 31, 2017

Service revenue		$970,000
Operating expenses, excluding depreciation	$624,000	
Depreciation expense	60,000	
Loss on disposal of equipment	16,000	700,000
Income before income taxes		270,000
Income tax expense		40,000
Net income		$230,000

Zumbrunn's balance sheet contained the comparative data at December 31, shown below.

	2017	2016
Accounts receivable	$75,000	$65,000
Accounts payable	46,000	28,000
Income taxes payable	11,000	7,000

Accounts payable pertain to operating expenses.

Instructions
Prepare the operating activities section of the statement of cash flows using the indirect method.

*__*P13-6A__* Data for Zumbrunn Company are presented in P13-5A.

Instructions
Prepare the operating activities section of the statement of cash flows using the direct method.

P13-7A The following are the financial statements of Nosker Company.

NOSKER COMPANY
Comparative Balance Sheets
December 31

Assets	2017	2016
Cash	$ 38,000	$ 20,000
Accounts receivable	30,000	14,000
Inventory	27,000	20,000
Equipment	60,000	78,000
Accumulated depreciation—equipment	(29,000)	(24,000)
Total	$126,000	$108,000

Liabilities and Stockholders' Equity	2017	2016
Accounts payable	$ 24,000	$ 15,000
Income taxes payable	7,000	8,000
Bonds payable	27,000	33,000
Common stock	18,000	14,000
Retained earnings	50,000	38,000
Total	$126,000	$108,000

NOSKER COMPANY
Income Statement
For the Year Ended December 31, 2017

Sales revenue		$242,000
Cost of goods sold		175,000
Gross profit		67,000
Operating expenses		24,000
Income from operations		43,000
Interest expense		3,000
Income before income taxes		40,000
Income tax expense		8,000
Net income		$ 32,000

Cash from operations
$318,000

Prepare the operating activities section—direct method.

(LO 4)

Cash from operations $318,000

Prepare a statement of cash flows—indirect method, and compute free cash flow.

(LO 2, 3)

Additional data:

1. Dividends declared and paid were $20,000.
2. During the year equipment was sold for $8,500 cash. This equipment cost $18,000 originally and had a book value of $8,500 at the time of sale.
3. All depreciation expense, $14,500, is in the operating expenses.
4. All sales and purchases are on account.

Instructions

(a) *Cash from operations $31,500*

(a) Prepare a statement of cash flows using the indirect method.
(b) Compute free cash flow.

Prepare a statement of cash flows—direct method, and compute free cash flow.

(LO 3, 4)

*P13-8A Data for Nosker Company are presented in P13-7A. Further analysis reveals the following.

1. Accounts payable pertain to merchandise suppliers.
2. All operating expenses except for depreciation were paid in cash.

Instructions

(a) Prepare a statement of cash flows for Nosker Company using the direct method.
(b) Compute free cash flow.

(a) *Cash from operations $31,500*

Prepare a statement of cash flows—indirect method.

(LO 2)

P13-9A Condensed financial data of Cheng Inc. follow.

CHENG INC.
Comparative Balance Sheets
December 31

Assets	2017	2016
Cash	$ 80,800	$ 48,400
Accounts receivable	92,800	33,000
Inventory	117,500	102,850
Prepaid expenses	28,400	26,000
Investments	143,000	114,000
Equipment	270,000	242,500
Accumulated depreciation—equipment	(50,000)	(52,000)
Total	$682,500	$514,750

Liabilities and Stockholders' Equity	2017	2016
Accounts payable	$112,000	$ 67,300
Accrued expenses payable	16,500	17,000
Bonds payable	110,000	150,000
Common stock	220,000	175,000
Retained earnings	224,000	105,450
Total	$682,500	$514,750

CHENG INC.
Income Statement
For the Year Ended December 31, 2017

Sales revenue		$392,780
Less:		
Cost of goods sold	$135,460	
Operating expenses, excluding depreciation	12,410	
Depreciation expense	46,500	
Income tax expense	27,280	
Interest expense	4,730	
Loss on disposal of plant assets	7,500	233,880
Net income		$158,900

Additional information:

1. New equipment costing $85,000 was purchased for cash during the year.
2. Old equipment having an original cost of $57,500 was sold for $1,500 cash.
3. Bonds matured and were paid off at face value for cash.
4. A cash dividend of $40,350 was declared and paid during the year.

Instructions

Prepare a statement of cash flows using the indirect method.

Cash from operations
$180,250

*P13-10A Data for Cheng Inc. are presented in P13-9A. Further analysis reveals that accounts payable pertain to merchandise creditors.

Prepare a statement of cash flows—direct method.

(LO 4)

Instructions

Prepare a statement of cash flows for Cheng Inc. using the direct method.

Cash from operations
$180,250

P13-11A The comparative balance sheets for Rothlisberger Company as of December 31 are presented below.

Prepare a statement of cash flows—indirect method.

(LO 2)

ROTHLISBERGER COMPANY
Comparative Balance Sheets
December 31

Assets	2017	2016
Cash	$ 81,000	$ 45,000
Accounts receivable	41,000	62,000
Inventory	151,450	142,000
Prepaid expenses	15,280	21,000
Land	105,000	130,000
Buildings	200,000	200,000
Accumulated depreciation—buildings	(60,000)	(40,000)
Equipment	221,000	155,000
Accumulated depreciation—equipment	(45,000)	(35,000)
Total	$709,730	$680,000

Liabilities and Stockholders' Equity	2017	2016
Accounts payable	$ 47,730	$ 40,000
Bonds payable	260,000	300,000
Common stock, $1 par	200,000	160,000
Retained earnings	202,000	180,000
Total	$709,730	$680,000

Additional information:

1. Operating expenses include depreciation expense of $42,000 and charges from prepaid expenses of $5,720.
2. Land was sold for cash at book value.
3. Cash dividends of $20,000 were paid.
4. Net income for 2017 was $42,000.
5. Equipment was purchased for $88,000 cash. In addition, equipment costing $22,000 with a book value of $10,000 was sold for $6,000 cash.
6. Bonds were converted at face value by issuing 40,000 shares of $1 par value common stock.

Instructions

Prepare a statement of cash flows for the year ended December 31, 2017, using the indirect method.

Cash from operations
$113,000

Prepare a worksheet—indirect method.

*P13-12A Condensed financial data of Oakley Company appear below.

(LO 5)

OAKLEY COMPANY
Comparative Balance Sheets
December 31

Assets	2017	2016
Cash	$ 82,700	$ 47,250
Accounts receivable	90,800	57,000
Inventory	126,900	102,650
Investments	84,500	87,000
Equipment	255,000	205,000
Accumulated depreciation—equipment	(49,500)	(40,000)
	$590,400	$458,900

Liabilities and Stockholders' Equity		
Accounts payable	$ 57,700	$ 48,280
Accrued expenses payable	12,100	18,830
Bonds payable	100,000	70,000
Common stock	250,000	200,000
Retained earnings	170,600	121,790
	$590,400	$458,900

OAKLEY COMPANY
Income Statement
For the Year Ended December 31, 2017

Sales revenue		$297,500
Gain on disposal of equipment		8,750
		306,250
Less:		
Cost of goods sold	$99,460	
Operating expenses (excluding depreciation expense)	14,670	
Depreciation expense	49,700	
Income tax expense	7,270	
Interest expense	2,940	174,040
Net income		$132,210

Additional information:

1. Equipment costing $97,000 was purchased for cash during the year.
2. Investments were sold at cost.
3. Equipment costing $47,000 was sold for $15,550, resulting in gain of $8,750.
4. A cash dividend of $83,400 was declared and paid during the year.

Instructions

Reconciling items total
$610,210

Prepare a worksheet for the statement of cash flows using the indirect method. Enter the reconciling items directly in the worksheet columns, using letters to cross-reference each entry.

PROBLEMS: SET B AND SET C

Visit the book's companion website, at **www.wiley.com/college/weygandt**, and choose the Student Companion site to access Problems: Set B and Set C.

CONTINUING PROBLEM

COOKIE CREATIONS

(*Note:* This is a continuation of the Cookie Creations problem from Chapters 1 through 12.)

CC13 Natalie has prepared the balance sheet and income statement of Cookie & Coffee Creations Inc. and would like you to prepare the statement of cash flows.

Go to the book's companion website, **www.wiley.com/college/weygandt**, *to see the completion of this problem.*

© leungchopan/
Shutterstock

BROADENING YOUR *PERSPECTIVE*

FINANCIAL REPORTING AND ANALYSIS

Financial Reporting Problem: Apple Inc.

BYP13-1 The financial statements of Apple Inc. are presented in Appendix A. Instructions for accessing and using the company's complete annual report, including the notes to the financial statements, are also provided in Appendix A.

Instructions
(a) What was the amount of net cash provided by operating activities for the year ended September 28, 2013? For the year ended September 29, 2012?
(b) What was the amount of increase or decrease in cash and cash equivalents for the year ended September 28, 2013? For the year ended September 29, 2012?
(c) Which method of computing net cash provided by operating activities does Apple use?
(d) From your analysis of the 2013 statement of cash flows, did the change in accounts and notes receivable require or provide cash? Did the change in inventories require or provide cash? Did the change in accounts payable and other current liabilities require or provide cash?
(e) What was the net outflow or inflow of cash from investing activities for the year ended September 28, 2013?
(f) What was the amount of income taxes paid in the year ended September 28, 2013?

Comparative Analysis Problem:
PepsiCo, Inc. vs. The Coca-Cola Company

BYP13-2 PepsiCo's financial statements are presented in Appendix B. Financial statements of The Coca-Cola Company are presented in Appendix C. Instructions for accessing and using the complete annual reports of PepsiCo and Coca-Cola, including the notes to the financial statements, are also provided in Appendices B and C, respectively.

Instructions
(a) Based on the information contained in these financial statements, compute free cash flow for each company.
(b) What conclusions concerning the management of cash can be drawn from these data?

Comparative Analysis Problem:
Amazon.com, Inc. vs. Wal-Mart Stores, Inc.

BYP13-3 Amazon.com, Inc.'s financial statements are presented in Appendix D. Financial statements of Wal-Mart Stores, Inc. are presented in Appendix E. Instructions for accessing and using the complete annual reports of Amazon and Wal-Mart, including the notes to the financial statements, are also provided in Appendices D and E, respectively.

Instructions
(a) Based on the information contained in these financial statements, compute free cash flow for each company.
(b) What conclusions concerning the management of cash can be drawn from these data?

Decision-Making Across the Organization

BYP13-4 Tom Epps and Mary Jones are examining the following statement of cash flows for Guthrie Company for the year ended January 31, 2017.

GUTHRIE COMPANY
Statement of Cash Flows
For the Year Ended January 31, 2017

Sources of cash	
From sales of merchandise	$380,000
From sale of capital stock	420,000
From sale of investment (purchased below)	80,000
From depreciation	55,000
From issuance of note for truck	20,000
From interest on investments	6,000
Total sources of cash	961,000
Uses of cash	
For purchase of fixtures and equipment	330,000
For merchandise purchased for resale	258,000
For operating expenses (including depreciation)	160,000
For purchase of investment	75,000
For purchase of truck by issuance of note	20,000
For purchase of treasury stock	10,000
For interest on note payable	3,000
Total uses of cash	856,000
Net increase in cash	$105,000

Tom claims that Guthrie's statement of cash flows is an excellent portrayal of a superb first year with cash increasing $105,000. Mary replies that it was not a superb first year. Rather, she says, the year was an operating failure, that the statement is presented incorrectly, and that $105,000 is not the actual increase in cash. The cash balance at the beginning of the year was $140,000.

Instructions
With the class divided into groups, answer the following.

(a) Using the data provided, prepare a statement of cash flows in proper form using the indirect method. The only noncash items in the income statement are depreciation and the gain from the sale of the investment.

(b) With whom do you agree, Tom or Mary? Explain your position.

Real-World Focus

BYP13-5 Purpose: Learn about the SEC.

Address: **www.sec.gov/index.html**, or go to **www.wiley.com/college/weygandt**

From the SEC homepage, choose **About the SEC**.

Instructions
Answer the following questions.

(a) How many enforcement actions does the SEC take each year against securities law violators? What are typical infractions?

(b) After the Depression, Congress passed the Securities Acts of 1933 and 1934 to improve investor confidence in the markets. What two "common sense" notions are these laws based on?

(c) Who was the President of the United States at the time of the creation of the SEC? Who was the first SEC Chairperson?

BYP13-6 Purpose: Use the Internet to view SEC filings.

Address: **biz.yahoo.com/i**, or go to **www.wiley.com/college/weygandt**

Steps:
1. Type in a company name.
2. Choose **Profile**.
3. Choose **SEC Filings**. (This will take you to Yahoo-Edgar Online.)

Instructions
Answer the following questions.

(a) What company did you select?
(b) Which filing is the most recent? What is the date?
(c) What other recent SEC filings are available for your viewing?

CRITICAL THINKING

Communication Activity

BYP13-7 Will Hardin, the owner-president of Computer Services Company, is unfamiliar with the statement of cash flows that you, as his accountant, prepared. He asks for further explanation.

Instructions
Write him a brief memo explaining the form and content of the statement of cash flows as shown in Illustration 13-13 (page 611).

Ethics Case

BYP13-8 Wesley Corp. is a medium-sized wholesaler of automotive parts. It has 10 stockholders who have been paid a total of $1 million in cash dividends for 8 consecutive years. The board's policy requires that, for this dividend to be declared, net cash provided by operating activities as reported in Wesley's current year's statement of cash flows must exceed $1 million. President and CEO Samuel Gunkle's job is secure so long as he produces annual operating cash flows to support the usual dividend.

At the end of the current year, controller Gerald Rondelli presents president Samuel Gunkle with some disappointing news: The net cash provided by operating activities is calculated by the indirect method to be only $970,000. The president says to Gerald, "We must get that amount above $1 million. Isn't there some way to increase operating cash flow by another $30,000?" Gerald answers, "These figures were prepared by my assistant. I'll go back to my office and see what I can do." The president replies, "I know you won't let me down, Gerald."

Upon close scrutiny of the statement of cash flows, Gerald concludes that he can get the operating cash flows above $1 million by reclassifying a $60,000, 2-year note payable listed in the financing activities section as "Proceeds from bank loan—$60,000." He will report the note instead as "Increase in payables—$60,000" and treat it as an adjustment of net income in the operating activities section. He returns to the president, saying, "You can tell the board to declare their usual dividend. Our net cash flow provided by operating activities is $1,030,000." "Good man, Gerald! I knew I could count on you," exults the president.

Instructions
(a) Who are the stakeholders in this situation?
(b) Was there anything unethical about the president's actions? Was there anything unethical about the controller's actions?
(c) Are the board members or anyone else likely to discover the misclassification?

All About You

BYP13-9 In this chapter, you learned that companies prepare a statement of cash flows in order to keep track of their sources and uses of cash and to help them plan for their future cash needs. Planning for your own short- and long-term cash needs is every bit as important as it is for a company.

Instructions
Read the article ("Financial Uh-Oh? No Problem") provided at **www.fool.com/personal-finance/ saving/index.aspx**, and answer the following questions. To access this article, it may be necessary to register at no cost.

(a) Describe the three factors that determine how much money you should set aside for short-term needs.
(b) How many months of living expenses does the article suggest to set aside?
(c) Estimate how much you should set aside based upon your current situation. Are you closer to Cliff's scenario or to Prudence's?

FASB Codification Activity

BYP13-10 If your school has a subscription to the FASB Codification, go to **http://aaahq.org/ ascLogin.cfm** to log in and prepare responses to the following. Use the Master Glossary to determine the proper definitions.

(a) What are cash equivalents?
(b) What are financing activities?
(c) What are investing activities?
(d) What are operating activities?
(e) What is the primary objective for the statement of cash flow? Is working capital the basis for meeting this objective?
(f) Do companies need to disclose information about investing and financing activities that do not affect cash receipts or cash payments? If so, how should such information be disclosed?

A Look at IFRS

LEARNING
OBJECTIVE **7**

Compare the procedures for the statement of cash flows under GAAP and IFRS.

As in GAAP, the statement of cash flows is a required statement for IFRS. In addition, the content and presentation of an IFRS statement of cash flows is similar to the one used for GAAP. However, the disclosure requirements related to the statement of cash flows are more extensive under GAAP. *IAS* 7 ("Cash Flow Statements") provides the overall IFRS requirements for cash flow information.

Relevant Facts

Following are the key similarities and differences between GAAP and IFRS as related to the statement of cash flows.

Similarities

- Companies preparing financial statements under IFRS must also prepare a statement of cash flows as an integral part of the financial statements.
- Both IFRS and GAAP require that the statement of cash flows should have three major sections—operating, investing, and financing activities—along with changes in cash and cash equivalents.
- Similar to GAAP, the statement of cash flows can be prepared using either the indirect or direct method under IFRS. In both U.S. and international settings, companies choose for the most part to use the indirect method for reporting net cash flows from operating activities.
- The definition of cash equivalents used in IFRS is similar to that used in GAAP. A major difference is that in certain situations, bank overdrafts are considered part of cash and cash equivalents under IFRS (which is not the case in GAAP). Under GAAP, bank overdrafts are classified as financing activities in the statement of cash flows and are reported as liabilities on the balance sheet.

Differences

- IFRS requires that noncash investing and financing activities be excluded from the statement of cash flows. Instead, these noncash activities should be reported elsewhere. This requirement is interpreted to mean that noncash investing and financing activities should be disclosed in the notes to the financial statements instead of in the financial statements. Under GAAP, companies may present this information on the face of the statement of cash flows.
- One area where there can be substantial differences between IFRS and GAAP relates to the classification of interest, dividends, and taxes. The following table indicates the differences between the two approaches.

Item	IFRS	GAAP
Interest paid	Operating or financing	Operating
Interest received	Operating or investing	Operating
Dividends paid	Operating or financing	Financing
Dividends received	Operating or investing	Operating
Taxes paid	Operating—unless specific identification with financing or investing activity	Operating

- Under IFRS, some companies present the operating section in a single line item, with a full reconciliation provided in the notes to the financial statements. This presentation is not seen under GAAP.

Looking to the Future

Presently, the FASB and the IASB are involved in a joint project on the presentation and organization of information in the financial statements. One interesting approach, revealed in a published proposal from that project, is that in the future the income statement and balance sheet would adopt headings similar to those of the statement of cash flows. That is, the income statement and balance sheet would be broken into operating, investing, and financing sections.

IFRS Practice

IFRS Self-Test Questions

1. Under IFRS, interest paid can be reported as:
   (a) only a financing activity.
   (b) a financing activity or an investing activity.
   (c) a financing activity or an operating activity.
   (d) only an operating activity.

2. IFRS requires that noncash items:
   (a) be reported in the section to which they relate, that is, a noncash investing activity would be reported in the investing section.
   (b) be disclosed in the notes to the financial statements.
   (c) do not need to be reported.
   (d) be treated in a fashion similar to cash equivalents.

3. In the future, it appears likely that:
   (a) the income statement and balance sheet will have headings of operating, investing, and financing, much like the statement of cash flows.
   (b) cash and cash equivalents will be combined in a single line item.
   (c) the IASB will not allow companies to use the direct approach to the statement of cash flows.
   (d) None of the above.

4. Under IFRS:
   (a) taxes are always treated as an operating activity.
   (b) the income statement uses the headings operating, investing, and financing.
   (c) dividends received can be either an operating or investing activity.
   (d) dividends paid can be either an operating or investing activity.

5. Which of the following is **correct?**
   (a) Under IFRS, the statement of cash flows is optional.
   (b) IFRS requires use of the direct approach in preparing the statement of cash flows.
   (c) The majority of companies following GAAP and the majority following IFRS employ the indirect approach to the statement of cash flows.
   (d) Under IFRS, companies offset financing activities against investing activities.

IFRS Exercises

IFRS13-1 Discuss the differences that exist in the treatment of bank overdrafts under GAAP and IFRS.

IFRS13-2 Describe the treatment of each of the following items under IFRS versus GAAP.
(a) Interest paid.   (c) Dividends paid.
(b) Interest received.   (d) Dividends received.

International Financial Reporting Problem: Louis Vuitton

IFRS13-3 The financial statements of Louis Vuitton are presented in Appendix F. Instructions for accessing and using the company's complete annual report, including the notes to its financial statements, are also provided in Appendix F.

Instructions
Use the company's annual report to answer the following questions.

(a) In which section (operating, investing, or financing) does Louis Vuitton report interest paid (finance costs)?
(b) In which section (operating, investing, or financing) does Louis Vuitton report dividends received?
(c) If Louis Vuitton reported under GAAP rather than IFRS, how would its treatment of bank overdrafts differ?

Answers to IFRS Self-Test Questions
1. c **2.** b **3.** a **4.** c **5.** c

Financial Statement Analysis

CHAPTER PREVIEW As the Feature Story below highlights, we can all learn an important lesson from Warren Buffett. Study companies carefully if you wish to invest. Do not get caught up in fads but instead find companies that are financially healthy. Using some of the decision tools presented in this textbook, you can perform a rudimentary analysis on any U.S. company and draw basic conclusions about its financial health. Although it would not be wise for you to bet your life savings on a company's stock relying solely on your current level of knowledge, we strongly encourage you to practice your new skills wherever possible. Only with practice will you improve your ability to interpret financial numbers.

Before unleashing you on the world of high finance, we present a few more important concepts and techniques, as well as provide you with one more comprehensive review of corporate financial statements. We use all of the decision tools presented in this textbook to analyze a single company— Macy's, Inc.—one of the country's oldest and largest retail store chains.

FEATURE STORY

It Pays to Be Patient

A recent issue of *Forbes* magazine listed Warren Buffett as the richest person in the world. His estimated wealth was $62 billion, give or take a few million. How much is $62 billion? If you invested $62 billion in an investment earning just 4%, you could spend $6.8 million per day—every day—forever.

So, how does Buffett spend his money? Basically, he doesn't! He still lives in the same house that he purchased in Omaha, Nebraska, in 1958 for $31,500. He still drives his own car (a Cadillac DTS). And, in case you believe that his kids are riding the road to Easy Street, think again. Buffett has committed to donate virtually all of his money to charity before he dies.

How did Buffett amass this wealth? Through careful investing. He applies the basic techniques he learned in the 1950s from the great value investor Benjamin Graham. Buffett looks for companies that have good long-term potential but are currently underpriced. He invests in companies that have low exposure to debt and that reinvest their earnings for future growth. He does not get caught up in fads or the latest trends.

For example, Buffett sat out on the dot-com mania in the 1990s. When other investors put lots of money into fledgling high-tech firms, Buffett didn't bite because the dot-com companies failed to meet his criteria. He didn't get to enjoy the stock price boom on the way up, but on the other hand, he didn't have to suffer the plummet back down to Earth. When the dot-com bubble burst, everyone else suffered from investment shock. Buffett swooped in and scooped up deals on companies that he had been following for years.

In 2012, when the stock market reached near record highs, Buffett's returns significantly lagged behind the market. Only 26% of his investments at that time were in stock, and he was sitting on $38 billion in cash. One commentator noted that "if the past is any guide, just when Buffett seems to look most like a loser, the party is about to end."

If you think you want to follow Buffett's example and transform your humble nest egg into a mountain of cash, be warned. His techniques have been widely circulated and emulated, but never practiced with the same degree of success. You should probably start by honing your financial analysis skills. A good way for you to begin your career as a successful investor is to master the fundamentals of financial analysis discussed in this chapter.

Source: Jason Zweig, "Buffett Is Out of Step," *Wall Street Journal* (May 7, 2012).

Daniel Acker/Bloomberg/Getty Images, Inc.

CHAPTER OUTLINE

Learning Objectives

1   Apply horizontal and vertical analysis to financial statements.

- Need for comparative analysis
- Tools of analysis
- Horizontal analysis
- Vertical analysis

DO IT!   **1**   Horizontal Analysis

2   Analyze a company's performance using ratio analysis.

- Liquidity ratios
- Profitability ratios
- Solvency ratios
- Summary of ratios

DO IT!   **2**   Ratio Analysis

3   Apply the concept of sustainable income.

- Discontinued operations
- Other comprehensive income

DO IT!   **3**   Unusual Items

Go to the **REVIEW AND PRACTICE** section at the end of the chapter for a review of key concepts and practice applications with solutions.

Visit **WileyPLUS with ORION** for additional tutorials and practice opportunities.

Analyzing financial statements involves evaluating three characteristics: a company's liquidity, profitability, and solvency. A **short-term creditor**, such as a bank, is primarily interested in liquidity—the ability of the borrower to pay obligations when they come due. The liquidity of the borrower is extremely important in evaluating the safety of a loan. A **long-term creditor**, such as a bondholder, looks to profitability and solvency measures that indicate the company's ability to survive over a long period of time. Long-term creditors consider such measures as the amount of debt in the company's capital structure and its ability to meet interest payments. Similarly, **stockholders** look at the profitability and solvency of the company. They want to assess the likelihood of dividends and the growth potential of the stock.

Need for Comparative Analysis

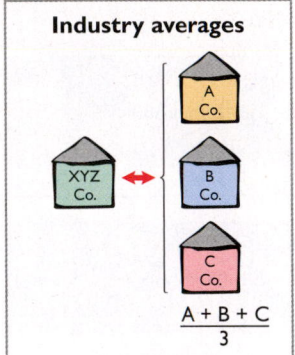

Every item reported in a financial statement has significance. When **Macy's, Inc.** reports cash and cash equivalents of $2.3 billion on its balance sheet, we know the company had that amount of cash on the balance sheet date. But, we do not know whether the amount represents an increase over prior years, or whether it is adequate in relation to the company's need for cash. To obtain such information, we need to compare the amount of cash with other financial statement data.

Comparisons can be made on a number of different bases. Three are illustrated in this chapter.

1. **Intracompany basis.** Comparisons within a company are often useful to detect changes in financial relationships and significant trends. For example, a comparison of Macy's current year's cash amount with the prior year's cash amount shows either an increase or a decrease. Likewise, a comparison of Macy's year-end cash amount with the amount of its total assets at year-end shows the proportion of total assets in the form of cash.

2. **Industry averages.** Comparisons with industry averages provide information about a company's relative position within the industry. For example, financial statement readers can compare Macy's financial data with the averages for its industry compiled by financial rating organizations such as **Dun & Bradstreet**, **Moody's**, and **Standard & Poor's**, or with information provided on the Internet by organizations such as **Yahoo!** on its financial site.

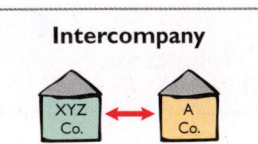

3. **Intercompany basis.** Comparisons with other companies provide insight into a company's competitive position. For example, investors can compare Macy's total sales for the year with the total sales of its competitors in retail, such as **J.C. Penney**.

Tools of Analysis

We use various tools to evaluate the significance of financial statement data. Three commonly used tools are as follows.

- **Horizontal analysis** evaluates a series of financial statement data over a period of time.

- **Vertical analysis** evaluates financial statement data by expressing each item in a financial statement as a percentage of a base amount.

- **Ratio analysis** expresses the relationship among selected items of financial statement data.

Horizontal analysis is used primarily in intracompany comparisons. Two features in published financial statements and annual report information facilitate this type of comparison. First, each of the basic financial statements presents comparative financial data for a minimum of two years. Second, a summary of selected financial data is presented for a series of five to 10 years or more. Vertical analysis is used in both intra- and intercompany comparisons. Ratio analysis is used in all three types of comparisons. In the following sections, we explain and illustrate each of the three types of analysis.

Horizontal Analysis

Horizontal analysis, also called **trend analysis**, is a technique for evaluating a series of financial statement data over a period of time. Its purpose is to determine the increase or decrease that has taken place. This change may be expressed as either an amount or a percentage. For example, Illustration 14-1 shows recent net sales figures of **Macy's, Inc.**

	MACY'S, INC. Net Sales (in millions)		
	2013	**2012**	**2011**
	$27,931	$27,686	$26,405

Illustration 14-1
Macy's, Inc.'s net sales

If we assume that 2011 is the base year, we can measure all percentage increases or decreases from this base period amount as follows.

$$\text{Change Since Base Period} = \frac{\text{Current Year Amount} - \text{Base Year Amount}}{\text{Base Year Amount}}$$

Illustration 14-2
Formula for horizontal analysis of changes since base period

For example, we can determine that net sales for Macy's increased from 2011 to 2012 approximately 4.9% [($27,686 − $26,405) ÷ $26,405]. Similarly, we can determine that net sales increased from 2011 to 2013 approximately 5.8% [($27,931 − $26,405) ÷ $26,405].

Alternatively, we can express current year sales as a percentage of the base period. We do this by dividing the current year amount by the base year amount, as shown below.

$$\text{Current Results in Relation to Base Period} = \frac{\text{Current Year Amount}}{\text{Base Year Amount}}$$

Illustration 14-3
Formula for horizontal analysis of current year in relation to base year

Illustration 14-4 presents this analysis for Macy's for a three-year period using 2011 as the base period.

	MACY'S, INC. Net Sales (in millions) in relation to base period 2011		
	2013	**2012**	**2011**
	$27,931	$27,686	$26,405
	105.8%	104.9%	100%

Illustration 14-4
Horizontal analysis of Macy's, Inc.'s net sales in relation to base period

BALANCE SHEET

To further illustrate horizontal analysis, we will use the financial statements of Quality Department Store Inc., a fictional retailer. Illustration 14-5 presents a horizontal analysis of its two-year condensed balance sheets, showing dollar and percentage changes.

Illustration 14-5
Horizontal analysis of balance sheets

QUALITY DEPARTMENT STORE INC. Condensed Balance Sheets December 31				
			Increase or (Decrease) during 2013	
	2013	2012	Amount	Percent
Assets				
Current assets	$1,020,000	$ 945,000	$ 75,000	7.9%
Plant assets (net)	800,000	632,500	167,500	26.5%
Intangible assets	15,000	17,500	(2,500)	(14.3%)
Total assets	$1,835,000	$1,595,000	$240,000	15.0%
Liabilities				
Current liabilities	$ 344,500	$ 303,000	$ 41,500	13.7%
Long-term liabilities	487,500	497,000	(9,500)	(1.9%)
Total liabilities	832,000	800,000	32,000	4.0%
Stockholders' Equity				
Common stock, $1 par	275,400	270,000	5,400	2.0%
Retained earnings	727,600	525,000	202,600	38.6%
Total stockholders' equity	1,003,000	795,000	208,000	26.2%
Total liabilities and stockholders' equity	$1,835,000	$1,595,000	$240,000	15.0%

The comparative balance sheets in Illustration 14-5 show that a number of significant changes have occurred in Quality Department Store's financial structure from 2012 to 2013:

- In the assets section, plant assets (net) increased $167,500, or 26.5%.
- In the liabilities section, current liabilities increased $41,500, or 13.7%.
- In the stockholders' equity section, retained earnings increased $202,600, or 38.6%.

These changes suggest that the company expanded its asset base during 2013 and **financed this expansion primarily by retaining income** rather than assuming additional long-term debt.

INCOME STATEMENT

Illustration 14-6 presents a horizontal analysis of the two-year condensed income statements of Quality Department Store Inc. for the years 2013 and 2012. Horizontal analysis of the income statements shows the following changes:

- Net sales increased $260,000, or 14.2% ($260,000 ÷ $1,837,000).
- Cost of goods sold increased $141,000, or 12.4% ($141,000 ÷ $1,140,000).
- Total operating expenses increased $37,000, or 11.6% ($37,000 ÷ $320,000).

Overall, gross profit and net income were up substantially. Gross profit increased 17.1%, and net income, 26.5%. Quality's profit trend appears favorable.

Illustration 14-6
Horizontal analysis of income statements

QUALITY DEPARTMENT STORE INC. Condensed Income Statements For the Years Ended December 31			Increase or (Decrease) during 2013	
	2013	**2012**	**Amount**	**Percent**
Sales revenue	$2,195,000	$1,960,000	**$235,000**	**12.0%**
Sales returns and allowances	98,000	123,000	**(25,000)**	**(20.3%)**
Net sales	2,097,000	1,837,000	**260,000**	**14.2%**
Cost of goods sold	1,281,000	1,140,000	**141,000**	**12.4%**
Gross profit	816,000	697,000	**119,000**	**17.1%**
Selling expenses	253,000	211,500	**41,500**	**19.6%**
Administrative expenses	104,000	108,500	**(4,500)**	**(4.1%)**
Total operating expenses	357,000	320,000	**37,000**	**11.6%**
Income from operations	459,000	377,000	**82,000**	**21.8%**
Other revenues and gains				
Interest and dividends	9,000	11,000	**(2,000)**	**(18.2%)**
Other expenses and losses				
Interest expense	36,000	40,500	**(4,500)**	**(11.1%)**
Income before income taxes	432,000	347,500	**84,500**	**24.3%**
Income tax expense	168,200	139,000	**29,200**	**21.0%**
Net income	$ 263,800	$ 208,500	**$ 55,300**	**26.5%**

Helpful Hint
Note that though the amount column is additive (the total is $55,300), the percentage column is not additive (26.5% is not the column total). A separate percentage has been calculated for each item.

RETAINED EARNINGS STATEMENT

Illustration 14-7 presents a horizontal analysis of Quality Department Store's comparative retained earnings statements. Analyzed horizontally, net income increased $55,300, or 26.5%, whereas dividends on the common stock increased only $1,200, or 2%. We saw in the horizontal analysis of the balance sheet that ending retained earnings increased 38.6%. As indicated earlier, the company retained a significant portion of net income to finance additional plant facilities.

Illustration 14-7
Horizontal analysis of retained earnings statements

QUALITY DEPARTMENT STORE INC. Retained Earnings Statements For the Years Ended December 31			Increase or (Decrease) during 2013	
	2013	**2012**	**Amount**	**Percent**
Retained earnings, Jan. 1	$525,000	$376,500	**$148,500**	**39.4%**
Add: Net income	263,800	208,500	**55,300**	**26.5%**
	788,800	585,000	**203,800**	
Deduct: Dividends	61,200	60,000	**1,200**	**2.0%**
Retained earnings, Dec. 31	$727,600	$525,000	**$202,600**	**38.6%**

Horizontal analysis of changes from period to period is relatively straightforward and is quite useful. But, complications can occur in making the computations. If an item has no value in a base year or preceding year but does have a value in the next year, we cannot compute a percentage change. Similarly, if a negative amount appears in the base or preceding period and a positive amount exists the following year (or vice versa), no percentage change can be computed.

Vertical Analysis

Vertical analysis, also called **common-size analysis**, is a technique that expresses each financial statement item as a percentage of a base amount. On a balance sheet, we might say that current assets are 22% of total assets—total assets being the base amount. Or on an income statement, we might say that selling expenses are 16% of net sales—net sales being the base amount.

BALANCE SHEET

Illustration 14-8 presents the vertical analysis of Quality Department Store Inc.'s comparative balance sheets. The base for the asset items is **total assets**. The base for the liability and stockholders' equity items is **total liabilities and stockholders' equity**.

Illustration 14-8
Vertical analysis of balance sheets

QUALITY DEPARTMENT STORE INC. Condensed Balance Sheets December 31				
	2013		**2012**	
	Amount	**Percent**	**Amount**	**Percent**
Assets				
Current assets	$1,020,000	**55.6%**	$ 945,000	**59.2%**
Plant assets (net)	800,000	**43.6%**	632,500	**39.7%**
Intangible assets	15,000	**0.8%**	17,500	**1.1%**
Total assets	$1,835,000	**100.0%**	$1,595,000	**100.0%**
Liabilities				
Current liabilities	$ 344,500	**18.8%**	$ 303,000	**19.0%**
Long-term liabilities	487,500	**26.5%**	497,000	**31.2%**
Total liabilities	832,000	**45.3%**	800,000	**50.2%**
Stockholders' Equity				
Common stock, $1 par	275,400	**15.0%**	270,000	**16.9%**
Retained earnings	727,600	**39.7%**	525,000	**32.9%**
Total stockholders' equity	1,003,000	**54.7%**	795,000	**49.8%**
Total liabilities and stockholders' equity	$1,835,000	**100.0%**	$1,595,000	**100.0%**

Helpful Hint
The formula for calculating these balance sheet percentages is:

$$\frac{\text{Each item on B/S}}{\text{Total assets}} = \%$$

Vertical analysis shows the relative size of each category in the balance sheet. It also can show the **percentage change** in the individual asset, liability, and stockholders' equity items. For example, we can see that current assets decreased from 59.2% of total assets in 2012 to 55.6% in 2013 (even though the absolute dollar amount increased $75,000 in that time). Plant assets (net) have increased from 39.7% to 43.6% of total assets. Retained earnings have increased from 32.9% to 39.7% of total liabilities and stockholders' equity. These results reinforce the earlier observations that **Quality Department Store is choosing to finance its growth through retention of earnings rather than through issuing additional debt**.

INCOME STATEMENT

Illustration 14-9 shows vertical analysis of Quality Department Store's income statements. Cost of goods sold as a percentage of net sales declined 1% (62.1% vs. 61.1%), and total operating expenses declined 0.4% (17.4% vs. 17.0%). As a result,

Illustration 14-9
Vertical analysis of income statements

QUALITY DEPARTMENT STORE INC.
Condensed Income Statements
For the Years Ended December 31

	2013		2012	
	Amount	Percent	Amount	Percent
Sales revenue	$2,195,000	104.7%	$1,960,000	106.7%
Sales returns and allowances	98,000	4.7%	123,000	6.7%
Net sales	2,097,000	100.0%	1,837,000	100.0%
Cost of goods sold	1,281,000	61.1%	1,140,000	62.1%
Gross profit	816,000	38.9%	697,000	37.9%
Selling expenses	253,000	12.0%	211,500	11.5%
Administrative expenses	104,000	5.0%	108,500	5.9%
Total operating expenses	357,000	17.0%	320,000	17.4%
Income from operations	459,000	21.9%	377,000	20.5%
Other revenues and gains				
Interest and dividends	9,000	0.4%	11,000	0.6%
Other expenses and losses				
Interest expense	36,000	1.7%	40,500	2.2%
Income before income taxes	432,000	20.6%	347,500	18.9%
Income tax expense	168,200	8.0%	139,000	7.5%
Net income	$ 263,800	12.6%	$ 208,500	11.4%

Helpful Hint
The formula for calculating these income statement percentages is:

$$\frac{\text{Each item on I/S}}{\text{Net sales}} = \%$$

it is not surprising to see net income as a percentage of net sales increase from 11.4% to 12.6%. Quality Department Store appears to be a profitable business that is becoming even more successful.

An associated benefit of vertical analysis is that it enables you to compare companies of different sizes. For example, suppose Quality Department Store's main competitor is a Macy's store in a nearby town. Using vertical analysis, we can compare the condensed income statements of Quality Department Store Inc. (a small retail company) with **Macy's, Inc.**[1] (a giant international retailer), as shown in Illustration 14-10.

Illustration 14-10
Intercompany income statement comparison

Condensed Income Statements
(in thousands)
For the Year Ended December 31, 2013

	Quality Department Store Inc.		Macy's, Inc.	
	Dollars	Percent	Dollars	Percent
Net sales	$2,097	100.0%	$27,931,000	100.0%
Cost of goods sold	1,281	61.1%	16,725,000	59.9%
Gross profit	816	38.9%	11,206,000	40.1%
Selling and administrative expenses	357	17.0%	8,440,000	30.2%
Income from operations	459	21.9%	2,766,000	9.9%
Other expenses and revenues (including income taxes)	195	9.3%	1,280,000	4.6%
Net income	$ 264	12.6%	$ 1,486,000	5.3%

[1]*2013 Annual Report,* Macy's, Inc. (Cincinnati, Ohio).

Macy's net sales are 13,320 times greater than the net sales of relatively tiny Quality Department Store. But vertical analysis eliminates this difference in size. The percentages show that Quality's and Macy's gross profit rates were comparable at 38.9% and 40.1%, respectively. However, the percentages related to income from operations were significantly different at 21.9% and 9.9%, respectively. This disparity can be attributed to Quality's selling and administrative expense percentage (17%) which is much lower than Macy's (30.2%). Although Macy's earned net income more than 5,629 times larger than Quality's, Macy's net income as a **percentage of each sales dollar** (5.3%) is only 42% of Quality's (12.6%).

DO IT! 1 Horizontal Analysis

Summary financial information for Rosepatch Company is as follows.

	December 31, 2017	December 31, 2016
Current assets	$234,000	$180,000
Plant assets (net)	756,000	420,000
Total assets	$990,000	$600,000

Compute the amount and percentage changes in 2017 using horizontal analysis, assuming 2016 is the base year.

Solution

Action Plan

 Find the percentage change by dividing the amount of the increase by the 2016 amount (base year).

	Increase in 2017	
	Amount	**Percent**
Current assets	$ 54,000	30% [($234,000 − $180,000) ÷ $180,000]
Plant assets (net)	336,000	80% [($756,000 − $420,000) ÷ $420,000]
Total assets	$390,000	65% [($990,000 − $600,000) ÷ $600,000]

Related exercise material: **BE14-2, BE14-3, BE14-5, BE14-6, BE14-7, E14-1, E14-3, E14-4, and DO IT! 14-1.**

LEARNING OBJECTIVE 2 Analyze a company's performance using ratio analysis.

Ratio analysis expresses the relationship among selected items of financial statement data. A **ratio** expresses the mathematical relationship between one quantity and another. The relationship is expressed in terms of either a percentage, a rate, or a simple proportion. To illustrate, in 2013 Nike, Inc. had current assets of $13,626 million and current liabilities of $3,926 million. We can find the relationship between these two measures by dividing current assets by current liabilities. The alternative means of expression are as follows.

Percentage:	Current assets are 347% of current liabilities.
Rate:	Current assets are 3.47 times current liabilities.
Proportion:	The relationship of current assets to liabilities is 3.47:1.

To analyze the primary financial statements, we can use ratios to evaluate liquidity, profitability, and solvency. Illustration 14-11 describes these classifications.

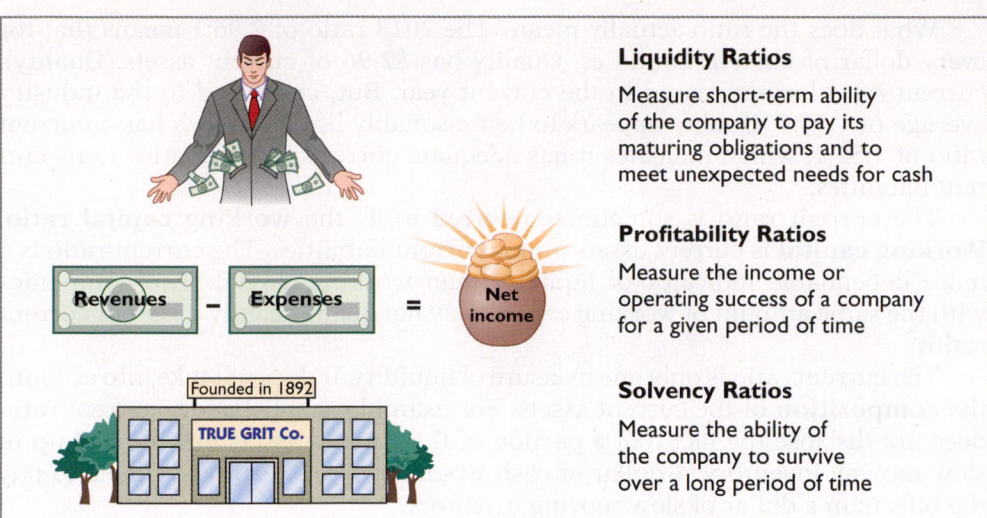

Illustration 14-11
Financial ratio classifications

Liquidity Ratios

Measure short-term ability of the company to pay its maturing obligations and to meet unexpected needs for cash

Profitability Ratios

Measure the income or operating success of a company for a given period of time

Solvency Ratios

Measure the ability of the company to survive over a long period of time

Ratios can provide clues to underlying conditions that may not be apparent from individual financial statement components. However, a single ratio by itself is not very meaningful. Thus, in the discussion of ratios we will use the following types of comparisons.

1. **Intracompany comparisons** for two years for Quality Department Store.
2. **Industry average comparisons** based on median ratios for department stores.
3. **Intercompany comparisons** based on Macy's, Inc. as Quality Department Store's principal competitor.

Liquidity Ratios

Liquidity ratios measure the short-term ability of the company to pay its maturing obligations and to meet unexpected needs for cash. Short-term creditors such as bankers and suppliers are particularly interested in assessing liquidity. The ratios we can use to determine the company's short-term debt-paying ability are the current ratio, the acid-test ratio, accounts receivable turnover, and inventory turnover.

1. CURRENT RATIO

The **current ratio** is a widely used measure for evaluating a company's liquidity and short-term debt-paying ability. The ratio is computed by dividing current assets by current liabilities. Illustration 14-12 shows the 2013 and 2012 current ratios for Quality Department Store and 2013 comparative data.

International Note

As more countries adopt international accounting standards, the ability of analysts to compare companies from different countries should improve. However, international standards are open to widely varying interpretations. In addition, some countries adopt international standards "with modifications." As a consequence, most cross-country comparisons are still not as transparent as within-country comparisons.

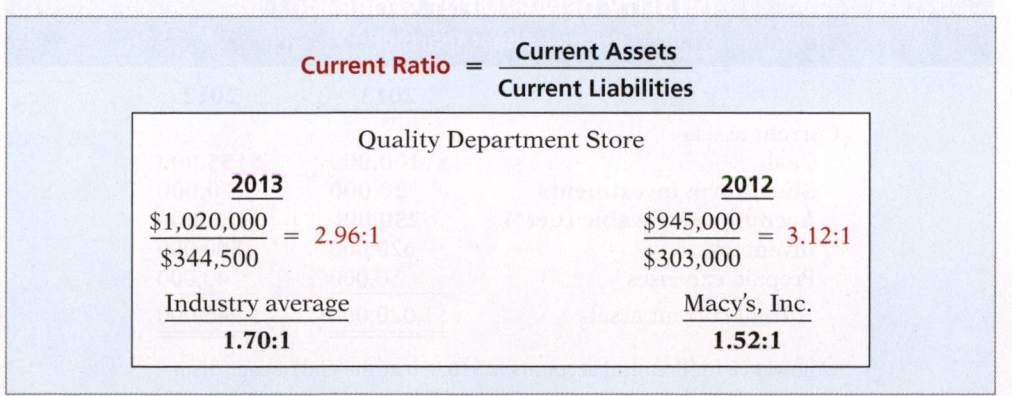

Illustration 14-12
Current ratio

$$\text{Current Ratio} = \frac{\text{Current Assets}}{\text{Current Liabilities}}$$

Quality Department Store

2013	2012
$\frac{\$1,020,000}{\$344,500} = 2.96:1$	$\frac{\$945,000}{\$303,000} = 3.12:1$
Industry average	Macy's, Inc.
1.70:1	**1.52:1**

What does the ratio actually mean? The 2013 ratio of 2.96:1 means that for every dollar of current liabilities, Quality has $2.96 of current assets. Quality's current ratio has decreased in the current year. But, compared to the industry average of 1.70:1, Quality appears to be reasonably liquid. Macy's has a current ratio of 1.52:1, which indicates it has adequate current assets relative to its current liabilities.

The current ratio is sometimes referred to as the **working capital ratio**. **Working capital** is current assets minus current liabilities. The current ratio is a more dependable indicator of liquidity than working capital. Two companies with the same amount of working capital may have significantly different current ratios.

The current ratio is only one measure of liquidity. It does not take into account the **composition** of the current assets. For example, a satisfactory current ratio does not disclose the fact that a portion of the current assets may be tied up in slow-moving inventory. A dollar of cash would be more readily available to pay the bills than a dollar of slow-moving inventory.

Investor Insight

SuperStock

How to Manage the Current Ratio

The apparent simplicity of the current ratio can have real-world limitations because adding equal amounts to both the numerator and the denominator causes the ratio to decrease.

Assume, for example, that a company has $2,000,000 of current assets and $1,000,000 of current liabilities. Thus, its current ratio is 2:1. If the company purchases $1,000,000 of inventory on account, it will have $3,000,000 of current assets and $2,000,000 of current liabilities. Its current ratio therefore decreases to 1.5:1. If, instead, the company pays off $500,000 of its current liabilities, it will have $1,500,000 of current assets and $500,000 of current liabilities. Its current ratio then increases to 3:1. Thus, any trend analysis should be done with care because the ratio is susceptible to quick changes and is easily influenced by management.

How might management influence a company's current ratio? (Go to **WileyPLUS** for this answer and additional questions.)

2. ACID-TEST RATIO

The **acid-test (quick) ratio** is a measure of a company's immediate short-term liquidity. We compute this ratio by dividing the sum of cash, short-term investments, and net accounts receivable by current liabilities. Thus, it is an important complement to the current ratio. For example, assume that the current assets of Quality Department Store for 2013 and 2012 consist of the items shown in Illustration 14-13.

Illustration 14-13
Current assets of Quality Department Store

QUALITY DEPARTMENT STORE INC.		
Balance Sheet (partial)		
	2013	**2012**
Current assets		
Cash	$ 100,000	$155,000
Short-term investments	20,000	70,000
Accounts receivable (net*)	230,000	180,000
Inventory	620,000	500,000
Prepaid expenses	50,000	40,000
Total current assets	$1,020,000	$ 945,000

*Allowance for doubtful accounts is $10,000 at the end of each year.

Cash, short-term investments, and accounts receivable (net) are highly liquid compared to inventory and prepaid expenses. The inventory may not be readily saleable, and the prepaid expenses may not be transferable to others. Thus, the acid-test ratio measures **immediate** liquidity. The 2013 and 2012 acid-test ratios for Quality Department Store and 2013 comparative data are as follows.

Illustration 14-14
Acid-test ratio

$$\text{Acid-Test Ratio} = \frac{\text{Cash + Short-Term Investments + Accounts Receivable (Net)}}{\text{Current Liabilities}}$$

Quality Department Store

2013	2012
$\dfrac{\$100,000 + \$20,000 + \$230,000}{\$344,500} = 1.02{:}1$	$\dfrac{\$155,000 + \$70,000 + \$180,000}{\$303,000} = 1.34{:}1$
Industry average	Macy's, Inc.
0.70:1	**0.47:1**

The ratio has declined in 2013. Is an acid-test ratio of 1.02:1 adequate? This depends on the industry and the economy. When compared with the industry average of 0.70:1 and Macy's of 0.47:1, Quality's acid-test ratio seems adequate.

3. ACCOUNTS RECEIVABLE TURNOVER

We can measure liquidity by how quickly a company can convert certain assets to cash. How liquid, for example, are the accounts receivable? The ratio used to assess the liquidity of the receivables is the **accounts receivable turnover**. It measures the number of times, on average, the company collects receivables during the period. We compute accounts receivable turnover by dividing net credit sales (net sales less cash sales) by the average net accounts receivable. Unless seasonal factors are significant, average net accounts receivable can be computed from the beginning and ending balances of the net accounts receivable.[2]

Assume that all sales are credit sales. The balance of net accounts receivable at the beginning of 2012 is $200,000. Illustration 14-15 shows the accounts receivable turnover for Quality Department Store and 2013 comparative data. Quality's accounts receivable turnover improved in 2013. However, the turnover of 10.2 times is substantially lower than Macy's 69.1 times and is also lower than the department store industry's average of 46.4 times.

Illustration 14-15
Accounts receivable turnover

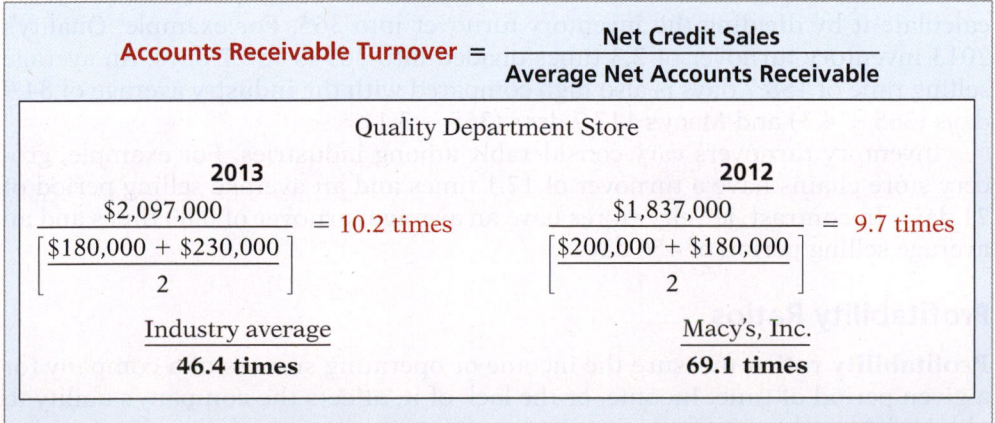

$$\text{Accounts Receivable Turnover} = \frac{\text{Net Credit Sales}}{\text{Average Net Accounts Receivable}}$$

Quality Department Store

2013	2012
$\dfrac{\$2,097,000}{\left[\dfrac{\$180,000 + \$230,000}{2}\right]} = 10.2 \text{ times}$	$\dfrac{\$1,837,000}{\left[\dfrac{\$200,000 + \$180,000}{2}\right]} = 9.7 \text{ times}$
Industry average	Macy's, Inc.
46.4 times	**69.1 times**

---

[2]If seasonal factors are significant, the average accounts receivable balance might be determined by using monthly amounts.

AVERAGE COLLECTION PERIOD A popular variant of the accounts receivable turnover is to convert it to an **average collection period** in terms of days. To do so, we divide the accounts receivable turnover into 365 days. For example, the accounts receivable turnover of 10.2 times divided into 365 days gives an average collection period of approximately 36 days. This means that accounts receivable are collected on average every 36 days, or about every 5 weeks. Analysts frequently use the average collection period to assess the effectiveness of a company's credit and collection policies. The general rule is that the collection period should not greatly exceed the credit term period (the time allowed for payment).

4. INVENTORY TURNOVER

Inventory turnover measures the number of times, on average, the inventory is sold during the period. Its purpose is to measure the liquidity of the inventory. We compute the inventory turnover by dividing cost of goods sold by the average inventory. Unless seasonal factors are significant, we can use the beginning and ending inventory balances to compute average inventory.

Assuming that the inventory balance for Quality Department Store at the beginning of 2012 was $450,000, its inventory turnover and 2013 comparative data are as shown in Illustration 14-16. Quality's inventory turnover declined slightly in 2013. The turnover of 2.3 times is low compared with the industry average of 4.3 and Macy's 3.1. Generally, the faster the inventory turnover, the less cash a company has tied up in inventory and the less chance a company has of inventory obsolescence.

Illustration 14-16
Inventory turnover

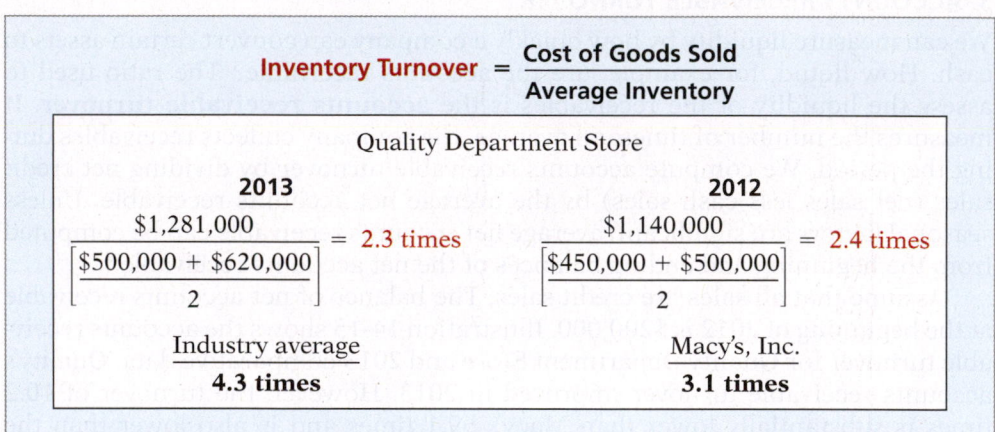

DAYS IN INVENTORY A variant of inventory turnover is the **days in inventory**. We calculate it by dividing the inventory turnover into 365. For example, Quality's 2013 inventory turnover of 2.3 times divided into 365 is 158.7 days. An average selling time of 158.7 days is also high compared with the industry average of 84.9 days (365 ÷ 4.3) and Macy's 117.7 days (365 ÷ 3.1).

Inventory turnovers vary considerably among industries. For example, grocery store chains have a turnover of 17.1 times and an average selling period of 21 days. In contrast, jewelry stores have an average turnover of 0.80 times and an average selling period of 456 days.

Profitability Ratios

Profitability ratios measure the income or operating success of a company for a given period of time. Income, or the lack of it, affects the company's ability to obtain debt and equity financing. It also affects the company's liquidity position and the company's ability to grow. As a consequence, both creditors and investors are interested in evaluating earning power—profitability. Analysts frequently use profitability as the ultimate test of management's operating effectiveness.

5. PROFIT MARGIN

Profit margin is a measure of the percentage of each dollar of sales that results in net income. We can compute it by dividing net income by net sales. Illustration 14-17 shows Quality Department Store's profit margin and 2013 comparative data.

Alternative Terminology
Profit margin is also called the *rate of return on sales*.

Illustration 14-17
Profit margin

$$\text{Profit Margin} = \frac{\text{Net Income}}{\text{Net Sales}}$$

Quality Department Store

2013	2012
$\dfrac{\$263,800}{\$2,097,000} = 12.6\%$	$\dfrac{\$208,500}{\$1,837,000} = 11.4\%$
Industry average	Macy's, Inc.
8.0%	**5.3%**

Quality experienced an increase in its profit margin from 2012 to 2013. Its profit margin is unusually high in comparison with the industry average of 8% and Macy's 5.3%.

High-volume (high inventory turnover) businesses, such as grocery stores (**Safeway** or **Kroger**) and discount stores (**Kmart** or **Wal-Mart**), generally experience low profit margins. In contrast, low-volume businesses, such as jewelry stores (**Tiffany & Co.**) or airplane manufacturers (**Boeing Co.**), have high profit margins.

6. ASSET TURNOVER

Asset turnover measures how efficiently a company uses its assets to generate sales. It is determined by dividing net sales by average total assets. The resulting number shows the dollars of sales produced by each dollar invested in assets. Unless seasonal factors are significant, we can use the beginning and ending balance of total assets to determine average total assets. Assuming that total assets at the beginning of 2012 were $1,446,000, the 2013 and 2012 asset turnover for Quality Department Store and 2013 comparative data are shown in Illustration 14-18.

Illustration 14-18
Asset turnover

$$\text{Asset Turnover} = \frac{\text{Net Sales}}{\text{Average Total Assets}}$$

Quality Department Store

2013	2012
$\dfrac{\$2,097,000}{\dfrac{\$1,595,000 + \$1,835,000}{2}} = 1.2 \text{ times}$	$\dfrac{\$1,837,000}{\dfrac{\$1,446,000 + \$1,595,000}{2}} = 1.2 \text{ times}$
Industry average	Macy's, Inc.
1.4 times	**1.3 times**

Asset turnover shows that in 2013 Quality generated sales of $1.20 for each dollar it had invested in assets. The ratio changed very little from 2012 to 2013. Quality's asset turnover is below the industry average of 1.4 times and Macy's ratio of 1.3 times.

Asset turnovers vary considerably among industries. For example, a large utility company like **Consolidated Edison** (New York) has a ratio of 0.4 times, and the large grocery chain **Kroger Stores** has a ratio of 3.4 times.

7. RETURN ON ASSETS

An overall measure of profitability is **return on assets**. We compute this ratio by dividing net income by average total assets. The 2013 and 2012 return on assets for Quality Department Store and 2013 comparative data are shown below.

Illustration 14-19
Return on assets

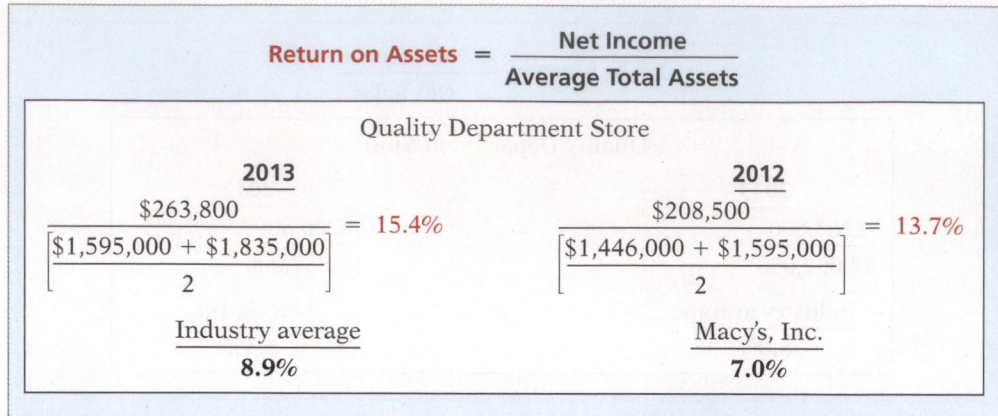

Quality's return on assets improved from 2012 to 2013. Its return of 15.4% is very high compared with the department store industry average of 8.9% and Macy's 7.0%.

8. RETURN ON COMMON STOCKHOLDERS' EQUITY

Another widely used profitability ratio is **return on common stockholders' equity**. It measures profitability from the common stockholders' viewpoint. This ratio shows how many dollars of net income the company earned for each dollar invested by the owners. We compute it by dividing net income by average common stockholders' equity. Assuming that common stockholders' equity at the beginning of 2012 was $667,000, Illustration 14-20 shows the 2013 and 2012 ratios for Quality Department Store and 2013 comparative data.

Illustration 14-20
Return on common stockholders' equity

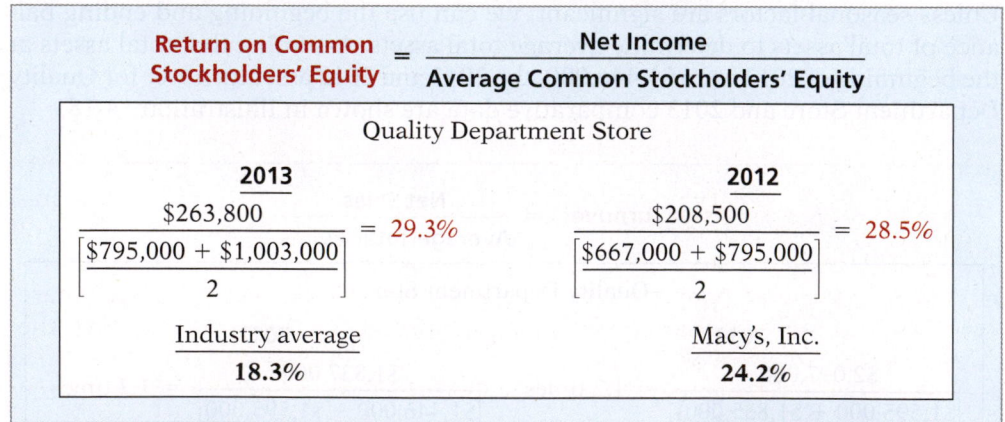

Quality's rate of return on common stockholders' equity is high at 29.3%, considering an industry average of 18.3% and a rate of 24.2% for Macy's.

WITH PREFERRED STOCK When a company has preferred stock, we must deduct **preferred dividend** requirements from net income to compute income available to common stockholders. Similarly, we deduct the par value of preferred stock (or call price, if applicable) from total stockholders' equity to determine the amount of common stockholders' equity used in this ratio. The ratio then appears as follows.

Illustration 14-21
Return on common stockholders' equity with preferred stock

$$\text{Return on Common Stockholders' Equity} = \frac{\text{Net Income} - \text{Preferred Dividends}}{\text{Average Common Stockholders' Equity}}$$

Note that Quality's rate of return on stockholders' equity (29.3%) is substantially higher than its rate of return on assets (15.4%). The reason is that Quality has made effective use of **leverage**. **Leveraging** or **trading on the equity** at a gain means that the company has borrowed money at a lower rate of interest than it is able to earn by using the borrowed money. Leverage enables Quality to use money supplied by nonowners to increase the return to the owners. A comparison of the rate of return on total assets with the rate of interest paid for borrowed money indicates the profitability of trading on the equity. Quality earns more on its borrowed funds than it has to pay in the form of interest. Thus, the return to stockholders exceeds the return on the assets, due to benefits from the positive leveraging.

9. EARNINGS PER SHARE (EPS)

Earnings per share (EPS) is a measure of the net income earned on each share of common stock. It is computed by dividing net income less preferred dividends by the number of weighted-average common shares outstanding during the year. A measure of net income earned on a per share basis provides a useful perspective for determining profitability. Assuming that there is no change in the number of outstanding shares during 2012 and that the 2013 increase occurred midyear, Illustration 14-22 shows the net income per share for Quality Department Store for 2013 and 2012, assuming no preferred dividends.

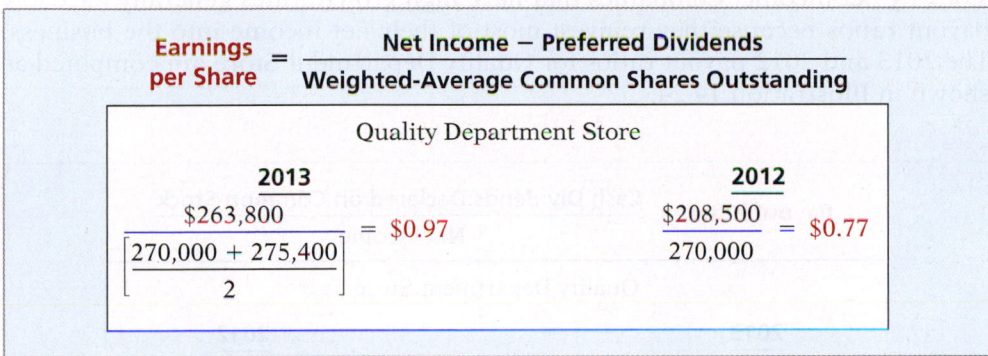

Illustration 14-22
Earnings per share

Note that no industry or specific competitive data are presented. Such comparisons are not meaningful because of the wide variations in the number of shares of outstanding stock among companies. The only meaningful EPS comparison is an intracompany trend comparison. Here, Quality's earnings per share increased 20 cents per share in 2013. This represents a 26% increase over the 2012 earnings per share of 77 cents.

The terms "earnings per share" and "net income per share" refer to the amount of net income applicable to each share of **common stock**. Therefore, in computing EPS, if there are preferred dividends declared for the period, we must deduct them from net income to determine income available to the common stockholders.

10. PRICE-EARNINGS RATIO

The **price-earnings (P-E) ratio** is a widely used measure of the ratio of the market price of each share of common stock to the earnings per share. The price-earnings (P-E) ratio reflects investors' assessments of a company's future earnings. We compute it by dividing the market price per share of the stock by earnings per share. Assuming that the market price of Quality Department Store stock is $8 in 2012 and $12 in 2013, the price-earnings ratio computation is computed as shown in Illustration 14-23 (page 674).

Illustration 14-23
Price-earnings ratio

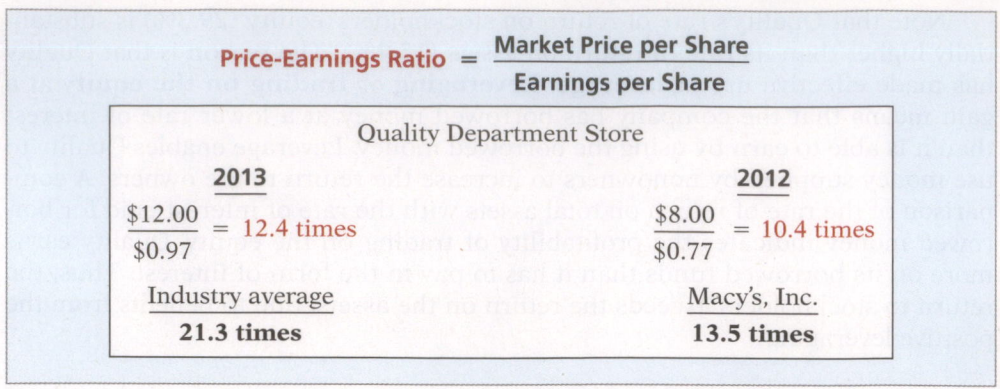

$$\text{Price-Earnings Ratio} = \frac{\text{Market Price per Share}}{\text{Earnings per Share}}$$

Quality Department Store

2013		**2012**	
$\dfrac{\$12.00}{\$0.97} = 12.4 \text{ times}$		$\dfrac{\$8.00}{\$0.77} = 10.4 \text{ times}$	
Industry average		Macy's, Inc.	
21.3 times		**13.5 times**	

In 2013, each share of Quality's stock sold for 12.4 times the amount that the company earned on each share. Quality's price-earnings ratio is lower than the industry average of 21.3 times but much closer to the ratio of 13.5 times for Macy's. For overall comparison to the market, the average price-earnings ratio for the stocks that constitute the Standard and Poor's 500 Index (500 largest U.S. firms) in mid-2014 was approximately 19.6 times.

11. PAYOUT RATIO

The **payout ratio** measures the percentage of earnings distributed in the form of cash dividends. We compute it by dividing cash dividends declared on common stock by net income. Companies that have high growth rates generally have low payout ratios because they reinvest most of their net income into the business. The 2013 and 2012 payout ratios for Quality Department Store are computed as shown in Illustration 14-24.

Illustration 14-24
Payout ratio

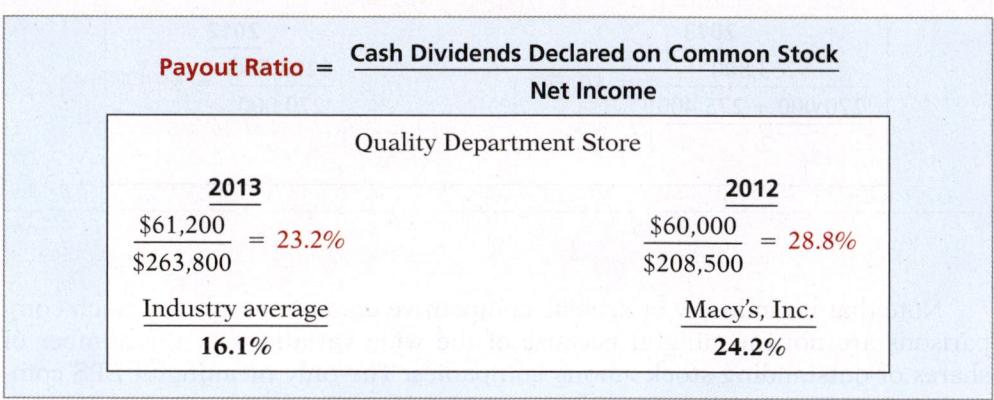

$$\text{Payout Ratio} = \frac{\text{Cash Dividends Declared on Common Stock}}{\text{Net Income}}$$

Quality Department Store

2013		**2012**	
$\dfrac{\$61,200}{\$263,800} = 23.2\%$		$\dfrac{\$60,000}{\$208,500} = 28.8\%$	
Industry average		Macy's, Inc.	
16.1%		**24.2%**	

Quality's payout ratio is higher than the industry average payout ratio of 16.1%.

Solvency Ratios

Solvency ratios measure the ability of a company to survive over a long period of time. Long-term creditors and stockholders are particularly interested in a company's ability to pay interest as it comes due and to repay the face value of debt at maturity. Debt to assets and times interest earned are two ratios that provide information about debt-paying ability.

12. DEBT TO ASSETS RATIO

The **debt to assets ratio** measures the percentage of the total assets that creditors provide. We compute it by dividing total liabilities (both current and long-term liabilities) by total assets. This ratio indicates the company's degree of leverage. It also provides some indication of the company's ability to withstand losses without impairing the interests of creditors. The higher the percentage of total liabilities to total assets, the greater the risk that the company may be unable to meet its maturing obligations. The 2013 and 2012 ratios for Quality Department Store and 2013 comparative data are as follows.

Illustration 14-25
Debt to assets ratio

$$\text{Debt to Assets Ratio} = \frac{\text{Total Liabilities}}{\text{Total Assets}}$$

Quality Department Store

2013	2012
$\dfrac{\$832,000}{\$1,835,000} = 45.3\%$	$\dfrac{\$800,000}{\$1,595,000} = 50.2\%$
Industry average	Macy's, Inc.
34.2%	**71.1%**

A ratio of 45.3% means that creditors have provided 45.3% of Quality Department Store's total assets. Quality's 45.3% is above the industry average of 34.2%. It is considerably below the high 71.1% ratio of Macy's. The lower the ratio, the more equity "buffer" there is available to the creditors. Thus, from the creditors' point of view, a low ratio of debt to assets is usually desirable.

The adequacy of this ratio is often judged in the light of the company's earnings. Generally, companies with relatively stable earnings (such as public utilities) have higher debt to assets ratios than cyclical companies with widely fluctuating earnings (such as many high-tech companies).

13. TIMES INTEREST EARNED

Times interest earned provides an indication of the company's ability to meet interest payments as they come due. We compute it by dividing the sum of net income, interest expense, and income tax expense by interest expense. Illustration 14-26 shows the 2013 and 2012 ratios for Quality Department Store and 2013 comparative data. Note that times interest earned uses net income before income tax expense and interest expense. This represents the amount available to cover interest. For Quality Department Store, the 2013 amount is computed by taking net income of $263,800 and adding back the $36,000 of interest expense and the $168,200 of income tax expense.

Alternative Terminology
Times interest earned is also called *interest coverage*.

Illustration 14-26
Times interest earned

$$\frac{\text{Times Interest}}{\text{Earned}} = \frac{\text{Net Income} + \text{Interest Expense} + \text{Income Tax Expense}}{\text{Interest Expense}}$$

Quality Department Store

2013	2012
$\dfrac{\$263,800 + \$36,000 + \$168,200}{\$36,000} = 13 \text{ times}$	$\dfrac{\$208,500 + \$40,500 + \$139,000}{\$40,500} = 9.6 \text{ times}$
Industry average	Macy's, Inc.
16.1 times	**6.9 times**

Quality's interest expense is well covered at 13 times. It is less than the industry average of 16.1 times but significantly exceeds Macy's 6.9 times.

Summary of Ratios

Illustration 14-27 summarizes the ratios discussed in this chapter. The summary includes the formula and purpose or use of each ratio.

Ratio	Formula	Purpose or Use
Liquidity Ratios		
1. Current ratio	$\dfrac{\text{Current assets}}{\text{Current liabilities}}$	Measures short-term debt-paying ability.
2. Acid-test (quick) ratio	$\dfrac{\text{Cash} + \text{Short-term investments} + \text{Accounts receivable (net)}}{\text{Current liabilities}}$	Measures immediate short-term liquidity.
3. Accounts receivable turnover	$\dfrac{\text{Net credit sales}}{\text{Average net accounts receivable}}$	Measures liquidity of accounts receivable.
4. Inventory turnover	$\dfrac{\text{Cost of goods sold}}{\text{Average inventory}}$	Measures liquidity of inventory.
Profitability Ratios		
5. Profit margin	$\dfrac{\text{Net income}}{\text{Net sales}}$	Measures net income generated by each dollar of sales.
6. Asset turnover	$\dfrac{\text{Net sales}}{\text{Average total assets}}$	Measures how efficiently assets are used to generate sales.
7. Return on assets	$\dfrac{\text{Net income}}{\text{Average total assets}}$	Measures overall profitability of assets.
8. Return on common stockholders' equity	$\dfrac{\text{Net income} - \text{Preferred dividends}}{\text{Average common stockholders' equity}}$	Measures profitability of owners' investment.
9. Earnings per share (EPS)	$\dfrac{\text{Net income} - \text{Preferred dividends}}{\text{Weighted-average common shares outstanding}}$	Measures net income earned on each share of common stock.
10. Price-earnings (P-E) ratio	$\dfrac{\text{Market price per share}}{\text{Earnings per share}}$	Measures the ratio of the market price per share to earnings per share.
11. Payout ratio	$\dfrac{\text{Cash dividends declared on common stock}}{\text{Net income}}$	Measures percentage of earnings distributed in the form of cash dividends.
Solvency Ratios		
12. Debt to assets ratio	$\dfrac{\text{Total liabilities}}{\text{Total assets}}$	Measures the percentage of total assets provided by creditors.
13. Times interest earned	$\dfrac{\text{Net income} + \text{Interest expense} + \text{Income tax expense}}{\text{Interest expense}}$	Measures ability to meet interest payments as they come due.

Illustration 14-27
Summary of liquidity, profitability, and solvency ratios

DO IT! ② Ratio Analysis

The condensed financial statements of John Cully Company, for the years ended June 30, 2017 and 2016, are presented below.

JOHN CULLY COMPANY
Balance Sheets
June 30

	(in thousands)	
Assets	**2017**	**2016**
Current assets		
Cash and cash equivalents	$ 553.3	$ 611.6
Accounts receivable (net)	776.6	664.9
Inventory	768.3	653.5
Prepaid expenses and other current assets	204.4	269.2
Total current assets	2,302.6	2,199.2
Investments	12.3	12.6
Property, plant, and equipment (net)	694.2	647.0
Intangibles and other assets	876.7	849.3
Total assets	$3,885.8	$3,708.1
Liabilities and Stockholders' Equity		
Current liabilities	$1,497.7	$1,322.0
Long-term liabilities	679.5	637.1
Stockholders' equity—common	1,708.6	1,749.0
Total liabilities and stockholders' equity	$3,885.8	$3,708.1

JOHN CULLY COMPANY
Income Statements
For the Year Ended June 30

	(in thousands)	
	2017	**2016**
Sales revenue	$6,336.3	$5,790.4
Costs and expenses		
Cost of goods sold	1,617.4	1,476.3
Selling and administrative expenses	4,007.6	3,679.0
Interest expense	13.9	27.1
Total costs and expenses	5,638.9	5,182.4
Income before income taxes	697.4	608.0
Income tax expense	291.3	232.6
Net income	$ 406.1	$ 375.4

Compute the following ratios for 2017 and 2016.

(a) Current ratio.

(b) Inventory turnover. (Inventory on 6/30/15 was $599.0.)

(c) Profit margin.

(d) Return on assets. (Assets on 6/30/15 were $3,349.9.)

(e) Return on common stockholders' equity. (Stockholders' equity on 6/30/15 was $1,795.9.)

(f) Debt to assets ratio.

(g) Times interest earned.

Action Plan

✔ Remember that the current ratio includes all current assets. The acid-test ratio uses only cash, short-term investments, and net accounts receivable.

✔ Use average balances for turnover ratios like inventory, accounts receivable, and return on assets.

Solution

	2017	2016
(a) Current ratio:		
$2,302.6 ÷ $1,497.7 =	1.5:1	
$2,199.2 ÷ $1,322.0 =		1.7:1
(b) Inventory turnover:		
$1,617.4 ÷ [($768.3 + $653.5) ÷ 2] =	2.3 times	
$1,476.3 ÷ [($653.5 + $599.0) ÷ 2] =		2.4 times
(c) Profit margin:		
$406.1 ÷ $6,336.3 =	6.4%	
$375.4 ÷ $5,790.4 =		6.5%
(d) Return on assets:		
$406.1 ÷ [($3,885.8 + $3,708.1) ÷ 2] =	10.7%	
$375.4 ÷ [($3,708.1 + $3,349.9) ÷ 2] =		10.6%
(e) Return on common stockholders' equity:		
($406.1 − $0) ÷ [($1,708.6 + $1,749.0) ÷ 2] =	23.5%	
($375.4 − $0) ÷ [($1,749.0 + $1,795.9) ÷ 2] =		21.2%
(f) Debt to assets ratio:		
($1,497.7 + $679.5) ÷ $3,885.8 =	56.0%	
($1,322.0 + $637.1) ÷ $3,708.1 =		52.8%
(g) Times interest earned:		
($406.1 + $13.9 + $291.3) ÷ $13.9 =	51.2 times	
($375.4 + $27.1 + $232.6) ÷ $27.1 =		23.4 times

Related exercise material: **BE14-9, BE14-10, BE14-12, BE14-13, E14-5, E14-6, E14-7, E14-8, E14-9, E14-10, E14-11, and DO IT! 14-2.**

LEARNING OBJECTIVE **3**

Apply the concept of sustainable income.

The value of a company like **Google** is a function of the amount, timing, and uncertainty of its future cash flows. Google's current and past income statements are particularly useful in helping analysts predict these future cash flows. In using this approach, analysts must make sure that Google's past income numbers reflect its **sustainable income**, that is, do not include unusual (out-of-the-ordinary) revenues, expenses, gains, and losses. **Sustainable income** is, therefore, the most likely level of income to be obtained by a company in the future. Sustainable income differs from actual net income by the amount of unusual revenues, expenses, gains, and losses included in the current year's income. Analysts are interested in sustainable income because it helps them derive an estimate of future earnings without the "noise" of unusual items.

Fortunately, an income statement provides information on sustainable income by separating operating transactions from nonoperating transactions. This statement also highlights intermediate components of income such as income from operations, income before income taxes, and income from continuing operations. In addition, information on unusual items such as gains or losses on discontinued items and components of other comprehensive income are disclosed.

Illustration 14-28 presents a statement of comprehensive income for Cruz Company for the year 2017. A statement of comprehensive income includes not only net income but a broader measure of income called comprehensive income. The two major unusual items in this statement are discontinued operations and other comprehensive income (highlighted in red). When estimating future cash flows, analysts must consider the implications of each of these components.

CRUZ COMPANY Statement of Comprehensive Income For the year ended 2017	
Sales revenue	$900,000
Cost of goods sold	650,000
Gross profit	250,000
Operating expenses	100,000
Income from operations	150,000
Other revenues (expenses) and gains (losses)	20,000
Income before income taxes	170,000
Income tax expense	24,000
Income from continuing operations	146,000
Discontinued operations (net of tax)	**30,000**
Net income	176,000
Other comprehensive income items (net of tax)	**10,000**
Comprehensive income	$186,000

Illustration 14-28
Statement of comprehensive income

In looking at Illustration 14-28, note that Cruz Company's two major types of unusual items, discontinued operations and other comprehensive income, are reported net of tax. That is, Cruz first calculates income tax expense before income from continuing operations. Then, it calculates income tax expense related to the discontinued operations and other comprehensive income. The general concept is, "Let the tax follow the income or loss." We discuss discontinued operations and other comprehensive income in more detail next.

Discontinued Operations

Discontinued operations refers to the disposal of a **significant component** of a business, such as the elimination of a major class of customers, or an entire activity. For example, to downsize its operations, General Dynamics Corp. sold its missile business to Hughes Aircraft Co. for $450 million. In its statement of comprehensive income, General Dynamics reported the sale in a separate section entitled "Discontinued operations."

Following the disposal of a significant component, the company should report on its statement both income from continuing operations and income (or loss) from discontinued operations. **The income (loss) from discontinued operations consists of two parts: the income (loss) from operations** and **the gain (loss) on disposal of the component**.

To illustrate, assume that during 2017 Acro Energy Inc. has income before income taxes of $800,000. During 2017, Acro discontinued and sold its unprofitable chemical division. The loss in 2017 from chemical operations (net of $60,000 taxes) was $140,000. The loss on disposal of the chemical division (net of $30,000 taxes) was $70,000. Assuming a 30% tax rate on income, Illustration 14-29 (page 680) shows Acro's statement of comprehensive income presentation.

Note that the statement uses the caption "Income from continuing operations" and adds a new section "Discontinued operations." **The new section reports both the operating loss and the loss on disposal net of applicable income taxes.** This presentation clearly indicates the separate effects of continuing operations and discontinued operations on net income.

Other Comprehensive Income

Most revenues, expenses, gains, and losses are included in net income. However, certain gains and losses bypass net income. Instead, companies record these items as direct adjustments to stockholders' equity. The FASB requires companies to report not only net income but also other comprehensive income.

Illustration 14-29
Statement presentation of
discontinued operations

Helpful Hint
Observe the dual
disclosures: (1) the results
of operation of the
discontinued division must
be eliminated from the
results of continuing
operations, and (2) the
company must also report
the disposal of the division.

ACRO ENERGY INC.		
Statement of Comprehensive Income (partial)		
For the Year Ended December 31, 2017		
Income before income taxes		$800,000
Income tax expense		240,000
Income from continuing operations		560,000
Discontinued operations		
Loss from operation of chemical division,		
net of $60,000 income tax savings	$140,000	
Loss from disposal of chemical division,		
net of $30,000 income tax savings	70,000	210,000
Net income		$350,000

Other comprehensive income includes all changes in stockholders' equity during a period except those changes resulting from investments by stockholders and distributions to stockholders.

ILLUSTRATION OF OTHER COMPREHENSIVE INCOME

Accounting standards require that companies adjust most investments in stocks and bonds up or down to their market price at the end of each accounting period. For example, assume that during 2017 Stassi Company purchased IBM stock for $10,000 as an investment. At the end of 2017, Stassi was still holding the investment, but the stock's market price was now $8,000. In this case, Stassi is required to reduce the recorded value of its IBM investment by $2,000. The $2,000 difference is an unrealized loss.

Should Stassi include this $2,000 unrealized loss in net income? It depends on whether Stassi classifies the IBM stock as a trading security or an available-for-sale security. A **trading security** is bought and held primarily for sale in the near term to generate income on short-term price differences. Companies report unrealized losses on trading securities in the "Other expenses and losses" section of the income statement. The rationale: It is likely that the company will realize the unrealized loss (or an unrealized gain), so the company should report the loss (gain) as part of net income.

If Stassi did not purchase the investment for trading purposes, it is classified as available-for-sale. **Available-for-sale securities** are held with the intent of selling them sometime in the future. Companies do not include unrealized gains or losses on available-for-sale securities in net income. Instead, they report them as part of "Other comprehensive income." Other comprehensive income is not included in net income. It bypasses net income and is recorded as a direct adjustment to stockholders' equity.

FORMAT

One format for reporting other comprehensive income is to report a statement of comprehensive income. For example, assuming that Stassi Company has a net income of $300,000, the unrealized loss would be reported below net income as follows.

Illustration 14-30
Lower portion of statement of
comprehensive income

STASSI CORPORATION	
Statement of Comprehensive Income (partial)	
For the Year Ended 2017	
Net income	$300,000
Unrealized loss on available-for-sale securities (net of tax)	2,000
Comprehensive income	**$298,000**

Companies also report the unrealized loss on available-for-sale securities as a separate component of stockholders' equity. To illustrate, assume Stassi Corporation has common stock of $3,000,000, retained earnings of $1,500,000, and an unrealized loss on available-for-sale securities of $2,000. Illustration 14-31 shows the balance sheet presentation of the unrealized loss.

Illustration 14-31
Unrealized loss in stockholders' equity section

Balance Sheet (partial)	
Stockholders' equity	
Common stock	$3,000,000
Retained earnings	1,500,000
Total paid-in capital and retained earnings	4,500,000
Less: Unrealized loss on available-for-sale securities	**2,000**
Total stockholders' equity	$4,498,000

Note that the presentation of the loss is similar to the presentation of the cost of treasury stock in the stockholders' equity section. (An unrealized gain would be added in this section of the balance sheet.) Reporting the unrealized gain or loss in the stockholders' equity section serves two important purposes: (1) it reduces the volatility of net income due to fluctuations in fair value, and (2) it informs the financial statement user of the gain or loss that would occur if the company sold the securities at fair value.

COMPLETE STATEMENT OF COMPREHENSIVE INCOME

The statement of comprehensive income for Pace Corporation in Illustration 14-32 presents the types of items found on this statement, such as net sales, cost of goods sold, operating expenses, and income taxes. In addition, it shows how companies report discontinued operations and other comprehensive income (highlighted in red).

Illustration 14-32
Complete statement of comprehensive income

PACE CORPORATION Statement of Comprehensive Income For the Year Ended December 31, 2017		
Net sales		$440,000
Cost of goods sold		260,000
Gross profit		180,000
Operating expenses		110,000
Income from operations		70,000
Other revenues and gains		5,600
Other expenses and losses		9,600
Income before income taxes		66,000
Income tax expense ($66,000 × 30%)		19,800
Income from continuing operations		46,200
Discontinued operations		
Loss from operation of Plastics Division, net of income tax savings $18,000 ($60,000 × 30%)	$42,000	
Gain on disposal of Plastics Division, net of $15,000 income taxes ($50,000 × 30%)	35,000	7,000
Net income		39,200
Unrealized gain on available-for-sale securities, net of income taxes ($15,000 × 30%)		10,500
Comprehensive income		$ 49,700

Investor Insight Cisco Systems

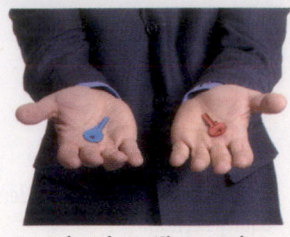

© gosphotodesign/Shutterstock

Another Measure of Sustainable Income?

Companies whose stock is publicly traded are required to present their income statement following GAAP. In recent years, many companies now report a second measure of income, called pro forma income. **Pro forma income** usually excludes items that the company thinks are unusual or nonrecurring. For example, in a recent year, Cisco Systems (a high-tech company) reported a quarterly net loss under GAAP of $2.7 billion. Cisco reported pro forma income for the same quarter as a profit of $230 million. This large difference in profits between GAAP income numbers and pro forma income is not unusual. For example, during one 9-month period, the 100 largest companies on the Nasdaq stock exchange reported a total pro forma income of $19.1 billion but a total loss as measured by GAAP of $82.3 billion—a difference of about $100 billion!

To compute pro forma income, companies generally exclude any items they deem inappropriate for measuring their performance. Many analysts and investors are critical of the practice of using pro forma income because these numbers often make companies look better than they really are. As the financial press noted, pro forma numbers might be called "earnings before bad stuff." Companies, on the other hand, argue that pro forma numbers more clearly indicate sustainable income because they exclude unusual items. "Cisco's technique gives readers of financial statements a clear picture of Cisco's normal business activities," the company said in a statement issued in response to questions about its pro forma income accounting.

Recently, the SEC provided some guidance on how companies should present pro forma information. Stay tuned: Everyone seems to agree that pro forma numbers can be useful if they provide insights into determining a company's sustainable income. However, many companies have abused the flexibility that pro forma numbers allow and have used the measure as a way to put their companies in a more favorable light.

*What incentive do companies have to report pro forma income? (Go to **WileyPLUS** for this answer and additional questions.)*

DO IT! 3 Unusual Items

In its proposed 2017 income statement, AIR Corporation reports income before income taxes $400,000, unrealized gain on available-for-sale securities $100,000, income taxes $120,000 (not including unusual items), loss from operation of discontinued flower division $50,000, and loss on disposal of discontinued flower division $90,000. The income tax rate is 30%. Prepare a correct statement of comprehensive income, beginning with "Income before income taxes."

Solution

Action Plan

 Show discontinued operations and other comprehensive income net of tax.

AIR CORPORATION Statement of Comprehensive Income (partial) For the Year Ended December 31, 2017		
Income before income taxes		$400,000
Income tax expense		120,000
Income from continuing operations		280,000
Discontinued operations		
Loss from operation of flower division, net of $15,000 income tax savings	$35,000	
Loss on disposal of flower division, net of $27,000 income tax savings	63,000	98,000
Net income		182,000
Unrealized gain on available-for-sale securities, net of $30,000 income taxes		70,000
Comprehensive income		$252,000

Related exercise material: **BE14-14, BE14-15, E14-12, E14-13, and DO IT! 14-3.**

REVIEW AND PRACTICE

LEARNING OBJECTIVES REVIEW

1 Apply horizontal and vertical analysis to financial statements. There are three bases of comparison: (1) intracompany, which compares an item or financial relationship with other data within a company; (2) industry, which compares company data with industry averages; and (3) intercompany, which compares an item or financial relationship of a company with data of one or more competing companies.

Horizontal analysis is a technique for evaluating a series of data over a period of time to determine the increase or decrease that has taken place, expressed as either an amount or a percentage. Vertical analysis is a technique that expresses each item within a financial statement in terms of a percentage of a relevant total or a base amount.

2 Analyze a company's performance using ratio analysis. The formula and purpose of each ratio is presented in Illustration 14-27 (page 676).

3 Apply the concept of sustainable income. Sustainable income analysis is useful in evaluating a company's performance. Sustainable income is the most likely level of income to be obtained by the company in the future. Discontinued operations and other comprehensive income are presented on the statement of comprehensive income to highlight their unusual nature. Items below income from continuing operations must be presented net of tax.

GLOSSARY REVIEW

Accounts receivable turnover A measure of the liquidity of accounts receivable; computed by dividing net credit sales by average net accounts receivable. (p. 669).

Acid-test (quick) ratio A measure of a company's immediate short-term liquidity; computed by dividing the sum of cash, short-term investments, and net accounts receivable by current liabilities. (p. 668).

Asset turnover A measure of how efficiently a company uses its assets to generate sales; computed by dividing net sales by average total assets. (p. 671).

Current ratio A measure used to evaluate a company's liquidity and short-term debt-paying ability; computed by dividing current assets by current liabilities. (p. 667).

Debt to assets ratio Measures the percentage of assets provided by creditors; computed by dividing total liabilities by total assets. (p. 674).

Discontinued operations The disposal of a significant component of a business. (p. 679).

Earnings per share (EPS) The net income earned on each share of common stock; computed by dividing net income minus preferred dividends (if any) by the number of weighted-average common shares outstanding. (p. 673).

Horizontal analysis A technique for evaluating a series of financial statement data over a period of time, to determine the increase (decrease) that has taken place, expressed as either an amount or a percentage. (p. 661).

Inventory turnover A measure of the liquidity of inventory; computed by dividing cost of goods sold by average inventory. (p. 670).

Leveraging See *Trading on the equity*. (p. 673).

Liquidity ratios Measures of the short-term ability of the company to pay its maturing obligations and to meet unexpected needs for cash. (p. 667).

Other comprehensive income Includes all changes in stockholders' equity during a period except those resulting from investments by stockholders and distributions to stockholders. (p. 680).

Payout ratio Measures the percentage of earnings distributed in the form of cash dividends; computed by dividing cash dividends declared on common stock by net income. (p. 674).

Price-earnings (P-E) ratio Measures the ratio of the market price of each share of common stock to the earnings per share; computed by dividing the market price per share by earnings per share. (p. 673).

Profit margin Measures the percentage of each dollar of sales that results in net income; computed by dividing net income by net sales. (p. 671).

Profitability ratios Measures of the income or operating success of a company for a given period of time. (p. 670).

Ratio An expression of the mathematical relationship between one quantity and another. The relationship may be expressed either as a percentage, a rate, or a simple proportion. (p. 666).

Ratio analysis A technique for evaluating financial statements that expresses the relationship between selected financial statement data. (p. 666).

Return on assets An overall measure of profitability; computed by dividing net income by average total assets. (p. 672).

Return on common stockholders' equity Measures the dollars of net income earned for each dollar invested by the owners; computed by dividing net income minus preferred dividends (if any) by average common stockholders' equity. (p. 672).

Solvency ratios Measures of the ability of the company to survive over a long period of time. (p. 674).

Sustainable income The most likely level of income to be obtained by a company in the future. (p. 678).

Times interest earned Measures a company's ability to meet interest payments as they come due; computed by dividing the sum of net income, interest expense, and income tax expense by interest expense. (p. 675).

Trading on the equity Borrowing money at a lower rate of interest than can be earned by using the borrowed money. (p. 673).

Vertical analysis A technique for evaluating financial statement data that expresses each item within a financial statement as a percentage of a base amount. (p. 664).

PRACTICE MULTIPLE-CHOICE QUESTIONS

(LO 1) **1.** Comparisons of data within a company are an example of the following comparative basis:
(a) Industry averages.   (c) Intercompany.
(b) Intracompany.   (d) Both (b) and (c).

(LO 1) **2.** In horizontal analysis, each item is expressed as a percentage of the:
(a) net income amount.
(b) stockholders' equity amount.
(c) total assets amount.
(d) base year amount.

(LO 1) **3.** Sammy Corporation reported net sales of $300,000, $330,000, and $360,000 in the years, 2015, 2016, and 2017, respectively. If 2015 is the base year, what is the trend percentage for 2017?
(a) 77%.   (c) 120%.
(b) 108%.   (d) 130%.

(LO 1) **4.** The following schedule is a display of what type of analysis?

	Amount	Percent
Current assets	$200,000	25%
Property, plant, and equipment	600,000	75%
Total assets	$800,000	

(a) Horizontal analysis.   (c) Vertical analysis.
(b) Differential analysis. (d) Ratio analysis.

(LO 1) **5.** In vertical analysis, the base amount for depreciation expense is generally:
(a) net sales.
(b) depreciation expense in a previous year.
(c) gross profit.
(d) fixed assets.

(LO 2) **6.** Which of the following measures is an evaluation of a firm's ability to pay current liabilities?
(a) Acid-test ratio.   (c) Both (a) and (b).
(b) Current ratio.   (d) None of the above.

(LO 2) **7.** A measure useful in evaluating the efficiency in managing inventories is:
(a) inventory turnover. (c) Both (a) and (b).
(b) days in inventory.   (d) None of the above.

Use the following financial statement information as of the end of each year to answer Questions 8-12.

	2017	2016
Inventory	$ 54,000	$ 48,000
Current assets	81,000	106,000
Total assets	382,000	326,000
Current liabilities	27,000	36,000
Total liabilities	102,000	88,000
Preferred stock	40,000	40,000
Common stockholders' equity	240,000	198,000
Net sales	784,000	697,000
Cost of goods sold	306,000	277,000
Net income	134,000	90,000
Income tax expense	22,000	18,000
Interest expense	12,000	12,000
Dividends paid to preferred stockholders	4,000	4,000
Dividends paid to common stockholders	15,000	10,000

8. Compute the days in inventory for 2017. (LO 2)
(a) 64.4 days.   (c) 6 days.
(b) 60.8 days.   (d) 24 days.

9. Compute the current ratio for 2017. (LO 2)
(a) 1.26:1.   (c) 0.80:1.
(b) 3.0:1.   (d) 3.75:1.

10. Compute the profit margin for 2017. (LO 2)
(a) 17.1%.   (c) 37.9%.
(b) 18.1%.   (d) 5.9%.

11. Compute the return on common stockholders' equity (LO 2) for 2017.
(a) 47.9%.   (c) 61.2%.
(b) 51.7%.   (d) 59.4%.

12. Compute the times interest earned for 2017. (LO 2)
(a) 11.2 times.   (c) 14.0 times.
(b) 65.3 times.   (d) 13.0 times.

13. In reporting discontinued operations, the statement of (LO 3) comprehensive income should show in a special section:
(a) gains and losses on the disposal of the discontinued component.

(b) other comprehensive income items.

(c) Both (a) and (b).

(d) None of these answer choices are correct.

(LO 3) **14.** Scout Corporation has income before taxes of $400,000 and a loss on discontinued operations of $100,000. If the income tax rate is 25% on all items, the statement of comprehensive income should show income from continuing operations and discontinued operations, respectively, of:

(a) $325,000 and $100,000.

(b) $325,000 and $75,000.

(c) $300,000 and $100,000.

(d) $300,000 and $75,000.

Solutions

1. (b) Comparisons of data within a company are called intracompany comparisons, not (a) industry averages, (c) intercompany comparisons, or (d) both intracompany and intercompany comparisons. Intercompany comparisons are among companies.

2. (d) Horizontal analysis converts each succeeding year's balance to a percentage of the base year amount, not (a) net income amount, (b) stockholders' equity amount, or (c) total assets amount.

3. (c) The trend percentage for 2017 is 120% ($360,000/$300,000), not (a) 77%, (b) 108%, or (d) 130%.

4. (c) The data in the schedule is a display of vertical analysis because the individual asset items are expressed as a percentage of total assets. The other choices are therefore incorrect. Horizontal analysis is a technique for evaluating a series of data over a period of time.

5. (a) In vertical analysis, net sales is used as the base amount for income statement items, not (b) depreciation expense in a previous year, (c) gross profit, or (d) fixed assets.

6. (c) Both the acid-test ratio and the current ratio measure a firm's ability to pay current liabilities. Choices (a) and (b) are correct but (c) is the better answer. Choice (d) is incorrect because there is a correct answer.

7. (c) Both inventory turnover and days in inventory measure a firm's efficiency in managing inventories. Choices (a) and (b) are correct but (c) is the better answer. Choice (d) is incorrect because there is a correct answer.

8. (b) Inventory turnover = Cost of goods sold/Average inventory [$306,000/($54,000 + $48,000)/2] = 6 times. Thus, days in inventory = 60.8 (365/6), not (a) 64.4, (c) 6, or (d) 24 days.

9. (b) Current ratio = Current assets/Current liabilities ($81,000/$27,000) = 3.0:1, not (a) 1.26:1, (c) 0.80:1, or (d) 3.75:1.

10. (a) Profit margin = Net income/Net sales ($134,000/$784,000) =17.1%, not (b) 18.1%, (c) 37.9%, or (d) 5.9%.

11. (d) Return on common stockholders' equity = Net income ($4,000) − Dividends to preferred stockholders ($4,000)/Average common stockholders' equity [($240,000 + $198,000)/2] = 59.4%, not (a) 47.9%, (b) 51.7%, or (c) 61.2%.

12. (c) Times interest earned = Net income + Interest expense + Income tax expense divided by Interest expense [($134,000 + $12,000 + $22,000)/$12,000] = 14.0 times, not (a) 11.2, (b) 65.3, or (d) 13.0 times.

13. (c) Gains and losses on the disposal of the discontinued segment and gains and losses from operations of the discontinued component are shown in the special section titled discontinued operations. Other comprehensive income items are reported in a separate section after net income on the statement of comprehensive income. Choices (a) and (b) are therefore correct but (c) is the better answer. Choice (d) is incorrect as there is a correct answer.

14. (d) Income tax expense = 25% × $400,000 = $100,000; therefore, income from continuing operations = $400,000 − $100,000 = $300,000. The loss on discontinued operations is shown net of tax, $100,000 × 75% = $75,000. The other choices are therefore incorrect.

PRACTICE EXERCISES

1. The comparative condensed balance sheets of Roadway Corporation are presented below.

Prepare horizontal and vertical analysis.

(LO 1)

ROADWAY CORPORATION
Condensed Balance Sheets
December 31

	2017	2016
Assets		
Current assets	$ 76,000	$ 80,000
Property, plant, and equipment (net)	99,000	90,000
Intangibles	25,000	40,000
Total assets	$200,000	$210,000
Liabilities and stockholders' equity		
Current liabilities	$ 40,800	$ 48,000
Long-term liabilities	143,000	150,000
Stockholders' equity	16,200	12,000
Total liabilities and stockholders' equity	$200,000	$210,000

Instructions

(a) Prepare a horizontal analysis of the balance sheet data for Roadway Corporation using 2016 as a base.

(b) Prepare a vertical analysis of the balance sheet data for Roadway Corporation in columnar form for 2017.

Solution

1. (a)

ROADWAY CORPORATION
Condensed Balance Sheets
December 31

	2017	2016	Increase (Decrease)	Percent Change from 2016
Assets				
Current assets	$ 76,000	$ 80,000	$ (4,000)	(5.0%)
Property, plant, and equipment (net)	99,000	90,000	9,000	10.0%
Intangibles	25,000	40,000	(15,000)	(37.5%)
Total assets	$200,000	$210,000	$(10,000)	(4.8%)
Liabilities and stockholders' equity				
Current liabilities	$ 40,800	$ 48,000	$ (7,200)	(15.0%)
Long-term liabilities	143,000	150,000	(7,000)	(4.7%)
Stockholders' equity	16,200	12,000	4,200	35.0%
Total liabilities and stockholders' equity	$200,000	$210,000	$(10,000)	(4.8%)

(b)

ROADWAY CORPORATION
Condensed Balance Sheet
December 31, 2017

	Amount	Percent
Assets		
Current assets	$ 76,000	38.0%
Property, plant, and equipment (net)	99,000	49.5%
Intangibles	25,000	12.5%
Total assets	$200,000	100.0%
Liabilities and stockholders' equity		
Current liabilities	$ 40,800	20.4%
Long-term liabilities	143,000	71.5%
Stockholders' equity	16,200	8.1%
Total liabilities and stockholders' equity	$200,000	100.0%

Compute ratios.

(LO 2)

2. Rondo Corporation's comparative balance sheets are presented below.

RONDO CORPORATION
Balance Sheets
December 31

	2017	2016
Cash	$ 5,300	$ 3,700
Accounts receivable	21,200	23,400
Inventory	9,000	7,000
Land	20,000	26,000
Buildings	70,000	70,000
Accumulated depreciation—buildings	(15,000)	(10,000)
Total	$110,500	$120,100

	2017	2016
Accounts payable	$ 10,370	$ 31,100
Common stock	75,000	69,000
Retained earnings	25,130	20,000
Total	$110,500	$120,100

Rondo's 2017 income statement included net sales of $120,000, cost of goods sold of $70,000, and net income of $14,000.

Instructions

Compute the following ratios for 2017.

(a) Current ratio.
(b) Acid-test ratio.
(c) Accounts receivable turnover.
(d) Inventory turnover.
(e) Profit margin.

(f) Asset turnover.
(g) Return on assets.
(h) Return on common stockholders' equity.
(i) Debt to assets ratio.

Solution

2. (a) ($5,300 + $21,200 + $9,000)/$10,370 = 3.42

(b) ($5,300 + $21,200)/$10,370 = 2.56

(c) $120,000/[($21,200 + $23,400)/2] = 5.38

(d) $70,000/[($9,000 + $7,000)/2] = 8.8

(e) $14,000/$120,000 = 11.7%

(f) $120,000/[($110,500 + $120,100)/2] = 1.04

(g) $14,000/[($110,500 + $120,100)/2] = 12.1%

(h) $14,000/[($100,130 + $89,000)/2] = 14.8%

(i) $10,370/$110,500 = 9.4%

PRACTICE PROBLEM

The events and transactions of Dever Corporation for the year ending December 31, 2017, resulted in the following data.

Prepare a statement of comprehensive income.

(LO 3)

Cost of goods sold	$2,600,000
Net sales	4,400,000
Other expenses and losses	9,600
Other revenues and gains	5,600
Selling and administrative expenses	1,100,000
Income from operations of plastics division	70,000
Gain from disposal of plastics division	500,000
Unrealized loss on available-for-sale securities	60,000

Analysis reveals the following:

1. All items are before the applicable income tax rate of 30%.

2. The plastics division was sold on July 1.

3. All operating data for the plastics division have been segregated.

Instructions

Prepare a statement of comprehensive income for the year.

Solution

DEVER CORPORATION
Statement of Comprehensive Income
For the Year Ended December 31, 2017

Net sales		$4,400,000
Cost of goods sold		2,600,000
Gross profit		1,800,000
Selling and administrative expenses		1,100,000
Income from operations		700,000
Other revenues and gains		5,600
Other expenses and losses		9,600
Income before income taxes		696,000
Income tax expense ($696,000 × 30%)		208,800
Income from continuing operations		487,200
Discontinued operations		
Income from operation of plastics division, net of $21,000		
income taxes ($70,000 × 30%)	49,000	
Gain from disposal of plastics division, net of $150,000		
income taxes ($500,000 × 30%)	350,000	399,000
Net income		886,200
Unrealized loss on available-for-sale securities, net of $18,000		
income tax savings ($60,000 × 30%)		42,000
Comprehensive income		$ 844,200

WileyPLUS Brief Exercises, Exercises, **DO IT!** Exercises, and Problems and many additional resources are available for practice in WileyPLUS

QUESTIONS

1. (a) Jose Ramirez believes that the analysis of financial statements is directed at two characteristics of a company: liquidity and profitability. Is Jose correct? Explain.
(b) Are short-term creditors, long-term creditors, and stockholders interested primarily in the same characteristics of a company? Explain.

2. (a) Distinguish among the following bases of comparison: (1) intracompany, (2) industry averages, and (3) intercompany.
(b) Give the principal value of using each of the three bases of comparison.

3. Two popular methods of financial statement analysis are horizontal analysis and vertical analysis. Explain the difference between these two methods.

4. (a) If Peoples Company had net income of $390,000 in 2017 and it experienced a 24.5% increase in net income for 2018, what is its net income for 2018?
(b) If six cents of every dollar of Peoples' revenue is net income in 2017, what is the dollar amount of 2017 revenue?

5. What is a ratio? What are the different ways of expressing the relationship of two amounts? What information does a ratio provide?

6. Name the major ratios useful in assessing (a) liquidity and (b) solvency.

7. Roberto Perez is puzzled. His company had a profit margin of 10% in 2017. He feels that this is an indication that the company is doing well. Julie Beck, his accountant, says that more information is needed to determine the firm's financial well-being. Who is correct? Why?

8. What do the following classes of ratios measure? (a) Liquidity ratios. (b) Profitability ratios. (c) Solvency ratios.

9. What is the difference between the current ratio and the acid-test ratio?

10. Hizar Company, a retail store, has an accounts receivable turnover of 4.5 times. The industry average is 12.5 times. Does Hizar have a collection problem with its accounts receivable?

11. Which ratios should be used to help answer the following questions?
(a) How efficient is a company in using its assets to produce sales?
(b) How near to sale is the inventory on hand?
(c) How many dollars of net income were earned for each dollar invested by the owners?
(d) How able is a company to meet interest charges as they fall due?

12. The price-earnings ratio of **General Motors** (automobile builder) was 8, and the price-earnings ratio of **Microsoft** (computer software) was 38. Which company did the stock market favor? Explain.

13. What is the formula for computing the payout ratio? Would you expect this ratio to be high or low for a growth company?

14. Holding all other factors constant, indicate whether each of the following changes generally signals good or bad news about a company.
(a) Increase in profit margin.
(b) Decrease in inventory turnover.
(c) Increase in the current ratio.
(d) Decrease in earnings per share.
(e) Increase in price-earnings ratio.
(f) Increase in debt to assets ratio.
(g) Decrease in times interest earned.

15. The return on assets for Zhang Corporation is 7.6%. During the same year, Zhang's return on common stockholders' equity is 12.8%. What is the explanation for the difference in the two rates?

16. Which two ratios do you think should be of greatest interest to:
(a) A pension fund considering the purchase of 20-year bonds?
(b) A bank contemplating a short-term loan?
(c) A common stockholder?

17. Why must preferred dividends be subtracted from net income in computing earnings per share?

18. (a) What is meant by trading on the equity?
(b) How would you determine the profitability of trading on the equity?

19. Lippert Inc. has net income of $160,000, weighted-average shares of common stock outstanding of 50,000, and preferred dividends for the period of $40,000. What is Lippert's earnings per share of common stock? Kate Lippert, the president of Lippert Inc., believes the computed EPS of the company is high. Comment.

20. Why is it important to report discontinued operations separately from income from continuing operations?

21. You are considering investing in Wingert Transportation. The company reports 2017 earnings per share of $6.50 on income from continuing operations and $4.75 on net income. Which EPS figure would you consider more relevant to your investment decision? Why?

22. RAF Inc. reported 2016 earnings per share of $3.20 and had no discontinued operations items. In 2017, EPS on income from continuing operations was $2.99, and EPS on net income was $3.49. Is this a favorable trend?

23. Identify the specific sections in **Apple**'s 2013 annual report where horizontal and vertical analyses of financial data are presented.

BRIEF EXERCISES

Follow the rounding procedures used in the chapter.

BE14-1 You recently received a letter from your Uncle Sammy. A portion of the letter is presented below.

Discuss need for comparative analysis.

(LO 1)

You know that I have a significant amount of money I saved over the years. I am thinking about starting an investment program. I want to do the investing myself, based on my own research and analysis of financial statements. I know that you are studying accounting, so I have a couple of questions for you. I have heard that different users of financial statements are interested in different characteristics of companies. Is this true and, if so, why? Also, some of my friends who are already investing have told me that comparisons involving a company's financial data can be made on a number of different bases. Can you explain these bases to me?

Instructions

Write a letter to your Uncle Sammy which answers his questions.

BE14-2 Schellhammer Corporation reported the following amounts in 2016, 2017, and 2018.

Identify and use tools of financial statement analysis.

(LO 1, 2)

	2016	2017	2018
Current assets	$200,000	$210,000	$240,000
Current liabilities	150,000	168,000	184,000
Total assets	500,000	600,000	620,000

Instructions

(a) Identify and describe the three tools of financial statement analysis. (b) Perform each of the three types of analysis on Schellhammer's current assets.

Prepare horizontal analysis.
(LO 1)

BE14-3 Using the following data from the comparative balance sheet of Goody Company, illustrate horizontal analysis.

	December 31, 2017	December 31, 2016
Accounts receivable	$ 520,000	$ 400,000
Inventory	840,000	600,000
Total assets	3,000,000	2,500,000

Prepare vertical analysis.
(LO 1)

BE14-4 Using the same data presented above in BE14-3 for Goody Company, illustrate vertical analysis.

Calculate percentage of change.
(LO 1)

BE14-5 Net income was $500,000 in 2016, $450,000 in 2017, and $522,000 in 2018. What is the percentage of change from (a) 2016 to 2017 and (b) 2017 to 2018? Is the change an increase or a decrease?

Calculate net income.
(LO 1)

BE14-6 If Sappington Company had net income of $585,000 in 2017 and it experienced a 20% increase in net income over 2016, what was its 2016 net income?

Calculate change in net income.
(LO 1)

BE14-7 Horizontal analysis (trend analysis) percentages for Dody Company's sales revenue, cost of goods sold, and expenses are shown below.

	2018	2017	2016
Sales revenue	96.2%	106.8%	100.0%
Cost of goods sold	102.0	97.0	100.0
Expenses	109.6	98.4	100.0

Did Dody's net income increase, decrease, or remain unchanged over the 3-year period?

Calculate change in net income.
(LO 1)

BE14-8 Vertical analysis (common size) percentages for Kochheim Company's sales revenue, cost of goods sold, and expenses are shown below.

	2018	2017	2016
Sales revenue	100.0%	100.0%	100.0%
Cost of goods sold	60.2	62.4	63.5
Expenses	25.0	25.6	27.5

Did Kochheim's net income as a percentage of sales increase, decrease, or remain unchanged over the 3-year period? Provide numerical support for your answer.

Calculate liquidity ratios.
(LO 2)

BE14-9 Selected condensed data taken from a recent balance sheet of Heidebrecht Inc. are as follows.

HEIDEBRECHT INC.
Balance Sheet (partial)

Cash	$ 8,041,000
Short-term investments	4,947,000
Accounts receivable	12,545,000
Inventory	14,814,000
Other current assets	5,571,000
Total current assets	$45,918,000
Total current liabilities	$40,644,000

What are the (a) working capital, (b) current ratio, and (c) acid-test ratio?

Calculate profitability ratios.
(LO 2)

BE14-10 Linebarger Corporation has net income of $11.44 million and net revenue of $95 million in 2017. Its assets are $14 million at the beginning of the year and $18 million at the end of the year. What are Linebarger's (a) asset turnover and (b) profit margin?

BE14-11 The following data are taken from the financial statements of Rainsberger Company.

Evaluate collection of accounts receivable.

(LO 2)

	2018	2017
Accounts receivable (net), end of year	$ 550,000	$ 520,000
Net sales on account	3,960,000	3,100,000
Terms for all sales are 1/10, n/60.		

(a) Compute for each year (1) the accounts receivable turnover and (2) the average collection period. At the end of 2016, accounts receivable (net) was $480,000.
(b) ▪━━━━ What conclusions about the management of accounts receivable can be drawn from these data?

BE14-12 The following data are from the income statements of Haskin Company.

Evaluate management of inventory.

(LO 2)

	2017	2016
Sales revenue	$6,420,000	$6,240,000
Beginning inventory	940,000	860,000
Purchases	4,340,000	4,661,000
Ending inventory	1,020,000	940,000

(a) Compute for each year (1) the inventory turnover and (2) the days in inventory.
(b) ▪━━━━ What conclusions concerning the management of the inventory can be drawn from these data?

BE14-13 Guo Company has stockholders' equity of $400,000 and net income of $66,000. It has a payout ratio of 20% and a return on assets of 15%. How much did Guo pay in cash dividends, and what were its average assets?

Calculate amounts from profitability ratios.

(LO 2)

BE14-14 An inexperienced accountant for Silva Corporation showed the following in the income statement: income before income taxes $450,000 and unrealized gain on available-for-sale securities (before taxes) $70,000. The unrealized gain on available-for-sale securities and income before income taxes are both subject to a 25% tax rate. Prepare a correct statement of comprehensive income.

Prepare statement of comprehensive income including unusual items.

(LO 3)

BE14-15 On June 30, Holloway Corporation discontinued its operations in Europe. During the year, the operating loss was $300,000 before taxes. On September 1, Holloway disposed of its European facilities at a pretax loss of $120,000. The applicable tax rate is 20%. Show the discontinued operations section of the statement of comprehensive income.

Prepare discontinued operations section of statement of comprehensive income.

(LO 3)

DO IT! Exercises

DO IT! 14-1 Summary financial information for Wolford Company is as follows.

Prepare horizontal analysis.

(LO 1)

	December 31, 2017	December 31, 2016
Current assets	$ 199,000	$ 220,000
Plant assets	821,000	780,000
Total assets	$1,020,000	$1,000,000

Compute the amount and percentage changes in 2017 using horizontal analysis, assuming 2016 is the base year.

Compute ratios.

(LO 2)

DO IT! 14-2 The condensed financial statements of Murawski Company for the years 2016 and 2017 are presented below. (Amounts in thousands.)

MURAWSKI COMPANY
Balance Sheets
December 31

	2017	2016
Current assets		
Cash and cash equivalents	$ 330	$ 360
Accounts receivable (net)	470	400
Inventory	460	390
Prepaid expenses	120	160
Total current assets	1,380	1,310
Investments	10	10
Property, plant, and equipment	420	380
Intangibles and other assets	530	510
Total assets	$2,340	$2,210
Current liabilities	$ 900	$ 790
Long-term liabilities	410	380
Stockholders' equity—common	1,030	1,040
Total liabilities and stockholders' equity	$2,340	$2,210

MURAWSKI COMPANY
Income Statements
For the Years Ended December 31

	2017	2016
Sales revenue	$3,800	$3,460
Costs and expenses		
Cost of goods sold	955	890
Selling & administrative expenses	2,400	2,330
Interest expense	25	20
Total costs and expenses	3,380	3,240
Income before income taxes	420	220
Income tax expense	126	66
Net income	$ 294	$ 154

Compute the following ratios for 2017 and 2016.

(a) Current ratio.
(b) Inventory turnover. (Inventory on 12/31/15 was $340.)
(c) Profit margin.
(d) Return on assets. (Assets on 12/31/15 were $1,900.)
(e) Return on common stockholders' equity. (Stockholders' equity on 12/31/15 was $900.)
(f) Debt to assets ratio.
(g) Times interest earned.

Prepare statement of comprehensive income including unusual items.

(LO 3)

DO IT! 14-3 In its proposed 2017 income statement, Hrabik Corporation reports income before income taxes $500,000, income taxes $100,000 (not including unusual items), loss on operation of discontinued music division $60,000, gain on disposal of discontinued music division $40,000, and unrealized loss on available-for-sale securities $150,000. The income tax rate is 20%. Prepare a correct statement of comprehensive income, beginning with income before income taxes.

EXERCISES

Follow the rounding procedures used in the chapter.

E14-1 Financial information for Kurzen Inc. is presented below.

Prepare horizontal analysis.

(LO 1)

	December 31, 2017	December 31, 2016
Current assets	$125,000	$100,000
Plant assets (net)	396,000	330,000
Current liabilities	91,000	70,000
Long-term liabilities	133,000	95,000
Common stock, $1 par	161,000	115,000
Retained earnings	136,000	150,000

Instructions

Prepare a schedule showing a horizontal analysis for 2017 using 2016 as the base year.

E14-2 Operating data for Navarro Corporation are presented below.

Prepare vertical analysis.

(LO 1)

	2017	2016
Net sales	$750,000	$600,000
Cost of goods sold	465,000	390,000
Selling expenses	105,000	66,000
Administrative expenses	60,000	54,000
Income tax expense	36,000	27,000
Net income	84,000	63,000

Instructions

Prepare a schedule showing a vertical analysis for 2017 and 2016.

E14-3 The comparative condensed balance sheets of Gurley Corporation are presented below.

Prepare horizontal and vertical analyses.

(LO 1)

GURLEY CORPORATION
Comparative Condensed Balance Sheets
December 31

	2017	2016
Assets		
Current assets	$ 74,000	$ 80,000
Property, plant, and equipment (net)	99,000	90,000
Intangibles	27,000	40,000
Total assets	$200,000	$210,000
Liabilities and stockholders' equity		
Current liabilities	$ 42,000	$ 48,000
Long-term liabilities	143,000	150,000
Stockholders' equity	15,000	12,000
Total liabilities and stockholders' equity	$200,000	$210,000

Instructions

(a) Prepare a horizontal analysis of the balance sheet data for Gurley Corporation using 2016 as a base.

(b) Prepare a vertical analysis of the balance sheet data for Gurley Corporation in columnar form for 2017.

Prepare horizontal and vertical analyses.
(LO 1)

E14-4 The comparative condensed income statements of Emley Corporation are shown below.

EMLEY CORPORATION
Comparative Condensed Income Statements
For the Years Ended December 31

	2017	2016
Net sales	$660,000	$600,000
Cost of goods sold	483,000	420,000
Gross profit	177,000	180,000
Operating expenses	125,000	120,000
Net income	$ 52,000	$ 60,000

Instructions

(a) Prepare a horizontal analysis of the income statement data for Emley Corporation using 2016 as a base. (Show the amounts of increase or decrease.)

(b) Prepare a vertical analysis of the income statement data for Emley Corporation in columnar form for both years.

Compute liquidity ratios and compare results.
(LO 2)

E14-5 Suppose Nordstrom, Inc., which operates department stores in numerous states, has the following selected financial statement data for a recent year.

NORDSTROM, INC.
Balance Sheet (partial)

(in millions)	End-of-Year	Beginning-of-Year
Cash and cash equivalents	$ 795	$ 72
Accounts receivable (net)	2,035	1,942
Inventory	898	900
Prepaid expenses	88	93
Other current assets	238	210
Total current assets	$4,054	$3,217
Total current liabilities	$2,014	$1,601

For the year, net sales were $8,258 and cost of goods sold was $5,328 (in millions).

Instructions

(a) Compute the four liquidity ratios at the end of the year.

(b) Using the data in the chapter, compare Nordstrom's liquidity with (1) that of Macy's, Inc., and (2) the industry averages for department stores.

Perform current and acid-test ratio analysis.
(LO 2)

E14-6 Keener Incorporated had the following transactions occur involving current assets and current liabilities during February 2017.

Feb.	3	Accounts receivable of $15,000 are collected.
	7	Equipment is purchased for $28,000 cash.
	11	Paid $3,000 for a 3-year insurance policy.
	14	Accounts payable of $12,000 are paid.
	18	Cash dividends of $5,000 are declared.

Additional information:

1. As of February 1, 2017, current assets were $110,000, and current liabilities were $50,000.
2. As of February 1, 2017, current assets included $15,000 of inventory and $2,000 of prepaid expenses.

Instructions

(a) Compute the current ratio as of the beginning of the month and after each transaction.

(b) Compute the acid-test ratio as of the beginning of the month and after each transaction.

E14-7 Frizell Company has the following comparative balance sheet data.

FRIZELL COMPANY
Balance Sheets
December 31

	2017	2016
Cash	$ 15,000	$ 30,000
Accounts receivable (net)	70,000	60,000
Inventory	60,000	50,000
Plant assets (net)	200,000	180,000
	$345,000	$320,000
Accounts payable	$ 50,000	$ 60,000
Mortgage payable (6%)	100,000	100,000
Common stock, $10 par	140,000	120,000
Retained earnings	55,000	40,000
	$345,000	$320,000

Additional information for 2017:

1. Net income was $25,000.
2. Sales on account were $410,000. Sales returns and allowances were $20,000.
3. Cost of goods sold was $198,000.

Instructions

Compute the following ratios at December 31, 2017.

(a) Current ratio.
(b) Acid-test ratio.

(c) Accounts receivable turnover.
(d) Inventory turnover.

E14-8 Selected comparative statement data for Queen Products Company are presented below. All balance sheet data are as of December 31.

	2017	2016
Net sales	$750,000	$720,000
Cost of goods sold	480,000	440,000
Interest expense	7,000	5,000
Net income	45,000	42,000
Accounts receivable	120,000	100,000
Inventory	85,000	75,000
Total assets	580,000	500,000
Total common stockholders' equity	430,000	325,000

Instructions

Compute the following ratios for 2017.

(a) Profit margin.
(b) Asset turnover.

(c) Return on assets.
(d) Return on common stockholders' equity.

E14-9 The income statement for Sutherland, Inc., appears below.

SUTHERLAND, INC.
Income Statement
For the Year Ended December 31, 2017

Net sales	$400,000
Cost of goods sold	230,000
Gross profit	170,000
Expenses (including $16,000 interest and $24,000 income taxes)	105,000
Net income	$ 65,000

Additional information:

1. The weighted-average common shares outstanding in 2017 were 30,000 shares.
2. The market price of Sutherland, Inc. stock was $13 in 2017.
3. Cash dividends of $26,000 were paid, $5,000 of which were to preferred stockholders.

Instructions

Compute the following ratios for 2017.

(a) Earnings per share.　　　　　　　(c) Payout ratio.
(b) Price-earnings ratio.　　　　　　(d) Times interest earned.

Compute amounts from ratios.

(LO 2)

E14-10 Lingenfelter Corporation experienced a fire on December 31, 2017, in which its financial records were partially destroyed. It has been able to salvage some of the records and has ascertained the following balances.

	December 31, 2017	December 31, 2016
Cash	$ 30,000	$ 10,000
Accounts receivable (net)	72,500	126,000
Inventory	200,000	180,000
Accounts payable	50,000	90,000
Notes payable	30,000	60,000
Common stock, $100 par	400,000	400,000
Retained earnings	113,500	101,000

Additional information:

1. The inventory turnover is 4.5 times.
2. The return on common stockholders' equity is 16%. The company had no additional paid-in capital.
3. The accounts receivable turnover is 8.8 times.
4. The return on assets is 12.5%.
5. Total assets at December 31, 2016, were $655,000.

Instructions

Compute the following for Lingenfelter Corporation.

(a) Cost of goods sold for 2017.　　　(c) Net income for 2017.
(b) Net sales (credit) for 2017.　　　(d) Total assets at December 31, 2017.

Compute ratios.

(LO 2)

E14-11 Wiemers Corporation's comparative balance sheets are presented below.

WIEMERS CORPORATION
Balance Sheets
December 31

	2017	2016
Cash	$ 4,300	$ 3,700
Accounts receivable (net)	21,200	23,400
Inventory	10,000	7,000
Land	20,000	26,000
Buildings	70,000	70,000
Accumulated depreciation—buildings	(15,000)	(10,000)
Total	$110,500	$120,100
Accounts payable	$ 12,370	$ 31,100
Common stock	75,000	69,000
Retained earnings	23,130	20,000
Total	$110,500	$120,100

Wiemers's 2017 income statement included net sales of $100,000, cost of goods sold of $60,000, and net income of $15,000.

Instructions

Compute the following ratios for 2017.

(a) Current ratio.　　　　　　　　　(f) Asset turnover.
(b) Acid-test ratio.　　　　　　　　(g) Return on assets.
(c) Accounts receivable turnover.　　(h) Return on common stockholders' equity.
(d) Inventory turnover.　　　　　　(i) Debt to assets ratio.
(e) Profit margin.

E14-12 For its fiscal year ending October 31, 2017, Haas Corporation reports the following partial data shown below.

Prepare a correct statement of comprehensive income.
(LO 3)

Income before income taxes	$540,000
Income tax expense (20% × $420,000)	84,000
Income from continuing operations	456,000
Loss on discontinued operations	120,000
Net income	$336,000

The loss on discontinued operations was comprised of a $50,000 loss from operations and a $70,000 loss from disposal. The income tax rate is 20% on all items.

Instructions
(a) Prepare a correct statement of comprehensive income beginning with income before income taxes.
(b) Explain in memo form why the income statement data are misleading.

E14-13 Trayer Corporation has income from continuing operations of $290,000 for the year ended December 31, 2017. It also has the following items (before considering income taxes).

Prepare statement of comprehensive income.
(LO 3)

1. An unrealized loss of $80,000 on available-for-sale securities.
2. A gain of $30,000 on the discontinuance of a division (comprised of a $10,000 loss from operations and a $40,000 gain on disposal).
3. A correction of an error in last year's financial statements that resulted in a $20,000 understatement of 2016 net income.

Assume all items are subject to income taxes at a 20% tax rate.

Instructions
Prepare a statement of comprehensive income, beginning with income from continuing operations.

EXERCISES: SET B AND CHALLENGE EXERCISES

Visit the book's companion website, at **www.wiley.com/college/weygandt**, and choose the Student Companion site to access Exercises: Set B and Challenge Exercises.

PROBLEMS

Follow the rounding procedures used in the chapter.

P14-1 Comparative statement data for Farris Company and Ratzlaff Company, two competitors, appear below. All balance sheet data are as of December 31, 2017, and December 31, 2016.

Prepare vertical analysis and comment on profitability.
(LO 1, 2)

	Farris Company		Ratzlaff Company	
	2017	**2016**	**2017**	**2016**
Net sales	$1,549,035		$339,038	
Cost of goods sold	1,080,490		241,000	
Operating expenses	302,275		79,000	
Interest expense	8,980		2,252	
Income tax expense	54,500		6,650	
Current assets	325,975	$312,410	83,336	$ 79,467
Plant assets (net)	521,310	500,000	139,728	125,812
Current liabilities	65,325	75,815	35,348	30,281
Long-term liabilities	108,500	90,000	29,620	25,000
Common stock, $10 par	500,000	500,000	120,000	120,000
Retained earnings	173,460	146,595	38,096	29,998

Instructions

(a) Prepare a vertical analysis of the 2017 income statement data for Farris Company and Ratzlaff Company in columnar form.

(b) ━━━━ Comment on the relative profitability of the companies by computing the return on assets and the return on common stockholders' equity for both companies.

Compute ratios from balance sheet and income statement.

(LO 2)

P14-2 The comparative statements of Painter Tool Company are presented below.

PAINTER TOOL COMPANY
Income Statement
For the Years Ended December 31

	2017	2016
Net sales	$1,818,500	$1,750,500
Cost of goods sold	1,011,500	996,000
Gross profit	807,000	754,500
Selling and administrative expenses	499,000	479,000
Income from operations	308,000	275,500
Other expenses and losses		
Interest expense	18,000	14,000
Income before income taxes	290,000	261,500
Income tax expense	87,000	77,000
Net income	$ 203,000	$ 184,500

PAINTER TOOL COMPANY
Balance Sheets
December 31

Assets	2017	2016
Current assets		
Cash	$ 60,100	$ 64,200
Short-term investments	69,000	50,000
Accounts receivable (net)	107,800	102,800
Inventory	133,000	115,500
Total current assets	369,900	332,500
Plant assets (net)	600,300	520,300
Total assets	$970,200	$852,800

Liabilities and Stockholders' Equity	2017	2016
Current liabilities		
Accounts payable	$160,000	$145,400
Income taxes payable	43,500	42,000
Total current liabilities	203,500	187,400
Bonds payable	200,000	200,000
Total liabilities	403,500	387,400
Stockholders' equity		
Common stock ($5 par)	280,000	300,000
Retained earnings	286,700	165,400
Total stockholders' equity	566,700	465,400
Total liabilities and stockholders' equity	$970,200	$852,800

All sales were on account.

Instructions
Compute the following ratios for 2017. (Weighted-average common shares in 2017 were 57,000.)

(a) Earnings per share.
(b) Return on common stockholders' equity.
(c) Return on assets.
(d) Current ratio.
(e) Acid-test ratio.

(f) Accounts receivable turnover.
(g) Inventory turnover.
(h) Times interest earned.
(i) Asset turnover.
(j) Debt to assets ratio.

P14-3 Condensed balance sheet and income statement data for Landwehr Corporation appear below.

Perform ratio analysis, and evaluate financial position and operating results.

(LO 2)

LANDWEHR CORPORATION
Balance Sheets
December 31

	2018	2017	2016
Cash	$ 25,000	$ 20,000	$ 18,000
Accounts receivable (net)	50,000	45,000	48,000
Other current assets	90,000	95,000	64,000
Investments	75,000	70,000	45,000
Plant and equipment (net)	400,000	370,000	358,000
	$640,000	$600,000	$533,000
Current liabilities	$ 75,000	$ 80,000	$ 70,000
Long-term debt	80,000	85,000	50,000
Common stock, $10 par	340,000	310,000	300,000
Retained earnings	145,000	125,000	113,000
	$640,000	$600,000	$533,000

LANDWEHR CORPORATION
Income Statement
For the Years Ended December 31

	2018	2017
Sales revenue	$740,000	$700,000
Less: Sales returns and allowances	40,000	50,000
Net sales	700,000	650,000
Cost of goods sold	420,000	400,000
Gross profit	280,000	250,000
Operating expenses (including income taxes)	235,000	220,000
Net income	$ 45,000	$ 30,000

Additional information:

1. The market price of Landwehr's common stock was $4.00, $5.00, and $8.00 for 2016, 2017, and 2018, respectively.
2. All dividends were paid in cash.

Instructions
(a) Compute the following ratios for 2017 and 2018.
  (1) Profit margin.
  (2) Asset turnover.
  (3) Earnings per share. (Weighted-average common shares in 2018 were 32,000 and in 2017 were 31,000.)
  (4) Price-earnings ratio.
  (5) Payout ratio.
  (6) Debt to assets ratio.
(b) ——— Based on the ratios calculated, discuss briefly the improvement or lack thereof in financial position and operating results from 2017 to 2018 of Landwehr Corporation.

Compute ratios, and comment on overall liquidity and profitability.

(LO 2)

P14-4 Financial information for Messersmith Company is presented below.

MESSERSMITH COMPANY
Balance Sheets
December 31

Assets	2017	2016
Cash	$ 70,000	$ 65,000
Short-term investments	52,000	40,000
Accounts receivable (net)	98,000	80,000
Inventory	125,000	135,000
Prepaid expenses	29,000	23,000
Land	130,000	130,000
Building and equipment (net)	180,000	175,000
	$684,000	$648,000

Liabilities and Stockholders' Equity		
Notes payable	$100,000	$100,000
Accounts payable	48,000	42,000
Accrued liabilities	50,000	40,000
Bonds payable, due 2020	150,000	150,000
Common stock, $10 par	200,000	200,000
Retained earnings	136,000	116,000
	$684,000	$648,000

MESSERSMITH COMPANY
Income Statement
For the Years Ended December 31

	2017	2016
Net sales	$850,000	$790,000
Cost of goods sold	620,000	575,000
Gross profit	230,000	215,000
Operating expenses	187,000	173,000
Net income	$ 43,000	$ 42,000

Additional information:

1. Inventory at the beginning of 2016 was $118,000.
2. Total assets at the beginning of 2016 were $630,000.
3. No common stock transactions occurred during 2016 or 2017.
4. All sales were on account. Accounts receivable, net at the beginning of 2016, were $88,000.
5. Notes payable are classified as current liabilities.

Instructions
(a) Indicate, by using ratios, the change in liquidity and profitability of Messersmith Company from 2016 to 2017. (*Note:* Not all profitability ratios can be computed.)
(b) Given below are three independent situations and a ratio that may be affected. For each situation, compute the affected ratio (1) as of December 31, 2017, and (2) as of December 31, 2018, after giving effect to the situation. Net income for 2018 was $50,000. Total assets on December 31, 2018, were $700,000.

Situation	Ratio
(1) 18,000 shares of common stock were sold at par on July 1, 2018.	Return on common stockholders' equity
(2) All of the notes payable were paid in 2018. The only change in liabilities was that the notes payable were paid.	Debt to assets ratio
(3) Market price of common stock was $9 on December 31, 2017, and $12.80 on December 31, 2018.	Price-earnings ratio

P14-5 Selected financial data of Target Corporation and Wal-Mart Stores, Inc. for a recent year are presented here (in millions).

Compute selected ratios, and compare liquidity, profitability, and solvency for two companies.
(LO 2)

	Target Corporation	Wal-Mart Stores, Inc.
Income Statement Data for Year		
Net sales	$61,471	$374,526
Cost of goods sold	41,895	286,515
Selling and administrative expenses	16,200	70,847
Interest expense	647	1,798
Other income (expense)	1,896	4,273
Income tax expense	1,776	6,908
Net income	$ 2,849	$ 12,731
Balance Sheet Data (End of Year)		
Current assets	$18,906	$ 47,585
Noncurrent assets	25,654	115,929
Total assets	$44,560	$163,514
Current liabilities	$11,782	$ 58,454
Long-term debt	17,471	40,452
Total stockholders' equity	15,307	64,608
Total liabilities and stockholders' equity	$44,560	$163,514
Beginning-of-Year Balances		
Total assets	$37,349	$151,587
Total stockholders' equity	15,633	61,573
Current liabilities	11,117	52,148
Total liabilities	21,716	90,014
Other Data		
Average net accounts receivable	$ 7,124	$ 3,247
Average inventory	6,517	34,433
Net cash provided by operating activities	4,125	20,354

Instructions
(a) For each company, compute the following ratios.
  (1) Current ratio.
  (2) Accounts receivable turnover.
  (3) Average collection period.
  (4) Inventory turnover.
  (5) Days in inventory.
  (6) Profit margin.
  (7) Asset turnover.
  (8) Return on assets.
  (9) Return on common stockholders' equity.
  (10) Debt to assets ratio.
  (11) Times interest earned.
(b) Compare the liquidity, profitability, and solvency of the two companies.

P14-6 The comparative statements of Corbin Company are presented below and on page 702.

Compute numerous ratios.
(LO 2)

CORBIN COMPANY
Income Statement
For the Years Ended December 31

	2017	2016
Net sales (all on account)	$595,000	$520,000
Expenses		
Cost of goods sold	415,000	354,000
Selling and administrative	120,800	114,800
Interest expense	7,800	6,000
Income tax expense	15,000	14,000
Total expenses	558,600	488,800
Net income	$ 36,400	$ 31,200

CORBIN COMPANY
Balance Sheets
December 31

Assets	2017	2016
Current assets		
Cash	$ 21,000	$ 18,000
Short-term investments	18,000	15,000
Accounts receivable (net)	91,000	74,000
Inventory	85,000	70,000
Total current assets	215,000	177,000
Plant assets (net)	423,000	383,000
Total assets	$638,000	$560,000

Liabilities and Stockholders' Equity	2017	2016
Current liabilities		
Accounts payable	$122,000	$110,000
Income taxes payable	23,000	20,000
Total current liabilities	145,000	130,000
Long-term liabilities		
Bonds payable	120,000	80,000
Total liabilities	265,000	210,000
Stockholders' equity		
Common stock ($5 par)	150,000	150,000
Retained earnings	223,000	200,000
Total stockholders' equity	373,000	350,000
Total liabilities and stockholders' equity	$638,000	$560,000

Additional data:

The common stock recently sold at $19.50 per share.

Instructions

Compute the following ratios for 2017.

(a) Current ratio.
(b) Acid-test ratio.
(c) Accounts receivable turnover.
(d) Inventory turnover.
(e) Profit margin.
(f) Asset turnover.
(g) Return on assets.

(h) Return on common stockholders' equity.
(i) Earnings per share.
(j) Price-earnings ratio.
(k) Payout ratio.
(l) Debt to assets ratio.
(m) Times interest earned.

Compute missing information given a set of ratios.

(LO 2)

P14-7 An incomplete income statement and an incomplete comparative balance sheet of Deines Corporation are presented below and on page 703.

DEINES CORPORATION
Income Statement
For the Year Ended December 31, 2017

Net sales	$11,000,000
Cost of goods sold	?
Gross profit	?
Operating expenses	1,665,000
Income from operations	?
Other expenses and losses	
Interest expense	?
Income before income taxes	?
Income tax expense	560,000
Net income	$?

DEINES CORPORATION
Balance Sheets
December 31

Assets	2017	2016
Current assets		
Cash	$ 450,000	$ 375,000
Accounts receivable (net)	?	950,000
Inventory	?	1,720,000
Total current assets	?	3,045,000
Plant assets (net)	4,620,000	3,955,000
Total assets	$?	$7,000,000

Liabilities and Stockholders' Equity	2017	2016
Current liabilities	$?	$ 825,000
Long-term notes payable	?	2,800,000
Total liabilities	?	3,625,000
Common stock, $1 par	3,000,000	3,000,000
Retained earnings	400,000	375,000
Total stockholders' equity	3,400,000	3,375,000
Total liabilities and stockholders' equity	$?	$7,000,000

Additional information:

1. The accounts receivable turnover for 2017 is 10 times.
2. All sales are on account.
3. The profit margin for 2017 is 14.5%.
4. Return on assets is 22% for 2017.
5. The current ratio on December 31, 2017, is 3.0.
6. The inventory turnover for 2017 is 4.8 times.

Instructions

Compute the missing information given the ratios above. Show computations. (*Note:* Start with one ratio and derive as much information as possible from it before trying another ratio. List all missing amounts under the ratio used to find the information.)

P14-8 Terwilliger Corporation owns a number of cruise ships and a chain of hotels. The hotels, which have not been profitable, were discontinued on September 1, 2017. The 2017 operating results for the company were as follows.

Prepare a statement of comprehensive income.

(LO 3)

Operating revenues	$12,850,000
Operating expenses	8,700,000
Operating income	$ 4,150,000

Analysis discloses that these data include the operating results of the hotel chain, which were operating revenues $1,500,000 and operating expenses $2,400,000. The hotels were sold at a gain of $200,000 before taxes. This gain is not included in the operating results. During the year, Terwilliger had an unrealized loss on its available-for-sale securities of $600,000 before taxes, which is not included in the operating results. In 2017, the company had other revenues and gains of $100,000, which are not included in the operating results. The corporation is in the 30% income tax bracket.

Instructions

Prepare a statement of comprehensive income.

P14-9 The ledger of Jaime Corporation at December 31, 2017, contains the following summary data.

Prepare a statement of comprehensive income.

(LO 3)

Net sales	$1,700,000	Cost of goods sold	$1,100,000
Selling expenses	120,000	Administrative expenses	150,000
Other revenues and gains	20,000	Other expenses and losses	28,000

Your analysis reveals the following additional information that is not included in the above data.

1. The entire Puzzles Division was discontinued on August 31. The income from operation for this division before income taxes was $20,000. The Puzzles Division was sold at a loss of $90,000 before income taxes.
2. The company had an unrealized gain on available-for-sale securities of $120,000 before income taxes for the year.
3. The income tax rate on all items is 25%.

Instructions
Prepare a statement of comprehensive income for the year ended December 31, 2017.

PROBLEMS: SET B

Visit the book's companion website, at **www.wiley.com/college/weygandt**, and choose the Student Companion site to access Problems: Set B.

CONTINUING PROBLEM

© leungchopan/
Shutterstock

COOKIE CREATIONS

(*Note:* This is a continuation of the Cookie Creations problem from Chapters 1 through 13.)

CC14 Natalie and Curtis have the balance sheet and income statement for the first year of operations for Cookie & Coffee Creations Inc. They have been told that they can use these financial statements to prepare horizontal and vertical analyses, and to calculate financial ratios, to determine how their business is doing and to make some decisions they have been considering.

Go to the book's companion website, **www.wiley.com/college/weygandt**, *to see the completion of this problem.*

BROADENING YOUR PERSPECTIVE

FINANCIAL REPORTING AND ANALYSIS

Financial Reporting Problem: Apple Inc.

BYP14-1 Your parents are considering investing in Apple Inc. common stock. They ask you, as an accounting expert, to make an analysis of the company for them. Apple's financial statements are presented in Appendix A. Instructions for accessing and using the company's complete annual report, including the notes to the financial statements, are also provided in Appendix A.

Instructions
(Follow the approach in the chapter for rounding numbers.)

(a) Make a 3-year trend analysis, using 2011 as the base year, of (1) net sales and (2) net income. Comment on the significance of the trend results.
(b) Compute for 2013 and 2012 the (1) profit margin, (2) asset turnover, (3) return on assets, and (4) return on common stockholders' equity. How would you evaluate Apple's profitability? Total assets at September 24, 2011, were $116,371 and total stockholders' equity at September 24, 2011, was $76,615.
(c) Compute for 2013 and 2012 the (1) debt to assets ratio and (2) times interest earned. How would you evaluate Apple's long-term solvency?
(d) What information outside the annual report may also be useful to your parents in making a decision about Apple?

Comparative Analysis Problem:
PepsiCo, Inc. vs. The Coca-Cola Company

BYP14-2 PepsiCo's financial statements are presented in Appendix B. Financial statements of The Coca-Cola Company are presented in Appendix C. Instructions for accessing and using the complete annual reports of PepsiCo and Coca-Cola, including the notes to the financial statements, are also provided in Appendices B and C, respectively.

Instructions

(a) Based on the information contained in these financial statements, determine each of the following for each company.
  (1) The percentage increase (decrease) in (i) net sales and (ii) net income from 2012 to 2013.
  (2) The percentage increase in (i) total assets and (ii) total common stockholders' (shareholders') equity from 2012 to 2013.
  (3) The basic earnings per share and price-earnings ratio for 2013. (For both PepsiCo and Coca-Cola, use the basic earnings per share.) Coca-Cola's common stock had a market price of $41.31 at the end of fiscal-year 2013, and PepsiCo's common stock had a market price of $82.71.
(b) What conclusions concerning the two companies can be drawn from these data?

Comparative Analysis Problem:
Amazon.com, Inc. vs. Wal-Mart Stores, Inc.

BYP14-3 Amazon.com, Inc.'s financial statements are presented in Appendix D. Financial statements of Wal-Mart Stores, Inc. are presented in Appendix E. Instructions for accessing and using the complete annual reports of Amazon and Wal-Mart, including the notes to the financial statements, are also provided in Appendices D and E, respectively.

Instructions

(a) Based on the information contained in these financial statements, determine each of the following for each company.
  (1) The percentage increase (decrease) in (i) net sales and (ii) net income from 2012 to 2013.
  (2) The percentage increase in (i) total assets and (ii) total common stockholders' (shareholders') equity from 2012 to 2013.
  (3) The basic earnings per share and price-earnings ratio for 2013. (For both Amazon and Wal-Mart, use the basic earnings per share.) Amazon's common stock had a market price of $398.79 at the end of fiscal-year 2013, and Wal-Mart's common stock had a market price of $74.68.
(b) What conclusions concerning the two companies can be drawn from these data?

Decision-Making Across the Organization

BYP14-4 As the CPA for Gandara Manufacturing Inc., you have been asked to develop some key ratios from the comparative financial statements. This information is to be used to convince creditors that the company is solvent and will continue as a going concern. The data requested and the computations developed from the financial statements follow.

	2017	2016
Current ratio	3.1 times	2.1 times
Acid-test ratio	.8 times	1.4 times
Asset turnover	2.8 times	2.2 times
Net income	Up 32%	Down 8%
Earnings per share	$3.30	$2.50

Instructions

With the class divided into groups, complete the following.

Gandara Manufacturing Inc. asks you to prepare a list of brief comments stating how each of these items supports the solvency and going-concern potential of the business. The company wishes to use these comments to support its presentation of data to its creditors. You are to prepare the comments as requested, giving the implications and the limitations of each item separately. Then prepare a collective inference that may be drawn from the individual items about Gandara's solvency and going-concern potential.

Real-World Focus

BYP14-5 The Management Discussion and Analysis section of an annual report addresses corporate performance for the year and sometimes uses financial ratios to support its claims.

Address: **www.ibm.com/investor/tools/index.phtml**, or go to **www.wiley.com/college/weygandt**

Steps
1. Choose **How to read annual reports** (in the Guides section).
2. Choose **Anatomy**.

Instructions
Using the information from the above site, answer the following questions.

(a) What are the optional elements that are often included in an annual report?
(b) What are the elements of an annual report that are required by the SEC?
(c) Describe the contents of the Management Discussion.
(d) Describe the contents of the Auditors' Report.
(e) Describe the contents of the Selected Financial Data.

CRITICAL THINKING

Communication Activity

BYP14-6 Abby Landis is the CEO of Pletcher's Electronics. Landis is an expert engineer but a novice in accounting. She asks you to explain the bases for comparison in analyzing Pletcher's financial statements.

Instructions
Write a letter to Abby Landis that explains the bases for comparison.

Ethics Case

BYP14-7 Dave Schonhardt, president of Schonhardt Industries, wishes to issue a press release to bolster his company's image and maybe even its stock price, which has been gradually falling. As controller, you have been asked to provide a list of 20 financial ratios along with some other operating statistics relative to Schonhardt Industries' first quarter financials and operations.

Two days after you provide the ratios and data requested, Steven Verlin, the public relations director of Schonhardt, asks you to prove the accuracy of the financial and operating data contained in the press release written by the president and edited by Steven. In the press release, the president highlights the sales increase of 25% over last year's first quarter and the positive change in the current ratio from 1.5:1 last year to 3:1 this year. He also emphasizes that production was up 50% over the prior year's first quarter.

You note that the press release contains only positive or improved ratios and none of the negative or deteriorated ratios. For instance, no mention is made that the debt to assets ratio has increased from 35% to 55%, that inventories are up 89%, and that while the current ratio improved, the acid-test ratio fell from 1:1 to 0.5:1. Nor is there any mention that the reported profit for the quarter would have been a loss had not the estimated lives of Schonhardt's plant and machinery been increased by 30%. Steven emphasizes, "The prez wants this release by early this afternoon."

Instructions
(a) Who are the stakeholders in this situation?
(b) Is there anything unethical in president Schonhardt's actions?
(c) Should you as controller remain silent? Does Steven have any responsibility?

All About You

BYP14-8 In this chapter, you learned how to use many tools for performing a financial analysis of a company. When making personal investments, however, it is most likely that you won't be buying stocks and bonds in individual companies. Instead, when most people want to invest in stock, they buy mutual funds. By investing in a mutual fund, you reduce your risk because the fund diversifies by buying the stock of a variety of different companies, bonds, and other investments, depending on the stated goals of the fund.

Before you invest in a fund, you will need to decide what type of fund you want. For example, do you want a fund that has the potential of high growth (but also high risk), or are you looking for lower risk and a steady stream of income? Do you want a fund that invests only in U.S. companies, or do you want one that invests globally? Many resources are available to help you with these types of decisions.

Instructions

Go to **http://web.archive.org/web/20050210200843/http://www.cnb1.com/invallocmdl.htm** and complete the investment allocation questionnaire. Add up your total points to determine the type of investment fund that would be appropriate for you.

FASB Codification Activity

BYP14-9 If your school has a subscription to the FASB Codification, go to **http://aaahq.org/ascLogin.cfm** to log in and prepare responses to the following. Use the Master Glossary for determining the proper definitions.

(a) Discontinued operations.
(b) Comprehensive income.

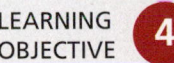

A Look at IFRS

LEARNING OBJECTIVE 4 **Compare financial statement analysis and income statement presentation under GAAP and IFRS.**

The tools of financial statement analysis, covered in the first section of this chapter, are the same throughout the world. Techniques such as vertical and horizontal analysis, for example, are tools used by analysts regardless of whether GAAP- or IFRS-related financial statements are being evaluated. In addition, the ratios provided in the textbook are the same ones that are used internationally.

The latter part of this chapter relates to the income statement and irregular items. As in GAAP, the income statement is a required statement under IFRS. In addition, the content and presentation of an IFRS income statement is similar to the one used for GAAP. *IAS 1* (revised), "Presentation of Financial Statements," provides general guidelines for the reporting of income statement information. In general, the differences in the presentation of financial statement information are relatively minor.

Relevant Facts

Following are the key similarities between GAAP and IFRS as related to financial statement analysis and income statement presentation. There are no significant differences between the two standards.

- The tools of financial statement analysis covered in this chapter are universal and therefore no significant differences exist in the analysis methods used.

- The basic objectives of the income statement are the same under both GAAP and IFRS. As indicated in the textbook, a very important objective is to ensure that users of the income statement can evaluate the sustainable income of the company. Thus, both the IASB and the FASB are interested in distinguishing normal levels of income from unusual items in order to better predict a company's future profitability.

- The basic accounting for discontinued operations is the same under IFRS and GAAP.

- The accounting for changes in accounting principles and changes in accounting estimates are the same for both GAAP and IFRS.

- Both GAAP and IFRS follow the same approach in reporting comprehensive income.

Looking to the Future

The FASB and the IASB are working on a project that would rework the structure of financial statements. Recently, the IASB decided to require a statement of comprehensive income, similar to what was required under GAAP. In addition, another part of this project addresses the issue of how to classify various items in the income statement. A main goal of this new approach is to provide information that better represents how businesses are run. In addition, the approach draws attention away from one number—net income.

IFRS Practice

IFRS Self-Test Questions

1. The basic tools of financial analysis are the same under both GAAP and IFRS **except** that:
   - (a) horizontal analysis cannot be done because the format of the statements is sometimes different.
   - (b) analysis is different because vertical analysis cannot be done under IFRS.
   - (c) the current ratio cannot be computed because current liabilities are often reported before current assets in IFRS statements of position.
   - (d) None of the above.

2. Presentation of comprehensive income must be reported under IFRS in:
   - (a) the statement of stockholders' equity.
   - (b) the income statement ending with net income.
   - (c) the notes to the financial statements.
   - (d) a statement of comprehensive income.

3. In preparing its income statement for 2017, Parmalane assembles the following information.

Sales revenue	$500,000
Cost of goods sold	300,000
Operating expenses	40,000
Loss on discontinued operations	20,000

   Ignoring income taxes, what is Parmalane's income from continuing operations for 2017 under IFRS?
   - (a) $260,000.
   - (b) $250,000.
   - (c) $240,000.
   - (d) $160,000.

International Financial Reporting Problem: Louis Vuitton

IFRS14-1 The financial statements of Louis Vuitton are presented in Appendix F. Instructions for accessing and using the company's complete annual report, including the notes to its financial statements, are also provided in Appendix F.

Instructions

Use the company's **2013 annual report** to answer the following questions.

(a) What was the company's profit margin for 2013? Has it increased or decreased from 2011?

(b) What was the company's operating profit for 2013?

(c) The company reported comprehensive income of €4,255 billion in 2013. What are the other comprehensive gains and losses recorded in 2013?

15 Managerial Accounting

CHAPTER PREVIEW This chapter focuses on issues illustrated in the Feature Story below about Current Designs and its parent company Wenonah Canoe. To succeed, the company needs to determine and control the costs of material, labor, and overhead, and understand the relationship between costs and profits. Managers often make decisions that determine their company's fate—and their own. Managers are evaluated on the results of their decisions. Managerial accounting provides tools to assist management in making decisions and to evaluate the effectiveness of those decisions.

FEATURE STORY

Just Add Water ... and Paddle

Mike Cichanowski grew up on the Mississippi River in Winona, Minnesota. At a young age, he learned to paddle a canoe so he could explore the river. Before long, Mike began crafting his own canoes from bent wood and fiberglass in his dad's garage. Then, when his canoe-making shop outgrew the garage, he moved it into an old warehouse. When that was going to be torn down, Mike came to a critical juncture in his life. He took out a bank loan and built his own small shop, giving birth to the company Wenonah Canoe.

Wenonah Canoe soon became known as a pioneer in developing techniques to get the most out of new materials such as plastics, composites, and carbon fibers—maximizing strength while minimizing weight.

In the 1990s, as kayaking became popular, Mike made another critical decision when he acquired Current Designs, a premier Canadian kayak manufacturer. This venture allowed Wenonah to branch out with new product lines while providing Current Designs with much-needed capacity expansion and manufacturing expertise. Mike moved Current Designs' headquarters to Minnesota and made a big (and

potentially risky) investment in a new production facility. Today, the company's 90 employees produce about 12,000 canoes and kayaks per year. These are sold across the country and around the world.

Mike will tell you that business success is "a three-legged stool." The first leg is the knowledge and commitment to make a great product. Wenonah's canoes and Current Designs' kayaks are widely regarded as among the very best. The second leg is the ability to sell your product. Mike's company started off making great canoes, but it took a little longer to figure out how to sell them. The third leg is not something that most of you would immediately associate with entrepreneurial success. It is what goes on behind the scenes—accounting. Good accounting information is absolutely critical to the countless decisions, big and small, that ensure the survival and growth of the company.

Bottom line: No matter how good your product is, and no matter how many units you sell, if you don't have a firm grip on your numbers, you are up a creek without a paddle.

Source: www.wenonah.com.

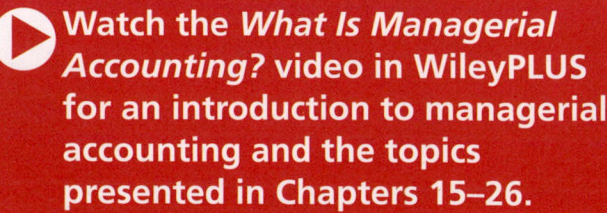

▶ Watch the *What Is Managerial Accounting?* video in WileyPLUS for an introduction to managerial accounting and the topics presented in Chapters 15–26.

© iNopparlal/Shutterstock

CHAPTER OUTLINE

Learning Objectives

1 Identify the features of managerial accounting and the functions of management.

- Comparing managerial and financial accounting
- Management functions
- Organizational structure

DO IT! **1** Managerial Accounting Overview

2 Describe the classes of manufacturing costs and the differences between product and period costs.

- Manufacturing costs
- Product vs. period costs
- Illustration of cost concepts

DO IT! **2** Managerial Cost Concepts

3 Demonstrate how to compute cost of goods manufactured and prepare financial statements for a manufacturer.

- Income statement
- Cost of goods manufactured schedule
- Balance sheet

DO IT! **3** Cost of Goods Manufactured

4 Discuss trends in managerial accounting.

- Service industries
- Value chain
- Balanced scorecard
- Business ethics
- Corporate social responsibility

DO IT! **4** Trends in Managerial Accounting

Go to the *REVIEW AND PRACTICE* section at the end of the chapter for a review of key concepts and practice applications with solutions.

Visit **WileyPLUS with ORION** for additional tutorials and practice opportunities.

Identify the features of managerial accounting and the functions of management.

Managerial accounting provides economic and financial information for managers and other internal users. The skills that you learn in this course will be vital to your future success in business. You don't believe us? Let's look at some examples of some of the crucial activities of employees at **Current Designs** and where those activities are addressed in this textbook.

In order to know whether it is making a profit, Current Designs needs accurate information about the cost of each kayak (Chapters 16, 17, and 18). To be profitable, Current Designs adjusts the number of kayaks it produces in response to changes in economic conditions and consumer tastes. It needs to understand how changes in the number of kayaks it produces impact its production costs and profitability (Chapters 19 and 20). Further, Current Designs' managers often consider alternative courses of action. For example, should the company accept a special order from a customer, produce a particular kayak component internally or outsource it, or continue or discontinue a particular product line (Chapter 21)? Finally, one of the most important and most difficult decisions is what price to charge for the kayaks (Chapter 22).

In order to plan for the future, Current Designs prepares budgets (Chapter 23), and it then compares its budgeted numbers with its actual results to evaluate performance and identify areas that need to change (Chapters 24 and 25). Finally, it sometimes needs to make substantial investment decisions, such as the building of a new plant or the purchase of new equipment (Chapter 26).

Someday, you are going to face decisions just like these. You may end up in sales, marketing, management, production, or finance. You may work for a company that provides medical care, produces software, or serves up mouth-watering meals. No matter what your position is and no matter what your product, the skills you acquire in this class will increase your chances of business success. Put another way, in business you can either guess or you can make an informed decision. As a CEO of **Microsoft** once noted: "If you're supposed to be making money in business and supposed to be satisfying customers and building market share, there are numbers that characterize those things. And if somebody can't speak to me quantitatively about it, then I'm nervous." This course gives you the skills you need to quantify information so you can make informed business decisions.

Comparing Managerial and Financial Accounting

There are both similarities and differences between managerial and financial accounting. First, each field of accounting deals with the economic events of a business. For example, *determining* the unit cost of manufacturing a product is part of managerial accounting. *Reporting* the total cost of goods manufactured and sold is part of financial accounting. In addition, both managerial and financial accounting require that a company's economic events be quantified and communicated to interested parties. Illustration 15-1 summarizes the principal differences between financial accounting and managerial accounting.

Management Functions

Managers' activities and responsibilities can be classified into three broad functions:

1. Planning.
2. Directing.
3. Controlling.

Feature	Financial Accounting	Managerial Accounting
Primary Users of Reports	External users: stockholders, creditors, and regulators.	Internal users: officers and managers.
Types and Frequency of Reports	Financial statements. Quarterly and annually.	Internal reports. As frequently as needed.
Purpose of Reports	General-purpose.	Special-purpose for specific decisions.
Content of Reports	Pertains to business as a whole. Highly aggregated (condensed). Limited to double-entry accounting and cost data. Generally accepted accounting principles.	Pertains to subunits of the business. Very detailed. Extends beyond double-entry accounting to any relevant data. Standard is relevance to decisions.
Verification Process	Audited by CPA.	No independent audits.

Illustration 15-1
Differences between financial and managerial accounting

In performing these functions, managers make decisions that have a significant impact on the organization.

Planning requires managers to look ahead and to establish objectives. These objectives are often diverse: maximizing short-term profits and market share, maintaining a commitment to environmental protection, and contributing to social programs. For example, **Hewlett-Packard**, in an attempt to gain a stronger foothold in the computer industry, greatly reduced its prices to compete with **Dell**. A key objective of management is to **add value** to the business under its control. Value is usually measured by the price of the company's stock and by the potential selling price of the company.

Directing involves coordinating a company's diverse activities and human resources to produce a smooth-running operation. This function relates to implementing planned objectives and providing necessary incentives to motivate employees. For example, manufacturers such as **Campbell Soup Company**, **General Motors**, and **Dell** need to coordinate purchasing, manufacturing, warehousing, and selling. Service corporations such as **American Airlines**, **Federal Express**, and **AT&T** coordinate scheduling, sales, service, and acquisitions of equipment and supplies. Directing also involves selecting executives, appointing managers and supervisors, and hiring and training employees.

The third management function, **controlling**, is the process of keeping the company's activities on track. In controlling operations, managers determine whether planned goals are met. When there are deviations from targeted objectives, managers decide what changes are needed to get back on track. Scandals at companies like **Enron**, **Lucent**, and **Xerox** attest to the fact that companies need adequate controls to ensure that the company develops and distributes accurate information.

How do managers achieve control? A smart manager in a very small operation can make personal observations, ask good questions, and know how to evaluate the answers. But using this approach in a larger organization would result in chaos. Imagine the president of **Current Designs** attempting to determine whether the company is meeting its planned objectives without some record of what has happened and what is expected to occur. Thus, large businesses typically use a formal system of evaluation. These systems include such features as budgets, responsibility centers, and performance evaluation reports—all of which are features of managerial accounting.

Decision-making is not a separate management function. Rather, it is the outcome of the exercise of good judgment in planning, directing, and controlling.

Management Insight   Louis Vuitton

© Camilia Wisbauer/iStockphoto

Even the Best Have to Get Better

Luxury-goods manufacturers used to consider stockouts to be a good thing. But recently, Louis Vuitton, a French manufacturer of high-end handbags, wallets, and suitcases, changed its attitude. The company adopted "lean" processes used by car manufacturers and electronics companies to speed up production of "hot" products. Work is done by flexible teams, with jobs organized based on how long a task takes. By reducing wasted time and eliminating bottlenecks, what used to take 20 to 30 workers eight days to do now takes only 6 to 12 workers one day.

Other efforts included organizing 10-person factory teams into U-shaped clusters. This arrangement freed up floor space, allowing Louis Vuitton to hire 300 additional employees. The company also selectively employs robots to bring items to human workers, saving valuable time. In addition, computer programs are now used to identify flaws in leather skins, enabling the company to identify the best way to cut pieces from the leather to increase quality and minimize waste.

Finally, Louis Vuitton stores around the world feed sales information to the company's headquarters in France. Production is then adjusted accordingly to ensure that would-be buyers aren't left empty-handed. With these new production processes, Louis Vuitton is already seeing improved results—returns of some products are down by two-thirds.

Sources: Christina Passariello, "Louis Vuitton Tries Modern Methods on Factory Lines," *Wall Street Journal* (October 9, 2006); and Christina Passariello, "At Vuitton, Growth in Small Batches," *Wall Street Journal* (June 27, 2011).

What are some of the steps that this company has taken in order to ensure that production meets demand? (Go to **WileyPLUS** for this answer and additional questions.)

Organizational Structure

Most companies prepare **organization charts** to show the interrelationships of activities and the delegation of authority and responsibility within the company. Illustration 15-2 shows a typical organization chart.

Illustration 15-2
A typical corporate organization chart

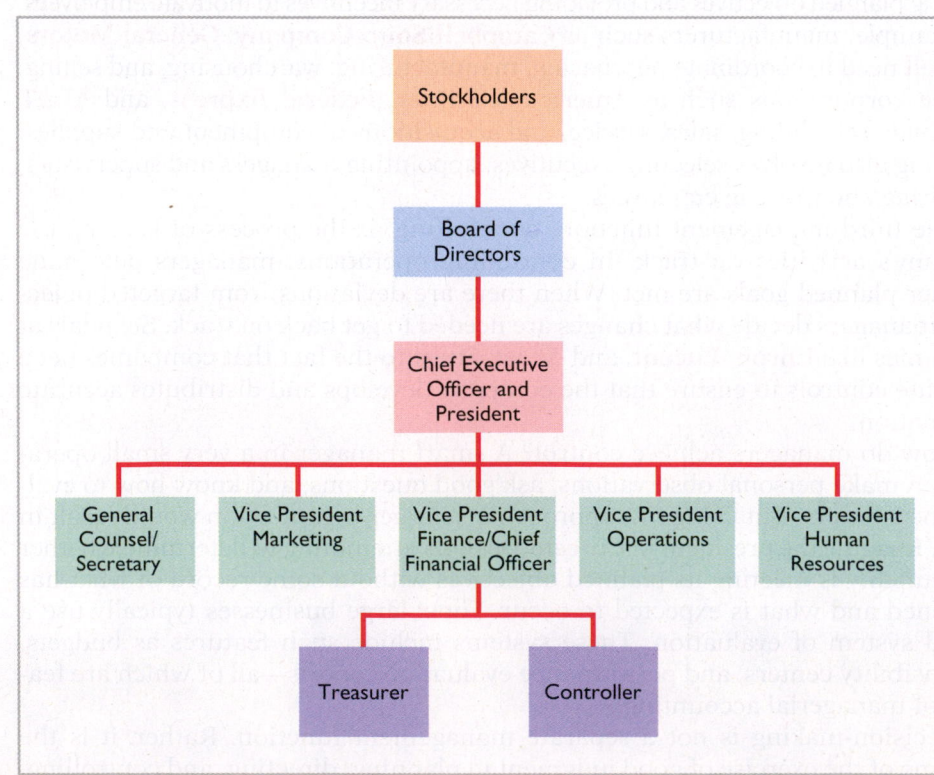

Stockholders own the corporation, but they manage it indirectly through a **board of directors** they elect. The board formulates the operating policies for the company or organization. The board also selects officers, such as a president and one or more vice presidents, to execute policy and to perform daily management functions.

The **chief executive officer (CEO)** has overall responsibility for managing the business. As the organization chart in Illustration 15-2 shows, the CEO delegates responsibilities to other officers.

Responsibilities within the company are frequently classified as either line or staff positions. Employees with **line positions** are directly involved in the company's primary revenue-generating operating activities. Examples of line positions include the vice president of operations, vice president of marketing, plant managers, supervisors, and production personnel. Employees with **staff positions** are involved in activities that support the efforts of the line employees. In a company like General Electric or Facebook, employees in finance, legal, and human resources have staff positions. While activities of staff employees are vital to the company, these employees are nonetheless there to serve the line employees who engage in the company's primary operations.

The **chief financial officer (CFO)** is responsible for all of the accounting and finance issues the company faces. The CFO is supported by the **controller** and the **treasurer**. The controller's responsibilities include (1) maintaining the accounting records, (2) ensuring an adequate system of internal control, and (3) preparing financial statements, tax returns, and internal reports. The treasurer has custody of the corporation's funds and is responsible for maintaining the company's cash position.

Also serving the CFO is the internal audit staff. The staff's responsibilities include reviewing the reliability and integrity of financial information provided by the controller and treasurer. Staff members also ensure that internal control systems are functioning properly to safeguard corporate assets. In addition, they investigate compliance with policies and regulations. In many companies, these staff members also determine whether resources are used in the most economical and efficient fashion.

The vice president of operations oversees employees with line positions. For example, the company might have multiple plant managers, each of whom reports to the vice president of operations. Each plant also has department managers, such as fabricating, painting, and shipping, each of whom reports to the plant manager.

DO IT! 1   Managerial Accounting Overview

Indicate whether the following statements are true or false. If false, explain why.

1. Managerial accountants have a single role within an organization: collecting and reporting costs to management.

2. Financial accounting reports are general-purpose and intended for external users.

3. Managerial accounting reports are special-purpose and issued as frequently as needed.

4. Managers' activities and responsibilities can be classified into three broad functions: cost accounting, budgeting, and internal control.

5. Managerial accounting reports must now comply with generally accepted accounting principles (GAAP).

Solution

1. False. Managerial accountants determine product costs. In addition, managerial accountants are now held responsible for evaluating how well the company employs its resources. As a result, when the company makes critical strategic decisions, managerial accountants serve as team members alongside personnel from production, marketing, and engineering.

Action Plan

✔ Understand that managerial accounting is a field of accounting that provides economic and financial information for managers and other internal users.

✔ Understand that financial accounting provides information for external users.

✔ Analyze which users require which different types of information.

2. True.

3. True.

4. False. Managers' activities are classified into three broad functions: planning, directing, and controlling. Planning requires managers to look ahead to establish objectives. Directing involves coordinating a company's diverse activities and human resources to produce a smooth-running operation. Controlling keeps the company's activities on track.

5. False. Managerial accounting reports are for internal use and thus do not have to comply with GAAP.

Related exercise material: **BE15-1, BE15-2, E15-1,** and **DO IT! 15-1.**

<table>
<tr><td>**LEARNING OBJECTIVE**</td><td>**2**</td><td>**Describe the classes of manufacturing costs and the differences between product and period costs.**</td></tr>
</table>

In order for managers at a company like **Current Designs** to plan, direct, and control operations effectively, they need good information. One very important type of information relates to costs. Managers should ask questions such as the following.

1. What costs are involved in making a product or performing a service?

2. If we decrease production volume, will costs decrease?

3. What impact will automation have on total costs?

4. How can we best control costs?

To answer these questions, managers obtain and analyze reliable and relevant cost information. The first step is to understand the various cost categories that companies use.

Manufacturing Costs

Manufacturing consists of activities and processes that convert raw materials into finished goods. Contrast this type of operation with merchandising, which sells products in the form in which they are purchased. Manufacturing costs are classified as direct materials, direct labor, and manufacturing overhead.

DIRECT MATERIALS

To obtain the materials that will be converted into the finished product, the manufacturer purchases raw materials. **Raw materials** are the basic materials and parts used in the manufacturing process.

Raw materials that can be physically and directly associated with the finished product during the manufacturing process are **direct materials**. Examples include flour in the baking of bread, syrup in the bottling of soft drinks, and steel in the making of automobiles. A primary direct material of many Current Designs' kayaks is polyethylene powder. Some of its high-performance kayaks use Kevlar®.

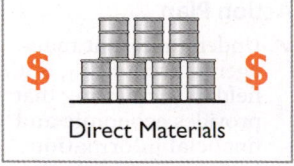

Direct Materials

Some raw materials cannot be easily associated with the finished product. These are called indirect materials. **Indirect materials** have one of two characteristics. (1) They do not physically become part of the finished product (such as polishing compounds used by Current Designs for the finishing touches on kayaks). Or, (2) they are impractical to trace to the finished product because their physical association with the finished product is too small in terms of cost (such as cotter pins and lock washers). Companies account for indirect materials as part of **manufacturing overhead**.

DIRECT LABOR

The work of factory employees that can be physically and directly associated with converting raw materials into finished goods is **direct labor**. Bottlers at Coca-Cola, bakers at Sara Lee, and equipment operators at Current Designs are employees whose activities are usually classified as direct labor. **Indirect labor** refers to the work of employees that has no physical association with the finished product or for which it is impractical to trace costs to the goods produced. Examples include wages of factory maintenance people, factory time-keepers, and factory supervisors. Like indirect materials, companies classify indirect labor as **manufacturing overhead**.

Direct Labor

MANUFACTURING OVERHEAD

Manufacturing overhead consists of costs that are indirectly associated with the manufacture of the finished product. Overhead costs also include manufacturing costs that cannot be classified as direct materials or direct labor. Manufacturing overhead includes indirect materials, indirect labor, depreciation on factory buildings and machines, and insurance, taxes, and maintenance on factory facilities.

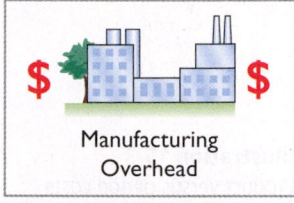

Manufacturing Overhead

One study of manufactured goods found the following magnitudes of the three different product costs as a percentage of the total product cost: direct materials 54%, direct labor 13%, and manufacturing overhead 33%. Note that the direct labor component is the smallest. This component of product cost is dropping substantially because of automation. Companies are working hard to increase productivity by decreasing labor. In some companies, direct labor has become as little as 5% of the total cost.

Alternative Terminology
Some companies use terms such as *factory overhead*, *indirect manufacturing costs*, and *burden* instead of manufacturing overhead.

Allocating direct materials and direct labor costs to specific products is fairly straightforward. Good recordkeeping can tell a company how much plastic it used in making each type of gear, or how many hours of factory labor it took to assemble a part. But allocating overhead costs to specific products presents problems. How much of the purchasing agent's salary is attributable to the hundreds of different products made in the same plant? What about the grease that keeps the machines humming, or the computers that make sure paychecks come out on time? Boiled down to its simplest form, the question becomes: Which products cause the incurrence of which costs? In subsequent chapters, we show various methods of allocating overhead to products.

Management Insight | Whirlpool

bikeriderlondon/Shutterstock

Why Manufacturing Matters for U.S. Workers

Prior to 2010, U.S. manufacturing employment fell at an average rate of 0.1% per year for 60 years. At the same time, U.S. factory output increased by an average rate of 3.4%. As manufacturers relied more heavily on automation, the number of people they needed declined. However, factory jobs are important because the average hourly wage of a factory worker is $22, twice the average wage of employees in the service sector. Fortunately, manufacturing jobs in the United States increased by 1.2% in 2010, and they were forecast to continue to increase through at least 2015. Why? Because companies like Whirlpool, Caterpillar, and Dow are building huge new plants in the United States to replace old, inefficient U.S. facilities. For many products that are ultimately sold in the United States, it makes more sense to produce them domestically and save on the shipping costs. In addition, these efficient new plants, combined with an experienced workforce, will make it possible to compete with manufacturers in other countries, thereby increasing export potential.

Sources: Bob Tita, "Whirlpool to Invest in Tennessee Plant," *Wall Street Journal Online* (September 1, 2010); and James R. Hagerty, "U.S. Factories Buck Decline," *Wall Street Journal Online* (January 19, 2011).

In what ways does the shift to automated factories change the amount and composition of product costs? (Go to **WileyPLUS** for this answer and additional questions.)

Product Versus Period Costs

Each of the manufacturing cost components—direct materials, direct labor, and manufacturing overhead—are product costs. As the term suggests, **product costs** are costs that are a necessary and integral part of producing the finished product. Companies record product costs, when incurred, as inventory. These costs do not become expenses until the company sells the finished goods inventory. At that point, the company records the expense as cost of goods sold.

Period costs are costs that are matched with the revenue of a specific time period rather than included as part of the cost of a salable product. These are non-manufacturing costs. Period costs include selling and administrative expenses. In order to determine net income, companies deduct these costs from revenues in the period in which they are incurred.

Illustration 15-3 summarizes these relationships and cost terms. Our main concern in this chapter is with product costs.

Illustration 15-3
Product versus period costs

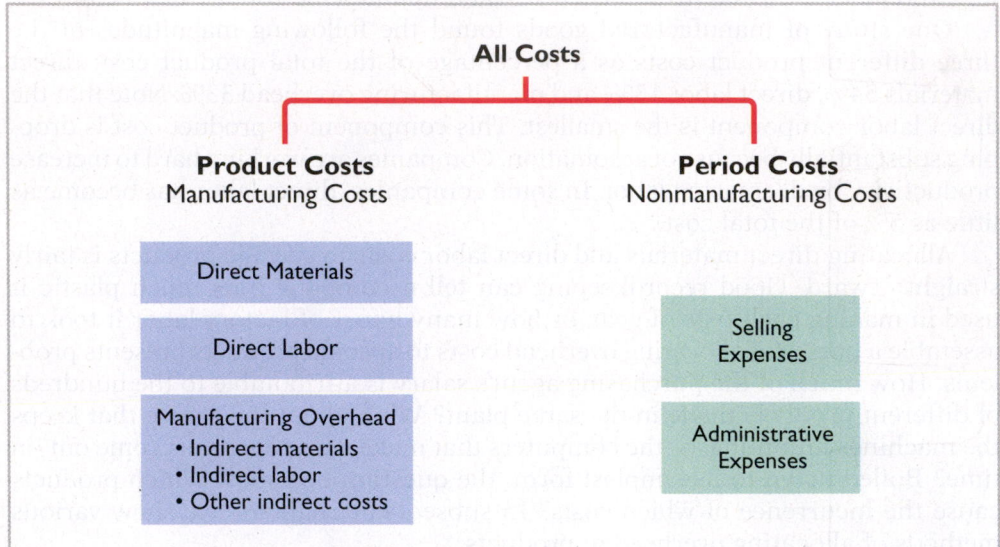

Illustration of Cost Concepts

To improve your understanding of cost concepts, we illustrate them here through an extended example. Suppose you started your own snowboard factory, Terrain Park Boards. Think that's impossible? **Burton Snowboards** was started by Jake Burton Carpenter, when he was only 23 years old. Jake initially experimented with 100 different prototype designs before settling on a final design. Then Jake, along with two relatives and a friend, started making 50 boards per day in Londonderry, Vermont. Unfortunately, while they made a lot of boards in their first year, they were only able to sell 300 of them. To get by during those early years, Jake taught tennis and tended bar to pay the bills.

Here are some of the costs that your snowboard factory would incur.

1. The materials cost of each snowboard (wood cores, fiberglass, resins, metal screw holes, metal edges, and ink) is $30.

2. The labor costs (for example, to trim and shape each board using jig saws and band saws) are $40.

3. Depreciation on the factory building and equipment (for example, presses, grinding machines, and lacquer machines) used to make the snowboards is $25,000 per year.

4. Property taxes on the factory building (where the snowboards are made) are $6,000 per year.

5. Advertising costs (mostly online and catalogue) are $60,000 per year.

6. Sales commissions related to snowboard sales are $20 per snowboard.

7. Salaries for factory maintenance employees are $45,000 per year.

8. The salary of the plant manager is $70,000.

9. The cost of shipping is $8 per snowboard.

Illustration 15-4 shows how Terrain Park Boards would assign these manufacturing and selling costs to the various categories.

Terrain Park Boards

| | Product Costs | | | |
Cost Item	Direct Materials	Direct Labor	Manufacturing Overhead	Period Costs
1. Material cost ($30 per board)	X			
2. Labor costs ($40 per board)		X		
3. Depreciation on factory equipment ($25,000 per year)			X	
4. Property taxes on factory building ($6,000 per year)			X	
5. Advertising costs ($60,000 per year)				X
6. Sales commissions ($20 per board)				X
7. Maintenance salaries (factory facilities, $45,000 per year)			X	
8. Salary of plant manager ($70,000 per year)			X	
9. Cost of shipping boards ($8 per board)				X

Illustration 15-4
Assignment of costs to cost categories

Total manufacturing costs are the sum of the **product costs**—direct materials, direct labor, and manufacturing overhead—incurred in the current period. If Terrain Park Boards produces 10,000 snowboards the first year, the total manufacturing costs would be $846,000, as shown in Illustration 15-5.

Cost Number and Item	Manufacturing Cost
1. Material cost ($30 × 10,000)	$300,000
2. Labor cost ($40 × 10,000)	400,000
3. Depreciation on factory equipment	25,000
4. Property taxes on factory building	6,000
7. Maintenance salaries (factory facilities)	45,000
8. Salary of plant manager	70,000
Total manufacturing costs	**$846,000**

Illustration 15-5
Computation of total manufacturing costs

Once it knows the total manufacturing costs, Terrain Park Boards can compute the manufacturing cost per unit. Assuming 10,000 units, the cost to produce one snowboard is $84.60 ($846,000 ÷ 10,000 units).

In subsequent chapters, we use extensively the cost concepts discussed in this chapter. So study Illustration 15-4 carefully. If you do not understand any of these classifications, go back and reread the appropriate section.

DO IT! 2   Managerial Cost Concepts

Action Plan

✔ Classify as direct materials any raw materials physically and directly associated with the finished product.

✔ Classify as direct labor the work of factory employees physically and directly associated with the finished product.

✔ Classify as manufacturing overhead any costs indirectly associated with the finished product.

A bicycle company has these costs: tires, salaries of employees who put tires on the wheels, factory building depreciation, advertising expenditures, lubricants, spokes, salary of factory manager, salary of accountant, handlebars, and salaries of factory maintenance employees. Classify each cost as direct materials, direct labor, overhead, or a period cost.

Solution

Tires, spokes, and handlebars are direct materials. Salaries of employees who put tires on the wheels are direct labor. Factory building depreciation, lubricants, salary of factory manager, and salary of factory maintenance employees are manufacturing overhead. Advertising expenditures and salary of accountant are period costs.

Related exercise material: **BE15-3, BE15-4, BE15-5, BE15-6, E15-2, E15-3, E15-4, E15-5, E15-6, E15-7, and DO IT! 15-2.**

LEARNING OBJECTIVE 3

Demonstrate how to compute cost of goods manufactured and prepare financial statements for a manufacturer.

The financial statements of a manufacturer are very similar to those of a merchandiser. For example, you will find many of the same sections and same accounts in the financial statements of **Procter & Gamble** that you find in the financial statements of **Dick's Sporting Goods**. The principal differences between their financial statements occur in two places: the cost of goods sold section in the income statement and the current assets section in the balance sheet.

Income Statement

Under a periodic inventory system, the income statements of a merchandiser and a manufacturer differ in the cost of goods sold section. Merchandisers compute cost of goods sold by adding the beginning inventory to the **cost of goods purchased** and subtracting the ending inventory. Manufacturers compute cost of goods sold by adding the beginning finished goods inventory to the **cost of goods manufactured** and subtracting the ending finished goods inventory. Illustration 15-6 shows these different methods.

A number of accounts are involved in determining the cost of goods manufactured. To eliminate excessive detail, income statements typically show only the total cost of goods manufactured. A separate statement, called a Cost of Goods Manufactured Schedule, presents the details. (See the discussion on page 722 and Illustration 15-9.)

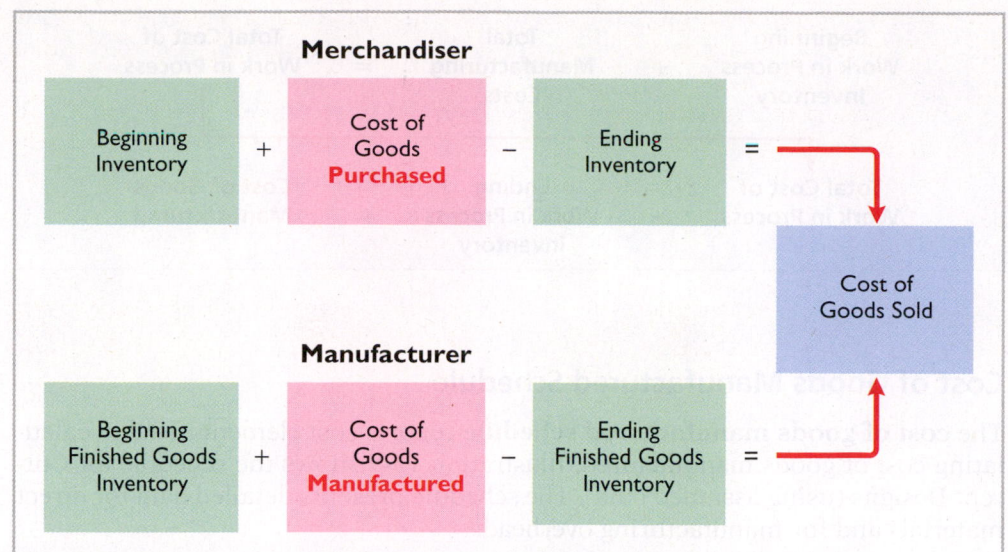

Illustration 15-6
Cost of goods sold components

Helpful Hint
We assume a periodic inventory system in this illustration.

Illustration 15-7 shows the different presentations of the cost of goods sold sections for merchandising and manufacturing companies. The other sections of an income statement are similar for merchandisers and manufacturers.

MERCHANDISING COMPANY Income Statement (partial) For the Year Ended December 31, 2017		MANUFACTURING COMPANY Income Statement (partial) For the Year Ended December 31, 2017	
Cost of goods sold		Cost of goods sold	
Inventory, Jan. 1	$ 70,000	Finished goods inventory, Jan. 1	$ 90,000
Cost of goods purchased	650,000	Cost of goods manufactured (see Illustration 15-9)	370,000
Cost of goods available for sale	720,000	Cost of goods available for sale	460,000
Less: Inventory, Dec. 31	400,000	Less: Finished goods inventory, Dec. 31	80,000
Cost of goods sold	$ 320,000	Cost of goods sold	$ 380,000

Illustration 15-7
Cost of goods sold sections of merchandising and manufacturing income statements

Cost of Goods Manufactured

An example may help show how companies determine the cost of goods manufactured. Assume that on January 1, **Current Designs** has a number of kayaks in various stages of production. In total, these partially completed units are called **beginning work in process inventory**. The costs the company assigns to beginning work in process inventory are based on the **manufacturing costs incurred in the prior period**.

Current Designs first incurs manufacturing costs in the current year to complete the work that was in process on January 1. It then incurs manufacturing costs for production of new orders. The sum of the direct materials costs, direct labor costs, and manufacturing overhead incurred in the current year is the **total manufacturing costs** for the current period.

We now have two cost amounts: (1) the cost of the beginning work in process and (2) the total manufacturing costs for the current period. The sum of these costs is the **total cost of work in process** for the year.

At the end of the year, Current Designs may have some kayaks that are only partially completed. The costs of these units become the cost of the **ending work in process inventory**. To find the **cost of goods manufactured**, we subtract this cost from the total cost of work in process. Illustration 15-8 (page 722) shows the formula for determining the cost of goods manufactured.

Illustration 15-8
Cost of goods manufactured
formula

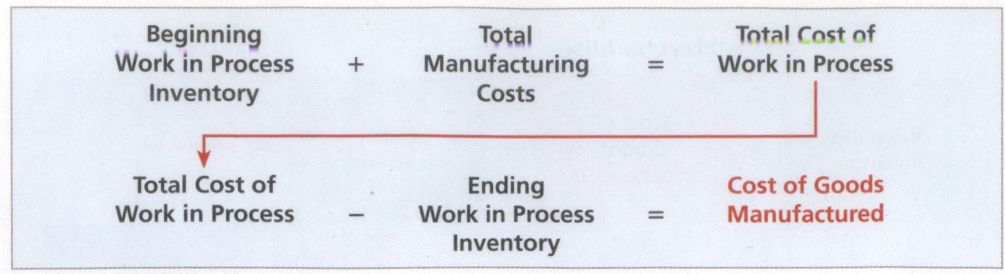

Cost of Goods Manufactured Schedule

The **cost of goods manufactured schedule** reports cost elements used in calculating cost of goods manufactured. Illustration 15-9 shows the schedule for Current Designs (using assumed data). The schedule presents detailed data for direct materials and for manufacturing overhead.

Illustration 15-9
Cost of goods manufactured
schedule

CURRENT DESIGNS Cost of Goods Manufactured Schedule For the Year Ended December 31, 2017			
Work in process, January 1			$ 18,400
Direct materials			
Raw materials inventory, January 1	$ 16,700		
Raw materials purchases	152,500		
Total raw materials available for use	169,200		
Less: Raw materials inventory, December 31	22,800		
Direct materials used		$146,400	
Direct labor		175,600	
Manufacturing overhead			
Indirect labor	14,300		
Factory repairs	12,600		
Factory utilities	10,100		
Factory depreciation	9,440		
Factory insurance	8,360		
Total manufacturing overhead		54,800	
Total manufacturing costs			**376,800**
Total cost of work in process			395,200
Less: Work in process, December 31			**25,200**
Cost of goods manufactured			**$370,000**

Review Illustration 15-8 and then examine the cost of goods manufactured schedule in Illustration 15-9. You should be able to distinguish between "Total manufacturing costs" and "Cost of goods manufactured." The difference is the effect of the change in work in process during the period.

Balance Sheet

The balance sheet for a merchandising company shows just one category of inventory. In contrast, the balance sheet for a manufacturer may have three inventory accounts, as shown in Illustration 15-10 for Current Designs' kayak inventory.

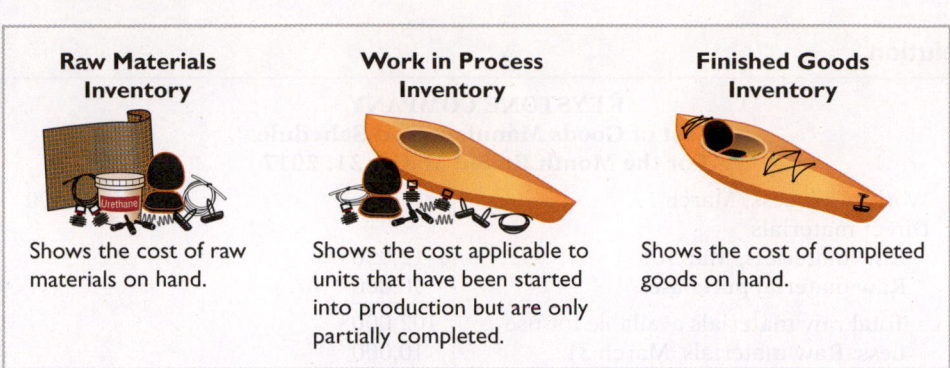

Illustration 15-10
Inventory accounts for a manufacturer

Finished Goods Inventory is to a manufacturer what Inventory is to a merchandiser. Each of these classifications represents the goods that the company has available for sale. The current assets sections presented in Illustration 15-11 contrast the presentations of inventories for merchandising and manufacturing companies. The remainder of the balance sheet is similar for the two types of companies.

Illustration 15-11
Current assets sections of merchandising and manufacturing balance sheets

MERCHANDISING COMPANY		MANUFACTURING COMPANY		
Balance Sheet		Balance Sheet		
December 31, 2017		December 31, 2017		
Current assets		Current assets		
Cash	$100,000	Cash		$180,000
Accounts receivable (net)	210,000	Accounts receivable (net)		210,000
Inventory	**400,000**	**Inventory**		
Prepaid expenses	22,000	**Finished goods**	**$80,000**	
Total current assets	$732,000	**Work in process**	**25,200**	
		Raw materials	**22,800**	**128,000**
		Prepaid expenses		18,000
		Total current assets		$536,000

Each step in the accounting cycle for a merchandiser applies to a manufacturer. For example, prior to preparing financial statements, manufacturers make adjusting entries. The adjusting entries are essentially the same as those of a merchandiser. The closing entries are also similar for manufacturers and merchandisers.

DO IT! 3 Cost of Goods Manufactured

The following information is available for Keystone Company.

		March 1	March 31
Raw materials inventory		$12,000	$10,000
Work in process inventory		2,500	4,000
Materials purchased in March	$ 90,000		
Direct labor in March	75,000		
Manufacturing overhead in March	220,000		

Prepare the cost of goods manufactured schedule for the month of March 2017.

Action Plan

✔ Start with beginning work in process as the first item in the cost of goods manufactured schedule.

✔ Sum direct materials used, direct labor, and manufacturing overhead to determine total manufacturing costs.

✔ Sum beginning work in process and total manufacturing costs to determine total cost of work in process.

✔ Cost of goods manufactured is the total cost of work in process less ending work in process.

Solution

KEYSTONE COMPANY Cost of Goods Manufactured Schedule For the Month Ended March 31, 2017			
Work in process, March 1			$ 2,500
Direct materials			
Raw materials, March 1	$ 12,000		
Raw material purchases	90,000		
Total raw materials available for use	102,000		
Less: Raw materials, March 31	10,000		
Direct materials used		$ 92,000	
Direct labor		75,000	
Manufacturing overhead		220,000	
Total manufacturing costs			387,000
Total cost of work in process			389,500
Less: Work in process, March 31			4,000
Cost of goods manufactured			$385,500

Related exercise material: **BE15-7, BE15-8, BE15-9, BE15-10, E15-8, E15-9, E15-10, E15-11, E15-12, E15-13, E15-14, E15-15, E15-16, E15-17, and DO IT! 15-3.**

LEARNING OBJECTIVE **4** **Discuss trends in managerial accounting.**

The business environment never stands still. Regulations are always changing, global competition continues to intensify, and technology is a source of constant upheaval. In this rapidly changing world, managerial accounting needs to continue to innovate in order to provide managers with the information they need.

Service Industries

Much of the U.S. economy has shifted toward an emphasis on services. Today, more than 50% of U.S. workers are employed by service companies. Airlines, marketing agencies, cable companies, and governmental agencies are just a few examples of service companies. How do service companies differ from manufacturing companies? One difference is that services are consumed immediately. For example, when a restaurant produces a meal, that meal is not put in inventory but is instead consumed immediately. An airline uses special equipment to provide its product, but again, the output of that equipment is consumed immediately by the customer in the form of a flight. And a marketing agency performs services for its clients that are immediately consumed by the customer in the form of a marketing plan. For a manufacturing company, like **Boeing**, it often has a long lead time before its airplane is used or consumed by the customer.

This chapter's examples featured manufacturing companies because accounting for the manufacturing environment requires the use of the broadest range of accounts. That is, the accounts used by service companies represent a subset of those used by manufacturers because service companies are not producing inventory. Neither the restaurant, the airline, or the marketing agency discussed above produces an inventoriable product. However, just like a manufacturer, each needs to keep track of the costs of its services in order to know whether it is generating a profit. A successful restaurateur needs to know the cost of each offering on the menu, an airline needs to know the cost of flight service to each destination, and a marketing agency needs to

ETHICS NOTE

Do telecommunications companies have an obligation to provide service to remote or low-user areas for a fee that may be less than the cost of the service?

know the cost to develop a marketing plan. Thus, the techniques shown in this chapter, to accumulate manufacturing costs to determine manufacturing inventory, are equally useful for determining the costs of performing services.

For example, let's consider the costs that **Hewlett-Packard (HP)** might incur on a consulting engagement. A significant portion of its costs would be salaries of consulting personnel. It might also incur travel costs, materials, software costs, and depreciation charges on equipment. In the same way that it needs to keep track of the cost of manufacturing its computers and printers, HP needs to know what its costs are on each consulting job. It could prepare a cost of services performed schedule similar to the cost of goods manufactured schedule in Illustration 15-9 (page 722). The structure would be essentially the same as the cost of goods manufactured schedule, but section headings would be reflective of the costs of the particular service organization.

Many of the examples we present in subsequent chapters will be based on service companies. To highlight the relevance of the techniques used in this course for service companies, we have placed a service company icon (see margin) next to those items in the text and end-of-chapter materials that relate to non-manufacturing companies.

Service Company Insight   Allegiant Airlines

© Stephen Strathdee/iStockphoto

Low Fares but Decent Profits

When other airlines were cutting flight service due to recession, Allegiant Airlines increased capacity by 21%. Sounds crazy, doesn't it? But it must know something because while the other airlines were losing money, it was generating profits. In fact, it often has the industry's highest profit margins. Consider also that its average one-way fare is only $83. So how does it make money? As a low-budget airline, it focuses on controlling costs.

Allegiant purchases used planes for $3 million each rather than new planes for $40 million. It flies out of small towns, so wages are low and competition is nonexistent. It minimizes hotel costs by having its flight crews finish their day in their home cities. The company also only flies a route if its 150-passenger planes are nearly full (it averages about 90% of capacity). The bottom line is that Allegiant knows its costs to the penny. Knowing what your costs are might not be glamorous, but it sure beats losing money.

Sources: Susan Carey, "For Allegiant, Getaways Mean Profits," *Wall Street Journal Online* (February 18, 2009); and Scott Mayerowitz, "Tiny Allegiant Air Thrives on Low Costs, High Fees," *http://bigstory.ap.org* (June 28, 2013).

What are some of the line items that would appear in the cost of services performed schedule of an airline? (Go to **WileyPLUS** for this answer and additional questions.)

Focus on the Value Chain

The **value chain** refers to all business processes associated with providing a product or performing a service. Illustration 15-12 depicts the value chain for a manufacturer. Many of the most significant business innovations in recent years

Illustration 15-12
A manufacturer's value chain

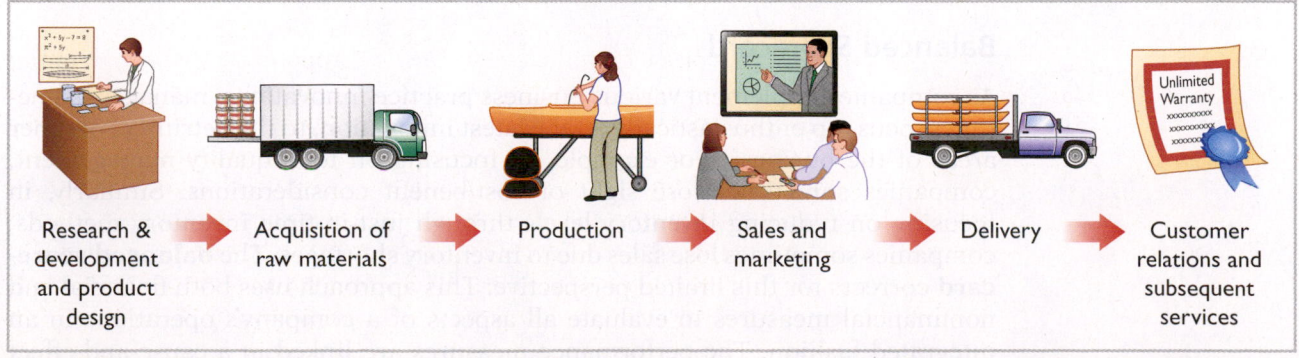

Research & development and product design → Acquisition of raw materials → Production → Sales and marketing → Delivery → Customer relations and subsequent services

have resulted either directly, or indirectly, from a focus on the value chain. For example, so-called **lean manufacturing**, originally pioneered by Japanese automobile manufacturer Toyota but now widely practiced, reviews all business processes in an effort to increase productivity and eliminate waste, all while continually trying to improve quality.

Just-in-time (JIT) inventory methods, which have significantly lowered inventory levels and costs for many companies, are one innovation that resulted from the focus on the value chain. Under the JIT inventory method, goods are manufactured or purchased just in time for sale. For example, Dell can produce and deliver a custom computer within 48 hours of a customer's order. However, JIT also necessitates increased emphasis on product quality. Because JIT companies do not have excess inventory on hand, they cannot afford to stop production because of defects or machine breakdowns. If they stop production, deliveries will be delayed and customers will be unhappy. For example, a design flaw in an Intel computer chip was estimated to cost the company $1 billion in repairs and reduced revenue. As a consequence, many companies now focus on **total quality management (TQM)** to reduce defects in finished products, with the goal of zero defects. The TQM philosophy has been employed by some of the most successful businesses to improve all aspects of the value chain.

Another innovation, the **theory of constraints**, involves identification of "bottlenecks"—constraints within the value chain that limit a company's profitability. Once a major constraint has been identified and eliminated, the company moves on to fix the next most significant constraint. General Motors found that by eliminating bottlenecks, it improved its use of overtime labor while meeting customer demand. An application of the theory of constraints is presented in Chapter 20.

Technology has played a big role in the focus on the value chain and the implementation of lean manufacturing. For example, **enterprise resource planning (ERP) systems**, such as those provided by SAP, provide a comprehensive, centralized, integrated source of information to manage all major business processes—from purchasing, to manufacturing, to sales, to human resources. ERP systems have, in some large companies, replaced as many as 200 individual software packages. In addition, the focus on improving efficiency in the value chain has also resulted in adoption of automated manufacturing processes. Many companies now use computer-integrated manufacturing. These systems often reduce the reliance on manual labor by using robotic equipment. This increases overhead costs as a percentage of total product costs.

As overhead costs increased because of factory automation, the accuracy of overhead cost allocation to specific products became more important. Managerial accounting devised an approach, called **activity-based costing (ABC)**, which allocates overhead based on each product's use of particular activities in making the product. In addition to providing more accurate product costing, ABC also can contribute to increased efficiency in the value chain. For example, suppose one of a company's overhead pools is allocated based on the number of setups that each product requires. If a particular product's cost is high because it is allocated a lot of overhead due to a high number of setups, management will be motivated to try to reduce the number of setups and thus reduce its overhead allocation. ABC is discussed further in Chapter 18.

Balanced Scorecard

As companies implement various business practice innovations, managers sometimes focus too enthusiastically on the latest innovation, to the detriment of other areas of the business. For example, by focusing on total quality management, companies sometimes lose sight of cost/benefit considerations. Similarly, in focusing on reducing inventory levels through just-in-time inventory methods, companies sometimes lose sales due to inventory shortages. The **balanced scorecard** corrects for this limited perspective: This approach uses both financial and nonfinancial measures to evaluate all aspects of a company's operations in an integrated fashion. The performance measures are linked in a cause-and-effect fashion to ensure that they all tie to the company's overall objectives. For example, to increase return on assets, the company could try to increase sales. To increase sales, the company could try to increase customer satisfaction. To increase customer satisfaction, the company could try to reduce product defects. Finally, to reduce product defects, the company could increase employee training. The balanced scorecard, which is discussed further in Chapter 25, is now used by many companies, including Hilton Hotels, Wal-Mart Stores, Inc., and HP.

Business Ethics

All employees within an organization are expected to act ethically in their business activities. Given the importance of ethical behavior to corporations and their owners (stockholders), an increasing number of organizations provide codes of business ethics for their employees.

CREATING PROPER INCENTIVES

Companies like Amazon.com, IBM, and Nike use complex systems to monitor, control, and evaluate the actions of managers. Unfortunately, these systems and controls sometimes unwittingly create incentives for managers to take unethical actions. For example, because budgets are also used as an evaluation tool, some managers try to "game" the budgeting process by underestimating their division's predicted performance so that it will be easier to meet their performance targets. On the other hand, if budgets are set at unattainable levels, managers sometimes take unethical actions to meet the targets in order to receive higher compensation or, in some cases, to keep their jobs.

For example, at one time, airline manufacturer Boeing was plagued by a series of scandals including charges of over-billing, corporate espionage, and illegal conflicts of interest. Some long-time employees of Boeing blamed the decline in ethics on a change in the corporate culture that took place after Boeing merged with McDonnell Douglas. They suggested that evaluation systems implemented after the merger to evaluate employee performance gave employees the impression that they needed to succeed no matter what actions were required to do so.

As another example, manufacturing companies need to establish production goals for their processes. Again, if controls are not effective and realistic, problems develop. To illustrate, Schering-Plough, a pharmaceutical manufacturer, found that employees were so concerned with meeting production quantity standards that they failed to monitor the quality of the product, and as a result the dosages were often wrong.

CODE OF ETHICAL STANDARDS

In response to corporate scandals, the U.S. Congress enacted the Sarbanes-Oxley Act (SOX) to help prevent lapses in internal control. One result of SOX was to clarify top management's responsibility for the company's financial statements. CEOs and CFOs are now required to certify that financial statements give a fair presentation of the company's operating results and its financial condition. In addition, top managers must certify that the company maintains an adequate system of internal controls to safeguard the company's assets and ensure accurate financial reports.

Another result of SOX is that companies now pay more attention to the composition of the board of directors. In particular, the audit committee of the board of directors must be comprised entirely of independent members (that is, non-employees) and must contain at least one financial expert. Finally, the law substantially increases the penalties for misconduct.

To provide guidance for managerial accountants, the Institute of Management Accountants (IMA) has developed a code of ethical standards, entitled *IMA Statement of Ethical Professional Practice*. Management accountants should not commit acts in violation of these standards. Nor should they condone such acts by others within their organizations. We include the IMA code of ethical standards in Appendix K. Throughout the textbook, we will address various ethical issues managers face.

Corporate Social Responsibility

The balanced scorecard attempts to take a broader, more inclusive view of corporate profitability measures. Many companies, however, have begun to evaluate not just corporate profitability but also **corporate social responsibility**. In addition to profitability, corporate social responsibility considers a company's efforts to employ sustainable business practices with regard to its employees, society, and the environment. This is sometimes referred to as the **triple bottom line** because it evaluates a company's performance with regard to **people, planet, and profit**. Recent reports indicate that over 50% of the 500 largest U.S. companies provide sustainability reports. Make no mistake, these companies are still striving to maximize profits—in a competitive world, they won't survive long if they don't. In fact, you might recognize a few of the names on a recent Forbes.com list of the 100 most sustainable companies in the world. Are you surprised that General Electric, adidas, Toyota, Coca-Cola, or Starbucks made the list? These companies have learned that with a long-term, sustainable approach, they can maximize profits while also acting in the best interest of their employees, their communities, and the environment. At various points within this textbook, we will discuss situations where real companies use the very skills that you are learning to evaluate decisions from a sustainable perspective, such as in the following Insight box.

People, Planet, and Profit Insight   Phantom Tac

Geanina Bechea/Shutterstock

People Matter

Many clothing factories in developing countries are known for unsafe buildings, poor working conditions, and wage and labor violations. One of the owners of Phantom Tac, a clothing manufacturer in Bangladesh, did make efforts to develop sustainable business practices. This owner, David Mayor, provided funding for a training program for female workers. He also developed a website to educate customers about the workers' conditions. But Phantom Tac also had to make a profit. Things got tight when one of its customers canceled orders because Phantom Tac failed a social compliance audit. The company had to quit funding the training program and the website.

Recently, Bangladesh's textile industry has seen some significant improvements in working conditions and safety standards. As Brad Adams, Asia director of Human Rights Watch, notes, "The (Dhaka) government has belatedly begun to register unions, which is an important first step, but it now needs to ensure that factory owners stop persecuting their leaders and actually allow them to function."

Sources: Jim Yardley, "Clothing Brands Sidestep Blame for Safety Lapses," *The New York Times Online* (December 30, 2013); and Palash Ghosh, "Despite Low Pay, Poor Work Conditions, Garment Factories Empowering Millions of Bangladeshi Women," *International Business Times* (March 25, 2014).

What are some of the common problems for many clothing factories in developing countries? (Go to **WileyPLUS** for this answer and additional questions.)

Sustainable business practices present numerous issues for management and managerial accountants. First, companies need to decide what items need to be measured, generally those that are of utmost importance to its stakeholders. For example, a particular company might be most concerned with minimizing water pollution or maximizing employee safety. Then, for each item identified, the company determines measurable attributes that provide relevant information regarding the company's performance with regard to that item, such as the amount of waste released into public waterways or the number of accidents per 1,000 hours worked. Finally, the company needs to consider the materiality of the item, the cost of measuring these attributes, and the reliability of the measurements. If the company uses this information to make decisions, then accuracy is critical. Of particular concern is whether the measurements can be verified by an outside third party.

Unlike financial reporting, which is overseen by the Financial Accounting Standards Board, the reporting of sustainable business practices currently has no agreed-upon standard-setter. A number of organizations have, however, published guidelines. The guidelines published by the **Global Reporting Initiative** are among the most widely recognized and followed. Illustration 15-13 provides a list of major categories provided by the Global Reporting Initiative for sustainability reporting and a sample of aspects that companies might consider within each category.

Illustration 15-13
Sample categories in Global Reporting Initiative guidelines

		Social			
Economic	**Environmental**	**Labor Practices and Decent Work**	**Human Rights**	**Society**	**Product Responsibility**
Economic performance Market presence Indirect economic impacts Procurement practices	Energy Biodiversity Effluents and waste Compliance	Occupational health and safety Training and education Diversity and equal opportunity Labor practices grievance mechanisms	Non-discrimination Child labor Indigenous rights Supplier human rights assessment	Anti-corruption Anti-competitive behavior Supplier assessment for impacts on society Grievance mechanisms for impacts on society	Customer health and safety Product and service labeling Marketing communications Customer privacy

Source: Global Reporting Initiative, G4 Sustainability Reporting Guidelines, p. 9. The full report is available at www.globalreporting.org.

DO IT! 4 | Trends in Managerial Accounting

Match the descriptions that follow with the corresponding terms.

Descriptions:

1. _____ All activities associated with providing a product or performing a service.

2. _____ A method of allocating overhead based on each product's use of activities in making the product.

3. _____ Systems implemented to reduce defects in finished products with the goal of achieving zero defects.

4. _____ A performance-measurement approach that uses both financial and nonfinancial measures, tied to company objectives, to evaluate a company's operations in an integrated fashion.

5. _____ Inventory system in which goods are manufactured or purchased just as they are needed for use.

6. _____ A company's efforts to employ sustainable business practices with regards to its employees, society, and the environment.

7. _____ A code of ethical standards developed by the Institute of Management Accountants.

Terms:

a. Activity-based costing
b. Balanced scorecard
c. Corporate social responsibility
d. Just-in-time (JIT) inventory
e. Total quality management (TQM)
f. Statement of Ethical Professional Practice
g. Value chain

Solution

1. g 2. a 3. e 4. b 5. d 6. c 7. f

Related exercise material: **BE15-11, E15-18, and DO IT! 15-4.**

Action Plan

✔ Develop a forward-looking view, in order to advise and provide information to various members of the organization.

✔ Understand current business trends and issues.

REVIEW AND PRACTICE

LEARNING OBJECTIVES REVIEW

1 Identify the features of managerial accounting and the functions of management. The *primary users* of managerial accounting reports, issued as frequently as needed, are internal users, who are officers, department heads, managers, and supervisors in the company. The purpose of these reports is to provide special-purpose information for a particular user for a specific decision. The content of managerial accounting reports pertains to subunits of the business. It may be very detailed, and may extend beyond the double-entry accounting system. The reporting standard is relevance to the decision being made. No independent audits are required in managerial accounting.

The functions of management are planning, directing, and controlling. Planning requires management to look ahead and to establish objectives. Directing involves coordinating the diverse activities and human resources of a company to produce a smooth-running operation. Controlling is the process of keeping the activities on track.

2 Describe the classes of manufacturing costs and the differences between product and period costs. Manufacturing costs are typically classified as either (1) direct materials, (2) direct labor, or (3) manufacturing overhead. Raw materials that can be physically and directly associated with the finished product during the manufacturing process are called direct materials. The work of factory employees that can be physically and directly associated with converting raw materials into finished goods is considered direct labor. Manufacturing overhead consists of costs that are indirectly associated with the manufacture of the finished product.

Product costs are costs that are a necessary and integral part of producing the finished product. Product costs are also called inventoriable costs. These costs do not become expenses until the company sells the finished goods inventory. Period costs are costs that are identified with a specific time period rather than with a salable product. These costs relate to nonmanufacturing costs and therefore are not inventoriable costs.

3 Demonstrate how to compute cost of goods manufactured and prepare financial statements for a manufacturer. Companies add the cost of the beginning work in process to the total manufacturing costs for the current year to arrive at the total cost of work in process for the year. They then subtract the ending work in process from the total cost of work in process to arrive at the cost of goods manufactured.

The difference between a merchandising and a manufacturing income statement is in the cost of goods sold section. A manufacturing cost of goods sold section shows beginning and ending finished goods inventories and the cost of goods manufactured.

The difference between a merchandising and a manufacturing balance sheet is in the current assets section. The current assets section of a manufacturing company's balance sheet presents three inventory accounts: finished goods inventory, work in process inventory, and raw materials inventory.

4 Discuss trends in managerial accounting. Managerial accounting has experienced many changes in recent years, including a shift toward service companies as well as an emphasis on ethical behavior. Improved practices include a focus on managing the value chain through techniques such as just-in-time inventory, total quality management, activity-based costing, and theory of constraints. The balanced scorecard is now used by many companies in order to attain a more comprehensive view of the company's operations. Finally, companies are now evaluating their performance with regard to their corporate social responsibility.

GLOSSARY REVIEW

Activity-based costing (ABC) A method of allocating overhead based on each product's use of activities in making the product. (p. 726).

Balanced scorecard A performance-measurement approach that uses both financial and nonfinancial measures, tied to company objectives, to evaluate a company's operations in an integrated fashion. (p. 726).

Board of directors The group of officials elected by the stockholders of a corporation to formulate operating policies and select officers who will manage the company. (p. 715).

Chief executive officer (CEO) Corporate officer who has overall responsibility for managing the business and delegates responsibilities to other corporate officers. (p. 715).

Chief financial officer (CFO) Corporate officer who is responsible for all of the accounting and finance issues of the company. (p. 715).

Controller Financial officer responsible for a company's accounting records, system of internal control, and preparation of financial statements, tax returns, and internal reports. (p. 715).

Corporate social responsibility The efforts of a company to employ sustainable business practices with regard to its employees, society, and the environment. (p. 728).

Cost of goods manufactured Total cost of work in process less the cost of the ending work in process inventory. (p. 721).

Direct labor The work of factory employees that can be physically and directly associated with converting raw materials into finished goods. (p. 717).

Direct materials Raw materials that can be physically and directly associated with manufacturing the finished product. (p. 716).

Enterprise resource planning (ERP) system Software that provides a comprehensive, centralized, integrated source of information used to manage all major business processes. (p. 726).

Indirect labor Work of factory employees that has no physical association with the finished product or for which it is impractical to trace the costs to the goods produced. (p. 717).

Indirect materials Raw materials that do not physically become part of the finished product or for which it is impractical to trace to the finished product because their physical association with the finished product is too small. (p. 716).

Just-in-time (JIT) inventory Inventory system in which goods are manufactured or purchased just in time for sale. (p. 726).

Line positions Jobs that are directly involved in a company's primary revenue-generating operating activities. (p. 715).

Managerial accounting A field of accounting that provides economic and financial information for managers and other internal users. (p. 712).

Manufacturing overhead Manufacturing costs that are indirectly associated with the manufacture of the finished product. (p. 717).

Period costs Costs that are matched with the revenue of a specific time period and charged to expense as incurred. (p. 718).

Product costs Costs that are a necessary and integral part of producing the finished product. (p. 718).

Sarbanes-Oxley Act (SOX) Law passed by Congress intended to reduce unethical corporate behavior. (p. 727).

Staff positions Jobs that support the efforts of line employees. (p. 715).

Theory of constraints A specific approach used to identify and manage constraints in order to achieve the company's goals. (p. 726).

Total cost of work in process Cost of the beginning work in process plus total manufacturing costs for the current period. (p. 721).

Total manufacturing costs The sum of direct materials, direct labor, and manufacturing overhead incurred in the current period. (p. 719).

Total quality management (TQM) Systems implemented to reduce defects in finished products with the goal of achieving zero defects. (p. 726).

Treasurer Financial officer responsible for custody of a company's funds and for maintaining its cash position. (p. 715).

Triple bottom line The evaluation of a company's social responsibility performance with regard to people, planet, and profit. (p. 728).

Value chain All business processes associated with providing a product or performing a service. (p. 725).

PRACTICE MULTIPLE-CHOICE QUESTIONS

(LO 1) **1.** Managerial accounting:
(a) is governed by generally accepted accounting principles.
(b) places emphasis on special-purpose information.
(c) pertains to the entity as a whole and is highly aggregated.
(d) is limited to cost data.

(LO 1) **2.** The management of an organization performs several broad functions. They are:
(a) planning, directing, and selling.
(b) planning, directing, and controlling.
(c) planning, manufacturing, and controlling.
(d) directing, manufacturing, and controlling.

(LO 2) **3.** Direct materials are a:

	Product Cost	Manufacturing Overhead Cost	Period Cost
(a)	Yes	Yes	No
(b)	Yes	No	No
(c)	Yes	Yes	Yes
(d)	No	No	No

4. Which of the following costs would a computer manufacturer include in manufacturing overhead? (LO 2)
(a) The cost of the disk drives.
(b) The wages earned by computer assemblers.
(c) The cost of the memory chips.
(d) Depreciation on testing equipment.

5. Which of the following is **not** an element of manufacturing overhead? (LO 2)
(a) Sales manager's salary.
(b) Plant manager's salary.
(c) Factory repairman's wages.
(d) Product inspector's salary.

6. Indirect labor is a: (LO 2)
(a) nonmanufacturing cost.
(b) raw material cost.
(c) product cost.
(d) period cost.

7. Which of the following costs are classified as a period cost? (LO 2)
(a) Wages paid to a factory custodian.
(b) Wages paid to a production department supervisor.

(c) Wages paid to a cost accounting department supervisor.

(d) Wages paid to an assembly worker.

(LO 3) 8. For the year, Redder Company has cost of goods manufactured of $600,000, beginning finished goods inventory of $200,000, and ending finished goods inventory of $250,000. The cost of goods sold is:
(a) $450,000. (b) $500,000.
(c) $550,000. (d) $600,000.

(LO 3) 9. Cost of goods available for sale is a step in the calculation of cost of goods sold of:
(a) a merchandising company but not a manufacturing company.
(b) a manufacturing company but not a merchandising company.
(c) a merchandising company and a manufacturing company.
(d) neither a manufacturing company nor a merchandising company.

(LO 3) 10. A cost of goods manufactured schedule shows beginning and ending inventories for:
(a) raw materials and work in process only.
(b) work in process only.
(c) raw materials only.
(d) raw materials, work in process, and finished goods.

(LO 3) 11. The formula to determine the cost of goods manufactured is:
(a) Beginning raw materials inventory + Total manufacturing costs − Ending work in process inventory.
(b) Beginning work in process inventory + Total manufacturing costs − Ending finished goods inventory.
(c) Beginning finished good inventory + Total manufacturing costs − Ending finished goods inventory.

(d) Beginning work in process inventory + Total manufacturing costs − Ending work in process inventory.

(LO 4) 12. After passage of the Sarbanes-Oxley Act:
(a) reports prepared by managerial accountants must by audited by CPAs.
(b) CEOs and CFOs must certify that financial statements give a fair presentation of the company's operating results.
(c) the audit committee, rather than top management, is responsible for the company's financial statements.
(d) reports prepared by managerial accountants must comply with generally accepted accounting principles (GAAP).

(LO 4) 13. Which of the following managerial accounting techniques attempts to allocate manufacturing overhead in a more meaningful fashion?
(a) Just-in-time inventory.
(b) Total quality management.
(c) Balanced scorecard.
(d) Activity-based costing.

(LO 4) 14. Corporate social responsibility refers to:
(a) the practice by management of reviewing all business processes in an effort to increase productivity and eliminate waste.
(b) an approach used to allocate overhead based on each product's use of activities.
(c) the attempt by management to identify and eliminate constraints within the value chain.
(d) efforts by companies to employ sustainable business practices with regard to employees and the environment.

Solutions

1. (b) Managerial accounting emphasizes special-purpose information. The other choices are incorrect because (a) financial accounting is governed by generally accepted accounting principles, (c) financial accounting pertains to the entity as a whole and is highly aggregated, and (d) cost accounting and cost data are a subset of management accounting.

2. (b) Planning, directing, and controlling are the broad functions performed by the management of an organization. The other choices are incorrect because (a) selling is performed by the sales group in the organization, not by management; (c) manufacturing is performed by the manufacturing group in the organization, not by management; and (d) manufacturing is performed by the manufacturing group in the organization, not by management.

3. (b) Direct materials are a product cost only. Therefore, choices (a), (c), and (d) are incorrect as direct materials are not manufacturing overhead or a period cost.

4. (d) Depreciation on testing equipment would be included in manufacturing overhead because it is indirectly associated with the finished product. The other choices are incorrect because (a) disk drives would be direct materials, (b) computer assembler wages would be direct labor, and (c) memory chips would be direct materials.

5. (a) The sales manager's salary is not directly or indirectly associated with the manufacture of the finished product. The other choices are incorrect because (b) the plant manager's salary, (c) the factory repairman's wages, and (d) the product inspector's salary are all elements of manufacturing overhead.

6. (c) Indirect labor is a product cost because it is part of the effort required to produce a product. The other choices are incorrect because (a) indirect labor is a manufacturing cost because it is part of the effort required to produce a product, (b) indirect labor is not a raw material cost because raw material costs only include direct materials and indirect materials, and (d) indirect labor is not a period cost because it is part of the effort required to produce a product.

7. (c) Wages paid to a cost accounting department supervisor would be included in administrative expenses and classified as a period cost. The other choices are incorrect because (a) factory custodian wages are indirect labor which is manufacturing overhead and a product cost, (b) production department supervisor wages are indirect labor which is manufacturing overhead and a product cost, and (d) assembly worker wages is direct labor and is a product cost.

8. (c) Cost of goods sold is computed as Beginning finished goods inventory ($200,000) + Cost of goods manufactured ($600,000) − Ending finished goods inventory ($250,000), or $200,000 + $600,000 − $250,000 = $550,000. Therefore, choices (a) $450,000, (b) $500,000, and (d) $600,000 are incorrect.

9. (c) Both a merchandising company and a manufacturing company use cost of goods available for sale to calculate cost of goods sold. Therefore, choices (a) only a merchandising company, (b) only a manufacturing company, and (d) neither a manufacturing company or a merchandising company are incorrect.

10. (a) A cost of goods manufactured schedule shows beginning and ending inventories for raw materials and work in process only. Therefore, choices (b) work in process only and (c) raw materials only are incorrect. Choice (d) is incorrect because it does not include finished goods.

11. (d) The formula to determine the cost of goods manufactured is Beginning work in process inventory + Total manufacturing costs − Ending work in process inventory. The other choices are incorrect because (a) raw material inventory, (b) ending finished goods inventory, and (c) beginning finished goods inventory and ending finished goods inventory are not part of the computation.

12. (b) CEOs and CFOs must certify that financial statements give a fair presentation of the company's operating results. The other choices are incorrect because (a) reports prepared by financial (not managerial) accountants must be audited by CPAs; (c) SOX clarifies that top management, not the audit committee, is responsible for the company's financial statements; and (d) reports by financial (not managerial) accountants must comply with GAAP.

13. (d) Activity-based costing attempts to allocate manufacturing overhead in a more meaningful fashion. Therefore, choices (a) just-in-time inventory, (b) total quality management, and (c) balanced scorecard are incorrect.

14. (d) Corporate social responsibility refers to efforts by companies to employ sustainable business practices with regard to employees and the environment. The other choices are incorrect because (a) defines lean manufacturing, (b) refers to activity-based costing, and (c) describes the theory of constraints.

▮ PRACTICE EXERCISES

1. Fredricks Company reports the following costs and expenses in May.

Determine the total amount of various types of costs.

(LO 2)

Factory utilities	$ 15,600	Direct labor	$89,100
Depreciation on factory		Sales salaries	46,400
equipment	12,650	Property taxes on factory	
Depreciation on delivery trucks	8,800	building	2,500
Indirect factory labor	48,900	Repairs to office equipment	2,300
Indirect materials	80,800	Factory repairs	2,000
Direct materials used	137,600	Advertising	18,000
Factory manager's salary	13,000	Office supplies used	5,640

Instructions

From the information, determine the total amount of:

(a) Manufacturing overhead.

(b) Product costs.

(c) Period costs.

Solution

1. (a)	Factory utilities	$ 15,600
	Depreciation on factory equipment	12,650
	Indirect factory labor	48,900
	Indirect materials	80,800
	Factory manager's salary	13,000
	Property taxes on factory building	2,500
	Factory repairs	2,000
	Manufacturing overhead	$175,450
(b)	Direct materials	$137,600
	Direct labor	89,100
	Manufacturing overhead	175,450
	Product costs	$402,150
(c)	Depreciation on delivery trucks	$ 8,800
	Sales salaries	46,400
	Repairs to office equipment	2,300
	Advertising	18,000
	Office supplies used	5,640
	Period costs	$ 81,140

Compute cost of goods manufactured and sold.

(LO 3)

2. Tommi Corporation incurred the following costs while manufacturing its product.

Materials used in product	$120,000	Advertising expense	$45,000
Depreciation on plant	60,000	Property taxes on plant	19,000
Property taxes on store	7,500	Delivery expense	21,000
Labor costs of assembly-line workers	110,000	Sales commissions	35,000
Factory supplies used	25,000	Salaries paid to sales clerks	50,000

Work-in-process inventory was $10,000 at January 1 and $14,000 at December 31. Finished goods inventory was $60,500 at January 1 and $50,600 at December 31.

Instructions

(a) Compute cost of goods manufactured.

(b) Compute cost of goods sold.

Solution

2. (a)	Work-in-process, 1/1			$ 10,000
	Direct materials used		$120,000	
	Direct labor		110,000	
	Manufacturing overhead			
	Depreciation on plant	$60,000		
	Factory supplies used	25,000		
	Property taxes on plant	19,000		
	Total manufacturing overhead		104,000	
	Total manufacturing costs			334,000
	Total cost of work-in-process			344,000
	Less: Ending work-in-process			14,000
	Cost of goods manufactured			$330,000
(b)	Finished goods, 1/1			$ 60,500
	Cost of goods manufactured			330,000
	Cost of goods available for sale			390,500
	Less: Finished goods, 12/31			50,600
	Cost of goods sold			$339,900

PRACTICE PROBLEM

Prepare a cost of goods manufactured schedule, an income statement, and a partial balance sheet.

(LO 3)

Superior Company has the following cost and expense data for the year ending December 31, 2017.

Raw materials, 1/1/17	$ 30,000	Insurance, factory	$ 14,000
Raw materials, 12/31/17	20,000	Property taxes, factory building	6,000
Raw materials purchases	205,000	Sales revenue	1,500,000
Indirect materials	15,000	Delivery expenses	100,000
Work in process, 1/1/17	80,000	Sales commissions	150,000
Work in process, 12/31/17	50,000	Indirect labor	90,000
Finished goods, 1/1/17	110,000	Factory machinery rent	40,000
Finished goods, 12/31/17	120,000	Factory utilities	65,000
Direct labor	350,000	Depreciation, factory building	24,000
Factory manager's salary	35,000	Administrative expenses	300,000

Instructions

(a) Prepare a cost of goods manufactured schedule for Superior Company for 2017.

(b) Prepare an income statement for Superior Company for 2017.

(c) Assume that Superior Company's accounting records show the balances of the following current asset accounts: Cash $17,000, Accounts Receivable (net) $120,000, Prepaid Expenses $13,000, and Short-Term Investments $26,000. Prepare the current assets section of the balance sheet for Superior Company as of December 31, 2017.

Solution

(a)

SUPERIOR COMPANY
Cost of Goods Manufactured Schedule
For the Year Ended December 31, 2017

Work in process, 1/1		$ 80,000
Direct materials		
Raw materials inventory, 1/1	$ 30,000	
Raw materials purchases	205,000	
Total raw materials available for use	235,000	
Less: Raw materials inventory, 12/31	20,000	
Direct materials used		$215,000
Direct labor		350,000
Manufacturing overhead		
Indirect labor	90,000	
Factory utilities	65,000	
Factory machinery rent	40,000	
Factory manager's salary	35,000	
Depreciation, factory building	24,000	
Indirect materials	15,000	
Insurance, factory	14,000	
Property taxes, factory building	6,000	
Total manufacturing overhead		289,000
Total manufacturing costs		854,000
Total cost of work in process		934,000
Less: Work in process, 12/31		50,000
Cost of goods manufactured		$ 884,000

(b)

SUPERIOR COMPANY
Income Statement
For the Year Ended December 31, 2017

Sales revenue		$1,500,000
Cost of goods sold		
Finished goods inventory, January 1	$110,000	
Cost of goods manufactured	884,000	
Cost of goods available for sale	994,000	
Less: Finished goods inventory,		
December 31	120,000	
Cost of goods sold		874,000
Gross profit		626,000
Operating expenses		
Administrative expenses	300,000	
Sales commissions	150,000	
Delivery expenses	100,000	
Total operating expenses		550,000
Net income		$ 76,000

(c)

SUPERIOR COMPANY
Balance Sheet (partial)
December 31, 2017

Current assets		
Cash		$ 17,000
Short-term investments		26,000
Accounts receivable (net)		120,000
Inventory		
Finished goods	$120,000	
Work in process	50,000	
Raw materials	20,000	190,000
Prepaid expenses		13,000
Total current assets		$366,000

WileyPLUS

Brief Exercises, Exercises, **DO IT!** Exercises, and Problems and many additional resources are available for practice in WileyPLUS

QUESTIONS

1. (a) "Managerial accounting is a field of accounting that provides economic information for all interested parties." Do you agree? Explain.

   (b) Joe Delong believes that managerial accounting serves only manufacturing firms. Is Joe correct? Explain.

2. Distinguish between managerial and financial accounting as to (a) primary users of reports, (b) types and frequency of reports, and (c) purpose of reports.

3. How do the content of reports and the verification of reports differ between managerial and financial accounting?

4. Linda Olsen is studying for the next accounting midterm examination. Summarize for Linda what she should know about management functions.

5. "Decision-making is management's most important function." Do you agree? Why or why not?

6. Explain the primary difference between line positions and staff positions, and give examples of each.

7. Tony Andres is studying for his next accounting examination. Explain to Tony what he should know about the differences between the income statements for a manufacturing and for a merchandising company.

8. Jerry Lang is unclear as to the difference between the balance sheets of a merchandising company and a manufacturing company. Explain the difference to Jerry.

9. How are manufacturing costs classified?

10. Mel Finney claims that the distinction between direct and indirect materials is based entirely on physical association with the product. Is Mel correct? Why?

11. Tina Burke is confused about the differences between a product cost and a period cost. Explain the differences to Tina.

12. Identify the differences in the cost of goods sold section of an income statement between a merchandising company and a manufacturing company.

13. The determination of the cost of goods manufactured involves the following factors: (A) beginning work in process inventory, (B) total manufacturing costs, and (C) ending work in process inventory. Identify the meaning of x in the following formulas:

   (a) $A + B = x$

   (b) $A + B - C = x$

14. Sealy Company has beginning raw materials inventory $12,000, ending raw materials inventory $15,000, and raw materials purchases $170,000. What is the cost of direct materials used?

15. Tate Inc. has beginning work in process $26,000, direct materials used $240,000, direct labor $220,000, total manufacturing overhead $180,000, and ending work in process $32,000. What are the total manufacturing costs?

16. Using the data in Question 15, what are (a) the total cost of work in process and (b) the cost of goods manufactured?

17. In what order should manufacturing inventories be listed in a balance sheet?

18. How does the output of manufacturing operations differ from that of service operations?

19. Discuss whether the product costing techniques discussed in this chapter apply equally well to manufacturers and service companies.

20. What is the value chain? Describe, in sequence, the main components of a manufacturer's value chain.

21. What is an enterprise resource planning (ERP) system? What are its primary benefits?

22. Why is product quality important for companies that implement a just-in-time inventory system?

23. Explain what is meant by "balanced" in the balanced scorecard approach.

24. In what ways can the budgeting process create incentives for unethical behavior?

25. What new rules were enacted under the Sarbanes-Oxley Act to address unethical accounting practices?

26. What is activity-based costing, and what are its potential benefits?

BRIEF EXERCISES

Distinguish between managerial and financial accounting.

(LO 1)

BE15-1 Complete the following comparison table between managerial and financial accounting.

	Financial Accounting	Managerial Accounting
Primary users of reports		
Types of reports		
Frequency of reports		
Purpose of reports		
Content of reports		
Verification process		

BE15-2 Listed below are the three functions of the management of an organization.
1. Planning   2. Directing   3. Controlling
Identify which of the following statements best describes each of the above functions.
(a) _____ requires management to look ahead and to establish objectives. A key objective of management is to add value to the business.
(b) _____ involves coordinating the diverse activities and human resources of a company to produce a smooth-running operation. This function relates to the implementation of planned objectives.
(c) _____ is the process of keeping the activities on track. Management determines whether goals are being met and what changes are necessary when there are deviations.

Identify the three management functions.

(LO 1)

BE15-3 Determine whether each of the following costs should be classified as direct materials (DM), direct labor (DL), or manufacturing overhead (MO).
(a) _____ Frames and tires used in manufacturing bicycles.
(b) _____ Wages paid to production workers.
(c) _____ Insurance on factory equipment and machinery.
(d) _____ Depreciation on factory equipment.

Classify manufacturing costs.

(LO 2)

BE15-4 Indicate whether each of the following costs of an automobile manufacturer would be classified as direct materials, direct labor, or manufacturing overhead.
(a) _____ Windshield.
(b) _____ Engine.
(c) _____ Wages of assembly line worker.
(d) _____ Depreciation of factory machinery.
(e) _____ Factory machinery lubricants.
(f) _____ Tires.
(g) _____ Steering wheel.
(h) _____ Salary of painting supervisor.

Classify manufacturing costs.

(LO 2)

BE15-5 Identify whether each of the following costs should be classified as product costs or period costs.
(a) _____ Manufacturing overhead.
(b) _____ Selling expenses.
(c) _____ Administrative expenses.
(d) _____ Advertising expenses.
(e) _____ Direct labor.
(f) _____ Direct materials.

Identify product and period costs.

(LO 2)

BE15-6 Presented below are Rook Company's monthly manufacturing cost data related to its tablet computer product.
(a) Utilities for manufacturing equipment $116,000
(b) Raw material (CPU, chips, etc.) $ 85,000
(c) Depreciation on manufacturing building $880,000
(d) Wages for production workers $191,000
Enter each cost item in the following table, placing an "X" under the appropriate headings.

Classify manufacturing costs.

(LO 2)

	Product Costs		
	Direct Materials	**Direct Labor**	**Factory Overhead**
(a)			
(b)			
(c)			
(d)			

BE15-7 Francum Company has the following data: direct labor $209,000, direct materials used $180,000, total manufacturing overhead $208,000, and beginning work in process $25,000. Compute (a) total manufacturing costs and (b) total cost of work in process.

Compute total manufacturing costs and total cost of work in process.

(LO 3)

BE15-8 In alphabetical order below are current asset items for Roland Company's balance sheet at December 31, 2017. Prepare the current assets section (including a complete heading).

Prepare current assets section.

(LO 3)

Accounts receivable	$200,000
Cash	62,000
Finished goods	91,000
Prepaid expenses	38,000
Raw materials	83,000
Work in process	87,000

Determine missing amounts in computing total manufacturing costs.

(LO 3)

BE15-9 Presented below are incomplete manufacturing cost data. Determine the missing amounts for three different situations.

	Direct Materials Used	Direct Labor Used	Factory Overhead	Total Manufacturing Costs
(1)	$40,000	$61,000	$ 50,000	?
(2)	?	$75,000	$140,000	$296,000
(3)	$55,000	?	$111,000	$310,000

Determine missing amounts in computing cost of goods manufactured.

(LO 3)

BE15-10 Use the same data from BE15-9 above and the data below. Determine the missing amounts.

	Total Manufacturing Costs	Work in Process (1/1)	Work in Process (12/31)	Cost of Goods Manufactured
(1)	?	$120,000	$82,000	?
(2)	$296,000	?	$98,000	$331,000
(3)	$310,000	$463,000	?	$715,000

Identify important regulatory changes.

(LO 4)

BE15-11 The Sarbanes-Oxley Act (SOX) has important implications for the financial community. Explain two implications of SOX.

DO IT! Exercises

Identify managerial accounting concepts.

(LO 1)

DO IT! 15-1 Indicate whether the following statements are true or false.

1. Managerial accounting reports focus on manufacturing and nonmanufacturing costs, but are also used in the budget process.

2. Financial accounting reports pertain to subunits of the business and are very detailed.

3. Managerial accounting reports must follow GAAP and are audited by CPAs.

4. Managers' activities and responsibilities can be classified into three broad functions: planning, directing, and controlling.

Identify managerial cost classifications.

(LO 2)

DO IT! 15-2 A music company has these costs:

Advertising	Paper inserts for CD cases
Blank CDs	CD plastic cases
Depreciation of CD image burner	Salaries of sales representatives
	Salaries of factory maintenance employees
Salary of factory manager	Salaries of employees who burn music onto CDs
Factory supplies used	

Classify each cost as a period or a product cost. Within the product cost category, indicate if the cost is part of direct materials (DM), direct labor (DL), or manufacturing overhead (MO).

Prepare cost of goods manufactured schedule.

(LO 3)

DO IT! 15-3 The following information is available for Tomlin Company.

	April 1	April 30
Raw materials inventory	$10,000	$14,000
Work in process inventory	5,000	3,500

Materials purchased in April	$ 98,000
Direct labor in April	80,000
Manufacturing overhead in April	160,000

Prepare the cost of goods manufactured schedule for the month of April.

DO IT! 15-4 Match the descriptions that follow with the corresponding terms.

Identify trends in managerial accounting.

(LO 4)

Descriptions:

1. _____ Inventory system in which goods are manufactured or purchased just as they are needed for sale.
2. _____ A method of allocating overhead based on each product's use of activities in making the product.
3. _____ Systems that are especially important to firms adopting just-in-time inventory methods.
4. _____ Provides guidelines for companies to describe their sustainable business practices to external parties.
5. _____ Part of the value chain for a manufacturing company.
6. _____ The U.S. economy is trending toward this.
7. _____ A performance-measurement approach that uses both financial and nonfinancial measures, tied to company objectives, to evaluate a company's operations in an integrated fashion.
8. _____ Requires that top managers certify that the company maintains an adequate system of internal controls.

Terms:

(a) Activity-based costing
(b) Balanced scorecard
(c) Total quality management (TQM)
(d) Research and development, and product design
(e) Service industries
(f) Just-in-time (JIT) inventory
(g) Sarbanes-Oxley Act (SOX)
(h) Global Reporting Initiative

EXERCISES

E15-1 Justin Bleeber has prepared the following list of statements about managerial accounting, financial accounting, and the functions of management.

Identify distinguishing features of managerial accounting.

(LO 1)

1. Financial accounting focuses on providing information to internal users.
2. Staff positions are directly involved in the company's primary revenue-generating activities.
3. Preparation of budgets is part of financial accounting.
4. Managerial accounting applies only to merchandising and manufacturing companies.
5. Both managerial accounting and financial accounting deal with many of the same economic events.
6. Managerial accounting reports are prepared only quarterly and annually.
7. Financial accounting reports are general-purpose reports.
8. Managerial accounting reports pertain to subunits of the business.
9. Managerial accounting reports must comply with generally accepted accounting principles.
10. The company treasurer reports directly to the vice president of operations.

Instructions

Identify each statement as true or false. If false, indicate how to correct the statement.

E15-2 Presented below is a list of costs and expenses usually incurred by Barnum Corporation, a manufacturer of furniture, in its factory.

Classify costs into three classes of manufacturing costs.

(LO 2)

1. Salaries for assembly line inspectors.
2. Insurance on factory machines.
3. Property taxes on the factory building.
4. Factory repairs.
5. Upholstery used in manufacturing furniture.
6. Wages paid to assembly line workers.
7. Factory machinery depreciation.
8. Glue, nails, paint, and other small parts used in production.
9. Factory supervisors' salaries.
10. Wood used in manufacturing furniture.

Instructions

Classify the above items into the following categories: (a) direct materials, (b) direct labor, and (c) manufacturing overhead.

Identify types of cost and explain their accounting.

(LO 2)

E15-3 Trak Corporation incurred the following costs while manufacturing its bicycles.

Bicycle components	$100,000	Advertising expense	$45,000
Depreciation on plant	60,000	Property taxes on plant	14,000
Property taxes on store	7,500	Delivery expense	21,000
Labor costs of assembly-line workers	110,000	Sales commissions	35,000
Factory supplies used	13,000	Salaries paid to sales clerks	50,000

Instructions

(a) Identify each of the above costs as direct materials, direct labor, manufacturing overhead, or period costs.

(b) Explain the basic difference in accounting for product costs and period costs.

Determine the total amount of various types of costs.

(LO 2)

E15-4 Knight Company reports the following costs and expenses in May.

Factory utilities	$ 15,500	Direct labor	$69,100
Depreciation on factory		Sales salaries	46,400
equipment	12,650	Property taxes on factory	
Depreciation on delivery trucks	3,800	building	2,500
Indirect factory labor	48,900	Repairs to office equipment	1,300
Indirect materials	80,800	Factory repairs	2,000
Direct materials used	137,600	Advertising	15,000
Factory manager's salary	8,000	Office supplies used	2,640

Instructions

From the information, determine the total amount of:

(a) Manufacturing overhead.

(b) Product costs.

(c) Period costs.

Classify various costs into different cost categories.

(LO 2)

E15-5 Gala Company is a manufacturer of laptop computers. Various costs and expenses associated with its operations are as follows.

1. Property taxes on the factory building.
2. Production superintendents' salaries.
3. Memory boards and chips used in assembling computers.
4. Depreciation on the factory equipment.
5. Salaries for assembly-line quality control inspectors.
6. Sales commissions paid to sell laptop computers.
7. Electrical components used in assembling computers.
8. Wages of workers assembling laptop computers.
9. Soldering materials used on factory assembly lines.
10. Salaries for the night security guards for the factory building.

The company intends to classify these costs and expenses into the following categories: (a) direct materials, (b) direct labor, (c) manufacturing overhead, and (d) period costs.

Instructions

List the items (1) through (10). For each item, indicate the cost category to which it belongs.

Classify various costs into different cost categories.

(LO 2)

E15-6 The administrators of Crawford County's Memorial Hospital are interested in identifying the various costs and expenses that are incurred in producing a patient's X-ray. A list of such costs and expenses is presented below.

1. Salaries for the X-ray machine technicians.
2. Wages for the hospital janitorial personnel.
3. Film costs for the X-ray machines.
4. Property taxes on the hospital building.
5. Salary of the X-ray technicians' supervisor.
6. Electricity costs for the X-ray department.
7. Maintenance and repairs on the X-ray machines.
8. X-ray department supplies.
9. Depreciation on the X-ray department equipment.
10. Depreciation on the hospital building.

The administrators want these costs and expenses classified as (a) direct materials, (b) direct labor, or (c) service overhead.

Instructions
List the items (1) through (10). For each item, indicate the cost category to which the item belongs.

E15-7 National Express reports the following costs and expenses in June 2017 for its delivery service.

Classify various costs into different cost categories.

(LO 2)

Indirect materials	$ 6,400	Drivers' salaries	$16,000
Depreciation on delivery equipment	11,200	Advertising	4,600
Dispatcher's salary	5,000	Delivery equipment repairs	300
Property taxes on office building	870	Office supplies	650
CEO's salary	12,000	Office utilities	990
Gas and oil for delivery trucks	2,200	Repairs on office equipment	180

Instructions
Determine the total amount of (a) delivery service (product) costs and (b) period costs.

E15-8 Lopez Corporation incurred the following costs while manufacturing its product.

Compute cost of goods manufactured and sold.

(LO 3)

Materials used in product	$120,000	Advertising expense	$45,000
Depreciation on plant	60,000	Property taxes on plant	14,000
Property taxes on store	7,500	Delivery expense	21,000
Labor costs of assembly-line		Sales commissions	35,000
workers	110,000	Salaries paid to sales	
Factory supplies used	23,000	clerks	50,000

Work in process inventory was $12,000 at January 1 and $15,500 at December 31. Finished goods inventory was $60,000 at January 1 and $45,600 at December 31.

Instructions
(a) Compute cost of goods manufactured.
(b) Compute cost of goods sold.

E15-9 An incomplete cost of goods manufactured schedule is presented below.

Determine missing amounts in cost of goods manufactured schedule.

(LO 3)

HOBBIT COMPANY
Cost of Goods Manufactured Schedule
For the Year Ended December 31, 2017

Work in process (1/1)		$210,000
Direct materials		
Raw materials inventory (1/1)	$?	
Add: Raw materials purchases	158,000	
Total raw materials available for use	?	
Less: Raw materials inventory (12/31)	22,500	
Direct materials used		$180,000
Direct labor		?
Manufacturing overhead		
Indirect labor	18,000	
Factory depreciation	36,000	
Factory utilities	68,000	
Total overhead		122,000
Total manufacturing costs		?
Total cost of work in process		?
Less: Work in process (12/31)		81,000
Cost of goods manufactured		$540,000

Instructions
Complete the cost of goods manufactured schedule for Hobbit Company.

Determine the missing amount of different cost items.

(LO 3)

E15-10 Manufacturing cost data for Copa Company are presented below.

	Case A	Case B	Case C
Direct materials used	$ (a)	$68,400	$130,000
Direct labor	57,000	86,000	(g)
Manufacturing overhead	46,500	81,600	102,000
Total manufacturing costs	195,650	(d)	253,700
Work in process 1/1/17	(b)	16,500	(h)
Total cost of work in process	221,500	(e)	337,000
Work in process 12/31/17	(c)	11,000	70,000
Cost of goods manufactured	185,275	(f)	(i)

Instructions

Indicate the missing amount for each letter (a) through (i).

Determine the missing amount of different cost items, and prepare a condensed cost of goods manufactured schedule.

(LO 3)

E15-11 Incomplete manufacturing cost data for Horizon Company for 2017 are presented as follows for four different situations.

	Direct Materials Used	Direct Labor Used	Manufac- turing Overhead	Total Manufac- turing Costs	Work in Process 1/1	Work in Process 12/31	Cost of Goods Manufac- tured
(1)	$117,000	$140,000	$ 87,000	$ (a)	$33,000	$ (b)	$360,000
(2)	(c)	200,000	132,000	450,000	(d)	40,000	470,000
(3)	80,000	100,000	(e)	265,000	60,000	80,000	(f)
(4)	70,000	(g)	75,000	288,000	45,000	(h)	270,000

Instructions

(a) Indicate the missing amount for each letter.

(b) Prepare a condensed cost of goods manufactured schedule for situation (1) for the year ended December 31, 2017.

Prepare a cost of goods manufactured schedule and a partial income statement.

(LO 3)

E15-12 Cepeda Corporation has the following cost records for June 2017.

Indirect factory labor	$ 4,500	Factory utilities	$ 400
Direct materials used	20,000	Depreciation, factory equipment	1,400
Work in process, 6/1/17	3,000	Direct labor	40,000
Work in process, 6/30/17	3,800	Maintenance, factory equipment	1,800
Finished goods, 6/1/17	5,000	Indirect materials	2,200
Finished goods, 6/30/17	7,500	Factory manager's salary	3,000

Instructions

(a) Prepare a cost of goods manufactured schedule for June 2017.

(b) Prepare an income statement through gross profit for June 2017 assuming sales revenue is $92,100.

Classify various costs into different categories and prepare cost of services performed schedule.

(LO 2, 3)

E15-13 Keisha Tombert, the bookkeeper for Washington Consulting, a political consulting firm, has recently completed a managerial accounting course at her local college. One of the topics covered in the course was the cost of goods manufactured schedule. Keisha wondered if such a schedule could be prepared for her firm. She realized that, as a service-oriented company, it would have no work in process inventory to consider.

Listed below are the costs her firm incurred for the month ended August 31, 2017.

Supplies used on consulting contracts	$ 1,700
Supplies used in the administrative offices	1,500
Depreciation on equipment used for contract work	900
Depreciation used on administrative office equipment	1,050
Salaries of professionals working on contracts	15,600
Salaries of administrative office personnel	7,700
Janitorial services for professional offices	700
Janitorial services for administrative offices	500
Insurance on contract operations	800
Insurance on administrative operations	900
Utilities for contract operations	1,400
Utilities for administrative offices	1,300

Instructions

(a) Prepare a schedule of cost of contract services performed (similar to a cost of goods manufactured schedule) for the month.

(b) For those costs not included in (a), explain how they would be classified and reported in the financial statements.

E15-14 The following information is available for Aikman Company.

Prepare a cost of goods manufactured schedule and a partial income statement.

(LO 3)

	January 1, 2017	2017	December 31, 2017
Raw materials inventory	$21,000		$30,000
Work in process inventory	13,500		17,200
Finished goods inventory	27,000		21,000
Materials purchased		$150,000	
Direct labor		220,000	
Manufacturing overhead		180,000	
Sales revenue		910,000	

Instructions

(a) Compute cost of goods manufactured.

(b) Prepare an income statement through gross profit.

(c) Show the presentation of the ending inventories on the December 31, 2017, balance sheet.

(d) How would the income statement and balance sheet of a merchandising company be different from Aikman's financial statements?

E15-15 University Company produces collegiate apparel. From its accounting records, it prepares the following schedule and financial statements on a yearly basis.

Indicate in which schedule or financial statement(s) different cost items will appear.

(LO 3)

(a) Cost of goods manufactured schedule.

(b) Income statement.

(c) Balance sheet.

The following items are found in its ledger and accompanying data.

1. Direct labor
2. Raw materials inventory, 1/1
3. Work in process inventory, 12/31
4. Finished goods inventory, 1/1
5. Indirect labor
6. Depreciation on factory machinery
7. Work in process, 1/1
8. Finished goods inventory, 12/31
9. Factory maintenance salaries
10. Cost of goods manufactured
11. Depreciation on delivery equipment
12. Cost of goods available for sale
13. Direct materials used
14. Heat and electricity for factory
15. Repairs to roof of factory building
16. Cost of raw materials purchases

Instructions

List the items (1)–(16). For each item, indicate by using the appropriate letter or letters, the schedule and/or financial statement(s) in which the item will appear.

E15-16 An analysis of the accounts of Roberts Company reveals the following manufacturing cost data for the month ended June 30, 2017.

Prepare a cost of goods manufactured schedule, and present the ending inventories on the balance sheet.

(LO 3)

Inventory	Beginning	Ending
Raw materials	$9,000	$13,100
Work in process	5,000	7,000
Finished goods	9,000	8,000

Costs incurred: raw materials purchases $54,000, direct labor $47,000, manufacturing overhead $19,900. The specific overhead costs were: indirect labor $5,500, factory insurance $4,000, machinery depreciation $4,000, machinery repairs $1,800, factory utilities $3,100, and miscellaneous factory costs $1,500. Assume that all raw materials used were direct materials.

Instructions

(a) Prepare the cost of goods manufactured schedule for the month ended June 30, 2017.

(b) Show the presentation of the ending inventories on the June 30, 2017, balance sheet.

Determine the amount of cost to appear in various accounts, and indicate in which financial statements these accounts would appear.

(LO 3)

E15-17 McQueen Motor Company manufactures automobiles. During September 2017, the company purchased 5,000 head lamps at a cost of $15 per lamp. McQueen withdrew 4,650 lamps from the warehouse during the month. Fifty of these lamps were used to replace the head lamps in autos used by traveling sales staff. The remaining 4,600 lamps were put in autos manufactured during the month.

Of the autos put into production during September 2017, 90% were completed and transferred to the company's storage lot. Of the cars completed during the month, 70% were sold by September 30.

Instructions

(a) Determine the cost of head lamps that would appear in each of the following accounts at September 30, 2017: Raw Materials, Work in Process, Finished Goods, Cost of Goods Sold, and Selling Expenses.

(b) •———— Write a short memo to the chief accountant, indicating whether and where each of the accounts in (a) would appear on the income statement or on the balance sheet at September 30, 2017.

Identify various managerial accounting practices.

(LO 4)

E15-18 The following is a list of terms related to managerial accounting practices.

1. Activity-based costing.
2. Just-in-time inventory.
3. Balanced scorecard.
4. Value chain.

Instructions

Match each of the terms with the statement below that best describes the term.

(a) _____ A performance-measurement technique that attempts to consider and evaluate all aspects of performance using financial and nonfinancial measures in an integrated fashion.

(b) _____ The group of activities associated with providing a product or performing a service.

(c) _____ An approach used to reduce the cost associated with handling and holding inventory by reducing the amount of inventory on hand.

(d) _____ A method used to allocate overhead to products based on each product's use of the activities that cause the incurrence of the overhead cost.

EXERCISES: SET B AND CHALLENGE EXERCISES

Visit the book's companion website, at **www.wiley.com/college/weygandt**, and choose the Student Companion site to access Exercises: Set B and Challenge Exercises.

PROBLEMS: SET A

Classify manufacturing costs into different categories and compute the unit cost.

(LO 2)

P15-1A Ohno Company specializes in manufacturing a unique model of bicycle helmet. The model is well accepted by consumers, and the company has enough orders to keep the factory production at 10,000 helmets per month (80% of its full capacity). Ohno's monthly manufacturing cost and other expense data are as follows.

Rent on factory equipment	$11,000
Insurance on factory building	1,500
Raw materials (plastics, polystyrene, etc.)	75,000
Utility costs for factory	900
Supplies for general office	300
Wages for assembly line workers	58,000
Depreciation on office equipment	800
Miscellaneous materials (glue, thread, etc.)	1,100
Factory manager's salary	5,700
Property taxes on factory building	400
Advertising for helmets	14,000
Sales commissions	10,000
Depreciation on factory building	1,500

Instructions

(a) Prepare an answer sheet with the following column headings.

	Product Costs			
Cost Item	Direct Materials	Direct Labor	Manufacturing Overhead	Period Costs

Enter each cost item on your answer sheet, placing the dollar amount under the appropriate headings. Total the dollar amounts in each of the columns.

(b) Compute the cost to produce one helmet.

(a) DM $75,000
DL $58,000
MO $22,100
PC $25,100

P15-2A Bell Company, a manufacturer of audio systems, started its production in October 2017. For the preceding 3 years, Bell had been a retailer of audio systems. After a thorough survey of audio system markets, Bell decided to turn its retail store into an audio equipment factory.

Classify manufacturing costs into different categories and compute the unit cost.

(LO 2)

Raw materials cost for an audio system will total $74 per unit. Workers on the production lines are on average paid $12 per hour. An audio system usually takes 5 hours to complete. In addition, the rent on the equipment used to assemble audio systems amounts to $4,900 per month. Indirect materials cost $5 per system. A supervisor was hired to oversee production; her monthly salary is $3,000.

Factory janitorial costs are $1,300 monthly. Advertising costs for the audio system will be $9,500 per month. The factory building depreciation expense is $7,800 per year. Property taxes on the factory building will be $9,000 per year.

Instructions

(a) Prepare an answer sheet with the following column headings.

(a) DM $111,000
DL $ 90,000
MO $ 18,100
PC $ 9,500

	Product Costs			
Cost Item	Direct Materials	Direct Labor	Manufacturing Overhead	Period Costs

Assuming that Bell manufactures, on average, 1,500 audio systems per month, enter each cost item on your answer sheet, placing the dollar amount per month under the appropriate headings. Total the dollar amounts in each of the columns.

(b) Compute the cost to produce one audio system.

P15-3A Incomplete manufacturing costs, expenses, and selling data for two different cases are as follows.

Indicate the missing amount of different cost items, and prepare a condensed cost of goods manufactured schedule, an income statement, and a partial balance sheet.

(LO 3)

	Case	
	1	2
Direct materials used	$ 9,600	$ (g)
Direct labor	5,000	8,000
Manufacturing overhead	8,000	4,000
Total manufacturing costs	(a)	16,000
Beginning work in process inventory	1,000	(h)
Ending work in process inventory	(b)	3,000
Sales revenue	24,500	(i)
Sales discounts	2,500	1,400
Cost of goods manufactured	17,000	24,000
Beginning finished goods inventory	(c)	3,300
Goods available for sale	22,000	(j)
Cost of goods sold	(d)	(k)
Ending finished goods inventory	3,400	2,500
Gross profit	(e)	7,000
Operating expenses	2,500	(l)
Net income	(f)	5,000

Instructions

(a) Indicate the missing amount for each letter.

(b) Prepare a condensed cost of goods manufactured schedule for Case 1.

(c) Prepare an income statement and the current assets section of the balance sheet for Case 1. Assume that in Case 1 the other items in the current assets section are as follows: Cash $3,000, Receivables (net) $15,000, Raw Materials $600, and Prepaid Expenses $400.

(b) Ending WIP $ 6,600
(c) Current assets $29,000

*Prepare a cost of goods
manufactured schedule, a
partial income statement,
and a partial balance sheet.*

(LO 3)

P15-4A The following data were taken from the records of Clarkson Company for the fiscal year ended June 30, 2017.

Raw Materials		Factory Insurance	$ 4,600
Inventory 7/1/16	$ 48,000	Factory Machinery	
Raw Materials		Depreciation	16,000
Inventory 6/30/17	39,600	Factory Utilities	27,600
Finished Goods		Office Utilities Expense	8,650
Inventory 7/1/16	96,000	Sales Revenue	534,000
Finished Goods		Sales Discounts	4,200
Inventory 6/30/17	75,900	Plant Manager's Salary	58,000
Work in Process		Factory Property Taxes	9,600
Inventory 7/1/16	19,800	Factory Repairs	1,400
Work in Process		Raw Materials Purchases	96,400
Inventory 6/30/17	18,600	Cash	32,000
Direct Labor	139,250		
Indirect Labor	24,460		
Accounts Receivable	27,000		

Instructions

(a) CGM $386,910

(a) Prepare a cost of goods manufactured schedule. (Assume all raw materials used were direct materials.)

(b) Gross profit $122,790
(c) Current assets $193,100

(b) Prepare an income statement through gross profit.

(c) Prepare the current assets section of the balance sheet at June 30, 2017.

*Prepare a cost of goods
manufactured schedule and a
correct income statement.*

(LO 3)

P15-5A Empire Company is a manufacturer of smart phones. Its controller resigned in October 2017. An inexperienced assistant accountant has prepared the following income statement for the month of October 2017.

EMPIRE COMPANY
Income Statement
For the Month Ended October 31, 2017

Sales revenue		$780,000
Less: Operating expenses		
Raw materials purchases	$264,000	
Direct labor cost	190,000	
Advertising expense	90,000	
Selling and administrative salaries	75,000	
Rent on factory facilities	60,000	
Depreciation on sales equipment	45,000	
Depreciation on factory equipment	31,000	
Indirect labor cost	28,000	
Utilities expense	12,000	
Insurance expense	8,000	803,000
Net loss		$ (23,000)

Prior to October 2017, the company had been profitable every month. The company's president is concerned about the accuracy of the income statement. As her friend, you have been asked to review the income statement and make necessary corrections. After examining other manufacturing cost data, you have acquired additional information as follows.

1. Inventory balances at the beginning and end of October were:

	October 1	October 31
Raw materials	$18,000	$29,000
Work in process	20,000	14,000
Finished goods	30,000	50,000

2. Only 75% of the utilities expense and 60% of the insurance expense apply to factory operations. The remaining amounts should be charged to selling and administrative activities.

Instructions
(a) Prepare a schedule of cost of goods manufactured for October 2017.
(b) Prepare a correct income statement for October 2017.

(a) CGM $581,800
(b) NI $ 2,000

PROBLEMS: SET B AND SET C

Visit the book's companion website, at **www.wiley.com/college/weygandt**, and choose the Student Companion site to access Problems: Set B and Set C.

CONTINUING PROBLEMS

(*Note:* Chapters 15–26 include a hypothetical exercise featuring **Current Designs**, the company described at the beginning of this chapter. Students can also work through this exercise following an **Excel tutorial** available in **WileyPLUS** and the book's companion website. Each chapter's tutorial focuses on a different Excel function or feature.)

CURRENT DESIGNS

EXCEL
TUTORIAL

CD15 Mike Cichanowski founded **Wenonah Canoe** and later purchased **Current Designs**, a company that designs and manufactures kayaks. The kayak-manufacturing facility is located just a few minutes from the canoe company's headquarters in Winona, Minnesota.

Current Designs makes kayaks using two different processes. (See *www.cdkayak.com/craftsmanship/index.php* for the details of each method.) The rotational molding process uses high temperature to melt polyethylene powder in a closed rotating metal mold to produce a complete kayak hull and deck in a single piece. These kayaks are less labor-intensive and less expensive for the company to produce and sell.

Its other kayaks use the vacuum-bagged composite lamination process (which we will refer to as the composite process). Layers of fiberglass or Kevlar® are carefully placed by hand in a mold and are bonded with resin. Then, a high-pressure vacuum is used to eliminate any excess resin that would otherwise add weight and reduce strength of the finished kayak. These kayaks require a great deal of skilled labor as each boat is individually finished. The exquisite finish of the vacuum-bagged composite kayaks gave rise to Current Designs' tag line, "A work of art, made for life."

Current Designs has the following managers:

Mike Cichanowski, CEO
Diane Buswell, Controller
Deb Welch, Purchasing Manager
Bill Johnson, Sales Manager
Dave Thill, Kayak Plant Manager
Rick Thrune, Production Manager for Composite Kayaks

Instructions
(a) What are the primary information needs of each manager?
(b) Name one special-purpose management accounting report that could be designed for each manager. Include the name of the report, the information it would contain, and how frequently it should be issued.
(c) When Diane Buswell, controller for Current Designs, reviewed the accounting records for a recent period, she noted the following items. Classify each item as a product cost or a period cost. If an item is a product cost, note if it is a direct materials, direct labor, or manufacturing overhead item.

	Current Designs.xls					
Home	Insert	Page Layout	Formulas	Data	Review	View

P18   fx

	A	B	C			D
1						
2			Product Costs			Period Costs
3	Payee	Purpose	Direct Materials	Direct Labor	Manufacturing Overhead	
4	Winona Agency	Property insurance for the manufacturing plant				
5	Bill Johnson (sales manager)	Payroll check—payment to sales manager				
6	Xcel Energy	Electricity for manufacturing plant				
7	Winona Printing	Price lists for salespeople				
8	Jim Kaiser (sales representative)	Sales commissions				
9	Dave Thill (plant manager)	Payroll check—payment to plant manager				
10	Dana Schultz (kayak assembler)	Payroll check—payment to kayak assembler				
11	Composite One	Bagging film used when kayaks are assembled; it is discarded after use				
12	Fastenal	Shop supplies—brooms, paper towels, etc.				
13	Ravago	Polyethylene powder which is the main ingredient for the rotational molded kayaks				
14	Winona County	Property taxes on manufacturing plant				
15	North American Composites	Kevlar® fabric for composite kayaks				
16	Waste Management	Trash disposal for the company office building				
17	None	Journal entry to record depreciation of manufacturing equipment				

WATERWAYS

(*Note:* The **Waterways problem** starts in this chapter and continues in the remaining chapters. You will find the complete problem for each chapter at the book's companion website.)

WP15 Waterways Corporation is a private corporation formed for the purpose of providing the products and the services needed to irrigate farms, parks, commercial projects, and private lawns. It has a centrally located factory in a U.S. city that manufactures the products it markets to retail outlets across the nation. It also maintains a division that performs installation and warranty servicing in six metropolitan areas.

The mission of Waterways is to manufacture quality parts that can be used for effective irrigation projects that also conserve water. By that effort, the company hopes to satisfy its customers, perform rapid and responsible service, and serve the community and the employees who represent them in each community.

The company has been growing rapidly, so management is considering new ideas to help the company continue its growth and maintain the high quality of its products.

Waterways was founded by Will Winkman, who is the company president and chief executive officer (CEO). Working with him from the company's inception is Will's brother, Ben, whose sprinkler designs and ideas about the installation of proper systems have been a major basis of the company's success. Ben is the vice president who oversees all aspects of design and production in the company.

The factory itself is managed by Todd Senter who hires his line managers to supervise the factory employees. The factory makes all of the parts for the irrigation systems. The purchasing department is managed by Helen Hines.

The installation and training division is overseen by vice president Henry Writer, who supervises the managers of the six local installation operations. Each of these local managers hires his or her own local service people. These service employees are trained by the home office under Henry Writer's direction because of the uniqueness of the company's products.

There is a small human resources department under the direction of Sally Fenton, a vice president who handles the employee paperwork, though hiring is actually performed by the separate departments. Teresa Totter is the vice president who heads the sales and marketing area; she oversees 10 well-trained salespeople.

The accounting and finance division of the company is run by Ann Headman, who is the chief financial officer (CFO) and a company vice president. She is a member of the Institute of Management Accountants and holds a certificate in management accounting. She has a small staff of accountants, including a controller and a treasurer, and a staff of accounting input operators who maintain the financial records.

A partial list of Waterways' accounts and their balances for the month of November follows.

Accounts Receivable	$ 275,000
Advertising Expenses	54,000
Cash	260,000
Depreciation—Factory Equipment	16,800
Depreciation—Office Equipment	2,400
Direct Labor	42,000
Factory Supplies Used	16,800
Factory Utilities	10,200
Finished Goods Inventory, November 30	68,800
Finished Goods Inventory, October 31	72,550
Indirect Labor	48,000
Office Supplies Expense	1,600
Other Administrative Expenses	72,000
Prepaid Expenses	41,250
Raw Materials Inventory, November 30	52,700
Raw Materials Inventory, October 31	38,000
Raw Materials Purchases	184,500
Rent—Factory Equipment	47,000
Repairs—Factory Equipment	4,500
Salaries	325,000
Sales Revenue	1,350,000
Sales Commissions	40,500
Work in Process Inventory, October 31	52,700
Work in Process Inventory, November 30	42,000

Instructions

(a) Based on the information given, construct an organizational chart of Waterways Corporation.

(b) A list of accounts and their values are given above. From this information, prepare a cost of goods manufactured schedule, an income statement, and a partial balance sheet for Waterways Corporation for the month of November.

BROADENING YOUR PERSPECTIVE

MANAGEMENT DECISION-MAKING

Decision-Making Across the Organization

BYP15-1 Wendall Company specializes in producing fashion outfits. On July 31, 2017, a tornado touched down at its factory and general office. The inventories in the warehouse and the factory were completely destroyed as was the general office nearby. Next morning, through a careful search of the disaster site, however, Bill Francis, the company's controller, and Elizabeth Walton, the cost accountant, were able to recover a small part of manufacturing cost data for the current month.

"What a horrible experience," sighed Bill "And the worst part is that we may not have enough records to use in filing an insurance claim."

"It was terrible," replied Elizabeth. "However, I managed to recover some of the manufacturing cost data that I was working on yesterday afternoon. The data indicate that our direct labor cost in July totaled $250,000 and that we had purchased $365,000 of raw materials. Also, I recall that the amount of raw materials used for July was $350,000. But I'm not sure this information will help. The rest of our records are blown away."

"Well, not exactly," said Bill. "I was working on the year-to-date income statement when the tornado warning was announced. My recollection is that our sales in July were $1,240,000 and our gross profit ratio has been 40% of sales. Also, I can remember that our cost of goods available for sale was $770,000 for July."

"Maybe we can work something out from this information!" exclaimed Elizabeth. "My experience tells me that our manufacturing overhead is usually 60% of direct labor."

"Hey, look what I just found," cried Elizabeth. "It's a copy of this June's balance sheet, and it shows that our inventories as of June 30 are Finished goods $38,000, Work in process $25,000, and Raw materials $19,000."

"Super," yelled Bill. "Let's go work something out."

In order to file an insurance claim, Wendall Company needs to determine the amount of its inventories as of July 31, 2017, the date of the tornado touchdown.

Instructions

With the class divided into groups, determine the amount of cost in the Raw Materials, Work in Process, and Finished Goods inventory accounts as of the date of the tornado touchdown.

Managerial Analysis

BYP15-2 Tenrack is a fairly large manufacturing company located in the southern United States. The company manufactures tennis rackets, tennis balls, tennis clothing, and tennis shoes, all bearing the company's distinctive logo, a large green question mark on a white flocked tennis ball. The company's sales have been increasing over the past 10 years.

The tennis racket division has recently implemented several advanced manufacturing techniques. Robot arms hold the tennis rackets in place while glue dries, and machine vision systems check for defects. The engineering and design team uses computerized drafting and testing of new products. The following managers work in the tennis racket division:

Jason Dennis, Sales Manager (supervises all sales representatives)
Peggy Groneman, Technical Specialist (supervises computer programmers)
Dave Marley, Cost Accounting Manager (supervises cost accountants)
Kevin Carson, Production Supervisor (supervises all manufacturing employees)
Sally Renner, Engineer (supervises all new-product design teams)

Instructions
(a) What are the primary information needs of each manager?
(b) Which, if any, financial accounting report(s) is each likely to use?
(c) Name one special-purpose management accounting report that could be designed for each manager. Include the name of the report, the information it would contain, and how frequently it should be issued.

Real-World Focus

BYP15-3 The Institute of Management Accountants (IMA) is an organization dedicated to excellence in the practice of management accounting and financial management.

Address: **www.imanet.org**, or go to **www.wiley.com/college/weygandt**

Instructions

At the IMA's home page, locate the answers to the following questions.

(a) How many members does the IMA have, and what are their job titles?
(b) What are some of the benefits of joining the IMA as a student?
(c) Use the chapter locator function to locate the IMA chapter nearest you, and find the name of the chapter president.

CRITICAL THINKING

Communication Activity

BYP15-4 Refer to P15-5A and add the following requirement.

Prepare a letter to the president of the company, Shelly Phillips, describing the changes you made. Explain clearly why net income is different after the changes. Keep the following points in mind as you compose your letter.

1. This is a letter to the president of a company, who is your friend. The style should be generally formal, but you may relax some requirements. For example, you may call the president by her first name.

2. Executives are very busy. Your letter should tell the president your main results first (for example, the amount of net income).

3. You should include brief explanations so that the president can understand the changes you made in the calculations.

Ethics Case

BYP15-5 Steve Morgan, controller for Newton Industries, was reviewing production cost reports for the year. One amount in these reports continued to bother him—advertising. During the year, the company had instituted an expensive advertising campaign to sell some of its slower-moving products. It was still too early to tell whether the advertising campaign was successful.

There had been much internal debate as how to report advertising cost. The vice president of finance argued that advertising costs should be reported as a cost of production, just like direct materials and direct labor. He therefore recommended that this cost be identified as manufacturing overhead and reported as part of inventory costs until sold. Others disagreed. Morgan believed that this cost should be reported as an expense of the current period, so as not to overstate net income. Others argued that it should be reported as prepaid advertising and reported as a current asset.

The president finally had to decide the issue. He argued that these costs should be reported as inventory. His arguments were practical ones. He noted that the company was experiencing financial difficulty and expensing this amount in the current period might jeopardize a planned bond offering. Also, by reporting the advertising costs as inventory rather than as prepaid advertising, less attention would be directed to it by the financial community.

Instructions
(a) Who are the stakeholders in this situation?
(b) What are the ethical issues involved in this situation?
(c) What would you do if you were Steve Morgan?

All About You

BYP15-6 The primary purpose of managerial accounting is to provide information useful for management decisions. Many of the managerial accounting techniques that you learn in this course will be useful for decisions you make in your everyday life.

Instructions
For each of the following managerial accounting techniques, read the definition provided and then provide an example of a personal situation that would benefit from use of this technique.

(a) Break-even point (page 895).
(b) Budget (page 1058).
(c) Balanced scorecard (page 1176).
(d) Capital budgeting (page 1204).

Considering Your Costs and Benefits

BYP15-7 As noted in this chapter, because of global competition, companies have become increasingly focused on reducing costs. To reduce costs and remain competitive, many companies are turning to outsourcing. Outsourcing means hiring an outside supplier to provide elements of a product or service rather than producing them internally.

Suppose you are the managing partner in a CPA firm with 30 full-time staff. Larger firms in your community have begun to outsource basic tax-return preparation work to India. Should you outsource your basic tax-return work to India as well? You estimate that you would have to lay off six staff members if you outsource the work. The basic arguments for and against are as follows.

YES: The wages paid to Indian accountants are very low relative to U.S. wages. You will not be able to compete unless you outsource.
NO: Tax-return data is highly sensitive. Many customers will be upset to learn that their data is being emailed around the world.

Instructions
Write a response indicating your position regarding this situation. Provide support for your view.

CHAPTER PREVIEW The Feature Story below about Disney describes how important accurate costing is to movie studios. In order to submit accurate bids on new film projects and to know whether it profited from past films, the company needs a good costing system. This chapter illustrates how costs are assigned to specific jobs, such as the production of *The Avengers 2*. We begin the discussion in this chapter with an overview of the flow of costs in a job order cost accounting system. We then use a case study to explain and illustrate the documents, entries, and accounts in this type of cost accounting system.

FEATURE STORY

Profiting from the Silver Screen

Have you ever had the chance to tour a movie studio? There's a lot going on! Lots of equipment and lots of people with a variety of talents. Running a film studio, whether as an independent company or part of a major corporation, is a complex and risky business. Consider Disney, which has produced such classics as *Snow White and the Seven Dwarfs* and such colossal successes as *Frozen*. The movie studio has, however, also seen its share of losses. Disney's *Lone Ranger* movie brought in revenues of $260 million, but its production and marketing costs were a combined $375 million—a loss of $115 million.

Every time Disney or another movie studio makes a new movie, it is creating a unique product. Ideally, each new movie should be able to stand on its own, that is, the film should generate revenues that exceed its costs. And in order to know whether a particular movie is profitable, the studio must keep track of all of the costs incurred to make and market the film. These costs include such items as salaries of the writers, actors, director, producer, and production team (e.g., film crew); licensing costs; depreciation on equipment; music; studio rental; and marketing and distribution costs. If you've ever watched the credits at the end of a movie, you know the list goes on and on.

The movie studio isn't the only one with an interest in knowing a particular project's profitability. Many of the people involved in making the movie, such as the screenwriters, actors, and producers, have at least part of their compensation tied to its profitability. As such, complaints about inaccurate accounting are common in the movie industry.

In particular, a few well-known and widely attended movies reported low profits, or even losses, once the accountants got done with them. How can this be? The issue is that a large portion of a movie's costs are overhead costs that can't be directly traced to a film, such as depreciation of film equipment and sets, facility maintenance costs, and executives' salaries. Actors and others often suggest that these overhead costs are overallocated to their movie and therefore negatively affect their compensation.

To reduce the risk of financial flops, many of the big studios now focus on making sequels of previous hits. This might explain why, shortly after losing money on the *Lone Ranger*, Disney announced plans to make *The Avengers 2*—a much safer bet.

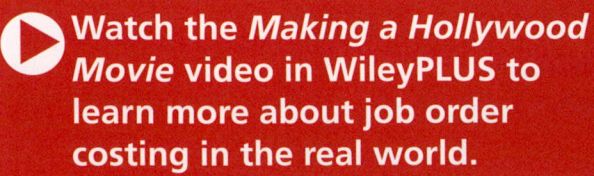
Watch the *Making a Hollywood Movie* video in WileyPLUS to learn more about job order costing in the real world.

© Pictorial Press Ltd/Alamy

CHAPTER OUTLINE

Learning Objectives

1 Describe cost systems and the flow of costs in a job order system.
- Process cost system
- Job order cost system
- Job order cost flow
- Accumulating costs

DO IT! 1 Accumulating Manufacturing Costs

2 Use a job cost sheet to assign costs to work in process.
- Raw materials costs
- Factory labor costs

DO IT! 2 Work in Process

3 Demonstrate how to determine and use the predetermined overhead rate.

DO IT! 3 Predetermined Overhead Rate

4 Prepare entries for manufacturing and service jobs completed and sold.
- Finished goods
- Cost of goods sold
- Summary
- Job order for service companies
- Pros and cons of job order costing

DO IT! 4 Completion and Sale of Jobs

5 Distinguish between under- and overapplied manufacturing overhead.
- Under- or overapplied manufacturing overhead

DO IT! 5 Applied Manufacturing Overhead

Go to the **REVIEW AND PRACTICE** section at the end of the chapter for a review of key concepts and practice applications with solutions.

Visit **WileyPLUS with ORION** for additional tutorials and practice opportunities.

Describe cost systems and the flow of costs in a job order system.

Cost accounting involves measuring, recording, and reporting product costs. Companies determine both the total cost and the unit cost of each product. The accuracy of the product cost information is critical to the success of the company. Companies use this information to determine which products to produce, what prices to charge, and how many units to produce. Accurate product cost information is also vital for effective evaluation of employee performance.

A **cost accounting system** consists of accounts for the various manufacturing costs. These accounts are fully integrated into the general ledger of a company. An important feature of a cost accounting system is the use of **a perpetual inventory system**. Such a system **provides immediate, up-to-date information on the cost of a product**.

There are two basic types of cost accounting systems: (1) a process cost system and (2) a job order cost system. Although cost accounting systems differ widely from company to company, most involve one of these two traditional product costing systems.

Process Cost System

A company uses a **process cost system** when it manufactures a large volume of similar products. Production is continuous. Examples of a process cost system are the manufacture of cereal by **Kellogg**, the refining of petroleum by **ExxonMobil**, and the production of ice cream by **Ben & Jerry's**. Process costing accumulates product-related costs **for a period of time** (such as a week or a month) instead of assigning costs to specific products or job orders. In process costing, companies assign the costs to departments or processes for the specified period of time. Illustration 16-1 shows examples of the use of a process cost system. We will discuss the process cost system further in Chapter 17.

Illustration 16-1
Process cost system

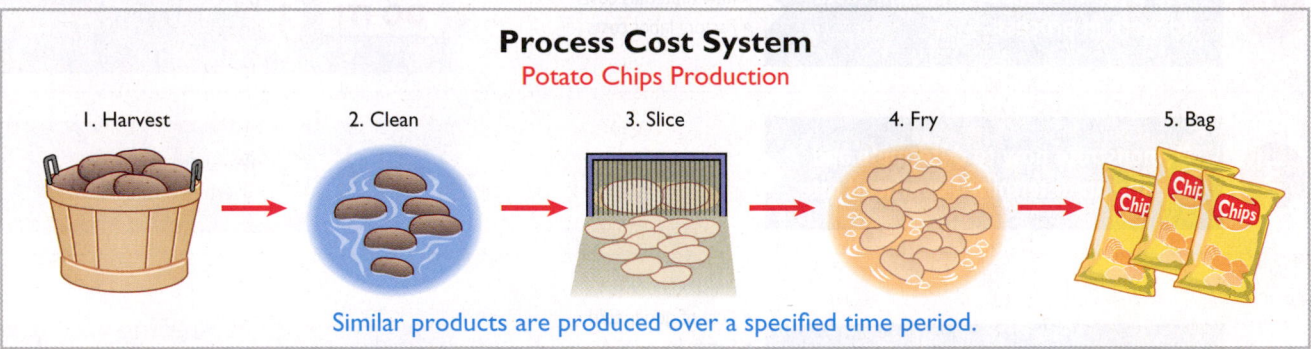

Process Cost System
Potato Chips Production

1. Harvest   2. Clean   3. Slice   4. Fry   5. Bag

Similar products are produced over a specified time period.

Job Order Cost System

Under a **job order cost system**, the company assigns costs to each **job** or to each **batch** of goods. An example of a job is the manufacture of a jet by **Boeing**, the production of a movie by **Disney**, or the making of a fire truck by **American LaFrance**. An example of a batch is the printing of 225 wedding invitations by a local print shop, or the printing of a weekly issue of *Fortune* magazine by a high-tech printer such as **Quad Graphics**.

An important feature of job order costing is that each job or batch has its own distinguishing characteristics. For example, each house is custom built, each consulting engagement by a CPA firm is unique, and each printing job is different. **The objective is to compute the cost per job.** At each point in manufacturing a product or performing a service, the company can identify the job and its associated costs. A job order cost system measures costs for each completed job, rather than for set time periods. Illustration 16-2 shows the recording of costs in a job order cost system for Disney as it produced two different films at the same time: an animated film and an action thriller.

Job Order Cost System
Two jobs: Animated Film and Action Thriller

- Computer programmers
- Musical composers
- Voice-over talent
- Animation talent

- Actors
- Stuntpeople
- Set design
- Food caterers
- Stuntperson insurance
- Location fees

Job #9501   Job #9502
Each job has distinguishing characteristics and related costs.

Illustration 16-2
Job order cost system for Disney

Can a company use both types of cost systems? Yes. For example, **General Motors** uses process cost accounting for its standard model cars, such as Malibus and Corvettes, and job order cost accounting for a custom-made limousine for the President of the United States.

The objective of both cost accounting systems is to provide unit cost information for product pricing, cost control, inventory valuation, and financial statement presentation.

Management Insight

© Tony Tremblay/iStockphoto

Jobs Won, Money Lost

Many companies suffer from poor cost accounting. As a result, they sometimes make products they should not be selling at all, or they buy product components that they could more profitably make themselves. Also, inaccurate cost data leads companies to misallocate capital and frustrates efforts by plant managers to improve efficiency.

For example, consider the case of a diversified company in the business of rebuilding diesel locomotives. The managers thought they were making money, but a consulting firm found that the company had seriously underestimated costs. The company bailed out of the business and not a moment too soon. Says the consultant who advised the company, "The more contracts it won, the more money it lost." Given that situation, a company cannot stay in business very long!

What type of costs do you think the company had been underestimating? (Go to **WileyPLUS** for this answer and additional questions.)

Job Order Cost Flow

The flow of costs (direct materials, direct labor, and manufacturing overhead) in job order cost accounting parallels the physical flow of the materials as they are converted into finished goods. As shown in Illustration 16-3 (page 756), companies first **accumulate** manufacturing costs in the form of raw materials, factory labor, or manufacturing overhead. They then **assign** manufacturing costs to the Work in Process Inventory account. When a job is completed, the company transfers the cost of the job to Finished Goods Inventory. Later when the goods are sold, the company transfers their cost to Cost of Goods Sold.

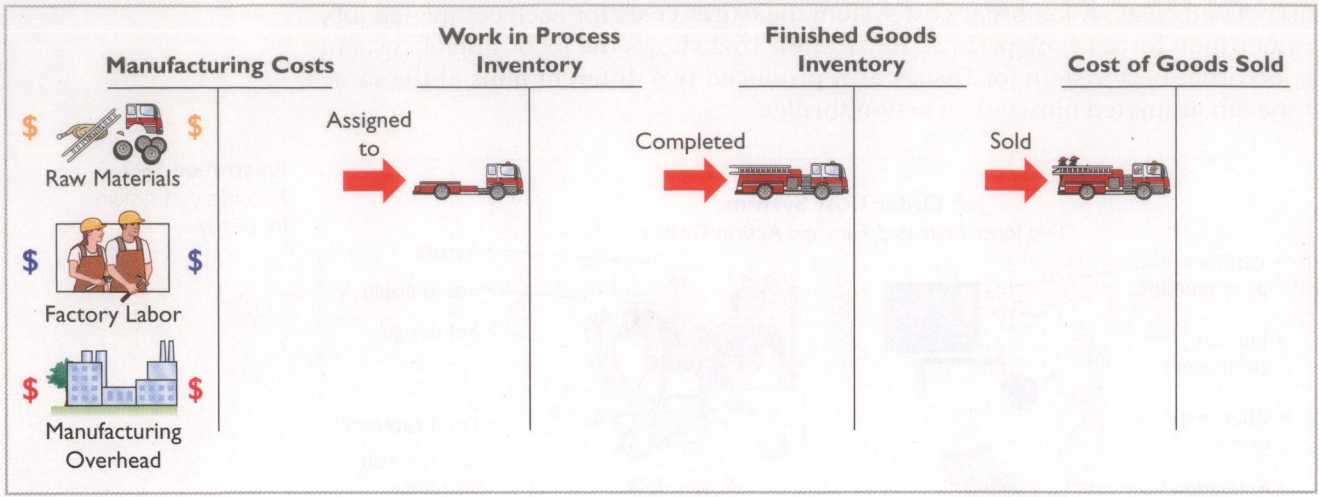

Manufacturing Costs	Work in Process Inventory	Finished Goods Inventory	Cost of Goods Sold

Illustration 16-3
Flow of costs in job order costing

Illustration 16-3 provides a basic overview of the flow of costs in a manufacturing setting for production of a fire truck. A more detailed presentation of the flow of costs is summarized near the end of this chapter in Illustration 16-15. There are two major steps in the flow of costs: (1) *accumulating* the manufacturing costs incurred, and (2) *assigning* the accumulated costs to the work done. The following discussion shows that the company accumulates manufacturing costs incurred by debits to Raw Materials Inventory, Factory Labor, and Manufacturing Overhead. When the company incurs these costs, it does not attempt to associate the costs with specific jobs. The company makes additional entries to assign manufacturing costs incurred to specific jobs. In the remainder of this chapter, we will use a case study to explain how a job order cost system operates.

Accumulating Manufacturing Costs

To illustrate a job order cost system, we will use the January transactions of Wallace Company, which makes custom electronic sensors for corporate safety applications (such as fire and carbon monoxide) and security applications (such as theft and corporate espionage).

RAW MATERIALS COSTS

When Wallace receives the raw materials it has purchased, **it debits the cost of the materials to Raw Materials Inventory**. The company debits this account for the invoice cost of the raw materials and freight costs chargeable to the purchaser. It credits the account for purchase discounts taken and purchase returns and allowances. Wallace makes **no effort at this point to associate the cost of materials with specific jobs or orders**.

To illustrate, assume that Wallace purchases 2,000 lithium batteries (Stock No. AA2746) at $5 per unit ($10,000) and 800 electronic modules (Stock No. AA2850) at $40 per unit ($32,000) for a total cost of $42,000 ($10,000 + $32,000). The entry to record this purchase on January 4 is:

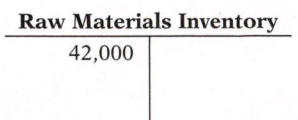

Raw Materials Inventory		
42,000		

(1)[1]

Jan. 4	Raw Materials Inventory		42,000	
	Accounts Payable			42,000
	(Purchase of raw materials on account)			

---

[1]The numbers placed above the entries for Wallace Company are used for reference purposes in the summary provided in Illustration 16-15.

At this point, Raw Materials Inventory has a balance of $42,000, as shown in the T-account in the margin. As we will explain later in the chapter, the company subsequently assigns direct raw materials inventory to work in process and indirect raw materials inventory to manufacturing overhead.

FACTORY LABOR COSTS

Some of a company's employees are involved in the manufacturing process, while others are not. As discussed in Chapter 15, wages and salaries of nonmanufacturing employees are expensed as period costs (e.g., Salaries and Wages Expense). Costs related to manufacturing employees are accumulated in Factory Labor to ensure their treatment as product costs. Factory labor consists of three costs: (1) gross earnings of factory workers, (2) employer payroll taxes on these earnings, and (3) fringe benefits (such as sick pay, pensions, and vacation pay) incurred by the employer. **Companies debit labor costs to Factory Labor as they incur those costs.**

To illustrate, assume that Wallace incurs $32,000 of factory labor costs. Of that amount, $27,000 relates to wages payable and $5,000 relates to payroll taxes payable in February. The entry to record factory labor for the month is:

	(2)		
Jan. 31	Factory Labor	32,000	
	Factory Wages Payable		27,000
	Employer Payroll Taxes Payable		5,000
	(To record factory labor costs)		

Factory Labor
32,000

At this point, Factory Labor has a balance of $32,000, as shown in the T-account in the margin. The company subsequently assigns direct factory labor to work in process and indirect factory labor to manufacturing overhead.

MANUFACTURING OVERHEAD COSTS

A company has many types of overhead costs. If these overhead costs, such as property taxes, depreciation, insurance, and repairs, relate to overhead costs of a nonmanufacturing facility, such as an office building, then these costs are expensed as period costs (e.g., Property Tax Expense, Depreciation Expense, Insurance Expense, and Maintenance and Repairs Expense). If the costs relate to the manufacturing process, then they are accumulated in Manufacturing Overhead to ensure their treatment as product costs.

Using assumed data, the summary entry for manufacturing overhead in Wallace Company is:

	(3)		
Jan. 31	Manufacturing Overhead	13,800	
	Utilities Payable		4,800
	Prepaid Insurance		2,000
	Accounts Payable (for repairs)		2,600
	Accumulated Depreciation		3,000
	Property Taxes Payable		1,400
	(To record overhead costs)		

Manufacturing Overhead
13,800

At this point, Manufacturing Overhead has a balance of $13,800, as shown in the T-account in the margin. The company subsequently assigns manufacturing overhead to work in process.

DO IT!   1   Accumulating Manufacturing Costs

During the current month, Ringling Company incurs the following manufacturing costs:

(a) Raw material purchases of $4,200 on account.

(b) Factory labor of $18,000. Of that amount, $15,000 relates to wages payable and $3,000 relates to payroll taxes payable.

(c) Factory utilities of $2,200 are payable, prepaid factory insurance of $1,800 has expired, and depreciation on the factory building is $3,500.

Prepare journal entries for each type of manufacturing cost.

Action Plan

✔ In accumulating manufacturing costs, debit at least one of three accounts: Raw Materials Inventory, Factory Labor, and Manufacturing Overhead.

✔ Manufacturing overhead costs may be recognized daily. Or, manufacturing overhead may be recorded periodically through a summary entry.

Solution

(a) Raw Materials Inventory	4,200	
Accounts Payable		4,200
(Purchases of raw materials on account)		
(b) Factory Labor	18,000	
Factory Wages Payable		15,000
Employer Payroll Taxes Payable		3,000
(To record factory labor costs)		
(c) Manufacturing Overhead	7,500	
Utilities Payable		2,200
Prepaid Insurance		1,800
Accumulated Depreciation		3,500
(To record overhead costs)		

Related exercise material: **BE16-1, BE16-2, E16-1, E16-7, E16-8, E16-11, and DO IT! 16-1.**

LEARNING OBJECTIVE   2

Use a job cost sheet to assign costs to work in process.

Assigning manufacturing costs to work in process results in the following entries.

1. **Debits** made to Work in Process Inventory.
2. **Credits** made to Raw Materials Inventory, Factory Labor, and Manufacturing Overhead.

An essential accounting record in assigning costs to jobs is a **job cost sheet**, as shown in Illustration 16-4. A **job cost sheet** is a form used to record the costs chargeable to a specific job and to determine the total and unit costs of the completed job.

Companies keep a separate job cost sheet for each job. The job cost sheets constitute the subsidiary ledger for the Work in Process Inventory account. A **subsidiary ledger** consists of individual records for each individual item—in this case, each job. The Work in Process account is referred to as a **control account** because it summarizes the detailed data regarding specific jobs contained in the job cost sheets. **Each entry to Work in Process Inventory must be accompanied by a corresponding posting to one or more job cost sheets.**

Illustration 16-4
Job cost sheet

Job Cost Sheet

Job No. _____   Quantity _____
Item _____   Date Requested _____
For _____   Date Completed _____

Date	Direct Materials	Direct Labor	Manufacturing Overhead

Cost of completed job
  Direct materials $ _____
  Direct labor   _____
  Manufacturing overhead   _____
Total cost $ _____
Unit cost (total dollars ÷ quantity) $ _____

Helpful Hint
Companies typically maintain job cost sheets as computer files.

Raw Materials Costs

Companies assign raw materials costs to jobs when their materials storeroom issues the materials in response to requests. Requests for issuing raw materials are made on a prenumbered **materials requisition slip**. The materials issued may be used directly on a job, or they may be considered indirect materials. As Illustration 16-5 shows, the requisition should indicate the quantity and type of materials withdrawn and the account to be charged. The company will charge direct materials to Work in Process Inventory, and indirect materials to Manufacturing Overhead.

Illustration 16-5
Materials requisition slip

Wallace Company
Materials Requisition Slip

Deliver to: _____ Assembly Department _____   Req. No.   R247
Charge to: _____ Work in Process—Job No. 101 _____   Date: _____ 1/6/17 _____

Quantity	Description	Stock No.	Cost per Unit	Total
200	Lithium batteries	AA2746	$5.00	$1,000

Requested by _Bruce Howart_   Received by _Herb Crowley_
Approved by _Kap Shin_   Costed by _Heather Remmers_

Helpful Hint
Note the specific job (in this case, Job No. 101) to be charged.

The company may use any of the inventory costing methods (FIFO, LIFO, or average-cost) in costing the requisitions **to the individual job cost sheets**.

Periodically, the company journalizes the requisitions. For example, if Wallace uses $24,000 of direct materials and $6,000 of indirect materials in January, the entry is:

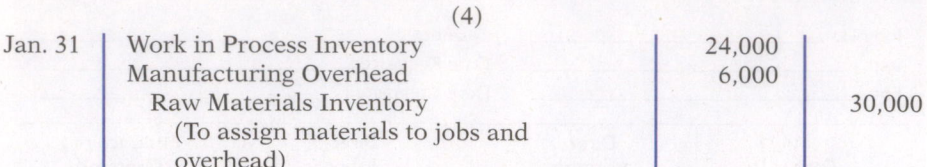

		(4)		
Jan. 31	Work in Process Inventory		24,000	
	Manufacturing Overhead		6,000	
	Raw Materials Inventory			30,000
	(To assign materials to jobs and overhead)			

This entry reduces Raw Materials Inventory by $30,000, increases Work in Process Inventory by $24,000, and increases Manufacturing Overhead by $6,000, as shown below.

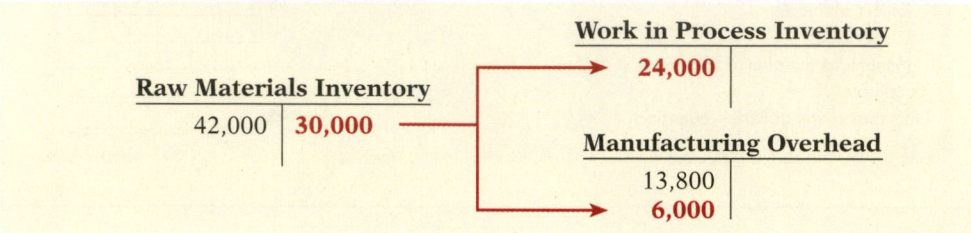

Illustration 16-6 shows the posting of requisition slip R247 to Job No. 101 and other assumed postings to the job cost sheets for materials. The requisition slips provide the basis for total direct materials costs of $12,000 for Job No. 101, $7,000 for Job No. 102, and $5,000 for Job No. 103. After the company has completed all postings, the sum of the direct materials columns of the job cost sheets (the

Illustration 16-6
Job cost sheets–posting of direct materials

Helpful Hint
Companies post to control accounts monthly, and post to job cost sheets daily.

Helpful Hint
Prove the $24,000 direct materials charge to Work in Process Inventory by totaling the charges by jobs:

101	$12,000
102	7,000
103	5,000
	$24,000

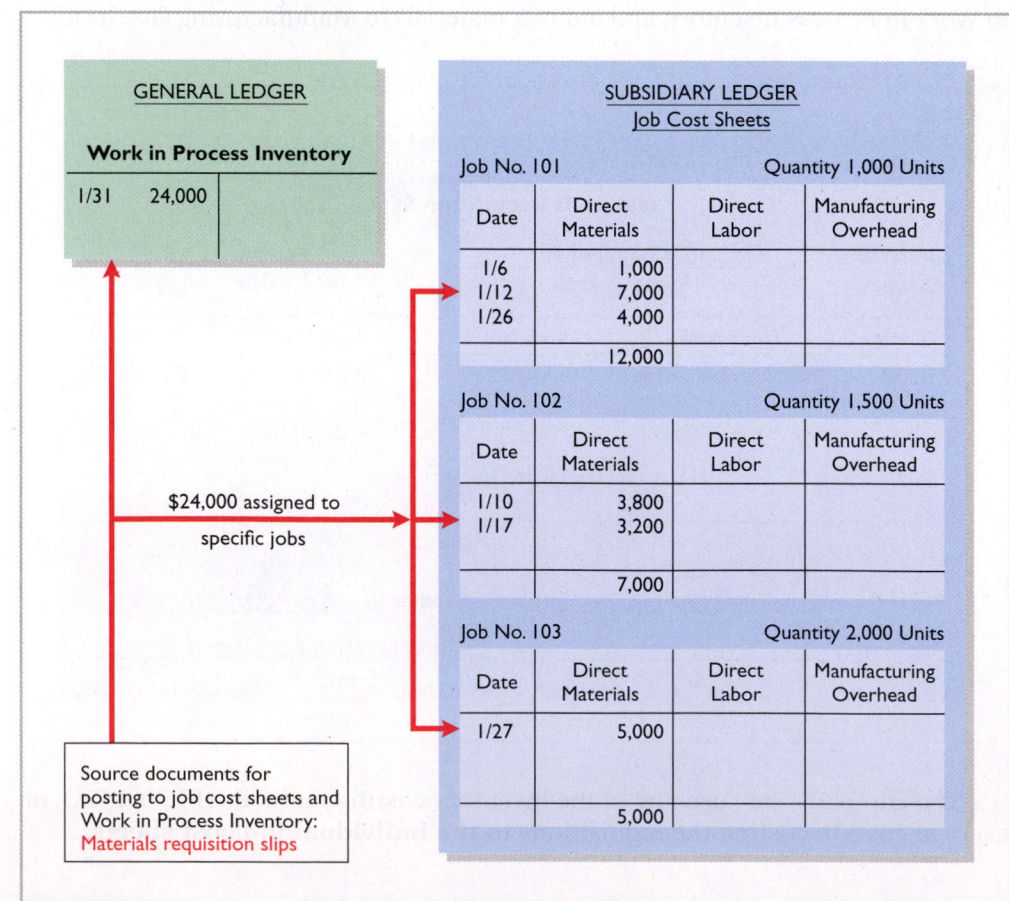

subsidiary account amounts of $12,000, $7,000, and $5,000) should equal the direct materials debited to Work in Process Inventory (the control account amount of $24,000).

Management Insight   iSuppli

© TommL/iStockphoto

The Cost of an iPhone? Just Tear One Apart

All companies need to know what it costs to make their own products—but a lot of companies would also like to know the cost of their competitors' products as well. That's where iSuppli steps in. For a price, iSuppli will tear apart sophisticated electronic devices to tell you what it would cost to replicate. In the case of smartphones, which often have more than 1,000 tiny components, that is no small feat. As shown in the chart to the right, the components of a recent iPhone model cost about $170. Assembly adds only about another $6.50. However, the difference between what you pay (about double the

total component cost) and the "cost" is not all profit. You also have to consider the additional nonproduction costs of research, design, marketing, patent fees, and selling costs.

Components	Apple iPhone[a]
Integrated circuits	$ 91.38
Display/touchscreen	34.65
Mechanical[b]	17.80
Camera	9.35
Battery	5.07
Other	11.82
Total	**$170.07**

[a]Latest data available.   [b]Includes electromechanical.
Source: iSuppli.

Source: "The Business of Dissecting Electronics: The Lowdown on Teardowns," *The Economist.com* (January 21, 2010).

What type of costs are marketing and selling costs, and how are they treated for accounting purposes? (Go to **WileyPLUS** for this answer and additional questions.)

Factory Labor Costs

Companies assign factory labor costs to jobs on the basis of time tickets prepared when the work is performed. The **time ticket** indicates the employee, the hours worked, the account and job to be charged, and the total labor cost. Many companies accumulate these data through the use of bar coding and scanning devices. When they start and end work, employees scan bar codes on their identification badges and bar codes associated with each job they work on. When direct labor is involved, the time ticket must indicate the job number, as shown in Illustration 16-7. The employee's supervisor should approve all time tickets.

Illustration 16-7
Time ticket

Wallace Company
Time Ticket

Date: 1/6/17

Employee: John Nash   Employee No. 124
Charge to: Work in Process   Job No. 101

Time			Hourly Rate	Total Cost
Start	Stop	Total Hours		
0800	1200	4	10.00	40.00

Approved by *Bob Kadler*   Costed by *M Cher*

The time tickets are later sent to the payroll department, which applies the employee's hourly wage rate and computes the total labor cost. Finally, the company journalizes the time tickets. It debits the account Work in Process Inventory for direct labor and debits Manufacturing Overhead for indirect labor. For example, if the $32,000 total factory labor cost consists of $28,000 of direct labor and $4,000 of indirect labor, the entry is:

(5)

Jan. 31	Work in Process Inventory	28,000	
	Manufacturing Overhead	4,000	
	Factory Labor		32,000
	(To assign labor to jobs and overhead)		

As a result of this entry, Factory Labor is reduced by $32,000 so it has a zero balance, and labor costs are assigned to the appropriate manufacturing accounts. The entry increases Work in Process Inventory by $28,000 and increases Manufacturing Overhead by $4,000, as shown below.

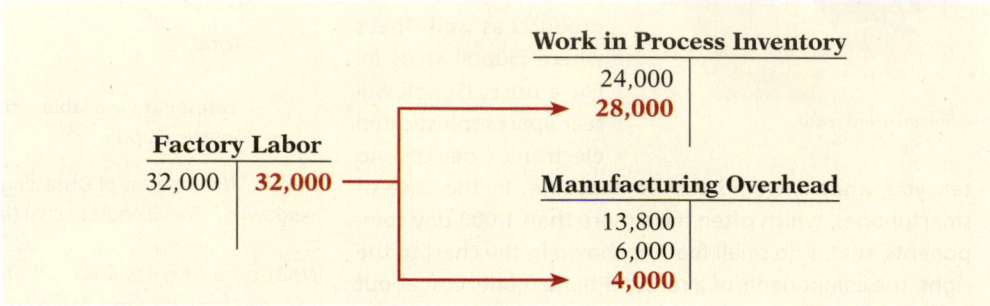

Let's assume that the labor costs chargeable to Wallace's three jobs are $15,000, $9,000, and $4,000. Illustration 16-8 shows the Work in Process Inventory

Illustration 16-8
Job cost sheets—direct labor

Helpful Hint
Prove the $28,000 direct labor charge to Work in Process Inventory by totaling the charges by jobs:

101	$15,000
102	9,000
103	4,000
	$28,000

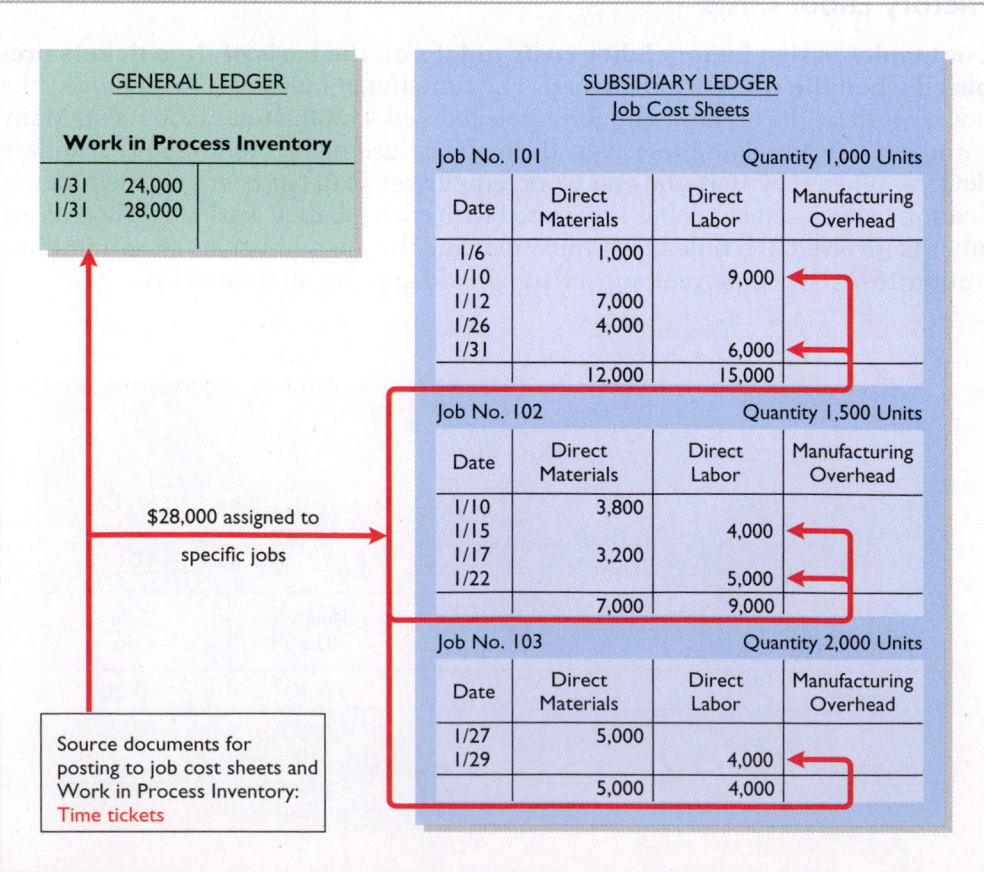

and job cost sheets after posting. As in the case of direct materials, the postings to the direct labor columns of the job cost sheets should equal the posting of direct labor to Work in Process Inventory.

DO IT! 2   Work in Process

Danielle Company is working on two job orders. The job cost sheets show the following:

> Direct materials—Job 120 $6,000; Job 121 $3,600
> Direct labor—Job 120 $4,000; Job 121 $2,000
> Manufacturing overhead—Job 120 $5,000; Job 121 $2,500

Prepare the three summary entries to record the assignment of costs to Work in Process from the data on the job cost sheets.

Solution

The three summary entries are:

Work in Process Inventory ($6,000 + $3,600)	9,600	
Raw Materials Inventory		9,600
(To assign materials to jobs)		
Work in Process Inventory ($4,000 + $2,000)	6,000	
Factory Labor		6,000
(To assign labor to jobs)		
Work in Process Inventory ($5,000 + $2,500)	7,500	
Manufacturing Overhead		7,500
(To assign overhead to jobs)		

Related exercise material: **BE16-3, BE16-4, BE16-5, E16-2, E16-7, E16-8, and DO IT! 16-2.**

Action Plan

✔ Recognize that Work in Process Inventory is the control account for all unfinished job cost sheets.

✔ Debit Work in Process Inventory for the materials, labor, and overhead charged to the job cost sheets.

✔ Credit the accounts that were debited when the manufacturing costs were accumulated.

LEARNING OBJECTIVE 3

Demonstrate how to determine and use the predetermined overhead rate.

Companies charge the actual costs of direct materials and direct labor to specific jobs. In contrast, manufacturing **overhead** relates to production operations **as a whole**. As a result, overhead costs cannot be assigned to specific jobs on the basis of actual costs incurred. Instead, companies assign manufacturing overhead to work in process and to specific jobs **on an estimated basis through the use of a predetermined overhead rate**.

The **predetermined overhead rate** is based on the relationship between estimated annual overhead costs and expected annual operating activity, expressed in terms of a common **activity base**. The company may state the activity in terms of direct labor costs, direct labor hours, machine hours, or any other measure that will provide an equitable basis for applying overhead costs to jobs. Companies establish the predetermined overhead rate at the beginning of the year. Small companies often use a single, company-wide predetermined overhead rate. Large companies often use rates that vary from department to department. The formula for a predetermined overhead rate is as follows.

Estimated Annual Overhead Costs	÷	Expected Annual Operating Activity	=	Predetermined Overhead Rate

Illustration 16-9
Formula for predetermined overhead rate

Overhead relates to production operations as a whole. To know what "the whole" is, the logical thing is to wait until the end of the year's operations. At that time, the company knows all of its costs for the period. As a practical matter, though, managers cannot wait until the end of the year. To price products effectively as they are completed, managers need information about product costs of specific jobs completed during the year. Using a predetermined overhead rate enables a cost to be determined for the job immediately. Illustration 16-10 indicates how manufacturing overhead is assigned to work in process.

Illustration 16-10
Using predetermined overhead rates

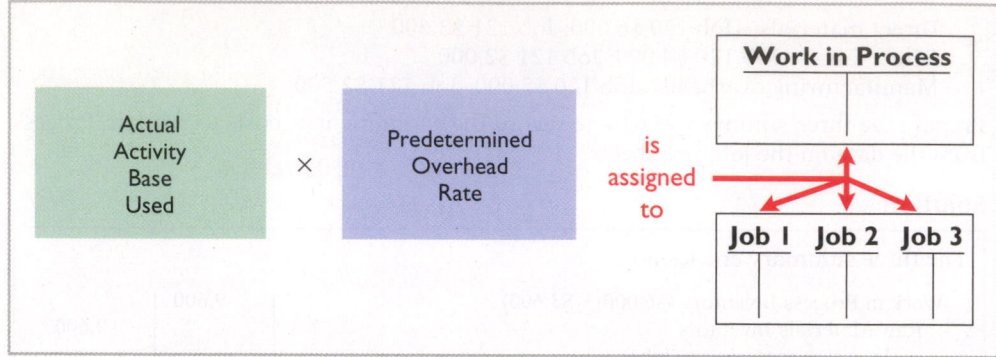

Wallace Company uses direct labor cost as the activity base. Assuming that the company expects annual overhead costs to be $280,000 and direct labor costs for the year to be $350,000, the overhead rate is 80%, computed as follows.

Illustration 16-11
Calculation of predetermined overhead rate

Estimated Annual Overhead Costs	÷	Expected Direct Labor Cost	=	Predetermined Overhead Rate
$280,000	÷	$350,000	=	80%

This means that for every dollar of direct labor, Wallace will assign 80 cents of manufacturing overhead to a job. The use of a predetermined overhead rate enables the company to determine the approximate total cost of each job **when it completes the job**.

Historically, companies used direct labor costs or direct labor hours as the activity base. The reason was the relatively high correlation between direct labor and manufacturing overhead. Today, more companies are using **machine hours as the activity base, due to increased reliance on automation in manufacturing operations**. Or, as mentioned in Chapter 15 (and discussed more fully in Chapter 18), many companies now use activity-based costing to more accurately allocate overhead costs based on the activities that give rise to the costs.

A company may use more than one activity base. For example, if a job is manufactured in more than one factory department, each department may have its own overhead rate. In the Feature Story, **Disney** might use two bases in assigning overhead to film jobs: direct materials dollars for indirect materials, and direct labor hours for such costs as insurance and supervisor salaries.

Wallace Company applies manufacturing overhead to work in process when it assigns direct labor costs. It also applies manufacturing overhead to specific jobs at the same time. For January, Wallace applied overhead of $22,400 in response to its assignment of $28,000 of direct labor costs (direct labor cost of $28,000 × 80%). The following entry records this application.

(6)

Jan. 31	Work in Process Inventory	22,400	
	Manufacturing Overhead		22,400
	(To assign overhead to jobs)		

This entry reduces the balance in Manufacturing Overhead and increases Work in Process Inventory by $22,400, as shown below.

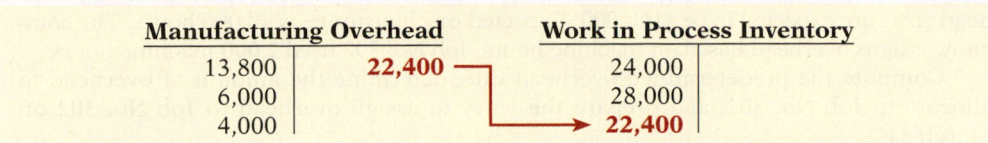

Manufacturing Overhead		Work in Process Inventory
13,800	**22,400**	24,000
6,000		28,000
4,000		**22,400**

The overhead that Wallace applies to each job will be 80% of the direct labor cost of the job for the month. Illustration 16-12 shows the Work in Process Inventory account and the job cost sheets after posting. Note that the debit of $22,400 to Work in Process Inventory equals the sum of the overhead applied to jobs: Job No. 101 $12,000 + Job No. 102 $7,200 + Job No. 103 $3,200.

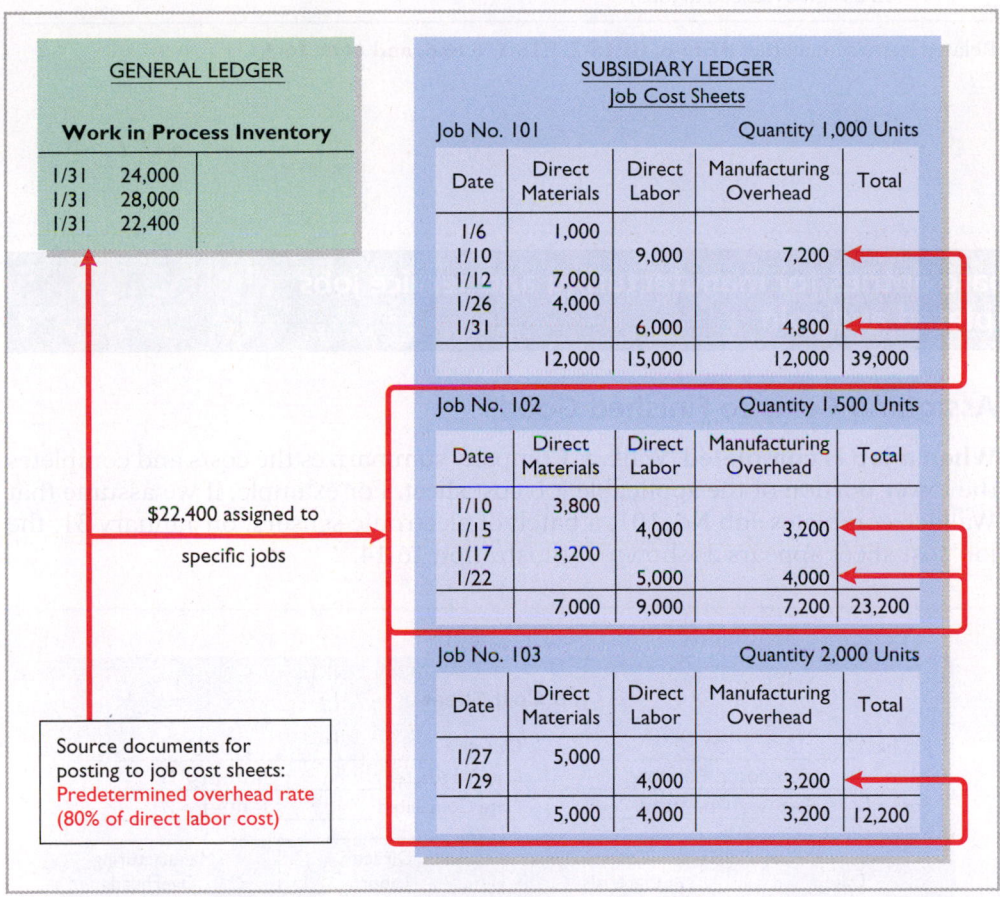

Illustration 16-12
Job cost sheets–manufacturing overhead applied

At the end of each month, the **balance in Work in Process Inventory should equal the sum of the costs shown on the job cost sheets of unfinished jobs**. Illustration 16-13 presents proof of the agreement of the control and subsidiary accounts in Wallace. (It assumes that all jobs are still in process.)

Work in Process Inventory		Job Cost Sheets	
Jan. 31	24,000	No. 101	$ 39,000
31	28,000	102	23,200
31	22,400	103	12,200
	74,400		**$74,400**

Illustration 16-13
Proof of job cost sheets to work in process inventory

DO IT! 3 Predetermined Overhead Rate

Action Plan

✔ Predetermined overhead rate is estimated annual overhead cost divided by expected annual operating activity.

✔ Assignment of overhead to jobs is determined by multiplying the actual activity base used by the predetermined overhead rate.

✔ The entry to record the assignment of overhead transfers an amount out of Manufacturing Overhead into Work in Process Inventory.

Stanley Company produces specialized safety devices. For the year, manufacturing overhead costs are expected to be $160,000. Expected machine usage is 40,000 hours. The company assigns overhead based on machine hours. Job No. 302 used 2,000 machine hours.

Compute the predetermined overhead rate, determine the amount of overhead to allocate to Job No. 302, and prepare the entry to assign overhead to Job No. 302 on March 31.

Solution

Predetermined overhead rate = $160,000 ÷ 40,000 hours = $4.00 per machine hour
Amount of overhead assigned to Job No. 302 = 2,000 hours × $4.00 = $8,000

The entry to record the assignment of overhead to Job No. 302 on March 31 is:

Work in Process Inventory	8,000	
Manufacturing Overhead		8,000
(To assign overhead to jobs)		

Related exercise material: **BE16-6, BE16-7, E16-5, E16-6, and DO IT! 16-3.**

LEARNING OBJECTIVE 4

Prepare entries for manufacturing and service jobs completed and sold.

Assigning Costs to Finished Goods

When a job is completed, Wallace Company summarizes the costs and completes the lower portion of the applicable job cost sheet. For example, if we assume that Wallace completes Job No. 101, a batch of electronic sensors, on January 31, the job cost sheet appears as shown in Illustration 16-14.

Illustration 16-14
Completed job cost sheet

Job Cost Sheet

Job No. 101   Quantity 1,000
Item Electronic Sensors   Date Requested January 5
For Tanner Company   Date Completed January 31

Date	Direct Materials	Direct Labor	Manufacturing Overhead
1/6	$ 1,000		
1/10		$ 9,000	$ 7,200
1/12	7,000		
1/26	4,000		
1/31		6,000	4,800
	$12,000	$15,000	$12,000

Cost of completed job
Direct materials $ 12,000
Direct labor   15,000
Manufacturing overhead   12,000
Total cost $ 39,000
Unit cost ($39,000 ÷ 1,000) $ 39.00

When a job is finished, Wallace makes an entry to transfer its total cost to finished goods inventory. The entry is as follows.

	(7)		
Jan. 31	Finished Goods Inventory	39,000	
	Work in Process Inventory		39,000
	(To record completion of		
	Job No. 101)		

This entry increases Finished Goods Inventory and reduces Work in Process Inventory by $39,000, as shown in the T-accounts below.

Work in Process Inventory		Finished Goods Inventory	
24,000	**39,000** ⟶	**39,000**	
28,000			
22,400			

Finished Goods Inventory is a control account. It controls individual finished goods records in a finished goods subsidiary ledger.

Assigning Costs to Cost of Goods Sold

Companies recognize cost of goods sold when each sale occurs. To illustrate the entries a company makes when it sells a completed job, assume that on January 31 Wallace Company sells on account Job No. 101. The job cost $39,000, and it sold for $50,000. The entries to record the sale and recognize cost of goods sold are:

	(8)		
Jan. 31	Accounts Receivable	50,000	
	Sales Revenue		50,000
	(To record sale of Job No. 101)		
31	Cost of Goods Sold	39,000	
	Finished Goods Inventory		39,000
	(To record cost of Job No. 101)		

This entry increases Cost of Goods Sold and reduces Finished Goods Inventory by $39,000, as shown in the T-accounts below.

Finished Goods Inventory		Cost of Goods Sold	
39,000	**39,000** ⟶	**39,000**	

Summary of Job Order Cost Flows

Illustration 16-15 shows a completed flowchart for a job order cost accounting system. All postings are keyed to entries 1–8 in the example presented in the previous pages for Wallace Company.

The cost flows in the diagram can be categorized as one of four types:

- **Accumulation.** The company first accumulates costs by (1) purchasing raw materials, (2) incurring labor costs, and (3) incurring manufacturing overhead costs.

- **Assignment to jobs.** Once the company has incurred manufacturing costs, it must assign them to specific jobs. For example, as it uses raw materials on specific jobs (4), the company assigns them to work in process or treats them as manufacturing overhead if the raw materials cannot be associated with a specific job. Similarly, the company either assigns factory labor (5) to work in process or treats it as manufacturing overhead if the factory labor cannot be associated with a specific job. Finally the company assigns manufacturing overhead (6) to work in process using a *predetermined overhead rate*. This deserves emphasis: **Do not assign overhead using actual overhead costs but instead use a predetermined rate.**

- **Completed jobs.** As jobs are completed (7), the company transfers the cost of the completed job out of work in process inventory into finished goods inventory.

- **When goods are sold.** As specific items are sold (8), the company transfers their cost out of finished goods inventory into cost of goods sold.

Illustration 16-15
Flow of costs in a job order cost system

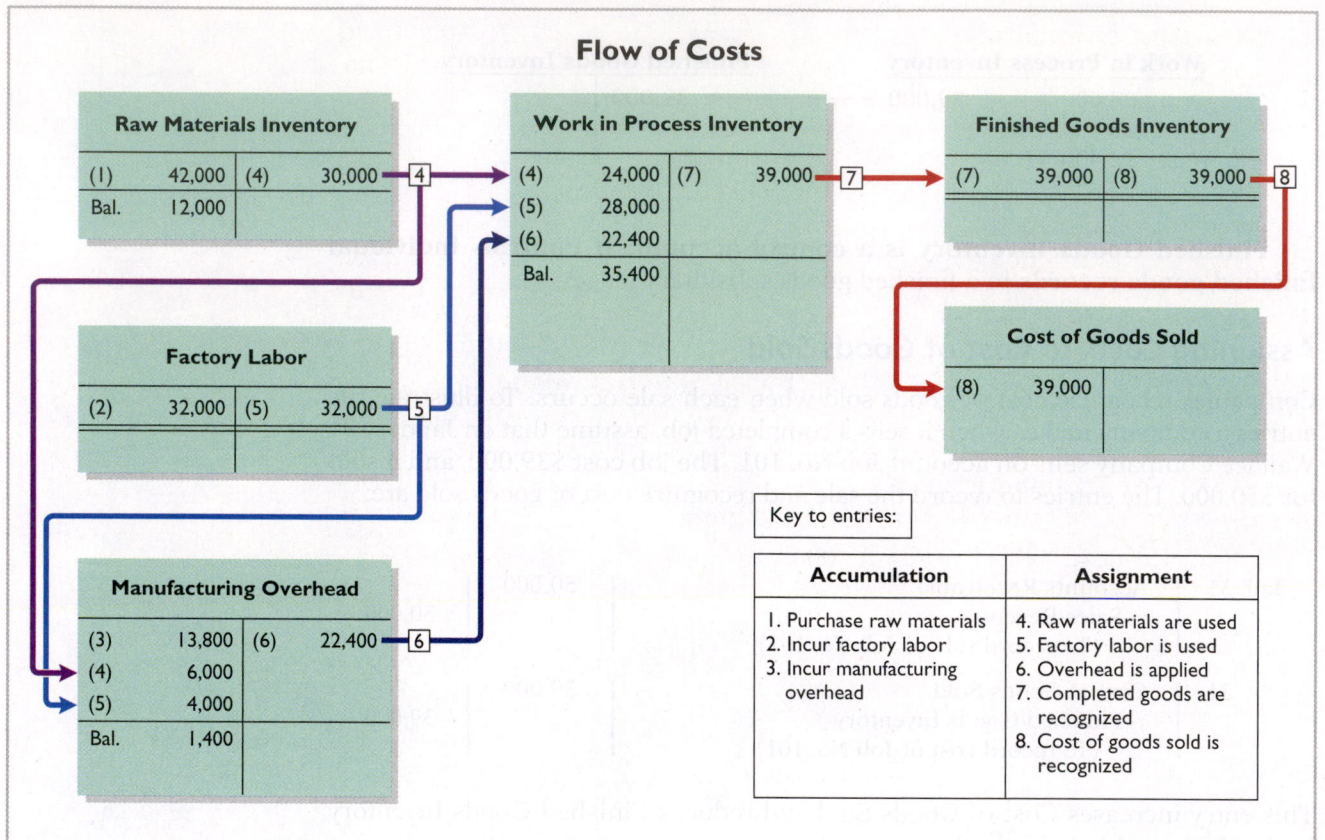

Illustration 16-16
Flow of documents in a job order cost system

Illustration 16-16 summarizes the flow of documents in a job order cost system.

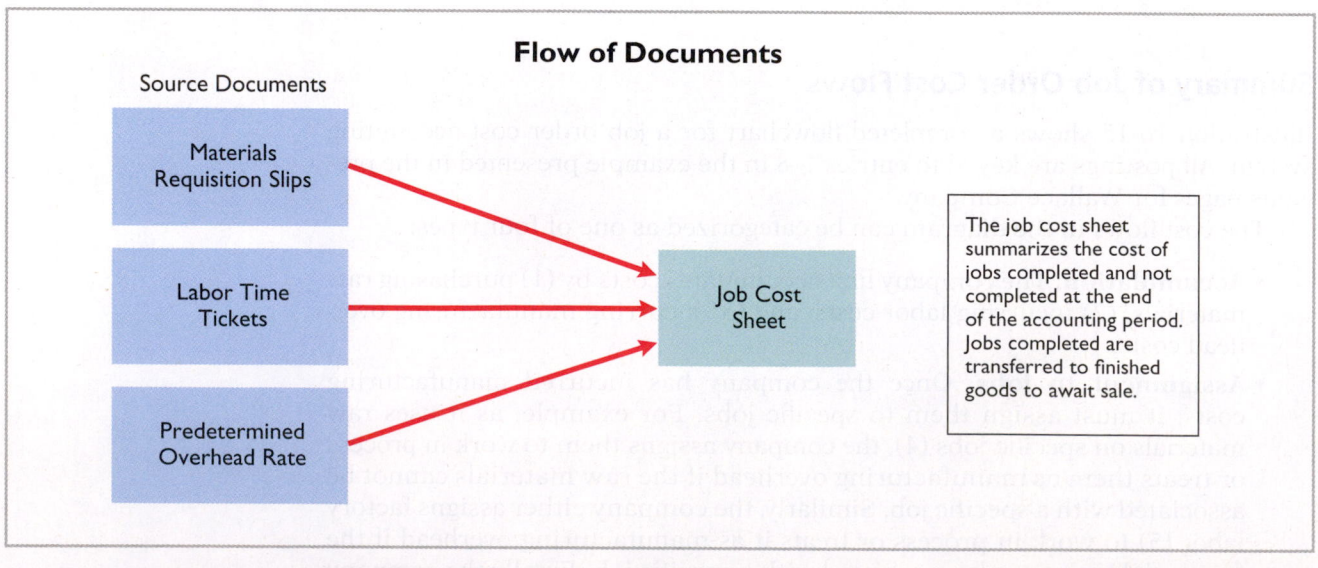

Job Order Costing for Service Companies

Our extended job order costing example focuses on a manufacturer so that you see the flow of costs through the inventory accounts. It is important to understand, however, that job order costing is also commonly used by service companies. While service companies do not have inventory, the techniques of job order costing are still quite useful in many service-industry environments. Consider, for example, the **Mayo Clinic** (healthcare), **PriceWaterhouseCoopers** (accounting), and **Goldman Sachs** (investment banking). These companies need to keep track of the cost of jobs performed for specific customers to evaluate the profitability of medical treatments, audits, or investment banking engagements.

Many service organizations bill their customers using cost-plus contracts (discussed more fully in Chapter 22). Cost-plus contracts mean that the customer's bill is the sum of the costs incurred on the job, plus a profit amount that is calculated as a percentage of the costs incurred. In order to minimize conflict with customers and reduce potential contract disputes, service companies that use cost-plus contracts must maintain accurate and up-to-date costing records. Up-to-date cost records enable a service company to immediately notify a customer of cost overruns due to customer requests for changes to the original plan or unexpected complications. Timely recordkeeping allows the contractor and customer to consider alternatives before it is too late.

A service company that uses a job order cost system does not have inventory accounts. It does, however, use an account similar to Work in Process Inventory, referred to here as Service Contracts in Process, to record job costs prior to completion. To illustrate the journal entries for a service company under a job order cost system, consider the following transactions for Dorm Decor, an interior design company. The entry to record the assignment of $9,000 of supplies to projects ($7,000 direct and $2,000 indirect) is:

Service Contracts in Process	7,000	
Operating Overhead	2,000	
Supplies		9,000
(To assign supplies to projects)		

The entry to record the assignment of service salaries and wages of $100,000 ($84,000 direct and $16,000 indirect) is:

Service Contracts in Process	84,000	
Operating Overhead	16,000	
Service Salaries and Wages		100,000
(To assign personnel costs to projects)		

Dorm Decor applies operating overhead at a rate of 50% of direct labor costs. The entry to record the application of overhead ($84,000 × 50%) based on the direct labor costs is:

Service Contracts in Process	42,000	
Operating Overhead		42,000
(To assign operating overhead to projects)		

Upon completion of a design project (for State University) the job cost sheet shows a total cost of $34,000. The entry to record completion of this project is:

Cost of Completed Service Contracts	34,000	
Service Contracts in Process		34,000
(To record completion of State University project)		

Job cost sheets for a service company keep track of materials, labor, and overhead used on a particular job similar to a manufacturer. Several exercises at the end of this chapter apply job order costing to service companies.

© Christian Lagereek/iStockphoto

Sales Are Nice, but Service Revenue Pays the Bills

Jet engines are one of the many products made by the industrial operations division of General Electric (GE). At prices as high as $30 million per engine, you can bet that GE does its best to keep track of costs. It might surprise you that GE doesn't make much profit on the sale of each engine. So why does it bother making them? For the service revenue. During one recent year, about 75% of the division's revenues came from servicing its own products. One estimate is that the $13 billion in aircraft engines sold during a recent three-year period will generate about $90 billion in service revenue over the 30-year life of the engines. Because of the high product costs, both the engines themselves and the subsequent service are most likely accounted for using job order costing. Accurate service cost records are important because GE needs to generate high profit margins on its service jobs to make up for the low margins on the original sale. It also needs good cost records for its service jobs in order to control its costs. Otherwise, a competitor, such as Pratt and Whitney, might submit lower bids for service contracts and take lucrative service jobs away from GE.

Source: Paul Glader, "GE's Focus on Services Faces Test," *Wall Street Journal Online* (March 3, 2009).

Explain why GE would use job order costing to keep track of the cost of repairing a malfunctioning engine for a major airline. (Go to **WileyPLUS** for this answer and additional questions.)

Advantages and Disadvantages of Job Order Costing

Job order costing is more precise in the assignment of costs to projects than process costing. For example, assume that a construction company, Juan Company, builds 10 custom homes a year at a total cost of $2,000,000. One way to determine the cost of the homes is to divide the total construction cost incurred during the year by the number of homes produced during the year. For Juan Company, an average cost of $200,000 ($2,000,000 ÷ 10) is computed. If the homes are nearly identical, then this approach is adequate for purposes of determining profit per home. But if the homes vary in terms of size, style, and material types, using the average cost of $200,000 to determine profit per home is inappropriate. Instead, Juan Company should use a job order cost system to determine the specific cost incurred to build each home and the amount of profit made on each. Thus, job order costing provides more useful information for determining the profitability of particular projects and for estimating costs when preparing bids on future jobs.

However, job order costing requires a significant amount of data entry. For Juan Company, it is much easier to simply keep track of total costs incurred during the year than it is to keep track of the costs incurred on each job (home built). Recording this information is time-consuming, and if the data is not entered accurately, then the product costs are incorrect. In recent years, technological advances, such as bar-coding devices for both labor costs and materials, have increased the accuracy and reduced the effort needed to record costs on specific jobs. These innovations expand the opportunities to apply job order costing in a wider variety of business settings, thus improving management's ability to control costs and make better informed decisions.

A common problem of all costing systems is how to allocate overhead to the finished product. Overhead often represents more than 50% of a product's cost, and this cost is often difficult to allocate meaningfully to the product. How, for example, is the salary of a project manager at Juan Company allocated to the various homes, which may differ in size, style, and cost of materials used? The accuracy of the job order cost system is largely dependent on the accuracy of the overhead allocation process. Even if the company does a good job of keeping track of the specific amounts of materials and labor used on each job, if the overhead costs are not allocated to individual jobs in a meaningful way, the product costing information is not useful. We address this issue in more detail in Chapter 18.

DO IT! 4   Completion and Sale of Jobs

During the current month, Onyx Corporation completed Job 109 and Job 112. Job 109 cost $19,000 and Job 112 cost $27,000. Job 112 was sold on account for $42,000. Journalize the entries for the completion of the two jobs and the sale of Job 112.

Solution

Finished Goods Inventory	46,000	
Work in Process Inventory		46,000
(To record completion of Job 109,		
costing $19,000 and Job 112,		
costing $27,000)		
Accounts Receivable	42,000	
Sales Revenue		42,000
(To record sale of Job 112)		
Cost of Goods Sold	27,000	
Finished Goods Inventory		27,000
(To record cost of goods sold for Job 112)		

Action Plan

✔ **Debit Finished Goods Inventory for the cost of completed jobs.**

✔ **Debit Cost of Goods Sold for the cost of jobs sold.**

Related exercise material: **BE16-9, BE16-10, E16-2, E16-3, E16-6, E16-7, E16-10, and DO IT! 16-4.**

LEARNING  5   Distinguish between under- and overapplied manufacturing overhead.
OBJECTIVE

At the end of a period, companies prepare financial statements that present aggregate data on all jobs manufactured and sold. The cost of goods manufactured schedule in job order costing is the same as in Chapter 15 with one exception: **The schedule shows manufacturing overhead applied, rather than actual overhead costs. The company adds this amount to direct materials and direct labor to determine total manufacturing costs.**

Companies prepare the cost of goods manufactured schedule directly from the Work in Process Inventory account. Illustration 16-17 (page 772) shows a condensed schedule for Wallace Company for January.

Helpful Hint
Companies usually prepare monthly financial statements for management use only.

Illustration 16-17
Cost of goods manufactured schedule

WALLACE COMPANY
Cost of Goods Manufactured Schedule
For the Month Ending January 31, 2017

Work in process, January 1		$ –0–
Direct materials used	$ 24,000	
Direct labor	28,000	
Manufacturing overhead applied	**22,400**	
Total manufacturing costs		74,400
Total cost of work in process		74,400
Less: Work in process, January 31		35,400
Cost of goods manufactured		$39,000

Note that the cost of goods manufactured ($39,000) agrees with the amount transferred from Work in Process Inventory to Finished Goods Inventory in journal entry No. 7 in Illustration 16-15 (page 768).

The income statement and balance sheet are the same as those illustrated in Chapter 15. For example, Illustration 16-18 shows the partial income statement for Wallace for the month of January.

Illustration 16-18
Partial income statement

WALLACE COMPANY
Income Statement (partial)
For the Month Ending January 31, 2017

Sales revenue		$50,000
Cost of goods sold		
Finished goods inventory, January 1	$ –0–	
Cost of goods manufactured (see Illustration 16-17)	**39,000**	
Cost of goods available for sale	39,000	
Less: Finished goods inventory, January 31	–0–	
Cost of goods sold		39,000
Gross profit		$11,000

Under- or Overapplied Manufacturing Overhead

Recall that overhead is applied based on an estimate of total annual overhead costs. This estimate will rarely be exactly equal to actual overhead incurred. Therefore, at the end of the year, after overhead has been applied to specific jobs, the Manufacturing Overhead account will likely have a remaining balance.

When Manufacturing Overhead has a **debit balance**, overhead is said to be underapplied. **Underapplied overhead** means that the overhead assigned to work in process is less than the overhead incurred. Conversely, when manufacturing overhead has a **credit balance**, overhead is overapplied. **Overapplied overhead** means that the overhead assigned to work in process is greater than the overhead incurred. Illustration 16-19 shows these concepts.

Illustration 16-19
Under- and overapplied overhead

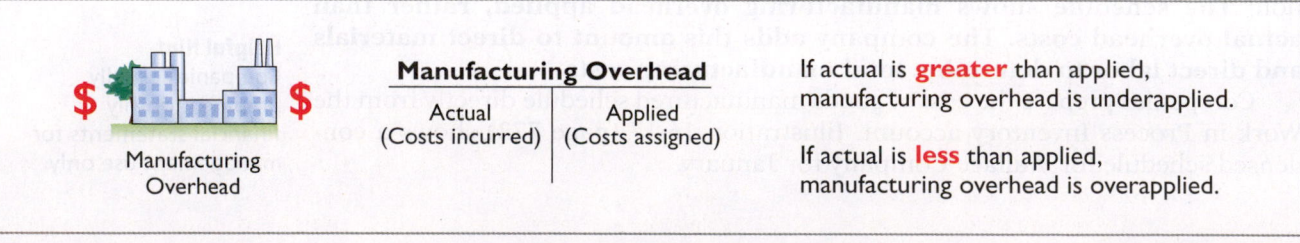

Manufacturing Overhead	
Actual (Costs incurred)	Applied (Costs assigned)

If actual is **greater** than applied, manufacturing overhead is underapplied.

If actual is **less** than applied, manufacturing overhead is overapplied.

YEAR-END BALANCE

At the end of the year, all manufacturing overhead transactions are complete. There is no further opportunity for offsetting events to occur. At this point, Wallace Company eliminates any balance in Manufacturing Overhead by an adjusting entry. It considers under- or overapplied overhead to be an **adjustment to cost of goods sold**. Thus, Wallace **debits underapplied overhead to Cost of Goods Sold. It credits overapplied overhead to Cost of Goods Sold**.

To illustrate, assume that Wallace has a $2,500 credit balance in Manufacturing Overhead at December 31. The adjusting entry for the overapplied overhead is:

Dec. 31	Manufacturing Overhead	2,500	
	Cost of Goods Sold		2,500
	(To transfer overapplied overhead to cost of goods sold)		

After Wallace posts this entry, Manufacturing Overhead has a zero balance. In preparing an income statement for the year, Wallace reports cost of goods sold **after adjusting it** for either under- or overapplied overhead.

Conceptually, some argue that under- or overapplied overhead at the end of the year should be allocated among ending work in process, finished goods, and cost of goods sold. The discussion of this possible allocation approach is left to more advanced courses.

DO IT! 5 | Applied Manufacturing Overhead

For Karr Company, the predetermined overhead rate is 140% of direct labor cost. During the month, Karr incurred $90,000 of factory labor costs, of which $80,000 is direct labor and $10,000 is indirect labor. Actual overhead incurred was $119,000.

Compute the amount of manufacturing overhead applied during the month. Determine the amount of under- or overapplied manufacturing overhead.

Solution

Manufacturing overhead applied = (140% × $80,000) = $112,000
Underapplied manufacturing overhead = ($119,000 − $112,000) = $7,000

Related exercise material: **BE16-10, E16-4, E16-5, E16-12, E16-13, and DO IT! 16-5.**

Action Plan

✔ Calculate the amount of overhead applied by multiplying the predetermined overhead rate by actual activity.

✔ If actual manufacturing overhead is greater than applied, manufacturing overhead is underapplied.

✔ If actual manufacturing overhead is less than applied, manufacturing overhead is overapplied.

REVIEW AND PRACTICE

LEARNING OBJECTIVES REVIEW

1 Describe cost systems and the flow of costs in a job order system. Cost accounting involves the procedures for measuring, recording, and reporting product costs. From the data accumulated, companies determine the total cost and the unit cost of each product. The two basic types of cost accounting systems are process cost and job order cost.

In job order costing, companies first accumulate manufacturing costs in three accounts: Raw Materials Inventory, Factory Labor, and Manufacturing Overhead. They then assign the accumulated costs to Work in Process Inventory and eventually to Finished Goods Inventory and Cost of Goods Sold.

2 Use a job cost sheet to assign costs to work in process. A job cost sheet is a form used to record the costs chargeable to a specific job and to determine the total and unit costs of the completed job. Job cost sheets constitute the subsidiary ledger for the Work in Process Inventory control account.

❸ Demonstrate how to determine and use the predetermined overhead rate. The predetermined overhead rate is based on the relationship between estimated annual overhead costs and expected annual operating activity. This is expressed in terms of a common activity base, such as direct labor cost. Companies use this rate to assign overhead costs to work in process and to specific jobs.

❹ Prepare entries for manufacturing and service jobs completed and sold. When jobs are completed, companies debit the cost to Finished Goods Inventory and credit it to Work in Process Inventory. When a job is sold, the entries are (a) debit Cash or Accounts Receivable and credit Sales Revenue for the selling price, and (b) debit Cost of Goods Sold and credit Finished Goods Inventory for the cost of the goods.

❺ Distinguish between under- and overapplied manufacturing overhead. Underapplied manufacturing overhead indicates that the overhead assigned to work in process is less than the overhead incurred. Overapplied overhead indicates that the overhead assigned to work in process is greater than the overhead incurred.

GLOSSARY REVIEW

Cost accounting An area of accounting that involves measuring, recording, and reporting product costs. (p. 754).

Cost accounting system Manufacturing-cost accounts that are fully integrated into the general ledger of a company. (p. 754).

Job cost sheet A form used to record the costs chargeable to a specific job and to determine the total and unit costs of the completed job. (p. 758).

Job order cost system A cost accounting system in which costs are assigned to each job or batch. (p. 754).

Materials requisition slip A document authorizing the issuance of raw materials from the storeroom to production. (p. 759).

Overapplied overhead A situation in which overhead assigned to work in process is greater than the overhead incurred. (p. 772).

Predetermined overhead rate A rate based on the relationship between estimated annual overhead costs and expected annual operating activity, expressed in terms of a common activity base. (p. 763).

Process cost system A cost accounting system used when a company manufactures a large volume of similar products. (p. 754).

Time ticket A document that indicates the employee, the hours worked, the account and job to be charged, and the total labor cost. (p. 761).

Underapplied overhead A situation in which overhead assigned to work in process is less than the overhead incurred. (p. 772).

PRACTICE MULTIPLE-CHOICE QUESTIONS

(LO 1) **1.** Cost accounting involves the measuring, recording, and reporting of:
  (a) product costs.
  (b) future costs.
  (c) manufacturing processes.
  (d) managerial accounting decisions.

(LO 1) **2.** A company is more likely to use a job order cost system if:
  (a) it manufactures a large volume of similar products.
  (b) its production is continuous.
  (c) it manufactures products with unique characteristics.
  (d) it uses a periodic inventory system.

(LO 1) **3.** In accumulating raw materials costs, companies debit the cost of raw materials purchased in a perpetual system to:
  (a) Raw Materials Purchases.
  (b) Raw Materials Inventory.
  (c) Purchases.
  (d) Work in Process.

(LO 1) **4.** When incurred, factory labor costs are debited to:
  (a) Work in Process.

  (b) Factory Wages Expense.
  (c) Factory Labor.
  (d) Factory Wages Payable.

5. The flow of costs in job order costing: (LO 1)
  (a) begins with work in process inventory and ends with finished goods inventory.
  (b) begins as soon as a sale occurs.
  (c) parallels the physical flow of materials as they are converted into finished goods.
  (d) is necessary to prepare the cost of goods manufactured schedule.

6. Raw materials are assigned to a job when: (LO 2)
  (a) the job is sold.
  (b) the materials are purchased.
  (c) the materials are received from the vendor.
  (d) the materials are issued by the materials storeroom.

7. The source of information for assigning costs to job (LO 2) cost sheets are:
  (a) invoices, time tickets, and the predetermined overhead rate.
  (b) materials requisition slips, time tickets, and the actual overhead costs.

(c) materials requisition slips, payroll register, and the predetermined overhead rate.

(d) materials requisition slips, time tickets, and the predetermined overhead rate.

(LO 2) **8.** In recording the issuance of raw materials in a job order cost system, it would be **incorrect** to:
(a) debit Work in Process Inventory.
(b) debit Finished Goods Inventory.
(c) debit Manufacturing Overhead.
(d) credit Raw Materials Inventory.

(LO 2) **9.** The entry when direct factory labor is assigned to jobs is a debit to:
(a) Work in Process Inventory and a credit to Factory Labor.
(b) Manufacturing Overhead and a credit to Factory Labor.
(c) Factory Labor and a credit to Manufacturing Overhead.
(d) Factory Labor and a credit to Work in Process Inventory.

(LO 3) **10.** The formula for computing the predetermined manufacturing overhead rate is estimated annual overhead costs divided by an expected annual operating activity, expressed as:
(a) direct labor cost.
(b) direct labor hours.
(c) machine hours.
(d) Any of the above.

(LO 3) **11.** In Crawford Company, the predetermined overhead rate is 80% of direct labor cost. During the month, Crawford incurs $210,000 of factory labor costs, of which $180,000 is direct labor and $30,000 is indirect labor. Actual overhead incurred was $200,000. The amount of overhead debited to Work in Process Inventory should be:
(a) $200,000.
(b) $144,000.
(c) $168,000.
(d) $160,000.

(LO 4) **12.** Mynex Company completes Job No. 26 at a cost of $4,500 and later sells it for $7,000 cash. A **correct** entry is:
(a) debit Finished Goods Inventory $7,000 and credit Work in Process Inventory $7,000.
(b) debit Cost of Goods Sold $7,000 and credit Finished Goods Inventory $7,000.

(c) debit Finished Goods Inventory $4,500 and credit Work in Process Inventory $4,500.
(d) debit Accounts Receivable $7,000 and credit Sales Revenue $7,000.

(LO 5) **13.** At the end of an accounting period, a company using a job order cost system calculates the cost of goods manufactured:
(a) from the job cost sheet.
(b) from the Work in Process Inventory account.
(c) by adding direct materials used, direct labor incurred, and manufacturing overhead incurred.
(d) from the Cost of Goods Sold account.

(LO 4) **14.** Which of the following statements is **true**?
(a) Job order costing requires less data entry than process costing.
(b) Allocation of overhead is easier under job order costing than process costing.
(c) Job order costing provides more precise costing for custom jobs than process costing.
(d) The use of job order costing has declined because more companies have adopted automated accounting systems.

(LO 5) **15.** At end of the year, a company has a $1,200 debit balance in Manufacturing Overhead. The company:
(a) makes an adjusting entry by debiting Manufacturing Overhead Applied for $1,200 and crediting Manufacturing Overhead for $1,200.
(b) makes an adjusting entry by debiting Manufacturing Overhead Expense for $1,200 and crediting Manufacturing Overhead for $1,200.
(c) makes an adjusting entry by debiting Cost of Goods Sold for $1,200 and crediting Manufacturing Overhead for $1,200.
(d) makes no adjusting entry because differences between actual overhead and the amount applied are a normal part of job order costing and will average out over the next year.

(LO 5) **16.** Manufacturing overhead is underapplied if:
(a) actual overhead is less than applied.
(b) actual overhead is greater than applied.
(c) the predetermined rate equals the actual rate.
(d) actual overhead equals applied overhead.

Solutions

1. (a) Cost accounting involves the measuring, recording, and reporting of product costs, not (b) future costs, (c) manufacturing processes, or (d) managerial accounting decisions.

2. (c) A job costing system is more likely for products with unique characteristics. The other choices are incorrect because a process cost system is more likely for (a) large volumes of similar products or (b) if production is continuous. (d) is incorrect because the choice of a costing system is not dependent on whether a periodic or perpetual inventory system is used.

3. (b) In a perpetual system, purchases of raw materials are debited to Raw Materials Inventory, not (a) Raw Materials Purchases, (c) Purchases, or (d) Work in Process.

4. (c) When factory labor costs are incurred, they are debited to Factory Labor, not (a) Work in Process, (b) Factory Wages Expense, or (d) credited to Factory Labor (they are debited to Factory Labor and credited to Factory Wages Payable).

5. (c) Job order costing parallels the physical flow of materials as they are converted into finished goods. The other choices are incorrect because job order costing begins (a) with raw materials, not work in process, and ends with finished goods; and (b) as soon as raw materials are purchased, not when the sale occurs. (d) is incorrect because the cost of goods manufactured schedule is prepared from the Work in Process account and is only a portion of the costs in a job order system.

6. (d) Raw materials are assigned to a job when the materials are issued by the materials storeroom, not when (a) the job is sold, (b) the materials are purchased, or (c) the materials are received from the vendor.

7. (d) Materials requisition slips are used to assign direct materials, time tickets are used to assign direct labor, and the predetermined overhead rate is used to assign manufacturing overhead to job cost sheets. The other choices are incorrect because (a) materials requisition slips, not invoices, are used to assign direct materials; (b) the predetermined overhead rate, not the actual overhead costs, is used to assign manufacturing overhead; and (c) time tickets, not the payroll register, are used to assign direct labor.

8. (b) Finished Goods Inventory is debited when goods are transferred from work in process to finished goods, not when raw materials are issued for a job. Choices (a), (c), and (d) are true statements.

9. (a) When direct factory labor is assigned to jobs, the entry is a debit to Work in Process Inventory and a credit to Factory Labor. The other choices are incorrect because (b) Work in Process Inventory, not Manufacturing Overhead, is debited; (c) Work in Process Inventory, not Factory Labor, is debited and Factory Labor, not Manufacturing Overhead, is credited; and (d) Work in Process Inventory, not Factory Labor, is debited and Factory Labor, not Work in Process Inventory, is credited.

10. (d) Any of the activity measures mentioned can be used in computing the predetermined manufacturing overhead rate. Choices (a) direct labor cost, (b) direct labor hours), and (c) machine hours can all be used in computing the predetermined manufacturing overhead rate, but (d) is a better answer.

11. (b) Work in Process Inventory should be debited for $144,000 ($180,000 × 80%), the amount of manufacturing overhead applied, not (a) $200,000, (c) $168,000, or (d) $160,000.

12. (c) When a job costing $4,500 is completed, Finished Goods Inventory is debited and Work in Process Inventory is credited for $4,500. Choices (a) and (b) are incorrect because the amounts should be for the cost of the job ($4,500), not the sale amount ($7,000). Choice (d) is incorrect because the debit should be to Cash, not Accounts Receivable.

13. (b) At the end of an accounting period, a company using a job costing system prepares the cost of goods manufactured from the Work in Process Inventory account, not (a) the job cost sheet; (c) by adding direct materials used, direct labor incurred, and manufacturing overhead incurred; or (d) from the Cost of Goods Sold Account.

14. (c) Job order costing provides more precise costing for custom jobs than process costing. The other choices are incorrect because (a) job order costing often requires significant data entry, (b) overhead allocation is a problem for all costing systems, and (d) the use of job order costing has increased due to automated accounting systems.

15. (c) The company would make an adjusting entry for the underapplied overhead by debiting Cost of Goods Sold for $1,200 and crediting Manufacturing Overhead for $1,200, not by debiting (a) Manufacturing Overhead Applied for $1,200 or (b) Manufacturing Overhead Expense for $1,200. Choice (d) is incorrect because at the end of the year, a company makes an entry to eliminate any balance in Manufacturing Overhead.

16. (b) Manufacturing overhead is underapplied if actual overhead is greater than applied overhead. The other choices are incorrect because (a) if actual overhead is less than applied, then manufacturing overhead is overapplied; (c) if the predetermined rate equals the actual rate, the actual overhead costs incurred equal the overhead costs applied, neither over- nor underapplied; and (d) if the actual overhead equals the applied overhead, neither over- nor underapplied occurs.

PRACTICE EXERCISES

Analyze a job cost sheet and prepare entries for manufacturing costs.

(LO 1, 2, 3, 4)

1. A job order cost sheet for Michaels Company is shown below.

Job No. 92			For 2,000 Units
Date	Direct Materials	Direct Labor	Manufacturing Overhead
Beg. bal. Jan. 1	3,925	6,000	4,200
8	6,000		
12		8,500	6,375
25	2,000		
27		4,000	3,000
	11,925	18,500	13,575

Cost of completed job:	
Direct materials	$11,925
Direct labor	18,500
Manufacturing overhead	13,575
Total cost	$44,000
Unit cost ($44,000 ÷ 2,000)	$ 22.00

Instructions

(a) Answer the following questions.
  (1) What was the balance in Work in Process Inventory on January 1 if this was the only unfinished job?
  (2) If manufacturing overhead is applied on the basis of direct labor cost, what overhead rate was used in each year?
(b) Prepare summary entries at January 31 to record the current year's transactions pertaining to Job No. 92.

Solution

1. (a) 1. $14,125, or ($3,925 + $6,000 + $4,200).

    2. Last year 70%, or ($4,200 ÷ $6,000); this year 75% (either $6,375 ÷ $8,500 or $3,000 ÷ $4,000).

(b) Jan. 31	Work in Process Inventory	8,000	
	Raw Materials Inventory		8,000
	($6,000 + $2,000)		
31	Work in Process Inventory	12,500	
	Factory Labor		12,500
	($8,500 + $4,000)		
31	Work in Process Inventory	9,375	
	Manufacturing Overhead		9,375
	($6,375 + $3,000)		
31	Finished Goods Inventory	44,000	
	Work in Process Inventory		44,000

2. Kwik Kopy Company applies operating overhead to photocopying jobs on the basis of machine hours used. Overhead costs are expected to total $290,000 for the year, and machine usage is estimated at 125,000 hours.

Compute the overhead rate and under- or overapplied overhead.

(LO 3, 5)

For the year, $295,000 of overhead costs are incurred and 130,000 hours are used.

Instructions

(a) Compute the service overhead rate for the year.
(b) What is the amount of under- or overapplied overhead at December 31?
(c) Assuming the under- or overapplied overhead for the year is not allocated to inventory accounts, prepare the adjusting entry to assign the amount to cost of jobs finished.

Solution

2. (a) $2.32 per machine hour ($290,000 ÷ 125,000).

    (b) ($295,000) − ($2.32 × 130,000 machine hours)
       $295,000 − $301,600 = $6,600 overapplied

(c) Operating Overhead	6,600	
Cost of Goods Sold		6,600

▍PRACTICE PROBLEM

Cardella Company applies overhead on the basis of direct labor costs. The company estimates annual overhead costs will be $760,000 and annual direct labor costs will be $950,000. During February, Cardella works on two jobs: A16 and B17. Summary data concerning these jobs are as follows.

Compute predetermined overhead rate, apply overhead, and calculate under- or overapplied overhead.

(LO 3, 5)

Manufacturing Costs Incurred

Purchased $54,000 of raw materials on account.
Factory labor $76,000, plus $4,000 employer payroll taxes.
Manufacturing overhead exclusive of indirect materials and indirect labor $59,800.

Assignment of Costs

Direct materials: Job A16 $27,000, Job B17 $21,000
Indirect materials: $3,000
Direct labor: Job A16 $52,000, Job B17 $26,000
Indirect labor: $2,000

The company completed Job A16 and sold it on account for $150,000. Job B17 was only partially completed.

Instructions

(a) Compute the predetermined overhead rate.

(b) Journalize the February transactions in the sequence followed in the chapter.

(c) What was the amount of under- or overapplied manufacturing overhead?

Solution

(a) Estimated annual overhead costs	÷	Expected annual operating activity	=	Predetermined overhead rate
$760,000	÷	$950,000	=	80%

(b)

(1)

Feb. 28	Raw Materials Inventory	54,000	
	Accounts Payable		54,000
	(Purchase of raw materials on account)		

(2)

28	Factory Labor	80,000	
	Factory Wages Payable		76,000
	Employer Payroll Taxes Payable		4,000
	(To record factory labor costs)		

(3)

28	Manufacturing Overhead	59,800	
	Accounts Payable, Accumulated Depreciation, and Prepaid Insurance		59,800
	(To record overhead costs)		

(4)

28	Work in Process Inventory	48,000	
	Manufacturing Overhead	3,000	
	Raw Materials Inventory		51,000
	(To assign raw materials to production)		

(5)

28	Work in Process Inventory	78,000	
	Manufacturing Overhead	2,000	
	Factory Labor		80,000
	(To assign factory labor to production)		

(6)

28	Work in Process Inventory	62,400	
	Manufacturing Overhead		62,400
	(To assign overhead to jobs— 80% × $78,000)		

(7)

28	Finished Goods Inventory	120,600	
	Work in Process Inventory		120,600
	(To record completion of Job A16: direct materials $27,000, direct labor $52,000, and manufacturing overhead $41,600)		

	(8)		
28	Accounts Receivable	150,000	
	Sales Revenue		150,000
	(To record sale of Job A16)		
28	Cost of Goods Sold	120,600	
	Finished Goods Inventory		120,600
	(To record cost of sale for Job A16)		

(c) Manufacturing Overhead has a debit balance of $2,400 as shown below.

Manufacturing Overhead

(3)	59,800	(6)	62,400
(4)	3,000		
(5)	2,000		
Bal.	2,400		

Thus, manufacturing overhead is underapplied for the month.

WileyPLUS

Brief Exercises, Exercises, **DO IT!** Exercises, and Problems and many additional resources are available for practice in WileyPLUS

QUESTIONS

1. (a) Mary Barett is not sure about the difference between cost accounting and a cost accounting system. Explain the difference to Mary.
   (b) What is an important feature of a cost accounting system?
2. (a) Distinguish between the two types of cost accounting systems.
   (b) Can a company use both types of cost accounting systems?
3. What type of industry is likely to use a job order cost system? Give some examples.
4. What type of industry is likely to use a process cost system? Give some examples.
5. Your roommate asks your help in understanding the major steps in the flow of costs in a job order cost system. Identify the steps for your roommate.
6. There are three inventory control accounts in a job order system. Identify the control accounts and their subsidiary ledgers.
7. What source documents are used in accumulating direct labor costs?
8. "Entries to Manufacturing Overhead normally are only made daily." Do you agree? Explain.
9. Stan Kaiser is confused about the source documents used in assigning materials and labor costs.

Identify the documents and give the entry for each document.
10. What is the purpose of a job cost sheet?
11. Indicate the source documents that are used in charging costs to specific jobs.
12. Explain the purpose and use of a "materials requisition slip" as used in a job order cost system.
13. Sam Bowden believes actual manufacturing overhead should be charged to jobs. Do you agree? Why or why not?
14. What elements are involved in computing a predetermined overhead rate?
15. How can the agreement of Work in Process Inventory and job cost sheets be verified?
16. Jane Neff believes that the cost of goods manufactured schedule in job order cost accounting is the same as shown in Chapter 15. Is Jane correct? Explain.
17. Matt Litkee is confused about under- and overapplied manufacturing overhead. Define the terms for Matt, and indicate the balance in the manufacturing overhead account applicable to each term.
18. "At the end of the year, under- or overapplied overhead is closed to Income Summary." Is this correct? If not, indicate the customary treatment of this amount.

BRIEF EXERCISES

BE16-1 Dieker Company begins operations on January 1. Because all work is done to customer specifications, the company decides to use a job order cost system. Prepare a flowchart of a typical job order system with arrows showing the flow of costs. Identify the eight transactions.

Prepare a flowchart of a job order cost accounting system and identify transactions.

(LO 1)

Prepare entries in accumulating manufacturing costs.

(LO 1)

BE16-2 During January, its first month of operations, Dieker Company accumulated the following manufacturing costs: raw materials $4,000 on account, factory labor $6,000 of which $5,200 relates to factory wages payable and $800 relates to payroll taxes payable, and utilities payable $2,000. Prepare separate journal entries for each type of manufacturing cost.

Prepare entry for the assignment of raw materials costs.

(LO 2)

BE16-3 In January, Dieker Company requisitions raw materials for production as follows: Job 1 $900, Job 2 $1,200, Job 3 $700, and general factory use $600. Prepare a summary journal entry to record raw materials used.

Prepare entry for the assignment of factory labor costs.

(LO 2)

BE16-4 Factory labor data for Dieker Company is given in BE16-2. During January, time tickets show that the factory labor of $6,000 was used as follows: Job 1 $2,200, Job 2 $1,600, Job 3 $1,400, and general factory use $800. Prepare a summary journal entry to record factory labor used.

Prepare job cost sheets.

(LO 2)

BE16-5 Data pertaining to job cost sheets for Dieker Company are given in BE16-3 and BE16-4. Prepare the job cost sheets for each of the three jobs. (*Note:* You may omit the column for Manufacturing Overhead.)

Compute predetermined overhead rates.

(LO 3)

BE16-6 Marquis Company estimates that annual manufacturing overhead costs will be $900,000. Estimated annual operating activity bases are direct labor cost $500,000, direct labor hours 50,000, and machine hours 100,000. Compute the predetermined overhead rate for each activity base.

Assign manufacturing overhead to production.

(LO 3)

BE16-7 During the first quarter, Francum Company incurs the following direct labor costs: January $40,000, February $30,000, and March $50,000. For each month, prepare the entry to assign overhead to production using a predetermined rate of 70% of direct labor cost.

Prepare entries for completion and sale of completed jobs.

(LO 4)

BE16-8 In March, Stinson Company completes Jobs 10 and 11. Job 10 cost $20,000 and Job 11 $30,000. On March 31, Job 10 is sold to the customer for $35,000 in cash. Journalize the entries for the completion of the two jobs and the sale of Job 10.

Prepare entries for service salaries and wages and operating overhead.

(LO 4)

BE16-9 Ruiz Engineering Contractors incurred service salaries and wages of $36,000 ($28,000 direct and $8,000 indirect) on an engineering project. The company applies overhead at a rate of 25% of direct labor. Record the entries to assign service salaries and wages and to apply overhead.

Prepare adjusting entries for under- and overapplied overhead.

(LO 5)

BE16-10 At December 31, balances in Manufacturing Overhead are Shimeca Company—debit $1,200, Garcia Company—credit $900. Prepare the adjusting entry for each company at December 31, assuming the adjustment is made to cost of goods sold.

DO IT! Exercises

Prepare journal entries for manufacturing costs.

(LO 1)

DO IT! 16-1 During the current month, Wacholz Company incurs the following manufacturing costs.

(a) Purchased raw materials of $18,000 on account.
(b) Incurred factory labor of $40,000. Of that amount, $31,000 relates to wages payable and $9,000 relates to payroll taxes payable.
(c) Factory utilities of $3,100 are payable, prepaid factory property taxes of $2,700 have expired, and depreciation on the factory building is $9,500.

Prepare journal entries for each type of manufacturing cost. (Use a summary entry to record manufacturing overhead.)

DO IT! 16-2 Milner Company is working on two job orders. The job cost sheets show the following.

Assign costs to work in process.

(LO 2)

	Job 201	Job 202
Direct materials	$7,200	$9,000
Direct labor	4,000	8,000
Manufacturing overhead	5,200	9,800

Prepare the three summary entries to record the assignment of costs to Work in Process from the data on the job cost sheets.

DO IT! 16-3 Washburn Company produces earbuds. During the year, manufacturing overhead costs are expected to be $200,000. Expected machine usage is 2,500 hours. The company assigns overhead based on machine hours. Job No. 551 used 90 machine hours. Compute the predetermined overhead rate, determine the amount of overhead to allocate to Job No. 551, and prepare the entry to assign overhead to Job No. 551 on January 15.

Compute and apply the predetermined overhead rate.

(LO 3)

DO IT! 16-4 During the current month, Standard Corporation completed Job 310 and Job 312. Job 310 cost $70,000 and Job 312 cost $50,000. Job 312 was sold on account for $90,000. Journalize the entries for the completion of the two jobs and the sale of Job 312.

Prepare entries for completion and sale of jobs.

(LO 4)

DO IT! 16-5 For Eckstein Company, the predetermined overhead rate is 130% of direct labor cost. During the month, Eckstein incurred $100,000 of factory labor costs, of which $85,000 is direct labor and $15,000 is indirect labor. Actual overhead incurred was $115,000. Compute the amount of manufacturing overhead applied during the month. Determine the amount of under- or overapplied manufacturing overhead.

Apply manufacturing overhead and determine under- or overapplication.

(LO 5)

EXERCISES

E16-1 The gross earnings of the factory workers for Larkin Company during the month of January are $76,000. The employer's payroll taxes for the factory payroll are $8,000. The fringe benefits to be paid by the employer on this payroll are $6,000. Of the total accumulated cost of factory labor, 85% is related to direct labor and 15% is attributable to indirect labor.

Prepare entries for factory labor.

(LO 1, 2)

Instructions
(a) Prepare the entry to record the factory labor costs for the month of January.
(b) Prepare the entry to assign factory labor to production.

E16-2 Stine Company uses a job order cost system. On May 1, the company has a balance in Work in Process Inventory of $3,500 and two jobs in process: Job No. 429 $2,000, and Job No. 430 $1,500. During May, a summary of source documents reveals the following.

Prepare journal entries for manufacturing costs.

(LO 1, 2, 3, 4)

Job Number	Materials Requisition Slips		Labor Time Tickets	
429	$2,500		$1,900	
430	3,500		3,000	
431	4,400	$10,400	7,600	$12,500
General use		800		1,200
		$11,200		$13,700

Stine Company applies manufacturing overhead to jobs at an overhead rate of 60% of direct labor cost. Job No. 429 is completed during the month.

Instructions
(a) Prepare summary journal entries to record (1) the requisition slips, (2) the time tickets, (3) the assignment of manufacturing overhead to jobs, and (4) the completion of Job No. 429.
(b) Post the entries to Work in Process Inventory, and prove the agreement of the control account with the job cost sheets. (Use a T-account.)

Analyze a job cost sheet and prepare entries for manufacturing costs.

(LO 1, 2, 3, 4)

E16-3 A job order cost sheet for Ryan Company is shown below.

Job No. 92			For 2,000 Units
Date	Direct Materials	Direct Labor	Manufacturing Overhead
Beg. bal. Jan. 1	5,000	6,000	4,200
8	6,000		
12		8,000	6,400
25	2,000		
27		4,000	3,200
	13,000	18,000	13,800

Cost of completed job:	
Direct materials	$13,000
Direct labor	18,000
Manufacturing overhead	13,800
Total cost	$44,800
Unit cost ($44,800 ÷ 2,000)	$22.40

Instructions

(a) On the basis of the foregoing data, answer the following questions.
  (1) What was the balance in Work in Process Inventory on January 1 if this was the only unfinished job?
  (2) If manufacturing overhead is applied on the basis of direct labor cost, what overhead rate was used in each year?
(b) Prepare summary entries at January 31 to record the current year's transactions pertaining to Job No. 92.

Analyze costs of manufacturing and determine missing amounts.

(LO 1, 5)

E16-4 Manufacturing cost data for Orlando Company, which uses a job order cost system, are presented below.

	Case A	Case B	Case C
Direct materials used	$ (a)	$ 83,000	$ 63,150
Direct labor	50,000	140,000	(h)
Manufacturing overhead applied	42,500	(d)	(i)
Total manufacturing costs	145,650	(e)	213,000
Work in process 1/1/17	(b)	15,500	18,000
Total cost of work in process	201,500	(f)	(j)
Work in process 12/31/17	(c)	11,800	(k)
Cost of goods manufactured	192,300	(g)	222,000

Instructions

Indicate the missing amount for each letter. Assume that in all cases manufacturing overhead is applied on the basis of direct labor cost and the rate is the same.

Compute the manufacturing overhead rate and under- or overapplied overhead.

(LO 3, 5)

E16-5 Ikerd Company applies manufacturing overhead to jobs on the basis of machine hours used. Overhead costs are expected to total $300,000 for the year, and machine usage is estimated at 125,000 hours.

For the year, $322,000 of overhead costs are incurred and 130,000 hours are used.

Instructions

(a) Compute the manufacturing overhead rate for the year.
(b) What is the amount of under- or overapplied overhead at December 31?
(c) Prepare the adjusting entry to assign the under- or overapplied overhead for the year to cost of goods sold.

E16-6 A job cost sheet of Sandoval Company is given below.

Job Cost Sheet

JOB NO. 469   Quantity 2,500
ITEM White Lion Cages   Date Requested 7/2
FOR Todd Company   Date Completed 7/31

Date	Direct Materials	Direct Labor	Manufacturing Overhead
7/10	700		
12	900		
15		440	550
22		380	475
24	1,600		
27	1,500		
31		540	675

Cost of completed job:
   Direct materials   _____
   Direct labor   _____
    Manufacturing overhead   _____
Total cost   _____
Unit cost   _____

Instructions
(a) Answer the following questions.
   (1) What are the source documents for direct materials, direct labor, and manufacturing overhead costs assigned to this job?
   (2) What is the predetermined manufacturing overhead rate?
   (3) What are the total cost and the unit cost of the completed job? (Round unit cost to nearest cent.)
(b) Prepare the entry to record the completion of the job.

E16-7 Crawford Corporation incurred the following transactions.

1. Purchased raw materials on account $46,300.
2. Raw materials of $36,000 were requisitioned to the factory. An analysis of the materials requisition slips indicated that $6,800 was classified as indirect materials.
3. Factory labor costs incurred were $59,900, of which $51,000 pertained to factory wages payable and $8,900 pertained to employer payroll taxes payable.
4. Time tickets indicated that $54,000 was direct labor and $5,900 was indirect labor.
5. Manufacturing overhead costs incurred on account were $80,500.
6. Depreciation on the company's office building was $8,100.
7. Manufacturing overhead was applied at the rate of 150% of direct labor cost.
8. Goods costing $88,000 were completed and transferred to finished goods.
9. Finished goods costing $75,000 to manufacture were sold on account for $103,000.

Instructions
Journalize the transactions. (Omit explanations.)

E16-8 Enos Printing Corp. uses a job order cost system. The following data summarize the operations related to the first quarter's production.

1. Materials purchased on account $192,000, and factory wages incurred $87,300.

2. Materials requisitioned and factory labor used by job:

Job Number	Materials	Factory Labor
A20	$ 35,240	$18,000
A21	42,920	22,000
A22	36,100	15,000
A23	39,270	25,000
General factory use	4,470	7,300
	$158,000	$87,300

3. Manufacturing overhead costs incurred on account $49,500.
4. Depreciation on factory equipment $14,550.
5. Depreciation on the company's office building was $14,300.
6. Manufacturing overhead rate is 90% of direct labor cost.
7. Jobs completed during the quarter: A20, A21, and A23.

Instructions

Prepare entries to record the operations summarized above. (Prepare a schedule showing the individual cost elements and total cost for each job in item 7.)

Prepare a cost of goods manufactured schedule and partial financial statements.

(LO 1, 5)

E16-9 At May 31, 2017, the accounts of Lopez Company show the following.

1. May 1 inventories—finished goods $12,600, work in process $14,700, and raw materials $8,200.
2. May 31 inventories—finished goods $9,500, work in process $15,900, and raw materials $7,100.
3. Debit postings to work in process were direct materials $62,400, direct labor $50,000, and manufacturing overhead applied $40,000.
4. Sales revenue totaled $215,000.

Instructions

(a) Prepare a condensed cost of goods manufactured schedule.
(b) Prepare an income statement for May through gross profit.
(c) Indicate the balance sheet presentation of the manufacturing inventories at May 31, 2017.

Compute work in process and finished goods from job cost sheets.

(LO 2, 4)

E16-10 Tierney Company begins operations on April 1. Information from job cost sheets shows the following.

Job Number	Manufacturing Costs Assigned			Month Completed
	April	May	June	
10	$5,200	$4,400		May
11	4,100	3,900	$2,000	June
12	1,200			April
13		4,700	4,500	June
14		5,900	3,600	Not complete

Job 12 was completed in April. Job 10 was completed in May. Jobs 11 and 13 were completed in June. Each job was sold for 25% above its cost in the month following completion.

Instructions

(a) What is the balance in Work in Process Inventory at the end of each month?
(b) What is the balance in Finished Goods Inventory at the end of each month?
(c) What is the gross profit for May, June, and July?

E16-11 The following are the job cost related accounts for the law firm of Colaw Associates and their manufacturing equivalents:

Prepare entries for costs of services provided.
(LO 1, 3, 4)

Law Firm Accounts	Manufacturing Firm Accounts
Supplies	Raw Materials
Salaries and Wages Payable	Factory Wages Payable
Operating Overhead	Manufacturing Overhead
Service Contracts in Process	Work in Process
Cost of Completed Service Contracts	Cost of Goods Sold

Cost data for the month of March follow.

1. Purchased supplies on account $1,800.
2. Issued supplies $1,200 (60% direct and 40% indirect).
3. Assigned labor costs based on time cards for the month which indicated labor costs of $70,000 (80% direct and 20% indirect).
4. Operating overhead costs incurred for cash totaled $40,000.
5. Operating overhead is applied at a rate of 90% of direct labor cost.
6. Work completed totaled $75,000.

Instructions
(a) Journalize the transactions for March. (Omit explanations.)
(b) Determine the balance of the Service Contracts in Process account. (Use a T-account.)

E16-12 Don Lieberman and Associates, a CPA firm, uses job order costing to capture the costs of its audit jobs. There were no audit jobs in process at the beginning of November. Listed below are data concerning the three audit jobs conducted during November.

Determine cost of jobs and ending balance in work in process and overhead accounts.
(LO 2, 3, 4)

	Lynn	Brian	Mike
Direct materials	$600	$400	$200
Auditor labor costs	$5,400	$6,600	$3,375
Auditor hours	72	88	45

Overhead costs are applied to jobs on the basis of auditor hours, and the predetermined overhead rate is $50 per auditor hour. The Lynn job is the only incomplete job at the end of November. Actual overhead for the month was $11,000.

Instructions
(a) Determine the cost of each job.
(b) Indicate the balance of the Service Contracts in Process account at the end of November.
(c) Calculate the ending balance of the Operating Overhead account for November.

E16-13 Tombert Decorating uses a job order cost system to collect the costs of its interior decorating business. Each client's consultation is treated as a separate job. Overhead is applied to each job based on the number of decorator hours incurred. Listed below are data for the current year.

Determine predetermined overhead rate, apply overhead, and determine whether balance under- or overapplied.
(LO 3, 5)

Estimated overhead	$960,000
Actual overhead	$982,800
Estimated decorator hours	40,000
Actual decorator hours	40,500

The company uses Operating Overhead in place of Manufacturing Overhead.

Instructions
(a) Compute the predetermined overhead rate.
(b) Prepare the entry to apply the overhead for the year.
(c) Determine whether the overhead was under- or overapplied and by how much.

EXERCISES: SET B AND CHALLENGE EXERCISES

Visit the book's companion website, at **www.wiley.com/college/weygandt**, and choose the Student Companion site to access Exercises: Set B and Challenge Exercises.

PROBLEMS: SET A

Prepare entries in a job order cost system and job cost sheets.

(LO 1, 2, 3, 4, 5)

P16-1A Lott Company uses a job order cost system and applies overhead to production on the basis of direct labor costs. On January 1, 2017, Job 50 was the only job in process. The costs incurred prior to January 1 on this job were as follows: direct materials $20,000, direct labor $12,000, and manufacturing overhead $16,000. As of January 1, Job 49 had been completed at a cost of $90,000 and was part of finished goods inventory. There was a $15,000 balance in the Raw Materials Inventory account.

During the month of January, Lott Company began production on Jobs 51 and 52, and completed Jobs 50 and 51. Jobs 49 and 50 were also sold on account during the month for $122,000 and $158,000, respectively. The following additional events occurred during the month.

1. Purchased additional raw materials of $90,000 on account.
2. Incurred factory labor costs of $70,000. Of this amount $16,000 related to employer payroll taxes.
3. Incurred manufacturing overhead costs as follows: indirect materials $17,000, indirect labor $20,000, depreciation expense on equipment $12,000, and various other manufacturing overhead costs on account $16,000.
4. Assigned direct materials and direct labor to jobs as follows.

Job No.	Direct Materials	Direct Labor
50	$10,000	$ 5,000
51	39,000	25,000
52	30,000	20,000

Instructions

(a) Calculate the predetermined overhead rate for 2017, assuming Lott Company estimates total manufacturing overhead costs of $840,000, direct labor costs of $700,000, and direct labor hours of 20,000 for the year.

(b) Open job cost sheets for Jobs 50, 51, and 52. Enter the January 1 balances on the job cost sheet for Job 50.

(c) Prepare the journal entries to record the purchase of raw materials, the factory labor costs incurred, and the manufacturing overhead costs incurred during the month of January.

(d) Prepare the journal entries to record the assignment of direct materials, direct labor, and manufacturing overhead costs to production. In assigning manufacturing overhead costs, use the overhead rate calculated in (a). Post all costs to the job cost sheets as necessary.

(e) Job 50, $69,000
Job 51, $94,000

(e) Total the job cost sheets for any job(s) completed during the month. Prepare the journal entry (or entries) to record the completion of any job(s) during the month.

(f) Prepare the journal entry (or entries) to record the sale of any job(s) during the month.

(g) What is the balance in the Finished Goods Inventory account at the end of the month? What does this balance consist of?

(h) What is the amount of over- or underapplied overhead?

P16-2A For the year ended December 31, 2017, the job cost sheets of Cinta Company contained the following data.

Prepare entries in a job order cost system and partial income statement.

(LO 1, 2, 3, 4, 5)

Job Number	Explanation	Direct Materials	Direct Labor	Manufacturing Overhead	Total Costs
7640	Balance 1/1	$25,000	$24,000	$28,800	$ 77,800
	Current year's costs	30,000	36,000	43,200	109,200
7641	Balance 1/1	11,000	18,000	21,600	50,600
	Current year's costs	43,000	48,000	57,600	148,600
7642	Current year's costs	58,000	55,000	66,000	179,000

Other data:

1. Raw materials inventory totaled $15,000 on January 1. During the year, $140,000 of raw materials were purchased on account.
2. Finished goods on January 1 consisted of Job No. 7638 for $87,000 and Job No. 7639 for $92,000.
3. Job No. 7640 and Job No. 7641 were completed during the year.
4. Job Nos. 7638, 7639, and 7641 were sold on account for $530,000.
5. Manufacturing overhead incurred on account totaled $120,000.
6. Other manufacturing overhead consisted of indirect materials $14,000, indirect labor $18,000, and depreciation on factory machinery $8,000.

Instructions

(a) Prove the agreement of Work in Process Inventory with job cost sheets pertaining to unfinished work. (*Hint:* Use a single T-account for Work in Process Inventory.) Calculate each of the following, then post each to the T-account: (1) beginning balance, (2) direct materials, (3) direct labor, (4) manufacturing overhead, and (5) completed jobs.

(b) Prepare the adjusting entry for manufacturing overhead, assuming the balance is allocated entirely to Cost of Goods Sold.

(c) Determine the gross profit to be reported for 2017.

(a) $179,000; Job 7642: $179,000

(b) Amount = $6,800

(c) $158,600

P16-3A Case Inc. is a construction company specializing in custom patios. The patios are constructed of concrete, brick, fiberglass, and lumber, depending upon customer preference. On June 1, 2017, the general ledger for Case Inc. contains the following data.

Prepare entries in a job order cost system and cost of goods manufactured schedule.

(LO 1, 2, 3, 4, 5)

Raw Materials Inventory $4,200   Manufacturing Overhead Applied $32,640
Work in Process Inventory $5,540   Manufacturing Overhead Incurred $31,650

Subsidiary data for Work in Process Inventory on June 1 are as follows.

Job Cost Sheets

Customer Job

Cost Element	Rodgers	Stevens	Linton
Direct materials	$ 600	$ 800	$ 900
Direct labor	320	540	580
Manufacturing overhead	400	675	725
	$1,320	$2,015	$2,205

During June, raw materials purchased on account were $4,900, and all wages were paid. Additional overhead costs consisted of depreciation on equipment $900 and miscellaneous costs of $400 incurred on account.

A summary of materials requisition slips and time tickets for June shows the following.

Customer Job	Materials Requisition Slips	Time Tickets
Rodgers	$ 800	$ 850
Koss	2,000	800
Stevens	500	360
Linton	1,300	1,200
Rodgers	300	390
	4,900	3,600
General use	1,500	1,200
	$6,400	$4,800

Overhead was charged to jobs at the same rate of $1.25 per dollar of direct labor cost. The patios for customers Rodgers, Stevens, and Linton were completed during June and sold for a total of $18,900. Each customer paid in full.

Instructions

(a) Journalize the June transactions: (1) for purchase of raw materials, factory labor costs incurred, and manufacturing overhead costs incurred; (2) assignment of direct materials, labor, and overhead to production; and (3) completion of jobs and sale of goods.
(b) Post the entries to Work in Process Inventory.
(c) Reconcile the balance in Work in Process Inventory with the costs of unfinished jobs.
(d) Prepare a cost of goods manufactured schedule for June.

(d) Cost of goods manufactured $14,740

Compute predetermined overhead rates, apply overhead, and calculate under- or overapplied overhead.

(LO 3, 5)

P16-4A Agassi Company uses a job order cost system in each of its three manufacturing departments. Manufacturing overhead is applied to jobs on the basis of direct labor cost in Department D, direct labor hours in Department E, and machine hours in Department K.

In establishing the predetermined overhead rates for 2017, the following estimates were made for the year.

	Department		
	D	**E**	**K**
Manufacturing overhead	$1,200,000	$1,500,000	$900,000
Direct labor costs	$1,500,000	$1,250,000	$450,000
Direct labor hours	100,000	125,000	40,000
Machine hours	400,000	500,000	120,000

During January, the job cost sheets showed the following costs and production data.

	Department		
	D	**E**	**K**
Direct materials used	$140,000	$126,000	$78,000
Direct labor costs	$120,000	$110,000	$37,500
Manufacturing overhead incurred	$ 99,000	$124,000	$79,000
Direct labor hours	8,000	11,000	3,500
Machine hours	34,000	45,000	10,400

Instructions

(a) Compute the predetermined overhead rate for each department.
(b) Compute the total manufacturing costs assigned to jobs in January in each department.
(c) Compute the under- or overapplied overhead for each department at January 31.

(a) 80%, $12, $7.50

(b) $356,000, $368,000, $193,500

(c) $3,000, $(8,000), $1,000

P16-5A Phillips Corporation's fiscal year ends on November 30. The following accounts are found in its job order cost accounting system for the first month of the new fiscal year.

Analyze manufacturing accounts and determine missing amounts.

(LO 1, 2, 3, 4, 5)

Raw Materials Inventory

Dec.	1	Beginning balance	(a)	Dec. 31	Requisitions	16,850
	31	Purchases	17,225			
Dec.	31	Ending balance	7,975			

Work in Process Inventory

Dec.	1	Beginning balance	(b)	Dec. 31	Jobs completed	(f)
	31	Direct materials	(c)			
	31	Direct labor	8,400			
	31	Overhead	(d)			
Dec.	31	Ending balance	(e)			

Finished Goods Inventory

Dec.	1	Beginning balance	(g)	Dec. 31	Cost of goods sold	(i)
	31	Completed jobs	(h)			
Dec.	31	Ending balance	(j)			

Factory Labor

Dec.	31	Factory wages	12,025	Dec. 31	Wages assigned	(k)

Manufacturing Overhead

Dec.	31	Indirect materials	2,900	Dec. 31	Overhead applied	(m)
	31	Indirect labor	(l)			
	31	Other overhead	1,245			

Other data:

1. On December 1, two jobs were in process: Job No. 154 and Job No. 155. These jobs had combined direct materials costs of $9,750 and direct labor costs of $15,000. Overhead was applied at a rate that was 75% of direct labor cost.
2. During December, Job Nos. 156, 157, and 158 were started. On December 31, Job No. 158 was unfinished. This job had charges for direct materials $3,800 and direct labor $4,800, plus manufacturing overhead. All jobs, except for Job No. 158, were completed in December.
3. On December 1, Job No. 153 was in the finished goods warehouse. It had a total cost of $5,000. On December 31, Job No. 157 was the only job finished that was not sold. It had a cost of $4,000.
4. Manufacturing overhead was $1,470 underapplied in December.

Instructions

List the letters (a) through (m) and indicate the amount pertaining to each letter.

(c) $13,950
(f) $52,450
(i) $53,450

PROBLEMS: SET B AND SET C

Visit the book's companion website, at **www.wiley.com/college/weygandt**, and choose the Student Companion site to access Problems: Set B and Set C.

CONTINUING PROBLEMS

CURRENT DESIGNS

CD16 Huegel Hollow Resort has ordered 20 rotomolded kayaks from Current Designs. Each kayak will be formed in the rotomolded oven, cooled, and then the excess plastic trimmed away. Then, the hatches, seat, ropes, and bungees will be attached to the kayak.

Dave Thill, the kayak plant manager, knows that manufacturing each kayak requires 54 pounds of polyethylene powder and a finishing kit (rope, seat, hardware, etc.). The polyethylene powder used in these kayaks costs $1.50 per pound, and the finishing kits cost $170 each. Each kayak will use two kinds of labor: 2 hours of more-skilled type I labor from people who run the oven and trim the plastic, and 3 hours of less-skilled type II labor from people who attach the hatches and seat and other hardware. The type I employees are paid $15 per hour, and the type II employees are paid $12 per hour. For purposes of this problem, assume that overhead is allocated to all jobs at a rate of 150% of direct labor costs.

Instructions

Determine the total cost of the Huegel Hollow order and the cost of each individual kayak in the order. Identify costs as direct materials, direct labor, or manufacturing overhead.

WATERWAYS

(*Note:* This is a continuation of the Waterways problem from Chapter 15.)

WP16 Waterways has two major public-park projects to provide with comprehensive irrigation in one of its service locations this month. Job J57 and Job K52 involve 15 acres of landscaped terrain which will require special-order sprinkler heads to meet the specifications of the project. This problem asks you to help Waterways use a job order cost system to account for production of these parts.

Go to the book's companion website, at **www.wiley.com/college/weygandt**, to find the completion of this problem.

COMPREHENSIVE CASE

Greetings Inc., a nationally recognized retailer of greeting cards and small gift items, decides to employ Internet technology to expand its sales opportunities. For this case, you will employ traditional job order costing techniques and then evaluate the resulting product costs.

Go to the book's companion website, at **www.wiley.com/college/weygandt**, for complete case details and instructions.

BROADENING YOUR PERSPECTIVE

MANAGEMENT DECISION-MAKING

Decision-Making Across the Organization

BYP16-1 Khan Products Company uses a job order cost system. For a number of months, there has been an ongoing rift between the sales department and the production department concerning a special-order product, TC-1. TC-1 is a seasonal product that is manufactured in batches of 1,000 units. TC-1 is sold at cost plus a markup of 40% of cost.

The sales department is unhappy because fluctuating unit production costs significantly affect selling prices. Sales personnel complain that this has caused excessive customer complaints and the loss of considerable orders for TC-1.

The production department maintains that each job order must be fully costed on the basis of the costs incurred during the period in which the goods are produced. Production personnel maintain that the only real solution is for the sales department to increase sales in the slack periods.

Andrea Parley, president of the company, asks you as the company accountant to collect quarterly data for the past year on TC-1. From the cost accounting system, you accumulate the following production quantity and cost data.

Costs	Quarter			
	1	**2**	**3**	**4**
Direct materials	$100,000	$220,000	$ 80,000	$200,000
Direct labor	60,000	132,000	48,000	120,000
Manufacturing overhead	105,000	153,000	97,000	125,000
Total	$265,000	$505,000	$225,000	$445,000
Production in batches	5	11	4	10
Unit cost (per batch)	$ 53,000	$ 45,909	$ 56,250	$ 44,500

Instructions

With the class divided into groups, answer the following questions.

(a) What manufacturing cost element is responsible for the fluctuating unit costs? Why?
(b) What is your recommended solution to the problem of fluctuating unit cost?
(c) Restate the quarterly data on the basis of your recommended solution.

Managerial Analysis

BYP16-2 In the course of routine checking of all journal entries prior to preparing year-end reports, Betty Eller discovered several strange entries. She recalled that the president's son Joe had come in to help out during an especially busy time and that he had recorded some journal entries. She was relieved that there were only a few of his entries, and even more relieved that he had included rather lengthy explanations. The entries Joe made were:

(1)

Work in Process Inventory	25,000	
Cash		25,000

(This is for materials put into process. I don't find the record that we paid for these, so I'm crediting Cash because I know we'll have to pay for them sooner or later.)

(2)

Manufacturing Overhead	12,000	
Cash		12,000

(This is for bonuses paid to salespeople. I know they're part of overhead, and I can't find an account called "Non-Factory Overhead" or "Other Overhead" so I'm putting it in Manufacturing Overhead. I have the check stubs, so I know we paid these.)

(3)

Wages Expense	120,000	
Cash		120,000

(This is for the factory workers' wages. I have a note that employer payroll taxes are $18,000. I still think that's part of wages expense and that we'll have to pay it all in cash sooner or later, so I credited Cash for the wages and the taxes.)

(4)

Work in Process Inventory	3,000	
Raw Materials Inventory		3,000

(This is for the glue used in the factory. I know we used this to make the products, even though we didn't use very much on any one of the products. I got it out of inventory, so I credited an inventory account.)

Instructions

(a) How should Joe have recorded each of the four events?

(b) If an entry was not corrected, which financial statements (income statement or balance sheet) would be affected? What balances would be overstated or understated?

Real-World Focus

BYP16-3 The Institute of Management Accountants sponsors a certification for management accountants, allowing them to obtain the title of Certified Management Accountant.

Address: **www.imanet.org**, or go to **www.wiley.com/college/weygandt**

Steps

1. Go to the site shown above.
2. Choose **CMA Certification**, then **Become a CMA**, and then **How to Get Started**. Answer part (a) below.
3. Choose **CMA Resource Center** and then **Continuing Education for CMAs**. Answer part (b) below.

Instructions

(a) What is the experience qualification requirement?

(b) How many hours of continuing education are required, and what types of courses qualify?

CRITICAL THINKING

Communication Activity

BYP16-4 You are the management accountant for Williams Company. Your company does custom carpentry work and uses a job order cost system. Williams sends detailed job cost sheets to its customers, along with an invoice. The job cost sheets show the date materials were used, the dollar cost of materials, and the hours and cost of labor. A predetermined overhead application rate is used, and the total overhead applied is also listed.

Nancy Kopay is a customer who recently had custom cabinets installed. Along with her check in payment for the work done, she included a letter. She thanked the company for including the detailed cost information but questioned why overhead was estimated. She stated that she would be interested in knowing exactly what costs were included in overhead, and she thought that other customers would, too.

Instructions

Prepare a letter to Ms. Kopay (address: 123 Cedar Lane, Altoona, KS 66651) and tell her why you did not send her information on exact costs of overhead included in her job. Respond to her suggestion that you provide this information.

Ethics Case

BYP16-5 LRF Printing provides printing services to many different corporate clients. Although LRF bids most jobs, some jobs, particularly new ones, are negotiated on a "cost-plus" basis. Cost-plus means that the buyer is willing to pay the actual cost plus a return (profit) on these costs to LRF.

Alice Reiley, controller for LRF, has recently returned from a meeting where LRF's president stated that he wanted her to find a way to charge more costs to any project that was on a cost-plus basis. The president noted that the company needed more profits to meet its stated goals this period. By charging more costs to the cost-plus projects and therefore fewer costs to the jobs that were bid, the company should be able to increase its profit for the current year.

Alice knew why the president wanted to take this action. Rumors were that he was looking for a new position and if the company reported strong profits, the president's opportunities would be enhanced. Alice also recognized that she could probably increase the cost of certain jobs by changing the basis used to allocate manufacturing overhead.

Instructions

(a) Who are the stakeholders in this situation?

(b) What are the ethical issues in this situation?

(c) What would you do if you were Alice Reiley?

All About You

BYP16-6 Many of you will work for a small business. Some of you will even own your own business. In order to operate a small business, you will need a good understanding of managerial accounting, as well as many other skills. Much information is available to assist people who are interested in starting a new business. A great place to start is the website provided by the Small Business Administration, which is an agency of the federal government whose purpose is to support small businesses.

Instructions

Go to **www.sba.gov/smallbusinessplanner/index.html** and in the Small Business Planner, Plan Your Business link, review the material under "Get Ready." Answer the following questions.

(a) What are some of the characteristics required of a small business owner?

(b) What are the top 10 reasons given for business failure?

Considering Your Costs and Benefits

BYP16-7 After graduating, you might decide to start a small business. As discussed in this chapter, owners of any business need to know how to calculate the cost of their products. In fact, many small businesses fail because they don't accurately calculate their product costs, so they don't know if they are making a profit or losing money—until it's too late.

Suppose that you decide to start a landscape business. You use an old pickup truck that you've fully paid for. You store the truck and other equipment in your parents' barn, and you store trees and shrubs on their land. Your parents will not charge you for the use of these facilities for the first two years, but beginning in the third year they will charge a reasonable rent. Your mother helps you by answering phone calls and providing customers with information. She doesn't charge you for this service, but she plans on doing it for only your first two years in business. In pricing your services, should you include charges for the truck, the barn, the land, and your mother's services when calculating your product cost? The basic arguments for and against are as follows.

YES: If you don't include charges for these costs, your costs are understated and your profitability is overstated.

NO: At this point, you are not actually incurring costs related to these activities; therefore, you shouldn't record charges.

Instructions

Write a response indicating your position regarding this situation. Provide support for your view.

17 Process Costing

FEATURE STORY

The Little Guy Who Could

It isn't easy for a small company to get a foothold in the bottled beverage business. The giants, The Coca-Cola Company and PepsiCo Inc., vigilantly defend their turf, constantly watching for new trends and opportunities. It is nearly impossible to get shelf space in stores, and consumer tastes can change faster than a bottle of soda can lose its fizz. But Jones Soda Co., headquartered in Seattle, has overcome these and other obstacles to make a name for itself. Its corporate motto is, "Run with the little guy . . . create some change."

The company started as a Canadian distributor of other companies' beverages. Soon, it decided to make its own products under the corporate name Urban Juice and Soda Company. Eventually, its name changed to Jones Soda—the name of its most popular product. From the very start, Jones Soda was different. It sold soda from machines placed in tattoo parlors and piercing shops, and it sponsored a punk rock band as well as surfers and snowboarders. At one time, the company's product was the official drink at the Seattle Seahawks' stadium and was served on Alaskan Airlines.

Today, Jones Soda makes a wide variety of products: soda-flavored candy, energy drinks, and product-promoting gear

that includes t-shirts, sweatshirts, caps, shorts, and calendars. Its most profitable product is still its multi-flavored, pure cane soda with its creative labeling. If you've seen Jones Soda on a store shelf, then you know that it appears to have an infinite variety of labels. The bottle labels are actually created by customers and submitted on the company's website. (To see some of the best labels from the past, see the Gallery at *www.jonessoda.com*.) If you would like some soda with a custom label of your own, you can design and submit a label and order a 12-pack.

Because Jones Soda has a dizzying array of product variations, keeping track of costs is of vital importance. Recently, management developed a reorganization plan that involved cost-cutting from top to bottom and eliminating unprofitable products. No matter how good your products are, if you don't keep your costs under control, you are likely to fail. Jones Soda's managers need accurate cost information regarding each primary product and each variation to ensure profitability. So while its marketing approach differs dramatically from the giants, Jones Soda needs the same kind of cost information as the big guys.

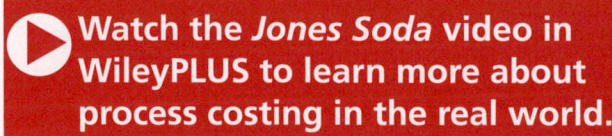

Watch the *Jones Soda* video in WileyPLUS to learn more about process costing in the real world.

Elaine Thompson/AP Photo

CHAPTER OUTLINE

Learning Objectives

1 Discuss the uses of a process cost system and how it compares to a job order system.

- Uses of process cost systems
- Process costing for service companies
- Comparing job order and process cost systems

DO IT! 1 Compare Job Order and Process Cost Systems

2 Explain the flow of costs in a process cost system and the journal entries to assign manufacturing costs.

- Process cost flow
- Assigning manufacturing costs

DO IT! 2 Manufacturing Costs in Process Costing

3 Compute equivalent units.

- Weighted-average method
- Refinements on the weighted-average method

DO IT! 3 Equivalent Units

4 Complete the four steps to prepare a production cost report.

- Physical unit flow
- Equivalent units of production
- Unit production costs
- Cost reconciliation schedule
- Production cost report

DO IT! 4 Cost Reconciliation Schedule

Go to the **REVIEW AND PRACTICE** section at the end of the chapter for a review of key concepts and practice applications with solutions.

Visit **WileyPLUS with ORION** for additional tutorials and practice opportunities.

Discuss the uses of a process cost system and how it compares to a job order system.

Uses of Process Cost Systems

Companies use **process cost systems** to apply costs to similar products that are mass-produced in a continuous fashion. **Jones Soda Co.** uses a process cost system: Production of the soda, once it begins, continues until the soda emerges. The processing is the same for the entire run—with precisely the same amount of materials, labor, and overhead. Each finished bottle of soda is indistinguishable from another.

A company such as **USX** uses process costing in the manufacturing of steel. **Kellogg** and **General Mills** use process costing for cereal production; **ExxonMobil** uses process costing for its oil refining. **Sherwin Williams** uses process costing for its paint products. At a bottling company like Jones Soda, the manufacturing process begins with the blending of ingredients. Next, automated machinery moves the bottles into position and fills them. The production process then caps, packages, and forwards the bottles to the finished goods warehouse. Illustration 17-1 shows this process.

Illustration 17-1
Manufacturing processes

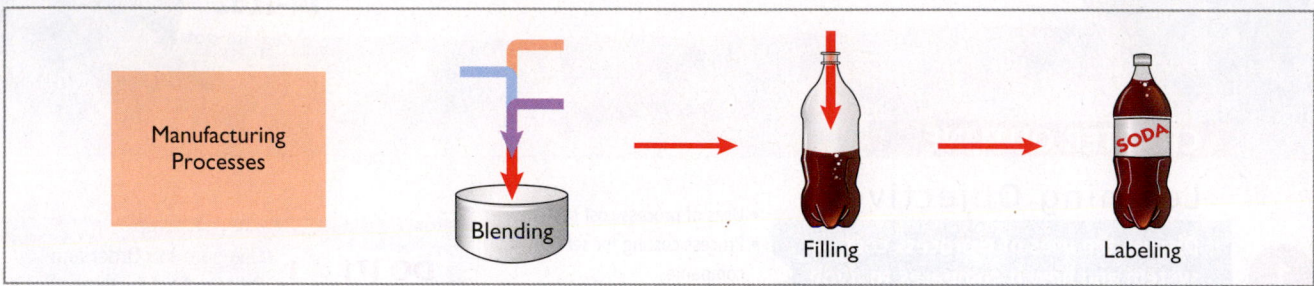

For Jones Soda, as well as the other companies just mentioned, once production begins, it continues until the finished product emerges. Each unit of finished product is like every other unit.

In comparison, a job order cost system assigns costs to a *specific job*. Examples are the construction of a customized home, the making of a movie, or the manufacturing of a specialized machine. Illustration 17-2 provides examples of companies that primarily use either a process cost system or a job order cost system.

Illustration 17-2
Process cost and job order cost companies and products

Process Cost System			Job Order Cost System		
Company	**Product**		**Company**	**Product**	
Jones Soda, PepsiCo	Soft drinks		Young & Rubicam, J. Walter Thompson	Advertising	
ExxonMobil, Royal Dutch Shell	Oil		Disney, Warner Brothers	Movies	
Intel, Advanced Micro Devices	Computer chips		Center Ice Consultants, Ice Pro	Ice rinks	
Dow Chemical, DuPont	Chemicals		Kaiser, Mayo Clinic	Patient health care	

Process Costing for Service Companies

When considering service companies, you might initially think of specific, non-routine tasks, such as rebuilding an automobile engine, consulting on a business acquisition, or defending a major lawsuit. However, many service companies perform repetitive, routine work. For example, Jiffy Lube regularly performs oil changes. H&R Block focuses on the routine aspects of basic tax practice. Service companies that perform individualized, nonroutine services will probably benefit from using a job order cost system. Those that perform routine, repetitive services will probably be better off with a process cost system.

Similarities and Differences Between Job Order Cost and Process Cost Systems

In a job order cost system, companies assign costs to each job. In a process cost system, companies track costs through a series of connected manufacturing processes or departments, rather than by individual jobs. Thus, companies use process cost systems when they produce a large volume of uniform or relatively homogeneous products. Illustration 17-3 shows the basic flow of costs in these two systems.

Illustration 17-3
Job order cost and process cost flow

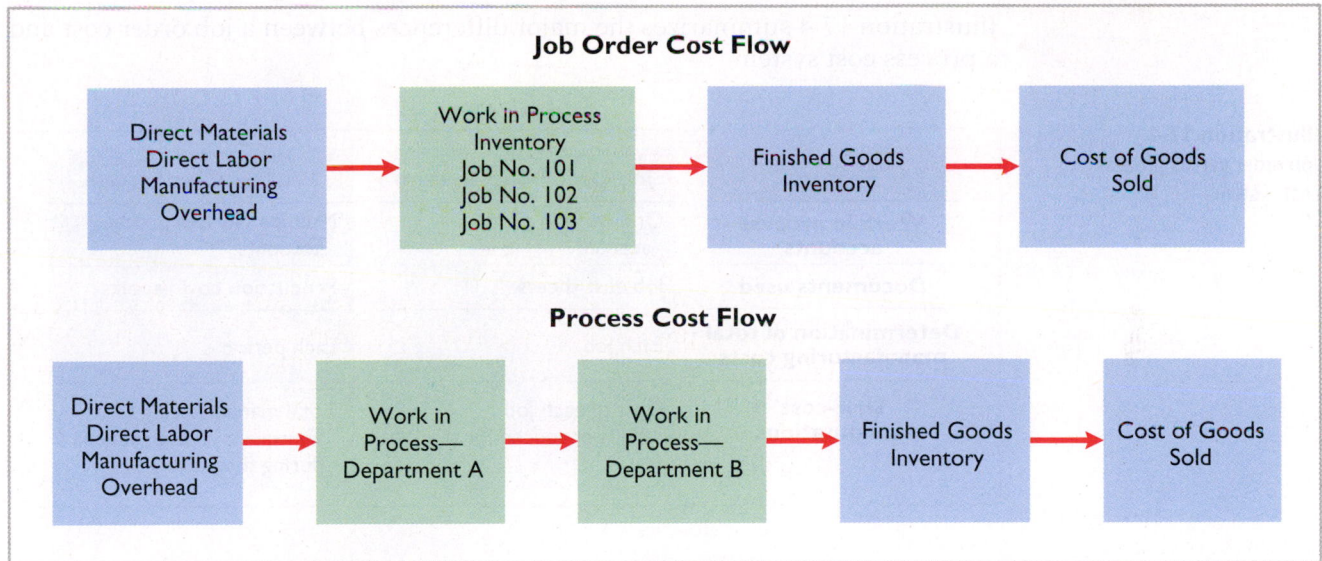

The following analysis highlights the basic similarities and differences between these two systems.

SIMILARITIES

Job order cost and process cost systems are similar in three ways:

1. **The manufacturing cost elements.** Both costing systems track three manufacturing cost elements—direct materials, direct labor, and manufacturing overhead.
2. **The accumulation of the costs of materials, labor, and overhead.** Both costing systems debit raw materials to Raw Materials Inventory, factory labor to Factory Labor, and manufacturing overhead costs to Manufacturing Overhead.

3. **The flow of costs.** As noted above, both systems accumulate all manufacturing costs by debits to Raw Materials Inventory, Factory Labor, and Manufacturing Overhead. Both systems then assign these costs to the same accounts—Work in Process, Finished Goods Inventory, and Cost of Goods Sold. **The methods of assigning costs, however, differ significantly.** These differences are explained and illustrated later in the chapter.

DIFFERENCES

The differences between a job order cost and a process cost system are as follows.

1. **The number of work in process accounts used.** A job order cost system uses only one work in process account. A process cost system uses multiple work in process accounts.

2. **Documents used to track costs.** A job order cost system charges costs to individual jobs and summarizes them in a job cost sheet. A process cost system summarizes costs in a production cost report for each department.

3. **The point at which costs are totaled.** A job order cost system totals costs when the job is completed. A process cost system totals costs at the end of a period of time.

4. **Unit cost computations.** In a job order cost system, the unit cost is the total cost per job divided by the units produced. In a process cost system, the unit cost is total manufacturing costs for the period divided by the equivalent units produced during the period.

Illustration 17-4 summarizes the major differences between a job order cost and a process cost system.

Illustration 17-4
Job order versus process cost systems

Feature	Job Order Cost System	Process Cost System
Work in process accounts	One work in process account	Multiple work in process accounts
Documents used	Job cost sheets	Production cost reports
Determination of total manufacturing costs	Each job	Each period
Unit-cost computations	Cost of each job ÷ Units produced for the job	Total manufacturing costs ÷ Equivalent units produced during the period

---

DO IT! 1 — Compare Job Order and Process Cost Systems

Indicate whether each of the following statements is true or false.

1. A law firm is likely to use process costing for major lawsuits.
2. A manufacturer of paintballs is likely to use process costing.
3. Both job order and process costing determine product costs at the end of a period of time, rather than when a product is completed.
4. Process costing does not keep track of manufacturing overhead.

Solution

1. False.   2. True.   3. False.   4. False.

Related exercise material: **E17-1 and 17-1.**

Action Plan
✔ Use job order costing in situations where unit costs are high, unit volume is low, and products are unique.
✔ Use process costing when there is a large volume of relatively homogeneous products.

LEARNING OBJECTIVE 2 **Explain the flow of costs in a process cost system and the journal entries to assign manufacturing costs.**

Process Cost Flow

Illustration 17-5 shows the flow of costs in the process cost system for Tyler Company. Tyler manufactures roller blade and skateboard wheels that it sells to manufacturers and retail outlets. Manufacturing consists of two processes: machining and assembly. The Machining Department shapes, hones, and drills the raw materials. The Assembly Department assembles and packages the parts.

Illustration 17-5
Flow of costs in process cost system

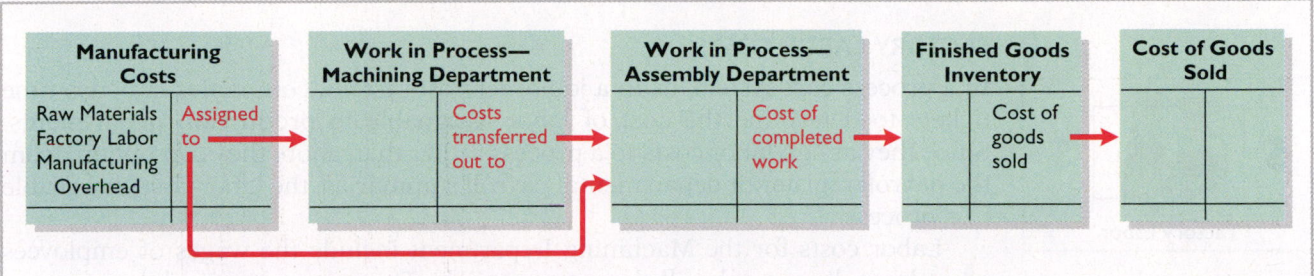

As the flow of costs indicates, the company can add materials, labor, and manufacturing overhead in both the Machining and Assembly Departments. When it finishes its work, the Machining Department transfers the partially completed units to the Assembly Department. The Assembly Department finishes the goods and then transfers them to the finished goods inventory. Upon sale, Tyler removes the goods from the finished goods inventory. Within each department, a similar set of activities is performed on each unit processed.

Assigning Manufacturing Costs—Journal Entries

As indicated, the accumulation of the costs of materials, labor, and manufacturing overhead is the same in a process cost system as in a job order cost system. That is, both systems follow these procedures:

- Companies debit all raw materials to Raw Materials Inventory at the time of purchase.
- They debit all factory labor to Factory Labor as the labor costs are incurred.
- They debit overhead costs to Manufacturing Overhead as these costs are incurred.

However, the assignment of the three manufacturing cost elements to Work in Process in a process cost system is different from a job order cost system. Here we'll look at how companies assign these manufacturing cost elements in a process cost system.

MATERIALS COSTS

All raw materials issued for production are a materials cost to the producing department. A process cost system may use materials requisition slips, but **it generally requires fewer requisitions than in a job order cost system. The materials are used for processes rather than for specific jobs** and therefore typically are for larger quantities.

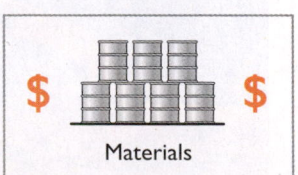

Materials

At the beginning of the first process, a company usually adds most of the materials needed for production. However, other materials may be added at various points. For example, in the manufacture of **Hershey** candy bars, the chocolate and other ingredients are added at the beginning of the first process, and the wrappers and cartons are added at the end of the packaging process. Tyler Company adds materials at the beginning of each process. Tyler makes the following entry to record the materials used.

Work in Process—Machining	XXXX	
Work in Process—Assembly	XXXX	
Raw Materials Inventory		XXXX
(To record materials used)		

Ice cream maker **Ben & Jerry's** adds materials in three departments: milk and flavoring in the mixing department, extras such as cherries and dark chocolate in the prepping department, and cardboard containers in the pinting (packaging) department.

FACTORY LABOR COSTS

Factory Labor

In a process cost system, as in a job order cost system, companies may use time tickets to determine the cost of labor assignable to production departments. Since they assign labor costs to a process rather than a job, they can obtain, from the payroll register or departmental payroll summaries, the labor cost chargeable to a process.

Labor costs for the Machining Department include the wages of employees who shape, hone, and drill the raw materials. The entry to assign labor costs to machining and assembly for Tyler Company is:

Work in Process—Machining	XXXX	
Work in Process—Assembly	XXXX	
Factory Labor		XXXX
(To assign factory labor to production)		

MANUFACTURING OVERHEAD COSTS

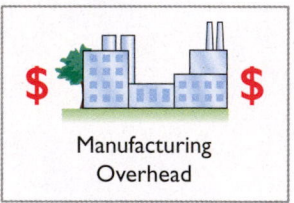

Manufacturing Overhead

The objective in assigning overhead in a process cost system is to allocate the overhead costs to the production departments on an objective and equitable basis. That basis is the activity that "drives" or causes the costs. A primary driver of overhead costs in continuous manufacturing operations is **machine time used**, not direct labor. Thus, companies **widely use machine hours** in allocating manufacturing overhead costs using predetermined overhead rates. Tyler Company's entry to allocate overhead to the two processes is:

Work in Process—Machining	XXXX	
Work in Process—Assembly	XXXX	
Manufacturing Overhead		XXXX
(To assign overhead to production)		

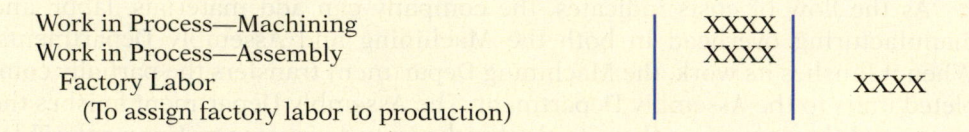

Management Insight · Caterpillar

Choosing a Cost Driver

© SweetyMommy/iStockphoto

In one of its automated cost centers, Caterpillar feeds work into the cost center, where robotic machines process it and transfer the finished job to the next cost center without human intervention. One person tends all of the machines and spends more time maintaining machines than operating them. In such cases, overhead rates based on direct labor hours may be misleading. Surprisingly, some companies continue to assign manufacturing overhead on the basis of direct labor despite the fact that there is no cause-and-effect relationship between labor and overhead.

*What is the result if a company uses the wrong "cost driver" to assign manufacturing overhead? (Go to **WileyPLUS** for this answer and additional questions.)*

TRANSFER TO NEXT DEPARTMENT

At the end of the month, Tyler Company needs an entry to record the cost of the goods transferred out of the Machining Department. In this case, the transfer is to the Assembly Department, and Tyler makes the following entry.

Work in Process—Assembly	XXXXX	
Work in Process—Machining		XXXXX
(To record transfer of units to the Assembly		
Department)		

TRANSFER TO FINISHED GOODS

When the Assembly Department completes the units, it transfers them to the finished goods warehouse. The entry for this transfer is as follows.

Finished Goods Inventory	XXXXX	
Work in Process—Assembly		XXXXX
(To record transfer of units to finished goods)		

TRANSFER TO COST OF GOODS SOLD

When Tyler Company sells the finished goods, it records the cost of goods sold as follows.

Cost of Goods Sold	XXXXX	
Finished Goods Inventory		XXXXX
(To record cost of units sold)		

DO IT! 2 Manufacturing Costs in Process Costing

Ruth Company manufactures ZEBO through two processes: blending and bottling. In June, raw materials used were Blending $18,000 and Bottling $4,000. Factory labor costs were Blending $12,000 and Bottling $5,000. Manufacturing overhead costs were Blending $6,000 and Bottling $2,500. The company transfers units completed at a cost of $19,000 in the Blending Department to the Bottling Department. The Bottling Department transfers units completed at a cost of $11,000 to Finished Goods. Journalize the assignment of these costs to the two processes and the transfer of units as appropriate.

Solution

The entries are:

Work in Process—Blending	18,000	
Work in Process—Bottling	4,000	
Raw Materials Inventory		22,000
(To record materials used)		
Work in Process—Blending	12,000	
Work in Process—Bottling	5,000	
Factory Labor		17,000
(To assign factory labor to production)		
Work in Process—Blending	6,000	
Work in Process—Bottling	2,500	
Manufacturing Overhead		8,500
(To assign overhead to production)		
Work in Process—Bottling	19,000	
Work in Process—Blending		19,000
(To record transfer of units to the Bottling		
Department)		
Finished Goods Inventory	11,000	
Work in Process—Bottling		11,000
(To record transfer of units to finished goods)		

Action Plan

✔ In process cost accounting, keep separate work in process accounts for each process.

✔ When the costs are assigned to production, debit the separate work in process accounts.

✔ Transfer cost of completed units to the next process or to Finished Goods.

Related exercise material: **BE17-1, BE17-2, BE17-3, E17-2, E17-4, and DO IT! 17-2.**

Compute equivalent units.

Suppose you have a work-study job in the office of your college's president, and she asks you to compute the cost of instruction per full-time equivalent student at your college. The college's vice president for finance provides the following information.

Illustration 17-6
Information for full-time student example

Costs:	
Total cost of instruction	$9,000,000
Student population:	
Full-time students	900
Part-time students	1,000

Part-time students take 60% of the classes of a full-time student during the year. To compute the number of full-time equivalent students per year, you would make the following computation.

Illustration 17-7
Full-time equivalent unit computation

Full-Time Students	+	Equivalent Units of Part-Time Students	=	Full-Time Equivalent Students
900	+	(1,000 × 60%)	=	1,500

The cost of instruction per full-time equivalent student is therefore the total cost of instruction ($9,000,000) divided by the number of full-time equivalent students (1,500), which is $6,000 ($9,000,000 ÷ 1,500).

A process cost system uses the same idea, called equivalent units of production. **Equivalent units of production** measure the work done during the period, expressed in fully completed units. Companies use this measure to determine the cost per unit of completed product.

Weighted-Average Method

The formula to compute equivalent units of production is as follows.

Illustration 17-8
Equivalent units of production formula

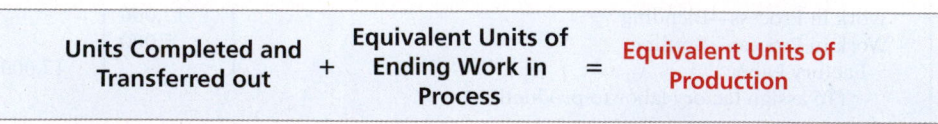

Units Completed and Transferred out	+	Equivalent Units of Ending Work in Process	=	Equivalent Units of Production

To better understand this concept of equivalent units, consider the following two separate examples.

Example 1. In a specific period, the entire output of Sullivan Company's Blending Department consists of ending work in process of 4,000 units which are 60% complete as to materials, labor, and overhead. The equivalent units of production for the Blending Department are therefore 2,400 units (4,000 × 60%).

Example 2. The output of Kori Company's Packaging Department during the period consists of 10,000 units completed and transferred out, and 5,000 units in ending work in process which are 70% completed. The equivalent units of production are therefore 13,500 [10,000 + (5,000 × 70%)].

This method of computing equivalent units is referred to as the **weighted-average method**. It considers the degree of completion (weighting) of the units completed and transferred out and the ending work in process.

Refinements on the Weighted-Average Method

Kellogg Company has produced Eggo® Waffles since 1970. Three departments produce these waffles: Mixing, Baking, and Freezing/Packaging. The Mixing Department combines dry ingredients, including flour, salt, and baking powder, with liquid ingredients, including eggs and vegetable oil, to make waffle batter. Illustration 17-9 provides information related to the Mixing Department at the end of June.

Illustration 17-9
Information for Mixing Department

MIXING DEPARTMENT			
		Percentage Complete	
	Physical Units	**Materials**	**Conversion Costs**
Work in process, June 1	100,000	100%	70%
Started into production	800,000		
Total units	900,000		
Units transferred out	700,000		
Work in process, June 30	200,000	100%	60%
Total units	900,000		

Helpful Hint
Separate unit cost computations are needed for materials and conversion costs whenever the two types of costs do not occur in the process at the same time.

Illustration 17-9 indicates that the beginning work in process is 100% complete as to materials cost and 70% complete as to conversion costs. **Conversion costs are the sum of labor costs and overhead costs.** In other words, Kellogg adds both the dry and liquid ingredients (materials) at the beginning of the waffle-making process, and the conversion costs (labor and overhead) related to the mixing of these ingredients are incurred uniformly and are 70% complete. The ending work in process is 100% complete as to materials cost and 60% complete as to conversion costs.

We then use the Mixing Department information to determine equivalent units. **In computing equivalent units, the beginning work in process is not part of the equivalent-units-of-production formula.** The units transferred out to the Baking Department are fully complete as to both materials and conversion costs. The ending work in process is fully complete as to materials, but only 60% complete as to conversion costs. We therefore need to make **two equivalent unit computations**: one for materials, and the other for conversion costs. Illustration 17-10 shows these computations.

ETHICS NOTE

An unethical manager might use incorrect completion percentages when determining equivalent units. This results in either raising or lowering costs. Since completion percentages are somewhat subjective, this form of income manipulation can be difficult to detect.

Illustration 17-10
Computation of equivalent units—Mixing Department

MIXING DEPARTMENT		
	Equivalent Units	
	Materials	**Conversion Costs**
Units transferred out	700,000	700,000
Work in process, June 30		
200,000 × 100%	200,000	
200,000 × 60%		120,000
Total equivalent units	900,000	820,000

We can refine the earlier formula used to compute equivalent units of production (Illustration 17-8, page 802) to show the computations for materials and for conversion costs, as follows.

Illustration 17-11
Refined equivalent units of production formula

Units Completed and Transferred Out— Materials	+	Equivalent Units of Ending Work in Process—Materials	=	**Equivalent Units of Production— Materials**
Units Completed and Transferred Out— Conversion Costs	+	Equivalent Units of Ending Work in Process—Conversion Costs	=	**Equivalent Units of Production— Conversion Costs**

People, Planet, and Profit Insight   General Electric

© Nicole Hofmann/iStockphoto

Haven't I Seen That Before?

For a variety of reasons, many companies, including General Electric, are making a big push to remanufacture goods that have been thrown away. Items getting a second chance include cell phones, computers, home appliances, car parts, vacuum cleaners, and medical equipment. Businesses have figured out that profit margins on remanufactured goods are significantly higher than on new goods. As commodity prices such as copper and steel increase, reusing parts makes more sense. Also, as more local governments initiate laws requiring that electronics

and appliances be recycled rather than thrown away, the cost of remanufacturing declines because the gathering of used goods becomes far more efficient. Besides benefitting the manufacturer, remanufacturing provides goods at a much lower price to consumers, reduces waste going to landfills, saves energy, reuses scarce resources, and reduces emissions. For example, it was estimated that a remanufactured car starter results in about 50% less carbon dioxide emissions than making a new one.

Source: James R. Hagerty and Paul Glader, "From Trash Heap to Store Shelf," *Wall Street Journal Online* (January 24, 2011).

In what ways might the relative composition (materials, labor, and overhead) of a remanufactured product's cost differ from that of a newly made product? (Go to **WileyPLUS** for this answer and additional questions.)

DO IT! 3   Equivalent Units

The Fabricating Department for Outdoor Essentials has the following production and cost data for the current month.

Beginning Work in Process	Units Transferred Out	Ending Work in Process
–0–	15,000	10,000

Materials are entered at the beginning of the process. The ending work in process units are 30% complete as to conversion costs. Compute the equivalent units of production for (a) materials and (b) conversion costs.

Action Plan

✔ To measure the work done during the period, expressed in fully completed units, compute equivalent units of production.

✔ Use the appropriate formula: Units completed and transferred out + Equivalent units of ending work in process = Equivalent units of production.

Solution

(a) Since materials are entered at the beginning of the process, the equivalent units of ending work in process are 10,000. Thus, 15,000 units + 10,000 units = 25,000 equivalent units of production for materials.

(b) Since ending work in process is only 30% complete as to conversion costs, the equivalent units of ending work in process are 3,000 (10,000 units × 30%). Thus, 15,000 units + 3,000 units = 18,000 equivalent units of production for conversion costs.

Related exercise material: **BE17-4, BE17-5, E17-5, E17-6, E17-8, E17-9, E17-10, E17-11, E17-13, E17-14, E17-15, and DO IT! 17-3.**

Complete the four steps to prepare a production cost report.

As mentioned earlier, companies prepare a production cost report for each department. A **production cost report** is the key document that management uses to understand the activities in a department; it shows the production quantity and cost data related to that department. For example, in producing Eggo® Waffles, **Kellogg Company** uses three production cost reports: Mixing, Baking, and Freezing/Packaging. Illustration 17-12 shows the flow of costs to make an Eggo® Waffle and the related production cost reports for each department.

Illustration 17-12
Flow of costs in making
Eggo® Waffles

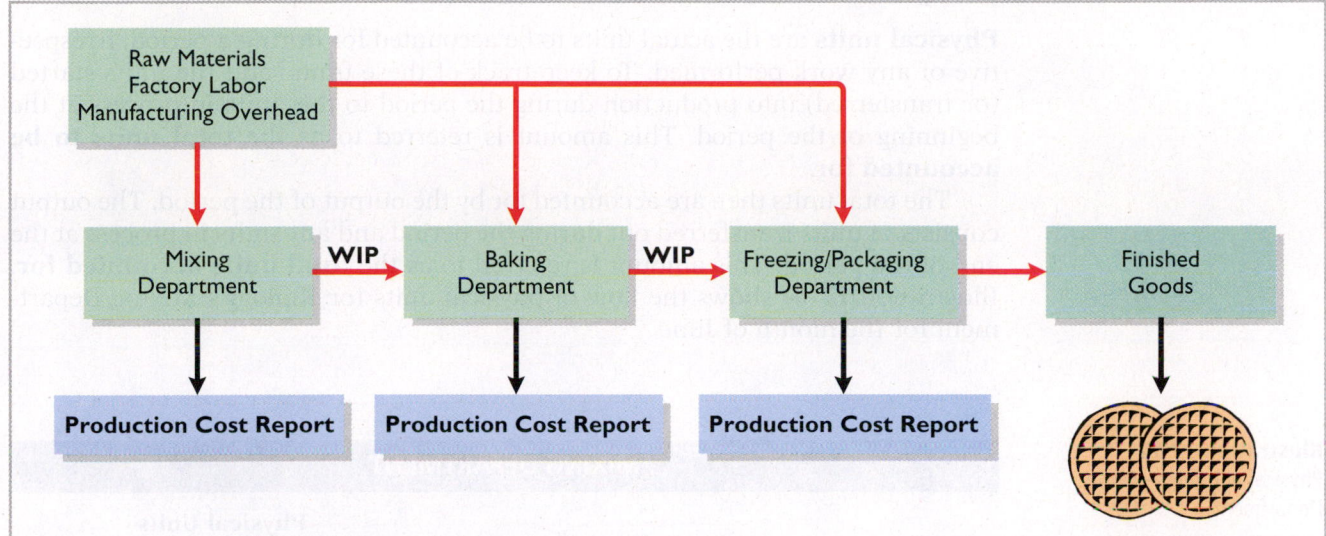

In order to complete a production cost report, the company must perform four steps, which as a whole make up the process cost system.

1. Compute the physical unit flow.
2. Compute the equivalent units of production.
3. Compute unit production costs.
4. Prepare a cost reconciliation schedule.

Illustration 17-13 shows assumed data for the Mixing Department at **Kellogg Company** for the month of June. We will use this information to complete a production cost report for the Mixing Department.

Illustration 17-13
Unit and cost data—Mixing
Department

MIXING DEPARTMENT	
Units	
Work in process, June 1	100,000
Direct materials: 100% complete	
Conversion costs: 70% complete	
Units started into production during June	800,000
Units completed and transferred out to Baking Department	700,000
Work in process, June 30	200,000
Direct materials: 100% complete	
Conversion costs: 60% complete	

Illustration 17-13
(cont'd.)

Costs	
Work in process, June 1	
Direct materials: 100% complete	$ 50,000
Conversion costs: 70% complete	35,000
Cost of work in process, June 1	$ 85,000
Costs incurred during production in June	
Direct materials	$400,000
Conversion costs	170,000
Costs incurred in June	$570,000

Compute the Physical Unit Flow (Step 1)

Physical units are the actual units to be accounted for during a period, irrespective of any work performed. To keep track of these units, add the units started (or transferred) into production during the period to the units in process at the beginning of the period. This amount is referred to as the **total units to be accounted for**.

The total units then are accounted for by the output of the period. The output consists of units transferred out during the period and any units in process at the end of the period. This amount is referred to as the **total units accounted for**. Illustration 17-14 shows the flow of physical units for Kellogg's Mixing Department for the month of June.

Illustration 17-14
Physical unit flow—Mixing Department

MIXING DEPARTMENT	
	Physical Units
Units to be accounted for	
Work in process, June 1	100,000
Started (transferred) into production	800,000
Total units	**900,000**
Units accounted for	
Completed and transferred out	700,000
Work in process, June 30	200,000
Total units	**900,000**

The records indicate that the Mixing Department must account for 900,000 units. Of this sum, 700,000 units were transferred to the Baking Department and 200,000 units were still in process.

Compute the Equivalent Units of Production (Step 2)

Helpful Hint
Materials are not always added at the beginning of the process. For example, materials are sometimes added uniformly during the process.

Once the physical flow of the units is established, Kellogg must measure the Mixing Department's productivity in terms of equivalent units of production. The Mixing Department adds materials at the beginning of the process, and it incurs conversion costs uniformly during the process. Thus, we need two computations of equivalent units: one for materials and one for conversion costs. The equivalent unit computation is as follows.

Illustration 17-15
Computation of equivalent units—Mixing Department

	Equivalent Units	
	Materials	**Conversion Costs**
Units transferred out	700,000	700,000
Work in process, June 30		
200,000 × 100%	200,000	
200,000 × 60%		120,000
Total equivalent units	**900,000**	**820,000**

Helpful Hint
Remember that we ignore the beginning work in process in this computation.

Compute Unit Production Costs (Step 3)

Armed with the knowledge of the equivalent units of production, we can now compute the unit production costs. **Unit production costs** are costs expressed in terms of equivalent units of production. When equivalent units of production are different for materials and conversion costs, we compute three unit costs: (1) materials, (2) conversion, and (3) total manufacturing.

The computation of total materials cost related to Eggo® Waffles is as follows.

Illustration 17-16
Total materials cost computation

Work in process, June 1	
Direct materials cost	$ 50,000
Costs added to production during June	
Direct materials cost	400,000
Total materials cost	**$450,000**

The computation of unit materials cost is as follows.

Illustration 17-17
Unit materials cost computation

Total Materials Cost	÷	Equivalent Units of Materials	=	Unit Materials Cost
$450,000	÷	900,000	=	$0.50

Illustration 17-18 shows the computation of total conversion costs.

Illustration 17-18
Total conversion costs computation

Work in process, June 1	
Conversion costs	$ 35,000
Costs added to production during June	
Conversion costs	170,000
Total conversion costs	**$205,000**

The computation of unit conversion cost is as follows.

Illustration 17-19
Unit conversion cost computation

Total Conversion Costs	÷	Equivalent Units of Conversion Costs	=	Unit Conversion Cost
$205,000	÷	820,000	=	$0.25

Total manufacturing cost per unit is therefore computed as shown in Illustration 17-20 (page 808).

Unit Materials Cost	+	Unit Conversion Cost	=	Total Manufacturing Cost per Unit
$0.50	+	$0.25	=	$0.75

Prepare a Cost Reconciliation Schedule (Step 4)

We are now ready to determine the cost of goods transferred out of the Mixing Department to the Baking Department and the costs in ending work in process. Kellogg charged total costs of $655,000 to the Mixing Department in June, calculated as follows.

Costs to be accounted for	
Work in process, June 1	$ 85,000
Started into production	570,000
Total costs	**$655,000**

The company then prepares a cost reconciliation schedule to assign these costs to (a) units transferred out to the Baking Department and (b) ending work in process.

MIXING DEPARTMENT
Cost Reconciliation Schedule

Costs accounted for		
Transferred out (700,000 × $0.75)		$ 525,000
Work in process, June 30		
Materials (200,000 × $0.50)	$100,000	
Conversion costs (120,000 × $0.25)	30,000	130,000
Total costs		**$655,000**

Kellogg uses the total manufacturing cost per unit, $0.75, in costing the **units completed** and transferred to the Baking Department. In contrast, the unit cost of materials and the unit cost of conversion are needed in costing **units in process**. The **cost reconciliation schedule** shows that the **total costs accounted for** (Illustration 17-22) equal the **total costs to be accounted for** (Illustration 17-21).

Preparing the Production Cost Report

At this point, Kellogg is ready to prepare the production cost report for the Mixing Department. As indicated earlier, this report is an internal document for management that shows production quantity and cost data for a production department. Illustration 17-23 shows the completed production cost report for the Mixing Department and identifies the four steps used in preparing it.

Production cost reports provide a basis for evaluating the productivity of a department. In addition, managers can use the cost data to assess whether unit costs and total costs are reasonable. By comparing the quantity and cost data with predetermined goals, top management can also judge whether current performance is meeting planned objectives.

Illustration 17-23
Production cost report

Mixing Department.xls

	A	B	C	D	E

MIXING DEPARTMENT
Production Cost Report
For the Month Ended June 30, 2017

		Physical Units	Materials	Conversion Costs	
4			Equivalent Units		
6	**Quantities**				
7	Units to be accounted for	Step 1	Step 2		
8	Work in process, June 1	100,000			
9	Started into production	800,000			
10	Total units	900,000			
11	Units accounted for				
12	Transferred out	700,000	700,000	700,000	
13	Work in process, June 30	200,000	200,000	120,000	(200,000 × 60%)
14	Total units	900,000	900,000	820,000	
15	**Costs**				

			Materials	Conversion Costs	Total
16	Unit costs Step 3				
17	Total cost	(a)	$450,000	$205,000	$655,000
18	Equivalent units	(b)	900,000	820,000	
19	Unit costs [(a) ÷ (b)]		$0.50	$0.25	$0.75
20	Costs to be accounted for				
21	Work in process, June 1				$ 85,000
22	Started into production				570,000
23	Total costs				$655,000
24	**Cost Reconciliation Schedule** Step 4				
25	Costs accounted for				
26	Transferred out (700,000 × $0.75)				$525,000
27	Work in process, June 30				
28	Materials (200,000 × $0.50)			$100,000	
29	Conversion costs (120,000 × $0.25)			30,000	130,000
30	Total costs				$655,000

Helpful Hint
The four steps in preparing a production cost report:
1. Compute the physical unit flow.
2. Compute the equivalent units of production.
3. Compute unit production costs.
4. Prepare a cost reconciliation schedule.

Costing Systems—Final Comments

Companies often use a combination of a process cost and a job order cost system. Called **operations costing**, this hybrid system is similar to process costing in its assumption that standardized methods are used to manufacture the product. At the same time, the product may have some customized, individual features that require the use of a job order cost system.

Consider, for example, **Ford Motor Company**. Each vehicle at a given plant goes through the same assembly line, but Ford uses different materials (such as seat coverings, paint, and tinted glass) for different vehicles. Similarly, **Kellogg's** Pop-Tarts® toaster pastries go through numerous standardized processes—mixing, filling, baking, frosting, and packaging. The pastry dough, though, comes in different flavors—plain, chocolate, and graham—and fillings include Smucker's® real fruit, chocolate fudge, vanilla creme, brown sugar cinnamon, and s'mores.

A cost-benefit trade-off occurs as a company decides which costing system to use. A job order cost system, for example, provides detailed information related to the cost of the product. Because each job has its own distinguishing characteristics, the system can provide an accurate cost per job. This information is useful in controlling costs and pricing products. However, the cost of implementing a job order cost system is often expensive because of the accounting costs involved.

On the other hand, for a company like Intel, is there a benefit in knowing whether the cost of the one-hundredth computer chip produced is different from the one-thousandth chip produced? Probably not. An average cost of the product will suffice for control and pricing purposes.

In summary, when deciding to use one of these systems or a combination system, a company must weigh the costs of implementing the system against the benefits from the additional information provided.

DO IT! 4 | Cost Reconciliation Schedule

In March, Rodayo Manufacturing had the following unit production costs: materials $6 and conversion costs $9. On March 1, it had no work in process. During March, Rodayo transferred out 12,000 units. As of March 31, 800 units that were 25% complete as to conversion costs and 100% complete as to materials were in ending work in process. Assign the costs to the units transferred out and in process.

Action Plan

✔ Assign the total manufacturing cost of $15 per unit to the 12,000 units transferred out.

✔ Assign the materials cost and conversion costs based on equivalent units of production to units in ending work in process.

Solution

The assignment of costs is as follows.

Costs accounted for		
Transferred out (12,000 × $15)		$180,000
Work in process, March 31		
Materials (800 × $6)	$4,800	
Conversion costs (200* × $9)	1,800	6,600
Total costs		$186,600
*800 × 25%		

Related exercise material: **BE17-6, BE17-7, BE17-8, BE17-9, E17-3, E17-5, E17-6, E17-7, E17-8, E17-9, E17-10, E17-11, E17-13, E17-14, E17-15, and** DO IT! **17-4.**

LEARNING
OBJECTIVE *5

APPENDIX 17A: Compute equivalent units using the FIFO method.

In this chapter, we demonstrated the weighted-average method of computing equivalent units. Some companies use a different method, referred to as the **first-in, first-out (FIFO) method**, to compute equivalent units. The purpose of this appendix is to illustrate how companies use the FIFO method to prepare a production cost report.

Equivalent Units Under FIFO

Under the FIFO method, companies compute equivalent units on a first-in, first-out basis. Some companies favor the FIFO method because the FIFO cost assumption usually corresponds to the actual physical flow of the goods. Under the FIFO method, companies therefore assume that the beginning work in process is completed before new work is started.

Using the FIFO method, equivalent units are the sum of the work performed to:

1. Finish the units of beginning work in process inventory.

2. Complete the units started into production during the period (referred to as the **units started and completed**).

3. Start, but only partially complete, the units in ending work in process inventory.

Normally, in a process cost system, some units will always be in process at both the beginning and end of the period.

ILLUSTRATION

Illustration 17A-1 shows the physical flow of units for the Assembly Department of Shutters Inc. In addition, it indicates the degree of completion of the work in process accounts in regard to conversion costs.

ASSEMBLY DEPARTMENT	
	Physical Units
Units to be accounted for	
Work in process, June 1 (40% complete)	500
Started (transferred) into production	8,000
Total units	**8,500**
Units accounted for	
Completed and transferred out	8,100
Work in process, June 30 (75% complete)	400
Total units	**8,500**

Illustration 17A-1
Physical unit flow—Assembly Department

In Illustration 17A-1, the units completed and transferred out (8,100) plus the units in ending work in process (400) equal the total units to be accounted for (8,500). Using FIFO, we then compute equivalent units as follows.

1. The 500 units of beginning work in process were 40% complete. Thus, 300 equivalent units (500 units × 60%) were required to complete the beginning inventory.

2. The units started and completed during the current month are **the units transferred out minus the units in beginning work in process**. For the Assembly Department, units started and completed are 7,600 (8,100 − 500).

3. The 400 units of ending work in process were 75% complete. Thus, equivalent units were 300 (400 × 75%).

Equivalent units for the Assembly Department are 8,200, computed as follows.

ASSEMBLY DEPARTMENT			
Production Data	Work Added Physical Units	Equivalent This Period	Units
Work in process, June 1	500	60%	**300**
Started and completed	7,600	100%	**7,600**
Work in process, June 30	400	75%	**300**
Total	8,500		**8,200**

Illustration 17A-2
Computation of equivalent units—FIFO method

Comprehensive Example

To provide a complete illustration of the FIFO method, we will use the data for the Mixing Department at **Kellogg Company** for the month of June, as shown in Illustration 17A-3 (page 812).

Illustration 17A-3
Unit and cost data—Mixing Department

MIXING DEPARTMENT	
Units	
Work in process, June 1	100,000
Direct materials: 100% complete	
Conversion costs: 70% complete	
Units started into production during June	800,000
Units completed and transferred out to Baking Department	700,000
Work in process, June 30	200,000
Direct materials: 100% complete	
Conversion costs: 60% complete	
Costs	
Work in process, June 1	
Direct materials: 100% complete	$ 50,000
Conversion costs: 70% complete	35,000
Cost of work in process, June 1	$ 85,000
Costs incurred during production in June	
Direct materials	$400,000
Conversion costs	170,000
Costs incurred in June	$570,000

COMPUTE THE PHYSICAL UNIT FLOW (STEP 1)

Illustration 17A-4 shows the physical flow of units for Kellogg's Mixing Department for the month of June.

Illustration 17A-4
Physical unit flow—Mixing Department

MIXING DEPARTMENT	
	Physical Units
Units to be accounted for	
Work in process, June 1	100,000
Started (transferred) into production	800,000
Total units	**900,000**
Units accounted for	
Completed and transferred out	700,000
Work in process, June 30	200,000
Total units	**900,000**

Under the FIFO method, companies often expand the physical units schedule, as shown in Illustration 17A-5, to explain the transferred-out section. As a result, this section reports the beginning work in process and the units started and completed. These two items further explain the completed and transferred-out section.

Illustration 17A-5
Physical unit flow (FIFO)—Mixing Department

MIXING DEPARTMENT	
	Physical Units
Units to be accounted for	
Work in process, June 1	100,000
Started (transferred) into production	800,000
Total units	**900,000**
Units accounted for	
Completed and transferred out	
Work in process, June 1	**100,000**
Started and completed	**600,000**
	700,000
Work in process, June 30	200,000
Total units	**900,000**

The records indicate that the Mixing Department must account for 900,000 units. Of this sum, 700,000 units were transferred to the Baking Department and 200,000 units were still in process.

COMPUTE EQUIVALENT UNITS OF PRODUCTION (STEP 2)

As with the method presented in the chapter, once they determine the physical flow of the units, companies need to determine equivalent units of production. The Mixing Department adds materials at the beginning of the process, and it incurs conversion costs uniformly during the process. Thus, Kellogg must make two computations of equivalent units: one for materials and one for conversion costs.

Helpful Hint
As noted earlier, materials are not always added at the beginning of the process. For example, companies sometimes add materials uniformly during the process.

EQUIVALENT UNITS FOR MATERIALS Since Kellogg adds materials at the beginning of the process, no additional materials costs are required to complete the beginning work in process. In addition, 100% of the materials costs has been incurred on the ending work in process. Thus, the computation of equivalent units for materials is as follows.

MIXING DEPARTMENT—MATERIALS			
Production Data	Physical Units	Materials Added This Period	Equivalent Units
Work in process, June 1	100,000	–0–	–0–
Started and finished	600,000	100%	600,000
Work in process, June 30	200,000	100%	200,000
Total	900,000		800,000

Illustration 17A-6
Computation of equivalent units—materials

EQUIVALENT UNITS FOR CONVERSION COSTS The 100,000 units of beginning work in process were 70% complete in terms of conversion costs. Thus, the Mixing Department required 30,000 equivalent units (100,000 units × 30%) of conversion costs to complete the beginning inventory. In addition, the 200,000 units of ending work in process were 60% complete in terms of conversion costs. Thus, the equivalent units for conversion costs is 750,000, computed as follows.

MIXING DEPARTMENT—CONVERSION COSTS			
Production Data	Physical Units	Work Added This Period	Equivalent Units
Work in process, June 1	100,000	30%	30,000
Started and finished	600,000	100%	600,000
Work in process, June 30	200,000	60%	120,000
Total	900,000		750,000

Illustration 17A-7
Computation of equivalent units—conversion costs

COMPUTE UNIT PRODUCTION COSTS (STEP 3)

Armed with the knowledge of the equivalent units of production, Kellogg can now compute the unit production costs. Unit production costs are costs expressed in terms of equivalent units of production. When equivalent units of production are different for materials and conversion costs, companies compute three unit costs: (1) materials, (2) conversion, and (3) total manufacturing.

Under the FIFO method, the unit costs of production are based entirely on the production costs incurred during the month. Thus, the costs in the beginning work in process are not relevant, because they were incurred on work done in the preceding month. As Illustration 17A-3 (page 812) indicated, the costs incurred during production in June were as follows.

Illustration 17A-8
Costs incurred during production in June

Direct materials	$400,000
Conversion costs	170,000
Total costs	$570,000

Illustration 17A-9 shows the computation of unit materials cost, unit conversion costs, and total unit cost related to Eggo® Waffles.

Illustration 17A-9
Unit cost formulas and computations—Mixing Department

(1)	Total Materials Cost	÷	Equivalent Units of Materials	=	Unit Materials Cost
	$400,000	÷	800,000	=	$0.50
(2)	Total Conversion Costs	÷	Equivalent Units of Conversion Costs	=	Unit Conversion Cost
	$170,000	÷	750,000	=	$0.227 (rounded)*
(3)	Unit Materials Cost	+	Unit Conversion Cost	=	Total Manufacturing Cost per Unit
	$0.50	+	$0.227	=	$0.727

*For homework problems, round unit costs to three decimal places.

As shown, the unit costs are $0.50 for materials, $0.227 for conversion costs, and $0.727 for total manufacturing costs.

PREPARE A COST RECONCILIATION SCHEDULE (STEP 4)

Kellogg is now ready to determine the cost of goods transferred out of the Mixing Department to the Baking Department and the costs in ending work in process. The total costs charged to the Mixing Department in June are $655,000, calculated as follows.

Illustration 17A-10
Costs charged to Mixing Department

Costs to be accounted for	
Work in process, June 1	$ 85,000
Started into production	570,000
Total costs	$655,000

Kellogg next prepares a cost reconciliation to assign these costs to (1) units transferred out to the Baking Department and (2) ending work in process. Under the FIFO method, the first goods to be completed during the period are the units in beginning work in process. Thus, the cost of the beginning work in process is always assigned to the goods transferred to the next department (or finished goods, if processing is complete). Under the FIFO method, ending work in process also will be assigned only the production costs incurred in the current period. Illustration 17A-11 shows a cost reconciliation schedule for the Mixing Department.

Illustration 17A-11
Cost reconciliation report

MIXING DEPARTMENT
Cost Reconciliation Schedule

Costs accounted for		
Transferred out		
Work in process, June 1		$ 85,000
Costs to complete beginning work in process		
Conversion costs (30,000 × $0.227)		6,810
Total costs		91,810
Units started and completed (600,000 × $0.727)		435,950*
Total costs transferred out		527,760
Work in process, June 30		
Materials (200,000 × $0.50)	$100,000	
Conversion costs (120,000 × $0.227)	27,240	127,240
Total costs		**$655,000**

*Any rounding errors should be adjusted in the "Units started and completed" calculation.

As you can see, the total costs accounted for ($655,000 from Illustration 17A-11) equal the total costs to be accounted for ($655,000 from Illustration 17A-10).

PREPARING THE PRODUCTION COST REPORT

At this point, Kellogg is ready to prepare the production cost report for the Mixing Department. This report is an internal document for management that shows production quantity and cost data for a production department.

As discussed on page 805, there are four steps in preparing a production cost report:

1. Compute the physical unit flow.
2. Compute the equivalent units of production.
3. Compute unit production costs.
4. Prepare a cost reconciliation schedule.

Illustration 17A-12 (page 816) shows the production cost report for the Mixing Department, with the four steps identified in the report.

As indicated in the chapter, production cost reports provide a basis for evaluating the productivity of a department. In addition, managers can use the cost data to assess whether unit costs and total costs are reasonable. By comparing the quantity and cost data with predetermined goals, top management can also judge whether current performance is meeting planned objectives.

Helpful Hint
The two self-checks in the report are (1) total physical units accounted for must equal the total units to be accounted for, and (2) total costs accounted for must equal the total costs to be accounted for.

FIFO and Weighted-Average

The weighted-average method of computing equivalent units has **one major advantage**: It is simple to understand and apply. In cases where prices do not fluctuate significantly from period to period, the weighted-average method will be very similar to the FIFO method. In addition, companies that have been using just-in-time procedures effectively for inventory control purposes will have minimal inventory balances. Therefore, differences between the weighted-average and the FIFO methods will not be material.

Conceptually, the FIFO method is superior to the weighted-average method because it measures **current performance** using only costs incurred in the current period. Managers are, therefore, not held responsible for costs from prior periods over which they may not have had control. In addition, the FIFO method

provides current cost information, which the company can use to establish **more accurate pricing strategies** for goods manufactured and sold in the current period.

Appendix 17A: FIFO Method for Compu...

Helpful Hint

The four steps in preparing a production cost report:

1. Compute the physical unit flow.

2. Compute the equivalent units of production.

3. Compute unit production costs.

4. Prepare a cost reconciliation schedule.

	A	B	C	D	E
			Mixing Department.xls		
	Home Insert Page Layout Formulas Data Review View				
	P18	fx			
1	**MIXING DEPARTMENT**				
2	**Production Cost Report**				
3	**For the Month Ended June 30, 2017**				
4		**Equivalent Units**			
5		Physical Units	Materials	Conversion Costs	
6	**Quantities**				
7	Units to be accounted for	Step 1	Step 2		
8	Work in process (WIP), June 1	100,000			
9	Started into production	800,000			
10	Total units	900,000			
11	Units accounted for				
12	Completed and transferred out				
13	Work in process, June 1	100,000	0	30,000	
14	Started and completed	600,000	600,000	600,000	
15	Work in process, June 30	200,000	200,000	120,000	
16	Total units	900,000	800,000	750,000	
17	**Costs**				
18	Unit costs Step 3		Materials	Conversion Costs	Total
19	Costs in June (excluding beginning WIP)	(a)	$400,000	$170,000	$570,000
20	Equivalent units	(b)	800,000	750,000	
21	Unit costs [(a) ÷ (b)]		$0.50	$0.227	$0.727
22	Costs to be accounted for				
23	Work in process, June 1				$ 85,000
24	Started into production				570,000
25	Total costs				$655,000
26	**Cost Reconciliation Schedule** Step 4				
27	Costs accounted for				
28	Transferred out				
29	Work in process, June 1				$ 85,000
30	Costs to complete beginning work in process				
31	Conversion costs (30,000 × $0.227)			6,810	$ 91,810
32	Units started and completed (600,000 × $0.727)*				435,950
33	Total costs transferred out				527,760
34	Work in process, June 30				
35	Materials (200,000 × $0.50)			100,000	
36	Conversion costs (120,000 × $0.227)			27,240	127,240
37	Total costs				$655,000
38	*Any rounding errors should be adjusted in the "Units started and completed"				
39					

Illustration 17A-12

Production cost report—FIFO method

REVIEW AND PRACTICE

LEARNING OBJECTIVES REVIEW

❶ Discuss the uses of a process cost system and how it compares to a job order system. Companies that mass-produce similar products in a continuous fashion use process cost systems. Once production begins, it continues until the finished product emerges. Each unit of finished product is indistinguishable from every other unit.

Job order cost systems are similar to process cost systems in three ways. (1) Both systems track the same cost elements—direct materials, direct labor, and manufacturing overhead. (2) Both accumulate costs in the same accounts—Raw Materials Inventory, Factory Labor, and Manufacturing Overhead. (3) Both assign accumulated costs to the same accounts—Work in Process, Finished Goods Inventory, and Cost of Goods Sold. However, the method of assigning costs differs significantly.

There are four main differences between the two cost systems. (1) A process cost system uses separate accounts for each department or manufacturing process, rather than only one work in process account used in a job order cost system. (2) A process cost system summarizes costs in a production cost report for each department. A job order cost system charges costs to individual jobs and summarizes them in a job cost sheet. (3) Costs are totaled at the end of a time period in a process cost system but at the completion of a job in a job order cost system. (4) A process cost system calculates unit cost as Total manufacturing costs for the period ÷ Units produced during the period. A job order cost system calculates unit cost as Total cost per job ÷ Units produced.

❷ Explain the flow of costs in a process cost system and the journal entries to assign manufacturing costs. A process cost system assigns manufacturing costs for raw materials, labor, and overhead to work in process accounts for various departments or manufacturing processes. It transfers the costs of partially completed units from one department to another as those units move through the manufacturing process. The system transfers the costs of completed work to Finished Goods Inventory. Finally, when inventory is sold, the system transfers the costs to Cost of Goods Sold.

Entries to assign the costs of raw materials, labor, and overhead consist of a credit to Raw Materials Inventory, Factory Labor, and Manufacturing Overhead, and a debit to Work in Process for each department. Entries to record the cost of goods transferred to another department are a credit to Work in Process for the department whose work is finished and a debit to the department to which the goods are transferred. The entry to record units completed and transferred to the warehouse is a credit to Work in Process for the department whose work is finished and a debit to Finished Goods Inventory. The entry to record the sale of goods is a credit to Finished Goods Inventory and a debit to Cost of Goods Sold.

❸ Compute equivalent units. Equivalent units of production measure work done during a period, expressed in fully completed units. Companies use this measure to determine the cost per unit of completed product. Equivalent units are the sum of units completed and transferred out plus equivalent units of ending work in process.

❹ Complete the four steps to prepare a production cost report. The four steps to complete a production cost report are as follows. (1) Compute the physical unit flow—that is, the total units to be accounted for. (2) Compute the equivalent units of production. (3) Compute the unit production costs, expressed in terms of equivalent units of production. (4) Prepare a cost reconciliation schedule, which shows that the total costs accounted for equal the total costs to be accounted for.

The production cost report contains both quantity and cost data for a production department. There are four sections in the report: (1) number of physical units, (2) equivalent units determination, (3) unit costs, and (4) cost reconciliation schedule.

*❺ Compute equivalent units using the FIFO method. Equivalent units under the FIFO method are the sum of the work performed to (1) finish the units of beginning work in process inventory, if any; (2) complete the units started into production during the period; and (3) start, but only partially complete, the units in ending work in process inventory.

GLOSSARY REVIEW

Conversion costs The sum of labor costs and overhead costs. (p. 803).

Cost reconciliation schedule A schedule that shows that the total costs accounted for equal the total costs to be accounted for. (p. 808).

Equivalent units of production A measure of the work done during the period, expressed in fully completed units. (p. 802).

Operations costing A combination of a process cost and a job order cost system in which products are

manufactured primarily by standardized methods, with some customization. (p. 809).

Physical units Actual units to be accounted for during a period, irrespective of any work performed. (p. 806).

Process cost system An accounting system used to apply costs to similar products that are mass-produced in a continuous fashion. (p. 796).

Production cost report An internal report for management that shows both production quantity and cost data for a production department. (p. 805).

Total units (costs) accounted for The sum of the units (costs) transferred out during the period plus the units (costs) in process at the end of the period. (p. 806).

Total units (costs) to be accounted for The sum of the units (costs) started (or transferred) into production during the period plus the units (costs) in process at the beginning of the period. (p. 806).

Unit production costs Costs expressed in terms of equivalent units of production. (p. 807).

Weighted-average method Method of computing equivalent units of production which considers the degree of completion (weighting) of the units completed and transferred out and the ending work in process. (p. 803).

PRACTICE MULTIPLE-CHOICE QUESTIONS

(LO 1) **1.** Which of the following items is **not** characteristic of a process cost system?
  (a) Once production begins, it continues until the finished product emerges.
  (b) The products produced are heterogeneous in nature.
  (c) The focus is on continually producing homogeneous products.
  (d) When the finished product emerges, all units have precisely the same amount of materials, labor, and overhead.

(LO 1) **2.** Indicate which of the following statements is **not** correct.
  (a) Both a job order and a process cost system track the same three manufacturing cost elements—direct materials, direct labor, and manufacturing overhead.
  (b) A job order cost system uses only one work in process account, whereas a process cost system uses multiple work in process accounts.
  (c) Manufacturing costs are accumulated the same way in a job order and in a process cost system.
  (d) Manufacturing costs are assigned the same way in a job order and in a process cost system.

(LO 2) **3.** In a process cost system, the flow of costs is:
  (a) work in process, cost of goods sold, finished goods.
  (b) finished goods, work in process, cost of goods sold.
  (c) finished goods, cost of goods sold, work in process.
  (d) work in process, finished goods, cost of goods sold.

(LO 2) **4.** In making journal entries to assign raw materials costs, a company using process costing:
  (a) debits Finished Goods Inventory.
  (b) often debits two or more work in process accounts.
  (c) generally credits two or more work in process accounts.
  (d) credits Finished Goods Inventory.

(LO 2) **5.** In a process cost system, manufacturing overhead:
  (a) is assigned to finished goods at the end of each accounting period.
  (b) is assigned to a work in process account for each job as the job is completed.
  (c) is assigned to a work in process account for each production department on the basis of a predetermined overhead rate.
  (d) is assigned to a work in process account for each production department as overhead costs are incurred.

(LO 3) **6.** Conversion costs are the sum of:
  (a) fixed and variable overhead costs.
  (b) labor costs and overhead costs.
  (c) direct material costs and overhead costs.
  (d) direct labor and indirect labor costs.

(LO 3) **7.** The Mixing Department's output during the period consists of 20,000 units completed and transferred out, and 5,000 units in ending work in process 60% complete as to materials and conversion costs. Beginning inventory is 1,000 units, 40% complete as to materials and conversion costs. The equivalent units of production are:
  (a) 22,600.　　　　　　(c) 24,000.
  (b) 23,000.　　　　　　(d) 25,000.

(LO 4) **8.** In RYZ Company, there are zero units in beginning work in process, 7,000 units started into production, and 500 units in ending work in process 20% completed. The physical units to be accounted for are:
  (a) 7,000.　　　　　　(c) 7,500.
  (b) 7,360.　　　　　　(d) 7,340.

(LO 4) **9.** Mora Company has 2,000 units in beginning work in process, 20% complete as to conversion costs, 23,000 units transferred out to finished goods, and 3,000 units in ending work in process $33\frac{1}{3}$% complete as to conversion costs.
  The beginning and ending inventory is fully complete as to materials costs. Equivalent units for materials and conversion costs are, respectively:
  (a) 22,000, 24,000.　　(c) 26,000, 24,000.
  (b) 24,000, 26,000.　　(d) 26,000, 26,000.

(LO 4) **10.** Fortner Company has no beginning work in process; 9,000 units are transferred out and 3,000 units in ending work in process are one-third finished as to conversion costs and fully complete as to materials cost. If total materials cost is $60,000, the unit materials cost is:
  (a) $5.00.
  (b) $5.45 rounded.
  (c) $6.00.
  (d) No correct answer is given.

(LO 4) **11.** Largo Company has unit costs of $10 for materials and $30 for conversion costs. If there are 2,500 units in ending work in process, 40% complete as to conversion costs, and fully complete as to materials cost, the total cost assignable to the ending work in process inventory is:

(a) $45,000.   (c) $75,000.
(b) $55,000.   (d) $100,000.

(LO 4) **12.** A production cost report:
(a) is an external report.
(b) shows both the production quantity and cost data related to a department.
(c) shows equivalent units of production but not physical units.
(d) contains six sections.

(LO 4) **13.** In a production cost report, units to be accounted for are calculated as:
(a) Units started into production + Units in ending work in process.
(b) Units started into production − Units in beginning work in process.
(c) Units transferred out + Units in beginning work in process.
(d) Units started into production + Units in beginning work in process.

(LO 5) *14. Hollins Company uses the FIFO method to compute equivalent units. It has 2,000 units in beginning work in process, 20% complete as to conversion costs, 25,000 units started and completed, and 3,000 units in ending work in process, 30% complete as to

conversion costs. All units are 100% complete as to materials. Equivalent units for materials and conversion costs are, respectively:

(a) 28,000 and 26,600.
(b) 28,000 and 27,500.
(c) 27,000 and 26,200.
(d) 27,000 and 29,600.

*15. KLM Company uses the FIFO method to compute (LO 5) equivalent units. It has no beginning work in process; 9,000 units are started and completed and 3,000 units in ending work in process are one-third completed. All material is added at the beginning of the process. If total materials cost is $60,000, the unit materials cost is:

(a) $5.00.
(b) $6.00.
(c) $6.67 (rounded).
(d) No correct answer is given.

*16. Toney Company uses the FIFO method to compute (LO 5) equivalent units. It has unit costs of $10 for materials and $30 for conversion costs. If there are 2,500 units in ending work in process, 100% complete as to materials and 40% complete as to conversion costs, the total cost assignable to the ending work in process inventory is:

(a) $45,000.   (c) $75,000.
(b) $55,000.   (d) $100,000.

Solutions

1. (b) The products produced are homogeneous, not heterogeneous, in nature. Choices (a), (c), and (d) are incorrect because they all represent characteristics of a process cost system.

2. (d) Manufacturing costs are not assigned the same way in a job order and in a process cost system. Choices (a), (b), and (c) are true statements.

3. (d) In a process cost system, the flow of costs is work in process, finished goods, cost of goods sold. Therefore, choices (a), (b), and (c) are incorrect.

4. (b) The debit is often to two or more work in process accounts, not (a) a debit to Finished Goods Inventory, (c) credits to two or more work in process accounts, or (d) a credit to Finished Goods Inventory.

5. (c) In a process cost system, manufacturing overhead is assigned to a work in process account for each production department on the basis of a predetermined overhead rate, not (a) a finished goods account, (b) as the job is completed, or (d) as overhead costs are incurred.

6. (b) Conversion costs are the sum of labor costs and overhead costs, not (a) the sum of fixed and variable overhead costs, (c) direct material costs and overhead costs, or (d) direct labor and indirect labor costs.

7. (b) The equivalent units of production is the sum of units completed and transferred out (20,000) and the equivalent units of ending work in process inventory (5,000 units × 60%), or 20,000 + 3,000 = 23,000 units, not (a) 22,600 units, (c) 24,000 units, or (d) 25,000 units.

8. (a) There are 7,000 physical units to be accounted for (0 units in beginning inventory + 7,000 units started), not (b) 7,360, (c) 7,500, or (d) 7,340.

9. (c) The equivalent units for materials are 26,000 (23,000 units transferred out plus 3,000 in ending work in process inventory). The equivalent units for conversion costs are 24,000 (23,000 transferred out plus 33⅓% of the ending work in process inventory or 1,000). Therefore, choices (a) 22,000, 24,000; (b) 24,000, 26,000; and (d) 26,000, 26,000 are incorrect.

10. (a) $60,000 ÷ (9,000 + 3,000 units) = $5.00 per unit, not (b) $5.45 (rounded), (c) $6.00, or (d) no correct answer is given.

11. (b) [(2,500 units × 100% complete) × $10] + [(2,500 units × 40% complete) × $30] or $25,000 + $30,000 = $55,000, not (a) $45,000, (c) $75,000, or (d) $100,000.

12. (b) A production cost report shows costs charged to a department and costs accounted for. The other choices are incorrect because a production cost report (a) is an internal, not external, report; (c) does show physical units; and (d) is prepared in four steps and does not contain six sections.

13. (d) In a production cost report, units to be accounted for are calculated as Units started in production + Units in beginning work in process, not (a) Units in ending work in process, (b) minus Units in beginning work in process, or (c) Units transferred out.

*14. (b) The equivalent units for materials are 28,000 [25,000 started and completed + (3,000 × 100%)]. The equivalent units for conversion costs are 27,500 [(2,000 × 80%) + 25,000 + (3,000 × 30%)]. Therefore, choices (a) 28,000, 26,600; (c) 27,000, 26,200; and (d) 27,000, 29,600 are incorrect.

*15. (a) Unit materials cost is $5.00 [$60,000 ÷ (9,000 + 3,000)]. Therefore, choices (b) $6.00, (c) $6.67 (rounded), and (d) no correct answer are incorrect.

*16. (b) The total cost assignable to the ending work in process is $55,000 [($10 × 2,500) + ($30 × 2,500 × 40%)]. Therefore, choices (a) $45,000, (c) $75,000, and (d) $100,000 are incorrect.

PRACTICE EXERCISES

Journalize transactions.

(LO 2)

1. Armando Company manufactures pizza sauce through two production departments: Cooking and Canning. In each process, materials and conversion costs are incurred evenly throughout the process. For the month of April, the work in process accounts show the following debits.

	Cooking	Canning
Beginning work in process	$ –0–	$ 4,000
Materials	25,000	8,000
Labor	8,500	7,500
Overhead	29,000	25,800
Costs transferred in		55,000

Instructions

Journalize the April transactions.

Solution

1. (a) April 30	Work in Process—Cooking		25,000	
	Work in Process—Canning		8,000	
	Raw Materials Inventory			33,000
30	Work in Process—Cooking		8,500	
	Work in Process—Canning		7,500	
	Factory Labor			16,000
30	Work in Process—Cooking		29,000	
	Work in Process—Canning		25,800	
	Manufacturing Overhead			54,800
30	Work in Process—Canning		55,000	
	Work in Process—Cooking			55,000

Prepare a production cost report.

(LO 3, 4)

2. The Sanding Department of Jo Furniture Company has the following production and manufacturing cost data for March 2017, the first month of operation.

Production: 11,000 units finished and transferred out; 4,000 units started that are 100% complete as to materials and 25% complete as to conversion costs.
Manufacturing costs: Materials $48,000; labor $42,000; and overhead $36,000.

Instructions

Prepare a production cost report.

Solution

2.

JO FURNITURE COMPANY
Sanding Department
Production Cost Report
For the Month Ended March 31, 2017

		Equivalent Units	
Quantities	**Physical Units**	**Materials**	**Conversion Costs**
Units to be accounted for			
Work in process, March 1	0		
Started into production	15,000		
Total units	15,000		
Units accounted for			
Transferred out	11,000	11,000	11,000
Work in process, March 31	4,000	4,000	1,000 (4,000 × 25%)
Total units	15,000	15,000	12,000

Costs	**Materials**	**Conversion Costs**	**Total**
Unit costs			
Costs in March	$48,000	$78,000*	$126,000
Equivalent units	15,000	12,000	
Unit costs [(a) + (b)]	$3.20	$6.50	$9.70
Costs to be accounted for			
Work in process, March 1			$ 0
Started into production			126,000
Total costs			$126,000

Cost Reconciliation Schedule

Costs accounted for		
Transferred out (11,000 × $9.70)		$106,700
Work in process, March 31		
Materials (4,000 × $3.20)	$12,800	
Conversion costs (1,000 × $6.50)	6,500	19,300
Total costs		$126,000

*$42,000 + $36,000

◼ PRACTICE PROBLEM

Karlene Industries produces plastic ice cube trays in two processes: heating and stamping. All materials are added at the beginning of the Heating Department process. Karlene uses the weighted-average method to compute equivalent units.

Prepare a production cost report and journalize.

(LO 3, 4)

On November 1, the Heating Department had in process 1,000 trays that were 70% complete. During November, it started into production 12,000 trays. On November 30, 2017, 2,000 trays that were 60% complete were in process.

The following cost information for the Heating Department was also available.

Work in process, November 1:		Costs incurred in November:	
Materials	$ 640	Material	$3,000
Conversion costs	360	Labor	2,300
Cost of work in process, Nov. 1	$1,000	Overhead	4,050

Instructions

(a) Prepare a production cost report for the Heating Department for the month of November 2017, using the weighted-average method.

(b) Journalize the transfer of costs to the Stamping Department.

Solution

(a)

KARLENE INDUSTRIES
Heating Department
Production Cost Report
For the Month Ended November 30, 2017

	Physical Units	Equivalent Units	
		Materials	Conversion Costs
Quantities	Step 1	Step 2	
Units to be accounted for			
Work in process, November 1	1,000		
Started into production	12,000		
Total units	13,000		
Units accounted for			
Transferred out	11,000	11,000	11,000
Work in process, November 30	2,000	2,000	1,200
Total units	13,000	13,000	12,200

Costs		Materials	Conversion Costs	Total
Unit costs Step 3				
Total cost	(a)	$ 3,640*	$ 6,710**	$10,350
Equivalent units	(b)	13,000	12,200	
Unit costs [(a) ÷ (b)]		$0.28	$0.55	$0.83
Costs to be accounted for				
Work in process, November 1				$ 1,000
Started into production				9,350
Total costs				$10,350

*$640 + $3,000
**$360 + $2,300 + $4,050

Cost Reconciliation Schedule Step 4

Costs accounted for			
Transferred out (11,000 × $0.83)			$ 9,130
Work in process, November 30			
Materials (2,000 × $0.28)		$560	
Conversion costs (1,200 × $0.55)		660	1,220
Total costs			$10,350

(b) Work in Process—Stamping	9,130	
Work in Process—Heating		9,130
(To record transfer of units to the Stamping Department)		

WileyPLUS Brief Exercises, Exercises, **DO IT!** Exercises, and Problems and many additional resources are available for practice in WileyPLUS

NOTE: All asterisked Questions, Exercises, and Problems relate to material in the appendix to the chapter.

QUESTIONS

1. Identify which costing system—job order or process cost—the following companies would primarily use: (a) Quaker Oats, (b) Jif Peanut Butter, (c) Gulf Craft (luxury yachts), and (d) Warner Bros. Motion Pictures.

2. Contrast the primary focus of job order cost accounting and of process cost accounting.

3. What are the similarities between a job order and a process cost system?

4. Your roommate is confused about the features of process cost accounting. Identify and explain the distinctive features for your roommate.

5. Sam Bowyer believes there are no significant differences in the flow of costs between job order cost accounting and process cost accounting. Is Bowyer correct? Explain.

6. (a) What source documents are used in assigning (1) materials and (2) labor to production in a process cost system?

    (b) What criterion and basis are commonly used in allocating overhead to processes?

7. At Ely Company, overhead is assigned to production departments at the rate of $5 per machine hour. In July, machine hours were 3,000 in the Machining Department and 2,400 in the Assembly Department. Prepare the entry to assign overhead to production.

8. Mark Haley is uncertain about the steps used to prepare a production cost report. State the procedures that are required in the sequence in which they are performed.

9. John Harbeck is confused about computing physical units. Explain to John how physical units to be accounted for and physical units accounted for are determined.

10. What is meant by the term "equivalent units of production"?

11. How are equivalent units of production computed?

12. Coats Company had zero units of beginning work in process. During the period, 9,000 units were completed, and there were 600 units of ending work in process. What were the units started into production?

13. Sanchez Co. has zero units of beginning work in process. During the period, 12,000 units were completed, and there were 500 units of ending work in process one-fifth complete as to conversion cost and 100% complete as to materials cost. What were the equivalent units of production for (a) materials and (b) conversion costs?

14. Hindi Co. started 3,000 units during the period. Its beginning inventory is 500 units one-fourth complete as to conversion costs and 100% complete as to materials costs. Its ending inventory is 300 units one-fifth complete as to conversion costs and 100% complete as to materials costs. How many units were transferred out this period?

15. Clauss Company transfers out 14,000 units and has 2,000 units of ending work in process that are 25% complete. Materials are entered at the beginning of the process and there is no beginning work in process. Assuming unit materials costs of $3 and unit conversion costs of $5, what are the costs to be assigned to units (a) transferred out and (b) in ending work in process?

16. (a) Ann Quinn believes the production cost report is an external report for stockholders. Is Ann correct? Explain.

    (b) Identify the sections in a production cost report.

17. What purposes are served by a production cost report?

18. At Trent Company, there are 800 units of ending work in process that are 100% complete as to materials and 40% complete as to conversion costs. If the unit cost of materials is $3 and the total costs assigned to the 800 units is $6,000, what is the per unit conversion cost?

19. What is the difference between operations costing and a process cost system?

20. How does a company decide whether to use a job order or a process cost system?

*21. Soria Co. started and completed 2,000 units for the period. Its beginning inventory is 800 units 25% complete and its ending inventory is 400 units 20% complete. Soria uses the FIFO method to compute equivalent units. How many units were transferred out this period?

*22. Reyes Company transfers out 12,000 units and has 2,000 units of ending work in process that are 25% complete. Materials are entered at the beginning of the process and there is no beginning work in process. Reyes uses the FIFO method to compute equivalent units. Assuming unit materials costs of $3 and unit conversion costs of $7, what are the costs to be assigned to units (a) transferred out and (b) in ending work in process?

BRIEF EXERCISES

BE17-1 Warner Company purchases $50,000 of raw materials on account, and it incurs $60,000 of factory labor costs. Journalize the two transactions on March 31, assuming the labor costs are not paid until April.

Journalize entries for accumulating costs.

(LO 2)

BE17-2 Data for Warner Company are given in BE17-1. Supporting records show that (a) the Assembly Department used $24,000 of raw materials and $35,000 of the factory labor, and (b) the Finishing Department used the remainder. Journalize the assignment of the costs to the processing departments on March 31.

Journalize the assignment of materials and labor costs.

(LO 2)

BE17-3 Factory labor data for Warner Company are given in BE17-2. Manufacturing overhead is assigned to departments on the basis of 160% of labor costs. Journalize the assignment of overhead to the Assembly and Finishing Departments.

Journalize the assignment of overhead costs.

(LO 2)

Compute equivalent units of production.

(LO 3)

BE17-4 Goode Company has the following production data for selected months.

Month	Beginning Work in Process	Units Transferred Out	Ending Work in Process	
			Units	% Complete as to Conversion Cost
January	–0–	35,000	10,000	40%
March	–0–	40,000	8,000	75
July	–0–	45,000	16,000	25

Compute equivalent units of production for materials and conversion costs, assuming materials are entered at the beginning of the process.

Compute equivalent units of production.

(LO 3)

BE17-5 The Smelting Department of Kiner Company has the following production data for November.

> Beginning work in process 2,000 units that are 100% complete as to materials and 20% complete as to conversion costs; units transferred out 9,000 units; and ending work in process 7,000 units that are 100% complete as to materials and 40% complete as to conversion costs.

Compute the equivalent units of production for (a) materials and (b) conversion costs for the month of November.

Compute unit costs of production.

(LO 4)

BE17-6 In Mordica Company, total materials costs are $33,000, and total conversion costs are $54,000. Equivalent units of production are materials 10,000 and conversion costs 12,000. Compute the unit costs for materials, conversion costs, and total manufacturing costs.

Assign costs to units transferred out and in process.

(LO 4)

BE17-7 Trek Company has the following production data for April: units transferred out 40,000, and ending work in process 5,000 units that are 100% complete for materials and 40% complete for conversion costs. If unit materials cost is $4 and unit conversion cost is $7, determine the costs to be assigned to the units transferred out and the units in ending work in process.

Compute unit costs.

(LO 4)

BE17-8 Production costs chargeable to the Finishing Department in June in Hollins Company are materials $12,000, labor $29,500, and overhead $18,000. Equivalent units of production are materials 20,000 and conversion costs 19,000. Compute the unit costs for materials and conversion costs.

Prepare cost reconciliation schedule.

(LO 4)

BE17-9 Data for Hollins Company are given in BE17-8. Production records indicate that 18,000 units were transferred out, and 2,000 units in ending work in process were 50% complete as to conversion costs and 100% complete as to materials. Prepare a cost reconciliation schedule.

Assign costs to units transferred out and in process.

(LO 5)

*BE17-10 Pix Company has the following production data for March: no beginning work in process, units started and completed 30,000, and ending work in process 5,000 units that are 100% complete for materials and 40% complete for conversion costs. Pix uses the FIFO method to compute equivalent units. If unit materials cost is $6 and unit conversion cost is $10, determine the costs to be assigned to the units transferred out and the units in ending work in process. The total costs to be assigned are $530,000.

Prepare a partial production cost report.

(LO 5)

*BE17-11 Using the data in BE17-10, prepare the cost section of the production cost report for Pix Company.

Compute unit costs.

(LO 5)

*BE17-12 Production costs chargeable to the Finishing Department in May at Kim Company are materials $8,000, labor $20,000, overhead $18,000, and transferred-in costs $67,000. Equivalent units of production are materials 20,000 and conversion costs 19,000. Kim uses the FIFO method to compute equivalent units. Compute the unit costs for materials and conversion costs. Transferred-in costs are considered materials costs.

DO IT! Exercises

DO IT! 17-1 Indicate whether each of the following statements is true or false.

1. Many hospitals use job order costing for small, routine medical procedures.
2. A manufacturer of computer flash drives would use a job order cost system.
3. A process cost system uses multiple work in process accounts.
4. A process cost system keeps track of costs on job cost sheets.

Compare job order and process cost systems.
(LO 1)

DO IT! 17-2 Kopa Company manufactures CH-21 through two processes: mixing and packaging. In July, the following costs were incurred.

	Mixing	Packaging
Raw materials used	$10,000	$28,000
Factory labor costs	8,000	36,000
Manufacturing overhead costs	12,000	54,000

Assign and journalize manufacturing costs.
(LO 2)

Units completed at a cost of $21,000 in the Mixing Department are transferred to the Packaging Department. Units completed at a cost of $106,000 in the Packaging Department are transferred to Finished Goods. Journalize the assignment of these costs to the two processes and the transfer of units as appropriate.

DO IT! 17-3 The Assembly Department for Right pens has the following production data for the current month.

Beginning Work in Process	Units Transferred Out	Ending Work in Process
–0–	20,000	10,000

Compute equivalent units.
(LO 3)

Materials are entered at the beginning of the process. The ending work in process units are 70% complete as to conversion costs. Compute the equivalent units of production for (a) materials and (b) conversion costs.

DO IT! 17-4 In March, Kelly Company had the following unit production costs: materials $10 and conversion costs $8. On March 1, it had no work in process. During March, Kelly transferred out 22,000 units. As of March 31, 4,000 units that were 40% complete as to conversion costs and 100% complete as to materials were in ending work in process.

Prepare cost reconciliation schedule.
(LO 4)

(a) Compute the total units to be accounted for.
(b) Compute the equivalent units of production.
(c) Prepare a cost reconciliation schedule, including the costs of materials transferred out and the costs of materials in process.

EXERCISES

E17-1 Robert Wilkins has prepared the following list of statements about process cost accounting.

Understand process cost accounting.
(LO 1)

1. Process cost systems are used to apply costs to similar products that are mass-produced in a continuous fashion.
2. A process cost system is used when each finished unit is indistinguishable from another.
3. Companies that produce soft drinks, movies, and computer chips would all use process cost accounting.
4. In a process cost system, costs are tracked by individual jobs.
5. Job order costing and process costing track different manufacturing cost elements.
6. Both job order costing and process costing account for direct materials, direct labor, and manufacturing overhead.
7. Costs flow through the accounts in the same basic way for both job order costing and process costing.
8. In a process cost system, only one work in process account is used.
9. In a process cost system, costs are summarized in a job cost sheet.
10. In a process cost system, the unit cost is total manufacturing costs for the period divided by the equivalent units produced during the period.

Journalize transactions.

(LO 2)

Instructions
Identify each statement as true or false. If false, indicate how to correct the statement.

E17-2 Harrelson Company manufactures pizza sauce through two production departments: Cooking and Canning. In each process, materials and conversion costs are incurred evenly throughout the process. For the month of April, the work in process accounts show the following debits.

	Cooking	**Canning**
Beginning work in process	$ –0–	$ 4,000
Materials	21,000	9,000
Labor	8,500	7,000
Overhead	31,500	25,800
Costs transferred in		53,000

Instructions
Journalize the April transactions.

Answer questions on costs and production.

(LO 2, 3, 4)

E17-3 The ledger of American Company has the following work in process account.

Work in Process—Painting

5/1	Balance	3,590	5/31	Transferred out	?
5/31	Materials	5,160			
5/31	Labor	2,530			
5/31	Overhead	1,380			
5/31	Balance	?			

Production records show that there were 400 units in the beginning inventory, 30% complete, 1,600 units started, and 1,700 units transferred out. The beginning work in process had materials cost of $2,040 and conversion costs of $1,550. The units in ending inventory were 40% complete. Materials are entered at the beginning of the painting process.

Instructions
(a) How many units are in process at May 31?
(b) What is the unit materials cost for May?
(c) What is the unit conversion cost for May?
(d) What is the total cost of units transferred out in May?
(e) What is the cost of the May 31 inventory?

Journalize transactions for two processes.

(LO 2)

E17-4 Schrager Company has two production departments: Cutting and Assembly. July 1 inventories are Raw Materials $4,200, Work in Process—Cutting $2,900, Work in Process—Assembly $10,600, and Finished Goods $31,000. During July, the following transactions occurred.

1. Purchased $62,500 of raw materials on account.
2. Incurred $60,000 of factory labor. (Credit Wages Payable.)
3. Incurred $70,000 of manufacturing overhead; $40,000 was paid and the remainder is unpaid.
4. Requisitioned materials for Cutting $15,700 and Assembly $8,900.
5. Used factory labor for Cutting $33,000 and Assembly $27,000.
6. Applied overhead at the rate of $18 per machine hour. Machine hours were Cutting 1,680 and Assembly 1,720.
7. Transferred goods costing $67,600 from the Cutting Department to the Assembly Department.
8. Transferred goods costing $134,900 from Assembly to Finished Goods.
9. Sold goods costing $150,000 for $200,000 on account.

Instructions
Journalize the transactions. (Omit explanations.)

E17-5 In Shady Company, materials are entered at the beginning of each process. Work in process inventories, with the percentage of work done on conversion costs, and production data for its Sterilizing Department in selected months during 2017 are as follows.

Compute physical units and equivalent units of production.

(LO 3, 4)

	Beginning Work in Process		Units Transferred Out	Ending Work in Process	
Month	Units	Conversion Cost%		Units	Conversion Cost%
January	–0–	—	11,000	2,000	60
March	–0–	—	12,000	3,000	30
May	–0–	—	14,000	7,000	80
July	–0–	—	10,000	1,500	40

Instructions
(a) Compute the physical units for January and May.
(b) Compute the equivalent units of production for (1) materials and (2) conversion costs for each month.

E17-6 The Cutting Department of Cassel Company has the following production and cost data for July.

Determine equivalent units, unit costs, and assignment of costs.

(LO 3, 4)

Production	Costs	
1. Transferred out 12,000 units.	Beginning work in process	$ –0–
2. Started 3,000 units that are 60%	Materials	45,000
complete as to conversion	Labor	16,200
costs and 100% complete as	Manufacturing overhead	18,300
to materials at July 31.		

Materials are entered at the beginning of the process. Conversion costs are incurred uniformly during the process.

Instructions
(a) Determine the equivalent units of production for (1) materials and (2) conversion costs.
(b) Compute unit costs and prepare a cost reconciliation schedule.

E17-7 The Sanding Department of Quik Furniture Company has the following production and manufacturing cost data for March 2017, the first month of operation.

Prepare a production cost report.

(LO 3, 4)

Production: 7,000 units finished and transferred out; 3,000 units started that are 100% complete as to materials and 20% complete as to conversion costs.

Manufacturing costs: Materials $33,000; labor $21,000; and overhead $36,000.

Instructions
Prepare a production cost report.

E17-8 The Blending Department of Luongo Company has the following cost and production data for the month of April.

Determine equivalent units, unit costs, and assignment of costs.

(LO 3, 4)

Costs:	
Work in process, April 1	
Direct materials: 100% complete	$100,000
Conversion costs: 20% complete	70,000
Cost of work in process, April 1	$170,000
Costs incurred during production in April	
Direct materials	$ 800,000
Conversion costs	365,000
Costs incurred in April	$1,165,000

Units transferred out totaled 17,000. Ending work in process was 1,000 units that are 100% complete as to materials and 40% complete as to conversion costs.

Instructions

(a) Compute the equivalent units of production for (1) materials and (2) conversion costs for the month of April.
(b) Compute the unit costs for the month.
(c) Determine the costs to be assigned to the units transferred out and in ending work in process.

Determine equivalent units, unit costs, and assignment of costs.

(LO 3, 4)

E17-9 Baden Company has gathered the following information.

Units in beginning work in process	–0–
Units started into production	36,000
Units in ending work in process	6,000
Percent complete in ending work in process:	
Conversion costs	40%
Materials	100%
Costs incurred:	
Direct materials	$72,000
Direct labor	$61,000
Overhead	$101,000

Instructions

(a) Compute equivalent units of production for materials and for conversion costs.
(b) Determine the unit costs of production.
(c) Show the assignment of costs to units transferred out and in process.

Determine equivalent units, unit costs, and assignment of costs.

(LO 3, 4)

E17-10 Overton Company has gathered the following information.

Units in beginning work in process	20,000
Units started into production	164,000
Units in ending work in process	24,000
Percent complete in ending work in process:	
Conversion costs	60%
Materials	100%
Costs incurred:	
Direct materials	$101,200
Direct labor	$164,800
Overhead	$184,000

Instructions

(a) Compute equivalent units of production for materials and for conversion costs.
(b) Determine the unit costs of production.
(c) Show the assignment of costs to units transferred out and in process.

Compute equivalent units, unit costs, and costs assigned.

(LO 3, 4)

E17-11 The Polishing Department of Major Company has the following production and manufacturing cost data for September. Materials are entered at the beginning of the process.

Production: Beginning inventory 1,600 units that are 100% complete as to materials and 30% complete as to conversion costs; units started during the period are 42,900; ending inventory of 5,000 units 10% complete as to conversion costs.

Manufacturing costs: Beginning inventory costs, comprised of $20,000 of materials and $43,180 of conversion costs; materials costs added in Polishing during the month, $175,800; labor and overhead applied in Polishing during the month, $125,680 and $257,140, respectively.

Instructions

(a) Compute the equivalent units of production for materials and conversion costs for the month of September.
(b) Compute the unit costs for materials and conversion costs for the month.
(c) Determine the costs to be assigned to the units transferred out and in process.

E17-12 David Skaros has recently been promoted to production manager. He has just started to receive various managerial reports, including the production cost report that you prepared. It showed that his department had 2,000 equivalent units in ending inventory. His department has had a history of not keeping enough inventory on hand to meet demand. He has come to you, very angry, and wants to know why you credited him with only 2,000 units when he knows he had at least twice that many on hand.

Explain the production cost report.

(LO 4)

Instructions

⊷ Explain to him why his production cost report showed only 2,000 equivalent units in ending inventory. Write an informal memo. Be kind and explain very clearly why he is mistaken.

E17-13 The Welding Department of Healthy Company has the following production and manufacturing cost data for February 2017. All materials are added at the beginning of the process.

Prepare a production cost report.

(LO 3, 4)

Manufacturing Costs			Production Data	
Beginning work in process			Beginning work in process	15,000 units
Materials	$18,000			1/10 complete
Conversion costs	14,175	$ 32,175	Units transferred out	55,000
Materials		180,000	Units started	51,000
Labor		67,380	Ending work in process	11,000 units
Overhead		61,445		1/5 complete

Instructions
Prepare a production cost report for the Welding Department for the month of February.

E17-14 Remington Inc. is contemplating the use of process costing to track the costs of its operations. The operation consists of three segments (departments): Receiving, Shipping, and Delivery. Containers are received at Remington's docks and sorted according to the ship they will be carried on. The containers are loaded onto a ship, which carries them to the appropriate port of destination. The containers are then off-loaded and delivered to the Receiving Department.

Remington wants to begin using process costing in the Shipping Department. Direct materials represent the fuel costs to run the ship, and "Containers in transit" represents work in process. Listed below is information about the Shipping Department's first month's activity.

Compute physical units and equivalent units of production.

(LO 3, 4)

Containers in transit, April 1	0
Containers loaded	1,200
Containers in transit, April 30	350, 40% of direct materials and 20% of conversion costs

Instructions
(a) Determine the physical flow of containers for the month.
(b) Calculate the equivalent units for direct materials and conversion costs.

E17-15 Santana Mortgage Company uses a process cost system to accumulate costs in its Application Department. When an application is completed, it is forwarded to the Loan Department for final processing. The following processing and cost data pertain to September.

Determine equivalent units, unit costs, and assignment of costs.

(LO 3, 4)

1. Applications in process on September 1: 100.	Beginning WIP:	
	Direct materials	$ 1,000
2. Applications started in September: 1,000.	Conversion costs	3,960
	September costs:	
3. Completed applications during September: 800.	Direct materials	$ 4,500
	Direct labor	12,000
4. Applications still in process at September 30: 100% complete as to materials (forms) and 60% complete as to conversion costs.	Overhead	9,520

Materials are the forms used in the application process, and these costs are incurred at the beginning of the process. Conversion costs are incurred uniformly during the process.

Instructions
(a) Determine the equivalent units of service (production) for materials and conversion costs.
(b) Compute the unit costs and prepare a cost reconciliation schedule.

Compute equivalent units, unit costs, and costs assigned.
(LO 5)

*E17-16 Using the data in E17-15, assume Santana Mortgage Company uses the FIFO method. Also, assume that the applications in process on September 1 were 100% complete as to materials (forms) and 40% complete as to conversion costs. Assume overhead costs were $9,620 instead of $9,520.

Instructions
(a) Determine the equivalent units of service (production) for materials and conversion costs.
(b) Compute the unit costs and prepare a cost reconciliation schedule.

Determine equivalent units, unit costs, and assignment of costs.
(LO 5)

*E17-17 The Cutting Department of Lasso Company has the following production and cost data for August.

Production	Costs	
1. Started and completed 10,000 units.	Beginning work in process	$ –0–
2. Started 2,000 units that are 40% completed at August 31.	Materials	45,000
	Labor	13,600
	Manufacturing overhead	16,100

Materials are entered at the beginning of the process. Conversion costs are incurred uniformly during the process. Lasso Company uses the FIFO method to compute equivalent units.

Instructions
(a) Determine the equivalent units of production for (1) materials and (2) conversion costs.
(b) Compute unit costs and show the assignment of manufacturing costs to units transferred out and in work in process.

Compute equivalent units, unit costs, and costs assigned.
(LO 5)

*E17-18 The Smelting Department of Polzin Company has the following production and cost data for September.

Production: Beginning work in process 2,000 units that are 100% complete as to materials and 20% complete as to conversion costs; units started and finished 9,000 units; and ending work in process 1,000 units that are 100% complete as to materials and 40% complete as to conversion costs.

Manufacturing costs: Work in process, September 1, $15,200; materials added $60,000; labor and overhead $132,000.

Polzin uses the FIFO method to compute equivalent units.

Instructions
(a) Compute the equivalent units of production for (1) materials and (2) conversion costs for the month of September.
(b) Compute the unit costs for the month.
(c) Determine the costs to be assigned to the units transferred out and in process.

Answer questions on costs and production.
(LO 5)

*E17-19 The ledger of Hasgrove Company has the following work in process account.

Work in Process—Painting

3/1	Balance	3,680	3/31	Transferred out	?
3/31	Materials	6,600			
3/31	Labor	2,400			
3/31	Overhead	1,150			
3/31	Balance	?			

Production records show that there were 800 units in the beginning inventory, 30% complete, 1,100 units started, and 1,500 units transferred out. The units in ending inventory were 40% complete. Materials are entered at the beginning of the painting process. Hasgrove uses the FIFO method to compute equivalent units.

Instructions

Answer the following questions.

(a) How many units are in process at March 31?
(b) What is the unit materials cost for March?
(c) What is the unit conversion cost for March?
(d) What is the total cost of units started in February and completed in March?
(e) What is the total cost of units started and finished in March?
(f) What is the cost of the March 31 inventory?

*E17-20 The Welding Department of Majestic Company has the following production and manufacturing cost data for February 2017. All materials are added at the beginning of the process. Majestic uses the FIFO method to compute equivalent units.

Prepare a production cost report for a second process.

(LO 5)

Manufacturing Costs		Production Data	
Beginning work in process	$ 32,175	Beginning work in process	15,000 units,
Costs transferred in	135,000		10% complete
Materials	57,000	Units transferred out	54,000
Labor	35,100	Units transferred in	64,000
Overhead	68,400	Ending work in process	25,000 units
			20% complete

Instructions

Prepare a production cost report for the Welding Department for the month of February. Transferred-in costs are considered materials costs.

EXERCISES: SET B AND CHALLENGE EXERCISES

Visit the book's companion website, at **www.wiley.com/college/weygandt**, and choose the Student Companion site to access Exercises: Set B and Challenge Exercises.

PROBLEMS: SET A

P17-1A Fire Out Company manufactures its product, Vitadrink, through two manufacturing processes: Mixing and Packaging. All materials are entered at the beginning of each process. On October 1, 2017, inventories consisted of Raw Materials $26,000, Work in Process—Mixing $0, Work in Process—Packaging $250,000, and Finished Goods $289,000. The beginning inventory for Packaging consisted of 10,000 units that were 50% complete as to conversion costs and fully complete as to materials. During October, 50,000 units were started into production in the Mixing Department and the following transactions were completed.

Journalize transactions.

(LO 2)

1. Purchased $300,000 of raw materials on account.
2. Issued raw materials for production: Mixing $210,000 and Packaging $45,000.
3. Incurred labor costs of $278,900.
4. Used factory labor: Mixing $182,500 and Packaging $96,400.
5. Incurred $810,000 of manufacturing overhead on account.
6. Applied manufacturing overhead on the basis of $23 per machine hour. Machine hours were 28,000 in Mixing and 6,000 in Packaging.
7. Transferred 45,000 units from Mixing to Packaging at a cost of $979,000.
8. Transferred 53,000 units from Packaging to Finished Goods at a cost of $1,315,000.
9. Sold goods costing $1,604,000 for $2,500,000 on account.

Instructions

Journalize the October transactions.

Complete four steps necessary
to prepare a production cost
report.

(LO 3, 4)

P17-2A Rosenthal Company manufactures bowling balls through two processes: Molding and Packaging. In the Molding Department, the urethane, rubber, plastics, and other materials are molded into bowling balls. In the Packaging Department, the balls are placed in cartons and sent to the finished goods warehouse. All materials are entered at the beginning of each process. Labor and manufacturing overhead are incurred uniformly throughout each process. Production and cost data for the Molding Department during June 2017 are presented below.

Production Data	June
Beginning work in process units	–0–
Units started into production	22,000
Ending work in process units	2,000
Percent complete—ending inventory	40%

Cost Data	
Materials	$198,000
Labor	53,600
Overhead	112,800
Total	$364,400

Instructions

(a) Prepare a schedule showing physical units of production.
(b) Determine the equivalent units of production for materials and conversion costs.
(c) Compute the unit costs of production.
(d) Determine the costs to be assigned to the units transferred out and in process for June.
(e) Prepare a production cost report for the Molding Department for the month of June.

(c) Materials $9.00
CC $8.00

(d) Transferred
out $340,000
WIP $ 24,400

Complete four steps necessary
to prepare a production cost
report.

(LO 3, 4)

P17-3A Thakin Industries Inc. manufactures dorm furniture in separate processes. In each process, materials entered at the beginning, and conversion costs are incurred uniformly. Production and cost data for the first process in making two products in two different manufacturing plants are as follows.

	Cutting Department	
	Plant 1	Plant 2
Production Data—July	T12-Tables	C10-Chairs
Work in process units, July 1	–0–	–0–
Units started into production	20,000	18,000
Work in process units, July 31	3,000	500
Work in process percent complete	60	80
Cost Data—July		
Work in process, July 1	$ –0–	$ –0–
Materials	380,000	288,000
Labor	234,400	110,000
Overhead	104,000	104,800
Total	$718,400	$502,800

(a) (3) T12:
Materials $19
CC $18
(4) T12:
Transferred
out $629,000
WIP $ 89,400

Instructions

(a) For each plant:
  (1) Compute the physical units of production.
  (2) Compute equivalent units of production for materials and for conversion costs.
  (3) Determine the unit costs of production.
  (4) Show the assignment of costs to units transferred out and in process.
(b) Prepare the production cost report for Plant 1 for July 2017.

P17-4A Rivera Company has several processing departments. Costs charged to the Assembly Department for November 2017 totaled $2,280,000 as follows.

Assign costs and prepare production cost report.

(LO 3, 4)

Work in process, November 1		
Materials	$79,000	
Conversion costs	48,150	$ 127,150
Materials added		1,589,000
Labor		225,920
Overhead		337,930

Production records show that 35,000 units were in beginning work in process 30% complete as to conversion costs, 660,000 units were started into production, and 25,000 units were in ending work in process 40% complete as to conversion costs. Materials are entered at the beginning of each process.

Instructions
(a) Determine the equivalent units of production and the unit production costs for the Assembly Department.
(b) Determine the assignment of costs to goods transferred out and in process.
(c) Prepare a production cost report for the Assembly Department.

(b) Transferred
   out $2,211,000
   WIP $ 69,000

P17-5A Polk Company manufactures basketballs. Materials are added at the beginning of the production process and conversion costs are incurred uniformly. Production and cost data for the month of July 2017 are as follows.

Determine equivalent units and unit costs and assign costs.

(LO 3, 4)

Production Data—Basketballs	Units	Percentage Complete
Work in process units, July 1	500	60%
Units started into production	1,000	
Work in process units, July 31	600	40%

Cost Data—Basketballs		
Work in process, July 1		
Materials	$750	
Conversion costs	600	$1,350
Direct materials		2,400
Direct labor		1,580
Manufacturing overhead		1,240

Instructions
(a) Calculate the following.
   (1) The equivalent units of production for materials and conversion costs.
   (2) The unit costs of production for materials and conversion costs.
   (3) The assignment of costs to units transferred out and in process at the end of the accounting period.
(b) Prepare a production cost report for the month of July for the basketballs.

(a) (2) Materials $2.10
      (3) Transferred
          out $4,590
          WIP $1,980

P17-6A Hamilton Processing Company uses a weighted-average process cost system and manufactures a single product—an industrial carpet shampoo and cleaner used by many universities. The manufacturing activity for the month of October has just been completed. A partially completed production cost report for the month of October for the Mixing and Cooking Department is shown on page 834.

Compute equivalent units and complete production cost report.

(LO 3, 4)

Instructions
(a) Prepare a schedule that shows how the equivalent units were computed so that you can complete the "Quantities: Units accounted for" equivalent units section shown in the production cost report, and compute October unit costs.
(b) Complete the "Cost Reconciliation Schedule" part of the production cost report.

(a) Materials $1.60
(b) Transferred
    out $282,000
    WIP $ 63,000

HAMILTON PROCESSING COMPANY
Mixing and Cooking Department
Production Cost Report
For the Month Ended October 31

Quantities	Physical Units	Equivalent Units Materials	Conversion Costs
Units to be accounted for			
Work in process, October 1			
(all materials, 70%			
conversion costs)	20,000		
Started into production	150,000		
Total units	170,000		
Units accounted for			
Transferred out	120,000	?	?
Work in process, October 31			
(60% materials, 40%			
conversion costs)	50,000	?	?
Total units accounted for	170,000	?	?

Costs

Unit costs	Materials	Conversion Costs	Total
Total cost	$240,000	$105,000	$345,000
Equivalent units	?	?	
Unit costs	$? +	$? =	$?
Costs to be accounted for			
Work in process, October 1			$ 30,000
Started into production			315,000
Total costs			$345,000

Cost Reconciliation Schedule

Costs accounted for		
Transferred out		$?
Work in process, October 31		
Materials	$?	
Conversion costs	?	?
Total costs		$?

Determine equivalent units and unit costs and assign costs for processes; prepare production cost report.

(LO 5)

*P17-7A Owen Company manufactures bicycles and tricycles. For both products, materials are added at the beginning of the production process, and conversion costs are incurred uniformly. Owen Company uses the FIFO method to compute equivalent units. Production and cost data for the month of March are as follows.

Production Data—Bicycles	Units	Percentage Complete
Work in process units, March 1	200	80%
Units started into production	1,000	
Work in process units, March 31	300	40%

Cost Data—Bicycles	
Work in process, March 1	$19,280
Direct materials	50,000
Direct labor	25,900
Manufacturing overhead	30,000

Production Data—Tricycles	Units	Percentage Complete
Work in process units, March 1	100	75%
Units started into production	1,000	
Work in process units, March 31	60	25%

Cost Data—Tricycles	
Work in process, March 1	$ 6,125
Direct materials	30,000
Direct labor	14,300
Manufacturing overhead	20,000

Instructions

(a) Calculate the following for both the bicycles and the tricycles.
    (1) The equivalent units of production for materials and conversion costs.
    (2) The unit costs of production for materials and conversion costs.
    (3) The assignment of costs to units transferred out and in process at the end of the accounting period.

(b) Prepare a production cost report for the month of March for the bicycles only.

(a) Bicycles:
    (1) Materials   1,000
    (2) Materials $50
    (3) Transferred
         out $102,380
         WIP $ 22,800

PROBLEMS: SET B AND SET C

Visit the book's companion website, at **www.wiley.com/college/weygandt**, and choose the Student Companion site to access Problems: Set B and Set C.

CONTINUING PROBLEMS

CURRENT DESIGNS

EXCEL TUTORIAL

CD17 Building a kayak using the composite method is a very labor-intensive process. In the Fabrication Department, the kayaks go through several steps as employees carefully place layers of Kevlar® in a mold and then use resin to fuse together the layers. The excess resin is removed with a vacuum process, and the upper shell and lower shell are removed from the molds and assembled. The seat, hatch, and other components are added in the Finishing Department.

At the beginning of April, Current Designs had 30 kayaks in process in the Fabrication Department. Rick Thrune, the production manager, estimated that about 80% of the materials costs had been added to these boats, which were about 50% complete with respect to the conversion costs. The cost of this inventory had been calculated to be $8,400 in materials and $9,000 in conversion costs.

During April, 72 boats were started. At the end of the month, the 35 kayaks in the ending inventory had 20% of the materials and 40% of the conversion costs already added to them.

A review of the accounting records for April showed that materials with a cost of $17,500 had been requisitioned by the Fabrication Department and that the conversion costs for the month were $39,600.

Instructions

Complete a production cost report for April 2017 for the Fabrication Department using the weighted-average method.

WATERWAYS

(*Note:* This is a continuation of the Waterways problem from Chapters 15–16.)

WP17 Because most of the parts for its irrigation systems are standard, Waterways handles the majority of its manufacturing as a process cost system. There are multiple process departments. Three of these departments are the Molding, Cutting, and Welding Departments. All items eventually end up in the Packaging Department, which prepares items for sale in kits or individually. This problem asks you to help Waterways calculate equivalent units and prepare a production cost report.

Go to the book's companion website, at **www.wiley.com/college/weygandt**, *to see the completion of this problem.*

BROADENING YOUR PERSPECTIVE

MANAGEMENT DECISION-MAKING

Decision-Making Across the Organization

BYP17-1 Florida Beach Company manufactures sunscreen, called NoTan, in 11-ounce plastic bottles. NoTan is sold in a competitive market. As a result, management is very cost-conscious. NoTan is manufactured through two processes: mixing and filling. Materials are entered at the beginning of each process, and labor and manufacturing overhead occur uniformly throughout each process. Unit costs are based on the cost per gallon of NoTan using the weighted-average costing approach.

On June 30, 2017, Mary Ritzman, the chief accountant for the past 20 years, opted to take early retirement. Her replacement, Joe Benili, had extensive accounting experience with motels in the area but only limited contact with manufacturing accounting. During July, Joe correctly accumulated the following production quantity and cost data for the Mixing Department.

Production quantities: Work in process, July 1, 8,000 gallons 75% complete; started into production 100,000 gallons; work in process, July 31, 5,000 gallons 20% complete. Materials are added at the beginning of the process.

Production costs: Beginning work in process $88,000, comprised of $21,000 of materials costs and $67,000 of conversion costs; incurred in July: materials $573,000, conversion costs $765,000.

Joe then prepared a production cost report on the basis of physical units started into production. His report showed a production cost of $14.26 per gallon of NoTan. The management of Florida Beach was surprised at the high unit cost. The president comes to you, as Mary's top assistant, to review Joe's report and prepare a correct report if necessary.

Instructions

With the class divided into groups, answer the following questions.

(a) Show how Joe arrived at the unit cost of $14.26 per gallon of NoTan.
(b) What error(s) did Joe make in preparing his production cost report?
(c) Prepare a correct production cost report for July.

Managerial Analysis

BYP17-2 Harris Furniture Company manufactures living room furniture through two departments: Framing and Upholstering. Materials are entered at the beginning of each process. For May, the following cost data are obtained from the two work in process accounts.

	Framing	Upholstering
Work in process, May 1	$ –0–	$?
Materials	450,000	?
Conversion costs	261,000	330,000
Costs transferred in	–0–	600,000
Costs transferred out	600,000	?
Work in process, May 31	111,000	?

Instructions

Answer the following questions.

(a) If 3,000 sofas were started into production on May 1 and 2,500 sofas were transferred to Upholstering, what was the unit cost of materials for May in the Framing Department?
(b) Using the data in (a) above, what was the per unit conversion cost of the sofas transferred to Upholstering?
(c) Continuing the assumptions in (a) above, what is the percentage of completion of the units in process at May 31 in the Framing Department?

Real-World Focus

BYP17-3 Paintball is now played around the world. The process of making paintballs is actually quite similar to the process used to make certain medical pills. In fact, paintballs were previously often made at the same factories that made pharmaceuticals.

Address: Go to www.youtube.com/watch?v=2hKrv60PJKE#t=129 to access the video.

Instructions

View that video at the site listed above and then answer the following questions.

(a) Describe in sequence the primary steps used to manufacture paintballs.

(b) Explain the costs incurred by the company that would fall into each of the following categories: materials, labor, and overhead. Of these categories, which do you think would be the greatest cost in making paintballs?

(c) Discuss whether a paintball manufacturer would use job order costing or process costing.

CRITICAL THINKING

Communication Activity

BYP17-4 Diane Barone was a good friend of yours in high school and is from your home town. While you chose to major in accounting when you both went away to college, she majored in marketing and management. You are now the accounting manager for the Snack Foods Division of Melton Enterprises. Your friend Diane was promoted to regional sales manager for the same division of Melton. Diane recently telephoned you. She explained that she was familiar with job cost sheets, which had been used by the Special Projects Division where she had formerly worked. She was, however, very uncomfortable with the production cost reports prepared by your division. She emailed you a list of her particular questions:

1. Since Melton occasionally prepares snack foods for special orders in the Snack Foods Division, why don't we track costs of the orders separately?

2. What is an equivalent unit?

3. Why am I getting four production cost reports? Isn't there one work in process account?

Instructions

Prepare a memo to Diane. Answer her questions and include any additional information you think would be helpful. You may write informally but do use proper grammar and punctuation.

Ethics Case

BYP17-5 R. B. Dillman Company manufactures a high-tech component used in Bluetooth speakers that passes through two production processing departments, Molding and Assembly. Department managers are partially compensated on the basis of units of products completed and transferred out relative to units of product put into production. This was intended as encouragement to be efficient and to minimize waste.

Jan Wooten is the department head in the Molding Department, and Tony Ferneti is her quality control inspector. During the month of June, Jan had three new employees who were not yet technically skilled. As a result, many of the units produced in June had minor molding defects. In order to maintain the department's normal high rate of completion, Jan told Tony to pass through inspection and on to the Assembly Department all units that had defects nondetectable to the human eye. "Company and industry tolerances on this product are too high anyway," says Jan. "Less than 2% of the units we produce are subjected in the market to the stress tolerance we've designed into them. The odds of those 2% being any of this month's units are even less. Anyway, we're saving the company money."

Instructions

(a) Who are the potential stakeholders involved in this situation?

(b) What alternatives does Tony have in this situation? What might the company do to prevent this situation from occurring?

Considering People, Planet, and Profit

BYP17-6 In a recent year, an oil refinery in Texas City, Texas, on the Houston Ship Channel exploded. The explosion killed 14 people and sent a plume of smoke hundreds of feet into the air. The blast started as a fire in the section of the plant that increased the octane of the gasoline that was produced at the refinery. The Houston Ship Channel is the main waterway that allows commerce to flow from the Gulf of Mexico into Houston.

The Texas Commission on Environmental Quality expressed concern about the release of nitrogen oxides, benzene, and other known carcinogens as a result of the blast. Neighbors of the plant complained that the plant had been emitting carcinogens for years and that the regulators had ignored their complaints about emissions and unsafe working conditions.

Instructions

Answer the following questions.

(a) Outline the costs that the company now faces as a result of the accident.

(b) How could the company have reduced the costs associated with the accident?

18

Activity-Based Costing

CHAPTER PREVIEW As indicated in the Feature Story below about Precor, the traditional costing systems described in earlier chapters are not the best answer for every company. Precor suspected that the traditional system was masking significant differences in its real cost structure, so it sought a new method of assigning costs. Similar searches by other companies for ways to improve operations and gather more accurate data for decision-making have resulted in the development of powerful new management tools, including **activity-based costing (ABC)**. The primary objective of this chapter is to explain and illustrate this concept.

FEATURE STORY

Precor Is on Your Side

Do you feel like the whole world is conspiring against your efforts to get in shape? Is it humanly possible to resist the constant barrage of advertisements and fast-food servers who pleasantly encourage us to "supersize" it? Lest we think that we have no allies in our battle against the bulge, consider Precor.

Ever since it made the first ergonomically sound rowing machine in 1980, Precor's sole mission has been to provide exercise equipment. It makes elliptical trainers, exercise bikes, rowing machines, treadmills, multi-station strength systems, and many other forms of equipment designed to erase the cumulative effects of a fast-food nation. Its equipment is widely used in Hilton hotels, Gold's Gym franchises, and even in Madonna's Hard Candy fitness center in Moscow.

Building high-quality fitness equipment requires sizable investments by Precor in buildings and machinery. For example, Precor recently moved its facilities from Valencia, California, to Greensboro, North Carolina. In order to reduce costs and minimize environmental impact, the company installed low-flow water fixtures, high-efficiency heating and cooling systems, and state-of-the-art lighting in its $26 million, 230,000-square-foot facility. As a result of these efforts, Precor's new facility received a Leadership in Energy and Efficient Design (LEED) CI Gold Certification.

Because of its huge investments in property, plant, and equipment, overhead costs represent a large percentage of the cost of Precor's exercise equipment. The combination of high overhead costs and a wide variety of products means that it is important that Precor allocates its overhead accurately to its various products. Without accurate cost information, Precor would not know whether its elliptical trainers and recumbent bicycles are making money, whether its AMT 100i adaptive motion trainer is priced high enough to cover its costs, or if its 240i Stretchtrainer is losing money.

To increase the accuracy of its costs, Precor uses a method of overhead allocation that focuses on identifying the types of activities that cause the company to incur costs. It then assigns more overhead to those products that rely most heavily on cost-incurring activities. By doing this, the allocation of overhead is less arbitrary than traditional overhead allocation methods. In short, before it can help us burn off the pounds, Precor needs to understand what drives its overhead costs.

Source: www.precor.com.

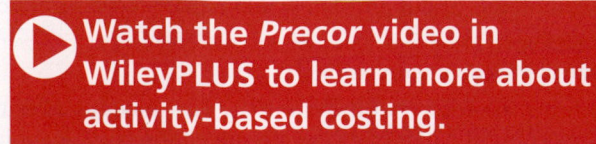

Watch the *Precor* video in WileyPLUS to learn more about activity-based costing.

© mediaphotos/iStockphoto

CHAPTER OUTLINE

Learning Objectives

1 Discuss the difference between traditional costing and activity-based costing.

- Traditional costing systems
- Illustration of a traditional system
- Need for a new approach
- Activity-based costing

DO IT! 1 Costing Systems

2 Apply activity-based costing to a manufacturer.

- Identify and classify activities and assign overhead
- Identify cost drivers
- Compute activity-based overhead rates
- Allocate overhead costs
- Comparing unit costs

DO IT! 2 Apply ABC to Manufacturer

3 Explain the benefits and limitations of activity-based costing.

- Advantage of multiple cost pools
- Advantage of enhanced cost control
- Advantage of better management decisions
- Limitations of ABC

DO IT! 3 Classify Activity Levels

4 Apply activity-based costing to service industries.

- Traditional costing example
- ABC example

DO IT! 4 Apply ABC to Service Company

Go to the **REVIEW AND PRACTICE** section at the end of the chapter for a review of key concepts and practice applications with solutions.

Visit **WileyPLUS with ORION** for additional tutorials and practice opportunities.

Discuss the difference between traditional costing and activity-based costing.

Traditional Costing Systems

It is probably impossible to determine the *exact* cost of a product or service. However, in order to achieve improved management decisions, companies strive to provide decision-makers with the most accurate cost estimates they can. The most accurate estimate of product cost occurs when the costs are traceable directly to the actual product or service. Direct materials and direct labor costs are the easiest to trace directly to the product through the use of material requisition forms and payroll time sheets. Overhead costs, on the other hand, are an indirect or common cost that generally cannot be easily or directly traced to individual products or services. Instead, companies use estimates to assign overhead costs to products and services.

Often, the most difficult part of computing accurate unit costs is determining the proper amount of **overhead cost** to assign to each product, service, or job. In our coverage of job order costing in Chapter 16 and of process costing in Chapter 17, we used a single or plantwide overhead rate throughout the year for the entire factory operation. That rate was called the **predetermined overhead rate**. For job order costing, we assumed that **direct labor cost** was the relevant activity base for assigning all overhead costs to jobs. For process costing, we assumed that **machine hours** was the relevant activity base for assigning all overhead to the process or department. Illustration 18-1 displays a simplified (one-stage) traditional costing system relying on direct labor to assign overhead.

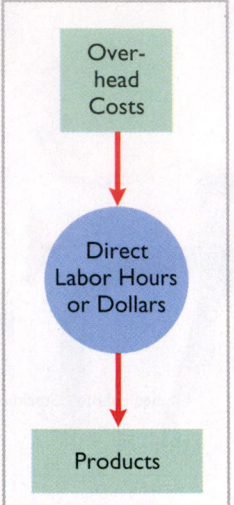

Illustration 18-1
Traditional one-stage costing system

Illustration of a Traditional Costing System

To illustrate a traditional costing system, assume that Atlas Company produces two abdominal fitness products—the Ab Bench and the Ab Coaster. Each year, the company produces 25,000 Ab Benches but only 5,000 Ab Coasters. Each unit produced requires one hour of direct labor, for a total of 30,000 labor hours (25,000 + 5,000). The direct labor cost is $12 per unit for each product.

The direct materials cost per unit is $40 for the Ab Bench and $30 for the Ab Coaster. Therefore, the total manufacturing costs (excluding overhead) is $52 for the Ab Bench and $42 for the Ab Coaster, as shown in Illustration 18-2.

Illustration 18-2
Direct costs per unit—traditional costing

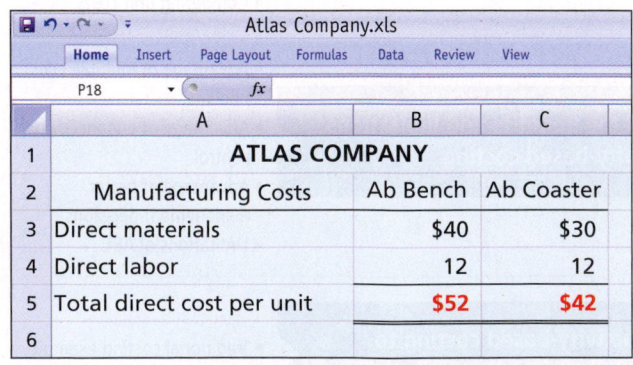

Manufacturing Costs	Ab Bench	Ab Coaster
ATLAS COMPANY		
Direct materials	$40	$30
Direct labor	12	12
Total direct cost per unit	**$52**	**$42**

Atlas also expects to incur annual manufacturing overhead costs of $900,000. Atlas allocates overhead using a single predetermined overhead rate based on the 30,000 direct labor hours it expects to use. Thus, the predetermined overhead rate is $30 per direct labor hour ($900,000/30,000 direct labor hours).

Since both products require one direct labor hour per unit, both products are allocated overhead costs of $30 per unit under traditional costing. Illustration 18-3 shows the total unit costs for the Ab Bench and the Ab Coaster.

	A	B	C
1	**ATLAS COMPANY**		
2	Manufacturing Costs	Ab Bench	Ab Coaster
3	Direct materials	$40	$30
4	Direct labor	12	12
5	Overhead	30	30
6	Total direct cost per unit	**$82**	**$72**
7			

Illustration 18-3
Total unit costs—traditional costing

The Need for a New Approach

As shown in Illustration 18-3, Atlas allocates the same amount of overhead costs per unit to both the Ab Bench and the Ab Coaster because these two products use the same amount of direct labor hours per unit. However, using a single rate based on direct labor hours may not be the best approach for Atlas to allocate its overhead.

Historically, the use of direct labor as the activity base made sense as direct labor made up a large portion of total manufacturing cost. Therefore, there was a high correlation between direct labor and the incurrence of overhead cost. Direct labor thus became the most popular basis for allocating overhead.

In recent years, however, manufacturers and service providers have experienced tremendous changes. Advances in computerized systems, technological innovations, global competition, and automation have altered the manufacturing environment drastically. As a result, the amount of direct labor used in many industries has greatly decreased, and total overhead costs resulting from depreciation on expensive equipment and machinery, utilities, repairs, and maintenance have significantly increased. When there is less (or no) correlation between direct labor and overhead costs incurred, plantwide predetermined overhead rates based on direct labor are misleading. Companies that use overhead rates based on direct labor when this correlation does not exist experience significant product cost distortions.

To minimize such distortions, many companies began to use machine hours instead of labor hours as the basis to allocate overhead in an automated manufacturing environment. But, even machine hours may not serve as a good basis for plantwide allocation of overhead costs. For example, product design and engineering costs are not correlated with machine hours but instead with the number of different items a company produces. Companies that have complex processes need to use multiple allocation bases to compute accurate product costs. An overhead cost allocation method that uses multiple bases is **activity-based costing**.

Activity-Based Costing

Activity-based costing (ABC) is an approach for allocating overhead costs. Specifically, ABC allocates overhead to multiple activity cost pools and then assigns the activity cost pools to products and services by means of cost drivers. In using ABC, you need to understand the following concepts.

Activity-based costing involves the following four steps, as shown in Illustration 18-4.

Illustration 18-4

The four steps of activity-based costing

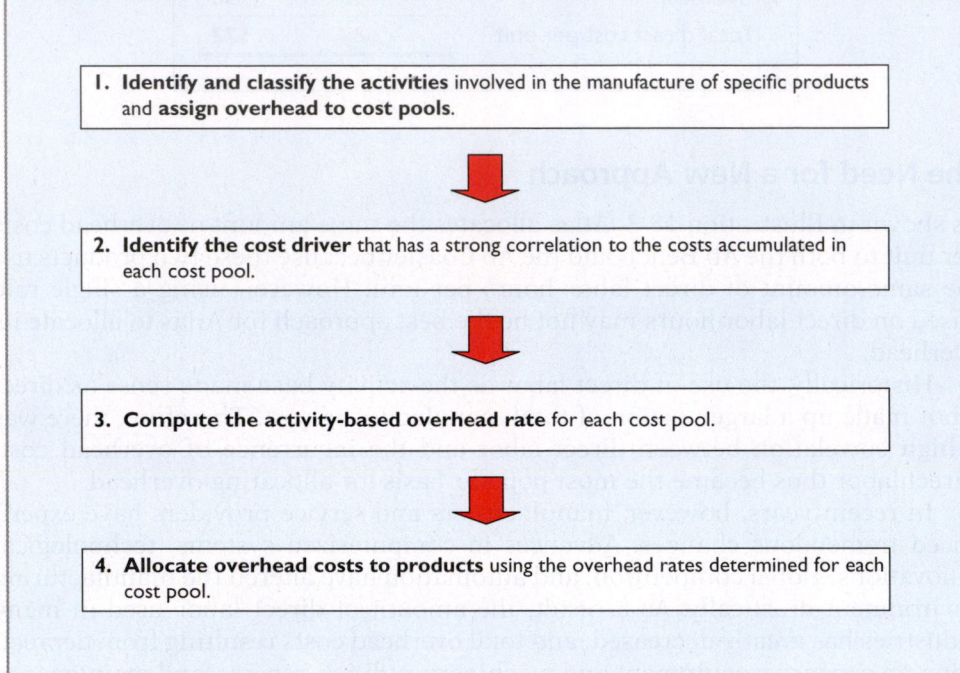

1. **Identify and classify the activities** involved in the manufacture of specific products and **assign overhead to cost pools**.

2. **Identify the cost driver** that has a strong correlation to the costs accumulated in each cost pool.

3. **Compute the activity-based overhead rate** for each cost pool.

4. **Allocate overhead costs to products** using the overhead rates determined for each cost pool.

ABC allocates overhead in a two-stage process. The first stage (Step 1) assigns overhead costs to activity cost pools. (Traditional costing systems, in contrast, allocate these costs to departments or to jobs.) Examples of overhead cost pools are ordering materials, setting up machines, assembling products, and inspecting products.

The second stage (Steps 2–4) allocates the overhead in the activity cost pools to products, using cost drivers. The cost drivers measure the number of individual activities undertaken to produce goods or perform services. Examples are number of purchase orders, number of setups, labor hours, and number of inspections. Illustration 18-5 shows examples of activities, and possible cost drivers to measure them, for a company that manufactures two types of abdominal exercise equipment—Ab Benches and Ab Coasters.

In the first step (as shown at the top of Illustration 18-5), the company assigns overhead costs to activity cost pools. In this simplified example, the company has identified four activity cost pools: purchasing, storing, machining, and supervising. After the costs are assigned to the activity cost pools, the company uses cost drivers to determine the costs to allocate to the individual products based on each product's use of each activity. For example, if Ab Benches require more activity by the purchasing department, as measured by the number of required purchase orders, then more of the overhead costs from the purchasing pool are allocated to the Ab Benches.

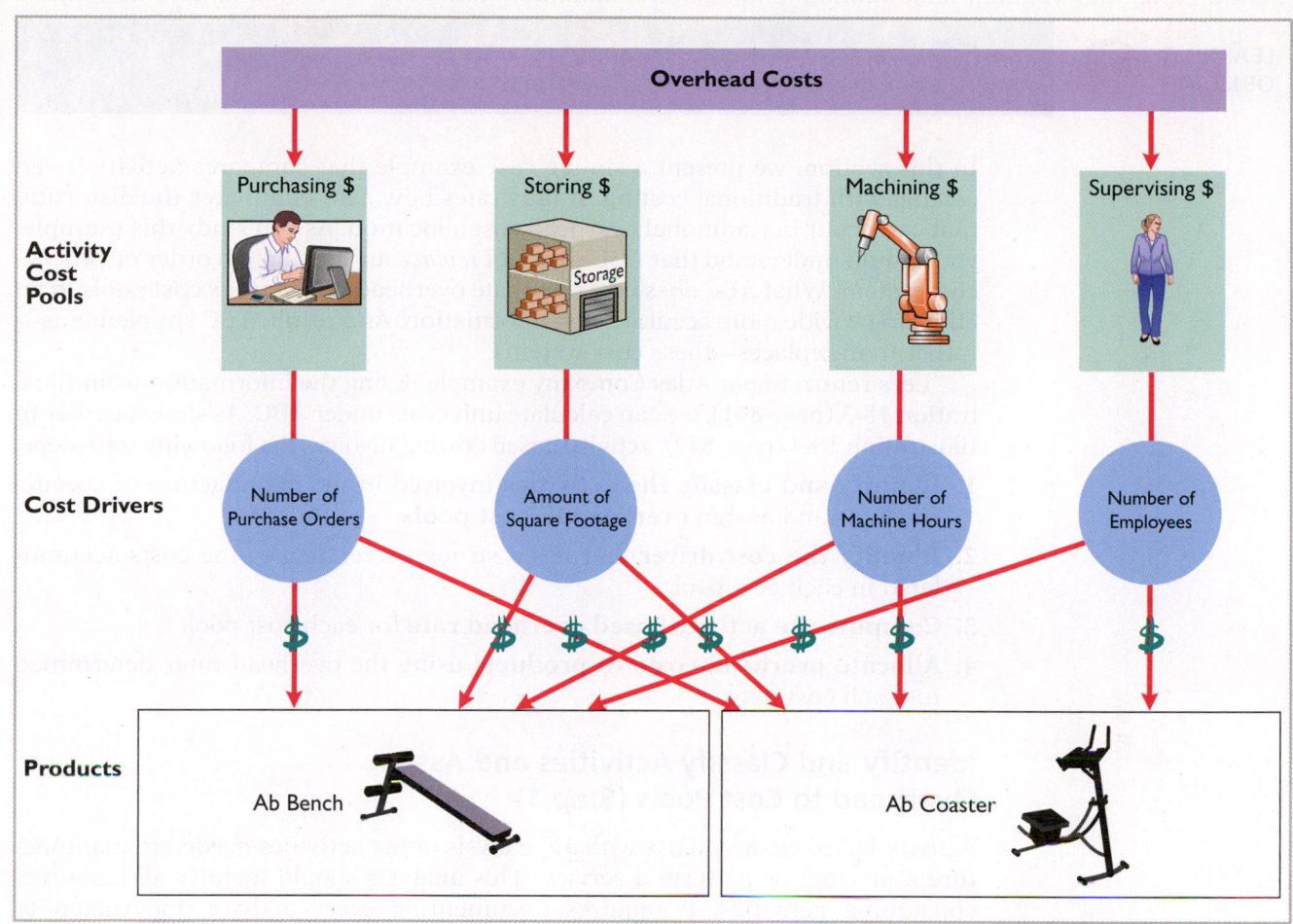

Illustration 18-5
Activities and related cost drivers

The more complex a product's manufacturing operation, the more activities and cost drivers it is likely to have. If there is little or no correlation between changes in the cost driver and consumption of the overhead cost, inaccurate product costs are inevitable.

DO IT!   1   Costing Systems

Indicate whether the following statements are true or false.

1. A traditional costing system allocates overhead by means of multiple overhead rates.
2. Activity-based costing allocates overhead costs in a two-stage process.
3. Direct materials and direct labor costs are easier to trace to products than overhead.
4. As manufacturing processes have become more automated, more companies have chosen to allocate overhead on the basis of direct labor costs.
5. In activity-based costing, an activity is any event, action, transaction, or work sequence that incurs cost when producing goods or performing services.

Solution

1. False.   2. True.   3. True.   4. False.   5. True.

Related exercise material: **BE18-1, BE18-2, E18-1, E18-2, and DO IT! 18-1.**

Action Plan

✔ Understand that a traditional costing system allocates overhead on the basis of a single predetermined overhead rate.

✔ Understand that an ABC system assigns overhead to identified activity cost pools and then allocates costs to products using related cost drivers that measure the resources consumed.

Apply activity-based costing to a manufacturer.

In this section, we present a simple case example that compares activity-based costing with traditional costing. It illustrates how ABC eliminates the distortion that can occur in traditional overhead cost allocation. As you study this example, you should understand that ABC does not *replace* an existing job order or process cost system. What ABC does is to segregate overhead into various cost pools in an effort to provide more accurate cost information. As a result, ABC supplements—rather than replaces—these cost systems.

Let's return to our Atlas Company example. Using the information from Illustration 18-3 (page 841), we can calculate unit costs under ABC. As shown earlier in Illustration 18-4 (page 842), activity-based costing involves the following four steps.

1. **Identify and classify the activities** involved in the manufacture of specific products and **assign overhead to cost pools**.

2. **Identify the cost driver** that has a strong correlation to the costs accumulated in each cost pool.

3. **Compute the activity-based overhead rate** for each cost pool.

4. **Allocate overhead costs to products** using the overhead rates determined for each cost pool.

Identify and Classify Activities and Assign Overhead to Cost Pools (Step 1)

Activity-based costing starts with an analysis of the activities needed to manufacture a product or perform a service. This analysis should identify all resource-consuming activities. It requires documenting every activity undertaken to accomplish a task. Atlas Company identifies five activity cost pools: manufacturing, setups, purchase ordering, product development, and property and plant.

Next, the company assigns overhead costs directly to the appropriate activity cost pool. For example, Atlas assigns all overhead costs directly associated with machine setups (such as salaries, supplies, and depreciation) to the setup cost pool. Illustration 18-6 shows the five cost pools, along with the estimated overhead assigned to each cost pool.

Illustration 18-6
Activity cost pools and estimated overhead

ATLAS COMPANY	
Activity Cost Pools	Estimated Overhead
Manufacturing	$500,000
Setups	100,000
Purchase ordering	50,000
Product development	200,000
Property and plant	50,000
Total	$900,000

Identify Cost Drivers (Step 2)

After costs are assigned to the activity cost pools, the company must identify the cost drivers for each cost pool. The cost driver must accurately measure the actual consumption of the activity by the various products. To achieve accurate costing, a **high degree of correlation** must exist between the cost driver and the actual consumption of the overhead costs in the cost pool.

Illustration 18-7 shows the cost drivers that Atlas Company identifies and their total expected use per activity cost pool.

Activity Cost Pools	Cost Drivers	Expected Use of Cost Drivers per Activity
Manufacturing	Machine hours	50,000 machine hours
Setups	Number of setups	2,000 setups
Purchase ordering	Number of purchase orders	2,500 purchase orders
Product development	Products developed	2 products developed
Property and plant	Square footage	25,000 square feet

Illustration 18-7
Cost drivers and their expected use

Availability and ease of obtaining data relating to the cost driver is an important factor that must be considered in its selection.

Compute Activity-Based Overhead Rates (Step 3)

Next, the company computes an **activity-based overhead rate** per cost driver by dividing the estimated overhead per activity by the number of cost drivers expected to be used per activity. Illustration 18-8 shows the formula for this computation.

$$\frac{\text{Estimated Overhead per Activity}}{\text{Expected Use of Cost Drivers per Activity}} = \frac{\text{Activity-Based}}{\text{Overhead Rate}}$$

Illustration 18-8
Formula for computing activity-based overhead rate

Atlas Company computes its activity-based overhead rates by using the estimated overhead per activity cost pool, shown in Illustration 18-6, and the expected use of cost drivers per activity, shown in Illustration 18-7. These computations are presented in Illustration 18-9.

	A	B	C	D	E	F
1		**ATLAS COMPANY**				
2	Activity Cost Pools	Estimated Overhead	÷	Expected Use of Cost Drivers per Activity	=	Activity-Based Overhead Rates
3	Manufacturing	$500,000		50,000 machine hours		$10 per machine hour
4	Setups	100,000		2,000 setups		$50 per setup
5	Purchase ordering	50,000		2,500 purchase orders		$20 per order
6	Product development	200,000		2 products developed		$100,000 per product
7	Plant and property	50,000		25,000 square feet		$2 per square foot
8	Total	**$900,000**				
9						

Illustration 18-9
Computation of activity-based overhead rates

Allocate Overhead Costs to Products (Step 4)

In allocating overhead costs, the company must know the expected use of cost drivers **for each product**. Because of its low volume and higher number of components, the Ab Coaster requires more setups and purchase orders than the

Ab Bench. Illustration 18-10 shows the expected use of cost drivers per product for each of Atlas Company's products.

Illustration 18-10
Expected use of cost drivers
per product

Activity Cost Pools	Cost Drivers	Expected Use of Cost Drivers per Activity	Expected Use of Cost Drivers per Product	
			Ab Bench	Ab Coaster
Manufacturing	Machine hours	50,000 machine hours	30,000	20,000
Setups	Number of setups	2,000 setups	500	1,500
Purchase ordering	Number of purchase orders	2,500 purchase orders	750	1,750
Product development	Products developed	2 products developed	1	1
Property and plant	Square feet	25,000 square feet	10,000	15,000

To allocate overhead costs to each product, Atlas multiplies the activity-based overhead rates per cost driver (Illustration 18-9) by the number of cost drivers expected to be used per product (Illustration 18-10). Illustration 18-11 shows the overhead cost allocated to each product.

Illustration 18-11
Allocation of activity cost pools
to products

Atlas Company.xls

	ATLAS COMPANY					
	Ab Bench			**Ab Coaster**		
Activity Cost Pools	Expected Use of Cost Drivers × per Product	Activity-Based Overhead Rates	= Cost Allocated	Expected Use of Cost Drivers × per Product	Activity-Based Overhead Rates	= Cost Allocated
Manufacturing	30,000	$10	$300,000	20,000	$10	$200,000
Setups	500	$50	25,000	1,500	$50	75,000
Purchase ordering	750	$20	15,000	1,750	$20	35,000
Product development	1	$100,000	100,000	1	$100,000	100,000
Property and plant	10,000	$2.00	20,000	15,000	$2.00	30,000
Total costs allocated (a)			$460,000			$440,000
Units produced (b)			25,000			5,000
Overhead cost per unit [(a)÷(b)], rounded			**$18.40**			**$88.00**

Under ABC, the overhead cost per unit is $18.40 for the Ab Bench and $88.00 for the Ab Coaster. We see next how this per unit amount substantially differs from that computed under a traditional costing system.

Comparing Unit Costs

Illustration 18-12 compares the unit costs for Atlas Company's Ab Bench and Ab Coaster under traditional costing and ABC.

The comparison shows that unit costs under traditional costing are different and often misleading. Traditional costing overstates the cost of producing the Ab Bench by $11.60 per unit and understates the cost of producing the Ab Coaster

Manufacturing Costs	Ab Bench		Ab Coaster	
	Traditional Costing	ABC	Traditional Costing	ABC
Direct materials	$40.00	$40.00	$30.00	$ 30.00
Direct labor	12.00	12.00	12.00	12.00
Overhead	30.00	18.40	30.00	88.00
Total direct cost per unit	**$82.00**	**$70.40**	**$72.00**	**$130.00**

Overstated **$11.60**   **Understated** **$58.00**

Illustration 18-12
Comparison of unit product costs

by $58 per unit. These differences are attributable to how Atlas allocates manufacturing overhead across the two systems. Using a traditional costing system, each product was allocated the same amount of overhead ($30) because both products use the same amount of the cost driver (direct labor hours). In contrast, ABC allocates overhead to products based on multiple cost drivers. For example, under ABC, Atlas allocates 75% of the costs of equipment setups to Ab Coasters because Ab Coasters were responsible for 75% (1,500 ÷ 2,000) of the total number of setups.

Note that activity-based costing does not change the amount of overhead costs. Under both traditional costing and ABC, Atlas spends the same amount of overhead—$900,000. However, ABC allocates overhead costs in a more accurate manner. Thus, ABC helps Atlas avoid some negative consequences of a traditional costing system, such as overpricing its Ab Benches and thereby possibly losing market share to competitors. Atlas has also been sacrificing profitability by underpricing the Ab Coaster.

Companies that move from traditional costing to ABC often have similar experiences as ABC shifts costs from high-volume products to low-volume products. This shift occurs because low-volume products are often more customized and require more special handling. Thus, low-volume products are frequently responsible for more overhead costs. In addition, ABC recognizes products' use of resources, which also increases the accuracy of product costs.

Management Insight

© CGinspiration/iStockphoto

ABC Evaluated

Surveys of companies often show ABC usage of approximately 50%. Yet, in recent years, articles about ABC have expressed mixed opinions regarding its usefulness. To evaluate ABC practices and user satisfaction with ABC, a survey was conducted of 348 companies worldwide. Some of the interesting findings included the following: ABC methods are widely used across the entire value chain, rather than being primarily used to allocate production-specific costs; only 25% of non-ABC companies think they are accurately tracing the costs of activities, while 70% of ABC companies think their company does this well; and respondents felt that ABC provides greater support for financial, operational, and strategic decisions. More than 87% of respondents said that their ideal costing system would include some form of ABC. Since this significantly exceeds the 50% of the respondents actually using it, ABC usage may well increase in the future.

Source: William Stratton, Denis Desroches, Raef Lawson, and Toby Hatch, "Activity-Based Costing: Is It Still Relevant?" *Management Accounting Quarterly* (Spring, 2009), pp. 31–39.

What might explain why so many companies say that ideally they would use ABC, but they haven't adopted it yet? (Go to **WileyPLUS** for this answer and additional questions.)

DO IT! 2 Apply ABC to Manufacturer

Casey Company has five activity cost pools and two products. It expects to produce 200,000 units of its automobile scissors jack and 80,000 units of its truck hydraulic jack. Having identified its activity cost pools and the cost drivers for each cost pool, Casey Company accumulated the following data relative to those activity cost pools and cost drivers.

| | | | | Expected Use of Cost Drivers per Product | |
Activity Cost Pools	Cost Drivers	Estimated Overhead	Expected Use of Cost Drivers per Activity	Scissors Jacks	Hydraulic Jacks
Ordering and receiving	Purchase orders	$ 200,000	2,500 orders	1,000	1,500
Machine setup	Setups	600,000	1,200 setups	500	700
Machining	Machine hours	2,000,000	800,000 hours	300,000	500,000
Assembling	Parts	1,800,000	3,000,000 parts	1,800,000	1,200,000
Inspecting and testing	Tests	700,000	35,000 tests	20,000	15,000
		$5,300,000			

Using the above data, do the following.

(a) Prepare a schedule showing the computations of the activity-based overhead rates per cost driver.

Action Plan

✔ Determine the activity-based overhead rate by dividing the estimated overhead per activity by the expected use of cost drivers per activity.

(b) Prepare a schedule assigning each activity's overhead cost to the two products.

(c) Compute the overhead cost per unit for each product.

(d) Comment on the comparative overhead cost per unit.

Solution

(a) Computations of activity-based overhead rates per cost driver:

Activity Cost Pools	Estimated Overhead	÷	Expected Use of Cost Drivers per Activity	=	Activity-Based Overhead Rates
Ordering and receiving	$ 200,000		2,500 purchase orders		$80 per order
Machine setup	600,000		1,200 setups		$500 per setup
Machining	2,000,000		800,000 machine hours		$2.50 per machine hour
Assembling	1,800,000		3,000,000 parts		$0.60 per part
Inspecting and testing	700,000		35,000 tests		$20 per test
	$5,300,000				

(b) Assignment of each activity's overhead cost to products using ABC:

| | Scissors Jacks | | | Hydraulic Jacks | | |
Activity Cost Pools	Expected Use of Cost Drivers per Product ×	Activity-Based Overhead Rates =	Cost Assigned	Expected Use of Cost Drivers per Product ×	Activity-Based Overhead Rates =	Cost Assigned
Ordering and receiving	1,000	$80	$ 80,000	1,500	$80	$ 120,000
Machine setup	500	$500	250,000	700	$500	350,000
Machining	300,000	$2.50	750,000	500,000	$2.50	1,250,000
Assembling	1,800,000	$0.60	1,080,000	1,200,000	$0.60	720,000
Inspecting and testing	20,000	$20	400,000	15,000	$20	300,000
Total assigned costs			$2,560,000			$2,740,000

(c) Computation of overhead cost per unit:

	Scissors Jack	Hydraulic Jack
Total costs assigned	$2,560,000	$2,740,000
Total units produced	200,000	80,000
Overhead cost per unit	$12.80	$34.25

(d) These data show that the total overhead assigned to 80,000 hydraulic jacks exceeds the overhead assigned to 200,000 scissors jacks. The overhead cost per hydraulic jack is $34.25, but it is only $12.80 per scissors jack.

Related exercise material: **BE18-3, BE18-4, BE18-5, BE18-6, BE18-7, E18-3, E18-4, E18-5, E18-6, E18-7, E18-8, and DO IT! 18-2.**

Action Plan (cont.)

✔ Assign the overhead of each activity cost pool to the individual products by multiplying the expected use of cost driver per product times the activity-based overhead rate.

✔ Determine overhead cost per unit by dividing the overhead assigned to each product by the number of units of that product.

LEARNING OBJECTIVE 3 — **Explain the benefits and limitations of activity-based costing.**

ABC has three primary benefits:

1. ABC leads to more cost pools and therefore more accurate product costing.
2. ABC leads to enhanced control over overhead costs.
3. ABC leads to better management decisions.

The Advantage of Multiple Cost Pools

The main mechanism by which ABC increases product cost accuracy is the use of multiple cost pools. Instead of one plantwide pool (or even several departmental pools) and a single cost driver, companies use numerous activity cost pools with more relevant cost drivers. Thus, costs are allocated more directly on the basis of the cost drivers used to produce each product.

Note that in the Atlas Company example, the *manufacturing* cost pool reflected multiple manufacturing activities, including machining, assembling, and painting. These activities were included in a single pool for simplicity. In many companies, the number of activities—and thus the number of pools—can be substantial. For example, **Clark-Hurth** (a division of **Clark Equipment Company**), a manufacturer of axles and transmissions, identified over 170 activities. **Compumotor** (a division of **Parker Hannifin**) identified over 80 activities in just the procurement function of its Material Control Department. Illustration 18-13 (page 850) shows a more likely "split" of the activities that were included in Atlas's manufacturing cost pool, reflecting separate pools and drivers for each of those activities.

CLASSIFICATION OF ACTIVITY LEVELS

To gain the full advantage of having multiple cost pools, the costs within the pool must be correlated with the driver. To achieve this, a company's managers often characterize activities as belonging to one of the following four activity-level groups when designing an ABC system.

1. **Unit-level activities** are performed for each unit of production. For example, the assembly of cell phones is a unit-level activity because the amount of assembly the company performs increases with each additional cell phone assembled.

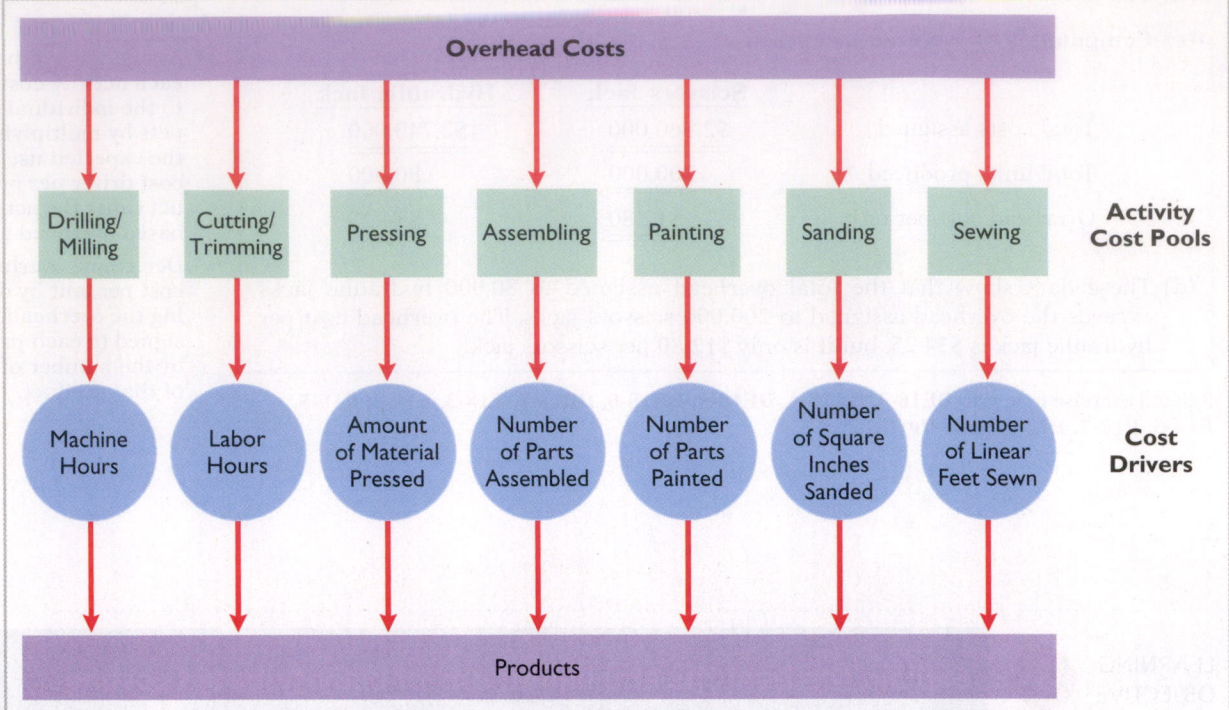

Illustration 18-13
A more detailed view of Atlas's
machining activities

2. **Batch-level activities** are performed every time a company produces another batch of a product. For example, suppose that to start processing a new batch of ice cream, an ice cream producer needs to set up its machines. The amount of time spent setting up machines increases with the number of batches produced, not with the number of units produced.

3. **Product-level activities** are performed every time a company produces a new type of product. For example, before a pharmaceutical company can produce and sell a new type of medicine, it must undergo very substantial product tests to ensure the product is effective and safe. The amount of time spent on testing activities increases with the number of products the company produces.

4. **Facility-level activities** are required to support or sustain an entire production process. Consider, for example, a hospital. The hospital building must be insured and heated, and the property taxes must be paid, no matter how many patients the hospital treats. These costs do not vary as a function of the number of units, batches, or products.

Companies may achieve greater accuracy in overhead cost allocation by recognizing these four different levels of activities and, from them, developing specific activity cost pools and their related cost drivers. Illustration 18-14 graphically displays this four-level activity hierarchy, along with the types of activities and examples of cost drivers for those activities at each level.

The Advantage of Enhanced Cost Control

ABC leads to enhanced control over overhead costs. Under ABC, companies can trace many overhead costs directly to activities—allowing some costs previously considered to be indirect costs to be identified as direct costs. In developing an ABC system, managers increase their awareness of the activities performed by the company in its production and supporting processes. This awareness helps managers classify activities as value-added or non-valued-added.

Four Levels	Types of Activities	Examples of Cost Drivers
Unit-Level Activities		
	Machine-related Drilling, cutting, milling, trimming, pressing	Machine hours
	Labor-related Assembling, painting, sanding, sewing	Direct labor hours or cost
Batch-Level Activities		
	Equipment setups	Number of setups or setup time
	Purchase ordering	Number of purchase orders
	Inspection	Number of inspections or inspection time
	Materials handling	Number of material moves
Product-Level Activities		
	Product design	Number of product designs
	Engineering changes	Number of changes
Facility-Level Activities		
	Plant management salaries	Number of employees managed
	Plant depreciation	Square footage
	Property taxes	Square footage
	Utilities	Square footage

There. This baby should keep the building cool.

Cutting Edge Apparel Company

Illustration 18-14
Hierarchy of activity levels

Value-added activities are those activities of **a company's operations** that increase the perceived value of a product or service to customers. Examples for the manufacture of Precor exercise equipment include engineering design, machining, assembly, and painting. Examples of value-added activities in a service company include performing surgery at a hospital, performing legal research at a law firm, or delivering packages by a freight company.

Non–value-added activities are those activities that, if eliminated, would not reduce the perceived value of a company's product or service. These activities simply **add cost to, or increase the time spent on, a product or service without increasing its perceived value**. One example is inventory storage. If a company **eliminated the need** to store inventory, it would not reduce the value of its product, but it would decrease its product costs. Other examples include moving materials, work in process, or finished goods from one location to another in the plant during the production process; waiting for manufacturing equipment to become available; inspecting goods; and fixing defective goods under warranty.

Companies often use **activity flowcharts** to help identify the ABC activities, such as the one shown in Illustration 18-15 (page 852). The top part of this flowchart identifies activities as value-added (highlighted in red) or non–value-added. Two rows in the lower part of the flowchart show the number of days spent on each activity. The first row shows the number of days spent on each activity under the current manufacturing process. The second row shows the number of days expected to be spent on each activity under management's proposed reengineered manufacturing process.

				Activities								
NVA	**NVA**	**NVA**	**NVA**	**VA**		**NVA**	**NVA**	**VA**	**NVA**	**NVA**	**NVA**	**VA**
Receive and Inspect Materials	Move and Store Materials	Move Materials to Production and Wait	Set Up Machines	Machining		Inspect	Move and Wait	Assembly	Inspect and Test	Move to Storage	Store Finished Goods	Package and Ship
				Drill	Lathe							

HEARTLAND COMPANY
Activity Flowchart

Current Days	1	12	2.5	1.5	2	1	0.2	6	2	0.3	0.5	14	1

Total Current Average Time = 44 days

Proposed Days	1	4	1.5	1.5	2	1	0.2	2	2	0.3	0.5	10	1

Total Proposed Average Time = 27 days

Proposed reduction in non–value-added time = 17 days

VA = Value-added   NVA = Non–value-added

Illustration 18-15
Analyzing non–value-added activities to improve operations

The proposed changes would reduce time spent on non–value-added activities by 17 days. This 17-day improvement is due entirely to moving inventory more quickly through the non–value-added processes—that is, by reducing inventory time in moving, storage, and waiting. Appendix 18A discusses a just-in-time inventory system, which some companies use to eliminate non–value-added activities related to inventory.

Not all activities labeled non–value-added are totally wasteful, nor can they be totally eliminated. For example, although inspection time is a non–value added activity from a customer's perspective, few companies would eliminate their quality control functions. Similarly, moving and waiting time is non–value added, but it would be impossible to completely eliminate. Nevertheless, when managers recognize the non–value-added characteristic of these activities, they are motivated to minimize them as much as possible. Attention to such matters is part of the growing practice of activity-based management, which helps managers concentrate on **continuous improvement** of operations and activities.

Management Insight   General Mills

© Action Sports Photography/ Shutterstock

What Does NASCAR Have to Do with Breakfast Cereal?

Often the best way to improve a process is to learn from observing a different process. Production-line technicians from food producer General Mills were flown to North Carolina to observe firsthand how race-car pit crews operate. In a NASCAR race, the value-added activity is driving toward the finish line; any time spent in the pit is non–value-added. Every split second saved in the pit increases the chances of winning. From what the General Mills' technicians learned at the car race, as well as other efforts, they were able to reduce setup time from 5 hours to just 20 minutes.

What are the benefits of reducing setup time? (Go to **WileyPLUS** for this answer and additional questions.)

The Advantage of Better Management Decisions

Some companies experiencing the benefits of activity-based costing have applied it to a broader range of management activities. **Activity-based management (ABM)** extends the use of ABC from product costing to a comprehensive management tool that focuses on reducing costs and improving processes and decision-making.

Managers extend the use of ABC via ABM for both strategic and operational decisions or perspectives. For example, returning to Atlas Company, its managers might use ABC information about its Ab Benches and Ab Coasters to improve the efficiency of its operations. For example, after realizing that both products require a high volume of setup hours—as well as the costs of these hours—they might want to reduce the hours required to set up production runs. Such information may lead managers to increase the number of units produced with each setup or to optimize production schedules for the two products.

ABC also helps managers evaluate employees, departments, and business units. Atlas, for example, might use ABC information about salespeople's activities related to customer visits, number of orders, and post-sales customer service. Such information informs managers about how much effort salespeople are exerting, as well as how efficient they are in dealing with customers. Similarly, Atlas might use ABC information about each department's use of shared resources, like inventory space. Such information lets managers know which departments are the most efficient, which in turn leads to sharing best-practices information within the company. ABC information also helps Atlas to establish **performance standards** within the company, as well as **benchmark** its performance against other companies.

The implications of ABC are not limited to operational decisions. The differences in profitability between the Ab Benches and Ab Coasters may suggest a need to change the company's product mix. Such considerations, in turn, have implications for Atlas's marketing strategy. ABM may guide managers in considering different target customer markets for the two products. Or, managers might consider bundling the two products into a "home gym" set. As another, more extreme, example, managers might consider outsourcing production for one of the products or dropping one of the product lines altogether.

It is often the case that ABM for one perspective has implications for another perspective. For instance, the strategic decision to drop a product line is usually followed by operational decisions regarding what to do with employees' time or the machinery and equipment originally used to manufacture the dropped product. Similarly, increases in employees' efficiency following from operational decisions often lead to changes in employee hiring and compensation strategy. The interrelated nature of the strategic and operational perspectives often means that a decision is not made until the cascading implications of that decision are also identified and considered.

Some Limitations and Knowing When to Use ABC

ABC can be very beneficial, but it is not without its limitations. **ABC can be expensive to use**. The increased cost of identifying multiple activities and applying numerous cost drivers discourages many companies from using ABC. ABC systems are also more complex than traditional systems. So companies must ask, is the cost of implementation greater than the benefit of greater accuracy? For some companies, there may be no need to consider ABC at all because their existing system is sufficient.

Further, ABC does not offer complete accuracy as **some arbitrary allocations remain**. Even though more overhead costs can be assigned directly to products through ABC, some overhead costs still need to be allocated by arbitrary cost drivers. For example, Atlas Company assigned $50,000 of overhead pertaining to insurance and property taxes to the property and plant cost pool. Atlas allocated this $50,000 using square footage used by each product (10,000 square feet for Ab Benches and 15,000 square feet for Ab Coasters). A more accurate driver of insurance costs might be replacement costs of production equipment for each product type. However, such information may not be readily available, and Atlas must make due with square footage.

In light of these limitations, how does a company know when to use ABC? The presence of one or more of the following factors would point to possible use:

1. Product lines differ greatly in volume and manufacturing complexity.

2. Product lines are numerous and diverse, requiring various degrees of support services.

3. Overhead costs constitute a significant portion of total costs.

4. The manufacturing process or the number of products has changed significantly, for example, from labor-intensive to capital-intensive due to automation.

5. Production or marketing managers are ignoring data provided by the existing system and are instead using "bootleg" costing data or other alternative data when pricing or making other product decisions.

Ultimately, it is important to realize that the redesign and installation of a product costing system is a significant decision that requires considerable costs and a major effort to accomplish. Therefore, financial managers need to be cautious and deliberate when initiating changes in costing systems. A key factor in implementing a successful ABC system is the support of top management, especially given that the benefits of ABC are not completely visible until *after* it has been implemented.

DO IT! 3 Classify Activity Levels

Action Plan

✔ You should use **unit-level** activities for each unit of product, **batch-level** activities for each batch of product, **product-level** activities for an entire product line, and **facility-level** activities for across the entire range of products.

Morgan Toy Company manufactures six primary product lines of toys in its Morganville plant. As a result of an activity analysis, the accounting department has identified eight activity cost pools. Each of the toy products is produced in large batches, with the whole plant devoted to one product at a time. Classify each of the following activities as either unit-level, batch-level, product-level, or facility-level: (a) engineering design, (b) machine setup, (c) toy design, (d) interviews of prospective employees, (e) inspections after each setup, (f) polishing parts, (g) assembling parts, and (h) health and safety.

Solution

(a) Product-level. (b) Batch-level. (c) Product-level. (d) Facility-level. (e) Batch-level. (f) Unit-level. (g) Unit-level. (h) Facility-level.

Related exercise material: **BE18-10, BE18-11, BE18-12, E18-12, E18-13, and DO IT! 18-3.**

LEARNING OBJECTIVE **4**

Apply activity-based costing to service industries.

Although initially developed and implemented by manufacturers, activity-based costing has been widely adopted in service industries as well. ABC is used by airlines, railroads, hotels, hospitals, banks, insurance companies, telephone companies, and financial services firms. The overall objective of ABC in service firms is no different than it is in a manufacturing company. That objective is to identify the key activities that generate costs and to keep track of how many of those activities are completed for each service performed (by job, service, contract, or customer).

 The general approach to identifying activities, activity cost pools, and cost drivers is the same for service companies and for manufacturers. Also, the labeling of activities as value-added and non–value-added, and the attempt to reduce or eliminate non–value-added activities as much as possible, is just as valid in service industries as in manufacturing operations. What sometimes makes implementation of activity-based costing difficult in service industries is that, compared to manufacturers, **a larger proportion of overhead costs are company-wide costs** that cannot be directly traced to specific services performed by the company.

To illustrate the application of activity-based costing to a service company contrasted to traditional costing, we use a public accounting firm. This illustration is applicable to any service firm that performs numerous services for a client as part of a job, such as a law firm, consulting firm, or architect.

Traditional Costing Example

Assume that the public accounting firm of Check and Doublecheck prepares the condensed annual budget shown in Illustration 18-16. The firm engages in a number of services, including audit, tax, and computer consulting.

<table>
<tr><td colspan="3">**CHECK AND DOUBLECHECK, CPAS**
Annual Budget</td></tr>
<tr><td>Revenue</td><td></td><td>$4,000,000</td></tr>
<tr><td>Direct labor</td><td>$1,200,000</td><td></td></tr>
<tr><td>Overhead (expected)</td><td>600,000</td><td></td></tr>
<tr><td>Total costs</td><td></td><td>1,800,000</td></tr>
<tr><td>Operating income</td><td></td><td>$2,200,000</td></tr>
</table>

$$\frac{\text{Estimated overhead}}{\text{Direct labor cost}} = \text{Predetermined overhead rate}$$

$$\frac{\$600,000}{\$1,200,000} = 50\%$$

Illustration 18-16
Condensed annual budget of a service firm under traditional costing

Direct labor is often the professional service performed. Under traditional costing, direct labor is the basis for overhead application to each job. As shown in Illustration 18-16, the predetermined overhead rate of 50% is calculated by dividing the total estimated overhead cost by the total direct labor cost. To determine the operating income earned on any job, Check and Doublecheck applies overhead at the rate of 50% of actual direct professional labor costs incurred. For example, assume that Check and Doublecheck records $140,000 of actual direct professional labor cost during its audit of Plano Molding Company, which was billed an audit fee of $260,000. Under traditional costing, using 50% as the rate for applying overhead to the job, Check and Doublecheck would compute applied overhead and operating income related to the Plano Molding Company audit as shown in Illustration 18-17.

<table>
<tr><td colspan="3">**CHECK AND DOUBLECHECK, CPAS**
Plano Molding Company Audit</td></tr>
<tr><td>Revenue</td><td></td><td>$260,000</td></tr>
<tr><td>Less: Direct professional labor</td><td>$140,000</td><td></td></tr>
<tr><td>Applied overhead (50% × $140,000)</td><td>70,000</td><td>210,000</td></tr>
<tr><td>Operating income</td><td></td><td>$ 50,000</td></tr>
</table>

Illustration 18-17
Overhead applied under traditional costing system

This example, under traditional costing, uses only one cost driver (direct labor cost) to determine the overhead application rate.

Activity-Based Costing Example

Illustration 18-18
Condensed annual budget of a service firm under activity-based costing

Under **activity-based costing**, Check and Doublecheck distributes its estimated annual overhead costs of $600,000 to three activity cost pools. The firm computes activity-based overhead rates per cost driver by dividing each activity overhead cost pool by the expected number of cost drivers used per activity. Illustration 18-18 shows an annual overhead budget using an ABC system.

CHECK AND DOUBLECHECK, CPAS					
Annual Overhead Budget					
Activity Cost Pools	**Cost Drivers**	**Estimated Overhead**	÷	**Expected Use of Cost Drivers per Activity** =	**Activity-Based Overhead Rates**
Administration	Number of partner-hours	$335,000		3,350	$100 per partner-hour
Customer development	Revenue billed	160,000		$4,000,000	$0.04 per $1 of revenue
Recruiting and training	Direct professional hours	105,000		30,000	$3.50 per hour
		$600,000			

The assignment of the individual overhead activity rates to the actual number of activities used in the performance of the Plano Molding Company audit results in total overhead assigned of $57,200, as shown in Illustration 18-19.

Illustration 18-19
Assigning overhead in a service company

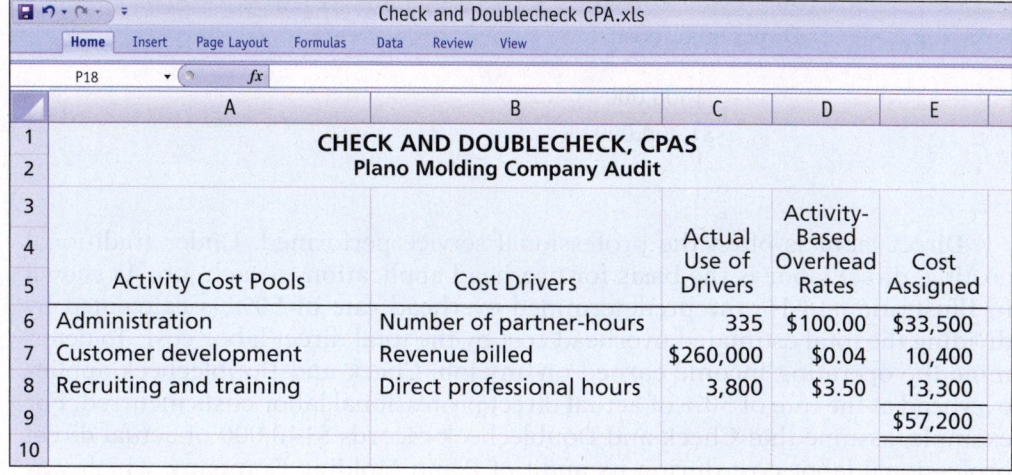

Under activity-based costing, Check and Doublecheck assigns overhead costs of $57,200 to the Plano Molding Company audit, as compared to $70,000 under traditional costing. Illustration 18-20 compares total costs and operating margins under the two costing systems.

Illustration 18-20
Comparison of traditional costing with ABC in a service company

CHECK AND DOUBLECHECK, CPAS		
Plano Molding Company Audit		
	Traditional Costing	**ABC**
Revenue	$260,000	$260,000
Expenses		
Direct professional labor	$140,000	$140,000
Applied overhead	70,000	57,200
Total expenses	210,000	197,200
Operating income	**$ 50,000**	**$ 62,800**
Profit margin	**19.2%**	**24.2%**

Illustration 18-20 shows that the assignment of overhead costs under traditional costing and ABC is different. The total cost assigned to performing the audit of Plano Molding Company is greater under traditional costing by $12,800 ($62,800 − $50,000), and the profit margin is significantly lower. Traditional costing understates the profitability of the audit.

Service Company Insight American Airlines

Oleksiy MaksymenkoPhotography/Alamy

Traveling Light

Have you flown on American Airlines since baggage fees have been implemented? Did the fee make you so mad that you swore that the next time you flew, you would pack fewer clothes so you could use a carry-on bag instead? That is exactly how American Airlines (and the other airlines that charge baggage fees) hoped that you would react. Baggage handling is extremely labor-intensive. All that tagging, sorting, loading on carts, loading in planes, unloading, and sorting again add up to about $9 per bag. Baggage handling also involves equipment costs: sorters, carts, conveyors, tractors, and storage facilities.

That's about another $4 of equipment-related overhead per bag. Finally, there is additional fuel cost of a 40-pound item—about $2 in fuel for a 3-hour flight. These costs add up to $15 ($9 + $4 + $2).

Since airlines have implemented their baggage fees, fewer customers are checking bags. Not only does this save the airlines money, it also increases the amount of space available for hauling cargo. An airline can charge at least $80 for hauling a small parcel for same-day delivery service.

Source: Scott McCartney, "What It Costs an Airline to Fly Your Luggage," *Wall Street Journal Online* (November 25, 2008).

Why do airlines charge even higher rates for heavier bags, bags that are odd shapes (e.g., ski bags), and bags with hazardous materials in them? (Go to WileyPLUS for this answer and additional questions.)

DO IT! 4   Apply ABC to Service Company

We Carry It, Inc. is a trucking company. It provides local, short-haul, and long-haul services. The company has developed the following three cost pools.

Activity Cost Pools	Cost Drivers	Estimated Overhead	Expected Use of Cost Drivers per Activity
Loading and unloading	Number of pieces	$ 70,000	100,000 pieces
Travel	Miles driven	250,000	500,000 miles
Logistics	Hours	60,000	2,000 hours

(a) Compute the activity-based overhead rate for each pool.

(b) Determine the overhead allocated to Job A1027 which has 150 pieces, requires 200 miles of driving, and 0.75 hours of logistics.

Solution

(a) The activity based overhead rates are as follows.

Activity Cost Pools	Estimated Overhead	÷	Expected Use of Cost Drivers per Activity	=	Activity-Based Overhead Rate
Loading and unloading	$ 70,000		100,000 pieces		$0.70 per piece
Travel	250,000		500,000 miles		$0.50 per mile
Logistics	60,000		2,000 hours		$30 per hour

(b) The overhead applied to job A1027 is (150 × $0.70) + (200 × $0.50) + (0.75 × $30) = $227.50

Action Plan

✔ Divide the estimated overhead by the expected use of cost driver per activity to determine activity-based overhead rate.

✔ Apply the activity-based overhead rate to jobs based on actual use of drivers.

Related exercise material: **BE18-12, E18-14, E18-15, E18-17, and DO IT! 18-4.**

APPENDIX 18A: Explain just-in-time (JIT) processing.

Traditionally, continuous process manufacturing has been based on a **just-in-case** philosophy: Inventories of raw materials are maintained *just in case* some items are of poor quality or a key supplier is shut down by a strike. Similarly, subassembly parts are manufactured and stored *just in case* they are needed later in the manufacturing process. Finished goods are completed and stored *just in case* unexpected and rush customer orders are received. This philosophy often results in a "**push approach**," in which raw materials and subassembly parts are pushed through each process. Traditional processing often results in the buildup of extensive manufacturing inventories.

Primarily in response to foreign competition, many U.S. firms have switched to **just-in-time (JIT) processing**. JIT manufacturing is dedicated to having the right amount of materials, parts, or products just as they are needed. JIT first hit the United States in the early 1980s when automobile companies adopted it to compete with foreign automakers. Many companies, including Dell, Caterpillar, and Harley-Davidson, now successfully use JIT. Under JIT processing, companies receive raw materials **just in time** for use in production, they complete subassembly parts **just in time** for use in finished goods, and they complete finished goods **just in time** to be sold. Illustration 18A-1 shows the sequence of activities in just-in-time processing.

Illustration 18A-1
Just-in-time processing

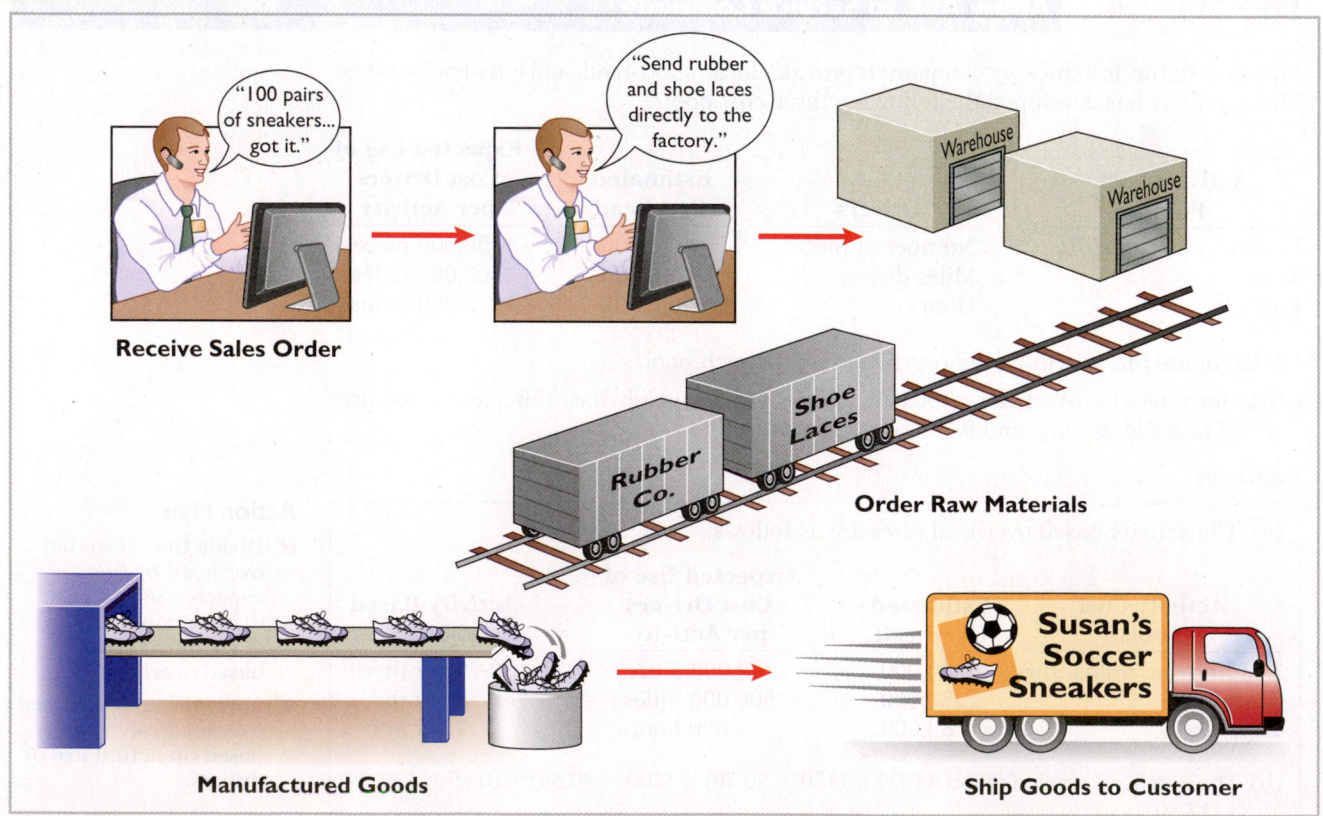

Objective of JIT Processing

A primary objective of JIT is to eliminate all manufacturing inventories. Inventories have an adverse effect on net income because they tie up funds and storage space that could be put to more productive uses. JIT strives to eliminate inventories by using a "**pull approach**" in manufacturing. This approach begins with the customer placing an order with the company, which starts the process of pulling the product through the manufacturing process. A computer at the final workstation sends a signal to the preceding workstation. This signal indicates the exact materials (parts and subassemblies) needed to complete the production of a specified product for a specified time period, such as an eight-hour shift. The next-preceding process, in turn, sends its signal to other processes back up the line. The goal is a smooth continuous flow in the manufacturing process, with no buildup of inventories at any point.

Elements of JIT Processing

There are three important elements in JIT processing:

1. **Dependable suppliers.** Suppliers must be willing to deliver on short notice exact quantities of raw materials according to precise quality specifications (even including multiple deliveries within the same day). Suppliers must also be willing to deliver the raw materials at specified workstations rather than at a central receiving department. This type of purchasing requires constant and direct communication. Such communication is facilitated by an online computer linkage between the company and its suppliers.

   Helpful Hint
   Buyer leverage is important in finding dependable suppliers. Companies like **GM** and **GE** have more success than smaller companies.

2. **A multiskilled work force.** Under JIT, machines are often strategically grouped into work cells or workstations. Much of the work is automated. As a result, one worker may operate and maintain several different types of machines.

3. **A total quality control system.** The company must establish total quality control throughout the manufacturing operations. Total quality control means **no defects**. Since the pull approach signals only required quantities, any defects at any workstation will shut down operations at subsequent workstations. Total quality control requires continuous monitoring by both line employees and supervisors at each workstation.

   Helpful Hint
   Without its emphasis on quality control, JIT would be impractical or even impossible. In JIT, quality is engineered into the production process.

Benefits of JIT Processing

The major benefits of implementing JIT processing are as follows.

1. Significant reduction or elimination of manufacturing inventories.
2. Enhanced product quality.
3. Reduction or elimination of rework costs and inventory storage costs.
4. Production cost savings from the improved flow of goods through the processes.

   The effects in many cases have been dramatic. For example, after using JIT for two years, a major division of **Hewlett-Packard** found that work in process inventories (in dollars) were down 82%, scrap/rework costs were down 30%, space utilization improved by 40%, and labor efficiency improved 50%. As indicated, JIT not only reduces inventory but also enables a company to manufacture a better product faster and with less waste.

   One of the major accounting benefits of JIT is the elimination of separate raw materials and work in process inventory accounts. These accounts are replaced by **one account**, Raw and In-Process Inventory. All materials and conversion costs are charged to this account. The reduction (or elimination) of in-process inventories results in a simpler computation of equivalent units of production.

REVIEW AND PRACTICE

LEARNING OBJECTIVES REVIEW

1 Discuss the difference between traditional costing and activity-based costing. A traditional costing system allocates overhead to products on the basis of predetermined plantwide or departmentwide rates such as direct labor or machine hours. An ABC system allocates overhead to identified activity cost pools and then assigns costs to products using related cost drivers that measure the activities (resources) consumed.

The development of an activity-based costing system involves the following four steps. (1) Identify and classify the major activities involved in the manufacture of specific products and assign overhead to cost pools. (2) Identify the cost driver that has a strong correlation to the costs accumulated in each cost pool. (3) Compute the activity-based overhead rate for each cost pool. (4) Allocate overhead costs to products using the overhead rates determined for each cost pool.

2 Apply activity-based costing to a manufacturer. To identify activity cost pools, a company must perform an analysis of each operation or process, documenting and timing every task, action, or transaction. Cost drivers identified for assigning activity cost pools must (a) accurately measure the actual consumption of the activity by the various products and (b) have related data easily available. The overhead assigned to each activity cost pool is divided by the expected use of cost drivers to determine the activity-based overhead rate for each pool. Overhead is allocated to products by multiplying a particular product's expected use of a cost driver by the activity-based overhead

rate. This is done for each activity cost pool and then summed.

3 Explain the benefits and limitations of activity-based costing. Features of ABC that make it a more accurate product costing system include (1) the increased number of cost pools used to assign overhead (including use of the activity-level hierarchy), (2) the enhanced control over overhead costs (including identification of non–value-added activities), and (3) the better management decisions it makes possible. The limitations of ABC are (1) the higher analysis and measurement costs that accompany multiple activity centers and cost drivers, and (2) the necessity still to allocate some costs arbitrarily.

4 Apply activity-based costing to service industries. The overall objective of using ABC in service industries is no different than for manufacturing industries—that is, improved costing of services performed (by job, service, contract, or customer). The general approach to costing is the same: analyze operations, identify activities, accumulate overhead costs by activity cost pools, and identify and use cost drivers to assign the cost pools to the services.

*5 Explain just-in-time (JIT) processing. JIT is a processing system dedicated to having on hand the right materials and products just at the time they are needed, thereby reducing the amount of inventory and the time inventory is held. One of the principal accounting effects is that one account, Raw and In-Process Inventory, replaces both the raw materials and work in process inventory accounts.

GLOSSARY REVIEW

Activity Any event, action, transaction, or work sequence that incurs costs when producing a product or performing a service. (p. 842).

Activity-based costing (ABC) A costing system that allocates overhead to multiple activity cost pools and assigns the activity cost pools to products or services by means of cost drivers. (p. 841).

Activity-based management (ABM) Extends ABC from product costing to a comprehensive management tool that focuses on reducing costs and improving processes and decision-making. (p. 852).

Activity cost pool The overhead cost attributed to a distinct type of activity or related activities. (p. 842).

Batch-level activities Activities performed for each batch of products rather than for each unit. (p. 850).

Cost driver Any factor or activity that has a direct cause–effect relationship with the resources consumed. In ABC, cost drivers are used to assign activity cost pools to products or services. (p. 842).

Facility-level activities Activities required to support or sustain an entire production process. (p. 850).

*Just-in-time (JIT) processing A processing system dedicated to having the right amount of materials, parts, or products arrive as they are needed, thereby reducing the amount of inventory. (p. 858).

Non–value-added activity An activity that, if eliminated, would not reduce the perceived value of a company's product or service. (p. 851).

Product-level activities Activities performed in support of an entire product line but not always performed every time a new unit or batch of products is produced. (p. 850).

Unit-level activities Activities performed for each unit of production. (p. 849).

Value-added activity An activity that increases the perceived value of a product or service to a customer. (p. 851).

PRACTICE MULTIPLE-CHOICE QUESTIONS

(LO 1) **1.** Activity-based costing (ABC):
    (a) can be used only in a process cost system.
    (b) focuses on units of production.
    (c) focuses on activities needed to produce a good or perform a service.
    (d) uses only a single basis of allocation.

(LO 1) **2.** Activity-based costing:
    (a) is the initial phase of converting to a just-in-time operating environment.
    (b) can be used only in a job order costing system.
    (c) is a two-stage overhead cost allocation system that identifies activity cost pools and cost drivers.
    (d) uses direct labor as its primary cost driver.

(LO 1, 2) **3.** Any activity that causes resources to be consumed is called a:
    (a) just-in-time activity.
    (b) facility-level activity.
    (c) cost driver.
    (d) non–value-added activity.

(LO 2) **4.** Which of the following would be the **best** cost driver for the assembling cost pool?
    (a) Number of product lines.
    (b) Number of parts.
    (c) Number of orders.
    (d) Amount of square footage.

(LO 2) **5.** The overhead rate for machine setups is $100 per setup. Products A and B have 80 and 60 setups, respectively. The overhead assigned to each product is:
    (a) Product A $8,000, Product B $8,000.
    (b) Product A $8,000, Product B $6,000.
    (c) Product A $6,000, Product B $6,000.
    (d) Product A $6,000, Product B $8,000.

(LO 2) **6.** Donna Crawford Co. has identified an activity cost pool to which it has allocated estimated overhead of $1,920,000. It has determined the expected use of cost drivers for that activity to be 160,000 inspections. Widgets require 40,000 inspections, gadgets 30,000 inspections, and targets 90,000 inspections. The overhead assigned to each product is:
    (a) Widgets $40,000, gadgets $30,000, targets $90,000.
    (b) Widgets $640,000, gadgets $640,000, targets $640,000.
    (c) Widgets $360,000, gadgets $480,000, targets $1,080,000.
    (d) Widgets $480,000, gadgets $360,000, targets $1,080,000.

(LO 3) **7.** A frequently cited limitation of activity-based costing is:
    (a) ABC results in more cost pools being used to assign overhead costs to products.

    (b) certain overhead costs remain to be allocated by means of some arbitrary volume-based cost driver such as labor or machine hours.
    (c) ABC leads to poorer management decisions.
    (d) ABC results in less control over overhead costs.

8. A company should consider using ABC if: **(LO 3)**
    (a) overhead costs constitute a small portion of total product costs.
    (b) it has only a few product lines that require similar degrees of support services.
    (c) direct labor constitutes a significant part of the total product cost and a high correlation exists between direct labor and changes in overhead costs.
    (d) its product lines differ greatly in volume and manufacturing complexity.

9. An activity that adds costs to the product but does not **(LO 3)** increase its perceived value is a:
    (a) value-added activity.
    (b) cost driver.
    (c) cost/benefit activity.
    (d) non–value-added activity.

10. The following activity is value-added: **(LO 3)**
    (a) Storage of raw materials.
    (b) Moving parts from machine to machine.
    (c) Shaping a piece of metal on a lathe.
    (d) All the answer choices are correct.

11. A relevant facility-level cost driver for heating costs is: **(LO 3)**
    (a) machine hours.   (c) square footage.
    (b) direct materials.   (d) direct labor cost.

12. The first step in the development of an activity-based **(LO 4)** costing system for a service company is:
    (a) identify and classify activities and allocate overhead to cost pools.
    (b) assign overhead costs to products.
    (c) identify cost drivers.
    (d) compute overhead rates.

*13. Under just-in-time processing: **(LO 5)**
    (a) raw materials are received just in time for use in production.
    (b) subassembly parts are completed just in time for use in assembling finished goods.
    (c) finished goods are completed just in time to be sold.
    (d) All the answer choices are correct.

*14. The primary objective of just-in-time processing **(LO 5)** is to:
    (a) accumulate overhead in activity cost pools.
    (b) eliminate or reduce all manufacturing inventories.
    (c) identify relevant activity cost drivers.
    (d) identify value-added activities.

Solutions

1. **(c)** Focusing on activities needed to produce a good or perform a service is an accurate statement about activity-based costing. The other choices are incorrect because ABC (a) can be used in either a process cost or a job order cost system; (b) focuses on activities performed to produce a product, not on units of production; and (d) uses multiple bases of allocation, not just a single basis of allocation.

2. **(c)** ABC is a two-stage overhead cost allocation system that identifies activity cost pools and cost drivers. The other choices are incorrect because ABC (a) is not necessarily part of the conversion to a just-in-time operating environment, (b) can be used in either a process cost or a job order cost system, and (d) uses other activities in addition to direct labor as cost drivers.

3. **(c)** Activities that cause resources to be consumed are called cost drivers, not (a) just-in-time activities, (b) facility-level activities, or (d) non–value-added activities.

4. **(b)** The number of parts would be the best cost driver for the assembling cost pool as it has a higher degree of correlation with the actual consumption of the overhead costs, that is, the assembling of parts, than (a) number of product lines, (c) number of orders, or (d) amount of square footage.

5. **(b)** The overhead assigned to Product A is $8,000 ($100 × 80) and to Product B is $6,000 ($100 × 60), not (a) $8,000, $8,000; (c) $6,000, $6,000; or (d) $6,000, $8,000.

6. **(d)** The overhead assigned to widgets is $480,000 [($1,920,000 ÷ 160,000) × 40,000], to gadgets is $360,000 [($1,920,000 ÷ 160,000) × 30,000], and to targets is $1,080,000 [($1,920,000 ÷ 160,000) × 90,000]. Therefore, choices (a) $40,000, $30,000, and $90,000; (b) $640,000, $640,000, and $640,000; and (c) $360,000, $480,000, and $1,080,000 are incorrect.

7. **(b)** A limitation of ABC is that certain overhead costs remain to be allocated by means of some arbitrary volume-based cost driver. The other choices are incorrect because (a) more cost pools is an advantage of ABC, (c) ABC can lead to better management decisions, and (d) ABC results in more control over overhead costs.

8. **(d)** A company should consider using ABC if its product lines differ greatly in volume and manufacturing complexity. For choices (a), (b), and (c), a traditional costing system should be sufficient and less expensive to implement.

9. **(d)** Non–value-added activities add costs to a product but do not increase its perceived value, not (a) value-added activities, (b) cost drivers, or (c) cost/benefit activities.

10. **(c)** Shaping a piece of metal on a lathe is a value-added activity as it is an integral part of manufacturing a product. Choices (a) and (b) are non–value-added activities, so therefore choice (d) is incorrect as well.

11. **(c)** Square footage is a relevant facility-level cost driver for heating costs. The other choices are incorrect because (a) machine hours, (b) direct materials, and (d) direct labor cost are all unit-level cost drivers.

12. **(a)** The first step in developing an ABC system is to identify and classify activities and allocate overhead to cost pools. The other choices are incorrect because (b) is Step 4, (c) is Step 2, and (d) is Step 3.

*13. **(d)** All of the choices are accurate statements about just-in-time processing.

*14. **(b)** Eliminating or reducing all manufacturing inventories is the primary objective of just-in-time processing. The other choices are incorrect because choices (a), (b), and (c) are part of the process of implementing an ABC system.

PRACTICE EXERCISES

Assign overhead using traditional costing and ABC.

(LO 1, 2)

1. Domestic Fabrics has budgeted overhead costs of $955,000. It has allocated overhead on a plantwide basis to its two products (wool and cotton) using direct labor hours which are estimated to be 477,500 for the current year. The company has decided to experiment with activity-based costing and has created two activity cost pools and related activity cost drivers. These two cost pools are Cutting (cost driver is machine hours) and Design (cost driver is number of setups). Overhead allocated to the Cutting cost pool is $400,000, and $555,000 is allocated to the Design cost pool. Additional information related to these pools is as follows.

	Wool	Cotton	Total
Machine hours	100,000	100,000	200,000
Number of setups	1,000	500	1,500

Instructions

(a) Determine the amount of overhead allocated to the wool product line and the cotton product line using activity-based costing.

(b) What is the difference between the allocation of overhead to the wool and cotton product lines using activity-based costing versus the traditional approach, assuming direct labor hours were incurred evenly between the wool and cotton?

Solution

1. (a)

Activity Cost Pools	**Cost Drivers**	**Estimated Overhead**
Cutting	Machine hours	$400,000
Design	Number of setups	555,000

Activity-based overhead rates:

Cutting	**Design**
$\dfrac{\$400,000}{200,000}$ = $2 per machine hour	$\dfrac{\$555,000}{1,500}$ = $370 per setup

	Wool	**Cotton**
Activity-based costing		
Cutting		
100,000 × $2	$200,000	
100,000 × $2		$200,000
Design		
1,000 × $370	370,000	
500 × $370		185,000
Total cost allocated	$570,000	$385,000

(b)

$\dfrac{\text{Estimated overhead}}{\text{Direct labors hours}} = \dfrac{\$955,000}{477,500}$ = $2 per direct labor hour

	Wool	**Cotton**
Traditional costing		
238,750* × $2	$477,500	
238,750 × $2		$477,500

*477,500 ÷ 2

The wool product line is allocated $92,500 ($570,000 − $477,500) more overhead cost when an activity-based costing system is used. As a result, the cotton product line is allocated $92,500 ($477,500 − $385,000) less.

---

2. Organic Products, Inc., uses a traditional product costing system to assign overhead costs uniformly to all products. To meet Food and Drug Administration (FDA) requirements and to assure its customers of safe, sanitary, and nutritious food, Organic engages in a high level of quality control. Organic assigns its quality-control overhead costs to all products at a rate of 20% of direct labor costs. Its direct labor cost for the month of June for its low-calorie dessert line is $55,000. In response to repeated requests from its financial vice president, Organic management agrees to adopt activity-based costing. Data relating to the low-calorie dessert line for the month of June are as follows.

Assign overhead using traditional costing and ABC; classify activities as value- or non–value-added.

(LO 1, 2, 3)

Activity Cost Pools	**Cost Drivers**	**Overhead Rate**	**Number of Cost Drivers Used per Activity**
Inspections of material received	Number of pounds	$ 0.70 per pound	6,000 pounds
In-process inspections	Number of servings	$ 0.35 per serving	10,000 servings
FDA certification	Customer orders	$13.00 per order	450 orders

Instructions

(a) Compute the quality-control overhead cost to be assigned to the low-calorie dessert product line for the month of June using (1) the traditional product costing system (direct labor cost is the cost driver), and (2) activity-based costing.

(b) By what amount does the traditional product costing system undercost or overcost the low-calorie dessert line?

(c) Classify each of the activities as value-added or non–value-added.

Solution

2. (a) (1) Traditional product costing system:

$55,000 × .20 = $11,000. Quality-control overhead costs assigned in June to the low-calorie dessert line are $11,000.

(2) Activity-based costing system:

Activity Cost Pools	Cost Drivers Used	×	Activity-Based Overhead Rate	=	Overhead Cost Assigned
Inspections of material received	6,000		$ 0.70		$ 4,200
In-process inspections	10,000		0.35		3,500
FDA certification	450		13.00		5,850
Total assigned cost for June					$13,550

(b) As compared to ABC, the traditional costing system undercosts the quality-control overhead cost assigned to the low-calorie dessert product line by $2,550 ($13,550 − $11,000) in the month of June. That is a 23.2% ($2,550 ÷ $11,000) understatement.

(c) All three activities, as quality-control related activities, are non–value-added activities.

PRACTICE PROBLEM

Assign overhead and compute unit costs.

(LO 2)

Spreadwell Paint Company manufactures two high-quality base paints: an *oil-based* paint and a *latex* paint. Both are housepaints and are manufactured only in a neutral white color. Spreadwell sells the white base paints to franchised retail paint and decorating stores where pigments are added to tint (color) the paint as the customer desires. The oil-based paint is made with organic solvents (petroleum products) such as mineral spirits or turpentine. The latex paint is made with water; synthetic resin particles are suspended in the water, and dry and harden when exposed to air.

Spreadwell uses the same processing equipment to produce both paints in different production runs. Between batches, the vats and other processing equipment must be washed and cleaned.

After analyzing the company's entire operations, Spreadwell's accountants and production managers have identified activity cost pools and accumulated annual budgeted overhead costs by pool as follows.

Activity Cost Pools	Estimated Overhead
Purchasing	$ 240,000
Processing (weighing and mixing, grinding, thinning and drying, straining)	1,400,000
Packaging (quarts, gallons, and 5-gallons)	580,000
Testing	240,000
Storage and inventory control	180,000
Washing and cleaning equipment	560,000
Total annual budgeted overhead	$3,200,000

Following further analysis, activity cost drivers were identified and their expected use by product and activity were scheduled as follows.

Activity Cost Pools	Cost Drivers	Expected Cost Drivers per Activity	Expected Use of Drivers per Product	
			Oil-Based	Latex
Purchasing	Purchase orders	1,500 orders	800	700
Processing	Gallons processed	1,000,000 gallons	400,000	600,000
Packaging	Containers filled	400,000 containers	180,000	220,000
Testing	Number of tests	4,000 tests	2,100	1,900
Storing	Avg. gals. on hand	18,000 gallons	10,400	7,600
Washing	Number of batches	800 batches	350	450

Spreadwell has budgeted 400,000 gallons of oil-based paint and 600,000 gallons of latex paint for processing during the year.

Instructions

(a) Prepare a schedule showing the computations of the activity-based overhead rates.

(b) Prepare a schedule assigning each activity's overhead cost pool to each product.

(c) Compute the overhead cost per unit for each product.

Solution

(a) Computations of activity-based overhead rates:

Activity Cost Pools	Estimated Overhead	÷	Expected Use of Cost Drivers	=	Activity-Based Overhead Rates
Purchasing	$ 240,000		1,500 orders		$160 per order
Processing	1,400,000		1,000,000 gallons		$1.40 per gallon
Packaging	580,000		400,000 containers		$1.45 per container
Testing	240,000		4,000 tests		$60 per test
Storing	180,000		18,000 gallons		$10 per gallon
Washing	560,000		800 batches		$700 per batch
	$3,200,000				

(b) Assignment of activity cost pools to products:

	Oil-Based Paint			Latex Paint		
Activity Cost Pools	Expected Use of Drivers	Overhead Rates	Cost Assigned	Expected Use of Drivers	Overhead Rates	Cost Assigned
Purchasing	800	$160	$ 128,000	700	$160	$ 112,000
Processing	400,000	$1.40	560,000	600,000	$1.40	840,000
Packaging	180,000	$1.45	261,000	220,000	$1.45	319,000
Testing	2,100	$60	126,000	1,900	$60	114,000
Storing	10,400	$10	104,000	7,600	$10	76,000
Washing	350	$700	245,000	450	$700	315,000
Total overhead assigned			$1,424,000			$1,776,000

(c) Computation of overhead cost assigned per unit:

	Oil-Based Paint	Latex Paint
Total overhead cost assigned	$1,424,000	$1,776,000
Total gallons produced	400,000	600,000
Overhead cost per gallon	$3.56	$2.96

WileyPLUS

Brief Exercises, Exercises, **DO IT!** Exercises, and Problems and many additional resources are available for practice in WileyPLUS

NOTE: All asterisked Questions, Exercises, and Problems relate to material in the appendix to the chapter.

QUESTIONS

1. Under what conditions is direct labor a valid basis for allocating overhead?

2. What has happened in recent industrial history to reduce the usefulness of direct labor as the primary basis for allocating overhead to products?

3. In an automated manufacturing environment, what basis of overhead allocation is frequently more relevant than direct labor hours?

4. What is generally true about overhead allocation to high-volume products versus low-volume products under a traditional costing system?

5. What are the principal differences between activity-based costing (ABC) and traditional product costing?

6. What is the formula for computing activity-based overhead rates?

7. What steps are involved in developing an activity-based costing system?
8. Explain the preparation and use of a value-added/non–value-added activity flowchart in an ABC system.
9. What is an activity cost pool?
10. What is a cost driver?
11. What makes a cost driver accurate and appropriate?
12. What is the formula for assigning activity cost pools to products?
13. What are the benefits of activity-based costing?
14. What are the limitations of activity-based costing?
15. Under what conditions is ABC generally the superior overhead costing system?

16. What refinement has been made to enhance the efficiency and effectiveness of ABC for use in managing costs?
17. Of what benefit is classifying activities as value-added and non–value-added?
18. In what ways is the application of ABC to service industries the same as its application to manufacturing companies?
19. What is the relevance of the classification of levels of activity to ABC?
*20. (a) Describe the philosophy and approach of just-in-time processing.
     (b) Identify the major elements of JIT processing.

BRIEF EXERCISES

Identify differences between costing systems.

(LO 1)

BE18-1 Digger Inc. sells a high-speed retrieval system for mining information. It provides the following information for the year.

	Budgeted	Actual
Overhead cost	$975,000	$950,000
Machine hours	50,000	45,000
Direct labor hours	100,000	92,000

Overhead is applied on the basis of direct labor hours. (a) Compute the predetermined overhead rate. (b) Determine the amount of overhead applied for the year. (c) Explain how an activity-based costing system might differ in terms of computing a predetermined overhead rate.

Identify differences between costing systems.

(LO 1)

BE18-2 Finney Inc. has conducted an analysis of overhead costs related to one of its product lines using a traditional costing system (volume-based) and an activity-based costing system. Here are its results.

	Traditional Costing	ABC
Sales revenue	$600,000	$600,000
Overhead costs:		
Product RX3	$ 34,000	$ 50,000
Product Y12	36,000	20,000
	$ 70,000	$ 70,000

Explain how a difference in the overhead costs between the two systems may have occurred.

Identify cost drivers.

(LO 2)

BE18-3 Splash Co. identifies the following activities that pertain to manufacturing overhead for its production of water polo balls: materials handling, machine setups, factory machine maintenance, factory supervision, and quality control. For each activity, identify an appropriate cost driver.

Identify cost drivers.

(LO 2)

BE18-4 Mason Company manufactures four products in a single production facility. The company uses activity-based costing. The following activities have been identified through the company's activity analysis: (a) inventory control, (b) machine setups, (c) employee training, (d) quality inspections, (e) materials orderings, (f) drilling operations, and (g) building maintenance.

For each activity, name a cost driver that might be used to assign overhead costs to products.

Compute activity-based overhead rates.

(LO 2)

BE18-5 Morgana Company identifies three activities in its manufacturing process: machine setups, machining, and inspections. Estimated annual overhead cost for each activity is $150,000, $375,000, and $87,500, respectively. The cost driver for each activity and the expected annual usage are number of setups 2,500, machine hours 25,000, and number of inspections 1,750. Compute the overhead rate for each activity.

BE18-6 Weisman, Inc. uses activity-based costing as the basis for information to set prices for its six lines of seasonal coats. Compute the activity-based overhead rates using the following budgeted data for each of the activity cost pools.

Compute activity-based overhead rates.

(LO 2)

Activity Cost Pools	Estimated Overhead	Expected Use of Cost Drivers per Activity
Designing	$ 450,000	10,000 designer hours
Sizing and cutting	4,000,000	160,000 machine hours
Stitching and trimming	1,440,000	80,000 labor hours
Wrapping and packing	336,000	32,000 finished units

BE18-7 Spud, Inc. a manufacturer of gourmet potato chips, employs activity-based costing. The budgeted data for each of the activity cost pools is provided below for the year 2017.

Compute activity-based overhead rates.

(LO 2)

Activity Cost Pools	Estimated Overhead	Expected Use of Cost Drivers per Activity
Ordering and receiving	$ 84,000	12,000 orders
Food processing	480,000	60,000 machine hours
Packaging	1,760,000	440,000 labor hours

For 2017, the company had 11,000 orders and used 50,000 machine hours, and labor hours totaled 500,000. What is the total overhead applied?

BE18-8 Rich Novelty Company identified the following activities in its production and support operations. Classify each of these activities as either value-added or non–value-added.

Classify activities as value- or non–value-added.

(LO 3)

(a) Machine setup.

(b) Design engineering.

(c) Storing inventory.

(d) Moving work in process.

(e) Inspecting and testing.

(f) Painting and packing.

BE18-9 Pine and Danner is an architectural firm that is contemplating the installation of activity-based costing. The following activities are performed daily by staff architects. Classify these activities as value-added or non–value-added: (a) designing and drafting, 3 hours; (b) staff meetings, 1 hour; (c) on-site supervision, 2 hours; (d) lunch, 1 hour; (e) consultation with client on specifications, 1.5 hours; and (f) entertaining a prospective client for dinner, 2 hours.

Classify service company activities as value- or non–value-added.

(LO 3, 4)

BE18-10 Kwik Pix is a large digital processing center that serves 130 outlets in grocery stores, service stations, camera and photo shops, and drug stores in 16 nearby towns. Kwik Pix operates 24 hours a day, 6 days a week. Classify each of the following activity costs of Kwik Pix as either unit-level, batch-level, product-level, or facility-level.

Classify activities according to level.

(LO 3)

(a) Color printing materials.

(b) Photocopy paper.

(c) Depreciation of machinery.

(d) Setups for enlargements.

(e) Supervisor's salary.

(f) Ordering materials.

(g) Pickup and delivery.

(h) Commission to dealers.

(i) Insurance on building.

(j) Loading developing machines.

BE18-11 FixIt, Inc. operates 20 injection molding machines in the production of tool boxes of four different sizes, named the Apprentice, the Handyman, the Journeyman, and the Professional. Classify each of the following costs as unit-level, batch-level, product-level, or facility-level.

Classify activities according to level.

(LO 3)

(a) First-shift supervisor's salary.

(b) Powdered raw plastic.

(c) Dies for casting plastic components.

(d) Depreciation on injection molding machines.

(e) Changing dies on machines.

(f) Moving components to assembly department.

(g) Engineering design.

(h) Employee health and medical insurance coverage.

Compute rates and activity levels.

(LO 3, 4)

BE18-12 Spin Cycle Architecture uses three activity pools to apply overhead to its projects. Each activity has a cost driver used to allocate the overhead costs to the projects. The activities and related overhead costs are as follows: initial concept formation $40,000, design $300,000, and construction oversight $100,000. The cost drivers and expected use are as follows.

Activities	Cost Drivers	Expected Use of Cost Drivers per Activity
Initial concept formation	Number of project changes	20
Design	Square feet	150,000
Construction oversight	Number of months	100

(a) Compute the predetermined overhead rate for each activity. (b) Classify each of these activities as unit-level, batch-level, product-level, or facility-level.

DO IT! Exercises

Identify characteristics of traditional and ABC systems.

(LO 1)

DO IT! 18-1 Indicate whether the following statements are true or false.

(a) The reasoning behind ABC cost allocation is that products consume activities and activities consume resources.
(b) Activity-based costing is an approach for allocating direct labor to products.
(c) In today's increasingly automated environment, direct labor is never an appropriate basis for allocating costs to products.
(d) A cost driver is any factor or activity that has a direct cause-effect relationship with resources consumed.
(e) Activity-based costing segregates overhead into various cost pools in an effort to provide more accurate cost information.

Compute activity-based overhead rates and assign overhead using ABC.

(LO 2)

DO IT! 18-2 Flynn Industries has three activity cost pools and two products. It expects to produce 3,000 units of Product BC113 and 1,500 of Product AD908. Having identified its activity cost pools and the cost drivers for each pool, Flynn accumulated the following data relative to those activity cost pools and cost drivers.

Annual Overhead Data			Expected Use of Cost Drivers per Product		
Activity Cost Pools	Cost Drivers	Estimated Overhead	Expected Use of Cost Drivers per Activity	Product BC113	Product AD908
Machine setup	Setups	$ 16,000	40	25	15
Machining	Machine hours	110,000	5,000	1,000	4,000
Packing	Orders	30,000	500	150	350

Using the above data, do the following:

(a) Prepare a schedule showing the computations of the activity-based overhead rates per cost driver.
(b) Prepare a schedule assigning each activity's overhead cost to the two products.
(c) Compute the overhead cost per unit for each product. (Round to nearest cent.)
(d) Comment on the comparative overhead cost per product.

Classify activities according to level.

(LO 3)

DO IT! 18-3 Adamson Company manufactures four lines of garden tools. As a result of an activity analysis, the accounting department has identified eight activity cost pools. Each of the product lines is produced in large batches, with the whole plant devoted to one product at a time. Classify each of the following activities or costs as either unit-level, batch level, product-level, or facility-level.

(a) Machining parts.
(b) Product design.
(c) Plant maintenance.
(d) Machine setup.

(e) Assembling parts.
(f) Purchasing raw materials.
(g) Property taxes.
(h) Painting.

DO IT! 18-4 | Ready Ride is a trucking company. It provides local, short-haul, and long-haul services. It has developed the following three cost pools.

Apply ABC to service company.

(LO 4)

Activity Cost Pools	Cost Drivers	Estimated Overhead	Expected Use of Cost Driver per Activity
Loading and unloading	Number of pieces	$ 90,000	90,000
Travel	Miles driven	450,000	600,000
Logistics	Hours	75,000	3,000

(a) Compute the activity-based overhead rates for each pool.
(b) Determine the overhead allocated to Job XZ3275 which has 150 pieces, requires 200 miles of driving, and 0.75 hours of logistics.

EXERCISES

E18-1 Saddle Inc. has two types of handbags: standard and custom. The controller has decided to use a plantwide overhead rate based on direct labor costs. The president has heard of activity-based costing and wants to see how the results would differ if this system were used. Two activity cost pools were developed: machining and machine setup. Presented below is information related to the company's operations.

Assign overhead using traditional costing and ABC.

(LO 1, 2)

	Standard	Custom
Direct labor costs	$50,000	$100,000
Machine hours	1,000	1,000
Setup hours	100	400

Total estimated overhead costs are $240,000. Overhead cost allocated to the machining activity cost pool is $140,000, and $100,000 is allocated to the machine setup activity cost pool.

Instructions
(a) Compute the overhead rate using the traditional (plantwide) approach.
(b) Compute the overhead rates using the activity-based costing approach.
(c) Determine the difference in allocation between the two approaches.

E18-2 Ayala Inc. has conducted the following analysis related to its product lines, using a traditional costing system (volume-based) and an activity-based costing system. Both the traditional and the activity-based costing systems include direct materials and direct labor costs.

Explain difference between traditional and activity-based costing.

(LO 1)

Products	Sales Revenue	Total Costs Traditional	ABC
Product 540X	$180,000	$55,000	$50,000
Product 137Y	160,000	50,000	35,000
Product 249S	70,000	15,000	35,000

Instructions
(a) For each product line, compute operating income using the traditional costing system.
(b) For each product line, compute operating income using the activity-based costing system.
(c) Using the following formula, compute the percentage difference in operating income for each of the product lines of Ayala: [Operating Income (ABC) − Operating Income (traditional cost)] ÷ Operating Income (traditional cost). (Round to two decimals.)
(d) Provide a rationale as to why the costs for Product 540X are approximately the same using either the traditional or activity-based costing system.

*Assign overhead using
traditional costing and ABC.*

(LO 1, 2)

E18-3 EcoFabrics has budgeted overhead costs of $945,000. It has allocated overhead on a plantwide basis to its two products (wool and cotton) using direct labor hours which are estimated to be 450,000 for the current year. The company has decided to experiment with activity-based costing and has created two activity cost pools and related activity cost drivers. These two cost pools are cutting (cost driver is machine hours) and design (cost driver is number of setups). Overhead allocated to the cutting cost pool is $360,000, and $585,000 is allocated to the design cost pool. Additional information related to these pools is as follows.

	Wool	Cotton	Total
Machine hours	100,000	100,000	200,000
Number of setups	1,000	500	1,500

Instructions

(a) Determine the amount of overhead allocated to the wool product line and the cotton product line using activity-based costing.

(b) What amount of overhead would be allocated to the wool and cotton product lines using the traditional approach, assuming direct labor hours were incurred evenly between the wool and cotton? How does this compare with the amount allocated using ABC in part (a)?

*Assign overhead using
traditional costing and ABC.*

(LO 1, 2)

E18-4 Altex Inc. manufactures two products: car wheels and truck wheels. To determine the amount of overhead to assign to each product line, the controller, Robert Hermann, has developed the following information.

	Car	Truck
Estimated wheels produced	40,000	10,000
Direct labor hours per wheel	1	3

Total estimated overhead costs for the two product lines are $770,000.

Instructions

(a) Compute the overhead cost assigned to the car wheels and truck wheels, assuming that direct labor hours is used to allocate overhead costs.

(b) Hermann is not satisfied with the traditional method of allocating overhead because he believes that most of the overhead costs relate to the truck wheels product line because of its complexity. He therefore develops the following three activity cost pools and related cost drivers to better understand these costs.

Activity Cost Pools	Expected Use of Cost Drivers	Estimated Overhead Costs
Setting up machines	1,000 setups	$220,000
Assembling	70,000 labor hours	280,000
Inspection	1,200 inspections	270,000

Compute the activity-based overhead rates for these three cost pools.

(c) Compute the cost that is assigned to the car wheels and truck wheels product lines using an activity-based costing system, given the following information.

Expected Use of Cost Drivers per Product		
	Car	Truck
Number of setups	200	800
Direct labor hours	40,000	30,000
Number of inspections	100	1,100

(d) What do you believe Hermann should do?

*Assign overhead using
traditional costing and ABC.*

(LO 1, 2)

E18-5 Perdon Corporation manufactures safes—large mobile safes, and large walk-in stationary bank safes. As part of its annual budgeting process, Perdon is analyzing the profitability of its two products. Part of this analysis involves estimating the amount of overhead to be allocated to each product line. The following information relates to overhead.

	Mobile Safes	Walk-In Safes
Units planned for production	200	50
Material moves per product line	300	200
Purchase orders per product line	450	350
Direct labor hours per product line	800	1,700

Instructions

(a) The total estimated manufacturing overhead was $260,000. Under traditional costing (which assigns overhead on the basis of direct labor hours), what amount of manufacturing overhead costs are assigned to:
  (1) One mobile safe?
  (2) One walk-in safe?
(b) The total estimated manufacturing overhead of $260,000 was comprised of $160,000 for materials handling costs and $100,000 for purchasing activity costs. Under activity-based costing (ABC):
  (1) What amount of materials handling costs are assigned to:
    (a) One mobile safe?
    (b) One walk-in safe?
  (2) What amount of purchasing activity costs are assigned to:
    (a) One mobile safe?
    (b) One walk-in safe?
(c) Compare the amount of overhead allocated to one mobile safe and to one walk-in safe under the traditional costing approach versus under ABC.

E18-6 Santana Corporation manufactures snowmobiles in its Blue Mountain, Wisconsin, plant. The following costs are budgeted for the first quarter's operations.

Identify activity cost pools and cost drivers.

(LO 2)

Machine setup, indirect materials	$ 4,000
Inspections	16,000
Tests	4,000
Insurance, plant	110,000
Engineering design	140,000
Depreciation, machinery	520,000
Machine setup, indirect labor	20,000
Property taxes	29,000
Oil, heating	19,000
Electricity, plant lighting	21,000
Engineering prototypes	60,000
Depreciation, plant	210,000
Electricity, machinery	36,000
Machine maintenance wages	19,000

Instructions

Classify the above costs of Santana Corporation into activity cost pools using the following: engineering, machinery, machine setup, quality control, factory utilities, maintenance. Next, identify a cost driver that may be used to assign each cost pool to each line of snowmobiles.

E18-7 Rojas Vineyards in Oakville, California, produces three varieties of non-alcoholic wine: merlot, viognier, and pinot noir. The winemaster, Russel Hansen, has identified the following activities as cost pools for accumulating overhead and assigning it to products.

Identify activity cost drivers.

(LO 2)

1. Culling and replanting. Dead or overcrowded vines are culled, and new vines are planted or relocated. (Separate vineyards by variety.)
2. Tying. The posts and wires are reset, and vines are tied to the wires for the dormant season.
3. Trimming. At the end of the harvest, the vines are cut and trimmed back in preparation for the next season.
4. Spraying. The vines are sprayed with organic pesticides for protection against insects and fungi.
5. Harvesting. The grapes are hand-picked, placed in carts, and transported to the crushers.

6. Stemming and crushing. Cartfuls of bunches of grapes of each variety are separately loaded into machines that remove stems and gently crush the grapes.
7. Pressing and filtering. The crushed grapes are transferred to presses that mechanically remove the juices and filter out bulk and impurities.
8. Fermentation. The grape juice, by variety, is fermented in either stainless-steel tanks or oak barrels.
9. Aging. The wines are aged in either stainless-steel tanks or oak barrels for one to three years depending on variety.
10. Bottling and corking. Bottles are machine-filled and corked.
11. Labeling and boxing. Each bottle is labeled, as is each nine-bottle case, with the name of the vintner, vintage, and variety.
12. Storing. Packaged and boxed bottles are stored awaiting shipment.
13. Shipping. The wine is shipped to distributors and private retailers.
14. Heating and air-conditioning of plant and offices.
15. Maintenance of buildings and equipment. Printing, repairs, replacements, and general maintenance are performed in the off-season.

Instructions
For each of Rojas Vineyards' 15 activity cost pools, identify a probable cost driver that might be used to assign overhead costs to its three wine varieties.

Identify activity cost drivers.

(LO 2)

E18-8 Wilmington, Inc. manufactures five models of kitchen appliances. The company is installing activity-based costing and has identified the following activities performed at its Mesa plant.

1. Designing new models.
2. Purchasing raw materials and parts.
3. Storing and managing inventory.
4. Receiving and inspecting raw materials and parts.
5. Interviewing and hiring new personnel.
6. Machine forming sheet steel into appliance parts.
7. Manually assembling parts into appliances.
8. Training all employees of the company.
9. Insuring all tangible fixed assets.
10. Supervising production.
11. Maintaining and repairing machinery and equipment.
12. Painting and packaging finished appliances.

Having analyzed its Mesa plant operations for purposes of installing activity-based costing, Wilmington, Inc. identified its activity cost centers. It now needs to identify relevant activity cost drivers in order to assign overhead costs to its products.

Instructions
Using the activities listed above, identify for each activity one or more cost drivers that might be used to assign overhead to Wilmington's five products.

Compute overhead rates and assign overhead using ABC.

(LO 2, 3)

E18-9 Air United, Inc. manufactures two products: missile range instruments and space pressure gauges. During April, 50 range instruments and 300 pressure gauges were produced, and overhead costs of $94,500 were estimated. An analysis of estimated overhead costs reveals the following activities.

Activities	Cost Drivers	Total Cost
1. Materials handling	Number of requisitions	$40,000
2. Machine setups	Number of setups	21,500
3. Quality inspections	Number of inspections	33,000
		$94,500

The cost driver volume for each product was as follows.

Cost Drivers	Instruments	Gauges	Total
Number of requisitions	400	600	1,000
Number of setups	200	300	500
Number of inspections	200	400	600

Instructions

(a) Determine the overhead rate for each activity.

(b) Assign the manufacturing overhead costs for April to the two products using activity-based costing.

(c) ━━━━━ Write a memorandum to the president of Air United explaining the benefits of activity-based costing.

E18-10 Kragan Clothing Company manufactures its own designed and labeled athletic wear and sells its products through catalog sales and retail outlets. While Kragan has for years used activity-based costing in its manufacturing activities, it has always used traditional costing in assigning its selling costs to its product lines. Selling costs have traditionally been assigned to Kragan's product lines at a rate of 70% of direct materials costs. Its direct materials costs for the month of March for Kragan's "high-intensity" line of athletic wear are $400,000. The company has decided to extend activity-based costing to its selling costs. Data relating to the "high-intensity" line of products for the month of March are as follows.

Assign overhead using traditional costing and ABC.

(LO 1, 2, 3)

Activity Cost Pools	Cost Drivers	Overhead Rate	Number of Cost Drivers Used per Activity
Sales commissions	Dollar sales	$0.05 per dollar sales	$900,000
Advertising—TV	Minutes	$300 per minute	250
Advertising—Internet	Column inches	$10 per column inch	2,000
Catalogs	Catalogs mailed	$2.50 per catalog	60,000
Cost of catalog sales	Catalog orders	$1 per catalog order	9,000
Credit and collection	Dollar sales	$0.03 per dollar sales	900,000

Instructions

(a) Compute the selling costs to be assigned to the "high-intensity" line of athletic wear for the month of March (1) using the traditional product costing system (direct materials cost is the cost driver), and (2) using activity-based costing.

(b) By what amount does the traditional product costing system undercost or overcost the "high-intensity" product line?

E18-11 Health 'R Us, Inc., uses a traditional product costing system to assign overhead costs uniformly to all its packaged multigrain products. To meet Food and Drug Administration requirements and to assure its customers of safe, sanitary, and nutritious food, Health 'R Us engages in a high level of quality control. Health 'R Us assigns its quality-control overhead costs to all products at a rate of 17% of direct labor costs. Its direct labor cost for the month of June for its low-calorie breakfast line is $70,000. In response to repeated requests from its financial vice president, Health 'R Us's management agrees to adopt activity-based costing. Data relating to the low-calorie breakfast line for the month of June are as follows.

Assign overhead using traditional costing and ABC; classify activities as value- or non–value-added.

(LO 1, 2, 3)

Activity Cost Pools	Cost Drivers	Overhead Rate	Number of Cost Drivers Used per Activity
Inspections of material received	Number of pounds	$0.90 per pound	6,000 pounds
In-process inspections	Number of servings	$0.33 per serving	10,000 servings
FDA certification	Customer orders	$12.00 per order	420 orders

Instructions

(a) Compute the quality-control overhead cost to be assigned to the low-calorie breakfast product line for the month of June (1) using the traditional product costing system (direct labor cost is the cost driver), and (2) using activity-based costing.

(b) By what amount does the traditional product costing system undercost or overcost the low-calorie breakfast line?

(c) Classify each of the activities as value-added or non–value-added.

E18-12 Having itemized its costs for the first quarter of next year's budget, Santana Corporation desires to install an activity-based costing system. First, it identified the activity cost pools in which to accumulate factory overhead. Second, it identified the relevant cost drivers. (This was done in E18-6.)

Classify activities by level.

(LO 3)

Instructions
Using the activity cost pools identified in E18-6, classify each of those cost pools as either unit-level, batch-level, product-level, or facility-level.

Classify activities by level.
(LO 3)

E18-13 William Mendel & Sons, Inc. is a small manufacturing company in La Jolla that uses activity-based costing. Mendel & Sons accumulates overhead in the following activity cost pools.

1. Hiring personnel.	6. Setting up equipment.
2. Managing parts inventory.	7. Training employees.
3. Purchasing.	8. Inspecting machined parts.
4. Testing prototypes.	9. Machining.
5. Designing products.	10. Assembling.

Instructions
For each activity cost pool, indicate whether the activity cost pool would be unit-level, batch-level, product-level, or facility-level.

Assign overhead using traditional costing and ABC.
(LO 4)

E18-14 Venus Creations sells window treatments (shades, blinds, and awnings) to both commercial and residential customers. The following information relates to its budgeted operations for the current year.

	Commercial		Residential	
Revenues		$300,000		$480,000
Direct materials costs	$ 30,000		$ 50,000	
Direct labor costs	100,000		300,000	
Overhead costs	85,000	215,000	150,000	500,000
Operating income (loss)		$ 85,000		($ 20,000)

The controller, Peggy Kingman, is concerned about the residential product line. She cannot understand why this line is not more profitable given that the installations of window coverings are less complex for residential customers. In addition, the residential client base resides in close proximity to the company office, so travel costs are not as expensive on a per client visit for residential customers. As a result, she has decided to take a closer look at the overhead costs assigned to the two product lines to determine whether a more accurate product costing model can be developed. Here are the three activity cost pools and related information she developed:

Activity Cost Pools	Estimated Overhead	Cost Drivers
Scheduling and travel	$85,000	Hours of travel
Setup time	90,000	Number of setups
Supervision	60,000	Direct labor cost

Expected Use of Cost Drivers per Product		
	Commercial	Residential
Scheduling and travel	750	500
Setup time	350	250

Instructions
(a) Compute the activity-based overhead rates for each of the three cost pools, and determine the overhead cost assigned to each product line.
(b) Compute the operating income for each product line, using the activity-based overhead rates.
(c) What do you believe Peggy Kingman should do?

Identify activity cost pools.
(LO 4)

E18-15 Snap Prints Company is a small printing and copying firm with three high-speed offset printing presses, five copiers (two color and three black-and-white), one collator, one cutting and folding machine, and one fax machine. To improve its pricing practices, owner-manager Terry Morton is installing activity-based costing. Additionally, Terry employs five employees: two printers/designers, one receptionist/bookkeeper, one salesperson/copy-machine operator, and one janitor/delivery clerk. Terry can operate any of the machines and, in addition to managing the entire operation, he performs the training, designing, selling, and marketing functions.

Instructions

As Snap Prints' independent accountant who prepares tax forms and quarterly financial statements, you have been asked to identify the activities that would be used to accumulate overhead costs for assignment to jobs and customers. Using your knowledge of a small printing and copying firm (and some imagination), identify at least 12 activity cost pools as the start of an activity-based costing system for Snap Prints Company.

E18-16 Lasso and Markowitz is a law firm that is initiating an activity-based costing system. Sam Lasso, the senior partner and strong supporter of ABC, has prepared the following list of activities performed by a typical attorney in a day at the firm.

Classify service company activities as value-added or non–value-added.

(LO 3)

Activities	Hours
Writing contracts and letters	1.5
Attending staff meetings	0.5
Taking depositions	1.0
Doing research	1.0
Traveling to/from court	1.0
Contemplating legal strategy	1.0
Eating lunch	1.0
Litigating a case in court	2.5
Entertaining a prospective client	1.5

Instructions

Classify each of the activities listed by Sam Lasso as value-added or non–value-added, and defend your classification. How much was value-added time and how much was non–value-added?

E18-17 Manzeck Company operates a snow-removal service. The company owns five trucks, each of which has a snow plow in the front to plow driveways and a snowthrower in the back to clear sidewalks. Because plowing snow is very tough on trucks, the company incurs significant maintenance costs. Truck depreciation and maintenance represents a significant portion of the company's overhead. The company removes snow at residential locations, in which case the drivers spend the bulk of their time walking behind the snowthrower machine to clear sidewalks. On commercial jobs, the drivers spend most of their time plowing. Manzeck allocates overhead based on labor hours. Total overhead costs for the year are $42,000. Total labor hours are 1,500 hours. The average residential property requires 0.5 hours of labor, while the average commercial property requires 2.5 hours of labor. The following additional information is available.

Apply ABC to service company.

(LO 4)

Activity Cost Pools	Cost Drivers	Estimated Overhead	Expected Use of Cost Drivers per Activity
Plowing	Square yards of surface plowed	$38,000	200,000
Snowthrowing	Linear feet of sidewalk cleared	$ 4,000	50,000

Instructions

(a) Determine the predetermined overhead rate under traditional costing.
(b) Determine the amount of overhead allocated to the average residential job using traditional costing based on labor hours.
(c) Determine the activity-based overhead rates for each cost pool.
(d) Determine the amount of overhead allocated to the average residential job using activity-based costing. Assume that the average residential job has 20 square yards of plowing and 60 linear feet of snowthrowing.
(e) Discuss your findings from parts (b) and (d).

EXERCISES: SET B AND CHALLENGE EXERCISES

Visit the book's companion website, at **www.wiley.com/college/weygandt**, and choose the Student Companion site to access Exercises: Set B and Challenge Exercises.

PROBLEMS: SET A

P18-1A Combat Fire, Inc. manufactures steel cylinders and nozzles for two models of fire extinguishers: (1) a home fire extinguisher and (2) a commercial fire extinguisher. The *home model* is a high-volume (54,000 units), half-gallon cylinder that holds 2 1/2 pounds of multi-purpose dry chemical at 480 PSI. The *commercial model* is a low-volume (10,200 units), two-gallon cylinder that holds 10 pounds of multi-purpose dry chemical at 390 PSI. Both products require 1.5 hours of direct labor for completion. Therefore, total annual direct labor hours are 96,300 or [1.5 hours × (54,000 + 10,200)]. Expected annual manufacturing overhead is $1,584,280. Thus, the predetermined overhead rate is $16.45 or ($1,584,280 ÷ 96,300) per direct labor hour. The direct materials cost per unit is $18.50 for the home model and $26.50 for the commercial model. The direct labor cost is $19 per unit for both the home and the commercial models.

The company's managers identified six activity cost pools and related cost drivers and accumulated overhead by cost pool as follows.

Activity Cost Pools	Cost Drivers	Estimated Overhead	Expected Use of Cost Drivers	Expected Use of Drivers by Product	
				Home	Commercial
Receiving	Pounds	$ 80,400	335,000	215,000	120,000
Forming	Machine hours	150,500	35,000	27,000	8,000
Assembling	Number of parts	412,300	217,000	165,000	52,000
Testing	Number of tests	51,000	25,500	15,500	10,000
Painting	Gallons	52,580	5,258	3,680	1,578
Packing and shipping	Pounds	837,500	335,000	215,000	120,000
		$1,584,280			

Instructions

(a) Under traditional product costing, compute the total unit cost of each product. Prepare a simple comparative schedule of the individual costs by product (similar to Illustration 18-3 on page 841).

(b) Under ABC, prepare a schedule showing the computations of the activity-based overhead rates (per cost driver).

(c) Prepare a schedule assigning each activity's overhead cost pool to each product based on the use of cost drivers. (Include a computation of overhead cost per unit, rounding to the nearest cent.)

(d) Compute the total cost per unit for each product under ABC.

(e) Classify each of the activities as a value-added activity or a non–value-added activity.

(f) Comment on (1) the comparative overhead cost per unit for the two products under ABC, and (2) the comparative total costs per unit under traditional costing and ABC.

P18-2A Schultz Electronics manufactures two ultra high-definition television models: the Royale which sells for $1,600, and a new model, the Majestic, which sells for $1,300. The production cost computed per unit under traditional costing for each model in 2017 was as follows.

Traditional Costing	Royale	Majestic
Direct materials	$ 700	$420
Direct labor ($20 per hour)	120	100
Manufacturing overhead ($38 per DLH)	228	190
Total per unit cost	$1,048	$710

In 2017, Schultz manufactured 25,000 units of the Royale and 10,000 units of the Majestic. The overhead rate of $38 per direct labor hour was determined by dividing total expected manufacturing overhead of $7,600,000 by the total direct labor hours (200,000) for the two models.

Under traditional costing, the gross profit on the models was Royale $552 ($1,600 − $1,048) and Majestic $590 ($1,300 − $710). Because of this difference, management is considering phasing out the Royale model and increasing the production of the Majestic model.

Before finalizing its decision, management asks Schultz's controller to prepare an analysis using activity-based costing (ABC). The controller accumulates the following information about overhead for the year ended December 31, 2017.

Activity Cost Pools	Cost Drivers	Estimated Overhead	Expected Use of Cost Drivers	Activity-Based Overhead Rate
Purchasing	Number of orders	$1,200,000	40,000	$30/order
Machine setups	Number of setups	900,000	18,000	$50/setup
Machining	Machine hours	4,800,000	120,000	$40/hour
Quality control	Number of inspections	700,000	28,000	$25/inspection

The cost drivers used for each product were:

Cost Drivers	Royale	Majestic	Total
Purchase orders	17,000	23,000	40,000
Machine setups	5,000	13,000	18,000
Machine hours	75,000	45,000	120,000
Inspections	11,000	17,000	28,000

Instructions
(a) Assign the total 2017 manufacturing overhead costs to the two products using activity-based costing (ABC) and determine the overhead cost per unit.
(b) What was the cost per unit and gross profit of each model using ABC?
(c) ✎▬▬▬ Are management's future plans for the two models sound? Explain.

(a) Royale $4,035,000

(b) Cost/unit—Royale $981.40

P18-3A Shaker Stairs Co. designs and builds factory-made premium wooden stairways for homes. The manufactured stairway components (spindles, risers, hangers, hand rails) permit installation of stairways of varying lengths and widths. All are of white oak wood. Budgeted manufacturing overhead costs for the year 2017 are as follows.

Assign overhead costs using traditional costing and ABC; compare results.

(LO 1, 2)

Overhead Cost Pools	Amount
Purchasing	$ 75,000
Handling materials	82,000
Production (cutting, milling, finishing)	210,000
Setting up machines	105,000
Inspecting	90,000
Inventory control (raw materials and finished goods)	126,000
Utilities	180,000
Total budgeted overhead costs	$868,000

For the last 4 years, Shaker Stairs Co. has been charging overhead to products on the basis of machine hours. For the year 2017, 100,000 machine hours are budgeted.

Jeremy Nolan, owner-manager of Shaker Stairs Co., recently directed his accountant, Bill Seagren, to implement the activity-based costing system that he has repeatedly proposed. At Jeremy Nolan's request, Bill and the production foreman identify the following cost drivers and their usage for the previously budgeted overhead cost pools.

Activity Cost Pools	Cost Drivers	Expected Use of Cost Drivers
Purchasing	Number of orders	600
Handling materials	Number of moves	8,000
Production (cutting, milling, finishing)	Direct labor hours	100,000
Setting up machines	Number of setups	1,250
Inspecting	Number of inspections	6,000
Inventory control (raw materials and finished goods)	Number of components	168,000
Utilities	Square feet occupied	90,000

Steve Hannon, sales manager, has received an order for 250 stairways from Community Builders, Inc., a large housing development contractor. At Steve's request, Bill prepares cost estimates for producing components for 250 stairways so Steve can submit a contract price per stairway to Community Builders. He accumulates the following data for the production of 250 stairways.

Direct materials	$103,600
Direct labor	$112,000
Machine hours	14,500
Direct labor hours	5,000
Number of purchase orders	60
Number of material moves	800
Number of machine setups	100
Number of inspections	450
Number of components	16,000
Number of square feet occupied	8,000

Instructions

(a) Compute the predetermined overhead rate using traditional costing with machine hours as the basis.

(b) What is the manufacturing cost per stairway under traditional costing? (Round to the nearest cent.)

(c) What is the manufacturing cost per stairway under the proposed activity-based costing? (Round to the nearest cent. Prepare all of the necessary schedules.)

(d) ✏—— Which of the two costing systems is preferable in pricing decisions and why?

(b) Cost/stairway $1,365.84

(c) Cost/stairway $1,139.80

Assign overhead costs using traditional costing and ABC; compare results.

(LO 1, 2)

P18-4A Benton Corporation produces two grades of non-alcoholic wine from grapes that it buys from California growers. It produces and sells roughly 3,000,000 liters per year of a low-cost, high-volume product called CoolDay. It sells this in 600,000 5-liter jugs. Benton also produces and sells roughly 300,000 liters per year of a low-volume, high-cost product called LiteMist. LiteMist is sold in 1-liter bottles. Based on recent data, the CoolDay product has not been as profitable as LiteMist. Management is considering dropping the inexpensive CoolDay line so it can focus more attention on the LiteMist product. The LiteMist product already demands considerably more attention than the CoolDay line.

Jack Eller, president and founder of Benton, is skeptical about this idea. He points out that for many decades the company produced only the CoolDay line and that it was always quite profitable. It wasn't until the company started producing the more complicated LiteMist wine that the profitability of CoolDay declined. Prior to the introduction of LiteMist, the company had basic equipment, simple growing and production procedures, and virtually no need for quality control. Because LiteMist is bottled in 1-liter bottles, it requires considerably more time and effort, both to bottle and to label and box than does CoolDay. The company must bottle and handle 5 times as many bottles of LiteMist to sell the same quantity as CoolDay. CoolDay requires 1 month of aging; LiteMist requires 1 year. CoolDay requires cleaning and inspection of equipment every 10,000 liters; LiteMist requires such maintenance every 600 liters.

Jack has asked the accounting department to prepare an analysis of the cost per liter using the traditional costing approach and using activity-based costing. The following information was collected.

	CoolDay	LiteMist
Direct materials per liter	$0.40	$1.20
Direct labor cost per liter	$0.50	$0.90
Direct labor hours per liter	0.05	0.09
Total direct labor hours	150,000	27,000

Activity Cost Pools	Cost Drivers	Estimated Overhead	Expected Use of Cost Drivers	Expected Use of Cost Drivers per Product	
				CoolDay	LiteMist
Grape processing	Cart of grapes	$ 145,860	6,600	6,000	600
Aging	Total months	396,000	6,600,000	3,000,000	3,600,000
Bottling and corking	Number of bottles	270,000	900,000	600,000	300,000
Labeling and boxing	Number of bottles	189,000	900,000	600,000	300,000
Maintain and inspect equipment	Number of inspections	240,800	800	350	450
		$1,241,660			

Instructions

Answer each of the following questions. (Round all calculations to three decimal places.)

(a) Under traditional product costing using direct labor hours, compute the total manufacturing cost per **liter** of both products.

(b) Under ABC, prepare a schedule showing the computation of the activity-based overhead rates (per cost driver).

(c) Prepare a schedule assigning each activity's overhead cost pool to each product, based on the use of cost drivers. Include a computation of overhead cost per liter.

(d) Compute the total manufacturing cost per liter for both products under ABC.

(e) ━━━━━ Write a memo to Jack Eller discussing the implications of your analysis for the company's plans. In this memo, provide a brief description of ABC as well as an explanation of how the traditional approach can result in distortions.

(a) Cost/liter—C.D. $1.251

(c) Cost/liter—C.D. $.241

P18-5A Lewis and Stark is a public accounting firm that offers two primary services, auditing and tax-return preparation. A controversy has developed between the partners of the two service lines as to who is contributing the greater amount to the bottom line. The area of contention is the assignment of overhead. The tax partners argue for assigning overhead on the basis of 40% of direct labor dollars, while the audit partners argue for implementing activity-based costing. The partners agree to use next year's budgeted data for purposes of analysis and comparison. The following overhead data are collected to develop the comparison.

Assign overhead costs to services using traditional costing and ABC; compute overhead rates and unit costs; compare results.

(LO 1, 2, 3, 4)

Activity Cost Pools	Cost Drivers	Estimated Overhead	Expected Use of Cost Drivers	Expected Use of Cost Drivers per Service	
				Audit	Tax
Employee training	Direct labor dollars	$216,000	$1,800,000	$1,100,000	$700,000
Typing and secretarial	Number of reports/ forms	76,200	2,500	800	1,700
Computing	Number of minutes	204,000	60,000	27,000	33,000
Facility rental	Number of employees	142,500	40	22	18
Travel	Per expense reports	81,300	Direct	56,000	25,300
		$720,000			

Instructions

(a) Using traditional product costing as proposed by the tax partners, compute the total overhead cost assigned to both services (audit and tax) of Lewis and Stark.

(b) (1) Using activity-based costing, prepare a schedule showing the computations of the activity-based overhead rates (per cost driver).

(2) Prepare a schedule assigning each activity's overhead cost pool to each service based on the use of the cost drivers.

(c) ━━━━━ Comment on the comparative overhead cost for the two services under both traditional costing and ABC.

(b) (2) Cost assigned—Tax $337,441

(c) Difference—Audit $57,441

PROBLEMS: SET B AND SET C

Visit the book's companion website, at **www.wiley.com/college/weygandt**, and choose the Student Companion site to access Problems: Set B and Set C.

CONTINUING PROBLEMS

CURRENT DESIGNS

CD18 As you learned in the previous chapters, Current Designs has two main product lines—composite kayaks, which are handmade and very labor-intensive, and rotomolded kayaks, which require less labor but employ more expensive equipment. Current Designs' controller, Diane Buswell, is now evaluating several different methods of assigning overhead to these products. It is important to ensure that costs are appropriately assigned to the company's products. At the same time, the system that is used must not be so complex that its costs are greater than its benefits.

Diane has decided to use the following activities and costs to evaluate the methods of assigning overhead.

Current Designs Activity Cost Pools.xls

	A	B
1		
2	Activities	Cost
3	Designing new models	$121,100
4	Creating and testing prototypes	152,000
5	Creating molds for kayaks	188,500
6	Operating oven for the rotomolded kayaks	40,000
7	Operating the vacuum line for the composite kayaks	28,000
8	Supervising production employees	180,000
9	Curing time (the time that is needed for the chemical processes to finish before the next step in the production process; many of these costs are related to the space required in the building)	190,400
10	Total	$900,000

As Diane examines the data, she decides that the cost of operating the oven for the rotomolded kayaks and the cost of operating the vacuum line for the composite kayaks can be directly assigned to each of these product lines and do not need to be allocated with the other costs.

Instructions

For purposes of this analysis, assume that Current Designs uses $234,000 in direct labor costs to produce 1,000 composite kayaks and $286,000 in direct labor costs to produce 4,000 rotomolded kayaks each year.

(a) One method of allocating overhead would allocate the common costs to each product line by using an allocation basis such as the number of employees working on each type of kayak or the amount of factory space used for the production of each type of kayak. Diane knows that about 50% of the area of the plant and 50% of the employees work on the composite kayaks, and the remaining space and other employees work on the rotomolded kayaks. Using this information and remembering that the cost of operating the oven and vacuum line have been directly assigned, determine the total amount to be assigned to the composite kayak line and the rotomolded kayak line, and the amount to be assigned to each of the units in each line.

(b) Another method of allocating overhead is to use direct labor dollars as an allocation basis. Remembering that the costs of the oven and the vacuum line have been assigned directly to the product lines, allocate the remaining costs using direct labor dollars as the allocation basis. Then, determine the amount of overhead that should be assigned to each unit of each product line using this method.

(c) Activity-based costing requires a cost driver for each cost pool. Use the following information to assign the costs to the product lines using the activity-based costing approach.

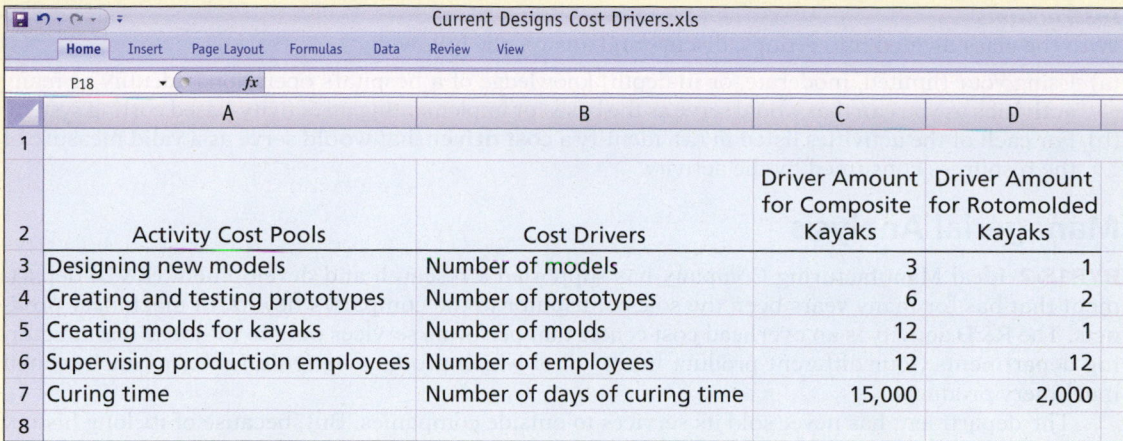

		Driver Amount for Composite Kayaks	Driver Amount for Rotomolded Kayaks
Activity Cost Pools	**Cost Drivers**		
Designing new models	Number of models	3	1
Creating and testing prototypes	Number of prototypes	6	2
Creating molds for kayaks	Number of molds	12	1
Supervising production employees	Number of employees	12	12
Curing time	Number of days of curing time	15,000	2,000

What amount of overhead should be assigned to each composite kayak using this method? What amount of overhead should be assigned to each rotomolded kayak using this method?

(d) Which of the three methods do you think Current Designs should use? Why?

WATERWAYS

(*Note:* This is a continuation of the Waterways problem from Chapters 15–17.)

WP18 Waterways looked into ABC as a method of costing because of the variety of items it produces and the many different activities in which it is involved. This problem asks you to help Waterways use an activity-based costing system to account for its production activities.

Go to the book's companion website, at **www.wiley.com/college/weygandt***, to find the completion of this problem.*

◼ COMPREHENSIVE CASE

In Chapter 16, you used job order costing techniques to help Greetings Inc., a retailer of greeting cards and small gift items, expand its operations. Your next task is to help the new unit, Wall Décor, become profitable through the use of activity-based costing. In this case, you will have the opportunity to discuss the cost/benefit trade-offs between simple ABC systems versus refined systems, and the potential benefit of using capacity rather than expected sales when allocating fixed overhead costs.

Go to the book's companion website, at **www.wiley.com/college/weygandt***, for complete case details and instructions.*

BROADENING YOUR *PERSPECTIVE*

MANAGEMENT DECISION-MAKING

Decision-Making Across the Organization

BYP18-1 East Valley Hospital is a primary medical care facility and trauma center that serves 11 small, rural midwestern communities within a 40-mile radius. The hospital offers all the medical/surgical services of a typical small hospital. It has a staff of 18 full-time doctors and 20 part-time visiting specialists. East Valley has a payroll of 150 employees consisting of technicians, nurses, therapists, managers, directors, administrators, dieticians, secretaries, data processors, and janitors.

Instructions

With the class divided into groups, discuss and answer the following.

(a) Using your (limited, moderate, or in-depth) knowledge of a hospital's operations, identify as many **activities** as you can that would serve as the basis for implementing an activity-based costing system.

(b) For each of the activities listed in (a), identify a **cost driver** that would serve as a valid measure of the resources consumed by the activity.

Managerial Analysis

BYP18-2 Ideal Manufacturing Company has supported a research and development (R&D) department that has for many years been the sole contributor to the company's new farm machinery products. The R&D activity is an overhead cost center that performs services only to in-house manufacturing departments (four different product lines), all of which produce agricultural/farm/ranch-related machinery products.

The department has never sold its services to outside companies. But, because of its long history of success, larger manufacturers of agricultural products have approached Ideal to hire its R&D department for special projects. Because the costs of operating the R&D department have been spiraling uncontrollably, Ideal's management is considering entertaining these outside approaches to absorb the increasing costs. However, (1) management doesn't have any cost basis for charging R&D services to outsiders, and (2) it needs to gain control of its R&D costs. Management decides to implement an activity-based costing system in order to determine the charges for both outsiders and the in-house users of the department's services.

R&D activities fall into four pools with the following annual costs.

Market analysis	$1,050,000
Product design	2,350,000
Product development	3,600,000
Prototype testing	1,400,000

Activity analysis determines that the appropriate cost drivers and their usage for the four activities are:

Activities	Cost Drivers	Total Estimated Drivers
Market analysis	Hours of analysis	15,000 hours
Product design	Number of designs	2,500 designs
Product development	Number of products	90 products
Prototype testing	Number of tests	500 tests

Instructions

(a) Compute the activity-based overhead rate for each activity cost pool.

(b) How much cost would be charged to an in-house manufacturing department that consumed 1,800 hours of market analysis time, was provided 280 designs relating to 10 products, and requested 92 engineering tests?

(c) How much cost would serve as the basis for pricing an R&D bid with an outside company on a contract that would consume 800 hours of analysis time, require 178 designs relating to 3 products, and result in 70 engineering tests?

(d) What is the benefit to Ideal Manufacturing of applying activity-based costing to its R&D activity for both in-house and outside charging purposes?

Real-World Focus

BYP18-3 An article in *Cost Management*, by Kocakulah, Bartlett, and Albin entitled "ABC for Calculating Mortgage Loan Servicing Expenses" (July/August 2009, p. 36), discusses a use of ABC in the financial services industry.

Instructions

Read the article and answer the following questions.

(a) What are some of the benefits of ABC that relate to the financial services industry?

(b) What are three things that the company's original costing method did not take into account?

(c) What were some of the cost drivers used by the company in the ABC approach?

CRITICAL THINKING

Ethics Case

BYP18-4 Curtis Rich, the cost accountant for Hi-Power Mower Company, recently installed activity-based costing at Hi-Power's St. Louis lawn tractor (riding mower) plant where three models—the 8-horsepower Bladerunner, the 12-horsepower Quickcut, and the 18-horsepower Supercut—are manufactured. Curtis's new product costs for these three models show that the company's traditional costing system had been significantly undercosting the 18-horsepower Supercut. This was due primarily to the lower sales volume of the Supercut compared to the Bladerunner and the Quickcut.

Before completing his analysis and reporting these results to management, Curtis is approached by his friend Ed Gray, who is the production manager for the 18-horsepower Supercut model. Ed has heard from one of Curtis's staff about the new product costs and is upset and worried for his job because the new costs show the Supercut to be losing, rather than making, money.

At first, Ed condemns the new cost system, where upon Curtis explains the practice of activity-based costing and why it is more accurate than the company's present system. Even more worried now, Ed begs Curtis, "Massage the figures just enough to save the line from being discontinued. You don't want me to lose my job, do you? Anyway, nobody will know."

Curtis holds firm but agrees to recompute all his calculations for accuracy before submitting his costs to management.

Instructions

(a) Who are the stakeholders in this situation?
(b) What, if any, are the ethical considerations in this situation?
(c) What are Curtis's ethical obligations to the company? To his friend?

All About You

BYP18-5 There are many resources available on the Internet to assist people in time management. Some of these resources are designed specifically for college students.

Instructions

Do an Internet search of Dartmouth's time-management video. Watch the video and then answer the following questions.

(a) What are the main tools of time management for students, and what is each used for?
(b) At what time of day are students most inclined to waste time? What time of day is the best for studying complex topics?
(c) How can employing time-management practices be a "liberating" experience?
(d) Why is goal-setting important? What are the characteristics of good goals, and what steps should you take to help you develop your goals?

Considering Your Costs and Benefits

BYP18-6 As discussed in the chapter, the principles underlying activity-based costing have evolved into the broader approach known as *activity-based management*. One of the common practices of activity-based management is to identify all business activities, classify each activity as either a value-added or a non–value-added activity, and then try to reduce or eliminate the time spent on non–value-added activities. Consider the implications of applying this same approach to your everyday life, at work and at school. How do you spend your time each day? How much of your day is spent on activities that help you accomplish your objectives, and how much of your day is spent on activities that do not add value?

Many "self-help" books and websites offer suggestions on how to improve your time management. Should you minimize the "non–value-added" hours in your life by adopting the methods suggested by these sources? The basic arguments for and against are as follows.

YES: There are a limited number of hours in a day. You should try to maximize your chances of achieving your goals by eliminating the time that you waste.

NO: Life is about more than working yourself to death. Being an efficiency expert doesn't guarantee that you will be happy. Schedules and daily planners are too constraining.

Instructions

Write a response indicating your position regarding this situation. Provide support for your view.

19

Cost-Volume-Profit

CHAPTER PREVIEW As the Feature Story below indicates, to manage any size business you must understand how costs respond to changes in sales volume and the effect of costs and revenues on profits. A prerequisite to understanding cost-volume-profit (CVP) relationships is knowledge of how costs behave. In this chapter, we first explain the considerations involved in cost behavior analysis. Then, we discuss and illustrate CVP analysis.

FEATURE STORY

Don't Worry—Just Get Big

It wasn't that Jeff Bezos didn't have a good job. He was a vice president at a Wall Street firm. But, he quit his job, moved to Seattle, and started an online retailer, which he named Amazon.com. Like any good entrepreneur, Jeff strove to keep his initial investment small. Operations were run out of his garage. And, to avoid the need for a warehouse, he took orders for books and had them shipped from other distributors' warehouses.

By its fourth month, Amazon was selling 100 books a day. In its first full year, it had $15.7 million in sales. The next year, sales increased eightfold. Two years later, sales were $1.6 billion.

Although its sales growth was impressive, Amazon's ability to lose money was equally amazing. One analyst nicknamed it *Amazon.bomb*, while another, predicting its demise, called it *Amazon.toast*. Why was it losing money? The company used every available dollar to reinvest in itself. It built massive warehouses and bought increasingly sophisticated (and expensive) computers and equipment to improve its distribution system. This desire to grow as fast as possible was captured in a T-shirt slogan at its company picnic, which read "Eat another hot dog, get big fast." This buying binge was increasing the

company's fixed costs at a rate that exceeded its sales growth. Skeptics predicted that Amazon would soon run out of cash. It didn't.

In the fourth quarter of 2010 (only 15 years after its world headquarters was located in a garage), Amazon reported quarterly revenues of $12.95 billion and quarterly income of $416 million. But, even as it announced record profits, its share price fell by 9%. Why? Because although the company was predicting that its sales revenue in the next quarter would increase by at least 28%, it predicted that its operating profit would fall by at least 2% and perhaps by as much as 34%. The company made no apologies. It explained that it was in the process of expanding from 39 distribution centers to 52. As Amazon's finance chief noted, "You're not as productive on those assets for some time. I'm very pleased with the investments we're making and we've shown over our history that we've been able to make great returns on the capital we invest in." In other words, eat another hot dog.

Sources: Christine Frey and John Cook, "How Amazon.com Survived, Thrived and Turned a Profit," *Seattle Post* (January 28, 2008); and Stu Woo, "Sticker Shock Over Amazon Growth," *Wall Street Journal Online* (January 28, 2011).

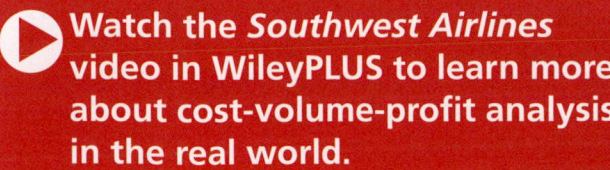

Watch the *Southwest Airlines* video in WileyPLUS to learn more about cost-volume-profit analysis in the real world.

Eric Gerrard/iStockphoto

Learning Objectives

1 Explain variable, fixed, and mixed costs and the relevant range.
- Variable costs
- Fixed costs
- Relevant range
- Mixed costs

DO IT! **1** Types of Costs

2 Apply the high-low method to determine the components of mixed costs.
- High-low method
- Identify variable and fixed costs

DO IT! **2** High-Low Method

3 Prepare a CVP income statement to determine contribution margin.
- Basic components
- CVP income statement

DO IT! **3** CVP Income Statement

4 Compute the break-even point using three approaches.
- Mathematical equation
- Contribution margin technique
- Graphic presentation

DO IT! **4** Break-Even Analysis

5 Determine the sales required to earn target net income and determine margin of safety.
- Target net income
- Margin of safety

DO IT! **5** Break-Even, Margin of Safety, and Target Net Income

Go to the *REVIEW AND PRACTICE* section at the end of the chapter for a review of key concepts and practice applications with solutions.

Visit **WileyPLUS with ORION** for additional tutorials and practice opportunities.

Explain variable, fixed, and mixed costs and the relevant range.

Cost behavior analysis is the study of how specific costs respond to changes in the level of business activity. As you might expect, some costs change, and others remain the same. For example, for an airline company such as **Southwest** or **United**, the longer the flight, the higher the fuel costs. On the other hand, **Massachusetts General Hospital**'s costs to staff the emergency room on any given night are relatively constant regardless of the number of patients treated. A knowledge of cost behavior helps management plan operations and decide between alternative courses of action. Cost behavior analysis applies to all types of entities.

The starting point in cost behavior analysis is measuring the key business activities. Activity levels may be expressed in terms of sales dollars (in a retail company), miles driven (in a trucking company), room occupancy (in a hotel), or dance classes taught (by a dance studio). Many companies use more than one measurement base. A manufacturer, for example, may use direct labor hours or units of output for manufacturing costs, and sales revenue or units sold for selling expenses.

For an activity level to be useful in cost behavior analysis, changes in the level or volume of activity should be correlated with changes in costs. The activity level selected is referred to as the activity (or volume) index. The **activity index** identifies the activity that causes changes in the behavior of costs. With an appropriate activity index, companies can classify the behavior of costs in response to changes in activity levels into three categories: variable, fixed, or mixed.

Variable Costs

Variable costs are costs that vary **in total** directly and proportionately with changes in the activity level. If the level increases 10%, total variable costs will increase 10%. If the level of activity decreases by 25%, variable costs will decrease 25%. Examples of variable costs include direct materials and direct labor for a manufacturer; cost of goods sold, sales commissions, and freight-out for a merchandiser; and gasoline in airline and trucking companies. A variable cost may also be defined as a cost that **remains the same** *per unit* **at every level of activity**.

To illustrate the behavior of a variable cost, assume that Damon Company manufactures tablet computers that contain $10 cameras. The activity index is the number of tablet computers produced. As Damon manufactures each tablet, the total cost of cameras used increases by $10. As part (a) of Illustration 19-1

Illustration 19-1
Behavior of total and unit variable costs

Helpful Hint
Variable costs per unit remain constant at all levels of activity.

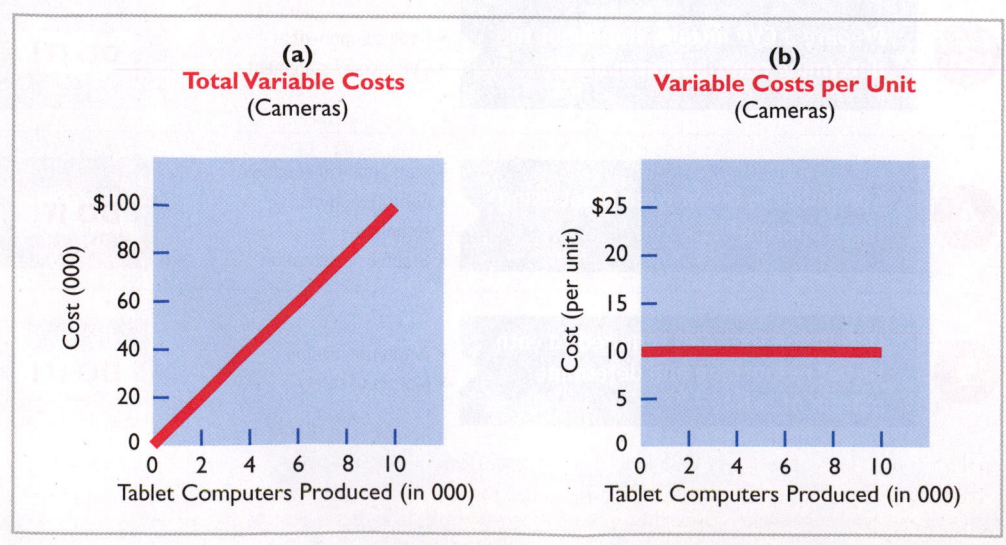

shows, total cost of the cameras will be $20,000 if Damon produces 2,000 tablets, and $100,000 when it produces 10,000 tablets. We also can see that a variable cost remains the same per unit as the level of activity changes. As part (b) of Illustration 19-1 shows, the unit cost of $10 for the cameras is the same whether Damon produces 2,000 or 10,000 tablets.

Companies that rely heavily on labor to manufacture a product, such as **Nike** or **Reebok**, or to perform a service, such as **Hilton** or **Marriott**, are likely to have many variable costs. In contrast, companies that use a high proportion of machinery and equipment in producing revenue, such as **AT&T** or **Duke Energy Co.**, may have few variable costs.

Fixed Costs

Fixed costs are costs that **remain the same in total** regardless of changes in the activity level. Examples include property taxes, insurance, rent, supervisory salaries, and depreciation on buildings and equipment. Because total fixed costs remain constant as activity changes, it follows that **fixed costs *per unit* vary inversely with activity: As volume increases, unit cost declines, and vice versa**.

To illustrate the behavior of fixed costs, assume that Damon Company leases its productive facilities at a cost of $10,000 per month. Total fixed costs of the facilities will remain constant at every level of activity, as part (a) of Illustration 19-2 shows. But, **on a per unit basis, the cost of rent will decline as activity increases**, as part (b) of Illustration 19-2 shows. At 2,000 units, the unit cost per tablet computer is $5 ($10,000 ÷ 2,000). When Damon produces 10,000 tablets, the unit cost of the rent is only $1 per tablet ($10,000 ÷ 10,000).

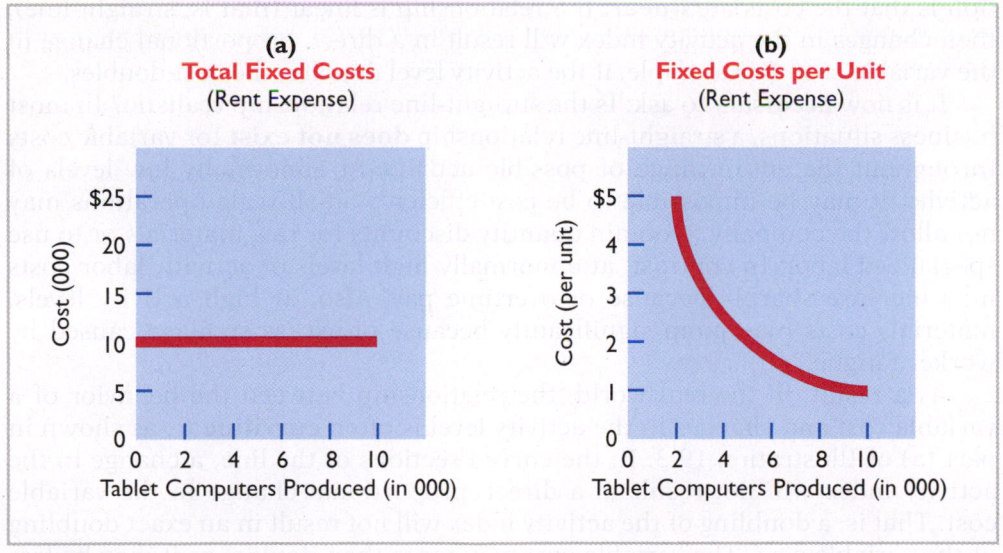

Illustration 19-2
Behavior of total and unit fixed costs

The trend for many manufacturers is to have more fixed costs and fewer variable costs. This trend is the result of increased use of automation and less use of employee labor. As a result, depreciation and lease charges (fixed costs) increase, whereas direct labor costs (variable costs) decrease.

People, Planet, and Profit Insight   BrightFarms

© Jani Bryson/iStockphoto

Gardens in the Sky

Because of population increases, the United Nations' Food and Agriculture Organization estimates that food production will need to increase by 70% by 2050. Also, by 2050, roughly 70% of people will live in cities, which means more food needs to be hauled further to get it to the consumer. To address the lack of farmable land and reduce the cost of transporting produce, some companies, such as New York-based BrightFarms, are building urban greenhouses.

This sounds great, but do the numbers work? Some variable costs would be reduced. For example, the use of pesticides, herbicides, fuel costs for shipping, and water would all drop. Soil erosion would be a non-issue since plants would be grown hydroponically (in a solution of water and minerals), and land requirements would be reduced because of vertical structures. But, other costs would be higher. First, there is the cost of the building. Also, any multistory building would require artificial lighting for plants on lower floors.

Until these cost challenges can be overcome, it appears that these urban greenhouses may not break even. On the other hand, rooftop greenhouses on existing city structures already appear financially viable. For example, a 15,000 square-foot rooftop greenhouse in Brooklyn already produces roughly 30 tons of vegetables per year for local residents.

Sources: "Vertical Farming: Does It Really Stack Up?" *The Economist* (December 9, 2010); and Jane Black, "BrightFarms Idea: Greenhouses That Cut Short the Path from Plant to Grocery Shelf," *The Washington Post* (May 7, 2013).

What are some of the variable and fixed costs that are impacted by hydroponic farming? (Go to **WileyPLUS** *for this answer and additional questions.)*

Relevant Range

In Illustration 19-1 part (a) (page 886), a straight line is drawn throughout the entire range of the activity index for total variable costs. In essence, the assumption is that the costs are **linear**. If a relationship is linear (that is, straight-line), then changes in the activity index will result in a direct, proportional change in the variable cost. For example, if the activity level doubles, the cost doubles.

It is now necessary to ask: Is the straight-line relationship realistic? In most business situations, a straight-line relationship **does not exist** for variable costs throughout the entire range of possible activity. At abnormally low levels of activity, it may be impossible to be cost-efficient. Small-scale operations may not allow the company to obtain quantity discounts for raw materials or to use specialized labor. In contrast, at abnormally high levels of activity, labor costs may increase sharply because of overtime pay. Also, at high activity levels, materials costs may jump significantly because of excess spoilage caused by worker fatigue.

As a result, in the real world, the relationship between the behavior of a variable cost and changes in the activity level is often **curvilinear**, as shown in part (a) of Illustration 19-3. In the curved sections of the line, a change in the activity index will not result in a direct, proportional change in the variable cost. That is, a doubling of the activity index will not result in an exact doubling of the variable cost. The variable cost may more than double, or it may be less than double.

Total fixed costs also do not have a straight-line relationship over the entire range of activity. Some fixed costs will not change. But it is possible for management to change other fixed costs. For example, in some instances, salaried employees (fixed) are replaced with freelance workers (variable). Illustration 19-3, part (b), shows an example of the behavior of total fixed costs through all potential levels of activity.

For most companies, operating at almost zero or at 100% capacity is the exception rather than the rule. Instead, companies often operate over a somewhat

Helpful Hint
Fixed costs that may be changeable include research, such as new product development, and management training programs.

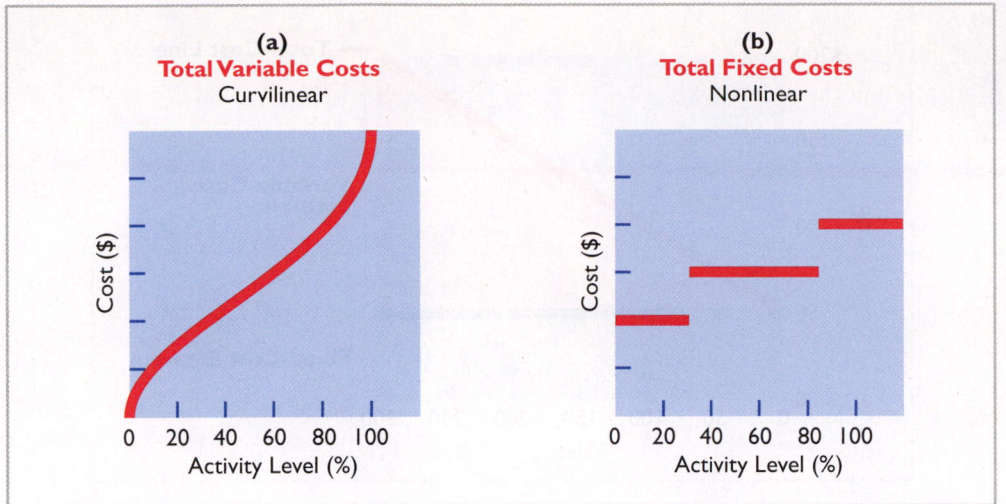

Illustration 19-3
Nonlinear behavior of variable
and fixed costs

narrower range, such as 40–80% of capacity. The range over which a company expects to operate during a year is called the **relevant range** of the activity index. Within the relevant range, as both diagrams in Illustration 19-4 show, a straight-line relationship generally exists for both variable and fixed costs.

Alternative Terminology
The relevant range is also
called the *normal* or *practical*
range.

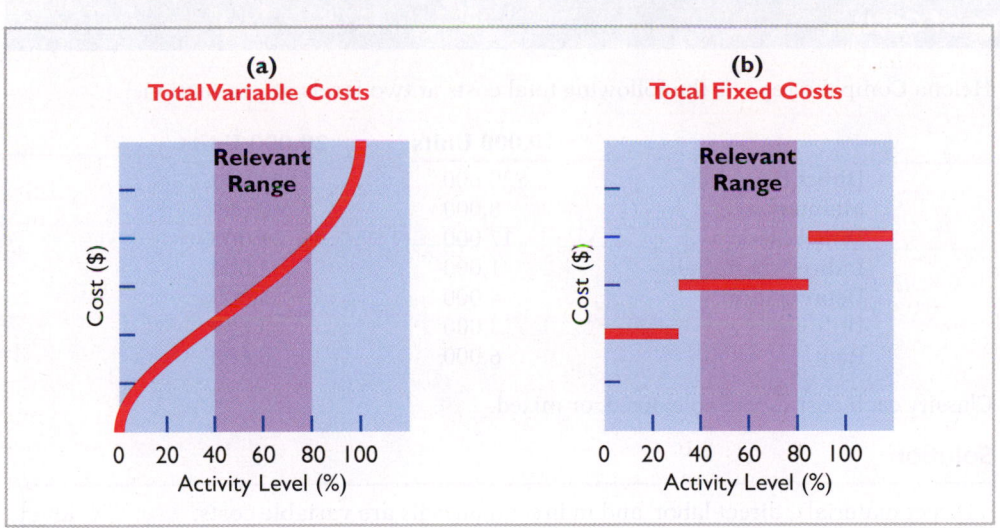

Illustration 19-4
Linear behavior within relevant
range

As you can see, although the linear (straight-line) relationship may not be completely realistic, **the linear assumption produces useful data for CVP analysis as long as the level of activity remains within the relevant range**.

Mixed Costs

Mixed costs are costs that contain both a variable- and a fixed-cost element. **Mixed costs, therefore, change in total but not proportionately with changes in the activity level.**

The rental of a U-Haul truck is a good example of a mixed cost. Assume that local rental terms for a 17-foot truck, including insurance, are $50 per day plus 50 cents per mile. When determining the cost of a one-day rental, the per day charge is a fixed cost (with respect to miles driven), whereas the mileage charge is a variable cost. The graphic presentation of the rental cost for a one-day rental is shown in Illustration 19-5 (page 890).

Illustration 19-5
Behavior of a mixed cost

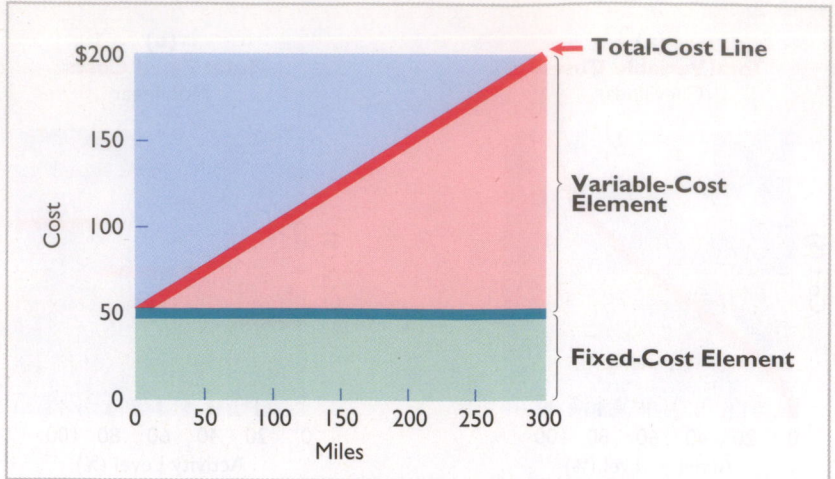

In this case, the fixed-cost element is the cost of having the service available. The variable-cost element is the cost of actually using the service. Utility costs such as for electricity are another example of a mixed cost. Each month the electric bill includes a flat service fee plus a usage charge.

DO IT! 1 | Types of Costs

Helena Company reports the following total costs at two levels of production.

	10,000 Units	20,000 Units
Direct materials	$20,000	$40,000
Maintenance	8,000	10,000
Direct labor	17,000	34,000
Indirect materials	1,000	2,000
Depreciation	4,000	4,000
Utilities	3,000	5,000
Rent	6,000	6,000

Action Plan

 Recall that a variable cost varies in total directly and proportionately with each change in activity level.

 Recall that a fixed cost remains the same in total with each change in activity level.

 Recall that a mixed cost changes in total but not proportionately with each change in activity level.

Classify each cost as variable, fixed, or mixed.

Solution

> Direct materials, direct labor, and indirect materials are variable costs.
> Depreciation and rent are fixed costs.
> Maintenance and utilities are mixed costs.

Related exercise material: **BE19-1, BE19-2, E19-1, E19-2, E19-4, E19-6, and DO IT! 19-1.**

LEARNING OBJECTIVE **2**

Apply the high-low method to determine the components of mixed costs.

For purposes of cost-volume-profit analysis, **mixed costs must be classified into their fixed and variable elements**. How does management make the classification? One possibility is to determine the variable and fixed components each time a mixed cost is incurred. But because of time and cost constraints, this approach is rarely followed. Instead, the usual approach is to collect data on the behavior of the mixed costs at various levels of activity. Analysts then identify the fixed- and variable-cost components. Companies use various types of analysis. One type of analysis, called the **high-low method**, is discussed next.

High-Low Method

The **high-low method** uses the total costs incurred at the high and low levels of activity to classify mixed costs into fixed and variable components. The difference in costs between the high and low levels represents variable costs, since only the variable-cost element can change as activity levels change.

The steps in computing fixed and variable costs under this method are as follows.

1. **Determine variable cost per unit from the following formula.**

Change in Total Costs	÷	High minus Low Activity Level	=	Variable Cost per Unit

Illustration 19-6
Formula for variable cost per unit using high-low method

To illustrate, assume that Metro Transit Company has the following maintenance costs and mileage data for its fleet of buses over a 6-month period.

Illustration 19-7
Assumed maintenance costs and mileage data

Month	Miles Driven	Total Cost	Month	Miles Driven	Total Cost
January	20,000	$30,000	April	50,000	$63,000
February	40,000	48,000	May	30,000	42,000
March	35,000	49,000	June	43,000	61,000

The high and low levels of activity are 50,000 miles in April and 20,000 miles in January. The maintenance costs at these two levels are $63,000 and $30,000, respectively. The difference in maintenance costs is $33,000 ($63,000 − $30,000), and the difference in miles is 30,000 (50,000 − 20,000). Therefore, for Metro Transit, variable cost per unit is $1.10, computed as follows.

$$\$33,000 \div 30,000 = \$1.10$$

2. **Determine the fixed costs by subtracting the total variable costs at either the high or the low activity level from the total cost at that activity level.**

For Metro Transit, the computations are shown in Illustration 19-8.

Illustration 19-8
High-low method computation of fixed costs

	Metro Transit.xls		
	Home Insert Page Layout Formulas Data Review View		
	P18 *fx*		
	A	B	C	D
1	**METRO TRANSIT**			
2			Activity Level	
3			High	Low
4	Total cost		$63,000	$30,000
5	Less:	Variable costs		
6		50,000 × $1.10	55,000	
7		20,000 × $1.10		22,000
8	Total fixed costs		$ 8,000	$ 8,000
9				
10				

Maintenance costs are therefore $8,000 per month of fixed costs plus $1.10 per mile of variable costs. This is represented by the following formula:

$$\text{Maintenance costs} = \$8{,}000 + (\$1.10 \times \text{Miles driven})$$

For example, at 45,000 miles, estimated maintenance costs would be $8,000 fixed and $49,500 variable ($1.10 × 45,000) for a total of $57,500.

The graph in Illustration 19-9 plots the 6-month data for Metro Transit Company. The red line drawn in the graph connects the high and low data points, and therefore represents the equation that we just solved using the high-low method. The red, "high-low" line intersects the y-axis at $8,000 (the fixed-cost level), and it rises by $1.10 per unit (the variable cost per unit). Note that a completely different line would result if we chose any two of the other data points. That is, by choosing any two other data points, we would end up with a different estimate of fixed costs and a different variable cost per unit. Thus, from this scatter plot, we can see that while the high-low method is simple, the result is rather arbitrary. A better approach, which uses information from all the data points to estimate fixed and variable costs, is called *regression analysis*. A discussion of regression analysis is provided in a supplement on the book's companion website.

Illustration 19-9
Scatter plot for Metro Transit Company

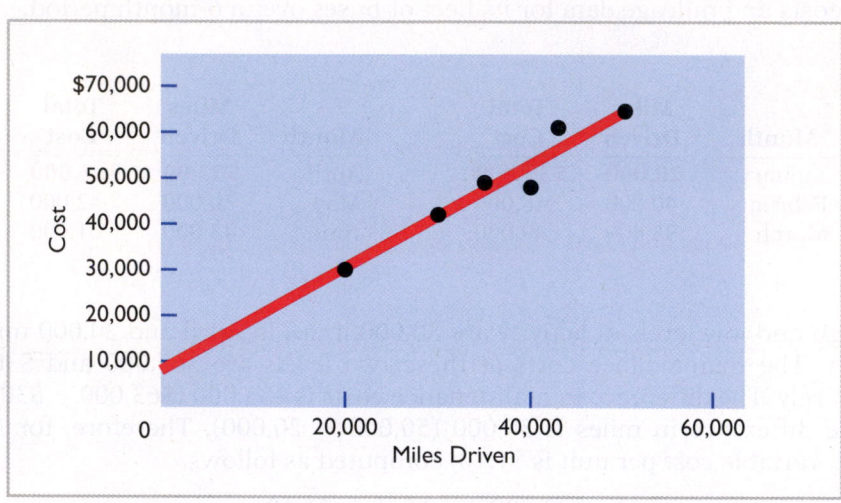

Management Insight   Tempur Sealy International

Bloomberg/Getty Images

Skilled Labor Is Truly Essential

The recent recession had devastating implications for employment. But one surprise was that for some manufacturers, the number of jobs lost was actually lower than in previous recessions. One of the main explanations for this was that in the years preceding the recession, many companies, such as Tempur Sealy International, adopted lean manufacturing practices. This meant that production relied less on large numbers of low-skilled workers and more on machines and a few highly skilled workers. As a result of this approach, a single employee supports far more dollars in sales. Thus, it requires a larger decline in sales before an employee would need to be laid-off in order for the company to continue to break even. Also, because the employees are highly skilled, employers are reluctant to lose them. Instead of lay-offs, many manufacturers now resort to cutting employees' hours when necessary.

Source: Timothy Aeppel and Justin Lahart, "Lean Factories Find It Hard to Cut Jobs Even in a Slump," *Wall Street Journal Online* (March 9, 2009).

Would you characterize labor costs as being a fixed cost, a variable cost, or something else in this situation? (Go to **WileyPLUS** for this answer and additional questions.)

Importance of Identifying Variable and Fixed Costs

Why is it important to segregate mixed costs into variable and fixed elements? The answer may become apparent if we look at the following four business decisions.

1. If **American Airlines** is to make a profit when it reduces all domestic fares by 30%, what reduction in costs or increase in passengers will be required?
   Answer: To make a profit when it cuts domestic fares by 30%, American Airlines will have to increase the number of passengers or cut its variable costs for those flights. Its fixed costs will not change.

2. If **Ford Motor Company** meets workers' demands for higher wages, what increase in sales revenue will be needed to maintain current profit levels?
   Answer: Higher wages at Ford Motor Company will increase the variable costs of manufacturing automobiles. To maintain present profit levels, Ford will have to cut other variable costs or increase the price of its automobiles.

3. If **United States Steel Corp.**'s program to modernize plant facilities through significant equipment purchases reduces the work force by 50%, what will be the effect on the cost of producing one ton of steel?
   Answer: The modernizing of plant facilities at United States Steel Corp. changes the proportion of fixed and variable costs of producing one ton of steel. Fixed costs increase because of higher depreciation charges, whereas variable costs decrease due to the reduction in the number of steelworkers.

4. What happens if **Kellogg's** increases its advertising expenses but cannot increase prices because of competitive pressure?
   Answer: Sales volume must be increased to cover the increase in fixed advertising costs.

DO IT! 2 High-Low Method

Byrnes Company accumulates the following data concerning a mixed cost, using units produced as the activity level.

	Units Produced	**Total Cost**
March	9,800	$14,740
April	8,500	13,250
May	7,000	11,100
June	7,600	12,000
July	8,100	12,460

(a) Compute the variable-cost and fixed-cost elements using the high-low method.

(b) Estimate the total cost if the company produces 8,000 units.

Solution

(a) Variable cost: ($14,740 − $11,100) ÷ (9,800 − 7,000) = $1.30 per unit
    Fixed cost: $14,740 − $12,740* = $2,000
        or $11,100 − $9,100** = $2,000

    *$1.30 × 9,800 units
    **$1.30 × 7,000 units

(b) Total cost to produce 8,000 units: $2,000 + $10,400 ($1.30 × 8,000 units) = $12,400

Related exercise material: **BE19-3, BE19-4, BE19-5, E19-3, E19-5, and DO IT! 19-2.**

Action Plan

✔ Determine the highest and lowest levels of activity.

✔ Compute variable cost per unit as Change in total costs ÷ (High − low activity level) = Variable cost per unit.

✔ Compute fixed cost as Total cost − (Variable cost per unit × Units produced) = Fixed cost.

Prepare a CVP income statement to determine contribution margin.

Cost-volume-profit (CVP) analysis is the study of the effects of changes in costs and volume on a company's profits. CVP analysis is important in profit planning. It also is a critical factor in such management decisions as setting selling prices, determining product mix, and maximizing use of production facilities.

Basic Components

CVP analysis considers the interrelationships among the components shown in Illustration 19-10.

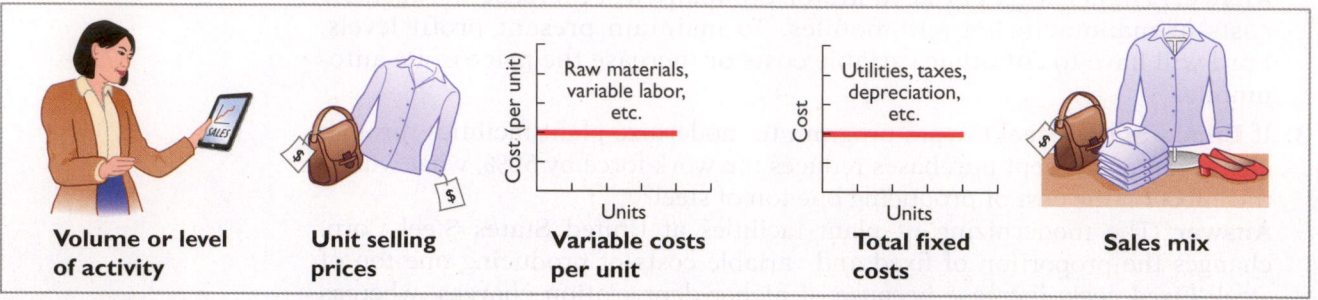

| Volume or level of activity | Unit selling prices | Variable costs per unit | Total fixed costs | Sales mix |

Illustration 19-10
Components of CVP analysis

The following assumptions underlie each CVP analysis.

1. The behavior of both costs and revenues is linear throughout the relevant range of the activity index.

2. Costs can be classified accurately as either variable or fixed.

3. Changes in activity are the only factors that affect costs.

4. All units produced are sold.

5. When more than one type of product is sold, the sales mix will remain constant. That is, the percentage that each product represents of total sales will stay the same. Sales mix complicates CVP analysis because different products will have different cost relationships. In this chapter, we assume a single product. In Chapter 20, however, we examine the sales mix more closely.

When these assumptions are not valid, the CVP analysis may be inaccurate.

CVP Income Statement

Because CVP is so important for decision-making, management often wants this information reported in a **cost-volume-profit (CVP) income statement** format for internal use. The CVP income statement classifies costs as variable or fixed and computes a contribution margin. **Contribution margin (CM)** is the amount of revenue remaining after deducting variable costs. It is often stated both as a total amount and on a per unit basis.

We will use Vargo Video Company to illustrate a CVP income statement. Vargo Video produces a high-definition digital camcorder with 15× optical zoom and a wide-screen, high-resolution LCD monitor. Relevant data for the camcorders sold by this company in June 2017 are as follows.

Illustration 19-11
Assumed selling and cost data for Vargo Video

Unit selling price of camcorder	$500
Unit variable costs	$300
Total monthly fixed costs	$200,000
Units sold	1,600

The CVP income statement for Vargo therefore would be reported as follows.

VARGO VIDEO COMPANY	
CVP Income Statement	
For the Month Ended June 30, 2017	

	Total
Sales (1,600 camcorders)	$ 800,000
Variable costs	480,000
Contribution margin	**320,000**
Fixed costs	200,000
Net income	**$120,000**

Illustration 19-12
CVP income statement, with net income

A traditional income statement and a CVP income statement both report the same net income of $120,000. However, a traditional income statement does not classify costs as variable or fixed, and therefore it does not report a contribution margin. In addition, sometimes per unit amounts and percentage of sales amounts are shown in separate columns on a CVP income statement to facilitate CVP analysis. *Homework assignments specify which columns to present.*

In the applications of CVP analysis that follow, we assume that the term "cost" includes all costs and expenses related to production and sale of the product. That is, cost includes manufacturing costs plus selling and administrative expenses.

UNIT CONTRIBUTION MARGIN

The formula for **unit contribution margin** and the computation for Vargo Video are as follows.

Unit Selling Price	−	Unit Variable Costs	=	Unit Contribution Margin
$500	−	$300	=	$200

Illustration 19-13
Formula for unit contribution margin

Unit contribution margin indicates that for every camcorder sold, the selling price exceeds the variable costs by $200. Vargo generates $200 per unit sold to cover fixed costs and contribute to net income. Because Vargo has fixed costs of $200,000, it must sell 1,000 camcorders ($200,000 ÷ $200) to cover its fixed costs.

At the point where total contribution margin exactly equals fixed costs, Vargo will report net income of zero. At this point, referred to as the **break-even point**, total costs (variable plus fixed) exactly equal total revenue. Illustration 19-14 shows Vargo's CVP income statement at the point where net income equals zero. It shows a contribution margin of $200,000, and a unit contribution margin of $200 ($500 − $300).

VARGO VIDEO COMPANY		
CVP Income Statement		
For the Month Ended June 30, 2017		

	Total	Per Unit
Sales (1,000 camcorders)	$ 500,000	$ 500
Variable costs	300,000	300
Contribution margin	**200,000**	**$200**
Fixed costs	200,000	
Net income	**$ –0–**	

Illustration 19-14
CVP income statement, with zero net income

It follows that for every camcorder sold above the break-even point of 1,000 units, **net income increases by the amount of the unit contribution margin, $200**. For example, assume that Vargo sold one more camcorder, for a total of 1,001 camcorders sold. In this case, Vargo reports net income of $200, as shown in Illustration 19-15.

Illustration 19-15
CVP income statement, with net income and per unit data

VARGO VIDEO COMPANY
CVP Income Statement
For the Month Ended June 30, 2017

	Total	Per Unit
Sales (1,001 camcorders)	$500,500	$ 500
Variable costs	300,300	300
Contribution margin	**200,200**	**$200**
Fixed costs	200,000	
Net income	**$ 200**	

CONTRIBUTION MARGIN RATIO

Some managers prefer to use a contribution margin ratio in CVP analysis. The contribution margin ratio is the contribution margin expressed as a percentage of sales, as shown in Illustration 19-16.

Illustration 19-16
CVP income statement, with net income and percent of sales data

VARGO VIDEO COMPANY
CVP Income Statement
For the Month Ended June 30, 2017

	Total	Percent of Sales
Sales (1,001 camcorders)	$500,500	100%
Variable costs	300,300	60
Contribution margin	**200,200**	**40%**
Fixed costs	200,000	
Net income	**$ 200**	

Alternatively, the **contribution margin ratio** can be determined by dividing the unit contribution margin by the unit selling price. For Vargo Video, the ratio is as follows.

Illustration 19-17
Formula for contribution margin ratio

Unit Contribution Margin	÷	Unit Selling Price	=	Contribution Margin Ratio
$200	÷	$500	=	40%

The contribution margin ratio of 40% means that Vargo generates 40 cents of contribution margin with each dollar of sales. That is, $0.40 of each sales dollar (40% × $1) is available to apply to fixed costs and to contribute to net income.

This expression of contribution margin is very helpful in determining the effect of changes in sales on net income. For example, if Vargo's sales increase $100,000, net income will increase $40,000 (40% × $100,000). Thus, by using the contribution margin ratio, managers can quickly determine increases in net income from any change in sales.

We can also see this effect through a CVP income statement. Assume that Vargo's current sales are $500,000 and it wants to know the effect of a $100,000 (200-unit) increase in sales. Vargo prepares a comparative CVP income statement analysis as follows.

Illustration 19-18
Comparative CVP income statements

VARGO VIDEO COMPANY
CVP Income Statements
For the Month Ended June 30, 2017

	No Change			With Change		
	Total	**Per Unit**	**Percent of Sales**	**Total**	**Per Unit**	**Percent of Sales**
Sales	$500,000	$500	100%	$600,000	$500	100%
Variable costs	300,000	300	60	360,000	300	60
Contribution margin	**200,000**	**$200**	**40%**	**240,000**	**$200**	**40%**
Fixed costs	200,000			200,000		
Net income	**$ –0–**			**$ 40,000**		

The $40,000 increase in net income can be calculated on either a unit contribution margin basis (200 units × $200 per unit) or using the contribution margin ratio times the increase in sales dollars (40% × $100,000). Note that the unit contribution margin and contribution margin as a percentage of sales remain unchanged by the increase in sales.

Study these CVP income statements carefully. The concepts presented in these statements are used extensively in this and later chapters.

DO IT! 3 CVP Income Statement

Ampco Industries produces and sells a cell phone-operated thermostat. Information regarding the costs and sales of thermostats during September 2017 are provided below.

Unit selling price of thermostat	$85
Unit variable costs	$32
Total monthly fixed costs	$190,000
Units sold	4,000

Prepare a CVP income statement for Ampco Industries for the month of September. Provide per unit values and total values.

Solution

AMPCO INDUSTRIES
CVP Income Statement
For the Month Ended September 30, 2017

	Total	Per Unit
Sales	$340,000	$85
Variable costs	128,000	32
Contribution margin	212,000	$53
Fixed costs	190,000	
Net income	$ 22,000	

Related exercise material: **BE19-6, BE19-7, E19-7, and DO IT! 19-3.**

Action Plan

✔ Provide a heading with the name of the company, name of statement, and period covered.

✔ Subtract variable costs from sales to determine contribution margin. Subtract fixed costs from contribution margin to determine net income.

✔ Express sales, variable costs and contribution margin on a per unit basis.

Compute the break-even point using three approaches.

A key relationship in CVP analysis is the level of activity at which total revenues equal total costs (both fixed and variable)—the **break-even point**. At this volume of sales, the company will realize no income but will suffer no loss. The process of finding the break-even point is called **break-even analysis**. Knowledge of the break-even point is useful to management when it considers decisions such as whether to introduce new product lines, change sales prices on established products, or enter new market areas.

The break-even point can be:

1. Computed from a mathematical equation.
2. Computed by using contribution margin.
3. Derived from a cost-volume-profit (CVP) graph.

The break-even point can be expressed either in **sales units** or **sales dollars**.

Mathematical Equation

The first line of Illustration 19-19 shows a common equation used for CVP analysis. When net income is set to zero, this equation can be used to calculate the break-even point.

Illustration 19-19
Basic CVP equation

Required Sales	−	Variable Costs	−	Fixed Costs	=	Net Income
$500Q	−	$300Q	−	$200,000	=	$0

As shown in Illustration 19-14 (page 895), net income equals zero when the contribution margin (sales minus variable costs) is equal to fixed costs.

To reflect this, Illustration 19-20 rewrites the equation with contribution margin (sales minus variable costs) on the left side, and fixed costs and net income on the right. We can compute the break-even point **in units** by **using unit selling prices** and **unit variable costs**. The computation for Vargo Video is as follows.

Illustration 19-20
Computation of break-even point in units

Required Sales	−	Variable Costs	−	Fixed Costs	=	Net Income
$500Q	−	$300Q	−	$200,000	=	$0
$500Q	−	$300Q	=	$200,000	+	$0
$200Q	=	$200,000				

$$Q = \frac{\$200,000}{\$200} = \frac{\textbf{\textcolor{red}{Fixed Costs}}}{\textbf{\textcolor{red}{Unit Contribution Margin}}}$$

$$Q = 1,000 \text{ units}$$

where

Q	=	sales volume in units
$500	=	selling price
$300	=	variable costs per unit
$200,000	=	total fixed costs

Thus, Vargo must sell 1,000 units to break even.

To find the amount of **sales dollars** required to break even, we multiply the units sold at the break-even point times the selling price per unit, as shown below.

$$1,000 \times \$500 = \$500,000 \text{ (break-even sales dollars)}$$

Contribution Margin Technique

Many managers employ the contribution margin to compute the break-even point.

CONTRIBUTION MARGIN IN UNITS

The final step in Illustration 19-20 divides fixed costs by the unit contribution margin (highlighted in red). Thus, rather than walk through all of the steps of the equation approach, we can simply employ this formula shown in Illustration 19-21.

Fixed Costs	÷	Unit Contribution Margin	=	Break-Even Point in Units
$200,000	÷	$200	=	1,000 units

Illustration 19-21
Formula for break-even point in units using unit contribution margin

Why does this formula work? The unit contribution margin is the net amount by which each sale exceeds the variable costs per unit. Every sale generates this much money to pay off fixed costs. Consequently, if we divide fixed costs by the unit contribution margin, we know how many units we need to sell to break even.

CONTRIBUTION MARGIN RATIO

As we will see in the next chapter, when a company has numerous products, it is not practical to determine the unit contribution margin for each product. In this case, using the contribution margin ratio is very useful for determining the break-even point in total dollars (rather than units). Recall that the contribution margin ratio is the percentage of each dollar of sales that is available to cover fixed costs and generate net income. Therefore, **to determine the sales dollars needed to cover fixed costs**, we divide fixed costs by the contribution margin ratio, as shown in Illustration 19-22.

Fixed Costs	÷	Contribution Margin Ratio	=	Break-Even Point in Dollars
$200,000	÷	40%	=	$500,000

Illustration 19-22
Formula for break-even point in dollars using contribution margin ratio

To apply this formula to Vargo Video, consider that its 40% contribution margin ratio means that for every dollar sold, it generates 40 cents of contribution margin. The question is, how many dollars of sales does Vargo need in order to generate total contribution margin of $200,000 to pay off fixed costs? We divide the fixed costs of $200,000 by the 40 cents of contribution margin generated by each dollar of sales to arrive at $500,000 ($200,000 ÷ 40%). To prove this result, if we generate 40 cents of contribution margin for each dollar of sales, then the total contribution margin generated by $500,000 in sales is $200,000 ($500,000 × 40%).

Service Company Insight | Flightserve

Digital Vision/Getty Images

Charter Flights Offer a Good Deal

The Internet is wringing inefficiencies out of nearly every industry. While commercial aircraft spend roughly 4,000 hours a year in the air, chartered aircraft are flown only 500 hours annually. That means that they are sitting on the ground—not making any money—about 90% of the time. One company, Flightserve, saw a business opportunity in that fact. For about the same cost as a first-class ticket, Flightserve matches up executives with charter flights in small "private jets." The executive gets a more comfortable ride and avoids the hassle of big airports. Flightserve noted that the average charter jet has eight seats. When all eight seats are full, the company has an 80% profit margin. It breaks even at an average of 3.3 full seats per flight.

Source: "Jet Set Go," *The Economist* (March 18, 2000), p. 68.

How did Flightserve determine that it would break even with 3.3 seats full per flight? (Go to **WileyPLUS** for this answer and additional questions.)

Graphic Presentation

An effective way to find the break-even point is to prepare a break-even graph. Because this graph also shows costs, volume, and profits, it is referred to as a **cost-volume-profit (CVP) graph**.

As the CVP graph in Illustration 19-23 shows, sales volume is recorded along the horizontal axis. This axis should extend to the maximum level of expected sales. Both total revenues (sales) and total costs (fixed plus variable) are recorded on the vertical axis.

Illustration 19-23
CVP graph

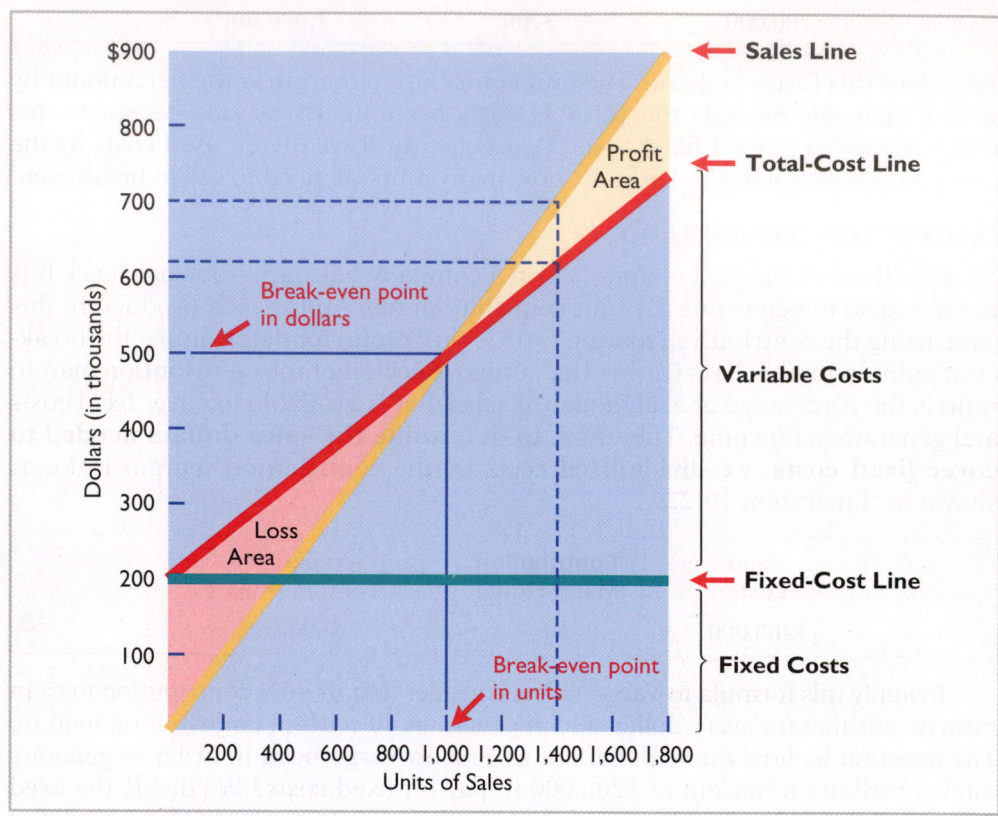

The construction of the graph, using the data for Vargo Video, is as follows.

1. Plot the sales line, starting at the zero activity level. For every camcorder sold, total revenue increases by $500. For example, at 200 units, sales are $100,000. At the upper level of activity (1,800 units), sales are $900,000. The revenue line is assumed to be linear through the full range of activity.

2. Plot the total fixed costs using a horizontal line. For the camcorders, this line is plotted at $200,000. The fixed costs are the same at every level of activity.

3. Plot the total-cost line. This starts at the fixed-cost line at zero activity. It increases by the variable costs at each level of activity. For each camcorder, variable costs are $300. Thus, at 200 units, total variable costs are $60,000 ($300 × 200) and the total cost is $260,000 ($60,000 + $200,000). At 1,800 units, total variable costs are $540,000 ($300 × 1,800) and total cost is $740,000 ($540,000 + $200,000). On the graph, the amount of the variable costs can be derived from the difference between the total-cost and fixed-cost lines at each level of activity.

4. Determine the break-even point from the intersection of the total-cost line and the sales line. The break-even point in dollars is found by drawing a horizontal line from the break-even point to the vertical axis. The break-even point in

units is found by drawing a vertical line from the break-even point to the horizontal axis. For the camcorders, the break-even point is $500,000 of sales, or 1,000 units. At this sales level, Vargo will cover costs but make no profit.

The CVP graph also shows both the net income and net loss areas. Thus, the amount of income or loss at each level of sales can be derived from the sales and total-cost lines.

A CVP graph is useful because the effects of a change in any element in the CVP analysis can be quickly seen. For example, a 10% increase in selling price will change the location of the sales line. Likewise, the effects on total costs of wage increases can be quickly observed.

DO IT! 4   Break-Even Analysis

Lombardi Company has a unit selling price of $400, variable costs per unit of $240, and fixed costs of $180,000. Compute the break-even point in units using (a) a mathematical equation and (b) unit contribution margin.

Solution

(a) The equation is $400Q − $240Q − $180,000 = $0; ($400Q − $240Q) = $180,000. The break-even point in units is 1,125. (b) The unit contribution margin is $160 ($400 − $240). The formula therefore is $180,000 ÷ $160, and the break-even point in units is 1,125.

Related exercise material: **BE19-8, BE19-9, E19-8, E19-9, E19-10, E19-11, E19-12, E19-13, E19-16, and DO IT! 19-4.**

Action Plan

✔ Apply the formula: Sales − Variable costs − Fixed costs = Net income.

✔ Apply the formula: Fixed costs ÷ Unit contribution margin = Break-even point in units.

LEARNING OBJECTIVE 5

Determine the sales required to earn target net income and determine margin of safety.

Target Net Income

Rather than simply "breaking even," management usually sets an income objective often called **target net income**. It then determines the sales necessary to achieve this specified level of income. Companies determine the sales necessary to achieve target net income by using one of the three approaches discussed earlier.

MATHEMATICAL EQUATION

We know that at the break-even point no profit or loss results for the company. By adding an amount for target net income to the same basic equation, we obtain the following formula for determining required sales.

Required Sales	−	Variable Costs	−	Fixed Costs	=	Target Net Income

Illustration 19-24
Formula for required sales to meet target net income

Recall that once the break-even point has been reached so that fixed costs are covered, each additional unit sold increases net income by the amount of the unit contribution margin. We can rewrite the equation with contribution margin (required sales minus variable costs) on the left-hand side, and fixed costs and target net income on the right. Assuming that target net income is $120,000 for Vargo Video, the computation of required sales in units is as shown in Illustration 19-25 (page 902).

Illustration 19-25
Computation of required sales

Required Sales	−	Variable Costs	−	Fixed Costs	=	Target Net Income
$500Q	−	$300Q	−	$200,000	=	$120,000
$500Q	−	$300Q		=	$200,000	+	$120,000

$$\$200Q = \$200,000 + \$120,000$$

$$Q = \frac{\$200,000 + \$120,000}{\$200} = \frac{\textbf{Fixed Costs + Target Net Income}}{\textbf{Unit Contribution Margin}}$$

$$Q = 1,600$$

where

$$Q = \text{sales volume}$$
$$\$500 = \text{selling price}$$
$$\$300 = \text{variable costs per unit}$$
$$\$200,000 = \text{total fixed costs}$$
$$\$120,000 = \text{target net income}$$

Vargo must sell 1,600 units to achieve target net income of $120,000. The sales dollars required to achieve the target net income is found by multiplying the units sold by the unit selling price [(1,600 × $500) = $800,000].

CONTRIBUTION MARGIN TECHNIQUE

As in the case of break-even sales, we can compute in either units or dollars the sales required to meet target net income. The formula to compute required sales in units for Vargo Video using the unit contribution margin can be seen in the final step of the equation approach in Illustration 19-25 (shown in red). We simply divide the sum of fixed costs and target net income by the unit contribution margin. Illustration 19-26 shows this for Vargo.

Illustration 19-26
Formula for required sales in units using unit contribution margin

(Fixed Costs + Target Net Income)	÷	Unit Contribution Margin	=	Required Sales in Units
($200,000 + $120,000)	÷	$200	=	1,600 units

To achieve its desired target net income of $120,000, Vargo must sell 1,600 camcorders.

The formula to compute the required sales in dollars for Vargo using the contribution margin ratio is shown below.

Illustration 19-27
Formula for required sales in dollars using contribution margin ratio

(Fixed Costs + Target Net Income)	÷	Contribution Margin Ratio	=	Required Sales in Dollars
($200,000 + $120,000)	÷	40%	=	$800,000

To achieve its desired target net income of $120,000, Vargo must generate sales of $800,000.

GRAPHIC PRESENTATION

We also can use the CVP graph in Illustration 19-23 (on page 900) to find the sales required to meet target net income. In the profit area of the graph, the distance between the sales line and the total-cost line at any point equals net income. We can find required sales by analyzing the differences between the two lines until the desired net income is found.

For example, suppose Vargo Video sells 1,400 camcorders. Illustration 19-23 shows that a vertical line drawn at 1,400 units intersects the sales line at $700,000 and the total-cost line at $620,000. The difference between the two amounts represents the net income (profit) of $80,000.

Margin of Safety

Margin of safety is the difference between actual or expected sales and sales at the break-even point. It measures the "cushion" that a particular level of sales provides. It tells us how far sales could fall before the company begins operating at a loss. The margin of safety is expressed in dollars or as a ratio.

The formula for stating the **margin of safety in dollars** is actual (or expected) sales minus break-even sales. Assuming that actual (expected) sales for Vargo Video are $750,000, the computation is as follows.

Actual (Expected) Sales	−	Break-Even Sales	=	Margin of Safety in Dollars
$750,000	−	$500,000	=	$250,000

Illustration 19-28
Formula for margin of safety in dollars

Vargo's margin of safety is $250,000. Its sales could fall $250,000 before it operates at a loss.

The **margin of safety ratio** is the margin of safety in dollars divided by actual (or expected) sales. Illustration 19-29 shows the formula and computation for determining the margin of safety ratio.

Margin of Safety in Dollars	÷	Actual (Expected) Sales	=	Margin of Safety Ratio
$250,000	÷	$750,000	=	33%

Illustration 19-29
Formula for margin of safety ratio

This means that the company's sales could fall by 33% before it operates at a loss.

The higher the dollars or the percentage, the greater the margin of safety. Management continuously evaluates the adequacy of the margin of safety in terms of such factors as the vulnerability of the product to competitive pressures and to downturns in the economy.

Service Company Insight   Rolling Stones

Yael/Retna

How a Rolling Stones' Tour Makes Money

Computations of break-even and margin of safety are important for service companies. Consider how the promoter for the Rolling Stones' tour used the break-even point and margin of safety. For example, say one outdoor show should bring 70,000 individuals for a gross of $2.45 million. The promoter guarantees $1.2 million to the Rolling Stones. In addition, 20% of gross goes to the stadium in which the performance is staged. Add another $400,000 for other expenses such as ticket takers, parking attendants, advertising, and so on. The promoter also shares in sales of T-shirts and memorabilia for which the promoter will net over $7 million during the tour. From a successful Rolling Stones' tour, the promoter could make $35 million!

*What amount of sales dollars are required for the promoter to break even? (Go to **WileyPLUS** for this answer and additional questions.)*

DO IT! 5   Break-Even, Margin of Safety, and Target Net Income

Zootsuit Inc. makes travel bags that sell for $56 each. For the coming year, management expects fixed costs to total $320,000 and variable costs to be $42 per unit. Compute the following: (a) break-even point in dollars using the contribution margin (CM) ratio; (b) the margin of safety and margin of safety ratio assuming actual sales are $1,382,400; and (c) the sales dollars required to earn net income of $410,000.

Action Plan

✔ Apply the formula for the break-even point in dollars.

✔ Apply the formulas for the margin of safety in dollars and the margin of safety ratio.

✔ Apply the formula for the required sales in dollars.

Solution

(a) Contribution margin ratio = [($56 − $42) ÷ $56] = 25%
    Break-even sales in dollars = $320,000 ÷ 25% = $1,280,000

(b) Margin of safety = $1,382,400 − $1,280,000 = $102,400
    Margin of safety ratio = $102,400 ÷ $1,382,400 = 7.4%

(c) Required sales in dollars = ($320,000 + $410,000) ÷ 25% = $2,920,000

Related exercise material: **BE19-10, BE19-11, BE19-12, E19-14, E19-15, E19-17, and DO IT! 19-5.**

REVIEW AND PRACTICE

LEARNING OBJECTIVES REVIEW

1 Explain variable, fixed, and mixed costs and the relevant range. Variable costs are costs that vary in total directly and proportionately with changes in the activity index. Fixed costs are costs that remain the same in total regardless of changes in the activity index.

The relevant range is the range of activity in which a company expects to operate during a year. It is important in CVP analysis because the behavior of costs is assumed to be linear throughout the relevant range.

Mixed costs change in total but not proportionately with changes in the activity level. For purposes of CVP analysis, mixed costs must be classified into their fixed and variable elements.

2 Apply the high-low method to determine the components of mixed costs. Determine the variable costs per unit by dividing the change in total costs at the highest and lowest levels of activity by the difference in activity at those levels. Then, determine fixed costs by subtracting total variable costs from the amount of total costs at either the highest or lowest level of activity.

3 Prepare a CVP income statement to determine contribution margin. The five components of CVP analysis are (1) volume or level of activity, (2) unit selling prices, (3) variable costs per unit, (4) total fixed costs, and (5) sales mix. Contribution margin is the amount of revenue remaining after deducting variable costs. It is identified in a CVP income statement, which classifies costs as variable or fixed. It can be expressed as a total amount, as a per unit amount, or as a ratio.

4 Compute the break-even point using three approaches. The break-even point can be (a) computed from a mathematical equation, (b) computed by using a contribution margin technique, and (c) derived from a CVP graph.

5 Determine the sales required to earn target net income and determine margin of safety. The general formula for required sales is Required sales − Variable costs − Fixed costs = Target net income. Two other formulas are (1) Required sales in units = (Fixed costs + Target net income) ÷ Unit contribution margin, and (2) Required sales in dollars = (Fixed costs + Target net income) ÷ Contribution margin ratio.

Margin of safety is the difference between actual or expected sales and sales at the break-even point. The formulas for margin of safety are (1) Actual (expected) sales − Break-even sales = Margin of safety in dollars, and (2) Margin of safety in dollars ÷ Actual (expected) sales = Margin of safety ratio.

GLOSSARY REVIEW

Activity index The activity that causes changes in the behavior of costs. (p. 886).

Break-even point The level of activity at which total revenue equals total costs. (p. 895).

Contribution margin (CM) The amount of revenue remaining after deducting variable costs. (p. 894).

Contribution margin ratio The percentage of each dollar of sales that is available to apply to fixed costs and contribute to net income; calculated as unit contribution margin divided by unit selling price. (p. 896).

Cost behavior analysis The study of how specific costs respond to changes in the level of business activity. (p. 886).

Cost-volume-profit (CVP) analysis The study of the effects of changes in costs and volume on a company's profits. (p. 894).

Cost-volume-profit (CVP) graph A graph showing the relationship between costs, volume, and profits. (p. 900).

Cost-volume-profit (CVP) income statement A statement for internal use that classifies costs as fixed or variable and reports contribution margin in the body of the statement. (p. 894).

Fixed costs Costs that remain the same in total regardless of changes in the activity level. (p. 887).

High-low method A mathematical method that uses the total costs incurred at the high and low levels of activity to classify mixed costs into fixed and variable components. (p. 891).

Margin of safety The difference between actual or expected sales and sales at the break-even point. (p. 903).

Mixed costs Costs that contain both a variable- and a fixed-cost element and change in total but not proportionately with changes in the activity level. (p. 889).

Relevant range The range of the activity index over which the company expects to operate during the year. (p. 889).

Target net income The income objective set by management. (p. 901).

Unit contribution margin The amount of revenue remaining per unit after deducting variable costs; calculated as unit selling price minus unit variable costs. (p. 895).

Variable costs Costs that vary in total directly and proportionately with changes in the activity level. (p. 886).

PRACTICE MULTIPLE-CHOICE QUESTIONS

(LO 1) **1.** Variable costs are costs that:
   (a) vary in total directly and proportionately with changes in the activity level.
   (b) remain the same per unit at every activity level.
   (c) Neither of the above.
   (d) Both (a) and (b) above.

(LO 1) **2.** The relevant range is:
   (a) the range of activity in which variable costs will be curvilinear.
   (b) the range of activity in which fixed costs will be curvilinear.
   (c) the range over which the company expects to operate during a year.
   (d) usually from zero to 100% of operating capacity.

(LO 2) **3.** Mixed costs consist of a:
   (a) variable-cost element and a fixed-cost element.
   (b) fixed-cost element and a controllable-cost element.
   (c) relevant-cost element and a controllable-cost element.
   (d) variable-cost element and a relevant-cost element.

(LO 2) **4.** Your cell phone service provider offers a plan that is classified as a mixed cost. The cost per month for 1,000 minutes is $50. If you use 2,000 minutes this month, your cost will be:
   (a) $50.   (c) more than $100.
   (b) $100.   (d) between $50 and $100.

(LO 2) **5.** Kendra Corporation's total utility costs during the past year were $1,200 during its highest month and $600 during its lowest month. These costs corresponded with 10,000 units of production during the high month and 2,000 units during the low month.

What are the fixed and variable components of its utility costs using the high-low method?
   (a) $0.075 variable and $450 fixed.
   (b) $0.120 variable and $0 fixed.
   (c) $0.300 variable and $0 fixed.
   (d) $0.060 variable and $600 fixed.

(LO 3) **6.** Which of the following is **not** involved in CVP analysis?
   (a) Sales mix.
   (b) Unit selling prices.
   (c) Fixed costs per unit.
   (d) Volume or level of activity.

(LO 3) **7.** When comparing a traditional income statement to a CVP income statement:
   (a) net income will always be greater on the traditional statement.
   (b) net income will always be less on the traditional statement.
   (c) net income will always be identical on both.
   (d) net income will be greater or less depending on the sales volume.

(LO 3) **8.** Contribution margin:
   (a) is revenue remaining after deducting variable costs.
   (b) may be expressed as unit contribution margin.
   (c) is selling price less cost of goods sold.
   (d) Both (a) and (b) above.

(LO 3) **9.** Cournot Company sells 100,000 wrenches for $12 a unit. Fixed costs are $300,000, and net income is $200,000. What should be reported as variable expenses in the CVP income statement?
   (a) $700,000.   (c) $500,000.
   (b) $900,000.   (d) $1,000,000.

(LO 4) **10.** Gossen Company is planning to sell 200,000 pliers for $4 per unit. The contribution margin ratio is 25%. If Gossen will break even at this level of sales, what are the fixed costs?

(a) $100,000. (c) $200,000.
(b) $160,000. (d) $300,000.

(LO 4) **11.** Brownstone Company's contribution margin ratio is 30%. If Brownstone's sales revenue is $100 greater than its break-even sales in dollars, its net income:

(a) will be $100.
(b) will be $70.
(c) will be $30.
(d) cannot be determined without knowing fixed costs.

(LO 5) **12.** The mathematical equation for computing required sales to obtain target net income is Required sales =

(a) Variable costs + Target net income.
(b) Variable costs + Fixed costs + Target net income.
(c) Fixed costs + Target net income.
(d) No correct answer is given.

13. Margin of safety is computed as: (LO 5)

(a) Actual sales − Break-even sales.
(b) Contribution margin − Fixed costs.
(c) Break-even sales − Variable costs.
(d) Actual sales − Contribution margin.

14. Marshall Company had actual sales of $600,000 when (LO 5) break-even sales were $420,000. What is the margin of safety ratio?

(a) 25%. (c) 33⅓%.
(b) 30%. (d) 45%.

Solutions

1. (d) Variable costs vary in total directly and proportionately with changes in the activity level and remain the same per unit at every activity level. Choices (a) and (b) are correct, but (d) is the better and more complete answer. Since (a) and (b) are both true statements, choice (c) is incorrect.

2. (c) The relevant range is the range over which the company expects to operate during a year. The other choices are incorrect because the relevant range is the range over which (a) variable costs are expected to be linear, not curvilinear, and (b) the company expects fixed costs to remain the same. Choice (d) is incorrect because this answer does not specifically define relevant range.

3. (a) Mixed costs consist of a variable-cost element and a fixed-cost element, not (b) a controllable-cost element, (c) a relevant-cost element or a controllable-cost element, or (d) a relevant-cost element.

4. (d) Your cost will include the fixed-cost component (flat service fee) which does not increase plus the variable cost (usage charge) for the additional 1,000 minutes which will increase your cost to between $50 and $100. Therefore, choices (a) $50, (b) $100, and (c) more than $100 are incorrect.

5. (a) Variable is $0.075 [($1,200 − $600) ÷ (10,000 − 2,000)] and fixed is $450 [($1,200 − ($0.075 × 10,000)]. Therefore, choices (b) $0.120 variable and $0 fixed, (c) $0.300 variable and $0 fixed, and (d) $0.060 variable and $600 fixed are incorrect.

6. (c) Total fixed costs, not fixed costs per unit, are involved in CVP analysis. Choices (a) sales mix, (b) unit selling prices, and (d) volume or level of activity are all involved in CVP analysis.

7. (c) Net income will always be identical on both a traditional income statement and a CVP income statement. Therefore, choices (a), (b), and (d) are incorrect statements.

8. (d) Contribution margin is revenue remaining after deducting variable costs and it may be expressed on a per unit basis. Choices (a) and (b) are accurate, but (d) is a better answer. Choice (c) is incorrect because it defines gross margin, not contribution margin.

9. (a) Contribution margin is equal to fixed costs plus net income ($300,000 + $200,000 = $500,000). Since variable expenses are the difference between total sales ($1,200,000) and contribution margin ($500,000), $700,000 must be the amount of variable expenses in the CVP income statement. Therefore, choices (b) $900,000, (c) $500,000, and (d) $1,000,000 are incorrect.

10. (c) Unit contribution margin is $1 ($4 × 25%). Fixed costs ÷ Unit contribution margin = Break-even point in units. Solving for fixed costs, 200,000 units × $1 per unit = $200,000, not (a) $100,000, (b) $160,000, or (d) $300,000.

11. (c) If Brownstone's sales revenue is $100 greater than its break-even sales in dollars, its net income will be $30 or ($100 × 30%), not (a) $100 or (b) $70. Choice (d) is incorrect because net income can be determined without knowing fixed costs.

12. (b) The correct equation is Required sales = Variable costs + Fixed costs + Target net income. The other choices are incorrect because (a) needs fixed costs added, (b) needs variable costs added, and (d) there is a correct answer given (b).

13. (a) Margin of safety is computed as Actual sales − Break-even sales. Therefore, choices (b) Contribution margin − Fixed costs, (c) Break-even sales − Variable costs, and (d) Actual sales − Contribution margin are incorrect.

14. (b) The margin of safety ratio is computed by dividing the margin of safety in dollars of $180,000 ($600,000 − $420,000) by actual sales of $600,000. The result is 30% ($180,000 ÷ $600,000), not (a) 25%, (c) 33⅓%, or (d) 45%.

PRACTICE EXERCISES

1. The controller of Teton Industries has collected the following monthly expense data for use in analyzing the cost behavior of maintenance costs.

Determine fixed and variable costs using the high-low method and prepare graph.

(LO 1, 2)

Month	Total Maintenance Costs	Total Machine Hours
January	$2,900	300
February	3,000	400
March	3,600	600
April	4,300	790
May	3,200	500
June	4,500	800

Instructions

(a) Determine the fixed-cost and variable-cost components using the high-low method.
(b) Prepare a graph showing the behavior of maintenance costs, and identify the fixed-cost and variable-cost elements. Use 200 unit increments and $1,000 cost increments.

Solution

1. (a) **Maintenance Costs:**

$$\frac{\$4,500 - \$2,900}{800 - 300} = \frac{\$1,600}{500} = \$3.20 \text{ variable cost per machine hour}$$

	800 Machine Hours	300 Machine Hours
Total costs	$4,500	$2,900
Less: Variable costs		
800 × $3.20	2,560	
300 × $3.20		960
Total fixed costs	$1,940	$1,940

Thus, maintenance costs are $1,940 per month plus $3.20 per machine hour.

(b)

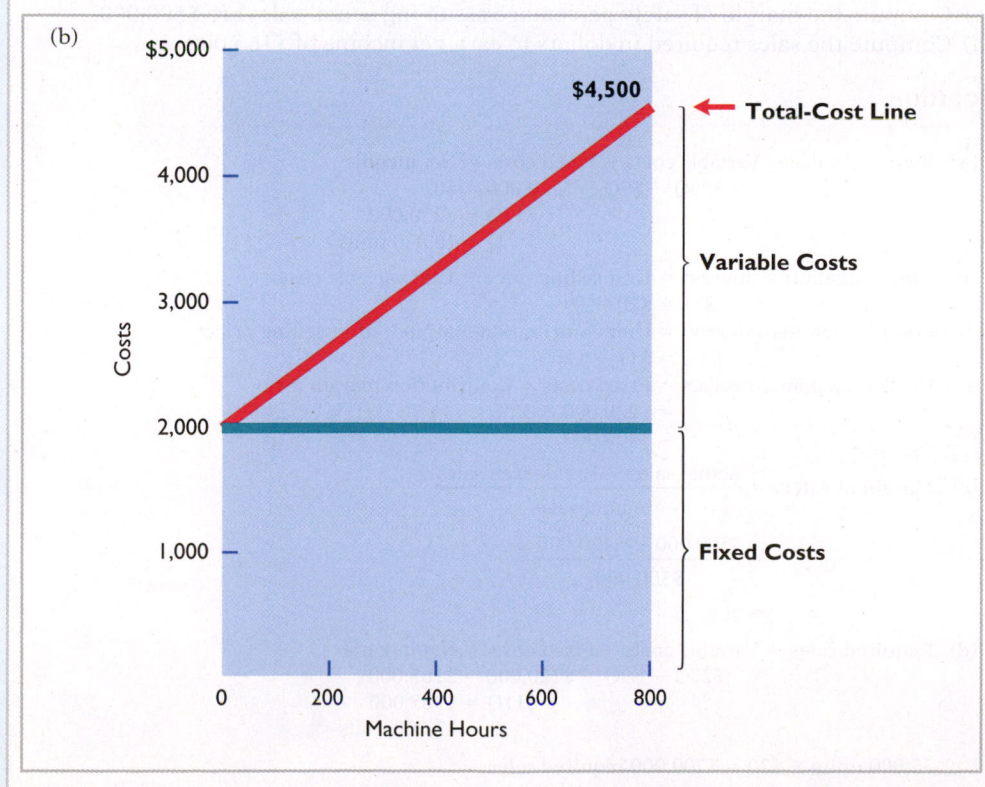

Determine contribution margin ratio, break-even point in dollars, and margin of safety.

(LO 3, 4, 5)

2. Zion Seating Co., a manufacturer of chairs, had the following data for 2017:

Sales	2,400 units
Sales price	$40 per unit
Variable costs	$15 per unit
Fixed costs	$19,500

Instructions

(a) What is the contribution margin ratio?

(b) What is the break-even point in dollars?

(c) What is the margin of safety in units and dollars?

(d) If the company wishes to increase its total dollar contribution margin by 40% in 2018, by how much will it need to increase its sales if all other factors remain constant?

(CGA adapted)

Solution

2. (a) Contribution margin ratio = Unit contribution margin ÷ Unit selling price
($40 − $15) ÷ $40 = 62.5%

(b) Break-even in dollars: $19,500 ÷ 62.5% = $31,200

(c) Margin of safety = (2,400 × $40) − $31,200 = $64,800
$64,800 ÷ $40 = 1,620 in units

(d) Current contribution margin is $40 − $15 = $25
Total contribution margin is $25 × 2,400 = $60,000
40% increase in contribution margin is $60,000 × 40% = $24,000
Total increase in sales required is $24,000 ÷ 62.5% = $38,400

PRACTICE PROBLEM

Compute break-even point, contribution margin ratio, margin of safety, and sales for target net income.

(LO 4, 5)

Mabo Company makes calculators that sell for $20 each. For the coming year, management expects fixed costs to total $220,000 and variable costs to be $9 per unit.

Instructions

(a) Compute break-even point in units using the mathematical equation.

(b) Compute break-even point in dollars using the contribution margin (CM) ratio.

(c) Compute the margin of safety percentage assuming actual sales are $500,000.

(d) Compute the sales required in dollars to earn net income of $165,000.

Solution

(a) Required sales − Variable costs − Fixed costs = Net income
$20Q − $9Q − $220,000 = $0
$11Q = $220,000
Q = 20,000 units

(b) Unit contribution margin = Unit selling price − Unit variable costs
$11 = $20 − $9
Contribution margin ratio = Unit contribution margin ÷ Unit selling price
55% = $11 ÷ $20
Break-even point in dollars = Fixed costs ÷ Contribution margin ratio
= $220,000 ÷ 55%
= $400,000

(c) Margin of safety = $\dfrac{\text{Actual sales − Break-even sales}}{\text{Actual sales}}$

$= \dfrac{\$500,000 − \$400,000}{\$500,000}$

= 20%

(d) Required sales − Variable costs − Fixed costs = Net income
$20Q − $9Q − $220,000 = $165,000
$11Q = $385,000
Q = 35,000 units

35,000 units × $20 = $700,000 required sales

Brief Exercises, Exercises, **DO IT!** Exercises, and Problems and many additional resources are available for practice in WileyPLUS

QUESTIONS

1. (a) What is cost behavior analysis?
 (b) Why is cost behavior analysis important to management?

2. (a) Scott Winter asks your help in understanding the term "activity index." Explain the meaning and importance of this term for Scott.
 (b) State the two ways that variable costs may be defined.

3. Contrast the effects of changes in the activity level on total fixed costs and on unit fixed costs.

4. J. P. Alexander claims that the relevant range concept is important only for variable costs.
 (a) Explain the relevant range concept.
 (b) Do you agree with J. P.'s claim? Explain.

5. "The relevant range is indispensable in cost behavior analysis." Is this true? Why or why not?

6. Adam Antal is confused. He does not understand why rent on his apartment is a fixed cost and rent on a Hertz rental truck is a mixed cost. Explain the difference to Adam.

7. How should mixed costs be classified in CVP analysis? What approach is used to effect the appropriate classification?

8. At the high and low levels of activity during the month, direct labor hours are 90,000 and 40,000, respectively. The related costs are $165,000 and $100,000. What are the fixed and variable costs at any level of activity?

9. "Cost-volume-profit (CVP) analysis is based entirely on unit costs." Do you agree? Explain.

10. Faye Dunn defines contribution margin as the amount of profit available to cover operating expenses. Is there any truth in this definition? Discuss.

11. Marshall Company's GWhiz calculator sells for $40. Variable costs per unit are estimated to be $26. What are the unit contribution margin and the contribution margin ratio?

12. "Break-even analysis is of limited use to management because a company cannot survive by just breaking even." Do you agree? Explain.

13. Total fixed costs are $26,000 for Daz Inc. It has a unit contribution margin of $15, and a contribution margin ratio of 25%. Compute the break-even sales in dollars.

14. Peggy Turnbull asks your help in constructing a CVP graph. Explain to Peggy (a) how the break-even point is plotted, and (b) how the level of activity and dollar sales at the break-even point are determined.

15. Define the term "margin of safety." If Revere Company expects to sell 1,250 units of its product at $12 per unit, and break-even sales for the product are $13,200, what is the margin of safety ratio?

16. Huang Company's break-even sales are $500,000. Assuming fixed costs are $180,000, what sales volume is needed to achieve a target net income of $90,000?

17. The traditional income statement for Pace Company shows sales $900,000, cost of goods sold $600,000, and operating expenses $200,000. Assuming all costs and expenses are 70% variable and 30% fixed, prepare a CVP income statement through contribution margin.

BRIEF EXERCISES

BE19-1 Monthly production costs in Dilts Company for two levels of production are as follows.

Classify costs as variable, fixed, or mixed.

(LO 1)

Cost	2,000 Units	4,000 Units
Indirect labor	$10,000	$20,000
Supervisory salaries	5,000	5,000
Maintenance	4,000	6,000

Indicate which costs are variable, fixed, and mixed, and give the reason for each answer.

BE19-2 For Lodes Company, the relevant range of production is 40–80% of capacity. At 40% of capacity, a variable cost is $4,000 and a fixed cost is $6,000. Diagram the behavior of each cost within the relevant range assuming the behavior is linear.

Diagram the behavior of costs within the relevant range.

(LO 1)

BE19-3 For Wesland Company, a mixed cost is $15,000 plus $18 per direct labor hour. Diagram the behavior of the cost using increments of 500 hours up to 2,500 hours on the horizontal axis and increments of $15,000 up to $60,000 on the vertical axis.

Diagram the behavior of a mixed cost.

(LO 1)

Determine variable- and fixed-cost elements using the high-low method.

(LO 2)

BE19-4 Bruno Company accumulates the following data concerning a mixed cost, using miles as the activity level.

	Miles Driven	Total Cost		Miles Driven	Total Cost
January	8,000	$14,150	March	8,500	$15,000
February	7,500	13,500	April	8,200	14,490

Compute the variable- and fixed-cost elements using the high-low method.

Determine variable- and fixed-cost elements using the high-low method.

(LO 2)

BE19-5 Markowis Corp. has collected the following data concerning its maintenance costs for the past 6 months.

	Units Produced	Total Cost
July	18,000	$36,000
August	32,000	48,000
September	36,000	55,000
October	22,000	38,000
November	40,000	74,500
December	38,000	62,000

Compute the variable- and fixed-cost elements using the high-low method.

Determine missing amounts for contribution margin.

(LO 3)

BE19-6 Determine the missing amounts.

	Unit Selling Price	Unit Variable Costs	Unit Contribution Margin	Contribution Margin Ratio
1.	$640	$352	(a)	(b)
2.	$300	(c)	$93	(d)
3.	(e)	(f)	$325	25%

Prepare CVP income statement.

(LO 3)

BE19-7 Russell Inc. had sales of $2,200,000 for the first quarter of 2017. In making the sales, the company incurred the following costs and expenses.

	Variable	Fixed
Cost of goods sold	$920,000	$440,000
Selling expenses	70,000	45,000
Administrative expenses	86,000	98,000

Prepare a CVP income statement for the quarter ended March 31, 2017.

Compute the break-even point.

(LO 4)

BE19-8 Rice Company has a unit selling price of $520, variable costs per unit of $286, and fixed costs of $163,800. Compute the break-even point in units using (a) the mathematical equation and (b) unit contribution margin.

Compute the break-even point.

(LO 4)

BE19-9 Presto Corp. had total variable costs of $180,000, total fixed costs of $110,000, and total revenues of $300,000. Compute the required sales in dollars to break even.

Compute sales for target net income.

(LO 5)

BE19-10 For Flynn Company, variable costs are 70% of sales, and fixed costs are $195,000. Management's net income goal is $75,000. Compute the required sales in dollars needed to achieve management's target net income of $75,000. (Use the contribution margin approach.)

Compute the margin of safety and the margin of safety ratio.

(LO 5)

BE19-11 For Astoria Company, actual sales are $1,000,000, and break-even sales are $800,000. Compute (a) the margin of safety in dollars and (b) the margin of safety ratio.

BE19-12 Deines Corporation has fixed costs of $480,000. It has a unit selling price of $6, unit variable costs of $4.40, and a target net income of $1,500,000. Compute the required sales in units to achieve its target net income.

Compute the required sales in units for target net income.

(LO 5)

DO IT! Exercises

DO IT! 19-1 Amanda Company reports the following total costs at two levels of production.

Classify types of costs.

(LO 1)

	5,000 Units	10,000 Units
Indirect labor	$ 3,000	$ 6,000
Property taxes	7,000	7,000
Direct labor	28,000	56,000
Direct materials	22,000	44,000
Depreciation	4,000	4,000
Utilities	5,000	8,000
Maintenance	9,000	11,000

Classify each cost as variable, fixed, or mixed.

DO IT! 19-2 Westerville Company accumulates the following data concerning a mixed cost, using units produced as the activity level.

Compute costs using high-low method and estimate total cost.

(LO 2)

	Units Produced	Total Cost
March	10,000	$18,000
April	9,000	16,650
May	10,500	18,580
June	8,800	16,200
July	9,500	17,100

(a) Compute the variable- and fixed-cost elements using the high-low method.
(b) Estimate the total cost if the company produces 9,200 units.

DO IT! 19-3 Cedar Grove Industries produces and sells a cell phone-operated home security control. Information regarding the costs and sales of security controls during May 2017 are provided below.

Prepare CVP income statement.

(LO 3)

Unit selling price of security control	$45
Unit variable costs	$22
Total monthly fixed costs	$120,000
Units sold	8,000

Prepare a CVP income statement for Cedar Grove Industries for the month of May. Provide per unit values and total values.

DO IT! 19-4 Snow Cap Company has a unit selling price of $250, variable costs per unit of $170, and fixed costs of $160,000. Compute the break-even point in units using (a) the mathematical equation and (b) unit contribution margin.

Compute break-even point in units.

(LO 4)

DO IT! 19-5 Presto Company makes radios that sell for $30 each. For the coming year, management expects fixed costs to total $220,000 and variable costs to be $18 per unit.

Compute break-even point, margin of safety ratio, and sales for target net income.

(LO 4, 5)

(a) Compute the break-even point in dollars using the contribution margin (CM) ratio.
(b) Compute the margin of safety ratio assuming actual sales are $800,000.
(c) Compute the sales dollars required to earn net income of $140,000.

EXERCISES

Define and classify variable, fixed, and mixed costs.

(LO 1)

E19-1 Bonita Company manufactures a single product. Annual production costs incurred in the manufacturing process are shown below for two levels of production.

	Costs Incurred			
Production in Units	5,000		10,000	
Production Costs	Total Cost	Cost/ Unit	Total Cost	Cost/ Unit
Direct materials	$8,000	$1.60	$16,000	$1.60
Direct labor	9,500	1.90	19,000	1.90
Utilities	2,000	0.40	3,300	0.33
Rent	4,000	0.80	4,000	0.40
Maintenance	800	0.16	1,400	0.14
Supervisory salaries	1,000	0.20	1,000	0.10

Instructions

(a) Define the terms variable costs, fixed costs, and mixed costs.
(b) Classify each cost above as either variable, fixed, or mixed.

Diagram cost behavior, determine relevant range, and classify costs.

(LO 1)

E19-2 Shingle Enterprises is considering manufacturing a new product. It projects the cost of direct materials and rent for a range of output as shown below.

Output in Units	Rent Expense	Direct Materials
1,000	$ 5,000	$ 4,000
2,000	5,000	7,200
3,000	8,000	9,000
4,000	8,000	12,000
5,000	8,000	15,000
6,000	8,000	18,000
7,000	8,000	21,000
8,000	8,000	24,000
9,000	10,000	29,300
10,000	10,000	35,000
11,000	10,000	44,000

Instructions

(a) Diagram the behavior of each cost for output ranging from 1,000 to 11,000 units.
(b) Determine the relevant range of activity for this product.
(c) Calculate the variable costs per unit within the relevant range.
(d) Indicate the fixed cost within the relevant range.

Determine fixed and variable costs using the high-low method and prepare graph.

(LO 1, 2)

E19-3 The controller of Norton Industries has collected the following monthly expense data for use in analyzing the cost behavior of maintenance costs.

Month	Total Maintenance Costs	Total Machine Hours
January	$2,700	300
February	3,000	350
March	3,600	500
April	4,500	690
May	3,200	400
June	5,500	700

Instructions

(a) Determine the fixed- and variable-cost components using the high-low method.
(b) Prepare a graph showing the behavior of maintenance costs, and identify the fixed- and variable-cost elements. Use 100-hour increments and $1,000 cost increments.

E19-4 Family Furniture Corporation incurred the following costs.

1. Wood used in the production of furniture.
2. Fuel used in delivery trucks.
3. Straight-line depreciation on factory building.
4. Screws used in the production of furniture.
5. Sales staff salaries.
6. Sales commissions.
7. Property taxes.
8. Insurance on buildings.
9. Hourly wages of furniture craftsmen.
10. Salaries of factory supervisors.
11. Utilities expense.
12. Telephone bill.

Classify variable, fixed, and mixed costs.

(LO 1)

Instructions
Identify the costs above as variable, fixed, or mixed.

E19-5 The controller of Hall Industries has collected the following monthly expense data for use in analyzing the cost behavior of maintenance costs.

Determine fixed and variable costs using the high-low method and prepare graph.

(LO 1, 2)

Month	Total Maintenance Costs	Total Machine Hours
January	$2,640	3,500
February	3,000	4,000
March	3,600	6,000
April	4,500	7,900
May	3,200	5,000
June	4,620	8,000

Instructions
(a) Determine the fixed- and variable-cost components using the high-low method.
(b) Prepare a graph showing the behavior of maintenance costs and identify the fixed- and variable-cost elements. Use 2,000-hour increments and $1,000 cost increments.

E19-6 PCB Corporation manufactures a single product. Monthly production costs incurred in the manufacturing process are shown below for the production of 3,000 units. The utilities and maintenance costs are mixed costs. The fixed portions of these costs are $300 and $200, respectively.

Determine fixed, variable, and mixed costs.

(LO 1)

Production in Units	3,000
Production Costs	
Direct materials	$ 7,500
Direct labor	18,000
Utilities	2,100
Property taxes	1,000
Indirect labor	4,500
Supervisory salaries	1,900
Maintenance	1,100
Depreciation	2,400

Instructions
(a) Identify the above costs as variable, fixed, or mixed.
(b) Calculate the expected costs when production is 5,000 units.

E19-7 Marty Moser wants Moser Company to use CVP analysis to study the effects of changes in costs and volume on the company. Marty has heard that certain assumptions must be valid in order for CVP analysis to be useful.

Explain assumptions underlying CVP analysis.

(LO 3)

Instructions
———— Prepare a memo to Marty Moser concerning the assumptions that underlie CVP analysis.

Compute break-even point in units and dollars.

(LO 3, 4)

E19-8 All That Blooms provides environmentally friendly lawn services for homeowners. Its operating costs are as follows.

Depreciation	$1,400 per month
Advertising	$200 per month
Insurance	$2,000 per month
Weed and feed materials	$12 per lawn
Direct labor	$10 per lawn
Fuel	$2 per lawn

All That Blooms charges $60 per treatment for the average single-family lawn.

Instructions

Determine the company's break-even point in (a) number of lawns serviced per month and (b) dollars.

Compute break-even point.

(LO 3, 4)

E19-9 The Palmer Acres Inn is trying to determine its break-even point during its off-peak season. The inn has 50 rooms that it rents at $60 a night. Operating costs are as follows.

Salaries	$5,900 per month
Utilities	$1,100 per month
Depreciation	$1,000 per month
Maintenance	$100 per month
Maid service	$14 per room
Other costs	$28 per room

Instructions

Determine the inn's break-even point in (a) number of rented rooms per month and (b) dollars.

Compute contribution margin and break-even point.

(LO 3, 4)

E19-10 In the month of March, Style Salon services 560 clients at an average price of $120. During the month, fixed costs were $21,024 and variable costs were 60% of sales.

Instructions

(a) Determine the contribution margin in dollars, per unit, and as a ratio.
(b) Using the contribution margin technique, compute the break-even point in dollars and in units.

Compute break-even point.

(LO 3, 4)

E19-11 Spencer Kars provides shuttle service between four hotels near a medical center and an international airport. Spencer Kars uses two 10-passenger vans to offer 12 round trips per day. A recent month's activity in the form of a cost-volume-profit income statement is shown below.

Fare revenues (1,500 fares)		$36,000
Variable costs		
Fuel	$ 5,040	
Tolls and parking	3,100	
Maintenance	860	9,000
Contribution margin		27,000
Fixed costs		
Salaries	15,700	
Depreciation	1,300	
Insurance	1,000	18,000
Net income		$ 9,000

Instructions

(a) Calculate the break-even point in (1) dollars and (2) number of fares.
(b) Without calculations, determine the contribution margin at the break-even point.

Compute variable costs per unit, contribution margin ratio, and increase in fixed costs.

(LO 3, 4)

E19-12 In 2016, Manhoff Company had a break-even point of $350,000 based on a selling price of $5 per unit and fixed costs of $112,000. In 2017, the selling price and the variable costs per unit did not change, but the break-even point increased to $420,000.

Instructions

(a) Compute the variable costs per unit and the contribution margin ratio for 2016.
(b) Compute the increase in fixed costs for 2017.

E19-13 Billings Company has the following information available for September 2017.

Unit selling price of video game consoles	$ 400
Unit variable costs	$ 280
Total fixed costs	$54,000
Units sold	600

Prepare CVP income statements.

(LO 3, 4)

Instructions

(a) Compute the unit contribution margin.
(b) Prepare a CVP income statement that shows both total and per unit amounts.
(c) Compute Billings' break-even point in units.
(d) Prepare a CVP income statement for the break-even point that shows both total and per unit amounts.

E19-14 Naylor Company had $210,000 of net income in 2016 when the selling price per unit was $150, the variable costs per unit were $90, and the fixed costs were $570,000. Management expects per unit data and total fixed costs to remain the same in 2017. The president of Naylor Company is under pressure from stockholders to increase net income by $52,000 in 2017.

Compute various components to derive target net income under different assumptions.

(LO 4, 5)

Instructions

(a) Compute the number of units sold in 2016.
(b) Compute the number of units that would have to be sold in 2017 to reach the stockholders' desired profit level.
(c) Assume that Naylor Company sells the same number of units in 2017 as it did in 2016. What would the selling price have to be in order to reach the stockholders' desired profit level?

E19-15 Yams Company reports the following operating results for the month of August: sales $400,000 (units 5,000), variable costs $240,000, and fixed costs $90,000. Management is considering the following independent courses of action to increase net income.

Compute net income under different alternatives.

(LO 5)

1. Increase selling price by 10% with no change in total variable costs or units sold.
2. Reduce variable costs to 55% of sales.

Instructions

Compute the net income to be earned under each alternative. Which course of action will produce the higher net income?

E19-16 Glacial Company estimates that variable costs will be 62.5% of sales, and fixed costs will total $600,000. The selling price of the product is $4.

Prepare a CVP graph and compute break-even point and margin of safety.

(LO 4, 5)

Instructions

(a) Prepare a CVP graph, assuming maximum sales of $3,200,000. (*Note:* Use $400,000 increments for sales and costs and 100,000 increments for units.)
(b) Compute the break-even point in (1) units and (2) dollars.
(c) Assuming actual sales are $2 million, compute the margin of safety in (1) dollars and (2) as a ratio.

E19-17 Felde Bucket Co., a manufacturer of rain barrels, had the following data for 2016:

Sales	2,500 units
Sales price	$40 per unit
Variable costs	$24 per unit
Fixed costs	$19,500

Determine contribution margin ratio, break-even point in dollars, and margin of safety.

(LO 3, 4, 5)

Instructions

(a) What is the contribution margin ratio?
(b) What is the break-even point in dollars?
(c) What is the margin of safety in dollars and as a ratio?
(d) If the company wishes to increase its total dollar contribution margin by 30% in 2017, by how much will it need to increase its sales if all other factors remain constant?

(CGA adapted)

EXERCISES: SET B AND CHALLENGE EXERCISES

Visit the book's companion website, at **www.wiley.com/college/weygandt**, and choose the Student Companion site to access Exercises: Set B and Challenge Exercises.

PROBLEMS: SET A

Determine variable and fixed costs, compute break-even point, prepare a CVP graph, and determine net income.

(LO 1, 2, 3, 4)

P19-1A Vin Diesel owns the Fredonia Barber Shop. He employs four barbers and pays each a base rate of $1,250 per month. One of the barbers serves as the manager and receives an extra $500 per month. In addition to the base rate, each barber also receives a commission of $4.50 per haircut.

Other costs are as follows.

Advertising	$200 per month
Rent	$1,100 per month
Barber supplies	$0.30 per haircut
Utilities	$175 per month plus $0.20 per haircut
Magazines	$25 per month

Vin currently charges $10 per haircut.

Instructions

(a) VC $5

(a) Determine the variable costs per haircut and the total monthly fixed costs.
(b) Compute the break-even point in units and dollars.
(c) Prepare a CVP graph, assuming a maximum of 1,800 haircuts in a month. Use increments of 300 haircuts on the horizontal axis and $3,000 on the vertical axis.
(d) Determine net income, assuming 1,600 haircuts are given in a month.

Prepare a CVP income statement, compute break-even point, contribution margin ratio, margin of safety ratio, and sales for target net income.

(LO 3, 4, 5)

P19-2A Jorge Company bottles and distributes B-Lite, a diet soft drink. The beverage is sold for 50 cents per 16-ounce bottle to retailers, who charge customers 75 cents per bottle. For the year 2017, management estimates the following revenues and costs.

Sales	$1,800,000	Selling expenses—variable	$70,000
Direct materials	430,000	Selling expenses—fixed	65,000
Direct labor	360,000	Administrative expenses—	
Manufacturing overhead—		variable	20,000
variable	380,000	Administrative expenses—	
Manufacturing overhead—		fixed	60,000
fixed	280,000		

Instructions

(a) Prepare a CVP income statement for 2017 based on management's estimates. (Show column for total amounts only.)

(b) (1) 2,700,000 units
(c) CM ratio 30%

(b) Compute the break-even point in (1) units and (2) dollars.
(c) Compute the contribution margin ratio and the margin of safety ratio. (Round to nearest full percent.)
(d) Determine the sales dollars required to earn net income of $180,000.

Compute break-even point under alternative courses of action.

(LO 4)

P19-3A Tanek Corp.'s sales slumped badly in 2017. For the first time in its history, it operated at a loss. The company's income statement showed the following results from selling 500,000 units of product: sales $2,500,000, total costs and expenses $2,600,000, and net loss $100,000. Costs and expenses consisted of the amounts shown below.

	Total	Variable	Fixed
Cost of goods sold	$2,140,000	$1,590,000	$550,000
Selling expenses	250,000	92,000	158,000
Administrative expenses	210,000	68,000	142,000
	$2,600,000	$1,750,000	$850,000

Management is considering the following independent alternatives for 2018.

1. Increase unit selling price 20% with no change in costs, expenses, and sales volume.
2. Change the compensation of salespersons from fixed annual salaries totaling $150,000 to total salaries of $60,000 plus a 5% commission on sales.

Instructions

(a) Compute the break-even point in dollars for 2017.
(b) Compute the break-even point in dollars under each of the alternative courses of action. (Round all ratios to nearest full percent.) Which course of action do you recommend?

(b) Alternative 1 $2,023,810

P19-4A Mary Willis is the advertising manager for Bargain Shoe Store. She is currently working on a major promotional campaign. Her ideas include the installation of a new lighting system and increased display space that will add $24,000 in fixed costs to the $270,000 currently spent. In addition, Mary is proposing that a 5% price decrease ($40 to $38) will produce a 20% increase in sales volume (20,000 to 24,000). Variable costs will remain at $24 per pair of shoes. Management is impressed with Mary's ideas but concerned about the effects that these changes will have on the break-even point and the margin of safety.

Compute break-even point and margin of safety ratio, and prepare a CVP income statement before and after changes in business environment.

(LO 3, 4, 5)

Instructions

(a) Compute the current break-even point in units, and compare it to the break-even point in units if Mary's ideas are used.
(b) Compute the margin of safety ratio for current operations and after Mary's changes are introduced. (Round to nearest full percent.)
(c) Prepare a CVP income statement for current operations and after Mary's changes are introduced. (Show column for total amounts only.) Would you make the changes suggested?

(b) Current margin of safety ratio 16%

P19-5A Viejol Corporation has collected the following information after its first year of sales. Sales were $1,600,000 on 100,000 units, selling expenses $250,000 (40% variable and 60% fixed), direct materials $490,000, direct labor $290,000, administrative expenses $270,000 (20% variable and 80% fixed), and manufacturing overhead $380,000 (70% variable and 30% fixed). Top management has asked you to do a CVP analysis so that it can make plans for the coming year. It has projected that unit sales will increase by 10% next year.

Compute contribution margin, fixed costs, break-even point, sales for target net income, and margin of safety ratio.

(LO 3, 4, 5)

Instructions

(a) Compute (1) the contribution margin for the current year and the projected year, and (2) the fixed costs for the current year. (Assume that fixed costs will remain the same in the projected year.)
(b) Compute the break-even point in units and sales dollars for the current year.
(c) The company has a target net income of $200,000. What is the required sales in dollars for the company to meet its target?
(d) If the company meets its target net income number, by what percentage could its sales fall before it is operating at a loss? That is, what is its margin of safety ratio?

(b) 120,000 units

P19-6A Kaiser Industries carries no inventories. Its product is manufactured only when a customer's order is received. It is then shipped immediately after it is made. For its fiscal year ended October 31, 2017, Kaiser's break-even point was $1.3 million. On sales of $1.2 million, its income statement showed a gross profit of $180,000, direct materials cost of $400,000, and direct labor costs of $500,000. The contribution margin was $180,000, and variable manufacturing overhead was $50,000.

Determine contribution margin ratio, break-even point, and margin of safety.

(LO 1, 3, 5)

Instructions

(a) Calculate the following:
  (1) Variable selling and administrative expenses.
  (2) Fixed manufacturing overhead.
  (3) Fixed selling and administrative expenses.
(b) Ignoring your answer to part (a), assume that fixed manufacturing overhead was $100,000 and the fixed selling and administrative expenses were $80,000. The marketing vice president feels that if the company increased its advertising, sales could be increased by 25%. What is the maximum increased advertising cost the company can incur and still report the same income as before the advertising expenditure?

(CGA adapted)

(a) (2) $70,000

■ PROBLEMS: SET B AND SET C

Visit the book's companion website, at **www.wiley.com/college/weygandt**, and choose the Student Companion site to access Problems: Set B and Set C.

■ CONTINUING PROBLEMS

EXCEL TUTORIAL

CURRENT DESIGNS

CD19 Bill Johnson, sales manager, and Diane Buswell, controller, at Current Designs are beginning to analyze the cost considerations for one of the composite models of the kayak division. They have provided the following production and operational costs necessary to produce one composite kayak.

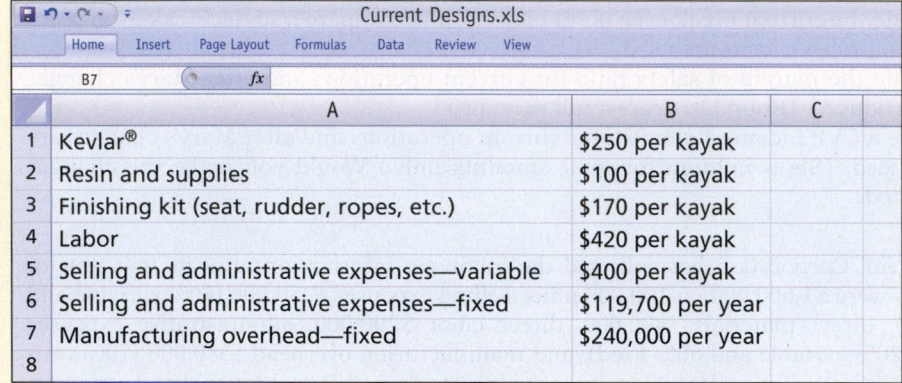

	A	B	C
1	Kevlar®	$250 per kayak	
2	Resin and supplies	$100 per kayak	
3	Finishing kit (seat, rudder, ropes, etc.)	$170 per kayak	
4	Labor	$420 per kayak	
5	Selling and administrative expenses—variable	$400 per kayak	
6	Selling and administrative expenses—fixed	$119,700 per year	
7	Manufacturing overhead—fixed	$240,000 per year	
8			

Bill and Diane have asked you to provide a cost-volume-profit analysis, to help them finalize the budget projections for the upcoming year. Bill has informed you that the selling price of the composite kayak will be $2,000.

Instructions

(a) Calculate variable costs per unit.

(b) Determine the unit contribution margin.

(c) Using the unit contribution margin, determine the break-even point in units for this product line.

(d) Assume that Current Designs plans to earn $270,600 on this product line. Using the unit contribution margin, calculate the number of units that need to be sold to achieve this goal.

(e) Based on the most recent sales forecast, Current Designs plans to sell 1,000 units of this model. Using your results from part (c), calculate the margin of safety and the margin of safety ratio.

WATERWAYS

(*Note:* This is a continuation of the Waterways problem from Chapters 15–18.)

WP19 The Vice President for Sales and Marketing at Waterways Corporation is planning for production needs to meet sales demand in the coming year. He is also trying to determine how the company's profits might be increased in the coming year. This problem asks you to use cost-volume-profit concepts to help Waterways understand contribution margins of some of its products and decide whether to mass-produce any of them.

Go to the book's companion website, **www.wiley.com/college/weygandt**, *to find the remainder of this problem.*

BROADENING YOUR PERSPECTIVE

MANAGEMENT DECISION-MAKING

Decision-Making Across the Organization

BYP19-1 Creative Ideas Company has decided to introduce a new product. The new product can be manufactured by either a capital-intensive method or a labor-intensive method. The manufacturing method will not affect the quality of the product. The estimated manufacturing costs by the two methods are as follows.

	Capital-Intensive	Labor-Intensive
Direct materials	$5 per unit	$5.50 per unit
Direct labor	$6 per unit	$8.00 per unit
Variable overhead	$3 per unit	$4.50 per unit
Fixed manufacturing costs	$2,524,000	$1,550,000

Creative Ideas' market research department has recommended an introductory unit sales price of $32. The incremental selling expenses are estimated to be $502,000 annually plus $2 for each unit sold, regardless of manufacturing method.

Instructions

With the class divided into groups, answer the following.

(a) Calculate the estimated break-even point in annual unit sales of the new product if Creative Ideas Company uses the:
   (1) Capital-intensive manufacturing method.
   (2) Labor-intensive manufacturing method.
(b) Determine the annual unit sales volume at which Creative Ideas Company would be indifferent between the two manufacturing methods.
(c) Explain the circumstance under which Creative Ideas should employ each of the two manufacturing methods.

(CMA adapted)

Managerial Analysis

BYP19-2 The condensed income statement for the Peri and Paul partnership for 2017 is as follows.

PERI AND PAUL COMPANY
Income Statement
For the Year Ended December 31, 2017

Sales (240,000 units)		$1,200,000
Cost of goods sold		800,000
Gross profit		400,000
Operating expenses		
Selling	$280,000	
Administrative	150,000	430,000
Net loss		$ (30,000)

A cost behavior analysis indicates that 75% of the cost of goods sold are variable, 42% of the selling expenses are variable, and 40% of the administrative expenses are variable.

Instructions

(Round to nearest unit, dollar, and percentage, where necessary. Use the CVP income statement format in computing profits.)

(a) Compute the break-even point in total sales dollars and in units for 2017.
(b) Peri has proposed a plan to get the partnership "out of the red" and improve its profitability. She feels that the quality of the product could be substantially improved by spending $0.25 more per

unit on better raw materials. The selling price per unit could be increased to only $5.25 because of competitive pressures. Peri estimates that sales volume will increase by 25%. What effect would Peri's plan have on the profits and the break-even point in dollars of the partnership? (Round the contribution margin ratio to two decimal places.)

(c) Paul was a marketing major in college. He believes that sales volume can be increased only by intensive advertising and promotional campaigns. He therefore proposed the following plan as an alternative to Peri's: (1) increase variable selling expenses to $0.59 per unit, (2) lower the selling price per unit by $0.25, and (3) increase fixed selling expenses by $40,000. Paul quoted an old marketing research report that said that sales volume would increase by 60% if these changes were made. What effect would Paul's plan have on the profits and the break-even point in dollars of the partnership?

(d) Which plan should be accepted? Explain your answer.

Real-World Focus

BYP19-3 The Coca-Cola Company hardly needs an introduction. A line taken from the cover of a recent annual report says it all: If you measured time in servings of Coca-Cola, "a billion Coca-Cola's ago was yesterday morning." On average, every U.S. citizen drinks 363 8-ounce servings of Coca-Cola products each year. Coca-Cola's primary line of business is the making and selling of syrup to bottlers. These bottlers then sell the finished bottles and cans of Coca-Cola to the consumer.

In the annual report of Coca-Cola, the information shown below was provided.

> ### THE COCA-COLA COMPANY
> #### Management Discussion
>
> Our gross margin declined to 61 percent this year from 62 percent in the prior year, primarily due to costs for materials such as sweeteners and packaging.
>
> The increases [in selling expenses] in the last two years were primarily due to higher marketing expenditures in support of our Company's volume growth.
>
> We measure our sales volume in two ways: (1) gallon shipments of concentrates and syrups and (2) unit cases of finished product (bottles and cans of Coke sold by bottlers).

Instructions

Answer the following questions.

(a) Are sweeteners and packaging a variable cost or a fixed cost? What is the impact on the contribution margin of an increase in the per unit cost of sweeteners or packaging? What are the implications for profitability?

(b) In your opinion, are Coca-Cola's marketing expenditures a fixed cost, variable cost, or mixed cost? Give justification for your answer.

(c) Which of the two measures cited for measuring volume represents the activity index as defined in this chapter? Why might Coca-Cola use two different measures?

BYP19-4 The May 21, 2010, edition of the *Wall Street Journal* includes an article by Jeffrey Trachtenberg entitled "E-Books Rewrite Bookselling."

Instructions

Read the article and answer the following questions.

(a) What aspect of Barnes and Noble's current structure puts it at risk if electronic books become a significant portion of book sales?

(b) What was Barnes and Noble's primary competitive advantage in a "paper book" world? How has this advantage been eliminated by e-books?

(c) What event do the authors say might eventually be viewed as the big turning point for e-books?

(d) What amount does Barnes and Noble earn on a $25 hardcover book? How much would it likely earn on an e-book version of the same title? What implications does this have for Barnes and Noble versus its competitors?

(e) What two mistakes does the author suggest that Barnes and Noble made that left it ill-prepared for an e-book environment?

CRITICAL THINKING

Communication Activity

BYP19-5 Your roommate asks for your help on the following questions about CVP analysis formulas.

(a) How can the mathematical equation for break-even sales show both sales units and sales dollars?
(b) How do the formulas differ for unit contribution margin and contribution margin ratio?
(c) How can contribution margin be used to determine break-even sales in units and in dollars?

Instructions
Write a memo to your roommate stating the relevant formulas and answering each question.

Ethics Case

BYP19-6 Scott Bestor is an accountant for Westfield Company. Early this year, Scott made a highly favorable projection of sales and profits over the next 3 years for Westfield's hot-selling computer PLEX. As a result of the projections Scott presented to senior management, the company decided to expand production in this area. This decision led to dislocations of some plant personnel who were reassigned to one of the company's newer plants in another state. However, no one was fired, and in fact the company expanded its workforce slightly.

Unfortunately, Scott rechecked his projection computations a few months later and found that he had made an error that would have reduced his projections substantially. Luckily, sales of PLEX have exceeded projections so far, and management is satisfied with its decision. Scott, however, is not sure what to do. Should he confess his honest mistake and jeopardize his possible promotion? He suspects that no one will catch the error because **PLEX** sales have exceeded his projections, and it appears that profits will materialize close to his projections.

Instructions

(a) Who are the stakeholders in this situation?
(b) Identify the ethical issues involved in this situation.
(c) What are the possible alternative actions for Scott? What would you do in Scott's position?

All About You

BYP19-7 Cost-volume-profit analysis can also be used in making personal financial decisions. For example, the purchase of a new car is one of your biggest personal expenditures. It is important that you carefully analyze your options.

Suppose that you are considering the purchase of a hybrid vehicle. Let's assume the following facts. The hybrid will initially cost an additional $4,500 above the cost of a traditional vehicle. The hybrid will get 40 miles per gallon of gas, and the traditional car will get 30 miles per gallon. Also, assume that the cost of gas is $3.60 per gallon.

Instructions
Using the facts above, answer the following questions.

(a) What is the variable gasoline cost of going one mile in the hybrid car? What is the variable cost of going one mile in the traditional car?
(b) Using the information in part (a), if "miles" is your unit of measure, what is the "contribution margin" of the hybrid vehicle relative to the traditional vehicle? That is, express the variable cost savings on a per-mile basis.
(c) How many miles would you have to drive in order to break even on your investment in the hybrid car?
(d) What other factors might you want to consider?

Cost-Volume-Profit Analysis: Additional Issues

CHAPTER PREVIEW
As the Feature Story below about Whole Foods Market suggests, the relationship between a company's fixed and variable costs can have a huge impact on its profitability. In particular, the trend toward cost structures dominated by fixed costs has significantly increased the volatility of many companies' net income. The purpose of this chapter is to demonstrate additional uses of cost-volume-profit analysis in making sound business decisions.

FEATURE STORY

Not Even a Flood Could Stop It

America has a reputation as a country populated with people who won't buy a restaurant meal unless it can be ordered from the driver's seat of a car. Customers want to receive said "meal" 30 seconds later from a drive-up window and then consume the bagged product while driving one-handed down an 8-lane freeway. This is actually a fairly accurate depiction of the restaurant preferences (and eating habits) of one of the authors of this textbook. However, given the success of Whole Foods Market, this certainly cannot be true of all Americans.

Whole Foods Market began humbly in 1978 as a natural-foods store called SaferWay. (Get it? A play on SafeWay grocery stores.) It was founded in Austin, Texas, by 25 year-old John Mackey (a self-described college dropout) and 21 year-old Renee Lawson Hardy. They financed the first store by borrowing $45,000 from family and friends. The early days were "interesting." First, John and Renee got kicked out of their apartment for storing grocery products there. No problem—they just moved into the store. They bathed in the store's dishwasher with an attached hose. They did whatever it took to keep their costs down and the store going.

Two years later, John and Renee merged SaferWay with another store to form the first Whole Foods Market. The store's first year was very successful. Well, that is until everything in the store was completely destroyed by Austin's biggest flood in more than 70 years. They lost $400,000 in goods—and they had no insurance. But within 28 days, with tons of volunteer work and understanding creditors and vendors, the store reopened.

Today, Whole Foods operates approximately 270 stores. The size of the average store has actually declined in recent years. While huge stores (up to 80,000 square feet) were successful in a few cities, in most locations the fixed costs of such a large facility made it hard to achieve profit targets. Then, when sales became sluggish during the recession, the company determined that it could reduce its fixed costs, such as rent and utility costs, by reducing its average store size by about 20%. However, with fewer square feet, managers must keep a close eye on the sales mix. They need to be aware of the relative contribution margins of each product line to maximize the profit per square foot while still providing the products its customers want.

Why is a company as successful as Whole Foods so concerned about controlling costs? The answer is that the grocery business runs on very thin margins. So while we doubt that anybody is bathing in the store's dishwashers anymore, Whole Foods is as vigilant about its costs today as it was during its first year of operations.

▶ **Watch the *Whole Foods Market* video in WileyPLUS to learn more about the use of cost-volume-profit analysis in a changing business environment.**

© bikeriderlondon/Shutterstock

CHAPTER OUTLINE

Learning Objectives

1 Apply basic CVP concepts.

- Basic concepts
- Basic computations
- Business environment

DO IT! **1** CVP Analysis

2 Explain the term sales mix and its effects on break-even sales.

- Break-even in units
- Break-even in dollars

DO IT! **2** Sales Mix Break-Even

3 Determine sales mix when a company has limited resources.

DO IT! **3** Sales Mix with Limited Resources

4 Indicate how operating leverage affects profitability.

- Contribution margin ratio
- Break-even point
- Margin of safety ratio
- Operating leverage

DO IT! **4** Operating Leverage

Go to the *REVIEW AND PRACTICE* section at the end of the chapter for a review of key concepts and practice applications with solutions.

Visit **WileyPLUS with ORION** for additional tutorials and practice opportunities.

Apply basic CVP concepts.

As indicated in Chapter 19, cost-volume-profit (CVP) analysis is the study of the effects of changes in costs and volume on a company's profit. CVP analysis is important to profit planning. It is also a critical factor in determining product mix, maximizing use of production facilities, and setting selling prices.

Basic Concepts

Because CVP is so important for decision-making, management often wants this information reported in a CVP income statement format for internal use. The CVP income statement classifies costs as variable or fixed, and computes a contribution margin. **Contribution margin** is the amount of revenue remaining after deducting variable costs. It is often stated both as a total amount and on a per unit basis.

Illustration 20-1 presents the CVP income statement for Vargo Video (which was shown in Illustration 19-12 on page 895). Note that Vargo's sold 1,600 camcorders at $500 per unit.

Illustration 20-1
Basic CVP income statement

VARGO VIDEO COMPANY
CVP Income Statement
For the Month Ended June 30, 2017

	Total	Per Unit
Sales (1,600 camcorders)	$ 800,000	$ 500
Variable costs	480,000	300
Contribution margin	**320,000**	**$200**
Fixed costs	200,000	
Net income	**$120,000**	

Companies often prepare detailed CVP income statements. The CVP income statement in Illustration 20-2 uses the same base information as that presented in Illustration 20-1 but provides more detailed information (using assumed data) about the composition of expenses.

Illustration 20-2
Detailed CVP income statement

VARGO VIDEO COMPANY
CVP Income Statement
For the Month Ended June 30, 2017

		Total	Per Unit
Sales		$ 800,000	$ 500
Variable expenses			
Cost of goods sold	$400,000		
Selling expenses	60,000		
Administrative expenses	20,000		
Total variable expenses		480,000	300
Contribution margin		**320,000**	**$200**
Fixed expenses			
Cost of goods sold	120,000		
Selling expenses	40,000		
Administrative expenses	40,000		
Total fixed expenses		200,000	
Net income		**$120,000**	

Helpful Hint
The appendix to this chapter provides additional discussion of income statements used for decision-making.

In the applications of CVP analysis that follow, we assume that the term "cost" includes all costs and expenses related to production and sale of the product. That is, **cost includes manufacturing costs plus selling and administrative expenses**.

Basic Computations

Before we introduce additional issues of CVP analysis, let's review some of the basic concepts that you learned in Chapter 19, specifically break-even analysis, target net income, and margin of safety.

BREAK-EVEN ANALYSIS

Vargo Video's CVP income statement (Illustration 20-2) shows that total contribution margin (sales minus variable expenses) is $320,000, and the company's unit contribution margin is $200. Recall that contribution margin can also be expressed in the form of the **contribution margin ratio** (contribution margin divided by sales), which in the case of Vargo is 40% ($200 ÷ $500).

Illustration 20-3 demonstrates how to compute Vargo's break-even point in units (using unit contribution margin).

Fixed Costs	÷	Unit Contribution Margin	=	Break-Even Point in Units
$200,000	÷	$200	=	1,000 units

Illustration 20-3
Break-even point in units

Illustration 20-4 shows the computation for the break-even point in dollars (using contribution margin ratio).

Fixed Costs	÷	Contribution Margin Ratio	=	Break-Even Point in Dollars
$200,000	÷	.40	=	$500,000

Illustration 20-4
Break-even point in dollars

When a company is in its early stages of operation, its primary goal is to break even. Failure to break even will lead eventually to financial failure.

TARGET NET INCOME

Once a company achieves break-even, it then sets a sales goal that will generate a target net income. For example, assume that Vargo's management has a target net income of $250,000. Illustration 20-5 shows the required sales in units to achieve its target net income.

(Fixed Costs + Target Net Income)	÷	Unit Contribution Margin	=	Required Sales in Units
($200,000 + $250,000)	÷	$200	=	2,250 units

Illustration 20-5
Target net income in units

Illustration 20-6 uses the contribution margin ratio to compute the required sales in dollars.

(Fixed Costs + Target Net Income)	÷	Contribution Margin Ratio	=	Required Sales in Dollars
($200,000 + $250,000)	÷	.40	=	$1,125,000

Illustration 20-6
Target net income in dollars

In order to achieve net income of $250,000, Vargo has to sell 2,250 camcorders, for a total price of $1,125,000.

MARGIN OF SAFETY

Another measure managers use to assess profitability is the margin of safety. The **margin of safety** tells us **how far sales can drop** before the company will be operating at a loss. Managers like to have a sense of how much cushion they have between their current situation and operating at a loss. This can be expressed in dollars or as a ratio. In Illustration 20-2 (page 924), for example, Vargo reported sales of $800,000. At that sales level, its margin of safety in dollars and as a ratio are as follows.

Illustration 20-7
Margin of safety in dollars

Actual (Expected) Sales	−	Break-Even Sales	=	Margin of Safety in Dollars
$800,000	−	$500,000	=	$300,000

As shown in Illustration 20-8, Vargo's sales could drop by $300,000, or 37.5%, before the company would operate at a loss.

Illustration 20-8
Margin of safety ratio

Margin of Safety in Dollars	÷	Actual (Expected) Sales	=	Margin of Safety Ratio
$300,000	÷	$800,000	=	37.5%

CVP and Changes in the Business Environment

To better understand how CVP analysis works, let's look at three independent situations that might occur at Vargo Video. Each case uses the original camcorder sales and cost data, which were as follows.

Illustration 20-9
Original camcorder sales and cost data

Unit selling price	$500
Unit variable cost	$300
Total fixed costs	$200,000
Break-even sales	$500,000 or 1,000 units

CASE I

A competitor is offering a 10% discount on the selling price of its camcorders. Management must decide whether to offer a similar discount.

Question: What effect will a 10% discount on selling price have on the break-even point for camcorders?

Answer: A 10% discount on selling price reduces the selling price per unit to $450 [$500 − ($500 × 10%)]. Variable costs per unit remain unchanged at $300. Thus, the unit contribution margin is $150. Assuming no change in fixed costs, break-even sales are 1,333 units, computed as follows.

Illustration 20-10
Computation of break-even sales in units

Fixed Costs	÷	Unit Contribution Margin	=	Break-Even Sales
$200,000	÷	$150	=	1,333 units (rounded)

For Vargo, this change requires monthly sales to increase by 333 units, or $33\frac{1}{3}$%, in order to break even. In reaching a conclusion about offering a 10%

discount to customers, management must determine how likely it is to achieve the increased sales. Also, management should estimate the possible loss of sales if the competitor's discount price is not matched.

CASE II

To meet the threat of foreign competition, management invests in new robotic equipment that will lower the amount of direct labor required to make camcorders. The company estimates that total fixed costs will increase 30% and that variable cost per unit will decrease 30%.

Question: What effect will the new equipment have on the sales volume required to break even?

Answer: Total fixed costs become $260,000 [$200,000 + (30% × $200,000)]. The variable cost per unit becomes $210 [$300 − (30% × $300)]. The new break-even point is approximately 897 units, computed as shown in Illustration 20-11.

Fixed Costs	÷	Unit Contribution Margin	=	Break-Even Sales
$260,000	÷	($500 − $210)	=	897 units (rounded)

Illustration 20-11
Computation of break-even sales in units

These changes appear to be advantageous for Vargo. The break-even point is reduced by approximately 10%, or 100 units.

CASE III

Vargo's principal supplier of raw materials has just announced a price increase. The higher cost is expected to increase the variable cost of camcorders by $25 per unit. Management decides to hold the line on the selling price of the camcorders. It plans a cost-cutting program that will save $17,500 in fixed costs per month. Vargo is currently realizing monthly net income of $80,000 on sales of 1,400 camcorders.

Question: What increase in units sold will be needed to maintain the same level of net income?

Answer: The variable cost per unit increases to $325 ($300 + $25). Fixed costs are reduced to $182,500 ($200,000 − $17,500). Because of the change in variable cost, the unit contribution margin becomes $175 ($500 − $325). The required number of units sold to achieve the target net income is computed as follows.

(Fixed Costs + Target Net Income)	÷	Unit Contribution Margin	=	Required Sales in Units
($182,500 + $80,000)	÷	$175	=	1,500

Illustration 20-12
Computation of required sales

To achieve the required sales, Vargo Video will have to sell 1,500 camcorders, an increase of 100 units. If this does not seem to be a reasonable expectation, management will either have to make further cost reductions or accept less net income if the selling price remains unchanged.

We hope that the concepts reviewed in this section are now familiar to you. We are now ready to examine additional ways that companies use CVP analysis to assess profitability and to help in making effective business decisions.

Management Insight Amazon.com

Warchi/iStockphoto

Don't Just Look— Buy Something

When analyzing an Internet business such as Amazon.com, analysts closely watch the so-called "conversion rate." This rate is calculated by dividing the number of people who actually take action at an Internet site (buy something) by the total number of people who visit the site. Average conversion rates are from 3% to 5%. A rate below 2% is poor, while a rate above 10% is great.

Conversion rates have an obvious effect on the break-even point. Suppose you spend $10,000 on your site, which then attracts 5,000 visitors. If you get a 2% conversion rate

(100 purchases), your site costs $100 per purchase ($10,000 ÷ 100). A 4% conversion rate lowers your cost to $50 per transaction, and an 8% conversion rate gets you down to $25. Studies show that conversion rates increase if the site has an easy-to-use interface, fast-performing screens, a convenient ordering process, and advertising that is both clever and clear.

Sources: J. William Gurley, "The One Internet Metric That Really Counts" *Fortune* (March 6, 2000), p. 392; and Milind Mody, "Chief Mentor: How Startups Can Win Customers Online," *Wall Street Journal Online,* (May 11, 2011).

Besides increasing their conversion rates, what steps can online merchants use to lower their break-even points? (Go to **WileyPLUS** for this answer and additional questions.)

DO IT! 1 CVP Analysis

Krisanne Company reports the following operating results for the month of June.

KRISANNE COMPANY
CVP Income Statement
For the Month Ended June 30, 2017

	Total	Per Unit
Sales (5,000 units)	$300,000	$60
Variable costs	180,000	36
Contribution margin	120,000	$24
Fixed expenses	100,000	
Net income	$ 20,000	

To increase net income, management is considering reducing the selling price by 10%, with no changes to unit variable costs or fixed costs. Management is confident that this change will increase unit sales by 25%.

Using the contribution margin technique, compute the break-even point in units and dollars and margin of safety in dollars (a) assuming no changes to sales price or costs, and (b) assuming changes to sales price and volume as described above. (c) Comment on your findings.

Solution

Action Plan

✔ Apply the formula for the break-even point in units.

✔ Apply the formula for the break-even point in dollars.

✔ Apply the formula for the margin of safety in dollars.

(a) Assuming no changes to sales price or costs:
Break-even point in units = 4,167 units (rounded) ($100,000 ÷ $24)
Break-even point in sales dollars = $250,000 ($100,000 ÷ .40[a])
Margin of safety in dollars = $50,000 ($300,000 − $250,000)
[a]$24 ÷ $60

(b) Assuming changes to sales price and volume:
Break-even point in units = 5,556 units (rounded) ($100,000 ÷ $18[b])
Break-even point in sales dollars = $300,000 ($100,000 ÷ ($18 ÷ $54[c]))
Margin of safety in dollars = $37,500 ($337,500[d] − $300,000)
[b]$60 − (.10 × $60) − 36 = $18
[c]$60 − (.10 × $60)
[d]5,000 + (.25 × 5,000) = 6,250 units, 6,250 units × $54 = $337,500

(c) The increase in the break-even point and the decrease in the margin of safety indicate that management should not implement the proposed change. The increase in sales volume will result in contribution margin of $112,500 (6,250 × $18), which is $7,500 ($120,000 − $112,500) less than the current amount.

Related exercise material: **BE20-3, BE20-4, BE20-5, BE20-6, E20-1, E20-2, E20-3, E20-4, E20-5, and DO IT! 20-1.**

LEARNING OBJECTIVE ❷ **Explain the term sales mix and its effects on break-even sales.**

To this point, our discussion of CVP analysis has assumed that a company sells only one product. However, most companies sell multiple products. When a company sells many products, it is important that management understand its sales mix.

Sales mix is the relative percentage in which a company sells its multiple products. For example, if 80% of **Hewlett Packard**'s unit sales are printers and the other 20% are PCs, its sales mix is 80% printers to 20% PCs.

Sales mix is important to managers because different products often have substantially different contribution margins. For example, **Ford**'s SUVs and F150 pickup trucks have higher contribution margins compared to its economy cars. Similarly, first-class tickets sold by **United Airlines** provide substantially higher contribution margins than coach-class tickets. **Intel**'s sales of computer chips for netbook computers have increased, but the contribution margin on these chips is lower than for notebook and desktop PCs.

Break-Even Sales in Units

Companies can compute break-even sales for a mix of two or more products by determining the **weighted-average unit contribution margin of all the products**. To illustrate, assume that Vargo Video sells not only camcorders but high-definition TVs as well. Vargo sells its two products in the following amounts: 1,500 camcorders and 500 TVs. The sales mix, expressed as a percentage of the 2,000 total units sold, is as follows.

Camcorders	TVs
1,500 units ÷ 2,000 units = 75%	500 units ÷ 2,000 units = 25%

Illustration 20-13
Sales mix as a percentage of units sold

That is, 75% of the 2,000 units sold are camcorders, and 25% of the 2,000 units sold are TVs.

Illustration 20-14 shows additional information related to Vargo. The unit contribution margin for camcorders is $200, and for TVs it is $500. Vargo's fixed costs total $275,000.

Unit Data	Camcorders	TVs
Selling price	$500	$1,000
Variable costs	300	500
Contribution margin	$200	$500
Sales mix—units	**75%**	**25%**
Fixed costs = $275,000		

Illustration 20-14
Per unit data—sales mix

To compute break-even for Vargo, we must determine the weighted-average unit contribution margin for the two products. We use the **weighted-average** contribution margin because Vargo sells three times as many camcorders as TVs. As a result, in determining an average unit contribution margin, three times as much weight should be placed on the contribution margin of the camcorders as on the TVs. Therefore, the camcorders must be counted three times for every TV sold. The weighted-average contribution margin for a sales mix of 75% camcorders and 25% TVs is $275, which is computed as follows.

Illustration 20-15
Weighted-average unit contribution margin

Camcorders				TVs				Weighted-Average
(Unit Contribution Margin	×	Sales Mix Percentage)	+	(Unit Contribution Margin	×	Sales Mix Percentage)	=	Unit Contribution Margin
($200	×	.75)	+	($500	×	.25)	=	$275

Similar to our calculation in the single-product setting, we can compute the break-even point in units by dividing the fixed costs by the weighted-average unit contribution margin of $275. The computation of break-even sales in units for Vargo Video, assuming $275,000 of fixed costs, is as follows.

Illustration 20-16
Break-even point in units

Fixed Costs	÷	Weighted-Average Unit Contribution Margin	=	Break-Even Point in Units
$275,000	÷	$275	=	1,000 units

Illustration 20-16 shows the break-even point for Vargo is 1,000 units—camcorders and TVs combined. Management needs to know how many of the 1,000 units sold are camcorders and how many are TVs. Applying the sales mix percentages that we computed previously of 75% for camcorders and 25% for TVs, these 1,000 units would be comprised of 750 camcorders (.75 × 1,000 units) and 250 TVs (.25 × 1,000). This can be verified by the computations in Illustration 20-17, which shows that the total contribution margin is $275,000 when 1,000 units are sold, which equals the fixed costs of $275,000.

Illustration 20-17
Break-even proof—sales units

Product	Unit Sales	×	Unit Contribution Margin	=	Total Contribution Margin
Camcorders	750	×	$200	=	$ 150,000
TVs	250	×	500	=	125,000
	1,000				**$275,000**

Management should continually review the company's sales mix. At any level of units sold, **net income will be greater if higher contribution margin units are sold rather than lower contribution margin units**. For Vargo, the TVs produce the higher contribution margin. Consequently, if Vargo sells 300 TVs and 700 camcorders, net income would be higher than in the current sales mix even though total units sold are the same.

An analysis of these relationships shows that a shift from low-margin sales to high-margin sales may increase net income even though there is a decline in total units sold. Likewise, a shift from high- to low-margin sales may result in a decrease in net income even though there is an increase in total units sold.

Break-Even Sales in Dollars

The calculation of the break-even point presented for Vargo Video in the previous section works well if a company has only a *small number* of products. In contrast, consider **3M**, the maker of Post-it Notes, which has more than 30,000 products. In order to calculate the break-even point for 3M using a weighted-average unit contribution margin, we would need to calculate 30,000 different unit contribution margins. That is not realistic.

Therefore, for a company with many products, we calculate the break-even point in terms of sales dollars (rather than units sold), using sales information for divisions or product lines (rather than individual products). This requires that we compute both sales mix as a percentage of total dollar sales (rather than units sold) and the contribution margin ratio (rather than unit contribution margin).

To illustrate, suppose that Kale Garden Supply Company has two divisions—Indoor Plants and Outdoor Plants. Each division has hundreds of different types of plants and plant-care products. Illustration 20-18 provides information necessary for determining the sales mix percentages for the two divisions of Kale Garden Supply.

	Indoor Plant Division	Outdoor Plant Division	Company Total
Sales	$ 200,000	$ 800,000	$1,000,000
Variable costs	120,000	560,000	680,000
Contribution margin	$ 80,000	$ 240,000	$ 320,000
Sales mix percentage (Division sales ÷ Total sales)	$\frac{\$200{,}000}{\$1{,}000{,}000} = .20$	$\frac{\$800{,}000}{\$1{,}000{,}000} = .80$	

Illustration 20-18
Cost-volume-profit data for Kale Garden Supply

As shown in Illustration 20-19, the contribution margin ratio for the combined company is 32%, which is computed by dividing the total contribution margin by total sales.

	Indoor Plant Division	Outdoor Plant Division	Company Total
Contribution margin ratio (Contribution margin ÷ Sales)	$\frac{\$80{,}000}{\$200{,}000} = .40$	$\frac{\$240{,}000}{\$800{,}000} = .30$	$\frac{\$320{,}000}{\$1{,}000{,}000} = .32$

Illustration 20-19
Contribution margin ratio for each division

It is useful to note that the contribution margin ratio of 32% for the total company is a weighted average of the individual contribution margin ratios of the two divisions (40% and 30%). To illustrate, in Illustration 20-20 we multiply each division's contribution margin ratio by its sales mix percentage, based on dollar sales, and then total these amounts. The calculation in Illustration 20-20 is useful because it enables us to determine how the break-even point changes when the sales mix changes.

Illustration 20-20
Calculation of weighted-average contribution margin

Indoor Plant Division		Outdoor Plant Division		Weighted-Average Contribution Margin Ratio
$\left(\begin{array}{c}\text{Contribution} \\ \text{Margin Ratio}\end{array} \times \begin{array}{c}\text{Sales Mix} \\ \text{Percentage}\end{array}\right)$	+	$\left(\begin{array}{c}\text{Contribution} \\ \text{Margin Ratio}\end{array} \times \begin{array}{c}\text{Sales Mix} \\ \text{Percentage}\end{array}\right)$	=	
(.40 × .20)	+	(.30 × .80)	=	.32

Kale Garden Supply's break-even point in dollars is then computed by dividing its fixed costs of $300,000 by the weighted-average contribution margin ratio of 32%, as shown in Illustration 20-21 (page 932).

Illustration 20-21
Calculation of break-even point in dollars

Fixed Costs	÷	Weighted-Average Contribution Margin Ratio	=	Break-Even Point in Dollars
$300,000	÷	.32	=	$937,500

The break-even point is based on the sales mix of 20% to 80%. We can determine the amount of sales contributed by each division by multiplying the sales mix percentage of each division by the total sales figure. Of the company's total break-even sales of $937,500, a total of $187,500 (.20 × $937,500) will come from the Indoor Plant Division, and $750,000 (.80 × $937,500) will come from the Outdoor Plant Division.

What would be the impact on the break-even point if a higher percentage of Kale Garden Supply's sales were to come from the Indoor Plant Division? Because the Indoor Plant Division enjoys a higher contribution margin ratio, this change in the sales mix would result in a higher weighted-average contribution margin ratio and consequently a lower break-even point in dollars. For example, if the sales mix changes to 50% for the Indoor Plant Division and 50% for the Outdoor Plant Division, the weighted-average contribution margin ratio would be 35% [(.40 × .50) + (.30 × .50)]. The new, lower, break-even point is $857,143 ($300,000 ÷ .35). The opposite would occur if a higher percentage of sales were expected from the Outdoor Plant Division. As you can see, the information provided using CVP analysis can help managers better understand the impact of sales mix on profitability.

Service Company Insight   Zoom Kitchen

dem10/iStockphoto

Healthy for You, and Great for the Bottom Line

Zoom Kitchen, a chain of restaurants in the Chicago area, was known for serving sizable portions of meat and potatoes. But the company's management was quite pleased when salad sales increased from 18% of its sales mix to 40%. Why were they pleased? Because the contribution margin on salads was much higher than on meat. The restaurant made a conscious effort to encourage people to buy more salads by offering an interesting assortment of salad ingredients including jicama, beets, marinated mushrooms, grilled tuna, and carved turkey. Management had to be very sensitive to contribution margin as opening up a new Zoom Kitchen restaurant was very costly.

Source: Amy Zuber, "Salad Sales 'Zoom' at Meat-and-Potatoes Specialist," *Nation's Restaurant News* (November 12, 2001), p. 26.

Why do you suppose restaurants are so eager to sell beverages and desserts? (Go to **WileyPLUS** for this answer and additional questions.)

DO IT! 2   Sales Mix Break-Even

Manzeck Bicycles International produces and sells three different types of mountain bikes. Information regarding the three models is shown below.

Action Plan

✔ The sales mix is the relative percentage of each product sold in units.

✔ The weighted-average unit contribution margin is the sum of the unit contribution margins multiplied by the respective sales mix percentage.

	Pro	Intermediate	Standard	Total
Units sold	5,000	10,000	25,000	40,000
Selling price	$800	$500	$350	
Variable costs	$500	$300	$250	

The company's total fixed costs to produce the bicycles are $7,500,000.

(a) Determine the sales mix as a function of units sold for the three products.

(b) Determine the weighted-average unit contribution margin.

(c) Determine the total number of units that the company must sell to break even.

(d) Determine the number of units of each model that the company must sell to break even.

Solution

(a) The sales mix percentages as a function of units sold are:

Pro	Intermediate	Standard
5,000/40,000 = 12.5%	10,000/40,000 = 25%	25,000/40,000 = 62.5%

(b) The weighted-average unit contribution margin is:

$$[.125 \times (\$800 - \$500)] + [.25 \times (\$500 - \$300)] + [.625 \times (\$350 - \$250)] = \$150$$

(c) The break-even point in units is:

$$\$7,500,000 \div \$150 = 50,000 \text{ units}$$

(d) The break-even units to sell for each product are:

Pro:	50,000 units × 12.5% =	6,250 units
Intermediate:	50,000 units × 25% =	12,500 units
Standard:	50,000 units × 62.5% =	31,250 units
		50,000 units

Related exercise material: **BE20-7, BE20-8, BE20-9, BE20-10, E20-6, E20-7, E20-8, E20-9, E20-10,** and **DO IT! 20-2.**

Action Plan (*cont.*)

✔ Determine the break-even point in units by dividing the fixed costs by the weighted-average unit contribution margin.

✔ Determine the number of units of each model to sell by multiplying the total break-even units by the respective sales mix percentage for each product.

LEARNING OBJECTIVE **3**   Determine sales mix when a company has limited resources.

In the previous discussion, we assumed a certain sales mix and then determined the break-even point given that sales mix. We now discuss how limited resources influence the sales-mix decision.

All companies have resource limitations. The limited resource may be floor space in a retail department store, or raw materials, direct labor hours, or machine capacity in a manufacturing company. When a company has limited resources, management must decide which products to make and sell in order to maximize net income.

To illustrate, recall that Vargo Video manufactures camcorders and TVs. The limiting resource is machine capacity, which is 3,600 hours per month. Relevant data consist of the following.

	Camcorders	TVs
Unit contribution margin	$200	$500
Machine hours required per unit	.2	.625

Illustration 20-22
Contribution margin and machine hours

The TVs may appear to be more profitable since they have a higher unit contribution margin ($500) than the camcorders ($200). However, the camcorders take fewer machine hours to produce than the TVs. Therefore, it is necessary to find the **contribution margin per unit of limited resource**—in this case, contribution margin per machine hour. This is obtained by dividing the unit contribution margin of each product by the number of units of the limited resource required for each product, as shown in Illustration 20-23.

Helpful Hint
CM alone is not enough to make this decision. The key factor is CM per unit of limited resource.

	Camcorders	TVs
Unit contribution margin (a)	$200	$500
Machine hours required (b)	0.2	0.625
Contribution margin per unit of limited resource [(a) ÷ (b)]	**$1,000**	**$800**

Illustration 20-23
Contribution margin per unit of limited resource

The computation shows that the camcorders have a higher contribution margin per unit of limited resource. This would suggest that, given sufficient demand for camcorders, Vargo should shift the sales mix to produce more camcorders or increase machine capacity.

As indicated in Illustration 20-23, the constraint for the production of the TVs is the larger number of machine hours needed to produce them. In addressing this problem, we have taken the limited number of machine hours as a given and have attempted to maximize the contribution margin given the constraint. One question that Vargo should ask, however, is whether this constraint can be reduced or eliminated. If Vargo is able to increase machine capacity from 3,600 hours to 4,200 hours, the additional 600 hours could be used to produce either the camcorders or TVs. The total contribution margin under each alternative is found by multiplying the machine hours by the contribution margin per unit of limited resource, as shown below.

Illustration 20-24
Incremental analysis—computation of total contribution margin

	Camcorders	**TVs**
Machine hours (a)	600	600
Contribution margin per unit of limited resource (b)	$ 1,000	$ 800
Contribution margin [(a) × (b)]	**$600,000**	**$480,000**

From this analysis, we can see that to maximize net income, all of the increased capacity should be used to make and sell the camcorders.

Vargo's manufacturing constraint might be due to a bottleneck in production or to poorly trained machine operators. In addition to finding ways to solve those problems, the company should consider other possible solutions, such as outsourcing part of the production, acquiring additional new equipment (discussed in Chapter 26), or striving to eliminate any non–value-added activities (see Chapter 18). As discussed in Chapter 15, this approach to evaluating constraints is referred to as the theory of constraints. The **theory of constraints** is a specific approach used to identify and manage constraints in order to achieve the company's goals. According to this theory, a company must continually identify its constraints and find ways to reduce or eliminate them, where appropriate.

Management Insight   Macy's

Something Smells

Liv Friis-Larsen/iStockphoto

When fragrance sales went flat, retailers such as Macy's turned up the heat on fragrance manufacturers. They reduced the amount of floor space devoted to fragrances, leaving fragrance manufacturers fighting each other for the smaller space. The retailer doesn't just choose the fragrance with the highest contribution margin. Instead, it chooses the fragrance with the highest contribution margin per square foot for a given period of time. In this game, a product with a lower contribution margin, but a higher turnover, could well be the winner.

What is the limited resource for a retailer, and what implications does this have for sales mix? (Go to WileyPLUS for this answer and additional questions.)

DO IT! 3   Sales Mix with Limited Resources

Carolina Corporation manufactures and sells three different types of high-quality sealed ball bearings for mountain bike wheels. The bearings vary in terms of their quality specifications—primarily with respect to their smoothness and roundness. They are referred to as Fine, Extra-Fine, and Super-Fine bearings. Machine time is limited. More machine time is required to manufacture the Extra-Fine and Super-Fine bearings. Additional information is provided below.

	Product		
	Fine	**Extra-Fine**	**Super-Fine**
Selling price	$6.00	$10.00	$16.00
Variable costs and expenses	4.00	6.50	11.00
Contribution margin	$2.00	$ 3.50	$ 5.00
Machine hours required	0.02	0.04	0.08

(a) Ignoring the machine time constraint, what strategy would appear optimal?

(b) What is the contribution margin per unit of limited resource for each type of bearing?

(c) If additional machine time could be obtained, how should the additional capacity be used?

Solution

(a) The Super-Fine bearings have the highest unit contribution margin. Thus, ignoring any manufacturing constraints, it would appear that the company should shift toward production of more Super-Fine units.

(b) The contribution margin per unit of limited resource (machine hours) is calculated as:

	Fine	**Extra-Fine**	**Super-Fine**
$\dfrac{\text{Unit contribution margin}}{\text{Limited resource consumed per unit}}$	$\dfrac{\$2}{.02} = \$100$	$\dfrac{\$3.5}{.04} = \$87.50$	$\dfrac{\$5}{.08} = \$62.50$

(c) The Fine bearings have the highest contribution margin per unit of limited resource even though they have the lowest unit contribution margin. Given the resource constraint, any additional capacity should be used to make Fine bearings.

Related exercise material: **BE20-11, BE20-12, E20-11, E20-12, E20-13, and DO IT! 20-3.**

Action Plan

✔ Calculate the contribution margin per unit of limited resource for each product.

✔ Apply the formula for the contribution margin per unit of limited resource.

✔ To maximize net income, shift sales mix to the product with the highest contribution margin per unit of limited resource.

LEARNING OBJECTIVE **4**   **Indicate how operating leverage affects profitability.**

Cost structure refers to the relative proportion of fixed versus variable costs that a company incurs. Cost structure can have a significant effect on profitability. For example, computer equipment manufacturer **Cisco Systems** has substantially reduced its fixed costs by choosing to outsource much of its production. By minimizing its fixed costs, Cisco is now less susceptible to economic swings. However, as the following discussion shows, its reduced reliance on fixed costs has also reduced its ability to experience the incredible profitability that it used to have during economic booms.

The choice of cost structure should be carefully considered. There are many ways that companies can influence their cost structure. For example, by acquiring sophisticated robotic equipment, many companies have reduced their use of manual labor. Similarly, some brokerage firms, such as **E*Trade**, have reduced their reliance on human brokers and have instead invested heavily in computers and online technology. In so doing, they have increased their reliance on fixed costs (through depreciation on the robotic equipment or computer equipment) and reduced their reliance on variable costs (the variable employee labor cost). Alternatively, some companies have reduced their fixed costs and increased their variable costs by outsourcing their production. **Nike**, for example, does very little manufacturing but instead outsources the manufacture of nearly all of its shoes. It has consequently converted many of its fixed costs into variable costs and therefore changed its cost structure.

Consider the following example of Vargo Video and one of its competitors, New Wave Company. Both make camcorders. Vargo uses a traditional, labor-intensive manufacturing process. New Wave has invested in a completely auto-mated system. The factory employees are involved only in setting up, adjusting, and maintaining the machinery. Illustration 20-25 shows CVP income statements for each company.

Illustration 20-25
CVP income statements for two companies

	Vargo Video	New Wave Company
Sales	$800,000	$800,000
Variable costs	480,000	160,000
Contribution margin	320,000	640,000
Fixed costs	200,000	520,000
Net income	$120,000	$120,000

Both companies have the same sales and the same net income. However, because of the differences in their cost structures, they differ greatly in the risks and rewards related to increasing or decreasing sales. Let's evaluate the impact of cost structure on the profitability of the two companies.

Effect on Contribution Margin Ratio

First let's look at the contribution margin ratio. Illustration 20-26 shows the computation of the contribution margin ratio for each company.

Illustration 20-26
Contribution margin ratio for two companies

	Contribution Margin	÷	Sales	=	Contribution Margin Ratio
Vargo Video	$320,000	÷	$800,000	=	.40
New Wave	$640,000	÷	$800,000	=	.80

Because of its lower variable costs, New Wave has a contribution margin ratio of 80% versus only 40% for Vargo Video. That means that with every dollar of sales, New Wave generates 80 cents of contribution margin (and thus an 80-cent increase in net income), versus only 40 cents for Vargo. However, it also means that for every dollar that sales decline, New Wave loses 80 cents in net income, whereas Vargo will lose only 40 cents. New Wave's cost structure, which relies more heavily on fixed costs, makes it more sensitive to changes in sales revenue.

Effect on Break-Even Point

The difference in cost structure also affects the break-even point. The break-even point for each company is calculated in Illustration 20-27.

Illustration 20-27
Computation of break-even point for two companies

	Fixed Costs	÷	Contribution Margin Ratio	=	Break-Even Point in Dollars
Vargo Video	$200,000	÷	.40	=	$500,000
New Wave	$520,000	÷	.80	=	$650,000

New Wave needs to generate $150,000 ($650,000 − $500,000) more in sales than Vargo Video before it breaks even. This makes New Wave riskier than Vargo because a company cannot survive for very long unless it at least breaks even.

Effect on Margin of Safety Ratio

We can also evaluate the relative impact that changes in sales would have on the two companies by computing the margin of safety ratio. Illustration 20-28 shows the computation of the **margin of safety ratio** for the two companies.

Illustration 20-28
Computation of margin of safety ratio for two companies

	(Actual Sales	−	Break-Even Sales)	÷	Actual Sales	=	Margin of Safety Ratio
Vargo Video	($800,000	−	$500,000)	÷	$800,000	=	.38
New Wave	($800,000	−	$650,000)	÷	$800,000	=	.19

The difference in the margin of safety ratio also reflects the difference in risk between the two companies. Vargo Video could sustain a 38% decline in sales before it would be operating at a loss. New Wave could sustain only a 19% decline in sales before it would be "in the red."

Operating Leverage

Operating leverage refers to the extent to which a company's net income reacts to a given change in sales. Companies that have higher fixed costs relative to variable costs have higher operating leverage. When a company's sales revenue is increasing, high operating leverage is a good thing because it means that profits will increase rapidly. But when sales are declining, too much operating leverage can have devastating consequences.

DEGREE OF OPERATING LEVERAGE

How can we compare operating leverage between two companies? The **degree of operating leverage** provides a measure of a company's earnings volatility and can be used to compare companies. Degree of operating leverage is computed by dividing contribution margin by net income. This formula is presented in Illustration 20-29 and applied to our two manufacturers of camcorders.

Illustration 20-29
Computation of degree of operating leverage

	Contribution Margin	÷	Net Income	=	Degree of Operating Leverage
Vargo Video	$320,000	÷	$120,000	=	2.67
New Wave	$640,000	÷	$120,000	=	5.33

New Wave's earnings would go up (or down) by about two times (5.33 ÷ 2.67 = 2.00) as much as Vargo Video's with an equal increase (or decrease) in sales. For example, suppose both companies experience a 10% decrease in sales. Vargo's net income will decrease by 26.7% (2.67 × 10%), while New Wave's will decrease by 53.3% (5.33 × 10%). Thus, New Wave's higher operating leverage exposes it to greater earnings volatility risk.

You should be careful not to conclude from this analysis that a cost structure that relies on higher fixed costs, and consequently has higher operating leverage, is necessarily bad. Some have suggested that Internet radio company **Pandora** has limited potential for growth in its profitability because it has very little operating leverage. When its revenues grow, its variable costs (fees it pays for the right to use music) grow proportionally. When used carefully, operating leverage can add considerably to a company's profitability. For example, computer equipment manufacturer **Komag** enjoyed a 66% increase in net income when its sales increased by only 8%. As one commentator noted, "Komag's fourth quarter illustrates the company's significant operating leverage; a small increase in sales leads to a big profit rise." However, as our illustration demonstrates, increased reliance on fixed costs increases a company's risk.

Service Company Insight Burlington Northern Railroad

Michele Wassell/Age Fotostock America, Inc.

There Is Something About a Train

A few years ago, Warren Buffett, arguably the most successful investor in history, bought a new train set—for $44 billion. The sage from Omaha bought Burlington Northern Railroad for a price that exceeded its fair value by 31%. At a time when the rest of the investing public was obsessed with technology companies like Facebook and Twitter, what could Buffett possibly see in a railroad? What he sees is a business whose costs are between 50–60% fixed. With such high fixed costs, railways have huge operating leverage. And because he bought the railroad at the bottom of a recession, when the economy turns around, Burlington could take off as well. Add to that the fact that railroad transport is very energy-efficient, and it has high barriers to entry. So, as energy prices increase, more people will turn to the rails, but there are a limited number of railways. Makes sense to me.

Source: Liam Denning, "Buffett's Unusual Train of Thought," *Wall Street Journal* (November 4, 2009).

Why did Warren Buffett think that this was a good time to invest in railroad stocks? (Go to **WileyPLUS** for this answer and additional questions.)

DO IT! 4 Operating Leverage

Rexfield Corp., a company specializing in crime scene investigations, is contemplating an investment in automated mass-spectrometers. Its current process relies on a high number of lab technicians. The new equipment would employ a computerized expert system. The company's CEO has requested a comparison of the old technology versus the new technology. The accounting department has prepared the following CVP income statements for use in your analysis.

	CSI Equipment	
	Old	New
Sales	$2,000,000	$2,000,000
Variable costs	1,400,000	600,000
Contribution margin	600,000	1,400,000
Fixed costs	400,000	1,200,000
Net income	$ 200,000	$ 200,000

Use the information provided above to do the following.

(a) Compute the degree of operating leverage for the company under each scenario.

(b) Discuss your results.

Solution

Action Plan

✔ Divide contribution margin by net income to determine degree of operating leverage.

✔ A higher degree of operating leverage will result in a higher change in net income with a given change in sales.

(a)

	Contribution Margin	÷	Net Income	=	Degree of Operating Leverage
Old	$600,000	÷	$200,000	=	3
New	$1,400,000	÷	$200,000	=	7

(b) The degree of operating leverage measures the company's sensitivity to changes in sales. By switching to a cost structure dominated by fixed costs, the company would significantly increase its operating leverage. As a result, with a percentage change in sales, its percentage change in net income would be 2.33 (7 ÷ 3) times as much with the new technology as it would under the old.

Related exercise material: **BE20-13, BE20-14, BE20-15, E20-14, E20-15, E20-16, and DO IT! 20-4.**

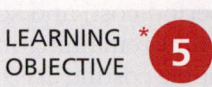

APPENDIX 20A: Explain the differences between absorption costing and variable costing.

In the earlier chapters, we classified both variable and fixed manufacturing costs as product costs. In job order costing, for example, a job is assigned the costs of direct materials, direct labor, and **both** variable and fixed manufacturing overhead. This costing approach is referred to as **full** or **absorption costing**. It is so named because all manufacturing costs are charged to, or absorbed by, the product. Absorption costing is the approach used for external reporting under generally accepted accounting principles.

An alternative approach is to use **variable costing**. Under variable costing, only direct materials, direct labor, and variable manufacturing overhead costs are considered product costs. Companies recognize fixed manufacturing overhead costs as period costs (expenses) when incurred. The difference between absorption costing and variable costing is shown graphically as follows.

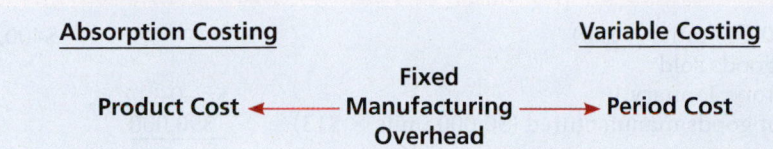

Illustration 20A-1
Difference between absorption costing and variable costing

Under both absorption and variable costing, selling and administrative expenses are period costs.

Companies may not use variable costing for external financial reports because generally accepted accounting principles require that fixed manufacturing overhead be accounted for as a product cost.

Example Comparing Absorption Costing with Variable Costing

To illustrate absorption and variable costing, assume that Premium Products Corporation manufactures a polyurethane sealant, called Fix-It, for car windshields. Relevant data for Fix-It in January 2017, the first month of production, are shown in Illustration 20A-2.

Selling price	$20 per unit.
Units	Produced 30,000; sold 20,000; beginning inventory zero.
Variable unit costs	Manufacturing $9 (direct materials $5, direct labor $3, and variable overhead $1).
	Selling and administrative expenses $2.
Fixed costs	Manufacturing overhead $120,000.
	Selling and administrative expenses $15,000.

Illustration 20A-2
Sealant sales and cost data for Premium Products Corporation

The per unit manufacturing cost under each costing approach is computed in Illustration 20A-3.

Type of Cost	Absorption Costing	Variable Costing
Direct materials	$ 5	$5
Direct labor	3	3
Variable manufacturing overhead	1	1
Fixed manufacturing overhead ($120,000 ÷ 30,000 units produced)	**4**	**0**
Manufacturing cost per unit	**$13**	**$9**

Illustration 20A-3
Computation of per unit manufacturing cost

The manufacturing cost per unit is $4 higher ($13 − $9) for absorption costing. This occurs because fixed manufacturing overhead costs are a product cost under absorption costing. Under variable costing, they are, instead, a period cost, and so they are expensed. Based on these data, each unit sold and each unit remaining in inventory is costed under absorption costing at $13 and under variable costing at $9.

ABSORPTION COSTING EXAMPLE

Illustration 20A-4 shows the income statement for Premium Products using absorption costing. It shows that cost of goods manufactured is $390,000, computed by multiplying the 30,000 units produced times the manufacturing cost per unit of $13 (see Illustration 20A-3). Cost of goods sold is $260,000, after subtracting ending inventory of $130,000. Under absorption costing, $40,000 of the fixed overhead (10,000 units × $4) is deferred to a future period as part of the cost of ending inventory.

Illustration 20A-4
Absorption costing income statement

Helpful Hint
The income statement format in Illustration 20A-4 is the same as that used under generally accepted accounting principles.

PREMIUM PRODUCTS CORPORATION		
Income Statement		
For the Month Ended January 31, 2017		
Absorption Costing		
Sales (20,000 units × $20)		$400,000
Cost of goods sold		
Inventory, January 1	$ –0–	
Cost of goods manufactured (30,000 units × $13)	390,000	
Cost of goods available for sale	390,000	
Less: Inventory, January 31 (10,000 units × $13)	130,000	
Cost of goods sold (20,000 units × $13)		260,000
Gross profit		140,000
Variable selling and administrative expenses		
(20,000 × $2)	40,000	
Fixed selling and administrative expenses	15,000	55,000
Net income		**$ 85,000**

VARIABLE COSTING EXAMPLE

As Illustration 20A-5 shows, companies use the cost-volume-profit format in preparing a variable costing income statement. The variable manufacturing cost of $270,000 is computed by multiplying the 30,000 units produced times variable manufacturing cost of $9 per unit (see Illustration 20A-3). As in absorption costing,

Illustration 20A-5
Variable costing income statement

Helpful Hint
Note the difference in the computation of the ending inventory: $9 per unit here, $13 per unit in Illustration 20A-4.

PREMIUM PRODUCTS CORPORATION		
Income Statement		
For the Month Ended January 31, 2017		
Variable Costing		
Sales (20,000 units × $20)		$400,000
Variable cost of goods sold		
Inventory, January 1	$ –0–	
Variable cost of goods manufactured		
(30,000 units × $9)	270,000	
Variable cost of goods available for sale	270,000	
Less: Inventory, January 31 (10,000 units × $9)	90,000	
Variable cost of goods sold	180,000	
Variable selling and administrative expenses		
(20,000 units × $2)	40,000	220,000
Contribution margin		180,000
Fixed manufacturing overhead	120,000	
Fixed selling and administrative expenses	15,000	135,000
Net income		**$ 45,000**

both variable and fixed selling and administrative expenses are treated as period costs.

There is one primary difference between variable and absorption costing: Under variable costing, companies charge the fixed manufacturing overhead as an expense in the current period. Fixed manufacturing overhead costs of the current period, therefore, are not deferred to future periods through the ending inventory. As a result, absorption costing will show a **higher net income number** than variable costing **whenever units produced exceed units sold**. This difference can be seen in the income statements in Illustrations 20A-4 and 20A-5. There is a $40,000 difference in the ending inventories ($130,000 under absorption costing versus $90,000 under variable costing). Under absorption costing, $40,000 of the fixed overhead costs (10,000 units × $4) has been deferred to a future period as part of inventory. In contrast, under variable costing, all fixed manufacturing costs are expensed in the current period.

As shown, when units produced exceed units sold, income under absorption costing is *higher*. When units produced are less than units sold, income under absorption costing is *lower*. When units produced and sold are the same, net income will be *equal* under the two costing approaches. In this case, there is no increase in ending inventory. So fixed overhead costs of the current period are not deferred to future periods through the ending inventory.

Net Income Effects

To further illustrate the concepts underlying absorption and variable costing, we will look at an extended example using Overbay Inc., a manufacturer of small airplane drones. We assume that production volume stays the same each year over the 3-year period, but the number of units sold varies each year.

2016 RESULTS

As indicated in Illustration 20A-6, the variable manufacturing cost per drone is $240,000, and the fixed manufacturing overhead cost per drone is $60,000 (assuming 10 drones). Total manufacturing cost per drone under absorption costing is therefore $300,000 ($240,000 + $60,000). Overbay also has variable selling and administrative expenses of $5,000 per drone. The fixed selling and administrative expenses are $80,000.

	2016	2017	2018
Volume information			
Drones in beginning inventory	0	0	2
Drones produced	10	10	10
Drones sold	10	8	12
Drones in ending inventory	0	2	0
Financial information			
Selling price per drone	$400,000		
Variable manufacturing cost per drone	$240,000		
Fixed manufacturing overhead for the year	$600,000		
Fixed manufacturing overhead per drone	$ 60,000 ($600,000 ÷ 10)		
Variable selling and administrative expenses per drone	$ 5,000		
Fixed selling and administrative expenses	$ 80,000		

Illustration 20A-6
Information for Overbay Inc.

An absorption costing income statement for 2016 for Overbay Inc. is shown in Illustration 20A-7.

OVERBAY INC.
Income Statement
For the Year Ended December 31, 2016
Absorption Costing

Sales (10 drones × $400,000)		$4,000,000
Cost of goods sold (10 drones × $300,000)		3,000,000
Gross profit		1,000,000
Variable selling and administrative expenses		
(10 drones × $5,000)	$50,000	
Fixed selling and administrative expenses	80,000	130,000
Net income		$ 870,000

Overbay reports net income of $870,000 under absorption costing.

Under a variable costing system, the income statement follows a cost-volume-profit (CVP) format. In this case, the manufacturing cost is comprised solely of the variable manufacturing costs of $240,000 per drone. The fixed manufacturing overhead costs of $600,000 for the year are expensed in 2016. As in absorption costing, the fixed and variable selling and administrative expenses are period costs expensed in 2016. A variable costing income statement for Overbay Inc. for 2016 is shown in Illustration 20A-8.

OVERBAY INC.
Income Statement
For the Year Ended December 31, 2016
Variable Costing

Sales (10 drones × $400,000)		$4,000,000
Variable cost of goods sold		
(10 drones × $240,000)	$2,400,000	
Variable selling and administrative expenses		
(10 drones × $5,000)	50,000	2,450,000
Contribution margin		1,550,000
Fixed manufacturing overhead	600,000	
Fixed selling and administrative expenses	80,000	680,000
Net income		$ 870,000

As shown in Illustration 20A-8, the variable costing net income of $870,000 is the same as the absorption costing net income computed in Illustration 20A-7. **When the numbers of units produced and sold are the same, net income is equal under the two costing approaches.** Because no increase in ending inventory occurs, no fixed manufacturing overhead costs incurred in 2016 are deferred to future periods using absorption costing.

2017 RESULTS

In 2017, Overbay produced 10 drones but sold only eight drones. As a result, there are two drones in ending inventory. The absorption costing income statement for 2017 is shown in Illustration 20A-9.

OVERBAY INC.
Income Statement
For the Year Ended December 31, 2017
Absorption Costing

Sales (8 drones × $400,000)		$3,200,000
Cost of goods sold (8 drones × $300,000)		2,400,000
Gross profit		800,000
Variable selling and administrative expenses		
(8 drones × $5,000)	$40,000	
Fixed selling and administrative expenses	80,000	120,000
Net income		$ 680,000

Under absorption costing, the ending inventory of two drones is $600,000 ($300,000 × 2). Each unit of ending inventory includes $60,000 of fixed manufacturing overhead. Therefore, fixed manufacturing overhead costs of $120,000 ($60,000 × 2 drones) are deferred until a future period.

The variable costing income statement for 2017 is shown in Illustration 20A-10.

OVERBAY INC.
Income Statement
For the Year Ended December 31, 2017
Variable Costing

Sales (8 drones × $400,000)		$3,200,000
Variable cost of goods sold		
(8 drones × $240,000)	$1,920,000	
Variable selling and administrative expenses		
(8 drones × $5,000)	40,000	1,960,000
Contribution margin		1,240,000
Fixed manufacturing overhead	600,000	
Fixed selling and administrative expenses	80,000	680,000
Net income		$ 560,000

As shown, when units produced (10) exceeds units sold (8), net income under absorption costing ($680,000) is higher than net income under variable costing ($560,000). The reason: The cost of the ending inventory is higher under absorption costing than under variable costing. In 2017, under absorption costing, fixed manufacturing overhead of $120,000 is deferred and carried to future periods as part of inventory. Under variable costing, the $120,000 is expensed in the current period and, therefore the difference in the two net income numbers is $120,000 ($680,000 − $560,000).

2018 RESULTS

In 2018, Overbay produced 10 drones and sold 12 (10 drones from the current year's production and 2 drones from the beginning inventory). As a result, there are no drones in ending inventory. The absorption costing income statement for 2018 is shown in Illustration 20A-11 (page 944).

Illustration 20A-11
Absorption costing income
statement—2018

OVERBAY INC.
Income Statement
For the Year Ended December 31, 2018
Absorption Costing

Sales (12 drones × $400,000)		$4,800,000
Cost of goods sold (12 drones × $300,000)		3,600,000
Gross profit		1,200,000
Variable selling and administrative expenses		
(12 drones × $5,000)	$60,000	
Fixed selling and administrative expenses	80,000	140,000
Net income		$1,060,000

Fixed manufacturing costs of $720,000 ($60,000 × 12 drones) are expensed as part of cost of goods sold in 2018. This $720,000 includes $120,000 of fixed manufacturing costs incurred during 2017 and included in beginning inventory, plus $600,000 of fixed manufacturing costs incurred during 2018. Given this result for the absorption costing statement, what would you now expect the result to be under variable costing? Let's take a look.

The variable costing income statement for 2018 is shown in Illustration 20A-12.

Illustration 20A-12
Variable costing income
statement—2018

OVERBAY INC.
Income Statement
For the Year Ended December 31, 2018
Variable Costing

Sales (12 drones × $400,000)		$4,800,000
Variable cost of goods sold		
(12 drones × $240,000)	$2,880,000	
Variable selling and administrative expenses		
(12 drones × $5,000)	60,000	2,940,000
Contribution margin		1,860,000
Fixed manufacturing overhead	600,000	
Fixed selling and administrative expenses	80,000	680,000
Net income		$1,180,000

When drones produced (10) are less than drones sold (12), net income under absorption costing ($1,060,000) is less than net income under variable costing ($1,180,000). This difference of $120,000 ($1,180,000 − $1,060,000) results because $120,000 of fixed manufacturing overhead costs in beginning inventory are charged to 2018 under absorption costing. Under variable costing, there is no fixed manufacturing overhead cost in beginning inventory.

Illustration 20A-13 summarizes the results of the three years.

Illustration 20A-13
Comparison of net income
under two costing approaches

	Net Income under Two Costing Approaches		
	2016	**2017**	**2018**
	Production = Sales	Production > Sales	Production < Sales
Absorption costing	$870,000	$ 680,000	$1,060,000
Variable costing	870,000	560,000	1,180,000
Difference	$ –0–	$120,000	$(120,000)

This relationship between production and sales and its effect on net income under the two costing approaches is shown graphically in Illustration 20A-14.

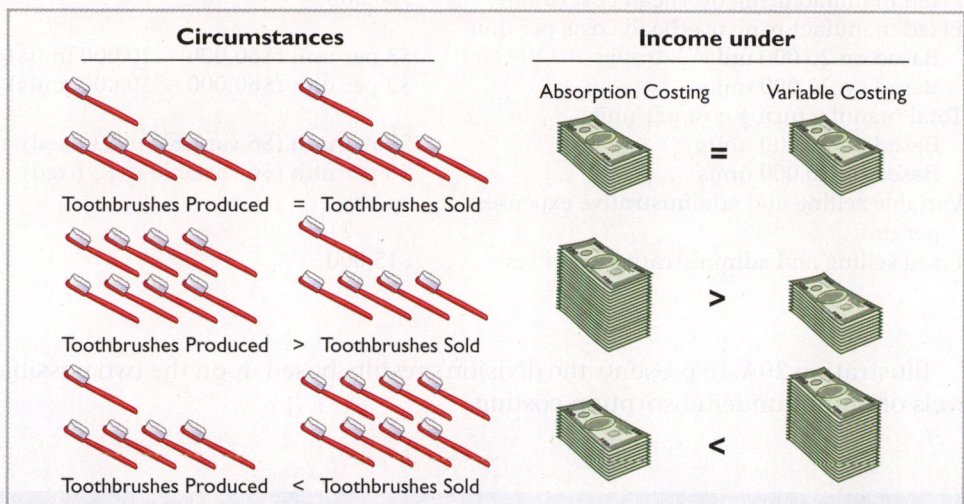

Decision-Making Concerns

Generally accepted accounting principles require that absorption costing be used for the costing of inventory for external reporting purposes. Net income measured under GAAP (absorption costing) is often used internally to evaluate performance, justify cost reductions, or evaluate new projects. Some companies, however, have recognized that net income calculated using GAAP does not highlight differences between variable and fixed costs and may lead to poor business decisions. Consequently, these companies use variable costing for internal reporting purposes. The following discussion and example highlight a significant problem related to the use of absorption costing for decision-making purposes.

When production exceeds sales, absorption costing reports a higher net income than variable costing. The reason is that some fixed manufacturing costs are not expensed in the current period but are deferred to future periods as part of inventory. As a result, management may be tempted to overproduce in a given period in order to increase net income. Although net income will increase, this decision to overproduce may not be in the company's best interest.

Suppose, for example, a division manager's compensation is based upon the division's net income. In such a case, the manager may decide to meet the net income targets by increasing production. While this overproduction may increase the manager's compensation, the buildup of inventories in the long run will lead to additional costs to the company. Variable costing avoids this situation because net income under variable costing is unaffected by changes in production levels, as the following illustration shows.

Warren Lund, a division manager of Walker Enterprises, is under pressure to boost the performance of the Lighting Division in 2017. Unfortunately, recent profits have not met expectations. The expected sales for this year are 20,000 units. As he plans for the year, Warren has to decide whether to produce 20,000 or 30,000 units. The following facts are available for the division.

Illustration 20A-15
Facts for Lighting
Division—2017

Beginning inventory	0
Expected sales in units	20,000
Selling price per unit	$15
Variable manufacturing cost per unit	$6
Fixed manufacturing overhead cost (total)	$60,000
Fixed manufacturing overhead costs per unit	
Based on 20,000 units	$3 per unit ($60,000 ÷ 20,000 units)
Based on 30,000 units	$2 per unit ($60,000 ÷ 30,000 units)
Total manufacturing cost per unit	
Based on 20,000 units	$9 per unit ($6 variable + $3 fixed)
Based on 30,000 units	$8 per unit ($6 variable + $2 fixed)
Variable selling and administrative expenses per unit	$1
Fixed selling and administrative expenses	$15,000

Illustration 20A-16 presents the division's results based upon the two possible levels of output under absorption costing.

Illustration 20A-16
Absorption costing income
statement—2017

LIGHTING DIVISION
Income Statement
For the Year Ended December 31, 2017
Absorption Costing

	20,000 Produced	30,000 Produced
Sales (20,000 units × $15)	$300,000	$ 300,000
Cost of goods sold	180,000*	160,000**
Gross profit	120,000	140,000
Variable selling and administrative expenses (20,000 units × $1)	20,000	20,000
Fixed selling and administrative expenses	15,000	15,000
Net income	**$ 85,000**	**$105,000**

*20,000 units × $9
**20,000 units × $8

If the Lighting Division produces 20,000 units, its net income under absorption costing is $85,000. If it produces 30,000 units, its net income is $105,000. By producing 30,000 units, the division has inventory of 10,000 units. This excess inventory causes net income to increase $20,000 because $20,000 of fixed costs (10,000 units × $2) are not charged to the current year, but are deferred to future periods.

What do you think Warren Lund might do in this situation? Given his concern about the profit numbers of the Lighting Division, he may be tempted to increase production. Although this increased production will increase 2017 net income, it may be costly to the company in the long run.

Now let's evaluate the same situation under variable costing. Illustration 20A-17 shows a variable costing income statement for production at both 20,000 and 30,000 units, using the information from Illustration 20A-15.

From this example, we see that under variable costing, net income is not affected by the number of units produced. Net income is $85,000 whether the division produces 20,000 or 30,000 units. Why? Because fixed manufacturing overhead is treated as a period expense. Unlike absorption costing, no fixed manufacturing overhead is deferred through inventory buildup. Therefore, under variable costing, production does not increase income; sales do. As a result, if the

Illustration 20A-17
Variable costing income
statement—2017

LIGHTING DIVISION Income Statement For the Year Ended December 31, 2017 Variable Costing	**20,000 Produced**	**30,000 Produced**
Sales (20,000 units × $15)	$300,000	$300,000
Variable cost of goods sold (20,000 units × $6)	120,000	120,000
Variable selling and administrative expenses (20,000 units × $1)	20,000	20,000
Contribution margin	160,000	160,000
Fixed manufacturing overhead	60,000	60,000
Fixed selling and administrative expenses	15,000	15,000
Net income	**$ 85,000**	**$ 85,000**

company uses variable costing, managers like Warren Lund cannot affect profitability by increasing production.

Potential Advantages of Variable Costing

Variable costing has a number of potential advantages relative to absorption costing:

1. Net income computed under variable costing is unaffected by changes in production levels. As a result, it is much easier to understand the impact of fixed and variable costs on the computation of net income when variable costing is used.

2. The use of variable costing is consistent with the cost-volume-profit material presented in Chapters 19 and 20.

3. Net income computed under variable costing is closely tied to changes in sales levels (not production levels) and therefore provides a more realistic assessment of the company's success or failure during a period.

4. The presentation of fixed and variable cost components on the face of the variable costing income statement makes it easier to identify these costs and understand their effect on the business. Under absorption costing, the allocation of fixed costs to inventory makes it difficult to evaluate the impact of fixed costs on the company's results.

Companies that use just-in-time processing techniques to minimize their inventories will not have significant differences between absorption and variable costing net income.

DO IT! 5 | Variable Costing

Franklin Company produces and sells tennis balls. The following costs are available for the year ended December 31, 2017. The company has no beginning inventory. In 2017, 8,000,000 units were produced, but only 7,500,000 units were sold. The unit selling price was $0.50 per ball. Costs and expenses were as follows.

Variable costs per unit	
Direct materials	$0.10
Direct labor	0.05
Variable manufacturing overhead	0.08
Variable selling and administrative expenses	0.02
Annual fixed costs and expenses	
Manufacturing overhead	$500,000
Selling and administrative expenses	100,000

(a) Compute the manufacturing cost of one unit of product using variable costing.

(b) Prepare a 2017 income statement for Franklin Company using variable costing.

Action Plan

✔ Recall that under variable costing, only variable manufacturing costs are treated as manufacturing (product) costs.

✔ Subtract all fixed costs, both manufacturing overhead and selling and administrative expenses, as period costs.

Solution

(a) The cost of one unit of product under variable costing would be:

Direct materials	$0.10
Direct labor	0.05
Variable manufacturing overhead	0.08
	$0.23

(b) The variable costing income statement would be as follows.

FRANKLIN COMPANY
Income Statement
For the Year Ended December 31, 2017
Variable Costing

Sales (7,500,000 × $0.50)		$3,750,000
Variable cost of goods sold (7,500,000 × $0.23)	$1,725,000	
Variable selling and administrative expenses		
(7,500,000 × .02)	150,000	1,875,000
Contribution margin		1,875,000
Fixed manufacturing overhead	500,000	
Fixed selling and administrative expenses	100,000	600,000
Net income		$1,275,000

Related exercise material: **BE20-16, BE20-17, BE20-18, BE20-19, E20-17, E20-18, and E20-19.**

REVIEW AND PRACTICE

LEARNING OBJECTIVES REVIEW

1 Apply basic CVP concepts. The CVP income statement classifies costs and expenses as variable or fixed and reports contribution margin in the body of the statement. Contribution margin is the amount of revenue remaining after deducting variable costs. It can be expressed as a per unit amount or as a ratio. The break-even point in units is fixed costs divided by unit contribution margin. The break-even point in dollars is fixed costs divided by the contribution margin ratio. These formulas can also be used to determine units or sales dollars needed to achieve target net income, simply by adding target net income to fixed costs before dividing by the contribution margin. Margin of safety indicates how much sales can decline before the company is operating at a loss. It can be expressed in dollar terms or as a percentage.

2 Explain the term sales mix and its effects on break-even sales. Sales mix is the relative proportion in which each product is sold when a company sells more than one product. For a company with a small number of products, break-even sales in units is determined by using the weighted-average unit contribution margin of all the products. If the company sells many different products, then calculating the break-even point using unit information is not practical. Instead, in a company with many products, break-even sales in dollars is calculated using the weighted-average contribution margin ratio.

3 Determine sales mix when a company has limited resources. When a company has limited resources, it is necessary to find the contribution margin per unit of limited resource. This amount is then multiplied by the units of limited resource to determine which product maximizes net income.

4 Indicate how operating leverage affects profitability. Operating leverage refers to the degree to which a company's net income reacts to a change in sales. Operating leverage is determined by a company's relative use of fixed versus variable costs. Companies with high fixed costs relative to variable costs have high operating leverage. A company with high operating leverage experiences a sharp increase (decrease) in net income with a given increase (decrease) in sales. The degree of operating leverage is measured by dividing contribution margin by net income.

*❺ **Explain the differences between absorption costing and variable costing.** Under absorption costing, fixed manufacturing costs are product costs. Under variable costing, fixed manufacturing costs are period costs.

If production volume exceeds sales volume, net income under absorption costing will exceed net income under variable costing by the amount of fixed manufacturing costs included in ending inventory that results from units produced but not sold during the period. If production volume is less than sales volume, net income under absorption costing will be less than under variable costing by the amount of fixed manufacturing costs included in the units sold during the period that were not produced during the period.

The use of variable costing is consistent with cost-volume-profit analysis. Net income under variable costing is unaffected by changes in production levels. Instead, it is closely tied to changes in sales. The presentation of fixed costs in the variable costing approach makes it easier to identify fixed costs and to evaluate their impact on the company's profitability.

GLOSSARY REVIEW

***Absorption costing** A costing approach in which all manufacturing costs are charged to the product. (p. 939).

Cost structure The relative proportion of fixed versus variable costs that a company incurs. (p. 935).

Degree of operating leverage A measure of the extent to which a company's net income reacts to a change in sales. It is calculated by dividing contribution margin by net income. (p. 937).

Operating leverage The extent to which a company's net income reacts to a change in sales. Operating leverage

is determined by a company's relative use of fixed versus variable costs. (p. 937).

Sales mix The relative percentage in which a company sells its multiple products. (p. 929).

Theory of constraints A specific approach used to identify and manage constraints in order to achieve the company's goals. (p. 934).

***Variable costing** A costing approach in which only variable manufacturing costs are product costs, and fixed manufacturing costs are period costs (expenses). (p. 939).

PRACTICE MULTIPLE-CHOICE QUESTIONS

(LO 1) 1. Which one of the following is the format of a CVP income statement?
   (a) Sales − Variable costs = Fixed costs + Net income.
   (b) Sales − Fixed costs − Variable costs − Operating expenses = Net income.
   (c) Sales − Cost of goods sold − Operating expenses = Net income.
   (d) Sales − Variable costs − Fixed costs = Net income.

(LO 1) 2. Croc Catchers calculates its contribution margin to be less than zero. Which statement is **true**?
   (a) Its fixed costs are less than the variable costs per unit.
   (b) Its profits are greater than its total costs.
   (c) The company should sell more units.
   (d) Its selling price is less than its variable costs.

(LO 1) 3. Which one of the following describes the break-even point?
   (a) It is the point where total sales equal total variable plus total fixed costs.
   (b) It is the point where the contribution margin equals zero.
   (c) It is the point where total variable costs equal total fixed costs.
   (d) It is the point where total sales equal total fixed costs.

(LO 1) 4. The following information is available for Chap Company.

Sales	$350,000
Cost of goods sold	$120,000
Total fixed expenses	$60,000
Total variable expenses	$100,000

   Which amount would you find on Chap's CVP income statement?
   (a) Contribution margin of $250,000.
   (b) Contribution margin of $190,000.

   (c) Gross profit of $230,000.
   (d) Gross profit of $190,000.

5. Gabriel Corporation has fixed costs of $180,000 and (LO 1) variable costs of $8.50 per unit. It has a target income of $268,000. How many units must it sell at $12 per unit to achieve its target net income?
   (a) 51,429 units.   (c) 76,571 units.
   (b) 128,000 units.   (d) 21,176 units.

6. Mackey Corporation has fixed costs of $150,000 and (LO 1) variable costs of $9 per unit. If sales price per unit is $12, what is break-even sales in dollars?
   (a) $200,000.   (c) $480,000.
   (b) $450,000.   (d) $600,000.

7. Sales mix is: (LO 2)
   (a) important to sales managers but not to accountants.
   (b) easier to analyze on absorption costing income statements.
   (c) a measure of the relative percentage of a company's variable costs to its fixed costs.
   (d) a measure of the relative percentage in which a company's products are sold.

8. Net income will be: (LO 2)
   (a) greater if more higher-contribution margin units are sold than lower-contribution margin units.
   (b) greater if more lower-contribution margin units are sold than higher-contribution margin units.
   (c) equal as long as total sales remain equal, regardless of which products are sold.
   (d) unaffected by changes in the mix of products sold.

(LO 3) **9.** If the unit contribution margin is $15 and it takes 3.0 machine hours to produce the unit, the contribution margin per unit of limited resource is:
  (a) $25.
  (b) $5.
  (c) $4.
  (d) None of the above are correct.

(LO 3) **10.** MEM manufactures two products. Product X has a contribution margin of $26 and requires 4 hours of machine time. Product Y has a contribution margin of $14 and requires 2 hours of machine time. Assuming that machine time is limited to 3,000 hours, how should it allocate the machine time to maximize its income?
  (a) Use 1,500 hours to produce X and 1,500 hours to produce Y.
  (b) Use 2,250 hours to produce X and 750 hours to produce Y.
  (c) Use 3,000 hours to produce only X.
  (d) Use 3,000 hours to produce only Y.

(LO 3) **11.** When a company has a limited resource, it should apply additional capacity of that resource to providing more units of the product or service that has:
  (a) the highest contribution margin.
  (b) the highest selling price.
  (c) the highest gross profit.
  (d) the highest unit contribution margin of that limited resource.

(LO 4) **12.** The degree of operating leverage:
  (a) can be computed by dividing total contribution margin by net income.
  (b) provides a measure of the company's earnings volatility.
  (c) affects a company's break-even point.
  (d) All of the answer choices are correct.

(LO 4) **13.** A high degree of operating leverage:
  (a) indicates that a company has a larger percentage of variable costs relative to its fixed costs.
  (b) is computed by dividing fixed costs by contribution margin.
  (c) exposes a company to greater earnings volatility risk.
  (d) exposes a company to less earnings volatility risk.

(LO 4) **14.** Stevens Company has a degree of operating leverage of 3.5 at a sales level of $1,200,000 and net income of $200,000. If Stevens' sales fall by 10%, Stevens can be expected to experience a:
  (a) decrease in net income of $70,000.
  (b) decrease in contribution margin of $7,000.
  (c) decrease in operating leverage of 35%.
  (d) decrease in net income of $175,000.

(LO 5) *15. Fixed manufacturing overhead costs are recognized as:
  (a) period costs under absorption costing.
  (b) product costs under absorption costs.
  (c) product costs under variable costing.
  (d) part of ending inventory costs under both absorption and variable costing.

(LO 5) *16. Net income computed under absorption costing will be:
  (a) higher than net income computed under variable costing in all cases.
  (b) equal to net income computed under variable costing in all cases.
  (c) higher than net income computed under variable costing when units produced are greater than units sold.
  (d) higher than net income computed under variable costing when units produced are less than units sold.

Solutions

1. (d) The format of a CVP income statement is Sales − Variable costs − Fixed costs = Net income. Therefore, choices (a), (b), and (c) are incorrect.

2. (d) If contribution margin is less than zero, selling price is less than variable costs. The other choices are incorrect because if contribution margin is less than zero (a) selling price, not fixed costs, is less than variable costs; (b) neither profits or total costs can be determined from the contribution margin amount; and (c) selling more units will only increase the negativity of the contribution margin.

3. (a) The break-even point is the point where total sales equal total variable costs plus total fixed costs. Choices (b), (c), and (d) are therefore incorrect.

4. (a) The CVP income statement would show Sales ($350,000) − Total variable expenses ($100,000) = Contribution margin ($250,000), not (b) contribution margin of $190,000. Choices (c) and (d) are incorrect because gross profit does not appear on a CVP income statement.

5. (b) Required sales in units to achieve net income = ($180,000 + $268,000)/($12 − $8.50) = 128,000 units, not (a) 51,429 units, (c) 76,571 units, or (d) 21,176 units.

6. (d) Fixed costs ($150,000) ÷ Contribution margin ratio ($3 ÷ $12) = $600,000, not (a) $200,000, (b) $450,000, or (c) $480,000.

7. (d) Sales mix is the relative percentage in which a company sells its multiple products. The other choices are incorrect because (a) sales mix is also important to accountants, and (b) absorption costing income statements are not needed. Choice (c) is an incorrect definition of sales mix.

8. (a) Net income will be greater if more higher contribution margin units are sold than lower contribution units. Choices (b), (c), and (d) are therefore incorrect statements.

9. (b) The contribution margin per unit of limited resource is Unit contribution margin ($15) ÷ Units of limited resource (3.0 machine hours) = $5, not (a) $25, (c) $4, or (d) none of the above.

10. (d) Unit contribution margin of Product X ($26 ÷ 4) < unit contribution margin of Product Y ($14 ÷ 2), so the machine time should be applied toward the product with the higher unit contribution margin. Choices (a), (b), and (c) are incorrect because these options will not maximize MEM's income.

11. (d) The company should apply additional capacity of the limited resource to providing more units of the product or service that has the highest unit contribution margin of that limited resource, not (a) the highest contribution margin, (b) the highest selling price, or (c) the highest gross profit.

12. (d) All of the above statements about operating leverage are true. So while choices (a), (b), and (c) are true statements, choice (d) is the better answer.

13. (c) A high degree of operating leverage exposes a company to greater earnings volatility risk. The other choices are incorrect because a high degree of operating leverage (a) means a company has higher fixed costs relative to variable costs, not vice versa; (b) is computed by dividing contribution margin by net income, not fixed costs by contribution margin; and (d) exposes a company to greater, not less, earnings volatility risk.

14. (a) Net income ($200,000) × Operating leverage (3.5) × Decrease in sales (10%) = decrease in net income of $70,000, not (b) decrease in contribution margin of $7,000, (c) decrease in operating leverage of 35%, or (d) decrease in net income of $175,000.

***15. (b)** Under absorption costing, fixed manufacturing overhead costs and variable manufacturing overhead costs are both product costs. The other choices are incorrect because (a) fixed manufacturing overhead costs are recognized as product costs under absorption costing, not period costs; (c) under variable costing, fixed manufacturing costs are recognized as period costs; and (d) fixed manufacturing costs are part of ending inventory under absorption costing only.

***16. (c)** Net income is higher under absorption costing than under variable costing when units produced exceed units sold, not (a) higher in all cases, (b) equal to net income under variable costing in all cases, or (d) higher when units produced are less than units sold.

PRACTICE EXERCISES

1. Yard-King manufactures lawnmowers, weed-trimmers, and chainsaws. Its sales mix and unit contribution margins are as follows.

Compute break-even point in units for a company with more than one product.

(LO 2)

	Sales Mix	Unit Contribution Margin
Lawnmowers	30%	$35
Weed-trimmers	50%	$25
Chainsaws	20%	$50

Yard-King has fixed costs of $4,620,000.

Instructions

Compute the number of units of each product that Yard-King must sell in order to break even under this product mix.

Solution

1.

	Sales Mix Percentage	Unit Contribution Margin	Weighted-Average Contribution Margin
Lawnmowers	30%	$35	$10.50
Weed-trimmers	50	25	12.50
Chainsaws	20	50	10.00
			$33.00

Total break-even sales in units = $4,620,000 ÷ $33.00 = 140,000 units

	Sales Mix Percentage		Total Break-Even Sales		Sales Needed per Product
Lawnmowers	30%	×	140,000 units	=	42,000 units
Weed-trimmers	50	×	140,000	=	70,000
Chainsaws	20	×	140,000	=	28,000
Total units					140,000 units

2. Rene Company manufactures and sells three products. Relevant per unit data concerning each product are given below.

Compute contribution margin and determine the product to be manufactured.

(LO 3)

	Product		
	A	B	C
Selling price	$12	$13	$15
Variable costs and expenses	$ 4	$ 8	$ 9
Machine hours to produce	2	1	2

Instructions

(a) Compute the contribution margin per unit of limited resource (machine hours) for each product.

(b) Assuming 4,500 additional machine hours are available, which product should be manufactured?

(c) Prepare an analysis showing the total contribution margin if the additional hours are (1) divided equally among the products, and (2) allocated entirely to the product identified in (b) above.

Solution

2. (a)

	Product		
	A	**B**	**C**
Unit contribution margin (a)	$8	$5	$6
Machine hours required (b)	2	1	2
Contribution margin per unit of limited resource (a) ÷ (b)	$4	$5	$3

(b) Product B should be manufactured because it results in the highest contribution margin per machine hour.

(c) (1)

	Product		
	A	**B**	**C**
Machine hours (a) (4,500 ÷ 3)	1,500	1,500	1,500
Contribution margin per unit of limited resource (b)	$ 4	$ 5	$ 3
Total contribution margin [(a)] × [(b)]	$6,000	$7,500	$4,500

The total contribution margin is $18,000 ($6,000 + $7,500 + $4,500).

(2)

	Product B
Machine hours (a)	4,500
Contribution margin per unit of limited resource (b)	$ 5
Total contribution margin [(a) × (b)]	$22,500

Compute degree of operating leverage and evaluate impact of alternative cost structures on net income.

(LO 4)

3. The CVP income statements shown below are available for Vericelli Company and Boone Company.

	Vericelli Co.	Boone Co.
Sales revenue	$600,000	$600,000
Variable costs	320,000	120,000
Contribution margin	280,000	480,000
Fixed costs	180,000	380,000
Net income	$100,000	$100,000

Instructions

(a) Compute the degree of operating leverage for each company and interpret your results.

(b) Assuming that sales revenue increases by 10%, prepare a variable costing income statement for each company.

(c) Discuss how the cost structure of these two companies affects their operating leverage and profitability.

Solution

3. (a)

	Contribution Margin	÷	Net Income	=	Degree of Operating Leverage
Vericelli	$280,000	÷	$100,000	=	2.8
Boone	480,000	÷	100,000	=	4.8

Boone has a higher degree of operating leverage. Its earnings would increase (decrease) by a greater amount than Vericelli if each experienced an equal increase (decrease) in sales.

(b)

	Vericelli Co.	Boone Co.
Sales revenue	$660,000*	$660,000
Variable costs	352,000**	132,000***
Contribution margin	308,000	528,000
Fixed costs	180,000	380,000
Net income	$128,000	$148,000

*$600,000 × 1.1   **$320,000 × 1.1   ***$120,000 × 1.1

(c) Each company experienced a $60,000 increase in sales. However, because of Boone's higher operating leverage, it experienced a $48,000 ($148,000 − $100,000) increase in net income while Vericelli experienced only a $28,000 ($128,000 − $100,000) increase. This is what we would have expected since Boone's degree of operating leverage exceeds that of Vericelli.

PRACTICE PROBLEM

Francis Corporation manufactures and sells three different types of water-sport wake-boards. The boards vary in terms of their quality specifications—primarily with respect to their smoothness and finish. They are referred to as Smooth, Extra-Smooth, and Super-Smooth boards. Machine time is limited. More machine time is required to manufacture the Extra-Smooth and Super-Smooth boards. Additional information is provided below.

Determine sales mix with limited resources.

(LO 3)

	Product		
	Smooth	Extra-Smooth	Super-Smooth
Selling price	$60	$100	$160
Variable costs and expenses	50	75	130
Contribution margin	$10	$ 25	$ 30
Machine hours required	0.25	0.40	0.60

Total fixed costs: $234,000

Instructions

Answer each of the following questions.

(a) Ignoring the machine time constraint, what strategy would appear optimal?
(b) What is the contribution margin per unit of limited resource for each type of board?
(c) If additional machine time could be obtained, how should the additional capacity be used?

Solution

(a) The Super-Smooth boards have the highest unit contribution margin. Thus, ignoring any manufacturing constraints, it would appear that the company should shift toward production of more Super-Smooth units.

(b) The contribution margin per unit of limited resource is calculated as follows.

	Smooth	Extra-Smooth	Super-Smooth
$\dfrac{\text{Unit contribution margin}}{\text{Limited resource consumed per unit}}$	$\dfrac{\$10}{.25} = \$40$	$\dfrac{\$25}{.40} = \$62.50$	$\dfrac{\$30}{.60} = \$50$

(c) The Extra-Smooth boards have the highest contribution margin per unit of limited resource. Given the resource constraint, any additional capacity should be used to make Extra-Smooth boards.

WileyPLUS

Brief Exercises, Exercises, **DO IT!** Exercises, and Problems and many additional resources are available for practice in WileyPLUS

NOTE: All asterisked Questions, Exercises, and Problems relate to material in the appendix to the chapter.

QUESTIONS

1. What is meant by CVP analysis?
2. Provide three examples of management decisions that benefit from CVP analysis.
3. Distinguish between a traditional income statement and a CVP income statement.
4. Describe the features of a CVP income statement that make it more useful for management decision-making than the traditional income statement that is prepared for external users.
5. The traditional income statement for Wheat Company shows sales $900,000, cost of goods sold $500,000, and operating expenses $200,000. Assuming all costs and expenses are 75% variable and 25% fixed, prepare a CVP income statement through contribution margin.
6. If management chooses to reduce its selling price to match that of a competitor, how will the break-even point be affected?
7. What is meant by the term sales mix? How does sales mix affect the calculation of the break-even point?
8. Performance Company sells two types of performance tires. The lower-priced model is guaranteed for only 50,000 miles; the higher-priced model is guaranteed for 150,000 miles. The unit contribution margin on the higher-priced tire is twice as high as that of the lower-priced tire. If the sales mix shifts so that the company begins to sell more units of the lower-priced tire, explain how the company's break-even point in units will change.
9. What approach should be used to calculate the break-even point of a company that has many products?
10. How is the contribution margin per unit of limited resource computed?
11. What is the theory of constraints? Provide some examples of possible constraints for a manufacturer.
12. What is meant by "cost structure?" Explain how a company's cost structure affects its break-even point.
13. What is operating leverage? How does a company increase its operating leverage?
14. How does the replacement of manual labor with automated equipment affect a company's cost structure? What implications does this have for its operating leverage and break-even point?
15. What is a measure of operating leverage, and how is it calculated?
16. Pine Company has a degree of operating leverage of 8. Fir Company has a degree of operating leverage of 4. Interpret these measures.
*17. Distinguish between absorption costing and variable costing.
*18. (a) What is the major rationale for the use of variable costing?
    (b) Discuss why variable costing may not be used for financial reporting purposes.
*19. Doc Rowan Corporation sells one product, its waterproof hiking boot. It began operations in the current year and had an ending inventory of 8,500 units. The company sold 20,000 units throughout the year. Fixed manufacturing overhead is $5 per unit, and total manufacturing cost per unit is $20 (including fixed manufacturing overhead costs). What is the difference in net income between absorption and variable costing?
*20. If production equals sales, what, if any, is the difference between net income under absorption costing versus under variable costing?
*21. If production is greater than sales, how does absorption costing net income differ from variable costing net income?
*22. In the long run, will net income be higher or lower under variable costing compared to absorption costing?

BRIEF EXERCISES

Determine missing amounts for contribution margin.

(LO 1)

BE20-1 Determine the missing amounts.

	Unit Selling Price	Unit Variable Costs	Unit Contribution Margin	Contribution Margin Ratio
1.	$250	$180	(a)	(b)
2.	$500	(c)	$200	(d)
3.	(e)	(f)	$330	30%

Prepare CVP income statement.

(LO 1)

BE20-2 Hamby Inc. has sales of $2,000,000 for the first quarter of 2017. In making the sales, the company incurred the following costs and expenses.

	Variable	Fixed
Cost of goods sold	$760,000	$600,000
Selling expenses	95,000	60,000
Administrative expenses	79,000	66,000

Prepare a CVP income statement for the quarter ended March 31, 2017.

BE20-3 Eastland Corp. had total variable costs of $150,000, total fixed costs of $120,000, and total revenues of $250,000. Compute the required sales in dollars to break even.

Compute the break-even point.
(LO 1)

BE20-4 Dilts Company has a unit selling price of $400, variable costs per unit of $250, and fixed costs of $210,000. Compute the break-even point in units using (a) the mathematical equation and (b) unit contribution margin.

Compute the break-even point.
(LO 1)

BE20-5 For Rivera Company, variable costs are 70% of sales, and fixed costs are $210,000. Management's net income goal is $60,000. Compute the required sales needed to achieve management's target net income of $60,000. (Use the mathematical equation approach.)

Compute sales for target net income.
(LO 1)

BE20-6 For Kosko Company, actual sales are $1,200,000 and break-even sales are $960,000. Compute (a) the margin of safety in dollars and (b) the margin of safety ratio.

Compute the margin of safety and the margin of safety ratio.
(LO 1)

BE20-7 NoFly Corporation sells three different models of a mosquito "zapper." Model A12 sells for $50 and has variable costs of $35. Model B22 sells for $100 and has variable costs of $70. Model C124 sells for $400 and has variable costs of $300. The sales mix of the three models is A12, 60%; B22, 15%; and C124, 25%. What is the weighted-average unit contribution margin?

Compute weighted-average unit contribution margin based on sales mix.
(LO 2)

BE20-8 Information for NoFly Corporation is given in BE20-7. If the company has fixed costs of $269,500, how many units of each model must the company sell in order to break even?

Compute break-even point in units for company with multiple products.
(LO 2)

BE20-9 Dixie Candle Supply makes candles. The sales mix (as a percentage of total dollar sales) of its three product lines is birthday candles 30%, standard tapered candles 50%, and large scented candles 20%. The contribution margin ratio of each candle type is shown below.

Compute break-even point in dollars for company with multiple product lines.
(LO 2)

Candle Type	Contribution Margin Ratio
Birthday	20%
Standard tapered	30%
Large scented	45%

(a) What is the weighted-average contribution margin ratio?
(b) If the company's fixed costs are $450,000 per year, what is the dollar amount of each type of candle that must be sold to break even?

BE20-10 Faune Furniture Co. consists of two divisions, Bedroom Division and Dining Room Division. The results of operations for the most recent quarter are:

Determine weighted-average contribution margin.
(LO 2)

	Bedroom Division	Dining Room Division	Total
Sales	$500,000	$750,000	$1,250,000
Variable costs	225,000	450,000	675,000
Contribution margin	$275,000	$300,000	$ 575,000

(a) Determine the company's sales mix.
(b) Determine the company's weighted-average contribution margin ratio.

BE20-11 In Marshall Company, data concerning two products are unit contribution margin— Product A $10, Product B $12; machine hours required for one unit—Product A 2, Product B 3. Compute the contribution margin per unit of limited resource for each product.

Show allocation of limited resources.
(LO 3)

BE20-12 Sage Corporation manufactures two products with the following characteristics.

Show allocation of limited resources.
(LO 3)

	Unit Contribution Margin	Machine Hours Required for Production
Product 1	$42	.15 hours
Product 2	$32	.10 hours

If Sage's machine hours are limited to 2,000 per month, determine which product it should produce.

Compute degree of operating leverage.

(LO 4)

BE20-13 Sam's Shingle Corporation is considering the purchase of a new automated shingle-cutting machine. The new machine will reduce variable labor costs but will increase depreciation expense. Contribution margin is expected to increase from $200,000 to $240,000. Net income is expected to be the same at $40,000. Compute the degree of operating leverage before and after the purchase of the new equipment. Interpret your results.

Compute break-even point with change in operating leverage.

(LO 4)

BE20-14 Presented below are variable costing income statements for Diggs Company and Doggs Company. They are in the same industry, with the same net incomes, but different cost structures.

	Diggs Co.	Doggs Co.
Sales	$200,000	$200,000
Variable costs	80,000	50,000
Contribution margin	120,000	150,000
Fixed costs	75,000	105,000
Net income	$ 45,000	$ 45,000

Compute the break-even point in dollars for each company and comment on your findings.

Determine contribution margin from degree of operating leverage.

(LO 4)

BE20-15 The degree of operating leverage for Montana Corp. and APK Co. are 1.6 and 5.4, respectively. Both have net incomes of $50,000. Determine their respective contribution margins.

Compute product costs under variable costing.

(LO 5)

*****BE20-16** The Rock Company produces basketballs. It incurred the following costs during the year.

Direct materials	$14,400
Direct labor	$25,600
Fixed manufacturing overhead	$12,000
Variable manufacturing overhead	$29,400
Selling costs	$21,000

What are the total product costs for the company under variable costing?

Compute product costs under absorption costing.

(LO 5)

*****BE20-17** Information concerning The Rock Company is provided in BE20-16. What are the total product costs for the company under absorption costing?

Determine manufacturing cost per unit under absorption and variable costing.

(LO 5)

*****BE20-18** Burns Company incurred the following costs during the year: direct materials $20 per unit; direct labor $14 per unit; variable manufacturing overhead $15 per unit; variable selling and administrative costs $8 per unit; fixed manufacturing overhead $128,000; and fixed selling and administrative costs $10,000. Burns produced 8,000 units and sold 6,000 units. Determine the manufacturing cost per unit under (a) absorption costing and (b) variable costing.

Compute net income under absorption and variable costing.

(LO 5)

*****BE20-19** ——— Harris Company's fixed overhead costs are $4 per unit, and its variable overhead costs are $8 per unit. In the first month of operations, 50,000 units are produced, and 46,000 units are sold. Write a short memo to the chief financial officer explaining which costing approach will produce the higher income and what the difference will be.

DO IT! Exercises

DO IT! 20-1 Victoria Company reports the following operating results for the month of April.

Compute the break-even point and margin of safety under different alternatives.

(LO 1)

VICTORIA COMPANY
CVP Income Statement
For the Month Ended April 30, 2017

	Total	Per Unit
Sales (9,000 units)	$450,000	$50
Variable costs	270,000	30
Contribution margin	180,000	$20
Fixed expenses	150,000	
Net income	$ 30,000	

Management is considering the following course of action to increase net income: Reduce the selling price by 4%, with no changes to unit variable costs or fixed costs. Management is confident that this change will increase unit sales by 20%.

Using the contribution margin technique, compute the break-even point in units and dollars and margin of safety in dollars:

(a) Assuming no changes to selling price or costs, and
(b) Assuming changes to sales price and volume as described above.

Comment on your findings.

DO IT! 20-2 Snow Cap Springs produces and sells water filtration systems for homeowners. Information regarding its three models is shown below.

Compute sales mix, weighted-average contribution margin, and break-even point.

(LO 2)

	Basic	Basic Plus	Premium	Total
Units sold	750	450	300	1,500
Selling price	$250	$400	$800	
Variable costs	$195	$285	$415	

The company's total fixed costs to produce the filtration systems are $180,700.

(a) Determine the sales mix as a function of units sold for the three products.
(b) Determine the weighted-average unit contribution margin.
(c) Determine the total number of units that the company must produce to break even.
(d) Determine the number of units of each model that the company must produce to break even.

DO IT! 20-3 Zoom Corporation manufactures and sells three different types of binoculars. They are referred to as Good, Better, and Best binoculars. Grinding and polishing time is limited. More time is required to grind and polish the lenses used in the Better and Best binoculars. Additional information is provided below.

Determine sales mix with limited resources.

(LO 3)

	Product		
	Good	Better	Best
Selling price	$90.00	$330.00	$900.00
Variable costs and expenses	50.00	180.00	480.00
Contribution margin	$40.00	$150.00	$420.00
Grinding and polishing time required	0.5 hrs	1.5 hrs	6 hrs

(a) Ignoring the time constraint, what strategy would appear to be optimal?
(b) What is the contribution margin per unit of limited resource for each type of binocular?
(c) If additional grinding and polishing time could be obtained, how should the additional capacity be used?

Determine operating leverage.

(LO 4)

DO IT! 20-4 Bergen Hospital is contemplating an investment in an automated surgical system. Its current process relies on the a number of skilled physicians. The new equipment would employ a computer robotic system operated by a technician. The company requested an analysis of the old technology versus the new technology. The accounting department has prepared the following CVP income statements for use in your analysis.

	Old	New
Sales	$3,000,000	$3,000,000
Variable costs	1,600,000	700,000
Contribution margin	1,400,000	2,300,000
Fixed costs	1,000,000	1,900,000
Net income	$ 400,000	$ 400,000

(a) Compute the degree of operating leverage for the company under each scenario.
(b) Discuss your results.

EXERCISES

Compute break-even point and margin of safety.

(LO 1)

E20-1 The Soma Inn is trying to determine its break-even point. The inn has 75 rooms that are rented at $60 a night. Operating costs are as follows.

Salaries	$10,600 per month
Utilities	2,400 per month
Depreciation	1,500 per month
Maintenance	800 per month
Maid service	8 per room
Other costs	34 per room

Instructions
(a) Determine the inn's break-even point in (1) number of rented rooms per month and (2) dollars.
(b) If the inn plans on renting an average of 50 rooms per day (assuming a 30-day month), what is (1) the monthly margin of safety in dollars and (2) the margin of safety ratio?

Compute contribution margin, break-even point, and margin of safety.

(LO 1)

E20-2 In the month of June, Jose Hebert's Beauty Salon gave 4,000 haircuts, shampoos, and permanents at an average price of $30. During the month, fixed costs were $16,800 and variable costs were 75% of sales.

Instructions
(a) Determine the contribution margin in dollars, per unit and as a ratio.
(b) Using the contribution margin technique, compute the break-even point in dollars and in units.
(c) Compute the margin of safety in dollars and as a ratio.

Compute net income under different alternatives.

(LO 1)

E20-3 Barnes Company reports the following operating results for the month of August: sales $325,000 (units 5,000); variable costs $210,000; and fixed costs $75,000. Management is considering the following independent courses of action to increase net income.

1. Increase selling price by 10% with no change in total variable costs or sales volume.
2. Reduce variable costs to 58% of sales.
3. Reduce fixed costs by $15,000.

Instructions
Compute the net income to be earned under each alternative. Which course of action will produce the highest net income?

E20-4 Comfi Airways, Inc., a small two-plane passenger airline, has asked for your assistance in some basic analysis of its operations. Both planes seat 10 passengers each, and they fly commuters from Comfi's base airport to the major city in the state, Metropolis. Each month, 40 round-trip flights are made. Shown below is a recent month's activity in the form of a cost-volume-profit income statement.

Compute break-even point and prepare CVP income statement.

(LO 1)

Fare revenues (400 passenger flights)		$48,000
Variable costs		
Fuel	$14,000	
Snacks and drinks	800	
Landing fees	2,000	
Supplies and forms	1,200	18,000
Contribution margin		30,000
Fixed costs		
Depreciation	3,000	
Salaries	15,000	
Advertising	500	
Airport hangar fees	1,750	20,250
Net income		$ 9,750

Instructions
(a) Calculate the break-even point in (1) dollars and (2) number of passenger flights.
(b) Without calculations, determine the contribution margin at the break-even point.
(c) If ticket prices were decreased by 10%, passenger flights would increase by 25%. However, total variable costs would increase by the same percentage as passenger flights. Should the ticket price decrease be adopted?

E20-5 Carey Company had sales in 2016 of $1,560,000 on 60,000 units. Variable costs totaled $900,000, and fixed costs totaled $500,000.

A new raw material is available that will decrease the variable costs per unit by 20% (or $3). However, to process the new raw material, fixed operating costs will increase by $100,000. Management feels that one-half of the decline in the variable costs per unit should be passed on to customers in the form of a sales price reduction. The marketing department expects that this sales price reduction will result in a 5% increase in the number of units sold.

Prepare a CVP income statement before and after changes in business environment.

(LO 1)

Instructions
Prepare a projected CVP income statement for 2017 (a) assuming the changes have not been made, and (b) assuming that changes are made as described.

E20-6 Yard Tools manufactures lawnmowers, weed-trimmers, and chainsaws. Its sales mix and unit contribution margin are as follows.

Compute break-even point in units for a company with more than one product.

(LO 2)

	Sales Mix	Unit Contribution Margin
Lawnmowers	20%	$30
Weed-trimmers	50%	$20
Chainsaws	30%	$40

Yard Tools has fixed costs of $4,200,000.

Instructions
Compute the number of units of each product that Yard Tools must sell in order to break even under this product mix.

E20-7 PDQ Repairs has 200 auto-maintenance service outlets nationwide. It performs primarily two lines of service: oil changes and brake repair. Oil change–related services represent 70% of its sales and provide a contribution margin ratio of 20%. Brake repair represents 30% of its sales and provides a 40% contribution margin ratio. The company's fixed costs are $15,600,000 (that is, $78,000 per service outlet).

Compute service line break-even point and target net income in dollars for a company with more than one service.

(LO 2)

Instructions
(a) Calculate the dollar amount of each type of service that the company must provide in order to break even.

(b) The company has a desired net income of $52,000 per service outlet. What is the dollar amount of each type of service that must be performed by each service outlet to meet its target net income per outlet?

Compute break-even point in dollars for a company with more than one service.

(LO 2)

E20-8 Express Delivery is a rapidly growing delivery service. Last year, 80% of its revenue came from the delivery of mailing "pouches" and small, standardized delivery boxes (which provides a 20% contribution margin). The other 20% of its revenue came from delivering non-standardized boxes (which provides a 70% contribution margin). With the rapid growth of Internet retail sales, Express believes that there are great opportunities for growth in the delivery of non-standardized boxes. The company has fixed costs of $12,000,000.

Instructions
(a) What is the company's break-even point in total sales dollars? At the break-even point, how much of the company's sales are provided by each type of service?
(b) The company's management would like to hold its fixed costs constant but shift its sales mix so that 60% of its revenue comes from the delivery of non-standardized boxes and the remainder from pouches and small boxes. If this were to occur, what would be the company's break-even sales, and what amount of sales would be provided by each service type?

Compute break-even point in units for a company with multiple products.

(LO 2)

E20-9 Tiger Golf Accessories sells golf shoes, gloves, and a laser-guided range-finder that measures distance. Shown below are unit cost and sales data.

	Pairs of Shoes	Pairs of Gloves	Range-Finder
Unit sales price	$100	$30	$260
Unit variable costs	60	10	200
Unit contribution margin	$ 40	$20	$ 60
Sales mix	35%	55%	10%

Fixed costs are $620,000.

Instructions
(a) Compute the break-even point in units for the company.
(b) Determine the number of units to be sold at the break-even point for each product line.
(c) Verify that the mix of sales units determined in (b) will generate a zero net income.

Determine break-even point in dollars for two divisions.

(LO 2)

E20-10 Personal Electronix sells iPads and iPods. The business is divided into two divisions along product lines. CVP income statements for a recent quarter's activity are presented below.

	iPad Division	iPod Division	Total
Sales	$600,000	$400,000	$1,000,000
Variable costs	420,000	260,000	680,000
Contribution margin	$180,000	$140,000	320,000
Fixed costs			120,000
Net income			$ 200,000

Instructions
(a) Determine sales mix percentage and contribution margin ratio for each division.
(b) Calculate the company's weighted-average contribution margin ratio.
(c) Calculate the company's break-even point in dollars.
(d) Determine the sales level in dollars for each division at the break-even point.

Compute contribution margin and determine the product to be manufactured.

(LO 3)

E20-11 Mars Company manufactures and sells three products. Relevant per unit data concerning each product are given below.

	Product		
	A	B	C
Selling price	$9	$12	$15
Variable costs and expenses	$3	$10	$12
Machine hours to produce	2	1	2

Instructions

(a) Compute the contribution margin per unit of limited resource (machine hours) for each product.

(b) Assuming 3,000 additional machine hours are available, which product should be manufactured?

(c) Prepare an analysis showing the total contribution margin if the additional hours are (1) divided equally among the products, and (2) allocated entirely to the product identified in (b) above.

E20-12 Dalton Inc. produces and sells three products. Unit data concerning each product is shown below.

	Product		
	D	**E**	**F**
Selling price	$200	$300	$250
Direct labor costs	30	80	35
Other variable costs	95	80	145

Compute contribution margin and determine the products to be manufactured.

(LO 3)

The company has 2,000 hours of labor available to build inventory in anticipation of the company's peak season. Management is trying to decide which product should be produced. The direct labor hourly rate is $10.

Instructions

(a) Determine the number of direct labor hours per unit.

(b) Determine the contribution margin per direct labor hour.

(c) Determine which product should be produced and the total contribution margin for that product.

E20-13 Helena Company manufactures and sells two products. Relevant per unit data concerning each product follow.

	Product	
	Basic	**Deluxe**
Selling price	$40	$52
Variable costs	$22	$24
Machine hours	0.5	0.8

Compute contribution margin and determine the products to be manufactured.

(LO 3)

Instructions

(a) Compute the contribution margin per machine hour for each product.

(b) If 1,000 additional machine hours are available, which product should Helena manufacture?

(c) Prepare an analysis showing the total contribution margin if the additional hours are:

(1) Divided equally between the products.

(2) Allocated entirely to the product identified in part (b).

E20-14 The CVP income statements shown below are available for Armstrong Company and Contador Company.

	Armstrong Co.	**Contador Co.**
Sales	$500,000	$500,000
Variable costs	240,000	50,000
Contribution margin	260,000	450,000
Fixed costs	160,000	350,000
Net income	$100,000	$100,000

Compute degree of operating leverage and evaluate impact of alternative cost structures on net income.

(LO 4)

Instructions

(a) Compute the degree of operating leverage for each company and interpret your results.

(b) Assuming that sales revenue increases by 10%, prepare a variable costing income statement for each company.

(c) Discuss how the cost structure of these two companies affects their operating leverage and profitability.

Compute degree of operating leverage and evaluate impact of alternative cost structures on net income and margin of safety.

(LO 4)

E20-15 Casas Modernas of Juarez, Mexico, is contemplating a major change in its cost structure. Currently, all of its drafting work is performed by skilled draftsmen. Rafael Jiminez, Casas' owner, is considering replacing the draftsmen with a computerized drafting system. However, before making the change, Rafael would like to know the consequences of the change, since the volume of business varies significantly from year to year. Shown below are CVP income statements for each alternative.

	Manual System	Computerized System
Sales	$1,500,000	$1,500,000
Variable costs	1,200,000	600,000
Contribution margin	300,000	900,000
Fixed costs	100,000	700,000
Net income	$ 200,000	$ 200,000

Instructions
(a) Determine the degree of operating leverage for each alternative.
(b) Which alternative would produce the higher net income if sales increased by $150,000?
(c) Using the margin of safety ratio, determine which alternative could sustain the greater decline in sales before operating at a loss.

Compute degree of operating leverage and impact on net income of alternative cost structures.

(LO 4)

E20-16 An investment banker is analyzing two companies that specialize in the production and sale of candied yams. Traditional Yams uses a labor-intensive approach, and Auto-Yams uses a mechanized system. CVP income statements for the two companies are shown below.

	Traditional Yams	Auto-Yams
Sales	$400,000	$400,000
Variable costs	320,000	160,000
Contribution margin	80,000	240,000
Fixed costs	30,000	190,000
Net income	$ 50,000	$ 50,000

The investment banker is interested in acquiring one of these companies. However, she is concerned about the impact that each company's cost structure might have on its profitability.

Instructions
(a) Calculate each company's degree of operating leverage. Determine which company's cost structure makes it more sensitive to changes in sales volume.
(b) Determine the effect on each company's net income if sales decrease by 15% and if sales increase by 10%. Do not prepare income statements.
(c) Which company should the investment banker acquire? Discuss.

Compute product cost and prepare an income statement under variable and absorption costing.

(LO 5)

*E20-17 Siren Company builds custom fishing lures for sporting goods stores. In its first year of operations, 2017, the company incurred the following costs.

Variable Costs per Unit	
Direct materials	$7.50
Direct labor	$3.45
Variable manufacturing overhead	$5.80
Variable selling and administrative expenses	$3.90

Fixed Costs per Year	
Fixed manufacturing overhead	$225,000
Fixed selling and administrative expenses	$210,100

Siren Company sells the fishing lures for $25. During 2017, the company sold 80,000 lures and produced 90,000 lures.

Instructions

(a) Assuming the company uses variable costing, calculate Siren's manufacturing cost per unit for 2017.
(b) Prepare a variable costing income statement for 2017.
(c) Assuming the company uses absorption costing, calculate Siren's manufacturing cost per unit for 2017.
(d) Prepare an absorption costing income statement for 2017.

*E20-18 Langdon Company produced 9,000 units during the past year, but only 8,200 of the units were sold. The following additional information is also available.

Determine ending inventory under variable costing and determine whether absorption or variable costing would result in higher net income.

(LO 5)

Direct materials used	$79,000
Direct labor incurred	$30,000
Variable manufacturing overhead	$21,500
Fixed manufacturing overhead	$45,000
Fixed selling and administrative expenses	$70,000
Variable selling and administrative expenses	$10,000

There was no work in process inventory at the beginning and end of the year, nor did Langdon have any beginning finished goods inventory.

Instructions

(a) What would be Langdon Company's finished goods inventory cost on December 31 under variable costing?
(b) Which costing method, absorption or variable costing, would show a higher net income for the year? By what amount?

*E20-19 Crate Express Co. produces wooden crates used for shipping products by ocean liner. In 2017, Crate Express incurred the following costs.

Compute manufacturing cost under absorption and variable costing and explain difference.

(LO 5)

Wood used in crate production	$54,000
Nails (considered insignificant and a variable expense)	$ 350
Direct labor	$43,000
Utilities for the plant:	
$1,500 each month,	
plus $0.50 for each kilowatt-hour used each month	
Rent expense for the plant for the year	$21,400

Assume Crate Express used an average 500 kilowatt-hours each month over the past year.

Instructions

(a) What is Crate Express's total manufacturing cost if it uses a variable costing approach?
(b) What is Crate Express's total manufacturing cost if it uses an absorption costing approach?
(c) What accounts for the difference in manufacturing costs between these two costing approaches?

▌EXERCISES: SET B AND CHALLENGE EXERCISES

Visit the book's companion website, at **www.wiley.com/college/weygandt**, and choose the Student Companion site to access Exercises: Set B and Challenge Exercises.

PROBLEMS: SET A

Compute break-even point under alternative courses of action.

(LO 1)

P20-1A Midlands Inc. had a bad year in 2016. For the first time in its history, it operated at a loss. The company's income statement showed the following results from selling 80,000 units of product: net sales $2,000,000; total costs and expenses $2,235,000; and net loss $235,000. Costs and expenses consisted of the following.

	Total	Variable	Fixed
Cost of goods sold	$1,568,000	$1,050,000	$ 518,000
Selling expenses	517,000	92,000	425,000
Administrative expenses	150,000	58,000	92,000
	$2,235,000	$1,200,000	$1,035,000

Management is considering the following independent alternatives for 2017.

1. Increase unit selling price 25% with no change in costs and expenses.
2. Change the compensation of salespersons from fixed annual salaries totaling $200,000 to total salaries of $40,000 plus a 5% commission on net sales.
3. Purchase new high-tech factory machinery that will change the proportion between variable and fixed cost of goods sold to 50:50.

Instructions

(a) Compute the break-even point in dollars for 2017.

(b) (2) $2,500,000

(b) Compute the break-even point in dollars under each of the alternative courses of action. (Round to the nearest dollar.) Which course of action do you recommend?

Compute break-even point and margin of safety ratio, and prepare a CVP income statement before and after changes in business environment.

(LO 1)

P20-2A Lorge Corporation has collected the following information after its first year of sales. Sales were $1,500,000 on 100,000 units; selling expenses $250,000 (40% variable and 60% fixed); direct materials $511,000; direct labor $290,000; administrative expenses $270,000 (20% variable and 80% fixed); and manufacturing overhead $350,000 (70% variable and 30% fixed). Top management has asked you to do a CVP analysis so that it can make plans for the coming year. It has projected that unit sales will increase by 10% next year.

Instructions

(a) Compute (1) the contribution margin for the current year and the projected year, and (2) the fixed costs for the current year. (Assume that fixed costs will remain the same in the projected year.)

(b) 157,000 units

(b) Compute the break-even point in units and sales dollars for the first year.

(c) The company has a target net income of $200,000. What is the required sales in dollars for the company to meet its target?

(d) If the company meets its target net income number, by what percentage could its sales fall before it is operating at a loss? That is, what is its margin of safety ratio?

(e) (3) $1,735,714

(e) The company is considering a purchase of equipment that would reduce its direct labor costs by $104,000 and would change its manufacturing overhead costs to 30% variable and 70% fixed (assume total manufacturing overhead cost is $350,000, as above). It is also considering switching to a pure commission basis for its sales staff. This would change selling expenses to 90% variable and 10% fixed (assume total selling expense is $250,000, as above). Compute (1) the contribution margin and (2) the contribution margin ratio, and recompute (3) the break-even point in sales dollars. Comment on the effect each of management's proposed changes has on the break-even point.

Determine break-even sales under alternative sales strategies and evaluate results.

(LO 2)

P20-3A The Grand Inn is a restaurant in Flagstaff, Arizona. It specializes in southwestern style meals in a moderate price range. Paul Weld, the manager of Grand, has determined that during the last 2 years the sales mix and contribution margin ratio of its offerings are as follows.

	Percent of Total Sales	Contribution Margin Ratio
Appetizers	15%	50%
Main entrees	50%	25%
Desserts	10%	50%
Beverages	25%	80%

Paul is considering a variety of options to try to improve the profitability of the restaurant. His goal is to generate a target net income of $117,000. The company has fixed costs of $1,053,000 per year.

Instructions

(a) Calculate the total restaurant sales and the sales of each product line that would be necessary to achieve the desired target net income.

(b) Paul believes the restaurant could greatly improve its profitability by reducing the complexity and selling price of its entrees to increase the number of clients that it serves. It would then more heavily market its appetizers and beverages. He is proposing to reduce the contribution margin ratio on the main entrees to 10% by dropping the average selling price. He envisions an expansion of the restaurant that would increase fixed costs by $585,000. At the same time, he is proposing to change the sales mix to the following.

(a) Total sales $2,600,000

(b) Total sales $3,375,000

	Percent of Total Sales	Contribution Margin Ratio
Appetizers	25%	50%
Main entrees	25%	10%
Desserts	10%	50%
Beverages	40%	80%

Compute the total restaurant sales, and the sales of each product line that would be necessary to achieve the desired target net income.

(c) Suppose that Paul reduces the selling price on entrees and increases fixed costs as proposed in part (b), but customers are not swayed by the marketing efforts and the sales mix remains what it was in part (a). Compute the total restaurant sales and the sales of each product line that would be necessary to achieve the desired target net income. Comment on the potential risks and benefits of this strategy.

P20-4A Tanek Industries manufactures and sells three different models of wet-dry shop vacuum cleaners. Although the shop vacs vary in terms of quality and features, all are good sellers. Tanek is currently operating at full capacity with limited machine time. Sales and production information relevant to each model follows.

Determine sales mix with limited resources.

(LO 3)

	Product		
	Economy	Standard	Deluxe
Selling price	$30	$50	$100
Variable costs and expenses	$16	$20	$46
Machine hours required	0.5	0.8	1.6

Instructions

(a) Ignoring the machine time constraint, which single product should Tanek Industries produce?

(b) What is the contribution margin per unit of limited resource for each product?

(c) If additional machine time could be obtained, how should the additional time be used?

(b) Economy $28

P20-5A The following CVP income statements are available for Blanc Company and Noir Company.

Compute degree of operating leverage and evaluate impact of operating leverage on financial results.

(LO 4)

	Blanc Company	Noir Company
Sales	$500,000	$500,000
Variable costs	280,000	180,000
Contribution margin	220,000	320,000
Fixed costs	170,000	270,000
Net income	$ 50,000	$ 50,000

Instructions

(a) Compute the break-even point in dollars and the margin of safety ratio (round to 3 places) for each company.

(b) Compute the degree of operating leverage for each company and interpret your results.

(c) Assuming that sales revenue increases by 20%, prepare a CVP income statement for each company.

(a) BE, Blanc $386,364
    BE, Noir $421,875

(b) DOL, Blanc 4.4
    DOL, Noir 6.4

(d) Assuming that sales revenue decreases by 20%, prepare a CVP income statement for each company.
(e) ⚬━━━━ Discuss how the cost structure of these two companies affects their operating leverage and profitability.

Determine contribution margin, break-even point, target sales, and degree of operating leverage.

(LO 1, 4)

P20-6A Bonita Beauty Corporation manufactures cosmetic products that are sold through a network of sales agents. The agents are paid a commission of 18% of sales. The income statement for the year ending December 31, 2017, is as follows.

BONITA BEAUTY CORPORATION
Income Statement
For the Year Ended December 31, 2017

Sales		$75,000,000
Cost of goods sold		
Variable	$31,500,000	
Fixed	8,610,000	40,110,000
Gross margin		34,890,000
Selling and marketing expenses		
Commissions	13,500,000	
Fixed costs	10,260,000	23,760,000
Operating income		$11,130,000

The company is considering hiring its own sales staff to replace the network of agents. It will pay its salespeople a commission of 8% and incur additional fixed costs of $7.5 million.

Instructions

(a) $47,175

(a) Under the current policy of using a network of sales agents, calculate the Bonita Beauty Corporation's break-even point in sales dollars for the year 2017.
(b) Calculate the company's break-even point in sales dollars for the year 2017 if it hires its own sales force to replace the network of agents.

(c) (2) 3.37

(c) Calculate the degree of operating leverage at sales of $75 million if (1) Bonita Beauty uses sales agents, and (2) Bonita Beauty employs its own sales staff. Describe the advantages and disadvantages of each alternative.
(d) Calculate the estimated sales volume in sales dollars that would generate an identical net income for the year ending December 31, 2017, regardless of whether Bonita Beauty Corporation employs its own sales staff and pays them an 8% commission or continues to use the independent network of agents.

(CMA-Canada adapted)

Prepare income statements under absorption costing and variable costing for a company with beginning inventory, and reconcile differences.

(LO 5)

***P20-7A** Jackson Company produces plastic that is used for injection-molding applications such as gears for small motors. In 2016, the first year of operations, Jackson produced 4,000 tons of plastic and sold 3,500 tons. In 2017, the production and sales results were exactly reversed. In each year, the selling price per ton was $2,000, variable manufacturing costs were 15% of the sales price of units produced, variable selling expenses were 10% of the selling price of units sold, fixed manufacturing costs were $2,800,000, and fixed administrative expenses were $500,000.

Instructions

(a) 2017 $2,700,000

(a) Prepare income statements for each year using variable costing. (Use the format from Illustration 20A-5.)

(b) 2017 $2,350,000

(b) Prepare income statements for each year using absorption costing. (Use the format from Illustration 20A-4.)
(c) Reconcile the differences each year in net income under the two costing approaches.
(d) ⚬━━━━ Comment on the effects of production and sales on net income under the two costing approaches.

*P20-8A Dilithium Batteries is a division of Enterprise Corporation. The division manu-
factures and sells a long-life battery used in a wide variety of applications. During the
coming year, it expects to sell 60,000 units for $30 per unit. Nyota Uthura is the division
manager. She is considering producing either 60,000 or 90,000 units during the period.
Other information is presented in the schedule.

*Prepare absorption and
variable costing income
statements and reconcile
differences between
absorption and variable
costing income statements
when sales level and
production level change.
Discuss relative usefulness
of absorption costing versus
variable costing.*

(LO 5)

Division Information for 2017

Beginning inventory	0
Expected sales in units	60,000
Selling price per unit	$30
Variable manufacturing costs per unit	$12
Fixed manufacturing overhead costs (total)	$540,000
Fixed manufacturing overhead costs per unit:	
Based on 60,000 units	$9 per unit ($540,000 ÷ 60,000)
Based on 90,000 units	$6 per unit ($540,000 ÷ 90,000)
Manufacturing costs per unit:	
Based on 60,000 units	$21 per unit ($12 variable + $9 fixed)
Based on 90,000 units	$18 per unit ($12 variable + $6 fixed)
Variable selling and administrative expenses	$2
Fixed selling and administrative expenses (total)	$50,000

Instructions

(a) Prepare an absorption costing income statement, with one column showing the results
if 60,000 units are produced and one column showing the results if 90,000 units are
produced.

(b) Prepare a variable costing income statement, with one column showing the results
if 60,000 units are produced and one column showing the results if 90,000 units are
produced.

(c) Reconcile the difference in net incomes under the two approaches and explain what
accounts for this difference.

(d) ✏——— Discuss the relative usefulness of the variable costing income statements
versus the absorption costing income statements for decision making and for evaluating the manager's performance.

(a) 90,000 units: NI $550,000

(b) 90,000 units: NI $370,000

PROBLEMS: SET B AND SET C

Visit the book's companion website, at **www.wiley.com/college/weygandt**, and choose the
Student Companion site to access Problems: Set B and Set C.

CONTINUING PROBLEMS

CURRENT DESIGNS

CD20 Current Designs manufactures two different types of kayaks, rotomolded kayaks and composite kayaks. The following information is available for each product line.

	Rotomolded	Composite
Sales price/unit	$950	$2,000
Variable costs/unit	$570	$1,340

The company's fixed costs are $820,000. An analysis of the sales mix identifies that rotomolded kayaks
make up 80% of the total units sold.

Instructions

(a) Determine the weighted-average unit contribution margin for Current Designs.

(b) Determine the break-even point in units for Current Designs and identify how many units of each
type of kayak will be sold at the break-even point. (Round to the nearest whole number.)

(c) Assume that the sales mix changes, and rotomolded kayaks now make up 70% of total units sold.
Calculate the total number of units that would need to be sold to earn a net income of $2,000,000

and identify how many units of each type of kayak will be sold at this level of income. (Round to the nearest whole number.)

(d) Assume that Current Designs will have sales of $3,000,000 with two-thirds of the sales dollars in rotomolded kayaks and one-third of the sales dollars in composite kayaks. Assuming $660,000 of fixed costs are allocated to the rotomolded kayaks and $160,000 to the composite kayaks, prepare a CVP income statement for each product line.

(e) Using the information in part (d), calculate the degree of operating leverage for each product line and interpret your findings. (Round to two decimal places.)

WATERWAYS

(*Note:* This is a continuation of the Waterways problem from Chapters 15–19.)

WP20 This problem asks you to perform break-even analysis based on Waterways' sales mix and to make sales mix decisions related to Waterways' use of its productive facilities. An optional extension of the problem (related to the chapter appendix) also asks you to prepare a variable costing income statement and an absorption costing income statement.

Go to the book's companion website, **www.wiley.com/college/weygandt**, *to find the remainder of this problem.*

BROADENING YOUR *PERSPECTIVE*

MANAGEMENT DECISION-MAKING

Decision-Making Across the Organization

 **BYP20-1** E-Z Seats manufactures swivel seats for customized vans. It currently manufactures 10,000 seats per year, which it sells for $500 per seat. It incurs variable costs of $200 per seat and fixed costs of $2,000,000. It is considering automating the upholstery process, which is now largely manual. It estimates that if it does so, its fixed costs will be $3,000,000, and its variable costs will decline to $100 per seat.

Instructions
With the class divided into groups, answer the following questions.

(a) Prepare a CVP income statement based on current activity.

(b) Compute contribution margin ratio, break-even point in dollars, margin of safety ratio, and degree of operating leverage based on current activity.

(c) Prepare a CVP income statement assuming that the company invests in the automated upholstery system.

(d) Compute contribution margin ratio, break-even point in dollars, margin of safety ratio, and degree of operating leverage assuming the new upholstery system is implemented.

(e) Discuss the implications of adopting the new system.

Managerial Analysis

BYP20-2 For nearly 20 years, Specialized Coatings has provided painting and galvanizing services for manufacturers in its region. Manufacturers of various metal products have relied on the quality and quick turnaround time provided by Specialized Coatings and its 20 skilled employees. During the last year, as a result of a sharp upturn in the economy, the company's sales have increased by 30% relative to the previous year. The company has not been able to increase its capacity fast enough, so Specialized Coatings has had to turn work away because it cannot keep up with customer requests.

Top management is considering the purchase of a sophisticated robotic painting booth. The booth would represent a considerable move in the direction of automation versus manual labor. If Specialized Coatings purchases the booth, it would most likely lay off 15 of its skilled painters. To analyze the decision, the company compiled production information from the most recent year and then prepared a parallel compilation assuming that the company would purchase the new equipment and lay off the workers. As shown in the following data, the company projects that during the last year it would have been far more profitable if it had used the automated approach.

	Current Approach	Automated Approach
Sales	$2,000,000	$2,000,000
Variable costs	1,500,000	1,000,000
Contribution margin	500,000	1,000,000
Fixed costs	380,000	800,000
Net income	$ 120,000	$ 200,000

Instructions
(a) Compute and interpret the contribution margin ratio under each approach.
(b) Compute the break-even point in sales dollars under each approach. Discuss the implications of your findings.
(c) Using the current level of sales, compute the margin of safety ratio under each approach and interpret your findings.
(d) Determine the degree of operating leverage for each approach at current sales levels. How much would the company's net income decline under each approach with a 10% decline in sales?
(e) At what level of sales would the company's net income be the same under either approach?
(f) Discuss the issues that the company must consider in making this decision.

Real-World Focus

BYP20-3 In a recent report, the Del Monte Foods Company reported three separate operating segments: consumer products (which includes a variety of canned foods including tuna, fruit, and vegetables); pet products (which includes pet food and snacks and veterinary products); and soup and infant-feeding products (which includes soup, broth, and infant feeding and pureed products).

In its annual report, Del Monte uses absorption costing. As a result, information regarding the relative composition of its fixed and variable costs is not available. We have assumed that $860.3 million of its total operating expenses of $1,920.3 million are fixed and have allocated the remaining variable costs across the three divisions. Sales data, along with assumed expense data, are provided below.

	(in millions)	
	Sales	Variable Costs
Consumer products	$1,031.8	$ 610
Pet products	837.3	350
Soup and infant-feeding products	302.0	100
	$2,171.1	$1,060

Instructions
(a) Compute each segment's contribution margin ratio and the sales mix.
(b) Using the information computed in part (a), compute the company's break-even point in dollars, and then determine the amount of sales that would be generated by each division at the break-even point.

BYP20-4 The external financial statements published by publicly traded companies are based on absorption cost accounting. As a consequence, it is very difficult to gain an understanding of the relative composition of the companies' fixed and variable costs. It is possible, however, to learn about a company's sales mix and the relative profitability of its various divisions. This exercise looks at the financial statements of FedEx Corporation.

Address: www.fedex.com/us/investorrelations, or go to www.wiley.com/college/weygandt

Steps
1. Go to the site above.
2. Under "Financial Information," choose "Annual Reports."
3. Choose "2013 Annual Report."

Instructions
(a) Read page 9 of the report under the heading "Description of Business." What are the three primary product lines of the company? What does the company identify as the key factors affecting operating results?

(b) Page 21 of the report lists the operating expenses of FedEx Ground. Assuming that rentals, depreciation, and "other" are all fixed costs, prepare a variable costing income statement for 2013, and compute the division's contribution margin ratio and the break-even point in dollars.

(c) Page 61, Note 14 ("Business segment information") provides additional information regarding the relative profitability of the business segments.

 (i) Calculate the sales mix for 2011 and 2013. (*Note:* Exclude "other" when you calculate total revenue.)

 (ii) The company does not provide the contribution margin for each division, but it does provide "operating margin" (operating income divided by revenues) on pages 21, 22, and 23 for three divisions. List these for each division for 2011 and 2013.

 (iii) Assuming that the "operating margin" (operating income divided by revenues) moves in parallel with each division's contribution margin, how has the shift in sales mix affected the company's profitability from 2011 to 2013?

BYP20-5 The June 8, 2009, edition of the *Wall Street Journal* has an article by JoAnn Lublin entitled "Smart Balance Keeps Tight Focus on Creativity."

Instructions
Read the article and answer the following questions.

(a) Describe Smart Balance's approach to employment and cost structure.
(b) What function does it keep "in-house"?
(c) Based on the discussion in this chapter, what are the advantages to Smart Balance's approach?
(d) Based on the discussion in this chapter, what are the disadvantages to Smart Balance's approach?

CRITICAL THINKING

Communication Activity

BYP20-6 Easton Corporation makes two different boat anchors—a traditional fishing anchor and a high-end yacht anchor—using the same production machinery. The contribution margin of the yacht anchor is three times as high as that of the other product. The company is currently operating at full capacity and has been doing so for nearly two years. Bjorn Borg, the company's CEO, wants to cut back on production of the fishing anchor so that the company can make more yacht anchors. He says that this is a "no-brainer" because the contribution margin of the yacht anchor is so much higher.

Instructions
Write a short memo to Bjorn Borg describing the analysis that the company should do before it makes this decision and any other considerations that would affect the decision.

Ethics Case

*BYP20-7 Brett Stern was hired during January 2017 to manage the home products division of Hi-Tech Products. As part of his employment contract, he was told that he would get $5,000 of additional bonus for every 1% increase that the division's profits exceeded those of the previous year.

Soon after coming on board, Brett met with his plant managers and explained that he wanted the plants to be run at full capacity. Previously, the plant had employed just-in-time inventory practices and had consequently produced units only as they were needed. Brett stated that under previous management the company had missed out on too many sales opportunities because it didn't have enough inventory on hand. Because previous management had employed just-in-time inventory practices, when Brett came on board there was virtually no beginning inventory. The selling price and variable costs per unit remained the same from 2016 to 2017. Additional information is provided below.

	2016	2017
Net income	$ 300,000	$ 525,000
Units produced	25,000	30,000
Units sold	25,000	25,000
Fixed manufacturing overhead costs	$1,350,000	$1,350,000
Fixed manufacturing overhead costs per unit	$ 54	$ 45

Instructions
(a) Calculate Brett's bonus based upon the net income shown above.
(b) Recompute the 2016 and 2017 results using variable costing.
(c) Recompute Brett's 2017 bonus under variable costing.
(d) Were Brett's actions unethical? Do you think any actions need to be taken by the company?

All About You

BYP20-8 Many of you will some day own your own business. One rapidly growing opportunity is no-frills workout centers. Such centers attract customers who want to take advantage of state-of-the-art fitness equipment but do not need the other amenities of full-service health clubs. One way to own your own fitness business is to buy a franchise. **Snap Fitness** is a Minnesota-based business that offers franchise opportunities. For a very low monthly fee ($26, without an annual contract), customers can access a Snap Fitness center 24 hours a day.

The Snap Fitness website (*www.snapfitness.com*) indicates that start-up costs range from $60,000 to $184,000. This initial investment covers the following pre-opening costs: franchise fee, grand opening marketing, leasehold improvements, utility/rent deposits, and training.

Instructions
(a) Suppose that Snap Fitness estimates that each location incurs $4,000 per month in fixed operating expenses plus $1,460 to lease equipment. A recent newspaper article describing no-frills fitness centers indicated that a Snap Fitness site might require only 300 members to break even. Using the information provided above and your knowledge of CVP analysis, estimate the amount of variable costs. (When performing your analysis, assume that the only fixed costs are the estimated monthly operating expenses and the equipment lease.)
(b) Using the information from part (a), what would monthly sales in members and dollars have to be to achieve a target net income of $3,640 for the month?
(c) Provide five examples of variable costs for a fitness center.
(d) Go to a fitness-business website, such as **Curves**, **Snap Fitness**, or **Anytime Fitness**, and find information about purchasing a franchise. Summarize the franchise information needed to decide whether entering into a franchise agreement would be a good idea.

Considering People, Planet, and Profit

BYP20-9 Many politicians, scientists, economists, and businesspeople have become concerned about the potential implications of global warming. The largest source of the emissions thought to contribute to global warming is from coal-fired power plants. The cost of alternative energy has declined, but it is still higher than coal. In 1980, wind-power electricity cost 80 cents per kilowatt hour. Using today's highly efficient turbines with rotor diameters of up to 125 meters, the cost can be as low as 4 cents (about the same as coal), or as much as 20 cents in places with less wind.

Some people have recently suggested that conventional cost comparisons are not adequate because they do not take environmental costs into account. For example, while coal is a very cheap energy source, it is also a significant contributor of greenhouse gases. Should environmental costs be incorporated into decision formulas when planners evaluate new power plants? The basic arguments for and against are as follows.

YES: As long as environmental costs are ignored, renewable energy will appear to be too expensive relative to coal.

NO: If one country decides to incorporate environmental costs into its decision-making process but other countries do not, the country that does so will be at a competitive disadvantage because its products will cost more to produce.

Instructions
Write a response indicating your position regarding this situation. Provide support for your view.

21 Incremental Analysis

CHAPTER PREVIEW An important purpose of management accounting is to provide managers with relevant information for decision-making. Companies of all sorts must make product decisions. Oral-B Laboratories opted to produce a new, higher-priced toothbrush. General Motors announced the closure of its Oldsmobile Division. Quaker Oats decided to sell off a line of beverages, at a price more than $1 billion less than it paid for that product line only a few years before.

This chapter explains management's decision-making process and a decision-making approach called incremental analysis. The use of incremental analysis is demonstrated in a variety of situations.

FEATURE STORY

Keeping It Clean

When you think of new, fast-growing, San Francisco companies, you probably think of fun products like smartphones, social networks, and game apps. You don't tend to think of soap. In fact, given that some of the biggest, most powerful companies in the world dominate the soap market (e.g., Proctor & Gamble, Clorox, and Unilever), starting a new soap company seems like an outrageously bad idea. But that didn't dissuade Adam Lowry and Eric Ryan from giving it a try. The long-time friends and former roommates combined their skills (Adam's chemical engineering and Eric's design and marketing) to start Method Products. Their goal: selling environmentally friendly soaps that actually remove dirt.

Within a year of its formation, the company had products on the shelves at Target stores. Within 5 years, Method was cited by numerous business publications as one of the fastest-growing companies in the country. It was easy—right? Wrong. Running a company is never easy, and given Method's commitment to sustainability, all of its business decisions are just a little more complex than usual. For example, the company wanted to use solar power to charge the batteries for the forklifts used in its factories. No problem, just put solar panels on the buildings. But because Method outsources its manufacturing, it doesn't actually own factory buildings. In fact, the company that does Method's manufacturing doesn't own the buildings either. Solution—

Method parked old semi-trailers next to the factories and installed solar panels on those.

Since Method insists on using natural products and sustainable production practices, its production costs are higher than companies that don't adhere to these standards. Adam and Eric insist, however, that this actually benefits them because they have to be far more careful about controlling costs and far more innovative in solving problems. Consider Method's most recently developed laundry detergent. It is 8 times stronger than normal detergent, so it can be sold in a substantially smaller package. This reduces both its packaging and shipping costs. In fact, when the cost of the raw materials used for soap production recently jumped by as much as 40%, Method actually viewed it as an opportunity to grab market share. It determined that it could offset the cost increases in other places in its supply chain, thus absorbing the cost much easier than its big competitors.

In these and other instances, Adam and Eric identified their alternative courses of action, determined what was relevant to each choice and what wasn't, and then carefully evaluated the incremental costs of each alternative. When you are small and your competitors have some of the biggest marketing budgets in the world, you can't afford to make very many mistakes.

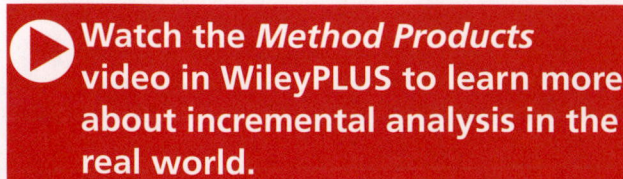

Watch the *Method Products* video in WileyPLUS to learn more about incremental analysis in the real world.

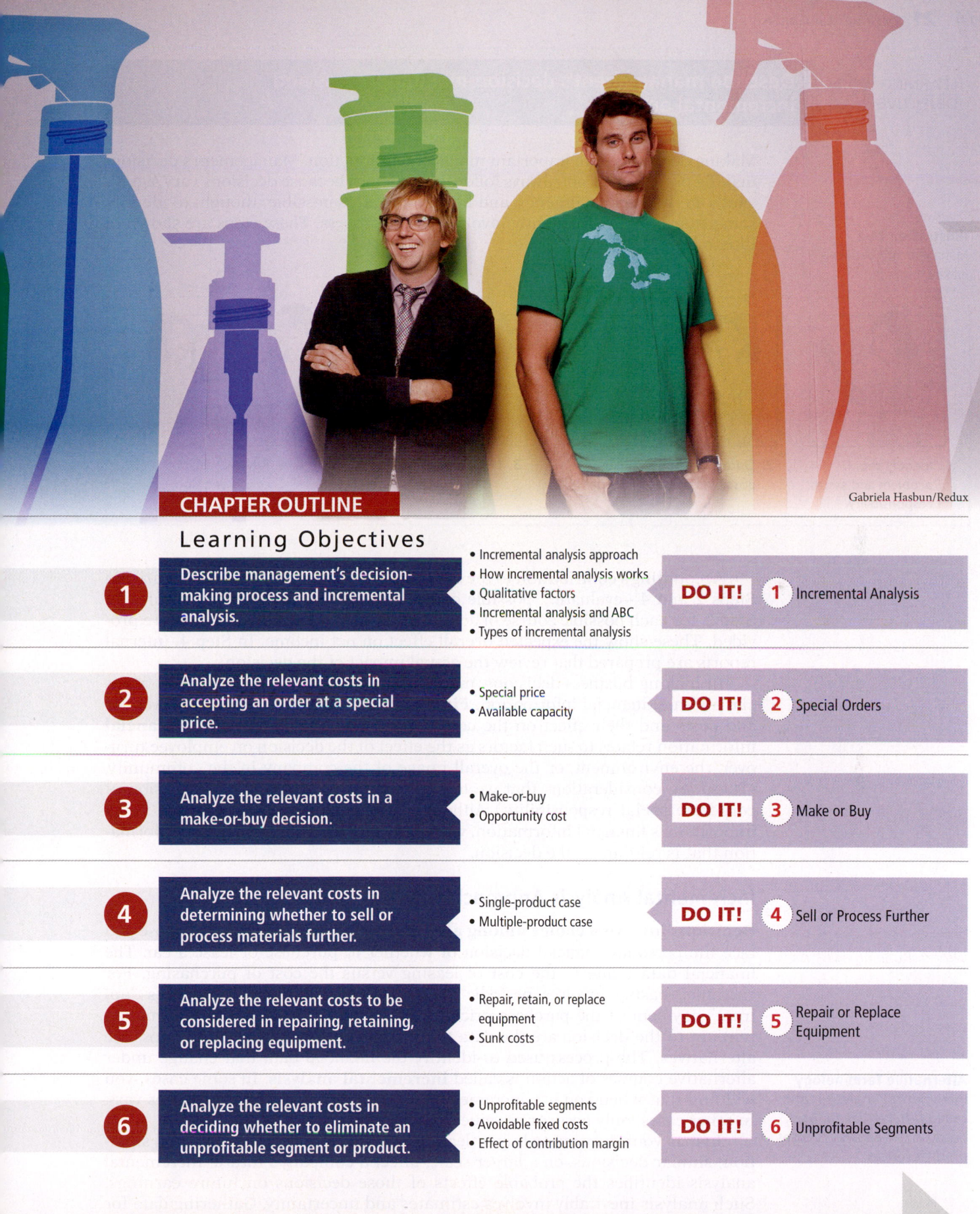

Gabriela Hasbun/Redux

CHAPTER OUTLINE

Learning Objectives

1 Describe management's decision-making process and incremental analysis.
- Incremental analysis approach
- How incremental analysis works
- Qualitative factors
- Incremental analysis and ABC
- Types of incremental analysis

DO IT! 1 Incremental Analysis

2 Analyze the relevant costs in accepting an order at a special price.
- Special price
- Available capacity

DO IT! 2 Special Orders

3 Analyze the relevant costs in a make-or-buy decision.
- Make-or-buy
- Opportunity cost

DO IT! 3 Make or Buy

4 Analyze the relevant costs in determining whether to sell or process materials further.
- Single-product case
- Multiple-product case

DO IT! 4 Sell or Process Further

5 Analyze the relevant costs to be considered in repairing, retaining, or replacing equipment.
- Repair, retain, or replace equipment
- Sunk costs

DO IT! 5 Repair or Replace Equipment

6 Analyze the relevant costs in deciding whether to eliminate an unprofitable segment or product.
- Unprofitable segments
- Avoidable fixed costs
- Effect of contribution margin

DO IT! 6 Unprofitable Segments

Go to the **REVIEW AND PRACTICE** section at the end of the chapter for a review of key concepts and practice applications with solutions.

Visit **WileyPLUS with ORION** for additional tutorials and practice opportunities.

Describe management's decision-making process and incremental analysis.

Making decisions is an important management function. Management's decision-making process does not always follow a set pattern because decisions vary significantly in their scope, urgency, and importance. It is possible, though, to identify some steps that are frequently involved in the process. These steps are shown in Illustration 21-1.

Illustration 21-1
Management's decision-making process

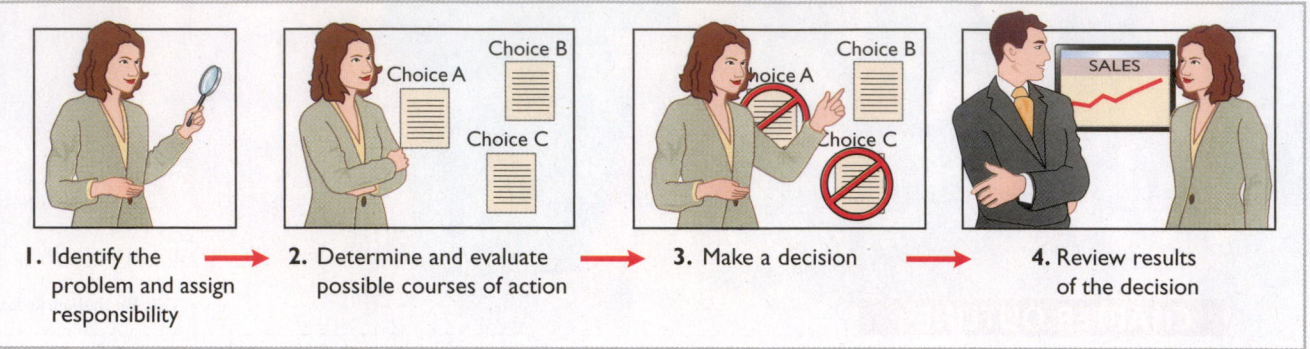

1. Identify the problem and assign responsibility → 2. Determine and evaluate possible courses of action → 3. Make a decision → 4. Review results of the decision

Accounting's contribution to the decision-making process occurs primarily in Steps 2 and 4—evaluating possible courses of action and reviewing results. In Step 2, for each possible course of action, relevant revenue and cost data are provided. These show the expected overall effect on net income. In Step 4, internal reports are prepared that review the actual impact of the decision.

In making business decisions, management ordinarily considers both financial and nonfinancial information. **Financial** information is related to revenues and costs and their effect on the company's overall profitability. **Nonfinancial** information relates to such factors as the effect of the decision on employee turnover, the environment, or the overall image of the company in the community. (These are considerations that we touched on in our Chapter 15 discussion of corporate social responsibility.) Although nonfinancial information can be as important as financial information, we will focus primarily on financial information that is relevant to the decision.

Incremental Analysis Approach

Decisions involve a choice among alternative courses of action. Suppose you face the personal financial decision of whether to purchase or lease a car. The financial data relate to the cost of leasing versus the cost of purchasing. For example, leasing involves periodic lease payments; purchasing requires "up-front" payment of the purchase price. In other words, the financial information relevant to the decision are the data that vary in the future among the possible alternatives. The process used to identify the financial data that change under alternative courses of action is called **incremental analysis**. In some cases, you will find that when you use incremental analysis, both costs **and** revenues vary. In other cases, only costs **or** revenues vary.

Alternative Terminology
Incremental analysis is also called *differential analysis* because the analysis focuses on differences.

Just as your decision to buy or lease a car affects your future financial situation, similar decisions, on a larger scale, affect a company's future. Incremental analysis identifies the probable effects of those decisions on future earnings. Such analysis inevitably involves estimates and uncertainty. Gathering data for incremental analyses may involve market analysts, engineers, and accountants. In quantifying the data, the accountant must produce the most reliable information available.

How Incremental Analysis Works

The basic approach in incremental analysis is illustrated in the following example.

Illustration 21-2
Basic approach in incremental analysis

	A	B	C	D
		Alternative A	Alternative B	Net Income Increase (Decrease)
2	Revenues	$125,000	$110,000	$ (15,000)
3	Costs	100,000	80,000	20,000
4	Net income	$ 25,000	$ 30,000	$ 5,000
5				

Incremental Analysis.xls — P18

This example compares Alternative B with Alternative A. The net income column shows the differences between the alternatives. In this case, incremental revenue will be $15,000 less under Alternative B than under Alternative A. But a $20,000 incremental cost savings will be realized.[1] Thus, Alternative B will produce $5,000 more net income than Alternative A.

In the following pages, you will encounter three important cost concepts used in incremental analysis, as defined and discussed in Illustration 21-3.

Illustration 21-3
Key cost concepts in incremental analysis

- **Relevant cost**   In incremental analysis, the only factors to be considered are those costs and revenues that differ across alternatives. Those factors are called **relevant costs**. Costs and revenues that do not differ across alternatives can be ignored when trying to choose between alternatives.

- **Opportunity cost**   Often in choosing one course of action, the company must give up the opportunity to benefit from some other course of action. For example, if a machine is used to make one type of product, the benefit of making another type of product with that machine is lost. This lost benefit is referred to as **opportunity cost**.

- **Sunk cost**   Costs that have already been incurred and will not be changed or avoided by any present or future decisions are referred to as **sunk costs**. For example, the amount you spent in the past to purchase or repair a laptop should have no bearing on your decision whether to buy a new laptop. **Sunk costs are not relevant costs.**

---

[1]Although income taxes are sometimes important in incremental analysis, they are ignored in the chapter for simplicity's sake.

Incremental analysis sometimes involves changes that at first glance might seem contrary to your intuition. For example, sometimes variable costs **do not change** under the alternative courses of action. Also, sometimes fixed costs **do change**. For example, direct labor, normally a variable cost, is not an incremental cost in deciding between two new factory machines if each asset requires the same amount of direct labor. In contrast, rent expense, normally a fixed cost, is an incremental cost in a decision whether to continue occupancy of a building or to purchase or lease a new building.

It is also important to understand that **the approaches to incremental analysis discussed in this chapter do not take into consideration the time value of money**. That is, amounts to be paid or received in future years are not discounted for the cost of interest. Time value of money is addressed in Chapter 26 and Appendix G.

Service Company Insight   American Express

Tina Spruce/iStockphoto

That Letter from AmEx Might Not Be a Bill

No doubt every one of you has received an invitation from a credit card company to open a new account—some of you have probably received three in one day. But how many of you have received an offer of $300 to close out your credit card account? American Express decided to offer some of its customers $300 if they would give back their credit card. You could receive the $300 even if you hadn't paid off your balance yet, as long as you agreed to give up your credit card.

Source: Aparajita Saha-Bubna and Lauren Pollock, "AmEx Offers Some Holders $300 to Pay and Leave," *Wall Street Journal Online* (February 23, 2009).

What are the relevant costs that American Express would need to know in order to determine to whom to make this offer? (Go to **WileyPLUS** for this answer and additional questions.)

Qualitative Factors

In this chapter, we focus primarily on the quantitative factors that affect a decision—those attributes that can be easily expressed in terms of numbers or dollars. However, many of the decisions involving incremental analysis have important qualitative features. Though not easily measured, they should not be ignored.

Consider, for example, the potential effects of the make-or-buy decision or of the decision to eliminate a line of business on existing employees and the community in which the plant is located. The cost savings that may be obtained from outsourcing or from eliminating a plant should be weighed against these qualitative attributes. One example would be the cost of lost morale that might result. Al "Chainsaw" Dunlap was a so-called "turnaround" artist who went into many companies, identified inefficiencies (using incremental analysis techniques), and tried to correct these problems to improve corporate profitability. Along the way, he laid off thousands of employees at numerous companies. As head of Sunbeam, it was Al Dunlap who lost his job because his Draconian approach failed to improve Sunbeam's profitability. It was reported that Sunbeam's employees openly rejoiced for days after his departure. Clearly, qualitative factors can matter.

Relationship of Incremental Analysis and Activity-Based Costing

In Chapter 18, we noted that many companies have shifted to activity-based costing to allocate overhead costs to products. The primary reason for using activity-based costing is that it results in a more accurate allocation of overhead. The concepts presented in this chapter are completely consistent with the use of activity-based costing. In fact, activity-based costing results in better identification of relevant costs and, therefore, better incremental analysis.

Types of Incremental Analysis

A number of different types of decisions involve incremental analysis. The more common types of decisions are whether to:

1. Accept an order at a special price.
2. Make or buy component parts or finished products.
3. Sell products or process them further.
4. Repair, retain, or replace equipment.
5. Eliminate an unprofitable business segment or product.

We consider each of these types of decisions in the following pages.

DO IT!   1   Incremental Analysis

Owen T Corporation is comparing two different options. The company currently follows Option 1, with revenues of $80,000 per year, maintenance expenses of $5,000 per year, and operating expenses of $38,000 per year. Option 2 provides revenues of $80,000 per year, maintenance expenses of $12,000 per year, and operating expenses of $32,000 per year. Option 1 employs a piece of equipment that was upgraded 2 years ago at a cost of $22,000. If Option 2 is chosen, it will free up resources that will increase revenues by $3,000.

Complete the following table to show the change in income from choosing Option 2 versus Option 1. Designate any sunk costs with an "S."

	Option 1	Option 2	Net Income Increase (Decrease)	Sunk (S)
Revenues				
Maintenance expenses				
Operating expenses				
Equipment upgrade				
Opportunity cost				

Solution

	Option 1	Option 2	Net Income Increase (Decrease)	Sunk (S)
Revenues	$80,000	$80,000	$ 0	
Maintenance expenses	5,000	12,000	(7,000)	
Operating expenses	38,000	32,000	6,000	
Equipment upgrade	22,000	0	0	S
Opportunity cost	3,000	0	3,000	
			$ 2,000	

Action Plan

✔ Past costs that cannot be changed are sunk costs.

✔ Benefits lost by choosing one option over another are opportunity costs.

Related exercise material: **BE21-1, BE21-2, E21-1, E21-18, and DO IT! 21-1.**

 LEARNING OBJECTIVE 2   Analyze the relevant costs in accepting an order at a special price.

Sometimes a company has an opportunity to obtain additional business if it is willing to make a price concession to a specific customer. To illustrate, assume that Sunbelt Company produces 100,000 Smoothie blenders per month, which is 80% of plant capacity. Variable manufacturing costs are $8 per unit. Fixed manufacturing costs are $400,000, or $4 per unit. The Smoothie blenders are normally sold directly to retailers at $20 each. Sunbelt has an offer from Kensington Co. (a foreign wholesaler) to purchase an additional 2,000 blenders at $11 per unit. Acceptance of the offer would not affect normal sales of the product, and the additional units can be manufactured without increasing plant capacity. What should management do?

If management makes its decision on the basis of the total cost per unit of $12 ($8 variable + $4 fixed), the order would be rejected because costs per unit ($12) exceed revenues per unit ($11) by $1 per unit. However, since the units can be produced within existing plant capacity, the special order **will not increase fixed costs**. Let's identify the relevant data for the decision. First, the variable manufacturing costs increase $16,000 ($8 × 2,000). Second, the expected revenue increases $22,000 ($11 × 2,000). Thus, as shown in Illustration 21-4, Sunbelt increases its net income by $6,000 by accepting this special order.

Incremental Analysis - Accepting an order at a special price.xls			
	Reject Order	**Accept Order**	**Net Income Increase (Decrease)**
Revenues	$0	$22,000	$ 22,000
Costs	0	16,000	(16,000)
Net income	$0	$ 6,000	$ 6,000

Illustration 21-4
Incremental analysis—accepting an order at a special price

Two points should be emphasized. First, we assume that sales of the product in other markets **would not be affected by this special order**. If other sales were affected, then Sunbelt would have to consider the lost sales in making the decision. Second, if Sunbelt is operating **at full capacity**, it is likely that the special order would be rejected. Under such circumstances, the company would have to expand plant capacity. In that case, the special order would have to absorb these additional fixed manufacturing costs, as well as the variable manufacturing costs.

DO IT! 2 Special Orders

Cobb Company incurs costs of $28 per unit ($18 variable and $10 fixed) to make a product that normally sells for $42. A foreign wholesaler offers to buy 5,000 units at $25 each. The special order results in additional shipping costs of $1 per unit. Compute the increase or decrease in net income Cobb realizes by accepting the special order, assuming Cobb has excess operating capacity. Should Cobb Company accept the special order?

Solution

Action Plan

✔ Identify all revenues that change as a result of accepting the order.

✔ Identify all costs that change as a result of accepting the order, and net this amount against the change in revenues.

	Reject	**Accept**	**Net Income Increase (Decrease)**
Revenues	$-0-	$125,000*	$125,000
Costs	-0-	95,000**	(95,000)
Net income	$-0-	$ 30,000	$ 30,000

*5,000 × $25
**(5,000 × $18) + (5,000 × $1)

The analysis indicates net income increases by $30,000; therefore, Cobb Company should accept the special order.

Related exercise material: **BE21-3, E21-2, E21-3, E21-4, and DO IT! 21-2.**

Analyze the relevant costs in a make-or-buy decision.

When a manufacturer assembles component parts in producing a finished product, management must decide whether to make or buy the components. The decision to buy parts or services is often referred to as outsourcing. For example, as discussed in the Feature Story, a company such as **Method Products** may either make or buy the soaps used in its products. Similarly, **Hewlett-Packard Corporation** may make or buy the electronic circuitry, cases, and printer heads for its printers. **Boeing** recently sold some of its commercial aircraft factories in an effort to cut production costs and focus on engineering and final assembly rather than manufacturing. The decision to make or buy components should be made on the basis of incremental analysis.

Baron Company makes motorcycles and scooters. It incurs the following annual costs in producing 25,000 ignition switches for scooters.

Direct materials	$ 50,000
Direct labor	75,000
Variable manufacturing overhead	40,000
Fixed manufacturing overhead	60,000
Total manufacturing costs	$225,000
Total cost per unit ($225,000 ÷ 25,000)	**$9.00**

Illustration 21-5
Annual product cost data

Instead of making its own switches, Baron Company might purchase the ignition switches from Ignition, Inc. at a price of $8 per unit. What should management do?

At first glance, it appears that management should purchase the ignition switches for $8 rather than make them at a cost of $9. However, a review of operations indicates that if the ignition switches are purchased from Ignition, Inc., *all* of Baron's variable costs but only $10,000 of its fixed manufacturing costs will be eliminated (avoided). Thus, $50,000 of the fixed manufacturing costs remain if the ignition switches are purchased. The relevant costs for incremental analysis, therefore, are as shown below.

Illustration 21-6
Incremental analysis—make or buy

	Make	Buy	Net Income Increase (Decrease)
2 Direct materials	$ 50,000	$ 0	$ 50,000
3 Direct labor	75,000	0	75,000
4 Variable manufacturing costs	40,000	0	40,000
5 Fixed manufacturing costs	60,000	50,000	10,000
6 Purchase price (25,000 × $8)	0	200,000	(200,000)
7 Total annual cost	$225,000	$250,000	$ (25,000)

This analysis indicates that Baron Company incurs $25,000 of additional costs by buying the ignition switches rather than making them. Therefore, Baron should continue to make the ignition switches even though the total manufacturing cost is $1 higher per unit than the purchase price. The primary cause of this result is that, even if the company purchases the ignition switches, it will still have fixed costs of $50,000 to absorb.

Opportunity Cost

The foregoing make-or-buy analysis is complete only if it is assumed that the productive capacity used to make the ignition switches cannot be converted to another purpose. If there is an opportunity to use this productive capacity in some other manner, then this opportunity cost must be considered. As indicated earlier, **opportunity cost** is the potential benefit that may be obtained by following an alternative course of action.

To illustrate, assume that through buying the switches, Baron Company can use the released productive capacity to generate additional income of $38,000 from producing a different product. This lost income is an additional cost of continuing to make the switches in the make-or-buy decision. This opportunity cost is therefore added to the "Make" column for comparison. As shown in Illustration 21-7, it is now advantageous to buy the ignition switches. The company's income would increase by $13,000.

Illustration 21-7
Incremental analysis—make or buy, with opportunity cost

Incremental Analysis - Make or buy with opportunity cost.xls

	A	B	C	D
1		Make	Buy	Net Income Increase (Decrease)
2	Total annual cost	$225,000	$250,000	$(25,000)
3	Opportunity cost	38,000	0	38,000
4	Total cost	$263,000	$250,000	$ 13,000
5				

The qualitative factors in this decision include the possible loss of jobs for employees who produce the ignition switches. In addition, management must assess the supplier's ability to satisfy the company's quality control standards at the quoted price per unit.

Service Company Insight Amazon.com

iStockphoto

Giving Away the Store?

In an earlier chapter, we discussed Amazon.com's incredible growth. However, some analysts have questioned whether some of the methods that Amazon uses to increase its sales make good business sense. For example, a few years ago, Amazon initiated a "Prime" free-shipping subscription program. For a $79 fee per year, Amazon's customers get free shipping on as many goods as they want to buy. At the time, CEO Jeff Bezos promised that the program would be costly in the short-term but benefit the company in the long-term. Six years later, it was true that Amazon's sales had grown considerably. It was also estimated that its Prime customers buy two to three times as much as non-Prime customers. But, its shipping costs rose from 2.8% of sales to 4% of sales, which is remarkably similar to the drop in its gross margin from 24% to 22.3%. Perhaps even less easy to justify is a proposal by Mr. Bezos to start providing a free Internet movie-streaming service to Amazon's Prime customers. Perhaps some incremental analysis is in order?

Source: Martin Peers, "Amazon's Prime Numbers," *Wall Street Journal Online* (February 3, 2011).

What are the relevant revenues and costs that Amazon should consider relative to the decision whether to offer the Prime free-shipping subscription? (Go to **WileyPLUS** for this answer and additional questions.)

DO IT! 3   Make or Buy

Juanita Company must decide whether to make or buy some of its components for the appliances it produces. The costs of producing 166,000 electrical cords for its appliances are as follows.

Direct materials	$90,000	Variable overhead	$32,000
Direct labor	$20,000	Fixed overhead	$24,000

Instead of making the electrical cords at an average cost per unit of $1.00 ($166,000 ÷ 166,000), the company has an opportunity to buy the cords at $0.90 per unit. If the company purchases the cords, all variable costs and one-fourth of the fixed costs are eliminated.

(a) Prepare an incremental analysis showing whether the company should make or buy the electrical cords. (b) Will your answer be different if the released productive capacity will generate additional income of $5,000?

Solution

(a)

	Make	Buy	Net Income Increase (Decrease)
Direct materials	$ 90,000	$ –0–	$ 90,000
Direct labor	20,000	–0–	20,000
Variable manufacturing costs	32,000	–0–	32,000
Fixed manufacturing costs	24,000	18,000*	6,000
Purchase price	–0–	149,400**	(149,400)
Total cost	$166,000	$167,400	$ (1,400)

*$24,000 × .75
**$166,000 × $0.90

This analysis indicates that Juanita Company will incur $1,400 of additional costs if it buys the electrical cords rather than making them.

(b)

	Make	Buy	Net Income Increase (Decrease)
Total cost	$166,000	$167,400	$(1,400)
Opportunity cost	5,000	–0–	5,000
Total cost	$171,000	$167,400	$ 3,600

Yes, the answer is different. The analysis shows that net income increases by $3,600 if Juanita Company purchases the electrical cords rather than making them.

Action Plan

✔ Look for the costs that change.

✔ Ignore the costs that do not change.

✔ Use the format in the chapter for your answer.

✔ Recognize that opportunity cost can make a difference.

Related exercise material: **BE21-4, E21-5, E21-6, E21-7, E21-8, and DO IT! 21-3.**

 LEARNING OBJECTIVE 4   **Analyze the relevant costs in determining whether to sell or process materials further.**

Many manufacturers have the option of selling products at a given point in the production cycle or continuing to process with the expectation of selling them at a later point at a higher price. For example, a bicycle manufacturer such as **Trek** could sell its bicycles to retailers either unassembled or assembled. A furniture manufacturer such as **Ethan Allen** could sell its dining room sets to furniture stores either unfinished or finished. The sell-or-process-further decision should be made on the basis of incremental analysis. The basic decision rule is: **Process**

further as long as the incremental revenue from such processing exceeds the incremental processing costs.

Single-Product Case

Assume, for example, that Woodmasters Inc. makes tables. It sells unfinished tables for $50. The cost to manufacture an unfinished table is $35, computed as follows.

Illustration 21-8
Per unit cost of unfinished table

Direct materials	$15
Direct labor	10
Variable manufacturing overhead	6
Fixed manufacturing overhead	4
Manufacturing cost per unit	**$35**

Helpful Hint
Current net income is known. Net income from processing further is an estimate. In making its decision, management could add a "risk" factor for the estimate.

Woodmasters currently has unused productive capacity that is expected to continue indefinitely. Some of this capacity could be used to finish the tables and sell them at $60 per unit. For a finished table, direct materials will increase $2 and direct labor costs will increase $4. Variable manufacturing overhead costs will increase by $2.40 (60% of direct labor). No increase is anticipated in fixed manufacturing overhead.

Should the company sell the unfinished tables, or should it process them further? The incremental analysis on a per unit basis is as follows.

	Sell Unfinished	Process Further	Net Income Increase (Decrease)
Sales price per unit	$50.00	$60.00	$10.00
Cost per unit			
Direct materials	15.00	17.00	(2.00)
Direct labor	10.00	14.00	(4.00)
Variable manufacturing overhead	6.00	8.40	(2.40)
Fixed manufacturing overhead	4.00	4.00	0.00
Total	35.00	43.40	(8.40)
Net income per unit	$15.00	$16.60	$ 1.60

Incremental Analysis - Sell or process further.xls

Illustration 21-9
Incremental analysis—sell or process further

It would be advantageous for Woodmasters to process the tables further. The incremental revenue of $10.00 from the additional processing is $1.60 higher than the incremental processing costs of $8.40.

Multiple-Product Case

Sell-or-process-further decisions are particularly applicable to processes that produce multiple products simultaneously. In many industries, a number of end-products are produced from a single raw material and a common production process. These multiple end-products are commonly referred to as **joint products**. For example, in the meat-packing industry, **Armour** processes a cow or pig into meat, internal organs, hides, bones, and fat products. In the petroleum industry, **ExxonMobil** refines crude oil to produce gasoline, lubricating oil, kerosene, paraffin, and ethylene.

Illustration 21-10 presents a joint product situation for Marais Creamery involving a decision **to sell or process further** cream and skim milk. Cream and skim milk are joint products that result from the processing of raw milk.

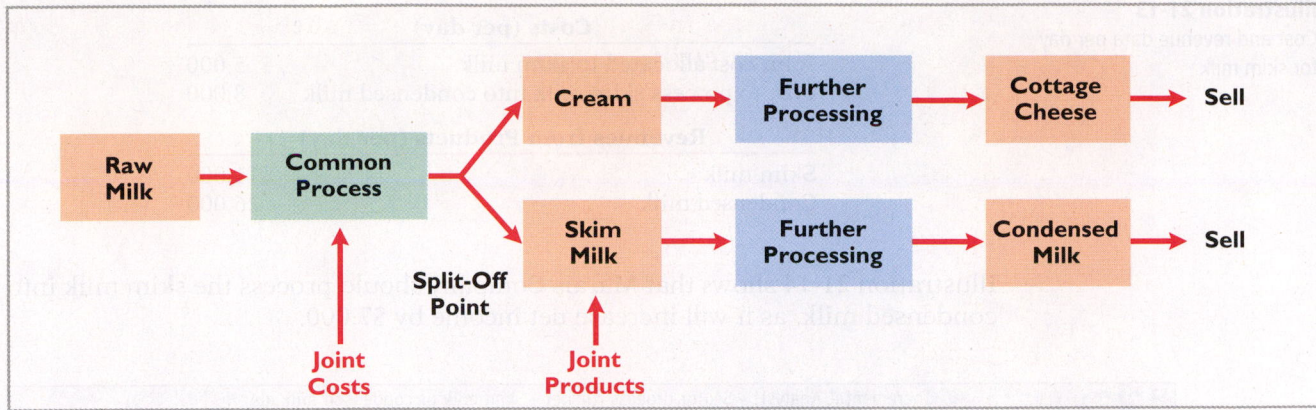

Illustration 21-10
Joint production process—
Creamery

Marais incurs many costs prior to the manufacture of the cream and skim milk. All costs incurred prior to the point at which the two products are separately identifiable (the **split-off point**) are called **joint costs**. For purposes of determining the cost of each product, joint product costs must be allocated to the individual products. This is frequently done based on the relative sales value of the joint products. While this allocation is important for determination of product cost, **it is irrelevant for any sell-or-process-further decisions**. The reason is that these **joint product costs are sunk costs**. That is, they have already been incurred, and they cannot be changed or avoided by any subsequent decision.

Illustration 21-11 provides the daily cost and revenue data for Marais Creamery related to cream and cottage cheese.

Illustration 21-11
Cost and revenue data per day
for cream

Costs (per day)	
Joint cost allocated to cream	$ 9,000
Cost to process cream into cottage cheese	10,000
Revenues from Products (per day)	
Cream	$19,000
Cottage cheese	27,000

From this information, we can determine whether the company should simply sell the cream or process it further into cottage cheese. Illustration 21-12 shows the necessary analysis. Note that the joint cost that is allocated to the cream is not included in this decision. It is not relevant to the decision because it is a sunk cost. It has been incurred in the past and will remain the same no matter whether the cream is subsequently processed into cottage cheese or not.

Illustration 21-12
Analysis of whether to sell
cream or process into cottage
cheese

	Incremental Analysis - Sell or process further - Cream or cottage cheese.xls			
	Home Insert Page Layout Formulas Data Review View			
	P18 fx			
	A	B	C	D
1		Sell	Process Further	Net Income Increase (Decrease)
2	Sales per day	$19,000	$27,000	$ 8,000
3	Cost per day to process cream into cottage cheese	0	10,000	(10,000)
4		$19,000	$17,000	**$ (2,000)**
5				

From this analysis, we can see that Marais should not process the cream further because it will sustain an incremental loss of $2,000.

Illustration 21-13 (page 984) provides the daily cost and revenue data for the company related to skim milk and condensed milk.

Illustration 21-13
Cost and revenue data per day
for skim milk

Costs (per day)	
Joint cost allocated to skim milk	$ 5,000
Cost to process skim milk into condensed milk	8,000
Revenues from Products (per day)	
Skim milk	$11,000
Condensed milk	26,000

Illustration 21-14 shows that Marais Company should process the skim milk into condensed milk, as it will increase net income by $7,000.

	A	B	C	D
		Sell	Process Further	Net Income Increase (Decrease)
2	Sales per day	$11,000	$26,000	$15,000
3	Cost per day to process skim milk into condensed milk	0	8,000	(8,000)
4		$11,000	$18,000	$ 7,000

Illustration 21-14
Analysis of whether to sell skim milk or process into condensed milk

Again, note that the $5,000 of joint cost allocated to the skim milk is irrelevant in deciding whether to sell or process further. Why? The joint cost remains the same, whether or not further processing is performed.

These decisions need to be reevaluated as market conditions change. For example, if the price of skim milk increases relative to the price of condensed milk, it may become more profitable to sell the skim milk rather than process it into condensed milk. Consider also oil refineries. As market conditions change, the companies must constantly re-assess which products to produce from the oil they receive at their plants.

DO IT! 4   Sell or Process Further

Action Plan

✔ Identify the revenues that change as a result of painting the rocking chair.

✔ Identify all costs that change as a result of painting the rocking chair, and net the amount against the revenues.

Easy Does It manufactures unpainted furniture for the do-it-yourself (DIY) market. It currently sells a child's rocking chair for $25. Production costs are $12 variable and $8 fixed. Easy Does It is considering painting the rocking chair and selling it for $35. Variable costs to paint each chair are expected to be $9, and fixed costs are expected to be $2.

Prepare an analysis showing whether Easy Does It should sell unpainted or painted chairs.

Solution

	Sell	Process Further	Net Income Increase (Decrease)
Revenues	$25	$35	$10
Variable costs	12	21[a]	(9)
Fixed costs	8	10[b]	(2)
Net income	$ 5	$ 4	$(1)

[a]$12 + $9   [b]$8 + $2

The analysis indicates that the rocking chair should be sold unpainted because net income per chair will be $1 greater.

Related exercise material: **BE21-5, BE21-6, E21-9, E21-10, E21-11, E21-12, and DO IT! 21-4.**

Analyze the relevant costs to be considered in repairing, retaining, or replacing equipment.

Management often has to decide whether to continue using an asset, repair, or replace it. For example, **Delta Airlines** must decide whether to replace old jets with new, more fuel-efficient ones. To illustrate, assume that Jeffcoat Company has a factory machine that originally cost $110,000. It has a balance in Accumulated Depreciation of $70,000, so the machine's book value is $40,000. It has a remaining useful life of four years. The company is considering replacing this machine with a new machine. A new machine is available that costs $120,000. It is expected to have zero salvage value at the end of its four-year useful life. If the new machine is acquired, variable manufacturing costs are expected to decrease from $160,000 to $125,000 annually, and the old unit could be sold for $5,000. The incremental analysis for the **four-year period** is as follows.

Illustration 21-15
Incremental analysis—retain or replace equipment

	Incremental Analysis - Retain or replace equipment.xls				
	Home Insert Page Layout Formulas Data Review View				
	P18	fx			
	A	B	C	D	E	F
1		Retain Equipment		Replace Equipment		Net Income Increase (Decrease)
2	Variable manufacturing costs	$640,000	a	$500,000	b	$140,000
3	New machine cost			120,000		(120,000)
4	Sale of old machine			(5,000)		5,000
5	Total	$640,000		$615,000		$ 25,000
6						
7	a(4 years × $160,000)					
8	b(4 years × $125,000)					
9						

In this case, it would be to the company's advantage to replace the equipment. The lower variable manufacturing costs due to replacement more than offset the cost of the new equipment. Note that the $5,000 received from the sale of the old machine is relevant to the decision because it will only be received if the company chooses to replace its equipment. In general, any trade-in allowance or cash disposal value of existing assets is relevant to the decision to retain or replace equipment.

One other point should be mentioned regarding Jeffcoat's decision: **The book value of the old machine does not affect the decision.** Book value is a **sunk cost**, which is a cost that cannot be changed by any present or future decision. **Sunk costs are not relevant in incremental analysis.** In this example, if the asset is retained, book value will be depreciated over its remaining useful life. Or, if the new unit is acquired, book value will be recognized as a loss of the current period. Thus, the effect of book value on cumulative future earnings is the same regardless of the replacement decision.

Sometimes, decisions regarding whether to replace equipment are clouded by behavioral decision-making errors. For example, suppose a manager spent $90,000 repairing a machine two months ago. Suppose that the machine now breaks down again. The manager might be inclined to think that because the company recently spent a large amount of money to repair the machine, the machine should be repaired again rather than replaced. However, the amount spent in the past to repair the machine is irrelevant to the current decision. It is a sunk cost.

Similarly, suppose a manager spent $5,000,000 to purchase a machine. Six months later, a new machine comes on the market that is significantly more efficient than the one recently purchased. The manager might be inclined to think that he or she should not buy the new machine because of the recent purchase.

In fact, the manager might fear that buying a different machine so quickly might call into question the merit of the previous decision. Again, the fact that the company recently bought a machine is not relevant. Instead, the manager should use incremental analysis to determine whether the savings generated by the efficiencies of the new machine would justify its purchase.

DO IT! 5   Repair or Replace Equipment

Rochester Roofing is faced with a decision. The company relies very heavily on the use of its 60-foot extension lift for work on large homes and commercial properties. Last year, the company spent $60,000 refurbishing the lift. It has just determined that another $40,000 of repair work is required. Alternatively, Rochester Roofing has found a newer used lift that is for sale for $170,000. The company estimates that both the old and new lifts would have useful lives of 6 years. However, the new lift is more efficient and thus would reduce operating expenses by about $20,000 per year. The company could also rent out the new lift for about $2,000 per year. The old lift is not suitable for rental. The old lift could currently be sold for $25,000 if the new lift is purchased. Prepare an incremental analysis that shows whether the company should repair or replace the equipment.

Action Plan

✔ Those costs and revenues that differ across the alternatives are relevant to the decision.

✔ Past costs that cannot be changed are sunk costs.

Solution

	Retain Equipment	Replace Equipment	Net Income Increase (Decrease)
Operating expenses	$120,000*		$120,000
Repair costs	40,000		40,000
Rental revenue		$ (12,000)**	12,000
New machine cost		170,000	(170,000)
Sale of old machine		(25,000)	25,000
Total cost	$160,000	$133,000	$ 27,000

*(6 years × $20,000)
**(6 years × $2,000)

The analysis indicates that purchasing the new machine would increase net income for the 6-year period by $27,000.

Related exercise material: **BE21-7, E21-13, E21-14, and DO IT! 21-5.**

LEARNING OBJECTIVE   **6**

Analyze the relevant costs in deciding whether to eliminate an unprofitable segment or product.

Management sometimes must decide whether to eliminate an unprofitable business segment or product. For example, in recent years, many airlines quit servicing certain cities or cut back on the number of flights. Goodyear quit producing several brands in the low-end tire market. Again, the key is to **focus on the relevant costs—the data that change under the alternative courses of action**. To illustrate, assume that Venus Company manufactures tennis racquets in three models: Pro, Master, and Champ. Pro and Master are profitable lines. Champ (highlighted in red in the table below) operates at a loss. Condensed income statement data are as follows.

Illustration 21-16
Segment income data

Helpful Hint
A decision to discontinue a segment based solely on the bottom line—net loss—is inappropriate.

	Pro	Master	Champ	Total
Sales	$800,000	$300,000	**$100,000**	$1,200,000
Variable costs	520,000	210,000	**90,000**	820,000
Contribution margin	280,000	90,000	**10,000**	380,000
Fixed costs	80,000	50,000	**30,000**	160,000
Net income	$200,000	$ 40,000	**$ (20,000)**	$ 220,000

You might think that total net income will increase by $20,000 to $240,000 if the unprofitable Champ line of racquets is eliminated. However, **net income may actually decrease if the Champ line is discontinued**. The reason is that if the fixed costs allocated to the Champ racquets cannot be eliminated, they will have to be absorbed by the other products. To illustrate, assume that the $30,000 of fixed costs applicable to the unprofitable segment are allocated ⅔ to the Pro model and ⅓ to the Master model if the Champ model is eliminated. Fixed costs will increase to $100,000 ($80,000 + $20,000) in the Pro line and to $60,000 ($50,000 + $10,000) in the Master line. The revised income statement is as follows.

	Pro	Master	Total
Sales	$800,000	$300,000	$1,100,000
Variable costs	520,000	210,000	730,000
Contribution margin	280,000	90,000	370,000
Fixed costs	**100,000**	**60,000**	160,000
Net income	$180,000	$ 30,000	$ 210,000

Illustration 21-17
Income data after eliminating unprofitable product line

Illustration 21-18
Incremental analysis—eliminating unprofitable segment with no reduction in fixed costs

Total net income has decreased $10,000 ($220,000 − $210,000). This result is also obtained in the following incremental analysis of the Champ racquets.

	A	B	C	D
1		Continue	Eliminate	Net Income Increase (Decrease)
2	Sales	$100,000	$ 0	$(100,000)
3	Variable costs	90,000	0	90,000
4	Contribution margin	10,000	0	(10,000)
5	Fixed costs	30,000	30,000	0
6	Net income	$(20,000)	$(30,000)	$ (10,000)
7				

The loss in net income is attributable to the Champ line's contribution margin ($10,000) that will not be realized if the segment is discontinued.

Assume the same facts as above, except now assume that $22,000 of the fixed costs attributed to the Champ line can be eliminated if the line is discontinued. Illustration 21-19 presents the incremental analysis based on this revised assumption.

Illustration 21-19
Incremental analysis—eliminating unprofitable segment with reduction in fixed costs

	A	B	C	D
1		Continue	Eliminate	Net Income Increase (Decrease)
2	Sales	$100,000	$ 0	$(100,000)
3	Variable costs	90,000	0	90,000
4	Contribution margin	10,000	0	(10,000)
5	Fixed costs	30,000	8,000	22,000
6	Net income	$ (20,000)	$(8,000)	$ 12,000
7				

In this case, because the company is able to eliminate some of its fixed costs by eliminating the division, it can increase its net income by $12,000. **This occurs because the $22,000 savings that results from the eliminated fixed costs exceeds the $10,000 in lost contribution margin by $12,000 ($22,000 − $10,000).**

In deciding on the future status of an unprofitable segment, management should consider the effect of elimination on related product lines. It may be possible for continuing product lines to obtain some or all of the sales lost by the discontinued product line. In some businesses, services or products may be linked—for example, free checking accounts at a bank, or coffee at a donut shop. In addition, management should consider the effect of eliminating the product line on employees who may have to be discharged or retrained.

Management Insight Buck Knives

Max Blain/iStockphoto

Time to Move to a New Neighborhood?

If you have ever moved, then you know how complicated and costly it can be. Now consider what it would be like for a manufacturing company with 260 employees and a 170,000-square-foot facility to move from southern California to Idaho. That is what Buck Knives did in order to save its company from financial ruin. Electricity rates in Idaho were half those in California, workers' compensation was one-third the cost, and factory wages were 20% lower. Combined, this would reduce manufacturing costs by $600,000 per year. Moving the factory would cost about $8.5 million, plus $4 million to move key employees. Offsetting these costs was the estimated $11 million selling price of the California property. Based on these estimates, the move would pay for itself in three years.

Ultimately, the company received only $7.5 million for its California property, only 58 of 75 key employees were willing to move, construction was delayed by a year which caused the new plant to increase in price by $1.5 million, and wages surged in Idaho due to low unemployment. Despite all of these complications, though, the company considers the move a great success.

Source: Chris Lydgate, "The Buck Stopped," *Inc. Magazine* (May 2006), pp. 87–95.

What were some of the factors that complicated the company's decision to move? How should the company have incorporated such factors into its incremental analysis? (Go to **WileyPLUS** for this answer and additional questions.)

DO IT!   Unprofitable Segments

Lambert, Inc. manufactures several types of accessories. For the year, the knit hats and scarves line had sales of $400,000, variable expenses of $310,000, and fixed expenses of $120,000. Therefore, the knit hats and scarves line had a net loss of $30,000. If Lambert eliminates the knit hats and scarves line, $20,000 of fixed costs will remain. Prepare an analysis showing whether the company should eliminate the knit hats and scarves line.

Solution

Action Plan

✔ Identify the revenues that change as a result of eliminating a product line.

✔ Identify all costs that change as a result of eliminating a product line, and net the amount against the revenues.

	Continue	Eliminate	Net Income Increase (Decrease)
Sales	$400,000	$ 0	$(400,000)
Variable costs	310,000	0	310,000
Contribution margin	90,000	0	(90,000)
Fixed costs	120,000	20,000	100,000
Net income	$ (30,000)	$(20,000)	$ 10,000

The analysis indicates that Lambert should eliminate the knit hats and scarves line because net income will increase $10,000.

Related exercise material: **BE21-8, E21-15, E21-16, E21-17, and DO IT! 21-6.**

REVIEW AND PRACTICE

LEARNING OBJECTIVES REVIEW

❶ Describe management's decision-making process and incremental analysis. Management's decision-making process consists of (a) identifying the problem and assigning responsibility for the decision, (b) determining and evaluating possible courses of action, (c) making the decision, and (d) reviewing the results of the decision. Incremental analysis identifies financial data that change under alternative courses of action. These data are relevant to the decision because they vary across the possible alternatives.

❷ Analyze the relevant costs in accepting an order at a special price. The relevant costs are those that change if the order is accepted. The relevant information in accepting an order at a special price is the difference between the variable manufacturing costs to produce the special order and expected revenues. Any changes in fixed costs, opportunity cost, or other incremental costs or savings (such as additional shipping) should be considered.

❸ Analyze the relevant costs in a make-or-buy decision. In a make-or-buy decision, the relevant costs are (a) the variable manufacturing costs that will be saved as well as changes to fixed manufacturing costs, (b) the purchase price, and (c) opportunity cost.

❹ Analyze the relevant costs in determining whether to sell or process materials further. The decision rule for whether to sell or process materials further is: Process further as long as the incremental revenue from processing exceeds the incremental processing costs.

❺ Analyze the relevant costs to be considered in repairing, retaining, or replacing equipment. The relevant costs to be considered in determining whether equipment should be repaired, retained, or replaced are the effects on variable costs and the cost of the new equipment. Also, any disposal value of the existing asset must be considered.

❻ Analyze the relevant costs in deciding whether to eliminate an unprofitable segment or product. In deciding whether to eliminate an unprofitable segment or product, the relevant costs are the variable costs that drive the contribution margin, if any, produced by the segment or product. Opportunity cost and reduction of fixed expenses must also be considered.

GLOSSARY REVIEW

Incremental analysis The process of identifying the financial data that change under alternative courses of action. (p. 974).

Joint costs For joint products, all costs incurred prior to the point at which the two products are separately identifiable (known as the **split-off point**). (p. 983).

Joint products Multiple end-products produced from a single raw material and a common production process. (p. 982).

Opportunity cost The potential benefit that is lost when one course of action is chosen rather than an alternative course of action. (p. 975).

Relevant costs Those costs and revenues that differ across alternatives. (p. 975).

Sunk cost A cost that cannot be changed or avoided by any present or future decision. (p. 975).

PRACTICE MULTIPLE-CHOICE QUESTIONS

(LO 1) **1.** Three of the steps in management's decision-making process are (1) review results of decision, (2) determine and evaluate possible courses of action, and (3) make the decision. The steps are prepared in the following order:
    (a) (1), (2), (3).   (c) (2), (1), (3).
    (b) (3), (2), (1).   (d) (2), (3), (1).

(LO 1) **2.** Incremental analysis is the process of identifying the financial data that:
    (a) do not change under alternative courses of action.
    (b) change under alternative courses of action.
    (c) are mixed under alternative courses of action.
    (d) No correct answer is given.

3. In making business decisions, management ordinarily **(LO 1)** considers:
    (a) quantitative factors but not qualitative factors.
    (b) financial information only.
    (c) both financial and nonfinancial information.
    (d) relevant costs, opportunity cost, and sunk costs.

4. A company is considering the following alternatives: **(LO 1)**

	Alternative A	Alternative B
Revenues	$50,000	$50,000
Variable costs	24,000	24,000
Fixed costs	12,000	15,000

Which of the following are relevant in choosing between these alternatives?
(a) Revenues, variable costs, and fixed costs.
(b) Variable costs and fixed costs.
(c) Variable costs only.
(d) Fixed costs only.

(LO 2) 5. It costs a company $14 of variable costs and $6 of fixed costs to produce product Z200 that sells for $30. A foreign buyer offers to purchase 3,000 units at $18 each. If the special offer is accepted and produced with unused capacity, net income will:
(a) decrease $6,000.   (c) increase $12,000.
(b) increase $6,000.   (d) increase $9,000.

(LO 2) 6. It costs a company $14 of variable costs and $6 of fixed costs to produce product Z200. Product Z200 sells for $30. A buyer offers to purchase 3,000 units at $18 each. The seller will incur special shipping costs of $5 per unit. If the special offer is accepted and produced with unused capacity, net income will:
(a) increase $3,000.   (c) decrease $12,000.
(b) increase $12,000.   (d) decrease $3,000.

(LO 3) 7. Jobart Company is currently operating at full capacity. It is considering buying a part from an outside supplier rather than making it in-house. If Jobart purchases the part, it can use the released productive capacity to generate additional income of $30,000 from producing a different product. When conducting incremental analysis in this make-or-buy decision, the company should:
(a) ignore the $30,000.
(b) add $30,000 to other costs in the "Make" column.
(c) add $30,000 to other costs in the "Buy" column.
(d) subtract $30,000 from the other costs in the "Make" column.

(LO 3) 8. In a make-or-buy decision, relevant costs are:
(a) manufacturing costs that will be saved.
(b) the purchase price of the units.
(c) the opportunity cost.
(d) All of the above.

(LO 3) 9. Derek is performing incremental analysis in a make-or-buy decision for Item X. If Derek buys Item X, he can use its released productive capacity to produce Item Z. Derek will sell Item Z for $12,000 and incur production costs of $8,000. Derek's incremental analysis should include an opportunity cost of:

(a) $12,000.   (c) $4,000.
(b) $8,000.   (d) $0.

(LO 4) 10. The decision rule in a sell-or-process-further decision is: process further as long as the incremental revenue from processing exceeds:
(a) incremental processing costs.
(b) variable processing costs.
(c) fixed processing costs.
(d) No correct answer is given.

(LO 4) 11. Walton, Inc. makes an unassembled product that it currently sells for $55. Production costs are $20. Walton is considering assembling the product and selling it for $68. The cost to assemble the product is estimated at $12. What decision should Walton make?
(a) Sell before assembly; net income per unit will be $12 greater.
(b) Sell before assembly; net income per unit will be $1 greater.
(c) Process further; net income per unit will be $13 greater.
(d) Process further; net income per unit will be $1 greater.

(LO 5) 12. In a decision to retain or replace equipment, the book value of the old equipment is a (an):
(a) opportunity cost.   (c) incremental cost.
(b) sunk cost.   (d) marginal cost.

(LO 6) 13. If an unprofitable segment is eliminated:
(a) net income will always increase.
(b) variable costs of the eliminated segment will have to be absorbed by other segments.
(c) fixed costs allocated to the eliminated segment will have to be absorbed by other segments.
(d) net income will always decrease.

(LO 6) 14. A segment of Hazard Inc. has the following data.

Sales	$200,000
Variable expenses	140,000
Fixed expenses	100,000

If this segment is eliminated, what will be the effect on the remaining company? Assume that 50% of the fixed expenses will be eliminated and the rest will be allocated to the segments of the remaining company.
(a) $120,000 increase.   (c) $50,000 increase.
(b) $10,000 decrease.   (d) $10,000 increase.

Solutions

1. (d) The order of the steps in the decision process is (2) determine and evaluate possible courses of action, (3) make the decision, and (1) review the results of decision. Choices (a), (b), and (c) list the steps in the incorrect order.

2. (b) Incremental analysis is the process of identifying the financial data that change under alternative courses of action, not the financial data that (a) do not change or (c) are mixed. Choice (d) is wrong as there is a correct answer given.

3. (c) Management ordinarily considers both financial and nonfinancial information in making business decisions. The other choices are incorrect because they are all limited to financial data and do not consider nonfinancial information.

4. (d) Fixed costs is the only relevant factor, that is, the only factor that differs across Alternatives A and B. The other choices are incorrect because they list either revenues, variable costs, or both, which are the same amounts for both alternatives.

5. (c) If the special offer is accepted and produced with unused capacity, variable cost per unit = $14, income per unit = ($18 − $14), so net income will increase by $12,000 (3,000 × $4), not (a) decrease $6,000, (b) increase $6,000, or (d) increase $9,000.

6. (d) If the special offer is accepted and produced with unused capacity, variable cost per unit = $19 ($14 variable + $5 shipping costs), income per unit = −$1 ($18 − $19), so net income will decrease by $3,000 (3,000 × −$1), not (a) increase $3,000, (b) increase $12,000, or (c) decrease $12,000.

7. (b) Jobart Company should add $30,000 to other costs in the "Make" column as it represents lost income of continuing to make the part in-house. The other choices are incorrect because the $30,000 (a) should not be ignored as it is an opportunity cost,

(c) represents potential lost income if the company continues to make the part instead of buying it so therefore should not be placed in the "Buy" column, and (d) should be added to, not subtracted from, the other costs in the "Make" column.

8. (d) All the costs in choices (a), (b), and (c) are relevant in a make-or-buy decision. So although choices (a), (b), and (c) are true statements, choice (d) is a better answer.

9. (c) Derek's opportunity cost in its make-or-buy decision is $12,000 (revenue for Item Z) − $8,000 (production costs for Item Z) = $4,000, not (a) $12,000, (b) $8,000, or (d) $0.

10. (a) The decision rule in a sell-or-process-further decision is to process further as long as the incremental revenue from such processing exceeds incremental processing costs, not (b) variable processing costs or (c) fixed processing costs. Choice (d) is wrong as there is a correct answer given.

11. (d) If Walton processes further, net income per unit will increase $13 ($68 − $55), which is $1 more than its additional production costs ($12). The other choices are therefore incorrect.

12. (b) In the decision to retain or replace equipment, the book value of the old equipment is a sunk cost (it reflects the original cost less accumulated depreciation, neither of which is relevant to the decision), not (a) an opportunity cost, (c) an incremental cost, or (d) a marginal cost.

13. (c) Even though the segment is eliminated, the fixed costs allocated to that segment will still have to be covered. This is done by having other segments absorb the fixed costs of that segment. Choices (a) and (d) are incorrect because net income can either increase or decrease if a segment is eliminated. Choice (b) is incorrect because when a segment is eliminated, the variable costs of that segment will also be eliminated and will not need to be absorbed by other segments.

14. (b) If the segment continues, net income = −$40,000 ($200,000 − $140,000 − $100,000). If the segment is eliminated, the contribution margin will also be eliminated but $50,000 ($100,000 × .50) of the fixed costs will remain. Therefore, the effect of eliminating the segment will be a $10,000 decrease not (a) a $120,000 increase, (c) a $50,000 increase, or (d) a $10,000 increase.

▮ PRACTICE EXERCISES

1. Maningly Inc. has been manufacturing its own lampshades for its table lamps. The company is currently operating at 100% of capacity. Variable manufacturing overhead is charged to production at the rate of 50% of direct labor cost. The direct materials and direct labor cost per unit to make the lampshades are $4 and $6, respectively. Normal production is 50,000 table lamps per year.

Use incremental analysis for make-or-buy decision.

(LO 3)

A supplier offers to make the lampshades at a price of $13.50 per unit. If Maningly accepts the supplier's offer; all variable manufacturing costs will be eliminated, but the $50,000 of fixed manufacturing overhead currently being charged to the lampshades will have to be absorbed by other products.

Instructions

(a) Prepare the incremental analysis for the decision to make or buy the lampshades.
(b) Should Maningly buy the lampshades?
(c) Would your answer be different in (b) if the productive capacity released by not making the lampshades could be used to produce income of $40,000?

Solution

1. (a)

	Make	Buy	Net Income Increase (Decrease)
Direct materials (50,000 × $4.00)	$200,000	$ 0	$ 200,000
Direct labor (50,000 × $6.00)	300,000	0	300,000
Variable manufacturing costs ($300,000 × 50%)	150,000	0	150,000
Fixed manufacturing costs	50,000	50,000	0
Purchase price (50,000 × $13.50)	0	675,000	(675,000)
Total annual cost	$700,000	$725,000	$ (25,000)

(b) No, Maningly should not purchase the lampshades. As indicated by the incremental analysis, it would cost the company $25,000 more to purchase the lampshades.

(c) Yes, by purchasing the lampshades, a total cost saving of $15,000 will result as shown below.

	Make	Buy	Net Income Increase (Decrease)
Total annual cost (from (a))	$700,000	$725,000	$(25,000)
Opportunity cost	40,000	0	40,000
Total cost	$740,000	$725,000	$ 15,000

Use incremental analysis for whether to sell or process materials further.

(LO 4)

2. A company manufactures three products using same production process. The costs incurred up to the split-off point are $200,000. These costs are allocated to the products on the basis of their sales value at the split-off point. The number of units produced, the selling prices per unit of the three products at the split-off point and after further processing, and the additional processing costs are as follows.

Product	Number of Units Produced	Selling Price at Split-Off	Selling Price after Processing	Additional Processing Costs
D	3,000	$11.00	$15.00	$14,000
E	6,000	12.00	16.20	16,000
F	2,000	19.40	24.00	9,000

Instructions

(a) Which information is relevant to the decision on whether or not to process the products further? Explain why this information is relevant.

(b) Which product(s) should be processed further and which should be sold at the split-off point?

(c) Would your decision be different if the company was using the quantity of output to allocate joint costs? Explain.

(CGA adapted)

Solution

2. (a) The costs that are relevant in this decision are the incremental revenues and the incremental costs associated with processing the material past the split-off point. Any costs incurred up to the split-off point are sunk costs and therefore irrelevant to this decision.

(b) Revenue after further processing:

Product D: $45,000 (3,000 units × $15.00 per unit)
Product E: $97,200 (6,000 units × $16.20 per unit)
Product F: $48,000 (2,000 units × $24.00 per unit)

Revenue at split-off:

Product D: $33,000 (3,000 units × $11.00 per unit)
Product E: $72,000 (6,000 units × $12.00 per unit)
Product F: $38,800 (2,000 units × $19.40 per unit)

	D	E	F
Incremental revenue	$ 12,000[a]	$ 25,200[b]	$ 9,200[c]
Incremental cost	(14,000)	(16,000)	(9,000)
Increase (decrease) in profit	$ (2,000)	$ 9,200	$ 200

[a]$45,000 − $33,000; [b]$97,200 − $72,000; [c]$48,000 − $38,800

Products E and F should be processed further.

(c) The decision would remain the same. It does not matter how the joint costs are allocated because joint costs are irrelevant to this decision.

3. Tek Enterprises uses a computer to handle its sales invoices. Lately, business has been so good that it takes an extra 3 hours per night, plus every third Saturday, to keep up with the volume of sales invoices. Management is considering updating its computer with a faster model that would eliminate all of the overtime processing.

Use incremental analysis for retaining or replacing equipment.

(LO 5)

	Current Machine	New Machine
Original purchase cost	$15,000	$25,000
Accumulated depreciation	6,000	—
Estimated operating costs	25,000	20,000
Useful life	6 years	6 years

If sold now, the current machine would have a salvage value of $5,000. If operated for the remainder of its useful life, the current machine would have zero salvage value. The new machine is expected to have zero salvage value after 6 years.

Instructions

Should the current machine be replaced? (Ignore the time value of money.)

Solution

3.

	Retain Machine	Replace Machine	Net Income Increase (Decrease)
Operating costs	$150,000*	$120,000**	$30,000
New machine cost (depr.)	0	25,000	(25,000)
Salvage value (old)	0	(5,000)	5,000
Total	$150,000	$140,000	$10,000

*$25,000 × 6
**$20,000 × 6

The current machine should be replaced. The incremental analysis shows that net income for the 6-year period will be $10,000 higher by replacing the current machine.

4. Benai Lorenzo, a recent graduate of Bonita's accounting program, evaluated the operating performance of Wasson Company's six divisions. Benai made the following presentation to the Wasson board of directors and suggested the Ortiz Division be eliminated. "If the Ortiz Division is eliminated," she said, "our total profits would increase by $23,870."

Use incremental analysis for elimination of division.

(LO 6)

	The Other Five Divisions	Ortiz Division	Total
Sales	$1,664,200	$ 96,200	$1,760,400
Cost of goods sold	978,520	76,470	1,054,990
Gross profit	685,680	19,730	705,410
Operating expenses	527,940	43,600	571,540
Net income	$ 157,740	$(23,870)	$ 133,870

In the Ortiz Division, cost of goods sold is $70,000 variable and $6,470 fixed, and operating expenses are $15,000 variable and $28,600 fixed. None of the Ortiz Division's fixed costs will be eliminated if the division is discontinued.

Instructions

Is Benai right about eliminating the Ortiz Division? Prepare a schedule to support your answer.

Solution

4.

	Continue	Eliminate	Net Income Increase (Decrease)
Sales	$ 96,200	$ 0	$(96,200)
Variable expenses			
Cost of goods sold	70,000	0	70,000
Operating expenses	15,000	0	15,000
Total variable	85,000	0	85,000
Contribution margin	11,200	0	(11,200)
Fixed expenses			
Cost of goods sold	6,470	6,470	0
Operating expenses	28,600	28,600	0
Total fixed	35,070	35,070	0
Net income (loss)	$(23,870)	$(35,070)	$(11,200)

Benai is incorrect. The incremental analysis shows that net income will be $11,200 less if the Ortiz Division is eliminated. This amount equals the contribution margin that would be lost by discontinuing the division.

PRACTICE PROBLEM

Use incremental analysis for a special order.

(LO 2)

Walston Company produces kitchen cabinets for homebuilders across the western United States. The cost of producing 5,000 cabinets is as follows.

Materials	$ 500,000
Labor	250,000
Variable overhead	100,000
Fixed overhead	400,000
Total	$1,250,000

Walston also incurs selling expenses of $20 per cabinet. Wellington Corp. has offered Walston $165 per cabinet for a special order of 1,000 cabinets. The cabinets would be sold to homebuilders in the eastern United States and thus would not conflict with Walston's current sales. Selling expenses per cabinet would be only $5 per cabinet. Walston has available capacity to do the work.

Instructions

(a) Prepare an incremental analysis for the special order.

(b) Should Walston accept the special order? Why or why not?

Solution

(a) Relevant costs per unit would be:

Materials	$500,000/5,000 = $100
Labor	250,000/5,000 = 50
Variable overhead	100,000/5,000 = 20
Selling expenses	5
Total relevant cost per unit	$175

	Reject Order	Accept Order	Net Income Increase (Decrease)
Revenues	$0	$165,000*	$165,000
Costs	0	175,000**	(175,000)
Net income	$0	$ (10,000)	$ (10,000)

*$165 × 1,000; **$175 × 1,000

(b) Walston should reject the offer. The incremental benefit of $165 per cabinet is less than the incremental cost of $175. By accepting the order, Walston's net income would actually decline by $10,000.

QUESTIONS

1. What steps are frequently involved in management's decision-making process?

2. Your roommate, Anna Polis, contends that accounting contributes to most of the steps in management's decision-making process. Is your roommate correct? Explain.

3. "Incremental analysis involves the accumulation of information concerning a single course of action." Do you agree? Why?

4. Sydney Greene asks for your help concerning the relevance of variable and fixed costs in incremental analysis. Help Sydney with her problem.

5. What data are relevant in deciding whether to accept an order at a special price?

6. Emil Corporation has an opportunity to buy parts at $9 each that currently cost $12 to make. What manufacturing costs are relevant to this make-or-buy decision?

7. Define the term "opportunity cost." How may this cost be relevant in a make-or-buy decision?

8. What is the decision rule in deciding whether to sell a product or process it further?

9. What are joint products? What accounting issue results from the production process that creates joint products?

10. How are allocated joint costs treated when making a sell-or-process-further decision?

11. Your roommate, Gale Dunham, is confused about sunk costs. Explain to your roommate the meaning of sunk costs and their relevance to a decision to retain or replace equipment.

12. Huang Inc. has one product line that is unprofitable. What circumstances may cause overall company net income to be lower if the unprofitable product line is eliminated?

BRIEF EXERCISES

BE21-1 The steps in management's decision-making process are listed in random order below. Indicate the order in which the steps should be executed.

_____ Make a decision

_____ Identify the problem and assign responsibility

_____ Review results of the decision

_____ Determine and evaluate possible courses of action

Identify the steps in management's decision-making process.

(LO 1)

BE21-2 Bogart Company is considering two alternatives. Alternative A will have revenues of $160,000 and costs of $100,000. Alternative B will have revenues of $180,000 and costs of $125,000. Compare Alternative A to Alternative B showing incremental revenues, costs, and net income.

Determine incremental changes.

(LO 1)

BE21-3 At Bargain Electronics, it costs $30 per unit ($20 variable and $10 fixed) to make an MP3 player that normally sells for $45. A foreign wholesaler offers to buy 3,000 units at $25 each. Bargain Electronics will incur special shipping costs of $3 per unit. Assuming that Bargain Electronics has excess operating capacity, indicate the net income (loss) Bargain Electronics would realize by accepting the special order.

Determine whether to accept a special order.

(LO 2)

BE21-4 Manson Industries incurs unit costs of $8 ($5 variable and $3 fixed) in making an assembly part for its finished product. A supplier offers to make 10,000 of the assembly part at $6 per unit. If the offer is accepted, Manson will save all variable costs but no fixed costs. Prepare an analysis showing the total cost saving, if any, Manson will realize by buying the part.

Determine whether to make or buy a part.

(LO 3)

BE21-5 Pine Street Inc. makes unfinished bookcases that it sells for $62. Production costs are $36 variable and $10 fixed. Because it has unused capacity, Pine Street is considering finishing the bookcases and selling them for $70. Variable finishing costs are expected to be $6 per unit with no increase in fixed costs. Prepare an analysis on a per unit basis showing whether Pine Street should sell unfinished or finished bookcases.

Determine whether to sell or process further.

(LO 4)

Determine whether to sell or process further, joint products.

(LO 4)

BE21-6 Each day, Adama Corporation processes 1 ton of a secret raw material into two resulting products, AB1 and XY1. When it processes 1 ton of the raw material, the company incurs joint processing costs of $60,000. It allocates $25,000 of these costs to AB1 and $35,000 of these costs to XY1. The resulting AB1 can be sold for $100,000. Alternatively, it can be processed further to make AB2 at an additional processing cost of $45,000, and sold for $150,000. Each day's batch of XY1 can be sold for $95,000. Or, it can be processed further to create XY2, at an additional processing cost of $50,000, and sold for $130,000. Discuss what products Adama Corporation should make.

Determine whether to retain or replace equipment.

(LO 5)

BE21-7 Bryant Company has a factory machine with a book value of $90,000 and a remaining useful life of 5 years. It can be sold for $30,000. A new machine is available at a cost of $400,000. This machine will have a 5-year useful life with no salvage value. The new machine will lower annual variable manufacturing costs from $600,000 to $500,000. Prepare an analysis showing whether the old machine should be retained or replaced.

Determine whether to eliminate an unprofitable segment.

(LO 6)

BE21-8 Lisah, Inc., manufactures golf clubs in three models. For the year, the Big Bart line has a net loss of $10,000 from sales $200,000, variable costs $180,000, and fixed costs $30,000. If the Big Bart line is eliminated, $20,000 of fixed costs will remain. Prepare an analysis showing whether the Big Bart line should be eliminated.

DO IT! Exercises

Determine incremental costs.

(LO 1)

DO IT! 21-1 Nathan T Corporation is comparing two different options. Nathan T currently uses Option 1, with revenues of $65,000 per year, maintenance expenses of $5,000 per year, and operating expenses of $26,000 per year. Option 2 provides revenues of $60,000 per year, maintenance expenses of $5,000 per year, and operating expenses of $22,000 per year. Option 1 employs a piece of equipment which was upgraded 2 years ago at a cost of $17,000. If Option 2 is chosen, it will free up resources that will bring in an additional $4,000 of revenue. Complete the following table to show the change in income from choosing Option 2 versus Option 1. Designate Sunk costs with an "S."

	Option 1	Option 2	Net Income Increase (Decrease)	Sunk (S)
Revenues				
Maintenance expenses				
Operating expenses				
Equipment upgrade				
Opportunity cost				

Evaluate special order.

(LO 2)

DO IT! 21-2 Maize Company incurs a cost of $35 per unit, of which $20 is variable, to make a product that normally sells for $58. A foreign wholesaler offers to buy 6,000 units at $30 each. Maize will incur additional costs of $4 per unit to imprint a logo and to pay for shipping. Compute the increase or decrease in net income Maize will realize by accepting the special order, assuming Maize has sufficient excess operating capacity. Should Maize Company accept the special order?

Evaluate make-or-buy opportunity.

(LO 3)

DO IT! 21-3 Wilma Company must decide whether to make or buy some of its components. The costs of producing 60,000 switches for its generators are as follows.

Direct materials	$30,000	Variable overhead	$45,000
Direct labor	$42,000	Fixed overhead	$60,000

Instead of making the switches at an average cost of $2.95 ($177,000 ÷ 60,000), the company has an opportunity to buy the switches at $2.70 per unit. If the company purchases the switches, all the variable costs and one-fourth of the fixed costs will be eliminated. (a) Prepare an incremental analysis showing whether the company should make or buy the switches. (b) Would your answer be different if the released productive capacity will generate additional income of $34,000?

DO IT! 21-4 Mesa Verde manufactures unpainted furniture for the do-it-yourself (DIY) market. It currently sells a table for $75. Production costs are $40 variable and $10 fixed. Mesa Verde is considering staining and sealing the table to sell it for $100. Variable costs to finish each table are expected to be $19, and fixed costs are expected to be $3. Prepare an analysis showing whether Mesa Verde should sell unpainted or finished tables.

Sell or process further.
(LO 4)

DO IT! 21-5 Darcy Roofing is faced with a decision. The company relies very heavily on the use of its 60-foot extension lift for work on large homes and commercial properties. Last year, Darcy Roofing spent $60,000 refurbishing the lift. It has just determined that another $40,000 of repair work is required. Alternatively, it has found a newer used lift that is for sale for $170,000. The company estimates that both lifts would have useful lives of 6 years. The new lift is more efficient and thus would reduce operating expenses by about $20,000 per year. Darcy Roofing could also rent out the new lift for about $10,000 per year. The old lift is not suitable for rental. The old lift could currently be sold for $25,000 if the new lift is purchased. Prepare an incremental analysis showing whether the company should repair or replace the equipment.

Repair or replace equipment.
(LO 5)

DO IT! 21-6 Gator Corporation manufactures several types of accessories. For the year, the gloves and mittens line had sales of $500,000, variable expenses of $370,000, and fixed expenses of $150,000. Therefore, the gloves and mittens line had a net loss of $20,000. If Gator eliminates the line, $38,000 of fixed costs will remain. Prepare an analysis showing whether the company should eliminate the gloves and mittens line.

Analyze whether to eliminate unprofitable segment.
(LO 6)

EXERCISES

E21-1 As a study aid, your classmate Pascal Adams has prepared the following list of statements about decision-making and incremental analysis.

Analyze statements about decision-making and incremental analysis.
(LO 1)

1. The first step in management's decision-making process is, "Determine and evaluate possible courses of action."
2. The final step in management's decision-making process is to actually make the decision.
3. Accounting's contribution to management's decision-making process occurs primarily in evaluating possible courses of action and in reviewing the results.
4. In making business decisions, management ordinarily considers only financial information because it is objectively determined.
5. Decisions involve a choice among alternative courses of action.
6. The process used to identify the financial data that change under alternative courses of action is called incremental analysis.
7. Costs that are the same under all alternative courses of action sometimes affect the decision.
8. When using incremental analysis, some costs will always change under alternative courses of action, but revenues will not.
9. Variable costs will change under alternative courses of action, but fixed costs will not.

Instructions
Identify each statement as true or false. If false, indicate how to correct the statement.

E21-2 Gruden Company produces golf discs which it normally sells to retailers for $7 each. The cost of manufacturing 20,000 golf discs is:

Use incremental analysis for special-order decision.
(LO 2)

Materials	$ 10,000
Labor	30,000
Variable overhead	20,000
Fixed overhead	40,000
Total	$100,000

Gruden also incurs 5% sales commission ($0.35) on each disc sold.

McGee Corporation offers Gruden $4.80 per disc for 5,000 discs. McGee would sell the discs under its own brand name in foreign markets not yet served by Gruden. If Gruden accepts the offer, its fixed overhead will increase from $40,000 to $46,000 due to the purchase of a new imprinting machine. No sales commission will result from the special order.

Instructions
(a) Prepare an incremental analysis for the special order.
(b) Should Gruden accept the special order? Why or why not?
(c) What assumptions underlie the decision made in part (b)?

*Use incremental analysis
for special order.*

(LO 2)

E21-3 Moonbeam Company manufactures toasters. For the first 8 months of 2017, the company reported the following operating results while operating at 75% of plant capacity:

Sales (350,000 units)	$4,375,000
Cost of goods sold	2,600,000
Gross profit	1,775,000
Operating expenses	840,000
Net income	$ 935,000

Cost of goods sold was 70% variable and 30% fixed; operating expenses were 80% variable and 20% fixed.

In September, Moonbeam receives a special order for 15,000 toasters at $7.60 each from Luna Company of Ciudad Juarez. Acceptance of the order would result in an additional $3,000 of shipping costs but no increase in fixed costs.

Instructions
(a) Prepare an incremental analysis for the special order.
(b) Should Moonbeam accept the special order? Why or why not?

*Use incremental analysis
for special order.*

(LO 2)

E21-4 Klean Fiber Company is the creator of Y-Go, a technology that weaves silver into its fabrics to kill bacteria and odor on clothing while managing heat. Y-Go has become very popular in undergarments for sports activities. Operating at capacity, the company can produce 1,000,000 Y-Go undergarments a year. The per unit and the total costs for an individual garment when the company operates at full capacity are as follows.

	Per Undergarment	Total
Direct materials	$2.00	$2,000,000
Direct labor	0.75	750,000
Variable manufacturing overhead	1.00	1,000,000
Fixed manufacturing overhead	1.50	1,500,000
Variable selling expenses	0.25	250,000
Totals	$5.50	$5,500,000

The U.S. Army has approached Klean Fiber and expressed an interest in purchasing 250,000 Y-Go undergarments for soldiers in extremely warm climates. The Army would pay the unit cost for direct materials, direct labor, and variable manufacturing overhead costs. In addition, the Army has agreed to pay an additional $1 per undergarment to cover all other costs and provide a profit. Presently, Klean Fiber is operating at 70% capacity and does not have any other potential buyers for Y-Go. If Klean Fiber accepts the Army's offer, it will not incur any variable selling expenses related to this order.

Instructions
Using incremental analysis, determine whether Klean Fiber should accept the Army's offer.

*Use incremental analysis
for make-or-buy decision.*

(LO 3)

E21-5 Pottery Ranch Inc. has been manufacturing its own finials for its curtain rods. The company is currently operating at 100% of capacity, and variable manufacturing overhead is charged to production at the rate of 70% of direct labor cost. The direct materials and direct labor cost per unit to make a pair of finials are $4 and $5, respectively. Normal production is 30,000 curtain rods per year.

A supplier offers to make a pair of finials at a price of $12.95 per unit. If Pottery Ranch accepts the supplier's offer, all variable manufacturing costs will be eliminated, but the $45,000 of fixed manufacturing overhead currently being charged to the finials will have to be absorbed by other products.

Instructions

(a) Prepare the incremental analysis for the decision to make or buy the finials.

(b) Should Pottery Ranch buy the finials?

(c) Would your answer be different in (b) if the productive capacity released by not making the finials could be used to produce income of $20,000?

E21-6 Jobs, Inc. has recently started the manufacture of Tri-Robo, a three-wheeled robot that can scan a home for fires and gas leaks and then transmit this information to a smartphone. The cost structure to manufacture 20,000 Tri-Robos is as follows.

Use incremental analysis for make-or-buy decision.

(LO 3)

	Cost
Direct materials ($50 per robot)	$1,000,000
Direct labor ($40 per robot)	800,000
Variable overhead ($6 per robot)	120,000
Allocated fixed overhead ($30 per robot)	600,000
Total	$2,520,000

Jobs is approached by Tienh Inc., which offers to make Tri-Robo for $115 per unit or $2,300,000.

Instructions

(a) Using incremental analysis, determine whether Jobs should accept this offer under each of the following independent assumptions.

(1) Assume that $405,000 of the fixed overhead cost can be avoided.

(2) Assume that none of the fixed overhead can be avoided. However, if the robots are purchased from Tienh Inc., Jobs can use the released productive resources to generate additional income of $375,000.

(b) Describe the qualitative factors that might affect the decision to purchase the robots from an outside supplier.

E21-7 Riggs Company purchases sails and produces sailboats. It currently produces 1,200 sailboats per year, operating at normal capacity, which is about 80% of full capacity. Riggs purchases sails at $250 each, but the company is considering using the excess capacity to manufacture the sails instead. The manufacturing cost per sail would be $100 for direct materials, $80 for direct labor, and $90 for overhead. The $90 overhead is based on $78,000 of annual fixed overhead that is allocated using normal capacity.

Prepare incremental analysis for make-or-buy decision.

(LO 3)

The president of Riggs has come to you for advice. "It would cost me $270 to make the sails," she says, "but only $250 to buy them. Should I continue buying them, or have I missed something?"

Instructions

(a) Prepare a per unit analysis of the differential costs. Briefly explain whether Riggs should make or buy the sails.

(b) If Riggs suddenly finds an opportunity to rent out the unused capacity of its factory for $77,000 per year, would your answer to part (a) change? Briefly explain.

(c) Identify three qualitative factors that should be considered by Riggs in this make-or-buy decision.

(CGA adapted)

E21-8 Innova uses 1,000 units of the component IMC2 every month to manufacture one of its products. The unit costs incurred to manufacture the component are as follows.

Prepare incremental analysis concerning make-or-buy decision.

(LO 3)

Direct materials	$ 65.00
Direct labor	45.00
Overhead	126.50
Total	$236.50

Overhead costs include variable material handling costs of $6.50, which are applied to products on the basis of direct material costs. The remainder of the overhead costs are applied on the basis of direct labor dollars and consist of 60% variable costs and 40% fixed costs.

A vendor has offered to supply the IMC2 component at a price of $200 per unit.

Instructions

(a) Should Innova purchase the component from the outside vendor if Innova's capacity remains idle?

(b) Should Innova purchase the component from the outside vendor if it can use its facilities to manufacture another product? What information will Innova need to make an accurate decision? Show your calculations.

(c) What are the qualitative factors that Innova will have to consider when making this decision?

(CGA adapted)

Use incremental analysis for further processing of materials decision.

(LO 4)

E21-9 Anna Garden recently opened her own basketweaving studio. She sells finished baskets in addition to the raw materials needed by customers to weave baskets of their own. Anna has put together a variety of raw material kits, each including materials at various stages of completion. Unfortunately, owing to space limitations, Anna is unable to carry all varieties of kits originally assembled and must choose between two basic packages.

The basic introductory kit includes undyed, uncut reeds (with dye included) for weaving one basket. This basic package costs Anna $16 and sells for $30. The second kit, called Stage 2, includes cut reeds that have already been dyed. With this kit the customer need only soak the reeds and weave the basket. Anna is able to produce the second kit by using the basic materials included in the first kit and adding one hour of her own time, which she values at $18 per hour. Because she is more efficient at cutting and dying reeds than her average customer, Anna is able to make two kits of the dyed reeds, in one hour, from one kit of undyed reeds. The Stage 2 kit sells for $36.

Instructions

Determine whether Anna's basketweaving studio should carry the basic introductory kit with undyed and uncut reeds or the Stage 2 kit with reeds already dyed and cut. Prepare an incremental analysis to support your answer.

Determine whether to sell or process further, joint products.

(LO 4)

E21-10 Stahl Inc. produces three separate products from a common process costing $100,000. Each of the products can be sold at the split-off point or can be processed further and then sold for a higher price. Shown below are cost and selling price data for a recent period.

	Sales Value at Split-Off Point	Cost to Process Further	Sales Value after Further Processing
Product 10	$60,000	$100,000	$190,000
Product 12	15,000	30,000	35,000
Product 14	55,000	150,000	215,000

Instructions

(a) Determine total net income if all products are sold at the split-off point.

(b) Determine total net income if all products are sold after further processing.

(c) Using incremental analysis, determine which products should be sold at the split-off point and which should be processed further.

(d) Determine total net income using the results from (c) and explain why the net income is different from that determined in (b).

Determine whether to sell or process further, joint products.

(LO 4)

E21-11 Kirk Minerals processes materials extracted from mines. The most common raw material that it processes results in three joint products: Spock, Uhura, and Sulu. Each of these products can be sold as is, or each can be processed further and sold for a higher price. The company incurs joint costs of $180,000 to process one batch of the raw material that produces the three joint products. The following cost and sales information is available for one batch of each product.

	Sales Value at Split-Off Point	Allocated Joint Costs	Cost to Process Further	Sales Value of Processed Product
Spock	$210,000	$40,000	$110,000	$300,000
Uhura	300,000	60,000	85,000	400,000
Sulu	455,000	80,000	250,000	800,000

Instructions

Determine whether each of the three joint products should be sold as is, or processed further.

E21-12 A company manufactures three products using the same production process. The costs incurred up to the split-off point are $200,000. These costs are allocated to the products on the basis of their sales value at the split-off point. The number of units produced, the selling prices per unit of the three products at the split-off point and after further processing, and the additional processing costs are as follows.

Prepare incremental analysis for whether to sell or process materials further.

(LO 4)

Product	Number of Units Produced	Selling Price at Split-Off	Selling Price after Processing	Additional Processing Costs
D	4,000	$10.00	$15.00	$14,000
E	6,000	11.60	16.20	20,000
F	2,000	19.40	22.60	9,000

Instructions

(a) Which information is relevant to the decision on whether or not to process the products further? Explain why this information is relevant.

(b) Which product(s) should be processed further and which should be sold at the split-off point?

(c) Would your decision be different if the company was using the quantity of output to allocate joint costs? Explain.

(CGA adapted)

E21-13 On January 2, 2016, Twilight Hospital purchased a $100,000 special radiology scanner from Bella Inc. The scanner had a useful life of 4 years and was estimated to have no disposal value at the end of its useful life. The straight-line method of depreciation is used on this scanner. Annual operating costs with this scanner are $105,000.

Use incremental analysis for retaining or replacing equipment decision.

(LO 5)

Approximately one year later, the hospital is approached by Dyno Technology salesperson, Jacob Cullen, who indicated that purchasing the scanner in 2016 from Bella Inc. was a mistake. He points out that Dyno has a scanner that will save Twilight Hospital $25,000 a year in operating expenses over its 3-year useful life. Jacob notes that the new scanner will cost $110,000 and has the same capabilities as the scanner purchased last year. The hospital agrees that both scanners are of equal quality. The new scanner will have no disposal value. Jacob agrees to buy the old scanner from Twilight Hospital for $50,000.

Instructions

(a) If Twilight Hospital sells its old scanner on January 2, 2017, compute the gain or loss on the sale.

(b) Using incremental analysis, determine if Twilight Hospital should purchase the new scanner on January 2, 2017.

(c) Explain why Twilight Hospital might be reluctant to purchase the new scanner, regardless of the results indicated by the incremental analysis in (b).

E21-14 Johnson Enterprises uses a computer to handle its sales invoices. Lately, business has been so good that it takes an extra 3 hours per night, plus every third Saturday, to keep up with the volume of sales invoices. Management is considering updating its computer with a faster model that would eliminate all of the overtime processing.

Use incremental analysis for retaining or replacing equipment decision.

(LO 5)

	Current Machine	New Machine
Original purchase cost	$15,000	$25,000
Accumulated depreciation	$ 6,000	—
Estimated annual operating costs	$25,000	$20,000
Remaining useful life	5 years	5 years

If sold now, the current machine would have a salvage value of $6,000. If operated for the remainder of its useful life, the current machine would have zero salvage value. The new machine is expected to have zero salvage value after 5 years.

Instructions

Should the current machine be replaced?

E21-15 Veronica Mars, a recent graduate of Bell's accounting program, evaluated the operating performance of Dunn Company's six divisions. Veronica made the following presentation to Dunn's board of directors and suggested the Percy Division be eliminated. "If the Percy Division is eliminated," she said, "our total profits would increase by $26,000."

Use incremental analysis concerning elimination of division.

(LO 6)

	The Other Five Divisions	Percy Division	Total
Sales	$1,664,200	$100,000	$1,764,200
Cost of goods sold	978,520	76,000	1,054,520
Gross profit	685,680	24,000	709,680
Operating expenses	527,940	50,000	577,940
Net income	$ 157,740	$ (26,000)	$ 131,740

In the Percy Division, cost of goods sold is $61,000 variable and $15,000 fixed, and operating expenses are $30,000 variable and $20,000 fixed. None of the Percy Division's fixed costs will be eliminated if the division is discontinued.

Instructions

Is Veronica right about eliminating the Percy Division? Prepare a schedule to support your answer.

Use incremental analysis for elimination of a product line.

(LO 6)

E21-16 Cawley Company makes three models of tasers. Information on the three products is given below.

	Tingler	Shocker	Stunner
Sales	$300,000	$500,000	$200,000
Variable expenses	150,000	200,000	145,000
Contribution margin	150,000	300,000	55,000
Fixed expenses	120,000	230,000	95,000
Net income	$ 30,000	$ 70,000	$ (40,000)

Fixed expenses consist of $300,000 of common costs allocated to the three products based on relative sales, and additional fixed expenses of $30,000 (Tingler), $80,000 (Shocker), and $35,000 (Stunner). The common costs will be incurred regardless of how many models are produced. The other fixed expenses would be eliminated if a model is phased out.

James Watt, an executive with the company, feels the Stunner line should be discontinued to increase the company's net income.

Instructions

(a) Compute current net income for Cawley Company.
(b) Compute net income by product line and in total for Cawley Company if the company discontinues the Stunner product line. (*Hint:* Allocate the $300,000 common costs to the two remaining product lines based on their relative sales.)
(c) Should Cawley eliminate the Stunner product line? Why or why not?

Prepare incremental analysis concerning keeping or dropping a product to maximize operating income.

(LO 6)

E21-17 Tharp Company operates a small factory in which it manufactures two products: C and D. Production and sales results for last year were as follows.

	C	D
Units sold	9,000	20,000
Selling price per unit	$95	$75
Variable cost per unit	50	40
Fixed cost per unit	24	24

For purposes of simplicity, the firm averages total fixed costs over the total number of units of C and D produced and sold.

The research department has developed a new product (E) as a replacement for product D. Market studies show that Tharp Company could sell 10,000 units of E next year at a price of $115; the variable cost per unit of E is $45. The introduction of product E will lead to a 10% increase in demand for product C and discontinuation of product D. If the company does not introduce the new product, it expects next year's results to be the same as last year's.

Instructions

Should Tharp Company introduce product E next year? Explain why or why not. Show calculations to support your decision.

(CMA-Canada adapted)

E21-18 The costs listed below relate to a variety of different decision situations.

Cost	Decision
1. Unavoidable fixed overhead	Eliminate an unprofitable segment
2. Direct labor	Make or buy
3. Original cost of old equipment	Equipment replacement
4. Joint production costs	Sell or process further
5. Opportunity cost	Accepting a special order
6. Segment manager's salary	Eliminate an unprofitable segment (manager will be terminated)
7. Cost of new equipment	Equipment replacement
8. Incremental production costs	Sell or process further
9. Direct materials	Equipment replacement (the amount of materials required does not change)
10. Rent expense	Purchase or lease a building

Instructions

For each cost listed above, indicate if it is relevant or not to the related decision. For those costs determined to be irrelevant, briefly explain why.

EXERCISES: SET B AND CHALLENGE EXERCISES

Visit the book's companion website, at **www.wiley.com/college/weygandt**, and choose the Student Companion site to access Exercises: Set B and Challenge Exercises.

PROBLEMS: SET A

P21-1A ThreePoint Sports Inc. manufactures basketballs for the Women's National Basketball Association (WNBA). For the first 6 months of 2017, the company reported the following operating results while operating at 80% of plant capacity and producing 120,000 units.

	Amount
Sales	$4,800,000
Cost of goods sold	3,600,000
Selling and administrative expenses	405,000
Net income	$ 795,000

Fixed costs for the period were cost of goods sold $960,000, and selling and administrative expenses $225,000.

In July, normally a slack manufacturing month, ThreePoint Sports receives a special order for 10,000 basketballs at $28 each from the Greek Basketball Association (GBA). Acceptance of the order would increase variable selling and administrative expenses $0.75 per unit because of shipping costs but would not increase fixed costs and expenses.

Instructions

(a) Prepare an incremental analysis for the special order.

(b) Should ThreePoint Sports Inc. accept the special order? Explain your answer.

(c) What is the minimum selling price on the special order to produce net income of $5.00 per ball?

(d) ——————— What nonfinancial factors should management consider in making its decision?

P21-2A The management of Shatner Manufacturing Company is trying to decide whether to continue manufacturing a part or to buy it from an outside supplier. The part, called CISCO, is a component of the company's finished product.

The following information was collected from the accounting records and production data for the year ending December 31, 2017.

1. 8,000 units of CISCO were produced in the Machining Department.
2. Variable manufacturing costs applicable to the production of each CISCO unit were: direct materials $4.80, direct labor $4.30, indirect labor $0.43, utilities $0.40.
3. Fixed manufacturing costs applicable to the production of CISCO were:

Cost Item	Direct	Allocated
Depreciation	$2,100	$ 900
Property taxes	500	200
Insurance	900	600
	$3,500	$1,700

All variable manufacturing and direct fixed costs will be eliminated if CISCO is purchased. Allocated costs will have to be absorbed by other production departments.
4. The lowest quotation for 8,000 CISCO units from a supplier is $80,000.
5. If CISCO units are purchased, freight and inspection costs would be $0.35 per unit, and receiving costs totaling $1,300 per year would be incurred by the Machining Department.

Instructions

(a) Prepare an incremental analysis for CISCO. Your analysis should have columns for (1) Make CISCO, (2) Buy CISCO, and (3) Net Income Increase/(Decrease).
(b) Based on your analysis, what decision should management make?
(c) Would the decision be different if Shatner Company has the opportunity to produce $3,000 of net income with the facilities currently being used to manufacture CISCO? Show computations.
(d) ———— What nonfinancial factors should management consider in making its decision?

(a) NI (decrease) $(1,160)

(c) NI increase $1,840

Determine if product should be sold or processed further.

(LO 4)

P21-3A Thompson Industrial Products Inc. (TIPI) is a diversified industrial-cleaner processing company. The company's Dargan plant produces two products: a table cleaner and a floor cleaner from a common set of chemical inputs (CDG). Each week, 900,000 ounces of chemical input are processed at a cost of $210,000 into 600,000 ounces of floor cleaner and 300,000 ounces of table cleaner. The floor cleaner has no market value until it is converted into a polish with the trade name FloorShine. The additional processing costs for this conversion amount to $240,000.

FloorShine sells at $20 per 30-ounce bottle. The table cleaner can be sold for $17 per 25-ounce bottle. However, the table cleaner can be converted into two other products by adding 300,000 ounces of another compound (TCP) to the 300,000 ounces of table cleaner. This joint process will yield 300,000 ounces each of table stain remover (TSR) and table polish (TP). The additional processing costs for this process amount to $100,000. Both table products can be sold for $14 per 25-ounce bottle.

The company decided not to process the table cleaner into TSR and TP based on the following analysis.

	Table Cleaner	Table Stain Remover (TSR)	Table Polish (TP)	Total
			Process Further	
Production in ounces	300,000	300,000	300,000	
Revenues	$204,000	$168,000	$168,000	$336,000
Costs:				
CDG costs	70,000*	52,500	52,500	105,000**
TCP costs	0	50,000	50,000	100,000
Total costs	70,000	102,500	102,500	205,000
Weekly gross profit	$134,000	$ 65,500	$ 65,500	$131,000

*If table cleaner is not processed further, it is allocated 1/3 of the $210,000 of CDG cost, which is equal to 1/3 of the total physical output.

**If table cleaner is processed further, total physical output is 1,200,000 ounces. TSR and TP combined account for 50% of the total physical output and are each allocated 25% of the CDG cost.

Instructions

(a) Determine if management made the correct decision to not process the table cleaner further by doing the following.

    (1) Calculate the company's total weekly gross profit assuming the table cleaner is not processed further.

    (2) Calculate the company's total weekly gross profit assuming the table cleaner is processed further.

    (3) Compare the resulting net incomes and comment on management's decision.

(b) Using incremental analysis, determine if the table cleaner should be processed further.

(CMA adapted)

(2) Gross profit $186,000

P21-4A Last year (2016), Richter Condos installed a mechanized elevator for its tenants. The owner of the company, Ron Richter, recently returned from an industry equipment exhibition where he watched a computerized elevator demonstrated. He was impressed with the elevator's speed, comfort of ride, and cost efficiency. Upon returning from the exhibition, he asked his purchasing agent to collect price and operating cost data on the new elevator. In addition, he asked the company's accountant to provide him with cost data on the company's elevator. This information is presented below.

Compute gain or loss, and determine if equipment should be replaced.

(LO 5)

	Old Elevator	New Elevator
Purchase price	$120,000	$160,000
Estimated salvage value	0	0
Estimated useful life	5 years	4 years
Depreciation method	Straight-line	Straight-line
Annual operating costs other than depreciation:		
Variable	$ 35,000	$ 10,000
Fixed	23,000	8,500

Annual revenues are $240,000, and selling and administrative expenses are $29,000, regardless of which elevator is used. If the old elevator is replaced now, at the beginning of 2017, Richter Condos will be able to sell it for $25,000.

Instructions

(a) Determine any gain or loss if the old elevator is replaced.

(b) Prepare a 4-year summarized income statement for each of the following assumptions:

    (1) The old elevator is retained.

    (2) The old elevator is replaced.

(c) Using incremental analysis, determine if the old elevator should be replaced.

(d) ✏ Write a memo to Ron Richter explaining why any gain or loss should be ignored in the decision to replace the old elevator.

(b) (2) NI $539,000
(c) NI increase $23,000

P21-5A Brislin Company has four operating divisions. During the first quarter of 2017, the company reported aggregate income from operations of $213,000 and the following divisional results.

Prepare incremental analysis concerning elimination of divisions.

(LO 6)

	Division			
	I	**II**	**III**	**IV**
Sales	$250,000	$200,000	$500,000	$450,000
Cost of goods sold	200,000	192,000	300,000	250,000
Selling and administrative expenses	75,000	60,000	60,000	50,000
Income (loss) from operations	$ (25,000)	$ (52,000)	$140,000	$150,000

Analysis reveals the following percentages of variable costs in each division.

	I	II	III	IV
Cost of goods sold	70%	90%	80%	75%
Selling and administrative expenses	40	60	50	60

Discontinuance of any division would save 50% of the fixed costs and expenses for that division. Top management is very concerned about the unprofitable divisions (I and II). Consensus is that one or both of the divisions should be discontinued.

Instructions

(a) I $80,000

(a) Compute the contribution margin for Divisions I and II.

(b) Prepare an incremental analysis concerning the possible discontinuance of (1) Division I and (2) Division II. What course of action do you recommend for each division?

(c) Income III $132,800

(c) Prepare a columnar condensed income statement for Brislin Company, assuming Division II is eliminated. (Use the CVP format.) Division II's unavoidable fixed costs are allocated equally to the continuing divisions.

(d) Reconcile the total income from operations ($213,000) with the total income from operations without Division II.

PROBLEMS: SET B AND SET C

Visit the book's companion website, at **www.wiley.com/college/weygandt**, and choose the Student Companion site to access Problems: Set B and Set C.

CONTINUING PROBLEMS

CURRENT DESIGNS

CD21 Current Designs faces a number of important decisions that require incremental analysis. Consider each of the following situations independently.

Situation 1

Recently, Mike Cichanowski, owner and CEO of Current Designs, received a phone call from the president of a brewing company. He was calling to inquire about the possibility of Current Designs producing "floating coolers" for a promotion his company was planning. These coolers resemble a kayak but are about one-third the size. They are used to float food and beverages while paddling down the river on a weekend leisure trip. The company would be interested in purchasing 100 coolers for the upcoming summer. It is willing to pay $250 per cooler. The brewing company would pick up the coolers upon completion of the order.

Mike met with Diane Buswell, controller, to identify how much it would cost Current Designs to produce the coolers. After careful analysis, the following costs were identified.

Direct materials	$80/unit	Variable overhead	$20/unit
Direct labor	$60/unit	Fixed overhead	$1,000

Current Designs would be able to modify an existing mold to produce the coolers. The cost of these modifications would be approximately $2,000.

Instructions

(a) Prepare an incremental analysis to determine whether Current Designs should accept this special order to produce the coolers.

(b) Discuss additional factors that Mike and Diane should consider if Current Designs is currently operating at full capacity.

Situation 2

Current Designs is always working to identify ways to increase efficiency while becoming more environmentally conscious. During a recent brainstorming session, one employee suggested to Diane Buswell, controller, that the company should consider replacing the current rotomold oven as a way to realize savings from reduced energy consumption. The oven operates on natural gas, using 17,000 therms of natural gas for an entire year. A new, energy-efficient rotomold oven would operate on 15,000 therms of natural gas for an entire year. After seeking out price quotes from a few suppliers, Diane determined that it would cost approximately $250,000 to purchase a new, energy-efficient roto-mold oven. She determines that the expected useful life of the new oven would be 10 years, and it would have no salvage value at the end of its useful life. Current Designs would be able to sell the current oven for $10,000.

Instructions

(a) Prepare an incremental analysis to determine if Current Designs should purchase the new rotomold oven, assuming that the average price for natural gas over the next 10 years will be $0.65 per therm.

(b) Diane is concerned that natural gas prices might increase at a faster rate over the next 10 years. If the company projects that the average natural gas price of the next 10 years could be as high as $0.85 per therm, discuss how that might change your conclusion in (a).

Situation 3

One of Current Designs' competitive advantages is found in the ingenuity of its owner and CEO, Mike Cichanowski. His involvement in the design of kayak molds and production techniques has led to Current Designs being recognized as an industry leader in the design and production of kayaks. This ingenuity was evident in an improved design of one of the most important components of a kayak, the seat. The "Revolution Seating System" is a one-of-a-kind, rotating axis seat that gives unmatched, full-contact, under-leg support. It is quickly adjustable with a lever-lock system that allows for a customizable seat position that maximizes comfort for the rider.

Having just designed the "Revolution Seating System," Current Designs must now decide whether to produce the seats internally or buy them from an outside supplier. The costs for Current Designs to produce the seats are as follows.

Direct materials	$20/unit	Direct labor	$15/unit
Variable overhead	$12/unit	Fixed overhead	$20,000

Current Designs will need to produce 3,000 seats this year; 25% of the fixed overhead will be avoided if the seats are purchased from an outside vendor. After soliciting prices from outside suppliers, the company determined that it will cost $50 to purchase a seat from an outside vendor.

Instructions

(a) Prepare an incremental analysis showing whether Current Designs should make or buy the "Revolution Seating System."

(b) Would your answer in (a) change if the productive capacity released by not making the seats could be used to produce income of $20,000?

WATERWAYS

(This is a continuation of the Waterways problem from Chapters 15–20.)

WP21 Waterways Corporation is considering various business opportunities. It wants to make the best use of its production facilities to maximize income. This problem asks you to help Waterways do incremental analysis on these various opportunities.

Go to the book's companion website, **www.wiley.com/college/weygandt**, *to find the remainder of this problem.*

BROADENING YOUR *PERSPECTIVE*

MANAGEMENT DECISION-MAKING

Decision-Making Across the Organization

BYP21-1 Aurora Company is considering the purchase of a new machine. The invoice price of the machine is $140,000, freight charges are estimated to be $4,000, and installation costs are expected to be $6,000. Salvage value of the new equipment is expected to be zero after a useful life of 5 years.

Existing equipment could be retained and used for an additional 5 years if the new machine is not purchased. At that time, the salvage value of the equipment would be zero. If the new machine is purchased now, the existing machine would have to be scrapped. Aurora's accountant, Lisah Huang, has accumulated the following data regarding annual sales and expenses with and without the new machine.

1. Without the new machine, Aurora can sell 12,000 units of product annually at a per unit selling price of $100. If the new machine is purchased, the number of units produced and sold would increase by 10%, and the selling price would remain the same.
2. The new machine is faster than the old machine, and it is more efficient in its usage of materials. With the old machine the gross profit rate will be 25% of sales, whereas the rate will be 30% of sales with the new machine.
3. Annual selling expenses are $180,000 with the current equipment. Because the new equipment would produce a greater number of units to be sold, annual selling expenses are expected to increase by 10% if it is purchased.
4. Annual administrative expenses are expected to be $100,000 with the old machine, and $113,000 with the new machine.
5. The current book value of the existing machine is $36,000. Aurora uses straight-line depreciation.

Instructions
With the class divided into groups, prepare an incremental analysis for the 5 years showing whether Aurora should keep the existing machine or buy the new machine. (Ignore income tax effects.)

Managerial Analysis

BYP21-2 MiniTek manufactures private-label small electronic products, such as alarm clocks, calculators, kitchen timers, stopwatches, and automatic pencil sharpeners. Some of the products are sold as sets, and others are sold individually. Products are studied as to their sales potential, and then cost estimates are made. The Engineering Department develops production plans, and then production begins. The company has generally had very successful product introductions. Only two products introduced by the company have been discontinued.

One of the products currently sold is a multi-alarm clock. The clock has four alarms that can be programmed to sound at various times and for varying lengths of time. The company has experienced a great deal of difficulty in making the circuit boards for the clocks. The production process has never operated smoothly. The product is unprofitable at the present time, primarily because of warranty repairs and product recalls. Two models of the clocks were recalled, for example, because they sometimes caused an electric shock when the alarms were being shut off. The Engineering Department is attempting to revise the manufacturing process, but the revision will take another 6 months at least.

The clocks were very popular when they were introduced, and since they are private-label, the company has not suffered much from the recalls. Presently, the company has a very large order for several items from Kmart Stores. The order includes 5,000 of the multi-alarm clocks. When the company suggested that Kmart purchase the clocks from another manufacturer, Kmart threatened to rescind the entire order unless the clocks were included.

The company has therefore investigated the possibility of having another company make the clocks for them. The clocks were bid for the Kmart order based on an estimated $6.90 cost to manufacture:

Circuit board, 1 each @ $2.00	$2.00
Plastic case, 1 each @ $0.80	0.80
Alarms, 4 @ $0.15 each	0.60
Labor, 15 minutes @ $12/hour	3.00
Overhead, $2.00 per labor hour	0.50

MiniTek could purchase clocks to fill the Kmart order for $10 from Trans-Tech Asia, a Korean manufacturer with a very good quality record. Trans-Tech has offered to reduce the price to $7.50 after MiniTek has been a customer for 6 months, placing an order of at least 1,000 units per month. If MiniTek becomes a "preferred customer" by purchasing 15,000 units per year, the price would be reduced still further to $4.50.

Omega Products, a local manufacturer, has also offered to make clocks for MiniTek. They have offered to sell 5,000 clocks for $5 each. However, Omega Products has been in business for only

6 months. They have experienced significant turnover in their labor force, and the local press has reported that the owners may face tax evasion charges soon. The owner of Omega Products is an electronic engineer, however, and the quality of the clocks is likely to be good.

If MiniTek decides to purchase the clocks from either Trans-Tech or Omega, all the costs to manufacture could be avoided, except a total of $1,000 in overhead costs for machine depreciation. The machinery is fairly new, and has no alternate use.

Instructions

(a) What is the difference in profit under each of the alternatives if the clocks are to be sold for $14.50 each to Kmart?

(b) What are the most important nonfinancial factors that MiniTek should consider when making this decision?

(c) What do you think MiniTek should do in regard to the Kmart order? What should it do in regard to continuing to manufacture the multi-alarm clocks? Be prepared to defend your answer.

Real-World Focus

BYP21-3 Founded in 1983 and foreclosed in 1996 **Beverly Hills Fan Company** was located in Woodland Hills, California. With 23 employees and sales of less than $10 million, the company was relatively small. In 1992, management felt that there was potential for growth in the upscale market for ceiling fans and lighting. They were particularly optimistic about growth in Mexican and Canadian markets.

Presented below is information from the president's letter in one of the company's last annual reports.

BEVERLY HILLS FAN COMPANY
President's Letter

An aggressive product development program was initiated during the past year resulting in new ceiling fan models planned for introduction this year. Award winning industrial designer Ron Rezek created several new fan models for the Beverly Hills Fan and L.A. Fan lines, including a new Showroom Collection, designed specifically for the architectural and designer markets. Each of these models has received critical acclaim, and order commitments for this year have been outstanding. Additionally, our Custom Color and special order fans continued to enjoy increasing popularity and sales gains as more and more customers desire fans that match their specific interior decors. Currently, Beverly Hills Fan Company offers a product line of over 100 models of contemporary, traditional, and transitional ceiling fans.

Instructions

(a) What points did the company management need to consider before deciding to offer the special-order fans to customers?

(b) How would have incremental analysis been employed to assist in this decision?

BYP21-4 Outsourcing by both manufacturers and service companies is becoming increasingly common. There are now many firms that specialize in outsourcing consulting.

Address: **www.alsbridge.com**, or go to **www.wiley.com/college/weygandt**

Instructions

Go to the website of Alsbridge, Inc. at the address shown above, and answer the following questions.

(a) What are some of the types of outsourcing for which the company provides assistance?

(b) What is insourcing?

(c) What are some of the potential benefits of insourcing?

CRITICAL THINKING

Communication Activity

BYP21-5 Hank Jewell is a production manager at a metal fabricating plant. Last night, he read an article about a new piece of equipment that would dramatically reduce his division's costs. Hank was very excited about the prospect, and the first thing he did this morning was to bring the article to his supervisor, Preston Thiese, the plant manager. The following conversation occurred:

Hank: Preston, I thought you would like to see this article on the new PDD1130; they've made some fantastic changes that could save us millions of dollars.

Preston: I appreciate your interest, Hank, but I actually have been aware of the new machine for two months. The problem is that we just bought a new machine last year. We spent $2 million on that machine, and it was supposed to last us 12 years. If we replace it now, we would have to write its book value off of the books for a huge loss. If I go to top management now and say that I want a new machine, they will fire me. I think we should use our existing machine for a couple of years, and then when it becomes obvious that we have to have a new machine, I will make the proposal.

Instructions

Hank just completed a course in managerial accounting, and he believes that Preston is making a big mistake. Write a memo from Hank to Preston explaining Preston's decision-making error.

Ethics Case

BYP21-6 Blake Romney became Chief Executive Officer of Peters Inc. two years ago. At the time, the company was reporting lagging profits, and Blake was brought in to "stir things up." The company has three divisions, electronics, fiber optics, and plumbing supplies. Blake has no interest in plumbing supplies, and one of the first things he did was to put pressure on his accountants to reallocate some of the company's fixed costs away from the other two divisions to the plumbing division. This had the effect of causing the plumbing division to report losses during the last two years; in the past it had always reported low, but acceptable, net income. Blake felt that this reallocation would shine a favorable light on him in front of the board of directors because it meant that the electronics and fiber optics divisions would look like they were improving. Given that these are "businesses of the future," he believed that the stock market would react favorably to these increases, while not penalizing the poor results of the plumbing division. Without this shift in the allocation of fixed costs, the profits of the electronics and fiber optics divisions would not have improved. But now the board of directors has suggested that the plumbing division be closed because it is reporting losses. This would mean that nearly 500 employees, many of whom have worked for Peters their whole lives, would lose their jobs.

Instructions

(a) If a division is reporting losses, does that necessarily mean that it should be closed?
(b) Was the reallocation of fixed costs across divisions unethical?
(c) What should Blake do?

All About You

BYP21-7 Managerial accounting techniques can be used in a wide variety of settings. As we have frequently pointed out, you can use them in many personal situations. They also can be useful in trying to find solutions for societal issues that appear to be hard to solve.

Instructions

Read the Fortune article, "The Toughest Customers: How Hardheaded Business Metrics Can Help the Hard-core Homeless," by Cait Murphy, available at *http://money.cnn.com/magazines/fortune/ fortune_archive/2006/04/03/8373067/index.htm*. Answer the following questions.

(a) How does the article define "chronic" homelessness?
(b) In what ways does homelessness cost a city money? What are the estimated costs of a chronic homeless person to various cities?
(c) What are the steps suggested to address the problem?
(d) What is the estimated cost of implementing this program in New York? What results have been seen?
(e) In terms of incremental analysis, frame the relevant costs in this situation.

Considering Your Costs and Benefits

BYP21-8 School costs money. Is this an expenditure that you should have avoided? A year of tuition at a public four-year college costs about $8,655, and a year of tuition at a public two-year college costs about $1,359. If you did not go to college, you might avoid mountains of school-related debt. In fact, each year, about 600,000 students decide to drop out of school. Many of them never return. Suppose that you are working two jobs and going to college, and that you are not making ends meet. Your grades are suffering due to your lack of available study time. You feel depressed. Should you drop out of school?

> **YES:** You can always go back to school. If your grades are bad and you are depressed, what good is school doing you anyway?
>
> **NO:** Once you drop out, it is very hard to get enough momentum to go back. Dropping out will dramatically reduce your long-term opportunities. It is better to stay in school, even if you take only one class per semester. While you cannot go back and redo your initial decision, you can look at some facts to evaluate the wisdom of your decision.

Instructions

Write a response indicating your position regarding this situation. Provide support for your view.

22 Pricing

FEATURE STORY

They've Got Your Size—and Color

Nick Swinmurn was shopping for a pair of shoes. He found a store with the right style, but not the right color. The next store had the right color, but not the right size. After visiting numerous stores, he went home, figuring he would buy them online. After all, it was 1999, so you could buy everything online, right? Well, apparently not shoes. After an exhaustive search, Nick still came up shoeless.

Nick lived in San Francisco, where in 1999 everybody with even half an idea started an Internet company and became a millionaire. Or so it seemed. So Nick started Zappos.com. The company is dedicated to providing the best selection in shoes in terms of brands, styles, colors, size, and, most importantly, service.

To make sure that Zappos had a fighting chance of evolving from a half-baked idea to a thriving business, Nick brought in Tony Hsieh. At the age of 24, Tony had developed and recently sold a business to Microsoft for $265 million. Tony then brought in Alfred Lin to manage the company's finances. Tony and Alfred first met when Tony was running a pizza business and Alfred was Tony's best pizza customer.

Together, Tony and Alfred have run Zappos based on 10 basic principles:

1. Deliver WOW through service.
2. Embrace and drive change.
3. Create fun and a little weirdness.
4. Be adventurous, creative, and open-minded.
5. Pursue growth and learning.
6. Build open and honest relationships with communication.
7. Build a positive team and family spirit.
8. Do more with less.
9. Be passionate and determined.
10. Be humble.

Are you looking for a pair of size 6 Giuseppe Zanotti heels for $1,295 or a pair of Keen size 17 sandals for $95? Zappos is committed to having what you want and getting it to you as fast as possible. Providing this kind of service is not cheap, however. It means having vast warehouses and sophisticated order processing systems. The company's price has to cover its costs and provide a reasonable profit yet still be competitive. If the price is too high, Zappos loses business. Too low and the company could lose its shirt (or in this case, shoes).

Source: www.zappos.com.

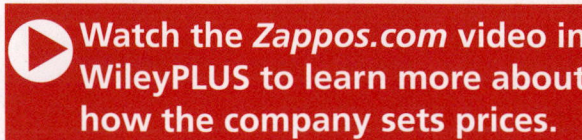

Watch the *Zappos.com* video in WileyPLUS to learn more about how the company sets prices.

© Tomasz Kobiela/iStockphoto

CHAPTER OUTLINE

Learning Objectives

1 Compute a target cost when the market determines a product price.
- Target costing

DO IT! 1 Target Costing

2 Compute a target selling price using cost-plus pricing.
- Cost-plus pricing
- Variable-cost pricing

DO IT! 2 Target Selling Price

3 Use time-and-material pricing to determine the cost of services provided.
- Calculate labor rate
- Calculate material loading charge

DO IT! 3 Time-and-Material Pricing

4 Determine a transfer price using the negotiated, cost-based, and market-based approaches.
- Negotiated transfer prices
- Cost-based transfer prices
- Market-based transfer prices
- Effect of outsourcing on transfer pricing
- Transfers between divisions in different countries

DO IT! 4 Transfer Pricing

Go to the **REVIEW AND PRACTICE** section at the end of the chapter for a review of key concepts and practice applications with solutions.

Visit **WileyPLUS with ORION** for additional tutorials and practice opportunities.

Compute a target cost when the market determines a product price.

Establishing the price for any good or service is affected by many factors. Take the pharmaceutical industry as an example. Its approach to profitability has been to spend heavily on research and development in an effort to find and patent a few new drugs, price them high, and market them aggressively. However, the AIDS crisis in Africa placed the drug industry under considerable pressure to lower prices on drugs used to treat the disease. For example, **Merck Co.** lowered the price of its AIDS drug Crixivan to $600 per patient in these countries. This compares with the $6,016 it typically charged in the United States.[1] As a consequence, individuals in the United States questioned whether prices in the U.S. market were too high. The drug companies countered that to cover their substantial financial risks to develop these products, they need to set the prices high. Illustration 22-1 indicates the many factors that can affect pricing decisions.

Illustration 22-1
Pricing factors

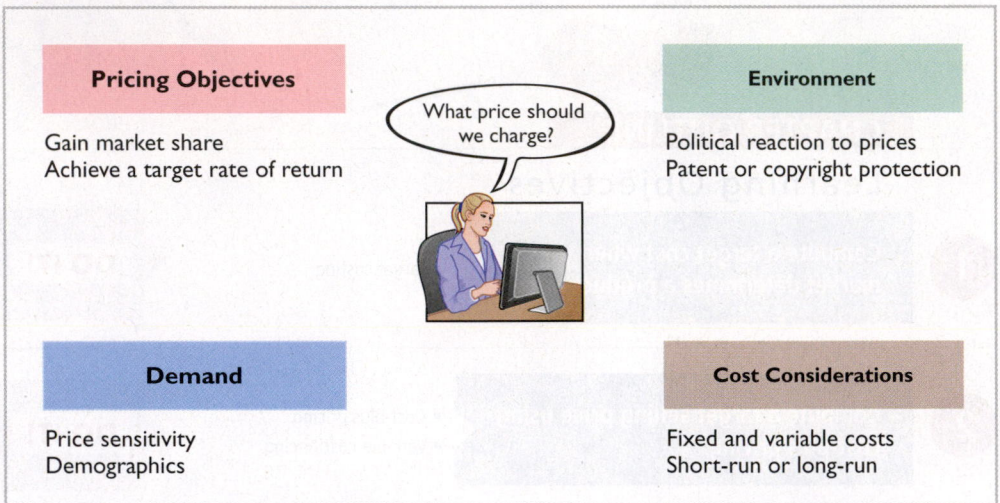

In the long run, a company must price its product to cover its costs and earn a reasonable profit. But to price its product appropriately, it must have a good understanding of market forces at work. In most cases, a company does not set the prices. Instead, the price is set by the competitive market (the laws of supply and demand). For example, a company such as **ChevronTexaco** or **Exxon-Mobil** cannot set the price of gasoline by itself. These companies are called **price takers** because the price of gasoline is set by market forces (the supply of oil and the demand by customers). This is the case for any product that is not easily differentiated from competing products, such as farm products (corn or wheat) or minerals (coal or sand).

In other situations, the company sets the prices. This would be the case where the product is specially made for a customer, as in a one-of-a-kind product such as a designer dress by **Versace** or **Armani**. A company also sets the price when there are few or no other producers capable of manufacturing a similar item. An example would be a company that has a patent or copyright on a unique process, such as the case of computer chips by **Intel**. Finally, a company can set prices when it effectively differentiates its product or service from others. Even in a competitive

---

[1]"AIDS Gaffes in Africa Come Back to Haunt Drug Industry at Home," *Wall Street Journal* (April 23, 2001), p. 1.

market like coffee, **Starbucks** has been able to differentiate its product and charge a premium for a cup of java.

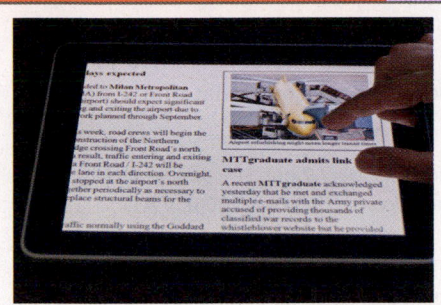

Target Costing

Automobile manufacturers like **Ford** or **Toyota** face a competitive market. The price of an automobile is affected greatly by the laws of supply and demand, so no company in this industry can affect the price to a significant degree. Therefore, to earn a profit, companies in the auto industry must focus on controlling costs. This requires setting a **target cost** that provides a desired profit. Illustration 22-2 shows the relationship of target cost to market price and desired profit.

Market Price − **Desired Profit** = **Target Cost**		

Illustration 22-2
Target cost as related to price and profit

Assuming it reaches sales targets, if **General Motors** can produce its automobiles for its target cost (or less), it will meet its profit goal. If it cannot achieve its target cost, it will fail to achieve the desired profit, which will disappoint its stockholders.

In a competitive market, a company chooses the segment of the market it wants to compete in—that is, its market niche. For example, it may choose between selling luxury goods or economy goods in order to focus its efforts on one segment or the other. Once the company has identified the segment of the market in which it wants to compete, it conducts market research. This determines the features its product should have, and what the market price is for a product with those features. Once the company has determined this price, it can determine its target cost by setting a desired profit. The difference between the market price and the desired profit is the target cost of the product (shown in Illustration 22-2). After the company determines the target cost, it assembles a team of employees with expertise in a variety of areas (production and operations, marketing, and finance). The team's task is to design and develop a product that can meet quality specifications while not exceeding the target cost. The target cost includes all product and period costs necessary to make and market the product or service.

Paul Hart/iStockphoto

Wal-Mart Says the Price Is Too High

"And the price should be $19 per pair of jeans instead of $23," said the retailer Wal-Mart Stores, Inc. to jean maker Levi Strauss.

What happened to Levi Strauss is what happens to many manufacturers who deal with Wal-Mart. Wal-Mart often sets the price, and the manufacturer has to figure out how to make a profit, given that price. In Levi Strauss's case, it revamped its distribution and production to serve Wal-

Mart and improve its overall record of timely deliveries. Producing a season of new jeans styles, from conception to store shelves, used to take Levi 12 to 15 months. Today, it takes just 10 months for Levi Strauss signature jeans; for regular Levi's, the time is down to 7 1/2 months. As the chief executive of Levi Strauss noted, "We had to change people and practice. It's been somewhat of a D-Day invasion approach."

Source: "In Bow to Retailers' New Clout, Levi Strauss Makes Alterations," *Wall Street Journal* (June 17, 2004), p A1.

What are some issues that Levi Strauss should consider in deciding whether it should agree to meet Wal-Mart's target price? (Go to **WileyPLUS** for this answer and additional questions.)

DO IT!   Target Costing

Fine Line Phones is considering introducing a fashion cover for its phones. Market research indicates that 200,000 units can be sold if the price is no more than $20. If Fine Line decides to produce the covers, it will need to invest $1,000,000 in new production equipment. Fine Line requires a minimum rate of return of 25% on all investments.

Determine the target cost per unit for the cover.

Solution

Action Plan

✔ Recall that Market price − Desired profit = Target cost.

✔ The minimum rate of return is a company's desired profit.

> The desired profit for this new product line is $250,000 ($1,000,000 × 25%).
>
> Each cover must result in $1.25 of profit ($250,000/200,000 units).
>
> | Market price | − | Desired profit | = | Target cost per unit |
> |---|---|---|---|---|
> | $20 | − | $1.25 | = | $18.75 per unit |

Related exercise material: **BE22-1, E22-1, E22-2, and DO IT! 22-1.**

LEARNING OBJECTIVE   **Compute a target selling price using cost-plus pricing.**

Cost-Plus Pricing

As discussed, in a competitive product environment, the price of a product is set by the market. In order to achieve its desired profit, the company focuses on achieving a target cost. In a less competitive environment, companies have a greater ability to set the product price. Commonly, when a company sets a product price, it does so as a function of, or relative to, the cost of the product or service. This is referred to as **cost-plus pricing**. Under cost-plus pricing, a company first determines a cost base and then adds a **markup** to the cost base to determine the **target selling price**.

If the cost base includes all of the costs required to produce and sell the product, then the markup represents the desired profit. This can be seen in Illustration 22-3, where the markup represents the difference between the selling price and cost—the profit on the product.

$$\text{Selling Price} \quad - \quad \text{Cost} \quad = \quad \text{Markup (Profit)}$$

Illustration 22-3
Relation of markup to cost and selling price

The size of the markup (profit) depends on the return the company hopes to generate on the amount it has invested. In determining the optimal markup, the company must consider competitive and market conditions, political and legal issues, and other relevant factors. Once the company has determined its cost base and its desired markup, it can add the two together to determine the target selling price. The basic cost-plus pricing formula is expressed as follows.

$$\text{Cost} \quad + \quad \text{Markup} \quad = \quad \text{Target Selling Price}$$

Illustration 22-4
Cost-plus pricing formula

To illustrate, assume that Thinkmore Products, Inc. is in the process of setting a selling price on its new video camera pen. It is a functioning pen that records up to 2 hours of audio and video. The per unit variable cost estimates for the video camera pen are as follows.

	Per Unit
Direct materials	$23
Direct labor	17
Variable manufacturing overhead	12
Variable selling and administrative expenses	8
Variable cost per unit	**$60**

Illustration 22-5
Variable cost per unit

To produce and sell its product, Thinkmore incurs fixed manufacturing overhead of $350,000 and fixed selling and administrative expenses of $300,000. To determine the cost per unit, we divide total fixed costs by the number of units the company expects to produce. Illustration 22-6 shows the computation of fixed cost per unit for Thinkmore, assuming the production of 10,000 units.

	Total Costs	÷	Budgeted Volume	=	Cost per Unit
Fixed manufacturing overhead	$350,000	÷	10,000	=	$35
Fixed selling and administrative expenses	300,000	÷	10,000	=	30
Fixed cost per unit					**$65**

Illustration 22-6
Fixed cost per unit, 10,000 units

Management is ultimately evaluated based on its ability to generate a high return on the company's investment. This is frequently expressed as a return on investment (ROI) percentage, calculated as income divided by the average amount invested in a product or service. A higher percentage reflects a greater success in generating profits from the investment in a product or service. Chapter 24 provides a more in-depth discussion of the use of ROI to evaluate the performance of investment center managers.

To achieve a desired return on investment percentage, a product's markup should be determined by calculating the desired return on investment (ROI) per unit. This is calculated by multiplying the desired ROI percentage times the amount invested to produce the product, and then dividing this by the number of units produced. Illustration 22-7 shows the computation used to determine a markup amount based on a desired ROI per unit for Thinkmore, assuming that the company desires a 20% ROI and that it has invested $2,000,000.

Illustration 22-7
Calculation of markup based on desired ROI per unit

$$\frac{\text{Desired ROI Percentage} \times \text{Amount Invested}}{\text{Units Produced}} = \text{Markup (Desired ROI per Unit)}$$

$$\frac{20\% \times \$2,000,000}{10,000 \text{ units}} = \$40$$

Thinkmore expects to receive income of $400,000 (20% × $2,000,000) on its $2,000,000 investment. On a per unit basis, the markup based on the desired ROI per unit is $40 ($400,000 ÷ 10,000 units). Given the per unit costs shown above, Illustration 22-8 computes the sales price to be $165.

Illustration 22-8
Computation of selling price, 10,000 units

	Per Unit
Variable cost	$ 60
Fixed cost	65
Total cost	125
Markup (desired ROI per unit)	40
Selling price per unit	**$165**

In most cases, companies like Thinkmore use a markup percentage on cost to determine the selling price. The formula to compute the markup percentage to achieve a desired ROI of $40 per unit is as follows.

Illustration 22-9
Computation of markup percentage

Markup (Desired ROI per Unit)	÷	Total Unit Cost	=	Markup Percentage
$40	÷	$125	=	32%

Using a 32% markup on cost, Thinkmore would compute the target selling price as follows.

Illustration 22-10
Computation of selling price— markup approach

Total Unit Cost	+	(Total Unit Cost	×	Markup Percentage)	=	Target Selling Price per Unit
$125	+	($125	×	32%)	=	$165

Thinkmore should set the price for its video camera pen at $165 per unit.

LIMITATIONS OF COST-PLUS PRICING

The cost-plus pricing approach has a major advantage: It is simple to compute. However, the cost model does not give consideration to the demand side. That is, will customers pay the price Thinkmore Products computed for its video camera pen? In addition, sales volume plays a large role in determining per unit costs. The lower the sales volume, for example, the higher the price Thinkmore must charge to meet its desired ROI. To illustrate, if the budgeted sales volume was 5,000 instead of 10,000, Thinkmore's variable cost per unit would remain the same. However, the fixed cost per unit would change as follows.

Illustration 22-11
Fixed cost per unit,
5,000 units

	Total Costs	÷	Budgeted Volume	=	Cost per Unit
Fixed manufacturing overhead	$350,000	÷	5,000	=	$70
Fixed selling and administrative expenses	300,000	÷	5,000	=	60
Fixed cost per unit					**$130**

As indicated in Illustration 22-6 (page 1017), the fixed cost per unit for 10,000 units was $65. However, at a lower sales volume of 5,000 units, the fixed cost per unit increases to $130. Thinkmore's desired 20% ROI now results in a $80 ROI per unit [(20% × $2,000,000) ÷ 5,000]. Thinkmore computes the selling price at 5,000 units as follows.

Illustration 22-12
Computation of selling price,
5,000 units

	Per Unit
Variable cost	$ 60
Fixed cost	130
Total cost	190
Markup (desired ROI per unit)	80
Selling price per unit	**$270**

As shown, the lower the budgeted volume, the higher the per unit price. The reason: Fixed costs and ROI are spread over fewer units, and therefore the fixed cost and ROI per unit increase. In this case, at 5,000 units, Thinkmore would have to mark up its total unit costs 42.11% to earn a desired ROI of $80 per unit, as shown below.

$$42.11\% = \frac{\$80 \text{ (desired ROI per unit)}}{\$190 \text{ (total unit cost)}}$$

The target selling price would then be $270, as indicated earlier:

$$\$190 + (\$190 \times 42.11\%) = \$270$$

The opposite effect will occur if budgeted volume is higher (say, at 12,000 units) because fixed costs and ROI can be spread over more units. As a result, the cost-plus model of pricing will achieve its desired ROI only when Thinkmore sells the quantity it budgeted. If actual volume is much less than budgeted volume, Thinkmore may sustain losses unless it can raise its prices.

Variable-Cost Pricing

In determining the target price for Thinkmore Products' video camera pen, we calculated the cost base by including all costs incurred. This approach is referred to as **full-cost pricing**. Instead of using full costs to set prices, some companies simply add a markup to their variable costs (thus excluding fixed manufacturing and fixed selling and administrative costs). Using **variable-cost pricing** as the basis for setting prices avoids the problem of using uncertain cost information (as discussed above for Thinkmore) related to fixed-cost-per-unit computations. Variable-cost pricing also is helpful in pricing special orders or when excess capacity exists.

The major disadvantage of variable-cost pricing is that managers may set the price too low and consequently fail to cover their fixed costs. In the long run, failure to cover fixed costs will lead to losses. As a result, companies that use variable-cost pricing must adjust their markups to make sure that the price set will provide a fair return. The use of variable costs as the basis for setting prices is discussed in Appendix 22A.

Management Insight | Parker Hannifin

Wesley VanDinter/iStockphoto

At Least It Was Simple

For nearly 90 years, Parker Hannifin used the same simple approach to price its industrial parts. It calculated the production cost, then added on a percentage of the cost (about 35%) to arrive at the price. It didn't matter if a product was a premium product or a standard product. And if Parker reduced its production costs, it then also cut the price for the product. The problem with this approach was that it made it difficult for the company to ever substantially increase its profit margins. So the company's CEO decided to break with tradition and implement strategic pricing schemes similar to those used by retailers. It determined that for about a third of its products, it had a competitive advantage that would allow it to charge a higher markup. For example, there might be limited competition for the product, or its product might be of higher quality, or it might have the ability to produce a product faster. The company determined that the price increases raised net income by $200 million—not bad considering that net income was $130 million before the price increases.

Source: Timothy Aeppel, "Changing the Formula: Seeking Perfect Prices, CEO Tears Up the Rules," *Wall Street Journal Online* (March 27, 2007).

What kind of help might the sales staff need in implementing this new approach? (Go to **WileyPLUS** for this answer and additional questions.)

DO IT! 2 | Target Selling Price

Air Corporation produces air purifiers. The following per unit cost information is available: direct materials $16, direct labor $18, variable manufacturing overhead $11, variable selling and administrative expenses $6. Fixed selling and administrative expenses are $50,000, and fixed manufacturing overhead is $150,000. Using a 45% markup percentage on total per unit cost and assuming 10,000 units, compute the target selling price.

Solution

Action Plan

✔ Calculate the total cost per unit.

✔ Multiply the total cost per unit by the markup percentage, then add this amount to the total cost per unit to determine the target selling price.

Direct materials	$16
Direct labor	18
Variable manufacturing overhead	11
Variable selling and administrative expenses	6
Fixed selling and administrative expenses	5*
Fixed manufacturing overhead	15**
Total unit cost	$71

$$\begin{pmatrix} \text{Total} \\ \text{unit cost} \end{pmatrix} + \begin{pmatrix} \text{Total} \\ \text{unit cost} \end{pmatrix} \times \begin{pmatrix} \text{Markup} \\ \text{percentage} \end{pmatrix} = \begin{pmatrix} \text{Target selling} \\ \text{price per unit} \end{pmatrix}$$

$$\$71 + (\$71 \times 45\%) = \$102.95$$

*$50,000 ÷ 10,000; **$150,000 ÷ 10,000

Related exercise material: **BE22-2, BE22-3, BE22-4, BE22-5, E22-3, E22-4, E22-5, E22-6, E22-7, and DO IT! 22-2.**

LEARNING OBJECTIVE **3**

Use time-and-material pricing to determine the cost of services provided.

Another variation on cost-plus pricing is **time-and-material pricing**. Under this approach, the company sets two pricing rates—one for the **labor** used on a job and another for the **material**. The labor rate includes direct labor time and other employee costs. The material charge is based on the cost of direct parts and materials used and a **material loading charge** for related overhead costs. Time-and-material pricing is widely used in service industries, especially professional firms such as public accounting, law, engineering, and consulting firms, as well as construction companies, repair shops, and printers.

To illustrate a time-and-material pricing situation, assume the following data for Lake Holiday Marina, a boat and motor repair shop.

Illustration 22-13
Total annual budgeted time and material costs

	Time Charges	Material Loading Charges*
LAKE HOLIDAY MARINA		
Budgeted Costs for the Year 2017		
Mechanics' wages and benefits	$103,500	—
Parts manager's salary and benefits	—	$11,500
Office employee's salary and benefits	20,700	2,300
Other overhead (supplies, depreciation, property taxes, advertising, utilities)	26,800	14,400
Total budgeted costs	$151,000	$28,200

*The material loading charges exclude the invoice cost of the materials.

Using time-and-material pricing involves three steps: (1) calculate the per hour labor charge, (2) calculate the charge for obtaining and holding materials, and (3) calculate the charges for a particular job.

STEP 1: CALCULATE THE LABOR RATE. The first step for time-and-material pricing is to determine a charge for labor time. The charge for labor time is expressed as a rate per hour of labor. This rate includes (1) the direct labor cost of the employees, including hourly pay rate plus fringe benefits; (2) selling, administrative, and similar overhead costs; and (3) an allowance for a desired profit or ROI per hour of employee time. In some industries, such as repair shops for autos and boats, the same hourly labor rate is charged regardless of which employee performs the work. In other industries, the rate that is charged is adjusted according to classification or level of the employee. A public accounting firm, for example, would charge different rates for the services of an assistant, senior, manager, or partner; a law firm would charge different rates for the work of a paralegal, associate, or partner.

Illustration 22-14 shows computation of the hourly charges for Lake Holiday Marina during 2017. The marina budgets 5,000 annual labor hours in 2017, and it desires a profit margin of $8 per hour of labor.

Illustration 22-14
Computation of hourly time-charge rate

	A	B	C	D	E	F
1	Per Hour	Total Cost	÷	Total Hours	=	Per Hour Charge
2	Hourly labor rate for repairs					
3	Mechanics' wages and benefits	$103,500	÷	5,000	=	$20.70
4	Overhead costs					
5	Office employee's salary and benefits	20,700	÷	5,000	=	4.14
6	Other overhead	26,800	÷	5,000	=	5.36
7	Total hourly cost	$151,000	÷	5,000	=	30.20
8	Profit margin					8.00
9	Rate charged per hour of labor					$38.20
10						

Lake Holiday Marina.xls

Home Insert Page Layout Formulas Data Review View

P18

To determine the labor charge for a job, the marina multiplies this rate of $38.20 by the number of hours of labor used.

STEP 2: CALCULATE THE MATERIAL LOADING CHARGE. The charge for materials typically includes the invoice price of any materials used on the job plus a material loading charge. The **material loading charge** covers the costs of purchasing, receiving, handling, and storing materials, plus any desired profit margin on the materials themselves. The material loading charge is expressed as a **percentage** of the total estimated costs of parts and materials for the year. To determine this percentage, the company does the following. (1) It estimates its total annual costs for purchasing, receiving, handling, and storing materials. (2) It divides this amount by the total estimated cost of parts and materials. (3) It adds a desired profit margin on the materials themselves.

Illustration 22-15 shows computation of the material loading charge used by Lake Holiday Marina during 2017. The marina estimates that the total invoice cost of parts and materials used in 2017 will be $120,000. The marina desires a 20% profit margin on the invoice cost of parts and materials.

Illustration 22-15
Computation of material loading charge

	A	B	C	D	E	F
1		Material Loading Charges	÷	Total Invoice Cost, Parts and Materials	=	Material Loading Percentage
2	Overhead costs					
3	Parts manager's salary and benefits	$11,500				
4	Office employee's salary	2,300				
5		13,800	÷	$120,000	=	11.50%
6						
7	Other overhead	14,400	÷	120,000	=	12.00%
8		$28,200	÷	120,000	=	23.50%
9	Profit margin					20.00%
10	Material loading percentage					43.50%
11						

The marina's material loading charge on any particular job is 43.50% multiplied by the cost of materials used on the job. For example, if the marina used $100 of parts, the additional material loading charge would be $43.50.

STEP 3: CALCULATE CHARGES FOR A PARTICULAR JOB. The charges for any particular job are the sum of (1) the labor charge, (2) the charge for the materials, and (3) the material loading charge. For example, suppose that Lake Holiday Marina prepares a price quotation to estimate the cost to refurbish a used 28-foot pontoon boat. Lake Holiday Marina estimates the job will require 50 hours of labor and $3,600 in parts and materials. Illustration 22-16 shows the marina's price quotation.

Illustration 22-16
Price quotation for time and material

LAKE HOLIDAY MARINA
Time-and-Material Price Quotation

Job: Marianne Perino, repair of 28-foot pontoon boat

Labor charges: 50 hours @ $38.20		$1,910
Material charges		
Cost of parts and materials	$3,600	
Material loading charge (43.5% × $3,600)	1,566	5,166
Total price of labor and material		$7,076

Included in the $7,076 price quotation for the boat repair are charges for labor costs, overhead costs, materials costs, materials handling and storage costs, and a profit margin on both labor and parts. Lake Holiday Marina used labor hours as a basis for computing the time rate. Other companies, such as machine shops, plastic molding shops, and printers, might use machine hours.

DO IT! 3   Time-and-Material Pricing

Presented below are data for Harmon Electrical Repair Shop for next year.

Repair-technicians' wages	$130,000
Fringe benefits	30,000
Overhead	20,000

The desired profit margin per labor hour is $10. The material loading charge is 40% of invoice cost. Harmon estimates that 8,000 labor hours will be worked next year. If Harmon repairs a TV that takes 4 hours to repair and uses parts costing $50, compute the bill for this job.

Solution

	Total Cost	÷	Total Hours	=	Per Hour Charge
Repair-technicians' wages	$130,000	÷	8,000	=	$16.25
Fringe benefits	30,000	÷	8,000	=	3.75
Overhead	20,000	÷	8,000	=	2.50
	$180,000	÷	8,000	=	22.50
Profit margin					10.00
Rate charged per hour of labor					$32.50

Job: Repair TV
Labor charges: 4 hours @ $32.50		$130
Material charges		
Cost of parts and materials	$50	
Material loading charge (40% × $50)	20	70
Total price of labor and material		$200

Action Plan
✔ Calculate the labor charge.
✔ Calculate the material loading charge.
✔ Compute the bill for specific repair.

Related exercise material: **BE22-6, E22-8, E22-9, E22-10, and DO IT! 22-3.**

LEARNING
OBJECTIVE **4**

Determine a transfer price using the negotiated, cost-based, and market-based approaches.

In today's global economy, growth is often vital to survival. Some companies grow "vertically," meaning they expand in the direction of either their suppliers or customers. For example, a manufacturer of bicycles like **Trek** may acquire a bicycle component manufacturer or a chain of bicycle shops. A movie production company like **Walt Disney** or **Time Warner** may acquire a movie theater chain or a cable television company.

In addition to customer sales, divisions within vertically integrated companies often transfer goods or services to other divisions in the company. When goods are transferred between divisions of the same company, the price used to record the transaction is the **transfer price**. Illustration 22-17 shows transfers between divisions for Aerobic Bicycle Company. As shown, the Component Division sells goods to the Company's Assembly Division, as well as to outside parties. Units sold to the Assembly Division are recorded at the transfer price.

Illustration 22-17
Transfer pricing example

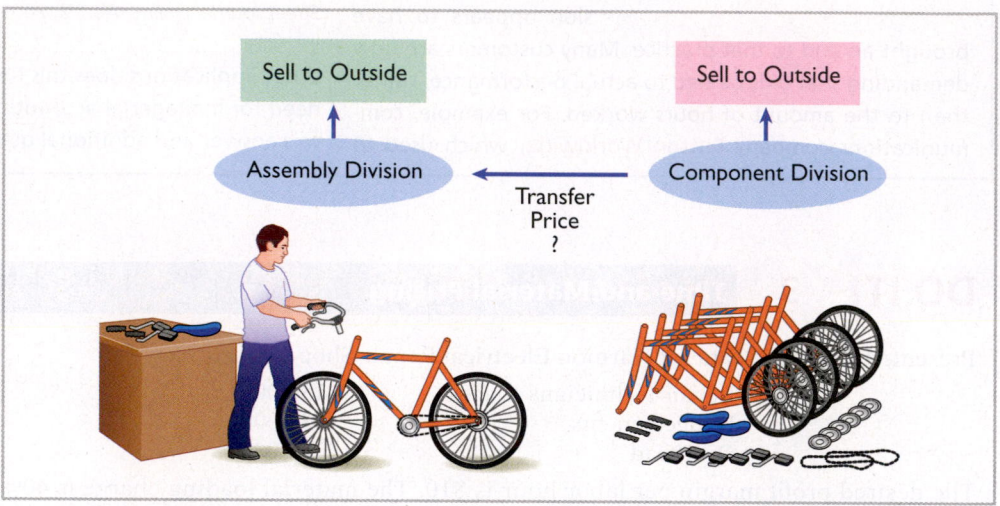

The primary objective of transfer pricing is the same as that of pricing a product to an outside party. The objective is to maximize the return to the company. An additional objective of transfer pricing is to measure divisional performance accurately. Setting a transfer price is complicated because of competing interests among divisions within the company. For example, in the case of the bicycle company shown in Illustration 22-17, setting the transfer price high will benefit the Component Division (the selling division) but will hurt the Assembly Division (the purchasing division).

There are three possible approaches for determining a transfer price:

1. Negotiated transfer prices.
2. Cost-based transfer prices.
3. Market-based transfer prices.

Conceptually, a negotiated transfer price should work best, but due to practical considerations, companies often use the other two methods.

Negotiated Transfer Prices

A **negotiated transfer price** is determined through agreement of division managers. To illustrate negotiated transfer pricing, we examine Alberta Company. Until recently, Alberta focused exclusively on making rubber soles for work boots and hiking boots. It sold these rubber soles to boot manufacturers. However, last year the company decided to take advantage of its strong reputation by expanding into the business of making hiking boots. As a consequence of this expansion, the company is now structured as two independent divisions, the Boot Division and the Sole Division. The company compensates the manager of each division based on achievement of profitability targets for that division.

The Boot Division manufactures leather uppers for hiking boots and attaches these uppers to rubber soles. During its first year, the Boot Division purchased its rubber soles from an outside supplier so as not to disrupt the operations of the Sole Division. However, top management now wants the Sole Division to provide at least some of the soles used by the Boot Division. Illustration 22-18 shows the computation of the contribution margin per unit for each division when the Boot Division purchases soles from an outside supplier.

Boot Division		Sole Division	
Selling price of boots	$90	Selling price of sole	$18
Variable cost of boot (not including sole)	35	Variable cost per sole	11
Cost of sole purchased from outside supplier	17	**Contribution margin**	
Contribution margin per unit	**$38**	**per unit**	**$ 7**
Total contribution margin per unit $45 ($38 + $7)			

Illustration 22-18
Computation of contribution margin for two divisions, when Boot Division purchases soles from an outside supplier

This information indicates that the contribution margin per unit for the Boot Division is $38 and for the Sole Division is $7. The total contribution margin per unit is $45 ($38 + $7).

Now let's ask the question, "What would be a fair transfer price if the Sole Division sold 10,000 soles to the Boot Division?" The answer depends on how busy the Sole Division is—that is, whether it has excess capacity.

NO EXCESS CAPACITY

As indicated in Illustration 22-18, the Sole Division charges outside customers $18 and derives a contribution margin of $7 per sole. The Sole Division has **no excess capacity** and produces and sells 80,000 units (soles) to outside customers. Therefore, the Sole Division must receive from the Boot Division a payment that will at least cover its variable cost per sole **plus** its lost contribution margin per sole. (This lost contribution margin is often referred to as **opportunity cost**.) If the Sole Division cannot recover that amount—called the **minimum transfer price**—it should not sell its soles to the Boot Division. The minimum transfer price that would be acceptable to the Sole Division is $18, as shown below.

Variable Cost	+	Opportunity Cost	=	Minimum Transfer Price
$11	+	$7	=	$18

Illustration 22-19
Minimum transfer price— no excess capacity

From the perspective of the Boot Division (the buyer), the most it will pay is what the sole would cost from an outside supplier. In this case, therefore, the Boot Division would pay no more than $17. As shown in Illustration 22-20 (page 1026), an acceptable transfer price is not available in this situation.

Illustration 22-20
Transfer price negotiations—
no deal

EXCESS CAPACITY

What happens if the Sole Division **has excess capacity**? For example, assume the Sole Division can produce 80,000 soles but can sell only 70,000 soles in the open market. As a result, it has available capacity of 10,000 units. Because it has excess capacity, the Sole Division could provide 10,000 units to the Boot Division without losing its $7 contribution margin on these units. Therefore, the minimum price it would now accept is $11, as shown below.

Illustration 22-21
Minimum transfer price
formula—excess capacity

Variable Cost	+	Opportunity Cost	=	Minimum Transfer Price
$11	+	$0	=	$11

In this case, the Boot Division and the Sole Division should negotiate a transfer price within the range of $11 to $17, as shown in Illustration 22-22.

Illustration 22-22
Transfer pricing
negotiations—deal

Given excess capacity, Alberta Company will increase its overall net income if the Boot Division purchases the 10,000 soles internally. This is true as long as the Sole Division's variable cost is less than the outside price of $17. The Sole Division will receive a positive contribution margin from any transfer price above its variable cost of $11. The Boot Division will benefit from any price below $17. At any transfer price above $17 the Boot Division will go to an outside supplier, a solution that would be undesirable to both divisions as well as to the company as a whole.

VARIABLE COSTS

In the minimum transfer price formula, **variable cost is defined as the variable cost of units sold *internally***. In some instances, the variable cost of units sold internally will differ from the variable cost of units sold externally. For example, companies often can avoid some variable selling expenses when units are sold internally. In this case, the variable cost of units sold internally will be lower than that of units sold externally.

Alternatively, the variable cost of units sold internally could be higher than normal if the internal division requests a special order that requires more expensive materials or additional labor. For example, assume that the Boot Division designs a new high-margin, heavy-duty boot. The sole for this boot will use denser rubber with an intricate lug design. Alberta Company is not aware of any supplier that currently makes such a sole, nor does it feel that any other supplier can meet its quality expectations. As a consequence, there is no available market price to use as the transfer price.

We can, however, employ the formula for the minimum transfer price to assist in arriving at a reasonable solution. After evaluating the special sole, the Sole Division determines that its variable cost would be $19 per sole. The Sole Division is at full capacity. The Sole Division's opportunity cost at full capacity is the $7 ($18 − $11) per sole that it earns producing the standard sole and selling it to an outside customer. Therefore, the minimum transfer price that the Sole Division would be willing to accept for the special-order sole is as follows.

Variable Cost	+	Opportunity Cost	=	Minimum Transfer Price
$19	+	$7	=	$26

Illustration 22-23
Minimum transfer price formula—special order

The transfer price of $26 provides the Sole Division with enough revenue to cover its increased variable cost and its opportunity cost (contribution margin on its standard sole).

SUMMARY OF NEGOTIATED TRANSFER PRICING

Under negotiated transfer pricing, the selling division establishes a minimum transfer price, and the purchasing division establishes a maximum transfer price. This system provides a sound basis for establishing a transfer price because both divisions are better off if the proper decision-making rules are used. However, companies often do not use negotiated transfer pricing because:

- Market price information is sometimes not easily obtainable.
- A lack of trust between the two negotiating divisions may lead to a breakdown in the negotiations.
- Negotiations often lead to different pricing strategies from division to division, which is cumbersome and sometimes costly to implement.

Many companies, therefore, often use simple systems based on cost or market information to develop transfer prices.

Cost-Based Transfer Prices

An alternative to negotiated transfer pricing is cost-based pricing. A **cost-based transfer price** is based on the costs incurred by the division producing the goods or services. A cost-based transfer price can be based on variable costs alone, or on variable costs plus fixed costs. Also, in some cases the selling division may add a markup.

The cost-based approach sometimes results in improper transfer prices. Improper transfer prices can reduce company profits and provide unfair evaluations of division performance. To illustrate, assume that Alberta Company requires the division to use a transfer price based on the variable cost of the sole.

Illustration 22-24
Cost-based transfer
price—10,000 units

With no excess capacity, the contribution margins per unit for the two divisions are as follows.

Boot Division		Sole Division	
Selling price of boots	$90	Selling price of sole	$11
Variable cost of boot (not including sole)	35	Variable cost per sole	11
Cost of sole purchased from sole division	11		
Contribution margin per unit	**$44**	**Contribution margin per unit**	**$ 0**
	Total contribution margin per unit $44 ($44 + $0)		

This cost-based transfer system is a bad deal for the Sole Division as it reports no profit on the transfer of 10,000 soles to the Boot Division. If the Sole Division could sell these soles to an outside customer, it would make $70,000 [10,000 × ($18 − $11)]. The Boot Division, on the other hand, is delighted: its contribution margin per unit increases from $38 to $44, or $6 per boot. Thus, this transfer price results in an unfair evaluation of these two divisions.

Further examination of this example reveals that this transfer price reduces the company's overall profits. The Sole Division lost a contribution margin per unit of $7 (Illustration 22-18, page 1025), and the Boot Division experiences only a $6 increase in its contribution margin per unit. Overall, Alberta Company loses $10,000 [10,000 boots × ($7 − $6)]. Illustration 22-25 illustrates this deficiency.

Illustration 22-25
Cost-based transfer price
results—no excess capacity

The overall results change if the Sole Division **has excess capacity**. In this case, the Sole Division continues to report a zero profit on these 10,000 units but does not lose the $7 per unit of contribution margin (because it had excess capacity). The Boot Division gains $6. So overall, the company is better off by $60,000 (10,000 × $6). However, with a cost-based system, the Sole Division continues to report a zero profit on these 10,000 units.

We can see that a cost-based system does not reflect the division's true profitability. What's more, **it does not provide adequate incentive for the Sole Division to control costs**. The division's costs are simply passed on to the next division.

Notwithstanding these disadvantages, the cost system is simple to understand and easy to use because the information is already available in the accounting system. In addition, market information is sometimes not available, so the only alternative is some type of cost-based system. As a result, it is the most common method used by companies to establish transfer prices.

Market-Based Transfer Prices

The **market-based transfer price** is based on existing market prices of competing goods or services. A market-based system is often considered the best approach because it is objective and generally provides the proper economic incentives. For example, if the Sole Division can charge the market price, it is indifferent as to whether soles are sold to outside customers or internally to the Boot Division— it does not lose any contribution margin. Similarly, the Boot Division pays a price for the soles that is at or reasonably close to market.

When the Sole Division has no excess capacity, the market-based system works reasonably well. The Sole Division receives market price, and the Boot Division pays market price.

If the Sole Division has excess capacity, however, the market-based system can lead to actions that are not in the best interest of the company. The minimum transfer price that the Sole Division should receive is its variable cost plus opportunity cost. If the Sole Division has excess capacity, its opportunity cost is zero. However, under the market-based system, the Sole Division transfers the goods at the market price of $18, for a contribution margin per unit of $7 ($18 − $11). The Boot Division manager has to accept the $18 sole price. This price may not accurately reflect a fair cost of the sole, given that the Sole Division had excess capacity. As a result, the Boot Division may overprice its boots in the market if it uses the market price of the sole plus a markup in setting the price of the boot. This action can lead to losses for Alberta overall.

As indicated earlier, in many cases, there simply is not a well-defined market for the good or service being transferred. When this is the case, a reasonable market value cannot be developed, so companies often resort to a cost-based system.

Effect of Outsourcing on Transfer Pricing

An increasing number of companies rely on **outsourcing**. Outsourcing involves contracting with an external party to provide a good or service, rather than performing the work internally. Some companies have taken outsourcing to the extreme by outsourcing all of their production. Many of these so-called **virtual companies** have well-established brand names though they do not manufacture any of their own products. Companies use incremental analysis (Chapter 21) to determine whether outsourcing is profitable. When companies outsource, fewer components are transferred internally between divisions. This reduces the need for transfer prices.

Transfers Between Divisions in Different Countries

As more companies "globalize" their operations, an increasing number of intercompany transfers are between divisions that are located in different countries. One estimate suggests that 60% of trade between countries is simply transfers between company divisions. Differences in tax rates across countries can complicate the determination of the appropriate transfer price. Appendix 22B discusses in more detail transfer pricing issues that occur when goods are exchanged between divisions in different countries.

DO IT! **4**   **Transfer Pricing**

The clock division of Control Central Corporation manufactures clocks and then sells them to customers for $10 per unit. Its variable cost is $4 per unit, and its fixed cost per unit is $2.50. Management would like the clock division to transfer 8,000 of these clocks to another division within the company at a price of $5. The clock division could avoid $0.50 per clock of variable packaging costs by selling internally.

(a) Determine the minimum transfer price, assuming the clock division is not operating at full capacity. (b) Determine the minimum transfer price, assuming the clock division is operating at full capacity.

Action Plan

✔ Determine whether the company is at full capacity or not.

✔ Determine variable cost and opportunity cost.

✔ Apply minimum transfer price formula.

Solution

(a) If the clock division is not operating at full capacity, the opportunity cost for the clocks is $0. Since internal sales will eliminate $0.50 of packaging costs, the variable cost per clock is $3.50 ($4 − $0.50).

Minimum transfer price	=	Variable cost	+	Opportunity cost
$3.50	=	$3.50	+	$0

(b) If the clock division is already operating at full capacity, the opportunity cost for the clocks is $6 ($10 − $4). Since internal sales will eliminate $0.50 of packaging costs, the variable cost per clock is $3.50 ($4 − $0.50).

Minimum transfer price	=	Variable cost	+	Opportunity cost
$9.50	=	$3.50	+	$6

Related exercise material: **BE22-7, BE22-8, BE22-9, E22-11, E22-12, E22-13, E22-14, E22-15, and** DO IT! **22-4.**

LEARNING OBJECTIVE *

APPENDIX 22A: Determine prices using absorption-cost pricing and variable-cost pricing.

In determining the target price for Thinkmore Products' video camera pen in the chapter, we calculated the cost base **by including all costs incurred**. This approach is referred to as **full-cost pricing**. Using total cost as the basis of the markup makes sense conceptually because, in the long run, the price must cover all costs and provide a reasonable profit. However, total cost is difficult to determine in practice. This is because period costs (selling and administrative expenses) are difficult to trace to a specific product. Activity-based costing can be used to overcome this difficulty to some extent.

In practice, companies sometimes use two other cost approaches: (1) absorption-cost pricing or (2) variable-cost pricing. Absorption-cost pricing is more popular than variable-cost pricing.[2] We illustrate both approaches because both have merit.

Absorption-Cost Pricing

Absorption-cost pricing is consistent with generally accepted accounting principles (GAAP). The reason: It includes both variable and fixed manufacturing costs as product costs. **It excludes from this cost base both variable and fixed selling and administrative costs.** Thus, companies must somehow provide for selling and administrative costs plus the target ROI. They do this through the markup.

The **first step** in absorption-cost pricing is to compute the unit **manufacturing cost**. For Thinkmore Products, this amounts to $87 per unit at a volume of 10,000 units, as shown in Illustration 22A-1.

Illustration 22A-1
Computation of unit manufacturing cost

	Per Unit
Direct materials	$23
Direct labor	17
Variable manufacturing overhead	12
Fixed manufacturing overhead ($350,000 ÷ 10,000)	35
Total unit manufacturing cost (absorption cost)	$87

---

[2]For a discussion of cost-plus pricing, see Eunsup Skim and Ephraim F. Sudit, "How Manufacturers Price Products," *Management Accounting* (February 1995), pp. 37–39; and V. Govindarajan and R.N. Anthony, "How Firms Use Cost Data in Pricing Decisions," *Management Accounting* (65, no. 1), pp. 30–36.

In addition, Thinkmore provides the following information regarding selling and administrative expenses per unit and desired ROI per unit.

Variable selling and administrative expenses	$ 8
Fixed selling and administrative expenses ($300,000 ÷ 10,000)	30
Total selling and administrative expenses per unit	$38
Desired ROI per unit (see Illustration 22-7)	$40

Illustration 22A-2
Other information

The **second step** in absorption-cost pricing is to compute the markup percentage using the formula in Illustration 22A-3. Note that when companies use manufacturing cost per unit as the cost base to compute the markup percentage, the **percentage must cover the desired ROI and also the selling and administrative expenses**.

Desired ROI per Unit	+	Selling and Administrative Expenses per Unit	=	Markup Percentage	×	Manufacturing Cost per Unit
$40	+	$38	=	**MP**	×	$87

Illustration 22A-3
Markup percentage—absorption-cost pricing

Solving, we find:

$$MP = (\$40 + \$38) \div \$87 = 89.66\%$$

The **third** and final **step** is to set the target selling price. Using a markup percentage of 89.66% and absorption-cost pricing, Thinkmore computes the target selling price as shown in Illustration 22A-4.

Manufacturing Cost per Unit	+	(Markup Percentage	×	Manufacturing Cost per Unit)	=	Target Selling Price
$87	+	(89.66%	×	$87)	=	$165

Illustration 22A-4
Computation of target price—absorption-cost pricing

Using a target price of $165 will produce the desired 20% return on investment for Thinkmore on its video camera pen at a volume level of 10,000 units, as shown in Illustration 22A-5.

Illustration 22A-5
Proof of 20% ROI—absorption-cost pricing

THINKMORE PRODUCTS, INC.
Budgeted Absorption-Cost Income Statement

Revenue (10,000 camera pens × $165)	$1,650,000
Cost of goods sold (10,000 camera pens × $87)	870,000
Gross profit	780,000
Selling and administrative expenses	
[10,000 camera pens × ($8 + $30)]	380,000
Net income	**$ 400,000**

Budgeted ROI

$$\frac{\text{Net income}}{\text{Invested assets}} = \frac{\$400,000}{\$2,000,000} = \mathbf{20\%}$$

Markup Percentage

$$\frac{\text{Net income} + \text{Selling and administrative expenses}}{\text{Cost of goods sold}} = \frac{\$400,000 + \$380,000}{\$870,000} = \mathbf{89.66\%}$$

Because of the fixed-cost element, if Thinkmore sells more than 10,000 units, the ROI will be greater than 20%. If it sells fewer than 10,000 units, the ROI will be less than 20%. The markup percentage is also verified by adding $400,000 (the net income) and $380,000 (selling and administrative expenses) and then dividing by $870,000 (the cost of goods sold or the cost base).

Most companies that use cost-plus pricing use either absorption cost or full cost as the basis. The reasons for this tendency are as follows.

1. Absorption-cost information is most readily provided by a company's cost accounting system. Because absorption-cost data already exist in general ledger accounts, it is cost-effective to use the data for pricing.

2. Basing the cost-plus formula on only variable costs could encourage managers to set too low a price to boost sales. There is the fear that if managers use only variable costs, they will substitute variable costs for full costs, which can lead to suicidal price cutting.

3. Absorption-cost or full-cost pricing provides the most defensible base for justifying prices to all interested parties—managers, customers, and government.

Variable-Cost Pricing

Under **variable-cost pricing**, the cost base consists of all of the **variable costs** associated with a product, including variable selling and administrative costs. **Because fixed costs are not included in the base, the markup must provide for all fixed costs (manufacturing, and selling and administrative) and the target ROI.** Variable-cost pricing is more useful for making short-run decisions because it considers variable-cost and fixed-cost behavior patterns separately.

The **first step** in variable-cost pricing is to compute the unit variable cost. For Thinkmore Products, this amounts to $60 per unit, as shown in Illustration 22A-6.

Illustration 22A-6
Computation of unit variable cost

	Per Unit
Direct materials	$23
Direct labor	17
Variable manufacturing overhead	12
Variable selling and administrative expense	8
Total unit variable cost	$60

The **second step** in variable-cost pricing is to compute the markup percentage. Illustration 22A-7 shows the formula for the markup percentage. For Thinkmore, fixed costs include fixed manufacturing overhead of $35 per unit ($350,000 ÷ 10,000) and fixed selling and administrative expenses of $30 per unit ($300,000 ÷ 10,000).

Illustration 22A-7
Computation of markup percentage—variable-cost pricing

Desired ROI per Unit	+	Fixed Cost per Unit	=	Markup Percentage	×	Variable Cost per Unit
$40	+	($35 + $30)	=	MP	×	$60

Solving, we find:

$$MP = \frac{\$40 + (\$35 + \$30)}{\$60} = 175\%$$

The **third step** is to set the target selling price. Using a markup percentage of 175% and the contribution approach, Thinkmore computes the selling price as shown in Illustration 22A-8.

Variable Cost per Unit	+	(Markup Percentage	×	Variable Cost per Unit)	=	Target Selling Price
$60	+	(175%	×	$60)	=	$165

Illustration 22A-8
Computation of target price—variable-cost pricing

Using a target price of $165 will produce the desired 20% return on investment for Thinkmore on its video camera pen at a volume level of 10,000 units, as shown in Illustration 22A-9.

Illustration 22A-9
Proof of 20% ROI—contribution approach

THINKMORE PRODUCTS, INC.
Budgeted Variable-Cost Income Statement

Revenue (10,000 camera pens × $165)		$1,650,000
Variable costs (10,000 camera pens × $60)		600,000
Contribution margin		1,050,000
Fixed manufacturing overhead (10,000 camera pens × $35)	$350,000	
Fixed selling and administrative expenses (10,000 camera pens × $30)	300,000	650,000
Net income		**$ 400,000**

Budgeted ROI

$$\frac{\text{Net income}}{\text{Invested assets}} = \frac{\$400,000}{\$2,000,000} = \textbf{20\%}$$

Markup Percentage

$$\frac{\text{Net income + Fixed costs}}{\text{Variable costs}} = \frac{\$400,000 + \$650,000}{\$600,000} = \textbf{175\%}$$

Under any of the three pricing approaches we have looked at (full-cost, absorption-cost, and variable-cost), the desired ROI will be attained only if the budgeted sales volume for the period is attained. None of these approaches guarantees a profit or a desired ROI. Achieving a desired ROI is the result of many factors, some of which are beyond the company's control, such as market conditions, political and legal issues, customers' tastes, and competitive actions.

Because absorption-cost pricing includes allocated fixed costs, it does not make clear how the company's costs will change as volume changes. To avoid blurring the effects of cost behavior on net income, some managers therefore prefer variable-cost pricing. The specific reasons for using variable-cost pricing, even though the basic accounting data are less accessible, are as follows.

1. Variable-cost pricing, being based on variable cost, is more consistent with cost-volume-profit analysis used by managers to measure the profit implications of changes in price and volume.

2. Variable-cost pricing provides the type of data managers need for pricing special orders. It shows the incremental cost of accepting one more order.

3. Variable-cost pricing avoids arbitrary allocation of common fixed costs (such as executive salaries) to individual product lines.

LEARNING
OBJECTIVE
*6

APPENDIX 22B: Explain issues involved in transferring goods between divisions in different countries.

Companies must pay income tax in the country where they generate the income. In order to maximize income and minimize income tax, many companies prefer to report more income in countries with low tax rates, and less income in countries with high tax rates. They accomplish this by adjusting the transfer prices they use on internal transfers between divisions located in different countries. They allocate more contribution margin to the division in the low-tax-rate country, and allocate less to the division in the high-tax-rate country.

To illustrate, suppose that Alberta's Boot Division is located in a country with a corporate tax rate of 10%, and the Sole Division is located in a country with a tax rate of 30%. Illustration 22B-1 compares the after-tax contribution margin to the company using a transfer price of $18 versus a transfer price of $11.

Illustration 22B-1
After-tax contribution margin per unit under alternative transfer prices

At $18 Transfer Price

Boot Division		Sole Division	
Selling price of boots	$90.00	Selling price of sole	$18.00
Variable cost of boot (not including sole)	35.00	Variable cost per sole	11.00
Cost of sole purchased internally	18.00		
Before-tax contribution margin	37.00	Before-tax contribution margin	7.00
Tax at 10%	3.70	Tax at 30%	2.10
After-tax contribution margin	$33.30	After-tax contribution margin	$ 4.90

Before-tax total contribution margin per unit to company = $37 + $7 = **$44**
After-tax total contribution margin per unit to company = $33.30 + $4.90 = **$38.20**

At $11 Transfer Price

Boot Division		Sole Division	
Selling price of boots	$90.00	Selling price of sole	$11.00
Variable cost of boot (not including sole)	35.00	Variable cost per sole	11.00
Cost of sole purchased internally	11.00		
Before-tax contribution margin	44.00	Before-tax contribution margin	0.00
Tax at 10%	4.40	Tax at 30%	0.00
After-tax contribution margin	$39.60	After-tax contribution margin	$ 0.00

Before-tax total contribution margin per unit to company = $44 + $0 = **$44**
After-tax total contribution margin per unit to company = $39.60 + $0 = **$39.60**

Note that the **before-tax** total contribution margin to Alberta Company is $44 regardless of whether the transfer price is $18 or $11. However, the **after-tax** total contribution margin to Alberta Company is $38.20 using the $18 transfer price and $39.60 using the $11 transfer price. The reason: When Alberta uses the $11 transfer price, more of the contribution margin is attributed to the division that is in the country with the lower tax rate, so it pays $1.40 less per shoe in taxes [($3.70 + $2.10) − $4.40].

As this analysis shows, Alberta Company would be better off using the $11 transfer price. However, this presents some concerns. First, the Sole Division manager will not be happy with an $11 transfer price. This price may lead to unfair evaluations of the Sole Division's manager. Second, the company must ask whether it is legal and ethical to use an $11 transfer price when the market price clearly is higher than that.

Additional consideration of international transfer pricing is discussed in advanced accounting courses.

REVIEW AND PRACTICE

■ LEARNING OBJECTIVES REVIEW

❶ Compute a target cost when the market determines a product price. To compute a target cost, the company determines its target selling price. Once the target selling price is set, it determines its target cost by setting a desired profit. The difference between the target price and desired profit is the target cost of the product.

❷ Compute a target selling price using cost-plus pricing. Cost-plus pricing involves establishing a cost base and adding to this cost base a markup to determine a target selling price. The cost-plus pricing formula is expressed as follows: Target selling price = Cost + (Markup percentage × Cost).

❸ Use time-and-material pricing to determine the cost of services provided. Under time-and-material pricing, two pricing rates are set—one for the labor used on a job and another for the material. The labor rate includes direct labor time and other employee costs. The material charge is based on the cost of direct parts and materials used and a material loading charge for related overhead costs.

❹ Determine a transfer price using the negotiated, cost-based, and market-based approaches. The negotiated price is determined through agreement of division managers. Under a cost-based approach, the transfer price may be based on variable cost alone or on variable costs plus fixed costs. Companies may add a markup to these numbers. The cost-based approach often leads to poor performance evaluations and purchasing decisions. The advantage of the

cost-based system is its simplicity. A market-based transfer price is based on existing competing market prices and services. A market-based system is often considered the best approach because it is objective and generally provides the proper economic incentives.

*❺ Determine prices using absorption-cost pricing and variable-cost pricing. Absorption-cost pricing uses total manufacturing cost as the cost base and provides for selling and administrative costs plus the target ROI through the markup. The target selling price is computed as: Manufacturing cost per unit + (Markup percentage × Manufacturing cost per unit).

Variable-cost pricing uses all of the variable costs, including selling and administrative costs, as the cost base and provides for fixed costs and target ROI through the markup. The target selling price is computed as: Variable cost per unit + (Markup percentage × Variable cost per unit).

*❻ Explain issues involved in transferring goods between divisions in different countries. Companies must pay income tax in the country where they generate the income. In order to maximize income and minimize income tax, many companies prefer to report more income in countries with low tax rates, and less income in countries with high tax rates. This is accomplished by adjusting the transfer prices they use on internal transfers between divisions located in different countries.

■ GLOSSARY REVIEW

*Absorption-cost pricing An approach to pricing that defines the cost base as the manufacturing cost; it excludes both variable and fixed selling and administrative costs. (p. 1030).

Cost-based transfer price A transfer price that uses as its foundation the costs incurred by the division producing the goods. (p. 1027).

Cost-plus pricing A process whereby a product's selling price is determined by adding a markup to a cost base. (p. 1016).

Full-cost pricing An approach to pricing that defines the cost base as all costs incurred. (p. 1019).

Market-based transfer price A transfer price that is based on existing market prices of competing products. (p. 1028).

Markup The amount added to a product's cost base to determine the product's selling price. (p. 1016).

Material loading charge A charge added to cover the cost of purchasing, receiving, handling, and storing materials, plus any desired profit margin on the materials themselves. (p. 1022).

Negotiated transfer price A transfer price that is determined by the agreement of the division managers. (p. 1024).

Outsourcing Contracting with an external party to provide a good or service, rather than performing the work internally. (p. 1029).

Target cost The cost that will provide the desired profit on a product when the seller does not have control over the product's price. (p. 1015).

Target selling price The selling price that will provide the desired profit on a product when the seller has the ability to determine the product's price. (p. 1016).

Time-and-material pricing An approach to cost-plus pricing in which the company uses two pricing rates, one for the labor used on a job and another for the material. (p. 1020).

Transfer price The price used to record the transfer of goods between two divisions of a company. (p. 1024).

Variable-cost pricing An approach to pricing that defines the cost base as all variable costs; it excludes both fixed manufacturing and fixed selling and administrative costs. (pp. 1019, 1032).

PRACTICE MULTIPLE-CHOICE QUESTIONS

(LO 1) **1.** Target cost related to price and profit means that:
  (a) cost and desired profit must be determined before selling price.
  (b) cost and selling price must be determined before desired profit.
  (c) price and desired profit must be determined before costs.
  (d) costs can be achieved only if the company is at full capacity.

(LO 1) **2.** Classic Toys has examined the market for toy train locomotives. It believes there is a market niche in which it can sell locomotives at $80 each. It estimates that it could sell 10,000 of these locomotives annually. Variable costs to make a locomotive are expected to be $25. Classic anticipates a profit of $15 per locomotive. The target cost for the locomotive is:
  (a) $80.   (c) $40.
  (b) $65.   (d) $25.

(LO 1) **3.** In a competitive, common-product environment, a seller would most likely use:
  (a) time-and-material pricing.
  (b) variable costing.
  (c) target costing.
  (d) cost-plus pricing.

(LO 2) **4.** Cost-plus pricing means that:
  (a) Selling price = Variable cost + (Markup percentage + Variable cost).
  (b) Selling price = Cost + (Markup percentage × Cost).
  (c) Selling price = Manufacturing cost + (Markup percentage + Manufacturing cost).
  (d) Selling price = Fixed cost + (Markup percentage × Fixed cost).

(LO 2) **5.** Adler Company is considering developing a new product. The company has gathered the following information on this product.

Expected total unit cost	$25
Estimated investment for new product	$500,000
Desired ROI	10%
Expected number of units to be produced and sold	1,000

Given this information, the desired markup percentage and selling price are:
  (a) markup percentage 10%; selling price $55.
  (b) markup percentage 200%; selling price $75.
  (c) markup percentage 10%; selling price $50.
  (d) markup percentage 100%; selling price $55.

(LO 2) **6.** Mystique Co. provides the following information for the new product it recently introduced.

Total unit cost	$30
Desired ROI per unit	$10
Target selling price	$40

What would be Mystique Co.'s percentage markup on cost?
  (a) 125%.   (c) 33⅓%.
  (b) 75%.   (d) 25%.

(LO 3) **7.** Crescent Electrical Repair has decided to price its work on a time-and-material basis. It estimates the following costs for the year related to labor.

Technician wages and benefits	$100,000
Office employee's salary and benefits	$ 40,000
Other overhead	$ 80,000

Crescent desires a profit margin of $10 per labor hour and budgets 5,000 hours of repair time for the year. The office employee's salary, benefits, and other overhead costs should be divided evenly between time charges and material loading charges. Crescent labor charge per hour would be:
  (a) $42.   (c) $32.
  (b) $34.   (d) $30.

(LO 3) **8.** Time-and-material pricing would most likely be used by a:
  (a) garden-fertilizer producer.
  (b) lawn-mower manufacturer.
  (c) tree farm.
  (d) lawn-care provider.

(LO 3) **9.** When a company uses time-and-material pricing, the material loading charge is expressed as a percentage of:
  (a) the total estimated labor costs for the year.

(b) the total estimated costs of parts and materials for the year.

(c) the total estimated overhead costs for the year.

(d) the total estimated costs of parts, materials, and labor for the year.

(LO 4) 10. The Plastics Division of Weston Company manufactures plastic molds and then sells them to customers for $70 per unit. Its variable cost is $30 per unit, and its fixed cost per unit is $10. Management would like the Plastics Division to transfer 10,000 of these molds to another division within the company at a price of $40. The Plastics Division is operating at full capacity. What is the minimum transfer price that the Plastics Division should accept?

(a) $10. (c) $40.

(b) $30. (d) $70.

(LO 4) 11. Assume the same information as Question 10, except that the Plastics Division has available capacity of 10,000 units for plastic moldings. What is the minimum transfer price that the Plastics Division should accept?

(a) $10. (c) $40.

(b) $30. (d) $70.

(LO 4) 12. The most common method used to establish transfer prices is the:

(a) negotiated transfer pricing approach.

(b) opportunity costing transfer pricing approach.

(c) cost-based transfer pricing approach.

(d) market-based transfer pricing approach.

(LO 5) *13. AST Electrical provides the following cost information related to its production of electronic circuit boards.

	Per Unit
Variable manufacturing cost	$40
Fixed manufacturing cost	$30
Variable selling and administrative expenses	$ 8
Fixed selling and administrative expenses	$12
Desired ROI per unit	$15

What is its markup percentage assuming that AST Electrical uses absorption-cost pricing?

(a) 16.67%. (c) 54.28%.

(b) 50%. (d) 118.75%.

*14. Assume the same information as Question 13 and **(LO 5)** determine AST Electrical's markup percentage using variable-cost pricing.

(a) 16.67%. (c) 54.28%.

(b) 50%. (d) 118.75%.

*15. Global Industries transfers parts between divisions in **(LO 6)** two countries, Eastland and Westland. Eastland's tax rate is 8%, and Westland's tax rate is 16%. To minimize tax payments and maximize net income, Global should establish transfer prices that:

(a) allocate contribution margin equally between Eastland and Westland.

(b) allocate more contribution margin to Eastland.

(c) allocate more contribution margin to Westland.

(d) allocate half as much contribution margin to Eastland as it does to Westland.

Solutions

1. (c) The selling price and the desired profit must be decided before costs are determined. Therefore, the other choices are incorrect.

2. (b) The target cost for the locomotive is selling price less desired profit or $80 − $15 = $65, not (a) $80, (c) $40, or (d) $25.

3. (c) A seller would most likely use target costing in a competitive common-product environment as the price is set by the market. In a less competitive environment, companies have a greater ability to set the product price and therefore could use (a) time-and-material pricing, (b) variable costing, or (d) cost-plus pricing.

4. (b) In cost-plus pricing, Selling price = Cost + (Markup percentage × Cost). The other choices are therefore incorrect.

5. (b) The desired markup percentage = [(.10 × $500,000) ÷ 1,000]/$25 = 200%. The selling price = $25 + $50 = $75. The other choices are therefore incorrect.

6. (c) The percentage markup on cost = ($10 ÷ $30) = 33⅓%, not (a) 125%, (b) 75%, or (d) 25%.

7. (a) The labor charge per hour = $10 + [[$100,000 + .5($40,000) + .5($80,000)] ÷ 5,000] = $42, not (b) $34, (c), $32, or (d) $30.

8. (d) A lawn-care provider would be most likely to use time-and-material pricing as it is a service company. The other choices are manufacturing companies.

9. (b) In time-and-material pricing, the material loading charge is expressed as a percentage of the total estimated costs of parts and materials for the year. Therefore, the other choices are incorrect.

10. (d) The minimum transfer price the Plastics Division should accept = Variable cost per unit + Opportunity cost per unit. Since the Plastics Division is operating at full capacity, the opportunity cost per unit is equal to the contribution margin per unit of $40 (selling price of $70 − variable cost per unit of $30). The minimum transfer price is therefore $30 + $40 = $70, not (a) $10, (b) $30, or (c) $40.

11. (b) Since we assume the Plastics Division has excess capacity of 10,000 units, the minimum transfer price is equal to the variable cost per unit of $30, not (a) $10, (c) $40, or (d) $70.

12. (c) The most common method to establish transfer prices is the cost-based transfer pricing approach as it is simple to use, easy to understand, and has available cost data. Negotiated transfer pricing and market-based transfer pricing are considered better approaches but often are not used because of lack of market price information or other considerations.

*13. (b) Using the absorption-cost approach, add the desired ROI per unit ($15) and selling and administrative expenses per unit ($20) = $35 per unit, then divide that by the manufacturing cost per unit ($70), which equals the markup percentage of 50%, not (a) 16.67%, (c) 54.28%, or (d) 118.75%.

*14. (d) Using variable-cost pricing, add the desired ROI per unit ($15), fixed manufacturing costs per unit ($30) and fixed selling and administrative expenses per unit ($12) = $57, then divide that by the total variable costs per unit ($40 + $8) = $57/$48 = 118.75%, not (a) 16.67%, (b) 50%, or (c) 54.28%.

*15. (b) To minimize tax payments and maximize net income, Global's transfer prices should allocate more contribution margin to Eastland as it has a lower tax rate. The other choices are therefore incorrect.

▮ PRACTICE EXERCISES

Use cost-plus pricing to determine various amounts.

(LO 2)

1. Notown Recording Studio rents studio time to musicians in 2-hour blocks. Each session includes the use of the studio facilities, a digital recorded CD of the performance, and a professional music producer/mixer. Anticipated annual volume is 1,000 sessions. The company has invested $2,300,000 in the studio and expects a return on investment (ROI) of 15%. Budgeted costs for the coming year are as follows.

	Per Session	Total
Direct materials (CDs, etc.)	$ 20	
Direct labor	$400	
Variable overhead	$ 50	
Fixed overhead		$950,000
Variable selling and administrative expenses	$ 40	
Fixed selling and administrative expenses		$540,000

Instructions

(a) Determine the total cost per session.
(b) Determine the desired ROI per session.
(c) Calculate the markup percentage on the total cost per session.
(d) Calculate the target price per session.

Solution

1. (a) Total cost per session:

	Per Session
Direct materials	$ 20
Direct labor	400
Variable overhead	50
Fixed overhead ($950,000 ÷ 1,000)	950
Variable selling & administrative expenses	40
Fixed selling & administrative expenses ($540,000 ÷ 1,000)	540
Total cost per session	$2,000

(b) Desired ROI per session = (15% × $2,300,000) ÷ 1,000 = $345

(c) Markup percentage on total cost per session = $345 ÷ $2,000 = 17.25%

(d) Target price per session = $2,000 + ($2,000 × 17.25%) = $2,345

Determine minimum transfer price.

(LO 4)

2. Mercury Corporation manufactures car audio systems. It is a division of Country-Wide Motors, which manufactures vehicles. Mercury sells car audio systems to other divisions of Country-Wide, as well as to other vehicle manufacturers and retail stores. The following information is available for Mercury's standard unit: variable cost per unit $31, fixed cost per unit $23, and selling price to outside customer $85. Country-Wide currently purchases a standard unit from an outside supplier for $80. Because of quality concerns and to ensure a reliable supply, the top management of Country-Wide has ordered Mercury to provide 200,000 units per year at a transfer price of $30 per unit. Mercury is already operating at full capacity. Mercury can avoid $2 per unit of variable selling costs by selling the unit internally.

Instructions

(a) What is the minimum transfer price that Mercury should accept?
(b) What is the potential loss to the corporation as a whole resulting from this forced transfer?
(c) How should the company resolve this situation?

Solution

---

2. (a) The minimum transfer price that Mercury should accept is:

Minimum transfer price = ($31 − $2) + ($85 − $31) = $83

(b) The lost contribution margin per unit to the company is:

Contribution margin lost by Mercury	
[($85 − $31) − [$30 − ($31 − $2)]]	$ 53
Increased contribution margin to vehicle division ($80 − $30)	(50)
Net loss in contribution margin	$ 3

Total lost contribution margin is $3 × 200,000 units = $600,000

(c) If management insists that it wants Mercury to provide the car audio systems and Mercury is operating at full capacity, then it must be willing to pay the minimum transfer price for those units. Otherwise, it will penalize the managers of Mercury by not giving them adequate credit for their contribution to the corporation's contribution margin.

 PRACTICE PROBLEM

Revco Electronics is a division of International Motors, an automobile manufacturer. Revco produces car radio/CD players. Revco sells its products to other divisions of International Motors, as well as to other car manufacturers and electronics distributors. The following information is available regarding Revco's car radio/CD player.

Determine minimum transfer price under different situations.

(LO 4)

Selling price of car radio/CD player to external customers	$49
Variable cost per unit	$28
Capacity	200,000 units

Instructions

Determine whether the goods should be transferred internally or purchased externally and what the appropriate transfer price should be under each of the following **independent** situations.

(a) Revco Electronics is operating at full capacity. There is a saving of $4 per unit for variable cost if the car radio is made for internal sale. International Motors can purchase a comparable car radio from an outside supplier for $47.

(b) Revco Electronics has sufficient existing capacity to meet the needs of International Motors. International Motors can purchase a comparable car radio from an outside supplier for $47.

(c) International Motors wants to purchase a special-order car radio/CD player with additional features. It needs 15,000 units. Revco Electronics has determined that the additional variable cost would be $12 per unit. Revco Electronics has no spare capacity. It will have to forgo sales of 15,000 units to external parties in order to provide this special order.

Solution

(a) Revco Electronics' opportunity cost (its lost contribution margin) would be $21 ($49 − $28). Using the formula for minimum transfer price, we determine:

Minimum transfer price = Variable cost + Opportunity cost
          $45   = ($28 − $4) + $21

Since this minimum transfer price is less than the $47 it would cost if International Motors purchases from an external party, internal transfer should take place. Revco Electronics and International Motors should negotiate a transfer price between $45 and $47.

(b) Since Revco Electronics has available capacity, its opportunity cost (its lost contribution margin) would be $0. Using the formula for minimum transfer price, we determine the following.

$$\text{Minimum transfer price} = \text{Variable cost} + \text{Opportunity cost}$$
$$\$28 \quad = \quad \$28 \quad + \quad \$0$$

Since International Motors can purchase the unit for $47 from an external party, the most it would be willing to pay would be $47. It is in the best interest of the company as a whole, as well as the two divisions, for a transfer to take place. The two divisions must reach a negotiated transfer price between $28 and $47 that recognizes the costs and benefits to each party and is acceptable to both.

(c) Revco Electronics' opportunity cost (its lost contribution margin per unit) would be $21 ($49 − $28). Its variable cost would be $40 ($28 + $12). Using the formula for minimum transfer price, we determine the following.

$$\text{Minimum transfer price} = \text{Variable cost} + \text{Opportunity cost}$$
$$\$61 \quad = \quad \$40 \quad + \quad \$21$$

Note that in this case Revco Electronics has no available capacity. Its management may decide that it does not want to provide this special order because to do so will require that it cut off the supply of the standard unit to some of its existing customers. This may anger those customers and result in the loss of customers.

WileyPLUS

Brief Exercises, Exercises, **DO IT!** Exercises, and Problems and many additional resources are available for practice in WileyPLUS

NOTE: All asterisked Questions, Exercises, and Problems relate to material in the appendices to the chapter.

QUESTIONS

1. What are the two types of pricing environments for sales to external parties?
2. In what situation does a company place the greatest focus on its target cost? How is the target cost determined?
3. What is the basic formula to determine the target selling price in cost-plus pricing?
4. Benz Corporation produces a filter that has a per unit cost of $18. The company would like a 30% markup. Using cost-plus pricing, determine the per unit selling price.
5. What is the basic formula for the markup percentage?
6. What are some of the factors that affect a company's desired ROI?
7. Stanley Corporation manufactures an electronic switch for dishwashers. The cost base per unit, excluding selling and administrative expenses, is $60. The per unit cost of selling and administrative expenses is $15. The company's desired ROI per unit is $6. Calculate its markup percentage on total unit cost.
8. Sheen Co. manufactures a standard cabinet for a Blu-ray player. The variable cost per unit is $16. The fixed cost per unit is $9. The desired ROI per unit is $6. Compute the markup percentage on total unit cost and the target selling price for the cabinet.
9. In what circumstances is time-and-material pricing most often used?
10. What is the material loading charge? How is it expressed?

11. What is a transfer price? Why is determining a fair transfer price important to division managers?
12. When setting a transfer price, what objective(s) should the company have in mind?
13. What are the three approaches for determining transfer prices?
14. Describe the cost-based approach to transfer pricing. What is the strength of this approach? What are the weaknesses of this approach?
15. What is the general formula for determining the minimum transfer price that the selling division should be willing to accept?
16. When determining the minimum transfer price, what is meant by the "opportunity cost"?
17. In what circumstances will a negotiated transfer price be used instead of a market-based price?
*18. What costs are excluded from the cost base when absorption-cost pricing is used to determine the markup percentage?
*19. Marie Corporation manufactures a fiber optic connector. The variable cost per unit is $16. The fixed cost per unit is $9. The company's desired ROI per unit is $3. Compute the markup percentage using variable-cost pricing.
*20. Explain how companies use transfer pricing between divisions located in different countries to reduce tax payments, and discuss the propriety of this approach.

BRIEF EXERCISES

BE22-1 Ortega Company manufactures computer hard drives. The market for hard drives is very competitive. The current market price for a computer hard drive is $45. Ortega would like a profit of $10 per drive. How can Ortega accomplish this objective?

Compute target cost.

(LO 1)

BE22-2 Mussatto Corporation produces snowboards. The following per unit cost information is available: direct materials $12, direct labor $8, variable manufacturing overhead $6, fixed manufacturing overhead $14, variable selling and administrative expenses $4, and fixed selling and administrative expenses $12. Using a 30% markup percentage on total per unit cost, compute the target selling price.

Use cost-plus pricing to determine selling price.

(LO 2)

BE22-3 Jaymes Corporation produces high-performance rotors. It expects to produce 50,000 rotors in the coming year. It has invested $10,000,000 to produce rotors. The company has a required return on investment of 12%. What is its ROI per unit?

Compute ROI per unit.

(LO 2)

BE22-4 Morales Corporation produces microwave ovens. The following per unit cost information is available: direct materials $36, direct labor $24, variable manufacturing overhead $18, fixed manufacturing overhead $40, variable selling and administrative expenses $14, and fixed selling and administrative expenses $28. Its desired ROI per unit is $30. Compute its markup percentage using a total-cost approach.

Compute markup percentage.

(LO 2)

BE22-5 During the current year, Chudrick Corporation expects to produce 10,000 units and has budgeted the following: net income $300,000, variable costs $1,100,000, and fixed costs $100,000. It has invested assets of $1,500,000. The company's budgeted ROI was 20%. What was its budgeted markup percentage using a full-cost approach?

Compute ROI and markup percentage.

(LO 2)

BE22-6 Rooney Small Engine Repair charges $42 per hour of labor. It has a material loading percentage of 40%. On a recent job replacing the engine of a riding lawnmower, Rooney worked 10.5 hours and used parts with a cost of $700. Calculate Rooney's total bill.

Use time-and-material pricing to determine bill.

(LO 3)

BE22-7 The Heating Division of Kobe International produces a heating element that it sells to its customers for $45 per unit. Its variable cost per unit is $25, and its fixed cost per unit is $10. Top management of Kobe International would like the Heating Division to transfer 15,000 heating units to another division within the company at a price of $29. The Heating Division is operating at full capacity. What is the minimum transfer price that the Heating Division should accept?

Determine minimum transfer price.

(LO 4)

BE22-8 Use the data from BE22-7 but assume that the Heating Division has sufficient excess capacity to provide the 15,000 heating units to the other division. What is the minimum transfer price that the Heating Division should accept?

Determine minimum transfer price with excess capacity.

(LO 4)

BE22-9 Use the data from BE22-7 but assume that the units being requested are special high-performance units and that the division's variable cost would be $27 per unit (rather than $25). What is the minimum transfer price that the Heating Division should accept?

Determine minimum transfer price for special order.

(LO 4)

*BE22-10 Using the data in BE22-4, compute the markup percentage using absorption-cost pricing.

Compute markup percentage using absorption-cost pricing.

(LO 5)

*BE22-11 Using the data in BE22-4, compute the markup percentage using variable-cost pricing.

Compute markup percentage using variable-cost pricing.

(LO 5)

DO IT! Exercises

Determine target cost.

(LO 1)

DO IT! 22-1 Maize Water is considering introducing a water filtration device for its 20-ounce water bottles. Market research indicates that 1,000,000 units can be sold if the price is no more than $3. If Maize Water decides to produce the filters, it will need to invest $2,000,000 in new production equipment. Maize Water requires a minimum rate of return of 16% on all investments.

Determine the target cost per unit for the filter.

Use cost-plus pricing to determine various amounts.

(LO 2)

DO IT! 22-2 Gundy Corporation produces area rugs. The following per unit cost information is available: direct materials $18, direct labor $9, variable manufacturing overhead $5, fixed manufacturing overhead $6, variable selling and administrative expenses $3, and fixed selling and administrative expenses $7.

Using a 30% markup on total per unit cost, compute the target selling price.

Use time-and-material pricing to determine bill.

(LO 3)

DO IT! 22-3 Presented below are data relating to labor for Verde Appliance Repair Shop.

Repair-technicians' wages	$110,000
Fringe benefits	40,000
Overhead	50,000

The desired profit margin per hour is $20. The material loading charge is 60% of invoice cost. Verde estimates that 5,000 labor hours will be worked next year. If Verde repairs a dishwasher that takes 1.5 hours to repair and uses parts of $70, compute the bill for the job.

Determine transfer prices.

(LO 4)

DO IT! 22-4 The fastener division of Southern Fasteners manufactures zippers and then sells them to customers for $8 per unit. Its variable cost is $3 per unit, and its fixed cost per unit is $1.50. Management would like the fastener division to transfer 12,000 of these zippers to another division within the company at a price of $3. The fastener division could avoid $0.20 per zipper of variable packaging costs by selling internally.

Determine the minimum transfer price (a) assuming the fastener division is not operating at full capacity, and (b) assuming the fastener division is operating at full capacity.

EXERCISES

Compute target cost.

(LO 1)

E22-1 Mesa Cheese Company has developed a new cheese slicer called Slim Slicer. The company plans to sell this slicer through its catalog, which it issues monthly. Given market research, Mesa believes that it can charge $20 for the Slim Slicer. Prototypes of the Slim Slicer, however, are costing $22. By using cheaper materials and gaining efficiencies in mass production, Mesa believes it can reduce Slim Slicer's cost substantially. Mesa wishes to earn a return of 40% of the selling price.

Instructions
(a) Compute the target cost for the Slim Slicer.
(b) When is target costing particularly helpful in deciding whether to produce a given product?

Compute target cost.

(LO 1)

E22-2 Eckert Company is involved in producing and selling high-end golf equipment. The company has recently been involved in developing various types of laser guns to measure yardages on the golf course. One small laser gun, called LittleLaser, appears to have a very large potential market. Because of competition, Eckert does not believe that it can charge more than $90 for LittleLaser. At this price, Eckert believes it can sell 100,000 of these laser guns. Eckert will require an investment of $8,000,000 to manufacture, and the company wants an ROI of 20%.

Instructions
Determine the target cost for one LittleLaser.

E22-3 Leno Company makes swimsuits and sells these suits directly to retailers. Although Leno has a variety of suits, it does not make the All-Body suit used by highly skilled swimmers. The market research department believes that a strong market exists for this type of suit. The department indicates that the All-Body suit would sell for approximately $100. Given its experience, Leno believes the All-Body suit would have the following manufacturing costs.

Compute target cost and cost-plus pricing.

(LO 1, 2)

Direct materials	$ 25
Direct labor	30
Manufacturing overhead	45
Total costs	$100

Instructions

(a) Assume that Leno uses cost-plus pricing, setting the selling price 25% above its costs. (1) What would be the price charged for the All-Body swimsuit? (2) Under what circumstances might Leno consider manufacturing the All-Body swimsuit given this approach?

(b) Assume that Leno uses target costing. What is the price that Leno would charge the retailer for the All-Body swimsuit?

(c) What is the highest acceptable manufacturing cost Leno would be willing to incur to produce the All-Body swimsuit, if it desired a profit of $25 per unit? (Assume target costing.)

E22-4 Kaspar Corporation makes a commercial-grade cooking griddle. The following information is available for Kaspar Corporation's anticipated annual volume of 30,000 units.

Use cost-plus pricing to determine selling price.

(LO 2)

	Per Unit	Total
Direct materials	$17	
Direct labor	$ 8	
Variable manufacturing overhead	$11	
Fixed manufacturing overhead		$300,000
Variable selling and administrative expenses	$ 4	
Fixed selling and administrative expenses		$150,000

The company uses a 40% markup percentage on total cost.

Instructions

(a) Compute the total cost per unit.

(b) Compute the target selling price.

E22-5 Schopp Corporation makes a mechanical stuffed alligator that sings the Martian national anthem. The following information is available for Schopp Corporation's anticipated annual volume of 500,000 units.

Use cost-plus pricing to determine various amounts.

(LO 2)

	Per Unit	Total
Direct materials	$ 7	
Direct labor	$11	
Variable manufacturing overhead	$15	
Fixed manufacturing overhead		$3,000,000
Variable selling and administrative expenses	$14	
Fixed selling and administrative expenses		$1,500,000

The company has a desired ROI of 25%. It has invested assets of $28,000,000.

Instructions

(a) Compute the total cost per unit.

(b) Compute the desired ROI per unit.

(c) Compute the markup percentage using total cost per unit.

(d) Compute the target selling price.

E22-6 Alma's Recording Studio rents studio time to musicians in 2-hour blocks. Each session includes the use of the studio facilities, a digital recording of the performance, and a professional music producer/mixer. Anticipated annual volume is 1,000 sessions. The

Use cost-plus pricing to determine various amounts.

(LO 2)

company has invested $2,352,000 in the studio and expects a return on investment (ROI) of 20%. Budgeted costs for the coming year are as follows.

	Per Session	Total
Direct materials (CDs, etc.)	$ 20	
Direct labor	$400	
Variable overhead	$ 50	
Fixed overhead		$950,000
Variable selling and administrative expenses	$ 40	
Fixed selling and administrative expenses		$500,000

Instructions
(a) Determine the total cost per session.
(b) Determine the desired ROI per session.
(c) Calculate the markup percentage on the total cost per session.
(d) Calculate the target price per session.

Use cost-plus pricing to determine various amounts.

(LO 2)

E22-7 Gibbs Corporation produces industrial robots for high-precision manufacturing. The following information is given for Gibbs Corporation.

	Per Unit	Total
Direct materials	$380	
Direct labor	$290	
Variable manufacturing overhead	$ 72	
Fixed manufacturing overhead		$1,500,000
Variable selling and administrative expenses	$ 55	
Fixed selling and administrative expenses		$ 324,000

The company has a desired ROI of 20%. It has invested assets of $54,000,000. It antici-pates production of 3,000 units per year.

Instructions
(a) Compute the cost per unit of the fixed manufacturing overhead and the fixed selling and administrative expenses.
(b) Compute the desired ROI per unit. (Round to the nearest dollar.)
(c) Compute the target selling price.

Use time-and-material pricing to determine bill.

(LO 3)

E22-8 Second Chance Welding rebuilds spot welders for manufacturers. The following budgeted cost data for 2017 is available for Second Chance.

	Time Charges	Material Loading Charges
Technicians' wages and benefits	$228,000	—
Parts manager's salary and benefits	—	$42,500
Office employee's salary and benefits	38,000	9,000
Other overhead	15,200	24,000
Total budgeted costs	$281,200	$75,500

The company desires a $30 profit margin per hour of labor and a 20% profit margin on parts. It has budgeted for 7,600 hours of repair time in the coming year, and estimates that the total invoice cost of parts and materials in 2017 will be $400,000.

Instructions
(a) Compute the rate charged per hour of labor.
(b) Compute the material loading percentage. (Round to three decimal places.)
(c) Pace Corporation has requested an estimate to rebuild its spot welder. Second Chance estimates that it would require 40 hours of labor and $2,000 of parts. Compute the total estimated bill.

E22-9 Rey Custom Electronics (RCE) sells and installs complete security, computer, audio, and video systems for homes. On newly constructed homes it provides bids using time-and-material pricing. The following budgeted cost data are available.

Use time-and-material pricing to determine bill.

(LO 3)

	Time Charges	Material Loading Charges
Technicians' wages and benefits	$150,000	—
Parts manager's salary and benefits	—	$34,000
Office employee's salary and benefits	30,000	15,000
Other overhead	15,000	42,000
Total budgeted costs	$195,000	$91,000

The company has budgeted for 6,250 hours of technician time during the coming year. It desires a $38 profit margin per hour of labor and an 80% profit on parts. It estimates the total invoice cost of parts and materials in 2017 will be $700,000.

Instructions
(a) Compute the rate charged per hour of labor.
(b) Compute the material loading percentage.
(c) RCE has just received a request for a bid from Buil Builders on a $1,200,000 new home. The company estimates that it would require 80 hours of labor and $40,000 of parts. Compute the total estimated bill.

E22-10 Wasson's Classic Cars restores classic automobiles to showroom status. Budgeted data for the current year are as follows.

Use time-and-material pricing to determine bill.

(LO 3)

	Time Charges	Material Loading Charges
Restorers' wages and fringe benefits	$270,000	
Purchasing agent's salary and fringe benefits		$ 67,500
Administrative salaries and fringe benefits	54,000	21,960
Other overhead costs	24,000	77,490
Total budgeted costs	$348,000	$166,950

The company anticipated that the restorers would work a total of 12,000 hours this year. Expected parts and materials were $1,260,000.

In late January, the company experienced a fire in its facilities that destroyed most of the accounting records. The accountant remembers that the hourly labor rate was $70.00 and that the material loading charge was 83.25%.

Instructions
(a) Determine the profit margin per hour on labor.
(b) Determine the profit margin on materials.
(c) Determine the total price of labor and materials on a job that was completed after the fire that required 150 hours of labor and $60,000 in parts and materials.

E22-11 Chen Company's Small Motor Division manufactures a number of small motors used in household and office appliances. The Household Division of Chen then assembles and packages such items as blenders and juicers. Both divisions are free to buy and sell any of their components internally or externally. The following costs relate to small motor LN233 on a per unit basis.

Determine minimum transfer price.

(LO 4)

Fixed cost per unit	$ 5
Variable cost per unit	$11
Selling price per unit	$35

Instructions
(a) Assuming that the Small Motor Division has excess capacity, compute the minimum acceptable price for the transfer of small motor LN233 to the Household Division.
(b) Assuming that the Small Motor Division does not have excess capacity, compute the minimum acceptable price for the transfer of the small motor to the Household Division.
(c) ———— Explain why the level of capacity in the Small Motor Division has an effect on the transfer price.

Determine effect on income from transfer price.

(LO 4)

E22-12 The Cycle Division of Ayala Company has the following per unit data related to its most recent cycle called Roadbuster.

Selling price		$2,200
Variable cost of goods sold		
Body frame	$300	
Other variable costs	900	1,200
Contribution margin		$1,000

Presently, the Cycle Division buys its body frames from an outside supplier. However Ayala has another division, FrameBody, that makes body frames for other cycle companies. The Cycle Division believes that FrameBody's product is suitable for its new Roadbuster cycle. Presently, FrameBody sells its frames for $350 per frame. The variable cost for FrameBody is $270. The Cycle Division is willing to pay $280 to purchase the frames from FrameBody.

Instructions

(a) Assume that FrameBody has excess capacity and is able to meet all of the Cycle Division's needs. If the Cycle Division buys 1,000 frames from FrameBody, determine the following: (1) effect on the income of the Cycle Division; (2) effect on the income of FrameBody; and (3) effect on the income of Ayala.

(b) Assume that FrameBody does not have excess capacity and therefore would lose sales if the frames were sold to the Cycle Division. If the Cycle Division buys 1,000 frames from FrameBody, determine the following: (1) effect on the income of the Cycle Division; (2) effect on the income of FrameBody; and (3) effect on the income of Ayala.

Determine minimum transfer price.

(LO 4)

E22-13 Benson Corporation manufactures car stereos. It is a division of Berna Motors, which manufactures vehicles. Benson sells car stereos to Berna, as well as to other vehicle manufacturers and retail stores. The following information is available for Benson's standard unit: variable cost per unit $37, fixed cost per unit $23, and selling price to outside customer $86. Berna currently purchases a standard unit from an outside supplier for $80. Because of quality concerns and to ensure a reliable supply, the top management of Berna has ordered Benson to provide 200,000 units per year at a transfer price of $35 per unit. Benson is already operating at full capacity. Benson can avoid $3 per unit of variable selling costs by selling the unit internally.

Instructions

Answer each of the following questions.

(a) What is the minimum transfer price that Benson should accept?

(b) What is the potential loss to the corporation as a whole resulting from this forced transfer?

(c) How should the company resolve this situation?

Compute minimum transfer price.

(LO 4)

E22-14 The Bathtub Division of Kirk Plumbing Corporation has recently approached the Faucet Division with a proposal. The Bathtub Division would like to make a special "ivory" tub with gold-plated fixtures for the company's 50-year anniversary. It would make only 5,000 of these units. It would like the Faucet Division to make the fixtures and provide them to the Bathtub Division at a transfer price of $160. If sold externally, the estimated variable cost per unit would be $140. However, by selling internally, the Faucet Division would save $6 per unit on variable selling expenses. The Faucet Division is currently operating at full capacity. Its standard unit sells for $50 per unit and has variable costs of $29.

Instructions

Compute the minimum transfer price that the Faucet Division should be willing to accept, and discuss whether it should accept this offer.

Determine minimum transfer price.

(LO 4)

E22-15 The Appraisal Department of Jean Bank performs appraisals of business properties for loans being considered by the bank and appraisals for home buyers that are financing their purchase through some other financial institution. The department charges $160 per home appraisal, and its variable costs are $130 per appraisal.

Recently, Jean Bank has opened its own Home-Loan Department and wants the Appraisal Department to perform 1,200 appraisals on all Jean Bank–financed home loans. Bank management feels that the cost of these appraisals to the Home-Loan Department should be $150. The variable cost per appraisal to the Home-Loan Department would be $8 less than those performed for outside customers due to savings in administrative costs.

Instructions

(a) Determine the minimum transfer price, assuming the Appraisal Department has excess capacity.

(b) Determine the minimum transfer price, assuming the Appraisal Department has no excess capacity.

(c) Assuming the Appraisal Department has no excess capacity, should management force the department to charge the Home-Loan Department only $150? Discuss.

E22-16 Crede Inc. has two divisions. Division A makes and sells student desks. Division B manufactures and sells reading lamps.

Each desk has a reading lamp as one of its components. Division A can purchase reading lamps at a cost of $10 from an outside vendor. Division A needs 10,000 lamps for the coming year.

Division B has the capacity to manufacture 50,000 lamps annually. Sales to outside customers are estimated at 40,000 lamps for the next year. Reading lamps are sold at $12 each. Variable costs are $7 per lamp and include $1 of variable sales costs that are not incurred if lamps are sold internally to Division A. The total amount of fixed costs for Division B is $80,000.

Determine minimum transfer price under different situations.

(LO 4)

Instructions

Consider the following independent situations.

(a) What should be the minimum transfer price accepted by Division B for the 10,000 lamps and the maximum transfer price paid by Division A? Justify your answer.

(b) Suppose Division B could use the excess capacity to produce and sell externally 15,000 units of a new product at a price of $7 per unit. The variable cost for this new product is $5 per unit. What should be the minimum transfer price accepted by Division B for the 10,000 lamps and the maximum transfer price paid by Division A? Justify your answer.

(c) If Division A needs 15,000 lamps instead of 10,000 during the next year, what should be the minimum transfer price accepted by Division B and the maximum transfer price paid by Division A? Justify your answer.

(CGA adapted)

E22-17 Twyla Company is a multidivisional company. Its managers have full responsibility for profits and complete autonomy to accept or reject transfers from other divisions. Division A produces a subassembly part for which there is a competitive market. Division B currently uses this subassembly for a final product that is sold outside at $2,400. Division A charges Division B market price for the part, which is $1,500 per unit. Variable costs are $1,100 and $1,200 for Divisions A and B, respectively.

The manager of Division B feels that Division A should transfer the part at a lower price than market because at market, Division B is unable to make a profit.

Determine minimum transfer price under different situations.

(LO 4)

Instructions

(a) Calculate Division B's contribution margin if transfers are made at the market price, and calculate the company's total contribution margin.

(b) Assume that Division A can sell all its production in the open market. Should Division A transfer the goods to Division B? If so, at what price?

(c) Assume that Division A can sell in the open market only 500 units at $1,500 per unit out of the 1,000 units that it can produce every month. Assume also that a 20% reduction in price is necessary to sell all 1,000 units each month. Should transfers be made? If so, how many units should the division transfer and at what price? To support your decision, submit a schedule that compares the contribution margins under the following three different alternatives. Alternative 1: maintain price, no transfers; Alternative 2: cut price, no transfers; and Alternative 3: maintain price and transfers.

(CMA-Canada adapted)

*E22-18 Information for Schopp Corporation is given in E22-5.

Compute total cost per unit, ROI, and markup percentages using absorption-cost pricing and variable-cost pricing.

(LO 5)

Instructions

Using the information given in E22-5, answer the following.

(a) Compute the total cost per unit.

(b) Compute the desired ROI per unit.

(c) Using absorption-cost pricing, compute the markup percentage.

(d) Using variable-cost pricing, compute the markup percentage.

Compute markup percentage using absorption-cost pricing and variable-cost pricing.

(LO 5)

*E22-19 Rap Corporation produces outdoor portable fireplace units. The following per unit cost information is available: direct materials $20, direct labor $25, variable manufacturing overhead $14, fixed manufacturing overhead $21, variable selling and administrative expenses $9, and fixed selling and administrative expenses $11. The company's ROI per unit is $24.

Instructions

Compute Rap Corporation's markup percentage using (a) absorption-cost pricing and (b) variable-cost pricing.

Compute various amounts using absorption-cost pricing and variable-cost pricing.

(LO 5)

*E22-20 Information for Gibbs Corporation is given in E22-7.

Instructions

Using the information given in E22-7, answer the following.

(a) Compute the cost per unit of the fixed manufacturing overhead and the fixed selling and administrative expenses.
(b) Compute the desired ROI per unit. (Round to the nearest dollar.)
(c) Compute the markup percentage and target selling price using absorption-cost pricing. (Round the markup percentage to three decimal places.)
(d) Compute the markup percentage and target selling price using variable-cost pricing. (Round the markup percentage to three decimal places.)

EXERCISES: SET B AND CHALLENGE EXERCISES

Visit the book's companion website, at **www.wiley.com/college/weygandt**, and choose the Student Companion site to access Exercises: Set B and Challenge Exercises.

PROBLEMS: SET A

Use cost-plus pricing to determine various amounts.

(LO 2)

P22-1A National Corporation needs to set a target price for its newly designed product M14–M16. The following data relate to this new product.

	Per Unit	Total
Direct materials	$25	
Direct labor	$40	
Variable manufacturing overhead	$10	
Fixed manufacturing overhead		$1,440,000
Variable selling and administrative expenses	$ 5	
Fixed selling and administrative expenses		$ 960,000

These costs are based on a budgeted volume of 80,000 units produced and sold each year. National uses cost-plus pricing methods to set its target selling price. The markup percentage on total unit cost is 40%.

Instructions

(a) Variable cost per unit $80

(a) Compute the total variable cost per unit, total fixed cost per unit, and total cost per unit for M14–M16.
(b) Compute the desired ROI per unit for M14–M16.
(c) Compute the target selling price for M14–M16.
(d) Compute variable cost per unit, fixed cost per unit, and total cost per unit assuming that 60,000 M14–M16s are produced and sold during the year.

Use cost-plus pricing to determine various amounts.

(LO 2)

P22-2A Lovell Computer Parts Inc. is in the process of setting a selling price on a new component it has just designed and developed. The following cost estimates for this new component have been provided by the accounting department for a budgeted volume of 50,000 units.

	Per Unit	Total
Direct materials	$50	
Direct labor	$26	
Variable manufacturing overhead	$20	
Fixed manufacturing overhead		$600,000
Variable selling and administrative expenses	$19	
Fixed selling and administrative expenses		$400,000

Lovell Computer Parts management requests that the total cost per unit be used in cost-plus pricing its products. On this particular product, management also directs that the target price be set to provide a 25% return on investment (ROI) on invested assets of $1,000,000.

Instructions
(Round all calculations to two decimal places.)
(a) Compute the markup percentage and target selling price that will allow Lovell Computer Parts to earn its desired ROI of 25% on this new component.
(b) Assuming that the volume is 40,000 units, compute the markup percentage and target selling price that will allow Lovell Computer Parts to earn its desired ROI of 25% on this new component.

(b) Target selling price
$146.25

P22-3A Sutton's Electronic Repair Shop has budgeted the following time and material for 2017.

Use time-and-material pricing to determine bill.

(LO 3)

SUTTON'S ELECTRONIC REPAIR SHOP
Budgeted Costs for the Year 2017

	Time Charges	Material Loading Charges
Shop employees' wages and benefits	$108,000	—
Parts manager's salary and benefits	—	$25,400
Office employee's salary and benefits	23,500	13,600
Overhead (supplies, depreciation, advertising, utilities)	26,000	16,000
Total budgeted costs	$157,500	$55,000

Sutton's budgets 5,000 hours of repair time in 2017 and will bill a profit of $10 per labor hour along with a 25% profit markup on the invoice cost of parts. The estimated invoice cost for parts to be used is $100,000.

On January 5, 2017, Sutton's is asked to submit a price estimate to fix a 72-inch flat-screen TV. Sutton's estimates that this job will consume 4 hours of labor and $200 in parts.

Instructions
(a) Compute the labor rate for Sutton's Electronic Repair Shop for the year 2017.
(b) Compute the material loading charge percentage for Sutton's Electronic Repair Shop for the year 2017.
(c) Prepare a time-and-material price quotation for fixing the flat-screen TV.

(c) $526

P22-4A Word Wizard is a publishing company with a number of different book lines. Each line has contracts with a number of different authors. The company also owns a printing operation called Quick Press. The book lines and the printing operation each operate as a separate profit center. The printing operation earns revenue by printing books by authors under contract with the book lines owned by Word Wizard, as well as authors under contract with other companies. The printing operation bills out at $0.01 per page, and a typical book requires 500 pages of print. A manager from Business Books, one of the Word Wizard's book lines, has approached the manager of the printing operation offering to pay $0.007 per page for 1,500 copies of a 500-page book. The book line pays outside printers $0.009 per page. The printing operation's variable cost per page is $0.004.

Determine minimum transfer price with no excess capacity and with excess capacity.

(LO 4)

Instructions
Determine whether the printing should be done internally or externally, and the appropriate transfer price, under each of the following situations.

(a) Assume that the printing operation is booked solid for the next 2 years, and it would have to cancel an obligation with an outside customer in order to meet the needs of the internal division.
(b) Assume that the printing operation has available capacity.
(c) ◄━━━ The top management of Word Wizard believes that the printing operation should always do the printing for the company's authors. On a number of occasions, it has forced the printing operation to cancel jobs with outside customers in order to meet the needs of its own lines. Discuss the pros and cons of this approach.
(d) Calculate the change in contribution margin to each division, and to the company as a whole, if top management forces the printing operation to accept the $0.007 per page transfer price when it has no available capacity.

(d) Loss to company ($750)

Determine minimum transfer price with no excess capacity.

(LO 4)

P22-5A Gutierrez Company makes various electronic products. The company is divided into a number of autonomous divisions that can either sell to internal units or sell externally. All divisions are located in buildings on the same piece of property. The Board Division has offered the Chip Division $21 per unit to supply it with chips for 40,000 boards. It has been purchasing these chips for $22 per unit from outside suppliers. The Chip Division receives $22.50 per unit for sales made to outside customers on this type of chip. The variable cost of chips sold externally by the Chip Division is $14.50. It estimates that it will save $4.50 per chip of selling expenses on units sold internally to the Board Division. The Chip Division has no excess capacity.

Instructions

(a) Calculate the minimum transfer price that the Chip Division should accept. Discuss whether it is in the Chip Division's best interest to accept the offer.

(b) Total loss to company
$160,000

(b) Suppose that the Chip Division decides to reject the offer. What are the financial implications for each division, and for the company as a whole, of this decision?

Determine minimum transfer price under different situations.

(LO 4)

P22-6A Comm Devices (CD) is a division of Worldwide Communications, Inc. CD produces pagers and other personal communication devices. These devices are sold to other Worldwide divisions, as well as to other communication companies. CD was recently approached by the manager of the Personal Communications Division regarding a request to make a special pager designed to receive signals from anywhere in the world. The Personal Communications Division has requested that CD produce 12,000 units of this special pager. The following facts are available regarding the Comm Devices Division.

Selling price of standard pager	$95
Variable cost of standard pager	$50
Additional variable cost of special pager	$30

Instructions

For each of the following independent situations, calculate the minimum transfer price, and discuss whether the internal transfer should take place or whether the Personal Communications Division should purchase the pager externally.

(a) The Personal Communications Division has offered to pay the CD Division $105 per pager. The CD Division has no available capacity. The CD Division would have to forgo sales of 10,000 pagers to existing customers in order to meet the request of the Personal Communications Division. (*Note:* The number of special pagers to be produced does not equal the number of existing pagers that would be forgone.)

(b) Minimum transfer
price $140

(b) The Personal Communications Division has offered to pay the CD Division $150 per pager. The CD Division has no available capacity. The CD Division would have to forgo sales of 16,000 pagers to existing customers in order to meet the request of the Personal Communications Division. (*Note:* The number of special pagers to be produced does not equal the number of existing pagers that would be forgone.

(c) The Personal Communications Division has offered to pay the CD Division $100 per pager. The CD Division has available capacity.

Compute the target price using absorption-cost pricing and variable-cost pricing.

(LO 5)

***P22-7A** Stent Corporation needs to set a target price for its newly designed product EverReady. The following data relate to this new product.

	Per Unit	Total
Direct materials	$20	
Direct labor	$40	
Variable manufacturing overhead	$10	
Fixed manufacturing overhead		$1,600,000
Variable selling and administrative expenses	$ 5	
Fixed selling and administrative expenses		$1,120,000

The costs shown above are based on a budgeted volume of 80,000 units produced and sold each year. Stent uses cost-plus pricing methods to set its target selling price. Because some managers prefer absorption-cost pricing and others prefer variable-cost pricing, the accounting department provides information under both approaches using a markup of 50% on absorption cost and a markup of 80% on variable cost.

Instructions

(a) Compute the target price for one unit of EverReady using absorption-cost pricing.

(b) Compute the target price for one unit of EverReady using variable-cost pricing.

(a) Markup $45

(b) Markup $60

*P22-8A Anderson Windows Inc. is in the process of setting a target price on its newly designed tinted window. Cost data relating to the window at a budgeted volume of 4,000 units are as follows.

Compute various amounts using absorption-cost pricing and variable-cost pricing.

(LO 5)

	Per Unit	Total
Direct materials	$100	
Direct labor	$ 70	
Variable manufacturing overhead	$ 20	
Fixed manufacturing overhead		$120,000
Variable selling and administrative expenses	$ 10	
Fixed selling and administrative expenses		$102,000

Anderson Windows uses cost-plus pricing methods that are designed to provide the company with a 25% ROI on its tinted window line. A total of $1,016,000 in assets is committed to production of the new tinted window.

Instructions

(a) Compute the markup percentage under absorption-cost pricing that will allow Anderson Windows to realize its desired ROI.

(b) Compute the target price of the window under absorption-cost pricing, and show proof that the desired ROI is realized.

(c) Compute the markup percentage under variable-cost pricing that will allow Anderson Windows to realize its desired ROI. (Round to three decimal places.)

(d) Compute the target price of the window under variable-cost pricing, and show proof that the desired ROI is realized.

(e) ———— Since both absorption-cost pricing and variable-cost pricing produce the same target price and provide the same desired ROI, why do both methods exist? Isn't one method clearly superior to the other?

(a) 45%

PROBLEMS: SET B AND SET C

Visit the book's companion website, at **www.wiley.com/college/weygandt**, and choose the Student Companion site to access Problems: Set B and Set C.

CONTINUING PROBLEMS

CURRENT DESIGNS

CD22 As a service to its customers, Current Designs repairs damaged kayaks. This is especially valuable to customers that have made a significant investment in the composite kayaks. To price the repair jobs, Current Designs uses time-and-material pricing with a desired profit margin of $20 per labor hour and a 50% materials loading charge.

Recently, Bill Johnson, Vice President of Sales and Marketing, received a phone call from a dealer in Brainerd, Minnesota. The dealer has a customer who recently damaged his composite kayak and would like an estimate of the cost to repair it. After the dealer emailed pictures of the damage, Bill reviewed the pictures with the repair technician and determined that the total materials charges for the repair would be $100. Bill estimates that the job will take 3 labor hours to complete. Following is the budgeted cost data for Current Designs:

EXCEL TUTORIAL

Repair technician wages	$30,000
Fringe benefits	$10,000
Overhead	$10,000

Current Designs has allocated 2,000 hours of repair time for the upcoming year. The customer has agreed to transport the kayak to the Winona production facility for the repairs.

Instructions

Determine the price that Current Designs would charge to complete the repairs for the customer.

WATERWAYS

(*Note:* This is a continuation of the Waterways problem from Chapters 15–21.)

WP22 Waterways Corporation competes in a market economy in which its products must be sold at market prices. Its emphasis is therefore on manufacturing its products at a cost that allows the company to earn its desired profit. This problem asks you to consider various pricing situations for Waterways' projects.

Go to the book's companion website, **www.wiley.com/college/weygandt**, *to find the remainder of this problem.*

COMPREHENSIVE CASE

Greetings, Inc., a retailer of greeting cards and small gift items, needs to change its transfer pricing strategy for its Wall Décor division. In this case, you will have the opportunity to evaluate profitability using two different transfer pricing approaches and comment on the terms of the proposed transfer pricing agreement.

Go to the book's companion website, at **www.wiley.com/college/weygandt**, *for complete case details and techniques.*

BROADENING YOUR PERSPECTIVE

MANAGEMENT DECISION-MAKING

Decision-Making Across the Organization

BYP22-1 Lanier Manufacturing has multiple divisions that make a wide variety of products. Recently, the Bearing Division and the Wheel Division got into an argument over a transfer price. The Wheel Division needed bearings for garden tractor wheels. It normally buys its bearings from an outside supplier for $25 per set. The company's top management recently initiated a campaign to persuade the different divisions to buy their materials from within the company whenever possible. As a result, Hank Sherril, the purchasing manager for the Wheel Division, received a letter from the vice president of Purchasing, ordering him to contact the Bearing Division to discuss buying bearings from this division.

To comply with this request, Hank from the Wheel Division called Mary Plimpton of the Bearing Division, and asked the price for 15,000 bearings. Mary responded that the bearings normally sell for $36 per set. However, Mary noted that the Bearing Division would save $3 on marketing costs by selling internally, and would pass this cost savings on to the Wheel Division. She further commented that they were at full capacity, and therefore would not be able to provide any bearings presently. In the future, if they had available capacity, they would be happy to provide bearings.

Hank responded indignantly, "Thanks but no thanks." He said, "We can get all the bearings we need from Falk Manufacturing for $25 per set." Mary snorted back, "Falk makes junk. It costs us $22 per set just to make our bearings. Our bearings can withstand heat of 2,000 degrees centigrade, and are good to within .00001 centimeters. If you guys are happy buying junk, then go ahead and buy from Falk."

Two weeks later, Hank's boss from the central office stopped in to find out whether he had placed an order with the Bearing Division. Hank responded that he would sooner buy his bearings from his worst enemy than from the Bearing Division.

Instructions

With the class divided into groups, prepare answers to the following questions.

(a) Why might the company's top management want the divisions to start doing more business with one another?

(b) Under what conditions should a buying division be forced to buy from an internal supplier? Under what conditions should a selling division be forced to sell to an internal division rather than to an outside customer?

(c) The vice president of Purchasing thinks that this problem should be resolved by forcing the Bearing Division to sell to the Wheel Division at its cost of $22. Is this a good solution for the Wheel Division? Is this a good solution for the Bearing Division? Is this a good solution for the company?

(d) Provide at least two other possible solutions to this problem. Discuss the merits and drawbacks of each.

Managerial Analysis

BYP22-2 Construction on the Bonita Full-Service Car Wash is nearing completion. The owner is Dave Kear, a retired accounting professor. The car wash is strategically located on a busy street that separates an affluent suburban community from a middle-class community. It has two state-of-the-art stalls. Each stall can provide anything from a basic two-stage wash and rinse to a five-stage luxurious bath. It is all "touchless," that is, there are no brushes to potentially damage the car. Outside each stall, there is also a 400 horse-power vacuum. Dave likes to joke that these vacuums are so strong that they will pull the carpet right out of your car if you aren't careful.

Dave has some important decisions to make before he can open the car wash. First, he knows that there is one drive-through car wash only a 10-minute drive away. It is attached to a gas station; it charges $5 for a basic wash, and $4 if you also buy at least 8 gallons of gas. It is a "brush"-type wash with rotating brush heads. There is also a self-serve "stand outside your car and spray until you are soaked" car wash a 15-minute drive away from Dave's location. He went over and tried this out. He went through $3 in quarters to get the equivalent of a basic wash. He knows that both of these locations always have long lines, which is one reason why he decided to build a new car wash.

Dave is planning to offer three levels of wash service—Basic, Deluxe, and Premium. The Basic is all automated; it requires no direct intervention by employees. The Deluxe is all automated except that at the end an employee will wipe down the car and will put a window treatment on the windshield that reduces glare and allows rainwater to run off more quickly. The Premium level is a "pampered" service. This will include all the services of the Deluxe, plus a special wax after the machine wax, and an employee will vacuum the car, wipe down the entire interior, and wash the inside of the windows. To provide the Premium service, Dave will have to hire a couple of "car wash specialists" to do the additional pampering.

Dave has pulled together the following estimates, based on data he received from the local Chamber of Commerce and information from a trade association.

	Per Unit	Total
Direct materials per Basic wash	$0.30	
Direct materials per Deluxe wash	$0.80	
Direct materials per Premium wash	$1.10	
Direct labor per Basic wash	na	
Direct labor per Deluxe wash	$0.40	
Direct labor per Premium wash	$2.40	
Variable overhead per Basic wash	$0.10	
Variable overhead per Deluxe and Premium washes	$0.20	
Fixed overhead		$117,000
Variable selling and administrative expenses all washes	$0.10	
Fixed selling and administrative expenses		$130,500

The total estimated number of washes of any type is 45,000. Dave has invested assets of $393,750. He would like a return on investment (ROI) of 20%.

Instructions

Answer each of the following questions.

(a) Identify the issues that Dave must consider in deciding on the price of each level of service of his car wash. Also discuss what issues he should consider in deciding on what levels of service to provide.

(b) Dave estimates that of the total 45,000 washes, 20,000 will be Basic, 20,000 will be Deluxe, and 5,000 will be Premium. Calculate the selling price, using cost-plus pricing, that Dave should use for each type of wash to achieve his desired ROI of 20%.

(c) During the first year, instead of selling 45,000 washes, Dave sold 43,000 washes. He was quite accurate in his estimate of first-year sales, but he was way off on the types of washes that he sold. He sold 3,000 Basic, 31,000 Deluxe, and 9,000 Premium. His actual total fixed expenses were as he expected, and his variable cost per unit was as estimated. Calculate Dave's actual net income and his actual ROI. (Round to two decimal places.)

(d) Dave is using a traditional approach to allocate overhead. As a consequence, he is allocating overhead equally to all three types of washes, even though the Basic wash is considerably less complicated and uses very little of the technical capabilities of the machinery. What should Dave do to determine more accurate costs per unit? How will this affect his pricing and, consequently, his sales?

Real-World Focus

BYP22-3 Merck & Co., Inc. is a global, research-driven pharmaceutical company that discovers, develops, manufactures, and markets a broad range of human and animal health products. The following are excerpts from the financial review section of the company's annual report.

MERCK & CO., INC.
Financial Review Section (partial)

In the United States, the Company has been working with private and governmental employers to slow the increase of health care costs.

Outside of the United States, in difficult environments encumbered by government cost containment actions, the Company has worked with payers to help them allocate scarce resources to optimize health care outcomes, limiting potentially detrimental effects of government actions on sales growth.

Several products face expiration of product patents in the near term.

The Company, along with other pharmaceutical manufacturers, received a notice from the Federal Trade Commission (FTC) that it was conducting an investigation into pricing practices.

Instructions

Answer each of the following questions.

(a) In light of the above excerpts from Merck's annual report, discuss some unique pricing issues faced by companies that operate in the pharmaceutical industry.

(b) What are some reasons why the same company often sells identical drugs for dramatically different prices in different countries? How can the same drug used for both humans and animals cost significantly different prices?

(c) Suppose that Merck has just developed a revolutionary new drug. Discuss the steps it would go through in setting a price. Include a discussion of the information it would need to gather, and the issues it would need to consider.

BYP22-4 Shopping "robots" have become very popular online. These are sites that will find the price of a specified product that is listed by retailers on the Internet ("e-tailers"). This allows the customer to search for the lowest possible price.

Address: www.dealtime.com or go to **www.wiley.com/college/weygandt**

Steps
1. Go to DealTime's website.
2. Under the heading "**Electronics**," click on **DVD players**.
3. Choose one of the models.

Instructions

(a) Write down the name of the retailer and the price of the two lowest-priced units and the two highest-priced units.

(b) As a consumer, what concerns might you have in clicking on the "buy" button?

(c) Why might a consumer want to purchase a unit from a retailer that isn't offering the lowest price?

(d) What implications does the existence of these sites have for retailers?

CRITICAL THINKING

Communication Activity

BYP22-5 Jane Fleming recently graduated from college with a degree in landscape architecture. Her father runs a tree, shrub, and perennial-flower nursery, and her brother has a business delivering topsoil, mulch, and compost. Jane has decided that she would like to start a landscape business. She believes that she can generate a nice profit for herself, while providing an opportunity for both her brother's and father's businesses to grow.

One potential problem that Jane is concerned about is that her father and brother tend to charge the highest prices of any local suppliers for their products. She is hoping that she can demonstrate that it would be in her interest, as well as theirs, for them to sell to her at a discounted price.

Instructions

Write a memo to Jane explaining what information she must gather, and what issues she must consider in working out an arrangement with her father and brother. In your memo, discuss how this situation differs from a "standard" transfer pricing problem, but also how it has many of the characteristics of a transfer pricing problem.

Ethics Case

BYP22-6 Jumbo Airlines operates out of three main "hub" airports in the United States. Recently, Econo Airlines began operating a flight from Reno, Nevada, into Jumbo's Metropolis hub for $190. Jumbo Airlines offers a price of $425 for the same route. The management of Jumbo is not happy about Econo invading its turf. In fact, Jumbo has driven off nearly every other competing airline from its hub, so that today 90% of flights into and out of Metropolis are Jumbo Airline flights. Econo is able to offer a lower fare because its pilots are paid less, it uses older planes, and it has lower overhead costs. Econo has been in business for only 6 months, and it services only two other cities. It expects the Metropolis route to be its most profitable.

Jumbo estimates that it would have to charge $210 just to break even on this flight. It estimates that Econo can break even at a price of $160. Within one day of Econo's entry into the market, Jumbo dropped its price to $140, whereupon Econo matched its price. They both maintained this fare for a period of 9 months, until Econo went out of business. As soon as Econo went out of business, Jumbo raised its fare back to $425.

Instructions
Answer each of the following questions.

(a) Who are the stakeholders in this case?
(b) What are some of the reasons why Econo's break-even point is lower than that of Jumbo?
(c) What are the likely reasons why Jumbo was able to offer this price for this period of time, while Econo couldn't?
(d) What are some of the possible courses of action available to Econo in this situation?
(e) Do you think that this kind of pricing activity is ethical? What are the implications for the stakeholders in this situation?

Considering Your Costs and Benefits

BYP22-7 The January 2011 issue of *Strategic Finance* includes an article by J. Lockhart, A. Taylor, K. Thomas, B. Levetsovitis, and J. Wise entitled "When a Higher Price Pays Off."

Instructions
Read the article and answer the following questions.

(a) Explain what is meant by a "low-cost" supplier versus a "low-priced" supplier.
(b) Clarus Technologies' products are typically priced significantly higher than its competitors' products. How is it able to overcome the initial "sticker shock"?
(c) List the five categories of costs that the authors used to compare the Tornado to competing products. Give examples of specific types of costs in each category.
(d) The article discusses full-cost accounting as developed by the Environmental Protection Agency (EPA). What are the characteristics of this approach, and what implications does the approach used in this article have for corporate social responsibility?

23 Budgetary Planning

CHAPTER PREVIEW   As the Feature Story below about BabyCakes NYC indicates, budgeting is critical to financial well-being. As a student, you budget your study time and your money. Families budget income and expenses. Governmental agencies budget revenues and expenditures. Businesses use budgets in planning and controlling their operations.

Our primary focus in this chapter is budgeting—specifically, how budgeting is used as a planning tool by management. Through budgeting, it should be possible for management to maintain enough cash to pay creditors as well as have sufficient raw materials to meet production requirements and adequate finished goods to meet expected sales.

FEATURE STORY

What's in Your Cupcake?

The best business plans often result from meeting a basic human need. Many people would argue that cupcakes aren't necessarily essential to support life. But if you found out that allergies were going to deprive you forever of cupcakes, you might view baked goods in a whole new light. Such was the dilemma faced by Erin McKenna. When she found that her wheat allergies prevented her from consuming most baked sweets, she decided to open a bakery that met her needs. Her vegan and kosher bakery, BabyCakes NYC, advertises that it is refined-sugar-free, gluten-free, wheat-free, soy-free, dairy-free, and egg-free. So if you're one of the more than 10 million Americans with a food allergy or some other dietary constraint, this is probably the bakery for you.

Those of you that have spent a little time in the kitchen might wonder what kind of ingredients BabyCakes uses. To avoid the gluten in wheat, the company uses Bob's Red Mill rice flour, a garbanzo/fava bean mix, or oat flours. How does BabyCakes get all those great frosting colors without artificial dyes? The company achieves pink with beets, green with

chlorophyll, yellow with turmeric, and blue/purple with red cabbage. To eliminate dairy and soy, the bakers use rice and coconut milk. And finally, to accomplish over-the-top deliciousness without refined sugar, BabyCakes uses agave nectar (a sweetener derived from cactus) and evaporated cane juice (often referred to as organic or unrefined sugar).

With cupcakes priced at over $3 per item and a brisk business, you might think that making money is easy for BabyCakes. But all of these specialty ingredients don't come cheap. In addition, BabyCakes' shops are located in Manhattan, Los Angeles, and Orlando, so rent isn't exactly inexpensive either. Despite these costs, Erin's first store made a profit its first year and did even better in later years. To achieve this profitability, Erin relies on careful budgeting. First, she needs to estimate how many items she will sell. Then, she determines her needs for materials, labor, and overhead. Prices for BabyCakes' materials can fluctuate significantly, so Erin needs to update her budget accordingly. Finally, she has to budget for other products such as her cookbooks, baking kits, and T-shirts. Without a budget, Erin's business might not be so sweet.

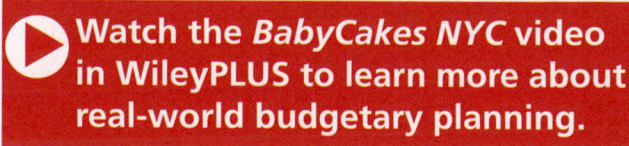

Watch the *BabyCakes NYC* video in WileyPLUS to learn more about real-world budgetary planning.

Deidre Schoo/The New York Times/Redux Pictures

CHAPTER OUTLINE

Learning Objectives

1 State the essentials of effective budgeting and the components of the master budget.
- Budgeting and accounting
- Benefits of budgeting
- Effective budgeting essentials
- Master budget

DO IT! 1 Budget Terminology

2 Prepare budgets for sales, production, and direct materials.
- Sales budget
- Production budget
- Direct materials budget

DO IT! 2 Sales, Production, and Direct Materials Budgets

3 Prepare budgets for direct labor, manufacturing overhead, and selling and administrative expenses, and a budgeted income statement.
- Direct labor budget
- Manufacturing overhead budget
- Selling and administrative expense budget
- Budgeted income statement

DO IT! 3 Budgeted Income Statement

4 Prepare a cash budget and a budgeted balance sheet.
- Cash budget
- Budgeted balance sheet

DO IT! 4 Cash Budget

5 Apply budgeting principles to nonmanufacturing companies.
- Merchandisers
- Service companies
- Not-for-profit organizations

DO IT! 5 Merchandise Purchases Budget

Go to the **REVIEW AND PRACTICE** section at the end of the chapter for a review of key concepts and practice applications with solutions.

Visit **WileyPLUS with ORION** for additional tutorials and practice opportunities.

State the essentials of effective budgeting and the components of the master budget.

One of management's major responsibilities is planning. As explained in Chapter 15, **planning** is the process of establishing company-wide objectives. A successful organization makes both long-term and short-term plans. These plans establish the objectives of the company and the proposed way of accomplishing them.

A **budget** is a formal written statement of management's plans for a specified future time period, expressed in financial terms. It represents the primary method of communicating agreed-upon objectives throughout the organization. Once adopted, a budget becomes an important basis for evaluating performance. It promotes efficiency and serves as a deterrent to waste and inefficiency. We consider the role of budgeting as a **control device** in Chapter 24.

Budgeting and Accounting

Accounting information makes major contributions to the budgeting process. From the accounting records, companies can obtain historical data on revenues, costs, and expenses. These data are helpful in formulating future budget goals.

Normally, accountants have the responsibility for presenting management's budgeting goals in financial terms. In this role, they translate management's plans and communicate the budget to employees throughout the company. They prepare periodic budget reports that provide the basis for measuring performance and comparing actual results with planned objectives. The budget itself and the administration of the budget, however, are entirely management responsibilities.

The Benefits of Budgeting

The primary benefits of budgeting are as follows.

1. It requires all levels of management to **plan ahead** and to formalize goals on a recurring basis.
2. It provides **definite objectives** for evaluating performance at each level of responsibility.
3. It creates an **early warning system** for potential problems so that management can make changes before things get out of hand.
4. It facilitates the **coordination of activities** within the business. It does this by correlating the goals of each segment with overall company objectives. Thus, the company can integrate production and sales promotion with expected sales.
5. It results in greater **management awareness** of the entity's overall operations and the impact on operations of external factors, such as economic trends.
6. It **motivates personnel** throughout the organization to meet planned objectives.

A budget is an aid to management; it is not a *substitute* for management. A budget cannot operate or enforce itself. Companies can realize the benefits of budgeting only when managers carefully administer budgets.

Essentials of Effective Budgeting

Effective budgeting depends on a **sound organizational structure**. In such a structure, authority and responsibility for all phases of operations are clearly defined. Budgets based on **research and analysis** are more likely to result in realistic goals that will contribute to the growth and profitability of a company. And, the effectiveness of a budget program is directly related to its **acceptance by all levels of management**.

Once adopted, the budget is an important tool for evaluating performance. Managers should systematically and periodically review variations between actual and expected results to determine their cause(s). However, individuals should not be held responsible for variations that are beyond their control.

LENGTH OF THE BUDGET PERIOD

The budget period is not necessarily one year in length. **A budget may be prepared for any period of time.** Various factors influence the length of the budget period. These factors include the type of budget, the nature of the organization, the need for periodic appraisal, and prevailing business conditions.

The budget period should be long enough to provide an attainable goal under normal business conditions. Ideally, the time period should minimize the impact of seasonal or cyclical fluctuations. On the other hand, the budget period should not be so long that reliable estimates are impossible.

The **most common budget period is one year**. The annual budget, in turn, is often supplemented by monthly and quarterly budgets. Many companies use **continuous 12-month budgets**. These budgets drop the month just ended and add a future month. One benefit of continuous budgeting is that it keeps management planning a full year ahead.

Accounting Across the Organization

Thinkstock/Comstock/Getty Images, Inc.

Businesses Often Feel Too Busy to Plan for the Future

A study by Willard & Shullman Group Ltd. found that fewer than 14% of businesses with less than 500 employees do an annual budget or have a written business plan. For many small businesses, the basic assumption is that, "As long as I sell as much as I can, and keep my employees paid, I'm doing OK." A few small business owners even say that they see no need for budgeting and planning. Most small business owners, though, say that they understand that budgeting and planning are critical for survival and growth. But given the long hours that they already work addressing day-to-day challenges, they also say that they are "just too busy to plan for the future."

Describe a situation in which a business "sells as much as it can" but cannot "keep its employees paid." (Go to **WileyPLUS** for this answer and additional questions.)

THE BUDGETING PROCESS

The development of the budget for the coming year generally starts several months before the end of the current year. The budgeting process usually begins with the collection of data from each organizational unit of the company. Past performance is often the starting point from which future budget goals are formulated.

The budget is developed within the framework of a **sales forecast**. This forecast shows potential sales for the industry and the company's expected share of such sales. Sales forecasting involves a consideration of various factors: (1) general economic conditions, (2) industry trends, (3) market research studies, (4) anticipated advertising and promotion, (5) previous market share, (6) changes in prices, and (7) technological developments. The input of sales personnel and top management is essential to the sales forecast.

In small companies like **BabyCakes NYC**, the budgeting process is often informal. In larger companies, a **budget committee** has responsibility for coordinating the preparation of the budget. The committee ordinarily includes the president, treasurer, chief accountant (controller), and management personnel from each of the major areas of the company, such as sales, production, and research. The budget committee serves as a review board where managers can defend their budget goals and requests. Differences are reviewed, modified if necessary, and reconciled. The budget is then put in its final form by the budget committee, approved, and distributed.

BUDGETING AND HUMAN BEHAVIOR

A budget can have a significant impact on human behavior. If done well, it can inspire managers to higher levels of performance. However, if done poorly, budgets can discourage additional effort and pull down the morale of managers. Why do these diverse effects occur? The answer is found in how the budget is developed and administered.

In developing the budget, each level of management should be invited to participate. This "bottom-to-top" approach is referred to as **participative budgeting**. One benefit of participative budgeting is that lower-level managers have more detailed knowledge of their specific area and thus are able to provide more accurate budgetary estimates. Also, when lower-level managers participate in the budgeting process, they are more likely to perceive the resulting budget as fair. The overall goal is to reach agreement on a budget that the managers consider fair and achievable, but which also meets the corporate goals set by top management. When this goal is met, the budget will provide positive motivation for the managers. In contrast, if managers view the budget as unfair and unrealistic, they may feel discouraged and uncommitted to budget goals. The risk of having unrealistic budgets is generally greater when the budget is developed from top management down to lower management than vice versa. Illustration 23-1 graphically displays the flow of budget data from bottom to top under participative budgeting.

Illustration 23-1
Flow of budget data under participative budgeting

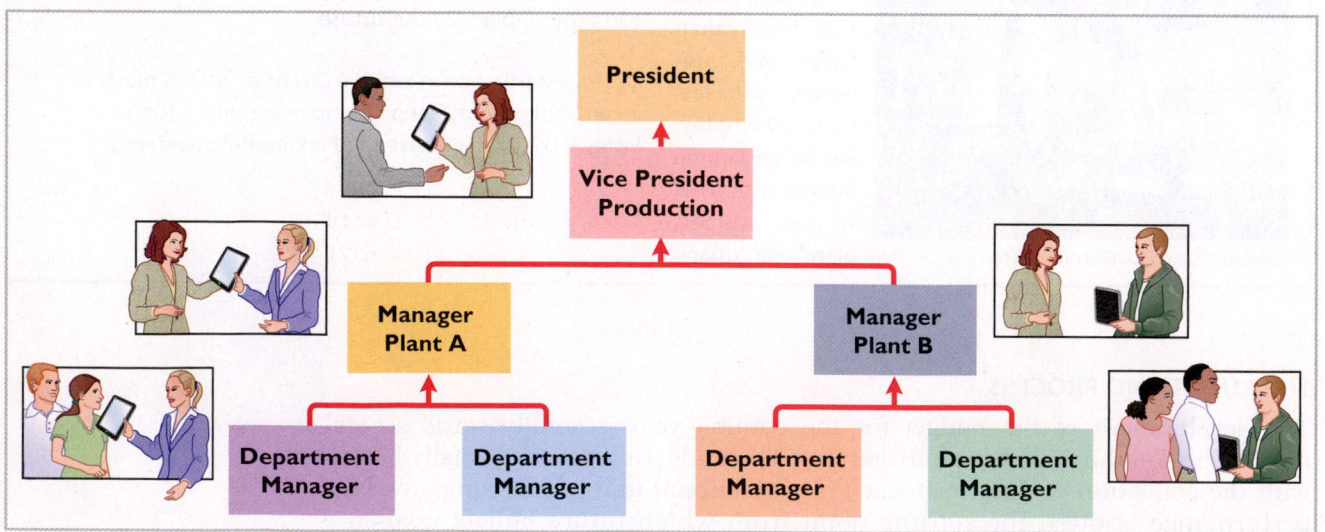

For example, at one time, in an effort to revive its plummeting stock price, **Time Warner's** top management determined and publicly announced bold new financial goals for the coming year. Unfortunately, these goals were not reached.

The next year, the company got a new CEO who said the company would now actually set reasonable goals that it could meet. The new budgets were developed with each operating unit setting what it felt were optimistic but attainable goals. In the words of one manager, using this approach created a sense of teamwork.

Participative budgeting does, however, have potential disadvantages. First, the "give and take" of participative budgeting is time-consuming (and thus more costly). Under a "top-down" approach, the budget is simply developed by top management and then dictated to lower-level managers. A second disadvantage is that participative budgeting can foster budgetary "gaming" through budgetary slack. **Budgetary slack** occurs when managers intentionally underestimate budgeted revenues or overestimate budgeted expenses in order to make it easier to achieve budgetary goals. To minimize budgetary slack, higher-level managers must carefully review and thoroughly question the budget projections provided to them by employees whom they supervise.

For the budget to be effective, top management must completely support the budget. The budget is an important basis for evaluating performance. It also can be used as a positive aid in achieving projected goals. The effect of an evaluation is positive when top management tempers criticism with advice and assistance. In contrast, a manager is likely to respond negatively if top management uses the budget exclusively to assess blame. A budget should not be used as a pressure device to force improved performance. In sum, a budget can be a manager's friend or foe.

> **ETHICS NOTE**
>
> Unrealistic budgets can lead to unethical employee behavior such as cutting corners on the job or distorting internal financial reports.

BUDGETING AND LONG-RANGE PLANNING

Budgeting and long-range planning are not the same. One important difference is the **time period involved**. The maximum length of a budget is usually one year, and budgets are often prepared for shorter periods of time, such as a month or a quarter. In contrast, long-range planning usually encompasses a period of at least five years.

A second significant difference is in **emphasis**. Budgeting focuses on achieving specific short-term goals, such as meeting annual profit objectives. **Long-range planning**, on the other hand, identifies long-term goals, selects strategies to achieve those goals, and develops policies and plans to implement the strategies. In long-range planning, management also considers anticipated trends in the economic and political environment and how the company should cope with them.

The final difference between budgeting and long-range planning relates to the **amount of detail presented**. Budgets, as you will see in this chapter, can be very detailed. Long-range plans contain considerably less detail. The data in long-range plans are intended more for a review of progress toward long-term goals than as a basis of control for achieving specific results. The primary objective of long-range planning is to develop the best strategy to maximize the company's performance over an extended future period.

> **Helpful Hint**
>
> In comparing a budget with a long-range plan, a budget has more detail and is more concerned with short-term goals, while a long-range plan is done for a longer period of time.

The Master Budget

The term "budget" is actually a shorthand term to describe a variety of budget documents. All of these documents are combined into a master budget. The **master budget** is a set of interrelated budgets that constitutes a plan of action for a specified time period.

The master budget contains two classes of budgets. **Operating budgets** are the individual budgets that result in the preparation of the budgeted income statement. These budgets establish goals for the company's sales and production personnel. In contrast, **financial budgets** focus primarily on the cash resources needed to fund expected operations and planned capital expenditures. Financial budgets include the capital expenditure budget, the cash budget, and the budgeted balance sheet.

Illustration 23-2 shows the individual budgets included in a master budget, and the sequence in which they are prepared. The company first develops the operating budgets, beginning with the sales budget. Then, it prepares the financial budgets. We will explain and illustrate each budget shown in Illustration 23-2 except the capital expenditure budget. That budget is discussed under the topic of capital budgeting in Chapter 26.

Illustration 23-2
Components of the master budget

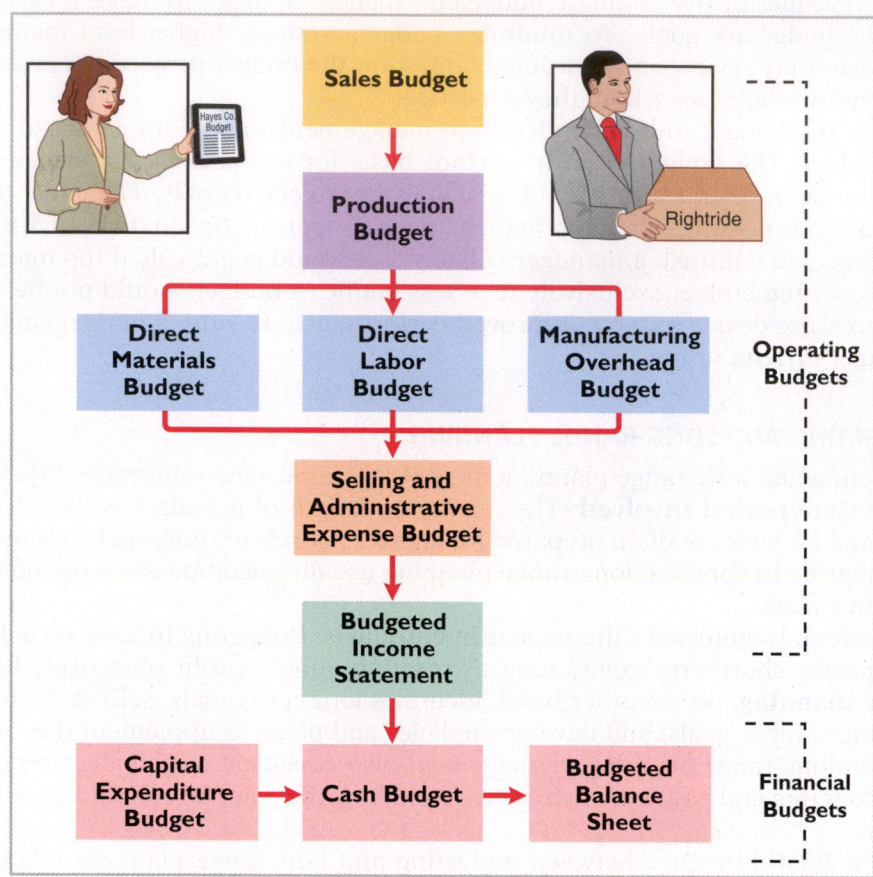

DO IT! 1   Budget Terminology

Use this list of terms to complete the sentences that follow.

Long-range planning   Participative budgeting
Sales forecast   Operating budgets
Master budget   Financial budgets

1. A _____ shows potential sales for the industry and a company's expected share of such sales.

2. _____ are used as the basis for the preparation of the budgeted income statement.

3. The _____ is a set of interrelated budgets that constitutes a plan of action for a specified time period.

4. _____ identifies long-term goals, selects strategies to achieve these goals, and develops policies and plans to implement the strategies.

5. Lower-level managers are more likely to perceive results as fair and achievable under a _____ approach.

6. _____ focus primarily on the cash resources needed to fund expected operations and planned capital expenditures.

Solution

1. Sales forecast.	**4.** Long-range planning.
2. Operating budgets.	**5.** Participative budgeting.
3. Master budget.	**6.** Financial budgets.

Related exercise material: **BE23-1, E23-1, and** **23-1.**

Action Plan

✔ **Understand the budgeting process, including the importance of the sales forecast.**

✔ **Understand the difference between an operating budget and a financial budget.**

✔ **Differentiate budgeting from long-range planning.**

✔ **Realize that the master budget is a set of interrelated budgets.**

LEARNING OBJECTIVE **2** **Prepare budgets for sales, production, and direct materials.**

We use a case study of Hayes Company in preparing the operating budgets. Hayes manufactures and sells a single product, an ergonomically designed bike seat with multiple customizable adjustments, called the Rightride. The budgets are prepared by quarters for the year ending December 31, 2017. Hayes Company begins its annual budgeting process on September 1, 2016, and it completes the budget for 2017 by December 1, 2016. The company begins by preparing the budgets for sales, production, and direct materials.

Sales Budget

As shown in the master budget in Illustration 23-2, **the sales budget is prepared first**. Each of the other budgets depends on the sales budget. The **sales budget** is derived from the sales forecast. It represents management's best estimate of sales revenue for the budget period. An inaccurate sales budget may adversely affect net income. For example, an overly optimistic sales budget may result in excessive inventories that may have to be sold at reduced prices. In contrast, an unduly pessimistic sales budget may result in loss of sales revenue due to inventory shortages.

For example, at one time **Amazon.com** significantly underestimated demand for its e-book reader, the Kindle. As a consequence, it did not produce enough Kindles and was completely sold out well before the holiday shopping season. Not only did this represent a huge lost opportunity for Amazon, but it exposed the company to potential competitors, who were eager to provide customers with alternatives to the Kindle.

Forecasting sales is challenging. For example, consider the forecasting challenges faced by major sports arenas, whose revenues depend on the success of the home team. **Madison Square Garden**'s revenues from April to June were $193 million during a year when the Knicks made the NBA playoffs. But revenues were only $133.2 million a couple of years later when the team did not make the playoffs. Or, consider the challenges faced by Hollywood movie producers in predicting the complicated revenue stream produced by a new movie. Movie theater ticket sales represent only 20% of total revenue. The bulk of revenue comes from global sales, DVDs, video-on-demand, merchandising products, and videogames, all of which are difficult to forecast.

The sales budget is prepared by multiplying the expected unit sales volume for each product by its anticipated unit selling price. Hayes Company expects sales volume to be 3,000 units in the first quarter, with 500-unit increases in each succeeding quarter. Illustration 23-3 (page 1064) shows the sales budget for the year, by quarter, based on a sales price of $60 per unit.

Helpful Hint
For a retail or manufacturing company, the sales budget is the starting point for the master budget. It sets the level of activity for other functions such as production and purchasing.

Illustration 23-3
Sales budget

		Quarter				
HAYES COMPANY						
Sales Budget						
For the Year Ending December 31, 2017						
	A	1	2	3	4	Year
Expected unit sales		3,000	3,500	4,000	4,500	15,000
Unit selling price		× $60	× $60	× $60	× $60	× $60
Total sales		$180,000	$210,000	$240,000	$270,000	$900,000

Some companies classify the anticipated sales revenue as cash or credit sales and by geographical regions, territories, or salespersons.

Service Company Insight

Marcela Barsse/iStockphoto

The Implications of Budgetary Optimism

Companies aren't the only ones that have to estimate revenues. Governments at all levels (e.g., local, state or federal) prepare annual budgets. Most are required to submit balanced budgets, that is, estimated revenues are supposed to cover anticipated expenditures. Unfortunately, estimating government revenues can be as difficult as, or even more difficult than, estimating company revenues. For example, during a recent year, the median state government overestimated revenues by 10.2%, with four state governments missing by more than 25%.

What makes estimation so difficult for these governments? Most states rely on income taxes, which fluctuate widely with economic gyrations. Some states rely on sales taxes, which are problematic because the laws regarding sales taxes haven't adjusted for the shift from manufacturing to service companies and from brick-and-mortar stores to online sales.

Source: Conor Dougherty, "States Fumble Revenue Forecasts," *Wall Street Journal Online* (March 2, 2011).

Why is it important that government budgets accurately estimate future revenues during economic downturns? (Go to **WileyPLUS** for this answer and additional questions.)

Production Budget

The **production budget** shows the number of units of a product to produce to meet anticipated sales demand. Production requirements are determined from the following formula.[1]

Illustration 23-4
Production requirements formula

Budgeted Sales Units	+	Desired Ending Finished Goods Units	−	Beginning Finished Goods Units	=	Required Production Units

---

[1]This formula ignores any work in process inventories, which are assumed to be nonexistent in Hayes Company.

A realistic estimate of ending inventory is essential in scheduling production requirements. Excessive inventories in one quarter may lead to cutbacks in production and employee layoffs in a subsequent quarter. On the other hand, inadequate inventories may result either in added costs for overtime work or in lost sales. Hayes Company believes it can meet future sales requirements by maintaining an ending inventory equal to 20% of the next quarter's budgeted sales volume. For example, the ending finished goods inventory for the first quarter is 700 units (20% × anticipated second-quarter sales of 3,500 units). Illustration 23-5 shows the production budget.

Units of Finished Goods Inventory	
Beg. Inv.	
Required Prod. Units	Sales
End. Inv.	

Hayes Company Production Budget.xls

Home Insert Page Layout Formulas Data Review View

P18   fx

	A	B	C	D	E	F	G	H	I	J
1		**HAYES COMPANY**								
2		**Production Budget**								
3		**For the Year Ending December 31, 2017**								
4		Quarter								
5		1		2		3		4		Year
6	Expected unit sales (Illustration 23-3)	3,000		3,500		4,000		4,500		
7	Add: Desired ending finished goods units[a]	700		800		900		1,000[b]		
8	Total required units	3,700		4,300		4,900		5,500		
9	Less: Beginning finished goods units	600[c]		700		800		900		
10	**Required production units**	**3,100**		**3,600**		**4,100**		**4,600**		**15,400**
11										
12	[a]20% of next quarter's sales									
13	[b]Expected 2018 first-quarter sales, 5,000 units × 20%									
14	[c]20% of estimated first-quarter 2017 sales units									

Units of Finished Goods Inventory	
600	
3,100	3,000
700	

Illustration 23-5
Production budget

The production budget, in turn, provides the basis for the budgeted costs for each manufacturing cost element, as explained in the following pages.

Direct Materials Budget

The **direct materials budget** shows both the quantity and cost of direct materials to be purchased. The quantities of direct materials are derived from the following formula.

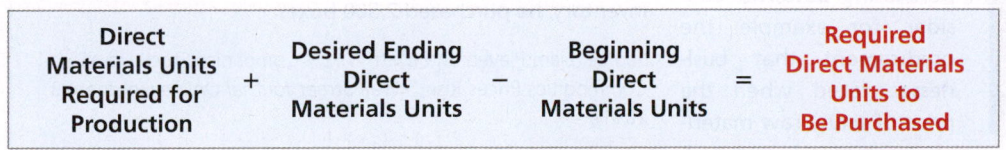

Illustration 23-6
Formula for direct materials quantities

After the company determines the number of units to purchase, it can compute the budgeted cost of direct materials to be purchased. It does so by multiplying the required units of direct materials by the anticipated cost per unit.

Units of Direct Materials

Beg. Inv.	
Direct Materials to Purchase	Direct Materials Required for Prod.
End. Inv.	

The desired ending inventory is again a key component in the budgeting process. For example, inadequate inventories could result in temporary shutdowns of production. Because of its close proximity to suppliers, Hayes Company maintains an ending inventory of raw materials equal to 10% of the next quarter's production requirements. The manufacture of each Rightride requires 2 pounds of raw materials, and the expected cost per pound is $4. Illustration 23-7 shows the direct materials budget. Assume that the desired ending direct materials amount is 1,020 pounds for the fourth quarter of 2017.

Illustration 23-7
Direct materials budget

Units of Direct Materials
(1st Qtr.)

620	
6,300	6,200
720	

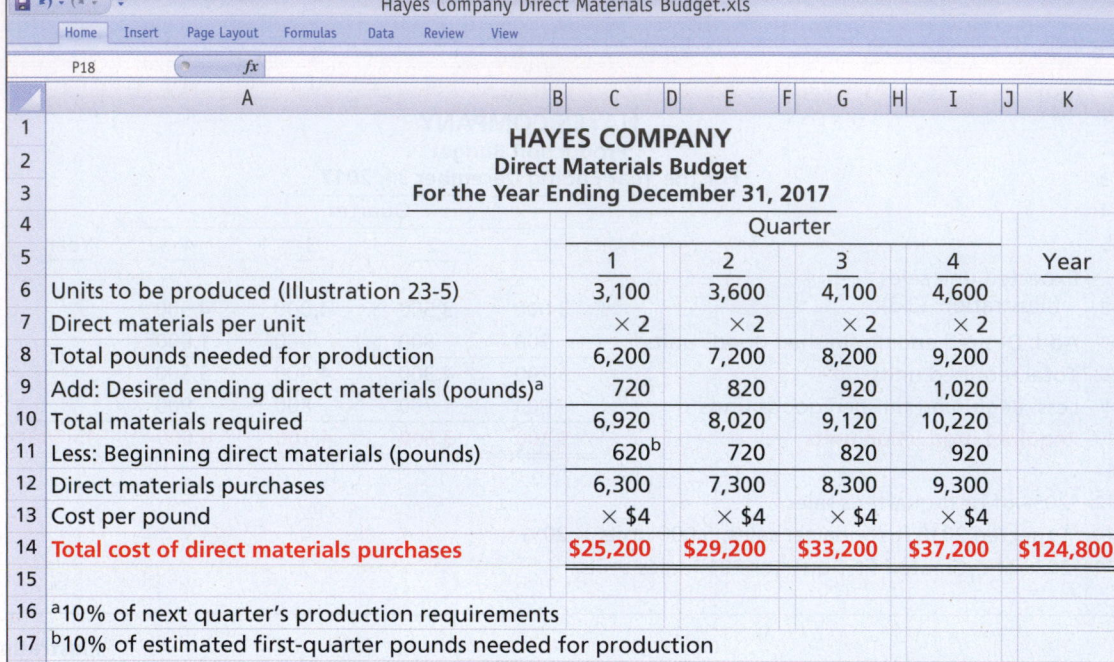

Hayes Company Direct Materials Budget.xls

P18

	A	B C D E F	G H	I J	K
1		**HAYES COMPANY**			
2		**Direct Materials Budget**			
3		**For the Year Ending December 31, 2017**			
4		Quarter			
5		1	2	3	4	Year
6	Units to be produced (Illustration 23-5)	3,100	3,600	4,100	4,600	
7	Direct materials per unit	× 2	× 2	× 2	× 2	
8	Total pounds needed for production	6,200	7,200	8,200	9,200	
9	Add: Desired ending direct materials (pounds)[a]	720	820	920	1,020	
10	Total materials required	6,920	8,020	9,120	10,220	
11	Less: Beginning direct materials (pounds)	620[b]	720	820	920	
12	Direct materials purchases	6,300	7,300	8,300	9,300	
13	Cost per pound	× $4	× $4	× $4	× $4	
14	**Total cost of direct materials purchases**	**$25,200**	**$29,200**	**$33,200**	**$37,200**	**$124,800**
15						
16	[a]10% of next quarter's production requirements					
17	[b]10% of estimated first-quarter pounds needed for production					
18						

Management Insight

© William Wang/iStockphoto

Betting That Prices Won't Fall

Sometimes things happen that cause managers to reevaluate their normal purchasing patterns. Consider, for example, the predicament that businesses faced when the price of many raw materials recently skyrocketed. Rubber, cotton, oil, corn, wheat, steel, copper, and spices—prices for seemingly everything were going straight up. Anticipating that prices might continue to go up, many managers decided to stockpile much larger quantities of raw materials to avoid paying even higher prices in the future. For example, after cotton prices rose 92%, one manager of a printed T-shirt manufacturer decided to stockpile a huge supply of plain T-shirts in anticipation of additional price increases. While he normally has about 30 boxes of T-shirts in inventory, he purchased 2,500 boxes.

Source: Liam Pleven and Matt Wirz, "Companies Stock Up as Commodities Prices Rise," *Wall Street Journal Online* (February 3, 2011).

What are the potential downsides of stockpiling a huge amount of raw materials? (Go to **WileyPLUS** for this answer and additional questions.)

DO IT! ② Sales, Production, and Direct Materials Budgets

Soriano Company is preparing its master budget for 2017. Relevant data pertaining to its sales, production, and direct materials budgets are as follows.

Sales. Sales for the year are expected to total 1,200,000 units. Quarterly sales, as a percentage of total sales, are 20%, 25%, 30%, and 25%, respectively. The sales price is expected to be $50 per unit for the first three quarters and $55 per unit beginning in the fourth quarter. Sales in the first quarter of 2018 are expected to be 10% higher than the budgeted sales for the first quarter of 2017.

Production. Management desires to maintain the ending finished goods inventories at 25% of the next quarter's budgeted sales volume.

Direct materials. Each unit requires 3 pounds of raw materials at a cost of $5 per pound. Management desires to maintain raw materials inventories at 5% of the next quarter's production requirements. Assume the production requirements for the first quarter of 2018 are 810,000 pounds.

Prepare the sales, production, and direct materials budgets by quarters for 2017.

Action Plan

✔ Know the form and content of the sales budget.

✔ Prepare the sales budget first, as the basis for the other budgets.

✔ Determine the units that must be produced to meet anticipated sales.

✔ Know how to compute the beginning and ending finished goods units.

✔ Determine the materials required to meet production needs.

✔ Know how to compute the beginning and ending direct materials units.

Solution

Soriano Company Sales Budget.xls

SORIANO COMPANY
Sales Budget
For the Year Ending December 31, 2017

	Quarter				
	1	2	3	4	Year
Expected unit sales	240,000	300,000	360,000	300,000	1,200,000
Unit selling price	× $50	× $50	× $50	× $55	
Total sales	$12,000,000	$15,000,000	$18,000,000	$16,500,000	$61,500,000

Soriano Company Production Budget.xls

SORIANO COMPANY
Production Budget
For the Year Ending December 31, 2017

	Quarter				
	1	2	3	4	Year
Expected unit sales	240,000	300,000	360,000	300,000	
Add: Desired ending finished goods units[a]	75,000	90,000	75,000	66,000[b]	
Total required units	315,000	390,000	435,000	366,000	
Less: Beginning finished goods units	60,000[c]	75,000	90,000	75,000	
Required production units	255,000	315,000	345,000	291,000	1,206,000

[a]25% of next quarter's unit sales
[b]Estimated first-quarter 2018 sales units: 240,000 + (240,000 × 10%) = 264,000: 264,000 × 25%
[c]25% of estimated first-quarter 2017 sales units (240,000 × 25%)

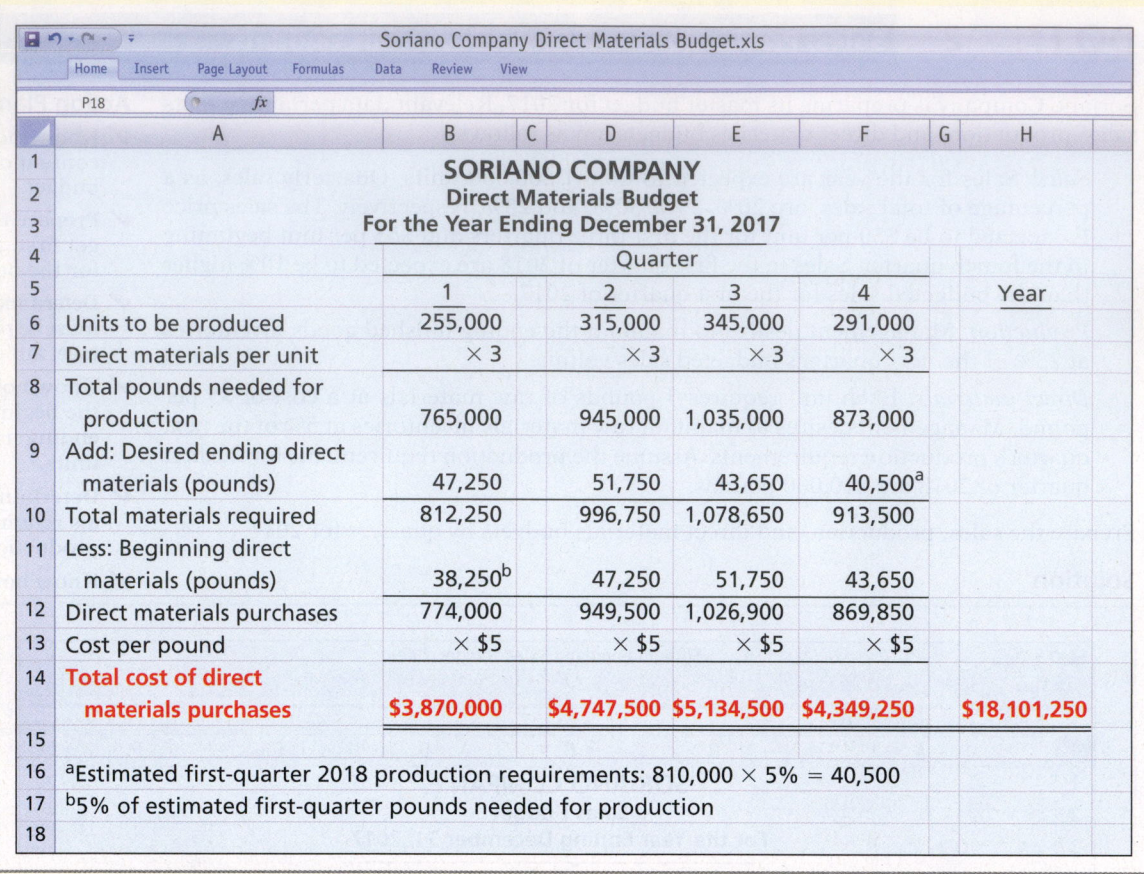

Soriano Company Direct Materials Budget.xls

| Home | Insert | Page Layout | Formulas | Data | Review | View |

P18   fx

	A	B	C	D	E	F	G	H
1		**SORIANO COMPANY**						
2		Direct Materials Budget						
3		For the Year Ending December 31, 2017						
4		Quarter						
5		1		2	3	4		Year
6	Units to be produced	255,000		315,000	345,000	291,000		
7	Direct materials per unit	× 3		× 3	× 3	× 3		
8	Total pounds needed for production	765,000		945,000	1,035,000	873,000		
9	Add: Desired ending direct materials (pounds)	47,250		51,750	43,650	40,500^a		
10	Total materials required	812,250		996,750	1,078,650	913,500		
11	Less: Beginning direct materials (pounds)	38,250^b		47,250	51,750	43,650		
12	Direct materials purchases	774,000		949,500	1,026,900	869,850		
13	Cost per pound	× $5		× $5	× $5	× $5		
14	**Total cost of direct materials purchases**	**$3,870,000**		**$4,747,500**	**$5,134,500**	**$4,349,250**		**$18,101,250**
15								
16	^{a}Estimated first-quarter 2018 production requirements: 810,000 × 5% = 40,500							
17	^{b}5% of estimated first-quarter pounds needed for production							
18								

Related exercise material: **BE23-2, BE23-3, BE23-4, E23-2, E23-3, E23-4, E23-5, E23-6, E23-7, E23-8, and DO IT! 23-2.**

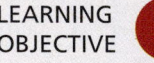
LEARNING OBJECTIVE **3**   **Prepare budgets for direct labor, manufacturing overhead, and selling and administrative expenses, and a budgeted income statement.**

As shown in Illustration 23-2 (page 1062), the operating budgets culminate with preparation of the budgeted income statement. Before we can do that, we need to prepare budgets for direct labor, manufacturing overhead, and selling and administrative expenses.

Direct Labor Budget

Like the direct materials budget, the **direct labor budget** contains the quantity (hours) and cost of direct labor necessary to meet production requirements. The total direct labor cost is derived from the following formula.

Illustration 23-8
Formula for direct labor cost

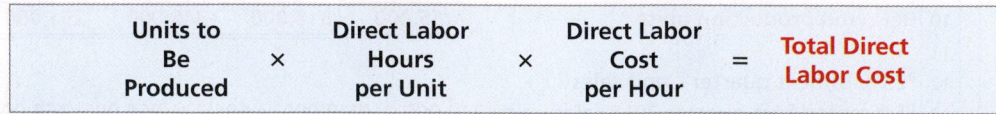

Units to Be Produced	×	Direct Labor Hours per Unit	×	Direct Labor Cost per Hour	=	**Total Direct Labor Cost**

Direct labor hours are determined from the production budget. At Hayes Company, two hours of direct labor are required to produce each unit of finished goods. The anticipated hourly wage rate is $10. Illustration 23-9 shows these data.

	Hayes Company Direct Labor Budget.xls								
Home	Insert	Page Layout	Formulas	Data	Review	View			

P18   fx

	A	B	C	D	E	F	G	H	I	J
1			**HAYES COMPANY**							
2			**Direct Labor Budget**							
3			**For the Year Ending December 31, 2017**							
4						Quarter				
5			1		2		3		4	Year
6	Units to be produced (Illustration 23-5)		3,100		3,600		4,100		4,600	
7	Direct labor time (hours) per unit		× 2		× 2		× 2		× 2	
8	Total required direct labor hours		6,200		7,200		8,200		9,200	
9	Direct labor cost per hour		× $10		× $10		× $10		× $10	
10	**Total direct labor cost**		**$62,000**		**$72,000**		**$82,000**		**$92,000**	**$308,000**
11										

Illustration 23-9
Direct labor budget

The direct labor budget is critical in maintaining a labor force that can meet the expected levels of production.

Manufacturing Overhead Budget

The **manufacturing overhead budget** shows the expected manufacturing overhead costs for the budget period. As Illustration 23-10 shows, **this budget distinguishes between variable and fixed overhead costs**. Hayes Company expects variable costs to fluctuate with production volume on the basis of the following rates per direct labor hour: indirect materials $1.00, indirect labor $1.40, utilities $0.40, and maintenance $0.20. Thus, for the 6,200 direct labor hours to produce 3,100 units, budgeted indirect materials are $6,200 (6,200 × $1), and budgeted indirect labor is $8,680 (6,200 × $1.40). Hayes also recognizes that some maintenance is fixed. The amounts reported for fixed costs are assumed for our example.

Helpful Hint
An important assumption in Illustration 23-9 is that the company can add to and subtract from its work force as needed so that the $10 per hour labor cost applies to a wide range of possible production activity.

	Hayes Company Manufacturing Overhead Budget.xls					
Home	Insert	Page Layout	Formulas	Data	Review	View

P18   fx

	A	B	C	D	E	F
1			**HAYES COMPANY**			
2			**Manufacturing Overhead Budget**			
3			**For the Year Ending December 31, 2017**			
4				Quarter		
5		1	2	3	4	Year
6	Variable costs					
7	Indirect materials ($1.00/hour)	$ 6,200	$ 7,200	$ 8,200	$ 9,200	$ 30,800
8	Indirect labor ($1.40/hour)	8,680	10,080	11,480	12,880	43,120
9	Utilities ($0.40/hour)	2,480	2,880	3,280	3,680	12,320
10	Maintenance ($0.20/hour)	1,240	1,440	1,640	1,840	6,160
11	Total variable costs	18,600	21,600	24,600	27,600	92,400
12	Fixed costs					
13	Supervisory salaries	20,000	20,000	20,000	20,000	80,000
14	Depreciation	3,800	3,800	3,800	3,800	15,200
15	Property taxes and insurance	9,000	9,000	9,000	9,000	36,000
16	Maintenance	5,700	5,700	5,700	5,700	22,800
17	Total fixed costs	38,500	38,500	38,500	38,500	154,000
18	**Total manufacturing overhead**	**$57,100**	**$60,100**	**$63,100**	**$66,100**	**$246,400**
	Direct labor hours					
19	**(Illustration 23-9)**	**6,200**	**7,200**	**8,200**	**9,200**	**30,800**
20	**Manufacturing overhead rate per direct labor hour ($246,400 ÷ 30,800)**					**$8**
21						

Illustration 23-10
Manufacturing overhead budget

The accuracy of budgeted overhead cost estimates can be greatly improved by employing activity-based costing.

At Hayes Company, overhead is applied to production on the basis of direct labor hours. Thus, as Illustration 23-10 shows, the budgeted annual rate is $8 per hour ($246,400 ÷ 30,800).

Selling and Administrative Expense Budget

Hayes Company combines its operating expenses into one budget, the **selling and administrative expense budget**. This budget projects anticipated selling and administrative expenses for the budget period. This budget (Illustration 23-11) also classifies expenses as either variable or fixed. In this case, the variable expense rates per unit of sales are sales commissions $3 and freight-out $1. Variable expenses per quarter are based on the unit sales from the sales budget (see Illustration 23-3, page 1064). For example, Hayes expects sales in the first quarter to be 3,000 units. Thus, sales commissions expense is $9,000 (3,000 × $3), and freight-out is $3,000 (3,000 × $1). Fixed expenses are based on assumed data.

Illustration 23-11
Selling and administrative expense budget

	A	B	C	D	E	F
1		HAYES COMPANY				
2		Selling and Administrative Expense Budget				
3		For the Year Ending December 31, 2017				
4				Quarter		
5		1	2	3	4	Year
6	Budgeted sales in units (Illustration 23-3)	3,000	3,500	4,000	4,500	15,000
7	Variable expenses					
8	Sales commissions ($3 per unit)	$ 9,000	$10,500	$12,000	$13,500	$ 45,000
9	Freight-out ($1 per unit)	3,000	3,500	4,000	4,500	15,000
10	Total variable expenses	12,000	14,000	16,000	18,000	60,000
11	Fixed expenses					
12	Advertising	5,000	5,000	5,000	5,000	20,000
13	Sales salaries	15,000	15,000	15,000	15,000	60,000
14	Office salaries	7,500	7,500	7,500	7,500	30,000
15	Depreciation	1,000	1,000	1,000	1,000	4,000
16	Property taxes and insurance	1,500	1,500	1,500	1,500	6,000
17	Total fixed expenses	30,000	30,000	30,000	30,000	120,000
18	Total selling and administrative expenses	$42,000	$44,000	$46,000	$48,000	$180,000
19						

Budgeted Income Statement

The **budgeted income statement** is the important end-product of the operating budgets. This budget indicates the expected profitability of operations for the budget period. The budgeted income statement provides the basis for evaluating company performance. Budgeted income statements often act as a call to action. For example, a board member at **XM Satellite Radio Holdings** felt that budgeted costs were too high relative to budgeted revenues. When management refused to cut its marketing and programming costs, the board member resigned. He felt that without the cuts, the company risked financial crisis.

As you would expect, the budgeted income statement is prepared from the various operating budgets. For example, to find the cost of goods sold, Hayes Company must first determine the total unit cost of producing one Rightride, as follows.

Illustration 23-12
Computation of total unit cost

Cost Element	Cost of One Rightride Illustration	Quantity	Unit Cost	Total
Direct materials	23-7	2 pounds	$ 4.00	$ 8.00
Direct labor	23-9	2 hours	$10.00	20.00
Manufacturing overhead	23-10	2 hours	$ 8.00	16.00
Total unit cost				**$44.00**

Hayes then determines cost of goods sold by multiplying the units sold by the unit cost. Its budgeted cost of goods sold is $660,000 (15,000 × $44). All data for the income statement come from the individual operating budgets except the following: (1) interest expense is expected to be $100, and (2) income taxes are estimated to be $12,000. Illustration 23-13 shows the budgeted multiple-step income statement.

Illustration 23-13
Budgeted multiple-step income statement

HAYES COMPANY
Budgeted Income Statement
For the Year Ending December 31, 2017

Sales (Illustration 23-3)	$900,000
Cost of goods sold (15,000 × $44)	660,000
Gross profit	240,000
Selling and administrative expenses (Illustration 23-11)	180,000
Income from operations	60,000
Interest expense	100
Income before income taxes	59,900
Income tax expense	12,000
Net income	$ 47,900

DO IT! 3   Budgeted Income Statement

Soriano Company is preparing its budgeted income statement for 2017. Relevant data pertaining to its sales, production, and direct materials budgets can be found in **DO IT! 2** (page 1067).

In addition, Soriano budgets 0.5 hours of direct labor per unit, labor costs at $15 per hour, and manufacturing overhead at $25 per direct labor hour. Its budgeted selling and administrative expenses for 2017 are $12,000,000.

(a) Calculate the budgeted total unit cost. (b) Prepare the budgeted multiple-step income statement for 2017. (Ignore income taxes.)

Solution

(a)

Cost Element	Quantity	Unit Cost	Total
Direct materials	3.0 pounds	$ 5	$ 15.00
Direct labor	0.5 hours	$15	7.50
Manufacturing overhead	0.5 hours	$25	12.50
Total unit cost			**$35.00**

Action Plan

✔ Recall that total unit cost consists of direct materials, direct labor, and manufacturing overhead.

Action Plan (cont.)

✔ Recall that direct materials costs are included in the direct materials budget.

✔ Know the form and content of the income statement.

✔ Use the total unit sales information from the sales budget to compute annual sales and cost of goods sold.

(b)

SORIANO COMPANY
Budgeted Income Statement
For the Year Ending December 31, 2017

Sales (1,200,000 units from sales budget, page 1067)	$61,500,000
Cost of goods sold (1,200,000 × $35.00/unit)	42,000,000
Gross profit	19,500,000
Selling and administrative expenses	12,000,000
Net income	$ 7,500,000

Related exercise material: **BE23-8, E23-11, E23-13, and DO IT! 23-3.**

LEARNING OBJECTIVE 4

Prepare a cash budget and a budgeted balance sheet.

As shown in Illustration 23-2 (page 1062), the financial budgets consist of the capital expenditure budget, the cash budget, and the budgeted balance sheet. We will discuss the capital expenditure budget in Chapter 26.

Cash Budget

The **cash budget** shows anticipated cash flows. Because cash is so vital, this budget is often considered to be the most important financial budget. The cash budget contains three sections (cash receipts, cash disbursements, and financing) and the beginning and ending cash balances, as shown in Illustration 23-14.

Illustration 23-14
Basic form of a cash budget

Helpful Hint
The cash budget is prepared after the other budgets because the information generated by the other budgets dictates the expected inflows and outflows of cash.

	A	B	C
	ANY COMPANY Cash Budget		
3	Beginning cash balance	$X,XXX	
4	Add: Cash receipts (itemized)	X,XXX	
5	Total available cash	X,XXX	
6	Less: Cash disbursements (itemized)	X,XXX	
7	Excess (deficiency) of available cash over cash disbursements	X,XXX	
8	Financing	X,XXX	
9	Ending cash balance	$X,XXX	

The **cash receipts section** includes expected receipts from the company's principal source(s) of revenue. These are usually cash sales and collections from customers on credit sales. This section also shows anticipated receipts of interest and dividends, and proceeds from planned sales of investments, plant assets, and the company's capital stock.

The **cash disbursements section** shows expected cash payments. Such payments include direct materials, direct labor, manufacturing overhead, and selling and administrative expenses. This section also includes projected payments for income taxes, dividends, investments, and plant assets.

The **financing section** shows expected borrowings and the repayment of the borrowed funds plus interest. Companies need this section when there is a cash deficiency or when the cash balance is below management's minimum required balance.

Data in the cash budget are prepared in sequence. The ending cash balance of one period becomes the beginning cash balance for the next period. Companies obtain data for preparing the cash budget from other budgets and from information provided by management. In practice, cash budgets are often prepared for the year on a monthly basis.

To minimize detail, we will assume that Hayes Company prepares an annual cash budget by quarters. Its cash budget is based on the following assumptions.

1. The January 1, 2017, cash balance is expected to be $38,000. Hayes wishes to maintain a balance of at least $15,000.

2. Sales (Illustration 23-3, page 1064): 60% are collected in the quarter sold and 40% are collected in the following quarter. Accounts receivable of $60,000 at December 31, 2016, are expected to be collected in full in the first quarter of 2017.

3. Short-term investment securities are expected to be sold for $2,000 cash in the first quarter.

4. Direct materials (Illustration 23-7, page 1066): 50% are paid in the quarter purchased and 50% are paid in the following quarter. Accounts payable of $10,600 at December 31, 2016, are expected to be paid in full in the first quarter of 2017.

5. Direct labor (Illustration 23-9, page 1069): 100% is paid in the quarter incurred.

6. Manufacturing overhead (Illustration 23-10, page 1069) and selling and administrative expenses (Illustration 23-11, page 1070): All items except depreciation are paid in the quarter incurred.

7. Management plans to purchase a truck in the second quarter for $10,000 cash.

8. Hayes makes equal quarterly payments of its estimated $12,000 annual income taxes.

9. Loans are repaid in the earliest quarter in which there is sufficient cash (that is, when the cash on hand exceeds the $15,000 minimum required balance).

In preparing the cash budget, it is useful to prepare schedules for collections from customers (assumption 2) and cash payments for direct materials (assumption 4). These schedules are shown in Illustrations 23-15 (below) and 23-16 (page 1074).

Illustration 23-15
Collections from customers

HAYES COMPANY					
Schedule of Expected Collections from Customers					
		Collections by Quarter			
	Sales[a]	1	2	3	4
Accounts receivable, 12/31/16		$ 60,000			
First quarter	$180,000	108,000[b]	$ 72,000[c]		
Second quarter	210,000		126,000	$ 84,000	
Third quarter	240,000			144,000	$ 96,000
Fourth quarter	270,000				162,000
Total collections		**$168,000**	**$198,000**	**$228,000**	**$258,000**

[a]Per Illustration 23-3; [b]$180,000 × .60; [c]$180,000 × .40

Illustration 23-16
Payments for direct materials

	A	B	C	D	E	F
			Hayes Company.xls			
	Home	Insert	Page Layout	Formulas	Data	Review	View
	P18		fx			
1			HAYES COMPANY			
2			Schedule of Expected Payments for Direct Materials			
3				Payments by Quarter		
4		Purchases[a]	1	2	3	4
5	Accounts payable, 12/31/16		$10,600			
6	First quarter	$25,200	12,600[b]	$12,600[c]		
7	Second quarter	29,200		14,600	$14,600	
8	Third quarter	33,200			16,600	$16,600
9	Fourth quarter	37,200				18,600
10	**Total payments**		**$23,200**	**$27,200**	**$31,200**	**$35,200**
11						
12	[a]Per Illustration 23-7; [b]$25,200 × .50; [c]$25,200 × .50					
13						

Illustration 23-17 shows the cash budget for Hayes Company. The budget indicates that Hayes will need $3,000 of financing in the second quarter to maintain a minimum cash balance of $15,000. Since there is an excess of available cash over disbursements of $22,500 at the end of the third quarter, the borrowing, plus $100 interest, is repaid in this quarter.

Illustration 23-17
Cash budget

	A	B	C	D	E	F	G	H	I	J
				Hayes Company Cash Budget.xls						
	Home	Insert	Page Layout	Formulas	Data	Review	View			
	P18		fx							
1			HAYES COMPANY							
2			Cash Budget							
3			For the Year Ending December 31, 2017							
4					Quarter					
5		Assumption	1		2		3		4	
6	Beginning cash balance	1	$ 38,000		$ 25,500		$ 15,000		$ 19,400	
7	**Add: Receipts**									
8	Collections from customers	2	168,000		198,000		228,000		258,000	
9	Sale of investment securities	3	2,000		0		0		0	
10	Total receipts		170,000		198,000		228,000		258,000	
11	Total available cash		208,000		223,500		243,000		277,400	
12	**Less: Disbursements**									
13	Direct materials	4	23,200		27,200		31,200		35,200	
14	Direct labor	5	62,000		72,000		82,000		92,000	
15	Manufacturing overhead	6	53,300[a]		56,300		59,300		62,300	
16	Selling and administrative expenses	6	41,000[b]		43,000		45,000		47,000	
17	Purchase of truck	7	0		10,000		0		0	
18	Income tax expense	8	3,000		3,000		3,000		3,000	
19	Total disbursements		182,500		211,500		220,500		239,500	
20	Excess (deficiency) of available cash over cash disbursements		25,500		12,000		22,500		37,900	
21	**Financing**									
22	Add: Borrowings		0		**3,000**		0		0	
23	Less: Repayments including interest	9	0		0		**3,100**		0	
24	Ending cash balance		$ 25,500		$ 15,000		$ 19,400		$ 37,900	
25										
26	[a]$57,100 − $3,800 depreciation									
27	[b]$42,000 − $1,000 depreciation									

A cash budget contributes to more effective cash management. It shows managers when additional financing is necessary well before the actual need arises. And, it indicates when excess cash is available for investments or other purposes.

Budgeted Balance Sheet

The **budgeted balance sheet** is a projection of financial position at the end of the budget period. This budget is developed from the budgeted balance sheet for the preceding year and the budgets for the current year. Pertinent data from the budgeted balance sheet at December 31, 2016, are as follows.

Buildings and equipment	$182,000	Common stock	$225,000
Accumulated depreciation	$ 28,800	Retained earnings	$ 46,480

Illustration 23-18 shows Hayes Company's budgeted classified balance sheet at December 31, 2017.

Illustration 23-18
Budgeted classified balance sheet

HAYES COMPANY
Budgeted Balance Sheet
December 31, 2017

Assets

Current assets		
Cash		$ 37,900
Accounts receivable		108,000
Finished goods inventory		44,000
Raw materials inventory		4,080
Total current assets		193,980
Property, plant, and equipment		
Buildings and equipment	$192,000	
Less: Accumulated depreciation	48,000	144,000
Total assets		$337,980

Liabilities and Stockholders' Equity

Liabilities		
Accounts payable		$ 18,600
Stockholders' equity		
Common stock	$225,000	
Retained earnings	94,380	
Total stockholders' equity		319,380
Total liabilities and stockholders' equity		$337,980

The computations and sources of the amounts are explained below.

Cash: Ending cash balance $37,900, shown in the cash budget (Illustration 23-17, page 1074).

Accounts receivable: 40% of fourth-quarter sales $270,000, shown in the schedule of expected collections from customers (Illustration 23-15, page 1073).

Finished goods inventory: Desired ending inventory 1,000 units, shown in the production budget (Illustration 23-5, page 1065) times the total unit cost $44 (shown in Illustration 23-12, page 1071).

Raw materials inventory: Desired ending inventory 1,020 pounds, times the cost per pound $4, shown in the direct materials budget (Illustration 23-7, page 1066).

Buildings and equipment: December 31, 2016, balance $182,000, plus purchase of truck for $10,000 (Illustration 23-17, page 1074).

Accumulated depreciation: December 31, 2016, balance $28,800, plus $15,200 depreciation shown in manufacturing overhead budget (Illustration 23-10, page 1069) and $4,000 depreciation shown in selling and administrative expense budget (Illustration 23-11, page 1070).

Accounts payable: 50% of fourth-quarter purchases $37,200, shown in schedule of expected payments for direct materials (Illustration 23-16, page 1074).

Common stock: Unchanged from the beginning of the year.

Retained earnings: December 31, 2016, balance $46,480, plus net income $47,900, shown in budgeted income statement (Illustration 23-13, page 1071).

After budget data are entered into the computer, Hayes prepares the various budgets (sales, cash, etc.), as well as the budgeted financial statements. Using spreadsheets, management can also perform "what if" (sensitivity) analyses based on different hypothetical assumptions. For example, suppose that sales managers project that sales will be 10% higher in the coming quarter. What impact does this change have on the rest of the budgeting process and the financing needs of the business? The impact of the various assumptions on the budget is quickly determined by the spreadsheet. Armed with these analyses, managers make more informed decisions about the impact of various projects. They also anticipate future problems and business opportunities. As seen in this chapter, budgeting is an excellent use of computer spreadsheets.

DO IT! 4   **Cash Budget**

Martian Company management wants to maintain a minimum monthly cash balance of $15,000. At the beginning of March, the cash balance is $16,500, expected cash receipts for March are $210,000, and cash disbursements are expected to be $220,000. How much cash, if any, must be borrowed to maintain the desired minimum monthly balance?

Solution

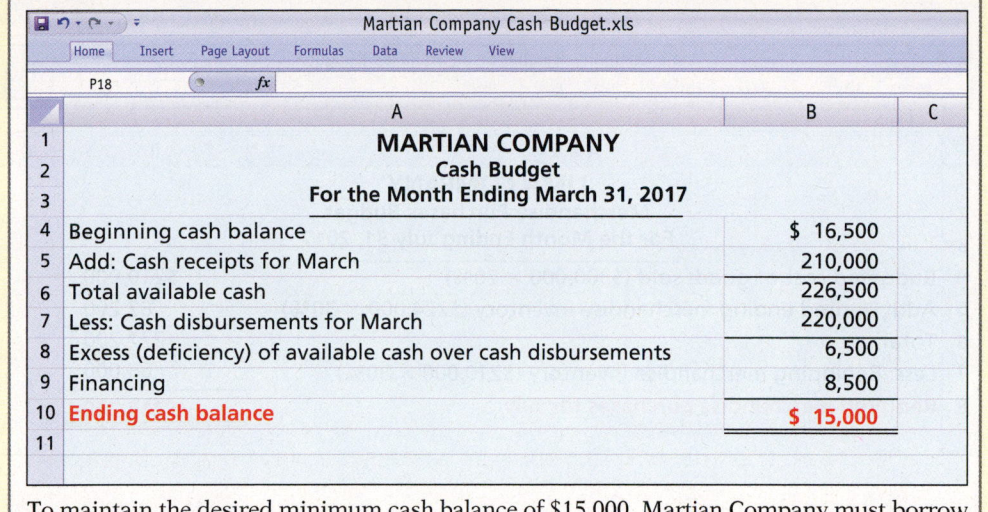

MARTIAN COMPANY
Cash Budget
For the Month Ending March 31, 2017

	A	B
4	Beginning cash balance	$ 16,500
5	Add: Cash receipts for March	210,000
6	Total available cash	226,500
7	Less: Cash disbursements for March	220,000
8	Excess (deficiency) of available cash over cash disbursements	6,500
9	Financing	8,500
10	**Ending cash balance**	**$ 15,000**

To maintain the desired minimum cash balance of $15,000, Martian Company must borrow $8,500 of cash.

Related exercise material: **BE23-9, E23-14, E23-15, E23-16, and DO IT! 23-4.**

LEARNING OBJECTIVE 5   **Apply budgeting principles to nonmanufacturing companies.**

Budgeting is not limited to manufacturers. Budgets are also used by merchandisers, service companies, and not-for-profit organizations.

Merchandisers

As in manufacturing operations, the sales budget for a merchandiser is both the starting point and the key factor in the development of the master budget. The major differences between the master budgets of a merchandiser and a manufacturer are as follows.

1. A merchandiser **uses a merchandise purchases budget instead of a production budget**.

2. A merchandiser **does not use the manufacturing budgets (direct materials, direct labor, and manufacturing overhead)**.

   The **merchandise purchases budget** shows the estimated cost of goods to be purchased to meet expected sales. The formula for determining budgeted merchandise purchases is as follows.

Budgeted Cost of Goods Sold	+	Desired Ending Merchandise Inventory	−	Beginning Merchandise Inventory	=	**Required Merchandise Purchases**

Illustration 23-19
Merchandise purchases formula

To illustrate, assume that the budget committee of Lima Company is preparing the merchandise purchases budget for July 2017. It estimates that budgeted sales will be $300,000 in July and $320,000 in August. Cost of goods sold is expected to be 70% of sales—that is, $210,000 in July (.70 × $300,000) and $224,000 in August (.70 × $320,000). The company's desired ending inventory is

30% of the following month's cost of goods sold. Required merchandise purchases for July are $214,200, computed as follows.

Illustration 23-20
Merchandise purchases budget

	A	B	C
	LIMA COMPANY		
	Merchandise Purchases Budget		
	For the Month Ending July 31, 2017		
4	Budgeted cost of goods sold ($300,000 × 70%)	$210,000	
5	Add: Desired ending merchandise inventory ($224,000 × 30%)	67,200	
6	Total	277,200	
7	Less: Beginning merchandise inventory ($210,000 × 30%)	63,000	
8	**Required merchandise purchases for July**	**$214,200**	

When a merchandiser is departmentalized, it prepares separate budgets for each department. For example, a grocery store prepares sales budgets and purchases budgets for each of its major departments, such as meats, dairy, and produce. The store then combines these budgets into a master budget for the store. When a retailer has branch stores, it prepares separate master budgets for each store. Then, it incorporates these budgets into master budgets for the company as a whole.

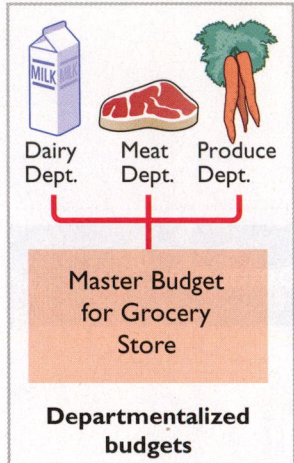

Departmentalized budgets

Service Companies

In a service company, such as a public accounting firm, a law office, or a medical practice, the critical factor in budgeting is **coordinating professional staff needs with anticipated services**. If a firm is overstaffed, several problems may result: Labor costs are disproportionately high. Profits are lower because of the additional salaries. Staff turnover sometimes increases because of lack of challenging work. In contrast, if a service company is understaffed, it may lose revenue because existing and prospective client needs for service cannot be met. Also, professional staff may seek other jobs because of excessive work loads.

Suppose that Stephan Lawn and Plowing Service estimates that it will service 300 small lawns, 200 medium lawns, and 100 large lawns during the month of July. It estimates its direct labor needs as 1 hour per small lawn, 1.75 hours for a medium lawn, and 2.75 hours for a large lawn. Its average cost for direct labor is $15 per hour. Stephan prepares a direct labor budget as follows.

Illustration 23-21
Direct labor budget for service company

	A	B	C	D	E
	STEPHAN LAWN AND PLOWING SERVICE				
	Direct Labor Budget				
	For the Month Ending July 31, 2017				
4		Small	Medium	Large	Total
5	Lawns to be serviced	300	200	100	
6	Direct labor time (hours) per lawn	× 1	× 1.75	× 2.75	
7	Total required direct labor hours	300	350	275	
8	Direct labor cost per hour	× $15	× $15	× $15	
9	**Total direct labor cost**	**$4,500**	**$5,250**	**$4,125**	**$13,875**

Service companies can obtain budget data for service revenue from **expected output** or **expected input**. When output is used, it is necessary to determine the expected billings of clients for services performed. In a public accounting firm, for example, output is the sum of its billings in auditing, tax, and consulting services. When input data are used, each professional staff member projects his or her billable time. The firm then applies billing rates to billable time to produce expected service revenue.

Not-for-Profit Organizations

Budgeting is just as important for not-for-profit organizations as for profit-oriented businesses. The budget process, however, is different. In most cases, not-for-profit entities budget **on the basis of cash flows (expenditures and receipts), rather than on a revenue and expense basis**. Further, the starting point in the process is usually expenditures, not receipts. For the not-for-profit entity, management's task generally is to find the receipts needed to support the planned expenditures. The activity index is also likely to be significantly different. For example, in a not-for-profit entity, such as a university, budgeted faculty positions may be based on full-time equivalent students or credit hours expected to be taught in a department.

For some governmental units, voters approve the budget. In other cases, such as state governments and the federal government, legislative approval is required. After the budget is adopted, it must be followed. Overspending is often illegal. In governmental budgets, authorizations tend to be on a line-by-line basis. That is, the budget for a municipality may have a specified authorization for police and fire protection, garbage collection, street paving, and so on. The line-item authorization of governmental budgets significantly limits the amount of discretion management can exercise. The city manager often cannot use savings from one line item, such as street paving, to cover increased spending in another line item, such as snow removal.

Service Company Insight | Museum of Contemporary Art

Budget Short-falls as Far as the Eye Can See

©ZUMA Press/Newscom/NewsCom

All organizations need to stick to budgets. The Museum of Contemporary Art in Los Angeles learned this the hard way. Over a 10-year period, its endowment shrunk from $50 million to $6 million as its newly hired director strove to build the museum's reputation through spending. The director consistently ran budget deficits, which eventually threatened the museum's survival.

The most recent recession created budgeting challenges for nearly all governmental agencies. Tax revenues dropped rapidly as earnings declined and unemployment skyrocketed. At the same time, sources of debt financing dried up. Even Princeton University, with the largest endowment per student of any U.S. university ($2 million per student), experienced a 25% drop in the value of its endowment when the financial markets plunged. Because the endowment supports 45% of the university's $1.25 billion budget, when the endowment fell the university had to make cuts. Many raises were capped at $2,000, administrative budgets were cut by 5%, and major construction projects were put on hold.

Sources: Edward Wyatt and Jori Finkel, "Soaring in Art, Museum Trips Over Finances," *Wall Street Journal Online* (December 4, 2008); Stu Woo, "California's Plans to Close Gap Become More Drastic," *Wall Street Journal Online* (January 8, 2009); and John Hechinger, "Princeton Cuts Budget as Endowment Slides," *Wall Street Journal Online* (January 9, 2009).

Why would a university's budgeted scholarships probably fall when the stock market suffers a serious drop? (Go to **WileyPLUS** for this answer and additional questions.)

DO IT! 5 — Merchandise Purchases Budget

Becker Company estimates that 2017 sales will be $15,000 in quarter 1, $20,000 in quarter 2, and $25,000 in quarter 3. Cost of goods sold is 80% of sales. Management desires to have ending finished goods inventory equal to 15% of the next quarter's expected cost of goods sold. Prepare a merchandise purchases budget by quarter for the first six months of 2017.

Solution

Action Plan

✔ Begin with budgeted cost of goods sold.

✔ Add desired ending merchandise inventory.

✔ Subtract beginning merchandise inventory.

Becker Company Merchandise Purchases Budget.xls

BECKER COMPANY
Merchandise Purchases Budget
For the Six Months Ending June 30, 2017

	Quarter		
	1	2	Six Months
Budgeted cost of goods sold (sales × .80)	$12,000	$16,000	
Add: Desired ending merchandise inventory (15% of next quarter's cost of goods sold)	2,400	3,000	
Total	14,400	19,000	
Less: Beginning merchandise inventory (15% this quarter's cost of goods sold)	1,800	2,400	
Required merchandise purchases	$12,600	$16,600	$29,200

Related exercise material: **BE23-10, E23-19, E23-20, E23-21, and DO IT! 23-5.**

REVIEW AND PRACTICE

LEARNING OBJECTIVES REVIEW

1 State the essentials of effective budgeting and the components of the master budget. The primary benefits of budgeting are that it (a) requires management to plan ahead, (b) provides definite objectives for evaluating performance, (c) creates an early warning system for potential problems, (d) facilitates coordination of activities, (e) results in greater management awareness, and (f) motivates personnel to meet planned objectives. The essentials of effective budgeting are (a) sound organizational structure, (b) research and analysis, and (c) acceptance by all levels of management.

The master budget consists of the following budgets: (a) sales, (b) production, (c) direct materials, (d) direct labor, (e) manufacturing overhead, (f) selling and administrative expense, (g) budgeted income statement, (h) capital expenditure budget, (i) cash budget, and (j) budgeted balance sheet.

2 Prepare budgets for sales, production, and direct materials. The sales budget is derived from sales forecasts. The production budget starts with budgeted

sales units, adds desired ending finished goods inventory, and subtracts beginning finished goods inventory to arrive at the required number of production units. The direct materials budget starts with the direct materials units (e.g., pounds) required for budgeted production, adds desired ending direct materials units, and subtracts beginning direct materials units to arrive at required direct materials units to be purchased. This amount is multiplied by the direct materials cost (e.g., cost per pound) to arrive at the total cost of direct materials purchases.

3 Prepare budgets for direct labor, manufacturing overhead, and selling and administrative expenses, and a budgeted income statement. The direct labor budget starts with the units to be produced as determined in the production budget. This amount is multiplied by the direct labor hours per unit and the direct labor cost per hour to arrive at the total direct labor cost. The manufacturing overhead budget lists all of the individual types of overhead costs, distinguishing between fixed and variable costs. The selling and administrative expense budget lists all of the individual types of selling and administrative expense items, distinguishing between fixed and variable costs. The budgeted income statement is prepared from the various operating budgets. Cost of goods sold is determined by calculating the budgeted cost to produce one unit, then multiplying this amount by the number of units sold.

❹ Prepare a cash budget and a budgeted balance sheet. The cash budget has three sections (receipts, disbursements, and financing) and the beginning and ending cash balances. Receipts and payments sec-

tions are determined after preparing separate schedules for collections from customers and payments to suppliers. The budgeted balance sheet is developed from the budgeted balance sheet from the preceding year and the various budgets for the current year.

❺ Apply budgeting principles to nonmanufacturing companies. Budgeting may be used by merchandisers for development of a merchandise purchases budget. In service companies, budgeting is a critical factor in coordinating staff needs with anticipated services. In not-for-profit organizations, the starting point in budgeting is usually expenditures, not receipts.

GLOSSARY REVIEW

Budget A formal written statement of management's plans for a specified future time period, expressed in financial terms. (p. 1058).

Budgetary slack The amount by which a manager intentionally underestimates budgeted revenues or overestimates budgeted expenses in order to make it easier to achieve budgetary goals. (p. 1061).

Budget committee A group responsible for coordinating the preparation of the budget. (p. 1060).

Budgeted balance sheet A projection of financial position at the end of the budget period. (p. 1075).

Budgeted income statement An estimate of the expected profitability of operations for the budget period. (p. 1070).

Cash budget A projection of anticipated cash flows. (p. 1072).

Direct labor budget A projection of the quantity and cost of direct labor necessary to meet production requirements. (p. 1068).

Direct materials budget An estimate of the quantity and cost of direct materials to be purchased. (p. 1065).

Financial budgets Individual budgets that focus primarily on the cash resources needed to fund expected operations and planned capital expenditures. (p. 1061).

Long-range planning A formalized process of identifying long-term goals, selecting strategies to achieve

those goals, and developing policies and plans to implement the strategies. (p. 1061).

Manufacturing overhead budget An estimate of expected manufacturing overhead costs for the budget period. (p. 1069).

Master budget A set of interrelated budgets that constitutes a plan of action for a specific time period. (p. 1061).

Merchandise purchases budget The estimated cost of goods to be purchased by a merchandiser to meet expected sales. (p. 1077).

Operating budgets Individual budgets that result in a budgeted income statement. (p. 1061).

Participative budgeting A budgetary approach that starts with input from lower-level managers and works upward so that managers at all levels participate. (p. 1060).

Production budget A projection of the units that must be produced to meet anticipated sales. (p. 1064).

Sales budget An estimate of expected sales revenue for the budget period. (p. 1063).

Sales forecast The projection of potential sales for the industry and the company's expected share of such sales. (p. 1059).

Selling and administrative expense budget A projection of anticipated selling and administrative expenses for the budget period. (p. 1070).

PRACTICE MULTIPLE-CHOICE QUESTIONS

(LO 1) **1.** Which of the following is **not** a benefit of budgeting?
   (a) Management can plan ahead.
   (b) An early warning system is provided for potential problems.
   (c) It enables disciplinary action to be taken at every level of responsibility.
   (d) The coordination of activities is facilitated.

(LO 1) **2.** A budget:
   (a) is the responsibility of management accountants.
   (b) is the primary method of communicating agreed-upon objectives throughout an organization.
   (c) ignores past performance because it represents management's plans for a future time period.

   (d) may promote efficiency but has no role in evaluating performance.

3. The essentials of effective budgeting do **not** include: (LO 1)
   (a) top-down budgeting.
   (b) management acceptance.
   (c) research and analysis.
   (d) sound organizational structure.

4. Compared to budgeting, long-range planning generally   (LO 1)
   has the:
   (a) same amount of detail.   (c) same emphasis.
   (b) longer time period.   (d) same time period.

(LO 2) 5. A sales budget is:
 (a) derived from the production budget.
 (b) management's best estimate of sales revenue for the year.
 (c) not the starting point for the master budget.
 (d) prepared only for credit sales.

(LO 2) 6. The formula for the production budget is budgeted sales in units plus:
 (a) desired ending merchandise inventory less beginning merchandise inventory.
 (b) beginning finished goods units less desired ending finished goods units.
 (c) desired ending direct materials units less beginning direct materials units.
 (d) desired ending finished goods units less beginning finished goods units.

(LO 2) 7. Direct materials inventories are kept in pounds in Byrd Company, and the total pounds of direct materials needed for production is 9,500. If the beginning inventory is 1,000 pounds and the desired ending inventory is 2,200 pounds, the total pounds to be purchased is:
 (a) 9,400.   (c) 9,700.
 (b) 9,500.   (d) 10,700.

(LO 3) 8. The formula for computing the direct labor budget is to multiply the direct labor cost per hour by the:
 (a) total required direct labor hours.
 (b) physical units to be produced.
 (c) equivalent units to be produced.
 (d) No correct answer is given.

(LO 3) 9. Each of the following budgets is used in preparing the budgeted income statement **except** the:
 (a) sales budget.
 (b) selling and administrative expense budget.
 (c) capital expenditure budget.
 (d) direct labor budget.

(LO 3) 10. The budgeted income statement is:
 (a) the end-product of the operating budgets.
 (b) the end-product of the financial budgets.
 (c) the starting point of the master budget.
 (d) dependent on cash receipts and cash disbursements.

11. The budgeted balance sheet is: **(LO 4)**
 (a) developed from the budgeted balance sheet for the preceding year and the budgets for the current year.
 (b) the last operating budget prepared.
 (c) used to prepare the cash budget.
 (d) All of the above.

12. The format of a cash budget is: **(LO 4)**
 (a) Beginning cash balance + Cash receipts + Cash from financing − Cash disbursements = Ending cash balance.
 (b) Beginning cash balance + Cash receipts − Cash disbursements +/− Financing = Ending cash balance.
 (c) Beginning cash balance + Net income − Cash dividends = Ending cash balance.
 (d) Beginning cash balance + Cash revenues − Cash expenses = Ending cash balance.

13. Expected direct materials purchases in Read Company are $70,000 in the first quarter and $90,000 in the second quarter. Forty percent of the purchases are paid in cash as incurred, and the balance is paid in the following quarter. The budgeted cash payments for purchases in the second quarter are: **(LO 4)**
 (a) $96,000.   (c) $78,000.
 (b) $90,000.   (d) $72,000.

14. The budget for a merchandiser differs from a budget for a manufacturer because: **(LO 5)**
 (a) a merchandise purchases budget replaces the production budget.
 (b) the manufacturing budgets are not applicable.
 (c) None of the above.
 (d) Both (a) and (b) above.

15. In most cases, not-for-profit entities: **(LO 5)**
 (a) prepare budgets using the same steps as those used by profit-oriented businesses.
 (b) know budgeted cash receipts at the beginning of a time period, so they budget only for expenditures.
 (c) begin the budgeting process by budgeting expenditures rather than receipts.
 (d) can ignore budgets because they are not expected to generate net income.

Solutions

1. (c) Budgeting does not necessarily enable disciplinary action to be taken at every level of responsibility. The other choices are all benefits of budgeting.

2. (b) A budget is the primary method of communicating agreed-upon objectives throughout an organization. The other choices are incorrect because (a) a budget is the responsibility of all levels of management, not management accountants; (c) past performance is not ignored in the budgeting process but instead is the starting point from which future budget goals are formulated; and (d) the budget not only may promote efficiency but is an important tool for evaluating performance.

3. (a) Top-down budgeting is not one of the essentials of effective budgeting. The other choices are true statements.

4. (b) Long-range planning generally encompasses a period of at least 5 years whereas budgeting usually covers a period of 1 year. The other choices are incorrect because budgeting and long-range planning (a) do not have the same amount of detail, (c) do not have the same emphasis, and (d) do not cover the same time period.

5. (b) A sales budget is management's best estimate of sales revenue for the year. The other choices are incorrect because a sales budget (a) is the first budget prepared and is the one budget that is not derived from any other budget, (c) is the starting point for the master budget, and (d) is prepared for both cash and credit sales.

6. (d) The formula for the production budget is budgeted sales in units plus desired ending finished goods units less beginning finished goods units. The other choices are therefore incorrect.

7. (d) Pounds to be purchased = Amount needed for production (9,500) + Desired ending inventory (2,200) − Beginning inventory (1,000) = 10,700, not (a) 9,400, (b) 9,500, or (c) 9,700.

8. (a) Direct labor cost = Direct labor cost per hour × Total required direct labor hours. The other choices are therefore incorrect.

9. (c) The capital expenditure budget is not used in preparing the budgeted income statement. The other choices are true statements.

10. (a) The budgeted income statement is the end-product of the operating budgets, not (b) the financial budgets, (c) the starting point of the master budget, or (d) dependent on cash receipts and cash disbursements.

11. (a) The budgeted balance sheet is developed from the budgeted balance sheet for the preceding year and the budgets for the current year. The other choices are therefore incorrect.

12. (b) The format of a cash budget is Beginning cash balance + Cash receipts − Cash disbursements +/− Financing = Ending cash balance. The other choices are therefore incorrect.

13. (c) Budgeted cash payments for the second quarter = Purchases for the first quarter ($42,000; $70,000 × 60%) + 40% of the purchases for the second quarter ($36,000; $90,000 × 40%) = $78,000, not (a) $96,000, (b) $90,000, or (d) $72,000.

14. (d) The budget for a merchandiser uses a merchandise purchases budget in place of a production budget, and the manufacturing budgets are not applicable for a merchandiser. Therefore, as both choices (a) and (b) are correct, choice (d) is the best answer.

15. (c) In most cases, not-for-profit entities begin the budgeting process by budgeting expenditures rather than receipts. The other choices are incorrect because in most cases not-for-profit entities (a) prepare budgets using different, not the same, steps as those used by profit-oriented enterprises; (b) budget for both expenditures and receipts; and (d) cannot ignore budgets.

PRACTICE EXERCISES

1. On January 1, 2017 the Heche Company budget committee has reached agreement on the following data for the 6 months ending June 30, 2017.

Prepare production and direct materials budgets by quarter for 6 months.

(LO 2)

Sales units:	First quarter 5,000; second quarter 6,000; third quarter 7,000
Ending raw materials inventory:	40% of the next quarter's production requirements
Ending finished goods inventory:	30% of the next quarter's expected sales units
Third-quarter 2017 production:	7,500 units

The ending raw materials and finished goods inventories at December 31, 2016, follow the same percentage relationships to production and sales that occur in 2017. Two pounds of raw materials are required to make each unit of finished goods. Raw materials purchased are expected to cost $5 per pound.

Instructions

(a) Prepare a production budget by quarters for the 6-month period ended June 30, 2017.
(b) Prepare a direct materials budget by quarters for the 6-month period ended June 30, 2017.

Solution

1. (a)

	Heche Company Production Budget.xls					
Home Insert Page Layout Formulas Data Review View						
P18		*fx*				
	A	B	C	D	E	F
1	**HECHE COMPANY**					
2	**Production Budget**					
3	**For the Six Months Ending June 30, 2017**					
4		Quarter				
5		1	2	Six Months		
6	Expected unit sales	5,000	6,000			
7	Add: Desired ending finished goods units	1,800[(1)]	2,100[(2)]			
8	Total required units	6,800	8,100			
9	Less: Beginning finished goods units	1,500[(3)]	1,800			
10	**Required production units**	**5,300**	**6,300**	**11,600**		
11						
12	[(1)]30% × 6,000; [(2)]30% × 7,000; [(3)]30% × 5,000					

(b)

	Heche Company Direct Materials Budget.xls					
	A	B	C	D	E	F
1	**HECHE COMPANY**					
2	**Direct Materials Budget**					
3	**For the Six Months Ending June 30, 2017**					
4		Quarter				
5		1		2		Six Months
6	Units to be produced	5,300		6,300		
7	Direct materials per unit	× 2		× 2		
8	Total pounds needed for production	10,600		12,600		
9	Add: Desired ending direct materials (pounds)	5,040$^{(1)}$		6,000$^{(2)}$		
10	Total materials required	15,640		18,600		
11	Less: Beginning direct materials (pounds)	4,240$^{(3)}$		5,040		
12	Direct materials purchase	11,400		13,560		
13	Cost per pound	× $5		× $5		
14	**Total cost of direct materials purchase**	**$57,000**		**$67,800**		**$124,800**
15						
16	$^{(1)}$40% × 12,600; $^{(2)}$7,500 × (2 × 40%); $^{(3)}$40% × 10,600					
17						

Prepare a cash budget for 2 months.

(LO 4)

2. Jake Company expects to have a cash balance of $45,000 on January 1, 2017. Relevant monthly budget data for the first 2 months of 2017 are as follows.

Collections from customers: January $100,000. February $160,000.

Payments for direct materials: January $60,000, February $80,000.

Direct labor: January $30,000, February $45,000. Wages are paid in the month they are incurred.

Manufacturing overhead: January $26,000, February $31,000. These costs include depreciation of $1,000 per month. All other overhead costs are paid as incurred.

Selling and administrative expenses: January $15,000. February $20,000. These costs are exclusive of depreciation. They are paid as incurred.

Sales of marketable securities in January are expected to realize $10,000 in cash. Jake Company has a line of credit at a local bank that enables it to borrow up to $25,000. The company wants to maintain a minimum monthly cash balance of $25,000.

Instructions

Prepare a cash budget for January and February.

Solution

2.

	A	B	C
	JAKE COMPANY		
	Cash Budget		
	For the Two Months Ending February 28, 2017		
		January	February
Beginning cash balance		$ 45,000	$ 25,000
Add: Receipts			
Collections from customers		100,000	160,000
Sale of marketable securities		10,000	0
Total receipts		110,000	160,000
Total available cash		155,000	185,000
Less: Disbursements			
Direct materials		60,000	80,000
Direct labor		30,000	45,000
Manufacturing overhead		25,000	30,000
Selling and administrative expenses		15,000	20,000
Total disbursements		130,000	175,000
Excess (deficiency) of available cash over cash			
Disbursements		25,000	10,000
Financing			
Borrowings		0	15,000
Repayments		0	0
Ending cash balance		$ 25,000	$ 25,000

PRACTICE PROBLEMS

Prepare sales and production budgets.

(LO 2)

1. Asheville Company is preparing its master budget for 2017. Relevant data pertaining to its sales and production budgets are as follows.

Sales. Sales for the year are expected to total 2,100,000 units. Quarterly sales, as a percentage of total sales, are 15%, 25%, 35%, and 25%, respectively. The sales price is expected to be $70 per unit for the first three quarters and $75 per unit beginning in the fourth quarter. Sales in the first quarter of 2018 are expected to be 10% higher than the budgeted sales volume for the first quarter of 2017.

Production. Management desires to maintain ending finished goods inventories at 20% of the next quarter's budgeted sales volume.

Instructions

Prepare the sales budget and production budget by quarters for 2017.

Solution

1.

	A	B	C	D	E	F	G	H

Asheville Company Sales Budget and Production Budget.xls

Home | Insert | Page Layout | Formulas | Data | Review | View

P18

ASHEVILLE COMPANY
For the Year Ending December 31, 2017
Sales Budget

	Quarter				
	1	2	3	4	Year
Expected unit sales	315,000	525,000	735,000	525,000	2,100,000
Unit selling price	× $70	× $70	× $70	× $75	
Total sales	$22,050,000	$36,750,000	$51,450,000	$39,375,000	$149,625,000

Production Budget

	1	2	3	4	
Expected unit sales	315,000	525,000	735,000	525,000	
Add: Desired ending finished goods units	105,000	147,000	105,000	69,300^a	
Total required units	420,000	672,000	840,000	594,300	
Less: Beginning finished goods units	63,000^b	105,000	147,000	105,000	
Required production units	**357,000**	**567,000**	**693,000**	**489,300**	**2,106,300**

^{a}Estimated first-quarter 2018 sales volume 315,000 + (315,000 × 10%) = 346,500; 346,500 × 20%
^{b}20% of estimated first-quarter 2017 sales units (315,000 × 20%)

Prepare budgeted cost of goods sold, income statement, and balance sheet.

(LO 3, 4)

2. Barrett Company has completed all operating budgets other than the income statement for 2017. Selected data from these budgets follow.

Sales: $300,000
Purchases of raw materials: $145,000
Ending inventory of raw materials: $15,000
Direct labor: $40,000
Manufacturing overhead: $73,000, including $3,000 of depreciation expense
Selling and administrative expenses: $36,000 including depreciation expense of $1,000
Interest expense: $1,000
Principal payment on note: $2,000
Dividends declared: $2,000
Income tax rate: 30%

Other information:

Assume that the number of units produced equals the number sold.
Year-end accounts receivable: 4% of 2017 sales.
Year-end accounts payable: 50% of ending inventory of raw materials.
Interest, direct labor, manufacturing overhead, and selling and administrative expenses other than depreciation are paid as incurred.
Dividends declared and income taxes for 2017 will not be paid until 2018.

BARRETT COMPANY
Balance Sheet
December 31, 2016

Assets

Current assets		
Cash		$20,000
Raw materials inventory		10,000
Total current assets		30,000
Property, plant, and equipment		
Equipment	$40,000	
Less: Accumulated depreciation	4,000	36,000
Total assets		$66,000

Liabilities and Stockholders' Equity

Liabilities
Accounts payable	$ 5,000	
Notes payable	22,000	
Total liabilities		$27,000

Stockholders' equity
Common stock	25,000	
Retained earnings	14,000	
Total stockholders' equity		39,000
Total liabilities and stockholders' equity		$66,000

Instructions

(a) Calculate budgeted cost of goods sold.
(b) Prepare a budgeted multiple-step income statement for the year ending December 31, 2017.
(c) Prepare a budgeted classified balance sheet as of December 31, 2017.

Solution

2. (a) Beginning raw materials + Purchases − Ending raw materials = Cost of direct materials
used ($10,000 + $145,000 − $15,000 = $140,000)
Direct materials used + Direct labor + Manufacturing overhead = Cost of goods sold
($140,000 + $40,000 + $73,000 = $253,000)

(b)

BARRETT COMPANY
Budgeted Income Statement
For the Year Ending December 31, 2017

Sales	$300,000
Cost of goods sold	253,000
Gross profit	47,000
Selling and administrative expenses	36,000
Income from operations	11,000
Interest expense	1,000
Income before income tax expense	10,000
Income tax expense (30%)	3,000
Net income	$ 7,000

(c)

BARRETT COMPANY
Budgeted Balance Sheet
December 31, 2017

Assets

Current assets		
Cash⁽¹⁾		$17,500
Accounts receivable (4% × $300,000)		12,000
Raw materials inventory		15,000
Total current assets		44,500
Property, plant and equipment		
Equipment	$40,000	
Less: Accumulated depreciation	8,000	32,000
Total assets		$76,500

⁽¹⁾Beginning cash balance	$ 20,000
Add: Collections from customers	
(96% × $300,000 sales)	288,000
Total available cash	308,000

Less: Disbursements		
Direct materials ($5,000 + $145,000 − $7,500)	$142,500	
Direct labor	40,000	
Manufacturing overhead	70,000	
Selling and administrative expenses	35,000	
Total disbursements		287,500
Excess of available cash over cash disbursements		20,500
Financing		
Less: Repayment of principal and interest		3,000
Ending cash balance		$ 17,500

Liabilities and Stockholders' Equity

Liabilities		
Accounts payable (50% × $15,000)	$ 7,500	
Income taxes payable	3,000	
Dividends payable	2,000	
Note payable	20,000	
Total liabilities		$32,500
Stockholders' equity		
Common stock	25,000	
Retained earnings[(2)]	19,000	
Total stockholders' equity		44,000
Total liabilities and stockholders' equity		$76,500

[(2)]Beginning retained earnings + Net income − Dividends declared = Ending retained earnings
($14,000 + $7,000 − $2,000 = $19,000)

WileyPLUS

Brief Exercises, Exercises, **DO IT!** Exercises, and Problems and many additional resources are available for practice in WileyPLUS

QUESTIONS

1. (a) What is a budget?
   (b) How does a budget contribute to good management?

2. Kate Cey and Joe Coulter are discussing the benefits of budgeting. They ask you to identify the primary benefits of budgeting. Comply with their request.

3. Jane Gilligan asks your help in understanding the essentials of effective budgeting. Identify the essentials for Jane.

4. (a) "Accounting plays a relatively unimportant role in budgeting." Do you agree? Explain.
   (b) What responsibilities does management have in budgeting?

5. What criteria are helpful in determining the length of the budget period? What is the most common budget period?

6. Lori Wilkins maintains that the only difference between budgeting and long-range planning is time. Do you agree? Why or why not?

7. What is participative budgeting? What are its potential benefits? What are its potential disadvantages?

8. What is budgetary slack? What incentive do managers have to create budgetary slack?

9. Distinguish between a master budget and a sales forecast.

10. What budget is the starting point in preparing the master budget? What may result if this budget is inaccurate?

11. "The production budget shows both unit production data and unit cost data." Is this true? Explain.

12. Alou Company has 20,000 beginning finished goods units. Budgeted sales units are 160,000. If management desires 15,000 ending finished goods units, what are the required units of production?

13. In preparing the direct materials budget for Quan Company, management concludes that required purchases are 64,000 units. If 52,000 direct materials units are required in production and there are 9,000 units of beginning direct materials, what is the desired units of ending direct materials?

14. The production budget of Justus Company calls for 80,000 units to be produced. If it takes 45 minutes to make one unit and the direct labor rate is $16 per hour, what is the total budgeted direct labor cost?

15. Ortiz Company's manufacturing overhead budget shows total variable costs of $198,000 and total fixed

costs of $162,000. Total production in units is expected to be 150,000. It takes 20 minutes to make one unit, and the direct labor rate is $15 per hour. Express the manufacturing overhead rate as (a) a percentage of direct labor cost, and (b) an amount per direct labor hour.

16. Everly Company's variable selling and administrative expenses are 12% of net sales. Fixed expenses are $50,000 per quarter. The sales budget shows expected sales of $200,000 and $240,000 in the first and second quarters, respectively. What are the total budgeted selling and administrative expenses for each quarter?

17. For Goody Company, the budgeted cost for one unit of product is direct materials $10, direct labor $20, and manufacturing overhead 80% of direct labor cost. If 25,000 units are expected to be sold at $65 each, what is the budgeted gross profit?

18. Indicate the supporting schedules used in preparing a budgeted income statement through gross profit for a manufacturer.

19. Identify the three sections of a cash budget. What balances are also shown in this budget?

20. Noterman Company has credit sales of $600,000 in January. Past experience suggests that 40% is collected in the month of sale, 50% in the month following the sale, and 10% in the second month following the sale. Compute the cash collections from January sales in January, February, and March.

21. What is the formula for determining required merchandise purchases for a merchandiser?

22. How may expected revenues in a service company be computed?

BRIEF EXERCISES

BE23-1 Maris Company uses the following budgets: balance sheet, capital expenditure, cash, direct labor, direct materials, income statement, manufacturing overhead, production, sales, and selling and administrative expense. Prepare a diagram of the interrelationships of the budgets in the master budget. Indicate whether each budget is an operating or a financial budget.

Prepare a diagram of a master budget.

(LO 1)

BE23-2 Paige Company estimates that unit sales will be 10,000 in quarter 1, 14,000 in quarter 2, 15,000 in quarter 3, and 18,000 in quarter 4. Using a sales price of $70 per unit, prepare the sales budget by quarters for the year ending December 31, 2017.

Prepare a sales budget.

(LO 2)

BE23-3 Sales budget data for Paige Company are given in BE23-2. Management desires to have an ending finished goods inventory equal to 25% of the next quarter's expected unit sales. Prepare a production budget by quarters for the first 6 months of 2017.

Prepare a production budget for 2 quarters.

(LO 2)

BE23-4 Perine Company has 2,000 pounds of raw materials in its December 31, 2016, ending inventory. Required production for January and February of 2017 are 4,000 and 5,000 units, respectively. Two pounds of raw materials are needed for each unit, and the estimated cost per pound is $6. Management desires an ending inventory equal to 25% of next month's materials requirements. Prepare the direct materials budget for January.

Prepare a direct materials budget for 1 month.

(LO 2)

BE23-5 For Gundy Company, units to be produced are 5,000 in quarter 1 and 7,000 in quarter 2. It takes 1.6 hours to make a finished unit, and the expected hourly wage rate is $15 per hour. Prepare a direct labor budget by quarters for the 6 months ending June 30, 2017.

Prepare a direct labor budget for 2 quarters.

(LO 3)

BE23-6 For Roche Inc., variable manufacturing overhead costs are expected to be $20,000 in the first quarter of 2017, with $5,000 increments in each of the remaining three quarters. Fixed overhead costs are estimated to be $40,000 in each quarter. Prepare the manufacturing overhead budget by quarters and in total for the year.

Prepare a manufacturing overhead budget.

(LO 3)

BE23-7 Elbert Company classifies its selling and administrative expense budget into variable and fixed components. Variable expenses are expected to be $24,000 in the first quarter, and $4,000 increments are expected in the remaining quarters of 2017. Fixed expenses are expected to be $40,000 in each quarter. Prepare the selling and administrative expense budget by quarters and in total for 2017.

Prepare a selling and administrative expense budget.

(LO 3)

BE23-8 North Company has completed all of its operating budgets. The sales budget for the year shows 50,000 units and total sales of $2,250,000. The total unit cost of making one unit of sales is $25. Selling and administrative expenses are expected to be $300,000. Interest is estimated to be $10,000. Income taxes are estimated to be $200,000. Prepare a budgeted multiple-step income statement for the year ending December 31, 2017.

Prepare a budgeted income statement for the year.

(LO 3)

Prepare data for a cash budget.

(LO 4)

BE23-9 Kaspar Industries expects credit sales for January, February, and March to be $220,000, $260,000, and $300,000, respectively. It is expected that 75% of the sales will be collected in the month of sale, and 25% will be collected in the following month. Compute cash collections from customers for each month.

Determine required merchandise purchases for 1 month.

(LO 5)

BE23-10 Moore Wholesalers is preparing its merchandise purchases budget. Budgeted sales are $400,000 for April and $480,000 for May. Cost of goods sold is expected to be 65% of sales. The company's desired ending inventory is 20% of the following month's cost of goods sold. Compute the required purchases for April.

DO IT! Exercises

Identify budget terminology.

(LO 1)

DO IT! 23-1 Use this list of terms to complete the sentences that follow.

Long-range plans	Participative budgeting
Sales forecast	Operating budgets
Master budget	Financial budgets

1. _____ establish goals for the company's sales and production personnel.

2. The _____ is a set of interrelated budgets that constitutes a plan of action for a specified time period.

3. _____ reduces the risk of having unrealistic budgets.

4. _____ include the cash budget and the budgeted balance sheet.

5. The budget is formed within the framework of a _____.

6. _____ contain considerably less detail than budgets.

Prepare sales, production, and direct materials budgets.

(LO 2)

DO IT! 23-2 Pargo Company is preparing its master budget for 2017. Relevant data pertaining to its sales, production, and direct materials budgets are as follows.

Sales. Sales for the year are expected to total 1,000,000 units. Quarterly sales are 20%, 25%, 25%, and 30%, respectively. The sales price is expected to be $40 per unit for the first three quarters and $45 per unit beginning in the fourth quarter. Sales in the first quarter of 2018 are expected to be 20% higher than the budgeted sales for the first quarter of 2017.

Production. Management desires to maintain the ending finished goods inventories at 25% of the next quarter's budgeted sales volume.

Direct materials. Each unit requires 2 pounds of raw materials at a cost of $12 per pound. Management desires to maintain raw materials inventories at 10% of the next quarter's production requirements. Assume the production requirements for first quarter of 2018 are 450,000 pounds.

Prepare the sales, production, and direct materials budgets by quarters for 2017.

Calculate budgeted total unit cost and prepare budgeted income statement.

(LO 3)

DO IT! 23-3 Pargo Company is preparing its budgeted income statement for 2017. Relevant data pertaining to its sales, production, and direct materials budgets can be found in **DO IT! 23-2**.

In addition, Pargo budgets 0.3 hours of direct labor per unit, labor costs at $15 per hour, and manufacturing overhead at $20 per direct labor hour. Its budgeted selling and administrative expenses for 2017 are $6,000,000.

(a) Calculate the budgeted total unit cost.

(b) Prepare the budgeted multiple-step income statement for 2017. (Ignore income taxes.)

Determine amount of financing needed.

(LO 4)

DO IT! 23-4 Batista Company management wants to maintain a minimum monthly cash balance of $25,000. At the beginning of April, the cash balance is $25,000, expected cash receipts for April are $245,000, and cash disbursements are expected to be $255,000. How much cash, if any, must be borrowed to maintain the desired minimum monthly balance?

Prepare merchandise purchases budget.

(LO 5)

DO IT! 23-5 Zeller Company estimates that 2017 sales will be $40,000 in quarter 1, $48,000 in quarter 2, and $58,000 in quarter 3. Cost of goods sold is 50% of sales. Management desires to have ending finished goods inventory equal to 10% of the next quarter's expected cost of goods sold. Prepare a merchandise purchases budget by quarter for the first 6 months of 2017.

EXERCISES

E23-1 Trusler Company has always done some planning for the future, but the company has never prepared a formal budget. Now that the company is growing larger, it is considering preparing a budget.

Explain the concept of budgeting.

(LO 1)

Instructions
Write a memo to Jim Dixon, the president of Trusler Company, in which you define budgeting, identify the budgets that comprise the master budget, identify the primary benefits of budgeting, and discuss the essentials of effective budgeting.

E23-2 Edington Electronics Inc. produces and sells two models of pocket calculators, XQ-103 and XQ-104. The calculators sell for $15 and $25, respectively. Because of the intense competition Edington faces, management budgets sales semiannually. Its projections for the first 2 quarters of 2017 are as follows.

Prepare a sales budget for 2 quarters.

(LO 2)

	Unit Sales	
Product	**Quarter 1**	**Quarter 2**
XQ-103	20,000	22,000
XQ-104	12,000	15,000

No changes in selling prices are anticipated.

Instructions
Prepare a sales budget for the 2 quarters ending June 30, 2017. List the products and show for each quarter and for the 6 months, units, selling price, and total sales by product and in total.

E23-3 Thome and Crede, CPAs, are preparing their service revenue (sales) budget for the coming year (2017). The practice is divided into three departments: auditing, tax, and consulting. Billable hours for each department, by quarter, are provided below.

Prepare a sales budget for 4 quarters.

(LO 2)

Department	Quarter 1	Quarter 2	Quarter 3	Quarter 4
Auditing	2,300	1,600	2,000	2,400
Tax	3,000	2,200	2,000	2,500
Consulting	1,500	1,500	1,500	1,500

Average hourly billing rates are auditing $80, tax $90, and consulting $110.

Instructions
Prepare the service revenue (sales) budget for 2017 by listing the departments and showing for each quarter and the year in total, billable hours, billable rate, and total revenue.

E23-4 Turney Company produces and sells automobile batteries, the heavy-duty HD-240. The 2017 sales forecast is as follows.

Prepare quarterly production budgets.

(LO 2)

Quarter	HD-240
1	5,000
2	7,000
3	8,000
4	10,000

The January 1, 2017, inventory of HD-240 is 2,000 units. Management desires an ending inventory each quarter equal to 40% of the next quarter's sales. Sales in the first quarter of 2018 are expected to be 25% higher than sales in the same quarter in 2017.

Instructions
Prepare quarterly production budgets for each quarter and in total for 2017.

Prepare a direct materials purchases budget.

(LO 2)

E23-5 DeWitt Industries has adopted the following production budget for the first 4 months of 2017.

Month	Units	Month	Units
January	10,000	March	5,000
February	8,000	April	4,000

Each unit requires 2 pounds of raw materials costing $3 per pound. On December 31, 2016, the ending raw materials inventory was 4,000 pounds. Management wants to have a raw materials inventory at the end of the month equal to 20% of next month's production requirements.

Instructions

Prepare a direct materials purchases budget by month for the first quarter.

Prepare production and direct materials budgets by quarters for 6 months.

(LO 2)

E23-6 On January 1, 2017, the Hardin Company budget committee has reached agreement on the following data for the 6 months ending June 30, 2017.

Sales units: First quarter 5,000; second quarter 6,000; third quarter 7,000.

Ending raw materials inventory: 40% of the next quarter's production requirements.

Ending finished goods inventory: 25% of the next quarter's expected sales units.

Third-quarter production: 7,200 units.

The ending raw materials and finished goods inventories at December 31, 2016, follow the same percentage relationships to production and sales that occur in 2017. Three pounds of raw materials are required to make each unit of finished goods. Raw materials purchased are expected to cost $4 per pound.

Instructions

(a) Prepare a production budget by quarters for the 6-month period ended June 30, 2017.
(b) Prepare a direct materials budget by quarters for the 6-month period ended June 30, 2017.

Calculate raw materials purchases in dollars.

(LO 2)

E23-7 Rensing Ltd. estimates sales for the second quarter of 2017 will be as follows.

Month	Units
April	2,550
May	2,675
June	2,390

The target ending inventory of finished products is as follows.

March 31	2,000
April 30	2,230
May 31	2,200
June 30	2,310

Two units of material are required for each unit of finished product. Production for July is estimated at 2,700 units to start building inventory for the fall sales period. Rensing's policy is to have an inventory of raw materials at the end of each month equal to 50% of the following month's production requirements.

Raw materials are expected to cost $4 per unit throughout the period.

Instructions

Calculate the May raw materials purchases in dollars.

(CGA adapted)

Prepare a production and a direct materials budget.

(LO 2)

E23-8 Fuqua Company's sales budget projects unit sales of part 198Z of 10,000 units in January, 12,000 units in February, and 13,000 units in March. Each unit of part 198Z requires 4 pounds of materials, which cost $2 per pound. Fuqua Company desires its ending raw materials inventory to equal 40% of the next month's production requirements, and its ending finished goods inventory to equal 20% of the next month's expected unit sales. These goals were met at December 31, 2016.

Instructions
(a) Prepare a production budget for January and February 2017.
(b) Prepare a direct materials budget for January 2017.

E23-9 Rodriguez, Inc., is preparing its direct labor budget for 2017 from the following production budget based on a calendar year.

Prepare a direct labor budget.
(LO 3)

Quarter	Units	Quarter	Units
1	20,000	3	35,000
2	25,000	4	30,000

Each unit requires 1.5 hours of direct labor.

Instructions
Prepare a direct labor budget for 2017. Wage rates are expected to be $16 for the first 2 quarters and $18 for quarters 3 and 4.

E23-10 Lowell Company makes and sells artistic frames for pictures. The controller is responsible for preparing the master budget and has accumulated the following information for 2017.

Prepare production and direct labor budgets.
(LO 2, 3)

	January	February	March	April	May
Estimated unit sales	12,000	14,000	13,000	11,000	11,000
Sales price per unit	$50.00	$47.50	$47.50	$47.50	$47.50
Direct labor hours per unit	2.0	2.0	1.5	1.5	1.5
Wage per direct labor hour	$8.00	$8.00	$8.00	$9.00	$9.00

Lowell has a labor contract that calls for a wage increase to $9.00 per hour on April 1. New labor-saving machinery has been installed and will be fully operational by March 1.

Lowell expects to begin the year with 17,600 frames on hand and has a policy of carrying an end-of-month inventory of 100% of the following month's sales, plus 40% of the second following month's sales.

Instructions
Prepare a production budget and a direct labor budget for Lowell Company by month and for the first quarter of the year. The direct labor budget should include direct labor hours.
(CMA-Canada adapted)

E23-11 Atlanta Company is preparing its manufacturing overhead budget for 2017. Relevant data consist of the following.

Prepare a manufacturing overhead budget for the year.
(LO 3)

Units to be produced (by quarters): 10,000, 12,000, 14,000, 16,000.

Direct labor: time is 1.5 hours per unit.

Variable overhead costs per direct labor hour: indirect materials $0.80; indirect labor $1.20; and maintenance $0.50.

Fixed overhead costs per quarter: supervisory salaries $35,000; depreciation $15,000; and maintenance $12,000.

Instructions
Prepare the manufacturing overhead budget for the year, showing quarterly data.

E23-12 Kirkland Company combines its operating expenses for budget purposes in a selling and administrative expense budget. For the first 6 months of 2017, the following data are available.

Prepare a selling and administrative expense budget for 2 quarters.
(LO 3)

1. Sales: 20,000 units quarter 1; 22,000 units quarter 2.
2. Variable costs per dollar of sales: sales commissions 5%, delivery expense 2%, and advertising 3%.
3. Fixed costs per quarter: sales salaries $12,000, office salaries $8,000, depreciation $4,200, insurance $1,500, utilities $800, and repairs expense $500.
4. Unit selling price: $20.

Instructions

Prepare a selling and administrative expense budget by quarters for the first 6 months of 2017.

Prepare a budgeted income statement for the year.

(LO 3)

E23-13 Fultz Company has accumulated the following budget data for the year 2017.

1. Sales: 30,000 units, unit selling price $85.
2. Cost of one unit of finished goods: direct materials 1 pound at $5 per pound, direct labor 3 hours at $15 per hour, and manufacturing overhead $5 per direct labor hour.
3. Inventories (raw materials only): beginning, 10,000 pounds; ending, 15,000 pounds.
4. Selling and administrative expenses: $170,000; interest expense: $30,000.
5. Income taxes: 30% of income before income taxes.

Instructions

(a) Prepare a schedule showing the computation of cost of goods sold for 2017.
(b) Prepare a budgeted multiple-step income statement for 2017.

Prepare a cash budget for 2 months.

(LO 4)

E23-14 Danner Company expects to have a cash balance of $45,000 on January 1, 2017. Relevant monthly budget data for the first 2 months of 2017 are as follows.

Collections from customers: January $85,000, February $150,000.

Payments for direct materials: January $50,000, February $75,000.

Direct labor: January $30,000, February $45,000. Wages are paid in the month they are incurred.

Manufacturing overhead: January $21,000, February $25,000. These costs include depreciation of $1,500 per month. All other overhead costs are paid as incurred.

Selling and administrative expenses: January $15,000, February $20,000. These costs are exclusive of depreciation. They are paid as incurred.

Sales of marketable securities in January are expected to realize $12,000 in cash. Danner Company has a line of credit at a local bank that enables it to borrow up to $25,000. The company wants to maintain a minimum monthly cash balance of $20,000.

Instructions

Prepare a cash budget for January and February.

Prepare a cash budget.

(LO 4)

E23-15 Deitz Corporation is projecting a cash balance of $30,000 in its December 31, 2016, balance sheet. Deitz's schedule of expected collections from customers for the first quarter of 2017 shows total collections of $185,000. The schedule of expected payments for direct materials for the first quarter of 2017 shows total payments of $43,000. Other information gathered for the first quarter of 2017 is sale of equipment $3,000, direct labor $70,000, manufacturing overhead $35,000, selling and administrative expenses $45,000, and purchase of securities $14,000. Deitz wants to maintain a balance of at least $25,000 cash at the end of each quarter.

Instructions

Prepare a cash budget for the first quarter.

Prepare cash budget for a month.

(LO 4)

E23-16 The controller of Trenshaw Company wants to improve the company's control system by preparing a month-by-month cash budget. The following information is for the month ending July 31, 2017.

June 30, 2017, cash balance	$45,000
Dividends to be declared on July 15*	12,000
Cash expenditures to be paid in July for operating expenses	40,800
Amortization expense in July	4,500
Cash collections to be received in July	90,000
Merchandise purchases to be paid in cash in July	56,200
Equipment to be purchased for cash in July	20,000

*Dividends are payable 30 days after declaration to shareholders of record on the declaration date.

Trenshaw Company wants to keep a minimum cash balance of $25,000.

Instructions

(a) Prepare a cash budget for the month ended July 31, 2017, and indicate how much money, if any, Trenshaw Company will need to borrow to meet its minimum cash requirement.

(b) Explain how cash budgeting can reduce the cost of short-term borrowing.

(CGA adapted)

E23-17 Nieto Company's budgeted sales and direct materials purchases are as follows.

Prepare schedules of expected collections and payments.

(LO 4)

	Budgeted Sales	Budgeted D.M. Purchases
January	$200,000	$30,000
February	220,000	36,000
March	250,000	38,000

Nieto's sales are 30% cash and 70% credit. Credit sales are collected 10% in the month of sale, 50% in the month following sale, and 36% in the second month following sale; 4% are uncollectible. Nieto's purchases are 50% cash and 50% on account. Purchases on account are paid 40% in the month of purchase, and 60% in the month following purchase.

Instructions

(a) Prepare a schedule of expected collections from customers for March.

(b) Prepare a schedule of expected payments for direct materials for March.

E23-18 Green Landscaping Inc. is preparing its budget for the first quarter of 2017. The next step in the budgeting process is to prepare a cash receipts schedule and a cash payments schedule. To that end the following information has been collected.

Prepare schedules for cash receipts and cash payments, and determine ending balances for balance sheet.

(LO 4)

Clients usually pay 60% of their fee in the month that service is performed, 30% the month after, and 10% the second month after receiving service.

Actual service revenue for 2016 and expected service revenues for 2017 are November 2016, $80,000; December 2016, $90,000; January 2017, $100,000; February 2017, $120,000; and March 2017, $140,000.

Purchases of landscaping supplies (direct materials) are paid 60% in the month of purchase and 40% the following month. Actual purchases for 2016 and expected purchases for 2017 are December 2016, $14,000; January 2017, $12,000; February 2017, $15,000; and March 2017, $18,000.

Instructions

(a) Prepare the following schedules for each month in the first quarter of 2017 and for the quarter in total:

  (1) Expected collections from clients.

  (2) Expected payments for landscaping supplies.

(b) Determine the following balances at March 31, 2017:

  (1) Accounts receivable.

  (2) Accounts payable.

E23-19 Pletcher Dental Clinic is a medium-sized dental service specializing in family dental care. The clinic is currently preparing the master budget for the first 2 quarters of 2017. All that remains in this process is the cash budget. The following information has been collected from other portions of the master budget and elsewhere.

Prepare a cash budget for 2 quarters.

(LO 4, 5)

Beginning cash balance	$ 30,000
Required minimum cash balance	25,000
Payment of income taxes (2nd quarter)	4,000
Professional salaries:	
1st quarter	140,000
2nd quarter	140,000
Interest from investments (2nd quarter)	7,000
Overhead costs:	
1st quarter	77,000
2nd quarter	100,000

Selling and administrative costs, including
$2,000 depreciation:

1st quarter	50,000
2nd quarter	70,000
Purchase of equipment (2nd quarter)	50,000
Sale of equipment (1st quarter)	12,000
Collections from patients:	
1st quarter	235,000
2nd quarter	380,000
Interest payments (2nd quarter)	200

Instructions
Prepare a cash budget for each of the first two quarters of 2017.

Prepare a purchases budget and budgeted income statement for a merchandiser.

(LO 5)

E23-20 In May 2017, the budget committee of Grand Stores assembles the following data in preparation of budgeted merchandise purchases for the month of June.

1. Expected sales: June $500,000, July $600,000.
2. Cost of goods sold is expected to be 75% of sales.
3. Desired ending merchandise inventory is 30% of the following (next) month's cost of goods sold.
4. The beginning inventory at June 1 will be the desired amount.

Instructions
(a) Compute the budgeted merchandise purchases for June.
(b) Prepare the budgeted multiple-step income statement for June through gross profit.

Prepare a direct labor budget for a service company.

(LO 5)

E23-21 Emeric and Ellie's Painting Service estimates that it will paint 10 small homes, 5 medium homes, and 2 large homes during the month of June 2017. The company estimates its direct labor needs as 40 hours per small home, 70 hours for a medium home, and 120 hours for a large home. Its average cost for direct labor is $18 per hour.

Instructions
Prepare a direct labor budget for Emeric and Ellie's Painting Service for June 2017.

EXERCISES: SET B AND CHALLENGE EXERCISES

Visit the book's companion website, at **www.wiley.com/college/weygandt**, and choose the Student Companion site to access Exercises: Set B and Challenge Exercises.

PROBLEMS: SET A

Prepare budgeted income statement and supporting budgets.

(LO 2, 3)

P23-1A Cook Farm Supply Company manufactures and sells a pesticide called Snare. The following data are available for preparing budgets for Snare for the first 2 quarters of 2017.

1. Sales: quarter 1, 40,000 bags; quarter 2, 56,000 bags. Selling price is $60 per bag.
2. Direct materials: each bag of Snare requires 4 pounds of Gumm at a cost of $3.80 per pound and 6 pounds of Tarr at $1.50 per pound.
3. Desired inventory levels:

Type of Inventory	January 1	April 1	July 1
Snare (bags)	8,000	15,000	18,000
Gumm (pounds)	9,000	10,000	13,000
Tarr (pounds)	14,000	20,000	25,000

4. Direct labor: direct labor time is 15 minutes per bag at an hourly rate of $16 per hour.
5. Selling and administrative expenses are expected to be 15% of sales plus $175,000 per quarter.
6. Interest expense is $100,000.
7. Income taxes are expected to be 30% of income before income taxes.

Your assistant has prepared two budgets: (1) the manufacturing overhead budget shows expected costs to be 125% of direct labor cost, and (2) the direct materials budget for Tarr shows the cost of Tarr purchases to be $297,000 in quarter 1 and $439,500 in quarter 2.

Instructions
Prepare the budgeted multiple-step income statement for the first 6 months and all required operating budgets by quarters. (*Note:* Use variable and fixed in the selling and administrative expense budget.) Do not prepare the manufacturing overhead budget or the direct materials budget for Tarr.

Net income $881,160
Cost per bag $33.20

P23-2A Deleon Inc. is preparing its annual budgets for the year ending December 31, 2017. Accounting assistants furnish the data shown below.

Prepare sales, production, direct materials, direct labor, and income statement budgets.

(LO 2, 3)

	Product JB 50	Product JB 60
Sales budget:		
Anticipated volume in units	400,000	200,000
Unit selling price	$20	$25
Production budget:		
Desired ending finished goods units	30,000	15,000
Beginning finished goods units	25,000	10,000
Direct materials budget:		
Direct materials per unit (pounds)	2	3
Desired ending direct materials pounds	30,000	10,000
Beginning direct materials pounds	40,000	15,000
Cost per pound	$3	$4
Direct labor budget:		
Direct labor time per unit	0.4	0.6
Direct labor rate per hour	$12	$12
Budgeted income statement:		
Total unit cost	$13	$20

An accounting assistant has prepared the detailed manufacturing overhead budget and the selling and administrative expense budget. The latter shows selling expenses of $560,000 for product JB 50 and $360,000 for product JB 60, and administrative expenses of $540,000 for product JB 50 and $340,000 for product JB 60. Interest expense is $150,000 (not allocated to products). Income taxes are expected to be 30%.

Instructions
Prepare the following budgets for the year. Show data for each product. Quarterly budgets should not be prepared.
(a) Sales.
(b) Production.
(c) Direct materials.
(d) Direct labor.
(e) Multiple-step income statement (*Note:* income taxes are not allocated to the products).

(a) Total sales $13,000,000
(b) Required production
    units: JB 50, 405,000
    JB 60, 205,000
(c) Total cost of direct
    materials purchases
    $4,840,000
(d) Total direct labor cost
    $3,420,000
(e) Net income $1,295,000

P23-3A Hill Industries had sales in 2016 of $6,800,000 and gross profit of $1,100,000. Management is considering two alternative budget plans to increase its gross profit in 2017.

Plan A would increase the selling price per unit from $8.00 to $8.40. Sales volume would decrease by 10% from its 2016 level. Plan B would decrease the selling price per unit by $0.50. The marketing department expects that the sales volume would increase by 100,000 units.

At the end of 2016, Hill has 40,000 units of inventory on hand. If Plan A is accepted, the 2017 ending inventory should be equal to 5% of the 2017 sales. If Plan B is accepted, the ending inventory should be equal to 60,000 units. Each unit produced will cost $1.80 in direct labor, $1.40 in direct materials, and $1.20 in variable overhead. The fixed overhead for 2017 should be $1,895,000.

Prepare sales and production budgets and compute cost per unit under two plans.

(LO 2)

Instructions
(a) Prepare a sales budget for 2017 under each plan.
(b) Prepare a production budget for 2017 under each plan.
(c) Compute the production cost per unit under each plan. Why is the cost per unit different for each of the two plans? (Round to two decimals.)
(d) Which plan should be accepted? (*Hint:* Compute the gross profit under each plan.)

(c) Unit cost: Plan A $6.88
    Plan B $6.35
(d) Gross profit:
    Plan A $1,162,800
    Plan B $1,092,500

Prepare cash budget for 2 months.

(LO 4)

P23-4A Colter Company prepares monthly cash budgets. Relevant data from operating budgets for 2017 are as follows.

	January	February
Sales	$360,000	$400,000
Direct materials purchases	120,000	125,000
Direct labor	90,000	100,000
Manufacturing overhead	70,000	75,000
Selling and administrative expenses	79,000	85,000

All sales are on account. Collections are expected to be 50% in the month of sale, 30% in the first month following the sale, and 20% in the second month following the sale. Sixty percent (60%) of direct materials purchases are paid in cash in the month of purchase, and the balance due is paid in the month following the purchase. All other items above are paid in the month incurred except for selling and administrative expenses that include $1,000 of depreciation per month.

Other data:

1. Credit sales: November 2016, $250,000; December 2016, $320,000.
2. Purchases of direct materials: December 2016, $100,000.
3. Other receipts: January—collection of December 31, 2016, notes receivable $15,000; February—proceeds from sale of securities $6,000.
4. Other disbursements: February—payment of $6,000 cash dividend.

The company's cash balance on January 1, 2017, is expected to be $60,000. The company wants to maintain a minimum cash balance of $50,000.

(a) January: collections
    $326,000 payments
    $112,000
(b) Ending cash balance:
    January $51,000
    February $50,000

Instructions

(a) Prepare schedules for (1) expected collections from customers and (2) expected payments for direct materials purchases for January and February.
(b) Prepare a cash budget for January and February in columnar form.

Prepare purchases and income statement budgets for a merchandiser.

(LO 5)

P23-5A The budget committee of Suppar Company collects the following data for its San Miguel Store in preparing budgeted income statements for May and June 2017.

1. Sales for May are expected to be $800,000. Sales in June and July are expected to be 5% higher than the preceding month.
2. Cost of goods sold is expected to be 75% of sales.
3. Company policy is to maintain ending merchandise inventory at 10% of the following month's cost of goods sold.
4. Operating expenses are estimated to be as follows:

Sales salaries	$35,000 per month
Advertising	6% of monthly sales
Delivery expense	2% of monthly sales
Sales commissions	5% of monthly sales
Rent expense	$5,000 per month
Depreciation	$800 per month
Utilities	$600 per month
Insurance	$500 per month

5. Interest expense is $2,000 per month. Income taxes are estimated to be 30% of income before income taxes.

(a) Purchases:
    May $603,000
    June $633,150
(b) Net income:
    May $36,470
    June $39,830

Instructions

(a) Prepare the merchandise purchases budget for each month in columnar form.
(b) Prepare budgeted multiple-step income statements for each month in columnar form. Show in the statements the details of cost of goods sold.

P23-6A Krause Industries' balance sheet at December 31, 2016, is presented below.

Prepare budgeted cost of goods sold, income statement, retained earnings, and balance sheet.

(LO 3, 4)

KRAUSE INDUSTRIES
Balance Sheet
December 31, 2016

Assets

Current assets		
Cash		$ 7,500
Accounts receivable		73,500
Finished goods inventory (1,500 units)		24,000
Total current assets		105,000
Property, plant, and equipment		
Equipment	$40,000	
Less: Accumulated depredation	10,000	30,000
Total assets		$135,000

Liabilities and Stockholders' Equity

Liabilities		
Notes payable		$ 25,000
Accounts payable		45,000
Total liabilities		70,000
Stockholders' equity		
Common stock	$40,000	
Retained earnings	25,000	
Total stockholders' equity		65,000
Total liabilities and stockholders' equity		$135,000

Budgeted data for the year 2017 include the following.

	2017	
	Quarter 4	**Total**
Sales budget (8,000 units at $32)	$76,800	$256,000
Direct materials used	17,000	62,500
Direct labor	12,500	50,900
Manufacturing overhead applied	10,000	48,600
Selling and administrative expenses	18,000	75,000

To meet sales requirements and to have 2,500 units of finished goods on hand at December 31, 2017, the production budget shows 9,000 required units of output. The total unit cost of production is expected to be $18. Krause uses the first-in, first-out (FIFO) inventory costing method. Interest expense is expected to be $3,500 for the year. Income taxes are expected to be 40% of income before income taxes. In 2017, the company expects to declare and pay an $8,000 cash dividend.

The company's cash budget shows an expected cash balance of $5,880 at December 31, 2017. All sales and purchases are on account. It is expected that 60% of quarterly sales are collected in cash within the quarter and the remainder is collected in the following quarter. Direct materials purchased from suppliers are paid 50% in the quarter incurred and the remainder in the following quarter. Purchases in the fourth quarter were the same as the materials used. In 2017, the company expects to purchase additional equipment costing $9,000. $4,000 of depreciation expense on equipment is included in the budget data and split equally between manufacturing overhead and selling and administrative expenses. Krause expects to pay $8,000 on the outstanding notes payable balance plus all interest due and payable to December 31 (included in interest expense $3,500, above). Accounts payable at December 31, 2017, includes amounts due suppliers (see above) plus other accounts payable of $7,200. Unpaid income taxes at December 31 will be $5,000.

Instructions
Prepare a budgeted statement of cost of goods sold, budgeted multiple-step income statement and retained earnings statement for 2017, and a budgeted classified balance sheet at December 31, 2017.

PROBLEMS: SET B AND SET C

Visit the book's companion website, at **www.wiley.com/college/weygandt**, and choose the Student Companion site to access Problems: Set B and Set C.

CONTINUING PROBLEMS

CURRENT DESIGNS

CD23 Diane Buswell is preparing the 2017 budget for one of **Current Designs'** rotomolded kayaks. Extensive meetings with members of the sales department and executive team have resulted in the following unit sales projections for 2017.

Quarter 1	1,000 kayaks
Quarter 2	1,500 kayaks
Quarter 3	750 kayaks
Quarter 4	750 kayaks

Current Designs' policy is to have finished goods ending inventory in a quarter equal to 20% of the next quarter's anticipated sales. Preliminary sales projections for 2018 are 1,100 units for the first quarter and 1,500 units for the second quarter. Ending inventory of finished goods at December 31, 2016, will be 200 rotomolded kayaks.

Production of each kayak requires 54 pounds of polyethylene powder and a finishing kit (rope, seat, hardware, etc.). Company policy is that the ending inventory of polyethylene powder should be 25% of the amount needed for production in the next quarter. Assume that the ending inventory of polyethylene powder on December 31, 2016, is 19,400 pounds. The finishing kits can be assembled as they are needed. As a result, Current Designs does not maintain a significant inventory of the finishing kits.

The polyethylene powder used in these kayaks costs $1.50 per pound, and the finishing kits cost $170 each. Production of a single kayak requires 2 hours of time by more experienced, type I employees and 3 hours of finishing time by type II employees. The type I employees are paid $15 per hour, and the type II employees are paid $12 per hour.

Selling and administrative expenses for this line are expected to be $45 per unit sold plus $7,500 per quarter. Manufacturing overhead is assigned at 150% of labor costs.

Instructions
Prepare the production budget, direct materials budget, direct labor budget, manufacturing overhead budget, and selling and administrative budget for this product line by quarter and in total for 2017.

WATERWAYS

(*Note:* This is a continuation of the Waterways problem from Chapters 15–22.)

WP23 Waterways Corporation is preparing its budget for the coming year, 2017. The first step is to plan for the first quarter of that coming year. The company has gathered information from its managers in preparation of the budgeting process. This problem asks you to prepare the various budgets that comprise the master budget for 2017.

Go to the book's companion website, at **www.wiley.com/college/weygandt**, *to see the completion of this problem.*

COMPREHENSIVE CASES

CC23-1 Auburn Circular Club is planning a major fundraiser that it hopes will become a successful annual event: sponsoring a professional rodeo. For this case, you will encounter many managerial accounting issues that would be common for a start-up business, such as CVP analysis (Chapter 19), incremental analysis (Chapter 21), and budgetary planning (Chapter 23).

Go to the book's companion website, at **www.wiley.com/college/weygandt**, *for complete case details and instructions.*

CC23-2 Sweats Galore is a new business venture that will make custom sweatshirts using a silk-screen process. In helping the company's owner, Michael Woods, set up his business, you will have the opportunity to apply your understanding of CVP relationships (Chapter 19) and budgetary planning (Chapter 23).

Go to the book's companion website, at **www.wiley.com/college/weygandt**, *for complete case details and instructions.*

BROADENING YOUR *PERSPECTIVE*

MANAGEMENT DECISION-MAKING

Decision-Making Across the Organization

BYP23-1 Palmer Corporation operates on a calendar-year basis. It begins the annual budgeting process in late August when the president establishes targets for the total dollar sales and net income before taxes for the next year.

The sales target is given first to the marketing department. The marketing manager formulates a sales budget by product line in both units and dollars. From this budget, sales quotas by product line in units and dollars are established for each of the corporation's sales districts. The marketing manager also estimates the cost of the marketing activities required to support the target sales volume and prepares a tentative marketing expense budget.

The executive vice president uses the sales and profit targets, the sales budget by product line, and the tentative marketing expense budget to determine the dollar amounts that can be devoted to manufacturing and corporate office expense. The executive vice president prepares the budget for corporate expenses. She then forwards to the production department the product-line sales budget in units and the total dollar amount that can be devoted to manufacturing.

The production manager meets with the factory managers to develop a manufacturing plan that will produce the required units when needed within the cost constraints set by the executive vice president. The budgeting process usually comes to a halt at this point because the production department does not consider the financial resources allocated to be adequate.

When this standstill occurs, the vice president of finance, the executive vice president, the marketing manager, and the production manager meet together to determine the final budgets for each of the areas. This normally results in a modest increase in the total amount available for manufacturing costs and cuts in the marketing expense and corporate office expense budgets. The total sales and net income figures proposed by the president are seldom changed. Although the participants are seldom pleased with the compromise, these budgets are final. Each executive then develops a new detailed budget for the operations in his or her area.

None of the areas has achieved its budget in recent years. Sales often run below the target. When budgeted sales are not achieved, each area is expected to cut costs so that the president's profit target can be met. However, the profit target is seldom met because costs are not cut enough. In fact, costs often run above the original budget in all functional areas (marketing, production, and corporate office).

The president is disturbed that Palmer has not been able to meet the sales and profit targets. He hired a consultant with considerable experience with companies in Palmer's industry. The consultant reviewed the budgets for the past 4 years. He concluded that the product line sales budgets were reasonable and that the cost and expense budgets were adequate for the budgeted sales and production levels.

Instructions
With the class divided into groups, answer the following.

(a) Discuss how the budgeting process employed by Palmer Corporation contributes to the failure to achieve the president's sales and profit targets.
(b) Suggest how Palmer Corporation's budgeting process could be revised to correct the problems.
(c) Should the functional areas be expected to cut their costs when sales volume falls below budget? Explain your answer.

(CMA adapted)

Managerial Analysis

BYP23-2 Elliot & Hesse Inc. manufactures ergonomic devices for computer users. Some of its more popular products include anti-glare filters and privacy filters (for computer monitors) and keyboard stands with wrist rests. Over the past 5 years, it experienced rapid growth, with sales of all products increasing 20% to 50% each year.

Last year, some of the primary manufacturers of computers began introducing new products with some of the ergonomic designs, such as anti-glare filters and wrist rests, already built in. As a result, sales of Elliot & Hesse's accessory devices have declined somewhat. The company believes that the privacy filters will probably continue to show growth, but that the other products will probably continue to decline. When the next year's budget was prepared, increases were built into research and development so that replacement products could be developed or the company could expand into some other product line. Some product lines being considered are general-purpose ergonomic devices including back supports, foot rests, and sloped writing pads.

The most recent results have shown that sales decreased more than was expected for the anti-glare filters. As a result, the company may have a shortage of funds. Top management has therefore asked that all expenses be reduced 10% to compensate for these reduced sales. Summary budget information is as follows.

Direct materials	$240,000
Direct labor	110,000
Insurance	50,000
Depreciation	90,000
Machine repairs	30,000
Sales salaries	50,000
Office salaries	80,000
Factory salaries (indirect labor)	50,000
Total	$700,000

Instructions
Using the information above, answer the following questions.

(a) What are the implications of reducing each of the costs? For example, if the company reduces direct materials costs, it may have to do so by purchasing lower-quality materials. This may affect sales in the long run.
(b) Based on your analysis in (a), what do you think is the best way to obtain the $70,000 in cost savings requested? Be specific. Are there any costs that cannot or should not be reduced? Why?

Real-World Focus

BYP23-3 Information regarding many approaches to budgeting can be found online. The following activity investigates the merits of "zero-based" budgeting, as discussed by Michael LaFaive, Director of Fiscal Policy of the Mackinac Center for Public Policy.

Address: **www.mackinac.org/5928**, or go to **www.wiley.com/college/weygandt**

Instructions
Read the article at the website and answer the following questions.

(a) How does zero-based budgeting differ from standard budgeting procedures?
(b) What are some potential advantages of zero-based budgeting?
(c) What are some potential disadvantages of zero-based budgeting?
(d) How often do departments in Oklahoma undergo zero-based budgeting?

CRITICAL THINKING

Communication Activity

BYP23-4 In order to better serve their rural patients, Drs. Joe and Rick Parcells (brothers) began giving safety seminars. Especially popular were their "emergency-preparedness" talks given to farmers. Many people asked whether the "kit" of materials the doctors recommended for common farm emergencies was commercially available.

After checking with several suppliers, the doctors realized that no other company offered the supplies they recommended in their seminars, packaged in the way they described. Their wives, Megan and Sue, agreed to make a test package by ordering supplies from various medical supply companies and assembling them into a "kit" that could be sold at the seminars. When these kits proved a runaway success, the sisters-in-law decided to market them. At the advice of their accountant, they organized this venture as a separate company, called Life Protection Products (LPP), with Megan Parcells as CEO and Sue Parcells as Secretary-Treasurer.

LPP soon started receiving requests for the kits from all over the country, as word spread about their availability. Even without advertising, LPP was able to sell its full inventory every month. However, the company was becoming financially strained. Megan and Sue had about $100,000 in savings, and they invested about half that amount initially. They believed that this venture would allow them to make money. However, at the present time, only about $30,000 of the cash remains, and the company is constantly short of cash.

Megan has come to you for advice. She does not understand why the company is having cash flow problems. She and Sue have not even been withdrawing salaries. However, they have rented a local building and have hired two more full-time workers to help them cope with the increasing demand. They do not think they could handle the demand without this additional help.

Megan is also worried that the cash problems mean that the company may not be able to support itself. She has prepared the cash budget shown below. All seminar customers pay for their products in full at the time of purchase. In addition, several large companies have ordered the kits for use by employees who work in remote sites. They have requested credit terms and have been allowed to pay in the month following the sale. These large purchasers amount to about 25% of the sales at the present time. LPP purchases the materials for the kits about 2 months ahead of time. Megan and Sue are considering slowing the growth of the company by simply purchasing less materials, which will mean selling fewer kits.

The workers are paid weekly. Megan and Sue need about $15,000 cash on hand at the beginning of the month to pay for purchases of raw materials. Right now they have been using cash from their savings, but as noted, only $30,000 is left.

LIFE PROTECTION PRODUCTS
Cash Budget
For the Quarter Ending June 30, 2017

	April	May	June
Cash balance, beginning	$15,000	$15,000	$15,000
Cash received			
From prior month sales	5,000	7,500	12,500
From current sales	15,000	22,500	37,500
Total cash on hand	35,000	45,000	65,000
Cash payments			
To employees	3,000	3,000	3,000
For products	25,000	35,000	45,000
Miscellaneous expenses	5,000	6,000	7,000
Postage	1,000	1,000	1,000
Total cash payments	34,000	45,000	56,000
Cash balance	$ 1,000	$ 0	$ 9,000
Borrow from savings	$14,000	$15,000	$ 1,000
Borrow from bank?	$ 0	$ 0	$ 5,000

Instructions

Write a response to Megan Parcells. Explain why LPP is short of cash. Will this company be able to support itself? Explain your answer. Make any recommendations you deem appropriate.

Ethics Case

BYP23-5 You are an accountant in the budgetary, projections, and special projects department of Fernetti Conductor, Inc., a large manufacturing company. The president, Richard Brown, asks you on very short notice to prepare some sales and income projections covering the next 2 years of the company's much heralded new product lines. He wants these projections for a series of speeches he is making while on a 2-week trip to eight East Coast brokerage firms. The president hopes to bolster Fernetti's stock sales and price.

You work 23 hours in 2 days to compile the projections, hand-deliver them to the president, and are swiftly but graciously thanked as he departs. A week later, you find time to go over some of your computations and discover a miscalculation that makes the projections grossly overstated. You quickly inquire about the president's itinerary and learn that he has made half of his speeches and has half yet to make. You are in a quandary as to what to do.

Instructions

(a) What are the consequences of telling the president of your gross miscalculations?
(b) What are the consequences of not telling the president of your gross miscalculations?
(c) What are the ethical considerations to you and the president in this situation?

All About You

BYP23-6 In order to get your personal finances under control, you need to prepare a personal budget. Assume that you have compiled the following information regarding your expected cash flows for a typical month.

Rent payment	$ 500	Miscellaneous costs	$210
Interest income	50	Savings	50
Income tax withheld	300	Eating out	150
Electricity bill	85	Telephone and Internet costs	125
Groceries	100	Student loan payments	375
Wages earned	2,500	Entertainment costs	250
Insurance	100	Transportation costs	150

Instructions

Using the information above, prepare a personal budget. In preparing this budget, use the format found at *http://financialplan.about.com/cs/budgeting/l/blbudget.htm*. Just skip any unused line items.

Considering Your Costs and Benefits

BYP23-7 You might hear people say that they "need to learn to live within a budget." The funny thing is that most people who say this haven't actually prepared a personal budget, nor do they intend to. Instead, what they are referring to is a vaguely defined, poorly specified collection of rough ideas of how much they should spend on various aspects of their lives. However, you can't live within or even outside of something that doesn't exist. With that in mind, let's take a look at one aspect of personal-budget templates.

Many personal-budget worksheet templates that are provided for college students treat student loans as an income source. See, for example, the template provided at *http://financialplan.about.com/cs/budgeting/l/blmocolbud.htm*. Based on your knowledge of accounting, is this correct?

YES: Student loans provide a source of cash, which can be used to pay costs. As the saying goes, "It all spends the same." Therefore, student loans are income.

NO: Student loans must eventually be repaid; therefore, they are not income. As the name suggests, they are loans.

Instructions
Write a response indicating your position regarding this situation. Provide support for your view.

24 Budgetary Control and Responsibility Accounting

CHAPTER PREVIEW In Chapter 23, we discussed the use of budgets for planning. We now consider how budgets are used by management to control operations. In the Feature Story below on the Tribeca Grand Hotel, we see that management uses the budget to adapt to the business environment. This chapter focuses on two aspects of management control: (1) budgetary control and (2) responsibility accounting.

FEATURE STORY

Pumpkin Madeleines and a Movie

Perhaps no place in the world has a wider variety of distinctive, high-end accommodations than New York City. It's tough to set yourself apart in the Big Apple, but unique is what the Tribeca Grand Hotel is all about.

When you walk through the doors of this triangular-shaped building, nestled in one of Manhattan's most affluent neighborhoods, you immediately encounter a striking eight-story atrium. Although the hotel was completely renovated, it still maintains its funky mid-century charm. Just consider the always hip Church Bar. Besides serving up cocktails until 2 a.m., Church's also provides food. These are not the run-of-the-mill, chain hotel, borderline edibles. Church's chef is famous for tantalizing delectables such as duck rillettes, sea salt baked branzino, housemade pappardelle, and pumpkin madeleines.

Another thing that really sets the Tribeca Grand apart is its private screening room. As a guest, you can enjoy plush leather seating, state-of-the-art projection, and digital surround sound, all while viewing a cult classic from the hotel's film series. In fact, on Sundays, free screenings are available to guests and non-guests alike on a first-come-first-served basis.

To attract and satisfy a discerning clientele, the Tribeca Grand's management incurs higher and more unpredictable costs than those of your standard hotel. As fun as it might be to run a high-end hotel, management can't be cavalier about spending money. To maintain profitability, management closely monitors costs and revenues to make sure that they track with budgeted amounts. Further, because of unexpected fluctuations (think Hurricane Sandy or a bitterly cold stretch of winter weather), management must sometimes revise forecasts and budgets and adapt quickly. To evaluate performance when things happen that are beyond management's control, the budget needs to be flexible.

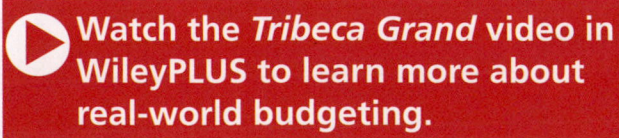

Watch the *Tribeca Grand* video in WileyPLUS to learn more about real-world budgeting.

Eviled/Shutterstock

CHAPTER OUTLINE

Learning Objectives

1 Describe budgetary control and static budget reports.
- Budgetary control
- Static budget reports

DO IT! **1** Static Budget Reports

2 Prepare flexible budget reports.
- Why flexible budgets?
- Developing the flexible budget
- Flexible budget—a case study
- Flexible budget reports

DO IT! **2** Flexible Budgets

3 Apply responsibility accounting to cost and profit centers.
- Controllable vs. noncontrollable revenues and costs
- Principles of performance evaluation
- Responsibility reporting system
- Types of responsibility centers

DO IT! **3** Profit Center Responsibility Report

4 Evaluate performance in investment centers.
- Return on investment (ROI)
- Responsibility report
- Judgmental factors in ROI
- Improving ROI

DO IT! **4** Performance Evaluation

Go to the **REVIEW AND PRACTICE** section at the end of the chapter for a review of key concepts and practice applications with solutions.

Visit **WileyPLUS with ORION** for additional tutorials and practice opportunities.

LEARNING OBJECTIVE ● 1

Describe budgetary control and static budget reports.

Budgetary Control

One of management's functions is to control company operations. Control consists of the steps taken by management to see that planned objectives are met. We now ask: How do budgets contribute to control of operations?

The use of budgets in controlling operations is known as **budgetary control**. Such control takes place by means of **budget reports** that compare actual results with planned objectives. The use of budget reports is based on the belief that planned objectives lose much of their potential value without some monitoring of progress along the way. Just as your professors give midterm exams to evaluate your progress, top management requires periodic reports on the progress of department managers toward their planned objectives.

Budget reports provide management with feedback on operations. The feedback for a crucial objective, such as having enough cash on hand to pay bills, may be made daily. For other objectives, such as meeting budgeted annual sales and operating expenses, monthly budget reports may suffice. Budget reports are prepared as frequently as needed. From these reports, management analyzes any differences between actual and planned results and determines their causes. Management then takes corrective action, or it decides to modify future plans. Budgetary control involves the activities shown in Illustration 24-1.

Illustration 24-1
Budgetary control activities

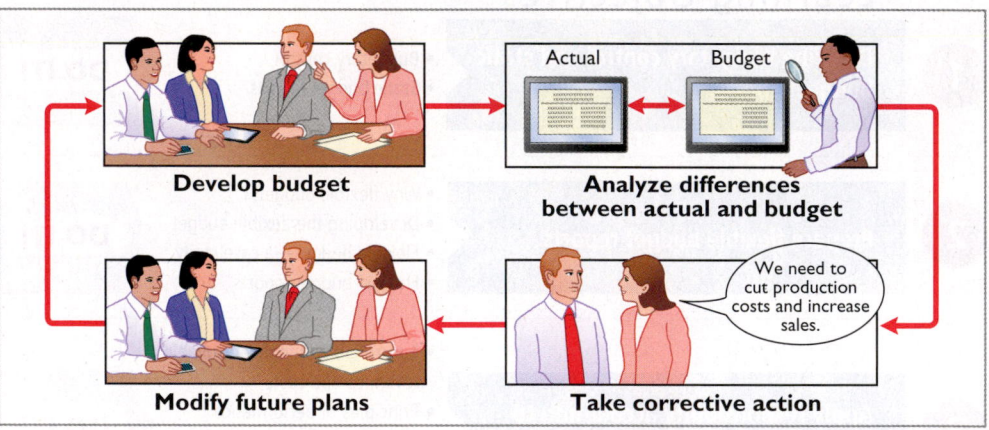

Budgetary control works best when a company has a formalized reporting system. The system does the following:

1. Identifies the name of the budget report, such as the sales budget or the manufacturing overhead budget.
2. States the frequency of the report, such as weekly or monthly.
3. Specifies the purpose of the report.
4. Indicates the primary recipient(s) of the report.

Illustration 24-2 provides a partial budgetary control system for a manufacturing company. Note the frequency of the reports and their emphasis on control. For example, there is a daily report on scrap and a weekly report on labor.

Name of Report	Frequency	Purpose	Primary Recipient(s)
Sales	Weekly	Determine whether sales goals are met	Top management and sales manager
Labor	Weekly	Control direct and indirect labor costs	Vice president of production and production department managers
Scrap	Daily	Determine efficient use of materials	Production manager
Departmental overhead costs	Monthly	Control overhead costs	Department manager
Selling expenses	Monthly	Control selling expenses	Sales manager
Income statement	Monthly and quarterly	Determine whether income goals are met	Top management

Illustration 24-2
Budgetary control reporting system

Static Budget Reports

You learned in Chapter 23 that the master budget formalizes management's planned objectives for the coming year. When used in budgetary control, each budget included in the master budget is considered to be static. A **static budget** is a projection of budget data **at one level of activity**. These budgets do not consider data for different levels of activity. As a result, companies always compare actual results with budget data at the activity level that was used in developing the master budget.

EXAMPLES

To illustrate the role of a static budget in budgetary control, we will use selected data prepared for Hayes Company in Chapter 23. Budget and actual sales data for the Rightride product in the first and second quarters of 2017 are as follows.

Sales	First Quarter	Second Quarter	Total
Budgeted	$180,000	$210,000	$390,000
Actual	179,000	199,500	378,500
Difference	$ 1,000	$ 10,500	$ 11,500

Illustration 24-3
Budget and actual sales data

The sales budget report for Hayes' first quarter is shown below. The right-most column reports the difference between the budgeted and actual amounts.

Illustration 24-4
Sales budget report—first quarter

Hayes Company Sales Budget Report.xls

	A	B	C	D
1		HAYES COMPANY		
2		Sales Budget Report		
3		For the Quarter Ended March 31, 2017		
4				Difference
5				Favorable F
6	Product Line	Budget	Actual	Unfavorable U
7	Rightride[a]	$180,000	$179,000	**$1,000 U**
8				
9	[a]In practice, each product line would be included in the report.			

The report shows that sales are $1,000 under budget—an unfavorable result. This difference is less than 1% of budgeted sales ($1,000 ÷ $180,000 = .0056). Top management's reaction to unfavorable differences is often influenced by the materiality (significance) of the difference. Since the difference of $1,000 is immaterial in this case, we assume that Hayes management takes no specific corrective action.

Alternative Terminology
The difference between budget and actual is sometimes called a *budget variance*.

Illustration 24-5 shows the budget report for the second quarter. It contains one new feature: cumulative year-to-date information. This report indicates that sales for the second quarter are $10,500 below budget. This is 5% of budgeted sales ($10,500 ÷ $210,000). Top management may now conclude that the difference between budgeted and actual sales requires investigation.

	Hayes Company Sales Budget Report.xls						
Home	Insert	Page Layout	Formulas	Data	Review	View	
P18		fx					
	A	B	C	D E	F	G	H

Product Line	Budget	Actual	Second Quarter — Difference Favorable F Unfavorable U	Budget	Actual	Year-to-Date — Difference Favorable F Unfavorable U
			HAYES COMPANY Sales Budget Report For the Quarter Ended June 30, 2017			
Rightride	$210,000	$199,500	$10,500 U	$390,000	$378,500	$11,500 U

Illustration 24-5
Sales budget report—second quarter

Management's analysis should start by asking the sales manager the cause(s) of the shortfall. Managers should consider the need for corrective action. For example, management may decide to spur sales by offering sales incentives to customers or by increasing the advertising of Rightrides. Or, if management concludes that a downturn in the economy is responsible for the lower sales, it may modify planned sales and profit goals for the remainder of the year.

USES AND LIMITATIONS

From these examples, you can see that a master sales budget is useful in evaluating the performance of a sales manager. It is now necessary to ask: Is the master budget appropriate for evaluating a manager's performance in controlling costs? Recall that in a static budget, data are not modified or adjusted, regardless of changes in activity. It follows, then, that a static budget is appropriate in evaluating a manager's effectiveness in controlling costs when:

1. The actual level of activity closely approximates the master budget activity level, and/or

2. The behavior of the costs in response to changes in activity is fixed.

A static budget report is, therefore, appropriate for **fixed manufacturing costs** and for **fixed selling and administrative expenses**. But, as you will see shortly, static budget reports may not be a proper basis for evaluating a manager's performance in controlling variable costs.

Static budgets report a single level of activity

Costs / Units

DO IT! 1 Static Budget Reports

Lawler Company expects to produce 5,000 units of product CV93 during the current month. Budgeted variable manufacturing costs per unit are direct materials $6, direct labor $15, and overhead $24. Monthly budgeted fixed manufacturing overhead costs are $10,000 for depreciation and $5,000 for supervision.

In the current month, Lawler actually produced 5,500 units and incurred the following costs: direct materials $33,900, direct labor $74,200, variable overhead $120,500, depreciation $10,000, and supervision $5,000.

Prepare a static budget report. (*Hint:* The Budget column is based on estimated production of 5,000 units while the Actual column is the actual costs incurred during the period.) Were costs controlled? Discuss limitations of this budget.

Solution

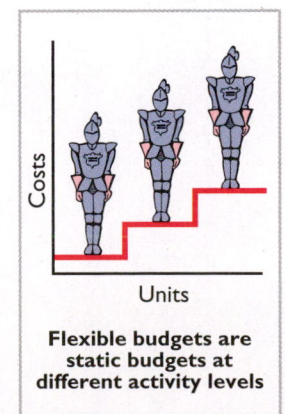

	Lawler Company.xls		
	Home Insert Page Layout Formulas Data Review View		
	P18	fx	
	A	B	C	D	
1				Difference	
2				Favorable - F	
3		Budget	Actual	Unfavorable - U	
4	Production in units	5,000	5,500		
5					
6	Variable costs				
7	Direct materials ($6)	$ 30,000	$ 33,900	$3,900	U
8	Direct labor ($15)	75,000	74,200	800	F
9	Overhead ($24)	120,000	120,500	500	U
10	Total variable costs	225,000	228,600	3,600	U
11					
12	Fixed costs				
13	Depreciation	10,000	10,000	0	
14	Supervision	5,000	5,000	0	
15	Total fixed costs	15,000	15,000	0	
16	Total costs	$240,000	$243,600	$3,600	U
17					
18					

The static budget indicates that actual variable costs exceeded budgeted amounts by $3,600. Fixed costs were exactly as budgeted. The static budget gives the impression that the company did not control its variable costs. However, the static budget does not give consideration to the fact that the company produced 500 more units than planned. As a result, the static budget is not a good tool to evaluate variable costs. It is, however, a good tool to evaluate fixed costs as those should not vary with changes in production volume.

Related exercise material: **BE24-1, BE24-2, E24-1, E24-2, and DO IT! 24-1.**

LEARNING OBJECTIVE **2** **Prepare flexible budget reports.**

In contrast to a static budget, which is based on one level of activity, a **flexible budget** projects budget data for various levels of activity. In essence, **the flexible budget is a series of static budgets at different levels of activity**. The flexible budget recognizes that the budgetary process is more useful if it is adaptable to changed operating conditions.

Flexible budgets can be prepared for each of the types of budgets included in the master budget. For example, **Marriott Hotels** can budget revenues and net income on the basis of 60%, 80%, and 100% of room occupancy. Similarly, **American Van Lines** can budget its operating expenses on the basis of various levels of truck-miles driven. **Duke Energy** can budget revenue and net income on the basis of estimated billions of kwh (kilowatt hours) of residential, commercial, and industrial electricity generated. In the following pages, we will illustrate a flexible budget for manufacturing overhead.

Why Flexible Budgets?

Assume that you are the manager in charge of manufacturing overhead in the Assembly Department of Barton Robotics. In preparing the manufacturing

Flexible budgets are static budgets at different activity levels

overhead budget for 2017, you prepare the following static budget based on a production volume of 10,000 units of robotic controls.

Illustration 24-6
Static overhead budget

BARTON ROBOTICS
Manufacturing Overhead Budget (Static)
Assembly Department
For the Year Ended December 31, 2017

Budgeted production in units (robotic controls)	10,000
Budgeted costs	
Indirect materials	$ 250,000
Indirect labor	260,000
Utilities	190,000
Depreciation	280,000
Property taxes	70,000
Supervision	50,000
	$1,100,000

Helpful Hint
The master budget described in Chapter 23 is based on a static budget.

Fortunately for the company, the demand for robotic controls has increased, and Barton produces and sells 12,000 units during the year rather than 10,000. You are elated! Increased sales means increased profitability, which should mean a bonus or a raise for you and the employees in your department. Unfortunately, a comparison of Assembly Department actual and budgeted costs has put you on the spot. The budget report is shown below.

Illustration 24-7
Overhead static budget report

BARTON ROBOTICS
Manufacturing Overhead Static Budget Report
For the Year Ended December 31, 2017

	Budget	Actual	Difference Favorable - F Unfavorable - U	
Production in units	10,000	12,000		
Costs				
Indirect materials	$ 250,000	$ 295,000	$ 45,000	U
Indirect labor	260,000	312,000	52,000	U
Utilities	190,000	225,000	35,000	U
Depreciation	280,000	280,000	0	
Property taxes	70,000	70,000	0	
Supervision	50,000	50,000	0	
	$1,100,000	$1,232,000	$132,000	U

This comparison uses budget data based on the original activity level (10,000 robotic controls). It indicates that the Assembly Department is significantly **over budget** for three of the six overhead costs. There is a total unfavorable difference of $132,000, which is 12% over budget ($132,000 ÷ $1,100,000). Your supervisor is very unhappy. Instead of sharing in the company's success, you may find yourself looking for another job. What went wrong?

When you calm down and carefully examine the manufacturing overhead budget, you identify the problem: The budget data are not relevant! At the time the budget was developed, the company anticipated that only 10,000 units would be produced, **not** 12,000. Comparing actual with budgeted variable costs is meaningless. As production increases, the budget allowances for variable costs should increase proportionately. The variable costs in this example are indirect materials, indirect labor, and utilities.

Analyzing the budget data for these costs at 10,000 units, you arrive at the following per unit results.

Helpful Hint
A static budget is not useful for performance evaluation if a company has substantial variable costs.

Illustration 24-8
Variable costs per unit

Item	Total Cost	Per Unit
Indirect materials	$250,000	$25
Indirect labor	260,000	26
Utilities	190,000	19
	$700,000	$70

Illustration 24-9 calculates the budgeted variable costs at 12,000 units.

Illustration 24-9
Budgeted variable costs, 12,000 units

Item	Computation	Total
Indirect materials	$25 × 12,000	$300,000
Indirect labor	26 × 12,000	312,000
Utilities	19 × 12,000	228,000
		$840,000

Because fixed costs do not change in total as activity changes, the budgeted amounts for these costs remain the same. Illustration 24-10 shows the budget report based on the flexible budget for **12,000 units** of production. (Compare this with Illustration 24-7.)

Illustration 24-10
Overhead flexible budget report

	A	B	C	D	E
1			BARTON ROBOTICS		
2			Manufacturing Overhead Flexible Budget Report		
3			For the Year Ended December 31, 2017		
4				Difference	
5		Budget	Actual	Favorable - F Unfavorable - U	
6	Production in units	12,000	12,000		
7					
8	Variable costs				
9	Indirect materials ($25)	$ 300,000	$ 295,000	$5,000	F
10	Indirect labor ($26)	312,000	312,000	0	
11	Utilities ($19)	228,000	225,000	3,000	F
12	Total variable costs	840,000	832,000	8,000	F
13					
14	Fixed costs				
15	Depreciation	280,000	280,000	0	
16	Property taxes	70,000	70,000	0	
17	Supervision	50,000	50,000	0	
18	Total fixed costs	400,000	400,000	0	
19	Total costs	$1,240,000	$1,232,000	$8,000	F
20					

This report indicates that the Assembly Department's costs are **under budget**—a favorable difference. Instead of worrying about being fired, you may be in line for a bonus or a raise after all! As this analysis shows, the only appropriate comparison is between actual costs at 12,000 units of production and budgeted costs at 12,000 units. Flexible budget reports provide this comparison.

Developing the Flexible Budget

The flexible budget uses the master budget as its basis. To develop the flexible budget, management uses the following steps.

1. Identify the activity index and the relevant range of activity.
2. Identify the variable costs, and determine the budgeted variable cost per unit of activity for each cost.
3. Identify the fixed costs, and determine the budgeted amount for each cost.
4. Prepare the budget for selected increments of activity within the relevant range.

The activity index chosen should significantly influence the costs being budgeted. For manufacturing overhead costs, for example, the activity index is usually the same as the index used in developing the predetermined overhead rate—that is, direct labor hours or machine hours. For selling and administrative expenses, the activity index usually is sales or net sales.

The choice of the increment of activity is largely a matter of judgment. For example, if the relevant range is 8,000 to 12,000 direct labor hours, increments of 1,000 hours may be selected. The flexible budget is then prepared for each increment within the relevant range.

Service Company Insight NBCUniversal

Fox BroadcastingCompany/
Album/Newscom

Just What the Doctor Ordered?

Nobody is immune from the effects of declining revenues—not even movie stars. When the number of viewers of the television show "House," a medical drama, declined by almost 20%, Fox Broadcasting said it wanted to cut the license fee that it paid to NBCUniversal by 20%. What would NBCUniversal do

in response? It might cut the size of the show's cast, which would reduce the payroll costs associated with the show. Or, it could reduce the number of episodes that take advantage of the full cast. Alternatively, it might threaten to quit providing the show to Fox altogether and instead present the show on its own NBC-affiliated channels.

Source: Sam Schechner, "Media Business Shorts: NBCU, Fox Taking Scalpel to 'House'," *Wall Street Journal Online* (April 17, 2011).

Explain how the use of flexible budgets might help to identify the best solution to this problem. (Go to **WileyPLUS** for this answer and additional questions.)

Flexible Budget—A Case Study

To illustrate the flexible budget, we use Fox Company. Fox's management uses a **flexible budget for monthly comparisons** of actual and budgeted manufacturing overhead costs of the Finishing Department. The master budget for the year ending December 31, 2017, shows expected **annual** operating capacity of 120,000 direct labor hours and the following overhead costs.

Illustration 24-11
Master budget data

Variable Costs		Fixed Costs	
Indirect materials	$180,000	Depreciation	$180,000
Indirect labor	240,000	Supervision	120,000
Utilities	60,000	Property taxes	60,000
Total	$480,000	Total	$360,000

The four steps for developing the flexible budget are applied as follows.

STEP 1. Identify the activity index and the relevant range of activity. The activity index is direct labor hours. The relevant range is 8,000–12,000 direct labor hours per **month**.

STEP 2. Identify the variable costs, and determine the budgeted variable cost per unit of activity for each cost. There are three variable costs. The variable cost per unit is found by dividing each total budgeted cost by the direct labor hours used in preparing the annual master budget (120,000 hours). Illustration 24-12 shows the computations for Fox Company.

Illustration 24-12
Computation of variable cost per direct labor hour

Variable Costs	Computation	Variable Cost per Direct Labor Hour
Indirect materials	$180,000 ÷ 120,000	**$1.50**
Indirect labor	$240,000 ÷ 120,000	2.00
Utilities	$ 60,000 ÷ 120,000	0.50
Total		**$4.00**

STEP 3. Identify the fixed costs, and determine the budgeted amount for each cost. There are three fixed costs. Since Fox desires **monthly budget data**, it divides each annual budgeted cost by 12 to find the monthly amounts. Therefore, the monthly budgeted fixed costs are depreciation $15,000, supervision $10,000, and property taxes $5,000.

STEP 4. Prepare the budget for selected increments of activity within the relevant range. Management prepares the budget in increments of 1,000 direct labor hours.

Illustration 24-13 shows Fox's flexible budget.

Illustration 24-13
Monthly overhead flexible budget

	Fox Company.xls				
	Home Insert Page Layout Formulas Data Review View				
	P18 fx				
	A	B	C	D	E	F

	A	B	C	D	E	F
1		FOX COMPANY				
2		Monthly Manufacturing Overhead Flexible Budget				
3		Finishing Department				
4		For Months During the Year 2017				
5	Activity level					
6	Direct labor hours	8,000	9,000	10,000	11,000	12,000
7	Variable costs					
8	Indirect materials ($1.50)ᵃ	$12,000ᵇ	$13,500	$15,000	$16,500	$18,000
9	Indirect labor ($2.00)ᵃ	16,000ᶜ	18,000	20,000	22,000	24,000
10	Utilities ($0.50)ᵃ	4,000ᵈ	4,500	5,000	5,500	6,000
11	Total variable costs	32,000	36,000	40,000	44,000	48,000
12	Fixed costs					
13	Depreciation	15,000	15,000	15,000	15,000	15,000
14	Supervision	10,000	10,000	10,000	10,000	10,000
15	Property taxes	5,000	5,000	5,000	5,000	5,000
16	Total fixed costs	30,000	30,000	30,000	30,000	30,000
17	Total costs	$62,000	$66,000	$70,000	$74,000	$78,000
18						
19	ᵃCost per direct labor hour; ᵇ8,000 x $1.50; ᶜ8,000 x $2.00; ᵈ8,000 x $0.50					

Fox uses the formula below to determine total budgeted costs at any level of activity.

Illustration 24-14
Formula for total budgeted costs

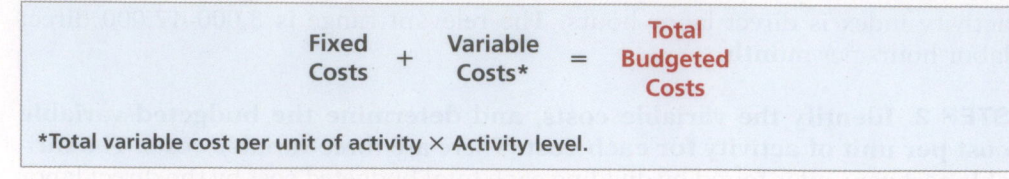

*Total variable cost per unit of activity × Activity level.

Helpful Hint
Using the data given for Fox, the amount of total costs to be budgeted for 10,600 direct labor hours would be $30,000 fixed + $42,400 variable (10,600 × $4) = $72,400 total.

For Fox, fixed costs are $30,000, and total variable cost per direct labor hour is $4 ($1.50 + $2.00 + $0.50). At 9,000 direct labor hours, total budgeted costs are $66,000 [$30,000 + ($4 × 9,000)]. At 8,622 direct labor hours, total budgeted costs are $64,488 [$30,000 + ($4 × 8,622)].

Total budgeted costs can also be shown graphically, as in Illustration 24-15. In the graph, the horizontal axis represents the activity index, and costs are indicated on the vertical axis. The graph highlights two activity levels (10,000 and 12,000). As shown, total budgeted costs at these activity levels are $70,000 [$30,000 + ($4 × 10,000)] and $78,000 [$30,000 + ($4 × 12,000)], respectively.

Illustration 24-15
Graphic flexible budget data highlighting 10,000 and 12,000 activity levels

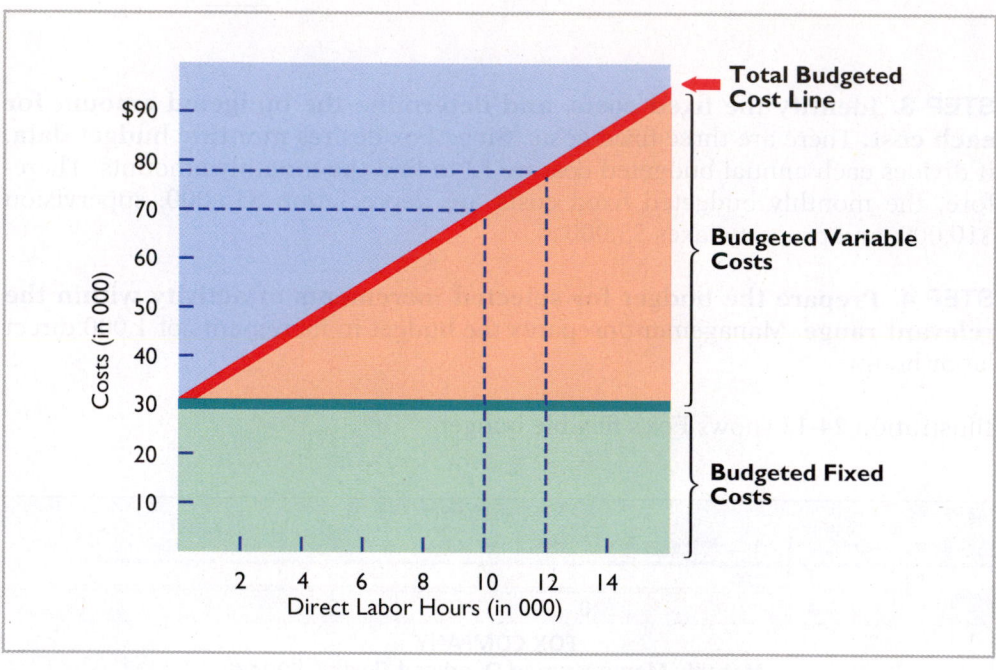

Flexible Budget Reports

Flexible budget reports are another type of internal report. The flexible budget report consists of two sections: (1) production data for a selected activity index, such as direct labor hours, and (2) cost data for variable and fixed costs. The report provides a basis for evaluating a manager's performance in two areas: production control and cost control. Flexible budget reports are widely used in production and service departments.

Illustration 24-16 shows a budget report for the Finishing Department of Fox Company for the month of January. In this month, 9,000 hours are worked. The budget data are therefore based on the flexible budget for 9,000 hours in Illustration 24-13 (page 1115). The actual cost data are assumed.

How appropriate is this report in evaluating the Finishing Department manager's performance in controlling overhead costs? The report clearly provides a reliable basis. Both actual and budget costs are based on the activity level worked during January. Since variable costs generally are incurred directly by the department, the difference between the budget allowance for those hours and the actual costs is the responsibility of the department manager.

Illustration 24-16
Overhead flexible budget report

			Fox Company.xls	
Home	Insert	Page Layout	Formulas	Data	Review	View
	P18		*fx*		

	A	B	C	D	E
1		FOX COMPANY			
2		Manufacturing Overhead Flexible Budget Report			
3		Finishing Department			
4		For the Month Ended January 31, 2017			
5				Difference	
6		Budget at	Actual costs at	Favorable - F	
7	Direct labor hours (DLH)	9,000 DLH	9,000 DLH	Unfavorable - U	
8					
9	Variable costs				
10	Indirect materials ($1.50)[a]	$13,500	$14,000	$ 500	U
11	Indirect labor ($2.00)[a]	18,000	17,000	1,000	F
12	Utilities ($0.50)[a]	4,500	4,600	100	U
13	Total variable costs	36,000	35,600	400	F
14					
15	Fixed costs				
16	Depreciation	15,000	15,000	0	
17	Supervision	10,000	10,000	0	
18	Property taxes	5,000	5,000	0	
19	Total fixed costs	30,000	30,000	0	
20	Total costs	$66,000	$65,600	$ 400	F
21					
22	[a]Cost per direct labor hour				

In subsequent months, Fox Company will prepare other flexible budget reports. For each month, the budget data are based on the actual activity level attained. In February that level may be 11,000 direct labor hours, in July 10,000, and so on.

Note that this flexible budget is based on a single cost driver. A more accurate budget often can be developed using the activity-based costing concepts explained in Chapter 18.

Service Company Insight | San Diego Zoo

Eric Isselée/iStockphoto

Budgets and the Exotic Newcastle Disease

Exotic Newcastle Disease, one of the most infectious bird diseases in the world, kills so swiftly that many victims die before any symptoms appear. When it broke out in Southern California, it could have spelled disaster for the San Diego Zoo. "We have one of the most valuable collections of birds in the world, if not *the* most valuable," says Paula Brock, CFO of the Zoological Society of San Diego, which operates the zoo.

Bird exhibits were closed to the public for several months (the disease, which is harmless to humans, can be carried on clothes and shoes). The tires of arriving delivery trucks were sanitized, as were the shoes of anyone visiting the zoo's nonpublic areas. Zookeeper uniforms had to be changed and cleaned daily. And ultimately, the zoo, with $150 million in revenues, spent almost half a million dollars on quarantine measures.

It worked: No birds got sick. Better yet, the damage to the rest of the zoo's budget was minimized by another protective measure: the monthly budget reforecast. "When we get a hit like this, we still have to find a way to make our bottom line," says Brock. Thanks to a new planning process Brock had introduced a year earlier, the zoo's scientists were able to raise the financial alarm as they redirected resources to ward off the disease. "Because we had timely awareness," she says, "we were able to make adjustments to weather the storm."

Source: Tim Reason, "Budgeting in the Real World," *CFO Magazine* (July 12, 2005), *www.cfodirect.com/cfopublic.nsf/vContentPrint/ 649A82C8FF8AB06B85257037004* (accessed July 2005).

*What is the major benefit of tying a budget to the overall goals of the company? (Go to **WileyPLUS** for this answer and additional questions.)*

DO IT! 2 — Flexible Budgets

In Strassel Company's flexible budget graph, the fixed cost line and the total budgeted cost line intersect the vertical axis at $36,000. The total budgeted cost line is $186,000 at an activity level of 50,000 direct labor hours. Compute total budgeted costs at 30,000 direct labor hours.

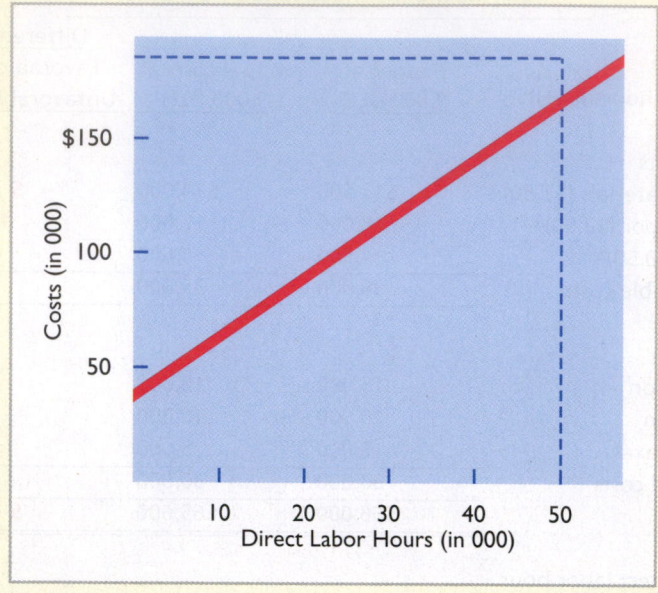

Action Plan

 Apply the formula: Fixed costs + Variable costs (Total variable cost per unit × Activity level) = Total budgeted costs.

Solution

Using the graph, fixed costs are $36,000, and variable costs are $3 per direct labor hour [($186,000 − $36,000) ÷ 50,000]. Thus, at 30,000 direct labor hours, total budgeted costs are $126,000 [$36,000 + ($3 × 30,000)].

Related exercise material: **BE24-4, E24-3, E24-5, and DO IT! 24-2.**

LEARNING OBJECTIVE 3

Apply responsibility accounting to cost and profit centers.

Like budgeting, responsibility accounting is an important part of management accounting. **Responsibility accounting** involves accumulating and reporting costs (and revenues, where relevant) on the basis of the manager who has the authority to make the day-to-day decisions about the items. Under responsibility accounting, a manager's performance is evaluated on matters directly under that manager's control. Responsibility accounting can be used at every level of management in which the following conditions exist.

1. Costs and revenues can be directly associated with the specific level of management responsibility.

2. The costs and revenues can be controlled by employees at the level of responsibility with which they are associated.

3. Budget data can be developed for evaluating the manager's effectiveness in controlling the costs and revenues.

Illustration 24-17 depicts levels of responsibility for controlling costs.

Under responsibility accounting, any individual who controls a specified set of activities can be a responsibility center. Thus, responsibility accounting may

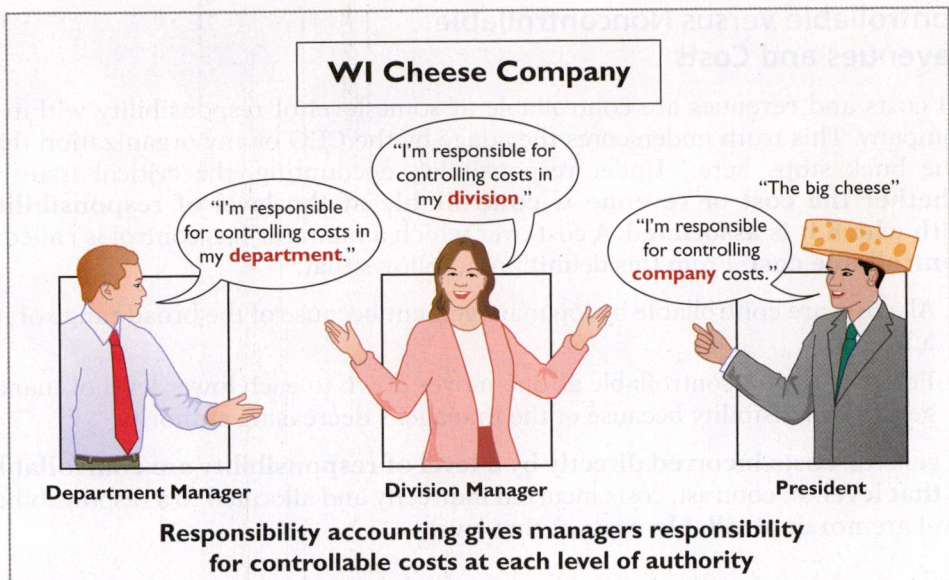

Illustration 24-17
Responsibility for controllable costs at varying levels of management

extend from the lowest level of control to the top strata of management. Once responsibility is established, the company first measures and reports the effectiveness of the individual's performance for the specified activity. It then reports that measure upward throughout the organization.

Responsibility accounting is especially valuable in a decentralized company. **Decentralization** means that the control of operations is delegated to many managers throughout the organization. The term **segment** is sometimes used to identify an area of responsibility in decentralized operations. Under responsibility accounting, companies prepare segment reports periodically, such as monthly, quarterly, and annually, to evaluate managers' performance.

Responsibility accounting is an essential part of any effective system of budgetary control. The reporting of costs and revenues under responsibility accounting differs from budgeting in two respects:

1. A distinction is made between controllable and noncontrollable items.

2. Performance reports either emphasize or include only items controllable by the individual manager.

Responsibility accounting applies to both profit and not-for-profit entities. For-profit entities seek to maximize net income. Not-for-profit entities wish to provide services as efficiently as possible.

Helpful Hint
All companies use responsibility accounting. Without some form of responsibility accounting, there would be chaos in discharging management's control function.

Management Insight | Procter & Gamble

Competition versus Collaboration

Khuong Hoang/iStockphoto

Many compensation and promotion programs encourage competition among employees for pay raises. To get ahead, you have to perform better than your fellow employees. While this may encourage hard work, it does not foster collaboration, and it can lead to distrust and disloyalty. Such negative effects have led some companies to believe that cooperation and collaboration, not competition, are essential in order to succeed in today's work environment.

As a consequence, many companies now explicitly include measures of collaboration in their performance measures. For example, Procter & Gamble measures collaboration in employees' annual performance reviews. At Cisco Systems, the assessment of an employee's teamwork can affect the annual bonus by as much as 20%.

Source: Carol Hymowitz, "Rewarding Competitors Over Collaboration No Longer Makes Sense," *Wall Street Journal* (February 13, 2006).

How might managers of separate divisions be able to reduce division costs through collaboration? (Go to **WileyPLUS** for this answer and additional questions.)

Controllable versus Noncontrollable Revenues and Costs

All costs and revenues are controllable at some level of responsibility within a company. This truth underscores the adage by the CEO of any organization that "the buck stops here." Under responsibility accounting, the critical issue is **whether the cost or revenue is controllable at the level of responsibility with which it is associated**. A cost over which a manager has control is called a **controllable cost**. From this definition, it follows that:

1. All costs are controllable by top management because of the broad range of its authority.
2. Fewer costs are controllable as one moves down to each lower level of managerial responsibility because of the manager's decreasing authority.

In general, **costs incurred directly by a level of responsibility are controllable at that level**. In contrast, costs incurred indirectly and allocated to a responsibility level are **noncontrollable costs** at that level.

Principles of Performance Evaluation

Performance evaluation is at the center of responsibility accounting. It is a management function that compares actual results with budget goals. It involves both behavioral and reporting principles.

MANAGEMENT BY EXCEPTION

Management by exception means that top management's review of a budget report is focused either entirely or primarily on differences between actual results and planned objectives. This approach enables top management to focus on problem areas. For example, many companies now use online reporting systems for employees to file their travel and entertainment expense reports. In addition to cutting reporting time in half, the online system enables managers to quickly analyze variances from travel budgets. This cuts down on expense account "padding" such as spending too much on meals or falsifying documents for costs that were never actually incurred.

Management by exception does not mean that top management will investigate every difference. For this approach to be effective, there must be guidelines for identifying an exception. The usual criteria are materiality and controllability.

MATERIALITY Without quantitative guidelines, management would have to investigate every budget difference regardless of the amount. Materiality is usually expressed as a percentage difference from budget. For example, management may set the percentage difference at 5% for important items and 10% for other items. Managers will investigate all differences either over or under budget by the specified percentage. Costs over budget warrant investigation to determine why they were not controlled. Likewise, costs under budget merit investigation to determine whether costs critical to profitability are being curtailed. For example, if maintenance costs are budgeted at $80,000 but only $40,000 is spent, major unexpected breakdowns in productive facilities may occur in the future. Alternatively, as discussed earlier, cost might be under budget due to budgetary slack.

Alternatively, a company may specify a single percentage difference from budget for all items and supplement this guideline with a minimum dollar limit. For example, the exception criteria may be stated at 5% of budget or more than $10,000.

CONTROLLABILITY OF THE ITEM Exception guidelines are more restrictive for controllable items than for items the manager cannot control. In fact, there may be no guidelines for noncontrollable items. For example, a large unfavorable difference between actual and budgeted property tax expense may not be flagged for investigation because the only possible causes are an unexpected increase in the tax rate or in the assessed value of the property. An investigation into the difference would be useless: The manager cannot control either cause.

BEHAVIORAL PRINCIPLES

The human factor is critical in evaluating performance. Behavioral principles include the following.

1. **Managers of responsibility centers should have direct input into the process of establishing budget goals of their area of responsibility.** Without such input, managers may view the goals as unrealistic or arbitrarily set by top management. Such views adversely affect the managers' motivation to meet the targeted objectives.

2. **The evaluation of performance should be based entirely on matters that are controllable by the manager being evaluated.** Criticism of a manager on matters outside his or her control reduces the effectiveness of the evaluation process. It leads to negative reactions by a manager and to doubts about the fairness of the company's evaluation policies.

3. **Top management should support the evaluation process.** As explained earlier, the evaluation process begins at the lowest level of responsibility and extends upward to the highest level of management. Managers quickly lose faith in the process when top management ignores, overrules, or bypasses established procedures for evaluating a manager's performance.

4. **The evaluation process must allow managers to respond to their evaluations.** Evaluation is not a one-way street. Managers should have the opportunity to defend their performance. Evaluation without feedback is both impersonal and ineffective.

5. **The evaluation should identify both good and poor performance.** Praise for good performance is a powerful motivating factor for a manager. This is especially true when a manager's compensation includes rewards for meeting budget goals.

REPORTING PRINCIPLES

Performance evaluation under responsibility accounting should be based on certain reporting principles. These principles pertain primarily to the internal reports that provide the basis for evaluating performance. Performance reports should:

1. Contain only data that are controllable by the manager of the responsibility center.

2. Provide accurate and reliable budget data to measure performance.

3. Highlight significant differences between actual results and budget goals.

4. Be tailor-made for the intended evaluation.

5. Be prepared at reasonable time intervals.

In recent years, companies have come under increasing pressure from influential shareholder groups to do a better job of linking executive pay to corporate performance. For example, software maker **Siebel Systems** unveiled a new incentive plan after lengthy discussions with the California Public Employees' Retirement System. One unique feature of the plan is that managers' targets will be publicly disclosed at the beginning of each year for investors to evaluate.

Management Insight   Honda

Kyodo/©AP/Wide World Photos

Flexible Manufacturing Requires Flexible Accounting

Flexible budgeting is useful because it enables managers to evaluate performance in light of changing conditions. But the ability to react quickly to changing conditions is even more important. Among automobile manufacturing facilities in the U.S., few plants are more flexible than Honda.

The manufacturing facilities of some auto companies can make slight alterations to the features of a vehicle in response to changes in demand for particular features. But for most plants, to switch from production of one type of vehicle to a completely different one typically takes months and costs hundreds of millions of dollars. At the Honda plant, however, the switch takes minutes. For example, it takes about five minutes to install different hand-like parts on the robots so they can switch from making Civic compacts to the longer, taller CR-V crossover. This ability to adjust quickly to changing demand gave Honda a huge advantage when gas prices surged and demand for more fuel-efficient cars increased quickly.

Source: Kate Linebaugh, "Honda's Flexible Plants Provide Edge," *Wall Street Journal Online* (September 23, 2008).

> What implications do these improvements in production capabilities have for management accounting information and performance evaluation within the organization? (Go to **WileyPLUS** for this answer and additional questions.)

Responsibility Reporting System

A **responsibility reporting system** involves the preparation of a report for each level of responsibility in the company's organization chart. To illustrate such a system, we use the partial organization chart and production departments of Francis Chair Company in Illustration 24-18.

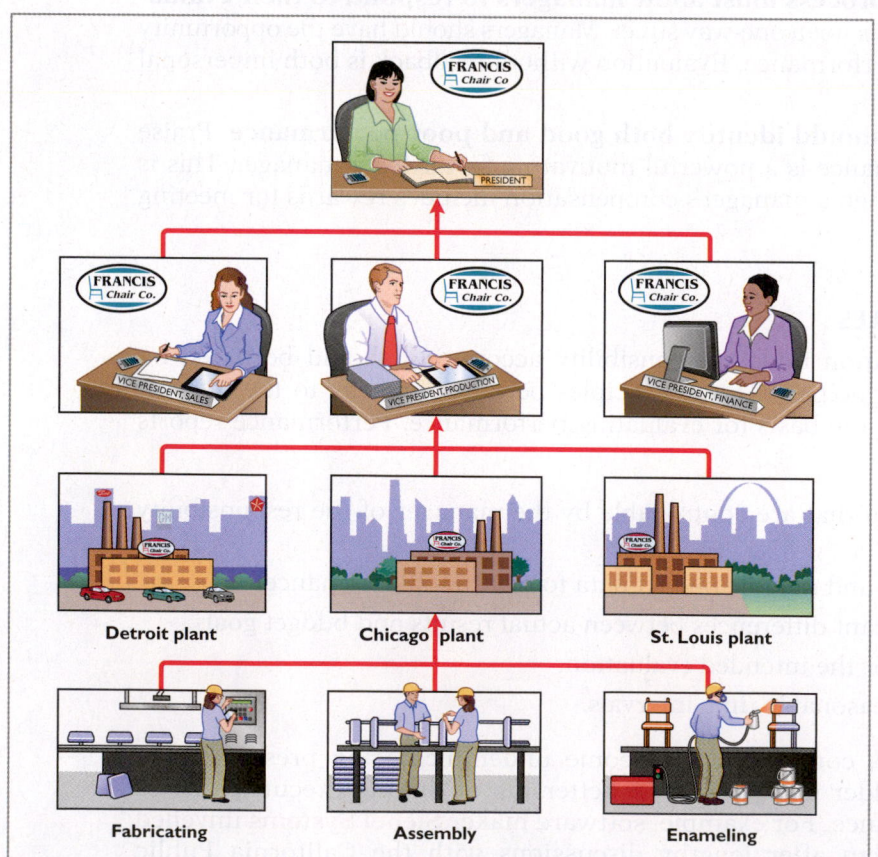

Report A
President sees summary data of vice presidents.

Report B
Vice president sees summary of controllable costs in his/her functional area.

Report C
Plant manager sees summary of controllable costs for each department in the plant.

Report D
Department manager sees controllable costs of his/her department.

Illustration 24-18
Partial organization chart

The responsibility reporting system begins with the lowest level of responsibility for controlling costs and moves upward to each higher level. Illustration 24-19 details the connections between levels.

Illustration 24-19
Responsibility reporting system

Report A
President sees summary data of vice presidents.

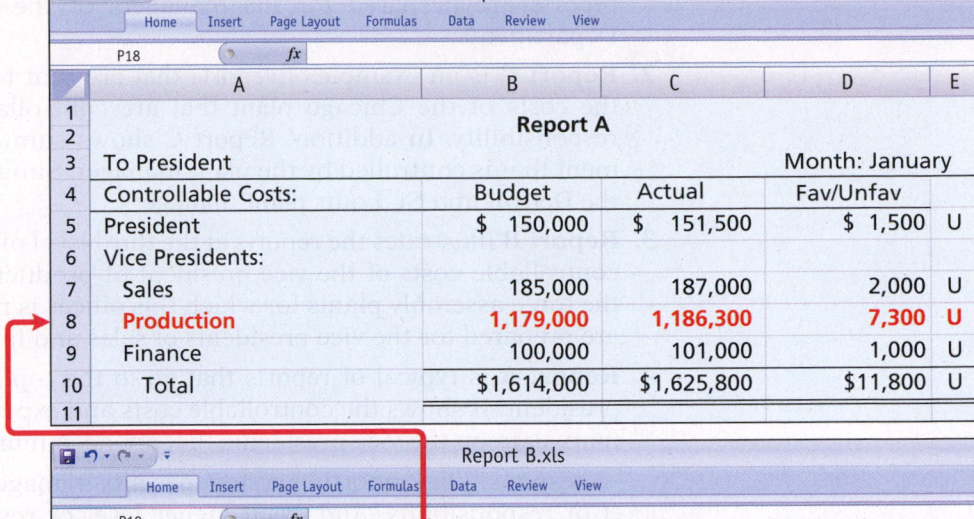

Report A.xls				
Report A				
To President			Month: January	
Controllable Costs:	Budget	Actual	Fav/Unfav	
President	$ 150,000	$ 151,500	$ 1,500	U
Vice Presidents:				
Sales	185,000	187,000	2,000	U
Production	**1,179,000**	**1,186,300**	**7,300**	**U**
Finance	100,000	101,000	1,000	U
Total	$1,614,000	$1,625,800	$11,800	U

Report B
Vice president sees summary of controllable costs in his/her functional area.

Report B.xls				
Report B				
To Vice President Production			Month: January	
Controllable Costs:	Budget	Actual	Fav/Unfav	
VP Production	$ 125,000	$ 126,000	$ 1,000	U
Assembly Plants:				
Detroit	420,000	418,000	2,000	F
Chicago	**304,000**	**309,300**	**5,300**	**U**
St. Louis	330,000	333,000	3,000	U
Total	$1,179,000	$1,186,300	$ 7,300	U

Report C
Plant manager sees summary of controllable costs for each department in the plant.

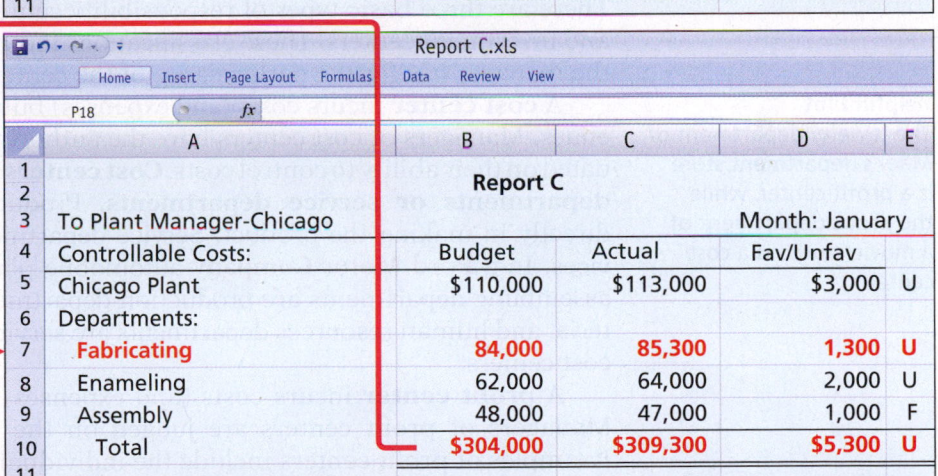

Report C.xls				
Report C				
To Plant Manager-Chicago			Month: January	
Controllable Costs:	Budget	Actual	Fav/Unfav	
Chicago Plant	$110,000	$113,000	$3,000	U
Departments:				
Fabricating	**84,000**	**85,300**	**1,300**	**U**
Enameling	62,000	64,000	2,000	U
Assembly	48,000	47,000	1,000	F
Total	$304,000	$309,300	$5,300	U

Report D
Department manager sees controllable costs of his/her department.

Report D.xls				
Report D				
To Fabricating Dept. Manager			Month: January	
Controllable Costs:	Budget	Actual	Fav/Unfav	
Direct Materials	$20,000	$20,500	$ 500	U
Direct Labor	40,000	41,000	1,000	U
Overhead	24,000	23,800	200	F
Total	$84,000	$85,300	$1,300	U

A brief description of the four reports for Francis Chair is as follows.

1. **Report D** is typical of reports that go to department managers. Similar reports are prepared for the managers of the Assembly and Enameling Departments.

2. **Report C** is an example of reports that are sent to plant managers. It shows the costs of the Chicago plant that are controllable at the second level of responsibility. In addition, Report C shows summary data for each department that is controlled by the plant manager. Similar reports are prepared for the Detroit and St. Louis plant managers.

3. **Report B** illustrates the reports at the third level of responsibility. It shows the controllable costs of the vice president of production and summary data on the three assembly plants for which this officer is responsible. Similar reports are prepared for the vice presidents of sales and finance.

4. **Report A** is typical of reports that go to the top level of responsibility—the president. It shows the controllable costs and expenses of this office and summary data on the vice presidents that are accountable to the president.

A responsibility reporting system permits management by exception at each level of responsibility. And, each higher level of responsibility can obtain the detailed report for each lower level of responsibility. For example, the vice president of production in Francis Chair may request the Chicago plant manager's report because this plant is $5,300 over budget.

This type of reporting system also permits comparative evaluations. In Illustration 24-19, the Chicago plant manager can easily rank the department managers' effectiveness in controlling manufacturing costs. Comparative rankings provide further incentive for a manager to control costs.

Types of Responsibility Centers

There are three basic types of responsibility centers: cost centers, profit centers, and investment centers. These classifications indicate the degree of responsibility the manager has for the performance of the center.

Helpful Hint
The jewelry department of Macy's department store is a profit center, while the props department of a movie studio is a cost center.

A **cost center** incurs costs (and expenses) but does not directly generate revenues. Managers of cost centers have the authority to incur costs. They are evaluated on their ability to control costs. **Cost centers are usually either production departments or service departments.** Production departments participate directly in making the product. Service departments provide only support services. In a **Ford Motor Company** automobile plant, the welding, painting, and assembling departments are production departments. Ford's maintenance, cafeteria, and human resources departments are service departments. All of them are cost centers.

A **profit center** incurs costs (and expenses) and also generates revenues. Managers of profit centers are judged on the profitability of their centers. Examples of profit centers include the individual departments of a retail store, such as clothing, furniture, and automotive products, and branch offices of banks.

Like a profit center, an **investment center** incurs costs (and expenses) and generates revenues. In addition, an investment center has control over decisions regarding the assets available for use. Investment center managers are evaluated on both the profitability of the center and the rate of return earned on the funds invested. Investment centers are often associated with subsidiary companies. Utility **Duke Energy** has operating divisions such as electric utility, energy trading, and natural gas. Investment center managers control or significantly influence investment decisions related to such matters as plant expansion and entry into new market areas. Illustration 24-20 depicts the three types of responsibility centers.

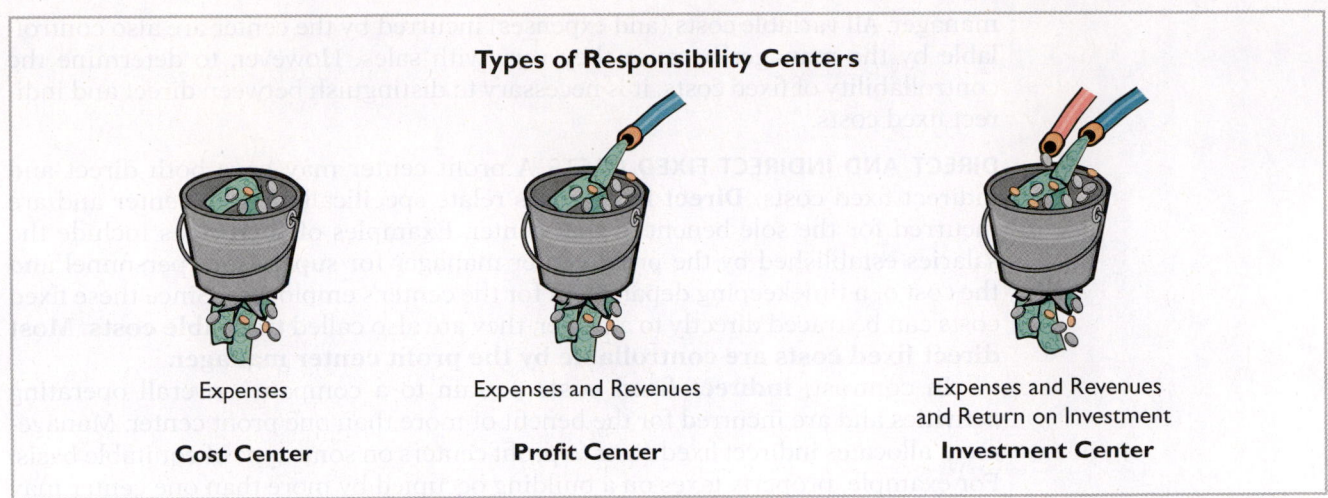

Types of Responsibility Centers

Expenses	Expenses and Revenues	Expenses and Revenues and Return on Investment
Cost Center	**Profit Center**	**Investment Center**

Illustration 24-20
Types of responsibility centers

RESPONSIBILITY ACCOUNTING FOR COST CENTERS

The evaluation of a manager's performance for cost centers is based on his or her ability to meet budgeted goals for controllable costs. **Responsibility reports for cost centers compare actual controllable costs with flexible budget data.**

Illustration 24-21 shows a responsibility report. The report is adapted from the flexible budget report for Fox Company in Illustration 24-16 (page 1117). It assumes that the Finishing Department manager is able to control all manufacturing overhead costs except depreciation, property taxes, and his own monthly salary of $6,000. The remaining $4,000 ($10,000 − $6,000) of supervision costs are assumed to apply to other supervisory personnel within the Finishing Department, whose salaries are controllable by the manager.

Illustration 24-21
Responsibility report for a cost center

Fox Company.xls

| Home | Insert | Page Layout | Formulas | Data | Review | View |

P18

	A	B	C	D	E
1		**FOX COMPANY**			
2		**Finishing Department**			
3		**Responsibility Report**			
4		**For the Month Ended January 31, 2017**			
5				Difference	
6	Controllable Costs	Budget	Actual	Favorable - F Unfavorable - U	
7	Indirect materials	$13,500	$14,000	$ 500	U
8	Indirect labor	18,000	17,000	$1,000	F
9	Utilities	4,500	4,600	100	U
10	**Supervision**	**4,000**	**4,000**	0	
11	Total	$40,000	$39,600	$ 400	F
12					

The report in Illustration 24-21 includes **only controllable costs**, and no distinction is made between variable and fixed costs. The responsibility report continues the concept of management by exception. In this case, top management may request an explanation of the $1,000 favorable difference in indirect labor and/or the $500 unfavorable difference in indirect materials.

RESPONSIBILITY ACCOUNTING FOR PROFIT CENTERS

To evaluate the performance of a profit center manager, upper management needs detailed information about both controllable revenues and controllable costs. The operating revenues earned by a profit center, such as sales, are controllable by the manager. All variable costs (and expenses) incurred by the center are also controllable by the manager because they vary with sales. However, to determine the controllability of fixed costs, it is necessary to distinguish between direct and indirect fixed costs.

DIRECT AND INDIRECT FIXED COSTS A profit center may have both direct and indirect fixed costs. **Direct fixed costs** relate specifically to one center and are incurred for the sole benefit of that center. Examples of such costs include the salaries established by the profit center manager for supervisory personnel and the cost of a timekeeping department for the center's employees. Since these fixed costs can be traced directly to a center, they are also called **traceable costs**. Most **direct fixed costs are controllable by the profit center manager.**

In contrast, **indirect fixed costs** pertain to a company's overall operating activities and are incurred for the benefit of more than one profit center. Management allocates indirect fixed costs to profit centers on some type of equitable basis. For example, property taxes on a building occupied by more than one center may be allocated on the basis of square feet of floor space used by each center. Or, the costs of a company's human resources department may be allocated to profit centers on the basis of the number of employees in each center. Because these fixed costs apply to more than one center, they are also called **common costs**. Most **indirect fixed costs are not controllable by the profit center manager.**

Helpful Hint

Recognize that we are emphasizing *financial* measures of performance. Companies are now making an effort to also stress *nonfinancial* performance measures such as product quality, labor productivity, market growth, materials' yield, manufacturing flexibility, and technological capability.

RESPONSIBILITY REPORT The responsibility report for a profit center shows budgeted and actual **controllable revenues and costs**. The report is prepared using the cost-volume-profit income statement explained in Chapter 19. In the report:

1. Controllable fixed costs are deducted from contribution margin.
2. The excess of contribution margin over controllable fixed costs is identified as **controllable margin**.
3. Noncontrollable fixed costs are not reported.

Illustration 24-22 shows the responsibility report for the manager of the Marine Division, a profit center of Mantle Company. For the year, the Marine Division also had $60,000 of indirect fixed costs that were not controllable by the profit center manager.

Illustration 24-22
Responsibility report for profit center

		Mantle Company.xls		
Home Insert Page Layout Formulas Data Review View				
P18 *fx*				
	A	B	C	D	E
1					
2		**MANTLE COMPANY**			
3		**Marine Division**			
		Responsibility Report			
4		**For the Year Ended December 31, 2017**			
5				Difference	
				Favorable - F	
6		Budget	Actual	Unfavorable - U	
7	Sales	$1,200,000	$1,150,000	$50,000	U
8	Variable costs				
9	Cost of goods sold	500,000	490,000	10,000	F
10	Selling and administrative	160,000	156,000	4,000	F
11	Total	660,000	646,000	14,000	F
12	Contribution margin	540,000	504,000	36,000	U
13	**Controllable fixed costs**				
14	Cost of goods sold	100,000	100,000	0	
15	Selling and administrative	80,000	80,000	0	
16	Total	180,000	180,000	0	
17	**Controllable margin**	**$ 360,000**	**$ 324,000**	**$36,000**	**U**
18					

Controllable margin is considered to be the best measure of the manager's performance **in controlling revenues and costs**. The report in Illustration 24-22 shows that the manager's performance was below budgeted expectations by 10% ($36,000 ÷ $360,000). Top management would likely investigate the causes of this unfavorable result. Note that the report does not show the Marine Division's noncontrollable fixed costs of $60,000. These costs would be included in a report on the profitability of the profit center.

Management also may choose to see **monthly** responsibility reports for profit centers. In addition, responsibility reports may include cumulative year-to-date results.

DO IT! 3   Profit Center Responsibility Report

Midwest Division operates as a profit center. It reports the following for the year:

	Budget	Actual
Sales	$1,500,000	$1,700,000
Variable costs	700,000	800,000
Controllable fixed costs	400,000	400,000
Noncontrollable fixed costs	200,000	200,000

Prepare a responsibility report for the Midwest Division for December 31, 2017.

Solution

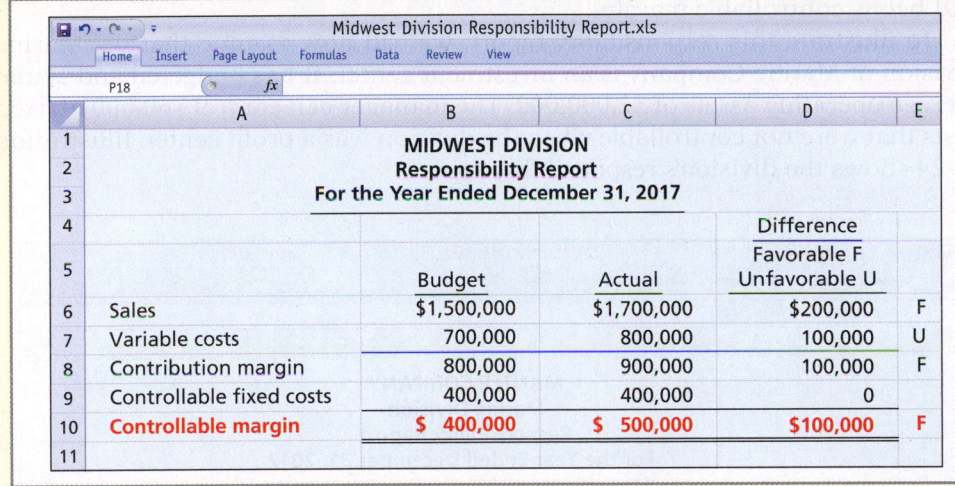

Action Plan

✔ Deduct variable costs from sales to show contribution margin.

✔ Deduct controllable fixed costs from the contribution margin to show controllable margin.

✔ Do not report noncontrollable fixed costs.

Related exercise material: **BE24-7, E24-15, and  24-3.**

LEARNING OBJECTIVE 4   Evaluate performance in investment centers.

As explained earlier, an investment center manager can control or significantly influence the investment funds available for use. Thus, the primary basis for evaluating the performance of a manager of an investment center is **return on investment (ROI)**. The return on investment is considered to be a useful performance measurement because it shows the **effectiveness of the manager in utilizing the assets at his or her disposal**.

Return on Investment (ROI)

The formula for computing ROI for an investment center, together with assumed illustrative data, is shown in Illustration 24-23 (page 1128).

Illustration 24-23
ROI formula

Controllable Margin	÷	Average Operating Assets	=	Return on Investment (ROI)
$1,000,000	÷	$5,000,000	=	20%

Both factors in the formula are controllable by the investment center manager. Operating assets consist of current assets and plant assets used in operations by the center and controlled by the manager. Nonoperating assets such as idle plant assets and land held for future use are excluded. Average operating assets are usually based on the cost or book value of the assets at the beginning and end of the year.

Responsibility Report

The scope of the investment center manager's responsibility significantly affects the content of the performance report. Since an investment center is an independent entity for operating purposes, **all fixed costs are controllable by its manager**. For example, the manager is responsible for depreciation on investment center assets. Therefore, more fixed costs are identified as controllable in the performance report for an investment center manager than in a performance report for a profit center manager. The report also shows budgeted and actual ROI below controllable margin.

To illustrate this responsibility report, we will now assume that the Marine Division of Mantle Company is an investment center. It has budgeted and actual average operating assets of $2,000,000. The manager can control $60,000 of fixed costs that were not controllable when the division was a profit center. Illustration 24-24 shows the division's responsibility report.

Illustration 24-24
Responsibility report for investment center

	A	B	C	D	E
1		**MANTLE COMPANY**			
2		**Marine Division**			
3		**Responsibility Report**			
4		**For the Year Ended December 31, 2017**			
5				Difference	
6		Budget	Actual	Favorable - F Unfavorable - U	
7	Sales	$ 1,200,000	$ 1,150,000	$ 50,000	U
8	Variable costs				
9	Cost of goods sold	500,000	490,000	10,000	F
10	Selling and administrative	160,000	156,000	4,000	F
11	Total	660,000	646,000	14,000	F
12	Contribution margin	540,000	504,000	36,000	U
13	**Controllable fixed costs**				
14	Cost of goods sold	100,000	100,000	0	
15	Selling and administrative	80,000	80,000	0	
16	**Other fixed costs**	**60,000**	**60,000**	**0**	
17	Total	240,000	240,000	0	
18	**Controllable margin**	$ 300,000	$ 264,000	$ 36,000	U
19	**Return on investment**	15.0%	13.2%	1.8%	U
20		(a)	(b)	(c)	
21					
22		(a) $ 300,000 / $2,000,000	(b) $ 264,000 / $2,000,000	(c) $ 36,000 / $2,000,000	
23					

The report shows that the manager's performance based on ROI was below budget expectations by 1.8% (15.0% versus 13.2%). Top management would likely want explanations for this unfavorable result.

Judgmental Factors in ROI

The return on investment approach includes two judgmental factors:

1. **Valuation of operating assets.** Operating assets may be valued at acquisition cost, book value, appraised value, or fair value. The first two bases are readily available from the accounting records.

2. **Margin (income) measure.** This measure may be controllable margin, income from operations, or net income.

Each of the alternative values for operating assets can provide a reliable basis for evaluating a manager's performance as long as it is consistently applied between reporting periods. However, the use of income measures other than controllable margin will not result in a valid basis for evaluating the performance of an investment center manager.

Improving ROI

The manager of an investment center can improve ROI by increasing controllable margin, and/or reducing average operating assets. To illustrate, we will use the following assumed data for the Laser Division of Berra Company.

Sales		$2,000,000
Variable costs		1,100,000
Contribution margin (45%)		900,000
Controllable fixed costs		300,000
Controllable margin (a)		$ 600,000
Average operating assets (b)		$5,000,000
Return on investment (a) ÷ (b)		**12%**

Illustration 24-25
Assumed data for Laser Division

INCREASING CONTROLLABLE MARGIN

Controllable margin can be increased by increasing sales or by reducing variable and controllable fixed costs as follows.

1. **Increase sales 10%.** Sales will increase $200,000 ($2,000,000 × .10). Assuming no change in the contribution margin percentage of 45%, contribution margin will increase $90,000 ($200,000 × .45). Controllable margin will increase by the same amount because controllable fixed costs will not change. Thus, controllable margin becomes $690,000 ($600,000 + $90,000). The new ROI is 13.8%, computed as follows.

$$\text{ROI} = \frac{\text{Controllable margin}}{\text{Average operating assets}} = \frac{\$690,000}{\$5,000,000} = \textbf{13.8\%}$$

Illustration 24-26
ROI computation—increase in sales

An increase in sales benefits both the investment center and the company if it results in new business. It would not benefit the company if the increase was achieved at the expense of other investment centers.

2. **Decrease variable and fixed costs 10%.** Total costs decrease $140,000 [($1,100,000 + $300,000) × .10]. This reduction results in a corresponding increase in controllable margin. Thus, controllable margin becomes $740,000 ($600,000 + $140,000). The new ROI is 14.8%, computed as follows.

$$\text{ROI} = \frac{\text{Controllable margin}}{\text{Average operating assets}} = \frac{\$740,000}{\$5,000,000} = \textbf{14.8\%}$$

Illustration 24-27
ROI computation—decrease in costs

This course of action is clearly beneficial when the reduction in costs is the result of eliminating waste and inefficiency. But, a reduction in costs that results from cutting expenditures on vital activities, such as required maintenance and inspections, is not likely to be acceptable to top management.

REDUCING AVERAGE OPERATING ASSETS

Assume that average operating assets are reduced 10% or $500,000 ($5,000,000 × .10). Average operating assets become $4,500,000 ($5,000,000 − $500,000). Since controllable margin remains unchanged at $600,000, the new ROI is 13.3%, computed as follows.

Illustration 24-28
ROI computation—decrease in operating assets

$$\text{ROI} = \frac{\text{Controllable margin}}{\text{Average operating assets}} = \frac{\$600,000}{\$4,500,000} = \mathbf{13.3\%}$$

Reductions in operating assets may or may not be prudent. It is beneficial to eliminate overinvestment in inventories and to dispose of excessive plant assets. However, it is unwise to reduce inventories below expected needs or to dispose of essential plant assets.

Accounting Across the Organization   Hollywood

brentmelissa/iStockphoto

Does Hollywood Look at ROI?

If Hollywood were run like a real business, where things like return on investment mattered, there would be one unchallenged, sacred principle that studio chieftains would never violate: Make lots of G-rated movies.

No matter how you slice the movie business—by star vehicles, by budget levels, or by sequels or franchises—by far the best return on investment comes from the not-so-glamorous world of G-rated films. The problem is, these movies represent only 3% of the total films made in a typical year.

On the flip side are the R-rated films, which dominate the total releases and yet yield the worst return on investment. A whopping 646 R-rated films were released in a recent year—69% of the total output—but only four of the top-20 grossing movies of the year were R-rated films.

This trend—G-rated movies are good for business but underproduced, R-rated movies are bad for business and yet overdone—is something that has been driving economists batty for the past several years.

Source: David Grainger, "The Dysfunctional Family-Film Business," *Fortune* (January 10, 2005), pp. 20–21.

What might be the reason that movie studios do not produce G-rated movies as much as R-rated ones? (Go to **WileyPLUS** for this answer and additional questions.)

DO IT! 4   Performance Evaluation

The service division of Metro Industries reported the following results for 2017.

Sales	$400,000
Variable costs	320,000
Controllable fixed costs	40,800
Average operating assets	280,000

Management is considering the following independent courses of action in 2018 in order to maximize the return on investment for this division.

1. Reduce average operating assets by $80,000, with no change in controllable margin.
2. Increase sales $80,000, with no change in the contribution margin percentage.
   (a) Compute the controllable margin and the return on investment for 2017.
   (b) Compute the controllable margin and the expected return on investment for each proposed alternative.

Solution

(a) Return on investment for 2017:

Sales	$400,000
Variable costs	320,000
Contribution margin	80,000
Controllable fixed costs	40,800
Controllable margin	$ 39,200

Return on investment $\dfrac{\$39,200}{\$280,000}$ = 14%

(b) Expected return on investment for alternative 1:

$\dfrac{\$39,200}{\$280,000 - \$80,000}$ = 19.6%

Expected return on investment for alternative 2:

Sales ($400,000 + $80,000)	$480,000
Variable costs ($320,000/$400,000 × $480,000)	384,000
Contribution margin	96,000
Controllable fixed costs	40,800
Controllable margin	$ 55,200

Return on investment $\dfrac{\$55,200}{\$280,000}$ = 19.7%

Related exercise material: **BE24-8, BE24-9, BE24-10, E24-16, E24-17, and DO IT! 24-4.**

Action Plan

✔ Recall key formulas: Sales − Variable costs = Contribution margin.

✔ Contribution margin ÷ Sales = Contribution margin percentage.

✔ Contribution margin − Controllable fixed costs = Controllable margin.

✔ Return on investment = Controllable margin ÷ Average operating assets.

LEARNING OBJECTIVE **5**

APPENDIX 24A: Explain the difference between ROI and residual income.

Although most companies use ROI to evaluate investment performance, ROI has a significant disadvantage. To illustrate, let's look at the Electronics Division of Pujols Company. It has an ROI of 20%, computed as follows.

Controllable Margin	÷	Average Operating Assets	=	Return on Investment (ROI)
$1,000,000	÷	$5,000,000	=	20%

Illustration 24A-1
ROI formula

The Electronics Division is considering producing a new product, a GPS device (hereafter referred to as Tracker) for its boats. To produce Tracker, operating assets will have to increase $2,000,000. Tracker is expected to generate an additional $260,000 of controllable margin. Illustration 24A-2 shows how Tracker will effect ROI.

	Without Tracker	Tracker	With Tracker
Controllable margin (a)	$1,000,000	$ 260,000	$1,260,000
Average operating assets (b)	$5,000,000	$2,000,000	$7,000,000
Return on investment [(a) ÷ (b)]	20%	13%	18%

Illustration 24A-2
ROI comparison

The investment in Tracker reduces ROI from 20% to 18%.

Let's suppose that you are the manager of the Electronics Division and must make the decision to produce or not produce Tracker. If you were evaluated using ROI, you probably would not produce Tracker because your ROI would drop from 20% to 18%. The problem with this ROI analysis is that it ignores an important variable: the minimum rate of return on a company's operating assets. The **minimum rate of return** is the rate at which the Electronics Division can cover its costs and earn a profit. Assuming that the Electronics Division has a minimum rate of return of 10%, it should invest in Tracker because its ROI of 13% is greater than 10%.

Residual Income Compared to ROI

To evaluate performance using the minimum rate of return, companies use the residual income approach. **Residual income** is the income that remains after subtracting from the controllable margin the minimum rate of return on a company's average operating assets. The residual income for Tracker would be computed as follows.

Illustration 24A-3
Residual income formula

Controllable Margin	−	Minimum Rate of Return × Average Operating Assets	=	Residual Income
$260,000	−	10% × $2,000,000	=	$60,000

As shown, the residual income related to the Tracker investment is $60,000. Illustration 24A-4 indicates how residual income changes as the additional investment is made.

Illustration 24A-4
Residual income comparison

	Without Tracker	Tracker	With Tracker
Controllable margin (a)	$1,000,000	$260,000	$1,260,000
Average operating assets × 10% (b)	500,000	200,000	700,000
Residual income [(a) − (b)]	$ 500,000	$ 60,000	$ 560,000

This example illustrates how performance evaluation based on ROI can be misleading and can even cause managers to reject projects that would actually increase income for the company. As a result, many companies such as **Coca-Cola**, **Briggs and Stratton**, **Eli Lilly**, and **Siemens AG** use residual income (or a variant often referred to as economic value added) to evaluate investment alternatives and measure company performance.

Residual Income Weakness

It might appear from the above discussion that the goal of any company should be to maximize the total amount of residual income in each division. This goal, however, ignores the fact that one division might use substantially fewer assets to attain the same level of residual income as another division. For example, we know that to produce Tracker, the Electronics Division of Pujols Company used $2,000,000 of average operating assets to generate $260,000 of controllable margin. Now let's say a different division produced a product called SeaDog, which used $4,000,000 to generate $460,000 of controllable margin, as shown in Illustration 24A-5.

Illustration 24A-5
Comparison of two products

	Tracker	SeaDog
Controllable margin (a)	$260,000	$460,000
Average operating assets × 10% (b)	200,000	400,000
Residual income [(a) − (b)]	$ 60,000	$ 60,000

If the performance of these two investments were evaluated using residual income, they would be considered equal: Both products have the same total residual income. This ignores, however, the fact that SeaDog required **twice** as many operating assets to achieve the same level of residual income.

REVIEW AND PRACTICE

▌ LEARNING OBJECTIVES REVIEW

❶ Describe budgetary control and static budget reports. Budgetary control consists of (a) preparing periodic budget reports that compare actual results with planned objectives, (b) analyzing the differences to determine their causes, (c) taking appropriate corrective action, and (d) modifying future plans, if necessary.

Static budget reports are useful in evaluating the progress toward planned sales and profit goals. They are also appropriate in assessing a manager's effectiveness in controlling costs when (a) actual activity closely approximates the master budget activity level, and/or (b) the behavior of the costs in response to changes in activity is fixed.

❷ Prepare flexible budget reports. To develop the flexible budget it is necessary to: (a) Identify the activity index and the relevant range of activity. (b) Identify the variable costs, and determine the budgeted variable cost per unit of activity for each cost. (c) Identify the fixed costs, and determine the budgeted amount for each cost. (d) Prepare the budget for selected increments of activity within the relevant range. Flexible budget reports permit an evaluation of a manager's performance in controlling production and costs.

❸ Apply responsibility accounting to cost and profit centers. Responsibility accounting involves accumulating and reporting revenues and costs on the basis of the individual manager who has the authority to make the day-to-day decisions about the items. The evaluation of a manager's performance is based on the matters directly under the manager's control. In responsibility accounting, it is necessary to distinguish between controllable and noncontrollable fixed costs and to identify three types of responsibility centers: cost, profit, and investment.

Responsibility reports for cost centers compare actual costs with flexible budget data. The reports show only controllable costs, and no distinction is made between variable and fixed costs. Responsibility reports show contribution margin, controllable fixed costs, and controllable margin for each profit center.

❹ Evaluate performance in investment centers. The primary basis for evaluating performance in investment centers is return on investment (ROI). The formula for computing ROI for investment centers is Controllable margin ÷ Average operating assets.

*❺ Explain the difference between ROI and residual income. ROI is controllable margin divided by average operating assets. Residual income is the income that remains after subtracting the minimum rate of return on a company's average operating assets. ROI sometimes provides misleading results because profitable investments are often rejected when the investment reduces ROI but increases overall profitability.

▌ GLOSSARY REVIEW

Budgetary control The use of budgets to control operations. (p. 1108).

Controllable cost A cost over which a manager has control. (p. 1120).

Controllable margin Contribution margin less controllable fixed costs. (p. 1126).

Cost center A responsibility center that incurs costs but does not directly generate revenues. (p. 1124).

Decentralization Control of operations is delegated to many managers throughout the organization. (p. 1119).

Direct fixed costs Costs that relate specifically to a responsibility center and are incurred for the sole benefit of the center. (p. 1126).

Flexible budget A projection of budget data for various levels of activity. (p. 1111).

Indirect fixed costs Costs that are incurred for the benefit of more than one profit center. (p. 1126).

Investment center A responsibility center that incurs costs, generates revenues, and has control over decisions regarding the assets available for use. (p. 1124).

Management by exception The review of budget reports by top management focused entirely or primarily on differences between actual results and planned objectives. (p. 1120).

Noncontrollable costs Costs incurred indirectly and allocated to a responsibility center that are not controllable at that level. (p. 1120).

Profit center A responsibility center that incurs costs and also generates revenues. (p. 1124).

*****Residual income** The income that remains after subtracting from the controllable margin the minimum rate of return on a company's average operating assets. (p. 1132).

Responsibility accounting A part of management accounting that involves accumulating and reporting

revenues and costs on the basis of the manager who has the authority to make the day-to-day decisions about the items. (p. 1118).

Responsibility reporting system The preparation of reports for each level of responsibility in the company's organization chart. (p. 1122).

Return on investment (ROI) A measure of management's effectiveness in utilizing assets at its disposal in an investment center. (p. 1127).

Segment An area of responsibility in decentralized operations. (p. 1119).

Static budget A projection of budget data at one level of activity. (p. 1109).

PRACTICE MULTIPLE-CHOICE QUESTIONS

(LO 1) **1.** Budgetary control involves all but one of the following:
(a) modifying future plans.
(b) analyzing differences.
(c) using static budgets but **not** flexible budgets.
(d) determining differences between actual and planned results.

(LO 1) **2.** Budget reports are prepared:
(a) daily.   (c) monthly.
(b) weekly.   (d) All of the above.

(LO 1) **3.** A production manager in a manufacturing company would most likely receive a:
(a) sales report.
(b) income statement.
(c) scrap report.
(d) shipping department overhead report.

(LO 1) **4.** A static budget is:
(a) a projection of budget data at several levels of activity within the relevant range of activity.
(b) a projection of budget data at a single level of activity.
(c) compared to a flexible budget in a budget report.
(d) never appropriate in evaluating a manager's effectiveness in controlling costs.

(LO 1) **5.** A static budget is useful in controlling costs when cost behavior is:
(a) mixed.   (c) variable.
(b) fixed.   (d) linear.

(LO 2) **6.** At zero direct labor hours in a flexible budget graph, the total budgeted cost line intersects the vertical axis at $30,000. At 10,000 direct labor hours, a horizontal line drawn from the total budgeted cost line intersects the vertical axis at $90,000. Fixed and variable costs may be expressed as:
(a) $30,000 fixed plus $6 per direct labor hour variable.
(b) $30,000 fixed plus $9 per direct labor hour variable.
(c) $60,000 fixed plus $3 per direct labor hour variable.
(d) $60,000 fixed plus $6 per direct labor hour variable.

(LO 2) **7.** At 9,000 direct labor hours, the flexible budget for indirect materials is $27,000. If $28,000 of indirect materials costs are incurred at 9,200 direct labor hours, the flexible budget report should show the following difference for indirect materials:
(a) $1,000 unfavorable.
(b) $1,000 favorable.
(c) $400 favorable.
(d) $400 unfavorable.

(LO 3) **8.** Under responsibility accounting, the evaluation of a manager's performance is based on matters that the manager:
(a) directly controls.
(b) directly and indirectly controls.
(c) indirectly controls.
(d) has shared responsibility for with another manager.

9. Responsibility centers include: (LO 3)
(a) cost centers.
(b) profit centers.
(c) investment centers.
(d) All of the above.

10. Responsibility reports for cost centers: (LO 3)
(a) distinguish between fixed and variable costs.
(b) use static budget data.
(c) include both controllable and noncontrollable costs.
(d) include only controllable costs.

11. The accounting department of a manufacturing company is an example of: (LO 3)
(a) a cost center.
(b) a profit center.
(c) an investment center.
(d) a contribution center.

12. To evaluate the performance of a profit center manager, upper management needs detailed information about: (LO 3)
(a) controllable costs.

(b) controllable revenues.
(c) controllable costs and revenues.
(d) controllable costs and revenues and average operating assets.

(LO 3) **13.** In a responsibility report for a profit center, controllable fixed costs are deducted from contribution margin to show:
(a) profit center margin.
(b) controllable margin.
(c) net income.
(d) income from operations.

(LO 4) **14.** In the formula for return on investment (ROI), the factors for controllable margin and operating assets are, respectively:
(a) controllable margin percentage and total operating assets.

(b) controllable margin dollars and average operating assets.
(c) controllable margin dollars and total assets.
(d) controllable margin percentage and average operating assets.

15. A manager of an investment center can improve (LO 4) ROI by:
(a) increasing average operating assets.
(b) reducing sales.
(c) increasing variable costs.
(d) reducing variable and/or controllable fixed costs.

Solutions

1. (c) Budgetary control involves using flexible budgets and sometimes static budgets. The other choices are all part of budgetary control.

2. (d) Budget reports are prepared daily, weekly, or monthly. The other choices are correct, but choice (d) is the better answer.

3. (c) A production manager in a manufacturing company would most likely receive a scrap report. The other choices are incorrect because (a) top management or a sales manager would most likely receive a sales report, (b) top management would most likely receive an income statement, and (d) a department manager would most likely receive a shipping department overhead report.

4. (b) A static budget is a projection of budget data at a single level of activity. The other choices are incorrect because a static budget (a) is a projection of budget data at a single level of activity, not at several levels of activity within the relevant range of activity; (c) is not compared to a flexible budget in a budget report; and (d) is appropriate in evaluating a manager's effectiveness in controlling fixed costs.

5. (b) A static budget is useful for controlling fixed costs. The other choices are incorrect because a static budget is not useful for controlling (a) mixed costs, (c) variable costs, or (d) linear costs.

6. (a) The intersection point of $90,000 is total budgeted costs, or budgeted fixed costs plus budgeted variable costs. Fixed costs are $30,000 (amount at zero direct labor hours), so budgeted variable costs are $60,000 [$90,000 (Total costs) − $30,000 (Fixed costs)]. Budgeted variable costs ($60,000) divided by total activity level (10,000 direct labor hours) gives the variable cost per unit of $6 per direct labor hour. The other choices are therefore incorrect.

7. (d) Budgeted indirect materials per direct labor hour (DLH) is $3 ($27,000/9,000). At an activity level of 9,200 direct labor hours, budgeted indirect materials are $27,600 (9,200 × $3 per DLH) but actual indirect materials costs are $28,000, resulting in a $400 unfavorable difference. The other choices are therefore incorrect.

8. (a) The evaluation of a manager's performance is based only on matters that the manager directly controls. The other choices are therefore incorrect as they include indirect controls and shared responsibility.

9. (d) Cost centers, profit centers, and investment centers are all responsibility centers. The other choices are correct, but choice (d) is the better answer.

10. (d) Responsibility reports for cost centers report only controllable costs; they (a) do not distinguish between fixed and variable costs; (b) use flexible budget data, not static budget data; and (c) do not include noncontrollable costs.

11. (a) The accounting department of a manufacturing company is an example of a cost center, not (b) a profit center, (c) an investment center, or (d) contribution center.

12. (c) To evaluate the performance of a profit center manager, upper management needs detailed information about controllable costs and revenues, not just (a) controllable costs or (b) controllable revenues. Choice (d) is incorrect because upper management does not need information about average operating assets.

13. (b) Contribution margin less controllable fixed costs is the controllable margin, not (a) the profit center margin, (c) net income, or (d) income from operations.

14. (b) The factors in the formula for ROI are controllable margin dollars and average operating assets. The other choices are therefore incorrect.

15. (d) Reducing variable or controllable fixed costs will cause the controllable margin to increase, which is one way a manager of an investment center can improve ROI. The other choices are incorrect because (a) increasing average operating assets will lower ROI; (b) reducing sales will cause contribution margin to go down, thereby decreasing controllable margin since there will be less contribution margin to cover controllable fixed costs and resulting in lower ROI; and (c) increasing variable costs will cause the contribution margin to be lower, thereby decreasing controllable margin and resulting in lower ROI.

PRACTICE EXERCISES

Prepare flexible manufacturing overhead budget.

(LO 2)

1. Felix Company uses a flexible budget for manufacturing overhead based on direct labor hours. Variable manufacturing overhead costs per direct labor hour are as follows.

Indirect labor	$0.70
Indirect materials	0.50
Utilities	0.40

Fixed overhead costs per month are supervision $4,000, depreciation $3,000, and property taxes $800. The company believes it will normally operate in a range of 7,000–10,000 direct labor hours per month.

Instructions

Prepare a monthly flexible manufacturing overhead budget for 2017 for the expected range of activity, using increments of 1,000 direct labor hours.

Solution

1.

FELIX COMPANY
Monthly Flexible Manufacturing Overhead Budget
For the Year 2017

Activity level				
Direct labor hours	7,000	8,000	9,000	10,000
Variable costs				
Indirect labor ($.70)	$ 4,900	$ 5,600	$ 6,300	$ 7,000
Indirect materials ($.50)	3,500	4,000	4,500	5,000
Utilities ($.40)	2,800	3,200	3,600	4,000
Total variable costs ($1.60)	11,200	12,800	14,400	16,000
Fixed costs				
Supervision	4,000	4,000	4,000	4,000
Depreciation	3,000	3,000	3,000	3,000
Property taxes	800	800	800	800
Total fixed costs	7,800	7,800	7,800	7,800
Total costs	$19,000	$20,600	$22,200	$23,800

Compute ROI for current year and for possible future changes.

(LO 4)

2. The White Division of Mesin Company reported the following data for the current year.

Sales	$3,000,000
Variable costs	2,400,000
Controllable fixed costs	400,000
Average operating assets	5,000,000

Top management is unhappy with the investment center's return on investment (ROI). It asks the manager of the White Division to submit plans to improve ROI in the next year. The manager believes it is feasible to consider the following independent courses of action.

1. Increase sales by $300,000 with no change in the contribution margin percentage.
2. Reduce variable costs by $100,000.
3. Reduce average operating assets by 4%.

Instructions

(a) Compute the return on investment (ROI) for the current year.

(b) Using the ROI formula, compute the ROI under each of the proposed courses of action. (Round to one decimal.)

Solution

2. (a) Controllable margin = ($3,000,000 − $2,400,000 − $400,000) = $200,000
ROI = $200,000 ÷ $5,000,000 = 4%

(b) (1) Contribution margin percentage is 20%, or ($600,000 ÷ $3,000,000)
     Increase in controllable margin = $300,000 × 20% = $60,000
     ROI = ($200,000 + $60,000) ÷ $5,000,000 = 5.2%
   (2) ($200,000 + $100,000) ÷ $5,000,000 = 6%
   (3) $200,000 ÷ [$5,000,000 − ($5,000,000 × .04)] = 4.2%

 PRACTICE PROBLEM

Glenda Company uses a flexible budget for manufacturing overhead based on direct labor hours. For 2017, the master overhead budget for the Packaging Department based on 300,000 direct labor hours was as follows.

Prepare flexible budget report.
(LO 2)

Variable Costs		Fixed Costs	
Indirect labor	$360,000	Supervision	$ 60,000
Supplies and lubricants	150,000	Depreciation	24,000
Maintenance	210,000	Property taxes	18,000
Utilities	120,000	Insurance	12,000
	$840,000		$114,000

During July, 24,000 direct labor hours were worked. The company incurred the following variable costs in July: indirect labor $30,200, supplies and lubricants $11,600, maintenance $17,500, and utilities $9,200. Actual fixed overhead costs were the same as monthly budgeted fixed costs.

Instructions

Prepare a flexible budget report for the Packaging Department for July.

Solution

GLENDA COMPANY
Manufacturing Overhead Budget Report (Flexible)
Packaging Department
For the Month Ended July 31, 2017

Direct labor hours (DLH)	Budget 24,000 DLH	Actual Costs 24,000 DLH	Difference Favorable F Unfavorable U
Variable costs			
Indirect labor ($1.20ᵃ)	$28,800	$30,200	$1,400 U
Supplies and lubricants ($0.50ᵃ)	12,000	11,600	400 F
Maintenance ($0.70ᵃ)	16,800	17,500	700 U
Utilities ($0.40ᵃ)	9,600	9,200	400 F
Total variable	67,200	68,500	1,300 U
Fixed costs			
Supervision	$ 5,000ᵇ	$ 5,000	–0–
Depreciation	2,000ᵇ	2,000	–0–
Property taxes	1,500ᵇ	1,500	–0–
Insurance	1,000ᵇ	1,000	–0–
Total fixed	9,500	9,500	–0–
Total costs	$76,700	$78,000	$1,300 U

ᵃ($360,000 ÷ 300,000; $150,000 ÷ 300,000; $210,000 ÷ 300,000; $120,000 ÷ 300,000).
ᵇAnnual cost divided by 12.

WileyPLUS

Brief Exercises, Exercises, DO IT! Exercises, and Problems and many additional resources are available for practice in WileyPLUS

NOTE: All asterisked Questions, Exercises, and Problems relate to material in the appendix to the chapter.

QUESTIONS

1. (a) What is budgetary control?
   (b) Fred Barone is describing budgetary control. What steps should be included in Fred's description?

2. The following purposes are part of a budgetary reporting system: (a) Determine efficient use of materials. (b) Control overhead costs. (c) Determine whether income objectives are being met. For each purpose, indicate the name of the report, the frequency of the report, and the primary recipient(s) of the report.

3. How may a budget report for the second quarter differ from a budget report for the first quarter?

4. Ken Bay questions the usefulness of a master sales budget in evaluating sales performance. Is there justification for Ken's concern? Explain.

5. Under what circumstances may a static budget be an appropriate basis for evaluating a manager's effectiveness in controlling costs?

6. "A flexible budget is really a series of static budgets." Is this true? Why?

7. The static manufacturing overhead budget based on 40,000 direct labor hours shows budgeted indirect labor costs of $54,000. During March, the department incurs $64,000 of indirect labor while working 45,000 direct labor hours. Is this a favorable or unfavorable performance? Why?

8. A static overhead budget based on 40,000 direct labor hours shows Factory Insurance $6,500 as a fixed cost. At the 50,000 direct labor hours worked in March, factory insurance costs were $6,300. Is this a favorable or unfavorable performance? Why?

9. Megan Pedigo is confused about how a flexible budget is prepared. Identify the steps for Megan.

10. Cali Company has prepared a graph of flexible budget data. At zero direct labor hours, the total budgeted cost line intersects the vertical axis at $20,000. At 10,000 direct labor hours, the line drawn from the total budgeted cost line intersects the vertical axis at $85,000. How may the fixed and variable costs be expressed?

11. The flexible budget formula is fixed costs $50,000 plus variable costs of $4 per direct labor hour. What is the total budgeted cost at (a) 9,000 hours and (b) 12,345 hours?

12. What is management by exception? What criteria may be used in identifying exceptions?

13. What is responsibility accounting? Explain the purpose of responsibility accounting.

14. Eve Rooney is studying for an accounting examination. Describe for Eve what conditions are necessary for responsibility accounting to be used effectively.

15. Distinguish between controllable and noncontrollable costs.

16. How do responsibility reports differ from budget reports?

17. What is the relationship, if any, between a responsibility reporting system and a company's organization chart?

18. Distinguish among the three types of responsibility centers.

19. (a) What costs are included in a performance report for a cost center? (b) In the report, are variable and fixed costs identified?

20. How do direct fixed costs differ from indirect fixed costs? Are both types of fixed costs controllable?

21. Jane Nott is confused about controllable margin reported in an income statement for a profit center. How is this margin computed, and what is its primary purpose?

22. What is the primary basis for evaluating the performance of the manager of an investment center? Indicate the formula for this basis.

23. Explain the ways that ROI can be improved.

24. Indicate two behavioral principles that pertain to (a) the manager being evaluated and (b) top management.

*25. What is a major disadvantage of using ROI to evaluate investment and company performance?

*26. What is residual income, and what is one of its major weaknesses?

BRIEF EXERCISES

Prepare static budget report.
(LO 1)

BE24-1 For the quarter ended March 31, 2017, Croix Company accumulates the following sales data for its newest guitar, The Edge: $315,000 budget; $305,000 actual. Prepare a static budget report for the quarter.

Prepare static budget report for 2 quarters.
(LO 1)

BE24-2 Data for Croix Company are given in BE24-1. In the second quarter, budgeted sales were $380,000, and actual sales were $384,000. Prepare a static budget report for the second quarter and for the year to date.

BE24-3 In Rooney Company, direct labor is $20 per hour. The company expects to operate at 10,000 direct labor hours each month. In January 2017, direct labor totaling $206,000 is incurred in working 10,400 hours. Prepare (a) a static budget report and (b) a flexible budget report. Evaluate the usefulness of each report.

Show usefulness of flexible budgets in evaluating performance.

(LO 2)

BE24-4 Gundy Company expects to produce 1,200,000 units of Product XX in 2017. Monthly production is expected to range from 80,000 to 120,000 units. Budgeted variable manufacturing costs per unit are direct materials $5, direct labor $6, and overhead $8. Budgeted fixed manufacturing costs per unit for depreciation are $2 and for supervision are $1. Prepare a flexible manufacturing budget for the relevant range value using 20,000 unit increments.

Prepare a flexible budget for variable costs.

(LO 2)

BE24-5 Data for Gundy Company are given in BE24-4. In March 2017, the company incurs the following costs in producing 100,000 units: direct materials $520,000, direct labor $596,000, and variable overhead $805,000. Actual fixed costs were equal to budgeted fixed costs. Prepare a flexible budget report for March. Were costs controlled?

Prepare flexible budget report.

(LO 2)

BE24-6 In the Assembly Department of Hannon Company, budgeted and actual manufacturing overhead costs for the month of April 2017 were as follows.

	Budget	Actual
Indirect materials	$16,000	$14,300
Indirect labor	20,000	20,600
Utilities	10,000	10,850
Supervision	5,000	5,000

All costs are controllable by the department manager. Prepare a responsibility report for April for the cost center.

Prepare a responsibility report for a cost center.

(LO 3)

BE24-7 Torres Company accumulates the following summary data for the year ending December 31, 2017, for its Water Division, which it operates as a profit center: sales—$2,000,000 budget, $2,080,000 actual; variable costs—$1,000,000 budget, $1,050,000 actual; and controllable fixed costs—$300,000 budget, $305,000 actual. Prepare a responsibility report for the Water Division.

Prepare a responsibility report for a profit center.

(LO 3)

BE24-8 For the year ending December 31, 2017, Cobb Company accumulates the following data for the Plastics Division which it operates as an investment center: contribution margin—$700,000 budget, $710,000 actual; controllable fixed costs—$300,000 budget, $302,000 actual. Average operating assets for the year were $2,000,000. Prepare a responsibility report for the Plastics Division beginning with contribution margin.

Prepare a responsibility report for an investment center.

(LO 4)

BE24-9 For its three investment centers, Gerrard Company accumulates the following data:

	I	II	III
Sales	$2,000,000	$4,000,000	$ 4,000,000
Controllable margin	1,400,000	2,000,000	3,600,000
Average operating assets	5,000,000	8,000,000	10,000,000

Compute the return on investment (ROI) for each center.

Compute return on investment using the ROI formula.

(LO 4)

BE24-10 Data for the investment centers for Gerrard Company are given in BE24-9. The centers expect the following changes in the next year: (I) increase sales 15%, (II) decrease costs $400,000, and (III) decrease average operating assets $500,000. Compute the expected return on investment (ROI) for each center. Assume center I has a controllable margin percentage of 70%.

Compute return on investment under changed conditions.

(LO 4)

*BE24-11 Sterling, Inc. reports the following financial information.

Average operating assets	$3,000,000
Controllable margin	$ 630,000
Minimum rate of return	10%

Compute the return on investment and the residual income.

Compute ROI and residual income.

(LO 5)

Compute ROI and residual income.

(LO 5)

*BE24-12 Presented below is information related to the Southern Division of Lumber, Inc.

Contribution margin	$1,200,000
Controllable margin	$ 800,000
Average operating assets	$4,000,000
Minimum rate of return	15%

Compute the Southern Division's return on investment and residual income.

DO IT! Exercises

Prepare and evaluate a static budget report.

(LO 1)

DO IT! 24-1 Wade Company estimates that it will produce 6,000 units of product IOA during the current month. Budgeted variable manufacturing costs per unit are direct materials $7, direct labor $13, and overhead $18. Monthly budgeted fixed manufacturing overhead costs are $8,000 for depreciation and $3,800 for supervision.

In the current month, Wade actually produced 6,500 units and incurred the following costs: direct materials $38,850, direct labor $76,440, variable overhead $116,640, depreciation $8,000, and supervision $4,000.

Prepare a static budget report. *Hint:* The Budget column is based on estimated production while the Actual column is the actual cost incurred during the period. (*Note:* You do not need to prepare the heading.) Were costs controlled? Discuss limitations of the budget.

Compute total budgeted costs in flexible budget.

(LO 2)

DO IT! 24-2 In Pargo Company's flexible budget graph, the fixed cost line and the total budgeted cost line intersect the vertical axis at $90,000. The total budgeted cost line is $350,000 at an activity level of 50,000 direct labor hours. Compute total budgeted costs at 65,000 direct labor hours.

Prepare a responsibility report.

(LO 3)

DO IT! 24-3 The Rockies Division operates as a profit center. It reports the following for the year.

	Budget	Actual
Sales	$2,000,000	$1,890,000
Variable costs	800,000	760,000
Controllable fixed costs	550,000	550,000
Noncontrollable fixed costs	250,000	250,000

Prepare a responsibility report for the Rockies Division at December 31, 2017.

Compute ROI and expected return on investments.

(LO 4)

DO IT! 24-4 The service division of Raney Industries reported the following results for 2017.

Sales	$500,000
Variable costs	300,000
Controllable fixed costs	75,000
Average operating assets	625,000

Management is considering the following independent courses of action in 2018 in order to maximize the return on investment for this division.

1. Reduce average operating assets by $125,000, with no change in controllable margin.
2. Increase sales $100,000, with no change in the contribution margin percentage.

(a) Compute the controllable margin and the return on investment for 2017. (b) Compute the controllable margin and the expected return on investment for each proposed alternative.

EXERCISES

Understand the concept of budgetary control.

(LO 1, 2)

E24-1 Connie Rice has prepared the following list of statements about budgetary control.

1. Budget reports compare actual results with planned objectives.
2. All budget reports are prepared on a weekly basis.
3. Management uses budget reports to analyze differences between actual and planned results and determine their causes.

4. As a result of analyzing budget reports, management may either take corrective action or modify future plans.
5. Budgetary control works best when a company has an informal reporting system.
6. The primary recipients of the sales report are the sales manager and the production supervisor.
7. The primary recipient of the scrap report is the production manager.
8. A static budget is a projection of budget data at one level of activity.
9. Top management's reaction to unfavorable differences is not influenced by the materiality of the difference.
10. A static budget is not appropriate in evaluating a manager's effectiveness in controlling costs unless the actual activity level approximates the static budget activity level or the behavior of the costs is fixed.

Instructions
Identify each statement as true or false. If false, indicate how to correct the statement.

E24-2 Crede Company budgeted selling expenses of $30,000 in January, $35,000 in February, and $40,000 in March. Actual selling expenses were $31,200 in January, $34,525 in February, and $46,000 in March.

Prepare and evaluate static budget report.

(LO 1)

Instructions
(a) Prepare a selling expense report that compares budgeted and actual amounts by month and for the year to date.
(b) What is the purpose of the report prepared in (a), and who would be the primary recipient?
(c) What would be the likely result of management's analysis of the report?

E24-3 Myers Company uses a flexible budget for manufacturing overhead based on direct labor hours. Variable manufacturing overhead costs per direct labor hour are as follows.

Prepare flexible manufacturing overhead budget.

(LO 2)

Indirect labor	$1.00
Indirect materials	0.70
Utilities	0.40

Fixed overhead costs per month are supervision $4,000, depreciation $1,200, and property taxes $800. The company believes it will normally operate in a range of 7,000–10,000 direct labor hours per month.

Instructions
Prepare a monthly manufacturing overhead flexible budget for 2017 for the expected range of activity, using increments of 1,000 direct labor hours.

E24-4 Using the information in E24-3, assume that in July 2017, Myers Company incurs the following manufacturing overhead costs.

Prepare flexible budget reports for manufacturing overhead costs, and comment on findings.

(LO 2)

Variable Costs		**Fixed Costs**	
Indirect labor	$8,800	Supervision	$4,000
Indirect materials	5,800	Depreciation	1,200
Utilities	3,200	Property taxes	800

Instructions
(a) Prepare a flexible budget performance report, assuming that the company worked 9,000 direct labor hours during the month.
(b) Prepare a flexible budget performance report, assuming that the company worked 8,500 direct labor hours during the month.
(c) ———— Comment on your findings.

E24-5 Fallon Company uses flexible budgets to control its selling expenses. Monthly sales are expected to range from $170,000 to $200,000. Variable costs and their percentage relationship to sales are sales commissions 6%, advertising 4%, traveling 3%, and delivery 2%. Fixed selling expenses will consist of sales salaries $35,000, depreciation on delivery equipment $7,000, and insurance on delivery equipment $1,000.

Prepare flexible selling expense budget.

(LO 2)

Prepare flexible budget reports for selling expenses.

(LO 2)

Instructions

Prepare a monthly flexible budget for each $10,000 increment of sales within the relevant range for the year ending December 31, 2017.

E24-6 The actual selling expenses incurred in March 2017 by Fallon Company are as follows.

Variable Expenses		Fixed Expenses	
Sales commissions	$11,000	Sales salaries	$35,000
Advertising	6,900	Depreciation	7,000
Travel	5,100	Insurance	1,000
Delivery	3,450		

Instructions

(a) Prepare a flexible budget performance report for March using the budget data in E24-5, assuming that March sales were $170,000.

(b) Prepare a flexible budget performance report, assuming that March sales were $180,000.

(c) ⬤▬▬▬ Comment on the importance of using flexible budgets in evaluating the performance of the sales manager.

Prepare flexible budget report.

(LO 2)

E24-7 Appliance Possible Inc. (AP) is a manufacturer of toaster ovens. To improve control over operations, the president of AP wants to begin using a flexible budgeting system, rather than use only the current master budget. The following data are available for AP's expected costs at production levels of 90,000, 100,000, and 110,000 units.

Variable costs	
Manufacturing	$6 per unit
Administrative	$4 per unit
Selling	$3 per unit
Fixed costs	
Manufacturing	$160,000
Administrative	$ 80,000

Instructions

(a) Prepare a flexible budget for each of the possible production levels: 90,000, 100,000, and 110,000 units.

(b) If AP sells the toaster ovens for $16 each, how many units will it have to sell to make a profit of $60,000 before taxes?

(CGA adapted)

Prepare flexible budget report; compare flexible and static budgets.

(LO 1, 2)

E24-8 Rensing Groomers is in the dog-grooming business. Its operating costs are described by the following formulas:

Grooming supplies (variable)	y = $0 + $5x
Direct labor (variable)	y = $0 + $14x
Overhead (mixed)	y = $10,000 + $1x

Milo, the owner, has determined that direct labor is the cost driver for all three categories of costs.

Instructions

(a) Prepare a flexible budget for activity levels of 550, 600, and 700 direct labor hours.

(b) ⬤▬▬▬ Explain why the flexible budget is more informative than the static budget.

(c) Calculate the total cost per direct labor hour at each of the activity levels specified in part (a).

(d) The groomers at Rensing normally work a total of 650 direct labor hours during each month. Each grooming job normally takes a groomer 1.3 hours. Milo wants to earn a profit equal to 40% of the costs incurred. Determine what he should charge each pet owner for grooming.

(CGA adapted)

Prepare flexible budget report, and answer question.

(LO 1, 2)

E24-9 As sales manager, Joe Batista was given the following static budget report for selling expenses in the Clothing Department of Soria Company for the month of October.

SORIA COMPANY
Clothing Department
Budget Report
For the Month Ended October 31, 2017

	Budget	Actual	Difference Favorable F Unfavorable U
Sales in units	8,000	10,000	2,000 F
Variable expenses			
Sales commissions	$ 2,400	$ 2,600	$ 200 U
Advertising expense	720	850	130 U
Travel expense	3,600	4,100	500 U
Free samples given out	1,600	1,400	200 F
Total variable	8,320	8,950	630 U
Fixed expenses			
Rent	1,500	1,500	–0–
Sales salaries	1,200	1,200	–0–
Office salaries	800	800	–0–
Depreciation—autos (sales staff)	500	500	–0–
Total fixed	4,000	4,000	–0–
Total expenses	$12,320	$12,950	$ 630 U

As a result of this budget report, Joe was called into the president's office and congratulated on his fine sales performance. He was reprimanded, however, for allowing his costs to get out of control. Joe knew something was wrong with the performance report that he had been given. However, he was not sure what to do, and comes to you for advice.

Instructions
(a) Prepare a budget report based on flexible budget data to help Joe.
(b) Should Joe have been reprimanded? Explain.

E24-10 Chubbs Inc.'s manufacturing overhead budget for the first quarter of 2017 contained the following data.

Prepare flexible budget and responsibility report for manufacturing overhead.

(LO 2, 3)

Variable Costs		Fixed Costs	
Indirect materials	$12,000	Supervisory salaries	$36,000
Indirect labor	10,000	Depreciation	7,000
Utilities	8,000	Property taxes and insurance	8,000
Maintenance	6,000	Maintenance	5,000

Actual variable costs were indirect materials $13,500, indirect labor $9,500, utilities $8,700, and maintenance $5,000. Actual fixed costs equaled budgeted costs except for property taxes and insurance, which were $8,300. The actual activity level equaled the budgeted level.

All costs are considered controllable by the production department manager except for depreciation, and property taxes and insurance.

Instructions
(a) Prepare a manufacturing overhead flexible budget report for the first quarter.
(b) Prepare a responsibility report for the first quarter.

E24-11 UrLink Company is a newly formed company specializing in high-speed Internet service for home and business. The owner, Lenny Kirkland, had divided the company into two segments: Home Internet Service and Business Internet Service. Each segment is run by its own supervisor, while basic selling and administrative services are shared by both segments.

Prepare and discuss a responsibility report.

(LO 2, 3)

Lenny has asked you to help him create a performance reporting system that will allow him to measure each segment's performance in terms of its profitability. To that end, the following information has been collected on the Home Internet Service segment for the first quarter of 2017.

	Budget	Actual
Service revenue	$25,000	$26,200
Allocated portion of:		
Building depreciation	11,000	11,000
Advertising	5,000	4,200
Billing	3,500	3,000
Property taxes	1,200	1,000
Material and supplies	1,600	1,200
Supervisory salaries	9,000	9,500
Insurance	4,000	3,900
Wages	3,000	3,250
Gas and oil	2,800	3,400
Equipment depreciation	1,500	1,300

Instructions

(a) Prepare a responsibility report for the first quarter of 2017 for the Home Internet Service segment.

(b) ▬▬▬ Write a memo to Lenny Kirkland discussing the principles that should be used when preparing performance reports.

State total budgeted cost formulas, and prepare flexible budget graph.

(LO 2)

E24-12 Venetian Company has two production departments, Fabricating and Assembling. At a department managers' meeting, the controller uses flexible budget graphs to explain total budgeted costs. Separate graphs based on direct labor hours are used for each department. The graphs show the following.

1. At zero direct labor hours, the total budgeted cost line and the fixed cost line intersect the vertical axis at $50,000 in the Fabricating Department and $40,000 in the Assembling Department.

2. At normal capacity of 50,000 direct labor hours, the line drawn from the total budgeted cost line intersects the vertical axis at $150,000 in the Fabricating Department, and $120,000 in the Assembling Department.

Instructions

(a) State the total budgeted cost formula for each department.

(b) Compute the total budgeted cost for each department, assuming actual direct labor hours worked were 53,000 and 47,000, in the Fabricating and Assembling Departments, respectively.

(c) Prepare the flexible budget graph for the Fabricating Department, assuming the maximum direct labor hours in the relevant range is 100,000. Use increments of 10,000 direct labor hours on the horizontal axis and increments of $50,000 on the vertical axis.

Prepare reports in a responsibility reporting system.

(LO 3)

E24-13 Fey Company's organization chart includes the president; the vice president of production; three assembly plants—Dallas, Atlanta, and Tucson; and two departments within each plant—Machining and Finishing. Budget and actual manufacturing cost data for July 2017 are as follows.

Finishing Department—Dallas: direct materials $42,500 actual, $44,000 budget; direct labor $83,400 actual, $82,000 budget; manufacturing overhead $51,000 actual, $49,200 budget.

Machining Department—Dallas: total manufacturing costs $220,000 actual, $219,000 budget.

Atlanta Plant: total manufacturing costs $424,000 actual, $420,000 budget.

Tucson Plant: total manufacturing costs $494,200 actual, $496,500 budget.

The Dallas plant manager's office costs were $95,000 actual and $92,000 budget. The vice president of production's office costs were $132,000 actual and $130,000 budget. Office costs are not allocated to departments and plants.

Instructions

Using the format shown in Illustration 24-19 (page 1123), prepare the reports in a responsibility system for:

(a) The Finishing Department—Dallas.

(b) The plant manager—Dallas.

(c) The vice president of production.

E24-14 The Mixing Department manager of Malone Company is able to control all overhead costs except rent, property taxes, and salaries. Budgeted monthly overhead costs for the Mixing Department, in alphabetical order, are:

Prepare a responsibility report for a cost center.

(LO 3)

Indirect labor	$12,000	Property taxes	$ 1,000
Indirect materials	7,700	Rent	1,800
Lubricants	1,675	Salaries	10,000
Maintenance	3,500	Utilities	5,000

Actual costs incurred for January 2017 are indirect labor $12,250; indirect materials $10,200; lubricants $1,650; maintenance $3,500; property taxes $1,100; rent $1,800; salaries $10,000; and utilities $6,400.

Instructions
(a) Prepare a responsibility report for January 2017.
(b) What would be the likely result of management's analysis of the report?

E24-15 Horatio Inc. has three divisions which are operated as profit centers. Actual operating data for the divisions listed alphabetically are as follows.

Compute missing amounts in responsibility reports for three profit centers, and prepare a report.

(LO 3)

Operating Data	Women's Shoes	Men's Shoes	Children's Shoes
Contribution margin	$270,000	(3)	$180,000
Controllable fixed costs	100,000	(4)	(5)
Controllable margin	(1)	$ 90,000	95,000
Sales	600,000	450,000	(6)
Variable costs	(2)	320,000	250,000

Instructions
(a) Compute the missing amounts. Show computations.
(b) Prepare a responsibility report for the Women's Shoes Division assuming (1) the data are for the month ended June 30, 2017, and (2) all data equal budget except variable costs which are $5,000 over budget.

E24-16 The Sports Equipment Division of Harrington Company is operated as a profit center. Sales for the division were budgeted for 2017 at $900,000. The only variable costs budgeted for the division were cost of goods sold ($440,000) and selling and administrative ($60,000). Fixed costs were budgeted at $100,000 for cost of goods sold, $90,000 for selling and administrative, and $70,000 for noncontrollable fixed costs. Actual results for these items were:

Prepare a responsibility report for a profit center, and compute ROI.

(LO 3, 4)

Sales	$880,000
Cost of goods sold	
Variable	408,000
Fixed	105,000
Selling and administrative	
Variable	61,000
Fixed	66,000
Noncontrollable fixed	90,000

Instructions
(a) Prepare a responsibility report for the Sports Equipment Division for 2017.
(b) Assume the division is an investment center, and average operating assets were $1,000,000. The noncontrollable fixed costs are controllable at the investment center level. Compute ROI.

E24-17 The South Division of Wiig Company reported the following data for the current year.

Compute ROI for current year and for possible future changes.

(LO 4)

Sales	$3,000,000
Variable costs	1,950,000
Controllable fixed costs	600,000
Average operating assets	5,000,000

Top management is unhappy with the investment center's return on investment (ROI). It asks the manager of the South Division to submit plans to improve ROI in the next year. The manager believes it is feasible to consider the following independent courses of action.

1. Increase sales by $300,000 with no change in the contribution margin percentage.
2. Reduce variable costs by $150,000.
3. Reduce average operating assets by 4%.

Instructions

(a) Compute the return on investment (ROI) for the current year.
(b) Using the ROI formula, compute the ROI under each of the proposed courses of action. (Round to one decimal.)

Prepare a responsibility report for an investment center.

(LO 4)

E24-18 The Dinkle and Frizell Dental Clinic provides both preventive and orthodontic dental services. The two owners, Reese Dinkle and Anita Frizell, operate the clinic as two separate investment centers: Preventive Services and Orthodontic Services. Each of them is in charge of one of the centers: Reese for Preventive Services and Anita for Orthodontic Services. Each month, they prepare an income statement for the two centers to evaluate performance and make decisions about how to improve the operational efficiency and profitability of the clinic.

Recently, they have been concerned about the profitability of the Preventive Services operations. For several months, it has been reporting a loss. The responsibility report for the month of May 2017 is shown below.

	Actual	Difference from Budget
Service revenue	$ 40,000	$1,000 F
Variable costs		
Filling materials	5,000	100 U
Novocain	3,900	100 U
Supplies	1,900	350 F
Dental assistant wages	2,500	–0–
Utilities	500	110 U
Total variable costs	13,800	40 F
Fixed costs		
Allocated portion of receptionist's salary	3,000	200 U
Dentist salary	9,800	400 U
Equipment depreciation	6,000	–0–
Allocated portion of building depreciation	15,000	1,000 U
Total fixed costs	33,800	1,600 U
Operating income (loss)	$ (7,600)	$ 560 U

In addition, the owners know that the investment in operating assets at the beginning of the month was $82,400, and it was $77,600 at the end of the month. They have asked for your assistance in evaluating their current performance reporting system.

Instructions

(a) Prepare a responsibility report for an investment center as illustrated in the chapter.
(b) ✏ Write a memo to the owners discussing the deficiencies of their current reporting system.

Prepare missing amounts in responsibility reports for three investment centers.

(LO 4)

E24-19 The Ferrell Transportation Company uses a responsibility reporting system to measure the performance of its three investment centers: Planes, Taxis, and Limos. Segment performance is measured using a system of responsibility reports and return on investment calculations. The allocation of resources within the company and the segment managers' bonuses are based in part on the results shown in these reports.

Recently, the company was the victim of a computer virus that deleted portions of the company's accounting records. This was discovered when the current period's responsibility reports were being prepared. The printout of the actual operating results appeared as follows.

	Planes	**Taxis**	**Limos**
Service revenue	$?	$500,000	$?
Variable costs	5,500,000	?	300,000
Contribution margin	?	250,000	480,000
Controllable fixed costs	1,500,000	?	?
Controllable margin	?	80,000	210,000
Average operating assets	25,000,000	?	1,500,000
Return on investment	12%	10%	?

Instructions

Determine the missing pieces of information above.

*E24-20 Presented below is selected information for three regional divisions of Medina Company.

Compare ROI and residual income.

(LO 5)

	Divisions		
	North	**West**	**South**
Contribution margin	$ 300,000	$ 500,000	$ 400,000
Controllable margin	$ 140,000	$ 360,000	$ 210,000
Average operating assets	$1,000,000	$2,000,000	$1,500,000
Minimum rate of return	13%	16%	10%

Instructions

(a) Compute the return on investment for each division.
(b) Compute the residual income for each division.
(c) Assume that each division has an investment opportunity that would provide a rate of return of 16%.
 (1) If ROI is used to measure performance, which division or divisions will probably make the additional investment?
 (2) If residual income is used to measure performance, which division or divisions will probably make the additional investment?

*E24-21 Presented below is selected financial information for two divisions of Samberg Brewing.

Fill in information related to ROI and residual income.

(LO 5)

	Lager	**Lite Lager**
Contribution margin	$500,000	$ 300,000
Controllable margin	200,000	(c)
Average operating assets	(a)	$1,200,000
Minimum rate of return	(b)	11%
Return on investment	16%	(d)
Residual income	$100,000	$ 204,000

Instructions

Supply the missing information for the lettered items.

EXERCISES: SET B AND CHALLENGE EXERCISES

Visit the book's companion website, at **www.wiley.com/college/weygandt**, and choose the Student Companion site to access Exercises: Set B and Challenge Exercises.

PROBLEMS: SET A

P24-1A Bumblebee Company estimates that 300,000 direct labor hours will be worked during the coming year, 2017, in the Packaging Department. On this basis, the following budgeted manufacturing overhead cost data are computed for the year.

Prepare flexible budget and budget report for manufacturing overhead.

(LO 2)

XLS

Fixed Overhead Costs		Variable Overhead Costs	
Supervision	$ 96,000	Indirect labor	$126,000
Depreciation	72,000	Indirect materials	90,000
Insurance	30,000	Repairs	69,000
Rent	24,000	Utilities	72,000
Property taxes	18,000	Lubricants	18,000
	$240,000		$375,000

It is estimated that direct labor hours worked each month will range from 27,000 to 36,000 hours.

During October, 27,000 direct labor hours were worked and the following overhead costs were incurred.

Fixed overhead costs: supervision $8,000, depreciation $6,000, insurance $2,460, rent $2,000, and property taxes $1,500.

Variable overhead costs: indirect labor $12,432, indirect materials $7,680, repairs $6,100, utilities $6,840, and lubricants $1,920.

Instructions

(a) Total costs: DLH 27,000,
$53,750; DLH 36,000,
$65,000
(b) Total $1,182 U

(a) Prepare a monthly manufacturing overhead flexible budget for each increment of 3,000 direct labor hours over the relevant range for the year ending December 31, 2017.

(b) Prepare a flexible budget report for October.

(c) •———— Comment on management's efficiency in controlling manufacturing overhead costs in October.

Prepare flexible budget, budget report, and graph for manufacturing overhead.

(LO 2)

P24-2A Zelmer Company manufactures tablecloths. Sales have grown rapidly over the past 2 years. As a result, the president has installed a budgetary control system for 2017. The following data were used in developing the master manufacturing overhead budget for the Ironing Department, which is based on an activity index of direct labor hours.

Variable Costs	Rate per Direct Labor Hour	Annual Fixed Costs	
Indirect labor	$0.40	Supervision	$48,000
Indirect materials	0.50	Depreciation	18,000
Factory utilities	0.30	Insurance	12,000
Factory repairs	0.20	Rent	30,000

The master overhead budget was prepared on the expectation that 480,000 direct labor hours will be worked during the year. In June, 41,000 direct labor hours were worked. At that level of activity, actual costs were as shown below.

Variable—per direct labor hour: indirect labor $0.44, indirect materials $0.48, factory utilities $0.32, and factory repairs $0.25.

Fixed: same as budgeted.

Instructions

(a) Total costs: 35,000 DLH,
$58,000; 50,000 DLH,
$79,000
(b) Budget $66,400
Actual $70,090

(a) Prepare a monthly manufacturing overhead flexible budget for the year ending December 31, 2017, assuming production levels range from 35,000 to 50,000 direct labor hours. Use increments of 5,000 direct labor hours.

(b) Prepare a budget report for June comparing actual results with budget data based on the flexible budget.

(c) Were costs effectively controlled? Explain.

(d) State the formula for computing the total budgeted costs for the Ironing Department.

(e) Prepare the flexible budget graph, showing total budgeted costs at 35,000 and 45,000 direct labor hours. Use increments of 5,000 direct labor hours on the horizontal axis and increments of $10,000 on the vertical axis.

State total budgeted cost formula, and prepare flexible budget reports for 2 time periods.

(LO 1, 2)

XLS

P24-3A Ratchet Company uses budgets in controlling costs. The August 2017 budget report for the company's Assembling Department is as follows.

RATCHET COMPANY
Budget Report
Assembling Department
For the Month Ended August 31, 2017

Manufacturing Costs	Budget	Actual	Difference Favorable F Unfavorable U
Variable costs			
Direct materials	$ 48,000	$ 47,000	$1,000 F
Direct labor	54,000	51,200	2,800 F
Indirect materials	24,000	24,200	200 U
Indirect labor	18,000	17,500	500 F
Utilities	15,000	14,900	100 F
Maintenance	12,000	12,400	400 U
Total variable	171,000	167,200	3,800 F
Fixed costs			
Rent	12,000	12,000	–0–
Supervision	17,000	17,000	–0–
Depreciation	6,000	6,000	–0–
Total fixed	35,000	35,000	–0–
Total costs	$206,000	$202,200	$3,800 F

The monthly budget amounts in the report were based on an expected production of 60,000 units per month or 720,000 units per year. The Assembling Department manager is pleased with the report and expects a raise, or at least praise for a job well done. The company president, however, is unhappy with the results for August because only 58,000 units were produced.

Instructions
(a) State the total monthly budgeted cost formula.
(b) Prepare a budget report for August using flexible budget data. Why does this report provide a better basis for evaluating performance than the report based on static budget data?
(c) In September, 64,000 units were produced. Prepare the budget report using flexible budget data, assuming (1) each variable cost was 10% higher than its actual cost in August, and (2) fixed costs were the same in September as in August.

(b) Budget $200,300

(c) Budget $217,400
Actual $218,920

P24-4A Clarke Inc. operates the Patio Furniture Division as a profit center. Operating data for this division for the year ended December 31, 2017, are as shown below.

Prepare responsibility report for a profit center.

(LO 3)

	Budget	Difference from Budget
Sales	$2,500,000	$50,000 F
Cost of goods sold		
Variable	1,300,000	41,000 F
Controllable fixed	200,000	3,000 U
Selling and administrative		
Variable	220,000	6,000 U
Controllable fixed	50,000	2,000 U
Noncontrollable fixed costs	70,000	4,000 U

In addition, Clarke incurs $180,000 of indirect fixed costs that were budgeted at $175,000. Twenty percent (20%) of these costs are allocated to the Patio Furniture Division.

Instructions
(a) Prepare a responsibility report for the Patio Furniture Division for the year.
(b) ———— Comment on the manager's performance in controlling revenues and costs.
(c) Identify any costs excluded from the responsibility report and explain why they were excluded.

(a) Contribution margin
$85,000 F
Controllable margin
$80,000 F

Prepare responsibility report for an investment center, and compute ROI.

(LO 4)

P24-5A Optimus Company manufactures a variety of tools and industrial equipment. The company operates through three divisions. Each division is an investment center. Operating data for the Home Division for the year ended December 31, 2017, and relevant budget data are as follows.

	Actual	Comparison with Budget
Sales	$1,400,000	$100,000 favorable
Variable cost of goods sold	665,000	45,000 unfavorable
Variable selling and administrative expenses	125,000	25,000 unfavorable
Controllable fixed cost of goods sold	170,000	On target
Controllable fixed selling and administrative expenses	80,000	On target

Average operating assets for the year for the Home Division were $2,000,000 which was also the budgeted amount.

Instructions

*(a) Controllable margin:
Budget $330;
Actual $360*

(a) Prepare a responsibility report (in thousands of dollars) for the Home Division.

(b) Evaluate the manager's performance. Which items will likely be investigated by top management?

(c) Compute the expected ROI in 2017 for the Home Division, assuming the following independent changes to actual data.

   (1) Variable cost of goods sold is decreased by 5%.

   (2) Average operating assets are decreased by 10%.

   (3) Sales are increased by $200,000, and this increase is expected to increase contribution margin by $80,000.

Prepare reports for cost centers under responsibility accounting, and comment on performance of managers.

(LO 3)

P24-6A Durham Company uses a responsibility reporting system. It has divisions in Denver, Seattle, and San Diego. Each division has three production departments: Cutting, Shaping, and Finishing. The responsibility for each department rests with a manager who reports to the division production manager. Each division manager reports to the vice president of production. There are also vice presidents for marketing and finance. All vice presidents report to the president.

In January 2017, controllable actual and budget manufacturing overhead cost data for the departments and divisions were as shown below.

Manufacturing Overhead	Actual	Budget
Individual costs—Cutting Department—Seattle		
Indirect labor	$ 73,000	$ 70,000
Indirect materials	47,900	46,000
Maintenance	20,500	18,000
Utilities	20,100	17,000
Supervision	22,000	20,000
	$183,500	$171,000
Total costs		
Shaping Department—Seattle	$158,000	$148,000
Finishing Department—Seattle	210,000	205,000
Denver division	678,000	673,000
San Diego division	722,000	715,000

Additional overhead costs were incurred as follows: Seattle division production manager—actual costs $52,500, budget $51,000; vice president of production—actual costs $65,000, budget $64,000; president—actual costs $76,400, budget $74,200. These expenses are not allocated.

The vice presidents who report to the president, other than the vice president of production, had the following expenses.

Vice President	Actual	Budget
Marketing	$133,600	$130,000
Finance	109,000	104,000

Instructions

(a) Using the format in Illustration 24-19 (page 1123), prepare the following responsibility reports.

    (1) Manufacturing overhead—Cutting Department manager—Seattle division.

    (2) Manufacturing overhead—Seattle division manager.

    (3) Manufacturing overhead—vice president of production.

    (4) Manufacturing overhead and expenses—president.

(b) Comment on the comparative performances of:

    (1) Department managers in the Seattle division.

    (2) Division managers.

    (3) Vice presidents.

(a) (1) $12,500 U
(2) $29,000 U
(3) $42,000 U
(4) $52,800 U

***P24-7A** Sentinel Industries has manufactured prefabricated houses for over 20 years. The houses are constructed in sections to be assembled on customers' lots. Sentinel expanded into the precut housing market when it acquired Jensen Company, one of its suppliers. In this market, various types of lumber are precut into the appropriate lengths, banded into packages, and shipped to customers' lots for assembly. Sentinel designated the Jensen Division as an investment center.

Compare ROI and residual income.

(LO 5)

    Sentinel uses return on investment (ROI) as a performance measure with investment defined as average operating assets. Management bonuses are based in part on ROI. All investments are expected to earn a minimum rate of return of 18%. Jensen's ROI has ranged from 20.1% to 23.5% since it was acquired. Jensen had an investment opportunity in 2017 that had an estimated ROI of 19%. Jensen management decided against the investment because it believed the investment would decrease the division's overall ROI.

    Selected financial information for Jensen are presented below. The division's average operating assets were $12,300,000 for the year 2017.

SENTINEL INDUSTRIES
Jensen Division
Selected Financial Information
For the Year Ended December 31, 2017

Sales	$24,000,000
Contribution margin	9,100,000
Controllable margin	2,460,000

Instructions

(a) Calculate the following performance measures for 2017 for the Jensen Division.

    (1) Return on investment (ROI).

    (2) Residual income.

(b) ⎯⎯⎯⎯ Would the management of Jensen Division have been more likely to accept the investment opportunity it had in 2017 if residual income were used as a performance measure instead of ROI? Explain your answer.

(CMA adapted)

▌PROBLEMS: SET B AND SET C

Visit the book's companion website, at **www.wiley.com/college/weygandt**, and choose the Student Companion site to access Problems: Set B and Set C.

▌CONTINUING PROBLEMS

CURRENT DESIGNS

CD24 The Current Designs staff has prepared the annual manufacturing budget for the rotomolded line based on an estimated annual production of 4,000 kayaks during 2017. Each kayak will require 54 pounds of polyethylene powder and a finishing kit (rope, seat, hardware, etc.). The polyethylene powder used in these kayaks costs $1.50 per pound, and the finishing kits cost $170 each. Each kayak

EXCEL
TUTORIAL

will use two kinds of labor—2 hours of type I labor from people who run the oven and trim the plastic, and 3 hours of work from type II workers who attach the hatches and seat and other hardware. The type I employees are paid $15 per hour, and the type II are paid $12 per hour.

Manufacturing overhead is budgeted at $396,000 for 2017, broken down as follows.

Variable costs	
Indirect materials	$ 40,000
Manufacturing supplies	53,800
Maintenance and utilities	88,000
	181,800
Fixed costs	
Supervision	90,000
Insurance	14,400
Depreciation	109,800
	214,200
Total	$396,000

During the first quarter, ended March 31, 2017, 1,050 units were actually produced with the following costs.

Polyethylene powder	$ 87,000
Finishing kits	178,840
Type I labor	31,500
Type II labor	39,060
Indirect materials	10,500
Manufacturing supplies	14,150
Maintenance and utilities	26,000
Supervision	20,000
Insurance	3,600
Depreciation	27,450
Total	$438,100

Instructions

(a) Prepare the annual manufacturing budget for 2017, assuming that 4,000 kayaks will be produced.

(b) Prepare the flexible budget for manufacturing for the quarter ended March 31, 2017. Assume activity levels of 900, 1,000, and 1,050 units.

(c) Assuming the rotomolded line is treated as a profit center, prepare a flexible budget report for manufacturing for the quarter ended March 31, 2017, when 1,050 units were produced.

WATERWAYS

(*Note:* This is a continuation of the Waterways problem from Chapters 15–23.)

WP24 Waterways Corporation is continuing its budget preparations. This problem gives you static budget information as well as actual overhead costs, and asks you to calculate amounts related to budgetary control and responsibility accounting.

Go to the book's companion website, at **www.wiley.com/college/weygandt**, *to find the completion of this problem.*

BROADENING YOUR PERSPECTIVE

MANAGEMENT DECISION-MAKING

Decision-Making Across the Organization

BYP24-1 Green Pastures is a 400-acre farm on the outskirts of the Kentucky Bluegrass, specializing in the boarding of broodmares and their foals. A recent economic downturn in the thoroughbred industry has led to a decline in breeding activities, and it has made the boarding business extremely competitive. To meet the competition, Green Pastures planned in 2017 to entertain clients, advertise more extensively, and absorb expenses formerly paid by clients such as veterinary and blacksmith fees.

The budget report for 2017 is presented below. As shown, the static income statement budget for the year is based on an expected 21,900 boarding days at $25 per mare. The variable expenses per mare per day were budgeted: feed $5, veterinary fees $3, blacksmith fees $0.25, and supplies $0.55. All other budgeted expenses were either semifixed or fixed.

During the year, management decided not to replace a worker who quit in March, but it did issue a new advertising brochure and did more entertaining of clients.[1]

GREEN PASTURES
Static Budget Income Statement
For the Year Ended December 31, 2017

	Actual	Master Budget	Difference
Number of mares	52	60	8 U
Number of boarding days	19,000	21,900	2,900 U
Sales	$380,000	$547,500	$167,500 U
Less: Variable expenses			
Feed	104,390	109,500	5,110 F
Veterinary fees	58,838	65,700	6,862 F
Blacksmith fees	4,984	5,475	491 F
Supplies	10,178	12,045	1,867 F
Total variable expenses	178,390	192,720	14,330 F
Contribution margin	201,610	354,780	153,170 U
Less: Fixed expenses			
Depreciation	40,000	40,000	–0–
Insurance	11,000	11,000	–0–
Utilities	12,000	14,000	2,000 F
Repairs and maintenance	10,000	11,000	1,000 F
Labor	88,000	95,000	7,000 F
Advertisement	12,000	8,000	4,000 U
Entertainment	7,000	5,000	2,000 U
Total fixed expenses	180,000	184,000	4,000 F
Net income	$ 21,610	$170,780	$149,170 U

Instructions

With the class divided into groups, answer the following.

(a) Based on the static budget report:
(1) What was the primary cause(s) of the loss in net income?
(2) Did management do a good, average, or poor job of controlling expenses?
(3) Were management's decisions to stay competitive sound?
(b) Prepare a flexible budget report for the year.
(c) Based on the flexible budget report, answer the three questions in part (a) above.
(d) What course of action do you recommend for the management of Green Pastures?

Managerial Analysis

BYP24-2 Lanier Company manufactures expensive watch cases sold as souvenirs. Three of its sales departments are Retail Sales, Wholesale Sales, and Outlet Sales. The Retail Sales Department is a profit center. The Wholesale Sales Department is a cost center. Its managers merely take orders from customers who purchase through the company's wholesale catalog. The Outlet Sales Department is an investment center because each manager is given full responsibility for an outlet store location. The

[1]Data for this case are based on Hans Sprohge and John Talbott, "New Applications for Variance Analysis," *Journal of Accountancy* (AICPA, New York), April 1989, pp. 137–141.

manager can hire and discharge employees, purchase, maintain, and sell equipment, and in general is fairly independent of company control.

Mary Gammel is a manager in the Retail Sales Department. Stephen Flott manages the Wholesale Sales Department. Jose Gomez manages the Golden Gate Club outlet store in San Francisco. The following are the budget responsibility reports for each of the three departments.

Budget

	Retail Sales	Wholesale Sales	Outlet Sales
Sales	$ 750,000	$ 400,000	$200,000
Variable costs			
Cost of goods sold	150,000	100,000	25,000
Advertising	100,000	30,000	5,000
Sales salaries	75,000	15,000	3,000
Printing	10,000	20,000	5,000
Travel	20,000	30,000	2,000
Fixed costs			
Rent	50,000	30,000	10,000
Insurance	5,000	2,000	1,000
Depreciation	75,000	100,000	40,000
Investment in assets	1,000,000	1,200,000	800,000

Actual Results

	Retail Sales	Wholesale Sales	Outlet Sales
Sales	$ 750,000	$ 400,000	$200,000
Variable costs			
Cost of goods sold	192,000	122,000	26,500
Advertising	100,000	30,000	5,000
Sales salaries	75,000	15,000	3,000
Printing	10,000	20,000	5,000
Travel	14,000	21,000	1,500
Fixed costs			
Rent	40,000	50,000	12,300
Insurance	5,000	2,000	1,000
Depreciation	80,000	90,000	56,000
Investment in assets	1,000,000	1,200,000	800,000

Instructions
(a) Determine which of the items should be included in the responsibility report for each of the three managers.
(b) Compare the budgeted measures with the actual results. Decide which results should be called to the attention of each manager.

Real-World Focus

BYP24-3 Computer Associates International, Inc., the world's leading business software company, delivers the end-to-end infrastructure to enable e-business through innovative technology, services, and education. Recently, Computer Associates had 19,000 employees worldwide and revenue of over $6 billion.

The following information is from the company's annual report.

The Company has experienced a pattern of business whereby revenue for its third and fourth fiscal quarters reflects an increase over first- and second-quarter revenue. The Company attributes this increase to clients' increased spending at the end of their calendar year budgetary periods and the culmination of its annual sales plan. Since the Company's costs do not increase proportionately with the third- and fourth-quarters' increase in revenue, the higher revenue in these quarters results in greater profit margins and income. Fourth-quarter profitability is traditionally affected by significant new hirings, training, and education expenditures for the succeeding year.

Instructions

(a) Why don't the company's costs increase proportionately as the revenues increase in the third and fourth quarters?

(b) What type of budgeting seems appropriate for the Computer Associates situation?

BYP24-4 There are many useful resources regarding budgeting available on websites. The following activity investigates the results of a comprehensive budgeting study.

Address: **http://www.accountingweb.com/whitepapers/centage_ioma.pdf**, or go to **www.wiley.com/college/weygandt**

Instructions

Go to the address above and then answer the following questions.

(a) What are cited as the two most common "pain points" of budgeting?

(b) What percentage of companies that participated in the survey said that they prepare annual budgets? Of those that prepare budgets, what percentage say that they start the budgeting process by first generating sales projections?

(c) What is the most common amount of time for the annual budgeting process?

(d) When evaluating variances from budgeted amounts, what was the most commonly defined range of acceptable tolerance levels?

(e) The study defines three types of consequences for varying from budgeted amounts. How does it describe "severe" consequences?

CRITICAL THINKING

Communication Activity

BYP24-5 The manufacturing overhead budget for Fleming Company contains the following items.

Variable costs		Fixed costs	
Indirect materials	$22,000	Supervision	$17,000
Indirect labor	12,000	Inspection costs	1,000
Maintenance expense	10,000	Insurance expense	2,000
Manufacturing supplies	6,000	Depreciation	15,000
Total variable	$50,000	Total fixed	$35,000

The budget was based on an estimated 2,000 units being produced. During the past month, 1,500 units were produced, and the following costs incurred.

Variable costs		Fixed costs	
Indirect materials	$22,500	Supervision	$18,400
Indirect labor	13,500	Inspection costs	1,200
Maintenance expense	8,200	Insurance expense	2,200
Manufacturing supplies	5,000	Depreciation	14,700
Total variable	$49,200	Total fixed	$36,500

Instructions

(a) Determine which items would be controllable by Fred Bedner, the production manager.

(b) How much should have been spent during the month for the manufacture of the 1,500 units?

(c) Prepare a flexible manufacturing overhead budget report for Mr. Bedner.

(d) Prepare a responsibility report. Include only the costs that would have been controllable by Mr. Bedner. Assume that the supervision cost above includes Mr. Bedner's salary of $10,000, both at budget and actual. In an attached memo, describe clearly for Mr. Bedner the areas in which his performance needs to be improved.

Ethics Case

BYP24-6 American Products Corporation participates in a highly competitive industry. In order to meet this competition and achieve profit goals, the company has chosen the decentralized form of organization. Each manager of a decentralized investment center is measured on the basis of profit contribution, market penetration, and return on investment. Failure to meet the objectives established by corporate management for these measures has not been acceptable and usually has resulted in demotion or dismissal of an investment center manager.

An anonymous survey of managers in the company revealed that the managers feel the pressure to compromise their personal ethical standards to achieve the corporate objectives. For example, at certain plant locations there was pressure to reduce quality control to a level which could not assure that all unsafe products would be rejected. Also, sales personnel were encouraged to use questionable sales tactics to obtain orders, including gifts and other incentives to purchasing agents.

The chief executive officer is disturbed by the survey findings. In his opinion, such behavior cannot be condoned by the company. He concludes that the company should do something about this problem.

Instructions

(a) Who are the stakeholders (the affected parties) in this situation?

(b) Identify the ethical implications, conflicts, or dilemmas in the above described situation.

(c) What might the company do to reduce the pressures on managers and decrease the ethical conflicts?

(CMA adapted)

All About You

BYP24-7 It is one thing to prepare a personal budget; it is another thing to stick to it. Financial planners have suggested various mechanisms to provide support for enforcing personal budgets. One approach is called "envelope budgeting."

Instructions

Read the article provided at **http://en.wikipedia.org/wiki/Envelope_budgeting**, and answer the following questions.

(a) Summarize the process of envelope budgeting.

(b) Evaluate whether you think you would benefit from envelope budgeting. What do you think are its strengths and weaknesses relative to your situation?

Considering Your Costs and Benefits

BYP24-8 Preparing a personal budget is a great first step toward control over your personal finances. It is especially useful to prepare a budget when you face a big decision. For most people, the biggest decision they will ever make is whether to purchase a house. The percentage of people in the United States who own a home is high compared to many other countries. This is partially the result of U.S. government programs and incentives that encourage home ownership. For example, the interest on a home mortgage is tax-deductible.

Before purchasing a house, you should first consider whether buying it is the best choice for you. Suppose you just graduated from college and are moving to a new community. Should you immediately buy a new home?

YES: If I purchase a home, I am making my housing cost more like a "fixed cost," thus minimizing increases in my future housing costs. Also, I benefit from the appreciation in my home's value. Although recent turbulence in the economy has caused home prices in many communities to decline, I know that over the long term, home prices have increased across the country.

NO: I just moved to a new town, so I don't know the housing market. I am new to my job, so I don't know whether I will like it or my new community. Also, if my job does go well, it is likely that my income will increase in the next few years, so I will able to afford a better house if I wait. Therefore, the flexibility provided by renting is very valuable to me at this point in my life.

Instructions

Write a response indicating your position regarding this situation. Provide support for your view.

25 Standard Costs and Balanced Scorecard

CHAPTER PREVIEW Standards are a fact of life. You met the admission standards for the school you are attending. The vehicle that you drive had to meet certain governmental emissions standards. The hamburgers and salads that you eat in a restaurant have to meet certain health and nutritional standards before they can be sold. As described in our Feature Story below, Starbucks has standards for the costs of its materials, labor, and overhead. The reason for standards in these cases is very simple: They help to ensure that overall product quality is high while keeping costs under control.

In this chapter, we continue the study of controlling costs. You will learn how to evaluate performance using standard costs and a balanced scorecard.

FEATURE STORY

80,000 Different Caffeinated Combinations

When Howard Schultz purchased a small Seattle coffee-roasting business in 1987, he set out to create a new kind of company. He thought the company should sell coffee by the cup in its store, in addition to the bags of roasted beans it already sold. He also saw the store as a place where you could order a beverage, custom-made to your unique tastes, in an environment that would give you the sense that you had escaped, if only momentarily, from the chaos we call life. Finally, Schultz believed that the company would prosper if employees shared in its success.

In a little more than 20 years, Howard Schultz's company, Starbucks, grew from that one store to over 17,000 locations in 54 countries. That is an incredible rate of growth, and it didn't happen by accident. While Starbucks does everything it can to maximize the customer's experience, behind the scenes it needs to control costs. Consider the almost infinite options

of beverage combinations and variations at Starbucks. The company must determine the most efficient way to make each beverage, it must communicate these methods in the form of standards to its employees, and it must then evaluate whether those standards are being met.

Schultz's book, *Onward: How Starbucks Fought for Its Life Without Losing Its Soul*, describes a painful period in which Starbucks had to close 600 stores and lay off thousands of employees. However, when a prominent shareholder suggested that the company eliminate its employee healthcare plan, as so many other companies had done, Schultz refused. The healthcare plan represented one of the company's most tangible commitments to employee well-being as well as to corporate social responsibility. Schultz feels strongly that providing health care to the company's employees is an essential part of the standard cost of a cup of Starbucks' coffee.

> ▶ In WileyPLUS, watch the *Starbucks* video to learn more about how the company sets standards, and watch the *Southwest Airlines* video to learn more about the real-world use of the balanced scorecard.

© Jeff Greenberg 5 of 6 / Alamy

CHAPTER OUTLINE

Learning Objectives

1   **Describe standard costs.**
- Distinguishing between standards and budgets
- Setting standard costs

DO IT!   **1**   Standard Costs

2   **Determine direct materials variances.**
- Analyzing and reporting variances
- Direct materials variances

DO IT!   **2**   Direct Materials Variances

3   **Determine direct labor and total manufacturing overhead variances.**
- Direct labor variances
- Manufacturing overhead variances

DO IT!   **3**   Labor and Manufacturing Overhead Variances

4   **Prepare variance reports and balanced scorecards.**
- Reporting variances
- Income statement presentation of variances
- Balanced scorecard

DO IT!   **4**   Reporting Variances

Go to the **REVIEW AND PRACTICE** section at the end of the chapter for a review of key concepts and practice applications with solutions.

Visit **WileyPLUS with ORION** for additional tutorials and practice opportunities.

Standards are common in business. Those imposed by government agencies are often called **regulations**. They include the Fair Labor Standards Act, the Equal Employment Opportunity Act, and a multitude of environmental standards. Standards established internally by a company may extend to personnel matters, such as employee absenteeism and ethical codes of conduct, quality control standards for products, and standard costs for goods and services. In managerial accounting, **standard costs** are predetermined unit costs, which companies use as measures of performance.

We focus on manufacturing operations in this chapter. But you should recognize that standard costs also apply to many types of service businesses as well. For example, a fast-food restaurant such as **McDonald's** knows the price it should pay for pickles, beef, buns, and other ingredients. It also knows how much time it should take an employee to flip hamburgers. If the company pays too much for pickles or if employees take too much time to prepare Big Macs, McDonald's notices the deviations and takes corrective action. Not-for-profit entities, such as universities, charitable organizations, and governmental agencies, also may use standard costs as measures of performance.

Standard costs offer a number of advantages to an organization, as shown in Illustration 25-1. The organization will realize these advantages only when standard costs are carefully established and prudently used. Using standards solely as

Illustration 25-1
Advantages of standard costs

Advantages of Standard Costs

Facilitate management planning

Promote greater economy by making employees more "cost-conscious"

Useful in setting selling prices

Contribute to management control by providing basis for evaluation of cost control

Useful in highlighting variances in management by exception

Simplify costing of inventories and reduce clerical costs

a way to place blame can have a negative effect on managers and employees. To minimize this effect, many companies offer wage incentives to those who meet the standards.

Distinguishing Between Standards and Budgets

Both **standards** and **budgets** are predetermined costs, and both contribute to management planning and control. There is a difference, however, in the way the terms are expressed. A standard is a **unit** amount. A budget is a **total** amount. Thus, it is customary to state that the **standard cost** of direct labor for a unit of product is, say, $10. If the company produces 5,000 units of the product, the $50,000 of direct labor is the **budgeted** labor cost. A standard is the budgeted **cost per unit** of product. A standard is therefore concerned with each individual cost component that makes up the entire budget.

There are important accounting differences between budgets and standards. Except in the application of manufacturing overhead to jobs and processes, budget data are not journalized in cost accounting systems. In contrast, as we illustrate in the appendix to this chapter, standard costs may be incorporated into cost accounting systems. Also, a company may report its inventories at standard cost in its financial statements, but it would not report inventories at budgeted costs.

Setting Standard Costs

The setting of standard costs to produce a unit of product is a difficult task. It requires input from all persons who have responsibility for costs and quantities. To determine the standard cost of direct materials, management consults purchasing agents, product managers, quality control engineers, and production supervisors. In setting the standard cost for direct labor, managers obtain pay rate data from the payroll department. Industrial engineers generally determine the labor time requirements. The managerial accountant provides important input for the standard-setting process by accumulating historical cost data and by knowing how costs respond to changes in activity levels.

To be effective in controlling costs, standard costs need to be current at all times. Thus, standards are under continuous review. They should change whenever managers determine that the existing standard is not a good measure of performance. Circumstances that warrant revision of a standard include changed wage rates resulting from a new union contract, a change in product specifications, or the implementation of a new manufacturing method.

IDEAL VERSUS NORMAL STANDARDS

Companies set standards at one of two levels: ideal or normal. **Ideal standards** represent optimum levels of performance under perfect operating conditions. **Normal standards** represent efficient levels of performance that are attainable under expected operating conditions.

Some managers believe ideal standards will stimulate workers to ever-increasing improvement. However, most managers believe that ideal standards lower the morale of the entire workforce because they are difficult, if not impossible, to meet. Very few companies use ideal standards.

Most companies that use standards set them at a normal level. Properly set, normal standards should be **rigorous but attainable**. Normal standards allow for rest periods, machine breakdowns, and other "normal" contingencies in the production process. In the remainder of this chapter, we will assume that standard costs are set at a normal level.

> **ETHICS NOTE**
>
> When standards are set too high, employees sometimes feel pressure to consider unethical practices to meet these standards.

A CASE STUDY

To establish the standard cost of producing a product, it is necessary to establish standards for each manufacturing cost element—direct materials, direct labor, and manufacturing overhead. The standard for each element is derived from the standard price to be paid and the standard quantity to be used.

To illustrate, we use an extended example. Xonic Beverage Company uses standard costs to measure performance at the production facility of its caffeinated energy drink, Xonic Tonic. Xonic produces one-gallon containers of concentrated syrup that it sells to coffee and smoothie shops, and other retail outlets. The syrup is mixed with ice water or ice "slush" before serving. The potency of the beverage varies depending on the amount of concentrated syrup used.

DIRECT MATERIALS The **direct materials price standard** is the cost per unit of direct materials that should be incurred. This standard is based on the purchasing department's best estimate of the **cost of raw materials**. This cost is frequently based on current purchase prices. The price standard also includes an amount for related costs such as receiving, storing, and handling. The materials price standard per pound of material for Xonic Tonic is as follows.

Illustration 25-2
Setting direct materials price standard

Item	Price
Purchase price, net of discounts	$ 2.70
Freight	0.20
Receiving and handling	0.10
Standard direct materials price per pound	**$3.00**

The **direct materials quantity standard** is the quantity of direct materials that should be used per unit of finished goods. This standard is expressed as a physical measure, such as pounds, barrels, or board feet. In setting the standard, management considers both the quality and quantity of materials required to manufacture the product. The standard includes allowances for unavoidable waste and normal spoilage. The standard quantity per unit for Xonic Tonic is shown in Illustration 25-3.

Item	Quantity (Pounds)
Required materials	3.5
Allowance for waste	0.4
Allowance for spoilage	0.1
Standard direct materials quantity per unit	**4.0**

The standard direct materials cost per unit is the standard direct materials price times the standard direct materials quantity. For Xonic, the standard direct materials cost per gallon of Xonic Tonic is $12.00 ($3 × 4 pounds).

DIRECT LABOR The **direct labor price standard** is the rate per hour that should be incurred for direct labor. This standard is based on current wage rates, adjusted for anticipated changes such as cost of living adjustments (COLAs). The price standard also generally includes employer payroll taxes and fringe benefits, such as paid holidays and vacations. For Xonic, the direct labor price standard is as follows.

Item	Price
Hourly wage rate	$ 12.50
COLA	0.25
Payroll taxes	0.75
Fringe benefits	1.50
Standard direct labor rate per hour	**$15.00**

The **direct labor quantity standard** is the time that should be required to make one unit of the product. This standard is especially critical in labor-intensive companies. Allowances should be made in this standard for rest periods, cleanup, machine setup, and machine downtime. Illustration 25-5 shows the direct labor quantity standard for Xonic.

Item	Quantity (Hours)
Actual production time	1.5
Rest periods and cleanup	0.2
Setup and downtime	0.3
Standard direct labor hours per unit	**2.0**

The standard direct labor cost per unit is the standard direct labor rate times the standard direct labor hours. For Xonic, the standard direct labor cost per gallon is $30 ($15 × 2 hours).

MANUFACTURING OVERHEAD For manufacturing overhead, companies use a **standard predetermined overhead rate** in setting the standard. This overhead rate is determined by dividing budgeted overhead costs by an expected standard activity index. For example, the index may be standard direct labor hours or standard machine hours.

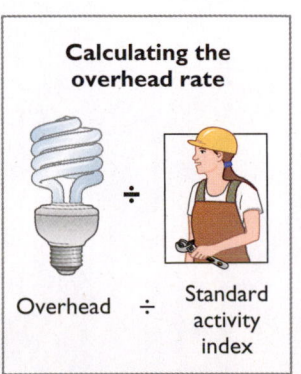

Calculating the overhead rate

Overhead ÷ Standard activity index

As discussed in Chapter 18, many companies employ activity-based costing (ABC) to allocate overhead costs. Because ABC uses multiple activity indices to allocate overhead costs, it results in a better correlation between activities and costs incurred than do other methods. As a result, the use of ABC can significantly improve the usefulness of standard costing for management decision-making.

Xonic uses standard direct labor hours as the activity index. The company expects to produce 13,200 gallons of Xonic Tonic during the year at normal capacity. **Normal capacity** is the average activity output that a company should experience over the long run. Since it takes two direct labor hours for each gallon, total standard direct labor hours are 26,400 (13,200 gallons × 2 hours).

At normal capacity of 26,400 direct labor hours, overhead costs are expected to be $132,000. Of that amount, $79,200 are variable and $52,800 are fixed. Illustration 25-6 shows computation of the standard predetermined overhead rates for Xonic.

Illustration 25-6
Computing predetermined overhead rates

Budgeted Overhead Costs	Amount	÷	Standard Direct Labor Hours	=	Overhead Rate per Direct Labor Hour
Variable	$ 79,200		26,400		$3.00
Fixed	52,800		26,400		2.00
Total	$132,000		26,400		**$5.00**

The standard manufacturing overhead cost per unit is the predetermined overhead rate times the activity index quantity standard. For Xonic, which uses direct labor hours as its activity index, the standard manufacturing overhead cost per gallon of Xonic Tonic is $10 ($5 × 2 hours).

TOTAL STANDARD COST PER UNIT After a company has established the standard quantity and price per unit of product, it can determine the total standard cost. The total standard cost per unit is the sum of the standard costs of direct materials, direct labor, and manufacturing overhead. The total standard cost per gallon of Xonic Tonic is $52, as shown on the following standard cost card.

Illustration 25-7
Standard cost per gallon of Xonic Tonic

Product: Xonic Tonic		Unit Measure: Gallon		
Manufacturing Cost Elements	Standard Quantity	× Standard Price	= Standard Cost	
Direct materials	4 pounds	$ 3.00	$12.00	
Direct labor	2 hours	$15.00	30.00	
Manufacturing overhead	2 hours	$ 5.00	10.00	
			$52.00	

The company prepares a standard cost card for each product. This card provides the basis for determining variances from standards.

DO IT!   1   Standard Costs

Action Plan

✔ Know that standard costs are predetermined unit costs.

✔ To establish the standard cost of producing a product, establish the standard for each manufacturing cost element—direct materials, direct labor, and manufacturing overhead.

✔ Compute the standard cost for each element from the standard price to be paid and the standard quantity to be used.

Ridette Inc. accumulated the following standard cost data concerning product Cty31.

Direct materials per unit: 1.5 pounds at $4 per pound
Direct labor per unit: 0.25 hours at $13 per hour.
Manufacturing overhead: allocated based on direct labor hours at a predetermined rate of $15.60 per direct labor hour.

Compute the standard cost of one unit of product Cty31.

Solution

Manufacturing Cost Element	Standard Quantity	×	Standard Price	=	Standard Cost
Direct materials	1.5 pounds		$ 4.00		$ 6.00
Direct labor	0.25 hours		$13.00		3.25
Manufacturing overhead	0.25 hours		$15.60		3.90
Total					$13.15

Related exercise material: **BE25-2, BE25-3, E25-1, E25-2, E25-3, and DO IT! 25-1.**

LEARNING OBJECTIVE 2   Determine direct materials variances.

Analyzing and Reporting Variances

One of the major management uses of standard costs is to identify variances from standards. **Variances** are the differences between total actual costs and total standard costs.

To illustrate, assume that in producing 1,000 gallons of Xonic Tonic in the month of June, Xonic incurred the following costs.

Alternative Terminology
In business, the term *variance* is also used to indicate differences between total budgeted and total actual costs.

Illustration 25-8
Actual production costs

Direct materials	$13,020
Direct labor	31,080
Variable overhead	6,500
Fixed overhead	4,400
Total actual costs	$55,000

Companies determine total standard costs by multiplying the units produced by the standard cost per unit. The total standard cost of Xonic Tonic is $52,000 (1,000 gallons × $52). Thus, the total variance is $3,000, as shown below.

Illustration 25-9
Computation of total variance

Actual costs	$55,000
Less: Standard costs	52,000
Total variance	**$ 3,000**

Note that the variance is expressed in total dollars, not on a per unit basis.

When actual costs exceed standard costs, the variance is **unfavorable**. The $3,000 variance in June for Xonic Tonic is unfavorable. An unfavorable variance has a negative connotation. It suggests that the company paid too much for one or more of the manufacturing cost elements or that it used the elements inefficiently.

If actual costs are less than standard costs, the variance is **favorable**. A favorable variance has a positive connotation. It suggests efficiencies in incurring manufacturing costs and in using direct materials, direct labor, and manufacturing overhead.

However, be careful: A favorable variance could be obtained by using inferior materials. In printing wedding invitations, for example, a favorable variance could result from using an inferior grade of paper. Or, a favorable variance might be achieved in installing tires on an automobile assembly line by tightening only half of the lug bolts. A variance is not favorable if the company has sacrificed quality control standards.

To interpret a variance, you must analyze its components. A variance can result from differences related to the cost of materials, labor, or overhead. Illustration 25-10 shows that the total variance is the sum of the materials, labor, and overhead variances.

Illustration 25-10
Components of total variance

Materials Variance + Labor Variance + Overhead Variance = **Total Variance**

In the following discussion, you will see that the materials variance and the labor variance are the sum of variances resulting from price differences and quantity differences. Illustration 25-11 shows a format for computing the price and quantity variances.

Illustration 25-11
Breakdown of materials or labor variance into price and quantity variances

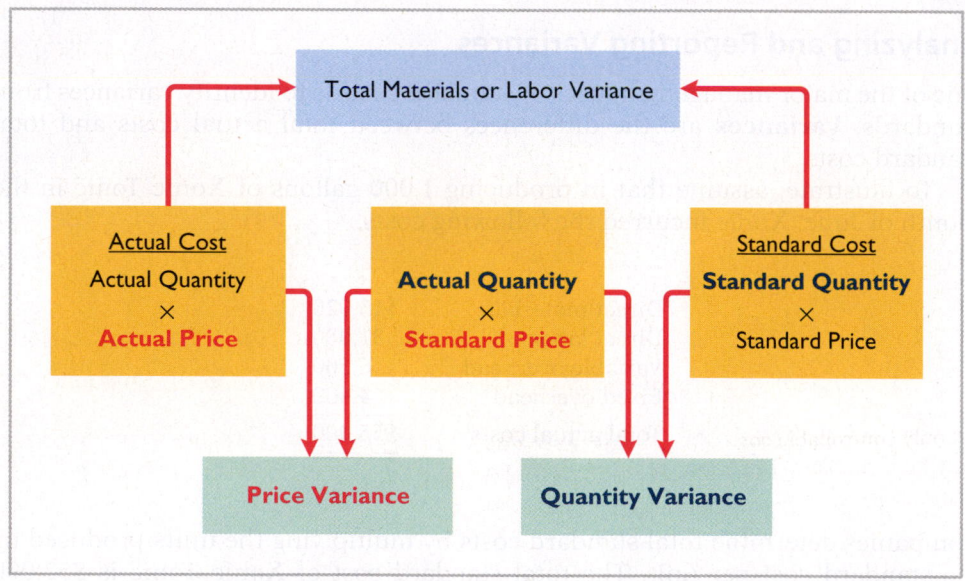

Note that the left side of the matrix is actual cost (actual quantity times actual price). The right hand is standard cost (standard quantity times standard price). The only additional element you need in order to compute the price and quantity variances is the middle element, the actual quantity at the standard price.

Direct Materials Variances

Part of Xonic's total variance of $3,000 is due to a materials variance. In completing the order for 1,000 gallons of Xonic Tonic, the company used 4,200 pounds of direct materials. The direct materials were purchased at a price of $3.10 per unit. From Illustration 25-3, we know that Xonic's standards require it to use 4 pounds of materials per gallon produced, so it should have only used 4,000 (4 × 1,000) pounds of direct materials to produce 1,000 gallons. Illustration 25-2 shows that the standard cost of each pound of direct materials is $3 instead of the $3.10 actually paid. Illustration 25-12 shows that the **total materials variance** is computed as the difference between the amount paid (actual quantity times actual price) and the amount that should have been paid based on standards (standard quantity times standard price of materials).

Actual Quantity × Actual Price	−	Standard Quantity × Standard Price	=	Total Materials Variance
(AQ) × (AP)		(SQ) × (SP)		(TMV)
(4,200 × $3.10)	−	(4,000 × $3.00)	=	$1,020 U

Illustration 25-12
Formula for total materials variance

Thus, for Xonic, the total materials variance is $1,020 ($13,020 − $12,000) unfavorable.

The total materials variance could be caused by differences in the price paid for the materials or by differences in the amount of materials used. Illustration 25-13 shows that the total materials variance is the sum of the materials price variance and the materials quantity variance.

Materials Price Variance + Materials Quantity Variance = Total Materials Variance

Illustration 25-13
Components of total materials variance

The materials price variance results from a difference between the actual price and the standard price. Illustration 25-14 shows that the **materials price variance** is computed as the difference between the actual amount paid (actual quantity of materials times actual price) and the standard amount that should have been paid for the materials used (actual quantity of materials times standard price).[1]

Actual Quantity × Actual Price	−	Actual Quantity × Standard Price	=	Materials Price Variance
(AQ) × (AP)		(AQ) × (SP)		(MPV)
(4,200 × $3.10)	−	(4,200 × $3.00)	=	$420 U

Illustration 25-14
Formula for materials price variance

For Xonic, the materials price variance is $420 ($13,020 − $12,600) unfavorable.

The price variance can also be computed by multiplying the actual quantity purchased by the difference between the actual and standard price per unit. The computation in this case is 4,200 × ($3.10 − $3.00) = $420 U.

As seen in Illustration 25-13, the other component of the materials variance is the quantity variance. The quantity variance results from differences between the amount of material actually used and the amount that should have been used. As shown in Illustration 25-15, the **materials quantity variance** is computed as the difference between the standard cost of the actual quantity (actual quantity times standard price) and the standard cost of the amount that should have been used (standard quantity times standard price for materials).

Helpful Hint
The alternative formula is:
$$\boxed{AQ} \times \boxed{AP - SP} = \boxed{MPV}$$

Actual Quantity × Standard Price	−	Standard Quantity × Standard Price	=	Materials Quantity Variance
(AQ) × (SP)		(SQ) × (SP)		(MQV)
(4,200 × $3.00)	−	(4,000 × $3.00)	=	$600 U

Illustration 25-15
Formula for materials quantity variance

---

[1]Assume that all materials purchased during the period are used in production and that no units remain in inventory at the end of the period.

Thus, for Xonic, the materials quantity variance is $600 ($12,600 − $12,000) unfavorable.

The quantity variance can also be computed by applying the standard price to the difference between actual and standard quantities used. The computation in this example is $3.00 × (4,200 − 4,000) = $600 U.

The total materials variance of $1,020 U, therefore, consists of the following.

Helpful Hint
The alternative formula is:
$$\boxed{SP} \times \boxed{AQ - SQ} = \boxed{MQV}$$

Illustration 25-16
Summary of materials variances

Materials price variance	$ 420 U
Materials quantity variance	600 U
Total materials variance	**$1,020 U**

Companies sometimes use a matrix to analyze a variance. **When the matrix is used, a company computes the amounts using the formulas for each cost element first and then computes the variances.** Illustration 25-17 shows the completed matrix for the direct materials variance for Xonic. The matrix provides a convenient structure for determining each variance.

Illustration 25-17
Matrix for direct materials variances

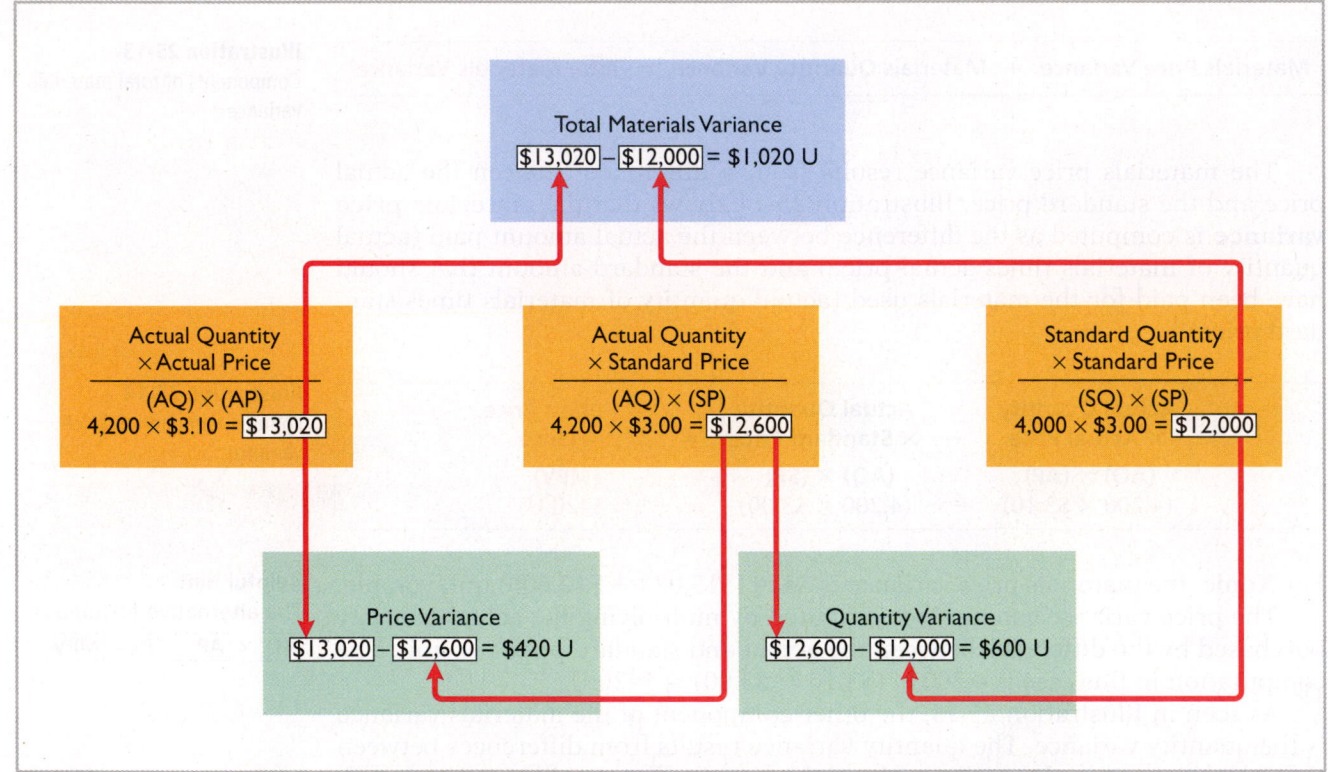

CAUSES OF MATERIALS VARIANCES

"What caused materials price variances?"

Purchasing Dept.

What are the causes of a variance? The causes may relate to both internal and external factors. The investigation of a **materials price variance usually begins in the purchasing department**. Many factors affect the price paid for raw materials. These include availability of quantity and cash discounts, the quality of the materials requested, and the delivery method used. To the extent that these factors are considered in setting the price standard, the purchasing department is responsible for any variances.

However, a variance may be beyond the control of the purchasing department. Sometimes, for example, prices may rise faster than expected. Moreover, actions by groups over which the company has no control, such as the OPEC nations' oil price increases, may cause an unfavorable variance. For example, during a recent year, **Kraft Foods** and **Kellogg Company** both experienced unfavorable materials price variances when the cost of dairy and wheat products jumped unexpectedly. There are also times when a production department may be responsible for the price variance. This may occur when a rush order forces the company to pay a higher price for the materials.

The starting point for determining the cause(s) of a significant **materials quantity variance is in the production department**. If the variances are due to inexperienced workers, faulty machinery, or carelessness, the production department is responsible. However, if the materials obtained by the purchasing department were of inferior quality, then the purchasing department is responsible.

"What caused materials quantity variances?"

Production Dept.

DO IT! 2 Direct Materials Variances

The standard cost of Wonder Walkers includes two units of direct materials at $8.00 per unit. During July, the company buys 22,000 units of direct materials at $7.50 and uses those materials to produce 10,000 Wonder Walkers. Compute the total, price, and quantity variances for materials.

Action Plan

Use the formulas for computing each of the materials variances:

Solution

Standard quantity = 10,000 × 2
Substituting amounts into the formulas, the variances are:

Total materials variance = (22,000 × $7.50) − (20,000 × $8.00) = $5,000 unfavorable
Materials price variance = (22,000 × $7.50) − (22,000 × $8.00) = $11,000 favorable
Materials quantity variance = (22,000 × $8.00) − (20,000 × $8.00) = $16,000 unfavorable

✔ Total materials variance = (AQ × AP) − (SQ × SP)

✔ Materials price variance = (AQ × AP) − (AQ × SP)

✔ Materials quantity variance = (AQ × SP) − (SQ × SP)

Related exercise material: **BE25-4, E25-5, and DO IT! 25-2.**

LEARNING OBJECTIVE 3 **Determine direct labor and total manufacturing overhead variances.**

Direct Labor Variances

The process of determining direct labor variances is the same as for determining the direct materials variances. In completing the Xonic Tonic order, the company incurred 2,100 direct labor hours at an average hourly rate of $14.80. The standard hours allowed for the units produced were 2,000 hours (1,000 gallons × 2 hours). The standard labor rate was $15 per hour.

The total labor variance is the difference between the amount actually paid for labor versus the amount that should have been paid. Illustration 25-18 shows that the **total labor variance** is computed as the difference between the amount actually paid for labor (actual hours times actual rate) and the amount that should have been paid (standard hours times standard rate for labor).

Illustration 25-18
Formula for total labor variance

Actual Hours × Actual Rate	−	Standard Hours × Standard Rate	=	Total Labor Variance
(AH) × (AR)		(SH) × (SR)		(TLV)
(2,100 × $14.80)	−	(2,000 × $15.00)	=	$1,080 U

The total labor variance is $1,080 ($31,080 − $30,000) unfavorable.

The total labor variance is caused by differences in the labor rate or difference in labor hours. Illustration 25-19 shows that the total labor variance is the sum of the labor price variance and the labor quantity variance.

Illustration 25-19
Components of total labor variance

Labor Price Variance	+	Labor Quantity Variance	=	Total Labor Variance

The labor price variance results from the difference between the rate paid to workers versus the rate that was supposed to be paid. Illustration 25-20 shows that the **labor price variance** is computed as the difference between the actual amount paid (actual hours times actual rate) and the amount that should have been paid for the number of hours worked (actual hours times standard rate for labor).

Illustration 25-20
Formula for labor price variance

Actual Hours × Actual Rate	−	Actual Hours × Standard Rate	=	Labor Price Variance
(AH) × (AR)		(AH) × (SR)		(LPV)
(2,100 × $14.80)	−	(2,100 × $15.00)	=	$420 F

Helpful Hint
The alternative formula is:
$$AH \times (AR - SR) = LPV$$

For Xonic, the labor price variance is $420 ($31,080 − $31,500) favorable.

The labor price variance can also be computed by multiplying actual hours worked by the difference between the actual pay rate and the standard pay rate. The computation in this example is 2,100 × ($15.00 − $14.80) = $420 F.

The other component of the total labor variance is the labor quantity variance. The labor quantity variance results from the difference between the actual number of labor hours and the number of hours that should have been worked for the quantity produced. Illustration 25-21 shows that the **labor quantity variance** is computed as the difference between the amount that should have been paid for the hours worked (actual hours times standard rate) and the amount that should have been paid for the amount of hours that should have been worked (standard hours times standard rate for labor).

Illustration 25-21
Formula for labor quantity variance

Actual Hours × Standard Rate	−	Standard Hours × Standard Rate	=	Labor Quantity Variance
(AH) × (SR)		(SH) × (SR)		(LQV)
(2,100 × $15.00)	−	(2,000 × $15.00)	=	$1,500 U

Helpful Hint
The alternative formula is:
$$SR \times (AH - SH) = LQV$$

Thus, for Xonic, the labor quantity variance is $1,500 ($31,500 − $30,000) unfavorable.

The same result can be obtained by multiplying the standard rate by the difference between actual hours worked and standard hours allowed. In this case, the computation is $15.00 × (2,100 − 2,000) = $1,500 U.

The total direct labor variance of $1,080 U, therefore, consists of the following.

Illustration 25-22
Summary of labor variances

Labor price variance	$ 420 F
Labor quantity variance	1,500 U
Total direct labor variance	**$1,080 U**

These results can also be obtained from the matrix in Illustration 25-23.

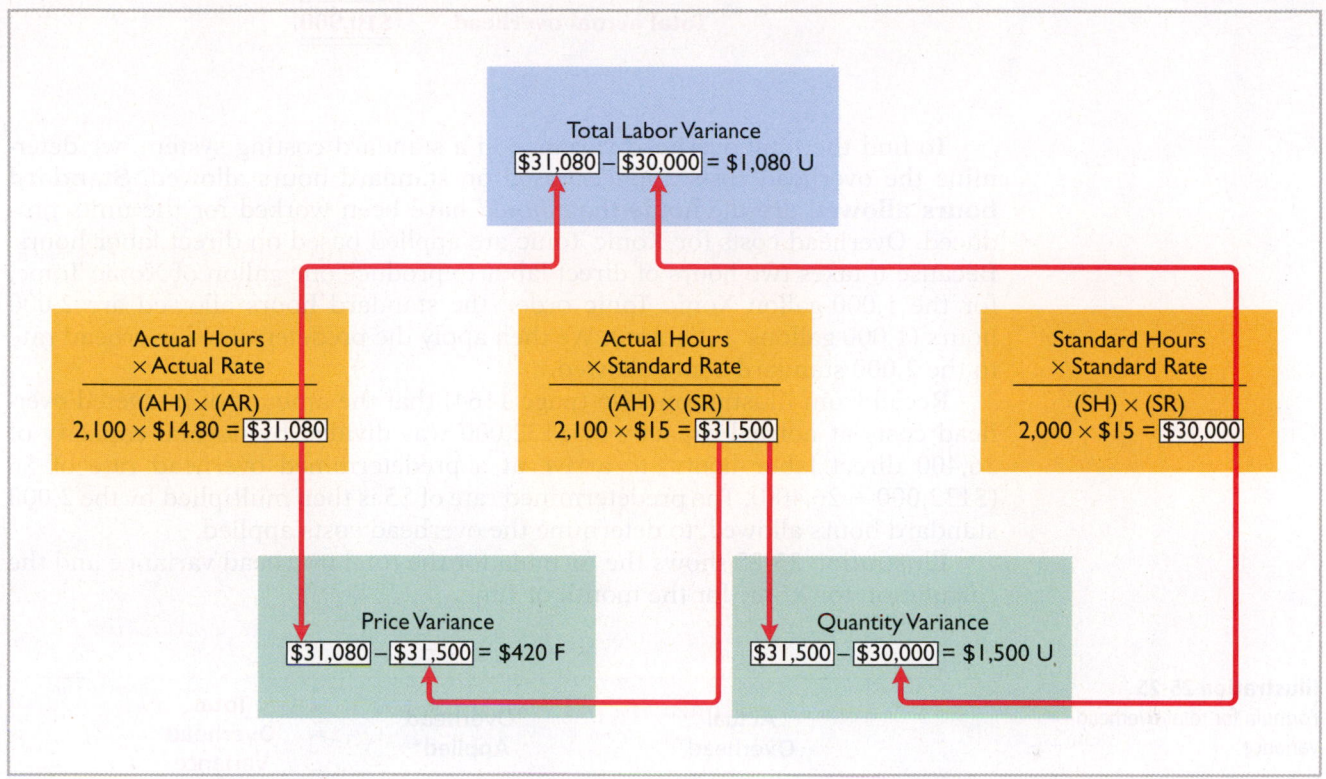

Illustration 25-23
Matrix for direct labor variances

CAUSES OF LABOR VARIANCES

Labor price variances usually result from two factors: (1) paying workers **different wages than expected**, and (2) **misallocation of workers**. In companies where pay rates are determined by union contracts, labor price variances should be infrequent. When workers are not unionized, there is a much higher likelihood of such variances. The responsibility for these variances rests with the manager who authorized the wage change.

Misallocation of the workforce refers to using skilled workers in place of unskilled workers and vice versa. The use of an inexperienced worker instead of an experienced one will result in a favorable price variance because of the lower pay rate of the unskilled worker. An unfavorable price variance would result if a skilled worker were substituted for an inexperienced one. The production department generally is responsible for labor price variances resulting from misallocation of the workforce.

Labor quantity variances relate to the **efficiency of workers**. The cause of a quantity variance generally can be traced to the production department. The causes of an unfavorable variance may be poor training, worker fatigue, faulty machinery, or carelessness. These causes are the responsibility of the **production department**. However, if the excess time is due to inferior materials, the responsibility falls outside the production department.

Manufacturing Overhead Variances

The **total overhead variance** is the difference between the actual overhead costs and overhead costs applied based on standard hours allowed for the amount of goods produced. As indicated in Illustration 25-8 (page 1165), Xonic incurred overhead costs of $10,900 to produce 1,000 gallons of Xonic Tonic in June. The computation of the actual overhead is comprised of a variable and a fixed component. Illustration 25-24 (page 1172) shows this computation.

Illustration 25-24
Actual overhead costs

Variable overhead	$ 6,500
Fixed overhead	4,400
Total actual overhead	**$10,900**

To find the total overhead variance in a standard costing system, we determine the overhead costs applied based on standard hours allowed. **Standard hours allowed** are the hours that *should* have been worked for the units produced. Overhead costs for Xonic Tonic are applied based on direct labor hours. Because it takes two hours of direct labor to produce one gallon of Xonic Tonic, for the 1,000-gallon Xonic Tonic order, the standard hours allowed are 2,000 hours (1,000 gallons × 2 hours). We then apply the predetermined overhead rate to the 2,000 standard hours allowed.

Recall from Illustration 25-6 (page 1164) that the amount of budgeted overhead costs at normal capacity of $132,000 was divided by normal capacity of 26,400 direct labor hours, to arrive at a predetermined overhead rate of $5 ($132,000 ÷ 26,400). The predetermined rate of $5 is then multiplied by the 2,000 standard hours allowed, to determine the overhead costs applied.

Illustration 25-25 shows the formula for the total overhead variance and the calculation for Xonic for the month of June.

Illustration 25-25
Formula for total overhead variance

Actual Overhead	−	Overhead Applied*	=	Total Overhead Variance
$10,900	−	$10,000	=	$900 U
($6,500 + $4,400)		($5 × 2,000 hours)		

*Based on standard hours allowed.

Thus, for Xonic, the total overhead variance is $900 unfavorable.

The overhead variance is generally analyzed through a price and a quantity variance. (These computations are discussed in more detail in advanced courses.) The name usually given to the price variance is the **overhead controllable variance**; the quantity variance is referred to as the **overhead volume variance**. Appendix 25B discusses how the total overhead variance can be broken down into these two variances.

CAUSES OF MANUFACTURING OVERHEAD VARIANCES

"What caused manufacturing overhead variances?"

Production Dept. or Sales Dept.

One reason for an overhead variance relates to over- or underspending on overhead items. For example, overhead may include indirect labor for which a company paid wages higher than the standard labor price allowed. Or, the price of electricity to run the company's machines increased, and the company did not anticipate this additional cost. Companies should investigate any spending variances to determine whether they will continue in the future. Generally, the responsibility for these variances rests with the production department.

The overhead variance can also result from the inefficient use of overhead. For example, because of poor maintenance, a number of the manufacturing machines are experiencing breakdowns on a consistent basis, leading to reduced production. Or, the flow of materials through the production process is impeded because of a lack of skilled labor to perform the necessary production tasks, due to a lack of planning. In both of these cases, the production department is responsible for the cause of these variances. On the other hand, overhead can also be underutilized because of a lack of sales orders. When the cause is a lack of sales orders, the responsibility rests outside the production department. For example, at one point **Chrysler** experienced a very significant unfavorable overhead variance because plant capacity was maintained at excessively high levels, due to overly optimistic sales forecasts.

People, Planet, and Profit Insight   Starbucks

Archer Colin/SIPA/NewsCom

What's Brewing at Starbucks?

It's easy for a company to say it's committed to corporate social responsibility. But **Starbucks** actually spells out measurable goals. Recently, the company published its annual *Global Responsibility Report* in which it describes its goals, achievements, and even its shortcomings related to corporate social responsibility. For example, Starbucks achieved its goal of getting more than 50% of its electricity from renewable sources. It also has numerous goals related to purchasing coffee from sources that are certified as responsibly grown and ethically traded; providing funds for loans to coffee farmers; and fostering partner-

ships with **Conservation International** to provide training to farmers on ecologically friendly growing.

The report also candidly explains that the company did not meet its goal to cut energy consumption by 25%. It also fell far short of its goal of getting customers to reuse their cups. In those instances where it didn't achieve its goals, Starbucks set new goals and described steps it would take to achieve them. You can view the company's *Global Responsibility Report* at *www.starbucks.com.*

Source: "Starbucks Launches 10th Global Responsibility Report," *Business Wire* (April 18, 2011).

What implications does Starbucks' commitment to corporate social responsibility have for the standard cost of a cup of coffee? (Go to **WileyPLUS** for this answer and additional questions.)

DO IT!   3   Labor and Manufacturing Overhead Variances

The standard cost of Product YY includes 3 hours of direct labor at $12.00 per hour. The predetermined overhead rate is $20.00 per direct labor hour. During July, the company incurred 3,500 hours of direct labor at an average rate of $12.40 per hour and $71,300 of manufacturing overhead costs. It produced 1,200 units.

(a) Compute the total, price, and quantity variances for labor. (b) Compute the total overhead variance.

Solution

> Substituting amounts into the formulas, the variances are:
>
> Total labor variance = (3,500 × $12.40) − (3,600 × $12.00) = $200 unfavorable
>
> Labor price variance = (3,500 × $12.40) − (3,500 × $12.00) = $1,400 unfavorable
>
> Labor quantity variance = (3,500 × $12.00) − (3,600 × $12.00) = $1,200 favorable
>
> Total overhead variance = $71,300 − $72,000* = $700 favorable
>
> *(1,200 × 3 hours) × $20.00

Related exercise material: **BE25-5, BE25-6, E25-4, E25-6, E25-7, E25-8, E25-11, and DO IT! 25-3.**

Action Plan

✔ Use the formulas for computing each of the variances:
Total labor variance = (AH × AR) − (SH × SR)
Labor price variance = (AH × AR) − (AH × SR) Labor quantity variance = (AH × SR) − (SH × SR) Total overhead variance = Actual overhead − Overhead applied*

*Based on standard hours allowed.

LEARNING OBJECTIVE   **4**   ## Prepare variance reports and balanced scorecards.

Reporting Variances

All variances should be reported to appropriate levels of management as soon as possible. The sooner managers are informed, the sooner they can evaluate problems and take corrective action.

The form, content, and frequency of variance reports vary considerably among companies. One approach is to prepare a weekly report for each department that has primary responsibility for cost control. Under this approach, materials price variances are reported to the purchasing department, and all other variances are reported to the production department that did the work. The following report for Xonic, with the materials for the Xonic Tonic order listed first, illustrates this approach.

Illustration 25-26
Materials price variance report

	XONIC				
	Variance Report—Purchasing Department				
	For Week Ended June 8, 2017				
Type of Materials	**Quantity Purchased**	**Actual Price**	**Standard Price**	**Price Variance**	**Explanation**
X100	4,200 lbs.	$3.10	$3.00	$ 420 U	Rush order
X142	1,200 units	2.75	2.80	60 F	Quantity discount
A85	600 doz.	5.20	5.10	60 U	Regular supplier on strike
Total price variance				**$420 U**	

The explanation column is completed after consultation with the purchasing department manager.

Variance reports facilitate the principle of "management by exception" explained in Chapter 24. For example, the vice president of purchasing can use the report shown above to evaluate the effectiveness of the purchasing department manager. Or, the vice president of production can use production department variance reports to determine how well each production manager is controlling costs. In using variance reports, top management normally looks for **significant variances**. These may be judged on the basis of some quantitative measure, such as more than 10% of the standard or more than $1,000.

Income Statement Presentation of Variances

In income statements **prepared for management** under a standard cost accounting system, **cost of goods sold is stated at standard cost and the variances are disclosed separately**. Unfavorable variances increase cost of goods sold, while favorable variances decrease cost of goods sold. Illustration 25-27 shows

Illustration 25-27
Variances in income statement for management

	XONIC	
	Income Statement	
	For the Month Ended June 30, 2017	
Sales revenue		$70,000
Cost of goods sold (at standard)		52,000
Gross profit (at standard)		18,000
Variances		
Materials price	$ 420 U	
Materials quantity	600 U	
Labor price	420 F	
Labor quantity	1,500 U	
Overhead	900 U	
Total variance unfavorable		3,000
Gross profit (actual)		15,000
Selling and administrative expenses		3,000
Net income		$12,000

the presentation of variances in an income statement. This income statement is based on the production and sale of 1,000 units of Xonic Tonic at $70 per unit. It also assumes selling and administrative costs of $3,000. Observe that each variance is shown, as well as the total net variance. In this example, variations from standard costs reduced net income by $3,000.

Standard costs may be used in financial statements prepared for stockholders and other external users. The costing of inventories at standard costs is in accordance with generally accepted accounting principles when there are no significant differences between actual costs and standard costs. Hewlett-Packard and Jostens, Inc., for example, report their inventories at standard costs. However, if there are significant differences between actual and standard costs, the financial statements must report inventories and cost of goods sold at actual costs.

It is also possible to show the variances in an income statement prepared in the variable costing (CVP) format. To do so, it is necessary to analyze the overhead variances into variable and fixed components. This type of analysis is explained in cost accounting textbooks.

Balanced Scorecard

Financial measures (measurement of dollars), such as variance analysis and return on investment (ROI), are useful tools for evaluating performance. However, many companies now supplement these financial measures with nonfinancial measures to better assess performance and anticipate future results. For example, airlines like Delta and United use capacity utilization as an important measure to understand and predict future performance. Companies that publish the *New York Times* and the *Chicago Tribune* newspapers use circulation figures as another measure by which to assess performance. Penske Automotive Group, the owner of 300 dealerships, rewards executives for meeting employee retention targets. Illustration 25-28 lists some key nonfinancial measures used in various industries.

Illustration 25-28
Nonfinancial measures used in various industries

Industry	Measure
Automobiles	Capacity utilization of plants. Average age of key assets. Impact of strikes. Brand-loyalty statistics.
Computer Systems	Market profile of customer end-products. Number of new products. Employee stock ownership percentages. Number of scientists and technicians used in R&D.
Chemicals	Customer satisfaction data. Factors affecting customer product selection. Number of patents and trademarks held. Customer brand awareness.
Regional Banks	Number of ATMs by state. Number of products used by average customer. Percentage of customer service calls handled by interactive voice response units. Personnel cost per employee. Credit card retention rates.

Source: Financial Accounting Standards Board, *Business Reporting: Insights into Enhancing Voluntary Disclosures* (Norwalk, Conn.: FASB, 2001).

Most companies recognize that both financial and nonfinancial measures can provide useful insights into what is happening in the company. As a result, many companies now use a broad-based measurement approach, called the **balanced scorecard**, to evaluate performance. The **balanced scorecard** incorporates financial and nonfinancial measures in an integrated system that links performance measurement with a company's strategic goals. Nearly 50% of the largest companies in the United States, including **Unilever**, **Chase**, and **Wal-Mart Stores Inc.**, are using the balanced scorecard approach.

The balanced scorecard evaluates company performance from a series of "perspectives." The four most commonly employed perspectives are as follows.

1. The **financial perspective** is the most traditional view of the company. It employs financial measures of performance used by most firms.

2. The **customer perspective** evaluates the company from the viewpoint of those people who buy its products or services. This view compares the company to competitors in terms of price, quality, product innovation, customer service, and other dimensions.

3. The **internal process perspective** evaluates the internal operating processes critical to success. All critical aspects of the value chain—including product development, production, delivery, and after-sale service—are evaluated to ensure that the company is operating effectively and efficiently.

4. The **learning and growth perspective** evaluates how well the company develops and retains its employees. This would include evaluation of such things as employee skills, employee satisfaction, training programs, and information dissemination.

Within each perspective, the balanced scorecard identifies objectives that contribute to attainment of strategic goals. Illustration 25-29 shows examples of objectives within each perspective.

Perspective		Objective
Financial		Return on assets.
		Net income.
		Credit rating.
		Share price.
		Profit per employee.
Customer		Percentage of customers who would recommend product.
		Customer retention.
		Response time per customer request.
		Brand recognition.
		Customer service expense per customer.
Internal Process		Percentage of defect-free products.
		Stockouts.
		Labor utilization rates.
		Waste reduction.
		Planning accuracy.
Learning and Growth		Percentage of employees leaving in less than one year.
		Number of cross-trained employees.
		Ethics violations.
		Training hours.
		Reportable accidents.

Illustration 25-29
Examples of objectives within the four perspectives of balanced scorecard

The objectives are linked across perspectives in order to tie performance measurement to company goals. The financial-perspective objectives are normally set first, and then objectives are set in the other perspectives in order to accomplish the financial goals.

For example, within the financial perspective, a common goal is to increase profit per dollars invested as measured by ROI. In order to increase ROI, a customer-perspective objective might be to increase customer satisfaction as measured by the percentage of customers who would recommend the product to a friend. In order to increase customer satisfaction, an internal-process-perspective objective might be to increase product quality as measured by the percentage of defect-free units. Finally, in order to increase the percentage of defect-free units, the learning-and-growth-perspective objective might be to reduce factory employee turnover as measured by the percentage of employees leaving in under one year.

Illustration 25-30 illustrates this linkage across perspectives.

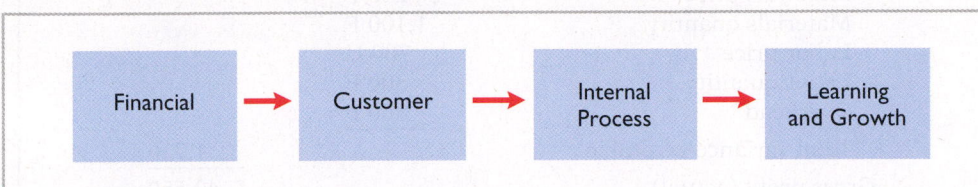

Illustration 25-30
Linked process across balanced scorecard perspectives

Through this linked process, the company can better understand how to achieve its goals and what measures to use to evaluate performance.

In summary, the balanced scorecard does the following:

1. Employs both **financial and nonfinancial measures**. (For example, ROI is a financial measure; employee turnover is a nonfinancial measure.)

2. **Creates linkages** so that high-level corporate goals can be communicated all the way down to the shop floor.

3. **Provides measurable objectives for nonfinancial measures** such as product quality, rather than vague statements such as "We would like to improve quality."

4. Integrates all of the company's goals into a single performance measurement system, so that **an inappropriate amount of weight will not be placed on any single goal**.

Service Company Insight   United Airlines

It May Be Time to Fly United Again

PhotoDisc, Inc./Getty Images

Many of the benefits of a balanced scorecard approach are evident in the improved operations at United Airlines. At the time it filed for bankruptcy, United had a reputation for some of the worst service in the airline business. But when Glenn Tilton took over as United's chief executive officer, he recognized that things had to change.

He implemented an incentive program that allows all of United's 63,000 employees to earn a bonus of 2.5% or more of their wages if the company "exceeds its goals for on-time flight departures and for customer intent to fly United again." After instituting this program, the company's on-time departures were among the best, its customer complaints were reduced considerably, and the number of customers who said that they would fly United again was at its highest level ever.

Sources: Susan Carey, "Friendlier Skies: In Bankruptcy, United Airlines Forges a Path to Better Service," *Wall Street Journal* (June 15, 2004); and Emre Serpen, "More to Maintain," *Airline Business* (November 2012), pp. 38–40.

Which of the perspectives of a balanced scorecard were the focus of United's CEO? (Go to **WileyPLUS** for this answer and additional questions.)

DO IT! 4   Reporting Variances

Polar Vortex Corporation experienced the following variances: materials price $250 F, materials quantity $1,100 F, labor price $700 U, labor quantity $300 F, and overhead $800 F. Sales revenue was $102,700, and cost of goods sold (at standard) was $61,900. Determine the actual gross profit.

Solution

Action Plan

✔ Gross profit at standard is sales revenue less cost of goods sold at standard.

✔ Adjust standard gross profit by adding a net favorable variance or subtracting a net unfavorable variance.

Sales revenue		$102,700
Cost of goods sold (at standard)		61,900
Standard gross profit		40,800
Variances		
Materials price	$ 250 F	
Materials quantity	1,100 F	
Labor price	700 U	
Labor quantity	300 F	
Overhead	800 F	
Total variance favorable		1,750
Gross profit (actual)		$ 42,550

Related exercise material: **E25-10, E25-14, E25-15, and DO IT! 25-4.**

LEARNING
OBJECTIVE **★5**

APPENDIX 25A: Identify the features of a standard cost accounting system.

A **standard cost accounting system** is a double-entry system of accounting. In this system, companies use standard costs in making entries, and they formally recognize variances in the accounts. Companies may use a standard cost system with either job order or process costing.

In this appendix, we will explain and illustrate a **standard cost, job order cost accounting system**. The system is based on two important assumptions:

1. Variances from standards are recognized at the earliest opportunity.

2. The Work in Process account is maintained exclusively on the basis of standard costs.

In practice, there are many variations among standard cost systems. The system described here should prepare you for systems you see in the "real world."

Journal Entries

We will use the transactions of Xonic to illustrate the journal entries. Note as you study the entries that the major difference between the entries here and those for the job order cost accounting system in Chapter 16 is the **variance accounts**.

1. Purchase raw materials on account for $13,020 when the standard cost is $12,600.

Raw Materials Inventory	12,600	
Materials Price Variance	420	
Accounts Payable		13,020
(To record purchase of materials)		

Xonic debits the inventory account for actual quantities at standard cost. This enables the perpetual materials records to show actual quantities. Xonic debits the price variance, which is unfavorable, to Materials Price Variance.

2. Incur direct labor costs of $31,080 when the standard labor cost is $31,500.

Factory Labor	31,500	
Labor Price Variance		420
Factory Wages Payable		31,080
(To record direct labor costs)		

Like the raw materials inventory account, Xonic debits Factory Labor for actual hours worked at the standard hourly rate of pay. In this case, the labor variance is favorable. Thus, Xonic credits Labor Price Variance.

3. Incur actual manufacturing overhead costs of $10,900.

Manufacturing Overhead	10,900	
Accounts Payable/Cash/Acc. Depreciation		10,900
(To record overhead incurred)		

The controllable overhead variance (see Appendix 25B) is not recorded at this time. It depends on standard hours applied to work in process. This amount is not known at the time overhead is incurred.

4. Issue raw materials for production at a cost of $12,600 when the standard cost is $12,000.

Work in Process Inventory	12,000	
Materials Quantity Variance	600	
Raw Materials Inventory		12,600
(To record issuance of raw materials)		

Xonic debits Work in Process Inventory for standard materials quantities used at standard prices. It debits the variance account because the variance is unfavorable. The company credits Raw Materials Inventory for actual quantities at standard prices.

5. Assign factory labor to production at a cost of $31,500 when standard cost is $30,000.

Work in Process Inventory	30,000	
Labor Quantity Variance	1,500	
Factory Labor		31,500
(To assign factory labor to jobs)		

Xonic debits Work in Process Inventory for standard labor hours at standard rates. It debits the unfavorable variance to Labor Quantity Variance. The credit to Factory Labor produces a zero balance in this account.

6. Apply manufacturing overhead to production $10,000.

Work in Process Inventory	10,000	
Manufacturing Overhead		10,000
(To assign overhead to jobs)		

Xonic debits Work in Process Inventory for standard hours allowed multiplied by the standard overhead rate.

7. Transfer completed work to finished goods $52,000.

Finished Goods Inventory	52,000	
Work in Process Inventory		52,000
(To record transfer of completed work to finished goods)		

In this example, both inventory accounts are at standard cost.

8. Sell the 1,000 gallons of Xonic Tonic for $70,000.

Accounts Receivable	70,000	
Cost of Goods Sold	52,000	
Sales		70,000
Finished Goods Inventory		52,000
(To record sale of finished goods and the		
cost of goods sold)		

The company debits Cost of Goods Sold at standard cost. Gross profit, in turn, is the difference between sales and the standard cost of goods sold.

9. Recognize unfavorable total overhead variance:

Overhead Variance	900	
Manufacturing Overhead		900
(To recognize overhead variances)		

Prior to this entry, a debit balance of $900 existed in Manufacturing Overhead. This entry therefore produces a zero balance in the Manufacturing Overhead account. The information needed for this entry is often not available until the end of the accounting period.

Ledger Accounts

Illustration 25A-1 shows the cost accounts for Xonic after posting the entries. Note that five variance accounts are included in the ledger. The remaining accounts are the same as those illustrated for a job order cost system in Chapter 16, in which only actual costs were used.

Illustration 25A-1
Cost accounts with variances

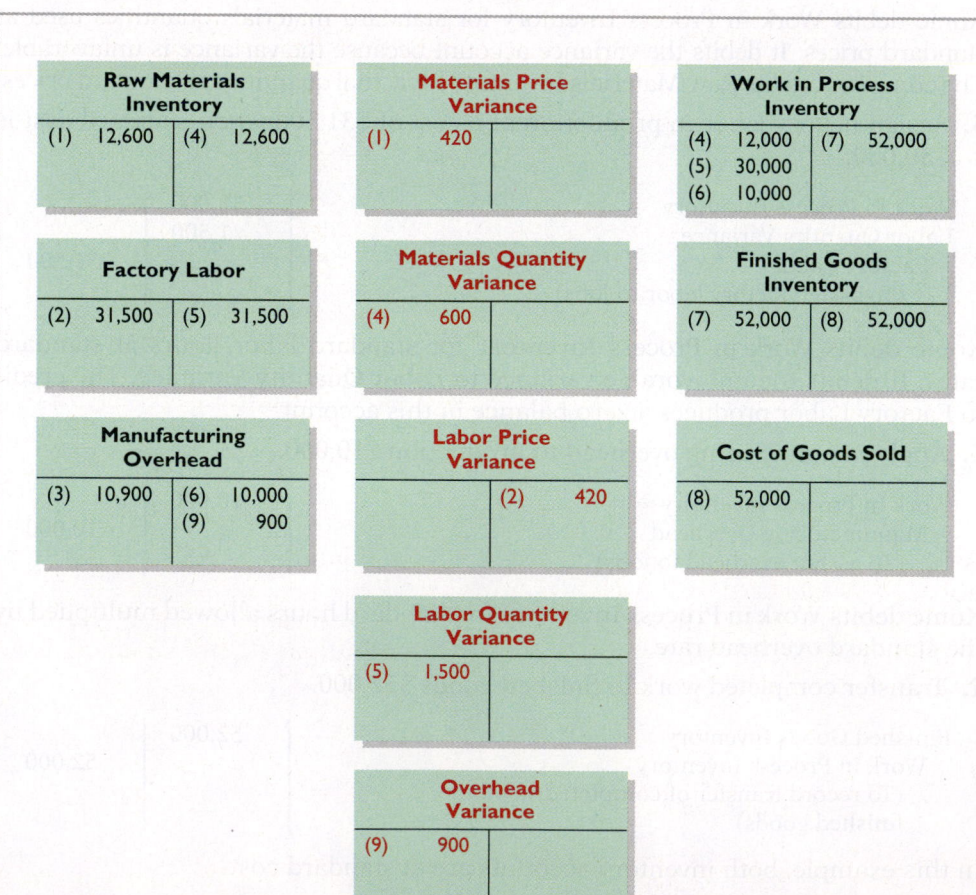

Helpful Hint
All debit balances in variance accounts indicate unfavorable variances; all credit balances indicate favorable variances.

LEARNING
OBJECTIVE   *6   **APPENDIX 25B: Compute overhead controllable and volume variances.**

As indicated in the chapter, the total overhead variance is generally analyzed through a price variance and a quantity variance. The name usually given to the price variance is the **overhead controllable variance**; the quantity variance is referred to as the **overhead volume variance**.

Overhead Controllable Variance

The **overhead controllable variance** shows whether overhead costs are effectively controlled. To compute this variance, the company compares actual overhead costs incurred with budgeted costs for the **standard hours allowed**. The budgeted costs are determined from a flexible manufacturing overhead budget. The concepts related to a flexible budget were discussed in Chapter 24.

For Xonic, the budget formula for manufacturing overhead is variable manufacturing overhead cost of $3 per hour of labor plus fixed manufacturing overhead costs of $4,400 ($52,800 ÷ 12, per Illustration 25-6 on page 1164). Illustration 25B-1 shows the monthly flexible budget for Xonic.

Illustration 25B-1
Flexible budget using standard direct labor hours

	Xonic.xls			
Home Insert Page Layout Formulas Data Review View				
P18	fx			
	A	B	C	D	E
1	**XONIC**				
2	**Flexible Manufacturing Overhead Monthly Budget**				
3	Activity Index				
4	Standard direct labor hours	1,800	**2,000**	2,200	2,400
5					
6	Costs				
7	Variable costs				
8	Indirect materials	$1,800	**$ 2,000**	$ 2,200	$ 2,400
9	Indirect labor	2,700	**3,000**	3,300	3,600
10	Utilities	900	**1,000**	1,100	1,200
11	Total variable costs	5,400	**6,000**	6,600	7,200
12					
13	Fixed costs				
14	Supervision	3,000	**3,000**	3,000	3,000
15	Depreciation	1,400	**1,400**	1,400	1,400
16	Total fixed costs	4,400	**4,400**	4,400	4,400
17	Total costs	$9,800	**$10,400**	$11,000	$11,600

As shown, the budgeted costs for 2,000 standard hours are $10,400 ($6,000 variable and $4,400 fixed).

Illustration 25B-2 shows the formula for the overhead controllable variance and the calculation for Xonic at 1,000 units of output (2,000 standard labor hours).

Illustration 25B-2
Formula for overhead controllable variance

Actual Overhead	−	Overhead Budgeted*	=	Overhead Controllable Variance
$10,900	−	$10,400	=	$500 U
($6,500 + $4,400)		($6,000 + $4,400)		

*Based on standard hours allowed.

The overhead controllable variance for Xonic is $500 unfavorable.

Most controllable variances are associated with variable costs, which are controllable costs. Fixed costs are often known at the time the budget is prepared and are therefore not as likely to deviate from the budgeted amount. In Xonic's case, all of the overhead controllable variance is due to the difference between the actual variable overhead costs ($6,500) and the budgeted variable costs ($6,000).

Management can compare actual and budgeted overhead for each manufacturing overhead cost that contributes to the controllable variance. In addition, management can develop cost and quantity variances for each overhead cost, such as indirect materials and indirect labor.

Overhead Volume Variance

The **overhead volume variance** is the difference between normal capacity hours and standard hours allowed times the fixed overhead rate. The overhead volume variance relates to whether fixed costs were under- or overapplied during the year. For example, the overhead volume variance answers the question of whether Xonic effectively used its fixed costs. If Xonic produces less Xonic Tonic than normal capacity would allow, an unfavorable variance results. Conversely, if Xonic produces more Xonic Tonic than what is considered normal capacity, a favorable variance results.

The formula for computing the overhead volume variance is as follows.

Illustration 25B-3
Formula for overhead volume variance

Fixed Overhead Rate	×	(Normal Capacity Hours	−	Standard Hours Allowed)	=	Overhead Volume Variance

To illustrate the fixed overhead rate computation, recall that Xonic budgeted fixed overhead cost for the year of $52,800 (Illustration 25-6 on page 1164). At normal capacity, 26,400 standard direct labor hours are required. The fixed overhead rate is therefore $2 per hour ($52,800 ÷ 26,400 hours).

Xonic produced 1,000 units of Xonic Tonic in June. The standard hours allowed for the 1,000 gallons produced in June is 2,000 (1,000 gallons × 2 hours). For Xonic, normal capacity for June is 1,100, so standard direct labor hours for June at normal capacity is 2,200 (26,400 annual hours ÷ 12 months). The computation of the overhead volume variance in this case is as follows.

Illustration 25B-4
Computation of overhead volume variance for Xonic

Fixed Overhead Rate	×	(Normal Capacity Hours	−	Standard Hours Allowed)	=	Overhead Volume Variance
$2	×	(2,200	−	2,000)	=	$400 U

In Xonic's case, a $400 unfavorable volume variance results. The volume variance is unfavorable because Xonic produced only 1,000 gallons rather than the normal capacity of 1,100 gallons in the month of June. As a result, it underapplied fixed overhead for that period.

In computing the overhead variances, it is important to remember the following.

1. Standard hours allowed are used in each of the variances.
2. Budgeted costs for the controllable variance are derived from the flexible budget.
3. The controllable variance generally pertains to variable costs.
4. The volume variance pertains solely to fixed costs.

REVIEW AND PRACTICE

LEARNING OBJECTIVES REVIEW

1 Describe standard costs. Both standards and budgets are predetermined costs. The primary difference is that a standard is a unit amount, whereas a budget is a total amount. A standard may be regarded as the budgeted cost per unit of product.

Standard costs offer a number of advantages. They (a) facilitate management planning, (b) promote greater economy, (c) are useful in setting selling prices, (d) contribute to management control, (e) permit "management by exception," and (f) simplify the costing of inventories and reduce clerical costs.

The direct materials price standard should be based on the delivered cost of raw materials plus an allowance for receiving and handling. The direct materials quantity standard should establish the required quantity plus an allowance for waste and spoilage.

The direct labor price standard should be based on current wage rates and anticipated adjustments such as COLAs. It also generally includes payroll taxes and fringe benefits. Direct labor quantity standards should be based on required production time plus an allowance for rest periods, cleanup, machine setup, and machine downtime.

For manufacturing overhead, a standard predetermined overhead rate is used. It is based on an expected standard activity index such as standard direct labor hours or standard machine hours.

2 Determine direct materials variances. The formulas for the direct materials variances are as follows.

$$\begin{pmatrix} \text{Actual quantity} \\ \times \text{ Actual price} \end{pmatrix} - \begin{pmatrix} \text{Standard quantity} \\ \times \text{ Standard price} \end{pmatrix} = \begin{matrix} \text{Total} \\ \text{materials} \\ \text{variance} \end{matrix}$$

$$\begin{pmatrix} \text{Actual quantity} \\ \times \text{ Actual price} \end{pmatrix} - \begin{pmatrix} \text{Actual quantity} \\ \times \text{ Standard price} \end{pmatrix} = \begin{matrix} \text{Materials} \\ \text{price} \\ \text{variance} \end{matrix}$$

$$\begin{pmatrix} \text{Actual quantity} \\ \times \text{ Standard price} \end{pmatrix} - \begin{pmatrix} \text{Standard quantity} \\ \times \text{ Standard price} \end{pmatrix} = \begin{matrix} \text{Materials} \\ \text{quantity} \\ \text{variance} \end{matrix}$$

3 Determine direct labor and total manufacturing overhead variances. The formulas for the direct labor variances are as follows.

$$\begin{pmatrix} \text{Actual hours} \\ \times \text{ Actual rate} \end{pmatrix} - \begin{pmatrix} \text{Standard hours} \\ \times \text{ Standard rate} \end{pmatrix} = \begin{matrix} \text{Total} \\ \text{labor} \\ \text{variance} \end{matrix}$$

$$\begin{pmatrix} \text{Actual hours} \\ \times \text{ Actual rate} \end{pmatrix} - \begin{pmatrix} \text{Actual hours} \\ \times \text{ Standard rate} \end{pmatrix} = \begin{matrix} \text{Labor} \\ \text{price} \\ \text{variance} \end{matrix}$$

$$\begin{pmatrix} \text{Actual hours} \\ \times \text{ Standard rate} \end{pmatrix} - \begin{pmatrix} \text{Standard hours} \\ \times \text{ Standard rate} \end{pmatrix} = \begin{matrix} \text{Labor} \\ \text{quantity} \\ \text{variance} \end{matrix}$$

The formula for the total manufacturing overhead variance is as follows.

$$\begin{pmatrix} \text{Actual} \\ \text{overhead} \end{pmatrix} - \begin{pmatrix} \text{Overhead} \\ \text{applied at} \\ \text{standard hours} \\ \text{allowed} \end{pmatrix} = \begin{matrix} \text{Total overhead} \\ \text{variance} \end{matrix}$$

4 Prepare variance reports and balanced scorecards. Variances are reported to management in variance reports. The reports facilitate management by exception by highlighting significant differences. Under a standard costing system, an income statement prepared for management will report cost of goods sold at standard cost and then disclose each variance separately.

The balanced scorecard incorporates financial and nonfinancial measures in an integrated system that links performance measurement and a company's strategic goals. It employs four perspectives: financial, customer, internal process, and learning and growth. Objectives are set within each of these perspectives that link to objectives within the other perspectives.

*5 Identify the features of a standard cost accounting system. In a standard cost accounting system, companies journalize and post standard costs, and they maintain separate variance accounts in the ledger.

*6 Compute overhead controllable and volume variances. The total overhead variance is generally analyzed through a price variance and a quantity variance. The name usually given to the price variance is the overhead controllable variance. The quantity variance is referred to as the overhead volume variance.

GLOSSARY REVIEW

Balanced scorecard An approach that incorporates financial and nonfinancial measures in an integrated system that links performance measurement and a company's strategic goals. (p. 1176).

Customer perspective A viewpoint employed in the balanced scorecard to evaluate the company from the perspective of those people who buy and use its products or services. (p. 1176).

Direct labor price standard The rate per hour that should be incurred for direct labor. (p. 1163).

Direct labor quantity standard The time that should be required to make one unit of product. (p. 1163).

Direct materials price standard The cost per unit of direct materials that should be incurred. (p. 1162).

Direct materials quantity standard The quantity of direct materials that should be used per unit of finished goods. (p. 1162).

Financial perspective A viewpoint employed in the balanced scorecard to evaluate a company's performance using financial measures. (p. 1176).

Ideal standards Standards based on the optimum level of performance under perfect operating conditions. (p. 1161).

Internal process perspective A viewpoint employed in the balanced scorecard to evaluate the effectiveness and efficiency of a company's value chain, including product development, production, delivery, and after-sale service. (p. 1176).

Labor price variance The difference between the actual hours times the actual rate and the actual hours times the standard rate for labor. (p. 1170).

Labor quantity variance The difference between actual hours times the standard rate and standard hours times the standard rate for labor. (p. 1170).

Learning and growth perspective A viewpoint employed in the balanced scorecard to evaluate how well a company develops and retains its employees. (p. 1176).

Materials price variance The difference between the actual quantity times the actual price and the actual quantity times the standard price for materials. (p. 1167).

Materials quantity variance The difference between the actual quantity times the standard price and the standard quantity times the standard price for materials. (p. 1167).

Normal capacity The average activity output that a company should experience over the long run. (p. 1164).

Normal standards Standards based on an efficient level of performance that are attainable under expected operating conditions. (p. 1161).

*Overhead controllable variance The difference between actual overhead incurred and overhead budgeted for the standard hours allowed. (p. 1181).

*Overhead volume variance The difference between normal capacity hours and standard hours allowed times the fixed overhead rate. (p. 1182).

*Standard cost accounting system A double-entry system of accounting in which standard costs are used in making entries, and variances are recognized in the accounts. (p. 1178).

Standard costs Predetermined unit costs which companies use as measures of performance. (p. 1160).

Standard hours allowed The hours that should have been worked for the units produced. (p. 1172).

Standard predetermined overhead rate An overhead rate determined by dividing budgeted overhead costs by an expected standard activity index. (p. 1163).

Total labor variance The difference between actual hours times the actual rate and standard hours times the standard rate for labor. (p. 1169).

Total materials variance The difference between the actual quantity times the actual price and the standard quantity times the standard price of materials. (p. 1167).

Total overhead variance The difference between actual overhead costs and overhead costs applied to work done, based on standard hours allowed. (p. 1171).

Variance The difference between total actual costs and total standard costs. (p. 1165).

PRACTICE MULTIPLE-CHOICE QUESTIONS

(LO 1) **1.** Standards differ from budgets in that:
  (a) budgets but not standards may be used in valuing inventories.
  (b) budgets but not standards may be journalized and posted.
  (c) budgets are a total amount and standards are a unit amount.
  (d) only budgets contribute to management planning and control.

(LO 1) **2.** Standard costs:
  (a) are imposed by governmental agencies.

  (b) are predetermined unit costs which companies use as measures of performance.
  (c) can be used by manufacturing companies but not by service or not-for-profit companies.
  (d) All of the above.

3. The advantages of standard costs include all of the (LO 1) following **except**:
  (a) management by exception may be used.
  (b) management planning is facilitated.
  (c) they may simplify the costing of inventories.
  (d) management must use a static budget.

(LO 1) 4. Normal standards:
    (a) allow for rest periods, machine breakdowns, and setup time.
    (b) represent levels of performance under perfect operating conditions.
    (c) are rarely used because managers believe they lower workforce morale.
    (d) are more likely than ideal standards to result in unethical practices.

(LO 1) 5. The setting of standards is:
    (a) a managerial accounting decision.
    (b) a management decision.
    (c) a worker decision.
    (d) preferably set at the ideal level of performance.

(LO 2) 6. Each of the following formulas is correct **except**:
    (a) Labor price variance = (Actual hours × Actual rate) − (Actual hours × Standard rate).
    (b) Total overhead variance = Actual overhead − Overhead applied.
    (c) Materials price variance = (Actual quantity × Actual price) − (Standard quantity × Standard price).
    (d) Labor quantity variance = (Actual hours × Standard rate) − (Standard hours × Standard rate).

(LO 2) 7. In producing product AA, 6,300 pounds of direct materials were used at a cost of $1.10 per pound. The standard was 6,000 pounds at $1.00 per pound. The direct materials quantity variance is:
    (a) $330 unfavorable.   (c) $600 unfavorable.
    (b) $300 unfavorable.   (d) $630 unfavorable.

(LO 3) 8. In producing product ZZ, 14,800 direct labor hours were used at a rate of $8.20 per hour. The standard was 15,000 hours at $8.00 per hour. Based on these data, the direct labor:
    (a) quantity variance is $1,600 favorable.
    (b) quantity variance is $1,600 unfavorable.
    (c) price variance is $3,000 favorable.
    (d) price variance is $3,000 unfavorable.

(LO 3) 9. Which of the following is **correct** about the total overhead variance?
    (a) Budgeted overhead and overhead applied are the same.
    (b) Total actual overhead is composed of variable overhead, fixed overhead, and period costs.
    (c) Standard hours actually worked are used in computing the variance.
    (d) Standard hours allowed for the work done is the measure used in computing the variance.

(LO 3) 10. The formula for computing the total overhead variance is:
    (a) actual overhead less overhead applied.
    (b) overhead budgeted less overhead applied.
    (c) actual overhead less overhead budgeted.
    (d) No correct answer is given.

(LO 4) 11. Which of the following is **incorrect** about variance reports?
    (a) They facilitate "management by exception."
    (b) They should only be sent to the top level of management.
    (c) They should be prepared as soon as possible.
    (d) They may vary in form, content, and frequency among companies.

(LO 4) 12. In using variance reports to evaluate cost control, management normally looks into:
    (a) all variances.
    (b) favorable variances only.
    (c) unfavorable variances only.
    (d) both favorable and unfavorable variances that exceed a predetermined quantitative measure such as a percentage or dollar amount.

(LO 4) 13. Generally accepted accounting principles allow a company to:
    (a) report inventory at standard cost but cost of goods sold must be reported at actual cost.
    (b) report cost of goods sold at standard cost but inventory must be reported at actual cost.
    (c) report inventory and cost of goods sold at standard cost as long as there are no significant differences between actual and standard cost.
    (d) report inventory and cost of goods sold only at actual costs; standard costing is never permitted.

(LO 4) 14. Which of the following would **not** be an objective used in the customer perspective of the balanced scorecard approach?
    (a) Percentage of customers who would recommend product to a friend.
    (b) Customer retention.
    (c) Brand recognition.
    (d) Earnings per share.

(LO 5) *15. Which of the following is **incorrect** about a standard cost accounting system?
    (a) It is applicable to job order costing.
    (b) It is applicable to process costing.
    (c) It reports only favorable variances.
    (d) It keeps separate accounts for each variance.

(LO 6) *16. The formula to compute the overhead volume variance is:
    (a) Fixed overhead rate × (Standard hours − Actual hours).
    (b) Fixed overhead rate × (Normal capacity hours − Actual hours).
    (c) Fixed overhead rate × (Normal capacity hours − Standard hours allowed).
    (d) (Variable overhead rate + Fixed overhead rate) × (Normal capacity hours − Standard hours allowed).

Solutions

1. (c) Budgets are expressed in total amounts, and standards are expressed in unit amounts. The other choices are incorrect because (a) standards, not budgets, may be used in valuing inventories; (b) standards, not budgets, may be journalized and posted; and (d) both budgets and standards contribute to management planning and control.

2. (b) Standard costs are predetermined units costs which companies use as measures of performance. The other choices are incorrect because (a) only those that are called regulations are imposed by governmental agencies, (c) standard costs can be used by all types of companies, and (d) choices (a) and (c) are incorrect.

3. (d) Standard costs are separate from a static budget. The other choices are all advantages of using standard costs.

4. (a) Normal standards allow for rest periods, machine breakdowns, and setup time. The other choices are incorrect because they describe ideal standards, not normal standards.

5. (b) Standards are set by management. The other choices are incorrect because setting standards requires input from (a) managerial accountants and (c) sometimes workers, but the final decision is made by management. Choice (d) is incorrect because setting standards at the ideal level of performance is uncommon because of the perceived negative effect on worker morale.

6. (c) Materials price variance = (Actual quantity × Actual price) − (Actual quantity (not Standard quantity) × Standard price). The other choices are correct formulas.

7. (b) The direct materials quantity variance is (6,300 × \$1.00) − (6,000 × \$1.00) = \$300. This variance is unfavorable because more material was used than prescribed by the standard. The other choices are therefore incorrect.

8. (a) The direct labor quantity variance is (14,800 × \$8) − (15,000 × \$8) = \$1,600. This variance is favorable because less labor was used than prescribed by the standard. The other choices are therefore incorrect.

9. (d) Standard hours allowed for work done is the measure used in computing the variance. The other choices are incorrect because (a) budgeted overhead is used to calculate the predetermined overhead rate while overhead applied is equal to standard hours allowed times the predetermined overhead rate, (b) overhead is a product cost and does not include period costs, and (c) standard hours allowed, not hours actually worked, are used in computing the overhead variance.

10. (a) Total overhead variance equals actual overhead less overhead applied. The other choices are therefore incorrect.

11. (b) Variance reports should be sent to the level of management responsible for the area in which the variance occurred so it can be remedied as quickly as possible. The other choices are correct statements.

12. (d) In using variance reports to evaluate cost control, management normally looks into both favorable and unfavorable variances that exceed a predetermined quantitative measure such as percentage or dollar amount. The other choices are therefore incorrect.

13. (c) GAAP allows a company to report both inventory and cost of goods sold at standard cost as long as there are no significant differences between actual and standard cost. The other choices are therefore incorrect.

14. (d) Earnings per share is not an objective used in the customer perspective of the balanced scorecard approach. The other choices are all true statements.

*15. (c) A standard cost accounting system reports both favorable and unfavorable variances. The other choices are all correct statements.

*16. (c) The formula to compute the overhead volume variance is Fixed overhead rate × (Normal capacity hours − Standard hours allowed). The other choices are therefore incorrect.

PRACTICE EXERCISES

Compute materials and labor variances.

(LO 2, 3)

1. Hector Inc., which produces a single product, has prepared the following standard cost sheet for one unit of the product.

Direct materials (6 pounds at \$2.50 per pound)	\$15.00
Direct labor (3.1 hours at \$12.00 per hour)	\$37.20

During the month of April, the company manufactures 250 units and incurs the following actual costs.

Direct materials purchased and used (1,600 pounds)	\$4,192
Direct labor (760 hours)	\$8,740

Instructions

Compute the total, price, and quantity variances for materials and labor.

Solution

1. Total materials variance:

$$
\begin{array}{ccccc}
(AQ \times AP) & - & (SQ \times SP) & & \\
(1{,}600 \times \$2.62^*) & & (1{,}500^{**} \times \$2.50) & & \\
\$4{,}192 & - & \$3{,}750 & = & \$442 \text{ U}
\end{array}
$$

*\$4,192 ÷ 1,600   **250 × 6

Materials price variance:

$$
\begin{array}{ccc}
(AQ \times AP) & - & (AQ \times SP) \\
(1,600 \times \$2.62) & & (1,600 \times \$2.50) \\
\$4,192 & - & \$4,000 & = \$192 \text{ U}
\end{array}
$$

Materials quantity variance:

$$
\begin{array}{ccc}
(AQ \times SP) & - & (SQ \times SP) \\
(1,600 \times \$2.50) & & (1,500 \times \$2.50) \\
\$4,000 & - & \$3,750 & = \$250 \text{ U}
\end{array}
$$

Total labor variance:

$$
\begin{array}{ccc}
(AH \times AR) & - & (SH \times SR) \\
(760 \times \$11.50^*) & & (775^{**} \times \$12.00) \\
\$8,740 & - & \$9,300 & = \$560 \text{ F}
\end{array}
$$

*$8,740 ÷ 760   **250 × 3.1

Labor price variance:

$$
\begin{array}{ccc}
(AH \times AR) & - & (AH \times SR) \\
(760 \times \$11.50) & & (760 \times \$12.00) \\
\$8,740 & - & \$9,120 & = \$380 \text{ F}
\end{array}
$$

Labor quantity variance:

$$
\begin{array}{ccc}
(AH \times SR) & - & (SH \times SR) \\
(760 \times \$12.00) & & (775 \times \$12.00) \\
\$9,120 & - & \$9,300 & = \$180 \text{ F}
\end{array}
$$

2. Manufacturing overhead data for the production of Product H by Yamato Company are as follows.

Compute overhead variances.
(LO 3)

Overhead incurred for 35,000 actual direct labor hours worked	$140,000
Overhead rate (variable $3; fixed $1) at normal capacity of 36,000 direct labor hours	$4
Standard hours allowed for work done	34,000

Instructions

Compute the total overhead variance.

Solution

2. Total overhead variance:

$$
\begin{array}{ccc}
\text{Actual Overhead} & - & \text{Overhead Applied} \\
\$140,000 & - & \$136,000 & = \$4,000 \text{ U} \\
& & (34,000 \times \$4)
\end{array}
$$

▌ PRACTICE PROBLEM

Manlow Company makes a cologne called Allure. The standard cost for one bottle of Allure is as follows.

Compute variances.
(LO 2, 3)

	Standard			
Manufacturing Cost Elements	**Quantity** ×	**Price**	=	**Cost**
Direct materials	6 oz.	× $ 0.90	=	$ 5.40
Direct labor	0.5 hrs.	× $12.00	=	6.00
Manufacturing overhead	0.5 hrs.	× $ 4.80	=	2.40
				$13.80

During the month, the following transactions occurred in manufacturing 10,000 bottles of Allure.

1. 58,000 ounces of materials were purchased at $1.00 per ounce.

2. All the materials purchased were used to produce the 10,000 bottles of Allure.

3. 4,900 direct labor hours were worked at a total labor cost of $56,350.

4. Variable manufacturing overhead incurred was $15,000 and fixed overhead incurred was $10,400.

The manufacturing overhead rate of $4.80 is based on a normal capacity of 5,200 direct labor hours. The total budget at this capacity is $10,400 fixed and $14,560 variable.

Instructions

(a) Compute the total variance and the variances for direct materials and direct labor elements.

(b) Compute the total variance for manufacturing overhead.

Solution

(a)
Total Variance

Actual costs incurred	
Direct materials	$ 58,000
Direct labor	56,350
Manufacturing overhead	25,400
	139,750
Standard cost (10,000 × $13.80)	138,000
Total variance	$ 1,750 U

Direct Materials Variances

Total	=	$58,000 (58,000 × $1.00)	− $54,000 (60,000* × $0.90)	=	$4,000 U
Price	=	$58,000 (58,000 × $1.00)	− $52,200 (58,000 × $0.90)	=	$5,800 U
Quantity	=	$52,200 (58,000 × $0.90)	− $54,000 (60,000 × $0.90)	=	$1,800 F

*10,000 × 6

Direct Labor Variances

Total	=	$56,350 (4,900 × $11.50*)	− $60,000 (5,000** × $12.00)	=	$3,650 F
Price	=	$56,350 (4,900 × $11.50)	− $58,800 (4,900 × $12.00)	=	$2,450 F
Quantity	=	$58,800 (4,900 × $12.00)	− $60,000 (5,000 × $12.00)	=	$1,200 F

*56,350 ÷ 4,900; **10,000 × 0.5

(b)
Overhead Variance

Total	=	$25,400 ($15,000 + $10,400)	− $24,000 (5,000 × $4.80)	=	$1,400 U

WileyPLUS

Brief Exercises, Exercises, **DO IT!** Exercises, and Problems and many additional resources are available for practice in WileyPLUS

NOTE: All asterisked Questions, Exercises, and Problems relate to material in the appendices to the chapter.

■ QUESTIONS

1. (a) "Standard costs are the expected total cost of completing a job." Is this correct? Explain.
   (b) "A standard imposed by a governmental agency is known as a regulation." Do you agree? Explain.

2. (a) Explain the similarities and differences between standards and budgets.
   (b) Contrast the accounting for standards and budgets.

3. Standard costs facilitate management planning. What are the other advantages of standard costs?

4. Contrast the roles of the management accountant and management in setting standard costs.

5. Distinguish between an ideal standard and a normal standard.

6. What factors should be considered in setting (a) the direct materials price standard and (b) the direct materials quantity standard?

7. "The objective in setting the direct labor quantity standard is to determine the aggregate time required to make one unit of product." Do you agree? What allowances should be made in setting this standard?

8. How is the predetermined overhead rate determined when standard costs are used?

9. What is the difference between a favorable cost variance and an unfavorable cost variance?

10. In each of the following formulas, supply the words that should be inserted for each number in parentheses.
    (a) (Actual quantity × (1)) − (Standard quantity × (2)) = Total materials variance
    (b) ((3) × Actual price) − (Actual quantity × (4)) = Materials price variance
    (c) (Actual quantity × (5)) − ((6) × Standard price) = Materials quantity variance

11. In the direct labor variance matrix, there are three factors: (1) Actual hours × Actual rate, (2) Actual hours × Standard rate, and (3) Standard hours × Standard rate. Using the numbers, indicate the formulas for each of the direct labor variances.

12. Mikan Company's standard predetermined overhead rate is $9 per direct labor hour. For the month of June, 26,000 actual hours were worked, and 27,000 standard hours were allowed. How much overhead was applied?

13. How often should variances be reported to management? What principle may be used with variance reports?

14. What circumstances may cause the purchasing department to be responsible for both an unfavorable materials price variance and an unfavorable materials quantity variance?

15. What are the four perspectives used in the balanced scorecard? Discuss the nature of each, and how the perspectives are linked.

16. Kerry James says that the balanced scorecard was created to replace financial measures as the primary mechanism for performance evaluation. He says that it uses only nonfinancial measures. Is this true?

17. What are some examples of nonfinancial measures used by companies to evaluate performance?

18. (a) How are variances reported in income statements prepared for management? (b) May standard costs be used in preparing financial statements for stockholders? Explain.

*19. (a) Explain the basic features of a standard cost accounting system. (b) What type of balance will exist in the variance account when (1) the materials price variance is unfavorable and (2) the labor quantity variance is favorable?

*20. If the $9 per hour overhead rate in Question 12 includes $5 variable, and actual overhead costs were $248,000, what is the overhead controllable variance for June? The normal capacity hours were 28,000. Is the variance favorable or unfavorable?

*21. What is the purpose of computing the overhead volume variance? What is the basic formula for this variance?

*22. Alma Ortiz does not understand why the overhead volume variance indicates that fixed overhead costs are under- or overapplied. Clarify this matter for Alma.

*23. John Hsu is attempting to outline the important points about overhead variances on a class examination. List four points that John should include in his outline.

BRIEF EXERCISES

BE25-1 Lopez Company uses both standards and budgets. For the year, estimated production of Product X is 500,000 units. Total estimated cost for materials and labor are $1,400,000 and $1,700,000. Compute the estimates for (a) a standard cost and (b) a budgeted cost.

Distinguish between a standard and a budget.
(LO 1)

BE25-2 Tang Company accumulates the following data concerning raw materials in making one gallon of finished product. (1) Price—net purchase price $2.30, freight-in $0.20, and receiving and handling $0.10. (2) Quantity—required materials 3.6 pounds, allowance for waste and spoilage 0.4 pounds. Compute the following.
(a) Standard direct materials price per gallon.
(b) Standard direct materials quantity per gallon.
(c) Total standard materials cost per gallon.

Set direct materials standard.
(LO 1)

BE25-3 Labor data for making one gallon of finished product in Bing Company are as follows. (1) Price—hourly wage rate $14.00, payroll taxes $0.80, and fringe benefits $1.20. (2) Quantity—actual production time 1.1 hours, rest periods and cleanup 0.25 hours, and setup and downtime 0.15 hours. Compute the following.
(a) Standard direct labor rate per hour.
(b) Standard direct labor hours per gallon.
(c) Standard labor cost per gallon.

Set direct labor standard.
(LO 1)

BE25-4 Simba Company's standard materials cost per unit of output is $10 (2 pounds × $5). During July, the company purchases and uses 3,200 pounds of materials costing $16,192 in making 1,500 units of finished product. Compute the total, price, and quantity materials variances.

Compute direct materials variances.
(LO 2)

BE25-5 Mordica Company's standard labor cost per unit of output is $22 (2 hours × $11 per hour). During August, the company incurs 2,150 hours of direct labor at an hourly cost of $10.80 per hour in making 1,000 units of finished product. Compute the total, price, and quantity labor variances.

Compute direct labor variances.
(LO 3)

BE25-6 In October, Pine Company reports 21,000 actual direct labor hours, and it incurs $118,000 of manufacturing overhead costs. Standard hours allowed for the work done is 20,600 hours. The predetermined overhead rate is $6 per direct labor hour. Compute the total overhead variance.

Compute total overhead variance.
(LO 3)

Match balanced scorecard perspectives.

(LO 4)

BE25-7 The four perspectives in the balanced scorecard are (1) financial, (2) customer, (3) internal process, and (4) learning and growth. Match each of the following objectives with the perspective it is most likely associated with: (a) plant capacity utilization, (b) employee work days missed due to injury, (c) return on assets, and (d) brand recognition.

Journalize materials variances.

(LO 5)

*BE25-8 Journalize the following transactions for Combs Company.
(a) Purchased 6,000 units of raw materials on account for $11,500. The standard cost was $12,000.
(b) Issued 5,600 units of raw materials for production. The standard units were 5,800.

Journalize labor variances.

(LO 5)

*BE25-9 Journalize the following transactions for Shelton, Inc.
(a) Incurred direct labor costs of $24,000 for 3,000 hours. The standard labor cost was $24,900.
(b) Assigned 3,000 direct labor hours costing $24,000 to production. Standard hours were 3,150.

Compute the overhead controllable variance.

(LO 6)

*BE25-10 Some overhead data for Pine Company are given in BE25-6. In addition, the flexible manufacturing overhead budget shows that budgeted costs are $4 variable per direct labor hour and $50,000 fixed. Compute the overhead controllable variance.

Compute overhead volume variance.

(LO 6)

*BE25-11 Using the data in BE25-6 and BE25-10, compute the overhead volume variance. Normal capacity was 25,000 direct labor hours.

DO IT! Exercises

Compute standard cost.

(LO 1)

DO IT! 25-1 Larkin Company accumulated the following standard cost data concerning product I-Tal.

Direct materials per unit: 2 pounds at $5 per pound
Direct labor per unit: 0.2 hours at $16 per hour
Manufacturing overhead: Allocated based on direct labor hours at a predetermined rate of $20 per direct labor hour

Compute the standard cost of one unit of product I-Tal.

Compute materials variance.

(LO 2)

DO IT! 25-2 The standard cost of product 777 includes 2 units of direct materials at $6.00 per unit. During August, the company bought 29,000 units of materials at $6.30 and used those materials to produce 16,000 units. Compute the total, price, and quantity variances for materials.

Compute labor and manufacturing overhead variances.

(LO 3)

DO IT! 25-3 The standard cost of product 5252 includes 1.9 hours of direct labor at $14.00 per hour. The predetermined overhead rate is $22.00 per direct labor hour. During July, the company incurred 4,000 hours of direct labor at an average rate of $14.30 per hour and $81,300 of manufacturing overhead costs. It produced 2,000 units.

(a) Compute the total, price, and quantity variances for labor. (b) Compute the total overhead variance.

Prepare variance report.

(LO 4)

DO IT! 25-4 Tropic Zone Corporation experienced the following variances: materials price $350 U, materials quantity $1,700 F, labor price $800 F, labor quantity $500 F, and overhead $1,200 U. Sales revenue was $92,100, and cost of goods sold (at standard) was $51,600. Determine the actual gross profit.

EXERCISES

Compute budget and standard.

(LO 1)

E25-1 Parsons Company is planning to produce 2,000 units of product in 2017. Each unit requires 3 pounds of materials at $5 per pound and a half-hour of labor at $16 per hour. The overhead rate is 70% of direct labor.

Instructions
(a) Compute the budgeted amounts for 2017 for direct materials to be used, direct labor, and applied overhead.
(b) Compute the standard cost of one unit of product.
(c) What are the potential advantages to a corporation of using standard costs?

E25-2 Hank Itzek manufactures and sells homemade wine, and he wants to develop a standard cost per gallon. The following are required for production of a 50-gallon batch.

Compute standard materials costs.

(LO 1)

   3,000 ounces of grape concentrate at $0.06 per ounce
   54 pounds of granulated sugar at $0.30 per pound
   60 lemons at $0.60 each
   50 yeast tablets at $0.25 each
   50 nutrient tablets at $0.20 each
   2,600 ounces of water at $0.005 per ounce

Hank estimates that 4% of the grape concentrate is wasted, 10% of the sugar is lost, and 25% of the lemons cannot be used.

Instructions
Compute the standard cost of the ingredients for one gallon of wine. (Carry computations to two decimal places.)

E25-3 Stefani Company has gathered the following information about its product.

Compute standard cost per unit.

(LO 1)

   Direct materials. Each unit of product contains 4.5 pounds of materials. The average waste and spoilage per unit produced under normal conditions is 0.5 pounds. Materials cost $5 per pound, but Stefani always takes the 2% cash discount all of its suppliers offer. Freight costs average $0.25 per pound.

   Direct labor. Each unit requires 2 hours of labor. Setup, cleanup, and downtime average 0.4 hours per unit. The average hourly pay rate of Stefani's employees is $12. Payroll taxes and fringe benefits are an additional $3 per hour.

   Manufacturing overhead. Overhead is applied at a rate of $7 per direct labor hour.

Instructions
Compute Stefani's total standard cost per unit.

E25-4 Monte Services, Inc. is trying to establish the standard labor cost of a typical oil change. The following data have been collected from time and motion studies conducted over the past month.

Compute labor cost and labor quantity variance.

(LO 3)

Actual time spent on the oil change	1.0 hour
Hourly wage rate	$12
Payroll taxes	10% of wage rate
Setup and downtime	20% of actual labor time
Cleanup and rest periods	30% of actual labor time
Fringe benefits	25% of wage rate

Instructions
(a) Determine the standard direct labor hours per oil change.
(b) Determine the standard direct labor hourly rate.
(c) Determine the standard direct labor cost per oil change.
(d) If an oil change took 1.6 hours at the standard hourly rate, what was the direct labor quantity variance?

E25-5 The standard cost of Product B manufactured by Pharrell Company includes three units of direct materials at $5.00 per unit. During June, 29,000 units of direct materials are purchased at a cost of $4.70 per unit, and 29,000 units of direct materials are used to produce 9,400 units of Product B.

Compute materials price and quantity variances.

(LO 2)

Instructions
(a) Compute the total materials variance and the price and quantity variances.
(b) Repeat (a), assuming the purchase price is $5.15 and the quantity purchased and used is 28,000 units.

Compute labor price and quantity variances.

(LO 3)

E25-6 Lewis Company's standard labor cost of producing one unit of Product DD is 4 hours at the rate of $12.00 per hour. During August, 40,600 hours of labor are incurred at a cost of $12.15 per hour to produce 10,000 units of Product DD.

Instructions
(a) Compute the total labor variance.
(b) Compute the labor price and quantity variances.
(c) Repeat (b), assuming the standard is 4.1 hours of direct labor at $12.25 per hour.

Compute materials and labor variances.

(LO 2, 3)

E25-7 Levine Inc., which produces a single product, has prepared the following standard cost sheet for one unit of the product.

Direct materials (8 pounds at $2.50 per pound)	$20
Direct labor (3 hours at $12.00 per hour)	$36

During the month of April, the company manufactures 230 units and incurs the following actual costs.

Direct materials purchased and used (1,900 pounds)	$5,035
Direct labor (700 hours)	$8,120

Instructions
Compute the total, price, and quantity variances for materials and labor.

Compute the materials and labor variances and list reasons for unfavorable variances.

(LO 2, 3)

E25-8 The following direct materials and direct labor data pertain to the operations of Laurel Company for the month of August.

Costs		Quantities	
Actual labor rate	$13 per hour	Actual hours incurred and used	4,150 hours
Actual materials price	$128 per ton	Actual quantity of materials purchased and used	1,220 tons
Standard labor rate	$12.50 per hour	Standard hours used	4,300 hours
Standard materials price	$130 per ton	Standard quantity of materials used	1,200 tons

Instructions
(a) Compute the total, price, and quantity variances for materials and labor.
(b) Provide two possible explanations for each of the unfavorable variances calculated above, and suggest where responsibility for the unfavorable result might be placed.

Determine amounts from variance report.

(LO 2, 3)

E25-9 You have been given the following information about the production of Usher Co., and are asked to provide the plant manager with information for a meeting with the vice president of operations.

	Standard Cost Card
Direct materials (5 pounds at $4 per pound)	$20.00
Direct labor (0.8 hours at $10)	8.00
Variable overhead (0.8 hours at $3 per hour)	2.40
Fixed overhead (0.8 hours at $7 per hour)	5.60
	$36.00

The following is a variance report for the most recent period of operations.

			Variances	
Costs	Total Standard Cost		Price	Quantity
Direct materials	$410,000		$2,095 F	$9,000 U
Direct labor	180,000		3,840 U	6,000 U

Instructions
(a) How many units were produced during the period?
(b) How many pounds of raw materials were purchased and used during the period?
(c) What was the actual cost per pound of raw materials?
(d) How many actual direct labor hours were worked during the period?
(e) What was the actual rate paid per direct labor hour?

(CGA adapted)

E25-10 During March 2017, Toby Tool & Die Company worked on four jobs. A review of direct labor costs reveals the following summary data.

Prepare a variance report for direct labor.

(LO 3, 4)

Job Number	Actual Hours	Actual Costs	Standard Hours	Standard Costs	Total Variance
A257	221	$4,420	225	$4,500	$ 80 F
A258	450	9,450	430	8,600	850 U
A259	300	6,180	300	6,000	180 U
A260	116	2,088	110	2,200	112 F
Total variance					$838 U

Analysis reveals that Job A257 was a repeat job. Job A258 was a rush order that required overtime work at premium rates of pay. Job A259 required a more experienced replacement worker on one shift. Work on Job A260 was done for one day by a new trainee when a regular worker was absent.

Instructions
Prepare a report for the plant supervisor on direct labor cost variances for March. The report should have columns for (1) Job No., (2) Actual Hours, (3) Standard Hours, (4) Quantity Variance, (5) Actual Rate, (6) Standard Rate, (7) Price Variance, and (8) Explanation.

E25-11 Manufacturing overhead data for the production of Product H by Shakira Company are as follows.

Compute overhead variance.

(LO 3)

Overhead incurred for 52,000 actual direct labor hours worked	$263,000
Overhead rate (variable $3; fixed $2) at normal capacity of 54,000 direct labor hours	$5
Standard hours allowed for work done	52,000

Instructions
Compute the total overhead variance.

E25-12 Byrd Company produces one product, a putter called GO-Putter. Byrd uses a standard cost system and determines that it should take one hour of direct labor to produce one GO-Putter. The normal production capacity for this putter is 100,000 units per year. The total budgeted overhead at normal capacity is $850,000 comprised of $250,000 of variable costs and $600,000 of fixed costs. Byrd applies overhead on the basis of direct labor hours.

Compute overhead variances.

(LO 3)

During the current year, Byrd produced 95,000 putters, worked 94,000 direct labor hours, and incurred variable overhead costs of $256,000 and fixed overhead costs of $600,000.

Instructions
(a) Compute the predetermined variable overhead rate and the predetermined fixed overhead rate.
(b) Compute the applied overhead for Byrd for the year.
(c) Compute the total overhead variance.

E25-13 Ceelo Company purchased (at a cost of $10,200) and used 2,400 pounds of materials during May. Ceelo's standard cost of materials per unit produced is based on 2 pounds per unit at a cost $5 per pound. Production in May was 1,050 units.

Compute variances for materials.

(LO 2, 3)

Instructions
(a) Compute the total, price, and quantity variances for materials.
(b) Assume Ceelo also had an unfavorable labor quantity variance. What is a possible scenario that would provide one cause for the variances computed in (a) and the unfavorable labor quantity variance?

E25-14 Picard Landscaping plants grass seed as the basic landscaping for business campuses. During a recent month, the company worked on three projects (Remington, Chang, and Wyco). The company is interested in controlling the materials costs, namely the grass seed, for these plantings projects.

Prepare a variance report.

(LO 2, 4)

In order to provide management with useful cost control information, the company uses standard costs and prepares monthly variance reports. Analysis reveals that the purchasing agent mistakenly purchased poor-quality seed for the Remington project.

The Chang project, however, received higher-than-standard-quality seed that was on sale. The Wyco project received standard-quality seed. However, the price had increased and a new employee was used to spread the seed.

Shown below are quantity and cost data for each project.

| | Actual | | Standard | | Total |
Project	Quantity	Costs	Quantity	Costs	Variance
Remington	500 lbs.	$1,200	460 lbs.	$1,150	$ 50 U
Chang	400	920	410	1,025	105 F
Wyco	550	1,430	480	1,200	230 U
Total variance					$175 U

Instructions

(a) Prepare a variance report for the purchasing department with the following columns: (1) Project, (2) Actual Pounds Purchased, (3) Actual Price per Pound, (4) Standard Price per Pound, (5) Price Variance, and (6) Explanation.

(b) Prepare a variance report for the production department with the following columns: (1) Project, (2) Actual Pounds, (3) Standard Pounds, (4) Standard Price per Pound, (5) Quantity Variance, and (6) Explanation.

Complete variance report.

(LO 4)

E25-15 Urban Corporation prepared the following variance report.

URBAN CORPORATION
Variance Report—Purchasing Department
For the Week Ended January 9, 2017

Type of Materials	Quantity Purchased	Actual Price	Standard Price	Price Variance	Explanation
Rogue11	? lbs.	$5.20	$5.00	$5,500 ?	Price increase
Storm17	7,000 oz.	?	3.30	1,050 U	Rush order
Beast29	22,000 units	0.40	?	660 F	Bought larger quantity

Instructions

Fill in the appropriate amounts or letters for the question marks in the report.

Prepare income statement for management.

(LO 4)

E25-16 Fisk Company uses a standard cost accounting system. During January, the company reported the following manufacturing variances.

Materials price variance	$1,200 U	Labor quantity variance	$750 U
Materials quantity variance	800 F	Overhead variance	800 U
Labor price variance	550 U		

In addition, 8,000 units of product were sold at $8 per unit. Each unit sold had a standard cost of $5. Selling and administrative expenses were $8,000 for the month.

Instructions

Prepare an income statement for management for the month ended January 31, 2017.

Identify performance evaluation terminology.

(LO 1, 4)

E25-17 The following is a list of terms related to performance evaluation.

1. Balanced scorecard
2. Variance
3. Learning and growth perspective
4. Nonfinancial measures

5. Customer perspective
6. Internal process perspective
7. Ideal standards
8. Normal standards

Instructions

Match each of the following descriptions with one of the terms above.

(a) The difference between total actual costs and total standard costs.

(b) An efficient level of performance that is attainable under expected operating conditions.

(c) An approach that incorporates financial and nonfinancial measures in an integrated system that links performance measurement and a company's strategic goals.

(d) A viewpoint employed in the balanced scorecard to evaluate how well a company develops and retains its employees.

(e) An evaluation tool that is not based on dollars.

(f) A viewpoint employed in the balanced scorecard to evaluate the company from the perspective of those people who buy its products or services.

(g) An optimum level of performance under perfect operating conditions.

(h) A viewpoint employed in the balanced scorecard to evaluate the efficiency and effectiveness of the company's value chain.

E25-18 Indicate which of the four perspectives in the balanced scorecard is most likely associated with the objectives that follow.

Identity balanced scorecard perspectives.

(LO 4)

1. Percentage of repeat customers.
2. Number of suggestions for improvement from employees.
3. Contribution margin.
4. Brand recognition.
5. Number of cross-trained employees.
6. Amount of setup time.

E25-19 Indicate which of the four perspectives in the balanced scorecard is most likely associated with the objectives that follow.

Identify balance scorecard perspectives.

(LO 4)

1. Ethics violations.
2. Credit rating.
3. Customer retention.
4. Stockouts.
5. Reportable accidents.
6. Brand recognition.

*E25-20 Vista Company installed a standard cost system on January 1. Selected transactions for the month of January are as follows.

Journalize entries in a standard cost accounting system.

(LO 5)

1. Purchased 18,000 units of raw materials on account at a cost of $4.50 per unit. Standard cost was $4.40 per unit.
2. Issued 18,000 units of raw materials for jobs that required 17,500 standard units of raw materials.
3. Incurred 15,300 actual hours of direct labor at an actual rate of $5.00 per hour. The standard rate is $5.50 per hour. (Credit Factory Wages Payable.)
4. Performed 15,300 hours of direct labor on jobs when standard hours were 15,400.
5. Applied overhead to jobs at the rate of 100% of direct labor cost for standard hours allowed.

Instructions
Journalize the January transactions.

*E25-21 Lopez Company uses a standard cost accounting system. Some of the ledger accounts have been destroyed in a fire. The controller asks your help in reconstructing some missing entries and balances.

Answer questions concerning missing entries and balances.

(LO 2, 3, 5)

Instructions
Answer the following questions.

(a) Materials Price Variance shows a $2,000 unfavorable balance. Accounts Payable shows $138,000 of raw materials purchases. What was the amount debited to Raw Materials Inventory for raw materials purchased?

(b) Materials Quantity Variance shows a $3,000 favorable balance. Raw Materials Inventory shows a zero balance. What was the amount debited to Work in Process Inventory for direct materials used?

(c) Labor Price Variance shows a $1,500 favorable balance. Factory Labor shows a debit of $145,000 for wages incurred. What was the amount credited to Factory Wages Payable?

(d) Factory Labor shows a credit of $145,000 for direct labor used. Labor Quantity Variance shows a $900 favorable balance. What was the amount debited to Work in Process for direct labor used?

(e) Overhead applied to Work in Process totaled $165,000. If the total overhead variance was $1,200 favorable, what was the amount of overhead costs debited to Manufacturing Overhead?

Journalize entries for materials and labor variances.

(LO 5)

*E25-22 Data for Levine Inc. are given in E25-7.

Instructions

Journalize the entries to record the materials and labor variances.

Compute manufacturing overhead variances and interpret findings.

(LO 6)

*E25-23 The information shown below was taken from the annual manufacturing overhead cost budget of Connick Company.

Variable manufacturing overhead costs	$34,650
Fixed manufacturing overhead costs	$19,800
Normal production level in labor hours	16,500
Normal production level in units	4,125
Standard labor hours per unit	4

During the year, 4,050 units were produced, 16,100 hours were worked, and the actual manufacturing overhead was $55,500. Actual fixed manufacturing overhead costs equaled budgeted fixed manufacturing overhead costs. Overhead is applied on the basis of direct labor hours.

Instructions

(a) Compute the total, fixed, and variable predetermined manufacturing overhead rates.

(b) Compute the total, controllable, and volume overhead variances.

(c) ✏—— Briefly interpret the overhead controllable and volume variances computed in (b).

Compute overhead variances.

(LO 6)

*E25-24 The loan department of Calgary Bank uses standard costs to determine the overhead cost of processing loan applications. During the current month, a fire occurred, and the accounting records for the department were mostly destroyed. The following data were salvaged from the ashes.

Standard variable overhead rate per hour	$9
Standard hours per application	2
Standard hours allowed	2,000
Standard fixed overhead rate per hour	$6
Actual fixed overhead cost	$12,600
Variable overhead budget based on standard hours allowed	$18,000
Fixed overhead budget	$12,600
Overhead controllable variance	$ 1,200 U

Instructions

(a) Determine the following.

  (1) Total actual overhead cost.

  (2) Actual variable overhead cost.

  (3) Variable overhead costs applied.

  (4) Fixed overhead costs applied.

  (5) Overhead volume variance.

(b) Determine how many loans were processed.

Compute variances.

(LO 6)

*E25-25 Seacrest Company's overhead rate was based on estimates of $200,000 for overhead costs and 20,000 direct labor hours. Seacrest's standards allow 2 hours of direct labor per unit produced. Production in May was 900 units, and actual overhead incurred in May was $19,500. The overhead budgeted for 1,800 standard direct labor hours is $17,600 ($5,000 fixed and $12,600 variable).

Instructions

(a) Compute the total, controllable, and volume variances for overhead.

(b) What are possible causes of the variances computed in part (a)?

■ EXERCISES: SET B AND CHALLENGE EXERCISES

Visit the book's companion website, at **www.wiley.com/college/weygandt**, and choose the Student Companion site to access Exercises: Set B and Challenge Exercises.

PROBLEMS: SET A

P25-1A Rogen Corporation manufactures a single product. The standard cost per unit of product is shown below.

Compute variances.

(LO 2, 3)

Direct materials—1 pound plastic at $7.00 per pound	$ 7.00
Direct labor—1.6 hours at $12.00 per hour	19.20
Variable manufacturing overhead	12.00
Fixed manufacturing overhead	4.00
Total standard cost per unit	$42.20

The predetermined manufacturing overhead rate is $10 per direct labor hour ($16.00 ÷ 1.6). It was computed from a master manufacturing overhead budget based on normal production of 8,000 direct labor hours (5,000 units) for the month. The master budget showed total variable costs of $60,000 ($7.50 per hour) and total fixed overhead costs of $20,000 ($2.50 per hour). Actual costs for October in producing 4,800 units were as follows.

Direct materials (5,100 pounds)	$ 36,720
Direct labor (7,400 hours)	92,500
Variable overhead	59,700
Fixed overhead	21,000
Total manufacturing costs	$209,920

The purchasing department buys the quantities of raw materials that are expected to be used in production each month. Raw materials inventories, therefore, can be ignored.

Instructions
(a) Compute all of the materials and labor variances.
(b) Compute the total overhead variance.

(a) MPV $1,020 U

P25-2A Ayala Corporation accumulates the following data relative to jobs started and finished during the month of June 2017.

Compute variances, and prepare income statement.

(LO 2, 3, 4)

Costs and Production Data	Actual	Standard
Raw materials unit cost	$2.25	$2.10
Raw materials units used	10,600	10,000
Direct labor payroll	$120,960	$120,000
Direct labor hours worked	14,400	15,000
Manufacturing overhead incurred	$189,500	
Manufacturing overhead applied		$193,500
Machine hours expected to be used at normal capacity		42,500
Budgeted fixed overhead for June		$55,250
Variable overhead rate per machine hour		$3.00
Fixed overhead rate per machine hour		$1.30

Overhead is applied on the basis of standard machine hours. Three hours of machine time are required for each direct labor hour. The jobs were sold for $400,000. Selling and administrative expenses were $40,000. Assume that the amount of raw materials purchased equaled the amount used.

Instructions
(a) Compute all of the variances for (1) direct materials and (2) direct labor.
(b) Compute the total overhead variance.
(c) Prepare an income statement for management. (Ignore income taxes.)

(a) LQV $4,800 F

P25-3A Rudd Clothiers is a small company that manufactures tall-men's suits. The company has used a standard cost accounting system. In May 2017, 11,250 suits were produced. The following standard and actual cost data applied to the month of May when normal capacity was 14,000 direct labor hours. All materials purchased were used.

Compute and identify significant variances.

(LO 2, 3, 4)

Cost Element	Standard (per unit)	Actual
Direct materials	8 yards at $4.40 per yard	$375,575 for 90,500 yards ($4.15 per yard)
Direct labor	1.2 hours at $13.40 per hour	$200,925 for 14,250 hours ($14.10 per hour)
Overhead	1.2 hours at $6.10 per hour (fixed $3.50; variable $2.60)	$49,000 fixed overhead $37,000 variable overhead

Overhead is applied on the basis of direct labor hours. At normal capacity, budgeted fixed overhead costs were $49,000, and budgeted variable overhead was $36,400.

Instructions

(a) MPV $22,625 F

(a) Compute the total, price, and quantity variances for (1) materials and (2) labor.
(b) Compute the total overhead variance.
(c) ──────── Which of the materials and labor variances should be investigated if management considers a variance of more than 4% from standard to be significant?

Answer questions about variances.

(LO 2, 3)

P25-4A Kansas Company uses a standard cost accounting system. In 2017, the company produced 28,000 units. Each unit took several pounds of direct materials and 1.6 standard hours of direct labor at a standard hourly rate of $12.00. Normal capacity was 50,000 direct labor hours. During the year, 117,000 pounds of raw materials were purchased at $0.92 per pound. All materials purchased were used during the year.

Instructions

(a) If the materials price variance was $3,510 favorable, what was the standard materials price per pound?

(b) 4.0 pounds

(b) If the materials quantity variance was $4,750 unfavorable, what was the standard materials quantity per unit?
(c) What were the standard hours allowed for the units produced?
(d) If the labor quantity variance was $7,200 unfavorable, what were the actual direct labor hours worked?
(e) If the labor price variance was $9,080 favorable, what was the actual rate per hour?

(f) $7.20 per DLH

(f) If total budgeted manufacturing overhead was $360,000 at normal capacity, what was the predetermined overhead rate?
(g) What was the standard cost per unit of product?
(h) How much overhead was applied to production during the year?
(i) Using one or more answers above, what were the total costs assigned to work in process?

Compute variances, prepare an income statement, and explain unfavorable variances.

(LO 2, 3, 4)

P25-5A Hart Labs, Inc. provides mad cow disease testing for both state and federal governmental agricultural agencies. Because the company's customers are governmental agencies, prices are strictly regulated. Therefore, Hart Labs must constantly monitor and control its testing costs. Shown below are the standard costs for a typical test.

Direct materials (2 test tubes @ $1.46 per tube)	$ 2.92
Direct labor (1 hour @ $24 per hour)	24.00
Variable overhead (1 hour @ $6 per hour)	6.00
Fixed overhead (1 hour @ $10 per hour)	10.00
Total standard cost per test	$42.92

The lab does not maintain an inventory of test tubes. As a result, the tubes purchased each month are used that month. Actual activity for the month of November 2017, when 1,475 tests were conducted, resulted in the following.

Direct materials (3,050 test tubes)	$ 4,270
Direct labor (1,550 hours)	35,650
Variable overhead	7,400
Fixed overhead	15,000

Monthly budgeted fixed overhead is $14,000. Revenues for the month were $75,000, and selling and administrative expenses were $5,000.

Instructions

(a) LQV $1,800 U

(a) Compute the price and quantity variances for direct materials and direct labor.
(b) Compute the total overhead variance.
(c) Prepare an income statement for management.
(d) Provide possible explanations for each unfavorable variance.

*P25-6A Jorgensen Corporation uses standard costs with its job order cost accounting system. In January, an order (Job No. 12) for 1,900 units of Product B was received. The standard cost of one unit of Product B is as follows.

Journalize and post standard cost entries, and prepare income statement.

(LO 2, 3, 4, 5)

Direct materials	3 pounds at $1.00 per pound	$ 3.00
Direct labor	1 hour at $8.00 per hour	8.00
Overhead	2 hours (variable $4.00 per machine hour;	
	fixed $2.25 per machine hour)	12.50
Standard cost per unit		$23.50

Normal capacity for the month was 4,200 machine hours. During January, the following transactions applicable to Job No. 12 occurred.

1. Purchased 6,200 pounds of raw materials on account at $1.05 per pound.
2. Requisitioned 6,200 pounds of raw materials for Job No. 12.
3. Incurred 2,000 hours of direct labor at a rate of $7.80 per hour.
4. Worked 2,000 hours of direct labor on Job No. 12.
5. Incurred manufacturing overhead on account $25,000.
6. Applied overhead to Job No. 12 on basis of standard machine hours allowed.
7. Completed Job No. 12.
8. Billed customer for Job No. 12 at a selling price of $65,000.

Instructions
(a) Journalize the transactions.
(b) Post to the job order cost accounts.
(c) Prepare the entry to recognize the total overhead variance.
(d) Prepare the January 2017 income statement for management. Assume selling and administrative expenses were $2,000.

(d) NI $15,890

*P25-7A Using the information in P25-1A, compute the overhead controllable variance and the overhead volume variance.

Compute overhead controllable and volume variances.

(LO 6)

*P25-8A Using the information in P25-2A, compute the overhead controllable variance and the overhead volume variance.

Compute overhead controllable and volume variances.

(LO 6)

*P25-9A Using the information in P25-3A, compute the overhead controllable variance and the overhead volume variance.

Compute overhead controllable and volume variances.

(LO 6)

*P25-10A Using the information in P25-5A, compute the overhead controllable variance and the overhead volume variance.

Compute overhead controllable and volume variances.

(LO 6)

PROBLEMS: SET B AND SET C

Visit the book's companion website, at **www.wiley.com/college/weygandt**, and choose the Student Companion site to access Problems: Set B and Set C.

CONTINUING PROBLEMS

CURRENT DESIGNS

CD25 The executive team at **Current Designs** has gathered to evaluate the company's operations for the last month. One of the topics on the agenda is the special order from Huegel Hollow, which was presented in CD2. Recall that Current Designs had a special order to produce a batch of 20 kayaks for a client, and you were asked to determine the cost of the order and the cost per kayak.

Mike Cichanowski asked the others if the special order caused any particular problems in the production process. Dave Thill, the production manager, made the following comments: "Since we wanted to complete this order quickly and make a good first impression on this new customer, we had some of our most experienced type I workers run the rotomold oven and do the trimming. They were very efficient and were able to complete that part of the manufacturing process even more quickly than the regular crew. However, the finishing on these kayaks required a different technique than what we usually use, so our type II workers took a little longer than usual for that part of the process."

Deb Welch, who is in charge of the purchasing function, said, "We had to pay a little more for the polyethylene powder for this order because the customer wanted a color that we don't usually stock. We also ordered a little extra since we wanted to make sure that we had enough to allow us to calibrate the equipment. The calibration was a little tricky, and we used all of the powder that we had purchased. Since the number of kayaks in the order was fairly small, we were able to use some rope and other parts that were left over from last year's production in the finishing kits. We've seen a price increase for these components in the last year, so using the parts that we already had in inventory cut our costs for the finishing kits."

Instructions

(a) Based on the comments above, predict whether each of the following variances will be favorable or unfavorable. If you don't have enough information to make a prediction, use "NEI" to indicate "Not Enough Information."

(1) Quantity variance for polyethylene powder.
(5) Quantity variance for type I workers.
(2) Price variance for polyethylene powder.
(6) Price variance for type I workers.
(3) Quantity variance for finishing kits.
(7) Quantity variance for type II workers.
(4) Price variance for finishing kits.
(8) Price variance for type II workers.

(b) Diane Buswell examined some of the accounting records and reported that Current Designs purchased 1,200 pounds of pellets for this order at a total cost of $2,040. Twenty (20) finishing kits were assembled at a total cost of $3,240. The payroll records showed that the type I employees worked 38 hours on this project at a total cost of $570. The type II finishing employees worked 65 hours at a total cost of $796.25. A total of 20 kayaks were produced for this order.

The standards that had been developed for this model of kayak were used in CD2 and are reproduced here. For each kayak:

54 pounds of polyethylene powder at $1.50 per pound

1 finishing kit (rope, seat, hardware, etc.) at $170

2 hours of type I labor from people who run the oven and trim the plastic at a standard wage rate of $15 per hour

3 hours of type II labor from people who attach the hatches and seat and other hardware at a standard wage rate of $12 per hour.

Calculate the eight variances that are listed in part (a) of this problem.

WATERWAYS

(This is a continuation of the Waterways problem from Chapters 15–24.)

WP25 Waterways Corporation uses very stringent standard costs in evaluating its manufacturing efficiency. These standards are not "ideal" at this point, but management is working toward that as a goal. This problem asks you to calculate and evaluate the company's variances.

Go to the book's companion website, at **www.wiley.com/college/weygandt**, *to find the completion of this problem.*

BROADENING YOUR *PERSPECTIVE*

MANAGEMENT DECISION-MAKING

Decision-Making Across the Organization

BYP25-1 Milton Professionals, a management consulting firm, specializes in strategic planning for financial institutions. James Hahn and Sara Norton, partners in the firm, are assembling a new strategic planning model for use by clients. The model is designed for use on most personal computers and replaces a rather lengthy manual model currently marketed by the firm. To market the new model, James and Sara will need to provide clients with an estimate of the number of labor hours and computer time needed to operate the model. The model is currently being test-marketed at five small financial institutions. These financial institutions are listed on the next page, along with the number of combined computer/labor hours used by each institution to run the model one time.

Financial Institutions	Computer/Labor Hours Required
Midland National	25
First State	45
Financial Federal	40
Pacific America	30
Lakeview National	30
Total	170
Average	34

Any company that purchases the new model will need to purchase user manuals for the system. User manuals will be sold to clients in cases of 20, at a cost of $320 per case. One manual must be used each time the model is run because each manual includes a nonreusable computer-accessed password for operating the system. Also required are specialized computer forms that are sold only by Milton. The specialized forms are sold in packages of 250, at a cost of $60 per package. One application of the model requires the use of 50 forms. This amount includes two forms that are generally wasted in each application due to printer alignment errors. The overall cost of the strategic planning model to clients is $12,000. Most clients will use the model four times annually.

Milton must provide its clients with estimates of ongoing costs incurred in operating the new planning model, and would like to do so in the form of standard costs.

Instructions

With the class divided into groups, answer the following.

(a) What factors should be considered in setting a standard for computer/labor hours?
(b) What alternatives for setting a standard for computer/labor hours might be used?
(c) What standard for computer/labor hours would you select? Justify your answer.
(d) Determine the standard materials cost associated with the user manuals and computer forms for each application of the strategic planning model.

Managerial Analysis

*BYP25-2 Ana Carillo and Associates is a medium-sized company located near a large metropolitan area in the Midwest. The company manufactures cabinets of mahogany, oak, and other fine woods for use in expensive homes, restaurants, and hotels. Although some of the work is custom, many of the cabinets are a standard size.

One such non-custom model is called Luxury Base Frame. Normal production is 1,000 units. Each unit has a direct labor hour standard of 5 hours. Overhead is applied to production based on standard direct labor hours. During the most recent month, only 900 units were produced; 4,500 direct labor hours were allowed for standard production, but only 4,000 hours were used. Standard and actual overhead costs were as follows.

	Standard (1,000 units)	Actual (900 units)
Indirect materials	$ 12,000	$ 12,300
Indirect labor	43,000	51,000
(Fixed) Manufacturing supervisors salaries	22,500	22,000
(Fixed) Manufacturing office employees salaries	13,000	12,500
(Fixed) Engineering costs	27,000	25,000
Computer costs	10,000	10,000
Electricity	2,500	2,500
(Fixed) Manufacturing building depreciation	8,000	8,000
(Fixed) Machinery depreciation	3,000	3,000
(Fixed) Trucks and forklift depreciation	1,500	1,500
Small tools	700	1,400
(Fixed) Insurance	500	500
(Fixed) Property taxes	300	300
Total	$144,000	$150,000

Instructions

(a) Determine the overhead application rate.
(b) Determine how much overhead was applied to production.
(c) Calculate the total overhead variance, controllable variance, and volume variance.
(d) Decide which overhead variances should be investigated.
(e) Discuss causes of the overhead variances. What can management do to improve its performance next month?

Real-World Focus

BYP25-3 Glassmaster Company is organized as two divisions and one subsidiary. One division focuses on the manufacture of filaments such as fishing line and sewing thread; the other division manufactures antennas and specialty fiberglass products. Its subsidiary manufactures flexible steel wire controls and molded control panels.

The annual report of Glassmaster provides the following information.

GLASSMASTER COMPANY
Management Discussion

Gross profit margins for the year improved to 20.9% of sales compared to last year's 18.5%. All operations reported improved margins due in large part to improved operating efficiencies as a result of cost reduction measures implemented during the second and third quarters of the fiscal year and increased manufacturing throughout due to higher unit volume sales. Contributing to the improved margins was a favorable materials price variance due to competitive pricing by suppliers as a result of soft demand for petrochemical-based products. This favorable variance is temporary and will begin to reverse itself as stronger worldwide demand for commodity products improves in tandem with the economy. Partially offsetting these positive effects on profit margins were competitive pressures on sales prices of certain product lines. The company responded with pricing strategies designed to maintain and/or increase market share.

Instructions
(a) Is it apparent from the information whether Glassmaster utilizes standard costs?
(b) Do you think the price variance experienced should lead to changes in standard costs for the next fiscal year?

BYP25-4 The **Balanced Scorecard Institute** *(www.balancedscorecard.org)* is a great resource for information about implementing the balanced scorecard. One item of interest provided at its website is an example of a balanced scorecard for a regional airline.

Address: **http://www.balancedscorecard.org/portals/0/pdf/regional_airline.pdf**, or go to **www.wiley.com/college/weygandt**

Instructions
Go to the address above and answer the following questions.

(a) What are the objectives identified for the airline for each perspective?
(b) What measures are used for the objectives in the customer perspective?
(c) What initiatives are planned to achieve the objective in the learning perspective?

BYP25-5 The December 22, 2009, edition of the *Wall Street Journal* has an article by Kevin Kelliker entitled "In Risky Move, GM to Run Plants Around Clock."

Instructions
Read the article and answer the following questions.

(a) According to the article, what is the normal industry standard for plants to be considered operating at full capacity?
(b) What ideal standard is the company hoping to achieve?
(c) What reasons are given in the article for why most companies do not operate a third shift? How does **GM** propose to overcome these issues?
(d) What are some potential drawbacks of the midnight shift? What implications does this have for variances from standards?
(e) What potential sales/marketing disadvantage does the third shift create?

CRITICAL THINKING

Communication Activity

BYP25-6 The setting of standards is critical to the effective use of standards in evaluating performance.

Instructions

Explain the following in a memo to your instructor.

(a) The comparative advantages and disadvantages of ideal versus normal standards.
(b) The factors that should be included in setting the price and quantity standards for direct materials, direct labor, and manufacturing overhead.

Ethics Case

BYP25-7 At Symond Company, production workers in the Painting Department are paid on the basis of productivity. The labor time standard for a unit of production is established through periodic time studies conducted by Douglas Management Consultants. In a time study, the actual time required to complete a specific task by a worker is observed. Allowances are then made for preparation time, rest periods, and cleanup time. Bill Carson is one of several veterans in the Painting Department.

Bill is informed by Douglas that he will be used in the time study for the painting of a new product. The findings will be the basis for establishing the labor time standard for the next 6 months. During the test, Bill deliberately slows his normal work pace in an effort to obtain a labor time standard that will be easy to meet. Because it is a new product, the Douglas representative who conducted the test is unaware that Bill did not give the test his best effort.

Instructions

(a) Who was benefited and who was harmed by Bill's actions?
(b) Was Bill ethical in the way he performed the time study test?
(c) What measure(s) might the company take to obtain valid data for setting the labor time standard?

All About You

BYP25-8 From the time you first entered school many years ago, instructors have been measuring and evaluating you by imposing standards. In addition, many of you will pursue professions that administer professional examinations to attain recognized certification. A federal commission presented proposals suggesting all public colleges and universities should require standardized tests to measure their students' learning.

Instructions

Read the article at **www.signonsandiego.com/uniontrib/20060811/news_1n11colleges.html**, and answer the following questions.

(a) What areas of concern did the panel's recommendations address?
(b) What are possible advantages of standard testing?
(c) What are possible disadvantages of standard testing?
(d) Would you be in favor of standardized tests?

Considering Your Costs and Benefits

BYP25-9 Do you think that standard costs are used only in making products like wheel bearings and hamburgers? Think again. Standards influence virtually every aspect of our lives. For example, the next time you call to schedule an appointment with your doctor, ask the receptionist how many minutes the appointment is scheduled for. Doctors are under increasing pressure to see more patients each day, which means the time spent with each patient is shorter. As insurance companies and employers push for reduced medical costs, every facet of medicine has been standardized and analyzed. Doctors, nurses, and other medical staff are evaluated in every part of their operations to ensure maximum efficiency. While keeping medical treatment affordable seems like a worthy goal, what are the potential implications for the quality of health care? Does a focus on the bottom line result in a reduction in the quality of health care?

A simmering debate has centered on a very basic question: To what extent should accountants, through financial measures, influence the type of medical care that you receive? Suppose that your local medical facility is in danger of closing because it has been losing money. Should the facility put in place incentives that provide bonuses to doctors if they meet certain standard-cost targets for the cost of treating specific ailments?

YES: If the facility is in danger of closing, then someone should take steps to change the medical practices to reduce costs. A closed medical facility is of no use to me, my family, or the community.
NO: I don't want an accountant deciding the right medical treatment for me. My family and I deserve the best medical care.

Instructions

Write a response indicating your position regarding this situation. Provide support for your view.

26 Planning for Capital Investments

CHAPTER PREVIEW Companies like Holland America Line (as discussed in the Feature Story below) must constantly determine how to invest their resources. Other examples: Dell announced plans to spend $1 billion on data centers for cloud computing. ExxonMobil announced that two wells off the Brazilian coast, which it had spent hundreds of millions of dollars to drill, would produce no oil. Renault and Nissan spent over $5 billion during a nearly 20-year period to develop electric cars, such as the Leaf.

The process of making such capital expenditure decisions is referred to as **capital budgeting**. Capital budgeting involves choosing among various capital projects to find those that will maximize a company's return on its financial investment. The purpose of this chapter is to discuss the various techniques used to make effective capital budgeting decisions.

FEATURE STORY

Floating Hotels

Do you own a boat? Maybe it's a nice boat, but how many swimming pools, movie theaters, shopping malls, or restaurants does it have on board? If you are in the cruise-line business, like Holland America Line, you need all of these amenities and more just to stay afloat. Holland America Line is considered by many to be the leader of the premium luxury-liner segment.

Carnival Corporation, which owns Holland America Line and other cruise lines, is one of the largest vacation companies in the world. During one recent three-year period, Carnival spent more than $3 billion per year on capital expenditures. That's a big number, but keep in mind that Carnival estimates that at any given time there are 270,000 people (200,000 customers and 70,000 crew) on its 100 ships somewhere in the world.

The cruise industry is a tricky business. When times are good, customers are looking for ways to splurge. But when times get tough, people are more inclined to take a trip in a minivan than a luxury yacht. So it's important to time your investment properly. For example, during one stretch of solid global economic growth, many cruise lines decided to add capacity. The industry built 14 new ships at a total price of $4.7 billion. (That's an average price of about $330 million.) But, it takes up to three years to build one of these giant vessels. Unfortunately, by the time the ships were completed, the economy was in a nose-dive.

To maintain passenger numbers, cruise prices had to be cut by up to 40%. While the lower prices attracted lots of customers, that wasn't enough to offset an overall decline in revenue of 10% in the middle of the recession. The industry had added capacity at just the wrong time.

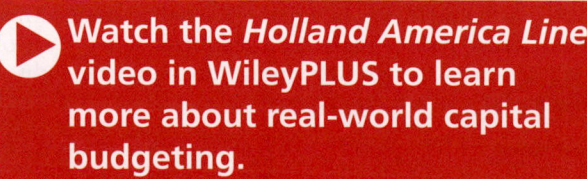

Watch the *Holland America Line* video in WileyPLUS to learn more about real-world capital budgeting.

© Engel & Gielen/Getty Images

CHAPTER OUTLINE

Learning Objectives

1 Describe capital budgeting inputs and apply the cash payback technique.
- Cash flow information
- Cash payback

DO IT! 1 Cash Payback Period

2 Use the net present value method.
- Equal annual cash flows
- Unequal annual cash flows
- Choosing a discount rate
- Simplifying assumptions
- Comprehensive example

DO IT! 2 Net Present Value

3 Identify capital budgeting challenges and refinements.
- Intangible benefits
- Profitability index for mutually exclusive projects
- Risk analysis
- Post-audit of investment projects

DO IT! 3 Profitability Index

4 Use the internal rate of return method.
- Comparing discounted cash flow methods

DO IT! 4 Internal Rate of Return

5 Use the annual rate of return method.
- Based on accrual-accounting data

DO IT! 5 Annual Rate of Return

Go to the **REVIEW AND PRACTICE** section at the end of the chapter for a review of key concepts and practice applications with solutions.

Visit **WileyPLUS with ORION** for additional tutorials and practice opportunities.

Describe capital budgeting inputs and apply the cash payback technique.

Many companies follow a carefully prescribed process in capital budgeting. At least once a year, top management requests proposals for projects from departments, plants, and authorized personnel. A capital budgeting committee screens the proposals and submits its findings to the officers of the company. The officers, in turn, select the projects they believe to be most worthy of funding. They submit this list of projects to the board of directors. Ultimately, the directors approve the capital expenditure budget for the year. Illustration 26-1 shows this process.

1. Project proposals are requested from departments, plants, and authorized personnel.

2. Proposals are screened by a capital budget committee.

3. Officers determine which projects are worthy of funding.

4. Board of directors approves capital budget.

Illustration 26-1
Corporate capital budget authorization process

The involvement of top management and the board of directors in the process demonstrates the importance of capital budgeting decisions. These decisions often have a significant impact on a company's future profitability. In fact, poor capital budgeting decisions can cost a lot of money. Such decisions have even led to the bankruptcy of some companies.

Cash Flow Information

In this chapter, we will look at several methods that help companies make effective capital budgeting decisions. Most of these methods employ **cash flow numbers**, rather than accrual accounting revenues and expenses. Remember from your financial accounting course that accrual accounting records **revenues** and **expenses**, rather than cash inflows and cash outflows. In fact, revenues and expenses measured during a period often differ significantly from their cash flow counterparts. Accrual accounting has advantages over cash accounting in many contexts. **For purposes of capital budgeting, though, estimated cash inflows and outflows are the preferred inputs.** Why? Because ultimately the value of all financial investments is determined by the value of cash flows received and paid.

Sometimes cash flow information is not available. In this case, companies can make adjustments to accrual accounting numbers to estimate cash flow. Often, they estimate net annual cash flow by adding back depreciation expense to net income. Depreciation expense is added back because it is an expense that does not require an outflow of cash. By adding depreciation expense back to net income, companies approximate net annual cash flow. Suppose, for example, that Reno Company's net income of $13,000 includes a charge for depreciation expense of $26,000. Its estimated net annual cash flow would be $39,000 ($13,000 + $26,000).

Illustration 26-2 lists some typical cash outflows and inflows related to equipment purchase and replacement.

Illustration 26-2
Typical cash flows relating to capital budgeting decisions

Cash Outflows

Initial investment
Repairs and maintenance
Increased operating costs
Overhaul of equipment

Cash Inflows

Sale of old equipment
Increased cash received from customers
Reduced cash outflows related to operating costs
Salvage value of equipment

These cash flows are the inputs that are considered relevant in capital budgeting decisions.

The capital budgeting decision, under any technique, depends in part on a variety of considerations:

- **The availability of funds:** Does the company have unlimited funds, or will it have to ration capital investments?
- **Relationships among proposed projects:** Are proposed projects independent of each other, or does the acceptance or rejection of one depend on the acceptance or rejection of another?
- **The company's basic decision-making approach:** Does the company want to produce an accept-reject decision or a ranking of desirability among possible projects?
- **The risk associated with a particular project:** How certain are the projected returns? The certainty of estimates varies with such issues as market considerations or the length of time before returns are expected.

Illustrative Data

To compare the results of the various capital budgeting techniques, we will use a continuing example. Assume that Stewart Shipping Company is considering an investment of $130,000 in new equipment. The new equipment is expected to last 10 years. It will have a zero salvage value at the end of its useful life. The annual cash inflows are $200,000, and the annual cash outflows are $176,000. Illustration 26-3 summarizes these data.

Illustration 26-3
Investment information for Stewart Shipping example

Initial investment	$130,000
Estimated useful life	10 years
Estimated salvage value	–0–
Estimated annual cash flows	
Cash inflows from customers	$200,000
Cash outflows for operating costs	176,000
Net annual cash flow	$ 24,000

In the following two sections, we will examine two popular techniques for evaluating capital investments: cash payback and the net present value method.

Cash Payback

The **cash payback technique** identifies the time period required to recover the cost of the capital investment from the net annual cash flow produced by the investment. Illustration 26-4 presents the formula for computing the cash payback period assuming equal annual cash flows.

Illustration 26-4
Cash payback formula

Cost of Capital Investment	÷	Net Annual Cash Flow	=	Cash Payback Period

Helpful Hint
Net annual cash flow can also be approximated by "Net cash provided by operating activities" from the statement of cash flows.

The cash payback period in the Stewart Shipping example is 5.42 years, computed as follows.

$$\$130,000 \div \$24,000 = 5.42 \text{ years}$$

The evaluation of the payback period is often related to the expected useful life of the asset. For example, assume that at Stewart Shipping a project is unacceptable if the payback period is longer than 60% of the asset's expected useful life. The 5.42-year payback period is 54.2% (5.42 ÷ 10) of the project's expected useful life. Thus, the project is acceptable.

It follows that when the payback technique is used to decide among acceptable alternative projects, **the shorter the payback period, the more attractive the investment**. This is true for two reasons: First, the earlier the investment is recovered, the sooner the company can use the cash funds for other purposes. Second, the risk of loss from obsolescence and changed economic conditions is less in a shorter payback period.

The preceding computation of the cash payback period assumes **equal** net annual cash flows in each year of the investment's life. In many cases, this assumption is not valid. In the case of **uneven** net annual cash flows, the company determines the cash payback period when the cumulative net cash flows from the investment equal the cost of the investment.

To illustrate, assume that Chen Company proposes an investment in a new website that is estimated to cost $300,000. Illustration 26-5 shows the proposed investment cost, net annual cash flows, cumulative net cash flows, and the cash payback period.

Illustration 26-5
Computation of cash payback period—unequal cash flows

Year	Investment	Net Annual Cash Flow	Cumulative Net Cash Flow
0	**$300,000**		
1		$ 60,000	$ 60,000
2		90,000	150,000
3		90,000	240,000
4		120,000	360,000
5		100,000	460,000

Cash payback period = 3.5 years

As Illustration 26-5 shows, at the end of year 3, cumulative net cash flow of $240,000 is less than the investment cost of $300,000, but at the end of year 4 the cumulative cash inflow of $360,000 exceeds the investment cost. The cash flow needed in year 4 to equal the investment cost is $60,000 ($300,000 − $240,000). Assuming the cash inflow occurred evenly during year 4, we then divide this amount by the net annual cash flow in year 4 ($120,000) to determine the point during the year when the cash payback occurs. Thus, we get 0.50 ($60,000/$120,000), or half of the year, and the cash payback period is 3.5 years.

The cash payback technique may be useful as an initial screening tool. It may be the most critical factor in the capital budgeting decision for a company that desires a fast turnaround of its investment because of a weak cash position. It also is relatively easy to compute and understand.

However, cash payback should not ordinarily be the only basis for the capital budgeting decision because it **ignores the expected profitability of the project**.

To illustrate, assume that Projects A and B have the same payback period, but Project A's useful life is double the useful life of Project B. Project A's earning power, therefore, is twice as long as Project B's. A further—and major—disadvantage of this technique is that it **ignores the time value of money**.

DO IT! 1   Cash Payback Period

Watertown Paper Corporation is considering adding another machine for the manufacture of corrugated cardboard. The machine would cost $900,000. It would have an estimated life of 6 years and no salvage value. The company estimates that annual cash inflows would increase by $400,000 and that annual cash outflows would increase by $190,000. Compute the cash payback period.

Solution

Estimated annual cash inflows	$400,000
Estimated annual cash outflows	190,000
Net annual cash flow	$210,000

Cash payback period = $900,000/$210,000 = 4.3 years.

Related exercise material: **BE26-1 and DO IT! 26-1.**

Action Plan

✔ Annual cash inflows − Annual cash outflows = Net annual cash flow.

✔ Cash payback period = Cost of capital investment/ Net annual cash flow.

LEARNING OBJECTIVE **2**   ## Use the net present value method.

Recognition of the time value of money can make a significant difference in the long-term impact of the capital budgeting decision. For example, cash flows that occur early in the life of an investment are worth more than those that occur later—because of the time value of money. Therefore, it is useful to recognize the timing of cash flows when evaluating projects.

Capital budgeting techniques that take into account both the time value of money and the estimated net cash flows from an investment are called **discounted cash flow techniques**. They are generally recognized as the most informative and best conceptual approaches to making capital budgeting decisions. The expected net cash flow used in discounting cash flows consists of the annual net cash flows plus the estimated liquidation proceeds (salvage value) when the asset is sold for salvage at the end of its useful life.

The primary discounted cash flow technique is the **net present value method**. A second method, discussed later in the chapter, is the **internal rate of return**. At this point, before you read on, **we recommend that you examine Appendix G** at the end of the book to review the time value of money concepts upon which these methods are based.

The **net present value (NPV) method** involves discounting net cash flows to their present value and then comparing that present value with the capital outlay required by the investment. The difference between these two amounts is referred to as **net present value (NPV)**. Company management determines what interest rate to use in discounting the future net cash flows. This rate, often referred to as the **discount rate** or **required rate of return**, is discussed in a later section.

The NPV decision rule is this: **A proposal is acceptable when net present value is zero or positive**. At either of those values, the rate of return on the investment equals or exceeds the **required rate of return**. This is the rate of return management expects on investments, sometimes called the discount rate or cost of capital. When net present value is negative, the project is unacceptable. Illustration 26-6 shows the net present value decision criteria.

Illustration 26-6
Net present value decision criteria

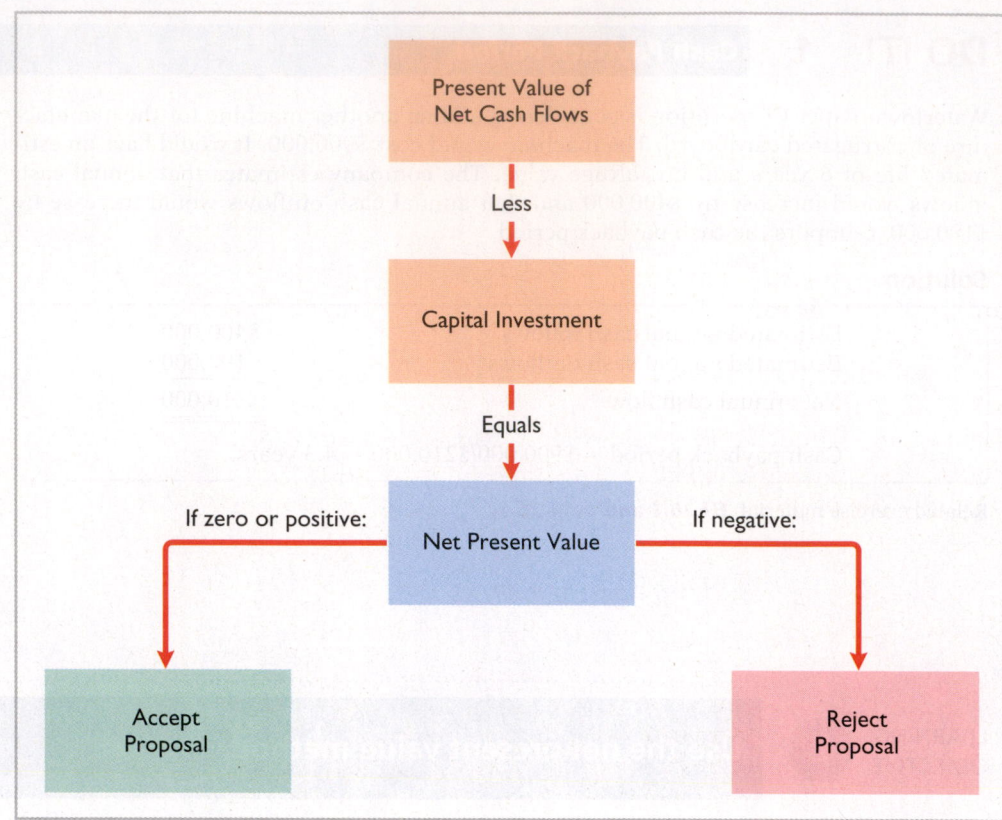

When making a selection among acceptable proposals, **the higher the positive net present value, the more attractive the investment**. The application of this method to two cases is described in the next two sections. In each case, we assume that the investment has no salvage value at the end of its useful life.

Equal Annual Cash Flows

In our Stewart Shipping Company example, the company's net annual cash flows are $24,000. If we assume this amount **is uniform over the asset's useful life**, we can compute the present value of the net annual cash flows by using the present value of an annuity of 1 for 10 payments (from Table 4, Appendix G). Assuming a discount rate of 12%, the present value of net cash flows are as shown in Illustration 26-7 (rounded to the nearest dollar).

Helpful Hint
The ABC Co. expects equal cash flows over an asset's 5-year useful life. The discount factor it should use in determining present values if management wants a 12% return is 3.60478 (using Table 4).

Illustration 26-7
Computation of present value of equal net annual cash flows

	Present Value at 12%
Discount factor for 10 periods	5.65022
Present value of net cash flows: $24,000 × 5.65022	**$135,605**

The analysis of the proposal by the net present value method is as follows.

	12%
Present value of net cash flows	$135,605
Less: Capital investment	130,000
Net present value	**$ 5,605**

Illustration 26-8
Computation of net present value—equal net annual cash flows

The proposed capital expenditure is acceptable at a required rate of return of 12% because the net present value is positive.

Unequal Annual Cash Flows

When net annual cash flows are unequal, we cannot use annuity tables to calculate their present value. Instead, we use tables showing the **present value of a single future amount for each annual cash flow**.

To illustrate, assume that Stewart Shipping Company expects the same total net cash flows of $240,000 over the life of the investment. But because of a declining market demand for the product over the life of the equipment, the net annual cash flows are higher in the early years and lower in the later years. The present value of the net annual cash flows is calculated as follows, using Table 3 in Appendix G.

Helpful Hint
Appendix G demonstrates the use of a financial calculator to solve time value of money problems.

Illustration 26-9
Computation of present value of unequal annual cash flows

Year	Assumed Net Annual Cash Flows	Discount Factor 12%	Present Value 12%
	(1)	(2)	(1) × (2)
1	$ 34,000	.89286	$ 30,357
2	30,000	.79719	23,916
3	27,000	.71178	19,218
4	25,000	.63552	15,888
5	24,000	.56743	13,618
6	22,000	.50663	11,146
7	21,000	.45235	9,499
8	20,000	.40388	8,078
9	19,000	.36061	6,852
10	18,000	.32197	5,795
	$240,000		**$144,367**

Therefore, the analysis of the proposal by the net present value method is as follows.

	12%
Present value of net cash flows	$144,367
Less: Capital investment	130,000
Net present value	**$ 14,367**

Illustration 26-10
Computation of net present value—unequal annual cash flows

In this example, the present value of the net cash flows is greater than the $130,000 capital investment. Thus, the project is acceptable at a 12% required rate of return. The difference between the present values using the 12% rate under equal cash flows ($135,605) and unequal cash flows ($144,367) is due to the pattern of the flows. Since more money is received sooner under this particular uneven cash flow scenario, its present value is greater.

Choosing a Discount Rate

Now that you understand how companies apply the net present value method, it is logical to ask a related question: How is a discount rate (required rate of return) determined in real capital budgeting decisions? In most instances, a company uses a required rate of return equal to its **cost of capital**—that is, the rate that it must pay to obtain funds from creditors and stockholders.

The cost of capital is a weighted average of the rates paid on borrowed funds as well as on funds provided by investors in the company's common stock and preferred stock. If management believes a project is riskier than the company's usual line of business, the discount rate should be increased. That is, the discount rate has two elements, a cost of capital element and a risk element. Often, companies assume the risk element is equal to zero.

Using an incorrect discount rate can lead to incorrect capital budgeting decisions. Consider again the Stewart Shipping example in Illustration 26-8, where we used a discount rate of 12%. Suppose that this rate does not take into account the fact that this project is riskier than most of the company's investments. A more appropriate discount rate, given the risk, might be 15%. Illustration 26-11 compares the net present values at the two rates. At the higher, more appropriate discount rate of 15%, the net present value is negative, and the company should reject the project (discount factors from Appendix G, Table 4).

Helpful Hint
Cost of capital is the rate that management expects to pay on all borrowed and equity funds. It does not relate to the cost of funding a *specific* project.

Illustration 26-11
Comparison of net present values at different discount rates

	Present Values at Different Discount Rates	
	12%	**15%**
Discount factor for 10 payments	5.65022	5.01877
Present value of net cash flows:		
$24,000 × 5.65022	$135,605	
$24,000 × 5.01877		$120,450
Less: Capital investment	130,000	130,000
Positive (negative) net present value	**$ 5,605**	**$ (9,550)**

The discount rate is often referred to by alternative names, including the **required rate of return**, the **hurdle rate**, and the **cutoff rate**. Determination of the cost of capital varies somewhat depending on whether the entity is a for-profit or not-for-profit business. Calculation of the cost of capital is discussed more fully in advanced accounting and finance courses.

Simplifying Assumptions

In our examples of the net present value method, we made a number of simplifying assumptions:

- **All cash flows come at the end of each year.** In reality, cash flows will come at uneven intervals throughout the year. However, it is far simpler to assume that all cash flows come at the end (or in some cases the beginning) of the year. In fact, this assumption is frequently made in practice.

- **All cash flows are immediately reinvested in another project that has a similar return.** In most capital budgeting situations, companies receive cash flows during each year of a project's life. In order to determine the return on the investment, some assumption must be made about how the cash flows are reinvested in the year that they are received. It is customary to assume that cash flows received are reinvested in some other project of similar return until the end of the project's life.

- **All cash flows can be predicted with certainty.** The outcomes of business investments are full of uncertainty, as the Holland America Line Feature Story shows. There is no way of knowing how popular a new product will be, how long a new machine will last, or what competitors' reactions might be to changes in a product. But, in order to make investment decisions, analysts must estimate future outcomes. In this chapter, we have assumed that future amounts are known with certainty.[1] In reality, little is known with certainty. More advanced capital budgeting techniques deal with uncertainty by considering the probability that various outcomes will occur.

Comprehensive Example

Best Taste Foods is considering investing in new equipment to produce fat-free snack foods. Management believes that although demand for fat-free foods has leveled off, fat-free foods are here to stay. The following estimated costs, cost of capital, and cash flows were determined in consultation with the marketing, production, and finance departments.

Initial investment	$1,000,000
Cost of equipment overhaul in 5 years	$200,000
Salvage value of equipment in 10 years	$20,000
Cost of capital (discount rate)	15%
Estimated annual cash flows	
Cash inflows received from sales	$500,000
Cash outflows for cost of goods sold	$200,000
Maintenance costs	$30,000
Other direct operating costs	$40,000

Illustration 26-12
Investment information for Best Taste Foods example

Remember that we are using cash flows in our analysis, not accrual revenues and expenses. Thus, for example, the direct operating costs would not include depreciation expense, since depreciation expense does not use cash. Illustration 26-13 presents the computation of the net annual cash flows of this project.

Cash inflows received from sales	$ 500,000
Cash outflows for cost of goods sold	(200,000)
Maintenance costs	(30,000)
Other direct operating costs	(40,000)
Net annual cash flow	**$230,000**

Illustration 26-13
Computation of net annual cash flow

---

[1]One exception is a brief discussion of sensitivity analysis later in the chapter.

Illustration 26-14 shows computation of the net present value for this proposed investment (discount factors from Appendix G, Tables 3 and 4).

Illustration 26-14
Computation of net present value for Best Taste Foods investment

Event	Time Period	Cash Flow	×	15% Discount Factor	=	Present Value
Net annual cash flow	1–10	$ 230,000	×	5.01877	=	$1,154,317
Salvage value	10	20,000		.24719		4,944
Less: Equipment purchase	0	1,000,000		1.00000		1,000,000
Less: Equipment overhaul	5	200,000		.49718		99,436
Net present value						**$ 59,825**

Because the net present value of the project is positive, Best Taste should accept the project.

DO IT! 2 Net Present Value

Watertown Paper Corporation is considering adding another machine for the manufacture of corrugated cardboard. The machine would cost $900,000. It would have an estimated life of 6 years and no salvage value. The company estimates that annual cash inflows would increase by $400,000 and that annual cash outflows would increase by $190,000. Management has a required rate of return of 9%. Calculate the net present value on this project and discuss whether it should be accepted.

Solution

Action Plan

✔ Estimated annual cash inflows − Estimated annual cash outflows = Net annual cash flow.

✔ Use the NPV technique to calculate the difference between net cash flows and the initial investment.

✔ Accept the project if the net present value is positive.

Estimated annual cash inflows	$400,000
Estimated annual cash outflows	190,000
Net annual cash flow	$210,000

	Cash Flow	9% Discount Factor	Present Value
Present value of net annual cash flows	$210,000	4.48592[a]	$942,043
Less: Capital investment			900,000
Net present value			$ 42,043

[a]Table 4, Appendix G, 9%, 6 years

Since the net present value is greater than zero, Watertown should accept the project.

Related exercise material: **BE26-2, BE26-3, E26-1, E26-2, E26-3, and DO IT! 26-2.**

LEARNING OBJECTIVE 3

Identify capital budgeting challenges and refinements.

Now that you understand how the net present value method works, we can add some "additional wrinkles." Specifically, these are the impact of intangible benefits, a way to compare mutually exclusive projects, refinements that take risk into account, and the need to conduct post-audits of investment projects.

Intangible Benefits

The NPV evaluation techniques employed thus far rely on tangible costs and benefits that can be relatively easily quantified. Some investment projects, especially high-tech projects, fail to make it through initial capital budget screens because only the project's tangible benefits are considered. **Intangible benefits** might include increased quality, improved safety, or enhanced employee loyalty. By ignoring intangible benefits, capital budgeting techniques might incorrectly eliminate projects that could be financially beneficial to the company.

To avoid rejecting projects that actually should be accepted, analysts suggest two possible approaches:

1. Calculate net present value ignoring intangible benefits. Then, if the NPV is negative, ask whether the project offers any intangible benefits that are worth at least the amount of the negative NPV.

2. Project rough, conservative estimates of the value of the intangible benefits, and incorporate these values into the NPV calculation.

EXAMPLE

Assume that Berg Company is considering the purchase of a new mechanical robot to be used for soldering electrical connections. Illustration 26-15 shows the estimates related to this proposed purchase (discount factor from Appendix G, Table 4).

Initial investment			$200,000	
Annual cash inflows			$ 50,000	
Annual cash outflows			20,000	
Net annual cash flow			**$ 30,000**	
Estimated life of equipment			10 years	
Discount rate			12%	

	Cash Flows	×	12% Discount Factor	=	Present Value
Present value of net annual cash flows	$30,000	×	5.65022	=	$ 169,507
Less: Initial investment					200,000
Net present value					**$(30,493)**

Illustration 26-15
Investment information for Berg Company example

Based on the negative net present value of $30,493, the proposed project is not acceptable. This calculation, however, ignores important information. First, the company's engineers believe that purchasing this machine will dramatically improve the quality of electrical connections in the company's products. As a result, future warranty costs will be reduced. Also, the company believes that this higher quality will translate into higher future sales. Finally, the new machine will be much safer than the previous one.

Berg can incorporate this new information into the capital budgeting decision in the two ways discussed earlier. First, management might simply ask whether the reduced warranty costs, increased sales, and improved safety benefits have an estimated total present value to the company of at least $30,493. If yes, then the project is acceptable.

Alternatively, analysts can estimate the annual cash flows of these benefits. In our initial calculation, we assumed each of these benefits to have a value of zero. It seems likely that their actual values are much higher than zero. Given the difficulty of estimating these benefits, however, conservative values should be assigned to them. If, after using conservative estimates, the net present value is positive, Berg should accept the project.

To illustrate, assume that Berg estimates that improved sales will increase cash inflows by $10,000 annually as a result of an increase in perceived quality. Berg also estimates that annual cost outflows would be reduced by $5,000 as a result of lower warranty claims, reduced injury claims, and missed work. Consideration of the intangible benefits results in the following revised NPV calculation (discount factor from Appendix G, Table 4).

Illustration 26-16
Revised investment information for Berg Company example, including intangible benefits

Initial investment	$200,000	
Annual cash inflows (revised)	$ 60,000	($50,000 + $10,000)
Annual cash outflows (revised)	15,000	($20,000 − $5,000)
Net annual cash flow	**$ 45,000**	
Estimated life of equipment	10 years	
Discount rate	12%	

	Cash Flows	×	12% Discount Factor	=	Present Value
Present value of net annual cash flows	$45,000	×	5.65022	=	$254,260
Less: Initial investment					200,000
Net present value					**$ 54,260**

Using these conservative estimates of the value of the additional benefits, Berg should accept the project.

Ethics Insight

Carol Gering/iStockphoto

It Need Not Cost an Arm and a Leg

Most manufacturers say that employee safety matters above everything else. But how many back up this statement with investments that improve employee safety? Recently, a woodworking hobbyist, who also happens to be a patent attorney with a Ph.D. in physics, invented a mechanism that automatically shuts down a power saw when the saw blade comes in contact with human flesh. The blade stops so quickly that only minor injuries result.

Power saws injure 40,000 Americans each year, and 4,000 of those injuries are bad enough to require amputation. Therefore, one might think that power-saw companies would be lined up to incorporate this mechanism into their saws. But, in the words of one power-tool company, "Safety doesn't sell." Since existing saw manufacturers were unwilling to incorporate the device into their saws, eventually the inventor started his own company to build the devices and sell them directly to businesses that use power saws.

Source: Melba Newsome, "An Edgy New Idea," *Time: Inside Business* (May 2006), p. A16.

In addition to the obvious humanitarian benefit of reducing serious injuries, how else might the manufacturer of this product convince potential customers of its worth?
(Go to **WileyPLUS** for this answer and additional questions.)

Profitability Index for Mutually Exclusive Projects

In theory, companies should accept all projects with positive NPVs. However, companies rarely are able to adopt all positive-NPV proposals. First, proposals often are **mutually exclusive**. This means that if the company adopts one proposal, it would be impossible or impractical also to adopt the other proposal. For example, a company may be considering the purchase of a new packaging machine and is looking at various brands and models. It needs only one packaging machine. Once the company has determined which brand and model to purchase, the others will not be purchased—even though they also may have positive net present values.

Even in instances where projects are not mutually exclusive, managers often must choose between various positive-NPV projects because of **limited resources**. For example, the company might have ideas for two new lines of business, each of which has a projected positive NPV. However, both of these proposals require skilled personnel, and the company determines that it will not be able to find enough skilled personnel to staff both projects. Management will have to choose the project it thinks is a better option.

When choosing between alternative proposals, it is tempting simply to choose the project with the higher NPV. Consider the following example of two mutually exclusive projects. Each is assumed to have a 10-year life and a 12% discount rate (discount factors from Appendix G, Tables 3 and 4). Illustration 26-17 shows the estimates for each project and the computation of the present value of the net cash flows.

Illustration 26-17
Investment information for mutually exclusive projects

	Project A	Project B
Initial investment	$40,000	$ 90,000
Net annual cash inflow	10,000	19,000
Salvage value	5,000	10,000
Present value of net cash flows		
($10,000 × 5.65022) + ($5,000 × .32197)	58,112	
($19,000 × 5.65022) + ($10,000 × .32197)		110,574

Illustration 26-18 computes the net present values of Project A and Project B by subtracting the initial investment from the present value of the net cash flows.

Illustration 26-18
Net present value computation

	Project A	Project B
Present value of net cash flows	$ 58,112	$110,574
Less: Initial investment	40,000	90,000
Net present value	**$18,112**	**$ 20,574**

As Project B has the higher NPV, it would seem that the company should adopt it. However, Project B also requires more than twice the original investment of Project A. In choosing between the two projects, the company should also include in its calculations the amount of the original investment.

One relatively simple method of comparing alternative projects is the **profitability index**. This method takes into account both the size of the original investment and the discounted cash flows. The profitability index is calculated by dividing the present value of net cash flows that occur after the initial investment by the amount of the initial investment, as Illustration 26-19 shows.

Illustration 26-19
Formula for profitability index

Present Value of Net Cash Flows	÷	Initial Investment	=	Profitability Index

The profitability index allows comparison of the relative desirability of projects that require differing initial investments. Note that any project with a positive NPV will have a profitability index above 1. The profitability index for each of the mutually exclusive projects is calculated in Illustration 26-20.

Illustration 26-20
Calculation of profitability index

$$\text{Profitability Index} = \frac{\text{Present Value of Net Cash Flows}}{\text{Initial Investment}}$$

Project A	Project B
$\dfrac{\$58,112}{\$40,000} = \mathbf{1.45}$	$\dfrac{\$110,574}{\$90,000} = \mathbf{1.23}$

In this case, the profitability index of Project A exceeds that of Project B. Thus, Project A is more desirable. Again, if these were not mutually exclusive projects and if resources were not limited, then the company should invest in both projects since both have positive NPVs. Additional considerations related to preference decisions are discussed in more advanced courses.

Risk Analysis

A simplifying assumption made by many financial analysts is that projected results are known with certainty. In reality, projected results are only estimates based upon the forecaster's belief as to the most probable outcome. One approach for dealing with such uncertainty is **sensitivity analysis**. Sensitivity analysis uses a number of outcome estimates to get a sense of the variability among potential returns. An example of sensitivity analysis was presented in Illustration 26-11 (page 1212), where we illustrated the impact on NPV of different discount rate assumptions. A higher-risk project would be evaluated using a higher discount rate.

Similarly, to take into account that more distant cash flows are often more uncertain, a higher discount rate can be used to discount more distant cash flows. Other techniques to address uncertainty are discussed in advanced courses.

Management Insight Sharp

Matjaz Boncina/iStockphoto

Wide-Screen Capacity

Building a new factory to produce 60-inch TV screens can cost $4 billion. But for more than 10 years, manufacturers of these screens have continued to build new plants. By building so many plants, they have expanded productive capacity at a rate that has exceeded the demand for big-screen TVs. In fact, during one recent year, the supply of big-screen TVs was estimated to exceed demand by 12%, rising to 16% in the future.

One state-of-the-art plant built by Sharp was estimated to be operating at only 50% of capacity. Experts say that the price of big-screen TVs will have to fall much further than they already have before demand may eventually catch up with productive capacity.

Source: James Simms, "Sharp's Payoff Delayed," *Wall Street Journal Online* (September 14, 2010).

What implications does the excess capacity have for the cash payback and net present value calculations of these investments? (Go to **WileyPLUS** for this answer and additional questions.)

Post-Audit of Investment Projects

Any well-run organization should perform an evaluation, called a **post-audit**, of its investment projects after their completion. A post-audit is a thorough evaluation of how well a project's actual performance matches the original projections. An example of a post-audit is seen in a situation that occurred at **Campbell Soup**. The company made the original decision to invest in the Intelligent Quisine line based on management's best estimates of future cash flows. During the development phase of the project, Campbell hired an outside consulting firm to evaluate the project's potential for success. Because actual results during the initial years were far below the estimated results and because the future also did not look promising, the project was terminated.

Performing a post-audit is important for a variety of reasons. First, if managers know that the company will compare their estimates to actual results, they will be more likely to submit reasonable and accurate data when they make investment proposals. This clearly is better for the company than for managers to submit overly optimistic estimates in an effort to get pet projects approved. Second, as seen with Campbell Soup, a post-audit provides a formal mechanism by which the company can determine whether existing projects should be supported or terminated. Third, post-audits improve future investment proposals because, by evaluating past successes and failures, managers improve their estimation techniques.

A post-audit involves the same evaluation techniques used in making the original capital budgeting decision—for example, use of the NPV method. The difference is that, in the post-audit, analysts insert actual figures, where known, and they revise estimates of future amounts based on new information. The managers responsible for the estimates used in the original proposal must explain the reasons for any significant differences between their estimates and actual results.

Post-audits are not foolproof. In the case of Campbell Soup, some observers suggested that the company was too quick to abandon the project. Industry analysts suggested that with more time and more advertising expenditures, the company might have enjoyed success.

DO IT! 3 Profitability Index

Taz Corporation has decided to invest in renewable energy sources to meet part of its energy needs for production. It is considering solar power versus wind power. After considering cost savings as well as incremental revenues from selling excess electricity into the power grid, it has determined the following.

	Solar	Wind
Present value of annual cash flows	$78,580	$168,450
Initial investment	$45,500	$125,300

Determine the net present value and profitability index of each project. Which energy source should it choose?

Solution

	Solar	Wind
Present value of annual cash flows	$78,580	$168,450
Less: Initial investment	45,500	125,300
Net present value	$33,080	$ 43,150
Profitability index	1.73*	1.34**

*$78,580 ÷ $45,500
**168,450 ÷ 125,300

While the investment in wind power generates the higher net present value, it also requires a substantially higher initial investment. The profitability index favors solar power, which suggests that the additional net present value of wind is outweighed by the cost of the initial investment. The company should choose solar power.

Action Plan

✔ Determine the present value of annual cash flows of each mutually exclusive project.

✔ Determine profitability index by dividing the present value of annual cash flows by the amount of the initial investment.

✔ Choose project with highest profitability index.

Related exercise material: **BE26-5, E26-4,** and **DO IT!** 26-3.

LEARNING OBJECTIVE **4**   **Use the internal rate of return method.**

The **internal rate of return method** differs from the net present value method in that it finds the **interest yield of the potential investment**. The **internal rate of return (IRR)** is the interest rate that will cause the present value of the proposed capital expenditure to equal the present value of the expected net annual cash flows (that is, NPV equal to zero). Because it recognizes the time value of money, the internal rate of return method is (like the NPV method) a discounted cash flow technique.

How do we determine the internal rate of return? One way is to use a financial calculator (see Appendix G) or electronic spreadsheet to solve for this rate. Or, we can use a trial-and-error procedure.

To illustrate, assume that Stewart Shipping Company is considering the purchase of a new front-end loader at a cost of $244,371. Net annual cash flows from this loader are estimated to be $100,000 a year for three years. To determine the internal rate of return on this front-end loader, the company finds the discount rate that results in a net present value of zero. As Illustration 26-21 shows, at a rate of return of 10%, Stewart Shipping has a positive net present value of $4,315. At a rate of return of 12%, it has a negative net present value of $4,188. At an 11% rate, the net present value is zero. Therefore, 11% is the internal rate of return for this investment (discount factors from Appendix G, Table 3).

Illustration 26-21

Estimation of internal rate of return

Year	Net Annual Cash Flows	Discount Factor 10%	Present Value 10%	Discount Factor 11%	Present Value 11%	Discount Factor 12%	Present Value 12%
1	$100,000	.90909	$ 90,909	.90090	$ 90,090	.89286	$ 89,286
2	$100,000	.82645	82,645	.81162	81,162	.79719	79,719
3	$100,000	.75132	75,132	.73119	73,119	.71178	71,178
			248,686		244,371		240,183
Less: Initial investment			244,371		244,371		244,371
Net present value			$ 4,315		$ -0-		$ (4,188)

An easier approach to solving for the internal rate of return can be used if the net annual cash flows are **equal**, as in the Stewart Shipping example. In this special case, we can find the internal rate of return using the following formula.

Illustration 26-22

Formula for internal rate of return—even cash flows

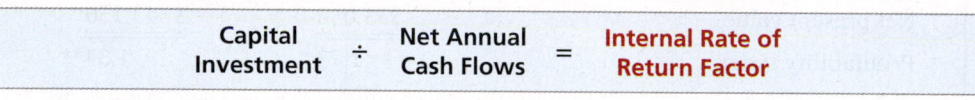

We then look up the factor 2.44371 in Table 4 of Appendix G in the three-payment row and find it under 11%. Row 3 is reproduced below for your convenience.

Applying this formula to the Stewart Shipping example, we find:

$$\$244,371 \div 100,000 = 2.44371$$

Table 4 Present Value of an Annuity of 1										
(n) Payments	4%	5%	6%	7%	8%	9%	10%	11%	12%	15%
3	2.77509	2.72325	2.67301	2.62432	2.57710	2.53130	2.48685	**2.44371**	2.40183	2.28323

Recognize that if the cash flows are **uneven**, then a trial-and-error approach or a financial calculator or computerized spreadsheet must be used.

Once managers know the internal rate of return, they compare it to the company's required rate of return (the discount rate). The IRR decision rule is as follows: **Accept the project when the internal rate of return is equal to or greater than the required rate of return. Reject the project when the internal rate of return is less than the required rate of return.** Illustration 26-23 shows these relationships. The internal rate of return method is widely used in practice, largely because most managers find the internal rate of return easy to interpret.

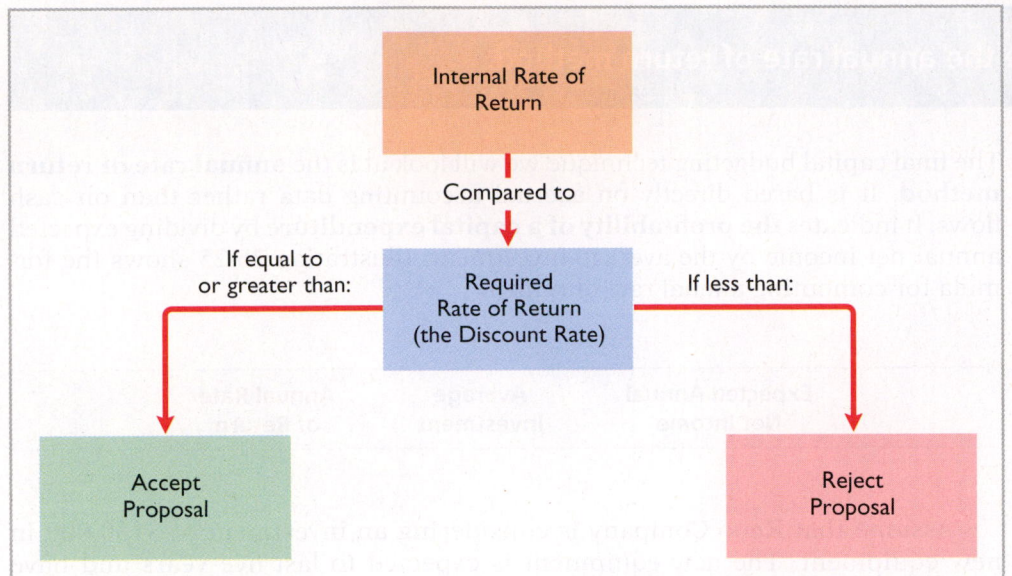

Illustration 26-23
Internal rate of return decision criteria

Comparing Discounted Cash Flow Methods

Illustration 26-24 compares the two discounted cash flow methods—net present value and internal rate of return. When properly used, either method will provide management with relevant quantitative data for making capital budgeting decisions.

	Net Present Value	**Internal Rate of Return**
1. Objective	Compute net present value (a dollar amount).	Compute internal rate of return (a percentage).
2. Decision Rule	If net present value is zero or positive, accept the proposal. If net present value is negative, reject the proposal.	If internal rate of return is equal to or greater than the required rate of return, accept the proposal. If internal rate of return is less than the required rate of return, reject the proposal.

Illustration 26-24
Comparison of discounted cash flow methods

DO IT! 4 — Internal Rate of Return

Watertown Paper Corporation is considering adding another machine for the manufacture of corrugated cardboard. The machine would cost $900,000. It would have an estimated life of 6 years and no salvage value. The company estimates that annual cash inflows would increase by $400,000 and that annual cash outflows would increase by $190,000. Management has a required rate of return of 9%. Calculate the internal rate of return on this project and discuss whether it should be accepted.

Solution

Estimated annual cash inflows	$400,000
Estimated annual cash outflows	190,000
Net annual cash flow	$210,000

$900,000/$210,000 = 4.285714. Using Table 4 of Appendix G and the factors that correspond with the six-payment row, 4.285714 is between the factors for 10% and 11%. Since the project has an internal rate that is greater than 10% and the required rate of return is only 9%, the project should be accepted.

Related exercise material: **BE26-7, BE26-8, E26-5, E26-6, E26-7, and DO IT! 26-4.**

Action Plan

✔ Estimated annual cash inflows − Estimated annual cash outflows = Net annual cash flow.

✔ Capital investment/Net annual cash flows = Internal rate of return factor.

✔ Look up the factor in the present value of an annuity table to find the internal rate of return.

✔ Accept the project if the internal rate of return is equal to or greater than the required rate of return.

The final capital budgeting technique we will look at is the **annual rate of return method**. It is based directly on accrual accounting data rather than on cash flows. It indicates **the profitability of a capital expenditure** by dividing expected annual net income by the average investment. Illustration 26-25 shows the formula for computing annual rate of return.

Illustration 26-25
Annual rate of return formula

Expected Annual Net Income	÷	Average Investment	=	Annual Rate of Return

Assume that Reno Company is considering an investment of $130,000 in new equipment. The new equipment is expected to last five years and have zero salvage value at the end of its useful life. Reno uses the straight-line method of depreciation for accounting purposes. The expected annual revenues and costs of the new product that will be produced from the investment are as follows.

Illustration 26-26
Estimated annual net income from Reno Company's capital expenditure

Sales		$200,000
Less: Costs and expenses		
Manufacturing costs (exclusive of depreciation)	$132,000	
Depreciation expense ($130,000 ÷ 5)	26,000	
Selling and administrative expenses	22,000	180,000
Income before income taxes		20,000
Income tax expense		7,000
Net income		$ 13,000

Reno's expected annual net income is $13,000. Average investment is derived from the formula shown below.

Illustration 26-27
Formula for computing average investment

$$\frac{\text{Original Investment} + \text{Value at End of Useful Life}}{2} = \text{Average Investment}$$

The value at the end of useful life is equal to the asset's salvage value, if any. For Reno, average investment is $65,000 [($130,000 + $0) ÷ 2]. The expected annual rate of return for Reno's investment in new equipment is therefore 20%, computed as follows.

$$\$13,000 \div \$65,000 = 20\%$$

Management then compares the annual rate of return with its **required rate of return** for investments of similar risk. The required rate of return is generally based on the company's cost of capital. The decision rule is: **A project is acceptable if its rate of return is greater than management's required rate of return. It is unacceptable when the reverse is true.** When companies use the rate of return technique in deciding among several acceptable projects, **the higher the rate of return for a given risk, the more attractive the investment**.

The principal advantages of this method are the simplicity of its calculation and management's familiarity with the accounting terms used in the computation. A major limitation of the annual rate of return method is that it does not consider the time value of money. For example, no consideration is given as to whether cash inflows will occur early or late in the life of the investment. As explained in Appendix G, recognition of the time value of money can make a significant difference between the future value and the discounted present value of an investment. A second disadvantage is that this method relies on accrual accounting numbers rather than expected cash flows.

> **Helpful Hint**
> A capital budgeting decision based on only one technique may be misleading. It is often wise to analyze an investment from a number of different perspectives.

DO IT! 5 | Annual Rate of Return

Watertown Paper Corporation is considering adding another machine for the manufacture of corrugated cardboard. The machine would cost $900,000. It would have an estimated life of 6 years and no salvage value. The company estimates that annual revenues would increase by $400,000 and that annual expenses excluding depreciation would increase by $190,000. It uses the straight-line method to compute depreciation expense. Management has a required rate of return of 9%. Compute the annual rate of return.

Solution

Revenues		$400,000
Less:		
Expenses (excluding depreciation)	$190,000	
Depreciation ($900,000/6 years)	150,000	340,000
Annual net income		$ 60,000

Average investment = ($900,000 + $0)/2 = $450,000.
Annual rate of return = $60,000/$450,000 = 13.3%.

Since the annual rate of return (13.3%) is greater than Watertown's required rate of return (9%), the proposed project is acceptable.

Related exercise material: **BE26-9, E26-8, E26-9, E26-10, E26-11, and DO IT! 26-5.**

> **Action Plan**
> ✔ Expected annual net income = Annual revenues − Annual expenses (including depreciation expense).
> ✔ Average investment = (Original investment + Value at end of useful life)/2.
> ✔ Annual rate of return = Expected annual net income/ Average investment.

REVIEW AND PRACTICE

LEARNING OBJECTIVES REVIEW

1 Describe capital budgeting inputs and apply the cash payback technique. Management gathers project proposals from each department; a capital budget committee screens the proposals and recommends worthy projects. Company officers decide which projects to fund, and the board of directors approves the capital budget. In capital budgeting, estimated cash inflows and outflows, rather than accrual-accounting numbers, are the preferred inputs.

The cash payback technique identifies the time period required to recover the cost of the investment. The formula when net annual cash flows are equal is Cost of capital investment ÷ Estimated net annual

cash flow = Cash payback period. The shorter the payback period, the more attractive the investment.

2 Use the net present value method. The net present value method compares the present value of future cash inflows with the capital investment to determine net present value. The NPV decision rule is: Accept the project if net present value is zero or positive. Reject the project if net present value is negative.

3 Identify capital budgeting challenges and refinements. Intangible benefits are difficult to quantify and thus are often ignored in capital budgeting decisions. This can result in incorrectly rejecting some projects. One method for considering intangible benefits is to calculate the NPV, ignoring intangible benefits. If the resulting NPV is below zero, evaluate whether the benefits are worth at least the amount of the negative net present value. Alternatively, intangible benefits can be incorporated into the NPV calculation, using conservative estimates of their value.

The profitability index is a tool for comparing the relative merits of alternative capital investment opportunities. It is computed as Present value of net cash flows ÷ Initial investment. The higher the index, the more desirable the project.

A post-audit is an evaluation of a capital investment's actual performance. Post-audits create an incentive for managers to make accurate estimates. Post-audits also are useful for determining whether a company should continue, expand, or terminate a

project. Finally, post-audits provide feedback that is useful for improving estimation techniques.

4 **Use the internal rate of return method.** The objective of the internal rate of return method is to find the interest yield of the potential investment, which is expressed as a percentage rate. The IRR decision rule is: Accept the project when the internal rate of return is equal to or greater than the required rate of return. Reject the project when the internal rate of return is less than the required rate of return.

5 **Use the annual rate of return method.** The annual rate of return uses accrual accounting data to indicate the profitability of a capital investment. It is calculated as Expected annual net income ÷ Amount of the average investment. The higher the rate of return, the more attractive the investment.

GLOSSARY REVIEW

Annual rate of return method The determination of the profitability of a capital expenditure, computed by dividing expected annual net income by the average investment. (p. 1222).

Capital budgeting The process of making capital expenditure decisions in business. (p. 1204).

Cash payback technique A capital budgeting technique that identifies the time period required to recover the cost of a capital investment from the net annual cash flow produced by the investment. (p. 1207).

Cost of capital The weighted-average rate of return that the firm must pay to obtain funds from creditors and stockholders. (p. 1212).

Discounted cash flow technique A capital budgeting technique that considers both the estimated net cash flows from the investment and the time value of money. (p. 1209).

Discount rate The interest rate used in discounting the future net cash flows to determine present value. (p. 1209).

Internal rate of return (IRR) The interest rate that will cause the present value of the proposed capital expenditure to equal the present value of the expected net annual cash flows. (p. 1219).

Internal rate of return (IRR) method A method used in capital budgeting that results in finding the interest yield of the potential investment. (p. 1219).

Net present value (NPV) The difference that results when the original capital outlay is subtracted from the discounted net cash flows. (p. 1209).

Net present value (NPV) method A method used in capital budgeting in which net cash flows are discounted to their present value and then compared to the capital outlay required by the investment. (p. 1209).

Post-audit A thorough evaluation of how well a project's actual performance matches the original projections. (p. 1218).

Profitability index A method of comparing alternative projects that takes into account both the size of the investment and its discounted net cash flows. It is computed by dividing the present value of net cash flows by the initial investment. (p. 1217).

Required rate of return The rate of return management expects on investments, sometimes called the discount rate or cost of capital. (p. 1210).

PRACTICE MULTIPLE-CHOICE QUESTIONS

(LO 1) **1.** Which of the following is **not** an example of a capital budgeting decision?
  (a) Decision to build a new plant.
  (b) Decision to renovate an existing facility.
  (c) Decision to buy a piece of machinery.
  (d) All of these are capital budgeting decisions.

2. What is the order of involvement of the following parties in the capital budgeting authorization process? (LO 1)
  (a) Plant managers, officers, capital budget committee, board of directors.
  (b) Board of directors, plant managers, officers, capital budget committee.

(c) Plant managers, capital budget committee, officers, board of directors.

(d) Officers, plant managers, capital budget committee, board of directors.

(LO 1) **3.** What is a weakness of the cash payback approach?

(a) It uses accrual-based accounting numbers.

(b) It ignores the time value of money.

(c) It ignores the useful life of alternative projects.

(d) Both (b) and (c) are true.

(LO 1) **4.** Siegel Industries is considering two capital budgeting projects. Project A requires an initial investment of $48,000. It is expected to produce net annual cash flows of $7,000. Project B requires an initial investment of $75,000 and is expected to produce net annual cash flows of $12,000. Using the cash payback technique to evaluate the two projects, Siegel should accept:

(a) Project A because it has a shorter cash payback period.

(b) Project B because it has a shorter cash payback period.

(c) Project A because it requires a smaller initial investment.

(d) Project B because it produces a larger net annual cash flow.

(LO 2) **5.** Which is a **true** statement regarding using a higher discount rate to calculate the net present value of a project?

(a) It will make it less likely that the project will be accepted.

(b) It will make it more likely that the project will be accepted.

(c) It is appropriate to use a higher rate if the project is perceived as being less risky than other projects being considered.

(d) It is appropriate to use a higher rate if the project will have a short useful life relative to other projects being considered.

(LO 2) **6.** A positive net present value means that the:

(a) project's rate of return is less than the cutoff rate.

(b) project's rate of return exceeds the required rate of return.

(c) project's rate of return equals the required rate of return.

(d) project is unacceptable.

(LO 2) **7.** Which of the following is **not** an alternative name for the discount rate?

(a) Hurdle rate.

(b) Required rate of return.

(c) Cutoff rate.

(d) All of these are alternative names for the discount rate.

(LO 3) **8.** If a project has intangible benefits whose value is hard to estimate, the best thing to do is:

(a) ignore these benefits, since any estimate of their value will most likely be wrong.

(b) include a conservative estimate of their value.

(c) ignore their value in your initial net present value calculation, but then estimate whether their potential value is worth at least the amount of the net present value deficiency.

(d) Either (b) or (c) is correct.

9. An example of an intangible benefit provided by a **(LO 3)** capital budgeting project is:

(a) the salvage value of the capital investment.

(b) a positive net present value.

(c) a decrease in customer complaints due to poor quality.

(d) an internal rate of return greater than zero.

10. The following information is available for a potential **(LO 3)** capital investment.

Initial investment	$80,000
Salvage value	10,000
Net annual cash flow	14,820
Present value of net annual cash flows	98,112
Net present value	18,112
Useful life	10 years

The potential investment's profitability index (rounded to two decimals) is:

(a) 5.40.   (c) 1.23.

(b) 1.19.   (d) 1.40.

11. A post-audit of an investment project should be **(LO 3)** performed:

(a) on all significant capital expenditure projects.

(b) on all projects that management feels might be financial failures.

(c) on randomly selected projects.

(d) only on projects that enjoy tremendous success.

12. A project should be accepted if its internal rate of **(LO 4)** return exceeds:

(a) zero.

(b) the rate of return on a government bond.

(c) the company's required rate of return.

(d) the rate the company pays on borrowed funds.

13. The following information is available for a potential **(LO 4)** capital investment.

Initial investment	$60,000
Net annual cash flow	15,400
Net present value	3,143
Useful life	5 years

The potential investment's internal rate of return is approximately:

(a) 5%.   (c) 4%.

(b) 10%.   (d) 9%.

14. Which of the following is **incorrect** about the annual **(LO 5)** rate of return technique?

(a) The calculation is simple.

(b) The accounting terms used are familiar to management.

(c) The timing of the cash inflows is not considered.

(d) The time value of money is considered.

15. The following information is available for a potential **(LO 5)** capital investment.

Initial investment	$120,000
Annual net income	15,000
Net annual cash flow	27,500
Salvage value	20,000
Useful life	8 years

The potential investment's annual rate of return is approximately:

(a) 21%.   (c) 30%.

(b) 15%.   (d) 39%.

Solutions

1. **(d)** Choices (a), (b), and (c) are all examples of capital budgeting decisions, so choice (d) is the best answer.

2. **(c)** The process of authorizing capital budget expenditures starts with plant managers, moves on to the capital budgeting committee, goes next to the officers of the firm and finally is acted upon by the board of directors. The other choices are therefore incorrect.

3. **(d)** Choices (b) and (c) are both correct; therefore, choice (d) is the best answer. Choice (a) is incorrect as the use of accrual-based accounting numbers is not a weakness of the cash payback approach.

4. **(b)** Project B ($75,000 ÷ $12,000) has a shorter cash payback period than Project A ($48,000 ÷ $7,000). The other choices are therefore incorrect.

5. **(a)** If a higher discount rate is used in calculating the net present value of a project, the resulting net present value will be lower and the project will be less likely to be accepted. The other choices are therefore incorrect.

6. **(b)** A positive net present value means that the project's rate of return exceeds the required rate of return. The other choices are therefore incorrect.

7. **(d)** Choices (a), (b), and (c) are all alternative names for the discount rate; therefore, choice (d) is the best answer.

8. **(d)** Choices (b) and (c) are both reasonable approaches to including intangible benefits in the capital budgeting process; therefore, choice (d) is the best answer. Choice (a) is incorrect because even though these intangible benefits may be hard to quantify, they should not be ignored in the capital budgeting process.

9. **(c)** A decrease in customer complaints due to poor quality is one example of an intangible benefit provided by a capital budgeting project. The other choices are incorrect because (a) salvage value, (b) net present value, and (d) internal rate of return are all quantitative measures, i.e., tangible.

10. **(c)** ($18,112+ $80,000) ÷ $80,000 = 1.23, not (a) 5.40, (b) 1.19, or (d) 1.40.

11. **(a)** A post-audit should be performed on all significant capital expenditure projects, not just on (b) financial failures, (c) randomly selected projects, or (d) tremendous successes, because the feedback gained will help to improve the process in the future and also will give managers an incentive to be more realistic in preparing capital expenditure proposals.

12. **(c)** A project should be accepted if its internal rate of return exceeds the company's required rate of return, not (a) zero, (b) the rate of return on a government bond, or (d) the rate the company pays on borrowed funds.

13. **(d)** ($60,000 ÷ $15,400) equals 3.8961, which corresponds with approximately 9% in Table 4 of Appendix G, not (a) 5%, (b) 10%, or (c) 4%.

14. **(d)** The time value of money is not considered when applying the annual rate of return method. The other choices are correct statements.

15. **(a)** $15,000 ÷ [($120,000 + $20,000) ÷ 2] = 21%, not (b) 15%, (c) 30%, or (d) 39%.

■ PRACTICE EXERCISES

Calculate payback period, internal rate of return, and apply decision rules.

(LO 1, 4)

1. BTMS Inc. wants to purchase a new machine for $30,000, excluding $1,500 of installation costs. The old machine was bought five years ago and had an expected economic life of 10 years without salvage value. This old machine now has a book value of $2,000, and BTMS Inc. expects to sell it for that amount. The new machine would decrease operating costs by $8,000 each year of its economic life. The straight-line depreciation method would be used for the new machine, for a five-year period with no salvage value.

Instructions

(a) Determine the cash payback period.

(b) Determine the approximate internal rate of return.

(c) Assuming the company has a required rate of return of 10%, state your conclusion on whether the new machine should be purchased.

(CGA adapted)

Solution

1. (a) Total net investment = $30,000 + $1,500 − $2,000 = $29,500
Annual net cash flow = $8,000
Payback period = $29,500 ÷ $8,000 = 3.7 years

(b) Net present value approximates zero when discount rate is 11%.

Item	Amount	Years	PV Factor	Present Value
Net annual cash flows	$8,000	1–5	3.69590	$29,567
Less: Capital investment				29,500
Net present value				$ 67

(c) Because the approximate internal rate of return of 11% exceeds the required rate of return of 10%, the investment should be accepted.

2. MCA Corporation is reviewing an investment proposal. The initial cost and estimates of the book value of the investment at the end of each year, the net cash flows for each year, and the net income for each year are presented in the schedule below. All cash flows are assumed to lake place at the end of the year. The salvage value of the investment at the end of each year is equal to its book value. There would be no salvage value at the end of the investment's life.

Calculate payback, annual rate of return, and net present value

(LO 1, 2, 5)

Investment Proposal

Year	Initial Cost and Book Value	Annual Cash Flows	Annual Net Income
0	$105,000		
1	70,000	$45,000	$16,000
2	42,000	40,000	18,000
3	21,000	35,000	20,000
4	7,000	30,000	22,000
5	0	25,000	24,000

MCA Corporation uses a 15% target rate of return for new investment proposals.

Instructions

(a) What is the cash payback period for this proposal?

(b) What is the annual rate of return for the investment?

(c) What is the net present value of the investment?

(CMA-Canada adapted)

Solution

2. (a)

	Year	Amount	Balance
Initial investment	0	$(105,000)	$(105,000)
Less: Cash flow	1	45,000	(60,000)
	2	40,000	(20,000)
	3	35,000	15,000

Payback period = 2 + ($20,000 ÷ $35,000) = 2.57

(b) Average annual net income = ($16,000 + $18,000 + $20,000 + $22,000 + $24,000) ÷ 5 = $20,000
Average investment = ($105,000 + $0) ÷ 2 = $52,500
Annual rate of return = $20,000 ÷ $52,500 = 38.10%

(c)

	Year	Discount Factor, 15%	Amount	Present Value
Net cash flows	1	0.86957	$45,000	$ 39,131
	2	0.75614	40,000	30,246
	3	0.65752	35,000	23,013
	4	0.57175	30,000	17,153
	5	0.49718	25,000	12,430
Present value of cash inflows				121,973
Less: Initial investment				105,000
Net present value				$ 16,973

▌ PRACTICE PROBLEM

Cornfield Company is considering a long-term capital investment project in laser equipment. This will require an investment of $280,000, and it will have a useful life of 5 years. Annual net income is expected to be $16,000 a year. Depreciation is computed by the straight-line method with no salvage value. The company's cost of capital is 10%. (*Hint:* Assume cash flows can be computed by adding back depreciation expense.)

Compute annual rate of return, cash payback, and net present value.

(LO 1, 2, 5)

Instructions

(Round all computations to two decimal places unless directed otherwise.)

(a) Compute the cash payback period for the project.

(b) Compute the net present value for the project. (Round to nearest dollar.)

(c) Compute the annual rate of return for the project.

(d) Should the project be accepted? Why?

Solution

(a) $280,000 ÷ $72,000 ($16,000 + $56,000) = 3.89 years

(b)

		Present Value at 10%
Discount factor for 5 payments		3.79079
Present value of net cash flows:		
$72,000 × 3.79079		$272,937
Less: Capital investment		280,000
Negative net present value		$ (7,063)

(c) $16,000 ÷ $140,000 ($280,000 ÷ 2) = 11.4%

(d) The annual rate of return of 11.4% is good. However, the cash payback period is 78% of the project's useful life, and net present value is negative. The recommendation is to reject the project.

WileyPLUS

Brief Exercises, Exercises, **DO IT!** Exercises, and Problems and many additional resources are available for practice in WileyPLUS

QUESTIONS

1. Describe the process a company may use in screening and approving the capital expenditure budget.

2. What are the advantages and disadvantages of the cash payback technique?

3. Tom Wells claims the formula for the cash payback technique is the same as the formula for the annual rate of return technique. Is Tom correct? What is the formula for the cash payback technique?

4. Two types of present value tables may be used with the discounted cash flow techniques. Identify the tables and the circumstance(s) when each table should be used.

5. What is the decision rule under the net present value method?

6. Discuss the factors that determine the appropriate discount rate to use when calculating the net present value.

7. What simplifying assumptions were made in the chapter regarding calculation of net present value?

8. What are some examples of potential intangible benefits of investment proposals? Why do these intangible benefits complicate the capital budgeting evaluation process? What might happen if intangible benefits are ignored in a capital budgeting decision?

9. What steps can be taken to incorporate intangible benefits into the capital budget evaluation process?

10. What advantages does the profitability index provide over direct comparison of net present value when comparing two projects?

11. What is a post-audit? What are the potential benefits of a post-audit?

12. Identify the steps required in using the internal rate of return method when the net annual cash flows are equal.

13. El Cajon Company uses the internal rate of return method. What is the decision rule for this method?

14. What are the strengths of the annual rate of return approach? What are its weaknesses?

15. Your classmate, Mike Dawson, is confused about the factors that are included in the annual rate of return technique. What is the formula for this technique?

16. Sveta Pace is trying to understand the term "cost of capital." Define the term and indicate its relevance to the decision rule under the internal rate of return technique.

BRIEF EXERCISES

BE26-1 Rihanna Company is considering purchasing new equipment for $450,000. It is expected that the equipment will produce net annual cash flows of $60,000 over its 10-year useful life. Annual depreciation will be $45,000. Compute the cash payback period.

Compute the cash payback period for a capital investment.

(LO 1)

BE26-2 Hsung Company accumulates the following data concerning a proposed capital investment: cash cost $215,000, net annual cash flows $40,000, and present value factor of cash inflows for 10 years 5.65 (rounded). Determine the net present value, and indicate whether the investment should be made.

Compute net present value of an investment.

(LO 2)

BE26-3 Thunder Corporation, an amusement park, is considering a capital investment in a new exhibit. The exhibit would cost $136,000 and have an estimated useful life of 5 years. It will be sold for $60,000 at that time. (Amusement parks need to rotate exhibits to keep people interested.) It is expected to increase net annual cash flows by $25,000. The company's borrowing rate is 8%. Its cost of capital is 10%. Calculate the net present value of this project to the company.

Compute net present value of an investment.

(LO 2)

BE26-4 Caine Bottling Corporation is considering the purchase of a new bottling machine. The machine would cost $200,000 and has an estimated useful life of 8 years with zero salvage value. Management estimates that the new bottling machine will provide net annual cash flows of $34,000. Management also believes that the new bottling machine will save the company money because it is expected to be more reliable than other machines, and thus will reduce downtime. How much would the reduction in downtime have to be worth in order for the project to be acceptable? Assume a discount rate of 9%. (*Hint:* Calculate the net present value.)

Compute net present value of an investment and consider intangible benefits.

(LO 2, 3)

BE26-5 McKnight Company is considering two different, mutually exclusive capital expenditure proposals. Project A will cost $400,000, has an expected useful life of 10 years, a salvage value of zero, and is expected to increase net annual cash flows by $70,000. Project B will cost $310,000, has an expected useful life of 10 years, a salvage value of zero, and is expected to increase net annual cash flows by $55,000. A discount rate of 9% is appropriate for both projects. Compute the net present value and profitability index of each project. Which project should be accepted?

Compute net present value and profitability index.

(LO 2, 3)

BE26-6 Quillen Company is performing a post-audit of a project completed one year ago. The initial estimates were that the project would cost $250,000, would have a useful life of 9 years, zero salvage value, and would result in net annual cash flows of $46,000 per year. Now that the investment has been in operation for 1 year, revised figures indicate that it actually cost $260,000, will have a total useful life of 11 years, and will produce net annual cash flows of $39,000 per year. Evaluate the success of the project. Assume a discount rate of 10%.

Perform a post-audit.

(LO 3)

BE26-7 Kanye Company is evaluating the purchase of a rebuilt spot-welding machine to be used in the manufacture of a new product. The machine will cost $176,000, has an estimated useful life of 7 years, a salvage value of zero, and will increase net annual cash flows by $35,000. What is its approximate internal rate of return?

Calculate internal rate of return.

(LO 4)

BE26-8 Viera Corporation is considering investing in a new facility. The estimated cost of the facility is $2,045,000. It will be used for 12 years, then sold for $716,000. The facility will generate annual cash inflows of $400,000 and will need new annual cash outflows of $150,000. The company has a required rate of return of 7%. Calculate the internal rate of return on this project, and discuss whether the project should be accepted.

Calculate internal rate of return.

(LO 4)

BE26-9 Swift Oil Company is considering investing in a new oil well. It is expected that the oil well will increase annual revenues by $130,000 and will increase annual expenses by $70,000 including depreciation. The oil well will cost $490,000 and will have a $10,000 salvage value at the end of its 10-year useful life. Calculate the annual rate of return.

Compute annual rate of return.

(LO 5)

DO IT! Exercises

Compute the cash payback period for an investment.

(LO 1)

DO IT! 26-1 Wayne Company is considering a long-term investment project called ZIP. ZIP will require an investment of $140,000. It will have a useful life of 4 years and no salvage value. Annual cash inflows would increase by $80,000, and annual cash outflows would increase by $40,000. Compute the cash payback period.

Calculate net present value of an investment.

(LO 2)

DO IT! 26-2 Wayne Company is considering a long-term investment project called ZIP. ZIP will require an investment of $120,000. It will have a useful life of 4 years and no salvage value. Annual cash inflows would increase by $80,000, and annual cash outflows would increase by $40,000. The company's required rate of return is 12%. Calculate the net present value on this project and discuss whether it should be accepted.

Compute profitability index.

(LO 3)

DO IT! 26-3 Ranger Corporation has decided to invest in renewable energy sources to meet part of its energy needs for production. It is considering solar power versus wind power. After considering cost savings as well as incremental revenues from selling excess electricity into the power grid, it has determined the following.

	Solar	Wind
Present value of annual cash flows	$52,580	$128,450
Initial investment	$39,500	$105,300

Determine the net present value and profitability index of each project. Which energy source should it choose?

Calculate internal rate of return.

(LO 4)

DO IT! 26-4 Wayne Company is considering a long-term investment project called ZIP. ZIP will require an investment of $120,000. It will have a useful life of 4 years and no salvage value. Annual cash inflows would increase by $80,000, and annual cash outflows would increase by $40,000. The company's required rate of return is 12%. Calculate the internal rate of return on this project and discuss whether it should be accepted.

Calculate annual rate of return.

(LO 5)

DO IT! 26-5 Wayne Company is considering a long-term investment project called ZIP. ZIP will require an investment of $120,000. It will have a useful life of 4 years and no salvage value. Annual revenues would increase by $80,000, and annual expenses (excluding depreciation) would increase by $41,000. Wayne uses the straight-line method to compute depreciation expense. The company's required rate of return is 12%. Compute the annual rate of return.

EXERCISES

Compute cash payback and net present value.

(LO 1, 2)

E26-1 Linkin Corporation is considering purchasing a new delivery truck. The truck has many advantages over the company's current truck (not the least of which is that it runs). The new truck would cost $56,000. Because of the increased capacity, reduced maintenance costs, and increased fuel economy, the new truck is expected to generate cost savings of $8,000. At the end of 8 years, the company will sell the truck for an estimated $27,000. Traditionally the company has used a rule of thumb that a proposal should not be accepted unless it has a payback period that is less than 50% of the asset's estimated useful life. Larry Newton, a new manager, has suggested that the company should not rely solely on the payback approach, but should also employ the net present value method when evaluating new projects. The company's cost of capital is 8%.

Instructions

(a) Compute the cash payback period and net present value of the proposed investment.

(b) Does the project meet the company's cash payback criteria? Does it meet the net present value criteria for acceptance? Discuss your results.

E26-2 Doug's Custom Construction Company is considering three new projects, each requiring an equipment investment of $22,000. Each project will last for 3 years and produce the following net annual cash flows.

Year	AA	BB	CC
1	$ 7,000	$10,000	$13,000
2	9,000	10,000	12,000
3	12,000	10,000	11,000
Total	$28,000	$30,000	$36,000

Compute cash payback period and net present value.

(LO 1, 2)

The equipment's salvage value is zero, and Doug uses straight-line depreciation. Doug will not accept any project with a cash payback period over 2 years. Doug's required rate of return is 12%.

Instructions
(a) Compute each project's payback period, indicating the most desirable project and the least desirable project using this method. (Round to two decimals and assume in your computations that cash flows occur evenly throughout the year.)
(b) Compute the net present value of each project. Does your evaluation change? (Round to nearest dollar.)

E26-3 Hillsong Inc. manufactures snowsuits. Hillsong is considering purchasing a new sewing machine at a cost of $2.45 million. Its existing machine was purchased five years ago at a price of $1.8 million; six months ago, Hillsong spent $55,000 to keep it operational. The existing sewing machine can be sold today for $250,000. The new sewing machine would require a one-time, $85,000 training cost. Operating costs would decrease by the following amounts for years 1 to 7:

Calculate net present value and apply decision rule.

(LO 2)

Year	1	$390,000
	2	400,000
	3	411,000
	4	426,000
	5	434,000
	6	435,000
	7	436,000

The new sewing machine would be depreciated according to the declining-balance method at a rate of 20%. The salvage value is expected to be $400,000. This new equipment would require maintenance costs of $100,000 at the end of the fifth year. The cost of capital is 9%.

Instructions
Use the net present value method to determine whether Hillsong should purchase the new machine to replace the existing machine, and state the reason for your conclusion.

(CGA adapted)

E26-4 BAK Corp. is considering purchasing one of two new diagnostic machines. Either machine would make it possible for the company to bid on jobs that it currently isn't equipped to do. Estimates regarding each machine are provided below.

Compute net present value and profitability index.

(LO 2, 3)

	Machine A	Machine B
Original cost	$75,500	$180,000
Estimated life	8 years	8 years
Salvage value	–0–	–0–
Estimated annual cash inflows	$20,000	$40,000
Estimated annual cash outflows	$5,000	$10,000

Instructions
Calculate the net present value and profitability index of each machine. Assume a 9% discount rate. Which machine should be purchased?

E26-5 Bruno Corporation is involved in the business of injection molding of plastics. It is considering the purchase of a new computer-aided design and manufacturing machine for $430,000. The company believes that with this new machine it will improve productivity

Determine internal rate of return.

(LO 4)

and increase quality, resulting in an increase in net annual cash flows of $101,000 for the next 6 years. Management requires a 10% rate of return on all new investments.

Instructions
Calculate the internal rate of return on this new machine. Should the investment be accepted?

Calculate cash payback period, internal rate of return, and apply decision rules.

(LO 1, 4)

E26-6 BSU Inc. wants to purchase a new machine for $29,300, excluding $1,500 of installation costs. The old machine was bought five years ago and had an expected economic life of 10 years without salvage value. This old machine now has a book value of $2,000, and BSU Inc. expects to sell it for that amount. The new machine would decrease operating costs by $7,000 each year of its economic life. The straight-line depreciation method would be used for the new machine, for a six-year period with no salvage value.

Instructions
(a) Determine the cash payback period.
(b) Determine the approximate internal rate of return.
(c) Assuming the company has a required rate of return of 10%, state your conclusion on whether the new machine should be purchased.

(CGA adapted)

Determine internal rate of return.

(LO 4)

E26-7 Iggy Company is considering three capital expenditure projects. Relevant data for the projects are as follows.

Project	Investment	Annual Income	Life of Project
22A	$240,000	$15,500	6 years
23A	270,000	20,600	9 years
24A	280,000	15,700	7 years

Annual income is constant over the life of the project. Each project is expected to have zero salvage value at the end of the project. Iggy Company uses the straight-line method of depreciation.

Instructions
(a) Determine the internal rate of return for each project. Round the internal rate of return factor to three decimals.
(b) If Iggy Company's required rate of return is 10%, which projects are acceptable?

Calculate annual rate of return.

(LO 5)

E26-8 Pierre's Hair Salon is considering opening a new location in French Lick, California. The cost of building a new salon is $300,000. A new salon will normally generate annual revenues of $70,000, with annual expenses (including depreciation) of $41,500. At the end of 15 years the salon will have a salvage value of $80,000.

Instructions
Calculate the annual rate of return on the project.

Compute cash payback period and annual rate of return.

(LO 1, 5)

E26-9 Legend Service Center just purchased an automobile hoist for $32,400. The hoist has an 8-year life and an estimated salvage value of $3,000. Installation costs and freight charges were $3,300 and $700, respectively. Legend uses straight-line depreciation.

The new hoist will be used to replace mufflers and tires on automobiles. Legend estimates that the new hoist will enable his mechanics to replace five extra mufflers per week. Each muffler sells for $72 installed. The cost of a muffler is $36, and the labor cost to install a muffler is $16.

Instructions
(a) Compute the cash payback period for the new hoist.
(b) Compute the annual rate of return for the new hoist. (Round to one decimal.)

Compute annual rate of return, cash payback period, and net present value.

(LO 1, 2, 5)

E26-10 Vilas Company is considering a capital investment of $190,000 in additional productive facilities. The new machinery is expected to have a useful life of 5 years with no salvage value. Depreciation is by the straight-line method. During the life of the investment, annual net income and net annual cash flows are expected to be $12,000 and

$50,000, respectively. Vilas has a 12% cost of capital rate, which is the required rate of return on the investment.

Instructions
(Round to two decimals.)
(a) Compute (1) the cash payback period and (2) the annual rate of return on the proposed capital expenditure.
(b) Using the discounted cash flow technique, compute the net present value.

E26-11 Drake Corporation is reviewing an investment proposal. The initial cost and estimates of the book value of the investment at the end of each year, the net cash flows for each year, and the net income for each year are presented in the schedule below. All cash flows are assumed to take place at the end of the year. The salvage value of the investment at the end of each year is equal to its book value. There would be no salvage value at the end of the investment's life.

Calculate payback, annual rate of return, and net present value.

(LO 1, 2, 5)

Investment Proposal

Year	Initial Cost and Book Value	Annual Cash Flows	Annual Net Income
0	$105,000		
1	70,000	$45,000	$10,000
2	42,000	40,000	12,000
3	21,000	35,000	14,000
4	7,000	30,000	16,000
5	0	25,000	18,000

Drake Corporation uses an 11% target rate of return for new investment proposals.

Instructions
(a) What is the cash payback period for this proposal?
(b) What is the annual rate of return for the investment?
(c) What is the net present value of the investment?

(CMA-Canada adapted)

■ EXERCISES: SET B AND CHALLENGE EXERCISES

Visit the book's companion website, at **www.wiley.com/college/weygandt,** and choose the Student Companion site to access Exercises: Set B and Challenge Exercises.

■ PROBLEMS: SET A

P26-1A U3 Company is considering three long-term capital investment proposals. Each investment has a useful life of 5 years. Relevant data on each project are as follows.

Compute annual rate of return, cash payback, and net present value.

(LO 1, 2, 5)

	Project Bono	Project Edge	Project Clayton
Capital investment	$160,000	$175,000	$200,000
Annual net income:			
Year 1	14,000	18,000	27,000
2	14,000	17,000	23,000
3	14,000	16,000	21,000
4	14,000	12,000	13,000
5	14,000	9,000	12,000
Total	$ 70,000	$ 72,000	$ 96,000

Depreciation is computed by the straight-line method with no salvage value. The company's cost of capital is 15%. (Assume that cash flows occur evenly throughout the year.)

Instructions
(a) Compute the cash payback period for each project. (Round to two decimals.)
(b) Compute the net present value for each project. (Round to nearest dollar.)

(b) E $(7,312); C $2,163

(c) Compute the annual rate of return for each project. (Round to two decimals.) (*Hint:* Use average annual net income in your computation.)

(d) Rank the projects on each of the foregoing bases. Which project do you recommend?

Compute annual rate of return, cash payback, and net present value.

(LO 1, 2, 5)

P26-2A Lon Timur is an accounting major at a midwestern state university located approximately 60 miles from a major city. Many of the students attending the university are from the metropolitan area and visit their homes regularly on the weekends. Lon, an entrepreneur at heart, realizes that few good commuting alternatives are available for students doing weekend travel. He believes that a weekend commuting service could be organized and run profitably from several suburban and downtown shopping mall locations. Lon has gathered the following investment information.

1. Five used vans would cost a total of $75,000 to purchase and would have a 3-year useful life with negligible salvage value. Lon plans to use straight-line depreciation.
2. Ten drivers would have to be employed at a total payroll expense of $48,000.
3. Other annual out-of-pocket expenses associated with running the commuter service would include Gasoline $16,000, Maintenance $3,300, Repairs $4,000, Insurance $4,200, and Advertising $2,500.
4. Lon has visited several financial institutions to discuss funding. The best interest rate he has been able to negotiate is 15%. Use this rate for cost of capital.
5. Lon expects each van to make ten round trips weekly and carry an average of six students each trip. The service is expected to operate 30 weeks each year, and each student will be charged $12.00 for a round-trip ticket.

Instructions

(a) (1) $5,000

(b) (1) 2.5 years

(a) Determine the annual (1) net income and (2) net annual cash flows for the commuter service.

(b) Compute (1) the cash payback period and (2) the annual rate of return. (Round to two decimals.)

(c) Compute the net present value of the commuter service. (Round to the nearest dollar.)

(d) ✏———— What should Lon conclude from these computations?

Compute net present value, profitability index, and internal rate of return.

(LO 2, 3, 4)

P26-3A Brooks Clinic is considering investing in new heart-monitoring equipment. It has two options. Option A would have an initial lower cost but would require a significant expenditure for rebuilding after 4 years. Option B would require no rebuilding expenditure, but its maintenance costs would be higher. Since the Option B machine is of initial higher quality, it is expected to have a salvage value at the end of its useful life. The following estimates were made of the cash flows. The company's cost of capital is 8%.

	Option A	Option B
Initial cost	$160,000	$227,000
Annual cash inflows	$71,000	$80,000
Annual cash outflows	$30,000	$31,000
Cost to rebuild (end of year 4)	$50,000	$0
Salvage value	$0	$8,000
Estimated useful life	7 years	7 years

Instructions

(a) (1) NPV A $16,709
    (3) IRR B 12%

(a) Compute the (1) net present value, (2) profitability index, and (3) internal rate of return for each option. (*Hint:* To solve for internal rate of return, experiment with alternative discount rates to arrive at a net present value of zero.)

(b) Which option should be accepted?

Compute net present value considering intangible benefits.

(LO 2, 3)

P26-4A Jane's Auto Care is considering the purchase of a new tow truck. The garage doesn't currently have a tow truck, and the $60,000 price tag for a new truck would represent a major expenditure. Jane Austen, owner of the garage, has compiled the estimates shown below in trying to determine whether the tow truck should be purchased.

Initial cost	$60,000
Estimated useful life	8 years
Net annual cash flows from towing	$8,000
Overhaul costs (end of year 4)	$6,000
Salvage value	$12,000

Jane's good friend, Rick Ryan, stopped by. He is trying to convince Jane that the tow truck will have other benefits that Jane hasn't even considered. First, he says, cars that need towing need to be fixed. Thus, when Jane tows them to her facility, her repair revenues will increase. Second, he notes that the tow truck could have a plow mounted on it, thus saving Jane the cost of plowing her parking lot. (Rick will give her a used plow blade for free if Jane will plow Rick's driveway.) Third, he notes that the truck will generate goodwill; people who are rescued by Jane's tow truck will feel grateful and might be more inclined to use her service station in the future or buy gas there. Fourth, the tow truck will have "Jane's Auto Care" on its doors, hood, and back tailgate—a form of free advertising wherever the tow truck goes. Rick estimates that, at a minimum, these benefits would be worth the following.

Additional annual net cash flows from repair work	$3,000
Annual savings from plowing	750
Additional annual net cash flows from customer "goodwill"	1,000
Additional annual net cash flows resulting from free advertising	750

The company's cost of capital is 9%.

Instructions

(a) Calculate the net present value, ignoring the additional benefits described by Rick. Should the tow truck be purchased?

(b) Calculate the net present value, incorporating the additional benefits suggested by Rick. Should the tow truck be purchased?

(c) Suppose Rick has been overly optimistic in his assessment of the value of the additional benefits. At a minimum, how much would the additional benefits have to be worth in order for the project to be accepted?

(a) NPV $(13,950)

(b) NPV $16,491

P26-5A Coolplay Corp. is thinking about opening a soccer camp in southern California. To start the camp, Coolplay would need to purchase land and build four soccer fields and a sleeping and dining facility to house 150 soccer players. Each year, the camp would be run for 8 sessions of 1 week each. The company would hire college soccer players as coaches. The camp attendees would be male and female soccer players ages 12–18. Property values in southern California have enjoyed a steady increase in value. It is expected that after using the facility for 20 years, Coolplay can sell the property for more than it was originally purchased for. The following amounts have been estimated.

Compute net present value and internal rate of return with sensitivity analysis.

(LO 2, 3, 4)

Cost of land	$300,000
Cost to build soccer fields, dorm and dining facility	$600,000
Annual cash inflows assuming 150 players and 8 weeks	$920,000
Annual cash outflows	$840,000
Estimated useful life	20 years
Salvage value	$1,500,000
Discount rate	8%

Instructions

(a) Calculate the net present value of the project.

(b) To gauge the sensitivity of the project to these estimates, assume that if only 125 players attend each week, annual cash inflows will be $805,000 and annual cash outflows will be $750,000. What is the net present value using these alternative estimates? Discuss your findings.

(c) Assuming the original facts, what is the net present value if the project is actually riskier than first assumed and an 10% discount rate is more appropriate?

(d) Assume that during the first 5 years, the annual net cash flows each year were only $40,000. At the end of the fifth year, the company is running low on cash, so management decides to sell the property for $1,332,000. What was the actual internal rate of return on the project? Explain how this return was possible given that the camp did not appear to be successful.

(a) NPV $207,277

(d) IRR 12%

PROBLEMS: SET B AND SET C

Visit the book's companion website, at **www.wiley.com/college/weygandt**, and choose the Student Companion site to access Problems: Set B and Set C.

CONTINUING PROBLEMS

CURRENT DESIGNS

CD26 A company that manufactures recreational pedal boats has approached Mike Cichanowski to ask if he would be interested in using **Current Designs'** rotomold expertise and equipment to produce some of the pedal boat components. Mike is intrigued by the idea and thinks it would be an interesting way of complementing the present product line.

One of Mike's hesitations about the proposal is that the pedal boats are a different shape than the kayaks that Current Designs produces. As a result, the company would need to buy an additional roto-mold oven in order to produce the pedal boat components. This project clearly involves risks, and Mike wants to make sure that the returns justify the risks. In this case, since this is a new venture, Mike thinks that a 15% discount rate is appropriate to use to evaluate the project.

As an intern at Current Designs, Mike has asked you to prepare an initial evaluation of this proposal. To aid in your analysis, he has provided the following information and assumptions.

1. The new rotomold oven will have a cost of $256,000, a salvage value of $0, and an 8-year useful life. Straight-line depreciation will be used.
2. The projected revenues, costs, and results for each of the 8 years of this project are as follows.

Sales		$220,000
Less:		
Manufacturing costs	$140,000	
Depreciation	32,000	
Shipping and administrative costs	22,000	194,000
Income before income taxes		26,000
Income tax expense		10,800
Net income		$ 15,200

Instructions

(a) Compute the annual rate of return. (Round to two decimal places.)
(b) Compute the payback period. (Round to two decimal places.)
(c) Compute the net present value using a discount rate of 9%. (Round to nearest dollar.) Should the proposal be accepted using this discount rate?
(d) Compute the net present value using a discount rate of 15%. (Round to nearest dollar.) Should the proposal be accepted using this discount rate?

WATERWAYS

(*Note:* This is a continuation of the Waterways problem from Chapters 15–25.)

WP26 Waterways Corporation puts much emphasis on cash flow when it plans for capital investments. The company chose its discount rate of 8% based on the rate of return it must pay its owners and creditors. Using that rate, Waterways then uses different methods to determine the best decisions for making capital outlays. Waterways is considering buying five new backhoes to replace the backhoes it now has. This problem asks you to evaluate that decision, using various capital budgeting techniques.

Go to the book's companion website, **www.wiley.com/college/weygandt**, *to find the remainder of this problem.*

COMPREHENSIVE CASES

CC26-1 For this case, revisit the Greetings Inc. company presented in earlier chapters. The company is now searching for new opportunities for growth. This case will provide you with the opportunity to evaluate a proposal based on initial estimates as well as conduct sensitivity analysis. It also requires evaluation of the underlying assumptions used in the analysis.

CC26-2 Armstrong Helmet Company needs to determine the cost for a given product. For this case, you will have the opportunity to explore cost-volume-profit relationships and prepare a set of budgets.

Go to the book's companion website, **at www.wiley.com/college/weygandt,** *for details and instructions for both cases.*

BROADENING YOUR PERSPECTIVE

MANAGEMENT DECISION-MAKING

Decision-Making Across the Organization

BYP26-1 Luang Company is considering the purchase of a new machine. Its invoice price is $122,000, freight charges are estimated to be $3,000, and installation costs are expected to be $5,000. Salvage value of the new machine is expected to be zero after a useful life of 4 years. Existing equipment could be retained and used for an additional 4 years if the new machine is not purchased. At that time, the salvage value of the equipment would be zero. If the new machine is purchased now, the existing machine would be scrapped. Luang's accountant, Lisa Hsung, has accumulated the following data regarding annual sales and expenses with and without the new machine.

1. Without the new machine, Luang can sell 10,000 units of product annually at a per unit selling price of $100. If the new unit is purchased, the number of units produced and sold would increase by 25%, and the selling price would remain the same.
2. The new machine is faster than the old machine, and it is more efficient in its usage of materials. With the old machine the gross profit rate will be 28.5% of sales, whereas the rate will be 30% of sales with the new machine. (*Note:* These gross profit rates do not include depreciation on the machines. For purposes of determining net income, treat depreciation expense as a separate line item.)
3. Annual selling expenses are $160,000 with the current equipment. Because the new equipment would produce a greater number of units to be sold, annual selling expenses are expected to increase by 10% if it is purchased.
4. Annual administrative expenses are expected to be $100,000 with the old machine, and $112,000 with the new machine.
5. The current book value of the existing machine is $40,000. Luang uses straight-line depreciation.
6. Luang's management has a required rate of return of 15% on its investment and a cash payback period of no more than 3 years.

Instructions
With the class divided into groups, answer the following. (Ignore income tax effects.)

(a) Calculate the annual rate of return for the new machine. (Round to two decimals.)
(b) Compute the cash payback period for the new machine. (Round to two decimals.)
(c) Compute the net present value of the new machine. (Round to the nearest dollar.)
(d) On the basis of the foregoing data, would you recommend that Luang buy the machine? Why?

Managerial Analysis

BYP26-2 Hawke Skateboards is considering building a new plant. Bob Skerritt, the company's marketing manager, is an enthusiastic supporter of the new plant. Lucy Liu, the company's chief financial officer, is not so sure that the plant is a good idea. Currently, the company purchases its skateboards from foreign manufacturers. The following figures were estimated regarding the construction of a new plant.

Cost of plant	$4,000,000	Estimated useful life	15 years
Annual cash inflows	4,000,000	Salvage value	$2,000,000
Annual cash outflows	3,540,000	Discount rate	11%

Bob Skerritt believes that these figures understate the true potential value of the plant. He suggests that by manufacturing its own skateboards the company will benefit from a "buy American" patriotism that he believes is common among skateboarders. He also notes that the firm has had numerous quality problems with the skateboards manufactured by its suppliers. He suggests that the inconsistent quality has resulted in lost sales, increased warranty claims, and some costly lawsuits. Overall, he believes sales will be $200,000 higher than projected above, and that the savings from lower warranty costs and legal costs will be $60,000 per year. He also believes that the project is not as risky as assumed above, and that a 9% discount rate is more reasonable.

Instructions
Answer each of the following.

(a) Compute the net present value of the project based on the original projections.
(b) Compute the net present value incorporating Bob's estimates of the value of the intangible benefits, but still using the 11% discount rate.
(c) Compute the net present value using the original estimates, but employing the 9% discount rate that Bob suggests is more appropriate.
(d) Comment on your findings.

Real-World Focus

BYP26-3 Tecumseh Products Company has its headquarters in Tecumseh, Michigan. It describes itself as "a global multinational corporation producing mechanical and electrical components essential to industries creating end-products for health, comfort, and convenience." The following was excerpted from the management discussion and analysis section of a recent annual report.

TECUMSEH PRODUCTS COMPANY
Management Discussion and Analysis

The company has invested approximately $50 million in a scroll compressor manufacturing facility in Tecumseh, Michigan. After experiencing setbacks in developing a commercially acceptable scroll compressor, the Company is currently testing a new generation of scroll product. The Company is unable to predict when, or if, it will offer a scroll compressor for commercial sale, but it does anticipate that reaching volume production will require a significant additional investment. Given such additional investment and current market conditions, management is currently reviewing its options with respect to scroll product improvement, cost reductions, joint ventures and alternative new products.

Instructions
Discuss issues the company should consider and techniques the company should employ to determine whether to continue pursuing this project.

BYP26-4 Campbell Soup Company is an international provider of soup products. Management is very interested in continuing to grow the company in its core business, while "spinning off" those businesses that are not part of its core operation.

Address: **www.campbellsoups.com**, or go to **www.wiley.com/college/weygandt**

Steps
1. Go to the home page of Campbell Soup Company at the address shown above.
2. Choose the current annual report.

Instructions
Review the financial statements and management's discussion and analysis, and answer the following questions.

(a) What was the total amount of capital expenditures in the current year, and how does this amount compare with the previous year? In your response, note what year you are using.
(b) What interest rate did the company pay on new borrowings in the current year?
(c) Assume that this year's capital expenditures are expected to increase cash flows by $50 million. What is the expected internal rate of return (IRR) for these capital expenditures? (Assume a 10-year period for the cash flows.)

CRITICAL THINKING

Communication Activity

BYP26-5 Refer back to E26-9 to address the following.

Instructions
Prepare a memo to Maria Fierro, your supervisor. Show your calculations from E26-9 (a) and (b). In one or two paragraphs, discuss important nonfinancial considerations. Make any assumptions you believe to be necessary. Make a recommendation based on your analysis.

Ethics Case

BYP26-6 NuComp Company operates in a state where corporate taxes and workers' compensation insurance rates have recently doubled. NuComp's president has just assigned you the task of preparing an economic analysis and making a recommendation relative to moving the entire operation to Missouri. The president is slightly in favor of such a move because Missouri is his boyhood home and he also owns a fishing lodge there.

You have just completed building your dream house, moved in, and sodded the lawn. Your children are all doing well in school and sports and, along with your spouse, want no part of a move to Missouri. If the company does move, so will you because the town is a one-industry community and you and your spouse will have to move to have employment. Moving when everyone else does will cause you to take a big loss on the sale of your house. The same hardships will be suffered by your coworkers, and the town will be devastated.

In compiling the costs of moving versus not moving, you have latitude in the assumptions you make, the estimates you compute, and the discount rates and time periods you project. You are in a position to influence the decision singlehandedly.

Instructions

(a) Who are the stakeholders in this situation?
(b) What are the ethical issues in this situation?
(c) What would you do in this situation?

All About You

BYP26-7 Numerous articles have been written that identify early warning signs that you might be getting into trouble with your personal debt load. You can find many good articles on this topic on the Web.

Instructions

Find an article that identifies early warning signs of personal debt trouble. Write up a summary of the article and bring your summary and the article to class to share.

Considering Your Costs and Benefits

BYP26-8 The March 31, 2011, edition of the *Wall Street Journal* includes an article by Russell Gold entitled "Solar Gains Traction—Thanks to Subsidies."

Instructions

Read the article and answer the following questions.

(a) What was the total cost of the solar panels installed? What was the "out-of-pocket" cost to the couple?
(b) Using the total annual electricity bill of $5,000 mentioned in the story, what is the cash payback of the project using the total cost? What is the cash payback based on the "out-of-pocket" cost?
(c) Solar panel manufacturers estimate that solar panels can last up to 40 years with only minor maintenance costs. Assuming no maintenance costs, a 6% rate of interest, a more conservative 20-year life, and zero salvage value, what is the net present value of the project based on the total cost? What is the net present value of the project based on the "out-of-pocket" cost?
(d) What was the wholesale price of panels per watt at the time the article was written? At what price per watt does the article say that subsidies no longer be needed? Does this price appear to be achievable?

Appendix A

Specimen Financial Statements: Apple Inc.

Once each year, a corporation communicates to its stockholders and other interested parties by issuing a complete set of audited financial statements. The **annual report**, as this communication is called, summarizes the financial results of the company's operations for the year and its plans for the future. Many annual reports are attractive, multicolored, glossy public relations pieces, containing pictures of corporate officers and directors as well as photos and descriptions of new products and new buildings. Yet the basic function of every annual report is to report financial information, almost all of which is a product of the corporation's accounting system.

The content and organization of corporate annual reports have become fairly standardized. Excluding the public relations part of the report (pictures, products, etc.), the following are the traditional financial portions of the annual report:

- Financial Highlights
- Letter to the Stockholders
- Management's Discussion and Analysis
- Financial Statements
- Notes to the Financial Statements

- Management's Responsibility for Financial Reporting
- Management's Report on Internal Control over Financial Reporting
- Report of Independent Registered Public Accounting Firm
- Selected Financial Data

The official SEC filing of the annual report is called a **Form 10-K**, which often omits the public relations pieces found in most standard annual reports. On the following pages, we present Apple Inc.'s financial statements taken from the company's 2013 Form 10-K. To access Apple's Form 10-K, including notes to the financial statements, follow these steps:

1. Go to **http://investor.apple.com**.
2. Select the Financial Information tab.
3. Select the 10-K annual report dated September 28, 2013.
4. The Notes to Consolidated Financial Statements begin on page 50.

CONSOLIDATED STATEMENTS OF OPERATIONS
(In millions, except number of shares which are reflected in thousands and per share amounts)

	Years ended		
	September 28, 2013	September 29, 2012	September 24, 2011
Net sales	$ 170,910	$ 156,508	$ 108,249
Cost of sales	106,606	87,846	64,431
Gross margin	64,304	68,662	43,818
Operating expenses:			
Research and development	4,475	3,381	2,429
Selling, general and administrative	10,830	10,040	7,599
Total operating expenses	15,305	13,421	10,028
Operating income	48,999	55,241	33,790
Other income/(expense), net	1,156	522	415
Income before provision for income taxes	50,155	55,763	34,205
Provision for income taxes	13,118	14,030	8,283
Net income	$ 37,037	$ 41,733	$ 25,922
Earnings per share:			
Basic	$ 40.03	$ 44.64	$ 28.05
Diluted	$ 39.75	$ 44.15	$ 27.68
Shares used in computing earnings per share:			
Basic	925,331	934,818	924,258
Diluted	931,662	945,355	936,645
Cash dividends declared per common share	$ 11.40	$ 2.65	$ 0.00

See accompanying Notes to Consolidated Financial Statements.

CONSOLIDATED STATEMENTS OF COMPREHENSIVE INCOME
(In millions)

	Years ended		
	September 28, 2013	September 29, 2012	September 24, 2011
Net income	$37,037	$41,733	$25,922
Other comprehensive income/(loss):			
Change in foreign currency translation, net of tax effects of $35, $13 and $18, respectively	(112)	(15)	(12)
Change in unrecognized gains/losses on derivative instruments:			
Change in fair value of derivatives, net of tax benefit/(expense) of $(351), $73 and $(50), respectively	522	(131)	92
Adjustment for net losses/(gains) realized and included in net income, net of tax expense/(benefit) of $255, $220 and $(250), respectively	(458)	(399)	450
Total change in unrecognized gains/losses on derivative instruments, net of tax	64	(530)	542
Change in unrealized gains/losses on marketable securities:			
Change in fair value of marketable securities, net of tax benefit/(expense) of $458, $(421) and $17, respectively	(791)	715	29
Adjustment for net losses/(gains) realized and included in net income, net of tax expense/(benefit) of $82, $68 and $(40), respectively	(131)	(114)	(70)
Total change in unrealized gains/losses on marketable securities, net of tax	(922)	601	(41)
Total other comprehensive income/(loss)	(970)	56	489
Total comprehensive income	$36,067	$41,789	$26,411

See accompanying Notes to Consolidated Financial Statements.

CONSOLIDATED BALANCE SHEETS
(In millions, except number of shares which are reflected in thousands)

	September 28, 2013	September 29, 2012
ASSETS:		
Current assets:		
Cash and cash equivalents	$ 14,259	$ 10,746
Short-term marketable securities	26,287	18,383
Accounts receivable, less allowances of $99 and $98, respectively	13,102	10,930
Inventories	1,764	791
Deferred tax assets	3,453	2,583
Vendor non-trade receivables	7,539	7,762
Other current assets	6,882	6,458
Total current assets	73,286	57,653
Long-term marketable securities	106,215	92,122
Property, plant and equipment, net	16,597	15,452
Goodwill	1,577	1,135
Acquired intangible assets, net	4,179	4,224
Other assets	5,146	5,478
Total assets	$ 207,000	$ 176,064
LIABILITIES AND SHAREHOLDERS' EQUITY:		
Current liabilities:		
Accounts payable	$ 22,367	$ 21,175
Accrued expenses	13,856	11,414
Deferred revenue	7,435	5,953
Total current liabilities	43,658	38,542
Deferred revenue – non-current	2,625	2,648
Long-term debt	16,960	0
Other non-current liabilities	20,208	16,664
Total liabilities	83,451	57,854
Commitments and contingencies		
Shareholders' equity:		
Common stock, no par value; 1,800,000 shares authorized; 899,213 and 939,208 shares issued and outstanding, respectively	19,764	16,422
Retained earnings	104,256	101,289
Accumulated other comprehensive income/(loss)	(471)	499
Total shareholders' equity	123,549	118,210
Total liabilities and shareholders' equity	$ 207,000	$ 176,064

See accompanying Notes to Consolidated Financial Statements.

CONSOLIDATED STATEMENTS OF SHAREHOLDERS' EQUITY
(In millions, except number of shares which are reflected in thousands)

	Common Stock		Retained Earnings	Accumulated Other Comprehensive Income/(Loss)	Total Shareholders' Equity
	Shares	Amount			
Balances as of September 25, 2010	915,970	$10,668	$ 37,169	$ (46)	$ 47,791
Net income	0	0	25,922	0	25,922
Other comprehensive income/(loss)	0	0	0	489	489
Share-based compensation	0	1,168	0	0	1,168
Common stock issued under stock plans, net of shares withheld for employee taxes	13,307	561	(250)	0	311
Tax benefit from equity awards, including transfer pricing adjustments	0	934	0	0	934
Balances as of September 24, 2011	929,277	13,331	62,841	443	76,615
Net income	0	0	41,733	0	41,733
Other comprehensive income/(loss)	0	0	0	56	56
Dividends and dividend equivalent rights declared	0	0	(2,523)	0	(2,523)
Share-based compensation	0	1,740	0	0	1,740
Common stock issued under stock plans, net of shares withheld for employee taxes	9,931	200	(762)	0	(562)
Tax benefit from equity awards, including transfer pricing adjustments	0	1,151	0	0	1,151
Balances as of September 29, 2012	939,208	16,422	101,289	499	118,210
Net income	0	0	37,037	0	37,037
Other comprehensive income/(loss)	0	0	0	(970)	(970)
Dividends and dividend equivalent rights declared	0	0	(10,676)	0	(10,676)
Repurchase of common stock	(46,976)	0	(22,950)	0	(22,950)
Share-based compensation	0	2,253	0	0	2,253
Common stock issued under stock plans, net of shares withheld for employee taxes	6,981	(143)	(444)	0	(587)
Tax benefit from equity awards, including transfer pricing adjustments	0	1,232	0	0	1,232
Balances as of September 28, 2013	899,213	$19,764	$104,256	$ (471)	$123,549

See accompanying Notes to Consolidated Financial Statements.

CONSOLIDATED STATEMENTS OF CASH FLOWS
(In millions)

	September 28, 2013	September 29, 2012	September 24, 2011
		Years ended	
Cash and cash equivalents, beginning of the year	$ 10,746	$ 9,815	$ 11,261
Operating activities:			
Net income	37,037	41,733	25,922
Adjustments to reconcile net income to cash generated by operating activities:			
Depreciation and amortization	6,757	3,277	1,814
Share-based compensation expense	2,253	1,740	1,168
Deferred income tax expense	1,141	4,405	2,868
Changes in operating assets and liabilities:			
Accounts receivable, net	(2,172)	(5,551)	143
Inventories	(973)	(15)	275
Vendor non-trade receivables	223	(1,414)	(1,934)
Other current and non-current assets	1,080	(3,162)	(1,391)
Accounts payable	2,340	4,467	2,515
Deferred revenue	1,459	2,824	1,654
Other current and non-current liabilities	4,521	2,552	4,495
Cash generated by operating activities	53,666	50,856	37,529
Investing activities:			
Purchases of marketable securities	(148,489)	(151,232)	(102,317)
Proceeds from maturities of marketable securities	20,317	13,035	20,437
Proceeds from sales of marketable securities	104,130	99,770	49,416
Payments made in connection with business acquisitions, net	(496)	(350)	(244)
Payments for acquisition of property, plant and equipment	(8,165)	(8,295)	(4,260)
Payments for acquisition of intangible assets	(911)	(1,107)	(3,192)
Other	(160)	(48)	(259)
Cash used in investing activities	(33,774)	(48,227)	(40,419)
Financing activities:			
Proceeds from issuance of common stock	530	665	831
Excess tax benefits from equity awards	701	1,351	1,133
Taxes paid related to net share settlement of equity awards	(1,082)	(1,226)	(520)
Dividends and dividend equivalent rights paid	(10,564)	(2,488)	0
Repurchase of common stock	(22,860)	0	0
Proceeds from issuance of long-term debt, net	16,896	0	0
Cash generated by/(used in) financing activities	(16,379)	(1,698)	1,444
Increase/(decrease) in cash and cash equivalents	3,513	931	(1,446)
Cash and cash equivalents, end of the year	$ 14,259	$ 10,746	$ 9,815
Supplemental cash flow disclosure:			
Cash paid for income taxes, net	$ 9,128	$ 7,682	$ 3,338

See accompanying Notes to Consolidated Financial Statements.

Specimen Financial Statements: PepsiCo, Inc.

PepsiCo, Inc. is a world leader in convenient snacks, foods, and beverages. The following are PepsiCo's financial statements as presented in its 2013 annual report. To access PepsiCo's complete annual report, including notes to the financial statements, follow these steps:

1. Go to **www.pepsico.com**.
2. Select Annual Reports and Proxy Information under the Investors tab.
3. Select the 2013 Annual Report.
4. The Notes to Consolidated Financial Statements begin on page 73.

Consolidated Statement of Income
PepsiCo, Inc. and Subsidiaries
Fiscal years ended December 28, 2013, December 29, 2012 and December 31, 2011
(in millions except per share amounts)

	2013	2012	2011
Net Revenue	$ 66,415	$ 65,492	$ 66,504
Cost of sales	31,243	31,291	31,593
Selling, general and administrative expenses	25,357	24,970	25,145
Amortization of intangible assets	110	119	133
Operating Profit	9,705	9,112	9,633
Interest expense	(911)	(899)	(856)
Interest income and other	97	91	57
Income before income taxes	8,891	8,304	8,834
Provision for income taxes	2,104	2,090	2,372
Net income	6,787	6,214	6,462
Less: Net income attributable to noncontrolling interests	47	36	19
Net Income Attributable to PepsiCo	$ 6,740	$ 6,178	$ 6,443
Net Income Attributable to PepsiCo per Common Share			
Basic	$ 4.37	$ 3.96	$ 4.08
Diluted	$ 4.32	$ 3.92	$ 4.03
Weighted-average common shares outstanding			
Basic	1,541	1,557	1,576
Diluted	1,560	1,575	1,597
Cash dividends declared per common share	$ 2.24	$ 2.1275	$ 2.025

See accompanying notes to consolidated financial statements.

Consolidated Statement of Comprehensive Income

PepsiCo, Inc. and Subsidiaries

Fiscal years ended December 28, 2013, December 29, 2012 and December 31, 2011

(in millions)

	2013		
	Pre-tax amounts	Tax amounts	After-tax amounts
Net income			$ 6,787
Other Comprehensive Income			
Currency translation adjustment	$ (1,303)	$ —	(1,303)
Cash flow hedges:			
Reclassification of net losses to net income	45	(17)	28
Net derivative losses	(20)	10	(10)
Pension and retiree medical:			
Net prior service cost	(23)	8	(15)
Net gains	2,540	(895)	1,645
Unrealized gains on securities	57	(28)	29
Other	—	(16)	(16)
Total Other Comprehensive Income	$ 1,296	$ (938)	358
Comprehensive income			7,145
Comprehensive income attributable to noncontrolling interests			(45)
Comprehensive Income Attributable to PepsiCo			$ 7,100

	2012		
	Pre-tax amounts	Tax amounts	After-tax amounts
Net income			$ 6,214
Other Comprehensive Income			
Currency translation adjustment	$ 737	$ —	737
Cash flow hedges:			
Reclassification of net losses to net income	90	(32)	58
Net derivative losses	(50)	10	(40)
Pension and retiree medical:			
Net prior service cost	(32)	12	(20)
Net losses	(41)	(11)	(52)
Unrealized gains on securities	18	—	18
Other	—	36	36
Total Other Comprehensive Income	$ 722	$ 15	737
Comprehensive income			6,951
Comprehensive income attributable to noncontrolling interests			(31)
Comprehensive Income Attributable to PepsiCo			$ 6,920

	2011		
	Pre-tax amounts	Tax amounts	After-tax amounts
Net income			$ 6,462
Other Comprehensive Loss			
Currency translation adjustment	$ (1,464)	$ —	(1,464)
Cash flow hedges:			
Reclassification of net losses to net income	5	4	9
Net derivative losses	(126)	43	(83)
Pension and retiree medical:			
Net prior service cost	(18)	8	(10)
Net losses	(1,468)	501	(967)
Unrealized losses on securities	(27)	19	(8)
Other	(16)	5	(11)
Total Other Comprehensive Loss	$ (3,114)	$ 580	(2,534)
Comprehensive income			3,928
Comprehensive income attributable to noncontrolling interests			(84)
Comprehensive Income Attributable to PepsiCo			$ 3,844

See accompanying notes to consolidated financial statements.

Consolidated Statement of Cash Flows
PepsiCo, Inc. and Subsidiaries
Fiscal years ended December 28, 2013, December 29, 2012 and December 31, 2011
(in millions)

	2013	2012	2011
Operating Activities			
Net income	$ 6,787	$ 6,214	$ 6,462
Depreciation and amortization	2,663	2,689	2,737
Stock-based compensation expense	303	278	326
Merger and integration costs	10	16	329
Cash payments for merger and integration costs	(25)	(83)	(377)
Restructuring and impairment charges	163	279	383
Cash payments for restructuring charges	(133)	(343)	(31)
Restructuring and other charges related to the transaction with Tingyi	—	176	—
Cash payments for restructuring and other charges related to the transaction with Tingyi	(26)	(109)	—
Non-cash foreign exchange loss related to Venezuela devaluation	111	—	—
Excess tax benefits from share-based payment arrangements	(117)	(124)	(70)
Pension and retiree medical plan contributions	(262)	(1,865)	(349)
Pension and retiree medical plan expenses	663	796	571
Deferred income taxes and other tax charges and credits	(1,058)	321	495
Change in accounts and notes receivable	(88)	(250)	(666)
Change in inventories	4	144	(331)
Change in prepaid expenses and other current assets	(51)	89	(27)
Change in accounts payable and other current liabilities	1,007	548	520
Change in income taxes payable	86	(97)	(340)
Other, net	(349)	(200)	(688)
Net Cash Provided by Operating Activities	9,688	8,479	8,944
Investing Activities			
Capital spending	(2,795)	(2,714)	(3,339)
Sales of property, plant and equipment	109	95	84
Acquisition of WBD, net of cash and cash equivalents acquired	—	—	(2,428)
Investment in WBD	—	—	(164)
Cash payments related to the transaction with Tingyi	(3)	(306)	—
Other acquisitions and investments in noncontrolled affiliates	(109)	(121)	(601)
Divestitures	133	(32)	780
Short-term investments, by original maturity			
More than three months – maturities	—	—	21
Three months or less, net	61	61	45
Other investing, net	(21)	12	(16)
Net Cash Used for Investing Activities	(2,625)	(3,005)	(5,618)
Financing Activities			
Proceeds from issuances of long-term debt	$ 4,195	$ 5,999	$ 3,000
Payments of long-term debt	(3,894)	(2,449)	(1,596)
Debt repurchase	—	—	(771)
Short-term borrowings, by original maturity			
More than three months – proceeds	23	549	523
More than three months – payments	(492)	(248)	(559)
Three months or less, net	1,634	(1,762)	339
Cash dividends paid	(3,434)	(3,305)	(3,157)
Share repurchases – common	(3,001)	(3,219)	(2,489)
Share repurchases – preferred	(7)	(7)	(7)
Proceeds from exercises of stock options	1,123	1,122	945
Excess tax benefits from share-based payment arrangements	117	124	70
Acquisition of noncontrolling interests	(20)	(68)	(1,406)
Other financing	(33)	(42)	(27)
Net Cash Used for Financing Activities	(3,789)	(3,306)	(5,135)
Effect of exchange rate changes on cash and cash equivalents	(196)	62	(67)
Net Increase/(Decrease) in Cash and Cash Equivalents	3,078	2,230	(1,876)
Cash and Cash Equivalents, Beginning of Year	6,297	4,067	5,943
Cash and Cash Equivalents, End of Year	$ 9,375	$ 6,297	$ 4,067

See accompanying notes to consolidated financial statements.

Consolidated Balance Sheet
PepsiCo, Inc. and Subsidiaries
December 28, 2013 and December 29, 2012
(in millions except per share amounts)

	2013	2012
ASSETS		
Current Assets		
Cash and cash equivalents	$ 9,375	$ 6,297
Short-term investments	303	322
Accounts and notes receivable, net	6,954	7,041
Inventories	3,409	3,581
Prepaid expenses and other current assets	2,162	1,479
Total Current Assets	22,203	18,720
Property, Plant and Equipment, net	18,575	19,136
Amortizable Intangible Assets, net	1,638	1,781
Goodwill	16,613	16,971
Other nonamortizable intangible assets	14,401	14,744
Nonamortizable Intangible Assets	31,014	31,715
Investments in Noncontrolled Affiliates	1,841	1,633
Other Assets	2,207	1,653
Total Assets	$ 77,478	$ 74,638
LIABILITIES AND EQUITY		
Current Liabilities		
Short-term obligations	$ 5,306	$ 4,815
Accounts payable and other current liabilities	12,533	11,903
Income taxes payable	—	371
Total Current Liabilities	17,839	17,089
Long-Term Debt Obligations	24,333	23,544
Other Liabilities	4,931	6,543
Deferred Income Taxes	5,986	5,063
Total Liabilities	53,089	52,239
Commitments and contingencies		
Preferred Stock, no par value	41	41
Repurchased Preferred Stock	(171)	(164)
PepsiCo Common Shareholders' Equity		
Common stock, par value $1^2/_3$¢ per share (authorized 3,600 shares, issued, net of repurchased common stock at par value: 1,529 and 1,544 shares, respectively)	25	26
Capital in excess of par value	4,095	4,178
Retained earnings	46,420	43,158
Accumulated other comprehensive loss	(5,127)	(5,487)
Repurchased common stock, in excess of par value (337 and 322 shares, respectively)	(21,004)	(19,458)
Total PepsiCo Common Shareholders' Equity	24,409	22,417
Noncontrolling interests	110	105
Total Equity	24,389	22,399
Total Liabilities and Equity	$ 77,478	$ 74,638

See accompanying notes to consolidated financial statements.

Consolidated Statement of Equity
PepsiCo, Inc. and Subsidiaries
Fiscal years ended December 28, 2013, December 29, 2012 and December 31, 2011
(in millions)

	2013		2012		2011	
	Shares	Amount	Shares	Amount	Shares	Amount
Preferred Stock	0.8 $	41	0.8 $	41	0.8 $	41
Repurchased Preferred Stock						
Balance, beginning of year	(0.6)	(164)	(0.6)	(157)	(0.6)	(150)
Redemptions	—	(7)	—	(7)	—	(7)
Balance, end of year	(0.6)	(171)	(0.6)	(164)	(0.6)	(157)
Common Stock						
Balance, beginning of year	1,544	26	1,565	26	1,582	26
Repurchased common stock	(15)	(1)	(21)	—	(17)	—
Balance, end of year	1,529	25	1,544	26	1,565	26
Capital in Excess of Par Value						
Balance, beginning of year		4,178		4,461		4,527
Stock-based compensation expense		303		278		326
Stock option exercises/RSUs and PEPUnits converted [a]		(287)		(431)		(361)
Withholding tax on RSUs converted		(87)		(70)		(56)
Other		(12)		(60)		25
Balance, end of year		4,095		4,178		4,461
Retained Earnings						
Balance, beginning of year		43,158		40,316		37,090
Net income attributable to PepsiCo		6,740		6,178		6,443
Cash dividends declared – common		(3,451)		(3,312)		(3,192)
Cash dividends declared – preferred		(1)		(1)		(1)
Cash dividends declared – RSUs		(26)		(23)		(24)
Balance, end of year		46,420		43,158		40,316
Accumulated Other Comprehensive Loss						
Balance, beginning of year		(5,487)		(6,229)		(3,630)
Currency translation adjustment		(1,301)		742		(1,529)
Cash flow hedges, net of tax:						
Reclassification of net losses to net income		28		58		9
Net derivative losses		(10)		(40)		(83)
Pension and retiree medical, net of tax:						
Reclassification of net losses to net income		230		421		133
Remeasurement of net liabilities and translation		1,400		(493)		(1,110)
Unrealized gains/(losses) on securities, net of tax		29		18		(8)
Other		(16)		36		(11)
Balance, end of year		(5,127)		(5,487)		(6,229)
Repurchased Common Stock						
Balance, beginning of year	(322)	(19,458)	(301)	(17,870)	(284)	(16,740)
Share repurchases	(37)	(3,000)	(47)	(3,219)	(39)	(2,489)
Stock option exercises	20	1,301	24	1,488	20	1,251
Other	2	153	2	143	2	108
Balance, end of year	(337)	(21,004)	(322)	(19,458)	(301)	(17,870)
Total PepsiCo Common Shareholders' Equity		24,409		22,417		20,704
Noncontrolling Interests						
Balance, beginning of year		105		311		312
Net income attributable to noncontrolling interests		47		36		19
Distributions to noncontrolling interests, net		(34)		(37)		(24)
Currency translation adjustment		(2)		(5)		65
Acquisitions and divestitures		(6)		(200)		(57)
Other, net		—		—		(4)
Balance, end of year		110		105		311
Total Equity		$ 24,389		$ 22,399		$ 20,899

(a) Includes total tax benefits of $45 million in 2013, $84 million in 2012 and $43 million in 2011.

See accompanying notes to consolidated financial statements.

Appendix C

Specimen Financial Statements: The Coca-Cola Company

The Coca-Cola Company is a global leader in the beverage industry. It offers hundreds of brands, including soft drinks, fruit juices, sports drinks and other beverages in more than 200 countries. The following are Coca-Cola's financial statements as presented in its 2013 annual report. To access Coca-Cola's complete annual report, including notes to the financial statements, follow these steps:

1. Go to **www.coca-colacompany.com**.
2. Select the Investors link near the bottom of the page, and then select Financial Reports & Information.
3. Select the 2013 Annual Report on Form 10-K.
4. The Notes to Consolidated Financial Statements begin on page 79.

THE COCA-COLA COMPANY AND SUBSIDIARIES
CONSOLIDATED STATEMENTS OF INCOME

Year Ended December 31,	2013	2012	2011
(In millions except per share data)			
NET OPERATING REVENUES	**$ 46,854**	$ 48,017	$ 46,542
Cost of goods sold	**18,421**	19,053	18,215
GROSS PROFIT	**28,433**	28,964	28,327
Selling, general and administrative expenses	**17,310**	17,738	17,422
Other operating charges	**895**	447	732
OPERATING INCOME	**10,228**	10,779	10,173
Interest income	**534**	471	483
Interest expense	**463**	397	417
Equity income (loss) — net	**602**	819	690
Other income (loss) — net	**576**	137	529
INCOME BEFORE INCOME TAXES	**11,477**	11,809	11,458
Income taxes	**2,851**	2,723	2,812
CONSOLIDATED NET INCOME	**8,626**	9,086	8,646
Less: Net income attributable to noncontrolling interests	**42**	67	62
NET INCOME ATTRIBUTABLE TO SHAREOWNERS OF THE COCA-COLA COMPANY	**$ 8,584**	$ 9,019	$ 8,584
BASIC NET INCOME PER SHARE[1]	**$ 1.94**	$ 2.00	$ 1.88
DILUTED NET INCOME PER SHARE[1]	**$ 1.90**	$ 1.97	$ 1.85
AVERAGE SHARES OUTSTANDING	**4,434**	4,504	4,568
Effect of dilutive securities	**75**	80	78
AVERAGE SHARES OUTSTANDING ASSUMING DILUTION	**4,509**	4,584	4,646

[1] Calculated based on net income attributable to shareowners of The Coca-Cola Company.

Refer to Notes to Consolidated Financial Statements.

THE COCA-COLA COMPANY AND SUBSIDIARIES
CONSOLIDATED STATEMENTS OF COMPREHENSIVE INCOME

Year Ended December 31,	2013	2012	2011
(In millions)			
CONSOLIDATED NET INCOME	$ 8,626	$ 9,086	$ 8,646
Other comprehensive income:			
Net foreign currency translation adjustment	(1,187)	(182)	(692)
Net gain (loss) on derivatives	151	99	145
Net unrealized gain (loss) on available-for-sale securities	(80)	178	(7)
Net change in pension and other benefit liabilities	1,066	(668)	(763)
TOTAL COMPREHENSIVE INCOME	8,576	8,513	7,329
Less: Comprehensive income (loss) attributable to noncontrolling interests	39	105	10
TOTAL COMPREHENSIVE INCOME ATTRIBUTABLE TO SHAREOWNERS OF THE COCA-COLA COMPANY	$ 8,537	$ 8,408	$ 7,319

Refer to Notes to Consolidated Financial Statements.

THE COCA-COLA COMPANY AND SUBSIDIARIES
CONSOLIDATED BALANCE SHEETS

December 31,	2013	2012
(In millions except par value)		
ASSETS		
CURRENT ASSETS		
Cash and cash equivalents	$ 10,414	$ 8,442
Short-term investments	6,707	5,017
TOTAL CASH, CASH EQUIVALENTS AND SHORT-TERM INVESTMENTS	17,121	13,459
Marketable securities	3,147	3,092
Trade accounts receivable, less allowances of $61 and $53, respectively	4,873	4,759
Inventories	3,277	3,264
Prepaid expenses and other assets	2,886	2,781
Assets held for sale	—	2,973
TOTAL CURRENT ASSETS	31,304	30,328
EQUITY METHOD INVESTMENTS	10,393	9,216
OTHER INVESTMENTS, PRINCIPALLY BOTTLING COMPANIES	1,119	1,232
OTHER ASSETS	4,661	3,585
PROPERTY, PLANT AND EQUIPMENT — net	14,967	14,476
TRADEMARKS WITH INDEFINITE LIVES	6,744	6,527
BOTTLERS' FRANCHISE RIGHTS WITH INDEFINITE LIVES	7,415	7,405
GOODWILL	12,312	12,255
OTHER INTANGIBLE ASSETS	1,140	1,150
TOTAL ASSETS	$ 90,055	$ 86,174
LIABILITIES AND EQUITY		
CURRENT LIABILITIES		
Accounts payable and accrued expenses	$ 9,577	$ 8,680
Loans and notes payable	16,901	16,297
Current maturities of long-term debt	1,024	1,577
Accrued income taxes	309	471
Liabilities held for sale	—	796
TOTAL CURRENT LIABILITIES	27,811	27,821
LONG-TERM DEBT	19,154	14,736
OTHER LIABILITIES	3,498	5,468
DEFERRED INCOME TAXES	6,152	4,981
THE COCA-COLA COMPANY SHAREOWNERS' EQUITY		
Common stock, $0.25 par value; Authorized — 11,200 shares;		
Issued — 7,040 and 7,040 shares, respectively	1,760	1,760
Capital surplus	12,276	11,379
Reinvested earnings	61,660	58,045
Accumulated other comprehensive income (loss)	(3,432)	(3,385)
Treasury stock, at cost — 2,638 and 2,571 shares, respectively	(39,091)	(35,009)
EQUITY ATTRIBUTABLE TO SHAREOWNERS OF THE COCA-COLA COMPANY	33,173	32,790
EQUITY ATTRIBUTABLE TO NONCONTROLLING INTERESTS	267	378
TOTAL EQUITY	33,440	33,168
TOTAL LIABILITIES AND EQUITY	$ 90,055	$ 86,174

Refer to Notes to Consolidated Financial Statements.

THE COCA-COLA COMPANY AND SUBSIDIARIES
CONSOLIDATED STATEMENTS OF CASH FLOWS

Year Ended December 31, (In millions)	2013	2012	2011
OPERATING ACTIVITIES			
Consolidated net income	$ 8,626	$ 9,086	$ 8,646
Depreciation and amortization	1,977	1,982	1,954
Stock-based compensation expense	227	259	354
Deferred income taxes	648	632	1,035
Equity (income) loss — net of dividends	(201)	(426)	(269)
Foreign currency adjustments	168	(130)	7
Significant (gains) losses on sales of assets — net	(670)	(98)	(220)
Other operating charges	465	166	214
Other items	234	254	(354)
Net change in operating assets and liabilities	(932)	(1,080)	(1,893)
Net cash provided by operating activities	10,542	10,645	9,474
INVESTING ACTIVITIES			
Purchases of investments	(14,782)	(14,824)	(4,798)
Proceeds from disposals of investments	12,791	7,791	5,811
Acquisitions of businesses, equity method investments and nonmarketable securities	(353)	(1,486)	(971)
Proceeds from disposals of businesses, equity method investments and nonmarketable securities	872	20	398
Purchases of property, plant and equipment	(2,550)	(2,780)	(2,920)
Proceeds from disposals of property, plant and equipment	111	143	101
Other investing activities	(303)	(268)	(145)
Net cash provided by (used in) investing activities	(4,214)	(11,404)	(2,524)
FINANCING ACTIVITIES			
Issuances of debt	43,425	42,791	27,495
Payments of debt	(38,714)	(38,573)	(22,530)
Issuances of stock	1,328	1,489	1,569
Purchases of stock for treasury	(4,832)	(4,559)	(4,513)
Dividends	(4,969)	(4,595)	(4,300)
Other financing activities	17	100	45
Net cash provided by (used in) financing activities	(3,745)	(3,347)	(2,234)
EFFECT OF EXCHANGE RATE CHANGES ON CASH AND CASH EQUIVALENTS	(611)	(255)	(430)
CASH AND CASH EQUIVALENTS			
Net increase (decrease) during the year	1,972	(4,361)	4,286
Balance at beginning of year	8,442	12,803	8,517
Balance at end of year	$ 10,414	$ 8,442	$ 12,803

Refer to Notes to Consolidated Financial Statements.

THE COCA-COLA COMPANY AND SUBSIDIARIES
CONSOLIDATED STATEMENTS OF SHAREOWNERS' EQUITY

Year Ended December 31, (In millions except per share data)	2013	2012	2011
EQUITY ATTRIBUTABLE TO SHAREOWNERS OF THE COCA-COLA COMPANY			
NUMBER OF COMMON SHARES OUTSTANDING			
Balance at beginning of year	**4,469**	4,526	4,583
Purchases of treasury stock	**(121)**	(121)	(127)
Treasury stock issued to employees related to stock compensation plans	**54**	64	70
Balance at end of year	**4,402**	4,469	4,526
COMMON STOCK	$ **1,760**	$ 1,760	$ 1,760
CAPITAL SURPLUS			
Balance at beginning of year	**11,379**	10,332	9,177
Stock issued to employees related to stock compensation plans	**569**	640	724
Tax benefit (charge) from stock compensation plans	**144**	144	79
Stock-based compensation	**227**	259	354
Other activities	**(43)**	4	(2)
Balance at end of year	**12,276**	11,379	10,332
REINVESTED EARNINGS			
Balance at beginning of year	**58,045**	53,621	49,337
Net income attributable to shareowners of The Coca-Cola Company	**8,584**	9,019	8,584
Dividends (per share — $1.12, $1.02 and $0.94 in 2013, 2012 and 2011, respectively)	**(4,969)**	(4,595)	(4,300)
Balance at end of year	**61,660**	58,045	53,621
ACCUMULATED OTHER COMPREHENSIVE INCOME (LOSS)			
Balance at beginning of year	**(3,385)**	(2,774)	(1,509)
Net other comprehensive income (loss)	**(47)**	(611)	(1,265)
Balance at end of year	**(3,432)**	(3,385)	(2,774)
TREASURY STOCK			
Balance at beginning of year	**(35,009)**	(31,304)	(27,762)
Stock issued to employees related to stock compensation plans	**745**	786	830
Purchases of treasury stock	**(4,827)**	(4,491)	(4,372)
Balance at end of year	**(39,091)**	(35,009)	(31,304)
TOTAL EQUITY ATTRIBUTABLE TO SHAREOWNERS OF THE COCA-COLA COMPANY	$ **33,173**	$ 32,790	$ 31,635
EQUITY ATTRIBUTABLE TO NONCONTROLLING INTERESTS			
Balance at beginning of year	$ **378**	$ 286	$ 314
Net income attributable to noncontrolling interests	**42**	67	62
Net foreign currency translation adjustment	**(3)**	38	(52)
Dividends paid to noncontrolling interests	**(58)**	(48)	(38)
Acquisition of interests held by noncontrolling owners	**(34)**	(15)	—
Contributions by noncontrolling interests	**6**	—	—
Business combinations	**25**	50	—
Deconsolidation of certain entities	**(89)**	—	—
TOTAL EQUITY ATTRIBUTABLE TO NONCONTROLLING INTERESTS	$ **267**	$ 378	$ 286

Refer to Notes to Consolidated Financial Statements.

Appendix D

Specimen Financial Statements: Amazon.com, Inc.

Amazon.com, Inc. is the world's largest online retailer. It also produces consumer electronics—notably the Kindle e-book reader and the Kindle Fire Tablet computer—and is a major provider of cloud computing services. The following are Amazon's financial statements as presented in the company's 2013 annual report. To access Amazon's complete annual report, including notes to the financial statements, follow these steps:

1. Go to **www.amazon.com**.
2. Select the Investor Relations link at the bottom of the page and then select the 2013 Annual Report under Annual Reports and Proxies.
3. The Notes to Consolidated Financial Statements begin on page 40.

AMAZON.COM, INC.

CONSOLIDATED STATEMENTS OF CASH FLOWS

(in millions)

	Year Ended December 31,		
	2013	2012	2011
CASH AND CASH EQUIVALENTS, BEGINNING OF PERIOD	$ 8,084	$ 5,269	$ 3,777
OPERATING ACTIVITIES:			
Net income (loss)	274	(39)	631
Adjustments to reconcile net income (loss) to net cash from operating activities:			
Depreciation of property and equipment, including internal-use software and website development, and other amortization	3,253	2,159	1,083
Stock-based compensation	1,134	833	557
Other operating expense (income), net	114	154	154
Losses (gains) on sales of marketable securities, net	1	(9)	(4)
Other expense (income), net	166	253	(56)
Deferred income taxes	(156)	(265)	136
Excess tax benefits from stock-based compensation	(78)	(429)	(62)
Changes in operating assets and liabilities:			
Inventories	(1,410)	(999)	(1,777)
Accounts receivable, net and other	(846)	(861)	(866)
Accounts payable	1,888	2,070	2,997
Accrued expenses and other	736	1,038	1,067
Additions to unearned revenue	2,691	1,796	1,064
Amortization of previously unearned revenue	(2,292)	(1,521)	(1,021)
Net cash provided by (used in) operating activities	5,475	4,180	3,903
INVESTING ACTIVITIES:			
Purchases of property and equipment, including internal-use software and website development	(3,444)	(3,785)	(1,811)
Acquisitions, net of cash acquired, and other	(312)	(745)	(705)
Sales and maturities of marketable securities and other investments	2,306	4,237	6,843
Purchases of marketable securities and other investments	(2,826)	(3,302)	(6,257)
Net cash provided by (used in) investing activities	(4,276)	(3,595)	(1,930)
FINANCING ACTIVITIES:			
Excess tax benefits from stock-based compensation	78	429	62
Common stock repurchased	—	(960)	(277)
Proceeds from long-term debt and other	394	3,378	177
Repayments of long-term debt, capital lease, and finance lease obligations	(1,011)	(588)	(444)
Net cash provided by (used in) financing activities	(539)	2,259	(482)
Foreign-currency effect on cash and cash equivalents	(86)	(29)	1
Net increase (decrease) in cash and cash equivalents	574	2,815	1,492
CASH AND CASH EQUIVALENTS, END OF PERIOD	$ 8,658	$ 8,084	$ 5,269
SUPPLEMENTAL CASH FLOW INFORMATION:			
Cash paid for interest on long-term debt	$ 97	$ 31	$ 14
Cash paid for income taxes (net of refunds)	169	112	33
Property and equipment acquired under capital leases	1,867	802	753
Property and equipment acquired under build-to-suit leases	877	29	259

See accompanying notes to consolidated financial statements.

AMAZON.COM, INC.

CONSOLIDATED STATEMENTS OF OPERATIONS

(in millions, except per share data)

	Year Ended December 31,		
	2013	**2012**	**2011**
Net product sales	$ 60,903	$ 51,733	$ 42,000
Net services sales	13,549	9,360	6,077
Total net sales	74,452	61,093	48,077
Operating expenses (1):			
Cost of sales	54,181	45,971	37,288
Fulfillment	8,585	6,419	4,576
Marketing	3,133	2,408	1,630
Technology and content	6,565	4,564	2,909
General and administrative	1,129	896	658
Other operating expense (income), net	114	159	154
Total operating expenses	73,707	60,417	47,215
Income from operations	745	676	862
Interest income	38	40	61
Interest expense	(141)	(92)	(65)
Other income (expense), net	(136)	(80)	76
Total non-operating income (expense)	(239)	(132)	72
Income before income taxes	506	544	934
Provision for income taxes	(161)	(428)	(291)
Equity-method investment activity, net of tax	(71)	(155)	(12)
Net income (loss)	$ 274	$ (39)	$ 631
Basic earnings per share	$ 0.60	$ (0.09)	$ 1.39
Diluted earnings per share	$ 0.59	$ (0.09)	$ 1.37
Weighted average shares used in computation of earnings per share:			
Basic	457	453	453
Diluted	465	453	461

---

(1) Includes stock-based compensation as follows:			
Fulfillment	$ 294	$ 212	$ 133
Marketing	88	61	39
Technology and content	603	434	292
General and administrative	149	126	93

See accompanying notes to consolidated financial statements.

AMAZON.COM, INC.

CONSOLIDATED STATEMENTS OF COMPREHENSIVE INCOME
(in millions)

| | Year Ended December 31, | | |
	2013	2012	2011
Net income (loss)	$ 274	$ (39)	$ 631
Other comprehensive income (loss):			
Foreign currency translation adjustments, net of tax of $(20), $(30), and $20	63	76	(123)
Net change in unrealized gains on available-for-sale securities:			
Unrealized gains (losses), net of tax of $3, $(3), and $1	(10)	8	(1)
Reclassification adjustment for losses (gains) included in "Other income (expense), net," net of tax of $(1), $3, and $1	1	(7)	(2)
Net unrealized gains (losses) on available-for-sale securities	(9)	1	(3)
Total other comprehensive income (loss)	54	77	(126)
Comprehensive income	$ 328	$ 38	$ 505

See accompanying notes to consolidated financial statements.

AMAZON.COM, INC.

CONSOLIDATED BALANCE SHEETS

(in millions, except per share data)

	December 31,	
	2013	**2012**
ASSETS		
Current assets:		
Cash and cash equivalents	$ 8,658	$ 8,084
Marketable securities	3,789	3,364
Inventories	7,411	6,031
Accounts receivable, net and other	4,767	3,817
Total current assets	24,625	21,296
Property and equipment, net	10,949	7,060
Goodwill	2,655	2,552
Other assets	1,930	1,647
Total assets	$ 40,159	$ 32,555
LIABILITIES AND STOCKHOLDERS' EQUITY		
Current liabilities:		
Accounts payable	$ 15,133	$ 13,318
Accrued expenses and other	6,688	4,892
Unearned revenue	1,159	792
Total current liabilities	22,980	19,002
Long-term debt	3,191	3,084
Other long-term liabilities	4,242	2,277
Commitments and contingencies		
Stockholders' equity:		
Preferred stock, $0.01 par value:		
Authorized shares — 500		
Issued and outstanding shares — none	—	—
Common stock, $0.01 par value:		
Authorized shares — 5,000		
Issued shares — 483 and 478		
Outstanding shares — 459 and 454	5	5
Treasury stock, at cost	(1,837)	(1,837)
Additional paid-in capital	9,573	8,347
Accumulated other comprehensive loss	(185)	(239)
Retained earnings	2,190	1,916
Total stockholders' equity	9,746	8,192
Total liabilities and stockholders' equity	$ 40,159	$ 32,555

See accompanying notes to consolidated financial statements.

AMAZON.COM, INC.

CONSOLIDATED STATEMENTS OF STOCKHOLDERS' EQUITY
(in millions)

	Common Stock		Treasury Stock	Additional Paid-In Capital	Accumulated Other Comprehensive Income (Loss)	Retained Earnings	Total Stockholders' Equity
	Shares	Amount					
Balance as of January 1, 2011	451	$ 5	$ (600)	$ 6,325	$ (190)	$ 1,324	$ 6,864
Net income	—	—	—	—	—	631	631
Other comprehensive income (loss)	—	—	—	—	(126)	—	(126)
Exercise of common stock options	5	—	—	7	—	—	7
Repurchase of common stock	(1)	—	(277)	—	—	—	(277)
Excess tax benefits from stock-based compensation	—	—	—	62	—	—	62
Stock-based compensation and issuance of employee benefit plan stock	—	—	—	569	—	—	569
Issuance of common stock for acquisition activity	—	—	—	27	—	—	27
Balance as of December 31, 2011	455	5	(877)	6,990	(316)	1,955	7,757
Net income (loss)	—	—	—	—	—	(39)	(39)
Other comprehensive income	—	—	—	—	77	—	77
Exercise of common stock options	4	—	—	8	—	—	8
Repurchase of common stock	(5)	—	(960)	—	—	—	(960)
Excess tax benefits from stock-based compensation	—	—	—	429	—	—	429
Stock-based compensation and issuance of employee benefit plan stock	—	—	—	854	—	—	854
Issuance of common stock for acquisition activity	—	—	—	66	—	—	66
Balance as of December 31, 2012	454	5	(1,837)	8,347	(239)	1,916	8,192
Net income	—	—	—	—	—	274	274
Other comprehensive income	—	—	—	—	54	—	54
Exercise of common stock options	5	—	—	4	—	—	4
Repurchase of common stock	—	—	—	—	—	—	—
Excess tax benefits from stock-based compensation	—	—	—	73	—	—	73
Stock-based compensation and issuance of employee benefit plan stock	—	—	—	1,149	—	—	1,149
Balance as of December 31, 2013	459	$ 5	$ (1,837)	$ 9,573	$ (185)	$ 2,190	$ 9,746

See accompanying notes to consolidated financial statements.

Appendix E

Specimen Financial Statements: Wal-Mart Stores, Inc.

The following are **Wal-Mart Stores, Inc.**'s financial statements as presented in the company's 2014 annual report. To access Wal-Mart's complete annual report, including notes to the financial statements, follow these steps:

1. Go to **http://corporate.walmart.com**.
2. Select Annual Reports under the Investors tab.
3. Select the 2014 Annual Report (Wal-Mart's fiscal year ends January 31).
4. The Notes to Consolidated Financial Statements begin on page 40.

Consolidated Statements of Income

	Fiscal Years Ended January 31,		
(Amounts in millions, except per share data)	**2014**	2013	2012
Revenues:			
Net sales	**$473,076**	$465,604	$443,416
Membership and other income	**3,218**	3,047	3,093
Total revenues	**476,294**	468,651	446,509
Costs and expenses:			
Cost of sales	**358,069**	352,297	334,993
Operating, selling, general and administrative expenses	**91,353**	88,629	85,025
Operating income	**26,872**	27,725	26,491
Interest:			
Debt	**2,072**	1,977	2,034
Capital leases	**263**	272	286
Interest income	**(119)**	(186)	(161)
Interest, net	**2,216**	2,063	2,159
Income from continuing operations before income taxes	**24,656**	25,662	24,332
Provision for income taxes:			
Current	**8,619**	7,976	6,722
Deferred	**(514)**	(18)	1,202
Total provision for income taxes	**8,105**	7,958	7,924
Income from continuing operations	**16,551**	17,704	16,408
Income (loss) from discontinued operations, net of income taxes	**144**	52	(21)
Consolidated net income	**16,695**	17,756	16,387
Less consolidated net income attributable to noncontrolling interest	**(673)**	(757)	(688)
Consolidated net income attributable to Walmart	**$ 16,022**	$ 16,999	$ 15,699
Basic net income per common share:			
Basic income per common share from continuing operations attributable to Walmart	**$ 4.87**	$ 5.03	$ 4.55
Basic income (loss) per common share from discontinued operations attributable to Walmart	**0.03**	0.01	(0.01)
Basic net income per common share attributable to Walmart	**$ 4.90**	$ 5.04	$ 4.54
Diluted net income per common share:			
Diluted income per common share from continuing operations attributable to Walmart	**$ 4.85**	$ 5.01	$ 4.53
Diluted income (loss) per common share from discontinued operations attributable to Walmart	**0.03**	0.01	(0.01)
Diluted net income per common share attributable to Walmart	**$ 4.88**	$ 5.02	$ 4.52
Weighted-average common shares outstanding:			
Basic	**3,269**	3,374	3,460
Diluted	**3,283**	3,389	3,474
Dividends declared per common share	**$ 1.88**	$ 1.59	$ 1.46

See accompanying notes.

Consolidated Statements of Comprehensive Income

(Amounts in millions)	Fiscal Years Ended January 31,		
	2014	2013	2012
Consolidated net income	**$16,695**	$17,756	$16,387
Less consolidated net income attributable to nonredeemable noncontrolling interest	**(606)**	(684)	(627)
Less consolidated net income attributable to redeemable noncontrolling interest	**(67)**	(73)	(61)
Consolidated net income attributable to Walmart	**16,022**	16,999	15,699
Other comprehensive income (loss), net of income taxes			
Currency translation and other	**(3,146)**	1,042	(2,758)
Derivative instruments	**207**	136	(67)
Minimum pension liability	**153**	(166)	43
Other comprehensive income (loss), net of income taxes	**(2,786)**	1,012	(2,782)
Less other comprehensive income (loss) attributable to nonredeemable noncontrolling interest	**311**	(138)	660
Less other comprehensive income (loss) attributable to redeemable noncontrolling interest	**66**	(51)	66
Other comprehensive income (loss) attributable to Walmart	**(2,409)**	823	(2,056)
Comprehensive income, net of income taxes	**13,909**	18,768	13,605
Less comprehensive income (loss) attributable to nonredeemable noncontrolling interest	**(295)**	(822)	33
Less comprehensive income (loss) attributable to redeemable noncontrolling interest	**(1)**	(124)	5
Comprehensive income attributable to Walmart	**$13,613**	$17,822	$13,643

See accompanying notes.

Consolidated Balance Sheets

(Amounts in millions)	As of January 31,	
	2014	2013
ASSETS		
Current assets:		
Cash and cash equivalents	**$ 7,281**	$ 7,781
Receivables, net	**6,677**	6,768
Inventories	**44,858**	43,803
Prepaid expenses and other	**1,909**	1,551
Current assets of discontinued operations	**460**	37
Total current assets	**61,185**	59,940
Property and equipment:		
Property and equipment	**173,089**	165,825
Less accumulated depreciation	**(57,725)**	(51,896)
Property and equipment, net	**115,364**	113,929
Property under capital leases:		
Property under capital leases	**5,589**	5,899
Less accumulated amortization	**(3,046)**	(3,147)
Property under capital leases, net	**2,543**	2,752
Goodwill	**19,510**	20,497
Other assets and deferred charges	**6,149**	5,987
Total assets	**$204,751**	$203,105
LIABILITIES, REDEEMABLE NONCONTROLLING INTEREST AND EQUITY		
Current liabilities:		
Short-term borrowings	**$ 7,670**	$ 6,805
Accounts payable	**37,415**	38,080
Accrued liabilities	**18,793**	18,808
Accrued income taxes	**966**	2,211
Long-term debt due within one year	**4,103**	5,587
Obligations under capital leases due within one year	**309**	327
Current liabilities of discontinued operations	**89**	—
Total current liabilities	**69,345**	71,818
Long-term debt	**41,771**	38,394
Long-term obligations under capital leases	**2,788**	3,023
Deferred income taxes and other	**8,017**	7,613
Redeemable noncontrolling interest	**1,491**	519
Commitments and contingencies		
Equity:		
Common stock	**323**	332
Capital in excess of par value	**2,362**	3,620
Retained earnings	**76,566**	72,978
Accumulated other comprehensive income (loss)	**(2,996)**	(587)
Total Walmart shareholders' equity	**76,255**	76,343
Nonredeemable noncontrolling interest	**5,084**	5,395
Total equity	**81,339**	81,738
Total liabilities, redeemable noncontrolling interest and equity	**$204,751**	$203,105

See accompanying notes.

Consolidated Statements of Shareholders' Equity

(Amounts in millions)	Common Stock		Capital in Excess of Par Value	Retained Earnings	Accumulated Other Comprehensive Income (Loss)	Total Walmart Shareholders' Equity	Nonredeemable Noncontrolling Interest	Total Equity	Redeemable Noncontrolling Interest
	Shares	Amount							
Balances as of February 1, 2011	3,516	$352	$ 3,577	$63,967	$ 646	$68,542	$2,705	$71,247	$ 408
Consolidated net income	—	—	—	15,699	—	15,699	627	16,326	61
Other comprehensive loss, net of income taxes	—	—	—	—	(2,056)	(2,056)	(660)	(2,716)	(66)
Cash dividends declared ($1.46 per share)	—	—	—	(5,048)	—	(5,048)	—	(5,048)	—
Purchase of Company stock	(113)	(11)	(229)	(5,930)	—	(6,170)	—	(6,170)	—
Nonredeemable noncontrolling interest of acquired entity	—	—	—	—	—	—	1,988	1,988	—
Other	15	1	344	3	—	348	(214)	134	1
Balances as of January 31, 2012	3,418	342	3,692	68,691	(1,410)	71,315	4,446	75,761	404
Consolidated net income	—	—	—	16,999	—	16,999	684	17,683	73
Other comprehensive income, net of income taxes	—	—	—	—	823	823	138	961	51
Cash dividends declared ($1.59 per share)	—	—	—	(5,361)	—	(5,361)	—	(5,361)	—
Purchase of Company stock	(115)	(11)	(357)	(7,341)	—	(7,709)	—	(7,709)	—
Nonredeemable noncontrolling interest of acquired entity	—	—	—	—	—	—	469	469	—
Other	11	1	285	(10)	—	276	(342)	(66)	(9)
Balances as of January 31, 2013	**3,314**	**332**	**3,620**	**72,978**	**(587)**	**76,343**	**5,395**	**81,738**	**519**
Consolidated net income	—	—	—	**16,022**	—	**16,022**	**595**	**16,617**	**78**
Other comprehensive loss, net of income taxes	—	—	—	—	(2,409)	(2,409)	(311)	(2,720)	(66)
Cash dividends declared ($1.88 per share)	—	—	—	**(6,139)**	—	**(6,139)**	—	**(6,139)**	—
Purchase of Company stock	**(87)**	**(9)**	**(294)**	**(6,254)**	—	**(6,557)**	—	**(6,557)**	—
Redemption value adjustment of redeemable noncontrolling interest	—	—	(1,019)	—	—	(1,019)	—	(1,019)	1,019
Other	**6**	—	**55**	**(41)**	—	**14**	**(595)**	**(581)**	**(59)**
Balances as of January 31, 2014	**3,233**	**$323**	**$ 2,362**	**$76,566**	**$(2,996)**	**$76,255**	**$5,084**	**$81,339**	**$1,491**

Consolidated Statements of Cash Flows

	Fiscal Years Ended January 31,		
(Amounts in millions)	2014	2013	2012
Cash flows from operating activities:			
Consolidated net income	$ 16,695	$ 17,756	$ 16,387
Income (loss) from discontinued operations, net of income taxes	(144)	(52)	21
Income from continuing operations	16,551	17,704	16,408
Adjustments to reconcile income from continuing operations to net cash provided by operating activities:			
Depreciation and amortization	8,870	8,478	8,106
Deferred income taxes	(279)	(133)	1,050
Other operating activities	938	602	468
Changes in certain assets and liabilities, net of effects of acquisitions:			
Receivables, net	(566)	(614)	(796)
Inventories	(1,667)	(2,759)	(3,727)
Accounts payable	531	1,061	2,687
Accrued liabilities	103	271	(935)
Accrued income taxes	(1,224)	981	994
Net cash provided by operating activities	23,257	25,591	24,255
Cash flows from investing activities:			
Payments for property and equipment	(13,115)	(12,898)	(13,510)
Proceeds from the disposal of property and equipment	727	532	580
Investments and business acquisitions, net of cash acquired	(15)	(316)	(3,548)
Other investing activities	105	71	(131)
Net cash used in investing activities	(12,298)	(12,611)	(16,609)
Cash flows from financing activities:			
Net change in short-term borrowings	911	2,754	3,019
Proceeds from issuance of long-term debt	7,072	211	5,050
Payments of long-term debt	(4,968)	(1,478)	(4,584)
Dividends paid	(6,139)	(5,361)	(5,048)
Dividends paid to and stock purchases of noncontrolling interest	(722)	(414)	(526)
Purchase of Company stock	(6,683)	(7,600)	(6,298)
Other financing activities	(488)	(84)	(71)
Net cash used in financing activities	(11,017)	(11,972)	(8,458)
Effect of exchange rates on cash and cash equivalents	(442)	223	(33)
Net increase (decrease) in cash and cash equivalents	(500)	1,231	(845)
Cash and cash equivalents at beginning of year	7,781	6,550	7,395
Cash and cash equivalents at end of year	$ 7,281	$ 7,781	$ 6,550
Supplemental disclosure of cash flow information:			
Income taxes paid	$ 8,641	$ 7,304	$ 5,899
Interest paid	2,362	2,262	2,346

See accompanying notes.

Louis Vuitton is a French company and is one of the leading international fashion houses in the world. Louis Vuitton has been named the world's most valuable luxury brand. Note that its financial statements are IFRS-based and are presented in euros (€). To access the company's complete financial statements, follow these steps:

1. Go to **www.lvmh.com/investor-relations**.
2. Select 2013 Annual report, and then select the Finance tab once the Intro has played.
3. Note that the comments (notes) to the financial statements are placed after each corresponding statement.

CONSOLIDATED BALANCE SHEET

ASSETS

(EUR millions)	2013	2012[1]	2011[1]
Brands and other intangible assets	11,458	11,510	11,482
Goodwill	9,959	7,806	6,957
Property, plant and equipment	9,602	8,769	8,017
Investments in associates	152	163	170
Non-current available for sale financial assets	7,080	6,004	5,982
Other non-current assets	432	519	478
Deferred tax	909	954	760
NON-CURRENT ASSETS	**39,592**	**35,725**	**33,846**
Inventories and work in progress	8,586	8,080	7,510
Trade accounts receivable	2,189	1,985	1,878
Income taxes	235	201	121
Other current assets	1,851	1,811	1,455
Cash and cash equivalents	3,221	2,196	2,303
CURRENT ASSETS	**16,082**	**14,273**	**13,267**
TOTAL ASSETS	**55,674**	**49,998**	**47,113**

(Continued.)

(Continued.)

LIABILITIES AND EQUITY

(EUR millions)	2013	2012[1]	2011[1]
Share capital	152	152	152
Share premium account	3,849	3,848	3,801
Treasury shares and LVMH-share settled derivatives	(451)	(414)	(485)
Cumulative translation adjustment	(8)	342	431
Revaluation reserves	3,900	2,731	2,637
Other reserves	15,817	14,341	12,770
Net profit, Group share	3,436	3,424	3,065
Equity, Group share	26,695	24,424	22,371
Minority interests	1,028	1,084	1,055
TOTAL EQUITY	27,723	25,508	23,426
Long term borrowings	4,159	3,836	4,132
Provisions	1,755	1,756	1,530
Deferred tax	3,934	3,960	3,925
Other non-current liabilities	6,403	5,456	4,506
NON-CURRENT LIABILITIES	16,251	15,008	14,093
Short term borrowings	4,688	2,976	3,134
Trade accounts payable	3,308	3,134	2,952
Income taxes	382	442	443
Provisions	322	335	349
Other current liabilities	3,000	2,595	2,716
CURRENT LIABILITIES	11,700	9,482	9,594
TOTAL LIABILITIES AND EQUITY	55,674	49,998	47,113

(1) The balance sheets as of December 31, 2012 and 2011 have been restated to reflect the retrospective application as of January 1, 2011 of IAS 19 Employee Benefits as amended.

CONSOLIDATED INCOME STATEMENT

——

(EUR millions, except for earnings per share)	2013	2012	2011
REVENUE	29,149	28,103	23,659
Cost of sales	(10,055)	(9,917)	(8,092)
GROSS MARGIN	19,094	18,186	15,567
Marketing and selling expenses	(10,849)	(10,101)	(8,360)
General and administrative expenses	(2,224)	(2,164)	(1,944)
PROFIT FROM RECURRING OPERATIONS	6,021	5,921	5,263
Other operating income and expenses	(127)	(182)	(109)
OPERATING PROFIT	5,894	5,739	5,154
Cost of net financial debt	(103)	(140)	(151)
Other financial income and expenses	(96)	126	(91)
NET FINANCIAL INCOME (EXPENSE)	(199)	(14)	(242)
Income taxes	(1,755)	(1,820)	(1,453)
Income (loss) from investments in associates	7	4	6
NET PROFIT BEFORE MINORITY INTERESTS	3,947	3,909	3,465
Minority interests	(511)	(485)	(400)
NET PROFIT, GROUP SHARE	3,436	3,424	3,065
BASIC GROUP SHARE OF NET EARNINGS PER SHARE (EUR)	6.87	6.86	6.27
Number of shares on which the calculation is based	500,283,414	499,133,643	488,769,286
DILUTED GROUP SHARE OF NET EARNINGS PER SHARE (EUR)	6.83	6.82	6.23
Number of shares on which the calculation is based	503,217,497	502,229,952	492,207,492

CONSOLIDATED STATEMENT OF COMPREHENSIVE GAINS AND LOSSES

——

(EUR millions)	2013	2012[1]	2011[1]
NET PROFIT BEFORE MINORITY INTERESTS	3,947	3,909	3,465
Translation adjustments	(346)	(99)	190
Tax impact	(48)	(18)	47
	(394)	(117)	237
Change in value of available for sale financial assets	963	(27)	1,634
Amounts transferred to income statement	(16)	(14)	(38)
Tax impact	(35)	(6)	(116)
	912	(47)	1,480
Change in value of hedges of future foreign currency cash flows	304	182	95
Amounts transferred to income statement	(265)	13	(168)
Tax impact	(17)	(50)	21
	22	145	(52)
GAINS AND LOSSES RECOGNIZED IN EQUITY, TRANSFERABLE TO INCOME STATEMENT	540	(19)	1,665
Change in value of vineyard land	369	85	25
Tax impact	(127)	(28)	(11)
	242	57	14
Employee benefit commitments: change in value resulting from actuarial gains and losses	80	(101)	(45)
Tax impact	(22)	29	13
	58	(72)	(32)
GAINS AND LOSSES RECOGNIZED IN EQUITY, NOT TRANSFERABLE TO INCOME STATEMENT	300	(15)	(18)
COMPREHENSIVE INCOME	4,787	3,875	5,112
Minority interests	(532)	(470)	(429)
COMPREHENSIVE INCOME, GROUP SHARE	4,255	3,405	4,683

(1) The consolidated statements of comprehensive gains and losses as of December 31, 2012 and 2011 have been restated to reflect the retrospective application as of January 1, 2011 of IAS 19 Employee Benefits as amended.

CONSOLIDATED CASH FLOW STATEMENT

———

(EUR millions)	2013	2012	2011
I. OPERATING ACTIVITIES AND OPERATING INVESTMENTS			
Operating profit	5,894	5,739	5,154
Net increase in depreciation, amortization and provisions	1,454	1,299	999
Other computed expenses	(29)	(62)	(45)
Dividends received	86	188	61
Other adjustments	(76)	(51)	(32)
CASH FROM OPERATIONS BEFORE CHANGES IN WORKING CAPITAL	7,329	7,113	6,137
Cost of net financial debt: interest paid	(112)	(154)	(152)
Income taxes paid	(1,979)	(1,970)	(1,544)
NET CASH FROM OPERATING ACTIVITIES BEFORE CHANGES IN WORKING CAPITAL	5,238	4,989	4,441
Change in working capital	(617)	(813)	(534)
NET CASH FROM OPERATING ACTIVITIES	4,621	4,176	3,907
Operating investments	(1,663)	(1,702)	(1,730)
NET CASH FROM OPERATING ACTIVITIES AND OPERATING INVESTMENTS (free cash flow)	2,958	2,474	2,177
II. FINANCIAL INVESTMENTS			
Purchase of non-current available for sale financial assets	(197)	(131)	(518)
Proceeds from sale of non-current available for sale financial assets	38	36	17
Impact of purchase and sale of consolidated investments	(2,158)	(45)	(785)[1]
NET CASH FROM (used in) FINANCIAL INVESTMENTS	(2,317)	(140)	(1,286)
III. TRANSACTIONS RELATING TO EQUITY			
Capital increases of LVMH	66	94	94[1]
Capital increases of subsidiaries subscribed by minority interests	7	8	3
Acquisition and disposals of treasury shares and LVMH-share settled derivatives	(113)	5	2
Interim and final dividends paid by LVMH	(1,501)	(1,447)	(1,069)
Interim and final dividends paid to minority interests in consolidated subsidiaries	(220)	(314)	(189)
Purchase and proceeds from sale of minority interests	(150)	(206)	(1,413)
NET CASH FROM (used in) TRANSACTIONS RELATING TO EQUITY	(1,911)	(1,860)	(2,572)
CHANGE IN CASH BEFORE FINANCING ACTIVITIES	(1,270)	474	(1,681)
IV. FINANCING ACTIVITIES			
Proceeds from borrowings	3,145	1,068	2,659
Repayment of borrowings	(1,099)	(1,526)	(1,005)
Purchase and proceeds from sale of current available for sale financial assets	101	(67)	6
NET CASH FROM (used in) FINANCING ACTIVITIES	2,147	(525)	1,660
V. EFFECT OF EXCHANGE RATE CHANGES	46	(42)	60
NET INCREASE (decrease) IN CASH AND CASH EQUIVALENTS (I+II+III+IV+V)	923	(93)	39
CASH AND CASH EQUIVALENTS AT BEGINNING OF PERIOD	1,988	2,081	2,042
CASH AND CASH EQUIVALENTS AT END OF PERIOD	2,911	1,988	2,081
Transactions included in the table above, generating no change in cash:			
– acquisition of assets by means of finance leases	7	5	3

(1) Not including the impact of the amount attributable to the acquisition of Bulgari remunerated by the capital increase of LVMH SA as of June 30, 2011, which did not generate any cash flows.

CONSOLIDATED STATEMENT OF CHANGES IN EQUITY

(EUR millions)	Number of shares	Share capital	Share premium account	Treasury shares and LVMH-share settled derivatives	Cumulative translation adjustment	Revaluation reserves				Net profit and other reserves	Total equity		
						Available for sale financial assets	Hedges of future foreign currency cash flows	Vineyard land	Employee benefit commitments		Group share	Minority interests	Total
AS OF DECEMBER 31, 2012 AFTER RESTATEMENT	508,163,349	152	3,848	(414)	342	1,943	118	758	(88)	17,765	24,424	1,084	25,508
Gains and losses recognized in equity					(350)	912	18	188	51		819	21	840
Net profit										3,436	3,436	511	3,947
COMPREHENSIVE INCOME		-	-		(350)	912	18	188	51	3,436	4,255	532	4,787
Stock option plan and similar expenses										31	31	3	34
Acquisition/disposal of treasury shares and LVMH-share settled derivatives				(103)						(7)	(110)	-	(110)
Exercise of LVMH share subscription options	1,025,418		67								67		67
Retirement of LVMH shares	(1,395,106)		(66)	66							-	-	-
Capital increase in subsidiaries											-	8	8
Interim and final dividends paid										(1,500)	(1,500)	(228)	(1,728)
Changes in control of consolidated entities										1	1	50	51
Acquisition and disposal of minority interests' shares										(73)	(73)	(76)	(149)
Purchase commitments for minority interests' shares										(400)	(400)	(345)	(745)
AS OF DECEMBER 31, 2013	507,793,661	152	3,849	(451)	(8)	2,855	136	946	(37)	19,253	26,695	1,028	27,723

Appendix G Time Value of Money

APPENDIX PREVIEW Would you rather receive $1,000 today or a year from now? You should prefer to receive the $1,000 today because you can invest the $1,000 and then earn interest on it. As a result, you will have more than $1,000 a year from now. What this example illustrates is the concept of the **time value of money**. Everyone prefers to receive money today rather than in the future because of the interest factor.

LEARNING OBJECTIVES

1 **Compute interest and future values.**
- Nature of interest
- Future value of a single amount
- Future value of an annuity

2 **Compute present values.**
- Present value variables
- Present value of a single amount
- Present value of an annuity
- Time periods and discounting
- Present value of a long-term note or bond

3 **Compute the present value in capital budgeting situations.**
- Using alternative discount rates

4 **Use a financial calculator to solve time value of money problems.**
- Present value of a single sum
- Present value of an annuity
- Useful financial calculator applications

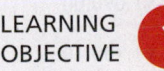

LEARNING OBJECTIVE **1** **Compute interest and future values.**

Nature of Interest

Interest is payment for the use of another person's money. It is the difference between the amount borrowed or invested (called the **principal**) and the amount repaid or collected. The amount of interest to be paid or collected is usually stated as a rate over a specific period of time. The rate of interest is generally stated as an annual rate.

The amount of interest involved in any financing transaction is based on three elements:

1. **Principal (p):** The original amount borrowed or invested.
2. **Interest Rate (i):** An annual percentage of the principal.
3. **Time (n):** The number of periods that the principal is borrowed or invested.

SIMPLE INTEREST

Simple interest is computed on the principal amount only. It is the return on the principal for one period. Simple interest is usually expressed as shown in Illustration G-1.

Illustration G-1
Interest computation

$$\text{Interest} = \frac{\text{Principal}}{p} \times \frac{\text{Rate}}{i} \times \frac{\text{Time}}{n}$$

For example, if you borrowed $5,000 for 2 years at a simple interest rate of 12% annually, you would pay $1,200 in total interest, computed as follows.

$$
\begin{aligned}
\text{Interest} &= p \times i \times n \\
&= \$5,000 \times .12 \times 2 \\
&= \$1,200
\end{aligned}
$$

COMPOUND INTEREST

Compound interest is computed on principal **and** on any interest earned that has not been paid or withdrawn. It is the return on (or growth of) the principal for two or more time periods. Compounding computes interest not only on the principal but also on the interest earned to date on that principal, assuming the interest is left on deposit.

To illustrate the difference between simple and compound interest, assume that you deposit $1,000 in Bank Two, where it will earn simple interest of 9% per year, and you deposit another $1,000 in Citizens Bank, where it will earn compound interest of 9% per year compounded annually. Also assume that in both cases you will not withdraw any cash until three years from the date of deposit. Illustration G-2 shows the computation of interest to be received and the accumulated year-end balances.

Illustration G-2
Simple versus compound interest

Bank Two				Citizens Bank		
Simple Interest Calculation	Simple Interest	Accumulated Year-End Balance		Compound Interest Calculation	Compound Interest	Accumulated Year-End Balance
Year 1 $1,000.00 × 9%	$ 90.00	$1,090.00		Year 1 $1,000.00 × 9%	$ 90.00	$1,090.00
Year 2 $1,000.00 × 9%	90.00	$1,180.00		Year 2 $1,090.00 × 9%	98.10	$1,188.10
Year 3 $1,000.00 × 9%	90.00	$1,270.00		Year 3 $1,188.10 × 9%	106.93	$1,295.03
	$ 270.00		$25.03 Difference		$ 295.03	

Note in Illustration G-2 that simple interest uses the initial principal of $1,000 to compute the interest in all three years. Compound interest uses the accumulated balance (principal plus interest to date) at each year-end to compute interest in the succeeding year—which explains why your compound interest account is larger.

Obviously, if you had a choice between investing your money at simple interest or at compound interest, you would choose compound interest, all other things—especially risk—being equal. In the example, compounding provides $25.03 of additional interest income. For practical purposes, compounding assumes that unpaid interest earned becomes a part of the principal, and the accumulated balance at the end of each year becomes the new principal on which interest is earned during the next year.

Illustration G-2 indicates that you should invest your money at the bank that compounds interest. Most business situations use compound interest. Simple interest is generally applicable only to short-term situations of one year or less.

Future Value of a Single Amount

The **future value of a single amount** is the value at a future date of a given amount invested, assuming compound interest. For example, in Illustration G-2, $1,295.03 is the future value of the $1,000 investment earning 9% for three years. The $1,295.03 is determined more easily by using the following formula.

$$FV = p \times (1 + i)^n$$

Illustration G-3
Formula for future value

where:

FV = future value of a single amount
p = principal (or present value; the value today)
i = interest rate for one period
n = number of periods

The $1,295.03 is computed as follows.

$$FV = p \times (1 + i)^n$$
$$= \$1,000 \times (1 + .09)^3$$
$$= \$1,000 \times 1.29503$$
$$= \$1,295.03$$

The 1.29503 is computed by multiplying $(1.09 \times 1.09 \times 1.09)$. The amounts in this example can be depicted in the time diagram shown in Illustration G-4.

Illustration G-4
Time diagram

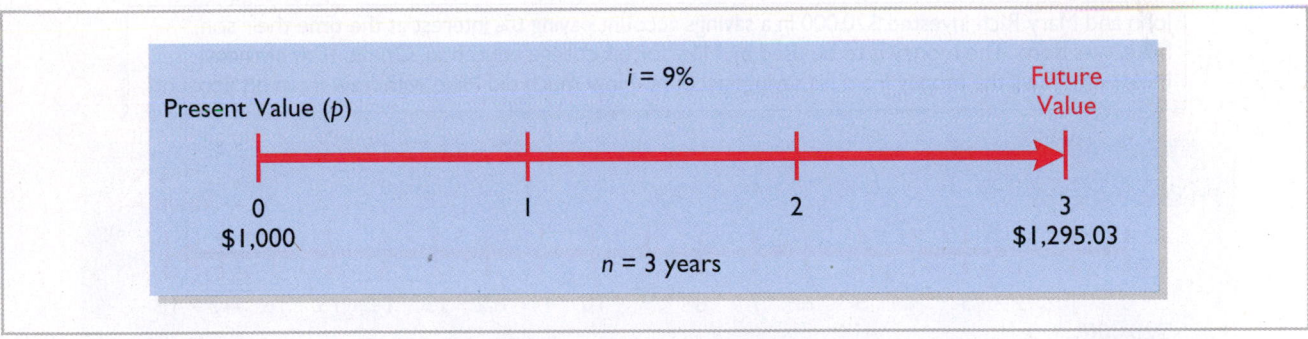

Another method used to compute the future value of a single amount involves a compound interest table. This table shows the future value of 1 for n periods. Table 1 (page G-4) is such a table.

In Table 1, n is the number of compounding periods, the percentages are the periodic interest rates, and the 5-digit decimal numbers in the respective columns are the future value of 1 factors. To use Table 1, you multiply the principal amount by the future value factor for the specified number of periods and interest rate. For example, the future value factor for two periods at 9% is 1.18810. Multiplying this factor by $1,000 equals $1,188.10—which is the accumulated balance at the end of year 2 in the Citizens Bank example in Illustration G-2. The $1,295.03 accumulated balance at the end of the third year is calculated from Table 1 by multiplying the future value factor for three periods (1.29503) by the $1,000.

The demonstration problem in Illustration G-5 shows how to use Table 1.

TABLE 1   Future Value of 1

(n) Periods	4%	5%	6%	7%	8%	9%	10%	11%	12%	15%
0	1.00000	1.00000	1.00000	1.00000	1.00000	1.00000	1.00000	1.00000	1.00000	1.00000
1	1.04000	1.05000	1.06000	1.07000	1.08000	1.09000	1.10000	1.11000	1.12000	1.15000
2	1.08160	1.10250	1.12360	1.14490	1.16640	1.18810	1.21000	1.23210	1.25440	1.32250
3	1.12486	1.15763	1.19102	1.22504	1.25971	1.29503	1.33100	1.36763	1.40493	1.52088
4	1.16986	1.21551	1.26248	1.31080	1.36049	1.41158	1.46410	1.51807	1.57352	1.74901
5	1.21665	1.27628	1.33823	1.40255	1.46933	1.53862	1.61051	1.68506	1.76234	2.01136
6	1.26532	1.34010	1.41852	1.50073	1.58687	1.67710	1.77156	1.87041	1.97382	2.31306
7	1.31593	1.40710	1.50363	1.60578	1.71382	1.82804	1.94872	2.07616	2.21068	2.66002
8	1.36857	1.47746	1.59385	1.71819	1.85093	1.99256	2.14359	2.30454	2.47596	3.05902
9	1.42331	1.55133	1.68948	1.83846	1.99900	2.17189	2.35795	2.55803	2.77308	3.51788
10	1.48024	1.62889	1.79085	1.96715	2.15892	2.36736	2.59374	2.83942	3.10585	4.04556
11	1.53945	1.71034	1.89830	2.10485	2.33164	2.58043	2.85312	3.15176	3.47855	4.65239
12	1.60103	1.79586	2.01220	2.25219	2.51817	2.81267	3.13843	3.49845	3.89598	5.35025
13	1.66507	1.88565	2.13293	2.40985	2.71962	3.06581	3.45227	3.88328	4.36349	6.15279
14	1.73168	1.97993	2.26090	2.57853	2.93719	3.34173	3.79750	4.31044	4.88711	7.07571
15	1.80094	2.07893	2.39656	2.75903	3.17217	3.64248	4.17725	4.78459	5.47357	8.13706
16	1.87298	2.18287	2.54035	2.95216	3.42594	3.97031	4.59497	5.31089	6.13039	9.35762
17	1.94790	2.29202	2.69277	3.15882	3.70002	4.32763	5.05447	5.89509	6.86604	10.76126
18	2.02582	2.40662	2.85434	3.37993	3.99602	4.71712	5.55992	6.54355	7.68997	12.37545
19	2.10685	2.52695	3.02560	3.61653	4.31570	5.14166	6.11591	7.26334	8.61276	14.23177
20	2.19112	2.65330	3.20714	3.86968	4.66096	5.60441	6.72750	8.06231	9.64629	16.36654

Illustration G-5

Demonstration problem—
Using Table 1 for *FV* of 1

John and Mary Rich invested $20,000 in a savings account paying 6% interest at the time their son, Mike, was born. The money is to be used by Mike for his college education. On his 18th birthday, Mike withdraws the money from his savings account. How much did Mike withdraw from his account?

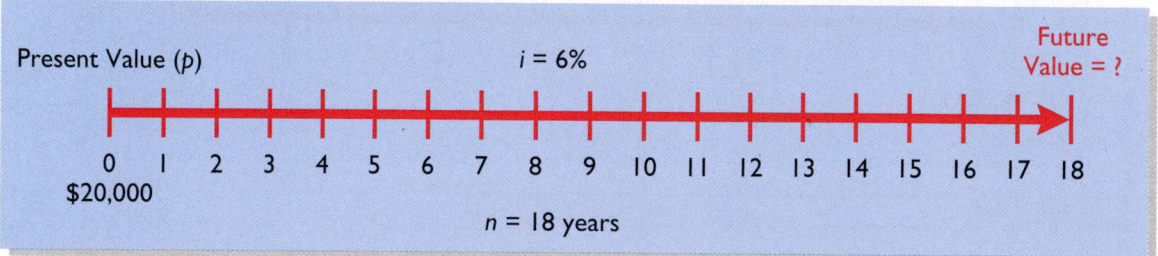

Present Value (p)   i = 6%   Future Value = ?

0 1 2 3 4 5 6 7 8 9 10 11 12 13 14 15 16 17 18

$20,000

n = 18 years

Answer: The future value factor from Table 1 is 2.85434 (18 periods at 6%). The future value of $20,000 earning 6% per year for 18 years is **$57,086.80** ($20,000 × 2.85434).

Future Value of an Annuity

The preceding discussion involved the accumulation of only a single principal sum. Individuals and businesses frequently encounter situations in which a

series of equal dollar amounts are to be paid or received at evenly spaced time intervals (periodically), such as loans or lease (rental) contracts. A series of payments or receipts of equal dollar amounts is referred to as an **annuity**.

The **future value of an annuity** is the sum of all the payments (receipts) plus the accumulated compound interest on them. In computing the future value of an annuity, it is necessary to know (1) the interest rate, (2) the number of payments (receipts), and (3) the amount of the periodic payments (receipts).

To illustrate the computation of the future value of an annuity, assume that you invest $2,000 at the end of each year for three years at 5% interest compounded annually. This situation is depicted in the time diagram in Illustration G-6.

Illustration G-6
Time diagram for a three-year annuity

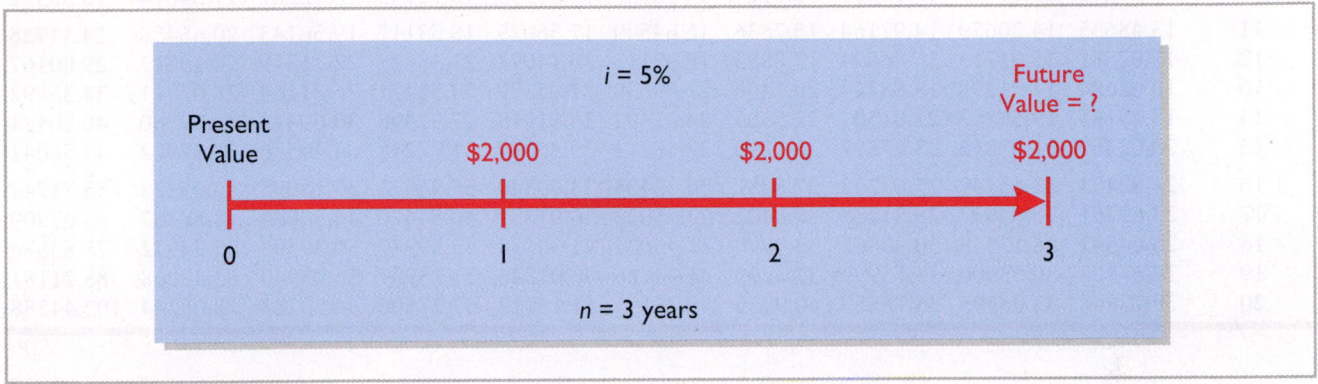

The $2,000 invested at the end of year 1 will earn interest for two years (years 2 and 3), and the $2,000 invested at the end of year 2 will earn interest for one year (year 3). However, the last $2,000 investment (made at the end of year 3) will not earn any interest. Using the future value factors from Table 1, the future value of these periodic payments is computed as shown in Illustration G-7.

Illustration G-7
Future value of periodic payment computation

Invested at End of Year	Number of Compounding Periods	Amount Invested	×	Future Value of 1 Factor at 5%	=	Future Value
1	2	$2,000		1.10250		$ 2,205
2	1	2,000		1.05000		2,100
3	0	2,000		1.00000		2,000
				3.15250		**$6,305**

The first $2,000 investment is multiplied by the future value factor for two periods (1.1025) because two years' interest will accumulate on it (in years 2 and 3). The second $2,000 investment will earn only one year's interest (in year 3) and therefore is multiplied by the future value factor for one year (1.0500). The final $2,000 investment is made at the end of the third year and will not earn any interest. Thus, $n = 0$ and the future value factor is 1.00000. Consequently, the future value of the last $2,000 invested is only $2,000 since it does not accumulate any interest.

Calculating the future value of each individual cash flow is required when the periodic payments or receipts are not equal in each period. However, when the periodic payments (receipts) are **the same in each period**, the future value can be computed by using a future value of an annuity of 1 table. Table 2 (page G-6) is such a table.

TABLE 2 Future Value of an Annuity of 1

(n) Payments	4%	5%	6%	7%	8%	9%	10%	11%	12%	15%
1	1.00000	1.00000	1.00000	1.0000	1.00000	1.00000	1.00000	1.00000	1.00000	1.00000
2	2.04000	2.05000	2.06000	2.0700	2.08000	2.09000	2.10000	2.11000	2.12000	2.15000
3	3.12160	3.15250	3.18360	3.2149	3.24640	3.27810	3.31000	3.34210	3.37440	3.47250
4	4.24646	4.31013	4.37462	4.4399	4.50611	4.57313	4.64100	4.70973	4.77933	4.99338
5	5.41632	5.52563	5.63709	5.7507	5.86660	5.98471	6.10510	6.22780	6.35285	6.74238
6	6.63298	6.80191	6.97532	7.1533	7.33592	7.52334	7.71561	7.91286	8.11519	8.75374
7	7.89829	8.14201	8.39384	8.6540	8.92280	9.20044	9.48717	9.78327	10.08901	11.06680
8	9.21423	9.54911	9.89747	10.2598	10.63663	11.02847	11.43589	11.85943	12.29969	13.72682
9	10.58280	11.02656	11.49132	11.9780	12.48756	13.02104	13.57948	14.16397	14.77566	16.78584
10	12.00611	12.57789	13.18079	13.8164	14.48656	15.19293	15.93743	16.72201	17.54874	20.30372
11	13.48635	14.20679	14.97164	15.7836	16.64549	17.56029	18.53117	19.56143	20.65458	24.34928
12	15.02581	15.91713	16.86994	17.8885	18.97713	20.14072	21.38428	22.71319	24.13313	29.00167
13	16.62684	17.71298	18.88214	20.1406	21.49530	22.95339	24.52271	26.21164	28.02911	34.35192
14	18.29191	19.59863	21.01507	22.5505	24.21492	26.01919	27.97498	30.09492	32.39260	40.50471
15	20.02359	21.57856	23.27597	25.1290	27.15211	29.36092	31.77248	34.40536	37.27972	47.58041
16	21.82453	23.65749	25.67253	27.8881	30.32428	33.00340	35.94973	39.18995	42.75328	55.71747
17	23.69751	25.84037	28.21288	30.8402	33.75023	36.97351	40.54470	44.50084	48.88367	65.07509
18	25.64541	28.13238	30.90565	33.9990	37.45024	41.30134	45.59917	50.39593	55.74972	75.83636
19	27.67123	30.53900	33.75999	37.3790	41.44626	46.01846	51.15909	56.93949	63.43968	88.21181
20	29.77808	33.06595	36.78559	40.9955	45.76196	51.16012	57.27500	64.20283	72.05244	102.44358

Table 2 shows the future value of 1 to be received periodically for a given number of payments. It assumes that each payment is made at the **end** of each period. We can see from Table 2 that the future value of an annuity of 1 factor for three payments at 5% is 3.15250. The future value factor is the total of the three individual future value factors as shown in Illustration G-7. Multiplying this amount by the annual investment of $2,000 produces a future value of $6,305. The demonstration problem in Illustration G-8 shows how to use Table 2.

Illustration G-8
Demonstration problem—
Using Table 2 for *FV* of an annuity of 1

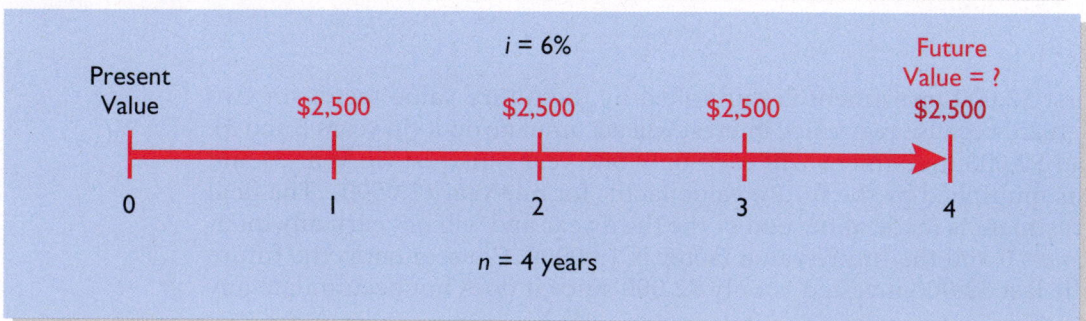

John and Char Lewis's daughter, Debra, has just started high school. They decide to start a college fund for her and will invest $2,500 in a savings account at the end of each year she is in high school (4 payments total). The account will earn 6% interest compounded annually. How much will be in the college fund at the time Debra graduates from high school?

Answer: The future value factor from Table 2 is 4.37462 (4 payments at 6%). The future value of $2,500 invested each year for 4 years at 6% interest is **$10,936.55** ($2,500 × 4.37462).

Present Value Variables

The **present value** is the value now of a given amount to be paid or received in the future, assuming compound interest. The present value, like the future value, is based on three variables: (1) the dollar amount to be received (future amount), (2) the length of time until the amount is received (number of periods), and (3) the interest rate (the discount rate). The process of determining the present value is referred to as **discounting the future amount**.

Present value computations are used in measuring many items. For example, the present value of principal and interest payments is used to determine the market price of a bond. Determining the amount to be reported for notes payable and lease liabilities also involves present value computations. In addition, capital budgeting and other investment proposals are evaluated using present value computations. Finally, all rate of return and internal rate of return computations involve present value techniques.

Present Value of a Single Amount

To illustrate present value, assume that you want to invest a sum of money today that will provide $1,000 at the end of one year. What amount would you need to invest today to have $1,000 one year from now? If you want a 10% rate of return, the investment or present value is $909.09 ($1,000 ÷ 1.10). The formula for calculating present value is shown in Illustration G-9.

Present Value (PV) = Future Value (FV) ÷ $(1 + i)^n$

Illustration G-9
Formula for present value

The computation of $1,000 discounted at 10% for one year is as follows.

$$
\begin{aligned}
PV &= FV \div (1 + i)^n \\
&= \$1,000 \div (1 + .10)^1 \\
&= \$1,000 \div 1.10 \\
&= \$909.09
\end{aligned}
$$

The future amount ($1,000), the discount rate (10%), and the number of periods (1) are known. The variables in this situation are depicted in the time diagram in Illustration G-10.

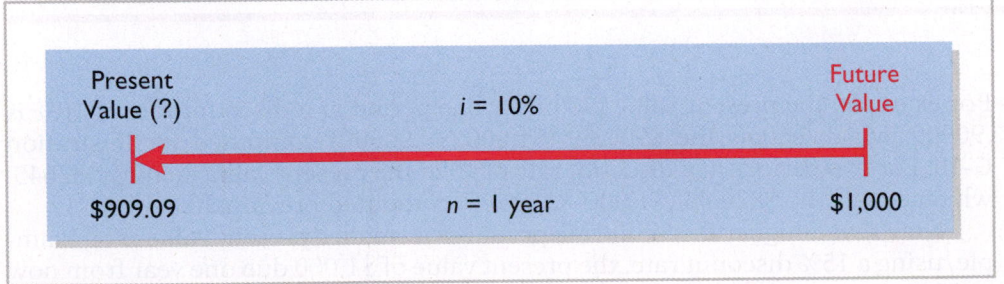

Illustration G-10
Finding present value if discounted for one period

Present Value (?)	$i = 10\%$	Future Value
$909.09	$n = 1$ year	$1,000

If the single amount of $1,000 is to be received **in two years** and discounted at 10% [$PV = \$1,000 \div (1 + .10)^2$], its present value is $826.45 [($1,000 ÷ 1.21), depicted in Illustration G-11 (page G-8).

Illustration G-11
Finding present value if
discounted for two periods

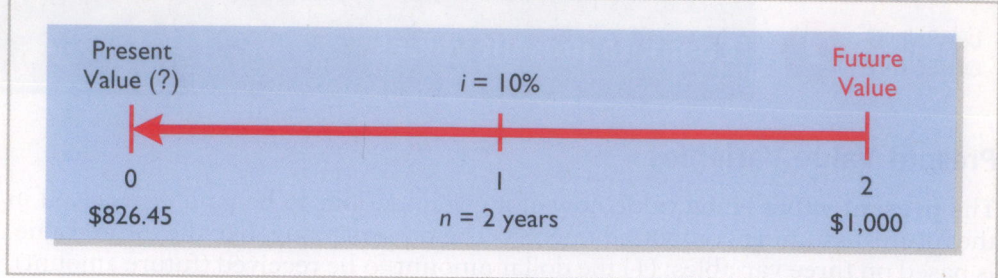

The present value of 1 may also be determined through tables that show the present value of 1 for *n* periods. In Table 3 (see below), *n* is the number of discounting periods involved. The percentages are the periodic interest rates or discount rates, and the 5-digit decimal numbers in the respective columns are the present value of 1 factors.

When using Table 3, the future value is multiplied by the present value factor specified at the intersection of the number of periods and the discount rate.

TABLE 3   Present Value of 1

(*n*) Periods	4%	5%	6%	7%	8%	9%	10%	11%	12%	15%
1	.96154	.95238	.94340	.93458	.92593	.91743	.90909	.90090	.89286	.86957
2	.92456	.90703	.89000	.87344	.85734	.84168	.82645	.81162	.79719	.75614
3	.88900	.86384	.83962	.81630	.79383	.77218	.75132	.73119	.71178	.65752
4	.85480	.82270	.79209	.76290	.73503	.70843	.68301	.65873	.63552	.57175
5	.82193	.78353	.74726	.71299	.68058	.64993	.62092	.59345	.56743	.49718
6	.79031	.74622	.70496	.66634	.63017	.59627	.56447	.53464	.50663	.43233
7	.75992	.71068	.66506	.62275	.58349	.54703	.51316	.48166	.45235	.37594
8	.73069	.67684	.62741	.58201	.54027	.50187	.46651	.43393	.40388	.32690
9	.70259	.64461	.59190	.54393	.50025	.46043	.42410	.39092	.36061	.28426
10	.67556	.61391	.55839	.50835	.46319	.42241	.38554	.35218	.32197	.24719
11	.64958	.58468	.52679	.47509	.42888	.38753	.35049	.31728	.28748	.21494
12	.62460	.55684	.49697	.44401	.39711	.35554	.31863	.28584	.25668	.18691
13	.60057	.53032	.46884	.41496	.36770	.32618	.28966	.25751	.22917	.16253
14	.57748	.50507	.44230	.38782	.34046	.29925	.26333	.23199	.20462	.14133
15	.55526	.48102	.41727	.36245	.31524	.27454	.23939	.20900	.18270	.12289
16	.53391	.45811	.39365	.33873	.29189	.25187	.21763	.18829	.16312	.10687
17	.51337	.43630	.37136	.31657	.27027	.23107	.19785	.16963	.14564	.09293
18	.49363	.41552	.35034	.29586	.25025	.21199	.17986	.15282	.13004	.08081
19	.47464	.39573	.33051	.27615	.23171	.19449	.16351	.13768	.11611	.07027
20	.45639	.37689	.31180	.25842	.21455	.17843	.14864	.12403	.10367	.06110

For example, the present value factor for one period at a discount rate of 10% is .90909, which equals the $909.09 ($1,000 × .90909) computed in Illustration G-10. For two periods at a discount rate of 10%, the present value factor is .82645, which equals the $826.45 ($1,000 × .82645) computed previously.

Note that a higher discount rate produces a smaller present value. For example, using a 15% discount rate, the present value of $1,000 due one year from now is $869.57, versus $909.09 at 10%. Also note that the further removed from the present the future value is, the smaller the present value. For example, using the same discount rate of 10%, the present value of $1,000 due in **five years** is $620.92. The present value of $1,000 due in **one year** is $909.09, a difference of $288.17.

The following two demonstration problems (Illustrations G-12 and G-13) illustrate how to use Table 3.

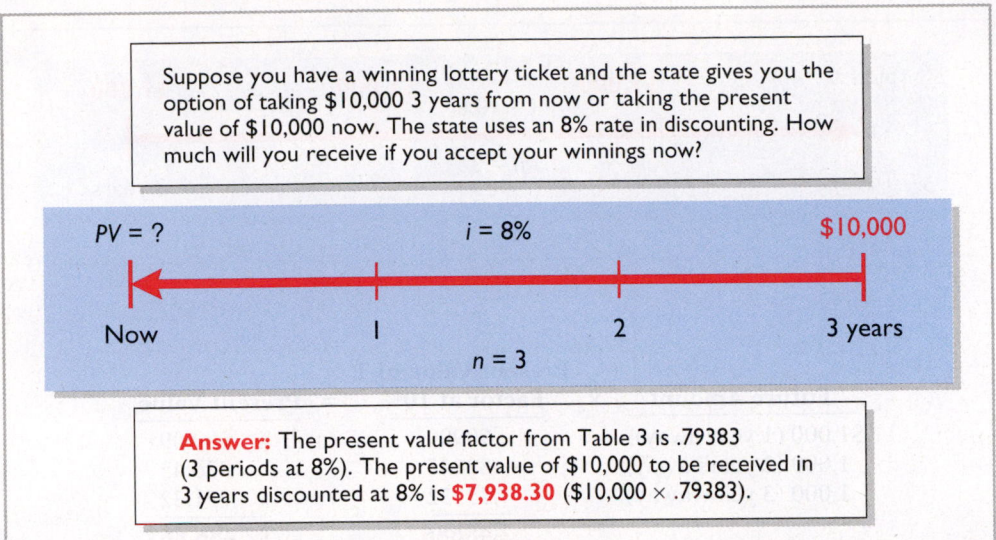

Illustration G-12
Demonstration problem—
Using Table 3 for *PV* of 1

Suppose you have a winning lottery ticket and the state gives you the option of taking $10,000 3 years from now or taking the present value of $10,000 now. The state uses an 8% rate in discounting. How much will you receive if you accept your winnings now?

PV = ?   *i* = 8% $10,000

Now   1   2   3 years
                n = 3

Answer: The present value factor from Table 3 is .79383 (3 periods at 8%). The present value of $10,000 to be received in 3 years discounted at 8% is **$7,938.30** ($10,000 × .79383).

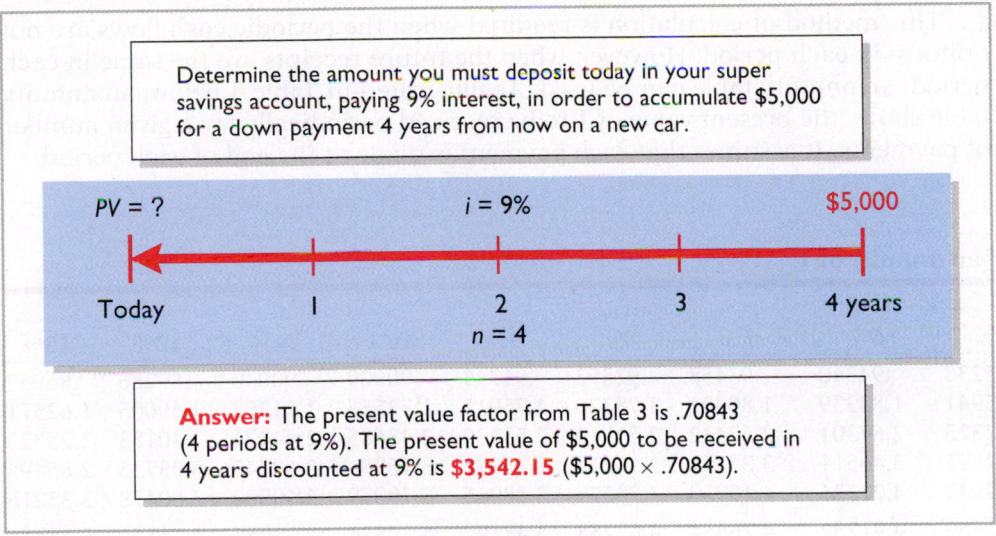

Illustration G-13
Demonstration problem—
Using Table 3 for *PV* of 1

Determine the amount you must deposit today in your super savings account, paying 9% interest, in order to accumulate $5,000 for a down payment 4 years from now on a new car.

PV = ?   *i* = 9% $5,000

Today   1   2   3   4 years
                  n = 4

Answer: The present value factor from Table 3 is .70843 (4 periods at 9%). The present value of $5,000 to be received in 4 years discounted at 9% is **$3,542.15** ($5,000 × .70843).

Present Value of an Annuity

The preceding discussion involved the discounting of only a single future amount. Businesses and individuals frequently engage in transactions in which a series of equal dollar amounts are to be received or paid at evenly spaced time intervals (periodically). Examples of a series of periodic receipts or payments are loan agreements, installment sales, mortgage notes, lease (rental) contracts, and pension obligations. As discussed earlier, these periodic receipts or payments are **annuities**.

The **present value of an annuity** is the value now of a series of future receipts or payments, discounted assuming compound interest. In computing the present value of an annuity, it is necessary to know (1) the discount rate, (2) the number of payments (receipts), and (3) the amount of the periodic receipts or payments. To illustrate the computation of the present value of an annuity, assume that you will receive $1,000 cash annually for three years at a time when the discount rate is 10%. This situation is depicted in the time diagram in Illustration G-14. Illustration G-15 shows the computation of its present value in this situation.

Illustration G-14
Time diagram for a three-year annuity

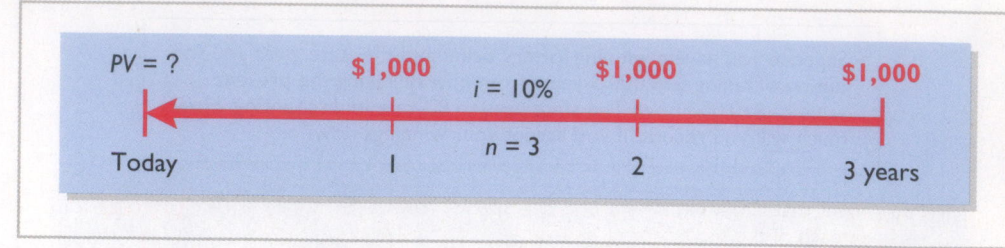

Illustration G-15
Present value of a series of future amounts computation

Future Amount	×	Present Value of 1 Factor at 10%	=	Present Value
$1,000 (1 year away)		.90909		$ 909.09
1,000 (2 years away)		.82645		826.45
1,000 (3 years away)		.75132		751.32
		2.48686		**$2,486.86**

This method of calculation is required when the periodic cash flows are not uniform in each period. However, when the future receipts are the same in each period, an annuity table can be used. As illustrated in Table 4 below, an annuity table shows the present value of 1 to be received periodically for a given number of payments. It assumes that each payment is made at the end of each period.

TABLE 4   Present Value of an Annuity of 1

(n) Payments	4%	5%	6%	7%	8%	9%	10%	11%	12%	15%
1	.96154	.95238	.94340	.93458	.92593	.91743	.90909	.90090	.89286	.86957
2	1.88609	1.85941	1.83339	1.80802	1.78326	1.75911	1.73554	1.71252	1.69005	1.62571
3	2.77509	2.72325	2.67301	2.62432	2.57710	2.53130	2.48685	2.44371	2.40183	2.28323
4	3.62990	3.54595	3.46511	3.38721	3.31213	3.23972	3.16986	3.10245	3.03735	2.85498
5	4.45182	4.32948	4.21236	4.10020	3.99271	3.88965	3.79079	3.69590	3.60478	3.35216
6	5.24214	5.07569	4.91732	4.76654	4.62288	4.48592	4.35526	4.23054	4.11141	3.78448
7	6.00205	5.78637	5.58238	5.38929	5.20637	5.03295	4.86842	4.71220	4.56376	4.16042
8	6.73274	6.46321	6.20979	5.97130	5.74664	5.53482	5.33493	5.14612	4.96764	4.48732
9	7.43533	7.10782	6.80169	6.51523	6.24689	5.99525	5.75902	5.53705	5.32825	4.77158
10	8.11090	7.72173	7.36009	7.02358	6.71008	6.41766	6.14457	5.88923	5.65022	5.01877
11	8.76048	8.30641	7.88687	7.49867	7.13896	6.80519	6.49506	6.20652	5.93770	5.23371
12	9.38507	8.86325	8.38384	7.94269	7.53608	7.16073	6.81369	6.49236	6.19437	5.42062
13	9.98565	9.39357	8.85268	8.35765	7.90378	7.48690	7.10336	6.74987	6.42355	5.58315
14	10.56312	9.89864	9.29498	8.74547	8.24424	7.78615	7.36669	6.98187	6.62817	5.72448
15	11.11839	10.37966	9.71225	9.10791	8.55948	8.06069	7.60608	7.19087	6.81086	5.84737
16	11.65230	10.83777	10.10590	9.44665	8.85137	8.31256	7.82371	7.37916	6.97399	5.95424
17	12.16567	11.27407	10.47726	9.76322	9.12164	8.54363	8.02155	7.54879	7.11963	6.04716
18	12.65930	11.68959	10.82760	10.05909	9.37189	8.75563	8.20141	7.70162	7.24967	6.12797
19	13.13394	12.08532	11.15812	10.33560	9.60360	8.95012	8.36492	7.83929	7.36578	6.19823
20	13.59033	12.46221	11.46992	10.59401	9.81815	9.12855	8.51356	7.96333	7.46944	6.25933

Table 4 shows that the present value of an annuity of 1 factor for three payments at 10% is 2.48685.[1] This present value factor is the total of the three individual present value factors, as shown in Illustration G-15. Applying this amount to the annual cash flow of $1,000 produces a present value of $2,486.85.

The following demonstration problem (Illustration G-16) illustrates how to use Table 4.

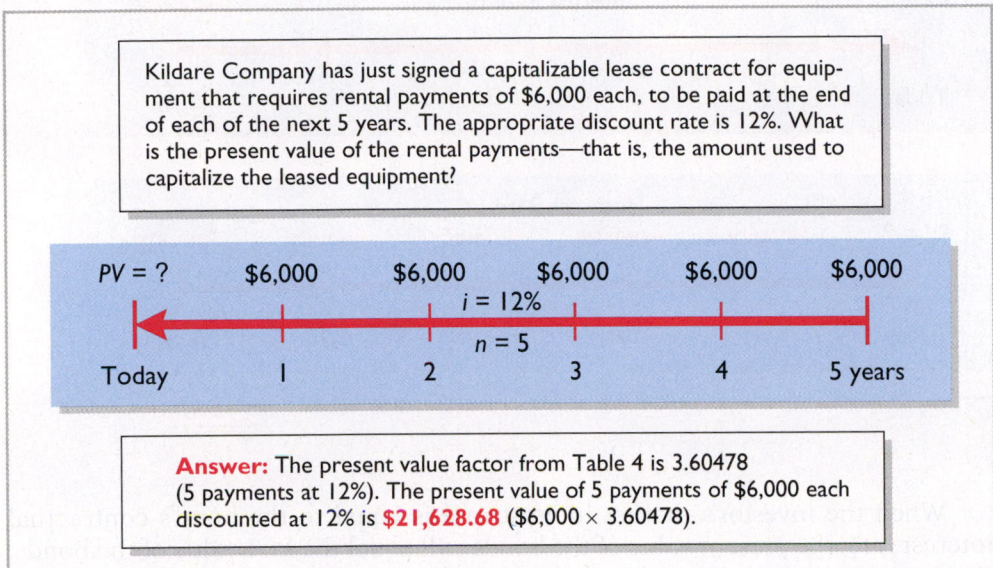

Illustration G-16
Demonstration problem—Using Table 4 for *PV* of an annuity of 1

Kildare Company has just signed a capitalizable lease contract for equipment that requires rental payments of $6,000 each, to be paid at the end of each of the next 5 years. The appropriate discount rate is 12%. What is the present value of the rental payments—that is, the amount used to capitalize the leased equipment?

PV = ? $6,000 $6,000 $6,000 $6,000 $6,000

i = 12%

n = 5

Today   1   2   3   4   5 years

Answer: The present value factor from Table 4 is 3.60478 (5 payments at 12%). The present value of 5 payments of $6,000 each discounted at 12% is **$21,628.68** ($6,000 × 3.60478).

Time Periods and Discounting

In the preceding calculations, the discounting was done on an annual basis using an annual interest rate. Discounting may also be done over shorter periods of time such as monthly, quarterly, or semiannually.

When the time frame is less than one year, it is necessary to convert the annual interest rate to the applicable time frame. Assume, for example, that the investor in Illustration G-14 received $500 **semiannually** for three years instead of $1,000 annually. In this case, the number of periods becomes six (3 × 2), the discount rate is 5% (10% ÷ 2), the present value factor from Table 4 is 5.07569 (6 periods at 5%), and the present value of the future cash flows is $2,537.85 (5.07569 × $500). This amount is slightly higher than the $2,486.86 computed in Illustration G-15 because interest is computed twice during the same year. That is, during the second half of the year, interest is earned on the first half-year's interest.

Present Value of a Long-Term Note or Bond

The present value (or market price) of a long-term note or bond is a function of three variables: (1) the payment amounts, (2) the length of time until the amounts are paid, and (3) the discount rate. Our example uses a five-year bond issue.

The first variable (dollars to be paid) is made up of two elements: (1) a series of interest payments (an annuity) and (2) the principal amount (a single sum). To

---

[1]The difference of .00001 between 2.48686 and 2.48685 is due to rounding.

compute the present value of the bond, both the interest payments and the principal amount must be discounted—two different computations. The time diagrams for a bond due in five years are shown in Illustration G-17.

Illustration G-17

Time diagrams for the present value of a bond

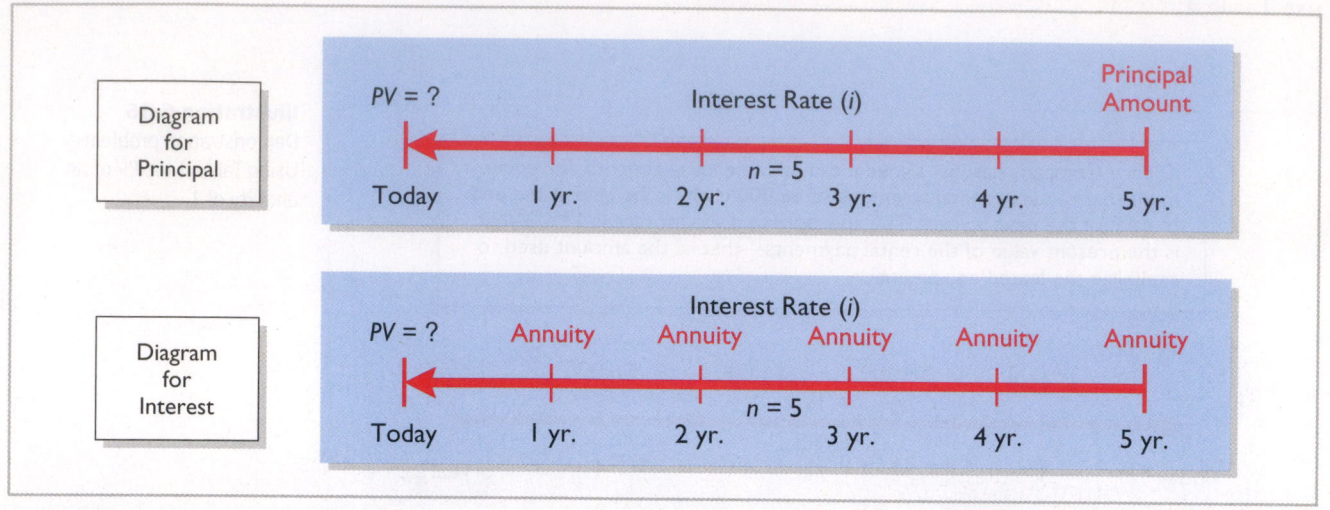

When the investor's market interest rate is equal to the bond's contractual interest rate, the present value of the bonds will equal the face value of the bonds. To illustrate, assume a bond issue of 10%, five-year bonds with a face value of $100,000 with interest payable **semiannually** on January 1 and July 1. If the discount rate is the same as the contractual rate, the bonds will sell at face value. In this case, the investor will receive (1) $100,000 at maturity and (2) a series of ten $5,000 interest payments [($100,000 × 10%) ÷ 2] over the term of the bonds. The length of time is expressed in terms of interest periods—in this case—10, and the discount rate per interest period, 5%. The following time diagram (Illustration G-18) depicts the variables involved in this discounting situation.

Illustration G-18

Time diagram for present value of a 10%, five-year bond paying interest semiannually

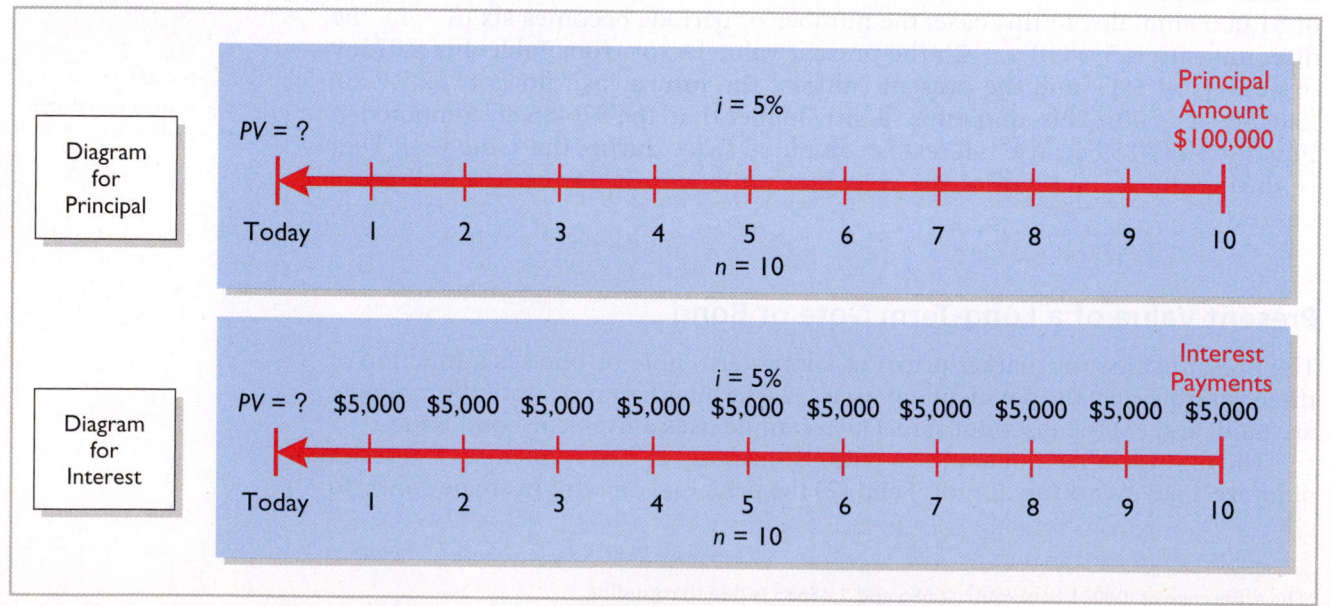

Illustration G-19 shows the computation of the present value of these bonds.

10% Contractual Rate—10% Discount Rate	
Present value of principal to be received at maturity	
$100,000 × *PV* of 1 due in 10 periods at 5%	
$100,000 × .61391 (Table 3)	$ 61,391
Present value of interest to be received periodically over the term of the bonds	
$5,000 × *PV* of 1 due periodically for 10 periods at 5%	
$5,000 × 7.72173 (Table 4)	38,609*
Present value of bonds	**$100,000**

*Rounded

Now assume that the investor's required rate of return is 12%, not 10%. The future amounts are again $100,000 and $5,000, respectively, but now a discount rate of 6% (12% ÷ 2) must be used. The present value of the bonds is $92,639, as computed in Illustration G-20.

10% Contractual Rate—12% Discount Rate	
Present value of principal to be received at maturity	
$100,000 × .55839 (Table 3)	$ 55,839
Present value of interest to be received periodically over the term of the bonds	
$5,000 × 7.36009 (Table 4)	36,800
Present value of bonds	**$92,639**

Conversely, if the discount rate is 8% and the contractual rate is 10%, the present value of the bonds is $108,111, computed as shown in Illustration G-21.

10% Contractual Rate—8% Discount Rate	
Present value of principal to be received at maturity	
$100,000 × .67556 (Table 3)	$ 67,556
Present value of interest to be received periodically over the term of the bonds	
$5,000 × 8.11090 (Table 4)	40,555
Present value of bonds	**$108,111**

The above discussion relied on present value tables in solving present value problems. Calculators may also be used to compute present values without the use of these tables. Many calculators, especially financial calculators, have present value (*PV*) functions that allow you to calculate present values by merely inputting the proper amount, discount rate, periods, and pressing the PV key. We discuss the use of financial calculators in a later section.

LEARNING
OBJECTIVE **3**

Compute the present value in capital budgeting situations.

The decision to make long-term capital investments is best evaluated using discounting techniques that recognize the time value of money. To do this, many companies calculate the present value of the cash flows involved in a capital investment.

To illustrate, Nagel-Siebert Trucking Company, a cross-country freight carrier in Montgomery, Illinois, is considering adding another truck to its fleet because of a purchasing opportunity. Navistar Inc., Nagel-Siebert's primary supplier of overland rigs, is overstocked and offers to sell its biggest rig for $154,000 cash payable upon delivery. Nagel-Siebert knows that the rig will produce a net cash flow per year of $40,000 for five years (received at the end of each year), at which time it will be sold for an estimated salvage value of $35,000. Nagel-Siebert's discount rate in evaluating capital expenditures is 10%. Should Nagel-Siebert commit to the purchase of this rig?

The cash flows that must be discounted to present value by Nagel-Siebert are as follows.

Cash payable on delivery (today): $154,000.

Net cash flow from operating the rig: $40,000 for 5 years (at the end of each year).

Cash received from sale of rig at the end of 5 years: $35,000.

The time diagrams for the latter two cash flows are shown in Illustration G-22.

Illustration G-22
Time diagrams for Nagel-Siebert Trucking Company

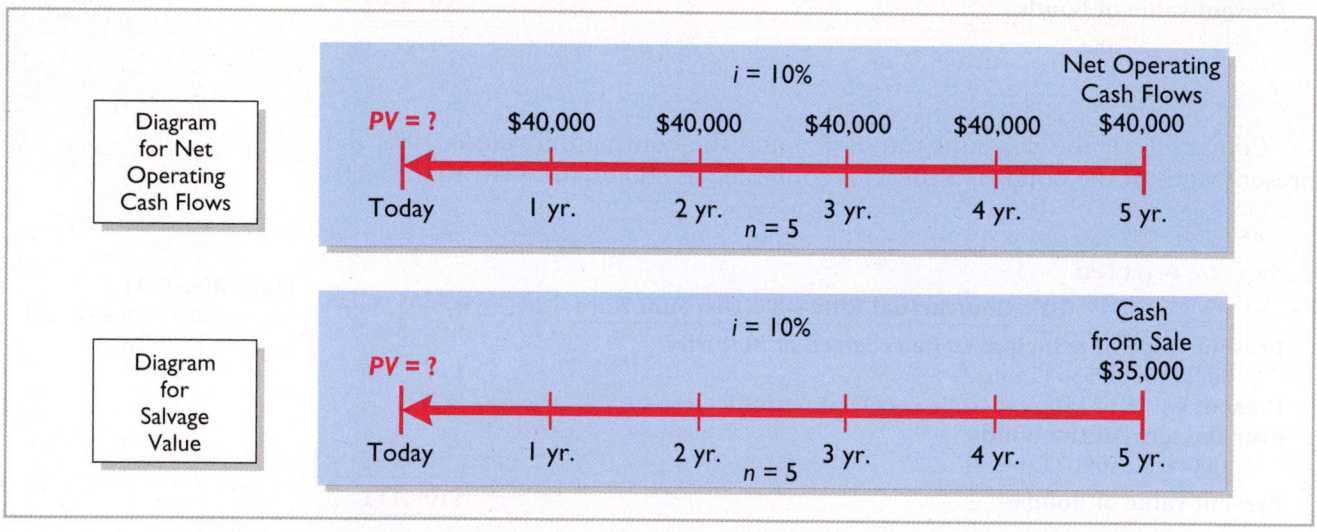

Notice from the diagrams that computing the present value of the net operating cash flows ($40,000 at the end of each year) is **discounting an annuity** (Table 4), while computing the present value of the $35,000 salvage value is **discounting a single sum** (Table 3). The computation of these present values is shown in Illustration G-23.

Present Values Using a 10% Discount Rate

Present value of net operating cash flows received annually over 5 years

$40,000 × PV of 1 received annually for 5 years at 10%

$40,000 × 3.79079 (Table 4) $ 151,631.60

Present value of salvage value (cash) to be received in 5 years

$35,000 × PV of 1 received in 5 years at 10%

$35,000 × .62092 (Table 3)   21,732.20

Present value of cash **inflows**   173,363.80

Present value of cash **outflows** (purchase price due today at 10%)

$154,000 × PV of 1 due today

$154,000 × 1.00000   (154,000.00)

Net present value   **$ 19,363.80**

Because the present value of the cash receipts (inflows) of $173,363.80 ($151,631.60 + $21,732.20) exceeds the present value of the cash payments (outflows) of $154,000.00, the net present value of $19,363.80 is positive, and **the decision to invest should be accepted**.

Now assume that Nagle-Siebert uses a discount rate of 15%, not 10%, because it wants a greater return on its investments in capital assets. The cash receipts and cash payments by Nagel-Siebert are the same. The present values of these receipts and cash payments discounted at 15% are shown in Illustration G-24.

Present Values Using a 15% Discount Rate

Present value of net operating cash flows received annually
over 5 years at 15%

$40,000 × 3.35216 (Table 4) $ 134,086.40

Present value of salvage value (cash) to be received in 5 years at 15%

$35,000 × .49718 (Table 3)   17,401.30

Present value of cash **inflows**   151,487.70

Present value of cash **outflows** (purchase price due today at 15%)

$154,000 × 1.00000   (154,000.00)

Net present value   **$ (2,512.30)**

Because the present value of the cash payments (outflows) of $154,000.00 exceeds the present value of the cash receipts (inflows) of $151,487.70 ($134,086.40 + $17,401.30), the net present value of $2,512.30 is negative, and **the investment should be rejected**.

The above discussion relied on present value tables in solving present value problems. As we show in the next section, calculators may also be used to compute present values without the use of these tables. Financial calculators have present value (PV) functions that allow you to calculate present values by merely identifying the proper amount, discount rate, periods, and pressing the PV key.

LEARNING OBJECTIVE **4**   **Use a financial calculator to solve time value of money problems.**

Business professionals, once they have mastered the underlying time value of money concepts, often use a financial calculator to solve these types of problems. In most cases, they use calculators if interest rates or time periods do not correspond with the information provided in the compound interest tables.

To use financial calculators, you enter the time value of money variables into the calculator. Illustration G-25 shows the five most common keys used to solve time value of money problems.[2]

Illustration G-25
Financial calculator keys

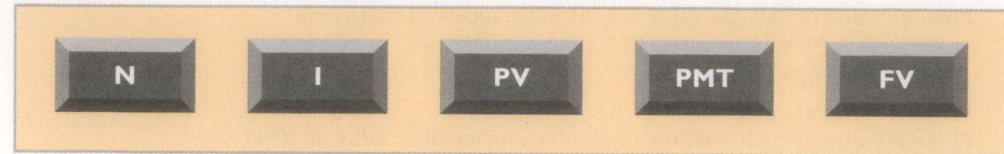

where:

N	=	number of periods
I	=	interest rate per period (some calculators use I/YR or i)
PV	=	present value (occurs at the beginning of the first period)
PMT	=	payment (all payments are equal, and none are skipped)
FV	=	future value (occurs at the end of the last period)

In solving time value of money problems in this appendix, you will generally be given three of four variables and will have to solve for the remaining variable. The fifth key (the key not used) is given a value of zero to ensure that this variable is not used in the computation.

Present Value of a Single Sum

To illustrate how to solve a present value problem using a financial calculator, assume that you want to know the present value of $84,253 to be received in five years, discounted at 11% compounded annually. Illustration G-26 depicts this problem.

Illustration G-26
Calculator solution for present value of a single sum

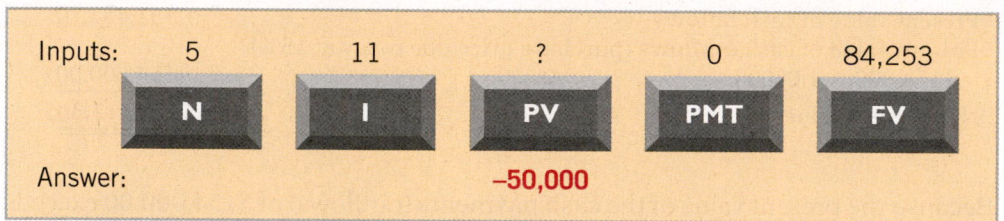

Illustration G-26 shows you the information (inputs) to enter into the calculator: N = 5, I = 11, PMT = 0, and FV = 84,253. You then press PV for the answer: −$50,000. As indicated, the PMT key was given a value of zero because a series of payments did not occur in this problem.

PLUS AND MINUS

The use of plus and minus signs in time value of money problems with a financial calculator can be confusing. Most financial calculators are programmed so that the positive and negative cash flows in any problem offset each other. In the present value problem above, we identified the $84,253 future value initial investment as a positive (inflow); the answer −$50,000 was shown as a negative amount, reflecting a cash outflow. If the 84,253 were entered as a negative, then the final answer would have been reported as a positive 50,000.

Hopefully, the sign convention will not cause confusion. If you understand what is required in a problem, you should be able to interpret a positive or negative amount in determining the solution to a problem.

---

[2]On many calculators, these keys are actual buttons on the face of the calculator; on others, they appear on the display after the user accesses a present value menu.

COMPOUNDING PERIODS

In the previous problem, we assumed that compounding occurs once a year. Some financial calculators have a default setting, which assumes that compounding occurs 12 times a year. You must determine what default period has been programmed into your calculator and change it as necessary to arrive at the proper compounding period.

ROUNDING

Most financial calculators store and calculate using 12 decimal places. As a result, because compound interest tables generally have factors only up to five decimal places, a slight difference in the final answer can result. In most time value of money problems, the final answer will not include more than two decimal places.

Present Value of an Annuity

To illustrate how to solve a present value of an annuity problem using a financial calculator, assume that you are asked to determine the present value of rental receipts of $6,000 each to be received at the end of each of the next five years, when discounted at 12%, as pictured in Illustration G-27.

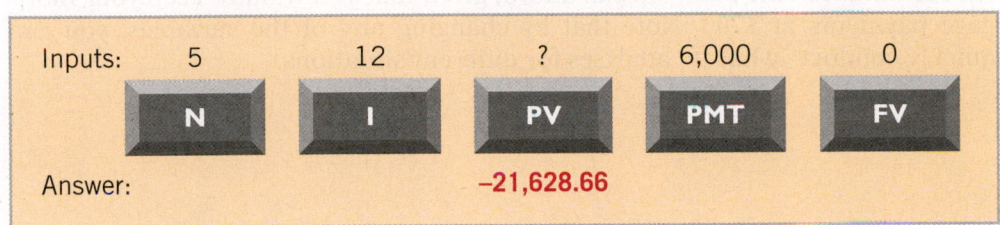

Illustration G-27
Calculator solution for present value of an annuity

In this case, you enter N = 5, I = 12, PMT = 6,000, FV = 0, and then press PV to arrive at the answer of −$21,628.66.

Useful Applications of the Financial Calculator

With a financial calculator, you can solve for any interest rate or for any number of periods in a time value of money problem. Here are some examples of these applications.

AUTO LOAN

Assume you are financing the purchase of a used car with a three-year loan. The loan has a 9.5% stated annual interest rate, compounded monthly. The price of the car is $6,000, and you want to determine the monthly payments, assuming that the payments start one month after the purchase. This problem is pictured in Illustration G-28.

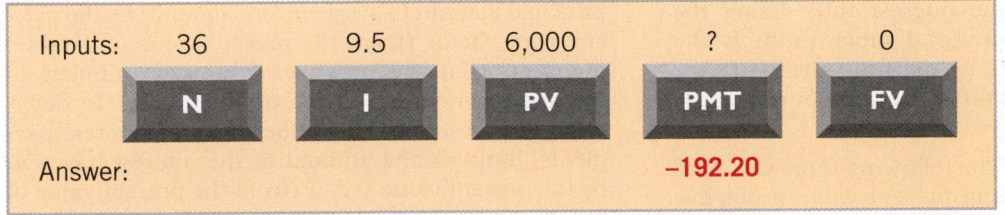

Illustration G-28
Calculator solution for auto loan payments

To solve this problem, you enter N = 36 (12 × 3), I = 9.5, PV = 6,000, FV = 0, and then press PMT. You will find that the monthly payments will be $192.20. Note that the payment key is usually programmed for 12 payments per year. Thus, you must change the default (compounding period) if the payments are other than monthly.

MORTGAGE LOAN AMOUNT

Say you are evaluating financing options for a loan on a house (a mortgage). You decide that the maximum mortgage payment you can afford is $700 per month. The annual interest rate is 8.4%. If you get a mortgage that requires you to make monthly payments over a 15-year period, what is the maximum home loan you can afford? Illustration G-29 depicts this problem.

Illustration G-29
Calculator solution for mortgage amount

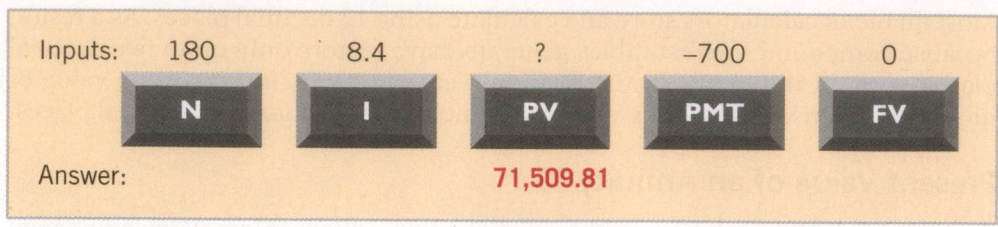

Inputs:	180	8.4	?	−700	0
	N	I	PV	PMT	FV

Answer: 71,509.81

You enter N = 180 (12 × 15 years), I = 8.4, PMT = −700, FV = 0, and press PV. With the payments-per-year key set at 12, you find a present value of $71,509.81— the maximum home loan you can afford, given that you want to keep your mortgage payments at $700. Note that by changing any of the variables, you can quickly conduct "what-if" analyses for different situations.

REVIEW

▌ LEARNING OBJECTIVES REVIEW

❶ Compute interest and future values. Simple interest is computed on the principal only, while compound interest is computed on the principal and any interest earned that has not been withdrawn.

To solve for future value of a single amount, prepare a time diagram of the problem. Identify the principal amount, the number of compounding periods, and the interest rate. Using the future value of 1 table, multiply the principal amount by the future value factor specified at the intersection of the number of periods and the interest rate.

To solve for future value of an annuity, prepare a time diagram of the problem. Identify the amount of the periodic payments (receipts), the number of payments (receipts), and the interest rate. Using the future value of an annuity of 1 table, multiply the amount of the payments by the future value factor specified at the intersection of the number of periods and the interest rate.

❷ Compute present value. The following three variables are fundamental to solving present value problems: (1) the future amount, (2) the number of periods, and (3) the interest rate (the discount rate).

To solve for present value of a single amount, prepare a time diagram of the problem. Identify the future amount, the number of discounting periods, and the discount (interest) rate. Using the present value of a single amount table, multiply the future amount by the present value factor specified at the intersection of the number of periods and the discount rate.

To solve for present value of an annuity, prepare a time diagram of the problem. Identify the amount of future periodic receipts or payments (annuities), the number of payments (receipts), and the discount (interest) rate. Using the present value of an annuity of 1 table, multiply the amount of the annuity by the present value factor specified at the intersection of the number of payments and the interest rate.

To compute the present value of notes and bonds, determine the present value of the principal amount and the present value of the interest payments. Multiply the principal amount (a single future amount) by the present value factor (from the present value of 1 table) intersecting at the number of periods (number of interest payments) and the discount rate. To determine the present value of the series of interest payments, multiply the amount of the interest payment by the present value factor (from the present value of an annuity of 1 table) intersecting at the number of periods (number of interest payments) and the discount rate. Add the present value of the principal amount to the present value of the interest payments to arrive at the present value of the note or bond.

❸ Compute the present value in capital budgeting situations. Compute the present values of all cash inflows and all cash outflows related to the capital budgeting proposal (an investment-type decision). If the **net** present value is positive, accept the proposal (make the investment). If the **net** present value is negative, reject the proposal (do not make the investment).

4 Use a financial calculator to solve time value of money problems. Financial calculators can be used to solve the same and additional problems as those solved with time value of money tables. Enter into the financial calculator the amounts for all of the known elements of a time value of money problem (periods, interest rate, payments, future or present value), and it solves for the unknown element. Particularly useful situations involve interest rates and compounding periods not presented in the tables.

GLOSSARY REVIEW

Annuity A series of equal dollar amounts to be paid or received at evenly spaced time intervals (periodically). (p. G-5).

Compound interest The interest computed on the principal and any interest earned that has not been paid or withdrawn. (p. G-2).

Discounting the future amount(s) The process of determining present value. (p. G-7).

Future value of an annuity The sum of all the payments (receipts) plus the accumulated compound interest on them. (p. G-5).

Future value of a single amount The value at a future date of a given amount invested, assuming compound interest. (p. G-3).

Interest Payment for the use of another person's money. (p. G-1).

Present value The value now of a given amount to be paid or received in the future, assuming compound interest. (p. G-7).

Present value of an annuity The value now of a series of future receipts or payments, discounted assuming compound interest. (p. G-9).

Principal The amount borrowed or invested. (p. G-1).

Simple interest The interest computed on the principal only. (p. G-2).

WileyPLUS

Brief Exercises and many additional resources are available for practice in WileyPLUS

BRIEF EXERCISES

(Use tables to solve exercises BEG-1 to BEG-23.)

BEG-1 Jozy Altidore invested $6,000 at 5% annual interest, and left the money invested without withdrawing any of the interest for 12 years. At the end of the 12 years, Jozy withdrew the accumulated amount of money. (a) What amount did Jozy withdraw, assuming the investment earns simple interest? (b) What amount did Jozy withdraw, assuming the investment earns interest compounded annually?

Compute the future value of a single amount.

(LO 1)

BEG-2 For each of the following cases, indicate (a) what interest rate columns and (b) what number of periods you would refer to in looking up the future value factor.

Use future value tables.

(LO 1)

(1) In Table 1 (future value of 1):

	Annual Rate	Number of Years Invested	Compounded
Case A	5%	3	Annually
Case B	12%	4	Semiannually

(2) In Table 2 (future value of an annuity of 1):

	Annual Rate	Number of Years Invested	Compounded
Case A	3%	8	Annually
Case B	8%	6	Semiannually

Compute the future value of a single amount.

(LO 1)

BEG-3 Liam Company signed a lease for an office building for a period of 12 years. Under the lease agreement, a security deposit of $9,600 is made. The deposit will be returned at the expiration of the lease with interest compounded at 4% per year. What amount will Liam receive at the time the lease expires?

Compute the future value of an annuity.

(LO 1)

BEG-4 Bates Company issued $1,000,000, 10-year bonds and agreed to make annual sinking fund deposits of $78,000. The deposits are made at the end of each year into an account paying 6% annual interest. What amount will be in the sinking fund at the end of 10 years?

Compute the future value of a single amount and of an annuity.

(LO 1)

BEG-5 Andrew and Emma Garfield invested $8,000 in a savings account paying 5% annual interest when their daughter, Angela, was born. They also deposited $1,000 on each of her birthdays until she was 18 (including her 18th birthday). How much was in the savings account on her 18th birthday (after the last deposit)?

Compute the future value of a single amount.

(LO 1)

BEG-6 Hugh Curtin borrowed $35,000 on July 1, 2017. This amount plus accrued interest at 8% compounded annually is to be repaid on July 1, 2022. How much will Hugh have to repay on July 1, 2022?

Use present value tables.

(LO 2)

BEG-7 For each of the following cases, indicate (a) what interest rate columns and (b) what number of periods you would refer to in looking up the discount rate.

(1) In Table 3 (present value of 1):

	Annual Rate	Number of Years Involved	Discounts per Year
Case A	12%	7	Annually
Case B	8%	11	Annually
Case C	10%	8	Semiannually

(2) In Table 4 (present value of an annuity of 1):

	Annual Rate	Number of Years Involved	Number of Payments Involved	Frequency of Payments
Case A	10%	20	20	Annually
Case B	10%	7	7	Annually
Case C	6%	5	10	Semiannually

Determine present values.

(LO 2)

BEG-8 (a) What is the present value of $25,000 due 9 periods from now, discounted at 10%?
(b) What is the present value of $25,000 to be received at the end of each of 6 periods, discounted at 9%?

Compute the present value of a single amount investment.

(LO 2)

BEG-9 Messi Company is considering an investment that will return a lump sum of $900,000 6 years from now. What amount should Messi Company pay for this investment to earn an 8% return?

Compute the present value of a single amount investment.

(LO 2)

BEG-10 Lloyd Company earns 6% on an investment that will return $450,000 8 years from now. What is the amount Lloyd should invest now to earn this rate of return?

Compute the present value of an annuity investment.

(LO 2)

BEG-11 Robben Company is considering investing in an annuity contract that will return $40,000 annually at the end of each year for 15 years. What amount should Robben Company pay for this investment if it earns an 8% return?

Compute the present value of an annual investment.

(LO 2)

BEG-12 Kaehler Enterprises earns 5% on an investment that pays back $80,000 at the end of each of the next 6 years. What is the amount Kaehler Enterprises invested to earn the 5% rate of return?

Compute the present value of bonds.

(LO 2)

BEG-13 Dempsey Railroad Co. is about to issue $400,000 of 10-year bonds paying an 11% interest rate, with interest payable semiannually. The discount rate for such securities is 10%. How much can Dempsey expect to receive for the sale of these bonds?

BEG-14 Assume the same information as BEG-13 except that the discount rate is 12% instead of 10%. In this case, how much can Dempsey expect to receive from the sale of these bonds?

Compute the present value of bonds.
(LO 2)

BEG-15 Neymar Taco Company receives a $75,000, 6-year note bearing interest of 4% (paid annually) from a customer at a time when the discount rate is 6%. What is the present value of the note received by Neymar?

Compute the present value of a note.
(LO 2)

BEG-16 Gleason Enterprises issued 6%, 8-year, $2,500,000 par value bonds that pay interest semiannually on October 1 and April 1. The bonds are dated April 1, 2017, and are issued on that date. The discount rate of interest for such bonds on April 1, 2017, is 8%. What cash proceeds did Gleason receive from issuance of the bonds?

Compute the present value of bonds.
(LO 2)

BEG-17 Frazier Company issues a 10%, 5-year mortgage note on January 1, 2017, to obtain financing for new equipment. Land is used as collateral for the note. The terms provide for semiannual installment payments of $48,850. What are the cash proceeds received from the issuance of the note?

Compute the present value of a note.
(LO 2)

BEG-18 If Colleen Mooney invests $4,765.50 now and she will receive $12,000 at the end of 12 years, what annual rate of interest will Colleen earn on her investment? (*Hint:* Use Table 3.)

Compute the interest rate on a single amount.
(LO 2)

BEG-19 Tim Howard has been offered the opportunity of investing $36,125 now. The investment will earn 11% per year and at the end of that time will return Tim $75,000. How many years must Tim wait to receive $75,000? (*Hint:* Use Table 3.)

Compute the number of periods of a single amount.
(LO 2)

BEG-20 Joanne Quick made an investment of $10,271.38. From this investment, she will receive $1,200 annually for the next 15 years starting one year from now. What rate of interest will Joanne's investment be earning for her? (*Hint:* Use Table 4.)

Compute the interest rate on an annuity.
(LO 2)

BEG-21 Kevin Morales invests $7,793.83 now for a series of $1,300 annual returns beginning one year from now. Kevin will earn a return of 9% on the initial investment. How many annual payments of $1,300 will Kevin receive? (*Hint:* Use Table 4.)

Compute the number of periods of an annuity.
(LO 2)

BEG-22 Barney Googal owns a garage and is contemplating purchasing a tire retreading machine for $12,820. After estimating costs and revenues, Barney projects a net cash inflow from the retreading machine of $2,700 annually for 7 years. Barney hopes to earn a return of 9% on such investments. What is the present value of the retreading operation? Should Barney Googal purchase the retreading machine?

Compute the present value of a machine for purposes of making a purchase decision.
(LO 3)

BEG-23 Snyder Company is considering purchasing equipment. The equipment will produce the following cash inflows: Year 1, $25,000; Year 2, $30,000; and Year 3, $40,000. Snyder requires a minimum rate of return of 11%. What is the maximum price Snyder should pay for this equipment?

Compute the maximum price to pay for a machine.
(LO 3)

BEG-24 Carly Simon wishes to invest $18,000 on July 1, 2017, and have it accumulate to $50,000 by July 1, 2027. Use a financial calculator to determine at what exact annual rate of interest Carly must invest the $18,000.

Determine interest rate.
(LO 4)

BEG-25 On July 17, 2016, Keith Urban borrowed $42,000 from his grandfather to open a clothing store. Starting July 17, 2017, Keith has to make 10 equal annual payments of $6,500 each to repay the loan. Use a financial calculator to determine what interest rate Keith is paying.

Determine interest rate.
(LO 4)

BEG-26 As the purchaser of a new house, Carrie Underwood has signed a mortgage note to pay the Nashville National Bank and Trust Co. $8,400 every 6 months for 20 years, at the end of which time she will own the house. At the date the mortgage is signed, the purchase price was $198,000 and Underwood made a down payment of $20,000. The first payment will be made 6 months after the date the mortgage is signed. Using a financial calculator, compute the exact rate of interest earned on the mortgage by the bank.

Determine interest rate.
(LO 4)

Various time value of money situations.

(LO 4)

BEG-27 Using a financial calculator, solve for the unknowns in each of the following situations.

(a) On June 1, 2016, Jennifer Lawrence purchases lakefront property from her neighbor, Josh Hutcherson, and agrees to pay the purchase price in seven payments of $16,000 each, the first payment to be payable June 1, 2017. (Assume that interest compounded at an annual rate of 7.35% is implicit in the payments.) What is the purchase price of the property?

(b) On January 1, 2016, Gerrard Corporation purchased 200 of the $1,000 face value, 8% coupon, 10-year bonds of Sterling Inc. The bonds mature on January 1, 2026, and pay interest annually beginning January 1, 2017. Gerrard purchased the bonds to yield 10.65%. How much did Gerrard pay for the bonds?

Various time value of money situations.

(LO 4)

BEG-28 Using a financial calculator, provide a solution to each of the following situations.

(a) Lynn Anglin owes a debt of $42,000 from the purchase of her new sport utility vehicle. The debt bears annual interest of 7.8% compounded monthly. Lynn wishes to pay the debt and interest in equal monthly payments over 8 years, beginning one month hence. What equal monthly payments will pay off the debt and interest?

(b) On January 1, 2017, Roger Molony offers to buy Dave Feeney's used snowmobile for $8,000, payable in five equal annual installments, which are to include 7.25% interest on the unpaid balance and a portion of the principal. If the first payment is to be made on December 31, 2017, how much will each payment be?

Company Index

A

Ace Hardware, 281
Adelphia, 10
adidas, 498, 728
Advanced Micro Devices, 505, 796
Ag-Chem, 333
Ahold NV, 148, 354
AIG, 7
Alaskan Airlines, 794
Allegiant Airlines, 725
Alliance Atlantis Communications Inc., 640
Aluminum Company of America (Alcoa), 547
Amazon.com, Inc., 4, 43, 88, 145, 198, 206, 208, 253, 302, 351, 391, 438, 493, 552, 594, 653, 705, 727, 884, 928, 980, 1063
American Airlines, 713, 857
American Cancer Society, 500
American Express, 361, 367, 444, 976
American LaFrance, 754
American Van Lines, 1111
Anheuser-Busch InBev, 274
Anytime Fitness, 971
Apple Inc., 4, 5, 10, 42, 78, 87, 144, 184, 197, 203, 239, 253, 289, 302, 340, 351, 381, 414, 438, 455, 492, 500, 529, 552, 554, 584, 594, 598, 639, 653, 689, 704, 1015
Armani, 1014
Armour, 982
AT&T, 4, 567, 713, 887
Avis, 396, 403

B

Baan NV, 148
BabyCakes NYC, 1056, 1060
Bank of America, 366
Bank One Corporation, 70
Barriques, 306
Ben & Jerry's, 754, 800
Berkshire Hathaway, 523
Best Buy, 9, 105, 121, 255, 413
Beverly Hills Fan Company, 1009
BHP Billiton, 413
Bill and Melinda Gates Foundation, 25

Bob's Red Mill, 1056
Boeing Capital Corporation, 401
Boeing Co., 410, 453, 671, 724, 727, 754, 979
Boise Cascade, 406
BorderStylo LLC, 416
Box, 612
BP, 271
Briggs and Stratton, 1132
BrightFarms, 888
Bristol-Myers Squibb, 269
Buck Knives, 988
Budget, 396
Burlington Northern Railroad, 938
Burton Snowboards, 718
Button Worldwide, 1023

C

Campbell Soup Company, 269, 405, 713, 1218, 1238
Capt'n Eli Root Beer Company, 198
Cargill Inc., 500
Carnival Corporation, 1204
Caterpillar Inc., 258, 260, 271, 464, 465, 500, 717, 800, 858
CBS, 415
Center Ice Consultants, 796
Chase, 70, 1176
Cheerwine, 198
Chevron, 406
ChevronTexaco, 1014
Chicago Bears, 53
Chicago Cubs, 53
Chrysler, 1173
Cisco Systems, 161, 302, 374, 682, 935, 1119
Citicorp, 11
Citigroup, 10
Clark Equipment Company, 849
Clark-Hurth, 849
Clarus Technologies, 1055
Clif Bar & Company, 2, 45
The Coca-Cola Company, 4, 43, 46, 88, 145, 198, 253, 302, 351, 391, 438, 493, 552, 578, 594, 653, 705, 717, 728, 794, 1132
Columbia Sportswear Company, 641
Commonwealth Edison, 518

Compumotor, 849
Computer Associates International, Inc., 98, 1154
ConAgra Foods, 222, 515
ConocoPhilips, 413
Conservation International, 1173
Consolidated Edison, 671
Continental Bank, 401
Cooper Tire & Rubber Company, 170
Costco Wholesale Corp., 216, 602
Countrywide Financial Corporation, 373
Craig Consumer Electronics, 262
Credit Suisse Group, 59
Crocs, Inc., 10
Current Designs, 710, 712, 713, 716, 717, 721, 747, 790, 835, 967, 1006, 1051, 1100, 1151, 1199, 1236
Curves, 971
Cyan, 612
Cypress Semiconductor Corporation, 640

D

Dell, 61, 260, 713, 726, 858, 1204
Dell Financial Services, 401
Del Monte Foods Company, 969
Delta Air Lines, 96, 104, 334, 410, 985, 1175
Dewey & LeBoeuf LLP, 8
Dick's Sporting Goods, 720
Discover, 366
Disney, *see* Walt Disney Company
Dow Chemical, 717, 796
Duke Energy Co., 887, 1111, 1124
Dun & Bradstreet, 660
DuPont Co., 358, 452, 454, 796

E

Earthlink, 517
Eastman Kodak, 562, 598
eBay, 223
Eli Lilly, 309, 1132
Enron, 7, 25, 223, 501, 713
Ethan Allen, 981
E*Trade, 935
ExxonMobil Corporation, 10, 271, 754, 796, 982, 1014, 1204

F

Facebook, 4, 715, 938
Fannie Mae, 70, 108
FedEx Corporation, 713, 969
Fiat/Chrysler, 46
Fireeye, 612
Flightserve, 899
Ford Motor Company, 10, 11, 207, 261, 274, 358, 413, 461, 809, 929, 1015, 1124
Fox Broadcasting, 415, 1114

G

Gap Inc., 10
General Dynamics Corp., 679
General Electric (GE), 6, 214, 358, 515, 715, 728, 770, 804
General Mills, 405, 796, 852
General Motors Corporation (GM), 5, 381, 451, 503, 562, 713, 726, 755, 972, 1015, 1202
Gillette Company, 566
Glassmaster Company, 1202
Global Reporting Initiative, 729
GM, *see* General Motors Corporation
Goldman Sachs, 11, 769
Gold's Gym, 838
Goodyear, 986
Google, 12, 25, 121, 416, 500, 505, 678, 1015
Green Bay Packers, 48, 89
Groupon, 94
Gulf Oil, 503

H

Hard Candy Fitness, 838
Harley-Davidson, 858
HealthSouth, 7
Hershey, 799
Hewlett-Packard Corporation (HP), 713, 725, 727, 859, 929, 979, 1175
Hilton, 401, 838, 887
Hilton Hotels, 727
Holland America Line, 1204, 1213
Home Depot, 4, 261, 281, 399
Honda, 1122
HP, *see* Hewlett-Packard Corporation
H&R Block, 797
Hughes Aircraft Co., 679

I

IBM, 223, 416, 500, 523, 727, 1162
Ice Pro, 796
Intel Corporation, 46, 358, 461, 726, 796, 810, 929, 1012, 1014
InterContinental, 401
International Outsourcing Services, LLC, 53
IT&T, 2

J

J. C. Penney Company, Inc., 359, 385, 602, 660

J. Crew, 10
J. Walter Thompson, 796
Jiffy Lube, 797
John Deere Capital Corporation, 401
Jones Soda Co., 794, 796
Jostens, Inc., 1175
J.P. Morgan Leasing, 401
JP Morgan Chase, 366

K

Kaiser, 796
Kellogg Company, 466, 752, 796, 803, 805, 809, 811, 1169
Kmart Stores, 671, 1008
Kohl's Corporation, 602
Komag, 937
Kraft Foods, 1169
Krispy Kreme, 98
Kroger Stores, 207, 269, 671

L

Leslie Fay, 262, 304
Levi Strauss, 1016
Lockheed Martin Corp., 161, 410
Loews Corporation, 506
Louis Vuitton Moët Hennessy, 4, 47, 93, 149, 203, 257, 305, 395, 443, 497, 557, 657, 709, 714
Lucent, 713

M

McDonald's Corporation, 11, 46, 414, 427, 462, 500, 646, 1160
McDonnell Douglas, 727
McKesson Corporation, 206, 304, 333
Macy's, Inc., 658, 660, 661, 665, 667, 934
Madison Square Garden, 1063
Major League Baseball Players Association, 7
Marcus Corporation, 171
Marriott Hotels, 401, 405, 887, 1111
Massachusetts General Hospital, 11, 886
MasterCard, 366, 367
Mayo Clinic, 769, 796
Medtronic, Inc., 455
Merck & Co., Inc., 1014, 1053
Merrill Lynch, 11
Method Products, 972, 979
MF Global Holdings Ltd, 48, 51, 69, 501
Microsoft Corporation, 5, 57, 214, 223, 413, 414, 598, 614, 1012
Minnesota Mining and Manufacturing Company (3M), 358, 383, 486, 931
Mitsubishi, 597
Mobile Iron, 612
Moody's, 660
Morgan Stanley, 569
Morrow Snowboards, Inc., 209
Motorola, 269
Museum of Contemporary Art, 1079

N

NBC, 415
NBCUniversal, 1114
NEC, 148
Nestlé, 46
NFL, 415
Nike, Inc., 4, 498, 500, 501, 504, 506, 507, 512, 515, 522, 666, 727, 887, 936
Nissan, 1204
Nordstrom, Inc., 173, 368, 694

O

Office Depot, 206
Oral-B Laboratories, 972
Owens-Illinois, 418

P

Pandora, 937
Parker Hannifin, 849, 1020
Parmalat, 354
Penske Automotive Group, 1175
PepsiCo, Inc., 4, 5, 12, 25, 43, 88, 96, 145, 198, 217, 253, 271, 302, 351, 391, 438, 493, 500, 517, 552, 594, 653, 705, 794, 796
P&G, *see* The Procter & Gamble Company
Phantom Tac, 728
Philip Morris International, 455
Pilgrim's Pride, 222
Pratt and Whitney, 770
Precor, 838, 851
PriceWaterhouseCoopers, 769
Princeton University, 1079
The Procter & Gamble Company (P&G), 11, 172, 417, 418, 507, 566, 720, 972, 1119, 1162
Prudential Real Estate, 11

Q

Quad Graphics, 754
Quaker Oats, 271, 972

R

Red Cross, 25
Reebok International Ltd., 269, 498, 887
REI (Recreational Equipment Incorporated), 204, 206, 210, 214
REL Consultancy Company, 172
Renault, 1204
Rent-A-Wreck, 396, 398, 399, 403, 414, 415
Republic Carloading, 167
Rhino Foods, Inc., 6, 150
Rite Aid, 358
Royal Ahold, 148, 354
Royal Dutch Shell, 271, 796

S

Safeway, 310, 671, 922
Salvation Army, 500

San Diego Zoo, 1117
SAP, 726
Sara Lee, 717
Satyam Computer Services, 354
Schering-Plough, 727
Seattle Seahawks, 794
Sharp, 1218
Shell, 415. *See also* Royal
    Dutch Shell
Sherwin-Williams, 796
Siebel Systems, 1121
Siemens AG, 1132
Simon Properties, 455
Skype, 223
Smart Balance, 970
Snap Fitness, 971
Sony, 46, 276
Southwest Airlines Co., 96, 104,
    168, 450, 886
Sports Illustrated, 450
Sprint Corporation, 447
Standard & Poor's, 493, 660
Stanley Black & Decker
    Manufacturing Company, 269
Starbucks, 25, 269, 728, 1158,
    1173
Subway, 415
Sunbeam, 976

T
Target Corporation, 261, 325, 429,
    602, 701, 972

Tecumseh Products Company, 1238
Tempur Sealy International, 892
Tesla, 7
3M, *see* Minnesota Mining and
    Manufacturing Company
Time Warner Inc., 6, 558, 564, 568,
    1024, 1060
Toyota, 46, 726, 728, 1015
Trek, 11, 981, 1024
Tribeca Grand Hotel, 1106
True Value Hardware, 261
Turner Broadcasting, 564
21st Century Fox, 558
Twitter, 938

U
U-Haul, 889
Unilever, 461, 972, 1176
United Airlines, 6, 104, 562, 598, 886,
    929, 1175, 1177
U.S. Navy, 1162
United Stationers, 206
US Bancorp Equipment
    Finance, 401
USX, 796

V
Verizon Communications Inc.,
    455, 1212
Versace, 1014
Visa, 366–368
Vodafone/Mannesmann, 46

W
Wachovia, 360
Walgreen Drugs, 206, 269
Wal-Mart Stores, Inc., 4, 10, 43, 88,
    145, 198, 204, 206, 253, 261, 281,
    302, 325, 351, 391, 438, 493, 552,
    594, 602, 653, 671, 701, 705, 727,
    1016, 1176
Walt Disney Company, 6, 96, 413,
    529, 752, 754, 764, 796, 1024
Warner Brothers, 796
Waste Management Inc., 70
Wells Fargo Bank, 308, 360, 366, 461
Wendy's International, 269
Wenonah Canoe, 710, 747
Whirlpool, 717
Whitehall-Robins, 356, 365
Whole Foods Market, 922
WorldCom, 7, 25, 315, 401, 501

X
Xerox, 713
XM Satellite Radio Holdings, 1070

Y
Yahoo! Inc., 170, 660
Yale Express, 167
Young & Rubicam, 796

Z
Zappos.com, 1012
Zoom Kitchen, 932

Subject Index

A

ABC, *see* Activity-based costing
ABM (activity-based management), 852–853
Absorption costing:
  deciding when to use, 945–947
  defined, 939
  example of, 940–945
  variable costing vs., 939–947
Absorption-cost pricing, 1030–1032
Accelerated-depreciation method, 407
Account(s), 50–55
  chart of, 61
  contra asset, 102–103, 457
  contra revenue, 216
  permanent, 157–158, 162, 163
  T-, 50, 629
  temporary, 157, 158, 163, 164
  three-column form of, 59
  uncollectible, 360–366
Accounting. *See also* Managerial accounting; Responsibility accounting
  accrual, 1206
  basic activities of, 4–5
  and budgeting, 1058
  building blocks of, 7–11
  and career opportunities, 11, 25–26
  cash, 1206
  cost, 754
  defined, 4
  financial, 712, 713
  as recruiting tool, 6
Accounting cycle, 165
Accounting data, users of, 5–7
Accounting reports, 4
Accounts payable, 12, 18–19, 608, 627, 1076
Accounts receivable, 1076
  defined, 358
  disposing of, 366–368
  recognizing, 358–360
  on statement of cash flows, 607–608, 626
  transaction analysis, 19
  valuing, 360–366

Accounts receivable turnover, 374, 669
Account titles (in journals), 56–57
Accruals, adjusting entries for, 98, 106–110
  accrued expenses, 108–110
  accrued revenues, 106–108
Accrual-basis accounting, 96, 1206
Accrued expenses, 108–110
Accrued interest, 108–109
Accrued revenues, 106–108
Accumulated depreciation, 170, 627, 1076
Accumulated profit or loss, 556
Accumulating manufacturing costs, 755–758, 767
  factory labor, 757
  in job order and process cost systems, 797
  overhead, 757
  raw materials, 756–757
Accuracy, 70
Acid-test (quick) ratio, 668–669
Acquisitions, depreciation of, 402
Activity(-ies), 842
  batch-level, 850, 851
  classification of, 849–851
  coordination of, 1058
  in cost behavior analysis, 886
  facility-level, 850, 851
  identification/classification of, 844
  non-value-added, 850–852
  product-level, 850, 851
  unit-level, 849, 851
  value-added, 850–852
  and variable/fixed costs, 886, 887
Activity bases, 763, 764
Activity-based costing (ABC), 726, 838–857
  and activity-based management, 852–853
  activity-based overhead rates, 845
  benefits of, 849–853
  classification of activity levels in, 849–851
  cost drivers in, 844–845
  and cost pools, 844, 849–850

  enhanced cost control with, 850–852
  and incremental analysis, 976–977
  limitations of, 853–854
  and overhead costs, 845–846, 1164
  in service industries, 854–857
  traditional costing vs., 840–843
  unit costs under, 844–849
  when to use, 853–854
Activity-based management (ABM), 852–853
Activity-based overhead rates, 844, 845
Activity cost pools, 841–844
Activity flowcharts, 851–852
Activity index, 886
  for flexible budgets, 1111, 1114, 1115
  relevant range of, 889
  for static budgets, 1109
Actual cost (in total variance), 1165–1166
Additional costs of borrowing, 458
Additional paid-in capital, 528
Additions and improvements, 400–401
Adjustable-rate mortgages, 462
Adjusted cash balance, 330
Adjusted cash balance per books, 330
Adjusted trial balance:
  defined, 113
  for merchandising operations, 232, 233
  preparation of, 113, 114
  preparing financial statements from, 114–117
  on worksheets, 153–155
Adjusting entries, 98–113
  for accruals, 106–110
    accrued expenses, 108–110
    accrued revenues, 106–108
  for bad debt, 365–366
  correcting vs., 166
  for deferrals, 98–106
    prepaid expenses, 100–103, 117–120
    unearned revenues, 104–105, 117–120

Adjusting entries (*Continued*)
  example of journalizing/posting, 111–112
  for merchandising operations, 218
  preparing, from worksheets, 157
  purpose of, 98
  reversing vs., 174
  types of, 98–99
Adjustments column (on worksheets), 153, 231, 232
Administrative expenses, *see* Selling and administrative expenses
Affiliated company (subsidiary company), 566
After-tax total contribution margin, 1034
Agents:
  collection, 447
  of corporations, 500
Aggregate, reporting data in, 4
Aging schedule, 365
Aging the accounts receivable, 365
AIR (Annals of Improbable Research), 354
Airline industry, 725, 857, 899, 1177
Allocation, valuation vs., 102
Allowance for Doubtful Accounts, 362, 364–366
Allowance method, 361–366
Amortization, 414
  of bond discount, 458
  of bond premium, 459–460, 473
  effective-interest method, 470–473
  straight-line method, 468–470
Analysis. *See also* Cost-volume-profit (CVP) analysis
  as accounting activity, 4
  break-even, 898–901, 904, 925
  cost behavior, 886–893
  and effective budgeting, 1058–1059
  incremental, 972–989, 1029
  regression, 892
  risk, 1218
  sensitivity, 1218
Annals of Improbable Research (AIR), 354
Annual depletion cost, 412–413
Annual rate, 370
Annual rate of return method, 1222–1223
Applications, pricing of, 1015
Assets, 12. *See also* Intangible assets; Plant assets
  current, 168–170, 446, 667–668
  debit and credit procedures, 51
  depreciable, 402
  fixed, 398, 614
  noncurrent, 610–611
  operating, 1129, 1130
  return on, 672
  total, 514, 517
Asset turnover, 418–419, 671

Assigning manufacturing costs, 758–763, 767–768, 799–801
  to cost of goods sold, 767, 801
  of factory labor, 761–762, 800
  to finished goods, 766–767, 801
  in job order costing, 758–763, 770, 798
  of manufacturing overhead, 763–766, 801
  to next department, 801
  in process costing, 755, 799–801
  of raw materials, 759–761, 799–800
Associate investment, 596
Assumptions:
  accounting, 9–11
  financial reporting, 121
Audit committees, 727
Auditing, 25
Auditors, internal, 315
Authorized stock, 505
Automation:
  and activity base for overhead, 764
  and cost structure, 935–936
  and CVP analysis, 927
  and fixed costs, 887
  and manufacturing in U.S., 717
  and the value chain, 726
Automobile industry, 1015, 1175
Available-for-sale securities, 569–571, 680–681
Available funds, 1207
Averages, industry, 660, 667
Average collection period, 374, 670
Average-cost method, 268, 279
Awareness of operations, management's, 1058

B

Backdating, sales, 98
Background checks, 315
Bad debt adjusting entry, 365–366
Bad Debt Expense, 360–361, 363
Bad loans, 373
Balanced scorecard, 726–727, 1175–1177
  defined, 1176
  perspectives employed with, 1176
Balanced Scorecard Institute, 1202
Balance sheet(s), 21–23, 722–723. *See also* Classified balance sheet
  from adjusted trial balance, 115, 116
  adjusting accounts on, 98, 106–107
  budgeted, 1075–1076
  consolidated, 575–578
  effects of cost flow methods on, 270–271
  effects of inventory errors on, 273
  horizontal analysis of, 662
  investments on, 569–570
  for merchandising operations, 233
  stockholders' equity section of, 528–529

  vertical analysis of, 664
  and write-offs, 363–364
Balancing amount, 628
Bank(s), 325–332, 1175
  deposits to, 325–326
  EFT systems of, 332
  and writing checks, 326–327
Bank accounts, reconciling, 325, 328–332
Bank memoranda, 330
Bank reconciliation, 325, 328–332
  entries from, 331
  example of, 330
  procedure for, 328–330
Bank service charges, 328, 331
Bank statements, 327–328
Barnum, P.T., 8
Basic accounting equation, 12–14
  business transactions' effects on, 14–20
  expansion of, 15, 54
Batches, 754
Batch-level activities, 850, 851
Before-tax total contribution margin, 1034
Beginning work in process inventory, 721
Behavior:
  and budgeting, 1060–1061
  and equipment retention/replacement, 985
  and performance evaluations, 1121
Benchmarks, 853
Best-efforts contracts, 506n.2
Bezos, Jeff, 884, 980
Big-screen televisions, 1218
Blank, Arthur, 4
Boards of directors, 715, 727
Bond(s), 452–462, 466–473
  amortization of, 458–460, 468–473
    effective-interest method, 470–473
    straight-line method, 468–470
  callable, 452
  common stock vs., 466–467, 562
  conversion of, to common stock, 461
  convertible, 452, 461, 496
  defined, 452
  determining market value of, 454
  discounting of, 456–458
  issuance of:
    accounting for, 456
    at discount, 457–458
    at face value, 456
    at premium, 459–460
    procedures for, 452–453
  premiums on, 457, 459–460
  recording acquisition of, 561
  recording interest from, 561
  recording sale of, 561–562
  redemption of:
    at maturity, 460
    before maturity, 460–461

retirement of, 460–461
secured, 452
trading of, 453–454
unsecured, 452
zero-interest, 454
Bond certificates, 453
Bond discount, 457–458
  amortization of, 458, 468–469,
    471–472
  defined, 457
Bonding, 315
Bond interest expense, 471
Bond interest paid, 471
Bonds payable, 610, 622, 627
Bond premium, 459–460
  amortization of, 459–460,
    469–470, 473
  defined, 457
Book errors, 331
Bookkeeping, 5
Book value (carrying value), 103,
    402, 985
  and consolidated balance
    sheets, 576
  of convertible bonds, 461
  and declining-balance
    depreciation, 406
  defined, 458
Book value method, 461
Book value per share, 531–533
Borrowing, costs of, 458, 459
Bottlenecks, 726
Bowerman, Bill, 498, 500
Break-even analysis, 898–901, 904
  contribution margin technique
    for, 899
  and CVP analysis, 898–901,
    904, 925
  and CVP graph, 900–901
  defined, 898
  equation for, 898
Break-even point, 895
  computing, 898–901
  and conversion rates, 928
  on CVP graph, 900–901
  defined, 895, 898
  formula for, 925
  identifying, 898
  in sales dollars, 898
  in sales units, 899
Brock, Paula, 1117
Budget(s), 1058. See also Budgeting
  cash, 1072–1077
  defined, 1058
  direct labor, 1068–1069
  direct materials, 1065–1068
  financial, 1061–1062, 1072–1077
  flexible, 1111–1118, 1122, 1125
  government, 1064, 1079
  manufacturing overhead,
    1069–1070
  master, 1061–1062, 1067–1068,
    1109–1110

merchandise purchases,
    1077–1078, 1080
  operating, 1063–1072
  production, 1064–1065, 1067
  sales, 1063–1064, 1067
  selling and administrative
    expense, 1070
  standards vs., 1161
  static, 1109–1113
Budgetary control, 1108–1118
  defined, 1108
  with flexible budgets, 1111–1118
  with static budget reports,
    1109–1111
Budgetary goals, 1121
Budgetary optimism, 1064
Budgetary planning, 1056–1080
  budgeting basics, 1058–1062
  financial budgets, 1072–1077
  in nonmanufacturing companies,
    1077–1080
  operating budgets, 1063–1072
Budgetary slack, 1061
Budget committees, 1060
Budgeted balance sheet, 1075–1076
Budgeted income statement,
    1070–1072
Budgeting, 1058–1062. See also
    Capital budgeting
  and accounting, 1058
  benefits of, 1058
  effective, 1058–1059
  human behavior affected by,
    1060–1061
  length of budget period, 1059
  long-range planning vs., 1061
  and master budget, 1061–1062
  for merchandisers, 1077–1078,
    1080
  for nonmanufacturing companies,
    1077–1080
  for not-for-profit
    organizations, 1079
  process of, 1059–1060
  responsibility accounting vs., 1119
  for service enterprises,
    1078–1079
Budget period, 1059
Budget reforecasting, 1117
Budget reports, 1108
  flexible, 1116–1118
  for responsibility accounting,
    1122–1124
  static, 1109–1111
Buffett, Warren, 523, 658, 938
Buildings, 399, 610, 622, 626, 1076
Burden, see Manufacturing overhead
Businesses. See also Service
    companies
  nonmanufacturing, 1077–1080
  small, 1059
  standards for, 1160–1162
  virtual, 1029

Business documents, 55, 214
Business environment, CVP analysis
    in, 926–927
Business ethics, 727
Business transactions, 14
Buswell, Diane, 747, 880, 918, 1006,
    1100, 1200
Buyers, freight costs incurred
    by, 211
By-laws, 503

C
Calendar year, 96
Callable bonds, 452
Canceled checks, 327
Capacity, 978, 1025–1026, 1164
Capital:
  ability of corporations to
    acquire, 501
  corporate, 507–508
  cost of, 1212
  legal, 506
  paid-in, 507, 509, 520, 522,
    525, 528
  for proprietorship, 10
  working, 172, 465, 668
Capital budgeting, 1204–1223
  annual rate of return method used
    in, 1222–1223
  authorization process, 1206
  and cash flow information,
    1206–1207
  cash payback technique used in,
    1207–1209
  defined, 1204
  intangible benefits in, 1214–1216
  internal rate of return method
    used in, 1219–1221
  with mutually exclusive projects,
    1216–1218
  net present value method used in,
    1209–1219, 1221
  and post-audits, 1218–1219
  and risk analysis, 1218
Capital expenditures, 401
Capital stock, 505, 528
Capital surplus, 529
Careers, accounting in, 11, 25–26
Carpenter, Jake Burton, 718
Carrying value, see Book value
Carrying value method, 461
Cash. See also Net cash
  in budgeted balance sheet, 1076
  change in, 611, 623, 628
  defined, 333
  and dividends, 515–516
  excess, 560
  net, 600, 616
  reporting, 333–334
  restricted, 333–334
Cash balance, 330
Cash-basis accounting, 96, 1206
Cash budget, 1072–1077

Cash controls, 317–325. *See also* Bank(s)
  disbursements, 320–324
    petty cash fund, 322–324
    voucher system, 321–322
  receipts, 318–320
    mail, 320
    over-the-counter, 318–319
Cash disbursements section (cash budget), 1072–1073
Cash dividends, 52, 515–519
Cash equivalents, 333, 354
Cash equivalent price, 510
Cash flow(s). *See also* Statement of cash flows
  and capital budgeting, 1206–1207
  classification of, 600–601
  discounted cash flow techniques, 1209–1221
  equal, 1210–1211, 1220
  free, 614–616
  future, 600
  inflows, 1206, 1207
  net annual, 1208
  in net present value method, 1213
  of not-for-profit organizations, 1079
  outflows, 1206, 1207
  statement of, *see* Statement of cash flows
  unequal, 1211, 1220
Cash flow numbers, 1206
"Cash Flow Statements" (*IAS* 7), 656
Cash inflow and cash outflow, 1206, 1207
  from financing/investing activities, 600, 610–611, 622–623
  from operating activities, 600–601, 604–613, 616–621
  on statement of cash flows, 624
Cash investments, 15–16, 62
Cash outflows, 1206, 1207
Cash payback technique, 1207–1209
Cash payments, 18–19, 66, 619–621
Cash prepayments, 63
Cash purchases, 16, 62
Cash (net) realizable value, 361–362, 371
Cash receipts, 318–320
  mail receipts, 320
  over-the counter receipts, 318–319
  and statement of cash flows, 616–618
Cash receipts section (cash budget), 1072
Cash registers, 310, 312
Cash register tapes, 214
Cash sales:
  credit card sales as, 368
  transaction analysis, 17–19
Cash value, net, 361–362, 371
Castle, Ted, 150
Casualty losses, 222

CEO (chief executive officer), 501, 715, 727
Certified public accountants (CPAs), 25
CFO (chief financial officer), 715, 727
Change in cash:
  net, 611, 623
  on statement of cash flows, 628
Charges:
  material loading, 1021, 1022
  in time-and-materials pricing, 1021–1023
Charter, 503
Chart of accounts, 61
Check(s):
  canceled, 327
  outstanding, 329–330
  writing, 326–327
Check register, 321
Chemical industry, 1175
Chief executive officer (CEO), 501, 715, 727
Chief financial officer (CFO), 715, 727
China, 170
Cichanowski, Mike, 710, 747, 1006, 1007, 1199, 1236
Classified balance sheet, 168–173
  current assets on, 168–170
  current liabilities on, 171–172
  GAAP vs. IFRS for, 200–202
  intangible assets on, 170–171
  long-term investments on, 170
  long-term liabilities on, 172, 173
  for merchandising operations, 224
  property, plant, and equipment on, 170
  stockholders' equity on, 172–173
  valuing/reporting of investments on, 573–574
Closing entries:
  journalizing of, 229–231
  for merchandising operations, 218–220
  posting of, 160–161, 229–231
  preparation of, 158–160
Closing the books, 157–164
  defined, 157
  and posting of closing entries, 160–161
  and preparation of closing entries, 158–160
  and preparation of post-closing trial balance, 162–164
CM, *see* Contribution margin
Codification, 45
COLAs (cost of living adjustments), 1163
Collaboration, 1119
Collections, schedule of expected, 1073
Collection agents, 447
Collection period, average, 374

Collusion, 317
Commercial substance (of plant asset exchange), 419
Common-size analysis, *see* Vertical analysis
Common stock, 13, 52, 509–511
  bonds vs., 466–467
  book value per share, 531–533
  on budgeted balance sheet, 1076
  cash dividend allocation, 519
  issuance of, 509–511
  no-par, 507, 510
  and owners' equity, 507–508
  par-value, 509
  for services or noncash assets, 510
  on statement of cash flows, 611, 622, 627
  and stockholder rights, 504
Common stock equity, 532
Common stockholders' equity, return on, 529, 672–673
Communication:
  of economic events, 4, 5
  in internal control, 309
Companies, *see* Businesses
Comparability (of financial information), 121
Comparative analysis, 660
Compensation, managers', 501
Compensation programs, 1119
Competitive advantage, 1020
Competitive markets, pricing in, 1014–1015
Complete information, 120
Completion percentages, 803
Component depreciation, 442
Components, cost of, 761
Composition (of current assets), 668
Compound entries, 57
Comprehensive income, 256, 555, 573, 708
Computer systems industry, 1175
Confirmatory value (of financial information), 120
Conservatism, 275
Consigned goods, 263
Consistency, 121, 271
Consolidated balance sheet, 575–578
Consolidated financial statements, 566–567
Consolidated income statement, 578
Constraints:
  financial reporting, 122
  theory of, 726, 934
Constructed buildings, 399
Continuous 12-month budgets, 1059
Continuous improvement, 852
Continuous life (of corporation), 501
Contra asset accounts, 102–103, 457
Contracts, best-efforts, 506n.2
Contractual interest rate, 452, 456
Contractual restrictions (on retained earnings), 525

Contra revenue accounts, 216
Contra stockholders' equity
    account, 513
Contribution margin (CM), 894–897,
    924, 932
  per unit, 895–896, 933
  ratios, 896–897, 899, 925, 936
  and tax rates, 1034
  of unprofitable segments/
    products, 987
  weighted-average, 929–932
Control(s). See also Budgetary
    control; Internal control(s)
  and activity-based costing,
    850–852
  with budgets, 1058
  cost, 1028
Control accounts, 758, 760, 767
Control activities, 309–310
Control environment (internal
    control), 309
Controllable costs, 1120–1121,
    1125, 1126
Controllable margin, 1126–1127,
    1129–1130
Controllable revenues, 1120,
    1126–1127
Controllable variance, 1172,
    1181–1182
Controller, 501, 715
Controlling, as management
    function, 713
Controlling interest, 566
Convergence, 9
Conversion costs, 803, 808, 813
Conversion rates, 928
Convertible bonds, 452, 461, 496
Copyrights, 415
Corporate assets, 505
Corporate capital, 507–508
Corporate reputation, 171
Corporate social responsibility, 24,
    530, 728–729, 1173
Corporate strategy, pricing in, 1015
Corporation(s), 10–11, 500–508
  book value per share of, 531–533
  characteristics of, 500–503
  classification of, 500
  corporate capital, 507–508
  defined, 10, 500
  formation of, 503–504
  issuance of stock by, 504–507
  ownership of, 504
Correct cash balance, 330
Correcting entries, 166–167
Cost(s), 716–720. See also specific
    types
  of ABC implementation, 853
  of borrowing, 458, 459
  in CVP analysis, 925
  depreciable, 403
  and equivalent units
    computations, 815

in financial statements, 720–724
  of intangible assets, 414
  of morale, 976
  organization, 503
  of plant assets, 398–400
  research and development, 416–417
  underestimating, 755
Cost accounting, 754
Cost accounting systems, 754,
    809–810
  absorption costing, 939–947
  activity-based, see Activity-based
    costing
  and cost-plus pricing, 1016–1019
  defined, 754
  job order costing, see Job order
    cost systems
  operations costing, 809–810
  process costing, see Process cost
    systems
  standard, 1178–1180
  target costing, 1015–1016
  traditional, 840–841, 855
  variable, see Variable costing
Cost-based transfer price, 1027–1028
Cost behavior analysis, 886–893
  fixed costs in, 887–888
  and identification of variable and
    fixed costs, 893
  mixed costs in, 889–893
  relevant range in, 888–889
  variable costs in, 886–887
Cost centers, 1124, 1125
Cost constraint, 122
Cost control, 1028
Cost determination, 712
Cost drivers, 800, 842–845
Cost flow(s):
  and job order costing, 770–771,
    797–798
  for merchandising company,
    207–209
  and process costing, 797–799
Cost flow assumptions, 265–269,
    277–279
Costing and costing systems, see Cost
    accounting systems
Cost method:
  and stock investments, 563
  for valuation of treasury stock, 512
Cost of capital, 1212
Cost of goods available for sale,
    265–266
Cost of goods manufactured,
    720–724
Cost of goods manufactured
    schedule, 720, 722–724, 772
Cost of goods purchased, 720
Cost of goods sold, 767, 773,
    801, 1174
  defined, 206
  under periodic system, 227–228
  recording, 214

Cost of living adjustments
    (COLAs), 1163
Cost of transfer to cost of goods
    sold, 801
Cost of transfer to finished goods, 801
Cost of transfer to next
    department, 801
Cost-plus pricing, 769, 1016–1019
Cost pools:
  and ABC, 844, 849–850
  activity, 841–844
  allocating overhead to, 844
  overhead, 842
Cost principle, see Historical cost
    principle
Cost reconciliation schedule, 808,
    814–815
Cost structures, 935–937
  and break-even point, 936–937
  and contribution margin ratio, 936
  and margin of safety ratio, 937
  and operating leverage, 937–938
Cost-volume-profit (CVP) analysis,
    894–904, 922–948
  absorption vs. variable costing in,
    939–947
  assumptions of, 894
  and break-even analysis, 898–901,
    904, 925
  and business environment,
    926–927
  components of, 894
  computations in, 925–926
  concepts in, 924–925
  cost structure and operating
    leverage in, 935–938
  margin of safety in, 903–904, 926
  and sales mix, 929–935
  and target net income, 901–904, 925
  and variances, 1175
Cost-volume-profit (CVP) graph,
    900–903
Cost-volume-profit (CVP) income
    statement, 894–897
  and contribution margin ratio,
    896–897
  and unit contribution margin,
    895–896
  variances on, 1175
Covenants, debt, 466
CPAs (certified public
    accountants), 25
Credits (Cr.), 50–55
  for assets and liabilities, 51
  general procedure, 51
  from manufacturing costs, 758
  for revenues and expenses, 53
  for stockholders' equity, 52–53
  summary of rules, 54
Credit balances, 50, 773
Credit cards:
  funding business with, 444
  sales via, 367–368

Credit crisis, 373
Crediting the account, 50
Credit memoranda, 328
Creditors:
  as internal users, 6
  long- vs. short-term, 660
Credit purchases:
  recording process, 64
  transaction analysis, 16, 17
Credit risk, 562
Credit sales, 17–18
Credit terms, 212
CRS (Financial Accounting
  Standards Board
  Codification Research
  System), 45
Cruise industry, 1204
Cumulative dividend, 518
Current assets:
  on classified balance sheet,
    168–170
  composition of, 668
  and current liabilities, 446
  noncash, 607–608
Current liabilities, 446–451
  changes in, 608–609
  on classified balance sheet,
    171–172
  and current assets, 446
  defined, 444, 446
  long-term debt, current maturities
    of, 451
  notes payable, 446–447
  payroll and payroll taxes payable,
    448–449
  sales taxes payable, 447–448
  statement presentation/analysis of,
    464–466
  unearned revenues, 450–451
Current maturities of long-term
    debt, 451
Current ratio, 465, 667–668
Curvilinear relationship (of cost and
    activity), 888
Customers:
  cash receipts from, 616–618
  as external users, 7
Customer perspective (balanced
    scorecard), 1176, 1177
Cutoff rate, 1212
CVP analysis, see Cost-volume-profit
    analysis
CVP (cost-volume-profit) graph,
    900–903
CVP income statement, see Cost-
    volume-profit income
    statement

D
Data entry (for job order costing),
    770
Days in inventory, 276, 670
Debenture bonds, 452

Debits (Dr.), 50–55
  for assets and liabilities, 51
  general procedure, 51
  from manufacturing costs, 758
  for revenues and expenses, 53
  for stockholders' equity, 52–53
  summary of rules, 54
Debit balance, 773
Debit balances, 50, 366
Debiting the account, 50
Debit memoranda, 328
Debt covenants, 466
Debt investments, 561–563
Debt to assets ratio, 466, 674–675
Decentralization, 1119
Decision-making process, 974–976
  as capital budgeting
    consideration, 1207
  make-or-buy decisions, 979–981
  sell-or-process-further decision,
    981–984
Declaration date, 516, 517
Declarations of dividends, 516
Declining-balance method, 406–407
Defects, 859
Deferrals, adjusting entries for,
    98–106
  prepaid expenses, 100–103,
    117–120
  unearned revenues, 104–105,
    117–120
Deferred revenue (unearned
    revenue), 104–105, 117–120,
    450–451
Deficits, 525
Degree of operating leverage,
    937–938
Departmental overhead costs
    (report), 1109
Depletion, 412–413
Depletion cost per unit of
    product, 412
Deposits, bank, 325–326
Deposits in transit, 329
Depreciable assets, 402
Depreciable cost, 403
Depreciation:
  accumulated, 170, 627, 1076
  component, 442
  declining-balance method of,
    406–407
  defined, 102, 402
  of plant assets, 402–409
    computation, 403–408
    and income taxes, 408
    methods, 403–408
    revisions in estimate of, 408–409
  as prepaid expense, 102–103
  straight-line method of, 404–405
  units-of-activity method of,
    405–406
Depreciation expense, 606, 620
Depreciation schedule, 404–405

Differential analysis, see Incremental
    analysis
Direct fixed costs, 1126
Directing, as management
    function, 713
Direct issue (of stock), 505
Direct labor, 717, 840, 1163
Direct labor budget, 1068–1069
Direct labor price standard (direct
    labor rate standard), 1163
Direct labor quantity standard
    (direct labor efficiency
    standard), 1163
Direct labor variances, 1169–1171
Direct materials, 716, 1163
Direct materials budget, 1065–1068
Direct materials price standard, 1162
Direct materials quantity standard,
    1162–1163
Direct materials variances,
    1167–1169
Direct method (of preparing
    statement of cash flows),
    604, 616–623
  investing/financing activities,
    622–623
  net change in cash, 623
  operating activities, cash provided/
    used by, 616–621
Direct write-off method, 361
Disbursements, cash, 320–324
  and petty cash fund, 322–324
  and voucher system, 321–322
Disclosure(s):
  financial, 223
  full disclosure principle, 122, 602
Discontinued operations, 679
Discount(s):
  bonds issued at, 457–458, 468–469,
    471–472
  purchase, 212–213, 229
  sales, 216, 229
  on selling price, 926–927
Discounted cash flow techniques:
  comparing, 1221
  defined, 1209
  internal rate of return method,
    1219–1221
  net present value method,
    1209–1219, 1221
Discount period, 212
Discount rate, 1209, 1212
Dishonored notes, 373
Disposal:
  of accounts receivable, 366–368
  of notes receivable, 372–373
  of plant assets, 409–412
    retirement, 410
    sale, 410–412
  of treasury stock, 513–514
Dividend(s), 52–53, 515–521
  ability to pay, 600
  cash, 52, 515–519

cumulative, 518
defined, 13, 515
dividend preference, 517–518
and free cash flow, 614
liquidating, 515
and net income, 160
preferred, 529, 672
recent changes in, 520
recording, 65, 564–566
stock, 520–521
stock splits, 522–524
transaction analysis, 19
Dividends in arrears, 518
Dividend preference, 517–518
Dividend revenue, 222
Documentation, cost system, 798
Documentation procedures,
   312–313, 401
Dollar signs, 70
Dollar-value LIFO, 265n.1
Dot-com companies, 658
Double-declining-balance
   method, 407
Double-entry system, 51
Double taxation, 502
Dr., see Debits
Dunlap, Al "Chainsaw," 976
Duties (of employees):
   rotating, 315
   segregation of, 311–312, 360

E

Early warning system, budgeting
   as, 1058
Earned surplus, 529
Earnings. See also Retained earnings;
   Retained earnings statement
   from investment income, 560
   managing, 222
   retained, 1076
Earnings per share (EPS), 673
Earnings statement, see Income
   statement
Ebbers, Bernie, 401
Economic downturns, 1064
Economic entity assumption,
   10–11, 121
Economic events, 4–5
Edmondson, David, 90–91
Effective-interest method, 470–473
Effective-interest rate, 471
Electronics, recycling of, 110
Electronic funds transfers (EFT), 332
Emphasis (of budgeting vs. long-
   range planning), 1061
Employees:
   bonding of, 315
   duties of, 311–312, 315, 360
   efficiency of, 1171
   evaluations of, 853
   hiring of, 65
   misallocation of, 1171
   safety of, 1216

skilled, 892, 1171
theft by, 324
Ending work in process
   inventory, 721
Endorsements, restrictive, 320
Enterprise resource planning (ERP)
   software systems, 726
EPS (earnings per share), 673
Equal Employment Opportunity
   Act, 1160
Equipment, 399–400, 610, 622,
   626–627
   on budgeted balance sheet, 1076
   incremental analysis for, 985–986
   replacement of, 985–986
   retention of, 985–986
Equity. See also Stockholders' equity
   common and preferred stock, 532
   trading on the, 673
Equity method, 564–565
Equivalent units of production,
   802–804, 810–816
   for conversion costs, 813
   FIFO method computation,
      810–816
   for materials, 813
   for process cost reports, 806–807
   weighted-average method
      computation, 802–804
Erickson, Gary, 2
ERP (enterprise resource planning)
   software systems, 726
Errors:
   on bank statements, 328, 330, 331
   in inventory, 272–273
      balance sheet effects, 273
      income statement effects,
         272–273
   irregularities vs., 69
   locating, with trial balance, 70
Estimation (of Allowance for
   Doubtful Accounts), 364–366
Ethics:
   and adjusting entries, 108
   and available-for-sale
      securities, 569
   and bond valuation, 569
   and budgeting, 1061
   business, 727
   and cash equivalents, 333
   and clarity of financial
      disclosures, 223
   and compensation of managers, 501
   defined, 8
   and depreciation of
      acquisitions, 402
   in determining equivalent units, 803
   and documentation, 55, 759
   and earnings numbers, 366
   and economic entity assumption,
      10, 121
   and employee theft, 324
   and errors vs. irregularities, 69

and fees, 724
and finance charges/interest
   rates, 358
and financial reporting, 7–8, 214
and incentives, 727
and inventory fraud, 261, 262, 272
and liabilities reporting, 465
and liquidity, 171
and make-or-buy decisions, 980
and managing earnings, 222
and petty cash, 322
and purchases of Treasury
   stock, 513
and receivables reporting, 358
and reported net income, 600
and restatements, 166
and revenue recognition
   principle, 98
and securities valuation, 59
and specific identification
   method, 264
and standards, 1161
Excess capacity, 1026
Exchange of plant assets, 419–420
   gain treatment, 420
   loss treatment, 419–420
Exclusive right of use, 171
Exotic Newcastle Disease, 1117
Expanded accounting equation,
   15, 54
Expected input and output, service
   revenue from, 1079
Expense(s), 53
   accrued, 108–110
   defined, 13
   and dividends, 13, 19
   operating, 221, 415
   "other expenses and losses," 222
   prepaid, 100–103, 117–120,
      608, 626
   selling and administrative, 1031,
      1070, 1109, 1110
   on single-step income
      statement, 22
Expense recognition principle, 97, 122
External sales, 1014–1020
   cost-plus pricing for, 1016–1019
   and target costing, 1015–1016
   time-and-material pricing for,
      1020–1023
   variable-cost pricing for,
      1019–1020
External transactions, 14
External users of accounting
   data, 6–7

F

Face value, 452, 453, 456
Facility-level activities, 850, 851
Factors, 367
Factory labor costs:
   accumulating, 757
   assigning, 761–762, 800

Factory overhead, *see* Manufacturing overhead
FAFSA form, 45
Fair Labor Standards Act, 1160
Fair value, 568–570
    book value vs., 103
    total, 569
Fair value of consideration given up, 510
Fair value of consideration received, 510
Fair value principle, 9, 122
Faithful representation, 9, 120
FASB, *see* Financial Accounting Standards Board
Favorable variances, 1166, 1174
Federal Bureau of Investigation (FBI), 4, 25–26
Feedback, 1121
FIFO method, *see* First-in, first-out method
Finance, careers in, 11
Finance charges, 358
Financial accounting, 6, 712, 713
Financial Accounting Standards Board (FASB), 9
    Accounting Standards Codification, 45
    conceptual framework for accounting standards project, 92, 120–121, 148–149, 496
    on debt and equity securities/instruments, 570
    financial statement presentation project, 202, 556, 656–657
    financial statement structure project, 256, 708
    intangible asset recognition project, 442
    other comprehensive income reporting, 679
    "principles-based" standards of, 354
    on reporting for financial instruments, 394, 597
    revenue recognition project, 148–149
Financial budgets, 1061–1062, 1072–1077
    and budgeted balance sheet, 1075–1076
    cash budget, 1072–1077
Financial disclosures, 223
Financial flexibility, 612
Financial information, 974
Financial markets, 46
Financial measures, 1177
Financial perspective (balanced scorecard), 1176–1177
Financial pressure, fraud and, 308
Financial reporting:
    assumptions in, 121

cost constraint, 122
    ethics in, 7–8
    principles in, 122
    useful information, 120–121
Financial statement(s), 4, 21–24.
    See also specific statements
    and adjusting accounts, 98
    analysis, 418–419, 658–682
        horizontal analysis, 660–664
        need for comparative analysis, 660
        ratio analysis, 666–678
        tools for, 660–661
        vertical analysis, 664–666
    cost of goods manufactured, 720–724
    cost of goods manufactured schedule, 720, 722–724, 772
    current liabilities on, 464–466
    depreciation on, 102–103
    inventories on:
        cost flow methods, 269–271
        presentation and analysis, 274–276
    job cost data on, 771–773
    long-term liabilities on, 464–466
    management's responsibility for, 727
    manufacturing costs reflected in, 720–724
    for merchandising operations, 220–224
        classified balance sheet, 224
        multiple-step income statement, 220–222
        single-step income statement, 223
    notes to the financial statement, 271, 274, 526
    over-/underapplied overhead on, 771–773
    paid-in capital and retained earnings on, 528–529
    preparing:
        from adjusted trial balance, 114–117
        from worksheets, 155–157
    presentation of, 202, 417–418
    receivables on, 373–374
    retained earnings statement, 526–527
    and social responsibility, 24
    standard costs and variances on, 1174–1175
Financing activities, cash inflow/outflow from, 600
    direct method, 622–623
    indirect method, 610–611
Financing section (cash budget), 1073–1074
Finished goods, 260
    assigning costs to, 766–767
    transfer to, 801
Finished goods inventory, 260, 767, 1076

First-in, first-out (FIFO) method, 266–267, 278, 810–816
    and cost reconciliation schedule, 814–815
    and equivalent units of production, 810–816
    and physical unit flow, 811–813
    and production cost report, 815, 816
    and unit production costs, 813–814
    weighted-average method vs., 815–816
Fiscal year, 96
FISH assumption, 267
Fixed assets, 398, 614. *See also* Plant assets
Fixed costs:
    in break-even analysis, 899
    computing, with high-low method, 891–892
    and controllable margin, 1129–1130
    in cost behavior analysis, 887–888
    on CVP graph, 900
    in flexible budgets, 1115–1116
    identifying, with cost behavior analysis, 893
    in incremental analysis, 976, 978
    overhead, 1069
    per unit, 1018–1019
    in responsibility accounting, 1126
    static budget for, 1110
Fixed-rate mortgages, 462
Flexible budget(s), 1111–1118, 1122
    budgetary control with, 1111–1118
    and budget reforecasting, 1117
    case study, 1114–1116
    for cost centers, 1125
    development of, 1114
    performance evaluations with, 1116–1118
    reasons to use, 1111–1114
Flexible budget reports, 1116–1118
Flexible manufacturing, 1122
Flowcharts, activity, 851–852
FOB (free on board), 211, 262
FOB destination, 211, 262
FOB shipping point, 211, 262
"For Deposit Only," 320
Forecasts:
    budget reforecasting, 1117
    sales, 1059–1060, 1063, 1173
Forensic accounting, 26
Fortune, 204, 558
Fragrance manufacturers, 934
Franchises, 415
Fraud, 308–316
    and documentation, 55
    and documentation procedures, 312–313, 401
    and establishment of responsibility, 310
    and human resource controls, 215, 316, 449

and independent internal verification, 315, 360, 401, 449, 522
inventory, 261–263, 272
and physical controls, 215, 314
and segregation of duties, 311–312, 360
Fraud triangle, 308
Free Application for Federal Student Aid (FAFSA) form, 45
Free cash flow, 614–616
Free on board, *see* FOB
Free-shipping subscriptions, 980
Freight costs, 210–211, 228
Full costing, *see* Absorption costing
Full-cost pricing, 1019, 1030
Full disclosure principle, 122, 602
Future cash flows, 600

G
GAAP, *see* Generally accepted accounting principles
Gains:
from exchange of assets, 420
"other revenues and gains," 222
from sale of property, plant, and equipment, 222
unrealized, 569, 572–573
Gain on disposal (gain on sale), 410–411
Geneen, Harold, 2
General journal, 56, 111, 158
General ledger, 57–59, 68, 112
Generally accepted accounting principles (GAAP), 9
and absorption-cost pricing, 1030
and allowance method, 362
and bond amortization, 471
and cash-basis accounting, 96
for classified balance sheet, 200–202
and effective-interest method, 471
for financial statement analysis, 707–708
and fraud, 354–355
IFRS vs., 46
for income statements, 682
for inventories, 304
for investments, 596–597
for liabilities, 495–496
for merchandising operations, 256
net income measured under, 945
for plant and intangible assets, 441–442
for publicly traded companies, 682
for receivables, 393–394
for recording process, 92
for revenue/expense recognition, 97, 148
for statement of cash flows, 656
for stockholders' equity, 555–556
General management, 11
Gift cards, 105

Globalization, 1029, 1034–1035
Global Reporting Initiative, 729
Global Responsibility Report, 1173
Going concern assumption, 121, 403
Goods in transit, 262
Goodwill, 414–416
Government:
accounting career opportunities in, 25–26
regulation of corporations by, 502
Government budgets, 1064, 1079
Graham, Benjamin, 658
Green bonds, 461
Gross profit, 221
Gross profit method (for estimating inventories), 280–281
Gross profit rate, 221
Growth, 884, 1024

H
Hardy, Renee Lawson, 922
Held-for-collection securities, 568
High-low method, 891–892
Hiring employees, 65
Historical cost principle, 9, 122, 510, 561
Honor (of notes receivable), 372
Horizontal analysis, 660–664
of balance sheet, 662
of income statement, 662–663
of retained earnings statement, 663–664
Hourly fees, 1023
"House" (television show), 1114
HR, *see* Human resources
Hsieh, Tony, 1012
Human behavior, *see* Behavior
Human element (in internal controls), 317
Human resources (HR), 6, 315–316
Human resource controls, 215, 449
Human Rights Watch, 728
Hurdle rate, 1212

I
IAASB (International Auditing and Assurance Standards Board), 355
IAS, *see* International Accounting Standards
IASB, *see* International Accounting Standards Board
Ideal standards, 1161
Identification of economic events, 4, 5
IFRS, *see* International Financial Reporting Standards
IFRS 9, 394
Ig Nobel Prizes, 354
IMA, *see* Institute of Management Accountants
IMA Statement of Ethical Professional Practice, 727

Immediate liquidity, 669
Imprest system, 322
Improvements:
additions and, 400–401
land, 399
Incentives, 727
Income. *See also* Net income
comprehensive, 256, 555, 573, 708
net, 21, 155, 160, 529, 565, 600, 607, 616
residual, 1131–1133
target net, 901–904, 925
Income (margin) measure, 1129
Income statement(s), 21–23, 720–721, 1109
from adjusted trial balance, 114, 115
adjusting accounts on, 98, 106–110
budgeted, 1070–1072
consolidated, 578
CVP, 894–897, 1175
effects of cost flow methods on, 269–270
effects of inventory errors on, 272–273
GAAP vs. IFRS for, 256
horizontal analysis of, 662–663
in job order costing, 772
for merchandising operations, 220–224, 231–233
multiple-step income statement, 220–222
single-step income statement, 223
sustainable income on, 678–679
variances disclosed on, 1174–1175
vertical analysis of, 664–666
Income Summary account, 158–160
Income taxes (income taxation):
cash payments for, 621
of corporations, 502
and depreciation of plant assets, 408
effects of cost flow methods on, 271
Income taxes payable, 608–609
Incremental analysis, 972–988
and activity-based costing, 976–977
approach used in, 974–976
defined, 974
for elimination of unprofitable segments, 986–988
for equipment retention/replacement, 985–986
for make-or-buy decision, 979–981
with orders at special prices, 977–978
for outsourcing, 1029
qualitative factors in, 976
for sell-or-process-further decision, 981–984
in virtual companies, 1029

Incremental overhead costs, 976
Indefinite lives, intangible assets with, 414
Independence (of capital projects), 1207
Independent internal verification, 263, 314–315, 360, 401, 449, 522
Indirect fixed costs, 1126
Indirect issue (of stock), 505–506
Indirect labor, 717
Indirect manufacturing costs, *see* Manufacturing overhead
Indirect materials, 716
Indirect method (statement of cash flows), 604–613
  investing/financing activities, 610–611
  net change in cash, 611
  operating activities, cash provided/used by, 606–610
  worksheets, using, 623–628
Industry averages, 660, 667
Information, in internal control, 309
Information technology, 46
Initial public offerings (IPOs), 503
In process inventories, 859
Institute of Management Accountants (IMA), 727, 750
Institutional Shareholder Services, 530
Insurance, as prepaid expense, 101, 102
Insurance payments, 64
Intangible assets, 414–417
  accounting for, 414–417
  amortization of, 414
  on classified balance sheet, 170–171
  copyrights, 415
  franchises and licenses, 415
  goodwill, 415–416
  patents, 414–415
  research and development costs, 416–417
  statement presentation/analysis of, 417–419
  trademarks and trade names, 415
Intangible benefits (net present value method), 1214–1216
Intended use, making land ready for, 398
Intent to convert, 571–572
Intercompany comparisons, 660, 667
Intercompany eliminations, 575, 576, 578
Intercompany transactions, 575, 578
Interest:
  accrued, 108–109
  on bonds, 467, 561
  cash payments for, 621
  on checking accounts, 328
  controlling, 566

  on notes receivable, 370–373
  and purchase discounts, 213
Interest expense, 222, 458, 459, 471
Interest paid, 471
Interest rates:
  and bond market, 562
  contractual, 452, 456
  and finance charges, 358
  market, 454, 456
Interest revenue, 222
Interim periods, 96
Internal auditors, 315
Internal audit staff, 715
Internal control(s), 308–317, 727, 759
  for cash, *see* Cash controls
  and documentation procedures, 312–313, 401
  and establishment of responsibility, 310
  in foreign countries, 98
  human resource controls, 215, 315–316, 449
  and independent internal verification, 314–315, 360, 401, 449, 522
  and inventory fraud, 263
  limitations of, 316–317
  physical controls, 215, 313–314
  primary components of systems for, 309
  principles of control activities, 309–310
  and Sarbanes-Oxley Act, 308–309
  and segregation of duties, 311–312, 360
  for sustainability reporting, 309
Internal process perspective (balanced scorecard), 1176, 1177
Internal rate of return (IRR), 1219–1221
Internal rate of return method, 1219–1221
  advantages of, 1223
  decision rule for, 1220–1221
  net present value method vs., 1221
Internal Revenue Service (IRS), 408
Internal sales, 1026–1027, 1029. *See also* Transfer pricing
Internal transactions, 14
Internal users of accounting data, 5–6
International accounting. *See also* International Financial Reporting Standards (IFRS)
  for debt and equity securities, 568
  double-entry accounting system, 51
  internal controls, 98
  interpretation of standards, 667
  and LIFO, 271
International Accounting Standards (IAS):

IAS 1 (revised) "Presentation of Financial Statements," 354, 707
IAS 7 "Cash Flow Statements," 656
International Accounting Standards Board (IASB), 9, 46
  conceptual framework for accounting standards project, 92, 120–121, 148–149, 496
  financial statement presentation project, 202, 556, 656–657
  financial statement structure project, 256, 708
  intangible asset recognition project, 442
  on reporting for financial instruments, 394, 597
  revenue recognition project, 148–149
International Auditing and Assurance Standards Board (IAASB), 355
International Financial Reporting Standards (IFRS), 9
  in China, 170
  for classified balance sheet, 200–202
  for financial statement analysis, 707–708
  and fraud, 354–355
  for inventories, 304
  for investments, 596–597
  for liabilities, 495–496
  for merchandising operations, 256
  need for, 46
  for plant and intangible assets, 441–442
  for receivables, 393–394
  for recording process, 92
  for revenue recognition, 148
  for statement of cash flows, 656
  for stockholders' equity, 555–556
Internet, 899, 928
Interpretation (of economic events), 4
Intracompany comparisons, 660, 667
Inventoriable costs, *see* Product cost(s)
Inventory(-ies), 250–282
  beginning work in process, 721
  classification of, 260–261
  costing of, 264–272
    average-cost method for, 268, 279
    and consistency principle, 271
    and cost flow assumption, 265–269
    FIFO method for, 266–267, 278
    financial statement effects, 269–271
      balance sheets, 270–271
      income statements, 269–270
      taxes, 271

LIFO method for, 267–268, 278–279

lower-of-cost-or-market for, 274–275

specific identification method for, 264–265

days in, 276, 670

determining quantities of, 261–263

and ownership of goods, 262–263

physical inventory, 261

in direct materials budgets, 1066

ending work in process, 721

errors in, 272–273

balance sheet effects, 273

income statement effects, 272–273

estimating, 280–282

gross profit method for, 280–281

retail inventory method for, 281–282

finished goods, 260, 767, 1076

GAAP vs. IFRS for, 256

just-in-time, 260–261

of merchandising and manufacturing companies, 722–723

in merchandising operations, 207–209, 227–231

perpetual inventory systems, 207–209, 227–231, 277–279, 754

in process, 859

product costs as, 718

in production budgets, 1065

raw materials, 756–757, 1076

on statement of cash flows, 608, 626

statement presentation and analysis of, 274–276

taking, 261

work in process, 758–759, 765

Inventory control, 276

Inventory fraud, 261–263, 272

Inventory methods:

just-in-time, 726

periodic, 720, 721

perpetual, 754

Inventory turnover, 275–276, 670

Investee, 563, 565

Investing activities, cash inflow/outflow from, 600

direct method, 622–623

indirect method, 610–611

Investments, 558–578

debt, 561–563

long-term, see Long-term investments

purchase of, by corporations, 560–561

short- vs. long-term, 571

stock, 563–567

between 20% and 50%, holdings of, 564–566

less than 20%, holdings of, 563–564

more than 50%, holdings of, 566, 567

valuing/reporting of, 568–578

available-for-sale securities, 569–571

on balance sheet, 571–572

on classified balance sheet, 573–574

consolidated financial statements, 575–578

realized/unrealized gain/loss presentation, 572–573

trading securities, 568, 569

Investment centers, 1124, 1127–1130

Investment portfolio, 563

Investors, 6

Invoice(s):

purchase, 209

sales, 214

iPhones, 761

IPOs (initial public offerings), 503

IRR (internal rate of return), 1219–1221

Irregularities, accounting, 69

IRS (Internal Revenue Service), 408

J

Japan, 857

Japanese automakers, 261

JIT (just-in-time) inventory method, 260–261, 726

JIT (just-in-time) processing, 858–859

Jobs:

in job order cost systems, 754–755

in time-and-materials pricing, 1021–1023

Job cost sheets, 758–759

Job order cost systems, 752–773, 809–810

accumulating costs in, 755–758, 767

advantages and disadvantages of, 770–771

assigning costs in, 758–763, 766–767, 770

and cost accounting systems, 754–755

features of, 754–755

flow of costs in, 755–766

journal entries in, 1178–1180

ledger accounts in, 1180

manufacturing costs, 756–766

and over-/underapplied overhead, 771–773

predetermined overhead rate, 763–766

process costing vs., 755, 796–798

recording of costs in, 755

reporting job cost data, 771–773

for service companies, 769–770

standard cost, 1178–1180

Johnson, Bill, 747, 918, 1051

Joint costs, 983–984

Joint products, 982–984

Journal, 56–57, 60–61, 111

Journal entries, 799–801, 1178–1180

Journalizing, 56–57, 67–68

of adjusting entries, 111

of bond trading, 453–454, 456

of closing entries, 158, 229–231

and intercompany eliminations, 576

of stock splits, 523

Just-in-case philosophy, 858

Just-in-time (JIT) inventory method, 260–261, 726

Just-in-time (JIT) processing, 858–859

K

Knight, Phil, 4, 498, 500, 501

L

Labor:

direct, 717, 840, 1068–1069, 1163

indirect, 717

and variable costs, 887

Labor costs:

direct, 840, 1163

factory, 757, 761–762, 800

in time-and-material pricing, 1020–1022

Labor price variances (LPVs), 1170–1171

Labor quantity variances, 1170–1171

Labor reports, 1109

Labor unions, 7

Labor variances, 1166, 1169–1171

Land, 398–399, 402, 622, 626

Land improvements, 399

Large stock dividend, 520

Last-in, first-out (LIFO) method, 267–268, 271, 278–279

LCM (lower-of-cost-or-market), 274–275

Leadership in Energy and Efficient Design (LEED) Certification, 838

Lean manufacturing, 726, 892

Learning and growth perspective (balanced scorecard), 1176, 1177

Leases, 401

Leasing, 401

Ledgers, 758, 1180. See also General ledger

LEED (Leadership in Energy and Efficient Design) Certification, 838

Legal capital, 506

Legal existence (of corporation), 500, 502

Legal restrictions (on retained earnings), 525
Leverage, 673
Leveraging, 673
Liabilities, 12, 444
  current, 446–451
    changes in, 608–609
    on classified balance sheet, 171–172
    and current assets, 446
    defined, 444, 446
    long-term debt, current maturities of, 451
    notes payable, 446–447
    payroll and payroll taxes payable, 448–449
    sales taxes payable, 447–448
    statement presentation/analysis of, 464–466
    unearned revenues, 450–451
  debit and credit procedures, 51
  long-term, 452–473
    bonds, 452–462, 466–473
    on classified balance sheet, 172, 173
    notes payable, long-term, 462–463
    statement presentation/analysis of, 464–466
  on statement of cash flows, 610–611
Liars' loans, 373
Licenses, 415, 503
Life, 558
LIFO conformity rule, 271
LIFO method, *see* Last-in, first-out method
Limited liability, 10, 500–501
Limited life, intangible assets with, 414
Limited resources, 933–935, 1216
Lin, Alfred, 1012
Linear cost assumption, 888, 889
Line positions, 715
Linkages (in balanced scorecard approach), 1177
Liquidating dividend, 515
Liquidation preference, 518
Liquidity, 172, 465, 669
Liquidity ratios, 667–670
  acid-test ratio, 668–669
  current ratio, 667–669
  inventory turnover, 670
  receivables turnover, 669
LISH assumption, 266
Loans, 373, 462–463
Long-range planning, 1061
Long-term creditors, 660
Long-term debt, current maturities of, 451
Long-term debt due within one year, 451
Long-term investments, 170, 571, 572

Long-term liabilities, 446, 452–473
  bonds, 452–462, 466–473
  on classified balance sheet, 172, 173
  notes payable, long-term, 462–463
  statement presentation/analysis of, 464–466
Long-term notes payable, 462–463
Losses:
  accumulated, 556
  casualty, 222
  from exchange of assets, 419–420
  net, 21, 155, 525
  "other expenses and losses," 222
  from sale of property, plant, and equipment, 222
  from strikes by employees, 222
  from uncollectible accounts, 361
  unrealized, 569, 572–573
Loss on disposal (loss on sale), 410, 411
Lower-of-cost-or-market (LCM), 274–275
Lowry, Adam, 972
LPVs (labor price variances), 1170–1171
Luxury goods, 714

M

Machine hours, 764, 800, 840
Machine time used, 800
McKenna, Erin, 1056
Mackey, John, 922
MACRS (Modified Accelerated Cost Recovery System), 408
Madoff, Bernard, 332
Mail receipts, 320
Make-or-buy decision:
  incremental analysis for, 979–981
  opportunity cost in, 980
Maker, 326, 369
Management (managers):
  awareness of operations, 1058
  decision-making process of, 974–976
  decisions of, 852–853
  and financial statements, 727
  functions of, 712–713
  in participative budgeting, 1060–1061
  usefulness of ABC for, 847
Management (of corporation), 501
Management, activity-based, 852–853
Management by exception, 1120–1121
Management consulting, 25
Managers, compensation of, 501
Managerial accounting, 6, 25, 712–716
  activities of, 712
  current trends in, 724–729
  defined, 712
  financial accounting vs., 712, 713

Manufacturing, 716
  automated factories in, 717
  flexible, 1122
  lean, 714, 726
  merchandising vs., 716
Manufacturing companies:
  deciding to move, 988
  financial statements for, 720, 722–723
Manufacturing costs, 716–720.
    See also Manufacturing overhead
  accumulating, 755–758, 767, 797
  assigning, *see* Assigning manufacturing costs
  calculating, for absorption-cost pricing, 1030
  direct labor, 717
  direct materials, 716
  in financial statements, 720–724
  in job order costing, 756–766, 797
  in process costing, 797, 799–801
  in static budget, 1110
  total, 721, 808
Manufacturing costs incurred in the prior period, 721
Manufacturing overhead, 717
  accumulating costs of, 757
  assigning costs of, 763–766, 801
  over-/underapplied, 771–773
  standard rate per unit, 1164
  in year-end balance, 772–773
Manufacturing overhead budget, 1069–1070
Manufacturing overhead variances, 1171–1173
Margin (income) measure, 1129
Margin of safety, 903–904, 926
Margin of safety ratio, 903, 926
Market-based transfer price, 1028–1029
Marketing, 11, 57, 217
Market interest rate, 454, 456
Market niche, 1015
Market value:
  of bonds, 454
  book value vs., 532–533
  of stock, 532–533
Markup, 1016–1018
  for absorption-cost pricing, 1031
  and competitive advantage, 1020
  for variable-cost pricing, 1032
Marshall, John, 500
Master budgets, 1061–1062, 1067–1068, 1109–1110
Matching principle, 97, 122
Material(s). *See also* Raw materials
  direct, 716, 1163
  equivalent units of production, 813
  indirect, 716
  pricing, 1020–1023
Materiality (materiality principle), 401, 1120

Material loading charge, 1021, 1022
Materials price variance (MPV), 1167–1169
Materials quantity variance, 1167–1169
Materials requisition slips, 759–761, 799
Materials variances, 1167–1169
Matrix, variance analysis, 1168, 1171
Maturity date:
  of bonds, 452
  of promissory notes, 369–370
Measurement principles, 9, 122
Merchandise inventory, 260
Merchandise purchases budget, 1077–1078, 1080
Merchandisers, 1077–1078, 1080
Merchandise transactions, in periodic system, 228
Merchandising, 716
Merchandising companies, 720, 722, 723
Merchandising operations, 204–233
  completing the accounting cycle for, 218–220
    adjusting entries, 218
    closing entries, 218–220
  financial statements for, 220–224
    classified balance sheet, 224
    income statement presentation of sales, 220
    multiple-step income statement, 220–222
    single-step income statement, 223
  flow of costs in, 207–209
  inventory systems in, 207–209
    periodic system, 208
    perpetual system, 207–209, 227–231
  operating cycles in, 206
  recording purchases of merchandise in, 209–213
    freight costs, 210–211
    purchase discounts, 212–213, 229
    purchase returns and allowances, 212, 228–229
  recording sales of merchandise in, 214–217
    sales discounts, 216, 229
    sales returns and allowances, 215–216, 229
Merchandising profit, 221
Mergers and acquisitions, 46
Minimum rate of return, 1132
Minimum transfer price, 1025–1027
Misallocation of workers, 1171
Mixed costs, 889–893
Modified Accelerated Cost Recovery System (MACRS), 408
Monetary unit assumption, 10, 121
Money, time value of, see Time value of money

Monitoring, in internal control, 309
Morale, cost of, 976
Mortgage bonds, 452
Mortgage loans, 462–463
Mortgage notes payable, 462
Motivation, 1058, 1121
Movie industry, 752, 1130
MPV (materials price variance), 1167–1169
Multinational corporations, 46
Multiple-step income statement, 220–222
Murdoch, Rupert, 558
Murdock, Wilbert, 444
Mutually exclusive projects, 1216–1218

N
Natural resources, 412–413, 417
Negotiable instruments, 326
Negotiated transfer prices, 1024–1027
  with excess capacity, 1026
  with no excess capacity, 1025–1026
  variable costs in, 1026–1027
Net annual cash flow, 1207–1208
Net cash, 600, 616
Net change in cash:
  direct method, 623
  indirect method, 611
Net income, 21
  and absorption vs. variable costing, 942–947
  and contribution margin, 930
  and dividends, 160
  of investee, 565
  and net cash for operating activities, 600
  net cash from converting, 616
  and noncash current assets, 607
  and sell-or-process-further decisions, 982
  sustainable income vs., 678
  target, 901–904, 925
  and unprofitable segments/products, 986–987
  on worksheets, 155
Net income available to common stockholders, 529
Net loss, 21, 155, 525
Net present value (NPV), 1209–1210
Net present value method, 1209–1219
  assumptions of, 1213
  for equal annual cash flows, 1210–1211
  example, 1213–1214
  intangible benefits in, 1214–1216
  internal rate of return method vs., 1221
  with mutually exclusive projects, 1216–1218
  and risk analysis, 1218
  for unequal annual cash flows, 1211

Net (cash) realizable value, 361–362, 371
Net sales, 221
Neutral information, 120
No excess capacity, 1025–1026
Nominal accounts (temporary accounts), 158, 163, 164
Noncash activities, significant, 601–602
Noncash current assets, changes in, 607–608
Noncontrollable costs, 1120, 1126
Noncurrent assets, changes in, 610–611
Nonfinancial information, 974
Nonfinancial measures, 1176–1177
Nonmanufacturing companies, 1077–1080
  merchandisers, 1077–1078, 1080
  not-for-profit organizations, 1079
  service enterprises, 1078–1079
Nonoperating activities, 220–222
Non-value-added activities, 850–852
No-par stock, 507, 510
Normal balance, 51–52, 55
Normal capacity, 1164
Normal range, 888–889
Normal standards, 1161
Norton, Terry, 356
Notes payable, 12, 446–447
Notes receivable, 369–373
  collection of, 331
  computing interest for, 370–373
  defined, 358
  disposing of, 372–373
  maturity date of, 369–370
  recognizing, 371
  valuing, 371
Notes to the financial statement, 271, 274, 526
Not-for-profit organizations, 500, 1079
NPV (net present value), 1209–1210. See also Net present value method
NSF (not sufficient funds), 328, 331

O
Obligations, ability to meet, 600
Obsolescence, 402–403
Olympic Games, 1075
Onward (Howard Schultz), 1158
Open Standards Benchmarking Collaborative, 1162
Operating activities:
  cash inflow/outflow from, 600–601
    direct method, 616–621
    indirect method, 606–610
  in multiple-step income statements, 220
  net cash provided/used by, 600
Operating assets, 1129, 1130

Operating budgets, 1063–1072
  and budgeted income statement,
    1070–1072
  defined, 1061
  direct labor budget, 1068–1069
  direct materials budget, 1065–1068
  manufacturing overhead budget,
    1069–1070
  preparation of, 1063–1072
  production budget, 1064–1065,
    1067
  sales budget, 1063–1064, 1067
  selling and administrative expense
    budget, 1070
Operating cycles, 168, 206
Operating expenses, 211, 221, 415
Operating leverage, 937–938
Operations costing, 809–810
Opportunity (for fraud), 308
Opportunity costs, 975
  in make-or-buy decision, 980
  and no excess capacity, 1025–1026
Optimism, budgetary, 1064
Orders:
  accepting, at special prices,
    977–978
  incremental analysis for, 977–978
Ordinary repairs, 400
Organizational structure, 714–715,
    1058
Organization charts, 714, 715
Organization costs, 503
Other assets, see Intangible assets
Other comprehensive income, 256,
    679–681
"Other expenses and losses," 222
Other receivables, 358
"Other revenues and gains," 222
Outsourcing:
  and cost structure, 935
  and transfer pricing, 1029
Outstanding checks, 329–330
Outstanding stock, 513
Overapplied overhead, 771–773
Overhead. See also Manufacturing
    overhead
  assigning, to products, 844–846
  departmental overhead costs, 1109
  and direct labor, 840
  inefficient use of, 1172–1173
  in job order costing, 771–773
  manufacturing overhead budget,
    1069–1070
  overapplied and underapplied,
    771–773
Overhead controllable variance,
    1172, 1181–1182
Overhead costs:
  and ABC, 849, 850
  assigning, to products, 845–846
  departmental, 1109
  incremental, 976
  in service industries, 855–857

Overhead cost pools, 842, 844
Overhead rates:
  activity-based, 844, 845
  computing, 845
  predetermined, 763–766, 768, 840,
    1163–1164
Overhead variance, 1171–1173,
    1181–1182
Overhead volume variance,
    1172, 1182
Overspending, 1079
Over-the counter receipts, 318–319
Owner's equity, see
    Stockholders' equity
Ownership:
  of corporations, 500
  of goods for inventories, 262–263
Ownership rights, 501, 504

P
Paid-in capital, 507, 509, 520, 522,
    525, 528–529
Paper (phantom) profit, 270
Parent company, 566, 567
Participative budgeting, 1060–1061
Partnerships, 10
Par-value stock, 506–507, 509
Patents, 414–415
Payback period, 1208, 1209
Payee, 326, 369
Payment date (dividends), 517
Payments, schedule of
    expected, 1074
Payout ratio, 674
Payroll, 448–449
Payroll taxes, 449
Payroll taxes payable, 449
PCAOB (Public Company Accounting
    Oversight Board), 308
People, 558
People, planet, profit, see Triple
    bottom line
P-E (price-earnings) ratio, 673–674
Percentage-of-receivables basis,
    365–366
Percentage-of-sales basis, 364–365
Performance, fees based on, 1023
Performance evaluation, 1120–1122,
    1127–1131
  with flexible budgets, 1116–1118
  with investment centers,
    1127–1130
  principles of, 1120–1122
  and residual income, 1131–1133
  with static budgets, 1110
Performance measures, 726–727,
    815–816, 1126–1127
Performance standards, 853
Period costs, 718
Periodic inventory system, 208,
    227–231, 720, 721
  closing of merchandise inventory
    in, 229–231

cost of goods sold under, 227–228
  merchandise purchases in,
    228–229
  merchandise sales in, 229
Periodicity assumption, 121
Permanent accounts, 157–158,
    162, 163
Perpetual inventory system(s),
    207–209, 754
  inventory cost flow methods in,
    277–279
  periodic vs., 227–231
Petty cash fund, 322–324
  establishment of, 322
  making payments from, 322–323
  replenishment of, 323–324
Phantom (paper) profit, 270
Pharmaceutical industry, 1014
Physical controls, 215, 313–314
Physical custody (of records), 312
Physical unit(s), 806
  and FIFO method, 811–813
  in process costing, 806, 811–813
Pickard, Thomas, 4
Planning. See also Budgetary
    planning
  and budgeting, 1058
  as management function, 713
Plant assets (plant and equipment),
    398–412
  buildings, 399
  defined, 398
  depreciation of, 402–409
    computation, 403–408
    and income taxes, 408
    methods, 403–408
    revisions in estimate of, 408–409
  determining cost of, 398–400
  disposal of, 409–412
    retirement, 410
    sale, 410–412
  equipment, 399–400
  exchange of, 419–420
    gain treatment, 420
    loss treatment, 419–420
  expenditures during useful life of,
    400–401
  land, 398–399
  land improvements, 399
  loss on sale of, 606–607, 620
  statement presentation and
    analysis, 417–419
Ponzi schemes, 332
Post-audits, 1218–1219
Post-closing trial balance, 162–164
Posting, 60–61, 68
  of adjusting entries, 112
  of closing entries, 158, 229–231
Practical range, 888–889
Predetermined overhead rates,
    763–766, 768, 840, 1163–1164
Predictive value (of financial
    information), 120

Preemptive right, 504
Preferred dividends, 529, 672
Preferred stock, 511, 517–519, 672
Preferred stock equity, 532
Premium, bonds issued at, 459–460
Prenumbered documents, 312
Prenumbering, 759
Prepaid expenses (prepayments), 100–103, 117–120, 608, 626
"Presentation of Financial Statements" (*IAS 1* [*revised*]), 354, 707
Present value, 454. *See also* Net present value method
Price-earnings (P-E) ratio, 673–674
Price takers, 1014
Pricing, 1012–1035
    absorption-cost, 1030–1032
    in competitive markets, 1014–1015
    in corporate strategy, 1015
    cost-plus costing, 769, 1016–1019
    and equivalent units computations, 815–816
    for external sales, 1014–1020
    full-cost, 1019, 1030
    for services, 1020–1023
    target costing, 1015–1016
    time-and-material, 1020–1023
    transfer, *see* Transfer pricing
    transfer prices, 1024–1030
    variable-cost, 1019–1020, 1032–1033
Principal, 467
"Principles-based" standards, 46
Prior period adjustments, 526
Private accounting, 25. *See also* Managerial accounting
Privately held corporations, 500
Process cost systems, 754, 794–816
    assigning manufacturing costs in, 799–801
    cost reconciliation schedule, preparation of, 808
    equivalent units of production, computation of, 802–804, 806–807, 810–816
    and flow of costs, 799
    job order costing vs., 755, 796–798
    operations costing, 809–810
    physical unit flow, computation of, 806
    preparing production cost report, 808–809
    and production cost report, 805–809
    for service companies, 797
    unit production costs, computation of, 807–808
    uses of, 796
Product cost(s), 717
    as inventory, 718
    in manufacturing costs, 719
    overhead as, 845–846

period costs vs., 718
    for service industries, 724–725
Production budget, 1064–1065, 1067
Production cost reports:
    and FIFO method, 815, 816
    in process costing, 805–809, 815, 816
Production department, 1169, 1171, 1172, 1174
Productive life, 403
Product-level activities, 850, 851
Profit:
    accumulated, 556
    gross, 221
    paper (phantom), 270
    as purpose of corporation, 500
    retained, 556
Profitability:
    of capital expenditure, 1222
    of capital projects, 1208–1209
    and growth, 884
Profitability index, 1217–1219
Profitability ratios, 670–674
    asset turnover, 671
    earnings per share, 673
    payout ratio, 674
    price-earnings ratio, 673–674
    profit margin, 671
    return on assets, 672
    return on common stockholders' equity, 672–673
Profit and loss statement, *see* Income statement
Profit centers, 1124–1127
Profit margin (profit margin percentage), 671
Pro forma income, 682
Promissory notes, 369–370
Property, plant, and equipment, 170. *See also* Plant assets
Proprietor, 10
Proprietorships, 10
Pro rata (term), 515
Prorating (of depreciation), 405
Public accounting, 25
Public Company Accounting Oversight Board (PCAOB), 308
Publicly held corporations, 500
"Pull approach," 859
Purchases, recording, 209–213
    discounts, 212–213, 229
    freight costs, 210–211
    returns and allowances, 212, 228–229
Purchase allowances, 212
Purchased buildings, 399
Purchase discounts, 212–213, 229
Purchase invoices, 209
Purchase returns, 212, 228–229
Purchasing activities, segregation of duties and, 311
Purchasing department, 57, 1168
"Push approach," 858

Q
Quick (acid-test) ratio, 668–669

R
Radio frequency identification (RFID), 276
Railroads, 942
Rapoport, Michael, 145
Rate of depreciation, 404–405
Ratio analysis, 660, 666–678
    liquidity ratios, 667–670
    margin of safety ratio, 903, 926
    profitability ratios, 670–674
    solvency ratios, 674–675
    summary of ratios, 676
Rationalization (of fraud), 308
Raw materials, 260, 716
    accumulating costs of, 756–757
    assigning costs of, 759–761, 799–800
    in direct materials standards, 1162
    stockpiling, 1066
Raw materials inventory, 756–757, 1076
R&D (research and development) costs, 416–417, 442
Readily marketable investments, 571
Real accounts (permanent accounts), 157–158, 162, 163
Real estate, 11
Real estate taxes payable, 12
Realizable value, net, 361–362, 371
Reasonable assurance (term), 316
Receipts, cash, *see* Cash receipts
Receivables, 356–375
    accounts receivable, 358–360
        disposing of, 366–368
        recognizing, 358–360
        valuing, 360–366
    defined, 358
    notes receivable, 369–373
        computing interest for, 370–373
        disposing of, 372–373
        maturity date of, 369–370
        recognizing, 371
        valuing, 371
    statement presentation/analysis for, 373–374
    trade, 358
    types of, 358
Receivables turnover (accounts receivable turnover ratio), 374, 669
Recessions, 272, 892, 1023
Reconciliation, *see* Bank reconciliation
Reconciliation method, *see* Indirect method (statement of cash flows)
Reconciling items, 626–628
Record date (dividends), 516, 517

Recording process, 48–71
    and accounts, 50–55
    illustrated example of, 62–68
    steps in, 55–61
        journalizing, 56–57
        posting, 60–61
        using ledger, 57–59
    and trial balance, 69–71
Record-keeping, 312
Recovery of uncollectible accounts,
    363–364
Recycling, electronics, 110
Regional banking industry, 1175
Regression analysis, 892
Regulations, 1160. See also
    Standards
Regulatory agencies, 6–7
Relevance of financial information,
    9, 120
Relevant costs, 975, 978, 979, 985
Relevant range:
    of activity index, 889
    in cost behavior analysis, 888–889
Remanufactured goods, 804
Rent payments, 63
Rent revenue, 222
Reporting:
    of cash, 333–334
    determining costs vs., 712
    financial, see Financial reporting
    performance evaluation, 1121
Reputation, corporate, 171
Required balance (in Allowance for
    Doubtful Accounts), 366
Required rate of return, 1209, 1212
Research (for effective budgeting),
    1058–1059
Research and development (R&D)
    costs, 416–417, 442
Reserves, 555
Residual claim, 504
Residual equity, see Stockholders'
    equity
Residual income, 1131–1133
Residual value, 441
Resources:
    ERP software systems, 726
    limited, 933–935, 1216
Responsibility, establishment
    of, 310
Responsibility accounting,
    1118–1131. See also
    Responsibility centers
    budgeting vs., 1119
    and collaboration, 1119
    conditions for, 1118
    with controllable vs.
        noncontrollable revenues
        and costs, 1120
    performance evaluation in,
        1120–1121
    reporting system for, 1122–1124

Responsibility centers, 1124–1131
    behavior affecting, 1121
    cost centers, 1124, 1125
    investment centers, 1127–1130
    profit centers, 1124–1127
Responsibility reporting system,
    1122–1124
    for investment centers, 1128–1129
    for profit centers, 1126–1127
Restricted cash, 333–334
Restrictive endorsements, 320
Résumes, inflating, 90–91
Retailers, 206
Retail inventory method, 281–282
Retained earnings, 13, 52, 507–508,
    524–527
    on budgeted balance sheet, 1076
    and cash dividends, 515
    defined, 524
    and prior period adjustments, 526
    restrictions on, 525–526
    statement of, 21–23, 526–527,
        663–664
    on statement of cash flows, 611,
        622, 627
    statement presentation/analysis of,
        528–529, 531
    and stock dividends, 520
    and stock splits, 522
Retained earnings restrictions,
    525–526
Retained earnings statement, 21–23
    from adjusted trial balance,
        114, 115
    of corporations, 526–527, 531
    horizontal analysis of, 663–664
Retained profits, 556
Retirement, of plant assets, 410
Returns and allowances:
    for merchandise purchases, 212,
        228–229
    for merchandise sales, 215–216, 229
Return on assets, 672
Return on common stockholders'
    equity, 529, 672–673
Return on investment (ROI),
    1127–1128
    and absorption-cost pricing,
        1031–1032
    and cost-plus pricing, 1017–1019
    disadvantage of, 1132
    improvement of, 1129–1130
    judgmental factors in, 1129
    for movie industry, 1130
    with positive or zero net present
        value, 1209–1210
    residual income vs., 1131–1133
    and variable-cost pricing, 1033
Revenue(s), 53
    accrued, 106–108
    controllable, 1120, 1126–1127
    defined, 13

"other revenues and gains," 222
    sales, 206, 220
    service, 1078, 1079
    on single-step income
        statement, 22
    and stockholders' equity, 17
    from stock investments, 565–566
    unearned, 104–105, 117–120,
        450–451
Revenue expenditures, 400
Revenue recognition, 97, 98, 122,
    148–149
Reversing entries, 165–167, 174–175
RFID (radio frequency
    identification), 276
Risk (in capital budgeting), 1207
Risk analysis, 1218
Risk assessment (in internal
    control), 309
Rodgers, Aaron, 48
ROI, see Return on investment
Rolling Stones, 903
Rowling, J.K., 414
"Rules-based" standards, 46
Ryan, Eric, 972

S
Safety:
    employee, 1216
    margin of, 903–904, 926
Salaries, 26, 109–110
Salaries and wages payable, 12
Salary payments, 66
Sale(s):
    of bonds, 561–562
    and controllable margin, 1129
    credit card, 367–368
    on CVP graph, 900
    external, 1014–1020
    internal, 1026–1027, 1029. See also
        Transfer pricing
    and margin of safety, 926
    net, 221
    of notes receivable, 373
    of plant assets, 410–412,
        606–607, 620
    of receivables, 367
    recording, 214–217
        discounts, 216, 229
        returns and allowances,
            215–216, 229
    of stock, 564
Sales activities, and segregation of
    duties, 311
Sales budgets, 1063–1064, 1067
Sales department, 1172–1173
Sales dollars:
    break-even point in, 898, 931–932
    for target net income, 902
Sales forecasts, 1059–1060,
    1063, 1173
Sales invoices, 214

Sales mix, 929–935
  and break-even analysis, 929–933
  defined, 929
  with limited resources, 933–935
Sales reports, 1109
Sales revenue, 206, 220
Sales taxes payable, 12, 447–448
Sales units:
  break-even point in, 899, 929–930
  for target net income, 901–902
Salvage value, 403, 406
Sarbanes-Oxley Act (SOX),
      7–8, 727
  and accounting errors, 70
  and human resources, 316
  and IFRS, 46
  and internal controls, 25, 98,
      308–309, 354
  and job of internal auditors, 25
  and management of
      corporations, 501
  and restatements, 166
Schedules:
  cost of goods manufactured, 720,
      722–724, 772
  cost reconciliation, 808, 814–815
  of expected payments and
      collections, 1073–1074
Schedules for noncash
      activities, 602
Schultz, Howard, 1158
Scrap reports, 1109
Secured bonds, 452
Securities and Exchange
      Commission (SEC), 9, 332,
      502, 569, 596, 682
Segregation of duties, 311–312, 360
Sellers, freight costs incurred
      by, 211
Selling and administrative expenses,
      1031, 1070, 1110
Selling and administrative expense
      budget, 1070
Selling expenses report, 1109
Selling price. See also Target
      selling price
  discounts on, 926–927
  unit, 898
Sell-or-process-further decision,
      981–984
  for multiple products, 982–984
  for single products, 982
Sensitivity analysis, 1218
Service charges, bank, 328, 331
Service companies:
  activity-based costing in, 854–857
  airline baggage handling costs, 857
  balanced scorecard approach
      in, 1176
  break-even and margin of safety
      in, 899, 903
  budgetary optimism in, 1064

budgeting in, 1075, 1078–1079,
      1114, 1117
  contribution margin in, 932
  credit card companies, 976
  fees of, 1023
  free-shipping subscriptions, 980
  job order costing for, 769–770
  operating leverage of, 937–938
  pricing, 1023
  process costing for, 797
  product costing for, 724–725
  standard costs in, 1160
  traditional costing in, 855
Service contracts, 770
Service life, 403
Shareholders' equity, see
      Stockholders' equity
Short-term creditors, 660
Short-term investments, 571
Short-term paper, 571n.4
Significant noncash activities,
      601–602
Significant variances, 1174
Simple entries, 57
Single-step income statement, 223
Sinking fund bond, 452
Skilled workers, 892, 1171
"Slush" funds, 322
Small businesses, 1059
Small stock dividend, 520
Social responsibility, 24, 171,
      728, 1173
Solvency ratios, 674–675
  debt to assets ratio, 674–675
  times interest earned, 675
SOX, see Sarbanes-Oxley Act
Specific identification method,
      264–265
Spending variance, 1172
Split-off point, 983
Sports Illustrated, 450, 558
Staff positions, 715
Stakeholders, 8
Standards:
  budgets vs., 1161
  need for, 1160
  normal vs. ideal, 1161
Standard costs, 1161–1175
  advantages of, 1160–1161
  defined, 1160
  direct labor standards, 1163
  and direct labor variances,
      1169–1171
  direct materials standards,
      1162–1163
  and direct materials variances,
      1167–1169
  on financial statements,
      1174–1175
  ideal vs. normal standards, 1161
  manufacturing overhead,
      1163–1164

and manufacturing overhead
      variances, 1171–1173
  and reporting variances,
      1173–1174
  setting, 1161–1164
  and statement presentation of
      variances, 1174–1175
  total standard cost per unit, 1164
  in total variance, 1166
  variances affecting, 1166–1167
Standard cost, job order cost
      accounting system,
      1178–1180
  journal entries, 1178–1180
  ledger accounts, 1180
Standard direct labor cost per
      unit, 1163
Standard direct materials cost per
      unit, 1163
Standard hours allowed,
      1172, 1181
Standard manufacturing overhead
      rate per unit, 1164
Standard predetermined overhead
      rate, 1163–1164
Stated rate (of bonds), 452
Stated value, 507, 510, 522
Statement of cash flows, 21–23,
      598–631
  classification of cash flows on,
      600–601
  direct method of preparing, 604,
      616–623
    investing/financing activities,
      622–623
    net change in cash, 623
    operating activities, 616–621
  evaluating a company using,
      614–616
  format of, 602–603
  indirect method of preparing,
      604–613
    investing/financing activities,
      610–611
    net change in cash, 611
    operating activities, 606–610
    worksheets, using, 623–628
  preparation of, 603–604,
      623–628
  and significant noncash activities,
      601–602
  T-account approach, 629–631
  usefulness of, 600
  worksheets in preparation of,
      623–628
Statement of comprehensive income,
      555, 678–679, 681
Statement of financial position, 201
Statement of operations, see Income
      statement
Static budget(s), 1109–1113. See also
      Master budgets

Static budget reports, 1109–1111
Stock:
  acquisition of, 564, 565
  authorized, 505
  book value of, 531–533
  capital, 505, 528
  common, 13, 52, 509–511
    bonds vs., 466–467, 562
    book value per share, 531–533
    cash dividend allocation, 519
    issuance of, 509–511
    no-par, 507, 510
    and owners' equity, 507–508
    par-value, 509
    for services or noncash
      assets, 510
    on statement of cash flows, 611,
      622, 627
    and stockholder rights, 504
  issuance of, 509–511
  market value of, 506, 532–533
  outstanding, 513
  par vs. no-par-value, 506–507,
    509–510
  preferred, 511, 517–519
  sale of, 564
  treasury, 512–515
    disposal of, 513–514
    purchase of, 512–513
Stock certificate, 504
Stock dividends, 520–521
Stockholders, 715
  financial statement analysis
    by, 660
  limited liability of, 500–501
  net income available to, 529
  ownership rights of, 504
Stockholders' equity, 12–14, 507–508
  accounts for, 52–53
  and available-for-sale
    securities, 570
  on balance sheet, 172–173,
    528–529
  and capital stock, 505
  and cash dividends, 517
  and corporate social
    responsibility, 530
  debits and credits for, 52–53
  impact of transactions on, 15–16
  relationships related to, 54
  return on common stockholders'
    equity, 529, 672–673
  and revenue, 17
  and sale of Treasury stock, 514
  and stock splits/dividends, 522
Stockholders' equity account,
  513, 521
Stockholders' equity statement, 531
Stock investments, 563–567
  between 20% and 50%, holdings
    of, 564–566

less than 20%, holdings of, 563–564
  more than 50%, holdings of,
    566, 567
Stockpiling of raw materials, 1066
Stock quotes, reading, 506
Stock splits, 522–524
Straight-line method, 404–405,
  468–470
Strategic investments, 560
Su, Vivi, 356
Subsidiary (affiliated) company, 566
Subsidiary ledger, 758
Sunk costs, 975, 983, 985
Supplementary schedules, 602
Suppliers:
  cash payments to, 619–620
  CVP analysis and price changes
    from, 927
  dependability of, 859
Supplies, as prepaid expense, 100–101
Surplus, 529
Sustainability:
  electronics recycling, 110
  green bonds, 461
  internal controls for sustainability
    reporting, 309
  marketing green, 217
  and shareholders' equity, 530
  social responsibility and financial
    statements, 24
  sustainability reports, 413
Sustainable business practices,
  728–729
Sustainable income, 678–682
Swinmum, Nick, 1012

T
T-account, 50, 629–631
Taking inventory, 261
Target costs, 1014–1016
Target net income, 901–904, 925
Target selling price, 1016–1020
  for absorption-cost pricing, 1031
  for variable-cost pricing, 1033
Taxes and taxation. *See also* Income
    taxes (income taxation);
    Payroll taxes
  as area of public accounting, 25
  corporate, 502
  global differences in rates, 1029,
    1034–1035
  payroll taxes, 449
  real estate taxes payable, 12
  sales taxes payable, 447–448
Taxing authorities, 6
Telecommunications companies, 724
Temporary accounts, 157, 158,
  163, 164
Theft:
  employee, 324
  of merchandise, 215

Theory of constraints, 726, 934
Thill, Dave, 747, 1199–1200
Three-column form of account, 59
Thrune, Rick, 747, 835
Tilton, Glenn, 1177
Time, 558
Time-and-material pricing,
  1020–1023
Time lags (for bank statements), 328
Timely information, 121
Time periods:
  budget, 1059
  for budgeting vs. long-range
    planning, 1061
  payback, 1208, 1209
  in process cost systems, 754
Time period assumption, 96,
  121, 148
Times interest earned, 466, 675
Time tickets, 761–762
Time value of money:
  and capital budgeting, 1209–1219
  and incremental analysis, 976
  and market value of bonds, 454
Timing issue(s), 96–98
  accrual- vs. cash-basis accounting
    as, 96
  fiscal/calendar years as, 96
  recognizing revenues/expenses as,
    97–98
TLV (total labor variance),
  1169–1170
TMV (total materials variance), 1167
Total assets, 514, 517
Total costs (on CVP graph), 900
Total costs accounted for, 808
Total cost of work in process, 721
Total costs to be accounted for, 808
Total fair value, 569
Totaling rule, 70
Total labor variance (TLV),
  1169–1170
Total manufacturing costs,
  719–721, 808
Total materials variance
  (TMV), 1167
Total overhead variance, 1171–1172
Total quality management (TQM)
  systems, 726, 859
Total standard cost per unit, 1164
Total units accounted for, 806
Total units to be accounted for, 806
Total variance, 1166
TQM (total quality management)
  systems, 726, 859
Traceable costs, *see* Fixed costs
Trademarks and trade names,
  415, 416
Trade receivables, 358
Trading on the equity, 673
Trading securities, 568, 569, 680

Traditional costing:
  activity-based costing vs., 840–843
  illustrated example of, 840–841
  in service industries, 855
  unit costs under, 846–847
Transactions, 14
Transaction analysis, 15–20, 62–67
Transfer, of corporate ownership rights, 501
Transfer prices, 1024–1030
Transfer pricing, 1024–1030
  cost-based, 1027–1028
  in global environment, 1029, 1034–1035
  market-based, 1028–1029
  negotiated, 1024–1027
  and outsourcing, 1029
  tax rates affecting, 1029, 1034–1035
Transit, goods in, 262
Transposition errors, 70
Treasurer, 501, 715
Treasury stock, 512–515
  disposal of, 513–514
  purchase of, 512–513
Trend analysis, see Horizontal analysis
Trial balance, 69–71
  adjusted, 232, 233
  and adjusting entries, 98
  defined, 69
  limitations of, 69–70
  locating errors in, 70
  for merchandising operations, 231–233
  post-closing, 162–164
  steps in preparation of, 69
  use of dollar signs in, 70
  on worksheets, 153
Triple bottom line (people, planet, profit):
  corporate social responsibility, 728
  remanufactured goods, 804
  at Starbucks, 1173
  vertical farming, 888
True cash balance, 330
Trustee (of bond), 452
Turnover:
  asset, 418–419, 671
  inventory, 275–276, 670
  receivables, 374, 669

U

Uncollectible accounts:
  allowance method for, 361–366
  direct write-off method for, 361
Underapplied overhead, 771–773
Underestimating costs, 755
Underlining, 70

Understandability (of financial information), 121
Underwriting, of stock issues, 505–506
Unearned revenue, 104–105, 117–120, 450–451
Unfavorable variances, 1165–1166, 1174
Unionized workers, 1171
Units completed, costing for, 808
Unit conversion cost, 808
Unit costs:
  with activity-based costing, 847
  calculating, for variable-cost pricing, 1032
  in job order and process cost systems, 798
  with traditional costing, 846–847
Units in process, costing for, 808
Unit-level activities, 849, 851
Unit materials cost, 808
Units-of-activity method, 405–406, 412
Units-of-production method, 405
Unit production costs:
  defined, 807
  with FIFO method, 813–814
  in process costing, 807–808, 813–814
Unit selling prices, 898
Units started and completed, 810
Unit variable costs, 898
Unprofitable segments, 986–988
Unrealized gains, 569, 572–573
Unrealized losses, 569, 572–573
Unsecured bonds, 452
Unskilled workers, 1171
Useful information (for financial reporting), 120–121
Useful life, 101, 403

V

Valuation:
  of accounts receivable, 360–366
  allocation vs., 102
  of notes receivable, 371
Value(s), 713. See also Book value
  adding, 713, 850–852
  measurement of, 713
  net present, 1209–1210
Value-added activities, 850–852
Value chain, 725–726
Value investing, 658
Variable cost(s):
  computing, with high-low method, 891–892
  and controllable margin, 1129–1130
  in cost behavior analysis, 886–887, 893
  on CVP graph, 900

in flexible budgets, 1115–1116
in incremental analysis, 976, 978
in negotiated transfer pricing, 1026–1027
overhead, 1069
unit, 898
Variable costing. See also specific topics, e.g. *Job costing
  absorption costing vs., 939–947
  deciding when to use, 945–947
  defined, 939
  example of, 940–945
  potential advantages of, 947
Variable cost per unit, 891
Variable-cost pricing, 1019–1020, 1032–1033
Variances:
  controllable, 1172, 1181–1182
  disclosing, 1174–1175
  favorable, 1166, 1174
  labor, 1166, 1169–1171
  and management by exception, 1174
  materials, 1167–1169
  overhead, 1171–1173, 1181–1182
  reporting, 1173–1174
  spending, 1172
  in standard cost accounting systems, 1178–1180
  total, 1166
  unfavorable, 1165–1166, 1174
Verifiable information, 121
Vertical analysis, 660, 664–666
  of balance sheet, 664
  of income statement, 664–666
Vertical farming, 888
Vertical growth, 1024
Vice president of operations, 715
Virtual close, 161
Virtual companies, 1029
Voluntary restrictions (on retained earnings), 525
Vouchers, 321–322
Voucher register, 321
Voucher systems, 321–322

W

Wages, 109–110
Wages and salaries payable, 448
Wages, 1171
Wear and tear, 402
Weighted-average contribution margin, 929–932
Weighted-average method, 802–804, 815–816
Weighted-average unit cost, 268
Welch, Deb, 747, 1200
Wholesalers, 206
Wireless service providers, 1212

Withholding taxes, 448–449.
     See also Payroll taxes
Work force (for JIT), 859
Working capital, 172, 465, 668
Work in process, 260
Work in process accounts, 798
Work in process inventory,
     758–759, 765
Worksheet(s), 150, 152–157
     defined, 152
     for merchandising operations,
          231–233

preparing adjusting entries
     from, 157
preparing financial statements
     from, 155–157
     consolidated balance sheets,
          576–578
     statement of cash flows,
          623–628
steps in preparation of,
     153–155
World Bank, 1162
Write-offs, 362–363

Y
Year-end balance, 772–773

Z
Zero-interest bonds, 454
Zuckerberg, Mark, 503

RAPID REVIEW
Chapter Content

BASIC ACCOUNTING EQUATION (Chapter 2)

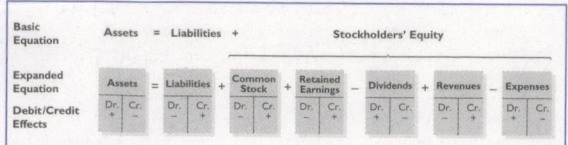

Basic Equation	Assets	=	Liabilities	+			Stockholders' Equity			

ADJUSTING ENTRIES (Chapter 3)

	Type		Adjusting Entry	
Deferrals	1. Prepaid expenses		Dr. Expenses	Cr. Assets
	2. Unearned revenues		Dr. Liabilities	Cr. Revenues
Accruals	1. Accrued revenues		Dr. Assets	Cr. Revenues
	2. Accrued expenses		Dr. Expenses	Cr. Liabilities

Note: Each adjusting entry will affect one or more income statement accounts and one or more balance sheet accounts.

Interest Computation

Interest = Face value of note × Annual interest rate × Time in terms of one year

CLOSING ENTRIES (Chapter 4)

Purpose: (1) Update the Retained Earnings account in the ledger by transferring net income (loss) and dividends to retained earnings. (2) Prepare the temporary accounts (revenue, expense, dividends) for the next period's postings by reducing their balances to zero.

Process

1. Debit each revenue account for its balance (assuming normal balances) and credit Income Summary for total revenues.
2. Debit Income Summary for total expenses and credit each expense account for its balance (assuming normal balances).

   STOP AND CHECK: Does the balance in your Income Summary account equal the net income (loss) reported in the income statement?

3. Debit (credit) Income Summary and credit (debit) Retained Earnings for the amount of net income (loss).
4. Debit Retained Earnings for the balance in the Dividends account and credit Dividends for the same amount.

   STOP AND CHECK: Does the balance in your Retained Earnings account equal the ending balance reported in the balance sheet and the retained earnings statement? Are all of your temporary account balances zero?

ACCOUNTING CYCLE (Chapter 4)

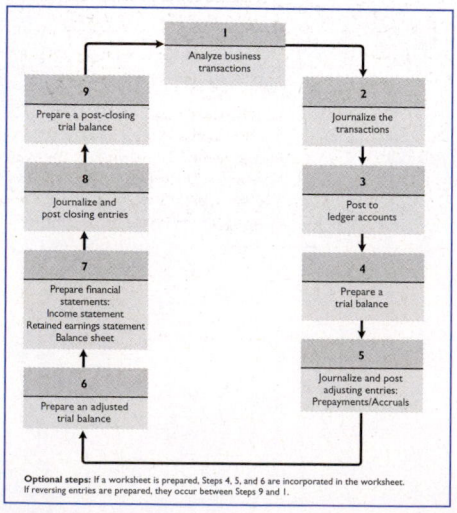

INVENTORY (Chapters 5 and 6)

Ownership

Freight Terms	Ownership of goods on public carrier resides with:	Who pays freight costs:
FOB shipping point	Buyer	Buyer
FOB destination	Seller	Seller

Perpetual vs. Periodic Journal Entries

Event	Perpetual	Periodic

Purchase of goods	Inventory
	   Cash (A/P)
		Purchases
		   Cash (A/P)

Freight (shipping point)	Inventory
	   Cash
		Freight-In
		   Cash

Return of goods	Cash (or A/P)
	   Inventory
		Cash (or A/P)
		   Purchase Returns and Allowances

Sale of goods	Cash (or A/R)
	   Sales Revenue
	Cost of Goods Sold
	   Inventory
		Cash (or A/R)
		   Sales Revenue
		No entry

End of period	No entry	Closing or adjusting entry required

Cost Flow Methods

- Specific identification
- First-in, first-out (FIFO)
- Weighted-average
- Last-in, first-out (LIFO)

FRAUD, INTERNAL CONTROL, AND CASH (Chapter 7)

The Fraud Triangle

Opportunity

Financial pressure △ Rationalization

Principles of Internal Control Activities

- Establishment of responsibility
- Segregation of duties
- Documentation procedures
- Physical controls
- Independent internal verification
- Human resource controls

Bank Reconciliation

Bank	Books
Balance per bank statement Add: Deposits in transit	Balance per books Add: Unrecorded credit memoranda from bank statement
Deduct: Outstanding checks	Deduct: Unrecorded debit memoranda from bank statement
Adjusted cash balance	Adjusted cash balance

Note: 1. Errors should be offset (added or deducted) on the side that made the error.
  2. Adjusting journal entries should only be made on the books.

STOP AND CHECK: Does the adjusted cash balance in the Cash account equal the reconciled balance?

RECEIVABLES (Chapter 8)

Methods to Account for Uncollectible Accounts

Direct write-off method	Record bad debt expense when the company determines a particular account to be uncollectible.
Allowance methods: Percentage-of-sales	At the end of each period, estimate the amount of credit sales uncollectible. Debit Bad Debt Expense and credit Allowance for Doubtful Accounts for this amount. As specific accounts become uncollectible, debit Allowance for Doubtful Accounts and credit Accounts Receivable.
Percentage-of-receivables	At the end of each period, estimate the amount of uncollectible receivables. Debit Bad Debt Expense and credit Allowance for Doubtful Accounts in an amount that results in a balance in the allowance account equal to the estimate of uncollectibles. As specific accounts become uncollectible, debit Allowance for Doubtful Accounts and credit Accounts Receivable.

PLANT ASSETS (Chapter 9)

Presentation

Tangible Assets	Intangible Assets
Property, plant, and equipment	Intangible assets (patents, copyrights, trademarks, franchises, goodwill)
Natural resources	

Computation of Annual Depreciation Expense

Straight-line	$\dfrac{\text{Cost} - \text{Salvage value}}{\text{Useful life (in years)}}$
Units-of-activity	$\dfrac{\text{Depreciable cost}}{\text{Useful life (in units)}} \times$ Units of activity during year
Declining-balance	Book value at beginning of year $\times$ Declining-balance rate* *Declining-balance rate = 1 ÷ Useful life (in years)

Note: If depreciation is calculated for partial periods, the straight-line and declining-balance methods must be adjusted for the relevant proportion of the year. Multiply the annual depreciation expense by the number of months expired in the year divided by 12 months.

BONDS (Chapter 10)

Premium	Market interest rate < Contractual interest rate
Face value	Market interest rate = Contractual interest rate
Discount	Market interest rate > Contractual interest rate

Computation of Annual Bond Interest Expense

Interest expense = Interest paid (payable) + Amortization of discount
(OR − Amortization of premium)

Straight-line amortization	$\dfrac{\text{Bond discount (premium)}}{\text{Number of interest periods}}$	
Effective-interest amortization (preferred method)	Bond interest expense	Bond interest paid
	Carrying value of bonds at beginning of period × Effective-interest rate	Face amount of bonds × Contractual interest rate

STOCKHOLDERS' EQUITY (Chapter 11)

No-Par Value vs. Par Value Stock Journal Entries

No-Par Value	Par Value

Cash
  Common Stock
	Cash
	  Common Stock (par value)
	  Paid-in Capital in Excess of Par

Comparison of Dividend Effects

	Cash	Common Stock	Retained Earnings
Cash dividend	↓	No effect	↓
Stock dividend	No effect	↑	↓
Stock split	No effect	No effect	No effect

Debits and Credits to Retained Earnings

Retained Earnings	
Debits (Decreases)	Credits (Increases)
1. Net loss 2. Prior period adjustments for overstatement of net income 3. Cash dividends and stock dividends 4. Some disposals of treasury stock	1. Net income 2. Prior period adjustments for understatement of net income

INVESTMENTS (Chapter 12)

Comparison of Long-Term Bond Investment and Liability Journal Entries

Event	Investor	Investee

Purchase / issue of bonds	Debt Investments
	  Cash
		Cash
		  Bonds Payable

Interest receipt / payment	Cash
	  Interest Revenue
		Interest Expense
		  Cash

Comparison of Cost and Equity Methods of Accounting for Long-Term Stock Investments

Event	Cost	Equity

Acquisition	Stock Investments
	  Cash
		Stock Investments
		  Cash

Investee reports earnings	No entry	Stock Investments Revenue from Stock Investments

Investee pays dividends	Cash
	  Dividend Revenue
		Cash
		  Stock Investments

Trading and Available-for-Sale Securities

Trading	Report at fair value with changes reported in net income.
Available-for-sale	Report at fair value with changes reported in the stockholders' equity section.

STATEMENT OF CASH FLOWS (Chapter 13)

Cash flows from operating activities (**indirect method**)

Net income		
Add:	Losses on disposals of assets	$ X
	Amortization and depreciation	X
	Decreases in noncash current assets	X
	Increases in current liabilities	X
Deduct:	Gains on disposals of assets	(X)
	Increases in noncash current assets	(X)
	Decreases in current liabilities	(X)
Net cash provided (used) by operating activities		$ X

Cash flows from operating activities (**direct method**)

Cash receipts
(Examples: from sales of goods and services to customers, from receipts of interest and dividends on loans and investments) $ X
Cash payments
(Examples: to suppliers, for operating expenses, for interest, for taxes)   (X)
Net cash provided (used) by operating activities $ X

PRESENTATION OF NON-TYPICAL ITEMS (Chapter 14)

Prior period adjustments (Chapter 11)	Retained earnings statement (adjustment of beginning retained earnings)
Discontinued operations	Income statement (presented separately after "Income from continuing operations")
Changes in accounting principle	In most instances, use the new method in current period and restate previous years' results using new method. For changes in depreciation and amortization methods, use the new method in the current period but do not restate previous periods.

RAPID REVIEW
Chapter Content

MANAGERIAL ACCOUNTING (Chapter 15)

Characteristics of Managerial Accounting

Primary users	Internal users
Reports	Internal reports issued as needed
Purpose	Special purpose for a particular user
Content	Pertains to subunits, may be detailed, use of relevant data
Verification	No independent audits

Types of Manufacturing Costs

Direct materials	Raw materials directly associated with finished product
Direct labor	Work of employees directly associated with turning raw materials into finished product
Manufacturing overhead	Costs indirectly associated with manufacture of finished product

JOB ORDER AND PROCESS COSTING (Chapters 16 and 17)

Types of Accounting Systems

Job order	Costs are assigned to each unit or each batch of goods
Process cost	Costs are applied to similar products that are mass-produced in a continuous fashion

Job Order and Process Cost Flow

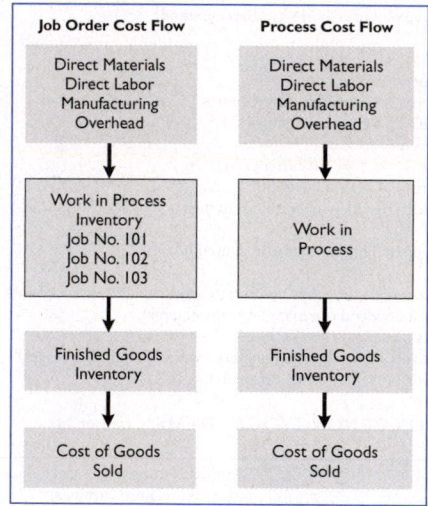

ACTIVITY-BASED COSTING (Chapter 18)

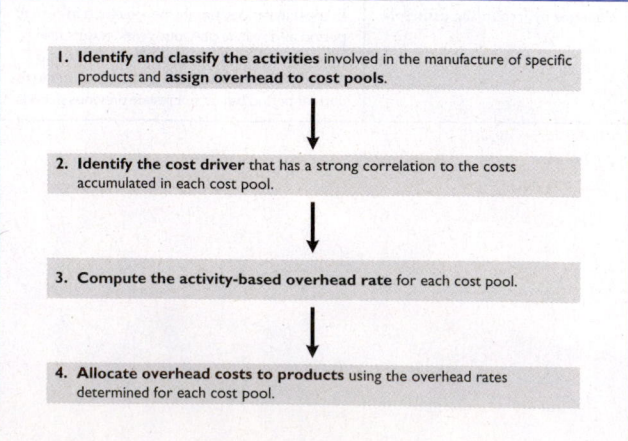

1. **Identify and classify the activities** involved in the manufacture of specific products and **assign overhead to cost pools**.

2. **Identify the cost driver** that has a strong correlation to the costs accumulated in each cost pool.

3. **Compute the activity-based overhead rate** for each cost pool.

4. **Allocate overhead costs to products** using the overhead rates determined for each cost pool.

COST-VOLUME-PROFIT (Chapters 19 and 20)

Types of Costs

Variable costs	Vary in total directly and proportionately with changes in activity level
Fixed costs	Remain the same in total regardless of change in activity level
Mixed costs	Contain both a fixed and a variable element

CVP Income Statement Format

	Total	Per Unit
Sales	$xx	$xx
Variable costs	xx	xx
Contribution margin	xx	$xx
Fixed costs	xx	
Net income	$xx	

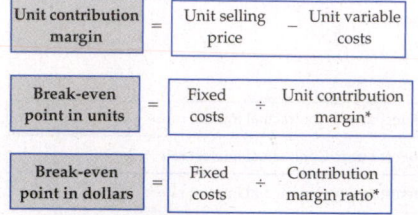

$$\text{Unit contribution margin} = \text{Unit selling price} - \text{Unit variable costs}$$

$$\text{Break-even point in units} = \text{Fixed costs} \div \text{Unit contribution margin*}$$

$$\text{Break-even point in dollars} = \text{Fixed costs} \div \text{Contribution margin ratio*}$$

$$\text{Required sales in units for target net income} = (\text{Fixed costs} + \text{Target net income}) \div \text{Unit contribution margin}$$

$$\text{Degree of operating leverage} = \text{Contribution margin} \div \text{Net income}$$

*For multiple products, use weighted-average.

INCREMENTAL ANALYSIS (Chapter 21)

1. Identify the relevant costs associated with each alternative. **Relevant costs** are those costs and revenues that differ across alternatives. Choose the alternative that maximizes net income.
2. **Opportunity costs** are those benefits that are given up when one alternative is chosen instead of another one. Opportunity costs are relevant costs.
3. **Sunk costs** have already been incurred and will not be changed or avoided by any future decision. Sunk costs are not relevant costs.

PRICING (Chapter 22)

External Pricing

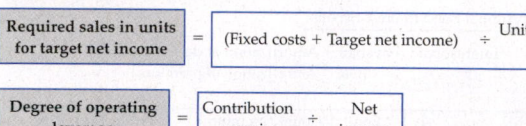

$$\text{Markup percentage} = \text{Desired ROI per unit} \div \text{Total unit cost}$$

$$\text{Target selling price per unit} = \text{Total unit cost} + \left(\text{Total unit cost} \times \text{Markup percentage}\right)$$

Transfer Pricing

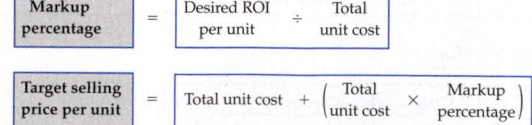

$$\text{Minimum transfer price} = \text{Variable cost} + \text{Opportunity cost}$$